The Oxford Handbook of Clinical Psychology

OXFORD LIBRARY OF PSYCHOLOGY

OXFORD LIBRARY OF PSYCHOLOGY

Editor-in-Chief PETER E. NATHAN

The Oxford Handbook of Clinical Psychology

Edited by

David H. Barlow

OXFORD
UNIVERSITY PRESS

2011

OXFORD
UNIVERSITY PRESS

Oxford University Press, Inc., publishes works that further Oxford University's
objective of excellence in research, scholarship, and education.

Oxford   New York
Auckland   Cape Town   Dar es Salaam   Hong Kong   Karachi
Kuala Lumpur   Madrid   Melbourne   Mexico City   Nairobi
New Delhi   Shanghai   Taipei   Toronto

With offices in
Argentina   Austria   Brazil   Chile   Czech Republic   France   Greece
Guatemala   Hungary   Italy   Japan   Poland   Portugal   Singapore
South Korea   Switzerland   Thailand   Turkey   Ukraine   Vietnam

Copyright © 2011 by Oxford University Press, Inc.

Published by Oxford University Press, Inc.
198 Madison Avenue, New York, New York 10016
www.oup.com

Oxford is a registered trademark of Oxford University Press

Library of Congress Cataloging-in-Publication Data
The Oxford handbook of clinical psychology / edited by David H. Barlow.
   p.; cm. – (Oxford library of psychology)
   Other title: Handbook of clinical psychology
   Includes bibliographical references and index.
   ISBN 978-0-19-536688-4 (hardcover) 1. Clinical psychology–Handbooks,
manuals, etc. I. Barlow, David H. II. Title: Handbook of clinical psychology.
III. Series: Oxford library of psychology.
   [DNLM: 1. Psychology, Clinical–methods. 2. Mental Disorders–diagnosis.
   3. Mental Disorders–therapy. 4. Psychotherapy–methods. WM 105 O98 2010]
   RC467.2.O94 2010
   616.89–dc22
                                                      2010004064
ISBN-13: 978-0-19-536688-4
ISBN-10: 0-19-531473-5

9 8 7 6 5 4 3 2 1

Printed in the United States of America on acid-free paper

CONTENTS

OXFORD LIBRARY OF PSYCHOLOGY

The *Oxford Library of Psychology*, a landmark series of handbooks, is published by Oxford University Press, one of the world's oldest and most highly respected publishers, with a tradition of publishing significant books in psychology. The ambitious goal of the *Oxford Library of Psychology* is nothing less than to span a vibrant, wide-ranging field and, in so doing, to fill a clear market need.

Encompassing a comprehensive set of handbooks, organized hierarchically, the *Library* incorporates volumes at different levels, each designed to meet a distinct need. At one level are a set of handbooks designed broadly to survey the major subfields of psychology; at another are numerous handbooks that cover important current focal research and scholarly areas of psychology in depth and detail. Planned as a reflection of the dynamism of psychology, the *Library* will grow and expand as psychology itself develops, thereby highlighting significant new research that will impact on the field. Adding to its accessibility and ease of use, the *Library* will be published in print and, later on, electronically.

The *Library* surveys psychology's principal subfields with a set of handbooks that capture the current status and future prospects of those major subdisciplines. This initial set includes handbooks of social and personality psychology, clinical psychology, counseling psychology, school psychology, educational psychology, industrial and organizational psychology, cognitive psychology, cognitive neuroscience, methods and measurements, history, neuropsychology, personality assessment, developmental psychology, and more. Each handbook undertakes to review one of psychology's major subdisciplines with breadth, comprehensiveness, and exemplary scholarship. In addition to these broadly conceived volumes, the *Library* also includes a large number of handbooks designed to explore in depth more specialized areas of scholarship and research, such as stress, health and coping, anxiety and related disorders, cognitive development, or child and adolescent assessment. In contrast to the broad coverage of the subfield handbooks, each of these latter volumes focuses on an especially productive, more highly focused line of scholarship and research. Whether at the broadest or most specific level, however, all of the *Library* handbooks offer synthetic coverage that reviews and evaluates the relevant past and present research and anticipates research in the future. Each handbook in the *Library* includes introductory and concluding chapters written by its editor to provide a roadmap to the handbook's table of contents and to offer informed anticipations of significant future developments in that field.

An undertaking of this scope calls for handbook editors and chapter authors who are established scholars in the areas about which they write. Many of the nation's and world's most productive and best-respected psychologists have agreed to edit *Library* handbooks or write authoritative chapters in their areas of expertise.

For whom has the *Oxford Library of Psychology* been written? Because of its breadth, depth, and accessibility, the *Library* serves a diverse audience, including graduate students in psychology and their faculty mentors, scholars, researchers, and practitioners in psychology and related fields. Each will find in the *Library* the information he or she seeks on the subfield or focal area of psychology in which they work or are interested.

Befitting its commitment to accessibility, each handbook includes a comprehensive index, as well as extensive references to help guide research. And because the *Library* was designed from its inception as an online as well as a print resource, its structure and contents will be readily and rationally searchable online. Further, once the *Library* is released online, the handbooks will be regularly and thoroughly updated.

In summary, the *Oxford Library of Psychology* will grow organically to provide a thoroughly informed perspective on the field of psychology, one that reflects both psychology's dynamism and its increasing interdisciplinarity. Once published electronically, the *Library* is also destined to become a uniquely valuable interactive tool, with extended search and browsing capabilities. As you begin to consult this handbook, we sincerely hope you will share our enthusiasm for the more than 500-year tradition of Oxford University Press for excellence, innovation, and quality, as exemplified by the *Oxford Library of Psychology*.

Peter E. Nathan
Editor-in-Chief
Oxford Library of Psychology

ABOUT THE EDITOR

David H. Barlow

David H. Barlow received his Ph.D. from the University of Vermont in 1969. He is a Professor of Psychology and Psychiatry at Boston University, where he founded the Center for Anxiety and Related Disorders and now serves as the Center's Director Emeritus.

Dr. Barlow is the recipient of the 2000 American Psychological Association (APA) Distinguished Scientific Award for the Applications of Psychology. He is also the recipient of the 2008 Career/Lifetime Achievement Award from the Association for Behavioral and Cognitive Therapies and the 2000 Distinguished Scientific Contribution Award from the Society of Clinical Psychology of the APA.

He is past-president of the Society of Clinical Psychology of the APA and the Association for Behavioral and Cognitive Therapies, past-editor of several journals, and currently Editor-in-Chief of the *Treatments That Work* series for Oxford University Press. He was Chair of the American Psychological Association Task Force of Psychological Intervention Guidelines, and was a member of the DSM-IV Task Force of the American Psychiatric Association. He is also a diplomat in clinical psychology for the American Board of Professional Psychology and maintains a private practice.

CONTRIBUTORS

Jonathan S. Abramowitz
Department of Psychology
University of North Carolina
Chapel Hill, NC

Lesley A. Allen
Department of Psychiatry
University of Medicine and Dentistry of
New Jersey
Robert Wood Johnson Medical School
Piscataway, NJ

Barbara L. Andersen
Department of Psychology
Ohio State University
Columbus, OH

Derek R. Anderson
Department of Psychology
Ohio State University
Columbus, OH

Martin M. Antony
Department of Psychology
Ryerson University
Toronto, ON

Allison J. Applebaum
Department of Psychology
Boston University
Boston, MA

Jacques P. Barber
Department of Psychiatry
University of Pennsylvania School of
Medicine
Philadelphia, PA

David H. Barlow
Center for Anxiety and Related
Disorders
Department of Psychology
Boston University
Boston, MA

Donald H. Baucom
Department of Psychology
University of North Carolina
Chapel Hill, NC

Adam Bernstein
Department of Psychology
University of California, Los Angeles
Los Angeles, CA

James F. Boswell
Department of Psychology
Pennsylvania State University
State College, PA

Andrea Bradford
Department of Family and Community
Medicine
Baylor College of Medicine
Houston, TX

Timothy A. Brown
Center for Anxiety and Related Disorders
Boston University
Boston, MA

Molly R. Butterworth
Psychology Department
University of Utah
Salt Lake City, UT

Jenna R. Carl
Center for Anxiety and Related Disorders
Department of Psychology
Boston University
Boston, MA

Louis G. Castonguay
Department of Psychology
Pennsylvania State University
State College, PA

Christine B. Cha
Department of Psychology
Harvard University
Cambridge, MA

Bruce F. Chorpita
Department of Psychology
University of California, Los Angeles
Los Angeles, CA

Lillian Comas-Díaz
Transcultural Mental Health Institute
Washington, DC

Jonathan S. Comer
Department of Psychiatry
Boston University
Boston, MA

Patrick H. DeLeon
Past President
American Psychological Association

David DeMatteo
Department of Psychology
Drexel University
Philadelphia, PA

Anne DePrince
Department of Psychology
University of Denver
Denver, CO

Lisa M. Diamond
Psychology Department
University of Utah
Salt Lake City, UT

Linda A. Dimeff
Behavioral Tech Research, Inc.
Seattle, WA

Halina J. Dour
Department of Psychology
Harvard University
Cambridge, MA

V. Mark Durand
Department of Psychology
University of South Florida, St. Petersburg
St. Petersburg, FL

Maryanne Edmundson
Department of Psychology
University of Kentucky
Lexington, KY

Charles F. Emery
Department of Psychology
Ohio State University
Columbus, OH

Norman B. Epstein
Marriage and Family Therapy Program
University of Maryland
College Park, MD

Mariana K. Falconier
Department of Human Development
Virginia Tech University
Blacksburg, VA

Dolores Gallagher-Thompson
Stanford University School of Medicine
Stanford, CA

Marvin R. Goldfried
Department of Psychology
Stony Brook University
Stony Brook, NY

Naomi Goldstein
Department of Psychology
Drexel University
Philadelphia, PA

Leslie S. Greenberg
Department of Psychology
York University
Toronto, ON

Catherine L. Grus
American Psychological Association
Washington, DC

Leonard J. Haas
Department of Family & Preventive
Medicine
University of Utah School of Medicine
Salt Lake City, UT

Allison Hart
Department of Psychology
Drexel University
Philadelphia, PA

Laurie Heatherington
Department of Psychology
Williams College
Williamstown, MA

Kirk Heilbrun
Department of Psychology
Drexel University
Philadelphia, PA

Justin M. Hill
VA Boston Healthcare System
Boston, MA

Jason M. Holland
VA Palo Alto Health Care System
Stanford University School of Medicine
Stanford, CA

Heather K. Hood
Department of Psychology
Ryerson University
Toronto, ON

John Hunsley
Department of Psychology
University of Ottawa
Ottawa, ON

Jonathan D. Huppert
Department of Psychology
The Hebrew University of Jerusalem
Jerusalem, Israel

Bradley E. Karlin
Department of Veterans Affairs
Central Office
Washington, DC

Terence M. Keane
VA National Center for Posttraumatic
Stress Disorder
Boston University School of Medicine
Boston, MA

Philip C. Kendall
Department of Psychology
Temple University
Philadelphia, PA

Mary Beth Kenkel
College of Psychology and Liberal Arts
Florida Institute of Technology
Melbourne, FL

Jennifer S. Kirby
Department of Psychology
University of North Carolina
Chapel Hill, NC

Phillip M. Kleespies
VA Boston Healthcare System
Boston, MA

Naomi Koerner
Department of Psychology
Ryerson University
Toronto, ON

Robert F. Krueger
Department of Psychology
University of Minnesota
Twin Cities

Beth A. Lewis
School of Kinesiology
University of Minnesota
Minneapolis, MN

Ovsanna Leyfer
Center for Anxiety and Related Disorders
Boston University
Boston, MA

Andrew K. Littlefield
Department of Psychological Sciences
Midwest Alcoholism Research Center
University of Missouri
Columbia, MO

Julie K. Lynch
Albany Neuropsychological Associates
Albany, NY

Brittain L. Mahaffey
Department of Psychology
University of North Carolina
Chapel Hill, NC

Stephanie Marcello Duva
University of Medicine and Dentistry
of New Jersey-University Behavioral
Health Care
Division of Schizophrenia Research
Piscataway, NJ

Bess H. Marcus
Program in Public Health
Brown University
Providence, RI

Julia A. Martinez
Department of Psychological Sciences
Midwest Alcoholism Research Center
University of Missouri
Columbia, MO

Brian P. Marx
VA National Center for Posttraumatic
Stress Disorder
Boston University School of Medicine
Boston, MA

Eric J. Mash
Department of Psychology
University of Calgary
Calgary, AB

Robert J. McCaffrey
University at Albany, SUNY
Albany Neuropsychological Associates
Albany, NY

Cindy M. Meston
Department of Psychology
University of Texas at Austin
Austin, TX

Jeanne Miranda
Department of Psychiatry and
Biobehavioral Sciences
University of California, Los Angeles
Los Angeles, CA

Kim T. Mueser
Department of Psychiatry
Dartmouth Medical School
Hanover, NH

Kelly Neville
Department of Preventive Medicine
Feinberg School of Medicine
Northwestern University
Evanston, IL

Matthew K. Nock
Department of Psychology
Harvard University
Cambridge, MA

Jill M. Oliveira Gray
I Ola Lahui, Inc.
Honolulu, HI

Thomas H. Ollendick
Child Study Center, Department of
Psychology
Virginia Polytechnic Institute and State
University
Blacksburg, VA

Thomas F. Oltmanns
Department of Psychology
Washington University
St. Louis, MO

Michael W. Otto
Department of Psychology
Boston University
Boston, MA

Andrew P. Paves
Behavioral Tech Research, Inc.
Seattle, WA

Kenneth S. Pope
Independent Practice
Norwalk, CT

Christina Riggs Romaine
Department of Psychology
Drexel University
Philadelphia, PA

Donald K. Routh
Department of Psychology
University of Miami
Coral Gables, FL

Morgan T. Sammons
California School of Professional
Psychology
Alliant International University
San Francisco, CA

Ritch C. Savin-Williams
Department of Human Development
Cornell University
Ithaca, NY

Sanjay Shah
Department of Psychology
Drexel University
Philadelphia, PA

Brian A. Sharpless
Department of Psychology
Drexel University
Philadelphia, PA

Kenneth J. Sher
Department of Psychological Sciences
Midwest Alcoholism Research Center
University of Missouri
Columbia, MO

Stephen R. Shirk
Department of Psychology
University of Denver
Denver, CO

Julie M. Skutch
Behavioral Tech Research, Inc.
Seattle, WA

Denise M. Sloan
VA National Center for Posttraumatic
Stress Disorder
Boston University School of Medicine
Boston, MA

Susan C. South
Department of Psychological Sciences
Purdue University
West Lafayette, IN

Bonnie Spring
Department of Preventive Medicine
Feinberg School of Medicine
Northwestern University
Chicago, IL

Eric Statt
School of Kinesiology
University of Minnesota
Minneapolis, MN

Robyn Sysko
Department of Psychiatry
Columbia University
College of Physicians & Surgeons &
Division of Clinical Therapeutics
New York State Psychiatric Institute
New York, NY

Holly James Westervelt
Warren Alpert Medical School
Brown University
Providence, RI

Roberta F. White
Department of Environmental Health
Boston University School of Public
Health
Boston, MA

Thomas A. Widiger
Department of Psychology
University of Kentucky
Lexington, KY

G. Terence Wilson
Graduate School of Applied and
Professional Psychology
Rutgers, The State University of
New Jersey
Piscataway, NJ

Eric A. Woodcock
Behavioral Tech Research, Inc.
Seattle, WA

Robert L. Woolfolk
Rutgers University
Princeton University
Princeton, NJ

Antonette M. Zeiss
Department of Veterans Affairs
Central Office
Washington, DC

CONTENTS

Part Five · Conclusion and Future Directions

PART 1

Overview and Introduction

A Prolegomenon to Clinical Psychology: Two 40-year Odysseys

David H. Barlow

Abstract

In 1969, David Shakow, generally acknowledged as the founding father of modern-day clinical psychology, recounted his 40-year odyssey in the field. He focused on advances in training, diagnosis and assessment, and treatment, and projected trends in these areas in the years to come. The author recounts his own 40-year odyssey, beginning in 1969, and reflects on the remarkable growth of clinical psychology, progress that has occurred in the areas of training, diagnosis and assessment, and treatment, and the extent to which Shakow's vision has been realized.

Keywords: Assessment, clinical psychology, diagnosis, psychological treatment, training

In 1969, two events occurred that would ultimately impact this handbook of clinical psychology. First, my career officially commenced with the conferral of a PhD. For me, this was the fulfillment of a dream that had begun in high school when I decided there was nothing else I wanted to be but a clinical psychologist. But a far more significant event caught the attention of most clinical psychologists. David Shakow, widely acclaimed as the father of modern clinical psychology, published a book of his collected papers entitled "Clinical Psychology as Science and Profession: A 40-Year Odyssey" (Shakow, 1969). At the time, Shakow had recently retired as the first chief of the Laboratory of Psychology in the Intramural Research Program of the National Institute of Mental Health (NIMH). Prior to that, his career included stints in both departments of psychiatry and psychology in major universities, as well as key leadership positions in prominent clinical settings, including McLean Hospital in Boston and Worcester State Hospital. Although he had officially retired in 1966, he continued going to work every day, where he would write and supervise research until he died suddenly one morning in his office, in 1981, at the age of 80 (Garmezy & Holzman, 1984).

Shakow is one of only two individuals to be honored by the American Psychological Association (APA) over the course of its history with two of its most prestigious awards: the Distinguished Scientific Contribution Award and the Distinguished Professional Contribution Award. Although he made enormous contributions to our research effort, much of it in the area of schizophrenia, it was Shakow's conceptualization of the role of modern-day clinical psychology that remains his most enduring legacy. He was an early president of the Division (now the Society) of Clinical Psychology of the APA and chaired the very influential Committee on Training in Clinical Psychology that made its report in 1947 defining the Scientist-Practitioner Model of training, a model that was endorsed, broadened, and deepened at the iconic Boulder Conference in 1949 (Raimy, 1950).

It is a coincidence that, as I write this prolegomenon in the summer of 2009, it has been another 40 years since the publication of Shakow's book in 1969, the year my career also commenced, and the field has expanded exponentially. Thus, it seems fitting to reflect on his views and his predictions for the future of the profession as put forth at the end of his 40-year odyssey and, with all humility, recount my own 40-year odyssey reviewing the major themes articulated by Shakow in 1969, and later elaborated in a major paper in 1976 (Shakow, 1976). These themes include training, diagnosis (by which he meant the broad area of psychological assessment), and therapy. I begin with a look at training.

Training in 1969

In 1969, Shakow observed:

> Present doctoral training . . . calls for a minimum program of four years, one year of which (preferably the third) consists of an internship. On a foundation of basic courses in theoretical clinical and dynamic psychology, practica, clerkships, and internships are organized. The type of training program now generally accepted was initially proposed by the Committee on Training in Clinical Psychology of the APA in its 1947 report, and, in its major outlines, further supported in conferences at Boulder (Raimy, 1950), Stanford (Strother, 1956) and Miami (Roe, Gustad, Moore, Ross, & Skodak, 1959). (A fourth conference was held in the spring of 1965.) The 1947 Report called for centering clinical training in existing university departments, and the integration of field training units and university programs. (*Shakow*, 1969, p. 39)

Shakow also recounted what he called the "phenomenal" growth in clinical psychology in the United States. As he noted:

> (1) membership in the Division of Clinical Psychology of the APA has risen from 787 in 1948 to 2,883 in 1964; (2) the number of schools fully approved by the Committee on Training in Clinical Psychology of the APA has increased from 30 in 1948 to 55 in 1963; (3) there were an estimated 742 graduate students enrolled in doctoral training in programs in clinical psychology in the academic year 1947–48 compared to 3,340 in 1962–63; (4) the number of clinical psychologists certified by the American Board of Examiners in Professional Psychology has increased from 234 in 1948 to 1,793 in 1963 (of the total, 1,116 are "grandfathers"); (5) 28 states, and four provinces in Canada have established some form of statutory control; 18 states have set up non-statutory control. (*Shakow*, 1969, p. 41)

But he noted that this "unusual growth" had not come about without much travail, and that this growth had given rise to a number of questions that would have to be answered forthrightly in the years to come. Some of these questions were:

1. Can psychology train persons with both professional and scientific goals in mind?
2. How much application can there be in a field where basic knowledge is still so meager?
3. Should not clinical psychologists be devoting more time to research?
4. Should training for research and teaching be separated from training for the applications of psychology? (Shakow, 1969, p. 41)

These questions, of course, reflected the continuing endorsement of the scientist-practitioner model of training of clinical psychologists as conceptualized by Shakow himself, with its emphasis on integration of science and practice, as articulated in various conferences on training sponsored by the APA, most notably the Boulder Conference mentioned earlier. And it is interesting to note that many of these questions raised in the 1960s still remain today, in 2009. But in fact, this philosophy of training psychologists had much deeper roots. Notably, Lightner Witmer, considered the first "clinical psychologist" by most, wrote "the pure and the applied sciences advance in a single front. What retards the progress of one, retards the progress of the other; what fosters one, fosters the other. But in the final analysis the progress of psychology, as of every other science, will be determined by the value and amount of its contributions to the advancement of the human race" (Witmer, 1907/1996, p. 2491; see also Routh, Chapter 2, this volume).

Despite the long history of this model of training for clinical psychology and the substantial amount of time and effort invested in articulating and implementing this model, the desired outcomes proved elusive. For example, in the report of the Boulder Conference itself it was noted, "too often, however, clinical psychologists have been trained in rigorous thinking about nonclinical subject matter and clinical problems have been dismissed as lacking in 'scientific' respectability. As a result, many clinicians have been unable to bridge the gap between their formal training and scientific thinking on the one hand, and the demands of practice on the other. As time passes and their skills become more satisfying to themselves and to others, the task of thinking systematically and impartially becomes more difficult" (Raimy, 1950, p. 86). Nevertheless, the Boulder Conference, under Shakow's influence and leadership, articulated a number of reasons why joint training in practice and research continued to be desirable:

1. Avoid narrowness of thinking associated with training in just research or practice and foster cross-fertilization by combined training.

2. Lack of dependable knowledge requires that research be a vital part of psychologists skills.

3. Substantial interest in field and the large number of applicants allows for accepting individuals with interests in both science and practice.

4. Direct involvement with clinical practice would highlight important research issues.

5. Effectively delivered service may generate financial support for the initiation and continuation of research and data collection.

It is interesting to reflect on this rationale for training after 60 years. Of course, few would dispute the necessity to avoid narrowness of thinking and to broaden perspectives on both research and practice. Similarly, Point 2 remains an important consideration despite the enormous advances in our understanding of psychopathology and behavior change over the ensuing last 60 years. Nevertheless, this particular point reflects the fact that even today a partnership between frontline clinicians who are actually objectively assessing the effects of their procedures, and clinical researchers responsible for developing and evaluating a variety of psychological procedures is essential if we are to move forward. There is also little question regarding Point 4, that some familiarity with the subject matter at hand through clinical practice greatly enriches the research effort. For Point 3, we are seeing somewhat less than universal agreement that one individual will have substantial and equal interest in both science and practice, nevertheless, this remains a goal of all scientist-practitioner programs that find their graduates either going on to clinical research careers, careers in practice with a more empirical bent, or perhaps some combination. Finally, Point 5 certainly came true with the advent of federal funding for development of psychological procedures that, in turn, provided financial support for training and research. Given the new strategic vision at the NIMH during the last several years (Insel, 2009), some direct connection to the practice effort is seen as a very important link to continued research funding.

As noted earlier, Shakow was a strong advocate of integrating clinical settings fully into doctoral clinical psychology programs. This arrangement was rare in those early years, since hardly any in-house training clinics existed, and sites for clinical practica were few and far between. And when they could be procured, psychologists were often limited to roles of administering routine psychological testing. Nevertheless, Shakow, in 1976, stipulated again a suggestion he had been making for 20 years. "My suggestion is that the university (or professional school) and the field-center training activities be as completely integrated as possible. Integration does not mean sameness, which results in a loss of vigor that comes with having the same point of view.... . The fundamental principal of the plan is that theory and practicum must be constantly associated and tied together, whether in the university or the field station, and that both types of activity—theory and practicum—start with the very beginning of the program. I would suggest as axiomatic: *the greater the degree of integration between theory and practice, and between university and field center, the more effective the program*" (Shakow, 1976, p. 556). On this point, it is clear that Shakow's wisdom has been recognized, as clinical psychology programs increasingly conduct training in captive clinics, often referred to as Psychological Service Centers, and increasingly, specialty clinics focusing on specific areas of psychopathology. Nevertheless, the necessity of completing internships in more fully organized clinical settings, still a requirement of all scientist-practitioner programs, is becoming increasingly problematic. There is a decreasing number of internship slots and at the same time a rapidly increasing number of applicants, resulting in a greater number of students each year unable to complete requirements for the PhD degree due to circumstances largely out of their control or that of their clinical psychology doctoral program. Clearly, this is an untenable situation and requires a new look at the admonitions made by Shakow over 40 years ago, recommending control of the entire clinical psychology training experience by the programs with the authority to conduct that training.

So after 40 years, what did Shakow conclude in 1969 about the future of clinical psychology, particularly in the context of training? First, he determined that it was crucial to train for research "... the content of research needs redefinition so it will encompass the most rigorous laboratory research, systematic naturalistic observation, and a serious attitude of inquiry leading to deliberate efforts to obtain answers to questions which arise during clinical operations" (Shakow, 1969, p. 42). This aspiration reflected, in part, a longstanding difficulty observed by the early leaders of clinical psychology that required research projects in doctoral training programs were conceptualized far too narrowly. That is, most required research efforts in clinical programs were concerned with only the most basic questions, often studying laboratory animals rather than taking advantage of the rich trove of clinical questions that could be addressed more directly in applied settings. Of course, as mentioned, most clinical psychologists in training in those days had little access to these settings.

Second, Shakow argued that clinical psychology training should occur in institutional and community settings, and that "the function of each of the training agencies and the way to integrate their work need careful spelling out" (Shakow, 1969, p. 42). Once again, as articulated earlier, Shakow was a firm believer in the integration of training directly into the clinical settings.

Third, Shakow proposed increased delineation of important areas for clinical research and practice. Toward fulfilling this goal, he suggested that "This calls for much imaginative thinking. New methods of therapy, new methods of diagnosis, and— particularly, preventive methods of education are becoming increasingly important… . It is clear that the personnel shortages in the area of mental health will be enormous and far from filled by present-day mental health professionals. Much thought and experimentation must go into making use of a much larger pool of persons, for example, younger persons with the ideals and resourcefulness represented in Peace Corps volunteers" (Shakow, 1969, p. 42). In this aspiration, Shakow correctly anticipated the greatly increased knowledge of the origins and course of psychopathology, the variety of new interventions both psychological and pharmacological that have occurred in the past 40 years, and the enormous upsurge in interest on the proper ways to deliver mental health services (Barlow, 2004; McHugh & Barlow, 2010). If anything, it is this latter area that is attracting the most attention as the reform of our healthcare delivery system in the United States gains traction, and as healthcare delivery in the rest of the developed world becomes more organized, efficient, and evidence-based. I return to this theme below.

Fourth, Shakow considered the proper place to locate training programs in clinical psychology. He underscored that the placement of clinical psychology programs in university settings should be carefully considered, so as to achieve his goals of integration in both the theory and application of practice, "The nature of the doctoral degree granted to clinical psychologists—with a strictly professional (say a PsyD) or a combined research degree (the PhD)—calls for special discussion. The place and nature of post-doctoral programs, particularly such programs for psychotherapy training should be given equal thought" (Shakow, 1969, p. 42).

In this era, professional degrees (PsyD) had just been conceptualized and were being initiated in a few university settings. Shakow did not seem to have a particular view on this development as long as they aspired to the same principles he outlined for ideal training in the field.

Finally, Shakow made observations on upgrading the standards for committees that evaluate training programs and the competency of individuals to practice psychology, noting in particular the potentially important role of the American Board of Professional Psychology, as well as state licensing and certification boards. In a prescient summary statement, Shakow concluded:

> The major problems of clinical psychology continue to lie within the parent field, psychology. Clinical psychology, after a long period spent as part of an academic discipline, has been through the early stages of becoming a profession as well. It is going through the natural disturbances and difficulties which attend a growth process of this kind. However, if it selects its students carefully, for personality as well as intellect; if it trains thoroughly, in spirit as well as letter; if it trains broadly, recognizing that narrowly educated specialists are not true clinical psychologists; if it remains flexible about its training and encourages experimentation; if it does not sacrifice remoter goals to the fulfillment of immediate needs; if it maintains its contact with its scientific background, remaining alert to the importance of theory as well as practice; if it keeps modest in the face of the complexity of its problems, rather than becoming pretentious—in short, if it finds good people and gives them good training—these disturbances and difficulties need not be of serious concern. Its future in society and as a profession is then assured.
> (*Shakow*, 1969, p. 43)

In summary, Shakow's odyssey led him to conclude that (1) science and practice should be integrated and related parts of training, but (2) that the focus of science in clinical psychology training should be on clinically relevant themes. (3) These training experiences should be firmly grounded in academic psychology, but should be fully integrated into front-line practice settings, with increased attention to organized methods for evaluating quality and competence. And (4), the field should be on the forefront of exploring new systems for delivering broad-based psychological services.

Training in 2009

Earlier in the chapter, Shakow recounted the "phenomenal" growth in clinical psychology, from the years 1948–64, but even he would be stunned by what has happened since then. To update some of the statistics from the early 1960s listed earlier, membership in the Division (Society) of Clinical Psychology (Division 12) has not only increased substantially, but has spawned numerous additional divisions within the APA. These include, but are not limited to, the Division of Psychotherapy (Division 29), the Society of Clinical Child & Adolescent Psychology (Division 52), and the Society of Pediatric Psychology (Division 53). In addition, many other divisions that exist today would have been subsumed under the Division of Clinical Psychology, such as Divisions 38 (Health Psychology), 39 (Psychoanalysis), 42 (Independent Practice), 40 (Clinical Neuropsychology), 49 (Group Psychology & Group Psychotherapy), and several others. The number of schools fully accredited by APA to offer doctoral-level training has grown from 55 in 1963, to 226 in the 2006 academic year (Grus, this volume). From 3,340 graduate students enrolled in doctoral training programs in clinical psychology in 1962–63, the number has jumped to 25,973 as of 2006 (Grus, this volume). In addition, the number of psychologists certified in clinical psychology by the American Board of Professional Psychology has increased from 1,793 in 1963 to 3,348 as of 2009. And, whereas clinical psychology was the only area in which certification was possible from this board in the early '60s, there are now 13 specialties (see Table 1.1).

Finally, psychologists are under some form of statutory control in every state and province in North America, up from approximately half of the states and provinces in the 1960s. Much more revealing data on the current status of clinical psychology, along with facts on training and credentialing of clinical psychologists, are available in Chapter 8.

Returning to Shakow's vision for the future of clinical psychology, particularly in the context of training, we can now evaluate his predictions in the ensuing 40-year period. One remarkable observation we can make is how little has changed in both underlying philosophy and the implementation of his vision for training. This is best exemplified by

Table 1.1 Specialty areas certified by the American Board of Professional Psychology

Clinical Psychology
Clinical Child & Adolescent Psychology
Clinical Health Psychology
Clinical Neuropsychology
Cognitive & Behavioral Psychology
Counseling Psychology
Couple & Family Psychology
Forensic Psychology
Group Psychology
Organizational & Business Psychology
Psychoanalysis in Psychology
Rehabilitation Psychology
School Psychology

the recent adoption of evidence-based practice (EBP) as policy by the APA (2006). Evidence-based practice has been defined by the APA as "the integration of the best available research with clinical expertise in the context of patient characteristics, culture, and preferences" (2006). This relatively broad definition of science and practice is perfectly in keeping with the spirit of Shakow's vision that we can now safely say has been realized. In addition, the model he espoused, the Scientist-Practitioner model, is still the most highly valued model for training in the field, despite the appearance of alternative and, in some cases seemingly competing models, as described later. His other recommendations for a greater focus of research on clinical issues, integrating the academy and the clinic, developing new and imaginative ways to deliver services, the location of training programs, and strengthening standards for evaluating competency have all come to pass or are in the process of being realized. We will describe each briefly in turn.

Integrating Science and Practice

It is remarkable how well the fundamental principles of the Scientist-Practitioner model have stood the test of time. As Grus (this volume) points out, from the vantage point of the APA, the three core training models that guide clinical psychology education and training programs "…all emphasize the role of science as it relates to practice." These models of training include, of course, the Scientist-Practitioner model, with its origins in the late 1940s and still employed by the majority of doctoral programs in clinical psychology today. The Practitioner-Scholar model was formulated at a conference held in Vail, Colorado, in 1973 (Korman, 1976), with the goal of placing greater emphasis on preparation for psychological practice that would, nevertheless, be informed by science. Finally, the Clinical Scientist model, as initially described by McFall (1991), emphasized, as implied in the title, the training of clinical psychologists to be primarily scientists, with a strong focus on mastering principles of the scientific method, discovery of new knowledge, and the critical thinking skills that go along with the process of science. Programs identifying with this model often discourage applicants who are interested, at least exclusively, in clinical practice.

Although a common emphasis on science might seem a stretch for some models, such as the Scholar-Practitioner model, the flexibility in the Scientist-Practitioner model in regard to strategies for integrating science and practice makes this focus very much a part of the type of training offered in at least the leading professional schools. Thus, mental health practitioners may function as scientist-practitioners in one or more of three ways (Barlow, Hayes, & Nelson, 1984; Hayes, Barlow, & Nelson-Gray, 1999). First, they may be consumers of science, in that they keep up with the latest scientific developments in their field and make use of the most current assessment and treatment procedures that would presently be referred to as "evidence-based." A firm foundation in the scientific aspects of clinical psychology would be necessary to evaluate the literature and keep abreast of these developments. Second, the same practitioners, as part of a responsible practice, may evaluate their own assessments or treatment procedures to assess effectiveness in a process now described as "outcomes assessment." In this way, they are accountable not only to their own patients, but also to third parties who may be paying for the services. This evaluative activity has also been encoded recently in principles of EBP, adopted by the APA (2006). Third, scientist-practitioners may conduct research in clinics, hospitals, or elsewhere for the purpose of creating new knowledge about treatments, assessment, or the nature of psychopathology. Much of this new knowledge would then find its way into the clinical psychology literature, where empirical reports are published. Thus, under the influence of EBP (discussed further later), at least two of these three distinct ways in

which one could function as a scientist-practitioner are endorsed by leading proponents of all models of training present today in clinical psychology (Barlow et al., 1984; Hayes et al., 1999).

Other evidence on the robustness of this model comes from data collected by Norcross, Karpiak, and Santoro (2005), who conducted one of the periodic surveys of members of the Society of Clinical Psychology that began in the 1960s. Their survey, conducted in late 2003, examined, among other things, the training models followed in clinical psychology graduate programs (restricted in this case to the Scientist-Practitioner or "Boulder" model or the Scholar-Professional or "Vail" model, since the Clinical Scientist model is still relatively new). These models were described rather narrowly, such that the Vail model was represented as focused largely on practice. The data are presented in Table 1.2 (Norcross et al., 2005).

From Table 1.2, one can see that, in 2003, the percentage of Division 12 psychologists hailing from Scientist-Practitioner model programs was slightly over 80%, a number that has remained steady since the 1980s. Looking at the bottom (total percent) row, 65% would prefer the "Boulder" or "Strongly Boulder" model of training if they were "doing over" their training, whereas only 4% would prefer training in a "Vail" or "Strongly Vail" model. In another statistic, only eight of the 463 clinical psychologists trained in Boulder model programs reported that they would prefer a Vail model program if they could do it over again, whereas half of the psychologists trained in the Vail model programs would remain firmly within the Vail model. This is all the more surprising since, as pointed out in Chapter 8, as of 2005, only 40% of the doctorates in clinical psychology earned a PhD, and 53% earned a professional degree, the PsyD. The answer to this discrepancy lies, to some extent, in the conclusion noted earlier, that all training programs these days, under the influence of EBP, are to some degree scientist-practitioner orientated, whether they award the PhD or the PsyD.

Research Focused on Clinically Relevant Themes in Integrated Practice Settings

Shakow's multifaceted vision is also clearly evident in the current focus of research training that exists in programs in clinical psychology. In the last 40 years, the focus of research, even for required dissertations, has shifted from the basic, nonapplied arena, to a very clear emphasis on clinical research. To accommodate the research productivity within clinical

Table 1.2 Model Trained in by Model Preference

Model trained in	Total %	Model preference (%)				
		SB	B	E	V	SV
Strongly Boulder (SB)	45	65	16	18	1	0
Boulder (B)	38	9	62	26	2	1
Equally Boulder & Vail (E)	13	4	4	87	1	4
Vail (V)	3	0	5	52	32	11
Strongly Vail (SV)	1	14	0	14	14	57
Total %		34	31	31	2	2

Adapted with permission from Norcross, J.C., Karpiak, C.P., & Santoro, S.O. (2005). Clinical psychologists across the years: The division of clinical psychology from 1960 to 2003. *Journal of Clinical Psychology, 61*(12), 1467–1483.

programs, including students and faculty, the number of journals publishing applied clinical research has proliferated over the past 40 years, beyond the imagination of leading psychologists from the 1960s, such as Shakow himself. In 1965, five psychological journals were publishing primarily clinical research (psychopathology and intervention). In 2009, most popular citation analyses include 87 journals in the category of clinical psychology. In many cases, this research has taken place in the context of entities set up to promote the integration of clinical work and research, as detailed later. And this kind of effort is taking place in both traditional psychology department–based clinical psychology programs, as well as in many (but certainly not all) of the leading professional schools. To illustrate these trends in part, I will briefly describe the example of one of our own research and training clinics at Boston University, the Center for Anxiety and Related Disorders (CARD), although the choice of this Center for description is based as much on familiarity and convenience as any other factor, since equally vibrant clinical research and training entities exist in other universities around the country.

CARD, originally founded at the State University of New York at Albany, relocated to Boston University in 1996. It is a clinical research and treatment facility, operating fully within the Department of Psychology, whose mission is to advance scientific knowledge on the nature and treatment of anxiety and its disorders, as well as of other emotional disorders as they relate to anxiety, and to disseminate this information widely. To this end, the Center pursues several objectives: it conducts research on the nature and origins of anxiety disorders, and on assessment and treatment outcomes for these disorders; it maintains a fundamental mission to educate and train doctoral students in clinical psychology; and it operates as a full-service clinic for the purpose of assessing and treating anxiety and related disorders from referrals by community health professionals.

To accomplish these goals, the Center admits between 500 and 600 new patients a year to its adult and child programs. "Admission" means that patients must first pass a phone screen to rule out obvious problems that are not the focus of CARD, such as current substance use or psychotic disorders. Individuals deemed appropriate are administered a full diagnostic and assessment battery before being referred either internally to one of the CARD clinics or treatment programs, or possibly to other community resources if the presenting problems are not within CARD's realm of expertise. The Center supports approximately 6,000 visits annually from patients receiving care.

The two fundamental goals of CARD are to support clinical training in its doctoral program and clinical research for both trainees and faculty. To accomplish these goals, it was decided at the outset that CARD must provide the best clinical care available. Most individuals would not attend a clinic if they thought that the clinicians were only interested in research and that they would be "guinea pigs" for this research. Rather, they come to alleviate their suffering and restore their functioning, and CARD has developed a reputation for fulfilling these goals. In fact, approximately 60% of patients admitted to CARD enter directly into usual and standard evidence-based clinical care, much of it provided by doctoral students in clinical psychology, but some provided by psychiatric residents, post-doctoral staff, and faculty. The remaining 40% of the patients (and this number varies considerably, depending on research projects ongoing) are offered the possibility of entering one or another clinical research protocol, in which interventions are evaluated in return for free treatment. CARD also has a clinic for eating disorders, a virtual reality laboratory, and a small program for sleep disorders. New programs are developed and some are discontinued, depending on resources available and the changing interests of faculty members. CARD supports between 30 and 40 full-time staff, including psychologists, psychiatrists, a nurse, and a number of clinic and research technicians. Some of the faculty associated with CARD are on tenure-track lines at the university, but the majority are supported with income generated by CARD through grants or patient fees. Annual income from patient fees and contracts runs between $500,000 and $700,000 a year, which is all fed back into the program for salaries or other resources.

In fiscal year 2009, CARD was supported by approximately $4.5 million in funds, most of it from the National Institutes of Health (NIH), but with some monies from other sources. Among the NIH monies are National Service Research Awards (NRSA), granted to doctoral students who have successfully competed for these funds. Examples of ongoing NRSA awards for doctoral students include a new innovative "summer camp" treatment for young children, aged 4–8, suffering from severe separation anxiety; a study utilizing functional magnetic resonance imaging (fMRI) technology to examine brain functioning during emotional processing among patients with emotional disorders; and a study examining an innovative new cognitive-behavioral treatment for women suffering from perinatal grief. Other funded projects among students include the development of a novel program to promote adjustment and prevent anxiety and depression among newly committed gay couples.

It should be noted that CARD is not the only clinical facility within the Department of Psychology, since the department also supports a more traditional Psychological Services Center that services a broader range of psychopathology, beyond the emotional and related disorders. These clinics work closely together.

Once again, facilities such as these are now widely available in graduate and professional schools across the country and provide the fullest realization

of Shakow's vision by clearly integrating theory and research with ongoing clinic work and providing a clear opportunity for a focus on clinical subject matter for required research projects. In this context, the imagination of trainees is given free rein and projects range from characterizing psychopathology and its various manifestations, to the full range of treatment development and evaluation.

Assessing Quality and Competence

Finally, reflecting on the last theme of Shakow's vision, developing more objective standards for evaluating competence, the field has come a long way. In Chapter 8, Grus describes the "competency initiatives" that are either in place or in development to evaluate training programs or individuals within those programs. Here one finds a decidedly growing emphasis on the measurement of learning outcomes among doctoral students within the framework of identified core competencies. These themes have been in development for a number of years now (Kaslow, 2004; Kaslow et al., 2006). Assessing quality of services through improvements in assessment and the development of "outcomes assessment" will be taken up in the next section. In summary, by 2009 Shakow's proposal for training in clinical psychology had been realized, or is well on its way to being realized.

Psychological Assessment in 1969

Shakow subsumed most aspects of psychological assessment under the term "diagnosis," but he makes it clear that, in addition to classification, the process includes descriptive and interpretive data gathered by the psychologists based largely on objective methods in the service of helping to understand both the individual and his or her disorder.

> On examination, this diagnostic contribution is found to be of three kinds: (1) The description of what the patient in his various conditions is like in certain relevant psychological functions, that is, *what he is*. (2) The implications that the psychological studies have for therapeutic (education, vocational, personality, etc.) policy, that is, *what to do*. (3) The determination of the effects of whatever therapy may have been used on psychological functions, that is, the evaluation of *what has been done*.
> (*Shakow*, 1969, p. 44)

As one can see, the general functions of psychological assessment outlined by Shakow are still very relevant today. Providing objective and psychometrically sound descriptions of psychopathology and related psychological functions, including personality and neuropsychological processes, remains an important aim of psychological assessment, as does Shakow's second goal of providing reasonable prognostic information and interventions likely to achieve desired results. But the third goal articulated by Shakow was often overlooked in those days; that is, monitoring the outcomes of interventions.

In fact, Shakow notes that, although the three overarching goals of assessment are distinct, psychologists in that era used essentially the same tests and strategies to collect data in each of the three areas, as reflected in the standard psychological test battery of the day. Typical issues that psychologists were asked to address, particularly in hospital settings, included IQ levels; assessment of cognitive deficits such as amnesia, aphasia, agnosia, etc.; the diagnosis of various types of psychoses; and, of course, the assessment of personality characteristics. Shakow also notes that much of psychological assessment went on in "departments" of psychology in hospitals, to which patients were referred by psychiatric staff. In these cases, patients would often be referred for "psychologicals" and other laboratory testing, with the understanding on the part of psychiatric staff that the results would be used by psychiatrists to make informed decisions on diagnosis and treatment. Shakow remarked that viewing the psychology laboratory as a purely technical service, like, for example "blood work," was a position that "should be discouraged and actively fought" (Shakow, 1969, p. 45). This was an all-too-common perception of the role of psychology in those days and one that the present author experienced (and actually fought) in a hospital setting in the early 1970s. Thus, whereas Shakow differentiated and articulated the goals of assessment in a thoughtful manner, the process of psychological assessment in that era was actually characterized by a largely undifferentiated, standardized battery of psychological tests that varied little from individual to individual and was viewed as just one more set of laboratory results to assist the psychiatrist in case formulation and treatment planning. Interestingly, the nomothetic concept of "diagnosis" as we know it today was an imprecise process widely viewed as providing little value to the case formulation process. This was due to the demonstrated unreliability and lack of validity of the second edition of the *Diagnostic and Statistical Manual of Mental Disorders* (DSM) (American Psychiatric Association, 1968).

Psychological Assessment in 2009

A quick perusal of the table of contents in this handbook reveals several chapters devoted exclusively to specialized psychological assessment. These chapters include discussions of interviewing and case formulation (Chapter 12), diagnosis and personality assessment (Chapter 13), clinical neuropsychology (Chapters 26 and 30), and tailored assessments within a variety of specialized contexts such as forensic and primary care settings (Chapters 27 and 29). But perhaps the most substantial development in recent years has been the extension of evidence-based concepts to the field of assessment, as described in some detail in Chapter 5 (Hunsley & Mash, this volume). Of course, considerable research ensued over the decades since 1969 on specific psychological tests and measures, and psychology became identified with a strong focus on psychometrics, a methodology that has been well worked out over the decades. Even for strategies that might seem less amenable to empirical evaluations, such as projective tests, there is substantial agreement within psychology on the importance of collecting and analyzing appropriate psychometric data, despite the fact that significant disagreements on the interpretation of those data may exist (Barlow, 2005; Exner, 2001; Wood, Nezworski, Garb, & Lilienfeld, 2001). Nevertheless, there was still something missing. What was missing was information and hard data on the usefulness of contemporary assessment practices for effectively formulating cases, planning treatment, or monitoring treatment outcomes. Thus, psychologists could choose psychometrically sound tests or assessment procedures, but there was little research on whether this process was actually contributing to desired outcomes.

This began to change over the past decade due to increased sensitivity to issues of accountability, as well as because of the need to conduct assessment research that is more directly related to treatment provision. All of this occurred, of course, in the context of the movement towards evidence-based health-care practices in general (APA, 2006; Institute of Medicine, 2001). As Hunsley and Mash (this volume) remark:

[Evidence-based assessment (EBA)] . . . is an approach to clinical evaluation that uses research and theory to guide the selection of constructs to be assessed for a specific assessment purpose, the methods and measures to be used in the assessment, and the manner in which the assessment process unfolds. Evidence-based assessment involves the recognition by the psychologist that, even when data from psychometrically strong measures are available, the assessment process is inherently a decision-making task in which the psychologist must iteratively formulate and test hypotheses by integrating data that may be incomplete or inconsistent. As a result, a truly evidence-based approach to assessment involves an evaluation of the accuracy and usefulness of this complex decision-making task in light of potential errors and biases in data synthesis and interpretation, the costs associated with the assessment process and, ultimately, the impact the assessment had on clinical outcomes for the person(s) being assessed.

In fact, EBP initially focused largely on interventions. But when applied to psychological assessment, EBP highlights two somewhat different issues that shift the focus from the data-based evaluation of assessment instruments using psychometrically sound procedures.

The first issue relates to the greatly increased focus on understanding the nature of various psychopathologies as part of an effort to develop new and more precisely targeted interventions. Thus, assessment procedures and strategies, beginning with newly developed semistructured diagnostic interviews, have now been adapted to assess more thoroughly the intricacies and subtleties of various forms of psychopathology as our understanding of the nature of psychopathology deepens. For example, domains for assessment in the anxiety disorders necessarily differ from domains that might be assessed among individuals with depression, schizophrenia, or personality disorders (Antony & Rowa, 2005; Widiger & Samuel, 2005). Even issues outside of the usual boundaries of psychopathology, at least as defined by DSM, such as couples stress, require a more focused, conceptually based framework for assessment (Snyder, Heyman, & Haynes, 2005). Obviously, this is a substantial departure from simply administering a standardized battery of tests to individuals presenting for treatment, without regard to presenting psychopathology.

The second issue underscores that these strategies are closely linked to existing treatment options, with the expectation that progress will be monitored in each of the crucial domains to the point of outcome. Again, this was a stated goal of assessment from Shakow's perspective in 1969, but because of the commonly accepted standardized battery of tests of that era, this goal was seldom achieved or even pursued. It is worth noting, however, that this emphasis on ongoing outcomes assessment facilitates an interactive process that will improve treatment outcome, and there is some evidence already that this occurs (Lambert et al., 2003).

In summary, we have progressed from assessment based on a generalized comprehensive battery of tests without regard, for the most part, to presenting issues or problems, to a more evidence-based assessment process highlighting close integration with emerging conceptions of psychopathology. In addition, broad-based, ongoing outcomes assessment systems are increasingly required for EBP on the part of health-care policy makers.

Advances in psychological assessment are also greatly dependent on a broader and deeper understanding of psychopathology or related psychological processes that are the subject of assessment. This broader and deeper understanding is most evident in the radical changes in widely accepted systems of nosology over the decades. In 1980, the third edition of the DSM (DSM III) (APA, 1980) was published, reflecting a more empirical approach to classification of psychopathology. This document was updated in 1987 (DSM III-R, APA), 1994 (DSM-IV, APA), and 2000 (DSM IV-TR, APA), and the fifth edition of the DSM (DSM V) will appear in 2013. It is noteworthy that psychologists have played an increasingly large role in the development of this diagnostic system; for example psychologists comprised approximately half of the membership of the various work groups writing DSM-IV, and four psychologists (including Peter Nathan, editor of the Oxford Library of Psychology, of which this handbook is one volume, as well as the author [David H. Barlow]) were members of the Task Force that made all final decisions (APA, 1994). For DSM V, psychologists have taken the lead in beginning to move the system away from a psychometrically unsatisfactory prototypical categorical approach to a more dimensional approach (Brown & Barlow, 2009; Leyfer & Brown, Chapter 14, this volume; Widiger & Edmundson, Chapter 13, this volume). Although this rather radical revision will not be complete for DSM V, a wide consensus exists that dimensional approaches to nosology represent the future, and that increasingly sophisticated, empirically based psychological approaches to diagnosis and assessment will comprise the major mechanism in achieving this goal.

Therapy in 1969

Interestingly, the practice of psychotherapy in 1969 was perhaps the most underdeveloped role for psychologists for several reasons (see also Routh,

Chapter 2, this volume). First, very few psychologists were allowed to practice psychotherapy, and when they did, it was often under the direct supervision of a psychiatrist or another physician. This reflected the widely held position at that time that, since one could not separate mind and body (an assumption that has proved increasingly true over the decades), then one must have comprehensive training in both basic biological sciences (e.g., anatomy, biochemistry) as well as psychiatry to practice psychotherapy (an assumption that very few would hold today). A second reason was that very little was known about psychotherapy in terms of the types of problems that would respond to therapy, the psychological techniques and procedures one would use to accomplish therapeutic goals, and the necessary and optimal therapist qualities. Thus, Shakow recognized at that time the well-established social need for psychotherapists, but wondered just what sort of training would be necessary, and if this training should be preferentially associated with one of the mental health professions.

> My fundamental position . . . is that the practice of psychotherapy should not be determined by a person's particular discipline. Many years of observation in this area have led me to believe that so far as psychotherapy is concerned, the order of importance of the three factors integrally involved is first, the personal qualities of the therapist; second, the nature of the patient and his problem; and, third, the nature and adequacy of the therapist's training, especially in areas related to human psychology and motivation. Particular professional identification is not necessarily involved in these three.
> (*Shakow*, 1969, p. 64)

He goes on to remark that, upon referring a friend for psychotherapy, he would rely far more on the personal qualities of the therapists than on their professional training, while admitting that it would be hard to define these personal qualities in a standard manner that would be useful for research. Although Shakow stipulated that one very important topic for research by psychologists should be psychotherapy, Shakow's preferred directions for psychotherapy research are perhaps least developed due, of course, to the clear emphasis in that era on the more highly developed area of psychological assessment and the construction of psychological tests. It would be another decade before psychologists were generally afforded the privilege of practicing psychotherapy independently, and even then this was seldom possible in hospital or other clinical settings, dominated as they were by the medical profession.

Shakow did have some ideas about the ideal training for psychotherapists that would occur in independent institutes, perhaps located within a university or other clinical setting, but he clung to the idea that this institute should be open to all professions with an interest in psychotherapy and that some of the didactic material would come from contributions of the humanities and the biological sciences, as well as the core mental health professions. Although Shakow himself identified with psychoanalytic thinking, as did most mental health professionals in those days, he regarded psychoanalytic institutes as narrowly construed and not an ideal model for training in psychotherapy. Of course, research on the variety of evidence-based psychological procedures that would find their way into the armamentarium of psychologists engaged in treatment was only just beginning.

In fact, results from some of the first research studies of psychotherapy at that time were very discouraging, in that therapy had relatively little effect either positive or negative when results from treatment groups and comparison groups not receiving therapy were examined (Barlow & Hersen, 1984; Bergin, 1966; Bergin & Strupp, 1972). Classic early studies, such as the Cambridge Somerville Youth Study (Powers & Witmer, 1951), which took decades to complete, arrived at this finding, as did other early efforts involving large numbers of patients treated in approximations of randomized, controlled clinical trials (Barron & Leary, 1955). More process-based research conducted on large numbers of outpatients to the point where outcomes were examined came to similar conclusions. The eminent psychotherapy researcher Lester Luborsky and his colleagues (1975) pointed out the lack of specificity of any psychotherapeutic procedures. In this era, Eysenck (1952; 1965) published his famously controversial thesis based on data from crude actuarial tables that outcomes from psychotherapy across a heterogeneous group of patients were no better than rates of "spontaneous" improvement without psychotherapeutic intervention over varying periods of time. Although this conclusion was outrageous to many who were convinced of the power of psychotherapy, in that it seemed to fly in the face of clinical experience, it was enormously impactful since it was difficult to rebut based on the dearth of evidence available.

Thus, advocates of psychotherapy in those early years were faced with a paradox. On the one hand, many psychologists assumed that training in psychotherapy was important, although as noted by Shakow, there was no consensus on how to do it. On the other hand, psychotherapy research of the day, such as it was, could not substantiate the assumption that psychotherapy had any effect whatsoever, either positive or negative.

This state of affairs began to change in 1966, with the publication of a seminal article by Allen Bergin (1966) in the *Journal of Abnormal Psychology* entitled "Some implications of psychotherapy research for therapeutic practice" (see Barlow, 2010). What Bergin concluded, based on a further analysis of some preliminary data first published in Bergin (1963) was that "Psychotherapy may cause people to become better or worse adjusted than comparable people who do not receive such treatment" (p. 235). Bergin found, as did Eysenck, that "Typically, control subjects improve somewhat with the varying amounts of change clustering around the mean." But, contrary to Eysenck's conclusions, Bergin observed, "On the other hand, experimental subjects are typically dispersed all the way from marked improvement to marked deterioration" (Bergin, 1963). Thus, the data indicated that psychotherapy could make some people considerably better off than comparable untreated patients. This was the first objective evidence against Eysenck's assertion that all changes associated with psychotherapy were due to spontaneous remission. As Bergin noted: "Consistently replicated, this is a direct and unambiguous refutation of the oft-cited Eysenckian position" (p. 237). From a historical perspective, this was a very important conclusion from the point of view of both science and policy, but did little to provide direction to the fledgling endeavor of psychotherapy.

Bergin (1966), in the process of articulating his influential argument, also described the substantial deficits in extant studies of psychotherapy at that time and, in so doing, began to pave the way for marked improvements in psychotherapy research methods to unfold in the coming decades (Barlow, 2010). He observed, for example, that experimental and control groups were often not well matched with differences in initial severity on various measures, a common finding. He also pointed out that individuals assigned to control groups were often subject to substantial nonexperimental influences, including therapeutic intervention of various sorts occurring outside the context of the clinical trial. To account for these influences, he suggested the need to carefully ascertain if control groups were indeed acting as controls and/or to directly measure the

effects of nonexperimental influences that might affect outcomes. He also presented some preliminary data showing that training was an important variable if therapists were indeed to deliver the treatment as intended, contributing to what we now refer to as *treatment integrity* of the intervention under study (Hayes et al., 1999). This issue arose in some earlier studies in which therapists had little or no training, and it was unclear just what they were doing (Powers & Witmer, 1951).

In addition to these critiques of existing studies, Bergin and Strupp, in 1972, went on to suggest more proactive recommendations on the future conduct of psychotherapy research, recommendations that were to have substantial impact. One of the observations focused on the substantial individual differences among patients in these studies, particularly patients with emotional or behavioral disorders. They suggested that attempts to answer basic questions on the effectiveness (or ineffectiveness) of a specific treatment for a specific individual would be impossible when applying broad-based and ill-defined treatments such as *psychotherapy* to a heterogeneous group of clients only vaguely described using such labels as *neurosis*. This heterogeneous approach also characterized meta-analyses in that era (Smith & Glass, 1977). Thus, Bergin's review suggested that asking "Is psychotherapy effective?" was probably the wrong question. Bergin and Strupp (1972) cited Gordon Paul (1967), who suggested that psychotherapy researchers must start defining their interventions more precisely and must ask the question, "What specific treatment is effective with a specific type of client under what circumstances?" (p. 112).

Therapy in 2009

Although Shakow foresaw EBP, even he would be greatly surprised by the radically different nature of psychotherapy and psychological treatments in 2009, much of it made possible by improvements in the methods of psychotherapy research. In addition to experimental design considerations, methodological improvements included a deeper understanding of psychopathology, allowing for the development of more targeted psychological treatments; a greater specification of psychological treatments, often in the form of flexible manuals to better define ongoing therapeutic operations; and a new emphasis on comparative effectiveness research. What follows is a brief discussion of the development of treatment manuals and clinical practice guidelines, and a growing emphasis on change in the individual versus average change in the group. To illustrate some of the trends in therapy research over the decades, I also present an account of the development of a new psychological treatment for panic disorder as it occurred over the last 20 years in our Center.

Treatment Manuals and Clinical Practice Guidelines

The initial impetus for the development of treatment manuals came from psychodynamic psychotherapy researchers who, in the early 1960s, began to test broadly the effectiveness of specific treatments in controlled outcome studies. Looking to demonstrate that psychological interventions could withstand rigorous scientific investigation, similar to that of existing pharmacological treatments (Luborsky & DeRubeis, 1984), scientist-practitioners realized that they needed treatment tools that would allow for systematic replication and comparison. Wilson (1996) more specifically pointed out that treatment manuals sought to eliminate any "substantial variability" associated with "clinical judgment" or intuition that might cause one therapist to proceed in a very different manner from another. Thus, to study the effectiveness of these therapies, treatments were condensed into manuals that could then be reviewed and used across studies. Many researchers hoped that by utilizing treatment manuals presented in this fashion, psychological interventions would be able to withstand the methodological constraints of research protocols. More specifically, it was thought, "treatment manuals help support the internal validity of a given study by ensuring that a specific set of treatment procedures exists, that procedures are identifiable, and that they can be repeated in other investigations" (Dobson & Shaw, 1988). This was in contrast to the conduct of treatment outcome research prior to manualization, during which time specific therapeutic techniques were often not explained and thus could not be compared to other treatments or be replicated by other investigative groups, as in early studies already described.

Another push to develop specific treatment manuals came from the founding of the Agency for Health Care Policy and Research in the United States in 1989 (now called the Agency for Health Care Research and Quality). The sole purpose of this Agency was to facilitate the identification of the effectiveness of specific treatment strategies for specific disorders, with the aim of increasing the quality and reducing the cost of health care (Barlow, 1996). One major mechanism of accomplishing this goal was the creation of clinical practice guidelines that

explicitly articulate the optimal strategies for assessing and treating a variety of psychological disorders based on an up-to-date review of evidence. In 1995, the APA promulgated a template for evaluating and setting minimum standards for these guidelines (Barlow, 1996), and these criteria were revised in 2002 (APA, 2002). Interventions recommended in these clinical practice guidelines are typically based on two specific factors as derived from the APA template: (a) *efficacy*, or internal validity of the specific treatment, the determination of which is based on the results of a systematic evaluation of the intervention in a controlled setting; and (b) *effectiveness*, or clinical utility of the treatment, which is based on the feasibility, general relevance, and cost effectiveness of the intervention actually being delivered in a local setting. Based on these equally important and rigorous bases of evidence, the development of treatment manuals that could produce the necessary evidence was encouraged. As a result, manual-based treatments were incorporated in early schemes as one of the major components of evidence-based service delivery (Barlow, 2004).

An Emphasis on the Individual

Although examples of evidenced-based psychological treatments for the full range of psychopathology can be found in appropriate chapters throughout this handbook, one concern frequently expressed focused on the "one size fits all" rigidity seemingly inherent in the administration of manualized treatment. This issue derived directly from the nature of psychotherapy research emphasizing, as it did, the average response of a treated group.

In fact, early on, leaders in psychotherapy research, such as Bergin and Strupp, suggested that a more valid tool for looking at the effects of psychotherapy would involve a more intensive study of the individual. "Among researchers as well as statisticians there is a growing disaffection from traditional experimental designs and statistical procedures which are held inappropriate to the subject matter under study" (Bergin & Strupp, 1972, p. 440). They recommended the individual experimental case study as one of the primary strategies that would move the field of psychotherapy research forward, since changes of clinical significance could be directly observed in the individual under study (followed by replication on additional individuals). In such a way, changes could be clearly and functionally related to specific therapeutic procedures. These ideas contributed to the development of single-case experimental designs for studying behavior change (Barlow, Nock, & Hersen,

2009; Hersen & Barlow, 1976). These designs, then and now, play an important role not only in delineating the positive effects of therapy but also in observing more readily any deleterious effects that may emerge, thus complementing efforts to extract information on individuals from the response of a group in a clinical trial (Kazdin, 2003).

This emphasis on individual change of clinical and practical importance contributed to a revision of the ways in which data from large between-group experimental designs (clinical trials) were analyzed (Kazdin, 2003). Specifically, over the ensuing decades, psychotherapy researchers began to move away from exclusive reliance on the overall average group response on measures of change and began highlighting the extent of change (effect sizes and confidence intervals), whether the change was "clinically significant," and the number or percentage of individuals who actually achieved some kind of satisfactory response (with a passing nod to those who did not do well) (Jacobson & Truax, 1991). Data-analytic techniques also became more sophisticated, powerful, and valid, with a move away from comparison of means among groups to multivariate random effects procedures, such as latent growth curve and multilevel modeling, which evaluate the extent, patterns, and predictors of individual differences in change (Brown, 2007).

In addition to improved delineation and definition of the actual psychotherapeutic procedures undergoing evaluation, as noted earlier, an equally important development was a greater specification of those psychopathological processes that most often comprised the targets of change efforts. Over the ensuing decades, the very nature of psychopathology in its various manifestations became increasingly well understood and defined, based on research in this area. This led to the appearance of nosological conventions through which psychotherapy researchers could begin to reliably agree on what was being treated and how to measure change, as described earlier (Barlow, 1991). Investigators increasingly made use of this information to assess both the process and outcomes of interventions (Elkin et al., 1989). Thus, by the 1980s, the field was now specifying and operationalizing psychotherapeutic procedures, as well as associated therapist, client, and relationship factors, and also specifying and measuring the targets of treatments in the form of identifiable psychopathology in a way that highlighted individual differences in response. By the 1990s, publications of large clinical trials, some begun 10 years prior to publication, rapidly grew in number. In the

clinic, this new emphasis facilitated greater attention to flexibility in the administration of evidenced-based manualized treatments based on case formulation and a move toward individualized treatment modules (Chorpita, Bernstein, & Miranda, Chapter 11, this volume; Spring & Neville, Chapter 7, this volume). These trends and strategies are next profiled in an account of the development of a psychological treatment for panic disorder in our Center (Craske & Barlow, 2008) and the relative efficacy of this treatment.

The Development of a Psychological Treatment for Panic Disorder

In the 1980s, a physical problem—some kind of a brain dysfunction—was thought to cause panic disorder. The best candidate was a "chemical imbalance," which was believed to cause heightened sensitivity in the brainstem. By the 1990s, research had ruled this out as the sole underlying cause (Barlow, 2002; Gorman et al., 1990), and investigators agreed that an interacting web of biological and psychological factors contributed to the onset of panic disorder (Bouton, Mineka, & Barlow, 2001).

When the cause of panic disorder was thought to be solely biological, drugs were the first choice for treatment. In the 1980s, the most popular drugs for panic disorder were high-potency tranquilizers, known by brand names such as Xanax and Klonopin. These drugs could be effective for panic disorder, but many patients developed dependence, such that attempts to stop taking them produced serious side effects. Because of this problem with dependence and addiction, other drugs, such as selective serotonin reuptake inhibitors (SSRIs), became the preferred drugs for treating panic disorder. These drugs include brand names such as Paxil and Prozac. Approximately 50% of patients with panic disorder respond at least somewhat (and some very well), as long as they continue to take the medication. But relapse rates are high once the medication is stopped (Craske & Barlow, 2008).

Around 1990, my colleague, Michelle Craske, and I developed a psychological treatment for panic disorder that focused directly on the sensitivity of these individuals to their own physical sensations, such as fluctuating heart rate, skin temperature, and dizziness (Barlow & Craske, 2007; Craske & Barlow, 2007). In people who are susceptible, these sensations are very frightening because they come to trigger the next panic attack through the psychological process of learning and association called *conditioning* (Bouton et al., 2001).

Based on this insight, we experimented with a treatment in which individuals with panic disorder were exposed to mild versions of the physical sensations. In the protected setting of our clinic, we had them exercise vigorously to produce fluctuations in heart rate, spin around in a chair to produce slight dizziness, and so forth. We decided which symptoms would be induced based on an assessment of the mix of physical sensations that were closely associated with a particular patient's panic attacks (these vary from one person to another).

In a psychological process called *extinction*, our patients learned, by experiencing these physical sensations repeatedly, that the sensations didn't lead to a terrible outcome, such as a heart attack. Of course, their rational self knew this all along, but the emotional brain, where these fear responses reside, tends to override the rational brain in cases of panic or any emotional disorder. Hence, these specialized treatments to reach the emotional brain.

To assist in strengthening the "rational brain," the patients' basic faulty attitudes and perceptions about the dangerousness of these sensations are also identified and modified. Patients might also be taught calming techniques, such as breathing and meditation, to help them cope with stress and anxiety in general. In a number of subsequent studies, we demonstrated that this treatment, a cognitive-behavioral approach called *panic control treatment* (PCT), is effective for panic disorder (Barlow & Lehman, 1996).

My colleagues and I then tested the hypothesis that combining drugs and psychological treatments might prove more effective than either individual treatment alone. We conducted a large clinical trial and treated 312 patients with panic disorder at four different sites. Two of these sites were known for their expertise with drug treatments, and two were known for their expertise with cognitive-behavioral therapy (CBT). Patients at all sites were administered either the psychological or drug treatment alone, or in combination, along with appropriate comparison conditions such as a drug placebo condition. The experiment was also double-blind, which means that neither the therapists nor the patients knew whether they were getting the actual medication or the placebo (sugar) capsule (Barlow, Gorman, Shear, & Woods, 2000).

We found that both the drug and the psychological treatments were effective, as we expected, with each better than the placebo. But, much to our surprise, the combination treatment was not any better than the individual treatments. Thus, our

hypothesis was not proven, and the widespread practice of administering both treatments simultaneously for panic disorder was called into question. Furthermore, after all treatments were stopped, the psychological treatment was found to be more durable. That is, fewer people relapsed over a period of 6 months after treatment was stopped in those patients who had the psychological treatment either alone, or combined with placebo. In the two conditions in which patients received an active drug (drug alone or drug plus psychological treatment), more people relapsed.

We concluded from this evidence that combining treatments offered no advantages and that, given a choice, the preference would be for the psychological treatment because it was more durable and less intrusive. (Drug treatments are almost always considered more intrusive than psychological treatments due to side effects or drug interactions that could occur.) Of course, some patients prefer to take a drug, or the cognitive-behavioral treatment may not be available, in which case drug treatment is a good alternative.

In a second study (Barlow, 2008), colleagues and I evaluated best strategies for maintaining long-term health after treatment. We began with the working hypothesis that once patients received CBT and were essentially cured, they would not need any further treatment sessions. We based this assumption on the view of most of our therapists that no further intervention was needed if patients had learned all the concepts that the therapists had taught them and had implemented them well in daily life.

But not all of our therapists agreed. Some argued that occasional booster sessions would prove useful in preventing relapse over the long-term in this chronic condition. To test this notion, we treated 256 patients with panic disorder and agoraphobia of varying degrees of severity, using the same CBT that we employed in our first study. Many of these patients (157, or 61.3%) did very well with treatment and were essentially cured. To evaluate the advantage of booster sessions, half of these patients ($n = 79$) went on to receive nine additional sessions, spaced every month for 9 months, and they then were followed for another year with no further treatment. The other half of the patients ($n = 78$) received no further treatment.

When the results were assessed after the 1-year period without any treatment, the majority view was proved wrong. That is, there *was* an advantage to having booster sessions. Among the group that did not have booster sessions, 18.0% had some relapse or recurrence of panic disorder during the 1-year follow-up and 82.0% stayed well. By contrast, only 2.7% of the group that experienced booster sessions evidenced a relapse or recurrence during that year, and fully 97.3% stayed well. This significant difference demonstrates the value of some continued attention to these patients, who are, after all, suffering from a chronic condition that waxes and wanes.

Of the remaining patients—individuals who did not meet our criteria for "responding" to treatment to the point at which they were essentially cured—some dropped out along the way for a variety of reasons, such as moving away or just feeling they didn't need treatment anymore. Others finished treatment with varying responses from just missing our criteria for being all but "cured" to having no benefit whatsoever. In this latter group, we evaluated the benefits of then giving them a medication for panic disorder (paroxetine) and, although the results haven't been fully analyzed yet, sequencing the treatments in this way looks like a promising treatment approach.

Scientific discoveries about the nature of panic disorder led us to develop a specifically tailored psychological treatment. The experiments I've described confirm that we have an effective psychological treatment for panic disorder—a treatment that has become a first-line choice based on recommendations from National Health Services around the world. Of course, we still have a long way to go to make our treatments powerful enough to benefit the largest number of people.

Interestingly, our studies also confirm that a number of our assumptions were incorrect. First, we proved ourselves wrong that combining drug and psychological treatments would be better than simply providing patients with one treatment or the other. Second, we now know that individuals who respond to treatment need further attention after treatment has ended to ensure that they have the best chance to stay well. Without close scientific examination of the effects of psychological treatments, we would have been unaware of these important treatment issues, and patients with panic disorder would not be getting the best care possible.

Conclusion

Clinical psychology was a work in progress in 1969, and it continues to be a work in progress today. I have chosen to recount David Shakow's vision in three areas—training, assessment, and therapy—since his views of clinical psychology on these issues

circa 1969 make for a fascinating perspective on directions and progress of clinical psychology over the ensuing 40 years. Generally, the accuracy of Shakow's vision for the future is remarkable and attests to his status as one of the founding fathers of clinical psychology. But, of course, he could not have foreseen the explosive growth of the field and the substantial changes that would evolve in all of their detail despite accurately forecasting the broad outlines of these changes. It is perhaps in the area of training that Shakow has come closest to the mark in that a more fully realized Scientist-Practitioner model of clinical practice dominates the field of training. As I noted, in view of the ascendance of EBP, it seems that this model of training for clinical practice will become an even more uniform template for the training of clinical psychologists in the years to come. But it should also be noted that this does not mean that psychologists emanating from Scientist-Practitioner programs will necessarily be trained in the intricacies of the scientific method to an extent necessary to become clinical scientists. Continuing to model Shakow, some of my own predictions for the future of our science and profession can be found in Chapter 39, the concluding chapter. There, my coauthor and I hazard what might seem to be some rather radical predictions for the development of training in clinical psychology.

In the area of assessment and diagnosis, a component of EBP, evidence-based assessment, is beginning to exert considerable influence and is very likely the wave of the future. Although Shakow did not envision the enormous influence psychologists would have on creating an empirically based nosology, nor did he necessarily envision the deep and broad increases in our knowledge of the nature of psychopathology and psychological processes, it is clear that his vision of the general function of assessment has stood the test of time. In Chapter 39, we also speculate on future developments to the relationship of the nomothetic process of diagnosis and classification to the more idiographic process of functional assessment. These two processes take us well beyond the status of psychological assessment in 1969, which was largely relegated to the development of psychometrically sound psychological tests, although this remains an extraordinarily important contribution of psychologists to this day.

Finally, the greatest change has occurred in the development of psychological treatments. The example of treating panic disorder described earlier in the chapter is but one of many equally fascinating examples of the development of evidence-based psychological treatments and was chosen simply because I am most familiar with it. Other excellent examples are found throughout this handbook and represent the most remarkable advances in my own 40-year odyssey. Of course, we are just at the beginning stages of the development of evidence-based psychological interventions. In Chapter 39, the concluding chapter, we also provide some predictions on the further recognition, development, and dissemination of psychological treatments and the kinds of efforts and trends that are likely to occur in service of these goals. To take one example, we suggest that the specific treatment of panic disorder developed in our clinic ("panic control treatment") is unlikely to be practiced in any kind of a systematic way in 10–15 years time. By that time, new psychological treatments based on our ever-deepening knowledge of psychopathology will likely focus on common therapeutic principles applicable to fundamental psychopathological processes found across the full range of emotional disorders. Similar developments will take place in other broad areas of psychopathology, which will increasingly be conceptualized along dimensions of traits and temperaments, suggesting new, more fundamental targets for treatment.

Of course, many of these developments are relatively new and do not yet characterize in any comprehensive sense the current practice of psychotherapy, which is very heterogeneous indeed. In the meantime, standing on the shoulders of the giants in our field over the past 40 years, the chapters in this handbook represent a breadth and depth of knowledge in the ever-expanding field of clinical psychology that would make David Shakow, and all of our forebears, proud.

References

American Psychiatric Association. (1968). *Diagnostic and statistical manual of mental disorders* (2nd ed.). Washington DC: Author.

American Psychiatric Association. (1980). *Diagnostic and statistical manual of mental disorders* (3rd ed.). Washington DC: Author.

American Psychiatric Association. (1987). *Diagnostic and statistical manual of mental disorders* (3rd, revised ed.). Washington DC: Author.

American Psychiatric Association. (1994). *Diagnostic and statistical manual of mental disorders* (4th ed.). Washington DC: Author.

American Psychiatric Association. (2000). *Diagnostic and statistical manual of mental disorders* (4th, text revision ed.). Washington DC: Author.

American Psychological Association. (2002). Criteria for evaluating treatment guidelines. *American Psychologist, 57,* 1052–1059.

American Psychological Association. (2006). Evidence-based practice in psychology. *American Psychologist, 61*(4), 271–285.

Antony, M. M., & Rowa, K. (2005). Evidence-based assessment of anxiety disorders in adults. *Psychological Assessment, 17*(3), 256–266.

Barlow, D. H. (1991). Introduction to the special Issue on diagnosis, dimensions, & DSM-IV: The science of classification. *Journal of Abnormal Psychology, 100,* 243–244.

Barlow, D. H. (1996). Health care policy, psychotherapy research, and the future of psychotherapy. *American Psychologist, 51*(10), 1050–1058.

Barlow, D. H. (2002). *Anxiety and its disorders: The nature and treatment of anxiety and panic* (2nd ed.). New York: The Guilford Press.

Barlow, D. H. (2004). Psychological treatments. *American Psychologist, 59*(9), 869–878.

Barlow, D. H. (2005). What's new about evidence-based assessment? *Psychological Assessment, 17*(3), 308–311.

Barlow, D. H. (2008, October). The power of psychological treatments: Implications for the future. *Invited address at the 5th World Congress on Psychotherapy.* Beijing, China.

Barlow, D. H. (2010). Negative effects from psychological treatments: A perspective. *American Psychologist, 65*(1), 13–20.

Barlow, D. H., & Craske, M. G. (2007). *Mastery of your anxiety and panic: Workbook* (4th ed.). New York: Oxford University Press.

Barlow, D. H., Gorman, J. M., Shear, M. K., & Woods, S. W. (2000). Cognitive-behavioral therapy, imipramine, or their combination for panic disorder: A randomized controlled trial. *JAMA, 283,* 2529–2536.

Barlow, D. H., Hayes, S. C., & Nelson, R. O. (1984). *The scientist-practitioner: Research and accountability in clinical settings.* New York: Pergamon Press.

Barlow, D. H., & Hersen, M. (1984). *Single case experimental designs: Strategies for studying behavior change* (2nd ed.). New York: Pergamon Press.

Barlow, D. H., & Lehman, C. L. (1996). Advances in the psychosocial treatment of anxiety disorders. Implications for national health care. *Archives of General Psychiatry, 53*(8), 727–735.

Barlow, D. H., Nock, M. K., & Hersen, M. (2009). *Single case experimental designs: Strategies for studying behavior change* (3rd ed.). Boston: Pearson Allyn & Bacon.

Barron, F., & Leary, T. F. (1955). Changes in psychoneurotic patients with and without psychotherapy. *Journal of Consulting Psychology, 19*(4), 239–245.

Bergin, A. E. (1963). The effects of psychotherapy: Negative results revisited. *Journal of Counseling Psychology, 10,* 224–250.

Bergin, A. E. (1966). Some implications of psychotherapy research for therapeutic practice. *Journal of Abnormal Psychology, 71*(4), 235–246.

Bergin, A. E., & Strupp, H. H. (1972). *Changing frontiers in the science of psychotherapy.* Chicago: Aldine Atherton Inc.

Bouton, M. E., Mineka, S., & Barlow, D. H. (2001). A modern learning theory perspective on the etiology of panic disorder. *Psychological Review, 108*(1), 4–32.

Brown, T. A. (2007). *Confirmatory factor analysis for applied research.* New York: Guilford Press.

Brown, T. A., & Barlow, D. H. (2009). A proposal for a dimensional classification system based on the shared features of the DSM-IV anxiety and mood disorders: Implications for assessment and treatment. *Psychological Assessment, 21*(3), 256–271.

Craske, M. G., & Barlow, D. H. (2007). *Mastery of your anxiety and panic: Therapist guide* (4th ed.). New York: Oxford University Press.

Craske, M. G., & Barlow, D. H. (2008). Panic disorder and agoraphobia. In D. H. Barlow (Ed.), *Clinical handbook of psychological disorders* (4th ed., pp. 1–64). New York: The Guilford Press.

Dobson, K. S., & Shaw, B. F. (1988). The use of treatment manuals in cognitive therapy: experience and issues. *Journal of Consulting and Clinical Psychology, 56*(5), 673–680.

Elkin, I., Shea, M. T., Watkins, J. T., Imber, S. D., Sotsky, S. M., Collins, J. F., et al. (1989). National Institute of Mental Health Treatment of Depression Collaborative Research Program. General effectiveness of treatments. *Archives of General Psychiatry, 46*(11), 971–982; discussion 983.

Exner, J. E. (2001). A comment on "The misperception of psychopathology: Problems with the norms of the Comprehensive System for the Rorschach." *Clinical Psychology: Science and Practice, 8,* 386–388.

Eysenck, H. J. (1952). The effects of psychotherapy: An evaluation. *Journal of Consulting Psychology, 16*(5), 319–324.

Eysenck, H. J. (1965). The effects of psychotherapy. *International Journal of Psychiatry, 1,* 99–178.

Garmezy, N., & Holzman, P. (1984). David Shakow (1901–1981). *American Psychologist, 39*(6), 698–699.

Gorman, J. M., Goetz, R. R., Dillon, D., Liebowitz, M. R., Fyer, A. J., Davies, S., et al. (1990). Sodium D-lactate infusion of panic disorder patients. *Neuropsychopharmacology, 3*(3), 181–189.

Hayes, S. C., Barlow, D. H., & Nelson-Gray, R. O. (1999). *The scientist-practitioner: Research and accountability in the age of managed care* (2nd ed.). Boston: Allyn & Bacon.

Hersen, M., & Barlow, D. H. (1976). *Single case experimental designs: Strategies for studying behavior change.* New York: Pergamon Press.

Insel, T. R. (2009). Translating scientific opportunity into public health impact: a strategic plan for research on mental illness. *Archives of General Psychiatry, 66*(2), 128–133.

Institute of Medicine. (2001). *Crossing the quality chasm: A new health system for the 21st century.* Washington DC: National Academy Press.

Jacobson, N. S., & Truax, P. (1991). Clinical significance: a statistical approach to defining meaningful change in psychotherapy research. *Journal of Consulting and Clinical Psychology, 59*(1), 12–19.

Kaslow, N. J. (2004). Competencies in professional psychology. *American Psychologist, 59*(8), 774–781.

Kaslow, N. J., Rubin, N. J., Leigh, I. W., Portnoy, S., Lichtenberg, J., Smith, I. L., et al. (2006). *American Psychological Association Task Force on the Assessment of Competence in Professional Psychology.* Washington DC: American Psychological Association.

Kazdin, A. (2003). *Research design in clinical psychology.* Boston: Allyn & Bacon.

Korman, M. (Ed.). (1976). *Levels and patterns of professional training in psychology.* Washington DC: American Psychological Association.

Lambert, M.J., Whipple, J.L., Hawkins, E.J., Vermeersch, D.A., Nielsen, S.L., & Smart, D.W. (2003). Is it time for clinicians to routinely track patient outcome? A meta-analyses. *Clinical Psychology: Science & Practice, 10,* 288–301.

Luborsky, L., & DeRubeis, R. J. (1984). The use of psychotherapy treatment manuals: A small revolution in psychotherapy research style. *Clinical Psychology Review, 4,* 5–14.

Luborsky, L., Singer, B., & Luborsky, L. (1975). Comparative studies of psychotherapies: Is it true that "everyone has won and all must have prizes"? *Archives of General Psychiatry, 32,* 995–1008.

McFall, R. M. (1991). Manifesto for a science of clinical psychology. *Clinical Psychologist, 44,* 75–88.

McHugh, R. K., & Barlow, D. H. (2010). Dissemination and implementation of evidence-based psychological treatments: A review of current efforts. *American Psychologist, 65*(2), 73–84.

Norcross, J. C., Karpiak, C. P., & Santoro, S. O. (2005). Clinical psychologists across the years: the division of clinical psychology from 1960 to 2003. *Journal of Clinical Psychology, 61*(12), 1467–1483.

Paul, G. L. (1967). Strategy of outcome research in psychotherapy. *Journal of Consulting Psychology, 31*(2), 109–118.

Powers, E., & Witmer, H. (1951). *An experiment in the prevention of delinquency: The Cambridge Somerville Youth Study.* New York: Columbia University Press.

Raimy, V. C. (Ed.). (1950). *Training in clinical psychology (Boulder Conference).* New York: Prentice Hall.

Roe, A., Gustad, J. W., Moore, B. V., Ross, S., & Skodak, M. (1959). *Graduate education in psychology. Report of the conference sponsored by the E&T Board.* Washington DC: American Psychological Association.

Shakow, D. (1969). *Clinical psychology as science and profession: A 40-year odyssey.* Chicago: Aldine.

Shakow, D. (1976). What is clinical psychology? *American Psychologist, 31*(8), 553–560.

Smith, M. L., & Glass, G. V. (1977). Meta-analysis of psychotherapy outcome studies. *American Psychologist, 32*(9), 752–760.

Snyder, D. K., Heyman, R. E., & Haynes, S. N. (2005). Evidence-based approaches to assessing couple distress. *Psychological Assessment, 17*(3), 288–307.

Strother, C. R. (1956). *Psychology and mental health.* Washington DC: American Psychological Association.

Widiger, T. A., & Samuel, D. B. (2005). Evidence-based assessment of personality disorders. *Psychological Assessment, 17*(3), 278–287.

Wilson, G. T. (1996). Manual-based treatments: the clinical application of research findings. *Behaviour Research and Therapy, 34*(4), 295–314.

Witmer, L. (1907/1996). Clinical psychology. *American Psychologist, 51,* 248–251.

Wood, J. M., Nezworski, M. T., Garb, H. N., & Lilienfeld, S. O. (2001). The misperception of psychopathology: Problems with the norms of the Comprehensive System for the Rorschach. *Clinical Psychology: Science and Practice, 8,* 350–373.

PART 2

History, Professional Issues, and Emerging Approaches to Psychopathology and Treatment

A History of Clinical Psychology

Donald K. Routh

Abstract

To be memorable, a history such as this might best be organized under a small number of headings. Accordingly, this chapter is structured around the work of seven pioneers who arguably had the greatest influence on the development of the field. Lightner Witmer is generally considered to have founded clinical psychology in 1896 (McReynolds, 1987, 1997; Routh, 1996; Watson, 1956). Hippocrates was the ancient Greek founder of medicine, always a close professional cousin of clinical psychology and a scientific model for psychology in general. Theodule Ribot led the development of psychology as an academic discipline in 19th-century France, as one primarily focused on clinical issues. Alfred Binet, also in France, devised the first practical "intelligence" test in 1905; administering such tests was among the most common activities of early clinical psychologists. Leta Hollingworth was an early practitioner who played a large role in the development of organized clinical psychology beginning in 1917 (Routh, 1994). Sigmund Freud founded psychoanalysis, the first influential form of psychotherapy practiced by clinical psychologists, among others. Finally, Hans Eysenck was among the earliest to conceptualize behavior therapy and to promote the use of what have come to be known as evidence-based methods of intervention in clinical psychology.

Keywords: Binet, Eysenck, Freud, Hippocrates, Hollingworth, Ribot, Witmer

Clinical psychologists have become familiar figures in America and in many countries around the world (Swierc & Routh, 2003). Indeed, clinical work now seems to be the most common activity of psychologists. They carry out psychotherapy or other interventions with individuals, groups, and families. They engage in various kinds of clinical assessment of the mental and behavioral aspects of health problems. Many collaborate with other health professionals or act as consultants in clinics and hospitals. Clinical psychologists are frequently involved in educational activities, teaching in colleges or universities, and many are also engaged in research. Despite its familiarity, this field had its origins in 1896, not much more than a century ago. This chapter attempts to provide a vivid portrait of its roots.

Hippocrates

To speak of "clinical" psychology is to invoke the medical metaphor of care at the bedside of the individual (the Greek word *klinein* refers to a couch or bed). In naming clinical psychology, Lightner Witmer thus alluded to the tradition of Hippocrates. Born on the Greek island of Cos about 460 BCE, Hippocrates is considered to be the founder of medicine. In using the word "clinical," Witmer implied that it is appropriate for psychology, like medicine, to attempt to help individuals.

Medicine is not only a profession but also a scientific field and, as such, served as a model for psychology in general. In comparing the Hippocratic writings to the previous Greek tradition of the god Asclepias, the most notable characteristic is Hippocrates' naturalism, the idea that the phenomena of human illnesses can be understood and explained in scientific terms. A famous example concerns epilepsy, often labeled in ancient Greece as a "sacred" disease. Seizures were thus explained as possession of the body by some invisible spirit. In contrast, Hippocrates and his followers believed that epilepsy was no more divine than any other illness and that its causes could be understood in natural terms (Temkin, 1994).

In addition to the name of Hippocrates, so familiar to accounts of Western medicine, the origins of modern scientific medicine can also be traced to various sources outside Europe, for example, ancient China, India, Egypt, and various smaller indigenous groups. In China, the best known ancient source of medical wisdom is the *Yellow Emperor's Classic of Internal Medicine*, probably written in the late first century BCE. This book discusses such well-known concepts as yin and yang; the Five Elements; the effects of diet, lifestyle, emotions, and the environment on health; how diseases develop; and the principles of acupuncture (Veith, 2002).

In ancient India, Ayurvedic medicine evolved over several millennia and appeared in writing about 2,000 years ago. The Sanskrit term, *ayur* means "life," and the term *veda*, "science or knowledge." The Ayurveda describes the constitution of the body (*prakriti*) and the operation of life forces (*doshas*), made up of the elements ether, air, fire, water, and earth. Ayurvedic treatments rely heavily on the use of herbs and plants (Lodha & Bagga, 2001).

Our knowledge of ancient Egyptian medicine is fragmentary. Examples of well-known sources include the Edwin Smith Papyrus and the Ebers Papyrus. The Edwin Smith Papyrus was written in about the 16th century BCE, based on material from perhaps a thousand years earlier. It outlines a series of 48 traumatic injury cases, including a discussion of the physical examination, treatment, and prognosis of each. Of special interest to psychologists are its descriptions of the cranial sutures, meninges, external surface of the brain, cerebral spinal fluid, and existence of a pulse in cerebral blood vessels (Breasted, 1922). The Ebers Papyrus, written in about 1550 BCE, includes a description of mental disorders, including depression and dementia. Like Hippocrates, the ancient Egyptians seemed to think of mental and physical disorders in much the same terms.

It seems that the culture of just about every human group includes concepts of health and illness, including what psychologists consider to be mental disorders, as well as ideas about how these problems should be managed. The Florida Seminole tribe, to give a modern example, considers the role of its medicine people an important one, which requires about eight years of intensive training to master and requires extensive knowledge of herbal treatments (West, 1998).

Many of the founders and influential researchers in the modern academic discipline of psychology, including Wilhelm Wundt, William James, Hermann Helmholtz, and Ivan Pavlov, were physicians by education, but they were scientists and scholars rather than practitioners of medicine. Wilhelm Wundt (Witmer's teacher at the University of Leipzig), who is generally credited with founding the first psychology laboratory in 1879, was medically trained, but not a practicing physician. Wundt carried out research in psychology, edited a journal, wrote books summarizing research in the field, and trained many of the first generation of experimental (or "physiological") psychologists, including Americans as well as Europeans (Benjamin, Durkin, Link, Vestal, & Accord, 1992). Although he was primarily devoted to basic research in psychology, Wundt maintained an interest in what today might be called mental health issues. Among Wundt's students and research collaborators was Emil Kraepelin, one of the leading psychiatrists of Germany during the late 19th and early 20th centuries (Kraepelin, 1962). Kraepelin studied manic-depressive disorder and conceptualized "dementia praecox" (the mental disorder now termed schizophrenia). He established psychology laboratories in mental hospitals under his direction, and studied experimentally the effects of alcohol and morphine on human reaction time.

William James, who is considered to be the founder of modern psychology in the United States, was also trained as a physician, but chose not to practice medicine. James spent his career teaching physiology, psychology, and philosophy at Harvard University, and wrote the classic two-volume textbook on *The Principles of Psychology* (James, 1890). Like Wundt, James maintained an academic interest in what we would now call mental health, as manifested by his 1896 Lowell Lectures on Exceptional Mental States (Taylor, 1983).

Another example of the influence of medicine on general psychology is provided by the work of Hermann Helmholtz. Helmholtz was born in Prussia in 1821, and he went on to become a world-recognized figure in several scientific fields, including physics, physiology, medicine, and psychology (Cahan, 1993). In terms of contributions to psychology and what is now called neuroscience, Helmholtz was the first to actually measure the speed of the nerve impulse in several different species. Some of his best-known scientific work on vision and hearing utilized his background in several areas, including mathematics, physics, physiology, and psychology. What is known as the Young-Helmholtz theory of color vision hypothesized the existence of three separate types of receptors in the retina for light of different wavelengths, corresponding to red, green, and violet. Subsequent research indeed demonstrated three different types of cone cells in the retina, with visual pigments responding to different wavelengths. In terms of the functioning of the auditory system, Helmholtz believed that the cochlea, the main sensory organ of the inner ear, worked something like a piano, with different strings vibrating to different frequency in sounds transmitted to it. Helmholtz also developed a theory of visual perception as an empirical process—in other words, one developed through experience. According to this theory, which continues to be influential, people engage in "unconscious inferences" in order to combine various cues about how far away objects are. During his time as a professor of physiology at the University of Heidelberg, Helmholtz served as supervisor to a younger colleague named Wilhelm Wundt. Thus, in effect, he taught some experimental psychology to the man who later became known as its "founder."

A final example of the influence of medicine on general psychology is provided by the career of the Russian scientist, Ivan Pavlov, who received the Nobel Prize for Medicine or Physiology in 1904, for his work on digestive processes. Born in 1849, Pavlov attended what was then called the Medical-Surgical Academy in St. Petersburg, the leading medical school of Russia. Rather than going into medical practice, though, Pavlov spent his career as a researcher. He developed a special chronic physiological procedure, isolating a separate pouch within a dog's stomach so that digestive juices could be collected from it. He was thus able to carry out a systematic program of research on the neural control of digestive processes in the dog. His laboratory worked out an arrangement in which about 15 medical students at a time seeking doctoral degrees could be employed as research collaborators, a veritable factory of physiologists (Todes, 2002). By about 1902, even before he received the Nobel Prize, Pavlov had decided to change the overall direction of his research toward work on what became known as "conditioned reflexes." Thus, he began what the world came to recognize as pioneering research in experimental psychology. Like humans and other animals, dogs do not just salivate when they actually eat, but as a result of just smelling the food, looking at it in a dish, or the appearance in the room of the person who is about to feed them. Pavlov used salivation to study processes now familiar to all psychologists, including conditioning, extinction, generalization, discrimination, and many others, including the disturbed behaviors called "experimental neuroses" that can be observed in the laboratory setting. His *Lectures on Conditioned Reflexes* were translated into English in 1927, and the concepts of conditioning have been influential throughout the world since that time.

Unquestionably, the psychological research of scientists such as Helmholtz and Pavlov has great "clinical" relevance, for example in ophthalmology and gastroenterology, but these workers are not usually regarded as clinical psychologists, because their work was not directly concerned with mental health, and they were not directly involved in trying to help individuals.

Theodule Ribot

Although clinical psychology as such did not originate there, France had a central role in the development of both psychiatry and neurology. French psychology, when it did develop under the leadership of Theodule Ribot (1839–1916), had its principal focus on the study of psychopathology (Nicolas & Murray, 1999). The French physician Philippe Pinel is generally considered to be the father of psychiatry as a medical specialty (Riese, 1969). Not long after the French Revolution of 1789, Pinel joined Jean-Baptiste Pussin in removing the chains from the mental patients in the Bicetre and Salpetriere hospitals in Paris. During the 19th century, the eminent neurologist Jean Charcot also worked at the Salpetriere Hospital, where he pioneered in the use of hypnosis in the treatment of patients with "hysteria" (Guillain, 1959). Ribot, the founder of French psychology, had Charcot as one of his teachers.

Ribot wrote an influential book about what was happening in psychology in Germany and England, and founded a journal to introduce his French colleagues to the psychological research going on in these countries. In 1881, Ribot published a second book, *Disorders of Memory*. Summarizing the existing research on memory, he developed the generalization now known as "Ribot's Law," stating that, in retrograde amnesia associated with brain damage, it is the most recent memories that tend to be lost, sparing the older ones. In some of his other writings, Ribot described the phenomenon of *anhedonia*, a loss of pleasure in daily activities, which is typical of persons experiencing mental depression and schizophrenia. In 1885, Ribot was made professor of psychology at the Sorbonne, and in 1888, he was given a chair in experimental and comparative psychology at the prestigious College de France.

The pattern in France was for any psychologist who wished to provide clinical services to individuals to go to medical school and become a neurologist or psychiatrist. Thus, Pierre Janet did his dissertation in psychology in 1889, under Ribot, and then completed a medical thesis under Charcot in 1892, on the mental states of persons with hysteria. It was Janet who coined the term "dissociation," and who first described multiple personality disorder. He also described "psychasthenia," better known today as obsessive-compulsive disorder. In addition, Janet developed a variety of psychotherapy techniques, considered by some to be an important rival of Freud's psychoanalysis (Janet, 1924).

Lightner Witmer

The term "clinical psychology" was first used in an article by Lightner Witmer (1867–1956), a psychology professor at the University of Pennsylvania, in the inaugural issue of a new journal he began to publish in 1907, *The Psychological Clinic*. Its 19th-century founders considered the modern discipline of psychology to be a science analogous to physiology; indeed, it was often labeled as "physiological psychology" for that reason. Witmer's idea was simply that if this new science was worthwhile, it ought to be possible to use its principles to help individuals with various problems. In other words, he thought that psychology should be an area of professional practice, as well as a science, and history has vindicated this concept.

The work of Witmer had some of its roots in France, but not in the work of Ribot or Janet. Witmer was most interested in the attempts of J. R. Pereira and J. M. Itard to teach language to nonverbal children, including the so-called Wild Boy of Aveyron, and the procedures developed by Edouard Seguin to remediate children with intellectual disabilities (Routh, del Barrio, & Carpintero, 1996).

Before going into psychology, Witmer taught English in a Philadelphia preparatory school (McReynolds, 1997). As a teacher, he encountered a student who was progressing poorly in his schoolwork. Witmer tried to help the youngster overcome these academic problems and learned that the boy had specific difficulty with language, including speaking and reading. The boy seemed to benefit from Witmer's efforts in his behalf.

Like many psychologists of his generation, Witmer went abroad to study and eventually obtained his doctorate under the direction of Wilhelm Wundt at the University of Leipzig. Wundt trained more American doctorate students in psychology than any other individual in the 19th century. When Witmer returned to the United States after his graduate training, he took a position as a faculty member in psychology at the University of Pennsylvania.

In 1896, Witmer founded the first psychology clinic at the University of Pennsylvania. Margaret McGuire, a student in one of his classes, was a schoolteacher with a student who had difficulty in learning to spell. She asked her professor if he could possibly help with this problem. Witmer reasoned that if this new scientific psychology was really worthwhile, it ought to be able to help with such problems. The boy was brought to Witmer and studied intensively, using various available psychological laboratory procedures. Many of these procedures, such as the study of reaction time, taken from Wundt's work, have not continued to be used clinically. In any case, on this basis, remedial educational strategies were devised and carried out. These seemed to be helpful. Soon, other individuals were brought to the new clinic, most of them children with problems of academic delay or deviant behavior. As the clinic grew, its staff came to involve PhD students in psychology and a social worker. Also, various physicians were asked to consult on the cases, including a neurologist and an ear, nose, and throat specialist. Witmer presented his ideas for the professional application of psychology to his colleagues at the American Psychological Association (APA) in December, 1896 (Witmer, 1897). Their reaction seemed to be lukewarm at best.

Witmer's graduate students in psychology at the University of Pennsylvania were offered professional training in diverse areas well beyond what might now be considered clinical psychology, branching out to include what is now considered school psychology, speech pathology (Twitmyer & Nathanson, 1932), vocational assessment and guidance (Brotemarkle, 1931), and industrial psychology (Viteles, 1932). His journal, the *Psychological Clinic*, begun in 1907, continued in publication irregularly into the 1930s, for a total of 23 volumes.

It is a historical curiosity that the professional specialty developed by Witmer more closely resembled the modern field of school psychology than what is now thought of as clinical psychology (Fagan, 1996). It is the APA Division of School Psychology, rather than the clinical division, that has chosen to give an annual Lightner Witmer Award. Witmer worked primarily with children, rather than adults and was more concerned with their academic and cognitive functioning than with their emotional life. He was not much influenced by the French clinical tradition pioneered by Charcot and Janet, and completely rejected the work of Sigmund Freud. Witmer favored educationally oriented interventions rather than psychotherapy or behavior therapy, and the medical procedure he most advocated was the surgical operation of removing a child's adenoids as a way of facilitating normal speech development.

Alfred Binet

Alfred Binet (1857–1911) was originally trained as a lawyer, and taught himself psychology on the basis of his own reading. He was influenced by individuals such as Ribot, the founder of French psychology, and the famous neurologist Charcot. Binet spent most of his career as an experimental psychologist, and founded an annual psychology journal, the first of its kind in France. In 1905, in response to a request from the ministry of education, Binet and his physician colleague Theodore Simon developed what became known as the first practical "intelligence test" for children (Binet & Simon, 1905). All of its items met the criterion of a demonstrated increase with age in the percent of children passing them, and the test thus enabled the examiner to estimate the child's "mental age" or level of intellectual maturity.

Binet's test materials continued to be used in France informally to gauge children's profiles of cognitive performance in different areas (Schneider, 1992). In English-speaking countries, though, the development and interpretation of the test took some different directions. For example, in Britain, its scores were interpreted in terms of Francis Galton's theory of intelligence as a mostly inherited personal characteristic (Galton, 1892). The concept of a ratio of mental age to chronological age, originating with the German psychologist William Stern (1912), was used to generate an "intelligence quotient" or IQ, although subsequently the ratio IQ was replaced by standard scores based on a comparison of the examinee to others the same age. Even before the development of Binet's test, Charles Spearman (1904) had noted the tendency of scores on cognitive test items to correlate with each other ("positive manifold"), and he interpreted their scores as a measure of general ability or "g," which he hypothesized as a single factor underlying test performance. The American psychologist Henry Goddard had Binet's

test translated into English and validated its ability to diagnose what is now called intellectual disability in children (Zenderland, 1998). Lewis Terman refined and standardized Binet's test in a version that became known as the "Stanford Binet" and provided quantitative norms for it based on a sizable sample of American children (Terman, 1916). Terman's subsequent research followed a group of "gifted" children (with exceptionally high Binet scores) throughout their lives and demonstrated that the test significantly predicted their academic and vocational accomplishments (Terman, 1975).

Soon, the most common activity for practitioners of the newly emerging profession of clinical psychologists in America came to be the administration of individual Binet tests, mostly to children, in clinics, schools, and hospitals. In 1908, the first formal psychology internship program began at the Vineland School, a New Jersey institution for those with intellectual disabilities (Routh, 2000).

Leta Hollingworth

On December 28, 1917, Leta Hollingworth, J. E. Wallace Wallin, and others founded a new professional organization, the American Association of Clinical Psychologists (AACP) (Routh, 1994). It was the first clinical psychology organization, and a direct ancestor of the present-day Society of Clinical Psychology (Division 12 of the APA). On a global level, clinical psychology shares representation as a division of the International Association of Applied Psychology, founded in 1920. Although Wallin was the president of the AACP in the United States and Hollingworth only the secretary, her name is better remembered today. Hollingworth (1886–1939) suggested in 1918 the possibility of a distinct professional degree for practitioners, which she labeled the PsD, or Doctor of Psychology. This suggestion foreshadowed the PsyD degree, now perhaps the most common type of training for clinical psychologists in the United States, and the DClinPsy degree for clinical psychologists in the United Kingdom, now offered by Oxford University, among other academic institutions. Hollingworth also argued for the legitimacy of clinical psychologists as expert witnesses in court.

The AACP only lasted for 2 years as an organization. In 1919, it was assimilated by the APA as its "Clinical Section," and met annually as part of the APA conventions. For a time, the APA tried to set up a procedure for certifying "consulting psychologists," but this did not work out very well and was soon discontinued. The APA Clinical Section dissolved itself in 1937, becoming one of the several sections of the new American Association for Applied Psychology. This group continued until 1945, when the AAAP and the APA were consolidated into a new version of the American Psychological Association, which kept the name of the old APA but adopted the structure of the AAAP. The Clinical Section of the AAAP thus became Division 12 of the APA, where it remains today, as the Society of Clinical Psychology. Other national organizations of clinical psychologists, such as that in Britain, mostly did not emerge until after World War II.

Leta Hollingworth is also remembered today as a pioneer advocate of women's rights. In her day, in the early 1900s, most of the clinical psychologists were men, but now most of them are women. A diary kept by Leta's mother reported her father's reaction to her birth in 1886: "I'd give a thousand dollars it if was a boy" (quoted in Klein, 2002, p. 17). Despite this unpromising reception, Leta Stetter was so precocious that she taught herself to read before she entered school. She became a freshman at the University of Nebraska at age 16, and graduated Phi Beta Kappa 4 years later, an occasion for which she was asked to write the class poem. She became a high school teacher and assistant principal. After her marriage to Harry Hollingworth, she moved to New York City, where he entered a PhD program in psychology at Columbia University. Her application for a job as a high school teacher was turned down because the New York City Board of Education had a rule against hiring married women as teachers. She began to take some graduate classes at Columbia, but was turned down for a fellowship because she was a woman. It is thus quite understandable that Leta Hollingworth then became active in the New York Suffrage Party, seeking the vote for women. Harry Hollingworth received his PhD in psychology in 1909, and began teaching at Barnard College, the women's branch of Columbia University. He was hired in 1911 by the Coca Cola Company to carry out research using double-blind procedures on the behavioral effects of caffeine. He hired Leta as assistant director of this project, thus initiating her scientific career in psychology. The funds from the Coca Cola project ultimately allowed Leta to enroll as a graduate student in psychology at Teachers College, Columbia University, where she later studied under Edward L. Thorndike. After receiving her master's degree, she took a part-time job administering Binet tests, an experience that introduced her to clinical psychology. Leta's research in this PhD program showed no relationship between women's menstrual status and their performance on tasks in the psychology laboratory. It also failed to support the hypothesis, then a popular one, that women's intellectual performance is more variable than that of men. After receiving her PhD, she moved on to a career as a professor at Teachers College, Columbia University, where she became a pioneer in the education of gifted schoolchildren (Klein, 2002).

The original rationale for the AACP organization centered on the role of clinical psychologists in administering and interpreting intelligence tests. Once Binet's test was translated into English, it came into wide use in the United States. Wallace Wallin and others argued that this test should only be used by persons who had both academic training in psychology and relevant supervised experience, not by schoolteachers untrained in psychology or by experimental psychologists with no practicum training. The hope was that the new organization would be able to certify and regulate these and other types of "consulting psychologists." The APA attempted for a time to set up such a professional certification procedure, but this did not work. It was not until 1977 that all U.S. states provided statutory licensing for psychologists.

Despite Lightner Witmer's initial emphasis on the importance of intervention and remediation, clinical psychologists during the era before World War II were primarily involved in assessment activities, using not only the Binet and other such intelligence tests, but also in the broader domain of personality. Lewis M. Terman, one of the original members of the AACP and a certified "consulting psychologist," did research further developing the Binet test. He refined and expanded the pool of Binet items, had them administered in a more standardized way, and collected systematic normative data on the performance of children of different ages, producing the "Stanford Binet" test in 1916, which came into common use internationally. Terman initiated important longitudinal research concerning the stability of such test scores and their value in predicting educational, vocational, and other outcomes throughout the lifespan (Terman, 1916, 1975).

Sigmund Freud

Sigmund Freud (1856–1939) did not originally intend to invent the new discipline he would labeled as "psychoanalysis," but arrived at it by a circuitous route. After a preliminary education including exposure to the Greek and Latin classics, he entered medical school. His goal was an academic career in the field presently called neuroscience. His prospects for ultimate employment in a university were thwarted, however, in part by Viennese prejudices against Jews. He went into medical practice instead, as a neurologist, so that he could afford to get married (Gay, 1988). To prepare for going into practice, he was awarded a fellowship to go to Paris to study under the most famous neurologist of the time, Jean Charcot. Thus, Freud began to use some of the techniques of hypnotism in treating patients with "hysterical" symptoms, but experience with an early patient led him to discontinue the use of hypnosis. Instead, he had patients "free associate," saying whatever came to mind, and he used the material produced in this way to try to reconstruct the origins of the presenting symptoms. He theorized that such an analysis could alleviate the patient's problems by detecting unconscious material and bringing it to conscious awareness, allowing the patient to cope with it rationally, hence the saying, "where id was, there shall ego be." An important aspect of treatment was the phenomenon of "transference," in which patients became unduly dependent upon their therapists; this was also the subject of the analyst's comments. In 1900, Freud published his famous book on the analysis of dreams as the "royal road to the unconscious" in psychoanalysis, marking the formal announcement of this new discipline.

Freud came to the United States only once, in 1909, at the invitation of psychologist G. Stanley Hall, to speak at the celebration of the 20th anniversary of the founding of Clark University in Worcester, Massachusetts. Although Freud did not particularly like the United States, it proved to be the country in which psychoanalysis achieved its greatest early recognition. The American Psychoanalytic Association was founded in 1911. As the Boston physician Morton Prince said afterward:

> Freudian psychology had flooded the field like a full rising tide and the rest of us were left submerged like clams in the sands at low water.
>
> (quoted by Hale, 1971, p. 434)

The standard method of educating new psychoanalysts, as it developed during the 1920s, came to consist of three parts: didactic instruction in basic principles, a personal psychoanalysis, and experience carrying out the psychoanalysis of patients under supervision. In Europe, the candidates accepted for such training were not necessarily physicians. In fact, no particular professional prerequisites were enforced, and thus a number of psychologists received psychoanalytic training. The European psychologist Theodore Reik, who worked as a psychoanalyst after

emerging from such training, was taken to court on charges of practicing medicine without a license. Freud, on the witness stand, testified that psychoanalysis was actually a part of psychology rather than of medicine, and thus Reik's use of psychoanalysis with his patients was legitimate. Reik won his case (Freud, 1927). Nevertheless, in 1938, the American Psychoanalytic Association began to enforce the rule that only physicians might be trained for the practice of psychoanalysis. Because Freud was struggling to leave Vienna in 1938 to escape the Nazis and died in London in 1939, he was hardly in any position to intervene personally in this American dispute. The controversial rule was not overturned until 50 years later, in 1988, when the case of *Welch v. American Psychoanalytic Association* (1985) was settled out of court. Now, psychologists may be accepted as candidates for psychoanalytic training in the United States, just as they always had been in other countries. By then, however, the use of psychoanalysis began to wane in the United States.

Before World War II, very few American psychologists worked as psychotherapists, psychoanalytic or otherwise. The same was true of U.S. psychiatrists, whose activities centered on the administration of mental hospitals and the care of psychotic or demented individuals. The war changed all that. For one thing, large numbers of European immigrants, including many psychoanalysts, arrived in the United States, fleeing Hitler. These European analysts formed a cadre for training others in this country. American psychiatrists were able to receive such training through the American Psychoanalytic Association, and psychologists wanting this kind of training were often able to obtain it in irregular ways, including via Theodor Reik's National Psychological Association for Psychoanalysis, in New York.

In addition, the U.S. Armed Forces required many clinicians to deal with the mental health problems that often accompany a war, including what is now labeled post-traumatic stress disorder. Not enough psychiatrists were available to carry out these duties, and thus many doctoral psychologists were brought into mental health–related work. The chief psychiatrist of the U.S. Army during World War II was Brigadier General William C. Menninger, a man strongly identified with psychoanalysis. After the war, the mental health problems of military veterans loomed large. The U.S. Veterans Administration began a massive program of financial support of training in all mental health fields, including psychiatry, psychology, social work, and nursing. The Department of Veterans' Affairs, as it is now known, is still the largest single employer of clinical psychologists in this country. At the same time, a new federal agency, the National Institute of Mental Health (NIMH) was organized as part of the National Institutes of Health, with responsibilities for supporting both research and training in mental health fields. In response to these federal initiatives, a conference on graduate training in clinical psychology was held in Boulder, Colorado, in 1949. The Boulder Conference (as described by Raimy, 1950) yielded the "scientist-practitioner" model for training clinical psychologists. The recommended curriculum closely followed the model elaborated by psychologist David Shakow, the first chief clinical psychologist at NIMH. Shakow's career was exemplary in its blend of scientific experimental psychology and a psychoanalytic orientation to clinical work. The Boulder Conference formed the basis of a system of graduate programs and internships operating under a new program of accreditation offered by the APA. Many of these new PhD programs in clinical psychology, for example the one at the University of Michigan, incorporated the psychoanalytic training model relatively fully, including didactic instruction, encouragement of personal psychoanalysis, and the supervision of psychotherapy by qualified psychoanalysts.

Meanwhile, clinical psychology was emerging as a discipline in several other countries. After World War II, the United Kingdom, the Scandinavian countries, and others were setting up government-supported national health services (rather than government-supported care for veterans alone). In each of these national health services, clinical psychologists became a mainstay of mental health care, and the psychoanalytic model was as influential in these places as it was in the United States at this time.

Psychoanalysis seems to have reached the peak of its influence in the United States in the mid-1960s. By that time, a large number of the departments of psychiatry in U.S. medical schools had hired psychoanalysts as chairs. After that, Freudian influences in mental health care appeared to wane. One factor in this decline was the reluctance of the psychoanalytic community to subject its treatments to rigorous research concerning their efficacy and effectiveness. A second factor was the cost of treatment, especially of the classical Freudian paradigm, in which patients were seen 5 days a week, sometimes for years on end. Third, by the 1950s, a number of lower-cost, more demonstrably effective pharmacological treatments were emerging for mental health problems, including neuroleptics for managing psychotic behavior,

antidepressants, mood stabilizers, anxiolytics, and others. Finally, alternative psychological treatments began to emerge, including the cognitive and behavioral therapies discussed under the next heading.

Hans Eysenck

Hans Eysenck (1916–1997) was important to clinical psychology as one of the founders of behavior therapy. The cognitive and behavioral therapies emerged during the latter half of the 20th century as credible alternatives to psychoanalysis. Eysenck was a German who was a firm opponent of the Nazis and soon emigrated to Great Britain. He received his PhD from the University of London, in psychometrics and experimental psychology, under Cyril Burt and was recruited by the prominent psychiatrist Aubrey Lewis to the Institute of Psychiatry at the Maudsley Hospital in London, to start a program in clinical psychology. Eysenck assumed at first that clinical psychologists should occupy themselves only with research and assessment activities, rather than treatment. He was a researcher, himself. In his work, he preferred to collect and analyze data and write articles and books, rather than deal directly with patients as a clinician. In 1949, Eysenck journeyed to the United States (to the University of Pennsylvania), where he began to realize and to agree with the commitment of the post-war generation of clinical psychologists to treatment, and not just assessment (Eysenck, 1949). However, he had no use for the psychoanalytic approaches in which so many of them were interested. He soon scandalized both psychiatrists and psychologists by publishing an article questioning the positive effects of psychotherapy (Eysenck, 1952). In his article, Eysenck described insurance company data that permitted a comparison between the outcomes of persons with neurotic problems who received psychotherapy and others who did not. He pointed out that the success rate of psychotherapy did not exceed the rate of "spontaneous remission" of the patients' difficulties without therapy. Although not a controlled study including random assignment of patients, it did point out the flaw in therapists' previous reasoning that if patients improved after treatment, the treatment must have been responsible.

Eysenck thought that psychological interventions should be based not on Freudian notions, but on ideas compatible with the theories and quantitative, experimental findings of the type of behavioral psychology that was typical of the academic psychology of his day. In his new Department of Psychology at the Institute of Psychiatry, he hired behaviorally oriented colleagues such as Gwynne Jones and began to train students like Stanley Rachman. Psychiatrist Aubrey Lewis objected to the direction being taken by Eysenck's program, but academic officials at the University of London supported the autonomy of the Psychology Department at the Institute of Psychiatry.

The Modern Era

What do these developments imply for the status of psychoanalysis? It is clear that Sigmund Freud was a powerful and persuasive writer, and that the cultural influence of his works to this day may be broader than that of any other individual in psychology. Freud's continuing influence within clinical psychology is also considerable. Yet Freud depended largely on the evidence of case histories, never did a psychological experiment, did not make use of quantitative methods, and generally ignored the research literature of nonpsychoanalytic psychology. Many of Freud's medical and psychological colleagues were critical of his approach from the beginning, a fact that is curiously portrayed in histories of psychoanalysis as an example of unconsciously motivated "resistance." Eysenck and his behavioral colleagues simply had the boldness to call the Freudians to account and to engage in much-needed critical thinking about the relevant evidence.

Meanwhile, support for the behavior therapy movement quickly appeared. A behavior modification conference was held in Charlottesville, Virginia, in 1962, and the first behavior therapy journal, *Behaviour Research and Therapy*, began publication in 1963. The interdisciplinary Association for the Advancement of Behavior Therapy first met in 1967, in Washington, D.C., and its name was changed in 2005 to the Association for Behavioral and Cognitive Therapies. Behavioral principles had a profound influence on research and the practice of therapy. In terms of research, pioneering work was carried out by physician Joseph Wolpe of South Africa, described in his 1958 book, *Psychotherapy by Reciprocal Inhibition*. A pioneer in the area of cognitive therapy was psychiatrist Aaron T. Beck (e.g., Beck, 1967). The Skinnerian version of intervention for behavioral problems is known as *applied behavior analysis* and has been particularly valuable in working with persons with intellectual and developmental disabilities, including those with autism (Baer, Wolf, & Risley, 1968).

By the 1980s, the larger scientific community finally began to realize the need for formal randomized clinical trials to evaluate the effectiveness of treatments for psychopathology. Elkin et al. (1989) reported the results of the NIMH Treatment of Depression Collaborative Research Program. Participants in this research were outpatients between the ages of 21 and 60 who met the current Research Diagnostic Criteria for major depressive disorder with specified scores on the Hamilton Depression Rating Scale. Those with other major psychiatric disorders, concurrent psychiatric treatment, or certain medical conditions were excluded, as were actively suicidal individuals. Of 250 potential subjects, 239 entered treatment, of whom 162 completed treatment. They were randomly assigned to either interpersonal psychotherapy, cognitive behavior therapy, imipramine plus clinical management, or pill placebo plus clinical management (medication was administered on a double-blind basis). The psychological treatments were carried out by 13 different therapists, in accordance with detailed treatment manuals. The results showed that the antidepressant medication and the two types of psychological treatment were all significantly more effective than pill placebo but were essentially equivalent to each other in their effects on depression. Critics of such research were quick to point out the additional need for studies on the "effectiveness," not just the "efficacy" of such treatments. In other words, the clinical trials with their formal manuals of procedure were not representative of typical clinical management, and the exclusion conditions made the patients studied also unrepresentative of the broad population of depressed patients. Nevertheless, it is clear that with the NIMH Collaborative Research and similar studies, a new era had arrived. The subsequent emphasis has been on the need for all therapists, when possible, to use "evidence-based" treatments of psychopathology, rather than procedures that have not been tested in a rigorous way. Similarly, the training of all mental health personnel should give priority to teaching treatments that are firmly grounded in the research literature. This is not to deny, however, that clinicians are constantly experiencing variations in the pictures presented by patients' problems, thus requiring a flexible adaptation of established principles.

Conclusion

This chapter has dealt with a number of strands in the development of Clinical Psychology with a "large C," including its psychoanalytic and cognitive-behavioral aspects. Many psychologists who deliver human services in the United States are specialists in other fields, and are thus are identifiable as clinicians "with a small c," so to speak. Among these areas are clinical child and adolescent psychology, clinical health psychology, clinical neuropsychology, counseling psychology, rehabilitation psychology, couple and family psychology, clinical geropsychology, school psychology, and in some jurisdictions, clinical psychopharmacology. Early on, in some cases, clinical psychology and school psychology were the same field, but later branched into distinct ones. The history of how each of these special areas developed would require many additional chapters. In many countries in Europe, Latin America, and in many other parts of the world, the patterns of training seen in psychology in the U.S. and the U.K. is not typical. Instead, university psychology graduates receive a diploma or licentiate degree, which is in itself legally sufficient for them to engage in the practice of psychology, although many supplement this by informal training in areas such as psychotherapy. In such countries, master's and doctoral degrees are considered to be preparation for an academic career, not for practice.

My largest effort toward studying the history of clinical psychology is the 1994 book on the history of the organization presently known as the Society of Clinical Psychology, a division of the APA. It was subtitled: "Science, Practice, and Organization," so perhaps these categories will serve in discussing the history of clinical psychology as a larger entity. Clinical psychologists seem to be well accepted as contributors to the scientific study of psychopathology, assessment, and treatment. Their progress in this respect can perhaps be tracked through the volumes of the *Annual Review of Clinical Psychology*, which began publication in 2005.

In terms of practice, doctoral-level clinical psychologists are prominent in the public sector, practicing in Veterans Affairs Hospitals and clinics in the United States and, the in national health services of Great Britain, the nations of the British Commonwealth, and Western Europe. Employment in private-sector mental health is highly competitive in such countries. Psychiatry, once the leading profession in this domain, has lost much of its turf to primary care physicians (and advanced practice nurses), who now write most of the prescriptions for psychotropic medications. Moreover, psychiatry has also lost professional turf to various kinds of nonmedical psychotherapists, including not only doctoral-level psychologists but also master's-level psychologists, social workers, mental health counselors, and many others. Current research does not support the idea that therapists with such different types and levels of professional preparation differ in their effectiveness in treating mental illness. And yet, despite all this professional activity, the mental health needs of the public still do not appear to be very well served. A study by Pratt and Brody (2008) of "depression in the United States household population, 2005–2006," might be taken as a snapshot of the status quo a few years before the beginning of the current world economic recession. A sample of about 5,000 persons representing the adult, civilian, noninstitutionalized U.S. population were given standardized interviews (National Health and Nutrition Examination Survey). Only 29% of those people considered to suffer from depression reported contacting a mental health professional (such as a psychologist, psychiatrist, psychiatric nurse, or clinical social worker) in the past year; of those with severe depression, only 39% reported such contact. Depression is considered a highly treatable condition, yet most people with depression in the United States were not treated. It is clear from such data that clinical psychologists and other mental health professionals have a long way to go to meet their goal of actually helping people even to a minimal extent.

Finally, in terms of organization, clinical psychologists in the United States have been represented by some kind of professional organization since 1917. Similar organizations began to appear in Great Britain, British Commonwealth countries, and in Western Europe, especially after the end of World War II. However, so far, international clinical psychology has not yet gone very far toward dealing with the kaleidoscope of world cultures in existence or achieving any kind of a coherent, organized voice. These remain as issues for the future.

Acknowledgments

I very much appreciate comments by colleagues on a preliminary version of this manuscript. These helpful early readers included David Barlow, John Cox, Nicola Foote, Christopher Green, Marjorie Sanfilippo Hardy, and Irvin D. S. Winsboro.

References

Baer, D. M., Wolf, M. M., & Tisley, T. R. (1968). Some current dimensions of applied behavior analysis. *Journal of Applied Behavior Analysis, 1,* 91–97.

Beck, A. T. (1967). *Depression: Clinical, experimental, and theoretical aspects.* New York: Hoeber Medical Division, Harper & Row.

Benjamin, L. T., Jr., Durkin, M., Link, M., Vestal, M., & Accord, T. (1992). Wundt's American doctoral students. *American Psychologist, 47,* 123–131.

Binet, A., & Simon, T. (1905). [A new method for the diagnosis of intellectual level of abnormal persons]. *Annee Psychologique, 11,* 191–244.

Breasted, J. H. (1922). *The Edwin Smith Papyrus*. New York: New York Historical Society.

Brotemarkle, R. A. (Ed.). (1931). *Clinical psychology: Studies in honor of Lightner Witmer*. Philadelphia: University of Pennsylvania Press.

Cahan, D. (Ed.). (1993). *Hermann Helmholtz and the foundations of nineteenth century science*. Berkeley, CA: University of California Press.

Elkin, I., Shea, T., Watkins, J. T., Imber, S. D., Sotsky, S. M., Collins, J. F., Glass, D. R., Pilkonis, P.A., Leber, W. R., Docherty, J. P., Fiester, S. J., & Parloff, M. B. (1989). National Institute of Mental Health Treatment of Depression Collaborative Research Program: General effectiveness of treatments. *Archives of General Psychiatry*, 46, 971–982.

Eysenck, H. J. (1949). Training in clinical psychology: An English point of view. *American Psychologist*, 4, 175–176.

Eysenck, H. J. (1952). The effects of psychotherapy: An evaluation. *Journal of Consulting Psychology*, 16, 319–324.

Fagan, T. K. (1996). Witmer's contribution to school psychological services. *American Psychologist*, 51, 241–243.

Freud, S. (1927). *The problem of lay analysis*. New York: Brentano's.

Galton, F. (1892). *Hereditary genius: An inquiry into its laws and consequences*. London: MacMillan.

Gay, P. (1988). *Freud: A life for our time*. New York: Norton.

Guillain, G. (1959). *J.-M. Charcot, 1825-1893; his life—his work*. Trans. Pearce Bailey. New York: Hoeber.

Hale, N. G., Jr. (1971). *Freud and the Americans*. (Vol. 1). *The beginnings of psychoanalysis in the United States, 1876–1917*. New York: Oxford University Press.

James, W. (1890). *The principles of psychology*. 2 vols. New York: Henry Holt.

Janet, P. (1924). *Principles of psychotherapy*. New York: MacMillan, 1924.

Klein, A. G. (2002). *A forgotten voice: A biography of Leta Stetter Hollingworth*. Scottsdale, AZ: Great Potential Press.

Kraepelin, E. (1962). *One hundred years of psychiatry*. W. Baskin, trans. New York: Philosophical Library.

Lodha, R., & Bagga, A. (2000). Traditional Indian systems of medicine. *Annals of the Academy of Medicine* (Singapore), 7, 36–42.

McReynolds, P. (1987). Lightner Witmer: Little-known founder of clinical psychology. *American Psychologist*, 42, 849–858.

McReynolds, P. (1997). *Lightner Witmer: His life and times*. Washington, D.C.: American Psychological Association.

Nicolas, D. S., & Murray, D. J. (1999). Theodule Ribot (1839–1916), founder of French psychology: A biographical introduction. *History of Psychology*, 2, 161–169.

Pratt, L. A., & Brody, D. J. (2008). Depression in the United States household population, 2005–2006. *National Center for Health Statistics Data Brief*, No. 7, 1–8.

Raimy, V. C. (Ed.). (1950). *Training in clinical psychology*. New York: Prentice-Hall.

Riese, W. (1969). *The legacy of Philippe Pinel: An inquiry into thought on mental alienation*. New York: Springer.

Routh, D. K. (1994). *Clinical psychology since 1917: Science, practice, and organization*. New York: Plenum.

Routh, D. K. (1996). Lightner Witmer and the first 100 years of clinical psychology. *American Psychologist*, 51, 244–247.

Routh, D. K. (2000). Clinical psychology training: A history of ideas and practices prior to 1946. *American Psychologist*, 55, 236–241.

Routh, D. K., del Barrio, V., & Carpintero, H. (1996). European roots of the first psychology clinic in North America. *European Psychologist*, 1, 44–50.

Schneider, W. H. (1992). After Binet: French intelligence testing, 1900–1950. *Journal of the History of the Behavioral Sciences*, 28, 111–132.

Spearman, C. (1904). "General intelligence," objectively determined and measured. *American Journal of Psychology*, 15, 201–293.

Stern, W. (1912). *The psychological methods of intelligence testing*. (G. Whipple, trans.). Baltimore: Warwick & York.

Swierc, S. F., & Routh, D. K. (2003). Introduction to the special issue on international clinical psychology. *Journal of Clinical Psychology*, 59, 631–634.

Taylor, E. (1983). *William James on exceptional mental states: The 1896 Lowell Lectures*. New York: Charles Scribner's Sons.

Temkin, O. (1994). *The falling sickness: A history of epilepsy from the Greeks to the beginning of modern neurology*. 2nd rev. ed. Baltimore: Johns Hopkins University Press.

Terman, L. M. (1916). *Measurement of intelligence*. Boston: Houghton Mifflin.

Terman, L. M. (1975). *Genius and stupidity*. New York: Arno Press.

Todes, D. P. (2002). *Pavlov's physiology factory: Experiment, interpretation, laboratory enterprise*. Baltimore, MD: Johns Hopkins University Press.

Twitmyer, E. B., & Nathanson, Y. S. (1932). *Correction of defective speech*. Philadelphia: Blakiston.

Veith, I. (2002). (trans.) *The Yellow Emperor's Classic of Internal Medicine*. Berkeley: University of California Press.

Viteles, M.S. (1932). *Industrial psychology*. New York; Norton.

Watson, R. I. (1956). Obituary: Lightner Witmer: 1867–1956. *American Journal of Psychology*, 69, 680–682.

Welch v. American Psychoanalytic Association, No. 85, Civ. 1651 (S.D.N.Y. 1985).

West, P. (1998). *The enduring Seminoles*. Gainesville: University Press of Florida.

Witmer, L. (1897). The organization of practical work in psychology. *Psychological Review*, 4, 116.

Witmer, L. (1907). Clinical psychology. *Psychological Clinic*, 1, 1–9.

Wolpe, J. (1958). *Psychotherapy by reciprocal inhibition*. Stanford, CA: Stanford University Press.

Zenderland, L. (1998). *Henry Herbert Goddard and the origins of American intelligence testing*. New York: Cambridge University Press.

Emerging Policy Issues for Psychology: A Key to the Future of the Profession

Patrick H. DeLeon, Mary Beth Kenkel, Jill M. Oliveira Gray, *and* Morgan T. Sammons

Abstract

Involvement in the public policy process is essential to the continued growth of the profession of psychology. The authors posit that five dimensions of involvement in the policy process are fundamental to ensuring the success of advocacy efforts: patience, persistence, the establishment of effective partnerships, emphasizing interpersonal relationships in the policy process, and the adoption of a long-term perspective. These key mediators are described in the context of current major public policy issues affecting psychology: mental health legislation in general, prescriptive authority, provision of psychological services in community health centers, expansion of the available treatments for autistic spectrum disorders, and recasting psychology as a primary health-care delivery profession. The authors suggest that policy makers will value the contributions of psychology only insofar as they are convinced of the profession's ability to improve the public weal.

Keywords: Autism interventions, community health centers, mental health legislation, prescriptive authority, public policy

Those of us who have been personally involved in the public policy process over the years have learned the critical importance of five key mediators of success: patience, persistence, partnerships, personal relationships, and a long-term perspective for the field (DeLeon, in press; DeLeon, Loftis, Ball, & Sullivan, 2006). In this chapter, we provide examples illustrating each of these factors and their contribution to recent policy initiatives affecting psychology. Sometimes one factor, such as the creation of strategic partnerships, is most important in effecting change in public policy. More commonly, however, significant change results from a combination of all these variables.

An immediate example of effective engagement in the public policy process is afforded by large professional advocacy organizations, such as the American Psychological Association (APA). APA has worked over a number of decades to have psychology's voice and expertise heard by those who establish our nation's domestic and foreign policies, and it can be justly proud of its role in successful passage of landmark legislation, such as the mental health parity bill enacted during the closing hours of the 110th Congress (discussed later). Such success has perhaps been one inspiration for the growing number of psychologists willing to run for elected office at both the local and national level (Sullivan, Groveman, Heldring, DeLeon, & Beauchamp, 1998; Sullivan & Reedy, 2005). Others have been appointed to high-level administrative positions, where they have the ability effectively bring the profession's data-based perspective to addressing society's most pressing needs. In spite of these successes, it remains true that very few, if any, of our current psychology training programs provide the type of "hands-on" exposure to the public policy world necessary to establish the foundation for our next generation of clinicians, educators, and scientists becoming effectively engaged in visionary legislative change (DeLeon, 2002; Kenkel,

DeLeon, Mantell, & Steep, 2005). It is also true that very few of our colleagues appreciate the historical roles that psychologists have had in shaping public policy; for example, that psychologist John Gardner served as Secretary of the then-Department of Health, Education, and Welfare (HEW) during the Great Society era of President Lyndon Johnson and had a major influence on the direction of health-care services. Psychology is a maturing profession, and it is critically important that our field appreciates its own history. Only through that lens we can see both what we have been capable of and the opportunities we have missed. We must find ways to educate current and future psychologists on both this history and in methods of effective engagement. We have no more potent mechanism for the profession to share its expertise for the betterment of society and the advancement of the field.

Learning About the Public Policy Process

Psychologists and most other health-care providers approach their professional lives from fundamentally different perspectives than do those who establish and implement our nation's health and education policies (DeLeon, Dubanoski, & Oliveira-Berry, 2005). Reflecting upon his year on Capitol Hill, former APA Congressional Science Fellow Neil Kirschner noted that:

> More often than not, research findings in the legislative arena are only valued if consistent with conclusions based upon the more salient political decision factors. Thus, within the legislative setting, research data are not used to drive decision-making decisions, but more frequently are used to support decisions made based upon other factors. As psychologists, we need to be aware of this basic difference between the role of research in science settings and the legislative world. It makes the role of the researcher who wants to put "into play" available research results into a public policy deliberation more complex. Data need to be introduced, explained, or framed in a matter cognizant of the political exigencies. Furthermore, it emphasizes the importance of efforts to educate our legislators on the importance and long-term effectiveness of basing decisions on quality research data . . . . If I've learned anything on the Hill, it is the importance of political advocacy if you desire a change in public policy.
> (*Kirschner, 2003*)

Psychologists involved in the public policy process also must appreciate the structural interrelationships between various congressional committees, their staffs and the personal interests of Congressmembers, and learn to look across federal agencies to systematically explore the range of federal involvement in matters pertaining to the science and profession of psychology. For example, why should the Secretary of the U.S. Department of Agriculture be supportive of investing in programs targeted toward encouraging women to become involved in science, technology, engineering, and math (STEM) initiatives (DeLeon, Eckert, & Wilkins, 2001)? This goal initially seems unrelated to agricultural concerns; however, those familiar with the jurisdiction of the Department of Agriculture would know that it has a broad mission to increase the quality of life for rural America, and historically has done so via funding of educational initiatives through Land Grant institutions. Broadening the focus to include much-needed STEM degrees is a reasonable extension, but it would only be obvious to those familiar with the Department's mission, jurisdiction, and priorities.

Educators, clinicians, and researchers in the field have never operated in a societal vacuum. And yet, very few psychology graduate programs have systematically exposed their students to the rich history of our involvement in such major health-care policy changes such as the community mental health center movement. Few programs have addressed the history and mission of the Centers for Medicare and Medicaid Services (CMS) and how it differs in orientation and programmatic priorities from the Health Resources and Services Administration (HRSA) and the Centers for Disease Control and Prevention (CDC). Very few of psychology's educators are aware of these agencies' different institutional personalities or their institutional affiliations within the Department of Health and Human Services (HHS). Similarly, we would rhetorically ask: How can our graduate students to be expected to appreciate how today's health psychology and integrated-care movements actually rest upon an important public health foundation envisioned by the Minister of National Health and Welfare of Canada in 1974 and President Carter's Surgeon General? (keen readers and students of history may find the answer on page 46)

As a maturing health-care profession, psychology's training programs have an institutional responsibility to educate our next generation regarding the public policy and public health context in which they will someday practice. It is equally important that the next generation of psychologists come to appreciate the public policy implications of the reality that the federal government has a long history of ensuring that those health-care practitioners for whom it provides training support will be appropriately recognized under each of its health service delivery programs. Perhaps, we would suggest, this vacuum will eventually be filled by psychology's professional schools, which seem to have a broad and global perspective on psychology's future and its potential clinical domain (DeLeon, Kenkel, & Belar, 2007; Kenkel, DeLeon, Albino, & Porter, 2003).

One of the most successful ways for psychologists to learn about the public policy process has been through congressional fellowship programs. The 2008–2009 Fellowship year marked the beginning of the 35th year of the APA Congressional Fellowship Program, with an incoming class of three fellows. APA senior policy advisor Ellen Garrison, also a previous congressional fellow, indicated that a number of psychologists, including herself and Ruby Takanishi (president of the Foundation for Child Development), obtained their Capitol Hill experience under the auspices of the Society for Research in Child Development (SRCD; Ellen Garrison, personal communication, October 23, 2008). A recent APA Fellow and current director of the Fellowship Program, Diane Elmore stated that:

> The APA Congressional Fellowship Program provides psychologists with an invaluable public policy learning experience, contributes to the more effective use of psychological knowledge in government, and broadens awareness about the value of psychology–government interaction among psychologists and within the federal government. As part of the larger Science and Technology Policy Fellowship Program at the American Association for the Advancement of Science (AAAS), APA Congressional Fellows benefit from the distinguished network of organizations dedicated to issues surrounding federal science and technology policy. Since 1974, APA has sponsored 107 Congressional Fellows who have represented the field with excellence and integrity. Participants in the program have gone on to make significant contributions to the field of psychology through clinical practice, research activities, work in the policy arena, and involvement in APA governance.
>
> (*Diane Elmore,* personal communication, October 19, 2008)

Some psychologists have gained a first-hand education in the public policy process by serving as members of Congress. At present, three psychologists are serving in the US Congress, including Rep Tim Murphy of Pennsylvania, Rep Brian Baird of Washington, and Rep Judy Chu of California (Congresswoman Chu also has the distinction of being the first Chinese-American female elected to the US Congress). At the beginning of every session of Congress, the Library of Congress Congressional Research Service develops an in-depth profile of the elected members. Recently, Congress (like the field of psychology) has become increasingly female and more ethnically diverse in its composition. Over the past three Congresses, a record number of women have served, and the 109th Congress also had an unprecedented number of African American members. The average age of the members of both houses is 57—among the oldest of any Congress in history. The overwhelming majority of elected officials have a college education, with 22 members of the House having doctoral degrees, and 13 members of the House and four Senators holding medical degrees. The dominant profession remains law, followed by public service/politics, and business. Of the 540 elected members of the 110th Congress, there were also ten health professionals (Library of Congress, 2008). Ted Strickland, the first psychologist to ever serve in the Congress, has now been elected governor of Ohio; again, being the first psychologist to serve in that capacity. Peter Newbould of the APA Practice Directorate reported that, during the 110th Congress (2007–2008), 14 psychologists were serving in various state House and Senate seats (Newbould, 2007). Given the fundamentally different ways in which members of the health professions and those with law and business professional backgrounds tend to address problems and conceptualize their personal priorities, it is especially important that a significant number of our next generation of psychologists be trained to understand the specific nuances of the legislative process and its highly unique culture, as expressed in its rules, language, and customs, if, as members of society's educated elite, we ever collectively decide to accept our societal responsibility to have a significant role in shaping our nation's priorities (DeLeon, 1986).

In addition to the fellowship program, psychologists and psychologists-in-training also have gained knowledge of the public policy process through advocacy training sponsored by APA and other national and state psychological associations. Each year, during the Educational Leadership Conference sponsored by the Education Directorate and the State Leadership Conference sponsored by the Practice Directorate, participants receive advocacy training and updates on legislative issues relevant to psychologists. They then travel over to Capitol Hill for scheduled appointments with legislators and aides, in order to establish crucial personal connections to better represent the meaning and potential effects of proposed legislation for society, psychologists, and the people we serve. These psychologists quickly learn that their advocacy efforts are most effective when legislators and staff are shown how proposed legislation will affect real people—clients, students, and the public at large—and how proposed changes will address persisting societal problems. Although research data are useful, a legislator's attention is more fully captured by actual accounts of people who have been helped or could be helped by a new bill or funded program. Psychologists' personal contacts with legislators expand these legislators' knowledge of the critical societal needs by showing them the world that psychologists experience daily—the struggles of individuals and their families, and the impact on individuals and communities from unmet social needs. Psychologists' personal contacts with legislators have been effectively increased through a number of public policy networks affiliated with APA, such as the Federal Educational Advocacy Coordinators (FEDAC) and the Public Policy Advocacy Network (PPAN), through which psychologists are mobilized to contact their legislators at times of important votes.

Although few in number, several academic programs and training councils have begun to highlight the importance of advocacy in their clinical psychology programs (Lating, Barnett, & Horowitz, 2009; Martin, 2006) and provide advocacy experiences for students. By doing so, students learn early on the importance of being involved in the public policy process for the good of their clients and their profession. By observing their professors and clinical supervisors involved in advocacy activities, students learn that advocacy is an important component of their professional roles. They also can become involved in advocacy activities through the APA Graduate Students' (APAGS) Advocacy Coordinating Team (ACT) (see their website, www.apa.org/apags/advocacy/act.html, for more information). Advocacy training materials with important information on the legislative process and effective communication as an advocate are available at the APA website: http://www.apa.org/ppo/ppan/guides.html.

Patience and Mental Health Parity Legislation

Perhaps one of the most taxing lessons to learn about public policy making is how long it takes to implement significant change, even if highly beneficial. The recently enacted, far-reaching mental health parity legislation (the Paul Wellstone and Pete Domenici Mental Health Parity and Addiction Equity Act of 2008; P.L. 110-343), took over a decade to come to fruition. It was back in April, 1996, when Senator Domenici told his Senate colleagues that "now is the time" to pass legislation requiring insurance companies to cover mental illness just as they did any other medical conditions, yet it took until 2008 for political forces and societal issues to come together to garner broad support for the legislation. Given his daughter's mental health diagnosis, this legislation also provides insight into how "the business of politics can be intensely personal" (Lueck, 2008). APA's senior legislative liaison, Marilyn Richmond, has been working diligently on this critical legislation since 1996, when the initial, albeit limited, federal mental health parity legislation was enacted.

Patience in the public policy process implies a commitment to long-term involvement. Just as psychologists must be lifelong learners to remain effective in their work, so must they have a lifelong presence in public policy processes to have a substantial effect on societal well-being. Patience, however, may be misconstrued as a more passive level of involvement, a "standing on the sidelines" approach. To ensure effective advocacy, patience must be combined with the next important factor—persistence. We illustrate the intersection of these two factors by describing one of psychology's major public policy initiatives of the past two decades: prescriptive authority for appropriately trained practitioners.

Persistence and Prescriptive Authority
The Prescriptive Authority (RxP) Agenda

From a public policy perspective, one of the fundamental health-care responsibilities of government is to test out promising and innovative models of health-care delivery, including exploring evolving roles for a range of health-care professionals (e.g., physician assistants and dental extenders). Without question, this has been the case for psychology's prescriptive authority initiative. Psychologists' quest for prescriptive authority vividly demonstrates the value of persistence in the public policy process.

In November 1984, U.S. Senator Daniel K. Inouye urged the membership of the Hawaii Psychological Association (HPA) to seek prescriptive authority (RxP) to improve the availability of comprehensive, quality mental health care. At that time, optometrists were authorized to utilize diagnostic drugs in 39 states (four states allowed therapeutic use), nurse practitioners in 18 states, and the contributions of clinical pharmacists were hardly ever considered (Burns, DeLeon, Chemtob, Welch, & Samuels, 1988; DeLeon, Fox, & Graham, 1991).

In 1991, at the request of the Congress, the Department of Defense (DoD) established a pilot training program at the Walter Reed Army Medical Center, under the auspices of the Uniformed Services University of the Health Sciences (USUHS). In June 1994, then-APA President Bob Resnick attended the graduation ceremonies for the first two DoD prescribing psychologists, including one of the current authors. Over the years, this particular program had been carefully evaluated and demonstrated for both psychology and for our nation's health policy experts that psychologists can be cost-effectively trained to provide high-quality, comprehensive psychopharmacological care (DeLeon, Dunivin, & Newman, 2002; Dunivin & Orabona, 1999; Newman, Phelps, Sammons, Dunivin, & Cullen, 2000). Ultimately, despite ferocious opposition, this program graduated ten prescribing psychologists until political maneuvering by organized medicine eliminated congressional funding in 1997. This program became the model upon which similar training programs in the civilian sector were established.

Notwithstanding objective findings, numerous arguments continue to be marshaled (largely by the psychiatric profession) in the policy process against prescriptive authority for psychologists. These arguments rest mainly on two assertions: that the training of psychologists is insufficient to allow them to provide psychopharmacological services, and that such providers would represent a "public health hazard" who will affirmatively harm their patients. Such arguments represent an extension of the reasoning that the medical profession has traditionally employed when any nonphysician health-care provider group seeks to expand its scope of practice into areas that were previously the exclusive domain of medical doctors: that patients will suffer if care is provided by non–medically trained personnel. This argument, however, has been repeatedly repudiated, as groups as diverse as nurses, podiatrists, dentists, and optometrists have rapidly expanded their professional scopes of practice to procedures including the administration of systemic drugs and surgery (Fox, DeLeon, Newman, Sammons, Dunivin & Baker, 2009; Sammons, 2003).

From an initial Board of Professional Affairs retreat in 1989 and the August 1990 Council of Representatives vote to establish a special task force, the various APA governance elements have intensively deliberated upon all aspects of psychology obtaining prescriptive authority (DeLeon, 2003). In 1995, the APA Council of Representatives voted overwhelmingly to endorse prescriptive authority for appropriately trained psychologists, as representing APA policy. Today, a number of programs within the civilian sector provide relevant training that meets the APA recommended standards, the majority of which are located within a university-based setting and grant a master's degree upon completion. To date, appropriately 190 post-doctoral graduates have taken the APA Psychopharmacology Examination for Psychologists (PEP exam), which has a passing rate of approximately 71% for first-time test takers (J. Ciuccio, personal communication, October 7, 2008).

The move to acquire prescriptive authority comes in the context of a dramatically altered landscape for all health professions. Optometrists and advance nurse practitioners have acquired prescriptive authority in all states, and clinical pharmacists, under varying conditions, in more than 40 states. Psychology has obtained prescriptive authority in New Mexico (2002) and Louisiana (2004); with Indiana (1993) and Guam (1998) enacting, but not implementing, relevant RxP statutes. Deborah Baker of the APA Practice Directorate reported that, every year, an increasing number of state psychological associations have introduced legislation (Deborah Baker, personal communications, Fall, 2008). In 2007, the Hawaii Psychological Association (HPA) passed such legislation; it was, however, ultimately vetoed by their governor. For 2008, there were a total of eight RxP-related bills, including two sponsored by major labor unions in California. In January 2009, the Hawaii Primary Care Association will sponsor the Hawaii RxP bill and launch their legislative agenda with prescriptive authority for psychologists as one of their top three initiatives. The Florida Psychological Association initiative was modified to become a request for a formal study, with the legislature's Joint Legislative Auditing Committee voting 7–3 to conduct such a study on whether there is a need and/or benefit for granting prescription privileges for psychologists. Historically, 70% of approved proposals from this group eventually become public law. Practice patterns in the jurisdictions that have passed enabling legislation for psychologists suggest that these laws work to expand public health services and do not endanger patients. As of early 2009, 48 medical psychologists have certificates of prescriptive authority in Louisiana. Psychologists have filled positions long left vacant by shortages of psychiatrists, and it is estimated that they have written more than 200,000 prescriptions. The Louisiana State Board of Examiners of Psychologists has not had a single complaint against a medical psychologist in the three years since the statute was implemented (Glenn Ally, personal communication, October 7, 2008).

The essence of psychology's prescriptive authority agenda rests on the assumption that psychopharmacological service provision from a nonpsychiatric perspective conveys unique benefits. In this "psychological model of pharmacologic service provision" medications are viewed almost always as adjunctive, with the ongoing relationship between therapist and patient assuming primacy. Because psychologists have a wide range of behavioral and psychosocially based interventions in addition to pharmacotherapy, it has also been posited that this integrated approach will lead to better patient outcomes (Sammons, 2001). Former APA Practice Directorate Executive Director and now Provost of Alliant International University Russ Newman predicted: "Prescribing psychologists will use medication in a qualitatively different manner than psychiatrists. They will use pharmacotherapy based on a psychological model of treatment, in contrast to a medical model. The implications of this difference may be profound. The psychological model of treatment can be described as a systems-oriented, holistic, integrative approach…. When other treatments are available, with a psychological model, the power to prescribe is also the power to unprescribe" (Newman, 2000, p. 45).

With persistence, psychologists have been able to gain prescriptive authority through an innovative program in the DoD, as well as in several states. That persistence was fueled by certitude that psychologists would be able to provide more efficacious and needed services with the ability to prescribe. This argument has convinced not only many critics within psychology but also policy-makers seeking to improve mental health services for their constituents. Continued persistence will be necessary to overcome the objections of organized psychiatry and enact prescriptive authority legislation in all the states.

Just as with prescriptive authority, over the past decade, significant progress has been made in ensuring that appropriately trained psychologists throughout the federal system have been able to effectively utilize their clinical skills, whether employed by the DoD, Indian Health Service, U.S. Public Health Service, or Department of Veterans Affairs. Interestingly, it has been our observation that, just as with prescriptive authority, the greatest obstacles this evolution has faced have been within the field of psychology itself; in this case, the institutional reticence on behalf of senior psychologists. Change is always unsettling and frequently takes more time than one might initially

expect (DeLeon, Brown, & Kupchella, 2003). Accordingly, interested students of the public policy process should probably not be surprised or discouraged by how persistent one must be and how long it is taking to fully implement psychology's vision of comprehensive, psychologically based health care (DeLeon, 1988; Kenkel et al., 2005).

Partnerships and Psychological Service Provision in Community Health Centers
Enhancing Psychological Service Provision in Community Health Centers

Today's societal problems are complex and multifaceted. Very few can be addressed comprehensively by only one profession, field, or strategy. Yet professional education rarely emphasizes collaborative skills or interdisciplinary approaches. Instead, educational silos exist (O'Neil, 2008) in which professionals become extremely knowledgeable about their own disciplines but have little idea how to talk with, much less work with, others from other professions.

Some psychologist educators, however, such as former Robert Wood Johnson Health Policy Fellow and now Kent State University Provost, Bob Frank, have come to appreciate, undoubtedly through their own personal experiences (i.e., by serving on Capitol Hill), the truly interdisciplinary nature of the public policy process, specifically the health policy process. Dr Frank has been instrumental in establishing health administration and public health training opportunities, so that psychology's graduate students and those of the other health professions have a viable vehicle for being exposed to the nuances and history of our nation's health-care system and the critical need for interdisciplinary cooperation.

More than 25 years ago, there were calls for more cooperation between health and general health providers. It was noted that primary care providers, even then, were charged with providing over 60% of care for those with discernible mental health disorders and that enhanced diagnosis, counseling, better-informed drug prescribing, and referral were key to ensuring high-quality services (Hamburg, Elliott, & Parron, 1982). Those authors also noted that primary care providers required training in discussing mental health issues with patients and called for alternative mechanisms for providing behavioral health-care services in primary care settings. Over 25 years later many of the deficiencies noted by Hamburg, Elliott, and Parron have yet to be addressed and, until recently, there have been few initiatives to promote greater partnerships between clinical psychologists and primary care providers. There are, however, some encouraging new partnerships, such as those being developed in community health centers (CHCs; DeLeon, Giesting, & Kenkel, 2003). At least four psychology training programs (three in Hawaii; one in Tennessee) are known to provide full-time, and/or, rotations, in pre- and/or post-doctoral training in CHCs (i.e., I Ola Lāhui Rural Hawaii Behavioral Health Training Program, Cherokee Health Systems, Tripler Army Medical Center (TAMC), and Waianae Coast Comprehensive Health Center). All are Association of Psychology Postdoctorate and Internship Centers (APPIC) members, with two being APA accredited (Cherokee Health Systems and TAMC) and one in the process of applying for APA accreditation (I Ola Lāhui). It is possible that this number is an *underestimate* given that other non-APA accredited programs may exist; there may be other CHC-based training programs with APPIC membership only; or, other training programs may have rotations in CHCs but are difficult to locate through existing search lists. In fact, a category specific to CHCs as a program setting is absent from the available list of APA or APPIC programs, which is hopefully something that will change in the near future as more CHC-based psychology training programs evolve.

From a training standpoint, CHCs offer a richness of diversity and complexity of patient populations. Mental health services are offered within the context of primary care, largely to medically underserved individuals. This imbues such sites with the capacity to create culturally competent, innovative, and resourceful psychologists capable of working collaboratively with general health providers and committed to serving the underserved, reducing health disparities, and advocating to reduce stigma and increase psychology's place as a front-line health-care profession (DeLeon, Giesting, & Kenkel, 2003). The challenge is that, at present the training programs that do exist are few and are difficult to develop given the harsh fiscal realities of many state health-care budgets. There is a significant need to establish creative and resourceful means to sustain psychological services and training initiatives in these settings, as well as to continue to develop within APA's framework the support and recognition necessary to expand, sustain, and validate training initiatives within CHCs.

Why should we emphasize the potential of CHCs? These federally qualified community health centers have been in existence serving our nation's most geographically isolated and medically underserved populations for more than 40 years (National Association of Community Health Centers, 2008). Between 1995 and 2004, the numbers of patients served in CHCs increased by more than 50%, from 8.6 to 15 million (Agency for Healthcare Research and Quality Conference Center [AHRQCC], 2005), and the number of uninsured individuals who received care rose from 2.2 to 4 million (DeLeon, Giesting, & Kenkel, 2003). In 2004, the Bureau of Primary Health Care reported that 70.5% of CHC patients were at or below the 100% federal poverty level, 85.3% were uninsured (40.1%) or received some form of public assistance (Medicaid, Medicare), and 63.5% were of a particular ethnic minority group. In addition, as one looks at various states where unique demographics and socioeconomic conditions exist, other medically underserved groups may become more prevalent, such as the homeless, immigrant, and/or migrant populations (Hawaii Primary Care Association, 2006).

Community health centers exist in all 50 states within the United States and are located in high-need communities in order to "provide comprehensive preventive and primary health services to all residents in the service area regardless of [their insurance status or] ability to pay" (AHRQCC, 2005, p. 3). Through this mission, CHCs accomplish impressive tasks to improve access to a range of medical and behavioral health-care services, and reduce health disparities in our nation's most medically underserved populations, including the unmet needs of our rural residents (DeLeon, Wakefield, & Hagglund, 2003). The most common diagnoses seen in CHCs include hypertension, diabetes mellitus, heart disease, asthma, depression, other mood disorders, all mental health, and substance abuse (NACHC, 2005). Approximately 72% and 48% of all health centers provide mental health and substance abuse treatment, respectively. Psychology definitely has multiple roles to play in the administrative, clinical, research, and program development aspects within the CHC model of health-care delivery and should continue to advocate for its role in this clinical setting, in order to provide integrative, whole-person health care for a significant majority of medically underserved populations across the nation.

Initiatives at the national and state levels have reinforced the relevance, benefits, involvement, and sustainability of psychologists in CHCs. The following excerpt, written more than a decade ago, from the Institute of Medicine's "Primary Care: American's Health in a New Era" (1996) speaks to the need for a profession such as psychology to expand beyond its traditional boundaries and definitions of practice and join with other health-care providers in attempts to improve the status quo of our nation's health-care system:

> Psychiatry itself, in its recent preoccupation with brain biology and psychopharmacology, has evolved in a way that is rather unhelpful to generalists. This is not to minimize the enormous value of this orientation, but to point out the vacuum that it has created. Primary care clinicians have lost a theoretical framework for understanding the human predicament and giving meaning to symptoms. Today, there is no coherent medical psychology that is taught in every medical school. With certain important exceptions, psychiatrists are most often called into service to prescribe or monitor psychotropic drugs or to make difficult diagnostic decisions about seriously disturbed patients. This leaves the primary care clinician without support when she or he is trying to understand and deal with the "ordinary" mental distress, disorders, and illnesses encountered in the daily practice of primary care. (Institute of Medicine, 1996, p. 299)

PSYCHOLOGISTS IN COMMUNITY HEALTH CENTERS

Psychologists who work in CHCs should be able to provide general, broad-based assessment and treatment services, as well as specialty care in the areas of health psychology, behavioral medicine, and psychopharmacology, in order to function effectively and efficiently (Garcia-Shelton & Vogel, 2002). As in other primary care settings, working in a CHC requires psychologists to possess skill sets that facilitate integrative and collaborative practice within a primary health care team often consisting of medical doctors, nurse practitioners, physician assistants, medical assistants, psychiatrists, social workers, and community outreach workers, as well as administrative, fiscal, and billing staff. A sizable literature on primary care psychology and integrated behavioral health care informs the practice of psychologists who work in CHCs (American Psychological Association, 1998; see special section reviews in Professional Psychology: Research and Practice, 2003, 2005; McDaniel, Belar, Schroeder, Hargrove, & Freeman, 2002; O'Donohue, Byrd, Cummings, & Henderson, 2005; Pruitt, Klapow, Epping-Jordan, & Dresselhaus, 1998; Robinson, 1998). A difference that may be unique to CHCs, however, is the focus on serving medically underserved populations who typically live in rural areas. Community health centers face multiple challenges, including but not limited to high turnover rates of providers, reduced access to specialty medical care, and patient populations that may be broadly compromised across a variety of health, cultural, and socioeconomic indices. Using Hawaii as an example, the Hawaii Primary Care Association (HPCA, 2006) described their CHC patient profile as: 29% Native Hawaiian, 20% Asian, 25% Caucasian, 14% other Pacific Islander. Fifteen percent of these patients needed interpreters when seeking care, 71% had incomes below federal poverty levels, 74% were rural, 30% were uninsured, and 40% were underinsured (Medicaid or QUEST); 10,700 of these patients were homeless. Anxiety, depression, and adjustment disorders—often in conjunction with domestic violence, substance abuse, homelessness, and chronic diseases—remain among the top mental/behavioral health problems treated. In 2005, the HPCA reported that 70% of Hawaii's CHC patients were in need of behavioral health interventions; however, only 11% actually received these services (demographic and clinical statistics across all 14 CHCs in Hawaii can be found at http://www.hawaiipca.net/chcs). Thus, although the knowledge and skills of psychologists working in primary care apply to CHCs, service planning and practice in such settings brings forth distinct challenges.

Behavioral health program objectives, service delivery, and integration models within Hawaii's CHCs are described in this section. These descriptions reveal that, although foundational elements exist to inform the services provided across CHCs, services provided in each CHC must be adapted to meet specific community needs. A saying made popular among those who have been involved in this expansion work is, "one size fits… only one size." Examples of specific foundational CHC/behavioral health program objectives have included the following: (a) to improve access to medical and behavioral health care, (b) to provide culturally appropriate services and, (c) to reduce health disparities in medically underserved populations. To carry out these objectives, behavioral health service delivery models strive to be evidence-based, accessible, and responsive to community and clinic needs. In most cases, service delivery models evolve over time as a psychologist "works in" to the clinic setting, conducts needs assessments, finds common interests, and builds and eventually assembles the behavioral health service delivery model into the most responsive, relevant, and reliable it can be for that particular CHC.

In general, Hawaiian CHCs have a combined primary behavioral model and colocated specialty model (Strosahl, 2005), given the "see all comers" and "from cradle to grave" philosophies that comprise CHC patient care. Typically, psychologists have had to begin with the colocated specialty model to initiate behavioral health services in order to generate revenue through traditional third-party reimbursements and then work in a primary behavioral model as CHC resources for behavioral health (namely, to hire more providers or trainees) increase. Ideally, a CHC should have one full-time equivalent (FTE) traditional psychologist and one FTE primary care psychologist per clinic (i.e., Adult, Women's, Pediatrics) within a small to moderate-sized health center (i.e., serving 1,500–3,000 patients per year).

A Week in the Life of a CHC psychologist

The following is an account of an actual week in the life of psychologists at the Waimanalo Health Center (WHC) in Hawaii (general information about WHC and the Integrated Behavioral Health [IBH] program can be found at http://www.waimanalohealth.com). According to the most recent Uniformed Data Services (UDS, 2008) report, 3,305 total patients were served at WHC (representing a 5% increase from 2007) by medical and behavioral health staff. Medical staff positions include family physicians (2.34 FTE), pediatrician (1.00), nurses (1.50), nurse practitioner (0.04), and other medical personnel (7.16). In addition, there is a nutritionist (0.42 FTE), case manager (1.01), patient community education specialist (0.97), outreach workers (1.51), and eligibility assistance workers (1.01). Of the patients served, 39.7% were male and 60.3% were female (report year January 1, 2008–December 31, 2008). WHC patients by race included, 47% Native Hawaiian, 20% White, 15% other Pacific Islander, 12% Asian, and 6% other. With regard to insurance status, 33% of the WHC patients served in 2008 were uninsured, 43% received Medicaid, 6% received Medicare, and 18% had private commercial insurance. There was a 12% increase in uninsured patients served compared to 2007. The most common medical diagnosis by encounter was for diabetes mellitus, followed by hypertension, asthma, and heart disease. Depression and/or other mood disorders was the primary mental health diagnosis by encounter, followed by anxiety (including post-traumatic stress disorder [PTSD]), and attention deficit-hyperactivity disorder (ADHD). There were 2,121 behavioral health clinical encounters for a total of 338 patients.

In IBH, there are two part-time staff psychologists (.6 FTE each), and one or two practicum students, one or two interns, and one or two post-doctoral fellows at any given point in time. Psychologists are colocated within the health center in a clinic that has a waiting area, an office manager, three individual offices, and one group conference room. This space allows psychologists to see patients for traditional appointments consisting of 30- to 45-minute sessions, while at the same time being steps away from the other primary care clinics (Adult, Women's, Pediatrics) to receive same-day, warm hand-off referrals. In addition, one psychologist or trainee is assigned to the three primary care clinics for 4-hour time blocks, which means that traditional therapy appointments are not made during this time, in order to have a behavioral health provider available to primary care physicians at all times throughout the week. The psychologist or trainee who is scheduled for primary care will not only be the first contact for a warm hand-off referral, but is also present in the primary care clinic to follow-up on all behavioral health screenings (i.e., depression, tobacco use), as well as chronic disease management initiatives that have identified behavioral health as an important part of the patient's care (i.e., diabetes, hypertension).

Clinical Care

As with any clinical practice, seeing patients is of utmost priority. WHC psychologists strive to see at least eight patients per day to provide general behavioral health service delivery, including traditional individual therapy, group interventions, and child and family interventions for mental health concerns, as well as primary care behavioral health including chronic disease management, smoking cessation, weight management, chronic pain management, psychopharmacology consultation, and medication monitoring. Collaborating and communicating with other primary care providers (namely, physicians, nurses, medical assistants, and outreach workers) happens frequently throughout the day (both in person and through the electronic medical record system) to support patient care in the form of bidirectional referrals, consultations, and following-up regarding important aspects of treatment. On average, primary care providers refer approximately two to four patients to IBH a day. During primary care blocks of time, psychologists conduct screening for depression and tobacco use, and undertake brief psychological interventions for either mental health or chronic disease management in conjunction with the patient's primary care visit. The screening and intervention focuses on identifying individuals in need who do not ordinarily access behavioral health services, utilizing motivational interviewing strategies to engage them in treatment in a way that circumvents the stigma of mental health services, providing early intervention to prevent the need for more intensive services, and keeping difficult-to-engage/treat individuals in needed behavioral health services until short- and/or long-term treatment goals are met. Depending on the patient's situation, ongoing visits can either occur in primary care exclusively or patients may schedule for follow-up appointments with the psychologist in behavioral health. One of the important benefits of providing this type of primary care intervention is the support it offers to primary care physicians who otherwise have to manage health care for individuals with complex psychosocial issues on their own. In this way, the integrated behavioral health intervention helps not only the patient, but also prevents primary care provider burnout.

Training and Supervision

The WHC has established memorandum of agreements with two local training programs, I Ola Lāhui and TAMC. Thus, WHC psychologists engage in both training and supervision of psychology trainees on a daily basis. As stated earlier, there are currently one to three trainees present on any given day, except Fridays. Psychologists share training and supervision responsibilities, and together will provide a total of 5 hours per week of direct supervision. Training often takes place in vivo, as there is not much time to set aside didactic training in addition to direct supervision in the primary care setting. Thus, trainees will observe psychologists conducting therapy with patients as needed, cofacilitating groups, and participating with psychologists in clinic/staff meetings.

Productivity data taken after the first year of I Ola Lāhui trainees alone (6-month, 3-day/week rotation at WHC) indicated services provided to over 274 individuals and families, with 1,080 total patient encounters. On average, patients attended an average of 3.9 sessions with trainees across all ethnic groups. Interestingly, although the research literature in this area would suggest that ethnic minority group members have higher attrition from behavioral health services, Native Hawaiian patients using these behavioral health services stayed for an average of 4.2 sessions. Trainees have also been well received by the WHC administration and clinical staff, who greatly value the work they perform and have been very supportive of continuing this training component for the past 8 years.

Clinical Research

Blocks of time are not scheduled for research only. However, because psychologists are invested in program development and evaluation, they do gather and track patient outcome data on a regular basis. These data are used both to inform clinical practice and to describe IBH productivity and patient outcomes.

Administration

Psychologists attend monthly staff meetings, provider meetings, provider huddles, and clinic huddles, which are all interdisciplinary and designed to enable discussions among providers and administrative staff regarding multiple topics, including clinic operations (i.e., policy and procedures), program development initiatives, health center updates, financial reports, quality improvement/quality assurance, and general announcements.

Thus, psychologists at WHC spend the majority of their week engaged in clinical patient care, 50% of which takes place within the primary care clinics, mainly Adult Medicine and Women's Health. To maximize work volume and maintain a workforce development training capacity, psychologists also supervise psychology trainees from two local psychology training programs on a weekly basis (totaling 4 days/week). Administrative responsibilities also assume dedicated blocks of time whereby psychologists engage with other health-center staff and providers to support daily center operations, as well as facilitate positive and productive working relationships. Finally, program development and evaluation is the type of research that characterizes this aspect of professional practice in the life of a CHC psychologist.

Hawaii CHC Initiatives

In the late 1990s, Hawaii's community health-care leaders and psychologists from the TAMC Department of Psychology, convened to discuss innovative ways that would combine federal and state resources to enable greater health-care access for Native Hawaiians in rural communities (Oliveira, Austin, Miyamoto, Kaholokula, Yano, & Lunasco, 2006). Native Hawaiians continue to suffer significant health disparities compared to other ethnic groups in Hawaii, largely due to risk factors that include acculturative stress and access to care challenges (Blaisdell, 1993; Braun, Yee, Browne, Mokuau, 2004; Hope & Hope, 2003; Johnson, Oyama, LeMarchand, & Wilkens, 2004). Native Hawaiians have high prevalence rates of certain chronic diseases such as obesity, diabetes, and cardiovascular disease; higher health risk behaviors such as tobacco and/or illicit drug use; and are overrepresented in the under- and uninsured, poverty, and homelessness groups, as well as in rural, medically underserved areas (Banks, Buki, Gallardo, & Yee, 2007; Oliveira et al., 2006). In 2000, the civilian post-doctoral psychology training program began at TAMC with the express interest of increasing access to culturally appropriate behavioral health care for Native Hawaiians in rural, medically underserved areas in order to enhance the existing health-care system and reduce significant health-care disparities that have plagued the indigenous population of Hawaii for decades (Hope & Hope, 2003).

Partnerships established between TAMC, Hawaii's CHCs, and Native Hawaiian Health Care System clinics (NHHCS) have led to successful outcomes from both service delivery and training perspectives. In terms of service delivery, psychologists have either started or expanded existing behavioral health services in 11 of the 14 CHCs and in one of the five NHHCS clinics. In 2009, 12 psychologists were employed in either a part- or full-time basis, and 13 psychologists in training were present. The TAMC training model was instrumental in the development of two additional full-time training programs in medically underserved communities via colocation and integration within CHCs and NHHCS: I Ola Lāhui Rural Hawaii Behavioral Health Program, and the Waianae Coast Comprehensive Health Center Psychology Training Program. Both programs are members of APPIC in good standing; the former also seeks APA accreditation and is currently in the accreditation process. One of the current authors is a faculty member of the I Ola Lāhui Rural Hawaii Behavioral Health Program and will thus further describe this training program to highlight an example of a nontraditional psychology training program that aims to be part of the systematic change necessary to address pressing cultural, economic, societal, and political issues that impact our nation's poorest and most vulnerable populations.

I Ola Lāhui Rural Hawaii Behavioral Health Program

I Ola Lāhui is a Hawaiian phrase that means, "So that the people will live and thrive." I Ola Lāhui is a clinical psychology training program whose mission is to provide culturally minded evidence-based behavioral health care that is responsive to the needs of medically underserved and predominantly Native Hawaiian rural communities. In recognition of Hawaii's urgent need for more quality behavioral/mental health care, I Ola Lāhui is committed not only to providing services but also to evaluating the effectiveness of the services provided and training future providers, with the hope of making a substantial contribution to the health and well-being of our Lāhui (people). I Ola Lāhui was incorporated in June 2007, and received its nonprofit 501(c)3 designation status on July 11, 2007. During the first year of internship training, I Ola Lāhui participated as a site in the APA accredited Argosy University/Honolulu Internship Consortium, and applied for its own APPIC membership in 2007. Official membership status was granted on November 27, 2007. Intake of the first cohort of interns as an independent training site occurred in June 2008 for the 2008–2009 training year. I Ola Lāhui sees the vital importance of offering training experiences for future psychologists that incorporate the domains expressed in this chapter, such as advocacy and public policy, interdisciplinary/primary care psychology, integrated behavioral health care, and prescriptive authority for psychologists. I Ola Lāhui is nontraditional in that it serves as both administrative and training functions, without being housed within a larger institutional setting, It is among the first of its kind to take psychology training beyond the proverbial four walls in order to answer the societal call to improve health provider shortages, access issues, and health disparities.

Personal Relationships
Advocating for Effective Treatment: Autistic Spectrum Disorders

Building personal relationships is critically important in the public policy process. This includes forming relationships with legislators and their staff, with directors and staff at federal and state agencies, with professionals with related goals, and with individuals who are looking for solutions to pressing problems. This skill should be easily acquired by clinical psychologists who are experts at building rapport, empathic listening, and establishing bonds with others.

What is the value of these relationships? First, they allow psychologists to learn about issues that are of concern to planners and recipients of health-care services. The psychologist has the opportunity to broaden a legislator's (who may have a personal interest, such as a family member or constituent struggling with mental illness) understanding of the issue and its impact on the people the legislator is trying to serve. The personal relationships also allow the psychologist to join in proposing and working on solutions on a more informal basis. Early involvement in the problem solution helps to ensure the consideration of factors important to psychology, such as the impact of proposed legislation/programs on different minority or disenfranchised groups. Personal contacts also allow the psychologist to gain credibility as a professional with information and expertise in areas of concern and one interested in assisting in the complex, rough-and-tumble, and sometimes frustrating process of public policy. Over time, through these personal contacts, psychologists can become known as reliable and informative advisors; as they acquire referent authority, they can have more influence when there are particular issues for which psychologists are advocating.

A network of personal relationships and professional contacts is key to getting things done, particularly in major initiatives involving large-scale shifts in policy or large budgets. This became exceedingly evident to one of the authors as she developed a center to provide autism services and research. Autism spectrum disorders (ASD) are neurodevelopmental disorders commonly diagnosed before the age of 3, now estimated to affect one in 110 children in the United States (Centers for Disease Control [CDC], 2009). The major characteristics of ASDs are impaired social and language skills and a restricted repertoire of activities and interests. In addition, many individuals with autism have mental retardation and may exhibit self-injurious, stereotypical, and/or aggressive behaviors. Because of the recent exceedingly rapid increase in the incidence of autism (CDC, 2007) many families, schools, health facilities, and social service agencies are increasingly overwhelmed by the treatment needs of this population. In general, such agencies have few resources to provide the intensive behavioral treatments and other interventions that have been shown to be the most efficacious with the disorder.

Clearly a need existed, and with a doctoral program in clinical psychology and a large master's program in applied behavior analysis (ABA), the School of Psychology at Florida Institute of Technology had a wealth of faculty and student resources that could be utilized to address significant needs of individuals with ASDs and those who care for them. It took an assemblage of many people working together—many with long-term personal relationships—to establish a center that would bring these resources to affected families. These included a trustee of the university and his wife, who had encountered the struggles of finding treatment for their son with ASD and who provided major funding for the center; the district's congressman, a physician committed to helping children with ASD who was made aware of the university's capabilities in this area and worked to secure Health Resources Services Administration (HRSA) funding for the center; a dedicated community advisory group, made up of parents and professionals caring for children with ASD, who helped develop the mission and vision of the center and build community awareness and support; school teachers, administrators, and other health-care professionals who flocked to training programs given by the center and provided vocal support for its establishment; and local media, who assisted the center in bringing information about autism to their readers/audiences and described the center as a valuable community asset.

With key input from the community it aimed to serve, the center developed a mission that was broader than it might have been if developed only by the university's school of psychology. There was a call for a "one-stop" center, which would include multidisciplinary services and a seamless transition among services—attributes that the public also are calling for in their general health-care settings.

The center has the benefit of being a major treatment center under the direction and control of a psychology program, with a priority on providing behavioral and psychological services, as opposed to more typically encountered programs housed in medical settings. This provides high visibility to the field of psychology as the primary profession for autism treatment, training, and applied research. This type of self-determinism is a hallmark of professions (Abbott, 1988; Larson, 1977) and is growing evidence of psychology's rising prominence as a "health" profession.

The center provides training to clinical psychology and behavior analysis students, and by doing so hopes to address the significant manpower shortage of professionals able to deliver autism services. The center also allows complete control of the training experiences provided to the students. This permits rapid adoption of new evidence-based treatment methods and the capability of developing and evaluating new programs to deal with this complex disorder.

Ongoing operation of the center requires a sustainable funding source. With this in mind, the school has been involved in recent legislative initiatives to require private insurance companies pay for autism services, specifically ABA interventions. With the strong backing of the advocacy group, *Autism Speaks*, by May 2010, these efforts have been successful in 19 states, including Florida (Autism Speaks, 2010). Through these advocacy efforts, stable funding is available not only for the Center but also for the services that the graduates of the school will provide in the future.

The autism center is an example of how psychology can be involved in multiple ways in the public policy process. A pressing societal need was identified; psychological resources were available and willing to be used to address it; a workable proposal was developed by the university and those affected by autism; contact with legislators informed them of the problem and possible solutions; community support was gathered and used to secure private and federal funding; partnerships with like-minded groups increased advocacy for support for autism services; and state and federal initiatives were obtained to develop and sustain the center. The network of personal relationships among the people involved in the center's development was critical to garnering support and action. It also required persistence and passion—and the next factor to be discussed: a long-term perspective for developing the center.

Long-term Perspectives: Moving Toward a Primary Health-care Profession

As previously stated, effective involvement in the policy process requires a long-term perspective. The profession must determine its long-term goals and plan and carry out the strategies to reach them. What is clinical psychology's long-term goal? There probably is no single answer that would be unanimously adopted by all in the field, but certain elements of a future vision would probably be agreed upon by many: being recognized as the most qualified behavioral health provider, having the resources to conduct psychological research and implement

psychological services, and inclusion as essential professionals in the solution of society's pressing problems. The more unified clinical psychology can be in the delineation of these long-term goals, the more effective the profession will be as a partner in the policy process.

We offer this long-term goal: that psychology be recognized as a front-line, primary health profession (DeLeon, Brown, & Kupchella, 2003). Such a perspective indicates that psychology be recognized as contributing not only to better mental health care, but also to better general health care, and it would be seen as an essential resource in efforts to improve healthy functioning. This perspective is not new, but has yet to be fully integrated into public policy.

Over 35 years ago, the government of Canada recognized the importance of good health for quality of life and the value of a broadened conceptualization of health care:

> Good health is the bedrock on which social progress is built. A nation of healthy people can do those things that make life worthwhile, and as the level of health increases so does the potential for happiness. The Governments of the Provinces and of Canada have long recognized that good physical and mental health are necessary for the quality of life to which everyone aspires. Accordingly, they have developed a health care system which, though short of perfection, is the equal of any in the world. For these environmental and behavioural threats to health, the organized health care system can do little more than serve as a catchment net for the victims. Physicians, surgeons, nurses and hospitals together spend much of their time in treating ills caused by adverse environmental factors and behavioural risks. . . . It is therefore necessary for Canadians themselves to be concerned with the gravity of environmental and behavioural risks before any real progress can be made. . . . The Government of Canada now intends to give human biology, the environment, and lifestyle as much attention as it has to the financing of the health care organization so that all four avenues to improved health are pursued with equal vigour. Its goal will continue to be not only to add years to our life but life to our years, so that all can enjoy the opportunities offered by increased economic and social justice.
> (*Lalonde*, 1974, pp. 5-6).

> Similar sentiments were expressed a few years later by the U.S. government:

> (L)et us make no mistake about the significance of this document. It represents an emerging

consensus among scientists and the health community that the Nation's health strategy must be dramatically recast to emphasize the prevention of disease.... But we are a long, long way from the kind of national commitment to good personal health habits that will be necessary to change drastically the statistics about chronic disease in America.... (U.S. Dept. of Health, Education, and Welfare [HEW], 1979, pp. vii, ix).

Prevention is an idea whose time has come. We have the scientific knowledge to begin to formulate recommendations for improved health.... (O)f the ten leading causes of death in the United States, at least seven could be substantially reduced if persons at risk improved just five habits: diet, smoking, lack of exercise, alcohol abuse, and use of antihypertensive medication.... (A)lthough people can take many actions to reduce risk of disease and injury through changes in personal behavior, the health consequences are seldom visible in the short run.... To imply, therefore, that personal behavior choices are entirely within the power of the individual is misleading.... (HEW, 1979, pp. 7, 14, 18).

Beginning in early childhood and throughout life, each of us makes decisions affecting our health. They are made, for the most part, without regard to, or contact with, the health care system. Yet their cumulative impact has a greater effect on the length and quality of life than all the efforts of medical care combined (*HEW,* 1979, p. 119).

Challenge To The Nation. Americans are becoming healthier people—but more can be achieved. This report has described and documented the potential for better health at each stage of life. It has set forth specific goals to be attained over the next decade, and a full agenda of possible actions to be taken. To reach these goals will require a national effort and the commitment of people extending far beyond what we traditionally consider the health sector. No single segment of society can accomplish them alone. Unnecessary death and disability can be prevented— and better health can be maintained—only through a partnership that involves the serious commitment of individual citizens, the communities in which they live, the employers for whom they work, voluntary agencies, and health professionals. Government agencies at all levels must encourage and bolster their efforts. How to move expeditiously toward the goals of prevention is the challenge for the years to come (*HEW,* 1979, p. 141).

The Institute of Medicine (IOM) was established in 1970 by the National Academy of Sciences to enlist distinguished members of the appropriate professions in the examination of policy matters pertaining to the health of the public. Acting as a health policy advisor to the federal government, it has recently issued a series of reports calling for major and unprecedented changes in both the structure and focus of our nation's health-care system.

The heaviest burdens of illness in the United States today are related to aspects of individual behavior, especially long-term patterns of behavior often referred to as 'lifestyle.' As much as 50% of mortality from the ten leading causes of death in the United States can be traced to lifestyle. Regardless of the health-risky behavior or the disease, treatment and prevention should be major research issues for the biobehavioral sciences. Attention is being given to methods of altering the burden of illness by changing behavior. This requires first that changes in behavior can be shown to result in improved health and second that effective methods be found to help large numbers of people to make such changes. Much remains to be learned, but the existing research base provides strong evidence that the biobehavioral sciences can make substantial and unique contributions to dealing with much of the disease that now constitutes the main burden of illness in this country.
(*Hamburg et al.* 1982, p.p. 3,16).

Psychology appears ready to respond to this broadened perspective on health care, as reflected in these statements by former APA President Ron Levant, formerly Dean of the Buchtel College of Arts and Sciences at the University of Akron:

Mind-Body dualism, is, in a word, bankrupt. We need to transform our biomedical health care system to one based on the biopsychosocial model, which will emphasize *collaboration* between medical and behavioral healthcare providers, and the *integration* of psychology into the very heart of health care. In order to reform the U.S. health-care system along these lines we must appeal directly to the public and to decision-makers, not alone, but in collaboration with other like-minded physician, provider, consumer, and policy groups. We need to articulate the public's dissatisfaction with the biomedical health-care system that results in their care provider not having time to listen to all of their concerns or offering what amounts to limited care. We need to put forth a vision of integrated care, a care system

that offers Health Care for the Whole Person. This was the second of my initiatives as President of APA. It is one very concrete example of how psychology can address urgent public needs and make psychology a household word.
(*Levant*, 2006, pp. 387–388).

The 21st century will be an era of educated consumers utilizing the most up-to-date technology to ensure that they and their loved ones will have timely access to data-based, objective standards of care, provided by technology-literate, interdisciplinary-oriented health-care providers. A recent report from the IOM concluded that not only is the health-care system in its current configuration incapable of engaging in effective future planning, inasmuch as we devote most of our energy toward the management, not the prevention of chronic disease. The lack of integration across provider groups and delivery settings was also seen as a significant impediment in the development of effective and economical health-care systems. The IOM saw behavioral interventions regarding diet, exercise, and substance abuse as key in a new mindset of prevention. Interdisciplinary coordination, using providers skilled in the latest in medical informatics to efficiently share information, track interventions and outcomes, and manage costs was also seen as essential (IOM, 2003a, 2003b).

Each year, more than 33 million Americans use health-care services for their mental health problems or conditions resulting from their use of alcohol, inappropriate use of prescription medications, or, less often, illegal drugs. In 2006, *Improving the Quality of Health Care for Mental and Substance-Use Conditions: Quality Chasm Series* was released, in which the IOM concluded that their Quality Chasm framework is, in fact, applicable to health care for mental and substance-use conditions. This newest report noted that these conditions are the leading cause of combined disability and death for women and the second highest for men. "Effective treatments exist and continually improve. However, as with general health care, deficiencies in care delivery prevent many from receiving appropriate treatments. That situation has serious consequences—for people who have the conditions; for their loved ones; for the workplace; for the education, welfare, and justice systems; and for our nation as a whole" (IOM, 2006, p. 1). Five psychologists served on the committee issuing this report, and the assistance of Jalie Tucker, then-Chair of the APA Board of Professional Affairs, was expressly noted.

Supporting this perspective, the President of the IOM declared: "As the Committee has concluded, improving our nation's general health, and the quality problems of our general health care system, depends upon equally attending to the quality problems in health care for mental and substance-use conditions…. Dealing equally with health care for mental, substance-use, and general health conditions requires a fundamental change in how we as a society and health-care system think about and respond to these problems and illnesses. Mental and substance-use problems and illnesses should not be viewed as separate from and unrelated to overall health and general health care. Building on this integrated concept, this report offers valuable guidance on how all can help to achieve higher-quality health care for people with mental or substance-use problems and illnesses. To this end, the Institute of Medicine will itself seek to incorporate attention to issues in health care for mental and substance-use problems and illnesses into its program of general health studies" (IOM, 2006, p. x).

Becoming front-line primary health professionals is our long-term perspective for the field. As just seen, voices from outside the profession are articulating the same need for such a front-line behavioral health professional. The time seems ripe for taking strides to achieve this vision. Many opportunities will exist for doing so as a new administration undertakes long-overdue structural changes in the American health-care system. Psychology must forcefully articulate its vital role in health care and what it can do to meet the current and future health-care challenges of the populace. Only by doing so can the profession be seen as an integral component of a new health-care delivery system.

Conclusion

The challenge for psychology's training and service delivery leaders in the 21st century will be designing clinical initiatives and training opportunities that are responsive to the unprecedented challenges that society at large will be facing. To do so effectively, psychologists must become more involved in the public policy process. As we have suggested, an important element of this role will be to ensure that those who establish our nation's health and educational policies become intimately aware of psychology's potential contributions to their underlying mission. Over the years, there have always been a number of specific legislative and administrative initiatives (e.g., inclusion in the Department of Defense CHAMPUS and later TRICARE reimbursement programs, the ability to bill under Medicare [most recently the expanded ability to bill for Evaluation and Management codes], Graduate Medical Education, and the federal Criminal Justice program) of definite and concrete interest to professional psychology. In addition to focusing on these specific programs, we would suggest that even more important in the long run for every health-care profession is building an institutional appreciation and capacity for understanding how government leaders (and increasingly those of the private sector) systematically seek to address society's most pressing needs. Such knowledge reveals past strategies and indicates how new initiatives could be designed. Participation in this decision-making process requires proactive leadership on the part of psychologists. And what better way to learn where proactive leadership is necessary than by studying the lessons of the past from our public health colleagues (DeLeon & Pallak, 1982)?

Clinical psychology can have a larger and stronger influence on public policy if such a role is embraced by the profession. As we have illustrated in this chapter, it will require patience while being persistent, forging partnerships and building personal relationships, and most importantly maintaining the long-term perspective of what clinical psychology can be and can contribute to society. It is a long-term commitment. The time to renew that commitment is now.

References

Abbott, A. (1988). *The system of professions: An essay on the division of expert labor*. Chicago: University of Chicago Press.

Agency for Healthcare Research and Quality Conference Center. (2005, December). The community health center model. Paper presented at meeting of the Health centers and the medically underserved: Building a research agenda. Rockville, MD.

American Psychological Association (1998). Interprofessional Health Care Services in Primary Care Settings: Implications for Professional Education and Training of Psychologists. Washington, D. C. SAMHSA/HRSA Project on Managed Behavioral Health Care and Primary Care, SAMHSA. Work order #97M220464.

Autism Speaks. (2010). Iowa autism news. Retrieved May 3, 2010 from http://www.autismvotes.org/site/c.frKNI3PCImE/b.4432767/k.BFA1/Iowa.htm

Banks, M. E., Buki, L. P., Gallardo, M., & Yee, B. W. K. (2007). Integrative healthcare and marginalized populations. In I. A. Serlin (General Ed.) & M. A. DiCowden (Volume Ed.), *Whole person healthcare: Vol. 1 Humanizing healthcare* (pp. 147–173). Westport, CT: Praeger Publishers.

Blaisdell, K. (1993). Historical and cultural aspects of Native Hawaiian health. *Social Process in Hawai'i, 31,* 37–57.

Braun, K., Yee, B. W. K., Browne, C. V., & Mokuau, N. (2004). Native Hawaiian and Pacific Islander elders. In K. E. Whitfield (Ed.), *Closing the gap: Improving the health minority elders*

in the new millennium (pp. 9–34). Washington, DC: Gerontological Society of America.

Burns, S. M., DeLeon, P. H., Chemtob, C. M., Welch, B. L., & Samuels, R. M. (1988). Psychotropic medication: A new technique for psychology? *Psychotherapy: Theory, research, practice, and training, 25,* 508–515.

Centers for Disease Control and Prevention (CDC). (2009). Prevalence of autism spectrum disorders — Autism and developmental disabilities monitoring network, United States, 2006. *MMWR Surveillance Studies, 58,* (S S10), 1–20. Retrieved May 3, 2010 from http://www.cdc.gov/mmwr/preview/mmwrhtml/ss5810a1.htm

DeLeon, P. H. (1986). Increasing the societal contribution of organized psychology. *American psychologist, 41,* 466–474.

DeLeon, P. H, (1988). Public policy and public service: Our professional duty. *American Psychologist, 43,* 309–315.

DeLeon, P. H. (2002). Presidential reflections – Past and future. *American Psychologist, 57*(6/7), 425–430.

DeLeon, P. H. (2003). Foreword – Reflections on prescriptive authority and the evolution of psychology in the 21st century. In M. T. Sammons, R. U. Paige, & R. F. Levant (Eds.), *Prescriptive authority for psychologists: A history and guide* (pp. xi–xxiv). Washington, DC: American Psychological Association.

DeLeon, P. H. (2008). Reflections upon a very rewarding journey: Almost a decade later. *Rehabilitation Psychology, 53*(4), 530–535.

DeLeon, P. H., Brown, K. S., & Kupchella, D. L. (2003). What will the 21st century bring? An emphasis on quality care. *International Journal of Stress Management, 10*(1), 5–15.

DeLeon, P. H., Dubanoski, R., & Oliveira-Berry, J. M. (2005). An education for the future. *Journal of Clinical Psychology, 61*(9), 1105–1109.

DeLeon, P. H., Dunivin, D. L., & Newman, R. (2002). Commentary – The tide rises. *Clinical Psychology: Science and Practice, 9*(3), 249–255.

DeLeon, P. H., Eckert, P. A., & Wilkins, L. R. (2001). Public policy formulation: A front line perspective. *The Psychologist Manager Journal, 5*(2), 155–163.

DeLeon, P. H., Fox, R. E., & Graham, S. R. (1991). Prescription privileges: Psychology's next frontier? *American Psychologist, 46,* 384–393.

DeLeon, P. H., Giesting, B., & Kenkel, M. B. (2003). Community health centers: Exciting opportunities for the 21st century. *Professional Psychology: Research and Practice, 34*(6), 579–585.

DeLeon, P. H., Kenkel, M. B., & Belar, C. (2007, May). [Shared Perspective] A window of opportunity: Community health centers can reduce health disparities and train the next generation of psychologists. *APA Monitor on Psychology, 38*(5), 24–25.

DeLeon, P. H., Loftis, C. W., Ball, V., & Sullivan, M. J. (2006). Navigating politics, policy, and procedure: A firsthand perspective of advocacy on behalf of the profession. *Professional Psychology: Research and Practice, 37*(2), 146–153.

DeLeon, P. H., & Pallak, M. S. (1982). Public health and psychology: An important, expanding interaction. *American Psychologist, 37,* 934–935.

DeLeon, P. H., Wakefield, M., & Hagglund, K. (2003). The behavioral health care needs of rural communities in the 21st century. In B. H. Stamm (Ed.), *Rural behavioral healthcare: An interdisciplinary guide* (pp. 23–31). Washington, DC: American Psychological Association.

Dunivin, D. L., & Orabona, E. (1999). Department of defense psychopharmacology demonstration project: Fellows' perspective on didactic curriculum. *Professional Psychology: Research and Practice, 30*(5), 510–518.

Fox, R. E., DeLeon, P. H., Newman, R., Sammons, M. T., Dunivin, D., & Baker, D (submitted). Prescriptive authority for psychologists: A status report. *American Psychologist, 64,* 257–268.

Garcia-Shelton, L., & Vogel, M. E. (2002). Primary care health psychology training: A collaborative model with family practice. *Professional Psychology: Research and Practice, 33(6), 546–556.*

Hamburg, D. A., Elliott, G. R., & Parron, D. L. (1982). *Health and behavior: Frontiers of research in the biobehavioral sciences.* Washington, DC: (IOM) National Academy Press.

Hawai'i Primary Care Association. (2006, October). The Hawai'i primary care directory: A directory of safety-net health services in Hawai'i. Honolulu: Author.

Hope, B. E., & Hope, J. H. (2003). Native Hawaiian health in Hawaii: Historical highlights. *Californian Journal of Health Promotion, 1,* 1–9.

Institute of Medicine (IOM). (1996). Primary care: America's health in a new era. Washington, DC: National Academy Press.

Institute of Medicine (IOM). (2003a). *Fostering rapid advances in health care: Learning from system demonstrations.* Washington, DC: National Academies Press.

Institute of Medicine (IOM). (2003b). *Health professions education: A bridge to quality.* Washington, DC: National Academies Press.

Institute of Medicine (IOM). (2006). *Improving the quality of health care for mental and substance-use conditions: Quality chasm series.* ISBN: 978-0-309-10044-1. Washington, DC: National Academies Press.

Johnson, D. B., Oyama, N., Le Marchand, L., & Wilkens, L. (2004). Native Hawaiian mortality, morbidity, and lifestyle: Comparing data from 1982, 1990, and 2000. *Pacific Health Dialog, 11,* 120–130.

Kenkel, M. B. (Ed.). (2003). Primary behavioral health care [Special section]. *Professional Psychology: Research and Practice, 34*(6), 579–594.

Kenkel, M. B. (Ed.). (2005). Primary behavioral health care [Special section]. *Professional Psychology: Research and Practice, 36*(2), 123–157.

Kenkel, M. B., DeLeon, P. H., Albino, J. E. N., & Porter, N. (2003). Challenges to professional psychology education in the 21st century: Response to Peterson. *American Psychologist, 58*(10), 801–805.

Kenkel, M. B., DeLeon, P. H., Mantell, E. O., & Steep, A. (2005, November). Divided no more: Psychology's role in integrated healthcare. *Canadian Psychology/Psychologie Canadienne, 46*(4), 189–202.

Kirschner, N. M. (2003, August). QMBs, SNFs and Notch Babies: A Hippie Banker Tour. Presentation at 111th APA Annual Convention, Toronto.

Lalonde, M. (1974). *A new perspective on the health care of Canadians: A working document.* Ottawa: Government of Canada.

Larson, M.S. (1977). *The rise of professionalism: A sociological analysis.* Berkeley: University of California Press.

Lating, J. M., Barnett, J.E., & Horowitz, M. (2009). Creating a culture of advocacy. In M. B. Kenkel & R. L. Peterson (Eds.), *Competency based education in professional psychology,* (pp xx). Washington, DC: American Psychological Association.

Levant, R. F. (2006). Making psychology a household word. *American Psychologist, 61*(5), 383–395.

Library of Congress. (2008, September). *CRS report for Congress: Membership of the 110th Congress: A profile.* (RS 22555). Washington, DC: Author.

Lueck, S. (2008, October 4–5). After 12-year quest, Domenici's mental-health bill succeeds. *The Wall Street Journal,* p. A2.

Martin, S. (2006, March). Lessons in advocacy. *GradPSYCH, 4* (2). Retrieved January 12, 2009 from http://gradpsych.apags. org/mar06/advocacy.html

McDaniel, S. H., Belar, C. D., Schroeder, C. S., Hargrove, D. S., & Freeman, E. L. (2002). A training curriculum for professional psychologists in primary care. *Professional Psychology: Research and Practice, 33,* 65–72.

National Association of Community Health Care Centers (NACHCC). (2008). Health Centers and Medicaid. Retrieved January 7, 2009, from http://www.nachc.com/research-factsheets.cfm

Newbould, P. (2007). Psychologists as legislators: Results of the 2006 elections. *Professional Psychology: Research and Practice, 38*(1), 3–6.

Newman, R. (2000, March). A psychological model for prescribing. *APA Monitor on Psychology, 31*(3), p. 45.

Newman, R., Phelps, R., Sammons, M. T., Dunivin, D. L., & Cullen, E. A. (2000). Evaluation of the psychopharmacology demonstration project: A retrospective analysis. *Professional Psychology: Research and Practice, 31*(6), 598–603.

O'Donohue, W. T., Byrd, M. R., Cummings, N. A., & Henderson, D. A. (Eds.). (2005). *Behavioral integrative care: Treatments that work in the primary care setting.* New York: Brunner-Routledge.

Oliveira, J. M., Austin, A., Miyamoto, R. E. S., Kaholokula, J. K., Yano, K. B., & Lunasco, T. (2006). The Rural Hawai'i Behavioral Health Program: Increasing access to primary care behavioral health for Native Hawaiians in rural settings. *Professional Psychology: Research and Practice, 37*(2), 174–182.

O'Neil, E. (2008, September). Centering on…Leadership. Center for Health Professions, Retrieved January 12, 2009 from http://futurehealth.ucsf.edu/archive/from_the_director_0908.htm

Pruitt, S. D., Klapow, J. D., Epping-Jordan, J. E., & Dresselhaus, T. R. (1998). Moving behavioral medicine to the front line: A model for the integration of behavioral and medical sciences in primary care. *Professional Psychology: Research and Practice, 29,* 230–236.

Robinson, P. (1998). Behavioral health services in primary care: A new perspective for treating depression. *Clinical Psychology Science & Practice, 5,* 77–93.

Sammons, M. T. (2001). Combined Treatments for mental disorders: Clinical Dilemmas. In M. T. Sammons & N. B. Schmidt (Eds.). *Combined treatments for mental disorders: Pharmacological and Psychological Interventions* (pp. 11–32). Washington: American Psychological Association.

Sammons, M. T. (2003). Some paradoxes and pragmatics surrounding the prescriptive authority movement. In M. T. Sammons, R. U. Paige, & R. F. Levant, (Eds.). *The evolution of prescribing psychology: A history and guide.* Washington: American Psychological Association.

Strosahl, K. (2005). Training behavioral health and primary care providers for integrated care: A core competencies approach.

In W. T. O'Donohou, M. R. Byrd, N. A. Cummings, & D. A. Henderson (Eds.), *Behavioral integrative care: Treatments that work in the primary care setting* (pp. 15–32). New York: Brunner-Rutledge.

Sullivan, M. J., & Reedy, S. D. (2005). Psychologists as legislators: Results of the 2004 elections. *Professional Psychology: Research and Practice, 36*(1), 32–36.

U.S. Department of Health, Education, and Welfare (HEW). (1979). *Healthy people: The surgeon general's report on health promotion and disease prevention.* DHEW Pub. No. (PHS) 79–55071. Washington, DC: U.S. Government Printing Office.

Research Methods in Clinical Psychology

Philip C. Kendall *and* Jonathan S. Comer

Abstract

This chapter describes methodological and design considerations central to the scientific evaluation of treatment efficacy and effectiveness. Matters of design, procedure, measurement, data analysis, and reporting are examined and discussed. The authors consider key concepts of controlled comparisons, random assignment, the use of treatment manuals, integrity and adherence checks, sample and setting selection, treatment transportability, handling missing data, assessing clinical significance, identifying mechanisms of change, and consolidated standards for communicating study findings to the scientific community. Examples from the treatment outcome literature are offered, and guidelines are suggested for conducting treatment evaluations that maximize both scientific rigor and clinical relevance.

Keywords: Measurement, random assignment, randomized clinical trial (RCT), treatment evaluation, treatment outcome

Central to research in clinical psychology is the evaluation of treatment outcomes. Research evaluations of the efficacy and effectiveness of therapeutic interventions have evolved from single-subject case histories to complex multimethod experimental investigations of carefully defined treatments applied to genuine clinical samples. The evolution is to be applauded.

In this chapter, we focus on how best to arrange these latter complex evaluations in a manner that maximizes both scientific rigor and clinical relevance. Although all of the ideals are rarely achieved in a single study, our discussions provide exemplars nonetheless. We encourage consistent attempts to incorporate these ideals into research designs, although we recognize that ethical and logistical constraints may compromise components of methodological rigor. We organize our chapter around the things that matter: (a) matters of design, (b) matters of procedure, (c) matters of measurement, (d) matters of data analysis, and (e) matters of reporting.

Matters of Design

To adequately assess the causal impact of a therapeutic intervention, clinical researchers use control procedures derived from experimental science. The objective is to separate the effects of the intervention from changes that result from other factors, which may include the passage of time, patient expectancies of change, therapist attention, repeated assessments, and simply regression to the mean. These extraneous factors must be "controlled" in order to have confidence that the intervention (i.e., the experimental manipulation) is responsible for any observed changes. To elaborate, we turn our attention to the selection of control conditions, random assignment, evaluation of response across time, and comparison of multiple treatments.

Selecting Control Condition(s)

Comparisons of persons randomly assigned to different treatment conditions are required to control for factors other than the treatment. In a "controlled" treatment evaluation, comparable persons are randomly placed into either the treatment condition (composed of those who receive the intervention) or the control condition (composed of those who do not receive the intervention), and by comparing the changes evidenced by the members of both conditions the efficacy of therapy over and above the outcome produced by extraneous factor (e.g., passage of time) can be determined. However, deciding the nature of the control condition (e.g., no-treatment, wait list, attention-placebo, standard treatment-as-usual) is not simple (see Table 4.1 for recent examples).

When comparison clients are assigned to a *no-treatment* control condition, they are administered the assessments on repeated occasions, separated by an interval of time equal in length to the therapy provided to those in the treatment condition. Any changes seen in the treated clients are compared to changes seen in the nontreated clients. When treated clients evidence significant improvements over nontreated clients, the treatment is credited with producing the changes. This no-treatment procedure eliminates several rival hypotheses (e.g., maturation, spontaneous remission, historical effects, regression to the mean). However, a no-treatment control condition does not guard against other potentially confounding factors, including client anticipation of treatment, client expectancy for change, and the act of seeing a therapist—independent of what specific

Table 4.1 Types of control conditions in treatment outcome research

Control condition	Definition	Recent example in literature	
		Description	Reference
No-treatment control	Control clients are administered assessments on repeated occasions, separated by an interval of time equal to the length of treatment.	Refugees in Uganda diagnosed with PTSD were randomly assigned to active trauma-focused treatments or a control condition. Individuals in the control condition received no treatment but were assessed on repeated occasions.	Neuner et al. (2008)
Waitlist control	Control clients are assessed before and after a designated duration of time, but receive the treatment following the waiting period. They may anticipate change due to therapy.	Anxious children and their parents were randomly assigned to group treatment, bibliotherapy, or a 12-week waitlist control condition.	Rapee et al. (2006)
Attention-placebo/ nonspecific control	Control clients receive a treatment that involves nonspecific factors (e.g., attention, contact with a therapist)	Children with anxiety disorders were randomly assigned to cognitive-behavioral treatments or a control condition in which they received weekly attention and psychoeducation.	Kendall et al. (2008)
Standard treatment/routine care control	Control clients receive an intervention that is the current practice for treatment of the problem under study.	Families were randomly assigned to either a parent-management training or a regular services comparison group.	Ogden & Hagen (2008)

treatment the therapist actually provided. Although a no-treatment control condition is sometimes useful in the earlier stages of evaluating a treatment, other control procedures are preferred.

Utilizing a *waitlist condition*—a variant of the no-treatment condition—provides some additional control. Clients in the waitlist condition expect that after a specified period of time they will be receiving treatment, and accordingly may anticipate changes due to this treatment, which may in turn affect the course of their symptoms. The changes that occur for wait-listed clients are evaluated at regular intervals, as are those of the clients who received therapy. If we assume the clients in the waitlist and treatment conditions are comparable (e.g., gender, age, ethnicity, severity of presenting problem, and motivation), then we can make inferences that the changes in the treated clients over and above those also manifested by the waitlist clients are likely due to the intervention rather than to any extraneous factors that were operative for both the treated and the waitlist conditions (e.g., expectations of change). The important demographic data are gathered so that statistical comparisons can be conducted to determine condition comparability. Waitlist conditions, like no-treatment conditions, are of less value for treatments that have already been examined versus somewhat "inactive" comparisons.

There are potential limitations associated with waitlist controls. First, a waitlist client might experience a life crisis that requires immediate professional attention. For ethical purposes, the status of control clients should be monitored to ensure that they are safely able to tolerate the treatment delay. In the event of an emergency, the provision of professional services will compromise the integrity of the waitlist condition. Second, it is preferable that the duration of the control condition be the same as the duration of the treatment condition(s). Comparable durations help to ensure that any differential changes between the conditions would not be due to the differential passage of time. However, suppose an 18-session treatment takes 4–5 months to provide—is it ethical to withhold treatment for 4–5 months as a wait period (see Bersoff & Bersoff, 1999)? With long waitlist durations, the probability of differential attrition arises, a situation that could have a compromising effect on study results. If rates of attrition from a waitlist condition are high, the sample in the control condition may be sufficiently different from the sample in the treatment condition, and no longer representative of the larger group (e.g., the smaller waitlist group at the end of the study now only represents clients who could tolerate and withstand a prolonged period without treatment).

No-treatment or waitlist controls provide initial evidence of treatment efficacy but are less important once a treatment has, in several evaluations, been found to be more effective than "inactive" control conditions. *Attention-placebo* (or nonspecific treatment) control conditions are an alternative to the waitlist control that rule out some threats to internal validity, and control for the effects that might be due simply to meeting with and getting the attention of a therapist. In addition, these participants receive a description of a treatment rationale (an explanation of the treatment procedures offered at the beginning of the intervention). The rationale provided to attention-placebo clients mobilizes an *expectancy* of positive gains. (For discussion of treatment elements separate from the proposed active components see Hollon & DeRubeis, 1981; Jacobson & Hollon, 1996a, 1996b).

Attention-placebo conditions enable clinical researchers to identify the changes produced by specific therapeutic strategies over and above nonspecific strategies. For example, in a recent randomized clinical trial (RCT) (Kendall et al., 2008), children with anxiety disorders received cognitive-behavioral treatment (CBT; either individual or family CBT) or a manualized family education, support, and attention (i.e., FESA) condition. Individual and family-based CBT was found to be superior to FESA in reducing the children's principal anxiety disorder. Given the nature of the FESA condition one was able to infer that the gains associated with receiving CBT are not likely attributed to "common therapy factors" such as learning about anxiety/emotions, experience with an understanding therapist, attention to and opportunities to discuss anxiety.

Despite the advantages of attention-placebo controls, they are not without limitations (Parloff, 1986). Attention placebos must be devoid of therapeutic techniques hypothesized to be effective, while at the same time instilling positive expectations in clients and providing professional contact. To offer such an intervention in the guise of effective therapy is acceptable when clients are fully informed in advance and sign informed consent forms acknowledging their willingness to take a chance on receiving either a psychosocial placebo condition. Even then, an attention-placebo condition may be difficult for the therapist to accomplish.

Methodologically, it is difficult to ensure that therapists who conduct attention-placebo conditions have the same degree of positive expectancy for client gains as do therapists conducting specific interventions (Kendall, Holmbeck, & Verduin, 2002; O'Leary & Borkovec, 1978). "Demand characteristics" would suggest that when therapists predict a favorable outcome, clients will tend to improve accordingly (Kazdin, 2003). Thus, therapist expectancies may not be equal for active and placebo conditions, reducing the interpretability of the findings. Similarly, clients in an attention-placebo condition may have high expectations at the start, but may grow disenchanted when no specific changes are emerging. If study results suggest that a therapy condition evidenced significantly better outcomes than a attention-placebo control condition, it is important that the researcher evaluate clients' perceptions of the credibility of the treatment and their expectations for change to confirm that clients in the attention-placebo condition perceived the treatment to be credible and expected to improve.

The use of a *standard treatment* (treatment-as-usual) as a comparison condition allows the researcher to evaluate an experimental treatment relative to the intervention that is currently available and being applied (i.e., an existing standard of care). When the standard care intervention and the therapy under study have comparable durations of treatment and client and therapist expectancies, the researcher can test the relative efficacy of the interventions. For example, in a recent RCT (Mufson et al., 2004), depressed adolescents were randomly assigned to interpersonal psychotherapy modified for depressed adolescents (IPT-A) or to "treatment-as-usual" in school-based mental health clinics. Adolescents treated with IPT-A compared to treatment-as-usual showed greater symptom reduction and improvement in overall functioning. Given the nature of their comparison group it can be inferred that the gains associated with IPT-A outperformed the existing standard of care for depressed adolescents in the community.

In standard treatment comparisons, it is important to ensure that both the standard (routine) treatment and the new treatment are implemented in a high-quality fashion (Kendall & Hollon, 1983). Using a standard treatment condition presents advantages over other conditions. Ethical concerns about no-treatment conditions are quelled, given that care is provided to all participants. Additionally, attrition is likely to be minimized and nonspecific factors are likely to be equated (Kazdin, 2003).

Random Assignment

After comparison conditions have been selected, procedures for assigning participants to conditions must be chosen. *Random assignment* ensures that every participant has an equal chance of being assigned to the active treatment condition or the control condition(s). Random assignment of participants to the active therapy or control conditions and random assignment to study therapists are essential steps toward achieving initial comparability between conditions. However, note that random assignment does not guarantee comparability across treatment conditions—one resultant group may be different on key variables (e.g., age, wealth, impairment) simply due to chance. Appropriate statistical tests can be applied to examine the comparability of participants across treatment conditions.

Problems can arise when random assignment is not applied. Consider a situation in which participants do not have an equal chance of being assigned to the active and control condition. Suppose a researcher were to allow depressed participants to decide for themselves whether to participate in the active treatment or in a waitlist condition. If participants in the active treatment condition subsequently evidenced greater symptom reductions than waitlist participants, one would be unable to rule out the possibility that symptom differences could have resulted from pre-study differences between the participants (e.g., selection bias). Waitlist participants who elected to delay treatment may be individuals not ready to initiate work on their depression symptoms.

Random assignment does not absolutely assure comparability of conditions on all measures, but it does maximize the likelihood of comparability. An alternative procedure, randomized blocks assignment, or assignment by stratified blocks, involves matching prospective clients in subgroups that (a) contain clients that are highly comparable on key dimensions (e.g., initial severity) and (b) contain the same number of clients as the number of conditions. For example, if the study requires two conditions (a standard treatment and a new treatment), clients can be paired off so that each pair is highly comparable. The members in each pair are then randomly assigned to either condition, thus increasing the likelihood that each condition will contain relatively mirror-image participants while retaining the randomization factor. When feasible, randomized blocks assignment of clients to conditions can be a wise research strategy.

Evaluating Response Across Time

To evaluate the effect of a treatment, it is essential to first evaluate the level of each client's functioning on the dependent variables before the intervention begins. Such pretreatment (or "baseline") assessments provide key data to inform whether clients are comparable at the beginning of treatment (i.e., between-groups comparisons), and whether clients' pretreatment levels of functioning differ significantly from functioning assessed at subsequent assessment points (i.e., within-groups comparisons).

Post-treatment assessments of clients are essential to examine the comparative efficacy of treatment versus control conditions. However, evidence of treatment efficacy immediately upon therapy completion may not be indicative of long-term success (maintenance). Treatment outcome may be appreciable at post-treatment but fail to exhibit maintenance of the effects at a follow-up assessment. It is highly recommended, and increasingly expected (Chambless & Hollon, 1998), that treatment outcome studies include a follow-up assessment. Follow-up assessments (e.g., 6 months, 1 year) are key to demonstrations of treatment efficacy and are a signpost of methodological rigor. For evidence of maintenance, the treatment must have produced results at the follow-up assessment that are comparable to those evident at post-treatment (i.e., improvements from pretreatment and an absence of detrimental change since post-treatment).

Follow-up evaluations can help to identify differential treatment effects. For example, the effects of two treatments may be comparable at the end of treatment, but one may be more effective in the prevention of relapse (see Greenhouse, Stangl, & Bromberg, 1989, for discussion of survival analysis). When two treatments are comparable at post-treatment, yet one has a higher relapse rate, the knowledge gained from the follow-up evaluation is a valuable rationale for selecting one treatment over another. For example, Brown and colleagues (1997) reported on a comparison of CBT and relaxation training as treatments for depression in alcoholism. Using the average (mean) days abstinent and drinks per day as dependent variables, measured at pretreatment and at 3 and 6 months post-treatment, the authors established that, although both treatments produced comparable initial gains, the cognitive-behavioral treatment was superior to relaxation training in maintaining gains.

Follow-up evaluations may also detect continued improvement—the benefits of some interventions may accumulate over time, and possibly expand to other domains of functioning. Researchers and policy-makers have become increasingly interested in expanding intervention research to consider potential indirect effects on the prevention of secondary problems. We followed-up individuals treated with a cognitive-behavioral treatment for childhood anxiety disorders roughly 7 years later (Kendall, Safford, Flannery-Schroeder & Webb, 2002). These data indicated that a meaningful percentage of treated participants had maintained improvements in anxiety and that positive responders, as compared with less-positive responders, had a reduced amount of substance-use involvement at long-term follow-up (see also Kendall & Kessler, 2002). It is important to note that gains identified at follow-up are best only attributed to the initial treatment after one determines that the participants did not seek or receive additional treatments during the follow-up interval.

As we learn more about the outcomes of treatment, we are intrigued by speculations about the process that takes place in achieving these outcomes. Some researchers are considering therapy process and outcome as intertwined and are assessing change during the course of treatment (i.e., intratreatment) as well as post-treatment and follow-up (e.g., Kazdin, Marciano, & Whitley, 2005; Kendall & Ollendick, 2004; Shirk, Gudmundsen, Kaplinski, & McMakin, 2008; Taft & Murphy, 2007). Repeated assessment of client symptoms and functional change suggests that the first several sessions of treatment constitute the period of most rapid positive change (Howard, Lueger, Maling, & Martiovich, 1993). However, change across several domains of functioning may be phasic and may require more extended treatment. Intratreatment assessments (see Lambert, Hansen, & Finch, 2001) not only permit a fine-grained mapping of the course of change in therapy, but also provide important clues (e.g., Jaycox, Foa, & Morral, 1998) to identify mediators (discussed later in this chapter) of positive or adverse outcomes.

Multiple Treatment Comparisons

To determine comparative (or relative) efficacy and effectiveness of therapeutic interventions, researchers use between-groups designs with more than one active treatment condition. Between-groups designs are more direct comparisons of one treatment with one or more alternative treatments. Note that sample size considerations are influenced by whether the comparison is between a treatment and a control condition or one treatment versus another known to be effective treatment (see Kazdin & Bass, 1989).

In multiple treatment comparisons, it is optimal when each client is randomly assigned to receive one and only one kind of therapy. The assignment of clients to conditions should result in the initial comparability of the clients receiving each intervention. As previously mentioned, a randomized block procedure, with participants blocked on an important variable (e.g., pretreatment severity), can be used. It is always wise to check the comparability of the clients in the different treatment conditions on other important variables (e.g., sociodemographic variables, prior therapy experience, treatment expectancies/ preferences) before continuing with the evaluation of the intervention. If not all participants are available at the outset of treatment, such as when participants come from consecutive clinic admissions, then the comparability of conditions can be checked at several intervals as the therapy outcome study progresses toward completion.

Comparability across therapists administering the different treatments is essential. Therapists conducting each type of treatment should be comparable in (a) training, (b) professional and clinical experience, (c) expertise in the intervention, (d) allegiance with the treatment, and (e) expectation that the intervention will be effective. One method to control for therapist effects has each therapist conduct each type of intervention with at least one client per intervention. Another viable option is *stratified blocking*, which assures that each intervention is conducted by several comparable therapists. The first method has random assignment of therapists, but is preferred only when therapists are equally expert and positively disposed toward each intervention. For example, it would probably not be a valid test to ask a group of psychodynamic therapists to conduct both a CBT (in which their expertise is low) and a psychodynamic therapy (in which their expertise is high). As is often the case, it is wise to gather data on therapist variables (e.g., expertise, allegiance) and examine their relationships to outcomes.

Comparing alternative treatments requires that the intervention procedures across treatments be equated for salient variables such as (a) duration; (b) length, intensity, and frequency of contacts with clients; (c) credibility of the treatment rationale; (d) setting in which treatment is to be provided; and (e) degree of involvement of persons significant to the client. In some cases, these factors may be the basis for two alternative therapies (e.g., conjoint vs. individual marital therapy; or child- vs. family-based treatment). In such cases, the variable is the experimental contrast rather than a matter for control.

What is the best method of measuring change when two alternative treatments are being compared? Clearly, measures should not be differentially sensitive to one or the other treatment. The measures should (a) cover the range of functioning that is a target for change, (b) tap the costs and possible negative side effects, and (c) be unbiased with respect to the alternate interventions. Comparisons of therapies may be misleading if the assessments are not equally sensitive to the types of changes that are most likely caused by each type of intervention.

When comparing alternative treatments, the "expected efficacy" of each therapy based on prior studies requires consideration. Consider, for example, that two treatments are compared and that therapy A is found to be superior to therapy B. The question can then arise, was therapy A superior, or did therapy B fail to be efficacious in this instance? It would be desirable in demonstrating the efficacy of therapy A if the results due to therapy B reflected the level of efficacy typically found in earlier demonstrations of therapy B's efficacy. Interpretations of the results of comparative studies are dependent on the level of efficacy of each therapy in relation to its expected (or standard) efficacy. Effect sizes are useful in making these comparisons and in reaching sound conclusions.

Although the issues discussed apply, comparisons of psychological and psychopharmacological treatments (e.g., Dobson et al., 2008; Marcus et al., 2007; MTA Cooperative Group, 1999; Pediatric OCD Treatment Study Team, 2004; Walkup et al, 2008) present special issues. For example, how and when should placebo medications be used in comparison to or with psychological therapy? How should expectancy effects be addressed? How should differential attrition be handled? How is it best to handle intrinsic differences in professional contact across psychological and pharmacologic interventions? Follow-ups become especially important after the active treatments are discontinued. The question is especially pertinent given that psychological treatment effects may persist after treatment, whereas the effects of medications may not persist when the medications are discontinued. (Readers interested in discussions of these issues are referred to Hollon, 1996; Hollon & DeRubeis, 1981; Jacobson & Hollon, 1996a, 1996b).

Matters of Procedure

We now consider procedural matters related to (a) defining the independent variable (the use of manual-based treatments), (b) checking the integrity of the independent variable (treatment fidelity checks), (c) selecting a sample, and (d) considering the research setting and the transportability of treatment.

Defining the Independent Variable: Manual-based Treatments

It is essential that a treatment be adequately described and detailed in order to replicate an evaluation of the treatment, or to be able to show and teach others how to conduct the treatment. Accordingly, there is the need for the use of treatment manuals. Treatment manuals enhance internal validity and treatment integrity, and afford comparison of treatments across contexts and formats, while reducing confounds (e.g., differences in the amount of contact, type and amount of training, time between sessions). Therapist manuals facilitate training and contribute meaningfully to replication (Dobson & Hamilton, 2002; Dobson & Shaw, 1988).

Not all agree on the merits of manuals. Debate has ensued regarding the use of manual-based treatments versus a more variable approach typically found in practice (see Addis, Cardemil, Duncan, & Miller, 2006; Addis & Krasnow, 2000; Westen, Novotny, & Thompson-Brenner, 2004). Some argue that manuals limit therapist creativity and place restrictions on the individualization that the therapists use (see also Waltz, Addis, Koerner, & Jacobson, 1993; Wilson, 1995). Some treatment manuals appear "cook-bookish," and some lack attention to the necessary clinical sensitivities needed for proper individualization and implementation, but our experience suggests that this is not the norm. An empirical evaluation from our laboratory found that the use of a manual-based treatment for child anxiety disorders (Kendall & Hedtke, 2006) did not restrict therapist flexibility (Kendall & Chu, 1999). Although it is not the goal of manual-based treatments to have practitioners perform treatment in a rigid manner, this misperception has influenced some practitioners' openness to the use of manual-based interventions (Addis & Krasnow, 2000).

The proper use of manual-based therapy requires interactive training, flexible application, and ongoing supervision (Kendall & Beidas, 2007). Professionals cannot become proficient in the administration of therapy simply by reading a manual. As Barlow (1989) noted, effective use of manual-based treatments must be preceded by adequate training.

Several contemporary treatment manuals allow the therapist to attend to each client's specific needs, concerns, and comorbid conditions without deviating from the treatment strategies detailed in the manual. The goal is to include provisions for standardized implementation of therapy while utilizing a personalized case formulation (Suveg, Comer, Furr, & Kendall, 2006). Importantly, using manual-based treatments does not eliminate the potential for differential therapist effects. Within the context of manual-based treatments, researchers are examining therapist variables (e.g., warmth, therapeutic relationship-building behaviors) that might be related to treatment outcome (Creed & Kendall, 2005; Karver et al., 2008; Shirk et al., 2008).

Checking the Integrity of the Independent Variable: Treatment Fidelity Checks

Quality experimental research includes checking the manipulated variable. In therapy outcome evaluations, the manipulated variable is typically treatment or a characteristic of treatment. By design, all clients are not treated the same. However, just because the study has been so designed does not guarantee that the independent variable (treatment) has been implemented as intended. In the course of a study—whether due to therapist variables, incomplete manual specification, poor therapist training, insufficient therapist monitoring, client demand characteristics, or simply error variance—the treatment that was assigned may not in fact be the treatment that was provided (see also Perepletchikova & Kazdin, 2005).

To help ensure that the treatments are indeed implemented as intended, it is wise to require that a treatment plan be followed, that therapists are trained carefully, and that sufficient supervision is available throughout. The researcher should conduct an independent check on the manipulation. For example, therapy sessions are audio- or videotaped, so that an independent rater can listen to/watch the tapes and conduct a manipulation check. Quantifiable judgments regarding key characteristics of the treatment provide the necessary check that the described treatment was indeed provided. Digital videotapes and audiotapes are inexpensive, can be used for subsequent training, and can be analyzed to answer other research questions. Tape recordings of the therapy sessions evaluated by outcome studies not only provide a check on the treatment within each separate study but also allow for a check on the comparability of treatments provided across studies. That is, the therapy provided as CBT in one clinician's study could be checked to determine its comparability to other clinician-researchers' CBT.

Procedures from a recently completed clinical trial from our research program comparing two active treatment conditions for child anxiety disorders against an active attention control condition (Kendall et al., 2008) can illustrate integrity checks. First, we developed a checklist of the content/strategies called for in each session by the respective manuals. A panel of expert clinicians serve as independent raters who used the checklists to rate randomly selected videotape segments from 20% of randomly selected cases. The panel of raters was trained on nonstudy cases until they reached an inter-rater reliability of .85 (Cohen's κ). Once reliable, the panel used the checklists to indicate whether the appropriate content was covered for randomly selected segments that were representative of all sessions, conditions, and therapists. A ratio was computed for each coded session: the number of checklist items covered by the therapist relative to the total number of items that should have been included. Results indicated that across the conditions, 85%–92% of intended content was in fact covered.

It is critical to also evaluate the *quality* of the treatment provided. A therapist may strictly adhere to the manual and yet fail to administer the therapy in an otherwise competent manner, or he or she may competently administer therapy while significantly deviating from the manual. In both cases, the operational definition of the independent variable (i.e., the treatment manual) has been violated, treatment integrity impaired, and replication rendered impossible (Dobson & Shaw, 1988). When a treatment fails to demonstrate expected gains, one can examine the adequacy with which the treatment was implemented (see Hollon, Garber, & Shelton, 2005). It is also of interest to study potential variations in treatment outcome that may be associated with differences in the *quality* of the treatment provided (Garfield, 1998; Kendall & Hollon, 1983). Expert judges are needed to make determinations of differential quality prior to the examination of differential outcomes for high- versus low-quality therapy implementation (see Waltz et al., 1993).

Sampling Issues

Choosing a sample to best represent the clinical population about which you are interested in making inferences requires consideration. Debate exists over the preferred samples for treatment outcome research. A *selected sample* refers to a sample of participants who may need service but who may otherwise only approximate clinically disordered individuals. Randomized controlled trials, by contrast, apply and evaluate treatments with actual clients who are seeking services. Consider a study investigating the effects of treatment X on depression. The researcher could use (a) a sample of clinically depressed clients diagnosed via structured interviews (*genuine clinical sample*), (b) a sample consisting of a group of adults who self-report dysphoric mood (an *analogue sample*), or (c) a sample of depressed persons after excluding cases with suicidal intent, economic stress, and family conflict (*highly select sample*). This last sample may meet diagnostic criteria for depression but are nevertheless highly selected.

The benefits of using analogue or select samples may include a greater ability to control various conditions and minimize threats to internal validity, and from a practical standpoint researchers may find it easier to recruit these samples over genuine clinical samples. On the other hand, select and analogue samples compromise external validity—these are not the same people seen in typical clinical practice. With respect to depression, for instance, many question whether depression in genuine clinical populations compares meaningfully to self-reported dysphoria in adults (e.g., Coyne, 1994; Krupnick, Shea, & Elkin, 1986; Tennen, Hall, & Affleck, 1995; see also Ruscio & Ruscio, 2002, 2008). Researchers consider how the study results will be interpreted and generalized when deciding whether to use clinical, analogue, or select samples.

Researchers consider *client diversity* when deciding which samples to study. Historically, research supporting the efficacy of psychological treatments was conducted with predominantly European American samples—although this is rapidly changing (see Huey & Polo, 2008). One can question the extent to which efficacy findings from European American samples can be generalized to ethnic minority samples (Bernal, Bonilla, & Bellido, 1995; Bernal & Scharron-Del-Rio, 2001; Hall, 2001; Sue, 1998). Investigations have also addressed the potential for bias in diagnoses and in the provision of mental health services to ethnic minority patients (e.g., Flaherty & Meaer, 1980; Homma-True, Green, Lopez, & Trimble, 1993; Lopez, 1989; Snowden, 2003).

A simple rule is that the research sample should reflect the population to which the results will be generalized. To generalize to a minority/diverse population, one must study a minority/diverse sample. Any barriers to care must be reduced and outreach efforts employed to inform minorities of available services (see Sweeney, Robins, Ruberu, & Jones, 2005; Yeh, McCabe, Hough, Dupuis, & Hazen, 2003). Walders and Drotar (2000) provide guidelines for recruiting and working with ethnically diverse samples.

Once sample diversity is accomplished, statistical analyses can examine potential differential outcomes (see Arnold et al., 2003; Treadwell, Flannery-Schroeder, & Kendall, 1994). Grouping and analyzing research participants by ethnic status is one approach. However, this approach is simplistic because it fails to address variations in individual client's degree of ethnic identity. It is often the degree to which an individual identifies with an ethnocultural group or community, and not simply his or her ethnicity itself, that may potentially moderate treatment outcome.

Setting

Research determines treatment efficacy, but it is not sufficient to demonstrate efficacy within a narrowly defined sample in a highly selective setting. The question of whether the treatment can be transported to other settings requires independent evaluation (Southam-Gerow, Ringeisen, & Sherrill, 2006). Treatment outcome studies conducted in some settings (settings in which clients may differ on important variables) may not generalize to other settings. Some have questioned whether the outcomes found at select research centers will transport to clinical practice settings. One should study, rather than assume, that a treatment found to be efficacious within a research clinical setting will be efficacious in a clinical service setting (see Hoagwood, 2002; Silverman, Kurtines, & Hoagwood, 2004; Southam-Gerow et al., 2006; Weisz, Donenberg, Han, & Weiss, 1995; Weisz, Weiss, & Donenberg, 1992).

Closing the gap between clinical research and practice requires transporting effective treatments (getting "what works" into practice) and identifying additional research into those factors (e.g., client, therapist, researcher, service delivery setting; see Kendall & Southam-Gerow, 1995; Silverman et al., 2004) that may be involved in successful transportation. Fishman (2000) suggested that an electronic journal of case studies be assembled so that patient, therapy, and environmental variables can be collected/compiled from within naturalistic therapy settings. Although the methodology has flaws (Stricker, 2000), information technology–based approaches may facilitate more seamless integration of research and practice and foster new waves of outcome research.

Matters of Measurement
Assessing the Dependent Variable(s)

No single measure serves as the sole indicator of clients' treatment-related gains. Rather, a variety of methods, measures, data sources, and sampling domains (e.g., symptomatic distress, functional impairment, quality of life) are used to assess therapy outcomes. A contemporary and rigorous study of the effects of therapy may use assessments of client self-report; client test/task performance; therapist judgments and ratings; archival or documentary records (e.g., health-care visit and costs, work and school records); observations by trained, unbiased, blinded observers; rating by significant people in the client's life; and independent judgments by professionals. Outcomes have more compelling impact when seen by independent (blind) evaluators than when based solely on the therapist's opinion or the client's self-reports.

The *multi-informant strategy*, in which data on variables of interest are collected from multiple reporters (e.g., client, family members, peers) can be particularly important when assessing children and adolescents. Features of cognitive development may compromise youth self-reports, and children may offer what they believe to be the desired responses. Thus, in RCTs with youth, collecting additional data from key adults in children's lives who observe them across different contexts (e.g., parents, teachers) is valued. However, because emotions and mood are partially internal phenomena, some symptoms may be less known to parents and teachers, and some observable symptoms may occur in situations outside the home or school.

An inherent concern with multi-informant assessment is that discrepancies among informants are to be expected (Comer & Kendall, 2004; Edelbrock, Costello, Dulcan, Conover, & Kalas, 1986). Research indicates low to moderate concordance rates among informants in the assessment of children and adolescents (Achenbach, McConaughy, & Howell, 1987; De Los Reyes & Kazdin, 2005). For example, cross-informant agreement in the assessment of childhood mood/anxiety can be low (Comer & Kendall, 2004; Grills & Ollendick, 2003).

A *multimodal strategy* relies on multiple inquiries to evaluate an underlying construct of interest. For example, assessing family functioning may include family members completing self-report forms on their perceptions of family relationships, as well as conducting structured behavioral observations of family members interacting (to later be coded by independent raters). Statistical packages can integrate data obtained from multimodal assessment strategies. The increasing availability of handheld communication devices and personal digital assistants allows researchers to incorporate experience sampling methodology (ESM), in which people report on their emotions and behavior in the actual situation (*in situ*). These ESM data provide naturalistic information on patterns in day-to-day functioning.

Treatment evaluations use multiple targets of assessment. For example, one can measure overall psychological adjustment, specific interpersonal skills, the presence of a diagnosis, self-report mood, cognitive functioning, life environment, vocational status, and the quality of interpersonal relationships. No one target captures all, and using multiple targets facilitates an examination of therapeutic changes when changes occur, and the absence of change when interventions are less beneficial.

Broadly speaking, evaluation of therapy-induced change can be appraised on two levels: the specifying level and the impact level (Kendall, Pellegrini, & Urbain, 1981). The *specifying level* refers to the exact skills, cognitive or emotional processes, or behaviors that have been modified during treatment (e.g., examining the number of positive spousal statements generated during a specific marital relationship task). In contrast, the *impact level* refers to the general level of functioning of the client (e.g., absence of a diagnosis, functional status of the client). A compelling demonstration of beneficial treatment would include change that occurs at both the level of specific discrete skills and behaviors, and the impact level of generalized functioning in which the client interacts differently within the larger environmental context.

Assessing *multiple domains* of functioning provides a comprehensive evaluation of treatment, but it is rarely the case that a treatment produces uniform effects across the domains assessed. Suppose treatment A, relative to a control condition, improves depressed clients' level of depression, but not their overall psychological well-being. In an RCT designed to evaluate improved level of depression and psychological well-being, should treatment A be deemed efficacious if only one of two measures found gains? De Los Reyes and Kazdin (2006) propose the Range of Possible Changes model, which calls for a multidimensional conceptualization of intervention

change. In this spirit, we recommend that researchers conducting RCTs be explicit about the domains of functioning expected to change and the relative magnitude of such expected changes. We also caution consumers of the treatment outcome literature against simplistic dichotomous appraisals of treatments as efficacious or not.

Matters of Data Analysis

Contrary to popular misguided perceptions, data do not "speak" for themselves. *Data analysis* is an active process in which we extract useful information from the data we have collected in ways that allow us to make statistical inferences about the larger population that a given sample was selected to represent. Although a comprehensive statistical discussion is beyond the present scope (the interested reader is referred to Jaccard & Guilamo-Ramos, 2002a, 2002b; Kraemer & Kupfer, 2006; Kraemer, Wilson, Fairburn, & Agras, 2002) in this section, we discuss four areas that merit consideration in the context of research methods in clinical psychology: (a) handling missing data and attrition, (b) assessing clinical significance (i.e., the persuasiveness of outcomes), (c) mechanisms of change (i.e., mediators and moderators), and (d) cumulative outcome analyses.

Handling Missing Data and Attrition

Given the time-intensive and ongoing nature of RCTs, not all clients who are assigned to treatment actually complete their participation in the study. A loss of research participants (*attrition*) may occur just after randomization, prior to post-treatment evaluation, or during the follow-up interval. Increasingly, clinical scientists are analyzing attrition and its predictors and correlates to elucidate the nature of treatment dropout, understand treatment tolerability, and to enhance the sustainability mental health services in the community (Kendall & Sugarman, 1997; Reis & Brown, 2006; Vanable, Carey, Carey, & Maisto, 2002). However, from a research methods standpoint, attrition can be problematic for data analysis, such as when there are large numbers of noncompleters or when attrition varies across conditions (Leon et al., 2006; Molenberghs et al., 2004).

No matter how diligently researchers work to prevent attrition, data will likely be lost. Although attrition rates vary across studies, Mason (1999) estimated that most researchers can expect nearly 20% of their sample to withdraw or be removed from a study before it is completed. To address this matter, researchers can conduct and report two sets of analyses: (a) analyses of outcomes for the treatment completers and (b) analyses of outcomes for all clients who were included at the time of randomization (i.e., the *intent-to-treat sample*). An analysis of completers involves the evaluation of only those who completed treatment and examines what the effects of treatment are when someone completes its full course. Treatment dropouts, treatment refusers, and clients who fail to adhere to treatment schedules would not be included in these outcome analyses. In such cases, reports of treatment outcome may be somewhat high because they represent the results for only those who adhered to and completed the treatment. Intent-to-treat analyses, a more conservative approach to addressing missing data, require the evaluation of outcomes for all participants involved at the point of randomization. Proponents of intent-to-treatment analyses will say, "once randomized, always analyzed."

When conducting intent-to-treat analyses, the method used to handle missing endpoint data requires consideration, because different methods can produce different outcomes. Delucchi and Bostrom (1999) summarized the effects of missing data on a range of statistical analyses. Researchers address missing endpoint data via one of several ways: (a) *last observation carried forward* (LOCF), (b) substituting pretreatment scores for post-treatment scores, (c) multiple imputation methods, and (d) mixed-effects models.

The following example illustrates these different methods. Suppose a researcher conducts a smoking cessation trial comparing a 12-week active treatment (treatment A) to a 12-week waitlist control condition, with mean number of daily cigarettes used over the course of the previous week as the dependent variable, and with four assessment points: pretreatment, week 4, week 8, and post-treatment. A LOCF analysis assumes that participants who attrit remain constant on the outcome variable from their last assessed point through the post-treatment evaluation. If a participant drops out at week 9, the data from the week 8 assessment would be substituted for their missing post-treatment assessment data. A LOCF approach can be problematic however, as the last data collected may not be representative of the dropout participant's ultimate progress or lack of progress at post-treatment, given that participants may change after dropping out of treatment (e.g., cigarette use may abruptly rise upon dropout, reversing initially assessed gains). The use of pretreatment data as post-treatment data (a conservative and not

recommended method) simply inserts pretreatment scores for cases of attrition as post-treatment scores, assuming that participants who attrit make no change from their initial baseline state.

Critics of the LOCF and the pretreatment data substitution methods argue that these crude methods introduce systematic bias and fail to take into account the uncertainty of post-treatment functioning (see Leon et al., 2006). Increasingly, journals are calling for missing data imputation methods to be grounded in statistical theory and to incorporate the uncertainty regarding the true value of the missing data. *Multiple imputation methods* impute a range of values for the missing data (incorporating the uncertainty of the true values of missing data), generating a number of nonidentical datasets (typically five is considered sufficient; Little & Rubin, 2002). After the researcher conducts analyses on the nonidentical datasets, the results are pooled and the resulting variability addresses the uncertainty of the true value of the missing data. Moreover, *mixed-effects modeling*, which relies on linear and/or logistic regression to address missing data in the context of random (e.g., participant) and fixed effects (e.g., treatment, age, sex) (see Hedeker & Gibbons, 1994, 1997; Laird & Ware, 1982), can be used (see Neuner et al., 2008 for an example). Mixed-effects modeling may be particularly useful in addressing missing data if numerous assessments are collected throughout a treatment trial (e.g., weekly symptom ratings).

Given a lack of consensus regarding the most appropriate way to address missing data in RCTs, we encourage researchers—if it is possible for non-completing participants to be contacted and evaluated at the time when the treatment protocol would have ended—to contact and reassess participants. This method controls for the passage of time, because both dropouts and treatment completers are evaluated over time periods of the same duration. If this method is used, however, it is important to determine whether dropouts sought and/or received alternative treatments in the interim.

Clinical Significance: Assessing the Persuasiveness of Outcomes

The data produced by research projects designed to evaluate the efficacy of therapy are submitted to statistical tests of significance. The mean scores for participants in each condition are compared, the within-group and between-group variability is considered, and the analysis produces a numerical figure, which is then checked against critical values. An outcome achieves *statistical* significance if the magnitude of the mean difference is beyond what could have resulted by chance alone (typically defined by convention as $p < .05$). Statistical analyses and statistical significance are essential for therapy evaluation because they inform us that the degree of change was likely not due to chance. However, statistical tests alone do not provide evidence of *clinical significance*.

Sole reliance on statistical significance can lead to perceiving differences (i.e., treatment gains) as potent when in fact they may not be clinically significant. For example, imagine that the results of a treatment outcome study demonstrate that mean Beck Depression Inventory (BDI) scores are significantly lower at post-treatment than pretreatment. An examination of the means, however, reveals only a small but reliable shift from a mean of 29 to a mean of 24. Given large sample sizes, this difference may well achieve statistical significance at the $p < .05$ level (i.e., over 95% chance that the finding is not due to chance alone), yet perhaps be of limited practical significance. At both pre- and post-treatment, the scores are within the range considered indicative of clinical levels of depressive distress (Kendall, Hollon, Beck, Hammen, & Ingram, 1987), and such a magnitude of change may have little effect on a person's perceived quality of life (Gladis, Gosch, Dishuk, & Crits-Christoph, 1990). Moreover, statistically meager results may disguise meaningful changes in client functioning. As Kazdin (1999) put it, sometimes a little can mean a lot, and vice versa.

Clinical significance refers to the meaningfulness or persuasiveness of the magnitude of change (Kendall, 1999). Whereas tests of statistical significance address the question "Were there treatment-related changes?" tests of clinical significance address the question "Were the treatment-related changes convincing and meaningful?" In the treatment of a depressive disorder, for example, clinically significant changes would have to be of the magnitude that, after therapy, the person no longer suffered from debilitating depression. Specifically, this can be made operational as changes on a measure of the presenting problem (e.g., depressive symptoms) that result in the client's being returned to within normal limits on that same measure. Several approaches for measuring clinically significant change have been developed, two of which are *normative sample comparison* and *reliable change index*.

NORMATIVE COMPARISONS

Clinically significant improvement can be identified using normative comparisons (Kendall & Grove,

1988), a method for operationalizing clinical significance testing. Normative comparisons (Kendall & Grove, 1988; Kendall, Marrs-Garcia, Nath, & Sheldrick, 1999) can be conducted in several steps. First, the researcher selects a normative group for post-treatment comparison. Given that several well-established measures provide normative data (e.g., the Beck Depression Inventory, the Child Behavior Checklist), investigators may choose to rely on these preexisting normative samples. However, when normative data do not exist, or when the treatment sample is qualitatively different on key factors (e.g., age, socioeconomic status), it may be necessary to collect one's own normative data.

In typical research, when using statistical tests to compare groups, the investigator assumes that the groups are equivalent (null hypothesis) and wishes to find that they are not (alternate hypothesis). However, when the goal is to show that treated individuals are equivalent to "normal" individuals on some factor (i.e., are indistinguishable from normative comparisons), traditional hypothesis-testing methods are inadequate. To circumvent this problem, one uses an equivalency testing method (Kendall, Marrs-Garcia, et al., 1999) that examines whether the difference between the treatment and normative groups is within some predetermined range. Used in conjunction with traditional hypothesis testing, this approach allows for conclusions about the equivalency of groups (see e.g., Jarrett, Vittengl, Doyle, & Clark, 2007; Kendall et al., 2008; Pelham et al., 2000; Westbrook & Kirk, 2007; for examples of normative comparisons), thus testing that post-treatment case are within a normative range on the measure of interest.

THE RELIABLE CHANGE INDEX

Another method to the examining clinically significant change is the Reliable Change Index (RCI; Jacobson, Follette, & Revenstorf, 1984; Jacobson & Traux, 1991). The RCI involves calculating the number of clients moving from a dysfunctional to a normative range. The RCI is a calculation of a difference score (post- minus pre-treatment) divided by the standard error of measurement (calculated based on the reliability of the measure). The RCI is influenced by the magnitude of change and the reliability of the measure (for a reconsideration of the interpretation of RCI, see Hsu, 1996). The RCI has been used in clinical psychological research, although its originators point out that it has at times been misapplied (Jacobson, Roberts, Berns, & McGlinchey, 1999). When used in conjunction with reliable measures and appropriate cutoff scores, it can be a valuable tool for assessing clinical significance.

CONCLUDING COMMENTS ON CLINICAL SIGNIFICANCE

Although progress has been made regarding the operationalization of clinical significance, some debate exists over how to improve its measurement (see Beutler & Moleiro, 2001; Blanton & Jaccard, 2006; Jensen, 2001). Whereas some researchers propose more advanced methods of normative comparison and analysis (e.g., using multiple normative samples), others suggest that clinical significance remain as a simple, client-focused, and practical adjunct to statistical significance results (Follette & Callaghan, 1996; Martinovich, Saunders, & Howard, 1996; Tingey, Lambert, Burlingame & Hansen, 1996).

Evaluations of statistical and clinical significance are most informative when used in conjunction with one another, and it is becoming more common for reports of RCTs to include evaluations of both. Statistically significant improvements are not equivalent to "cures," and clinical significance is a complementary, not a substitute, evaluative strategy. Statistical significance is required to document that changes were beyond those that could be expected due to chance alone—yet, it is also useful to consider if the changes returned dysfunctional clients to within normative limits on the measures of interest.

Evaluating Mechanisms of Change: Mediators and Moderators of Treatment Response

When evaluating treatment efficacy, it is of interest to identify (a) the conditions that dictate when a treatment is more or less effective, and (b) the processes through which a treatment produces change. Addressing such issues necessitates the specification of *moderator* and *mediator* variables (Baron & Kenny, 1986; Holmbeck, 1997; Kraemer et al., 2002; Shadish & Sweeney, 1991). A moderator is a variable that delineates the conditions under which a given treatment is related to an outcome. Conceptually, moderators identify *on whom* and *under what circumstances* treatments have different effects (Kraemer et al., 2002). Functionally, a moderator is a variable that influences either the direction or the strength of a relationship between an independent variable (treatment) and a dependent variable (outcome). For example, if a given treatment were found to be more effective with women than with

men, gender would be considered a moderator of the association between treatment and outcome. A mediator, on the other hand, is a variable that serves to explain the process by which a treatment impacts on an outcome. Conceptually, mediators identify *how* and *why* treatments have effects (Kraemer et al., 2002). If an effective treatment for child conduct problems was found to impact on the parenting behavior of mothers and fathers, which in turn were found to have a significant impact on child problem behavior, then parent behavior would be considered to mediate the treat-to-outcome relationship (provided certain statistical criteria were met; see Holmbeck, 1997). Let's take a closer look at each of these notions.

MODERATORS

Treatment moderators help clarify for clinicians (and other consumers of the treatment outcome literature) which clients might be most responsive to a particular treatment (and for which clients alternative treatment might be sought). They have historically received more attention in the research literature than mediators of effectiveness. Moderator variables that have received the most attention include client age, client ethnicity, client gender, problem type, problem severity, therapist training, mode of delivery (e.g., individual, group, family), setting, and type and source of outcome measure (e.g., Dimidjian et al., 2006; Kolko, Brent, Baugher, Bridge, & Birmaher, 2000; McBride, Atkinson, Quilty, & Bagby, 2006; Owens et al., 2003; Shadish & Sweeney, 1991; Weisz, Weiss, Han, Granger, & Morton, 1995).

How does one test for the presence of a moderator effect? A moderator effect is an interaction effect (Holmbeck, 1997) and can be evaluated using multiple regression analyses or analyses of variance (ANOVA). When using multiple regression, the predictor (e.g., treatment vs. no treatment) and proposed moderator (e.g., age of client) are main effects and are entered into the regression equation first, followed by the interaction of the predictor and the moderator. Alternatively, if one is *only* interested in testing the significance of the interaction effect, all of these terms can be entered simultaneously (see Aiken & West, 1991). If one is using ANOVA, the significance of the interaction between two main effects is tested in an analogous manner: a moderator, like an interaction effect, documents that the effects of one variable (e.g., treatment) are different across different levels of another variable (i.e., the moderator).

The presence of a significant interaction tells us that there is significant moderation (i.e., that the association between the treatment variable and the outcome variable differs significantly across different levels of the moderator). Unfortunately, it tells us little about the specific conditions that dictate whether or not the treatment is significantly related to the outcome. For example, if a treatment-by-age interaction effect is significant in predicting treatment-related change, we know that the effect of the treatment for older clients differs from the effect of the treatment for younger clients, but we do not know whether the treatment effect is statistically significant for either age group. One would not yet know, based on the initial significant interaction effect, whether the relationship between treatment and outcome was significant for the older group, the younger group, or both groups.

Thus, when testing for moderation of treatment effects, statistically significant interactions must be further scrutinized. One such *post-hoc probing* approach is to plot and test the significance of simple slopes of regression lines for high and low values of the moderator variable (Aiken & West, 1991; Kraemer et al., 2002). Alternatively, one can test the significance of simple main effects via ANOVA procedures when the predictor (e.g., treatment vs. no treatment) and moderator (e.g., gender) are both categorical variables.

MEDIATORS

A *mediator* is that variable that specifies the process through which a particular outcome is produced. The mediator effect elucidates the mechanism by which the independent variable (e.g., treatment) is related to outcome (e.g., treatment-related changes). Thus, mediational models are inherently causal models, and in the context of an experimental design (i.e., random assignment), significant mediational pathways are suggestive of causal relationships. As noted by Collins, Maccoby, Steinberg, Hetherington, and Bornstein (2000), studies of parenting interventions inform us not only about the effectiveness (or lack thereof) of such interventions, but also about causal relations between potential parenting mediators and child outcomes. For example, Forgatch and DeGarmo (1999) administered a parent training treatment to a sample of recently divorced mothers (as well as controls) and found that treatment was associated with positive (or less-negative) changes in parenting behavior—and that changes in parenting behavior were linked with

changes in child behavior. This work not only provides preliminary evidence for the utility of a particular treatment approach, but also demonstrates that a prospective (and perhaps causal) link exists in the direction of parenting impacting on child outcome.

When testing for meditational effects, the researcher is usually interested in whether a variable "mediates" the association between a treatment and an outcome, such that the mediator accounts for (i.e., attenuates) part or all of this association. To test for mediation, one examines whether the following are significant: (1) the association between the predictor (e.g., treatment) and the outcome, (2) the association between the predictor and the mediator, and (3) the association between the mediator and the outcome, after controlling for the effect of the predictor. If these three conditions are first met, one then examines (4) whether the predictor-to-outcome effect is less after controlling for the mediator. A corollary of the first condition is that there initially should be a significant relationship between the treatment and the outcome for a mediator to serve its mediating role. If the treatment and outcome are not significantly associated, there is no effect to mediate. Such a bivariate association between treatment and outcome is not required for moderated effects.

The three prerequisite conditions for testing mediational effects can be tested with three multiple regression analyses (Baron & Kenny, 1986). The significance of the treatment-to-outcome path (condition 1 above) is examined in the first regression. The significance of the treatment-to-mediator path (condition 2) is examined in the second regression. Finally, the treatment and mediator variable are simultaneously employed as predictors (via simultaneous entry) in the third equation, where the outcome is the dependent variable. Baron and Kenny (1986) recommend using simultaneous entry (rather than hierarchical entry) in this third equation, so that the effect of the mediator on the outcome is examined after controlling for the treatment and the effect of the treatment on the outcome is examined after controlling for the mediator (borrowing from path analytic methodology; Cohen & Cohen, 1983). The significance of the mediator-to-outcome path in this third equation is a test of condition 3. The relative effect of the treatment on the outcome in this equation (when the mediator is controlled) in comparison to the effect of the treatment on the outcome in the first equation (when the mediator is not controlled) is the test of the fourth condition. Specifically, the treatment should be less associated with the outcome in the third equation than was the case in the first equation (i.e., the association between treatment and the dependent variable is attenuated in the presence of the proposed mediator variable).

Consider the following example: Within a cognitive-behavioral treatment for childhood anxiety disorders, what changes within the clients mediate the identified positive outcomes? To test for mediation, Kendall and Treadwell (2007) computed three regression equations for each dependent variable. In the first, it was established that treatment condition (CBT) predicted the dependent variable (e.g., change on an established anxiety measure). The second equation established that treatment condition predicted the proposed mediator (i.e., changes in children's self-statements during the trial). In the third equation, it was established that changes in children's self-statements (i.e., the proposed mediator) independently predicted the dependent variable. Finally, the meditational hypothesis was confirmed when the independent variable (treatment) no longer significantly predicted the dependent variable when change in self-statements was entered into the equation. This study (Kendall & Treadwell, 2007) provided support that change in children's self-talk mediates the effects of cognitive-behavior treatment for childhood anxiety.

How much reduction in the total effect is necessary to support the presence of mediation? Some researchers have reported whether the treatment-to-outcome effect drops from significance (e.g., $p < .05$) to nonsignificance (e.g., $p > .05$) after the mediator is introduced into the model. This strategy may be flawed, however, because a drop from significance to nonsignificance may occur, for example, when a regression coefficient drops from .28 to .27, but may not occur when it drops from .75 to .35. In other words, it is possible that significant mediation *has not* occurred when the test of the treatment-to-outcome effect drops from significance to nonsignificance after taking the mediator into account. On the other hand, it is also possible that significant mediation *has* occurred even when statistical test of the treatment-to-outcome effect continues to be significant after taking the mediator into account. Thus, it has been recommended when reporting mediational tests to also include a significance test that examines whether the drop in the treatment-to-outcome effect achieves statistical significance when accounting for the impact of the proposed

mediator (see MacKinnon & Dwyer, 1993; Sobel, 1988 for details).

Cumulative Outcome Analyses: From Qualitative Reviews to Meta-Analytic Evaluations

The literature examining the outcomes of diverse therapies is vast, and there is a need to integrate that which we have learned in a systematic, coherent, and meaningful manner. Several major cumulative analyses have undertaken the challenging task of reviewing and reaching conclusions with regard to the effects of psychological therapy. Some of the reviews are strictly qualitative and are based on subjective conclusions, whereas others have used tabulations of the number of studies favoring one type of intervention versus that of competing interventions (e.g., Beutler, 1979; Luborsky, Singer, & Luborsky, 1975). This approach uses a "box score" summary of the findings, and reviewers would compare rates of treatment success to draw conclusions about outcomes. Still other reviewers have used multidimensional analyses of the impact of potential causal factors on therapy outcome: *meta-analysis* (Smith & Glass, 1977).

Meta-analytic procedures provide a quantitative, accepted, and respected approach to the synthesis of a body of empirical literature. Literature reviews are increasingly moving away from the qualitative summary of studies to the quantitative analysis of the reported findings of the studies (e.g., Cooper & Hedges, 1994; Cooper & Rosenthal, 1980; Durlak, 1999; Rosenthal, 1984). By summarizing the magnitude of overall relationships found across studies, determining factors associated with variations in the magnitude of such relationships, and establishing relationships by aggregate analysis, meta-analytic procedures provide more systematic, exhaustive, objective, and representative conclusions than do qualitative reviews (Rosenthal, 1984). To understand the effects of psychological treatments, as well as the factors associated with variations in these effects, meta-analysis is a preferred tool with which to inform funding decisions, service delivery, and public policy.

Meta-analytic techniques are highly informative because they synthesize findings across multiple studies by converting the results of each investigation into a common metric (e.g., the effect size). The outcomes of different types of treatments can then be compared with respect to the aggregate magnitude of change reflected in such statistics across studies. The effect size is typically derived by computing the difference between the reported means of the treatment group and control group at post-treatment, then dividing this difference by the pooled standard deviation of the two groups (Durlak, 1995). The more rigorous scientific journals now require authors to include effect sizes in their reports.

Assuming that one has decided to conduct a meta-analytic review, what are the steps involved in conducting a meta-analysis? After determining that a particular research area has matured to the point at which a meta-analysis is possible and the results of such an analysis would be of interest to the field, one conducts a literature search. Multiple methods of searching are often used (e.g., computer database searches, reviews of reference sections from relevant article, sending a table of studies to be included to known experts in the area to review for potential missing citations). A word of advice to the meta-analyzer: Do not rely solely on computer searches, because they routinely omit several important studies.

A decision that often arises at this point is whether studies of varying quality should be included (Kendall, Flannery-Schroeder, & Ford, 1999; Kendall & Maruyama, 1985). On the one hand, one could argue that studies of poor quality should not be included in the review, since such studies would not ordinarily be used to draw conclusions about the effectiveness of a given psychological therapy. On the other hand, decisions concerning whether a study is of poor versus good quality are often not straightforward. A study may have certain exemplary features and other less desirable features. By including studies that vary in quality, one can examine whether certain "quality" variables (e.g., select vs. genuine clinical cases) are associated with differential outcomes. For example, in a recent meta-analysis (Furr, Comer, Edmunds, & Kendall, 2008), studies were rated in terms of their methodological rigor: one point for addressing missing data, one point for including appropriate comparison groups, one point for using psychometrically sound measures, etc. The research can then examine the extent to which methodological quality is related to results.

Coding the results of specific studies is an important part of a meta-analysis. Decisions need to be made regarding what types of variables will be coded and how inter-rater reliability among coders will be assessed. For example, in a study that examined the outcomes of a psychological therapy, one might code the nature of the intervention, whether the treatment was conducted in clinically representative conditions (Shadish, Matt, Navarro, & Phillips, 2000), the number of sessions, the types of participants, the diagnoses of the participants, the age range, the gender distribution, the therapy administration method (e.g., group vs. individual), the qualifications of the therapists, the various features of the research design, and types of outcomes. Once variables such as these have been coded, the effect sizes are then computed. The methods employed to compute effect sizes should be specified. Another consideration is whether effect sizes will be weighted (for example, based on the sample sizes of the studies reviewed, methodological rigor of studies, etc.). Using sample size to weight study findings has historically been employed in meta-analyses as a way to approximate the reliability of findings (i.e., larger samples would expectedly yield more reliable estimates than smaller samples). However, researchers are increasingly weighting studies by inverse variance weights (i.e., $1/(SE)^2$), where SE = standard error), rather than sample size, as this provides a more direct weighting of study findings by reliability. By weighting by inverse variance weights, the researcher is weighting by precision—the smaller the SE, the more precise the effect size, and consequently the greater you want to represent that effect size when aggregating it with other effect sizes.

After computing the effect sizes and inverse variance weights across studies, and then computing an overall *weighted mean effect size* (and confidence interval) based on the inverse variance weights associated with each effect size, the researcher evaluates the adequacy of the mean effect size in representing the entire distribution of effects via homogeneity testing (i.e., homogeneity statistic, Q). This consists of comparing the observed variability in the effect size values with the estimate of variance that is expected from subject-level sampling error alone (Lipsey & Wilson, 2000). A stem-and-leaf plot can also be useful in determining the distribution of effect sizes. Often a researcher will specifically hypothesize that effect sizes will be significantly heterogenous, given that multiple factors (e.g., sample characteristics, study methodology, etc.) can systematically exert influences on documented treatment effects. If the distribution is not found to be homogeneous, the studies likely estimate different population mean effect sizes, and alternative procedures are required that are beyond the scope of this chapter (see Lipsey & Wilson, 2000).

The merits of integration and summation of the results of related outcome studies are recognized, yet some cautions must be exercised in any meta-analysis. As noted earlier, one must check on the quality of the studies, eliminating those that cannot contribute meaningful findings due to basic inadequacies (Kraemer, Gardner, Brooks, & Yesavage, 1998). Consider the following: Would you accept the recommendation that one treatment approach is superior to another if the recommendation was based on inadequate research? Probably not. If the research evidence is methodologically unsound, it is insufficient evidence for a recommendation; it remains inadequate as a basis for either supporting or refuting treatment recommendations, and therefore it should not be included in cumulative analyses. If a study is methodologically sound, then regardless of the outcome, it must be included.

Caution is paramount in meta-analyses in which various studies are said to provide evidence that treatment is superior to controls. The exact nature of the control condition in each specific study must be examined, especially in the case of attention-placebo control conditions. This caution arises from the indefinite definition of attention-placebo control conditions. As has been noted, one researcher's attention-placebo control condition may be serving as another researcher's therapy condition! Meta-analyzers cannot tabulate the number of studies in which treatment was found to be efficacious in relation to controls without examining the nature of the control condition.

Currently, major efforts are being made to identify and examine those psychological treatments that can be considered empirically supported. These efforts take a set of "criteria" that have been proposed as required for a treatment to be considered empirically supported and review the reported research literature in search of studies that can be used to meet the criteria. Such reviews (e.g., Baucom, Shoham, Mueser, Daiuto, & Stickle, 1998; Compas, Haaga, Keefe, Leitenberg, & Williams, 1998; DeRubeis & Crits-Christoph, 1998; Kazdin & Weisz, 1998; Weisz, Jensen-Doss, & Hawley, 2006; Weisz, McCarty, & Valeri, 2006) and reactions to the approach (e.g., Beutler, 1998; Borkovec & Castonguay, 1998; Garfield, 1998; Goldfried & Wolfe, 1998) document not only that this approach is being applied, but also that there are treatments that meet the criteria of having been supported by empirical research.

Matters of Reporting

Communicating study findings to the scientific community is the final stage of conducting an evaluation of treatment. A well-constructed and quality report will discuss findings in the context of previous related work (e.g., discussing how the findings build on and support previous work; discussing the ways in which findings are discrepant from previous work and why this may be the case), as well as consider limitations and shortcomings that can direct future theory and empirical efforts in the area.

When preparing a quality report, the researcher provides all of the relative information for the reader to critically appraise, interpret, and/or replicate study findings. Historically, there have been some inadequacies in the reporting of RCTs (see Westen et al., 2004 for a critique of past practices). In fact, inadequacies in the reporting of RCTs can result in bias in estimating the effectiveness of interventions (Moher, Schulz, & Altman, 2001; Shulz, Chalmers, Hayes, & Altman, 1995). To maximize transparency in the reporting of RCTs, an international group of epidemiologists, statisticians, and journal editors developed a set of consolidated standards of reporting trials (i.e., CONSORT; see Begg et al., 1996), consisting of a 22-item checklist of study features that can bias estimates of treatment effects, or that are critical to judging the reliability or relevance of study findings, and consequently should be included in a comprehensive research report. A quality report will address each of these 22 items. For example, the title and abstract are to include how participants were allocated to interventions (e.g., randomly assigned), the methods must clearly detail eligibility criteria (i.e., inclusion/exclusion criteria) and how the sample size was determined, the procedures must indicate whether or not evaluators were blind to treatment assignment, and baseline demographic characteristics must be included for all participants. Importantly, participant flow must be characterized at each stage. The researcher reports the specific numbers of participants randomly assigned to each treatment condition, who received treatments as assigned, who participated in post-treatment evaluations, and who participated in follow-up evaluations (see Figure 4.1 for an example from Kendall et al., 2008). It has become standard practice for scientific journals to require a CONSORT flow diagram.

When the researcher has prepared a quality report that he or she deems is ready to be communicated to the academic community, the next decision is where to submit the report. When communicating the results of a clinical evaluation to the scientific community, the researcher should only consider submitting the report of their findings to a peer-reviewed journal.

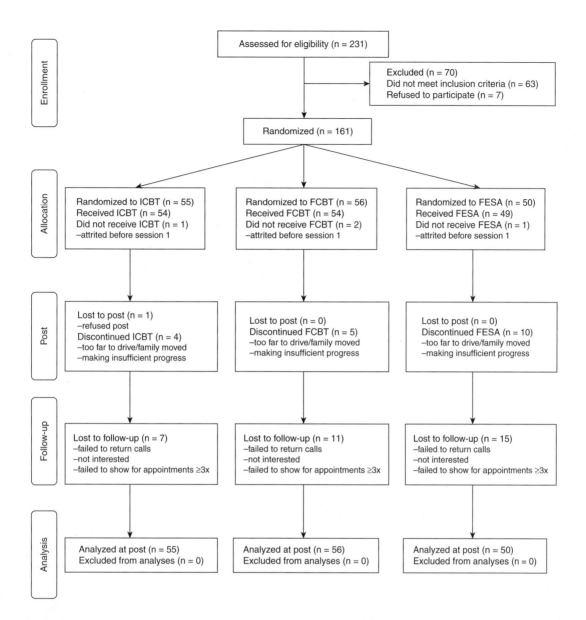

Figure 4.1 Example of flow diagram used in reporting to depict participant flow at each stage of a study. From Kendall, P. C., Hudson, J.L., Gosch, E., Flannery-Schroeder, E., & Suveg, C. (2008). Cognitive-behavioral therapy for anxiety disordered youth: A randomized clinical trial evaluating child and family modalities. *Journal of Consulting and Clinical Psychology, 76*, 282–297. Reprinted with permission of the publisher, the American Psychological Association (APA).

Publishing the outcomes of a study in a refereed journal (i.e., one that employs the peer-review process) signals that the work has been accepted and approved for publication by a panel of qualified and impartial reviewers (i.e., independent scientists knowledgeable in the area but not involved with the study). Consumers should be highly cautious of studies published in journals that do not place manuscript submissions through a rigorous peer-review process.

Although the peer-review process slows down the speed with which one is able to communicate study results (much to the chagrin of the excited researcher who just completed an investigation), it is nonetheless one of the indispensable safeguards that we have to ensure that our collective knowledge base is drawn from studies meeting acceptable standards. Typically, the review process is "blind," meaning that the authors of the article do not know the identities of the peer-reviewers who are considering their manuscript. Many journals employ a double-blind peer-review process, in which the identities of study authors are also not known to the peer-reviewers.

Conclusion

Having reviewed matters of design, procedure, measurement, data analysis, and reporting that are pertinent, one recognizes that no one single study, even with optimal design and procedures, can answer the relevant questions about the efficacy and effectiveness of therapy. Rather, a series and collection of studies, with varying approaches, is necessary. The criteria for determining empirically supported treatments have been proposed, and the quest for identification of such treatments continues. The goal is for the research to be rigorous, with the end goal being that the most promising procedures serve professional practice and those in need of services.

Therapy outcome research plays a vital role in facilitating a dialogue between scientist-practitioners and the public and private sector (e.g., Department of Health and Human Services, insurance payers, policy-makers). Outcome research is increasingly being examined by both managed care organizations and professional associations with the intent of formulating practice guidelines for cost-effective psychological care that provides maximal service to those in need. There is the risk that psychological science and practice will be co-opted and exploited in the service only of cost-containment and profitability: Therapy outcome research must retain scientific rigor while enhancing the ability of practitioners to deliver effective procedures to individuals in need.

References

Achenbach, T. M., McConaughy, S. H., & Howell, C. T. (1987). Child/adolescent behavioral and emotional problems: Implication of cross-informant correlations for situational specificity. *Psychological Bulletin, 101,* 213–232.

Addis, M., Cardemil, E. V., Duncan, B., & Miller, S. (2006). Does manualization improve therapy outcomes? In J. C. Norcross, L. E. Beutler, & R. F. Levant (Eds.), *Evidence-based practices in mental health* (pp. 131–160). Washington, DC: American Psychological Association.

Addis, M., & Krasnow, A. (2000). A national survey of practicing psychologists' attitudes toward psychotherapy treatment manuals. *Journal of Consulting and Clinical Psychology, 68,* 331–339.

Aiken, L. S., & West, S. G. (1991). *Multiple regression: Testing and interpreting interactions.* Newbury Park, CA: Sage.

Arnold, L. E., Elliott, M., Sachs, L., Bird, H., Kraemer, H. C., Wells, K. C., et al. (2003). Effects of ethnicity on treatment attendance, stimulant response/dose, and 14-month outcome in ADHD. *Journal of Consulting and Clinical Psychology, 71,* 713–727.

Barlow, D. H. (1989). Treatment outcome evaluation methodology with anxiety disorders: Strengths and key issues. *Advances in Behavior Research and Therapy, 11,* 121–132.

Baron, R. M., & Kenny, D. A. (1986). The mediator-moderator variable distinction in social psychological research: Conceptual, strategic, and statistical consideration. *Journal of Personality and Social Psychology, 51,* 1173–1182.

Baucom, D., Shoham, V., Mueser, K., Daiuto, A., & Stickle, T. (1998). Empirically supported couple and family interventions for marital distress and adult mental health problems. *Journal of Consulting and Clinical Psychology, 66,* 53–88.

Begg, C. B., Cho, M. K., Eastwood, S., Horton, R., Moher, D., Olkin, I., et al. (1996). Improving the quality of reporting of randomized controlled trials: The CONSORT statement. *JAMA, 276,* 637–639.

Bernal, G., Bonilla, J., & Bellido, C. (1995). Ecological validity and cultural sensitivity for outcome research: Issues for the cultural adaptation and development of psychosocial treatments with Hispanics. *Journal of Abnormal Child Psychology, 23,* 67–82.

Bersoff, D. M., & Bersoff, D. N. (1999). Ethical perspectives in clinical research. In P. C. Kendall, J. Butcher, & G. Holmbeck (Eds.), *Handbook of research methods in clinical psychology* (pp. 31–55).

Bernal, G., & Scharron-Del-Rio, M. R. (2001). Are empirically supported treatments valid for ethnic minorities? Toward an alternative approach for treatment research. *Cultural Diversity and Ethnic Minority Psychology, 7,* 328–342.

Beutler, L. (1979). Toward specific psychological therapies for specific conditions. *Journal of Consulting and Clinical Psychology, 47,* 882–897.

Beutler, L. (1998). Identifying empirically supported treatments: What if we didn't? *Journal of Consulting and Clinical Psychology, 66,* 37–52.

Beutler, L. E., & Moleiro, C. (2001). Clinical versus reliable and significant change. *Clinical Psychology: Science and Practice, 8,* 441–445.

Borkovec, T., & Castonguay, L. (1998). What is the scientific meaning of empirically supported therapy? *Journal of Consulting and Clinical Psychology, 54,* 136–142.

Blanton, H., & Jaccard, J. (2006). Arbitrary metrics in psychology. *American Psychologist, 61,* 27–41.

Brown, R. A., Evans, M., Miller, I., Burgess, E., & Mueller, T. (1997). Cognitive-behavioral treatment for depression in alcoholism. *Journal of Consulting and Clinical Psychology, 65,* 715–726.

Chambless, D. L., & Hollon, S. D. (1998). Defining empirically supported therapies. *Journal of Consulting and Clinical Psychology, 66,* 7–18.

Cohen, J., & Cohen, P. (1983). *Applied multiple regression/correlation analysis for the behavioral sciences* (2nd edition). Hillsdale, NJ: Erlbaum.

Collins, W. A., Maccoby, E. E., Steinberg, L., Hetherington, E. M., & Bornstein, M. H. (2000). Contemporary research on parenting: The case for nature and nurture. *American Psychologist, 55,* 218–232.

Comer, J. S., & Kendall, P. C. (2004). A symptom-level examination of parent-child agreement in the diagnosis of anxious youths. *Journal of the American Academy of Child and Adolescent Psychiatry, 43,* 878–886.

Compas, B., Haaga, D., Keefe, F., Leitenberg, H., & Williams, D. (1998).Sampling of empirically supported psychological treatments from health psychology: Smoking, chronic pain, cancer, and bulimia nervosa. *Journal of Consulting and Clinical Psychology, 66,* 89–112.

Cooper, H., & Hedges, L. V. (1994). *The handbook of research synthesis.* New York: Russell Sage.

Cooper, H. M., & Rosenthal, R. (1980). Statistical versus traditional procedures for summarizing research findings. *Psychological Bulletin, 87,* 442–449.

Coyne, J. C. (1994). Self-reported distress: Analog or ersatz depression? *Psychological Bulletin, 116,* 29–45.

Creed, T. A., & Kendall, P. C. (2005). Therapist alliance-building behavior within a cognitive-behavioral treatment for anxiety in youth. *Journal of Consulting and Clinical Psychology, 73,* 498–505.

De Los Reyes, A., & Kazdin, A. E. (2005). Informant discrepancies in the assessment of childhood psychopathology: A critical review, theoretical framework, and recommendations for further study. *Psychological Bulletin, 131,* 483–509.

De Los Reyes, A., & Kazdin, A. E. (2006). Conceptualizing changes in behavior in intervention research: The range of possible changes model. *Psychological Review, 113,* 554–583.

Delucchi, K., & Bostrom, A. (1999). Small sample longitudinal clinical trials with missing data: A comparison of analytic methods. *Psychological Methods, 4,* 158–172.

DeRubeis, R., & Crits-Christoph, P. (1998). Empirically supported individual and group psychological treatments for adult mental disorders. *Journal of Consulting and Clinical Psychology, 66,* 27–52.

Dimidjian, S., Hollon, S. D., Dobson, K. S., Schmaling, K. B., Kohlenberg, R. J., & Addis, M. E. (2006). Randomized trial of behavioral activation, cognitive therapy, and antidepressant medication in the acute treatment of adults with major depression. *Journal of Consulting and Clinical Psychology, 74,* 658–*670.*

Dobson, K. S., & Hamilton, K. E. (2002). The stage model for psychotherapy manual development: A valuable tool for promoting evidence-based practice. *Clinical Psychology: Science and Practice, 9,* 407–409.

Dobson, K. S., Hollon, S. D., Dimidjian, S., Schmaling, K. B., Kohlenberg, R. J., Gallop, R. J., et al. (2008). Randomized trial of behavioral activation, cognitive therapy, and antidepressant medication in the prevention of relapse and recurrence in major depression. *Journal of Consulting and Clinical Psychology, 76,* 468–477.

Dobson, K. S., & Shaw, B. (1988). The use of treatment manuals in cognitive therapy. Experience and issues. *Journal of Consulting and Clinical Psychology, 56,* 673–682.

Durlak, J. A. (1995). Understanding meta-analysis. In L. G. Grimm, & P. R. Yarnold (Eds.), *Reading and understanding multivariate statistics* (pp. 319–352). Washington, DC: American Psychological Association.

Durlak, J. A. (1999). Meta-analytic research methods. In P. C. Kendall, J. N. Butcher, & G. N. Holmbeck (Eds.), *Research methods in clinical psychology* (pp. 419–429). New York: John Wiley & Sons.

Edelbrock, C., Costello, A. J., Dulcan, M. K., Conover, N. C., & Kalas, R. (1986). Parent-child agreement on psychiatric symptoms assessed via a structured interview. *Journal of Child Psychology and Psychiatry, 27,* 181–190.

Fishman, D.B. (2000). Transcending the efficacy versus effectiveness research debate: Proposal for a new, electronic "Journal of Pragmatic Case Studies." *Prevention and Treatment, 3,* ArtID8.

Follette, W. C., & Callaghan, G. M. (1996). The importance of the principle of clinical significance—defining significant to whom and for what purpose: A response to Tingey, Lambert, Burlingame, and Hansen. *Psychotherapy Research, 6,* 133–143.

Forgatch, M. S., & DeGarmo, D. S. (1999). Parenting through change: An effective prevention program for single mothers. *Journal of Consulting and Clinical Psychology, 67,* 711–724.

Flaherty, J. A., & Meaer, R. (1980). Measuring racial bias in inpatient treatment. *American Journal of Psychiatry, 137,* 679–682.

Furr, J. M., Comer, J. S., Edmunds, J., & Kendall, P. C. (2008, November). Disasters and Youth: A Meta-Analytic Examination of Posttraumatic Stress. Paper presented at the annual meeting of the Association for Behavioral and Cognitive Therapies, Orlando, FL.

Garfield, S. (1998). Some comments on empirically supported psychological treatments. *Journal of Consulting and Clinical Psychology, 66,* 121–125.

Goldfried, M., & Wolfe, B. (1998). Toward a more clinically valid approach to therapy research. *Journal of Consulting and Clinical Psychology, 66,* 143–150.

Gladis, M. M., Gosch, E. A., Dishuk, N. M., & Crits-Cristoph, P. (1999). Quality of Life: Exampling the scope of clinical significance. *Journal of Consulting and Clinical Psychology, 67,* 320–331.

Greenhouse, J., Stangl, D., & Bromberg, J. (1989). An introduction to survival analysis: Statistical methods for analysis of clinical trial data. *Journal of Consulting and Clinical Psychology, 57,* 536–544.

Grills, A. E., & Ollendick, T. H. (2003). Multiple informant agreement and the Anxiety Disorders Interview Schedule for Parents and Children. *Journal of the American Academy of Child and Adolescent Psychiatry, 42,* 30–40.

Hall, G. C. N. (2001). Psychotherapy research with ethnic minorities: Empirical, ethnical, and conceptual issues. *Journal of Consulting and Clinical Psychology, 69,* 502–510.

Havik, O. E., & VandenBos, G. R. (1996). Limitations of manualized psychotherapy for everyday clinical practice. *Clinical Psychology: Science and Practice, 3,* 264–267.

Hedeker, D., & Gibbons, R. D. (1994). A random-effects ordinal regression model for multilevel analysis. *Biometrics, 50,* 933–944.

Hedeker, D., & Gibbons, R. D. (1997). Application of random-effects pattern-mixture models for missing data in longitudinal studies. *Psychological Methods, 2,* 64–78.

Hoagwood, K. (2002). Making the translation from research to its application: The je ne sais pas of evidence-based practices. *Clinical Psychology: Science and Practice, 9,* 210–213.

Hollon, S. D. (1996). The efficacy and effectiveness of psychotherapy relative to medications. *American Psychologist, 51,* 1025–1030.

Hollon, S. D., & DeRubeis, R. J. (1981). Placebo-psychotherapy combinations: Inappropriate representation of psychotherapy in drug-psychotherapy comparative trials. *Psychological Bulletin, 90,* 467–477.

Hollon, S. D., Garber, J., & Shelton, R. C. (2005). Treatment of depression in adolescents with cognitive behavior therapy and medications: A commentary on the TADS project. *Cognitive and Behaviowral Practice, 12,* 149–155.

Holmbeck, G. N. (1997). Toward terminological, conceptual, and statistical clarity in the study of mediators and moderators: Examples from the child-clinical and pediatric psychology literatures. *Journal of Consulting and Clinical and Clinical Psychology, 65,* 599–610.

Homma-True, R., Greene, B., Lopez, S. R., & Trimble, J. E. (1993). Ethnocultural diversity in clinical psychology. *Clinical Psychologist, 46*, 50–63.

Howard, K. I., Lueger, R., Maling, M., & Martinovich, Z. (1993). A phase model of psychotherapy. *Journal of Consulting and Clinical Psychology, 61*, 678–685.

Hsu, L. (1996). On the identification of clinically significant changes: Reinterpretation of Jacobson's cut scores. *Journal of Psychopathology and Behavior Assessment, 18*, 371–386.

Huey, S. J., & Polo, A. J. (2008). Evidence-based psychosocial treatments for ethnic minority youth. *Journal of Clinical Child and Adolescent Psychology, 37*, 262–301.

Jaccard, J., & Guilamo-Ramos, V. (2002a). Analysis of variance frameworks in clinical child and adolescent psychology: Issues and recommendations. *Journal of Clinical Child and Adolescent Psychology, 31*, 130–146.

Jaccard, J., & Guilamo-Ramos, V. (2002b). Analysis of variance frameworks in clinical child and adolescent psychology: Advanced issues and recommendations. *Journal of Clinical Child and Adolescent Psychology, 31*, 278–294.

Jacobson, N. S., Follette, W. C., & Revenstorf, D. (1984). Psychotherapy outcome research: Methods for reporting variability and evaluating clinical significance. *Behavior Therapy, 15*, 336–352.

Jacobson, N. S., & Hollon, S. D. (1996a). Cognitive-behavior therapy versus pharmacotherapy: Now that the jury's returned its verdict, it's time to present the rest of the evidence. *Journal of Consulting and Clinical Psychology, 74*, 74–80.

Jacobson, N. S., & Hollon, S. D. (1996b). Prospects for future comparisons between drugs and psychotherapy: Lessons from the CBT-versus-pharmacotherapy exchange. *Journal of Consulting and Clinical Psychology, 64*, 104–108.

Jacobson, N. S., Roberts, L. J., Berns, S. B., & McGlinchey, J. B. (1999). Methods for defining and determining the clinical significance of treatment effects. Description, application, and alternatives. *Journal of Consulting and Clinical Psychology, 67*, 300–307.

Jacobson, N. S., & Traux, P. (1991). Clinical significance: A statistic approach to defining meaningful change in psychotherapy research. *Journal of Consulting and Clinical Psychology, 59*, 12–19.

Jarrett, R. B., Vittengl, J. R., Doyle, K., & Clark, L. A. (2007). Changes in cognitive content during and following cognitive therapy for recurrent depression: Substantial and enduring, but not predictive of change in depressive symptoms. *Journal of Consulting and Clinical Psychology, 75*, 432–446.

Jaycox, L., Foa, E., & Morral, A. (1998). Influence of emotional engagement and habituation on exposure therapy for PTSD. *Journal of Consulting and Clinical Psychology, 66*, 185–192.

Jensen, P. S. (2001). Clinical equivalence: A step, a misstep, or just a misnomer? *Clinical Psychology: Science and Practice, 8*, 436–440.

Karver, M., Shirk, S., Handelsman, J. B., Fields, S., Crisp, H., Gudmundsen, G., & McMakin, D. (2008). Relationship processes in youth psychotherapy: Measuring alliance, alliance-building behaviors, and client involvement. *Journal of Emotional and Behavioral Disorders, 16*, 15–28.

Kazdin, A. E. (1999). The meanings and measurement of clinical significance. *Journal of Consulting and Clinical Psychology, 67*, 332–339.

Kazdin, A. E. (2003). *Research design in clinical psychology, 4th ed.* Boston, MA: Allyn and Bacon.

Kazdin, A. E., & Bass, D. (1989). Power to detect differences between alternative treatments in comparative psychotherapy outcome research. *Journal of Consulting and Clinical Psychology, 57*, 138–147.

Kazdin, A. E., Marciano, P. L., & Whitley, M. K. (2005). The therapeutic alliance in cognitive-behavioral treatment of children referred for oppositional, aggress, and antisocial behavior. *Journal of Consulting and Clinical Psychology, 73*, 726–730.

Kazdin, A. E., & Weisz, J. R. (1998). Identifying and developing empirically supported child and adolescent treatments. *Journal of Consulting and Clinical Psychology, 66*, 19–36.

Kendall, P. C. (1999). Introduction to the special section: Clinical Significance. *Journal of Consulting and Clinical Psychology, 67*, 283–284.

Kendall, P. C., & Beidas, R. S. (2007). Smoothing the trail for dissemination of evidence-based practices for youth: Flexibility within fidelity. *Professional Psychology: Research and Practice, 38*, 13–20.

Kendall, P. C., & Chu, B. (1999). Retrospective self-reports of therapist flexibility in a manual-based treatment for youths with anxiety disorders. *Journal of Clinical Child Psychology, 29*, 209–220.

Kendall, P. C., Flannery-Schroeder, E., & Ford, J. (1999). Therapy outcome research methods (330–363). In P. C. Kendall, J. Butcher, & G. Holmbeck (Eds.). *Handbook of research methods in clinical psychology (2nd ed.).* New York: Wiley.

Kendall, P. C., & Grove, W. (1988). Normative comparisons in therapy outcome. *Behavioral Assessment, 10*, 147–158.

Kendall, P. C., & Hedtke, K. A. (2006). *Cognitive-behavioral therapy for anxious children,* 3rd edition. Ardmore, PA: Workbook Publishing. www.WorkbookPublishing.com

Kendall, P. C., & Hollon, S. D. (1983). Calibrating therapy: Collaborative archiving of tape samples from therapy outcome trials. *Cognitive Therapy and Research, 7*, 199–204.

Kendall, P. C., Hollon, S., Beck, A. T., Hammen, C., & Ingram, R. (1987). Issues and recommendations regarding use of the Beck Depression Inventory. *Cognitive Therapy and Research, 11*, 289–299.

Kendall, P. C., Holmbeck, G., & Verduin, T. L. (2002). Methodology, design, and evaluation in psychotherapy research. In M. Lambert, A. Bergin, & S. Garfield (Eds.), *Handbook of psychotherapy and behavior change,* 5th ed. New York: Wiley.

Kendall, P. C., Hudson, J. L., Gosch, E., Flannery-Schroeder, E., & Suveg, C. (2008). Cognitive-behavioral therapy for anxiety disordered youth: A randomized clinical trial evaluating child and family modalities. *Journal of Consulting and Clinical Psychology, 76*, 282–297.

Kendall, P. C., & Kessler, R. C. (2002). The impact of childhood psychopathology interventions on subsequent substance abuse: Policy implications, comments, and recommendations. *Journal of Consulting and Clinical Psychology, 70*, 1303–1306.

Kendall, P. C., Marrs-Garcia, A., Nath, S. R., & Sheldrick, R. C. (1999). Normative comparisons for the evaluation of clinical significance. *Journal of Consulting and Clinical Psychology, 67*, 285–299.

Kendall, P. C., & Maruyama, G. (1985). Meta-analysis: On the road to synthesis of knowledge? *Clinical Psychology Review, 5*, 79–89.

Kendall, P. C., & Ollendick, T. H. (2004). Setting the research and practice agenda for anxiety in children and adolescence: A topic comes of age. *Cognitive and Behavioral Practice, 11*, 65–74.

Kendall, P. C., Pellegrini, D. S., & Urbain, E. S. (1981). Approaches to assessment for cognitive-behavioral interventions with children. In P. C. Kendall & S. D. Hollon (Eds.), *Assessment strategies for cognitive-behavioral interventions.* New York: Academic Press.

Kendall, P. C., Safford, S., Flannery-Schroeder, E., & Webb, A. (2002). Child anxiety treatment: Outcomes in adolescence and impact on substance use and depression at 7.4-year follow-up. *Journal of the Consulting and Clinical Psychology, 72*, 276–287.

Kendall, P. C., Southam-Gerow, M. A. (1995). Issues in the transportability of treatment: The case of anxiety disorders in youth. *Journal of Consulting and Clinical Psychology, 63*, 702–708.

Kendall, P. C., & Sugarman, A. (1997). Attrition in the treatment of childhood anxiety disorders. *Journal of Consulting and Clinical Psychology, 65,* 883–888.

Kendall, P. C., & Treadwell, K. R. H. (2007). The role of self-statements as a mediator in treatment for youth with anxiety disorders. *Journal of Consulting and Clinical Psychology, 75*, 380–389.

Kolko, D. J., Brent, D. A., Baugher, M., Bridge, J., & Birmaher, B. (2000). Cognitive and family therapies for adolescent depression: Treatment specificity, mediation, and moderation. *Journal of Consulting and Clinical Psychology, 68*, 603–614.

Kraemer, H. C., Gardner, C., Brooks, J., & Yesavage, J. (1998). Advantages of excluding underpowered studies in meta-analysis: Inclusionist versus exclusionist viewpoints. *Psychological Methods, 3*, 23–31.

Kraemer, H. C., & Kupfer, D. J. (2006). Size of treatment effects and their importance to clinical research and practice. *Biological Psychiatry, 59*, 990–996.

Kraemer, H. C., Wilson, G. T., Fairburn, C. G., & Agras, W. S. (2002). Mediators and moderators of treatment effects in randomized clinical trials. *Archives of General Psychiatry, 59*, 877–883.

Krupnick, J., Shea, T., & Elkin, I. (1986). Generalizability of treatment studies utilizing solicited patients. *Journal of Consulting and Clinical Psychology, 54*, 68–78.

Laird, N. M., & Ware, J. H. (1982). Random-effects models for longitudinal data. *Biometrics, 38*, 963–974.

Lambert, M. J., Hansen, N. B., & Finch, A. E. (2001). Patient-focused research: Using patient outcome data to enhance treatment effects. *Journal of Consulting and Clinical Psychology, 69*, 159–172.

Leon, A. C., Mallinckrodt, C. H., Chuang-Stein, C., Archibald, D. G., Archer, G. E., & Chartier, K. (2006). Attrition in randomized controlled clinical trials: Methodological issues in psychopharmacology. *Biological Psychiatry, 59*, 1001–1005.

Lipsey, M. W., & Wilson, D. B. (2000). Practical meta-analysis. *Applied social research methods series* (Vol. 49). Thousand Oaks, CA: Sage Publications.

Little, R. J. A., & Rubin, D. (2002). *Statistical analysis with missing data*, 2nd ed. New York: Wiley.

Lopez, S. R. (1989). Patient variable biases in clinical judgment: Conceptual overview and methodological considerations. *Psychological Bulletin, 106*, 184–204.

Luborsky, L., Singer, B., & Luborsky, L. (1975). Comparative studies of psychotherapy. *Archives of General Psychiatry, 32*, 995–1008.

MacKinnon, D. P., & Dwyer, J. H. (1993). Estimating mediated effects in prevention studies. *Evaluation Review, 17*, 144–158.

Marcus, S. M., Gorman, J., Shea, M. K., Lewin, D., Martinez, J., Ray, S. et al. (2007). A comparison of medication side effect reports by panic disorder patients with and without concomitant cognitive behavior therapy. *American Journal of Psychiatry, 164*, 273–275.

Martinovich, Z., Saunders, S., & Howard, K. (1996). Some comments on "Assessing clinical significance." *Psychotherapy Research, 6*, 124–132.

Mason, M. J. (1999). A review of procedural and statistical methods for handling attrition and missing data. *Measurement and Evaluation in Counseling and Development, 32*, 111–118.

McBride, C., Atkinson, L., Quilty, L. C., & Bagby, R. M. (2006). Attachment as moderator of treatment outcome in major depression: A randomized control trial of interpersonal psychotherapy versus cognitive behavior therapy. *Journal of Consulting and Clinical Psychology, 74*, 1041–1054.

Moher, D., Schulz, K. F., & Altman, D. (2001). The CONSORT Statement: Revised recommendations for improving the quality of reports of parallel-group randomized trials. *JAMA, 285*, 1987–1991.

Molenberghs, G., Thijs, H., Jansen, I., Beunckens, C., Kenward, M. G., Mallinckrodt, C., & Carroll, R. (2004). Analyzing incomplete longitudinal clinical trial data. *Biostatistics, 5*, 445–464.

MTA Cooperative Group. (1999). A 14-month randomized clinical trial of treatment strategies for attention-deficit/hyperactivity disorder. *Archives of General Psychiatry, 56*, 1088–1096.

Mufson, L., Dorta, K. P., Wickramaratne, P., Nomura, Y., Olfson, M., & Weissman, M. M. (2004). A randomized effectiveness trial of interpersonal psychotherapy for depressed adolescents. *Archives of General Psychiatry, 61*, 577–584.

Neuner, F., Onyut, P. L., Ertl, V., Odenwald, M., Schauer, E., & Elbert, T. (2008). Treatment of posttraumatic stress disorder by trained lay counselors in an African refugee settlement: A randomized controlled trial. *Journal of Consulting and Clinical Psychology, 76*, 686–694.

Ogden, T., & Hagen, K. A. (2008). Treatment effectiveness of parent management training in Norway: A randomized controlled trial of children with conduct problems. *Journal of Consulting and Clinical Psychology, 76*, 607–621.

O'Leary, K. D., & Borkovec, T. D. (1978). Conceptual, methodological, and ethical problems of placebo groups in psychotherapy research. *American Psychologist, 33*, 821–830.

Owens, E. B., Hinshaw, S. P., Kraemer, H. C., Arnold, L. E., Abikoff, H. B., Cantwell, D. P., et al. (2003). Which treatment for whom for ADHD? Moderators of treatment response in the MTA. *Journal of Consulting and Clinical Psychology, 71*, 540–552.

Parloff, M. B. (1986). Placebo controls in psychotherapy research: A sine qua non or a placebo for research problems? *Journal of Consulting and Clinical Psychology, 54*, 79–87.

Pediatric OCD Treatment Study (POTS) Team. (2004). Cognitive-behavior therapy, sertraline, and their combination for children and adolescents with obsessive-compulsive disorder: The Pediatric OCD Treatment Study (POTS) randomized controlled trial. *JAMA, 292*, 1969–1976.

Pelham, W. E., Jr., Gnagy, E. M., Greiner, A. R., Hoza, B., Hinshaw, S. P., Swanson, J. M., et al. (2000). Behavioral versus behavioral and psychopharmacological treatment in

ADHD children attending a summer treatment program. *Journal of Abnormal Child Psychology, 28*, 507–525.

Perepletchikova, F., & Kazdin, A. E. (2005). Treatment integrity and therapeutic change: Issues and research recommendations. *Clinical Psychology: Science and Practice, 12*, 365–383.

Rapee, R. M., Abbott, M. J., & Lyneham, H. J. (2006). Bibliotherapy for children with anxiety disorders using written materials for parents: A randomized controlled trial. *Journal of Consulting and Clinical Psychology, 74*, 436–444.

Reis, B. F., & Brown, L. G. (2006). Preventing therapy dropout in the real world: The clinical utility of videotape preparation and client estimate of treatment duration. *Professional Psychology: Research and Practice, 37*, 311–316.

Rosenthal, R. (1984). Meta-analytic procedures for social research. Beverly Hils, CA: Sage.

Ruscio, A. M., & Ruscio, J. (2002). The latent structure of analogue depression: Should the Beck Depression Inventory be used to classify groups? *Psychological Assessment, 14*, 135–145.

Ruscio, J., & Ruscio, A. M. (2008). Categories and dimensions: Advancing psychological science through the study of latent structure. *Current Directions in Psychological Science, 17*, 203–207.

Shadish, W. R., & Sweeney, R. B. (1991). Mediators and moderators in meta-analysis: There's a reason we don't let dodo birds tell us which psychotherapies should have prizes. *Journal of Consulting and Clinical Psychology, 59*, 883–893.

Shadish, W. R., Matt, G. E., Navarro, A. M., & Phillips, G. (2000). The effects of psychological therapies under clinically representative conditions: A meta-analysis. *Psychological Bulletin, 126*, 512–529.

Shirk, S. R., Gudmundsen, G., Kaplinski, H., & McMakin, D. L. (2008). Alliance and outcome in cognitive-behavioral therapy for adolescent depression. *Journal of Clinical Child and Adolescent Psychology, 37*, 631–639.

Shulz, K. F., Chalmers, I., Hayes, R. J., & Altman, D. G. (1995). Empirical evidence of bias: Dimensions of methodological quality associated with estimates of treatment effects in clinical trials. *JAMA, 273*, 408–412.

Silverman, W. K., Kurtines, W. M., & Hoagwood, K. (2004). Research progress on effectiveness, transportability, and dissemination of empirically supported treatments: Integrating theory and research. *Clinical Psychology: Science and Practice, 11*, 295–299.

Smith, M.L., & Glass, G.V. (1977). Meta-analysis of psychotherapy outcome studies. *American Psychologist, 32*, 752–760.

Snowden, L. R. (2003). Bias in mental health assessment and intervention: Theory and evidence. *American Journal of Public Health, 93*, 239–243.

Sobel, M. E. (1988). Direct and indirect effects in linear structural equation models. In J. S. Long (Ed.), *Common problems/proper solutions: Avoiding error in quantitative research* (pp. 46–64). Beverly Hills, CA: Sage.

Southam-Gerow, M. A., Ringeisen, H. L., & Sherrill, J. T. (2006). Integrating interventions and services research: Progress and prospects. *Clinical Psychology: Science and Practice, 13*, 1–8.

Stricker, G. (2000). What is a scientist-practitioner anyway? *Journal of Clinical Psychology, 58*, 1277–1283.

Sue, S. (1998). In search of cultural competence in psychotherapy and counseling. *American Psychologist, 53*, 440–448.

Suveg, C., Comer, J. S., Furr, J. M., & Kendall, P. C. (2006). Adapting manualized CBT for a cognitively delayed child with multiple anxiety disorders. *Clinical Case Studies, 5*, 488–510.

Sweeney, M., Robins, M., Ruberu, M., & Jones, J. (2005). African-American and Latino families in TADS: Recruitment and treatment considerations. *Cognitive and Behavioral Practice, 12*, 221–229.

Taft, C. T., & Murphy, C. M. (2007). The working alliance in intervention for partner violence perpetrators: Recent research and theory. *Journal of Family Violence, 22*, 11–18.

Tennen, H., Hall, J. A., & Affleck, G. (1995). Depression research methodologies in the *Journal of Personality and Social Psychology*: A review and critique. *Journal of Personality and Social Psychology, 68*, 870–884.

Tingey, R. C., Lambert, M. J., Burlingame, G. M., & Hansen, N. B. (1996). Assessing clinical significance: Proposed extensions to method. *Psychotherapy Research, 6*, 109–123.

Treadwell, K., Flannery-Schroeder, E. C., & Kendall, P. C. (1994). Ethnicity and gender in a sample of clinic-referred anxious children: Adaptive functioning, diagnostic status, and treatment outcome. *Journal of Anxiety Disorders, 9*, 373–384.

Vanable, P. A., Carey, M. P., Carey, K. B., & Maisto, S. A. (2002). Predictors of participation and attrition in a health promotion study involving psychiatric outpatients. *Journal of Consulting and Clinical Psychology, 70*, 362–368.

Walders, N., Drotar, D. (2000). Understanding cultural and ethnic influences in research with child clinical and pediatric psychology populations. In D. Drotar (Ed.), *Handbook of research in pediatric and clinical child psychology* (pp. 165–188).

Walkup, J.T., Albano, A.M., Piacentini, J., Birmaher, B., Compton, S.N., et al. (2008). Cognitive behavioral therapy, sertraline, or a combination in childhood anxiety. *New England Journal of Medicine, 359*, 1–14.

Waltz, J., Addis, M. E., Koerner, K., & Jacobson, N. S. (1993). Testing the integrity of a psychotherapy protocol: Assessment of adherence and competence. *Journal of Consulting and Clinical Psychology, 61*, 620–630.

Weisz, J., Donenberg, G. R., Han, S. S., & Weiss, B. (1995). Bridging the gap between laboratory and clinic in child and adolescent psychotherapy. *Journal of Consulting and Clinical Psychology, 63*, 688–701.

Weisz, J. R., Jensen-Doss, A., & Hawley, K. M. (2006). Evidence-based youth psychotherapies versus usual clinical care: A meta-analysis of direct comparisons. *American Psychologist, 61*, 671–689.

Weisz, J. R., McCarty, C. A., & Valeri, S. M. (2006). Effects of psychotherapy for depression in children and adolescents: A meta-analysis. *Psychological Bulletin, 132*, 132–149.

Weisz, J. R., Weiss, B., & Donenberg, G. R. (1992). The lab versus the clinic: Effects of child and adolescent psychotherapy. *American Psychologist, 47*, 1578–1585.

Weisz, J. R., Weiss, B., Han, S. S., Granger, D. A., & Morton, T. (1995). Effects of psychotherapy with children and adolescents revisited: A meta-analysis of treatment outcome studies. *Psychological Bulletin, 117*, 450–468.

Westbrook, D., & Kirk, J. (2007). The clinical effectiveness of cognitive behaviour therapy: Outcome for a large sample of adults treated in routine practice. *Behaviour Research and Therapy, 43*, 1243–1261.

Westen, D., Novotny, C., & Thompson-Brenner, H. (2004). The empirical status of empirically supported psychotherapies: Assumptions, findings, and reporting in controlled clinical trials. *Psychological Bulletin, 130*, 631–663.

Wilson, G. T. (1995). Empirically validated treatments as a basis for clinical practice: Problems and prospects. In S. C. Hayes, V. M. Follette, R. D. Dawes, & K. Grady (Eds.), *Scientific standards of psychological practice: Issues and recommendations* (pp. 163–196). Reno, NV: Context Press.

Yeh, M., McCabe, K., Hough, R. L., Dupuis, D., & Hazen, A. (2003). Racial and ethnic differences in parental endorsement of barriers to mental health services in youth. *Mental Health Services Research, 5*, 65–77.

Evidence-based Assessment

John Hunsley *and* Eric J. Mash

Abstract

Evidence-based assessment relies on research and theory to inform the selection of constructs to be assessed for a specific assessment purpose, the methods and measures to be used in the assessment, and the manner in which the assessment process unfolds. An evidence-based approach to clinical assessment necessitates the recognition that, even when evidence-based instruments are used, the assessment process is a decision-making task in which hypotheses must be iteratively formulated and tested. In this chapter, we review (a) the progress that has been made in developing an evidence-based approach to clinical assessment in the past decade and (b) the many challenges that lie ahead if clinical assessment is to be truly evidence-based.

Keywords: Assessment, evidence-based assessment, evidence-based instruments, clinical decision-making

Assessment is ubiquitous in our society. At birth, babies are weighed, measured, and evaluated. In educational systems, students are assessed virtually every day from the time they begin school until they complete their education many years later. In the employment domain, people are repeatedly evaluated, either formally or informally, for myriad reasons, such as determining whether they should be offered a job, allowed to continue in the job, receive promotions, and receive salary increases. Every appointment with a health-care professional, including dentists, optometrists, and physicians, involves an evaluation of the patient's health, presenting complaints, and potential for rehabilitation, amelioration of symptoms, or cure. Assessment, in one form or another, is a central and inescapable aspect of our lives in the 21st century.

There can be no doubt about the critical role that assessment has in psychology. For many psychologists, core elements of the discipline include (a) our heritage of striving to accurately measure and evaluate a host of human phenomena and (b) our development of strategies, tools, and statistics to achieve these goals (Benjamin, 2005). Likewise, for many clinical psychologists, expertise in clinical assessment is seen as a unique and defining feature of the profession, one that sets us apart from other disciplines involved in providing health-care services (Krishnamurthy et al., 2004). Historically, assessment was an integral component in the development of the profession of clinical psychology, and it remains one that is clearly evident in the contemporary practice of clinical psychology. Indeed, it is hard to conceive of assessment *not* occurring in situations in which psychological services are provided, research is conducted, or psychological policy decisions are made.

The fact that something is ubiquitous and integral to some aspect of life does not mean that it is always valued as highly or examined as closely as it should be. As an example, we tend to take for granted having ready access to electricity to power our homes, offices, and numerous electronic devices. It may be only when storms disrupt the electrical transmission grid, or when blackouts occur for other reasons, that our reliance on electricity to run our personal and professional lives comes into sharp focus. The very centrality of electrical power in our lives makes us rather complacent about its value and importance, and probably leads us to be rather unquestioning in our acceptance of our need for it. From our perspective, the very successful history of measurement, test development, and assessment within psychology, generally, and clinical psychology, specifically, has, likewise, left psychologists complacent about the nature and value of psychological assessment methods and processes. Because of the assumptions, at least among psychologists, that psychological assessment is important and that clinical psychologists are well-equipped to conduct assessments that inform psychological services, the usefulness of contemporary assessment instruments and practices has rarely been questioned. For example, there is little solid evidence to support the usefulness of assessment for improving treatment outcomes, and many commonly used assessment methods have limited or contradictory empirical support (e.g., Fletcher, Francis, Morris, & Lyon, 2005; Neisworth & Bagnato, 2004; Norcross, Koocher, & Garofalo, 2006). As a result, at this point in time, any requests from program administrators, third-party payers, or clients to justify the professional time and costs associated with psychological assessment cannot be convincingly addressed with empirical data.

The neglect of such a basic question as the usefulness of current assessment practices in professional practice also reflects the influence of other factors, including (a) a belief in the intrinsic worth of many established and commonly used assessment methods (e.g., intelligence tests and projective personality tests) and (b) a lack of clarity regarding the kinds of evidence and criteria needed to evaluate the utility of assessment methods and processes. As a result, systematic evaluations of the way in which clinicians integrate and use assessment information in case formulation, treatment planning, or treatment monitoring activities are only infrequently conducted (Fernandez-Ballesteros et al., 2001). Thus, rather than having a cumulative scientific literature on psychological assessment, we currently have an impressive and extremely large body of research on assessment instruments and instrument subscales. However, research on psychological measures is not the same as research on the more complicated task of psychological assessment, a task that involves integrating test results (including data from self-report measures, behavioral observations, performance tasks, and biologically based indices), life history information, and collateral data into a coherent description of the client being assessed. Research on psychological instruments is a necessary component of, but not a substitute for, research on psychological assessment (Hunsley, 2002; McGrath, 2001), a point we will return to later in the chapter.

Fortunately, over the past decade, a modest but noticeable shift has occurred in the assessment literature, one that involves scientifically and professionally informed critical appraisals of the way in which psychological assessment research is conducted and psychological assessments are used to guide practice. This shift is due to many factors, including concerns about accountability of psychological services (e.g., Wood et al., 2002), the need to base assessment practices more fully on scientific evidence (e.g., Hunsley & Mash, 2005), the need for assessment research that is directly relevant to the practice of assessment (e.g., McGrath, 2001), the need to more fully consider assessment issues in treatment research and treatment provision (e.g., Mash & Hunsley, 2005), and, more broadly, the move toward evidence-based health-care practices (e.g., Institute of Medicine, 2001). One of the main results of the confluence of these factors has been the development of evidence-based assessment (EBA).

As we have written elsewhere (Hunsley & Mash, 2007), EBA is an approach to clinical evaluation that uses research and theory to guide the selection of constructs to be assessed for a specific assessment purpose, the methods and measures to be used in the assessment, and the manner in which the assessment process unfolds. Evidence-based assessment involves the recognition by the psychologist that, even when data from psychometrically strong measures are available, the assessment process is inherently a decision-making task in which the psychologist must iteratively formulate and test hypotheses by integrating data that may be incomplete or inconsistent. As a result, a truly evidence-based approach to assessment involves an evaluation of the accuracy and usefulness of this complex decision-making task in light of potential errors and biases in data synthesis and interpretation, the costs associated with the assessment process and, ultimately, the impact the assessment had on clinical outcomes for the person(s) being assessed. Defined in this manner, EBA is part of the larger evidence-based practice (EBP) movement that stresses the use of an amalgamation of systematically collected data, clinical expertise, and patient preferences by decision makers (including, but not limited to, clinicians) when considering services options for individual patients or subgroups of the population (e.g., American Psychological Association Presidential Task Force on Evidence-Based Practice, 2006; Sackett et al., 1996).

Building on our previous work (e.g., Hunsley & Mash, 2007, 2008b; Mash & Hunsley, 2005), in this chapter we present the current state of development of EBA. We begin by highlighting the reasons that EBA is needed in clinical psychology, including problems with commonly used instruments and the lack of data on clinical utility. We then review efforts to conceptualize EBA and recent attempts to operationalize criteria for EBA. This is followed by an examination of how differences in these criteria affect whether an instrument is classified as being evidence-based. Finally, we discuss some of the challenges the field must address in building a truly evidence-based approach to clinical assessment.

Some Current Problems and Limitations in Clinical Assessment

As just discussed, it appears that the weight of scientific evidence is not being used to its fullest extent in a number of areas in the domain of psychological assessment. In the following sections, we present some examples of the problems that underscore the importance of promoting an evidence-based approach to clinical assessment. We hasten to add that these problems do not mean that clinical assessment, in general, is lacking in merit or without value in the provision of health-care services to those being assessed. Rather, by focusing on problems associated with some frequently used instruments and common assessment practices, our intention to is to demonstrate ways in which clinical psychologists can improve upon their efforts to deliver high-quality care to the patients they serve and to provide scientifically based education to the trainees they teach and supervise.

Scientific Limitations of Some Commonly Used Clinical Instruments

Over the years, there have been numerous surveys of the instruments most commonly used by clinical psychologists and taught in graduate training programs and internships. Despite some rather important advances in measurement and test development having occurred, the general patterns of instrument usage and the relative rankings of specific instruments have changed very little over at least 30 years (Piotrowski, 1999). These surveys indicate that, among the most commonly used and taught instruments are a number of assessment tools that have either little or mixed research support. As we describe

in the following paragraphs, although many of these scientifically questionable tests are projective instruments, there are also problems with other types of frequently used measures.

The Rorschach inkblot test has been the focus of a number of literature reviews during the past decade (e.g., Hunsley & Bailey, 2001, Meyer & Archer, 2001; Wood, Nezworski, Lilienfeld & Garb, 2003). The Comprehensive System (CS; Exner, 1993) is now considered by Rorschach proponents as the principal scoring system for the Rorschach. The Rorschach is a very complex measure to administer, score, and interpret, and the CS provides very clear directions on its administration and scoring. Unfortunately, research indicates that even if these directions are followed, relatively innocuous contextual factors in Rorschach administration, such as the layout of the testing room and the appearance of the assessor, influence the responses produced by examinees (Masling, 1992). Moreover, the CS system can be very difficult to follow correctly. Guarnaccia, Dill, Sabatino, and Southwick (2001) found that both graduate students and psychologists made numerous errors in scoring the Rorschach. In fact, these errors were so extensive that the overall mean accuracy in scoring the main aspects of the CS was only 65%.

A longstanding concern with the CS norms is that they tend to overpathologize normal individuals, something that has been found in both child and adult research samples (Wood, Nezworski, Garb, & Lilienfeld, 2001). The nature of the concern is best illustrated by Hamel, Shaffer, and Erdberg's (2000) study involving data from 100 children who were selected for the absence of psychopathology and behavior problems based on historical information and assessment of current functioning. When the Rorschach data from these children were scored and interpreted according to CS norms, many of them scored in the clinical range on Rorschach indices of psychopathology. As Hamel and colleagues wrote (p. 291): "(T)hese children may be described as grossly misperceiving and misinterpreting their surroundings and having unconventional ideation and significant cognitive impairment. Their distortion of reality and faulty reasoning approach psychosis. These children would also be described as having significant problems establishing and maintaining interpersonal relationships and coping within a social context." However, based on the extensive data used to select these children for the study, none had had psychological problems in the past, none were currently experiencing psychological distress, and all were doing very well in school and in social activities.

Questions about the CS norms resulted in efforts to develop norms that meet the standards required of psychological tests. A series of norms, called the International Reference Samples, were published for the CS, based on data from over 5,800 people from 16 countries (Shaffer, Erdberg, & Meyer, 2007). Taken together, these norms are now recommended for scoring and interpreting adults' responses to the Rorschach (Meyer, Erdberg, & Shaffer, 2007). Although many of the problems with the previous adult norms are said to have been addressed with these new norms, major problems arose in trying to develop norms for youth. Substantial and erratic differences in CS scores occurred both within and across samples from the various countries. This resulted in the main researchers in the international norming effort recommending against using available norms for Rorschach responses from children and adolescents (Meyer et al., 2007). This means that, essentially, the Rorschach should not be used as a psychological test with youth. The scientifically appropriate position taken by these researchers stands in direct contrast with frequent claims that using the Rorschach with youth is consistent with ethical and professional standards for psychological test usage (Hughes, Gacono, & Owens, 2007).

Another example of an instrument that is frequently used by clinical psychologists despite the lack of evidence for its reliability or validity is the Thematic Apperception Test (TAT; Murray, 1943). Although reliable and valid scoring systems for apperceptive tests are employed in research contexts (e.g., Spangler, 1992), they have not been adopted in clinical practice. Very little has changed over several decades of TAT research: There continues to be enormous variability in the manner in which the test is administered, scored, and interpreted, and there is no cumulative evidence that supports the test's reliability and validity (Rossini & Moretti, 1997). Most importantly, for a clinical instrument, there are repeated negative findings in the literature that many approaches to scoring the TAT are simply incapable of differentiating between research participants with mental disorders and those with no mental disorders (Lilienfeld, Wood, & Garb, 2000). Despite its popularity with some psychologists, the TAT is clearly a psychological test that falls well short of professional standards for tests.

A very similar set of problems, in terms of scoring systems and the lack of established reliability and validity, is encountered with the various types of projective drawing tests. In his review of the literature, Lally (2001) concluded that the most frequently used approaches to scoring projective drawings failed to meet legal standards for a scientifically valid technique. Commenting on the scoring systems for projective drawings developed within research contexts, he indicated that they fared somewhat better than other systems. Nevertheless, he summarized their scientific status in the following manner: "(a)lthough their validity is weak, their conclusions are limited in scope, and they appear to offer no additional information over other psychological tests, it can at least be argued that they cross the relatively low hurdle of admissibility (p. 146)." For clinicians looking to provide scientifically based assessments for their clients, this is certainly damning with faint praise.

Thus far, we have focused on commonly used projective tests, but there are also problems, albeit less serious ones, evident in other types of psychological tests. For example, the Symptom Checklist 90-Revised (Derogatis, 1992) is frequently used in a range of clinical settings to assess patients' psychological problems and symptoms. It has nine subscales assessing primary symptom dimensions such as depression, phobic anxiety, psychoticism, and interpersonal sensitivity, along with three summary scores that assess overall symptom levels and distress. It has been known for well over two decades that the factor structure of the test is not consistent with the use and interpretation of the subscales (Cyr, McKenna-Foley, & Peacock, 1985), and more recent studies continue to indicate that there is a single underlying general factor evident in the test (e.g., Holi, Sammallahti, & Aalberg, 1998; Olsen, Mortensen, & Bech, 2004). The repeated finding of this single factor, best conceptualized as a broad dimension of distress, strongly indicates that interpreting the subscales in a substantive manner (i.e., as indicating the presence of elevated of symptoms of depression, phobic anxiety) is unlikely to be appropriate. Without a clear sense of how best to interpret the validity of the scales of this self-report measure, there may be considerable problems with the construct validity of the various short-form versions of this test—a concern that is not unique among the plethora of short forms developed for psychological measures (Smith, 2000).

Problems with Instrument Selection and Interpretation

Even if clinical psychologists refrain from using instruments that have limited scientific support, they must still ensure that the instruments they choose to use are appropriate for the assessment task and are interpreted in accordance with the scientific evidence. Although these would seem to be rather self-evident requirements, there are numerous examples in the professional literature in which these requirements are not met or are simply ignored. As assessments conducted by clinical psychologists often have substantial impact on the people who are assessed (e.g., psychoeducational assessments that will largely determine access to additional educational supports and resources and disability assessments that will affect the possible awarding of disability pensions), it is critical that instruments are selected and used in a professionally responsible manner.

Many clinical psychologists conduct evaluations that are used to inform the courts in determining child custody decisions. These evaluations are expected to provide fair and balanced information about all parties relevant to child custody decisions, and guidelines for conducting these assessments have been available to psychologists and other health professionals for many years (e.g., American Academy of Child and Adolescent Psychiatry, 1997; American Psychological Association, 1994). However, there continue to be many problems with the way in which some clinical psychologists undertake these assessments. One survey of psychologists who frequently conducted child custody evaluations found that projective tests were often used to assess child adjustment (Ackerman & Ackerman, 1997). As described in the previous section, these types of tests rarely have appropriate levels of reliability and validity, and are unlikely to have valid norms. Without evidence of strong psychometric properties, it is all but impossible to make accurate determinations about the psychological adjustment of those tested. For reasons such as these, the recent guidelines of the Association of Family and Conciliation Courts (AFCC, 2006) stressed the need for assessors to use assessment methods that are empirically based and warn against using instruments with questionable reliability or validity. As valuable as such guidelines may be, there is compelling evidence that professional guidelines are not always closely followed. Horvath, Logan, and Walker (2002) examined child custody evaluation reports included in court records and conducted content analyses to determine the extent to which key aspects of these guidelines were met in the evaluations. They found evidence of many gaps in the reports as, for example, evaluators often failed to assess general parenting abilities and the ability of each parent to meet his or her child's needs—key elements of any assessment intended to provide guidance on the issue of child custody.

Fortunately, in some assessment areas there is clear evidence that practices are being influenced by research findings. Lally (2003) surveyed experts in forensic assessment to derive recommendations for which psychological tests should be used for assessment tasks such as malingering, mental state at the time of the criminal offence, risk for future violence or sexual violence, competency to stand trial, and competency to waive rights regarding self-incrimination. For most of these assessment tasks, among the instruments that were recommended or deemed acceptable were recently developed tests designed to specifically address the assessment question and repeatedly validated for that purpose (such as the Violence Risk Appraisal Guide [Rice & Harris, 1995] for the prediction of future violence and the Test of Memory Malingering [Rees, Tombaugh, Gansler, & Moczynski, 1998] for the assessment of malingering). On the other hand, consistent with the scientific evidence in this area, projective tests were routinely described as unacceptable for these forensic assessment tasks.

Even when a psychometrically robust measure is used, challenges can still arise in accurately interpreting the test data. This fact is abundantly evident in the literature on the Wechsler intelligence scales, tests that are among the psychometrically strongest psychological instruments available. A wealth of information exists on the importance of using country-specific norms for the interpretation of the Wechsler intelligence scales. For example, Kamieniecki and Lynd-Stevenson (2002) found that Australian children obtained slightly higher IQ scores than did American children of a similar age. This means that, as was typically done in the past, using American norms in the assessment of giftedness or mental retardation among Australian children would result in some classification errors. Similarly, the use of American norms, rather than the Canadian norms, for the adult intelligence scale leads to a significant underestimation of the extent of cognitive impairment experienced by Canadian patients with substantial neuropsychological problems (Iverson, Lange, & Viljoen, 2006). Findings such as these underscore the importance of recent efforts to develop country-specific norms for the Wechsler scales in English-speaking countries outside of the United States.

Beyond the use of appropriate norms, there is another problem with the interpretation of the Wechsler intelligence scales that is likely quite widespread.

Many of the professional books used by clinical psychologists as an aid to the interpretation of the scales recommend that, following a consideration of the full scale IQ score, the verbal and performance IQ scores, and the factor scores, the next interpretive step should be to examine the variability between and within subtests (e.g., Flanagan & Kaufman, 2004; Kaufman & Lichtenberger, 1999). There are at least two problems with such a recommendation. First, as the internal consistency of each subtest is lower than that associated with the IQ and factor scores, the ability assessed by each subtest is measured less precisely, which means that there will be an increased likelihood of false positive and false negative conclusions drawn about the ability measured by the subtest. Second, beyond the issue of measurement and decision-making errors, there is substantial evidence over several decades that the information contained in subtest profiles adds little to the prediction of either learning behaviors or academic achievement once IQ scores and factor scores have been taken into account (Watkins, 2003).

Limited Evidence for Clinical Utility of Commonly Used Instruments

The concept of clinical utility is being used increasingly in evaluations of the value of both diagnostic systems (e.g., First et al., 2004; Kendell & Jablensky, 2003) and psychological assessment instruments (e.g., Hunsley & Bailey, 1999; McFall, 2005; Yates & Taub, 2003). In the context of diagnostic systems, utility refers to the extent to which a classification system provides nontrivial information about prognosis or treatment outcome and/or provides testable propositions about variables associated with a patient's diagnosis (Kendell & Jablensky, 2003). With respect to psychological instruments, clinical utility refers to whether the use of test data improve upon typical clinical decision-making and treatment outcome or, in other ways, make a difference in terms of the client's functioning as a result of clinical services informed by the test data (Hunsley & Bailey, 1999). Although the definitions vary, a common emphasis is placed on garnering evidence regarding actual improvements in both decisions made by clinicians and service outcomes experienced by patients. To date, despite thousands of studies on the psychometric properties of psychological instruments, only scant attention is paid to matters of utility in the assessment research literature (McGrath, 2001). In other words, we have very little evidence that psychological assessment data have a direct impact on the improved provision and outcome of clinical services.

In the past two decades, many authors have commented on the limited attention paid to the utility of widely used assessment instruments and methods with respect to treatment process and outcome (e.g., Hayes, Nelson & Jarrett, 1987). Diagnosis has some utility in determining the best treatment options for clients (i.e., by guiding clinicians to the evidence base on what treatments are most efficacious and effective for patients with the diagnosis or diagnoses in question). However, most psychologists consider diagnostic information as providing only one aspect of what is necessary in assessing clients seeking treatment. At this point, there is extremely little replicated evidence regarding the extent to which other data gathered in a clinical assessment contributes to beneficial treatment outcomes (Nelson-Gray, 2003). A study by Lima et al. (2005) illustrates the way in which research can begin to address the important set of questions inherent in the concept of clinical utility. In this study, clients completed the Minnesota Multiphasic Personality Inventory-2 (MMPI-2) prior to commencing treatment; half the treating clinicians then received feedback on their client's MMPI-2 data, half did not. The clients involved in the study presented with a range of diagnoses, including anxiety disorders, mood disorders, substance-related disorders, adjustment disorders, eating disorders, and personality disorders. To address questions of utility, the researchers conducted between-group comparisons on variables related to treatment outcome. They found that providing clinicians with the MMPI-2 results as a potential aid in treatment planning had no discernible impact on variables such as client improvement ratings or premature termination rates. These results illustrate that, even for instruments that have been extensively researched, such as the MMPI-2, an instrument should not automatically be assumed to possess utility for all the tasks for which it is commonly used.

Conceptualizing and Evaluating Evidence-based Assessment

The current era of evidence-based health-care practices both requires and depends upon the use of scientifically sound assessment methods, instruments, and strategies (Barlow, 2005). Without accurate assessment data, it is impossible to determine the psychosocial functioning of patients, monitor the treatments they are provided, evaluate the impact of these services at completion, evaluate the broader program in which the treatments are provided, or conduct ongoing quality assurance in order to enhance the functioning of the clinicians working in the program. Recent efforts to develop a consensus cognitive battery of tests to evaluate cognitive deficits in schizophrenia nicely illustrate this point. The lack of such a commonly accepted and used battery of tests, and the standardized evaluations it could provide, has been described as a major impediment to the development and regulatory approval of treatments designed to enhance cognitive functioning in patients with schizophrenia (Green et al., 2008; Nuechterlein, Green, Kern, Baade, Barch, Cohen, et al., 2008). The National Institute of Mental Health's Measurement and Treatment Research to Improve Cognition in Schizophrenia (MATRICS) study was designed to develop, test, and norm such a battery. The MATRICS initiative has reached the stage at which the battery of tests is now available for use in clinical trials (Kern et al., 2008), a necessary first step in the development of cognition-enhancing drugs for schizophrenia and related disorders.

Considerable attention has recently been focused in the professional literature on the development, dissemination, and use of evidence-based treatments (EBTs) (Nathan & Gorman, 2007; Silverman & Hinshaw, 2008). Although EBTs have been hailed by many psychologists as the best option for providing optimal treatments to patients, a number of concerns about their general applicability and relevance remain. Recently, Kazdin (2008) summarized several fundamental issues that must be confronted in using EBTs in light of the nature of clinical practice. These included, for EBTs, variability in classification criteria used to designate a treatment as evidence-based or empirically supported, the real-world meaning of scores on psychological measures and the extent of changes on these measures necessary to indicate a clinically relevant change in functioning, and variability in the extent of treatment-related change observed in the multiple outcome measures used in any given treatment study. With respect to routine clinical practice, Kazdin noted that considerable progress needs to be made on the use of clinical expertise and decision-making to guide treatment formulation and provision, the manner in which clinical experience can be meaningfully and systematically used to inform service provision, and the use of systematic measurement to evaluate the impact of psychological services. Even a cursory review of these issues indicates that most, if not all, are essentially issues of measurement and the application of assessment data to inform clinical practice.

Yet, relative to the attention devoted to EBTs, matters pertinent to EBA have received scant attention.

As Achenbach (2005) emphasized, the failure to draw upon the scientific literature on psychological assessment in developing and promoting EBTs is like constructing a magnificent house without bothering to build a solid foundation. Indeed, as the evaluation of, and, ultimately, the identification of EBTs rests entirely on the assessment data, ignoring the quality of psychological assessment instruments and the manner in which they are used places the promotion of evidence-based psychological practice in jeopardy. As an example, for a number of psychological disorders, research-derived treatment benchmarks can now provide clinicians with meaningful and attainable targets for their intervention services (Hunsley & Lee, 2007; Minami et al., 2008; Weersing, 2005). But, to be meaningful, these benchmarks must be based on reliable and valid measures, and to employ these benchmarks in routine practice, clinical psychologists must use assessment tools that have strong scientific support and are appropriate for the task at hand. Moreover, the decision-making processes surrounding how to determine relevant and appropriate benchmarks, obtain client data, and compare these data to the benchmarks must, themselves, be reliable and valid.

Across mental health professions, clinicians are seeking assessment tools they can use to determine a client's level of pretreatment functioning and to develop, monitor, and evaluate the services received by the client (Barkham et al., 2001; Bickman et al., 2000; Hatfield & Ogles, 2004). In their continuing efforts to improve the quality of mental health assessments, the American Psychiatric Association published the second edition of its *Practice Guideline for the Psychiatric Evaluation of Adults* (2006). Drawing from both current scientific knowledge and the realities of clinical practice, this guideline addresses both the content and process of psychiatric evaluations. It also builds upon the *Handbook of Psychiatric Measures* (American Psychiatric Association, 2000), a publication that offers information to mental health professionals on the availability of self-report measures, clinician checklists, and structured interviews relevant to the provision of clinical services. For each measure reviewed, there is a brief summary of its intended purpose, psychometric properties, likely clinical utility, and the practical issues likely to be encountered in its use.

With respect to children and adolescents, the American Academy of Child and Adolescent Psychiatry and American Academy of Pediatrics have been active in developing practice guidelines for assessment instruments (e.g., self-report instruments) and contexts (e.g., family assessment), as well as for the assessment of specific childhood disorders (e.g., autistic spectrum disorders). These guidelines are based on the scientific literature and clinical consensus, and describe generally accepted approaches to assess specific disorders (e.g., Johnson, Myers, & the Council on Children with Disabilities, 2007). Thus, the need for developing EBA practices is apparent not only in clinical psychology but across a variety of health disciplines that, in some areas, may be further along in this enterprise than professional psychology.

Clinical psychology has a long and impressive history of measure development and validation. However, with the recent exception of the Society for Pediatric Psychology initiative we describe in the next section, no professional organization in clinical psychology, or psychology more generally, has undertaken the task of formulating and disseminating psychological assessment guidelines in professional psychology. This may simply be another example of organized psychology's apparent reluctance, relative to other health professions, to operationalize and promote practice guidelines and requirements. It is also, at least partially, due to the extremely limited attention to the foundational role that assessment activities play in evidence-based psychological services (cf. Cohen, La Greca, Blount, Kazak, Holmbeck, & Lemanek, 2008).

The *Standards for Educational and Psychological Testing* (American Educational Research Association, American Psychological Association, & National Council on Measurement in Education, 1999) set out generic standards to be followed in developing and using psychological instruments, but they offer no guidance on the level of psychometric adequacy an instrument should have. Psychometric characteristics are not properties of an instrument per se but, rather, are properties of an instrument when used for a specific purpose with a specific sample. Accordingly, assessment scholars, psychometricians, and test developers have typically been reluctant to set the minimum psychometric criteria necessary for specifying when an instrument is scientifically sound (cf. Streiner & Norman, 2003). Although understandable, this is of little aid to clinicians, who must make decisions about what assessment tools to use in their practices, how best to use and combine the various forms of information they obtain in their assessment, and how to integrate assessment activities into other necessary aspects of clinical service. Fortunately, some initial efforts have been made to operationalize the criteria necessary for

designating psychological instruments and assessment processes as evidence-based. It is to these efforts that we now turn our attention.

Evidence-based Assessment Initiatives and Criteria

In this section, we review three approaches to operationalize evidence-based psychological instruments. As we will illustrate, these initiatives differed in the criteria used to identify best available instruments, the scope of the search strategies used to develop a pool of instruments to be evaluated, and the manner in which the criteria were systematically applied to the pool of instruments. As will become apparent, all three approaches have their strengths and limitations. However, one major limitation, at least for the promotion of EBP, is that all developed criteria for evidence-based *instruments*, not for evidence-based *assessments*. As we described previously in this chapter and elsewhere (Hunsley & Mash, 2007; Mash & Hunsley, 2005), this reflects the state of our (limited) scientific knowledge of the processes, outcomes, and utility of psychological assessments. Accordingly, it is perhaps more accurate to describe these three initiatives as focusing on evidence-based instruments (EBI) rather than EBA per se.

The first comprehensive effort to develop and apply criteria for evaluating clinical instruments of which we are aware is that of Bickman, Nurcombe, Townsend, Belle, Schut, and Karver (1999). As part of the Australian government's effort to reform mental health services, these researchers conducted a thorough review of outcome measures for use in child and adolescent mental health services. Based on their efforts, they recommended that a modular outcome measurement system be implemented in which brief, easily administered and interpreted measures are used in each of three assessment modules. These modules were focused on (a) background assessment (i.e., measuring factors in the youth and family's background that are likely to influence treatment), (b) baseline and follow-up assessment (i.e., measuring aspects of the youth's and family's mental health prior to treatment and at subsequent points in service delivery), and (c) concurrent assessment (i.e., monitoring key variables throughout the course of treatment).

Database searches were conducted to relevant articles, chapters, and books published in the period 1990–1998, and a list of 188 measures was extracted from these sources. All available published information was then obtained and reviewed for these measures. Each measure was then rated on the basis of

29 criteria, which are presented in Table 5.1. Although many of the criteria involved simple yes/no ratings or similar ratings (e.g., number of minutes to administer the test), they also developed specific criteria for determining specific levels of reliability and validity (such as unacceptable, barely acceptable, and highly acceptable). A detailed list of coding keys for each criterion is available in Bickman et al. (1999).

After this initial coding, the research group developed 18 evaluation requirements that were most relevant for their task of determining the best measures for a modular outcome measurement system. Among these 18, five were designated as being the most important: these were that the test took less than 10 minutes to complete, required less than 2 hours of training for the person administering and interpreting the test, required no specialized background for using the test, had evidence of convergent validity coefficients greater than .50, and had known groups validity. None of the 188 measures met all 18 requirements, but ten measures met the reduced set of five requirements. To ensure full coverage of the necessary domains for the measurement system, additional measures were included that best satisfied the selection requirements, resulting in a battery of 31 measures.

There are several noteworthy aspects to the Bickman et al. work. They include the use of systematic search strategies to generate an initial list of tests to be evaluated, the use of appropriate and justifiable evaluation criteria (including both scientific and practice-relevant criteria), the presentation of specific requirements of psychometric adequacy, and the identification of key elements necessary for a test to be included in their measurement system. Of course, there are some limitations, the most notable being that (a) the sheer volume of work involved in their literature search and subsequent coding of criteria means that their approach to determining the best available measures cannot be easily implemented by psychologists reviewing the measures available for other assessment purposes and other client populations, and (b) the requirements set for their measurement system likely mean that their conclusions about the best available measures may not be applicable to other clinical psychology practice contexts.

The work presented in a recent volume by Hunsley and Mash (2008a) has some similarities to the Bickman et al. initiative, inasmuch as explicit criteria were used to evaluate the adequacy of psychological instruments. The scope of the Hunsley and

Table 5.1 Bickman et al. (1999) criteria for rating outcome measures for use in child and adolescent mental health services

Cultural Sensitivity:	Evidence of bias
	Cultural norms
	Used in Australia
Suitability:	Cost
	Time required
	Training required
	Degree/experience required to administer
	Reading level
	Computer software available
Reliability:	Test–retest reliability within a 2-week period
	Test–retest coefficient
	Internal consistency
	Cross-informant agreement
	Inter-rater agreement
Content validity:	Theory-based items
	Expert judgment used in item evaluation
	Respondent feedback used in item evaluation
	Factor analytic findings
Construct validity:	Convergent validity
	Divergent validity
	Social desirability
	Group differences
	Sensitivity/specificity
Norms:	Current norms available
	Number of normative samples
Developmental sensitivity:	Number of forms for specific age groups
	Age effects
	Norms across ages and/or age groups

Mash volume is, however, much broader, with measures used in the assessment of the most commonly encountered disorders or conditions among children, adolescents, adults, older adults, and couples (e.g., anxiety disorders, mood disorders, disruptive behavior disorders, sexual disorders, couple distress, sleep disorders, personality disorders, self-injurious thoughts and behaviors, substance-use disorders, pain). To ensure the clinical relevance of the review of EBIs, reviews by subject-area experts focused on three clinically important assessment purposes: diagnosis, case conceptualization and treatment planning, and treatment monitoring and evaluation. With these purposes in mind, subject-area experts focused on assessment measures and strategies that had either demonstrated their utility in clinical settings or have a substantial likelihood of being clinically useful. Thus, the measures reviewed in the volume were selected to be among the best measures currently available. The experts considered the full range of relevant assessment methods (i.e., interviews, self-report, observation, performance tasks, computer-based methods, physiological, etc.), but considerations of scientific evidence and clinical feasibility were used to guide decisions about which instruments to review in detail. Some authors (e.g., Green, Worden, Menges, & McCrady, 2008) reported developing and following a systematic methodology for identifying possible measures for inclusion in their review. The ways in which age, gender, ethnicity, and other relevant patient characteristics influence both the assessment measures and the process of assessment for the disorder/condition were also examined.

Criteria developed by Hunsley and Mash (2008b) were used to evaluate all instruments reviewed in the volume. These criteria were explicitly designed to allow for the determination of measures that were "good enough" for clinical and research use. Rather than focusing on standards that defined ideal criteria for a measure, the intent was to have criteria that would indicate the minimum evidence sufficient to warrant the use of a measure for specific assessment purposes and clinical problems. In operationalizing the "good enough" principle, we developed specific rating criteria to be used across categories of psychometric properties that have clear clinical relevance.

The rating framework focused on nine criterion categories: norms, internal consistency, inter-rater reliability, test–retest reliability, content validity, construct validity, validity generalization, sensitivity to treatment change, and clinical utility. Each of these categories was examined in relation to a specific assessment purpose (e.g., case conceptualization and treatment planning) in the context of a specific disorder or clinical condition (e.g., eating disorders, obsessive-compulsive disorder, late life depression), and factors such as gender, ethnicity, and age were considered in making ratings within these categories. For each criterion category, a rating of less than adequate, adequate, good, excellent, unavailable, or not applicable was possible based upon the invited expert's appraisal of the preponderance of available evidence. The precise nature of what constituted adequate, good, and excellent varied from category to category. In general, a rating of adequate indicated that the instrument meets a minimal level of scientific rigor, good indicated that the instrument would generally be seen as possessing solid scientific support, and excellent indicated there was extensive, high-quality supporting evidence. A rating of less than adequate indicated that the instrument did not meet the minimum level set out in the criteria. A rating of unavailable indicated that research on the psychometric property under consideration had not yet been conducted or published. A rating of not applicable indicated that the psychometric property under consideration was not relevant to the instrument (e.g., inter-rater reliability for a self-report symptom rating scale). Precise details about these specific criteria are presented in Tables 5.2 and 5.3.

On the basis of their evaluations, subject-area experts indicated instruments that are the best measures currently available to clinicians for specific purposes and disorders and, thus, are highly recommended for clinical use. Given the considerable differences in the state of the assessment literature for different disorders/conditions, there was some variability among experts in precisely operationalizing the rating of *highly recommended*. That being said, a moderate level of consistency in these ratings, at least, was ensured by the requirement that a highly recommended rating could only be considered for those instruments that had achieved ratings of good or excellent in the majority of their rated psychometric categories. Not surprisingly, there were more highly recommended instruments for the assessment of some disorders than for others. For example, in the assessment of schizophrenia, two assessment instruments were rated as highly recommended for diagnostic purposes, 12 for case conceptualization and treatment planning purposes, and 13 for treatment monitoring and outcome evaluation purposes (Mueser & Glynn, 2008). In contrast, for bipolar disorder, three instruments were identified as highly recommended for diagnosis, none for case conceptualization and treatment planning, and only two for treatment monitoring and outcome evaluation (Johnson, Miller, & Eisner, 2008).

The major strengths of the Hunsley and Mash (2008a) work include the use of subject-area experts to identify and rate assessment instruments, a focus on clinically meaningful assessment purposes, the presentation of specific requirements of psychometric

Table 5.2 Hunsley & Mash (2008b) criteria for rating assessment instruments: Norms and reliability

NORMS

Adequate = Measures of central tendency and distribution for the total score (and subscores if relevant) based on a large, relevant, clinical sample are available

Good = Measures of central tendency and distribution for the total score (and subscores if relevant) based on several large, relevant samples (must include data from both clinical and nonclinical samples) are available

Excellent = Measures of central tendency and distribution for the total score (and subscores if relevant) based on one or more large, *representative* samples (must include data from both clinical and nonclinical samples) are available

INTERNAL CONSISTENCY

Adequate = Preponderance of evidence indicates alpha values of .70–.79

Good = Preponderance of evidence indicates alpha values of .80–.89

Excellent = Preponderance of evidence indicates alpha values $\geq$.90

INTER-RATER RELIABILITY

Adequate = Preponderance of evidence indicates κ values of .60–.74; the preponderance of evidence indicates Pearson correlation or intraclass correlation values of .70–.79

Good = Preponderance of evidence indicates κ values of .75–.84; the preponderance of evidence indicates Pearson correlation or intraclass correlation values of .80–.89

Excellent = Preponderance of evidence indicates κ values $\geq$.85; the preponderance of evidence indicates Pearson correlation or intraclass correlation values $\geq$.90

TEST–RETEST RELIABILITY

Adequate = Preponderance of evidence indicates test–retest correlations of at least .70 over a period of several days to several weeks

Good = Preponderance of evidence indicates test–retest correlations of at least .70 over a period of several months

Excellent = Preponderance of evidence indicates test–retest correlations of at least .70 over a period of a year or longer

adequacy, and the broad range of clinical conditions addressed in reviews of the assessment literature. Some of the limitations of this initiative are the flip side of the strengths. For example, the use of experts to select and rate instruments (rather than using systematic literature review strategies and independent coders) means that some solid instruments may have been overlooked and that the ratings of psychometric adequacy could have been affected by subjective biases (including our own biases in inviting the contributors to the volume). Similarly, the focus on specific assessment purposes, although enhancing the clinical relevance of the assessment reviews, may have resulted in important and scientifically supported instruments not being represented (e.g., broadband measures such as the MMPI-2 and MMPI-A did not appear as highly recommended for any disorder/condition–assessment purpose combination). Finally, the overall ratings for some

dimensions (e.g., clinical utility) were necessarily based on a smaller evidence base than those for other dimensions (e.g., reliability and validity).

A very different approach to classifying EBIs was taken in a recent task force initiative of the APA Society of Pediatric Psychology (Cohen et al., 2008). The task force steering committee and a set of expert working groups identified measures that fell into one of eight areas of broad interest: quality of life, family functioning, psychosocial functioning and psychopathology, social support and peer relations, treatment adherence, pain, stress and coping, and cognitive functioning. A survey that included all 367 instruments was posted on the Society's listserve, and an additional 56 measures were added to the list of measures to be considered for the designation of evidence-based. Work groups for each area were instructed to focus on reviewing the most widely used and researched instruments and to use

Table 5.3 Hunsley & Mash (2008b) criteria for rating assessment instruments: Validity and utility

CONTENT VALIDITY

Adequate = The test developers clearly defined the domain of the construct being assessed and ensured that selected items were representative of the entire set of facets included in the domain.

Good = In addition to the criteria used for an Adequate rating, all elements of the instrument (e.g., instructions, items) were evaluated by judges (e.g., by experts, by pilot research participants).

Excellent = In addition to the criteria used for a Good rating, multiple groups of judges were employed and quantitative ratings were used by the judges.

CONSTRUCT VALIDITY

Adequate = Some independently replicated evidence of construct validity (e.g., predictive validity, concurrent validity, convergent and discriminant validity)

Good = Preponderance of independently replicated evidence, across multiple types of validity (e.g., predictive validity, concurrent validity, convergent and discriminant validity), is indicative of construct validity.

Excellent = In addition to the criteria used for a Good rating, evidence of incremental validity with respect to other clinical data

VALIDITY GENERALIZATION

Adequate = Some evidence supports the use of this instrument with either (a) more than one specific group (based on sociodemographic characteristics such as age, gender, and ethnicity) or (b) in multiple contexts (e.g., home, school, primary care setting, inpatient setting)

Good = Preponderance of evidence supports the use of this instrument with either (a) more than one specific group (based on sociodemographic characteristics such as age, gender, and ethnicity) or (b) in multiple settings (e.g., home, school, primary care setting, inpatient setting)

Excellent = Preponderance of evidence supports the use of this instrument with more than one specific group (based on sociodemographic characteristics such as age, gender, and ethnicity) *and* across multiple contexts (e.g., home, school, primary care setting, inpatient setting)

TREATMENT SENSITIVITY

Adequate = Some evidence of sensitivity to change over the course of treatment

Good = Preponderance of independently replicated evidence indicates sensitivity to change over the course of treatment

Excellent = In addition to the criteria used for a Good rating, evidence of sensitivity to change across different types of treatments

CLINICAL UTILITY

Adequate = Taking into account practical considerations (e.g., costs, ease of administration, availability of administration and scoring instructions, duration of assessment, availability of relevant cutoffs scores, acceptability to patients), the resulting assessment data are likely to be clinically useful.

Good = In addition to the criteria used for an Adequate rating, there is some published evidence that the use of the resulting assessment data confers a demonstrable clinical benefit (e.g., better treatment outcome, lower treatment attrition rates, greater patient satisfaction with services).

Excellent = In addition to the criteria used for an Adequate rating, there is *independently replicated* published evidence that the use of the resulting assessment data confers a demonstrable clinical benefit.

a combination of the results of the survey, the current literature, and their own expertise in selecting instruments to be reviewed.

The criteria that were developed to determine whether an instrument was evidence-based were based on those used to identify empirically supported treatments. Thus, depending on the extent of the empirical support, any measure presented in the peer-reviewed literature could be designated as promising, approaching well-established, and well-established. The precise criteria are presented in Table 5.4. Along with these criteria, the work groups were asked to evaluate the clinical and research utility of the measures and to identify which measures could be used with various ethnic and linguistic minority populations.

The decision in the Society of Pediatric Psychology initiative to have an initial pool of possible EBIs generated by those working in the field of pediatric psychology ensures that the pool contained many measures that were both scientifically sound and clinically useful, although the lack of a systematic review strategy may have resulted in some relevant measures being overlooked. As with the Hunsley and Mash (2008a) effort, the use of subject-area experts has both strengths and weaknesses: It ensures that knowledgeable individuals were involved in examining possible EBIs, but subjective biases may have affected both the generation of the list of instruments to be considered and the manner in which criteria were applied. The choice of empirically supported treatment-like criteria was an interesting one. On the one hand, the consistency with treatment criteria provides a kind of face validity to the criteria; on the other hand, given that assessments can be undertaken for a range of purposes, the voluminous nature of the psychological assessment

literature, and the psychometric sophistication evident in many assessment articles, these criteria may be both too nonspecific and too lax to provide a thorough and meaningful evaluation of an instrument's evidence base. For example, in the area of psychopathology and psychosocial functioning, which we use for comparison purposes in the next section, nearly all of the instruments reviewed were designated as evidence-based. Finally, although the work groups were provided psychometric descriptions and references to guide their evaluations, the lack of precise requirements for what constitutes "good" validity and reliability limits the transparency of decisions made about psychometric adequacy.

Evidence-based Instruments: Current Status and Issues

The three initiatives just described all attempted to apply standardized criteria for determining the extent and quality of the evidence base supporting psychological measures. Despite a common goal, the three differed substantially in the methods used for identifying and evaluating potential EBIs. Although the availability of multiple frameworks for methods and criteria is probably appropriate at this early juncture in the operationalization of EBA, it does raise questions about the comparability and validity of the various efforts. Do the three approaches simply provide different routes to the same outcome (i.e., do they all identify a similar set of EBIs?), or do they provide different routes *and* different outcomes (i.e., is there little consistency across frameworks in the instruments identified as evidence-based?)? If similar instruments are identified regardless of the framework used, then parsimony of methods and criteria should prevail in determining the best framework to use in subsequent work.

Table 5.4 Cohen et al. (2008) criteria for rating assessment instruments

Well-established assessment
- Measure presented in two or more peer-reviewed articles by different investigators/investigatory teams
- Details about measure are available, thus allowing critical evaluation and replication
- Detailed information indicating good reliability and validity in at least one peer-reviewed article

Approaching Well-established assessment
- Measure presented in two or more peer-reviewed articles, possibly by the same investigator/investigatory team
- Details about measure are available, thus allowing critical evaluation and replication
- Validity and reliability data are moderate, or information presented only in vague terms

Promising assessment
- Measure presented in at least one peer-reviewed article
- Details about measure are available, thus allowing critical evaluation and replication
- Validity and reliability data are moderate or information presented only in vague terms

However, if there is little overlap among instruments identified as evidence-based, then essential questions about what constitutes an EBI must be addressed.

To begin to answer these types of questions, we compared the results of the Society for Pediatric Psychology and the Hunsley and Mash (2008a) work. For both, measures of psychopathology and adjustment were examined for child and adolescent populations. Although Bickman et al. (1999) also examined these types of instruments, the particular requirements for their initiative (e.g., brief administration time, no specialized background required for administering the instrument) generated a list of recommended instruments that was not directly comparable to those from the other two frameworks. Therefore, in Table 5.5, we present a list of instruments, including specific internalizing or externalizing problems and broadband measures of symptoms and adjustment, that received the highest ratings in the two evaluation systems. These measures were either rated as well-established by the psychosocial adjustment and psychopathology work group (Holmbeck et al., 2008; Table 5, column 1) or as evidence-based by the authors of chapters in Hunsley and Mash (2008a) that focused on youth-related disorders (Dougherty, Klein, Olino, & Laptook, 2008; Frick & McMahon, 2008; Johnston & Mah, 2008; Silverman & Ollendick, 2008; Table 5, column 2). Because of our focus on instruments to assess psychopathology, we did not include measures of self-esteem or self-perception rated by Holmbeck et al.

Table 5.5 clearly demonstrates that a wide range of measures are available for assessing youth psychopathology and psychosocial functioning. These include both measures assessing specific problems and more general symptom and adjustment measures. However, it is also apparent that the two frameworks used to determine generated lists of EBIs resulted in only modest overlap. Of the 26 psychopathology measures rated by Holmbeck et al. as well-established, only 16 were seen as sufficiently evidence-based to be included by the authors in the Hunsley and Mash volume. Likewise, of the 29 instruments rated as evidence-based by the Hunsley and Mash authors, only 16 were rated as well-established by Holmbeck et al. Clearly, not all roads lead to the same list of EBIs. The emphasis on a pediatric context in the Holmbeck et al. review, compared to an emphasis on a general clinical context in the other reviews, probably contributed to these discrepancies. However, the extent and nature of the

discrepancies are such that we believe other factors played a contributing role in the differences observed in Table 5.5.

By examining the nature of the instruments listed in the table and the material provided by the authors whose reviews provided the information therein, it is evident that at least two main factors were responsible for the discrepancies between the two frameworks. First, the instruments identified by Holmbeck et al. were almost entirely self-report measures, whereas the Hunsley and Mash authors were more likely to include interview and observational methods in their set of recommended instruments. Second, many of the measures identified by Holmbeck et al., but not by authors in the Hunsley and Mash volume, were ones identified as commonly used *research* measures in the Society of Pediatric Psychology survey. Of course, differences in the number of required studies supporting each measure ("two or more" vs. "the preponderance of published evidence") and the precision of criteria for establishing psychometric adequacy may also have contributed to the discrepant outcome. This is especially likely as Holmbeck et al. reported that many of the instruments rated as well-established had psychometric weaknesses, such as a lack of full psychometric data on reliability and validity, poor internal consistency, limited content validity, inconsistent factor structure across studies, and high correlations with measures of social desirability. This also suggests that their criteria may, indeed, have been too general and too lenient.

In discussions of how to best operationalize EBAs or EBIs, it is worth noting that the evaluation frameworks described in the previous section all differ from the approach that is typically taken in evaluating services in evidence-based medicine (EBM). As recently discussed by Youngstrom (2008), it may be appropriate to consider explicitly adopting the evidence hierarchy approach used in EBM. In general, based largely on internal validity considerations, evidence hierarchies place expert opinion on the lowest level of the hierarchy, followed by case studies, group research designs that have shortcomings in addressing threats to internal validity, and group research designs that have a high degree of internal validity. At the top of the hierarchy are systematic reviews of well-designed studies (including meta-analyses). Clinicians searching the scientific literature to locate information that could aid service delivery efforts are explicitly encouraged to use the evidence hierarchy, turning to evidence at a lower level in the hierarchy only if the evidence at

Table 5.5 Applying Cohen et al. (2008) and Hunsley and Mash (2008b) criteria to instruments for assessing psychopathology in youth

Type of Instrument		
Cohen et al.	Hunsley & Mash	
Internalizing or Externalizing Problems		
ADHD Rating Scale-IV		
Yes	Yes	
Antisocial Process Screening Device		
No	Yes	
Behavioral Tasks (including avoidance, self-evaluation)		
No	Yes	
Beck Anxiety Inventory		
Yes	No	
Beck Depression Inventory		
Yes	No	
Behavioral Coding System		
No	Yes	
Center for Epidemiologic Studies Depression Scale		
Yes	No	
Child Anxiety Sensitivity Index		
Yes	Yes	
Children's Depression Inventory		
Yes	Yes	
Children's Depression Rating Scale–Revised		
No	Yes	
Children's Somatization Inventory		
Yes	No	
Dyadic Parent–Child Interaction Coding System		
No	Yes	
Eyberg Child Behavior Inventory		
No	Yes	
Fear Survey Schedule for Children Revised		
Yes	Yes	
Mood and Feelings Questionnaire		
No	Yes	
Multidimensional Anxiety Scale for Children		
Yes	Yes	
Parent Daily Report		
No	Yes	
Positive and Negative Affect Schedule for Children		
Yes	No	
Revised Children's Manifest Anxiety Scale		
Yes	Yes	
Reynold's Adolescent Depression Scale, 2nd ed.		
Yes	Yes	
Screen for Child Anxiety-related Emotional Problems		
Yes	Yes	
Social Anxiety Scale for Adolescents		
Yes	No	
Social Anxiety Scale for Children (including revised scale)		
Yes	Yes	
Social Phobia and Anxiety Inventory for Children		
Yes	Yes	
State-Trait Anxiety Inventory for Children		
Yes	Yes	
Broadband		
Achenbach System of Empirically Based Assessment		
Yes	Yes	
Anxiety Disorders Interview Schedule		
No	Yes	
Behavior Assessment System for Children (including 2nd ed.)		
Yes	Yes	
Brief Symptom Inventory		
Yes	No	
Child and Adolescent Functional Assessment Scale		
Yes	Yes	
Child and Adolescent Psychiatric Assessment		
No	Yes	
Children's Global Assessment Scale		
Yes	Yes	
Conners' Rating Scales–Revised		
Yes	Yes	
Diagnostic Interview Schedule for Children		
No	Yes	
Minnesota Multiphasic Personality Inventory–Adolescent		
Yes	No	
Schedule for Affective Disorders and Schizophrenia in School-age Children		
No	Yes	
Social Adjustment Scale–Self-report		
Yes	No	

Table 5.5 Applying Cohen et al. (2008) and Hunsley and Mash (2008b) criteria to instruments for assessing psychopathology in youth *(Cont'd)*

Broadband *(Cont'd)*

Symptom Checklist-90–Revised	
Yes	No
Therapy Attitude Inventory	
No	Yes

Note: For the Cohen et al. column, Yes indicates that an instrument was rated as well-established or approaching well-established, and No indicates that the instrument was not reviewed. For the Hunsley & Mash column, Yes indicates that an instrument was evaluated as evidence-based, and No means that the instrument was not reviewed.

the highest available level is insufficient or not applicable to the situation at hand.

In reviewing the literature to develop an evidence hierarchy, two aspects are critical. First, a systematic search of the peer-reviewed literature should be undertaken: Although this strategy was used by Bickman et al., neither the Society for Pediatric Psychology nor the Hunsley and Mash (2008a) initiatives used this strategy. Second, reliance on the best available evidence is encouraged (i.e., results from the highest level of the hierarchy). All three frameworks we reviewed encouraged this and attempted to operationalize this, albeit in different ways. This illustrates the fact that, although conceptually clear and straightforward, operationally defining steps in the evidence hierarchy is neither an obvious nor a simple task. Similarly, although it may be relatively easy to conduct a literature search for evidence about which treatments "work" for a disorder like agoraphobia, searching the literature on the assessment of agoraphobia is a much more complex task. For example, if a psychologist is searching for information on conducting assessments as part of the monitoring of treatment provision, the resulting literature will be substantially different than would be the case if the search was for the purpose of diagnosing agoraphobia. Therefore, although a systematic literature search strategy may be the optimal approach, the search will need to be sensitive to the specific purposes of the assessment task under consideration.

Building a Truly Evidence-based Psychological Assessment

As we have indicated in the proceeding sections, some progress has been made in developing the foundation for EBA. Having discussed the question

regarding appropriate criteria for EBIs, in this section we highlight some of the other issues that need to be addressed in order for psychological assessment to be truly evidence-based. These include the meaning of scores and change scores on psychological instruments, the role of incremental validity in optimizing assessment procedures, the need for evidence on clinical utility, the importance of moving beyond EBIs to consider how best to integrate data and make scientifically sound clinical decisions, and, finally, the relation between EBA and EBT.

The Meaningfulness of Instrument Metrics and Change Scores

Unlike information about weight or height, scores on psychological instruments do not, of themselves, convey much information about a person's functioning (Blanton & Jaccard, 2006). Knowing that someone obtained a score of 20 tells us nothing unless we know the range of possible scores, norms for the instrument and, in the case of clinical instruments, the cut-score value(s) that indicate whether a score is in the "clinical" or "normal" range. Because of the diverse range of clients for which instruments may be used, it is critical that nationally representative norms be available that are sensitive to possible gender and age influences (Achenbach, 2005). Although clinical cutoffs are reported for many clinical instruments, either in a test manual or in the research literature, the manner in which the cut-scores were derived may be problematic (Meehl & Rosen, 1955). Specifically, using a cut-score derived from samples in which clinical cases are overrepresented compared to usual base rates will usually result in frequent classification errors (e.g., determining that a person scored in the clinical range of functioning when, in fact, the person's difficulties are not that extreme). The best solution is to use signal detection theory and receiver operating characteristic curves to operationalize multiple cut-scores that can take into account base rate information (e.g., McFall & Treat, 1999). Although such analyses are increasingly being used to derive clinical cutoffs, many instruments do not yet have cut-scores derived in this manner.

Just as a score itself usually has no intrinsic meaning, a change in a person's scores over time is also meaningless without a standardized way of interpreting the magnitude of the change. This is a key concern for clinical psychologists, as monitoring changes in functioning via self-report and observational instruments provides us with information about the impact of our treatments (cf. Kazdin, 2006). To this end, it is necessary to determine whether the observed change in scores is (a) more than simply a matter of measurement error and (b) substantial enough to indicate that improvement has occurred. Such factors are considered in a set of statistics designed to evaluate clinically significant changes in scores (for a recent summary, see Lambert, Hansen, & Bauer, 2008). For any instrument for which basic psychometric information is available, it is possible to derive a value to determine the minimum changes in scores necessary to indicate that a client is no longer functioning in the clinical range (for an example applied to the Beck Depression Inventory, see Seggar, Lambert, & Hansen, 2002).

Incremental Validity and Evidence-based Assessment

Incremental validity addresses the question of whether data from an instrument (or other source of data) adds to the prediction of a criterion above what can be predicted by other sources of data (Hunsley & Meyer, 2003; Sechrest, 1963). Given the plethora of available clinical instruments, shockingly little information is available on the extent to which data from an instrument improves upon what can be obtained from simple sociodemographic characteristics or other psychological instruments. Evidence of incremental validity is important for a host of reasons, both conceptual (e.g., does an instrument measure a construct better than similar measures?) and practical (e.g., is it cost-efficient to obtain extensive assessment data from multiple informants?).

Clinical psychologists often gather data from multiple measures and multiple informants, yet there is little evidence in the empirical literature to aid in determining which measures to use, how to combine them, and what to do if conflicting results are obtained with some measures. Progress is being made in some areas. For example, Pelham, Fabiano, and Massetti (2005) reported that, in diagnosing attention-deficit/hyperactivity disorder in youth, structured diagnostic interviews do not possess incremental validity over rating scales and, therefore, are likely to have little value in clinical settings. More such research is necessary before clinical psychologists will be able to make scientifically informed decisions about which instruments to use in an assessment (and which may be redundant and cost *in*effective).

Clinical Utility and Evidence-based Assessment

Evidence about enhancements to decisions made by clinicians and/or service outcomes experienced by patients are central aspects of clinical utility, regardless of whether the focus of the evidence is on diagnostic systems (e.g., First et al., 2004), psychological instruments (e.g., McFall, 2005), or intervention strategies (e.g., American Psychological Association Presidential Task Force on Evidence-Based Practice, 2006). Attention to clinical utility has grown in recent years but, unfortunately, there is still little evidence that bears on the question of the extent to which EBIs or EBA have clinical utility. For example, there is some evidence that functional analyses can have added value over other clinical data in some treatment contexts (Haynes, Leisen, & Blaine, 1997) and that the Outcome-Questionnaire-45 (OQ-45), a self-report measure of distress, interpersonal relations, and social functioning, has considerable clinical utility.

The OQ-45 research provides an excellent example that could be used in designing clinical utility studies for other instruments. Specifically, Lambert, Whipple, Hawkings, Vermeersch, Nielsen, and Smart (2003) conducted a meta-analysis of three utility studies in which more than 2,500 adult clients completed the instrument after each therapy session. Clinicians in the control condition did not receive information about the client scores; clinicians in the experimental condition received feedback about the scores that was limited to an indication of whether clients, based on normative data, were making adequate treatment gains, making less-than-adequate treatment gains, or experiencing so few benefits from treatment that they were at risk for negative treatment outcomes. By the end of treatment, based on OQ-45 data, 21% of clients in the control condition had experienced a deterioration of functioning and 21% had improved in their functioning. In the experimental condition, only 13% of clients had deteriorated and 35% had improved. Such results provide a very compelling indication of the clinical utility of the instrument.

Integration of Data and Clinical Decision-making: From Evidence-based Instrument to Evidence-based Assessment

As we indicated early in this chapter, EBA must involve the recognition that psychological assessment is a complex decision-making task. Decisions must be made about which constructs to assess and which instruments should be used to assess these constructs. The data obtained from instruments must be then integrated and interpreted, and the impact of potential errors and biases in this process must be considered. However, as we have illustrated, reviews of EBAs to date to appear to be primarily lists of EBIs.

It is possible that this may simply reflect the early stage of development of EBA and that, over time, increased attention will be paid to the pressing question of how data from EBIs can contribute to a truly evidence-based assessment. Although we know a great deal about how clinical decision-making can go wrong (Garb, 1998), we have only a limited sense of how results of nomothetic research can be used to guide the integration and interpretation of data for a specific patient (see, for example, Haynes, 2008; McGrath, 2008; and Persons, 2006). Accordingly, for the foreseeable future, the most scientifically sound option available may be to ensure that assessments are conducted with EBIs in a manner that is informed by the research evidence regarding key constructs to assess for specific patient conditions and assessment purposes.

The Relation Between Evidence-based Assessment and Evidence-based Treatment

All EBPs rely on gathering data from different sources, integrating data, and making service decisions based on these data. As we have discussed, EBA and EBT are inextricably related, and most likely represent different parts of the same overall process. Whether a treatment is designated as evidence based in the first place depends on the quality of data used to evaluate its outcome. If these data are derived using flawed assessment instruments or processes, then designating a treatment as evidence-based has little meaning. In addition, since EBTs are designed for specific disorders and problems, their effective use requires that these disorders and problems be assessed using instruments and processes that are evidence-based for the purpose of identifying and diagnosing these problems. A failure at the level of assessment may very well lead to the inappropriate or ineffective use of EBT if a treatment is paired with a target problem for which it has not been evaluated (Weisz & Gray, 2008).

Despite recognition of the critical synergy between EBA and EBT, EBT continues to generate considerable attention, whereas EBA receives little to none. For example, a comprehensive 2008 Special Issue of the *Journal of Clinical Child and Adolescent Psychology* (Silverman & Hinshaw, 2008) on evidence-based psychosocial treatments for children and adolescents is virtually silent on the role of assessment in EBT. This is so despite the fact that considerable attention was given to EBA in an earlier Special Section of the same journal (Mash & Hunsley, 2005).

The operational rule here, and in other reviews of EBT, seems to be that the quality of outcome data underlying EBT recommendations is assumed to be high, despite evidence to the contrary. Moreover, we know very little about how assessments and the data they generate are being used in the context of EBT. The tacit acceptance of the status quo and the continuing use of many assessment instruments that are problematic and lacking in clinical utility is clearly a concern, but one that appears to be unrecognized. As pointed out by Kazdin (1988) such "unfelt problems are dangerous because they are likely to be neglected and ignored" (p. 9). Thus, despite progress on the psychotherapy front, research into evidence-based psychological assessment is characterized by a lack of clarity regarding the kinds of evidence needed to evaluate the utility of assessment methods and processes, and limited progress in the field. Hopefully, the beginning efforts to specify criteria for EBA that we have described in this chapter will begin to redress this problem.

Conclusions

As outlined in this chapter, some important initial steps have been taken in establishing specific criteria for EBIs and in addressing the scope of issues that must be addressed if EBA is to develop. Some useful guidelines and lists of instruments are now available for clinical psychologists to apply in their assessment activities. That being said, with only limited consensus on how EBA should be operationalized and an assessment literature that is largely focused on providing evidence of only basic psychometric properties (i.e., not incremental validity, evidence of utility, or testing of decision-making models), there is much more work to be accomplished to develop EBA. In many ways, the current situation is reminiscent of Paul's (1967, p. 111) famous question about psychotherapy from over 40 years ago: "*What* treatment, by *whom*, is most effective for *this* individual, with *that* specific problem, and under *what* specific set of circumstances?" With respect to EBA, we must ask what assessment data, from which informant, is most valid and clinically useful for this individual, with these specific problems, and under what specific set of life circumstances. Given the obvious connection between clinical assessment and clinical treatment, answering the assessment question is a necessary step in fully answering the treatment question.

Future Directions

From our perspective, the main issues outlined in this chapter that need to be addressed in future research efforts are (a) clarifying the meaning of scores and change scores on psychological instruments, (b) increasing the role of incremental validity in optimizing assessment procedures, (c) developing the evidence base for the clinical utility of psychological instruments, and (d) developing a consensus about what constitutes EBA and, therefore, which set of criteria, guidelines, parameters, or list of assessment instruments a professional clinician should use as a reference for assessment activities.

There are, however, a number of other important issues that must be addressed in order to develop a truly evidence-based approach to psychological assessment. First, although there is much information on EBIs, we know very little about the assessment process in the context of clinical decision making. Thus, even when instruments are reliable and valid, the ways in which they are used in clinical practice may not be. There is clearly a need to move beyond EBIs, to consider how best to integrate data and make scientifically sound clinical decisions. Second, the content and procedures of usual psychological assessment practices are not well known. Usual assessment practices have typically been assessed via surveys that provide information about the percentage of clinicians using particular assessment instruments. However, such surveys tell us little about how assessment instruments are being used and integrated into clinical decision making. Despite longstanding recognition of a lack of knowledge in this area, our understanding remains quite limited.

Third, as we have discussed, the relation between EBA and EBT involves much more than simply matching a valid diagnosis and selecting a designated EBT for this problem. Evidence should be used to guide both the assessment and treatment process from identifying and diagnosing a target problem, monitoring treatment progress and outcomes in relation to an EBT, and making ongoing adjustments in treatment procedures as needed. Weisz, Chu, and Polo (2004) have noted how the dialectic of assess→treat→reassess→adjust treatment→reassess is not well articulated in relation to current clinical practice. Operationalizing how this process is to proceed presents a major challenge for evidence-based health practices. Finally, the dissemination of EBTs also requires the dissemination of EBAs. This poses a problem, as we don't yet have an agreed-upon list of EBAs. Although the current list of instruments that appear in the sources cited in this chapter would be a good starting point, many recommended instruments (e.g., structured diagnostic interviews) are lengthy and complex to administer,

thus making them difficult to use in clinical practice. On the other hand, more practice-feasible instruments may not provide the information needed to meet service system requirements (e.g., DSM diagnosis).

References

Achenbach, T. M. (2005). Advancing assessment of children and adolescents: Commentary on evidence-based assessment of child and adolescent disorders. *Journal of Clinical Child and Adolescent Psychology, 34,* 541–547.

Ackerman, M. J., & Ackerman, M. C. (1997). Custody evaluation practices: A survey of experienced professionals (revisited). *Professional Psychology: Research and Practice, 29,* 137–145.

American Academy of Child and Adolescent Psychiatry. (1997). Practice parameters for custody evaluation. *Journal of the American Academy of Child and Adolescent Psychiatry, 36*(Supplement), 57S–68S.

American Educational Research Association, American Psychological Association, National Council on Measurement in Education. (1999). *Standards for educational and psychological testing.* Washington, DC: American Educational Research Association.

American Psychiatric Association. (2000). *Handbook of psychiatric measures.* Washington, DC: American Psychiatric Publishing.

American Psychiatric Association. (2006). *Practice guideline for the psychiatric evaluation of adults* (2nd ed.). Retrieved on June 24, 2008 from http://www.psychiatryonline.com/pracGuide/pracGuideTopic_1.aspx

American Psychological Association. (1994). Guidelines for child custody evaluations in divorce proceedings. *American Psychologist, 49,* 677–680.

American Psychological Association Presidential Task Force on Evidence-Based Practice. (2006). Evidence-based practice in psychology. *American Psychologist, 61,* 271–285.

Association of Family and Conciliation Courts. (2006). *Model standards of practice for child custody evaluation.* Retrieved on June 24, 2008 from http://www.afccnet.org/pdfs/

Barkham, M., Margison, F., Leach, C., Lucock, M., Mellor-Clark, J., et al. (2001). Service profiling and outcomes benchmarking using the CORE-OM: Toward practice-based evidence in the psychological therapies. *Journal of Consulting and Clinical Psychology, 69,* 184–196.

Barlow, D. H. (2005). What's new about evidence based assessment? *Psychological Assessment, 17,* 308–311.

Bickman, L., Nurcombe, B., Townsend, C., Belle, M., Schut, J., & Karver, M. (1999). *Consumer measurement systems in child and adolescent mental health.* Canberra, ACT: Department of Health and Family Services.

Bickman, L., Rosof-Williams, J., Salzerm, M. S., Summerfelt, W. T., Noser, K., et al. (2000). What information do clinicians value for monitoring adolescent client progress and outcomes? *Professional Psychology: Research and Practice, 31,* 70–74.

Benjamin, L. T. Jr. (2005). A history of clinical psychology as a profession in America (and a glimpse at its future). *Annual Review of Clinical Psychology, 1,* 1–30.

Blanton, H., & Jaccard, J. (2006). Arbitrary metrics in psychology. *American Psychologist, 61,* 27–41.

Cohen, L. L., La Greca, A. M., Blount, R. L., Kazak, A. E., Holmbeck, G. N., & Lemanek, K. L. (2008). Introduction to the special issue: Evidence-based assessment in pediatric psychology. *Journal of Pediatric Psychology, 33,* 911–915.

Cyr, J. J., McKenna-Foley, J. M., & Peacock, E. (1985). Factor structure of the SCL-90-R: Is there one? *Journal of Personality Assessment, 49,* 571–578.

Derogatis, L. R. (1992). *SCL-90-R: Administration, scoring and procedures manual—II.* Baltimore, MD: Clinical Psychometric Research.

Dougherty, L. R., Klein, D. N., Olino, T. M., & Laptook, R. S. (2008). Depression in children and adolescents. In J. Hunsley & E. J. Mash (Eds.), *A guide to assessments that work* (pp. 69–95). New York: Oxford University Press.

Exner, J. E. (1993). *The Rorschach: A comprehensive system. Vol. I. Basic foundations* (3rd ed.). New York: John Wiley & Sons.

Fernandez-Ballesteros, R., De Bruyn, E. E. J., Godoy, A., Hornke, L. F., Ter Laak, J., Vizcarro, C., et al. (2001). Guidelines for the Assessment Process (GAP): A proposal for discussion. *European Journal of Psychological Assessment, 17,* 187–200.

First, M. B., Pincus, H. A., Levine, J. B., Williams, J. B. W., Ustun, B., & Peele, R. (2004). Clinical utility as a criterion for revising psychiatric diagnoses. *American Journal of Psychiatry, 161,* 946–954.

Flanagan, D. P., & Kaufman, A. S. (2004). *Essentials of WISC-IV assessment.* New York: John Wiley & Sons.

Fletcher, J. M., Francis, D. J., Morris, R. D., & Lyon, G. R. (2005). Evidence-based assessment of learning disabilities in children and adolescents. *Journal of Clinical Child and Adolescent Psychology, 34,* 506–522.

Frick, P. J., & McMahon, R. J. (2008). Child and adolescent conduct problems. In J. Hunsley & E. J. Mash (Eds.), *A guide to assessments that work* (pp. 41–66). New York: Oxford University Press.

Garb, H. N. (1998). *Studying the clinician: Judgment research and psychological assessment.* Washington, DC: American Psychological Association.

Green, M. F., Nuechterlein, K. H., Kern, R. S., Baade, L. E., Fenton, W. S., Gold, J. M., et al. (2008). Functional co-primary measures for clinical trials in schizophrenia: Results from the MATRICS psychometric and standardization study. *American Journal of Psychiatry, 165,* 221–228.

Green, K., Worden, B., Menges, D., & McCrady, B. (2008). Alcohol use disorders. In J. Hunsley & E. J. Mash (Eds.), *A guide to assessments that work* (pp. 339–369). New York: Oxford University Press.

Guarnaccia, V., Dill, C. A., Sabatino, S., & Southwick, S. (2001). Scoring accuracy using the Comprehensive System for the Rorschach. *Journal of Personality Assessment, 77,* 464–474.

Hamel, M., Shaffer, T. W., & Erdberg, P. (2000). A study of nonpatient preadolescent Rorschach protocols. *Journal of Personality Assessment, 75,* 280–294.

Hatfield, D. R., & Ogles, B. M. (2004). The use of outcome measures by psychologists in clinical practice. *Professional Psychology: Research and Practice, 35,* 485–491.

Hayes, S. C., Nelson, R. O., & Jarrett, R. B. (1987). The treatment utility of assessment: A functional approach to evaluating assessment quality. *American Psychologist, 42,* 963–974.

Haynes, S. N. (2008). Empirical foundations of case formulation: Causal diagrams for clinical case formulation. Paper presented at the 29th International Congress of Psychology, Berlin.

Haynes, S. N., Leisen, M. B., & Blaine, D. D. (1997). Design of individualized behavioral treatment programs using functional

analytic clinical case methods. *Psychological Assessment, 9,* 334–348.

Holi, M. M., Sammallahti, P. R., & Aalberg, V. A. (1998). A Finnish validation study of the SCL-90. *Acta Psychiatrica Scandinavica, 97,* 42–46.

Holmbeck, G. N., Thill, A. W., Bachanas, P., Garber, J., Miller, K. B., Abad, M., et al. (2008). Evidence-based assessment in pediatric psychology: Measures of psychosocial adjustment and psychopathology. *Journal of Pediatric Psychology, 33,* 958–980.

Horvath, L. S., Logan, T. K., & Walker, R. (2002). Child custody cases: A content analysis of evaluations in practice. *Professional Psychology: Research and Practice, 33,* 557–563.

Hughes, T. L., Gacono, C. B., & Owen, P. F. (2007). Current status of Rorschach assessment: Implications for the school psychologist. *Psychology in the Schools, 44,* 281–291.

Hunsley, J. (2002). Psychological testing and psychological assessment: A closer examination. *American Psychologist, 57,* 139–140.

Hunsley, J., & Bailey, J. M. (1999). The clinical utility of the Rorschach: Unfulfilled promises and an uncertain future. *Psychological Assessment, 11,* 266–277.

Hunsley, J., & Bailey, J.M. (2001). Whither the Rorschach? An analysis of the evidence. *Psychological Assessment, 13,* 472–485.

Hunsley, J., & Lee, C. M. (2007). Research-informed benchmarks for psychological treatments: Efficacy studies, effectiveness studies, and beyond. *Professional Psychology: Research and Practice, 38,* 21–33.

Hunsley, J., & Mash, E. J. (2005). Introduction to the special section on developing guidelines for the evidence-based assessment (EBA) of adult disorders. *Psychological Assessment, 17,* 251–255.

Hunsley, J., & Mash, E. J. (2007). Evidence-based assessment. *Annual Review of Clinical Psychology, 3,* 29–51.

Hunsley, J., & Mash, E. J. (Eds.). (2008a). *A guide to assessments that work.* New York: Oxford University Press.

Hunsley, J., & Mash, E. J. (2008b). Developing criteria for evidence-based assessment: An introduction to assessments that work. In J. Hunsley & E. J. Mash (Eds.), *A guide to assessments that work* (pp. 3–14). New York: Oxford University Press.

Hunsley, J., & Meyer, G. J. (2003). The incremental validity of psychological testing and assessment: Conceptual, methodological, and statistical issues. *Psychological Assessment, 15,* 446–455.

Institute of Medicine. (2001). *Crossing the quality chasm: A new health system for the 21st century.* Washington, DC: National Academy Press.

Iverson, G. L., Lange, R. T., & Viljoen, H. (2006). Comparing the Canadian and American WAIS-III normative systems in inpatient neuropsychiatry and forensic psychiatry. *Canadian Journal of Behavioural Science, 38,* 348–353.

Johnson, C. P., Myers, S. M., & the Council on Children with Disabilities. (2007). Identification and evaluation of children with autism spectrum disorders. *Pediatrics, 120,* 1183–1215.

Johnson, S. L., Miller, C., & Eisner, L. (2008). Bipolar disorder. In J. Hunsley & E. J. Mash (Eds.), *A guide to assessments that work* (pp. 121–137). New York: Oxford University Press.

Johnston, C., & Mah, J. W. T. (2008). Child attention-deficit/hyperactivity disorder. In J. Hunsley & E. J. Mash (Eds.), *A guide to assessments that work* (pp. 17–40). New York: Oxford University Press.

Kamieniecki, G. W., & Lynd-Stevenson, R. M. (2002). Is it appropriate to use United States norms to assess the "intelligence" of Australian children? *Australian Journal of Psychology, 54,* 67–78.

Kaufman, A. S., & Lichtenberger, E. O. (1999). *Essentials of WAIS-III assessment.* New York: John Wiley & Sons.

Kazdin, A. E. (1988). *Child psychotherapy: Developing and identifying effective treatments.* New York: Pergamon.

Kazdin, A. E. (2006). Arbitrary metrics: Implications for identifying evidence-based treatments. *American Psychologist, 61,* 42–49.

Kazdin, A. E. (2008). Evidence-based treatment and practice: New opportunities to bridge clinical research and practice, enhance the knowledge base, and improve patient care. *American Psychologist, 63,* 146–159.

Kern, R. S., Nuechterlein, K. H., Green, M. F., Baade, L. E., Fenton, W. S., Gold, J. M., et al. (2008). The MATRICS consensus cognitive battery, Part 2: Co-norming and standardization. *American Journal of Psychiatry, 165,* 214–220.

Kendell, R., & Jablensky, A. (2003). Distinguishing between the validity and utility of psychiatric diagnoses. *American Journal of Psychiatry, 160,* 4–12.

Krishnamurthy, R., VandeCreek, L., Kaslow, N. J., Tazeau, Y. N., Miville, M. L., Kerns, R., et al. (2004). Achieving competency in psychological assessment: Directions for education and training. *Journal of Clinical Psychology, 60,* 725–739.

Lally, S. J. (2001). Should human figure drawings be admitted into the court? *Journal of Personality Assessment, 76,* 135–149.

Lally, S. J. (2003). What tests are acceptable for use in forensic evaluations? A survey of experts. *Professional Psychology: Research and Practice, 34,* 491–498.

Lambert, M. J., Hansen, N. B., & Bauer, S. (2008). Assessing the clinical significance of outcome results. In A. M. Nezu & C. M. Nezu (Eds.), *Evidence-based outcome research: A practical guide to conducting randomized controlled trials for psychosocial interventions* (pp. 359–378). New York: Oxford University Press.

Lambert, M. J., Whipple, J. L., Hawkings, E. J., Vermeersch, D., Nielsen, S. L., Smart, D. W. (2003). Is it time to track patient outcome on a routine basis? A meta-analysis. *Clinical Psychology: Science and Practice, 10,* 288–301.

Lilienfeld, S. O., Wood, J. M., & Garb, H. N. (2000). The scientific status of projective techniques. *Psychological Science in the Public Interest, 1,* 27–66.

Lima, E. N., Stanley, S., Kaboski, B., Reitzel, L. R., Richey, J. A., et al. (2005). The incremental validity of the MMPI-2: When does therapist access not enhance treatment outcome? *Psychological Assessment, 17,* 462–468.

Mash, E. J., & Hunsley, J. (2005). Evidence-based assessment of child and adolescent disorders: Issues and challenges. *Journal of Clinical Child and Adolescent Psychology, 34,* 362–379.

Mash, E. J., & Hunsley, J. (2007). Assessment of child and family disturbance: A developmental-systems approach. In E. J. Mash & R. A. Barkley (Eds.), *Assessment of childhood disorders* (4th ed., pp. 3–50). New York: Guilford.

Masling, J. M. (1992). The influence of situation and interpersonal variables in projective testing. *Journal of Personality Assessment, 59,* 616–640.

McFall, R. M. (2005). Theory and utility—key themes in evidence-based assessment comment on the special section. *Psychological Assessment, 17,* 312–323.

McFall, R. M., & Treat, T. A. (1999). Quantifying the information value of clinical assessments with signal detection theory. *Annual Review of Psychology, 50,* 215–241.

McGrath, R. E. (2001). Toward more clinically relevant assessment research. *Journal of Personality Assessment, 77,* 307–332.

McGrath, R. E. (2008). Predictor combination in binary decision-making situations. *Psychological Assessment, 20,* 195–205.

Meehl, P. E., & Rosen, A. (1955). Antecedent probability and the efficiency of psychometric signs, patterns, or cutting scores. *Psychological Bulletin, 52,* 194–216.

Meyer, G.J., & Archer, R. P. (2001). The hard science of Rorschach research: What do we know and where do we go? *Psychological Assessment, 13,* 486–502.

Meyer, G. J., Erdberg, P., & Shaffer, T. W. (2007). Toward international normative reference data for the Comprehensive System. *Journal of Personality Assessment, 89,* S201–S216.

Minami, T., Wampold, B. E., Serlin, R. C., Hamilton, E. G., Brown, G. S., et al. (2008). Benchmarking the effectiveness of psychotherapy treatment for adult depression in a managed care environment: A preliminary study. *Journal of Consulting and Clinical Psychology, 76,* 116–124.

Mueser, K. T., & Glynn, S. M. (2008). Schizophrenia. In J. Hunsley & E. J. Mash (Eds.), *A guide to assessments that work* (pp. 391–412). New York: Oxford University Press.

Murray, H. A. (1943). *Thematic Apperception Test manual.* Cambridge, MA: Harvard University Press.

Nathan, P. E., & Gorman, J. M. (Eds.). (2007). *A guide to treatments that work* (3rd ed.). New York: Oxford University Press.

Neisworth, J. T., & Bagnato, S. J. (2000). Recommended practices in assessment. In S. Sandall, M. E. McLean, & B. J. Smith (Eds.), *DEC recommended practices in early intervention/early child special education* (pp. 17–27). Longmont, CO: Sopris West.

Nelson-Gray, R. O. (2003). Treatment utility of psychological assessment. *Psychological Assessment, 15,* 521–531.

Norcross, J. C., Koocher, G. P., & Garofalo, A. (2006). Discredited psychological treatments and tests: A Delphi poll. *Professional Psychology: Research and Practice, 37,* 515–522.

Nuechterlein, K. H., Green, M. F., Kern, R. S., Baade, L. E., Barch, D. M., Cohen, J. D., et al. (2008). The MATRICS consensus cognitive battery, Part 1: Test selection, reliability, and validity. *American Journal of Psychiatry, 165,* 203–213.

Olsen, L. R., Mortensen, E. L., & Bech, P. (2004). The SCL-90 and SCL-90R versions validated by item response models in a Danish community sample. *Acta Psychiatrica Scandinavica, 110,* 225–229.

Paul, G. L. (1967). Strategy of outcome research in psychotherapy. *Journal of Consulting Psychology, 31,* 109–118.

Pelham, W. E., Fabiano, G. A., & Massetti, G. M. (2005). Evidence-based assessment of attention deficit hyperactivity disorder in children and adolescents. *Journal of Clinical Child and Adolescent Psychology, 34,* 449–476.

Persons, J. B. (2006). Case formulation-driven psychotherapy. *Clinical Psychology: Science and Practice, 13,* 167–170.

Piotrowski, C. (1999). Assessment practices in the era of managed care: Current status and future directions. *Journal of Clinical Psychology, 55,* 787–796.

Rees, L. M., Tombaugh, T. N., Gansler, D. A., & Moczynski, N. P. (1998). Five validation experiments of the Test of Memory Malingering (TOMM). *Psychological Assessment, 10,* 10–20.

Rice, M. E., & Harris, G. T. (1995). Violent recidivism: Assessing predictive validity. *Journal of Consulting and Clinical Psychology, 63,* 737–748.

Rossini, E. E., & Moretti, R. J. (1997). Thematic Apperception Test (TAT) interpretation: Practice recommendations from a survey of clinical psychology doctoral programs accredited by the American Psychological Association. *Professional Psychology: Research and Practice, 28,* 393–398.

Sackett, D. L., Rosenberg, W. M. C., Gray, J. A. M., Haynes, R. B., & Richardson, W. S. (1996). Evidence based medicine: What it is and what it isn't. *British Medical Journal, 312,* 71–72.

Sechrest, L. (1963). Incremental validity: A recommendation. *Educational and Psychological Measurement, 23,* 153–158.

Seggar, L. B., Lambert, M. J., & Hansen, N. B. (2002). Assessing clinical significance: Application to the Beck Depression Inventory. *Behavior Therapy, 33,* 253–269.

Shaffer, T. W., Erdberg, P., & Meyer, G. J. (2007). Introduction to the *JPA* special supplement on the international reference samples for the Rorschach Comprehensive System. *Journal of Personality Assessment, 89,* S2–S6.

Silverman, W. K., & Hinshaw, S. P. (Eds.). (2008). Special issue: Evidence-based psychosocial treatments for children and adolescents: A ten-year update. *Journal of Clinical Child and Adolescent Psychology, 37* (Whole No. 1), 1–301.

Silverman, W. K., & Ollendick, T. H. (2008). Child and adolescent anxiety disorders. In J. Hunsley & E. J. Mash (Eds.), *A guide to assessments that work* (pp. 181–206). New York: Oxford University Press.

Smith, G. T. (2000). On the sins of short form development. *Psychological Assessment, 12,* 102–111.

Spangler, W.D. (1992). Validity of questionnaire and TAT measures of need for achievement: Two meta-analyses. *Psychological Bulletin, 112,* 140–154.

Streiner, D. L, & Norman, G. R. (2003). *Health measurement scales: A practical guide to their development and use* (3rd ed.). New York: Oxford University Press.

Watkins, M. W. (2003). IQ subtest analysis: Clinical acumen or clinical illusion? *Scientific Review of Mental Health Practice, 2,* 118–141.

Weersing, V. R. (2005). Benchmarking the effectiveness of psychotherapy: Program evaluation as a component of evidence-based practice. *Journal of the American Academy of Child and Adolescent Psychiatry, 44,* 1058–1062.

Weisz, J. R., Chu, B. C., Polo, A. J. (2004). Treatment dissemination and evidence-based practice: Strengthening intervention through clinician-researcher collaboration, *Clinical Psychology: Science and Practice, 11,* 300–307.

Weisz, J. R., & Gray, J. S. (2008). Evidence-based psychotherapy for children and adolescents: Data from the present and a model for the future. *Child and Adolescent Mental Health, 13,* 54–65.

Wood, J. M., Garb, H. N., Lilienfeld, S. O., & Nezworski, M. T. (2002). Clinical assessment. *Annual Review of Psychology, 53,* 519–543.

Wood, J. M., Nezworski, M. T., Garb, H. N., & Lilienfeld, S. O. (2001). The misperception of psychopathology: Problems with the norms of the Comprehensive System for the Rorschach. *Clinical Psychology: Science and Practice, 8,* 350–373.

Wood, J. M., Nezworski, M. T., Lilienfeld, S. O., & Garb, H. N. (2003). *What's wrong with the Rorschach?* San Francisco: Jossey-Bass.

Yates, B. T., & Taub, J. (2003). Assessing the costs, benefits, cost-effectiveness, and cost-benefit of psychological assessment: We should, we can, and here's how. *Psychological Assessment, 15,* 478–495.

Youngstrom, E. (2008). Evidence-based assessment in not evidence-based medicine—Commentary on evidence-based assessment of cognitive functioning in pediatric psychology. *Journal of Pediatric Psychology, 33,* 1015–1020.

Schools of Psychotherapy and the Beginnings of a Scientific Approach

James F. Boswell, Brian A. Sharpless, Leslie S. Greenberg, Laurie Heatherington, Jonathan D. Huppert, Jacques P. Barber, Marvin R. Goldfried, *and* Louis G. Castonguay

Abstract

The theoretical, clinical, and empirical foundations of psychotherapy come from five primary movements that still exist today, continue to evolve, and remain scientifically productive: psychodynamic, cognitive-behavioral, humanistic, systemic, and integrative. The goal of this chapter is to examine the philosophical, clinical, and scientific underpinnings of each of these major traditions in detail. Experts in these five approaches will describe: (a) the model of psychopathology (especially focusing upon etiological and maintenance factors emphasized in assessment and case formulation); (b) the focus and specific techniques used in treatment planning and implementation; (c) the hypothesized therapeutic mechanisms of change; and (d) the outcome literature/empirical support for each modality. We conclude with a look toward the future of the science of psychotherapy and the scientist-practitioner model of psychotherapy.

Keywords: Cognitive-behavior therapy, humanistic therapy, integrative therapy, psychodynamic therapy, psychotherapy, systemic therapy

If defined as a "talking cure," psychotherapy has a very long history. The moral therapy that Pinel developed in the 18th century included not only the unchaining of patients (as it is often portrayed in undergraduate abnormal psychology textbooks), but also involved establishing safe and comforting relationships at both a personal and institutional level. As part of their therapeutic responsibilities, staff members of the asylums were asked to walk with, listen to, and talk with patients, with the ultimate goal of helping them find solace from the social afflictions that were believed to be partly responsible for their mental conditions. A similar philosophy toward mental disorders can be traced back to ancient Greece, where temples were created to help individuals restore a balance in what Hippocrates designated the major bodily "humors." In addition to the prescription of rest and music, the restorative treatments might well have involved meaningful (and hopefully soothing) verbal exchanges, if only as

a reflection of Hippocrates' belief that an intimate relationship between patient and healer was important to health. Arguably, however, the foundation of modern talking cures resides in Breuer and Freud's (1893) cathartic method, where successful treatment was assumed to require three conditions: (1) the patient remembering the traumatic event at the origin of his or her symptoms; (2) the patient re-experiencing the emotions felt during this traumatic event; and (3) the patient expressing both the event and emotional experiences to the therapist (Nisole, 1977). These three conditions, interestingly, are very consistent with today's leading treatment (exposure therapy) for post-traumatic stress disorder.

Although the cathartic method is no longer used (at least as originally prescribed by Freud and Breuer), it directly led to Freud's development of psychoanalysis proper. Although still practiced today, Freud's classical psychoanalysis did not remain static, but also spurred the development of several other important treatment approaches that are linked by a common goal of uncovering and understanding the (often unconscious) conflicts and early developmental experiences associated with the client's symptoms.

However, as early as the 1920s, opposition to psychoanalytic thinking and methods also served to galvanize the beginning of a second major tradition or school of therapy. Born in laboratories and intimately linked with animal research (e.g., Pavlov's and Seligman's dogs, Watson's rats, Skinner's pigeons, and Wolpe's cats), behavioral and later cognitive-behavioral approaches represented an effort to understand and treat abnormal behavior that used techniques based on the implementation of methods derived from the physical sciences.

With the 1950s came the genesis of another movement, often called the "third force" in psychology. It was in large part a reaction to several of the deterministic assumptions shared by psychodynamic and behavioral orientations. Rejecting the notion that human behaviors could be fully understood as the result of past learning or developmental conflicts, scholars and clinicians associated with humanistic, existential, and experiential traditions constructed models and therapeutic interventions focused on notions of emotional awareness, the creation of meaning, a person's capacity for choice, and human tendencies toward healthy growth and the actualization of potential.

A fourth movement was born in the late 1960s and early 1970s. This group of systemic and family-centered approaches emphasized the many complex and subtle interpersonal processes that shape and control human behaviors at least as much as (if not more than) the intrapersonal forces (e.g., intrapsychic conflict, classical and operant conditioning, actualization of potentialities) at the core of the previous three traditions.

As discussed here, these four movements still exist today, continue to evolve, and remain both theoretically and empirically productive. As it seems clear that many, if not most, of currently available forms of therapy can be linked in some way to these four traditions, the goal of this chapter is to examine them in detail. Experts in these four approaches will describe: the model of psychopathology (especially focusing upon etiological and maintenance factors emphasized in assessment and case formulation); the focus and specific techniques used in treatment planning and implementation; the hypothesized therapeutic mechanisms of change;

and the outcome literature and empirical support for each modality.[1]

Although we believe that each of these major approaches to psychotherapy is here to stay, it is also clear that the majority of practicing psychotherapists (at least in the United States) define themselves as eclectic or integrative (Norcross, 2005). As an attempt to improve psychotherapy based on points of convergences and complementarities between different schools, the integration movement has been described as a Zeitgest (Lecomte, 1987) in the literature. In our effort to provide a complete (as much as possible) picture of the contemporary landscape of psychotherapy, this chapter will offer a brief history of the integration movement, as well as a description of its current trends and empirical contributions.

As a way to further establish the scientific foundation of psychotherapy, the chapter will end with a plea for more research on the process and outcome of current approaches (including the integrative movement), as well as on principles of change that cut across most of them. It will also be argued that the future growth of the Scientist-Practitioner model underlying modern psychotherapy will likely benefit from research conducted with active collaborations between researchers and clinicians.

Psychodynamic Approach

"Psychodynamic therapy" is a broad term used to encompass the many approaches for fostering understanding and alleviating human suffering that were directly influenced by Sigmund Freud, the intellectual father of psychodynamic therapy. Like all children, Freud's progeny have made choices that, although individual and autonomous, are nonetheless reflective of his influence. Some have decided to adhere closely to Freud's original formulations, others intensively focused upon one or more aspects, and several reacted against core principles while retaining others. This rich heterogeneity eventuated in a multitude of approaches with which therapists can flexibly

---

[1] The section on the psychodynamic approach was written by Brian A. Sharpless and Jacques P. Barber. The section on the cognitive-behavioral approach was written by Jonathan D. Huppert. The section on the humanistic approach was written by Leslie S. Greenberg. The section on the systemic approach was written by Laurie Heatherington. The section on psychotherapy integration was written by James Boswell, Louis Castonguay, and Marvin Goldfried

treat the vicissitudes of human psychopathology, but also had the unintended consequence of making it particularly difficult to summarize across modalities without gross oversimplification or error. While acknowledging this risk, we will attempt to broadly describe the current state of the field. Prior to discussing specific content, it will be helpful to cast this modality in sharper relief by briefly describing what some have termed the psychodynamic "sensibility" (e.g., McWilliams, 2004).

This sensibility has many components. Psychodynamic therapists could be described as operating under a "hermeneutic of suspicion" (Ricoeur, 1970). Specifically, the superficial or manifest contents of speech, actions, and symptoms are often not taken at face value, but are instead openly questioned in the hope of revealing other meanings/values that may have been lost, disavowed, or never fully considered. Such meanings (although somewhat hidden) are nevertheless thought to possess relevance for, and impact on, the patient's present life, level of distress, and understandings of self and other. A corollary of this is a belief in, and overriding respect for, the complexity of human thought, action, emotion, and behavior in all of its many varieties and shades. This can be seen in Wäelder's (1936) concepts of "over-determination" (i.e., the belief that every mental event has many causes) and "multiple function" (i.e., that every action/symptom intended to solve one psychological conflict or problem is simultaneously an attempt to solve other problems). Further, understanding oneself and increasing freedom from the many determinisms present in life requires a high level of honesty and self-exploration (for both patient and therapist). What is *not* said can be as important as what is, and therapists strive to attend to the multiple levels of verbal and nonverbal communication; for, as Freud wrote in 1905, "betrayal oozes out of… every pore." Finally, the dynamic sensibility could also be characterized by a profound recognition of the human psyche's fragility. Namely, no one is immune from falling ill, psychopathology exists on a continuum (and in normal life), and we are all more vulnerable than we think. This can clearly be seen in dynamic therapy's proposed etiologies.

Models of Function and Dysfunction

Although psychodynamic theories of pathology can diverge markedly, they are unanimous in viewing both psychopathology and health in developmental terms. This emphasis on the formative role of early experiences in current functioning is evident in two of the main psychodynamic subtypes. For instance,

traditional drive and ego psychologists typically conceptualize patients in terms of psychosexual development and conflict. Early experiences influence and shape characteristic conflicts between sexual and aggressive wishes/impulses, external reality, and internalized societal prohibitions. As a result, certain *compromises* between these conflicts arise, some of which are maladaptive (e.g., depressive symptoms), as a means of attempting to cope with them. In contrast, healthier individuals who have successfully passed developmental challenges, or who have undergone psychotherapy, presumably possess more effective compromises (i.e., they are regulated by more developmentally mature defenses, such as the sublimation of aggressive urges) that elicit minimal anxiety. Thus, these individuals may be more flexible and better able to satisfy their needs using multiple adaptive behaviors.

Another important school of dynamic thought has been termed the *object relational approach*. Object relation theorists, influenced by Klein, Winnicott, and Fairbairn, believe that *relationships* (especially early ones) constitute the building blocks of both our character and our adult relational patterns. This shift away from emphasizing the primacy of sexual and aggressive drives and toward relationships (and relatedness itself) represented a significant theoretical modification from both classical psychoanalysis and ego psychology. *Objects* (an unfortunate choice of words meaning "that to which a subject relates"—usually other people) are internalized (i.e., psychically "taken in") over the course of human development. If a person does not have "good enough" caregivers who adequately meet his or her physical and emotional needs, and therefore does not have opportunities to internalize *adaptive* objects, a future of interpersonal conflicts and an inability to maintain psychic homeostasis is often, but not always, the result (e.g., the borderline conditions). Further, inordinate levels of either dependence or independence in relationships (instead of healthy adult interdependent mutuality and respect) can also be a sequela.

Psychopathology viewed in object relational terms is a necessary adaptation to deficient environmental, innate, and interpersonal conditions. In contrast, the achievement of both a stable identity and object constancy (i.e., the capacity to tolerate loving and hostile feelings for the same person, view people as unique, and not use others instrumentally) is indicative of healthy object relations. The environment, one's biology, and one's parents need not be perfect, of course, but must allow for the healthy development of these more nuanced views of self and other. Further, the work of therapy (and the therapeutic relationship itself) can move individuals toward healthier functioning. In ending this section, it is important to note that, in spite of all dynamic theories' emphasis on early development, they all seriously consider genetic and temperamental contributions to the development of psychopathology.

In line with the diversity and complexity of factors involved in dynamic models of health and psychopathology, the assessment process is a multi-layered one. Although some therapists decry the use of the predominant nosological systems (i.e., DSM-IV-TR and ICD-10), many find it very important to possess an accurate and complete symptom topography. However, most dynamic therapists do not find these phenomenological descriptions sufficient in isolation, and they are usually supplemented with additional assessments. For instance, therapists try to understand their patient's character structure (i.e., neurotic, borderline, or psychotic), developmental and interpersonal histories, characteristic expressions (and non-expressions) of affect, and coping styles (e.g., defenses).

In addition, dynamic therapists attempt to listen to three complementary levels of discourse/communication. First, they try to be "objective" and realistic observers of their patients and their problems without being clouded by personal reactions, prejudgments, or preferences. Second, dynamic therapists attempt to fully *resonate* with their patients' idiosyncratic experiences. It is held to be of the utmost importance to understand (and subjectively capture) events in the world as they are colored through their patients' eyes. Third, the therapist's own idiosyncratic human reactions to the patient's experiences must be closely attended to. This not only provides crucial information about how others likely react to the patient, but also may serve to circumvent certain interpersonal "pulls" that may be less than therapeutic. The combination of these three different levels of communication (and the corresponding tension between subjective–objective and participant–observer) allows the therapist to triangulate relevant problem areas. Data derived from observations at these three levels also lend focus to the complex process of psychodynamic psychotherapy.

The Process of Therapy
TARGETS OF DYNAMIC PSYCHOTHERAPY
In a quote attributed to Freud (but not found in his corpus) it is stated that the capacity to love and work are indicators of mental health and, therefore,

preeminent targets of treatment (Erikson, 1963). These goals possess a commonsense and intuitive appeal, and further seem to converge with the *realistic* worldview of the psychodynamic therapies.

This willingness to realistically interpret oneself and the world with neither "rose-colored" nor "dark-colored" glasses pervades several other targets of therapy. For instance, attaining a realistic sense of self and other is a principal focus of many dynamic approaches (e.g., object relational and self psychologies). This necessarily entails a recognition (and possibly acceptance) of traits and qualities that may be unattractive or unflattering, yet nonetheless real. Relatedly, helping to instill a sense of realistic hope for patients is also important, as is an acceptance of the many determinants in life (e.g., including much of what would fall under Heidegger's concept of "thrownness," or the fact that we exist, that we exist in a particular time, that we have particular parents or, put another way, that we were "thrown" into a world not of our choosing). We would argue that the acceptance of that which cannot be changed and an ability to take pride and enjoyment in who and what one is are both strong indicators of psychological health. Further, these factors are also conducive to the attainment of authentic senses of meaning and purpose.

Along with these somewhat more abstract targets, dynamic therapies also share clinical goals with other modalities. Symptom relief is often emphasized, especially in short-term psychodynamic psychotherapies (e.g., Milrod, Busch, Copper, & Shapiro, 1997), where longer-term goals (e.g., significant personality modification) may be inappropriate or unrealistic. Dynamic therapies also assist patients in freeing themselves from repetitive patterns (interpersonal or otherwise) that inevitably only lead to despair, pain, and thwarted potential. As with behavior therapy, there is a desire to help patients adapt to their particular environmental demands and contingencies. And, as is probably universal among the many talk therapies, there is a general belief that flexibility is good and rigidity is undesirable.

THERAPIST TECHNIQUES AND THE EMERGENT PROPERTIES IN THERAPY
Most interventions contained in the armamentarium of dynamic therapists (e.g., see Thoma & Kachele, 1994) can be roughly divided into expressive and supportive techniques (Luborsky, 1984); the former focuses on uncovering relevant clinical material, as well as in increasing self-understanding and self-attunement. Expressive techniques are

epitomized by "interpretations," in which observable thoughts, feelings, or behaviors are directly linked to the dynamic content that are assumed to give rise to them. It is important to note that expressive techniques are not merely arid intellectual exercises, but must take place with affective urgency (and relatedness) in order to be effective.

In contrast, supportive techniques are intended to bolster and support adaptive defenses, shore up ego boundaries, make the patient feel more comfortable and more accepting of themselves, and facilitate the development of a positive therapeutic alliance. Some authors also consider interventions to be supportive if they facilitate the therapeutic process itself and enable patients to "open up." However, supportive techniques do not lead to or encourage regression, but instead are typically intended to combat immediate distress and return patients to their level of baseline functioning.

We term the many subtle forms of interaction arising between patient and therapist "emergent properties." This would include constructs such as the therapeutic alliance, transferences, countertransferences, and the "real" relationship. The therapeutic alliance has received much discussion (e.g., Hatcher & Barends, 2006), and will not be described further here. The current status of key dynamic constructs as transference (the attributing of qualities from earlier life relationships/experiences onto the therapist) and countertransference (the therapist's subjective experiences that are triggered by patient material) differ in some significant ways from Freud's original formulations, and definitions remain both in flux and hotly contested. In general, though, whereas transference was once seen as primarily a contributor of grist for the analytic mill, it has been increasingly viewed as important on its own terms, due to its many relational implications. Further, countertransference has ceased being viewed as merely a negative indicator of unresolved therapist issues, and is more often seen as an important font of clinical information in its own right. Finally, there is the "real" relationship, which has typically been considered how patient and therapist relate on their own terms and not as "parent substitute or working partner" (de Jonghe, Rijnierse, & Janssen, 1991, p. 696). It is important to note, however, that these various distinctions between relational constructs may not be as clear cut as they seem, for a therapist's "real" character traits may serve as "hooks" upon which they can more plausibly hang their transference reactions (e.g., an obese therapist may engender particular transferences, Baudry, 1991). Further, all

of these may have a direct (e.g., alliance) or indirect (e.g., interpretation of the transference leading to self-understanding) impact on outcome.

Taken together, the application of expressive and supportive techniques in a judicious manner (taking into account the idiosyncratic character, context, and strengths of the patient), when utilized in conjunction with the above-mentioned emergent properties, all join together to set the stage for work toward dynamic targets. However, we have yet to discuss the various therapeutic actions that may mediate dynamic therapy outcome.

THERAPEUTIC ACTIONS
Although therapeutic actions have been discussed in the literature, and several edited volumes on the topic exist (e.g., Lifson, 1996), empirical work and evidence have significantly lagged behind theory. We group therapeutic actions into increases in self-understanding (SU) and the attainment of corrective emotional experiences (CEE).

We have found it useful to conceptually subdivide "global" SU into specific subtypes, and we will briefly describe five of them here. First, the exploration of conflicts (both intrapersonal and interpersonal) is considered to be a core focus of dynamic therapy leading to greater self-understanding and positive outcome. Second, a patient's characteristic defense mechanisms or "character armor" (Reich, 1933) are held to be expressions of these very same unconscious conflicts, motivations, and desires. And, consonant with classical psychoanalysis, understanding and changing defenses are primary foci in psychodynamic therapy. Third, the exploration of a patient's object relations and capacity for object relatedness is thought to increase self-understanding, as well as contribute to therapy outcome. This often takes place in the context of the transference. Fourth, therapists who adopt a more hermeneutic approach to therapy look to narrative change as a means for increasing SU. In this, self/life-narratives are explored (and often co-written) in order to make them more coherent, comprehensible, nuanced, and capable of reflecting and encompassing the many complexities of lived human experience. A greater understanding of self and other is thought to result. Finally, reflective functioning is also related to SU. Reflective functioning, also termed *mentalization* (Fonagy, 2002), is the capacity to understand the behavior of oneself (and others) in terms of internal mental states (i.e., beliefs, thoughts, and emotions).

Corrective emotional experiences, or "reexperiencing the old, unsettled conflict but with a new ending" (Bridges, 2006, p. 551) may be another important therapeutic action. As one prototypical example of a CEE, a patient becomes angry with the therapist and holds the expectation that the therapist (like others) will respond to anger with rejection and more anger. However, the therapist's different-than-expected responses to anger (e.g., curiosity and empathy) provides the patient with a novel experience that holds the potential to modify rigid schemas, foster interpersonal flexibility, and even (if powerful enough) modify psychic structure. Whereas some early theorists toyed with directly influencing the therapeutic environment in order to elicit these experiences (e.g., Alexander & French, 1946), most today would view CEEs more broadly and less manipulatively. Corrective emotional experiences can occur without the therapist necessarily deviating from "normal" dynamic therapy protocol. In this conception of CEEs, the empathic mode of non-judgmental listening, interpersonal reliability, and therapeutic structure can provide patients with reparative experiences. Further, the very act of feeling understood and accepted by another can elicit profound changes, as can the presence of an important individual in one's life who acts in ways (as just described) that do not "fit the pattern" one expects.

Empirical Support

Whereas other schools of therapy (e.g., behavior therapy) developed hand-in-hand with an empirical and experimental approach, dynamic therapy arose from within a different methodological tradition. Historically, psychodynamic research focused primarily upon the intensive study of individual patients (i.e., the case study) instead of large-scale trials. The latter were likely hindered by a popular belief that dynamic therapy could not really be accurately studied because any operationalization of dynamic constructs into therapy manuals (a prerequisite for clinical trials) ineluctably made them enervated and sterile. There was also a widespread belief that existing measures of patient change were inadequate to capture dynamic change. However, several researchers began exploring the efficacy and mechanisms of dynamic treatments in the 1970s (e.g., Malan, Luborsky, and Strupp, to name a few).

In fact, evidence for the effectiveness of different forms of dynamic therapy exists. In longer dynamic treatments, evidence is consistent with the idea that lengthier and more intensive (e.g., Sandell, Blomberg, & Lazar, 1997) treatments evince better outcomes. With regard to short-term approaches, meta-analyses indicate that dynamic therapy is as effective as cognitive-behavioral therapy in treating Axis I and personality disorders (Liechsenring & Leibing, 2003; Leichsenring, Rabung, & Leibing, 2004). Although these findings are supportive of the effectiveness of dynamic therapy and the fact that it is at least equivalent to other approaches, additional research is needed, especially using the methodology of randomized clinical trials in order to compare it to well-established therapies for clearly defined disorders.

In addition to outcome literature and research into *general* processes of therapy that may exist *across* modalities (e.g., the therapeutic alliance, a construct also shown to have a causal role in patients' improvement in dynamic therapy [Barber, Connolly, Crits-Christoph, Gladis, & Siqueland, 2000]), several *dynamic-specific* constructs and therapeutic actions have received empirical attention and support, and three will be discussed here. First, dynamic interpretations have been found to be generally beneficial (Orlinsky, Rønnestad, & Willutzki 2004) and, more specifically, accurate and appropriate interpretations are associated with outcome (e.g., Crits-Christoph, Cooper, & Luborsky, 1988). However, this relationship between interpretations and outcome may be moderated by a patient's quality of object relations, although the direction of the relationship is unclear (e.g., Connolly et al., 1999; Hoglend et al. 2006). Second, dynamic therapy has been found to improve adaptive defensive functioning (e.g., Hersoug, Sexton, & Høglend, 2002), and these changes are also associated with outcome (e.g., Coleman, 2005). Interestingly, one study demonstrated that treatment continued past symptom recovery led to a normalization of defenses (Akkerman, Lewin, & Carr, 1999). Third, Levy et al. (2006) have shown that one year of expressive dynamic therapy (but not supportive dynamic therapy or dialectical behavior therapy) was associated with significant increases in reflective functioning in patients with severe personality disorders. These and other findings are promising, but additional elucidation of dynamic constructs (and their complex relation to outcome) is needed.

In closing, although high-quality research into dynamic therapy has begun, many more questions than answers remain, and certain core constructs (e.g., narcissistic vulnerabilities, internalization of the therapist as an object) have yet to be rigorously evaluated. However, it is heartening that many scholars have worked to operationalize their concepts and manualize their therapies (see Table 6.1 for examples). This makes it possible to both reliably

Table 6.1 Examples of Psychodynamic Treatment Guides/Manuals for Specific Disorders

Source	Disorder	Source	Disorder
Busch et al. (2004)	Depression	Milrod et al. (1997)	Panic Disorder
Luborsky et al. (1995)	Depression	Leichsenring et al. (2007)	Social Phobia
Crits-Christoph et al. (1995)	Generalized Anxiety Disorder	Yeomans et al. (2002)	Borderline Personality Disorder

train new psychodynamic therapists and adequately replicate empirical findings.

Cognitive Behavioral Approach

Cognitive-behavioral therapy (CBT) is probably better called *cognitive and behavioral therapies*, given that many treatments and traditions fall under the rubric of CBT. These therapies emphasize different theories or integrations of theories (e.g., cognitive vs. behavioral). Historically, behavior therapy developed out of the learning theory traditions of Pavlov (1927) and Skinner (1953), both of whom considered animal models of learning and their implications for psychopathology. More direct examinations of behavioral principles as applied to clinical theory were first developed by Mowrer (1939), Watson and Rayner (1920), and later by Wolpe (1952) and many others. The integration of notions of cognitive concepts with behavior therapy included work by Beck (1976), Ellis (1962), Goldfried and Davison (1976), and Meichenbaum (1977) in the 1960s and '70s.

From its outset, cognitive therapy was built on principles included in behavior therapy (see Beck, 1976), but with a focus on using such principles to facilitate the modification of cognitive distortions that were proposed to be the primary factor involved in the maintenance of depressive and other symptoms. In the last 30 years, significant progress has been made in understanding the cognitive and behavioral maintenance factors related to psychopathology in general (Harvey, Watkins, Mansell, & Shafran, 2004), and specific disorders in particular (e.g., Clark & Wells, 1995; Dalgeish, 2004; Mathews & Mackintosh, 1998; Mogg & Bradley, 1998), although there is still much to understand. In addition to the increased sophistication and empirical study of behavioral and cognitive mechanisms involved in psychopathology, an increasing emphasis has been placed on emotion as an important construct within these theories (Barlow, 2002; Power & Dalgleish, 1997; Samoilov & Goldfried, 2000; Teasdale & Barnard, 1993). In line with these and other recent developments, the current status of CBT theories can be viewed as an integrative approach, considering cognitive, behavioral, emotional, and interpersonal factors in treatment, as well as biological issues. The advances in treatments will be described further here.

Models of Function and Dysfunction

The basic tenets of CBT theory of human functioning and mental illness is that psychopathology is comprised of maladaptive associations among thoughts, behaviors, and emotions that are maintained by cognitive (attention, interpretation, memory) and behavioral processes (avoidance, reinforcement, etc.). Within CBT theories, there are different emphases on aspects of the characteristics of psychopathology and their maintenance mechanisms (e.g., Beck, 1996; Brewin, 2006; Foa, Huppert, & Cahill, 2006; Mineka & Zinbarg, 2006; Teasdale & Barnard, 1993). In general, CBT theories are stronger in their hypotheses regarding maintenance than etiology, and most interventions are aimed at interrupting or modifying cognitive, behavioral, emotional, and physiological processes and/or altering pathological beliefs, emotions, and behaviors that are involved in the maintenance of maladaptive or problematic behaviors.

It is beyond the scope of the current chapter to describe all of the various CBT theories of pathology and treatment in detail (some of these are books in and of themselves; e.g., Barlow, 2002; Power & Dalgleish, 1997). Instead, the common intersections of most of these theories will be described, with some examples from various theories used to illustrate the principles. Early behavioral theories suggested that associations between stimuli (S–S relationships) and between stimuli and responses (S–R relationships) led to learning maladaptive behaviors that underlie psychopathology (Mowrer, 1939; Watson & Raynor, 1920). Early cognitive theories proposed that idiosyncratic negative cognitive schemas underlay the cognitive, behavioral, and physiological symptoms of depression and other pathology (Beck, 1976). Interventions that targeted both dysfunctional interpretations and predictions, as well as underlying beliefs (schemas) would therefore alleviate such pathology. Theories have expanded on the early cognitive and behavioral theories to create idiographic cognitive models for most disorders of psychopathology (Clark, 1986; Clark & Wells, 1995; Ehlers & Clark, 2000; Fairburn, Cooper, & Shafran, 2003; Salkovsksis, 1999; Rapee & Heimberg, 1997, etc.). Each of these models attempt to explain the core symptoms of specific disorders by developing a model of interacting cognitions, behaviors, and physiological responses that are maintained through lower- and higher-level cognitive processes including attention, interpretation, memory, and appraisal processes.

Cognitive and behavioral theories were not only integrated, but cognitive theories were also developed to explain many behavioral models of psychopathology, including the revised helplessness model of depression (Abramson, Seligman, & Teasdale, 1978) and emotional processing theories of anxiety and habituation (Foa & Kozak, 1986). The helplessness model of depression suggested that attribution of negative events to personal, permanent, and pervasive factors maintains depressogenic beliefs and may account for the depressive states caused by inescapable aversive situations, as described in the original behavioral account of learned helplessness (Abramson et al., 1978). Emotional processing theory (Foa & Kozak, 1986) followed Lang (1977) by suggesting that fear structures are propositional networks that contain information about stimuli; verbal, behavioral, and physiological responses; and the meaning of the stimuli and responses. Further, Foa and Kozak (1986) proposed that, for modification of a fear structure to occur, there are two necessary components: activation of the fear structure and incorporation of new, disconfirmatory information into the fear structure. Thus, cognitive processes were proposed to account for both within- and between-session habituation. Similarly, Barlow (1988) integrated cognitive appraisals of control and predictability into Gray's biobehavioral emotion theory account of anxiety to advance theory and treatment. These types of theorizing helped to create a dominance of cognitive theory within CBT, acquiring significant empirical support as well as clinical utility in advancing treatments.

In the last two decades, these theories have been expanded upon and refined based on accumulating evidence. Some of these theories have undergone significant revision to accommodate new findings (Abramson, Metalsky, & Alloy, 1989), while others have worked on updating the theories without a complete revision (Barlow, 2002; Beck, 1996; Foa et al., 2006). Many of these updates include the incorporation of recent information regarding the nature of the same processes that were originally discussed, such as learning, memory, attention, and extinction, as well as the advancement of newer findings regarding emotion regulation and similar constructs (Gross, 1998). Some newer theories have focused specifically on the accumulation of information on competing information in memory (e.g., Brewin, 2006), while others have attempted to understand psychopathology in terms of multiple levels of information processing that occur in both benign and emotional circumstances (Beevers, 2005; Power & Dalgleish, 1997; Teasdale & Barnard, 1993). One of the earliest multilevel theories was the Interactive Cognitive Subsystems (ICS) of Teasdale and Barnard (1993). The ICS theory proposes that there are multiple codes (various forms of information), which are stored at two levels of meaning: generic and specific. These codes can be converted to one another, but are stored in separate memory systems. Emotion-related schematic models contain features of protypical situations that have elicited the emotion in the past. Generic meanings typically activate such schema and are overgeneralized and maintained in a cognitive loop in most forms of psychopathology. This model has been further expanded by Power and Dalgleish (1997, 2008), incorporating substantial information from emotion theory (attempting to account for most forms of psychopathology via the five basic emotions), and cognitive theory (in a highly complex model including four levels of representations of information).

The empirical status of CBT theories is strong and developing further. Recent studies have suggested the potential causal role in attentional and interpretive biases in developing anxiety (see Mathews & MacLeod, 2005). Longitudinal studies are demonstrating the importance of specific forms of cognition on the development of psychopathology (Bryant & Guthrie, 2007; Huppert, Foa, McNally, & Cahill, 2008) and, as described later, a number of studies have demonstrated that changes in cognitive and behavioral mechanisms proposed to be core aspects of CBT theories are related to symptom improvement (Huppert et al., 2008; Ingram, 2007). Overall, current CBT theories of psychopathology have incorporated findings from many areas of experimental psychopathology, basic areas of psychology, and neuroscience, allowing for further development of current notions of psychological processes in our understanding of the nature and treatment of psychopathology.

The Process of Therapy

Prior to discussing the specific CBT focus, techniques, and processes it is important to note that the CBT focus on techniques, although essential, is conducted within the context of a therapeutic relationship. In many forms of CBT, the therapeutic relationship is established during the initial evaluation and sessions. Data suggest that the therapeutic alliance in CBT is quite strong and positive, and that therapists are seen as warm, caring, and authoritative (although not authoritarian) (Keijsers, Schaap, & Hoogduin, 2000), which is indeed the goal. In addition, the therapeutic stance is one of genuineness, transparency (the therapist provides a general framework of what will happen in therapy, and discusses the plan for each session at the beginning of the session), and collaborative empiricism (explicitly working together toward a common goal of understanding the patient's problems by testing out hypotheses generated by the patient and therapist). Socratic questioning is used, with the goal of having patients contemplate and process information fully, making them more likely to remember and apply it. Most CBT therapies do not emphasize discussions of the therapeutic relationship as a facilitator of change unless there are reasons to believe that ignoring such issues will interfere with the treatment from the outset (e.g., Linehan, 1993; McCullough, 2003; Young, Klosko, & Weishaar, 2003). In fact, data suggest that the improvements in the therapeutic alliance in CBT may follow cognitive change and symptom reduction rather than precede them, at least in some forms of CBT (e.g., Tang & DeRubeis, 1999). At the same time, since the beginning of CBT, the context of a positive therapeutic relationship has been emphasized (c.f., Chapter 3 in Beck, Rush, Shaw, & Emory, 1979), and other data suggest that patients' perceptions of therapist empathy predicted changes in outcome, whereas changes in outcome did not predict perceptions of therapist empathy (Burns & Nolen-Hoeksema, 1992). Overall, the role of the therapeutic relationship in CBT is seen as important, but not the essential ingredient (see Castonguay, Constantino, McAleavey, & Goldfried, in press). This is also demonstrated by the efficacy of self-help using CBT for a number of disorders (Newman, Erickson, Przeworski, & Dzus, 2003).

The basic focus in most forms of CBT is on the thoughts, behaviors, physical sensations, and emotions experienced by the patient, which are typically related to their presenting complaint or form of psychopathology. The main concept is to understand the context of problematic situations for the patient by examining recent situations in which the individual experienced an extreme or excessive emotional or behavioral response (fear, shame, embarrassment, depression, anger, etc.). The thoughts, appraisals, and beliefs, behavioral responses (typically in order to cope by avoiding, suppressing, distracting, etc.), and physiological responses are examined in a detailed fashion in order to understand the pattern of responses that the patient engages in, in response to such situations (i.e., a careful functional analysis).

Most forms of CBT encourage a process of emotional engaging in the memory of the situation (to facilitate "hot cognitions" or "emotional processing") followed by some level of distancing. The distancing may be in the form of cognitive challenging (reevaluating the thoughts that occurred in the situation), or examining the alternative behaviors that could have been engaged in (exposure to feared experiences).

All forms of CBT ultimately attempt to actively create new learning experiences (modify associations of meaning within the multiple levels of schemata), although different streams of CBT will emphasize different methods of doing so. More behavioral forms of treatment (such as exposure therapy for anxiety disorders or behavioral activation for depression) will emphasize changes in behavior to facilitate new learning, whereas cognitive approaches will emphasize methods of testing predictions and thoughts via cognitive challenging and behavioral experiments. Ultimately, most schools of CBT incorporate behavioral strategies with cognitive strategies, oftentimes within the same exercise. The therapist's goal is to use the power of the relationship and the power of persuasion to help the patient engage in experiences that challenge his beliefs about himself, the world, and the future.

A number of techniques are common to most (although not all) forms of CBT. These include psychoeducation, monitoring, cognitive restructuring, in-vivo exposure, imaginal exposure, behavioral activation, and homework assignments. These techniques are tailored to the individual patient, to target the core problems that appear to be maintaining pathological emotions, thoughts, and behaviors. An individualized case conceptualization is essential, where one takes into consideration both the presenting disorders and the patients' unique contributions to the problems they are experiencing.

Ultimately, the information and techniques utilized in the therapy office are seen as mechanisms to facilitate learning and that need to be generalized to real-world situations. Most cognitive, behavioral, emotional patterns of living cannot be changed via treatment occurring one hour a week. At times, this means doing therapy outside of the office (especially with exposures) to facilitate generalization, but it most commonly includes completing homework assignments, one of *the sine qua non* of CBT. Homework's importance has been researched relatively thoroughly and shown to be a significant predictor of outcome in CBT (Kazantzis, Deane, & Ronan, 2000). Conceptually, the use of homework in CBT is similar to that of learning a new language. As such, one needs to immerse oneself in the language if one is to be fluent enough to use it difficult situations. Although the therapy sessions may provide the basics of grammar and vocabulary for the language, only by using it in every opportunity can one truly master it and be able to use it independently even long after treatment. This metaphor is often provided directly to the patient as homework rationale.

Empirical Support

Over the last 30 years, there have been many advances and developments in both behavioral and cognitive aspects of the treatment, including an abundance of treatment outcome studies demonstrating CBT's efficacy for most forms of psychopathology including anxiety disorders, depression, eating disorders, schizophrenia, personality disorders, and more (for a review of meta-analyses see Butler, Chapman, Forman, & Beck, 2006). In fact, outcome research on CBT comprises the lion's share of the empirical evidence for the effectiveness of psychotherapy via randomized clinical trials. There has also been substantial progress in demonstrating the durability of CBT over long periods of time, from 1 to 10 years for many treatments (Hollon, Stewart, & Strunk, 2006), and that outcomes in practice are similar to those obtained in randomized trials (Stewart & Chambless, 2009). These studies have included careful studies of mechanisms, randomized trials versus medications, placebos, and therapy controls. Results of these trials have had major implications in various health-care environments throughout the world. First, the majority of treatments considered to be empirically supported are CBT-oriented (c.f., Barlow, 2008; Nathan & Gorman, 2007). Second, health-care systems (whether insurance or governmental) have begun to allocate significant funding to the dissemination of CBT treatments, with the

notion that such dissemination will ease both burden of illness (e.g., unemployment, time off from work, etc.) as well as decrease service utilization (for two examples, see the National Institute for Clinical Excellence in the UK, www.nice.org.uk and the USA Veterans' Affairs Central Office Initiative (http://www.avapl.org/pub/2009%20Conference/Presentations/AVAPL%202009%20-%20Karlin.pdf). Finally, given the results of clinical trials showing the equivalent effectiveness or superiority of CBT over medications for some conditions, psychiatric guidelines are increasingly calling for CBT to be a first-line treatment for many disorders, including anxiety disorders, eating disorders, and affective disorders (see http://www.psychiatryonline.com/pracGuide/pracGuidehome.aspx).

In addition to the substantial body of research supporting the efficacy and effectiveness of CBT, research has also supported the importance of many of the main tenets of the theories and use of many of the specific techniques. For example, a number of studies have demonstrated the relationship between cognitive change and symptom change (see Huppert et al., 2008 or Ingram, 2007 for reviews, or Tang & DeRubeis, 1999 for a specific example). In addition, numerous studies have shown the relationship between exposure techniques and outcome (see Foa et al., 2006), and between homework and outcome (Kazantzis et al., 2000). More sophisticated data-analytic procedures continue to provide specific tests of CBT theories (see Ingram, 2007). Although data are overall supportive, results are far from definitive, and more research examining CBT theories is clearly warranted.

Cognitive-behavioral therapy is a rich, creative, and effective set of treatments that have been developed over the last 50-plus years. The demand in CBT for assessment, application of idiographically tailored empirically validated techniques (followed by further assessment), and the desire to help achieve maximal benefit for the therapy is reflected both on the local (case-by-case therapeutic stance) and macro (treatment studies) levels. Thus, there is constant work on evaluating what is working within CBT and how it can be improved.

Humanisitic / Experiential Approach

The most central characteristics of humanistic approaches to psychotherapy are promoting in-therapy *experiencing*, a belief in the uniquely human *capacity for reflective consciousness* plus a *positive view* of human functioning based on the operation of some form of *growth tendency*. Humanistic approaches adopt a consistently *person-centered* view that involves concern and real respect for each person. Major approaches within this orientation are person-centered, Gestalt, psychodrama, and existential. Some more contemporary experiential therapies, such as emotion-focused (Greenberg, 2002) and experiential therapy (Gendlin 1996; Mahrer 2005), based on a neo-humanistic reformulation of the earlier classic humanistic values, have emerged. In these, the traditional humanistic assumptions have been expanded to incorporate modern views on emotion, dynamic systems, constructivism, and the importance of a process view of functioning to help clarify the humanistic views of growth and self-determination.

Models of Function and Dysfunction

A general principle that has united all experientially oriented theorists is that people are wiser than their intellects alone. In an experiencing organism, consciousness is seen as being at the peak of a pyramid of nonconscious organismic functioning. Of central importance is that tacit experiencing is seen as potentially available to awareness, as an important guide to conscious experience, and is fundamentally adaptive. In addition, behavior is seen as the goal-directed attempt of people to satisfy their perceived needs, to maintain consistency (Rogers, 1951; Perls, Hefferline, & Goodman, 1951) and, more recently, to regulate affect (Greenberg, 2008).

Internal tacit experiencing is most readily available to awareness, when the person turns his or her attention internally within the context of a supportive interpersonal relationship. Interpersonal safety and support are thus viewed as key elements in enhancing the amount of attention available for self-awareness and exploration. Experiments in directed awareness, in addition, help focus and concentrate attention on unformed experience and intensify its vividness. The classical humanistic–experiential theories of functioning posited two main structural constructs, self-concept and organismic experience, as well as one major motivational construct, a growth tendency. An additional important concept was that of an organismic valuing process.

Rogers developed the most systematic self-theory and equated the self with the self-concept. For Rogers, the self was viewed as an organized *conceptual* system consisting of the individual's perceptions of self, of self in relation, as well as the perceived *values* attached to these perceptions. Needs were seen as important determiners of behavior, but a need was thought to be satisfied only through the selection and use of behavior that was consistent with the self-concept. In contrast to the self-concept, Rogers (1959) defined experience as all that is "going on" within the organism that at any moment is potentially available to awareness. Awareness of in-the-moment embodied "goings-on" was thought essential to being able to access the information implicit in organismic intelligence.

Experiential theorists posit a core human tendency toward growth. Rogers defined an actualizing tendency as the "inherent tendency of the organism to develop all its capacities in ways which serve to maintain or enhance the organism" (Rogers, 1959, p. 196). This view asserted that the person was not solely guided by regulating internal deficiencies, but also was a proactive and self-creative being organized to grow. Neither Rogers nor Perls saw actualization as the unfolding of a genetic blueprint. Rather, they were committed to the concept of an inherent organismic tendency toward increased levels of organization and evolution of ability. Maslow's (1954) concept of hierarchy of needs, from survival to being needs, was also incorporated into the humanistic understanding of motivation.

Rogers explicitly, and Perls implicitly, also proposed an *organismic valuing* process, believing that experience provided an embodied, felt access to this organismic valuing capacity. Organismic valuation is thought to measure how present events are consistent with, respect, and serve important organismic needs. This proposed organismic evaluation does not provide a logical valuation of truth or falseness, but rather a global apprehension of the meaning of events in relation to lived well-being. This valuing process was proposed to be the governor of functioning.

Humanistic theorists see the self as central in explaining human functioning. A central assumption is that to avoid anxiety the person must "maintain" the experience of consistency between an acceptable self-concept and both organismic experience and behavior, and that individuals limit awareness of current feelings and needs that may motivate self-inconsistent behavior. This disowning of feelings and needs is viewed in the long run to lead to maladjustment and to the thwarting of actualization.

Additional concepts recently introduced by neo-humanistic perspectives are affect regulation as a core motive, emotion schemes as central structures, and "voices of self-organizations" as aspects of functioning (Greenberg, 2002; Stiles 1999). Behavior is then seen as being motivated by the desire to have the emotions one wants and not have the emotions one does not want. Emotion schemes are internal organizations of past lived emotional experience that, when activated, produce current emotional experience. People are seen as multivocal, with many different interacting self-organizations, and the inter-linked traces of experiences into emotion schemes, when activated, form a *community of voices* within the person. Unintegrated voices tend to be problems, whereas assimilated voices are resources, available when circumstances call for their unique features and capacities.

HEALTHY FUNCTIONING

All humanistic/experiential theorists view the person as a complex self-organizing system. The greater the awareness of experience of the self, and the field or environment in which the person is operating, the greater the integration of all aspects of experience and the more engagement with the environment. In this view, it is the integration in awareness of all facets and levels of experience (Greenberg & Safran, 1986; Mahrer, 2005; Perls, 1969; Resnick, 1995; Rogers, 1961; Schneider & May, 1995; Yalom, 1980) that is seen as important in healthy function-ing. When functioning well, people can access well-differentiated aspects of self as an immediate felt referent, and use it as an online source of informa-tion to inform present and subsequent behavior (Gendlin, 1962; Rogers, 1957, 1959).

These traditional humanistic assumptions have been expanded by neo-humanistic perspectives to help clarify the humanistic views of growth and self-determination (Greenberg, Rice, & Elliott 1993; Greenberg Watson, & Leitaer 1998). Contemporary *emotion theory* (Frijda 1986; Greenberg & Paivio, 1997; Greenberg & Safran, 1986) holds that emo-tion is a biologically adaptive system that provides rapid appraisals of the significance of situations to peoples' well-being and, therefore, guides adaptive action. Emotion thus provides a process by which the growth tendency and the organismic valuing process function (Greenberg, 2002). In this view, emotion helps the organism to process complex situational information rapidly and automatically, in order to produce action appropriate to meeting important organismic needs (e.g., self-protection, support).

In addition, humanistic perspectives on subjec-tivity and perception have been connected to *constructivist* epistemology and views of functioning. Within this framework, people are seen as dynamic systems in which various elements continuously interact to produce experience and action (Greenberg & Pascual-Leone, 1995, 2001; Greenberg & van Balen, 1998). These multiple interacting self-organizations

can be described metaphorically as "voices" or parts of self (Elliott & Greenberg, 1997; Mearns & Thorne, 1988; Stiles, 1999). In this view, the "I" is an agentic self-aspect or self-narrating voice that constructs a coherent story of the self by integrating different aspects of experience in a given situation; however, this voice has no special status as an "executive self."

In a neo-humanistic view, growth is seen as emerging, not only through the self-organization of some type of biological tendency, but also from gen-uine dialogue with another person. In such an I–Thou dialogue (Buber, 1978), each person is made present to and by the other. In therapy, the therapist both *contacts* and *confirms* the client by focusing on particular aspects of the client's experiencing. Contact involves a continual empathic focus by the therapist on the client's subjective experience, confirming the person as an authentic source of experience and strengthening the self. Confirmation validates the other and, by focusing on strengths and internal resources, promotes growth. It is the therapist's focus on subjective experience and strengths that helps facilitate client growth and development.

DYSFUNCTION

In general, experiential approaches viewed pathology as resulting from the inability to integrate certain experiences into existing self-organization. From the experiential perspective, what is unacceptable to the self is dealt with, not by expelling it from con-sciousness but by failing to own experience as belonging to one's self (i.e., not experiencing it). In addition, what is disowned is not by definition pathogenic. Therefore, in the experiential perspec-tive, because healthy experiences and feelings may be seen as unacceptable by other self-organizations, they are as likely to be disowned as are unhealthy feelings or trauma. Experiential theory therefore sees dysfunction as occurring both from the disown-ing of healthy growth-oriented resources and needs, as well as from the avoidance of painful emotions.

In the neo-humanistic process view, it is the *inability to integrate* aspects of functioning into coherent harmonious internal relations that is viewed as a major source of dysfunction, rather than incongruence between self-concept and experience. Thus, different voices in the self representing one's wishes and fears, one's strengths and vulnerabilities, or one's autonomy and dependence may at any moment be in conflict and at any moment in danger of being disowned. Notice that conflict here is between different self-organizations, not conscious versus unconscious, or moral versus immoral.

The second central source of dysfunction is the *inability to symbolize bodily felt experience* in awareness. Thus, one may not be aware or be able to make sense of the increasing tension in one's body, of the anxiety one feels, or of unexpressed resentment, and this will lead to being out of touch with how one feels and, therefore, disoriented and unable to act most adaptively. A third major source of dysfunction involves the activation of *core maladaptive emotion schemes*, often trauma-based (Greenberg & Paivio, 1997). This leads to painful emotions and emotional memories and to maladaptive emotional experience and expression or the avoidance of these. The operation of this process implies that not all basic internal experience is an adaptive guide, and that, in addition to the benefits of becoming aware of basic experience, basic experience itself sometimes requires therapeutic change.

The above three general processes of dysfunction are supplemented by the operation of a large variety of more specific cognitive/affective processing difficulties that help explain different types of dysfunctional experiential states. A variety of particular experiential difficulties have been described by Greenberg, Ford, Alden, and Johnson (1993). Difficulties such as problematic reactions, in which one's view of an experience and one's reaction don't fit; self-evaluative splits, in which one part of the self negatively evaluates another; unfinished business, involving unresolved emotional memories; and statements of vulnerability involving a fragile sense of self. All involve different types of underlying emotion-schematic processing problems. Each state requires different interventions designed to deal with the specific emotional processing problems. This focus on different problematic in-session states offers a differential view of dysfunction in which current determinants and maintainers of disorders are identified by a form of process diagnosis in which therapists identify markers of in-session opportunities for implementing specific types of interventions and change processes.

The Process of Therapy

In the most general terms, humanistic–experiential therapy is based on two basic principles: first, the importance of the relationship; and, second, the consistent and gentle promotion of the deepening of the client's experience.

THE RELATIONSHIP

The relationship is seen as both curative, in and of itself, and as facilitating of the main task of therapy; that is, the deepening of client experiencing.

The relationship is built on a genuinely prizing empathic stance and on the therapist guiding clients' experiential processing toward their internal experience. An active collaboration is created between client and therapist, in which neither feels led, or simply followed by the other. Instead, the ideal is an easy sense of co-exploration. Although the relationship is collaborative, when disjunction or disagreement does occur, the therapist defers to the client as the expert on his or her own experience. Thus, therapist interventions are offered in a nonimposing, tentative manner, as conjectures, perspectives, "experiments," or offers, rather than as expert pronouncements or statements of truth. Interventions are construed as offering tasks on which clients who are active agents can work, if they so choose. Maintaining a responsive relational bond always takes precedence over the pursuit of a task. Although the therapist may be an expert on the possible therapeutic steps that might facilitate task resolution, it is made clear that the therapist is a facilitator of client discovery, not a provider of "truth," nor a psycho-educator. Experiential therapy thus recognizes both the power of the understanding relationship and the importance of different in-therapy tasks in promoting different types of therapeutic change.

STRATEGIES AND INTERVENTIONS

In experiential therapy, deepening experiential processing and subsequent meaning construction is accomplished by (a) creating a safe, trusting environment conducive to experiential processing and providing emotion coaching that models approach, valuing, and acceptance of emotion; (b) providing words for understanding and symbolizing a person's unformulated experience to help the client both regulate and express experience; (c) directing the client's attentional resources to the edges of awareness; (d) using empathic exploration and evocation to activate tacit meanings, bring them emotionally alive, and explore what is at the periphery of awareness; and, finally, (e) using emotion-stimulating interventions to activate emotional experience to help the client access and express alternative adaptive emotional resources (Greenberg, 2002).

The purpose of deepening emotional processing in experiential therapy is to activate internal emotional resources in the client; that is, the client's adaptive tendencies and resources toward adaptive growth (Gendlin, 1962; Greenberg 2002; Rogers, 1957). As clients access an experience of their feelings, they will also experience related needs, as well as action tendencies that may actualize the meeting of these needs in the world. Although accessing internal emotional resources is thought by some to occur sufficiently in a person-centered relationship, experiential therapists work toward accessing alternate emotional resources of the client in more focused ways by the use of specific techniques. These may include experiments in attention, focusing, working directly with embodied expression, and by empty-chair and two-chair dialogues (Greenberg et al., 1993; Greenberg & Watson, 2006).

EXPERIENTIAL THERAPY AS PROCESS THEORY

An important distinguishing characteristic of experiential therapy is that it offers a process theory of how to facilitate experiential knowledge, and rather than a content theory of personality or psychopathology, it offers a process theory that specifies both the moment-by-moment steps in the client's process of change and the therapist interventions that will facilitate these steps. The emphasis in each step always is on how to promote the direct sensing of what is concretely felt in the moment to create new meaning and how to promote a next processing step.

The key to experiential therapy is to have clients experience content in a new way, so that this new experience will produce a change in the way they view themselves, others, and the world. Experiential therapy thus emphasizes that symbols, schemes, and even behavior must interact with the body-based, experiential, level of existence in order to produce change (Gendlin, 1996). It thus offers a process theory of how body and symbol interact, and a set of methods for promoting this process.

Case formulation in this approach involves an unfolding, co-constructive process of establishing a focus on the key components of the presenting problems (Greenberg & Goldman, 2007). Formulation emphasizes making process diagnoses of current in-session states and exploring these until a clear focus on underlying determinants emerge through the exploratory process. In developing a case formulation, the therapist focuses first on salient poignant feelings and meanings, follows the client's emotional pain, and notices the client's initial manner of cognitive-affective processing and what will be needed to help the client focus internally. Then, working together, client and therapist develop a shared understanding of the underlying emotional determinants of the presenting problem, the main therapeutic tasks and, finally, of the client's emerging foci and themes. Case formulation emerges from this dialogue and is a shared construction involving deeper understandings of the problem and goals of treatment. The defining feature of an experiential approach to case formulation and assessment is that it is *process-diagnostic and marker-focused* (Greenberg et al., 1993) rather than person-diagnostic. Diagnostic focus is on in-session problematic processes in which clients are currently engaged.

Differential process-diagnosis involves the therapist attending to a variety of different *in-session markers* of in-the-moment problematic states. Problematic states are then addressed by interventions designed to address the specific difficulty. These processes may include process markers of clients' emotional processing style, such as being externally focused or emotionally dysregulated, or of particular problem states, such as self-critical conflict or unresolved bad feelings toward a significant other. Attention is paid to *how* clients are presenting their experiences in addition to *what* they are saying. Formulation and intervention are therefore constantly and intimately connected, span the entire course of treatment, and occur constantly at many levels.

Empirical Support

A series of meta–analyses of controlled and uncontrolled studies on the outcome of humanistic-experiential therapies have demonstrated their effectiveness (Greenberg, Elliott, & Lietaer, 1994). Elliott, Greenberg, and Lietaer (2005) presented a meta-analysis of 64 studies of experiential therapies. Eighteen examined emotion-focused individual therapy (EFT); ten evaluated EFT for couples; ten studied Gestalt therapy, 11 investigated encounter/sensitivity groups, and 15 looked at the outcome of various other experiential–humanistic therapies (e.g., focusing-oriented, psychodrama, or integrative). The average pre–post effect size was .99, considered large. Clients maintained or perhaps even increased their post-treatment gains over the post-therapy period, with largest effects obtained at early follow-up. Control-referenced effect sizes of pre–post differences in the 42 treated groups in which experiential treatments were compared to waitlist or no-treatment controls were also considered large.

Results of 74 comparisons between experiential and nonexperiential therapies showed no overall difference between experiential and nonexperiential treatments. In 60% of the comparisons, no significant differences were found. In 18% of comparisons, clients in nonexperiential treatments did significantly better; whereas in 22% of comparisons, experientially treated clients did significantly better. A subsample of 46 studies compared effects between experiential and CBT. In general, experiential therapies and CBT therapies were shown to be equally effective.

As an example of a humanistic approach that has been empirically studied, process experiential emotion-focused (PE/EFT) therapy, was found to be highly effective in treating depression in three separate trials. In two studies PE/EFT was compared to a purely relational empathic treatment, and one study compared PE/EFT to a cognitive behavioral treatment. All three treatments were found highly effective in reducing depression. Process experiential emotion-focused therapy was found to be more effective than a pure relational empathic treatment in reducing interpersonal problems, in symptom reduction, and in preventing relapse (Goldman, Greenberg, & Pos, 2005; Greenberg & Watson, 1998). Watson, Gordon, Stermac, Kalogerakos, and Steckley (2003) found no significant differences in symptom improvement between PE/EFT and CBT for the treatment of major depression. However, clients in PE/EFT therapy reported being significantly more self-assertive and less overly accommodating at the end of treatment than did clients in the CBT treatment. In addition, EFT has been shown to be effective in treating childhood trauma, abuse, and interpersonal injuries (Paivio & Greenberg 1995; Paivio, Hall, Holowaty, Jellis, & Tran, 2001).

The majority of research on experiential psychotherapy has focused on whether depth of experiencing relates to outcome. Hendriks (2002) has reviewed 91 of these studies. Experiential processing was explored within various treatments (not solely experiential) for varied diagnostic categories, from schizophrenia, to marital discord, to depression. The vast majority of studies found that the higher experiencing levels measured related to better psychotherapy outcomes, as measured by a variety of outcome measures.

Systemic Approach

The essence of the systemic approaches to psychotherapy is their focus on contextually defining and conceptualizing clients' psychological problems. Most often, the context or frame of interest is the couple or the family, but it may also be a broader context, such as an extended family or classroom of students and teacher. Although assessment and case conceptualizations are informed by this perspective, in practice, specific interventions are directed not only at the family or couple but may also be directed at an individual. As discussed later, there are numerous approaches to systemic therapy. What specifically, then, defines a systemic approach to therapy,

and how do systemic approaches differ from other approaches? To fully answer these questions, we consider both the defining features of systemic therapy models and their evolution as a distinct approach to treatment. This is followed by a detailed description of selected systemic therapy approaches, followed by a summary of outcome and change process research.

Models of Function and Dysfunction

Although systemic therapies can differ from each other substantially in practice, they share certain common philosophical and conceptual features that distinguish them from other therapy approaches. Most importantly, systemic therapies focus not solely on *intra*personal or individual dynamics, but rather on the *inter*personal and *inter*actional dynamics that shape and maintain problems in one or more members of the system. A system (e.g., couple, family) is a set of dynamic elements (e.g., people) that mutually act upon, and are acted upon, by the others. For example, in a couple, the emotional or physical avoidance of one partner may "cause" the other to approach the partner, which in turn begets more avoidance behavior by the partner, then more approach behavior by the first person, and so on. Although the partners themselves often punctuate this ongoing sequence in a linear way that blames the other and exonerates themselves ("she started it," "I wouldn't bug him if he didn't avoid me"), the systemic therapist takes a "metaperspective," focusing instead on circular causal explanations of the ways in which the couples' joint pattern of interacting sustains their unhappiness.

The same is true in the family context. Systemic therapists assess a child's problem behavior by considering it, not in isolation, but within the context of the family system. For instance, a child's externalizing behaviors may function to draw a distant parent into more contact with the other parent and the child, or to deflect conflict between the parents onto the child. Each person's behavior is part of a web of elements in which the whole is more than the sum of its parts. Thus, explanations of psychopathology in an individual require an expansion of the frame of reference: "If a person exhibiting disturbed behavior (psychopathology) is studied in isolation, then the inquiry must be concerned with the *nature* of the condition and, in a wider sense, with the *nature* of the human mind. If the limits of the inquiry are extended to include the effect of this behavior on others, their reactions to it, and the context in which all of this takes place, the focus shifts from the artificially isolated monad to the *relationship* between parts of the system. The observer of human behavior then turns from an inferential study of the mind to the study of the observable manifestations of relationship" (Watzlawick, Beavin, & Jackson, 1967, p. 21).

Early theorizing and clinical observation yielded a number of heuristically rich corollaries that provide the underpinnings for systemic models. The first assumption is that communication is the vehicle by which relationships (both healthy and disturbed) are defined, and thus much is learned from a study of not just *what* people within a system say to each other, but *how* they say it. Tone of voice, sarcasm, humor, interruptions, kinesics, even silence, communicate information about not only the content of the communication and how to "read" it, but also about the relationship itself. Another assumption is that family and other human systems have a kind of psychological equilibrium that is maintained by positive and negative feedback to the system. Negative feedback is information that signals a deviation from the steady state (homeostasis) and the necessity of some self-regulating adjustments (e.g., when an adolescent's emerging needs for independence feeds conflict and results in shifts in established family patterns of interaction). Positive feedback is information that signals, "we are on course, no change is needed." Since, in a family system, the behavior of each person continually provides feedback to the others, the result is a complex and dynamic system in which "concepts of pattern and information" (Watzlawick et al., 1967, p. 32) are the focus of clinical assessment. This stands in contrast to most other psychotherapy approaches, in which characteristics of individuals—intrapsychic drives and conflicts, problematic affective states, or distorted cognitions—are the focus.

At the time it was developed, in the late 1960s, the systemic model was a radical shift from the psychoanalytic, psychodynamic, and humanistic psychotherapy approaches that were dominant; it developed in parallel, however, with the emerging behavioral therapies that were applied to families. Some of these assumptions have subsequently been challenged or refined in newer systemic therapy approaches. However, they served to further define the transformative nature of the systemic approach. Although systemic approaches are now firmly established, they continue to present interesting challenges to traditional assumptions and habits of thinking on questions such as: Who is the client? How should change be measured? How can we classify and assess distressed relationships and family systems? (See Kaslow, 1996; Kaslow & Patterson, 2006, for discussion of relational diagnosis.)

Current systemic therapies must be understood within the context of their evolution (see Becvar, 2003, for an excellent summary). From the beginning, systemic therapy has had broad interdisciplinary roots. It was born of the exchange of ideas and in some cases, actual collaborations between those interested in general systems theory in the biological sciences, mathematicians, communications researchers, anthropologists, and psychiatrists (Ruesch & Bateson, 1968; von Bertalanffy, 1950; Watzlawick et al., 1967; Watzlawick, Weakland, & Fisch, 1974; Weiner, 1948). Translation and use of these ideas in clinical settings and early forms of family therapy in the 1960s and 1970s were powerful, generative, and occasionally misguided, as in the case of the double-bind theory of schizophrenia (Bateson, Jackson, Haley & Weakland, 1956). The fact that this *was* a radically different view of psychological problems no doubt accounted for the development, in some of its applications, of a singular, if not zealous, focus on the system to the exclusion of the individual, leading some to question whether the "self" had been lost in the system (Nichols, 1987). As major advances were made in the 1980s and 1990s, in understanding the role of cognition and emotion in psychopathology, the role of attachment in adult relational problems, and the ways in which brain biochemistry both affects and is affected by experience, these developments became incorporated into the newer evolving forms of systemic family and couples therapies. As will become clear shortly, these newer approaches integrate both individual-level and systems-level dynamics in their theories and practice.

The Process of Therapy

Current systemic therapy interventions draw heavily on the foundations established by the "classic" approaches, e.g., behavioral family therapy (Falloon, 1991; Patterson, 1971), structural family therapy (Colapinto, 1991; Minuchin, 1974), strategic therapy (Haley, 1963, 1973; Madanes, 1981), and interactional/MRI approaches (Segal, 1991; Watzlawick et al., 1974). They are, however, more integrative and more cognizant of the ways in which systems outside the nuclear family and the forces of gender, race, culture, and socioeconomics interact with the family system. And there are a few models that marry systemic thinking with postmodern philosophy, the "social construction therapies"

(Anderson, 2003). Two systemic approaches are described in some detail here. They were chosen from the many current approaches (see Gurman & Jacobson, 2002, and Lebow, 2005) as illustrations of the variety of interventions that characterize systems treatments, and because they each have strong empirical support.

Brief Strategic Family Therapy

Brief strategic family therapy (BSFT; Santisteban, Szapocznik, Perez-Vidal, Kurtines, Murray, & LaPerriere, 1996); Szapocznik & Kurtines, 1989; Szapocznik, Perez-Vidal, Hervis, Brickman, & Kurtines, 1990) is a set of interventions for families of adolescents with externalizing behavior problems, such as conduct disorder and delinquency, as well as substance abuse. Brief strategic family therapy focuses on the dysfunctional family relationship patterns that are associated with these (often, co-occurring) problems. It also targets the school and peer systems. Brief strategic family therapy entails three steps, each equally important (Horigian et al., 2005). *Joining* is the first step, and BSFT has pioneered techniques that work for engaging difficult families, including (a) consultation by phone, even before therapy starts to get family members to come in; (b) forming an early alliance with each family member to learn what his or her goals are to enable work toward them; and (c) successfully joining the family system by working within existing structures at first. The therapist's goal is to become a trusted, temporary leader of the family, one who is seen by each member as both respectful and capable of helping them resolve their problems. The therapy was developed with Hispanic families and is especially attuned to cultural considerations, including respect for the most powerful family members.

In the next step, *diagnostic assessment,* the therapist creates enactments in the sessions that allow him or her to assess the family's typical patterns of interactions by observing them *in vivo* rather than just hearing accounts of them. The BSFT therapist studies their organization (leadership, subsystems, communication), resonance (emotional connections between them), and their developmental stage as a family. He or she also notes which member is the "identified patient" and the family's conflict resolution style. This assessment allows the therapist to develop a formulation of how the family interactions are sustaining the problem behaviors and from that, to launch the third step, *restructuring* their maladaptive styles of interaction to healthier ones. Working with the family conjointly, the BSFT

engages the family in active work on the here-and-now process of how they interact with each other during the sessions. Brief strategic family therapy training and the therapy manual (Szapocznik, Hervis, & Schwartz, 1993) provide directions for orchestrating change via techniques of reframing, assignments that create shifts in boundaries and alliances, and tasks within the therapy session and (once they have been successfully completed there) outside of it; for example, parents talk together to establish a curfew. Treatment typically lasts 12–16 sessions, with booster sessions as needed, and it ends when both family functioning and the adolescent problem behavior are significantly improved. There is also a one-person form of BSFT for those families that cannot be engaged as a whole (Szapocznik, Kurtines, Foote, & Perez-Vidal, 1986).

Emotionally Focused Couple Therapy

Emotionally focused couple therapy (EFT; Greenberg & Goldman, 2008; Greenberg & Johnson, 1988; Johnson, 1996; Johnson & Greenberg, 1994; 1985; Johnson et al., 2005) is also a brief, structured treatment that focuses on emotion and relational bonds together, in order to decrease couple distress and dissatisfaction. Specifically, EFT interventions are targeted at "identifying the negative cycles of interaction, accessing the emotions that are both a response to and organizers of these cycles, and reprocessing these emotions to create new responses that shape secure bonding events and new cycles of trust and security" (Woolley & Johnson, 2005, p. 387). The therapy proceeds through three stages: *deescalation of negative cycles, restructuring interactional positions toward secure connection,* and *consolidation and integration.* Although these are articulated sequentially, the work proceeds in an iterative fashion, and setbacks may require some backtracking, so that in actual practice, the couple and therapist may be working on more than one step at once. *Deescalation* is accomplished by active involvement of the therapist, beginning with building an alliance with each partner individually (there may be long stretches where the therapist is talking with one person empathically while the other just listens) to establish safety and security within the therapeutic relationship. As in BSFT, the therapist then observes the clients' relational behavior to identify the negative interaction cycle; with couples, this is often a pattern such as pursue/withdraw, blame/placate, criticize/defend. The therapist then uses gentle but persistent experience-focused questions to access and bring out the previously unacknowledged attachment emotions that underlie the patterned interactions (e.g., feelings of being unworthy, fear of abandonment). The other partner, of course, is a witness to this work but is enjoined from jumping in to defend him or herself, to invalidate the others' emotional experience, etc. This stage culminates in the therapist articulating a construction of the problem in terms of how each partner's underlying emotions and attachment needs are related to their negative and jointly created interactional cycle. This is done matter-of-factly, avoiding blame, and striving to keep each partner feeling understood and supported by the therapist as the second stage is entered.

Here, the work deepens, as the therapist focuses in on the disowned emotional needs and works toward the central change events, "withdrawer reengagement" and "blamer softening." Theoretically, the outcome of this work—although it may take a while—is the partner's acceptance of the other's emotional experiences and resulting shifts in interactional positions that allow partners to share their needs and wants directly, becoming closer and more emotionally engaged as a couple. This undermines the rigid, conflictual patterns of relating. In the final stage, the work is about consolidating the new ways of relating and integrating them reliably into their life together beyond the therapy sessions.

Empirical Support

There is strong empirical support for the efficacy of couple and family systems therapies as a class of therapy (Pinsof & Wynne, 1995; Sexton, Alexander & Mease, 2004). But because these therapies are myriad and diverse, the better question is, *which* approaches have empirical support? In general, solid empirical support is strongest, but not limited to, those therapies with a strong behavioral or cognitive behavioral focus.

In the couples' therapy domain, behavioral couple therapy (BCT: Jacobson & Margolin, 1979) and integrative behavioral couple therapy (IBCT), which adds an acceptance component to traditional behavioral couple therapy (Baucom, Christensen & Yi, 2005; Christensen & Jacobson, 1998), insight-oriented marital therapy (IOCT; Snyder, 1999; Synder & Wills, 1989), and EFT have been demonstrated in clinical trials to be more effective than no treatment and about equally effective as each other (Sexton et al., 2004). However, a robust finding in this literature is that couples' therapy of *any* kind results in significant improvements in relationship satisfaction for under 50% of couples and that, even

for those couples, gains in relationship satisfaction erode significantly within a year after treatment (Snyder, Castellani, & Whisman, 2006).

In the family therapy domain, again, certain approaches have strong empirical support. These include: functional family therapy (FFT; Sexton & Alexander, 2003), multisystemic family therapy (MST; Henggeler, Schoenwald, Borduin, Rowland, & Cunningham, 1998), multidimensional family therapy (MDFT; Liddle, 1995), and BSFT (Szapocznick & Kurtines, 1989). Attachment-based family therapy for depressed adolescents (ABFT) has good preliminary empirical support as an effective, distinct model (Diamond, Diamond, & Hogue, 2007; Diamond, Siqueland, & Diamond, 2003). With the exception of the latter, these all share a focus on families with delinquent or substance-abusing adolescents. Other empirically supported family treatments include parent management training for child conduct disorders (Brestan & Eyberg, 1998); psychoeducational family interventions for schizophrenia (Lam, 1991) and bipolar disorder (Miklowitz, George, Richards, Simoneau, & Suddath, 2003; Rea et al., 2003); and systemic treatments for substance-abuse problems (O'Farrell, 1993; Stanton & Shadish, 1997) and adults dually diagnosed with substance-abusing and other Axis I disorders (Moore, 2005).

However, other popular family therapy approaches have simply not yet been adequately tested, and family therapy efficacy research focuses primarily on externalizing disorders of youth. Meanwhile, other approaches, such as strategic therapy (Fisch, Weakland, & Segal, 1982; Madanes, 1981), solution-focused therapy (de Shazer, 1985, 1991), and postmodern social construction therapies, including narrative therapy (White & Epston, 1990) and collaborative therapy (Anderson & Goolishian, 1988), continue to be practiced and developed. Progress in outcome research continues (Sprenkle, 2002), as do ongoing debates about the best ways to assess outcomes and study the process of therapy in a manner compatible with a systemic perspective (Sprenkle, 2002; Sprenkle & Piercy, 2005).

Research on the change process of change is just beginning (Friedlander & Tuason, 2000; Heatherington, Friedlander, & Greenberg, 2005) and is greatly needed. Although the treatments reviewed here are diverse, they share common features and (theoretically) some common change mechanisms that are specific to a systemic approach. These mechanisms should include processes between therapist and clients and also *between the clients* within the couple or family, as well as *within* individual members of the system. Articulating these mechanisms or "principles of effective change" (Castonguay & Beutler, 2006) and testing them empirically is key to the healthy growth and future of systemic therapies. Christensen, Doss, and Atkins (2005) provide a good illustration of how to articulate transtheoretical, testable principles of change in the couples therapy domain. An example is an "evocative intervention," that, theoretically, facilitates corrective experiences for the couple. In EFT and IBCT (Cordova, Jacobson, & Christensen, 1998), for example, the therapist elicits emotional, less-defensive, more honest, and vulnerable reactions in a partner which, ideally, are processed by the other partner; a "softening" on one person's part feeds "accessibility" on the other's part and, as each person experiences a different sense of self, and a different sense of the other, they draw closer. Evidence supports this theorized change process (Bradley & Furrow, 2004; Greenberg et al., 1993). Another transtheoretical process that has received empirical support is transforming or reframing the clients' construction of the presenting problem. This includes the kind of reframing done in BSFT, the transformation of an individual narrative about the problem to an interpersonal, systemic one in constructivist family therapy (Coulehan, Friedlander, & Heatherington, 1998; Sluzki, 1992), and "relational reframing" of an adolescent's depression as a schism or rupture of trust in the adolescent–parent subsystem in ABFT (Diamond et al., 2003). The evocative intervention and the reframing interventions are good examples of the ways in which contemporary systemic approaches explicitly incorporate individual processes (emotion and cognition, respectively) into theory and therapy practice, in tandem with attention to interpersonal processes. They also illustrate the ways in which systemic thinking continues to be cross-disciplinary, and the ways in which many current approaches have built clinically grounded, testable propositions into the theory itself.

Psychotherapy Integration

Although a substantial number of psychotherapists identify themselves as eclectic or integrative (Norcross & Goldfried, 2005; Orlinsky & Rønnestad, 2005), the acceptance of psychotherapy integration was a process that evolved over several decades. A seed for psychotherapy integration was first planted by Alexander French, in his address of the 1932 meeting of the American Psychiatric Association (later published as French, 1933). In this address, French drew parallels between psychoanalysis and Pavlovian conditioning (e.g., the similarities between repression and extinction). Subsequently, the potential for psychotherapy integration received attention from only a handful of authors between 1932 and 1960 (e.g., Dollard & Miller, 1950; Rosenzweig, 1936), and did not emerge as a latent theme until the 1960s and 1970s, beginning with Frank's (1961) *Persuasion and Healing*. This book addressed itself to the commonalities cutting across varying attempts at personal influence and healing in general. Soon after, the important concept of "technical eclecticism" was introduced in 1967, by Lazarus, who argued that clinicians could use techniques from various therapeutic systems without necessarily accepting the theoretical underpinnings associated with these approaches. By this time, many clinicians were arguing that, rather than being irreconcilable, techniques from divergent approaches could be viewed as complementary. For example, Wachtel (1975) maintained that many instances of relapse following behavior therapy might possibly be linked to the client's maladaptive patterns that might more readily be identified when reviewed from within a psychodynamic framework.

In 1976, Garfield and Kurtz published findings indicating that approximately 55% of clinical psychologists in the United States considered themselves eclectic (also see Garfield & Kurtz, 1977). Prochaska (1979), in a textbook describing diverse systems of psychotherapy, concluded with a chapter that made the case for developing a transtheoretical orientation that would encompass what had been found to be effective across different approaches to psychotherapy. With these developments, psychotherapy integration became a bona fide movement in the 1980s. An important contribution was made in a seminal paper by Goldfried (1980), who, noting past attempts to find commonalities across psychotherapies, argued that a fruitful level of abstraction at which such a comparative analysis might take place would be somewhere between the specific techniques and theoretical explanations for their potential effectiveness. Goldfried (1980) maintained that it is at this intermediate level of abstraction—the level of clinical strategy—that potential points of overlap may exist.

Another significant event in the history of psychotherapy integration was the formation of an international organization devoted specifically to this endeavor. Formed in 1983, the Society for the

Exploration of Psychotherapy Integration (SEPI) was established as a way of bringing together the growing number of professionals interested in this area. In the mid to late 1980s, in order to provide forums for these many voices, new journals appeared that directly addressed clinical and research issues pertinent to integration. One journal was the *International Journal of Eclectic Psychotherapy*, later renamed the *Journal of Integrative and Eclectic Psychotherapy* in 1987. The 1990s witnessed a continued growth of writing on psychotherapy integration, as well as a continued trend toward more therapists identifying themselves as eclectic/integrative. In 1991, SEPI began publishing its own journal, *Journal of Psychotherapy Integration*. The first edition of the *Handbook of Psychotherapy Integration* (edited by Norcross and Goldfried) was published in 1992, followed by the *Comprehensive Handbook of Psychotherapy Integration* (Stricker & Gold, 1993). These handbooks and journals, as well as the establishment of SEPI, are clear signs that psychotherapy integration has grown from being an idea (or dream) evoked by a few visionaries (and/or heretics within their own schools of thought) to becoming nothing less than a *leitmotif* in psychotherapy textbooks and training programs. For a more comprehensive review of the history of psychotherapy integration, see Goldfried (2005).

Factors Contributing to Psychotherapy Integration

Although the majority of therapists (at least in the United States) identify themselves as integrative or eclectic (Norcross, 2005), psychotherapy integration has only developed into a defined area of interest in the past 20 years. Of the many factors that have fostered this movement, a number of empirical findings have led numerous scholars and therapists to consider the contributions of a plurality of theoretical orientations in their attempt to both understand and improve psychotherapy (see Castonguay, Reid, Halperin, & Goldfried, 2003).

• Although psychotherapy works, some clients fail to fully improve, others terminate prematurely, and yet others deteriorate.
• Although some treatments (e.g., CBT) appear to be more effective than others for particular clinical problems (e.g., obsessive-compulsive disorder), major forms of psychotherapy tend to have equivalent outcomes.
• Descriptions and observations of psychotherapists (including leading figures such as Freud, Rogers, and Wolpe) suggest that there are differences between their theoretical writings and clinical practice (see Castonguay, 1997; Castonguay et al., in press; Castonguay & Goldfried, 1994).
• Process research suggests that, in their regular clinical practice, therapists of different orientations can show more similarities than differences (e.g., Goldfried, Raue, & Castonguay, 1998).
• Process research not only demonstrates that factors that are common to different approaches (e.g., the alliance) predict client improvement, but that some variables typically associated with one orientation (e.g., emotional deepening, exploration of attachment to early significant figures) are associated with positive outcome in other orientations (e.g., CBT) (Castonguay et al., 1996; Hayes, Goldfried, & Castonguay, 1996).

In addition to these empirical findings, leaders of major orientations have voiced serious criticisms of their preferred theoretical approaches, while encouraging an open-minded attitude toward other orientations. Strupp (1976), for instance, denounced the "closed-shop" mentality that prevailed in the psychoanalytic milieux and urged his colleagues to consider the contributions of learning theories and research in their conceptualization of therapy. Similarly, Thorensen and Coates (1978) lamented that a complacent orthodoxy was bred within behavioral therapies and that a critical revision of its conceptual rationale (including the consideration of the "purpose of life") was needed.

Furthermore, clinicians of different orientations recognized that their approaches did not provide them with the clinical repertoire sufficient to address the diversity of clients and their presenting problems. For example, Goldfried and Castonguay (1993) argued that CBT has paid limited attention to the therapeutic relationship and emotion. Integrating contributions from psychodynamic, interpersonal, and humanistic approaches, they argued that the examination of the way in which clients interact during sessions, as well as the use of emotional deepening techniques, could help CBT therapists to identify and modify core schemas and maladaptive patterns of interpersonal behavior.

Pathways of Psychotherapy Integration

There are a number of routes to psychotherapy integration, and these multiple pathways are typically understood to fall into one of four categories: technical eclecticism, theoretical integration, common factors, and assimilative integration. Research by Norcross, Karpiak, and Lister (2005) reveals that each of these is embraced by a significant number of self-identified eclectics and integrationists.

TECHNICAL ECLECTICISM

The least theoretical of these pathways, technical eclecticism, seeks to select the best intervention for the person and the problem, based on the best available data. Thus, the foundation is more empirical than theoretical. Examples of technical eclecticism include Lazarus's (2005) multimodal therapy and Beutler's (see Beutler, Consoli, & Lane, 2005) systematic treatment selection and prescriptive psychotherapy (STS). Technical eclectics utilize interventions from different sources without necessarily identifying with the theories that generated them. Unlike theoretical integrationists, there is less interest in the convergence between disparate systems and their connection with specific techniques.

THEORETICAL INTEGRATION

The most theoretical of these pathways, theoretical integration, seeks to integrate two or more therapies with the intention of developing an overlapping theoretical system that improves upon the constituent therapies alone. An emphasis is placed on integrating the underlying models, along with their theory-specific techniques into an overarching framework. Examples of this approach include Wachtel, Kruk, and McKinney's (2005) effort to integrate psychoanalytic and behavioral theories with cyclical dynamics, and Ryle's (2005) cognitive-analytic therapy. As noted by Norcross (2005) "the primary distinction between technical eclecticism and theoretical integration is that of empirical pragmatism and theoretical flexibility" (p. 9).

COMMON FACTORS

Stemming from the work of Frank (1961) and Garfield (1980), a common factors approach seeks to elucidate the core ingredients that different therapies share in common. This method is predicated on accumulating research that commonalities across treatments (e.g., the working alliance) may be at least as important in accounting for psychotherapy outcome as the unique factors that differentiate among them. However, it is widely recognized that the debate between common and unique factors in psychotherapy represents a false dichotomy, and these factors must be integrated to maximize effectiveness.

ASSIMILATIVE INTEGRATION

Assimilative integration was defined by Messer (2001) as "the incorporation of attitudes, perspectives, or techniques from an auxiliary therapy into a therapist's primary, grounding approach" (p. 1). This form of integration calls for a firm grounding in one system of psychotherapy, with a willingness to incorporate practices and views from other systems. This entails adherence to a single, coherent theoretical system that assimilates techniques and interventions from multiple systems into this system. Examples of this approach to integration include Castonguay, Newman, Borkovec, Grosse Holtforth, and Maramba's (2005) cognitive-behavioral assimilative integration and Stricker and Gold's (2005) assimilative psychodynamic therapy. It has been argued that assimilative integration does not represent its own integration pathway; rather, it serves as a prime example of how the above approaches are not mutually exclusive, and in clinical work, the distinctions among them are not so apparent (Norcross, 2005). Assimilative integration may be conceptualized as a bridge between technical eclecticism and theoretical integration, and this is often accomplished through the lens of common factors. One specific method for building this bridge is based on a theory of change involving change principles, such as those identified by Goldfried (1980) (see Boswell, Nelson, Nordberg, McAleavey, & Castonguay, 2010).

Theories of Change

As previously described, a significant source of motivation for integration stems from clinicians' dissatisfaction with single-theory systems that do not fully explain, or cannot be applied to a diverse set of clients and presenting problems. Integration becomes an attempt to grapple with the inherent complexity of psychopathology and its treatment. An integrative theory of change can take many forms. However, two major, complementary systems have been advocated: principles of change, or core clinical strategies that cut across divergent theoretical orientations, and the transtheoretical model.

CHANGE PRINCIPLES

Change principles are general guidelines of intervention that cut across different theoretical orientations. As described by Goldfried (1980), such principles (e.g., facilitation of a corrective experience, expectation that therapy can be helpful, participation in a therapeutic relationship, obtaining a new perspective of self and other, and opportunity for repeated reality testing) are found at a level of abstraction between specific techniques and the theoretical models developed to explain why these techniques work. As argued by Goldfried (1980; Goldfried & Padawer, 1982), given this intermediate level of abstraction, change principles can be used as an implicit guide, or heuristic, for therapists in addressing a diverse number of clients and presenting problems.

It is important to note that these levels (theory, technique, and common change principles) interrelate. One who is technically eclectic cannot disregard theory, just as one who is a theoretical integrationist cannot disregard techniques, and common change principles would not be possible in the absence of both. According to Goldfried, techniques are parameters to facilitate change processes. For example, techniques such as interpretation and cognitive restructuring are viewed as particular manipulations of the same general principle of change: providing a new perspective. As argued by Castonguay (2000), however, principles or strategies of change need to be framed within an articulated theory of human functioning and change. Whether it is integrative or closely related to one of the four pathways described in this chapter, this theory is necessary to help clinicians decide when and how to foster a principle of intervention.

A complementary approach to understanding change processes has been the conceptualization of stages of change (see Prochaska & DiClemente, 2005). Individuals are assumed to progress through a series of stages as behavior is modified. These stages include: pre-contemplation, contemplation, preparation, action, and maintenance. Clinical experience and research evidence (e.g., Rosen, 2000) indicate that change processes (e.g., interventions and their mechanisms) are differentially effective, depending on the client's stage of change. For example, individuals judged to be in the contemplation stage are thought to benefit from interventions that raise their consciousness around problem behaviors, impacts, and other individuals; whereas individuals judged to be in the action stage are thought to benefit more from interventions that directly address behavioral processes (e.g ., counterconditioning and contingency management).

Empirical Support

Despite being the focus of a large theoretical and clinical literature, empirical research on psychotherapy integration has been slow to progress.

However, evidence has begun to accumulate in recent years for factors that support and/or contribute to integration and treatments that fall under most of the major categories of psychotherapy integration (see Schottenbauer, Glass, & Arnkoff, 2005 for a comprehensive review).

A number of common factors have also received empirical support (see Weinberger & Rasco, 2007). The therapeutic relationship, for example, has been extensively studied across a number of treatment approaches and specific disorders and has been shown to be a robust and consistent predictor of positive treatment outcome (Castonguay, Constantino, & Grosse Holtforth, 2006; Martin, Garske, & Davis, 2000). Empirical support has also been found for client expectancies of treatment effectiveness (Baskin, Tierney, Minami, & Wampold, 2003; Frank, Nash, Stone, & Imber, 1963; Howard, Kopta, Krause, & Orlinsky, 1986; Kirsch & Henry, 1977). Although the area of focus and the specific techniques used may differ between approaches, exposure is another common therapeutic factor with significant research support (Franklin & Foa, 2002; Heimberg et al., 1990; Roth & Fonagy, 2005).

In terms of eclecticism, the work of Beutler and colleagues has provided useful guidelines for prescribing specific types of interventions for certain types of clients (e.g., clients with high vs. low levels of reactance), leading to the development of systematic treatment selection and prescriptive psychotherapy. This system has accumulated the greatest empirical support for client–treatment matching (see Beutler et al., 2005 for a review).

Several treatments developed from an assimilative integration approach have garnered empirical support. For example, Greenberg and colleagues developed a process–experiential therapy (EFT) that has been tested in both individual and couples modalities. This therapy integrates process-directive and experiential interventions for specific client markers within a person-centered framework (Greenberg & Watson, 1998) and has been shown to be effective in the treatment of depression. Also from an assimilative integration perspective, in an effort to increase the effectiveness of a previously supported treatment, Castonguay designed and tested an integrative cognitive treatment for depression (ICT; Castonguay et al., 2004), which uses techniques from humanistic and interpersonal therapies to help repair alliance ruptures in traditional cognitive therapy, and has been shown to be superior to a waitlist control group in a randomized trial for depression.

In a replication trial, Constantino et al. (2008) found that clients in the ICT condition evidenced greater post-treatment improvement than did clients who received traditional cognitive therapy, and they also reported higher alliance and therapist empathy ratings across treatment. Other examples of integrative treatments with some empirical support include cognitive-behavioral assimilative therapy for generalized anxiety disorder (Newman, Castonguay, Borkovec, Fisher, & Nordberg, 2008), and mindfulness-based cognitive therapy for depression (MBCT; Segal, Teasdale, & Williams, 2002).

Examples of theoretically driven integrative treatments with empirical support also exist (e.g., Ryle's [2005] cognitive analytic therapy). Transtheoretical psychotherapy, based on the Transtheoretical Model (TTM; Prochaska & DiClemente, 2005), as mentioned, posits five stages of change (precontemplative, contemplation, preparation, action, and maintenance), with specific processes of change and related interventions to be used at specific stages. The transtheoretical psychotherapy model has been applied and tested in a variety of problem areas, for both health behaviors and mental disorders, and has been shown to be significantly related to change processes and outcome (Prochaska & DiClemente, 2005; Schottenbauer et al., 2005). Perhaps the most well-studied integrative treatment to date is Linehan's dialectic-behavior therapy (DBT) for borderline personality disorder. A number of process findings and efficacy studies have been conducted that lend support to this treatment and its assumptions regarding client change (Linehan, Cochran, & Cochran, 2001).

Conclusion

Psychotherapy is a vibrant domain of theoretical, applied, and empirical knowledge that has benefited over more than a century from contributions of many mental health professions (e.g., psychology, psychiatry, social work). The vitality of this field is reflected by a large variety of psychotherapeutic treatments which, as we suggested in this chapter, can be clustered into four major contemporary orientations (psychodynamic, cognitive-behavioral, humanistic, and systemic) and one movement aimed at fostering different pathways of integration between them.

Each of the four specific systems of therapy is based on a model of human health and maladaptive functioning and each emphasizes a number of interventions and mechanisms of change to foster and explain the process of therapy. Consistent with an argument made almost three decades ago (Goldfried, 1980), not many similarities can be found in the conceptual models underlying these four major systems. However, also in line with Goldfried (1980), a number of strategies or principles of intervention appear to cut across most if not all of them, such as the importance of establishing a therapeutic relationship and the facilitation of new and corrective experiences. As we described earlier, these principles of change, along with other common factors, reflect one of the current pathways of integration.

All of the contemporary approaches to psychotherapy, "pure-form" or integrative, have also generated research. The willingness of psychotherapy scholars to submit their claims of success (and some of their hypotheses regarding the process of change) to empirical investigation has provided the field with some solid scientific foundations. But we would like to argue that we are only witnessing the beginning of psychotherapy as a scientific approach. Consistent with its epistemological bases, and reflecting its predominance in the list of ESTs, CBT has demonstrated a longer and more systematic commitment to empirical scrutiny than other orientations. The lag between clinical (and/or theoretical) contributions and research support seems to be particularly wide within the integration movement (Castonguay et al., 2003). This is most unfortunate, not only because most therapists (at least in North America) currently identify themselves as integrationists, but also, as Goldfried (2009) recently reminded us, SEPI was created to facilitate the integration of different schools of therapy, as well as the integration of research and practice.

If attended to carefully, however, the unfortunate level of enthusiasm toward research in psychotherapy integration can actually address what has been viewed by many as the most important problem of the field of contemporary psychotherapy: The shaky state of the Scientist-Practitioner model upon which it is assumed to rest. As argued elsewhere, clinicians are more likely to pay attention to research findings if they are involved in research (Castonguay in Lampropoulos et al., 2002); and since a large number of clinicians are integrative in their approach, one could expect that their increased engagement in research will lead to more empirical attention given to integrative issues. To maximize the probability of this occurring, however, we would argue that clinicians need to be involved in all aspects of research—its design, implementation, and the dissemination of results (rather than simply being asked to hand out questionnaires or apply a treatment protocol, as is too frequently the case in current research).

In other words, for psychotherapy to reach its full potential as a scientific field, we believe that it should cease its almost exclusive reliance on what has been called "empirical imperialism" (Castonguay, in Lampropoulous et al., 2002), where researchers (most of them seeing only a few clients) dictate what to study and how to study it. A full and equal collaboration between researchers and clinicians, as aimed at by recent practice research networks (see Castonguay et al., in press a, b), may instead be a more fruitful way to provide the field with clinically relevant and scientifically rigorous research.

References

Abramson, L. Y., Metalsky, G. I., & Alloy, L. B. (1989). Hopelessness depression: A theory-based subtype of depression. *Psychological Review, 96,* 358–372.

Abramson, L. Y., Seligman, M. P., & Teasdale, J. D. (1978). Learned helplessness in humans: Critique and reformulation. *Journal of Abnormal Psychology, 87,* 49–74.

Akkerman, K., Lewin, T. J., & Carr, V. J. (1999). Long-term changes in defense style among patients recovering from major depression. *The Journal of Nervous and Mental Disease, 187,* 80–87.

Alexander, F., & French, T. M. (1946). *Psychoanalytic therapy.* New York: The Ronald Press Company.

Anderson, H. (2003). Postmodern social construction therapies. In T. L. Sexton, G. R. Weeks, & M. S. Robbins (Eds.), *Handbook of family therapy* (pp. 125–146). New York: Brunner-Routledge.

Anderson, H., & Goolishian, H. A. (1988). Human systems as linguistic sysems: Evolving ideas about the implications for theory and practice. *Family Process, 27,* 371–393.

Barber, J. P., Connolley, M. B., Crits-Christoph, P., Gladis, L., & Siqueland, L. (2000). Alliance predicts patients' outcome beyond in-treatment change in symptoms. *Journal of Consulting and Clinical Psychology, 68,* 1027–1032.

Barlow, D. H. (1988). *Anxiety and its disorders: The nature and treatment of anxiety and panic.* New York: Guilford Press.

Barlow, D. H. (2002). *Anxiety and its disorders: The nature and treatment of anxiety and panic* (2nd ed.). New York: Guilford Press.

Barlow, D. H. (Ed.). (2008). *Clinical handbook of psychological disorders* (4th ed.) New York, NY: Guilford Press.

Baskin, T. W., Tierney, S. C., Minami, T., & Wampold, B. E. (2003). Establishing specificity in psychotherapy: A meta-analysis of structural equivalence of placebo controls. *Journal of Consulting and Clinical Psychology, 71,* 973–979.

Bateson, G., Jackson, D. D., Haley, J., & Weakland, J. (1956). Toward a theory of schizophrenia. *Behavioral Science, 1,* 251–264.

Baucom, B., Christensen, A., & Yi, J. C. (2005). Integrative behavioral couple therapy. In J. L. Lebow (Ed.), *Handbook of clinical family therapy* (pp. 329–352). Hoboken, NJ: John Wiley & Sons.

Baudry, E. (1991). The relevance of the analyst's character and attitudes to his work. *Journal of the American Psychoanalytic Association, 39,* 917–938.

Beck, A. T. (1976). *Cognitive therapy and the emotional disorders.* New York: New American Library.

Beck A. T. (1996). Beyond belief: A theory of modes, personality and psychopathology. In P. M. Salkovskis (Ed.), *Frontiers of cognitive therapy* (pp. 1–25). New York: Guilford Press.

Beck, A. T., Rush, A. J., Shaw, B. F., & Emery, G. (1979). *Cognitive therapy of depression.* New York: The Guilford Press.

Becvar, D. S. (2003). Eras of epistemology: A survey of family therapy thinking and theorizing. In T. L. Sexton, G. R. Weeks, & M. S. Robbins (Eds.), *Handbook of family therapy* (pp. 3–20). New York: Brunner-Routledge.

Beevers, C. G. (2005). Cognitive vulnerability to depression: A dual process model. *Clinical Psychology Review, 25,* 975–1002.

Beutler, L. E., Consoli, A. J., & Lane, G. (2005). In J. C. Norcross, & M. R. Goldfried (Eds.), *Handbook of psychotherapy integration* (2nd ed., pp. 121–143). New York: Basic Books.

Boswell, J. F., Nelson, D. L., Nordberg, S. S., McAleavey, A. A., & Castonguay, L. G. (2010). Competency in integrative psychotherapy: Perspectives on training and supervision. *Psychotherapy: Theory, Research, Practice, Training, 47,* 3–11.

Bradley, B., & Furrow, J. L. (2004). Toward a mini-theory of the blamer softening event: Tracking the moment-by-moment process. *Journal of Marital and Family Therapy, 30,* 1–12.

Brestan, E. V., & Eyberg, S. M. (1998). Effective psychosocial treatments of conduct-disordered children and adolescents: 29 years, 82 studies, and 5,272 kids. *Journal of Clinical Child and Adolescent Psychology, 27,* 180–189.

Breuer, J., & Freud, S. (1893). *Studies on hysteria.* Standard edition Vol. 2 (pp. 3–305).

Brewin, C. R. (2006). Understanding cognitive behaviour therapy: A retrieval competition account. *Behaviour Research and Therapy, 44,* 765–784.

Bridges, M. (2006). Activating the corrective emotional experience. *Journal of Clinical Psychology, 62,* 551–568.

Bryant, R. A., & Guthrie, R. M. (2007). Maladaptive self-appraisals before trauma exposure predict posttraumatic stress disorder. *Journal of Consulting and Clinical Psychology, 75,* 812–815.

Buber, M. (1978). *I and thou.* New York: Scribner.

Burns, D. D., & Nolen-Hoeksema, S. (1992). Therapeutic empathy and recovery from depression in cognitive-behavioral therapy: A structural equation model. *Journal of Consulting and Clinical Psychology, 60,* 441–449.

Busch, F. N., Rudden, M., & Shapiro, T. (2004). *Psychodynamic treatment of depression.* Washington, DC: American Psychiatric Publishing.

Butler A. C., Chapman J. E., Forman E. M., & Beck A. T. (2006). The empirical status of cognitive-behavioral therapy: A review of meta-analyses. *Clinical Psychology Review, 26,* 17–31.

Castonguay, L. G. (1997). Support in psychotherapy: A common factor in need of empirical data, conceptual clarification, and clinical input. *Journal of Psychotherapy Integration, 7,* 99–103.

Castonguay, L. G. (2000). A common factors approach to psychotherapy training. *Journal of Psychotherapy Integration, 10,* 263–282.

Castonguay, L. G., & Beutler, L. E. (Eds.) (2006). *Principles of therapeutic change that work.* New York: Oxford Press.

Castonguay, L. G., Boswell, J. F., Zack, S., Baker, S., Boutselis, M., Chiswick, N., et al. (in press a). Helpful and hindering events in psychotherapy: A practice research network study. *Psychotherapy: Theory, Research, Practice, Training.*

Castonguay, L. G., Constantino, M. J., & Grosse Holtforth, M. (2006). The working alliance: Where are we and where should we go? *Psychotherapy: Theory, Research, Practice, Training, 43,* 271–279.

Castonguay, L. G., Constantino, M. J., McAleavey, A. A., & Goldfried, M. R. (in press). The alliance in cognitive-behavioral therapy. In J. P. Barber & J. C. Muran (Eds.), *The therapeutic alliance: An evidence-based approach to practice and training.* New York: Guilford Press.

Castonguay, L. G., & Goldfried, M. R. (1994). Psychotherapy integration: An idea whose time has come. *Applied and Preventive Psychology, 3,* 159–172.

Castonguay, L. G., Goldfried, M. R., Wiser, S., Raue, P. J., and Hayes, A. H. (1996). Predicting outcome in cognitive therapy for depression: A comparison of unique and common factors. *Journal of Consulting and Clinical Psychology, 64,* 497–504.

Castonguay, L., Nelson, D., Boutselis, M,. Chiswick, N., Damer, D., Hemmelstein, N., et al. (in press b). Clinicians and/or researchers? A qualitative analysis of therapists' experiences in a Practice Research Network. *Psychotherapy: Theory, Research, Practice, Training.*

Castonguay, L. G., Newman, M. G., Borkovec, T. D., Grosse Holtforth, M., & Maramba, G. G. (2005). Cognitive-behavioral assimilative integration. In J. C. Norcross and M. R. Goldfried (Eds.), *Handbook of psychotherapy integration* (2nd ed., pp. 241–260). New York: Basic Books.

Castonguay, L. G., Reid, J. J., Halperin, G. S., & Goldfried, M. R. (2003). Psychotherapy integration. In G. Stricker, & T. A. Widiger (Eds.), *Comprehensive handbook of Psychology, Vol. 8: Clinical psychology.* New York: Wiley.

Castonguay, L. G., Schut, A. J., Aikins, D., Constantino, M. J., Laurenceau, J. P., Bologh, L., & Burns, D. D. (2004). Repairing alliance ruptures in cognitive therapy: A preliminary investigation of an integrative therapy for depression. *Journal of Psychotherapy Integration, 14,* 4–20.

Christensen, A., Doss, B. D., & Atkins, D. C. (2005). A science of couple therapy: For what should we seek empirical support? In W. M. Pinsof, & J. L. Lebow (Eds.), *Family psychology: The art of the science* (pp. 43–63). New York: Oxford University Press.

Christensen, A., & Jacobson, N. S. (1998). *Acceptance and change in couple therapy: A therapist's guide to transforming relationships.* New York: Norton.

Clark, D. M. (1986). A cognitive approach to panic. *Behaviour Research and Therapy, 24,* 461–470.

Clark, D. M., & Wells, A. (1995). A cognitive model of social phobia. In R. Heimberg, M. Liebowitz, D. A. Hope, & F. Scheiner (Eds.), *Social phobia: Diagnosis, assessment, and treatment* (pp. 69–93). New York: Guilford Press.

Colapinto, J. (1991). Structural family therapy. In A. S. Gurman, & D. P. Kniskern (Eds.), *Handbook of family therapy: Vol. 2* (pp. 417–443). New York: Brunner/Mazel.

Coleman D. (2005). Psychodynamic and cognitive mechanisms of change in adult therapy: A pilot study. *Bulletin of the Menninger Clinic, 69,* 206–219.

Connolly, M. B., Crits-Christoph, P., Shappell, S., Barber, J. P., Luborsky, L., Shaffer, C. (1999). Relation of transference interpretations to outcome in the early session of brief supportive-expressive psychotherapy. *Psychotherapy Research, 9,* 485–495.

Constantino, M. J., Marnell, M., Haile, A. J., Kanther-Sista, S. N., Wolman, K., Zappert, L., & Arnow, B. A. (2008). Integrative cognitive therapy for depression: A randomized pilot comparison. *Psychotherapy: Theory, Research, Practice, Training, 45,* 122–134.

Cordova, J. V., Jacobson, N. S., & Christensen, A. (1998). Acceptance versus change interventions in behavioral couple therapy: Impact on couples' in-session communications. *Journal of Marital and Family Therapy, 24,* 437–455.

Coulehan, R., Friedlander, M. L., & Heatherington, L. (1998). Transforming narratives: A change event in constructivist family therapy. *Family Process, 37,* 17–33.

Crits-Christoph, P., Cooper, A., & Luborsky, L. (1988). The accuracy of therapists' interpretations and the outcome of dynamic psychotherapy. *Journal of Consulting and Clinical Psychology, 56, 490*–495.

Crits-Christoph, P., Crits-Christoph, K., Wolf-Pacio, D., Fichter, M. & Rudick, D. (1995). Brief supportive-expressive psychodynamic therapy for generalized anxiety disorder. In J. P Barber, & Crits-Christoph (Eds.) *Dynamic therapies for psychiatric disorders (Axis-I)* (pp. 43–83). New York: Basic Books.

Dalgleish, T. (2004). Cognitive theories of posttraumatic stress disorder: The evolution of multi-representational theorizing. *Psychological Bulletin, 130,* 228–260.

de Jonghe, E., Rijnierse, P. & Janssen, R. (1991). Aspects of the analytic relationship. *International Journal of Psycho-Analysis, 72,* 693–707.

de Shazer, S. (1985). *Keys to solution in brief therapy.* New York: Norton.

de Shazer, S. (1991). *Putting difference to work.* New York: Norton.

Diamond, G. M., Diamond, G. S., & Hogue, A. (2007). Attachment-based family therapy: Adherence and differentiation. *Journal of Marital and Family Therapy, 33,* 177–191.

Diamond, G., Siqueland, L., & Diamond, G. M. (2003). Attachment-based family therapy for depressed adolescents: Programmatic treatment development. *Clinical Child and Family Psychology Review, 6,* 107–127.

Dollard, J., & Miller, N. (1950). *Personality and psychotherapy: An analysis in terms of learning, thinking, and culture.* New York: McGraw-Hill.

Ehlers, A., & Clark, D. M. (2000). A cognitive model of post-traumatic stress disorder. *Behaviour Research and Therapy, 38,* 319–345.

Elliott, R., & Greenberg, L. S. (1997). Multiple voices in process-experiential therapy: Dialogues between aspects of the self. *Journal of Psychotherapy Integration, 7,* 225–239.

Elliott, R., Greenberg, L. S., & Lietaer, G. (2005). Research on experiential psychotherapies. In M. Lambert, Q. E. Bergin, & S. L. Garfield (Eds.), *Handbook of psychotherapy and behavior change* (5th ed., p. 493–539). New York: Wiley & Sons.

Ellis, A. (1962). *Reason and emotion in psychotherapy.* New York: Lyle Stuart.

Erikson, E. H. (1963). *Childhood and society* (2nd ed.). New York: Norton.

Fairburn, C. G., Cooper, Z., & Shafran, R. (2003). Cognitive behaviour therapy for eating disorders: A "transdiagnostic" theory and treatment. *Behaviour Research and Therapy, 41,* 509–528.

Falloon, I. R. H. (1991). Behavioral family therapy. In A. S. Gurman & D. P. Kniskern (Eds.), *Handbook of family therapy,* Vol. 2 (pp. 65–95). New York: Brunner/Mazel.

Fisch, R., Weakland, J. H., & Segal, L. (1982). *The tactics of change: Doing therapy briefly.* San Francisco: Jossey-Bass.

Foa, E. B., Huppert, J. D., & Cahill, S. P. (2006). Update on emotional processing theory. In B. O. Rothbaum, B. O. (Ed.), *The nature and treatment of pathological anxiety* (pp. 3–24). New York: Guilford Press.

Foa, E. B., & Kozak, M. J. (1986). Emotional processing of fear: Exposure to corrective information. *Psychological Bulletin, 99,* 20–35.

Fonagy, P. (2002). Understanding of mental states, mother-infant interaction, and the development of the self. In J. M. Maldonado-Durán (Ed.), *Infant and toddler mental health: Models of clinical intervention with infants and their families* (pp. 57–74). Arlington, VA: American Psychiatric Publishing.

Frank, J. D. (1961). *Persuasion and healing.* Baltimore: Johns Hopkins University Press.

Frank, J. D., Nash, E. H., Stone, A. R., & Imber, S. D. (1963). Immediate and long-term symptomatic course of psychiatric outpatients. *American Journal of Psychiatry, 120,* 429–439.

Franklin, M. E. & Foa, E. B. (2002). Cognitive-behavioral treatments for obsessive compulsive disorder. In P. E. Nathan & J. M. Gorman (Eds.), *A guide to treatments that work* (2nd ed., pp. 367–385). New York: Oxford University Press.

French, T. M. (1933). Interrelations between psychoanalysis and the experimental work of Pavlov. *Americana Journal of Psychiatry, 89,* 1165–1203.

Freud, S. (1905). Fragment of an analysis of a case of hysteria. In J. E. Strachey's (Ed. and Trans.), *The standard edition of the complete psychological works of Sigmund Freud* (Vol. 21). London: Hogarth Press.

Freidlander, M. L., & Tuason, M. T. (2000). Processes and outcomes in couples and family therapy. In S. Brown & R. Lent (Eds.), *Handbook of counseling psychology* (3rd ed.; pp. 797–824). New York: Wiley.

Frijda, N. H. (1986). *The emotions.* New York: Cambridge University Press.

Garfield, S. L. (1980). *Psychotherapy: An eclectic approach.* New York: Wiley.

Garfield, S. L., & Kurtz, R. (1976). Clinical psychologists in the 1970s. *American Psychologist, 31,* 1–9.

Garfield, S. L., & Kurtz, R. (1977). A study of eclectic views. *Journal of Consulting and Clinical Psychology, 45,* 78–83.

Gendlin, E. T. (1962). *Experiencing and the creation of meaning.* New York: Free Press of Glencoe.

Gendlin, E. (1996). *Focusing-oriented psychotherapy: A manual of the experiential method.* New York: Guildford Press.

Goldfried, M. R. (1980). Toward the delineation of therapeutic change principles. *American Psychologist, 35,* 991–999.

Goldfried, M. R. (2005). A history of psychotherapy integration. In J. C. Norcross and M. R. Goldfried (Eds.), *Handbook of psychotherapy integration* (2nd ed., pp. 24–60). New York: Basic Books.

Goldfried, M. R. (2009). Making evidence-based practice work: The future of psychotherapy integration. *Psychotherapy Bulletin, 44,* 25–28.

Goldfried, M. R., and Castonguay, L. G. (1993). Behavior therapy: redefining clinical strengths and limitations. *Behavior Therapy, 24,* 505–526.

Goldfried, M. R., & Davison, G. C. (1976). *Clinical behavior therapy.* New York: Holt, Rinehart, & Winston.

Goldfried, M. R., & Padawer, W. (1982). Current status and future directions in psychotherapy. In M. R. Goldfried (Ed.), *Converging themes in psychotherapy* (pp. 3–49). New York: Springer.

Goldfried, M. R., Raue, P. J., & Castonguay, L. G. (1998). The therapeutic focus in significant sessions of master therapists: A comparison of cognitive-behavioral and psychodynamic-interpersonal interventions. *Journal of Consulting and Clinical Psychology, 66,* 803–811.

Goldman, R. N., Greenberg, L. S., & Pos, A. E. (2005). Depth of emotional experience and outcome. *Psychotherapy Research, 15,* 248–260.

Greenberg, L. S. (2002). *Emotion-focused therapy: Coaching clients to work through their feelings.* Washington, DC: American Psychological Association.

Greenberg, L. (2008). The clinical application of emotion in therapy. In M. Lewis, J. M. Haviland Jones, & L. Feldman Barret (Eds.), *Handbook of emotions* (pp. 88–101). New York: Guilford Press.

Greenberg, L. S., Elliott, R., & Lietnaer, G. (1994). Research on experiential psychotherapies. In A. E. Bergin, & S. L. Garfield (Eds.), *Handbook of psychotherapy and behavior change* (4th ed., pp. 509–539). Oxford, UK: John Wiley & Sons.

Greenberg, L. S., Ford, C. L., Alden, L., & Johnson, S. M. (1993). In-session change in emotionally focused therapy. *Journal of Consulting and Clinical Psychology, 61,* 78–84.

Greenberg L. S. & Goldman R. N. (2008). *Emotion-focused couples therapy: The dynamics of emotion, love and power.* Washington, DC: American Psychological Association Press.

Greenberg, L. S., & Goldman, R. N. (2007). Case formulation in emotion-focused therapy. In T. Ells (Ed.), *Handbook of psychotherapy case formulation* (pp. 379–412). New York: Guilford Press.

Greenberg, L. S., & Johnson, S. M. (1988). *Emotionally focused therapy for couples.* New York: Guilford Press.

Greenberg, L. S., & Paivio, S. C. (1997). *Working with emotions in psychotherapy.* New York: Guildford.

Greenberg, L. S., & Pascual-Leone, J. (1995). A dialectical constructivist approach to experiential change. In R. Neimeyer, & M. Mahoney (Eds.), *Constructivism in Psychotherapy* (pp. 169–194). Washington, DC: American Psychological Association Press.

Greenberg, L. S., & Pascual-Leone, J. (2001). A dialectical constructivist view of the creation of personal meaning. *Journal of Constructivist Psychology, 14,* 165–186.

Greenberg, L. S., Rice, L. N., & Elliott, R. K. (1993). *Facilitating emotional change: The moment-by-moment process.* New York: Guilford Press.

Greenberg, L. S., & Safran, J. D. (1986). *Emotion in psychotherapy: Affect, cognition, and the process of change.* New York: Guilford Press.

Greenberg, L. S., & Watson, J. C. (1998). Experiential therapy of depression: Differential effects of client-centered relationship conditions and process-experiential interventions. *Psychotherapy Research, 8,* 210–224.

Greenberg, L. S., & Watson, J. C. (2006). *Emotion-focused therapy for depression.* Washington, DC: American Psychological Association.

Greenberg, L. S., Watson, J. C., & Lietaer, G. (Eds.). (1998). *Handbook of experiential psychotherapy.* New York: Guilford Press.

Greenberg, L. S. & van Balen. (1998). Theory of Experience Centered Therapy. In L. S. Greenberg, J. C. Watson, & G. Lietaer, (Eds.), *Handbook of experiential psychotherapy: Foundations and differential treatment,* (pp. 28–57). New York: Guilford Press.

Gross, J. J. (1998). The emerging field of emotion regulation: An integrative review. *Review of General Psychology, 2,* 271–299.

Gurman, A. S., & Jacobson, N. S. (Eds.). (2002). *Clinical handbook of couple therapy.* New York: Guilford Press.

Haley, J. (1963). *Strategies of psychotherapy.* New York: Grune & Stratton.

Haley, J. (1973). *Uncommon therapy: The psychiatric techniques of Milton H. Erickson, M. D.* New York: Norton.

Harvey, A., Watkins, E., Mansell, W., & Shafran, R. (2004). *Cognitive behavioural processes across psychological disorders.* New York: Oxford University Press.

Hatcher, R. L., & Barends, A. W. (2006). How a return to theory could help alliance research. *Psychotherapy: Theory, Research, Practice, Training, 43,* 292–299.

Hayes, A. H., Castonguay, L. G., & Goldfried, M. R. (1996). The effectiveness of targeting the vulnerability factors of depression in cognitive therapy. *Journal of Consulting and Clinical Psychology, 64,* 623–627.

Heatherington, L., Friedlander, M. L., & Greenberg, L. (2005). Change process research in couple and family therapy: Methodological challenges and opportunities. *Journal of Family Psychology, 19,* 18–27.

Heimberg, R. G., Dodge, C. S., Hope, D. A., Kennedy, C. R., Zallo, L., & Becker, R. E. (1990). Cognitive-behavioral group treatment for social phobia: Comparison to a credible placebo control. *Cognitive Therapy and Research, 14,* 1–23.

Hendriks, M. N. (2002). Focusing-oriented/experiential psychotherapy. In D. Cain (Ed.), *Humanistic psychotherapy: Handbook of research and practice* (pp. 221–256). Washington, DC: American Psychological Association.

Henggeler, S. W., Schoenwald, S. K., Borduin, C. M., Rowland, M. D., & Cunningham, P. B. (1998). *Multisystemic treatment of antisocial behavior in children and adolescents.* New York: Guilford.

Hersoug, A. G., Sexton, H. C., & Hoglend, P. (2002). Contribution of defensive functioning to the quality of working alliance and psychotherapy outcome. *American Journal of Psychotherapy, 56,* 539–554.

Høglend, P., Amlo, S., Marble, A., Bogwald, K. P., Sorbye, O., Sjaastad, M. C., et al. (2006). Analysis of the patient-therapist relationship in dynamic psychotherapy: An experimental study of transference interpretations. *American Journal Psychiatry, 163,* 1739–1746.

Hollon, S. D., Stewart, M. O., & Strunk, D. (2006). Cognitive behavior therapy has enduring effects in the treatment of depression and anxiety. *Annual Review of Psychology, 57,* 285–315.

Horigian, V. E., Suarez-Morales, L., Robbins, M. S., Zarate, M., Mayorga, C. C., Mitrani, V. B, et al. (2005). Brief strategic family therapy for adolescents with behavior problems. In J. L. Lebow (Ed.) *Handbook of clinical family therapy* (pp. 73–102). Hoboken, NJ: Wiley.

Howard, K. I., Kopta, S. M., Krause, M. S., & Orlinsky, D. E. (1986). The dose-effect relationship in psychotherapy. *American Psychologist, 41,* 159–164.

Huppert, J. D., Foa, E. B., McNally, R. J., & Cahill, S. P. (2008). The role of cognition in stress and fear-circuitry disorders. In G. Andrews, D. Charney, P. Sirovatka, & D. A. Regier (Eds.) *Stress-induced and fear circuitry disorders: Refining the research agenda for DSM-5* (pp. 193–212). Arlington, VA, American Psychiatric Association.

Ingram, R. E. (2007). Introduction to the special section on cognitive processes and psychotherapy. *Journal of Consulting and Clinical Psychology, 75,* 359–362.

Jacobson, N. S., & Margolin, G. (1979). *Marital therapy: Strategies based on social learning and behavior exchange principles.* New York: Brunner/Mazel.

Johnson, S. M. (1996). *Creating connections: The practice of emotionally-focused couple therapy.* New York: Brunner-Mazel.

Johnson, S. & Greenberg, L. S. (Eds.). (1994). *The heart of the matter. Emotion in marriage and marital therapy.* New York: Bruner-Mazel.

Johnson, S. M., & Greenberg, L. S. (1985). Differential effects of experiential and problem solving interventions in resolving marital conflicts. *Journal of Consulting and Clinical Psychology, 53,* 175–184.

Johnson, S., Bradley, B., Furrow, J., Lee, A., Palmer, G., Tiley, D., & Wooley, S. (2005). *Becoming an emotionally focused couple therapist: The workbook.* New York: Routledge.

Kaslow, F. W. (Ed.). (1996). *Handbook of relational diagnosis and dysfunctional family patterns.* New York: Wiley.

Kaslow, F., & Patterson, T. (2006) Relational diagnosis: A retrospective synopsis. *Contemporary Family Therapy, 28,* 269–284.

Kazantzis, N., Deane, F. P., Ronan, K. R. (2000). Homework assignments in cognitive and behavioral therapy: A meta-analysis. *Clinical Psychology: Science & Practice, 7,* 189–202.

Keijsers, G. P. J., Schaap, C. P. D. R, & Hoogduin, C. A. L. (2000). The impact of interpersonal patient and therapist behavior on outcome in cognitive-behavioral therapy. *Behavior Modification, 24,* 264–297.

Kirsch, I., & Henry, D. (1977). Extinction vs. credibility in the desensitization of speech anxiety. *Journal of Consulting and Clinical Psychology, 45,* 1052–1059.

Lang, P. J. (1977). Imagery in therapy: An information processing analysis of fear. *Behavior Therapy, 8,* 862–886.

Lam, D. H. (1991). Psychosocial family intervention in schizophrenia: A review of empirical studies. *Psychological Medicine, 21,* 423–441.

Lampropulous, G. K., Goldfried, M. R., Castonguay, L. G., Lambert, M. J., Stiles, W. B., Nestoros, J. N. (2002). What kind of research can we realistically expect from the practitioner? *Journal of Clinical Psychology, 58,* 1241–1264.

Lazarus, A. A. (1967). In support of technical eclecticism. *Psychological Reports, 21,* 415–416.

Lazarus, A. A. (2005). *Multimodal therapy.* In J. C. Norcross and M. R. Goldfried (Eds.), *Handbook of psychotherapy integration* (2nd ed., pp. 105–120). New York: Basic Books.

Lebow, J. (2005). *Handbook of clinical family therapy.* New York: Wiley.

Lecomte, C. (1987). Mythes et realites de l'eclectisme en psychotherapie. In C. Lecomte & L. G. Castonguay (Eds.), *Rapprochement et integration en psychotherapy: Psychanalyse, behaviorisme, et humanisme* (pp. 23–38). Chicoutimi, Quebec: Gaetan Morin.

Liechsenring, F. & Leibing, E. (2003). The effectiveness of psychodynamic therapy and cognitive behavior therapy in the treatment of personality disorders: A meta-analysis. *American Journal of Psychiatry, 160,* 1223–1232.

Leichsenring, F., Rabung, S., & Leibing, R. (2004). The efficacy of short-term psychodynamic psychotherapy in specific psychiatric disorders: A meta-analysis. *Archives of General Psychiatry, 61,* 1208–1216.

Leichsenring, F., Beutel, M., & Leibing, E. (2007). Psychodynamic psychotherapy for social phobia: A treatment manual based on supportive-expressive therapy. *Bulletin of the Menninger Clinic, 71,* 56–83.

Levy, K. L., Meehan, K. B., Kelly, K. M., Reynoso, J. S., Weber, M., Clarkin, J. F., et al. (2006). Change in attachment patterns and reflective functioning in a randomized control trial of transference-focused psychotherapy for borderline personality disorder. *Journal of Consulting and Clinical Psychology, 74,* 1027–1040.

Liddle, H. A. (1995). Conceptual and clinical dimensions of a multidimensional multisystems engagement strategy in family-based adolescent treatment. *Psychotherapy: Theory, Research, Practice, Training, 32*, 39–58.

Lifson, L. L. (Ed.). (1996). *Understanding therapeutic action: Psychodynamic concepts of cure*. London: The Analytic Press.

Linehan, M. M. (1993). *Cognitive behavioral treatment of borderline personality disorder*. New York: Guilford Press.

Linehan, M. M., Cochran, B. N., & Cochran, C. A. (2001). Dialectical behavior therapy for borderline personality disorder. In D. Barlow (Ed.), *Clinical handbook of psychological disorders: A step-by-step treatment manual* (3rd ed., pp. 470–522). New York: Guilford Press.

Luborsky, L. (1984). *Principles of psychoanalytic psychotherapy: A manual for supportive-expressive treatment*. New York: Basic Books.

Luborsky, L., Mark, D., Hole, A. V., Popp, C., Goldsmith, B., & Cacciola, J. (1995). Supportive-expressive psychotherapy of depression, a time-limited version. In J. P. Barber, & Crits-Christoph (Eds.), *Dynamic therapies for psychiatric disorders (Axis-I)* (pp. 13–42). New York: Basic Books.

Madanes, C. (1981). *Strategic family therapy*. San Francisco: Jossey-Bass.

Mahrer, A. (2005). Experiential psychotherapy. In R. J. Corsini & D. Wedding (Eds.), *Current psychotherapies* (pp. 439–474). Belmont, CA: Thomson/Brooks/Cole.

Martin, D. J., Garske, J. P., & Davis, M. K. (2000). Relation of the therapeutic alliance with outcome and other variables. A meta-analytic review. *Journal of Consulting and Clinical Psychology, 68*, 438–450.

Maslow, A. H. (1954). *Motivation and personality*. New York: Harper.

Mathews, A., & Mackintosh, B. (1998). A cognitive model of selective processing in anxiety, *Cognitive Therapy and Research, 22*, 539–560.

Mathews, A., & MacLeod, C. (2005). Cognitive vulnerability to emotional disorders. *Annual Review of Clinical Psychology, 1*, 167–195.

McCullough, J. P Jr. (2003). *Treatment for chronic depression: Cognitive Behavioral Analysis System of Psychotherapy (CBASP)*. New York: Guilford Press.

McWilliams, N. (2004). *Psychoanalytic psychotherapy: A practitioner's guide*. New York: Guilford Press.

Mearns, D., & Thorne, B. (1988). *Person-centered counseling in action*. Thousand Oaks, CA: Sage Publications.

Meichenbaum, D. (1977). *Cognitive behavior modification: An integrative approach*. New York: Plenum Press.

Messer, S. B. (2001). Introduction to the special issue on assimilative integration. *Journal of Psychotherapy Integration, 11*, 1–4.

Milrod, B. L., Busch, F. N., Cooper, A. M. & Shapiro, T. (1997). *Manual of panic-focused psychodynamic psychotherapy*. Washington, DC: American Psychiatric Press.

Mineka, S., & Zinbarg, R. (2006). A contemporary learning theory perspective on the etiology of anxiety disorders: It's not what you thought it was. *American Psychologist, 61*, 10–26.

Minuchin, S. (1974). *Families and family therapy*. Cambridge, MA: Harvard University Press.

Miklowitz, D. J., George, E. L., Richards, J. A., Simoneau, T. L. & Suddath, R. L. (2003). A randomized study of family-focused psychoeducation and pharmacotherapy in the outpatient management of bipolar disorder. *Archives of General Psychiatry, 60*, 904–912.

Mogg, K. & Bradley, B. P. (1998). A cognitive-motivational analysis of anxiety. *Behaviour Research and Therapy, 36*, 809–848.

Moore, B. C. (2005). Empirically supported family and peer interventions for dual disorders. *Research on Social Work Practice, 15*, 231–245.

Mowrer, O. H. (1939). A stimulus-response analysis of anxiety and its role as a reinforcing agent. *Psychology Review, 46*, 553–565.

Nathan, P. E., & Gorman, J. M. (Eds.). (2007). *A guide to treatments that work* (3rd ed.). New York: Oxford University Press.

Newman, M. G., Castonguay, L. G., Borkovec, T. D., Fisher, A. J., & Nordberg, S. S. (2008). An open trial of integrative therapy for generalized anxiety disorder. *Psychotherapy: Theory, Research, Practice, Training, 45*, 135–147.

Newman, M. G., Erickson, T., Przeworski, A., & Dzus, E. (2003). Self-help and minimal-contact therapies for anxiety disorders: Is human contact necessary for therapeutic efficacy? *Journal of Clinical Psychology, 59*, 251–274.

Nichols, M. P. (1987). *The self in the system: Expanding the limits of family therapy*. New York: Brunner/Mazel.

Nisole, J. A. (1977). *Mise en question de la psychotherapie*. Montreal: Les editions de l'aurore.

Norcross, J. C. (2005). A primer on psychotherapy integration. In J. C. Norcross and M. R. Goldfried (Eds.), *Handbook of psychotherapy integration* (2nd ed., pp. 3–23). New York: Basic Books.

Norcross, J. C., & Goldfried, M. R. (Eds.). (1992). *Handbook of psychotherapy integration* (2nd ed.). New York: Basic Books.

Norcross, J. C., & Goldfried, M. R. (Eds.). (2005). *Handbook of psychotherapy integration* (2nd ed.). New York: Basic Books.

Norcross, J. C., Karpiak, C. P., & Lister, K. M. (2005). What's an integrationist? A study of self-identified integrative and (occasionally) eclectic psychologists. *Journal of Clinical Psychology. 61*, 1587–1594.

O'Farrell, T. J. (Ed.). (1993). *Treating alcohol problems: Marital and family interventions*. New York: Guilford.

Orlinsky, D. E., & Rønnestad, M. H. (Eds.). (2005). *How psychotherapists develop: A study of therapeutic work and professional growth*. Washington, DC: American Psychological Association.

Orlinsky, D. E., Rønnestad, M. H., Willutzki, U. (2004). Fifty year of psychotherapy process-outcome research: Continuity and change. In Lambert, M. J. (Ed.), *Handbook of psychotherapy and behavior change* (pp. 307–389). New York: John Wiley & Sons.

Paivio, S. C., & Greenberg, L. S. (1995). Resolving "unfinished business": Efficacy of experiential therapy using empty-chair dialogue. *Journal of Consulting and Clinical Psychology, 63*, 419–425.

Paivio, S. C., Hall, I. E., Holowaty, K. A. M., Jellis, J. B., & Tran, N. (2001). Imaginal confrontation for resolving child abuse issues. *Psychotherapy Research, 11*, 56–68.

Patterson, G. R. (1971). *Families: Applications of social learning to family life*. Champaign, IL: Research Press.

Pavlov, I. P. (1927). *Conditioned reflexes*. London: Oxford University Press.

Perls, F. S. (1969). *Gestalt therapy verbatim*. Mohab, UT: Real People Press.

Perls, F. S., Hefferline, R., & Goodman, P. (1951). *Gestalt therapy*. New York: Dell.

Pinsof, W. M., & Wynne, L. C. (1995). The efficacy of marital and family therapy: An empirical overview, conclusions, and recommendations. *Journal of Marital and Family Therapy, 21,* 585–613.

Power, M. J., & Dalgleish, T. (1997). *Cognition and emotion: From order to disorder.* Hove, UK: Psychology Press.

Power, M. J., & Dalgleish, T. (2008). *Cognition and emotion: From order to disorder* (2nd ed.). New York: Psychology Press.

Prochaska, J. O. (1979). *Systems of psychotherapy: A transtheoretical analysis.* Homewood, IL: Dorsey.

Prochaska, J. O., & DiClemente, C. C. (2005). The transtheoretical approach. In J. C. Norcross and M. R. Goldfried (Eds.), *Handbook of psychotherapy integration* (2nd ed., pp. 147–171). New York: Basic Books.

Rapee, R. M., & Heimberg, R. G. (1997). A cognitive-behavioural model of anxiety in social phobia. *Behaviour Research and Therapy, 35,* 741–756.

Rea, M. M., Tompson, M. C., Milowitz, D. J., Goldstein, M. J., Hwang, S. & Mintz, J. (2003). Family-focused treatment versus individual treatment for bipolar disorder: Results of a randomized clinical trial. *Journal of Consulting and Clinical Psychology, 71,* 482–492.

Reich, W. (1933). *Character analysis.* New York: Farrar, Straus, & Giroux.

Resnick, R. (1995). Gestalt therapy: Principles, prisms and perspectives. *British Gestalt Journal 4,* 3–13.

Ricoeur, P. (1970). *Freud and philosophy: An essay on interpretation* (D. Savage, Trans.). New Haven, CT: Yale University Press.

Rogers, C. R. (1951). *Client-centered therapy: Its current practice, implications, and theory.* Oxford, England: Houghton Mifflin.

Rogers, C. R. (1957). The necessary and sufficient conditions of therapeutic personality change. *Journal of Consulting Psychology, 21,* 95–103.

Rogers, C. R. (1959). Person or science? *Pastoral Psychology, 10,* 25–36.

Rogers, C. R. (1961). The place of the person in the new world of the behavioral sciences. *Personnel & Guidance Journal, 39,* 442–451.

Rosen, C. S. (2000). Is the sequencing of change processes by stage consistent across health problems? A meta-analysis. *Health Psychology, 19,* 593–604.

Rosenzweig, S. (1936). Some implicit common factors in diverse methods in psychotherapy. "At last the Dodo said, "Everybody has won and all must have prizes." *American Journal of Orthopsychiatry, 6,* 412–415.

Roth, A., & Fonagy, P. (2005). *What works for whom: A critical review of psychotherapy research* (2nd ed.). New York: Guilford.

Ruesch, J., & Bateson, G. (1968). *Communication: The social matrix of psychiatry.* New York: Norton.

Ryle, A. (2005). Cognitive analytic therapy. In J. C. Norcross and M. R. Goldfried (Eds.), *Handbook of psychotherapy integration* (2nd ed., pp. 196–217). New York: Basic Books.

Salkovskis, P. M. (1999). Understanding and treating obsessive-compulsive disorder. *Behaviour Research and Therapy, 37,* s29–s52.

Samoilov, A., & Goldfried, M. R. (2000). Role of emotion in cognitive-behavior therapy. *Clinical Psychology: Science and Practice, 7,* 373–385.

Sandell, R., Blomberg, J., & Lazar, A. (1997). When reality doesn't fit the blueprint: Doing research on psychoanalysis and long-term psychotherapy in a public health service program. *Psychotherapy Research, 7,* 333–344.

Santisteban, D. A., Szapocznik, J., Perez-Vidal, A., Kurtines, W. M., Murray, E. J., & LaPerriere, A. (1996). Engaging behavior problem drug abusing youth and their families in treatment: An investigation of the efficacy of specialized engagement interventions and factors that contribute to differential effectiveness. *Journal of Family Psychology, 10,* 35–44.

Schottenbauer, M. A., Glass, C. R., & Arnkoff, D. B. (2005). Outcome research on psychotherapy integration. In J. C. Norcross and M. R. Goldfried (Eds.), *Handbook of psychotherapy integration* (2nd ed., pp. 459–493). New York: Basic Books.

Schneider, K., & May R. (1995). *The psychology of existence: An integrative clinical perspective.* New York: McGraw Hill.

Segal, L. (1991). Brief therapy: The MRI approach. In A. S. Gurman & D. P. Kniskern (Eds.), *Handbook of family therapy,* Vol. 2 (pp. 171–199). New York: Brunner/Mazel.

Segal, Z. V., Teasdale, J. D., & Williams, J. M. G. (2002). The mindfulness-based cognitive therapy adherence scale: Inter-rater reliability, adherence to protocol and treatment distinctiveness. *Clinical Psychology and Psychotherapy, 9,* 131–138.

Sexton, T. L., & Alexander, J. F. (2003). Functional family therapy: A mature clinical model for working with at-risk adolescents and their families. In T. L. Sexton, G. R. Weeks, & M. S. Robbins (Eds.), *Handbook of Family Therapy* (pp. 323–348). New York: Brunner-Routledge.

Sexton, T. L., Alexander, J. F., & Mease, A. L. (2004). Levels of evidence for the models and mechanisms of therapeutic change in family and couple therapy. In M. J. Lambert (Ed.), *Bergin and Garfield's Handbook of psychotherapy and behavior change* (4th ed., pp. 590–646). New York: Wiley.

Skinner, B. F. (1953). *Science and human behavior.* New York: Macmillan.

Sluzki, C. (1992). Transformations: A blueprint for narrative change in therapy. *Family Process, 31,* 217–230.

Snyder, D. K. (1999). Affective reconstruction in the context of a pluralistic approach to couples therapy. *Clinical Psychology: Science and Practice, 6,* 348–365.

Snyder, D. K., Castellani, A. M., & Whisman, M. A. (2006). Current status and future directions in couple therapy. *Annual Review of Psychology, 57,* 317–344.

Snyder, D. K., & Wills, R. M. (1989). Behavioral versus insight-oriented marital therapy: Effects on individual and inter-spousal functioning. *Journal of Consulting and Clinical Psychology, 57,* 39–46.

Sprenkle, D. H. (Ed.). (2002). *Effectiveness research in marriage and family therapy.* Alexandria, VA: American Association for Marriage and Family Therapy.

Sprenkle, D. H., & Piercy, F. P. (Eds.). (2005). *Research methods in family therapy* (2nd ed.). New York: Guilford Press.

Stanton, M. D., & Shadish, W. R. (1997). Outcome, attrition, and family-couples treatment for drug abuse: A meta-analysis and review of the controlled, comparative studies. *Psychological Bulletin, 122,* 170–191.

Stewart, R. E., & Chambless, D. L. (2009). Cognitive–behavioral therapy for adult anxiety disorders in clinical practice: A meta-analysis of effectiveness studies. *Journal of Consulting and Clinical Psychology, 77,* 595–606.

Stiles, W. B. (1999). Signs and voices in psychotherapy. *Psychotherapy Research, 9,* 1–21.

Stricker, G., & Gold, J. R. (1993). *Comprehensive handbook of psychotherapy integration*. New York: Plenum Press.

Stricker, G., & Gold, J. R. (2005). Assimilative psychodynamic therapy. In J. C. Norcross and M. R. Goldfried (Eds.), *Handbook of psychotherapy integration* (2nd ed., pp. 221–240). New York: Basic Books.

Strupp, H. H. (1976). Some critical comments on the future of psychoanalytic therapy. *Bulletin of the Menninger Clinic, 40,* 238–254.

Szapocznik, J., Hervis, O. E., & Schwartz, S. (2003). *Brief strategic family therapy for adolescent drug abuse (NIDA therapy manuals for drug addiction series)*. Rockville, MD: NIDA.

Szapocznik, J. & Kurtines, W. (1989). *Breakthroughs in family therapy with drug abusing problem youth*. New York: Springer.

Szapocznik, J., Kurtines, W. M., Foote, F., & Perez-Vidal, A. (1986). Conjoint versus one-person family therapy: Further evidence for the effectiveness of conducting family therapy through one person. *Journal of Consulting and Clinical Psychology, 54,* 395–397.

Szapocznik, J., Perez-Vidal, A., Hervis, O. E., Brickman, A. L., & Kurtines, W. M. (1990). Innovations in family therapy: Overcoming resistance to treatment. In R. A. Wells, & V. A. Gianetti (Eds.), *Handbook of brief psychotherapy* (pp. 93–114). New York: Plenum.

Tang, T. Z., & DeRubeis, R. J. (1999). Sudden gains and critical sessions in cognitive behavioral therapy for depression. *Journal of Consulting and Clinical Psychology, 67,* 894–904.

Teasdale, J., & Barnard, P. (1993). *Affect, cognition and change*. Hillsdale, NJ: Lawrence Erlbaum Associates.

Thoma, H., & Kachele, H. (1994). *Psychoanalytic practice*. Northvale, NJ: Jason Aronson Inc.

Thorensen, C. E., & Coates, T. J. (1978). What does it mean to be a behavior therapist? *Counseling Psychologist, 7,* 3–20.

von Bertalanffy, L. (1950). An outline of general system theory. *British Journal of the Philosophy of Science, 1,* 134–165.

Wachtel, P. L. (1975). Behavior therapy and the facilitation of psychoanalytic exploration. *Psychotherapy: Theory, Research, and Practice, 12,* 68–72.

Wachtel, P. L., Kruk, J. C., & McKinney, M. K. (2005). Cyclical psychodynamics and integrative relational psychotherapy.

In J. C. Norcross and M. R. Goldfried (Eds.), *Handbook of psychotherapy integration* (2nd ed., pp. 172–195). New York: Basic Books.

Wäelder, R. (1936). The principle of multiple function: Observations on over-determination. *Psychoanalytic Quarterly, 5,* 45–62.

Watson, J. B. & Raynor, R. (1920). Conditioned emotional reactions. *Journal of Experimental Psychology, 3,* 1–14.

Watson, J. C., Gordon, L. B., Stermac, L., Kalogerakos, F., & Steckley, P. (2003). Comparing the effectiveness of process-experiential with cognitive-behavioral psychotherapy in the treatment of depression. *Journal of Consulting and Clinical Psychology, 71,* 773–781.

Watzlawick, P., Beavin, J. H., & Jackson, D. D. (1967). *Pragmatics of human communication: A study of interactional patterns, pathologies, and paradoxes*. New York: Norton.

Watzlawick, P., Weakland, J. H., & Fisch, R. (1974). *Change: Principles of problem formation and problem resolution*. New York: Norton.

Weinberger, J., & Rasco, C. (2007). Empirically supported common factors. In S. G. Hofman & J. Weinberger (Eds.), *The art and science of psychotherapy* (pp. 103–129). New York: Routledge.

Weiner, N. (1948). *Cybernetics: Or control and communication in the animal and the machine*. New York: Wiley.

White, M, & Epston, E. (1990). *Narrative means to therapeutic ends*. New York: Norton.

Wolpe, J. (1952). Experimental neuroses as learned behavior. *British Journal of Psychology, 43,* 243–268.

Woolley, S. R., & Johnson, S. M. (2005). Creating secure connections: Emotionally focused couples therapy. In J. L. Lebow (Ed.), *Handbook of clinical family therapy* (pp. 384–405). Hoboken, NJ: Wiley.

Yalom, I. D. (1980). *Existential psychotherapy*. New York: Basic Books.

Yeomans, F. E., Clarkin, J. F., & Kernberg, O. F. (2002). *A primer of transference-focused psychotherapy for the borderline patient*. London, Jason Aronson Inc.

Young, J. E., Klosko, J. S., & Weishaar, M. E. (2003). *Schema Therapy: A practitioner's guide*. New York: Guilford Press.

CHAPTER 7

Evidence-based Practice in Clinical Psychology

Bonnie Spring *and* Kelly Neville

Abstract

The Institute of Medicine identifies evidence-based practice (EBP) as a core competence for all 21st century health professionals (Greiner & Knebel, 2003). Psychology is a relative newcomer to the evidence-based movement, having just adopted EBP as policy in 2005 (www2.apa.org/practice/ ebpstatement.pdf). Evidence-based practice is both a conceptual model and a process for basing clinical decision-making on the integration of research, client characteristics, and resource considerations. We describe the evolution of models of EBP across the health disciplines and discuss how the concepts and methods of EBP apply in clinical psychology. Psychologists' roles in relation to EBP are as creators, synthesizers, and consumers of evidence. We consider implications of EBP's adoption for clinical psychology training, and describe learning resources that support clinical psychologists in mastering EBP.

Keywords: Behavioral science training, clinical psychology, decision-making, empirically supported treatment, evidence-based practice

Evidence-based practice (EBP) is both a conceptual model and a process involving "the conscientious, explicit, judicious use of current best evidence in making decisions about the care of individual patients" (Haynes, Sackett, Gray, Cook, & Guyatt, 1996; Sackett, Rosenberg, Gray, Haynes, & Richardson, 1996). The conceptual model, elaborated below, depicts "three circles" or data streams to be integrated when making clinical decisions. One circle represents research; the second is client characteristics (including preferences and values); the third is resource considerations (including practitioner expertise or skills). Performing the EBP process, to be described later, entails carrying out a sequence of five steps. After assessing the presenting problem, the practitioner: (1) asks key questions, (2) acquires evidence to answer them, (3) appraises its quality and contextual relevance, (4) applies the evidence via shared decision-making that integrates client characteristics and resources, and, after reassessing, (5) analyzes outcomes and adjusts practice accordingly.

All major health professions have now endorsed EBP. The Institute of Medicine identifies EBP as a core competence for all 21st-century health professionals (Greiner & Knebel, 2003). Psychology is a relative newcomer to the evidence-based movement, having just adopted EBP as policy in 2005 (www2. apa.org/practice/ebpstatement.pdf). The purposes of this chapter are, therefore, to: (a) discuss how the concepts and methods of evidence-based practice apply to clinical psychology, (b) consider implications of EBP adoption for clinical psychology training, and (c) describe relevant learning resources for EBP.

Rationale for Evidence-based Practice
Health-care Quality

Since its first emergence in medicine a century ago, the evidence-based movement has been about finding ways to distinguish quackery from valid health practices. An important context for that aspiration is that it was not possible to identify legitimate medical procedures until the start of the 20th century. Only then did the good outcomes of antiseptic surgery, vaccination, and public sanitation provide examples of scientifically derived practices that were differentiable from specious ones. During the preceding era when, as it were, one form of snake oil was as good as any other, numerous proprietary, for-profit schools of medicine did a brisk, profitable business in training physicians. Many date the onset of the evidence-based movement to the 1910 publication of the Flexner Report, which challenged the quality of that era's medical training. In work commissioned by the American Medical Association and the Carnegie Foundation, Abraham Flexner surveyed all 155 existing medical schools. His charge was to identify and root out those whose curricula failed to be based on science and rigorous clinical training. By 1935, as a result of the Flexner Report, more than half of all medical schools had been closed (Beck, 2004).

The EBP movement has continued to press for rational, systematic provision of high-quality care. To achieve that objective, the first problem that needed to be resolved was to find a basis on which to judge the quality of alternative care options. In Flexner's era, the best available science came from systematic observation and plausible inference based upon underlying pathophysiology. Then, in 1972, Archibald Cochrane, an epidemiologist well-known for population-wide descriptive studies, published a book championing the randomized controlled trial (RCT) as the most reliable, unbiased method to determine whether a treatment works. The RCT (discussed further later) is a kind of experiment in which patients are allocated randomly to experimental or comparable control treatments whose effects are contrasted on a limited number of pre-declared primary clinical outcomes.

Cochrane became convinced that the British National Health Service could be vastly improved if RCTs were used to test treatments, because that methodology would provide the most valid evidence about whether a treatment works (Cochrane & Blythe, 1989). That the RCT sits high on the hierarchy of best available evidence to determine the efficacy of treatments is a core tenet of EBP. In most accounts, the only form of evidence that sits higher still is a systematic review that examines the synthesized results of multiple RCTs. Named in Archibald's honor, the Cochrane Collaboration, launched in 1992, is an international voluntary organization dedicated to conducting systematic reviews of RCTs.

Accountability and Health-care Policy

In his prescient 1972 book, entitled *Effectiveness and Efficiency: Random Reflections on Health Services*, Cochrane laid out an argument that equates EBP with accountable health-care policy. He noted that economic resources will always be limited. Therefore, he advocated, they should be divided equitably and spent wisely only on treatments that have demonstrable worth. The value of a treatment, he proposed, should be determined by high-quality RCTs, because this method provides the most valid, least biased estimate of treatment effectiveness. Health-care policy in the United Kingdom mirrors Cochrane's viewpoint (Norheim, 2008). When trying to determine whether a procedure should be paid for by the National Health Service (NHS), the United Kingdom's National Institute of Clinical Excellence (NICE) commissions a systematic evidence review. Treatments found effective are covered by NHS; those found ineffective are not. Those for which evidence is insufficient to make a determination are recommended to receive additional research.

In the United States, some health-care policy determinations are based upon synthesized research evidence. Systematic evidence reviews are used to determine coverage of specific procedures by Veterans Affairs/Department of Defense (cf., http://www.hsrd.research.va.gov/publications/esp/), Centers for Medicaid and Medicare (cf., www.cms.hhs.gov/mcd/ncpc_view_document.asp?id=7), and a growing number of private insurers. Increasing calls for transparency, equity, and accountability in health-care policies (Laupacis, 2006) may signal that evidence-based policy decisions will increase. Already, the National Guidelines Clearinghouse (www.guidelines.gov), sponsored by the Agency for Health Research and Quality, posts more than 2,000 EBP guidelines. Practice guidelines are sets of recommendations or principles to help health professionals and patients make decisions about screening, prevention, and treatment of specific health conditions. Only guidelines that are evidence-based are eligible for posting on the National Guidelines Clearinghouse website. To be considered evidence-based, a guideline must be documentably derived from a systematic literature search and review of existing scientific evidence published in peer-reviewed journals.

Upon what basis other than evidence can care be allocated? In the United States, at present, a driving force is market supply. For the past 30 years, it has been demonstrated repeatedly that U.S. medical expenditures increase in direct proportion to the medical resources that exist in a geographic area

(Wennberg, Fisher, & Skinner, 2002; Wennberg & Gittelsohn, 1973). Moreover, greater spending does not necessarily translate into better health outcomes (Wennberg, Fisher, & Skinner, 2002; Wennberg, Fisher, Stukel, & Sharp, 2004). Indeed, regions that spend more and provide more intensive services often achieve worse health outcomes than do areas that spend less and provide less care. International comparative data bear out the reality that greater U.S. spending on health care often fails to translate into better health. The United States currently spends $2 trillion on health care—far more than any other country (World Health Organization [WHO], 2000). Yet the WHO ranks the performance of the U.S. health system 37th relative to all other nations (WHO, 2000). The performance indicators are neither subtle nor abstract: the United States ranks only 26th among industrialized countries on infant mortality and 24th on life expectancy (WHO, 2000).

Clearly, there is a problem in accountability to the public for U.S. health-care investments. The root causes lie both in the current market drivers of health expenditures and in the lack of systems to establish rational spending. Influential, well-funded initiatives by drug and device manufacturers and guilds promote the use of expensive treatments. Often, there is a lack of good evidence about which treatments work best and most cost-effectively. Moreover, the process of deriving and disseminating such evidence can be fraught with political peril. When the federal Agency for Health Care Policy and Research (AHCPR) was formed in 1989, one of its goals was to formulate clinical practice guidelines by evaluating the outcomes of various diagnostic and treatment procedures. In 1994, the AHCPR issued evidence-based guidelines suggesting that most back surgery performed in the U.S. was unnecessary. The ensuing, well-orchestrated uproar by back surgeons led to the end of AHCPR's guidelines program in 1996 and to de-funding of the agency by Congress. When the Agency was reestablished in 1999, it was under a new name: the Agency for Health Research and Quality (AHRQ). Deletion of the word "Policy" from the name clearly disassociated AHRQ from an influence on U.S. health-care policies.

The U.S. Congress recently authorized new research on comparative effectiveness. Such research entails head-to-head comparisons to test which treatments work best and at what relative costs. A body of evidence on comparative effectiveness would potentially provide a basis for both evidence-based practice and policy. To become a firmly established component of evidence-based health care, psychological treatments need to be evaluated in comparative effectiveness research, both on their own and in combination with pharmacotherapy.

Growth of the Evidence Base About Psychological Treatments

One of the greatest challenges faced by EBP stems from gaps in the research literature. Insufficiencies are especially stark in the areas of nondrug treatment and preventive care (Maciosek et al., 2006; Moyer et al., 2005). The U.S. Preventive Services Task Force (USPTF) has addressed this issue with particular eloquence. USPTF members note the disparity between the abundant quality and availability of evidence demonstrating the impact of behavioral risk factors for disease, versus the meager quality and availability of evidence supporting the efficacy, impact, and risk–benefit ratio of clinical preventive services to modify these risk factors (Maciosek et al., 2006).

For psychological treatments to become standard of care, it is critically important that trials testing their efficacy be included in systematic evidence reviews. Often, incomplete reporting or inadequacies in research design and implementation cause clinical trials of psychological treatments to be excluded from research syntheses (Spring, Pagoto, Knatterud, Kozak, & Hedeker, 2007). Lack of inclusion of psychological treatments in research syntheses deprives psychology's evidence of an opportunity to influence policy.

Policy-making bodies often find too little high-quality evidence to recommend for or against the delivery of many nonmedical interventions. Of course, absence of evidence is not the same as evidence of absence of an effect. Nonetheless, many policy-making bodies assign a grade of "I" for "insufficient evidence." Usually, a guidelines panel cannot advise for or against practices whose support is limited to expert consensus or less rigorous evidence (Moyer et al., 2005). The fact that systematic reviewers apply the same evaluative criteria when considering trials of medical and nonmedical treatments levels the playing field for psychological interventions. Inclusion in international databases like the Cochrane Library offers an opportunity to disseminate and enhance the evidence base for psychological interventions.

Transdisciplinary Collaboration

The National Institutes of Health (NIH) Roadmap encourages transdisciplinary collaboration because progress is often made at the interface of preexisting disciplines (Abrams, 2006; Zerhouni, 2005). Yet, even though boundary spanning has undeniable advantages, vast differences between disciplines in vocabularies and frames of reference can impede progress (Ruggill & McAllister, 2006). That EBP has come to provide shared vocabulary across health disciplines offers tremendous advantages for communication. Learning EBP vocabulary and methods affords psychologists invaluable opportunities to participate in transdisciplinary collaboration.

Just as future science will be increasingly transdisciplinary, future health-care teams will be increasingly interprofessional. The shared EBP framework supports jointly held foundational assumptions, vocabulary, and practice principles for psychologists who participate in interprofessional teams (Greiner & Knebel, 2003; Satterfield et al., 2009).

Lifelong Learning

The methods of EBP were developed as a way to close the research-to-practice gap and foster lifelong learning (Institute of Medicine [IOM], 2001; Miller, 2005). A well-documented chasm exists between what research shows to be effective and what is done in usual clinical practice (Dubinsky & Ferguson, 1990; Field & Lohe, 1992; IOM, 2001). Often, practitioners continue to implement practices they learned during training (Isaacs & Fitzgerald, 1999; Turner, 2001), even when few of those practices were ever based upon evidence (Booth, 2007) and some have been supplanted by new evidence.

The research evidence base relevant to health professionals proliferates at an astonishing rate. There exist approximately 23,000 clinical journals that publish more than 2 million articles annually (Goodman, 2003). It is difficult to imagine how a practitioner could keep up to date with this primary literature (Koonce, Giuse, & Todd, 2004; Swinglehurst, Pierce, & Fuller, 2001). A growing set of databases of secondary, synthesized literature has evolved to meet practitioners' needs. One important resource already mentioned is the Cochrane Collaboration's online database of Systematic Reviews of health-care practices (www.cochrane. org). Other more clinically oriented resources to address practical questions are available online and/ or on a hand-held device. These tools, based upon continually updated evidence reviews, offer pithy evidence synopses, clinical practice guidelines, and structured abstracts. Examples are UpToDate (www. uptodate.com), MD Consult (www.mdconsult. com), ACP Journal Club (www.acpjc.org), Clinical

Evidence (www.clinicalevidence.com), InfoPOEMS (www.infopoems.com), and Clin-eguide (www. clineguide.com).

At McMaster University in Canada, in the early 1980s, there developed a critical mass of faculty with an ambitious agenda: to close the research-to-practice gap. The group wrote many journal articles and books about how to keep up with and understand the research literature (Guyatt & Rennie, 2002; Haynes et al., 1986; McKibbon, Eady, & Marks, 2000). They wanted to develop a method that let practitioners find and apply evidence that answered their questions in real time, during the actual clinical encounter. The idea was to make it a habit to routinely ask questions, consult research, and integrate knowledge from three data strands (research, clinical experience, and the patient) when making clinical decisions. The rationale was that routinely performing such integration would overcome old, automatic decision-making biases and cultivate new learning. Gordon Guyatt coined the phrase "evidence-based medicine" to describe the EBP process. The new name represented a departure from the older term, "scientific medicine," which omitted the clinician's and patient's contribution to decision-making and overemphasized making inferences based on pathophysiology. The basic premise of EBP is that there should be no learning disjuncture between graduate school and subsequent professional life. While in school, just as afterward, engaging in EBP involves finding and implementing those practices that are supported by best available current research evidence. It is to be hoped that scientific progress supplants older best practices with newer and better ones, and that the evidence-based practitioner will continue to find the best evidence and upgrade respectively.

One can only marvel at the McMaster group's temerity. Just imagine trying to train practitioners to do library searching and critical appraisal of research at the bedside, in real time, before the advent of the internet. Having rapid access to the research evidence base at the point of care became critically important. Such access became feasible as the emergence of large electronic data sets brought library resources to the desktop. Perhaps not surprisingly, the McMaster group has played a key role in developing the health informatics that are needed to store, retrieve, manage, and use health information at the time and place that decisions need to be made. The science of informatics addresses resources, devices, and structures (e.g., treatment algorithms, practice guidelines, systematic evidence reviews, and electronic medical records) that are needed to store, retrieve, manage, and use evidence at the point of care. The phrase, "evidence-based capitulation" is sometimes used pejoratively to describe practitioner reliance on filtered, synthesized evidence resources rather than primary research studies. However, use of such infrastructure is in keeping with the voluminous realities of contemporary science and practice.

Framework for Evidence-based Practice
Conceptual Models of Evidence-based Practice: The Three Circles

The root conceptual model for EBP depicts three interlinked circles (i.e., data strands) that must be integrated in order to determine optimal client care. Here, we review the evolution of EBP models in medicine, psychology, and allied health professions, leading to the most current transdisciplinary model. Research evidence has consistently remained a circle as the EBP models evolved over time. The contents of the other two circles have changed somewhat. Also varying has been the presence or absence of an interior circle that functionally ties the elements together into a three-legged stool.

EVIDENCE-BASED MEDICINE

The original three-circles model was introduced in 1992 as a "new paradigm" for the practice of medicine (Evidence-based Medicine Working Group, 1992) and a way to incorporate research findings into clinical care. Evidence-based practice was defined as "the conscientious and judicious use of current best evidence from clinical care research in the management of individual patients" (Haynes et al., 1996; Sackett et al., 1996). The proffered model depicted one circle labeled "clinical expertise" sitting atop and interlinked with two equal-sized circles labeled "research evidence" and "patient preferences." The intent of EBP was to promote an explicit and rational process for clinical decision-making that de-emphasized intuition and unsystematic clinical expertise, while highlighting consideration of best research evidence. Facetiously, EBP was contrasted with alternative forms of medical management: eminence-based, vehemence-based, eloquence-based, nervousness-based, and so forth (Isaacs & Fitzgerald, 1999). Evidence-based medicine explicitly de-emphasized the role of expert authority and endorsed a transparent, rational decision-making process that could be taught and applied by all clinicians. Placement of clinical expertise as the top circle was meaningful in stating the

policy that clinical expertise may override research evidence under some conditions, as may patient preferences.

The first three-circles model was subsequently revised to address certain concerns (Haynes, Devereaux, & Guyatt, 2002a, 2002b). It can be noted, though, that the earlier model remains better-known and served as the template for the American Psychological Association's (APA) 2006 EBP conceptualization. The original 1996 (Haynes et al., 1996) three-circles model offered a vague definition of clinical expertise and no guidance about how to address discrepancies between the research evidence and either patient preferences or clinical opinion. The updated model attempted to address these concerns. A "clinical state and circumstances" circle replaced the original circle containing clinical expertise. Instead, clinical expertise was depicted as an interior circle that tied together evidence, patient preferences, and clinical state. Retaining clinical expertise as the central integrating circle expressed respect for the practitioner's pivotal role. Notably, clinical expertise was defined in terms of skill in performing the EBP process; that is, the abilities to elicit, appropriately appraise, and ultimately integrate the three potentially disparate sources of data (Haynes et al., 2002a, 2002b).

Proponents of EBM have always been clear in stating that all three EBP circles are of equal importance. Research is seen as a necessary but not sufficient component of clinical decision-making. However, the vast majority of the literature and teaching on EBM has addressed critical appraisal of published research. One respected resource is *The Users' Guides to the Medical Literature* series, first released as a series of articles in the *Journal of the American Medical Association* and then in online and book versions. The series addresses 25 separate topics in appraising and applying the results of studies focused on questions about therapy, diagnosis, prognosis, and harm. For teaching EBP in medicine, the main text is a small coat-pocket–sized book called *Evidence-Based Medicine: How to Practice and Teach EBM*. Lead-authored by David Sackett through its second edition (Sackett, Strauss, Richardson, Rosenberg, & Haynes, 2000), the third edition of the volume is now led by Sharon Strauss (Strauss, Richardson, Glasziou, & Haynes, 2005).

Certain principles are expressed as core tenets of EBP as it has been taught in medicine (Guyatt & Rennie, 2007; Strauss et al., 2005). The first principle is that of the hierarchy of evidence. The higher-up a research methodology is ranked on the evidence pyramid, the more robust and closer to the truth its results are considered to be. Most versions of the hierarchy for treatment questions place systematic reviews of multiple RCTs at the top. Single RCTs come next, as the RCT design is considered the most valid way of removing bias and contrasting comparable groups. Lower down come observational studies without randomization, and at the bottom of the hierarchy come anecdote and opinion.

A second principle of EBM is that all clinical decisions need to attend to the preferences and values of the informed patient. Understanding of patient preferences has continued to be underdeveloped in EBP, but is now benefiting from work ongoing in the field of shared decision-making (Strauss et al., 2005). A third principle endorses an EBP process: a clear sequence of steps to be followed in integrating research into the care of a patient (Strauss et al., 2005; Bhandari & Giannoudis, 2006).

EVIDENCE-BASED PRACTICE IN OTHER HEALTH DISCIPLINES

Following after medicine (Sackett et al., 1996), the EBP movement was embraced by nursing (Craig & Smyth, 2002), social work (Gibbs, 2003), and public health (Brownson, Baker, Leet, & Gillespie., 2003). Each discipline retained research evidence as one of the three circles, but otherwise adapted the model to its own context and introduced improvements (Satterfield et al., 2009). Evidence-based nursing moved beyond EBM by increasing the integration of patient experiences and preferences into clinical decision-making. Partly because there is a dearth of RCT evidence in nursing, EBP in nursing gave greater emphasis to qualitative data, patient satisfaction, QI data, and cost-effectiveness (Newhouse, Dearholt, Poe, Pugh, & White, 2007; Stetler, 2001; Titler et al., 2001).

Contextual influences on EBP have received heightened attention in recent social work models of EBP (cf., Regehr, Stern, & Shlonsky, 2007). Social workers' roles in management and policy in addition to clinical practice draw them into intimate contact with external constraints and facilitators. Consequently, the EBP conceptualization emphasizes sensitivity to surrounding socio-historic, political, economic, organizational, and community influences.

Public health's model of EBP focuses on the well-being of a population rather than an individual. The prevailing model, put forward by Kohatsu, Robinson, and Torner (2004), is adapted from the thinking of Sir Muir Gray (1997), Chief Knowledge Officer of Britain's National Health Service. In public health's EBP model, the patient circle became population needs, values, and preferences; the research circle was retained. However, as in nursing, few RCTs are available to guide front-line public health practice, resulting in greater reliance on observational studies, time series analyses, and quasi-experiments. Finally, the third circle became resources. That revision acknowledges the reality that resource considerations usually emerge front and center in public health decision-making. Especially in the constraint-ridden world of public health, where overtaxed systems are often insufficient to meet population needs, resources set constraints on an intervention's feasibility.

TRANSDISCIPLINARY MODEL OF EVIDENCE-BASED PRACTICE

In 2006, the NIH Office of Behavioral and Social Science Research (OBSSR) commissioned a 5-year project to harmonize the EBP approach and support communication and collaboration across health disciplines. The resulting multidisciplinary Council and Advisory Board for Training on Evidence-Based Behavioral Practice (EBBP), chaired by the first author, includes EBP experts from medicine, nursing, psychology, social work, public health, and library sciences (www.ebbp.org). The transdisciplinary model of EBP, depicted in Figure 7.1, incorporates the most important advances made within each profession and reflects an emphasis on shared decision-making.

The transdisciplinary EBP model depicts three data streams to be integrated when deciding upon a course of action: evidence, client characteristics, and resources. Best available scientific evidence remains one of the three circles. Client values, preferences, and characteristics remain a second circle. Reflecting a conceptual advance from public health, the third circle is resources, which includes practitioner expertise. Decision-making is the central concept of the model and the action that ties the three data streams together in EBP. The transdisciplinary EBP model is grounded in an ecological framework (McLeroy, Bibeau, Steckler, & Glanz, 1988) that suggests a need to understand the environmental and organizational context for a problem and address influences at multiple levels. Consequently, the model depicts the decision-making process in the surrounding environmental and institutional context that frames it.

Fig. 7.1 Elements that need integration in evidence-based practice

Best Research Evidence

Evidence is comprised of research findings derived from the systematic collection of data through observation and experiment, and the formulation of questions and testing of hypotheses. What constitutes best research evidence depends upon the question needing to be addressed (Sackett & Wennberg, 1997). For example, for questions about etiology or prognosis, the optimum research design is often a longitudinal cohort study. For questions concerning the efficacy and effectiveness of treatments, the research design least prone to bias or error is the RCT. Topping the evidence pyramid for a question about treatment is the systematic review, which synthesizes the findings from many treatment trials (Oxford Center for Evidence Based Medicine, 2001). Recently there have been renewed calls for contextualized research evidence that is directly relevant to the specific patient and practice context (Weaver et al., 2005; Westfall, Mold, & Fagnan, 2007). Accordingly, some presentations of the evidence hierarchy place at the apex of the evidence pyramid an $N = 1$, single-case experimental design study that tests the treatment of interest with the target patient (Guyatt et al., 1986; Mahon et al., 1996).

Resources

The resources circle depicts the skills and infrastructure support that are needed to offer EBPs. Resources include the physical, technological, personnel, and financial assets needed to deliver treatments (e.g., space, time, technological support, finances including insurance reimbursement, and expert practitioners trained in EBP). Other needed resources may involve institutional endorsement by higher administration and agreement from other system components.

Universally, resources are a variable that factors into evidence-based decisions. The most efficacious treatment is irrelevant to any but theoretical EBP if there is no trained practitioner accessible to deliver treatment or no resources to pay. The creation of resource-sensitive practice guidelines is a new development in EBP (cf., Fried et al., 2008). Such guidelines review the quality of evidence supporting alternative practice recommendations that fit the resources available. Decision-makers can use the guideline to gauge the level of intervention intensity that makes best use of accessible infrastructure, human capital, and financial wherewithal.

The transdisciplinary EBP model incorporates practitioner expertise within the broader circle that depicts needed resources. In earlier models of EBP, the circle named practitioner expertise generated the greatest controversy and underwent several revisions (Spring et al., 2005). In part, the difficulty reflected ambiguity in medicine's original EBP model (Haynes et al., 1996), which sometimes led practitioner expertise to be misconstrued as opinion or unquestioned intuition (McFall, 1991; Meehl, 1973; Thornton, 2006). Later versions of the EBP model in medicine (Haynes et al., 2002a;) operationalized expertise as skill in performing the steps of the EBP process (e.g., asking questions, acquiring evidence, critically appraising research), etc.

In the transdisciplinary EBP model, practitioner expertise entails four categories of skills:

1. *Assessment skills* pertain to the appraisal of client characteristics, problems, values and expectations, and environmental context. Competency in assessment also applies to the practitioner's ability to assess in an unbiased manner his or her own level of expertise to

implement techniques and the outcomes of those techniques once implemented.

2. *Evidence-based practice process skills* involve competency at performing the steps of the EBP process: ask well-formulated questions, acquire best available research evidence, appraise evidence for quality and relevance, apply evidence by engaging in shared decision-making with those who will be affected, analyze change, and adjust practice accordingly.

3. *Communication and collaboration skills* entail the ability to convey information clearly and appropriately, and to listen, observe, adjust, and negotiate as appropriate to achieve understanding and agreement on a course of action.

4. *Engagement and intervention skills* involve proficiency at motivating interest, constructive involvement, and positive change from individuals, groups, organizations, communities, and others who may be affected by health decisions. Interventions vary in the degree of training, experience, and skill required to implement them competently.

Client Characteristics, State, Needs, Values and Preferences

Except for single-case studies, research evidence describes the average responses of individuals or groups. The core challenge addressed by EBP is how to apply the averaged data to an individual client. The evidence needs to be appraised in relation to the particular circumstances at hand. Client characteristics are one key set of contextualizing factors that need to be taken into account. Relevant client attributes include state and trait variation in condition, needs, history of treatment response, values, and preferences. To decide whether available research evidence is truly relevant to the client, a judgment must be made about the comparability between the client and the study population. Some tailoring (e.g., literacy level of materials) can often enhance treatment feasibility and acceptability, without undermining fidelity to core treatment elements that make a treatment effective (National Cancer Institute, 2006).

Client preferences warrant special mention as a contextualizing variable. Preferences are the lynchpin of shared decision-making, but are also the least-developed aspect of the EBP model. The rationale for shared decision-making is to engage patients more fully in self-managing their own wellness and health care. For shared decision-making to become a reality, there are two needed preconditions. One is

departure from a paternalistic care model, in which the provider makes decisions on the patient's behalf. The other is progress toward a more culturally informed shared model of care. The idea is for providers to respect and help patients clarify their own values and treatment preferences.

The need to systematize an approach to patient preferences is inescapable and complex. How patients weigh out the relative risks and benefits of treatment alternatives is personally distinctive, subjective, and often not previously considered by the patient. Effective deliberation also requires information that may be unknown to the patient, such as the range of treatment alternatives, including no treatment, and their potential inconveniences and risks. For many psychological conditions, patients need to determine whether they prefer to be treated pharmacologically, psychosocially, or both. The availability of insurance coverage for specific treatments also factors in, as do such logistical considerations as geographic access to trained therapists, scheduling, transportation, and child care.

Evidence-based practice has done much to highlight the importance of shared decision-making in the health-care delivery process (Edwards et al., 2005; Gravel, Legare, & Graham, 2006; Krahn & Naglie, 2008). Engaging clients in decision-making that acknowledges their preferences is justifiable on sociopolitical grounds of equity. Shared decision-making is also justified on evidentiary grounds because of the association between shared decision-making and improved health outcomes (Say & Thomson, 2003; Spring, 2008).

EVIDENCE-BASED PRACTICE IN PSYCHOLOGY

The need to align psychology with other health professions led the APA to form an Evidence-Based Task Force in 2005. The Task Force's definition of EBP modeled the original three-circles model from medicine (APA Presidential Task Force on Evidence-based Practice, 2006; Haynes et al., 1996). However, although the APA Task Force acknowledged that some research designs are better than others, they did not endorse a hierarchy of evidence. The APA did improve upon the original three-circles model in two primary ways. First, the Task Force proposed a number of competences (e.g., assessment, diagnostic judgment, systematic case formulation, and treatment planning) to operationalize clinical expertise. Second, as incorporated in the Transdisciplinary EBP model, they elaborated the patient preference circle to include patient characteristics, values, and context.

In addition to noting relevant contextual factors (e.g., social support), they outlined a comprehensive portfolio of personal and sociocultural factors germane to clinical decision-making (e.g., age, gender, ethnicity, social class, religion, income, functional status, readiness to change, and developmental history).

It is ironic that psychology is among the last health professions to adopt the EBP framework, because clinical psychologists first contemplated a version of EBP before the movement took root in medicine. In fact, clinical psychologists actually proposed an approach to EBP a year earlier than the McMaster group published their influential initial papers on EBM (Haynes et al., 1996). In 1995, the American Psychological Association's Society of Clinical Psychology (Division 12) released the first report of its Task Force on Promotion and Dissemination of Psychological Procedures, chaired by Dianne Chambless (Chambless et al., 1996). Division 12's Task Force aimed to establish standards of evidence that could be applied to select which psychological treatments warranted inclusion in psychology training programs. Treatments identified as having strong research support were initially called *empirically validated*; ultimately, they were called *empirically supported treatments* (ESTs). In transparently publishing its evidentiary criteria,

clinical psychology anticipated the general policy of critical appraisal that EBM would later implement to select best practices for endorsement in treatment guidelines.

Table 7.1 shows how the 1998 Division 12 Task Force classified different levels of research support for various psychological treatments (Chambless et al., 1998). Those evaluative criteria remain unchanged in a 2008 update recently published online at www.psychology.sunysb.edu/eklonsky-/division12. Treatments judged to be "well-established" or "probably efficacious" require a treatment manual, specification of participant characteristics, and replication by an independent investigator. The "strong evidence" that is considered to warrant designation as a "well-established treatment" consists of two or more good group experiments showing superiority or equivalence of a treatment to a matched intervention that controls for attention and expectations. The Division 12 website now improves upon the original published criteria by clarifying that an RCT is what is meant by a "good group design." Criteria for judging the quality of an RCT are not specified. Also, in addition to RCT evidence, the Task force accepts as strong evidence nine single-case experiments. To qualify as "probably efficacious" the Task Force requires "modest evidence." The Task Force characterizes modest research evidence as involving

Table 7.1 Criteria for empirically validated treatments

Well-established Treatments

   I. At least two good between-group design experiments demonstrating efficacy in one or more of the following ways:
      A. Superior (statistically significantly so) to pill or psychological placebo or to another treatment.
      B. Equivalent to an already-established treatment in experiments with adequate sample sizes.
OR
   II. A large series of single-case design experiments ($n > 9$) demonstrating efficacy. These experiments must have:
      A. Used good experimental designs and
      B. Compared the intervention to another treatment as in IA.
Further Criteria for Both I and II:
   III. Experiments must be conducted with treatment manuals.
   IV. Characteristics of the client samples must be clearly specified.
   V. Effects must have been demonstrated by at least two different investigators or investigating teams.

Probably Efficacious Treatments

   I. Two experiments showing the treatment is superior (statistically significantly so) to a waiting-list control group.
OR
   II. One or more experiments meeting the Well-Established Treatment Criteria IA or IB, III, and IV, but not V.
OR
   III. A small series of single-case design experiments ($n > 3$) otherwise meeting Well-Established Treatment

From Chambless, D. L., Baker, M. J., Baucom, D. H., Beutler, L. E., Calhoun, K. S., Crits-Cristoph, P., et al. (1998). Update on empirically validated therapies, II. *The Clinical Psychologist, 51*(1), 3–16. Reprinted with permission.

well-designed experiments lacking independent replication, comparison to a waitlist (rather than attention control) comparison group, or support from fewer than nine single-case experiments.

The 1996 Task Force identified 18 treatments as "empirically supported" (Chambless et al., 1996). Based on a later report, 16 ESTs were then widely disseminated to clinical psychology training programs across the country (Chambless et al., 1998). The number of psychological treatments that the Division 12 Task Force considers empirically supported has more than doubled in the past decade. The Society of Clinical Psychology website now lists 38 treatments as having strong support.

The ESTs generated enthusiasm, and they also stimulated controversy (Norcross, Beutler, & Levant, 2005; Spring et al., 2005, Wampold, 2001). Many objected to a perceived neglect of clinician variables, a criticism that had also been leveled against "scientific medicine" (Sackett et al., 1996; G. Guyatt, personal communication, 2008). To some, the provision of therapy based on research-tested treatment manuals gave the appearance of "cookbook" therapy. Others noted a lack of evidence that specific psychotherapies work best for specific disorders (Luborsky, Singer, & Luborsky, 1975). They suggested that nonspecific therapeutic elements, such as positive expectations and a therapeutic alliance, account for the efficacy of most psychological treatments (Wampold, 2001). Bias was seen in the fact that most of the originally selected ESTs were grounded in either a cognitive or behavioral theoretical orientation. Some even argued that psychotherapy could not be appropriately studied via an RCT design because results could not be generalized to real-world practice (Goldfried & Wolfe, 1996). Throughout the debate, the elephant in the room was fear that EBP really meant cost-cutting and restriction of clinician autonomy (Spring et al., 2005; Pagoto et al., 2007).

As the 21st century arrived, most health professionals faced shrinking reimbursements on the one hand, and increased demands for care quality and accountability on the other. Concerns about curtailment of practice were ubiquitous and reasonable under such circumstances. Many professions responded by formulating clinical practice guidelines that justified reimbursement of best practices by documenting the evidence that established their efficacy. Psychology, however, took a very different approach. Given ongoing controversy about ESTs, the APA opted for an unusual solution. First, an APA Task Force drew an idiosyncratic verbal distinction between "practice guidelines," defined as addressing the general conduct of practitioners, and "treatment guidelines," defined as providing recommendations about interventions to be offered to patients (APA, 2002). Second, the Association formulated policy stating that the APA would formulate practice but not treatment guidelines. Instead, APA's Task Force proposed criteria for evaluating the treatment guidelines developed by other organizations (APA, 2002).

It is interesting to compare the pace of adoption of EBP policy in psychology to that in other disciplines. Certainly, controversies also surrounded adoption of EBP in other health professions (Sackett et al., 1996; Spring et al., 2005), but they resolved more quickly. The core objection was the same in most fields: the argument that science should not dictate practice (Goldfried & Wolfe, 1996; Wampold, 2001; Bohart, 2005). Medicine responded to this critique by renaming their approach "evidence-based medicine" rather than "scientific medicine," and by supplementing research data with input from clinician and patient. In contrast, clinical psychology has, until very recently, retained an EBP model that includes only one circle: research. Accordingly, many students of clinical psychology continue to reduce the concept of EBP to ESTs (Luebbe, Radcliffe, Callands, Green, & Thorn, 2007).

In wondering whether the exclusive focus on ESTs has helped or hindered the progress of EBP in clinical psychology, we suspect that the answer is, "both." A tremendous accomplishment of Division 12's Dissemination Task Force was to achieve the uptake of ESTs into the curricula of all accredited U.S. training programs in clinical psychology. Increased practical skill training in EST delivery remains needed (Weissman et al., 2006), but at least didactic coverage of ESTs has been extensively incorporated into graduate training. Psychology's success in disseminating research-supported practices into the graduate curriculum outstrips that of most other health professions. Another achievement probably brought about by focusing on ESTs has been to stimulate growth of the evidence base for psychological treatments. That success, suggested by a doubling of the number of efficacious ESTs in less than 10 years, can be considered a major accomplishment. Its importance should not be underestimated, particularly since insufficiencies in the evidence base represent one of the most significant impediments to EBP in all health disciplines.

On the other hand, there appear also to have been some drawbacks associated with an exclusive focus on research as the sole consideration for EBP.

Drawing a sharp bifurcation between research data and other kinds of data from the clinical encounter may have heightened polarization between more science-oriented and more practice-oriented constituencies of clinical psychologists. A consequence is that our field has now spawned two separate accrediting bodies for clinical psychology training programs. Clinical scientist training programs will soon seek accreditation through the Academy of Psychological Clinical Science, whereas scientist-practitioner and practitioner-scientist training programs will continue to seek accreditation through the APA. Perhaps in no other health discipline has a cultural gap between researchers and practitioners emerged quite so strongly.

Psychologists' Roles in Evidence-based Practice

As depicted in Figure 7.2, psychologists have three main roles in relation to EBP. In each role, the psychologist is chiefly a consumer of data from some EBP circles and a contributor to others (Spring, 2007). First, as primary researchers, psychologists contribute directly to creating the evidence base. They design, conduct, analyze, and report research that characterizes the risk factors, course, and causal influences on a wide range of health problems. Psychologists validate instruments to assess clinical conditions, and they develop and test treatments to alleviate psychological and other health problems. The evidence that psychologists create as primary researchers is used by both systematic reviewers and practitioners.

Second, as systematic reviewers, psychologists use primary research that has been created by others to create syntheses that are used by clinicians and policy-makers. They locate the primary research that addresses a practical question, and they critically appraise, extract, and synthesize the information to provide an answer. Systematic reviewing is itself a sophisticated and evolving form of research methodology that is increasingly becoming the basis for health policies.

Third, as clinicians, psychologists have the most challenging role in EBP. The clinician extracts and uses data from each of the three circles of EBP.

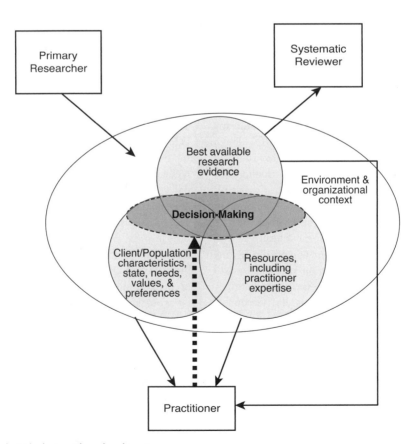

Fig. 7.2 Psychologists' roles in evidence-based practice

Clinicians are research consumers: they access research evidence and appraise its quality and relevance for their context. In the practitioner role, the psychologist also acquires and parses data about client characteristics, including developmental course, treatment response history, needs, values, and preferences. Additionally, the psychologist as clinician assesses available resources, including his or her own personal training and skill in delivering relevant ESTs.

Training for Evidence-based Practice

Several forms of learning will enhance psychologists' abilities to participate fully in the EBP movement as creators, synthesizers, or consumers of research evidence (Spring, 2007). The discussion below describes content not presently well-covered in the clinical psychology curriculum and suggests available resources that might be considered to provide coverage.

Primary Research: Evidence Creation

As noted earlier, the RCT design is considered the gold standard for testing whether a treatment works. Increasingly, RCTs are aggregated in systematic reviews and analyzed to determine coverage policy. For psychological treatments to become standard of care, it is critically important that the RCTs testing them be included and fare well in systematic evidence reviews. Often, incomplete reporting or inadequacies in research design and implementation causes behavioral clinical trials to be excluded from research syntheses (Davidson et al., 2003; Spring et al., 2007). Lack of inclusion in research syntheses deprives psychology's evidence of an opportunity to influence policy.

DESIGN AND IMPLEMENTATION OF THE RANDOMIZED CONTROLLED TRIAL

A number of key features define an experiment as an RCT. First, in an RCT, participants are allocated randomly to the active experimental treatment or to an inactive control condition that is comparable in important respects (e.g., credibility, attention, therapist contact, and incentives). A second key feature to prevent selection bias is *allocation concealment*. It is critically important that both clinicians and patients remain in the dark about upcoming treatment assignments. If the allocation sequence can be deciphered, the researcher's decision to accept or reject a study candidate or the participant's decision to give informed consent can be influenced in a manner that subverts randomization (Schulz & Grimes, 2002).

A third feature that defines an experiment as an RCT is that only a small number of primary outcomes (e.g., between one and three) on which the treatment's effects will be measured is selected and declared in advance of beginning the trial. Registering these primary outcomes in the database at www.ClinicalTrials.gov (a service of the U.S. NIH) serves to protect the evidence base against findings that capitalize on chance. Otherwise, when a treatment fails to show predicted effects on primary outcomes, there may be temptation to "fish" or "cherry-pick." The dangers being addressed are the joint product of publication pressure upon researchers and editorial bias imposed by journals more inclined to publish positive than null results. Preselection and advance declaration of primary outcomes guards against trial reporting of successful secondary outcomes rather than the primary outcomes that were preselected as the treatment's proving ground.

A fourth property of RCTs is *blinding*. Under ideal double-blind conditions, both patients and interventionists are kept in the dark about which treatment the patient has received. Since double-blinding is rarely feasible (or even appropriate) in trials of psychological treatments, alternative procedures are usually adopted. For example, the desirability and credibility of the experimental and control treatments is equated to the extent possible, and the outcome is assessed by independent assessors who are kept blind to treatment assignment. A fifth property of RCTs concerns the data-analytic policy of *intent to treat*. Under intent-to-treat analysis, patients are retained and analyzed in the treatment to which they were randomized regardless of whether they received the intended treatment.

It is very rare for clinical psychologists to receive graduate training specifically devoted to clinical trial methodology. Students learn group comparison methods in coursework on experimental design and statistics. Consequently, it is natural for psychologists to conceptualize RCTs as simple experiments (as they are in many respects). However, the experimental tradition in psychology derives from laboratory research that affords very tight control over the experimental stimulus and most extraneous sources of variation (Maher, 1968; Wilson, 1981). Stimulus intensity and duration, diet, time of day, presence of others, and the like can all be regulated. The experimental manipulation is often simple and able to be characterized exactly. Measurement of the outcome usually occurs after a brief assessment interval, and there are ordinarily few or no missing data.

Contrast that with the usual scenario in a trial comparing a psychological treatment to a control intervention. Rather than being a loud noise or a short audiotaped message or a film, the experimental stimulus now becomes a complex intervention that transpires between two or more human beings over an extended period of time. The very first challenge is to establish whether the experimental stimulus even occurred—a task more challenging than it sounds. The question is addressed by coding directly observed or recorded treatment sessions to measure *treatment fidelity* (whether the intended treatment was delivered as planned).

If one considers an RCT to be identical to a laboratory experiment, the rationale for intent-to-treat analysis policy is especially challenging to understand. In a laboratory experiment, if a mishap occurs and an animal escapes or a human quits the study, it is logical to replace the lost case. Because the missing subject was not exposed to either intervention condition, including the person in the analysis would appear to compromise the internal validity of the experiment. Viewed from that perspective, a "completer analysis" that retains only those participants exposed fully to their assigned treatment conditions would seem the most valid approach. Perhaps that mistaken assumption explains why trials of psychological interventions reported in the behavioral research literature continue to show deficiencies in intent-to-treat analysis and in other aspects of the handling of missing data (Pagoto et al., 2009; Spring et al., 2007).

Epidemiologists understand RCTs as tests of whether a treatment constitutes sound public policy. Framed in that manner, a treatment that is declined or deserted in midstream by many individuals is a poor treatment, regardless of whether it has outstanding efficacy among the subset that continues to adhere. From a public health perspective, the treatment's viability needs to be evaluated by considering outcomes for the entire group of people that was assigned to receive it. Hence, the policy, "Once randomized, always analyzed."

RESOURCES FOR LEARNING ABOUT RANDOMIZED CONTROLLED TRIALS

A number of good textbooks on randomized controlled trials exist. These include Steven Piantadosi's (2005) Comprehensive *Clinical Trials: A Methodological Perspective* (2nd ed.), S. J. Pocock's (1984) *Clinical Trials: A Practical Approach,* and the paperback *Fundamentals of Clinical Trials* by Lawrence M. Friedman, Curt D. Furberg, and David L. DeMets (1999).

An excellent in-person training opportunity is the annual 2-week Summer Institute for Randomized Clinical Trials Involving Behavioral Interventions, sponsored by OBSSR. Also available and helpful are the many scales that have been published to evaluate the quality of clinical trials (cf., Jüni et al., 2001). Examining these quality scales when designing and executing an RCT enables a trialist to begin with the end in mind. Remaining mindful of the criteria that systematic reviewers will use to determine whether a trial passes threshold for inclusion in a research synthesis can improve the quality of the RCT.

REPORTING OF RANDOMIZED CONTROLLED TRIALS: THE CONSORT STATEMENT

It is not enough for an RCT to be designed and conducted well. It also needs to be reported well and transparently, so that it can influence practice and policy. A useful tool to support reporting of RCTs was created by an international group of epidemiologists, statisticians, journal editors, and trialists known as the Consolidated Standards of Reporting Trials (CONSORT) Group. The CONSORT Statement and reporting guidelines (Altman et al., 2001; Moher, Schulz, & Altman, 2001) have been endorsed by many leading journals in the medical (e.g., *The Journal of the American Medical Association [JAMA], The Lancet*) and behavioral sciences (e.g., *Journal of Consulting and Clinical Psychology, Health Psychology, Annals of Behavioral Medicine*). The CONSORT Group's website (www.consort-statement.org) provides a checklist of 22 items that should be reported when presenting an RCT, and a flow diagram that depicts participants' progress through the trial. The aim of the CONSORT statement is to standardize and make more transparent the research process, so that evidence users and synthesizers can clearly evaluate validity and relevance for their context.

Several checklist items are of particular relevance to psychologists because they represent areas in which our reporting of trials is often incomplete (Pagoto et al., 2009; Spring et al., 2007; Stinson, McGrath, & Yamada, 2003). One example involves specifying the study eligibility criteria and their impact on enrollment (important for appraising external validity). A second is describing how the sample size was determined. A third involves detailing how the randomization sequence was generated, concealed, and implemented. A fourth concerns describing whether any blinding was implemented and how its success was evaluated, including blinding assessors of the study outcomes. A fifth area in which reporting of psychosocial intervention trials often falls down involves specifying, in advance, clear primary and secondary outcomes, so that a priori hypothesis testing can be discriminated from subsequent cherry-picking. Finally, improvement is needed in providing enough information about the number of cases analyzed in each group to enable readers to tell whether comparisons were conducted on an intent-to-treat basis. Exposure to the CONSORT statement is useful for clinical psychologists, regardless of whether they wish to appraise, create, or synthesize research evidence about the effectiveness of treatments.

SYSTEMATIC REVIEW: EVIDENCE SYNTHESIS

As noted, systematic reviews are an increasingly vital part of the infrastructure needed to perform EBP. Some scientific journals (e.g., JAMA) no longer accept traditional narrative literature reviews, but continue to welcome systematic evidence reviews. The distinctive features of a systematic review stem from the care that is taken to avoid bias in gathering and summarizing the literature (Dickersin, 2002; Pai et al., 2004). One key tool is the prespecified search protocol. The protocol states the question to be answered by the review. The question is phrased in PICO language, which specifies the target *Population, Intervention, Comparison*, and study *Outcomes* (primary and secondary dependent variables). Also specified are clear criteria for including or excluding studies, and all key words and terms that will be used to guide the search.

To minimize bias, the approach in conducting searches for a systematic review is to be as inclusive and transparent as possible. The search protocol declares which databases will be examined and by which search engines. The protocol also states whether gray literature (e.g., unpublished manuscripts, conference proceedings, etc.) will be scrutinized and whether articles written in certain languages will be filtered out. The selection of databases to be searched has important practical and substantive implications. Key indexing terms differ across databases (e.g., PubMED uses MeSH terms; psycINFO uses the Thesaurus of Psychological Index Terms). Additionally, EMBASE (Medline's European counterpart) and CINAHL (a database used extensively by nurses and other allied health

professionals) include many journals that are not included in either MEDLINE or psycINFO. As compared to Medline or psychINFO, searching EMBASE, the Cochrane Database of Systematic Reviews, and the Cochrane Controlled Clinical Trials Registry is more likely to yield reports of null or negative findings which can, in turn, influence a review's conclusions (Sampson et al., 2003). The Cochrane Database of Systematic Reviews and the Cochrane Controlled Clinical Trials Registry may also yield unique citations, and sometimes unpublished studies, identified by Cochrane reviewers. The assistance of a trained librarian can be invaluable throughout the search process.

Once the initial pool of articles has been assembled (usually at least several hundred), two or more raters sort the articles for relevance and quality using prespecified criteria. Most rating scales for trial quality offer separate items to code internal validity, external validity, and analytic quality. Of the many available rating scales for methodological quality, Jadad et al.'s (1996) is the most widely used, but its emphasis on double-blinding is inappropriate for many behavioral trials. The PEDRO and SIGN rating systems apply well to behavioral clinical trials (Bhogal, Teasell, Foley, & Speechley, 2005; www.sign.ac.uk/guidelines). It can be noted, though, that at our field's present stage of development, few high-quality RCTs exist. The scarcity of high-quality trials is such that, for many psychosocial interventions, implementing quality considerations beyond whether a study used randomization leaves too few remaining studies to synthesize quantitatively (cf., Spring et al., 2007).

The next step in systematic reviewing is design of a data extraction form and extraction of data on the primary outcomes. At this juncture, a decision usually needs to be made about whether to contact study authors to obtain data not available in their published reports. Data synthesis via meta-analysis comes next and requires decision-making about the handling of study heterogeneity. Nearly all systematic reviews of treatment reflect heterogeneity; a key question is whether it is so great as to preclude quantification of effects across studies.

An essential point is that not all systematic reviews synthesize data quantitatively via meta-analysis. Some systematic reviews explore reasons for heterogeneity on a purely qualitative basis. The optimal approach to handling heterogeneity is a very active area of investigation in systematic review science (Viechtbauer, 2007), as are questions of how to adequately reflect data on harms (Chou & Helfand, 2005) or synthesize qualitative information (Dixon-Woods et al., 2007).

RESOURCES FOR LEARNING ABOUT
SYSTEMATIC REVIEWS

A semester-long course on systematic review is offered in most graduate training programs in public health, but such courses are rarely taught in psychology. Usually, meta-analysis is covered as part of statistics training. However, the remaining content—systematic reviewing, per se—is omitted, and warrants consideration for inclusion in psychology training.

Two online learning courses available free of charge at www.ebbp.org/training.html offer an introduction and background relevant to systematic reviews. The "Search for Evidence Module" provides an overview of how to acquire evidence. It is rich in information about useful search strategies and the extensive roster of databases relevant to psychologists. The "Systematic Review Module" covers topics such as judging the quality of a review, how and why high-quality reviews can reach different conclusions, and steps in conducting a systematic review. For those who want more in-depth coverage, the Cochrane Collaboration has recently published their comprehensive handbook for systematic reviewers (Higgins & Green, 2008).

PRACTICAL DECISION-MAKING:
EVIDENCE USE

When psychologists integrate research evidence to engage in evidence-based decision-making with their clients, they act as consumers of the research evidence. Figure 7.1 might make it appear that integration of the three spheres involved in EBP could occur simultaneously, but that is not the case. Engaging in the EBP process entails performing a specific sequence of five steps (5 A's) that is known as the *evidence-based practice process*.

The Evidence-based Practice Process

The five steps of the EBP process are depicted in Table 7.2. Also, an interactive learning module that walks learners through the five steps is freely accessible at www.ebbp.org/training.html. After assessing the problem, the clinician performs the following sequence: (1) *A*sk a question, (2) *A*cquire the evidence, (3) *A*ppraise the evidence, (4) *A*pply the evidence, and (5) *A*nalyze and *A*djust practice. Each step, described in greater detail below, is an integral component of the EBP process and represents a competency or skill to be mastered by the practitioner. Note that, rather than being considered a formal step in the EBP process, assessment is assumed to precede the onset of the process and to recur throughout it.

Ask: Asking Questions

After assessing the client, the clinician poses important, practical questions in order to inform decisions about management or treatment of the presenting condition. Asking effective clinical questions involves formulating them in a manner that allows them to be readily answerable. Skill at framing "well-built" questions is an acquired competency (Council for Training in Evidence-Based Behavioral Practice, 2008).

Table 7.2 Steps in the evidence-based practice process

Step 1	Ask client-oriented, relevant, answerable questions about the health status and context of individuals or communities.
Step 2	Acquire the best available evidence to answer the question.
Step 3	Appraise the evidence critically for validity and applicability to the problem at hand.
Step 4	Apply the evidence by engaging in collaborative health decision-making with the affected individual(s). Appropriate decision-making integrates the context, values, and preferences of the recipient of the health intervention, as well as consideration of available resources, including professional expertise. Implement the health practice.
Step 5	Analyze the effects of the health practice and Adjust practice. Evaluate implications for future decision-making, disseminate the results, and identify new informational needs.

From Satterfield, J.M., B. Spring, R.C. Brownson, E.J. Mullen, R.P. Newhouse, B.B. Walker, and E.P. Whitlock. (2009). Toward a Transdisciplinary Model of Evidence-Based Practice. *The Milbank Quarterly, 87*(2), 368–390. © Milbank Memorial Fund. Reprinted with permission.

Numerous kinds of uncertainty arise in clinical practice. The major types of uncertainty can be framed as questions about:

- *Assessment.* Questions about best ways of measuring, describing, or diagnosing a condition.
- *Treatment.* Questions that address interventions to prevent, contain, or improve biopsychosocial difficulties.
- *Etiology.* Questions about influences that cause or contribute to the onset of a health problem.
- *Prognosis.* Questions about the probable course and outcome of a health condition.
- *Harm.* Questions that concern potential adverse effects of interventions.
- *Cost-effectiveness.* Questions comparing the expenditures relative to outcomes yielded by two or more alternative clinical courses of action.

Because many questions will be generated for each client, prioritization of the most important ones needs to proceed in an efficient fashion. The chief criterion for prioritization usually concerns the impact of potential courses of action on the client's function or quality of life, or the perceived significance of the issue to the client (Council for Training in Evidence-Based Behavioral Practice, 2008).

Trainees learning to practice EBP are taught to differentiate two formats of question: background (general) and foreground (specific). Background questions aim to acquire general information about a condition, class of treatments, and the like. A well-formulated background question is comprised of two parts: (1) a question root (What, Who, How, etc.) including a verb, and (2) a disorder, treatment, or other health issue. Training in EBM devotes almost no attention to background questions. Such questions are too diffuse and yield too many citations to be used efficiently in the very brief time that most physicians have available for each patient. Clinical psychologists usually have longer to spend with each client. Additionally, in the authors' experience, many psychologists ask background questions in order to update their knowledge when first preparing to see a client. Subsequently, after having assessed the client in context, the practitioner proceeds to pose more focused and efficient foreground questions.

An example of a background question is: "What are effective treatments for binge eating disorder (BED)?" A clinical psychologist preparing to see a new client with BED might pose such a question

in order to ensure that her knowledge of current best-treatment options is up to date. A subsequent foreground question might be, "In adults with BED: (P) Does interpersonal therapy (I) compared to cognitive-behavioral therapy (C) reduce the frequency of binge episodes (O). The better-focused foreground question will yield cites that specifically inform a decision about whether to proceed with interpersonal or cognitive-behavioral therapy, assuming the clinician is trained to provide both and both are acceptable to the client.

Acquire: Acquisition of Evidence

Once a well-built question has been formulated, the next step is to acquire the evidence to answer it. This step requires the practitioner to translate the question into an efficient search plan. Help can be found at www.ebbp.org's online tutorial on searching, or via consultation from a librarian or other professional with expertise in information science. Navigating the sheer bulk of existing primary research can be daunting and time-consuming. Consequently, it is expected and advantageous that busy practitioners will turn first to the secondary, synthesized literature to answer their questions. Practice guidelines based on systematic reviews can be found at www.guidelines.gov or at the UK's National Institute of Clinical Excellence (www.nice.org.uk/Guidance/CG/Published). Useful search strategies for retrieving systematic reviews have also been published (Montori et al., 2005). The authors of a systematic review will already have compiled and critically appraised the quality of the primary research literature to answer many frequently asked questions. However, the clinician will still need to appraise the quality and relevance of the systematic review (Hunt & McKibbon, 1997).

APPRAISE: CRITICAL APPRAISAL OF QUALITY AND RELEVANCE

The next step in the EBP process is to critically appraise two aspects of the obtained evidence: its quality and its applicability to the client and circumstances at hand. In evaluating research on interventions, the key parameter to be appraised is internal validity: whether the research was designed and conducted in a manner that allows psychological or behavioral change to be attributed causally to the intervention rather than to extraneous influences. Applicability or relevance refers to the clinician's judgment about whether the research results can be generalized to the specific client, interventionist, and circumstances at hand.

The appraisal of relevance is challenging. Applying either overly stringent or overly lax criteria to judge applicability may have adverse consequences. If the body of evidence is seen as having no relevance to new groups and circumstances, then old, ineffective practices may continue to constitute usual care for many understudied and underserved populations. On the other hand, if interventions are assumed to be universally applicable, then the need to adapt treatment to attain client acceptance may be ignored. Given the limited body of research for psychosocial interventions, few treatments have been evaluated fully to determine their efficacy across demographic and cultural groups.

What should the clinician do when considering the prospect of delivering a well-established treatment to a patient from a demographic subgroup whose response to the intervention has not been fully characterized? One possibility is to search the primary research literature for evidence of treatment × subgroup interactions indicative of differential benefit or harm. Finding no evidence of treatment interaction, and assuming the client finds the treatment acceptable, the best available evidence suggests going ahead to implement the treatment. Of course, the necessary next step is to assess the results and adjust treatment accordingly. That "analyze and adjust" step, to be discussed shortly, is no less necessary when treating an individual from a well-studied population.

Apply: Decision-making and Action

The "apply" step is at the heart of the EBP process. "Apply" is also the most complex and least described step in the EBP process model. During the apply phase, the clinician integrates knowledge from best available, relevant research with consideration of patient characteristics and resources to arrive at an action decision. After finding and appraising the evidence, the interventionist assesses the resources available to offer what research shows to be the intervention best supported by evidence. The considered resources include finances, linguistically appropriate materials, trained practitioners, client's ability to attend sessions, and other factors. The clinician also considers the likely acceptability and uptake of the best-supported treatment by the client. She evaluates the client's values and preferences by proactively engaging the individual in the process of collaborative decision-making. In some instances, other stake-holders (e.g., family members) may also be included in decision-making.

Resource appraisal usually requires the clinician to self-assess whether personal training and skills are adequate to implement best clinical practices. A challenge for EBP in clinical psychology is that, once an evidence-based intervention is identified, practitioners may not have the skills needed to implement the intervention. A decision then needs to be made, collaboratively, about whether to implement an alternative EBP in which the clinician is trained, or whether to refer (if a clinician skilled in the best practice is available and amenable).

For EBPs to be disseminated and implemented, practitioners need to know how to search for training resources. Materials are now readily available on many Internet sites. For example, the Substance Abuse and Mental Health Services Administration (SAMHSA) and its Center for Mental Health Services (CMHS) provides six Evidence-Based Practice Implementation Resource Kits to encourage the use of EBPs in mental health (Center for Mental Health Services, 2008).

Analyze and Adjust: Evaluation, Dissemination, and Follow-up

A clinician engaging in evidence-based practice performs continuous practice-based quality improvement (Greiner & Knebel, 2003). During and after applying an evidence-based intervention, the practitioner analyzes outcomes and adjusts practice accordingly. The clinician engages the client and sometimes other stakeholders (e.g., family members) in the process of evaluation and quality improvement. Results are then used to refine local decision-making policies, generate new questions, and identify needed research.

The analyze and adjust step makes EBP an iterative process. Performing the step requires ongoing assessment, followed by realignment of treatment based upon local data from the patient. It is usually possible to perform such realignments within the scope of an EST without compromising the core features integral to the therapy. Analyze and adjust simply reminds the clinician of the need to monitor progress. However, in some instances the EST appraised as having highest quality and relevance may fail to help a particular client. To continue administering the same EST months after the client's condition has deteriorated would no longer constitute EBP. The clinician practicing EBP would analyze the deterioration and adjust course, probably by offering an alternative EST.

As noted earlier, the www.ebbp.org website offers an online experiential module to learn the EBP process. The EBP process module presents two alternative cases in which a practitioner addresses tobacco use with a client. In one case, the client is an individual. In the other case, the client is a community. For those who prefer in-person training, conference workshops on EBP are offered at the Society of Behavioral Medicine, Association of Behavioral and Cognitive Therapy, and American Psychological Association. More extended courses on EBM are taught at several locales. Best known are the annual summer workshop on "How to Teach Evidence-Based Clinical Practice" taught at McMaster University in Canada, and courses by the Center on Evidence-Based Medicine at Oxford University in the UK.

Conclusion

Engaging in EBP entails a process of lifelong learning as the evidence about best practices continues to evolve. Attaining mastery of skills needed to perform the EBP process is a process and not an event with an endpoint. The complexities of real-world practice, the proliferation of the research evidence base, the changing sociocultural and health-care contexts, and rapidly evolving health information technologies require ongoing engagement in the EBP process (McCourt, 2005; Michel, 2007).

Much is to be gained from engagement of psychology's research and practice communities in the EBP process. Ultimately, the goal of EBP is the provision of best-tested, most effective care to the public in a manner that reflects shared decision-making and mutual involvement in continuing to enrich the evidence base.

Psychology has a long tradition of excellence in research methodology. Indeed, clinical psychologists proposed a form of EBP based on empirically supported treatments before publication of the major initial papers on EBM. Inclusion of ESTs in the didactic curriculum of accredited clinical psychology programs has been a major achievement in the dissemination of evidence-based psychological treatments. Now, work is needed to increase further the availability of hands-on, supervised training in ESTs.

Also needed to participate fully in the EBP movement is increased education of psychologists in clinical trial and research synthesis methodologies. These methodologies are applied across health disciplines to evaluate the quality of support for preventive and treatment interventions. Provision of evidence from high-quality RCTs is likely to become increasingly important as a means by which policy-makers will make coverage decisions. Conducting well-designed, carefully implemented, well-reported

clinical trials, and synthesizing the evidence in systematic reviews are two ways that psychologists can contribute to EBP. Growth and dissemination of the evidence base for psychological treatments are vital in helping to ensure that the public continues to have access to the psychological treatments best supported by evidence. Clinical psychologists can contribute to EBP by acquiring the training and clinical skills needed to implement ESTs. Finally and critically important is the need for psychologists to master the steps of the EBP process in order to stay up-to-date as the evidence for best-supported psychological practices continues to evolve.

Future Directions

• Gaps in the evidence base are a major impediment to EBP. How can psychology, as a discipline, prioritize which gaps warrant research attention most urgently in order to guide policy and practice?

• Psychological treatments represent a viable alternative or increment to medical–surgical treatments for many health problems, and psychological treatments are often preferred by patients. Inclusion of psychological treatments in comparative effectiveness trials would yield a sounder basis for coverage policies.

• Reasonable agreement has emerged about standards to appraise the quality of research evidence. Greater ambiguity surrounds the appraisal of whether research is relevant to the client and the context at hand. Can psychologists systematize a process for taking context into account when critically appraising whether evidence is relevant? For example, can decisional algorithms be derived and validated to judge the degree to which evidence derived from majority populations is applicable to cultural subgroups?

• How to implement the "apply" step of the EBP process remains undefined. Exactly how should the clinician integrate research evidence, client characteristics, and resources? How should the apply step be systematized? Will the optimal systematization take the form of practice guidelines, decisional algorithms, or something different?

• A vital component of EBP is the infrastructure needed to actively disseminate (i.e., "push") regularly updated syntheses of evidence to practicing clinicians. Will psychology as a discipline invest in creating infrastructure to support EBP? Will clinical psychology go it alone on creating infrastructure for EBP, or will we partner with other psychological specialties and/or other health disciplines that offer psychosocial treatment?

Acknowledgments

Preparation of this material was supported in part by the National Institutes of Health Office of Behavioral and Social Science Research contract N01-LM-6-3512, "Resources for Training in Evidence-Based Behavioral Practice." Appreciation is expressed to the members of the Council on Evidence-Based Behavioral Practice (Ross Brownson, Jason Satterfield, Robin Newhouse, Edward Mullen, Evelyn Whitlock).

References

Abrams, D. B. (2006). Applying transdisciplinary research strategies to understanding and eliminating health disparities. *Health Education & Behavior, 33*(4), 515–531.

Altman, D. G., Schulz, K. F., Moher, D., Egger, M., Davidoff, F., Elbourne, D., et al. (2001). The revised CONSORT statement for reporting randomized trials: Explanation and elaboration. *Annals of Internal Medicine, 134*(8), 663–694.

American Psychological Association. (2002). Criteria for evaluating treatment guidelines. *American Psychologist, 57*, 1052–1059.

American Psychological Association, Presidential Task Force on Evidence-Based Practice. (2006). Evidence-based practice in psychology. *American Psychologist, 61*(4), 271–285.

Beck, A. H. (2004). The Flexner Report and the standardization of medical education. *Journal of the American Medical Association, 291*, 2139–2140.

Bhandari, M., & Giannoudis, P. V. (2006). Evidence-based medicine: What it is and what it is not. *Injury, 37*(4), 302–306.

Bhogal, S. K., Teasell, R. W., Foley, N. C., & Speechley, M. R. (2005). The PEDro scale provides a more comprehensive measure of methodological quality than the Jadad scale in stroke rehabilitation literature. *Journal of Clinical Epidemiology, 58*(7), 668–673.

Bohart, A. C. (2005). Evidence-based psychotherapy means evidence-informed, not evidence-driven. *Journal of Contemporary Psychotherapy, 35*, 39–53.

Booth, A. (2007). What proportion of healthcare is evidence based? Resource guide. Accessed March 1, 2007 at http://www.shef.ac.uk/scharr/ir/percent.html

Brownson, R. C., Baker, E. A., Leet, T. L., & Gillespie, K. N. (2003). *Evidence-based public health*. Oxford: Oxford University Press.

Center for Mental Health Services. (n.d.). *About evidence-based practices: Shaping mental health services toward recovery*. Substance Abuse and Mental Health Services Administration, U.S. Department of Health and Human Services. Retrieved January 28, 2008, from at http://mentalhealth.samhsa.gov/cmhs/communitysupport/toolkits/about.asp

Chambless, D. L., Baker, M. J., Baucom, D. H., Beutler, L. E., Calhoun, K. S., Crits-Cristoph, P., et al. (1998). Update on empirically validated therapies, II. *The Clinical Psychologist, 51*(1), 3–16.

Chambless, D. L., Sanderson, W. C., Shoham, V., Bennett Johnson, S., Pope, K. S, Crits-Christoph, P., et al. (1996). An update on empirically validated therapies. *The Clinical Psychologist, 49*(2), 5–18.

Chou, R., & Helfand, M. (2005). Challenges in systematic reviews that assess treatment harms. *Annals of Internal Medicine, 142*(12 Pt 2), 1090–1099.

Cochrane, A. (1972). *Effectiveness and efficiency: Random reflections on health services*. London: Royal Society of Medicine Press.

Cochrane, A. L., with Blythe M. (1989). *One man's medicine: An autobiography of Professor Archie Cochrane*. London: BMJ Books.

Council for Training in Evidence-Based Behavioral Practice. (2008). White Paper on Definition and Competencies for Evidence-based Behavioral Practice. Retrieved May 23, 2010, from http://www.ebbp.org

Craig, J. V. & Smyth, R. L. (2002). *The evidence-based practice manual for nurses*. London: Churchill Livingstone.

Davidson, K. W., Goldstein, M., Kaplan, R. M., Kaufmann, P. G., Knatterud, G. L., Orleans, C. T., et al. (2003). Evidence-based behavioral medicine: What is it and how do we achieve it? *Annals of Behavioral Medicine, 26*(3), 161–171.

Dickersin, K. (2002). Systematic reviews in epidemiology: Why are we so far behind? *International Journal of Epidemiology, 31*(1), 6–12.

Dixon-Woods, M., Sutton, A., Shaw, R., Miller, T., Smith, J., Young, B., et al. (2007). Appraising qualitative research for inclusion in systematic reviews: A quantitative and qualitative comparison of three methods. *Journal of Health Services & Research Policy, 12*(1), 42–47.

Dubinsky, M., & Ferguson, J. H. (1990). Analysis of the national institutes of health medicare coverage assessment. *International Journal of Technology Assessment in Health Care, 6*(3), 480–488.

Edwards, A., Elwyn, G., Wood, F., Atwell, C., Prior, L., & Houston, H. (2005). Shared decision making and risk communication in practice: A qualitative study of GPs' experiences. *British Journal of General Practice, 55*, 6–13.

Evidence-Based Medicine Working Group. (1992). Evidence-based medicine. A new approach to teaching the practice of medicine. *Journal of the American Medical Association, 268*(17), 2420–2425.

Field, M. J., & Lohe, K. N. (Eds.). (1992). *Guidelines for clinical practice: From development to use by Committee on Clinical Practice Guidelines*. Washington, DC: National Academy of Science, Institute of Medicine.

Fried, M., Quigley, E. M., Hunt, R. H., Guyatt, G., Anderson, B. O., Bjorkman, D. J., et al. (2008). Can global guidelines change health policy? *Nature Clinical Practice Gastroenterology & Hepatology, 5*(3), 120–121.

Friedman, L. M., Furberg, C. D., & DeMets, D. L. (1999). *Fundamentals of clinical trials*. New York: Springer Publishing.

Gibbs, L. E. (2003). *Evidence-based practice for the helping professions: A practical guide with integrated multimedia*. Pacific Grove, CA: Brooks/Cole-Thompson Learning.

Goldfried, M. R., & Wolfe, B.E. (1996). Psychotherapy practice and research: Repairing a strained alliance. *American Psychologist, 51*, 1007–1016.

Goodman, K. W. (2003). *Ethics and evidence-based medicine: Fallibility and responsibility in clinical science*. New York: Cambridge University Press.

Gravel, K., Legare, F., & Graham, I. D. (2006). Barriers and facilitators to implementing shared decision-making in clinical practice: A systematic review of health professionals' perceptions. *Implementation Science, 1,* 1–16.

Greiner, A. C., & Knebel, E. (Eds.). (2003). *Health professions education: A bridge to quality.* Washington, DC: National Academies Press.

Guyatt, G., & Rennie, D. (2002). *Users guides to the medical literature: Essentials of evidence-based clinical practice.* Washington, DC: American Medical Association.

Guyatt, G. H., & Rennie, D. (2007). *Users' guides to the medical literature: A manual for evidence-based clinical practice.* Chicago: American Medical Association.

Guyatt, G., Sackett, D., Taylor, D. W, Chong, J., Roberts, R., & Pugsley, S. (1986). Determining optimal therapy – Randomized trials in individual patients. *New England Journal of Medicine, 314*(14), 889–892.

Haynes, R. B., Devereaux, P. J., & Guyatt, G. H. (2002a). Clinical expertise in the era of evidence-based medicine and patient choice. *ACP Journal Club, 136*(2), A11–4.

Haynes, R. B., Devereaux, P. J., & Guyatt, G. H. (2002b). Physicians' and patients' choices in evidence based practice. *British Medical Journal, 324*(7350), 1350.

Haynes, R. B., McKibbon, K. A., Fitzgerald, D., Guyatt, G. H., Walker, C. J., & Sackett, D. L. (1986). How to keep up with the medical literature: I. Why try to keep up and how to get started. *Annals of Internal Medicine, 105,* 149–153.

Haynes, R. B., Sackett, D. L., Gray, J. A., Cook, D. L., & Guyatt, G. H. (1997). Transferring evidence from research into practice: 2. Getting the evidence straight. *ACP Journal Club, 126*(1), A14–6.

Haynes, R. B., Sackett, D. L., Gray, J. M., Cook, D. J., & Guyatt, G. H. (1996). Transferring evidence from research into practice: 1. The role of clinical care research evidence in clinical decisions. *ACP Journal Club, 125*(3), A14–16.

Higgins, J. P. T., & Green, S. (2008). *Cochrane handbook for systematic reviews of interventions.* New York: Wiley Cochrane Series.

Hunt, D. L., & McKibbon, K. A. (1997). Locating and appraising systematic reviews. *Annals of Internal Medicine, 126*(7), 532–538.

Institute for Healthcare Improvement. (n.d.). Measures. Retrieved December 11, 2007, from http://www.ihi.org/IHI/Topics/Improvement/ImprovementMethods/Measures/

Institute of Medicine. (2001). *Crossing the quality chasm a new health system for the 21st century.* Washington, DC: National Academy Press.

Isaacs, D., & Fitzgerald, D. (1999). Seven alternatives to evidence based medicine. *British Medical Journal, 319*(7225), 1618.

Jadad, A. R., Moore, R. A., Carroll, D., Jenkinson, C., Reynolds, D. J., Gavaghan, D. J., et al. (1996). Assessing the quality of reports of randomized clinical trials: Is blinding necessary? *Controlled Clinical Trials, 17,* 1–12.

Jüni, P., Altman, D. G., & Egger, M. (2001). Systematic reviews in health care: Assessing the quality of controlled clinical trials. *British Medical Journal, 323,* 42–46.

Kohatsu, N. D., Robinson, J. G., & Torner, J. C. (2004). Evidence-based public health: An evolving concept. *American Journal of Preventive Medicine, 27*(5), 417–421.

Koonce, T. Y., Giuse, N. B., & Todd, P. (2004). Evidence-based databases versus primary medical literature: An in-house investigation on their optimal use. *Journal of the Medical Library Association, 92*(4), 407–411.

Krahn, M., & Naglie, G. (2008). The next step in guideline development: Incorporating patient preferences. *Journal of the American Medical Association, 300*(4), 436–438.

Laupacis, A. (2006). On bias and transparency in the development of influential recommendations, *Canadian Medical Association Journal, 174,* 335–336.

Luborsky, L., Singer, B., & Luborsky, L. (1975). Comparative studies of psychotherapies. Is it true that "everywon has one and all must have prizes"? *Archives of General Psychiatry, 32*(8), 995–1008.

Luebbe, A. M., Radcliffe, A. M., Callands, T. A., Green, D., & Thorn, B. E. (2007). Evidence-based practice in psychology: Perceptions of graduates students in scientist-practitioner programs. *Journal of Clinical Psychology, 63*(7), 643–655.

Maciosek, M. V., Coffield, A. B., Edwards, N. M., Flottemesch, T. J., Goodman, M. J., & Solberg, L. I. (2006). Priorities among effective clinical preventive services: Results of a systematic review and analysis. *American Journal of Preventive Medicine, 31*(1), 52–61.

Maher, B. (1968). *Principles of psychopathology: An experimental approach.* New York: McGraw-Hill.

Mahon, J., Laupacis, A., Donner, A., & Wood, T. (1996). Randomised study of n of 1 trials versus standard practice. *British Medical Journal, 312,* 1069–1074.

McCourt, C. (2005). Research and theory for nursing and midwifery: Rethinking the nature of evidence. *Worldviews on Evidence-Based Nursing, 2*(2), 75–83.

McFall, R. M. (1991). Manifesto for a science of clinical psychology. *The Clinical Psychologist, 44,* 75–88.

McKibbon, A., Eady, A., & Marks, S. (2000). *PDQ evidence-based principles and practice.* New York: BC Decker Inc.

McLeroy, K. R., Bibeau, D., Steckler, A., & Glanz, K. (1988). An ecological perspective on health promotion programs. *Health Education Quarterly, 15*(4), 351–377.

McMaster University. (n.d.). How to teach evidence-based clinical practice. Retrieved March 3, 2009, from http://ebm.mcmaster.ca/

Meehl, P. E. (1973). *Psychodiagnosis: Selected papers.* Minneapolis: University of Minnesota Press.

Michel, L. A. (2007). The epistemology of evidence-based medicine. *Surgical Endoscopy, 21*(2), 145–151.

Miller, S. H. (2005). American board of medical specialties and repositioning for excellence in lifelong learning: Maintenance of certification. *Journal of Continuing Education in the Health Professions, 25*(3), 151–156.

Moher, D., Schulz, K. F., & Altman, D. (2001). The CONSORT statement: Revised recommendations for improving the quality of reports of parallel-group randomized trials. *Journal of the American Medical Association, 285*(15), 1987–1991.

Montori, V. M., Wilczynski, N. L., Morgan, D., & Haynes, R. B. for the Hedges Team. (2005). Optimal search strategies for retrieving systematic reviews from Medline: Analytical survey. *British Medical Journal, 330,* 68–73.

Moyer, V. A., Klein, J. D., Ockene, J. K., Teutsch, S. M., Johnson, M. S., & Allan, J. D. Childhood Obesity Working Group, US Preventive Services Task Force. (2005). Screening for overweight in children and adolescents: Where is the evidence? A commentary by the childhood obesity working group of the US preventive services task force. *Pediatrics, 116*(1), 235–238.

Muir Gray, J. A., Haynes, R. B., Sackett, D. L., Cook, D. J., & Guyatt, G. H. (1997). Transferring evidence from research into practice: 3. Developing evidence-based clinical policy. *ACP Journal Club, 126*(2), A14–16.

National Cancer Institute. (2006). *Using what works: Adapting evidence-based programs to fit your needs.* NIH Publication No. 06-5874. Washington DC: USDHHS.

Newhouse, R. P., Dearholt, S., Poe, S., Pugh, L. C., & White, K. (2007). *Johns Hopkins nursing evidence-based practice model and guidelines.* Indianapolis: Sigma Theta Tau International.

Norcross, J.C., Beutler, L. E., & Levant, R.F. (2005). *Evidence-based practices in mental health:Debate and dialogue on the fundamental questions.* Washington, DC: American Psychological Association.

Norheim, O. F. (2008). Moving forward on rationing. *British Medical Journal, 337*(1846), 903–904.

Oxford Center for Evidence-Based Medicine. (2001, May). Levels of evidence. Retrieved March 1, 2007, from http://www.cebm.net/levels_of_evidence.asp

Pagoto, S. L., Kozak, A. T., John, P., Bodenlos, J. S., Hedeker, D., Spring, B., et al. (2009). Intention to treat analyses in behavioral medicine randomized clinical trials. *International Journal of Behavioral Medicine, 16*(4), 316–322.

Pagoto, S. L., Spring, B., Coups, E. J., Mulvaney, S., Coutu, M., & Ozakinci, G. (2007). Barriers and facilitators of evidence-based practice perceived by behavioral science health professionals. *Journal of Clinical Psychology, 63*(7), 695–705.

Pai, M., McCulloch, M., Gorman, JD., Pai, N., Enanoria, W., Kennedy, G., et al. (2004). Systematic reviews and meta-analyses: An illustrated, step-by-step guide. *The National Medical Journal of India, 17*(2), 86–95.

Piantadosi, S. (2005). Comprehensive *clinical trials: A methodological perspective* (2nd ed.). New York: John Wiley & Sons.

Pocock, S. J. (1984). *Clinical trials: A practical approach.* New York: John Wiley & Sons.

Regehr, C., Stern, S., & Shlonsky, A. (2007). Operationalizing evidence-based practice: The development of an institute for evidence-based social work. *Research on Social Work Practice, 17*(3), 408–416.

Ruggill, J., & McAllister, K. (2006). The wicked problem of collaboration, *M/C Journal, 9(2).* Retrieved March 4, 2007 from http://journal.media-culture.org.au/0605/07-ruggillmcallister.php

Sackett, D. L., Rosenberg, W. M., Gray, J. A., Haynes, R. B., & Richardson, W. S. (1996). Evidence based medicine: What it is and what it isn't. *British Medical Journal, 312*(7023), 71–72.

Sackett, D. L., Strauss, S. E., Richardson, W. S., Rosenberg, W. M., & Haynes, R. B. (2000). *Evidence-based medicine: How to practice and teach EBM.* Edinburgh: Churchill Livingstone.

Sackett, D. L., & Wennberg, J. E. (1997). Choosing the best research design for each question. *British Medical Journal, 315,* 1636.

Sampson, M., Barrowman, N. J., Moher, D., Klassen, T. P., Pham, B., Platt, R., et al. (2003). Should meta-analysts search Embase in addition to Medline? *Journal of Clinical Epidemiology, 56,* 943–55.

Satterfield, J. M., Spring, B., Brownson, R. C., Mullen, E. J., Newhouse, R. P., Walker, B. B., et al. (2009). Toward a transdisciplinary model of evidence-based practice. *The Milbank Quarterly, 82*(2), 368–390.

Say, R. E., & Thomson, R. (2003). The importance of patient preferences in treatment decisions: Challenges for doctors. *British Medical Journal, 327*(7414), 542–545.

Schultz, K. F., & Grimes, D. A. (2002). Allocation concealment in randomised trials: Defending against deciphering, *The Lancet, 359*(9306), 614–618.

Spring, B. (2007). Evidence-based practice in clinical psychology: What it is, why it matters; what you need to know. *Journal of Clinical Psychology, 63*(7), 611–631.

Spring, B. (2008). Health decision making: Lynchpin of evidence-based practice. *Medical Decision Making, 28*(6), 866–874.

Spring, B., Pagoto, S., Kaufmann, P. G., Whitlock, E. P., Glasgow, R. E., Smith, T. W., et al. (2005). Invitation to a dialogue between researchers and clinicians about evidence-based behavioral medicine. *Annals of Behavioral Medicine, 30*(2), 125–137.

Spring, B., Pagoto, S., Knatterud, G., Kozak, A., & Hedeker, D. (2007). Examination of the analytic quality of behavioral health randomized clinical trials. *Journal of Clinical Psychology, 63*(1), 53–71.

Stetler, C. B. (2001). Updating the Stetler model of research utilization to facilitate evidence-based practice. *Nursing Outlook, 49*(6), 272–279.

Stinson, J. N., McGrath, P. J., & Yamada, J. T. (2003). Clinical trials in the Journal of Pediatric Psychology: Applying the CONSORT Statement. *Journal of Pediatric Psychology, 28,* 159–167.

Strauss, S. E., Richardson, W. S., Glasziou, P., & Haynes, R. B. (2005). *Evidence-based medicine: How to practice and teach EBM* (3rd ed.). New York: Elsevier.

Swinglehurst, D. A., Pierce, M., & Fuller, J. C. (2001). A clinical informaticist to support primary care decision making. *Quality in Health Care, 10*(4), 245–249.

Thornton, T. (2006). Tacit knowledge as the unifying factor in evidence based medicine and clinical judgment. *Philosophy, Ethics, & Humanities in Medicine, 1*(1), E2.

Titler, M. G., Kleiber, C., Steelman, V. J., Rakel, B. A., Budreau, G., Everett, L. Q., et al. (2001). The Iowa model of evidence-based practice to promote quality care. *Critical Care Nursing Clinics of North America, 13*(4), 497–509.

Turner, P. (2001). Evidence-based practice and physiotherapy in the 1990s. *Physiotherapy Theory and Practice, 17,* 107–121.

Viechtbauer, W. (2007). Confidence intervals for the amount of heterogeneity in meta-analysis. *Statistics in Medicine, 26,* 37–52.

Wampold, B. E. (2001). *The great psychotherapy debate: Models, methods, and findings.* Hillsdale, NJ: Lawrence Erlbaum Associates Publishers.

Weaver, C. A., Warren, J. J., & Delaney, C. for the International Medical Informatics Association Nursing Informatics Special Interest Group (IMIA-NI) Evidence-Based Practice Working Group. (2005). Bedside, classroom and bench: Collaborative strategies to generate evidence-based knowledge for nursing practice. *International Journal of Medical Informatics, 74,* 989–999.

Weissman, M. M., Verdeli, H., Gameroff, M. J., Bledsoe, S. E., Betts, K., Mufson, L., et al. (2006). National survey of psychotherapy training in psychiatry, psychology, and social work. *Archives of General Psychiatry, 63,* 925–934.

Wennberg, J., & Gittelsohn. (1973). Small area variations in health care delivery. *Science, 182*(117), 1102–1108.

Wennberg, J. E., Fisher, E. S., & Skinner, J. S. (2002). Geography and the debate over Medicare reform. *Health Affairs, Supplemental Web Exclusives,* W96–114.

Wennberg, J. E., Fisher, E. S., Stukel, T. A., & Sharp, S. M. (2004). Use of Medicare claims data to monitor provider-specific performance among patients with severe chronic illness. *Health Affairs, Supplemental Web Exclusives,* VAR5–18.

Westfall, J. M., Mold, J., & Fagnan, L. (2007). Practice-based research—"Blue Highways" on the NIH Roadmap. *Journal of the American Medical Association, 297,* 403–406.

Wilson, G. T. (1981). Relationships between experimental and clinical psychology: The case of behavior therapy. *International Journal of Psychology, 16,* 323–341.

World Health Organization. (2000). *The World Health Report 2000 – Health systems: Improving performance.* Geneva: World Health Organization.

Zerhouni, E. A. (2005). Translational and clinical science—time for a new vision. *New England Journal of Medicine, 353*(15), 1621–1623.

Training, Credentialing, and New Roles in Clinical Psychology: Emerging Trends

Catherine L. Grus

Abstract

This chapter provides an overview of key developments in the education, training, and credentialing of clinical psychologists; new roles in the field; and intersecting issues across these domains. Emerging issues highlighted within education and training include the move toward the assessment of competence in trainees, accreditation developments, and the doctoral internship match imbalance. Changes in licensing laws, mobility, and the degree of coordination between education and training and credentialing systems are described. Expanded roles for clinical psychologist, such as in health-care settings and public health, are reviewed. Finally, emerging developments such workforce analyses conducted within and across health-care professions and the relationship of issues such to national policy initiatives that are and will impact the future of clinical psychology are presented.

Keywords: Competency, credentialing, health care, licensure, training, workforce

Clinical psychology is the largest subfield of psychology at the doctoral level. Over 49.8% of doctoral degrees awarded in 2006–2007 were in clinical psychology, to a total of 2,483 individuals (APA, 2008c). This is not new: Clinical psychology has long been the subfield in which more individuals earn a doctoral degree among all others in the field; in 2001, 50% of doctorates earned were in clinical psychology (APA, 2003). A majority of the doctorates awarded in psychology are to women, as many as 72% in 2005, whereas minorities account for 19% (APA, 2005). The number of individuals earning PsyD degrees has been steadily increasing and now number more than those earning PhD degrees. In 2005, 47% of doctorates in clinical psychology earned were a PhD degree, and 53% earned a PsyD degree (APA, 2008c; APA Center for Workforce Studies [CWS], 2007a).

Doctoral programs in clinical psychology accredited by the American Psychological Association also have grown in the past 10 years. As of the 2005–2006 academic year, there were 226 accredited

doctoral programs in clinical psychology, which comprised 61.7% of all accredited programs (APA Committee on Accreditation, 2006). This is an increase of 39 accredited programs over 10 years. These clinical psychology programs were responsible for the education and training of 77.4% of all students enrolled in professional psychology doctoral programs, an increase from 74.4% in 2001 (APA Committee on Accreditation, 2001). Correspondingly, student enrollment has also increased. In 2001, there were 16,528 students enrolled in APA-accredited doctoral programs in clinical psychology; as of 2006, this number jumped to 25,973—an increase of 57.1% (APA Committee on Accreditation, 2001; APA Committee on Accreditation, 2006). Thus, clinical psychology continues to be a thriving and growing area within the field.

This chapter describes emerging trends in clinical psychology, with a focus on education, training, credentialing, and new roles. An overview of key issues for the field will be reviewed across these domains. Education and training prepares the individual for credentialing and practice, and serves as the cornerstone for entry into the profession. Education and training, in turn, should be guided by developments in the profession, including emerging roles, to ensure that students are properly prepared for the settings in which they will be working and the types of services they will provide. To that end, the linkages that are or should be occurring across these domains will be addressed with a focus on next steps for clinical psychology.

Education and Training in Clinical Psychology

Education and training in clinical psychology is at the forefront of several exciting initiatives and issues, many of which are broadly facing professional psychology. A strong focus continues to be on mechanisms for enhancing quality in education and training, which will be discussed in light of developments in the areas of competency-based education and training, and accreditation. A particular challenge that will be discussed is the internship match imbalance—the number of students seeking internship training compared to the number of internship training positions available. Emerging issues in education and training include evidence-based practice (EBP) in education and training, the role of technology in education, links between undergraduate and graduate education in psychology, student debt load, and issues with respect to practicum training.

Competency Initiatives

Perhaps one of the most significant developments in clinical psychology education and training—and, in fact, within professional psychology training more broadly—is the growing focus on measurement of student learning outcomes using the framework of competencies. The articulation of core competencies for professional psychologists dates back over two decades to a model developed by the National Council of Schools and Programs of Professional Psychology (NCSPP), which, in 1986, articulated six core competency areas (Peterson, Peterson, Abrams, & Stricker, 1997). However, in recent years, several major initiatives have taken place that have broadened the awareness and use of competency-based models of education and training in professional psychology. This series of events has been termed as a shift to a "culture of competence" (Roberts, Borden, Christiansen, & Lopez, 2005). Fundamentally, this shift represents a significant pedagogical change in which traditional models of education and training that were driven by curriculum and course objectives

are being replaced with a model in which the desired student learning outcomes, defined as competencies, shape the design of the learning experience (Nelson, 2006). The growing emphasis on competence as an outcome of education and training is not unique to professional psychology and, in fact, is occurring in other health-care disciplines, such as medicine, nursing, dentistry, and pharmacy (Medical School Objectives Writing Group, 1999; Spielman, Fulmer, Eisenberg, & Alfano, 2005; Watson, Stimpson, Topping, & Porock, 2002). Graduate medical education has moved to requiring all accredited programs to design their curriculum around, and measure student learning outcomes based on, six established core competencies (Accreditation Council for Graduate Medical Education, 2007).

The shift toward this culture of competence was accelerated and informed by psychology's 2002 Competencies Conference: Future Directions in Education and Credentialing. The outcome of that conference included agreement as to core competencies in professional psychology and a discussion of those methods of education and training leading to competence, including strategies for the assessment of competence (Kaslow, 2004; Kaslow et al., 2004). A further outcome of that conference was the conceptualization of a three-dimensional or "cube" model of competence development (Rodolfa, Bent, Eisman, Nelson, Rehm, & Ritchie, 2005). The model proposes that there are foundational competencies, which refer to the knowledge, skills, attitudes, and values that serve as the foundation for the functions a psychologist is expected to carry out, and these competencies are cross-cutting (e.g. reflective practice, ethics). There are also functional competencies that encompass the major functions that a psychologist is expected to carry out (e.g., assessment, intervention). The foundational and functional competencies intersect with one another and also vary by stage of professional development (e.g., doctoral level, internship, postdoctoral). This model has been widely embraced within professional psychology education and training, and has served as the guiding framework for two subsequent initiatives that have also had a significant impact on education and training: the Competency Benchmarks and the Competency Assessment Toolkit for Professional Psychology (Fouad et al., 2009; Kaslow et al., 2009).

The Competency Benchmarks is a document developed by a 32-member work group that met for 2 days in 2006; following this meeting, detailed revisions and enhancements were made during following 2 years (Fouad, et al., 2009). The document outlines 15 core foundational (professionalism, reflective practice, scientific knowledge and methods, relationships, individual and cultural diversity, ethical and legal standards and policy, interdisciplinary systems) and functional (assessment, intervention, consultation, research and evaluation, supervision, teaching, administration, and advocacy) competencies. Each of the core competencies is defined and then their essential components are further elaborated in detail. As an example, one of the core functional competencies is consultation, defined as the ability to provide expert guidance or professional assistance in response to a client's needs or goals. Consultation is comprised of four subdomains, for which essential components are articulated, specific to each stage of education and training: role of consultation, addressing the referral question, communication of findings, and application of methods (of consultation). For example, at the readiness-to-enter-practice level, the essential component of the role of the consultant is: "Determines situations that require different role functions and shift roles accordingly." Each essential component, in turn, has a series of benchmarks or operational definitions of the essential component, termed *behavioral anchors*. These behavioral anchors address the question, "What would this essential component look like if it were observed?" Essential components and their behavioral anchors are presented at three levels of the professional development sequence—readiness for practicum, readiness for internship, and readiness for entry to practice—and are graduated to reflect the development of competence across the sequence of education and training. Following the readiness-to-enter-practice example given previously, the behavioral anchors are: (1) recognizes situations in which consultation is appropriate and (2) demonstrates capability to shift functions and behavior to meet referral needs.

Defining and operationalizing the core competencies, across the developmental sequence of education and training, was a significant step in this shift to the culture of competence. However, also necessary to the assessment of competence is the establishment of approaches to best practices. The Competency Assessment Toolkit for Professional Psychology (Kaslow, et al., 2009) will address this need by developing a toolkit for the assessment of competence. The Toolkit was informed by similar efforts in general medicine (Accreditation Council for Graduate Medical Education and American Board of Medical Specialties; 2000). Further, the

work on the Toolkit was guided by efforts of the APA Board of Educational Affairs (BEA) Task Force on Assessment of Competence in Professional Psychology, which was convened in 2004 (Kaslow et al., 2006). The report of the task force and subsequent publications provide an overview of the competencies movement within professional psychology (Rubin et al., 2007), assessment models from other health professions (Leigh et al., 2007), challenges in the assessment of competence (Lichtenberg et al., 2007), and guiding principles for the assessment of competence (Kaslow et al., 2007).

Components of the toolkit include a series of fact sheets that describe 15 different assessment methods (e.g., rating forms, portfolios, standardized patients, etc.) of relevance to psychology education and training. Each fact sheet describes the method, its application to the assessment of competence, its implementation, and notes the available psychometric data, and it describes the strengths and challenges of the method. Further components of the toolkit include a grid that provides recommendations as to which assessment methods are best suited to assess specific core competences and their associated essential components, a glossary of terms, suggested references for further information, and a historical review of the competency movement in psychology.

Applying models of education and training that are based on the assessment of competence will pose several challenges for the field. New assessment tools need to be developed, and existing measures must be adapted for use in the assessment of competence. The role of assessment in education and training will require broadening to include regular use of formative evaluation (used to guide students toward ongoing development), as well as the use of summative evaluation to ascertain readiness to move to the next level in the sequence of training. Another challenge is posed by the fact that competence is developmental—expectations differ over time, and may not be demonstrated consistently across situations; two factors that must be addressed in both the design and interpretation of assessment results. Further, those charged with conducting the assessment of competence must be trained in the appropriate use of such methods, as well as how to optimally give student feedback in ways that meaningfully shape the education and training process.

Despite these challenges, given the focused effort that has been devoted to defining and assessing competence in professional psychology (as evidenced by the number of large-scale national initiatives), it seems unlikely that this will be a short-lived trend. The adoption of similar models by other health-care disciplines, as well as a focus at the national level on the importance of measuring student learning outcomes, also supports the continued role that competency-based education and training will play in psychology. Specialty-specific models have been developed, building on the cube model, for both geropsychology and clinical health psychology (Borrayo, 2006; France et al., 2008). Further, as will be discussed in later sections of this chapter, the developments within education and training on defining and measuring competence have relevance to efforts within credentialing, which has as its fundamental premise the assessment and awarding of a credential to those who demonstrate competence.

Developments in Accreditation of Education and Training Programs in Clinical Psychology

The APA Commission on Accreditation serves as the oversight body charged with evaluating and recognizing quality education and training programs in professional psychology—including clinical psychology—and for doctoral, internship, and postdoctoral programs. Although the Commission engages in ongoing discussion and takes action to enhance quality through its policies and procedures, three key events will be highlighted: the 1996 revisions to the Guidelines and Principles for Accreditation, the accreditation of programs in "developed practice areas," and the recent transition of the Committee on Accreditation to the Commission on Accreditation.

In 1996, revisions to the Guidelines and Principles for Accreditation of Programs in Professional Psychology were approved. One of the key changes was to move away from documenting the curriculum of the training program to an emphasis on outcomes assessment (Nelson, 2007). Specifically, programs are now required to declare a program model or philosophy of training and to demonstrate relevant outcomes, including the acquisition of competence across the broad and general domains of professional psychology. Although a number of training models have been broadly promulgated within professional psychology, clinical psychology programs have tended to identify with four models: Scientist-Practitioner, Practitioner-Scholar, Clinical Scientist, and Local Clinical Scholar.

The Scientist-Practitioner model is the model employed by the majority of doctoral programs in clinical psychology (Belar & Perry, 1992) and traces its origins to the Boulder Conference held in 1949, which was prompted by a need to better articulate what was, at that time, an emerging model of training in clinical psychology in which doctoral-level psychologists were beginning to be trained as service providers (Raimy, 1950). The Scientist-Practitioner model described the balance of preparing students for careers as both scientists and providers of services, a stark contrast from psychology's earlier history of focusing solely on research. In 1990, a national conference was held for the purpose of articulating the key features of the Scientist-Practitioner model, and delegates to that conference reaffirmed the importance of this model in the education and training of psychologists (Belar & Perry, 1992). The model, as articulated in the conference policy statement, involves the development of integrated skills within science and practice and is responsive to the changing knowledge and practice base within the field (Belar & Perry, 1992).

The Practitioner-Scholar model emerged as the outcome of another national training conference held in Vail, in 1973 (Korman, 1976). The impetus for the conference was dissatisfaction by some with training under the Scientist-Practitioner model, particularly in the area of how social issues were addressed (Belar, 1992). The Practitioner-Scholar model emphasizes the preparation for psychological practice that is informed by science. The Vail conference made a specific endorsement of the doctorate of psychology, and the participants recommended that the PsyD degree be awarded upon completion of the doctoral degree in a professional psychology program, given the training emphasis in these programs on the direct delivery of services and the evaluation of the efficacy of such (Korman, 1976).

The Local Clinical Scientist model notes that the clinician functions as a scientist, but in the local setting in which services are provided, thus the setting serves as a "metaphorical scientific laboratory" for the clinician (Stricker & Trierweiler, 2006). According to the Local Clinical Scientist model, data are gathered and combined with observations of the setting and the experience of the practitioner. Critical, scientific thinking is encouraged, as well as the application of scientific knowledge to clinical issues. Further, the model notes that the clinician is an active scientist and not acting as an applied scientist (Stricker & Trierweiler, 2006).

Clinical psychology also developed an education and training model specific to clinical psychology, known as the Clinical Scientist model, which also grew out of discontent with the Scientist-Practitioner model (McFall, 1991). A specific criticism raised against the Scientist-Practitioner model was that it does not promote the unification of science and practice; further, the goal of doctoral education is not to train individuals to work in specific settings, but to train scientists. McFall (1991) raised concern that the focus of education and training had shifted to mastering techniques and demonstrating that one had acquired knowledge. What was missing was critical thinking, mastery of scientific principles, and the solution of new problems by the independent application of scientific knowledge, principles, and methods. The Clinical Scientist model holds that the overarching goal of doctoral training is to produce competent clinical scientists who will practice as scientists.

Each of these models has a distinct origin and focus, and they are prominent constructs in education and training programs in clinical psychology. The decision to require education and training programs to identify a model of training and then to allow the model to be identified by the program for accreditation purposes has been criticized by some. It has been argued that such proliferation has allowed for a (continued) diffusion of the core identity of professional psychology (Benjamin, 2001). Nonetheless, the continued recognition of these models and their importance to the broadening definition of the field is attested to by their codification in the APA's procedures for accreditation of programs in professional psychology.

A second major policy development in accreditation was the establishment of criteria and a mechanism to accredit doctoral and internship programs in developed practice areas, which went into effect in 2007. Historically, accreditation was limited to programs in the broad specialty areas of clinical, counseling, or school psychology, or a combination of these. A developed practice area must have been recognized by an appropriate national organization, have a body of knowledge providing empirical support for the practice area, have a national training council that is recognized and active, develop and disseminate education and training guidelines, exist within established education and training programs, and have practitioners in the practice area who are geographically dispersed (APA Commission on Accreditation, 2008). Although no developed practice areas have as yet been recognized, this offers an expansion in the scope of programs eligible for accreditation. Such areas as clinical child psychology, for example, have long argued their distinctiveness (Roberts, 2006).

Finally, in 2008, the Committee on Accreditation became the Commission on Accreditation, increasing from 21 members to 32 (APA, 2008c). This change was approved by the APA Council of Representatives in 2006, based on recommended changes proposed at what is known as the "Snowbird Summit," which was convened in 2005, and based upon several years of due-diligence review of the accreditation structure. The increased number of members allows for a commission that more closely mirrors the representation of the diversity of professional psychology in terms of specialty training areas (e.g., clinical, counseling, school, NCSPP, the Academy of Psychological Clinical Science, the Council of Specialties), as well as in terms of levels of training (doctoral, internship, and postdoctoral). Further, in the future, accreditation of programs will be conducted by panels consisting of several members from a specific doctoral training model (as described earlier), with the intent of enhancing the quality of the review process by having specific expertise applied to the review of programs using a specific model.

Doctoral Internship Match

The doctoral internship required for completion of the doctoral degree in clinical psychology has been a focus of attention within clinical psychology and more broadly across all programs preparing the next generation of health-service providers. Specifically, recent years have seen large and increasing numbers of students failing to obtain an internship through the internship match process sponsored by the Association of Psychology Postdoctoral and Internship Centers (APPIC). In that process, students rank-order their preference for training sites, and training sites rank-order their preference for students. At a given date, the lists are "matched" and students are thereby chosen for their internship placement. Although the number of internship positions increased by 174 to a total of 3,058 in the 2008 APPIC internship match, this growth was insufficient to meet the demands of the 3,492 students seeking an internship, resulting in an overall match rate of 79% (APPIC, 2008). Although this figure is slightly better than the 75% match rate in 2007, it represents 743 and 842 individuals who went unmatched in the 2008 and 2007 APPIC internship matches, respectively. The number of students who did not obtain an internship in the match in 2007 was the largest in any year since the inception of the computerized match in 1999. Survey data collected by APPIC of students who participated in the 2007 match indicates that students from clinical psychology programs matched at rates comparable to other specialty areas (79% vs. 78% for counseling, 84% for school, 80% for combined) (APPIC, 2007).

Although the numbers of students who do not obtain an internship through the APPIC match process has increased to record levels, there is a long history of imbalance in the match (Kaslow & Keilin, 2006). National attention was focused on the internship match imbalance at a 1997 meeting co-sponsored by the APA and APPIC titled, "Supply and Demand: Training and Employment Opportunities in Professional Psychology" (Pederson, DePiano, Kaslow, Klepac, Hargrove, & Vasquez, 1997). This working conference focused on the supply-and-demand issues in professional psychology, with the goal of developing action steps that would better prepare psychology students at all levels of training for the changing employment market. Several resolutions were passed by the participants, such as a request for greater attention to systematic data collection, gathering more information about students seeking internship, and a recommendation that APA and APPIC should work together to develop and publicize data sets that are national, regional, and program-specific. As two of the national organizations most directly concerned with the internship match imbalance, APPIC and APA have both engaged in additional and ongoing efforts related to the internship match imbalance. The APPIC has provided mentorship to and consultation with new and developing internship programs and educational outreach to students and training faculty. Both groups have been involved in efforts to provide data about match outcomes to the public to both inform and assure transparency in the process. The APPIC has been collecting and disseminating comprehensive statistical data on match outcomes on its website (Baker, McCutcheon, & Keilin, 2007). The APA now collects and publishes data about specific program match outcomes in its publication *Graduate Study in Psychology*, which is also available in an online version. The creation, in 2006, of the APA Center for Workforce Studies, described in detail later in this chapter, will provide a data-based perspective of the field of psychology that is necessary to understand possible pathways toward improvement (Rozensky, Grus, Belar, Nelson, & Kohout, 2007). Further, the APA engages in advocacy initiatives to raise awareness about the critical need for funding for psychology education and training. For example, the Graduate Psychology

Education Program (GPE), which was established in 2002, was funded by the U.S. Congress at $1.8 million in 2007 and 2008, and hopes to be funded at $4 million in 2009 (APA, 2008a). The GPE grants provide support to education and training programs whose students provide services to underserved populations in interdisciplinary settings.

Despite these and other efforts to address the APPIC internship match imbalance, it has persisted. In recognition of this, in 2007, a special issue of the *Journal of Training and Education in Professional Psychology* was published, in which articles addressing this issue were written by the various doctoral training councils, APPIC, APA, and the American Psychological Association of Graduate Students (APAGS). Each article offered observations on the nature of the internship match imbalance and proposed efforts to address the imbalance. Collins, Callahan, and Klonoff (2007), providing a perspective from the Scientist-Practitioner model, proposed a "Stairway to Competency" model, and urged the focus of the field to shift away from a focus on the attainment of an internship and to those methods by which competence is developed in students and to the role that internship training and the program–internship match play in the development of competencies. Entry-level competence, which is at the top of the stairway model, is built upon trainee characteristics, the doctoral program, and the internship year. Hutchings, Mangione, Dobbins, and Wechsler (2007), representing the perspective of NSCPP note three factors contributing to the internship match imbalance: decreased financial support for internship training, a relative lack of connectivity between doctoral programs and internships, and that internships tend to be housed in traditional settings and have not yet moved into the breadth of practice settings in which psychologists are employed. They advocate for expanding internship sites and positions as one of the more viable pathways to improve the internship match imbalance. Other suggestions include the need for ongoing advocacy initiatives aimed at securing funding for internship training, looking at innovative ways to support training, and for examining the sequence and structure of doctoral training.

Concerns have been raised about the impact of the internship match imbalance on the quality of internship training that students receive. These include students failing to develop the necessary competencies for entry-level to practice (Collins, Callahan, & Klonoff, 2007) and a possible push to lower standards for internship training or eliminate the doctoral internship altogether (Baker, McCutcheon, & Keilin, 2007; Keilin, Baker, McCutcheon, & Peranson, 2007). This is a significant issue for clinical psychology (and all of professional psychology), and will require ongoing attention and efforts directed toward pathways that will address the internship match imbalance.

Emerging Trends in Education and Training

Several emerging trends relevant to education and training in clinical psychology will be mentioned. These include training in EBP, the role of technology in education, linkages between undergraduate and graduate education and training, the balance between preparing students for practice and for the production of scientific knowledge, practicum training, and debt loads for those earning doctorates in psychology.

TRAINING IN EVIDENCE-BASED PRACTICE

The scientific foundations of practice in psychology are a required component of the doctoral curriculum for programs accredited by the APA (Belar, 2003). All four training models that are typically employed by clinical psychology education and training programs emphasize the role of science as it relates to practice (Hunsely, 2007). So, although not a new focus for education and training, the use of EBP has become a large-scale conversation across health professions in recent years, including policy statements advocating for the use of EBP issued by both psychology and medicine (APA, 2005; Institute of Medicine [IOM], 2001, p. 147). Evidence-based practice, as defined by APA policy is, "the integration of the best available research with clinical expertise in the context of patient characteristics, culture, and preferences" (APA, 2005). Medicine adopted a similar statement in 2000 (IOM, 2001). Some of the challenges for education and training programs seeking to provide training in EBP include finding a balance between instruction in the science behind a method without neglecting attention to the patient as an individual (Belar, 2003). It is also necessary to train students in self-assessment, such that self-directed study can occur and prepare students to engage in lifelong learning (Belar, 2003; Hunsely, 2007). Further evidence must be gathered about best teaching methods to train in EBP, and supervisors need to model the use of EBP to their trainees (Belar, 2003). Challenges identified by training directors include the need to clarify if the intent of training is to teach a specific protocol

versus training in the principles of EBP, lack of time, lack of trained supervisors, lack of an evidence-base for all clinical issues that students will be expected to confront in practice, and opposition to the approach, as it can be perceived to limit one's autonomy as a provider (Woody, Weisz, & McClean, 2005). These challenges must be addressed by education and training programs in clinical psychology, both now and in the future.

TECHNOLOGY IN EDUCATION

The role of technology in education and training has become greater, offering both challenges and opportunities for clinical psychology. Technology has become infused in education and training across all levels and settings, and includes classroom-based tools and technology to capture student performance for evaluation purposes, as well as its application in supervision and distance learning programs. The delivery of quality education and training using distance learning methods and the use of technology to evaluate and supervise clinical training are tools that are being used in education and training at the doctoral level in psychology.

Distance education is increasingly popular across other health professions and in education in general. Distance education programs are diverse, and can vary from students gathering at a satellite location to those programs that are primarily Internet-based with little in-person, face-to-face interaction (Murphy, Levant, Hall, & Glueckauf, 2007). For psychology, the application of traditional models for quality assurance of education and training programs to distance education programs poses a challenge that has yet to be resolved (Murphy, Levant, Hall, & Glueckauf, 2007). Specific areas that will require continued focus include the roles of mentorship, pedagogy, and residency in distance education (Nelson et al., 2008, pp. 30-31). Distance education may offer opportunities to enhance education and training through improved communication with students on internship, to present courses with low enrollment at one site to students across many sites, and to broaden exposure to cultural diversity (Murphy et al., 2007). Technology, in the form of *telehealth*, offers additional opportunities for education and training in psychology, particularly in rural settings. Telehealth can reduce barriers to face-to-face supervision secondary to distance between practice settings (Wood, Miller, & Hargrove, 2005). Further, it is likely that computer technology will serve an increasing role in the assessment of competence for professional practice in both education and training, and at the level of licensure (Nelson, 2007).

LINK TO UNDERGRADUATE CURRICULUM

Another future challenge for clinical psychology is fostering better linkages across levels of education and training. Although efforts, such as the communication guidelines developed by the Council of Chairs of Training Councils (CCTC, 2007), to address the perceived lack of continuity between doctoral and internship programs, limited systematic attention has been given to the connection between undergraduate and doctoral education in psychology. Interestingly, attention to issues of quality in education and training advanced through the assessment of competence now pervades discussion in both groups, although, to date, these discussions have occurred independently. Guidelines developed for the undergraduate psychology major outline ten goals and learning objectives applicable across educational settings (APA, 2007). The guidelines articulate the knowledge, skills, and values to be acquired with respect to the science and application of psychology, and with respect to a liberal arts education, that are then further developed in psychology. Future directions would include mapping the undergraduate guidelines and the benchmark documents onto each other to look for overlap, continuity, and opportunities to enhance that continuity.

BALANCE BETWEEN PREPARING STUDENTS FOR PRACTICE AND FOR THE PRODUCTION OF SCIENTIFIC KNOWLEDGE

As noted in the discussion of the common education and training models employed by clinical psychology doctoral programs, all emphasize the role of a background in science and practice as necessary for those training to practice clinical psychology. Although psychology has its historical roots as a science-based profession, growing numbers of individuals are choosing to focus their careers on the practice of psychology and less on the production of new scientific knowledge, as exemplified by the growing popularity of doctoral programs leading to the PsyD. Further, this balance may be influenced by students who are seeking to enhance their "competitiveness" in the APPIC internship match through ever-increasing hours of training (Kaslow & Keilin, 2006; Miville, Adams, & Juntunen (2007).

Merlo, Collins, and Bernstein (2008) offer data that suggest that clinical psychology education and training programs have been able to maintain a balance between training to produce scientific knowledge and practice training. In a sample of clinical psychology programs that emphasized science and practice training, students using a 5-point scale to report the rating of the mix of practice and science training rated their programs at 3.53 (5 = primarily research focused). Students reported spending an average of 37% of their time in research training activities, as compared to 29% in clinical training activities. Overall, students, on average, reported optimal levels of training. In contrast, in a survey of counseling psychology doctoral programs, Miville, Adams, and Juntunen (2007) reported that 36% of their sample reported decreased emphasis on research training as result of increased focus on helping students with the internship match process.

Although the current internship match imbalance may be highlighting the balance of training for practice and for the production of scientific knowledge in clinical psychology, these concerns were raised early on by participants in the Vail Conference (Korman, 1976), which recommended that a clear delineation should be set between the PsyD and PhD degrees in psychology. The PhD degree was appropriate for those programs whose focus was on education and training to develop new knowledge in psychology. The PsyD degree should be awarded to those programs that prepare students for the practice of psychology. More recently, L.W. Craighead and W.E. Craighead (2006) proposed that clinical psychology doctoral programs should offer a joint PhD and PsyD degree if their intent is to train researchers and clinicians who would go on to seek licensure. In contrast, the PhD degree should be awarded solely as a research degree. The field will likely continue to struggle with the balance between preparation for practice and for the production of scientific knowledge in the education and training of clinical psychologists. As Benjamin (2001) noted, the field cannot answer the question, "what is a psychologist," in that we have neither defined the field nor identified a core curriculum.

PSYCHOLOGY PRACTICUM TRAINING

Another issue in professional psychology education and training that has been emerging more recently relates to the quality, quantity, and details of psychology practicum training. Increases in the numbers of practicum training hours are occurring, with students accruing more hours in hopes that this will enhance their standing as an intern applicant (Kaslow & Keilin, 2006; Ko & Rodolfa, 2005; Rodolfa, Ko, & Peterson, 2004). Ko and Rodolfa (2005) reported that a majority of academic, internship, and postdoctoral training directors felt that there should be a minimum required number of practicum hours prior to internship. However, academic training directors reported a significantly lower number of minimum hours than the other two groups. Respectively, the mean number of hours reported as optimal prior to internship were 1,094, 1,255, and 1,233 for academic, internship, and postdoctoral program directors, respectively. These are all well below the average number of hours that students are reporting—with an average of 1,941 reported for 1989–1999; 2,199 for 2002; and 1,896 in 2003 (Ko & Rodolfa, 2005).

In an effort to address the issue of quality practicum training as assessed through attending to the competencies students acquire, Hatcher and Lassiter (2007) report on the development of the Practicum Competencies Outline, which was prepared by a work group formed by the Association of Directors of Psychology Training Clinics (ADPTC) whose members are directly involved in psychology training clinics offering practicum training. The efforts of this work group were later folded into efforts of a work group formed by CCTC, which approved a final document in 2005 (Hatcher & Lassiter, 2007). The intent of this project was to approach the issue of practicum competencies from a developmental and training-focused perspective. Specific goals were (a) to define the knowledge, skills, and attitudes needed prior to beginning practicum training; (b) articulate the domains of competency in professional psychology; and (c) define the level of competence that would reasonably be expected to occur at the completion of practicum training. The Practicum Competencies Outline provides a structure for the assessment of competence in students as they prepare to enter practicum training and as move through their practicum training experiences, thus offering an alternative to existing models of education and training that have focused on obtaining hours of training in absence of attention to the outcome of the training, as measured in the assessment of competence (Kaslow & Keilin, 2006).

DEBT LOAD

With more than 70% of doctoral degree recipients in clinical psychology reporting that it takes 5–6 years to complete their degree, financing graduate education is a significant issue (APA, 2008b). Loans, student earnings, and family financial support were reported to make up 69.4% of support for students enrolled in clinical psychology doctoral programs. In contrast, 50.8% of those earning doctorates in research or other subfields of psychology reported research/teaching assistantships as their primary source of financial support (as contrasted to 22.9% of clinical psychology students) (APA CWS, 2007b). Students in clinical psychology doctoral programs are more likely to incur debt than are their counterparts in research and other subfields of psychology (79% vs. 52%), with an average debt of over $82,000 at the time of receipt of their doctorate (APA CWS, 2007b).

The setting in which students obtain their doctorate appears to be a primary factor in regard to the amount of debt incurred. Rapoport, Kohout, and Wicherski (2000) note that, during the period from 1993 to 1996, PhD degree recipients from professional schools of psychology (as compared to traditional universities) were more likely (41% vs. 15%) to have debt in excess of $30,000. As noted previously, over 50% of clinical psychology doctorates are PsyD degrees, and a majority of PsyD programs are located within professional schools of psychology. When compared to other science and engineering PhD degree recipients, the debt incurred by psychology doctoral students exceeds that of all other fields, with an excess of $30,000 of debt reported by 19% of all doctoral recipients in psychology. The next closest field was social science at 8% (Rapoport, Kohout, & Wicherski, 2000).

The implications of debt load on the future of clinical psychology remain unclear, although enrollments are up and more programs continue to become accredited by the APA, thus suggesting that it remains a popular career option. The interplay of the debt load issue and the internship imbalance remain contemporary problems in need of discipline-wide attention.

Credentialing

Just as with education and training, credentialing in clinical psychology is also confronting several emerging and ongoing issues. This section addresses issues such as changes to licensing laws specific to when license eligibility occurs, mobility for psychologists, specialty board certification, and the Examination for Professional Practice in Psychology (EPPP). Emerging opportunities in credentialing will be discussed, focusing on the intersection and linkages between education, training, and credentialing in psychology.

Changes in Psychology Licensing Laws

In some jurisdictions, 2007 and 2008 ushered in significant changes to psychology licensing laws, relative to the point in the training sequence at which one is eligible to seek licensure. These changes are secondary to a 2006 policy statement approved by the APA that addresses when in the sequence of education and training an individual might be considered eligible to become licensed:

> The American Psychological Association recommends that for admission to licensure applicants demonstrate that they have completed a sequential, organized, supervised professional experience equivalent to 2 years of full-time training that can be completed prior or subsequent to the granting of the doctoral degree. For applicants prepared for practice in the health services domain of psychology, one of those 2 years of supervised professional experience shall be a pre-doctoral internship.
>
> (*APA*, 2006)

This policy is a significant departure from previous guidelines, which stated that a period of postdoctoral training was needed prior to seeking licensure for independent practice, as reflected in documents such as the APA Model Act for Licensure (Office of Professional Affairs APA, 1987) and the ASPPB Model Act for Licensure of Psychologists (Rodolfa, Ko, & Peterson, 2004). In 2004, a majority of states (92%) required postdoctoral experience prior to being eligible for licensure (Rodolfa, Ko & Peterson, 2004). The policy had its origins in the APA Commission on Education and Training Leading to Licensure in Psychology that was convened in 2000, in response to the difficulties experienced by students seeking postdoctoral supervised hours for licensure (Olvey, Hogg, & Counts, 2002). The Commission drafted a report maintaining that 2 years of experience should be required for licensure, but it recommended flexibility in the timing and sequence of 2 two years. One of those years should be the doctoral internship, the second could either be completed as practicum or in a postdoctoral fellowship. After the report was received, it was decided that no action would be taken for a period of 5 years from the meeting of the Commission. In 2005, the APA Board of Directors Work Group met to review progress within the field relevant to the Recommendations of the Commission as a context for considering any change to APA policy. The report of the Work Group led to the policy statement that was passed in 2006. Although there have been misperceptions that the intent of the policy is to eliminate postdoctoral training, the policy does make an explicit statement on the continued importance of postdoctoral education in training.

In the United States and Canada, each jurisdiction has its own psychology licensing laws, thus each will have to decide whether to seek changes within its jurisdiction. So far, the policy statement has led to changes in state licensing laws in Washington state and Utah, with a bill proposing changes pending in Ohio. Several other states are discussing the possibility of making changes. One consequence of these changes in licensing laws is that changes are being made in the education and training requirements for licensure, most evident with respect to increased specificity about the nature of practicum experiences that are acceptable to count toward licensure. As a result, the Association of State and Provincial Psychology Licensing Boards (ASPPB, 2008b) convened a Practicum Task Force that met in 2007 to craft model statutory language that could be used by state licensing boards concerning the practicum training experiences used to qualify for licensure. The task force was convened as several jurisdictions had or were seeking to make changes consistent with the 2006 APA policy statement. By drafting model language, the ASPPB sought to encourage the use of consistent standards across jurisdictions. A final draft of the model regulations is expected to be approved (ASPPB, 2008b). Such changes raise another credentialing issue of significance for professional psychology, including clinical psychologists: the issue of mobility for those seeking licensure in other jurisdictions at a later point in their career.

Licensure and Mobility

With each jurisdiction in the United States and Canada having different requirements for licensure, and as psychologists broaden their practice settings to work in multiple jurisdictions, mobility for psychologists is increasingly discussed (Hall & Boucher, 2003). Although attempts at automatic reciprocity have not been successful, three vehicles exist that facilitate mobility for licensed psychologists seeking licensure in a different jurisdiction: (1) "banking" one's credentials with the National Register of Health Service Providers in Psychology (National Register), (2) the Certificate of Professional Qualifications in Psychology (CPQ) available through the ASPPB, and (3) specialty board certification by the American Board of Professional Psychology (ABPP). Each of these mechanisms offers endorsement of one's credentials, which facilitates the licensure process, but does not supplant the state- or jurisdiction-based process (Hall & Boucher, 2003).

The National Register is a credentialing organization that verifies that health-service providers have obtained a doctoral degree in psychology, completed supervised experience, and possess an active, unrestricted license to practice at the independent level with no disciplinary sanctions (Hall & Boucher, 2003). The CPQ also includes verification of one's credentials, certifying that one has meet the criteria for license eligibility, but has the additional requirement of licensure for at least 5 years (DeMers & Jonason, 2006). Agreements to accept the CPQ have been reached in 39 jurisdictions, with eight others in process, and eight that "recognize" the CPQ (ASPPB, 2008a). The ASPPB also maintains a credentials bank. Being able to bank one's credentials is an important concept for students. Both the programs by the National Register and ASPPB offer students the opportunity to submit documentation of the components required for licensure as they are completed and, by banking one's credentials with one of these organizations, they are more readily available if needed later in one's career (DeMers & Jonason, 2006; Hall & Boucher, 2003). Specialty board certification by the ABPP, which will be described in detail in a later section, requires the applicant to submit documentation of his or her education and training qualifications as part of the specialty certification process. Many jurisdictions will accept the ABPP as verification that the education and training requirements for licensure have been met (Hall & Boucher, 2003). There are costs involved for the student or licensed professional who chooses to use these services to maintain documentation of their credentials.

In Canada, the Mutual Recognition Agreement (MRA) has been successful in facilitating mobility for psychologists who seek licensure in a province or territory other than the one in which they are currently licensed. Further, the MRA is a model of how the assessment of competence can be used in the credentialing process for psychology (Nelson, 2007). Development of the MRA was triggered by a 1994 agreement by federal, provincial, and territorial governments to reduce barriers to mobility for workers, goods, services, and capital between the territories and provinces of Canada. The MRA, which was signed in 2001, defines parameters that allow for a psychologist who is licensed at the independent level to have his or her qualifications in one jurisdiction recognized in another. A key feature of the MRA is that it is a competency-based agreement, with applicants required to demonstrate competency in five core areas using a variety of sources and methods (Gauthier, 2002). These competency areas are interpersonal relationships, assessment and diagnosis, intervention and consultation, research, and ethics and standards.

A future challenge in credentialing is the issue of global mobility, as more psychologists extend their practice outside the United States and Canada, consistent with the increasing globalization of society. Opportunities exist for psychologists to provide services either physically in other countries or virtually through the use of technology (Hall & Lunt, 2005). As a result, there is a growing desire for a global mobility process that is both easy and efficient. For several reasons (including the varying educational requirements to become a psychologist across different countries) efforts are being directed toward advocating for mechanisms by which endorsements of credentials can be recognized across countries, as opposed to attempting the daunting feat of trying to reach consistency among the credentials awarded (Hall & Lunt, 2005). To date, efforts have not moved beyond the level of developing the framework by which international mobility for psychologists might be facilitated. Developing standards remains to be done, and presents a future challenge for the field (Hall & Lunt, 2005).

Advanced Credentialing and Specialization

Licensure for a psychologist is an entry-level credential and generic in scope (i.e., one is licensed as a psychologist and not, for example, as a clinical psychologist) in the majority of jurisdictions (Dattilio, 2002). Advanced credentialing, in the form of board certification, is a method by which the public and other professionals can be assured that a psychologist has demonstrated the skills and qualifications required to practice in a specialty area (Dattilio, 2002). Board certification, after initial licensure, is the model routinely employed in medicine for physicians. The oldest and most recognized entity offering specialty board certification to psychologists is the ABPP, which has been in existence since 1947 and recognizes and certifies 13 specialty areas (Packard & Simon, 2006) including cognitive and behavioral psychology, clinical psychology, clinical child and adolescent psychology, clinical health psychology, clinical neuropsychology, counseling psychology, family psychology, forensic psychology, group psychology, psychoanalysis in psychology, rehabilitation psychology, school psychology, and organizational and business consulting psychology. Board certification is a voluntary process, offering the psychologist the opportunity to document specialized expertise in a specific domain. Board certification by ABPP requires all applicants to have earned a doctoral degree from an APA or Canadian Psychological Association accredited program or a program designated by the National Register, and to be licensed at the independent-practice level. Each of the specialty boards in turn has a board-specific examination that typically includes submission of representative work samples and an oral examination.

Despite the potential advantages for the field, as well as for the individual provider, offered by obtaining board certification, the numbers of psychologists certified by the ABPP is relatively low compared to the overall number of licensed psychologists. Estimates suggest that less than 3.5% of licensed psychologists or just over 3,300 have obtained board certification through the ABPP (Dattilio, 2002). Possible reasons include the costs associated with seeking board certification, time, misperception about the pass rates, and questions about the value added by board certification. However, in some employment settings, such as hospitals, board certification is required or expected (as it is within medicine) and in others, such as the Veteran's Administration and the military, bonuses are offered to psychologists who have board certification (Dattilio, 2002).

Recently, the ABPP began an Early Entry Option program that allows students enrolled in doctoral programs (as well as interns and postdoctoral fellows) to begin to bank a record of completion of each requirement for the ABPP at a reduced cost and without having to declare which specialty board certification they are planning to seek. The requirements for credentials review will be the same for all applicants, regardless if they seek the early entry option or not (ABPP, 2008).

Examination for Professional Practice in Psychology and Practice Analysis

The Examination for Professional Practice in Psychology (EPPP), the national licensing examination for psychology, is offered by the ASPPB and administered through the Professional Examination Service (PES). First administered in 1965, the EPPP is developed with oversight by an examination committee appointed by the ASPPB (Terris, 1973). The examination was created for the purpose of assessing

the knowledge, understanding, and judgment deemed important to the practice of psychology (Terris, 1973). The EPPP sets a minimum standard for use for licensure with a set pass/fail point; it is not intended to identify excellence (Terris, 1973). The PES conducts periodic studies, or practice analyses, in which licensed psychologists in the United States and Canada are surveyed regarding the practice of professional psychology and the knowledge needed for such, in order to assess the validity of the content domains of the EPPP and update it as warranted. The ASPPB recently began a new practice analysis to update those done in 2003 and 1995. Of note, a focus of the current practice analysis will be to identify underlying professional competencies and to identify methods best suited to assess these.

Linkages Between Education and Training and Credentialing/Regulatory Organizations

As Nelson (2007) notes, professional psychology education and training and credentialing/licensure systems developed independently of one another, although each continues to struggle with issues of quality assurance. Historically, there have been efforts by these two diverse communities to engage in shared conversations. Two examples of how this has occurred in formal context are the Council of Credentialing Organizations in Professional Psychology (CCOPP) and the CCTC.

The CCOPP was formed in 1996, in response to the establishment of a formal recognition process for specialties in professional psychology by the APA through the creation of the Commission for the Recognition of Specialties and Proficiencies in Professional Psychology (CRSPPP). The intent was to convene organizations to discuss the impact of specialty recognition on the profession and its education, training, and credentialing practices. It was hoped that the CCOPP could serve to promote open lines of communication and reduce policy conflict on issues of specialty and proficiency recognition, accreditation, and credentialing. The CCOPP was not formed as a decision- or policy-making entity independent from its member organizations. Rather, through shared expertise and information, it would serve to analyze, from different perspectives, issues that may have policy implications. Original membership in the CCOPP included credentialing and regulatory organizations in both the United States and Canada. To enhance the discussions, early in its history, a decision was made to include liaison representation from the doctoral training councils, those groups formed for the purpose of organizing and promoting education and training within a specialty area of psychology (e.g., clinical, counseling psychology).

Further, the CCTC was developed to foster communication across diverse constituent groups within professional psychology's education and training communities, but to also include in the conversation representation from regulatory and credentialing organizations. The CCTC was formed in the mid 1980s. A mission statement was developed in the late 1990s that articulated the role of the CCTC in promoting discussion, encouraging communication, developing recommendations, and providing comment, thus providing a more active charge to the group beyond that of sharing information. Both the ASPPB and the National Register were active liaisons to the CCTC from its inception, and the CCTC has provided a unique context in which shared conversations occur among education and training groups and credentialing bodies (Nelson, 2007).

Recent events suggest that the exemplars of collaborative interaction among education and training groups and regulatory/credentialing bodies will continue and likely become more critical in the future. One key example was the recent ASPPB Practicum Task Force, noted in an earlier section. The ASPPB invited eight representatives from the education and training community, with expertise specific to defining and measuring competence, to attend the task force meeting and inform the discussion (ASPPB, 2008). This process helped to ensure that the proposed regulations used language and constructs consistent with models of professional psychology education and training. In addition, inviting representation from education and training was helpful in terms of achieving mutual acceptance of the product of such a working group, in that the education and training programs (for example, graduate departments and internship programs) would likely have to make changes to their existing program requirements and practices if they were going to enable their students to meet any changes in the requirements for licensure. Additionally, the ASPPB has made a formal commitment to establishing connections with the professional psychology education and training community by appointing a liaison to the major training councils (ASPPB, 2008b). The intent is to provide information about the licensure process to education and training groups, which would serve both students and the licensing boards by producing applicants better prepared to go through the steps of the licensure process.

One of the key forces driving this convergence is the continued and increasing conversations about the definition of and methods used to assess competence in professional psychologists. Although each community has had a longstanding investment in the construct, recently collaboration has expanded with the involvement of both groups in national initiatives such as the Competencies Conference (Kaslow et al., 2004) and the APA Benchmarks and Toolkit work groups (Fouad, et al., 2009; Kaslow, et al., 2009). As Nelson (2007) notes, "it is as common now as it was uncommon 30–50 years ago for those who represent these different roles and perspectives of professional responsibility to engage with one another in trying to address the challenges we face" (p. 8).

As the shift to a culture of competence moves forward in professional psychology education, training, and credentialing, the need for the assessment of competence must be infused throughout the sequence of education and training. This will ensure a best-practice approach to the assessment of competence. As Nelson (2007) notes, high-stakes summative evaluations, such as the licensing examination, must not only have fidelity with regards to actual practice, but also must reflect the education and training of the person being assessed.

New Roles for Clinical Psychologists
Health-service Provider

An emerging, or rather, increasing trend for clinical psychology will be expanded numbers of clinical psychologists providing services in health-care settings. Although psychologists practicing in health-care settings are not new, this trend represents an emerging opportunity for clinical psychology (Rozensky, 2008). Clinical psychologists seeking to expand their practice into health-care settings can benefit from the framework for this type of practice found in the literature of clinical health psychology, a long-established domain within the field that traces its roots back to 1969. A division of the APA representing clinical health psychology was formed in 1978. Clinical health psychology was recognized by the ABPP as a specialty in 1991, and by the APA in 1997 (Belar, 2008). Further, in 2001, the word "health" was added to the bylaws and mission statement of the APA, adding further emphasis to the roles that psychologists play in promoting health (Rozensky, 2008).

Clinical health psychology is recognized as a distinctive and encompassing specialty, and offers a definition of psychology practice that expands beyond that of a mental health profession to a health profession (Belar, 2008). Clinical health psychology focuses on both the psychological aspects of illness and treatment, as well as on the promotion of health and prevention of illness (Vandenbos, DeLeon, & Belar, 1991). Psychology's role in providing services in health-care settings has been expanding. Its influence is reflected in the development of special billing codes (known as health and behavior codes) specific to those psychological services provided to patients with medical problems but without psychiatric diagnoses (Belar, 2008). Models of education and training in clinical health psychology are well established, having first been articulated by the Arden House Conference in 1983, and the more recent competency model for clinical health psychology (France et. al., 2008).

In 1991, Vandenbos, DeLeon, and Belar noted the relevance of psychology's research and practice base to health-care settings and issues, and how this led to increased practice opportunities. Deleon, Kenkel, and Belar (2007) also noted the need and opportunity for psychologists to become more integrated into the culture of health-care settings, specifically primary care. Embedding education and training in community health centers offers exciting training opportunities, including working within the context of a team-based approach to health care, the opportunity for greater understanding of the unique skills and knowledge psychology brings to the health-care setting, and exhibiting how those who receive services benefit from such psychological interventions. Belar (2007) noted that psychology has a way to go to meet this opportunity with respect to educating and training a workforce prepared to function within health-care settings. She noted that about 10% of accredited psychology internship programs are in medical schools, and only about ten of the 375 accredited doctoral programs are in such settings. Belar (2007) urges psychology to expand research and training opportunities in those settings, with attention paid to training both future psychologists, as well to training individuals from other health-care disciplines to work with psychology.

An emerging role for psychology within the arena of health care is found within the sphere of public health (Rozensky, 2008). This represents a shift toward providing interventions that are prevention-based as opposed to treatment-oriented. Specifically, there are opportunities for the field to expand the range of services provided to the public health sector and make unique contributions. Rozensky (2008) notes that several of the leading health indicators listed in Healthy People 2010 are behavioral health issues that impact public health (e.g., physical activity, overweight and obesity; and tobacco and substance use). In addition, such a model of service delivery entails a population-based, community-oriented approach, an arena in which psychology has had relatively little involvement to date.

Workforce Analysis and the Future of Clinical Psychology

Future roles for clinical psychologist depend on the extent and quality of information available about the workforce. Psychology has been debating for some time the societal needs for the psychology workforce, and in what types of settings psychologists are needed, at what numbers, and where emerging employment opportunities are located. A major reason that no definitive conclusions have been reached about the size and nature of the psychology workforce is largely due to the historical approach to data gathering conducted within the field. Isolated samples (snapshots) of the psychology workforce were taken as opposed to a comprehensive approach that integrates multiple sources of data across many venues and over time (Rozensky et al., 2007).

Robiner (1991) and Robiner, Ax, Stamm, and Harowski (2002) argue that, given the dramatic increases in the number of psychologists being trained and subsequently entering the workforce, it would only be a matter of time before the workforce would have more psychologists than needed. Robiner's conclusions were challenged by VandenBos, DeLeon, and Belar (1991), noting that psychology's increasing presence as a health-care profession had not been adequately accounted for. Further, employment forecasts for psychologists from the Bureau of Labor Statistics estimate that the need for clinical, counseling, and school psychologists will increase from approximately 167,000 in 2004 to 199,000 in 2014, a 19% increase; although these data do not include those earning a PsyD degree (Commission on Professionals in Science and Technology, 2006).

The employment picture in the academy suggests that faculty are being hired increasingly into part-time and\or non–tenure track positions (Barker & Kohout, 2003). For psychology specifically, a similar trend was observed from the mid 1980s to the late 1990s, in which part-time employment in colleges and universities among those with doctorates in psychology has risen from 7% to 10%. The overall number of faculty with a degree in psychology increased from 18,730 to 19,320 between 1992 and 1998. Of those, the number with doctorates increased from 11,810 to 12,130, indicating that half of the new positions in psychology were for those with doctorates (Barker & Kohout, 2003). Those with a doctorate were also more likely to have a standard (regular, full-time) position. Women were just as likely to be in standard versus nonstandard jobs, whereas for men, standard employment was more likely. With regard to tenure-line positions, Barker and Kohout reported that 43.5% of those with doctorates were in positions or institutions that did not offer tenure, with an overall increase from 39.9% of positions being ineligible for tenure in 1992 to 44.5% in 1998.

The need to expand the number of ethnic minority faculty in psychology is a further significant challenge for the field. Faculty from minority backgrounds continue to be represented at low levels (approximately 11.5%), although this represents an increase from figures in the early 1980s (Barker and Kohout, 2003). This need was specifically addressed and identified as a priority for psychology by the APA Commission on Ethnic Minority Recruitment, Retention, and Training in Psychology (CEMRRAT; CEMRRAT2, 2007). Major findings included in their report are that ethnic minority representation has increased at all levels of psychology's education since the first report of the Commission, issued in 1997. However, the number of ethnic minority doctoral recipients increased by only 16.6% between 1996 and 2004; ethnic minorities received 20.1% of EdD and PhD degrees in psychology in 2004, and comprised 19.9% of new enrollees in PsyD programs in 2003. The report makes a series of recommendations to address the need to increase ethnic minority representation in psychology at all levels of the pipeline and to ensure this occurs, as well as to address the service and research needs to communities of color.

A workforce analysis is needed to provide comprehensive data and to accurately predict the future of the psychology workforce. Workforce analysis is an empirical approach that answers questions about the need for individuals trained within a discipline, and gives a full picture of the profession from entry to education and training systems to practicing professionals, and including those preparing to leave the workforce. This is done in the context of an environmental scan that identifies key societal issues and trends that will impact the need for professionals in a particular discipline. From the integration of these sources of data, a picture of the relationship between the numbers of available providers to need for providers can be discerned and predictions made about future workforce needs based upon societal need, educational requirements to meet those needs, and employment opportunities (Rozensky et al., 2007). Workforce analysis is a tool that is routinely used by other health-care professions, such as medicine, nursing, and pharmacy, to document need for training providers, as well to advocate for funding to develop the needed workforce (Rozensky et al., 2007). Psychology has recognized this need for workforce analysis through the creation of a newly funded Center for Workforce Studies within the APA, which is currently engaged in data collection as it relates to conducting a workforce analysis.

National Health-care Policy Initiatives and Clinical Psychology

In the United States, at a national level, the broader health-care workforce has been the focus of attention, and key initiatives of relevance to clinical psychology will be noted in this section, as they suggest emerging roles for psychology in the context of larger health-care policy initiatives. In 2008, the Association of Academic Health Centers (AAHC), of which psychology is represented as a member through the APA, released a report, "Out of Order, Out of Time" (AAHC, 2008). The report calls attention to the critical need for a coordinated national health workforce planning initiative. A strong statement is made that health-care professions must work together to overcome the problems that have developed in the health-care system secondary to a decentralized approach to education and training, planning, development, and policymaking. The report recommends that stakeholders work together to make policy issues related to the U.S. health workforce a priority, to address workforce issues immediately in light of potential crises in workforce capacity and infrastructure, to move away from a decentralized approach to health workforce policy and instead adopt an integrated and comprehensive approach, and to create a health workforce planning body. The tasks of such a body would include developing a national health workforce agenda; working for greater consistency in standards and requirements for providers across jurisdictions; addressing issues of entry into the health professions and factors affecting the ability of academic institutions to train the workforce; and confronting any inconsistencies among public or private policies, standards, or requirements that may have an adverse impact. The increased demands on the U.S health-care system in light of an aging population in need of and asking for health care, coupled with retirements from the health-care workforce outpacing entry by new professionals, argues for the importance and timeliness of such an agenda (AAHC, 2008). Psychology's involvement in such national initiatives is critical so that resulting policy actions will include psychology in its role as a health-care profession. Such inclusion will provide opportunities for continued and expanded roles for the profession within the larger health-care system, thus ensuring a strong future for the field.

Further, the need for policy that supports the development of a competent behavioral health-care workforce is a key recommendation of a report from the Annapolis Coalition for the Behavioral Health Workforce (Annapolis Coalition, 2007) titled, "An Action Plan for Behavioral Health Workforce Development." The need to focus on issues of both the supply and training of behavioral health workers is highlighted in this report. The Annapolis Coalition was commissioned by the Substance Abuse and Mental Health Services Administration (SAMHSA) with the charge to propose an action plan addressing these workforce needs that is both encompassing of the breadth of behavioral health and national in scope. The report notes evidence insufficient numbers of providers and a failure to train providers to address issues such as health promotion and prevention. Seven strategic goals are presented, addressing the need to broaden the concept of workforce, strengthen the workforce, and develop structures to support the workforce. The report of the Annapolis Coalition makes a strong statement in support of the need for national attention to mechanisms through which quality education and training can lead to increasing the numbers of skilled behavioral health professionals. Attention is given to the need for education and training to continue to promote models of competency-based education and training, and stresses that more collaboration across disciplines must occur to meet these goals of an adequately prepared and sufficiently large behavioral health workforce.

A final national initiative of significance to psychology is the report issued by the Institute of Medicine 2003, Health Professions Education: A Bridge to Quality (IOM, 2003). A key recommendation in that report is that, to promote quality in education and training across all health professions, five core competencies are required within each health-care discipline (IOM, 2003). These include the ability to provide patient-centered care, work in interdisciplinary teams, employ EBP, apply quality improvement strategies, and utilize informatics. Psychology must be in a position to coordinate its efforts across its training models, specialties, and regulatory bodies to incorporate such competencies into its education and practice if it wishes to be seen as part of the broader health-care community.

Reports such as these are routinely used to develop national policy initiatives that, in turn, may be used to advocate for support of existing or new educational and training programs and new clinical services, in order to realize the goal of the stated policy. Although psychology has established itself as a health-care discipline and is recognized in many national policy reports, the discipline must continue to advocate for its role in health-care settings through involvement in groups developing such initiatives and collecting the data used to inform the products of such policies.

Conclusion

Clinical psychology, as the largest doctoral subfield in the discipline of psychology in general and within professional psychology specifically, is engaged in efforts to ensure its future through enhancing quality in education, training, and credentialing, and in identifying and exploring new roles. Attention to quality, as demonstrated in the competence of clinical psychologists, is a major focus for both those in the education and training communities and those with credentialing or regulatory roles. Clinical psychology must address some challenges to its future, such as the difficulties students face obtaining doctoral internships, the high levels of debt incurred by students, and the complexity resulting from licensure laws that vary in their requirements across jurisdictions and the impact this has on both the initial credentialing and the mobility of psychologists. The emerging ability of the discipline to engage in workforce analysis is a key tool to better predict the future needs of society, so that the discipline can be responsive with education and training opportunities to prepare future generations to meet those needs. The future of clinical psychology is strengthened by involvement in federal policy initiatives looking at the need for increasing the health-care workforce and ensuring that those entering the workforce have the requisite skills to provide quality services.

Future Directions

This chapter raises several questions as the clinical psychology profession looks to the future: How will clinical psychology respond to the growing emphasis on competency assessment in students and providers? In what ways might a competency-based approach be infused in the education, training, and credentialing processes? Can the growing collaboration between educators and regulatory groups be actualized in a sequential approach to competency assessment, one that is inclusive of the phases in professional development? How can the challenge raised by licensing laws that vary by jurisdiction, and the impact that this variability has on those entering the profession and those seeking mobility, be met? How will clinical psychology ensure its continued vibrancy by developing a workforce prepared for roles in emerging health care settings and public health? How can this approach be informed and enhanced by data obtained from a psychology or health-care workforce analysis? Finally, how will clinical psychology assure that workforce data and a competency-based approach to education and practice are utilized in national policy initiatives that support funding for education and training, as well as for clinical services provided?

References

Accreditation Council for Graduate Medical Education (2007, February 13). Common Program Requirements: General Competencies. Retrieved August 24, 2008 from http://www.acgme.org/outcome/comp/GeneralCompetencies Standards21307.pdf.

Accreditation Council for Graduate Medical Education and American Board of Medical Specialties. (2000). *Toolbox of assessment methods: A product of the joint initiative of the ACGME Outcome Project of the Accreditation Council for Graduate Medical Education (ACGME) and the American Board of Medical Specialties (ABMS), version 1.1.* Chicago: Accreditation Council for Graduate Medical Education and American Board of Medical Specialties.

American Board of Professional Psychology. (2008). A message from the president. Retrieved August, 24, 2008 from http://www.abpp.org/abpp_home_more.htm#about_abpp.

American Psychological Association. (2003). *Graduate Study in Psychology.* Washington, DC: Author.

American Psychological Association. (2006). Doctorate as minimum entry into the practice of psychology. Retrieved August 24, 2008 from http://www.apa.org/governance/cpm/chapter4b.html#7.

American Psychological Association. (2005, August). American Psychological Association policy statement on evidence-based practice in psychology. Retrieved September 1, 2008 from http://www2.apa.org/practice/ebpstatement.pdf.

American Psychological Association. (2007). *APA guidelines for the undergraduate psychology major.* Washington, DC: Author. Retrieved August 24, 2008 from www.apa.org/ed/resources.html.

American Psychological Association (2008a). GPE gets significant boost in the house. Retrieved August 24, 2008 from http://www.apa.org/ppo/education/gpe0608.html.

American Psychological Association. (2008b). *Graduate Study in Psychology.* Washington, DC: Author.

American Psychological Association. (2008c, August). Moving forward with the transition to a commission. Retrieved August 25, 2008 from http://www.apa.org/ed/accreditation/transitionupdate.html.

American Psychological Association Center for Workforce Studies. (2007a, August). Doctoral level data. Retrieved August 24, 2008 from http://research.apa.org.

American Psychological Association Center for Workforce Studies (2007b, November). 2005 doctoral employment survey. Retrieved August 24, 2008 from http://research.apa.org.

American Psychological Association Commission on Accreditation. (2008). *Accreditation operating procedures of the commission on accreditation.* Washington, DC: Author.

American Psychological Association Commission on Ethnic Minority Recruitment, Retention and Training in Psychology Task Force (CEMRRAT2). (2007). The APA/CEMRRAT Plan for Ethnic Minority Recruitment, Retention, and Training in Psychology. The Progress Report 1997–2005. Retrieved April 20, 2007 from http://www.apa.org/pi/oema/programs/cemrrat_report.html

American Psychological Association Committee on Accreditation. (2001). *2001 annual report.* Washington, DC: Author.

American Psychological Association Committee on Accreditation. (2006). *2006 annual report.* Washington, DC: Author.

Annapolis Coalition on the Behavioral Health Workforce. (2007). An action plan for behavioral health workforce development. Retrieved August 27, 2008 http://208.106.217.45/pages/images/WorkforceActionPlan.pdf.

Association of Academic Health Centers. (2008, July 17). Out of order out of time: The state of the nation's health workforce. Retrieved July 17, 2008 from www.aahcdc.org.

Association of State and Provincial Psychology Boards. (2008a, July 28). ASPPB mobility program. Retrieved August 25, 2008 from http://www.asppb.net/files/public/CPQ_lists_July_2008.pdf.

Association of State and Provincial Psychology Boards. (2008b). ASPPB report of activities. Retrieved August 25, 2008 from http://www.asppb.org/about/pdf/1312.pdf

Association of Psychology Postdoctoral and Internship Centers. (2007, June 6). 2007 Match survey of intern applicants. Retrieved August 26, 2008 from http://www.appic.org/match/5_2_2_4_9b_match_about_statistics_surveys_2007b.htm.

Association of Psychology Postdoctoral and Internship Centers. (2008, February 25). 2008 APPIC match statistics. Retrieved August 26, 2008 from http://www.appic.org/match/5_2_2_1_10_match_about_statistics_general_2008.html.

Baker, J., McCutcheon, S., & Keilin, W.G. (2007). The internship supply-demand imbalance: The APPIC perspective. *Training and Education in Professional Psychology, 1,* 287–293.

Barker, K., & Kohout, J. (2003). Contemporary employment in psychology and future trends. In M.J. Prinstein and M.D. Patterson (Eds.). *The portable mentor: Expert guide to a successful career in psychology.* Washington, DC: American Psychological Association.

Belar, C. (1992). Education and training conferences in graduate education. In A.E. Puente, J.R. Matthews & C.L. Brewer (Eds.), *Teaching psychology in America: A history.* Washington, DC: Author.

Belar, C. (2003). Training for evidence-based practice. *Monitor on Psychology, 34*, 57.

Belar, C. (2007). Academic health centers: Preparing our health work force. *Monitor on Psychology, 38*, 60.

Belar, C. (2008). Clinical health psychology: A health care specialty in professional psychology. *Professional Psychology: Research and Practice, 39*, 229–233.

Belar, C.D., & Perry, N.W. (1992). National conference on scientist-practitioner education and training for the professional practice of psychology. *American Psychologist*, 71–75.

Benjamin, L.T. (2001). American Psychology's Struggles with its curriculum. Should a thousand flowers bloom? *American Psychologist, 56*, 735–742.

Borrayo, E.A., (2006, Winter). Report on the National Conference on Training in Professional Geropsychology. *Focus, 18*, 19–20.

Collins, F.L., Jr., Callahan, J.L., & Klonoff, E.A. (2007). A scientist-practitioner perspective of the internship match imbalance: The stairway to competence. *Training and Education in Professional Psychology, 1*, 267–275.

Commission on Professionals in Science and Technology (2006). STEM workforce data project: Report No.7: STEM employment forecasts and distributions among employment sectors. Retrieved August 27, 2008 from www.cpst.org.

Council of Chairs of Training Councils. Council of Chairs of Training Councils (CCTC). (2008). A historical view. Retrieved August 26, 2008 from http://www.psychtraining-councils.org/pubs/CCTC-%20Background.pdf

Council of Chairs of Training Councils. (2007, November 1). Council of Chairs of Training Councils (CCTC): Recommendations for communication. Retrieved August 26, 2008 from http://www.psychtrainingcouncils.org/pubs/CCTC%20Recommendations%20for%20Communication.pdf.

Craighead, L.W., & Craighead, W.E. (2006). Ph.D. training in clinical psychology: Fix it before it breaks. *Clinical Psychology: Science and Practice, 13*, 235–241.

Dattilio, F.M. (2002). Board certification in psychology: Is it really necessary? *Professional Psychology: Research and Practice, 33*, 54–57.

Deleon, P.H., Kenkel, M.B., & Belar, C. (2007). A window of opportunity: Community health centers can reduce the health disparities and train the next generation of psychologists. *Monitor on Psychology, 38*, 24–25.

DeMers, S.T., & Jonason, K.R. (2006). The ASPPB credentials bank and certificate of professional qualification in psychology: Comprehensive solutions to mobility obstacles. In T.J. Vaughn (Ed.), *Psychology licensure and certification. What students need to know* (pp. 107–116). Washington, DC: American Psychological Association.

Fouad, N.A., Grus, C.L., Hatcher, R.L., Kaslow, N.J. Hutchings, P.S., Madson, M., Collins, F.L., Jr. & Crossman, R.E. (2009). Competency Benchmarks: A Developmental Model for Understanding and Measuring Competence in Professional Psychology. *Training and Education in Professional Psychology. 3(4, Suppl)*, Nov 2009, S5–S26.

France C.R., Masters, K.S. Belar, C.D., Kerns, R.D., Klonoff, E.A., Larkin, K.E., et al. (2008). Application of the competence model to clinical health psychology, *Professional Psychology: Research and Practice, 39*, 573–580.

Gauthier, J.G. (September, 2002). Facilitating mobility for psychologists through a competency-based approach for regulation and accreditation: The Canadian experiment. *European Psychologist, 7*, 203–212.

Hall, J.E., & Boucher A.P. (2003). Professional mobility for psychologists: Multiple choices, multiple opportunities. *Professional Psychology: Research and Practice, 34*, 463–467.

Hall, J.E., & Lunt, I. (2005). Global mobility for psychologists. The role of psychology organizations in the United States, Canada, Europe and other regions. *American Psychologist, 60*, 713–726.

Hatcher, R.L., & Lassiter K.D. (2007). Initial training in professional psychology: The practicum competencies outline. *Training and Education in Professional Psychology, 1*, 49–63.

Hunsely, J. (2007). Training psychologists for evidence-based practice. *Canadian Psychology, 48*, 32–42.

Hutchings, P.S., Mangione, L., Dobbins, J.E., & Wechsler, F.S. (2007). A critical analysis of systemic problems with psychology pre-doctoral internship training: Contributing factors and collaborative solutions. *Training and Education in Professional Psychology, 5*, 276–286.

Institute of Medicine. (2001). *Crossing the quality chasm: A new health system for the 21st century*. Washington, DC: National Academy Press.

Institute of Medicine. (2003). Health professions education: A bridge to quality. Washington, DC: National Academies Press.

Kaslow, N. J. (2004). Competencies in professional psychology. *American Psychologist, 59*, 774–781.

Kaslow, N. J., Borden, K. A., Collins, F. L., Forrest, L., Illfelder-Kaye, J., Nelson, P. D., Rallo, J. S., Vasquez, M. J. T., & Willmuth, M. E. (2004). Competencies Conference: Future directions in education and credentialing in professional psychology. *Journal of Clinical Psychology, 80*, 699–712.

Kaslow, N.J., Grus, C.L., Campbell, L.F., Fouad, N.A., Hatcher, R.L., Rodolfa, E.R. (2009). Competency Assessment Toolkit for Professional Psychology. *Training and Education in Professional Psychology. 3(4, Suppl)*, Nov 2009, S27–S45.

Kaslow, N.J., & Keilin, W.G. (2006). Internship training in clinical psychology: Looking into our crystal ball. *Clinical Psychology: Science and Practice, 13*, 242–248.

Kaslow, N. J., Rubin, N. J., Bebeau, M., Leigh, I. W., Lichtenberg, J., Nelson, P. D., Portnoy, S., & Smith, I. L. (2007). Guiding principles and recommendations for the assessment of competence. *Professional Psychology: Research and Practice, 38*, 441–451.

Kaslow, N. J., Rubin, N. J., Leigh, I. W., Portnoy, S., Lichtenberg, J., Smith, I. L., Bebeau, M., & Nelson, P. D. (2006). *American Psychological Association Task Force on the Assessment of Competence in Professional Psychology*. Washington, D.C.: American Psychological Association.

Keilin, W.G., Baker, J., McCutcheon, S., & Perason, E. (2007). A growing bottleneck: The internship supply-demand imbalance in 2007 and its impact on psychology training. *Training and Education in Professional Psychology, 1*, 229–237.

Ko, S.F., & Roldofa, E. (2005). Psychology training directors' views of number of practicum hours necessary prior to internship application. *Professional Psychology: Research and Practice, 36*, 318–322.

Korman, M. (1976). *Levels and patterns of professional training in psychology*. Washington, DC: American Psychological Association.

Leigh, I. W., Smith, I. L., Bebeau, M., Lichtenberg, J., Nelson, P. D., Portnoy, S., Rubin, N. J., & Kaslow, N. J. (2007). Competency assessment models. *Professional Psychology: Research and Practice, 38*, 463–473.

Lichtenberg, J., Portnoy, S., Bebeau, M., Leigh, I. W., Nelson, P. D., Rubin, N. J., Smith, I. L., & Kaslow, N. J. (2007). Challenges to the assessment of competence and competencies. *Professional Psychology: Research and Practice, 38*, 474–478.

McFall, R.M. (1991). Manifesto for a science of clinical psychology. *The Clinical Psychologist, 44*, 75–88.

Medical School Objectives Writing Group. (1999). Learning objectives for medical student education - Guidelines for medical schools: Report I of the Medical School Objectives Project. *Academic Medicine, 74*, 13–18.

Merlo, L.J., Collins, A., & Bernstein, J. (2008). CUDCP-affiliated clinical psychology student views of their science training. *Training and Education in Professional Psychology, 2*, 58–65.

Miville, M.L., Adams, E.M., & Juntunen, C. L. (2007). Counseling psychology perspectives on the predoctoral internship supply-demand imbalance: Strategies for problem definition and resolution. *Training and Education in Professional Psychology, 1*, 258–266.

Murphy, M.J., Levant, R.F., Hall, J.E., & Glueckauf, R.L. (2007). Distance education in professional training in psychology. *Professional Psychology: Research and Practice, 38*, 97–103.

Nelson, P. D. (2007). Striving for competence in the assessment of competence: Psychology's professional education and credentialing journey of public accountability. *Training and Education in Professional Psychology, 1*, 3–12.

Nelson, P.D., Belar, C.D., Grus, C.L., & Zlotlow, S. (2008). Quality assessment in higher education through accreditation. In Hall & Altmair (Eds.), *Global promise: Quality assurance and accountability in professional psychology* (pp. 16–37). New York: Oxford University Press.

Office of Professional Affairs American Psychological Association. (1987). Model act for state licensure of psychologists. *American Psychologist, 42*, 696–703.

Olvey, C.D., Hogg, A., & Counts, W. (2002). Licensure requirements: Have we raised the bar too far? *Professional Psychology: Research and Practice, 33*, 323–329.

Packard, T., & Simon, N.P. (2006). Board certification by the American Board of Professional Psychology. In T.J. Vaugh (Ed.), *Psychology licensure and certification. What students need to know* (pp. 117–126). Washington, DC: American Psychological Association.

Pederson, S.L., DePiano, F., Kaslow, N., Klepac, R.K., Hargrove, D.S., & Vasquez, M. (1997). *Proceedings from the national working conference on supply and demand: Training and opportunities in professional psychology.* Washington, DC: American Psychological Association and Association of Psychology Postdoctoral and Internship Centers.

Peterson, R.L., Peterson, D.R., Abrams, J.C., & Stricker, G. (1997). The National Council of Schools and Programs of Professional Psychology education model. *Professional Psychology: Research and Practice, 28*, 373–386.

Raimy, V. C. (Ed.). (1950). *Training in clinical psychology.* New York: Prentice Hall.

Rapoport, A.I., Kohout, J., & Wicherski, M. (2000). Psychology doctorate recipients: How much financial debt at graduation? Retrieved September 19, 2007 from http://www/nsf.gov/statistics/issuebrf/sib00321.htm.

Roberts, M.D. (2006). Essential tension: Specialization with broad and general training in psychology. *American Psychologist, 61*, 862–870.

Roberts, M. C., Borden, K. A., Christiansen, M. D., & Lopez, S. J. (2005). Fostering a culture shift: Assessment of competence in the education and careers of professional psychologists. *Professional Psychology: Research and Practice, 36*, 355–361.

Robiner, W.N. (1991). How many psychologists are needed? A call for a national psychology resource agenda. *Professional Psychology: Research and Practice, 22*, 427–440.

Robiner, W.N., Ax, R.K., Stamm, B.H., & Harowski, K. (2002). Addressing the supply of psychologists in the workforce: Is focusing principally on demand sound economics. *Journal of Clinical Psychology in Medical Settings, 9*, 273–285.

Rodolfa, E. R., Bent, R. J., Eisman, E., Nelson, P. D., Rehm, L., & Ritchie, P. (2005). A cube model for competency development: Implications for psychology educators and regulators. *Professional Psychology: Research and Practice, 36*, 347–354.

Rodolfa, E.R., Ko, S.F., & Peterson, L. (2004). Psychology training directors' views of trainees' readiness to practice independently. *Professional Psychology: Research and Practice, 35*, 397–404.

Rozensky, R.H. (2008, August). Issues and barrier to overcome when working in both psychology and public health. In D. Kimmel (Chair), *Empowering Psychology's Contributions to Public Health through Research, Practice and Policy.* Symposium conducted at the annual meeting of the American Psychological Association, Boston, MA.

Rozensky, R.H., Grus, C., Belar, C., Nelson, P., & Kohout (2007). Using workforce analysis to answer questions related to the "internship imbalance" and career pipeline in professional psychology. *Journal of Training and Education in Professional Psychology, 1*, 238–248.

Rubin, N. J., Bebeau, M., Leigh, I. W., Lichtenberg, J., Smith, I. L., Nelson, P. D., Portnoy, S., & Kaslow, N. J. (2007). The competency movement within psychology: An historical perspective. *Professional Psychology: Research and Practice, 38*, 452–462.

Spielman, A. I., Fulmer, T., Eisenberg, E. S., & Alfano, M. C. (2005). Dentistry, nursing, and medicine: A comparison of core competencies. *Journal of Dental Education, 69*, 1257–1271.

Stricker, G., & Trierweiler, S.J. (2006). The local clinical scientist: A bridge between science and practice. *Training and Education in Professional Psychology, 5*, 37–47.

Terris, L.D. (1973). The national licensing examination. *Professional Psychology, 4*, 386–391.

VandenBos, G., DeLeon, P.H., & Belar, C.D. (1991). How many psychological practitioners are needed? It's too early to know! *Professional Psychology: Research and Practice, 22*, 441–448.

Watson, R., Stimpson, A., Topping, A., & Porock, D. (2002). Clinical competence assessment in nursing: A systematic review of the literature. *Advanced Nursing, 39*, 421–431.

Wood, J.A.V., Miller, T.W., & Hargrove, D.S. (2005). Clinical supervision in rural settings: A telehealth model. *Professional Psychology: Research and Practice, 36*, 173–179.

Woody, S.R., Weisz, J., & McLean, C. (2005). Empirically supported treatments: 10 years later. *The Clinical Psychologist, 58*, 5–11.

The Role of Psychology in Emerging Federal Health-care Plans

Antonette M. Zeiss *and* Bradley E. Karlin

Abstract

Professional psychology plays a prominent role at a number of key levels in the federal mental health-care system. This chapter examines the increasing impact professional psychology has had in recent years on two major and evolving federal mental health-care systems: the Veterans Health Administration (VHA) and the Medicare program. Within the VHA, professional psychology has helped to promote the expansion and transformation of evidence-based and recovery-oriented mental health care at the levels of policy, practice, and research. As the largest integrated health-care system in the nation, mental health-care transformation within the VHA and psychology's contributions to this major effort may help to inform other private and public mental health-care systems. Similarly, important changes within the Medicare program designed to promote mental health-care access, coverage, and quality portend that professional psychology will have an increasingly prominent role within Medicare. These developments provide unprecedented opportunities for psychologists to influence the future practice of psychology and the mental health-care landscape of the nation.

Keywords: Federal, Medicare, mental health, psychology, Veterans Health Administration

Professional psychology has had an increasingly important and diverse role in the federal mental health-care system in recent years. The federal mental health-care system in the United States is, in actuality, comprised of multiple systems that often interact but have significant distinctions in terms of their clinical landscapes, policies, and operations. Professional psychology has become a central component of each of these systems. In this chapter, we examine psychology's significant impact and expanding role in two major federal mental health-care systems: the Department of Veterans Affairs (VA) health-care system and the Medicare Program. In recent years, psychology has had particularly profound growth and impact in the delivery of mental health care in the VA health-care system, where the profession has recently helped to foster mental health-care integration, interdisciplinary practice, recovery-oriented care, and service innovation. In so doing, the profession has helped promote new models of mental health-care practice. Psychology has also been a critical part of mental health-care delivery in the Medicare Program. Recent developments and changes to Medicare in the coming years will greatly increase psychology's stake in the federal health insurance program.

Department of Veterans Affairs

The VA is the largest employer of psychologists in the United States, as of the end of 2009, with over 3,200 psychologists employed at that time. The VA provides health care to over 5 million veterans, of whom over 1.5 million have at least one mental-health diagnosis. Psychology is vitally involved in all aspects of health care for veterans, including mental health-care and health psychology care for those with medical illness without mental health diagnoses. Psychology also plays important roles in VA research, education, and administration. Psychology historically has helped to shape VA health care and policies, and continues to do so as the VA strives to provide evidence-based, accessible, sensitive care to all eligible Veterans.

The VA as a Health-care System

The original incarnation of the agency now titled the "Department of Veterans Affairs" (VA) was established July 21, 1930, as the "Veterans Administration." It was created to consolidate and coordinate government activities affecting war veterans. The mission of the VA was expressed inspiringly by President Abraham Lincoln in his second inaugural address, speaking of military veterans of the Civil War: "With malice toward none, with charity for all, with firmness in the right as God gives us to see the right, let us strive on to finish the work we are in, to bind up the nation's wounds, to care for him who shall have borne the battle and for his widow and his orphan, to do all which may achieve and cherish a just and lasting peace among ourselves and with all nations" (Abraham Lincoln, Second Inaugural Address, Saturday, March 4, 1865).

Mental heath services have always been a part of the VA, but the VA was a fairly small operation from its inception in 1931—until World War II led to a dramatic expansion of VA benefits, including passage, in 1944, of the Servicemen's Readjustment Act (P.L. 78-346), commonly known as the G.I. Bill of Rights, which authorized occupational, educational, and health assistance for veterans. The VA became a Cabinet-level department in 1989, and, as such, its title was changed to the Department of Veterans Affairs.

The VA has many responsibilities, including provision of financial benefits such as pensions, educational funding support, and home loans. The specific focus in this chapter is on the Veterans Health Administration (VHA)—the specific component of the VA that is responsible for providing comprehensive health care to eligible veterans.

The VHA is a complete health-care environment, offering the full spectrum of health-care services in a variety of settings. The VHA's health-care system includes over 1,200 points of care, and 155 medical centers provide the full spectrum of care from primary care to tertiary care. In addition, over 700 community based outpatient clinics provide primary care and outpatient mental health care in settings that are typically closer to the veteran's home than the nearest medical center. One-hundred thirty-five nursing homes (now called "Community Living Centers" in the VA) serve older veterans and others who have significant physical disability and need extended care services. Over 230 Vet Centers, "storefront" operations that provide walk-in services in the community, provide readjustment counseling services to combat veterans and their families.

The VA has over 260,000 employees, making it the second largest Cabinet-level department. In the United States, there are 23.8 million veterans; of these, 7.8 million are enrolled with the VA system, and at least 5.2 million enrolled veterans come for health-care services in any year. Of those receiving care, 1.6 million have at least one mental health diagnosis, including over 400,000 with post-traumatic stress disorder (PTSD) and 360,000 with an alcohol or other substance use diagnosis.

History of Psychology in the Department of Veterans Affairs

Psychology has played a key role in the VA since its early development. In 1945, soon after passage of the G.I. Bill of Rights, the VA opened its first mental hygiene clinic for outpatient mental health services at the Regional Office in Los Angeles. In that same year, General Omar Bradley, Administrator of the VA, appointed George A. Kelly, PhD, as the first VA psychology consultant, to help design the new VA psychology program. Kelly, who later developed personal construct psychology (Kelly, 1955), had accepted a post in the aviation psychology branch of the U.S. Navy during World War II, and following the war, he taught briefly at the University of Maryland, while also leading the development of psychology as an integral component of VA health-care. Kelly was a consultant rather than a VA psychologist per se; during his period of consultation, James Grier Miller, MD, PhD, was appointed the first chief clinical psychologist for the Psychology Section in the Neuropsychiatry Division in the VA Central Office. Since then, there has been continuous psychology leadership in the VA Central Office.

Several professional organizations have been created for VA psychology. A main organization has been a section specifically for VA psychologists within Division 18 (Psychologists in Public Service) of the American Psychological Association (APA); this section was created in 1977. Another organization also was created in 1977, known originally as the Association of VA Chief Psychologists. As the organization of VA health-care changed in the 1990s, not all sites had separate psychology sections, and often psychologists were in other leadership positions not titled "psychology service chief." In response to these changes, and because of an experienced need for mutual support and mentoring, that organization evolved into the Association of Veterans Affairs Psychology Leaders (AVAPL) in 1997. This organization is a free-standing association, separate from VA institutional lines of authority. Any psychologist with a leadership role of some kind in their facility, or in other contexts such as APA governance, is welcomed as a member. The AVAPL has become a vital organization; their website (www.avapl.org) describes the organization as follows:

> The Association of VA Psychologist Leaders (AVAPL) is a nonprofit organization with a voluntary membership of psychologists with various leadership roles within the Department of Veterans Affairs (DVA). Our purpose is to address the professional needs and concerns of VA psychologists. Our primary goal is to help provide the highest quality of patient care to our nation's Veterans. We are likewise committed to excellence in training and the advancement of clinical care through both program development and research.

The APA has been a supporter and partner of VA psychology since the beginning of VA health care. As one example of such support, the practice directorate of the APA has partnered with AVAPL since 1998 in offering an annual conference for VA psychology leaders, and Division 18 of APA also now co-sponsors this conference. Similarly, the VA has recognized and supported the APA. VA members have taken key roles in APA governance, and VA psychology holds two meetings annually at the APA convention—a meeting of AVAPL psychologists, and an update by VA Central Office psychology leadership. The APA accreditation process also has been valued by the VA, as it ensures that psychologists have been trained in peer-reviewed, well-organized programs. Based on legislation passed in 1979, the VA requires the following criteria to be eligible to be hired as a VA psychologist:

- U.S. citizenship
- A doctoral degree in clinical or counseling psychology from a graduate school approved by the APA
- An APA-approved internship
- State licensure or certification as a psychologist within 2 years of appointment

VA psychology thrived from the 1940s through the early 1990s. In addition to continuous leadership of psychologists in the VA Central Office, a growing number of psychology staff was involved in an expanding array of clinical services, training opportunities, and research initiatives. However, in the 1990s, the VA faced an array of funding and leadership challenges that affected psychology, as well as other mental health professions and programs.

The graph in Figure 9.1 shows the decline in VA psychology staffing numbers from fiscal year 1995, a historic high point, up to the end of fiscal year 2002. The decline in mental health staffing is depicted for psychology in this graph. The top line shows the actual number of psychologists hired cumulatively across the Government Service (GS) grade levels (11–15) relevant for psychologists. The bottom line shows the total amount of staff time, accounting for part-time versus full-time status (expressed as Full Time Employee Equivalent, or FTEE). Both show the same pattern—a marked decline in the number of VA psychology staff beginning in fiscal year 1996.

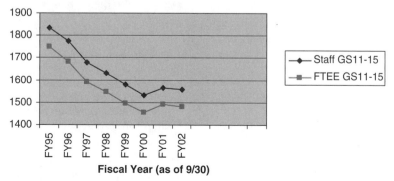

Fig. 9.1 VA psychology staffing through fiscal year 2002

Thus, psychology's history in the VA has been as a vital component of the development of an effective health-care system to serve our nation's military veterans. Although VA care has been excellent, leading it to be called *The Best Care Anywhere* in a recent book (Longman, 2007), challenges emerged in the mid-1990s to psychology and to mental health services generally. These challenges have been faced and overcome, beginning in the early years of the 21st century; we turn now to that story.

The VA's Implementation of Strategic Plans for Providing Mental Health Care

In 2003, the VA recommitted to enhancing mental health services. The decline in the VA's mental health care resources was recognized by new top leadership in the VA, including the under secretary for health and the chief consultant for patient care services. In addition, the emerging and projected needs for mental health care of new veterans from the war in Afghanistan and Iraq necessitated a revitalized system.

A catalyst and guide for designing a new approach to mental health care in the VA came from the report of the president's New Freedom Commission on Mental Health (2003), "Achieving the Promise: Transforming Mental Health Care in America," released in 2003. This Commission did not focus on the VA; its charge was to look broadly at mental health care in the United States. However, a VA ex-officio member attended meetings of the Commission, and the VA took great interest in the findings as a guide—a road map—to how mental health care might optimally be organized and delivered.

This Commission grappled with the current state of mental health care in the United States, and their report began with the sobering, but candid, words, "The system is fragmented and in disarray." The report went on to say, "To improve access to quality care and services, the Commission recommends fundamentally transforming how mental health care is delivered in America." Their recommendations for creating that transformation of mental health care in the United States were built around six goals:

- Goal 1. Americans understand that mental health is essential to overall health.
- Goal 2. Mental health care is consumer and family driven.
- Goal 3. Disparities in mental health services are eliminated.
- Goal 4. Early mental health screening, assessment, and referral to services are common practice.

- Goal 5. Excellent mental health care is delivered and research is accelerated.
- Goal 6. Technology is used to access mental health care and information.

In the fall of 2003, a VA work group was established to create an action agenda to implement the president's New Freedom Commission on Mental Health report as adapted to be relevant for VA. That work group's report, "Action Agenda: Achieving the Promise, Transforming Mental Health Care in VA," was released in December 2003 (Department of Veterans Affairs, 2003). That action plan then evolved further into a comprehensive strategic plan, the VA Mental Health Strategic Plan. The strategic plan was developed by an interdisciplinary group of mental health professionals, with psychology well-represented among them. It was completed in 2004 and approved as official VA policy by the secretary of the Department of Veterans Affairs in November 2004 (Department of Veterans Affairs, 2004). The strategic plan presented over 250 action items designed to enhance VA mental health care. These were organized into the same categories as the president's New Freedom Commission on Mental Health report, but with content specific to revitalizing VA mental health care. For example, the plan presented actions designed to:

- Close gaps in VA mental health care, with the guiding principle that mental health care should be treated with the same urgency as physical health care
- Transform the VA's culture of care to one of psychosocial rehabilitation with a recovery orientation, moving beyond an emphasis only on symptom reduction
- Transform the delivery system to integrate primary care and mental health services in the VA
- Provide care that integrates science and practice, resulting in delivery of evidence-based mental health care responsive to emerging research findings
- Enhance suicide prevention activities
- Provide accessible, timely services to meet the mental health needs of newly returning veterans from Afghanistan and Iraq

The VA made significant financial support available for implementation of the Mental Health Strategic Plan. Over the first 4 years of its implementation, federal government fiscal years 2005 through 2008 (October 1, 2004 through September 31, 2008), over $850 million dollars cumulatively was committed specifically to implement the strategic plan and enhance VA mental health services. This focused use of mental health enhancement funding was above and beyond the basic recurring VA mental health budget, which was over $3 billion in fiscal year 2008.

Most of the additional funding provided for mental health enhancement was used to hire new VA mental health staff. As part of the implementation of the VA's comprehensive Mental Health Strategic Plan, over 6,500 additional mental health positions have been hired for mental health service delivery (as of October 31, 2009), primarily professional staff for direct service delivery, along with appropriate support staff. The new positions were distributed among all of the mental health professions, with psychology well included, as shown in Table 9.1.

With this hiring, the VA's total mental health workforce is now over 19,000 staff nationwide. This is a historic high point for VA mental heath staffing. Most significant is that these staff are increasingly devoted to implementing the kind of care envisioned by the president's New Freedom Commissions on Mental Health and by the VA's adaptation of it to the strategic plan: care that is accessible and without major gaps, evidence-based, focused on recovery, integrated with primary care, including intensive suicide prevention efforts, and including services to meet the needs of returning veterans. (Edwards, 2008)

Based on the success of efforts over the last 4 years in implementing the Mental Health Strategic

Plan, the VA has now begun a next effort, designed be its culmination: the creation of a uniform mental health services package to ensure the availability of a broad continuum of accessible, evidence-based and recovery-oriented mental health services for all veterans throughout the national VA health-care system. This effort has resulted in an official VA handbook, "Uniform Mental Health Services in VA Medical Centers and Clinics" (VHA Directive 1160.01), that delineates the essential components of mental health care that is to be implemented nationally. The handbook defines the essential components of a comprehensive mental health system of care. The focus is veteran-centric—the handbook defines what services must be available to all veterans. Decisions about how those services will be utilized for the care of any specific veteran need to be made in active collaboration between the veteran and the VA mental health providers. The handbook provides guidance for local and regional VA health-care leadership in analyzing their current services in relation to the comprehensive requirements of the mental health services handbook, and it can be used to plan how to augment and reconfigure their current services to reach full adherence to the system of care delineated in the handbook. Implementation of the mental health services handbook began at the start of fiscal year 2009 (October 1, 2008) and is proceeding as of this writing.

Current Scope of Mental Health in the VA

Implementation of the VA's Mental Health Strategic Plan has clearly turned around the decline in overall mental health care, and changes in staffing levels for psychology provide a dramatic index of that overall turn-around. This is shown in Figure 9.2, which extends Figure 9.1 up to the end of October of fiscal year 2009 (October 31, 2009); this graph is simplified to show only the number of individuals hired; the number of FTEE is not shown, but remains in close parallel with the total number of staff, as in Figure 9.1. This table also shows month-by-month progress, beginning in December 2007; thus, what may at first appear to be a reduction in the rate of growth for fiscal year 2008 is simply a more detailed layout of continued rapid growth. The overall number of psychologists now in the Veterans Health Administration, as of the end of October of FY10 (October 31, 2009), is 3,233, well above the prior historic high of 1,832 in 1995.

Psychology's roles in the VA system have expanded, along with the total number of staff. The following sections describe some of the important

Table 9.1 New VA mental health positions hired between January 2005 and September 30, 2009

Discipline	Number hired by September 30, 2009
Psychiatrists	594
Psychologists	1,325
Nurses	816
Social Workers	2,052
Addiction Therapist	239
Health Technicians	422
Peer Positions	201
Rehabilitation & Therapy Positions	216
Administration & Other	923
Total	**6,788**

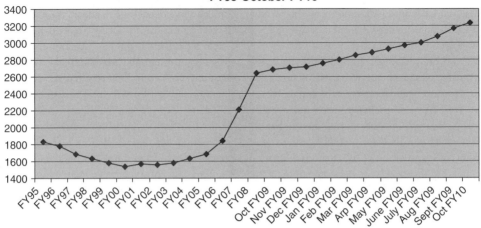

VA Psychologists GS11-GS15 by Fiscal Year, FY95-October FY10

Fig. 9.2 VA psychology staffing through October of fiscal year 2010 (October 31, 2009)

contexts in which VA psychologists function. These span working as an integral team member in the provision of health care to veterans, guiding and participating in research, providing training to the next generation of psychologists, and providing a variety of program development and leadership functions.

VA Settings in Which Psychologists Provide Health Care

Psychologists in the VA work in a wide array of health-care settings. Psychology has helped to promote mental health service innovation and to create new models of practice in the VA to ensure mental health services are consistently available. The system is designed to include the provision of basic mental health services, and also to create services appropriate for those who are in need, but less likely to receive care, such as older veterans or homeless veterans.

Most settings are organized as interdisciplinary teams, with psychology functioning in a collaborative, integrated manner with health-care providers of other disciplines—physicians, nurses, social workers, pharmacists, physical therapists, and occupational therapists, to name just some of the participants. In these roles, psychologists respect the unique skills and knowledge of other health-care providers and seek to add value through the particular expertise of psychology.

The following is a sampling of care settings in which psychologists play an integral role; it is not an exhaustive listing of all the settings and types of care to which psychologists contribute in the VA.

INPATIENT AND OUTPATIENT MENTAL HEALTH

Psychologists in the VA are well-represented in traditional mental health-care settings: inpatient mental health units and outpatient mental health clinics. All VA medical facilities have outpatient mental health clinics, and most VA medical centers have mental health inpatient units. In addition, the VA requires that mental health staff be available in all of its emergency departments; these are based in medical centers, with the intensity of emergency department coverage guided by the size and complexity of the medical facility. Although it is not required that the mental health staff include psychologists (or any other specific profession), psychologists commonly provide such emergency department coverage.

Most VA community-based outpatient clinics also provide mental heath services, and larger clinics typically have at least one psychologist on staff. Those that do not may still provide psychology care through telemental health, in which a veteran at a VA community-based clinic is seen by a primary care provider or health technician, who arranges more complex mental health services to be delivered using secure tele-video contact with a VA clinician at the medical center overseeing the community-based clinic.

INTENSIVE OUTPATIENT MENTAL HEALTH CARE

Psychologists provide more specialized recovery-oriented outpatient care in a variety of VA intensive care settings. For example, Mental Health Intensive Care Management (MHICM) teams, based on the community Assertive Community Treatment (ACT) program (Dixon, 2000), have been shown to improve the ability of adults with serious mental illness (typically psychosis) to function, live, work, and participate in relationships in the community, with reduced likelihood of need for inpatient mental health hospitalizations. Another intensive outpatient program serving veterans with serious mental illness is the Psychosocial Rehabilitation and Recovery Center (PRRC) program. This is a transformation of the older Day Hospital concept; the new model is designed to be much more active in defining patient goals and promoting self-directed activity to reestablish community participation, with appropriate professional and peer support. Psychologists are staff members, and frequently team leaders, for these PRRC programs.

INTEGRATION OF PRIMARY CARE AND MENTAL HEALTH

The VA has established model programs for the integration of mental health into the primary care setting across the country. As part of the implementation of the Uniform Mental Health Services in VA Medical Centers and Clinics Handbook, all VA primary care clinics will be expected to complete such integration. The VA requires that integrated care teams include a care management component—typically a nurse who can follow psychoactive medication for depression or possibly other mental health problems—and additionally a co-located, collaborative mental health provider, commonly a psychologist. The co-located mental health provider is required to focus, at least, on depression, co-occurring anxiety, and problem drinking in patients seen in primary care, and to provide services in the primary care context for these concerns, referring only complex cases to specialty mental health. Typically, the role is much broader, as the co-located mental health provider assumes an active, collaborative role with the primary care provider.

The VA screens all new patients for depression, PTSD, problem drinking, military sexual trauma, and traumatic brain injury (TBI). If either the depression or PTSD screen is positive, a clinician in the primary care setting is also required to evaluate suicide risk. Many of these screens are repeated at yearly intervals. Clearly, psychology can play a major role in conducting screening, following up on positive screens, establishing mental heath care when needed, and determining when a referral to specialty mental health care is needed. The psychologist also provides consultation to primary care providers regarding the implications of any mental health problems for care of other health problems being followed in primary care. In addition, psychologists in the primary care setting often provide health psychology services, including psychological care for pain, sleep problems, stress management, and improved adherence to medical treatment regimens.

POST-TRAUMATIC STRESS DISORDER

The VA has, of necessity, been a leader in development of effective treatment for PTSD. Not all veterans who have experienced combat develop PTSD, but combat is a powerful stressor that clearly raises vulnerability. Post-traumatic stress disorder came into focus as a disorder after the Viet Nam war, although it has been recognized by some name after every war (battle shock, combat fatigue, "soldier's heart", etc.). The VA offers outpatient specialized care for veterans with PTSD at every one of its medical facilities. The VA also has a large network of inpatient and residential rehabilitation programs that allow more extensive care for those with more severe PTSD-related problems. As of 2009, the VA's programs for women veterans with PTSD were expanding, as more women veterans of combat returned from Iraq and Afghanistan and sought VA care.

In addition to clinical care, the VA operates the National Center for PTSD (http://ncptsd.va.gov), a Congressionally mandated program to conduct research on PTSD and its treatment, and to provide education and consultation throughout the VA system on care for PTSD. The Center is a national resource for promoting effective treatment for PTSD outside the VA system, with seven divisions across the country, each with a specific focus of activity. The VA also has established in recent years, as a result of Congressional legislation, three additional Centers of Excellence for the treatment of PTSD and other mental heath concerns in currently returning veterans from Iraq and Afghanistan.

The VA is engaged in broad dissemination of two types of care: Cognitive Processing Therapy (CPT; e.g., Monson et al., 2006) and Prolonged Exposure Therapy (PE; e.g., Schnurr et al., 2007). These psychotherapies currently have the strongest evidence for their effectiveness in treating PTSD, compared to both current psychoactive medications and other psychotherapeutic approaches, according to the Institute of Medicine (IOM, 2007). The VA is funding training nationally in both these approaches, to ensure that staff are available at every VA medical facility to offer these therapies. As of November 2009, there were already over 2,500 therapists in the

VA trained in one of these therapies, with training efforts continuing.

Psychologists have been leaders in all of the activities described here. They lead clinical programs, they provide direct clinical care, they conduct research, and they are leaders in the National Center for PTSD and other VA mental health centers of excellence. In addition, psychologist have been leaders in the efforts to disseminate CPT and PE therapies, and most of the staff trained to provide these treatments have been psychologists.

PSYCHOGERIATRIC CARE

A large number of veterans served by the VA are older adults; as of 2008, 57% of veterans receiving care from the VA were over age 60. Psychologists play important roles in geriatric care nationally (American Psychological Association, 2008), and the same is true in the VA. Psychologists in the VA have been key in developing innovative approaches to providing mental health care to older veterans, which is critical considering that older adults are often highly unlikely to receive needed mental health care through traditional models of care (Karlin, Duffy, & Gleaves, 2008; Karlin & Zeiss, in press).

The VA has pioneered an important health-care program to support veterans who are home-bound because of illness that allows them to continue living at home. This program, Home Based Primary Care (HBPC), goes well beyond community home health programs; it provides primary care, nursing care, rehabilitation care, social work, pharmacy, and mental health care, organized in a well-coordinated, interdisciplinary model of care. All team members meet regularly at the medical center that is their base, share assessment and treatment response information, and continuously develop and refine treatment plans for these veterans. All disciplines make home visits and support each other's efforts.

In 2007, the VA began integrating mental health care into HBPC. Every HBPC team in the VA is now mandated to include a full-time mental health provider. A psychologist is in place for all teams, except a handful where, because of hiring difficulties or other special circumstances, another mental health profession is involved. Serving as the HBPC mental health provider, the psychologist serves as a core member of the interdisciplinary HBPC team, providing a range of psychological and brief cognitive evaluation services, capacity assessments, evidence-based psychotherapy, behavior management services, caregiver and family-oriented interventions, and team-focused activities. Comparable to the other team members, the HBPC mental health provider travels to veterans enrolled in the HBPC program and provides clinical services in veterans' homes. In addition, the psychologist provides consultation to other team members to improve their interactions and communications with patients to enhance the treatment process.

In addition, the VA operates extended care settings, primarily for geriatric patients. These were termed Nursing Home Care Units until 2008, when the name was changed to Community Living Centers (CLCs), to underscore that the goal is to create a home-like, person-centered environment for older adults that nurtures as much independence and functionality as possible while also providing the necessary level of nursing care and other health care. All CLCs were mandated in October 2008 to hire a mental health professional by the end of September 2009, also optimally a psychologist.

Among the primary responsibilities of the CLC mental health providers is to help serve as leaders in culture transformation in CLCs and to promote the delivery of evidence-based psychosocial services for behavioral and other neuropsychiatric symptoms associated with dementia or serious mental illness. This is a notable opportunity for psychologists to bring effective nonpharmacological approaches (which have largely remained in the proverbial laboratory) to the treatment setting, with the goal of reducing the use of those antipsychotic medications that have been found to have a death risk associated with their use with older patients with dementia. The CLC mental health provider also provides direct individual psychological and cognitive assessment and treatment services. Significantly, the rate of new episodes of depression for those moving from a home in the community to a nursing home has been estimated to be at least 50%. Such a high rate cannot be accounted for by the health status of those entering the nursing home care environment: Much of it is the result of the depressogenic environment at many traditional nursing home settings (Zeiss, 2005). Psychologists can work with nursing staff and other providers in the CLC to transform the environment, as envisioned in this new model, and as shown in prior research to be less mentally demoralizing (e.g., Bergman-Evans, 2004; Hamilton & Tesh, 2002).

Psychologists also serve older veterans in a variety of other settings: hospice, palliative care, geriatric primary care clinics, dementia clinics, and inpatient rehabilitation settings, for example for post-stroke rehabilitation. Psychologist can offer direct clinical care in all such settings, and they also provide consultation to other interdisciplinary staff, particularly regarding mental health co-occurring disorders or when problem behaviors are exhibited. One area of great interest, but without a research base to guide care, is the experience of veterans with PTSD (often undiagnosed earlier in life) during late-life and in hospice care.

RESIDENTIAL REHABILITATION

In addition to locked inpatient units serving those with the most severe mental health problems, the VA supports a large network of residential rehabilitation treatment settings. Veterans live at these programs for weeks to months, while participating in intensive mental health therapeutic activities. Units are not locked, and most medication is self-managed by the veterans while in the program. These programs are valuable for multiple populations, because they offer care in a secure environment for those who do not require and would not be willing to stay in a locked inpatient environment. They provide an intermediate step for those who need sustained care before returning to independent community living after inpatient care. They also offer the opportunity for more rural veterans to engage in intensive therapy while living at the medical facility, rather than having to travel long distances every day for intensive outpatient care. Psychologists are part of the staff at residential rehabilitation programs, they often have leadership positions, and they participate in research and program evaluation focused on these programs.

SUBSTANCE USE DISORDER AND DUAL DIAGNOSIS CARE

The VA provides a full array of substance abuse treatment services, including inpatient and outpatient detoxification support, intensive outpatient programs, residential rehabilitation programs focused on substance use disorder, dual diagnosis programs for those with other co-occurring mental health problems along with substance use disorder, care for problem drinking in the primary care team context, opioid substitution programs (using either methadone or buprenorphine), and individual and group treatment in outpatient clinics. Psychologists participate at every level of all these programs as clinicians, administrators, researchers, and program evaluators.

HOMELESS SERVICES

In 2008, there were an estimated 154,000 homeless veterans; this was down from prior years, and efforts continue to address homelessness in veterans. Most homeless veterans have longstanding mental health and substance use problems, so that services need to be more than finding housing—these veteran needs to be linked to the full array of VA physical and mental health services. The VA provides housing in multiple ways, through residential rehabilitation programs, including domiciliaries that specifically target the homeless; through nonprofit community-based transitional housing funded by VA through grant and per diem programs; and through a new joint program of VA and the Department of Housing and Urban Development that provides permanent housing for veterans and their family members. The VA also does extensive outreach to identify homeless veterans and encourage them to use these services. One outreach program involves annual "Stand Downs" at VA facilities, which are open houses when homeless veterans can get dental care, personal care (such as haircuts or clothing), and connect with other resources the VA can provide.

Social work has taken a lead role in the VA in coordinating programs for homeless veterans, but psychologists also have been involved. In particular, psychologists serve as a lynchpin between providing the basic social services needed and linking veterans to the right level of mental health care.

MILITARY SEXUAL TRAUMA

The VA screens all veterans for a possible history of sexual trauma while in the military or in training for military duty. Military sexual trauma (MST) is defined in the VA as psychological trauma, which in the judgment of a VA mental health professional, resulted from a physical assault of a sexual nature, battery of a sexual nature, or sexual harassment that occurred while the veteran was serving on active duty or active duty for training. Sexual harassment is further defined as repeated, unsolicited verbal or physical contact of a sexual nature that is threatening in character. About 20% of female veterans and about 1.1% of male veterans screen positively for MST, although not all need or request care for problems resulting from the MST.

If a veteran presents a history of sexual trauma and has physical or mental health issues judged to be a result of the trauma or exacerbated by the trauma, the VA provides free care for those problems for the length of time needed, regardless of the veteran's eligibility otherwise for free care. Every VA facility has staff trained to work with veterans who present with MST-related mental health problems. The VA also has a national network of residential rehabilitation programs specifically developed to treat veterans with mental health problems deemed to be related to MST. Although PTSD is the most common mental health diagnosis for those with a history of MST, a full array of other diagnoses also is relevant, including depression, substance use disorder, and psychotic disorders (in which there is presumably a genetic component, but in which the experience of MST impacts the resulting level of disorder severity). These programs have separate cohorts of male or female veterans, in order to ensure an environment that is psychologically safe and secure for treatment, as well as physically safe.

Psychologists take a lead role in providing MST care in the VA. A national MST Resource Center, led by psychologists, provides education and consultation across the VA system, using national conference calls, an e-mail network, VA intranet information sharing, and national conferences. The MST Resource Center also collects data on MST, and psychologists in the Center conduct research on MST. Many clinical staff providing mental heath care in outpatient and residential rehabilitation programs also are psychologists, working along with nurses, psychiatrist, social workers, and other valued mental health staff. Finally, psychologists have been involved in working with the national dissemination of training to conduct CPT and PE for treatment of PTSD, to ensure that components of the training address PTSD related to a history of MST.

SUICIDE PREVENTION
Suicide prevention is the bottom line for all mental health care. Suicide prevention requires a public health approach, in which knowledge of suicidal risk is broadly disseminated and those at potential risk receive early care before a suicidal crisis develops. Suicide prevention also requires crisis care and specific clinical approaches that can be immediately, intensely available at the point where it is urgently needed. The VA's overall plans for mental health care address both of these needs. The wide array of services defined in the Mental Health Strategic Plan in 2004 and in the Uniform Mental Health Services Handbook in 2008, which have guided the use of the VA's greatly expanding budget for mental health care, define the public health approach to ensuring excellent basic services that prevent suicidal crisis. In addition, the VA provides crisis care services for those who do not seek earlier care, or who become suicidal despite clinical efforts. Two major components of crisis care are a suicide hotline, available 24 hours per day, 7 days per week, staffed by mental health professionals, and a team of suicide-prevention resource staff at every VA medical center, who also are responsible for veterans served by the facility's community-based outpatient clinics. Psychologists have also been key in adapting and disseminating Safety Planning for Veterans, a brief intervention for suicidal patients, as well as in developing and providing training in suicide risk assessment.

Social work and nursing have taken lead roles with the crisis components of the VA's suicide prevention efforts, although they work closely with psychologists and other mental health professionals in linking those in crisis to appropriate mental health care. This ongoing care links back to all the levels of care described earlier, in which psychologists are integral members of the team and often program leaders.

Services Provided by Psychologists
Considering all of the settings described here, VA psychologists offer the full range of services that professional psychologists are trained and licensed to provide. The relative level and the specific content of services, of course, varies by site and patient population. For example, the particular approach to assessment or the specific psychotherapy offered will depend on typical presenting problems, age, and other demographics of the veterans served in the setting.

Assessment roles are important for VA psychologists. The VA employs neuropsychologists, who work in a variety of settings. Currently, the two components of the veteran population most in need of neuropsychological assessment are older veterans with cognitive changes ranging from mild cognitive impairment to dementia, and veterans returning from active combat in Iraq or Afghanistan who have suffered TBI. VA psychologists also conduct a wide array of other assessments. A computer-based system, the Mental Health Assistant, makes most well-validated personality and psychopathology assessment instruments available online. Patients can complete the instrument online, and results are scored and sent electronically to the psychologist who ordered the test. Behavioral assessment—observing behavior in clinically meaningful situations—also is widely done.

VA psychologists offer individual and group psychotherapy, using a wide array of techniques. Since 2007, the VA has conducted, and continues to expand, a comprehensive staff training program to ensure the wide availability of expertise in evidence-based psychotherapies. These evidence-based psychotherapies are required to be available to all veterans for whom they are relevant. Evidence-based psychotherapy may be sufficient to meet the needs of some veterans; for others, these therapies complement and support the delivery of other psychotherapy and medication-based therapy. Training in CPT and PE for PTSD were mentioned earlier; full training and ongoing consultation are also provided in Cognitive Behavioral Therapy (CBT) and Acceptance and Commitment Therapy (ACT) for depression. Relevant staff also are trained to be able to provide social skills training (Bellack, Mueser, Gingerich, & Agresta, 2004) for veteran patients with serious mental illness. Psychologists have taken the lead in providing and receiving most of the training in delivery of evidence-based psychotherapy, although social workers, nurses, and psychiatrists also are involved.

Psychologists working in medical settings, such as primary care setting, geriatric care clinics, and pain clinics, provide behavioral medicine services. In these settings, they typically work as an interdisciplinary team member, coordinating psychological care with medical and surgical care. Frequent targets of such services include chronic pain, sleep problems, problems with adherence to medical regimens, improved diet and other health promotion behaviors, and management of disruptive behavior in those with dementia.

Psychologists also play many roles in the VA that go beyond direct service delivery. They are often leaders in designing new and innovative programs, usually working with other professions to design interdisciplinary service delivery. Because of the research and evaluation experience integral to psychology graduate training, psychologists also are very often the designers of evaluation components for new and existing programs. They can help VA facilities track data for required performance measures, such as meeting the requirement that any new referral for mental health care be evaluated and have treatment initiated within 15 days of the referral. Psychologists also often function as supervisors of other mental health staff in service delivery. Most VA sites have a lead psychologist who has professional oversight responsibilities for the other psychology staff at that facility and its community-based outpatient clinics. In addition, the VA requires that any mental health leadership position (i.e., a position that involves direct supervision of staff from multiple professions) be advertised for all of the core mental health professions. Thus, psychologists may also direct interdisciplinary clinical programs, having responsibility for effective program functioning and

for direct supervision of multiple program staff. Finally, many psychologists function in key national leadership roles in the Department of Veterans Affairs Central Office in Washington, D.C. The first author of this chapter serves as the lead psychologist nationally for VA, in addition to being the deputy chief for the Office of Mental Health Services (OMHS) in VA Central Office. In addition, as of 2009, over ten other psychologists had key roles in the OMHS or in other components of national leadership for the VA.

VA psychologists also work in research settings. These include ten Mental Illness Research, Education, and Clinical Centers (MIRECCs), which function collaboratively with an affiliated university to conduct research relevant to improving mental health care and disseminating important findings. The VA has numerous other mental health Centers of Excellence established by Congress, including three specifically created to conduct and disseminate research relevant to the mental health needs of veterans returning from Iraq and Afghanistan. Psychologists also play key roles in the VA's National Center for PTSD (NCPTSD). This congressionally established program has seven divisions at different VA sites across the Untied States. As with the other Centers of Excellence, its mission is to conduct research—in this care, relevant to a better understanding of PTSD and improved treatment for it. The NCPTSD also conducts extensive training and consultation within the VA on PTSD care and hosts a complex website with massive amounts of information on PTSD and its treatment. Finally, the NCPTSD is a national and international resource for promoting better understanding of PTSD and effective utilization of that understanding. In addition to these Centers of Excellence, the VA funds and conducts a large amount of research through the Office of Research Development; many VA psychology staff obtain research funding from this source.

VA Training of Psychologists

The VA supports a large and thriving training program for all health professions. One component of that program, the psychology training program, ensures the largest single source of psychology training in the United States. The VA's internship and fellowship training programs have thrived for many years, and recently have grown considerably. As of 2009, VA funds 435 psychology internship slots in 90 sites and 171 postdoctoral fellowship slots in 54 sites. All of these sites are required to obtain APA accreditation within 3 years of obtaining funding.

All psychology training sites are required to obtain APA accreditation within 3 years of obtaining funding. Training occurs primarily in clinical settings and is designed to prepare psychologists who will become part of the workforce that provides direct clinical care for the "VA and for the nation." In addition, MIRECC and other Centers of Excellence train postdoctoral fellows in research on mental health care. Currently, the VA trains 17% of all psychology interns in the United States.

The VA benefits from committing significant resources to training. In recent years, 75% of new psychologists hired had received some VA training. The extensive hiring that was done to implement VA's MHSP, which will continue with its Uniform Mental Health Services Handbook, likely could not have been accomplished without the well-trained pool of new psychologists coming from the VA's internship and postdoctoral programs.

In recognition of the importance of psychology training, in 2008 the VA created a Psychology Training Council. Training directors of all VA psychology internship and postdoctoral programs are members of this Training Council. The chair of VA's Training Council is a member of the Council of Chairs of Training Councils (CCTC), participating fully in discussions with other chairs, who are primarily from graduate programs. The VA has an interest in encouraging attention in the CCTC to address important issues that allow greater dialogue and understanding between the graduate school level of training and the internship and postdoctoral levels.

Medicare

The Medicare Program, established in 1965 by the Social Security Act, is the United States federal health insurance program for individuals age 65 and older and for other Americans with certain disabilities. Medicare is administered by the Centers for Medicare and Medicaid Services, and has four main components: (1) Medicare Part A, which provides hospital benefits and limited extended care coverage; (2) Medicare Part B, which is optional and covers outpatient medical and professional services; (3) Medicare Part C, also referred to as "Medicare Advantage," an optional capitated program that Medicare beneficiaries may elect in place of Medicare Parts A and B, which are fee-for-service programs; and (4) Medicare Part D, which became effective in 2006, an optional program that provides coverage of outpatient prescription medications.

Medicare is very different from the VA healthcare system in a number of significant respects.

For one, Medicare is not an integrated health-care system. Thus, services are often highly fragmented. Medicare has also traditionally had high cost-sharing requirements for mental health services. These aspects of the Medicare Program have contributed to significant mental health care access difficulties among Medicare beneficiaries. Medicare Part A provides coverage for inpatient psychiatric services up to a lifetime limit of 190 days. There is no such limit on psychiatric or medical care provided in general hospitals. Under Part B, Medicare reimburses outpatient psychological treatment services at a rate of only 50%, compared to 80% for general outpatient medical care services. This has greatly limited the practice and provision of psychological services to Medicare beneficiaries, who often cannot afford the high co-payment requirements. Moreover, the overwhelming majority of Medicare beneficiaries do not have supplemental "Medigap" insurance coverage, which picks up the costs Medicare does not cover for Medicare-approved claims. Making matters worse, significant restrictions in funding for Medicaid (the government health insurance for indigent individuals) in many states have greatly limited coverage of Medicare co-payments and deductibles for individuals who are enrolled in both Medicare and Medicaid. Traditionally, Medicaid has covered Medicare cost-sharing requirements for mental health services of individuals dually eligible for both programs. The limited coverage of mental health services under Medicare and the decreasing availability of Medicaid funding have served as significant disincentives to the delivery of psychological services under Medicare.

Beyond limited reimbursement of psychological services, professional psychology's involvement in Medicare has been tumultuous. It was not until 1989 that psychologists became recognized as independent providers under Medicare and were able to bill the government health insurance program. Although strongly advocated for and welcomed by psychologists, the granting of professional autonomy to professional psychology did not have nearly the anticipated impact in improving the role of psychology in Medicare. The cost-sharing requirements under Medicare have rendered psychotherapy and other psychosocial services prohibitive for many. It is partly for this reason that older adults continue to significantly underutilize mental health services (Karlin, Duffy, & Gleaves, 2008).

Psychology's role and the day-in day-out business of providing psychological services in Medicare is significantly shaped by local coverage policies, known as "local coverage determinations" (LCDs; formerly known as "local medical review policies"). By statute, services provided to Medicare beneficiaries must be "medically necessary." However, Medicare statutes do not precisely define what is "medically necessary" or delineate the specific services that may be provided; rather, this standard is operationalized by LCDs, which are developed by insurance companies who contract with Medicare to manage the daily administration of the Medicare Program. These contractors (known as "fiscal intermediaries" under Part A and "carriers" under Part B) develop LCDs that are to be consistent with medical science and standard practice. Unfortunately, many contractors have developed psychological service delivery LCDs that have often been highly restrictive, variable from one contractor to another, and, in some cases, directly inconsistent with medical science and standard practice (Karlin & Duffy, 2004). As a result of such policies, many psychologists and other mental health providers have been denied claims. Moreover, professional psychology has historically been relatively absent in LCD development and revision processes, even though their input should be considered.

The good news is that the role of psychology and the state of psychological service delivery in the Medicare Program has improved considerably in very recent years and will likely see unprecedented positive opportunities and developments in the years ahead. In 2002, Medicare adopted six new Health and Behavior Assessment and Intervention (H&B) CPT codes that significantly extend the role of psychologists and psychological services in Medicare. These new codes allow for the provision of behavioral health assessment and interventions for problems related to physical health conditions in the absence of a mental illness.

In addition, there is real and unprecedented opportunity for incorporating mental health prevention and early identification into Medicare, in light of recent political, policy, societal, and program developments, as we have examined in detail elsewhere (Karlin & Humphreys, 2007). Such a development could transform where, when, and how psychological services are provided, as well as enhance public welfare and promote the status of the profession. Moreover, since Medicare typically sets the trend that the private insurance industry follows, the incorporation of mental health prevention and early identification could have impact well beyond Medicare. Significantly, Medicare has recently established coverage for tobacco cessation counseling and alcohol and drug screening and brief intervention.

One of the most significant changes to Medicare and mental health care since the creation of the government health insurance program over 40 years ago will soon take effect, and it will, undoubtedly, promote the interest, opportunity, and involvement of professional psychology in Medicare. After many years of unsuccessful legislative proposals, 2008 witnessed the passage of landmark legislation that established mental health parity in Medicare. On July 15, 2008, the Medicare Improvements for Patients and Providers Act of 2008 (Public Law No. 110-275) was enacted over presidential veto, calling for the gradual phasing down of copayment rates for outpatient mental health services from 50% to 20%, beginning in 2010 and continuing through 2014, as follows:

Year	Cost-Sharing Requirement
2010 and 2011	45%
2012	40%
2013	35%
2014 and thereafter	20%

In addition to promoting financial access to mental health services, the creation of mental health parity in Medicare may have profound secondary benefits. Specifically, mental health parity in Medicare may likely elevate the status of mental health and psychological services, thereby reducing stigma and increasing "psychological access" to services. Mental health parity in Medicare is likely to also increase psychology's participation in and impact on the government health insurance program. Moreover, the leveling of the playing field between physical health and mental health care in Medicare may help to reduce fragmentation and promote coordination of services.

Another significant development in Medicare that will likely bode particularly well for mental health care in general and psychology specifically are the planned changes to reform Medicare's contracting process to promote provider and beneficiary satisfaction, pursuant to the Medicare Prescription Drug, Improvement, and Modernization Act of 2003. By 2011, the carriers and fiscal intermediaries with which Medicare contracts to help administer the Medicare Program will be replaced by 15 Medicare Administrative Carriers that will administer both Part A and Part B claims. This will lead to fewer LCDs, which is likely to promote consistency.

The CMS will also consider which new LCDs should be implemented nationally.

Finally, in looking to the future, the writing on the wall suggests that the psychological service landscape in Medicare may look somewhat different from what it traditionally has. Over the last few years, the CMS has developed a number of Pay for Performance (P4P) initiatives within Medicare to promote improved quality of care to Medicare beneficiaries and to enhance efficiency of care. These initiatives tend to focus on services for patients with chronic conditions. Given the nature and scope of the current initiatives and some evidence of success, it is reasonable to believe that the CMS's increasing focus on performance and outcomes will soon impact how mental health services are provided in Medicare, especially given the expansion in the mental health benefit in Medicare that parity will provide.

Conclusion

Psychology plays key and growing roles in national health care throughout the Veterans Health Administration, the component of the VA that provides health-care services. After a period of struggle in the 1990s and very early 2000s, psychology has been thriving, with increased numbers of psychologists hired, increased involvement in diverse clinical and research settings, and increased training positions. Typically, psychology functions as part of an interdisciplinary provision of care in VA facilities, offering the full range of psychological services that are well-coordinated with the services of other health-care professions.

At the same time that professional psychology experienced a period of decline in the VA in the 1990s, psychologists faced significant challenges in the Medicare Program, shortly after gaining recognition as independent providers in Medicare. The granting of professional autonomy to psychologists in the late 1980s was a watershed moment for the profession; however, psychologists and patients confronted significant mental health care access and reimbursement challenges in the ensuing decade that prevented psychology from fully achieving the possibilities that being part of the government health insurance program offered. Now, approximately 20 years after becoming recognized by Medicare, psychologists face a new dawn on the horizon. New regulatory and legislative changes in the Medicare Program, including the expansion of the Medicare mental health benefit, provide unprecedented opportunities for psychologists—changes that could help to further shape the practice of professional psychology.

Future Directions

Some questions that face the future of psychological care under government systems include:

• Can VA expansion generally—and psychology specifically—be sustained in the current economic climate?

• Will a national health-care system be developed in the United States, and if so, what can it learn from VA accomplishments?

• What can mental health care in the United States learn from the VA's experiences with dissemination of evidence-based psychotherapy?

• What impact will the reduction in Medicare's co-payment requirement have on utilization of psychological treatment services by older Americans?

• How can psychology in the VA and Medicare continue to innovate and respond to new research findings, as mental health care continues to evolve?

• How can behavioral health service delivery be enhanced in the VA and Medicare?

References

American Psychological Association. (2008). Blueprint for change: Achieving integrated health care for an aging population. Washington, DC: Author.

Bellack, A.S., Mueser, K. T., Gingerich, S., & Agresta, J. (2004). Social skills training for schizophrenia: A step-by-step guide. New York: Guilford.

Bergman-Evans, B. (2004). Beyond the basics: Effects of the Eden Alternative model on quality of life issues. Journal of Gerontological Nursing, 30, 27–34.

Department of Veterans Affairs. (2003). Action agenda: Achieving the promise, transforming mental health care in VA. Washington, DC: Author.

Department of Veterans Affairs. (2004). A Comprehensive Veterans Health Administration Strategic Plan for Mental Health. Washington, DC: Author.

Dixon, L. (2000). Assertive community treatment: Twenty-five years of gold. Psychiatric Services, 51, 759–765.

Edwards, D. J. (2008). Transforming the VA. Behavioral Healthcare, 28, 15–17.

Hamilton, N., & Tesh, A.S. (2002). The North Carolina Eden Coalition: Facilitating environmental transformation. Journal of Gerontological Nursing, 28, 35–40.

Institute of Medicine. (2007). Treatment of posttraumatic stress disorder: An assessment of the evidence. Washington, DC: National Academies Press.

Kelly, G.A. (1955). The Psychology of personal constructs. New York: Norton.

Longman, P. (2007). The best care anywhere: Why VA health care is better than yours. Sausalito, CA: PoliPointPress.

Karlin, B. E., & Duffy, M. (2004). Geriatric mental health policy: Impact on service delivery and directions for effecting change. Professional Psychology: Research and Practice, 35, 509–519.

Karlin, B. E., Duffy, M., & Gleaves, D. H. (2008). Patterns and predictors of mental health service use and mental illness among older and younger adults in the United States. *Psychological Services, 5*, 275–294.

Karlin, B. E., & Humphreys, K. (2007). Improving Medicare coverage of psychological services for older Americans. *American Psychologist, 62*, 637–649.

Karlin, B. E., & Zeiss, A. M. (in press). Transforming mental healthcare for older veterans in the Veterans Health Administration. Generations.

New Freedom Commission on Mental Health. (2003). Achieving the promise: Transforming mental health care in America. Retrieved March 31, 2010 from http://www.mentalhealth-commission.gov.

Monson, C. M., Schnurr, P. P., Resick, P. A., Friedman, M. J., Young-Xu, Y., & Stevens, S. P. (2006). Cognitive Processing Therapy for veterans with military-related Posttraumatic Stress Disorder. *Journal of Consulting and Clinical Psychology, 74*, 898–907.

Schnurr, P.P., Friedman, M.J., Engel, C.C, Foa, E.B., Shea, M.T., Chow, B.K., et al. (2007). Cognitive-behavioral therapy for posttraumatic stress disorder in women: A randomized controlled trial. *Journal of the American Medical Association, 297*, 820–830.

Zeiss, A.M. (2005). Depression in long term care: Contrasting a disease model with attention to environmental impact. *Clinical Psychology: Science and Practice, 12*, 300–302.

Ethical Issues in Clinical Psychology

Kenneth S. Pope

Abstract

This chapter examines how ethical issues are approached differently by two prominent psychological associations, how they are encountered by psychologists, the formal complaints they give rise to, and how they can be approached systematically to avoid missteps. Included are basic assumptions about ethics; the unique approaches to developing a ethics code taken by the American Psychological Association (APA) and the Canadian Psychological Association (CPA), and what each of these two codes provides; empirical data about what ethical problems psychologists encounter and what formal complaints they face; four major sets of ethical issues that are particularly complex and challenging (confidentiality, informed consent, competence, and boundaries); an area of major controversy (clinical psychology and national security); steps in ethical decision-making; and four possible lines of future research.

Keywords: Boundaries, competence, confidentiality, ethics, ethical decision-making, formal complaints, informed consent

You're screening a patient for whom treatment is desperately needed and may be literally life-saving. However, her health insurance covers a very limited range of diagnoses. The only way she can afford treatment is for you to provide a false diagnosis.

***

The clinic director instructs you to begin using a new battery of psychological tests, developed by his cousin, to screen all new patients. You diplomatically suggest that the clinic might use other tests, because the battery's tests have not been studied and lack validity and reliability data. The director refuses to rescind his order. You and your family live in a tight job market, you are unlikely to be able to find another position, and you are already barely able to pay the rent.

***

During your dream internship, you work under the supervision of a famous psychologist, seeing patients as part of his large study. One day, you happen to see on

a secretary's desk the reports filed with the granting agency. Your supervisor has reported that you have been seeing over twice as many patients as you've actually seen. During a subsequent private discussion, when you raise the issue, your supervisor assures you that you were mistaken and that should you spread libel, not only would you face a lawsuit but that it would be impossible to certify your internship hours or write you the planned glowing job recommendation. The next day, a letter informs you that, due to unexpected new funding sources, your internship stipend had been doubled.

***

When you arrive at your psychological services clinic, Department of Homeland Security officials are waiting for you. They believe there may be bombings planned for your area, and one of your therapy clients likely has specific information about when and where the bombs would be placed. The officials must have immediate access to your client's records, so that they can be faxed to the field office to assist in investigation and interrogation. They also want to know anything you can tell them that might help them quickly obtain information from your client. They instruct you not to tell anyone, including the client, of this matter.

***

Exhausted as you prepare to the leave your office and—already late!—rush to the airport, so that you don't miss the flight that will carry you and your family to that long-awaited vacation, you discover that your patient has left a message for you in an envelope taped to the outer door of your office: Convinced he will never find work to support his family, he is taking steps to end it all tonight.

***

A new teenage patient tells you that her father got drunk and sexually assaulted her, but that if you tell anyone she will deny it, tell them that you made it up because she had refused to have sex with you, and then kill herself. You believe her.

Each day clinical psychologists confront almost countless ethical issues, from the routine to the one-of-a-kind. They range from the trivial to matters of life or death. Responding to the almost infinite variety of these issues is an essential, inescapable part of the work. This chapter examines the ethical aspects of clinical psychology.

The first section following this introduction makes explicit some basic assumptions about ethics. Because ethical decision-making occurs in the context of a formal code of ethics, the second and third sections of the chapter describe the unique approaches to developing such a code taken by the American Psychological Association (APA) and the Canadian Psychological Association (CPA), and what each of these two codes provides. The fourth section presents empirical data about what ethical problems psychologists encounter and what formal complaints they face. The next four sections focus on major sets of ethical issues that are particularly complex and challenging: confidentiality, informed consent, competence, and boundaries. The final section presents a set of steps that clinical psychologists may find helpful when thinking through ethical decisions.

Basic Assumptions

Too often "ethics" may come across as a dry or forbidding abstraction. A heavy coat of misleading stereotypes can hide its nature. It may seem a set of authoritarian do's and don'ts to be passively followed or mechanically applied; a set of answers "out there" somewhere, if we can only find the right one at the

right time from the right source (a book, an attorney, someone on an ethics committee). Ethics may seem a nightmarish area in which an angry patient can file a baseless complaint against us and we will have to defend ourselves against a potentially hostile ethics committee while colleagues wonder if we've done something horrible; or ethics may be a way to protect ourselves, by burying our work under layers of risk micro-management and psychology's version of "defensive medicine." The following basic assumptions, which are adapted from Pope and Vasquez (2010), are intended to sweep away some of these misconceptions:

- Responding effectively to ethical issues is a process of active, creative decision-making rather than passive rule-following or finding some book or expert to tell us what to do. Ethics codes, administrative regulations, legal requirements, and those with expert knowledge of these documents can inform our decisions, but they cannot make those decisions for us. They may underscore essential responsibilities, such as informed consent, but they cannot identify how each of us—with different patterns of skills, theoretical orientations, and resources—can best meet those responsibilities with diverse patients from diverse backgrounds, each with different patterns of strengths, weaknesses, and clinical needs. Codes, regulations, requirements, and authorities cannot do our thinking for us.
- Sound ethical decision-making depends on maintaining awareness of the ethical implications of what we do. The rush of events—the next patient, phone calls to return, and overdue paperwork—can distract us. Fatigue, financial pressures, family conflicts, worries about the future, and so many other stresses can dim our awareness. None of us is immune to these factors.
- None of us is perfect, so our decisions are often imperfect. We must make some ethical decisions on the basis of inadequate information, perhaps lacking adequate time, resources, and options. Despite limitations, we are individually responsible for doing the best we can, and we must assume personal responsibility for our actions. In light of our fallibility, it is always worth asking ourselves: Can I come up with a more creative, effective approach to this ethical issue, one that better serves those who are affected?
- Our ability to identify the approach that makes the most sense ethically, practically, and

clinically depends to some extent on maintaining awareness of evolving research, theory, and practice. No matter how authoritative, widely accepted, or consistent with our expectations, the claims emerging from scientific and professional articles do not deserve passive or reflexive acceptance, but warrant thoughtful, informed questioning and active engagement.

• Sound ethical decision-making may often be consistent with sound risk-management, but ethical decision-making is different from risk-management and may lead clinical psychologists to consider placing their income, reputations, referral sources, jobs, or psychology licenses at risk. A classic article, "The Psychologist As Whistleblower," documented how a psychologist's steadfast refusal to follow instructions to quickly discharge patients from a Veterans Administration program because he believed precipitous discharge would endanger their health and safety ultimately led to his being fired (Simon, 1978). Pope and Gutheil (2009b; see also Pope & Bajt, 1988) discussed the implications of the APA ethics code's approach to risks that arise when psychologists encounter laws that are in conflict with their ethical responsibilities.

• All of us have ethical blind spots, and the respectful, direct intervention of colleagues can save us from making or compounding ethical blunders. We are valuable resources for each other. However, most of us probably find it more interesting and convenient to question our colleagues' ethical beliefs, reasoning, or behavior than our own. We need to spend at least as much time, energy, and creativity—probably more—in questioning our own thoughts and actions as we do in challenging others.

• When questioning ourselves, it is probably easier to focus on those things we aren't so sure of, assumptions and conclusions we have not developed a strong allegiance to, ideas and possibilities we are still trying on for size. It can be equally important—and often more revealing—to question that which we have always taken for granted, which we are most sure of, or which seems beyond question. This form of rigorous questioning often takes considerable courage, sometimes raising possibilities that may be exceptionally unpopular and viewed by ourselves and others as taboo, "politically incorrect," or "psychologically incorrect" (Pope, Sonne, & Greene, 2006).

The American Psychological Association's Approach to an Ethics Code

The APA existed for 60 years without an ethics code. Early accounts trace the APA's founding to a July 8, 1892, organizational meeting attended by Stanley Hall, George Fullerton, Joseph Jastrow, William James, George Ladd, James Cattell, and Mark Baldwin at Clark University (Fernberger, 1932). It is worth noting that a psychologist writing a history of the organization attempted to gather and verify information about this meeting. Finding that two of psychologists who allegedly attended the meeting (Cattell and Jastrow) denied attending, and unable to locate any supportive evidence, he concluded that there is no evidence that the meeting actually occurred and that "all of this leads to a possible conclusion—and I say this as an ex-Secretary of the Association—that one cannot always trust the printed minutes . . . as evidence of what actually happened at any meeting" (Fernberger, 1943, p. 35).

Whatever its actual beginnings, the APA created its first Committee on Scientific and Professional Ethics (CSPE) several decades later, in 1938. When someone made a formal complaint about an APA member, the CPSE discussed the matter privately and attempted to agree on an informal approach to resolving the matter. Working without a written ethics code, the CPSE had to reach of consensus and then rely on persuasion.

The initial ethical challenges encountered by APA members were neither varied nor complex. Rich wrote that ethical problems in the APA's early years were fairly simple because the organization's membership consisted mainly of college professors. "The only ethical problems which seemed to present themselves were those of plagiarism and of academic freedom" (1952, p. 440).

However, as the ethical problems grew in diversity and complexity, the APA charged the committee, in 1939, with assessing whether an ethics code would be helpful. Eight years later, the CPSE concluded that the APA needed a written code, in part because an "unwritten code is tenuous, elusive, and unsatisfactory" ("A little recent history," 1952). The APA created a Committee on Ethical Standards, chaired by Edward Tolman, to develop an ethics code for psychologists.

Not all members thought that an ethics code was a good idea. Various members—some of them exceptionally prominent—argued vigorously against the APA adopting a written code of ethical standards. Calvin Hall, for example, believed that even the most carefully developed written code of ethics favored the crooked psychologist, who examines an ethics code "to see how much he can get away with . . . and since any code is bound to be filled with ambiguities and omissions, he can rationalize his unethical conduct" (Hall, 1952, p. 430).

The CPSE recommended a method for developing an ethics code that was remarkable and unprecedented, sharply different from the customary and accepted methods used previously by more than 500 professional and business associations (Hobbs, 1948). They wanted to avoid what Hobbs termed the "armchair approach" (p. 82) in which a committee of those presumably most qualified would study the available codes, pressing issues, and relevant literature; then issue general calls for input or comments in various publications, but not contact members individually.

They decided that the code's development must be based on the methods of psychological science, specifically empirical survey research. The APA would contact its members individually, sending each a letter that would ask about the psychologist's personal experiences. This method of reaching out to members individually could establish a direct connection between the committee and each member that would be more effective than running a general announcement in some of the APA publications that members might or might not happen to notice. It conveyed the seriousness with which the committee was seeking input from all members, rather than the relative few who participated actively in the APA, and the weight that the committee accorded to each member's individual views. Contacting the members individually and asking for personal experience would give all members, rather than just a sampling of the membership, a stake in the code. Members would know that their views and experiences were part of the *primary* data on which the code was based. Nicholas Hobbs wrote that this method would produce "a code of ethics truly indigenous to psychology, a code that could be lived" (Hobbs, 1948).

The APA adopted the CPSE's recommendation and appointed a new committee, chaired by Hobbs, to conduct the research and create a code (APA, 1949). Each of the 7,500 APA members received a letter in 1948. The letter invited the member "to share his experiences in solving ethical problems by describing the specific circumstances in which someone made a decision that was ethically critical" (APA, 1949). More than 1,000 critical incidents became the empirical base of APA's first ethics code. The committee assessed and categorized the responses,

and began publishing the results of their work in 1950.

The APA Board of Directors had asked the committee to address what they believed to be an urgent concern: the growing number of psychological tests and other assessment instruments that were questionable in terms of validity and reliability, along with the increase in psychologists and others who were conducting psychological assessments but who lacked appropriate education, training, and experience. Noting that, in 1944 alone, around 20,000,000 U.S. citizens took around 60,000,000 psychological tests, the committee produced a set of 18 "Ethical Standards for the Distribution of Psychological Tests and Diagnostic Aids," which the APA quickly adopted (APA Committee on Ethical Standards, 1950).

In 1951, the committee published six separate sets of draft ethical standards, each accompanied by relevant critical incidents (APA Committee on Ethical Standards, 1951a,b,c,d). The six topic areas were:

- Ethical standards and public responsibility
- Ethical standards in professional relationships
- Ethical standards in client relationships
- Ethical standards in research
- Ethical standards in writing and publishing
- Ethical standards in teaching

After extensive discussion and several revisions, the APA adopted its first ethics code in 1952 and published it in 1953 (APA, 1953). Amazingly—at least from the perspective of subsequent revisions—the first code ran 171 pages!

The APA adopted nine subsequent revisions of the code in 1959, 1963, 1968, 1977, 1979, 1981, 1990, 1992, and 2002, although in 2010 APA Council voted to change several sentences in the Introduction and sections 1.02 and 1.03 that were relevant to the Nuremberg Ethic ("Amending the Ethics Code," 2010). The Nuremberg Ethic and its relationship to the APA ethics code is discussed in a subsequent section of this chapter, "An Area of Major Controversy: Clinical Psychology and National Security."

The latest version of the APA ethics code includes an introduction, preamble, five general principles, and specific ethical standards. The preamble and the general principles—which include beneficence and nonmaleficence, fidelity and responsibility, integrity, justice, and respect for people's rights and dignity—are nonenforceable aspirational goals to guide psychologists toward the highest ideals of psychology. The subsequent 89 ethical standards are enforceable rules for conduct. The ethical standards fall into ten major categories:

- Resolving ethical issues
- Competence
- Human relations
- Privacy and confidentiality
- Advertising and other public statements
- Record keeping and fees
- Education and training
- Research and publication
- Assessment
- Therapy

Each revision of the code was to be based on similar surveys mailed to the membership to gather "additional critical incidents of controversial behavior" (Holtzman, 1960, p. 247). By sending an individual survey form to each member, as was done with the original code, subsequent revisions would maintain this unique empirical approach, preserve the stake that *all* members had in a code, reflect the concerns and expertise of the full range of membership, and foster loyalty to the code.

The conviction that revisions should be based on survey forms sent to the membership also rested on beliefs about empowerment, management style, group process, and allegiance (e.g., Golann, 1969; Hobbs, 1948; Holzman, 1960). The two ways of developing a revision were considered to create very different outcomes. The first approach, unique to psychology, began by actively seeking, through a formal mail survey, the observations, ideas, and questions from those working "on the front lines" in diverse specialties, settings, and circumstances. These survey responses form the primary data for the revision. The second approach, used by virtually all other professional and business associations, centered on the work of a committee that would use many sources of data, perhaps including a published call for input or a survey of a sample of the membership. The first approach was considered (a) to empower all members by involving them meaningfully and individually (through the mailed survey) from the start, (b) benefit from better group or organizational dynamics by creating a psychological sense of community among all members, and (c) produce a better revision.

The most valuable attribute of the APA's empirically based code of ethics was that it was "based upon the day-to-day decisions made by psychologists in the practice of their profession, rather than prescribed by a committee" (Golann, 1969, p. 454). Surveying all members individually was considered

essential to maintain an ethics code "close enough to the contemporary scene to win the genuine acceptance of the majority who are most directly affected by its principles" (Holzman, 1960, p. 250). To date, none of the revisions of the APA's ethics code has been based on crucial incident survey forms sent individually to the full membership.

The Canadian Psychological Association's Approach to an Ethics Code

The CPA was formed in 1939, and existed for over two decades without a formal ethics code. Incorporating under the Canada Corporations Act, Part II, in 1950, the organization represented the relatively small number of Canadian psychologists scattered across a very large country. As the need for a formal code became apparent, so did the daunting challenges of bringing together psychologists from diverse regions often enough to develop the basis, methodology, organization, and wording of a formal code. Consequently, CPA chose "to adopt the 1959 . . . APA code for a 3-year trial. This was followed by adoptions (with minor wording changes) of the 1963 and 1977 APA revised codes" (Sinclair & Pettifor, 2001).

CPA members soon began to grow discontent with the APA code, but it was only in 1977, when the APA released that year's revision of the code, that the discontent reached a critical point (Sinclair, N. P. Simon, & Pettifor, 1996). A central concern was that the APA's new code ran "ran the risk of changing the nature of the professional relationship from a primarily fiduciary contract to a commercial one" (Sinclair et al., 1996).

Sinclair (1998) notes that the CPA established four goals for its new code:

- Conceptual coherence, which would make it better suited to use in education
- Inclusiveness, so that it would embrace more new areas of psychological practice
- Explicitness, so that it would provide clearer guidelines for what to do when two or more ethical values were in conflict
- Usefulness, so that it would include helpful rules for the ethical decision-making process

To provide an empirical basis for the code, the CPA sent 37 ethical dilemmas to its members (Truscott & Crook, 2004). The dilemmas were designed to cover each of the principles—and the conflicts among those principles—in the APA's current code, as well as newer areas of practice including creative approaches that as yet lacked empirical support. The survey not only invited participants to describe what they would do when confronting each dilemma but also asked them a series of questions created to clarify the ethical decision-making process that led up to that action. A content analysis found that the participants were relying on four fundamental ethical principles (Canadian Psychological Association [CPA], 1986):

- Respect for the dignity of persons
- Responsible caring
- Integrity in relationships
- Responsibility to society

The CPA's first ethics code set forth those four principles, and included a set of seven steps for ethical decision-making. The CPA adopted the most recent revision of the code in 2000. The third edition of the Canadian Code of Ethics for Psychologists (CPA, 2000) includes a preamble, four ethical principles, statements of values that are embodied in each of the ethical principles, ethical standards that show how the principles and values are applied to psychologists' activities, and a set of ten steps in ethical decision-making. (Note: A subsequent section of this chapter discusses steps in ethical decision-making.)

The current code also includes sections discussing:

- The code's uses
- Nine specific responsibilities of the individual psychologist (e.g., to discuss ethical issues with colleagues regularly; to take seriously the concerns of others about one's own ethically questionable behavior; to avoid being provocative or vicious when voicing or responding to concerns about ethically questionable behavior)
- The code's relationship to personal behavior
- The code's relationship to provincial regulatory agencies
- Definitions

Empirical Data About What Ethical Problems Psychologists Encounter and What Formal Complaints They Face

This section reviews some data that shed light on which ethical dilemmas psychologists seem to face most often and what ethical issues are the most frequent sources of formal complaints against psychologists.

Ethical Incidents That Are Challenging or Troubling

Fifty years after the original membership survey that formed the basis of the APA's original ethics code, a limited replication appeared in *American Psychologist* (Pope & Vetter, 1992). Because the survey was funded by two individuals without a grant or other external financial resources, the replication was limited to only a sample, rather than the full APA membership. A random sample of 1,319 APA members received survey forms asking them to describe incidents that they found ethically challenging or troubling. Over half (679) of the psychologists provided 703 incidents falling into 23 categories.

Here are the eight largest categories of critical incidents, along with examples of the incidents. The percentage of reported incidents in each category appears in parentheses.

- *Confidentiality* (18%):
  One of the psychologist's patients is a psychologist who tells the therapist he has committed an ethics violation but confidentiality prevents the therapist from reporting it.

  A clinic's executive director reads the charts of patients who are members of his church, saying that it helps him in his clerical role.

  One client tells the psychologist that she was raped but the police do not believer her because of a history of psychological problems. Another client tells the same psychologist how he raped that woman.
- *Blurred, dual, or conflictual relationships* (17%):
  The psychologist lives in a rural setting and must offer psychotherapy to other members of her tightly knit spiritual community because there is no one else to provide appropriate psychological services.

  A psychologist's patient, whom she had been working with for 3 years, fell in love with the psychologist's oldest and best friend. The psychologist obtained clinical, legal, and ethical consultations and, as a result, arranged a gradual transfer to another therapist and told her friend that she would need to suspend contact temporarily. She was currently considering when and under what conditions she could see the new couple socially.
- *Payment sources, plans, settings, and methods* (14%):
  The psychologist evaluated a young boy who had been severely sexually abused and was depressed. He recommended 6 months of therapy. However, the managed care company approved ten sessions to be conducted by a nonprofessional. The psychologist noted that there is no ten-session treatment for a young boy in such

circumstances that has shown evidence of effectiveness.

A managed care organization stopped coverage of therapy and advised the psychologist's patient to terminate. The organization then referred the patient to another therapist, whose managed care contract specified a lower fee.

The psychologist works for a private hospital that generally provides good clinical services. However, the motivation to maximize profits is so intense that it often overrules clinical concerns and results in decisions that harm patients. Patient complaints tend to be attributed to their psychopathology, and the psychologist feels he can't speak openly with his patients about the hospital's financial decisions overshadowing clinical concerns.

• *Academic settings, teaching dilemmas, and concerns about training* (8%):

The psychologist, who employs over 600 other psychologists, finds it disturbing that some of them have marginal ethics and competence, and that these problems were not addressed in graduate school and were no barrier to graduation.

• *Forensic psychology* (5%):

The psychologist describes a forensic psychologist in his community who is widely known (to lawyers and others) to give whatever testimony that the retaining lawyer requires. He has a great courtroom presence and is very persuasive. The side that retains him often wins because of his testimony, so that lawyers often hire him.

The psychologist describes another psychologist whose forensic assessment reports or testimony go far beyond the psychologist's competence or what the data support. The survey respondent does not know whether or how to handle the matter.

The psychologist is uncomfortable providing sensitive information about a client in a deposition or in court, even though the client has given informed consent for the testimony.

• *Research* (4%):

The psychologist is a co-investigator on a research grant who happened to see on a secretary's desk the principal investigator's interim report to the funding source. The report states that the current data were based on twice as many subjects as had actually participated.

The psychologist listed three concerns: a study that involved deception that was not disclosed; using a data video in a public presentation without the consent of one of the subjects in the video (the subject was in the presentation's audience); and performing an experimental manipulation in the assignment of course homework without informing the students.

The psychologist was consultant at a prominent medical school for drug research in which there were violations of random selection of participants.

• *Conduct of colleagues* (4%):

The psychologist referred a child patient to a community medical center for hospitalization, contacting a psychiatrist whom the mother wanted involved to make the arrangements. The psychiatrist hospitalized the child and then informed the psychologist that, as the admitting professional, he would take over the treatment and would assign the child to another psychologist who worked in his office.

The psychologist worked at a facility whose director had emotional problems that adversely affected patient care and staff morale. The director refused to seek professional help.

The psychologist sees foster children whose case workers have little time or interest in them. The psychologist does not know how to maintain effective working relationships with the case workers under those conditions.

The psychologist had trouble dealing with a fellow faculty member after many students complained about the colleague.

• *Sexual issues* (4%):

The psychologist's supervisee reported that her prior supervisor had forced her to perform sexual acts and had threatened to refuse to validate her supervision hours if she refused or reported him.

The psychologist's patient is a psychiatrist who has been having sex with his own patient for the past 6 years. He now would like to bring what he calls "the affair" to an end but is afraid of what will happen if he does.

The remaining categories and percentages were: assessment (4%), questionable or harmful interventions (3%), competence (3%), ethics (and related) codes and committees (2%), school psychology (2%), publishing (2%), helping the financially stricken (2%), supervision (2%), advertising and (mis)representation (2%), industrial–organizational psychology (1%), medical issues (1%), termination (1%), ethnicity (1%), treatment records (1%), and miscellaneous (1%).

Sources of Formal Complaints Against Psychologists

Drawing on the annual data made available by the American Association of State and Provincial Psychology Boards, the APA, CPA, and the APA Insurance Trust, Pope and Vasquez (2010) presented multiyear data on ethics, licensing, and malpractice complaints against psychologists in the United States and Canada. These data suggest areas of particular difficulty for psychologists.

ETHICS COMPLAINTS

Ethics cases opened by the APA are assigned a primary category, which is the technical basis for processing that particular care. However, cases are also assigned "multiple categories," which indicate the underlying behaviors. For example, a case may be opened because a member was expelled from a state psychological association, so the expulsion would be the primary category. But the expulsion may have been based on sexual misconduct with an adult, working outside areas of competence, and a breach of confidentiality—the multiple categories. During a 5-year period, the multiple categories with the largest number of newly opened cases (with the number of instances appearing in parentheses) included: loss of licensure (92); sexual misconduct with an adult (59); inappropriate practice involving child custody (25); nonsexual dual relationship (24); inappropriate practice involving insurance or fees (18); other (nonspecified) adjudications in other jurisdictions (14); other (nonspecified) inappropriate professional practice (11); confidentiality (10); felony convictions (8); response to ethics committee (7); sexual misconduct with a minor (3); inappropriate response to a crisis (3); and inappropriate termination/supervision (3).

It is extremely rare that the CPA receives ethics complaints against its members. During the same 5-year period, the CPA had taken no action against any member.

STATE AND PROVINCIAL PSYCHOLOGY LICENSING BOARD DISCIPLINARY ACTIONS

Over a 22-year period, psychology licensing boards in the United States took 3,471 disciplinary actions. The major causes of the 2,858 cases for which causes were reported (with the percentage of total identified causes indicated in parentheses) were sexual or nonsexual dual relationship with a patient (30%); unprofessional, unethical, or negligent practice (29.5%); criminal conviction (9%); fraudulent acts (6%); inadequate or improper record keeping (5.5%); noncompliance with continuing educational requirements (4.5%); breaching confidentiality (4.5%); inadequate or improper supervision (4%); psychological impairment affecting practice (4%); and fraud in applying for a license (2%).

During the same period, Canadian psychology licensing boards took 142 disciplinary actions. The major causes of the 109 cases for which causes were reported include (because the total is 109 and most categories have only between one and four cases, absolute numbers rather than percentages will be included in parentheses): unprofessional, unethical, or negligent practice (39); sexual/dual relationship with patient (35); breach of confidentiality (5); malpractice (4); conviction of crimes (4); failure to meet conditions of candidacy (3); improper termination of therapy (3); failure to adhere to standards (3); improper/inadequate record keeping (2); fraud in application for license (2); fraudulent acts (2); improper experimental treatment (2) impairment (1); failure to timely report child abuse (1); boundary violations (1); improper or inadequate supervision (1); and practice outside scope (1).

PROFESSIONAL LIABILITY SUITS

Multiyear statistical data on categories for professional liability suits filed against Canadian psychologists were unavailable. However, 10 years' worth of data on psychologists in the United States suggest the following areas of difficulty, based on the amount in claims paid out for such suits (with the percentage of claims paid out in parentheses): ineffective treatment/failure to consult/failure to refer (29%); failure to diagnose/improper diagnosis (16%); custody dispute (10%); sexual intimacy/sexual harassment and/or sexual misconduct (95); breach of confidentiality (8%); suicide (4%); and supervisory issues, conflict of interest or improper multiple relationships (3%).

Confidentiality, Privacy, and Privilege

Confidentiality allows psychotherapy patients to tell their therapists secrets they might tell no one else. Even with confidentiality, it can take great courage for some patients to mention what to them is almost impossible to speak aloud: humiliating failures, sexual longings, loss of religious faith, betrayal of a partner, hatred of a new child, shame about looks or abilities, cheating to get ahead, thoughts of killing themselves, fears and anxieties they've kept hidden from others. But without confidentiality, these patients might not speak at all.

The sensitive nature of what many patients tell clinical psychologists places a great ethical responsibility on psychologists not to breach patients' trust, even unintentionally. An initial step is to understand three often confused terms: privacy, confidentiality, and privilege.

Privacy is the individual's right to decide how much personal information or private values, beliefs, preferences, or behavior should be known by anyone else, particularly government officials or agencies. In a law review article, and later in his court decisions, Louis Brandeis discussed the nature and importance of privacy. In his dissent in *Olmstead v. U.S.* (1928), he wrote:

> The makers of our Constitution undertook to secure conditions favorable to the pursuit of happiness. They recognized the significance of man's spiritual nature, of his feelings and of his intellect . . . They sought to protect Americans in their beliefs, their thoughts, their emotions, and their sensations. They conferred as against the government the right to be left alone—the most comprehensive of rights and the right most valued . . . .

The U.S. Constitution addresses basic privacy rights—such as freedom from unreasonable search and seizure—in the Fourth, Fifth, and Fourteen Amendments. The Canadian government addresses privacy rights in the Privacy Act of 1982, the Personal Information and Electronic Documents Act (PIPEDA), and Section 8 of the Canadian Charter of Rights and Freedoms (1982).

Privilege defines the information that is protected from disclosure in trials or other legal procedures. The courts, particularly in criminal trials where someone's liberty and sometimes life is at stake, place an almost absolute value on considering all relevant facts. However, the importance and benefits of some forms of communication—for example, between lawyers and their clients or therapists and their patients—are considered so valuable that they are protected against disclosure. The privilege virtually always belongs to the patient, rather than to the clinical psychologist, and the psychologist who is asked to reveal privileged information about a patient is generally required to claim the privilege on behalf of the patient. If, however, the client waives privilege, the psychologist can, under most circumstances, be required to testify in regard to previously protected information.

The status of psychotherapist–client privilege differs among the states, provinces, and federal court systems. After the various appellate courts in the federal districts handed down contradictory decisions, the U.S. Supreme Court considered the issue in the form of a case posing the question: Are a client's communications to a licensed clinical social worker privileged in federal court?

In *Jaffee v. Redmond* (1996), the Court recognized the privilege. Justice Stevens provided the majority's reasoning in his opinion:

> Like the spousal and attorney client privileges, the psychotherapist patient privilege is "rooted in the imperative need for confidence and trust." . . . Treatment by a physician for physical ailments can often proceed successfully on the basis of a physical examination, objective information supplied by the patient, and the results of diagnostic tests. Effective psychotherapy, by contrast, depends upon an atmosphere of confidence and trust in which the patient is willing to make a frank and complete disclosure of facts, emotions, memories, and fears. Because of the sensitive nature of the problems for which individuals consult psychotherapists, disclosure of confidential communications made during counseling sessions may cause embarrassment or disgrace. For this reason, the mere possibility of disclosure may impede development of the confidential relationship necessary for successful treatment.
> (*Jaffee v. Redmond*, 1996)

Although the reasoning of the majority prevailed, it is worth noting the scathing skepticism expressed by Justice Scalia, who was joined by the Chief Justice in his dissent:

> When is it, one must wonder, that the psychotherapist came to play such an indispensable role in the maintenance of the citizenry's mental health? For most of history, men and women have worked out their difficulties by talking to, inter alios, parents, siblings, best friends and bartenders—none of whom was awarded a privilege against testifying in court. Ask the average citizen: Would your mental health be more significantly impaired by preventing you from seeing a psychotherapist, or by preventing you from getting advice from your mom? I have little doubt what the answer would be. Yet there is no mother–child privilege.
> (*Jaffee v. Redmond*, 1996)

Confidentiality refers to a clinical psychologist's duty not to reveal information about a client to anyone else unless the client provides voluntary informed consent or unless a valid legal authority allows or requires the disclosure. The nature and scope of confidentiality can be defined by legislation, by a court in the form of case law, by psychology licensing board regulations and other forms of administrative law, and by the ethical standards of professional organizations.

Sometimes, psychologists may or must set aside confidentiality. Some common exceptions include:

- When patients provide informed consent for the psychologist to disclose confidential information to third parties (e.g., to a health insurance company covering some of the costs of therapy, to another provider of clinical services)
- When patients place their psychological state at issue before the court through filing a lawsuit or related claim. For example, a patient who has been hit by a car may develop post-traumatic stress disorder (PTSD) and sue the car's driver for damages, including the cost of therapy to address the PTSD. Filing a suit in which the patient's claim of suffering PTSD and needing treatment will be at issue can constitute a waiver of both confidentiality and privilege.
- When patients become a danger to self, a danger to others, or gravely psychologically disabled, a jurisdiction may allow or require clinicians to take steps—which can include breaching confidentiality—to protect the patient or third parties.

Such exceptions differ among the different states, provinces, and federal systems. A disclosure that is permitted in one jurisdiction may be required in another and prohibited in a third. Changes can occur within a particular jurisdiction as the legislature enacts new laws, the appellate courts recognize new duties or overturn prior requirements, and as licensing boards change their regulations. It is crucial that psychologists remain aware of the evolving requirements within the relevant jurisdictions.

Ethical missteps can occur through lack of awareness of current legal requirements in a particular jurisdiction, but can also happen when a legal analysis becomes a substitute for—rather than a supplement to—ethical analysis. In a detailed analysis, M. A. Fisher (2008) wrote that an overemphasis on legal aspects has tended to shift the focus from the therapist's concern for the client's welfare to how therapists can avoid legal problems and manage risks to themselves (instead of to their patients). Consequently, attorneys have emerged as the perceived experts on confidentiality in psychotherapy. According to Fisher, the increasing dominance of attorney-led workshops on risk-management, compliance with confidentiality requirements, and so on have replaced psychologists' own clinical and ethical language with legal terminology and drawn

psychologists' focus to avoiding "risks to themselves, when what they need is a clearer focus on their ethical obligations and the potential risks to clients" (M. A. Fisher, 2008).

The tendency of legislatures and courts to impose more exceptions to confidentiality and additional mandated reporting duties on therapists has sparked controversy among psychologists concerned with unintended consequences. Gonsiorek (2008), for example, noted that confidentiality was becoming more porous, particularly regarding mandated reporting statutes, and wrote that "as health care professionals become deputized as agents of the state—without consent, compensation, or training—for a broadening array of functions, the net effect may undermine the core of the health-care relationship" (p. 374).

In many cases, violations of confidentiality are unrelated to legal complexities and mandated exceptions but occur through the clinician's lack of attention. Here are a few sources of careless violations discussed in more detail by Pope and Vasquez (Pope & Vasquez, 2010):

- Providing confidential information to an insurance company, managed care company, or similar organization without prior informed consent
- Discussing a patient's progress in treatment with a referral source without obtaining the patient's informed consent
- Consulting a colleague about a patient without the patient's informed consent
- Consulting a colleague about a patient when others might overhear (e.g., in a hallway, elevator, cafeteria)
- Leaving charts unattended
- Unintentionally revealing confidential information when talking with the patient's family
- Unintentionally revealing confidential information when talking to one's own family or friends
- Unintentionally revealing confidential information to others in phone, fax, or e-mail messages to patients
- Failing to anticipate and address the many ways in which confidential information stored in or transmitted by computer can be compromised

Informed Consent
Informed consent respects the autonomy of the individual patient and the patient's right to make informed choices about what psychological assessments or

treatments, if any, to receive. The right is not absolute. In emergencies and other exceptional circumstances, the right may be temporarily limited.

A Relatively Recent Concept

The health-care professions were relatively late in recognizing the right of informed consent. The concept is nowhere to be found in the Hippocratic Oath, which assumed that the physician knew best. On what basis could patients, who lacked understanding of diagnosis and treatment, make decisions that required years of specialty education? It was only in the 20th century that this paternalistic view began to give way to recognition of the patient's right to choose, a shift prompted by the courts.

Although the case had little impact for decades, *Schloendorff v. Society of New York Hospital* (1914) clearly stated the contemporary view of informed consent as a basic right. Judge Benjamin Cordozo, later a justice of the U.S. Supreme Court, wrote that "every human being of adult years and sound mind has a right to determine what shall be done with his own body" (p. 93).

The major change in thinking about informed consent occurred after World War II, when evidence emerged of the horrors inflicted by physicians, psychologists, and others in the name of treatment or research under the Nazi regime (Cocks, 1997; Geuter, 1992; Lifton, 2000; Proctor, 1988). The Nuremberg trials—especially those in which doctors were defendants—and the Nuremberg Declaration gave the individual a basic right to veto the treatment or research plans suggested by a professional (Annas & Grodin, 1995; T. Taylor, 1993, 1997).

The increasing number of legal cases setting standards for informed consent prompted professionals to address these issues in their ethics codes. The APA devotes several sections to addressing responsibilities (3.10a, b, c, &d; 9.03a & b; 10.01a, b, & c; 10.02a; 10.03; 10.04), and Truscott and Crook (2004) note that "informed consent is the most represented value in the Canadian Code of Ethics for Psychologists" (p. 55).

The Patient's Competence

For the process of informed consent to be meaningful, the patient must be competent to consent to or refuse treatment (Appelbaum, 2007; Berner, 1998). The psychologist must assess whether the patient can adequately:

• Understand the current situation (e.g., why treatment is indicated), the recommended

treatment, the available alternatives, and the consequences of agreeing to or refusing treatment
• Engage in decision-making
• Make a choice free of coercion (i.e., the consent or refusal is voluntary)
• Communicate that choice

Helpful Information

What information do clinical psychologists need to provide, so that patients can make informed decisions? The content will vary significantly depending on many factors, including the setting (e.g., inpatient, outpatient, day treatment), modality (e.g., individual, couple, family, or group therapy), and patient's prior knowledge and cognitive abilities. However, many patients will find clear answers to the following questions useful in making a truly informed decision:

• *Why am I here?* Many patients will have sought therapy and scheduled an initial appointment or will have been referred and understood the reason for the referral. But a surprising number may have been referred by an internist concerned about the patient's depression or impaired cognition, an attorney who wishes them to receive a psychological assessment or to be in therapy related to pending litigation, or a family member who is insistent that "you need to talk to a therapist." These patients may know that someone believes it important that they talk with you and may have even scheduled an appointment for them, but they do not understand why.

• *Who are you?* New patients may have no idea whether the person they are meeting with is a practicum student, an intern, or licensed clinical psychologist. Do you have the qualifications and experience to help them?

• *Who will be involved in the treatment?* Will the person conducting the initial interview provide the therapy, or is one purpose of the screening interview to decide which psychologist, intern, etc., within an organization is the best qualified to help this particular patient? Will the therapist be supervised?

• *What treatment is recommended, what does it involve, and what is the basis for the recommendation?* What evidence, if any, suggests that this treatment will likely be effective for this problem?

• *How much does each session cost?* Is the fee covered in whole or in part by private insurance, managed care, an employee assistance plan, or other source? Will the patient be charged for missed or cancelled appointments?

- *To what extent is what the patient tells the psychologist confidential?* What are the limits to confidentiality? Are there any circumstances that would require the psychologist to breach confidentiality? A patient who learns for the first time that a psychologist must contact authorities *after* making a disclosure in the expectation of confidentiality has not been accorded informed consent.

- *What external factors, if any, are likely to affect the therapy?* Does a managed care contract limit the number of sessions to ten in the absence of a life-threatening situation? Is the therapist scheduled to complete an internship and move on some time within the likely course of therapy, so that a new therapist will be assigned to this patient?

Cognition, Communication, and Decision-making

Research in cognitive psychology and related areas has increased understanding of how people make decisions, and how decisions are affected by age, heuristics, and other factors (Birnbaum, 2008; Dijkstra, Jaspers, & van Zwieten, 2008; Doya, 2008; Fischhoff, 2008; Gatz, 2006; Gilovich, Griffin, & Kahneman, 2002; Reyna & Rivers, 2008; Sinz, Zamarian, Benke, Wenning, & Delazer, 2008; Tversky & Kahneman, 2004, 2005; Williams-Piehota, McCormack, Treiman, & Bann, 2008; Zikmund-Fisher, Lacey, & Fagerlin, 2008). Staying abreast of this research enables psychologists to present information in ways that are best suited to the cognitive capacities and styles of the individual patient and that take into account the nature of the relevant information that the patient needs to make an adequately informed decision.

Presenting the same basic information but in a different format can profoundly affect the patient's decision-making process. A classic study at a Harvard Medical School hospital provides an example. McNeil and her colleagues (McNeil, Pauker, Sox, & Tversky, 1982) presented people with a choice of two possible treatments. The information she provided to help them make a decision was actuarial data of previous outcomes. Patients with lung cancer had chosen either surgery or radiation. When the patients had chosen surgery, 10% had died during the surgery, and another 22% died less than a year after the operation. Thirty-four percent died between 1 year and 5 years after surgery. None of the lung cancer patients who had decided to undergo radiation therapy died during the radiation sessions, but 23% died less than a year later, and 55% died between 1 and 5 years after the radiation sessions.

These actuarial data were presented in the form of mortality: how many patients died at each stage. Presented with these mortality statistics, well over a third of the study participants (42%) reported that they would choose radiation therapy. However, when the same actuarial data were presented in the form of survivability (e.g., of those who chose radiation treatment, 100% survived the radiation treatments, 77% survived at least a year, and 22% survived at least 5 years), the percentage of participants who chose radiation treatment dropped to 25%. Whether the same actuarial statistics were presented in terms of mortality or survival significantly affected the decision-making process.

The decisions patients make—for example, whether to begin psychotherapy and if so, what kind; whether to take psychotropic medications; or whether to voluntarily begin inpatient treatment—can have profound and lasting effects for themselves and for others. To make adequately informed decisions to consent to or refuse treatment, they need to understand the relevant information. Maintaining awareness of the evolving research on how people receive and process information in arriving at decisions helps psychologists to provide the relevant information in a clear, fair, and helpful way.

Forms

Forms for informed consent can serve an important purpose. Their precise wording can avoid the misstatements of oral presentations. Both patient and therapist can save a copy, so that neither will have to trust to the potential glitches of memory regarding what, exactly, was consented to.

But forms also can tempt therapists to believe a comforting fallacy: that words on paper can handle the complex ethical responsibility of making sure that the patient understands the information and is giving consent both knowingly and voluntarily. Even when forms are used, psychologists must discuss the information with the client, assessing the patient's understanding.

Psychologists must also assess the forms. Are they readable? Grundner (1980) observed long ago that great attention is paid to making sure that all the right content goes into consent forms but relatively little effort is made to see whether people can understand the forms. He used standardized readability assessment instruments to study five consent forms. He reported that all required the reading abilities of advanced undergraduates or graduate students, and that all but one were "written at the level of a scientific journal, and the fifth at the level of a specialized academic magazine" (p. 900). Unfortunately, readability is still a hurdle for many patients, although research is increasing our understanding of readability issues and how forms can be improved (Aleligay, Worrall, & Rose, 2008; Christopher, Foti, Roy-Bujnowski, & Appelbaum, 2007; Collins, Novotny, & Light, 2006; Hochauser, 1997; Martin, 2005; Paasche-Orlow, H. A. Taylor, & Brancati, 2003; Walfish & Ducey, 2007; Wallace et al., 2008).

Some patients, of course, may not be able to read even the most seemingly readable form. It is important for psychologists to know if the patient can read and whether English (or whatever language the form is written in) is appropriate for the patient.

Many forms—especially those for clinics, hospitals, and similar organizations—will be carefully reviewed by an attorney, a risk-management specialist, an administrator, and other nonpsychologists. This is good practice to make sure that the form meets legal and administrative standards. However, there is some risk that when the review process exclusively focuses on legal and administrative needs, the legitimate needs of patients may be overlooked. Akkad and her colleagues' study of patient perceptions of consent forms found that many did not perceive the purpose of the forms to be protecting their interests or finding out what interventions they wanted but, consistent with prior studies, "many thought the primary function of the form was to protect the hospital" (2006, p. 529). One way to help make sure that the primary focus of a consent form is the legitimate rights and needs of patients is to ask a few friends—particularly those who are not psychologists—to take a look at the form and critique it. If they were a patient, would they feel that the form speaks clearly to their legitimate rights and needs? Is anything missing? How would they improve it? Another way is to use the Golden Rule when reviewing the form: If you yourself went to another clinical psychologist for assessment or therapy and were handed this form, what would your reaction be?

Links to sample forms for informed consent from diverse sources including the APA Insurance Trust; excerpts addressing informed consent from the standards and guidelines (with links to the original documents) of 18 professional associations including the APA, the CPA, European Federation of Psychologists' Associations, and the Psychological Society of Ireland; and quotes about informed consent from diverse articles, books, and studies are available online at http://kspope.com/consent/index.php.

Beyond Forms: Informed Consent as a Continuing Process

The focus on forms as an important key to obtaining informed consent can mislead us into thinking of obtaining consent as a one-time event—the signing of a form—that occurs at the beginning of therapy. It is as if, once we have the signed form, we can check "informed consent" off our mental checklist of responsibilities. But truly informed consent is a process of both patient and therapist coming to agree on a shared venture. The CPA's "Code of Ethics for Psychologists" emphasizes that psychologists "[r]ecognize that informed consent is the result of a process of reaching an agreement to work collaboratively, rather than of simply having a consent form signed" (CPA, 2000).

O'Neil discusses this process as *negotiation* in his book *Negotiating Consent in Psychotherapy*. He emphasizes the potential benefits to therapists—such as clearing up the misconceptions about a patient—as well as to patients. "An open dialogue can make the therapist aware of features of the case that depart from both the therapist's model and his or her previous experience, and thus it serves as a corrective to the representativeness and availability biases" (O'Neill, 1998, p. 176).

Finally, the process can continue throughout the course of therapy. The patient's condition can change significantly (if not, perhaps the treatment plan needs rethinking) or events in the patient's life may shift the focus away from the original presenting problem(s). These and other factors may prompt therapist and patient to renegotiate their original agreement, and the patient may provide or withhold informed consent for the new possibilities.

Competence

An ethic of competence is a cornerstone for any profession. How many readers would consider entrusting themselves or their loved ones to an incompetent surgeon, attorney, or psychotherapist?

Ethics Codes

The ethics codes emphasize competence as a fundamental ethical responsibility. Ethical Standard 2.01a of APA's "Ethical Principles of Psychologists and Code of Conduct" states: "Psychologists provide services, teach, and conduct research with populations and only within the boundaries of their competence, based on their education, training, supervised experience, or appropriate professional experience" (APA, 2002, p. 1063). Ethical Standard II.6 of the "Canadian Code of Ethics for Psychologists" states that, in adhering to the Principle of Responsible Caring, psychologists perform without supervision any activity only if "they have established their competence to [perform that activity] to the benefit of others" (CPA, 2000).

Learning Competence

Graduate school, practica, and internship help us acquire basic competence in clinical psychology. We learn about theory, research, and practice, and how to apply critical thinking skills to evaluate them. We learn, under careful supervision, how to conduct assessments and a range of psychological treatments (Barlow, 2004). We learn to evaluate our work and its consequences, to seek and consider feedback from others. We develop sound professional judgment.

Training in clinical psychology also involves acquiring what Pope and Brown termed *emotional competence for therapy* (Pope & Brown, 1996; Pope, Sonne, & Greene, 2006; Pope & Vasquez, 2010). Emotional competence is in part an active awareness of the emotional aspects of providing clinical services, the ways in which the work can be stressful, and the need to recognize when we have reached, however briefly, the limits of our emotional competence. Pope and Vasquez (2010), for example, reviewed national surveys of psychologists in which:

• Over half of the respondents reported crying in the presence of a patient
• Almost a third reported hating a patient
• Almost one-fifth reported having been physically attacked by a patient
• Almost four-fifths reported having been afraid that a client would attack them
• About one-fourth reported having summoned police or security personnel to protect them from a patient
• Almost all reported being afraid that a patient would commit suicide
• Over half reported becoming sexually aroused in the presence of a patient
• About nine-tenths reported feeling fear because a patient's condition became suddenly or seriously worse
• Almost nine-tenths reported having felt afraid that a colleague would be critical of their work
• About two-thirds reported feeling afraid that a patient would file a formal complaint against them

Some areas of practice may tend to involve more intense emotional reactions. Pope and Garcia-Peltoniemi (1991), for example, described the emotional responses experienced by many who provide psychological treatments to victims of torture.

Formal training fosters a growing awareness that competence must be evaluated for each situation. A psychologist who is exceptionally skilled at working, for example, with adults, with people suffering from schizophrenia, with individual psychotherapy, or with airline pilots might lack basic competence in working with children, with people suffering from performance anxiety, with group therapy, or with war refugees. These limitations on the generalization of competence can pose difficult challenges for clinical psychologists in small communities, when the closest professional with the necessary competence for a specific patient may be many hours away. Psychologists facing those dilemmas often have no alternative if the patient's needs are urgent than to undertake the psychological treatment, if possible, while obtaining long-distance supervision from a qualified professional.

Competence and Methods of Assessment and Intervention

Psychologists must evaluate not only their own competence but also the competence of the methods that they use. Although difficult challenges remain, the field has made great progress in this area. As recently as the landmark Boulder Conference, psychology was still struggling just to define what psychotherapy was, so that graduate schools could teach it effectively. APA president Carl Rogers created a committee, chaired by David Shakow, to report on what psychotherapy was and what training students needed in order to achieve competence. The 1947 APA convention adopted the Shakow report, which laid the ground work for the Boulder Conference in 1949. George Lehner, the recorder for the Boulder Conference task force charged with providing a formal definition for psychotherapy and specific recommendations for the training to ensure competence, offered this summary of their work: "We have left therapy as an undefined technique which is applied to unspecified problems with a nonpredictable outcome. For this technique we recommend rigorous training" (1952, p. 547).

Just as the APA returned to its scientific and empirical roots to construct a unique ethics code based on the experience of its members, psychology returned to those same roots to address questions of competence related to psychotherapy and other psychological treatments. The field began to focus on research that explored the effects caused by various interventions with various populations under various conditions. Singer's (1980) classic article, "The Scientific Basis of Psychotherapeutic Practice: A Question of Values and Ethics," exemplified the growing recognition that psychologists had ethical as well as practical reasons for staying abreast of the empirical basis of their methods of psychological assessment and treatment. Ethically, it was hard to justify ignoring evidence that some techniques were less effective than others under the same circumstances, and that some could cause harm. Stricker emphasized this ethical responsibility: "[A]lthough it may not be unethical to practice in the absence of knowledge, it is unethical to practice in the face of knowledge . . . . [T]here is no excuse for ignoring contradictory data" (1992, p. 564). Barlow noted how research has challenged conventional wisdom and practices, and brought sweeping changes in the field. "Stunning developments in health care have occurred during the last several years. Widely accepted health-care strategies have been brought into question by research evidence as not only lacking benefit but also, perhaps, as inducing harm" (Barlow, 2004, 2005a, 2005b; Huppert, Fabbro, & Barlow, 2006).

The strengths of empiricism have enabled psychology to progress in identifying aspects of competence and how they can be learned with greater precision than was possible at the Boulder Conference. For example, the *Mutual Recognition Agreement of the Regulatory Bodies for Professional Psychologists in Canada* (2004) focused on five core aspects of competence:

- Assessment and evaluation
- Ethics and standards
- Interpersonal relationships
- Intervention and consultation
- Research

The *2002 Competencies Conference: Future Directions in Education and Credentialing in Professional Psychology* (Kaslow, 2004; Kaslow et al., 2004) focused on how to assess and teach eight domains of core competence:

- Consultation and interprofessional collaboration
- Ethical and legal issues
- Individual and cultural diversity
- Intervention
- Professional development
- Psychological assessment
- Scientifically minded practice
- Supervision

The *Competencies Conference* led to the APA Task Force on Assessment of Competence in Professional Psychology and other advancements in defining, assessing, and teaching competence (Kaslow, Rubin, Bebeau, et al., 2007; Kaslow, Rubin, Forrest, et al., 2007).

Challenges persist in the midst of this substantial progress. Kazdin (2006), for example, noted that "[p]sychotherapy outcome research has been dominated by randomized controlled trials . . . . However, pivotal features of these trials make them not very relevant for clinical practice" (see also Goodheart, 2006; Sternberg, 2006). He also observed that the number of psychological treatments continues to grow rapidly—over 550 in his specialty of child and adolescent therapy—and that only a small minority of them had been studied in any kind of research trials (Kazdin, 2008).

When focusing on the progress and remaining challenges of a clinical psychology that is informed by research, it is important to remain aware that an evidence-based practice does *not* mean that professional judgment and experience are set aside in order to reflexively apply research findings, as if that were possible. Professional expertise is essential. The APA Presidential Task Force on Evidence-Based Practice underscored "the need to integrate clinical expertise with the best available research" (APA Presidential Task Force on Evidence-Based Practice, 2006, p. 282).

Boundaries

Handled with appropriate professional judgment and care, nonsexual boundary crossings can play a positive—sometimes seemingly key—role in psychological treatment. However, they also have the potential to sabotage the treatment plan and harm the client.

Consider these hypothetical scenarios:

- "My attorney is depressed, wants to start therapy, and says I am the only one she would trust with her problems—should I accept her as a patient?"
- "One day a week the last patient of the day needs a ride home—is there any reason I shouldn't provide it?"
- "A patient is about to lose his house because he is short on his mortgage payment and has been unable to secure a loan—I can easily afford to lend him the money and would like to, but am uncertain if I should."
- "A client has invited me to replace the pianist who has just left his jazz trio that plays weekends at

a local nightclub—this is a once-in-a-lifetime opportunity for me but I wonder if I should accept."

• "My infant son needs life-saving surgery that I can't afford and the only way to pay for it is to ask a wealthy patient who is always telling me how much therapy is helping her and that I should just ask if I even need anything. Is it OK to ask her to for a loan? What if the reason I need the money is for a Paris vacation because I am totally burnt out, have never been to Paris, and am sure I would return refreshed and a better therapist?"

Situations like these ignited one of the most vigorous controversies in clinical psychology, reaching its peak in the period from the beginnings of the 1980s to the mid-1990s, and continuing to challenge the field today. In the 15 years beginning in 1980, a wealth of individual journal articles and journal special issues challenged or endorsed virtually every possible prohibition involving different nonsexual boundaries (Pope & Keith-Spiegel, 2008; Pope & Vasquez, 2010). Thoughtful articles examined the issues in light of diverse perspectives, values, and theoretical orientations. Research during that period explored the ways in which therapists' beliefs and behavior in regard to nonsexual boundaries were significantly associated with such factors as therapist gender, patient gender, size of the local community, profession, practice setting (e.g., hospital vs. solo practice), and theoretical orientation.

Much of the discussion focused on how the ethics code section addressing nonsexual boundary issues might be changed. For example, on the basis of their replication of the critical incident study that formed the basis of the original APA ethics code, Pope and Vetter (1992) recommended that the current APA ethics code be changed to

• Provide a more precise definition of dual relationships and specify when they might be appropriate
• Take account of the realities of psychological practice in geographically isolated areas, small communities, etc.
• Clarify the differences between dual relationships that the psychologist enters into by choice and those which are unavoidable or occur by chance

Two factors may have made it harder to address nonsexual boundary issues realistically. First, the discomfort with sexual boundary issues that many therapists experienced may have generalized into a discomfort with nonsexual boundary issues as well. The prohibition against violating sexual boundaries with patients dates back to the Hippocratic Oath and even to the more ancient Code of the Nigerian Healing Arts. That prohibition, as pertains specifically to psychotherapy, dates back to Freud. As the judge in a widely cited mid-1970s case wrote: "Thus from [Freud] to the modern practitioner we have common agreement of the harmful effects of sensual intimacies between patient and therapist" (*Roy v. Hartogs*, 1976). Nevertheless, surveys of therapists in different disciplines found that a majority of respondents reported that simply experiencing sexual attraction to a patient made the therapists feel anxious, guilty, or confused (Pope, Sonne, & Holroyd, 1993; see also Pope et al., 2006).

Second, the concept of clear, helpful, ethical boundaries may have become confused with the concept of inflexible boundaries. Some of the discussion seemed to have an all-or-none absolutist quality. Either a particular boundary—such as nonsexual touch, dual roles, or out-of-the-office meetings with patients—should be completely prohibited, or it was always acceptable.

A landmark article, "The Concept of Boundaries in Clinical Practice" (Gutheil & Gabbard, 1993) helped transform this area, providing a practical framework for clinicians to use in considering boundary decisions. After observing that many of those who endorsed inflexible boundaries cited Freud as a model and influence, the authors pointed out that Freud loaned books to his patients, gave gifts to them, told them about his family, shared a walk with a patient through the countryside during a treatment session, met a patient for a meal while he was on vacation, and conduced a psychoanalysis of Anna, his daughter.

Gutheil and Gabbard avoided an absolutist approach to any nonsexual boundary decision, arguing that any decision must be based on a case-by-case analysis of the specific facts and clinical context. Their framework identified the concepts of *boundary crossing* and *boundary violation*. A boundary crossing is a neutral descriptive term to indicate an instance when a therapist decides not to observe a particular boundary. A boundary crossing can be therapeutic, can harm the patient, or can produce no significant impact, depending on the specific situation and clinical context. Boundary crossings that were harmful were termed boundary violations. The article provided examples of therapeutic or acceptable boundary crossings, and of boundary violations involving boundaries of role, time, place and space, money, gifts, services, clothing, language, self-disclosure, and physical contact.

A subsequent article, which had a similar influence on the field, examined how the concept of boundaries was sometimes misunderstood and misused by licensing boards and others who enforce formal policies (Gutheil & Gabbard, 1998).

These and similar articles tended to shift the focus in this area away from general rules that approved or prohibited large classes of nonsexual boundary crossings toward sets of useful steps clinicians could take in thinking through whether to cross a specific boundary with a specific client in a specific situation. Here are a variety of decision-making guides for nonsexual boundary issues, some of which are available on the web:

- "A guide to violating an injunction in psychotherapy: On seeing acquaintances as patients" (Roll & Millen, 1981)—a nine-step model
- "Avoiding exploitive dual relationships: A decision-making model" (Gottlieb, 1993) a five-step model
- "Managing multiple relationships in rural communities" (Faulkner & Faulkner, 1997) multilevel guidelines
- "Sexual and nonsexual boundary violations involving psychologists, clients, supervisees, and students: Implications for professional practice" (Lamb & Catanzaro 1998—a six-step model
- "Ethical decision-making and dual relationships" (Younggren, 2002)—an eight-step model
- "Acknowledging the inevitable: Understanding multiple relationships in rural practice" (Campbell & Gordon, 2003)—a five-step model
- "Addressing multiple relationships between clients and therapists in lesbian, gay, bisexual, and transgender communities" (Kessler & Waehler, 2005)—a six-step model
- "Nonsexual multiple relationships: A practical decision-making model for clinicians" (Sonne, 2005)—a multilevel approach
- "A practical approach to boundaries in psychotherapy: Making decisions, bypassing blunders, and mending fences" (Pope & Keith-Spiegel, 2008)—a nine-step model

Additional resources for considering boundary decisions are available at http://kspope.com/dual/index.php. These include excerpts on boundaries from the ethics codes of 29 professional associations (e.g., APA, CPA, Australian Psychological Society, Psychological Society of Ireland, European Federation of Psychologists' Associations, British Association for Counselling & Psychotherapy) with links to the complete codes, excerpts from books and articles addressing boundary issues, and links to articles on boundaries.

An Area of Major Controversy: Clinical Psychology and National Security

Psychology's involvement in national security efforts following the terrorist attack on the United States on September 11, 2001 sparked major controversy and raised complex ethical questions. As the scenario about Homeland Security officials asking a clinical psychologist for a patient's records at the start of this chapter illustrated, one set of questions asks under what circumstances and to what extent should therapy patients' records be made available to third parties if they might lead to information about terrorist attacks or serve other national security purposes? Should therapy and other clinical records be made available to those conducting detainee interrogations? Should therapy or other clinical services be used as a pretext to gain information related to national security? Should psychologists help plan or implement the interrogation of individual detainees?

The APA's approach to detainee interrogations, which was based on the work of the Presidential Task Force on Psychological Ethics and National Security (APA, 2005), emphasized that psychologists' rightly assumed a key role in interrogations in part because interrogations were an inherently psychological process requiring psychological expertise. The "Statement of the American Psychological Association on Psychology and Interrogations Submitted to the United States Senate Select Committee on Intelligence" emphasized:

> Conducting an interrogation is inherently a psychological endeavor . . . . Psychology is central to this process because an understanding of an individual's belief systems, desires, motivations, culture, and religion likely will be essential in assessing how best to form a connection and facilitate educing accurate, reliable, and actionable intelligence. Psychologists have expertise in human behavior, motivations, and relationships . . . . Psychologists have valuable contributions to make toward . . . protecting our nation's security through interrogation processes.
> (APA, 2007)

This special expertise set psychologists apart from psychiatrists and other physicians, who lacked competence in this area, according to the APA. The Director of the APA Ethics Office wrote: "This difference, which stems from psychologists' unique competencies, represents an important distinction between what role psychologists and physicians may take in interrogations" (Behnke, 2006, p. 6).

The contrast with physicians was striking, though physician associations stated that the difference was not one of competence but of ethics. The American Medical Association prohibited participation in detainee interrogations to such a degree that they banned even monitoring an interrogation with an intent to intervene (Moran, 2006; Ray, 2006). Commenting on the American Psychiatric Association's prohibition (American Psychiatric Association, 2006), the American Psychiatric Association president Steven Sharfstein (2006) wrote: "I told the generals that psychiatrists will not participate in the interrogation of persons held in custody. Psychologists, by contrast, had issued a position statement allowing consultations in interrogations. If you were ever wondering what makes us different from psychologists, here it is. This is a paramount challenge to our ethics and our Hippocratic training … . Our profession is lost if we play any role … ." (p. 1713).

The difference in ethical policies among the professions led to differences in involvement. As the *New York Times* reported:

> Pentagon officials said Tuesday they would try to use only psychologists, not psychiatrists, to help interrogators devise strategies to get information from detainees at places like Guantánamo Bay, Cuba. The new policy follows by little more than 2 weeks an overwhelming vote by the American Psychiatric Association discouraging its members from participating in those efforts. Stephen Behnke, director of ethics for the counterpart group for psychologists, the American Psychological Association, said psychologists knew not to participate in activities that harmed detainees. But he also said the group believed that helping military interrogators made a valuable contribution . . . .
> (Lewis, 2006; see also Hausman, 2006)

The APA provided a compelling rationale for psychologists' involvement in detainee interrogations, emphasizing important benefits such as psychologists' "valuable contributions" toward "protecting our nation's security through interrogation processes" and their inherent knowing "not to participate in activities that harmed detainees." The 2007 president of the APA wrote: "The Association's position is rooted in our belief that having psychologists

consult with interrogation teams makes an important contribution toward keeping interrogations safe and ethical."

Nevertheless, psychologists' involvement was controversial. Eban (2007; see also Goodman, 2007) was among those who documented ways in which "psychologists weren't merely complicit in America's aggressive new interrogation regime. Psychologists, working in secrecy, had actually designed the tactics and trained interrogators in them … . " Having published a series of investigative reports on the nature of psychologists' involvement in interrogations, the *Boston Globe* (2008) stated: "From the moment U.S. military and civilian officials began detaining and interrogating Guantanamo Bay prisoners with methods that the Red Cross has called tantamount to torture, they have had the assistance of psychologists … . " In April 2009, an American Civil Liberties Union (ACLU) Freedom of Information request led the U.S. Justice Department to release documents previously classified as top secret. These documents revealed the significant number and wide range of psychologists involved directly or indirectly with what had come to be called extreme interrogations. For example, they noted the roles played not only by "on-site psychologists" but also by "outside psychologists" in justifying the use of waterboarding and other techniques. (American Civil Liberties Union, 2009). The prominence of this ethical controversy was exemplified by the cover of the May 16, 2009 *British Medical Journal* (vol. 338, No. 7704), which showed an photograph from Abu Ghraib and the words: "Interrogating Detainees: Why Psychologists Participate and Doctors Don't."

It is important to note that some physicians were also involved in detainee interrogations (Lifton & Xenakis, 2006). However, physicians who conducted, directly participated in, or monitored an interrogation with an intent to intervene did so *despite* the American Medical Association's and the American Psychiatric Association's explicit ethical prohibition and formal statements condemning such involvement. In contrast, the APA's public statements emphasized that psychologists (unlike physicians) were uniquely qualified, that interrogations were inherently a psychological process, that psychologists "knew not to participate in activities that harmed detainees," and that psychologists were making important contributions to national security and to keeping the interrogations safe and ethical. Commenting on the striking differences between APA and the medical professional associations,

Professor of Medicine and Bioethics Steven Miles, author of *Oath Betrayed: America's Torture Doctors*, wrote: "The American Psychological Association was unique among US health professional associations in providing policy cover for abusive interrogations…" (2009). Amnesty International, Physicians for Human Rights, and 11 other organizations sent an open letter to APA ("Open letter," 2009) about what it termed APA's "grievous mismanagement of this issue"; APA's "providing ethical cover for psychologists' participation in detainee abuse"; and APA's handling of the detainee interrogation issue creating "the greatest ethical crisis" in the profession's history and making a "terrible stain on the reputation of American psychology."

The controversy over complex questions about the relationship of ethics to national security—Is it ethical for the clinical psychologist in the scenario at the beginning of this chapter to hand over the client's records to Homeland Security and help them design an interrogation? Is it ethical for the psychologist to refuse in light of the massive loss of lives that might occur as a result of refusing?—was heightened by a change in ethical policy regarding the relationship of ethical responsibilities to the authority of the state.

The ethics code had stated that psychologists' ethical responsibilities might conflict with governmental authority. In the year following the terrorist attacks of September 2001, however, the APA added a new statement to Section 1.02 of the code's enforceable ethical standards: "If psychologists' ethical responsibilities conflict with law, regulations, or other governing legal authority, psychologists make known their commitment to the Ethics Code and take steps to resolve the conflict" (APA, 1992, p. 1600). The editor of the *British Medical Journal* was among those who criticized this abandonment of the Nuremberg ethic:

> Just obeying the rules has long been insufficient for doctors. The judges at Nuremberg made clear that obeying commands from superiors didn't remove personal accountability. Doctors couldn't deviate from their ethical obligations even if a country's laws allowed or demanded otherwise. The World Medical Association is meeting as I write. Its most noteworthy contribution has been the drafting of the Helsinki Declaration on Ethical Principles for Medical Research Involving Human Subjects. Both this and the World Medical Association's International Code of Ethics contain the crucial statement that a doctor's or investigator's conscience and duty of care must

transcend national laws. So deeply ingrained is this ethic in health care that it's surprising, even shocking, to find that the same code isn't shared by psychologists, at least in the United States.
> (*Godlee*, 2009)

Writing in the British Psychological Society's *The Psychologist*, Burton and Kagan wrote that "the APA allows its members the 'Nuremberg defence' that 'I was only following orders'…. The implication is that psychologists are permitted to assist in torture and abuse if they can claim that they first tried to resolve the conflict between their ethical responsibility and the law, regulations or government legal authority. Otherwise they can invoke the Nuremberg defence…" (p. 485).

It is impossible to overemphasize the deep and daunting complexity of these issues, for which there are no simple answers. Thinking them through requires careful review of the available documents (not just the few brief excerpts quoted here), openness to the arguments and evidence on each side, willingness to respect and consider contrary views, and the weighing of conflicting values, needs, and responsibilities. Some works presenting basic data, documentation, reviews, and analysis include those by the APA (2005, 2007), Eidelson, (2009), Hutson (2006), Koocher (2006), Levine (2007), Lifton (2008), Olson and Miles (2009), Pope & Gutheil (2009a, 2009b), and Soldz (2009). A comprehensive online archive of over 360 citations of articles, chapters, and books representing the full range of views of the controversy over psychologists, psychiatrists, and other health-care professionals participating in the planning or implementation of detainee interrogations is available at http://kspope.com/interrogation/index.php.

Steps in Ethical Decision-making

This chapter has emphasized an approach to ethical issues that is active and creative rather than passive rule-following, reflexive application of a code, or looking for a one-size-fits-all "answer" from an authority. This final section suggests a set of steps that may be helpful in thinking through situations, problems, or issues.

Such steps have always been a focus of the CPA ethics code. The original CPA code included seven steps (CPA, 1986), and the revisions have included ten steps (CPA, 1991, 2000). Fisher (C. B. Fisher, 2003), Haas and Malouf (2005), Koocher and Keith-Spiegel (2008), and Welfel (2005) are among those who have published thoughtful sets of steps in ethical decision-making for psychologists. (See Cottone & Claus, 2000, for a review of other decision-making guides.) These guides tend to be consistent with one another, but with varied structures, perspectives, and emphases.

The following set of steps is adapted from Pope and Vasquez (2010). Some steps may not be relevant to a particular situation, problem, or issue, or may need to be adapted.

1. *Defining the problem.* What exactly is the problem, situation, or issue that serves as the focus of ethical decision-making? Can it be stated clearly and directly without euphemisms, jargon, or bias?

2. *Recognizing those whom your actions will affect.* Most of our ethical decisions affect more than one person. A client may begin to show signs of cognitive impairment that would likely affect driving skills and yet refuse to discuss finding other ways to get around. A managed care administrator may refuse to approve clinical services that seem essential for a patient with extremely violent tendencies. A colleague may show signs of abusing alcohol in a way that interferes with professional functioning. The buildings or services at a clinic may be inaccessible to those with certain physical disabilities. A fellow graduate student, intern, or licensed psychologist may be encountering discrimination based on race, religion, gender, age, sexual orientation, physical disability, or other factors. What we choose to do or avoid doing in such situations may affect many people.

3. *Identifying the client.* If the situation involves a psychologist–client relationship, is it clear who the client is? Are there any actual or potential conflicts of interest that might affect our responsibilities to our client? For example, if a managed care company or family member is paying the fee for psychological treatment, how, if at all, might that affect our work? If a company facing large damage claims from a class action suit alleging harm from a product offers us over half a million—along with hints of future assignments should they like our work—to evaluate the plaintiffs and then testify whether each has suffered psychological harm because of the company's product, would our assessment and testimony be free of bias?

4. *Assessing competence.* What kinds of competence are needed to addresses this situation, problem, or issue, and are they present? Are there practical ways in which we could improve our ability to be effective?

5. *Reviewing formal ethical standards.* Does the ethics code provide guidance in this matter? Does it speak clearly to the situation, problem, or issue? Does the matter at hand involve conflicting values within the code or conflicts between the guidance offered by the code and other sources of responsibilities, such as legal mandates or licensing board regulations? Does the ethics code's guidance seem appropriate or inappropriate in this instance?

6. *Reviewing legal requirements.* Do legislation and case law provide guidance in this matter? Do they speak clearly to the situation, problem, or issue? Do the legal requirements seem to support or permit the most ethical decision and action in this instance?

7. *Reviewing relevant research and theory.* What research and theory are relevant and helpful to the decision-making process? Are there new findings and ideas in that literature since the last time we took a look? Is there relevant work outside our own theoretical orientation and specialties that might have escaped our notice?

8. *Considering personal reactions.* Does the situation, problem, or issue evoke personal feeling that might cloud or complicate the process of ethical decision-making? Does the matter make us uncomfortable in some way? Are we concerned about pleasing, offending, angering, disappointing, or alienating someone? Are we worried because the most ethical response places at risk our income, professional advancement, popularity, job recommendations, psychology license, or safety? These are normal—and *very* common—human reactions and tend to cause problems only when they aren't honestly and openly acknowledged.

9. *Considering cultural, religious, and spiritual factors.* In what ways could cultural, religious, or spiritual factors affect our understanding of the matter at hand or the possible options? Could these factors be the cause of conflicts or miscommunications? What is viewed as ethical, appropriate, and helpful in one society or tradition may be viewed as misguided, offensive, and damaging in another context. It is important to remain aware of not only how these factors affect our clients but also of how our own cultural, religious, or spiritual contexts affect us. *The Spirit Catches You and You Fall Down: A Hmong Child, Her American Doctors, and the Collision of Two Cultures* (Fadiman, 1998) discussed the tragic consequences of failing to take such contexts into account when a California hospital and Laotian refugee family tried help to a Hmong child

diagnosed with epilepsy. Medical anthropologist Arthur Kleinman described how those involved failed to take adequate account not only the Hmong culture but also of the culture of biomedicine. He wrote: "If you can't see that your own culture has its own set of interests… and biases, how can you expect to deal successfully with someone else's culture?" (p. 261). Comas-Diaz (2006), Hansen, Randazzo, Schwartz, and colleagues (2006); Derald Wing Sue and David Sue (Sue & Sue, 2007); Stanley Sue, Zane, Levant, and colleagues (S. Sue et al., 2006); and Vasquez (2007) provide valuable resources in this area.

10. *Considering consultation.* Other perspectives and second (and third) opinions can be invaluable. Are there those with more knowledge or experience in the relevant areas? Sometimes the following hypothetical is helpful: If you imagine the worst possible case scenario resulting from an ethical decision you make regarding this situation, problem, or issue, who would you wish you'd consulted before taking action?

11. *Searching for possible responses.* Are there alternative methods of problem-solving or courses of action that have been overlooked? Often, when beginning to think through a situation, problem, or issue, a few obvious possibilities will present themselves, and these may seem adequate or perhaps appear to be the only possibilities that exist. More persistent searching for creative alternatives, rather than settling for the first arrivals, can result in better ethical decision-making.

12. *Evaluating the alternatives.* What is the most likely outcome of the various alternatives for those who will be affected? What is the best possible outcome and what is the worst possible case scenario? What are the risks, costs, and the benefits? When our actions affect others in significant ways, often the short- and long-term outcomes include unintended consequences—what could those unintended consequences be in this instance?

13. *Adopting the perspective of others.* It is worth trying to imagine what those who will be affected by our actions would view as the most ethical response to a challenging situation. This approach may broaden, deepen, and in some instances significantly change our understanding. It may also correct the distortions that viewing a situation, problem, or issue from a single limited perspective can cause. One form of this distortion is what Jones (1979; see also Blanchard-Fields, Chen,

Horhota, & Wang, 2007; Gawronski, 2003) identified as "correspondence bias": We tend to attribute our own behavior in a particular instance to situational factors while attributing the behavior of others to internal dispositions. In his classic essay "Why I Do Not Attend Case Conferences," Meehl (1989) identified another form of this distortion as the "double-standard of morals" (p. 232): We tend to subject the explanations of others to skeptical and rigorous scientific scrutiny that we avoid applying to our own explanations.

14. *Deciding on a course of action and then reconsidering it.* If time allows, it can be useful once an initial decision is made to second-guess it. Once other alternatives are eliminated, sometimes previously unnoticed flaws, costs, consequences, or implications will become evident.

15. *Taking action and assuming personal responsibility for our choices and behavior.* For some situations, problems, or issues, weighing options and making a decision are the real challenge. Having reached a decision, taking action is relatively easy. The reverse can also occur: Identifying the most ethical response is easy, but convincing ourselves to follow that path can be almost impossible. (And sometimes we simply cannot bring ourselves to "do the right thing.") When we avoid what we know or suspect is the most ethical response, it is a normal human reaction for any of us to be tempted to blur, shift, deny, or otherwise escape responsibility for our decisions and acts.

16. *Assessing the consequences.* What were the results of our actions? Did they achieve what we'd hoped? Were there unexpected consequences? How did these actions affect the clinical needs of the patient? Does the treatment plan need to be changed in any way? With the benefit of hindsight, would we do the same thing again, or would we decide on a different response?

17. *Assuming personal responsibility for mistakes.* If it becomes apparent that, despite the best of intentions, we have made the wrong decision or made mistakes in implementing what we still believe was the right decision, what steps, if any, do we need to take in assuming personal responsibility?

18. *Learning from the experience.* What can we learn from this experience that will enable us to improve our work in the future? What practical steps might be helpful? Do we need to make any changes in our policies, procedures, or the ways in which we approach certain situations?

Conclusion

Future Directions

• What research would provide the most accurate understanding of how clinical psychologists make ethical decisions in the context of providing psychological treatment (rather than confronting fictional scenarios representing hypothetical situations)?

• What research would provide the most useful guidance in developing ethics codes that are realistic (i.e., reflect the realities of clinical work), helpful, and based on the values of those who will be using the code?

• What research would best identify the personal and situational factors associated with clinical psychologists intentionally or unintentionally violating an ethics code?

• What research would provide the most valid assessment of the degree to which the steps that a professional association, graduate training program, internship, clinic, or other agency takes to identify and support ethical behavior are effective, irrelevant, or counterproductive?

References

A little recent history. (1952). *American Psychologist*, 7(8), 426–428.

Akkad, A., Jackson, C., Kenyon, S., Dixon-Woods, M., Taub, N., & Habiba, M. (2006). Patients' perceptions of written consent: questionnaire study. *BMJ (Clinical Research Ed.)*, 333(7567), 528.

Aleligay, A., Worrall, L. E., & Rose, T. A. (2008). Readability of written health information provided to people with aphasia. *Aphasiology*, 22(4), 383–407.

"Amending the Ethics Code." (2010). *Monitor on Psychology*, 41(4), 64.

American Civil Liberties Union. (2009). Transcripts of four previously classified U.S. Department of Justice memoranda. Retrieved May 7, 2010, from http://www.aclu.org/safefree/general/olc_memos.html

American Psychiatric Association. (2006, May). Psychiatric participation in interrogation of detainees: position statement. Retrieved May 7, from http://archive.psych.org/edu/other_res/lib_archives/archives/200601.pdf

American Psychological Association. (1949). Developing a code of ethics for psychologists; A first report of progress. *American Psychologist*, 4(1), 17.

American Psychological Association. (1953). *Ethical standards of psychologists*. Washington, DC: American Psychological Association.

American Psychological Association, Ethics Committee, Washington, DC, US (1992). Ethical Principles of Psychologists and Code of Conduct. *American Psychologist*, 47, 1597–1611. doi: 10.1037/0003-066X.47.12.1597

American Psychological Association. (2002). Ethical Principles of Psychologists and Code of Conduct. *American Psychologist*, 57, 1060–1073. doi: 10.1037/0003-066X.57.12.1060

American Psychological Association. (2005, June). Report of the American Psychological Association Presidential Task Force on Psychological Ethics and National Security. Retrieved May 10, 2010, from http://www.apa.org/pubs/info/reports/pens.pdf

American Psychological Association. (2007, September 21). Statement of the American Psychological Association on Psychology and Interrogations submitted to the United States Senate Select Committee on Intelligence. [document on the Internet]. Retrieved May 10, 2010, from http://www.apa.org/ethics/programs/position/legislative/senate-select.aspx

American Psychological Association Committee on Ethical Standards. (1950). Ethical standards for the distribution of psychological tests and diagnostic aids. *American Psychologist*, 5(11), 620–626.

American Psychological Association Committee on Ethical Standards. (1951a). Ethical standards for psychology; section 1, ethical standards and public responsibility; section 6, ethical standards in teaching. *American Psychologist*, 6(11), 626–661.

American Psychological Association Committee on Ethical Standards. (1951b). Ethical standards for psychology: Section 2–Ethical standards in professional relationships; Section 4–Ethical standards in research; Section 5–Ethical standards in writing and publishing. *American Psychologist*, 6(8), 427–452.

American Psychological Association Committee on Ethical Standards. (1951c). Ethical standards in clinical and consulting relationships: Part I. *American Psychologist*, 6(2), 57–64.

American Psychological Association Committee on Ethical Standards. (1951d). Ethical standards in clinical and consulting relationships: Section 3, parts II-V. *American Psychologist*, 6(5), 145–166.

American Psychological Association Presidential Task Force on Evidence-Based Practice. (2006). Evidence-based practice in psychology. *American Psychologist*, 61(4), 271–285.

Annas, G. J., & Grodin, M. A. (1995). *The Nazi doctors and the Nuremberg Code: Human rights in human experimentation*. New York: Oxford University Press.

Appelbaum, P. S. (2007). Assessment of patient's competence to consent to treatment. *New England Journal of Medicine*, 357, 1834–1849,

Barlow, D. H. (2004). Psychological treatments. *American Psychologist*, 59(9), 869–878.

Barlow, D. H. (2005a). Clarification on psychological treatments and psychotherapy. *American Psychologist*, 60(7), 734–735.

Barlow, D. H. (2005b). What's new about evidence-based assessment? *Psychological Assessment*, 17(3), 308–311.

Behnke, S. (2006). Ethics and interrogations: Comparing and contrasting the American Psychological, American Medical and American Psychiatric Association positions. *Monitor on Psychology*, 37(7), 66.

Berner, M. (1998). Informed consent. In Lifson, L. E. & Simon, R. I. (Eds.), *Mental health practitioners and the law: A comprehensive handbook* (pp. 23–43). Cambridge, MA: Harvard University Press.

Birnbaum, M. H. (2008). New paradoxes of risky decision making. *Psychological Review*, 115(2), 463–501.

Blanchard-Fields, F., Chen, Y., Horhota, M., & Wang, M. (2007). Cultural differences in the relationship between aging and the correspondence bias. *Journals of Gerontology: Series B: Psychological Sciences and Social Sciences*, 62(6), P362–P365.

Boston Globe. (2008, August 30). Boston Globe Editorial: Psychologists and torture. *Boston Globe*. Retrieved May 7, 2010, from http://bit.ly/c1t0mK

Burton, M., & Kagan, C. (2007). Psychologists and torture: More than a question of interrogation. *The Psychologist, 20*, 484–487.

Campbell, C. D., & Gordon, M. C. (2003). Acknowledging the inevitable: Understanding multiple relationships in rural practice. *Professional Psychology: Research and Practice, 34*(4), 430–434.

Canadian Charter of Rights and Freedoms. Constitution Act, 1982 (Canada). Retrieved May 7, 2010, from http://laws.justice.gc.ca/en/charter

Canadian Psychological Association. (1986). *Canadian code of ethics for psychologists*. Ottawa, Ontario: Canadian Psychological Association.

Canadian Psychological Association. (1991). *Canadian code of ethics for psychologists, 2nd edition*. Ottawa, Ontario: Canadian Psychological Association.

Canadian Psychological Association. (2000). *Canadian code of ethics for psychologists, 3rd edition*. Retrieved May 10, 2010, from http://www.cpa.ca/publications.

Christopher, P. P., Foti, M. E., Roy-Bujnowski, K., & Appelbaum, P. S. (2007). Consent form readability and educational levels of potential participants in mental health research. *Psychiatric Services, 58*(2), 227–232.

Cocks, G. (1997). *Psychotherapy in the Third Reich, 2nd Edition*. Piscataway, NJ: Transaction Publishers.

Collins, N., Novotny, N. L., & Light, A. (2006). A cross-section of readability of Health Information Portability and Accountability Act authorizations required with health care research. *Journal of Allied Health, 35*(4), 223–225.

Comas-Diaz, L. (2006). Cultural variation in the therapeutic relationship. In C. D. Goodheart, A. E. Kazdin, & R. J. Sternberg (Eds.), *Evidence-based psychotherapy: Where practice and research meet*. (pp. 81–105). Washington, DC: American Psychological Association.

Cottone, R. R., & Claus, R. E. (2000). Ethical decision-making models: A review of the literature. *Journal of Counseling & Development, 78*(3), 275–283.

Dijkstra, A., Jaspers, M., & van Zwieten, M. (2008). Psychiatric and psychological factors in patient decision making concerning antidepressant use. *Journal of Consulting and Clinical Psychology, 76*(1), 149–157.

Doya, K. (2008). Modulators of decision making. *Nature Neuroscience, 11*(4), 410–416.

Eban, K. (2007, July 17). Rorschach and awe. *Vanity Fair*. Retrieved May 7, 2010, from http://bit.ly/9p28E4

Eidelson, R. (2009). No place to hide: Torture, psychologists, and the APA – A 10 Minute Video. Retrieved May 7, 2010, from http://www.youtube.com/watch?v=o84RE-9023U.

Fadiman, A. (1998). *The spirit catches you and you fall down*. New York: Farrar, Straus and Giroux.

Faulkner, K. K., & Faulkner, T. A. (1997). Managing multiple relationships in rural communities: Neutrality and boundary violations. *Clinical Psychology: Science and Practice, 4*(3), 225–234.

Fernberger, S. W. (1932). The American Psychological Association: a historical summary, 1892–1930. *Psychological Bulletin, 29*(1), 1–89.

Fernberger, S. W. (1943). The American Psychological Association: 1892–1942. *Psychological Review, 50*(1), 33–60.

Fischhoff, B. (2008). Assessing adolescent decision-making competence. *Developmental Review, 28*(1), 12–28.

Fisher, C. B. (2003). *Decoding the ethics code: A practical guide for psychologists*. Thousand Oaks, CA: Sage Publications, Inc.

Fisher, M. A. (2008). Protecting confidentiality rights: The need for an ethical practice model. *American Psychologist, 63*(1), 1–13.

Gatz, M. (2006). Cognitive capacities of older adults who are asked to consent to medical treatment or to clinical research. *Behavioral Sciences & the Law, 24*(4), 465–468.

Gawronski, B. (2003). Implicational schemata and the correspondence bias: On the diagnostic value of situationally constrained behavior. *Journal of Personality and Social Psychology, 84*(6), 1154–1171.

Geuter, U. (1992). *The professionalization of psychology in Nazi Germany*. Cambridge: Cambridge University Press.

Gilovich, T., Griffin, D., & Kahneman, D. (2002). *Heuristics and biases: The psychology of intuitive judgment*. Cambridge: Cambridge University Press.

Godlee, F. (2009, May 16). Rules of conscience. *British Medical Journal, 338*(7704).

Golann, S. E. (1969). Emerging areas of ethical concern. *American Psychologist, 24*(4), 454–459.

Gonsiorek, J. C. (2008). Informed consent can solve some confidentiality dilemmas, but others remain. *Professional Psychology: Research and Practice, 39*(3), 374–375.

Goodheart, C. D. (2006). Evidence, endeavor, and expertise in psychology practice. In C. D. Goodheart, A. E. Kazdin, & R. J. Sternberg (Eds.), *Evidence-based psychotherapy: Where practice and research meet*. (pp. 37–61). Washington, DC: American Psychological Association.

Goodman, A. (2007, June 8). Psychologists implicated in torture. *Seattle Post-Intelligencer*. Retrieved May 7, 2010, from http://seattlepi.nwsource.com/opinion/318745_amy07.html

Gottlieb, M. C. (1993). Avoiding exploitive dual relationships: A decision-making model. *Psychotherapy: Theory, Research, Practice, Training, 30*(1), 41–48.

Grundner, T. M. (1980). On the readability of surgical consent forms. *The New England Journal of Medicine, 302*(16), 900–902.

Gutheil, T. G., & Gabbard, G. O. (1993). The concept of boundaries in clinical practice: Theoretical and risk-management dimensions. *American Journal of Psychiatry, 150*(2), 188–196.

Gutheil, T. G., & Gabbard, G. O. (1998). Misuses and misunderstandings of boundary theory in clinical and regulatory settings. *American Journal of Psychiatry, 155*(3), 409–414.

Haas, L. J., & Malouf, J. L. (2005). *Keeping up the good work: A practitioner's guide to mental health ethics*, 4th edition. Sarasota, FL: Professional Resource Press.

Hall, C. (1952). Crooks, codes, and cant. *American Psychologist, 7*(8), 430–431.

Hansen, N. D., Randazzo, K. V., Schwartz, A., Marshall, M., Kalis, D., Frazier, R., et al. (2006). Do we practice what we preach? An exploratory survey of multicultural psychotherapy competencies. *Professional Psychology: Research and Practice, 37*(1), 66–74.

Hausman, K. (2006). Military looks to psychologists for advice on interrogations. *Psychiatric News, 41*(13), 4.

Hobbs, N. (1948). The development of a code of ethical standards for psychology. *American Psychologist, 3*(3), 80–84.

Hochauser, M. (1997). Some overlooked aspects of consent form readability. *IRB: A Review of Human Subjects Research, 19*(5), 5–9.

Holtzman, W. H. (1960). Some problems of defining ethical behavior. *American Psychologist, 15*(4), 247–250.

Huppert, J. D., Fabbro, A., & Barlow, D. H. (2006). Evidence-based practice and psychological treatments. In C. D. Goodheart, A. E. Kazdin, & R. J. Sternberg (Eds.), *Evidence-based psychotherapy: Where practice and research meet.* (pp. 131–152). Washington, DC: American Psychological Association.

Hutson, M. (2006, November 1). Keeping interrogation clean: Should therapists be involved in prisoner interrogations? Two experts go head to head. *Psychology Today.* Retrieved May 7, 2010, from http://bit.ly/9f7zeg

Jaffee v. Redmond, 518 U.S. 1 (1996).

Jones, E. E. (1979). The rocky road from acts to dispositions. *American Psychologist, 34*(2), 107–117.

Kaslow, N. J. (2004). Competencies in professional psychology. *American Psychologist, 59*(8), 774–781.

Kaslow, N. J., Borden, K. A., Collins Jr., F. L., Forrest, L., Illfelder-Kaye, J., Nelson, P. D., et al. (2004). Competencies conference: Future directions in education and credentialing in professional psychology. *Journal of Clinical Psychology, 60*(7), 699–712.

Kaslow, N. J., Rubin, N. J., Bebeau, M. J., et al. (2007). Guiding principles and recommendations for the assessment of competence. *Professional Psychology: Research and Practice, 38*(5), 441–451.

Kaslow, N. J., Rubin, N. J., Forrest, L., et al. (2007). Recognizing, assessing, and intervening with problems of professional competence. *Professional Psychology: Research and Practice, 38*(5), 479–492.

Kazdin, A. E. (2006). Assessment and evaluation in clinical practice. In C. D. Goodheart, A. E. Kazdin, & R. J. Sternberg (Eds.), *Evidence-based psychotherapy: Where practice and research meet.* Washington, DC: American Psychological Association. Retrieved August 23, 2008.

Kazdin, A. E. (2008). Evidence-based treatment and practice: New opportunities to bridge clinical research and practice, enhance the knowledge base, and improve patient care. *American Psychologist, 63*(3), 146–159.

Kessler, L. E., & Waehler, C. A. (2005). Addressing multiple relationships between clients and therapists in lesbian, gay, bisexual, and transgender communities. *Professional Psychology: Research and Practice, 36*(1), 66–72.

Koocher, G. K. (2006 July/August). President's column: Varied and valued roles. *Monitor on Psychology, 37(7),* 5.

Koocher, G. P., & Keith-Spiegel, P. C. (2008). *Ethics in psychology and the mental health professions: Standards and cases, 3rd Edition.* Cambridge: Oxford University Press.

Lamb, D. H., & Catanzaro, S. J. (1998). Sexual and nonsexual boundary violations involving psychologists, clients, supervisees, and students: Implications for professional practice. *Professional Psychology: Research and Practice, 29,* 498–503. doi: 10.1037/0735-7028.29.5.498

Lehner, G. F. J. (1952). Comment: Defining Psychotherapy. *American Psychologist, 7*(9), 547.

Levine, A. (2007, January-February). Collective unconscionable: How psychologists, the most liberal of professionals, abetted torture. *Washington Monthly.* Retrieved May 7, 2010, from http://www.washingtonmonthly.com/features/2007/0701.levine.html

Lewis A. (2006, June 7). Psychologists preferred for detainees. *New York Times.* Retrieved May 7, 2010, from http://bit.ly/ahd9L9

Lifton, R. J. (2000). *The Nazi doctors: Medical killing and the psychology of genocide.* New York: Basic Books.

Lifton, R. J. (2008, August 11). Robert Jay Lifton on the American Psychological Association and torture. Video. Producer/Director: Hermine Muskat. Studio: Back Bay Films, LLC. Retrieved May 7, 2010, from http://video.google.com/videoplay?docid=752182170409437361.

Lifton, R. J., & Xenakis, S. N. (2006, June 8). Doctors must be healers, not interrogators. *Los Angeles Times.* Retrieved July May 7, 2010, from http://articles.latimes.com/2006/jun/08/opinion/oe-lifton8

Martin, D. A. (2005). Readability of informed consent forms and sufficient opportunity for patients to ask questions: Relationship with psychologists' perceived benefit of informed consent to psychotherapy. *Dissertation Abstracts International: Section B: The Sciences and Engineering. 66(4-B), 2005, 2311.,* 66(4-B), 2311.

McNeil, B., Pauker, S., Sox, H., & Tversky, A. (1982). On the elucidation of preferences for alternative therapies. *New England Journal of Medicine, 306,* 1259–1262.

Meehl, P. (1989). Why I do not attend case conferences. In Meehl, Paul (Ed.), *Psychodiagnosis: Selected papers.* New York: Norton. (Originally published 1973).

Miles, S. H. (2009) Psychologists and torture. *British Medical Journal (BMJ).* (May 1). Retrieved May 7, 2010, from http://bmj.com/cgi/eletters/338/apr30_2/b1653#213065.

Moran M. (2006). American Medical Association interrogation policy similar to American Psychiatric Association's position. *Psychiatric News, 41*(13), 1–5. Retrieved May 7, 2010, from http://pn.psychiatryonline.org/cgi/content/full/41/13/1

Mutual Recognition Agreement of the Regulatory Bodies for Professional Psychologists in Canada (amended). (2004, June). Canadian Psychological Association. Retrieved May 7, 2010, from http://www.cpa.ca/documents/MRA.pdf.

Olmstead v. United States, 277 U.S. 438 (1928).

Olson B., & Miles S. H. (2009). The American Psychological Association and war on terror interrogations. In S. H. Miles (Ed.), *Oath betrayed: America's torture doctors, 2nd Edition* (pp. 186–198). Berkeley: University of California Press.

O'Neill, P. (1998). *Negotiating consent in psychotherapy.* New York: NYU Press.

"Open letter in response to the American Psychological Association Board." (2009, June 29). Retrieved May 7, 2010, from http://bit.ly/Y2bFj

Paasche-Orlow, M. K., Taylor, H. A., & Brancati, F. L. (2003). Readability standards for informed-consent forms as compared with actual readability. *New England Journal of Medicine, 348*(8), 721–726.

Pope, K. S., & Bajt, T. R. (1988). When laws and values conflict: A dilemma for psychologists. *American Psychologist, 43*(10), 828–829.

Pope, K. S., & Brown, L. S. (1996). *Recovered memories of abuse: Assessment, therapy, forensics.* Washington, DC: American Psychological Association.

Pope, K. S., & Garcia-Peltoniemi, R. E. (1991). Responding to victims of torture: Clinical issues, professional responsibilities, and useful resources. *Professional Psychology: Research and Practice, 22*(4), 269–276. Retrieved May 7, 2010, from http://kspope.com/torvic/torture1.php

Pope, K. S., & Gutheil, T. G. (2009a, May 16). Contrasting ethical policies of physicians & psychologists concerning detainee interrogation. *British Medical Journal, 338*(7704),

1178–1180. Retrieved May 7, 2010, from http://kspope.com/detainee/interrogation.php

Pope, K. S., & Gutheil, T. G. (2009b, May-June). Psychologists abandon the Nuremberg ethic. *International Journal of Law & Psychiatry*, *32*(4), 161–166. Retrieved May 7, 2010, from http://kspope.com/nuremberg.php

Pope, K. S., & Keith-Spiegel, P. C. (2008). A practical approach to boundaries in psychotherapy: Making decisions, bypassing blunders, and mending fences. *Journal of Clinical Psychology: In Session*, *64*(5), 638–652. Retrieved May 7, 2010, from http://kspope.com/ethics/boundary.php

Pope, K. S., Sonne, J. L., & Greene, B. (2006). *What therapists don't talk about and why: Understanding taboos that hurt us and our clients*. Washington, DC: American Psychological Association.

Pope, K. S., Sonne, J. L., & Holroyd, J. (1993). *Sexual feelings in psychotherapy: Explorations for therapists and therapists-in-training*. Washington, DC: American Psychological Association.

Pope, K. S., & Vasquez, M. J. T. (2010). *Ethics in psychotherapy and counseling: A practical guide, 4rd edition*. San Francisco, CA: Jossey-Bass/John Wiley.

Pope, K. S., & Vetter, V. A. (1992). Ethical dilemmas encountered by members of the American Psychological Association: A national survey. *American Psychologist*, *47*(3), 397–411. Retrieved May 7, 2010, from http://kspope.com/ethics/ethics2.php

Proctor, R. (1988). *Racial hygiene: Medicine under the Nazis*. Cambridge, MA: Harvard University Press.

Ray P. (2006, June 12). New AMA ethical policy opposes direct physician participation in interrogation. American Medical Association news release [document on the Internet]. Retrieved July 20, 2009, from http://www0.ama-assn.org/ama/pub/category/16446.html

Reyna, V. F., & Rivers, S. E. (2008). Current theories of risk and rational decision making. *Developmental Review*, *28*(1), 1–11.

Rich, G. J. (1952). A new code of ethics is needed. *American Psychologist*, *7*(8), 440–441.

Roll, S., & Millen, L. (1981). A guide to violating an injunction in psychotherapy: On seeing acquaintances as patients. *Psychotherapy: Theory, Research & Practice*, *18*(2), 179–187.

Roy v. Hartogs. (1976). 381 N.Y.S.2d 587, 85 Misc. 2d 891.

Schloendorff v. Society of New York Hospital. (1914). 211 N.Y. 125, 105 N.E. 92.

Sharfstein, S. (2006). Presidential address: Advocacy as leadership. *American Journal of Psychiatry*, *163*(10), 1711–1715 (Retrieved May 7, 2010, from http://ajp.psychiatryonline.org/cgi/content/full/163/10/1711

Simon, G. C. (1978). The psychologist as whistle blower: A case study. *Professional Psychology*, *9*(2), 322–340.

Sinclair, C. (1998). Nine unique features of the Canadian Code of Ethics for Psychologists. *Canadian Psychology/Psychologie Canadienne*, *39*(3), 167–176.

Sinclair, C. M., & Pettifor, J. (2001). Introduction and acknowledgements. In C. M. Sinclair & J. Pettifor (Eds.), *Companion manual to the Canadian Code of Ethics for Psychologists, 3rd edition* (pp. i–iv). Ottawa, Ontario: Canadian Psychological Association.

Sinclair, C. M., Simon, N. P., & Pettifor, J. (1996). Professional conduct and discipline in psychology. In L. J. Bass, S. T. DeMers, J. R. P. Ogloff, C. Peterson, J. L. Pettifor, R. P. Reaves, T. Retfalvi, N. Simon, C. Sinclair, & R. Topton

(Eds.), *Professional conduct and discipline in psychology* (pp. 1–15). Washington, DC: American Psychological

Singer, J. L. (1980). The scientific basis of psychotherapeutic practice: A question of values and ethics. *Psychotherapy: Theory, Research & Practice*, *17*(4), 372–383.

Sinz, H., Zamarian, L., Benke, T., Wenning, G. K., & Delazer, M. (2008). Impact of ambiguity and risk on decision making in mild Alzheimer's disease. *Neuropsychologia*, *46*(7), 2043–2055.

Soldz, S. (2009). Closing eyes to atrocities: U.S. psychologists, detainee interrogations, and the response of the American Psychological Association. In Goodman, R. & Roseman, M.J. (Eds.), *Interrogations, forced feedings, and the role of health professionals: New perspectives on international human rights, humanitarian law and ethics* (Harvard Law School Human Rights Program series). Cambridge, MA: Harvard University Press. Retrieved May 7, 2010, from http://tinyurl.com/cc9yw4

Sonne, J. L. (2005). Nonsexual multiple relationships: A practical decision-making model for clinicians. Retrieved May 7, 2010, from http://kspope.com/site/multiple-relationships.php

Sternberg, R. J. (2006). Evidence-based practice: Gold standard, gold plated, or fool's gold? In C. D. Goodheart, A. E. Kazdin, & R. J. Sternberg (Eds.), *Evidence-based psychotherapy: Where practice and research meet*. (pp. 261–271). Washington, DC: American Psychological Association.

Stricker, G. (1992). The relationship of research to clinical practice. *American Psychologist*, *47*(4), 543–549.

Sue, D. W., & Sue, D. (2007). *Counseling the culturally diverse: Theory and practice, 5th edition*. New York: Wiley.

Sue, S., Zane, N., Levant, R. F., Silverstein, L. B., Brown, L. S., Olkin, R., & Taliafero, G. (2006). How well do both evidence-based practices and treatment as usual satisfactorily address the various dimensions of diversity? In J. Norcross, L. Beutler, & R. Levant (Eds.), *Evidence-based practices in mental health: Debate and dialogue on the fundamental questions*. (pp. 329–374). Washington, DC: American Psychological Association: Washington.

Taylor, T. (1993). *The anatomy of the Nuremberg trials: A personal memoir*. New York: Little Brown & Co.

Taylor, T. (1997). *Final report to the secretary of the army on the Nuremberg War Crimes Trials under Control Council Law No. 10*. Buffalo, NY: William S. Hein & Company.

Truscott, D., & Crook, K. H. (2004). *Ethics for the practice of psychology in Canada*. Edmonton: University of Alberta Press.

Tversky, A., & Kahneman, D. (2004). Framing of decisions and the psychology of choice. In D. Balota & E. Marsch (Eds.), *Cognitive psychology: Key readings*. (pp. 621–630). New York: Psychology Press.

Tversky, A., & Kahneman, D. (2005). Judgment under uncertainty: Heuristics and biases. In M. H. Bazerman (Ed.), *Negotiation, decision making and conflict management, Vol. 1–3*. (pp. 251–258). Northampton: Edward Elgar Publishing.

Vasquez, M. J. T. (2007). Cultural difference and the therapeutic alliance: An evidence-based analysis. *American Psychologist*, *62*(8), 878–885.

Walfish, S., & Ducey, B. B. (2007). Readability level of Health Insurance Portability and Accountability Act notices of privacy practices utilized by academic medical centers. *Professional Psychology: Research and Practice*, *38*(2), 203–207.

Wallace, L. S., Keenum, A. J., Roskos, S. E., Blake, G. H., Colwell, S. T., & Weiss, B. D. (2008). Suitability and readability of consumer medical information accompanying prescription medication samples. *Patient Education and Counseling, 70*(3), 420–425.

Welfel, E. R. (2005). *Ethics in counseling and psychotherapy: Standards, research, and emerging issues, 3rd Edition.* Pacific Grove, CA: Brooks Cole.

Williams-Piehota, P. A., McCormack, L. A., Treiman, K., & Bann, C. M. (2008). Health information styles among participants in a prostate cancer screening informed decision-making intervention. *Health Education Research, 23*(3), 440–453.

Younggren, J. N. (2002). Ethical decision-making and dual relationships. Retrieved August 27, 2008, from http://kspope.com/dual/younggren.php

Zikmund-Fisher, B. J., Lacey, H. P., & Fagerlin, A. (2008). The potential impact of decision role and patient age on end-of-life treatment decision making. *Journal of Medical Ethics, 34*(5), 327–331.

Creating Public Health Policy: The Dissemination of Evidenced-based Psychological Interventions

Bruce F. Chorpita, Jeanne Miranda, *and* Adam Bernstein

Abstract

In recent years, clinical psychology has made significant contributions to mental health policy through its increasing focus on the notion of evidence-based practice and an empirical approach to clinical decision-making. These developments have not been without challenges, however. Most notable are issues with the acceptability of treatment design among practitioners and the difficulty of implementing and sustaining high-quality practices in real-world contexts. Two specific barriers central to these challenges are discussed, namely, the highly specialized architecture of most research-based mental health treatments and the unavailability of a dedicated supervisory and training infrastructure. Solutions are proposed that suggest the need to rethink both the way treatments are packaged and the way they are supported in real-world practice.

Keywords: Clinical psychology, evidence-based practice, mental health, mental health policy, public health policy

Historical Background

Some of the earliest mental health policy in the United States emerged as a result of the activism of Dorathea Dix, in the mid-19th century. Her work was primarily concerned with the absence of any standard of care for impoverished and indigent people with mental health needs. The country soon entered an era of state-run institutions that provided shelter and treatment for such individuals. This policy of exceptionalism—the notion of creating special services and institutions for people with mental health needs—lasted roughly 100 years, until the emergence of a movement toward deinstitutionalizing and mainstreaming occurred in the middle of the 20th century. This mainstreaming era saw an emphasis not only on developing services in the community but also on serving more than just seriously mentally ill individuals, with an increased role of the federal government in shaping policy. The National Mental Health Act, signed in 1946, created a National Mental Health

Advisory Council and the National Institute of Mental Health (NIMH). The latter group focused on research and training that ultimately led to the development of community alternatives to hospitalization. The NIMH at that time sought to help individuals with mental health needs by developing resources directly in the community (Felix, 1949). Legislation followed in the late 1950s and early 1960s that promoted the development of Community Mental Health Centers, and debate grew regarding whether the evidence favored hospital-based or community-based treatment (e.g., NIMH, 1962).

The resulting 20 years of deinstitutionalization were characterized by controversy among policy makers and fragmentation of the service system. Many of the individuals for whom community centers had been created were not being served appropriately, while a newly identified population of individuals with less intensive mental health needs drew on those services. In 1977, President

Carter established the President's Commission on Mental Health, in the hopes of understanding and improving the existing mental health system. This Commission, however, was plagued by bureaucratic rivalries and ultimately did not produce the revolutionary and lasting change that was hoped for.

The next 10–15 years was characterized by numerous incremental gains in improving access to care, as well as system integration between hospitals and community services. During this time, funding for mental health services improved, largely through increased use of nonspecialty mental health sources, such as Medicaid. This shifted funding for mental health to agencies for which mental health was not the major concern. In 1992, there was a division within federal programs, with NIMH focusing primarily on research, and the Substance Abuse and Mental Health Services Administration being created for service development and policy functions. Around this time, federal focus increased on specific actions to create coordination and integration of care—including the now well-known demonstration project for children's mental health services in Ft. Bragg, North Carolina (e.g., Bickman et al., 1995).

A long-running theme over this nearly 150-year period of mental health policy involved a focus on equitable access to the best available services. Although debate often raged about the most appropriate methods, the primary focus of mental health policy in the United States has been to facilitate outcomes related primarily to community benefit and safety.

The Influence of Psychology: Service Quality

The profession of psychology has played its own part in influencing mental health policy, emanating most recently from work in the early 1990s that was related to increasing pressure in the managed care environment to justify the costs of mental health services. In the midst of a long period of productivity on issues related to access to and coordination of mental health services, as well as parity to medical health, the 1990s saw an additional and initially somewhat independent focus on service quality and cost effectiveness. In the interest of establishing a working definition of service quality, in 1992, the American Psychological Association (APA) established the Task Force on Psychological Intervention Guidelines, chaired by David H. Barlow. This task force outlined a template for measuring the quality of psychosocial treatments, with the eventual goal of establishing guidelines for selecting the most appropriate mental

health treatments. The task force outlined two dimensions—now widely known—along which treatments should be evaluated: (1) efficacy (i.e., how reliably a treatment is known to bring about change in a target disorder in clinical research), and (2) effectiveness (i.e., how well a treatment is expected to perform in a "real world" setting). These terms have been defined and discussed in detail elsewhere (e.g., Chambless & Hollon, 1998; Task Force on Psychological Intervention Guidelines, 1995).

As this APA task force concluded, Dr. Barlow requested that the Clinical Division of the APA build on this important foundation by establishing the Division 12 Task Force on Promotion and Dissemination of Psychological Procedures, chaired by Dianne Chambless. This Division 12 Task Force outlined a detailed definition of efficacy and developed an initial list of those psychosocial treatments with the best empirical support. The Division 12 Task Force published the first official list of empirically supported treatments in 1995 (Task Force on Promotion and Dissemination of Psychological Procedures, 1995), and has since published several updates (Chambless et al., 1996; Chambless et al., 1998). Eventually ushering in a national dialogue on *evidence-based practice* (EBP) in psychosocial treatment, these efforts within psychology have been profound and enduring in their influence on the nature of subsequent clinical training, research, and policy (Chambless & Hollon, 1998; Elliott, 1998; Glass & Arnkoff, 1996; Kazdin, 1996, 1998; Kendall, 1999; Kendall & Chambless, 1998; Nathan & Gorman, 1998; Nathan, Stuart, & Dolan, 2000; VandenBos, 1996; Weisz, Hawley, Pilkonis, Woody, & Follette, 2000).

Explicit in the early definition of EBP (initially described as "empirically validated treatments") were several important study features that afforded their treatments higher status: experimental control, replication, the use of treatment manuals, and clearly defined populations. Some of these features later came to embody significant controversy as the EBP paradigm began to shape practice policy, as will be reviewed later.

Benefits

The benefits of this work by the APA and its Clinical Division have been substantial, laying the groundwork for policy and decision-making grounded in evidence and an increasing level of objectivity and accountability in a variety of domains. First and foremost are the implications for the diffusion of information about promising practices. The initial list of treatments identified by the Division 12 Task Force has since spawned multiple successive movements and a diversity of evidence-based lists and registries (Chorpita et al., 2002; Lonigan, Elbert, & Bennet-Johnson, 1998; Silverman & Hinshaw, 2008; Substance Abuse and Mental Health Services Administration, 2008). Practitioners, researchers, and the public are now inundated with choices regarding how to select or identify an EBP, whether in books, chapters, state guidelines, federal guidelines, or online public and private registries and databases.

In terms of research, there is a new lexicon for establishing evidence of producing reliable outcomes—with most researchers now designing studies explicitly to meet the criteria for efficacy issued in 1995 (e.g., use of treatment manuals, randomized designs, independent replication). The result has been an improvement in many aspects of the quality of clinical research and research reporting over the past 15 years (see also Moher, Schultz, & Altman, 2001). Federal agencies are increasingly focused on research designs that build on this set of definitions and have, in many ways, sought to make EBPs a larger focus of the federal mental health agenda (e.g., U.S. Department of Health and Human Services, 1999; National Advisory Mental Health Council Workgroup on Services Research and Clinical Epidemiology, 2006; NIMH, 2008).

Challenges

Although these developments with respect to service quality have been positive at the policy level, their practical implications have met with a host of challenges. For example, research has shown that treatment manuals—a core part of the definition of EBPs—have raised concerns on the part of many practitioners, who feel that manuals limit therapeutic rapport and the ability to flexibly tailor case conceptualization on an individual level (Addis & Krasnow, 2000). Interestingly, Nelson and Steele (2007) found that therapists' concerns with EBPs were not a function of negative attitudes toward research (viz. quality per se), but focused instead on reduced opportunity for clinical judgment and fears that research-based protocols do not fully address the complexity of real-world cases. Such findings suggest that practitioner objections are less a function of the direct emphasis on scientific support and more likely to be a side effect of the proposed definition of what constitutes a testable treatment (cf. Borntrager, Chorpita, Higa-McMillan, & Weisz, 2009).

Over time, a detailed array of arguments and concerns about EBPs and their policy implications

developed into a significant antitheses, perhaps best summarized by Westen, Novotny, and Thompson-Brenner (2004). Longstanding concerns about the representativeness of clinical research and over-reliance on psychiatric diagnosis were combined with new concerns about the single-disorder architecture of most treatment manuals, inattention to comorbidity, inadequate control groups, and the perceived inflexibility of most evidence-based manuals (Norcross, Beutler, & Levant, 2006; Persons, 1991; Westen et al., 2004; Wolpe, 1989).

While the EBP movement and countermovement engaged in this healthy debate, national policy recommendations continued to emerge, whose integration with EBPs is often unclear. In 1999, the Office of the Surgeon General issued a report on mental health in the United States arguing, among other things, that promising treatments tested by science needed to be more available. At the same time, that report called for increased individualization of care and a need for services to be more consumer-driven, notions that could be considered difficult to integrate with manualized evidence-based treatments and sanctioned lists of scientifically approved interventions. Similar sets of recommendations followed in nearly every major national report or action agenda on mental health (and health more broadly) in the past 10 years (Hogan, 2003; Institute of Medicine, 2001; National Advisory Mental Health Council Workgroup on Child and Adolescent Mental Health Intervention Development and Deployment, 2001; National Advisory Mental Health Council Workgroup on Services Research and Clinical Epidemiology, 2006; Substance Abuse and Mental Health Services Administration, 2006).

Federal agencies are beginning to direct resources toward research on implementation and dissemination strategies (NIMH, 2008), in order to understand better what forces are involved with the successful impact of research-based treatments on communities. Similar to the dialectic regarding institutional and community-based care that characterized much of the policy discussions of the late 20th century, the current policy climate involves an interplay between two sets of ideals: (1) the objectivity, quality, and accountability associated with research-based protocols; and (2) the emphasis on consumer needs (e.g., occupational and social functioning), parity, access, and decision-making. Although both sets of ideals have the best interest of the public at heart, the pathway to their successful integration remains unclear, given the current structure of mental health delivery systems and laboratories that produce and test interventions. In the remaining pages, we hope to outline what we see as two particularly compelling points of controversy, in the hopes of identifying strategies to address them, and we provide some example illustrations of possible ways forward.

Problem 1: Organization and Emphasis of Research Findings

One fundamental goal of research is to serve public welfare in the long term by producing findings that are *cumulative*, such that one set of advances serves as a foundation for further work. To a significant degree, the history reviewed earlier demonstrates successful cumulative growth, and over a century-long span can be viewed as a gradual march toward equitable access to the best available services, adequately funded. Additionally, over the past 15 years, major advances have emanated from the efficacy criteria issued in 1995. The design standards enacted by these criteria make for enhanced comparability of results from diverse studies and prioritize independent replication, a necessarily cumulative endeavor. The resulting growth of the field has been powered in part by the decision of federal agencies to fund research designs that utilize these definitions.

However, to date, a major emphasis of the research community has also been on individual innovation. This emphasis is reflected in mental health by the proliferation of numerous successful treatment protocols (e.g., over 200 in children's mental health; Chorpita & Daleiden, 2009). The result is a fragmentation of innovation that stems from the complexity of using the evidence base as a guide to selecting a quality treatment protocol for the purpose of training staff or treating an average client. Hundreds of randomized clinical trials exist to inform such decisions; however, these trials have produced a comparably large number of successful protocols that are unique in the strict sense of scientific replication (see Chorpita, Daleiden, & Weisz, 2005a). These various protocols each have evidence of efficacy only with certain populations. Selecting a protocol with the goal of maximizing the fit of the intervention with the problem and context of an individual client or the client population typically served by an agency thus involves making difficult decisions. Given the large number of similar but unique protocols, interpretation of the evidence base depends on discerning which approaches are sufficiently similar such that their findings can be aggregated. To illustrate with an example, one might ask whether findings in a trial of a leading youth anxiety protocol, the Coping Cat (Kendall, Kane,

Howard, & Siqueland, 1990), can be aggregated with those of an adapted Australian version, the Coping Koala (Barrett, Dadds, & Rapee, 1991), or whether those findings can also be aggregated with those of other studies testing youth anxiety protocols based upon similar cognitive behavioral principals and strategies (e.g., Barrington, Prior, Richardson, & Allen, 2005; Masia-Warner et al., 2005). There is, at present, no policy regarding a uniform standard for aggregating scientific information to inform mental health practice, and this affects not only the ability to leverage existing federally funded research, but also the quality of ongoing and future research reporting.

A major question to be addressed is, thus, whether the current emphasis on individual innovation in the treatment development area continues to serve the long-term goal of serving public welfare via cumulative growth of the field. First, it is important to recognize that the current incentive structures reward researchers and developers for specialization, and that many of these contingencies are influenced, directly or indirectly, by federal research policy. For example, tenure, promotion, and grant resources are attained through voluminous research output and demonstration of expertise, both of which are most readily achieved via specialization: the crafting of a niche area of endeavor, and replication of success within that area. In mental health treatment research, this often involves the design of a new treatment, incorporating many elements of existing treatments, but adding new elements as well, and packaging them into a unique whole. Incentive structures implicitly encourage this creation of new treatments even when a large number of effective protocols already exist in a particular area. Studies replicating the success of an existing treatment created by another researcher afford relatively less reward or opportunity; whereas the creation of a new treatment that proves successful in a clinical trial may offer the opportunity for further study by its designer, as well as additional opportunities if the treatment is eventually adopted by others. Mental health treatment researchers are thus generally rewarded for creating a new treatment, studying that treatment, and promoting it as distinct and superior to other existing treatments.

This individual-specialization model has been useful to the field, in that it has produced a large number of efficacious and sophisticated treatment technologies. However, a problem with the emphasis on individual innovation is that it tends to create relatively isolated "silos" of research, and ultimately silos of treatment technology available for consumers.

Certainly, investigators do incorporate aspects of others' advances into their own work. However, the incentive structures described here encourage researchers to emphasize the differences between their own and others' work, without a balanced emphasis on the commonalities and compatibilities. Additionally, career success may be maximized by protecting one's own research product, replicating success only in safe environments, producing further investigation within a controlled, restricted realm, or looking mainly at measures most sensitive to change (i.e., symptoms) regardless of their importance to consumers. Efforts to protect such work may also expand to preventing it from being adapted into the work of others or tested in ways that expose weaknesses. The cost to the field here is the relative isolation and even irrelevance of the resulting lines of research. Towering advances exist, but they stand as silos, separated from other areas of research that will ultimately be essential to advancing real-world applications for the public benefit.

To be clear, the isolation of treatment research from dissemination and implementation know-how is not specific to any protocol but rather endemic throughout the field, affected in part by a federal research policy that has not fully anticipated the changing landscape of accumulating treatment research. At the very least, it is a lack of a policy addressing the consequences of specialization that has played a role. This potential for inefficiency is especially salient in the context of a field that generally sees a 15 to 20-year gap between research innovations and changes in practice (Institute of Medicine, 2001).

Potential Solutions: Emphasis on Collaboration, Compatibility, and Common Architecture

An alternative to the emphasis on individual innovation, design, and replication is a new, more rigorous emphasis on cooperation and compatibility. One method of combating fragmentation is via research *networks*, in which researchers collaboratively design programs of broader scope and greater scale than can be achieved by any individual laboratory alone. Although informal collaboration among small groups of researchers is common throughout the field, the majority of treatments available did not emanate from formal collaborative networks. Exceptions do exist. In the private sector, the Resource for Advancing Children's Health Institute's (REACH) is a nonprofit organization with a focus on treatment dissemination in children's mental health. Its members participate in the associated Integrated Psychotherapy Consortium

(IPC), a collaboration of many leading treatment developers and researchers. Additionally, the MacArthur Foundation, one of the nation's largest private granting agencies, has sponsored a number of research networks in mental health areas, including Youth Mental Health, Mental Health Policy Research, Mind–Body Interactions, and Psychopathology and Development. An example of a federally organized collaboration is the National Child Traumatic Stress Network, which combines academic and community-based service centers with the mission of raising the standard of care and improving access to services for traumatized children via training, direct provision of clinical services, and collaboration with established systems of care.

The most significant obstacles to the success of these types of networks relate to the issues of incentive structures mentioned earlier. A natural difficulty concerns compromises about the research designs, as well as significant increases in time and complexity associated with collaborative networks. Planning and coordinating a large integrated operation, often across long distances, entails ongoing, complex communication, much beyond that associated with research in an individual laboratory. However, little direct reward comes from excellence in these areas per se; indeed, effective communication may easily be neglected amid efforts to satisfy more immediate demands of developing and testing mental health treatments. As explored further later, for research networks to be more a widespread and common part of the landscape, incentive structures have to change on a broad scale.

A second way in which cumulative research progress can be achieved through an emphasis on cooperation is through the use of common standards or common architecture. The principle here is that consumers tend to benefit when developers can agree on a design standard. Common standards can be either proprietary or open, and examples are quite common in areas outside of mental health treatment. An example of a proprietary standard is the Blu-ray digital disc format. Recent de facto agreement on Blu-ray as the next-generation disc format has allowed producers of discs and disc players to commit to the format, producing a wider array of compatible products at a substantially lower cost than was previously possible, thus creating benefit for consumers. Other examples of proprietary standards and architectures include proprietary computer operating systems, radiological image storage and viewing systems, and selected digital media file formats, as well as a plethora of more mundane products ranging from vacuum cleaner filters to razor blades to printer ink cartridges.

Examples of open standards are those published by the World Wide Web Consortium (W3C), an international group that develops standards and guidelines with the mission of preventing fragmentation of the Web by promoting interoperability (World Wide Web Consortium, 2008). The W3C is organized as a consortium, with paying member organizations obtaining a seat on an advisory committee and participating in other capacities of standards development. Standards published by the W3C include HyperText Markup Language (HTML), the predominant means of structuring text and forms on Web pages, as well as a large number of compatible and widely used open technologies such as media formats and standards for Web applications and security. The existence of these standards has been instrumental to the rapid growth of the Internet (Branscomb & Kahin, 1995). Other examples of open standards and architectures include the Unix (and Unix-like) computer operating systems, voltage and socket standards for U.S. appliances, and television and radio broadcast standards. Notably, the use of open standards does not indicate that a market is noncommercial. Rather, as with the proliferation of commerce on the Web, businesses may thrive by selling unique products that function via compatibility with an open architecture.

Applying common standards or common architecture to the design of mental health treatments may also hold potential for major benefits to consumers. A common standard or common architecture for treatment protocols could take a variety of forms. One model is provided by the integrated approach to manual design of the REACH Institute, mentioned earlier. REACH offers manuals for each of four common youth disorder areas (e.g., Integrated Psychotherapy Consortium, 2005). These manuals feature an integrated design with standardization of session organization, terms, and techniques across manuals. Additionally, each manual includes a small list of additional sessions from the other problem areas that may be utilized as needed to supplement treatment (e.g., a session titled "Changing Negative Thoughts" from the depression protocol may be used to supplement the anxiety protocol). The manuals can thus be used in combination to address comorbidities with greater ease than is possible with stand-alone single-disorder manuals.

REACH's integrated approach offers potentially significant advantages in terms of compatibility and transferability of competencies. These advantages could be multiplied were the architecture to become a widely adopted standard. Wide adoption by other treatment designers could mean compatibility across a greater number of problem areas and multiple compatible manual options within single problem areas, allowing providers to choose preferred manuals without sacrificing compatibility. However, despite these potential advantages, some of the drawbacks associated with traditional standalone manuals remain. Notably, the REACH manuals are subject to the common problem of updating material: changing its content requires creating a new version of an entire manual (or perhaps of multiple compatible manuals) and thus can be undertaken only rarely.

We have argued elsewhere that greater steps toward achieving common architecture can be taken through the use of a modular approach to treatment design, as opposed to the conventional, or integral, approach represented by most manuals today (Chorpita, Daleiden, & Weisz, 2005b). In modular treatment design, a complex treatment is organized into smaller subcomponents, referred to as *modules*. Key features of a modular design include the fact that each module has a specific function (e.g., a relaxation module aims to reduce autonomic arousal), and each module implements a standardized interface to allow smooth connection with other modules (e.g., communicating information required for reviewing assigned homework in the following session). Additionally, modules can be of two types: (1) content modules, that represent the building blocks of the intervention, describing the therapeutic activities to be performed (e.g., teaching relaxation) and are similar to procedural descriptions in typical therapy manuals, and (2) coordination modules, that outline the decision-making algorithms regarding whether and when to apply the various content modules. Although modular design has a wide array of potential advantages, as well as disadvantages, in comparison to integral design (Chorpita et al., 2005b), most relevant here is the ease of incremental improvement. Whereas changing an integral design requires examining a treatment procedure from beginning to end, a modular design allows updating of a single piece. Thus, a researcher could contribute a module representing a particular innovation—say a new relaxation technique—with minimal design overhead. This potential advantage makes modular frameworks strong candidates for a common architecture, and potentially organizes innovation in such a way as to impact consumers more quickly and effectively.

A common architecture could be achieved in a modular framework via specification of an interface for all intervention components (content and coordination modules) to implement. For content modules, the interface would indicate the types of information the modules must be capable of communicating (e.g., the type of homework assigned, if any, and how it is to be reviewed), as well as the structure of the therapeutic activities to be performed (e.g., each step listed with a title, a brief summary, and detailed description if appropriate). The interface may also specify certain required components that the content module must implement (e.g., when appropriate, bridge from previous session and review homework). Additionally, the interface may provide a format for types of "meta-data," (ADL, 2003) or information about the module itself, to be included. Examples of meta-data are description of a module's purpose, the age or cultural limitations of its application, constraints regarding its sequencing within a protocol, references, and information regarding ownership/authorship (Chorpita Daleiden, & Weisz, 2005b). For coordination modules, in addition to structuring meta-data similar to that of the content modules, the interface may define the manner for representing information, such as the sequencing of content modules, the decision points in sequencing, and the information sources used to guide decisions.

Returning to a broader level of discussion, it is important to emphasize that the goal of a common architecture is to encourage more cumulative growth of mental health treatment knowledge by allowing contributions from different designers to be combined in meaningful and effective ways and by providing a framework for collaboration and shared incentives for treatment developers. The potential advantages that modular treatment design frameworks offer in comparison to integral frameworks, particularly the efficiency-related advantages of reusability and ease of updating, reorganizing, and combining modules, seem to make modular frameworks well suited for this goal.

However, even with a modular framework, significant challenges would have to be overcome to create and maintain an open architecture that serves this goal. For example, the most common method of disseminating mental health treatment procedures to practitioners remains published books and manuals (unfortunately, a major incentive for treatment developers). These are by nature more challenging to update and/or aggregate. At present, no clear standard exists for how to codify treatment procedures efficiently that allows for incremental updates as well as multiauthor collaboration.

As noted earlier, shifting the field's research emphasis from individual innovation to cooperation and collaboration will require significant change to incentive structures. Within academic research institutions, increasing recognition would need to be given for collaboration and work supporting cumulative growth. Encouragement of collaboration through research networks would require some shift in funding priorities from government agencies and private foundations. Similarly, for common architectures to flourish, grant-funding priorities would need to emphasize projects that are compatible with a consensually defined common set of standards. Achieving consensus on such a standard would be a great challenge. A standard could be imposed in a "top-down" manner via government intervention or via the recommendation of a consortium of relevant stakeholders (similar to the W3C described earlier). Alternately, a standard could evolve in a "bottom-up" manner via demand from mental health provider organizations for treatments compatible with their existing investments in staff training, instrumentation, and technology.

Problem 2: Scaling for Implementation

Aside from problems that stem from research principles and policies that continue to privilege specialization and individualism over coordinated standards, an entirely separate problem remains regarding the lack of a dedicated product dissemination network in mental health.

As discussed in the introduction, nearly every major national report or action agenda on mental health in the past 10 years has emphasized that promising treatments tested by science need to be made more available. Although federal agencies are now beginning to direct resources toward research on implementation and dissemination strategies (NIMH, 2008), the field is still in the early stages of gathering knowledge regarding the challenges involved in bringing research-based treatments to communities. A major open question, then, is how to scale practices effectively from the research level to the national level (see Fixsen, Naoom, Blase, Friedman, & Wallace, 2005).

Before considering how to guide policy to encourage scaling practices for implementation, it is valuable to consider the ways in which practices are scaled in the current mental health landscape. The most common paradigm for treatment production and scaling in recent years centers around manual publication. The routine chain of steps and corresponding incentives involved in dissemination involve the development and testing of a treatment in an academic research laboratory, often utilizing public funding via granting agencies. Incentives for this work exist for the academic investigator who develops the treatment and conducts the research. A second step is for the successfully tested treatment to be published as a manual, then distributed and promoted via existing channels (e.g., stocking on bookstore shelves and promotion at research conferences and via mailings). The incentive for this step is profit from sales for both the publishing house and the treatment manual's author(s).

In many cases, the current chain breaks down at this second step. To begin with, provider concerns about treatment manuals (e.g., Addis, Wade, & Hatgis, 1999) may be a disincentive to learning new treatments through this medium. Further, most treatment developers acknowledge that the purchase and application of a treatment manual is insufficient for one to learn a new practice (e.g., Henggeler & Schoenwald, 2002), and most research on adult learning demonstrates the importance of coaching and supervision/feedback for new practices to take hold. Thus, the end-product of much federally sponsored research designed to improve the quality of mental health services ends up on clinicians' bookshelves (or worse, unsold in bookstores), and rarely makes its way to affecting the lives of mental health consumers.

In places where exceptions exist, it is often through highly entrepreneurial and ambitious efforts on the part of developers who have successfully commercialized their approaches, despite a lack of policy-based incentives for doing so. Multisystemic therapy (MST; Henggeler, Schoenwald, Borduin, Rowland, & Cunningham, 1998) is perhaps the strongest example of successful diffusion for an evidence-based treatment (Drake, Skinner, & Goldman, 2008). Multisystemic therapy is a family-based treatment for youths with severe antisocial and other clinical problems, delivered in the home and community. First developed and evaluated around 1990, MST has spread to currently serve 16,000 families a year in 32 states and 10 countries (Drake, et al., 2008). This scaling success has been achieved in part via the creation of a technology transfer organization, MST Services, Inc., which is affiliated with the treatment's university research center of origin. MST Services, Inc. has established many high-fidelity implementation sites by engaging in a long list of implementation activities, including site assessment, orientation training at a central location, weekly telephone consultation and quarterly booster trainings, evaluation of monthly adherence data, and support with both administrative and larger system issues, such as interagency collaboration (Schoenwald, Brown, & Henggeler, 2000).

This success in producing numerous high-fidelity implementation sites provides a valuable example. However, it is important also to note that, despite this success, after nearly two decades, MST adoption remains small in relation to need. Drake and colleagues (Drake et al., 2008) identify both financial and system compatibility barriers to MST's greater diffusion. Regarding financial barriers, the cost of training and financing the intervention are formidable. Although MST has been associated with overall cost savings, incentives may encourage agencies to shift relevant youth to others' budgets rather than serving as an authority for these difficult cases.

Regarding system compatibility barriers, Drake and colleagues note that MST imposes strong requirements for new skills and business practices, and may present a real threat to existing programs and systems of care. Additionally, as Henggeler and Schoenwald (2002) indicate, a large set of problematic contingencies act on providers of care at the practitioner, organizational, and community levels. Examples include productivity measures based primarily upon hours of face-to-face therapist–client contact, and reimbursement mechanisms favoring group and facility-based treatment over individualized evidence-based and intensive community-based treatments. These forces limit the range of sites that can be considered for MST implementation without major structural changes.

A critical aspect to highlight from the example of MST is that a great deal of effort, resourcefulness, and ingenuity was required to conceive of and build its complex implementation organization. MST Services, Inc. states that this effort was undertaken when "the burden of disseminating the MST model to interested communities began to have a detrimental impact on the research productivity" (MST Services Inc., 2008). The MST research team engineered a way to transform this burden into a successful implementation arm dedicated to the intricacies of the technology transfer process. However, in the face of similarly burdensome obstacles to dissemination and implementation, many treatment research teams have instead fallen back on academic travel-and-train approaches, with insufficient time and personnel resources to have a truly large or lasting impact—even with treatments that are quite promising and likely to serve the mission of increased service reliability. There are many understandable reasons for such a choice. Indeed, the incentive structures discussed earlier pressure researchers to pursue specialization, and efforts directed at implementation are outside most treatment researcher's area of expertise. However, the need for the invention of MST's implementation arm should also draw attention to the absence of an existing structure for scaling many effective treatments for other populations.

Although both state and federal infrastructure exists to support treatment developers in dissemination and implementation (e.g., Substance Abuse and Mental Health Services Administration and the California Institute for Mental Health), such mechanisms have not entirely addressed the training workforce problems, instead choosing to promote and support those approaches that have independently developed training divisions. These groups must "reinvent the wheel" to build a dissemination solution. The absence of a dedicated workforce for dissemination is exemplified by EBP's most widely researched treatment modality, cognitive behavioral therapy (CBT). No authoritative large-scale resource exists to service institutions that want to train their staff to provide adult CBT. One notable resource, the Beck Institute, provides workshops and year-long programs for therapists and supervisors, and features training from one of CBT's founding figures, Aaron T. Beck. However, like other existing training programs, the Beck Institute can serve only a small population.

For evidence-based treatments to become widely available, the task of dissemination and implementation will have to be transformed from a treatment-developer's burden to a sophisticated enterprise, leveraging broad networks of knowledge and support. Ways to approach this goal are explored below.

Potential Solutions: Dialogue on a "Practice-Centered" Approach, Implementation Workforce, and Economic Incentives

Summarizing the problem just described, the current paradigm for dissemination of high-quality treatments represents a broken chain, terminating at the link of manual publication. Few structures or support systems exist to provide scaffolding for dissemination and implementation efforts. Instead, treatment producers seeking to reach communities must reinvent the wheel, undertaking major efforts outside their areas of expertise. Few have succeeded in this difficult task.

Solutions to such problems require a shift in policy, from emphasizing development of quality treatments, as noted earlier, to installing and implementing them in a sustainable manner. Such a shift has significant implications for the culture of training and service delivery. For example, Fixsen et al. (2005) characterize the status quo in mental health as being "practitioner-centered" as opposed to "practice-centered." By that, they mean that the services available to consumers are largely a function of each individual provider's unique training history and experiences. By contrast, Fixsen et al. describe a "program-centered" or "practice-centered" approach as one that involves systems characterized by well-defined practices, theory, and values, in which practitioners are participants. In the practice-centered approach, it is the agencies and systems that define and sustain what services are delivered, rather than the sum of individual practitioners. Thus, the system defines the standard of care, and the practitioner is hired to participate as an agent in the delivery of that care.

Within psychology, this is a radical shift in philosophy within graduate training and continuing education programs, which implicitly position practitioners to be individualist-experts rather than agents of a larger professional system. Although the Individual-Expert Model has served the field and the public well for the past 50 years, the field has changed in terms of the availability of mature, integrated evidence-based service programs. In light of these new developments, the models that characterize many of the field's best training programs now may overemphasize the role of clinician as developer and tester (e.g., the Scientist-Practitioner Model). Given the developing stock of robust, high-quality treatments, at least an equal emphasis may be needed to prepare psychologists to understand better the implementation processes and clinical management structures of common EBPs. The workforce demands of the future are more likely to require individuals who can participate in delivering, training, evaluating, and sustaining practice models that are already highly developed. Given how the field has evolved, federally sponsored agendas should be developed to explore and define training models that are more conducive to the changing ecology of mental health service delivery, much in the way the Scientist-Practitioner Model was established and then promoted in the mid 20th century.

Aside from the need to address problems with an increasingly outmoded culture of professional training, there is an even greater need to develop an implementation industry in its own right. Making high-quality, evidence-based treatments widely available will require the creation of a support system. Addressing this very topic, Fixsen et al. (2005) drew a striking analogy in the area of computer science. As hardware and software continued to develop and improve in the computer industry, government and businesses began to adopt particular platforms, invest in refinements and improvements, and staff a workforce for maintaining and sustaining such platforms. It is now standard practice for government agencies and all but the smallest businesses to have information technology (IT) departments or divisions, which are dedicated to the continual upgrading, refinement, and problem-free operation of the latest technologies. This professional architecture is largely absent from mental health services, with the majority of innovation occurring de facto due to the often incidental hiring of new staff into leadership or supervisor/trainer roles. Simply put, there needs to be a dedicated arm of the workforce—whether seated in government, third-party payers, or service agencies—that plays the innovation and sustainability function analogous to IT departments in most industries. The "software" of mental health services, its evidence-based practices and programs, has matured to a point similar to where operating systems, word processing, and statistical spreadsheet software were in the late 1980s.

This raises the question of where an implementation and maintenance workforce will come from, and what precise form it will take. Indeed, in much the same way that the IT support industry has developed a diversified and robust career trajectory for computer science majors, such a pathway will need to come into better focus in mental health. The current state of affairs is that such responsibilities for implementation and maintenance continue to fall to the treatment developer. That is, the largest and most successful evidence-based programs have developed implementation arms to their research and development programs. Such a strategy may ultimately run up against issues of scale, and is analogous to having a software developer such as Microsoft handling the installation of its own software and the management of local technical support. In the ideal world, the highest-quality practices would be available on a scale far too great for developers to play a significant role. It is plausible that no treatment developer currently has the capacity to initiate and staff a national implementation agenda for its programs, let alone to make sense of how those programs will mesh with other programs being adopted (as reviewed earlier). A whole new industry is needed to implement and coordinate the massive-scale implementation efforts needed to close the gap between science and practice.

Some early indications of such independent implementation structures have emerged, although it remains to be seen what will define an industry standard. For example, California has had a government-sponsored structure in place for 16 years—the California Institute of Mental Health (CIMH)—dedicated to promoting excellence and innovation in the state's mental health services. In 2001, the CIMH began efforts to introduce EBPs into the state system. The Institute has recently established a development model, the Community Development Team Model (Sosna & Marsenich, 2006), that established a statewide structure with the aims of providing information on EBPs, providing technical assistance to agencies implementing those practices, consulting directly with developers on best strategies for dissemination and innovation efforts, supporting social networks for continued communication about practices, and creating mechanisms for sustainability of adopted practices. A major benefit of this approach is that it houses much of the responsibility for implementation within a single organization, rather than with developers whose focus may be on treatment innovation, research, and evaluation, or with providers whose focus is first and foremost on service delivery. Many other initiatives exist across the nation, with each taking a somewhat different shape. For example, Ohio has established a Center for Evidence Based Practices within Case Western Reserve University, charged with fostering implementation of evidence-based approaches, whereas New York's Office of Mental Health and Hawaii's Department of Health, for example, have government-driven initiatives that leverage local university partnerships. Other models continue to emerge, but the larger message with respect to policy is that a national dialogue has come due on which of these structures are proving to be most useful, a dialogue that should include input from researchers and experts in system change and organizational innovation, both in mental health and in other fields.

Finally, there is the issue of incentives. Profitability is thus often an engine for overcoming informational barriers through advertisements and other promotional activities. Drake and colleagues (2008) cite the example of naltrexone, a drug used in the treatment of alcoholism, whose story demonstrates a failure of diffusion in the absence of profitability. This drug is available in generic preparations and thus incentives for marketing are absent. Despite efficacy having been demonstrated in 29 placebo-control trials (Pettinati et al., 2006), and over a million Americans receiving treatment for alcoholism in medical care settings, the average number of naltrexone prescriptions per month was 14,000. Drake and colleagues (2008) point out that the lure of profitability can also lead to problematic wide adoption in the absence of good evidence, as in the case of second-generation antipsychotic medications for schizophrenia. Prior to the availability of well-designed trials to compare the second-generation antipsychotics to the first-generation medications, the pharmaceutical industry convinced government agencies to pay for these drugs at the expense of diminished funding for evidenced-based services such as housing programs. When evidence matured, the new second-generations medications were found to be no more effective than the older antipsychotics (Lieberman et al., 2006). Thus, incentives play an important role in determining what services reach the consumer. An open dialogue regarding these issues is difficult, given that profitability and economic incentives are somewhat taboo topics within academic mental health, and yet a new paradigm needs to emerge that supplants or extends the current approaches of (a) publication of book-length treatment manuals in exchange for royalties, (b) time-limited government sponsorship of isolated dissemination efforts, or (c) university clinical laboratories acting as dissemination agents. Again, it is not clear what shape that new paradigm will take, but it is clear that a nationally sponsored dialogue on the issue is overdue.

Conclusion

The long history of mental health policy in the United States has principally served the issues of availability, access, and parity of mental health services, with an increasing focus on the real-life outcomes that matter to consumers and structures of delivery that reflect the values of community- and family-centered approaches. While dealing with the questions of where, to whom, and how much, mental health policy has yet to play the same significant role with respect to the question "of what quality?" This relative neglect is an understandable consequence of the still very recent EBP revolution and its implication for service quality. This revolution is our generation's policy battle, just as the creation of asylums for the indigent and mentally ill was in the late 1800s and just as deinstitutionalization was in the mid-1900s. The complexity of leveraging science to optimizing or even just improve service has proven to be substantial,

and we inherit training, service delivery, insurance, and government structures that were not originally developed with these new aims in mind. We are fortunate that such a problem confronts the field—there are now more high-quality, evidence-based practices and programs than can be successfully integrated and for which there is a workforce to implement. The pace of progress in treatment development and refinement is likely only to increase, so it is time to turn our attention nationally to how best to take advantage of such bounty, especially now when most of those quality programs and practices still never make it to the consumer.

References

Addis, M. E., & Krasnow, A. D. (2000). A national survey of practicing psychologists' attitudes toward psychotherapy treatment manuals. *Journal of Consulting and Clinical Psychology, 68*, 331–339.

Addis, M. E., Wade, W. A., & Hatgis, C. (1999). Barriers to dissemination of evidence-based practices: Addressing practitioners' concerns about manual-based psychotherapies. *Clinical Psychology: Science and Practice, 6*(4), 430–430.

ADL. (2003). ADL SCORM Version 1.3 application profile. Advanced distributed learning co-laboratories. Retrieved in 2005 from: www.adlnet.org [2003, 11-05-03]

Barrett, P. M., Dadds, M. R., & Rapee, R. M. (1991). *The coping koala: Treatment manual*. Unpublished manuscript, The University of Queensland, Queensland, Australia.

Barrington, J., Prior, M., Richardson, M., & Allen, K. (2005). Effectiveness of CBT versus standard treatment for childhood anxiety disorders in a community clinic setting. *Behaviour Change, 22*, 29–43.

Bickman, L., Guthrie, P. R., Foster, E. M., Lambert, E. W., Summerfelt, W. T., Breda, C. S., Heflinger, C. A. (1995). *Evaluating managed mental health services: The Fort Bragg experiment*. New York: Plenum Press.

Borntrager, C. F., Chorpita, B. F., Higa-McMillan, C., & Weisz, J. R. (2009). Provider attitudes toward evidence-based practices: Are the concerns with the evidence or with the manuals? *Psychiatric Services, 60*(5), 677–681.

Branscomb, L. M., & Kahin, B. (1995). Standards processes and objectives for the national information infrastructure. In B. Kahin & J. Abbate (Eds.), *Standards policy for information infrastructure* (pp. 3–31). Cambridge, MA: MIT Press.

Chambless, D. L., & Hollon, S. D. (1998). Defining empirically supported therapies. *Journal of Consulting and Clinical Psychology, 66*, 7–18.

Chambless, D. L., Baker, M. J., Baucom, D. H., Beutler, L. E., Calhoun, K. S., Crits-Christoph, P., et al. (1998). Update on empirically validated therapies II. *The Clinical Psychologist, 51*, 3–16.

Chambless, D. L., Sanderson, W. C., Shoham, V., Johnson, S. B., Pope, K. S., Crits-Christoph, P., et al. (1996). An update on empirically validated therapies. *The Clinical Psychologist, 49*, 5–18.

Chorpita, B. F., Yim, L. M., Donkervoet, J. C., Arensdorf, A., Amundsen, M. J., McGee, C., et al. (2002). Toward large-scale implementation of empirically supported treatments for children: A review and observations by the Hawaii

Empirical Basis to Services Task Force. *Clinical Psychology: Science and Practice, 9,* 165–190.

Chorpita, B. F., & Daleiden, E. L. (2009). Mapping evidence-based treatments for children and adolescents: Application of the distillation and matching model to 615 treatments from 322 randomized trials. *Journal of Consulting and Clinical Psychology, 77*(3), 566–579.

Chorpita, B. F., Daleiden, E., & Weisz, J. R. (2005a). Identifying and selecting the common elements of evidence based interventions: A distillation and matching model. *Mental Health Services Research, 7,* 5–20.

Chorpita, B. F., Daleiden, E. L., & Weisz, J. R. (2005b). Modularity in the design and application of therapeutic interventions. *Applied and Preventive Psychology, 11,* 141–156.

Drake, R., Skinner, J., & Goldman, H. H. (2008). What explains the diffusion of treatments for mental illness? *The American Journal of Psychiatry, 165*(11), 1385–1392.

Elliott, R. (Ed.). (1998). The empirically supported treatments controversy [special section]. *Psychotherapy Research, 8,* 115–170.

Glass, C. R., & Arnkoff, D. B. (1996). Psychotherapy integration and empirically validated treatments: Introduction to the special series. *Journal of Psychotherapy Integration, 6*(3), 183–189.

Felix, R. H. (1949). Mental disorders as a public health problem. *American Journal of Psychiatry, 106,* 401–406.

Fixsen, D. L., Naoom, S. F., Blase, K. A., Friedman, R. M., & Wallace, F. (2005). *Implementation research: A synthesis of the literature.* Tampa, FL: University of South Florida, Louis de la Parte Florida Mental Health Institute, The National Implementation Research Network.

Henggeler, S. W. & Schoenwald, S. K. (2002). Treatment manuals: Necessary, but far from sufficient. *Clinical Psychology: Science and Practice, 9,* 419–420.

Henggeler, S. W., Schoenwald, S. K., Borduin, C. M., Rowland, M. D., & Cunningham, P. B. (1998). *Multisystemic treatment for antisocial behavior in children and adolescents.* New York: Guilford Press.

Institute of Medicine. (2001). *Crossing the quality chasm: A new health system for the 21st century.* Washington, DC: National Academy Press.

Integrated Psychotherapy Consortium. (2005). Project Liberty Enhanced Services Program: Anxiety symptoms intervention manual. New York: State Office of Mental Health.

Kazdin, A. E. (Ed.). (1996). Validated treatments: Multiple perspectives and issues [special section]. *Clinical Psychology: Science and Practice, 3,* 216–267.

Kazdin, A. E. (Ed.). (1998). Treatment manuals in clinical practice [special section]. *Clinical Psychology: Science and Practice, 5,* 361–407.

Kendall, P. C. (1999). Clinical significance [special section]. *Journal of Consulting and Clinical Psychology, 67,* 283–339.

Kendall, P. C., Chambless, D. L. (Eds.). (1998). Empirically supported psychological therapies [special section]. *Journal of Consulting and Clinical Psychology, 66,* 3–167.

Kendall, P. C., Kane, M., Howard, B., & Siqueland, L. (1990). *Cognitive-behavioral therapy for anxious children: Treatment manual.* Ardmore, PA: Workbook Publishers.

Lieberman, J. A., Stroup, T. S., McEvoy, J. P., Swartz, M. S., Rosenheck, R. A., Perkins, D. O., et al. (2006). Effectiveness of antipsychotic drugs in patients with chronic schizophrenia. *New England Journal of Medicine, 353,* 1209–1223.

Lonigan, C. J., Elbert, J. C., & Bennett Johnson, S. (1998). Empirically supported psychosocial interventions for children: An overview. *Journal of Clinical Child Psychology, 27,* 138–145.

Masia-Warner, C., Klein, R. G., Dent, H. C., Fisher, P. H., Alvir, J., et al. (2005). School-based intervention for adolescents with social anxiety disorder: Results of a controlled study. *Journal of Abnormal Child Psychology, 33,* 707–722.

Moher, D., Schultz, K. F., & Altman, D. (2001). The CONSORT statement: Revised recommendations for improving the quality of reports of parallel-group randomized trials. *JAMA, 285,* 1987–1991.

MST Services, Inc. (2008). *Organizational Biography.* Retrieved December 10, 2008, from http://www.mstservices.com/organizational_biography.php

Nathan, P. E., & Gorman, J. M. (Eds.). (1998). *A guide to treatments that work.* New York: Oxford University Press.

Nathan, P. E., Stuart, S. P., & Dolan, S. L. (2000). Research on psychotherapy efficacy and effectiveness: Between Scylla and Charybdis? *Psychological Bulletin, 126,* 964–981.

National Advisory Mental Health Council Workgroup on Child and Adolescent Mental Health Intervention Development and Deployment. (2001). *Blueprint for change: Research on child and adolescent mental health.* Washington, DC: Author.

National Advisory Mental Health Council Workgroup on Services Research and Clinical Epidemiology. (2006). *The road ahead: Research partnerships to transform services.* Washington, DC: Author.

National Institute of Mental Health. (1962). *Report of the task force on the status of state mental hospitals in the United States.* Bethesda, MD: Author.

National Institute of Mental Health. (2008). *National Institute of Mental Health strategic plan.* Bethesda: MD: Author.

Nelson, T. D., & Steele, R. G. (2007). Predictors of practitioner self-reported use of evidence-based practices: Practitioner training, clinical setting, and attitudes toward research. *Administration and Policy in Mental Health and Mental Health Services Research, 34*(4), 319–319.

Norcross, J. C., Beutler, L. E., & Levant, R. F. (2006). *Evidence-based practices in mental health: Debate and dialogue on the fundamental questions.* Washington, DC: American Psychological Association.

Persons, J. B. (1991). Psychotherapy outcome studies do not accurately represent current models of psychotherapy: A proposed remedy. *American Psychologist, 46,* 99–106.

Pettinati, H. M., O'Brien, C. P., Rabinowitz, A. R., Wortman, S. M., Oslin, D. W., Kampman, K. M., & Dackis, C. A. (2006). The status of naltrexone in the treatment of alcohol dependence: specific effects on heavy drinking, *Journal of Clinical Psychopharmacology, 26,* 610–625.

Hogan, M. (2003). The President's New Freedom Commission: Recommendations to transform mental health care in America. *Psychiatric Services, 54*(11), 1467–1474.

Schoenwald, S. K., Brown, T. L., & Henggeler, S. W. (2000). Inside multisystemic therapy: Therapist, supervisory, and program practices. *Journal of Emotional and Behavioral Disorders, 8*(2), 113–127.

Silverman, W. K., Hinshaw, S. P. (2008). The second special issue on evidence-based psychosocial treatments for children and adolescents: A 10-year update. *Journal of Clinical Child and Adolescent Psychology. Special Issue: Evidence-based psychosocial treatments for children and adolescents: A ten year update, 37,* 1–7.

Sosna, T., & Marsenich, L. (2006). Community development team model: Supporting the model adherent implementation of programs and practices. Retrieved from http://www.cimh. org/downloads/CDT_report.pdf.

Substance Abuse and Mental Health Services Administration. (2006). *From exclusion to belonging: Transforming mental health care in America*. Rockville, MD: Author.

Substance Abuse and Mental Health Services Administration. (2008). National registry of effective programs and practices. Available on the internet at: http://nrepp.samhsa.gov/.

Task Force on Promotion and Dissemination of Psychological Procedures, Division of Clinical Psychology, American Psychological Association. (1995). Training in and dissemination of empirically validated psychological treatments: Report and recommendations. *The Clinical Psychologist, 48*, 3–23.

Task Force on Psychological Intervention Guidelines, American Psychological Association. (1995). *Template for developing guidelines: Interventions for mental disorders and psychosocial aspects of physical disorders*. Washington, DC: American Psychological Association.

U.S. Department of Health and Human Services. (1999). *Mental health: A report of the surgeon general*. Rockville, MD: U.S. Department of Health and Human Services, Substance Abuse and Mental Health Services Administration, Center for Mental Health Services, National Institutes of Health, National Institute of Mental Health.

VandenBos, G. R., (Ed.). (1996). Outcome assessment of psychotherapy [special issue]. *American Psychologist, 51*, 1005–1006.

Weisz, J. R., Hawley, K. M., Pilkonis, P. A., Woody, S. R., & Follette W. C. (2000). Stressing the (other) three Rs in the search for empirically supported treatments: Review procedures, research quality, relevance to practice and the public interest. *Clinical Psychology: Science and Practice, 7*, 243–258.

Westen, D., Novotny, C. M., Thompson-Brenner, H. (2004). The empirical status of empirically supported psychotherapies: Assumptions, findings, and reporting in controlled clinical trials. *Psychological Bulletin, 130*, 631–663.

Wolpe, J. (1989). The derailment of behavior therapy: A tale of conceptual misdirection. *Journal of Behaviour Therapy and Experimental Psychiatry, 20*, 3–15.

World Wide Web Consortium. (2008). About the World Wide Web Consortium. Retrieved December 10, 2008, from http://www.w3.org/Consortium/

PART 3

Unified and
Transdiagnostic
Conceptions and
Treatments for
Psychopathology and
Pathophysiology

Interviewing and Case Formulation

Naomi Koerner, Heather K. Hood, *and* Martin M. Antony

Abstract

The main objective of this chapter is to provide an overview of clinical interviewing. Although clinical interviewing is often referred to as an art (Shea, 2007), the information in this chapter highlights the science of clinical interviewing as well. The chapter opens with a discussion of the general structure and content of clinical interviews that are typically conducted in mental health contexts. The reader is introduced to a variety of interviews that are used in the assessment of Axis I and Axis II conditions, including their psychometric properties; guidelines for the assessment of suicidality are also presented. This is followed by an overview of interviewing skills. Specifically discussed are ways in which information processing limitations, verbal and nonverbal cues, and style of questions can influence the clinical interview. We then turn to a discussion of case formulation, a core component of the clinical interview. Empirical research on the impact of training on quality of case conceptualization and on the association between case formulation and treatment outcome is summarized. The chapter closes with a brief overview of issues that may arise when interviewing certain populations, in particular, couples, individuals from diverse populations, and young individuals.

Keywords: Case formulation, clinical interviewing, couples, diagnostic interviews, diverse populations, interviewing skills, suicide risk assessment, young clients

The Clinical Interview: An Introduction

The clinical interview is one of the most essential elements of psychological care. Although it is just one component of a comprehensive assessment, it is often the first opportunity for client contact and is the foundation for subsequent treatment. Unlike many other assessment tools, the interview allows the clinician to explore the idiographic or unique nature of an individual's experience, including any or all of the following: symptoms; observable behavioral features; degree of distress and functional impairment; development and course of the problem; relevant personal and family history; and goals for treatment. The richness of data collected may aid in matching the client to treatment, increasing the likelihood that the client will receive the most effective intervention (Yates & Taub, 2003). Sommers-Flanagan and Sommers-Flanagan

(2009) suggest that it is "ill-advised, unprofessional, and potentially dangerous" (p. 7) to initiate treatment without first conducting a suitable assessment. In fact, research suggests that the clinical interview itself may confer some psychological benefits to the client (Finn & Tonsager, 1997).

The prominent role of clinical interviewing in the management of psychological distress highlights the need for an understanding of the nature of the clinical interview. The interview is multidimensional in nature, integrating intrapersonal, interpersonal, and theoretical factors. One's clinical judgment and, therefore, the validity of the clinical interview can be enhanced by an awareness of intrapersonal factors including, but not limited to, personal biases, overconfidence in one's diagnosis, and tendency to search for information that confirms this diagnosis

(Arkes, 1981). Concurrently, the clinician must be mindful of the interpersonal dynamic with the client. Establishing good rapport and obtaining accurate information in part depends on the client's feeling that the information conveyed is done so in an atmosphere of confidentiality, understanding, and respect (Kremer & Gesten, 1998; Turner, Hersen, & Heiser, 2003). Finally, an accurate assessment requires the clinician to be knowledgeable about psychopathology and the psychological conditions being assessed. Balancing these factors, while remaining aware of the purpose of the interview, requires a high degree of skill, knowledge, and training on the part of the clinician.

The clinical interview may be a diagnostic, risk-management, treatment, or research tool, or any combination thereof. Thus, the purpose of the interview is highly dependent on the setting in which it occurs. The clinical interview in a hospital emergency room or crisis center will look much different than one conducted in an outpatient clinic or private practice. In emergency situations, the priority is often to quickly assess the risk of violence or suicide, perhaps with the goal of making a determination about the need for hospitalization or immediate medical intervention, rather than a precise diagnosis. Conversely, clients presenting to an outpatient treatment and research clinic often receive a comprehensive assessment, in which the clinical interview may be accompanied by self-report questionnaires, monitoring diaries, behavioral assessments, and physiological measures (Antony & Rowa, 2005). Interviews for the purposes of long-term therapy planning may span several sessions aimed at developing the therapeutic relationship and obtaining a detailed personal history and thorough understanding of the client's presenting problems. Although the precise purpose of the clinical interview will depend on the setting in which it is conducted, the goal is always to develop a greater understanding of the client's experience and level of psychological functioning.

The purpose of the interview and the setting in which it is conducted largely determine the type of interview to be used. Unstructured interviews, also referred to as traditional interviews, engage clients in a flexible manner. The course of the interview is variable; the questions are selected entirely at the discretion of the clinician, who is guided by the responses of the client to explore areas of interest and determine a diagnosis (Summerfeldt & Antony, 2002). This approach has been credited with increasing rapport with the client, enabling quick decision-making in crisis situations, and validating the client's

experience (Groth-Marnat, 2003). However, the lack of standardization has been criticized for compromising reliability and validity. Research has shown that inter-rater reliability is low with unstructured interviews; that is, two clinicians with similar training often assign different diagnoses (Ward, Beck, Mendelson, Mock, & Erbaugh, 1962). The phrasing, focus, and sequencing of questions affect a client's interpretation and response, introducing a considerable amount of variance into the process (Rogers, 2001; Ward et al., 1962). Further, although the unstructured interview explores some symptoms in depth, it often lacks breadth of questioning, resulting in an increased risk of missed diagnoses (Rogers, 2001; Zimmerman & Mattia, 1999a).

The structured interview, on the other hand, is a systematic approach to interviewing that uses standardized questions and responses options. This format resolves many of the psychometric limitations of unstructured interviews, and it has been argued that it improves the diagnostic utility of the clinical interview (Rogers, 2001). For example, Ruegg, Ekstrom, Evans, and Golden (1990) found that the use of structured mental status exams resulted in higher-quality and more comprehensive assessments compared to the unstructured format.

Structured clinical interviews are often organized according to symptom clusters, allowing the clinician to quickly screen for the presence or absence of symptoms or disorders, and to focus the interview on specific areas of interest (Summerfeldt & Antony, 2002). The efficiency of this method increases the breadth of the assessment, obtaining the most relevant information needed to make an accurate diagnosis in the least amount of time. Structured interviews also vary greatly in their degree of structure. In highly structured interviews, such as the *Diagnostic Interview Schedule* (DIS-IV; Robins, Cottler, Bucholz, & Compton, 1995), questions are read verbatim from the manual and responses are coded according to the available response options. The interviewer is not permitted to include follow-up questions, aside from those provided in the administration manual. Critics of structured interviews suggest that such a format may overlook the "idiosyncrasies and richness of the person" (Groth-Marnat, 2003, p. 77) and interfere with rapport; however, others argue that this may only be the case if the interviewer is unskilled in the administration of the test (Rogers, 2001).

As the name implies, semi-structured interviews are an amalgamation of traditional and structured interviews, capitalizing on the psychometric strengths of the structured format while maintaining the flexibility to include additional probes as necessary. Such interviews are common in research settings, and are becoming more common in clinical settings because of the quality of the information obtained (Summerfeldt & Antony, 2002). All means of interviewing have assets and limitations, and it is therefore unwise to dismiss out of hand any one format. The perception that one must choose between structured and unstructured formats represents a false dichotomy, or what Rogers (2001) refers to as the "either/or" fallacy. Structured and unstructured interviews provide useful information for an accurate assessment of the individual.

The clinical interview is critical to the mental health care process. It is multidimensional in nature and thus requires a high degree of skill and knowledge on the part of the clinician. The information provided in this chapter will aid clinicians in selecting the appropriate type of interview to meet their needs, using interview data for case formulation, exploring strategies and skills to enhance the clinical interview, and in discussing ethical and professional issues relevant to the interviewing process.

Overview of the Interview Structure

Although the format, content, and flow of the interview are determined by the type of interview, all clinical interviews share common elements. Variations in the structure of interviews have been proposed (e.g., Foley & Sharf, 1981; Shea, 1998), but there is general agreement that assessment sessions consist of an *opening*, *body*, and *closing*. Prior to the session, several preliminary steps set the stage for a successful interview.

Initial Steps

The assessment process begins at the moment of first contact with the client, often at the time of scheduling the appointment. Whether conducted by administrative personnel or by the individual carrying out the interview, this is the first step in developing rapport; therefore, it should be done in a professional and collaborative manner. Managing first impressions is critical at the beginning of the interview. As the clinician presents his or her credentials, it is an opportunity to establish authority, instill confidence, and set boundaries for the remainder of the session. This can be particularly challenging for clinicians-in-training. Generally, clinicians are advised to use their first and last name when introducing themselves and to follow this with a brief description of their credentials (e.g., "Hello, my

name is Pat Smith; I am a psychology intern here at Clinic X, and my supervisor is Dr. Brown, a licensed clinical psychologist"). Students are encouraged to present their credentials in a confident and straightforward manner; however, they should be careful not to overstate or misrepresent their qualifications, as this constitutes an ethical violation (Sommers-Flanagan & Sommers-Flanagan, 2009). Students should be direct and honest in their presentation of their experience and current status (e.g., "I am in my second year of a master's degree in clinical psychology and this is my second psychology placement"; "I am in the third year of a doctoral program in clinical psychology, and I am working here at Clinic X as part of my training").

Many clinicians in the early stages of their training may not be sure how to address their client. The most prudent approach is to address clients by their title and last name (as in, "Mr. Jones" or "Ms. Lee"), rather than addressing them immediately by their first name. Some clients may readily indicate that they would prefer to be called by their first name, while others may not. Clinicians can ask clients about their preferences if they are uncertain (e.g., "Would you prefer that I address you as Ms. Lee, or Sam?").

The physical space also contributes to a client's first impression of the upcoming session. Although the physical space will be determined in large part by the clinical setting, some features of the room may facilitate the interview process. At the very least, privacy is crucial, and interruptions should be avoided. This reaffirms the confidentiality of the procedure and increases client self-disclosure (Sommers-Flanagan & Sommers-Flanagan, 2009). In addition, the interviewer should have control of the environment, in order to establish professional boundaries, although the client should have minor choices such as seating arrangements (Sommers-Flanagan & Sommers-Flanagan, 2009). Some recommend a 90-to-120-degree angle seating arrangement (Sommers-Flanagan & Sommers-Flanagan, 2009), which allows for flexible eye contact for both parties. Others prefer a face-to-face arrangement for the intake interview, with a desk between the interviewer and client, thus differentiating an assessment from a therapy session.

Opening

The goals of the opening phase of the interview are to convey essential information (such as confidentiality), to obtain informed consent, to alleviate anxiety, to develop rapport, and to set the tone of the interview. Confidentiality is a right afforded to all clients as mandated by law, and clinicians are not permitted to disclose information obtained during the assessment without the client's consent. However, there are conditions under which the clinician is ethically and legally obligated to break confidentiality. The specific conditions are established by one's professional governing body (e.g., American Psychological Association [APA], 2002) and legislative guidelines. It is the responsibility of the interviewer to be familiar with these before initiating any dialogue with the client, and to convey this information at the outset of the assessment. In fact, an honest discussion of confidentiality may contribute to the validity of the assessment. Research indicates that clients are more likely to disclose personal and potentially critical diagnostic information when confidentiality, and its limits, are clear (Kremer & Gesten, 1998).

Informed consent refers to sufficient disclosure of information about the nature of the assessment so that a competent person can make a voluntary decision to continue (APA, 2002). This is frequently provided both orally and in writing, using clear and understandable language. Informed consent is not only mandatory, but also facilitates the interview process. Clients become actively engaged in the assessment because they are aware of what to expect, the potential risks and benefits, and they agree to accept shared liability and responsibility for the interview (Beahrs & Gutheil, 2001).

Moving from communicating standard information to discussing the client's presenting problems signals a transition to the information collection phase of the interview. Most interviews begin with an open-ended question and then proceed with more direct questions throughout the session to obtain targeted information. Often, the interviewer is interested in hearing, in the client's own words, what led him or her to seek treatment at that time (e.g., "Tell me what brings you to therapy at this time"; Sommers-Flanagan & Sommers-Flanagan, 2009, p. 155). This puts the client at ease, and allows the interviewer to make important behavioral observations, regarding such variables as the client's ability to organize his or her thoughts, tone of voice, energy level, body language, and interpersonal style (Sommers-Flanagan & Sommers-Flanagan, 2009). Although this may be done with varying degrees of formality depending on the type and structure of the interview, in essence, this portion sets the tone for the remainder of the assessment.

Body

The body of the interview is generally the most variable section, defined by the depth, breadth, and structure of the assessment. It is a process of information gathering, in which hypotheses are formed and refined, and a complete picture of the client is developed. The format of this section is based almost entirely on the type of interview conducted. Some interviews may cover a breadth of psychological disorders, whereas others will focus on a specific area of interest in some depth. For example, the *Structured Clinical Interview for DSM-IV* (SCID-IV; First, Spitzer, Gibbon, & Williams, 2007) is a comprehensive assessment of the most prevalent Axis I disorders, whereas the *Anxiety Disorders Interview Schedule for DSM-IV* (ADIS-IV; Brown, Di Nardo, & Barlow, 1994) assesses in depth the presence and severity of anxiety disorder symptoms, as well as disorders that often occur in the context of anxiety disorders. The body of the interview will also depend on the degree of structure. Structured interviews contain primarily closed questions with specified response options. On the other hand, unstructured interviews often allow the client to describe difficulties in his or her own words. Information regarding the body of the clinical interview is discussed for each interview reviewed later in this chapter.

Throughout the interview, the clinician should be aware of inconsistencies in reported symptoms and behavior. The implicit assumption is that the client and interviewer work together to obtain complete and accurate information. However, some clients may adopt response styles that interfere with this process. For example, a client may overendorse symptoms in an effort to "fake bad," as in malingering, or provide socially desirable responses in order to "fake good" (Rogers, 2001). Interpreting these inconsistencies may be more difficult with unstructured interviews, as they may be an artifact of the question form or sequence (Rogers); however, it is the task of the interviewer to resolve the discrepancies when making diagnostic conclusions and treatment recommendations. Several strategies may be useful, such as using counterbalanced and neutral questions, seeking corroborative data, and using clinical judgment to assess the plausibility of the client self-reports (Rogers, 2001).

Closing

At the end of the session, the interviewer should reserve time to summarize the main themes of the assessment, address any questions or concerns, and discuss the next steps. In most jurisdictions, communicating a diagnosis is considered a controlled act requiring a minimum level of professional competence; therefore, when summarizing and organizing reported symptoms, the interviewer should be mindful of relevant legal restrictions. Once the information has been summarized and presented to the client, the client should always have an opportunity to confirm the conclusions. Occasionally, the interviewer may recommend treating a different problem than the client wishes to focus on in treatment. Unless the client is at risk of endangering himself or herself, or someone else, the client is ultimately responsible for determining the course of treatment. Often, the clinician will provide some basic psychoeducation regarding the nature of the client's difficulties as well as treatment options. The interview typically concludes with a clear description of the next steps in the process, such as when and how results and recommendations will be communicated to both the referral source and the client, and resolution of payment, as established at the outset of the session.

Content of the Interview
Unstructured Clinical Interviews

Unstructured interviews are used to collect information about client problems and goals, background and personal history, symptoms, level of functioning, and behavioral observations. The significance of each piece of information is weighted by the referral question, and by the confidence that the clinician has in the information obtained. In a crisis mental health care setting, for instance, the interviewer may be particularly interested in behavioral observations, including the client's appearance and emotional state, such as signs of anxiety, agitation, frustration, or anger. Although these pieces of information are important in all assessments, other settings may focus more on other aspects of an individual's symptoms.

Time constraints, coupled with an open-ended question style, produces an interview focused on depth rather than breadth of diagnostic coverage. Although this remains one of the largest criticisms of unstructured interviews because of the potential for missed diagnoses (Zimmerman & Mattia, 1999a), they have also been credited with focusing on the client's primary concerns and thus enhancing rapport (Miller, 2003). The format of the interview is inherently structured to develop rapport.

Using open-ended questions early in the interview then transitioning to questions targeting specific symptoms encourages a feeling of being understood (Beutler & Groth-Marnat, 2005). Moving from less-sensitive to more difficult topics is useful, particularly for clients who are somewhat guarded or unsure of the interview procedure (Beutler & Groth-Marnat). Although the goal of the clinical interview is to obtain information necessary for diagnosis and treatment, a pragmatic yet empathic stance serves to bolster the validity of the assessment outcome.

Client Problems and Goals

The unstructured interview should begin by defining the client's presenting problems and goals. Allowing the client to describe, in his or her own words, what led him or her to seek treatment at that time orients the clinician to preliminary working hypotheses and suggests how to direct the remaining interview. Additional information is indirectly obtained regarding the client's emotional and cognitive state, degree of insight about one's symptoms, and motivation for treatment. Although some clients may have a high degree of insight into their symptoms and be able to articulate their concerns, others may benefit from a more facilitative approach on the part of the interviewer, using reflective listening and frequent paraphrasing. It is worth noting that many psychological terms have become colloquial, and may not carry the same meaning for a patient as a clinician. For example, many people describe experiencing a "depression," although this often refers to feelings of low mood and may not be accompanied by the additional symptom and duration criteria required for a diagnosis of major depressive disorder. Terms such as "paranoid," "obsession," "compulsion," and "psychotic," also tend to have different meanings when used colloquially versus the way they are defined by mental health professionals. An explorative dialogue is necessary to make a confident diagnosis.

It is useful to ask the client for a summary of his or her concerns at the beginning of the assessment. Most unstructured interviews are conducted in a 50–60-minute session, and a failure to be clear about the client's concerns at the outset could lead to unproductive lines of questioning and inefficient use of limited time. In addition, it may introduce threats to the therapeutic relationship if the clinician has failed to truly understand what the client has expressed.

Background and Historical Information

Obtaining a complete picture of the individual, including personal and family history, and the development and course of the problems is most easily and accurately accomplished in an unstructured interview than through any other means (Beutler & Groth-Marnat, 2005). Although the interview can only capture the person's functioning at a single moment in time, a thorough personal history collects information about the biological and psychosocial factors affecting the client's current condition. In some cases, establishing a long-standing pattern of behavior is essential for assigning a diagnosis that takes into account the timing of a problem. For example, a personality disorder diagnosis can only be made if symptoms are present beginning in adolescence or early adulthood (APA, 2000). Similarly, a diagnosis of dysthymic disorder can only be assigned after considering the temporal relationship between the symptoms of dysthymic mood and any past major depressive episodes that may have occurred (APA, 2000). Thus, the historical information takes on added significance for certain diagnostic categories.

Typically, information about the individual's social and family history, symptom onset and course, and treatment history are collected. Other common areas of inquiry include educational attainment, employment history, peer and romantic relationships, medical and health history, and patterns of alcohol and drug use. The extent of background information collected and the domains explored will depend on the purpose of the interview. For example, some crisis settings may focus on the course and treatment history of the presenting problem, whereas therapy settings may be more likely to collect a broader personal and family history. Understanding the onset and course of the presenting problem requires information about life events at the time of symptom onset, the frequency and duration of the symptoms, and how the symptoms have changed over time (Beutler & Groth-Marnat, 2005). The course of the disorder should be considered alongside the individual's family and social history, to identify possible contributing factors and consequences of the symptoms.

Treatment history and coping strategies (e.g., noting what has and has not provided symptom relief in the past), provide a clearer picture of the nature of the problem and the client's personality, and are useful in case formulation. Importantly, a pattern of excessive treatment-seeking may be indicative of a tendency toward dependence and low self-efficacy (Beutler & Groth-Marnat, 2005). On the other hand, success in previous treatment may suggest a high degree of motivation to obtain help for one's difficulties (Beutler & Groth-Marnat, 2005). A careful examination of precipitating factors and treatment outcome is recommended before current treatment recommendations are made.

Behavioral Observations

Behavioral observations are an important part of the clinical interview. During the clinical interview, assessors will typically take note of the client's appearance, behavior, mood and affect, motor activity, and quality of thought and speech. Such observations are made in an unobtrusive manner and provide important information over and above client self-reports. The client's verbal and nonverbal behavior during the assessment can provide corroborating information for reported symptoms, but may also alert the clinician to inconsistencies. For example, a client who reports being deeply depressed yet displays positive affect and normal motor activity may suggest the possibility of low insight or malingering.

The mental status examination (MSE) is a system by which clinicians can categorize their observations. The MSE is used primarily to make inferences about cognitive functioning. Generally, MSEs include the following categories of observations (Sommers-Flanagan & Sommers-Flanagan, 2009):

- Appearance (e.g., grooming, weight)
- Physical movements (e.g., avoidance of eye contact)
- Attitude toward the assessor (e.g., hostile, cooperative)
- Mood and affect (e.g., euphoric, irritable)
- Thought and speech (e.g., flight of ideas, tangential speech)
- Delusions and hallucinations
- Orientation and consciousness (i.e., awareness of who one is, where one is, and what day it is)
- Memory and intelligence (e.g., memory for facts, problem-solving ability)
- Reliability (e.g., vague self-report; inconsistency across multiple assessments), judgment (e.g., impulsive decision-making), and insight (e.g., belief that one's psychological problems are due exclusively to a medical problem)

Behavioral observations are subjective. The clinician is comparing the client's presentation to a prototype that has been developed through clinical experience to determine if the presentation deviates from the "norm." Therefore, when making diagnostic determinations or reporting to a referral source, specific examples of behavioral observations are critical to support one's clinical impressions. These important pieces of information are also useful for determining suitability for particular treatment modalities. Inappropriate affect may disrupt the group dynamic in group therapy, and a patient who demonstrates low cognitive abilities may not benefit fully from certain types of therapy (Mohlman & Gorman, 2005; Sams, Collins, & Reynolds, 2006).

Summary

The unstructured interview has several advantages. It provides maximum flexibility for the clinician to formulate questions, develop and test hypotheses, and to establish a diagnosis. One of the primary strengths of this format is that the majority of questions are tailored to the client's presenting problems, creating a more conversational flow, which has been credited with enhancing rapport (Miller, 2003). In addition, administration time is typically shorter than for more structured formats, making unstructured interviews a potentially efficient tool in the assessment process.

Despite these benefits, unstructured interviews have been subject to criticism, primarily because of their inability to produce consistent and accurate diagnoses. The psychometric properties of unstructured interviews are generally unsatisfactory. Research has found that traditional interviews are able to adequately and consistently detect the presence of clinically significant symptoms only about half of the time (Beck, Ward, Mendelson, Mock, & Erbaugh, 1962; Tiemens, VonKorff, & Linn, 1999). Validity and reliability are complicated by the reliance on patient reports and clinician interpretation. There is often little agreement between patient questionnaire data and the information obtained in the interview (Beutler & Groth-Marnat, 2005). In addition, clinical judgment is fallible, subject to subtle and unintentional biases that may color the interview process (Arkes, 1981; Garb, 1998). This may account for the low inter-rater reliability, as two similarly trained clinicians frequently reach different conclusions (Ward et al., 1962).

An extensive literature has explored the phenomenon of underdiagnosis with traditional interviews, resulting in missed diagnoses and potentially inappropriate treatment recommendations (Tiemens, VonKorff, & Linn, 1999; Zimmerman & Mattia, 1999a). Clinicians are often more aware of and
comfortable assessing for disorders frequently seen in clinical practice, thus underdiagnosing uncommon disorders (Zimmerman & Mattia, 1999a). Further, it is not uncommon for clinicians to stop after reaching the first diagnosis, thus missing potential comorbidity (Rogers, 2003). This tendency to seek diagnostic information that confirms one's initial clinical impressions is minimized with structured interviews because symptoms are assessed for a range of psychological disorders. It is therefore recommended that unstructured interviews be used to screen clients for subsequent, more thorough, assessments should they be warranted, and to obtain information to supplement and corroborate that obtained from other sources, such as self-report measures, structured interviews, and other informants.

Structured and Semi-Structured Interviews for Assessment of Axis I Disorders
Overview of Structured and Semi-Structured Interviews

Over the years, changes in diagnostic nomenclature have served to reduce the subjectivity of unstructured assessments by incorporating more specific and reliable diagnostic criteria (Rogers, 2001). Imposing a greater degree of structure has naturally led to the development of structured interview formats reflecting the diagnostic categories outlined in the American Psychiatric Association's *Diagnostic and Statistical Manual of Mental Disorders* (DSM) and the World Health Organization's (WHO) *International Classification of Diseases* (ICD). Introducing standard questions and response formats has, generally speaking, had the intended effect. Reliability improves as the degree of structure increases, with fully structured interviews resulting in the greatest test–retest and inter-rater reliability (Rogers, 2001; Wood, Garb, Lilienfeld, & Nezworski, 2002). Similarly, structured assessments tend to be characterized by stronger validity than unstructured formats for both Axis I and Axis II diagnoses (Basco et al., 2000; Miller, Dasher, Collins, Griffiths, & Brown, 2001; Widiger, 2002).

The reasons for this may seem obvious. Standardization removes much of the variability introduced by the idiosyncratic nature of unstructured interviews discussed earlier. Ward, Beck, Mendelson, Mock, and Erbaugh (1962) analyzed sources of diagnostic variability in unstructured interviews and determined that most of the variance is introduced by the clinician. *Information variance*, or differences in the amount and type of information collected by the clinician, and *criterion variance*, the interpretation of that information in making clinical diagnoses, accounted for 95% of the variability in diagnoses between psychiatrists, whereas, only 5% of the variability was due to *patient variance*, or inconsistent presentation on the part of the client. Structured and semi-structured interviews minimize information and criterion variance by standardizing the question wording, coverage, sequencing, and response interpretation uncontrolled for in unstructured interviews. Semi-structured interviews are considered the "gold standard" in psychiatric diagnostic interviewing because of their ability to produce reliable, accurate, and complete diagnoses (Miller, Dasher, Collins, Griffiths, & Brown, 2001; Zimmerman, 2003).

Diagnostic Interview Schedule

The Diagnostic Interview Schedule (DIS) was one of the first fully structured diagnostic interviews designed to standardize psychological assessment procedures for use in epidemiological research (a review of the evolution of the DIS can be found in Helzer and Robins, 1988). The current version, the DIS-IV (Robins et al., 1995), is oriented around DSM-IV diagnostic criteria (American Psychiatric Association, 2000), assessing a broad range of Axis I disorders, including mood and anxiety disorders, substance use disorders, and, to a lesser extent, disorders first diagnosed in infancy, childhood, and adolescence. A strength of the DIS is that it obtains information regarding age of onset, demographic risk factors, and possible organic etiology of each disorder assessed, as well as cognitive impairment. Initial questions screen for the presence of symptoms, and affirmative responses are followed by additional probes specified by a *Probe Flow Chart*. Questions are read verbatim, and unstructured follow-up questions are not permitted, aside from the additional probe questions provided in the manual. A diagnostic determination is made by a computer scoring system that assigns diagnoses based on reported symptoms and etiology. The high degree of structure also lends itself to computer administration, with versions of the DIS available in computerized formats for use by patients and clinicians.

The highly structured format allows administration by both professionals and trained nonprofessionals, and has produced moderate inter-rater agreement between these groups (Robins, Helzer, Ratcliff, & Seyfried, 1982). However, studies of the validity of the DIS are less encouraging. Concordance between diagnoses made by psychiatrists and the DIS is typically poor (Anthony et al., 1985; Folstein et al., 1985), and a review of several studies indicates that the DIS shows poor concurrent validity with other diagnostic measures (Rogers, 2001). A comprehensive review of psychometric properties of the DIS can be found elsewhere (Rogers, 2001; Summerfeldt & Antony, 2002). The somewhat questionable psychometric properties suggest that the DIS should not be used for clinical diagnosis, but may be useful to screen individuals for subsequent, more comprehensive assessments.

Diagnostic Interview Schedule for Children

The Diagnostic Interview Schedule for Children (DISC; Costello, Edelbrock, Dulcan, Kalas, & Klaric, 1984), like its adult counterpart, is a fully structured clinical interview designed to assess a broad range of current and lifetime psychiatric disorders. Developed by the National Institute of Mental Health for epidemiological purposes, the most recent version, the DISC-IV, is used in both research and clinical settings (Shaffer, Fisher, Lucas, Dulcan, & Schwab-Stone, 2000). The interview questions closely correspond to both DSM-IV and ICD-10 diagnostic criteria for over 30 diagnoses assessed in six modules, including anxiety disorders, mood disorders, disruptive disorders (e.g., attention-deficit hyperactivity disorder, conduct disorder), substance use disorders, schizophrenia, and miscellaneous disorders (e.g., eating, elimination, and tic disorders). Like the SCID, each module is self-contained and may be skipped if no symptoms are present, without affecting the overall validity of the assessment.

Two parallel versions of the DISC-IV are intended for use with children (DISC-C for children aged 9–17) and parents (DISC-P for parents of children aged 6–17). Both versions follow the same highly structured "stem-and-branching tree" format as other structured interviews, but have shorter sentences and simplified wording to be understandable to both children and adults (Edelbrock, Costello, Dulcan, Kalas, & Conover, 1985). Reliability studies indicate that there is moderate agreement between parent and child scores (Edelbrook et al., 1985); however, the child version has lower test–retest reliability (Edelbrook et al., 1985; Schwab-Stone, Fisher, Piacentini, Shaffer, Davies, & Briggs, 1993) and sensitivity (Fisher et al., 1993) than does the parent version. Further, test–retest reliabilities are sensitive to age; that is, younger children tend to have lower reliability estimates than do older children (Edelbrook et al., 1985). Therefore, it is recommended that the clinician weight the outcome of the parent version more than the child version when making diagnostic decisions (Rogers, 2001). Nevertheless, reliability studies suggest moderate to excellent overall reliability for current diagnoses (Rogers, 2001). Validity studies indicate that the DISC is best conceptualized as a measure of general impairment, as it has only modest convergent and concurrent validity at the level of individual diagnosis. For a thorough review of the psychometric properties of the DISC, see Rogers (2001).

Composite International Diagnostic Interview

The Composite International Diagnostic Interview (CIDI; World Health Organization, 1997) was designed primarily for use in cross-cultural epidemiological research, using the DIS as a template while incorporating more culturally diverse items (Robins et al., 1988). The CIDI has undergone several revisions; the most recent version, the CIDI 3.0 (Kessler & Üstün, 2004), directly corresponds with both DSM-IV and ICD-10 diagnostic criteria. Like the DIS, the CIDI is a fully structured diagnostic interview suitable for administration by both professionals and trained lay persons. Although the question wording has changed slightly for some items, the CIDI retains every item from the DIS and the identical response format.

Although the DIS was once the most widely used assessment tool in epidemiological research, the CIDI has been the most frequently used instrument for this purpose for over a decade because of its greater applicability across cultures, compared to the DIS. To illustrate, the CIDI has been translated into 32 languages (Kobak, Skodol, & Bender, 2008) and has undergone validation studies for many of these translations. In addition to research applications, the CIDI-Primary Health Care Version (CIDI-PHC) can be used as a diagnostic tool in clinical practice, although this application is less common. Other versions exist for self- or clinician administration, 12-month and lifetime assessment, and paper-and-pencil and computer administration.

Most research regarding the psychometric properties of the CIDI has been conducted for version 2.1 or earlier. Generally, reliability statistics are impressive, with inter-rater reliability estimates of .90 or greater, and good to excellent test–retest reliability for most diagnoses (Andrews & Peters, 1998). However, many reliability and validity studies are confounded by using the DIS, which comprises much of the CIDI, as a comparison measure (Rogers, 2001).

Nevertheless, recent studies have found high concurrent validity of CIDI 3.0 and SCID-IV diagnoses, despite the somewhat more conservative prevalence estimates detected by the CIDI (Haro et al., 2006; Kessler et al., 2006). For a comprehensive and balanced review of the psychometric properties of the CIDI see Andrews and Peters (1998), and Rogers (2001).

Structured Clinical Interview for DSM-IV

The SCID (First, Spitzer, Gibbon, & Williams, 2007) is a semi-structured diagnostic interview that assesses a broad range of DSM-IV Axis I disorders. To reflect changes to the DSM, the SCID has undergone several revisions, beginning with the first edition in 1985 for the DSM-III to the DSM-IV version first published in 1996, and most recently updated in 2007. Importantly, it has remained true to the DSM's multiaxial assessment system, collecting information about the historical, medical, psychosocial, and environmental factors possibly contributing to the individual's presenting problems.

There are several versions of the SCID-IV, each with differing breadth and depth of inquiry. The SCID-I (First, Spitzer, Gibbon, & Williams, 2007) is intended for a research audience and provides the broadest coverage of Axis I disorders. The SCID-CV (First, Spitzer, Gibbon, & Williams, 1996) is a briefer version, intended for clinical settings, that does not collect the depth of information in the research version and eliminates questions regarding course specifiers unless required for a diagnosis (e.g., mood disorders). Further, the SCID-CV does not assess disorders rarely seen in clinical practice, such as minor depressive disorder, acute stress disorder, and binge eating disorder. Separate tests designed to supplement the SCID have been developed to assess dissociative disorders (SCID-D; Steinberg, 1994) and Axis II personality disorders (SCID-II; First, Gibbon, Spitzer, Williams, & Benjamin, 1997) independently.

The format of the SCID also parallels that of the DSM-IV. The test manual is organized into modules according to symptom clusters and disorders, allowing the interviewer to skip sections that are not relevant for a particular client. An optional screening module early in the interview identifies the presence of symptoms requiring further investigation, and suggests which modules may be omitted. This saves time in administration, as the clinician is not unnecessarily querying symptoms of little relevance. However, this may have the unintended consequence of failing to alert the clinician to subtle or atypical symptoms, resulting in missed diagnoses (Rogers, 2001). Anticipating such a problem, the SCID also includes skip-out rules when assessing for each disorder, so that the interviewer may proceed to the next module if the client does not endorse symptoms. Thus, the SCID can be administered in its entirety, while still eliminating unnecessary questioning.

The SCID is organized into a three-column format, with the left column containing the questions, the middle column containing the corresponding diagnostic criteria, and the right column containing the response options and branching rules. The questions are read verbatim, with probes provided to clarify the client's responses. The interviewer is permitted to generate additional probes to elicit adequate information and relevant examples. Responses are recorded on a 3-point categorical scale based on the diagnostic criteria, where 1 indicates the symptom is absent, 2 indicates that the symptom is present at a subthreshold level, and 3 indicates the symptom is present. If criteria are met for a particular disorder, a severity rating may be provided, based on the clinical judgment of the interviewer.

Generally, the SCID has demonstrated adequate psychometric properties with clinical samples. Space constraints do not allow us to review the extent of research available regarding the reliability and validity of the SCID; for a comprehensive review of the literature see Rogers (2001). Rogers (2001) reported moderately high to superb inter-rater reliability for current diagnoses, although studies have shown that reliability statistics vary by disorder. For example, in the largest and most thorough reliability study to date (Williams et al., 1992), test–retest reliability of the SCID-I for DSM-III was found to be high for bulimia but considerably lower for dysthymia, and there was substantial site-to-site variation (κ ranged from .37 to .82 for major depressive disorder). Similarly, studies of the SCID-I for DSM-IV indicate that reliability statistics vary by disorder, with the highest test–retest and inter-rater reliability for alcohol and substance use disorders, and the lowest reliability estimates for dysthymic disorder and generalized anxiety disorder. In addition, reliability statistics have tended to be much lower in nonclinical samples (Zanarini et al., 2000). Studies of the validity of the SCID have largely been limited to concurrent validity, and have rarely assessed criterion-related validity because of its high concordance with the DSM. The SCID has generally demonstrated

moderate levels of concurrent validity for current diagnoses with the CIDI (Haro et al., 2006) and the *Mini International Neuropsychiatric Interview* (MINI; Sheehan et al., 1997). Compared to disorder-specific measures, the SCID has demonstrated adequate convergent validity for PTSD, depression, and substance abuse, but is less than impressive for panic disorder and psychotic disorders (Rogers, 2001).

In summary, the SCID is a commonly used instrument in both research and clinical settings and is designed to assess for a range of Axis I and Axis II disorders. After adequate training, many clinicians are comfortable with the administration because of the close resemblance to the DSM-IV. Finally, the adequate psychometric properties of the SCID ensure that a skilled clinician can be reasonably confident in the validity of his or her assessment.

Anxiety Disorders Interview Schedule for DSM-IV

The Anxiety Disorders Interview Schedule for DSM-IV (ADIS-IV; Brown et al., 1994) provides a detailed assessment of symptoms for DSM-IV anxiety disorders and also includes sections for the diagnosis of mood, substance use, psychotic, and somatoform disorders. For each of the anxiety disorders assessed (panic disorder, social phobia, specific phobias, obsessive-compulsive disorder, post-traumatic stress disorder, and generalized anxiety disorder), information is obtained regarding the specific symptom presentation, and the intensity of fear and avoidance, as well as age of onset and possible etiology. Like other semi-structured interviews, the ADIS-IV is designed to be administered only by trained professionals and is suitable for use in both research and clinical settings. The flexibility of the semi-structured interview permits the clinician to ask unstructured follow-up questions and to probe for relevant examples, where appropriate, to aid with diagnosis and treatment planning. The lifetime version (ADIS-IV-L; Di Nardo, Brown, & Barlow, 1994) expands on the standard version to query about both lifetime and current diagnoses, as well as symptom course. An adaptation of the ADIS-IV is also available for children (ADIS-IV-C) and their parents (ADIS-IV-P; Silverman & Albano, 1996).

Most studies on the reliability of the ADIS have been conducted for earlier versions. In a large-scale study assessing the reliability of the ADIS-IV, reliability was found to be in the range of good to excellent for all disorders except dysthymic disorder

(Brown, Di Nardo, Lehman, & Campbell, 2001). Although few studies have evaluated the validity of the ADIS, Rogers (2001) concluded, based on limited available evidence, that convergent validity is in the moderate range. The child and parent versions of the ADIS-IV have demonstrated excellent interrater reliability (Lyneham, Abbott, & Rapee, 2007), test–retest reliability (Silverman, Saavedra, & Pina, 2001), and strong concurrent validity at the disorder level (Wood, Piacentini, Bergman, McCracken, & Barrios, 2002). It should be noted that most studies on the properties of the ADIS-IV and ADIS-C/P have found lower reliability estimates for generalized anxiety disorder (GAD), possibly because of the high diagnostic overlap with other disorders (Brown et al., 2001; Wood et al., 2002).

Mini-International Neuropsychiatric Interview

The Mini-International Neuropsychiatric Interview (MINI; Sheehan et al., 1997) is a brief semi-structured diagnostic interview for the assessment of DSM-IV and ICD-10 disorders. Although designed for research use, the MINI is also used as a screening measure in clinical contexts, largely because of its relatively brief administration time (15–20 minutes) and broad diagnostic coverage. It is designed to assess the current, but not lifetime, diagnosis of 15 Axis I disorders, including anxiety, mood, substance use, eating, and psychotic disorders, and antisocial personality disorder. In addition to the original MINI, there are three other versions: the MINI-Screen, an abbreviated version of the original for use in primary care settings; the MINI-Plus, to include assessment of lifetime diagnoses; and the MINI-Kid, for use with children. The MINI has been translated into 43 languages, and has demonstrated impressive reliability and validity, making it an ideal tool for cross-cultural epidemiological research. A review of the development and psychometric properties of the MINI can be found in Sheehan et al. (1998) and Lecrubier et al. (1997).

Disorder-specific Interviews

The interviews described in the previous sections generally provide broad diagnostic coverage for situations in which the nature of the presenting problem is unknown, or to obtain information of interest for researchers. In many cases, the goal of the clinical interview is to obtain detailed information about the complexities of a particular disorder. Disorder-specific measures also vary in their depth and breadth of coverage; however, they typically focus on a single disorder or domain. The reader is referred to Table 12.1 for examples of measures that are commonly used in both research and clinical settings. Detailed information to help determine which disorder-specific interview may be most appropriate for a particular application may be found elsewhere (e.g., Antony & Barlow, 2002; Hunsley & Mash, 2008).

Structured and Semi-Structured Interviews for Assessment of Axis II Disorders

Personality disorders are rarely the primary reason that a person is seen for an assessment; rather, individuals are likely to seek treatment for Axis I conditions. Personality disorders are characterized by maladaptive and inflexible ways of thinking, feeling, and behaving, but it is precisely these features that treatment aims to change. Thus, if a personality disorder is present and undetected prior to initiating treatment, it may have the unintended consequence of interfering with the course of treatment, and often with a successful outcome (Widiger, 2002). However, personality disorders are modifiable if appropriately detected and targeted for treatment. Several inventories are available in the form of self-report personality questionnaires, such as the Minnesota Multiphasic Personality Inventory (MMPI-2; Colligan, Morey, & Offord, 1994) and the NEO PI-R (Costa & McCrae, 1992), which do not provide a targeted assessment of personality disorders per se, but provide response profiles characteristic of personality disorders in the scoring manual. Self-report questionnaires and unstructured interviews alone often provide inaccurate and unreliable diagnoses, whereas structured and semi-structured interviews have been found to be the most efficient and accurate assessment tools for Axis II disorders (Widiger & Samuel, 2005). Unfortunately, unstructured interviews are the norm in clinical practice (Zimmerman & Mattia, 1999b). Below is a brief review of three commonly used clinical interviews for Axis II personality disorders: the Structured Interview for DSM-IV Personality Disorders (SIDP-IV; Pfohl, Blum, & Zimmerman, 1997), the International Personality Disorder Examination (IPDE; Loranger, 1999), and the Structured Clinical Interview for DSM-IV Axis II Personality Disorders (SCID-II; First et al., 1997). A review of all interview measures is beyond the scope of this chapter; for a thorough review of measures and psychometric data, see Rogers (2001).

Table 12.1 Interview-based Symptom Measures

	Name of measure	What it assesses	Administration time	Psychometric properties
Anxiety Disorders	Yale-Brown Obsessive Compulsive Scale (Y-BOCS; Goodman et al., 1989a, 1989b. Y-BOCS-II; Goodman, Rasmussen, Price, & Storch, 2006; Storch et al., 2010a, 2010b)	Severity and nature of OCD symptoms	45 minutes	Good to excellent inter-rater reliability, internal consistency, and test-retest reliability; limited information regarding test validity, but preliminary information indicates adequate validity
	Liebowitz Social Anxiety Scale (LSAS; Liebowitz, 1987)	Measures fear and avoidance of social and performance situations	10 minutes	Demonstrated adequate psychometric properties
	Clinician-Administered PTSD Scale for DSM-IV (CAPS; Blake, Weathers, Nagy, Kaloupek, Charney, & Keane, 1998)	Current and lifetime PTSD symptoms	45–60 minutes	Good to excellent psychometric properties
Depression	Hamilton Rating Scale for Depression (HRSD; Hamilton, 1960, 1967)	Severity of depressive symptoms	30+ minutes	Good inter-rater reliability and moderate internal consistency; good convergent validity but inconclusive concurrent and discriminant validity
	Brief Psychiatric Rating Scale (BPRS; Overall & Gorham, 1962)	Presence and severity of Schizophrenia and Mood Disorder symptoms	10–40 minutes	High inter-rater reliability, and concurrent and construct validity
Substance Use Disorders	Comprehensive Drinker Profile (CDP; Miller & Marlatt, 1984)	Extent of substance use, related psychosocial problems, and motivation for change	120 minutes	Excellent inter-rater reliability, and good predictive and convergent validity; moderate agreement between interviewer and client reports
	Addiction Severity Index (ASI; McLellan, Luborsky, Woody, & O'Brien, 1980)	Overview of problems related to substance use	45 minutes	Generally excellent reliability estimates; modest convergent validity
Eating Disorders	Eating Disorders Examination (EDE; Fairburn & Cooper, 1993)	Presence and frequency of bulimia symptoms	30–60 minutes	Adequate internal consistency and excellent inter-rater reliability; good construct and discriminant validity; distinguishes people with bulimia from people with other eating disorders. Considered the gold standard for ED diagnosis

Table 12.1 Interview-based Symptom Measures *(Cont'd)*

	Name of measure	What it assesses	Administration time	Psychometric properties
Eating Disorders *(Cont'd)*	Interview for the Diagnosis of Eating Disorders-IV (IDED-IV; Kutlesic, Williamson, Gleaves, Barbin, & Murphy-Eberenz, 1998)	Initial assessment of severity and frequency of eating disorder symptoms	30–90 minutes	Excellent reliability and good convergent, content, and discriminant validity
Schizophrenia	BPRS most commonly used			
	Comprehensive Assessment of Symptoms and History (CASH; Andreason, 1987)	Positive and negative symptoms of schizophrenia	120 minutes	Adequate reliability estimates; preliminary validity data are promising

For recommendations regarding selecting an appropriate measure, see Widiger (2002).

Structured Interview for DSM-IV Personality Disorders

The SIDP-IV (Pfohl, Blum, & Zimmerman, 1997) is a clinician-administered semi-structured diagnostic interview whose items correspond closely with DSM-IV criteria. The questions are organized by ten areas of an individual's life, (e.g., interests and activities, work style, relationships, emotions, and social perception), rather than diagnostic categories; therefore, face validity of the items is low, minimizing the possibility of being confounded by particular response sets. Further, the organization of the questions progresses from less threatening to more intrusive, which creates a more conversational flow and is useful in developing rapport. An optional third-party interview is available to corroborate the information obtained in the patient version of the SIDP-IV, if the clinician deems it necessary. Possibly because of a lack of insight characteristic of personality disorders, or because many do not see their symptoms as distressing or impairing, the informant interview has been found to increase the accuracy of clinical diagnoses (Berstein et al., 1997).

The SIDP-IV has received good empirical support, with several studies reporting reliability and validity in the good to high range (Rogers, 2001). Rogers concludes that "the SIDP is an excellent Axis II interview that should be strongly considered in a wide range of clinical settings" (p. 383). Despite the lengthy administration time (60–90 minutes), the strong psychometric properties and suitability for use with patients presenting with both Axis I and

Axis II disorders make this is an ideal instrument for use in clinical practice.

International Personality Disorders Examination

The IPDE (Loranger, 1999) is a clinician-administered semi-structured interview that uses both dimensional and categorical ratings to provide information about the presence and severity of personality disorders. It is unique among personality disorder assessments in that it includes a self-administered paper-and-pencil screening questionnaire to detect the possible presence of a personality disorder before proceeding with the clinical interview. The IPDE is a modification of its predecessor, the PDE (Loranger, 1988), to include a module for assessment of ICD-10 personality disorders, as well as the DSM-IV. It should be noted that some questions related to DSM-IV criteria are used to assess for ICD-10 diagnoses despite sometimes substantial differences in the diagnostic criteria between the classification systems. However, the strong psychometric properties of the IPDE, and the cross-national validation, suggest that it is an acceptable standardized diagnostic tool for use worldwide.

Like the SIDP-IV, questions on the IPDE are organized according to life domains and can be used with both patient and informant interviews. However, unlike the SIDP-IV, the IPDE items are relatively transparent and therefore vulnerable to distortion in client reports, somewhat limiting its validity (Boyle, 1998). This appears to be only a minor consideration, as studies have demonstrated that the reliability and validity of the IPDE are generally moderate to excellent (Rogers, 2001).

Structured Clinical Interview for DSM-IV Personality Disorders

The SCID-II (First et al., 1997) is a semi-structured interview designed to be used as a companion to the SCID-I. Items are organized by diagnostic modules, rather than life domains (as in other personality disorder interviews) for all ten DSM-IV Axis II personality disorders, as well as depressive personality disorder, passive-aggressive personality disorder, and personality disorder not otherwise specified. The response format is very similar to that of the SCID-I in that a response of 1 indicates the symptom is absent, a score of 2 refers to a symptom that is present at a subthreshold level, and a score of 3 indicates the symptom is present. Its similarity to the SCID-I increases the ease of administration. In addition, a relatively short administration time (30 minutes) makes this a practical instrument for use in clinical settings. Unlike the SCID-I, there are no skip-out rules or branching options; however, the stand-alone modules can be administered independently without impacting the validity of the assessment. Importantly, it also asks the client to provide several examples when endorsing items because symptoms of personality disorders are, by definition, present in many areas of an individual's life.

The SCID-II has demonstrated adequate reliability and validity for most personality disorders (First & Gibbon, 2004; Maffei et al., 1997). The validity of the SCID-II, because of its close adherence to the DSM-IV criteria, is complicated by the questioned validity of personality disorder diagnoses (Bornstein, 1998; Farmer, 2000). This may, in part, reflect a failure to meet the impairment and distress criteria for some personality disorders, particularly histrionic and obsessive-compulsive personality disorders (Ryder, Costa, & Bagby, 2007). Nonetheless, it has been recommended for use in clinical practice because of its ease of use and its acceptable empirical support (Widiger, 2002; Widiger & Samuel, 2005). Importantly, diagnostic accuracy increases substantially when self-report questionnaires are used in combination with semi-structured interviews, with unstructured interviews contributing little to the diagnosis (Widiger & Samuel, 2005; Zimmerman & Mattia, 1999b).

Summary

Ultimately, structured and semi-structured interviews rely on client self-report; therefore, their validity rests, in part, on the degree of clients' insight and self-disclosure. This may be particularly relevant for conditions that are characterized by low insight regarding the presence of symptoms and degree of impairment, such as bipolar disorder and schizophrenia (Eaton, Neufeld, Chen, & Cai, 2000). In addition, people may intentionally misrepresent their symptoms for purposes of malingering or to appear less impaired. However, the bulk of empirical evidence suggests that structured interviews are superior to both self-report and unstructured interviews in the assessment of both Axis I and Axis II disorders. Although the reliability of an assessment interview may increase as the degree of structure increases, semi-structured interviews have been considered the "gold standard" in clinical interviewing because of their typically strong psychometric properties and comprehensiveness, and their ability to facilitate rapport with the client. A thorough assessment is the first step in the treatment process, and provides the basis for case formulation and treatment planning.

Assessing Suicide Risk

Client suicidality can be one of the most stressful and intimidating experiences for health professionals, particularly for beginning or inexperienced clinicians and in cases where the client is not known to the clinician or interviewer (e.g., as in the case of an independent assessment). In one study, approximately 19% of psychology interns reported that, during their clinical training, they had a client who attempted suicide, and 11% reported that they had a client who completed suicide (Kleespies, Penk, & Forsyth, 1993). In a study on stress and clinical work, suicide attempts and expressions of suicidality were among the top three stressful client behaviors reported by psychology interns, clinical psychologists, and counselors (Rodolfa, Kraft, & Reilley, 1988). The majority of clinical psychologists actually receive minimal instruction in suicide risk assessment during their training (Dexter-Mazza & Freeman, 2003; Knox, Burkard, Jackson, Schaack, & Hess, 2006), which likely contributes to clinicians' discomfort with this form of clinical interviewing. In the following paragraphs, risk and protective factors for suicide will be described, and this will be followed with an overview of recommended components of suicide risk assessment.

Clinicians and assessors are advised to be highly familiar with the demographic, clinical, and behavioral risk factors for suicidal ideation (i.e., wanting or wishing to be dead), planning, attempt, and completion, as the need to assess for these could arise at any time (Dexter-Mazza & Korslund, 2007). The WHO World Mental Health Survey Initiative has provided data on the risk factors for suicide in 17 countries (Nock et al., 2008). In terms of demographic factors, the findings suggest that being female, being younger, being unmarried, and having fewer years of formal education are all risk factors for suicidal ideation, planning, and attempt. In a recent review, Paris (2006) noted that the profiles of suicide attempters and suicide completers are considerably different, with suicide completers (as opposed to suicide attempters) tending to be male, older, and to use means that are more lethal. In terms of clinical variables, the findings of the WHO study indicate that a diagnosis of a DSM-IV impulse control disorder or mood disorder is also associated with elevated risk of suicidal behavior. In the case of mood disorder, the risk is particularly elevated when it is characterized by anhedonia, hopelessness, or neurovegetative symptoms that are severe, or when psychotic symptoms are present (Dexter-Mazza & Korslund, 2007). The WHO study also revealed that a diagnosis of an anxiety disorder or substance use disorder is associated with an elevated risk of suicidal behavior. In terms of behavioral indicators of suicide risk, the WHO study findings indicate that, among individuals who report suicide ideation, the likelihood of developing a suicide plan and attempting suicide are highest within the first year of ideation onset (Nock et al., 2008).

Dexter-Mazza and Korslund (2007) also note that a history of suicide attempts, in particular attempts that are more serious as defined by clear intent or medically-serious outcomes, also confers risk for suicide. A family history of suicidal behavior has also been shown to be a predictor of suicide; however, it is not known whether this risk is transmitted biologically or whether it is transmitted indirectly, via modeling (Dexter-Mazza & Korslund, 2007). Finally, a diagnosis of schizophrenia is associated with increased risk of suicide, with the risk being highest at the time individuals are first diagnosed and in the period following initial hospitalization (Dexter-Mazza & Korslund, 2007).

In addition to risk factors, the clinician must also inquire about *protective factors*, that is, factors that prevent an individual from considering suicide (Rutter, Freedenthal, & Osman, 2008), as the estimate of suicide risk is determined by a balance of risk factors (particularly the behavioral indicators) and protective factors, and not solely by the presence of risk factors. Examples of protective factors include having loved ones to whom the client feels responsible (e.g., family, spouse, children, and pets), as well as other social supports that are important to the client. However, it should be noted that data from a large-scale epidemiological study (Borges, Angst, Nock, Ruscio, & Kessler, 2008) indicate that, although the presence of young children in the home is associated with a reduced risk of suicide attempt, it has been, on the other hand, linked with *increased* risk of ideation among individuals who engage in suicide ideation, which suggests that stress is an important factor for clinicians to assess and monitor (Borges et al., 2008). A high level of self-efficacy and an expression of hope for the future have also been identified as protective factors (Dexter-Mazza & Korslund, 2007). Some clients also report that they would not consider suicide as an option because it is proscribed within their religion or culture. The reader is directed to Dexter-Mazza and Korslund (2007) for additional information on risk and protective factors for suicide.

A suicide risk assessment allows the clinician to assess the *possibility* (i.e., risk) of suicide; however, it is important to note that it cannot be used to *predict* whether a specific individual will actually carry out the act (Dexter-Mazza & Korslund, 2007). The prediction of who will and will not complete suicide is made complicated by the fact that the majority of individuals with suicidal ideation do not attempt suicide and, in turn, only a minority of attempters complete suicide (Paris, 2006).

As noted earlier, the clinician uses information about risk and protective factors derived from the empirical and clinical literature to arrive at a determination of a client's estimated risk for suicide. As such, the suicide risk assessment should contain questions that elicit information about both types of factors. Dexter-Mazza and Korslund (2007) and Shea (2004) provide examples of key questions that should be asked to assess suicide potential. The interviewer must gather information about (a) demographic and clinical factors that place the client in a high-risk or low-risk category for suicidal behavior (as discussed earlier), (b) the client's history of intentional self-harm and suicide attempts, (c) current behavioral indicators of imminent suicide, and (d) factors that could dissuade the client from considering suicide.

Asking about past instances of self-harm and suicidal behavior will enable the clinician to gain an understanding of the function of these behaviors. Clients should be asked about events or factors that precipitated episodes of self-harm and/or suicidal behavior; the means used to engage in the behaviors, including how they were obtained (Dexter-Mazza & Korslund, 2007; p. 104); the extent to which the behavior was planned; the client's feelings at the time he or she was engaging in the behaviors; and the desired outcome (e.g., relief) (Dexter-Mazza & Korslund, 2007).

In terms of behavioral indicators, there are key questions that clinicians and interviewers must ask to assess *imminent* risk of suicidal behavior. Determining the imminence of suicide potential is critical, as there is an ethical and legal obligation to take steps to reduce imminent risk when it is identified (Sommers-Flanagan & Sommers-Flanagan, 2009). Once it has been established that the client is experiencing suicidal ideation, the clinician or interviewer must ask the client whether he or she has a plan for how the suicide might be completed (Dexter-Mazza & Korslund, 2007). If the client indicates that he or she has a plan, the means with which the client intends to execute the plan and the client's access to those means need to be assessed. The clinician should also pay attention to and assess for indicators that the client is preparing to attempt suicide (e.g., giving away of possessions; preparation of a will). It is important for the clinician to elicit reasons for living. A critical part of suicide risk assessment involves helping the client to develop a "crisis plan" in the event that she or he experiences the urge to act on suicidal ideation (Dexter-Mazza & Korslund, 2007).

Many health professionals report being intimidated by suicide risk assessment because they are afraid that asking questions about suicide might inadvertently "plant the seed of suicide" in a vulnerable individual who is not currently suicidal (Pearson, Stanley, King, & Fisher, 2001). Dexter-Mazza and Korslund (2007) note that there is no evidence to indicate that client suicidality increases after a suicide risk assessment; on the contrary, such an assessment may actually disencumber clients of their private thoughts and feelings about suicide (Dexter-Mazza & Korslund, 2007).

Finally, it should be noted that, for a number of reasons (e.g., embarrassment, fear that disclosure of ideation will result in hospitalization), clients may not readily communicate their suicidal thoughts to the clinician or interviewer (Shea, 2004). Writings on suicide risk assessment often focus on strategies for assessing suicidal *intent*; however, there is not sufficient discussion of strategies for eliciting suicidal *ideation*, even though ideation and intent go hand in hand. The reader is referred to Shea (2004) for a detailed description of the *Chronological Assessment of Suicide Events* (CASE), an interview designed to assess suicidal ideations, intent, and behavior.

Interviewing: Strategies and Skills
Interviewer Bias
Human information processing is fallible and largely heuristic; as such, clinicians must be aware of thinking errors (i.e., cognitive biases) that influence their clinical decision-making. With reference to clinical psychologists, Chapman and Chapman (1982) noted that "clinicians are subject to the same illusions as everyone else" and suggested that direct training in cognitive heuristics and biases should be a requirement for graduate students in clinical psychology. Garb and Grove (2005) stated that the ability to identify and safeguard against biases does not come with clinical experience; but rather, with training. In a recent survey of 200 American Psychological Association (APA)-accredited graduate programs in clinical psychology, Harding (2007) found that, although 79% of programs offered at least one course with a section on clinical judgment and decision-making only *one* program offered an entire course on the topic. It appears that although psychologists agree that acquiring skills in clinical decision-making is important, formal training in clinical decision-making is not explicitly built into graduate programs in clinical psychology.

Representativeness heuristic, availability heuristic, confirmation bias, and *illusory correlations* are a few examples of cognitive heuristics that have been shown to affect medical decision-making and may also be the same cognitive processes that promote biases in clinical judgment in a mental health context (Harding, 2007). In the following paragraphs, we will discuss ways in which these heuristics may affect clinical interviewing, diagnostic impressions, and case formulation.

Kahneman and Tversky (1972) defined representativeness as a cognitive error whereby an event is judged to be "similar in essential properties to its parent population." Judgment by representativeness can influence judgments that are made about individuals. If an individual appears to fit some sort of larger category, there is an increased chance that the individual will be viewed as a member of that category. In the "Tom W." problem popularized by Kahneman and Tversky (1973), a man is described as highly intelligent, lacking in creativity, having a need for order, having a writing style that is "dull and mechanical," and having little sympathy for, and a lack of interest in interacting with, others. When respondents are presented with this description and are asked to indicate his occupation, the majority report that Tom W. is most likely an engineering student and that he is least likely to be a student in social work or the social sciences, even if the objective likelihood is higher that he would be a student in social work or the social sciences. Garb (1998) notes that in a clinical context, representativeness can affect the way in which clinicians diagnose psychological conditions. Specifically, it is not uncommon for clinicians to compare clients to some prototype or exemplar when formulating a diagnostic impression (Garb, 1998). There are risks in making clinical judgments based on representativeness. If the clinician is relying on his or her personal experience with past clients who have features that are similar to those of the individual being assessed, this would constitute a comparison to exemplars who may or may not be representative of the population of interest. In other words, the clinician may be drawing on a limited "sample size" to inform his or her diagnoses. If, however, the client being assessed is being compared to a prototype (i.e., a theoretical standard; Garb, 1998), this may not be as problematic, unless the validity of the prototype can be called into question. If the prototype is invalid, the findings of a diagnostic interview may also be invalid.

Dumont (1993) notes that a clinician's diagnostic impression and case formulation is influenced, in part, by the information he or she can remember after the interview; in other words, information that is *available*. The ease with which one calls up information from memory depends on a number of factors. The vividness or salience of the information (Garb, 1998) and the mood that one is in when listening and processing the information (Dumont, 1993) are both factors that influence what one is able to recall.

Clinical interviewers must also be attentive to *confirmation bias*. Clinicians may enter the assessment with a working hypothesis of the nature of a client's difficulties (based on the referral question or a brief review of a psychological record, for example), which may lead them to inadvertently structure the interview in a manner that confirms their initial hypothesis. As a result, interviewers may be inclined to arrive at diagnostic impressions prematurely, before all the information has been gathered (Dumont, 1993). For example, if an individual is having difficulty returning to work following a serious industrial accident, it should not be readily assumed that

the individual has post-traumatic stress disorder. Meehl (1960) reported that clinical impressions that are derived from 2 to 4 hours of clinical interviewing tend to remain unrevised over the course of treatment. Furthermore, once an impression has been formulated, clinicians tend to perseverate with it, even when disconfirming information is made available to them (Dumont, 1993). Gilovich (1993) notes that, generally, when individuals are presented with disconfirming information, they do not ignore it; but rather, they "shape" the information and incorporate it into their existing clinical conceptualization ("theory salvaging"; Dumont, 1993).

Clinicians' thinking is also susceptible to covariation bias, known also as *illusory correlation*. Humans are "pattern detectors"; as such, we often attempt to draw causal connections between events, even when none exists (Dumont, 1993). Peterson and Beach (1967) and others (e.g., Gilovich, 1993) have discussed problems associated with the "present-present" bias. When individuals are presented with data in a 2×2 contingency table crossing psychological condition (present-absent) with a putative antecedent (present-absent) and are asked to determine whether there is an association between the two, individuals will tend to concentrate on data in the present-present cell of the table, while ignoring data in the other three cells. McNally (2003), for example, pointed out that the perceived link between sexual abuse in childhood and dissociative disorders in adulthood could be attributed to the present-present bias. A considerable number of individuals with recurrent dissociative experiences may also report a history of childhood sexual abuse; however, this finding cannot be interpreted without information about the number of individuals who report having recurrent dissociative experiences, but *do not* have a history of childhood sexual abuse; such cases may represent the majority. Likewise, the number of individuals with a history of childhood sexual abuse but who *do not* have dissociative experiences may exceed the number of individuals in whom both are present.

Garb (1998) provides a number of suggestions for minimizing the impact of cognitive biases on clinical decision-making. One way by which clinicians can increase the accuracy of their judgments is by actively considering *alternative explanations* for behavior. Garb also recommends that clinicians should document their observations and clients' reports, and review their notes to reduce reliance on their memory, as memory is fallible and susceptible to distortion.

Attending

Sommers-Flanagan and Sommers-Flanagan (2009) note that the majority of clinicians, regardless of their clinical orientation, agree that learning how to attend in session is an essential clinical skill. Attending behavior is mainly nonverbal and includes eye contact, body language, and vocalizations.

A considerable amount of information can be gleaned from an individual's nonverbal communication. The following are generally considered to be *positive* attending behaviors (Sommers-Flanagan & Sommers-Flanagan, 2009): leaning slightly toward the client when speaking with or listening to the client; maintaining a relaxed but "alert" posture; keeping hand gestures to a minimum; sitting at a distance of an arm's length from the client; arranging the furniture so that there are no physical barriers (e.g., a desk) between the clinician and the client; and maintaining eye contact with the client.

Clinicians should also be aware of *negative* attending behavior. Body language that may communicate defensiveness (e.g., sitting with arms folded across the chest) or lack of interest (e.g., noticeable and repeated checking of the time) should be avoided. Making too little or too much eye contact can be off-putting. When used excessively, positive attending behaviors can come to be perceived by the client as bothersome or even offensive. For example, use of head nods and "uh huh" statements, although well-intentioned, may be perceived as irritating if they are used excessively. *Selective* use of particular nonverbal behaviors can also have an influence on what the client chooses to discuss in session. If the clinician displays considerable interest (e.g., by leaning forward, nodding frequently) when the discussion turns to a particular topic, this may inadvertently lead a client to stop talking about subjects or problems that he or she perceives to not be of interest to the clinician (Sommers-Flanagan & Sommers-Flanagan, 2009).

Asking Questions

The clinical interview should not come across as an interrogation; however, as Sommers-Flanagan and Sommers-Flanagan (2009) note, there are times when the interviewer does take on the role of investigator. The particular manner in which questions are asked can have an important impact on the quality and quantity of information that the interviewer acquires during the interview.

Sommers-Flanagan and Sommers-Flanagan (2009) describe five types of questions: open, closed, swing, implied (also known as indirect), and projective.

Open questions "are designed to facilitate verbal output" (Sommers-Flanagan & Sommers-Flanagan, 2009, p. 84). For example, questions beginning with *how* foster responses that extend beyond one-word responses. Sommers-Flanagan and Sommers-Flanagan (2009) advise clinicians to be judicious in their use of *why* questions, as these can be experienced by clients as critical and attacking, particularly when rapport has not been established (e.g., "Why haven't you returned to work?"; "Why did you drop out of college?").

Closed questions, commonly used in diagnostic interviews, can be responded to with a "yes" or "no" answer (e.g., "Do you experience difficulty bringing your worry under control?"). Questions beginning with *who* (e.g., "Who assists you with activities around the house?), *where* ("Where were you when you experienced your first panic attack?"), or *when* ("When did you first notice that you were having problems managing your anxiety?") are also examples of closed ended questions. Other examples include *do* questions ("Do you become anxious in many social situations, or only in specific ones?") and *are* questions ("Are you having difficulty concentrating?"). Closed questions are easier to formulate than are open-ended questions, which might be why it is not uncommon for beginner interviewers to inadvertently use closed questions where there is the potential to transform them into open questions.

Swing questions begin with *could* (e.g., "Could you tell me about your worst panic attack?"; "Could you tell me what it was like to assert yourself to your co-worker?"). Swing questions appear to elicit either a yes or a no response, but actually draw elaborate responses and facilitate discussion. The tentative quality of *could* questions also makes it less likely that they will be experienced as interrogative.

Implied questions are used when an interviewer is interested in receiving more information about a client's thoughts or emotions, but does not want to come across as intrusive. *I wonder* (e.g., "I wonder how you are feeling about the recent job cuts at your workplace.") is an example of an implied question.

Finally, *projective questions* are designed to elicit information about a client's goals, desires, and values. Examples of projective questions include, "Where do you see yourself in a few years from now?", "What, if anything, would you do differently the next time around?", and "If you could wave a magic wand and make your symptoms disappear, how would things be different for you?" Projective questions in the form of a hypothetical scenario can also provide insight into a client's decision-making processes (e.g., "If you were stuck in a desert for 24 hours, what measures might you take to survive?" (Sommers-Flanagan and Sommers-Flanagan, 2009, p. 217).

Case Formulation

In the previous sections, the purpose and content of clinical interviewing were discussed, and a detailed description of the types of interviews that are used in clinical practice was provided. This portion of the chapter will focus on *case formulation*—a component of clinical interviewing that is considered a "core therapy skill" (Kendjelic & Eells, 2007). Case formulation is considered to be an integral component of clinical assessment, which is reflected in the proliferation of books (recent examples include Kuyken, Padesky, & Dudley, 2009; Persons, 2008) and scientific articles on the topic in the last 15 years.

Case Formulation: Definition and Elements

Case formulation refers to the construction of an idiographic or individualized explanatory model of the factors that may have caused and precipitated the onset of a client's emotional or behavioral problems and of the factors that may be contributing to their maintenance. It consists of hypotheses about the mechanisms that may underlie a client's presenting problem and predictions about the client's thoughts, emotions, and behaviors in a particular set of situations. Regardless of a clinician's therapeutic orientation, case formulation is considered to be a core aspect of clinical assessment, as it helps both the clinician and client to identify goals for treatment; enables the clinician to devise a treatment plan that is focused and relevant to the client's concerns; and guides clinical decision-making during the course of treatment (Kendjelic & Eells, 2007; Persons, 2006). A well-developed case formulation can also facilitate the early identification of factors that may impede progress in treatment (Eells, 2007; Persons, 2008).

Contributions of Different Schools of Psychotherapy to Case Formulation

Bieling and Kuyken (2003) noted that clinicians generally agree that organizing the client's presenting problems and the factors underlying those problems into a framework or structure is important for clinical assessment and treatment, irrespective of one's psychotherapy orientation. Eells (2007) discusses the contributions of four "schools" of psychotherapy

to current approaches to clinical interviewing and case formulation.

Eells (2007) suggests that the *psychoanalytic* approach, as popularized by Freud, brought to the fore the importance of considering the role of personality in psychopathology. Freud's approach to clinical assessment also represented a radical departure from the medical approaches that dominated psychiatry at the time in at least two ways. First, Freud observed that clients often "enacted" their psychological problems during the clinical interview. He suggested that an astute clinician could learn a considerable amount about a client's interpersonal difficulties by paying attention to their verbal and nonverbal behaviors and overall style of interaction during the interview. Eells notes that psychoanalysts rarely mention actual psychiatric diagnoses in their case formulations and focus instead on describing processes or dynamics. The *humanistic* approach (Rogers, 1951) is known for its client-centered focus and emphasizes the importance of collaboration within the clinician–client relationship and of idiographic (as opposed to nomothetic) approaches to formulation. *Cognitive approaches* underscore the contributions of schemata, information processing biases, and negative automatic thoughts to psychopathology. Until recently, a common approach for cognitive therapists was to use general cognitive formulations of psychological disorders to inform treatment planning. For example, a clinician might have used Beck's cognitive theory of depression (see Clark, Beck, & Alford, 1999) to devise a treatment plan for an individual with depression (Eells, 2007). Similarly, Beck and Clark's information processing model of anxiety (1997) describes various cognitive processes that are common across anxiety disorders and is a generic model that can be applied to most forms of anxiety. In recent years, disorder-specific models have proliferated in the clinical and empirical literature. For example, Dugas and colleagues have constructed and tested a cognitive model of generalized anxiety disorder that has led to the development of a psychological treatment that targets each of the components of the model (Dugas & Robichaud, 2007). Eells (2007) noted that there has been an increasing movement in cognitive therapy toward idiographic case formulation. However, it is not known whether there are any substantial benefits to using individualized cognitive formulations over general formulations; this remains an empirical question (Eells, 2007; Persons & Tomkins, 2007). Central to the *behavioral approach* to case formulation is the *functional analysis*.

A functional analysis attempts to identify those factors that are reinforcing a client's problematic behavior. Returning to the example of depression, a clinician working from a more behavioral perspective would concentrate on identifying behaviors that may inadvertently be maintaining the client's difficulties, such as reassurance-seeking and avoidance. Similarly, behavioral formulations of anxiety disorders underscore the roles of escape and avoidance in the maintenance of fear. Eells (2007) discusses three contributions that the behavioral approach has made to current case formulation methods. According to Eells, a relatively unique feature of the behavioral approach to case formulation is that it views maladaptive behaviors as symptoms of psychopathology in and of themselves; therefore, interventions aimed at changing problematic behaviors are, in effect, targeting symptoms of disorder directly. She also proposes that behavioral formulations of psychopathology are grounded in basic experimental research. However, we would contend that these two features are not unique to behavioral approaches; they are also characteristic of cognitive formulations of psychopathology, particularly more recent models that have led to the development of corresponding treatments. Eells proposes that a third important feature of behavioral functional analysis is its explicit emphasis on the identification of external factors (e.g., stressors) that may be contributing to and reinforcing the client's problematic behavior.

The Role of Case Formulation in Psychological Treatment: Parallels with the Scientific Method

A number of parallels exist between case formulation–driven psychological treatment and the *scientific method* (Persons, 2006). One of the cornerstones of the scientific method is the *hypothesis*. In the process of designing a new experiment, a researcher formulates a tentative, yet informed a priori prediction of what he or she expects to observe in an experiment. To derive this hypothesis, the researcher typically looks to findings documented in the empirical literature, as well as observations that he or she has made in other studies. The first steps in clinical work are not dissimilar from the initial steps that are taken when conducting a scientific study. Before the clinician enters the clinical interview, he or she usually has a minimal amount of information about the client's presenting problem, obtained from a written referral or an existing clinical record. Based on the available information, the clinician devises a preliminary

or "working" hypothesis about the nature of the client's difficulties. The working hypothesis might be based on the clinician's past experiences working with clients with similar characteristics or presenting problems, or may be derived from the empirical literature, if the client's stated presenting problem is not one with which the clinician has experience.

During the clinical assessment, the clinician collects data with the aim of testing initial, working hypotheses and developing a more elaborate "theory" of the nature of the client's psychological difficulties that includes possible causes, as well as precipitating and maintaining factors. The clinical interview is the clinician's principal tool for collecting data.

Just as science is "self-correcting," so is the process of case formulation. Over the course of treatment, many of the clinician's observations are likely to be consistent with the original case formulation; however, the clinician may also make observations that run counter to his or her original formulation. Just as scientists are expected to re-examine and revise theories and hypotheses in light of inconsistent data, clinicians are similarly expected to be prepared and open to the possibility that their original formulation of the nature of the client's problems was inaccurate and requires revision. Clinicians ought not to feel compelled to adhere to their initial case conceptualizations for the duration of treatment; flexibility is key. Although the clinical interview does produce a considerable amount of data regarding the client's difficulties, it should be viewed as a strong starting point, as it almost never captures the full range of the client's experience. As such, it is important that clinicians continue to collect data throughout treatment and adjust their case formulations and treatment plans accordingly (Persons, 2006).

Elements of a Good Case Formulation

Clinicians generally hold the view that a reliable case formulation contributes to the effectiveness of psychological treatment (Persons, Mooney, & Padesky, 1995); however, there is currently little consensus as to what constitutes a "good" case formulation (Flitcroft, James, Freeston, & Wood-Mitchell, 2007). A small number of studies have examined clinicians' beliefs about what amounts to an effective cognitive-behavioral case formulation. In a study by Persons and colleagues (1995), 46 clinicians attending a case formulation workshop listened to an audiotaped portion of a clinical interview with two anxious and depressed clients and constructed a cognitive-behavioral case formulation using a well-known protocol by Persons (1989). The case formulation protocol included the following components: identification of the client's actual problem and symptoms (e.g., difficulty functioning at work) and identification of the mechanisms underlying the client's difficulties (e.g., beliefs about the self, world, and others). The findings revealed that there was only a moderate level of agreement in clinicians' identification of clients' actual problems. Agreement between clinicians' conceptualizations of underlying mechanisms was not as high as would be expected, given that all participants were following the same case formulation guidelines.

In a recent extension of the Persons and colleagues study, Flitcroft and colleagues (2007) presented seven clinicians, who identified themselves as cognitive-behavioral therapists, with a clinical case vignette of a man with depressive symptoms. Participants were given a list of 86 features that are characteristics of a cognitive-behavioral case formulation and were asked to indicate which aspects they believed were the most and least essential to a case formulation for depression. Examples of case formulation aspects included, "it identifies precipitating events," "it explains depression at an individual level," and "it identifies typical negative automatic thoughts relating to the self." The findings revealed that there was a high level of agreement that "factual" or descriptive information (e.g., demographic information and medical history) was least essential in the construction of an effective case formulation. On the other hand, there were three distinct views as to what constituted essential features of the formulation: (1) that it have sufficient explanatory power to allow for situation-specific predictions, (2) that it be functional and practical, and (3) that it capture trait-level or dispositional features that may be contributing to the client's difficulties.

Does Case Formulation Improve Treatment Efficacy?

Although case formulation is not a formal component of the majority of standardized protocols for empirically supported treatments, most clinicians operate on the assumption that case formulation improves treatment outcomes and view it as an important component of clinical assessment and treatment for this reason (Bieling & Kuyken, 2003). Interestingly, only a small number of studies have been conducted to test the validity and clinical utility of case formulations (Mumma, 2004; Mumma & Mooney, 2007a; 2007b). Bieling and Kuyken (2003) reviewed the findings of three studies that examined the relationship between cognitive case formulation

and treatment outcome, and none of the studies provided evidence of a link. Since their review, a few other studies have examined the relationship of case formulation to treatment outcome. These have focused exclusively (to our knowledge) on cognitive or cognitive-behavioral case formulation and treatment. The studies will be described in a considerable amount of detail in the following paragraphs, as they illustrate a range of methodologies that have been employed to test the validity of case formulations.

Using a single-case design methodology, Mumma (2004) assessed the clinical validity of cognitive case formulation for a female client with comorbid mood and anxiety disorders. Mumma conducted an idiographic assessment of the client's cognitive schema using a semi-structured interview that was designed to elicit automatic thoughts and beliefs relevant to her current problems (see Mumma, 2001). The client's verbatim statements were then classified into four categories of depression- and anxiety-related beliefs. The client also completed *standardized* self-report measures of dysfunctional beliefs (e.g., the *Dysfunctional Attitudes Scale*; Weissman, 1979). To validate the hypothesized belief categories derived from the idiographic assessment, Mumma constructed a questionnaire comprised of items derived from the client's verbatim statements in the idiographic assessment, items from the standardized self-report measures, and items from the *Mood and Anxiety Symptoms Questionnaire* (Watson & Clark, 1991). For each item, the client was asked to indicate, using an 11-point scale, the extent to which it was relevant to her experience. The client was asked to complete the questionnaire daily for 90 days.

A factor analysis was performed on the belief items that were derived from the idiographic assessment and revealed a factor structure that supported the four hypothesized categories of cognitions. The four factors derived from the idiographic assessment predicted daily variation in depressive and anxiety symptoms, over and above variation accounted for by the standardized cognitive measures. These findings provide support for the incremental validity of cognitive case formulation.

In a recent investigation, Persons, Roberts, Zalecki, and Brechwald (2006) examined the effectiveness of case-formulation–driven cognitive-behavioral treatment for comorbid mood and anxiety disorders in a sample of 58 clients who received treatment at a private practice clinic specializing in cognitive-behavioral therapy (CBT). Prior to the start of treatment, individualized cognitive-behavioral case formulations were constructed for each client, using a protocol developed by Persons (see Persons & Tomkins, 1997, 2007). Individualized treatment plans were developed based on the idiographic formulations, and treatment strategies were drawn from empirically supported cognitive-behavioral treatment protocols. Clients received approximately 18 sessions of treatment on average. Each client's case formulation and treatment plan were reviewed every three to four sessions and revised as appropriate. Clients completed self-report measures of depressive and anxiety symptoms at each session. Outcomes for case formulation–driven CBT were compared with outcomes from published randomized controlled trials of treatments for individual mood and anxiety disorders (based on the presumption that protocols tested in such trials did not have case formulation as an explicit component). The findings revealed that there were statistically significant reductions in depressive and anxiety symptoms from pre-treatment to post-treatment. Furthermore, the reductions in depressive symptoms were comparable to those documented in published randomized controlled trials of treatments for major depressive disorder. Mean reductions in depression and anxiety were smaller overall for clients who received case formulation treatment relative to means reported in efficacy trials; however, this was likely due to the lower baseline severity of depression and anxiety symptoms in clients in the naturalistic study, as compared with baseline severities reported in the literature.

Impact of Training on Case Formulation

There appears to be a consensus that providing formalized training in case formulation to beginning therapists is important, the assumption being that such training will enhance clinical decision-making (Kendjelic & Eells, 2007). A small number of studies have examined whether it is possible to train therapists in case formulation and whether such training has an appreciable impact on clinical decision-making. Eells and colleagues (2005) presented novice, experienced, and expert therapists who self-identified as psychodynamic or cognitive-behavioral therapists with 2-minute audiotaped clinical case vignettes describing clients with symptoms that were consistent with generalized anxiety disorder, major depressive disorder, or borderline personality disorder. Using a "think aloud" procedure, therapists spent 5 minutes developing a case conceptualization and an additional 2 minutes discussing how they would treat the clients. The formulations and treatment plans were recorded and later transcribed and coded. The results showed

that expert therapists produced higher-quality formulations relative to the novice and experienced therapists. Specifically, expert formulations were characterized by a higher degree of comprehensiveness, more detailed and nuanced inferences regarding possible mechanisms underlying clients' psychological difficulties, and treatment plans that were more closely linked to formulations. The authors proposed that experts may have employed specific "cognitive skills" when constructing their formulations and treatment plans; however, this was not assessed in the study. The study was unable to identify the skills that may have differentiated the expert therapists from the novice and experienced therapists.

Kendjelic and Eells (2007) recently examined the impact of training on quality of case formulations. Clinicians (75% of whom were trainees) participated in a 2-hour workshop on case formulation that employed a transtheoretical approach developed by the authors, based on a comprehensive review of the literature. The training consisted of education on generic case formulation, which consists of components that were found through the review to be common across psychodynamic, interpersonal, cognitive, and behavioral therapy approaches: identification of symptoms and self-identified problems, identification of predisposing events and conditions, identification of precipitating stressors, and identification of hypothesized mechanisms underlying putative associations between the other three components. Workshop participants also learned strategies for enhancing case formulation. At the end of the session, clinicians were presented with a case vignette and were asked to construct a case formulation.

Trained raters subsequently rated case formulations for quality, complexity, degree of inference, and precision of language. Participants in the training group produced case formulations that were of higher quality, more comprehensive in terms of their representation of the four formulation components, more idiographic, and that contained more information about possible mechanisms than did participants in the no-training condition. Although the findings are preliminary, they suggest that a relatively brief training session on case formulation may improve beginning therapists' skills. The authors proposed that a next step would be to examine whether the quality of case formulation predicts treatment outcome.

In summary, irrespective of a clinician's theoretical orientation, case formulation is an integral component of assessment that informs efficient and effective treatment planning. Data suggest that training in case formulation improves clinicians' conceptualizations and may contribute to treatment outcome; however, more research is needed to test whether explicit case formulation has a significant impact on treatment efficacy.

Interviewing Special Populations

In this final section, we will provide an overview of considerations when interviewing special populations. Because of the scope of this chapter, the focus is on considerations as they pertain to couples, individuals from diverse populations, and young individuals.

Interviewing Couples

The main advantage of the couple interview is that it provides the clinician with the opportunity to observe a couple's interactions, particularly their communication style, in vivo (Duman, Grodin, Cespedes, Fine, Otilingham, & Margolin, 2007). The couple interview can provide richer information than might be obtained if partners were interviewed separately, or if clinicians had access only to clients' self-report of couple difficulties (Duman et al., 2007). The couple interview is an opportunity to observe, "online," verbal and nonverbal exchanges that may be contributing to the couple's problem areas.

A number of considerations present themselves in a multi-individual interview. First, the clinician must create an atmosphere of collaboration, so that partners enter the interview on a "level playing field." Duman et al. (2007) note that the clinician can set the stage for collaboration before the interview begins by positioning chairs so that both partners are sitting at an equal distance from the clinician, at angles that also allow them to face one another. There are two situations in which a couple might be interviewed together: (1) when two partners are seeking treatment and (2) when one partner is brought in to assist with some aspect of the other partner's treatment (e.g., exposure-based therapy). During any couple interview, it is generally important for the clinician to ensure that the couple does not perceive that the clinician is taking the side of one partner versus the other. The clinician can safeguard against this by making certain that both partners are being attended to equally during the interview. The clinician should ensure, for example, that he or she is making eye contact with both partners and that both partners are given an equal opportunity to speak and share their concerns and points of view.

When one partner is invited to participate in an interview to facilitate the other partner's treatment, the clinician's approach to the interview will differ from when a couple is being interviewed as a part of a couple intervention. In cases in which one member of the couple is in treatment, typically, the client's partner is asked to attend only one or two sessions, during which the clinician may ask questions to gain the partner's perspective on the client's difficulties. For example, the partner of a client with obsessive-compulsive disorder might be able to provide additional information about subtle safety behaviors that the client may not be fully aware of, or might be in a position to provide additional information about the extent of the client's functional impairment. The partner is introduced into treatment only if he or she is identified by the client as a trusted and supportive individual who is aware of the client's difficulties and who can provide instrumental support with certain treatment strategies. For example, it is not uncommon to introduce the client's partner into treatment as a "helper" in exposure-based treatment for an anxiety disorder. When the client's partner is introduced into treatment in a facilitative role, the clinician must ensure that the client's partner does not assume a "co-therapist" role, as the client may perceive this as invalidating or even collusive, which could place the therapeutic alliance at risk. Ruptures to the therapeutic alliance can be avoided by having a discussion with the client about the purpose and potential advantages of the partner's involvement in treatment, before the joint interview. The discussion should be transparent, and the clinician should be attentive to and address any misunderstandings regarding the role of the client's partner in the client's treatment. Before the joint interview, the clinician and client should discuss how confidentiality will be handled. Given that the clinician has an obligation to the client to maintain confidentiality, clinicians are advised to consult with clients about topics that are "off-limits" for the joint session; this discussion should be documented in a progress note in the client's clinical record. In many cases, clients will report that they have no concerns about the clinician disclosing information as they have "nothing to hide" from their partner. However, the clinician should not presume that there are no boundaries to confidentiality; because it is the clinician's legal and ethical responsibility to maintain confidentiality, nothing should be taken for granted. Another way to ensure that the client's goals and needs do not take a backseat in the joint interview is to elicit the active participation of the client during the session, to the extent that the client is comfortable. For example, when a "helper" is brought into treatment to assist the client with exposure practices, part of the meeting is spent providing education to the helper about the client's anxiety disorder. If the psychoeducation is delivered by both the clinician and client, this communicates that the client is "in charge" of his or her own treatment.

Interviewing Individuals from Diverse Populations

Although a thorough discussion of considerations in multicultural assessment is beyond the scope of this chapter, an overview of some of the main ones will be provided in the following paragraphs. The reader is referred to Aronson Fontes (2008) for a detailed discussion of issues pertaining to multicultural assessment.

During their training, clinicians are made aware of the importance of "considering the role of culture" in clinical assessment and treatment; however, what exactly does it mean to "consider" cultural factors? Before clinicians can begin to consider how cultural factors may be influencing a client's psychological experiences and the communication of those experiences, they must first examine their own understanding of culture. The APA (2003) has adopted a broad stance on diversity that includes the dimensions of race, ethnicity, language, sexual orientation, gender, age, disability, class status, education, religious/spiritual orientation, and "other cultural dimensions." According to this definition, culture and diversity are likely to be a consideration when working with most clients.

Multicultural clinical interviewing proceeds in much the same way as has already been described in this chapter, with an additional focus on the collection of cultural data. As clinicians prepare for the interview, relevant cultural factors should be factored into the preparation. For example, the clinician or interviewer should ensure that any paperwork or forms to be administered to the client are available in the client's language. If materials are not available in the client's language, arrangements should be made for a professional interpreter or translator to attend the assessment. Aronson Fontes (2008) notes that this is an especially important consideration when clinicians are obtaining clients' consent to participate in the interview. Even if a client indicates his or her consent to the clinical assessment by signing the consent form, it should not be taken for granted that the client has understood the purpose and conditions of his or her participation in the interview or that he or she even read the consent

form, for that matter. In some cultures, taking the time to read a consent form would constitute a display of distrust toward the clinician (Aronson Fontes, 2008). If an interviewer decides to employ the services of an interpreter, it is important to prepare him or her for the clinical interview, even if the interpreter is experienced and has worked in the same clinical setting as the interviewer in the past. The reader is directed to Aronson Fontes (2008) for a thorough discussion of considerations related to interpreters.

During the actual interview, it is important for clinicians to adopt an unpresumptuous approach when asking questions (Ridley, Li, & Hill, 1998). This is an especially important consideration when a clinician is from the same cultural group as the client, as the clinician might be less inclined to ask the client to elaborate on his or her experiences or might overlook potentially important information. By the same token, the clinician should not bombard the client with questions about his or her cultural group, as this could, paradoxically make the clinician appear unprepared. The onus should not have to be on the client to "educate" the clinician; as such, in preparation for the interview, the clinician should obtain information about the client's cultural group from existing clinical records and from credible Internet sites and books (Aronson Fontes, 2008). Aronson Fontes (2008) also notes that the client's cultural affiliation is not determined by the clinician, but rather by the client. For example, if a client reports that he or she is married to an opposite-sex individual, it should not be assumed that he or she identifies as heterosexual. Such an assumption might preclude the interviewer from asking potentially important questions about the client's sexual practices, resulting in inaccurate information about the client's sexual orientation and sexual identity. As part of the interview, the clinician will also want to obtain information on the degree to which the client has acculturated into the majority culture. See Aronson Fontes (2008) for a list of questions that can be used to assess acculturation, as well as for guidelines on how to ask questions in a noninterrogative style.

During the interview, the clinician is also encouraged to be aware of his or her style of questions. When the client's primary language is different from interviewer's, the interviewer should minimize use of closed-ended questions that invite responses of "yes" or "no," as there is little way of knowing whether the client truly understood the questions. Whenever possible, the clinician should use terms that are concrete and elicit information about experiences at a behavioral level (e.g., "Have you stopped doing things that you used to enjoy?" versus "Have you been feeling down?"). The clinician is also advised to be mindful of and eliminate behaviors that may be offensive to the client (e.g., speaking in an excessively loud voice with clients whose primary language is not the same as the clinician's).

Interviewing Young Clients

A number of challenges present themselves when interviewing younger clients. The most notable one is the fact that young clients are typically referred for a clinical interview by their parent, guardian/caretaker, or teacher (Sommers-Flanagan & Sommers-Flanagan, 2009). As such, young clients are usually interviewed with their caretakers present. Sommers-Flanagan and Sommers-Flanagan (2009) note that the manner in which the initial interview with the young client and his or her caretaker is arranged can convey a strong message to both parties; as such, the clinician is advised to be mindful of a number of considerations. First, the clinician should inform the caretaker of the plan for the interview right from the outset. Specifically, the clinician should inform the caretaker that he or she will be interviewed with the young client. The clinician can expect that, if the client is an adolescent or preadolescent, the caretaker may request to speak with the clinician alone first, before beginning the joint interview. If the clinician accepts this request, the young client might gather from this that the clinician and caretaker are colluding, which could have a negative impact on the interview. On the other hand, the caregiver may have a legitimate need to share information with the clinician that is not appropriate to divulge in front of the child. If the child is the "primary client" (Sommers-Flanagan & Sommers-Flanagan, 2009), then the clinician must act in accordance with this and make this clear to the caretaker. For example, the clinician may inform the caretaker at the outset that he or she may share the information that the caretaker provides, as appropriate and at the discretion of the clinician.

Sommers-Flanagan and Sommers-Flanagan (2009) note that clinicians should approach the task of interviewing a younger client as they would the task of interviewing a client from a different cultural background. One of the considerations that should be in the forefront of the clinician's mind while preparing to interview a younger client is the client's stage of development. Clinicians should familiarize themselves with the cognitive, emotional, and behavioral features that characterize different stages of development and modify their interviewing practices accordingly. The reader is referred to Sommers-Flanagan and Sommers-Flanagan (2009) for a detailed comparison of clinical interviewing with young clients versus adult clients.

Conclusion

As Hunsley and Mash (this volume) note, psychological assessment "is seen as a unique and defining feature of the profession, one that sets us apart from other disciplines involved in providing health-care services." Although clinical assessment has long held a revered place in psychology, there has been a call to re-examine current approaches and procedures in an effort to render them more evidence-based. In their discussion of the limitations of current approaches to clinical assessment, Hunsley and Mash (this volume) argue that, generally, research on psychological assessment has prioritized the construction and validation of empirically derived, psychometrically sound assessment instruments, with insufficient focus on the *incremental validity* and *clinical utility* of these instruments. In this chapter, we have similarly noted that more research is needed on case conceptualization, a core component of clinical interviewing. Specifically, questions still remain as to whether training in case conceptualization increases the quality of formulations, whether explicit case conceptualization enhances treatment efficacy, and whether idiographic case conceptualizations are superior to "generic" variants. Like Hunsley and Mash (this volume), we are also of the view that research on clinical assessment should focus on addressing questions about the reliability, incremental validity, and clinical utility of current assessment approaches, if the field is to move forward.

References

American Psychiatric Association. (2000). *Diagnostic and statistical manual of mental disorders* (4th ed., text revision). Washington, DC: Author.

American Psychological Association. (2002). Ethical principles of psychologists and code of conduct. *American Psychologist, 57,* 1060–1073.

American Psychological Association. (2003). Guidelines on multicultural education, training, research, practice, and organizational change for psychologists. *American Psychologist, 58,* 377–402.

Andreason, N. C. (1987). *Comprehensive assessment of symptoms and history.* Iowa City: University of Iowa College of Medicine.

Andrews, G., & Peters, L. (1998). The psychometric properties of the Composite International Diagnostic Interview. *Social Psychiatry and Psychiatric Epidemiology, 33*, 80–88.

Anthony, J. C., Folstein, M., Romanoski, A. J., Von Korff, M. R., Nestadt, F. R., Chahal, R., et al. (1985). Comparison of the lay Diagnostic Interview Schedule and a standardized psychiatric diagnosis. *Archives of General Psychiatry, 42*, 667–675.

Antony, M. M., & Barlow, D. H. (2002). *Handbook of assessment and treatment planning for psychological disorders.* New York: Guilford Press.

Antony, M. M., & Rowa, K. (2005). Evidence-based assessment of anxiety disorders in adults. *Psychological Assessment, 17*, 256–266.

Arkes, H. R. (1981). Impediments to accurate clinical judgment and possible ways to minimize their impact. *Journal of Consulting and Clinical Psychology, 49*, 323–330.

Aronson Fontes, L. (2008). *Interviewing clients across cultures: A practitioner's guide.* New York: Guilford Press.

Basco, M. R., Bostic, J. Q., Davies, D., Rush, A. J., Witte, B., Hendrickse, W., et al. (2000). Methods to improve diagnostic accuracy in a community mental health setting. *American Journal of Psychiatry, 157*, 1599–1605.

Beahrs, J. O., & Gutheil, T. G. (2001). Informed consent in psychotherapy. *American Journal of Psychiatry, 158*, 4–10.

Beck, A. T., & Clark, D. A. (1997). An information processing model of anxiety: Automatic and strategic processes. *Behaviour Research and Therapy, 35*, 49–58.

Beck, A. T., Ward, C. H., Mendelson, M., Mock, J. E., & Erbaugh, J. K. (1962). Reliability of psychiatric diagnoses 2: A study of consistency of clinical judgments and ratings. *American Journal of Psychiatry, 119*, 351–357.

Berstein, D. P., Kasapis, C., Bergman, A., Weld, E., Mitropoulou, V., Horvath, T., et al. (1997). Assessing Axis II disorders by informant interview. *Journal of Personality Disorders, 11*, 158–167.

Beutler, L. E., & Groth-Marnat, G. (2005). *Integrative assessment of adult personality.* New York: Guilford Press.

Bieling, P. J., & Kuyken, W. (2003). Is cognitive case formulation science or science fiction? *Clinical Psychology: Science and Practice, 10,* 52–69.

Blake, D. D., Weathers, F., Nagy, L. M., Kaloupek, D. G., Charney, D. S., & Keane, T. M. (1998). *Clinician-Administered PTSD Scale for DSM-IV.* Boston, MA: National Center for Posttraumatic Stress Disorder.

Borges, G., Angst, J., Nock, M. K., Ruscio, A. M., & Kessler, R. C. (2008). Risk factors for the incidence and persistence of suicide-related outcomes: A 10-year follow-up study using the National Comorbidity Surveys. *Journal of Affective Disorders, 105*, 25–33.

Bornstein, R. F. (1998). Reconceptualizing personality disorder diagnosis in the DSM-V: The discriminant validity challenge. *Clinical Psychology: Science and Practice, 5*, 333–343.

Boyle, G. J. (1998). Schizotypal personality traits: Extension of previous psychometric investigations. *Australian Journal of Psychology, 50*, 114–118.

Brown, T. A., Di Nardo, P. A., & Barlow, D. H. (1994). *Anxiety Disorders Interview Schedule for DSM-IV (ADIS-IV).* New York: Oxford University Press.

Brown, T. A., Di Nardo, P. A., Lehman, C. L., & Campbell, L. A. (2001). Reliability of DSM-IV anxiety and mood disorders: Implications for the classification of emotional disorders. *Journal of Abnormal Psychology, 110*, 49–58.

Chapman, L. J., & Chapman, J. (1982). Test results are what you think they are. In D. Kahneman, P. Slovic, & A. Tversky, A. (Eds.), *Judgment under uncertainty: Heuristics and biases.* Cambridge, UK: Cambridge University Press.

Clark, D. A., Beck, A. T., & Alford, B. A. (1999). *Scientific foundations of cognitive theory and therapy for depression.* New York: John Wiley & Sons, Inc.

Colligan, R. C., Morey, L. C., & Offord, K. P. (1994). MMPI/MMPI-2 personality disorder scales: Contemporary norms for adults and adolescents. *Journal of Clinical Psychology, 50*, 168–200.

Costa, P. T., & McCrae, R. R. (1992). *Revised NEO Personality Inventory (NEOPI-R) and NEO Five-Factor Inventory (NEO-FFI) professional manual.* Odessa, FL: Psychological Assessment Resources.

Costello, A. J., Edelbrock, C. S., Dulcan, M. K., Kalas, R., & Klaric, S. H. (1984). *Development and testing of the NIMH Diagnostic Interview Schedule for Children on a clinical population: Final report.* Rockville, MD: Center for Epidemiological Studies, National Institute of Mental Health.

Dexter-Mazza, E. T., & Freeman, K. A. (2003). Graduate training and the treatment of suicidal clients: The students' perspective. *Suicide and Life Threatening Behavior, 33*, 211–218.

Dexter-Mazza, E. T., & Korslund, K. E. (2007). Suicide risk assessment. In M. Hersen and J. C. Thomas (Eds.), *Handbook of clinical interviewing with adults* (pp. 95-113). Thousand Oaks, CA: Sage Publications.

Di Nardo, P. A., Brown, T. A., & Barlow, D. H. (1994). *Anxiety Disorders Interview Schedule for DSM-IV: Lifetime Version.* New York: Oxford University Press.

Duman, S., Grodin, J., Céspedes, Y. M., Fine, E., Otilingham, P., & Margolin, G. (2007). Couples. In M. Hersen and J. C. Thomas (Eds.), *Handbook of clinical interviewing with adults* (pp. 340–357). Thousand Oaks, CA: Sage Publications.

Dumont, F. (1993). Inferential heuristics in clinical problem formulation: Selective review of their strengths and weaknesses. *Professional Psychology: Research and Practice, 24*, 196–205.

Dugas, M. J., & Robichaud, M. (2007). *Cognitive-behavioral treatment for generalized anxiety disorder: From science to practice.* New York: Routledge/Taylor & Francis Group.

Eaton, W. W., Neufeld, K., Chen, L., & Cai, G. (2000). A comparison of self-report and clinical diagnostic interviews for depression. *Archives of General Psychiatry, 57*, 217–222.

Edelbrock, C., Costello, A. J., Dulcan, M. K., Kalas, R., & Conover, N. C. (1985). Age differences in the reliability of the psychiatric interview of the child. *Child Development, 56*, 265–275.

Eells, T.D. (2007). *Handbook of psychotherapy case formulation* (2nd edition). New York: Guilford Press.

Eells, T. D., Lombart, K. G., Kendjelic, E. M., Turner, C., & Lucas, C. P. (2005). The quality of psychotherapy case formulations: A comparison of expert, experienced, and novice cognitive-behavioral and psychodynamic therapists. *Journal of Consulting and Clinical Psychology, 73*, 579–589.

Fairburn, C. G., & Cooper, Z. (1993). The Eating Disorders Examination (12th ed.). In C. G. Fairburn & G. T. Wilson (Eds.), *Binge eating: Nature, assessment, and treatment* (pp. 317–360). New York: Guilford Press.

Farmer, R. F. (2000). Issues in the assessment and conceptualization of personality disorders. *Clinical Psychology Review, 20*, 823–851.

Finn, S. E., & Tonsager, M. E. (1997). Information-gathering and therapeutic models of assessment: Complementary paradigms. *Psychological Assessment, 9*, 374–385.

First, M. B., & Gibbon, M. (2004). The Structured Clinical Interview for DSM-IV Axis I disorders (SCID-I) and the Structured Clinical Interview for DSM-IV Axis II disorders (SCID-II). In M. J. Hilsensorth & D. L. Segal (Eds.), *Comprehensive handbook of psychological assessment, Vol. 2: Personality assessment* (pp. 134–143). Hoboken, NJ: John Wiley & Sons, Inc.

First, M. B., Gibbon, M., Spitzer, R. L., Williams, J. B. W., & Benjamin, L. S. (1997). *Structured Clinical Interview for DSM-IV Axis II Personality Disorders* (SCID-II). Washington, D. C.: American Psychiatric Press.

First, M. B., Spitzer, R. L, Gibbon, M. & Williams, J. B. W. (2007). *Structured Clinical Interview for DSM-IV-TR Axis I Disorders, Research Version, Patient Edition.* (SCID-I/P) New York: Biometrics Research, New York State Psychiatric Institute.

First, M. B., Spitzer, R. L, Gibbon, M., & Williams, J. B. W. (1996). *Structured Clinical Interview for DSM-IV Axis I Disorders, Clinician Version* (SCID-CV). Washington, DC: American Psychiatric Press, Inc.

Fisher, P. W., Shaffer, D., Piacentini, J., Lapkin, J., Kafantaris, V., Leonard, H., et al. (1993). Sensitivity of the Diagnostic Interview Schedule for Children, 2nd edition (*DISC*-2.1) for specific diagnoses of children and adolescents. *Journal of the American Academy of Child & Adolescent Psychiatry, 32*, 666–673.

Flitcroft, A., James, I. A., Freeston, M., & Wood-Mitchell, A. (2007). Determining what is important in a good formulation. *Behavioural and Cognitive Psychotherapy, 35*, 325–333.

Foley, R., & Sharf, B. F. (1981). The five interviewing strategies most often overlooked by primary care physicians. *Behavioral Medicine, 8*, 26–31.

Folstein, M. F., Romanoski, A. J., Nestadt, G., Chahal, R., Merchant, A., Shapiro, S., et al. (1985). Brief report on the clinical reappraisal of the Diagnostic Interview Schedule carried out at the Johns Hopkins site of the Epidemiological Catchment Area Program of the NIMH. *Psychological Medicine, 15*, 809–814.

Garb, H. N. (1998). *Studying the clinician: Judgment research and psychological assessment.* Washington, DC: American Psychological Association.

Garb, H. N., & Grove, W. M. (2005). On the merits of clinical judgment. *American Psychologist, 60*, 658–659.

Gilovich, T. (1993). *How we know what isn't so: The fallibility of human reason in everyday life.* New York: The Free Press.

Goodman, W. K., Price, L. H., Rasmussen, S. A., Mazure, C., Fleischmann, R. L., Hill, C. L., Heninger, G. R., & Charney, D. S. (1989a). The Yale-Brown Obsessive Compulsive Scale: I. Development, use, and reliability. *Archives of General Psychiatry, 46*, 1006–1011.

Goodman, W. K., Price, L. H., Rasmussen, S. A., Mazure, C., Delgado, P., Heninger, G. R., & Charney, D. S. (1989b). The Yale-Brown Obsessive Compulsive Scale: II. Validity. *Archives of General Psychiatry, 46*, 1012–1016.

Goodman, W. K., Rasmussen, S. A., Price, L. H., & Storch, E. A. (2006). *Yale-Brown Obsessive-Compulsive Scale-Second Edition.* Unpublished manuscript.

Groth-Marnat, G. (2003). *Handbook of psychological assessment* (4th ed.). Hoboken, NJ: John Wiley and Sons.

Hamilton, M. (1960). A rating scale for depression. *Journal of Neurology, Neurosurgery and Psychiatry, 23*, 56–62.

Hamilton, M. (1967). Development of a rating scale for primary depressive illness. *British Journal of Social and Clinical Psychology, 6*, 278–296.

Harding, T. P. (2007). Clinical decision-making: How prepared are we? *Training and Education in Professional Psychology, 1*, 95–104.

Haro, J. M., Arbabzadeh-Bouchez, S., Brugha, T. S., de Girolamo, G., Guyer, M. E., et al. (2006). Concordance of the Composite International Diagnostic Interview Version 3.0 (CIDI 3.0) with standardized clinical assessments WHO World Mental Health Surveys. *International Journal of Methods in Psychiatric Research, 15*, 167–180.

Helzer, J. E., & Robins, L. N. (1988). The Diagnostic Interview Schedule: Its development, evolution, and use. *Social Psychiatry and Psychiatric Epidemiology, 23*, 6–16.

Hunsley, J., & Mash, E. J. (2008). *A guide to assessments that work.* New York: Oxford University Press.

Kahneman, D., & Tversky, A. (1972). Subjective probability: A judgment of representativeness. *Cognitive Psychology, 3*, 430–454.

Kahneman, D., & Tversky, A. (1973). On the psychology of prediction. *Psychological Review, 80*, 237–251.

Kendjelic, E. M., & Eells, T. D. (2007). Generic psychotherapy case formulation training improves formulation quality. *Psychotherapy: Theory, Research, Practice, Training, 44*, 66–77.

Kessler, R. C., Akiskal, H. S., Angst, J., Guyer, M., Hirschfeld, R. M. A., Marikangas, K. R., et al. (2006). Validity of the assessment of bipolar spectrum disorders in the WHO CIDI 3.0. *Journal of Affective Disorders, 96*, 259–269.

Kessler, R. C., Üstün, T. B. (2004). The World Mental Health (WMH) survey initiative version of the World Health Organization (WHO) Composite International Diagnostic Interview (CIDI). *International Journal of Methods in Psychiatric Research, 13*, 93–121.

Kleespies, P. M., Penk, W. E., & Forsyth, J. P. (1993). The stress of patient suicidal behavior during clinical training: Incidence, impact, and recovery. *Professional Psychology: Research and Practice, 24*, 293–303.

Knox, S., Burkard, A. W., Jackson, J. A., Schaack, A. M., & Hess, S. A. (2006). Therapists-in-training who experience a client suicide: Implications for supervision. *Professional Psychology: Research and Practice, 37*, 547–557.

Kobak, K. A., Skodol, A. E., & Bender, D. S. (2008). Diagnostic measures for adults. In J. Rush, M. B. First, and D. Blacker (Eds.), *Handbook of psychiatric measures*, 2nd edition, (pp. 35–60). Arlington, VA: American Psychiatric Publishing, Inc.

Kremer, T. G., & Gesten, E. L. (1998). Confidentiality limits of managed care and clients' willingness to self-disclose. *Professional Psychology: Research and Practice, 29*, 553–558.

Kutlesic, V., Williamson, D. A., Gleaves, D. H., Barbin, J. M., & Murphy-Eberenz, K. P. (1998). The Interview for the Diagnosis of Eating Disorders-IV: Application to DSM-IV diagnostic criteria. *Psychological Assessment, 10*, 41–48.

Kuyken, W., Padesky, C. A., & Dudley, R. (2009). *Collaborative case conceptualization: Working effectively with clients in cognitive-behavioral therapy.* New York: Guilford Press.

Lecrubier, Y., Sheehan, D. V., Weiller, E., Amorim, P., Bonora, I., Sheehan, K. H., et al. (1997). The Mini International Neuropsychiatric Interview (MINI). A short diagnostic structured interview: Reliability and validity according to the CIDI. *European Psychiatry, 12*, 224–231.

Liebowitz, M. R. (1987). Social phobia. *Modern Problems in Pharmacopsychiatry, 22*, 141–173.

Loranger, A. W. (1988). *Personality Disorder Examination (PDE) manual.* Yonkers, NY: DV Communications.

Loranger, A. W. (1999). *IPDE: International Personality Disorder Examination: DSM-IV and ICD-10 Interviews.* Odessa, FL: Psychological Assessment Resources.

Lyneham, H. J., Abbott, M. J., & Rapee, R. M. (2007). Interrater reliability of the anxiety disorders interview schedule for DSM-IV: Child and parent version. *Journal of the American Academy of Child and Adolescent Psychiatry, 46,* 731–736.

Maffei, C., Fossati, A., Agostoni, I., Barraco, A., Bagnato, M., Donati, D., et al. (1997). Interrater reliability and internal consistency of the Structured Clinical Interview for DSM-IV Axis II Personality Disorders (SCID-II), version 2.0. *Journal of Personality Disorders, 11,* 279–284.

McLellan, A. T., Luborsky, L., Woody, G. E., & O'Brien, C. P. (1980). An improved diagnostic evaluation instrument for substance abuse patients: The Addiction Severity Index. *Journal of Nervous and Mental Disorders, 168,* 26–33.

McNally, R. J. (2003). Progress and controversy in the study of posttraumatic stress disorder. *Annual Review of Psychology, 54,* 229–252.

Meehl, P. E. (1960). The cognitive activity of the clinician. *American Psychologist, 15,* 19–27.

Miller, C. (2003). Interviewing strategies. In M. Hersen, & S. M. Turner (Eds.), *Diagnostic interviewing* (pp. 3–20). New York: Springer.

Miller, P. R., Dasher, R., Collins, R., Griffiths, P., & Brown, F. (2001). Inpatient diagnostic assessments: 1. Accuracy of structured vs. unstructured interviews. *Psychiatry Research, 105,* 255–264.

Miller, W. R., & Marlatt, G. A. (1984). *Manual for the Comprehensive Drinker Profile.* Odessa, FL: Psychological Assessment Resources.

Mohlman, J., & Gorman, J. M. (2005). The role of executive functioning in CBT: A pilot study with anxious older adults. *Behaviour Research and Therapy, 43,* 447–465.

Mumma, G. H. (2001). Increasing accuracy in clinical decision making: Toward an integration of nomothetic-aggregate and intraindividual-idiographic approaches. *Behavior Therapist, 24,* 77–94.

Mumma, G. H. (2004). Validation of idiosyncratic cognitive schema in cognitive case formulations: An intraindividual idiographic approach. *Psychological Assessment, 16,* 211–230.

Mumma, G. H., & Mooney, S. R. (2007a). Comparing the validity of alternative cognitive case formulations: A latent variable, multivariate time series approach. *Cognitive Therapy and Research, 31,* 451–481.

Mumma, G. H., & Mooney, S. R. (2007b). Incremental validity of cognitions in a clinical case formulation: An intraindividual test in a case example. *Journal of Psychopathology and Behavioral Assessment, 29,* 17–28.

Nock, M. K., Borges, G., Bromet, E. J., Alonso, J., Angermeyer, M., Beautrais, A., Bruffaerts, R., et al. (2008). Cross-national prevalence and risk factors for suicidal ideation, plans, and attempts. *British Journal of Psychiatry, 192,* 98–105.

Overall, J. E., & Gorham, D. R. (1962). The Brief Psychiatric Rating Scale. *Psychological Reports, 10,* 79–812.

Paris, J. (2006). Predicting and preventing suicide: Do we know enough to do either? *Harvard Review of Psychiatry, 14,* 233–240.

Pearson, J. L., Stanley, B., King, C. A., & Fisher, C. B. (2001). Intervention research with persons at high risk for suicidality: Safety and ethical considerations. *Journal of Clinical Psychiatry, 62,* 17–26.

Persons, J. B. (1989). *Cognitive therapy in practice: A case formulation approach.* New York: W W Norton & Co.

Persons, J. B. (2006). Case formulation-driven psychotherapy. *Clinical Psychology: Science and Practice, 13,* 167–170.

Persons, J. B. (2008). *The case formulation approach to cognitive-behavior therapy.* New York: Guilford Press.

Persons, J. B., Mooney, K. A., & Padesky, C. A. (1995). Interrater reliability of cognitive-behavioral case formulations. *Cognitive Therapy and Research, 19,* 21–34.

Persons, J. B., Roberts, N. A., Zalecki, C. A., & Brechwald, W. A. G. (2006). Naturalistic outcome of case formulation-driven cognitive-behavior therapy for anxious depressed outpatients. *Behaviour Research and Therapy, 44,* 1041–1051.

Persons, J. B., & Tomkins, M. A. (1997). Cognitive-behavioral case formulation. In T. D. Eells (Ed.), *Handbook of psychotherapy case formulation* (pp. 314–339). New York: Guilford Press.

Persons, J. B., & Tomkins, M. A. (2007). Cognitive-behavioral case formulation. In T. D. Eells (Ed.), *Handbook of psychotherapy case formulation* (2nd edition). New York: Guilford Press.

Peterson, C. R., & Beach, L. R. (1967). Man as an intuitive statistician. *Psychological Bulletin, 68,* 29–46.

Pfohl, B., Blum, N., & Zimmerman, M., (1997). *Structured Interview for DSM-IV Personality.* Washington, DC: American Psychiatric Press.

Ridley, C. R., Li, L. C., & Hill, C. L. (1998). Multicultural assessment: Reexamination, reconceptualization, and practical application. *Counseling Psychologist, 26,* 827–910.

Robins, L. N., Cottler, L., Bucholz, K., & Compton, W. (1995). *The Diagnostic Interview Schedule, Version 4.* St. Louis, MO: Washington University.

Robins, J. N., Wing, J., Wittchen, H. U., Helzer, J. E., Babor, T. E., Burke, J., et al. (1988). The Composite International Diagnostic Interview: An epidemiologic instrument suitable for use in conjunction with different diagnostic systems and in different cultures. *Archives of General Psychiatry, 45,* 1069–1077.

Robins, L. N., Helzer, J. E., Ratcliff, K. S., & Seyfried, W. (1982). Validity of the diagnostic interview schedule, version II: DSM-III diagnoses. *Psychological Medicine, 12,* 855–870.

Rodolfa, E. R., Kraft, W. A., & Reilley, R. R. (1988). Stressors of professionals and trainees at APA-approved counseling and VA medical center internship sites. *Professional Psychology: Research and Practice, 19,* 43–49.

Rogers, C. R. (1951). *Client-centered therapy: Its current practice, implications and theory.* Boston, MA: Houghton Mifflin.

Rogers, R. (2001). *Handbook of diagnostic and structured interviewing.* New York: Guilford Press.

Rogers, R. (2003). Standardizing DSM-IV diagnoses: The clinical applications of structured interviews. *Journal of Personality Assessment, 81,* 220–225.

Ruegg, R. G., Ekstrom, D., Evans, D. L., & Golden, R. N. (1990). Introduction of a standardized report form improves the quality of mental status examination reports by psychiatric residents. *Academic Psychiatry, 14,* 157–163.

Rutter, P. A., Freedenthal, S., & Osman, A. (2008). Assessing protection from suicidal risk: Psychometric properties of the suicide resilience inventory. *Death Studies, 32,* 142–153.

Ryder, A. G., Costa, P. T., & Bagby, R. M. (2007). Evaluation of the SCID-II personality disorder traits for DSM-IV: Coherence, discrimination, relations with general personality traits, and functional impairment. *Journal of Personality Disorders, 21*, 626–637.

Sams, K., Collins, S., & Reynolds, S. (2006). Cognitive therapy abilities in people with learning disabilities. *Journal of Applied Research in Intellectual Abilities, 19*, 25–33.

Schwab-Stone, M., Fisher, P., Piacentini, J., Shaffer, D., Davies, M., & Briggs, M. (1993). The Diagnostic Interview Schedule for Children-Revised version (DISC-R): II. Test-retest reliability. *Journal of American Academy of Child and Adolescent Psychiatry, 32*, 651–657.

Shaffer, D., Fisher, P., Lucas, C., Dulcan, M., & Schwab-Stone, M. (2000). NIMH Diagnostic Interview Schedule for Children, Version IV (NIMH DISC-IV): Description, differences from previous versions, and reliability of some common diagnoses. *Journal of the American Academy of Child and Adolescent Psychiatry, 39*, 28–38.

Shea, S. C. (1998). *Psychiatric interviewing: The art of understanding* (2nd ed.). Philadelphia, PA: Saunders.

Shea, S. C. (2004). The delicate art of eliciting suicidal ideation. *Psychiatric Annals, 34*, 385–400.

Sheehan, D. V., Lecrubier, Y., Sheehan, K. H, Amorim, P., Janavas, J., Weiller, E., et al. (1998). The Mini-International Neuropsychiatric Interview (M. I. N. I): The development and validation of a structured diagnostic psychiatric interview for DSM-IV and ICD-10. *Journal of Clinical Psychiatry, 59*, 22–33.

Sheehan, D. V., Lecrubier, Y., Sheehan, K. H., Janavas, J., Weiller, E., Keskiner, A., et al. (1997). The validity of the Mini International Neuropsychiatric Interview (MINI) according to the SCID-P and its reliability. *European Psychiatry, 12*, 232–241.

Silverman W. K., & Albano, A. M. (1996). *Anxiety Disorders Interview Schedule for DSM-IV Child Version (ADIS-IV-Child)*. New York: Oxford University Press.

Silverman, W. K., Saavedra, L. M., & Pina, A. A. (2001). Test-retest reliability of anxiety symptoms and diagnoses with the Anxiety Disorders Interview Schedule for DSM-IV: Child and parent versions. *Journal of the American Academy of Child & Adolescent Psychiatry, 40*, 937–944.

Sommers-Flanagan, J., & Sommers-Flanagan, R. (2009). *Clinical Interviewing* (4th ed.). Hoboken, NJ: John Wiley & Sons.

Steinberg, M. (1994). *Interviewer's guide to the Structured Clinical Interview for DSM-IV Dissociative Disorders (SCID-D)*. Washington, DC: American Psychiatric Press.

Storch, E. A., Larson, M. J., Price, L. H., Rasmussen, S. A., Murphy, T. K., & Goodman, W. K. (2010a). Psychometric analysis of the Yale-Brown Obsessive-Compulsive Scale Second Edition Symptom Checklist. *Journal of Anxiety Disorders, 24*, 650–656.

Storch, E. A., Rasmussen, S. A., Price, L. H., Larson, M. J., Murphy, T. K., & Goodman, W. K. (2010b). Development and psychometric evaluation of the Yale-Brown Obsessive-Compulsive Scale – Second Edition. *Psychological Assessment, 22*, 223–232.

Summerfeldt, L. J., & Antony, M. M. (2002). Structured and semi-structured diagnostic interviews. In M. M. Antony & D. H. Barlow (Eds.), *Handbook of assessment and treatment planning for psychological disorders* (pp. 3–37). New York: Guilford Press.

Tiemens, B. G., VonKorff, M., & Linn, E. H. B. (1999). Diagnosis of depression by primary care physicians versus a structured diagnostic interview: Understanding discordance. *General Hospital Psychiatry, 21*, 87–96.

Turner, S. M., Hersen, M., & Heiser, N. (2003). The interviewing process. In M. Hersen, & S. M. Turner (Eds.), *Diagnostic Interviewing* (pp. 3–20). New York: Springer.

Ward, C. H., Beck, A. T., Mendelson, M., Mock, J. E., & Erbaugh, J. K. (1962). Psychometric nomenclature: Reasons for diagnostic disagreement. *Archives of General Psychiatry, 7*, 198–295.

Watson, D., & Clark, L. A. (1991). *The Mood and Anxiety Symptoms Questionnaire*. Unpublished manuscript, University of Iowa, Department of Psychology, Iowa City.

Weissman, A. (1979). *Dysfunctional Attitude Scale: A validation study*. Unpublished doctoral dissertation, University of Pennsylvania, Philadelphia.

Widiger, T. A. (2002). Personality disorders. In M. M. Antony & D. H. Barlow (Eds.), *Handbook of assessment and treatment planning for psychological disorders* (pp. 3–37). New York: Guilford Press.

Widiger, T. A., & Samuel, D. B. (2005). Evidence-based assessment of personality disorders. *Psychological Assessment, 17*, 278–287.

Williams, J. B. W., Gibbon, M., First, M. B., Spitzer, R. L., Davies, M., Borus, J., et al. (1992). The Structured Clinical Interview for the DSM-III-R (SCID): II. Multi-site test-retest reliability. *Archives of General Psychiatry, 49*, 630–636.

Wood, J. J., Piacentini, J. C., Bergman, R. L., McCracken, J., & Barrios, V. (2002). Concurrent validity of the anxiety disorders section of the Anxiety Disorders Interview Schedule for DSM-IV: Child and parent versions. *Journal of Clinical Child and Adolescent Psychology, 31*, 335–342.

Wood, J. M., Garb, H. N., Lilienfeld, S. O., & Nezworski, M. T. (2002). Clinical assessment. *Annual Review of Psychology, 53*, 519–543.

World Health Organization (1997). *The Composite International Diagnostic Interview (Version 2, 12 month)*. Geneva: Author.

Yates, B. T., & Taub, J. (2003). Assessing the costs, benefits, cost-effectiveness, and cost-benefit of psychological assessment: We should, we can, and here's how. *Psychological Assessment, 15*, 478–495.

Zanarini, M. C., Skodol, A. E., Bender, D., Dolan, R., Sanislow, C., Schaefer, E., et al. (2000). The Collaborative Longitudinal Personality Disorders Study: Reliability of Axis I and II diagnoses. *Journal of Personality Disorders, 14*, 291–299.

Zimmerman, M. (2003). What should the standard of care for psychiatric diagnostic evaluations be? *Journal of Nervous and Mental Disease, 191*, 281–286.

Zimmerman, M., & Mattia, J. I. (1999a). Psychiatric diagnosis in clinical practice: Is comorbidity being missed? *Comprehensive Psychiatry, 40*, 182–191.

Zimmerman, M., & Mattia, J. I. (1999b). Differences between research and clinical practices in diagnosing borderline personality disorder. *American Journal of Psychiatry, 156*, 1570–1574.

Diagnoses, Dimensions, and DSM-5

Thomas A. Widiger *and* Maryanne Edmundson

Abstract

The *Diagnostic and Statistical Manual of Mental Disorders, Third Edition* (DSM-III) is often said to have provided a significant paradigm shift in how psychopathology is diagnosed. The authors of DSM-5 have the empirical support and the opportunity to lead the field of psychiatry to a comparably bold new future in diagnosis and classification. The purpose of this chapter is to address the validity of the categorical and dimensional models for the classification and diagnosis of psychopathology. Considered in particular will be research concerning substance use disorders, mood disorders, and personality disorders. Limitations and concerns with respect to a dimensional classification of psychopathology are also considered. The chapter concludes with a recommendation for a conversion to a more quantitative, dimensional classification of psychopathology.

Keywords: Categorical, classification, diagnosis, dimensional, DSM-5, validity

The *Diagnostic and Statistical Manual of Mental Disorders* (DSM) is the classification of psychopathology developed under the authority of the American Psychiatric Association (APA), the current version of which is DSM-IV-TR (APA, 2000). The primary purpose of an official diagnostic nomenclature is to provide a common language of communication (Kendell, 1975; Sartorius et al., 1993), the absence of which essentially incapacitates communication among clinicians and researchers. Official diagnostic nomenclatures, however, can be exceedingly powerful, impacting many important social, scientific, forensic, clinical, and other professional decisions (Schwartz & Wiggins, 2002). Persons think in terms of their language, and the predominant language of psychopathology is DSM-IV-TR. As such, DSM-IV-TR has a substantial impact on how clinicians, scientists, and the general public conceptualize aberrant, problematic, and maladaptive behavior.

"DSM-IV is a categorical classification that divides mental disorders into types based on criterion sets with defining features" (APA, 2000, p. xxxi).

The categorical model of classification is consistent with a medical tradition in which it is believed (and often confirmed in other areas of medicine) that disorders have specific etiologies, pathologies, and treatments (Guze, 1978; Guze & Helzer, 1987; Zachar & Kendler, 2007). Clinicians, following this lead, diagnose and conceptualize the conditions presented in DSM-IV-TR as disorders that are qualitatively distinct from normal functioning and from one another. Clinicians devote initial time with a new patient to identify, through differential diagnosis, which specific disorder best explains a patient's presenting complaints. Authors of the diagnostic manual devote a considerable amount of time writing, revising, and researching diagnostic criteria to improve differential diagnosis, and scientists may devote their careers to attempting to identify the specific etiology, pathology, or treatment for a respective diagnostic category.

The principal model for the validation of distinct diagnostic categories was provided by Robins and Guze (1970), who articulated five fundamental phases: clinical description, laboratory study, delimitation from other disorders, follow-up, and family studies. However, the question of whether mental disorders are in fact discrete clinical conditions or arbitrary distinctions along continuous dimensions of functioning has been a longstanding issue (Kendell, 1975) and its significance is escalating with the growing recognition of the limitations of the categorical model (Widiger & Clark, 2000; Widiger & Samuel, 2005). As expressed by the Vice Chair of DSM-5, "the failure of DSM-III criteria to specifically define individuals with only one disorder served as an alert that the strict neo-Kraepelinian categorical approach to mental disorder diagnoses advocated by Robins and Guze (1970), Spitzer, Endicott, & Robins (1978), and others could have some serious problems" (Regier, 2008, p. xxi).

In 1999, a DSM-5 Research Planning Conference was held under joint sponsorship of the APA and the National Institute of Mental Health (NIMH), the purpose of which was to set research priorities that would optimally inform future classifications. An impetus for this effort was the frustration with the existing nomenclature (Kupfer, First, & Regier, 2002). At this conference, DSM-5 Research Planning Work Groups were formed to develop white papers that would set an effective research agenda for the forthcoming revision of the diagnostic manual. The Nomenclature Work Group, charged with addressing fundamental assumptions of the diagnostic system, concluded that it will be "important that consideration be given to advantages and disadvantages of basing part or all of DSM-5 on dimensions rather than categories" (Rounsaville et al., 2002, p. 12).

The white papers developed by the DSM-5 Research Planning Work Groups were followed by a series of international conferences whose purpose was to further enrich the empirical data base in preparation for the eventual development of DSM-5 (a description of this conference series can be found at http://www.dsm5.org). The first conference was devoted to shifting personality disorders to a dimensional model of classification (Widiger, Simonsen, Krueger, Livesley, & Verheul, 2005). The final conference was devoted to dimensional approaches across the diagnostic manual, including substance use disorders, major depressive disorder, psychoses, anxiety disorders, and developmental psychopathology, as well as the personality disorders (Helzer, Kraemer, et al., 2008).

The purpose of this chapter is to address the validity of the categorical and dimensional models for the classification and diagnosis of psychopathology.

Considered in particular will be research concerning substance use disorders, mood disorders, and personality disorders. Limitations and concerns with respect to a dimensional classification of psychopathology are also considered. The chapter concludes with a recommendation for a conversion to a more quantitative, dimensional classification of psychopathology.

Dimensional Models for DSM-5

One of the more problematic findings for the validity of the DSM-IV-TR categorical model of classification has been the excessive comorbidity among diagnoses (Krueger & Markon, 2006; Maser & Patterson, 2002; Widiger & Clark, 2000). The term "comorbidity" refers to the co-occurrence of distinct disorders, apparently interacting with one another, and each presumably with its own etiology, pathology, and treatment implications (Feinstein, 1970). However, in the case of psychopathology, comorbidity may be saying more about the invalidity of existing diagnostic distinctions than the presence of multiple conditions (Krueger, 2002).

DSM-IV-TR provides diagnostic criterion sets to help guide clinicians toward a purportedly correct diagnosis and an additional supplementary section devoted to differential diagnosis that indicates "how to differentiate [the] disorder from other disorders that have similar presenting characteristics" (APA, 2000, p. 10). The intention of the diagnostic manual is to help the clinician determine which particular mental disorder is present, the selection of which would presumably indicate the presence of a specific pathology that will explain the occurrence of the symptoms and suggest a specific treatment that will ameliorate the patient's suffering (Frances, First, & Pincus, 1995; Kendell, 1975). Considerable effort is spent by the authors of each edition of the diagnostic manual to further buttress each disorder's criterion set, trying to shore up discriminant validity and distinctiveness, following the rubric of Robins and Guze (1970) that the validity of a diagnosis rests in large part on its "delimitation from other disorders" (p. 108). "These criteria should ... permit exclusion of borderline cases and doubtful cases (an undiagnosed group) so that the index group may be as homogeneous as possible" (Robins & Guze, 1970, p. 108). Indeed, as acknowledged more recently by Kendell and Jablensky (2003), "if no detectable discontinuities in symptoms are found in large tracts of the territory of psychiatric disorder, it is likely that, sooner or later, our existing typology will be abandoned and replaced by a dimensional classification" (p. 8).

In an effort to force differential diagnosis, a majority of diagnoses in DSM-III (APA, 1980) contained exclusionary criteria specifying that a respective disorder could not be diagnosed if it could in fact be due to another disorder. These exclusions by fiat did not prove to be at all effective (Boyd et al., 1984) and many were deleted in DSM-III-R (APA, 1987). As expressed at the time by Maser and Cloninger (1990), "It is clear that the classic Kraepelinian model in which all psychopathology is comprised of discrete and mutually exclusive diseases must be modified or rejected" (p. 12).

Many DSM-IV-TR diagnostic criterion sets, however, continue to contain exclusionary criteria that attempt to force clinicians to make largely arbitrary choices among competing diagnoses (APA, 2000), and it is also evident that there is a highly problematic rate of diagnostic co-occurrence (Kessler, Chiu, Dember, & Walters, 2005). If one considers the entire diagnostic manual (which has not yet been done by any epidemiologic study), it would likely be exceedingly rare for any single patient to meet the criteria for just one disorder, and the comorbidity rises even further if one considers co-occurrence of lifetime disorders. Brown, Campbell, Lehman, Grisham, and Mancill (2001) reported that 95% of individuals in a clinical setting who meet criteria for lifetime major depression or dysthymia also meet criteria for a current or past anxiety disorder.

"The greatest challenge that the extensive comorbidity data pose to the current nosological system concerns the validity of the diagnostic categories themselves—do these disorders constitute distinct clinical entities?" (Mineka, Watson, & Clark, 1998, p. 380). Diagnostic comorbidity has become so prevalent that some researchers have argued for an abandonment of the term "comorbidity" in favor of a term (e.g., "co-occurrence") that is more simply descriptive and does not imply the presence of distinct clinical entities (Lilienfeld, Waldman, & Israel, 1994). There are instances in which the presence of multiple diagnoses do suggest the presence of distinct yet comorbid psychopathologies, but in most instances the presence of co-occurring diagnoses does appear to suggest the presence of a common, shared pathology (Clark, 2005; Krueger & Markon, 2006; Watson, 2005; Widiger & Clark, 2000). "Comorbidity may be trying to show us that many current treatments are not so much treatments for transient 'state' mental disorders of affect and anxiety as they are treatments for core processes, such as negative affectivity, that span normal and abnormal variation as well as undergird multiple mental disorders" (Krueger, 2002, p. 44).

New diagnostic categories are added to the nomenclature in large part to decrease clinicians' reliance on the nonspecific, wastebasket label of "not otherwise specified" (NOS). NOS is among the most frequent disorders within clinical populations (Clark, Watson, & Reynolds, 1995; Verheul & Widiger, 2004). Diagnostic criteria are developed and modified in order to construct a disorder that is as homogeneous as possible, thereby facilitating the likelihood of identifying a specific etiology, pathology, and treatment (Robins & Guze, 1970). However, the typical result of this effort is to leave many cases unaccounted for. In addition, despite the best effort to construct homogeneous and distinct syndromes, DSM-IV-TR is still replete with heterogeneous conditions with overlapping boundaries (Smith & Combs, in press). The function of most of the new disorders that are added to the diagnostic manual doesn't appear to involve the identification of uniquely new forms of psychopathology. Their purpose is generally instead to fill problematic gaps. Notable examples of DSM-IV included bipolar II (filling a gap between DSM-III-R bipolar and cyclothymic mood disorders), mixed anxiety-depressive disorder (a gap between anxiety and mood disorders), depressive personality disorder (personality and mood disorders), and postpsychotic depressive disorder of schizophrenia (schizophrenia and major depression) (Frances et al., 1995).

When new diagnoses are added to fill the gaps, they have the ironic effect of creating additional boundary problems, thereby making the problem of differential diagnosis even worse (Phillips, Price, Greenburg, & Rasmussen, 2003; Pincus, McQueen, & Elinson, 2003). One must ask whether it is really meaningful or useful to argue or decide whether mixed anxiety-depressive disorder is a mood or an anxiety disorder, whether schizoaffective disorder is a mood disorder or a form of schizophrenia (Craddock & Owen, 2005), whether postpsychotic depressive disorder of schizophrenia is a form of depression or schizophrenia, whether early-onset dysthymia is a mood or a personality disorder (Widiger, 2003), whether acute stress disorder is an anxiety or a dissociative disorder (Cardena, Butler, & Spiegel, 2003), whether hypochondriasis is an anxiety disorder or a somatoform disorder, whether body dysmorphic disorder is an anxiety, eating, or somatoform disorder, and whether generalized social phobia is an anxiety or a personality disorder (Widiger, 2001a). Yet these arbitrary and procrustean decisions must be made by the authors of a categorical diagnostic manual, and a considerable amount of effort and research is conducted to guide their decision, followed by further discussion and research to refute and debate whatever particular categorical decision was made.

Internalization and Externalization

As stated in DSM-IV-TR, "a categorical approach to classification works best when all members of a diagnostic class [e.g., mood disorder] are homogeneous, when there are clear boundaries between classes [e.g., mood and anxiety disorders], and when the different classes are mutually exclusive" (APA, 2000, p. xxxi). Nevertheless, it is quite evident from the comorbidity research that much diagnostic co-occurrence cuts across the major classes of anxiety, mood, substance use, psychotic, and personality disorders (Mineka et al., 1998). Achenbach and colleagues, quite a number of years ago, identified and subsequently validated two fundamental dimensions of psychopathology, internalization and externalization, that cut across and largely explained the co-occurrence among existing diagnostic categories of childhood (Achenbach, 1966; Achenbach & Edelbrock, 1978, 1984). Internalizing disorders included shy, anxious, depressive, inhibited, over-controlled behaviors, whereas externalizing involved aggressive, impulsive, acting-out, and conduct disordered behaviors. Achenbach and colleagues suggested that these two broad dimensions, along with empirically identified facets within each, would likely have more support as endophenotypic latent constructs with specific treatment implications than the existing diagnostic categories. These dimensions of Achenbach continue to have a strong impact on the study and understanding of childhood psychopathology (e.g., Lahey et al., 2004).

The internalization-externalization distinction of Achenbach and colleagues has been more recently applied to adult disorders of psychopathology, perhaps now to a much more receptive audience. Krueger and colleagues in particular have replicated the existence of these two broad domains using a variety of methods and sampling from a wide variety of populations. As suggested by Achenbach, internalizing is distinguished by prominent problems with negative emotion, and it influences liability to disorders such as major depression, generalized anxiety disorder, phobias, panic disorder, obsessive-compulsive disorder, and post-traumatic stress disorder. Externalizing also involves negative affectivity, along with disinhibition or impulsivity, and influences liability to disorders such as substance abuse

and dependence, antisocial personality disorder, and conduct disorder. As Achenbach had predicted, these superordinate dimensions have been successful in accounting for relationships among common forms of psychopathology (Krueger & Markon, 2006) and in helping to explain their etiology (Krueger, 2002). Kendler, Prescott, Myers, and Neale (2003), for instance, demonstrated that the comorbidity across major depression, generalized anxiety disorder, phobia, alcohol dependence, drug abuse and dependence, antisocial personality disorder, and conduct disorder does appear to concern a shared variance with individual differences in genetic structure. The "results suggest strongly that genetic factors are largely responsible for the pattern of comorbidity that results in the two frequently co-occurring clusters of internalizing and externalizing disorders" (Kendler et al., 2003, p. 253).

There is, of course, much that still need to be done with respect to these two broad constructs. For one, it isn't yet really clear how the APA diagnostic manual could in fact be re-organized with respect to internalization and externalization. The numerical coding system of the DSM-IV-TR may not even be able to provide any official recognition of a construct that cuts across different classes of disorders (Frances et al., 1995). In addition, there are many mood, anxiety, and personality disorder constructs that have typically been left out of the analyses, and many disorders outside of these broad classes of psychopathology that have been largely neglected (e.g., psychotic disorders, impulse dyscontrol disorders, paraphilias, and sex dysfunctions).

Perhaps most importantly, the explanatory power of the internalization and externalization constructs is not really clear. The constructs of internalization and externalization sound quite distinct, but they are typically highly correlated (e.g., Krueger et al., 1998; Lahey et al., 2008) and may not be that well distinguished conceptually. Krueger and Tackett (2003) suggest that the labels "make psychological sense... the internalizing disorders are associated with negative emotionality, whereas the externalizing disorders are associated with negative emotionality and a lack of constraint" (p. 121). However, it is perhaps problematic for their conceptual understanding and distinction to have both dimensions be heavily saturated with neuroticism or negative affectivity. The dimensions do not in fact appear to be well distinguished with respect to fundamental temperaments, which would presumably provide an important foundation and disposition toward the development of the respective DSM-IV-TR disorders

(Clark & Watson, 2008). Lahey et al. in fact noted that major depressive disorder and generalized anxiety disorder loaded on "externalizing" as well as "internalizing." They suggest that their "findings are consistent with the idea that dimensions of DSM-IV symptoms are hierarchically organized within such broad 'internalizing' and 'externalizing' dimensions (Krueger, 1999), but the nature of those broad dimensions will need to be reconsidered" (p. 203).

It might be useful if scales were developed to assess internalization and externalization rather than simply reproducing them in a somewhat different manner with each new study that organizes DSM-IV-TR disorders and/or symptoms in terms of the two respective dimensions. Researchers could then conduct studies that are more specifically concerned with their construct validity (Smith & Combs, in press). Achenbach and colleagues did develop instruments and scales for their assessment in children and adolescents (Achenbach, 1991; Achenbach & Rescorla, 2001) and perhaps their lead should again be followed in the further development and validation of these same constructs within adulthood.

Just as a factor analysis of heterogeneous scales or items will lack clear meaning, so will a factor analysis of a set of heterogeneous disorders. It would be useful to further differentiate each heterogeneous disorder (e.g., depression, borderline personality disorder) into its homogeneous components, and then factor analyze those components. This would more likely result in meaningful higher-order dimensions (Smith & Combs, in press). The purpose of an empirically derived hierarchical model of classification is not simply to provide a means with which to reproduce fundamentally flawed diagnostic categories that represent constellations of heterogeneous and overlapping symptoms, but to instead replace these flawed diagnoses with more specific and clearly defined constructs that are then more likely to have specific etiologies, pathologies, and treatment implications (Clark, 2007). Some progress in this area has begun (e.g., the distinction between distress and fear within the internalization domain; Watson, 2005). Indeed, homogeneous dimensions for many DSM-IV-TR disorders have been identified (Smith & Combs, in press).

Intellectual Disability

Many persons write as if a shift to a dimensional classification represents a new, fundamental change to the diagnostic manual (e.g., Regier, 2008; Rounsaville et al., 2002), and for much of the manual, diagnosing mental disorders on a continuum that shades imperceptibly into normal psychological functioning would certainly represent a fundamental change in how mental disorders are conceptualized and classified (Guze, 1978; Guze & Helzer, 1987; Robins & Guze, 1970). Nevertheless, there is a clear precedent for a dimensional classification of psychopathology already included within DSM-IV-TR: the diagnosis of mental retardation (APA, 2000).

Mental retardation in DSM-IV-TR is diagnosed along a continuum of intellectual and social functioning; more specifically, "significantly subaverage intellectual functioning: an IQ [intelligence quotient] of approximately 70 or below" (APA, 2000, p. 49), along with related deficits or impairments in adaptive functioning. An IQ of 70 does not carve nature at a discrete joint or identify the presence of a qualitatively distinct condition, disease, or disorder. On the contrary, it is a quantitatively arbitrary cutoff point along a continuum of functioning. An IQ of 70 is simply two standard deviations below the mean of an appropriate assessment instrument (American Association on Mental Retardation [AAMR], 2002).

Intelligence involves the ability to reason, plan, solve problems, think abstractly, comprehend complex ideas, learn quickly, and learn from experience (AAMR, 2002). It is distributed as a hierarchical, multifactorial continuous variable, as most persons' levels of intelligence, including most of those with mental retardation, is the result of a complex interaction of multiple genetic, fetal, and infant development, and environmental influences (Deary, Spinath, & Bates, 2006; Gray & Thompson, 2004). There are no discrete breaks in its distribution that would provide an absolute distinction between normal and abnormal intelligence. The point of demarcation for the diagnosis of an intellectual disability (the more current term for the disorder; Schalock et al., 2007) is an arbitrary, quantitative distinction along the normally distributed levels of hierarchically and multifactorially defined intelligence (i.e., two standard deviations below the normative mean). This point of demarcation is arbitrary in the sense that it does not correspond with a distinct, natural joint, but neither was it randomly or mindlessly chosen. It is a defensible selection that was informed by the impairments in functioning commonly associated with an IQ of 70 or below (AAMR, 2002).

In addition, the disorder of mental retardation is not diagnosed simply by the presence of an IQ of 70 or below. It must be accompanied by a documented impairment to functioning. "Mental retardation is a disability characterized by significant limitation in both intellectual functioning and in adaptive behavior as expressed in conceptual, social, and practical adaptive skills" (AAMR, 2002, p. 23). The purpose of the diagnosis is not to suggest that a specific pathology is present, but to identify persons who, on the basis of their intellectual disability, would be eligible for services and benefits to help them overcome or compensate for their relatively lower level of intelligence.

IQ scores, of course, must always be considered in light of the standard error of measurement, which for most IQ tests is approximately 5, and so an IQ as high as 75 may also be diagnosed. In addition, the diagnosis of mental retardation must also be considered relative to the adaptive behaviors the persons must learn to function in their everyday lives, not with respect to a notion of a maximal or absolute performance (AAMR, 2002). Those with IQ scores lower than 70 who can function effectively would not be diagnosed; hence, the diagnosis is understood in the context of the social, practical requirements of everyday functioning that must be met by the person (Luckasson & Reeve, 2001).

It is certainly the case that many instances of intellectual disability are due to specific etiologies, such as tuberous sclerosis, microcephaly, von Recklinghausen disease, trisomy 21, mosaicism, Prader-Willi syndrome, and many, many more (Kendell & Jablensky, 2003). Nevertheless, the disorders that result from these specific etiologies are generally understood as medical conditions, an associated feature of which is an intellectual disability that would be diagnosed concurrently and independently as mental retardation. The intellectual disability that is diagnosed as a mental disorder within DSM-IV-TR is itself a multifactorially determined and heterogeneous dimensional construct falling along the broad continuum of intellectual functioning. "The causes of intellectual disabilities are typically complex interactions of biological, behavioral/psychological, and sociocultural factors" (Naglieri, Salter, & Rojahn, 2008, p. 409). An important postnatal cause for intellectual disability is "simply" psychosocial deprivation, resulting from poverty, chaotic living environment, and/or child abuse or neglect. As expressed in DSM-IV-TR, "in approximately 30%–40% of individuals seen in clinical settings, no clear etiology for the mental retardation can be determined despite extensive evaluation efforts" (APA, 2000, p. 45). In sum, in the classification of intellectual disability (mental retardation), one diagnoses a multifactorial disorder

on the basis of a normative cutoff point and level of impairment without any implication of there being a qualitative distinction.

Alcohol Abuse and Dependence

One of the sections of the DSM-IV-TR for which a categorical model of classification and conceptualization has had a long and firmly entrenched tradition is the substance use disorders. Alcoholism in particular has a long tradition of being conceptualized as a qualitatively distinct disease (Garbutt, 2008; Goodwin & Guze, 1996; Jellinek, 1960). A significant change to its diagnosis and conceptualization occurred with DSM-III-R (APA, 1987) when it shifted from being understood as a purely physiological dependence to a broader and less specific behavioral dependence (Carroll, Rounsaville, & Bryant,1994; Edwards & Gross, 1976). "Dependence is seen as a complex process that reflects the central importance of substances in an individual's life, along with a feeling of compulsion to continue taking the substance and subsequent problems controlling use" (Schuckit et al., 1999, p. 41). To many, the diagnosis does still refer to a disease, but one that is developed through a social learning history (Kandel, 1998). It is perhaps time for a further fundamental shift in how this disorder is diagnosed and conceptualized.

One of the difficulties plaguing the diagnoses of alcohol dependence and abuse is the lack of a meaningful distinction between these two diagnostic categories. Abuse is generally considered to be simply a residual category and/or a less severe form of dependence (Saunders, 2006). Some of the diagnostic criteria for abuse are contained with the criterion set for dependence (e.g., interference with social, occupational, or recreational activities), which is always a problem for disorders that would be considered to be qualitatively distinct conditions. A related problem for the alcohol use disorder diagnoses (as well as for other substance use disorders) is the failure of either diagnostic category to adequately capture or cover a number of additional dyscontrolled and harmful patterns of alcohol use (Saunders, 2006). These failings could all reflect limitations that will be inherent to any effort to impose categorical diagnostic distinctions onto what is more validly understood to be a continuum of dyscontrolled and impairing alcohol usage (Widiger & Smith, 1994).

The diagnostic criteria for alcohol dependence were written largely in an effort to describe a prototypic case of this disorder, a practice that is largely followed for all but a few of the disorders in DSM-IV-TR

(Frances et al., 1995). However, prototypic cases are typically understood to be the most severe cases and/or those cases that involve all possible features or symptoms of the disorder (First & Westen, 2007). The diagnosis of an individual involves either counting up the number of features of these prototypic (most severe) cases that are present in the individual (Spitzer, Williams, & Skodol, 1980) or more subjectively matching the actual case to these prototypes (First & Westen, 2007).

The construction of diagnostic criterion sets in terms of prototypic cases does work to an extent, but it will also fail to adequately describe many of the actual cases, the subthreshold cases, and perhaps even the typical cases, depending upon the distribution of features and symptomatology within the general population. This approach is comparable to confining the description and diagnosis of mental retardation to the most severe variant of intellectual disability, and then attempting to apply this description to all of the less-severe variants; a method of diagnosis that would obviously be sorely limited. The limitations of this approach are now becoming more closely appreciated in the diagnosis of dyscontrolled substance use and, more specifically, alcohol use disorders, in which the existing criterion sets are failing to adequately describe dyscontrolled and impairing alcohol usage in adolescents (Crowley, 2006) and other "diagnostic orphans" (Saunders, 2006).

The limitation is perhaps most clearly demonstrated in studies using item response theory (IRT) methodology. Item response theory allows the researcher to investigate the fidelity with which items are measuring a latent trait along the length of its continuum, contrasting, for instance, the amount of information that different diagnostic criteria provide at different levels of a latent trait underlying the diagnostic construct (Muthen, 2006). A number of IRT analyses have now been conducted, and the findings are quite consistent (Reise & Waller, 2009. The existing diagnostic criterion sets (and/or symptoms currently assessed in existing instruments) cluster around the high end of the disorder, as opposed to being spread out across the entire range of the continuum (e.g., Kahler & Strong, 2006; Krueger et al., 2004; Langenbucher et al., 2004; Muthen, 2006; Proudfoot, Baillie, & Teesson, 2006; Saha, Chou, & Grant, 2006). This consistent pattern of results is in stark contrast to what is traditionally found in cognitive ability testing, where IRT analyses have been largely developed and previously applied (Reise & Waller, 2009. It is also worth noting that

the diagnostic criteria for abuse are not consistently providing information for a lower level of alcoholism severity (when compared to diagnostic criteria for dependence), and are at times providing more information than some dependency criteria at the higher levels of severity for the disorder (Kahler & Strong, 2006; Saha et al., 2006).

It is evident from the IRT analyses that the existing diagnostic criterion sets are sorely inadequate in characterizing the lower and even middle range of substance use dysfunction, consistent with the DSM-IV-TR description being confined to a prototypic case (of the presumably qualitatively distinct disorder). If alcohol usage was conceptualized along a continuum, the job of the authors of the diagnostic manual would be instead to construct a description and measurement of the disorder that adequately represents each of the levels or degrees to which the disorder appears along this continuum. Instead, the existing criterion sets are confined to only the most severe cases and are not describing well a large proportion of persons with clinically significant alcohol use dysfunction, and, as a result, clinicians must continue to rely on the nondescriptive, wastebasket diagnosis of NOS (Saunders, 2006).

Reise and Waller (2009) suggest that the IRT anomaly for substance use and other areas of psychopathology is a reflection of a "quasi-trait" status for many diagnostic constructs, by which they mean that the trait is unipolar (i.e., relevant only in one direction). Variation at the low end is relatively less informative because persons at the low end simply lack any meaningful variation with respect to the construct (e.g., absence of alcohol use symptomatology). This interpretation, however, might in fact be understood as being inconsistent with a dimensional understanding of the latent construct (i.e., the continuum only reflects a severity of dysfunction among persons with the disorder, rather than a broader continuum within the general population). One taxometric study has supported a latent categorical taxon for alcoholism (Walters, 2008). However, the bulk of the existing research does appear to be most consistent with the hypothesis that alcohol use disorders are best understood as a continuous distribution shading imperceptibly into normal, relatively nonharmful alcohol usage (Hasin, Liu, Alderson, & Grant, 2006; Muthen, 2006).

Further research, however, should perhaps explore the precise nature of the latent trait underlying the substance use continuum, particularly the trait that is being modeled in existing IRT and related research; more specifically, the extent to which the continuum may reflect simply a severity of impairment rather than a degree of dyscontrolled usage (Widiger & Smith, 1994). All mental disorders can be ranked along a common level of impairment (e.g., Axis IV of DSM-IV-TR; APA, 2000), and each disorder within each class of disorder (e.g., substance use) can be similarly ranked along this common continuum. For example, embedded within indicators of dyscontrol (e.g., drinking more than originally intended) are indicators of impairment secondary to this dyscontrol (e.g., problems with relationships, employment, arrests, and costs to physical health). These indicators of impairment will be seen in other disorders (i.e., level of impairment is a dimension common across all disorders). It is possible that the latent trait being identified and analyzed for different mental disorders in IRT analyses are not actually specific to each particular disorder (reflecting a continuum of that respective disorder), but perhaps measure instead the fact that all disorders vary in level of severity (even those that could in fact be qualitatively distinct medical conditions).

Depression

The mood disorders is a section of the APA diagnostic manual for which the presence of qualitatively distinct conditions is difficult to defend, particularly for the primary diagnoses of dysthymia and major depressive disorder. Discussed here will be early-onset dysthymia, the continuum of depression, and subthreshold major depression, along with more general points concerning the boundary between Axis I and Axis II disorders.

Early-onset Dysthymia

There is no meaningful distinction between early-onset dysthymia, an officially recognized mood disorder diagnosis, and depressive personality disorder, a proposed diagnosis within an appendix to DSM-IV-TR (APA, 2000). In fact, much of the empirical and conceptual basis for adding dysthymia to the DSM-III (APA, 1980) came from research and clinical literature concerning depressive personality (Keller, 1989). As acknowledged by the principal architects of DSM-III, dysthymia is "roughly equivalent to the concept of depressive personality" (Spitzer, Williams, & Skodol, 1980, p. 159). Depressive personality disorder was included within the mood disorders section of DSM-III despite the recommendations to recognize its existence as a personality disorder (Klerman, Endicott, Spitzer, & Hirschfeld, 1979) because it resembled the symptomatology of other mood disorders (i.e., depressed mood) more than it resembled the symptoms of other personality disorders (e.g., schizoid). However, whereas mood disorders are defined largely by similarity in content (i.e., mood being the predominant feature; APA, 2000), the personality disorders are defined largely by form (i.e., early onset, pervasive, and chronic), often with quite different content (e.g., schizoid also shares little resemblance to histrionic personality disorder).

After DSM-III was published, it became evident that many of the persons who were consistently and characteristically pessimistic, gloomy, cheerless, glum, and sullen (i.e., dysthymic) had been that way since childhood and that, in many cases, no apparent or distinct age of onset could be established. DSM-III-R therefore added an early-onset subtype (APA, 1987) and acknowledged that "this disorder usually begins in childhood, adolescence, or early adult life, and for this reason has often been referred to as a Depressive Personality" (APA, 1987, p. 231).

Personality disorder researchers made a further proposal for the inclusion of a depressive personality disorder (DPD) for DSM-IV. They were told that, in order for it to be included, it needed to be distinguished from the already established diagnosis of early-onset dysthymia, a task that might be considered rather difficult, if not unfair, given that the latter construct was based in large part on the former construct. Nevertheless, the DSM-IV Personality Disorders Work Group developed a proposed diagnostic criterion set that placed relatively more emphasis on cognitive features not currently included within the criterion set for dysthymia, as well as excluding somatic features (Task Force, 1991). This criterion set was provided to the DSM-IV Mood Disorders Work Group to include within their DSM-IV field trial to determine empirically whether it was indeed possible to demarcate any area of functioning not yet covered by early-onset dysthymia or at least identify persons not yet meeting diagnostic criteria for early-onset dysthymia.

The proposed criterion set was in fact successful in reaching this goal (Phillips et al., 1998), which perhaps should not be surprising, as no criterion set for a categorical diagnosis appears to be entirely successful in covering all cases. However, the Mood Disorders Work Group was equally impressed with the potential utility of the DPD diagnostic criteria for further describing and expanding the coverage of dysthymia (Keller et al., 1995) and therefore incorporated much of the proposed criteria for DPD into their proposed revisions for dysthymia

(Task Force, 1993). The DSM-IV Task Force recognized that it might be problematic to now require the personality disorder researchers to further redefine DPD to distinguish it from this further revision of dysthymia. The DSM-IV Task Force decided instead to include both criterion sets in the appendix to DSM-IV (along with the original criterion set for dysthymia within the mood disorders section), with the acknowledgment that there may not be any meaningful distinction between them (APA, 2000 Frances et al., 1995).

The issues and concerns that plague any distinction between early-onset dysthymia and depressive personality disorder are also readily apparent for many other boundaries between the personality disorders and Axis I disorders (Krueger, 2005), particularly the distinction between generalized social phobia and avoidant personality disorder (Schneider, Blanco, Anita, & Liebowitz, 2002; Widiger, 2003). In fact, many, if not most, of the personality disorders can be understood, in part, as early-onset variants of Axis I disorders (Krueger, 2005; Widiger, 2003). In addition to the avoidant and depressive personality disorders, borderline personality disorder could be reconceptualized as an affective dysregulation disorder (Linehan, 2000); schizoid as an early-onset and chronic variant of the negative (anhedonic) symptoms of schizophrenic pathology (Miller, Useda, Trull, Burrs, & Minks-Brown, 2001; Parnas, Licht, & Bovet, 2005); paranoid personality disorder by an early onset, chronic, and milder variant of a delusional disorder; obsessive-compulsive personality disorder by a generalized and chronic variant of obsessive-compulsive anxiety disorder (although there is in fact only weak evidence to support a close relationship between the obsessive-compulsive anxiety and personality disorders; Costa, Samuels, Bagby, Daffin, & Norton, 2005); and antisocial personality disorder by an adult variant of conduct (disruptive behavior) disorder. The World Health Organization's (WHO) International Classification of Diseases (ICD-10; WHO, 1992), the parent classification to the APA diagnostic manual, already includes schizotypal personality disorder within the section of the manual for disorders of schizophrenia, not recognizing the existence of DSM-IV-TR schizotypal personality disorder. There is a good possibility that the authors of DSM-5 will follow this lead (First et al., 2002; Siever & Davis, 1991).

Support for conceptualizing schizotypal personality disorder as a form of schizophrenia includes that it is genetically related to schizophrenia, most of its neurobiological risk factors and psychophysiological correlates are shared with schizophrenia (e.g., eye tracking, orienting, startle blink, and neurodevelopmental abnormalities), and the treatments that are effective in ameliorating schizotypal symptoms overlap with treatments used for persons with Axis I schizophrenia (Lenzenweger, 2006). Nevertheless, inconsistent with the ICD-10 classification of schizotypal personality disorder as a form of schizophrenia is that it is far more comorbid with other personality disorders than it is with psychotic disorders, persons with schizotypal personality disorder rarely go on to develop schizophrenia, and schizotypal symptomatology is seen in quite a number of persons who appear to lack a genetic association with schizophrenia and would not be at all well described as being schizophrenic (Raine, 2006).

An additional concern with reformulating personality disorders as early-onset and chronic variants of Axis I disorders, including dysthymia, beyond the fundamental consideration that the diagnostic manual would no longer recognize the existence of maladaptive personality functioning, is that it might create more problems than it solves. It does appear to be true that persons have constellations of maladaptive personality traits that are not well described by just one or even multiple personality disorder diagnoses (Widiger & Trull, 2007). These constellations of maladaptive personality traits would be even less well described by multiple Axis I diagnoses across broad classes of anxiety, mood, impulsive dyscontrol, delusional, disruptive behavior, and schizophrenic disorders (Widiger & Smith, 2008).

The DSM-IV-TR as a categorical model of classification has a fundamental difficulty in resolving these boundary disputes. The boundaries are quite distinct in theory, yet in reality they appear to be very fluid, arbitrary, and even illusory. The coverage within a diagnostic class literally becomes a territory defended by work group members, fending off threats to their borders, at the same time attempting to annex new territory within their sphere of influence. Clinicians devote considerable amounts of time attempting to make differential diagnoses, and researchers spend time, funds, and journal space arguing whether early-onset dysthymia is a personality disorder or a mood disorder (Huprich, 2003; Ryder, Bagby, & Schuller, 2002; Vachon Sellbom, Ryder, Miller & Bagby, in press). It is perhaps time to recognize that there is no clear answer to such questions or, minimally, to allow both perspectives comparable representation.

The Continuum of Depression

Even the namesake for the neo-Kraepelinian approach to diagnosis appears to have known that it doesn't really work. Kraepelin (1917) himself acknowledged that "wherever we try to mark out the frontier between mental health and disease, we find a neutral territory, in which the imperceptible change from the realm of normal life to that of obvious derangement takes place" (p. 295). A simple inspection of the diagnostic criteria for major depressive disorder would not lend confidence to a conceptualization of this disorder as a condition that is qualitatively distinct from normal depression or sadness (Andrews et al., 2008). The diagnostic criteria include depressed mood, loss of interest or pleasure, weight loss (or gain), insomnia (or hypersomnia), psychomotor retardation (or agitation), loss of energy, feelings of worthlessness, and/or diminished capacity to make decisions. Each of these diagnostic criteria is readily placed along a continuum of severity that would shade imperceptibly into what would be considered a normal sadness or depression. DSM-IV-TR, therefore, includes specific thresholds for each of them, but they are clearly arbitrary attempts to demarcate simply a relatively high level of severity (e.g., "nearly every day" or "markedly diminished," and at least a "2-week" period; APA, 2000). The diagnosis itself requires five of the nine criteria, with no apparent rationale for this threshold other than it would appear to be severe enough to be defensible to be titled as a "major" depressive episode, as distinguished from a "minor" depressive episode, which is then distinguished from "normal" sadness (APA, 2000).

Depression does appear to shade imperceptibly into "normal" sadness (Andrews et al., 2008). Ustun and Sartorius (1995) conducted a study of 5,000 primary care attendees in 14 countries and reported a linear relationship between disability and number of depressive symptoms. Kessler, Zhao, Blazer, and Swartz (1997) examined the distribution of minor and major symptoms of depression using data from the National Comorbidity Survey. They examined the relationship of these symptoms with parental history of mental disorder, number and duration of depressive episodes, and comorbidity with other forms of psychopathology. Relationship increased with increasing number of symptoms, with no clear, distinct break in relationships. Sakashita, Slade, and

Andrews (2007) examined the relationship between the number of symptoms of depression and four measures of impairment using data from the Australian National Survey of Mental Health and Well-Being, and found that the relationship was again simply linear, with no clear or natural discontinuity to support the selection of any particular cutoff point.

Taxometrics refers to a series of related statistical techniques to detect whether a set of items is optimally understood as describing (assessing) a dimensional or a categorical construct (Beauchaine, 2007; Ruscio & Ruscio, 2004). Other statistical techniques, such as cluster or factor analyses, presume that the construct is either categorical or dimensional (respectively) and then determines how best to characterize the variables or items in either a categorical or dimensional format (respectively). Taxometric analyses are uniquely intriguing in providing a direct test of which structural model is most valid in characterizing the set of items or variables.

A number of taxometric studies have been conducted on various symptoms and measures of depression. The first was provided by Ruscio and Rusio (2000) in their taxometric analyses of items from the Beck Depression Inventory and, independently, items from the Zung Self-Rating Depression Scale in a sample of 996 male veterans who had received a diagnosis of post-traumatic stress disorder but also had a high prevalence rate of major depressive disorder, as well as a sample of 8,045 individuals (60% female) who completed the items from the Depression scale of the Minnesota Multiphasic Personality Inventory (MMPI). They indicated that "results of both studies, drawing on three widely used measures of depression, corroborated the dimensionality of depression" (Ruscio & Ruscio, 2000, p. 473).

The taxometric findings of Ruscio and Ruscio (2000) have been subsequently replicated, including taxometric analyses of (a) structured interview assessments of DSM-IV-TR major depressive disorder symptoms and, independently, items from the Beck Depression Inventory in a sample of 960 psychiatric outpatients (Slade, 2007); (b) major depressive disorder diagnostic criteria assessed in the 1,933 persons who endorsed at least one criterion in the Australian National Survey of Mental Health and Well-Being (Slade & Andrews, 2005); (c) self- and parent reported depressive symptoms in 845 children and adolescents drawn from the population-based

Georgia Health and Behavior Study (Hankin, Fraley, Lahey, & Waldman, 2005); (d) responses to MMPI-2 depression scales completed by 2,000 psychiatric inpatients and outpatients (Franklin, Strong, & Greene, 2002); (e) epidemiologic survey of depressive symptoms within 392 college students (Baldwin & Shean, 2007); (f) Beck Depression Inventory items reported by 2,260 college students (Ruscio & Ruscio, 2002); and (g) depression items in the Composite International Diagnostic Interview, as administered in the National Comorbidity Survey to 4,577 participants who endorsed the item concerning a lifetime occurrence of sad mood or loss of interest (Prisciandoro & Roberts, 2005). However, in contrast to the findings from these eight taxometric studies, three taxometric studies have supported a latent class taxon, including semistructured interview assessments of DSM-IV-TR major depressive disorder symptoms in 1,800 psychiatric outpatients (Ruscio, Zimmerman, McGlinchey, Chelminski, & Young, 2007), interview and self-report assessments of depression in 1,400 high school students (Solomon, Ruscio, Seeley, & Lewinsohn, 2006), and self-report and interview data on depression in 378 adolescents receiving treatment for depression (Ambrosini, Bennett, Cleland, & Haslam, 2002). In sum, the bulk of the evidence does appear to support a dimensional understanding of depression, but there is some ambiguity and inconsistency in the taxometric findings (Beach & Amir, 2003; Beauchaine, 2007; Widiger, 2001b).

Subthreshold Major Depression

Depression is a section of the diagnostic manual that does have considerable difficulty identifying or defining a clear boundary with "normal" sadness. Subthreshold cases of depression (i.e., persons with depressive symptoms below the threshold for a DSM-IV-TR mental disorder diagnosis) are clearly responsive to pharmacologic interventions, do seek treatment for their sadness, and are often being treated within primary care settings (Judd, Schettler, & Akiskal, 2002; Magruder & Calderone, 2000; Pincus, McQueen, & Elinson, 2003). These facts contributed to the proposal to include within DSM-IV the diagnosis of "minor depressive disorder" for which it is simply acknowledged "can be difficult to distinguish from periods of sadness that are an inherent part of everyday life" (APA, 2000, p. 776).

Wakefield (2007) has been critical of the DSM-IV-TR criteria for major depressive disorder for including an inconsistently applied exclusion criterion. The diagnosis excludes most instances of depressive reactions to the loss of a loved one (i.e., uncomplicated bereavement). Depression after the loss of a loved one can be considered a mental disorder if "the symptoms persist for longer than 2 months" (APA, 2000, p. 356). Allowing just 2 months to grieve before one is diagnosed with a mental disorder does appear to be rather arbitrary. Perhaps more importantly, it is also unclear if depression in response to other losses should not also then be comparably excluded, such as depression secondary to the loss of a job or physical health (Wakefield, Schimtz, First, & Horwitz, 2007).

One could also argue alternatively that all exclusion criteria should be removed. Perhaps the problem is not that depression in response to a loss of a job or physical disorder should not be a disorder, analogous to bereavement (Wakefield, 2007); perhaps the problem is that bereavement should be a mental disorder (Bonanno et al., 2007; Forstmeier & Maercker, 2007; Widiger & Miller, 2008). What is currently considered to be a normal depression in response to the loss of a loved one does often, if not always, include pain and suffering, meaningful impairment to functioning, and is outside of the ability of the bereaved person to fully control, the essential hallmarks of a mental disorder (Widiger & Sankis, 2000). The depression is a reasonable response to the loss of a loved one, but many physical disorders and injuries are reasonable and understandable responses to viruses and accidents. The loss is part of the etiology for the disorder, not a reason for which the disorder is not present (Widiger, 2008).

Personality Disorders

Rounsaville et al. (2002) suggested that the first section of the APA diagnostic manual to shift to a dimensional classification should be the personality disorders (ignoring for the moment that mental retardation is already dimensional). They did not provide a reason for identifying personality disorders as a likely first place for such a fundamental shift, but one reason would be that personality disorders have been among the most problematic of disorders to be diagnosed categorically (First et al., 2002). Personalities are generally understood to involve constellations of adaptive and maladaptive personality traits that are not well summarized in just one word, the etiologies for which appear to involve complex interactions of an array of genetic dispositions and environmental experiences unfolding over time. The personality disorder diagnostic categories of DSM-IV-TR do not appear to be functioning well as a descriptive model, being stricken with significant diagnostic heterogeneity, excessive diagnostic co-occurrence, lack of stable or meaningful diagnostic thresholds, inadequate coverage, and a weak scientific foundation (Clark, 2007; Trull & Durrett, 2005; Widiger & Trull, 2007).

However, a more positive reason for personality disorders being potentially the first to shift to a dimensional model of classification is that there already exists a well-developed and empirically supported dimensional classification of general personality structure with which the APA personality disorders can be readily integrated: the five-factor model (Widiger & Trull, 2007). The five-factor model (FFM) consists of five broad domains of general personality functioning: neuroticism (or emotional instability), extraversion versus introversion, openness versus closedness, agreeableness versus antagonism, and conscientiousness. The FFM was derived originally through empirical studies of the trait terms within the English language. Language can be understood as a sedimentary deposit of the observations of persons over the thousands of years of the language's development and transformation. The most important domains of personality functioning are those with the most number of trait terms to describe and differentiate the various manifestations and nuances of a respective domain, and the structure of personality is suggested by the empirical relationships among these trait terms. The initial lexical studies with the English language converged well onto a five-factor structure (Ashton & Lee, 2001). Subsequent lexical studies have been conducted on many additional languages (e.g., German, Dutch, Czech, Polish, Russian, Italian, Spanish, Hebrew, Hungarian, Turkish, Korean, and Filipino), and these have confirmed well the existence of the five broad domains (Ashton & Lee, 2001; Church, 2001). The five broad domains have been differentiated into more specific facets by Costa and McCrae (1992) on the basis of their development of and research with the NEO Personality Inventory-Revised (NEO PI-R), by far the most commonly used and heavily researched measure of the FFM.

Studies have also now well documented that all of the DSM-IV-TR personality disorder symptomatology are readily understood as maladaptive variants of the domains and facets of the FFM (O'Connor, 2002, 2005; Samuel & Widiger, 2008; Saulsman & Page, 2004; Widiger & Costa, 2002). As acknowledged by Livesley (2001b), "all categorical diagnoses of DSM can be accommodated within the five-factor framework" (p. 24). As expressed by Clark (2007), a long advocate of an alternative three-factor model (Clark, 2005), "the five-factor model of personality is widely accepted as representing the higher-order structure of both normal and abnormal personality traits" (p. 246). Huprich (2003), Ryder et al. (2002), and Vachon et al. (in press) disagree as to the inclusion of depressive personality disorder in DSM-5, but they do agree that it is best understood from the perspective of the FFM.

However, the purpose of an FFM of personality disorder is not simply to describe the diagnostic categories of DSM-IV-TR. It is instead to replace the DSM-IV-TR diagnostic categories with a more clinically useful, feasible, and empirically validated classification. The FFM of personality disorder would cover both normal and abnormal personality functioning within a single, common structure, bringing to an understanding of personality disorders a considerable amount of basic science research supporting behavior genetics (Yamagata et al., 2006), molecular genetics for neuroticism (Munafo, Clark, & Flint, 2005), childhood antecedents (Caspi, Roberts, & Shiner, 2005; Mervielde, De Clerq, De Fruyt, & Van Leeuwen, 2005), temporal stability across the life span (Roberts & DelVecchio, 2000), and universality (Allik, 2005; Ashton & Lee, 2001). This is a scientific foundation that is sorely lacking for the existing nomenclature (Blashfield & Intoccia, 2000; Widiger & Trull, 2007).

Widiger, Costa, and McCrae (2002) proposed a four-step procedure for the diagnosis of a personality disorder from the perspective of the FFM that is quite comparable to the current procedure for the diagnosis of mental retardation. The first step is to obtain a hierarchical and multifactorial description of an individual's general personality structure in terms of the five domains and 30 facets of the FFM. Widiger and Lowe (2007) provide a discussion of optimal instruments for this assessment. The second step is to identify problems in living associated with elevated scores. Problems in living associated with each of the 60 poles of the 30 facets of the FFM are provided in Widiger et al. (2002) and McCrae, Loeckenhoff, and Costa (2005). Each of these problems is considered within the social-cultural context in which the person must function, as some personality traits can be quite adaptive within some contexts but maladaptive within others (Wakefield, 2008; Widiger & Costa, 1994). The third step is to determine whether the impairments reach a clinically significant level that would warrant a diagnosis of personality disorder. This can be done through simply a sum of the impairments associated with each facet or through a more inferential consideration of the configuration or interaction of traits (Wakefield, 2008). The latter is more consistent with traditional personality disorder theory, but the former would be simpler and perhaps more reliable. The fourth step is optional: a quantitative matching of the individual's FFM personality profile to prototypic profiles of diagnostic constructs (e.g., Miller & Lynam 2003; Trull, Widiger, Lynam, & Costa, 2003). An illustration of this four-step procedure was provided by Widiger and Lowe (2007). Further discussions of this proposal are provided by Widiger and Lowe (2008) and Widiger and Mullins-Sweatt (2009).

The FFM of personality disorder has substantially more construct validity than the existing diagnostic categories (Skodol et al., 2005; Widiger & Trull, 2007). However, an FFM diagnosis might at first blush appear to involve a considerable amount of work (step four is, though, optional). Clinicians may understandably find it daunting to conceive of having to become familiar with both the adaptive and maladaptive variants of all 60 poles of all 30 facets of the FFM (Widiger et al., 2002). A lengthy, complicated profile concerning 60 poles of 30 facets is perhaps unlikely to be used reliably (Ruscio, 2008). Consider, for instance, the original Framingham Index for indexing dimensionally the risk for cardiac problems (Kraemer, 2008). The weighting of age, gender, smoking status, high blood pressure medication, high-density lipoprotein cholesterol, and so forth provided a highly valid measure of cardiac risk but did not become a routine measure in general clinical practice due to being considered overly cumbersome. A simplified version was therefore created and is now frequently used.

Figure 13.1 provides an abbreviated version of the FFM of personality disorder (Widiger & Mullins-Sweatt, 2009; Widiger & Lowe, 2008). The FFM classification of personality disorder provided in Figure 13.1 is a simplification in a number of ways. First, the adaptive behaviors are confined to just the five broad domains, rather than the 30 facets. In addition, the maladaptive facets have been reduced from 60 to just 26. This reduction was achieved in part by eliminating poles of facets that were considered to be too infrequent or obscure for most clinical use (e.g., maladaptively high openness to aesthetics).

Figure 13.2 provides draft diagnostic criteria for the extraversion versus introversion domain, and for the four respective maladaptive facets for that domain included within the abbreviated version. A patient is first assessed with respect to the six facets of the FFM. Each facet is rated on a 1 to 5 Likert scale, consistent with existing research with the Five-Factor Model Rating Form (FFMRF; Mullins-Sweatt, Jamerson, Samuel, Olson, & Widiger, 2006). If the person receives an elevated score, then the clinician would assess for the presence of the two maladaptive variants of high extraversion (i.e., reckless sensation-seeking and intense attachment). If the person receives a low score, then the clinician would assess for maladaptive variants of introversion. Space limitations prohibit the presentation of all of the diagnostic criteria for all five domains and the 26 facets, but these can obtained on request from the first author. If the person receives a score within the middle range, then no further assessment would typically be necessary (exceptions to this are discussed below).

The presence of 26 facets might still seem daunting. However, it is important to appreciate that each of the FFM clinical constructs are substantially easier to assess than the DSM-IV-TR personality disorders, as the latter constitute complex combinations and constellations of these constructs (Clark, 2007; Livesley, 2001b; Lynam & Widiger, 2001; Widiger & Trull, 2007). A classification system that abandons the fruitless effort to make illusory differential diagnoses among overlapping diagnostic categories in favor of a more straightforward description of each individual's unique personality profile will likely be much easier to use than the existing diagnostic categories (Widiger & Lowe, 2007). In addition, the maladaptive facets are only assessed if there is an elevation on a respective domain. One first begins with the description of the person in terms of general personality functioning at the level of the five broad domains. If the person is assessed to be high in agreeableness (for instance), one would then assess for the maladaptive variants of deference and meekness, and one would not need to assess for the maladaptive variants of suspiciousness, manipulation, aggression, or arrogance. In this way, the five broad domains serve in part as a screening process, identifying whether particular maladaptive traits need to be assessed (exceptions to this rule of thumb can occur if a person is both extremely high and extremely low on facets within the same domain). An FFM assessment of personality disorder generally takes half the amount of time than an assessment of the DSM-IV-TR personality disorders, as much of the administration of a DSM-IV-TR personality disorder semistructured interview is spent in the assessment of diagnostic criteria that are not present (Widiger & Lowe, 2007). This considerable amount of time is diminished substantially by the

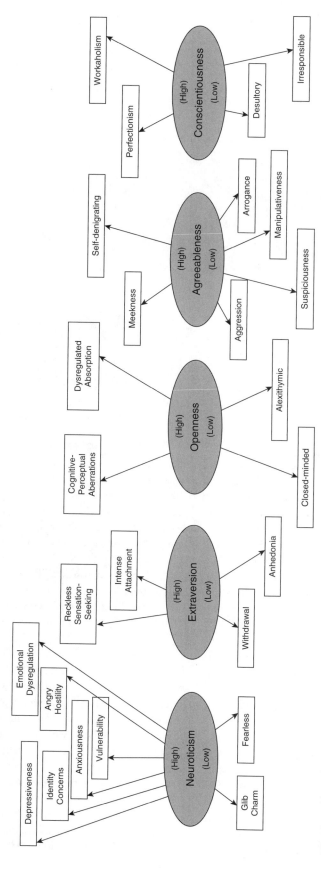

Fig. 13.1 Abbreviated Version of FFM Proposal for DSM-5

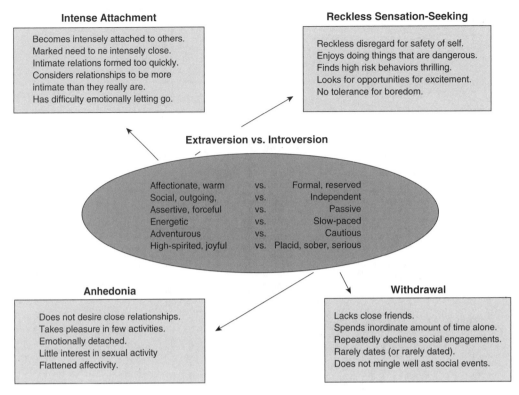

Intense Attachment

Becomes intensely attached to others.
Marked need to ne intensely close.
Intimate relations formed too quickly.
Considers relationships to be more
intimate than they really are.
Has difficulty emotionally letting go.

Reckless Sensation-Seeking

Reckless disregard for safety of self.
Enjoys doing things that are dangerous.
Finds high risk behaviors thrilling.
Looks for opportunities for excitement.
No tolerance for boredom.

Extraversion vs. Introversion

Affectionate, warm	vs.	Formal, reserved
Social, outgoing,	vs.	Independent
Assertive, forceful	vs.	Passive
Energetic	vs.	Slow-paced
Adventurous	vs.	Cautious
High-spirited, joyful	vs.	Placid, sober, serious

Anhedonia

Does not desire close relationships.
Takes pleasure in few activities.
Emotionally detached.
Little interest in sexual activity
Flattened affectivity.

Withdrawal

Lacks close friends.
Spends inordinate amount of time alone.
Repeatedly declines social engagements.
Rarely dates (or rarely dated).
Does not mingle well ast social events.

Fig. 13.2 FFM Diagnosis of Maladaptive Extraversion Versus Introversion

FFM through the screening process of assessing whether the person is high or low in the five broad domains of general personality functioning.

The abbreviated version does naturally fail to include all of the maladaptive traits present within the FFM (Widiger et al., 2002; Widiger & Lowe, 2008). Missing from the abbreviated version, for instance, are such maladaptive variants as attention-seeking (high gregariousness), gullibility (high trust), guilelessness (high straightforwardness), exploitativeness and greed (low altruism), callousness (high tough-mindedness), ruminative indecisiveness (high deliberation), hedonism (low self-discipline), and aimlessness (low achievement-striving). Nevertheless, even in the abbreviated version, clinicians would be alerted to the potential presence of the additional maladaptivity through elevations on specifically relevant facet scales within each of the five domains. For example, with respect to Figure 13.2, a person could receive the highest (or lowest) possible score on a respective facet for which no maladaptive variant is provided (e.g., a score of 5 on gregariousness, suggesting the potential presence of attention-seeking, or a score of 1 on warmth suggesting the possibility of interpersonal coldness). These specific facets of

maladaptive personality functioning could then be assessed, if wished, through an implementation of the more complete, full version of the FFM of personality disorder. A number of instruments have been developed to facilitate this more complete and comprehensive assessment (Widiger & Lowe, 2007), including the NEO PI-R (Costa & McCrae, 1992), which will assess well the normal range, as well as the Structured Interview Assessment of the Five-Factor Model (Trull & Widiger, 1997) and the FFMRF (Mullins-Sweatt et al., 2006).

Discussion

The diagnosis of mental disorders has been largely within the domain of medicine, which has used since the days of Hippocrates a categorical model of classification (Kendell, 1975). Many clinicians identify themselves as being within a branch of medicine, treating pathologies that are qualitatively distinct from normal functioning. A reformulation of mental disorders as shading imperceptibly into normal psychological functioning could complicate the perceived identity of the profession (Guze, 1978; Guze & Helzer, 1987). This concern has perhaps been best expressed by Wakefield (2008), when he raised a foreboding alarm that a shift to a dimensional classification of personality disorder "has the potential to undermine some of the progress that has been made in relegitimizing psychiatry after the disastrous years of the antipsychiatry movement" (p. 383). One might ask, though, what in fact he is defending. As expressed by Drs. Kupfer, First, and Regier (two of whom are the Chair and Vice Chair of DSM-5):

> In the more than 30 years since the introduction of the Feighner criteria by Robins and Guze, which eventually led to DSM-III, the goal of validating these syndromes and discovering common etiologies has remained elusive. Despite many proposed candidates, not one laboratory marker has been found to be specific in identifying any of the DSM-defined syndromes. Epidemiologic and clinical studies have shown extremely high rates of comorbidities among the disorders, undermining the hypothesis that the syndromes represent distinct etiologies. Furthermore, epidemiologic studies have shown a high degree of short-term diagnostic instability for many disorders. With regard to treatment, lack of treatment specificity is the rule rather than the exception.
>
> (*Kupfer, First, & Regier*, 2002, p. xviii)

A much greater threat to the credibility of the profession perhaps is the perpetuation of an inherently flawed and failing diagnostic system that continues to try to impose a tradition that is simply inadequate to the task at hand. The diagnostic system is currently failing in many ways, including an absence of a provision of reliably distinct boundaries, an absence of a credible rationale for diagnostic thresholds, an inadequate coverage of existing clinical populations, and the absence of specific etiologies and treatments (Kupfer et al., 2002; Regier et al., 1998; Widiger & Trull, 2007).

Kraemer, Noda, and O'Hara (2004) argue that "a categorical diagnosis is necessary" (p. 21). "Clinicians who must decide whether to treat or not treat a patient, to hospitalize or not, to treat a patient with a drug or with psychotherapy, or what type, must inevitably use a categorical approach to diagnosis" (Kraemer et al., 2004, p. 12). This is not actually correct. In many of these common clinical situations, the decision is not in fact categorical in nature, as there is usually a decision of degree of medication dosage, frequency of therapy sessions, and even degree of hospitalization (e.g., day hospital, partial hospitalization, residential program, and traditional hospitalization). Even more importantly, it is evident that these many different clinical decisions

will not be well informed by a categorical diagnosis, particularly if one considers as well other important social and professional decisions (e.g., disability and insurance coverage). A dimensional model would likely increase the credibility of mental disorder classification by providing the means with which to identify more explicitly and reliably precise points along respective continua that would be optimal for these different decisions, rather than assuming that a single diagnostic threshold—that is itself largely arbitrary—is optimal for all of the different decisions that must be made. The current diagnostic thresholds are not set at a point that is optimal for any particular social and clinical decision, and yet are used to inform most to all of them (Regier & Narrow, 2002). A diagnostic system with the flexibility to set different thresholds for alternative social and clinical decisions could indeed be considerably more useful and credible than the current system. The credibility of the profession is being undermined most by the problems and errors generated by a model that claims to carve psychological or neurochemical functioning at discrete joints but yet clearly fails to do so. A dimensional model of classification could be preferable to governmental, social, and professional agencies because it would provide more reliable, valid, and explicitly defined bases for making important social and clinical decisions.

It is stated in the first paragraph of the introduction to DSM-IV-TR that "our highest priority has been to provide a helpful guide to clinical practice" (APA, 2000, p. xxiii). As First (2005) argued in his rejoinder to proposals for shifting the diagnostic manual into a dimension model, "the most important obstacle standing in the way of its implementation in DSM-5 (and beyond) is questions about clinical utility" (p. 561). Nevertheless, one must again question whether the existing diagnostic manual has appreciable clinical utility. "Apologists for categorical diagnoses argue that the system has clinical utility being easy to use and valuable in formulating cases and planning treatment [but] there is little evidence for these assertions" (Livesley, 2001a, p. 278). First (2005) suggested in one context that "the current categorical system of DSM has clinical utility with regard to the treatment of individuals" (p. 562), yet within another context stated that "with regard to treatment, lack of treatment specificity is the rule rather than the exception" (Kupfer, First, & Regier, 2002, p. xviii). The heterogeneity of diagnostic membership, the lack of precision in description, the excessive diagnostic co-occurrence, the failure to lead to a specific diagnosis, the reliance on the "not otherwise specified" wastebasket diagnosis, and the unstable and arbitrary diagnostic boundaries of the DSM-IV-TR diagnostic categories (Clark, 2007; Trull & Durrett, 2005; Widiger & Trull, 2007), are matters of clinical utility that present a source of considerable frustration for clinicians.

Consider, for example, the personality disorder diagnoses. It is telling that it has been over 10 years since the American Psychiatric Association has been publishing practice guidelines for the diagnostic categories of DSM-IV-TR and, as yet, treatment guidelines have been developed for only one of the ten personality disorder diagnostic categories (i.e., APA, 2001). The reason is perhaps straightforward: there have been no adequate empirical studies on the treatment of (for instance) the avoidant, schizoid, paranoid, histrionic, narcissistic, obsessive-compulsive, or dependent personality disorders. It would be difficult to even find researchers attempting to develop manualized treatment programs for these personality disorders. One reason is perhaps because the DSM-IV-TR personality disorders are generally not well suited for specific and explicit treatment manuals, as each disorder involves a complex constellation of an array of maladaptive personality traits. Persons meeting the diagnostic criteria for the same personality disorder may not even share many of the same traits (Trull & Durrett, 2005).

What is evident from the personality disorder treatment research is that treatment does not address or focus on the entire personality structure (Paris, 2006). Clinicians treat, for instance, the affective instability, the behavioral dyscontrol, or the self-mutilation of persons diagnosed with borderline personality disorder, which are specific facets of the FFM of personality disorder (see Figure 13.1). Effective change occurs with respect to these components, rather than to the entire, global construct. One of the empirically supported treatments for borderline personality disorder (APA, 2001) is dialectical behavior therapy (DBT). Research has demonstrated that DBT is an effective treatment for many of the components of this personality disorder, but it is evident to even the proponents of this clinical approach that the treatment is not entirely comprehensive in its effectiveness (Linehan, 2000). DBT has been particularly effective with respect to decreasing self-harm and angry hostility, but not with other aspects of borderline psychopathology, such as hopelessness (Scheel, 2000), components readily identified in the FFM of personality disorder. It is difficult to imagine clinicians not finding useful a classification system

that concerns explicitly their focus of treatment, such as cognitive-perceptual aberrations, anxiousness, emotional dysregulation, intense attachment, meekness, or workaholism (see Figure 13.1).

The factor analytic development of the FFM provides a more conceptually (as well as empirically) coherent structure than the syndromal constellations of traits within DSM-IV-TR (Lynam & Widiger, 2001). Extraversion and agreeableness are domains of interpersonal relatedness, neuroticism is a domain of emotional instability and dysregulation, conscientiousness is a domain of work-related behavior and responsibility, and openness is a domain of cognitive intellect, curiosity, and creativity (Costa & McCrae, 1992; Mullins-Sweatt & Widiger, 2006). Extraversion and agreeableness are confined specifically to social, interpersonal dysfunction, an area of functioning that is relevant to relationship quality both outside and within the therapy office. Interpersonal models of therapy, marital-family therapy, and group therapy would be confined largely to these two domains, or at least they would have the most specific and explicit implications for this domain. In contrast, neuroticism provides information with respect to mood, anxiety, and emotional dyscontrol, often targets for pharmacologic interventions (as well as cognitive, behavioral, and psychodynamic interventions). There are very clear pharmacologic implications for mood and anxiety dysregulation and emotional instability (e.g., anxiolytic, antidepressants, and/or mood stabilizers), but little to none for maladaptive antagonism or introversion, the interpersonal domains of the FFM. Maladaptively high openness implies cognitive–perceptual aberrations, which would have pharmacologic implications (i.e., neuroleptics) that are quite different from those of neuroticism. The domain of conscientiousness is, in contrast to agreeableness and extraversion, the domain of most specific relevance to occupational dysfunction, or impairments concerning work and career. Maladaptively high levels involve workaholism, perfectionism, and compulsivity; low levels involve laxness, negligence, and irresponsibility. There might be specific pharmacologic treatment implications for low conscientiousness (e.g., methylphenidates) although, as yet, none for maladaptively high conscientiousness. Perhaps there never will be a pharmacotherapy for high conscientiousness, but the point is that the structure of the FFM is commensurate with much more specific treatment implications than the existing diagnostic categories. Empirical support for the perceived utility of the

FFM relative to DSM-IV-TR for treatment decisions (and other matters of clinical utility) is provided in studies by Samuel and Widiger (2006) and Lowe and Widiger (2009).

Conclusion

Most (if not all) mental disorders appear to be the result of a complex interaction of an array of interacting biological vulnerabilities and dispositions with a number of significant environmental, psychosocial events that often exert their effects over a progressively developing period of time (Rutter, 2003). The symptoms and pathologies of mental disorders appear to be highly responsive to a wide variety of neurobiological, interpersonal, cognitive, and other mediating and moderating variables that help to develop, shape, and form a particular individual's psychopathology profile. This complex etiological history and individual psychopathology profile are unlikely to be well described by single diagnostic categories that attempt to make distinctions at nonexistent discrete joints along the continuous distributions (Widiger & Samuel, 2005). The publication of DSM-III provided a significant, major advance in the diagnosis and classification of psychopathology (Klerman, 1983). As Craddock and Owen (2002) suggest, perhaps it is time to move on.

The Robins and Guze (1970) paradigm for the validation of categorical diagnosis has been widely influential within psychiatry (Klerman, 1983; Kupfer et al., 2002; Spitzer, Endicott, & Robins, 1975; Spitzer et al., 1978). In 1989, L. Robins and Barrett (1989) edited a text in honor of this classic paper. Kendell (1989) provided the final word in his closing chapter. His conclusions, however, were curiously negative. "Ninety years have now elapsed since Kraepelin first provided the framework of a plausible classification of mental disorders. Why then, with so many potential validators available, have we made so little progress since that time?" (Kendell, 1989, p. 313). He answered his rhetorical question in the next paragraph: "One important possibility is that the discrete clusters of psychiatric symptoms we are trying to delineate do not actually exist but are as much a mirage as discrete personality types" (Kendell, 1989, p. 313).

Work is now beginning on DSM-5, and it is evident that a primary goal is to shift the manual toward a dimensional classification (Helzer, Wittchen, Krueger, & Kraemer, 2008). Nevertheless, it also appears to be the case that the shifts likely to be taken in DSM-5 will neither be fundamental nor significant. The effort is likely to fall considerably short of a true paradigm shift. Current proposals appear, for the most part, to be quite tentative, if not timid. "What is being proposed for DSM-5 is not to substitute dimensional scales for categorical diagnoses, but to add a dimensional option to the usual categorical diagnoses for DSM-5" (Kraemer, 2008, p. 9).

As acknowledged by Helzer, Kraemer, and Krueger (2006) "our proposal not only preserves categorical definitions but also does not alter the process by which these definitions would be developed. Those charged with developing criteria for specific mental disorders would operate just as their predecessors have" (p. 1675). In other words, work groups will continue to develop diagnostic criteria to describe prototypic cases in a manner that will maximize homogeneity (Robins & Guze, 1970; Spitzer et al., 1980), thereby continuing to fail to adequately describe typical cases and again leaving many patients to receive the diagnosis of NOS.

Dimensional proposals for DSM-5 were presented in a conference sponsored by the APA and NIMH that was the capstone to ten earlier conferences devoted to identifying "the future of psychiatric diagnosis" (Regier, 2008, p. xvii). The purpose of the conference was to present "a set of suggestions for developing dimensional alternatives for DSM-5 categorical diagnoses" (Helzer, Wittchen, et al., 2008, p. 116). In the end, however, the proposals were to construct "supplementary dimensional approaches to the categorical definitions that would also relate back to the categorical definitions in an unambiguous way" (Helzer, Wittchen, et al., 2008, p. 116). The proposals were confined simply to constructing a standardized quantitative dimensional assessment rating system for severity of substance use disorders (Helzer, Bucholz, & Gossop, 2008), a supplementary dimensional measure of depression to aid in the identification of major depressive disorder and facilitate assessment of treatment response (Andrews et al., 2008), the identification of dimensions of psychotic symptomatology (e.g., positive symptoms, negative symptoms, and disorganization) to be used in conjunction with the categorical diagnoses (Allardyce, Suppes, & Os, 2008), adding cross-cutting dimensions and stages of disorder that would supplement the assessment of the anxiety disorder diagnostic categories (Shear, Bjelland, Beesdo, Gloster, & Wittchen, 2008), and supplementary dimensional scales to assist in the assessment of the existing categorical diagnoses of childhood (Hudziak, Achenbach,

Althoff, & Pine, 2008). All DSM-5 work groups will be asked to "proceed as they always have in creating the phenomenological definitions for DSM" (Helzer, Wittchen, et al., 2008, p. 123) but to also indicate, if possible, how each respective diagnostic category can be rated on a scale of severity (it is perhaps worth noting that DSM-IV-TR already includes a method for rating the severity of each disorder: APA, 2000, p. 2). In sum, "what is being proposed for DSM-5 is not to substitute dimensional scales for categorical diagnoses, but to add a dimensional option to the usual categorical diagnoses for DSM-5" (Kraemer, 2008, p. 9).

DSM-III was highly innovative in many important respects (Kendell, 1983; Klerman, 1983; Spitzer, Williams, & Skodol, 1980). It would appear that the same innovative vision may fail to occur for DSM-5. The difficulty is evident in part by two caveats outlined by Kraemer (2008). She stated that "to achieve what is hoped from [the] addition of a dimensional diagnosis into DSM-5, there are certain criteria that would have to be met" (p. 14). The first criterion is that "it is crucial that a DSM-5 dimensional diagnosis correspond well with its categorical diagnosis" (p. 14). The second was that "the dimensional diagnosis … must show good … clinical validity, and withstand more demanding challenges to validity" (p. 15). These would not appear to be particularly compatible goals, as the existing diagnostic categories have already been shown to be grossly inadequate with respect to clinical validity and withstanding challenges to their validity (Kupfer et al., 2002).

This is perhaps most clearly evident with respect to the personality disorders. The most likely shift in the official classification of personality disorders is to provide a dimensional profile in terms of the existing (or somewhat revised) diagnostic categories (Oldham & Skodol, 2000). A personality disorder would be characterized as prototypic if all of the diagnostic criteria are met, moderately present if one or two criteria beyond the threshold are present, threshold if the patient just barely meets the diagnostic threshold, subthreshold if symptoms are present but are just below diagnostic threshold, traits if no more than one to three symptoms are present, and absent if no diagnostic criteria are present. This proposal was in fact made for DSM-IV (Widiger, 1996) but, at the time, it was considered to be too radical of a shift (Gunderson, 1998).

A fundamental limitation of this revision is that clinicians would continue to be describing patients in terms of markedly heterogeneous and overlapping constructs. A profile description of a patient in terms

of the antisocial, borderline, dependent, histrionic, and other DSM-IV (or DSM-5) constructs would essentially reify the excessive diagnostic co-occurrence that is currently being obtained (Clark, 2007; Trull & Durrett, 2005; Widiger & Mullins-Sweatt, 2005). In other words, the problem of excessive diagnostic co-occurrence would not in fact be solved. It would simply be accepted as an inherent limitation of the diagnostic manual. This is comparable to the decision made by the authors of DSM-III-R (APA, 1987) to address the problematic heterogeneity of the diagnostic categories by abandoning monothetic criterion sets that required homogeneity and converting to polythetic criterion sets that accepted the existence of the problematic heterogeneity (Widiger, Frances, Spitzer, & Williams, 1988).

It is likely that a more significant, meaningful, and valid shift in the classification of personality disorders will be included in an appendix to DSM-5, analogous to the alternative dimensional classification of psychosis already included in an appendix to DSM-IV-TR (APA, 2000, p. 765). However, it may not involve an integration of the classification of personality disorders with the dimensional classification of FFM personality structure. The proposal, to date, is confined simply to a reorganization of personality disorder symptomatology in terms of four broad domains (Krueger, Skodol, Livesley, Shrout, & Huang, 2008). These four broad domains can be coordinated with four of the five domains of the FFM (Widiger, 1998), but there was no effort to make this connection within the published proposal. In fact, the proposal for DSM-5 was distinguished from the FFM proposal (Krueger et al., 2008).

DSM-III is often said to have provided a significant paradigm shift in how psychopathology is diagnosed (Kendell & Jablensky, 2003; Klerman, 1983; Regier, 2008). Much of the credit for the innovative nature and success of DSM-III is due to the foresight, resolve, and perhaps even courage of its Chair, Dr. Robert Spitzer. The authors of DSM-5 have the empirical support and the opportunity to lead the field of psychiatry to a comparably bold new future in diagnosis and classification.

Future Directions

• How would a future edition of the diagnostic manual be reorganized dimensionally? This reorganization should be comprehensive, covering all of the existing categorical diagnoses (or more accurately the symptoms covered by each respective diagnosis) currently included within the diagnostic manual (e.g., psychotic disorders, mental retardation, mood disorders, sexual dysfunctions, and so forth).

• How should each section of the diagnostic manual (e.g., mood disorders, anxiety disorders, sexual dysfunctions, dissociative disorders) be optimally reorganized dimensionally? This reorganization would operate under the questionable assumption that a dimensional restructure of psychopathology would retain the existing sections.

• What would be the optimal diagnostic thresholds on each respective dimension for different clinical and social decisions? This would most likely be based on level of impairment and need for professional services.

Acknowledgment

The authors express their appreciation to Sara Boyd and Greg Smith for their comments on earlier draft.

References

Achenbach, T. M. (1966). The classification of children's psychiatric symptoms: A factor analytic study. *Psychological Monographs, 80,* 37.

Achenbach, T. M. (1991). *Manual for the Child Behavior Checklist/4–18 and 1991 Profile.* Burlington: University of Vermont, Department of Psychiatry.

Achenbach, T. M., & Edelbrock, C. S. (1978). The classification of child psychopathology: A review and analysis of empirical efforts. *Psychological Bulletin, 85,* 1275–1301.

Achenbach, T. M., & Edelbrock, C. S. (1984). Psychopathology of childhood. *Annual Review of Psychology, 35,* 227–256.

Achenbach, T. M., & Rescorla, L. A. (2001). *Manual for the ASEBA school-age forms & profiles.* Burlington: University of Vermont, Research Center for Children, Youth, & Families.

Allardyce, J., Suppes, T., & van Os, J. (2008). Dimensions and the psychosis phenotype. In J. E. Helzer, H. C. Kraemer, R. F. Krueger, H-U. Wittchen, P. J. Sirovatka, & D. A. Regier (Eds.), *Dimensional approaches to diagnostic classification. Refining the research agenda for DSM-5* (pp. 53–64). Washington, DC: American Psychiatric Association.

Allik, J. (2005). Personality dimensions across cultures. *Journal of Personality Disorders, 19,* 212–232.

Ambrosini, P. J., Bennett, D. S., Cleland, C. M., & Haslam, N. (2002). *Journal of Psychiatric Research, 36,* 247–256.

American Association on Mental Retardation. (2002). *Mental retardation: Definition, classification, and systems of support* (10th ed.). Washington, DC: Author.

American Psychiatric Association. (1980). *Diagnostic and statistical manual of mental disorders* (3rd ed.). Washington, DC: Author.

American Psychiatric Association. (1987). *Diagnostic and statistical manual of mental disorders* (3rd ed., rev. ed.). Washington, DC: Author.

American Psychiatric Association. (2000). *Diagnostic and statistical manual of mental disorders. Text Revision* (4th ed., rev. ed.). Washington, DC: Author.

American Psychiatric Association. (2001). *Practice guidelines for the treatment of patients with borderline personality disorder.* Washington, DC: Author.

Andrews, G., Brugha, T., Thase, M., Duffy, F. F., Rucci, P., & Slade, T. (2008). Dimensionality and the category of major depressive episode. In J. E. Helzer, H. C. Kraemer, R. F. Krueger, H-U. Wittchen, P. J. Sirovatka, & D. A. Regier (Eds.), *Dimensional approaches to diagnostic classification. Refining the research agenda for DSM-5* (pp. 35–51). Washington, DC: American Psychiatric Association.

Ashton, M. C., & Lee K. (2001). A theoretical basis for the major dimensions of personality. *European Journal of Personality, 15,* 327–353.

Baldwin, G., & Shean, G. D. (2006). A taxometric study of the Center for Epidemiological Studies depression scale. *Genetic, Social, and General Psychology Monographs, 132,* 101–128.

Beach, S. R. H., & Amir, N. (2003). Is depression taxonic, dimensional, or both? *Journal of Abnormal Psychology, 112,* 2228–236.

Beauchaine, T. P. (2007). A brief taxometrics primer. *Journal of Clinical Child and Adolescent Psychology, 36,* 654–676.

Blashfield, R. K, & Intoccia, V. (2000). Growth of the literature on the topic of personality disorders. *American Journal of Psychiatry, 157,* 472–473.

Bonanno, G. A., Neria, Y., Mancini, A., Coifman, K. G., Litz, B., & Insel, B. (2007). Is there more to complicated grief than depression and posttraumatic stress disorder? A test of incremental validity. *Journal of Abnormal Psychology, 116,* 342–351.

Boyd, J. H., Burke, J. D. Jr., Gruenberg, E., Holzer, C. E. III, Rae, D. S., George, L. K., et al. (1984). Exclusion criteria of DSM-III: A study of co-occurrence of hierarchy-free syndromes. *Archives of General Psychiatry, 41,* 983–989.

Brown, T. A., Campbell, L. A., Lehman, C. L., Grisham, J. R., & Mancill, R. B. (2001). Current and lifetime comorbidity of the DSM-IV anxiety and mood disorders in a large clinical sample. *Journal of Abnormal Psychology, 110,* 585–599.

Cardena, E., Butzler, L. D., & Spiegel, D. (2003). Stress disorders. In I. Weiner, G. Stricker, & T. A. Widiger (Eds.), *Handbook of psychology. Volume 8. Clinical psychology* (pp. 229–249). New York: John Wiley & Sons.

Carroll, K. M., Rounsaville, B. J., & Bryant, K. J. (1994). Should tolerance and withdrawal be required for substance dependence disorder? *Drug and Alcohol Dependence, 36,* 15–20.

Caspi, A., Roberts, B. W., & Shiner, R. L. (2005). Personality development: Stability and change. *Annual Review of Psychology, 56,* 453–484.

Church, A. T. (2001). Personality measurement in cross-cultural perspective. *Journal of Personality, 69,* 979–1006.

Clark, L. A. (2005). Temperament as a unifying basis for personality and psychopathology. *Journal of Abnormal Psychology, 114,* 505–521.

Clark, L. A. (2007). Assessment and diagnosis of personality disorder. Perennial issues and an emerging reconceptualization. *Annual Review of Psychology, 58,* 227–257.

Clark, L. A., & Watson, D. (2008). Temperament: An organizing paradigm for trait psychology. In O. P. John, R. W. Robins, & L. A. Pervin (Eds.), *Handbook of personality. Theory and research* (3rd, ed., pp. 265–286). New York: Guilford Press.

Clark, L. A., Watson, D., & Reynolds, S. (1995). Diagnosis and classification of psychopathology: Challenges to the current system and future directions. *Annual Review of Psychology, 46,* 121–153.

Costa, P. T., & McCrae, R. R. (1992). *Revised NEO Personality Inventory (NEO-PI-R) and NEO Five-Factor Inventory (NEO-FFI) professional manual.* Odessa, FL: Psychological Assessment Resources.

Costa, P. T., Samuels, J., Bagby, M., Daffin, L., & Norton, H. (2005). Obsessive-compulsive personality disorder: A review. In M. Maj, H. S. Akiskal, J. E. Mezzich, & A. Okasha (Eds.), *Personality disorders* (pp. 405–439). New York: Wiley.

Craddock, N., & Owen, M. J. (2005). The beginning of the end for the Kraepelinian dichotomy. *British Journal of Psychiatry, 186,* 364–366.

Crowley, T. J. (2006). Adolescents and substance-related disorders: Research agenda to guide decisions on Diagnostic and Statistical Manual Disorders, fifth edition (DSM-5). *Addiction, 101 (supplement 1),* 115–124.

Deary, I. J., Spinath, F. M., & Bates, T. C. (2006). Genetics of intelligence. *European Journal of Human Genetics, 14,* 690–700.

Edwards, G., & Gross, M. (1976). Alcohol dependence: Provisional description of a clinical syndrome. *British Medical Journal, 1,* 1058–1061.

Feinstein, A. R. (1970). The pre-therapeutic classification of co-morbidity in chronic disease. *Chronic Disease, 23,* 455–468.

First, M. B. (2005). Clinical utility: A prerequisite for the adoption of a dimensional approach in DSM. *Journal of Abnormal Psychology, 114,* 560–564.

First, M. B., & Westen, D. (2007). Classification for clinical practice: How to make ICD and DSM better able to serve clinicians. *International Review of Psychiatry, 19,* 473–481.

First, M. B., Bell, C. B., Cuthbert, B., Krystal, J. H., Malison, R., Offord, D. R., et al. (2002). Personality disorders and relational disorders: A research agenda for addressing crucial gaps in DSM. In D. J. Kupfer, M. B. First, & D. A. Regier (Eds.), *A research agenda for DSM-5* (pp. 123–199). Washington, DC: American Psychiatric Association.

Forstmeier S., & Maercker, A. (2007). Comparison of two diagnostic systems for complicated grief. *Journal of Affective Disorders, 99,* 203–211.

Frances, A. J., First, M. B., & Pincus, H. A. (1995). *DSM-IV guidebook.* Washington, DC: American Psychiatric Press.

Franklin, C. L., Strong, D. R., & Greene, R. L. (2002). A taxometric analysis of the MMPI-2 depression scales. *Journal of Personality Assessment, 79,* 110–121.

Garbutt, J. C. (2008). Alcoholism. In S. H. Fatemi & P. J. Clayton (Eds.), *The medical basis of psychiatry* (3rd ed., pp. 227–249). Totowa, NJ: Humana Press.

Goodwin, D. W., & Guze, S. B. (1996). *Psychiatric diagnosis* (5th ed.). New York: Oxford University Press.

Gray, J. R., & Thompson, P. M. (2004). Neurobiology of intelligence: Science and ethics. *Nature Reviews: Neuroscience, 5,* 471–482.

Gunderson, J. G. (1998). DSM-IV personality disorders: Final overview. In T. A. Widiger, A. J. Frances, H. A. Pincus, R. Ross, M. B., First, W. Davis, & M. Kline (Eds.), *DSM-IV Sourcebook,* (Vol. 4. pp. 1123–1140). Washington, DC: American Psychiatric Association.

Guze, S. B. (1978). Nature of psychiatric illness: Why psychiatry is a branch of medicine. *Comprehensive Psychiatry, 19,* 295–307.

Guze, S. B., & Helzer, J. E. (1987). The medical model and psychiatric disorders. In R. Michels & J. Cavenar (Eds.), *Psychiatry* (Vol. 1, Ch. 51, pp. 1–8). Philadelphia, PA: J. B. Lippincott.

Hankin, B. L., Fraley, R. C., Lahey, B. B., Waldman, I. D. (2005). Is depression best viewed as a continuum or discrete category? A taxometric analysis of childhood and adolescent depression in a population-based sample. *Journal of Abnormal Psychology, 114,* 96–110.

Hasin, D. S., Liu, X., Alderson, D., & Grant, B. F. (2006). DSM-IV alcohol dependence: A categorical or dimensional phenotype? *Psychological Medicine, 36,* 1695–1705.

Helzer, J. E., Bucholz, K. K., & Gossop, M. (2008). A dimensional option for the diagnosis of substance dependence in DSM-5. In J. E. Helzer, H. C. Kraemer, R. F. Krueger, H-U. Wittchen, P. J. Sirovatka, & D. A. Regier (Eds.), *Dimensional approaches to diagnostic classification. Refining the research agenda for DSM-5* (pp. 19–34). Washington, DC: American Psychiatric Association.

Helzer, J. E., Kraemer, H. C, & Krueger, R. F. (2006). The feasibility and need for dimensional psychiatric diagnoses. *Psychological Medicine, 36,* 1671–1680.

Helzer, J. E., Kraemer, H. C., Krueger, R. F., Wittchen, H-U., Sirovatka, P. J., & Regier, D. A. (Eds.). (2008). *Dimensional approaches in diagnostic classification.* Washington, DC: American Psychiatric Association.

Helzer, J. E., Wittchen, H-U., Krueger, R. F., & Kraemer, H. C. (2008). Dimensional options for DSM-5: The way forward. In J. E. Helzer, H. C. Kraemer, R. F. Krueger, H-U. Wittchen, P. J. Sirovatka, & D. A. Regier (Eds.), *Dimensional approaches to diagnostic classification. Refining the research agenda for DSM-5* (pp. 115–127). Washington, DC: American Psychiatric Association.

Hudziak, J. J., Achenbach, T. M., Althoff, R. R., & Pine, D. S. (2008). A dimensional approach to developmental psychopathology. In J. E. Helzer, H. C. Kraemer, R. F. Krueger, H-U. Wittchen, P. J. Sirovatka, & D. A. Regier (Eds.), *Dimensional approaches to diagnostic classification. Refining the research agenda for DSM-5* (pp. 101–114). Washington, DC: American Psychiatric Association.

Huprich, S. K. (2003). Evaluating facet-level predictions and construct validity of depressive personality disorder. *Journal of Personality Disorders, 17,* 219–232.

Jellinek, E. M. (1960). *The disease concept of alcoholism.* New Haven, CT: Hillhouse Press.

Judd, L. L., Schettler, P. J., & Akiskal, H. S. (2002). The prevalence, clinical relevance, and public health significance of subthreshold depressions. *Psychiatric Clinics of North America, 25,* 685–698.

Kahler, C. W., & Strong, D. R. (2006). A Rasch model analysis of DSM-IV alcohol abuse and dependence items in the National Epidemiological Survey on Alcohol and Related Conditions. *Alcoholism: Clinical and Experimental Research, 30,* 1165–1175.

Kandel, E. R. (1998). A new intellectual framework for psychiatry. *American Journal of Psychiatry, 155,* 457–469.

Keller, M. (1989). Current concepts in affective disorders. *Journal of Clinical Psychiatry, 50,* 157–162.

Keller, M. B., Klein, D. N., Hirschfeld, R. M. A., Kocsis, J. H., McCullough, J. P., Miller, I., et al. (1995). Results of the DSM-IV mood disorders field trial. *American Journal of Psychiatry, 152,* 843–849.

Kendell, R. E. (1975). *The role of diagnosis in psychiatry.* Oxford, England: Blackwell Scientific Publications.

Kendell, R. E. (1983). DSM-III: A major advance in psychiatric nosology. In R. L. Spitzer, J. B. W. Williams, & A. E. Skodol (Eds.), *International perspectives on DSM-III* (pp. 55–68). Washington, DC: American Psychiatric Press.

Kendell, R. E. (1989). Clinical validity. In L. N. Robins & J. E. Barrett (Eds.), *The validity of psychiatric diagnosis* (pp. 305–321). New York: Raven Press.

Kendell, R. E., & Jablensky, A. (2003). Distinguishing between the validity and utility of psychiatric diagnosis. *American Journal of Psychiatry, 160,* 4–12.

Kendler, K. S., Prescott, C. A., Myers, J., & Neale, M. C. (2003). The structure of genetic and environmental risk factors for common psychiatric and substance use disorders in men and women. *Archives of General Psychiatry, 60,* 929–937.

Kessler, R. C., Chiu, W. T., Dember, O., & Walters, E. E. (2005). Prevalence, severity, and comorbidity of 12-month DSM-IV disorders in the National Comorbidity Survey replication. *Archives of General Psychiatry, 62,* 617–627.

Kessler, R. C., Zhao, S., Blazer, D. G., & Swartz, M. (1997). Prevalence, correlates, and course of minor depression and major depression in the National Comorbidity Survey. *Journal of Affective Disorders, 45,* 19–30.

Klerman, G. L. (1983). The significance of DSM-III in American psychiatry. In R. L. Spitzer, J. B. W. Williams, & A. E. Skodol (Eds.), *International perspectives on DSM-III* (pp. 3–26). Washington, DC: American Psychiatric Press.

Klerman, G. L., Endicott, J., Spitzer, R. L., & Hirschfeld, R. M. (1979). Neurotic depressions: A systematic analysis of multiple criteria and meanings. *American Journal of Psychiatry, 136,* 57–61.

Kraemer, H. C. (2008). DSM categories and dimensions in clinical and research contexts. In J. E. Helzer, H. C. Kraemer, R. F. Krueger, H-U. Wittchen, P. J. Sirovatka, & D. A. Regier (Eds.), *Dimensional approaches to diagnostic classification. Refining the research agenda for DSM-5* (pp. 5–17). Washington, DC: American Psychiatric Association.

Kraemer, H. C., Noda, A., & O'Hara, R. (2004). Categorical versus dimensional approaches to diagnosis: Methodological challenges. *Journal of Psychiatric Research, 38,* 17–25.

Kraepelin, E. (1917). *Lectures on clinical psychiatry* (3rd ed.). New York: William Wood.

Krueger, R. F. (1999). The structure of common mental disorders. *Archives of General Psychiatry, 56,* 921–926.

Krueger, R. F. (2002). Psychometric perspectives on comorbidity. In J. E. Helzer & J. J. Hudziak (Eds.), *Defining psychopathology in the 21st century. DSM-5 and beyond* (pp. 41–54). Washington, DC: American Psychiatric Publishing.

Krueger, R. F. (2005). Continuity of Axes I and II: Toward a unified model of personality, personality disorders, and clinical disorders. *Journal of Personality Disorders, 19,* 233–261.

Krueger, R. F., Caspi, A., Moffitt, T. E., & Silva, P. A. (1998). The structure and stability of common mental disorders (DSM-III-R): A longitudinal-epidemiological study. *Journal of Abnormal Psychology, 107,* 216–227.

Krueger, R. F., & Markon, K. E. (2006). Reinterpreting comorbidity: A model-based approach to understanding and classifying psychopathology. *Annual Review of Clinical Psychology, 2,* 111–133.

Krueger, R. F., Nichol, P. E., Hicks, B. M., Markon, K. E., Patrick, C. J., Iacono, W. G., McGue, M. (2004). Using latent trait modeling to conceptualize an alcohol problems continuum. *Psychological Assessment, 16,* 107–119.

Krueger, R. F., Skodol, A. E., Livesley, W. J., Shrout, P. E., & Huang, Y. (2008). Synthesizing dimensional and categorical approaches to personality disorders: Refining the research agenda for DSM-IV Axis II. In J. E. Helzer, H. C. Kraemer, R. F. Krueger, H-U. Wittchen, P. J. Sirovatka, & D. A. Regier (Eds.), *Dimensional approaches to diagnostic classification. Refining the research agenda for DSM-5* (pp. 85–100). Washington, DC: American Psychiatric Association.

Krueger, R. F., & Tackett, J. L. (2003). Personality and psychopathology: Working toward the bigger picture. *Journal of Personality Disorders, 17,* 109–1128.

Kupfer, D. J., First, M. B., & Regier, D. A. (Eds.). (2002). Introduction. In D. J. Kupfer, M. B. First, & D. A. Regier (Eds.), *A research agenda for DSM-5* (pp. xv–xxiii). Washington, DC: American Psychiatric Association.

Lahey, B. B., Applegate, B., Waldman, I. D., Loft, J. D., Hankin, B. L., & Rick, J. (2004). The structure of child and adolescent psychopathology: Generating new hypotheses. *Journal of Abnormal Psychology, 113,* 358–385.

Langenbucher, J. W., Labouvie, E., Martin, C. S., Sanjuan, P. M., Bavly, L., Kirisci, L., & Chung, T. (2004). Application of item response theory analysis to alcohol, cannabis, and cocaine criteria in DSM-IV. *Journal of Abnormal Psychology, 113,* 72–80.

Lenzenweger, M. F. (2006). Schizotypy: An organizing framework for schizophrenia research. *Current Directions in Psychological Science, 15,* 162–166.

Lilienfeld, S. O., Waldman, I. D., & Israel, A. C. (1994). A critical examination of the use of the term "comorbidity" in psychopathology research. *Clinical Psychology: Science and Practice, 1,* 71–83.

Linehan, M. (2000). The empirical basis of dialectical behavior therapy: Development of new treatments versus evaluation of existing treatments. *Clinical Psychology: Science and Practice, 7,* 113–119.

Livesley, W. J. (2001a). Commentary on reconceptualizing personality disorder categories using trait dimensions. *Journal of Personality, 69,* 277–286.

Livesley, W. J. (2001b). Conceptual and taxonomic issues. In W. J. Livesley (Ed.), *Handbook of personality disorders. Theory, research, and treatment* (pp. 3–38). New York: Guilford.

Lowe, J. R., & Widiger, T. A. (2009). Clinicians' judgments of clinical utility: A comparison of the DSM-IV with dimensional models of personality disorder. *Journal of Personality Disorders, 23,* 211–229.

Luckasson, R., & Reeve, A. (2001). Naming, defining, and classifying in mental retardation. *Mental Retardation, 39,* 47–52.

Lynam, D. R., & Widiger, T. A. (2001). Using the five factor model to represent the DSM-IV personality disorders: An expert consensus approach. *Journal of Abnormal Psychology, 110,* 401–412.

Magruder, K. M., & Calderone, G. E. (2000). Public health consequences of different thresholds for the diagnosis of mental disorders. *Comprehensive Psychiatry, 41,* 14–18.

Maser, J. D., & Cloninger, C. R. (1990). Comorbidity of anxiety and mood disorders: Introduction and overview. In J. D. Maser & C. R. Cloninger (Eds.), *Comorbidity of mood and anxiety disorders* (pp. 3–12). Washington, DC: American Psychiatric Press.

Maser, J. D., & Patterson, T. (2002). Spectrum and nosology: Implications for DSM-5. *Psychiatric Clinics of North America, 25,* 855–885.

McCrae, R. R., Loeckenhoff, C. E., & Costa, P. T., Jr. (2005). A step toward DSM-5: Cataloguing personality-related problems in living. *European Journal of Personality, 19,* 269–286.

Mervielde, I., De Clercq, B., De Fruyt, F., & Van Leeuwen, K. (2005). Temperament, personality, and developmental psychopathology as childhood antecedents of personality disorders. *Journal of Personality Disorders, 19*, 171–201.

Miller, J. D, & Lynam, D. R. (2003). Psychopathy and the five-factor model of personality: A replication and extension. *Journal of Personality Assessment, 81*, 168–178.

Miller, M. B., Useda, J. D., Trull, T. J., Burr, R. M., & Minks Brown, C. (2001). Paranoid, schizoid, and schizotypal personality disorders. In P. B. Sutker & H. E. Adams (Eds.), *Comprehensive handbook of psychopathology* (3rd ed., pp. 535–558). New York: Plenum Publishers.

Mineka, S., Watson, D., & Clark, L. A. (1998). Comorbidity of anxiety and unipolar mood disorders. *Annual Review of Psychology, 49*, 377–412.

Mullins-Sweatt, S. N., Jamerson, J. E., Samuel, S. B., Olson, D. R., & Widiger, T. A. (2006). Psychometric properties of an abbreviated instrument for the assessment of the five factor model. *Assessment, 13*, 119–137.

Mullins-Sweatt, S. N., & Widiger, T. A. (2006). The five-factor model of personality disorder: A translation across science and practice. In R. Krueger & J. Tackett (Eds.), *Personality and psychopathology: Building bridges* (pp. 39–70). New York: Guilford.

Munafo, M. R., Clark, T., & Flint, J. (2005). Does measurement instrument moderate the association between the serotonin transporter gene and anxiety-related personality traits? A meta-analysis. *Molecular Psychiatry, 10*, 415–419.

Muthen, B. (2006). Should substance use disorders be considered as categorical or dimensional? *Addiction, 101 (supplement 1)*, 6–16.

Naglieri, J., Salter, C., & Rojahn, J. (2008). Cognitive disorders of childhood. Specific learning and intellectual disabilities. In J. E. Maddux & B. A. Winstead (Eds.), *Psychopathology. Foundations for a contemporary understanding* (2nd ed., pp. 401-416). Mahwah, NJ: Lawrence Erlbaum.

O'Connor, B. P. (2002). A quantitative review of the comprehensiveness of the five-factor model in relation to popular personality inventories. *Assessment, 9*, 188–203.

O'Connor, B. P. (2005). A search for consensus on the dimensional structure of personality disorders. *Journal of Clinical Psychology, 61*, 323–345.

Oldham, J. M., & Skodol, A. E. (2000). Charting the future of Axis II. *Journal of Personality Disorders, 14*, 17–29.

Paris, J. (2006, May). *Personality disorders: Psychiatry's stepchildren come of age.* Invited lecture presented at the 159th Annual Meeting of the American Psychiatric Association, Toronto, Canada.

Parnas, J., Licht, D., & Bovet, P. (2005). Cluster A personality disorders: A review. In M. Maj, H. S. Akiskal, J. E. Mezzich, & A. Okasha (Eds.), *Personality disorders* (pp. 1–74). New York: Wiley.

Phillips, K. A., Gunderson, J. G., Triebwasser, J., Kimble, C. R., Faedda, G., Lyoo, I. K., & Renn, J. (1998). Reliability and validity of depressive personality disorder. *American Journal of Psychiatry, 155*, 1044–1048.

Phillips, K. A., Price, L. H., Greenburg, B. D., & Rasmussen, S. A. (2003). Should the DSM diagnostic groupings be changed? In K. A. Phillips, M. B. First, & H. A. Pincus (Eds.), *Advancing DSM. Dilemmas in psychiatric diagnosis* (pp. 57–84). Washington, DC: American Psychiatric Association.

Pincus, H. A., McQueen, L. E., & Elinson, L. (2003). Subthreshold mental disorders: Nosological and research recommendations. In K. A. Phillips, M. B. First, & H. A. Pincus (Eds.), *Advancing DSM. Dilemmas in psychiatric diagnosis* (pp. 129–144). Washington, DC: American Psychiatric Association.

Prisciandaro, J. J., & Roberts, J. E. (2005). A taxometric investigation of unipolar depression in the National Comorbidity Survey. *Journal of Abnormal Psychology, 114*, 718–728.

Proudfoot, H., Baillie, A. J., & Teesson, M. (2006). The structure of alcohol dependence in the community. *Drug and Alcohol Dependence, 81*, 21–26.

Raine, A. (2006). Schizotypal personality: Neurodevelopmental and psychosocial trajectories. *Annual Review of Clinical Psychology, 2*, 291–326.

Regier, D. A. (2008). Forward: Dimensional approaches to psychiatric classification. In J. E. Helzer, H. C. Kraemer, R. F. Krueger, H-U. Wittchen, P. J. Sirovatka, & D. A. Regier (Eds.), *Dimensional approaches to diagnostic classification. Refining the research agenda for DSM-5* (pp. xvii–xxiii). Washington, DC: American Psychiatric Association.

Regier, D. A., Kaelber, C. T., Rae, D. S., Farmer, M. E., Knauper, B., Kessler, R. C., & Norquist, G. S. (1998). Limitations of diagnostic criteria and assessment instruments for mental disorders. Implications for research and policy. *Archives of General Psychiatry, 55*, 109–15.

Regier, D. A., & Narrow, W. E. (2002). Defining clinically significant psychopathology with epidemiologic data. In J. E. Helzier & J. J. Hudziak (Eds.), *Defining psychopathology in the 21st century. DSM-5 and beyond* (pp. 19–30). Washington, DC: American Psychiatric Publishing.

Reise, S. P., & Waller, N. G. (2009). Item response theory and clinical measurement. *Annual Review of Clinical Psychology, 5*, 27–48.

Roberts, B. W., & DelVecchio, W. F. (2000). The rank-order consistency of personality traits from childhood to old age: A quantitative review of longitudinal studies. *Psychological Bulletin, 126*, 3–25.

Robins, E., & Guze, S. B. (1970). Establishment of diagnostic validity in psychiatric illness: Its application to schizophrenia. *American Journal of Psychiatry, 126*, 107–111.

Robins, L. N., & Barrett, J. E. (Eds.). *The validity of psychiatric diagnosis.* New York: Raven Press.

Rounsaville, B. J., Alarcon, R. D., Andrews, G., Jackson, J. S., Kendell, R. E., & Kendler, K. (2002). Basic nomenclature issues for DSM-5. In D. J. Kupfer, M. B. First, & D. E. Regier (Eds.), *A research agenda for DSM-5* (pp. 1–29). Washington, DC: American Psychiatric Association.

Ruscio, A. M. (2008). Important questions remain to be addressed before adopting a dimensional classification of mental disorders. *American Psychologist, 63*, 61–62.

Ruscio, A. M., & Ruscio, J. (2002). The latent structure of analogue depression: Should the Beck Depression Inventory be used to classify groups? *Psychological Assessment, 14*, 135–145.

Ruscio, J., & Ruscio, A. M. (2000). Informing the continuity controversy: A taxometric analysis of depression. *Journal of Abnormal Psychology, 109*, 473–487.

Ruscio, J., & Ruscio, A. M. (2004). Clarifying boundary issues in psychopathology: The role of taxometrics in a comprehensive program of structural research. *Journal of Abnormal Psychology, 113*, 24–38.

Ruscio, J., Zimmerman, M., McGlinchey, J. B., Chelminski, I., & Young, D. (2007). Diagnosing major depressive disorder XI. A taxometric investigation of the structure underlying

DSM-IV symptoms. *Journal of Nervous and Mental Disease, 195*, 10–19.

Rutter, M. (2003, October). *Pathways of genetic influences on psychopathology*. Zubin Award Address at the 18th Annual Meeting of the Society for Research in Psychopathology, Toronto, Ontario.

Ryder, A. G., Bagby, R. M., & Schuller, D. R. (2002). The overlap of depressive personality disorder and dysthymia: A categorical problem with a dimensional solution. *Harvard Review of Psychiatry, 10*, 337–353.

Saha, T. D., Chou, S. P., & Grant, B. F. (2006). Toward an alcohol use disorder continuum using item response theory: Results from the National Epidemiologic Survey on Alcohol and Related Conditions. *Psychological Medicine, 36*, 931–941.

Sakashita, C., Slade, T., & Andrews, G. (2007). An empirical analysis of two assumptions in the diagnosis of DSM-IV major depressive episode. *Australian and New Zealand Journal of Psychiatry, 41*, 17–23.

Samuel, D. B., & Widiger, T. A. (2006). Clinicians' judgments of clinical utility: A comparison of the DSM-IV and five factor models. *Journal of Abnormal Psychology, 115*, 298–308.

Samuel, D. B., & Widiger, T. A. (2008). A meta-analytic review of the relationships between the five-factor model and DSM-IV-TR personality disorders: A facet level analysis. *Clinical Psychology Review, 28*, 1326–1342.

Sartorius, N., Kaelber, C. T., Cooper, J. E., Roper, M., Rae, D. S., Gulbinat, W., et al. (1993). Progress toward achieving a common language in psychiatry. *Archives of General Psychiatry, 50*, 115–124.

Saulsman, L. M., & Page, A. C. (2004). The five-factor model and personality disorder empirical literature: A meta-analytic review. *Clinical Psychology Review, 23*, 1055–1085.

Saunders, J. B. (2006). Substance dependence and non-dependence in the Diagnostic and Statistical Manual of Mental Disorders (DSM) and the International Classification of Diseases (ICD): Can an identical conceptualization be achieved? *Addiction, 101* (Suppl 1), 48–48.

Schalock, R. L., Luckasson, R. A., Shogren, K. A., Borthwick, D. S., Bradley, V., Buntinx, W. H. E., et al. (2007). The renaming of mental retardation: Understanding the change to the term intellectual disability. *Intellectual and Developmental Disabilities, 45*, 116–124.

Scheel, K. R. (2000). The empirical basis of dialectical behavior therapy: Summary, critique, and implications. *Clinical Psychology: Science Practice, 7*, 68–86.

Schneider, F. R., Blanco, C., Anita, S., & Liebowitz, M. R. (2002). The social anxiety spectrum. *Psychiatric Clinics of North America, 25*, 757–774.

Schuckit, M. A., Daeppen, J-B., Danko, G. P., Tripp, M. L., Smith, T. L., Li, T-K., et al. (1999). Clinical implications for four drugs of the DSM-IV distinction between substance dependence with and without a physiological component. *American Journal of Psychiatry, 156*, 41–49.

Schwartz, M. A., & Wiggins, O. P. (2002). The hegemony of the DSMs. In J. Sadler (Ed.), *Descriptions and prescriptions: Values, mental disorders, and the DSM* (pp. 199–209). Baltimore, MD: Johns Hopkins University Press.

Shear, M. K., Bjelland, I., Beesdo, K., Gloster, A. T., & Wittchen, H-U. (2008). Supplementary dimensional assessment in anxiety disorders. In J. E. Helzer, H. C. Kraemer, R. F. Krueger, H-U. Wittchen, P. J. Sirovatka, & D. A. Regier (Eds.), *Dimensional approaches to diagnostic classification.*

Refining the research agenda for DSM-5 (pp. 65–84). Washington, DC: American Psychiatric Association.

Siever, L. J., & Davis, K. L. (1991). A psychobiological perspective on the personality disorders. *American Journal of Psychiatry, 148*, 1647–1658.

Skodol, A. E., Gunderson, J. G., Shea, M. T., McGlashan, T. H., Morey, L. C., Sanislow, C. A., et al. (2005). The Collaborative Longitudinal Personality Disorders Study (CLPS): Overview and implications. *Journal of Personality Disorders, 19*, 487–504.

Slade, T. (2007). Taxometric investigation of depression: Evidence of consistent latent structure across clinical and community samples. *Australian and New Zealand Journal of Psychiatry, 41*, 403–410.

Slade, T., & Andrews, G. (2005). Latent structure of depression in a community sample: A taxometric analysis. *Psychological Medicine, 35*, 489–497.

Smith, G. T., & Combs, J. (in press). Issues of construct validity in psychological diagnoses. In T. Millon, R. F. Krueger, and E. Simonsen (Eds.), *Contemporary Directions in Psychopathology: Toward the DSM-5 and ICD-11*. New York: Guilford Press.

Solomon, A., Ruscio, J., Seeley, J. R., & Lewinsohn, P. M. (2006). A taxometric investigation of unipolar depression in a large community sample. *Psychological Medicine, 36*, 973–985.

Spitzer, R. L., Endicott, J., & Robins E. (1975). Clinical criteria for psychiatric diagnosis and DSM-III. *American Journal of Psychiatry, 132*, 1187–1192.

Spitzer, R. L., Endicott, J., & Robins E. (1978). Research diagnostic criteria: Rationale and reliability. *Archives of General Psychiatry, 35*, 773–782.

Spitzer, R. L., Williams, J. B. W., & Skodol, A. E. (1980). DSM-III: The major achievements and an overview. *American Journal of Psychiatry, 137*, 151–164.

Task Force on DSM-IV. (1991, September). *DSM-IV options book: Work in progress*. Washington, DC: American Psychiatric Association.

Task Force on DSM-IV. (1993, March). *DSM-IV draft criteria*. Washington, DC: American Psychiatric Association.

Trull, T. J., & Durrett, C. A. (2005). Categorical and dimensional models of personality disorder. *Annual Review of Clinical Psychology, 1*, 355–380.

Trull, T. J., & Widiger, T. A. (1997). *Structured interview for the five factor model of personality*. Odessa, FL: Psychological Assessment Resources.

Trull, T. J., Widiger, T. A., Lynam, D. R., & Costa, P. T. (2003). Borderline personality disorder from the perspective of general personality functioning. *Journal of Abnormal Psychology, 112*, 193–202.

Ustun, T. B., & Sartorius, N. (Eds.). (1995). *Mental illness in general health care: An international study*. London: John Wiley & Sons.

Vachon, D., Sellbom, M., Ryder, A. G., Miller, J. D., & Bagby, R. M. (in press). A five-factor model description of depressive personality disorder. *Journal of Personality Disorders*.

Verheul, R., & Widiger, T. A. (2004). A meta-analysis of the prevalence and usage of the personality disorder not otherwise specified (PDNOS) diagnosis. *Journal of Personality Disorders, 18*, 309–319.

Wakefield, J. C. (2007). The concept of mental disorder: Diagnostic implications of the harmful dysfunction analysis. *World Psychiatry, 6*, 149–156.

Wakefield, J. C. (2008). The perils of dimensionalization: Challenges in distinguishing negative traits from personality disorders. *Psychiatric Clinics of North America, 31*, 379–393.

Wakefield, J. C., Schmitz, M. F., First, M. B., & Horwitz, A. V. (2007). Extending the bereavement exclusion for major depression to other losses - Evidence from the National Comorbidity Survey. *Archives of General Psychiatry, 64*, 433–440.

Walters, G. D. (2008). The latent structure of alcohol use disorders: A taxometric analysis of structured interview data obtained from male federal prison inmates. *Alcohol and Alcoholism, 43*, 326–333.

Watson, D. (2005). Rethinking the mood and anxiety disorders: A quantitative hierarchical model for DSM-5. *Journal of Abnormal Psychology, 114*, 522–536.

Widiger, T. A. (1996). Personality disorder dimensional models. In T. A. Widiger, A. J. Frances, H. A. Pincus, R. Ross, M. B. First, & W. W. Davis (Eds.), *DSM-IV sourcebook* (Vol. 2, pp. 789–798). Washington, DC: American Psychiatric Association.

Widiger, T. A. (1998). Four out of five ain't bad. *Archives of General Psychiatry, 55*, 865–866.

Widiger, T. A. (2001a). Social anxiety, social phobia, and avoidant personality disorder. In W. R. Corzier & L. Alden (Eds.), *International handbook of social anxiety* (pp. 335–356). New York: Wiley.

Widiger, T. A. (2001b). What can we learn from taxometric analyses? *Clinical Psychology: Science and Practice, 8*, 528–533.

Widiger, T. A. (2003). Personality disorder and Axis I psychopathology: The problematic boundary of Axis I and Axis II. *Journal of Personality Disorders, 17*, 90–108.

Widiger, T. A. (2008). Classification and diagnosis: Historical development and contemporary issues. In J. Maddux and B. Winstead (Eds.), *Psychopathology: Foundations for a contemporary understanding* (2nd ed., pp. 83–101). Lawrence Erlbaum Associates, Inc.

Widiger, T. A., & Clark, L. A. (2000). Toward DSM-5 and the classification of psychopathology. *Psychological Bulletin, 126*, 946–963.

Widiger, T. A., & Costa, P. T. (1994). Personality and personality disorders. *Journal of Abnormal Psychology, 103*, 78–91.

Widiger, T. A., & Costa, P. T. (2002). FFM personality disorder research. In P. T. Costa & T. A. Widiger (Eds.), *Personality disorders and the five factor model of personality* (2nd ed., pp. 59–87). Washington, DC: American Psychological Association.

Widiger, T. A., Costa, P. T., & McCrae, R. R. (2002). Proposal for Axis II: Diagnosing personality disorders using the five factor model. In P. T. Costa & T. A. Widiger (Eds.), *Personality disorders and the five factor model of personality* (2nd ed., pp. 431–456). Washington, DC: American Psychological Association.

Widiger, T. A., Frances, A. J., Spitzer, R. L., & Williams, J. B. W. (1988). The DSM-III-R personality disorders: An overview. *American Journal of Psychiatry, 145*, 786–795.

Widiger, T. A., & Lowe, J. (2007). Five factor model assessment of personality disorder. *Journal of Personality Assessment, 89*, 16–29.

Widiger, T. A., & Lowe, J. (2008). A dimensional model of personality disorder: Proposal for DSM-5. *Psychiatric Clinics of North America, 31*, 363–378.

Widiger, T. A., & Miller, J. D. (2008). Psychological diagnosis. In D. Richard & S. Huprich (Eds.), *Clinical psychology, assessment, treatment, and research* (pp. 69–88). Oxford, England: Elsevier.

Widiger, T. A., & Mullins-Sweatt, S. (2005). Categorical and dimensional models of personality disorder. In J. Oldham, A. Skodol, & D. Bender (Eds.), *Textbook of Personality Disorders* (pp. 35–53). Washington, DC: American Psychiatric Press.

Widiger, T. A., & Mullins-Sweatt, S. (2009). Five-factor model of personality disorder: A proposal for DSM-5. *Annual Review of Clinical Psychology, 5,* 115–138.

Widiger, T. A., & Samuel, D. B. (2005). Diagnostic categories or dimensions: A question for DSM-5. *Journal of Abnormal Psychology, 114*, 494–504.

Widiger, T. A., & Sankis, L. (2000). Adult psychopathology: Issues and controversies. *Annual Review of Psychology, 51*, 377–404.

Widiger, T. A., Simonsen, E., Krueger, R. F., Livesley, W. J., & Verheul, R. (2005). Personality disorder research agenda for the DSM-5. *Journal of Personality Disorders, 19*, 317–340.

Widiger, T. A., & Smith, G. T. (1994). Substance use disorder: Abuse, dependence, and dyscontrol. *Addiction, 89*, 267–282.

Widiger, T. A., & Smith, G. T. (2008). Personality and psychopathology. In O. P. John, R. Robins, & L. A. Pervin (Eds.), *Handbook of personality: Theory and research* (3rd edition, pp. 743–769). New York: Guilford.

Widiger, T. A., & Trull, T. J. (2007). Plate tectonics in the classification of personality disorder: Shifting to a dimensional model. *American Psychologist, 62*, 71–83.

World Health Organization. (1992). *The ICD-10 classification of mental and behavioural disorders. Clinical descriptions and diagnostic guidelines.* Geneva, Switzerland: Author.

Yamagata, S., Suzuki, A., Ando, J., One, Y., Kijima, N., Yoshimura, K., et al. (2006). Is the genetic structure of human personality universal? A cross-cultural twin study from North America, Europe, and Asia. *Journal of Personality and Social Psychology, 90*, 987–998.

Zachar, P., & Kendler, K. S. (2007). Psychiatric disorders: A conceptual taxonomy. *American Journal of Psychiatry, 164*, 557–565.

The Anxiety-Depression Spectrum

Ovsanna Leyfer *and* Timothy A. Brown

Abstract

The *Diagnostic and Statistical Manual of Mental Disorders* (DSM) has undergone considerable revisions since its first publication, with a continuous increase in the number of the anxiety and mood disorder categories. However, many researchers have expressed concern that the expansion of our nosology has resulted in less consideration of the overlapping features of emotional disorders. The purpose of this chapter is to review current issues and empirical evidence pertinent to the classification of anxiety and mood disorders and the relevance of these issues to treatment planning. It discusses discriminant validity, including diagnostic reliability and comorbidity, reviews the existing hierarchical models of emotional disorders, proposes a dimensional approach for classification of anxiety and mood disorders, and reviews transdiagnostic treatments of emotional disorders.

Keywords: Anxiety disorders, assessment, comorbidity, diagnostic reliability, dimensional classification, hierarchical models, mood disorders, overlap, transdiagnostic treatment

The *Diagnostic and Statistical Manual of Mental Disorders* (*DSM*) has undergone considerable revisions since its first publication, with a continuous increase in the number of the anxiety and mood disorder categories. The fourth edition of the *DSM* (*DSM-IV*; American Psychiatric Association [APA], 1994) specifies 12 anxiety disorder categories and ten mood disorder categories. The anxiety disorders are panic disorder, panic disorder with agoraphobia (PDA), agoraphobia without a history of panic disorder, social phobia, specific phobia, generalized anxiety disorder (GAD), obsessive-compulsive disorder (OCD), post-traumatic stress disorder (PTSD), acute stress disorder, anxiety disorder due to a general medical condition, substance-induced anxiety disorder, and anxiety disorder not otherwise specified (NOS). A 13th category, mixed anxiety-depressive disorder, was considered for inclusion in *DSM-IV*, but it is currently included in the appendix of disorders in need of further study for *DSM-5* (cf. Zinbarg et al., 1994). The mood disorder

categories includes major depressive disorder (MDD), dysthymic disorder, depressive disorder NOS, bipolar I and bipolar II disorders, bipolar disorder NOS, cyclothymic disorder, mood disorder due to a general medical condition, substance-induced mood disorder, and mood disorder NOS. Table 14.1 summarizes key diagnostic features for major anxiety and mood disorders.

This increase could be due to expansion of knowledge of the nature of psychopathology and classification of disorders. However, many researchers (e.g., Andrews, 1996; Brown & Barlow, 2002; Tyrer, 1989) have expressed concern that the expansion of our nosology has resulted in less consideration of the overlapping features of emotional disorders, which may have more significance in explaining their etiology, course, and treatment response than the "unique" features of specific disorders. In fact, many anxiety disorders share fundamental processes, such as apprehension of situations or objects, and differ mostly in content of apprehension (e.g., worry about

Table 14.1 Overview of key features of major anxiety and depressive disorders in *DSM-IV*

Disorder	Key feature(s)
Panic Disorder	Recurrent, unexpected panic attacks and persistent worry/concern about additional attacks or their consequences
Panic Disorder with Agoraphobia	Meets criteria for panic disorder Agoraphobia: fear/avoidance of situations where panic attacks might occur
Social Phobia	Marked fear/avoidance of social situations due to possibility of embarrassment or humiliation
Specific Phobia	Marked fear/avoidance of specific objects or situations (e.g., animals, heights, receiving injections)
Generalized Anxiety Disorder	Chronic excessive, uncontrollable worry about a number of events or activities (e.g., job performance, finances)
Obsessive-Compulsive Disorder	Recurrent, intrusive thoughts, images or impulses (e.g., excessive doubting, thoughts of contamination)
Posttraumatic Stress Disorder	Persistent reexperiencing (e.g., dreams), distress, and avoidance of stimuli associated with prior exposure to extreme stress (e.g., combat)
Acute Stress Disorder	Short-term reexperiencing, dissociation, distress, and avoidance of stimuli associated with exposure to extreme stress
Major Depressive Disorder	At least one 2-week episode of persistent depressed mood or loss of interest
Dysthymic Disorder	Persistent depressed mood for at least 2 years
Bipolar I Disorder	Occurrence of a manic episode characterized by at least 1-week period of persistent expansive mood or a mixed episode, characterized by 1 week of both mania and major depression symptoms, and major depressive episodes
Bipolar II Disorder	At least one major depressive episode and at least one hypomanic episode, characterized by at least a 4-day period of persistent expansive mood
Cyclothymic Disorder	At least 2 years of multiple periods of hypomanic symptoms and periods of depressive symptoms

DSM-IV = Diagnostic and statistical manual of mental disorders, 4th edition (APA, 1994).

contamination in OCD, worry about several events or activities in GAD). The question arises whether these manifestations are sufficiently distinct to warrant separate diagnostic categories. The purpose of this chapter is to review current issues and empirical evidence pertinent to the classification of anxiety and mood disorders and the relevance of these issues to treatment planning.

Indeed, a great deal of evidence has led to questioning the discriminant validity of the anxiety and depressive disorder categories. Findings of unfavorable inter-rater agreement (diagnostic reliability) and a high degree of covariance between anxiety and mood disorders at diagnostic, symptom, and genetic levels (e.g., Brown, Campbell, Lehman, Grisham, & Mancill, 2001; Hettema, Neale, & Kendler, 2001) have been cited in support of these concerns.

Diagnostic Reliability

With the increase in specificity and complexity of diagnostic criteria for anxiety and mood disorders, the use of standardized diagnostic measures became more important. Such instruments are essential for establishing the reliability of diagnostic categories. Several instruments have been developed, including the Structured Clinical Interview for *DSM-IV* Axis I disorders (SCID-I; First, Spitzer, Gibbon, & Williams, 1997) and the Schedule for Affective Disorders and Schizophrenia–Lifetime Anxiety Version (SADS-LA; Fyer, Endicott, Mannuzza, & Klein, 1985). However, these and some other structured diagnostic interviews do not cover sufficient information to allow for making differential diagnoses among anxiety and mood disorders. For example, the SCID-I and SADS-LA are useful for screening for a broad range of psychopathology, but they collect the minimum amount of information necessary for each of the *DSM-IV* disorders, in the interest of time. Therefore, these instruments are not as valuable for the purposes of detailed inquiry into anxiety and depressive disorders.

Anxiety Disorders Interview Schedule

The first edition of the Anxiety Disorder Interview Schedule (ADIS; Di Nardo, O'Brien, Barlow, Waddell, & Blanchard, 1983) was developed specifically for anxiety disorders, to advance research on their classification. It was revised several times, using the experience and revisions of the *DSM*. In 1988, the Anxiety Disorders Interview Schedule – Revised (ADIS-R) was published, corresponding to *DSM-III-R*, to include all anxiety and mood disorders and selected somatoform disorders (Di Nardo & Barlow, 1988). The current version, the Anxiety Disorders Interview Schedule for *DSM-IV*: Lifetime Version (ADIS-IV-L), was published in 1994 to correspond to *DSM-IV* criteria. Unlike its predecessors, the ADIS-IV-L (Di Nardo, Brown, & Barlow, 1994) also included assessment of lifetime disorders, as well as a diagnostic timeline to facilitate the determination of the onset, remission, and temporal sequence of these conditions. It additionally included assessment of substance and alcohol use disorders, as well as a dimensional assessment of the key and associated features of disorders, regardless of whether they meet the criteria for a particular *DSM-IV* diagnosis. These ratings can serve in research on treatment outcome and as dimensional indicators in studies of latent structure (e.g., Brown, 2007). These ratings are also in agreement with the position that it may be more informative to classify features of emotional disorders on a continuum rather than in a categorical fashion (Brown & Barlow, 2005). For each current and lifetime diagnosis, ADIS-IV-L interviewers assign a clinical severity rating from 0 to 8, to indicate the degree of distress and impairment associated with the disorder. A principal diagnosis is assigned to reflect the disorder that causes most impairment and distress.

Reliability Studies

Diagnostic reliability refers to the extent to which two (or more) independent interviewers agree on the presence or absence of a given diagnosis. The approach to studying diagnostic reliability of the anxiety and mood disorders usually has utilized one of two methods—test–retest or simultaneous—both involving the use of structured clinical interviews such as the ADIS-IV-L (Di Nardo et al., 1994).

Test–retest involves the patient being interviewed by different independent evaluators on two separate occasions (e.g., Brown, Di Nardo, Lehman, & Campbell, 2001; Di Nardo, Moras, Barlow, Rapee, & Brown, 1993). The simultaneous method suggests that a diagnostic interview is video- or audiotaped and rated by an independent evaluator (e.g., Riskind, Beck, Berhick, Brown, & Steer, 1987). In both approaches, the most widely used index of inter-rater agreement is the κ *statistic* (Fleiss, Nee, & Landis, 1979), which ranges in value from 0 (poor agreement) to 1 (perfect agreement). The strategy of interviewing patients on separate occasions is the more stringent approach to estimating diagnostic reliability because it introduces several potential sources of disagreement not found in the single-interview method (e.g., variation in patient report, change in clinical status). The single-interview method also has been criticized for its potential of providing an overly optimistic estimation of diagnostic reliability (e.g., the independent evaluator's judgments may be strongly influenced by the nature and extent of follow-up questions asked by the initial interviewer).

Large-scale reliability studies based on *DSM-III-R* and *DSM-IV* definitions of anxiety and mood disorder categories have indicated that these diagnoses are associated with differential levels of agreement (Brown, Di Nardo, et al., 2001; Di Nardo et al., 1993; Mannuzza et al., 1989; Williams et al., 1992). Results of one large-scale study of the *DSM-IV* anxiety disorders and three of the *DSM-III-R* anxiety and mood disorders are summarized in Table 14.2 for current diagnoses. All four studies employed the test–retest method, but differed on the structured interview used; Brown, Di Nardo, et al. (2001) used the ADIS-IV-L; Di Nardo et al. (1993) used the ADIS-R; Mannuzza et al. (1989) used the SADS-LA, and Williams et al. (1992) used the Structured Clinical Interview for *DSM-III-R* Axis I. The following guidelines were used in the interpretation of κ: κ > .75 = excellent agreement; κ between .60 and .74 = good agreement; κ between .40 and .59 = fair agreement; κ < .40 = poor agreement (Shrout, Spitzer, & Fleiss, 1987), indicating that panic disorder with agoraphobia, social phobia, specific phobia, OCD, and GAD had good to excellent reliability in the *DSM-IV* study (Brown, Di Nardo, et al., 2001). However, certain categories (e.g., MDD, dysthymia) were associated with fair or poor agreement. The reliability of GAD improved in the *DSM-IV* study in comparison to the previous studies, which is probably due to the revision of its criteria in *DSM-IV*, including the addition of the criterion of uncontrollable worry, specification of worries across "a number of events/activities" as opposed to "at least two worry spheres," and the reduction of the associated symptoms from 18 to six (APA, 1987, 1994). The inter-rater agreement for dysthymia remained poor across the studies.

The factors contributing to unreliability have varied substantially across the anxiety and mood disorders. For example, in the study by Brown, Di Nardo, et al. (2001), the majority of discrepancy involving social phobia, specific phobia, and OCD (62%–67%) resulted from interviewer disagreement on whether the disorder should be rated at a clinical or subclinical level. This, however, was a relatively rare source of disagreement for GAD, MDD, and dysthymia. The most common reason for disagreements across studies has been "information variance" (patients providing different information to the two interviewers), which accounted for 22%–100% of the discrepancies in the Brown, Di Nardo, et al. (2001) study.

The frequency with which other disorders were involved in diagnostic disagreements varied across categories (Brown, Di Nardo, et al., 2001). Disagreement was rather frequent for disorders with overlapping definitional criteria, such as dysthymia, GAD, and MDD (64%–74%). For GAD, 63% of disagreements involving another disorder were with mood disorders. It was also frequent for anxiety and depressive disorders NOS. In the presence of two or more potential diagnoses, the risk for disagreement is increased by the fact that interviewers may not agree as to whether the features of one disorder should be subsumed under another disorder. Indeed, this source of diagnostic disagreement is related to another issue concerning the potentially poor discriminant validity among emotional disorders—their high rate of comorbidity.

Comorbidity

Consistent evidence of high comorbidity among anxiety and mood disorders is frequently cited to question the distinguishability of the emotional disorders (Andrews, 1990; Brown & Barlow, 2002). Comorbidity studies based on *DSM-III-R* criteria have demonstrated that at least 50% of patients with a principal anxiety disorder have one or more additional diagnoses at the time of assessment (e.g., Brown & Barlow, 1992; Kessler et al., 1994). Similar findings were obtained in a large-scale study ($N = 1,127$) of the *DSM-IV* categories, with patients presenting to an anxiety disorders specialty clinic (Table 14.2; Brown, Campbell, et al., 2001). The nature of exclusion and inclusion criteria for this study (e.g., active substance use disorders and

Table 14.2 Summary of inter-rater reliability studies for *DSM-IV* and *DSM-III-R* anxiety and mood disorders

	Brown et al. (2001)		Di Nardo et al. (1993)		Mannuzza et al. (1989)		Williams et al. (1992)	
	n	κ	n	κ	n	κ	n	κ
PD	22	.56	44	.39	53	.79	—	—
PDA	102	.81	53	.71	34	.81	35	.58a
GAD	113	.65	108	.53	11	.27	8	.56
Social phobia	152	.77	84	.66	51	.68	23	.47
Specific phobia	100	.71	47	.63	30	.29	20	.52
OCD	60	.75	24	.75	13	.91	27	.59
PTSD	14	.59	8	.55	—	—	—	—
MDD	111	.59	46	.55	—	—	121	.64
Dysthymia	53	.31	25	.35	—	—	23	.40

DSM-IV = Diagnostic and statistical manual of mental disorders, 4th edition (APA, 1994); *DSM-III-R = Diagnostic and statistical manual of mental disorders,* revised 3rd edition (APA, 1987); PD, panic disorder; PDA, panic disorder with agoraphobia; GAD, generalized anxiety disorder; OCD, obsessive-compulsive disorder; PTSD, post-traumatic stress disorder; *n,* number of cases in which diagnosis was assigned by one or both raters; *κ,* all kappas pertain to current clinical diagnoses (collapsing across principal and additional diagnoses). aPD and PDA were collapsed under the same category in this study.

presence of suicidality were exclusion criteria) and its outpatient setting, similar to previous studies, limited its generalizability and probably rendered conservative estimates of diagnostic co-occurrence. Nevertheless, comorbidity rates for many categories were quite high. Similar to earlier findings, 55% of patients with a principal anxiety or mood disorder had at least one additional anxiety or depressive disorder at the time of the assessment. This rate increased to 76% for lifetime diagnoses. The principal diagnoses of PTSD, MDD, dysthymia, and GAD had the highest comorbidity rates. The lowest comorbidity rates were found for the principal diagnosis of specific phobia. The most commonly occurring additional diagnoses were social phobia (22%) and MDD (20%).

However, the findings of comorbidity alone do not have substantial implications for establishing or refuting the discriminant validity of the emotional disorder constructs. There are multiple conceptual explanations for diagnostic comorbidity (e.g., Andrews, 1996; Brown & Barlow, 2002; Frances, Widiger, & Fyer, 1990). Accounts for comorbidity that challenge current *DSM* classification system include the possibility that disorders co-occur in part because they share overlapping definitional criteria, or that they represent variations of a broader underlying syndrome that has been erroneously separated by the classification system. For example, in regard to the first explanation, the associated symptom criteria for *DSM-IV* GAD diagnosis almost entirely overlap with those of major depression and dysthymia (e.g., sleep disturbance, fatigue, concentration difficulties, restlessness). In fact, this overlap contributed to findings of an exceptionally high comorbidity rate of GAD and mood disorders (e.g., 82%; Brown and Barlow 1992), in studies based on *DSM-III-R* criteria. Currently, the *DSM-IV* attempts to adjust for this with a hierarchy rule stating that GAD should not be assigned if its features occur exclusively during the course of a mood disorder.

Explanations for comorbidity that do not suggest problems in the current classification systems include the possibility that features of one disorder can be risk factors for another, or that they emerge from the same diathesis. In regard to the first explanation, the results from the Brown, Campbell, et al. (2001) study indicated that the presence of PTSD was associated with a significantly elevated risk of PDA, and that, in the majority of the cases, PTSD preceded panic disorder. These findings can be interpreted to suggest that the high autonomic arousal

and low perception of personal control associated with PTSD, perhaps combined with a preexisting trait such as anxiety sensitivity, may have served as precipitants to PDA. The second explanation is in accord with current theories of emotional disorders, which assert that anxiety and mood disorders share genetic, biological, and psychosocial vulnerabilities (e.g., Barlow, 2002; Clark, Watson, & Mineka, 1994).

Hierarchical Models

The current models of emotion disorders suggest that, whereas anxiety and mood disorders emanate from the same core vulnerabilities, these vulnerabilities are manifested heterogeneously because of different environmental exposures and other biological and genetic factors (e.g., Barlow, 2002). For example, a genetically based trait of neuroticism can underlie both depression and social phobia, but whether one or both disorders become manifest may depend on environmental experience factors such as a direct experience with rejection, social humiliation, or others.

Two genetically based core dimensions of temperament have been suggested as instrumental in the etiology and course of anxiety and depressive disorders: neuroticism/negative affectivity and extraversion/positive affectivity. Research indicates that these constructs are heritable (e.g., Hettema, Prescott, & Kendler, 2004), and they may account for the onset, overlap, and maintenance of anxiety and depression (e.g., Brown, Chorpita, & Barlow, 1998).

Several conceptual models of anxiety and depression have been developed and subsequently reformulated in accordance with growing research evidence. Clark and Watson (1991) proposed a tripartite structure of anxiety and depression consisting of *negative affect* (i.e., symptoms of general distress such as worry, irritability, tension); *positive affect*, defined as a level of pleasurable engagement with the environment and characterized by features such as cheerfulness, sociability, energetic nature, and enthusiasm; and *autonomic hyperarousal*, characterized by symptoms such as rapid heart rate, shortness of breath, and trembling. This model posited that negative affect is a shared feature of anxiety and mood disorders (i.e., symptoms of tension, worry, irritability, etc., are present in both anxiety and depression). Absence of positive affect (anhedonia) was considered unique to mood disorders, whereas autonomic hyperarousal was viewed as specific to anxiety. However, this model did not account for the diversity of symptoms of anxiety disorders. Subsequent research (e.g., Brown et al., 1998) found that the higher-order dimensions of negative and positive affect accounted for all the covariance among latent variables, corresponding to the *DSM-IV* constructs of unipolar depression, social phobia, GAD, OCD, and PDA. However, autonomic arousal was not specific to all anxiety disorders but was uniquely related to panic disorder. The same study (Brown et al., 1998) found that the absence of positive affect was related not only to depression but also to social phobia. Comorbidity and genetic study findings (e.g., Brown, Campbell, et al., 2001; Kessler, Stang, Wittchen, Stein, & Walters, 1999) also reveal a relationship between unipolar depression and social phobia that may be suggestive of a higher-order vulnerability dimension specific to these two disorders. To address these shortcomings, the tripartite model was reformulated as the hierarchical model of anxiety and depression, in which each disorder consists of both a shared and a unique component (Mineka, Watson, & Clark, 1998). The shared component corresponds to individual differences in general distress and negative affect, representing a higher-order factor common to both anxiety and mood disorders. The unique component for each disorder consists of the specific features that distinguish it from the other disorders.

Barlow (2000, 2002) has formulated a triple vulnerability model of emotional disorders that integrates genetics, personality, cognitive and neuroscience, and emotion and learning theories. The first diathesis, "generalized biological vulnerability," corresponds to the genetically based core dimensions of temperament (e.g., neuroticism). The second, "generalized psychological vulnerability," refers to the perceived sense of uncontrollability, which is manifested as one's tendency to process failures and perceived flaws as an indication of an inability to cope with unpredictable negative events. This propensity may be learned from certain early life experiences, such as overcontrolling parenting style (Chorpita & Barlow, 1998).

Together, generalized biological and psychological vulnerabilities may produce an emotional disorder. However, there is also a third set of "specific psychological vulnerabilities," which, in combination with the other two diatheses, contribute to the development of specific emotional disorders. These vulnerabilities also emerge from early learning experiences, and they refer to one's tendency to focus anxious apprehension on the perceived danger of specific events, thoughts, or objects. For example, "thought–action fusion," conceptualized as a specific psychological vulnerability for OCD, may develop when individuals learn from parents or other important caregivers to equate dangerous thoughts with dangerous actions. Similarly, "anxiety sensitivity," conceptualized as a specific psychological vulnerability for panic disorder (Taylor, 1999), may appear when individuals learn early on that unexplained somatic sensations are dangerous and could indicate illness or death.

Genetic evidence is consistent with the models of emotion disorders. For example, in a study of 1,033 blindly assessed female–female twin pairs, Kendler, Neale, Kessler, Heath, and Eaves (1992a) estimated 30% heritability for GAD (the remainder of the variance may be accounted for nonshared environmental factors). Subsequent research in all-female and mixed-set twin sample (e.g., Kendler, 1996; Kendler, Gardner, Gatz, & Pedersen, 2007; Kendler, Neale, Kessler, Heath, & Eaves, 1992b) has found that a genetic influence exists in GAD and that the genetic factors in GAD are completely shared with major depression. Although these findings may be interpreted as further indication of the overlap in anxiety and depression, empirical evidence suggests otherwise. For example, Kendler et al. (1992b) found that, although GAD and major depression share genetic factors, their environmental determinants are distinct.

In summary, evidence and predictions stemming from the current models of emotional disorders (e.g., Barlow, 2002) and genetic studies (e.g., Kendler et al., 2007) propose that although most constructs of the *DSM-IV* anxiety and mood disorders are relatively distinct (e.g., Brown, 2007), a certain degree of overlap exists between these categories. This overlap may include features such as neuroticism and behavioral inhibition, which represent genetic/biological vulnerability dimensions. Other explanations are also possible for this overlap, including erroneous splitting of a broader syndrome into categories and overlap in the diagnostic criteria. Hence, more research is needed to determine the validity of these positions.

Studies have begun to emerge that examine the relations of the *DSM-IV* disorder constructs with vulnerability dimensions. For example, Brown and colleagues (1998) examined the structural relations of unipolar depression, GAD, panic disorder/agoraphobia, OCD, and social phobia, and the dimensions of negative affect, positive affect, and autonomic arousal in a cross-sectional study. A sample of 350 patients with *DSM-IV* anxiety and mood disorders were assessed using a variety of questionnaires and clinician ratings. A confirmatory factor analysis of the latent structural dimensions of key features of the aforementioned five *DSM-IV* disorders demonstrated the discriminant validity of *DSM-IV* for these constructs; the five-factor model (i.e., mood disorders, GAD, panic disorder/agoraphobia, OCD, social phobia) provided the best fit for the data. Interestingly, model fit decreased significantly when indicators of mood disorders and GAD were collapsed into a single factor, hence supporting the differentiation of these constructs. However, the GAD factor was most strongly correlated with the mood disorder latent factor ($r = .63$), suggesting that the features of GAD have the most overlap with the mood disorders.

As noted earlier, this study also evaluated relations among the five *DSM-IV* disorder latent factors and the latent factors of negative affect, positive affect, and autonomic arousal, finding that the higher-order dimensions of negative affect and positive affect explained almost all of the covariance among latent variables, corresponding to the *DSM-IV* disorder factors. Although all paths from negative affect to the *DSM-IV* disorder factors were statistically significant, corresponding to the predictions that negative affect is a shared feature of emotional disorders, the strongest paths from negative affect were to GAD and mood disorders (path coefficients = .74 and .67, respectively), thus supporting the arguments that GAD and depression are associated with the highest levels of negative affect.

In a more recent study, Brown (2007) expanded on previous findings, examining the temporal course and temporal structural relationships of latent dimensions of temperament (i.e., neuroticism/behavioral inhibition and behavioral activation/positive affect) with a focus on three disorder constructs—unipolar depression, GAD, and social phobia—in a sample of 606 patients with anxiety and mood disorders. Confirmatory factor analyses indicated that the latent factors of neuroticism/behavioral inhibition and behavioral activation/positive affect were distinct from GAD, social phobia, and depression. Neuroticism/behavioral inhibition and behavioral activation/positive affect accounted for most of the covariance among the *DSM-IV* disorder constructs. Neuroticism/behavioral inhibition had the strongest relationship with GAD and depression. Behavioral activation/positive affect was more strongly related to depression and social phobia than to GAD, similar to the findings of Brown et al. (1998). The findings on the temporal course of latent dimensions of

temperament and the disorder constructs are discussed elsewhere in this chapter.

Dimensional Versus Categorical Classification

Thus far, research literature reviewed in this chapter demonstrates a considerable overlap among the anxiety and mood disorders. This is evident in studies of comorbidity (e.g., Brown, Campbell, et al., 2001), nonspecificity of treatment response (e.g., Tyrer, Seivewright, Murphy, Ferguson, Kingdon, Barczak, et al., 1988), and the remission of comorbid conditions following treatment of psychosocial disorder (e.g., Brown, Antony, & Barlow, 1995). On the other hand, there is evidence that the dimensional features of the *DSM* anxiety and mood disorders are distinct, despite some overlap (e.g., Brown, 2007). Moreover, this overlap can be accounted for by a higher-order dimension of neuroticism/negative affect. However, most of these studies relevant to the classification of anxiety and depressive disorders have a significant design problem. Specifically, the majority of these studies have been conducted at the diagnostic level (e.g., family and twin studies, Kendler et al., 2007). This approach presents notable limitations (e.g., Brown & Barlow, 2005). For example, reliability, comorbidity, family, and genetic studies conducted at the diagnostic level are restricted to the disorder definitions specified by the classification system. Additionally, data at the diagnostic level reduce information by artificially collapsing variability above and below an arbitrary threshold, such as presence or absence of a *DSM-IV* disorder. This, in turn, reduces statistical power and introduces additional measurement error.

The limitations of a categorical approach to classification have been apparent in many studies. For example, as previously mentioned, in the reliability study of Brown, Di Nardo, et al. (2001), one of the major sources of unreliability was interviewer disagreement on whether the disorder met the *DSM* threshold. This problem can manifest in two different ways. In some cases, both raters agree that the key features of the disorder are present, but they disagree on whether they cause sufficient impairment or distress to meet the *DSM-IV* threshold for a disorder. This is also apparent in disagreements involving "not otherwise specified" diagnoses, when both raters concur that clinical features of the disorder are present, but they disagree on the number and duration of symptoms that are sufficient to meet the criteria. Similarly, this problem is evident in diagnostic disagreements involving MDD and dysthymia, as core features of depression are noted by both raters, but disagreement occurs with regard to the severity or duration of these symptoms. Finally, although dimensional ratings of the severity of depression are reliable ($r = .74$), a poor level of agreement has been found for the *DSM-IV* categorical severity specifiers ($\kappa = .30$; Brown, Di Nardo, et al., 2001).

Additionally, imposing categories on dimensional phenomena leads to loss of valuable information. For example, *DSM* does not cover clinically significant symptom presentations that do not meet criteria for formal diagnostic categories (Widiger & Samuel, 2005). This is reflected in the high rate with which NOS diagnoses are assigned (Brown, Campbell, et al., 2001). The *DSM* also does not provide a mechanism to record the severity of disorders (e.g., the severity of a comorbid mood disorder rather than merely its presence may be more relevant to the course and treatment outcome of an anxiety disorder). Information is also lost because of adherence to the hierarchical exclusions and differential diagnostic decision rules posed by the *DSM*. These rules are in place to avoid excessive comorbidity and to increase diagnostic reliability. For example, according to the *DSM-IV*, a diagnosis of GAD should not be assigned if its features occur exclusively within the course of a mood disorder. Adherence to such rules may lead to misleading findings about comorbidity of disorders. For example, in the Brown, Campbell, et al. (2001) comorbidity study, the comorbidity rate of GAD and dysthymia was only 5% when the *DSM* hierarchical rules were followed. This result contradicts the evidence pointing to substantial genotypic and phenotypic overlap of GAD and mood disorders (e.g., Brown et al., 1998; Kendler et al., 1992b). Indeed, when this diagnostic hierarchy rule was ignored, the comorbidity rate of GAD and dysthymia rose to 90%. Artifacts of *DSM-IV* differential diagnosis rules are also evident in other patterns of comorbidity, such as lower estimates of PDA co-occurrence with social and specific phobia (Brown, Campbell et al., 2001). While decreasing undue comorbidity, the *DSM* differential diagnostic rules obscure important clinical information about the nature of one's symptoms and overall level of functioning, which may have important implications for treatment planning and prognosis. Clinical information may be potentially presented more completely if dimensional systems are utilized.

Although the utility of dimensional classification has been recognized, no strong proposals have been made about how dimensional classification can be included in the *DSM*. First (2005) argues that a purely dimensional classification system may complicate clinical assessment, as well as the communication between mental health professionals. The question then becomes how dimensional elements can be incorporated into the categorical system. Brown and Barlow (2005) suggest introducing dimensional ratings of severity to the present diagnostic categories and their symptom criteria, a method similar to the one utilized in the ADIS-IV-L. This appears to be a practical alternative, as it would allow the categorical system to remain intact, and the dimensional rating can be optional for settings in which its implementation is less feasible (e.g., primary care). This approach may help address some of the problems with the present system, such as its inability to convey the severity of a disorder or clinical characteristics that may be significant, but are either subsumed by another disorder (e.g., GAD occurring exclusively within the course of a mood disorder) or do not meet the severity or the number of symptoms defined by the *DSM* (e.g., subclinical or NOS diagnoses). Because dimensional ratings would be added to the current diagnostic categories, this approach would have several advantages, including its basis on a preexisting and well-studied set of constructs, as well as its ability to retain the functional analytic and temporal aspects of a diagnosis that are difficult to be conveyed using a purely psychometric approach. Inclusion of the dimensional ratings would also provide a standardized assessment system that would allow for across-site comparability in a study of dimensional models of psychopathology. This approach may be the initial step that would help determine the reliability and feasibility of more complex dimensional systems, such as quantifying higher-order dimensions of temperament.

However, despite its usefulness, such an approach would leave some of the main problems with the categorical classification system unresolved, including poor reliability and high comorbidity. For example, the previously mentioned information variance (i.e., the difference in the patient's report of information), which is the most common reason for disagreements in reliability studies (e.g., Brown, Di Nardo et al., 2001), would remain the case with dimensional assessment as well. However, if diagnostic classification was focused at higher-order dimensions, these problems might be improved.

Indeed, it has been suggested that the classification system be driven by dimensions corresponding to biologically and environmentally based constructs of temperament and personality (e.g., Clark, 2005). This is in line with the aforementioned theories and empirical evidence that the overlap in anxiety and mood disorders may be due to the fact that these disorders share biologic-genetic and psychosocial diatheses (e.g., Barlow, 2002). There is accumulating empirical evidence pointing to the importance of these higher-order dimensions and their implications in long-term treatment outcomes (e.g., Kasch, Rottenberg, Arnow, & Gotlib, 2002). If these broader dimensions of temperament were incorporated, the *DSM* would cease being a descriptive instrument and would become relevant to the prevention of mental disorders.

Treatment of Anxiety and Depressive Disorders

The classification of anxiety and mood disorders has had a significant impact on treatment development. The increase in diagnostic categories across *DSM* editions has led to the development of disorder-specific interventions. The revision of agoraphobia and GAD criteria are examples of how classification

can drive treatment development. In the *DSM-III* (APA, 1980), panic disorder was regarded as different from agoraphobia, which was considered a "phobic disorder." However, a later series of studies suggested a relationship between panic disorder and agoraphobia (e.g., Thyer & Himle, 1985; Zitrin, Klein, Woerner, & Ross, 1983). The higher prevalence of agoraphobia with panic attacks in comparison to agoraphobia without panic attacks (Di Nardo et al., 1983) also supported this relationship. These findings led to the redefinition of agoraphobia as a condition secondary to panic disorder in *DSM-III-R* (APA, 1987). This change in the classification of agoraphobia and its conceptualization as apprehension about situations in which one may experience panic-like symptoms, led to a refinement of cognitive-behavioral therapy for PDA, to include exposure to anxiety-provoking situations and physical sensations (e.g., Craske & Barlow, 2007).

Similarly, GAD could not be diagnosed in *DSM-III* in the presence of any other mental disorder. However, its revision from a residual condition to a formal diagnostic category in *DSM-III-R* and *DSM-IV* led to the development of specific treatment

Table 14.3 Additional current diagnoses among patients with principal anxiety and mood disorders

Additional diagnosis	DSM-IV principal diagnosis							
	PD (*n* = 36)	PDA (*n* = 324)	SOC (*n* = 186)	GAD (*n* = 120)	OCD (*n* = 77)	SPEC (*n* = 110)	MDD (*n* = 81)	Overall *a*
Any diagnosis	42	62	46	68	57	34	69	57
PD			1	3	1	0	4	1
PDA			3	15	3	5	15	9
SOC	8	15		36	26	9	41	22
GAD	19	16	13		12	5	5	13
OCD	6	7	8	4		3	9	7
SPEC	8	15	8	12	12	15	15	13
MDD	8	24	14	26	22	3		20
DYS	8	7	13	6	10	4	11	8
MDD or DYS	11	17	20	29	40	4	0	18

PD, panic disorder; PDA, panic disorder with agoraphobia; SOC, social phobia; GAD, generalized anxiety disorder; OCD, obsessive-compulsive disorder; SPEC, specific phobia; MDD, major depressive disorder; DYS, dysthymia.

a, Overall frequency in which category was assigned as an additional diagnosis.

Adapted from Brown, T. A., Campbell, L. A., Lehman, C. L., Grisham, J. R., & Mancill, R. B. (2001). Current and lifetime comorbidity of the *DSM-IV* anxiety and mood disorders in a large clinical sample. *Journal of Abnormal Psychology, 11*, 592, with permission of the publisher, APA.

protocols focusing on the key feature of the disorder—excessive and uncontrollable worry (e.g., Zinbarg, Craske, & Barlow, 2006).

Indeed, disorder-specific psychological treatment protocols have now been developed for each anxiety disorder. However, the cognitive-behavioral interventions bear a lot of similarities in their components, including elements of exposure, cognitive restructuring, and between-sessions practice, and vary mostly on content to match the specific features of each disorder. Although these differentiations are helpful in addressing the nature of the disturbance, the question then becomes whether these treatments have become too specific.

Treatment Specificity

Evidence demonstrates that anxiety and depressive disorders respond similarly to the same psychological or medical treatment. For example, a wide range of emotional disorders, including major depression, OCD, panic disorder, and GAD, have responded similarly to selective serotonin reuptake inhibitors (Hudson & Pope, 1990). Similar evidence has been obtained for benzodiazepines, tricyclic antidepressants, and monoamine oxidase inhibitors (Bandelow, Zohar, Hollander, Kasper, & Moller, 2002). In a large study, Tyrer et al. (1988) treated 210 outpatients with GAD, panic disorder, and dysthymia with diazepam, dothiepin, placebo, cognitive-behavioral therapy, or a self-help program. No difference was found in treatment response between the diagnostic groups, leading Tyrer et al. (1988) to conclude that differential diagnosis of anxiety and mood disorders was not essential for treatment planning.

Additionally, evidence suggests that psychological treatment of a specific anxiety disorder leads to a decline in other anxiety and mood disorders not addressed in treatment (e.g., Borkovec, Abel, & Newman, 1995; Brown et al., 1995). For example, Brown et al. (1995) examined the course of additional diagnoses in a sample of 126 patients in a short-term psychological treatment program for panic disorder with minimal agoraphobic avoidance. At pre-treatment, 40% of the patient had an additional diagnosis. This rate decreased to 17% at post-treatment. However, at 2-year follow-up, the rate of comorbidity increased to 30%, which was no longer significantly different from pre-treatment. These findings could be interpreted in accord with the explanation for comorbidity and theoretical models stating that disorders emerge from the same vulnerabilities. It is possible that while cognitive-behavioral therapy was effective in reducing the symptoms of panic disorder, it was not sufficient to reduce the general predispositional features such as neuroticism, which left patients vulnerable to other disorders.

However, these conclusions are speculative, because the above-mentioned studies did not measure vulnerability traits. It is possible that that the temperamental dimensions of neuroticism/negative affect and extraversion/positive affect are temporally stable and less responsive to treatment. Longitudinal studies are starting to emerge examining the temporal course of dimensions of temperament. Kasch et al. (2002) examined the temporal stability of behavioral inhibition and behavioral activation in 41 individuals with major depression over a period of 8 months; most of these individuals received treatment during the follow-up period. Lower behavioral activation at Time 1 predicted poorer clinical outcome for depression at the 8-month assessment. The self-report measures of behavioral inhibition and behavioral activation were highly stable over time, regardless of the presence of depression at the follow-up.

The aforementioned study by Brown (2007) also examined the temporal course and temporal structural relationships of dimensions of neuroticism/ behavioral inhibition and behavioral activation/ positive affect and *DSM-IV* constructs on unipolar depression, GAD, and social phobia, reassessing the participants at 1-year and 2-year follow-ups. Because the majority of the study participants (76%) received psychotherapy following their intake, the rate of anxiety and mood disorders decreased significantly between the intake (100%) and the 2-year follow-up (58%). Behavioral activation/positive affect evidenced a very high degree of temporal stability, consistent with its conceptualization as a trait vulnerability construct that is relatively unaffected by treatment. Neuroticism, on the other hand, evidenced the greatest amount of temporal change of the five constructs examined (Cohen's d = .70), inconsistent with previous findings (e.g., Kasch et al., 2002), and it was associated with the largest treatment effect (d = -.98). However, it is possible that the self-report of temperament is affected by mood state (e.g., Clark, Vittengl, Kraft, & Jarrett, 2003). Hence, the measurement of neuroticism/behavioral inhibition may consist of some combination of stable temperament variance and variability due to generalized distress, which is likely to be temporally less stable and to covary with changes in the severity of disorders. Other studies have also demonstrated that scores on measure of temperament change from pre- to post-treatment (e.g., Clark et al., 2003). Moreover, Clark et al. (2003) implemented multivariate statistical procedures to differentiate between trait and state components of their measure of temperament. They found that changes of depression severity at post-treatment correlated with changes in the state component of the measure, but not with the trait scores.

Additionally, Brown (2007) demonstrated that neuroticism/behavioral activation operated differently than the *DSM-IV* disorder constructs. Whereas, for the disorder constructs, higher initial severity was associated with greater symptom decreases over time, the finding was opposite for neuroticism/behavioral inhibition; patients with higher initial levels of neuroticism/behavioral activation showed less change in it over time. Hence, it appeared that, unlike the *DSM-IV* disorders, the stability of neuroticism/behavioral inhibition increased as a function of initial severity.

Because dimensions of temperament have been conceptualized as risk factors for emotional disorders, studies have examined whether pre-treatment levels of these dimensions are related to treatment response and long-term course of emotional disorders. Previous studies have yielded contradictory results for depression, some showing that higher pre-treatment scores on temperament measures were associated with poorer treatment outcome (e.g., Geerts & Bouhuys, 1998; Kasch et al., 2002), whereas other studies reported no such effects (e.g., Boyce & Parker, 1985; Clark et al., 2003). Brown (2007) examined directional effects among temperament and disorder constructs over 2-year follow-up. Higher levels of neuroticism/behavioral inhibition were associated with less improvement in GAD and social phobia. Lower levels of behavioral activation/positive affect were associated with poorer outcome for the social phobia construct. However, this effect was no longer significant when neuroticism/behavioral inhibition was included in the analyses. No temporal relations were obtained for the *DSM-IV* construct of depression. The *DSM-IV* disorders did not have directional effects on dimensions of temperament. Moreover, change in neuroticism/behavioral inhibition accounted for all the temporal covariance of the *DSM-IV* disorder constructs. This suggests that either neuroticism may be affected by therapy, or a reduction in disorder severity is associated with a reduction in general distress, a feature shared by all emotional disorders. Overall, the results of this study demonstrate in a longitudinal context the role of neuroticism/behavioral inhibition

as a unifying construct accounting for the covariance among the emotional disorders.

Transdiagnostic Treatments

The emerging evidence on commonalities among the anxiety and mood disorders, including their overlapping key features and comorbidity, has led to the development of transdiagnostic approaches to the treatment of emotional disorders. It has been noted that virtually all specialized treatments for anxiety and mood disorders consist of similar components: psychoeducation, cognitive reappraisal, changing behaviors associated with the particular emotion, and exposure. Although some variations are disorder-specific, the general principles are similar. Furthermore, the earlier cited evidence on improvement of comorbid disorders after cognitive-behavioral treatment for one disorder (e.g., Brown et al., 1995) have suggested that there may be an underlying mechanism to emotional disorders that could be the focus of treatment.

Several transdiagnostic treatment approaches have been developed, based on the processes common to emotional disorders. For example, Barlow, Allen, and Choate (2004) have developed a unified protocol for treatment of anxiety and depression that suggests that maladaptive emotional regulation strategies such as suppression and avoidance are a component of all emotional disorders. This protocol begins with psychoeducation about the nature and purpose of emotions, and how they become "disordered." It then focuses on cognitive reappraisal, changing emotion-driven behaviors, and preventing emotional avoidance. As in other cognitive-behavioral treatments, exposures are an essential part of treatment. However, in the unified protocol, they are not designed to target a particular disorder; they are rather defined as "emotion exposures," the focus of treatment being emotional avoidance as opposed to the symptoms associated with a specific disorder.

Hayes and colleagues (1996) have argued that categorical classification of disorders, such as that implemented in the *DSM-IV*, does not adequately convey pathological processes underlying the disorders. They have suggested the dimension of experiential avoidance (i.e., engaging in maladaptive behaviors to avoid other psychological experiences) may be central to many forms of psychopathology. Based on this theory, Hayes, Strosahl, and Wilson (1999) developed *acceptance and commitment therapy*, which incorporates acceptance of emotional experience, mindfulness, and behavioral change that is accordance with one's values.

Several other transdiagnostic approaches have been developed, with an emphasis on enhancing treatment effectiveness and facilitating treatment dissemination. Most of them have focused on providing group cognitive-behavioral treatment to individuals with various anxiety and depressive disorders. For example, Erickson, Janeck, and Tallman (2007) reported a medium-size effect in a randomized waitlist controlled study of group cognitive-behavioral therapy (CBT) for various anxiety disorders. Erickson (2004) reported medium to large effect sizes in an uncontrolled trial of group CBT for anxiety disorders. In a randomized waitlist controlled study, Norton, Hayes, and Hope (2004) found a significant decrease in depressive symptoms following a transdiagnostic group treatment for anxiety. More recently, McEvoy and Nathan (2007), in a benchmarking study, demonstrated that effects of group transdiagnostic treatment for emotional disorders are similar to those of diagnosis-specific treatments. Overall, these studies provide support for the transdiagnostic cognitive-behavioral treatment of anxiety and depressive disorders. However, unlike Barlow's unified protocol and Hayes and colleagues' acceptance and commitment therapy, these approaches do not offer a unified theory about the processes common to emotional disorders.

Transdiagnostic approaches to treatment of anxiety and depression present several advantages over the use of disorder-specific treatments. First, they reflect the recent advances in our understanding of etiology and maintenance of emotional disorders. Some of these approaches view symptoms of the disorders as manifestations of this vulnerability and attempt to address it instead of the specific symptoms. Additionally, such approaches may facilitate treatment dissemination, but condense available interventions into a more widely applicable form. Despite these benefits, further research is needed to evaluate the efficacy of these treatments. It will also be important to investigate the effects of such treatments on the higher-order dimensions of vulnerability, such as neuroticism.

Conclusion

This chapter focused on issues pertaining to the classification of anxiety and mood disorders and the relevance of these issues to treatment planning. The extant literature points to considerable overlap among the various anxiety and mood disorders. This is evident in studies demonstrating high rates of current and lifetime comorbidity at the diagnostic level (e.g., Brown, Campbell, et al., 2001), nonspecificity

of treatment response (e.g., Tyrer et al., 1989), and the remission of comorbid conditions following psychosocial treatment of the principal disorder (e.g., Brown et al., 1995). On the other hand, evidence suggests that the dimensional key features of the *DSM* anxiety and mood disorders display a high level of discriminant validity, despite a certain degree of overlap (e.g., Brown, 2007; Brown et al., 1998). Moreover, most of the shared variance of these emotional disorder constructs can be accounted for by a higher-order dimension of general distress/ neuroticism.

The principal position outlined in the chapter was that overlap in anxiety and mood disorders may provide important clues to understanding the origins and maintenance of these syndromes and be of importance in treatment planning. This position is consistent with one potential explanation of comorbidity that high co-occurrence of disorders at the descriptive level is the result of their common etiological roots.

Future Directions

This hypothesis awaits future research to further refine issues on the classification of emotional disorders. Several suggestions can help refine the research in this direction. First, as noted previously in the chapter, greater emphasis on dimensional measures of psychopathological phenomena and disorders will help further clarify the latent structure of these measures and the relationship between them. The increased use of latent variable approaches to data analysis will provide the advantage of adjusting for measurement error and will allow for statistical comparison of models reflecting competing theories of causality or classification. Finally, by incorporating multiple measures associated with the higher-order vulnerability dimensions (e.g., negative affect, behavioral inhibition, perceived control), researchers could examine issues such as the prediction of the emergence of specific disorders and the extent to which the defining features of emotional disorders overlap with these traits. This latter focus also would address suggestions made by researchers for increased empirical consideration of those common traits of emotional disorders that may hold strong predictive value to the prevention, etiology, course, and treatment response of emotional disorders.

It is hoped that these methodological refinements will be increasingly applied to three other important avenues of classification and pathogenesis research—genetic, longitudinal, and treatment outcome studies. Greater emphasis on dimensional assessment of psychopathology (e.g., latent disorder constructs) in twin studies, combined with the use of latent variable approaches, could lead to important advances beyond evidence on the heritability and familial aggregation of disorders focused at the diagnostic level, where estimates of genetic liability are influenced by increased measurement error and diminished statistical power associated with collapsing dimensional variability above and below the *DSM* threshold.

There are several important potential directions for longitudinal research. Studies of at-risk and large nonclinical samples will allow investigators to identify the contribution of dimensions implicated as vulnerability factors (e.g., neuroticism) in the prediction of emotional disorders and to determine whether these higher-order traits are more explanatory than the constructs suggested to be disorder-specific (e.g., thought–action fusion for OCD). Additionally, large-scale clinical studies addressing issues such as the temporal stability and covariation of disorders and their underlying constructs, and effects of life stress on the relationship between temperament and psychopathology are crucial for increasing the understanding of the direction of the relationship among disorders and vulnerability constructs. For instance, given the evidence that the effects of vulnerability on psychopathology may be affected by stressful life events (Kendler, Kuhn, & Prescott, 2004), the Brown (2007) study may have underestimated the influence of neuroticism/behavioral inhibition and behavioral activation/positive affect on the course of the *DSM-IV* disorder constructs. Finally, large-scale clinical studies focusing on the bidirectional influence of temperament and *DSM-IV* disorders during the course of psychosocial treatment, as well as the effects of transdiagnostic treatments on the higher-order dimensions of vulnerability, will provide further evidence for determining the direction of the relationship among disorders and vulnerability constructs. These questions await longitudinal study in twin, community, at-risk, and clinical samples.

List of Abbreviations

APA	American Psychiatric Association
ADIS	Anxiety Disorders Interview Schedule
ADIS-IV-L	Diagnostic and Statistical Manual of Mental Disorders, 3rd edition
ADIS-R	Anxiety Disorders Interview Schedule – Revised
DSM	Diagnostic and Statistical Manual of Mental Disorders
DSM-III	Diagnostic and Statistical Manual of Mental Disorders, 3rd edition
DSM-III-R	Diagnostic and Statistical Manual of Mental Disorders, 3rd edition, revised
DSM-IV	Diagnostic and Statistical Manual of Mental Disorders, 4th edition
DSM-5	Diagnostic and Statistical Manual of Mental Disorders, 5th edition
GAD	Generalized anxiety disorder
MDD	Major depressive disorder
NOS	Not otherwise specified
OCD	Obsessive-compulsive disorder
PDA	Panic disorder with agoraphobia
PTSD	Post-traumatic stress disorder
SADS-LA	Schedule for Affective Disorders and Schizophrenia – Lifetime Anxiety Version
SCID-I	Structured Clinical Interview for *DSM-IV* Axis I Disorders

References

Andrews, G. (1996). Comorbidity in neurotic disorders: The similarities are more important than the differences. In R. M. Rapee (Ed.), *Current controversies in the anxiety disorders* (pp. 3–20). New York: Guilford Press.

American Psychiatric Association. (1980). *Diagnostic and statistical manual of mental disorders, 3rd edition (DSM-III)*. Washington, DC: Author.

American Psychiatric Association. (1987). *Diagnostic and statistical manual of mental disorders, 3rd edition, revised (DSM-III-R)*. Washington, DC: Author.

American Psychiatric Association. (1994). *Diagnostic and statistical manual of mental disorders, 4th edition, (DSM-IV)*. Washington, DC: Author.

Bandelow, B., Zohar, J., Hollander, E., Kasper, S., & Moller, H. J. (2002). World Federation of Societies of Biological Psychiatry (WFSBP) guidelines for the pharmacological treatment of anxiety, obsessive-compulsive and posttraumatic stress disorders. *World Journal of Biological Psychiatry, 3,* 171–199.

Barlow, D. H. (2000). Unraveling the mysteries of anxiety and its disorders from the perspective of emotion theory. *American Psychologist, 55,* 1247–1263.

Barlow, D. H. (2002). *Anxiety and its disorders: The nature and treatment of anxiety and panic* (2nd ed.). New York: Guilford Press.

Barlow, D. H., Allen, L. B., & Choate, M. L. (2004). Toward a unified treatment for emotional disorders. *Behavior Therapy, 35,* 205–230.

Borkovec, T. D., Abel, J. L., & Newman, H. (1995). Effects of psychotherapy on comorbid conditions in generalized anxiety disorder. *Journal of Consulting and Clinical Psychology, 63*, 479–483.

Boyce, P., & Parker, G. (1985). Neuroticism as a predictor of outcome in depression. *Journal of Nervous and Mental Disease, 173*, 685–688.

Brown, T. A. (2007). Temporal course and structural relationships among dimensions of temperament and DSM-IV anxiety and mood disorder constructs. *Journal of Abnormal Psychology, 116*, 313–328.

Brown, T. A., Antony, M. M., & Barlow, D. H. (1995). Diagnostic comorbidity in panic disorder: Effect on treatment outcome and course of comorbid diagnoses following treatment. *Journal of Consulting and Clinical Psychology, 63*, 408–418.

Brown, T. A., & Barlow, D. H. (2005). Categorical *vs* dimensional classification of mental disorders in DSM-5 and beyond. *Journal of Abnormal Psychology, 114*, 551–556.

Brown, T. A., & Barlow, D. H. (2002). Classification of anxiety and mood disorders. In D. H. Barlow, *Anxiety and its disorders: The nature and treatment of anxiety and panic* (2nd ed., pp. 292–327). New York: Guilford Press.

Brown, T. A., & Barlow, D. H. (1992). Comorbidity among anxiety disorders: Implications for treatment and DSM-IV. *Journal of Consulting and Clinical Psychology, 60*, 835–844.

Brown, T. A., Campbell, L. A., Lehman, C. L., Grisham, J. R., & Mancill, R. B. (2001). Current and lifetime comorbidity of the DSM-IV anxiety and mood disorders in a large clinical sample. *Journal of Abnormal Psychology, 110*, 585–599.

Brown, T. A., Chorpita, B. F., & Barlow, D. H. (1998). Structural relationships among dimensions of the DSM-IV anxiety and mood disorders and dimensions of negative affect, positive affect, and autonomic arousal. *Journal of Abnormal Psychology, 107*, 179–192.

Brown, T. A., Di Nardo, P. A., Lehman, C. L., & Campbell, L. A. (2001). Reliability of DSM-IV anxiety and mood disorders: Implications for the classification of emotional disorders. *Journal of Abnormal Psychology, 110*, 49–58.

Chorpita, B. F., & Barlow, D. H. (1998). The development of anxiety: The role of control in the early environment. *Psychological Bulletin, 124*, 3–21.

Clark, L. A. (2005). Temperament as a unifying basis for personality and psychopathology. *Journal of Abnormal Psychology, 114*, 505–521.

Clark, L. A., Vittengl, J. R., Kraft, D., & Jarrett, R. B. (2003). Shared, not unique, components of personality and psychosocial functioning predict depression severity after acute-phase cognitive therapy. *Journal of Personality Disorders, 17*, 406–430.

Clark, L. A., & Watson, D. (1991). Tripartite model of anxiety and depression: Psychometric evidence and taxonomic implications. *Journal of Abnormal Psychology, 100*, 316–336.

Clark, L. A., Watson, D., & Mineka, S. (1994). Temperament, personality, and the mood and anxiety disorders. *Journal of Abnormal Psychology, 103*, 103–116.

Craske, M. G., & Barlow, D. H. (2007). *Mastery of your anxiety and panic: Therapist guide (4th ed.).* New York, New York: Oxford University Press.

Di Nardo, P. A., & Barlow, D. H. (1988). *Anxiety Disorders Interview Schedule-Revised.* Albany, NY: Graywind Publications.

Di Nardo, P. A., Brown, T. A., & Barlow, D. H. (1994). *Anxiety Disorders Interview Schedule for DSM-IV: Lifetime Version (ADIS-IV-L).* New York: Oxford University Press.

Di Nardo, P. A., O'Brien, G. T., Barlow, D. H., Waddell, M. T., & Blanchard, E. B. (1983). Reliability of *DSM-III* anxiety disorder categories using a new structured interview. *Archives of General Psychiatry, 40*, 1070–1074.

Di Nardo, P. A., Moras, K., Barlow, D. H., Rapee, R. M., & Brown, T. A. (1993). Reliability of *DSM-III-R* anxiety disorder categories using the Anxiety Disorders Interview Schedule-Revised (ADIS-R). *Archives of General Psychiatry, 50*, 251–256.

Erickson, D. H. (2004). Group cognitive behavioral therapy for heterogeneous anxiety disorders. *Cognitive Behavior Therapy, 32*, 179–186.

Erickson, D. H., Janeck, A. S., & Tallman, K. (2007). A cognitive-behavioral group for patients with various anxiety disorders. *Psychiatric Services, 58*, 1205–1211.

First, M. B. (2005). Clinical utility: A prerequisite for the adoption of a dimensional approach in *DSM. Journal of Abnormal Psychology, 114*, 560–564.

First, M. B., Spitzer, R. L., Gibbon, M., Williams, J. B. (1997). *Structured Clinical Interview for* DSM-IV *Axis I Disorders (SCID).* Washington, DC: American Psychiatric Press.

Fleiss J. L., Nee, J. C., Landis, J. R. (1979). Large sample variance of kappa in the case of different sets of raters. *Archives of General Psychiatry, 86*, 974–977.

Frances, A., Widiger, T., & Fyer, M. R. (1990). The influence of classification methods on comorbidity. In J. D. Maser, C. R. Cloninger (Eds.). *Comorbidity of mood and anxiety disorders* (pp. 41–59). Washington, DC: American Psychiatric Press.

Fyer, A. J., Endicott, J., Mannuzza, S., & Klein, D. F. (1985). *Schedule for Affective Disorders and Schizophrenia – Lifetime Anxiety Version.* New York: Anxiety Disorders Clinic, New York State Psychiatric Institute.

Geerts, E., & Bouhuys, A. L. (1998). Multi-level prediction of short-term outcome of depression: The role of non-verbal interpersonal and cognitive processes and of personality traits. *Psychiatry Research, 79*, 59–72.

Hayes, S. C., Strosahl, K., & Wilson, K. G. (1999). *Acceptance and commitment therapy: An experiential approach to behavior change.* New York: Guilford Press.

Hayes, S. C., Wilson, K. G., Gifford, E. V., Follette, V. M., & Strosahl, K. (1996). Experiential avoidance and behavioral disorders: A functional dimensional approach to diagnosis and treatment. *Journal of Consulting and Clinical Psychology, 64*, 1152–1168.

Hettema, J. M., Neale, M. C., & Kendler, K. S. (2001). A review and meta-analysis of the genetic epidemiology of anxiety disorders. *American Journal of Psychiatry, 158*, 1568–1578.

Hettema, J. M., Prescott, C. A., & Kendler, K. S. (2004). Genetic and environmental sources of covariation between generalized anxiety disorder and neuroticism. *American Journal of Psychiatry, 161*, 1581–1587.

Hudson, J. I., & Pope, H. G., Jr. (1990). Affective spectrum disorder: does antidepressant response identify a family of disorders with a common pathophysiology? *American Journal of Psychiatry, 147*, 552–564.

Kasch, K. L., Rottenberg, J., Arnow, B. A., & Gotlib, I. H. (2002). Behavioral activation and inhibition systems and the severity and course of depression. *Journal of Abnormal Psychology, 111*, 589–597.

Kendler, K. S. (1996). Major depression and generalized anxiety disorder. Same genes, (partly) different environments – revisited. *British Journal of Psychiatry, 168 (Suppl. 30)*, 68–75.

Kendler, K. S., Gardner, C. O., Gatz, M., & Pedersen, N. L. (2007). The sources of comorbidity between major depression and generalized anxiety disorder in a Swedish national twin sample. *Psychological Medicine, 37,* 453–462.

Kendler, K. S., Kuhn, J., Prescott, C. A. (2004). The interrelationship of neuroticism, sex, and stressful life events in the prediction of episodes of major depression. *American Journal of Psychiatry, 161,* 631–636.

Kendler, K. S., Neale, M. C., Kessler, R. C., Heath, A. C., & Eaves, L. J. (1992a). Generalized anxiety disorder in women: A population-based twin study. *Archives of General Psychiatry, 9,* 267–272.

Kendler, K. S., Neale, M. C., Kessler, R. C., Heath, A. C., & Eaves, L. J. (1992b). Major depression and generalized anxiety disorder: Same genes, (partly) different environments? *Archives of General Psychiatry, 49,* 716–722.

Kessler, R. C., McGonagle, K. A., Zhao, S., Nelson, C. B., Hughes, M., Eshleman, S., et al. (1994). Lifetime and 12-month prevalence of *DSM-III-R* psychiatric disorders in the United States: Results from the National Comorbidity Survey. *Archives of General Psychiatry, 51,* 8–19.

Kessler, R. C., Stang, P., Wittchen, H. U., Stein, M., & Walters, E. E. (1999). Lifetime comorbidities between social phobia and mood disorders in the U. S. National Comorbidity Survey. *Psychological Medicine, 29,* 555–567.

Mannuzza, S., Fyer, A. J., Martin, L. Y., Gallops, M. S., Endicott, J., Gorman, J. M., et al. (1989). Reliability of anxiety assessment I: Diagnostic agreement. *Archives of General Psychiatry, 46,* 1093–1101.

McEvoy, P. M., & Nathan, P. (2007). Effectiveness of cognitive-behavioral therapy for diagnostically heterogeneous groups: A benchmarking study. *Journal of Consulting and Clinical Psychology, 75,* 344–350.

Mineka, S., Watson, D., & Clark, L. A. (1998). Comorbidity of anxiety and unipolar mood disorders. *Annual Review of Psychology, 49,* 377–412.

Norton, P., Hayes, S., & Hope, D. (2004). Effects of a transdiagnostic group treatment for anxiety on secondary depression. *Depression and Anxiety, 20,* 198–202.

Riskind, J. H., Beck, A. T., Berchick, R. J., Brown, G., & Steer, R. A. (1987). Reliability of the *DSM-III-R* diagnoses for major depression and generalized anxiety disorder using the Structured Clinical Interview for *DSM-III-R*. *Archives of General Psychiatry, 44,* 817–820.

Shrout, P. E., Spitzer, R. L., & Fleiss, J. L. (1987). Quantification of agreement in psychiatric diagnosis revisited. *Archives of General Psychiatry, 44,* 172–177.

Taylor, S. (1999). *Anxiety sensitivity: Theory, research, and treatment of the fear of anxiety.* New York: Guilford Press.

Thyer, B. A., & Himle, J. (1985). Temporal relationship between panic attack onset and phobic avoidance in agoraphobia. *Behaviour Research and Therapy, 23,* 607–608.

Tyrer, P.J. (1989). *Classification of neurosis.* Chichester, England: Wiley.

Tyrer, P.J., Seivewright, N., Murphy, S., Ferguson, B., Kingdon, D., Barczak, B. et al. (1988). The Nottingham study of neurotic disorder: comparison of drug and psychological treatments. *Lancet, 2,* 235–240.

Widiger, T. A., & Samuel, D. B. (2005). Diagnostic categories or dimensions? A question for the diagnostic and statistical manual of mental disorders–fifth edition. *Journal of Abnormal Psychology, 114,* 494–504.

Williams, J. B. W., Gibbon, M., First, M. B., Spitzer, R. L., Davies, M., Borus, J., et al. (1992). The Structured Clinical Interview for *DSM-III-R* (SCID), II: Multisite test-retest reliability. *Archives of General Psychiatry, 49,* 630–636.

Zinbarg, R. E., Barlow, D. H., Liebowitz, M. R., Street, L., Broadhead, E., & Katon, W. (1994). The DSM-IV field trial for mixed anxiety depression. *American Journal Psychiatry, 151,* 1153–1162.

Zinbarg, R. E., Craske, M. G., & Barlow, D. H. (2006). *Mastery of your anxiety and worry: Therapist guide (2nd ed.).* New York, NY: Oxford University Press.

Zitrin, C. M., Klein, D. F., Woerner, M. G., & Ross, D. C. (1983). Treatment of phobias, I: Comparison of imipramine hydrochloride and placebo. *Archives of General Psychiatry, 40,* 125–138.

The Nature and Treatment of Bipolar Disorder and the Bipolar Spectrum

Michael W. Otto *and* Allison J. Applebaum

Abstract

In this chapter, we review the nature and treatment of bipolar disorder. We first present a perspective on the disorder, based on the dominant bipolar I and II classifications, and review the current state of medication and empirically supported psychosocial interventions (e.g., cognitive-behavioral therapy, family-focused therapy, interpersonal and social rhythm therapy, and group treatment), including factors that lead to poor treatment response. Given the increased attention to how bipolar I and II may lie at one end of a continuum of patterns of mood instability, we subsequently address spectrum conceptualizations of bipolar disorder. The proposed spectrum models are presented and then considered in relation to revised prevalence rates and treatment implications.

Keywords: Bipolar disorder, bipolar spectrum, cognitive-behavioral therapy, family-focused therapy, interpersonal and social rhythm therapy

Bipolar disorder is a disabling, chronic, and prevalent condition. The disorder is defined by periods of mood instability and is most frequently characterized by repeated episodes of depression and at least one manic or hypomanic episode. A full manic episode is defined by a period of 1 week (unless interrupted by treatment or other factors) of feeling euphoric, irritable, or high, along with three or more of the following symptoms: exaggerated feelings of importance, racing thoughts, distractibility, little need for sleep, pressured speech, and reckless behavior (American Psychiatric Association, 2000). Hypomanic episodes are similar to manic episodes, except that they are less severe and impairing. The bipolar I subtype of bipolar disorder is defined by at least one episode of mania, whereas the bipolar II subtype refers to individuals who have had at least one hypomanic, but not full manic, episode and one or more depressive episodes.

Although there is variation in the pattern of episodes, in the most common presentation, bipolar patients typically experience several episodes of depression before the emergence of the initial manic episode (Lish et al., 1994; Suppes et al., 2001), and depressive symptoms are generally present more often than manic/hypomanic symptoms (Colom, Vieta, Daban, Pacchiarotti, & Sanchez-Moreno, 2006; Judd et al., 2003). For example, Judd et al. (2003) found that a sample of bipolar I patients felt depressed three times as many weeks compared to manic/hypomanic patients, and bipolar II patients had depressive symptoms 37 times more frequently than hypomanic symptoms. A predominance of depressive episodes was also reported by Colom et al. (2006). Of the smaller number of individuals who present initially with a manic episode, evidence suggests that this pattern may be more characteristic of men than women (Suppes et al., 2001).

Rates of relapse are high over the long term. Studies indicate that three-quarters of patients can be expected to relapse within 4–5 years, with half of these relapses occurring in the first year (Gitlin, Swendsen, Heller, & Hammen, 1995; O'Connell, Mayo, Flatlow, Cuthbertson, & O'Brien, 1991;

Tohen, Waternaux, & Tsuang, 1990). Moreover, impairment in role functioning and continued bipolar symptoms are common between episodes (Keck et al., 1998).

Attention to a potential spectrum of bipolar disorders dates back to Aristotle, over two millennia ago (Pies, 2007), but received further clarity in the writings of Kraepelin in the early 1900s. Kraeplin discussed a continuum of bipolar illness that ranged from cyclothymia to full manic-depressive patterns (see Brieger & Marneros, 1997), with the identification of cyclothymia as a milder form of, or a predisposition to, full bipolar disorder. A potential benefit of a continuum approach is the greater inclusion of diverse patterns of pathology under a single organizing principle—the cyclic mood instability that defines bipolar disorder—and, accordingly, the extension of treatment strategies based on bipolar disorder to more patients (Angst et al., 2003; Dunner, 2003; Moreno & Andrade, 2005). On the other hand, a liability of this approach is the potential overdiagnosis of varied subsyndromal characteristics that should not be integrated under the rubric of bipolar disorder nor share interventions with it. This tension between a continuum approach and concerns about overdiagnosis was present in the time of Kraepelin (Brieger & Marneros, 1997) and continues into the present, with proposals of new ways to expand the conceptualization of bipolar spectrum disorders (e.g., Akiskal, 2003).

In this chapter, the nature and treatment of bipolar disorder is considered, first from the perspective of the dominant bipolar I and II designations, with subsequent consideration of treatment implications associated with a spectrum conceptualization of bipolar disorder.

Nature and Course of Bipolar I and II

Bipolar disorder has been estimated to affect between 1% and 3% of the population (Kessler, Chiu, Demlers, & Walters, 2005; Regier et al., 1990), although higher rates have been reported in select studies and for bipolar spectrum (e.g., including cyclothymia) disorders (see below). The average age of onset for bipolar disorder is in the mid-teens, with evidence of a worse course for individuals with an earlier age of onset (Perlis et al., 2004). Women and men are equally likely to receive a diagnosis of the disorder (Kessler et al., 1994), although sex differences have been found for the rapid cycling course (i.e., four or more mood episodes a year), with more women meeting criteria for a rapid-cycling subtype (Schneck et al., 2004).

Many factors are associated with an increased likelihood of mood episodes. Stressful life events that disrupt the daily routine and sleep–wake rhythms—such as the termination of a relationship—are linked with the precipitation of a mood episode (Bebbington et al., 1993; Healy & Williams, 1988, 1989) and are associated with delayed recovery and elevated relapse rates (Ellicott, Hammen, Gitlin, Brown, & Jameson, 1990; Johnson & Miller, 1997). Moreover, stressful family environments, characterized by high levels of expressed emotion and/or negative interactional patterns, have been linked to higher relapse rates (Miklowitz, Goldstein, Nuechterlein, Snyder, & Mintz, 1988; see also Prieb, Wildgrube, & Muller-Oerlinghausen, 1989). As noted, an early age of onset of bipolar disorder is also associated with a more chronic course, with fewer periods of recovery, more psychotic features, and greater suicidal ideation and role disruption (Perlis et al., 2004). Likewise, greater anxiety comorbidity has been linked with a lower likelihood of recovering from mood episodes and more frequent relapses (Otto et al., 2006), as well as poorer role functioning (Simon et al., 2004).

Pharmacotherapy

For decades, pharmacotherapy has been the principal treatment option for individuals with bipolar disorder, with a primary intervention strategy of chronic treatment with one or more mood stabilizers. Mood stabilizers are ideally characterized by efficacy in ameliorating episodes of both mania and depression, as well as by preventing these episodes without increasing the risk of cycling into another mood state (Keck et al., 2004). Lithium (brand names Eskalith, Lithobid) most closely meets this definition and has been used as a mood stabilizer for 30 years in the United States. Anticonvulsants, such as divalproex (brand name Depakote), carbamazepine (brand name Tegretol), and lamotrigine (brand name Lamictal), and some atypical antipsychotic medications, such as aripiprazole (Abilify), olanzapine (Zyprexa), quetiapine (Seroquel), risperidone (Risperdal), and ziprasidone (Geodon) also provide elements of mood stabilization and, in some cases, depression treatment (Calabrese et al., 2004; Gao, Gajwani, Elhaj, & Calabrese, 2005; Thase et al., 2006; Tohen et al., 2003).

Given the prominence of the depressive pole in bipolar disorder, there is ample motivation to boost mood stabilizer efficacy by also treating with antidepressants. This treatment has been a standard strategy in the management of bipolar disorder (Keck et al.,

2004), but its utility is now being questioned. Despite the popularity of antidepressant prescriptions to treat bipolar depression, two recent studies have called into question the efficacy of this approach. In the first, Nemeroff et al. (2001) examined the combination of paroxetine or imipramine as an adjunct to ongoing lithium therapy for the treatment of acute bipolar depression; 117 outpatients with bipolar disorder who were suffering from a major depressive episode and had been treated with lithium for at least 6 weeks were enrolled. Results of 10 weeks of treatment indicated that the additional antidepressant treatment was not helpful for patients who maintained high lithium levels, but was helpful for those with low serum levels (i.e., the mean changes on depression rating scales from baseline to week 10 were statistically significant only among the low serum lithium level patients). The benefit of augmentation with paroxetine or imipramine for the treatment of bipolar depression may therefore only be realized among select patients who have low serum lithium levels or who cannot tolerate high serum lithium levels.

In perhaps the largest investigation of the efficacy of combined mood stabilizer and antidepressive treatment, Sachs et al. (2007) conducted a multicenter double-blind, randomized, placebo-controlled, parallel-group study of standard antidepressants (either bupropion or paroxetine) as adjuncts to treatment with mood stabilizers (lithium, valproate, carbamazepine, or other approved antimanic agents) at 22 centers in the United States (STEP-BD, protocol described later). Subjects had bipolar I or II disorder and were treated for up to 26 weeks to evaluate the effectiveness, safety, and tolerability of the adjunctive use of antidepressant medication. There were no significant differences in the percentage of patients meeting the criteria for a durable recovery (defined as eight consecutive weeks of euthymia) between those who received a mood stabilizer and an antidepressant and those who received a mood stabilizer and placebo. Rates of treatment-emergent mania or hypomania observed prospectively were similar in both groups. The results suggest that monotherapy provides as much benefit as treatment with mood stabilizers combined with a standard antidepressant for the treatment of bipolar depression. Together, the studies by Sachs et al. (2007) and Nemeroff et al. (2001) provide converging evidence that one of the primary pharmacologic strategies for intervening with bipolar depression—adding antidepressants to mood stabilizers—may offer little efficacy. In addition, there is a more longstanding concern that the addition of an antidepressant will promote a manic episode (Moller & Grunze, 2000), although this risk appears to be less apparent for some of the more selectively serotonergic versus noradrenergic antidepressants (i.e., tricyclics; Gijsman, Geddes, Rendell, Nolen, & Goodwin, 2004; Leverich et al., 2006).

For managing bipolar depression, there is some encouraging evidence for the use of atypical antipsychotics. For example, there have been positive trials of the efficacy of quetiapine (Thase et al., 2006), as well as the efficacy of the combination of olanzapine-fluoxetine (Brown et al., 2006). However, the side-effect profile of these agents is concerning (as discussed later). As a pharmacologic alternative, there is only minimal evidence supporting the use of anticonvulsants (e.g., carbamazepine, valproate, lamotrigine) in the treatment of bipolar depression (e.g., Post, Uhde, Roy & Joffe, 1986; Sachs et al., 2002). For example, although data supports the use of lamotrigine as a relapse prevention strategy, in four out of five placebo-controlled trials, lamotrigine monotherapy failed to demonstrate efficacy for the treatment of bipolar depression (Calabrese et al., 2008). However, a pilot study suggests that lamotrigine, when added to another mood stabilizer, may have beneficial effects on comorbid anxiety disorders (Maina, Albert, Rosso, & Bogetto, 2008).

Treatments applied to bipolar disorder also include the use of benzodiazepines applied as a strategy to calm hypomanic symptoms, manage sleep and overactivity, and treat comorbid anxiety disorders. However, there is little evidence of the efficacy of this approach for managing the emergence or length of bipolar episodes (Moller & Nasrallah, 2003; American Psychiatric Association, 2002; Simon et al., 2004a).

It is also important to note that pharmacologic treatment of bipolar disorder is associated with significant problems of medication adherence (Johnson & McFarland, 1996; Keck et al., 1996, 1998). Some of these problems may arise due to the challenging side-effect profiles associated with the mood stabilizers. For example, a range of significant side effects—including weight gain with risk of diabetes, cognitive slowing, somnolence, and extrapyramidal symptoms—are common to at least some of the atypical antipsychotics (Allison & Casey, 2001; Gao et al., 2008a, 2008b; Newcomer, 2005), as well as for anticonvulsant and lithium treatment (Bowden et al., 2002; Goodwin & Jamison, 2007; Macritchie, Geddes, Scott, Haslam, & Goodwin, 2001). Comorbid substance use appears to further reduce medication adherence (Manwani et al., 2007). Moreover, remaining on medications long term is a daunting prospect independent of specific side effects for some patients; regardless of the source of noncompliance, approximately half of samples of patients have discontinued their mood stabilizer medications within 2 months (e.g., Johnson & McFarland, 1996; Keck et al., 1996, 1998; Scott & Pope, 2002). Discontinuation of mood stabilizers brings with it the risk of relapse, particularly when the medication is rapidly terminated (Perlis et al., 2002). Furthermore, despite the advances in pharmacotherapy for bipolar disorder, recurrences of mood episodes appear to be the norm even with medication use (Gelenberg et al., 1989; Gitlin et al., 1995; Otto et al., 2006). For all of these reasons, consideration of alternatives to medication treatments is important.

Psychosocial Treatments

In the last decade, psychosocial treatment strategies have emerged as a new and important force for the management of bipolar disorder (Otto & Miklowitz, 2004). Prior to this recent period of research growth, psychosocial treatment for bipolar disorder was relegated to a supportive role (Callahan & Bauer, 1999) or used as a strategy to enhance medication adherence (Cochran, 1984). Encouraged both by the limits of the efficacy of pharmacotherapy alone, and by evidence of a significant role for psychosocial stress and interpersonal issues in altering the course of bipolar disorder, new structured and focused psychosocial treatments for bipolar disorder emerged (Miklowitz et al., 2007; Otto & Miklowitz, 2004).

These new treatments were derived from very different theoretical orientations, but nonetheless show a striking degree of similarity in the strategies applied to the treatment of bipolar disorder. Specifically, recent randomized controlled trials of cognitive behavioral therapy (CBT), family-focused therapy (FFT), interpersonal and social rhythm therapy (IPSRT), and a comprehensive group treatment approach share a number of treatment elements, which include (a) psychoeducation designed to provide patients and (in the case of FFT) family members with a model of the nature and course of bipolar disorder, including risk and protective factors such as the role of sleep and lifestyle regularity, stress management, and medication adherence; (b) communication and/or problem-solving training aimed at reducing familial and external stress; and (c) a review of strategies for the early detection and intervention for mood episodes, including intensified pharmacotherapy, the activation of increased support, and more-frequent treatment sessions. These interventions may also be combined with cognitive restructuring, thought and activity monitoring, treatment contracting, and other interventions in individual, group, and family settings (Otto & Miklowitz, 2004).

Cognitive Behavioral Therapy

Cognitive behavioral therapy is an effective psychosocial treatment for bipolar disorder. In early applications, it was directed successfully toward medication adherence in a brief session format (Cochran, 1984). Following this success, much more general applications of CBT have been adopted that focus on both relapse prevention and the treatment of bipolar depression. These broader protocols of treatment generally involve a combination of psychoeducation about bipolar disorder, cognitive restructuring, activity and lifestyle management, and active monitoring of mood states, with plans for early interventions.

For example, Perry, Tarrier, Morriss, McCarthy, and Limb (1999) emphasized the role of 12 sessions of individual CBT in the early detection and formulation of an action plan for prodromal bipolar symptoms in 69 outpatients who had a relapse during the past 12 months. This intervention was compared to treatment as usual, and the results indicated a significant difference in the length of time until manic relapse. However, the treatment was not effective in reducing depressive relapses over the 18-month study and follow-up period. Perry et al. (1999) hypothesized that the prodromal symptoms of mania are more distinct than those of depression, and therefore more easily identifiable to patients.

Lam and colleagues (2000, 2003) examined a brief program of individual CBT (12–18 sessions within the first 6 months and two booster sessions in the second 6 months of care) relative to usual care alone. Following the promising results of the pilot study (Lam et al., 2000), Lam et al. (2003) conducted a randomized controlled study of CBT in 103 bipolar patients. Patients who received CBT had significantly fewer bipolar episodes, higher social functioning, and decreased mood symptoms and fluctuation in manic symptoms during the 12-month study period than did patients in the control group. Moreover, although the participants were not experiencing an acute bipolar episode at recruitment, more than 56% had mild to moderate levels of depression at study entry, and the results indicated that CBT significantly reduced these residual symptoms of depression.

Relapse prevention was the primary focus of a study by Scott, Garland, and Moorhead (2001). The key elements of their intervention included psychoeducation, training in medication adherence, stress management, cognitive restructuring, and regulation of activities and sleep. After 6 months of treatment, patients who received CBT had significantly greater improvements in depressive symptoms and global functioning than did patients in the waitlist condition. Furthermore, patients in the CBT group showed a 60% reduction in relapse rates at the 18-month follow-up point.

Finally, Scott et al. (2006) examined the impact of 22 sessions of CBT versus treatment as usual in 253 patients with severe and recurrent bipolar disorder over 18 months. The overall results were disappointing; there were no differences between the groups for time to recurrence of an episode and symptom severity ratings. However, post-hoc analyses revealed an interaction between treatment efficacy and the number of previous episodes. Those patients with greater than 12 episodes showed no benefit from CBT, whereas a benefit was evident for those with fewer episodes. Although it is not clear whether this finding will be replicated, these results encourage the *early* application of CBT.

Interpersonal and Social Rhythm Therapy

The theoretical basis of IPSRT comes from the instability model of bipolar disorder (Goodwin & Jameson, 1990) that identifies three potential precursors to recurrence of a bipolar episode: (1) medication noncompliance; (2) disruption in social rhythms; and (3) stressful life events. Interpersonal and social rhythm therapy addresses all three of these potential precursors (Frank et al., 1997). The treatment is derived from interpersonal therapy for depression (Klerman, Weissman, Rounsaville, & Chevron, 1984) and targets the interpersonal context within which manic and depressive symptoms arise.

Similar to traditional interpersonal therapy, IPSRT focuses on four problem areas: grief over loss (and grief over the "lost healthy self"), interpersonal conflicts, role transitions (i.e., changes in one's employment situation as a result of a mood episode), and interpersonal deficits. Unlike traditional interpersonal therapy, IPSRT includes an additional focus on the impact of stressful life events on patients' social and circadian rhythms.

Frank et al. (1997) examined the impact of individual IPSRT on relapse prevention. Their treatment included four phases that focused on the following: (1) personal history, identification of problem areas and education about bipolar disorder; (2) the identification and resolution of personal problems and typical triggers of rhythm disruption; (3) the establishment of the patient's confidence in the use of IPSRT techniques; and (4) termination, with an emphasis on signs of episodes and vulnerabilities, and a plan for the future. Patients received either IPSRT or clinical status and symptoms review treatment (CSSRT, Frank et al., 1990), which provided support and education while assessing the presence of depressive or manic symptoms and medication side effects. The results indicated that, after 1 year, patients assigned to IPSRT showed significantly greater stability of daily routines than those in CSSRT.

Frank et al. (1999) examined the effects of changing treatment modality on the onset of bipolar episodes. Participants were assigned to one of the following four conditions, each representing the intervention used during the acute and preventative phases over two years: CM (clinical management)/CM, CM/IPSRT, IPSRT/IPSRT, and IPSRT/CM. Seven out of 40 patients assigned to stable (versus altered) treatments experienced a recurrence, compared to 17 out of 42 patients assigned to altered treatment. There was no clear benefit of one treatment modality over another. However, changing treatment modality was strongly correlated with recurrence. The results indicated that stability of treatment is more important than the particular treatment modality administered, which is consistent with evidence that significant life changes can precipitate a bipolar episode (Goodwin & Jameson, 1990). In a 2-year outcome study of the same protocol (Frank et al., 2005), 175 acutely ill bipolar I patients were randomized into the four previously mentioned conditions. The results indicated that there was no difference between treatment types in time to stabilization, but patients assigned to IPSRT in the acute treatment phase survived longer without a new affective episode, regardless of the maintenance treatment to which they were assigned. The authors concluded that IPSRT—administered particularly during the acute phase—promotes a stability of social rhythms that is protective against future relapse.

Family-focused Therapy

Family-focused therapy is grounded in the conceptualization that the symptoms of bipolar disorder are exacerbated by high levels of familial expressed emotion and life events that are disruptive to a regular daily routine. Not only are bipolar episodes often precipitated by significant life events (i.e., those that disrupt the regularity of the daily sleep–wake cycle), but patients who return to a stressful family environment following hospitalization were more likely to relapse (Miklowitz et al., 1988). Family-focused therapy is based upon skills-oriented family interventions that have been applied effectively to delay relapses in schizophrenia (e.g., Falloon et al., 1985; Hogarty et al., 1991; Leff, Kupfers, Berkowitz, & Sturgeon, 1985; Tarrier et al., 1988). Family-focused therapy includes psychoeducation about bipolar illness; communication enhancement training, in which patients rehearse the expression of positive and negative feelings, active listening, and requesting changes in others' behaviors; and problem-solving skills training, in which patients learn to identify, define, and solve specific family problems that are related to the course of bipolar disorder (Miklowitz & Goldstein, 1997).

Miklowitz, George, Richards, Simoneau, and Suddath (2003) examined the impact of FFT and pharmacotherapy on the management of bipolar disorder. They enrolled 101 patients in FFT or less intensive crisis management (CM) and evaluated them every 3 to 6 months for 2 years. All participants were maintained on their prestudy medication regimen. The treatment involved all available family members and was administered in 21 one-hour sessions (12 weekly, 6 biweekly). Patients assigned to FFT remained remitted or partially remitted for longer intervals than did those assigned to CM, and they showed greater reduction in mood disorder symptoms and better adherence to their medication regimens.

Rea et al. (2003) conducted a randomized clinical trial of FFT versus individual treatment. Participants were 53 recently manic, bipolar patients receiving mood stabilizers who were assigned to either a 9-month manual-based FFT or an individually focused treatment. Patients were assessed every 3 months for 1 year of treatment and 1 year of follow-up. The results indicated that patients who received FFT were less likely to be rehospitalized during the study and experienced fewer mood disorder relapses. However, the impact of FFT was strongest after completion of the treatment protocol. The authors hypothesized that the skills and coping strategies gained by patients and family members may require a period of absorption and may be realized only through the active management of the illness.

Simoneau, Miklowitz, Richards, Saleem, and George (1999) examined the impact of FFT on communication between family members of those with bipolar disorder. The authors compared 9 months of FFT to crisis management with naturalistic follow-up (CMNF, which consisted of two sessions of home-based family education and ongoing crisis intervention and supportive problem solving as needed). Members of families who received FFT showed more positive nonverbal, but not less negative nonverbal, interactional behavior 1 year after treatment had been completed. Moreover, patients in FFT who became more nonverbally positive over the year showed greater improvements in mood. The results suggest the importance of positive nonverbal engagement with others as an index of mood stability.

Finally, Clarkin, Carpenter, Hull, Wilner, and Glick (1998) examined the impact of 15 sessions of marital therapy and medication management (mood stabilizers, antidepressants, and antipsychotics) for 11 months on medication adherence and mood in 19 patients who were either married or living with a significant other for more than 6 months at study entry. There was no effect of the intervention for time to recurrence or symptomatic status, but patients who received the intervention showed improvements in global functioning and increased medication adherence.

Group Treatment

Group treatment, a potentially cost-effective alternative to individual or family therapy, has also been found to prevent recurrences in patients with bipolar I and II disorder. In addition to focused psychoeducation and skill-building interventions, the group format affords members the opportunity to learn illness management skills from other members, and provides them with an arena in which to practice problem-solving and effective communication skills. For example, in an open treatment trial, Bauer, McBride, Chase, Sachs, and Shea (1998) examined a two-phase manual-based group approach (the "Life Goals" program), which consisted of five weekly group sessions that focused first on relapse prevention, and then on problem-solving around social and occupational goals. At the end of treatment, patients showed increases in their knowledge about the disorder, and 70% reached their first self-identified behaviorally based life goal (e.g., finding a job).

In a much larger study, Colom et al. (2003) examined the impact of group psychotherapy in 120 bipolar I and II outpatients in remission. Patients were randomized to receive standard psychiatric care with standard pharmacologic treatment, and either a structured group-based "psychoeducation" or a nondirective group therapy. Although termed psychoeducation by the authors, the treatment was a comprehensive series of 21 sessions that included interventions that demonstrated efficacy individually (i.e., a focus on the early detection of prodromal symptoms [e.g., Perry et al., 1999]; the enhancement of treatment compliance [Cochran, 1984]; and induction of lifestyle regularity [Frank et al., 1999]), and education about avoiding alcohol and street drugs and coping with the interpersonal consequences of past and future episodes. The group treatment significantly reduced the number of relapsed patients and the number of recurrences per patient, and increased the time to depressive, manic, hypomanic, and mixed recurrences. The number and length of hospitalizations per patient were also lower in patients who received group treatment.

Bipolar Depression and Psychotherapy

Given recent evidence for the low efficacy of antidepressant treatments for bipolar depression (Nemeroff et al., 2001; Sachs et al., 2007), the potential for psychosocial treatments for this phase of the disorder emerges as a particularly important issue. In the large-scale National Institute of Mental Health (NIMH)-sponsored Systematic Treatment Enhancement Program for Bipolar Disorder (STEP-BD) protocol, this issue was examined at 15 study sites where patients were randomized to receive intensive psychosocial treatment (up to 30 sessions of CBT, IPSRT, or FFT over 9 months), or a minimal psychosocial intervention (collaborative care [CC], consisting of three sessions over 6 weeks). All four interventions included psychoeducation about bipolar disorder, relapse prevention planning, and illness management interventions. Collaborative care provided a brief version of common psychosocial strategies shown to be beneficial for bipolar disorder (Miklowitz, 2006; Miklowitz & Otto, 2006), whereas the intensive treatments were enhanced versions of CBT, IPSRT, and FFT, with additional treatment targets, including cognitive distortions and activity and skill deficits in CBT; disturbances in interpersonal relationships and social rhythms in IPSRT; and disturbances in family relationships and communication in FFT (Miklowitz et al., 2007). Results from the STEP-BD protocol supported the efficacy of all three psychotherapy approaches and indicated that these intensive psychosocial treatments

are more effective than collaborative care in enhancing recovery from bipolar depression and increasing the likelihood of remaining well (e.g., Miklowitz et al., 2007). Recovery rates were significantly greater (64.4% vs. 51.5%), and time to recovery was significantly shorter, among patients who received intensive psychotherapy plus pharmacotherapy, than among patients who received collaborative care plus pharmacotherapy. Also, it is noteworthy that the intensive psychotherapies succeeded where antidepressant medications failed. That is, the intensive treatments were associated with efficacy in largely the same cohort of patients who failed to respond to randomized antidepressant treatment (Sachs et al., 2007).

In further analyses of the same data set, Miklowitz et al. (2007) examined the impact of intensive psychosocial treatment and pharmacotherapy on role functioning. Patients who were assigned to one of the intensive psychosocial treatments had better overall functioning, relationship functioning, and life satisfaction scores over the 9-month study period, than did patients who received CC. These results indicated that the intensive psychosocial treatments were more effective than brief psychoeducation in enhancing these functional outcomes.

Factors That Lead to Poor Treatment Response

Comorbidity with other disorders is frequent among patients with bipolar disorder. The prevalence of comorbid anxiety disorders in epidemiologic and clinical studies ranges from 7.8% to 47.2% for social anxiety disorder, 7% to 40% for post-traumatic stress disorder, 10.6% to 62.5% for panic disorder, 7% to 32% for generalized anxiety disorder, and 3.2% to 35% for obsessive-compulsive disorder (for a review, see Simon et al., 2004b). Studies of clinical populations (Brady, Castro, Lydiard, Malcolm, & Arana, 1991; Goldberg, Garno, Leon, Kocsis, & Portera, 1999) and community samples (Kessler et al., 1997; Regier et al., 1990) have revealed high rates of substance use disorder (SUD) comorbidity, with prevalence rates ranging from 21% to 45%. There is also evidence that bipolar disorder is comorbid with eating disorders (McElroy et al., 2001) and attention-deficit disorder (Nierenberg et al., 2005).

Comorbidity in general is associated with a poorer course of illness (McElroy et al., 2001). For example, comorbid anxiety and bipolar disorder has been linked with a greater likelihood of being in a mood episode, poorer role functioning and quality of life, decreased likelihood of recovery from a mood episode, poorer response to some medications, and a greater likelihood of suicide attempts (Henry et al. 2003; Otto et al., 2006; Simon et al., 2004). Moreover, comorbid panic disorder and/or high levels of somatic anxiety have been found to be predictors of poor response to IPSRT (Feske et al., 2000). Studies have also found that comorbidity with attention-deficit hyperactivity disorder in children and adolescents with bipolar disorder is predictive of poor treatment response (Masi et al., 2004; Strober et al., 1998). Decreased medication compliance (Goldberg et al., 1999; Keck et al., 1996), hospitalization (Brady et al., 1991; Reich, Davies, & Himmelhoch, 1974), and poorer recovery (Keller et al, 1986; Tohen, Waternaux, & Tsuang, 1990) are also common among bipolar patients with comorbid substance use disorders.

Suicide is particularly associated with bipolar disorder, with lifetime prevalence rates of attempts as high as 30% in some samples (Chen & Dilsaver, 1996; Oquendo et al., 2000; Oquendo & Mann, 2001). In one study that evaluated suicidal outcomes over 20 years in a sample of 7,000 psychiatric outpatients (Brown, Beck, Steer, & Grisham, 2000), bipolar patients were found to have the highest risk for completed suicide and nearly a four-fold increase in suicide risk, as compared to the other psychiatric patients in the sample. The risk for suicide is particularly elevated in patients with comorbid bipolar and substance use disorders (Dalton, Cate-Carter, Mundo, Parikh, & Kennedy, 2003).

Comorbid personality disorders are also considered predictors of poor treatment response. Personality disorders have been associated with increased rates of psychiatric symptoms, decreased response to lithium treatment, and poorer treatment outcome, including poorer social and occupational functioning (Carpenter, Clarkin, Glick, & Wilner, 1995; Dunayevich et al., 2000; Kutcher, Maton, & Korenblum, 1990). One study (Kay, Altshuler, Ventura, & Mintz, 2002) found that male bipolar disorder patients with a comorbid personality disorder were prescribed more medications, were less likely to have been employed in the last 6 months, and more frequently had a history of a substance use disorder than did patients without Axis II pathology.

Finally, an early onset of bipolar disorder has been found to increase the risk for a severe course and poor treatment outcome (Carter, Mundo, Parikh, & Kennedy, 2003; Perlis et al., 2004). Early age of onset is also a risk factor for rapid cycling, suicidal ideation, and comorbidity with substance use disorders

(Perlis et al., 2004; Tohen, Greenfield, Weiss, Zarate, & Vagge, 1998; Tsai et al, 2001).

Consideration of Bipolar Spectrum Disorders

Treatment-outcome research has been organized around the diagnostic categories of bipolar I and bipolar II disorder. Nonetheless, commensurate with greater attention to dimensional approaches throughout psychopathology research (Krueger, Watson, & Barlow, 2005), over the last decade increasing attention has been paid to elucidating how bipolar I and II disorder may lie at one end of a continuum of patterns of mood instability. Although this recent attention has not embraced a fully dimensional approach, it has sought to clarify additional categories of diagnoses along a continuum of severity.

A helpful starting point in this process is to first consider the lower severity disorder, cyclothymia. As compared to bipolar disorder, cyclothymic disorder is defined as a chronic (at least 2 years in duration), fluctuating mood disturbance involving numerous periods of hypomanic and depressive symptoms, which are insufficient in number, severity, pervasiveness, or duration to fulfill the criteria for a manic episode or major depressive episode, respectively (American Psychiatric Association, 2000). Cyclothymia has been largely ignored in psychopathology studies, despite calls for greater attention a decade ago (Brieger & Marneros, 1997).

An additional approach to considering the bipolar spectrum concerns diagnostic criteria and the discrimination between disorder and nondisorder. For example, according to current DSM definitions (*Diagnostic and Statistical Manual of Mental Disorders, Fourth Edition, Text Revision*, DSM-IV-TR; American Psychiatric Association, 2000), a duration of 4 days is needed for an active state to be considered a hypomanic episode. Angst and associates (2003), however, have found that the mean duration of hypomanic episodes is 1–3 days, and therefore many hypomanic episodes miss the threshold required by the DSM and are subsequently not diagnosed (Akiskal et al., 2000). Moreover, DSM-IV-TR requires that an individual have either euphoric or irritable mood in order to be labeled hypomanic. Yet, patients rarely seek treatment as a result of these symptoms of hypomania (instead the symptoms of depression typically bring patients into treatment, Benazzi, 1999), and the diagnosis of bipolar II based upon patient report of past symptoms may be unreliable (Rice et al., 1986). Perugi and Akiskal (2002) assert that the accurate diagnosis of bipolar II depends on the extent to which clinicians query both patients and family members about past hypomanic episodes, with a focus on overactive behavior and increased productivity.

This emphasis on overactivity is reflected in a study that sought to determine the frequency of bipolar spectrum disorder in remitted depressed outpatients. Benazzi (2003b) included subsyndromal hypomania (as defined by an episode of overactivity and at least two hypomanic symptoms) in the diagnostic criteria. In the sample of 111 patients presenting with major depressive disorder, subsyndromal hypomania was present in 39.5% of the cases, and the frequency of bipolar spectrum disorder was 76.5%. The author concluded that by focusing more on overactivity than mood change, and including subsyndromal hypomania, diagnostic criteria can better capture an essential cohort of patients in need of treatment.

Angst et al. (2003) sought to test the diagnostic criteria for DSM-IV hypomania and to validate the criteria for a definition of softer expressions of bipolar disorder by examining data from a 20-year prospective community cohort study of 4,547 young adults. Their results suggested that symptoms of overactivity should be included in the principal criteria of hypomania, whereas episode duration should not be a criterion as long as three of seven signs/symptoms are present, and that a change in functioning should remain necessary for a rigorous diagnosis. Angst and associates also note that below this threshold, "hypomanic symptoms only" associated with major or mild depression are important indicators of bipolarity. Their proposed framework is one of the broadest definitions of the bipolar spectrum, which includes the following:

- *Bipolar I*. Hospitalized mania plus major depression
- *Hard Bipolar II*. Major depressive episodes associated with a hypomanic syndrome (euphoria, irritability or overactivity), the experience of consequences from these symptoms, and three of seven signs and symptoms of DSM-IV hypomania
- *Soft Bipolar II*. Major depressive episodes associated with hypomanic symptoms only
- *Minor Bipolar Disorder (MinBP)*. Dysthymia, minor depression, or recurrent brief depression associated with a hypomanic syndrome or hypomanic symptoms only
- *Pure Hypomania*. A hypomanic syndrome without any diagnosis of depression, or hypomanic symptoms only

Given this proposed revision of the diagnostic criteria for hypomania, Angst et al. (2003) report that the altered criterion led to a doubling of the proportion of bipolar II diagnoses, from 5.3% to 11%, based on their community sample.

Rethinking Unipolar Depression

According to the conceptualization of Perugi and Akiskal (2002), the term "bipolar spectrum" refers not only to a continuum of substhreshold and threshold cases (with a duration as brief as 1 day), but includes patients who experience major depressive episodes that are superimposed on cyclothymic or hyperthymic temperamental characteristics. Perugi and Akiskal (2002) propose the enlargement of the current bipolar II disorders to include a spectrum of conditions (ranging from mood, anxiety, impulse control, and eating disorders) caused by such a cyclothymic-anxious-sensitive disposition, with mood reactivity and interpersonal sensitivity. This approach would result in the reclassification of patients originally diagnosed with unipolar depression along the bipolar spectrum.

Benazzi examined the potential role of unipolar major depression and co-occurring anger (Benazzi, 2003a) and racing thoughts (Benazzi, 2005) in defining mood episodes that may be more aptly placed on a continuum with bipolar disorder. Clinical criteria that were used to support the inclusion of major depression with anger or racing thoughts on the bipolar spectrum were age of onset, major depressive episode recurrences, atypical features of depression (e.g., overeating, oversleeping, rejection sensitivity), depressive mixed state (major depressive episode and three or more hypomanic symptoms), and bipolar family history. In each of these studies, patients with anger and racing thoughts were separately compared to depressed patients without these characteristics and patients with bipolar II disorder. Both major depression with anger and major depression with racing thoughts were significantly associated with atypical depression, as well as with early age of onset, mixed state, and bipolar family history. Although Benazzi (2003a, 2005) concludes that major depression with anger or racing thoughts may lie on a bipolar spectrum midway between major depression without anger or racing thoughts and bipolar II, it is far from clear whether these features really signify subtypes of the disorder that reflect a bipolar spectrum. Moreover, it should be noted that it is mood reactivity and rejection sensitivity that, in part, defines the atypical subtype of depression. Furthermore, the presence of anger in major depression appears to confer little treatment relevance; these patients appear to respond like those without anger to monotherapy with antidepressants (Benazzi, 2003a).

Akiskal and Benazzi (2005) examined the potential of atypical depression (DSM-IV-TR criteria for the atypical specifier require mood reactivity plus overeating or weight gain, oversleeping, leaden paralysis, and interpersonal rejection sensitivity [at least two], and absence of melancholic or catatonic features) as a marker for bipolar spectrum disorder. The authors compared 348 bipolar II and 254 outpatients presenting with major depressive episodes on bipolar validators, which included age of onset, high depressive recurrence, depressed mixed state, and bipolar family history (types I and II). The results indicated that patients with atypical depression had significantly higher rates of bipolar II and that atypical depression was significantly associated with all of the proposed bipolar validators, particularly family history. The authors conclude that atypical depression may be viewed as a variant of bipolar II, and that patients who present with major depressive episodes with atypical features should be considered for a bipolar II diagnosis. In considering this proposition, it is important to note that atypical depression accounts for up to one-third or more of many outpatient samples of treatment-seeking patients with major depression (McGrath et al., 2000), and the data suggest that those with atypical depression may preferentially respond to monoamine oxidase inhibitor (MAO-I) pharmacology (Quitkin et al., 1990) has done little to inform pharmacologic treatment of bipolar patients.

Categorizing the Bipolar Spectrum

One result of research on the bipolar spectrum has been the expansion of categorical considerations that may exist along a spectrum of mood instability. Although validating studies are still pending, Akiskal and Pinto (1999) have proposed one such system that illustrates both a more detailed discrimination of potential subgroups and a much broader consideration of symptom profiles within a bipolar classification scheme:

• *Bipolar I½, depression with protracted hypomania.* This subgroup of patients is defined by the presence of protracted hypomanic periods, which cause patients and their significant others difficulty without reaching the destructive potential of a full manic episode. This category is described as one that accounts for the difficulty with demarcating the end of hypomania and beginning of mania, with bipolar I½ patients existing between these extremes.

• *Bipolar II, depression with hypomania.* By DSM-IV-TR definition, these patients have moderately to severely impairing major depressions, interspersed with hypomanic periods of at least 4 days' duration without marked impairment. Although these patients' behavior can be characterized by elated mood, confidence, and optimism, their judgment is relatively preserved compared with patients with mania. However, the course of bipolar II may involve periods of significant dysfunction, including suicide attempts. The authors note that a growing number of patients do not meet criteria for this category, as a result of their hypomanic episodes lasting less than the 4 days indicated by DSM-IV.

• *Bipolar II½, cyclothymic depressions.* This category refers to patients who have short hypomanic episodes (i.e., less than 4 days) and a recurrent pattern of periods of excitement followed by "mini-depressions," thereby fulfilling criteria for cyclothymic disorder. In a comparative analysis of the different subgroups within the bipolar spectrum using the French National EPIDEP study, Akiskal et al. (2006) found that BP II½ accounted for 33% of all major depressive episodes and emerged as the most prevalent and severe expression of the bipolar spectrum.

• *Bipolar III, antidepressant-associated hypomania.* This category refers to patients who develop manic or hypomanic episodes during treatment with an antidepressant. They also often have early-onset dysthymia, with a family history of bipolar I disorder.

• *Bipolar III½, bipolarity masked—and unmasked—by stimulant abuse.* This category refers to patients whose periods of excitement are so closely linked with substance or alcohol use and abuse that it is difficult to determine if these periods would have occurred in the absence of such use and abuse. The inclusion of this category may bring the potential benefit of mood stabilization to patients who otherwise might be classified as having substance-induced or substance withdrawal–induced mood disorders. Camacho and Akiskal (2005) note that premorbid cyclothymic and hyperthymic traits, a family history of bipolarity, and the presence of subthreshold bipolar signs during periods of protracted sobriety are common to these patients. On the other hand, clinicians are often met with the challenge of differentiating mood swings that are related to mania or hypomania from those that result from substance use and/or withdrawal, and it is possible that patients with substance use disorders may be misdiagnosed and unnecessarily treated for mood disorders (e.g., Hirschfeld, 2001; Hirschfeld & Vornik, 2004).

• *Bipolar IV, hyperthymic depression.* This category includes patients who experience clinical depression later in life that is superimposed on a lifelong hyperthymic temperament (which the authors describe as part of the long-term functioning of the individual, as opposed to being episode bound). Patients are typically men in their fifties whose life-long drive, ambition, high energy, confidence, and extroverted interpersonal skills helped them to advance and achieve success in their life. Unlike the brief hypomanias of bipolar II and III, the hyperthymic traits of these individuals are maintained for much of their lives at a more or less stable level.

Bipolar Disorder and Borderline Personality Disorder

Another diagnostic group that is under examination for reclassification as a bipolar spectrum disorder is borderline personality disorder. Comorbidity between the disorders is high (e.g., Deltito et al., 2001; Paris, Gunderson, & Weinberg, 2007), and there is evidence that diagnostic reliability is aided by examination of interepisode functioning. For example, George, Miklowitz, Richards, Simoneau, and Taylor (2003) examined patients with bipolar disorder who were currently in remission and found that personality disorders were diagnosed in 28.8% of the sample. Cluster B (dramatic, emotionally erratic) and cluster C (fearful, avoidant) personality disorders were more common than cluster A (odd, eccentric). Moreover, patients with personality disorders had more severe residual mood symptoms, even during remission, than did patients without personality disorders. However, this diagnostic clarity is muddled for patients with chronic but less clear-cut mood symptoms (i.e., bipolar II versus bipolar I disorder), including rapid mood changes that are hard to differentiate from the situation-specific mood disturbances that may be part of a personality disorder. Akiskal and Pinto (1999) hypothesize that the overlap between bipolar and borderline personality disorder is situated within their conceptualization of bipolar II½. In particular, they propose that, because cyclothymic patients may present with depressive moodiness characterized by brief depressive mood swings instead of exhibiting clear cut hypomanic features, they are easily misdiagnosed with borderline personality disorder.

Revised Prevalence

As might be expected, the expansion of symptoms considered to be within a bipolar spectrum leads to much higher prevalence rates than the 1%–2% associated with traditional bipolar I and II. When the full spectrum of bipolar disorders is considered, current data suggest lifetime prevalence rates as high as 11% for community samples (Angst et al., 2003; Judd & Akiskal, 2003; Lewinsohn, Klein, & Seeley, 1995; Moreno & Andrade, 2005; Szadoczky, Papp, Vitrai, Rihmer, & Furedi, 1998). For example, in a reanalysis of the Epidemiological Catchment Area (ECA) study, Judd and Akiskal (2003) raised the lifetime prevalence from 1.3% to 6.4% by including a subgroup of patients with subsyndromal symptoms of mania.

One effect of using a spectrum approach is not just the identification of undiagnosed cases, but a reclassification of unipolar depression as bipolar spectrum. Indeed, as part of the French National EPIDEP study, Akiskal et al. (2006) examined the prevalence of the soft bipolar spectrum disorders and concluded that, when considered together, the spectrum (bipolar I, II, II½, III, III½, IV) accounted for 65% of all major depressive episode cases, making unipolar depression less prevalent than bipolar disorder, as redefined by these researchers.

Bipolar Spectrum Disorders: Treatment Implications

Research on bipolar spectrum classification systems has made it clear that limited hypomanic symptoms are common among individuals with unipolar depression, and are also common among individuals with comorbid Axis I and II disorders (e.g., borderline personality disorder or substance dependence). However, it is not known whether the presence of these symptoms has meaning relative to treatment. Regarding pharmacotherapy, it is not clear whether the use of mood-stabilizing agents—lithium, anticonvulsants, and atypical antipsychotics—would be appropriate for the subsyndromal characteristics that define many bipolar II spectrum patients. Moreover, for patients with unipolar depression, consideration of mood-stabilizing agents is already part of treatment algorithms (e.g., Crossley & Bauer, 2007), and it is unclear whether the bipolar spectrum designation would lead to earlier discrimination of those likely to fail antidepressants alone and need such augmentation. In fact, preliminary evidence suggests that subsyndromal bipolar features do not discriminate depressed patients who are more likely to respond to this treatment approach (Hantouche, Akiskal, Lancrenon, & Chatenêt-Duchêne, 2005). Furthermore, the utility of spectrum classification schemes will be competing in the future with alternative (e.g., genetic) strategies for identifying responsive and nonresponsive cohorts for given medications (e.g., Stamm et al., 2008).

Similar considerations are apt for the overlap between bipolar spectrum and borderline personality disorder. Application of mood stabilizers is already under way for some of the core symptoms of borderline personality disorder, with some evidence for their efficacy for affect instability and aggressive behavior (Diaz-Marsa et al., 2008; Herpertz et al., 2007), although, as might be expected, they had little effect on unstable relationships, impulsivity, suicidality, and global functioning. Similar outcomes were evident for antidepressant treatment (Nosè, Cipriani, Biancosino, Grassi, & Barbui, 2006).

Regarding the impact of bipolar spectrum disorders relative to treatment with psychotherapy, research suggests that patients with subsyndromal characteristics are well represented in psychosocial practice. Specifically, Stirman, DeRubeis, Crits-Christoph, and Rothman (2005) examined patients in clinical practice relative to entry criteria for clinical trials. They found that a prominent reason for the divergence between patients studied in clinical trials of psychotherapy and patients seen in clinic practice was the over-representation of patients who did not meet duration or severity criteria for disorders in clinical trials. Also, it is important to note that some of the strategies for CBT for bipolar disorder (e.g., Otto et al., 2009) represent an extension of those traditionally applied to unipolar depression (see also Totterdell & Kellett, 2008; Zaretsky, Segal, & Gemar, 1999). Furthermore, given the role assigned to atypical depression in identifying patients who are relegated to a bipolar spectrum diagnosis (Akiskal & Benazzi, 2005), it is promising that the efficacy of CBT for this subtype of depressed patients compares well to the preferred pharmacotherapy for this cohort (Jarrett et al., 1999). Nonetheless, recent successful treatment trials for bipolar disorder (Miklowitz et al., 2007) may help expand the interventions used by clinicians for these subsyndromal patients.

Conclusion

At this time, treatment outcome research for bipolar disorder has been marked by two important findings. First, recent studies have provided cautions about the efficacy of antidepressant medications for bipolar depression. This finding may bring about a new search for efficacious alternatives, while helping physicians refrain from prescribing antidepressant agents that may add little efficacy while increasing the side-effect and treatment-adherence burden. Second, in the face of this limiting evidence for one popular pharmacologic strategy for bipolar depression, recent studies have shown that psychosocial treatments can have a significant and meaningful impact on bipolar depression and the course of bipolar disorder. These data help end the longstanding assumption that effective treatment of bipolar disorder lies exclusively in the realm of somatic interventions. It is now clear that psychosocial treatments, and the individuals who offer them, have a crucial role in providing patients greater control over their disorder.

Future Directions

Confidence in the efficacy of focused psychosocial treatments for bipolar disorder is only now growing among experts in the field (Keck et al., 2004), and hence dissemination of these successful strategies to more clinicians is a central issue for psychosocial strategies for bipolar disorder. Further validation and expansion of psychosocial treatment for bipolar disorder is an area of expected growth for treatment research and intervention over the next decade. Likewise, future studies are likely to attend to the treatment of bipolar spectrum patients, with particular attention to whether consideration of a broader cohort of patients under the "bipolar" rubric truly aids treatment conceptualization and outcome for these individuals in need. Important questions to be addressed by future studies include the following:

• Is the reclassification of unipolar depressives as part of the bipolar spectrum useful for understanding the course and prognosis of mood disorders?

• Will the psychosocial treatment of bipolar depression emerge as a standard strategy for a disorder once assumed to require biological intervention?

• Will the bipolar spectrum approach lead to better treatment by expanding traditional interventions for bipolar disorder to more individuals?

• What treatments will replace the tendency to use antidepressant medications for bipolar depression?

• Will psychosocial treatment for bipolar disorder be expanded to the treatment of comorbid conditions (e.g., anxiety and substance use disorders) in individuals with bipolar disorder?

• What is the true relationship between borderline personality disorder and bipolar II disorder?

References

Akiskal, H. (2003). Validating "hard" and "soft" phenotypes within the bipolar spectrum: Continuity or discontinuity? *Journal of Affective Disorders, 73*, 1–5.

Akiskal, H., Akiskal, K., Lancrenon, S., Hantouche, E., Fraud, J., Gury, C., et al. (2006). Validating the bipolar spectrum in the French National EPIDEP Study: Overview of the phenomenology and relative prevalence of its clinical prototypes. *Journal of AffectiveDisorders, 96*, 197–205.

Akiskal, H., & Benazzi, F. (2005). Atypical depression: A variant of bipolar II or a bridge between unipolar and bipolar II? *Journal of Affective Disorders, 84*, 209–217.

Akiskal, H., Bourgeois, M., Angst, J., Post, R., Moller, J., & Hirschfeld, R. (2000). Re-evaluation the prevalence of and diagnostic composition within the broad clinical spectrum of bipolar disorders. *Journal of Affective Disorders, 59* (Suppl 1), 5s–30s.

Akiskal, H., & Pinto, O. (1999). The l: Prototypes I, II, III, and IV. *The Psychiatric Clinics of North America, 22*, 517–534.

Allison, D., & Casey, D. (2001). Antipsychotic-induced weight gain: A review of the literature. *Journal of Clinical Psychiatry, 62*(Suppl 7), 22–31.

American Psychiatric Association. (2000). *Diagnostic and statistical manual of mental disorders, 4th ed.* (Text Revision) (DSM-IV-TR). Washington, DC: American Psychiatric Press.

American Psychiatric Association. (2002). Practice guideline for the treatment of patients with bipolar disorder (revision). *American Journal of Psychiatry, 159* (Suppl. 4), 1–50.

Angst, J., Gamma, A., Benazzi, F., Ajdacic, V., Eich, D., & Rossler, W. (2003). Toward a re-definition of subthreshold bipolarity: Epidemiology and proposed criteria for bipolar-II, minor bipolar disorders and hypomania. *Journal of Affective Disorders, 73*, 133–146.

Bauer, M., McBride, L., Chae, C., Sachs, G., & Shea, N. (1998). Manual-based group psychotherapy for bipolar disorder: A feasibility study. *Journal of Clinical Psychiatry, 59*, 449–455.

Bebbington, P., Wilkins, S., Jones, P., Forrester, A., Murray, R., Tooner, B., & Lewis, S. (1993). Life events and psychosis: Initial results from the Camberwell Collaborative Psychosis Study. *British Journal of Psychiatry, 162*, 72–79.

Benazzi, F. (1999). Prevalence of bipolar II disorder in atypical depression. *European Archives of Psychiatry and Clinical Neuroscience, 249*, 62–65.

Benazzi, F. (2003a). Major depressive disorder with anger: A bipolar spectrum disorder? *Psychotherapy and Psychosomatics, 72*, 300–306.

Benazzi, F. (2003b). Frequency of bipolar spectrum in 111 private practice depression outpatients. *European Archives of Psychiatry and Clinical Neurosciences, 253*, 203–208.

Benazzi, F. (2005). Unipolar depression with racing thoughts: A bipolar spectrum disorder? *Psychiatry and Clinical Neurosciences, 59*, 570–575.

Bowden, C., Asnis, G., Ginsberg, L., Benley, B., Leadbetter, R., & White, R. (2002). Safety and tolerability of lamotrigine for bipolar disorder. *Drug Safety, 27*, 173–184.

Brady, K., Castro, S., Lydiard, R., Malcolm, R., & Arana, G. (1991). Substance abuse in an inpatient psychiatric sample. *American Journal of Drug and Alcohol Abuse, 17*, 389–397.

Brieger, P., & Marneros, A. (1997). Dysthymia and cyclothymia: Historical origins and contemporary development. *Journal of Affective Disorders, 45*, 117–126.

Brown, G., Beck, A., Steer, R., & Grisham, J. (2000). Risk factors for suicide in psychiatric outpatients: A 20-year prospective study. *Journal of Consulting and Clinical Psychology, 68*, 371–377.

Brown, E., McElroy, S., Keck, P., Jr., Deldar, A., Adams, D., Tohen, M., et al. (2006). A 7-week, randomized, double-blind trial of olanzapine/fluoxetine combination versus lamotrigine in the treatment of bipolar I depression. *Journal of Clinical Psychiatry, 67*, 1025–1033.

Calabrese, J., Huffman, R., White, R., Edwards, S., Thompson, T., Ascher, J., et al. (2008). Lamotrigine in the acute treatment of bipolar depression: Results of five double-blind, placebo-controlled clinical trials. *Bipolar Disorders, 10*, 323–333.

Calabrese, J., McFadden, W., McCoy, R., Minkwitz, M., Wilsen, E., & Mullen, J. (2004). Double-blind, placebo-controlled study of quetiapine in bipolar depression. Abstract presented at APA 2004, New York City.

Callahan, M., & Bauer, M. (1999). Psychosocial interventions for bipolar disorder. *Psychiatric Clinics of North America, 22*, 675–688.

Camacho, A., & Akiskal, H. (2005). Proposal for a bipolar-stimulant spectrum: Temperament, diagnostic validation and therapeutic outcomes with mood stabilizers. *Journal of Affective Disorders, 85*, 217–230.

Carpenter, D., Clarkin, J., Glick, I., & Wilner, P. (1995). Personality pathology among married adults with bipolar disorder. *Journal of Affective Disorders, 34*, 269–274.

Carter, T., Mundo, E., Parikh, S., & Kennedy, J. (2003). Early age at onset as a risk factor for poor outcome of bipolar disorder. *Journal of Psychiatric Research, 37*, 297–303.

Chen, Y., & Dilsaver, S. (1996). Lifetime rates of suicide attempts among subjects with bipolar and unipolar disorders relative to subjects with other Axis I disorders. *Biological Psychiatry, 39*, 896–899.

Clarkin J., Carpenter, D., Hull, J., Wilner, P., & Glick I. (1998). Effects of a psychoeducational intervention for married patients with bipolar disorder and their spouses. *Psychiatric Services, 49*, 531–533.

Cochran, S. (1984). Preventing medical noncompliance in the outpatient treatment of bipolar affective disorders. *Journal of Consulting and Clinical Psychology, 52*, 873–878.

Colom, F., Vieta, E., Daban, C., Pacchiarotti, I., & Sanchez-Moreno, J. (2006). Clinical and therapeutic implications of predominant polarity in bipolar disorder. *Journal of Affective Disorders, 93*, 13–17.

Colom, F., Vieta, E., Martinez-Aran, A., Reinares, M., Goikolea, J., Benabarre, A., et al. (2003). A randomized trial on the efficacy of group psychoeducation in the prophylaxis of recurrences in bipolar patients whose disease is in remission. *Archives of General Psychiatry, 60*, 402–407.

Crossley, N., & Bauer, M. (2007). Acceleration and augmentation of antidepressants with lithium for depressive disorders: Two meta-analyses of randomized, placebo-controlled trials. *Journal of Clinical Psychiatry, 68,* 935–940.

Dalton, J., Cate-Carter, T., Mundo, E., Parikh, S., & Kennedy, J. (2003). Suicide risk in bipolar patients: The role of comorbid substance use disorders. *Bipolar Disorders, 5,* 58–61.

Deltito, J., Martin, L., Riefkohl, J., Austria, B., Kissilenko, A., Corless, C., & Morse, P. (2001). Do patients with borderline personality disorder belong to the bipolar spectrum? *Journal of Affective Disorders, 56,* 221–228.

Diaz-Marsa, M., Gonzalez Bardanca, S., Tajima, K., Garcia-Albea, J., Navas, M., & Carrasaco, J. (2008). Psychopharmacological treatment in borderline personality disorder. *Actas Espanolas de Psiquiatria, 36,* 39–49.

Dunayevich, E., Sax, K., Keck, P., McElroy, S., Sorten, M., McConville, B., et al. (2000). Twelve-month outcome in bipolar patients with and without personality disorders. *Journal of Clinical Psychiatry, 61,* 134–139.

Dunner, D. (2003). Clinical consequences of under-recognized bipolar spectrum disorder. *Bipolar Disorder, 5,* 456–463.

Ellicott, A., Hammen, C., Gitlin, M., Brown, G., & Jameson, K. (1990). Life events and the course of bipolar disorder. *American Journal of Psychiatry, 147,* 1194–1198.

Falloon, I., Boyd, J., McGill, C., Williamson, M. Razani, J., Moss, H., et al. (1985). Family management in the prevention of morbidity of schizophrenia. *Archives of General Psychiatry, 42,* 887–896.

Feske, U., Frank, E., Mallinger, A., Houck, P., Faglioni, A., Shear, M., et al. (2000). Anxiety as a correlate of response to the acute treatment of bipolar I disorder. *American Journal of Psychiatry, 157,* 956–962.

Frank, E., Hlastala, S., Ritenour, A., Houck, P., Tu, X., Monk, T., et al. (1997). Inducing lifestyle regularity in recovering bipolar disorder patients: Results from the maintenance therapies in bipolar disorder protocol. *Biological Psychiatry, 41,* 1165–1173.

Frank, E., Kupfer, D., Perel, J., Cornes, C., Jarrett, D., Mallinger, A., et al. (1990). Three-year outcomes for maintenance therapy in recurrent depression. *Archives of General Psychiatry, 47,* 1093–1099.

Frank, E., Kupfer, D., Thase, M., Mallinger, A., Swartz, H., Fagiolini, A., et al. (2005). Two-year outcomes for interpersonal and social rhythm therapy in individuals with bipolar I disorder. *Archives of General Psychiatry, 62,* 996–1004.

Frank E., Swartz H., Mallinger A., Thase M., Weaver E., & Kupfer, D. (1999). Adjunctive psychotherapy for bipolar disorder: Effects of changing treatment modality. *Journal of Abnormal Psychology, 108,* 579–87.

Gao, K., Gajwani, P., Elhaj, O., & Calabrese, J. (2005). Typical and atypical antipsychotics in bipolar depression. *Journal of Clinical Psychiatry, 66,* 1376–85.

Gao, K., Ganocy, S., Gajwani, P., Muzina, D., Kemp, D., & Calabrese, J. (2008a). A review of sensitivity and tolerability of antipsychotics in patients with bipolar disorder or schizophrenia: Focus on somnolence. *Journal of Clinical Psychiatry, 69,* 302–309.

Gao, K., Kemp, D., Ganocy, S., Gajwani, P., Xia, G., & Calabrese, J. (2008b). Antipsychotic-induced extrapyramidal side effects in bipolar disorder and schizophrenia: A systematic review. *Journal of Clinical Psychopharmacology, 28,* 203–209.

Gelenberg, A., Kane, J., Keller, M., Lavori, P., Rosenbaum, J., Cole, K., & Lavelle, J. (1989). Comparison of standard and low serum levels of lithium for maintenance treatment of bipolar disorders. *New England Journal of Medicine, 321,* 1489–1493.

George, E., Miklowitz, D., Richards, J., Simoneau, T., & Taylor, D. (2003). The comorbidity of bipolar disorder and axis II personality disorders: Prevalence and clinical correlates. *Bipolar Disorders, 5,* 115–122.

Gijsman, H., Gedses, J., Rendell, J., Nolen, W., & Goodwin, G. (2004). Antidepressants for bipolar depression: A systematic review of randomized, controlled trials. *American Journal of Psychiatry, 161,* 1537–1547.

Gitlin, M., Swendsen, J., Heller, T., & Hammen, C. (1995). Relapse and impairment in bipolar disorder. *American Journal of Psychiatry, 152,* 1635–1640.

Goldberg, J., Garno, J., Leon, A., Kocsis, J., & Portera, L. (1999). A history of substance abuse complicates remission from acute mania in bipolar disorder. *The Journal of Clinical Psychiatry, 60,* 733–40.

Goodwin, F., & Jamison, K. (1990). *Manic-depressive illness.* London: Oxford University Press.

Goodwin, F., & Jamison, K. (2007). *Manic-Depressive Illness: Bipolar Disorders and Recurrent Depression* (2nd ed.). New York: Oxford University Press.

Hantouche, E., Akiskal, H., Lancrenon, S., & Chatenêt-Duchêne, L. (2005). Mood stabilizer augmentation in apparently "unipolar" MDD: Predictors of response in the naturalistic French national EPIDEP study. *Journal of Affective Disorders, 84,* 243–249.

Healy, D., & Williams, J. (1988). Dysthymia, dysphoria and depression: The interaction of learned helplessness and circadian dysthymia in the pathogenesis of depression. *Psychological Bulletin, 103,* 163–178.

Healy D., & Williams, J. (1989). Moods, misattributions and mania: An interaction of biological and psychological factors in the pathogenesis of mania. *Psychiatric Developments, 1,* 49–70.

Henry, C., Van den Bulke, D., Bellivier, F., Etain, B., Rouillon, F., & Leboyer, M. (2003). Anxiety disorders in 318 bipolar patients: Prevalence and impact on illness severity and response to mood stabilizer. *Journal of Clinical Psychiatry, 64,* 331–335.

Herpertz, S., Zanarini, M., Schulz, C., Siever, L., Lieb, K., Moller, H., et al. (2007). World Federation of Societies of Biological Psychiatry (WFSBP) guidelines for biological treatment of personality disorders. *World Journal of Biological Psychiatry, 8,* 212–244.

Hirschfeld, R. (2001). Bipolar spectrum disorder: Improving its recognition and diagnosis. *Journal of Clinical Psychiatry, 62*(Suppl 14), 5–9.

Hirschfeld, R., & Vornik, L. (2004). Recognition and diagnosis of bipolar disorder. *Journal of Clinical Psychiatry, 15,* 5–9.

Hogarty, G., Anderson, C., Reiss, D., Kornblith, S., Greenwald, D., Ulrich, R., & Carter, M. (1991). Family psychoeducation, social skills training, and maintenance chemotherapy in the aftercare of schizophrenia. *Archives of General Psychiatry, 48,* 340–347.

Jarrett, R., Schaffer, M., McIntire, D., Witt-Browder, A., Kraft, D., & Risser, R. (1999). Treatment of atypical depression with cognitive therapy or phenelzine: A double-blind, placebo-controlled trial. *Archives of General Psychiatry, 56,* 431–437.

Johnson, S, & Miller, I. (1997). Negative life events and time to recovery from episodes of bipolar disorder. *Journal of Abnormal Psychology, 106,* 449–457.

Johnson, R., & McFarland, B. (1996). Lithium use and discontinuation in a health maintenance organization. *American Journal of Psychiatry, 153*, 993–1000.

Judd, L., & Akiskal, J. (2003). The prevalence and disability of bipolar spectrum disorders in the US population: Re-analysis of the ECA database taking into account subthreshold cases. *Journal of Affective Disorders, 73*, 123–131.

Judd, L., Akiskal, H., Schettler, P., Coryel, W., Maser, J., Rice, J., et al. (2003). The comparative clinical phenotype and long term longitudinal episode course of bipolar I and II: A clinical spectrum or distinct disorders? *Journal of Affective Disorders, 73*, 19–32.

Kay, J., Altshuler, K., Ventura, J., & Mintz, J. (2002). Impact of axis II comorbidity on the course of bipolar illness in men: A retrospective chart review. *Bipolar Disorders, 4*, 237–242.

Keck, P., McElroy, S., Strakowski, S., Stanton, S., Kizer, D., Balistreri, T. et al. (1996). Factors associated with pharmacologic noncompliance in patients with mania. *Journal of Clinical Psychiatry, 57*, 292–297.

Keck, P., McElroy, S., Strakowski, S., West, S., Sax, K., Hawkins, J. et al. (1998). Twelve-month outcome of patients with bipolar disorder following hospitalization for a manic or mixed episode. *American Journal of Psychiatry, 155*, 646–652.

Keck, P., Perlis, R., Otto, M., Carpenter, D., Docherty, J., & Ross, R. (2004). Expert consensus guideline series: Treatment of bipolar disorder. *A Postgraduate Medicine Special Report*, December, 1–108.

Keller, M., Lavori, P., Coryell, W., Andreasen, N., Endicott, J., Clayton, P., et al. (1986). Differential outcome of pure manic, mixed/cycling, and pure depressive episodes in patients with bipolar illness. *Journal of the American Medical Association, 255*, 3138–3142.

Kessler, R., Chiu, W., Demler, O., & Walters, E. (2005). Prevalence, severity, and comorbidity of twelve-month DSM-IV disorders in the National Comorbidity Survey Replication (NCS-R). *Archives of General Psychiatry, 62*, 617–27.

Kessler, R., Crum, R., Warner, L., Nelson, C., Schulenberg, J., & Anthony, J. (1997). Lifetime co-occurrence of DSM-III-R alcohol abuse and dependence with other psychiatric disorders in the National Comorbidity Survey. *Archives of General Psychiatry, 54*, 313–321.

Kessler, R., McGonagle, K., Zhao, S., Nelson, C., Hughes, M., Eshleman, S., et al. (1994). Lifetime and 12-month prevalence of DSM-III-R psychiatric disorders in the United States: Results from the National Comorbidity Survey. *Archives of General Psychiatry, 51*, 8–19.

Klerman, G., Weissman, M., Rounsaville, B., & Chevron, E. (1984). *Interpersonal psychotherapy for depression*. New York: Basic Books.

Krueger, R., Watson, D., & Barlow, D. (2005). Introduction to the special section: Toward a dimensionally based taxonomy of psychopathology. *Journal of Abnormal Psychology, 114*, 491–493.

Kutcher, S., Maton, P., & Korenblum, M. (1990). Adolescent bipolar illness and personality disorder. *Journal of the American Academy of Child and Adolescent Psychiatry, 29*, 355–358.

Lam, D., Bright, J., Jones, S., Hayward, P., Schuck, D., Chisholm, D., & Sham, P. (2000). Cognitive therapy for bipolar illness-A pilot study of relapse prevention. *Cognitive therapy and Research, 24*, 503–520.

Lam, D., Watkins, E., Hayward, P., Bright, J., Wright, K., Kerr, N., et al. (2003). A randomized controlled study of cognitive therapy for relapse prevention for bipolar affective disorder: Outcome of the first year. *Archives of General Psychiatry, 60*, 145–152.

Leff, J., Kupfers, L., Berkowitz, R., & Sturgeon, D. (1985). A controlled trial of social intervention in the families of schizophrenic patients: Two-year follow-up. *British Journal of Psychiatry, 146*, 594–600.

Leverich, G., Altshuler, L., Frye, M., Suppes, T., McElroy, S., Keck, P., Jr., et al. (2006). Risk of switch in mood polarity to hypomania or mania in patients with bipolar depression during acute and continuation trials of venlafaxine, sertraline, and bupropion as adjuncts to mood stabilizers. *American Journal of Psychiatry, 163*, 232–239.

Lewinsohn, P., Klein, D., & Seeley, J. (1995). Bipolar disorder in a community sample of older adolescents: Prevalence, phenomenology, comorbidity, and course. *Journal of the American Academy of Child and Adolescent Psychiatry, 34*, 454–463.

Lish, J., Dime-Meenan, S., Whybrow, P., Price, R., & Hirschfeld, R. (1994). The National Depressive and Manic-depressive Association (DMDA) survey of bipolar members. *Journal of Affective Disorders, 31*, 281–294.

Macritchie, K., Geddes, J., Scott, J., Haslam, D., & Goodwin, G. (2001). Valproic acid, valproate and divalproex in the maintenance treatment of bipolar disorder. *Cochrane Database of Systematic Reviews, 3*, CD003196.

Maina, G., Albert, U., Rosso, G., & Bogetto, F. (2008). Olanzapine or lamotrigine addition to lithium in remitted bipolar disorder patients with anxiety disorder comorbidity: A randomized, single-blind, pilot study. *Journal of Clinical Psychiatry, 20*, e1–e8.

Manwani, S., Szilagyi, K., Zablotsky, B., Hennen, J., Griffin, M., & Weiss, R. (2007). Adherence to pharmacotherapy in bipolar disorder patients with and without co-occurring substance use disorders. *Journal of Clinical Psychiatry, 68*, 1172–1176.

Masi, G., Perugi, G., Toni, C., Millepiedi, S., Mucci, M., Bertini, N., et al. (2004). Predictors of treatment nonresponse in bipolar children and adolescents with manic or mixed episodes. *Journal of Child and Adolescent Psychopharmacology, 14*, 395–404.

McElroy, S., Altshuler, L., Suppes, T., Keck, P., Frye, M., Denikoff, K., et al. (2001). Axis I psychiatric comorbidity and its relationship to historical illness variables in 288 patients with bipolar disorder. *American Journal of Psychiatry, 158*, 420–426.

McGrath, P., Stewart, J., Janal, M., Petkova, E., Quitkin, F., & Klein, D. (2000). A placebo-controlled study of fluoxetine versus imipramine in the acute treatment of atypical depression. *American Journal of Psychiatry, 157*, 344–350.

Miklowitz, D. (2006). A review of evidence-based psychosocial interventions for bipolar disorder. *Journal of Clinical Psychiatry, 67*, 28–33.

Miklowitz, D., George, E., Richards, J., Simoneau, T., & Suddath, R. (2003). A randomized study of family-focused psychoeducation and pharmacotherapy in the outpatient management of bipolar disorder. *Archives of General Psychiatry, 60*, 904–912.

Miklowitz, D., & Goldstein, M. (1997). *Bipolar disorder: A family-focused treatment approach*. New York: Guilford Press.

Miklowitz, D., Goldstein, M., Nuechterlein, K., Snyder, K., & Mintz, J. (1988). Family factors and the course of bipolar affective disorder. *Archives of General Psychiatry, 45*, 225–231.

Miklowitz, D., & Otto, M. (2006). New psychosocial interventions for bipolar disorder: A review of literature and introduction of the Systematic Treatment Enhancement Program. *Journal of Cognitive Psychotherapy, 20*, 215–230.

Miklowkitz, D., Otto, M., Frank, E., Reilly-Harrington, N., Wisniewski, S., Kogan, J., et al. (2007). A 1-year randomized trial from the systematic treatment enhancement program. *Archives of General Psychiatry, 64*, 419–426.

Moller, H., & Grunze, H. (2000). Have some guidelines for the treatment of acute bipolar depression gone too far in the restriction of antidepressants? *European Archives of Psychiatry and Clinical Neurosciences, 250*, 57–68.

Moller, H., & Nasrallah, H. (2003). Treatment of bipolar disorder. *Journal of Clinical Psychiatry, 64*(Suppl 6), 9–16.

Moreno, D., & Andrade, L. (2005). The lifetime prevalence, health services utilization and risk of suicide of bipolar spectrum subjects, including subthreshold categories in the Sao Paulo ECA study. *Journal of Affective Disorders, 87*, 231–241.

Nemeroff, C., Evans, D., Gyulai, L., Sachs, G., Bowden, C., Gergel, I., Oakes, R., & Pitts, D. (2001). Double-blind, placebo-controlled comparison of imipramine and paroxetine in the treatment of bipolar depression. *American Journal of Psychiatry, 158*, 906–912.

Newcomer, J. (2005). Second-generation (atypical) antipsychotics and metabolic effects: A comprehensive literature review. *CNS Drugs, 19*(Suppl 1), 1–93.

Nierenberg, A., Miyahara, S., Spencer, T., Wisniewski, S., Otto, M., Simon, N., et al. (2005). Clinical and diagnostic implications of lifetime attention deficit/hyperactivity disorder comorbidity in adults with bipolar disorder: Data from the first 1000 STEP-BD participants. *Biological Psychiatry, 57*, 1467–1473.

Nosè, M., Cipriani, A., Biancosino, B., Grassi, L., & Barbui, C. (2006). Efficacy of pharmacotherapy against core traits of borderline personality disorder: Meta-analysis of randomized controlled trials. *International Clinical Psychopharmacology, 21*, 345–353.

O'Connell, R., Mayo, J., Flatlow, L., Cuthbertson, B., & O'Brien, B. (1991). Outcome of bipolar disorder on long-term treatment with lithium. *British Journal of Psychiatry, 159*, 123–129.

Oquendo, M., Waternaux, C., Brodsky, B., Parsons, B., Haas, G., Malone, K., & Mann, J. (2000). Suicidal behavior in bipolar mood disorder: Clinical characteristics of attempters and nonattempters. *Journal of Affective Disorders, 59*, 107–117.

Oquendo, M., & Mann, J. (2001). Identifying and managing suicide risk in bipolar patients. *Journal of Clinical Psychiatry, 62*(Suppl 5), 31–34.

Otto, M., & Miklowitz, D. (2004). The role and impact of psychotherapy in the management of bipolar disorder. *CNS Spectrums, 9*(11 Suppl 12), 27–32.

Otto, M., Reilly-Harrington, N., Knauz, R., Henin, A., Kogan, J., & Sachs, G. (2009). *Managing bipolar disorder: A cognitive behavioral approach (Therapists guide).* New York: Oxford University Press.

Otto, M., Simon, N., Wisniewski, S., Miklowitz, D., Kogan, J., Reilly-Harrington, N., et al. (2006). Prospective 12-month course of bipolar disorder in outpatients with and without comorbid anxiety disorders. *British Journal of Psychiatry, 189*, 20–25.

Paris, J., Gunderson, J., & Weinberg, I. (2007). The interface between borderline personality disorder and bipolar spectrum disorders. *Comparative Psychiatry, 48*, 145–154.

Perlis, R., Miyahara, S., Marangell, L., Wisniewski, S., Ostacher, M., DelBello, M., et al. (2004). Long-term implications of early onset in bipolar disorder: Data from the first 1000 participants in the systematic treatment enhancement program for bipolar disorder (STEP-BD). *Biological Psychiatry, 55*, 875–881.

Perlis, R., Sachs, G., Lafer, B., Otto, M., Faraone, S., & Rosenbaum, J. (2002). Effect of abrupt change from standard to low serum lithium levels: A reanalysis of double-blind lithium maintenance data. *American Journal of Psychiatry, 159*, 1155–1159.

Perry, A., Tarrier, N., Morriss, R., McCarthy, E., & Limb, K. (1999). Randomized controlled trial of efficacy of teaching patients with bipolar disorder to identify early warning signs or relapse and obtain treatment. *British Medical Journal, 318*, 149–153.

Perugi, G., & Akiskal, H. (2002). The soft bipolar spectrum redefined: Focus on the cyclothymic, anxious-sensitive, impulse dyscontrol, and binge-eating connection in BPII and related conditions. *Psychiatric Clinics of North America, 25*, 713–737.

Pies, R. (2007). The historical roots of the "bipolar spectrum": Did Aristotle anticipate Kraepelin's broad concept of manic-depression? *Journal of Affective Disorders, 100*, 7–11.

Post, R., Uhde, T., Roy, B., & Joffe, R. (1986). Antidepressant effects of carbamazepine. *American Journal of Psychiatry, 143*, 29–34.

Priebe, S., Wildgrube C., & Muller-Oerlinghausen, B. (1989). Lithium prophylaxis and expressed emotion. *British Journal of Psychiatry, 154*, 396–399.

Quitkin, F., McGrath, P., Stewart, J., Harrison, W., Tricamo, E., Wager, S., et al. (1990). Atypical depression, panic attacks, and response to imipramine and phenelzine. A replication. *Archives of General Psychiatry, 47*, 935–941.

Rea, M., Tompson, M., Miklowitz, D., Goldstein, M., Hwang, S., & Mintz, J. (2003). Family-focused treatment versus individual treatment for bipolar disorder: Results of a randomized clinical trial. *Journal of Consulting and Clinical Psychology, 71*, 482–492.

Regier, D., Farmer, M., Rae, D., Locke, B., Keith, S., Judd., L., et al. (1990). Comorbidity of mental disorders with alcohol and other drug abuse: Results from the Epidemiologic Catchment Area (ECA) study. *Journal of the American Medical Association, 264*, 2511–2518.

Reich, L., Davies, R., & Himmelhoch, J. (1974). Excessive alcohol use in manic-depressive illness. *American Journal of Psychiatry, 131*, 83–86.

Rice, J., McDonald-Scott, P., Endicott, J., Corywell, W., Grove, W., Keller, M., et al. (1986). The stability of diagnosis with an application to bipolar II disorder. *Psychiatry Research, 19*, 285–296.

Sachs, G., Collins, M., Altshuler, L., Ketter, T., Suppes, T., Rasgon, N., et al. (2002). Divalproex sodium versus placebo for the treatment of bipolar depression. *APA 2002 Syllabus and Proceedings Summary*.

Sachs, G., Nierenberg, A., Calabrese, J., Marangel, L., Wisniewski, S., Gyulai, L., et al. (2007). Effectiveness of adjunctive antidepressant treatment for bipolar depression. *The New England Journal of Medicine, 356*, 1711–1722.

Schneck C., Miklowitz, D., Calabrese, J., Allen, M., Thomas, M., Wisniewski, S., et al. (2004). Phenomenology of rapid-cycling bipolar disorder: Data from the first 500 participants in the Systematic Treatment Enhancement Program. *American Journal of Psychiatry, 161*, 1902–1908.

Scott, J., Garland, A., & Moorhead, S. (2001). A pilot study of cognitive therapy in bipolar disorders. *Psychological Medicine, 31*, 459–467.

Scott, J., Paykey, E., Morriss, R., Bentall, R., Kinderman, P., Johnson, T., et al. (2006). Cognitive-behavioral therapy for severe and recurrent bipolar disorders. *British Journal of Psychiatry, 188*, 313–320.

Scott, J., & Pope, M. (2002). Nonadherence with mood stabilizers: Prevalence and predictors. *Journal of Clinical Psychiatry, 65*, 384–390.

Simon, N., Otto, M., Weiss, R., Bauer, M., Miyahara, S., Wisniewski, S., et al. (2004a). Pharmacotherapy for bipolar disorder and comorbid conditions: Baseline data from STEP-BD. *Journal of Clinical Psychopharmacology, 24*, 512–520.

Simon, N., Otto, M., Wisniewski, S., Fossey M., Sagduyu, K., Frank, E., et al. (2004b). Anxiety disorder comorbidity in bipolar disorder: Data from the first 500 STEP-BD participants. *American Journal of Psychiatry, 161*, 2222–2229.

Simoneau, T., Miklowitz D., Richards, J., Saleem R., & George, E. (1999). Bipolar disorder and family communication: Effects of a psychoeducational treatment program. *Journal of Abnormal Psychology, 108*, 588–597.

Stamm, T., Adli, M., Kirchheiner, J., Smolka, M., Kaiser, R., Tremblay, P., & Bauer, M. (2008). Serotonin transporter gene and response to lithium augmentation in depression. *Psychiatric Genetics, 18*, 92–7.

Stirman, S., DeRubeis, R., Crits-Christoph, P., & Rothman, A. (2005). Can the randomized controlled trial literature generalize to nonrandomized patients? *Journal of Consulting and Clinical Psychology, 73*, 127–135.

Strober, M., DeAntonio, M., Schmidt-Lackner, S., Freeman, R., Lampert, C., & Diamon, J. (1998). Early childhood attention deficit hyperactivity disorder predicts poorer response to acute lithium therapy in adolescent mania. *Journal of Affective Disorders, 51*, 145–151.

Suppes, T., Leverich, G., Keck, P., Nolen, W., Denicoff, K., Altshuler, L. et al. (2001). The Stanley Foundation Bipolar Treatment Outcome Network. II. Demographics and illness characteristics of the first 261 patients. *Journal of Affective Disorders, 67*, 45–59.

Szadoczky, E., Papp, Z., Vitrai, J., Rihmer, Z., & Furedi, J. (1998). The prevalence of major depressive and bipolar disorders in Hungary: Results from a national epidemiologic survey. *Journal of Affective Disorders, 50*, 153–169.

Tarrier, N., Barrowclough, C., Vaughn, C., Bamrah, J., Porceddu, K., Watts, S., & Freeman H. (1988). The community management of schizophrenia: A controlled trial of a behavioral intervention with families to reduce relapse. *British Journal of Psychiatry, 153*, 532–542.

Thase, M., Macfadden, W., Weisler, R., Chang, W., Paulsson, B., Khan, A., et al. (2006). Efficacy of quetiapine monotherapy in bipolar I and II depression: A double blind, placebo-controlled study (the BOLDER II study). *Journal of Clinical Psychopharmacology, 26*, 600–609.

Tohen, M., Greenfield, S., Weiss, R., Zarate, C., & Vagge, L. (1998). The effect of comorbid substance use disorders on the course of bipolar disorder: A review. *Harvard Review of Psychiatry, 6*, 133–141.

Tohen, M., Vieta, E., Calabrese, J., Ketter, T., Sachs, G., Bowden, C., et al. (2003). Efficacy of olanzapine and olanzapine-fluoxetine combination in the treatment of bipolar I depression. *Archives of General Psychiatry, 60*, 1079–1088.

Tohen, M., Waternaux, C., & Tsuang. M. (1990). Outcome in mania: A 4-year prospective follow-up of 75 patients utilizing survival analysis. *Archives of General Psychiatry, 47*, 1106–1111.

Totterdell, P., & Kellett, S. (2008). Restructuring mood in cyclothymia using cognitive behavior therapy: An intensive time-sampling study. *Journal of Clinical Psychology, 64*, 501–518.

Tsai, S., Chen, C., Kuo, C., Lee, J., Lee, H., & Strakowski, M. (2001). 15-year outcome of treated bipolar disorder. *Journal of Affective Disorders, 63*, 215–220.

Zaretsky, A., Segal, Z., & Gemar, M. (1999). Cognitive therapy for bipolar depression: A pilot study. *Canadian Journal of Psychiatry, 44*, 491–494.

The Obsessive-Compulsive Disorder Spectrum

Jonathan S. Abramowitz *and* Brittain L. Mahaffey

Abstract

This chapter presents a comprehensive overview of the nature, psychological conceptualization, assessment, and treatment of obsessive-compulsive disorder (OCD) and related conditions. First, we describe the symptoms of OCD and the proposal that numerous other disorders overlap with this condition. We critically review this proposal, and conclude that the number of overlapping conditions is somewhat smaller than some authors have suggested. From there, we turn to a review of the empirically supported psychological models of OCD and these related conditions. A discussion of the assessment and treatment of these disorders then follows.

Keywords: Anxiety disorders, CBT, cognitive-behavioral therapy, diagnosis, ERP, exposure and response prevention, obsessive compulsive disorder, obsessive compulsive spectrum, OCD, OCSDs

Obsessive-compulsive disorder (OCD) has captured the attention of clinicians for over a century. Despite its somewhat low prevalence rate relative to other anxiety disorders, the presentation of OCD is usually severe and often crippling, with symptoms that frequently prevent normal functioning at school or work, within social relationships, and in basic life activities (e.g., eating, personal hygiene). Further, the relatively complex psychopathology of OCD initially made the development and implementation of effective treatments difficult. Sufferers appear to struggle against unwanted thoughts and urges that are consciously recognized as senseless on the one hand and yet are perceived as signs of danger on the other. The wide array and intricate associations between thoughts and behaviors can bewilder even the most experienced and astute of clinicians.

Fortunately, since the 1970s, research on OCD has increased exponentially, leading to a better understanding of the course of this condition, its symptom heterogeneity, its boundaries with and relationship to other syndromes, and the development of increasingly refined theoretical models.

Perhaps most importantly, research has led to advances in assessment and treatment to the point where OCD is now considered one of the most treatable psychological disorders.

This chapter begins with an overview of the nature and course of OCD. It has recently been proposed that between 10 and 20 other psychological and neurological disorders, with seemingly overlapping symptoms, comprise a spectrum of obsessive-compulsive disorders. However, this proposal is not reflected in the *Diagnostic and Statistical Manual of Mental Disorders* (DSM-IV; American Psychiatric Association [APA], 2000), nor is it uniformly supported by those in the field (Mataix-Cols et al., 2007). We will critically examine the basis for this spectrum approach and, based on empirical evidence, define it much more narrowly than some of its proponents. We then turn to a critical discussion of the various conceptual models proposed to explain the symptoms of OCD and related problems. Finally, we discuss the assessment of these conditions, describe empirically supported treatment methods, and discuss the research supporting the effectiveness of these interventions.

Definition of Obsessive-Compulsive Disorder

In the DSM-IV-TR (APA, 2000) OCD is classified as an anxiety disorder characterized by two main symptoms: *obsessions* or *compulsions*. Obsessions are persistent intrusive thoughts, ideas, images, impulses, or doubts that an individual experiences as unwanted, unacceptable, or senseless. The intrusions also evoke subjective distress (e.g., anxiety, fear, doubt) and are not simply everyday worries about work, relationships, or finances. Although highly specific to the individual, obsessions often concern themes such as (a) germs, contamination, and illness (e.g., "I'll get AIDS if I use a public restroom"); (b) responsibility for harm, disasters, mistakes, or bad luck ("What if I left the stove on and there's a fire?" "What if I hit someone with my car without realizing it?"); (c) sex and morality (e.g., senseless doubts about one's sexual orientation); (d) violence (e.g., "What if I shake my baby?"); (e) religion (e.g., "What if I've offended God?"); and (f) symmetry, order, and exactness (e.g., "It's just not right unless I take an even number of steps"). Most individuals with OCD evidence multiple types of obsessions. Table 16.1 presents some examples of common obsessions.

To control their anxiety, individuals with OCD attempt to avoid situations, thoughts, and other stimuli that trigger obsessions (e.g., using the iron or stove in the case of obsessions about causing a fire). If such situations cannot be avoided, the individual may engage in compulsive rituals. Compulsive rituals are defined as behavioral or mental acts that are formulated according to a set of idiosyncratic personal "rules." Rituals are generally deliberate, yet clearly senseless or excessive in relation to the obsession they are designed to neutralize (e.g., scrubbing one's hands for 30 minutes after using the restroom, testing smoke detectors 10 times before leaving the house). As with obsessions, rituals are unique to the individual. Common *behavioral* rituals include excessive decontamination (e.g., cleaning), counting, repeating routine actions (e.g., turning the light switch off and on several times, getting dressed five times), checking (e.g., door locks, lights), and repeatedly seeking reassurance. Some examples of *mental* rituals include internally repeating special "safe" numbers or phrases (e.g., "God is great") to neutralize obsessional thoughts, and trying to mentally review one's actions to reassure oneself, for example, that one didn't cheat on her partner without realizing. Table 16.2 presents examples of common rituals.

Typically, a fair amount of variance occurs between individuals with regard to insight into the senselessness of their obsessions and compulsive rituals. Some patients easily acknowledge the irrationality of their obsessive cognitions and compulsive rituals, whereas others are firmly convinced that they are entirely rational. An individual's degree of insight may change over time, and can vary between his or her obsessions. For example, an individual may recognize that his obsessive thoughts about physically abusing his children are senseless, and yet

Table 16.1 Examples of common obsessions

Category	Example
Contamination	Fear of germs from urine or feces What if the money I handled had germs?
Responsibility for harm	If I don't warn people that the floor is slippery, it will be my fault if they get hurt. What if I hit someone with my car without realizing it?
Sex and morality	Unwanted images of incestuous relationships Unwanted impulses to stare at someone's crotch
Violence	Impulse to stab a loved one Thoughts of verbally abusing an innocent or undeserving person Images of death or dismemberment
Religion	What if I offended God by mistake? Images of Jesus with an erection on the cross
Symmetry and order	The sense that odd numbers are "not right" The thought that everything has to be arranged "just right"

Table 16.2 Examples of common compulsive rituals

Category	Case example
Decontamination	Handwashing for 15 minutes at a time after taking off one's shoes Wiping down all mail and groceries brought into the house for fear of germs from the grocery store clerks
Checking	Driving back to recheck that no accidents were caused at the intersection Checking locks, appliances, electrical outlets, and windows
Repeating routine activities	Turning the light switch off and on 18 times
Ordering/arranging	Saying the word "left" whenever one hears the word "right" Rearranging the books on the bookshelf until they are "just right"
Mental rituals	Cancelling a "bad" thought by thinking of a "good" thought Repeating a prayer until it is said "just right"

he may have poor insight into the irrationality of his religious obsessions.

It is critical to note that obsessions and compulsions are *functionally related*; meaning that the compulsive ritual is indeed a response to the obsessional distress—an attempt to reduce this distress. For example, an obsession with accidently leaving a door unlocked to intruders would *increase* subjective distress, and a subsequent compulsive ritual such as checking door locks a prescribed number of times would temporarily *reduce* the distress caused by the obsession. Research indicates that certain obsessions and rituals tend to co-occur in the following patterns: (a) obsessions about responsibility for harm and mistakes are associated with checking rituals; (b) symmetry obsessions occur along with ordering and counting rituals; (c) contamination obsessions co-occur with washing and cleaning rituals; (d) religious, sexual, and violent obsessions often trigger mental rituals and reassurance-seeking; and (e) hoarding-related obsessions (e.g., "What if I discard something very important by mistake?") trigger saving compulsions (e.g., McKay et al., 2004). The latter group, hoarding, deserves special mention. Although hoarding has traditionally been considered a form of OCD (e.g., APA, 2000), the differences between hoarding and the other symptom subgroups are compelling enough that most researchers now consider it to be a separate disorder (e.g., Abramowitz, Wheaton, & Storch, 2008).

The Obsessive-Compulsive Spectrum

Recently, some authors have argued that OCD is incorrectly classified as an anxiety disorder and should be removed from this category and, instead, integrated into a grouping to be known as the obsessive-compulsive spectrum disorders (OCSDs). This category would contain numerous conditions located on a continuum of compulsivity and impulsivity (Hollander et al., 2005). Table 16.3 lists the proposed OCSDs, which fall into three main categories: impulse control disorders, disorders focused on appearance and bodily sensations, and neurological disorders that feature repetitive behaviors. Although the OCSD was initially conceived on the basis of apparent overlaps in overt symptom presentation among these disorders (e.g., repetitive thinking and repetitive behavior), proponents of the OCSD approach currently assert that the various disorders also overlap in terms of their neurobiology, patterns of comorbidity, familial patterns, and effective treatments (e.g., Hollander, Kim, Khanna, & Pallanti, 2007).

Both the general creation of an OCSD category and the way in which it is defined here are widely contested by clinicians and researchers on both conceptual and empirical grounds. For example, in a survey by Mataix-Cols et al. (2007), although 60% of 187 clinicians and researchers who specialize in OCD agreed with shifting OCD out of the anxiety disorders category, the majority of those who agreed with the shift to an OCSD model believed that the spectrum is much narrower in scope than is displayed in Table 16.3 (including the author of this chapter). The next section discusses specific problems with the OCSD approach as just outlined, and proposes—on the basis of empirical evidence—that if an obsessive-compulsive spectrum exists, it is indeed quite narrow compared to the model proposed by Hollander et al. (2005).

Table 16.3 Proposed obsessive-compulsive spectrum disorders

Impulse control disorders	Appearance/bodily sensations	Neurological disorders characterized by repetitive behaviors
• Intermittent explosive disorder • Pyromania • Kleptomania • Pathological gambling • Trichotillomania • Paraphilias and nonparaphilic compulsive sexual behavior • Impulsive and aggressive personality disorders such as borderline, narcissistic, and antisocial personality disorders	• Body dysmorphic disorder • Hypochondriasis • Depersonalization disorder • Anorexia nervosa • Bulimia nervosa	• Autism • Asperger syndrome • Tourette syndrome • Sydenham chorea

A Critical Review of the OCSD Approach

FOCUS ON REPETITIVE BEHAVIOR

Proponents of the broader OCSD model argue that a broad range of disorders should be subsumed by the model because they all involve similar repetitive thinking or behavior patterns. A problem with this argument, however, is that in most of the OCSDs, the repetitive symptoms are not functionally related in the same way that obsessions and compulsions are related in OCD. Repetitive impulsive behavior, for example, such as that which characterizes impulse control disorders (ICDs; i.e., pathological gambling, trichotillomania), does not serve the purpose of reducing obsessional anxiety. Rather it is pleasure-seeking. Individuals with ICDs generally feel a rush of excitement when performing their impulsive behavior (Grant & Potenza, 2004). Also, neurological disorders such as autism and Tourette syndrome sometimes involve repetitive behaviors, but these are more akin to pointless muscle movements rather than anxiety-reducing behaviors. Finally, the lack of evidence of a relationship between impulsivity and compulsivity (e.g., Bienvenu et al., 2000; Summerfeldt, Hood, Antony, Richter, & Swinson, 2004) is a compelling mark against a broadly defined OCSDs category that includes impulse control disorders.

There are, however, two disorders for which there may be a legitimate argument for inclusion in an OCSDs category on the basis of overlaps in behavioral features: body dysmorphic disorder (BDD) and hypochondriasis. In these conditions, the individual experiences anxiety-provoking thoughts (i.e., of poor appearance in BDD; of medical problems in hypochondriasis) and avoids or performs repetitive, excessive, and sometimes rule-driven behaviors to alleviate this anxiety (i.e., checking, masking, or reassurance-seeking in BDD; checking with doctors and seeking assurances in hypochondriasis; e.g., Abramowitz & Moore, 2007). Because of their bodily focus, BDD and hypochondriasis are traditionally known as somatoform disorders; however, the intrusion, distress, ritual, and relief cycle seen in these disorders is strikingly similar, if not identical, to that seen in OCD. Further similarities will be discussed later in this chapter.

NEUROBIOLOGY

Some studies have reported differences in neurobiological variables (e.g., brain functioning) between individuals with and without OCD and some of the putative OCSDs. Some authors (e.g., Hollander et al., 2005) have interpreted such findings as confirming that some common "abnormality," "imbalance," or "defect" is responsible for *causing* OCD or OCSDs. However, neurobiological studies are generally cross-sectional and therefore only describe *differences* between people with and without the disorder in question and do not allow for causal or etiological inferences to be drawn. Indeed, alterations in brain functioning could be the cause of OCD, but having OCD could also be responsible for such changes. Finally, both OCD and the brain alterations could be linked to one or more third variables. Thus, the origin of such neurobiological differences remains unclear.

The results of neurobiological research on OCD have also been highly inconsistent. Therefore, this body of research fails to provide convincing evidence of common neurological deficits or dysfunctions in OCD and the proposed OCSDs. In a meta-analysis of 13 neuroimaging (e.g., magnetic resonance imaging [MRI] of the brain) studies of OCD patients, for example, Whiteside, Port, and Abramowitz (2004) found that most results could not be replicated across studies. In addition, few studies have addressed the neurobiology of proposed OCSDs, and those in existence largely report results that are inconsistent with the findings for OCD (e.g., O'Sullivan, Rauch, & Brieter, 1997; Stein, Coetzer, & Lee., 1997, in trichotillomania). Thus, it is "premature to bring neurobiology into the formal classification of mental disorders" (Hyman, 2007, pp. 731).

PATTERNS OF COMORBIDITY

Although OCSD proponents have argued that OCD and the spectrum conditions are often comorbid with one another, several large-scale studies do not support this notion. For example, Bienvenu et al. (2000) reported the following rates of proposed OCSDs among 80 individuals with OCD: anorexia nervosa, 9%; bulimia, 4%; trichotillomania, 4%; kleptomania, 3%; pathologic gambling, 0%; and pyromania, 0%. In contrast, hypochondriasis (16%) and BDD (15%) were more likely to be comorbid with OCD, supporting the position that these two disorders might be part of an OC spectrum. Other studies have reported largely similar results (e.g., Jaisoorya, Reddy, & Srinath 2003). These findings indicate that, other than BDD and hypochondriasis, the proposed OCSDs are quite uncommon among individuals with OCD. In contrast, OCD is more often comorbid with other anxiety disorders (e.g., Jaisoorya et al., 2003).

FAMILY PATTERNS

It is thought that if OCSDs occur frequently in relatives of people with OCD, then such problems are related and share a common genetic underpinning. The available research, however, does not support this contention. For example, Bienvenu et al. (2000) reported the following lifetime prevalence rates of OCSDs in first-degree relatives of adults with OCD: 1% for trichotillomania, 0% for kleptomania, 9% for pathologic gambling, 0% for pyromania, and 4% for any eating disorder.

TREATMENT RESPONSE

Proponents of the broadly defined OCSD model also argue that OCD and the proposed OCSD respond to the same psychological and pharmacological treatments, thereby suggesting the presence of a spectrum. As we discuss further later, research has established the effectiveness of cognitive-behavioral

therapy (CBT) using exposure and response prevention (ERP) techniques, and pharmacotherapy using serotonin reuptake inhibitor (SRI) medications (e.g., clomipramine and selective serotonin reuptake inhibitors [SSRIs], e.g., Prozac) for the treatment of OCD (e.g., Abramowitz, 1997). However, among the OCSDs, response to ERP and to SRIs is highly variable; and in some cases, these are *not* recommended treatments. For example, several studies of trichotillomania have shown no beneficial effect of SRIs relative to placebo (Christenson, Mackenzie, Mitchell, & Callies, 1991; Ninan et al., 2000; Streichenwein &Thornby, 1995; van Minnen, Hoogduin, Keijsers, Hellenbrand, & Hendriks, 2005). In fact, non-SRIs are often helpful for many of the proposed OCSDs, such as kleptomania (McElroy, Keck, Pope, & Hudson, 1989), compulsive shopping (McElroy, Hudson, Pope, & Keck, 1991), and pathological gambling (Moskowitz, 1980) to name a few. Also, neuroleptic medications (e.g., Haldol) that are ineffective as monotherapies for OCD are often used in the treatment of Tourette syndrome (Leckman et al., 1991). Psychological treatment for impulse control disorders also involves techniques such as habit reversal that are not used for OCD (e.g., van Minnen et al., 2003). Thus, overall, there are insufficient data to support any linkage among OCD and the putative OCSDs as a function of treatment response. We'll return to a discussion of the treatment of OCD, BDD, and hypochondriasis later in this chapter.

Conclusions: Body Dysmorphic Disorder and Hypochondriasis as Possible OCSDs

As mentioned previously, although most of the disorders placed within the OCSDs category (e.g., Table 16.3) appear to be a poor fit, BDD and hypochondriasis are the exceptions. Based on the nature of their essential psychopathology and treatment response, BDD and hypochondriasis do appear to be closely related to OCD. In both of these conditions, we find compulsive-like behavior (e.g., checking in mirrors in BDD; checking with doctors for reassurance in hypochondriasis) that are phenomenologically linked to intrusive thoughts and (obsession-like) fears (e.g., regarding appearance in BDD; regarding one's medical health in hypochondriasis). These presentations are similar to OCD, the common underlying process being the perception that some feared catastrophe will occur at some time in the future, requiring the use of avoidance or ritualistic strategies to avert such negative outcomes and reduce anxiety and fear. Moreover, BDD and hypochondriasis respond preferentially to many of the same CBT (and pharmacological) interventions used for the treatment of OCD. Based on the sum of this evidence, it could be appropriate to include BDD and hypochondriasis in a category with OCD. Therefore, the remainder of this chapter focuses on a narrowly defined OCD spectrum that incorporates only these two spectrum conditions along with OCD per se.

Models of Psychopathology
Models Based on Conditioning and Learning Theory
Until the 1980s, clinical researchers relied on conditioning models based on learning theory to understand OCD and other anxiety-based disorders. The most well articulated of these models was Mowrer's (1960) two-factor model of fear, which proposed that obsessional fears were acquired by classical conditioning and maintained by operant conditioning. To illustrate, an obsessional fear of the number "666" could arise from an incident in which the person had an aversive experience (the unconditioned stimulus) in the presence of this number (the conditioned stimulus), leading to a classically conditioned fear. The obsessional fear was then said to be maintained by negative reinforcement; that is, the anxiety-reducing effects of avoiding or escaping from distress (e.g., by avoidance of the number 666) or by engaging in compulsive rituals such as mentally "replacing" the number with a "safe" number, or repeating a behavior until the number is out of one's consciousness.

Exposure and response prevention, which remains the most effective treatment for OCD, developed largely as a result of conditioning models such as Mowrer's (1960). Exposure and response prevention involves gradual confrontation with stimuli that, although realistically safe, provoke obsessional fear (e.g., touching a stair rail, thinking about or viewing the number "666"), while resisting compulsive urges to perform rituals to reduce anxiety (e.g., refraining from washing, resisting mental rituals). Despite the effectiveness of ERP and other treatments developed from the conditioning paradigm, these types of models have some limitations. First, most people with OCD do not report the kinds of conditioning experiences these models credit with obsession formation. Second, behavioral models have difficulty explaining the emergence, persistence, and content of repugnant sexual, religious, and violent obsessions (e.g., Why do some people with OCD experience obsessional images of Jesus masturbating on the cross?). Third, this model

fails to explain why the focus of obsessions and the nature of compulsions sometimes shift over time (e.g., the patient who previously had obsessions about Jesus now has obsessions about molesting his infant). These and other limitations led researchers to consider the role cognitive processes play in the development and persistence of OCD.

General Cognitive Deficit Models
Research in the area of cognitive deficits has primarily taken two directions. The first main area of research approach focuses on dysfunctions or deficits in cognitive processing, which may have neurobiological or neuropsychological origins. The idea that individuals with OCD suffer from cognitive processing deficits is intuitively appealing. For example, it seems plausible that individuals with checking rituals have a memory problem and cannot remember whether they have locked the door. Alternately, the individual could have a deficit in his ability to accurately recall whether he actually turned off the oven or merely imagined doing so (i.e., a *reality monitoring* deficit). Research findings, however, provide weak and inconsistent support for these types of memory problems in OCD. In fact, the most consistent finding has been that individuals with OCD have less confidence in their own memory than do individuals without OCD (e.g., Foa, Amir, Gershuny, Molnar, & Kozak, 1997; McNally & Kohlbeck, 1993; Woods, Vevea, Chambless, & Bayen, 2002). Research has also examined whether the intrusive, repetitive, and seemingly uncontrollable quality of obsessional thoughts is the result of cognitive inhibition deficits. Research in this domain posits that individuals with OCD are relatively less able than nondisordered individuals to forget or dismiss thoughts about extraneous mental stimuli. For example, when individuals with OCD are given tests of recall and recognition, they have more difficulty forgetting *negative* material and material related to their particular OCD concerns, relative to positive and neutral material, whereas healthy control subjects do not show this bias (e.g., Tolin, Hamlin, & Foa, 2002; Wilhelm, McNally, Baer, & Florin, 1996).

Poor cognitive inhibition might explain the high frequency of obsessional thoughts, yet the idea that OCD arises from general cognitive deficits does not add to our understanding of or our ability to treat the disorder. It seems likely that apparent memory and processing deficits are better accounted for by *cognitive biases*, in which obsessional anxiety leads to preferential processing of threat-relevant stimuli.

For example, an individual who possesses a biased perception that she is responsible for negative events or outcomes may have reduced confidence in her memory and fear that her perceived memory problems may lead to misfortune. Consequently the individual may engage in compulsive checking. Therefore, checking compulsions may function as a way of reducing doubts that have arisen because of mistaken beliefs about one's memory and ability to manage uncertainty, and pathological overestimates of responsibility for harm. These types of mistaken beliefs are the focus of the cognitive specificity hypothesis of OCD.

Cognitive Specificity Models

The second, cognitive approach to OCD proposes that this (and related) disorders arise from particular types of dysfunctional cognitions (i.e., beliefs and interpretations). Such models are based on Beck's (1976) cognitive specificity hypothesis, which posits that each type of psychopathology is associated with a distinct type or pattern of dysfunctional beliefs. Depression, for example, is said to arise from overly negative beliefs about oneself, the world, and the future (e.g., "I'm a loser"). Panic disorder is thought to be associated with catastrophic misinterpretations of the physical sensations that accompany normal anxiety (fight–flight) response (e.g., "When my heart races, I think I'm having a heart attack"). With respect to OCD, particular dysfunctional beliefs have been theoretically linked to particular types of symptoms. For example, beliefs about inflated personal responsibility have been conceptually linked to obsessions about harm and mistakes, and checking compulsions (Salkovskis, 1985). Further, beliefs about the overimportance of one's intrusive thoughts (e.g., "Bad thoughts mean I'm a bad person") have been linked to violent, sexual, and religious obsessions (e.g., Frost & Steketee, 2002).

Given the heterogeneity of OCD symptoms, it is not surprising that a number of similar cognitive approaches have expanded on Beck's (1976) initial model. Among the most well-articulated of these is Salkovskis' (1985, 1989) cognitive approach. This model begins with the well-established research finding that most people experience unwanted intrusive thoughts (i.e., thoughts, images, and impulses that intrude into consciousness; e.g., Rachman & de Silva, 1978). These "nonclinical" obsessions tend to be less frequent, less distressing, and shorter in duration than the "clinical" obsessions of individuals with OCD. Clinical and nonclinical obsessions, however, have similar themes such as violence, contamination,

sex, and doubts. Thus, a comprehensive model of OCD must explain why almost everyone experiences intrusive thoughts, yet only a minority of people experience frequent, distressing, and persistent clinical obsessions.

Salkovskis argues that intrusive thoughts reflect the person's current concerns and are triggered by internal or external cues that remind the person of their concerns. For example, intrusive thoughts about accidentally hitting pedestrians with an automobile may be triggered by driving past people walking on the side of the road. Salkovskis asserted that nonclinical intrusive thoughts only escalate into obsessions when they are evaluated or *appraised* as posing a threat for which the individual is personally responsible. To illustrate, consider the intrusive image of shaking a baby. Most people experiencing such an intrusion would regard it as a meaningless cognitive event with no harm-related implications (i.e., "mental noise"). Such an intrusion might develop into a clinical obsession if the person appraises it as indicating that he or she has the responsibility for causing or preventing disastrous consequences. For example, if the person made an appraisal such as the following: "Thinking about hurting my baby means that I'm a dangerous and bad parent who must take extra care to ensure that I don't lose control." Such appraisals evoke distress and motivate the person to try to suppress or remove the unwanted intrusion (e.g., by replacing it with a "good" thought), and to attempt to prevent the content of the intrusion from actually occurring (e.g., by avoiding the baby). Thus, compulsive rituals are cast in this model as efforts to remove intrusions and to prevent any perceived harmful consequences.

Why, then, do some people, but not others, interpret and appraise their intrusive thoughts in terms of harm and responsibility? Beck (1976) proposed that our life experiences shape the basic assumptions we hold about ourselves and the world, including beliefs about personal responsibility, and about the significance of unwanted thoughts (e.g., beliefs that all our thoughts are significant). Such beliefs may be acquired from a strict moral or religious upbringing, or from other experiences that teach the person extreme or rigid codes of conduct and responsibility (Salkovskis, Shafran, Rachman, & Freeston, 1999).

But if obsessions are unrealistic, senseless thoughts, why doesn't the person with OCD recognize this and move on? Why, instead, do they engage in useless and time-consuming rituals? Salkovskis proposed that rituals develop and persist as coping strategies for obsessional thoughts for two reasons. First, compulsive rituals are reinforced by the immediate (albeit temporary) reduction in obsessional distress that they often produce (i.e., negative reinforcement, as in the conditioning model). Second, they maintain obsessions by preventing the person from learning that his or her beliefs and appraisals are unrealistic. That is, when a person ritualizes, he or she fails to learn that obsessional thoughts and situations aren't dangerous and, instead, he or she continues to think that without the ritual a disaster would have occurred. Other authors (e.g., Rachman, 2003) have also proposed that compulsive rituals increase the frequency and repetitiveness of obsessions by serving as reminders of (retrieval cues) intrusions, and thereby triggering their reoccurrence. For example, compulsive reassurance-seeking can remind the person of his or her obsessional doubts. Therefore, attempts to distract one's self from obsessional thoughts can paradoxically *increase* the frequency of these thoughts and images. Rituals can also strengthen one's perceived responsibility. For example, when the feared consequences of thinking a violent thought do not occur after performing a mental ritual, it strengthens the person's belief that he is indeed solely responsible for removing the potential threat.

In summary, the cognitive model of OCD proposes that obsessions and compulsions develop when a person habitually interprets normal intrusive thoughts as posing a threat for which he or she is personally responsible. This leads to distress and attempts to remove the intrusion, to alleviate discomfort and prevent the feared consequences. But, this response paradoxically increases the frequency of intrusions. Thus, the intrusions become persistent and distressing, and they escalate into clinical obsessions. Compulsive rituals maintain the obsessions and prevent the person from evaluating the accuracy of his or her interpretations. Avoidance is analogous to compulsive rituals, in that avoidance functions as a strategy for reducing anxiety. Avoidance and rituals differ in that avoidance is a passive anxiety-reduction strategy and ritual use is an active strategy.

Salkovskis' model emphasizes the role of responsibility appraisals of intrusive thoughts. Other authors, however, have developed additional cognitive models by expanding on the types of dysfunctional beliefs and appraisals that contribute to OCD. Although these cognitive models differ in some ways, they are more similar than they are different.

Most of the differences between these models relate to the emphasis that they give to certain types of dysfunctional beliefs. Rachman (1998), for example, focuses on beliefs concerning the significance of intrusive thoughts (e.g., "If I think an immoral thought, it means I'm an immoral person"). Thus, for Rachman, obsessions arise when the person misinterprets the intrusive thought as implying that he or she is bad, mad, or dangerous. *Thought–action fusion* is an important concept in this model (Shafran, Thordarson, & Rachman, 1996). Thought–action fusion is defined as beliefs that one's unwanted thoughts will inevitably be translated into actions (e.g., "I might cause my father to have a car accident just by thinking about it"), or beliefs that thoughts are the moral equivalent of actions (e.g., "Thinking about cursing at someone is just as bad as actually doing it").

The most comprehensive contemporary cognitive model of OCD was developed collaboratively by members of the Obsessive Compulsive Cognitions Working Group (OCCWG; Frost & Steketee, 2002), an international assembly of over 40 investigators with interests in the cognitive aspects of OCD. Table 16.4 lists the various domains of dysfunctional beliefs identified by the OCCWG. The OCCWG model accounts for the heterogeneity of OCD symptoms by proposing that particular beliefs (or patterns of beliefs) are important for specific types of OCD symptoms.

IMPLICATIONS OF COGNITIVE SPECIFICITY MODELS

The cognitive-behavioral approach provides a logical and consistent account of OCD symptoms that assumes intact learning (conditioning) processes and normally functioning (albeit biased and maladaptive) cognitive processes. It is parsimonious in that there is no appeal to "chemical imbalances" or disease states to explain OCD symptoms. Further, the hypothesized maladaptive beliefs and appraisals are viewed as "errors" rather than "disease processes." Additionally, the use of avoidance and compulsive behaviors to reduce perceived threats could be considered adaptive if harm was indeed likely. However, OCD patients' obsessive fears and rituals cease to be adaptive because they are out of proportion to the actual threat of the situation. Therefore, such avoidance and rituals are not only irrational, but highly problematic, since they perpetuate a vicious cycle of intrusion → misappraisal → anxiety, and so on.

Table 16.4 Domains of dysfunctional beliefs associated with obsessive-compulsive disorder

Belief domain	Description
Excessive responsibility	Belief that one has the special power to cause, and/or the duty to prevent, negative outcomes
Overimportance of thoughts	Belief that the mere presence of a thought indicates that the thought is significant; for example, the belief that the thought has ethical or moral ramifications, or that thinking the thought increases the probability of the corresponding behavior or event
Need to control thoughts	Belief that complete control over one's thoughts is both necessary and possible
Overestimation of threat	Belief that negative events are especially likely and would be especially awful
Perfectionism	Belief that mistakes and imperfection are intolerable
Intolerance for uncertainty	Belief that it is necessary and possible to be completely certain that negative outcomes will not occur

The model also suggests that successful treatment for OCD symptoms must accomplish two things: (a) the correction of maladaptive beliefs and appraisals and (b) the termination of avoidance and compulsive rituals that prevent the self-correction of maladaptive beliefs and a consequent extinction of anxiety. In short, the task of cognitive therapy is to foster an evaluation of obsessional stimuli as nonthreatening and therefore not demanding of further action. Patients must come to understand their problem not in terms of the risk of feared consequences, but in terms of how they are thinking and behaving in response to stimuli that objectively pose a low risk of harm.

To illustrate, consider a patient who has recurrent doubts that she's spilled her medication on the floor and will be responsible for a child who has poisoned himself with it. She keeps her pill bottles tightly wrapped in several plastic bags and counts the pills compulsively to reassure herself that she hasn't dropped any. This individual overestimates the likelihood of danger and holds the belief that she is solely responsible for causing (and preventing) the disaster she obsesses about. To challenge this belief, the patient and therapist can create a more realistic belief (e.g., "My bottle wrapping and counting have no influence on the feared disaster") and then devise a behavioral experiment to test the new belief. A behavioral experiment in this situation might involve deliberately opening her pill bottle in a candy store and then evaluating the consequences. Cognitive restructuring methods derived from Beck's cognitive therapy (e.g., Beck & Emery, 1985) are also used to challenge OCD-related beliefs and appraisals.

EMPIRICAL STATUS

The cognitive specificity approach to OCD is supported by data from three lines of evidence: self-report questionnaire research, laboratory experiments, and naturalistic longitudinal studies. Results from questionnaire studies consistently indicate that people with OCD are more likely than those without to overestimate the probability of harm and interpret intrusive thoughts as meaningful, threatening, or in terms of responsibility for harm (e.g., Abramowitz, Whiteside, Lynam, & Kalsy, 2003; Freeston, Ladouceur, Gagon, & Thibodeau, 1993; Obsessive Compulsive Working Group [OCCWG], 2003; Salkovskis et al., 2000; Shafran et al., 1996). Although such studies clearly suggest a relationship between OCD and cognitive variables, these correlational data do not address whether cognitive biases play a causal role in OCD onset. Thus, it cannot be ruled out that dysfunctional beliefs result *from* the presence of OCD symptoms. Results from experimentally controlled studies must be examined for evidence of causal directionality.

Several laboratory experiments have addressed the effects of interpretations of intrusive thoughts on OCD symptoms (Ladouceur et al., 1995; Lopatka & Rachman, 1995; Rassin, Merckelbach, Muris, & Spaan, 1999). In one particularly clever study, Rassin et al. (1999) connected 45 psychologically naïve participants to electrical equipment that, participants were told, would monitor their thoughts for 15 minutes. To induce dysfunctional appraisals, participants who had been randomly assigned to the experimental condition were told that thinking the word "apple" would automatically result in a mild electric shock to another person (a confederate of the experimenter) whom they had met earlier. Participants were also informed that by pressing a certain button immediately after having an "apple" thought, they could prevent the shock—this was intended to simulate a compulsive ritual. At the same time, a group of subjects in the control group were told only that the electrical equipment would monitor their thoughts. Results indicated that, during the 15-minute monitoring period, the experimental group reported more intrusive "apple" thoughts, more guilt, greater subjective discomfort, and more intense resistance to thoughts about apples compared to the control group. Moreover, there was a strong association between the number of reported "apple" thoughts and the number of button presses. These data suggest that intrusive thoughts and compulsive behaviors can indeed be evoked by experimentally manipulating participants' beliefs about the significance and harmfulness of intrusive thoughts.

Although the results of this experiment suggest that beliefs can cause OCD symptoms in a *laboratory* setting, it cannot speak to the development of OCD in naturalistic settings. Thus, longitudinal studies in which individuals are assessed for cognitive variables and then followed up after some critical event are apt to be particularly informative. Because pregnancy and the postpartum period represent periods of increased vulnerability to OCD onset, this life event provides an opportune time to examine hypotheses about potential cognitive determinants of OCD: In particular, will the presence of OCD-related cognitive distortions be related to postpartum OCD symptoms? To examine this question, we (Abramowitz, Khandker, Nelson, Deacon, & Rygwall, 2006; Abramowitz, Nelson, Rygwall, & Khandker, 2007) administered measures of OCD-related dysfunctional beliefs to two samples of first-time expecting parents (mothers- and fathers-to-be) during the third trimester of pregnancy. Between 2 and 3 months after childbirth, these new parents were again contacted and assessed for the presence and intensity of unwanted intrusive thoughts about their newborn. Not surprisingly, 75% of these new parents reported unwanted infant-related thoughts ("nonclinical obsessions"; e.g., an image of dropping the child down the stairs or off the balcony). Moreover, after controlling for baseline levels of OC symptoms and trait anxiety, the pre-childbirth strength of OCD-related dysfunctional beliefs was a significant predictor of OC symptom intensity in the postpartum period. These data lend support to the cognitive-behavioral model and suggest that the

tendency to overestimate the chances of harm and significance of intrusive thoughts is a risk factor for the development of more severe OC symptoms.

Despite the fact that dysfunctional beliefs (as posited by cognitive models) do appear to cause OC symptoms in both laboratory and natural settings, existing cognitive models of OCD may yet remain incomplete. For example, in a sample of new parents, dysfunctional beliefs only accounted for a small proportion of OC symptom variance. Thus, other factors must also be involved in determining the onset of OC problems. Additionally, a small group of individuals with OCD do not show the types of dysfunctional beliefs thought to be tied to OCD onset (Taylor, Asmundson, & Coons, 2005). Finally, cognitive therapy techniques, which are derived from cognitive models, do not appear to be more effective than behavioral therapy techniques (e.g., Abramowitz, Franklin, & Foa, 2002). Generally, cognitive specificity models probably hold some validity, yet require modification (rather than abandonment, as in the general cognitive-deficit models). Specifically, future models should define additional etiologically relevant variables, and "boundaries" should be more clearly identified (i.e., defining the types of OCD symptoms they can and cannot account for).

Conceptual Models of OCSDs

As discussed previously, BDD and hypochondriasis are the conditions that appear most closely related to OCD from a conceptual and empirical standpoint. The next sections provide an overview of the contemporary conceptual models of psychopathology in these disorders.

Body Dysmorphic Disorder

Classified as a somatoform disorder in DSM-IV (APA, 2000), BDD involves imagined or exaggerated concerns about physical defects, such as obsessions about the shape or size of facial features. These appearance preoccupations are similar to obsessions in OCD in that both trigger anxiety or distress. Similarly, in individuals with BDD, the avoidance and excessive behaviors designed to conceal, correct, check, or seek reassurance about the imagined defects, as with the compulsive rituals of OCD, serve the purpose of anxiety and distress reduction. For instance, some individuals with BDD check their appearance for prolonged periods of time; looking in mirrors, windows, and so forth. Others go so far as to avoid all reflective surfaces. Additional compulsive behaviors can include dieting, comparing oneself to others, skin-picking, measuring the "flawed" body parts, and seeking a cure (e.g., dental, dermatological, cosmetic, etc.) for the perceived defect (Perugi & Frare, 2005).

CONCEPTUAL MODEL

The most well-thought-out conceptual model of BDD is the cognitive model proposed by Veale (2004). This model proposes that episodes of heightened concern with body image in BDD are often precipitated by "external representations" of the individual's appearance—such as seeing one's reflection—which trigger a defective mental image. Through selective attention to appearance-related details, the individual experiences heightened awareness of specific characteristics within the image. This, in turn, offers faulty information on how the individual appears to others from an observer perspective. This imagery is then associated with greater self-focused attention, to the extent that, in more severe cases of BDD, all of the individuals' attention may be focused on the distorted image and the poor self-evaluation.

In addition to his or her distorted self-appraisals and maladaptive degree of self-focused attention, the individual with BDD also typically holds dysfunctional beliefs and assumptions about the importance of physical appearance. The individual may endorse beliefs such as, "If I'm unattractive, then life isn't worth living." Core beliefs regarding feelings of inadequacy, worthlessness, abnormality, and rejection are also activated. The individual then compares his or her "defective" features with the ideal, which leads to feelings of self-disgust, social anxiety and the fear of embarrassment or rejection, depression, and anger at oneself. These emotional responses trigger urges to perform defensive behaviors, such as avoidance or active escape and concealment of the imagined defect, intended to prevent feared outcomes and to reduce distress. Although these safety behaviors may temporarily alleviate distress, they tend to generally maintain the self-consciousness, preoccupation with the imagined defect, and negative self-appraisal.

EMPIRICAL SUPPORT

Generally, empirical findings support Veale's model (see Buhlmann & Wilhelm, 2004, for a review). First, evidence from the emotional Stroop test supports the hypothesis that people with BDD deploy selective attention toward minute details and features, rather than on global figures. This may explain why individuals with BDD focus on specific appearance-related details while ignoring more global features. For example, Buhlmann, McNally, Wilhelm,

and Florin (2002) found that BDD patients selectively attend to emotional BDD-related stimuli (both positive and negative); thus, they are concerned about both beauty and their own perceived ugliness. Interestingly, studies of cognitive inhibition suggest that, although persons with BDD experience distressing, intrusive thoughts about their appearance, they generally do not try to suppress them because they are perceived as valid (Wilhelm, Buhlmann, & McNally, 2003).

Second, there also appear to be a number of interpretive biases present in BDD that overlap with social phobia. For example, individuals with BDD tend to interpret ambiguous social situations as threatening, have difficulty recognizing others' emotional expression, and tend to be biased toward interpreting others' facial expression as negative in valence (Grocholewski, Henry, & Lingnau, 2007). Relative to people without BDD, those with this condition also tend to rate attractive facial photographs of others as more attractive. Thus, in general, those with BDD may be highly sensitive to beauty and aesthetics.

Hypochondriasis

Although long believed to represent a form of personality pathology, depression, or attention-seeking behavior, contemporary models of hypochondriasis cast this problem as a form of excessive health anxiety. There is an intuitive appeal to such a classification, given that hypochondriasis is characterized by a preoccupation with fears of having, or the idea that one has, a serious disease, based on a misinterpretation of bodily sensations (APA, 2000). These preoccupations also persist despite appropriate medical evaluation and reassurance from physicians. As with BDD, the psychopathology of and efficacious treatments for hypochondriasis are very similar to those of OCD. In fact, hypochondriasis can reasonably be viewed as a variant of OCD in which the individual is exclusively obsessed with health and disease.

CONCEPTUAL MODEL

Recently, several etiological theories for health anxiety have been proposed (Abramowitz & Braddock, 2008; Taylor & Asmundson, 2004). The first theory we will discuss, the biopsychosocial approach, is a general theory that describes physiological, cognitive, behavioral processes. The biopsychosocial approach posits that excessive health anxiety arises from and is maintained by dysfunctional beliefs about sickness and health, including beliefs that lead people to misinterpret the significance of and overestimate the dangerousness of normal bodily sensations and perturbations. Bodily sensations are common occurrences in healthy people (Pennebaker, 1982) and may occur for a variety of reasons, such as benign strains, minor diseases, or autonomic arousal arising from stress. People with excessive health anxiety interpret bodily changes and sensations as threatening and fear some health-related catastrophic consequence (Warwick & Salkovskis, 1990). For example, simple constipation may be misinterpreted as evidence of colon cancer and impending death, or a headache may be taken as evidence of a malignant brain tumor. Other types of beliefs held by people with excessive health anxiety include the idea that they are healthy only when they do not have *any* bodily sensations, that doctors and medical tests can't be trusted, and that worrying about their health will keep them safe (Taylor & Asmundson, 2004). Retrospective studies suggest that these beliefs arise from learning experiences, particularly childhood experiences, about health and disease (Taylor & Asmundson, 2004).

Dysfunctional beliefs are thought to persist in people with excessive health anxiety for many reasons. For example, as with compulsive rituals in OCD, behaviors performed with the aim of alleviating health worries also serve to perpetuate elevated levels of health anxiety by providing cues that prompt more worries and by preventing the individual from learning that his worries are unfounded. Common maladaptive coping behaviors include persistent reassurance seeking (from physicians or family), other forms of repetitive checking (e.g., bodily checking, searching the Internet for health information), and avoidance of behaviors that elicit bodily sensations (e.g., physical exertion). These behaviors persist because they are reinforced by reduced anxiety in the short-term. In the long-term, however, they are not only ineffective in producing lasting reductions in anxiety, but they actually serve to perpetuate health anxiety (Lucock, White, Peake, & Morley, 1998). For example, checking the Internet might increase a person's preoccupation with disease and expose them to frightening information about the symptoms and risks of other health conditions. Additionally, rituals may have other negative consequences. For instance, reassurance-seeking may reduce the individual's sense of independence (e.g., by repeatedly turning to others for help). Also, seeking additional treatment and tests can produce iatrogenic effects, such as side effects of medications, pain from unnecessary invasive procedures, and the like (see Abramowitz &

Braddock, 2006, and Taylor & Asmundson, 2004 for a discussion).

EMPIRICAL SUPPORT

Consistent with the biopsychosocial model, research suggests that people with excessive health anxiety more frequently tend to misinterpret their bodily sensations as indicative of disease than do nonanxious individuals (Haenen, Schmidt, Schoenmakers, & van den Hout, 1998). These anxious individuals are also more likely to overestimate the probability of contracting a disease and the seriousness of diseases (Ditto, Jemmott, & Darley, 1988; Easterling & Leventhal, 1989). The fact that environmental factors (e.g., learning experiences) account for most of the individual differences in scores of health anxiety (63%–90% of the variance) whereas genetic factors played a significant but less important role (10%–37% of the variance) is also consistent with the biopsychosocial model (Taylor, Thordarson, Jang, & Asmundson, 2006). Other psychosocial factors implicated in the etiology of health anxiety include early learning experiences (e.g., childhood history of disease, reinforcement or receiving special attention when sick), which contribute to dysfunctional beliefs about the dangerousness of bodily changes and that one's body is weak (e.g., Robbins & Kirmayer, 1996; Whitehead et al., 1994). Research has also demonstrated that performing checking, reassurance-seeking, and other ritualistic behaviors results in a decrease in health worries (Abramowitz & Moore, 2007).

Assessment

Proper assessment of OCD and related disorders is guided by the conceptual models of psychopathology discussed in the previous sections. Because of the consistent empirical support for behaviorally and cognitively oriented models, such models are use as a framework for determining which parameters are appropriate to assess. Methodologies for a comprehensive assessment of OCD, BDD, and hypochondriasis are discussed in this section.

Clinical Interviews

STRUCTURED DIAGNOSTIC INTERVIEWS

Three psychometrically validated structured clinical interviews exist for the diagnosis of OCD and related disorders. The *Anxiety Disorders Interview Schedule for DSM-IV* (ADIS-IV; Di Nardo, Brown, & Barlow, 1994) is a clinician-administered, semi-structured interview developed to allow for differential diagnosis among the anxiety disorders based on DSM-IV criteria. The ADIS-IV begins with demographic questions and items related to general functioning and life stress. Sections for assessing each anxiety, mood disorder, and two somatoform disorders (hypochondriasis and somatization disorder) appear next. The OCD and hypochondriasis sections each begin with a screening question; a positive answer to this question triggers more detailed questions about specific symptoms based on DSM criteria.

Studies demonstrate that the ADIS-IV modules have very good inter-rater reliability, with the main sources of unreliability stemming from the occasional assignment of a subclinical OCD diagnosis (rather than a different anxiety disorder) (e.g., Brown, Campbell, Lehman, Grisham, & Mancill, 2001). Although no studies have directly examined the validity of the ADIS-IV OCD section, many studies do show that OCD samples diagnosed with this instrument have higher scores on other measures of OCD severity than do non-OCD samples. This provides some indirect evidence for the validity of the ADIS-IV OCD section. The semistructured format of the ADIS-IV is also advantageous because it allows the clinician to collect more detailed information. The dimensional rating of symptom severity provided in this interview is also frequently useful. One drawback of the ADIS-IV is that administration of the full instrument can be time-consuming. However, it should be noted that the OCD module itself is relatively short.

The *Structured Clinical Interview for DSM-IV Axis I Disorders* (SCID; First, Spitzer, Gibbon, & Williams, 2002) is a second clinician-administered interview. However, the SCID, unlike the ADIS-IV, was developed for the purpose of diagnosing a range of DSM-IV Axis I disorders. Consequently, the SCID contains modules designed for the assessment of OCD, BDD, and hypochondriasis. Each section includes probe questions about the presence of obsessions, compulsions, or bodily or health preoccupations. Next to each probe appear the corresponding DSM-IV diagnostic criteria, which are rated as absent (false), subthreshold, or present (true). Thus, ratings relate to diagnostic criteria rather than interviewees' responses. Relative to the ADIS-IV, the SCID affords the clinician less opportunities to collect qualitative information about clients.

Finally, the *Mini International Neuropsychiatric Interview* (MINI; Sheehan et al., 1998) is a brief structured interview for the major Axis I psychiatric disorders in DSM-IV. Validation and reliability studies show that the MINI is comparable to the SCID, yet can be administered in a much shorter period of time than the instruments just discussed. Although the MINI can be used to assess the presence of OCD, it does not have modules for assessing BDD or hypochondriasis.

YALE-BROWN OBSESSIVE COMPULSIVE SCALE
The Yale-Brown Obsessive Compulsive Scale (YBOCS; Goodman et al., 1989a, 1989b) is considered the "gold standard" instrument for assessing the range and severity of OCD symptoms. The scale is divided into three parts. The first section provides definitions of obsessions and compulsions that are read to the patient. The second part contains a rationally derived checklist of over 50 common obsessions and compulsive rituals. The clinician reviews the list with the client and asks whether or not they are currently experiencing or have ever experienced the symptom. The most prominent obsessions, compulsions, and OCD-related avoidance behaviors are then identified from those endorsed by the patient.

Although the YBOCS checklist is currently the gold standard of assessment for OCD, there are several drawbacks to the measure. First, the YBOCS attempts to be comprehensive in scope, yet it merely assesses the *form* of the patient's obsessions and rituals without examining the relationship between these symptoms. For example, there are no questions relating to how rituals are used to reduce obsessional fears (later in this chapter, a functional approach to assessing OCD symptoms that has incremental validity over the YBOCS is described). Another limitation of the checklist is that it contains too few items assessing some sorts of symptoms (i.e., mental rituals) and includes other items assessing phenomena that are not symptoms of OCD (e.g., self-injurious behavior). Although the YBOCS was primarily developed to assess obsessions and compulsions in OCD, the checklist also contains items that assess BDD (e.g., obsessions about appearance) and hypochondriasis (e.g., checking rituals related to somatic obsessions).

The third part of the YBOCS is a severity scale that contains ten items (five that assess obsessions and five that assess compulsions), each of which is rated on a 5-point scale from 0 (no symptoms) to 4 (extremely severe). Items address (a) the time occupied by current symptoms, (b) interference with functioning, (c) associated distress, (d) attempts to resist obsessions and compulsions, and (e) the degree of control over symptoms. Scores on each of the ten items are summed to produce a total score ranging from 0 to 40. In most instances, scores of 0 to 7 represent subclinical OCD symptoms, those from 8 to 15 represent mild symptoms, scores of 16 to 23 relate to moderate symptoms, scores from 24 to 31 suggest severe symptoms, and scores of 32 to 40 imply extreme symptoms. The YBOCS severity scale can easily be adapted to assess the severity of BDD and hypochondriacal symptoms. Specifically, the intrusive thoughts (i.e., "somatic obsessions") and compulsive behaviors in these conditions can be rated on the obsessions and compulsions YBOCS items respectively.

INSIGHT INTO THE SENSELESSNESS OF SYMPTOMS

The degree of insight a client has into the senselessness of his or her obsession and compulsion provides a fair amount of prognostic value for treatment outcome. Therefore, it is extremely useful to assess insight where possible. The *Brown Assessment of Beliefs Scale* (BABS; Eisen et al., 1998) is a seven-item interview that provides a continuous measure of insight into the senselessness of OCD symptoms. It can also be used to assess insight into beliefs about appearance in BDD, and beliefs about feared medical conditions in hypochondriasis. Administration begins with the interviewer and patient identifying one or two of the patient's specific obsessional fears that have been of significant concern over the past week (e.g., "Everyone thinks I'm ugly because my nose is too big"). Next, specific items assess the patient's (a) conviction in the validity of the fear, (b) perceptions of how others view the validity of the fear, (c) explanation for why others hold a different view, (d) willingness to challenge the fear, (e) attempts to disprove the fear, (f) insight into whether the fear is part of a psychological/psychiatric problem, and (g) ideas/delusions of reference. Only the first six items are summed to produce a total score.

Self Reported OCD Symptoms

DIMENSIONAL OBSESSIVE COMPULSIVE SCALE

It is also important to obtain patient self-ratings of the severity of the current symptoms. A newly published instrument, the Dimensional Obsessive Compulsive Scale (DOCS; Abramowitz et al., 2010) is ideally suited for assessing the severity of the four most empirically supported OCD symptom domains as mentioned previously: (a) contamination and washing, (b) responsibility for harm and checking, (c) order, symmetry, and completeness, and (d) unacceptable sexual, religious, and violent obsessional thoughts. The DOCS is a 20-item questionnaire with four subscales (corresponding to the four OCD symptom domains). To accommodate the heterogeneity of OCD symptoms, and the presence of obsessions and rituals within each symptom dimension, each subscale begins with a description of the symptom dimension along with examples of representative obsessions and rituals. The examples clarify the form and function of each dimension's fundamental obsessional fears, compulsive rituals, and avoidance behaviors. Within each symptom dimension, five items (rated 0 to 4) assess the following parameters of severity (over the past month): (a) time occupied by obsessions and rituals, (b) avoidance behavior, (c) associated distress, (d) functional interference, and (e) difficulty disregarding the obsessions and refraining from the compulsions. The DOCS subscales have excellent reliability in clinical samples (α = .94-.96) and the measure converges well with other measures of OC symptoms (Abramowitz et al., 2010).

Assessment of Patient-Specific Symptoms: Functional Analysis

In OCD (and to a lesser extent with BDD and hypochondriasis) there is a great deal of individual difference relating to specific fear triggers and strategies for managing anxiety. Therefore, to best understand a particular patient's problems, it is necessary to conduct a thorough investigation of the specific fears and coping mechanisms (i.e., rituals) that are present (e.g., Abramowitz, 2006). The cognitive and behavioral models described earlier provide a framework for collecting this patient-specific information. The collection of such information is critical for deriving a treatment plan. The present section therefore describes the phenomena to be assessed in a *functional analysis*.

FEAR TRIGGERS

It is important to catalogue all of the external and internal triggers that evoke the patient's obsessional fear. Because of the idiosyncratic nature of fear cues in OCD and related disorders, there is virtually an endless number of potential fear cues. However, triggers typically fall into three domains: situational triggers, intrusive thoughts, and interoceptive cues.

Situational triggers include objects, situations, places, etc. that evoke obsessional fear and general urges to ritualize. In relation to OCD, examples of situational triggers include toilets, knives, completing paperwork, religious icons, feared numbers (e.g., 13 or 666), leaving the house, and so on. In BDD, situational triggers often include looking in the mirror and noticing the perceived disfigurement, social situations, pictures of oneself, etc. With hypochondriasis, triggers are often reminders of the feared illness, such as magazine articles or shows about the illness, hospitals, and the like.

Intrusive thoughts can also trigger obsessional fears across all three of these disorders. As already discussed, in OCD, these thoughts are typically unwanted or upsetting images, doubts, or ideas that the person finds unacceptable, intrusive, or disturbing. Examples include images of becoming ill or contaminated, impulses to harm loved ones, thoughts of blasphemy, doubts about one's sexual preference, and thoughts of loved ones being injured. In BDD, intrusions may relate to highly distorted images of how one appears to others. In hypochondriasis, the intrusions often focus on the feared medical conditions, such as images of tumors growing inside the body, thoughts about ones' own funeral, doubts about whether the illness is present, and thoughts of missing out on life once one had died.

Bodily sensations may or may not trigger obsessional fear in OCD and BDD, but they clearly play a central role in generating anxiety in hypochondriasis. The clinician must therefore learn about all of the internal sensations, feelings, signs, perturbations, and variations of such sensations that trigger health concerns and worries. Specific examples include loose bowel movements, unexplained stomach pain, headaches, feelings of lightheadedness, rapid heartbeat, chest pain, chronic fatigue, sensations associated with respiration or swallowing, and the like.

COGNITIVE FEATURES

Based on Beck's (1976) idea that anxiety arises from one's beliefs and interpretations of fear cues, information ought to be obtained about the cognitive basis of the individual's fears. This means understanding the consequences that the individual associates with the fear triggers (e.g., "I am afraid of public restrooms because I believe I will get AIDS," "If there are 13 people at a dinner table, I will have bad luck"). In addition to assessing this information in a semistructured way (e.g., by asking, "What exactly is it that you fear about _____"), a number of psychometrically sound self-report instruments exist for the purposes of assessing feared catastrophes and the dysfunctional beliefs that underlie them. For example, the Obsessive Beliefs Questionnaire (OBQ; OCCWG, 2005) and Interpretation of Intrusions Inventory (III; OCCWG, 2005) assess cognitions

found to be related to OCD. Analogous measures, such as the Short Health Anxiety Inventory (SHAI; Salkovskis et al., 2002) and Cognitions About Body and Health Questionnaire (CBHQ; Rief, Hiller, & Margraf, 1998) have been developed to measure key dysfunctional cognitions in hypochondriasis. Unfortunately, no such measure is presently available for individuals with BDD.

AVOIDANCE STRATEGIES

In an attempt to prevent feared catastrophes, most individuals with OCD, BDD, and hypochondriasis avoid situations and stimuli that may trigger their fears and obsessions. Avoidance might be overt, such as the evasion of certain people (e.g., cancer patients, the homeless, popular people), places (e.g., public washrooms, hospitals, school), situations (e.g., using pesticides, giving oneself a breast exam, going to a party), or certain words (e.g., "sex," "cancer"). Alternately, avoidance can be more subtle, such as staying away from the *most often touched* part of the door handle and refraining from listening to loud music while driving. In addition to understanding *what* the person is avoiding, it is important to assess *why* he or she avoids it. For example, a man with hypochondriasis avoided giving himself testicular exams because he worried he might discover that he has testicular cancer. A young woman with BDD avoided wearing eye makeup because she felt others would be starring at her disproportionately sized breasts. A man with OCD refused to listen to the radio while driving because he felt it would distract him and cause him to hit pedestrians.

COMPULSIVE RITUALS

The frequently ubiquitous nature of the external stimuli, intrusive thoughts, and bodily sensations associated OCD and related conditions can be make triggers difficult to successfully avoid. Thus, patients use rituals as "active avoidance" strategies that provide a means of *escape* from fear that could not be avoided. Often, these rituals are overt behaviors performed repetitively and in accordance with certain self-prescribed rules (e.g., checking exactly 10 times, washing for 40 seconds). Other rituals may be more subtle, brief, or performed only mentally (e.g., holding the steering wheel tightly, compulsive praying, wearing makeup to cover up a blemish, etc.). As with avoidance, the clinician should assess the function or purpose of the ritual: Why does the person need to perform the behavior at all, and what consequence do they fear would occur as a result of failing to perform the ritual?

SELF-MONITORING

Self-monitoring is an information gathering strategy in which the clinician asks the client with OCD, BDD, or hypochondriasis to record the occurrence of rituals in "real-time." Specifically, the clinician instructs the client to log the following parameters using a form with corresponding column headers: (a) the date and time of the ritual, (b) the fear trigger (situation, thought, bodily sensation) that evoked anxiety and the need to ritualize, and (c) a description of the ritual itself and the length of time spent performing the behavior. Self-monitoring helps the clinician and client gain a clearer picture of the way in which (obsessional) fear and rituals are related, and how much time is consumed by such episodes. Figure 16.1 contains an example of one patient's OCD self-monitoring form.

Treatment

In this section, we discuss empirically supported psychological treatments for OCD, BDD, and hypochondriasis. These interventions are generally based in the behavioral and cognitive traditions as described earlier. The procedure for each individual intervention is delineated, and then a brief review of the supporting research is presented.

Before the 1960s, OCD was largely considered a highly treatment-resistant disorder. The most widely used treatment was psychodynamic psychotherapy, in which the therapist attempted to determine the "root" cause of the patient's obsessions and compulsions by uncovering evidence of unconscious conflict. Although BDD did not exist as an official diagnosis until the publication of DSM-III-R (APA, 1987), unrealistic concerns about appearance were addressed in a similar fashion. Hypochondriasis, a well-known problem for centuries, was often considered pathological attention-seeking behavior (i.e., for being in the sick role) and was dealt with via similar therapeutic approaches. Unfortunately, there is little systematic research on the efficacy of psychodynamic treatment approaches to these disorders. However, the fact that OCD was reputed to be treatment-refractory suggests that psychodynamic therapy was generally ineffective in producing long-term treatment gains.

Exposure-based Therapy

Troubled by the disappointing results of psychodynamic treatments, behaviorally oriented clinical researchers in the 1960s and 1970s began to apply learning and conditioning models to the treatment of fear-based problems such as OCD. Victor Meyer (1966) is credited with being the first to report a systematic study of the effects of behavioral treatment for OCD. Meyer encouraged patients hospitalized with OCD to deliberately confront, for 2 hours each day, situations and stimuli they usually avoided (e.g., toilets, door knobs). The purpose of confrontation was to induce obsessional fears and urges to perform compulsive rituals. Once such fears and urges were elicited, patients were instructed to refrain from performing their rituals (e.g., no washing or cleaning allowed). Ten of Meyer's 15 patients responded extremely well to this therapy, and the remainder showed partial improvement.

Date and time	Activity or thought that triggered the ritual	Ritual	Time ritualizing
June 11 at 8:05	Taking out the garbage	Hand washing	1 min 45 sec
June 11 at 9:30	Leaving the house for work	Checking electrical appliances	23 min
June 11 at 12:15	Intrusive thought that my house is on fire	Go home to check the house	45 min
June 11 at 3:35	See a red spot on the carpet, thoughts about blood	Change clothes and shower	30 min

Fig. 16.1 Self-monitoring form for an individual with OCD

Follow-up studies conducted several years later found that only two of those who were successfully treated had relapsed (Meyer, Levy, & Schnurer, 1974). These techniques would eventually be adopted worldwide, and become known as *exposure and response prevention* (i.e., ERP).

Contemporary ERP, which is used (at least in part) in the treatment of OCD, BDD, and hypochondriasis, entails therapist-guided systematic repeated and prolonged exposure to the fear triggers identified during the functional assessment. Abstinence from compulsive and ritualistic behaviors is also required. This might occur in the form of repeated physical confrontation with feared low-risk situations (i.e., in vivo exposure), in the form of imaginal confrontation with anxiety-provoking intrusive thoughts (imaginal exposure), or in the form of deliberate provocation of distressing (but harmless) internal bodily sensations (interoceptive exposure; e.g., drinking caffeine to produce feelings of jitters, or squinting one's eyes to provoke a tension headache). In the case of an individual with OCD who has contamination obsessions triggered by restrooms, the client would practice touching restroom surfaces such as door knobs, toilets, and sinks. Generally, the client would be asked to work her way up from touching less-disturbing surfaces (e.g. walls and door knobs) to more disturbing surfaces (e.g., flush handles, toilet seats, and even the interior of the toilet bowl). She might also practice imaginal exposure to the idea of having "restroom germs" on her hands and then spreading these germs and becoming ill. For someone with BDD, exposure might entail not wearing any makeup and going to a social event. For a person with hypochondriacal fears of leukemia, exposure might entail reading a book about leukemia sufferers.

Refraining from compulsive rituals (response prevention) is a vital component of effective treatment because the performance of rituals to reduce fear would prematurely discontinue exposure and consequently prevent the client from learning that (a) the fear trigger is not realistically dangerous, and (b) anxiety subsides on its own even if the ritual is not performed. Thus, successful ERP requires that the patient remain in the exposure situation until the anxiety or distress decreases naturally (i.e., without using standby rituals to artificially reduce the distress via avoidance or escape). Continuing on with the exposure examples just described, the person with OCD would refrain from washing or showering, the person with BDD would refrain from checking or applying makeup, and the person

with hypochondriasis would resist the urge to seek reassurance or additional medical testing about whether or not he has leukemia.

Practically speaking, the therapist typically supervises exposure therapy practices during the treatment session, and then assigns additional exposure practices to be completed as homework. Depending on the individual's specific fear triggers and the practicality of confronting actual feared situations, treatment sessions might involve varying amounts of actual, imaginal, and interoceptive exposure practice.

Treatment usually begins with a functional assessment, as described in detail earlier. Before actual treatment begins, the therapist also provides the client with a clear rationale for how ERP is expected to be helpful in reducing obsessional and compulsive symptoms. This is an important step in therapy because it helps to motivate the client and increase his tolerance to the distress that typically accompanies exposure practice. A helpful rationale includes information about how ERP involves the provocation and reduction of distress during prolonged exposure. Information gathered during the assessment is then used to plan, collaboratively with the patient, the specific exposure exercises that will be pursued.

In addition to explaining and planning a hierarchy of exposure exercises, the educational stage of ERP must also acquaint the patient with response prevention procedures. Importantly, the term "response prevention" does not imply that the therapist actively prevents the patient from performing rituals. Instead, the therapist must convince patients to resist urges to perform rituals on their own. Self-monitoring of rituals is often used in support of this goal.

The exposure exercises typically begin with moderately distressing situations, stimuli, and images, and escalate to increasingly distressing situations. The full hierarchy of stimuli should be confronted during treatment. Beginning with less anxiety-evoking exposure tasks increases the likelihood that the client will learn to manage her distress and complete the exposure exercise successfully. Moreover, having success with initial exposures increases the client's confidence in the treatment and reduces the likelihood of treatment dropout. At the end of each session, the therapist instructs the patient to continue exposure for several hours and in different environmental contexts, without the therapist. It is often effective to place exposure to the most anxiety-evoking situations mid-way through a session rather than at the end. This strategy allows the client ample opportunity to repeat exposure to the most difficult situations in different contexts, to allow generalization of treatment effects. During the later treatment sessions, the therapist emphasizes the importance of continuing to apply the ERP procedures learned during treatment. The details of how to use ERP in the treatment of OCD, BDD, and hypochondriasis can be found in resources such as Abramowitz (2006), Rosen (1999), and Abramowitz & Braddock (2008), respectively.

Mechanisms of Action in Exposure and Response Prevention

Three mechanisms are thought to be involved in the reduction of fear and rituals during ERP. First, from a conditioning perspective, ERP provides an opportunity for the extinction of conditioned fear responses. Specifically, repeated and uninterrupted exposure to feared stimuli produces habituation—an inevitable natural decrease in conditioned fear. Response prevention fosters habituation by blocking the performance of anxiety-reducing rituals which, left unchecked, usually foil the habituation process. Extinction occurs when the once-feared obsessional stimulus is repeatedly paired with the nonoccurrence of feared consequences and the eventual reduction of anxiety. From a cognitive perspective, ERP is effective because it corrects dysfunctional beliefs that underlie fear and anxiety by presenting the client with disconfirmatory evidence. For example, when a client confronts feared situations and refrains from rituals, he or she finds out that (a) fear declines naturally (habituation) and (b) feared negative consequences are unlikely to happen. This evidence is processed and incorporated into the client's belief system. Thus, rituals to reduce anxiety and prevent feared disasters become unnecessary. Finally, ERP helps clients gain self-efficacy by helping them to master their fears without having to rely on avoidance or compulsive rituals. The importance of this sense of mastery is an oft-overlooked effect of ERP.

Foa and Kozak (1986) have drawn attention to three indicators of change during exposure-based treatment. First, physiological arousal and subjective fear must be evoked during exposure. Second, the fear responses gradually diminish *during* the exposure session (within-session habituation). Third, the initial fear response at the beginning of each exposure session declines *across* sessions (between-sessions habituation).

EFFICACY OF EXPOSURE AND RESPONSE PREVENTION

Most of the research examining the effects of ERP has been conducted with OCD. A number of carefully designed controlled studies have provided particularly strong evidence of the superiority of ERP over credible control therapies, such as progressive muscle relaxation training (e.g., Fals-Stewart, Marks, & Shaffer, 1993), anxiety management training (Lindsay, Crino, & Andrews, 1997), and pill placebo (Foa et al., 2005). Of particular interest, ERP has also been found more effective than antidepressant medications used in the treatment of OCD (e.g., Foa et al., 2005). For clients receiving ERP, symptom reductions typically exceed 50%–60% at post-treatment. However, most patients evince mild to moderate residual symptoms. Therefore, despite clinically significant improvement in symptoms, patients with OCD rarely achieve complete symptom remission with ERP.

Only a handful of studies have examined the effects of ERP for BDD (e.g., Campsi, 1995) and hypochondriasis (e.g., Taylor, Asmundson, & Coons, 2005). Two reviews of the BDD literature suggest that ERP produces large effects from pre- to post-treatment, with post-test scores on a version of the Y-BOCS adapted for BDD typically in the "moderate" range (e.g., Cororve & Gleaves, 2001; Williams, Hadjistavropoulous, & Sharpe, 2006). Relating to hypochondriasis, the efficacy of ERP is demonstrated by a number of small trials (Logsdail, Lovell, Warwick, & Marks, 1991; Visser & Bouman, 1992; Warwick & Marks, 1988). A larger controlled study found that ERP was significantly more effective than a waitlist control condition, with gains maintained at 7 months follow-up (Visser & Bouman, 2001). In a meta-analytic review by Taylor et al. (2005), ERP was associated with large short- and long-term effect sizes, however, this estimate included only two studies.

Cognitive Therapy

Although often effective, ERP depends upon patients making the decision to face their fears and provoke anxiety, and then resist using the coping strategies that have become entrenched as fear reduction crutches. Needless to say this is a daunting proposition, and many individuals with OCD and related disorders refuse ERP or discontinue treatment prematurely. Consequently, some clinicians and researchers have turned to cognitive therapy approaches that incorporate less prolonged exposure to fear cues and have proven useful in the treatment of other anxiety disorders, such as panic disorder and social phobia. Cognitive therapy is based on the rational and evidence-based challenging and correction of faulty and dysfunctional thoughts and beliefs that are thought to underlie pathological fear, as described in detail earlier (e.g., Clark, 1999). In practice, behavioral techniques (i.e., ERP) are commonly implemented alongside of cognitive therapy strategies. The term *cognitive behavioral therapy* (CBT) was coined in response to the notion that cognitive therapy and ERP are complementary because they both affect change on the behavioral and cognitive levels.

As with ERP, cognitive therapy typically begins with the therapist presenting a treatment rationale that incorporates Beck's (1976) cognitive specificity model; the concept that one's *beliefs and appraisals* of situations and stimuli (not the situations and stimuli themselves) determine how one feels and acts. Patients are taught to examine their own beliefs and appraisals and appreciate how beliefs and interpretations influence their emotions and behaviors. Additionally, they are taught how modifying (or *correcting*) faulty beliefs and appraisals can help to alleviate their problems with anxiety and rituals.

Psychoeducation is an extremely important part of cognitive therapy because it is assumed that anxious patients lack objective knowledge about the true danger (or safety) of feared stimuli. For instance, in OCD, psychoeducation focuses on teaching the patient that his or her obsessional thoughts are in fact harmless—that is, they are not personally significant, indicative of responsibility for harm, signs of moral failing, or the like. Patients are taught to understand how misappraisal of such intrusions leads to preoccupation with the unwanted thought (as well as responses, such as avoidance and compulsive rituals), which unwittingly maintain the obsessional preoccupation and anxiety. In an analogous fashion, individuals with hypochondriasis are taught about the ubiquity of bodily sensations (e.g., Abramowitz & Braddock, 2008; Taylor & Asmundson, 2004). Generally, psychoeducation promotes therapeutic alliance by fostering an environment in which the client is active in identifying and conceptualizing the nature of his or her own problems and helps to facilitate willingness to correct mistaken beliefs in the next stage of treatment.

Various techniques are used to help clients correct their erroneous beliefs and appraisals, such as didactic presentation of additional educational material, Socratic dialogue aimed at helping patients recognize and correct dysfunctional thinking patterns, and gathering more objective evidence about feared stimuli. "Behavioral experiments," in which the patient enters and observes situations that exemplify his or her fears, are often used to facilitate the collection of information that will allow the patient to revise his or her judgments about the degree of risk associated with his or her fears and obsessions.

An example of a cognitive technique used in the treatment of OCD is the "pie technique" (Clark, 2004), which involves the client giving an initial estimate of the percent responsibility that would be attributable to them if a feared consequence were to occur. Next, the client generates a list of the parties (other than him- or herself) who would also have some responsibility for the feared consequence. They then draw a pie chart, each slice of which represents one of the responsible parties identified. Finally, the client labels all parties' slices according to their percent responsibility and labels her own slice last. By the exercise's end, it is generally clear to the patient that the majority of the responsibility for the feared event would not be her own.

For patients with BDD, a behavior experiment might involve striking up a conversation with someone and noticing how much the person appears preoccupied with the imagined defect, or how often the other individual stares at the imagined flaw. When these feared consequences don't actually occur (or occur less than anticipated), this can be used to help the patient reevaluate the likelihood that his or her beliefs about his or her appearance are accurate. In the case of hypochondriasis, a behavioral experiment might involve delaying reassurance seeking about bodily sensations to see that these sensations will naturally dissipate with time (along with the associated anxiety). Such a technique can be used to change catastrophic misperceptions of such sensations as malignant or long-term. This latter experiment resembles the type of interoceptive exposure and response prevention often used for individual with panic disorder. In turn, this raises the point that although there is some procedural overlap between many behavioral experiments and ERP, conceptually, these techniques are different. Behavioral experiments are primarily aimed at modifying dysfunctional beliefs, whereas ERP exercises are traditionally intended to bring about extinction of classically conditioned fear.

EFFICACY OF COGNITIVE THERAPY

Given the established effects of ERP, researchers interested in advancing cognitive therapy as a treatment that entails less direct exposure to fear triggers have conducted side-by-side horse-race comparisons of these two treatments. Largely, the results of these studies suggest that ERP and cognitive therapy have similar efficacy (e.g., Emmelkamp & Beens, 1991). However, interpretation of these results as indicating equivalent success for these two types of treatment is questionable. Exposure and response prevention and cognitive therapy both yield minimal improvements in the majority of studies (e.g., 30%–40% symptom reduction). One plausible explanation for this is that, in some of these studies, exposure practice was conducted exclusively as homework, without therapist supervision. Consequently, treatment outcome was likely attenuated and not representative of a complete treatment protocol. Moreover, the cognitive therapy programs in the aforementioned studies could have been enhanced by behavioral experiments, which likely have similar effects as supervised exposure. Using meta-analytic methods, Abramowitz, Franklin, and Foa (2002) found that behavioral experiments improve the efficacy of cognitive therapy for OCD. In other studies of OCD that incorporated in-session exposure within ERP protocols, the treatment based on behavioral theory appears to be superior to cognitive therapy.

A small number of case reports and controlled studies suggest that cognitive therapy (some involving behavioral techniques; i.e. CBT) can be effective for BDD (e.g., Rosen, Reiter, & Orosan, 1995). In their meta-analysis, Williams et al. (2006) reported a large treatment effect that was not significantly different from the effects found in ERP studies with BDD.

There is strong evidence that CBT, which combines cognitive therapy and exposure techniques, is an effective treatment for hypochondriasis (Taylor, Asmundson, & Coons, 2005). Several controlled studies demonstrate clinically significant and lasting improvements (e.g., Barsky & Ahern, 2004; Clark et al., 1998; Visser & Bouman, 2001). In a waitlist-controlled study, Warwick and colleagues (1996) found that CBT produced significant reductions in reassurance-seeking, overall health anxiety, and checking frequency. General anxiety was reduced by approximately 70%, and depressive symptoms by 53%. Moreover, CBT was acceptable to clients: only 6% of those recruited into the study refused to begin therapy, and another 6% dropped out of treatment prematurely.

In a study evaluating the relative effects of cognitive therapy and ERP, Visser and Bouman (2001) found that both treatments produced significant improvement relative to waiting list. Immediately following treatment, there were no differences between ERP and cognitive therapy. Improvement was also durable: at the 7-month follow-up assessment, patients remained improved, without significant differences between active treatments. Thus, the available evidence does not suggest substantial differences in the efficacy of ERP and cognitive therapy approaches for hypochondriasis. As we discussed earlier, with respect to OCD, a likely explanation for this is that these treatments incorporate elements of each other. That is, the effective implementation of ERP requires the implicit modification of dysfunctional beliefs that underlie anxiety and fear; and cognitive therapy typically involves exposure-like behavioral experiments in which patients confront feared situations to disconfirm dysfunctional beliefs and attitudes (Deacon & Abramowitz, 2004).

Conclusion

In the last hundred years, a great deal of progress has been made toward understanding the nature and origin of OCD, and in developing effective treatment for this condition. There has been a firm push by some members of the research community for the creation of an OCD spectrum of conditions thought to be strongly related to OCD proper. Although superficially it may seem appealing to conceptualize disorders such as compulsive gambling, Tourette syndrome, and trictollomania as variants or relatives of OCD, a deeper investigation into the relationship between these disorders and OCD reveals a cosmetic relationship at best. On the other hand, BDD and hypochondriasis do appear to be meaningfully related to OCD, both in terms of symptom presentation and treatment response. Although questions remain to be answered, cognitive and behavioral models of OCD, BDD, and hypochondriasis provide an empirically consistent account of the maintenance of these conditions, and researchers are working toward better understanding their (likely multifaceted) etiologies. Diagnostic tools, assessment strategies, and treatments based on research in the cognitive and behavioral traditions have also proven successful in properly identifying affected individuals, targets of treatment, and alleviating the symptoms of these disorders. Moreover, procedures such as ERP and cognitive therapy have demonstrated success in producing both short- and long-term treatment gains.

References

Abramowitz, J. S. (1997). Effectiveness of psychological and pharmacological treatments for obsessive-compulsive disorder: A quantitative review. *Journal of Consulting and Clinical Psychology, 65*, 44–52.

Abramowitz, J. S. (2006). *Understanding and treating obsessive-compulsive disorder: A cognitive-behavioral approach.* Mahwah, NJ: Erlbaum.

Abramowitz, J. S., & Braddock, A. E. (2008). *Psychological treatment of hypochondriasis and health anxiety: A biopsychosocial approach.* Cambridge, MA: Hogrefe & Huber.

Abramowitz, J. S., Deacon, B., Olatunji, B. O., Wheaton, M. G., Berman, N. C., Losardo, D. L. et al. (2010). Assessment of obsessive-compulsive symptoms: Development and evaluation of the Dimensional Obsessive-Compulsive Scale. *Psychological Assessment, 22*, 180–198.

Abramowitz, J. S., Franklin, M. E., & Foa, E. B. (2002). Empirical status of cognitive-behavioral therapy for obsessive-compulsive disorder: A meta-analytic review. *Romanian Journal of Cognitive and Behavioural Psychotherapies, 2*, 89–104.

Abramowitz, J. S., Nelson, C. A., Rygwall, & Khandker, M. (2007). The cognitive mediation of obsessive-compulsive symptoms: a longitudinal study. *Journal of Anxiety Disorders, 21*, 91–104.

Abramowitz, J. S., Khandker, M., Nelson, C., Deacon, B., & Rygwall, R. (2006). The role of cognitive factors in the pathogenesis of obsessions and compulsions: A prospective study. *Behaviour Research and Therapy, 44*, 1361–1374.

Abramowitz, J. S., & Moore, E. L. (2007). An experimental analysis of hypochondriasis. *Behaviour Research and Therapy, 45*, 413–424.

Abramowitz, J. S., Nelson, C. A., Rygwall, R., & Khandker, M. (2007). The cognitive mediation of obsessive-compulsive symptoms: a longitudinal study. *Journal of Anxiety Disorders, 21*, 91–104.

Abramowitz, J. S., Wheaton, M., & Storch, E. A. (2008). The status of hoarding as a symptom of obsessive-compulsive disorder. *Behaviour Research and Therapy, 46*, 1026–1033.

Abramowitz, J. S., Whiteside, S. P., Lynam, D., & Kalsy, S. A. (2003). Is thought-action fusion specific to obsessive-compulsive disorder: A mediating role of negative affect. *Behaviour Research and Therapy, 41*, 1069–1079.

American Psychiatric Association. (1987). *Diagnostic and statistical manual of mental disorders* (3rd ed., revised). Washington, DC: American Psychiatric Association.

American Psychiatric Association. (2000). *Diagnostic and statistical manual of mental disorders* (4th ed., text revision). Washington, DC: American Psychiatric Association.

Barsky, A.J., & Ahern, D.K. (2004). Cognitive behaviour therapy for hypochondriasis: A randomized controlled trial. *The Journal of the American Medical Association, 291(12)*, 1464–1470.

Beck, A. T. (1976). *Cognitive therapy of the emotional disorders.* New York: International Universities Press.

Beck, A. T., & Emery, G. (1985). *Anxiety disorders and phobias: a cognitive perspective.* New York: Basic Books.

Bienvenu O. J., Samuels, J. F., Riddle, M. A., Hoehn-Saric, R., Liang, K. Y., Cullen, B.A., et al. (2000). The relationship of obsessive-compulsive disorder to possible spectrum disorders: results from a family study. *Biological Psychiatry, 48*, 287–293.

Brown, T. A., Campbell, L. A., Lehman, C. L., Grisham, J. R., & Mancill, R. B. (2001). Current and lifetime comorbidity of the DSM-IV anxiety and mood disorders in a large clinical sample. *Journal of Abnormal Psychology, 110*, 585–599.

Buhlmann, U., McNally, R. J., Wilhelm, S., & Florin, I. (2002). Selective processing of emotional information in body Dysmorphic disorder. *Journal of Anxiety Disorders, 16*, 289–298.

Buhlmann, U., & Wilhelm, S. (2004). Cognitive factors in body dysmorphic disorder. *Psychiatric Annals, 34*, 922–926.

Campsi, T. A. (1995). Exposure and response prevention in the treatment of body dysmorphic disorder. *Dissertation abstracts international: Section B: The sciences and engineering, 56*, 7036.

Cororve, M. B., & Gleaves, D. H. (2001). Body dysmorphic disorder: A review of conceptualizations, assessment, and treatment strategies. *Clinical Psychology Review, 21*, 949–970.

Christenson, G. A., Mackenzie, T. B., Mitchell, J. E., Callies, A. L. (1991). A placebo controlled, double-blind crossover study of fluoxetine in trichotillomania. *American Journal of Psychiatry, 148*, 1566–1571.

Clark, D. A. (2004). *Cognitive-behavioral therapy for OCD.* New York: The Guilford Press.

Clark, D. M. (1999). Anxiety disorders: why they persist and how to treat them. *Behaviour Research & Therapy, 37*, S5–S27.

Clark, D.M., Salkovskis, P.M., Hackmann, A., Wells, A., Fennell, M., Ludgate, J., et al. (1998). Two psychological treatments for hypochondriasis: A randomized controlled trial. *British Journal of Psychiatry, 173*, 218–225.

Deacon, B.J., & Abramowitz, J.S. (2004). Cognitive and behavioral treatments for anxiety disorders: A review of meta-analytic findings. *Journal of Clinical Psychology, 60(4)*, 429–441.

Di Nardo, P., Brown, T., & Barlow, D. H. (1994). *Anxiety Disorders Interview Schedule for DSM-IV: Lifetime Version (ADIS-IV-LV).* San Antonio, TX: The Psychological Corporation.

Ditto, P. H., Jemmott, J. B., & Darley, J. M. (1988). Appraising the threat of illness: A mental representational approach. *Health Psychology, 7*, 183–201.

Easterling, D. V., & Leventhal, H. (1989). Contribution of concrete cognition to emotion: Neutral symptoms as elicitors of worry about cancer. *Journal of Applied Psychology, 74*, 787–796.

Eisen, J. L., Phillips, K. A., Baer, L., Beer, D. A., Atala, K. D., & Rasmussen, S. A. (1998). The Brown Assessment of Beliefs Scale: reliability and validity. *American Journal of Psychiatry, 155*, 102–108.

Emmelkamp, P. M. G., & Beens, H. (1991). Cognitive therapy with obsessive-compulsive disorder: A comparative evaluation. *Behaviour Research and Therapy, 29*, 293–300.

Fals-Stewart, W., Marks, A. P., & Schafer, J. (1993). A comparison of behavioral group therapy and individual behavior therapy in treating obsessive-compulsive disorder. *The Journal of Nervous and Mental Disease, 181*, 189–193.

First, M. B., Spitzer, R. L., Gibbon, M., & Williams, J. B.W. (2002). *Structured Clinical Interview for DSM-IV-TR Axis I Disorders.* New York: Biometrics Research, New York State Psychiatric Institute.

Foa, E. B., Amir, N., Gershuny, B., Molnar, C., & Kozak, M. (1997). Implicit and explicit memory in obsessive-compulsive disorder. *Journal of Anxiety Disorders, 11*, 119–129.

Foa, E. B., Liebowitz, M. R., Kozak, M. J., Davies, S., Campeas, R., Franklin, M. E., et al. (2005). Treatment of obsessive-compulsive disorder by exposure and ritual prevention, clomipramine, and their combination: A randomized, placebo controlled trial. *American Journal of Psychiatry, 162,* 151–161.

Foa, E. B., & Kozak, M. J. (1986). Emotional processing of fear: Exposure to corrective information. *Psychological Bulletin, 99,* 20–35.

Freeston, M. H., Ladouceur, R., Gagnon, F., & Thibodeau, N. (1993). Beliefs about obsessional thoughts. *Journal of Psychopathology and Behavioral Assessment, 15,* 1–21.

Frost, R. O., & Steketee, S. (2002). *Cognitive approaches to obsessions and compulsions: Theory, assessment, and treatment.* Oxford: Elsevier.

Goodman, W. K., Price, L. H., Rasmussen, S. A., Mazure, C., Delgado, P., Heninger, G. R., & Charney, D. S. (1989a). The Yale-Brown Obsessive Compulsive Scale: Validity. *Archives of General Psychiatry, 46,* 1012–1016.

Goodman, W. K., Price, L. H., Rasmussen, S. A., Mazure, C., Fleischmann, R. L., Hill, C. L., et al. (1989b). The Yale-Brown Obsessive Compulsive Scale: Development, use, and reliability. *Archives of General Psychiatry, 46,* 1006–1011.

Grant, J. E., & Potenza, M. N. (2004). Impulse control disorders: clinical characteristics and pharmacological management. *Annals of Clinical Psychiatry, 16,* 27–34.

Grocholewski A., Henry N., & Lingnau A. (2007). Selective attention in the facial area for people with a cosmetic medical treatment wishes. *Journal of Clinical Psychology and Psychotherapy, 36,* 57–66.

Haenen, M. A., Schmidt, A. J. M., Schoenmakers, M., & van den Hout, M. A. (1998). Quantitative and qualitative aspects of cancer knowledge: Comparing hypochondriacal subjects and healthy controls. *Psychology and Health, 13,* 1005–1014.

Hollander, E., Friedberg, J. P., & Wasserman, S. (2005). The Case for the OCD Spectrum. In J. S. Abramowitz, A. C. Houts (Eds.), *Concepts and controversies in obsessive-compulsive disorder* (pp. 95–118). New York: Springer Science.

Hollander, E., Kim, S., Khanna, S., & Pallanti, S. (2007). Obsessive-compulsive disorder and obsessive-compulsive spectrum disorders: Diagnostic and dimensional issues. *CNS Spectrums, 12,* 5–13.

Hyman, S. E. (2007). Can neuroscience be integrated into the DSM-5? *Nature Reviews: Neuroscience, 8,* 725–732.

Jaisoorya, T.S., Reddy, Y.C., & Srinath, S. (2003). The relationship of obsessive-compulsive disorder to putative spectrum disorders: results from an Indian study. *Comprehensive Psychiatry, 44,* 317–323.

Ladouceur, R., Rheaume, J., Freeston, M. H., Aublet, F., Jean, K., Lachance, S., et al. (1995). Experimental manipulations of responsibility: an analogue test for models of obsessive-compulsive disorder. *Behaviour Research and Therapy, 33,* 937–946.

Leckman, J. F., Hardin, M. T., Riddle, M. A., Stevenson, J., Ort, S. I., & Cohen, D. J. (1991). Clonidine treatment of Gilles de la Tourette's syndrome. *Archives of General Psychiatry, 48,* 324–328.

Lindsay, M., Crino, R., & Andrews, G. (1997). Controlled trial of exposure and response prevention in obsessive-compulsive disorder. *British Journal of Psychiatry, 171,* 135–139.

Logsdail, S., Lovell, K., Warwick, H., & Marks, I. (1991). Behavioral treatment of AIDS-focused illness phobia. *British Journal of Psychiatry, 159,* 422–425.

Lopatka, C., & Rachman, S. (1995). Perceived responsibility and compulsive checking: an experimental analysis. *Behaviour Research and Therapy, 33,* 673–684.

Lucock, M., White, C., Peake, M., & Morley, S. (1998). Biased perception and recall of reassurance in medical patients. *British Journal of Health Psychology, 3,* 237–243.

Mataix-Cols, D., Pertusa, A., & Leckman, J.F. (2007). Issues for DSM-5: How should obsessive-compulsive and related disorders be classified? *American Journal of Psychiatry,* 164(9), 1313–1314. [editorial]

McElroy, S. L., Hudson, J. I., Pope, H. G., Keck, P. E. (1991). Kleptomania: clinical characteristics and associated psychopathology. *Psychological Medicine, 21,* 93–108.

McElroy, S. L., Keck, P. E. Jr., Pope, H. G. Jr., & Hudson, J. I. (1989). Pharmacological treatment of kleptomania and bulimia nervosa. *Journal of Clinical Psychopharmacology, 9,* 358–60.

McKay, D., Abramowitz, J. S., Calamari, J., Kyrios, M., Sookman, D., Taylor, S., & Wilhelm, S. (2004). A critical evaluation of obsessive-compulsive disorder subtypes: Symptoms versus mechanisms. *Clinical Psychology Review, 24,* 283–313.

McNally, R. J., & Kohlbeck, P. A. (1993). Reality monitoring in obsessive-compulsive disorder. *Behaviour Research and Therapy, 31,* 249–253.

Meyer, V. (1966). Modification of expectations in cases with obsessional rituals. *Behaviour Research and Therapy, 4,* 273–280.

Meyer, V., Levy, R., & Schnurer, A. (1974). The behavioral treatment of obsessive-compulsive disorders. In H. R. Beech (Ed.), *Obsessional states* (pp. 233–258). London: Methuen.

Moskowitz, J.A. (1980). Lithium and lady luck: Use of lithium carbonate in compulsive gambling. *NY State Journal of Medicine, 80,* 785–788.

Mowrer, O. H. (1960). *Learning theory and behavior.* New York: Wiley.

Ninan, P. T., Rothbaum, B. O., Marsteller, F. A., Knight, B. T., & Eccard, M. B. (2000). A placebo-controlled trial of cognitive-behavioral therapy and clomipramine in trichotillomania. *Journal of Clinical Psychiatry, 61,* 47–50.

Obsessive Compulsive Cognitions Working Group. (2003). Psychometric validation of the Obsessive Beliefs Questionnaire and the Interpretation of Intrusions Inventory: Part I. *Behaviour Research & Therapy, 41,* 863–878.

Obsessive Compulsive Cognitions Working Group. (2005). Psychometric validation of the Obsessive Beliefs Questionnaire and the Interpretation of Intrusions Inventory: Part 2. *Behaviour Research and Therapy.*

O'Sullivan, R. L., Rauch, S. L., Brieter, H. C. (1997). Reduced basal ganglia volumes in trichotillomania measured via morphometric MRI. *Biological Psychiatry, 42,* 39–45.

Pennebaker, J. W. (1982). *The psychology of physical symptoms.* New York: Springer-Verlag.

Perugi, G., & Frare, F. (2005). Body dysmorphic disorder. In M. Maj, H.S. Akiskal, J.E. Mezzich, and A. Okasha (Eds.) Evidence and experience in psychiatry (pp. 191–221; Vol. 9). Chichester: Wiley.

Rachman, S. (1998). A cognitive theory of obsessions: elaborations. *Behaviour Research and Therapy, 36,* 385–401.

Rachman, S. (2003). *The treatment of obsessions.* Oxford, New York: Oxford University Press.

Rachman, S., & de Silva, P. (1978). Abnormal and normal obsessions. *Behaviour Research and Therapy, 16,* 233–248.

Rassin, E., Merckelbach, H., Muris, P., & Spaan, V. (1999). Thought-action fusion as a causal factor in the development of intrusions. *Behaviour Research and Therapy, 37,* 231–237.

Rief, W., Hiller, W., & Margraf, J. (1998). Cognitive aspects of hypochondriasis and the somatization syndrome. *Journal of Abnormal Psychology, 107*, 587–595.

Robbins, J. M., & Kirmayer, L. J. (1996). Transient and persistent hypochondriacal worry in primary care. *Psychological Medicine, 26*, 575–589.

Rosen, J. C. (1999). Cognitive-behavior therapy for body dysmorphic disorder. In V. E. Caballo (Ed.). *International handbook of cognitive and behavioral treatments for psychological disorders* (pp. 363–391). Oxford: Pergamon.

Rosen, J.C., Reiter, J., & Orosan, P. (1995). Cognitive–behavioral therapy for body dysmorphic disorder. *Journal of Consulting and Clinical Psychology, 63*, 263–269.

Salkovskis, P. M. (1985). Obsessional-compulsive problems: a cognitive-behavioural analysis. *Behaviour Research and Therapy, 23*, 571–583.

Salkovskis, P. M. (1989). Cognitive-behavioural factors and the persistence of intrusive thoughts in obsessional problems. *Behaviour Research and Therapy, 27*, 677–682.

Salkovskis, P. M., Rimes, K. A., Warwick, H. M., & Clark, D. M. (2002). The Health Anxiety Inventory: Development and validation of scales for the measurement of health anxiety and hypochondriasis. *Psychological Medicine, 32*, 843–853.

Salkovskis, P. M., Shafran, R., Rachman, S., & Freeston, M. H. (1999). Multiple pathways to inflated responsibility beliefs in obsessional problems: possible origins and implications for therapy and research. *Behaviour Research and Therapy, 37*, 1055–1072.

Salkovskis, P. M., Wroe, A. L., Gledhill, A., Morrison, N., Forrester, E., Richards, C., et al. (2000). Responsibility attitudes and interpretations are characteristic of obsessive compulsive disorder. *Behaviour Research and Therapy, 38*, 347–372.

Shafran, R., Thordarson, D. S., & Rachman, S. (1996). Thought-action fusion in obsessive compulsive disorder. *Journal of Anxiety Disorders, 10*, 379–391.

Sheehan, D., Lecrubier, Y, Harnett-Sheehan, K., Amoriam, P., Janavs, J., Weiller, E., et al. (1998). The Mini International Neuropsychiatric Interview (M.I.N.I.): The development and validation of a structured diagnostic interview for DSM-IV and ICD-10. *Journal of Clinical Psychiatry, 59 (Suppl 20)*, 22–33.

Stein, D. J., Coetzer, R., & Lee, M. (1997). Magnetic resonance brain imaging in women with obsessive-compulsive disorder and trichotillomania. *Psychiatry Research, 74*, 177–182.

Streichenwein, S. M., & Thornby, J. I. (1995). A long-term, double-blind, placebo-controlled crossover trial of the efficacy of fluoxetine for trichotillomania. *American Journal of Psychiatry, 152*, 1192–1196.

Summerfeldt, L., Hood, K., Antony, M., Richter, M., & Swinson, R. (2004). Impulsivity in obsessive-compulsive disorder: Comparisons with other anxiety disorders and within tic-related subgroups. *Personality and Individual Differences, 36*, 539–553.

Taylor, S., & Asmundson, G. (2004). *Treating health anxiety: A cognitive-behavioral approach.* New York: Guilford.

Taylor, S., Asmundson, G., & Coons, M. (2005). Current directions in the treatment of hypochondriasis. *Journal of Cognitive Psychotherapy, 19*, 285–304.

Taylor, S., Thordarson, D. S., Jang, K. L., & Asmundson, G. J. G. (2006). Genetic and environmental origins of health anxiety: A twin study. *World Psychiatry, 5*, 47–50.

Tolin, D. F., Hamlin, C., & Foa, E. B. (2002). Directed forgetting in obsessive-compulsive disorder: Replication and extension. *Behaviour Research and Therapy, 40*, 792–803.

Van Minnen, A., Hoogduin, K. A., Keijsers, G. P., Hellenbrand, I., & Hendriks, G. J. (2003). Treatment of trichotillomania with behavioral therapy or fluoxetine: a randomized, waiting-list controlled study. *Archives of General Psychiatry, 60*, 517–522.

Veale, D. (2004). Advances in a cognitive behavioral model of body dysmorphic disorder. *Body Image, 1*, 113–125.

Visser, S., & Bouman, T.K. (1992). Cognitive-behavioral approaches in the treatment of hypochondriasis: Six single case cross-over studies. *Behavior Research and Therapy, 30*, 301–306.

Visser, S., & Bouman, T.K. (2001). The treatment of hypochondriasis: Exposure plus response prevention vs. cognitive therapy. *Behavior Research and Therapy, 39*, 423–442.

Warwick, H.M., Clark, D.M., Cobb, A.M., & Salkovskis, P.M. (1996). A controlled trial of cognitive-behavioral treatment of hypochondriasis. *British Journal of Psychiatry, 169*, 189–195.

Warwick, H.M., & Marks, I.M. (1988). Behavioural treatment of illness phobia and hypochondriasis: A pilot study of 17 cases. *British Journal of Psychiatry, 152*, 239–241.

Warwick, H., & Salkovskis, P. (1990). Hypochondriasis. *Behaviour Research and Therapy, 28*, 105–117.

Whitehead, W. E., Crowell, M. D., Heller, B. R., Robinson, J. C., Schuster, M. M., & Horn, S. (1994). Modeling and reinforcement of the sick role during childhood predicts adult illness behavior. *Psychosomatic Medicine, 56*, 541–550.

Whiteside, S. P., Port, J. D., & Abramowitz, J. S. (2004). A meta-analysis of functional neuroimaging in obsessive-compulsive disorder. *Psychiatry Research, 32*, 69–79.

Wilhelm, S., Buhlmann, U., & McNally, R. J. (2003). Negative priming for threatening versys nonthreatening information in body dysmorphic disorder. *Acta Neuropsychiatrica, 1*, 180–183.

Wilhelm, S., McNally, R., Baer, L., & Florin, I. (1996). Directed forgetting in obsessive-compulsive disorder. *Behaviour Research and Therapy, 34*, 633–641.

Williams, J., Hadjistavropolous, T., & Sharpe, D. (2006). A mete-analysis of psychological and pharmacological treatments for body dysmorphic disorder. *Behaviour Research and Therapy, 44*, 99–111.

Woods, C. M., Vevea, J. L., Chambless, D. L., & Bayen, U. J. (2002). Are compulsive checkers impaired in memory? a meta-analytic review. *Clinical Psychology: Science and Practice, 9*, 353–366.

Somatoform and Physical Disorders

Robert L. Woolfolk *and* Lesley A. Allen

Abstract

This chapter provides an overview of the treatment of somatoform and related disorders. A brief history of the disorder is provided, along with a sociocultural framework in which to conceptualize somatization. The epidemiology of somatoform disorders is discussed. Empirical research evaluating psychosocial treatments for somatoform disorders, including the functional somatic syndromes, is reviewed and critiqued. The rather substantial assortment of treatment options available to clinicians is compared and contrasted, and their level of empirical support evaluated. The limitations of the empirical literature, as well as the treatment implications that can be drawn, are discussed.

Keywords: Cognitive-behavioral therapy, functional somatic syndromes, medically unexplained physical symptoms, mind-body, psychosomatic, psychotherapy, somatization, somatoform

Somatization is among the most puzzling phenomena that health-care workers encounter. In somatization, physical symptoms occur in the absence of any identifiable bodily mechanism. The causes of somatization that we are able to implicate are neither proximate nor identifiably somatic. Patients presenting with medically unexplained physical symptoms (MUPS) provide significant challenges to health-care providers. These patients tend to overuse health-care services, derive little benefit from treatment, and experience protracted impairment, often lasting many years (Smith, Monson, & Ray, 1986a). Often, MUPS patients are dissatisfied with the medical services they receive and repeatedly change physicians (Lin et al., 1991). These "treatment-resistant" patients frustrate physicians with their frequent complaints and dissatisfaction with treatment (Hahn, 2001; Lin et al., 1991). Because standard medical care has been relatively unsuccessful in treating somatoform and factitious disorders, alternative treatments have been developed.

The chapter summarizes and evaluates the treatment of various somatoform and factitious disorders.

All the somatoform and factitious disorders are characterized by the presence of physical symptom(s) that suggest a general medical condition but are not fully explained by a general medical condition. Somatoform disorders differ from factitious disorders in the extent to which the symptoms are intentionally produced or feigned. Symptoms related to a factitious disorder are intentionally produced or feigned in order to assume the sick role. Symptoms related to a somatoform disorder are not under voluntary control.

Background: Historical and Theoretical

The history of somatization begins with hysteria, first described 4,000 years ago by the Egyptians and later elaborated and named by the Greeks. Typical cases involved pain in the absence of any injury or pathology in the location of the pain. The Greco-Egyptian formulation reveals two noteworthy features: that the disorder was primarily observed in females, and that there was something thought to be essentially female about the disorder. Foucault (1961/1965) suggests that, by the end of the 18th century, hysteria and hypochondria were beginning to be viewed as "diseases of the nerves," akin to such recognized mental disorders as melancholia. Before the 19th century, because of the heterogeneous nature of hysterical symptoms and the hypothesized connection with the emotions, physicians had begun to allege that these symptoms were feigned or imagined (Woolfolk & Allen, 2007). The unsympathetic attitudes of contemporary health-care workers toward somatizers and the tendency to regard these patients as malingerers can be traced to this period in the history of medicine.

A landmark in the descriptive psychopathology of somatization was the seminal monograph of Paul Briquet (1859), *Triate Clinique et Therapeutique de L'hysterie*. Our current conception of somatization disorder derives directly from this paper. Briquet's meticulous and exhaustive listing of the symptomatology of hysteria remains unsurpassed. Briquet, in fact, described three related syndromes: conversion phenomena, hysterical personality, and multiple chronic unexplained somatic symptoms (Dongier, 1983; Mai & Merskey, 1980). These three syndromes overlapped in symptomatology somewhat, and they often were observed to co-occur. Briquet's perspicuous work was revived by Purtell, Robins, and Cohen (1951) and developed further by members of the illustrious Washington University department of psychiatry. Perley and Guze (1962) published a list of 57 symptoms, commonly reported by women diagnosed with hysteria, symptoms that were clustered in ten different areas. These investigators were the first to suggest specific criteria for the diagnosis of hysteria: the presence of 25 symptoms from at least nine of the ten symptom areas (Guze, 1967). Later, this list of 57 symptoms was expanded to include 59 symptoms and the term *Briquet's syndrome* was adopted (Guze, Woodruff, & Clayton, 1972). The criteria for Briquet's syndrome were incorporated into the Feighner criteria (Feighner, Robins, Guze, Woodruff, Winokur, & Munoz, 1972), the precursor to the symptom set that appeared in the third edition of the *Diagnostic and Statistical Manual of Mental Disorders* (DSM-III; American Psychiatric Association [APA], 1980). In that volume, the theoretically neutral term, *somatization*, was preferred over the more traditional terminology. Although some of the traditional language remains in the fourth edition of the DSM (e.g., "conversion disorder"), the word "hysteria" no longer appears (DSM-IV; APA, 1994). The ninth edition of the World Health Organization's International Classification of Diseases (ICD-9; WHO, 1979), a more cosmopolitan nosology of somatic and mental disorders published a year earlier than DSM-III, retains much of the perennial terminology, including not only hysteria but also "neurasthenia."[1] ICD-10 (World Health Organization, 1993) has shifted in the direction of the American volume, although without banishing every bit of the classical vocabulary.

Psychodynamic Roots

Many of Sigmund Freud's early patients were hysterics. His first book, co-authored with Breuer, was entitled *Studies in Hysteria* (1895/1974), in which Breuer and Freud developed the concept of "conversion," a process whereby intrapsychic activity putatively brings about somatic symptoms. This work also introduced the notion of a physical symptom as an unconscious form of communication, as a device for securing secondary gain, or as a means for avoiding emotional pain.

Franz Alexander (1950) was a contributor to the psychoanalytic literature and an important figure in what was, in the mid 20th century, called "psychosomatic medicine." He distinguished between two types of psychosomatic symptoms: those cases in which psychological conflict was "converted" and communicated symbolically through physical symptoms, and those cases in which the somatic symptoms resulted from the direct and indirect physiological effects of emotional arousal. This second kind of psychosomatic mechanism required few, if any, psychoanalytic assumptions and was quite compatible with mainstream scientific research, especially the work of Cannon, Seyle, and others on psychosocial stress. As psychoanalysis declined in influence, psychosomatic medicine declined also. Today, the term "psychosomatic," which was faddish in the 1950s, is no longer in vogue. Many of the problems once treated within the context of psychosomatic medicine now fall under the purview of what is, in some sense, its successor discipline, behavioral medicine.

---

[1] ICD-10 *Neurasthenia* is defined as persistent and distressing feelings of exhaustion after minor mental or physical effort accompanied by one or more of the following symptoms: muscular aches or pains, dizziness, tension headache, sleep disturbance, inability to relax, and irritability. The term was coined in 1856, by Robert Mayne and popularized by the American neurologist George Beard during the second half of the 19th century (Gijswijt-Hofstra & Porter, 2001).

Sociocultural and Conceptual Issues

Historically, in Western psychiatry, a mental disorder has been posited in one of two instances. The first of these occurs when there exists a theory of psychogenesis, such as psychoanalysis, that hypothesizes mental entities to be the underlying causes of the symptoms of a disorder. The second instance involves the presence of symptoms in the absence of a physicalistic explanation. In this second instance, psychogenic etiology may be inferred solely from the absence of a known underlying physical mechanism, thus revealing a tacit dualism that originated even before Paracelsus and that continues to underlie Western medicine: Disease entities, whether they be causes or symptoms, belong to one and only one of two categories, either the physical or the mental—these two categories being mutually exclusive (Robinson, 1996). Symptoms of almost any variety that cannot be linked to a scientifically explained physical pathology are assumed to be psychogenic. Individuals afflicted with multiple sclerosis, Wilson disease, temporal lobe epilepsy, and numerous other maladies currently within the purview of somatic medicine were once regarded as mentally ill. Through the course of medical progress, mental illness has served as a residual category wherein poorly understood or refractory illness has been placed, often temporarily, only to exit when medical science established the physical mechanisms underlying the disorder (Grob, 1991).

Dualistic assumptions operate not so subtly within DSM-IV. In DSM-IV, two principal classes of disease entities are posited: general medical conditions and primary mental disorders. Contradistinct from the most paradigmatic mental disorders contained in DSM-IV are mental symptoms resulting from a "general medical condition" (read physical illness). Such symptoms arising from such causes, indeed, imply the absence of a mental disorder. Of course, DSM-IV's authors claim that the distinction between primary mental disorders and those stemming from a general medical condition should not be taken to imply that there are fundamental differences between mental disorders and general medical conditions (APA, 1994, p. 165). But the volume is careful to distinguish symptoms deriving from a general medical disorder from those that emanate from a primary mental disorder. This distinction is drawn so sharply that symptoms of organic origin are exclusionary for the diagnosis of such paradigmatic disorders as schizophrenia. The locution of the volume instantiates not only dualism, but also logical circularity, in that a general medical condition is defined as a medical condition

other than a primary mental disorder, and a primary mental disorder is defined as something other than the result of a general medical condition. The distinction drawn here, whether nominal or substantive, is old Cartesian wine in a new bottle, that venerable distinction between the functional and the organic. In its language, DSM-IV also stipulates, as a kind of axiom, the historical role of psychiatry as a processor of aberrations within the category of illness. Mental illnesses are abnormal, poorly understood illnesses that normal physicians do not treat.

The biopsychosocial concept of illness, proposed by George Engel (1977) and to which the authors of this chapter subscribe, suggests that illness is a complex entity involving the interplay of physical, psychological, and cultural factors. In particular, many illnesses cannot be adequately comprehended without taking into account the social contexts in which they develop, are manifested, diagnosed, and treated. What phenomena that societies come to label "illness" or how human suffering is expressed and presented to healers are complicated matters that can be conceptualized at several different levels, levels that involve variables that interact causally.

Research on psychopathology in countries outside of North America and Europe frequently is used to argue that cultural factors are crucial in determining the manner in which human suffering is experienced and, more specifically, to support the view that non-Western societies are prone to generate somatic expressions of distress. One distinction that is made in cross-cultural theory is that between somatization and "psychologization." The former refers to the experience of bodily aspects of distress, whereas the latter refers to the experience of the psychic, social, and mental aspect of distress (Kirmayer, 1984; White, 1982). According to this formulation, either somatization or psychologization could serve as alternative modalities through which a negative emotional reaction is experienced and as alternative "idioms of distress" through which emotional pain is communicated. It has been suggested that psychologization is compatible with Western, Euro American concepts of selfhood and with an individualistic, psychologically minded world view that emphasizes causal explanations implicating individual persons and their traits as sources of events (Kihlstrom & Canter Kihlstrom, 1999; Kirmayer, Young, & Robbins, 1994). Somatization, in contrast, has been associated with the more sociocentric cultural views of selfhood, wherein self-reflection and self-examination are de-emphasized or disvalued; here, behavior is more often viewed as caused by the external environment, rather than by qualities of the person, such as psychological traits or will-power. Other factors that might influence the ratio of psychologization to somatization are the stigma attached to psychological symptoms and the degree to which a desired treatment is obtained through either a psychological or a somatic presentation (Kirmayer, 2001). According to this view, a culture's background assumptions about illness or its "idiom of distress" is crucial to determining whether a disruption of homeostasis is experienced as physical rather than mental. An individual can learn to attend to and express physical discomfort, rather than psychological distress, especially if an idiom of affect is not available. Thus, the theory has it that somatization conditions can be shaped through processes of selective attention to physical symptoms and by learning a vocabulary of somatic symptomatology.

Whether there are cultures that foster somatization is still a complex and controversial question. The World Health Organization's international collaborative study of Psychological Problems in General Health Care (Gureje, Simon, Ustun, & Goldberg, 1997) did not find the disparity in somatization disorders between East and West that might have been predicted from the early formulations of medical anthropologists. Nor did the ratio of somatic to psychological symptoms of depression vary across cultures in a systematic or expected fashion. However, the data were, to some degree, consistent with the cultural hypothesis. For example, somatization rates were significantly higher in Latin America than in the rest of the world, and rates of somatization were higher in China than in the United States (Simon, VonKorff, Piccinelli, Fullerton, & Ormel, 1999). Cultural variation in psychopathology results not only from differences in how psychiatric labels are applied, but from the fact that different societies seem to produce different forms of psychopathology. Many specific syndromes are unique to particular cultural contexts, such as *ataque de nervios*, *koro*, or *taijin kyofusho*.[2] The epidemics of anorexia nervosa and bulimia in the contemporary West are unprecedented, but are spreading to middle and upper classes around the world, along with Westernization and its current aesthetic ideal of a slender female body (Ung & Lee, 1999). Writers such as Ian Hacking (1995; 1999) have argued persuasively that some mental disorders (e.g., multiple

personality disorder) are roles that are created by the theories and practices of the mental health professions and subsequently enacted by patients. The articulation and dissemination of information about psychopathology through professional activities and by the media provide a symptom set and patient profile that can be assimilated by disturbed individuals who possess sufficient psychic malleability (Woolfolk, 1998).

Models of Somatization

It has not been since the psychoanalytic era that somatization was viewed as a well-understood phenomenon. In some sense, we have not progressed very far beyond Breuer and Freud's psychodynamic theory of conversion hysteria. Currently, there is widespread admission among authorities that no adequate theory of somatization exists. Indeed, one might argue that, with the exception of the oft-criticized and scientifically beleaguered psychoanalytic theory, there are no well-developed theories of somatization, rather merely some fragmentary models or speculation.

In evaluating models of somatization, one needs to be mindful of the logical pitfalls that abound in the territory of mind–body relationships. As we have seen in conjecture about the cause of somatization, such phrases as "emotional distress expressed as physical symptoms" or a "somatic idiom of distress" or a tendency to "somatize rather than psychologize" are invoked. Such locutions are problematic and bespeak the poverty of our theories, as they invariably risk the possibility of emerging as either pseudo-explanatory or tautologous. Such formulations often fail to explain because they leave key terms undefined and unexplained. We have seen this kind of fallacious logic before in psychiatric discourse that utilizes the notion of "chemical imbalance" in explanations of the treatment of depression (i.e., a prior chemical imbalance being inferred from a presumptive "balancing" of neurochemistry by antidepressants). Key concepts that are unexplained can result in circular reasoning, illustrated by Moliere's physician who attributed the effect of a soporific to its "dormative powers." A cogent explanation of somatization must spell out exactly what is denoted by the "emotional distress" that is putatively "expressed" somatically and also include valid and reliable methods for measuring it. Can the emotional distress thought to underlie somatization be identified independently of the somatic expression of it? If not, what is the epistemological status of our model or theory? Are we simply assuming a priori that there is some

---

[2] Each of these "culture specific syndromes" comprises somatic and psychological symptoms.

emotional basis for any unexplained physical symptom? If so, we have engaged in question begging rather than explanation.

Fortunately for scientists, health-care providers, and patients, various diagnoses and the forms of psychotherapy and pharmacotherapy applied are warranted, for the most part, by practical, empirical results. There are few cases in psychiatry in which a treatment can be shown to produce clinical benefits because it affects a well-understood mechanism that is implicated conclusively in pathogenesis. We simply do not have theories or models of mental disorders that have been validated in the manner of our theories of, for example, infectious diseases. Our technologies of healing typically are legitimized, not by the verification of the underlying theory, but by the efficacies of these technologies. Research on treatments for mental disorders is much more akin to industrial practices of "product testing" than to theory-based applied science. Fortunately for all of us, effective clinical interventions need not wait upon validated scientific theories of psychiatric disorder. We and our colleagues of today, as did the empirics of old, put our money on pragmatic, observable results of interventions, as opposed to armchair speculation about the true nature of things.

Somatization Disorder and Subthreshold Somatization
Overview of Diagnostic Criteria and Prevalence

Somatization disorder is the contemporary conceptualization of a syndrome that was once labeled hysteria and, more recently, Briquet's syndrome. The criteria for Briquet's syndrome were symptoms associated with a diagnosis of hystera and were incorporated into the Feighner diagnostic criteria (Feighner et al., 1972) that were the precursor to DSM-III. According to the current DSM (DSM-IV, APA, 1994), somatization disorder is characterized by a lifetime history of at least four unexplained pain complaints (e.g., in the back, chest, joints), two unexplained nonpain gastrointestinal complaints (e.g., nausea, bloating), one unexplained sexual symptom (e.g., sexual dysfunction, irregular menstruation), and one pseudoneurological symptom (e.g., seizures, paralysis, numbness). For a symptom to be counted toward the diagnosis of somatization disorder, its presence must be medically unexplained or its degree of severity be substantially in excess of the associated medical pathology. Also, each symptom must either prompt the seeking of medical care or interfere with

the patient's functioning. In addition, at least some of the somatization symptoms must have occurred prior to the patient's 30th birthday (APA, 1994). The course of somatization disorder tends to be characterized by symptoms that wax and wane, remitting only to return later and/or be replaced by new unexplained physical symptoms. Thus, somatization disorder is a chronic, polysymptomatic disorder whose requisite symptoms need not be manifested concurrently.

Epidemiological research suggests that somatization disorder is relatively rare. The prevalence of somatization disorder in the general population has been estimated to be 0.1%–0.7% (Faravelli et al., 1997; Robins & Reiger, 1991; Weissman, Myers, & Harding, 1978). When patients in primary care, specialty medical, and psychiatric settings are assessed, the rate of somatization is higher than in the general population, with estimates ranging from 1% to 5% (Altamura et al., 1998; Fabrega, Mezzich, Jacob, & Ulrich, 1988; Fink, Steen Hansen, & S ndergaard, 2005; Gureje, Simon et al., 1997; Kirmayer & Robbins, 1991; Peveler, Kilkenny, & Kinmonth, 1997).

Although somatization disorder is classified as a distinct disorder in DSM-IV, it has been argued that somatization disorder represents the extreme end of a somatization continuum (Escobar, Burnam, Karno, Forsythe, & Golding, 1987; Kroenke et al., 1997). Research suggests that the number of unexplained physical symptoms reported correlates positively with the patient's degree of emotional distress and functional impairment (Katon, Lin, Von Korff, Russo, Lipscomb, & Bush, 1991). A broadening of the somatization construct has been advocated by those wishing to underscore the many patients encumbered by unexplained symptoms that are not numerous enough to meet criteria for full somatization disorder (Escobar, Burnham et al., 1987; Katon et al., 1991; Kroenke et al., 1997).

DSM-IV includes a residual diagnostic category for subthreshold somatization cases. *Undifferentiated somatoform disorder* is a diagnosis characterized by one or more medically unexplained physical symptom(s) lasting for at least 6 months (APA, 1994). Long considered a category that is too broad because it includes patients with only one unexplained symptom, as well as those with many unexplained symptoms, undifferentiated somatoform disorder never has been well-validated or widely applied (Kroenke, Sharpe, & Sykes, 2007).

Two research teams have suggested categories for subthreshold somatization using criteria less restrictive and requiring less extensive symptomatology than the standards for DSM-IV's full somatization disorder.

Escobar and colleagues proposed the label *abridged somatization* to be applied to men experiencing four or more unexplained physical symptoms or to women experiencing six or more unexplained physical symptoms (Escobar, Burnam et al., 1987). Kroenke et al. suggested the category of *multisomatoform disorder* to describe men or women currently experiencing at least three unexplained physical symptoms and reporting a 2-year history of somatization (Kroenke et al., 1997).

Both of these subthreshold somatization categories appear to be significantly more prevalent than is *somatization disorder* as defined by DSM-IV. Abridged somatization has been observed in 4% of community samples (Escobar, Burnam et al., 1987) and 16%–22% of primary care samples (Escobar, Waitzkin, Silver, Gara, & Holman, 1998; Gureje, Simon et al., 1997; Kirmayer & Robbins, 1991). The occurrence of multisomatoform disorder has been estimated at 8% of primary care patients (Kroenke et al., 1997; Jackson & Kroenke, 2008).

Demographic and Clinical Characteristics

The demographic characteristic most often associated with somatization is gender. In the Epidemiological Catchment Area (ECA) study, women were ten times more likely to meet criteria for somatization disorder than were men (Swartz, Landermann, George, Blazer, & Escobar, 1991). Higher rates of occurrence in women, although not as extreme, also have been found in most studies employing subthreshold somatization categories, such as Escobar's abridged somatization or Kroenke's multisomatoform disorder (Escobar, Rubio-Stipec, Canino, & Karno, 1989; Kroenke et al., 1997). A more complex picture of the association between gender and somatization was suggested by the WHO's Cross-National study, in which female primary care patients were more likely to meet criteria for full somatization disorder, but no more likely to meet Escobar's abridged somatization criteria than were their male counterparts (Gureje, Simon, et al., 1997). On the severe end of the continuum, somatization disorder is uncommon in men. Gender differences are less obvious in the various subthreshold syndromes.

Ethnicity, race, and education have been associated with somatization disorder and subthreshold somatization. Epidemiological research has shown somatization patients more likely to be female, non-white, and less educated than nonsomatizers (Gureje, Simon, et al., 1997; Robins & Reiger, 1991). Findings on ethnicity have been less consistent across studies.

In the ECA study, Hispanics were no more likely to meet criteria for somatization disorder than were non-Hispanics (Robins & Reiger, 1991). The WHO study, conducted in 14 different countries, revealed a higher incidence of both somatization, as defined by either ICD-10 or Escobar's abridged criteria, in Latin American countries than in the United States (Gureje, Simon et al., 1997).

Much attention has focused on somatization patients' illness behavior and the resulting impact of that behavior on the health-care system. These patients disproportionately use and misuse health-care services. When standard diagnostic evaluations fail to uncover organic pathology, somatization patients tend to seek additional medical procedures, often from several different physicians. Patients may even subject themselves to unnecessary hospitalizations and surgeries, which introduce the risk of iatrogenic illness (Fink, 1992). One study found that somatization disorder patients, on average, incurred nine times the U.S. per capita health-care cost (Smith et al., 1986a). Abridged somatization and multisomatoform disorder also have been associated with significant health-care utilization (Kroenke et al., 1997; Escobar, Golding, Hough, Karno, Burnam, & Wells, 1987).

The abnormal illness behavior of somatizing patients extends beyond medical offices and hospitals to patients' workplaces and households. Somatizers withdraw from both productive and pleasurable activities because of discomfort, fatigue, and/or fears of exacerbating their symptoms. In a study assessing the efficacy of cognitive behavior therapy (CBT) for somatization disorder, we found 19% of patients meeting DSM-IV criteria for somatization disorder to be receiving disability payments from either their employers or the government (Allen, Woolfolk, Escobar, Gara, & Hamer, 2006). Estimates of unemployment among somatization disorder patients range from 36% to 83% (Allen et al., 2006; Smith et al., 1986a; Yutzy et al., 1995). Whether working outside their homes or not, these patients report substantial functional impairment. Some investigators have found that somatization disorder patients report being bedridden for 2 to 7 days per month (Katon et al., 1991; Smith et al., 1986a). Likewise, high levels of functional impairment have been associated with subthreshold somatization (Allen, Gara, Escobar, Waitzkin, Cohen-Silver, 2001; Escobar, Golding, Hough, Karno, Burnam, & Wells, 1987; Gureje, Simon, et al., 1997; Jackson & Kroenke, 2008; Kroenke et al., 1997).

In addition to their physical complaints, many somatization patients complain of psychiatric distress. As many as 80% of patients meeting criteria for somatization disorder or subthreshold somatization meet DSM criteria for another lifetime Axis I disorder, usually an anxiety or mood disorder (Smith et al., 1986a; Swartz, Blazer, George, & Landerman, 1986). When investigators consider only current psychiatric diagnoses, rates of psychiatric comorbidity associated with somatization are closer to 50% (Allen et al., 2001; Simon & VonKorff, 1991). Also, overall severity of psychological distress, defined as the number of psychological symptoms reported, correlates positively with the number of functional somatic symptoms reported (Katon et al., 1991; Simon & VonKorff, 1991).

Treatment

Several different psychosocial interventions have been used to treat somatization, some administered by mental health providers and others administered by non–mental health providers. All approaches seem to have been theoretically grounded in social learning theory. The studies are reviewed below.

Three studies have compared the efficacy of individually administered CBT with standard medical care for patients manifesting a diverse set of unexplained physical symptoms. Only one study has been published treating patients meeting DSM-IV criteria for full somatization disorder (Allen et al., 2006). Two studies were conducted in primary care settings with patients who were diagnosed with subthreshold somatization, defined as abridged somatization in one study (Escobar et al., 2007) and defined as five or more unexplained physical symptoms in the other (Sumathipala, Hewege, Hanwella, & Mann, 2000).

All three studies showed that individual CBT coincided with greater reductions in somatic complaints than did standard medical care (Allen et al., 2006; Escobar et al., 2007; Sumathipala et al., 2000). Allen et al. found that 40% of their CBT-treated participants, versus 7% of the control group, were judged to have achieved clinically significant improvement, defined as being "very much improved" or "much improved" on a clinician-rated scale of somatization severity (Allen et al., 2006). Also, CBT was associated with enhanced physical functioning in that study (Allen et al., 2006) and reduced health-care utilization in two studies (Allen et al., 2006; Sumathipala et al., 2000). Long-term maintenance of symptom relief was demonstrated in two studies; one showed significant differences in

somatization symptomatology 6 months after treatment completion (Escobar et al., 2007), and the other showed that symptom improvement lasted for 12 months after the treatment phase of the study (Allen et al., 2006).

Two groups of investigators have conducted controlled treatment trials assessing the efficacy of CBT with a less severely disturbed group of patients, those complaining of at least one "psychosomatic" symptom. In one study, patients treated with individual CBT showed greater improvement in their psychosomatic complaints than did patients treated with standard medical care (Speckens et al., 1995). The other study found group CBT, led by a trained physician, superior to a waiting-list control condition in reducing physical symptoms and hypochondriacal beliefs (Lidbeck, 1997). In both studies, improvements were observed after treatment as well as 6 months later (Lidbeck, 1997; Speckens et al., 1995). Lidbeck's CBT participants seemed to maintain reductions in somatization and hypochondriacal beliefs 18 months after treatment (Lidbeck, 2003).

Other approaches to the treatment of somatization have been focused on primary care physicians' behavior. Smith and colleagues sent a psychiatric consultation letter to patients' primary care physicians, describing somatization disorder and providing recommendations to guide primary care (Smith, Monson, & Ray, 1986b). The recommendations to physicians were straightforward: (a) to schedule somatizers' appointments every 4–6 weeks, instead of "as needed" appointments, (b) to conduct a physical examination in the organ system or body part relevant to the presenting complaint, (c) to avoid diagnostic procedures and surgeries unless clearly indicated by underlying somatic pathology, and (d) to avoid making disparaging statements, such as "your symptoms are all in your head." Patients whose primary physicians had received the consultation letter experienced better health outcomes (physical functioning and cost of medical care) than did those whose physicians had not received the letter. The results were replicated in three additional studies, one study using patients meeting criteria for full somatization disorder (Rost, Kashner, & Smith, 1994) and two studies using patients with subthreshold somatization (Dickinson, Dickinson, deGruy, Main, Candib, & Rost, 2003; Smith, Rost, & Kashner, 1995).

One other study examined the effect of group psychotherapy conducted in the primary care setting on the physical and emotional functioning of patients meeting DSM criteria for full somatization disorder. In this study, the group treatment was developed to provide peer support, psychoeducation, and coping skills, and to encourage emotional expression. This group intervention, in combination with standard medical care augmented by the psychiatric consultation letter described earlier, was associated with significantly greater improvements in physical functioning and mental health than was the control condition—that is, standard medical treatment augmented by the psychiatric consultation letter (Kashner, Rost, Cohen, Anderson, & Smith, 1995).

Given the success of this consultation letter, the success of CBT, and the difficulties involved in distinguishing between medically explained and medically unexplained symptoms, some investigators have attempted to train primary care physicians to better detect somatization and to incorporate cognitive-behavioral techniques into their treatment of these patients. Three groups have reported controlled clinical trials on the effects of such physician training (Larisch, Schweickhardt, Wirsching, & Fritzsche, 2004; Rief, Martin, Rauh, Zech, & Bender, 2006; Rosendal et al., 2007). The one study providing the most extensive physician training (25 hours) resulted in no association between physician training and patients' symptomatology, functioning, or quality of life (Rosendal et al., 2007). Two other studies found less intensive physician training programs, 12 hours (Larisch et al., 2004) or 1 day (Rief, Martin, Rauh, Zech, & Bender, 2006) to coincide with no clear improvement in somatization symptomatology. However, Rief and colleagues did find their training to result in fewer health-care visits for the 6 months subsequent to training (Rief, Martin, Rauh, Zech, & Bender, 2006).

One additional study examined the effect of training primary care clinicians to identify and treat somatization using a biopsychosocial model (Smith et al., 2006). In this study, nurse practitioners were trained to provide a multidimensional intervention in primary care. The treatment incorporated biopsychosocial conceptualizations, behavioral recommendations, and medication management of somatization. The nurses' training program was intensive, entailing 84 hours over 10 weeks. Patients who received treatment from these trained nurses reported modest improvements on self-report scales of mental health (e.g., mood, energy) and physical functioning. A post hoc analysis was interpreted by the study's investigators as suggesting that improvements were attributable to more frequent and appropriate use of antidepressant medication among patients of nurses who received the training (Smith et al., 2006).

Summary

The extraordinary financial costs of somatization, along with the associated suffering and disability, make it a public health concern. Initial findings on the characteristics of somatizing patients support a cognitive behavioral rationale for treatment. Six controlled clinical trials suggest that CBT may reduce physical discomfort, functional limitations, and physician visits. Additional research is required to replicate these findings. Studies designed to alter primary care treatment have had mixed results. Smith et al.'s psychiatric consultation letter, providing treatment recommendations for specific patients and labeling their symptoms as somatization, has repeatedly been shown to produce reductions in medical utilization. However, extensive training of physicians aimed at broadly affecting their approaches to working with somatization patients in their practices has had minimal effects on patient symptomatology and behavior.

Conversion Disorder
Overview of Diagnostic Criteria and Prevalence

Conversion symptoms (also described as pseudoneurological symptoms) are abnormalities or deficits in voluntary motor or sensory function that are medically unexplained. Some of the most common pseudoneurological symptoms are pseudoseizures, pseudoparalysis, and psychogenic movement disorders. According to DSM-IV, conversion disorder is characterized by the presence of one or more pseudoneurological symptoms that are associated with psychological stressor(s) or conflict(s) (APA, 1994). The diagnosis of conversion disorder requires a thorough psychiatric evaluation, as well as a physical examination to rule out organic neurological illness. Patients presenting with conversion symptoms typically have normal reflexes and normal muscle tone.

The course of conversion disorder appears to be different from that of somatization disorder, which tends to be chronic (Kent, Tomasson, & Coryell, 1995). The onset and course of conversion disorder often take the form of an acute episode. Symptoms may remit within a few weeks of an initial episode, and they may recur in the future. Some research indicates that a brief duration of symptoms prior to treatment is associated a better prognosis (Crimlisk et al., 1998; Hafeiz, 1980; Ron, 2001).

Estimates of the prevalence of conversion disorder have varied widely, ranging from 11/100,000 to 0.3% in the community (Faravelli et al., 1997; Stefansson, Messina, & Meyerowitz, 1979). As is the case with the other somatoform disorders, conversion disorder is much more common in medical and psychiatric practices than in community samples. As many as 25% of neurology clinic patients may present for treatment of a medically unexplained neurological symptom (Creed et al., 1990; Perkin, 1989).

Demographic and Clinical Characteristics

The demographic characteristics of conversion disorder have not been investigated extensively. Nevertheless, there is some evidence that conversion disorder is more common among women (Deveci et al., 2007; Faravelli et al., 1997), non-whites (Stefansson, Messina, & Meyerowitz, 1979), and individuals from lower socioeconomic classes (Folks, Ford, & Regan, 1984; Stefansson, Messina, & Meyerowitz, 1979). Comorbid psychiatric distress in patients with pseudoneurological symptoms is high; it has been estimated that 30%–90% of patients seeking treatment for pseudoneurological symptoms also meet criteria for at least one other psychiatric disorder, typically somatoform disorders, affective disorders, anxiety disorders, or personality disorders (Binzer, Andersen, & Kullgren, 1997; Crimlisk et al., 1998; Mokleby et al., 2002; Sar, Akyuz, Kundakci, Kiziltan, & Dogan, 2004). A comorbid personality disorder diagnosis has been found to indicate poor prognosis of conversion disorder (Mace & Trimble, 1996).

Like somatization disorder, conversion disorder is costly to the health-care system, especially when symptoms are chronic (Mace & Trimble, 1996). Patients with longstanding conversion symptoms are likely to submit themselves to unnecessary diagnostic and medical procedures. Martin, Bell, Hermann, & Mennemeyer, (2003) report an average of $100,000 being spent per year per conversion disorder patient.

Treatment

Conversion disorders have been treated with various approaches, including hypnosis, CBT, biofeedback, family therapy, spa treatment, pharmacotherapy, surgery, electroconvulsive therapy (ECT), physiotherapy, and inpatient psychiatric care. However, only three randomized controlled trials (RCTs) on the treatment of conversion disorder have been published: two assessing the efficacy of hypnosis (Moene, Spinhoven, Hoogduin, & van Dyck, 2002; 2003) and one assessing the efficacy of paradoxical intention therapy (Ataoglu, Ozcetin, Icmeli, & Ozbulut, 2003).

In their first study on hypnosis, Moene et al. (2002) compared the efficacy of adding hypnotherapy to an inpatient treatment for patients with motor-type conversion symptoms. All study participants were inpatients receiving a multidisciplinary treatment including group therapy, problem-solving and social skills training, exercise, physiotherapy, and bedrest. Twenty-four patients were randomly assigned to receive one hypnotherapy preparatory session and eight weekly 1-hour hypnotherapy sessions. The hypnotherapy strategies were aimed at direct symptom alleviation using suggestions designed to alter conditioned cues to motor symptoms, and emotional expression/insight involving age regression to explore factors implicated in the development of the symptoms. Also, hypnotherapy-treated participants were instructed to practice self-hypnosis for 30 minutes/day. The control comparison condition consisted of one preparatory session and eight weekly 1-hour therapy sessions "aimed at optimizing nonspecific or common therapy factors." Participants were encouraged to think and write about therapy sessions for homework. Assessments conducted 8 months after enrollment suggested that the motor symptoms of both groups had improved following baseline. However, there were no between-group differences (Moene et al., 2002).

In a second study, the same group of investigators treated outpatients diagnosed with motor-type conversion disorder. In this study, a slightly longer hypnotherapy intervention (including one preparatory session and ten weekly 1-hour sessions) was associated with better outcomes than was a waitlist control condition (Moene et al., 2003). The content of the hypnotherapy strategies and homework were the same as in their previous study (Moene et al., 2002). Experimental patients received significantly lower scores on the Video Rating Scale for Motor Symptoms and on an interviewer-based measure of physical limitations (ICIDH: International Classification of Impairments, Disabilities and Handicaps – subscale for physical activities) than did those randomized to the control waitlist condition (Moene et al., 2003). The treatment effect sizes were $d = 1.55$ for the Video Rating Scale for Motor Symptoms, and $d = 0.30$ for the ICIDH. Because these findings are based on treatment completers, not the intent-to-treat sample, they probably overestimate true differences between the treatment and control sample.

A third study compared paradoxical intention therapy provided as a part of a 3-week inpatient program with a 7-week outpatient pharmacotherapy intervention using diazepam (5–15 mg/day) combined with four outpatient medication management sessions. The paradoxical intention therapy was administered twice per day and involved asking patients to imagine anxiety-provoking situations and/or experiences. The aim was to trigger conversion attacks by helping patients reexperience putative underlying trauma (Ataoglu et al., 2003). At the end of treatment, there were no differences in the number of conversion symptoms between the groups, although the paradoxical intention group did report greater reductions in anxiety than did the diazepam group. Nevertheless, the study's findings have little validity because the differences between groups may have been attributable to other differences in treatment (i.e., inpatient versus outpatient, medication versus talk therapy) rather than to the paradoxical intention therapy itself (Ataoglu et al., 2003).

Summary

At present, there is little evidence supporting the efficacy of any treatment for conversion disorder. The only three published randomized controlled trials contain significant methodological flaws. Before any guidelines for treatment can be formulated, there is a need for well-designed randomized controlled trials to assess the efficacy of interventions with this population.

Pain Disorder

Pain disorder is characterized by clinically significant pain that is judged to be affected by psychological factors (APA, 1994). Very little research has been conducted that addresses pain disorder as defined by DSM-IV (or its DSM-III-R counterpart, Somatoform Pain Disorder) as a discrete diagnostic category. Instead, researchers have tended to formulate research based on the anatomical site and the chronicity of the pain. Thus, there is a voluminous literature on distinct pain conditions (e.g., back pain, chest pain, pelvic pain, headaches). In none of these studies have investigators attempted to distinguish between pain that was "affected by psychological factors" and pain that was not, presumably because such a distinction is too difficult to make. Many experts have suggested the elimination of the pain disorder category from future versions of DSM (Birket-Smith & Mortenson, 2002; Kroenke, Sharpe, & Sykes, 2007; Sullivan, 2000). Given the paucity of research on pain disorder and the uncertainty of

its future as a diagnostic category, we will not address the topic further. We have, however, addressed related conditions in the functional somatic syndrome section of this chapter (pages 347–351).

Hypochondriasis
Overview of Diagnostic Criteria and Prevalence
According to DSM-IV, hypochondriasis is defined as a "preoccupation with fears of having, or the idea that one has, a serious disease based on the person's misinterpretation of bodily symptoms" (APA, 1994). This preoccupation must persist despite medical evaluation and physician reassurance and cause significant distress or impairment in one's functioning (APA, 1994). Thus, unlike in somatization, where the distress and dysfunction experienced is due to the physical symptoms themselves, in hypochondriasis the distress and dysfunction is due to the patient's interpretation of the meaning of his or her symptoms. The course of hypochondriasis is often chronic; as many as 50% of patients meeting DSM criteria for hypochondriasis have excessive health concerns for many years (Barsky, Fama, Bailey, & Ahern, 1998; Barsky, Wyshak, Klerman, & Latham, 1990).

Only a few epidemiological studies have examined the prevalence of hypochondriasis. Studies that have utilized a clinical interview to assess prevalence have suggested that hypochondriasis occurs rarely in the general population. Such estimates range from 0.02% to 1.6% (Faravelli et al., 1997; Looper & Kirmayer, 2001; Martin & Jacobi, 2006). In primary care, estimates range from 0.8% to 6.3% (Barsky et al., 1990; Escobar et al., 1998; Gureje, Ustun, & Simon, 1997).

Demographic and Clinical Characteristics
Unlike somatization disorder, hypochondriasis does not appear to be related to gender (Barsky et al., 1990; Gureje, Ustun, & Simon, 1997; Looper & Kirmayer, 2001). Men are as likely to meet DSM criteria for hypochondriasis as are women. Findings have been inconsistent on whether hypochondriasis is related to education, socioeconomic status, and ethnicity.

Like patients with somatization disorder and milder versions of somatization disorder, those with hypochondriasis exhibit abnormal illness behavior. They overutilize health care (Gureje, Ustun, & Simon, 1997; Looper & Kirmayer, 2001), subjecting themselves to multiple physician visits and multiple diagnostic procedures. They report great dissatisfaction with their medical care (Barksy, 1996;

Noyes et al., 1993). In addition, patients diagnosed with hypochondriasis report substantial physical impairment and functional limitations related to employment (Escobar et al., 1998; Gureje, Ustun, & Simon, 1997; Looper & Kirmayer, 2001; Noyes et al., 1993). Also, hypochondriasis frequently co-occurs with other Axis I disorders, such as mood, anxiety, or other somatoform disorders (Gureje, Ustun, & Simon, 1997; Noyes et al., 1994).

Treatment

Psychosocial treatments for hypochondriasis have been examined in six randomized controlled trials. The interventions in all six studies were theoretically grounded in social learning theory and were administered on an individual basis.

The interventions labeled as cognitive therapy (CT) for hypochondriasis (Clark et al., 1998; Visser & Bouman, 2001) are procedurally similar to the point of being indistinguishable from those labeled CBT for hypochondriasis (Barsky & Ahern, 2004; Greeven et al., 2007; Warwick, Clark, Cobb, & Salkovskis, 1996). All of these interventions focused on identifying and challenging patients' misinterpretations of physical symptoms, as well as on constructing more realistic interpretations of them. Barsky and Ahern (2004) state that, in addition to restructuring cognitions, they attempted to reduce patients' tendency to amplify physical symptoms and to alter patients' illness behaviors. Warwick et al.'s CBT (1996) and Clark et al.'s CT (1998) combined cognitive restructuring with exposure to interoceptive and/or external stimuli along with response prevention after exposure. What differed most among these interventions was their duration. Barsky and Ahern's (2004) treatment entailed six 90-minute sessions. Visser and Bouman's (2001) intervention consisted of 12 weekly sessions (each presumably lasting 1 hour, although session duration was not indicated). The duration of Greeven et al.'s (2007) CBT, which was "based on Visser and Bouman's intervention," ranged from 6 to 16 sessions. Both Clark et al.'s (1998), and Warwick et al.'s (1996) treatments involved 16 one-hour sessions.

All CT and CBT interventions were associated with significantly greater reductions in hypochondriacal symptoms than was the comparable waitlist control condition (Barsky & Ahern, 2004; Clark et al., 1998; Greeven et al., 2007; Visser & Bouman, 2001; Warwick et al., 1996). Barsky and Ahern's study was the only one that examined long-term differences between the waiting list group and the treated group. Their data show that, 10 months after treatment completion, patients enrolled in CBT reported a greater decline in hypochondriacal cognitions than did controls. Also, Barsky and Ahren's CBT-treated patients reported a significantly greater increase in daily activities than did controls, even 10 months after treatment (Barsky & Ahern, 2004).

In their study, Visser and Bouman (2001) also assessed the efficacy of a largely behavioral intervention, exposure plus response prevention. Patients receiving this treatment constructed hierarchies of their own hypochondriacal fears and avoidance behavior patterns (e.g., checking, reassurance seeking, avoidance of interoceptive and/or external stimuli). Afterward, they were given assignments of in vivo exposure and response prevention. Patients treated with exposure reported significantly greater reductions in their hypochondriacal symptoms than did waitlist control participants. Although Visser and Bouman also compared exposure plus response prevention to their CT intervention (described earlier), the study was not powered sufficiently to distinguish between the two groups.

Clark et al. (1998) created a psychosocial alternative to CT, behavioral stress management (BSM), that did not directly address hypochondriacal concerns. It was intended to address anxiety related to hypochondriasis by training patients in relaxation, problem-solving, assertiveness training, and time management. Clark et al. found behavioral stress management significantly more effective in alleviating hypochondriacal concerns than was a waiting list. Clark et al. also compared this treatment to their CT described earlier. At post-treatment CT-treated participants experienced greater reductions in their hypochondriacal cognitions than did BSM-treated participants. Nevertheless, 12 months after the post-treatment assessment, these differences were not observed (Clark et al., 1998).

Finally, Fava et al. examined the efficacy of explanatory therapy (Kellner, 1983) for hypochondriasis, in hopes of identifying a beneficial treatment that is less complex and easier to administer than CBT (Fava, Grandi, Rafanelli, Fabbri, & Cazzaro, 2000). Explanatory therapy is a physician-administered individual therapy consisting of patient education, reassurance, and training in selective attention (i.e., reducing somatic attention). Like the cognitive and behavioral treatments described earlier, explanatory therapy was found to result in greater reductions in worry about illness than was the waiting list (Fava et al., 2000). Although explanatory therapy was also associated with greater reductions in physician visits than was the control group, the mean reduction in visits was minimal (three visits) considering that the treatment group received eight additional visits as part of their explanatory therapy (Fava et al., 2000).

The one study comparing a psychosocial intervention with a pharmacological intervention demonstrated that CBT was more effective than a placebo pill, but no more effective than paroxetine, in reducing hypochondriacal beliefs and health anxiety (Greeven et al., 2007). Despite the statistical significance of these findings, the clinical significance of changes observed in this study suggests that patients experienced only modest improvement. Instead of using Jacobson's recommendation of a change of 1.96 standard deviations from the pretreatment mean as an index of clinically significant change, the investigators judged as clinically significant a change of 1.0 standard deviation. Using this more lenient criterion, 45% of CBT recipients and 30% of paroxetine recipients versus 14% of waiting list controls responded to treatment at "clinically significant" levels (Greeven et al., 2007).

Summary

Although the findings from controlled trials on behavioral treatment for hypochondriasis suggest that these interventions are effective in reducing hypochondriacal concerns, conclusions remain uncertain. Long-term benefits have only been assessed relative to a control condition in one study. None of the studies demonstrates that treatment has meaningful effects on measures of health-care utilization. Also inadequately examined is the impact of treatment on the functional impairment so often observed in hypochondriasis. Clinically meaningful change has not been observed. In addition, it has yet to be demonstrated that one intervention appears more potent than the others. An internal analysis of the data from a meta-analysis on psychotherapy for hypochondriasis revealed that the total amount of time with a therapist was highly correlated with the effect size as measured by standardized mean difference (r^2 = 0.93, r = 0.090 (95% CI 0.056–0.124) p = 0.002) (Thomson & Page, 2007).

Also noteworthy is the setting where studies on the treatment of hypochondriasis have been conducted. In each study, except that of Barsky and Ahern, patients were referred to mental health clinics by their general practitioner or mental health professional. Thus, not one of these treatments was specifically designed to be conducted in a primary care medical setting, where hypochondriasis is frequently

first observed and where psychological interventions might be most advantageously applied. Because the participants in the studies described here were willing to participate in treatment in a mental health facility, they may not be representative of the majority of hypochondriacal patients who are seeking treatment for physical, not psychological symptomatology.

Body Dysmorphic Disorder
Overview of Diagnostic Criteria and Prevalence

Body dysmorphic disorder (BDD) is characterized by a preoccupation with an imagined defect in appearance. If a slight physical irregularity is present, the person's concern must be excessive to meet criteria for BDD. Also required for a diagnosis of BDD is significant distress or impairment caused by this preoccupation (APA, 1994). Typically, patients are concerned about their skin or complexion, the size of the nose or head, or the attractiveness of the hair. However, the preoccupation may concern any body part.

Body dysmorphic disorder tends to be chronic; in one study Phillips at al. found only a 0.09 probability of full remission and 0.2 probability of partial remission over the course of a year (Phillips, Pagano, Menard, & Stout, 2006).

The prevalence of BDD is uncertain. Research conducted in community settings has produced varying estimates: a prevalence of 0.7% in a community setting in Italy (Faravelli et al., 1997), 1.7 % in a national survey of German adolescents and adults (Rief, Buhlmann, Wilhelm, Borkenhagen, & Brähler, 2006), and 2.4% in a telephone survey of U.S. adults (Koran, Abujaoude, Large, & Serpe, 2008). The prevalence of BDD in medical practices has been found to be substantially higher than that found in the general population: 4% of general medicine patients (Phillips, 1996), 3%–16% of cosmetic surgery patients (Sarwer & Crerand, 2008), and 8%–15% of dermatology patients (Sarwer & Crerand, 2008).

Demographic and Clinical Characteristics

Very little research has been conducted on sex and cultural differences in BDD. Phillips and Diaz found that women and men were equally likely to meet criteria for BDD (Phillips & Diaz, 1997). We are aware of no systematic investigation of race and culture in BDD, although the condition has been described in various cultures around the world (Phillips, 1996).

Patients meeting criteria for BDD have been shown to have substantial functional impairment

(Phillips, 2000). Negative thoughts about one's appearance interfere with concentration at work and the social lives of patients. In addition, individuals with BDD are so afraid of exposing their flaw to others that they go to great lengths to hide it. They may spend substantial amounts of time camouflaging their perceived defect or avoiding activities in which they will be conspicuous (Phillips, McElroy, Keck, Pope, & Hudson, 1993). Avoidance of social activities and work is common (Phillips et al., 1993).

Health-care use associated with BDD tends to be directed toward seeking various appearance-enhancing medical treatments, especially cosmetic surgery and dermatological procedures. For patients with BDD, these treatments typically fail to alleviate distress (Crerand, Phillips, Menard, & Fay, 2005; Phillips, Grant, Siniscalchi, & Albertini, 2001). Investigators have found that 48%–76% of patients with BDD sought cosmetic surgery, dermatological treatment, or dental procedures (Crerand et al., 2005; Phillips, Grant, Siniscalchi, & Albertini, 2001; Veale, Boocock, et al., 1996), and 26% received multiple procedures (Veale, Boocock, et al., 1996).

Patients meeting criteria for BDD experience an enormous amount of emotional distress and psychiatric comorbidity (Phillips, Menard, Fay, & Weisberg, 2005; Veale, Boocock, et al., 1996). Depression and suicidal thoughts are frequently reported (Gunstad & Phillips, 2003; Phillips & Menard, 2006). Also common in this population is social phobia and obsessive-compulsive disorder (Gunstad & Phillips, 2003). Often, compulsions are related to the perceived physical defect, such as checking mirrors or brushing one's hair. Many of these patients also admit to substance, particularly alcohol, use and dependence disorders (Grant, Menard, Pagano, Fay, & Phillips, 2005; Gunstad & Phillips, 2003).

Many patients preoccupied with an imagined defect in their physical appearance have such inaccurate perceptions of their appearance that they meet DSM-IV criteria for delusional disorder, somatic type. About 50% of clinical samples meeting criteria for BDD also meet criteria for delusional disorder, somatic type (Phillips, McElroy, & Keck, 1994). However, instead of considering this somatic type of delusional disorder a comorbid condition with BDD, a growing body of research suggests psychotic variants of BDD are simply a more severe form of nonpsychotic BDD and are, therefore, best conceived as on the same continuum. It seems that nonpsychotic and psychotic BDD share the same demographic characteristics, clinical characteristics, and response to treatment (Phillips, 2004). Further evidence

suggests that the cognitions of BDD patients involving such matters as the degree of conviction with which these patients hold their beliefs are more indicative of a dimensional rather than a categorical structure (Phillips, 2004). Thus, the research data suggest a dimensional model of BDD with varying levels of insight indicating severity of the condition.

Treatment

Only two randomized controlled trials have been published on the efficacy of psychosocial treatment for BDD (Rosen, Reiter, & Orosan, 1995; Veale, Gournay, et al., 1996). Both assessed the efficacy of cognitive-behavioral interventions, those involving the restructuring dysfunctional beliefs about one's body and exposure to avoided situations plus response prevention (e.g., preventing checking behavior and reassurance seeking). Whereas Rosen et al.'s treatment was administered in eight 2-hour group sessions, Veale et al. administered treatment in 12 weekly individual sessions. Both groups of investigators compared the effects of CBT with those of a waitlist control condition.

Both studies provided strong evidence for the short-term efficacy of CBT for BDD. Rosen et al. found that 81.5% of treated participants and 7.4% of control participants experienced clinically significant improvement, in that their scores on the Body Dysmorphic Disorder Examination (BDDE) dropped more than 2 standard deviations *and* they no longer met criteria for BDD. The effect size on the BDDE was substantial ($d = 2.81$) (Rosen et al., 1995). Follow-up assessment, occurring 4.5 months after treatment, was conducted with only CBT participants, 74% of whom continued to have achieved clinically meaningful gains (Rosen et al., 1995). Veale et al. reported that at post-treatment 77.8% of the treatment group either had absent or subclinical BDD symptomatology, whereas all waiting-list participants still met criteria for BDD. Furthermore, Veale's effect sizes on the BDDE and on a BDD-modified Yale-Brown Obsessive Compulsive Scale were also noteworthy ($d = 2.65$ and $d = 1.81$, respectively) (Veale, Gournay, et al., 1996). Follow-up was not investigated in this study.

Although the potency of the treatments described in these two well-designed controlled trials is noteworthy, a number of questions remain about the efficacy of CBT for BDD. No additional RTCs have been published. Cognitive-behavioral therapy has not been compared with alternative treatments nor with an attention control. It is unclear whether the treatment gains reported here could be attributable to nonspecific aspects of therapy. Also, long-term follow-up has not been adequately studied. Other important outcomes, such as physical and social functioning and health-care use, have not been assessed. Finally, the generalizability of these findings is unclear. Between the two studies, only 36 patients have been treated. Rosen et al.'s sample consisted of women, 83% of whom had body weight and shape concerns. Veale et al.'s sample specifically excluded potential participants with body weight and shape concerns.

Related Conditions: Functional Somatic Syndromes
Overview of Diagnostic Criteria and Prevalence

The term *functional somatic syndrome* is used to describe groups of co-occurring symptoms that are medically unexplained. Each area of medicine identifies at least one functional somatic syndrome for patients who present with symptoms that are common in that area of medicine, but have uncertain pathology and a poor prognosis. Three polysymptomatic functional somatic syndromes frequently encountered by both mental health and primary care practitioners are irritable bowel syndrome (IBS), chronic fatigue syndrome (CFS), and fibromyalgia. As will be discussed here, they all share many of the characteristics of the somatoform disorders.

Irritable bowel syndrome is characterized by persistent abdominal pain along with altered bowel habits and abdominal distension that cannot be explained by organic pathology (Thompson, Dotevall, Drossman, Heaton, & Kruis, 1989). It has been estimated that 8%–20% of the U.S. population, 12% of primary care patients (Drossman, Whitehead, & Camilleri, 1997), and 22%–28% of gastroenterologists' patients are afflicted with IBS (Harvey, Salih, & Read, 1983; Thompson & Heaton, 1980).

Chronic fatigue syndrome is characterized by unexplained fatigue, lasting at least 6 months, that causes substantial reductions in activities. At least four of the following symptoms must have co-occurred with the fatigue: significant memory impairment or concentration difficulties, sore throat, tender lymph nodes, muscle pain, joint pain, headache, nonrestorative sleep, and postexertional fatigue (Fukuda et al., 1994). The prevalence of CFS has been estimated to be 0.002%–0.6% in the general population and 2.6% in primary care settings (Jason et al., 1999; Reyes et al., 2003; Wessely, Chadler, Hirsch, Wallace, & Wright, 1997).

A diagnosis of *fibromyalgia* is given for chronic widespread pain and multiple tender points that have no known biological basis and are accompanied by nonrestorative sleep, fatigue, and malaise (Wolfe et al., 1990). Fibromyalgia has been estimated to occur in about 2% of the U.S. population and in 6%–20% of general medical outpatients (Wolfe, Ross, Anderson, Russell, & Hebert, 1995).

Demographic and Clinical Characteristics

Women are more likely than men to suffer from all three syndromes: IBS (Drossman et al., 1993), CFS (Jason et al., 1999; Reyes et al., 2003), and fibromyalgia (Wolfe et al., 1995). Although the incidence of CFS and fibromyalgia have been shown to be elevated in minority groups in the United States, larger epidemiological studies are required to confirm these findings (Gansky & Plesh, 2007; Jason et al., 1999).

Our decision to include the research on CFS, fibromyalgia, and IBS in this chapter on somatoform disorders may invite controversy. Some medical specialists, focusing upon the bodily organ or somatic system of their specialization, assume these disorders have distinct pathophysiological causes and draw sharp distinctions among these syndromes. Other authorities suggest these syndromes should be viewed as one disorder. After all, many patients diagnosed with one functional somatic syndrome meet diagnostic criteria for one or more of the other functional somatic syndromes, resulting in multisystem comorbid functional syndromes (Buchwald & Garrity, 1994; Goldenberg, Simms, Geiger, & Komaroff, 1990; Veale, Kavanagh, Fielding, & Fitzgerald, 1991; Yunus, Masi, & Aldag, 1989). Also, investigators have noted similarities in the illness behaviors, illness beliefs, and psychological functioning of patients diagnosed with one of these functional somatic syndromes and those diagnosed with a somatoform disorder (Barsky & Borus, 1999; Rief, Hiller, & Margraf, 1998; Wessely, Nimnuan, & Sharpe, 1999). As discussed earlier regarding patients with somatoform disorders, patients with functional somatic syndromes tend to adopt a sick role (Parsons, 1951), overutilizing medical services and withdrawing from their normal activities. They tend to assume their symptoms are signs of a serious, disabling illness that is likely to worsen; they think "catastrophically" about their health. They frequently suffer from concurrent emotional disorders (see Woolfolk & Allen, 2007, for further review).

Treatment

Various psychosocial interventions have been used to treat the functional somatic syndromes. Short-term dynamic therapy, relaxation training, exercise regimens, behavior therapy, cognitive therapy, and CBT have been tested in controlled studies with one or more of the patient groups described. The studies are reviewed here. A more detailed examination of this literature can be found elsewhere (Allen, Escobar, Lehrer, Gara, & Woolfolk, 2002).

SHORT-TERM DYNAMIC THERAPY

Psychodynamic theory has proposed that unexplained physical symptoms are produced to protect the patient from traumatic, frightening, and/or depressing emotional experiences. If an individual fails to process a trauma adequately, it is hypothesized, the original affect later may be converted into physical symptoms (Engel, 1959). Short-term dynamically oriented treatments that explore the stress and emotional distress associated with physical symptoms have been studied systematically with IBS patients. In one study, a short-term dynamic therapy, aimed at "modifying maladaptive behaviour and finding new solutions to problems," resulted in significantly greater improvement in IBS symptoms than did a standard medical care condition. Differences between groups were observed after treatment as well as 1 year later (Svedlund, Sjodin, Ottosson, & Dotevall, 1983). Another trial examined the efficacy of a short-term dynamic therapy aimed at helping participants explore the links between IBS symptoms and emotional factors. The treatment was supplemented by audiotape-administered relaxation methods that participants were instructed to use at home. Immediately after the 3-month intervention phase, participants receiving psychotherapy reported significantly greater improvements in IBS symptoms than did participants receiving standard medical care (Guthrie, Creed, Dawson, & Tomenson, 1991). This second intervention (psychodynamic therapy plus relaxation training) was more recently compared to pharmacotherapy with paroxetine and to standard medical care for IBS. Although there were no differences among the three treatment conditions in patient-reported abdominal pain, both dynamic therapy and paroxetine coincided with greater improvement in physical functioning than did standard medical care a year after treatment. Furthermore, psychotherapy, but not paroxetine, was associated with greater reductions in health-care costs during the year after treatment (Creed et al., 2003).

RELAXATION TRAINING

Psychophysiologists have described several mechanisms that produce somatic symptoms in the absence of organic pathology (Clauw, 1995; Gardner & Bass, 1989). These mechanisms include overactivity or dysregulation of the autonomic nervous system, smooth muscle contractions, endocrine overactivity, and hyperventilation. Miscellaneous techniques, directed at reducing physiological arousal and physical discomfort associated with unexplained physical symptoms, have been studied within controlled experimental designs. Small studies have shown that relaxation techniques, such as electromyogram (EMG)-biofeedback and guided imagery, reduce pain associated with fibromyalgia more effectively than do sham relaxation treatments (Ferraccioli et al., 1987; Fors, Sexton, & Gotestam, 2002). In another small trial, patients treated with progressive muscle relaxation reported greater relief in their irritable bowel symptoms than did patients in a control comparison treatment condition (Blanchard, Greene, Scharff, & Schwarz-McMorris, 1993).

Hypnotherapy, designed to produce generalized relaxation and control of intestinal motility, has been successfully applied to IBS as well as to fibromyalgia. In three different studies, hypnotherapy was associated with less abdominal pain and fewer abnormal bowel habits than was either of two comparison conditions, supportive psychotherapy combined with a placebo pill (Whorwell, Prior, & Farragher, 1984) or a symptom-monitoring condition (Galovski & Blanchard, 1998; Palsson, Turner, Johnson, Burnett, & Whitehead, 2002). The one study assessing the efficacy of hypnotherapy for fibromyalgia found it to be associated with greater pain relief than was physical therapy (Haanen et al., 1991). In an attempt to examine the mechanism of improvement, Palsson et al. showed that improvements seen in IBS symptoms after hypnotherapy were related to improvements in somatization and in anxiety, but not related to physiological measures of rectal pain threshold, rectal smooth muscle tone, or autonomic functioning (Palsson et al., 2002).

EXERCISE TREATMENTS

Exercise interventions have been developed for CFS and fibromyalgia, in accordance with evidence suggesting that exercise improves mood, pain thresholds, and sleep (Minor, 1991; Weyerer & Kupfer, 1994). One theory explaining the benefits of exercise proposes that exercise produces increases in serum levels of β-endorphin-like immunoreactivity, adrenocorticotropic hormone, prolactin, and growth hormone (Harber & Sutton, 1984). In most studies, graded exercise treatments have coincided with improvements in physical functioning, fatigue, and global perceived well-being in patients diagnosed with CFS or fibromyalgia (Fulcher & White, 1997; Martin et al., 1996; McCain, Bell, Mai, & Halliday, 1988; Powell, Bentall, Nye, & Edwards, 2001; Richards & Scott, 2002). Some trials have even shown exercise to outperform relaxation and/or stretching comparison interventions (Fulcher & White, 1997; Martin et al., 1996; McCain, Bell, Mai, & Halliday, 1988; Richards & Scott, 2002). Although both statistically and clinically significant gains have been reported, the findings reported here probably are not generalizable to all CFS and fibromyalgia patients. First, some investigators have not found an association between exercise treatments and symptom relief (King, Wessel, Bhambhani, Sholter, & Maksymowych, 2002; Mengshoel, Komnaes, & Forre, 1992). Second, many patients are disinclined to exercise and, thus, are unlikely to enroll in exercise studies. Finally, some studies have produced high attrition rates (Martin et al., 1996; Wearden et al., 1998) indicating that even those patients who agree to undergo an exercise regimen may not adhere to it.

BEHAVIOR THERAPY

Operant behavior therapy manipulates the consequences of patients' illness behavior with the aim of alleviating the associated pain and impairment. Recipients of operant behavior therapy are rewarded as they display "healthy behaviors" and increased activity levels; additional activities are expected to result in positive interactions with the outside world, experiences of joy, and a sense of productivity. Pain behaviors, such as taking medication, wincing, complaining, and seeking treatment, are identified, labeled, and consequated. A recent study compared the efficacy of an inpatient, operant behavioral treatment to that of inpatient physical therapy for fibromyalgia (Thieme, Gromnica-Ihle, & Flor, 2003). Operant behavior therapy was conducted in groups of five to seven patients for 5 weeks. Immediately after treatment, as well as 6 and 15 months after treatment, behavior therapy was associated with substantial reductions in pain intensity, use of medication, and physician visits (Thieme et al., 2003). The only other randomized controlled study of behavior therapy for a functional somatic syndrome was conducted with outpatients diagnosed with IBS. In this study, patients who received six to 15 sessions of individual behavior therapy reported no more improvement than did control participants (Corney, Stanton, Newell, Clare, & Fairclough, 1991).

Discrepancies in findings from these two studies may be related to differences in patient populations (fibromyalgia vs. IBS; inpatient vs. outpatient) or the mode of administration of the intervention (group vs. individual). Additional research on the efficacy of behavior therapy for functional somatic syndromes is required before such interventions can be endorsed.

COGNITIVE THERAPY

Cognitive therapy focuses on and attempts to alter faulty thinking patterns associated with functional somatic symptoms. Three trials with IBS patients have shown individual cognitive therapy to be associated with greater reductions in IBS symptoms than were either a waiting-list control condition or a support group (Greene & Blanchard, 1994; Payne & Blanchard, 1994; Vollmer & Blanchard, 1998).

COGNITIVE-BEHAVIORAL THERAPY

Cognitive-behavioral therapy aims to alter dysfunctional thoughts and behaviors associated with somatic symptoms. With IBS patients, CBT usually has included a relaxation component. Controlled trials of CBT interventions for IBS have produced inconsistent results. Five trials showed CBT, administered individually, relieved bowel symptoms more effectively than did standard medical care (Heymann-Monnikes et al., 2000; Shaw et al., 1991), an educational attention-control condition (Drossman et al., 2003), or a waiting list (Lynch & Zamble, 1989; Neff & Blanchard, 1987). In a sixth study, CBT administered as a group treatment resulted in greater improvements in IBS symptoms than did a waiting list control condition (Van Dulmen, Fennis, & Bleijenberg, 1996). Four other investigations found no difference between individual CBT and a control condition (Bennett & Wilkinson, 1985; Blanchard, Schwarz, Suls, Gerardi, & Scharff, 1992a; Blanchard, Schwarz, Suls, Gerardi, & Scharff, 1992b; Boyce, Talley, Balaam, Koloski, & Truman, 2003).

Studies of CBT for IBS have not yielded a consistent pattern of results. Discrepancies in the findings of the earliest studies were to be expected, given their lack of methodological rigor. Findings that have emerged from the two most recently published and methodologically sound studies on CBT for IBS also are not congruent (Boyce et al., 2003; Drossman et al., 2003). Identifiable differences between the more recent studies' designs and outcome measures potentially provide some insight into the discrepancies in findings. Whereas Drossman et al. found

CBT more effective than an educational intervention, Boyce et al. found CBT no more effective than an 8-week relaxation treatment (Boyce et al., 2003; Drossman et al., 2003). Because Boyce's comparison treatment condition, a relaxation intervention, has been demonstrated in past studies to reduce IBS symptoms (Blanchard et al., 1993), it was likely to have been more "active" than was Drossman al.'s control condition. Drossman et al.'s primary outcome measure was a composite of the following variables: satisfaction with treatment, global well-being, diary abdominal pain scores, and health-related quality of life (Drossman et al., 2003). Boyce et al., on the other hand, measured outcome with the Bowel Symptom Severity Scale, a measure of frequency, disability, and distress caused by each of eight gastrointestinal symptoms. Treatment satisfaction and global well-being were not assessed in the Boyce et al. study (2003). The results of these two studies suggest that CBT may help patients with IBS cope with their symptoms and with their lives better than would educational sessions, but may not relieve specific IBS symptoms any better than would relaxation treatments.

When CBT has been administered to CFS patients, it has not included relaxation training. Instead, encouragement to increase activities, including exercise, has been a key component of these interventions. In one study, CBT was no more effective than the control treatment (Lloyd et al., 1993), whereas in three other studies CBT reduced fatigue significantly more than did relaxation (Deale, Chalder, Marks, & Wessely, 1997), support groups (Prins et al., 2001), or standard medical care (Sharpe et al., 1996). One study found the superiority of CBT over relaxation to be maintained for 5 years after treatment (Deale, Kaneez, Chalder, & Wessely, 2001). The trials that found CBT to be efficacious employed more intensive treatments than did the one unsuccessful trial. The clinical impact achieved in the successful trials, coupled with the methodological quality of the trials, lends further support to the use of CBT with CFS patients.

For fibromyalgia, the efficacy of *group CBT*, but not of *individually administered CBT*, has been studied in controlled trials with fibromyalgia patients. Patients treated with a six-session group CBT reported significantly more improvement in physical functioning, but not in pain, 12 months after baseline when compared with patients who had received standard medical care (Williams et al., 2002). Another trial, comparing the efficacy of a group CBT to that of group relaxation training (autogenic training), showed no differences between the conditions at post-treatment. However, 4 months later, CBT participants reported a greater reduction in pain intensity than did the autogenic training participants (Keel, Bodoky, Gerhard, & Muller, 1998). Two trials comparing a CBT/education group with a discussion/education group found no differences in pain complaints or functioning between the two treatment conditions (Nicassio et al., 1997; Vlaeyen et al., 1996). The findings of a less-than-powerful impact of CBT on fibromyalgia may reflect the ineffectiveness of group-administered treatment for this population. The benefits of individual CBT have yet to be explored with fibromyalgia patients.

SUMMARY

As a whole, psychosocial interventions have been moderately effective in reducing the physical symptoms associated with functional somatic syndromes. Investigators who reported long-term outcome data suggest that benefits persist as much as a year after treatment. Although detailed descriptions of most interventions are not provided in research articles, close scrutiny of the studies' methods sections suggests a great deal of overlap among the interventions. For example, one of the dynamically oriented therapies included a relaxation component. The other dynamic treatment involved directive interventions: encouraging patients to change maladaptive behavior and to engage in problem-solving exercises. Cognitive-behavioral training often incorporated relaxation training or homework assignments directing patients to engage in physical exercise. With so much overlap among treatments, perhaps it is not surprising that none of the interventions appears to be more potent than any of the others.

PSYCHOSOCIAL VERSUS PHARMACOLOGICAL TREATMENTS

A few studies have compared the efficacy of a psychosocial intervention with a pharmacological treatment for functional somatic syndromes. Chronic fatigue syndrome patients who participated in an exercise treatment reported greater improvements in fatigue and functional capacity than did CFS patients treated with fluoxetine (Wearden et al., 1998). Guided imagery produced superior results in fibromyalgia pain than did amitriptyline (Fors, Sexton, & Gotestam, 2002). And, Svedlund et al.'s (1983) psychodynamic treatment outperformed the control treatment, which included physician-prescribed bulking agents, anticholinergic drugs, antacids, and minor tranquilizers. These last two studies, those of Fors et al. and Svedlund et al., suggest a psychosocial intervention might be more effective than the medications most frequently prescribed for fibromyalgia and IBS, respectively. Nevertheless, too few studies have made the kinds of comparisons that would allow this conclusion to be asserted with certitude. Additional research is needed to examine the relative efficacy, and also the combined efficacy, of pharmacological and behavioral interventions with functional somatic syndromes and with somatoform disorders.

Factitious Disorder
Overview of Diagnostic Criteria and Prevalence

A diagnosis of factitious disorder is made when a patient intentionally produces, feigns, or exaggerates physical or psychological symptoms in order to assume the sick role. Identifiable external incentives, as would be the case when a person malingers for a specific purpose, are not present in factitious disorder (APA, 1994). Patients meeting DSM-IV criteria for factitious disorder with predominantly physical signs and symptoms are represented in most fields of medicine. Symptoms may be fabricated (e.g., claiming blindness when vision is unimpaired), intentionally produced (e.g., hematuria when patient intentionally pricks a finger to add blood to his or her urine), or exaggerated (e.g., exaggerations of pain). In factitious disorder with predominantly psychological signs or symptoms, patients may feign, exaggerate, or intentionally produce (e.g., such as with psychoactive substances) psychiatric symptoms, often psychosis.

The prevalence of factitious disorder has not been systematically investigated. Verification of the diagnosis is particularly difficult. Not only do organic explanations have to be excluded, but also the patient's role in and motivation for creating the symptom has to be determined. Physicians may be reluctant to consider factitious disorder as a potential differential diagnosis (Krahn, Li, & O'Connor, 2003). One study surveying physicians in internal medicine, neurology, dermatology, and surgery for their estimates of the prevalence of factitious disorder with predominantly physical symptoms in their practices found a range of from 0.0001% to 15%, with an average of 1.3% (Fliege et al., 2007).

Demographic and Clinical Characteristics

The scientific literature on factitious disorder consists of only case studies and clinical record reviews. At present, the demographic and clinical characteristics of factitious disorder are unknown.

Treatment

Treatment approaches for factitious disorder also have not been investigated systematically. Some clinicians have suggested that treatment should include confrontation of the patient (van der Feltz-Cornelis, 2002), whereas others recommend supportive, nonconfrontational treatment (Eisendrath, Rand, & Feldman, 1996). Many patients discontinue treatment when confronted directly with the diagnosis (Krahn et al., 2003). At present, we have no evidence to guide our treatment of factitious disorders.

Conclusion

An evaluation of the empirical research on psychosocial treatments for somatoform and related disorders suggests that, in some respects, it mirrors the literature on evaluating the efficacy of psychotherapy with generic mental disorders. A number of different focused psychosocial treatments have been shown to be superior to various control conditions, especially waiting lists or standard medical treatment. Effect sizes are respectable, relative to other medical or quasi-medical interventions. There is little evidence that one form of treatment is superior to any other. Treatments that are appropriately conceived as forms of CBT are the most frequently studied, have a creditable record of success, and, by the sheer volume of data, would appear to be the best candidates for a designation of "empirically supported" treatments.

Although the literature on the specific somatoform and factitious disorders is relatively small, a few global conclusions can be posited. Cognitive-behavioral therapy for somatization, hypochondriasis, IBS, and CFS is moderately effective, probably with some lasting effects. However, there is little data on the impact of treatment on health-care utilization, especially when the cost of a psychosocial intervention, such as those described earlier, is factored into the equation. There is inadequate data on the treatment of conversion disorder, pain disorder, or factitious disorder to make any conclusion. The data on CBT's efficacy on BDD is the most powerful. Effect sizes are large, and the vast majority of patients appear to have made clinically meaningful gains from treatment. However, the two groups of investigators who have systematically studied CBT's efficacy in BDD acknowledge residual symptoms persist and argue for a longer, more intensive treatment before these patients are likely to resolve their difficulties. Longer-term treatments for other somatoform disorders have been recommended by others as well (Woolfolk & Allen, 2007).

We have very little data on the mechanisms by which efficacious psychosocial treatments may have their impact upon somatoform disorders. There are multiple reasons for this. First, the "mediators and moderators" style of research has not been extensively applied to research on somatization. Second, the treatments studied have not been disassembled into discrete components and those constituents systematically assessed. Evidence that might shed some light on this issue, pertaining to differential efficacy of treatment, is also scant. This absence of evidence, to some extent, is the result of much overlap among treatments. Even treatments with very different labels (e.g., brief psychodynamic therapy and CBT) turn out to be similar procedurally—for example, both identifying stressors and providing training in relaxation. When reading the somatoform treatment literature, careful attention must be paid to methods sections, as the labeling of treatments can often be somewhat misleading.

Somatoform researchers as a whole recommend treatment for these conditions be administered in primary care settings. It has been estimated that 50%–80% of patients with somatoform disorders who are referred for mental health services fail to seek mental health treatment (Escobar, Waitzkin, Silver, Gara & Holman, 1998; Regier et al., 1988). Barriers to following through with psychiatric referrals occur at both the systemic level (e.g., lack of collaboration between and proximity of primary care physicians and mental health practitioners, lack of mental health training for primary care physicians, inadequate mental health insurance) and individual level (e.g., concerns about the stigma of having a psychiatric disorder, resistance to psychiatric diagnosis, health beliefs that lead to somatic presentations, pessimism, and fatigue) (Pincus, 2003). The efficacy of CBT conducted in primary care has not been studied adequately for hypochondriasis or BDD.

The treatment of somatoform and factitious disorders via psychosocial methods is very much in its infancy. The methodological quality of the early research has been uneven. Nevertheless, there is sufficient evidence to believe that psychosocial interventions have therapeutic value for a number of these disorders. For somatization, hypochondriasis, BDD, and many of the functional somatic syndromes, CBT is likely the treatment of choice by default, in that no other intervention has demonstrated efficacy.

References

Alexander, F. (1950). *Psychosomatic medicine*. New York: Norton.

Allen, L. A., Escobar, J. I., Lehrer, P. M., Gara, M. A., & Woolfolk, R. L. (2002). Psychosocial treatments for multiple unexplained physical symptoms: A review of the literature. *Psychosomatic Medicine, 64*, 939–950.

Allen, L. A., Gara, M. A., Escobar, J. I., Waitzkin, H., & Cohen-Silver, R. (2001). Somatization: A debilitating syndrome in primary care. *Psychosomatics, 42*, 63–67.

Allen, L. A., Woolfolk, R. L., Escobar, J. I., Gara, M. A., & Hamer, R. M. (2006). Cognitive-behavioral therapy for somatization disorder: A randomized controlled trial. *Archives of Internal Medicine, 166*, 1512–1518.

Altamura, A. C., Carta, M. G., Tacchini, G., Musazzi, A., Pioli, M. R., & the Italian Collaborative Group on Somatoform Disorders. (1998). Prevalence of somatoform disorders in a psychiatric population: An Italian nationwide survey. *European Archives of Psychiatry and Clinical Neuroscience, 248*, 267–271.

American Psychiatric Association. (1980). *Diagnostic and statistical manual of mental disorders* (3rd ed.). Washington, DC: Author.

American Psychiatric Association. (1994). *Diagnostic and statistical manual of mental disorders* (4th ed.). Washington, DC: Author.

Ataoglu, A., Ozcetin, A., Icmeli, C., & Ozbulut, O. (2003). Paradoxical therapy in conversion reaction. *Journal of Korean Medicine, 18*, 581–584.

Barsky, A. J. (1996). Hypochondriasis: Medical management and psychiatric treatment. *Psychosomatics, 37*, 48–56.

Barsky, A. J., & Ahern, D. K. (2004). Cognitive behavior therapy for hypochondriasis: A randomized controlled trial. *Journal of the American Medical Association, 291*, 1464–1470.

Barsky, A. J., & Borus, J. F. (1999). Functional somatic syndromes. *Annals of Internal Medicine, 130*, 910–921.

Barsky, A. J., Fama, J. M., Bailey, E., D., & Ahern, D. K. (1998). A prospective 4- to 5-year study of DSM-III-R hypochondriasis. *Archives of General Psychiatry, 55*, 737–744.

Barsky, A. J., Wyshak, G., Klerman, G. L., & Latham, K. S. (1990). The prevalence of hypochondriasis in medical outpatients. *Social Psychiatry and Psychiatric Epidemiology, 25*, 89–94.

Bennett, P., & Wilkinson, S. (1985). A comparison of psychological and medical treatment of the irritable bowel syndrome. *British Journal of Clinical Psychology, 24*, 215–216.

Binzer, M., Andersen, P. M., & Kullgren, G. (1997). Clinical characteristics of patients with motor disability due to conversion disorder: A prospective control group study. *Journal of Neurology Neurosurgery and Psychiatry, 63*, 83–88.

Birket-Smith, M., & Mortensen, E. L. (2002). Pain in somatoform disorders: Is somatoform pain disorder a valid diagnosis? *Acta Psychiatrica Scandanavica, 106*, 103–108.

Blanchard, E. B., Greene, B., Scharff, L., & Schwarz-McMorris, S. P. (1993). Relaxation training as a treatment for irritable bowel syndrome. *Biofeedback and Self Regulation, 18*, 125–132.

Blanchard, E. B., Schwarz, S. P., Suls, J. M., Gerardi, M. A., Scharff, L., Greene, B., et al. (1992a). Two controlled evaluations of multi-component psychological treatment of irritable bowel syndrome (study 1). *Behaviour Research and Therapy, 30*, 175–189.

Blanchard, E. B., Schwarz, S. P., Suls, J. M., Gerardi, M. A., Scharff, L., Greene, B., et al. (1992b). Two controlled evaluations of multi-component psychological treatment of irritable bowel syndrome (study 2). *Behaviour Research and Therapy, 30*, 175–189.

Boyce, P. M., Talley, N. J., Balaam, B., Koloski, N. A., & Truman, G. (2003). A randomized controlled trial of cognitive behavioral therapy, relaxation training, and routine clinical care for the irritable bowel syndrome. *American Journal of Gastroenterology, 98*, 2209–2218.

Breuer, J., & Sigmund, F. (1895/1974). *Studies on hysteria.* (J. Strachey & A. Strachey, Trans.). Harmondsworth: Penguin. (Original work published 1895).

Briquet, P. (1859). *Traité clinique et thérapeutique de l'hystérie.* Paris: Bailliére & Fils.

Buchwald, D., & Garrity, D. (1994). Comparison of patients with chronic fatigue syndrome, fibromyalgia, and multiple chemical sensitivities. *Archives of Internal Medicine, 154*, 2049–2053.

Clark, D. M., Salkovskis, P. M., Hackmann, A., Wells, A., Fennell, M., Ludgate, J., et al. (1998). Two psychological treatments for hypochondriasis: A randomised controlled trial. *British Journal of Psychiatry, 173*, 218–225.

Clauw, D. J. (1995). The pathogenesis of chronic pain and fatigue syndromes, with special reference to fibromyalgia. *Medical Hypotheses, 44*, 369–378.

Corney, R. H., Stanton, R., Newell, R., Clare, A., & Fairclough, P. (1991). Behavioural psychotherapy in the treatment of irritable bowel syndrome. *Journal of Psychosomatic Research, 35*, 461–469.

Creed, F., Fernandes, L., Guthrie, E., Palmer, S., Ratcliffe, J., Read, N., et al. (2003). The cost-effectiveness of psychotherapy and paroxetine for severe irritable bowel syndrome. *Gastroenterology, 124*, 303-317.

Creed, F., Firth, D., Timol, M., Metcalfe, R., & Pollock, S. (1990). Somatization and illness behaviour in a neurology ward. *Journal of Psychosomatic Research, 34*, 427–437.

Crerand, C. E., Phillips, K. A., Menard, W., & Fay, C. (2005). Nonpsychiatric medical treatment of body dysmorphic disorder. *Psychosomatics, 46*, 549–555.

Crimlisk, H. L., Bhatia, K., Cope, H., David, A., Marsden, C. D., & Ron, M. A. (1998). Slater revisited: 6-year follow-up study of patients with medically unexplained motor symptoms. *British Medical Journal, 316*, 582–586.

Deale, A., Chalder, T., Marks, I., & Wessely, S. (1997). Cognitive behavior therapy for chronic fatigue syndrome: A randomized controlled trial. *American Journal of Psychiatry, 154*, 408–414.

Deale, A., Kaneez, A., Chalder, T., & Wessely S. (2001). Long-term outcome of cognitive behavior therapy versus relaxation therapy for chronic fatigue syndrome: A 5-year follow-up study. *American Journal of Psychiatry, 158*, 2038–2041.

Deveci, A., Taskin, O., Dinc, G., Yilmaz, H., Demet, M. M., Erbay-Dundar, P., et al. (2007). Prevalence of pseudoneurological conversion disorder in an urban community in Manisa, Turkey. *Social Psychiatry and Psychiatric Epidemiology, 42*, 857–864.

Dickinson, W. P., Dickinson, L. M., deGruy, F. V., Main, D. S., Candib, L. M., & Rost, (2003). A randomized clinical trial of a care recommendation letter intervention for somatization in primary care. *Annals of Family Medicine, 1*, 228–235.

Dongier, M. (1983). Briquet and Briquet's syndrome viewed from France. *Canadian Journal of Psychiatry, 6*, 422–427.

Drossman, D. A., Li, Z., Andruzzi, E., Temple, R. D., Talley, N. J., Thompson, W. G., et al. (1993). U.S. householder survey of functional gastrointestinal disorders: Prevalence, sociodemography and health impact. *Digestive Disease Science, 38*, 1569–1580.

Drossman, D. A., Toner, B. B., Whitehead, W. E., Diamant, N. E., Dalton, C. B., Duncan, S., et al. (2003). Cognitive-behavioral therapy versus education and desipramine versus placebo for moderate to severe functional bowel disorders. *Gastroenterology, 125*, 19–31.

Drossman, D. A., Whitehead, W. E., & Camilleri, M. (1997). Medical position statement: Irritable bowel syndrome. *Gastroenterology, 112*, 2118–2119.

Eisendrath, S. J., Rand, D. C., & Feldman, M. D. (1996). Factitious disorders and litigation. In M. D. Feldman & S. J. Eisendrath (Eds.), *The spectrum of factitious disorders* (pp. 65–81). Washington, DC: American Psychiatric Publishing.

Engel, G. L. (1959). Psychogenic pain and the pain-prone patient. *American Journal of Medicine, 26*, 899–918.

Engel G. L. (1977). The need for a new medical model: A challenge for biomedicine. *Science, 196*, 129–136.

Escobar, J. I., Burnam, A., Karno, M., Forsythe, A., & Golding J. M. (1987). Somatization in the community. *Archives of General Psychiatry, 44*, 713-718.

Escobar, J. I., Gara, M. I., Diaz-Martinez, A. M., Interian, A., Warman, M., Allen, L. A., et al. (2007). Effectiveness of a time-limited cognitive behavior therapy–type intervention among primary care patients with medically unexplained symptoms. *Annals of Family Medicine, 5*, 328–335.

Escobar, J. I., Gara, M., Waitzkin, H., Silver, R. C., Holman, A., & Compton, W. (1998). DSM-IV hypochondriasis in primary care. *General Hospital Psychiatry, 20*, 155–159.

Escobar, J. I., Golding, J. M., Hough, R. L., Karno, M., Burnam, M. A., & Wells, K. B. (1987). Somatization in the community: Relationship to disability and use of services. *American Journal of Public Health, 77*, 837–840.

Escobar, J. I., Rubio-Stipec, M., Canino, G., & Karno, M. (1989). Somatic symptom index (SSI): A new and abridged somatization construct. Prevalence and epidemiological correlates in two large community samples. *Journal of Nervous & Mental Disease, 177*, 140–146.

Escobar, J. I., Waitzkin, H., Silver, R. C., Gara, M., & Holman, A. (1998). Abridged somatization: A study in primary care. *Psychosomatic Medicine, 60*, 466–472.

Fabrega, H., Mezzich, J., Jacob, R., & Ulrich, R. (1988). Somatoform disorder in a psychiatric setting: Systematic comparisons with depression and anxiety disorders. *Journal of Nervous and Mental Disease, 176*, 431–439.

Faravelli, C., Salvatori, S., Galassi, F., Aiazzi, L., Drei, C., & Cabras, P. (1997). Epidemiology of somatoform disorders: A community survey in Florence. *Social Psychiatry and Psychiatric Epidemiology, 32*, 24–29.

Fava, G. A., Grandi, S., Rafanelli, C., Fabbri, S., & Cazzaro, M. (2000). Explanatory therapy in hypochondriasis. *Journal of Clinical Psychiatry, 61*, 317–322.

Feighner, J. P., Robins, E., Guze, S. B., Woodruff, R. A., Winokur, R., & Munoz, R. (1972). Diagnostic criteria for use in psychiatric research. *Archives of General Psychiatry, 26*, 57–63.

Ferraccioli, G., Ghirelli, L., Scita, F., Nolli, M., Mozzani, M., Fontana, S., et al. (1987). EMG-biofeedback training in fibromyalgia syndrome. *Journal of Rheumatology, 14*, 820–825.

Fink, P. (1992). Surgery and medical treatment in persistent somatizing patients. *Journal of Psychosomatic Research, 36*, 439–447.

Fink, P., Steen Hansen, M., & S ndergaard, L. (2005). Somatoform disorders among first-time referrals to a neurology service. *Psychosomatics, 46*, 540–548.

Fliege, H., Grimm, A., Eckhardt-Henn, A., Gieler, U., Martin, K., & Klapp, B. F. (2007). Frequency of ICD-10 factitious disorder: Survey of senior hospital consultants and physicians in private practice. *Psychosomatics, 48*, 60–64.

Folks, D. G., Ford, C. V., & Regan, W. M. (1984). Conversion symptoms in a general hospital. *Psychosomatics, 25*, 285–295.

Fors, E. A., Sexton, H., & Gotestam, K. G. (2002). The effect of guided imagery and amitriptyline on daily fibromyalgia pain: A prospective, randomized, controlled trial. *Journal of Psychiatric Research, 36*, 179–187.

Foucault, M. (1961/1965). *Madness and civilization: A history of insanity in the age of reason.* (R. Howard, Trans.). New York: Pantheon. (Original work published 1961).

Fukuda, K., Straus, S. E., Hickie, I., Sharpe, M. C., Dobbins, J. G., & Komaroff, A. (1994). The chronic fatigue syndrome: A comprehensive approach to its definition and study. *Annals of Internal Medicine, 121*, 953–959.

Fulcher, K. Y., & White, P. D. (1997). Randomised controlled trial of graded exercise in patients with the chronic fatigue syndrome. *British Medical Journal, 341*, 1647–1652.

Galovski, T. E., & Blanchard, E. B. (1998). The treatment of irritable bowel syndrome with hypnotherapy. *Applied Psychophysiology and Biofeedback, 23*, 219–232.

Gansky, S. A., & Plesh, O. (2007). Widespread pain and fibromyalgia in a biracial cohort of young women. *Journal of Rheumatology, 34*, 810–817.

Gardner, W. N., & Bass, C. (1989). Hyperventilation in clinical practice. *British Journal of Hospital Medicine, 41*, 73–81.

Gijswijt-Hofstra, M., & Porter, R. (Eds.). (2001). *Cultures of neurasthenia: From Beard to the First World War.* Amsterdam: Rodopi.

Goldenberg, D. L., Simms, R. W., Geiger, A., & Komaroff, A. K. (1990). High frequency of fibromyalgia in patients with chronic fatigue seen in a primary care practice. *Arthritis and Rheumatism, 33*, 381–387.

Grant, J. E., Menard, W., Pagano, M. E., Fay, C., & Phillips, K. A. (2005). Substance use disorders in individuals with body dysmorphic disorder. *Journal of Clinical Psychiatry, 66*, 309–316.

Greene, B., & Blanchard, E. D. (1994). Cognitive therapy for irritable bowel syndrome. *Journal of Consulting and Clinical Psychology, 62*, 576–582.

Greeven A., van Balkom, A. J., Visser, S., Merkelbach, J. W., vanRood, Y. R., van Dyck, R., et al. (2007). Cognitive behavior therapy and paroxetine in the treatment of hypochondriasis: A randomized controlled trial. *American Journal of Psychiatry, 164*, 91–9.

Grob, G. N. (1991). *From asylum to community. Mental health policy in modern America.* Princeton, NJ: Princeton University Press.

Gunstad, J., & Phillips, K. A. (2003). Axis I comorbidity in body dysmorphic disorder. *Comprehensive Psychiatry, 44*, 270–276.

Gureje, O., Simon, G. E., Ustun, T., Goldberg, D. P. (1997). Somatization in cross-cultural perspective: A World Health Organization study in primary care. *American Journal of Psychiatry, 154*, 989–995.

Gureje, O., Ustun, T. G., & Simon, G. E. (1997). The syndrome of hypochondriasis: A cross-national study in primary care. *Psychological Medicine, 27*, 1001–1010.

Guthrie, E., Creed, F., Dawson, D., & Tomenson, B. (1991). A controlled trial of psychological treatment for the irritable bowel syndrome. *Gastroenterology, 100*, 450–457.

Guze, S. B. (1967). The diagnosis of hysteria: What are we trying to do? *American Journal of Psychiatry, 124*, 491–498.

Guze, S. B., & Perley, M. J. (1963). Observations on the natural history of hysteria. *American Journal of Psychiatry, 119*, 960–965.

Guze, S. B., Woodruff, R. A., & Clayton, P. J. (1972). Sex, age, and the diagnosis of hysteria (Briquet's syndrome). *American Journal of Psychiatry, 129*, 745–748.

Haanen, H. C. M., Hoenderdos, H. T. W., van Romunde, L. K. J., Hop, W. C. J., Mallee, C., Terwiel, J. P., & Hekster, G. B. (1991). Controlled trial of hypnotherapy in the treatment of refractory fibromyalgia. *Journal of Rheumatology, 18*, 72–75.

Hacking, I. (1995). *Rewriting the soul: Multiple personality and the sciences of memory.* Princeton, NJ: Princeton University Press.

Hacking, I. (1999). *The social construction of what?* Cambridge, MA: Harvard University Press.

Hafeiz, H. B. (1980). Hysterical conversion: A prognostic study. *British Journal of Psychiatry, 136*, 548-551.

Hahn, S. R. (2001). Physical symptoms and physician-experienced difficulty in the physician-patient relationship. *Annals of Internal Medicine, 134*, 897–904.

Harber, V. J., & Sutton, J. R. (1984). Endorphins and exercise. *Sports Medicine, 1*, 154–171.

Harvey, R. F., Salih, S. Y., & Read, A. E. (1983). Organic and functional disorders in 2000 gastroenterology outpatients. *Lancet, 1*, 632–634.

Heymann-Monnikes, I., Arnold, R., Florin, I., Herda, C., Melfsen, S., & Monnikes, H. (2000). The combination of medical treatment plus multicomponent behavioral therapy is superior to medical treatment alone in the therapy of irritable bowel syndrome. *American Journal of Gastroenterology, 95*, 981–994.

Jackson, J. L., & Kroenke, K. (2008). Prevalence, impact, and prognosis of multisomatoform disorder in primary care: A 5-year follow-up study. *Psychosomatic Medicine, 70*, 430–434.

Jason, L. A., Richman, J. A., Rademaker, A. W., Jordan, K. M., Plioplys, A. V., Taylor, R. R., et al. (1999). A community-based study of chronic fatigue syndrome. *Archives of Internal Medicine, 159*, 2129– 2137.

Katon, W., Lin, E., Von Korff, M., Russo, J., Lipscomb, P., & Bush, T. (1991). Somatization: A spectrum of severity. *American Journal of Psychiatry, 148*, 34–40.

Keel, P. J., Bodoky, C., Gerhard, U., & Muller, W. (1998). Comparison of integrated group therapy and group relaxation training for fibromyalgia. *Clinical Journal of Pain, 14*, 232–238.

Kellner, R. (1983). Prognosis of treated hypochondriasis. *Acta Psychiatrica Scandanavica, 67*, 69–76.

Kent, D. A., Tomasson, K., Coryell, W. (1995). Course and outcome of conversion and somatization disorder. A four-year follow-up. *Psychosomatics, 36*, 138–144.

Kihlstrom, J. F., & Canter Kihlstrom, L. (1999). Self, sickness, somatization, and systems of care. In R. J. Contrada & R. D. Ashmore (Eds.), *Self, identity, and physical health: Interdisciplinary exploration* (pp. 23–42). New York: Oxford University Press.

King, S. J., Wessel, J., Bhambhani, Y., Sholter, D., & Maksymowych, W. (2002). The effects of exercise and education, individually or combined, in women with fibromyalgia. *Journal of Rheumatology, 29*, 2620–2627.

Kirmayer, L. J. (1984). Culture, affect and somatization, I & II. *Transcultural Psychiatric Research Review 21*, 159–188, 237–262.

Kirmayer, L. J. (2001). Cultural variations in the clinical presentation of depression and anxiety: Implications for diagnosis and treatment. *Journal of Clinical Psychiatry, 62* (Suppl. 13), 22–28.

Kirmayer, L. J., & Robbins, J. M. (1991). Three forms of somatization in primary care: Prevalence, co-occurrence, and sociodemographic characteristics. *Journal of Nervous and Mental Disease, 179*, 647–655.

Kirmayer, L. J., Young, A., & Robbins, J. M. (1994). Symptom attribution in cultural perspective. *Canadian Journal of Psychiatry, 39*, 584–595.

Koran, L. M., Abujaoude, E., Large, M.D., & Serpe, R. T. (2008). The prevalence of body dysmorphic disorder in the United States adult population. *CNS Spectrums, 13*, 316–322.

Krahn, L. E., Li, H., & O'Connor, M. K. (2003). Patients who strive to be ill: factitious disorder with physical symptoms. *American Journal of Psychiatry, 160*, 1163–1168.

Kashner, T. M., Rost, K., Cohen, B., Anderson, M., & Smith, G. R. (1995). Enhancing the health of somatization disorder patients: Effectiveness of short-term group therapy. *Psychosomatics, 36*, 462–470.

Kroenke, K., Sharpe, M., & Sykes, R. (2007). Revising the classification of somatoform disorders: Key questions and preliminary recommendations. *Psychosomatics, 48*, 277–285.

Kroenke, K., Spitzer, R. L., deGruy, F. V., Hahn, S. R., Linzer, M., Williams, J. B., et al. (1997). Multisomatoform disorder: An alternative to undifferentiated somatoform disorder for the somatizing patient in primary care. *Archives of General Psychiatry, 54*, 352–358.

Larisch, A., Schweickhardt, A., Wirsching, M., & Fritzsche, K. (2004). Psychosocial interventions for somatizing patients by the general practitioner: A randomized controlled trial. *Journal of Psychosomatic Research, 57*, 507–514.

Lidbeck, J. (1997). Group therapy for somatization disorders in general practice: Effectiveness of a short cognitive-behavioural treatment model. *Acta Psychiatrica Scandinavica, 96*, 14–24.

Lidbeck, J. (2003). Group therapy for somatization disorders in primary care: Maintenance of treatment goals of short cognitive-behavioural treatment one-and-a-half-year follow-up. *Acta Psychiatrica Scandinavica, 107*, 449–456.

Lin, E. H., Katon, W., Von Korff, M., Bush T., Lipscomb P., Russo J., et al. (1991). Frustrating patients: Physician and patient perspectives among distressed high users of medical services. *Journal of General Internal Medicine, 6*, 241–246.

Lloyd, A. R., Hickie, I., Brockman, A., Hickie, C., Wilson, A., Dwyer, J., & Wakefield, (1993). Immunologic and psychologic therapy for patients with chronic fatigue syndrome: A double-blind, placebo-controlled trial. *American Journal of Medicine, 94*, 197–203.

Looper, K. J., & Kirmayer, L. J. (2001). Hypochondriacal concerns in a community population. *Psychological Medicine, 31*, 577–584.

Lynch, P. M., & Zamble, E. (1989). A controlled behavioral treatment study of irritable bowel syndrome. *Behavior Therapy, 20*, 509–523.

Mace, C. J., & Trimble, M. R. (1996). Ten-year prognosis of conversion disorder. *British Journal of Psychiatry, 169*, 282–288.

Mai, F. M., & Merskey, H. (1980). Briquet's treatise on hysteria. A synopsis and commentary. *Archives of General Psychiatry, 37*, 1401–1405.

Martin, A., & Jacobi, F. (2006). Features of hypochondriasis and illness worry in the general population in Germany. *Psychosomatic Medicine, 68*, 770–777.

Martin, L., Nutting, A., Macintosh, B. R., Edworthy, S. M., Butterwick, D., & Cook, J. (1996). An exercise program in the treatment of fibromyalgia. *Journal of Rheumatology, 23*, 1050–1053.

Martin, R., Bell, B., Hermann, B., & Mennemeyer, S. (2003). Non epileptic seizures and their costs: The role of neuropsychology. In G. P. Pritigano & N. H. Pliskin (Eds.), *Clinical neuropsychology and cost outcome research: A beginning* (pp. 235–258). New York: Psychology Press.

McCain, G. A., Bell, D. A., Mai, F. M., & Halliday, P. D. (1988). A controlled study of the effects of a supervised cardiovascular fitness training program on the manifestations of primary fibromyalgia. *Arthritis and Rheumatism, 31*, 1135–1141.

Mengshoel, A. M., Komnaes, H. B., & Forre, O. (1992). The effects of 20 weeks of physical fitness training in female patients with fibromyalgia. *Clinical and Experimental Rheumatology, 10*, 345–349.

Minor, M. A. (1991). Physical activity and management of arthritis. *Annals of Behavioral Medicine, 13*, 117–124.

Moene, F. C., Spinhoven, P., Hoogduin, K. A., & van, D. R. (2002). A randomized controlled clinical trial on the additional effect of hypnosis in a comprehensive treatment programme for in-patients with conversion disorder of the motor type. *Psychotherapy and Psychosomatics, 71*, 66–76.

Moene, F. C., Spinhoven, P., Hoogduin, K. A., & van, D. R. (2003). A randomized controlled clinical trial of a hypnosis-based treatment for patients with conversion disorder, motor type. *International Journal of Clinical and Experimental Hypnosis, 51*, 29–50.

Mokleby, K., Blomhoff, S., Malt, U. F., Dahlström, A., Tauböll, E., & Gjerstad, L. (2002). Psychiatric comorbidity and hostility in patients with psychogenic nonepileptic seizures compared with somatoform disorders and healthy controls. *Epilepsia, 43*, 193–198.

Neff, D. F., & Blanchard, E. B. (1987). A multi-component treatment for irritable bowel syndrome. *Behavior Therapy, 18*, 70–83.

Nicassio, P. M., Radojevic, V., Weisman, M. H., Schuman, C., Kim, J., Schoenfeld-Smith, K., & Krall, T. (1997). A comparison of behavioral and educational interventions for fibromyalgia. *Journal of Rheumatology, 24*, 2000–2007.

Noyes, R., Kathol, R. G., Fisher, M. M., Phillips, B. M., Suelzer, M. T., & Holt, C. S. (1993). The validity of DSM-III-R hypochondriasis. *Archives of General Psychiatry, 50*, 961–970.

Noyes, R., Kathol, R. G., Fisher, M. M., Phillips, B. M., Suelzer, M. T., & Woodman, C. (1994). Psychiatric comorbidity among patients with hypochondriasis. *General Hospital Psychiatry, 16*, 78–87.

Palsson, O. S., Turner, M. J., Johnson, D. A., Burnett, C. K., & Whitehead, W. E. (2002). Hypnosis treatment for severe irritable bowel syndrome: Investigation of mechanism and effects on symptoms. *Digestive Diseases and Sciences, 47*, 2605–2614.

Parsons, T. (1951). Illness and the role of the physician: A sociological perspective. *American Journal of Orthopsychiatry, 21*, 452-460.

Payne, A., & Blanchard, E. B. (1994). A controlled comparison of cognitive therapy and self-help support groups in the treatment of irritable bowel syndrome. *Journal of Consulting and Clinical Psychology, 63*, 779–786.

Perkin, G. D. (1989). An analysis of 7,836 successive new outpatient referrals. *Journal of Neurology, Neurosurgery, and Psychiatry, 52*, 447–448.

Perley, M. J., & Guze, S. B. (1962). Hysteria-the stability and usefulness of clinical criteria. *New England Journal of Medicine, 266*, 421–426.

Peveler, R., Kilkenny, L., & Kinmonth A. L. (1997). Medically unexplained physical symptoms in primary care: A comparison of self-report screening questionnaires and clinical opinion. *Journal of Psychosomatic Research, 42*, 245–252.

Phillips, K. A. (1996). *The broken mirror: Understanding and treating body dysmorphic disorder.* New York, NY: Oxford University Press.

Phillips, K. A. (2000). Quality of life for patients with body dysmorphic disorder. *Journal of Nervous & Mental Disease, 188*, 170–175.

Phillips, K. A. (2004). Psychosis in body dysmorphic disorder. *Journal of Psychiatric Research, 38*, 63–72.

Phillips, K. A., & Diaz, S. (1997). Gender differences in body dysmorphic disorder. *Journal of Nervous & Mental Disease, 185*, 570–577.

Phillips, K. A., Grant, J., Siniscalchi, J., & Albertini, R. S. (2001). Surgical and nonpsychiatric medical treatment of patients with body dysmorphic disorder. *Psychosomatics, 42*, 504–510.

Phillips, K. A., McElroy, S. L., & Keck, P. E. Jr. (1994). A comparison of delusional and nondelusional body dysmorphic disorder in 100 cases. *Psychopharmacological Bulletin, 30*, 179–186.

Phillips, K. A., McElroy, S. L., Keck, P. E. Jr., Pope, H. G. Jr., & Hudson, J. I. (1993). Body dysmorphic disorder: 30 cases of imagined ugliness. *American Journal of Psychiatry, 150*, 302–308.

Phillips, K. A., & Menard, W. (2006). Suicidality in body dysmorphic disorder: A prospective study. *American Journal of Psychiatry, 163*, 1280–1282.

Phillips, K. A., Menard, W., Fay, C., & Weisberg, R. (2005). Demographic characteristics, phenomenology, comorbidity, and family history in 200 individuals with body dysmorphic disorder. *Psychosomatics, 46*, 317–325.

Phillips, K. A., Pagano, M. E., Menard, W., & Stout, R. L. (2006). A 12-month follow-up study of the course of body dysmorphic disorder. *American Journal of Psychiatry, 163*, 907–912.

Pincus, H. A. (2003). The future of behavioral health and primary care: Drowning in the mainstream or left on the bank? *Psychosomatics, 44*, 1–11.

Powell, P., Bentall, R. P., Nye, F. J., & Edwards, R. H. T. (2001). Randomised controlled trial of patient education to encourage graded exercise in chronic fatigue syndrome. *British Medical Journal, 322*, 387–390.

Prins, J. B., Bleijenberg, G., Bazelmans, E., Elving, L. D., de Boo, T. M., Severens, J. L., et al. (2001). Cognitive behaviour therapy for chronic fatigue syndrome: A multicentre randomized controlled trial. *Lancet, 357*, 841–847.

Purtell, J. J., Robins, E., & Cohen, M. E. (1951). Observations on clinical aspects of hysteria: A quantitative study of 50 hysteria patients and 156 control subjects. *Journal of the American Medical Association, 146*, 902–909.

Regier, D., Boyd, J., Burke, J., Rae, D. S., Myers, J. K., Kramer, M., et al. (1988). One-month prevalence of mental disorders in the US: based on five epidemiological catchment area sites. *Archives of General Psychiatry, 45*, 977–986.

Reyes, M., Nisenbaum, R., Hoaglin, D. C., Unger, E. R., Emmons, C., Randall, B., et al. (2003). Prevalence and incidence of chronic fatigue syndrome in Wichita, Kansas. *Archives of Internal Medicine, 163*, 1530–1536.

Richards, S. C. M., & Scott, D. L. (2002). Prescribed exercise in people with fibromyalgia: Parallel group randomised controlled trial. *British Medical Journal, 325*, 185–189.

Rief, W., Buhlmann, U., Wilhelm, S., Borkenhagen, A., & Brähler, E. (2006). The prevalence of body dysmorphic disorder: A population-based survey. *Psychological Medicine, 36*, 877–885.

Rief, W., Hiller, W., & Margraf, J. (1998). Cognitive aspects of hypochondriasis and the somatization syndrome. *Journal of Abnormal Psychology, 107*, 587–595.

Rief, W., Martin, A., Rauh, E., Zech, T., & Bender, A. (2006). Evaluation of general practitioners' training: How to manage patients with unexplained physical symptoms. *Psychosomatics, 47*, 304–311.

Robins, L. N., & Reiger, D. (1991). *Psychiatric disorders in America: The epidemiological catchment area study.* New York: Free Press.

Robinson, D. N. (1996). *Wild beasts and idle humours: The insanity defense from antiquity to the present.* Cambridge, MA: Harvard University Press.

Ron, M. (2001). The prognosis of hysteria/somatization disorder. *Contemporary approaches to the study of hysteria.* Oxford: Oxford University Press.

Rosen, J. C., Reiter, J., & Orosan, P. (1995). Cognitive-behavioral body image therapy for body dysmorphic disorder. *Journal of Consulting and Clinical Psychology, 63*, 263–269.

Rosendal, M., Olesen, F., Fink, P., Toft, T., Sokolowski, I., & Bro, F. (2007). A randomized controlled trial of brief training in the assessment and treatment of somatization in primary care: Effects on patient outcome. *General Hospital Psychiatry, 29*, 364–373.

Rost, K., Kashner, T. M., & Smith, G. R. (1994). Effectiveness of psychiatric intervention with somatization disorder patients: Improved outcomes at reduced costs. *General Hospital Psychiatry, 16*, 381–387.

Sar, V., Akyuz, G., Kundakci, T., Kiziltan, E., & Dogan, O. (2004). Childhood trauma, dissociation, and psychiatric comorbidity in patients with conversion disorder. *American Journal of Psychiatry, 161*, 2271–2276.

Sarwer, D. B., & Crerand, C. E. (2008). Body dysmorphic disorder and appearance enhancing medical treatments. *Body Image, 5*, 50–58.

Sharpe, M., Hawton, K., Simkin, S., Surawy, C., Hackmann, A., Klimes, I., et al. (1996). Cognitive behaviour therapy for the chronic fatigue syndrome: A randomised controlled trial. *British Medical Journal, 312*, 22–26.

Shaw, G., Srivastava, E. D., Sadlier, M., Swann, P., James, J. Y., & Rhodes, J. (1991). Stress management for irritable bowel syndrome: A controlled trial. *Digestion, 50*, 36–42.

Simon, G. E., & VonKorff, M. (1991). Somatization and psychiatric disorder in the NIMH Epidemiologic Catchment Area Study. *American Journal of Psychiatry, 148*, 1494–1500.

Simon, G. E., VonKorff, M., Piccinelli, M., Fullerton, C., & Ormel, J. (1999). An international study of the relation between somatic symptoms and depression. *The New England Journal of Medicine, 341*, 1329–1335.

Smith, G. R., Monson, R. A., Ray, D. C. (1986a). Patients with multiple unexplained symptoms: Their characteristics, functional health, and health care utilization. *Archives of Internal Medicine, 146*, 69–72.

Smith, G. R., Monson, R. A., & Ray, D. C. (1986b). Psychiatric consultation letter in somatization disorder. *New England Journal of Medicine, 314*, 1407–1413.

Smith, G. R., Rost, K., & Kashner, M. (1995). A trial of the effect of a standardized psychiatric consultation on health outcomes and costs in somatizing patients. *Archives of General Psychiatry, 52,* 238–243.

Smith, R. C., Lyles, J. S., Gardiner, J. C., Sirbu, C., Hodges, A., Collins, C., et al. (2006). Primary care clinicians treat patients with medically unexplained symptoms: A randomized controlled trial. *Journal of General Internal Medicine, 21,* 671–677.

Speckens, A. E. M., van Hemert, A. M., Spinhoven, P., Hawton, K. E., Bolk, J. H., & Rooijmans, G. M. (1995). Cognitive behavioural therapy for medically unexplained physical symptoms: A randomised controlled trial. *British Medical Journal, 311,* 1328–1332.

Stefansson, J. G., Messina, J. A., & Meyerowitz, S. (1979). Hysterical neurosis, conversion type: Clinical and epidemiological considerations. *Acta Psychiatrica Scandanavica, 53,* 119–138.

Sullivan, M. D. (2000). DSM-IV Pain Disorder: A case against the diagnosis. *International Review of Psychiatry, 12,* 91–98.

Sumathipala, A., Hewege, S., Hanwella, R., & Mann, A. H. (2000). Randomized controlled trial of cognitive behaviour therapy for repeated consultations for medically unexplained complaints: a feasibility study in Sri Lanka. *Psychological Medicine, 30,* 747–757.

Svedlund, J., Sjodin, I., Ottosson, J. O., & Dotevall, G. (1983). Controlled study of psychotherapy in irritable bowel syndrome. *Lancet, 2,* 589–592.

Swartz, M., Blazer, D., George, L., & Landerman, R. (1986). Somatization disorder in a community population. *American Journal of Psychiatry, 143,* 1403–1408.

Swartz, M., Landermann, R., George, L., Blazer, D., & Escobar, J. (1991). Somatization. In L. N. Robins & D. Reiger (Eds.), *Psychiatric disorders in America* (pp. 220–257). New York: Free Press.

Thieme, K., Gromnica-Ihle, E., & Flor, H. (2003). Operant behavioral treatment of fibromyalgia: A controlled study. *Arthritis Care and Research, 49,* 314–320.

Thomson, A. B., & Page, L. A. (2007). Psychotherapies for hypochondriasis. *Cochrane Database of Systematic Reviews, 4,* CD006520.

Thompson, W. G., Dotevall, G., Drossman, D. A., Heaton, K. W., & Kruis, W. (1989). Irritable bowel syndrome: Guidelines for the diagnosis. *Gastroenterology International, 2,* 92–95.

Thompson, W. G., & Heaton, K. W. (1980). Functional bowel disorders in apparently healthy people. *Gastroenterology, 79,* 283–288.

Ung, E. K., & Lee, D. S-W. (1999). Thin desires and fat realities. *Singapore Medical Journal, 40,* 495–497.

van der Feltz-Cornelis, C. (2002). The impact of factitious disorder on the physician-patient relationship. An epistemological model. *Medicine, Health Care, & Philosophy, 5,* 253–261.

Van Dulmen, A. M., Fennis, J. F. M., & Bleijenberg, G. (1996). Cognitive-behavioral group therapy for irritable bowel syndrome: Effects and long-term follow-up. *Psychosomatic Medicine, 58,* 508–514.

Veale, D., Boocock, A., Goumay, E., Dryden, W., Shah, R., Willson, R., & Walburn, J. (1996). Body dysmorphic disorder. A survey of fifty cases. *British Journal of Psychiatry, 169,* 196–201.

Veale, D., Gournay, K., Dryden, W., Boocock, A., Shah, F., Willson, R., & Walburn, J. (1996). Body dysmorphic disorder: A cognitive behavioural model and pilot randomised controlled trial. *Behaviour Research and Therapy, 34,* 717–729.

Veale, D., Kavanagh, G., Fielding, J. F., & Fitzgerald, O. (1991). Primary fibromyalgia and the irritable bowel syndrome: Different expressions of a common pathogenetic process. *British Journal of Rheumatology, 30,* 220–222.

Visser, S., & Bouman, T. K. (2001). The treatment of hypochondriasis: Exposure plus response prevention vs. cognitive therapy. *Behaviour Research & Therapy, 39,* 423–442.

Vlaeyen, J. W. S., Teeken-Gruben, N. J. G., Goossens, M. E. J. B., Rutten-van Molken, M. P. M. H., Pelt, R. A. G. B., van Eek, H., & Heuts, P. H. T. G. (1996). Cognitive-educational treatment of fibromyalgia: A randomized clinical trial. I. Clinical effects. *Journal of Rheumatology, 23,* 1237–1245.

Vollmer, A., & Blanchard, E. B. (1998). Controlled comparison of individual versus group cognitive therapy for irritable bowel syndrome. *Behavior Therapy, 29,* 19–33.

Warwick, H. M. C., Clark, D. M., Cobb, A. M., & Salkovskis, P. M. (1996). A controlled trial of cognitive-behavioural treatment of hypochondriasis. *British Journal of Psychiatry, 169,* 189–195.

Wearden, A. J., Morris, R. K., Mullis, R., Strickland, P. L., Pearson, D. J., Appleby, L., et al. (1998). Randomized, double-blind, placebo-controlled treatment trial of fluoxetine and graded exercise for chronic fatigue syndrome. *British Journal of Psychiatry, 172,* 485–490.

Weissman, M. M., Myers, J. K., & Harding, P. S. (1978). Psychiatric disorders in a U.S. urban community: 1975–1976. *American Journal of Psychiatry, 135,* 459–462.

Wessely, S., Chadler, T., Hirsch, S., Wallace, P., & Wright, D. (1997). The epidemiology of chronic fatigue and chronic fatigue syndrome: A prospective primary care study. *American Journal of Public Health, 87,* 1449–1455.

Wessely, S., Nimnuan, C., & Sharpe, M. (1999). Functional somatic syndromes: One or many? *Lancet, 354,* 936–939.

Weyerer, S., & Kupfer, B. (1994). Physical exercise and psychological health. *Sports Medicine, 17,* 108–116.

White, G. M. (1982). The role of cultural explanations in "somatization" and "psychologization." *Social Science and Medicine, 16,* 1519–1530.

Whorwell, P. J., Prior, A., & Farragher, E. B. (1984). Controlled trial of hypnotherapy in the treatment of severe refractory irritable bowel syndrome. *Lancet, 2,* 1232–1234.

Williams, D. A., Cary, M. A., Groner, K. H., Chaplin, W., Glazer, L. J., Rodriguez, A. M., & Clauw, D. J. (2002). Improving physical functional status in patients with fibromyalgia: A brief cognitive behavioral intervention. *Journal of Rheumatology, 29,* 1280–1286.

Wolfe, F., Ross, K., Anderson, J., Russell, I. J., & Hebert, L. (1995). The prevalence and characteristics of fibromyalgia in the general population. *Arthritis and Rheumatism, 38,* 19–28.

Wolfe, F., Smythe, H. A., Yunus, M. B., Bennett, R. M., Bombardier, C., Goldenberg, D. L., et al. (1990). The American College of Rheumatology 1990 criteria for the classification of fibromyalgia: Report of the Multicenter Criteria Committee. *Arthritis and Rheumatism, 33,* 160–172.

Woolfolk, R. L. (1998). *The cure of souls: Science, values, and psychotherapy.* San Francisco, CA: Jossey-Bass.

Woolfolk, R. L., & Allen, L. A. (2007). *Treating Somatization: A Cognitive-Behavioral Approach.* New York: Guilford Press.

World Health Organization. (1979). *The ICD-9 classification of mental and behavioural disorders: Diagnostic criteria for research*. Geneva, Switzerland: Author.

World Health Organization. (1993). *The ICD-10 classification of mental and behavioural disorders: Diagnostic criteria for research*. Geneva, Switzerland: Author.

Yunus, M. B., Masi, A. T., & Aldag, J. C. (1989). A controlled study of primary fibromyalgia syndrome: Clinical features and association with other functional syndromes. *Journal of Rheumatology, 16* (Suppl. 19), 62–71.

Yutzy, S. H., Cloninger, R., Guze, S. B., Pribor, E. F., Martin, R. L., Kathol, R. G., et al. (1995). DSM-IV field trial: Testing a new proposal for somatization disorder. *American Journal of Psychiatry, 152*, 97–101.

Trauma, Dissociation, and Post-traumatic Stress Disorder

Terence M. Keane, Brian P. Marx, Denise M. Sloan, *and* Anne DePrince

Abstract

Worldwide, post-traumatic stress disorder (PTSD) is among the most common psychological disorders; over the past three decades researchers have made considerable progress in understanding the prevalence of PTSD and its psychological and biological underpinnings, while developing methods for its assessment and treatment. Only included in the diagnostic nomenclature since 1980, the history of PTSD extends as far back as the oldest literature in Western civilization. Homer's *Iliad* and *Odyssey* capture the impact of war on combatants and civilians, as do many of the works of writers and artists across the centuries. The focus of this chapter is on the integration of contemporary work on traumatic stress exposure, psychological dissociation, and the development of PTSD, a disorder characterized by concurrent high levels of anxiety and depression and, in many instances, considerable chronicity and disability. More than 50 randomized controlled treatment outcome studies suggest that cognitive-behavioral treatments are especially effective, and support the use of exposure therapy, stress management therapy, cognitive therapy, cognitive processing therapy, and eye movement desensitization and reprocessing in treating PTSD. All these approaches constitute key evidence-based psychological treatments for PTSD. Future work will determine which treatments used by which therapists are best for patients with specific symptoms and concomitant conditions.

Keywords: Dissociation, post-traumatic stress disorder, stress, trauma

The earliest cultural works of Western civilization describe the devastating personal impact of exposure to violence, war, and related trauma. The psychological consequences of these experiences are well captured in the art, literature, and theatrical plays that describe the human condition throughout the centuries. Eloquent descriptions of trauma sequelae can be found in reference to the Civil War (e.g., Stephen Crane's description in *The Red Badge of Courage*), the presence of "irritable heart" among soldiers (Da Costa, 1871), Page's (1883) conception of railroad spine (distress following train crashes in the United Kingdom), the psychological consequences of the disastrous 1666 Great Fire of London (Daly, 1983), and even the Trojan War (e.g., the story of Ulysses in Homer's *Iliad*). Anxiety as a specific

response to severe or traumatic life stress is described by Oppenheim (1892; cited by Kraepelin, 1896), who labeled this response as "traumatic neurosis," and by Kraepelin (1896) who labeled it "Schreckneurose" (i.e., fright neurosis). Each of these early contributors to diagnostic nomenclature recognized something special and perhaps distinct about the psychological disorders that emerge from exposure to traumatic life events.

Despite these common observations throughout history, the scientific study of traumatic responses is a recent enterprise. After World Wars I and II, studies of psychological distress among combatants and concentration camp survivors set the stage for the recognition of the long-term negative effects of trauma exposure. Terms such as "shell shock," "combat fatigue," and "war neurosis" all seemed to capture the essence of war-related post-traumatic stress disorder (PTSD), but the psychological effects of other traumatic life stressors were not recognized in the research literature until Ann Burgess at the famed Boston City Hospital observed the impact of rape on women (Burgess & Holmstrom, 1974). Once advocates for rape survivors and Vietnam veterans teamed with scholars who had studied and treated World War II veterans and concentration camp survivors, the diagnosis of PTSD emerged in the *Diagnostic and Statistical Manual of Mental Disorders* (DSM) of the American Psychiatric Association (APA, 1980).

Given the consistent historical precedence associated with the notion of a trauma condition, it is somewhat surprising that controversy regarding its validity emerged during the 1970s and '80s (Figley, 1978; Goodwin & Guze, 1984). Although much of the initial controversy about PTSD's validity has ceased, the nature of the disorder still instigates considerable debate in the field (see Brewin, 2003; Weathers & Keane, 2007). Conceptual issues still exist about the precise definition of PTSD, about which symptoms should define the disorder, and the proposition that PTSD is simply a social construction, not a psychiatric disorder (McNally, 2004).

Dissociation is a more modern term that developed from the 19th-century origins of contemporary psychiatry. Pierre Janet, of the Salpetriere in Paris, discussed the cognitive and behavioral consequences of exposure to traumatic events. He described many of the basic phenomena that we now characterize as dissociative through his interviews with patients who were then viewed as suffering from hysteria. Alterations in consciousness, observed defects in attention and memory, and suggestibility are key components of dissociation. Theories of psychopathology proposed by the Europeans Charcot (1887), Janet (1909), and Freud (1896) all relied upon the storage of emotionally laden material in an altered level of consciousness (dissociated state) that adversely influenced the individual's behavior, cognition, and affect. This stored material affected one's view of the world, the way one interacted with the world, and the emotional state in which one lived.

More recent views of dissociation directly connect dissociative states to the field of psychological trauma and PTSD. Although some authorities state that traumatic events spawn the development of dissociative experiences as a direct function of the overwhelming emotions associated with the event (van der Kolk & Fisler, 1995), others propose that dissociation at the time of the event (peritraumatic

dissociation) is a potent biopsychological phenomenon that is an important etiological variable in the ultimate development of PTSD (Marmar et al., 1994; Ozer, Best, Lipsey, & Weiss, 2003). In the former conceptualization, the stress is so extreme that a protective splitting from reality into fantasy mitigates the impact of the event. In the latter formulation, dissociation at the time of the event appears to function as a protective mechanism immediately, but ultimately results in the development of the very disabling condition we know as PTSD. These findings suggest that dissociation is a cognitive mechanism that precludes the adaptive processing of the emotional concomitants of the traumatic experience.

Freyd (1996) and her colleagues (DePrince & Freyd, 1999; 2004; Freyd, Klest, & Allard, 2005) studied what might amount to the most challenging area of research in the field of trauma: failure to recall highly significant traumatic life events such as childhood sexual abuse or even combat events. In 1994, Linda Williams reported on a cohort of women who were sexually abused as children, and learned that a high percentage of these women didn't recall the index episode of sexual abuse. This study, and observations by clinicians nationwide, instigated an intense debate about whether it is possible for people to forget the memories associated with such a significant life event. Freyd's premise, termed "Betrayal Trauma Theory" relied upon Darwinian survival notions to help us understand why children exposed to incest or violence in the home might not recall such experiences. The greater the reliance upon responsible caretakers and the closer the abuser is to the abused, the less likely the individual is to bring this abuse into consciousness. This betrayal by a needed caretaker results in motivation for the abused to not recall the events by the abuser. To do so might threaten the abused person's very survival. Freyd's work established a scientific foundation for understanding the cognitive and motivational aspects of one form of dissociative experience: the absence of recall of significant aspects of a traumatic event.

In its current conception of psychological trauma, the DSM-IV (American Psychiatric Association [APA], 1994) defines PTSD as necessarily stemming from an event in which one is exposed to serious threat of injury or death and then experiences extreme fear, helplessness, or horror. Three symptom clusters define the disorder. In addition to recurrent and intrusive recollections and dreams of the event, the "reexperiencing" cluster includes the experience of "flashback" episodes wherein an individual experiences a recurrence of at least a portion of the trauma.

"Hyperarousal" symptoms are characterized by an enhanced startle reaction and difficulty sleeping, concentrating, and controlling anger, as well as hypervigilance for danger and a sense of a foreshortened future. Extreme distress and avoidance of cues or reminders of the trauma, as well as an inability to remember aspects of the event, also can accompany this disorder. Additional "avoidance" symptoms include emotional numbing, described as an inability to feel any positive emotions such as love, contentment, satisfaction, or happiness.

The interpersonal, psychosocial, physical health, and societal consequences of PTSD are considerable. Those with PTSD are more likely to divorce, report trouble raising their children, engage in intimate partner aggression, experience depression and other psychological problems, report poorer life satisfaction and physical health problems, become involved with the legal system, earn less, and change jobs frequently (Jordan et al., 1992; Koss, Woodruff, & Koss, 1991; Kulka et al. 1990; Schnurr & Green, 2004; Walker et al., 2003). These findings suggest that PTSD constitutes a major problem for the public health of this nation and the world, and highlight the importance of prevention and intervention efforts. As with many conditions, to date we've accomplished more in terms of treatment than in prevention, although progress in this domain is beginning to emerge in the literature and especially with respect to the military (Adler, Bliese, McGurk, Hoge, & Castro, 2009). The purpose of this chapter is to highlight the interrelationships among trauma exposure, dissociative phenomena, and the development of PTSD and related psychological conditions. In it, we will highlight progress in both the assessment and treatment of PTSD, as well as provide an understanding the prevalence of this disorder.

Trauma Spectrum

In multiple venues, we have proposed the creation of a category of *trauma spectrum disorders* (Keane, 2008; Keane & Miller, 2009) as a result of new evidence that PTSD and its related conditions don't appear to fit with other anxiety disorders. In addition, it was our premise that, conceptually, it is more appropriate for disorders that occur in proximity to exposure to an extreme life event are best classified together. For our purposes, we considered clustering together the following psychological conditions: PTSD, acute stress disorder (ASD), adjustment disorder, dissociative disorders, trauma-related phobias, grief, bereavement, and trauma-related personality disorders.

Our thinking on this issue is related to several converging sources of information. First, it is clear that anxiety or fear is only one aversive emotion that can lead to PTSD. Other intense emotional experiences can lead to PTSD, such as rage, horror, guilt, and shame. Second, PTSD is only one of several possible outcomes of exposure to a traumatic event. Other Axis I and Axis II conditions can emerge: depression, phobias, substance abuse, and personality disorders are common.

Third, those disorders that are conditional on exposure to a precipitating traumatic event seem logically to share common elements. For example, PTSD, ASD, adjustment disorder, pathological grief, and bereavement all share a proximal instigating event and attendant emotional responses, whether these were fear, loss, or shame. Fourth, PTSD doesn't appear to aggregate with other items in the anxiety disorders. For example, Slade and Watson (2006) found that in the structure of common mental disorders, PTSD was more strongly associated with major depression, dysthymia, and generalized anxiety disorder rather than with the other key anxiety disorders like panic, social phobia, agoraphobia, and obsessive-compulsive disorder all of which were more highly correlated with one another. Similarly, Miller, Fogler, Wolf, Kaloupek, and Keane (2008) found that PTSD in combat veterans was more strongly related to major depression and alcohol abuse than it was to panic disorder, agoraphobia, and obsessive-compulsive disorder. Thus, trauma-related psychopathology shares more in common with other conditions than it does with the anxiety disorders.

Fifth, we feel that the causal influence of PTSD on the high rates of comorbidity often observed in people with PTSD (cf., Keane & Wolfe, 1990) are important new findings in this literature. For example, PTSD typically leads to depression or substance abuse, but the inverse relationship doesn't appear to be as strong. Breslau, Davis, Peterson, and Schultz (2000) first demonstrated this in their longitudinal cohort of young adults in the Detroit metropolitan area. In a related series of analyses, Brown, Campbell, Lehman, Grisham, and Mancill (2001) found that when they examined the onset of comorbid depression, obsessive-compulsive disorder, panic disorder, alcohol abuse, and drug abuse in cases of PTSD, these disorders were far more likely to develop once PTSD was present. This causal influence of PTSD on comorbid psychopathology suggests a distinct phenomenology that should be reflected in its diagnostic class membership within the DSM. Constructing a spectrum of trauma-induced disorders appears to be one viable solution for the most appropriate placement of PTSD and related conditions.

Finally, Miller, Resick, and Keane (2008) reviewed studies of adult psychopathology that assert that childhood and/or adolescent anxiety disorders foreshadow the emergence of adult anxiety problems. Post-traumatic stress disorder departs from the other anxiety disorders in this realm too; adults with PTSD often display externalizing disorders as children (rather than the more typical internalizing precedents in anxiety disorders; Gregory et al., 2007). This represents more evidence that PTSD may actually be better situated with other disorders of stress exposure rather than with anxiety.

Further DSM Considerations

Irrespective of the placement of PTSD in the DSM, the diagnostic criteria for PTSD need modification. Weathers and Keane (2007) reviewed the literature with respect to the bifurcation of Criterion A into A1 – trauma event exposure, and A2 – trauma event response. We found that this exposure–response distinction did very little to tighten the entrance into the diagnosis, as was initially intended. As a result, most authorities are recommending the combining of A1 and A2 into a single dimension of exposure.

Other issues pertain to the existing criteria. In particular, confirmatory factor analytic studies (e.g., King, Leskin, King, & Weathers, 1998) find four latent factors underlying the existing symptom criteria of PTSD, rather than the three conceptual factors that appear in the diagnostic criteria (i.e., intrusion, numbing/avoidance, and hyperarousal). Most typically, in factor analytic studies, the avoidance and numbing symptoms are found to be distinct factors. Adjusting the factors so that they represent how the symptoms are found naturally seems to be an obvious course for future modifications for the DSM.

Most of the concerns expressed about these diagnostic criteria, however, are based on the fact that, although patients with PTSD meet the diagnostic criteria, they do not seem to resemble these criteria. This has led to many variations, such as complex PTSD, which focuses greatly on issues of emotional lability and instability, impaired interpersonal relations, and self-esteem. These latter symptoms can actually characterize many patients who've experienced trauma and have developed PTSD. For instance, when examined concurrently, the vast majority of people with PTSD also met diagnostic criteria for disorders of extreme stress or complex

PTSD (Newman, Orsillo, Herman, Niles, & Litz, 1995). Thus, there is considerable overlap between PTSD and the constructs proposed as distinct entities.

Finally, it is valuable to understand that, in any classification scheme in science, one tries to employ the fewest number of items to discriminate one condition from the next. If we were trying to describe PTSD by the diagnostic criteria, we would most assuredly lead with anxiety and depression. Yet neither of these symptoms provides any discriminatory power to the diagnostic criteria in segregating PTSD from either mood or anxiety conditions. The symptoms of intrusion, hyperarousal, numbing, and avoidance provide the greatest levels of distinction of PTSD from similar psychological conditions.

The Interrelationship of Trauma and Dissociation

Among the complex issues involved in understanding PTSD is its relationship with dissociation. Dissociative experiences overlap considerably with PTSD, leading to at least three dominant explanations for their co-occurrence. First, co-occurring PTSD and dissociation may reflect complex adaptations to trauma, particularly traumas that occur early in child development, when regulation systems are still developing (e.g., van der Kolk et al., 1996). For example, PTSD, dissociation, somatization, and affect dysregulation were highly interrelated in a sample of 395 treatment-seeking and 125 non–treatment seeking individuals exposed to trauma. Second, high (or pathological) levels of dissociation may characterize a specific subtype of PTSD (e.g., Putnam, 1997). For example, adult rape survivors who scored high on measures of dissociation 2 weeks post-rape were more likely to meet symptom criteria for PTSD *and* show suppressed autonomic physiological responses in the lab (Griffin, Resick, & Mechanic, 1997). Because PTSD is usually thought of as associated with greater physiological reactivity, the suppressed physiological finding is particularly noteworthy. Putnam, Carlson, Ross, and Anderson (1996) examined dissociative tendencies (as measured by the Dissociative Experiences Scale; DES) and PTSD among 1,566 individuals who comprised three groups: psychiatric patients, neurological patients, or typical adolescents or adults. Half of the participants diagnosed with PTSD scored in the extreme range on the DES and half in the normal range. Similarly, Briere, Scott, and Weathers (2005) reported that approximately 44% of participants diagnosed with PTSD did not have clinically elevated scores on a dissociation measure.

Third, PTSD symptoms can be conceptualized as dissociative symptoms. For example, van der Hart, Nijenhuis, and Steele (2005) propose that dissociation is not only a central feature of PTSD, but that PTSD can be reconceptualized into two categories of dissociative symptoms: positive (e.g., traumatic memories and nightmares) and negative (e.g., loss of affect, loss of memory). By this logic, high correlations between PTSD and dissociation should not be surprising, as they are part of the same underlying construct.

Still other theorists and researchers remain agnostic with regard to the reason for the relationship between concurrent PTSD and dissociation symptoms, but note the importance of dissociative responses in understanding PTSD trajectories (e.g., Halligan, Michael, Clark, & Ehlers, 2003).

Prevalence Issues

When initially delineated in the DSM-III, PTSD was considered to be a relatively rare condition, and traumatic events were considered to be outside the range of normal human experience. In the past two decades, there has been an explosion of growth in our knowledge of exposure to traumatic events, the development of PTSD, and the conditional probability of developing PTSD if one is exposed to a specific life event. Recent epidemiological studies document high prevalence rates of exposure to traumatic events in the general population and confirm that PTSD occurs following a wide range of aversive life events. Most important, though, are the consistent findings that suggest that although exposure to potentially traumatic events is quite common, development of PTSD is relatively rare. Elucidation of the factors responsible for some people developing PTSD while others exposed to similar threatening events do not may inform our understanding of key variables in the etiology of this condition. These factors are termed risk and resilience variables.

Post-traumatic Stress Disorder in the U.S. Population

Perhaps the most complete general U.S. population studies are those conducted by Kessler and colleagues. In the original National Comorbidity Survey (NCS; Kessler, Sonnega, Bromet, Hughes, & Nelson, 1995), a nationally representative sample of 5,877 individuals aged 15–54 years were interviewed using a structured diagnostic inventory. An overall lifetime PTSD prevalence rate of 7.8% was found, with rates for women (10.4%) more than twice that for men (5.0%). Trauma exposure estimates indicated

that about 61% of men and 51% of women were exposed to one or more traumatic events. In the National Comorbidity Survey Replication (NCS-R; Kessler et al., 2005), a nationally representative sample of 5,692 individuals were interviewed based on the Composite International Diagnostic Interview. Similar to the rates reported in the NCS, an overall lifetime PTSD prevalence rate of 6.8% was found.

Compared to the NCS and NCS-R, similar or slightly higher PTSD rates were obtained in selected, specialized samples. For example, among 21–30-year-old members of a Detroit area HMO, 39% reported experiencing a trauma and 9% met PTSD criteria (11% of women and 6% of men; Breslau, Davis, Andreski, & Peterson, 1991). Similarly, among former Miami–Dade public school students aged 18–23, 11.5% met lifetime PTSD criteria (15.5% of women and 7.5% of men; Lloyd & Turner, 2003). Further, among two American Indian tribes, lifetime PTSD rates were 14% and 16%, whereas past year rates were 5% and 6%, with higher rates consistently found among women compared to men (Beals et al., 2005).

Emphasizing the impact of sexual assault and other criminal acts, several epidemiological studies focused on documenting PTSD in women. For example, Kilpatrick, Edmunds, and Seymour (1992), in a nationally representative sample of women, learned that 13% of 4,008 participants reported a completed rape. Of those who were raped, lifetime and current PTSD rates were 32% and 12%, respectively. Importantly, Kilpatrick and his group (2008) conducted a similar survey 10 years later to learn that the prevalence of rape in the general population of women rose significantly to 18%. These rates were especially disappointing, given the implementation of policies to address date rape in the intervening decade between these two epidemiological surveys. Finally, using a national probability sample, Resnick, Kilpatrick, Dansky, Saunders, and Best (1993) estimated that 36% of women had been criminally victimized, with 14% experiencing attempted rape or molestation and 12% experiencing a completed rape. They estimated lifetime and current PTSD rates to be 12% and 5%, respectively. Among those who were exposed to criminal victimization, rates of lifetime and current PTSD were 26% and 10%.

Clearly, the prevalence of exposure to traumatic events in the United States is far more common than anticipated in 1980, when the diagnosis of PTSD was incorporated into the diagnostic nomenclature. Even more surprising are findings indicating that the rate of current PTSD in the general population falls only behind major depression, attention-deficit hyperactivity disorder, specific phobia, and social phobia—making PTSD the fifth most common psychiatric condition in the United States (Kessler et al., 2005).

POST-TRAUMATIC STRESS DISORDER AMONG U.S. COMBATANTS

Soldiers whom we send to fight wars and to keep peace are among those most at risk for trauma exposure and the development of PTSD. Despite the high frequency of military action and war worldwide, few countries have ever estimated the psychological toll of war. The major exception to this was the National Vietnam Veterans Readjustment Study (NVVRS; Kulka et al., 1990), which included a representative sample of 1,632 Vietnam Theater Veterans (VTVs), a matched sample of 716 Vietnam Era Veterans (VEVs), and 668 civilian comparison subjects. More than 15% of male VTVs and 9% of female VTVs met criteria for current PTSD; this survey was conducted more than 15 years after the most intense fighting in the Vietnam Theater.

In a painstaking reanalysis of the clinical data from the NVVRS, Dohrenwend et al. (2006) examined military records, newspapers, and other sources of information to confirm the reports of combat trauma among theater veterans. The purpose of the study was to reduce or eliminate recall bias of combat exposure. Using only the strictest of definitions of combat exposure (confirmed by a source other than the study participant), they found PTSD rates that were at least twice those found in the general population of American males.

Peacekeeping has its own set of stressors associated with it, including being instructed to not fire unless fired upon while instructed to guard areas that are often under tenuous control. Litz, Orsillo, Friedman, Ehlich, and Batres (1997) examined a sample of 3,461 active-duty peacekeeping military troops who served in Somalia. Shortly after their return to the United States, 8% of these soldiers reported PTSD, a rate that did not differ for men and women. Eighteen months after their return, 7% of a subsample of 1,040 veterans met criteria for delayed-onset PTSD (Gray, Bolton, & Litz, 2004).

Several studies examined the impact of service in Persian Gulf War I. For instance, Wolfe, Brown, and Kelley (1993) conducted a longitudinal study of 2,344 Gulf War I veterans and found PTSD prevalence rates of 4% for men and 9% for women. Studies using smaller convenience and reservist samples found PTSD rates in the range of 16%–19%

(Perconte, Wilson, Pontius, Dietrick, & Spiro, 1993; Sutker, Uddo, Brailey, & Allain, 1993). Among soldiers deployed during Operation Iraqi Freedom and Operation Enduring Freedom, Hoge et al. (2004) found that 6% of the Army soldiers met screening criteria for PTSD after deployment to Afghanistan, and 12% met criteria after deployment to Iraq. Among the Marine Corps soldiers deployed to Iraq, 12% met screening criteria for PTSD. More recent studies from this same group indicate that prevalence rates among returning groups are reaching 15%–20% of those deployed, with higher rates among those with multiple deployments (Bliese et al., 2008).

Given the notably high prevalence rates of PTSD among combatants, as well as findings indicating that PTSD symptoms among Vietnam veterans typically do not remit (Schnurr, Lunney, Sengupta, & Waelde, 2003), continued study of combatants is a national priority. Further substantiating the chronic course and nature of combat-related PTSD is the detailed study of the military's testing of mustard gas on soldiers during World War II. Although this testing was not commonly known until the 1990s, fully 32% of those exposed continued to exhibit full PTSD symptomatology a half century later.

After the appearance of the NVVRS in the late 1980s, there was great interest in the prevalence of PTSD among other minority groups who were involved in that war. In the Matsunaga Vietnam Veterans Project, prevalence rates of PTSD were 45% among Southwest Plains Indians, 57% for Northern Plains Indians, 38% for Native Hawaiians, and 9% among Americans of Japanese extraction; these differences appear to be largely a function of differences in war zone stress exposure (Beals et al., 2002; Friedman, Schnurr, Sengupta, Holmes, & Ashcraft, 2004). These remarkably high rates of PTSD led to multiple changes in public policy that provided additional services to many of these minority communities.

POST-TRAUMATIC STRESS DISORDER ACROSS THE GLOBE

With increasing recognition of the health and economic costs associated with psychological morbidity across the world (Murray & Lopes, 1994), there is a growing acknowledgment of the need for regional and world estimates of psychiatric disorders, including PTSD.

Economically developed countries often observe a wide range of PTSD prevalence, perhaps owing to differences in culture, language, experiences, and study methodology. The lowest rates of PTSD were found in Iceland among a cohort of half the birth population in the year 1931 (i.e., lifetime rate of 0.6%, with no men meeting criteria; Líndal & Stefánsson, 1993). In addition, among a representative sample of 10,641 Australian adults, past-year PTSD prevalence was estimated at 1.5%, with similar rates among women and men. Among the 57% of the sample who experienced a traumatic event, higher rates of PTSD were found among women (4%) than men (2.0%), potentially because experiencing rape or sexual molestation were the traumas most likely to result in PTSD (Creamer, Burgess, & McFarlane, 2001; Rosenman, 2002). Among Australian male Gulf War I veterans, 5% were found to have developed PTSD after the war, whereas only 1.4% of a comparison sample of veterans who did not deploy to the Gulf developed PTSD during that time (Ikin et al., 2004).

Post-traumatic stress disorder prevalence rates in less economically developed countries tend to be higher than in more developed countries. For example, among a geographically diverse sample of Mexican adults, lifetime PTSD prevalence was estimated to be 19% (Norris, Murphy, Baker, & Perilla, 2004). In addition, among adult Israeli residents, Bleich, Gelkopf, and Solomon (2003) found that 9% met criteria for current PTSD, with higher rates among women (16%) than men (2.4%). Finally, in a Palestinian sample, Punamäki, Komproe, Qouta, El-Masri, and de Jong (2005) found PTSD prevalence rates of 22% and 13% for men and women, respectively.

Substantially higher rates of PTSD are observed in those countries that are non-Western and developing. Many of these estimates were derived following periods of war and political turmoil. Examining large, fairly representative samples of men and women age 16 or older living in post-conflict, low-income countries such as Algeria, Cambodia, Ethiopia, and Gaza, de Jong et al. (2001) found high rates of PTSD in each sample (37%, 28%, 16%, and 18%, respectively). In Algeria and Cambodia, and consistent with findings in the United States, women had higher rates of PTSD than men (44% vs. 32% and 34% vs. 21%, respectively). In contrast, in Ethiopia and Gaza, women possessed similar or lower rates of PTSD compared to men (15% vs. 17% and 14% vs. 23%, respectively).

Following the bombing raids launched by the United States on Afghanistan, as well as a long history of war, conflict, and drought, Lopes Cardozo et al. (2004) studied a representative sample of disabled and nondisabled Afghan people age 15 or older. Similarly high rates of PTSD were found among the disabled and nondisabled samples (i.e., 42% and 43%, respectively). Women in both groups exhibited higher rates of PTSD than men, findings that were attributed to the widespread restrictions placed on women during the Taliban regime. Near this same time, and using a similar methodology, Scholte et al. (2004) found that 20% of persons age 15 or older in the Nangarhar province of eastern Afghanistan met criteria for PTSD, with much higher rates found among women (32%) than men (8%).

In a sample of Rwandans living in four diverse communes eight years after the 1994 genocide in that country, Pham, Weinstein, and Longman (2004) reported a 25% prevalence rate of PTSD, with higher rates again found among women than men. Interestingly, participants in this study reported particularly high rates of avoidance symptoms, an approach to anxiety management consistent with Rwandan cultural discouragement of open displays of emotion.

Norris and Slone (2007) suggest that the most significant limitations of the PTSD epidemiological literature is a lack of research in developing countries, particularly since they appear to be at elevated risk for experiencing trauma. Although international studies of trauma continue to grow, much more work is necessary. Clearly, it is unlikely that research conducted in the United States and other developed countries can be readily generalized to the developing world. Differences in experiences, cultures, resources, social structures, and coping behaviors may significantly influence the prevalence and course of PTSD among peoples.

REFUGEES

Fazel, Wheeler, and Danesh (2005) summarized the data across multiple studies, including a total of 5,499 adult refugees resettled in Western countries. They found substantial variability in prevalence rates (range = 3%–44%). When restricting analyses to more rigorously designed studies including at least 200 participants, the average PTSD prevalence rate was 9%.

Sack, McSharry, Clarke, and Kinney (1994) reported that 100% of 209 Cambodian adolescent refugees were exposed to atrocities such as witnessing executions and being separated from family. Kuterovac, Dyregrov, and Stuvland (1994) found similar rates among 134 youths living in Croatia.

Although long overlooked, the needs of children in war zones are now receiving considerable attention due to these ground-breaking studies of war zone exposure and its consequences.

POST-TRAUMATIC STRESS DISORDER FOLLOWING DISASTER AND TERRORISM

A burgeoning literature suggests that a wide range of natural and man-made disasters can lead to the development of chronic PTSD. Green and colleagues found that 44% of survivors of the collapse of the Buffalo Creek Dam in West Virginia in the late 1970s met criteria for PTSD, and 28% of the sample still met diagnostic criteria 14 years later (Green, Lindy, Grace, & Gleser, 1990; Green, Lindy, Grace, Gleser, Leonard, et al., 1990). Similarly, McFarlane (1989) studied the effects of Australian brush fires on a sample of firefighters; PTSD prevalence rates were estimated at 32%, 27%, and 30% respectively at 4, 11, and 29 months post disaster.

Norris, Murphy, Baker, and Perilla (2004) studied the devastating 1999 floods and mudslides in Mexico. Interviewing a representative sample of 561 drawn from two affected cities, they found a combined prevalence of 24% PTSD in these two cities some 6 months following the disaster. Rates of current PTSD decreased sharply, however, as the investigators continued to monitor psychological outcomes over the next 2 years. Yet, at the 2-year mark, the prevalence of PTSD still exceeded that of the general population.

In recent years, concern regarding the psychological consequences of terrorist attacks has increased substantially. In a review of studies reporting PTSD prevalence rates following terrorist attacks, Gidron (2002) reported a mean rate of 28%. However, these studies varied greatly in subject sampling and in the timing of assessments. Following the September 11, 2001 terrorist attacks on the World Trade Center (WTC) and the Pentagon, telephone and web-based methodologies were employed to examine levels of resultant PTSD symptoms throughout the United States. Rates of PTSD generally were higher based upon regional proximity to the attacks. For example, Schlenger et al. (2002) found the prevalence of probable PTSD to be 11% in the New York City metropolitan area, but much lower in Washington D.C. (3%), other metropolitan areas (4%), and the remainder of the country (4%). In a sample of adults residing in an area of Manhattan closest to the World Trade Center, 7.5% reported symptoms consistent with a PTSD diagnosis, and 20.0% of a subsample residing closest to the WTC reported such symptoms (Galea et al., 2002).

These are just a few of the many different types of disasters examined to date. Overall, the epidemiological literature strongly suggests that various types of disasters contribute substantially to the development of PTSD, that the prevalence is high, and that the effects for some can be long-lasting.

Theoretical Models

A great number of PTSD models have been proposed. A few of the models that have empirical support will be described here.

Barlow's Model of Anxiety

Keane and Barlow (2002) adapted Barlow's (2002) model of anxiety and panic to promote an understanding of the variables involved in the development of PTSD. This conceptual model suggests that both biological and psychological vulnerabilities may underlie the development of PTSD. Each of these variables may exert independent effects or may interact to increase the likelihood of exposure to a traumatic event; these factors constitute those variables responsible for the vulnerability of some to developing disorder upon trauma exposure. Extrapolating from this model, when an individual is exposed to a traumatic life event, a biological and psychological alarm occurs that leads to both conditioning of stimuli present at the time of the event and to the development of cognitions, such as anxious apprehension of a recurrence of the traumatic event. The conditioned cues and the apprehension that another event like this might occur contribute to the maintenance of symptoms (i.e., a learned alarm). These emotionally charged cues then promote the development of avoidance strategies in order to effectively minimize the experience of aversive emotional reactions. The emergence of PTSD is a function of these variables; if an individual experiences high levels of social support or he or she possesses positive coping abilities, these may influence whether PTSD develops or the severity of the PTSD when it does.

Keane and his colleagues first conceptualized PTSD using a conditioning and avoidance model of the disorder (Keane & Kaloupek, 1982; Keane, Zimering, & Caddell, 1985). Wirtz and Harrell (1987) provided some empirical support for the process of classical conditioning (i.e., learned alarms) within PTSD. They observed that victims of physical assault were less distressed 6 months after the assault if they had experienced exposure to situations or stimuli that were part of (or resembled) the context of the original assault without experiencing another assault. Survivors who had not had the advantage of this exposure, on the other hand, maintained their distress until the 6-month measurement. This is what one would expect in classical conditioning. Other investigators have noted the importance of conditioning in the development of PTSD (Keane, Fairbank, Caddell, Zimering & Bender, 1985; Orr et al., 2000), whether the trauma is combat-related, involves a physical or sexual assault (e.g., Holmes & St. Lawrence, 1983; Kilpatrick et al., 1985; Orr, Meyerhoff, Edwards, & Pitman, 1998), or is the consequence of terrorism (Shalev et al., 2000).

In PTSD, the emotions themselves are avoided to some extent; we refer to this as a numbing of emotional responsiveness. This numbing in PTSD may very well represent avoidance of aversive emotional reactions or, in terms of Barlow's theory, avoidance of the learned emotional alarm (cf., Jones & Barlow 1991; Litz, 1992; Litz, Orsillo, Kaloupek, & Weathers, 2000). The importance of the use of the term "alarm" here is related to the distinct possibility that the event has biological and psychological concomitants. The intensity of the emotional alarm may precipitate the experience of a dissociative state, as noted earlier. It also is likely that the alarm that the individual experiences is comparable to panicking, wherein the concurrent psychological experiences may actually be, in part, dissociative in nature. Although the focus in past etiological work on this topic is on fear and the feared stimulus, future work may well focus upon a broader understanding of the psychobiological concomitants of the exposure itself. It may well be true that the alarm is more than fear and include a complex range of emotional responses.

In any case, the experience of alarm or other intense emotions in and of itself is not sufficient for the development of PTSD. Much as in other disorders, one must develop anxiety or the sense that these events, and one's own emotional reactions to them, are proceeding in an unpredictable, uncontrollable manner. When negative affect and a sense of uncontrollability occur in conjunction with one another, it increases the likelihood that anxious apprehension and rumination occurs and, thus, PTSD emerges.

As in many disorders, anxiety and related affective states can be moderated to some extent by the use of adaptive coping skills and the presence of structural and functional social support systems. In PTSD,

evidence already exists that these moderating variables play a role in determining whether the disorder develops or not. Therefore, these factors are represented explicitly in the Barlow (2002) and Keane and Barlow (2002) model of PTSD. Although it is likely that the use of adaptive coping skills and support systems mitigate many psychological disorders, the data supporting this assertion in the area of psychological trauma are especially convincing (Keane, Scott, Chavoya, Lamparski, & Fairbank 1985).

Cognitive Model

Ehlers and Clark's (2000) cognitive model of PTSD emphasizes perceptions of threat in the onset and maintenance of PTSD symptoms. With an emphasis on appraisal processes, the authors argue that individuals suffering from persistent PTSD (relative to trauma-exposed peers without PTSD) are "unable to see the trauma as a time-limited event that does not have global negative implications for their future" (p. 320). Thus, appraisals of external and/or internal experiences lead to perceptions of ongoing threat. In turn, appraisals (e.g., "bad things always happen to me") increase avoidant behaviors, initiating a cycle in which overgeneralized fears are maintained in response to avoidance. Appraisals of post-trauma reactions can also create or maintain ongoing threat. For example, common post-trauma responses (e.g., disruptions in concentration, intrusive recollections, and irritability) may be interpreted as signs of threat to one's mental or physical well-being. Appraisals of stress responses as threatening in and of themselves can lead to efforts to suppress experiences, which paradoxically increase the feared responses. A growing number of studies document prospectively links between appraisals (e.g., negative beliefs about the self and world) and PTSD symptoms (Dunmore, Clark, & Ehlers, 2001; Ehring, Ehlers, & Glucksman, 2008). With its focus on appraisal processes, this theory lends itself nicely to cognitive interventions (Dalgleish, 2004).

In addition to appraisals, the cognitive model also highlights the role that memory problems can play in ongoing perceptions of threat (see Halligan et al., 2003). For example, trauma memories may be poorly integrated in autobiographical memory and may be less elaborate, leading to decreased associations with other thematically related material that would otherwise assist the individual with meaning-making. Problems in integration and elaboration may result in frequent triggering of intrusive memories in response to sensory (rather than thematic) cues (Halligan et al., 2003). Further, dissociation at the time of the event may disrupt encoding of the event as it occurs. Because intrusive memories may contain sensory-specific characteristics related to how the memory was encoded (e.g., smells, body sensations), sensory cues may trigger intrusive memories. The cognitive model also suggests that stimuli from the traumatic event are closely connected to one another, as are individual responses to those stimuli. Therefore, when an individual encounters a trauma-relevant stimulus in the present, the closely connected response is also triggered. Avoidance strategies may lessen the individual's perception of threat in the short run, but block cognitive change and contribute to the maintenance of PTSD in the long run. Several empirical studies support the cognitive model's emphasis on disorganized trauma memories in PTSD. Using both cross-sectional and prospective methods, disorganized trauma memories predicted concurrent and prospective PTSD symptoms in adult assault survivors, even after controlling for event severity (Halligan et al., 2003). Further, encoding that focuses on sensory and perceptual dimensions of events with relatively less elaboration and meaning-making has been associated with PTSD symptom development among motor vehicle accident survivors (Murray, Ehlers, & Mayou, 2002).

Dual Representation Theory of Post-traumatic Stress Disorder

The dual representation theory (DRT) of PTSD (e.g., Brewin, 2001, 2003; Brewin, Dalgleish, & Joseph, 1996) has important implications for understanding the nature of PTSD experiences, particularly the oscillation between seemingly inaccessible trauma-related information and all-too-accessible intrusive memories. Implying the existence of multiple memory systems (Brewin, 2001), the DRT proposes that trauma-related memories for emotionally arousing events are stored in at least two representational formats: as verbally accessible and situationally accessible memories (VAMs and SAMs). Verbally accessible memories comprise trauma narratives that the individual can consciously bring into awareness and about which the person can make statements (generally referred to as declarative memory). Because information stored in VAMs is integrated with other autobiographical information, VAMs can interact with other information about the self. Importantly, VAMs can be updated and recognized as existing at a particular point in time relative to the past, present, and future.

Situationally accessible memories are not verbally accessible (i.e., nondeclarative). Therefore, SAMs are unavailable for the sort of integration and meaning-making characteristic of representations in VAMS. Situationally accessible memories are theorized to include lower-level perceptual information about the trauma scene and/or about somatic experiences during the trauma. These lower-level perceptual memories do not get updated based on other information in autobiographical memory, time, or context (e.g., relative to the past, present, and future), making them essentially time-locked. Exposure, therefore, to traumatic reminders in the form of sights, sounds, and smells makes it difficult for the individual to control SAMs. When SAMs are activated, the accompanying emotions are likely to be those experienced at the time of the event.

From a DRT perspective, the intrusive memories that are characteristic of PTSD are represented in SAMs, disconnected from other aspects of autobiographical memory and verbal expression. Brewin et al. (1996) suggest that premature inhibition of processing trauma memories may result in impaired memory for the trauma or trauma-related material. Thus, the dual representation view of PTSD provides an important framework for understanding inconsistencies in memory (too much and too little access) that can otherwise appear inconsistent within a single individual. For example, when trauma representations are activated in SAM, the memory will be sensory in nature, disintegrated from higher-level representations, and relatively fixed in time. Further, the unprocessed emotions from the original traumatic event will be activated. A series of creative laboratory studies provide empirical support for the DRT model (e.g., Holmes, Brewin, & Hennessey, 2004).

In his 2001 review, Brewin places the DRT in the context of the neuroscience of memory, fear, and PTSD, particularly in relation to the hippocampus and amygdala, key elements in the limbic system. Brewin argues that flashbacks in the immediate aftermath of trauma exposure provide opportunities to transfer perceptual information from the SAM system to the VAM system. For example, if the individual focuses on perceptual details in flashbacks while the trauma-related representations are active in working memory, information can be recoded into VAMs, mediated by the hippocampus. As this information is recoded, contextual and temporal information can be integrated with support from the hippocampus. As the perceptual information is recoded to provide temporal information indicating that the danger is in the past (assuming the present is safe), the hippocampus and prefrontal cortex can inhibit amygdala activity, thus stopping the fear response. As these representations are repeatedly activated in the hippocampus, information can be consolidated in the cortex, which is otherwise slow to update and integrate radically new information (such as what a trauma represents). Failure to create VAMs renders sensory and perceptual information isolated in the SAM system. Because representations in the SAM system are prone to activation following trauma cues, activation of the amygdala and fear response would be expected to continue. Further, the slow-changing, higher-level cortical systems cannot integrate the SAM-mediated information, leading to a lack of inhibition from the cortical structures to the amygdala. This model fits nicely with recent hippocampal findings (see the section "Abnormalities in Brain Structure and Function").

To the extent that working memory is implicated in the transfer of information from the SAM to VAM system (Brewin, 2001), deficits in executive function may place individuals at risk for PTSD. Consistent with this view is a growing body of work documenting disruptions in executive function among trauma-exposed adults (El-Hage, Gaillard, Isingrini, & Belzung, 2006; Navalta, Polcari, Webster, Boghossian, & Teicher, 2006; Stein, Kennedy, & Twamley, 2002), including those who report PTSD (e.g., Foa, Feske, Murdock, & Kozak, 1991; Kremen et al., 2007; McKenna & Sharma, 1995; Parslow & Jorm, 2007; Uddo, Vasterling, Brailey, & Sutker, 1993) and dissociative (e.g., DePrince & Freyd, 1999; Simeon et al., 2006) symptoms. Working memory deficits have also been documented among children in relation to violence exposure (DePrince, Weinzierl, & Combs, in press), PTSD diagnosis (Beers & De Bellis, 2002), and dissociative symptoms (Cromer, Stevens, DePrince, & Pears, 2006). Brewin's model provides a framework for how such deficits in executive function might affect consolidation and integration of trauma memories, and in turn, the development and maintenance of PTSD.

The Schematic, Propositional, Analogue, and Associative Representational Systems Model

Like the DRT model, the Schematic, Propositional, Analogue, and Associative Representational Systems (SPAARS) model of PTSD is a multirepresentational model (Dalgleish, 2004). The SPAARS framework points to two critical characteristics of events that lead to PTSD. These events are: (1) significantly inconsistent or discrepant with existing schema of the self and world; and (2) likely to evoke intense emotion, particularly fear, either automatically or via appraisal processes (Dalgleish & Power, 2004). Because events are discrepant with existing schemas (or beliefs, representations) of the self and world, the representation of the trauma remains active in an effort to integrate this information via assimilation and accommodation into preexisting schemas; reexperiencing symptoms result from ongoing activation of the trauma representations. In turn, people attempt to avoid trauma-related cues and representations to mitigate the reexperiencing symptoms and related distress. As this process unfolds, the representation continues to elicit trauma-related emotions that lead to the hyperarousal symptom of PTSD. Further, the SPAARS model specifies different levels (propositional, analogical, and schematic) at which representations can be encoded. Associative representations then link information across these levels. Repeated analysis of the incompatibility of these lower-level representation levels with higher-level schemas likely contributes to the maintenance of an ongoing sense of threat.

Betrayal Trauma Theory

While the Cognitive, DRT, and SPAARS models emphasize fear and threat, betrayal trauma theory (BTT) highlights the importance of social relationships in understanding post-traumatic outcomes (Freyd, 1994, 1996, 2001; Freyd, DePrince, & Gleaves, 2007). The theory was initially developed as a framework for understanding *why* victims of abuse would report disruptions in memory for the event, particularly memory impairment. As noted by Freyd et al. (2007), "the phrase *betrayal trauma* refers to a social dimension of trauma, independent of the individual's reaction to the trauma" (p. 297). Betrayal Trauma Theory proposes that the way in which events are processed and remembered will be related to the degree to which a negative event represents a betrayal by a trusted, needed other (Sivers, Schooler, Freyd, 2002). In recent years, the theory has been extended and developed, and other responses such as alexithymia, depression, and anxiety have been considered (e.g., Goldsmith & Freyd, 2005).

Betrayal Trauma Theory (Freyd, 1996) offers an important framework to help us understand key PTSD findings. For example, women, relative to men are more likely to report interpersonal traumas perpetrated by close others (Goldberg & Freyd, 2006), and to meet criteria for PTSD (Norris, Foster, & Weisshaar, 2002). Betrayal Trauma Theory predicts that higher levels of dissociation should be associated with interpersonal traumas perpetrated by close others relative to other types of events (see Freyd et al., 2007). In turn, the Ehlers and Clark cognitive model links dissociation to disorganized memories involved in the onset of PTSD (Halligan et al., 2003). Thus, to the extent that closeness to the perpetrator is linked to dissociative responses (e.g., Chu & Dill, 1990; DePrince, 2005; Plattner et al., 2003), the cognitive model can help explain how that dissociative response relates to disorganized memories and PTSD.

Betrayal Trauma Theory also implicates shareability theory (see Freyd, 1996), which is relevant to the DRT model. The DRT model highlights the importance of recoding and integration of SAM-mediated information into the VAM system (Brewin, 2001). Such recoding requires activating the trauma representations in working memory and sustained attention to the content (Brewin, 2001). By extension, avoidance processes would inhibit or preclude such recoding. Complementing this view, shareability theory (see Freyd, 1996) points to the importance of sharing information for the structure of mental representations. In order to share information, Freyd argued that we recode fine-grained perceptual information about events to more discrete and abstract forms. Shareability theory, then, predicts that memory for events that have never been discussed will be qualitatively different from those that have been shared with others. According to BTT, traumas high in betrayal are less likely to be shared (see Foynes, Freyd, & DePrince, 2009). In the absence of sharing, the original perceptual information is likely to remain intact without the recoding that occurs when memories are shared. Consistent with a DRT perspective, perceptual information may remain as a SAM, where it is easily activated by trauma-related perceptual cues.

Thus, multiple theories are proposed to understand the development and maintenance of PTSD. Each theory provides a unique perspective, one that emphasizes aspects of the condition. Each theory also points to directions for intervening to promote recovery and lasting change.

Psychopathology
Cognitive Science
ATTENTION AND POST-TRAUMATIC STRESS DISORDER

The modulation of attention to emotional (particularly threat-related) stimuli has garnered a great deal of interest in the PTSD literature. In several studies, adults diagnosed with PTSD show difficulty controlling interference from trauma-related stimuli in the emotional Stroop task, relative to control groups (McKenna & Sharma, 1995, Foa et al., 1991; Williams, Watts, MacLeod, & Mathews, 1997). In this task, participants are asked to name the colors in which words are printed while ignoring the words themselves. A positive emotional Stroop effect happens when participants are slower to name the color of trauma-relevant words relative to a baseline condition, compared to their peers. Recently, Kimble et al. (2009) argued that the robustness of the Stroop effect may be overstated because of failure to publish null findings. Using dissertation abstracts to address the "file drawer" problem in meta-analysis, Kimble demonstrated that the rates of positive findings that make their way into the literature are significantly higher than in well-implemented, but unpublished, dissertations.

Regardless of the size of the Stroop effect, attentional biases among adults diagnosed with PTSD are generally assumed to maintain a sense of ongoing threat (see Ehlers and Clark, 2000 for a discussion of the consequences of ongoing threat). This premise is supported by the observation that trauma exposure in the absence of symptoms does not appear to be associated with attentional biases in adults. For example, Elsesser, Sartory, and Tackenberg (2005) found no evidence that the trauma-exposed adults show biases toward threat images relative to non–trauma exposed controls. Children diagnosed with PTSD or high levels of dissociative symptoms also appear to process threat-related information differently than do comparison groups (e.g., Becker-Blease, Freyd, & Pears, 2004; Dalgleish, Moradi, Taghavi, Neshat-Doost, & Yule, 2001; Moradi, Taghavi, Neshat-Doost, Yule, & Dalgleish, 1999). For example, Dalgleish and colleagues (2001) have documented Stroop interference caused by trauma-related information among children with PTSD.

EXPLICIT MEMORY AND POST-TRAUMATIC STRESS DISORDER

Cognitive scientists have also examined memory performance in the laboratory, documenting explicit memory deficits for neutral information in relation to PTSD. For example, individuals diagnosed with PTSD related to a range of trauma types (e.g., combat, abuse) perform worse on measures of explicit memory performance on standardized neuropsychological tests relative to no-PTSD and non–trauma exposed peers (e.g., Bremner, Randall, Scott, Capelli, et al., 1995; Bremner et al., 2003a; Sutker, Winstead,

Galina, & Allain, 1991; Yehuda, Keefe, Harvey, & Levengood, 1995). However, we do not know whether explicit memory impairments in adults are a consequence of *or* a risk factor for PTSD. Although relatively little work has examined basic memory functioning in children, at least one study demonstrates that children diagnosed with PTSD show deficits in memory relative to a no-trauma comparison group (Beers & De Bellis, 2002). This study suggests that PTSD-related explicit memory deficits may occur fairly early in development.

Explicit memory for trauma-relevant information appears to be heightened among adults diagnosed with PTSD in laboratory tasks (e.g., Litz et al., 1996; Paunovic, Lundh, & Öst, 2002; Vrana, Roodman, & Beckham, 1995). For example, Holocaust survivors diagnosed with PTSD recalled fewer paired-associates overall (consistent with the literature on poor explicit memory reviewed earlier), but more Holocaust-related word pairs than neutral word pairs, relative to Holocaust-exposed control participants without PTSD whose recall was unaffected by word type (Golier, Yehuda, Lupien, & Harvey, 2003). Thus, PTSD is associated with both general deficits in explicit memory performance and heightened memory for trauma-related stimuli in laboratory tasks. How laboratory tasks correspond to autobiographical memory in PTSD remains unclear. In a related review, Brewin (2007) noted the importance of distinguishing between voluntary (intentional, conscious recollection) and involuntary (memory intrusions and flashbacks) autobiographical memory for trauma in clinical and nonclinical populations. This distinction is likely important in interpreting heightened voluntary memory in lab tasks relative to voluntary and involuntary autobiographical memories in daily life.

PHYSIOLOGICAL REACTIVITY

Psychophysiological symptoms are a prominent feature of PTSD. According to criteria outlined in the DSM-IV (APA, 1994), there are several ways in which heightened psychophysiological activity would be expected in PTSD. First, an exaggerated startle response to startling sounds would be predicted. Second, a heightened psychophysiological activity during resting periods would be expected, which would be consistent with the hyperarousal symptom cluster of the disorder. Third, elevated psychophysiological reactivity would be expected during exposure to cues (either internal or external) that symbolize or resemble an aspect of the traumatic event, consistent with the reexperiencing

symptom cluster of PTSD and specifically relevant to the DSM-IV (APA, 1994) PTSD symptom of physiological reactivity on exposure to trauma cues.

A wealth of literature investigates whether elevations in psychophysiological activity and reactivity is associated with PTSD. Indeed, there have been consistent findings demonstrating that individuals with PTSD show elevated psychophysiological activity (e.g., heart rate, skin conductance, facial electromyography) during resting periods, heightened psychophysiological reactivity (e.g., eye blink startle reflex, heart rate, skin conductance, and slower skin conductance habituation) to startling sounds, and heightened psychophysiological responding (e.g., heart rate, skin conductance, systolic blood pressure, facial electromyography) to trauma cues relative to individuals without PTSD, including individuals who have had similar trauma exposure but have not developed PTSD (Keane et al., 1998; Malloy, Fairbank, & Keane, 1983).

An excellent quantitative review of this literature was recently conducted by Pole (2007). Pole's meta-analysis included 58 resting baseline studies, 25 standardized cue studies, and 22 idiographic trauma cue studies that compared adults with and without PTSD on a variety of psychophysiological measures. Findings indicated reliable associations between PTSD and laboratory measures of psychophysiological activity and reactivity. Specifically, PTSD was associated with aggregate indices of higher resting arousal (unweighted mean effect size $r = .16$). Post-traumatic stress disorder was also associated with aggregate indices of larger responses to startling sounds (unweighted mean effect size $r = .24$). As expected, PTSD was associated with aggregate indices of larger responses to standardized trauma cues and larger responses to idiographic trauma cues (unweighted mean effect size $r = .37$ for both standardized and ideographic trauma cues). It should be noted that large effect sizes were observed for psychophysiological responding to trauma cues, whereas effect sizes were small for resting psychophysiological activity and startle responding.

There is some evidence that psychophysiological symptoms in PTSD may be affected by several factors, including PTSD symptom severity (Orr & Roth, 2000). In his meta-analysis, Pole examined moderators that might affect psychophysiological responding in PTSD. Findings indicated that greater PTSD symptom severity was associated with larger effect sizes and greater diagnostic sensitivity of diagnostic prediction. This finding likely reflects the fact that there is considerable heterogeneity among PTSD samples.

Psychophysiological symptoms do not need to be endorsed in order to meet diagnostic criteria for PTSD. However, the more symptoms endorsed, the great the likelihood that psychophysiological symptoms will be endorsed.

Another factor that has been speculated to influence psychophysiological responding is the manner in which PTSD is diagnosed. Pole observed that larger effect sizes and greater diagnostic specificity were obtained when earlier versions of the DSM were applied. The critical change in PTSD criteria from the DSM-III to the DSM-IV is how a traumatic event is defined. In DSM-III, a traumatic event would involve direct threat to oneself. In contrast, the definition of a traumatic event in DSM-IV has been expanded to include threats to physical integrity of the self and witnessing serious injury or harm to others (APA, 1994). Given that psychophysiological abnormalities that are observed in PTSD are thought to reflect psychophysiological responses that occurred at the time of the trauma, it is reasonable to assume that learning about an injury of another person would produce less psychophysiological responding than a direct life threat. On the other hand, technical advances in psychophysiological assessment may account for the differences in effect sizes between earlier and later studies.

Contrary to prior speculation, Pole found that anticipatory anxiety does not account for the elevated resting psychophysiological activity observed in PTSD individuals. Specifically, Pole reported that effect sizes were larger when baseline was followed by no challenge than when it was followed by personal trauma reminders. Another noteworthy finding from this review is that psychoactive medication did not influence the aggregate psychophysiological effects. Pole was unable to examine the effect of dissociation on psychophysiological symptoms, as studies did not typically include characterization of their sample in terms of dissociation. This is unfortunate because there is some evidence that high levels of dissociation are related to reduced psychophysiological responding (e.g., Griffin et al., 1997; Pole, 2007). Another potential moderating factor that Pole did not examine is comorbid depression. There is some evidence that the presence of comorbid depression produces attenuated psychophysiological reactivity in individuals with PTSD (Cuthbert et al., 2003), which is important given the high rate of comorbid depression among PTSD samples (Keane & Wolfe, 1990; Kulka et al., 1990).

Importantly, individuals with anxiety disorders other than PTSD do not show heightened psychophysiological reactivity to trauma cues, including cues to traumas they have experienced, such as combat (e.g., Pitman et al., 1990). Moreover, relative to individuals without PTSD, individuals with PTSD do not show heightened psychophysiological reactivity to nontrauma stressful or fear-evoking stimuli (Cuthbert et al., 2003; Orr, Meyerhoff, Edwards & Pitman, 1998; Shalev, Orr, & Pitman, 1993). Thus, the heightened psychophysiological response pattern to trauma cues for PTSD individuals does not appear to be attributable to a nonspecific sensitivity to stress and/or fear cues.

Heightened psychophysiological responding also appears to be useful in predicting the development and persistence of PTSD. For example, Shalev and colleagues (1998) found that elevated heart rate in the emergency room immediately following trauma exposure was predictive of the development of PTSD. Blanchard et al. (1996) found that individuals with PTSD that did not remit within 1 year of a motor vehicle accident (MVA) had elevated heart rate during a trauma recall task that took place within the first 4 months following the MVA, compared to individuals who remitted within the first year following the MVA.

Taken together, psychophysiological symptoms (particularly heightened reactivity) are prominent features of PTSD and represent several diagnostic criteria of the disorder. Moreover, the empirical literature supports the existence of these psychophysiological symptoms in PTSD, and there is some evidence that heightened psychophysiological responding to trauma cues is predictive of the development and persistence of the disorder. Yet, within clinical practice and research there is little to no actual use of psychophysiological measurement.

Psychobiology of Post-traumatic Stress Disorder
Psychobiological Abnormalities
Key psychobiological mechanisms that are impaired in PTSD include sympathetic nervous system (SNS) activation, hypothalamic-pituitary-adrenocortical (HPA) mobilization, acoustic startle response, and fear conditioning. Sympathetic nervous system activation has been referred to as the "fight-or-flight response" and is a reaction in which muscular systems are mobilized to react to a significant threat. Individuals with PTSD exhibit abnormal increases in SNS reactivity, as well as in adrenergic dysregulation. Specifically, they exhibit autonomic hyper-responsiveness to both neutral and trauma-related stimuli, they show elevated urinary catecholamine levels, a downregulation of β- and α_2-adrenergic

receptors, and they display increased reactivity to an α_2-antagonist, yohimbine, which can provoke panic attacks and flashbacks in individuals with PTSD, but not in non-PTSD individuals (Shiromani, Keane, & LeDoux, 2009).

The HPA mobilization response is another fundamental response that promotes successful coping with stressful events and is dysregulated in PTSD (Yehuda, 2001). Specific abnormalities in individuals with PTSD include lower urinary cortisol levels, elevated lymphocyte glucocorticoid receptor levels, and dexamethasone supersuppression.

The acoustic startle response is a sequence of muscular and autonomic responses that alert an organism of impending threat and, thus, promotes survival. As noted previously, an exaggerated startle response is one of the diagnostic symptoms of PTSD, and individuals with PTSD display shorter latency and increased amplitude of the acoustic startle response, significant loss of the normal inhibitory modulation of the startle response, and resistance to habituation of the startle response (Orr & Roth, 2000).

Abnormalities in fear conditioning are also found commonly in individuals with PTSD. Fear conditioning is an adaptive mechanism whereby organisms learn to preserve information about previous threats in order to promote future survival. Several brain structures and functions have been shown to play a critical role in normal fear conditioning, and evidence indicates abnormalities in these structures and functions in PTSD. These abnormalities are described here.

ABNORMALITIES IN BRAIN STRUCTURE AND FUNCTION

Over the past decade, neuroimaging studies have substantially advanced our understanding of the key brain systems in the pathophysiology of PTSD. As noted previously, the three brain regions that have emerged as critical in PTSD include the amygdala, medial prefrontal cortex, and the hippocampus. The amygdala is involved in the assessment of threat-related stimuli and/or biologically relevant ambiguity, and is necessary for the process of fear conditioning (Fendt & Fanselow, 1999; LeDoux, 2000). Individuals with PTSD are hypervigilant to potential threats in their environment, and they display relatively heightened acquisition of conditioned fear. Consequently, there has been speculation that the amygdala is hyperresponsive in PTSD, and functional neuroimaging studies support this speculation (e.g., Bryant et al., 2005; Driessen et al., 2004; Hendler et al., 2003; Shin et al., 2004).

The medial prefrontal cortex includes the anterior cingulated cortex, subcallosal cortex, and medial frontal gyrus. The medial frontal cortex is well connected to the amygdala in primates (e.g., Chiba, Kayahara, & Nakano, 2001; Ghashghaei & Barbas, 2002) and is involved in the process of extinction of fear conditioning and the retention of extinction (Morgan, Romanski, & LeDoux, 1993; Quirk, Russo, Barron, & Lebron, 2000). However, extinction does not occur normally when the medial frontal cortex is damaged. Given that individuals with PTSD display persistently inappropriate fear responses and diminished extinction of conditioned fear responding in the laboratory (e.g., Orr et al., 2000; Rothbaum, Kozak, Foa, & Whitaker, 2001), some have proposed that the medial prefrontal cortex is impaired in PTSD. Neuroimaging studies have found reduced cortical volumes and neuronal integrity (e.g., Rauch et al., 2003; Woodward et al., 2006; Yamasue et al., 2003), and decreased function in medial prefrontal structures among individuals with PTSD. It is notable that individuals with PTSD who dissociated during traumatic narratives show greater activation of medial prefrontal cortex relative to non-PTSD control participants. In contrast, PTSD participants who did not dissociate during a trauma narrative display relatively less activation of prefrontal medial cortex relative to the control participants (Lanius et al., 2002; Lanius et al., 2001). These findings underscore the importance of examining how brain abnormalities might be different for PTSD individuals with and without dissociative symptoms.

The third brain region of interest in PTSD is the hippocampus. The hippocampus is involved in explicit memory processes and the encoding of context during fear conditioning (Corcoran & Maren, 2001; Eichenbaum, 2000). There is also evidence that the hippocampus interacts with the amygdala during the encoding of emotional memories (e.g., Dolcos, LaBar, & Cabeza, 2004). Animal research suggests that hippocampal damage and memory impairment can result from extreme stress and high levels of stress-related hormones, such as cortisol (e.g., Sapolsky, Uno, Rebert, & Finch, 1990; Watanabe, Gould, & McEwen, 1992). Neuroimaging studies demonstrate that PTSD is associated with memory impairment, reduced hippocampal volumes, and abnormal hippocampal function (e.g., Bremner, Randall, Scott, & Bronen, 1995; Bremner et al., 2003a; Gurvits et al., 1996; Villarreal et al., 2002; Winter & Irle, 2004). Recent hippocampal studies using twin methods indicate that hippocampal irregularities may act as risk factors for (rather than consequences of) trauma exposure (Pitman et al., 2006). Although specific hippocampal volume reductions have not replicated consistently in children, maltreated children (particularly those diagnosed with PTSD) appear to have smaller total brain and/or cerebral volumes than their peers (Watts-English, Fortson, Gibler, Hooper, & De Bellis, 2006). See Watts-English and colleagues (2006) for a review of developmental issues in brain maturation and trauma.

Based on the available evidence, the neurocircuitry model of PTSD posits that the amygdala is hyper-responsive, the medial prefrontal cortex is hyporesponsive, and the medial prefrontal cortex and the hippocampus fail to inhibit the amygdala. Although substantial advances have been made in our understanding of the neurocircuitry of PTSD, many issues need to be addressed. For instance, neuroimaging studies have typically compared individuals with PTSD to individuals without PTSD. As a result, we know very little about the specificity of brain abnormalities to PTSD versus comorbid psychiatric disorders or other anxiety disorders. There is some evidence that PTSD individuals with dissociative symptoms may display different brain abnormalities compared to those without dissociative symptoms (e.g., Lanius et al., 2002). However, only a handful of studies have investigated how dissociation might influence brain abnormalities in PTSD. It would also be useful to examine whether brain abnormalities observed in PTSD resolve with effective treatment. The functional relationship between brain structures in PTSD also needs additional investigation. Another area needing further investigation is whether the brain structure, chemistry, and function vary during the course of the disorder. Moreover, it remains uncertain whether the brain abnormalities observed in PTSD represent a preexisting risk factor for the development of PTSD, or whether these brain abnormalities represent markers for the disorder. Longitudinal and twin studies will be critical in providing information in these areas.

Risk and Resiliency Trajectories

A major challenge for the trauma field has been to identify the individual, social, and cultural factors that increase risk for chronic PTSD and related impairment in functioning. Previous studies (Brewin et al., 2000; Ehring et al., 2006; King, King, Foy, Keane, & Fairbank, 1999; Nemeroff et al., 2006; Ozer et al., 2003; Sharkansky et al., 2000; Wolfe, Erickson, Sharkansky, King, & King 1999; Vogt &

Tanner, 2007) highlight the complexity of predicting who will and will not develop long-term PTSD.

Risk and resilience factors include, but are not limited to, the quality of the victim's early family environment, age at trauma exposure, history of prior adversity, severity of trauma exposure, breadth and strength of the social support network, exposure to additional life stressors, and individual difference characteristics such as coping repertoires, hardiness, and neurobiology. Studies also convincingly demonstrate that preexisting psychopathology may increase the risk for PTSD following exposure to a traumatic event (Bowman, 1997; Kessler et al., 1995; Kessler et al., 1999; Schlenger et al., 1992).

Two meta-analyses of the predictors of PTSD have been published (Brewin, Andrews, & Valentine, 2000; Ozer et al., 2003). With respect to historical or static predictors, both Brewin et al. (2000) and Ozer et al. (2003) found that family history of psychopathology, gender, age, race, and prior trauma exposure generally predicted a small but significant amount of variance of PTSD (average weighted effect sizes ranging from $r = .05$ to .19). With respect to trauma severity and psychological processes occurring during or immediately after the trauma, Brewin et al. (2000) found a small to medium weighted effect size of $r = .23$ for the association between trauma severity and PTSD severity, and Ozer et al. (2003) found a small to medium average weighted effect size of $r = .26$ for the strength of the relationship between perceived life threat and PTSD. Ozer et al. (2003) separately examined the relation between peritraumatic emotional response (e.g., fear, helplessness, horror, guilt, shame) and PTSD and found a similar effect size ($r = .26$). Ozer et al. (2003) also found a medium average weighted effect size ($r = .35$) for the strength of the relation between peritraumatic dissociation and PTSD. Regarding the contribution of post-trauma factors to the development and maintenance of PTSD, Ozer et al. (2003) learned that perceived social support following the traumatic event was associated with PTSD symptoms, with an average effect size falling in the small to medium range ($r = -.28$). Similarly, Brewin et al. (2000) found an average weighted medium effect size ($r = -.40$) for the relations between social support and PTSD symptoms.

Although we have learned a great deal about predictors of PTSD from the studies on which these meta-analyses are based, a serious limitation of the existing research is that most of these studies employed a cross-sectional methodology. As such, results of these studies are not able to provide definitive information regarding whether the aforementioned variables are actually causal risk factors and the true extent to which these variables confer risk for PTSD. Prospective methodologies allow for stronger causal inferences to be made regarding the role of various risk and resilience variables in the etiology of PTSD. Recently, numerous investigators employed prospective methods to further examine the role of a few mechanisms thought to be particularly important to the development and maintenance of PTSD in the wake of trauma. More specifically, these investigations focused upon the importance of the emergence of ASD following trauma, peritraumatic dissociation, physiological reactivity immediately following trauma, neuropsychological functioning, and cognitive style.

With respect to the predictive importance of ASD, although initial findings from prospective studies supported the contention that an ASD diagnosis may confer risk for subsequent PTSD, a recent multisite prospective investigation showed that the majority of those who were admitted to hospital trauma centers and go on to develop PTSD do not initially meet criteria for ASD (Bryant, Creamer, O'Donnell, Silove, & McFarlane, 2008). This finding suggests that the ASD diagnosis may have limited utility in predicting subsequent PTSD.

Regarding the role of peritraumatic dissociation, Shalev, Peri, Canetti, and Schreiber (1996) found that degree of peritraumatic dissociation predicted a diagnosis of PTSD 6 months after the trauma, over and above all other predictors. More recently, though, Hagenaars, van Minnen, and Hoogduin (2007) demonstrated that the influence of peritraumatic dissociation disappeared after controlling for initial PTSD symptoms. These results are consistent with other research showing that the predictive power of peritraumatic dissociation is significantly reduced once initial PTSD symptoms are accounted for (Marshall & Schell, 2002; Marx & Sloan, 2005). It may not be the dissociative aspects of the experience at all, but rather the terrifying elements of the alarm associated with panic.

With respect to the prospective role of psychophysiological reactivity in the development of PTSD, Shalev et al. (1998) examined the heart rate and blood pressure of civilian trauma survivors upon admission to a hospital emergency room. Results showed that elevated heart rate upon admission as well as 1 week later significantly predicted later PTSD status. These results are consistent with other research with adult trauma survivors (e.g., Bryant, Harvey,

Guthrie, & Moulds, 2000, 2003; Kuhn, Blanchard, Fuse, Hickling, & Broderick, 2006), as well as more recent research showing that elevated heart rate at emergency room admission among children predicted PTSD symptoms 6 months later (De Young, Kenardy, & Spence, 2007). Guthrie and Bryant (2005) examined the extent to which pretrauma startle response prospectively predicted post-trauma PTSD symptomatology among firefighters. Findings showed that pretrauma startle response predicted both post-trauma startle responding and that pretrauma skin conductance response to startle predicted post-trauma PTSD symptom severity.

In the first prospective investigation of the relationship between pre-trauma neuropsychological functioning and PTSD symptoms, Parslow and Jorm (2007) indicated that greater pre-trauma verbal working memory was associated with lower post-trauma PTSD symptoms among a civilian sample of natural disaster survivors. However, pre-trauma PTSD symptom levels were not assessed in this study, and the measure that was used to assess PTSD symptomatology did not assess PTSD avoidance or emotional numbing symptoms. Further, Parslow and Jorm did not assess visual memory performance. More recently, Marx, Doron-LaMarca, Proctor, and Vasterling (2009) examined the influence of predeployment memory performance on postdeployment PTSD symptom outcomes in a sample of deployed active-duty Army soldiers. As part of a larger longitudinal study, each participant completed baseline measures of visual and verbal memory and baseline and postdeployment self-report measures of PTSD symptom severity. Results revealed that pre-trauma immediate recall of visual information was associated with postdeployment PTSD symptom severity, even after controlling for predeployment PTSD symptom levels, combat intensity, age, gender, and test–retest interval. Marx et al. also reported an interaction between predeployment PTSD symptom severity and predeployment immediate visual recall and verbal learning, indicating that neurocognitive performances were more strongly (and negatively) associated with residualized postdeployment PTSD symptoms at higher levels of predeployment PTSD symptoms. These findings highlight the potential role of pre-trauma neurocognitive functioning in moderating the effects of trauma exposure on PTSD symptoms.

Other prospective studies also support the notion that cognitive style factors may be crucial to the onset and maintenance of PTSD following trauma exposure in both children and adults (e.g., Bryant,

Salmon, Sinclair, & Davidson, 2007; Kleim, Ehlers, & Glucksman, 2007; O'Donnell, Elliott, Wolfgang, & Creamer, 2007). Specifically, research demonstrates that data-driven processing during the trauma, negative interpretations of intrusive memories, rumination, and thought suppression are all important predictors of post-trauma psychopathology (Ehlers, Mayou, & Bryant, 2003; Mayou, Ehlers, & Bryant, 2002). Another recent study by Ehring, Ehlers, and Glucksman (2008) even showed that various cognitive variables predicted PTSD and depression in disorder-specific ways.

Assessment Methods and Prediction of Post-traumatic Stress Disorder

With elevated prevalence rates and the debilitating nature of PTSD, mental health professionals have directed efforts to the development of measures to evaluate the presence and severity of PTSD. As a result of these efforts, we now have numerous psychometrically sound self-report scales (e.g., Posttraumatic Stress Diagnostic Scale; Foa, Cashman, Jaycox, & Perry, 1997, and the PTSD Checklist; Weathers, Litz, Herman, Huska, & Keane, 1993) and interview-based instruments (e.g., Clinician-Administered PTSD Scale; Blake et al., 1995; Weathers, Keane, & Davidson, 2001, and the PTSD Symptom Scale-Interview; Foa, Riggs, Dancu, & Rothbaum, 1993) for assessing PTSD with excellent sensitivity and specificity. These measures generally produce diagnostic utility rates of around .90.

Many of these self-report instruments are helpful in screening for the possible presence of PTSD in primary care and other nonspecialty health-care settings. Such instruments are useful in the context of mass trauma, and have important implications for providing services that may ultimately prevent the development of PTSD following trauma exposure. In his excellent review of PTSD screening measures, Brewin (2005) noted that screening with a few items referring to core PTSD symptoms may be effective in screening for PTSD, and that measures with fewer items, simpler response scales, and simpler methods of scoring do as well as or better than other measures in screening for PTSD. Since Brewin's review, additional research has explored the extent to which successful screening for PTSD can occur using even shorter screening instruments (Kimerling et al., 2006; Lang & Stein, 2005). For example, Bliese et al. (2008) assessed the diagnostic efficiency of the four-item Primary Care Posttraumatic Stress Disorder Screen (PC-PTSD) as a screening tool for deployed active-duty soldiers. Results showed that both the PC-PTSD and PTSD Checklist had sound diagnostic efficiency rates.

Importantly, symptom-based screening measures are inherently limited in their ability to promote the prevention of PTSD due to their reliance on the presence or absence of current symptoms. Measures that quantify information about risk and resilience factors that influence long-term adjustment to trauma exposure may be employed to actually identify those who may be prone to develop PTSD following trauma before symptoms actually manifest. Such a tool would be useful from a true primary prevention perspective and would reduce overall health-care utilization by PTSD patients. In a recent example of such an approach, O'Donnell and colleagues (2008) developed and validated a screening instrument that identifies, during hospitalization, adults at high risk for developing PTSD and/or major depression. Participants completed a pool of questions representing 13 constructs of vulnerability during hospitalization and were then reassessed for PTSD and major depression 12 months later. The data were then split into two subsamples, with data from the first subsample used in factor analyses to derive the test items. These test items were then cross-validated on the second subsample. Receiver–operating characteristic curves showed that the resulting Posttraumatic Adjustment Scale had a sensitivity of .82 and a specificity of .84 when predicting PTSD, and a sensitivity of .72 and a specificity of .75 in predicting post-traumatic major depression.

In another recent effort, Marx et al. (2008) developed and tested a similar screening instrument for combat-related PTSD. Data were taken from the responses of 1,081 Vietnam era veterans who participated in VA Cooperative Study (see Keane et al., 1998). Participants were administered a comprehensive assessment battery, including structured interviews and self-report measures. They supplied information on a broad array of topics related to prewar background and functioning, military and war zone experiences, and postwar circumstances, life events, and mental health status. Drawing on the findings of King et al. (1999), Marx et al. focused on those risk-resilience factors that were found to have the strongest relations with combat-related PTSD status. The entire sample was then divided into three equal subsamples, matched on PTSD diagnosis as well as on PTSD symptom severity. Two of these subsamples were used to derive and identify variables that significantly differentiated between individuals with and without PTSD. In order for a variable to be included in the instrument, the variable must have significantly predicted PTSD diagnostic status, as well as attained a medium to large effect size in both derivation subsamples. A total of 12 variables met or exceeded the selection criterion. Marx et al. then derived empirically based cutoffs for each item that was not already dichotomous by using the risk difference statistic to determine which cutoff point best distinguished between those with and without PTSD. Because all 12 items met or exceeded the selection criterion in both derivation subsamples, subsequent analyses were conducted on the combined subsamples. The resulting instrument, the PTSD Statistical Prediction Instrument (PSPI), displayed strong internal consistency (Cronbach's α = .84), and excellent sensitivity (.90) and good specificity (.80).

Despite the exceptional success in developing methods to assess for PTSD, all of the current methods have inherent limitations. For example, both self-report scales and interview-based methods may be vulnerable to response bias (Frueh, Elhai, & Hamner, 2003). Further, reliance on a single assessment methodology or instrument may lead to an inaccurate diagnosis. As a result of these limitations, it has become standard practice to employ multiple methods and measures to better inform diagnostic decisions (see Keane, Wolfe, & Taylor, 1987). Such multimethod assessment of PTSD takes advantage of each measure's relative strengths, overcoming the psychometric limitations of any single instrument and maximizing correct diagnostic decisions.

Treatment

Although PTSD is a relatively new psychiatric disorder, more than 50 randomized clinical trials (RCTs) examine treatments for the disorder. The treatment literature has been evaluated by conducting meta-analyses (e.g., Bisson & Andrew, 2006; Bradley, Greene, Russ, Dutra, & Westen, 2005), as well as by expert committees formed by the International Society for Traumatic Stress Studies (Foa, Keane, Friedman, & Cohen, 2009), Division 12 of the American Psychological Association (APA Presidential Task Force on Evidence-Based Practice, 2006) and the Institute of Medicine (Institute of Medicine, 2008). There is general consensus that cognitive-behavioral treatments, particularly treatments that include an exposure component, are effective in treating PTSD (see Keane & Kaloupek, 1982).

To date, no psychopharmacological treatment has been identified as effective in the treatment of PTSD. The U.S. Food and Drug Administration (FDA) approved the selective serotonin reuptake inhibitors sertraline and paroxetine for treating PTSD.

However, the approval was regulatory in nature and based on a risk–benefit analysis, which differs from the more rigorous standards used to define effective treatments for psychiatric disorders. Furthermore, approval by the FDA is generally not reconsidered except when new safety data emerges.

In terms of the cognitive-behavioral interventions, several evidence-based treatments for PTSD have been identified. These treatments include prolonged exposure (PE), cognitive processing therapy (CPT), and eye movement and desensitization reprocessing (EMDR).

Prolonged exposure involves the confrontation of the traumatic memory, as well as hierarchical in vivo (i.e., in person) exposure to objects, environments, and situations that remind the client of the trauma (Foa, Hembree, & Rothbaum, 2007). Exposure to the trauma memory occurs in session (i.e., imaginal exposure). These sessions are recorded, and the client is requested to listen to the recorded trauma account several times before the next session. In vivo exposures typically take place in between sessions as well. The purpose of the imaginal exposure is to allow the client to fully process the traumatic event, and to teach the patient that the traumatic memory is not inherently dangerous and is not the same as experiencing the trauma again. Confrontation of the trauma memory and in vivo exposures also allows the client the opportunity to experience her fear and anxiety without the need to escape or avoid. The treatment consists of up to twelve 90- to 120-minute sessions. Although a number of randomized controlled trials have demonstrated the efficacy of PE in the treatment of PTSD, the majority of these trials have examined female sexual assault survivors. Thus, there is some concern whether the observed efficacy of PE would be similar with other trauma samples, such as veterans with combat-related PTSD. In addition, PE tends to have a relatively high dropout rate (i.e., as much as 40%). One other concern is that the majority of randomized trials examining the efficacy of PE have been conducted by the same investigator or investigative team that developed the protocol, and this has led some to question the generalizability of the reported findings.

Cognitive processing therapy primarily focuses on challenging and changing distorted beliefs and self-blame regarding the traumatic event through Socratic questioning (Resick & Schnicke, 1992). An exposure component is also included in the protocol, such that clients are asked to provide a written account of the trauma event. Cognitive processing therapy consists of twelve 60-minute weekly sessions. A recent study conducted by Resick and colleagues (2008) found that participants randomly assigned to a treatment condition that only included the cognitive restructuring component of CPT, and participants assigned to a treatment condition that only included the written account component of CPT benefited equally compared with participants randomly assigned to the full CPT protocol. However, participants who were assigned to the cognitive restructuring-only condition improved at a faster rate (i.e., within the first few weeks of treatment) than did participants who were assigned to the written account-only condition. This is an important finding, given the relatively large percentage of clients who drop out of PTSD treatment early in the course of treatment, and participants generally report greater distress to the exposure component of PTSD treatment (Foa, Zoellner, Feeny, Hembree, & Alvarez-Conrad, 2002). As with PE, the majority of the randomized trials of CPT have examined female sexual assault victims, although a recent study by Monson et al. (2006) found CPT to possess efficacy with male veterans diagnosed with chronic PTSD.

Eye movement and desensitization reprocessing pairs eye movements with cognitive processing of the traumatic memories (Shapiro, 1995). The initial phases of EMDR involve affect management techniques, such as relaxation. During the processing stage of therapy, the patient describes the traumatic memory and identifies and labels the images, beliefs, and physiological symptoms elicited by it. The patient is instructed to focus on these aspects of the traumatic memory while moving his or her eyes back and forth by tracking the therapists' finger (although other bilateral stimulation, such as finger-tapping, is used). The theoretical basis for EMDR is that PTSD symptoms result from insufficient processing/integration of sensory, cognitive, and affective elements of the traumatic memory. The bilateral eye movements are proposed to facilitate information processing and integration, allowing clients to fully process traumatic memories (Shapiro, 1995). There has been substantial controversy regarding the use of EMDR and the underlying mechanism of this treatment. There is some evidence that the mechanism of change is exposure, and that the eye movements are an unnecessary addition (Cahill, Carrigan, & Frueh, 1999; Davidson & Parker, 2001). Although some have concluded that there is sufficient evidence to recommend EMDR as an effective treatment for PTSD (e.g., APA Presidential Task Force on Evidence-Based Practice, 2006), others have concluded that

there is insufficient evidence to recommend it (e.g., Institute of Medicine, 2008).

Although we have made significant strides in our understanding of how best to treat those with PTSD, there are still some substantial gaps in our knowledge. Most trials exclude substance abuse, chronic pain, and traumatic brain injury. Given the high prevalence rate of these comorbid conditions in PTSD (e.g., Kessler et al., 1995), it is important to demonstrate whether these treatments are also effective in treating PTSD when these comorbid conditions are present.

An issue mentioned previously is that a large majority of RCTs focus on the treatment of female sexual assault survivors. Post-traumatic stress disorder resulting from other traumatic events, such as combat, may differ in terms of associated features (e.g., remorse related to committing acts of abusive violence, bereavement and loss, survivor guilt). Whether these types of issues are addressed in PE, CPT, and EMDR is an empirical question. As pointed out by the recent IOM committee report (2008), few RCTs have focused on veterans diagnosed with PTSD, one of the largest consumers of PTSD treatment. Another area in which the field needs to advance is conducting RCTs for group therapy for PTSD. Although group therapy is frequently used in clinical settings, there are currently no evidence-based group therapies for PTSD and the group RCTs that have been conducted are fraught with methodological shortcomings (Shea, McDevitt-Murphy, Ready, & Schnurr, 2009; Sloan, Feinstein, Beck, & Keane, 2009). Similarly, our knowledge of early interventions for PTSD is also very limited.

Another important area of investigation that has received limited attention to date is understanding how the evidence-based treatments for PTSD work (i.e., what are the mechanisms of action). Although the basic assumptions of some of these interventions are based upon the findings from basic research on learning and behavior in humans and nonhuman animals, mechanisms of action are rarely tested in RCTs. This is unfortunate, as understanding how or why a given therapy may work would help to identify the essential components of the treatment protocol, which could, in turn, facilitate the streamlining of treatment protocols and improve treatment outcomes.

Conclusion

Work in the field of psychological trauma, PTSD, and dissociative processes is accelerating at unprecedented rates. Soon a sixth specialty journal will join the field, just one indicator of the level of productivity in this clinical and research area. Articles on psychological trauma are now routinely published in the most prestigious journals in all of research, including *Science*, the *New England Journal of Medicine*, *Lancet*, the *Journal of the American Medical Association*, and *Nature*. This is an indication of the importance of the area in understanding human development, psychopathology, and health.

Future Directions

Future studies in this area will be characterized by mixed models, methods, and measures (Keane, 2009) that will elevate the importance of the field. Investigators and clinicians are beginning to conduct integrative studies that examine risk and resiliency variables in the hope of understanding the key factors associated with the question of why some develop PTSD in the face of adversity while others do not. Studies that incorporate genetic methods, developmental strategies, physiological and psychophysiological measurement, and state-of-the-art assessment measures are gaining momentum in this field and are already beginning to influence the models and perspectives for understanding the development of PTSD and related conditions.

Studies are now ongoing in the developing as well as the developed world to establish that PTSD and dissociative constructs exist across races, cultures, languages, and other boundaries. This is dramatic progress and represents three decades of serious science, debate, and scholarly work. Although controversy may always surround the notion of psychological trauma, those of us involved in the scientific study of trauma exposure, PTSD, and dissociative reactions are gratified at the widespread acceptance of the importance of psychological trauma among the public, those in academia, governmental authorities, and policy makers (Gerrity, Keane, & Tuma 2001; Green et al., 2003).

References

Adler, A., Bliese, P., McGurk, D., Hoge, C., & Castro, C. (2009). Battlemind debriefing and battlemind training as early interventions with soldiers returning from Iraq: Randomization by platoon. *Journal of Consulting and Clinical Psychology, 77,* 928–940.

American Psychiatric Association. (1980). *Diagnostic and statistical manual of mental disorders* (3rd ed.). Washington, DC: Author.

American Psychiatric Association. (1994). *Diagnostic and statistical manual of mental disorders* (4th ed.). Washington, DC: Author.

APA Presidential Task Force on Evidence-Based Practice. (2006). Evidence-based practice in psychology. *American Psychologist, 61,* 271–285.

Barlow, D. (2002). *Anxiety and its disorders: The nature and treatment of anxiety and panic* (2nd ed.). New York, NY US: Guilford Press.

Beals, J., Manson, S., Whitesell, N., Mitchell, C., Novins, D., Simpson, S., et al. (2005). Prevalence of major depressive episode in two American Indian reservation populations: Unexpected findings with a structured interview. *The American Journal of Psychiatry, 162,* 1713–1722.

Becker-Blease, K. A., Freyd, J. J., Pears, K. C. (2004). Preschoolers' memory for threatening information depends on trauma history and attentional context: Implications for the development of dissociation. *Journal of Trauma and Dissociation, 5,* 113–131.

Beers, S. R., & De Bellis, M. D. (2002). Neuropsychological function in children with maltreatment-related posttraumatic stress disorder. *American Journal of Psychiatry, 159,* 483–486.

Bisson, J., & Andrew, M. (2006). Psychological treatment of post-traumatic stress disorder (PTSD). *Cochrane Database of Systematic Reviews, 3*:CD003388.

Blake, D. D., Weathers, F. W., Nagy, L. M., Kaloupek, D. M., Gusman, F. D., Charney, D. S., et al. (1995). The development of a Clinician-Administered PTSD Scale. *Journal of Traumatic Stress, 8,* 75–90.

Blanchard, E. B., Hickling, E. J., Buckley, T. C., Taylor, A. E., Vollmer, A., & Loos, W. R. (1996). Psychophysiology of posttraumatic stress disorder related to motor vehicle accidents: Replication and extension. *Journal of Consulting and Clinical Psychology, 64,* 742–751.

Bleich, A., Gelkopf, M., & Solomon, Z. (2003). Exposure to Terrorism, Stress-Related Mental Health Symptoms, and Coping Behaviors Among a Nationally Representative Sample in Israel. *Journal of the American Medical Association, 290,* 612–620.

Bliese, P., Wright, K., Adler, A., Cabrera, O., Castro, C., & Hoge, C. (2008). Validating the Primary Care Posttraumatic Stress Disorder Screen and the Posttraumatic Stress Disorder Checklist with soldiers returning from combat. *Journal of Consulting and Clinical Psychology, 76,* 272–281.

Bowman, M. L. (1997). *Individual differences in posttraumatic response: Problems with the adversity-distress connection.* Mahwah, NJ: Lawrence Erlbaum Associates Publishers.

Bradley, R., J. Greene, E. Russ, L. Dutra, & Westen, D. (2005). A multidimensional meta-analysis of psychotherapy for PTSD. *American Journal of Psychiatry, 162,* 214–227.

Bremner, J. D., Randall, P., Scott, T. M., & Bronen, R. A. (1995). MRI-based measurement of hippocampal volume in patients with combat-related posttraumatic stress disorder. *American Journal of Psychiatry, 152,* 973–981.

Bremner, J. D., Randall, P., Scott, T. M., Capelli, S., Delaney, R., McCarthy, G., et al. (1995). Deficits in short-term memory in adult survivors of childhood abuse. *Psychiatry Research, 59,* 97–107.

Bremner, J. D., Vermetten, E. Afzal, N., & Vythilingam, M. (2003a). Deficits in verbal declarative memory function in women with childhood sexual abuse-related posttraumatic stress disorder. *Journal of Nervous and Mental Disease, 192,* 643–649.

Bremner, J. D., Vythilingam, M., Vermetten, E., Southwick, S. M., McGlashan, T., Nazeer, A., et al. (2003b). MRI and PET study of deficits in hippocampal structure and function in women with childhood sexual abuse and posttraumatic stress disorder. *American Journal of Psychiatry, 160,* 924–932.

Bremner, J. D., Vythilingam, M., Vermetten, E., Southwick, S. M., McGlashan, T., Staib, L. H., et al. (2003c). Neural correlates of declarative memory for emotionally valenced words in women with posttraumatic stress disorder related to early childhood sexual abuse. *Biological Psychiatry, 53,* 879–889.

Breslau, N., Davis, G., Andreski, P., & Peterson, E. (1991). Traumatic events and posttraumatic stress disorder in an urban population of young adults. *Archives of General Psychiatry, 48,* 216–222.

Breslau, N., Davis, G., Peterson, E., & Schultz, L. (2000). A second look at comorbidity in victims of trauma: The posttraumatic stress disorder–major depression connection. *Biological Psychiatry, 48,* 902–909.

Brewin, C. R. (2001). A cognitive neuroscience account of posttraumatic stress disorder and its treatment. *Behaviour Research and Therapy, 39,* 373–393.

Brewin, C. R. (2003). *Posttraumatic Stress Disorder: Malady or Myth?* New Haven, CT: Yale University Press.

Brewin, C. R. (2005). Systematic review of screening instruments for adults at risk of PTSD. *Journal of Traumatic Stress, 18,* 53–62.

Brewin, C. R. (2007). Autobiographical memory for trauma: Update on four controversies. *Memory, 15,* 227–248.

Brewin, C. R., Andrews, B., & Valentine, J. D. (2000). Meta-analysis of risk factors for posttraumatic stress disorder in trauma-exposed adults. *Journal of Consulting and Clinical Psychology, 68,* 748–766.

Brewin, C.R., Dalgleish, T., & Joseph, S. (1996). A dual representation theory of post traumatic stress disorder. *Psychological Review, 103,* 670–686.

Briere, J., Scott, C., & Weathers, F. (2005). Peritraumatic and persistent dissociation in the presumed etiology of PTSD. *American Journal of Psychiatry, 162,* 2295–2301.

Brown, T., Campbell, L., Lehman, C., Grisham, J., & Mancill, R. (2001). Current and lifetime comorbidity of the DSM-IV anxiety and mood disorders in a large clinical sample. *Journal of Abnormal Psychology, 110,* 585–599.

Bryant, R. A., Creamer, M., O'Donnell, M. L., Silove, D., & McFarlane, A. C. (2008). A multisite study of the capacity of acute stress disorder diagnosis to predict posttraumatic stress disorder. *Journal of Clinical Psychiatry, 69,* 923–929.

Bryant, R. A., Felmingham, K. L., Kemp, A. H., Barton, M., Peduto, A. S., Rennie, C., et al. (2005). Neural networks of information processing in posttraumatic stress disorder: A functional magnetic resonance imaging study. *Biological Psychiatry, 58,* 111–118.

Bryant, R. A., Harvey, A. G., Guthrie, R. M., & Moulds, M. L. (2000). A prospective study of psychophysiological arousal, acute stress disorder, and posttraumatic stress disorder. *Journal of Abnormal Psychology, 109,* 341–344.

Bryant, R. A., Harvey, A. G., Guthrie, R. M., & Moulds, M. L. (2003). Acute psychophysiological arousal and posttraumatic stress disorder: A two-year prospective study. *Journal of Traumatic Stress, 16,* 439–443.

Bryant, R. A., Salmon, K., Sinclair, E., & Davidson, P. (2007). A prospective study of appraisals in childhood posttraumatic stress disorder. *Behaviour Research and Therapy, 45,* 2502–2507.

Burgess, A., & Holmstrom, L. (1974). Rape trauma syndrome. *The American Journal of Psychiatry, 131,* 981–986.

Cahill. S. P., Carrigan. M. H., & Freuh, B. C. (1999). Does EMDR work? And if so, why?: A critical review of controlled outcome and dismantling research. *Journal of Anxiety Disorders, 13,* 5–33.

Charcot, J.M. (1887) Lecons sur les maladies du systeme nerveux faites a la Salpetriere [Lessons on the nervous system held at the Salpetriere](vol.3). Paris: Proges Medical en A. Delahaye & E. Lecrosnie.

Chiba, T., Kayahara, T., & Nakano, K. (2001). Efferent projections of infralimbic and prelimbic areas of the medial prefrontal cortex in the Japanese monkey, *Macaca fuscata. Brain Research, 888,* 83–101.

Chu, J. A. & Dill, D. L. (1990). Dissociative symptoms in relation to childhood physical and sexual abuse. *American Journal of Psychiatry, 147,* 887–892.

Corcoran, K. A., & Maren, S. (2001). Hippocampal inactivation disrupts contextual retrieval of fear memory after extinction. *Journal of Neuroscience, 21,* 1720–1726.

Creamer, M., Burgess, P., & McFarlane, A. (2001). Post-traumatic stress disorder: Findings from the Australian National Survey of Mental Health and Well-Being. *Psychological Medicine, 31,* 1237–1247.

Cromer, L. D., Stevens, C., DePrince, A. P., & Pears, K. (2006). The relationship between executive attention and dissociation in children. *Journal of Trauma and Dissociation, 7,* 135–154.

Cuthbert, B. N., Lang, P. J., Strauss, C., Drobes, D., Patrick, C. J., & Bradley, M. M. (2003). The psychophysiology of anxiety disorder: Fear memory imagery. *Psychophysiology, 40,* 407–422.

Da Costa, J.M. (1871). On irritable heart: A clinical study of a form of functional cardiac disorder and its consequences. *American Journal of the Medical Sciences, 61,* 17–52.

Dalgleish, T. (2004). Cognitive approaches to posttraumatic stress disorder: The evolution of multirepresentational theorizing. *Psychological Bulletin, 130,* 228–260.

Dalgleish, T., Moradi, A. R., Taghavi, M. R., Neshat-Doost, H. T., & Yule, W. (2001). An experimental investigation of hypervigilance for threat in children and adolescents with posttraumatic stress disorder. *Psychological Medicine, 31,* 541–547.

Dalgleish, T. & Power, M. J. (2004). Emotion-specific and emotion-non-specific components of posttraumatic stress disorder (PTSD): Implications for a taxonomy of related psychopathology. *Behaviour Research and Therapy, 42,* 1069–1088.

Daly, R.J. (1983). Samuel Pepys and post-traumatic stress disorder. *British Journal of Psychiatry, 143,* 64–68.

Davidson, P. R., & Parker, K. C. H. (2001). Eye movement desensitization and reprocessing (EMDR): A meta-analysis. *Journal of Consulting and Clinical Psychology, 69,* 305–316.

De Jong, de J. T., Komproe, I. H., Van Ommeren, M., El Masri M., Araya, M., Khaled, M., et al. (2001). Lifetime events and posttraumatic stress disorder in 4 post conflict settings. *Journal of the American Medical Association, 286,* 555–562.

DePrince, A. P. (2005). Social cognition and revictimization risk. *Journal of Trauma and Dissociation, 6,* 125–141.

DePrince, A. P., & Freyd, J. J. (1999). Dissociative tendencies, attention, and memory. *Psychological Science, 10,* 449–452.

DePrince, A., & Freyd, J. (2004). Forgetting Trauma Stimuli. *Psychological Science, 15,* 488–492.

DePrince, A. P., Weinzierl, K. M., & Combs, M. D. (2009). Executive function performance and trauma exposure in a community sample of children. *Child Abuse and Neglect: the International Journal, 33,* 353–361.

De Young, A. C., Kenardy, J. A., & Spence, S. H. (2007). Elevated heart rate as a predictor of PTSD six months following accidental pediatric injury. *Journal of Traumatic Stress, 20,* 1–6.

Dohrenwend, B., Turner, J., Turse, N., Adams, B., Koenen, K., & Marshall, R. (2006). The psychological risks of Vietnam for U.S. veterans: A revisit with new data and methods. *Science, 313,* 979–982.

Dolcos, F., LaBar, K. S., & Cabeza, R. (2004). Interaction between the amygdala and the medial temporal lobe memory system predicts better memory for emotional events. *Neuron, 42,* 855–863.

Driessen, M., Beblo, T., Mertens, M., Piefke, M., Rullkoetter, N., Silva-Saavedra, A., et al. (2004). Posttraumatic stress disorder and fMRI activation patterns of traumatic memory in patients with borderline personality disorder. *Biological Psychiatry, 55,* 603–611.

Dunmore, E., Clark, D.M., & Ehlers, A. (2001). A prospective investigation of the role of cognitive factors in persistent Posttraumatic Stress Disorder (PTSD) after physical or sexual assault. *Behaviour Research and Therapy, 39,* 1063–1084.

Ehlers, A. & Clark, D.M. (2000). A cognitive model of post-traumatic stress disorder. *Behaviour Research and Therapy, 38,* 319–345.

Ehlers, A., Mayou, R. A., & Bryant, B. (2003). Cognitive predictors of posttraumatic stress disorder in children: Results of a prospective longitudinal study. *Behaviour Research and Therapy, 41,* 1–10.

Ehring, T., Ehlers, A., & Glucksman, E. (2006). Contribution of cognitive factors to the prediction of post-traumatic stress disorder, phobia and depression after motor vehicle accidents. *Behaviour Research and Therapy, 44,* 1699–1716.

Ehring, T., Ehlers, A., & Glucksman, E. (2008). Do cognitive models help in predicting the severity of posttraumatic stress disorder, phobia, and depression after motor vehicle accidents? A prospective longitudinal study. *Journal of Consulting and Clinical Psychology, 76,* 219–230.

Eichenbaum, H. (2000). A cortical-hippocampal system for declarative memory. *Nature Reviews Neuroscience, 1,* 41–50.

El-Hage, W., Gaillard, P., Isingrini, M., & Belzung, C. (2006). Trauma-related deficits in working memory. *Cognitive Neuropsychiatry, 11,* 33–46.

Elsesser, K., Sartory, G., & Tackenberg, A. (2005). Initial symptoms and reactions to trauma-related stimuli and the development of posttraumatic stress disorder. *Depression and Anxiety, 21,* 61–70.

Fazel, M., Wheeler, J., & Danesh, J. (2005). Prevalence of serious mental disorder in 7000 refugees resettled in western countries: A systematic review. *The Lancet, 365,* 1309–1314.

Fendt, M. & Fanselow, M. S. (1999). The neuroanatomical and neurochemical basis of conditioned fear. *Neuroscience and Biobehavioral Reviews, 23,* 743–760.

Figley, C. (1978). *Stress disorders among Vietnam veterans: Theory, research, and treatment implications.* New York: Brunner/Mazel.

Foa, E. B., Cashman, L., Jaycox, L., & Perry, K. (1997). The validation of a self-report measure of posttraumatic stress disorder: The Posttraumatic Diagnostic Scale. *Psychological Assessment, 9,* 445–451.

Foa, E. B., Feske, U., Murdock, T. B., & Kozak, M. J. (1991). Processing of threat-related information in rape victims. *Journal of Abnormal Psychology, 100,* 156–162.

Foa, E. B., Hembree, E. A., Rothbaum, B. O. (2007). *Prolonged exposure therapy for PTSD: Emotional processing of traumatic experiences: Therapist guide.* New York: Oxford University Press.

Foa, E.B., Keane, T.M., Friedman, M.J., & Cohen, J.A. (Eds.). (2009). *Effective treatments for PTSD: Practice guidelines from the International Society for Traumatic Stress Studies* (2nd ed.). New York: Guilford Press.

Foa, E. B., Riggs, D. S., Dancu, C. V., & Rothbaum, B. O. (1993). Reliability and validity of a brief instrument for assessing post-traumatic stress disorder. *Journal of Traumatic Stress, 6,* 459–473.

Foa, E. B., Zoellner, L. A., Feeny, N. C., Hembree, E. A., & Alvarez-Conrad, J. (2002). Does imaginal exposure exacerbate PTSD symptoms? *Journal of Consulting and Clinical Psychology, 70,* 1022–1028.

Foynes, M., Freyd, J. J., & DePrince, A. P. (2009). Child abuse: Betrayal and disclosure. Manuscript under review.

Freud, S. (1896). Further remarks on the neuro-psychoses of defense. *Neurologisches Zentralblat, 15,* 434–48.

Freyd, J. J. (1994). Betrayal trauma: Traumatic amnesia as an adaptive response to childhood abuse. *Ethics & Behavior, 4,* 307–329.

Freyd, J. J. (1996). *Betrayal trauma: The logic of forgetting childhood abuse.* Cambridge, MA: Harvard University Press.

Freyd, J. J. (2001). Memory and dimensions of trauma: Terror may be "all–too-well remembered" and betrayal buried. In J.R. Conte (Ed.), *Critical Issues in Child Sexual Abuse: Historical, Legal, and Psychological Perspectives* (pp. 139–173). Thousand Oaks, CA: Sage Publications.

Freyd, J. J., DePrince, A. P., & Gleaves, D. H. (2007). The state of betrayal trauma theory: Reply to McNally – Conceptual issues and future directions. *Memory, 15,* 295–311.

Freyd, J., Klest, B., & Allard, C. (2005). Betrayal trauma: Relationship to physical health, psychological distress, and a written disclosure intervention. *Journal of Trauma & Dissociation, 6,* 83–104.

Friedman, M., Schnurr, P., Sengupta, A., Holmes, T., & Ashcraft, M. (2004). The Hawaii Vietnam Veterans Project: Is minority status a risk factor for posttraumatic stress disorder?. *Journal of Nervous and Mental Disease, 192,* 42–50.

Frueh, B. C., Elhai, J. D., & Hamner, M. B. (2003). Post-traumatic stress disorder (combat). In M. Hersen & S. M. Turner (Eds.), *Diagnostic interviewing (3rd ed.)* (pp. 321–343). New York, NY: Kluwer Academic/Plenum Publishers.

Galea, S., Ahern, J., Resnick, H., Kilpatrick, D., Bucuvalas, M., Gold, J., et al. (2002). Psychological sequelae of the September 11 terrorist attacks in New York City. *The New England Journal of Medicine, 346,* 982–987.

Gerrity, E., Keane, T. M., & Tuma, F. (Eds.). (2001). *The mental health consequences of torture.* Dordrecht, Netherlands: Kluwer Academic Publishers.

Ghashghaei, H. T., & Barbas, H. (2002). Pathways for emotion: interactions of prefrontal and anterior temporal pathways in the amygdala of the rhesus monkey. *Neuroscience, 115,* 1261–1279.

Gidron, Y. (2002). Posttraumatic stress disorder after terrorist attacks: A review. *Journal of Nervous and Mental Disease, 190,* 118–121.

Goldberg, L. R., & Freyd, J. J. (2006). Self-reports of potentially traumatic experiences in an adult community sample: Gender differences and test-retest stabilities of the items in a Brief Betrayal-Trauma Survey. *Journal of Trauma & Dissociation, 7,* 39–63.

Goldsmith, R. E., & Freyd, J. J. (2005). Awareness for emotional abuse. *Journal of Emotional Abuse, 5,* 95–123.

Golier, J. A., Yehuda, R., Lupien, S. J., & Harvey, P. D. (2003). Memory for trauma-related information in Holocaust survivors with PTSD. *Psychiatry Research, 121,* 133–143.

Goodwin, D. W. & Guze, S. B. (1984). *Psychiatric diagnosis*. New York: Oxford University Press.

Gray, M., Bolton, E., & Litz, B. (2004). A longitudinal analysis of PTSD symptom course: Delayed-onset PTSD in Somalia peacekeepers. *Journal of Consulting and Clinical Psychology, 72*, 909–913.

Green, B. L., Friedman, M. J., de Jong, J. T. V. M., Solomon, S. D., Keane, T. M., et al. (Eds.). (2003). *Trauma interventions in war and peace*. New York, NY: Kluwer Academic/Plenum Publishers.

Green, B., Grace, M., Lindy, J., & Gleser, G. (1990). Buffalo Creek survivors in the second decade: Comparison with unexposed and nonlitigant groups. *Journal of Applied Social Psychology, 20*, 1033–1050.

Green, B., Lindy, J., Grace, M., Gleser, G., Leonard, A., Korol, M., et al. (1990). Buffalo Creek survivors in the second decade: Stability of stress symptoms. *American Journal of Orthopsychiatry, 60*, 43–54.

Gregory, A., Caspi, A., Moffitt, T., Koenen, K., Eley, T., & Poulton, R. (2007). Juvenile mental health histories of adults with anxiety disorders. *The American Journal of Psychiatry, 164*, 301–308.

Griffin, M. G., Resick, P. A., & Mechanic, M. B. (1997). Objective assessment of peritraumatic dissociation: Psychophysiological indicators. *American Journal of Psychiatry, 154*, 1081–1088.

Gurvits, T. V., Shenton, M. E., Hokoma, H., Ohta, H., Lasko, N., Gilbertson, M., et al. (1996). Magnetic resonance imaging study of hippocampal volume in chronic, combat-related posttraumatic stress disorder. *Biological Psychiatry, 40*, 1091–1099.

Guthrie, R. M. & Bryant, R. A. (2005). Auditory startle response in firefighters before and after trauma exposure. *American Journal of Psychiatry, 162*, 283–290.

Hagenaars, M. A., van Minnen, A., & Hoogduin, K. A. L. (2007). Peritraumatic psychological and somatoform dissociation in predicting PTSD symptoms: A prospective study. *Journal of Nervous and Mental Disease, 195*, 952–954.

Halligan, S. L., Michael, T., Clark, D. M., & Ehlers, A. K. (2003). Posttraumatic stress disorder following assault: The role of cognitive processing, trauma memory, and appraisals. *Journal of Consulting and Clinical Psychology, 71*, 419–431.

Hendler, T., Rotshtein, P., Yeshurun, Y., Weizmann, T., Kahn, I., Ben-Bashat, D., et al. (2003). Sensing the invisible: Differential sensitivity of visual cortex and amygdala to traumatic context. *Neuroimage, 19*, 587–600.

Hoge, C., Castro, C., Messer, S., McGurk, D., Cotting, D., & Koffman, R. (2004). Combat Duty in Iraq and Afghanistan, Mental Health Problems, and Barriers to Care. *The New England Journal of Medicine, 351*, 13–22.

Holmes, E., Brewin, C.R., & Hennessey, R. (2004). Trauma films, information processing, and intrusive memory development. *Journal of Experimental Psychology: General, 133*, 3–22.

Holmes, M., & St. Lawrence, J. (1983). Treatment of rape-induced trauma: Proposed behavioral conceptualization and review of the literature. *Clinical Psychology Review, 3*, 417–433.

Ikin, J., Sim, M., Creamer, M., Forbes, A., McKenzie, D., Kelsall, H., et al. (2004). War-related psychological stressors and risk of psychological disorders in Australian veterans of the 1991 Gulf War. *British Journal of Psychiatry, 185*, 116–126.

Institute of Medicine (2008). *Treatment of Posttraumatic Stress Disorder: An assessment of the evidence*. Washington, DC: National Academies Press. Retrieved April 20, 2009 from http://www.nap.edu/catalog/11955.html.

Janet, P. (1909). *Les nervosas*. Paris: Flammarion.

Jones, J., & Barlow, D. (1990). The etiology of posttraumatic stress disorder. *Clinical Psychology Review, 10*, 299–328.

Jordan, B., Marmar, C., Fairbank, J., Schlenger, W., Kulka, R., Hough, R., et al. (1992). Problems in families of male Vietnam veterans with posttraumatic stress disorder. *Journal of Consulting and Clinical Psychology, 60*, 916–926.

Keane, T.M. (2008) Should there be a Traumatic Stress Category in the DSM-5? Paper presented in plenary symposium on the DSM-5 at the Anxiety Disorders Association of America, Savannah, GA.

Keane, T.M. (2009). Improving models, methods, and measures: Understanding CITRM's contributions to the study of psychological trauma. *Journal of Traumatic Stress, 22*, 632–633.

Keane, T. M. & Barlow, D. H. (2002). Posttraumatic stress disorder. In D. H. Barlow (Ed.), *Anxiety and Its Disorders (2nd ed.)* (pp. 418–453). New York: Guilford Press.

Keane, T. M., Fairbank, J. A., Caddell, J. M., Zimering, R. T., & Bender, M. E. (1985). A behavioral approach to assessing and treating PTSD in Vietnam veterans. In C. R. Figley (Ed.), *Trauma and its wake* (pp. 257–297). New York: Brunner-Mazel.

Keane, T. M., & Kaloupek, D. G. (1982). Imaginal flooding in the treatment of a posttraumatic stress disorder. *Journal of Consulting and Clinical Psychological, 50*, 138–140.

Keane, T. M., Kolb, L. C., Kaloupek, D. G., Orr, S. P., Blanchard, E. B., Thomas, R. G., et al. (1998). Utility of psychophysiology measurement in the diagnosis of posttraumatic stress disorder: Results from a department of Veteran's Affairs cooperative study. *Journal of Consulting and Clinical Psychology, 66*, 914–923.

Keane, T.M. & Miller, M.W. (2009) Is PTSD an Anxiety Disorder? Paper presented at the meetings of the American Psychological Association. Boston, MA.

Keane, T., Scott, W., Chavoya, G., Lamparski, D., & Fairbank, J. (1985). Social support in Vietnam veterans with posttraumatic stress disorder: A comparative analysis. *Journal of Consulting and Clinical Psychology, 53*, 95–102.

Keane, T., & Wolfe, J. (1990). Comorbidity in post-traumatic stress disorder: An analysis of community and clinical studies. *Journal of Applied Social Psychology, 20*, 1776–1788.

Keane, T. M., Wolfe, J., & Taylor, K. L. (1987). Post-traumatic stress disorder: Evidence for diagnostic validity and methods of psychological assessment. *Journal of Clinical Psychology, 43*, 32–43.

Keane, T., Zimering, R., & Caddell, J. (1985). A behavioral formulation of posttraumatic stress disorder in Vietnam veterans. *The Behavior Therapist, 8*, 9–12.

Kessler, R., Berglund, P., Demler, O., Jin, R., Merikangas, K., & Walters, E. (2005). Lifetime prevalence and age-of-onset distributions of DSM-IV disorders in the National Comorbidity Survey Replication. *Archives of General Psychiatry, 62*, 593–602.

Kessler, R. C., Sonnega, A., Bromet, E., Hughes, M., & Nelson, C. B. (1995). Posttraumatic stress disorder in the National Comorbidity Survey. *Archives of General Psychiatry, 52*, 1048–1060.

Kessler, R. C., Sonnega, A., Bromet, E., Hughes, M., Nelson, C. B., & Breslau, N. (1999). Epidemiological risk factors for trauma and PTSD. In R. Yehuda (Ed.), *Risk factors for posttraumatic stress disorder* (pp. 23–59). Washington, DC: American Psychiatric Association.

Kilpatrick, D., Best, C., Veronen, L., Amick, A., Villeponteaux, L., & Ruff, G. (1985). Mental health correlates of criminal victimization: A random community survey. *Journal of Consulting and Clinical Psychology, 53,* 866–873.

Kilpatrick, D. G., Edmunds, C. N., & Seymour, A. K. (1992). Rape in America: A report to the nation. Arlington, VA: National Victim Center.

Kilpatrick, D.G. (2008) *Prevalence rates of rape related PTSD among women in the United States.* Paper presented at the annual meetings of the Anxiety Disorders Association of America, Savannah, GA.

Kimble, M., Frueh, B. C., & Marks, L. (2009). Does the modified Stroop effect exist in PTSD? Evidence from dissertation abstracts and the peer reviewed literature. *Journal of Anxiety Disorders, 23,* 650–655.

Kimerling, R., Ouimette, P., Prins, A., Nisco, P., Lawler, C., Cronkite, R., et al. (2006). Utility of a short screening scale for DSM-IV PTSD in primary care. *Journal of General Internal Medicine, 21,* 65–67.

King, D. W., King, L. A., Foy, D. W., Keane, T. M., & Fairbank, J. A. (1999). Posttraumatic stress disorder in a national sample of female and male Vietnam veterans: Risk factors, war-zone stressors, and resilience-recovery variables. *Journal of Abnormal Psychology, 108,* 164–170.

King, D., Leskin, G., King, L., & Weathers, F. (1998). Confirmatory factor analysis of the clinician-administered PTSD Scale: Evidence for the dimensionality of posttraumatic stress disorder. *Psychological Assessment, 10,* 90–96.

Kleim, B., Ehlers, A., & Glucksman, E. (2007). Early predictors of chronic post-traumatic stress disorder in assault survivors. *Psychological Medicine, 37,* 1457–1467.

Koss, M., Woodruff, W., & Koss, P. (1991). Criminal victimization among primary care medical patients: Prevalence, incidence, and physician usage. *Behavioral Sciences & the Law, 9,* 85–96.

Kraepelin, E. (1896). *Psychiatrie:* Vol. 5 Auflage. Leipzig: Barth.

Kremen, W. S., Koenen, K. C., Boake, C., Purcell, S., Eisen, S. A., Franz, C. E., et al. (2007). Pretrauma cognitive ability and risk for posttraumatic stress disorder. *Archives of General Psychiatry, 64,* 361–368.

Kuhn, E., Blanchard, E. B., Fuse, T., Hickling, E. J., & Broderick, J. (2006). Heart rate of motor vehicle accident survivors in the emergency department, peritraumatic psychological reactions, ASD, and PTSD severity: A 6-month prospective study. *Journal of Traumatic Stress, 19,* 735–740.

Kulka, R., Schlenger, W., Fairbank, J., Hough, R., Jordan, B., Marmar, C., et al. (1990). *Trauma and the Vietnam war generation: Report of findings from the National Vietnam Veterans Readjustment Study.* Philadelphia, PA US: Brunner/Mazel.

Kuterovac, G., Dyregrov, A., & Stuvland, R. (1994). Children in war: A silent majority under stress. *British Journal of Medical Psychology, 67,* 363–375.

Lang, A. J., & Stein, M. B. (2005). An abbreviated PTSD checklist for use as a screening instrument in primary care. *Behaviour Research and Therapy, 43,* 585–594.

Lanius, R. A., Williamson, P. C., Boksman, K., Densmore, M., Gupta, M., Neufeld, R. W. J., et al. (2002). Brain activation during script-driven imagery induced dissociative responses in PTSD: A functional magnetic resonance imaging investigation. *Biological Psychiatry, 52,* 305–311.

Lanius, R. A., Williamson, P. C., Densmore, M., Boksman, K., Gupta, M. A., Neufeld, R. W., et al. (2001). Neural correlates of traumatic memories in posttraumatic stress disorder: A functional MRI investigation. *American Journal of Psychiatry, 158,* 1920–1922.

LeDoux, J., E. (2000). Emotion circuits in the brain. *Annual Review of Neuroscience, 23,* 155–184.

Líndal, E., & Stefánsson, J. (1993). The lifetime prevalence of anxiety disorders in Iceland as estimated by the US National Institute of Mental Health Diagnostic Interview Schedule. *Acta Psychiatrica Scandinavica, 88,* 29–34.

Lopes Cardozo, B., Bilukha, O., Gotway Crawford, C., Shaikh, I., Wolfe, M., Gerber, M., et al. (2004). Mental Health, Social Functioning, and Disability in Postwar Afghanistan. *Journal of the American Medical Association, 292,* 575–584.

Litz, B. (1992). Emotional numbing in combat-related posttraumatic stress disorder: A critical review and reformulation. *Clinical Psychology Review, 12,* 417–432.

Litz, B., Orsillo, S., Friedman, M., Ehlich, P., & Batres, A. (1997). Posttraumatic stress disorder associated with peacekeeping duty in Somalia for U.S. military personnel. *The American Journal of Psychiatry, 154,* 178–184.

Litz, B., Orsillo, S., Kaloupek, D., & Weathers, F. (2000). Emotional processing in posttraumatic stress disorder. *Journal of Abnormal Psychology, 109,* 26–39.

Litz, B. T., Weathers, F. W., Monaco, V., Herman, D. S., Wulfsohn, M., Marx, B., et al. (1996). Attention, arousal, and memory in posttraumatic stress disorder. *Journal of Traumatic Stress, 9,* 497–520.

Lloyd, D., & Turner, R. (2003). Cumulative adversity and posttraumatic stress disorder: Evidence from a diverse community sample of young adults. *American Journal of Orthopsychiatry, 73,* 381–391.

Malloy, P. F., Fairbank, J. A., & Keane, T. M. (1983). Validation of a multimethod assessment of posttraumatic stress disorders in Vietnam veterans. *Journal of Consulting and Clinical Psychology, 51,* 488–494.

Marmar, C. R., Weiss, D. S., Schlenger, W. E., Fairbank, J. A., Jordan, B. K., Kulka, R. A., et al. (1994). Peritraumatic dissociation and posttraumatic stress in male Vietnam theater veterans. *The American Journal of Psychiatry, 151,* 902–907.

Marshall, G. N. & Schell, T. L. (2002). Reappraising the link between peritraumatic dissociation and PTSD symptom severity: Evidence from a longitudinal study of community violence survivors. *Journal of Abnormal Psychology, 111,* 626–636.

Marx. B. P., Doron-Lamarca, Proctor, S., & Vasterling, J. (2009). The influence of pre-delopyment neurocognitive functioning on post-deployment PTSD symptom outcome among Iraq-deployed Army soldiers. *Journal of the International Neuropsychological Society, 15,* 840–852.

Marx, B. P., Humphreys, K. L., Weathers, F. W., Martin, E. K., Sloan, D. M., Grove, W. M., et al. (2008). Development and initial validation of a statistical prediction instrument for assessing combat-related posttraumatic stress disorder. *Journal of Nervous and Mental Disease, 196,* 605–611.

Marx, B. P. & Sloan, D. M. (2005). Peritraumatic dissociation and experiential avoidance as predictors of posttraumatic stress symptomatology. *Behaviour Research and Therapy, 43,* 569–583.

Mayou, R. A., Ehlers, A., & Bryant, B. (2002). Posttraumatic stress disorder after motor vehicle accidents: 3-year follow-up of a prospective longitudinal study. *Behaviour Research and Therapy, 40,* 665–675.

McFarlane, A. (1989). The treatment of post-traumatic stress disorder. *British Journal of Medical Psychology, 62*, 81–90.

McKenna, F. P. & Sharma, D. (1995). Intrusive cognitions: An investigation of the emotional Stroop task. *Journal of Experimental Psychology: Learning, Memory, & Cognition, 21*, 1595–1607.

McNally, R. (2004). Has clinical psychology gone astray?. *PsycCRITIQUES, 49*, 555–557.

Miller, M.W., Fogler, J., Wolf, E., Kaloupek, D., & Keane, T. (2008). The internalizing and externalizing structure of psychiatric comorbidity in combat veterans. *Journal of Traumatic Stress, 21*, 58–65.

Miller, M.W., Resick, P.A., & Keane, T.M. (2008) Should there be a Traumatic Stress Disorder Category in DSM-5? *British Journal of Psychiatry*

Monson, C. M., Schnurr, P. P., Resick, P. A., Friedman, M. J., Young-Xu, Y. & Stevens, S. P. (2006). Cognitive processing therapy for veterans with military-related posttraumatic stress disorder. *Journal of Consulting and Clinical Psychology, 74*, 898–907.

Moradi, A. R., Taghavi, M. R., Neshat-Doost, H. T., Yule, W., & Dalgleish, T. (1999). Performance of children and adolescents with PTSD on the Stroop colour-naming task. *Psychological Medicine, 29*, 415–419.

Morgan, M. A., Romanski, L. M., & LeDoux, J. E. (1993). Extinction of emotional learning: Contribution of medial prefrontal cortex. *Neuroscience Letters, 163*, 109–113.

Murray, E.J. & Lopes, A.D. (1996). *The Global Burden of Disease.* Cambridge, MA.: Harvard University Press.

Murray, J., Ehlers, A., & Mayou, R.A. (2002). Dissociation and posttraumatic stress disorder: Two prospective studies of motor vehicle accident survivors. *British Journal of Psychiatry, 180*, 363–368.

Navalta, C. P., Polcari, A., Webster, D. M., Boghossian, A., & Teicher, M. H. (2006). Effects of childhood sexual abuse on neuropsychological and cognitive function in college women. *Journal of Neuropsychiatry and Clinical Neurosciences, 18*, 45–53.

Nemeroff, C. B., Bremner, J. D., Foa, E. B., Mayberg, H. S., North, C. S., & Stein, M. B. (2006). Posttraumatic stress disorder: A state-of-the-science review. *Journal of Psychiatric Research, 40*, 1–21.

Newman, E., Orsillo, S.M., Herman, D.S., Niles, B.L., & Litz, B. T. (1995). The clinical presentation of disorders of extreme stress in combat veterans. *Journal of Nervous and Mental Disease, 183*, 628–632.

Norris, F. H., Foster, J. D., & Weisshaar, D. L. (2002). The epidemiology of sex differences in PTSD across developmental, societal, and research contexts. In R. Kimmerling, P. Ouimette, & J. Wolfe (Eds.), *Gender and PTSD* (pp. 3–42). New York, NY: Guilford Press.

Norris, F., Murphy, A., Baker, C., & Perilla, J. (2004). Postdisaster PTSD over four waves of a panel study of Mexico's 1999 flood. *Journal of Traumatic Stress, 17*, 283–292.

Norris, F., & Slone, L. (2007). The epidemiology of trauma and PTSD. In M. J. Friedman, T. M. Keane, & P. A. Resick (Eds.), *Handbook of PTSD: Science and practice* (pp. 78–98). New York, NY: Guilford Press.

O'Donnell, M. L., Creamer, M. C., Parslow, R., Elliot, P., Holmes, A. C. N., Ellen, S., et al. (2008). A predictive screening index for posttraumatic stress disorder and depression following traumatic injury. *Journal of Consulting and Clinical Psychology, 76*, 923–932.

O'Donnell, M. L., Elliott, P., Wolfgang, B. J., & Creamer, M. (2007). Posttraumatic appraisals in the development and persistence of posttraumatic stress symptoms. *Journal of Traumatic Stress, 20*, 173–182.

Orr, S., Lasko, N., Metzger, L., Berry, N., Ahern, C., & Pitman, R. (1998). Psychophysiologic assessment of women with posttraumatic stress disorder resulting from childhood sexual abuse. *Journal of Consulting and Clinical Psychology, 66*, 906–913.

Orr, S. P., Metzger, L. J., Lasko, N. B., Macklin, M. L., Peri, T., & Pitman, R. K. (2000). De novo conditioning in trauma exposed individuals with and without posttraumatic stress disorder. *Journal of Abnormal Psychology, 109*, 290–298.

Orr, S. P., Meyerhoff, J. L., Edwards, J. V., & Pitman, R. K. (1998). Heart rate and blood pressure resting levels and responses to generic stressors in Vietnam veterans with posttraumatic stress disorder. *Journal of Traumatic Stress, 11*, 155–164.

Orr, S., & Roth, W. (2000). Psychophysiological assessment: Clinical applications for PTSD. *Journal of Affective Disorders, 61*, 225–240.

Ozer, E., Best, S., Lipsey, T., & Weiss, D. (2003). Predictors of posttraumatic stress disorder and symptoms in adults: A meta-analysis. *Psychological Bulletin, 129*, 52–73.

Page, H. W. (1883). *Injuries of the spine and spinal cord without apparent mechanical lesion and nervous shock, in their surgical and medico-legal aspects.* London: J & A Churchill.

Parslow, R. A., & Jorm, A. F. (2007). Pretrauma and posttrauma neurocognitive functioning and PTSD symptoms in a community sample of young adults. *American Journal of Psychiatry, 164*, 509–515.

Paunovic, N., Lundh, L.-G., & Öst, L.-G. (2002). Attentional and memory bias for emotional information in crime victims with acute posttraumatic stress disorder (PTSD). *Journal of Anxiety Disorders, 16*, 675–692.

Perconte, S., Wilson, A., Pontius, E., Dietrick, A., & Spiro, K. J. (1993). Psychological and war stress symptoms among deployed and non-deployed reservists following the Persian Gulf War. *Military Medicine, 158*, 516–521.

Pham, P., Weinstein, H., & Longman, T. (2004). Trauma and PTSD symptoms in Rwanda: Implications for attitudes toward justice and reconciliation. *Journal of the American Medical Association, 292*, 602–612.

Pitman, R. K., Orr, S. P., Forgue, D. F., Altman, B., de Jong, J. B., & Herz, L. R. (1990). Psychophysiologic responses to combat imagery of Vietnam veterans with post-traumatic stress disorder versus other anxiety disorders. *Journal of Abnormal Psychology, 99*, 49–54.

Pitman, R. K., Gilbertson, M. W., Gurvits, T. V., May, F. S., Lasko, N. B., Metzger, L. J., et al. (2006). Clarifying the origin of biological abnormalities in PTSD through the study of identical twins discordant for combat exposure. In R. Yehuda (Ed.), *Psychobiology of Posttraumatic Stress Disorder: A Decade of Progress* (pp. 242–254). Malden, MA: Blackwell Publishing.

Plattner, B., Silvermann, M. A., Redlich, A. D., Carrion, V. G., Feucht, M., Friedrich, M. H., et al. (2003). Pathways to dissociation: Intrafamilial versus extrafamilial trauma in juvenile delinquents. *The Journal of Nervous and Mental Disease, 191*, 781–788.

Pole, N. (2007). The psychophysiology of posttraumatic stress disorder: A meta-analysis. *Psychological Bulletin, 133*, 725–746.

Punamäki, R., Komproe, I., Qouta, S., El-Masri, M., & de Jong, J. (2005). The deterioration and mobilization effects of trauma on social support: Childhood maltreatment and adulthood military violence in a Palestinian community sample. *Child Abuse & Neglect, 29*, 351–373.

Putnam, F. (1997). *Dissociation in children and adolescents: A developmental perspective*. New York, NY US: Guilford Press.

Putnam, F., Carlson, E., Ross, C., & Anderson, G. (1996). Patterns of dissociation in clinical and nonclinical samples. *Journal of Nervous and Mental Disease, 184*, 673–679.

Quirk, G. J., Russo, G. K., Barron, J. L., & Lebron, K. (2000). The role of ventromedial prefrontal cortex in the recovery of extinguished fear. *Journal of Neuroscience, 20*, 6225–6231.

Rauch, S. L., Shin, L. M., Segal, E., Pitman, R. K., Carson, M. A., McMullin, K., et al. (2003). Selectively reduced regional cortical volumes in post-traumatic stress disorder. *Neuroreport, 14*, 913–916.

Resick, P. A., Galovski, T. E., Uhlmansiek, M. O., Scher, C. D., Clum, G. A., & Young-Xu, Y. (2008). A randomized clinical trial to dismantle components of cognitive processing therapy for posttraumatic stress disorder in female victims of interpersonal violence. *Journal of Consulting and Clinical Psychology, 76*, 243–248.

Resick, P. A., & Schnicke, M. K. (1992). Cognitive processing therapy for sexual assault survivors. *Journal of Consulting and Clinical Psychology, 60*, 748–756.

Resnick, H., Kilpatrick, D., Dansky, B., Saunders, B., & Best, C. (1993). Prevalence of civilian trauma and posttraumatic stress disorder in a representative national sample of women. *Journal of Consulting and Clinical Psychology, 61*, 984–991.

Rosenman, S. (2002). Trauma and posttraumatic stress disorder in Australia: Findings in the population sample of the Australian National Survey of Mental Health and Wellbeing. *Australian and New Zealand Journal of Psychiatry, 36*, 515–520.

Rothbaum, B. O., Kozak, M. J., Foa, E. B., & Whitaker, D. J. (2001). Posttraumatic stress disorder in rape victims: Autonomic habituation to auditory stimuli. *Journal of Traumatic Stress, 14*, 283–293.

Sack, W., McSharry, S., Clarke, G., & Kinney, R. (1994). The Khmer Adolescent Project: I. Epidemiologic findings in two generations of Cambodian refugees. *Journal of Nervous and Mental Disease, 182*, 387–395.

Sapolsky, R. M., Uno, H., Rebert, C. S., & Finch, C. E. (1990). Hippocampal damage associated with prolonged glucocorticoid exposure in primates. *Journal of Neuroscience, 10*, 2897–2902.

Schlenger, W. E., Caddell, J. M., Ebert, L., Jordan, K., Rourke, K. M., Wilson, D., et al. (2002). Psychological reactions to terrorist attacks: Findings from the National Study of Americans' Reactions to September 11. *Journal of the American Medical Association, 288*, 581–588.

Schlenger, W. E., Kulka, R. A., Fairbank, J. A., Hough, R. L., Jordan, B. K., Marmar, C. R., et al. (1992). The prevalence of post-traumatic stress disorder in the Vietnam generation: A multimethod, multisource assessment of psychiatric disorder. *Journal of Traumatic Stress, 5*, 333–363.

Schnurr, P., & Green, B. (2004). Understanding relationships among trauma, post-traumatic stress disorder, and health outcomes. *Advances in Mind-Body Medicine, 20*, 18–29.

Schnurr, P., Lunney, C., Sengupta, A., & Waelde, L. (2003). A descriptive analysis of PTSD chronicity in Vietnam veterans. *Journal of Traumatic Stress, 16*, 545–553.

Scholte, W. F., Olff, M., Ventevogel, P., de Vries, G.-J., Jansveld, E., Lopes Cardozo, B., et al. (2004). Mental health symptoms following war and repression in Eastern Afghanistan. *Journal of the American Medical Association, 292*, 585–593.

Shalev, A. Y., Orr, S. P., & Pitman, R. K. (1993). Psychophysiologic assessment of traumatic imagery in Israeli civilian patients with posttraumatic stress disorder. *American Journal of Psychiatry, 150*, 620–624.

Shalev, A., Peri, T., Brandes, D., Freedman, S., Orr, S., & Pitman, R. (2000). Auditory startle response in trauma survivors with posttraumatic stress disorder: A prospective study. *The American Journal of Psychiatry, 157*, 255–261.

Shalev, A. Y., Peri, T., Canetti, L., & Schreiber, S. (1996). Predictors of PTSD in injured trauma survivors: A prospective study. *American Journal of Psychiatry, 153*, 219–225.

Shalev, A. Y., Sahar, T., Freedman, S., Peri, T., Glick, N., Brandes, D., et al. (1998). A prospective study of heart rate response following trauma and the subsequent development of post-traumatic stress disorder. *Archives of General Psychiatry, 55*, 553–559.

Shapiro. F. (1995). *Eye movement desensitization and reprocessing: Basic principles, protocols and procedures*. New York: Guilford Press.

Sharkansky, E. J., King, D. W., King, L. A., Wolfe, J., Erickson, D. J., & Stokes, L. R. (2000). Coping with Gulf War combat stress: Mediating and moderating effects. *Journal of Abnormal Psychology, 109*, 188–197.

Shea, M. T., McDevitt-Murphy, M., Ready, D. J., & Schnurr, P. P. (2009). Group therapy. In E. B. Foa, T. M. Keane, M. J. Friedman, & J. A. Cohen (Eds.), *Effective treatments for PTSD: Practice guidelines from the International Society for Traumatic Stress Studies (2nd ed.)* (pp. 306–326). New York: Guilford Press.

Shin, L. M., Orr, S. P., Carson, M. A., Rauch, S. L., Macklin, M. L., Lasko, N. B., et al. (2004). Regional cerebral blood flow in the amygdala and medial prefrontal cortex during traumatic imagery in male and female Vietnam veterans with PTSD. *Archives of General Psychiatry, 61*, 168–176.

Shiromani, P. J., Keane, T. M., & LeDoux, J. E. (Eds.). (2009). *Post-traumatic stress disorder: Basic science and clinical practice*. Totowa, NJ: Humana Press.

Simeon, D., Knutelska, M.E., Putnam, F., Yehuda, R., Schmeidler, J., & Smith, L. (2006). Attention and memory in dissociative disorders, posttraumatic stress disorder, and healthy volunteers. Annual Meeting, International Society for Traumatic Stress Studies, Hollywood, CA, November 5–7, 2006.

Sivers, H., Schooler, J., & Freyd, J. J. (2002). Recovered memories. In V.S. Ramachandran (Ed.) *Encyclopedia of the Human Brain, Volume 4*. (pp 169–184). San Diego, California and London: Academic Press.

Slade, T., & Watson, D. (2006). The structure of common DSM-IV and ICD-10 mental disorders in the Australian general population. *Psychological Medicine, 36*, 1593–1600.

Sloan, D. M., Feinstein, B., Beck, J. G., & Keane, T. M. (2009). Efficacy of group treatment for posttraumatic stress symptoms: A meta-analysis. Manuscript under review.

Stein, M. B., Kennedy, C. M., & Twamley, E. W. (2002). Neuropsychological function in female victims of intimate partner violence with and without posttraumatic stress disorder. *Biological Psychiatry, 52*, 1079–1088.

Sutker, P., Uddo, M., Brailey, K., & Allain, A. (1993). War-zone trauma and stress-related symptoms in Operation Desert Shield/Storm (ODS) returnees. *Journal of Social Issues, 49*, 33–50.

Sutker, P. B., Winstead, D. K., Galina, Z. H., & Allain, A. N. (1991). Cognitive deficits and psychopathology among former prisoners of war and combat veterans of the Korean conflict. *American Journal of Psychiatry, 148,* 67–72.

Uddo, M., Vasterling, J. J., Brailey, K., & Sutker, P. B. (1993). Memory and attention in combat-related post-traumatic stress disorder (PTSD). *Journal of Psychopathology and Behavioral Assessment, 15,* 43–52.

van der Hart, O., Nijenhuis, E., & Steele, K. (2005). Dissociation: An Insufficiently Recognized Major Feature of Complex Posttraumatic Stress Disorder. *Journal of Traumatic Stress, 18,* 413–423.

van der Kolk, B., & Fisler, R. (1995). Dissociation and the fragmentary nature of traumatic memories: Overview and exploratory study. *Journal of Traumatic Stress, 8,* 505–525.

van der Kolk, Pelcovitz, D., Roth, S., Mandel, F. S., McFarlane, A., & Herman, J. (1996). Dissociation, somatization, and affect dysregulation: The complexity of trauma. *American Journal of Psychiatry, 153,* 83–93.

Villarreal, G., Hamilton, D. A., Petropoulos, H., Driscoll, I., Rowland, L. M., Griego, J. A., et al. (2002). Reduced hippocampal volume and total white matter volume in posttraumatic stress disorder. *Biological Psychiatry, 52,* 119–125.

Vogt, D. S. & Tanner, L. R. (2007). Risk and resilience factors for posttraumatic stress symptomatology in Gulf War I veterans. *Journal of Traumatic Stress, 20,* 27–38.

Vrana, S. R., Roodman, A., & Beckham, J. C. (1995). Selective processing of trauma-relevant words in posttraumatic stress disorder. *Journal of Anxiety Disorders, 9,* 515–530.

Walker, E., Katon, W., Russo, J., Ciechanowski, P., Newman, E., & Wagner, A. (2003). Health care costs associated with post-traumatic stress disorder symptoms in women. *Archives of General Psychiatry, 60,* 369–374.

Watanabe, T., Gould, E., & McEwen, B. S. (1992). Stress induces atrophy of apical dendrites of hippocampal CA3 pyramidal neurons. *Brain Research, 588,* 341–345.

Watts-English, T., Fortson, B.L., Gibler, N., Hooper, S.R., & De Bellis, M.D. (2006). The psychobiology of maltreatment in childhood. *Journal of Social Issues, 62,* 717–736.

Weathers, F., & Keane, T. (2007). The crucial role of criterion A: A response to Maier's commentary. *Journal of Traumatic Stress, 20,* 917–919.

Weathers, F. W., Keane, T. M., Davidson, J. R. T. (2001). Clinician-Administered PTSD Scale: A review of the first ten years of research. *Depression and Anxiety, 13,* 132–156.

Weathers, F. W., Litz, B. T., Herman, D. S., Huska, J. A., & Keane, T. M. (1993, October). *The PTSD Checklist: Reliability, validity, and diagnostic utility.* Paper presented at the annual meeting of the International Society for Traumatic Stress Studies, San Antonio, TX.

Williams, L. (1994). Recall of childhood trauma: A prospective study of women's memories of child sexual abuse. *Journal of Consulting and Clinical Psychology, 62,* 1167–1176.

Williams, J. M. G., Watts, F. N., MacLeod, C., & Mathews, A. (1997). *Cognitive psychology and emotional disorders* (2nd ed.). Chichester: Wiley.

Winter, H., & Irle, E. (2004). Hippocampal volume in adult burn patients with and without posttraumatic stress disorder. *American Journal of Psychiatry, 161,* 2194–2200.

Wirtz, P., & Harrell, A. (1987). Effects of postassault exposure to attack-similar stimuli on long-term recovery of victims. *Journal of Consulting and Clinical Psychology, 55,* 10–16.

Wolfe, J., Brown, P., & Kelley, J. (1993). Reassessing war stress: Exposure and the Persian Gulf War. *Journal of Social Issues, 49,* 15–31.

Wolfe, J., Erickson, D. J., Sharkansky, E. J., King, D. W., & King, L. A. (1999). Course and predictors of posttraumatic stress disorder among Gulf War veterans: A prospective analysis. *Journal of Consulting and Clinical Psychology, 67,* 520–528.

Woodward, S. H., Kaloupek, D. G., Streeter, C. C., Martinez, C., Schaer, M., & Eliez, S. (2006). Decreased anterior cingulate volume in combat-related PTSD. *Biological Psychiatry, 59,* 582–587.

Yamasue, H., Kasai, K., Iwanami, A., Ohtani, T., Yamada, H., Abe, O., et al. (2003). Voxel-based analysis of MRI reveals anterior cingulate gray-matter volume reduction in posttraumatic stress disorder due to terrorism. *Proceedings of the National Academy of Sciences of the United States of America, 100,* 9039–9043.

Yehuda, R. (2001). Biology of posttraumatic stress disorder. *Journal of Clinical Psychiatry, 62,* 41–46.

Yehuda, R., Keefe, R. S. E., Harvey, P. D., & Levengood, R. A. (1995). Learning and memory in combat veterans with post-traumatic stress disorder. *American Journal of Psychiatry, 152,* 137–139.

Eating Disorders

Robyn Sysko *and* G. Terence Wilson

Abstract

The Diagnostic and Statistical Manual of Mental Disorders (DSM-IV; American Psychiatric Association, 1994) describes two eating disorder diagnoses, anorexia nervosa (AN) and bulimia nervosa (BN). Provisional criteria are also provided in DSM-IV for binge eating disorder (BED), which is an example of an eating disorder not otherwise specified. This chapter presents a summary and synthesis of research related to the clinical features and treatment of AN, BN, and BED, including studies of prevalence, common comorbidities, and treatment efficacy. Both psychological and pharmacological treatments are reviewed, including cognitive-behavioral therapy, interpersonal psychotherapy, family therapy, and the use of antidepressant medications. Recommendations are made for future research across the eating disorders.

Keywords: Anorexia nervosa, bulimia nervosa, binge eating disorder, cognitive-behavioral therapy, antidepressant medication

This chapter presents a comprehensive overview of empirical research on eating disorders. General information is provided about the diagnostic criteria for eating disorders, prevalence and incidence of eating disorders, common comorbidities, treatment efficacy, and future directions for research in eating disorders. *The Diagnostic and Statistical Manual of Mental Disorders, Fourth Edition* (DSM-IV; American Psychiatric Association [APA], 1994) describes only two main eating disorder diagnoses, anorexia nervosa (AN) and bulimia nervosa (BN). However, provisional criteria for binge eating disorder (BED) are provided in the Appendix of DSM-IV, and as this diagnosis has generated a significant amount of attention and research since the publication of DSM-IV (Walsh, 2007), it will also be covered in the sections that follow.

Anorexia Nervosa

Individuals meeting the diagnostic criteria for AN have a body weight below a minimally normal weight for age and height (e.g., less than 85% of expected); endorse a fear of weight gain or becoming fat; demonstrate a disturbance in body shape or weight, or the overvaluation of body shape and weight, or deny the seriousness of their current weight; and for postmenarchal females, experience amenorrhea for at least 3 months (APA, 1994). In the absence of regular binge eating and purging episodes, individuals are diagnosed with AN, restricting type (AN-R), whereas individuals with binge eating and purging behaviors (e.g., self-induced vomiting, laxative misuse) are classified as AN, binge-eating/purging type (AN-B/P; APA, 1994). This chapter summarizes information related to the presentation and treatment of AN, and suggests future directions for research on this disorder. Although the studies described in this chapter provide important information about the clinical course and outcome of patients with AN, a number of limitations are also evident, and are described in greater detail in upcoming sections. Additional research is needed to better characterize the optimal treatment interventions for patients with AN.

Anorexia nervosa is a serious psychiatric disorder associated with significant morbidity and mortality (Sullivan, 1995; Steinhausen, 2002). Patients with AN are at risk for a range of medical complications, including cardiac abnormalities (e.g., bradycardia, hypotension, QT interval prolongation, QT dispersion, etc.), electrolyte abnormalities, osteopenia or osteoporosis, and endocrine disturbances (Mehler, Birmingham, Crow, & Jahraus, 2010). Long-term outcomes for individuals with AN are concerning, with less than half of the patients experiencing a full recovery, approximately one-third considered improved, and another 20% demonstrating a chronic course after a 4- to 10-year follow-up period (Steinhausen, 2002). Further, a recent study documented a six-fold increased mortality rate in comparison to the general population among individuals with AN, and 20 years or more after their first hospitalization, standardized mortality ratios for natural and unnatural causes were still high among patients with AN (Papadopoulous, Ekbom, Brandt, & Ekselius, 2009).

Prevalence

Anorexia nervosa is a severe psychiatric disorder, but it is also a relatively rare condition. Hoek and van Hoeken (2003) reviewed epidemiologic studies of eating disorders, including AN, and found the average total number of cases in the population, or prevalence rate, was 0.29% (range of 0.0%–0.9%), with higher prevalence rates observed for subthreshold AN. A recent study examining AN among twins in Finland found an incidence, or number of new cases, of 270 per 100,000 person-years for individuals aged 15–19, and a lifetime prevalence of 2.2% for DSM-IV AN, and increased incidence and prevalence for broader definitions of AN (Keski-Rahkonen et al., 2007). Data documenting the incidence of AN among males are limited, but the female-to-male ratio of cases is estimated at 10:1 (Hoek & van Hoeken, 2003). The majority of studies related to epidemiology and treatment of AN focus on girls or women, and consequently much less is known about the clinical presentation of males with AN. Estimates of the incidence and prevalence of AN are further complicated by both the rarity of this disorder, which necessitates recruiting very large sample sizes, and patient characteristics, including secrecy and denial of patients, which interfere with the reporting of eating disorder symptoms (Grilo, 2006). Thus, it is not known whether these studies are accurately estimating the true prevalence and incidence rates for AN.

The prevalence of AN appears similar in Western and non-Western countries, suggesting that the effects of Western culture may be less prominent for AN than for other eating disorders (i.e., bulimia nervosa; Keel & Klump, 2003). Debate continues about whether the incidence of AN in the community has increased during the 20th century, or if other factors account for increases in the incidence of AN among youth, especially for 15- to 24-year-old females; however, larger numbers of identified cases have resulted in an increased need for treatment (Hoek & van Hoeken, 2003).

Comorbidities

Patients with AN often describe symptoms consistent with other Axis I disorders. Clinical assessments of other psychiatric disorders are complicated by the presence of symptoms that may be secondary to low body weight or indicate an independent mood or anxiety disorder (e.g., depressed mood, low energy, obsessions, etc.). Patients with AN-R and AN-B/P report a prevalence of lifetime anxiety disorders of 33%–72% and 55%, respectively (Godart, Flament, Perdereau, & Jeammet, 2002). The prevalence of lifetime major depressive disorder ranges between 9.5% and 64.7% for patients with AN-R, and 50%–71% for patients with AN-B/P (Godart et al., 2007). Difficulties in differentiating Axis I mood or anxiety symptoms among patients with AN from the consequences of achieving a low body weight may explain some of the variability in these estimates. A substantial proportion of patients with AN also endorse a lifetime substance use disorder (Hudson, Hiripi, Pope, & Kessler, 2007), with a higher prevalence of alcohol or drug problems observed among individuals who binge eat (AN-B/P; Braun, Sunday, & Halmi, 1994; Bulik, Sullivan, & Slof, 2004; Herzog, Keller, Sacks, Yeh, & Lavori, 1992; Wiederman & Pryor, 1996). Recently, Root and colleagues (2010) observed higher rates of lifetime substance use disorders among a large sample of patients with a lifetime history of AN (n = 731) than did previous research (e.g., Braun et al., 1994; Herzog et al., 1992); however, patients with either alcohol or substance abuse or dependence were included in the analyses. With this broader definition of substance use, Root et al. (2010) also documented higher lifetime rates of alcohol and substance abuse and dependence among patients with binge eating or purging behaviors in comparison to those patients with a history of AN characterized by restricting without purging.

Treatment Efficacy

Consistent with the low prevalence of AN, only a small number of controlled trials have evaluated treatments for this disorder, and the majority of these studies have focused on younger patients. Challenges in conducting research on patients with AN, such as the egosyntonic nature of the symptoms (Vitousek, Watson, & Wilson, 1998), high costs associated with more intensive treatment interventions (Agras et al., 2004), and significant medical complications that may necessitate withdrawing patients from treatment (Halmi et al., 2005), also slow the progress of research. Additionally, a number of different treatment options are needed for patients with AN (e.g., inpatient hospitalization, partial hospitalization/day treatment, outpatient treatment), and practitioners often use a combination of psychological and pharmacological interventions (Fairburn, 2005), which further complicates the process of conducting treatment research.

In general, research on psychological and pharmacological interventions for AN focuses on either acute treatment or the prevention of relapse to a low weight. Many of the trials described here have methodological flaws, including small sample sizes, short treatment durations or a small number of treatment sessions, limited follow-up, and others (Pike, 2009). Treatment trials for AN can be characterized by low rates of treatment acceptance (e.g., agreeing to participate in the trial), high rates of dropout, and questionable compliance with treatment (Halmi et al., 2005). Further, there is a notable risk that individuals with AN may need to be withdrawn from outpatient treatment studies to receive a higher level of care (Bulik, Berkman, Brownley, Sedway, & Lohr, 2007). However, despite these challenges, these patients are at risk for significant morbidity and mortality, and additional research to develop effective treatments is urgently needed.

PSYCHOLOGICAL TREATMENTS
Family Therapy

The greatest proportion of studies for the treatment of AN have examined the utility of family therapy. One particular form of family therapy, called the Maudsley form of family therapy (Lock, le Grange, Agras, & Dare, 2001), is the most commonly studied (Wilson, Grilo, & Vitousek, 2007). Initially, this approach involves the therapist training parents to function in a manner similar to that of inpatient staff, whereby the parents are entirely in control of their child's eating and weight (Lock et al., 2001). Subsequently, as the child gains weight, the second phase of the treatment allows the child greater autonomy and control, and the parents are less directly involved in refeeding (Lock et al., 2001).

The first investigation of Maudsley family therapy compared it to an eclectic supportive individual psychotherapy for preventing posthospitalization relapse among patients with AN (Russell, Szmukler, Dare, & Eisler, 1987). Russell and colleagues (1987) observed that, for younger patients with a shorter duration of illness, family therapy was superior to individual treatment; however, for patients older than 19 years of age with a longer duration of illness, the data suggested that individual treatment was more effective. In a 5-year follow-up of the Russell et al. (1987) report, Eisler and colleagues (1997) found evidence that these effects endured, as the benefits of family or individual therapy continued to be apparent for patients who were younger with a short duration of illness and older patients with a more chronic illness, respectively. Subsequent studies examining the Maudsley form of family therapy for adolescents with AN has focused on comparisons of varying types of the Maudsley approach (Wilson et al., 2007). Conclusions about the efficacy of family therapy for adolescents with AN are complicated by the possibility that patients under the age of 18 with a shorter duration of illness are more likely to respond, and by questions of whether family treatment is specifically beneficial or if other treatment interventions would show similar results (Fairburn, 2005).

Cognitive-Behavioral Therapy

Cognitive-behavioral therapy (CBT) has been evaluated for the acute treatment of AN among outpatients in a small number of controlled trials. Garner and Vitousek first described a version of CBT for AN (Garner & Bemis, 1982, 1985; Garner, Vitousek, & Pike, 1997) that is similar to CBT as developed for BN (described later), but with a greater emphasis on issues related to low weight, weight gain (Garner et al., 1997), and increasing motivation for change and collaboration (Vitousek et al., 1998). The amount of time patients spend in treatment also differs substantially between CBT for AN and BN, with a recommendation of 1–2 years of treatment for patients with acute AN, and about 1 year for relapse prevention among individuals who enter treatment after weight restoration (Wilson et al., 2007).

Two studies utilizing CBT cannot be interpreted due to serious methodological issues, with the first noting a 100% dropout rate from the comparison treatment (nutritional counseling; Serfaty, Turkington, Heap, Ledsham, & Jolley, 1999), and the second retaining less than 40% of patients across all groups (Halmi et al., 2005). A few studies have observed no differences in outcome for patients receiving CBT and other comparison therapies, including Channon and colleagues (1989), who examined the efficacy of three brief treatments, including CBT, a behavioral exposure treatment, and an eclectic control treatment. After 6 months of treatment, few significant differences were observed among the groups (Channon, DeSilva, Hemsley, & Perkins, 1989). Additionally, the authors noted that, although overall improvements were observed, the majority of patients were not weight restored and continued to experience eating-disordered symptoms (Channon et al., 1989). Ball and Mitchell (2004) compared CBT and behavioral family therapy for a younger sample of patients (ages 13–23), and in a completer analysis, observed no differences in weight or menstrual status between the treatment groups. For patients with broadly defined AN, McIntosh and colleagues (2005) compared CBT, interpersonal psychotherapy (IPT), and nonspecific supportive clinical management over 20 weeks. For the primary outcome measure of global AN rating, patients receiving nonspecific supportive clinical management demonstrated significantly better outcomes than the IPT group; however, other comparisons between treatments were not significantly different.

All three aforementioned studies included fewer treatment sessions than suggested by experts in CBT and utilized a form of CBT for AN that differed from what is recommended by the field (Wilson et al., 2007). Additional limitations include the small number of patients with AN (24–56), the inclusion of some individuals with a higher entry body mass index (McIntosh et al., 2005), and the fact that a significant proportion of patients did not complete a full course of therapy and/or did not demonstrate clinically significant improvements at the end of treatment.

Data supporting a specific effect of CBT are found in two studies focusing on the prevention of posthospitalization relapse among patients with AN. Pike and colleagues (2003) randomized patients to receive CBT or a nutritional counseling intervention over the year following discharge from an inpatient unit. At the end of treatment, significantly more patients in the nutritional counseling group met criteria for relapse (53%) in comparison to CBT (22%), and CBT was also superior when considering rates of premature dropout and percent of patients achieving a good outcome (Pike et al., 2003). More recently,

a nonrandomized study also found support for the superiority of CBT over community treatment as usual (Carter et al., 2009). Carter et al. (2009) observed that time to relapse, when defined as either a body mass index of 17.5 or less for 3 months or the resumption of regular binge eating and/or purging behaviors, was significantly longer for patients receiving CBT than for the treatment-as-usual group. Taken together, and in light of limitations similar to those described earlier, these studies suggest that nutritional counseling is not effective in preventing relapse among patients with AN and, although CBT has more promise for posthospitalization treatment, more data are needed.

PHARMACOLOGICAL TREATMENTS
A number of small studies have evaluated the role of medications in facilitating weight restoration among patients with AN. For patients with acute AN, studies have examined antipsychotic medications such as chlorpromazine, pimozide, and sulpiride; antidepressants including clomipramine, amitriptyline, nortriptyline, and fluoxetine; and other medications including cisapride, an opiate antagonist (naltrexone), an antihypertensive (clonidine), hormones (testosterone, human growth hormone, estrogen/progestin), lithium, a serotonin antagonist (cyproheptadine), tetrahydrocannabinol, and zinc (Attia & Schroeder, 2005; Bulik et al., 2007; Crow, Mitchell, Roerig, & Steffen, 2009).

In general, the results of these studies were disappointing, with few suggesting any notable impact on weight gain; however, research evaluating pharmacological treatments for patients with AN typically utilize small sample sizes, are of short duration, and utilize medications primarily targeting appetite stimulation and comorbid symptoms of anxiety and depression (Attia & Schroeder, 2005; Crow et al., 2009). Additionally, the high percentage of patients with AN who will not accept a medication-only treatment, in combination with high dropout rates, has led some to argue that providing medication alone is not sufficient treatment for these individuals (Halmi et al., 2005). The failure to demonstrate a difference between active medication and placebo for either eating disordered or mood symptoms among patients with AN stands in contrast to studies of BN, which are described more fully later. However, newer agents may offer more promise for patients with AN. A recent study examined olanzapine, an atypical antipsychotic, versus placebo among 34 individuals attending a day treatment program in Canada (Bissada, Tasca, Barber, & Bradwejn, 2008).

Over the 13 weeks of the trial, all of the patients with AN gained weight, but patients randomized to olanzapine showed greater increases in body mass index, and a greater percentage achieved weight restoration in comparison to patients receiving placebo (Bissada et al., 2008). As the patients in the Bissada and colleagues (2008) study all participated in day treatment during the trial, additional studies are needed to evaluate the role of olanzapine without the addition of an intensive psychological intervention.

Two placebo-controlled studies have evaluated the utility of fluoxetine to prevent relapse following an inpatient hospitalization. In the first study (Kaye et al., 2001), some patients also received psychological treatment, which was not standardized, and in the second (Walsh et al., 2006), all patients received CBT in addition to fluoxetine or placebo. Kaye and colleagues (2001) found that fluoxetine-treated patients were more likely to complete the trial (63% completed) in comparison to patients receiving placebo (16% completed, p = .0001), and patients who completed the trial tended to experience more weight gain and psychological improvement than patients who did not complete the trial. In the largest controlled medication trial for individuals with AN, Walsh and colleagues (2006) randomized 93 women to receive either fluoxetine or placebo. All of the patients were also provided with a CBT intervention, consisting of 50 individual treatment sessions. On almost all of the measures, the authors found little evidence for any significant benefit of fluoxetine compared to placebo (Walsh et al., 2006). In contrast to the Kaye et al. (2001) findings, Walsh et al. (2006) observed that fluoxetine did not affect time-to-relapse regardless of how dropouts from the study were classified, and the authors suggest that antidepressant medication is "unlikely to provide substantial benefit for most patients with anorexia nervosa" (p. 2611).

In summarizing the extant data on medication, Crow and colleagues (2009) state "at present, there is no convincing evidence of efficacy for any drug treatment for AN in either the acute or chronic phase of the illness" (p. 1). Crow et al. (2009) suggest a number of possible explanations for the lack of efficacy of psychopharmacological treatments for AN, including: medication compliance, complications from the impact of starvation (e.g., nutritional deficits, problems with cognitive function), use of medication monotherapy, the choices of outcome measures and treatment targets, few animal models of AN, limited attention from pharmaceutical companies, and the possibility that AN is not responsive to medication treatment. To address these limitations, Crow and colleagues (2009) propose solutions such as considering alternative targets for medications (e.g., fear conditioning), utilizing different measures (e.g., laboratory measures of feeding behavior), conducting shorter pilot trials of medication, identifying new strategies for drug development, focusing on the symptoms that most affect functioning and outcome among patients with AN, and modifying the existing clinical trials system to increase recruitment. The studies of pharmacological treatments to date have not been promising, but options do exist for continuing to examine medication options for patients with AN.

Early Response
Body weight, body composition, and nutritional status appear to be important in the prevention of relapse among patients with AN. A few recent studies have highlighted the specific importance of early changes in these domains in predicting individuals with AN who will subsequently relapse or maintain a normal weight after inpatient hospitalization. Schebendach and colleagues (2008) examined dietary choices and the food intake of inpatients after reaching 90% ideal body weight in predicting outcome, as measured by the Morgan-Russell criteria (Morgan & Russell, 1975), following discharge from the hospital. Although there were no differences in total calorie intake between the successful and unsuccessful groups, individuals classified as treatment failures as outpatients were found to report a lower total fat intake and measures of diet energy density and diet variety (Schebendach et al., 2008). The authors suggested that patients with AN who consume a large proportion of their calories from low-energy-density foods (e.g., fruits, vegetables), and eat a limited range of foods as inpatients may have difficulty maintaining a diet with sufficient calories (Schebendach et al., 2008). In addition, body composition, and specifically percent body fat, measured after acute inpatient weight restoration has also been identified as a significant predictor of later outcome by Morgan-Russell criteria (Mayer et al., 2007). The Mayer et al. (2007) study found no differences in body mass index (kg/m^2) between groups of patients with AN considered to be "treatment successes" or "treatment failures" after discharge from the hospital, but body fat, as measured by dual-energy x-ray absorptiometry, differed between the two groups. Thus, this study suggests that the failure to restore patients with AN to a level of body fat similar to that of healthy women during an inpatient hospitalization

may increase the risk for relapse. Finally, a secondary analysis of the data from the Walsh, Kaplan, and colleagues (2006) study of fluoxetine and CBT found that patients with a higher body mass index and a lower rate of weight loss in the first month after hospitalization predicted successful weight maintenance after 6 months (Kaplan et al., 2009). Taken together, these studies suggest that, to increase the likelihood of success after inpatient treatment, prior to leaving the hospital, patients with AN should have a normal percentage of body fat and a higher body mass index and a diet that includes both a range of foods and calorie-dense foods. Further, body weight in the first month following inpatient treatment should be carefully monitored, as more intensive treatment interventions may be required for patients with AN who are rapidly losing weight.

Future Directions

Additional research on AN is a priority due to both the notable morbidity associated with this disorder and the limited extant data (Agras et al., 2004). However, the rarity of AN and the challenges associated with enrolling patients in treatment trials makes progress very difficult. Many patients with AN are hospitalized to manage the serious medical risk associated with this disorder; however, no controlled studies suggest how to determine the appropriate level of care. The use of a stepped-care approach is one possibility (Agras et al., 2004). In addition, at this time, studies of pharmacological treatments have not identified substantial benefit for patients with AN, but there are emerging agents that offer possibilities for future research. Identifying effective psychotherapies for patients with AN will likely be challenging (Wilson, 2010a), and the development of individual treatments, given the extant data on family therapy, should be a priority (Wilson et al., 2007).

Bulimia Nervosa

Patients with DSM-IV BN experience episodes of binge eating and inappropriate compensatory behavior on average twice per week over a 3-month period (APA, 1994). The DSM-IV definition specifies that binge eating episodes consist of eating in a distinct period of time an amount of food that is larger than others would eat in similar circumstances, along with a sense of loss of control over eating. This chapter summarizes information related to the presentation and treatment of BN, and suggests future directions for research on this disorder. In contrast to the literature described earlier for patients with AN, more consistent and positive results are identified in treatment studies of BN; however, challenges, such as dissemination and implementation of empirically based approaches, remain.

Individuals with BN are also at risk for medical complications from their eating disorder, such as dental erosion, swollen salivary glands, esophageal tearing, and electrolyte abnormalities (Mehler et al., 2010). Consequently, a medical assessment by a clinician familiar with the potential medical complications resulting from BN is recommended for patients at the beginning of treatment (Mehler et al., 2010). The measurement of clinical outcome among patients with BN is complicated by the lack of standardized definitions for remission, recovery, or relapse from this disorder (Shapiro et al., 2007). However, using available data, Steinhausen and Weber (2009) observed mean recovery rates of 45%, mean improvement rates of 27%, and mean chronicity rates of 23% for patients with BN among 27 studies classifying outcome using these three categories. These rates for recovery, improvement, and chronicity are similar to a prior review by Steinhausen (2002) examining studies of AN; however, the mean crude mortality rate for individuals with BN (0.32%; Steinhausen & Weber, 2009) was lower than that observed for AN (5%; Steinhausen, 2002).

Prevalence

Extant data on the prevalence and incidence of BN in the population suggest that this disorder is more common than AN, but still relatively rare. The aforementioned review by Hoek and van Hoeken (2003) found an aggregated prevalence rate for BN of 1.0%, with a range of 0.0%–4.5% from 12 studies identified in the literature since 1990 and, similar to AN, higher prevalence rates are observed for subthreshold cases of BN. A longitudinal study of twins in Finland identified a similar lifetime prevalence of DSM-IV BN (1.7%), with a small proportion (21%) classified with nonpurging BN (Keski-Rahkonen et al., 2009). Similar to the trends previously described for AN, few studies examine the prevalence of BN among males. The available data suggest an estimate for the lifetime prevalence of 15- to 65-year-old men of 0.1% (Hoek & van Hoeken, 2003). Although the identification of AN in the population is complicated by the rarity of the disorder, research on the incidence of BN is influenced by the fact that earlier versions of the DSM and International Classification of Diseases (ICD-9; World Health Organization, 1978) did not provide a specific diagnostic code for this disorder (Hoek & van Hoeken, 2003).

Comorbidities

Many treatment-seeking individuals with BN are also diagnosed with co-occurring psychiatric disorder, including mood and anxiety disorders. Approximately 20%–80% of patients with BN are classified with a lifetime major depressive disorder, and lifetime prevalence rates for anxiety disorders are between 41% and 75% (Godart et al., 2007; Godart et al., 2002). In treatment trials for BN, a significant proportion of patients have a diagnosis of major depressive disorder, but treatment with CBT or medication typically results in significant improvements in these comorbid symptoms of depression (Walsh, Fairburn, Mickley, Sysko, & Parides, 2004; Wilson & Fairburn, 2002). Estimates of the co-occurrence of BN and substance use disorders are also greater than chance, with between 3% and 50% of patients with eating disorders estimated to have a comorbid diagnosis of substance abuse or dependence (Bulik, Sullivan, & Slof, 2004), with a median prevalence of 22.9% (Holderness, Brooks-Gunn, & Warren, 1994).

Treatment Efficacy

PSYCHOLOGICAL TREATMENTS

Cognitive-Behavioral Therapy

The model underlying CBT for BN emphasizes the critical role of both cognitive and behavioral factors in maintaining bulimic symptoms. The overvaluation of an idealized body weight and shape is of critical importance and leads to rigid dietary restriction. Dietary restriction subsequently produces a vulnerability to periodic binge eating episodes, which are characterized by a loss of control over eating. Attempts to counteract the effects of binge eating, such as self-induced vomiting and other extreme weight control behaviors, also maintain binge eating by reducing anxiety about weight gain and disrupting the development of satiety. Binge eating and purging cause distress and low self-esteem, which reinforce circumstances that will lead to continued dietary restraint and binge eating (Fairburn, 1997a; Fairburn, Cooper, & Shafran, 2003). Cognitive-behavioral therapy assists in the development of a regular pattern of eating and problem-solving skills for coping with high-risk situations, modifying problematic shape and weight concerns, and preventing relapse (Fairburn, Marcus, & Wilson, 1993).

Extant data on the efficacy of CBT for patients with BN, including typical remission rates for binge eating and purging of 30%–50% (Wilson et al., 2007), led the National Institute for Health and Clinical Excellence (NICE, 2004) to designate this type of treatment as the treatment of choice for adults. Further, CBT has been shown to be superior to other psychological treatments in the short-term (Wilson & Fairburn, 2007) and antidepressant medications for achieving abstinence from bulimic symptoms (Wilson et al., 2007). The effects of manual-based CBT for BN are seen not only for improvements in binge eating and purging, but also for other psychiatric comorbidities (e.g., depression), self-esteem, and social functioning (Wilson, 2010a). Although CBT is a robust treatment with long-lasting effects, improvements are still needed, as a significant portion of patients remain symptomatic after receiving 16–20 sessions of treatment.

Fairburn (2008) has developed an enhanced version of CBT (CBT-E) that promises to be the most effective treatment available. CBT-E is "trans-diagnostic" in that it focuses on the commonalities among the eating disorders rather than exclusively directing treatment toward DSM-IV eating disorders. Consistent with this focus, CBT-E provides for a highly individualized form of treatment that emphasizes personalized treatment formulations. The core treatment consists mainly of the earlier Fairburn et al. (1993) manual, with two major changes. The first is a reformulated strategy and method for addressing dysfunctional body weight and shape concerns, and the second is the addition of an explicit treatment module for what is called "mood intolerance" as a specific trigger of binge eating and purging. The primary focus on eating disorder symptoms is supplemented by the flexible use of additional treatment modules designed to address common maintaining mechanisms, namely, core low self-esteem, clinical perfectionism, and interpersonal functioning. The first controlled evaluation of CBT-E for BN indicated that it appears to be a more effective treatment for complex cases of BN (Fairburn et al., 2009).

Interpersonal Psychotherapy

Interpersonal psychotherapy (IPT) was adapted for BN by Fairburn (1997b) from the short-term treatment for depression developed by Klerman, Weissman, Rounsaville, and Chevron (1984). In contrast to CBT for BN, IPT for BN does not directly focus on the modification of binge eating, purging, other disturbed eating, or overconcern with body shape and weight. Instead, IPT for BN focuses exclusively on interpersonal issues and construes eating disturbances as a way to understand the interpersonal context, which is assumed to be maintaining bulimic symptoms. Two large randomized-controlled studies of patients with BN found IPT to be significantly less effective than CBT at the end of treatment (Agras, Walsh, Fairburn, Wilson, & Kraemer, 2000; Fairburn, Jones, et al., 1993). Differences between the two treatments were no longer statistically significant at the 1-year follow-up. As these studies did not include any form of a control treatment, the improvement associated with IPT cannot be associated with a specific treatment effect. However, in a study by Fairburn et al. (1995), both IPT and CBT demonstrated significant improvements over a comparison treatment (a form of behavior therapy without the cognitive features of CBT) for individuals with BN over the course of follow-up. This single study provides specific evidence of the efficacy of IPT for BN.

Family Therapy

Two studies have evaluated the Maudsley form of family therapy for adolescents with BN. In the first, Le Grange and colleagues (2007) examined family therapy and supportive psychotherapy, and found equivalent improvements from pre- to post-treatment for most eating disorder symptoms, self-esteem, and depressive symptoms. However, in comparison to supportive psychotherapy, family therapy produced significantly higher rates of remission from eating disorder symptoms post-treatment. The second study, by Schmidt and colleagues (2007), compared family therapy to a cognitive-behavioral self-care treatment, and found a significantly larger proportion of adolescents receiving cognitive-behavioral self-help to be abstinent from binge eating at the end of treatment. The two treatments were similarly efficacious with regard to abstinence from self-induced vomiting (Schmidt et al., 2007). On the basis of these studies, it appears that family therapy is useful for younger patients with BN, but the Schmidt et al. (2007) results suggest that this type of treatment may not be more effective than other treatments, such as a self-help form of CBT, which is discussed next.

Guided Self-Help

Despite the effectiveness of CBT in the treatment of BN, access to this type of treatment in the United States is limited. Variables affecting the availability of CBT include the amount of time needed to administer CBT (20 50-minute sessions over 4–5 months); challenges related to training and supervising therapists to administer CBT; and the small number of available CBT therapists (Sysko & Walsh, 2007). Self-help programs using the principles and procedures of CBT were developed to help overcome these barriers. Guided self-help (CBTgsh)

combines a self-help manual with a limited number (e.g., 8–10) of brief therapy sessions (Fairburn, 1995) with therapists who may vary widely in terms of experience and expertise (Fairburn, 1995).

Several studies have shown that CBTgsh is effective with at least a subset of patients with BN (Wilson, 2010a). For example, Banasiak et al. (2005) found that primary care physicians trained and supervised in CBTgsh obtained significantly superior results as compared with a delayed treatment control condition. The results were maintained at a 6-month follow-up, and rivaled the outcomes of more standard manual-based CBT. The aforementioned study by Schmidt and colleagues (2007) compared family therapy (based on the Maudsley model) with CBTgsh, consisting of ten weekly sessions, three monthly follow-up sessions, and two optional sessions with a "close other." Both treatments resulted in significant improvement in binge eating and purging at the end of treatment (6 months) and a follow-up at 12 months, but CBTgsh resulted in significantly more rapid reduction in binge eating. Moreover, CBTgsh was associated with greater acceptability and a lower cost than family therapy. Questions still remain regarding the level of training, degree of supervision, and type of setting that is needed for the effective implementation of CBTgsh (Sysko & Walsh, 2007). Widely varying results have been reported across different studies, and inexperienced and unsupervised healthcare providers with minimal training in CBTgsh are ineffective. Nevertheless, even though the successful use of CBTgsh requires specific therapist selection, training, and supervision, it still provides a briefer, less costly, and more readily disseminable intervention to a wider range of health-care providers than does formal, manual-based CBT.

PHARMACOLOGICAL TREATMENTS

A recent systematic review of medication studies for the treatment of BN identified 12 trials that were given a quality rating of "good" (Shapiro et al., 2007). Half of the trials in the Shapiro et al. (2007) review compared fluoxetine and placebo, which is currently the only medication approved by the U.S. Food and Drug Administration (FDA) for the treatment of BN. Most of these studies found significant decreases in binge eating and purging resulted from the administration of 60 mg of fluoxetine. Other positive medication trials included the antidepressants fluvoxamine, desipramine, trazodone, and brofaromine; the anticonvulsant topiramate; and a $5HT_3$ antagonist (ondansetron; Shapiro et al., 2007). Although some effective medication treatments have been identified, there are a number of limitations to the existing literature. For example, there are few studies examining selective serotonin reuptake inhibitors other than fluoxetine, few data on the use of antidepressants for adolescents with BN, and the optimal duration of treatment with medications is not known (Broft, Berner, & Walsh, 2010).

Early Response

The time course of response to CBT and antidepressant medications has been examined for patients with BN. Wilson et al. (1999) analyzed the time to treatment response in a study in which patients were randomly assigned to one of five treatment groups (Walsh et al., 1997). Four of the groups received a combination of psychotherapy (CBT or supportive psychotherapy) and antidepressant medication or placebo under double-blind conditions. A survival analysis was used to identify the time to improvement among the four treatment conditions (CBT + medication, CBT + placebo, supportive psychotherapy + medication, supportive psychotherapy + placebo), with response defined as a 75% reduction in binge eating or vomiting from baseline for a minimum of 2 weeks. A significant main effect was observed for CBT in comparison to supportive psychotherapy, indicating that CBT produced significantly more rapid reductions in binge eating and vomiting than did supportive psychotherapy. Sixty-one percent of patients receiving CBT across medication conditions were early responders for binge eating, and 61% were early responders for vomiting, in comparison to 27% for binge eating and 30% for vomiting among patients receiving supportive psychotherapy across medication conditions. These data suggested that the response to CBT in BN begins in the first few weeks after beginning treatment.

A second study by Wilson and colleagues (2002) examined the time to response in a study of women with BN randomized to receive either CBT or interpersonal psychotherapy (IPT; Agras et al., 2000). Similar to the findings of Wilson et al. (1999), rapid improvements were observed among patients receiving CBT, with 62% of the post-treatment improvement evident by the sixth week of treatment. The pattern of early response observed by Wilson et al. (2002) was further explored by Fairburn and colleagues (2004). Using a classification tree analysis, Fairburn et al. (2004) examined predictors of response at the end of acute treatment and outcome 8 months after the end of treatment and found that early change in the frequency of purging (after 4 weeks) in both types of treatment was a significant predictor of post-treatment response. Surprisingly, early change in purging was also a predictor of outcome 8 months after the termination of treatment. Response to psychological treatments for BN begins in the first few weeks, and early response is predictive of longer-term outcome.

Similar findings are also observed when examining antidepressant response among patients with BN, including one study that suggested that individuals who do not respond to antidepressant medication can be reliably identified early in treatment (Walsh, Sysko, & Parides, 2006). Specifically, 80%–85% of patients would be correctly identified as eventual nonresponders to desipramine by the second week of treatment. However, this study had several notable limitations, including the relatively small sample of patients with BN ($n = 77$) and the now infrequent use of desipramine to treat BN. In a more recent study of the antidepressant fluoxetine (Sysko, Sha, Wang, Duan, & Walsh, 2010), a majority of patients with BN who do not respond could be identified early in treatment, specifically by the third week. At week 3, if fluoxetine was discontinued for patients with less than a 60% reduction in binge eating, approximately 73% would be correctly classified as eventual non-responders to fluoxetine and 23% of patients who would eventually respond to fluoxetine would be misclassified as non-responders. For patients with less than a 60% decrease in vomiting at week three, approximately 72% would be correctly classified as non-responders and 22% would be misclassified.

Future Directions

Although effective treatments are available for patients with BN, additional research is needed to assist those patients who fail to respond to the existing empirically supported treatments. Wilson and colleagues (2007) suggest that treatment efficacy for patients with BN could potentially be improved in a number of ways, including identifying robust moderators of outcome; combining or sequencing antidepressant medications with CBT; combining or sequencing CBT with other theoretically compatible treatments, such as dialectical behavior therapy; and enhancing existing manual-based CBT. Further, Wilson (2010b) suggests focusing on variables that have been identified as clinically useful predictors of outcome in studies of BN, including negative affect and early response. Although it is important to improve existing treatments for BN, the most significant research questions relate to how best to disseminate these treatments to individuals for whom access to specialty care is limited.

Training in empirically supported treatments is scarce, and there is limited information about how to provide training, supervision, and ensure the fidelity of these treatments (Wilson, 2010b). Further, empirically supported treatments should be simplified to allow their use by a wider range of mental health professionals, such as by employing self-help versions of these interventions (Wilson, 2010b).

Eating Disorder Not Otherwise Specified

Eating disorder not otherwise specified (EDNOS) is a heterogeneous and poorly specified diagnostic category in DSM-IV that consists mainly of variations of AN, BN, or mixed disorders containing features of both AN and BN. As discussed here, the exception is BED, for which provisional diagnostic were published (APA, 1994). EDNOS is the most common eating disorder diagnosis health-care professionals encounter in routine clinical practice. Disorders within this category are as clinically severe as AN and BN (Fairburn, Cooper, et al., 2007). For example, a longitudinal assessment of mortality in a large sample of individuals with eating disorders found that those with EDNOS had elevated mortality risks, similar to those seen in AN (Crow, Peterson, et al., 2009). Moreover, the same study revealed an increased risk of suicide across the different eating disorder diagnoses.

Fairburn and colleagues (2009) reported the only treatment study enrolling a wide range of normal-weight individuals with an EDNOS. The treatment provided in this study was CBT-E, as summarized in the previous section on BN, and as CBT-E is based on a transdiagnostic model that assumes that all eating disorders have common underlying mechanisms, CBT-E seems well-suited to treating EDNOS. Fairburn (2008) describes two main versions of CBT-E for the full range of eating disorder patients, namely, a "focused" (CBT-Ef) and a "broad" treatment (CBT-Eb). The former is very similar to the Fairburn et al. (1993) manual as described earlier, with the two main changes consisting of a reformulated strategy and method for addressing dysfunctional body weight and shape concerns, the addition of an explicit treatment module for what is called "mood intolerance" as a specific trigger of binge eating and purging. CBT-Eb is based on a broader model of the processes that are hypothesized to maintain BN, and incorporates an expanded range of strategies for treating these additional maintaining mechanisms.

In this study, Fairburn, Cooper, et al. (2009) compared CBT-Ef with CBT-Eb and a waiting-list control condition in the treatment of 154 patients with BN or EDNOS. Consistent with previous research on BN, the waiting-list control condition showed little change. Both forms of CBT-E resulted in significant improvement at post-treatment and at a 60-week follow-up. More than half of the overall sample had a level of eating disorder psychopathology, assessed via the Eating Disorder Examination (EDE; Fairburn & Cooper, 1993), less than 1 standard deviation above the community mean. The rate of remission from both binge eating and purging in the BN patients was 45.6% at follow-up, a figure higher than that obtained with the earlier version of CBT (e.g., Agras et al., 2000). Treatment outcome was comparable for both BN and EDNOS patients. In a novel finding, exploratory moderator analyses indicated that CBT-Eb, as predicted, appeared to be more effective than CBT-Ef with patients characterized by at least two of the hypothesized maintaining mechanisms of mood intolerance, perfectionism, low self-esteem, and interpersonal difficulties. By contrast, the reverse pattern was obtained in the remaining patients. These promising results suggest that CBT-E is broadly effective with a range of eating disorders other than BN itself.

Binge Eating Disorder

The provisional criteria for BED in DSM-IV characterize this disorder as recurrent binge eating, but without the regular use of inappropriate compensatory weight control methods that are required in BN. Several behavioral indicators are described by the diagnostic criteria to help evaluate a patient's subjective sense of loss of control during binge episode, in addition to the requirement that the overeating consists of large quantities of food. The criteria also require that the binge eating is associated with emotional distress, occurs regularly (at least 2 days per week), and is persistent (at least 6 months). Unlike AN and BN, there is no diagnostic criterion requiring undue influence of body weight or shape on self-evaluation; however, a growing body of research has shown that patients with BED have similar levels of overvaluation as those with BN, and that overvaluation signals a more disturbed variant of this disorder (Goldschmidt et al., 2010; Grilo et al., 2008). On the basis of these findings, some experts have recommended that the overvaluation of body weight and shape be included as a diagnostic specifier for BED in DSM-5 (e.g., Grilo, Masheb, & White, 2010).

Binge eating disorder has several features in common with other eating disorders, such as binge eating and overvaluation of body weight and shape (see earlier discussion). Evidence for BED as a distinctive and valid clinical category comes from well-documented differences between individuals with BED and other eating disorders. Compared with other eating disorders, BED is marked by less dietary restraint, a significant association with obesity, different gender and racial distributions, and diagnostic stability and response to treatment (Wonderlich, Gordon, Mitchell, Crosby, & Engel, 2009). Although closely linked with obesity, BED differs from weight-matched individuals without BED on several counts. For example, individuals with BED consume more calories in single eating episodes, have significantly more eating disorder psychopathology and psychiatric comorbidity in general, and have a lower quality of life (Wonderlich et al., 2009). The prevalence of BED (estimated to be roughly 3% of adults) also appears higher than the prevalence documented for AN or BN.

Comorbidities

Individuals with BED have multiple comorbid problems, including depression, anxiety, personality disorders, and low self-esteem. The severity of co-occurring problems is often comparable to that found in AN and BN (Striegel-Moore & Franko, 2007; Wonderlich et al., 2009).

Treatment Efficacy

SPECIALTY PSYCHOLOGICAL TREATMENT

Cognitive Behavior Therapy

Research studies evaluating CBT for BED to date have typically been based on the Fairburn et al. (1993) manual developed for BN. The NICE (National Institute for Clinical Excellence, 2004) guidelines specify that CBT is the treatment of choice for BED, and this clinical recommendation was assigned a methodological grade of A, indicating strong empirical support from RCTs. In general, studies have shown that manual-based CBT results in remission rates in binge eating of between 55% and 70% at post-treatment that are generally well-maintained at a 1-year follow-up. The treatment also reliably results in a reduction in specific eating disorders and general psychopathology (Wilson et al., 2007).

Cognitive-behavioral therapy has proved more effective than pharmacological treatments for the treatment of BED. For example, a study by Grilo, Masheb, and Wilson (2005) found that CBT was

significantly more effective than either fluoxetine or pill placebo, with remission rates of 61% for CBT plus pill placebo compared with 22% for fluoxetine. Using a different design, Devlin et al. (2005) showed that a combination of CBT with behavioral weight loss (BWL) treatment was more effective than adding fluoxetine to BWL.

Cognitive-behavioral therapy has also been shown to be superior to BWL treatment. A well-controlled study by Grilo et al. (2007) found that, at post-treatment, CBT was associated with a significantly greater binge eating remission rate (60%) than was BWL (31%). At the 1-year follow-up, the rates were 51% and 36%, respectively. Munsch et al. (2007) similarly showed that CBT for obese patients with BED was significantly more effective than BWL in producing remission from binge eating.

Interpersonal Psychotherapy

Two studies have shown that group manual-based IPT was as effective as CBT delivered in a group format (Wilfley et al., 1993, Wilfley et al., 2002). In the second of these studies, Wilfley et al. (2002) obtained remission rates of 79% and 73% for CBT and IPT, respectively, at post-treatment, and 59% and 62% at a 1-year follow-up. Both treatments produced significant reductions in eating disorder and associated general psychopathology. The equivalent effects of these two treatments for BED contrasts sharply with the findings observed among patients with BN (Agras et al., 2000). The NICE (2004) guidelines assigned a grade of B to IPT, presumably because of the limited empirical support for this type of treatment in comparison to the large number of studies on manual-based CBT by diverse groups of investigators in different countries.

In the largest controlled outcome study to date, Wilson, Wilfley, Agras, and Bryson (2010) compared 20 sessions of individual IPT to 20 sessions of BWL and to ten sessions of guided self-help based on cognitive-behavioral principles (CBTgsh). No differences were evident at post-treatment, but at 2-year follow-up both IPT and CBTgsh were significantly more effective than BWL in eliminating binge eating. A noteworthy finding was the very low attrition rate in IPT (7%) versus the other treatments (28% and 30%, respectively). Exploratory moderator analyses indicated that BWL fared less well than IPT in patients with low self-esteem at the 2-year follow-up. Interpersonal therapy was also superior to CBTgsh in patients with low self-esteem and high global EDE scores. The finding that global

EDE scores moderated treatment outcome is consistent with a latent class and latent transition analysis of the BED patients, in which four different latent classes were observed within the sample, with two of the classes showing a differential treatment response (Sysko, Hildebrandt, Wilson, Wilfley, & Agras, in press). In this analysis, IPT was the most effective treatment for those patients characterized by the most severe specific eating disorder psychopathology.

Guided Self-Help
Similar to that previously described for BN, guided self-help based on the CBT model for BN and BED (CBTgsh), and using the Fairburn (1995) manual, has been studied extensively in the treatment of BED. The NICE guidelines assigned CBTgsh a methodological grade of B, recommending that it might be a good first-step treatment for many patients. Subsequent studies, however, have provided evidence that CBTgsh might be as effective as specialty psychological treatments, at least for a specific subset of patients. Specifically, Grilo and Masheb (2005) compared CBTgsh (Fairburn, 1995) to a guided-help program for weight loss derived from Brownell's (2000) LEARN manual and to a control condition, which consisted of self-monitoring of eating. CBTgsh resulted in a 50% remission rate, compared with less than 20% in either of the comparison conditions. A second study by Grilo, Masheb, and Salant (2005) replicated the efficacy of CBTgsh in eliminating binge eating in obese BED patients. In the Wilson et al. (2010) multisite study referenced earlier, ten sessions of CBTgsh administered by beginning clinical psychology graduate students with little therapy experience proved to be as effective as 20 sessions of IPT delivered by intensively trained and supervised doctoral-level clinical psychologists both at post-treatment and at 2-year follow-up. No differences between the treatments were observed on the EDE subscales or measures of depression and self-esteem, and both treatments were superior to BWL.

CBTgsh has also been evaluated in the treatment of patients with recurrent binge eating among a population of members of a large Health Maintenance Organization in the United States (Striegel-Moore, Wilson, DeBar et al., 2010). In a sample of 123 participants, 55 were diagnosed with BED, and 56 reported binge eating once a week on average for the previous 3 months. CBTgsh was significantly more effective than treatment-as-usual (TAU) in eliminating binge eating and in producing improvements on specific measures of eating disorder psychopathology,

depression, and quality of life at a 1-year follow-up. CBTgsh in this setting was very acceptable to participants and significantly more cost-effective than TAU (Lynch et al., 2010).

Weight Loss in Overweight and Obese Binge Eating Disorder Patients
As summarized earlier, specialty psychological therapies and CBTgsh are broadly effective in eliminating binge eating, reducing associated psychopathology, and improving quality of life. Neither, however, is effective in reducing body weight. Patients who cease binge eating by post-treatment typically show a statistically significant weight loss compared with those who continue to binge, although the magnitude is modest (Wilfley et al., 2002; Wilson et al., 2010).

The evidence is mixed as to whether the presence of BED predicts less short-term weight loss in obesity treatments (Wonderlich et al., 2009). Early studies of BWL treatment produced results ranging from no effect to a negative impact, but these studies were limited by small sample sizes and less-than-optimal assessments of binge eating. Recent studies have found that BWL results in disappointingly small weight losses compared with studies of obese non-BED patients (Grilo et al., 2007; Wilson et al., 2010). A meta-analysis in which studies of BED patients were matched with other studies of obese non-BED individuals showed that the presence of BED resulted in significantly less weight loss (Blaine & Rodman, 2007). A limitation of this meta-analysis is that BED and non-BED samples were not directly compared in the same study (Wonderlich et al., 2009).

PHARMACOLOGICAL TREATMENT
A variety of medications have been used in the treatment of BED, including antidepressants (e.g., fluoxetine), antiobesity drugs (e.g., sibutramine), and antiepileptic medications (e.g., topiramate). As described previously, CBT has been shown to be significantly more effective than fluoxetine in two well-controlled RCTs (Devlin et al., 2005; Grilo et al., 2005). A recent, comprehensive meta-analysis of available studies of the pharmacological treatment of BED indicated that medications do not differ from pill placebo in terms of attrition, but are significantly more effective in producing remission from binge eating (48.7% vs. 28.5%) and short-term weight loss, although the latter is minimal (Reas & Grilo, 2008). Combining medication with psychological treatment does not enhance outcome in terms of binge eating, although two specific drugs (orlistat and topiramate) may enhance weight loss to a modest degree.

Perhaps the most striking conclusion of the Reas and Grilo (2008) meta-analysis is the total absence of any long-term, controlled evaluation of the effects of pharmacological treatments. Given the absence of long-term data, and the evidence that both CBTgsh and specialty psychological therapies reliably result in sustained reductions in binge eating, pharmacological treatments cannot be recommended as a first-line therapy for BED.

PREDICTORS AND MODERATORS OF TREATMENT OUTCOME

Manual-based CBT for BED produces more successful outcomes in the treatment of eating disorder symptoms for patients with BED than BN. Nevertheless, there is still room for improvement. Identifying predictors and, ideally, moderators of therapeutic change would allow for the development of more targeted and possibly effective treatments. No evidence of reliable pretreatment or of either predictors or moderators of pharmacological treatments are currently available; however, research has identified two pre-treatment predictors of outcome. One is negative affect, as measured by the Beck Depression Inventory (BDI; Beck & Steer, 1987). Higher ratings of negative affect resulted in worse outcomes for individuals receiving CBT (Stice et al., 2001) or CBTgsh (Masheb & Grilo, 2008; Wilson et al., 2010). In the latter two studies negative affect predicted the reduction in the frequency of binge eating episodes but not remission, the more important index of improvement. A second predictor is overvaluation of body shape and weight as measured by the EDE (Fairburn & Cooper, 1993). Higher scores on this variable have been shown to predict lower reductions in the frequency of binge eating in CBTgsh among patients with BED, and overvaluation of shape and weight (Masheb & Grilo, 2008) and significantly lower remission rates not only in CBT but also in BWL (Grilo, Masheb, & White, 2010).

Neither negative affect nor the overvaluation of body shape and weight moderate treatment outcome (Grilo, 2009), and the only evidence to date for moderators is based on exploratory analyses that found both self-esteem and a composite score of the EDE subscales moderated treatment outcome at the 2-year follow-up (Wilson et al., 2010). Low self-esteem undermined the effects of BWL in eliminating binge eating, but had no influence on IPT. CBTgsh was unaffected by low self-esteem in patients with low global EDE scores, but was less effective in interaction with high EDE scores. The finding that global EDE moderated treatment outcome is consistent with a latent class analysis of the same sample of patients. Sysko et al. (in press) found four different latent classes within the sample, and the class characterized by the most specific eating disorder psychopathology (i.e., most severe objective and subjective bulimic episodes and highest body shape and weight concerns), which would be reflected in high global EDE scores, responded the most to IPT. CBTgsh was the most effective treatment for the "pure" binge eating class. Should these findings be replicated, they would have important implications for future treatment. It may be that CBTgsh is the treatment of choice for that subset of BED patients with symptoms defined mainly by binge eating. However, those patients with severe associated eating disorder psychopathology, such as body shape and weight overconcern, would benefit from a specialty therapy like IPT or CBT. CBT-E has yet to be applied to BED patients, but as Fairburn, Cooper, and Waller (2008) propose, it might be well-suited to "those patients with obesity who have prominent eating disorder psychopathology such as mood-triggered eating or extreme concerns about appearance" (p. 254).

RAPID RESPONSE

Similar to the findings regarding early response for BN, rapid response to treatment—defined as a quick and clinically meaningful change in symptoms—has been found to be a clinically significant predictor of treatment outcome in CBT and pharmacological therapy for patients with BED. Grilo et al. (2006) found that individuals experiencing a rapid response, defined by a 65% reduction in binge eating by the fourth week of treatment, had a different prognostic significance and time course across different treatments for BED. Rapid response predicted remission rates of 73% for manual-based CBT versus 46% for fluoxetine. Whereas rapid response to CBT predicted improvement that was sustained over the remaining course of treatment, in the fluoxetine condition some of the improvement eroded. Clinically important findings were also observed for patients without a rapid response to treatment. In CBT, patients without a rapid response showed a subsequent pattern of continued improvement throughout treatment, although it did not reach the high levels of improvement achieved by the rapid responders. Clinically, these findings suggest that continuing CBT for patients who are not rapid responders—rather than switching to another intervention—may be best. Consistent with this conclusion, Eldredge et al. (1997) found that extending CBT for initial nonresponders was an effective option. In the case of antidepressant treatment, the absence of a rapid response to antidepressant pharmacotherapy for BED suggests that the patient is quite unlikely to eventually respond to that medication and may suggest the need to try a different intervention. Masheb and Grilo (2007) similarly found that rapid response predicted greater improvement in overall eating psychopathology and depression in CBTgsh and guided self-help BWL (BWLgsh) for obese BED patients. In terms of binge eating, however, patients receiving CBTgsh, but not BWLgsh, did equally well regardless of whether they experienced rapid response.

Future Directions

Reliably effective treatments for BED have been developed. Nonetheless, a significant minority of patients do not respond. A research priority must be the identification of moderators of treatment outcome—what specific treatment works for which subgroups of patients. Preliminary findings indicate that CBTgsh may be recommended as the first-step treatment for a majority of BED patients, but that specialty psychological treatments, such as IPT or full CBT, might be required for patients with more complex eating disorder psychopathology. The efficacy of CBT-E for BED remains to be evaluated. As a robust predictor of treatment outcome, rapid and early response will need additional experimental analysis, so that it is possible to capitalize on its implications for treatment planning. Finally, as with the other eating disorders, improved dissemination and implementation of evidence-based psychological treatments remains a priority.

Reviews of the BED literature typically conclude with calls for more effective means for producing weight loss. The problem, however, extends beyond just obese patients with an eating disorder. Effective treatments for producing long-term weight loss do not exist. The majority of individuals who lose weight in the short-term eventually relapse (Cooper et al., 2010). As this holds true for obese individuals free of any psychiatric comorbidity, it must be expected that obese patients with BED will fare at least as poorly. Future research must focus on improved methods for preventing and managing obesity in general.

Conclusion

The next version of the *Diagnostic and Statistical Manual of Mental Disorders* (DSM-5) is scheduled for publication in 2012. Modest (e.g., Attia & Roberto, 2009; Peat, Mitchell, Hoek, & Wonderlich, 2009; van Hoeken et al., 2009; Wilson & Sysko, 2009) and more substantial changes (e.g., Wonderlich et al., 2009; Walsh & Sysko, 2009) to the existing classification of eating disorders have been proposed. It is not yet known what alterations, if any, will be made to the nosology of eating disorders in DSM-5; however, it is clear that regardless of the specific form of the diagnoses, treatment research for any of these disorders should be a priority. For patients with AN, an effective treatment must be identified. Among individuals with BN or BED, the dissemination of existing effective treatments is needed. Recently, means for aiding treatment dissemination have been developed through innovative computer-assisted technology, including telemedicine (Mitchell et al., 2008) or Internet-based CBT (Andersson, 2009). Finally, as clinicians in the community begin to implement manual-based CBT for individuals with BN or BED more frequently, researchers will be able to obtain additional information regarding the generalizability of RCTs and better understand how existing manuals should be adapted and changed (Wilson, 2010a).

References

Agras, W. S., Brandt, H. A., Bulik, C. M., Dolan-Sewell, R., Fairburn, C. G., Halmi, K. A., et al. (2004). Report of the National Institutes of Health workshop on overcoming barriers to treatment research in anorexia nervosa. *International Journal of Eating Disorders, 35*, 509–521.

Agras, W. S., Walsh, B. T., Fairburn, C. G., Wilson, G. T., & Kraemer, H. C. (2000). A multicenter comparison of cognitive-behavioral therapy and interpersonal psychotherapy for bulimia nervosa. *Archives of General Psychiatry, 57*, 459–466.

American Psychiatric Association. (1994). *Diagnostic and statistical manual of mental disorders*, 4th ed. Washington, DC: American Psychiatric Association.

Andersson, G. (2009). Using the internet to provide cognitive behavior therapy. *Behaviour Research and Therapy, 47*, 175–180.

Attia, E., & Roberto, C. A. (2009). Should amenorrhea be a diagnostic criterion for anorexia nervosa? *International Journal of Eating Disorders, 42*, 581–589.

Attia, E., & Schroeder, L. (2005). Pharmacologic treatment of anorexia nervosa: Where do we go from here? *International Journal of Eating Disorders, 37*, S60–63.

Ball, J., & Mitchell, P. (2004). A randomized controlled study of cognitive behavior therapy and behavioral family therapy for anorexia nervosa patients. *Eating Disorders, 12*, 303–314.

Banasiak, S. J., Paxton, S. J., & Hay, P. (2005). Guided self-help for bulimia nervosa in primary care: A randomized controlled trial. *Psychological Medicine, 35*, 1283–1294.

Beck, A., & Steer, R. (1987). *Manual for the Beck Depression Inventory*. San Antonio, Texas: Psychological Corporation.

Bissada, H., Tasca, G. A., Barber, A. M., & Bradwejn, J. (2008). Olanzapine in the treatment of low body weight and obsessive thinking in women with anorexia nervosa: A randomized, double-blind, placebo-controlled trial. *American Journal of Psychiatry, 165*, 1281–1288.

Blaine, B., & Rodman, J. (2007). Responses to weight loss treatment among obese individuals with and without BED: A matched-study meta-analysis. *Eating and Weight Disorders, 12*, 54–60.

Braun, D. L., Sunday, S. R., & Halmi, K. A. (1994). Psychiatric comorbidity in patients with eating disorders. *Psychological Medicine, 24*, 859–867.

Broft, A., Berner, L. A., & Walsh, B. T. (2010). Pharmacotherapy for bulimia nervosa. In C. M. Grilo & J. E. Mitchell (Eds.), *The treatment of eating disorders: A clinical handbook* (pp. 388–401). New York: Guilford Press.

Brownell, K. D. (2000). *The LEARN Program for Weight Management (10th edition)*. American Dallas, Texas: Health Publishing Company.

Bulik, C. M., Berkman, N. D., Brownley, K. A., Sedway, J. A., & Lohr, K. N. (2007). Anorexia nervosa treatment: A systematic review of randomized controlled trials. *International Journal of Eating Disorders, 40*, 310–320.

Bulik, C. M., Sullivan, P. F., & Slof, M. C. T. (2004). Comorbidity of eating disorders and substance-related disorders. In H. R. Kranzler, & J. A. Tinsley (Eds.), *Dual diagnosis and psychiatric treatment: Substance abuse and comorbid disorders* (2nd ed., pp. 317–348). New York: Taylor and Francis.

Carter, J. C., McFarlane, T. L., Bewell, C., Olmsted, M. P., Woodside, D. B., Kaplan, A. S., et al. (2009). Maintenance treatment for anorexia nervosa: A comparison of cognitive behavior therapy and treatment as usual. *International Journal of Eating Disorders, 42*, 202–207.

Channon, S., De Silva, P., Helmsley, D., & Perkins, R. (1989). A controlled trial of cognitive behavioural and behavioural treatment of anorexia nervosa. *Behaviour Research and Therapy, 27*, 529–535.

Cooper, Z., Doll, H., Hawker, D. M., Byrne, S., Bonner, G., Eeley, E., et al. (2010). Testing a new cognitive behavioural treatment for obesity: A randomized controlled trial with three year follow-up. *Behaviour Research and Therapy, 48*, 706–713.

Crow, S. J., Mitchell, J. E., Roerig, J. D., & Steffen, K. (2009). What potential role is there for medication treatment in anorexia nervosa? *International Journal of Eating Disorders, 42*, 1–8.

Crow, S. J., Peterson, C. B., Swanson, S. A., Raymond, N., Specker, S., Eckert, E., et al. (2009). Increased mortality in bulimia nervosa and other eating disorders. *American Journal of Psychiatry, 166*, 1342–1346.

Devlin, M. J., Goldfein, J. A., Petkova, E., Jiang, H., Raizman, P. S., Wolk, S., et al. (2005). Cognitive behavioral therapy and fluoxetine as adjuncts to group behavioral therapy for binge eating disorder. *Obesity Research, 13*, 1077–1088.

Eisler, I., & Dare, C. (1997). Family and individual therapy in anorexia nervosa. A 5-year follow-up. *Archives of General Psychiatry, 54*, 1025–1030.

Eldredge, K. L., Agras, W. S., Arnow, B., Telch, C. F., Bell, S., Castonguay, L., et al. (1997). The effects of extending cognitive-behavioral therapy for binge eating disorder among initial treatment nonresponders. *International Journal of Eating Disorders, 21*, 347–352.

Fairburn, C. G. (1995). *Overcoming binge eating*. New York: Guilford Press.

Fairburn, C. G. (1997a). Eating disorders. In D. M. Clark & C. G. Fairburn (Eds.), *The science and practice of cognitive behaviour therapy* (pp. 209–242). Oxford: Oxford University Press.

Fairburn, C. G. (1997b). Interpersonal psychotherapy for bulimia nervosa. In D. M. Garner & P. E. Garfinkel (Eds.), *Handbook of treatment for eating disorders* (pp. 278–294). New York: Guilford Press.

Fairburn, C. G. (2005). Evidence-based treatment of anorexia nervosa. *International Journal of Eating Disorders, 37*, S26–S30.

Fairburn, C. G. (2008). *Cognitive behavior therapy and eating disorders*. New York: Guilford Press.

Fairburn, C. G., Agras, W. S., Walsh, B. T., Wilson, G. T., & Stice, E. (2004). Prediction of outcome in bulimia nervosa by early change in treatment. *American Journal of Psychiatry, 161*, 2322–2324.

Fairburn, C. G., & Cooper, Z. (1993). The eating disorder examination. In C. G. Fairburn, & G.T. Wilson (Eds.), *Binge eating: Nature, assessment, and treatment* (pp. 361–404). New York: Guilford Press.

Fairburn, C. G., Cooper, Z., Bohn, K., O'Connor, M. E., Doll, H. A., & Palmer, R. L. (2007). The severity and status of eating disorder NOS: Implications for DSM-5. *Behaviour Research and Therapy, 45*, 1705–1715.

Fairburn, C. G., Cooper, Z., Doll, H. A., O'Connor, M., Bohn, K., Hawker, D., et al. (2009). Transdiagnostic cognitive-behavioral therapy for patients with eating disorders: A two-site trial with 60-week follow-up. *American Journal of Psychiatry, 166*, 311–319.

Fairburn, C. G., Cooper, Z., & Shafran, R. (2003). Cognitive behaviour therapy for eating disorders: A "transdiagnostic" theory and treatment. *Behaviour Research and Therapy, 41*, 509–529.

Fairburn, C. G., Cooper, Z., & Waller, D. (2008). "Complex" cases and comorbidity. In C. G. Fairburn (Ed.), *Cognitive behavior therapy and eating disorders* (pp.245–258). New York: Guilford Press.

Fairburn, C. G., Jones, R., Peveler, R. C., Hope, R. A., & O'Connor, M. (1993). Psychotherapy and bulimia nervosa: The longer-term effects of interpersonal psychotherapy, behaviour therapy and cognitive behaviour therapy. *Archives of General Psychiatry, 50*, 419–428.

Fairburn, C. G., Marcus, M. D., & Wilson, G. T. (1993). Cognitive-behavioral therapy for binge eating and bulimia nervosa: A comprehensive treatment manual. In C. G. Fairburn & G. T. Wilson (Eds.), *Binge eating: Nature, assessment and treatment* (pp. 361–404). New York: Guilford Press.

Fairburn, C. G., Norman, P. A., Welch, S. L., O'Connor, M. E., Doll, H. A., & Peveler, R. C. (1995). A prospective study of outcome in bulimia nervosa and the long term effects of three psychological treatments. *Archives of General Psychiatry, 52*, 304–312.

Garner, D. M., & Bemis, K. M. (1982). A cognitive-behavioral approach to anorexia nervosa. *Cognitive Therapy and Research, 6*, 123–150.

Garner, D. M., & Bemis, K. M. (1985). Cognitive therapy for anorexia nervosa. In D. M. Garner & P. E. Garfinkel (Eds.), *Handbook of psychotherapy for anorexia nervosa and bulimia* (pp. 107–146). Chichester, England: Wiley.

Garner, D. M., Vitousek, K., & Pike, K. M. (1997). Cognitive behavioral therapy for anorexia. In D. M. Garner & P. E. Garfinkel (Eds.), *Handbook of treatment for eating disorders* (2nd ed., pp. 91–144). Chichester, England: Wiley.

Godart, N. T., Flament, M. F., Perdereau, F., & Jeammet, P. (2002). Comorbidity between eating disorders and anxiety disorders: A review. *International Journal of Eating Disorders, 32*, 253–270.

Godart, N. T., Perdereau, F., Rein, Z., Berthoz, S., Wallier, J., Jeammet, P. et al. (2007). Comorbidity studies of eating disorders and mood disorders: Critical review of the literature. *Journal of Affective Disorders, 97*, 37–49.

Goldschmidt, A. B., Hilbert, A., Manwaring, J. L., Wilfley, D. E., Pike, K. M., Fairburn, C. G., et al. (2010). The significance of overvaluation of shape and weight in binge eating disorder. *Behaviour Research and Therapy, 48*, 187–193.

Grilo, C. M. (2006). *Eating and weight disorders. Hove,* United Kingdom: Psychology Press.

Grilo, C. M. (2009, November). *Clinical and prognostic significance of overvaluation of shape/weight in binge eating disorder.* Paper presented at Association of Behavioral and Cognitive Therapies, New York, NY.

Grilo, C. M., Hrabosky, J. I., White, M. A., Allison, K. C., Stunkard, A. J., & Masheb, R. (2008). Overvaluation of shape and weight in binge eating disorder and overweight controls: Refinement of a diagnostic construct. *Journal of Abnormal Psychology, 117*, 414–419.

Grilo, C. M., & Masheb, R. M. (2005). A randomized controlled comparison of guided self-help cognitive behavioral therapy and behavioral weight loss for binge eating disorder. *Behaviour Research and Therapy, 43*, 1509–1525.

Grilo, C. M., Masheb, R. M., & Salant, S. L. (2005). Cognitive behavioral therapy guided self-help and orlistat for the treatment of binge eating disorder: A randomized, double-blind, placebo-controlled trial. *Biological Psychiatry, 57*, 1193–1201.

Grilo, C. M., Masheb, R., Brownell, K. D., & White, M. A. (2007, July). *Randomized comparison of cognitive behavioral therapy and behavioral weight loss treatments for obese patients with binge eating disorder: 12-month outcomes.* Paper presented at the World Congress of Behavioural and Cognitive Therapy, Barcelona, Spain.

Grilo, C. M., Masheb, R. M., & White, M. A. (2010). Significance of overvaluation of shape/weight in binge-eating disorder: Comparative study with overweight and bulimia nervosa. *Obesity, 18*, 499–504.

Grilo, C. M., Masheb, R. M., & Wilson, G. T. (2005). Efficacy of cognitive behavioral therapy and fluoxetine for the treatment of binge eating disorder: a randomized double-blind placebo-controlled comparison. *Biological Psychiatry, 57*, 301–309.

Grilo, C. M., Masheb, R. M., & Wilson, G. T. (2006). Rapid response to treatment for binge eating disorder. *Journal of Consulting and Clinical Psychology, 74*, 602–613.

Halmi, K. A., Agras, W. S., Crow, S., Mitchell, J., & Wilson, G. T., Bryson, S. W., et al. (2005). Predictors of treatment acceptance and completion in anorexia nervosa: Implications for future study designs. *Archives of General Psychiatry, 62*, 776–781.

Herzog, D. B., Keller, M. B., Sacks, N. R., Yeh, C. J., & Lavori, P. W. (1992). Psychiatric comorbidity in treatment-seeking anorexics and bulimics. *Journal of the American Academy of Child and Adolescent Psychiatry, 31*, 810–818.

Hoek, H. W., & van Hoeken, D. (2003). Review of the prevalence and incidence of eating disorders. *International Journal of Eating Disorders, 34*, 383–396.

Holderness, C. C., Brooks-Gunn, J., & Warren, M. P. (1994). Co-morbidity of eating disorders and substance abuse review of the literature. *International Journal of Eating Disorders, 16,* 1–34.

Hudson, J. I., Hiripi, E., Pope, H. G. Jr., & Kessler, R. C. (2007). The prevalence and correlates of eating disorders in the National Comorbidity Survey Replication. *Biological Psychiatry, 61,* 348–358.

Kaplan, A. S., Walsh, B. T., Olmsted, M., Attia, E., Carter, J. C., Devlin, M. J., et al. (2009). The slippery slope: Prediction of successful weight maintenance in anorexia nervosa. *Psychological Medicine, 39,* 1037–1045.

Kaye, W. H., Nagata, T., Weltzin, T. E., Hsu, L. K., Sokol, M. S., McConaha, C., et al. (2001). Double-blind placebo-controlled administration of fluoxetine in restricting- and restricting-purging-type anorexia nervosa. *Biological Psychiatry, 49,* 644–652.

Keel, P. K., & Klump, K. L. (2003). Are eating disorders culture-bound syndromes? Implications for conceptualizing their etiology. *Psychological Bulletin, 129,* 747–769.

Keski-Rahkonen, A., Hoek, H. W., Linna, M. S., Raevuori, A., Sihvola, E., Bulik, C. M., et al. (2009). Incidence and outcomes of bulimia nervosa: A nationwide population-based study. *Psychological Medicine, 39,* 823–831.

Klerman, G. L., Weissman, M. M., Rounsaville, B. J. & Chevron, E. S. (1984). *Interpersonal psychotherapy of depression.* New York: Basic Books.

Le Grange, D., Crosby, R. D., Rathouz, P. J., & Leventhal, B. L. (2007). A randomized controlled comparison of family-based treatment and supportive psychotherapy for adolescent bulimia nervosa. *Archives of General Psychiatry, 64,* 1049–1056.

Lock, J., le Grange, D., Agras, W. S., & Dare, C. (2001). *Treatment manual for anorexia nervosa: A family-based approach.* New York: Guilford Press.

Lynch, F. L., Dickerson, J., Perrin, N., DeBar, L., Wilson, G. T., Kraemer, H., et al. (2010). Cost-effectiveness of treatment for recurrent binge eating. *Journal of Consulting and Clinical Psychology, 78,* 322–333.

Masheb, R. M., & Grilo, C. M. (2008). Examination of predictors and moderators for self-help treatments of binge-eating disorder. *Journal of Consulting and Clinical Psychology, 76,* 900–904.

Masheb, R. M., & Grilo, C. M. (2007). Rapid response predicts treatment outcomes in binge eating disorders: Implications for stepped care. *Journal of Consulting and Clinical Psychology, 75,* 639–644.

Mayer, L. E., Roberto, C. A., Glasofer, D. R., Etu, S. F., Gallagher, D., Wang, J., et al. (2007). Does percent body fat predict outcome in anorexia nervosa? *American Journal of Psychiatry, 164,* 970–972.

McIntosh, V. V. W., Jordan, J., Carter, F. A., Luty, S. E., McKenzie, J. M., Bulik, C. M., et al. (2005). Three psychotherapies for anorexia nervosa: A randomized, controlled trial. *American Journal of Psychiatry, 162,* 741–747.

Mehler, P. S., Birmingham, C. L., Crow, S. J., & Jahraus, J. P. (2010). Medical complications of eating disorders. In C. M. Grilo & J. E. Mitchell (Eds.), *The treatment of eating disorders: A clinical handbook* (pp. 66–80). New York: Guilford Press.

Mitchell, J. E., Crosby, R. D., Wonderlich, S. A., Crow, S., Lancaster, K., Simonich, H., et al. (2008). A randomized trial comparing the efficacy of cognitive behavioral therapy for bulimia nervosa delivered via telemedicine versus face-to-face. *Behaviour Research and Therapy, 46,* 581–592.

Morgan, H. G., & Russell, G. F. (1975). Value of family background and clinical features as predictors of long-term outcome in anorexia nervosa: Four-year follow-up study of 41 patients. *Psychological Medicine, 5,* 355–371.

Munsch. S., Biedert, E., Meyer, A., Michael, T., Schlup, B., Tuch, A., et al. (2007). A randomized comparison of cognitive behavioral therapy and behavioral weight loss treatment for overweight individuals with binge eating disorder. *International Journal of Eating Disorders, 40,* 102–13.

National Institute for Clinical Excellence. (2004). *Eating disorders—Core interventions in the treatment and management of anorexia nervosa, bulimia nervosa and related eating disorders.* NICE Clinical Guideline No. 9. London: NICE. www.nice.org.uk

Papadopoulos, F. C., Ekbom, A., Brandt, L., & Ekselius, L. (2009). Excess mortality, causes of death and prognostic factors in anorexia nervosa. *British Journal of Psychiatry, 194,* 10–17.

Peat, C., Mitchell, J. E., Hoek, H. W., & Wonderlich, S. A. (2009). Validity and utility of subtyping anorexia nervosa. *International Journal of Eating Disorders, 42,* 590–594.

Pike, K. M. (2009). Half full or half empty?: Commentary of maintenance treatment for anorexia nervosa by Jacqueline C. Carter et al. *International Journal of Eating Disorders, 42,* 208–209.

Pike, K. M., Walsh, B. T., Vitousek, K., Wilson, G. T., & Bauer, J. (2003). Cognitive behavior therapy in the posthospitalization treatment of anorexia nervosa. *American Journal of Psychiatry, 160,* 2046–2049.

Reas, D. L., & Grilo, C. M. (2008). Review and meta-analysis of pharmacotherapy for binge eating disorder. *Obesity, 16,* 2024–2038.

Root, T. L., Poyastro Pinheiro, A. P., Thornton, L., Strober, M., Fernandez-Aranda, F., Brandt, H., et al. (2010). Substance use disorders in women with anorexia nervosa. *International Journal of Eating Disorders, 43,* 14–21.

Russell, G. F. M., Szmukler, G. I., Dare, C., & Eisler, I. (1987). An evaluation of family therapy in anorexia nervosa and bulimia nervosa. *Archives of General Psychiatry, 44,* 1047–1056.

Schebendach, J. E., Mayer, L. E., Devlin, M. J., Attia, E., Contento, I. R., Wolf, R. L., et al. (2008). Dietary energy density and diet variety as predictors of outcome in anorexia nervosa. *American Journal of Clinical Nutrition, 87,* 810–816.

Schmidt, U., Lee, S., Beecham, J., Perkins, S., Treasure, J., Yee, I., et al. (2007). A randomized controlled trial of family therapy and cognitive behavioral therapy guided self help for adolescents with bulimia nervosa and related conditions. *American Journal of Psychiatry, 164,* 591–598.

Serfaty, M. A., Turkington, D., Heap, M., Ledsham, L., & Jolley, E. (1999). Cognitive therapy versus dietary counselling in the outpatient treatment of anorexia nervosa: Effects of the treatment phase. *European Eating Disorders Review, 7,* 334–350.

Shapiro, J. R., Berkman, N. D., Brownley, K. A., Sedway, J. A., Lohr, K. N., & Bulik, C. M. (2007). Bulimia nervosa treatment: A systematic review of randomized controlled trials. *International Journal of Eating Disorders, 40,* 321–336.

Steinhausen, H. C. (2002). The outcome of anorexia nervosa in the 20th century. *American Journal of Psychiatry, 159,* 1284–1293.

Steinhausen, H. C., & Weber, S. (2009). The outcome of bulimia nervosa: Findings from one-quarter century of research. *American Journal of Psychiatry, 166,* 1331–1341.

Stice, E., Agras, W. S., Telch, C. F., Halmi, C., Mitchell, J., & Wilson, G. T. (2001). Subtyping binge eating disordered women along dietary restraint and negative affect dimensions. *International Journal of Eating Disorders, 30,* 11–27.

Striegel-Moore, R., & Franko, D. (2007). Should binge eating disorder be included in the DSM-5? A critical review of the state of the evidence. *Annual Review of Clinical Psychology, 4,* 305–324.

Striegel-Moore, R., Wilson, G.T., DeBar, L., Perrin, N., Lynch, F., Rosselli, F., et al. (2010). Guided self-help for the treatment of recurrent binge eating. *Journal of Consulting and Clinical Psychology, 78,* 312–321.

Sullivan, P. F. (1995). Mortality in anorexia nervosa. *American Journal of Psychiatry, 152,* 1073–1074.

Sysko, R., Hildebrandt, T., Wilson, G. T., Wilfley, D. E., & Agras, W. S. (in press). Heterogeneity Moderates Treatment Response among Patients with Binge Eating Disorder. *Journal of Consulting and Clinical Psychology.*

Sysko, R., Sha, N., Wang, Y., Duan, N., & Walsh, B. T. (2010). Early response to antidepressant treatment in bulimia nervosa. *Psychological Medicine, 40,* 999–1005.

Sysko, R., & Walsh, B. T. (2007). Guided self-help for bulimia nervosa. In J. D. Latner & G. T. Wilson (Eds.), *Self-help approaches for obesity and eating disorders: Research and practice* (pp. 92–117). New York: Guilford Press.

Van Hoeken, D., Veling, W., Sinke, S., Mitchell, J. E., & Hoek, H. W. (2009). The validity and utility of subtyping bulimia nervosa. *International Journal of Eating Disorders, 42,* 595–602.

Vitousek, K. M., Watson, S., & Wilson, G. T. (1998). Enhancing motivation for change in treatment-resistant eating disorders. *Clinical Psychology Review, 18,* 391–420.

Walsh, B. T. (2007). DSM-5 from the perspective of the DSM-IV experience. *International Journal of Eating Disorders, 40,* S3–S7.

Walsh, B. T., Fairburn, C. G., Mickley, D., Sysko, R., & Parides, M. K. (2004). Treatment of bulimia nervosa in a primary care setting. *American Journal of Psychiatry, 161,* 556–561.

Walsh, B. T., Kaplan, A. S., Attia, E., Olmsted, M., Parides, M., Carter, J. C., et al. (2006). Fluoxetine after weight restoration in anorexia nervosa - A randomized controlled trial. *JAMA, 295,* 2605–2612.

Walsh, B. T., & Sysko, R. (2009). Broad categories for the diagnosis of eating disorders (BCD-ED): An alternative system for classification. *International Journal of Eating Disorders, 42,* 754–164.

Walsh, B. T., Sysko, R., & Parides, M. K. (2006). Early response to medication among women with bulimia nervosa. *International Journal of Eating Disorders, 39,* 72–75.

Walsh, B. T., Wilson, G. T., Loeb, K. L., Devlin, M. J., Pike, K. M., Roose, S. P., et al. (1997). Medication and psychotherapy in the treatment of bulimia nervosa. *American Journal of Psychiatry, 154,* 523–531.

Wiederman, M. W., & Pryor, T. (1996). Substance use among women with eating disorders. *International Journal of Eating Disorders, 20,* 163–168.

Wilfley, D. E., Agras, W. S., Telch, C. F., Rossiter, E. M., Schneider, J. A., Cole, A. G., et al. (1993). Group cognitive-behavioral therapy and group interpersonal psychotherapy for the nonpurging bulimic individual: A controlled comparison. *Journal of Consulting and Clinical Psychology, 61,* 296–305.

Wilfley, D. E., Welch, R. R., Stein, R. I., Spurrell, E. B., Cohen, L. R., Saelens, B. E., et al. (2002). A randomized comparison of group cognitive-behavioral therapy and group interpersonal psychotherapy for the treatment of overweight individuals with binge eating disorder. *Archives of General Psychiatry, 59,* 713–721.

Wilson, G. T. (2010a). Cognitive behavioral therapy for eating disorders. In W. S. Agras (Ed.), *The Oxford Handbook of Eating Disorders*. New York: Oxford University Press.

Wilson, G. T. (2010b). What treatment research is needed for bulimia nervosa? In C. M. Grilo & J. E. Mitchell (Eds.), *The treatment of eating disorders: A clinical handbook* (pp. 544–553). New York: Guilford Press.

Wilson, G. T., & Fairburn, C. G. (2002). Treatments for eating disorders. In P.E. Nathan and J.M. Gorman (Eds.), *Treatments that work* (2nd edition; pp. 559–592). Oxford University Press: New York.

Wilson, G. T., & Fairburn, C. G. (2007). Treatments for eating disorders. In P.E. Nathan and J.M. Gorman (Eds.), *Treatments that work* (3rd edition; pp. 579–610). Oxford University Press: New York.

Wilson, G. T., Fairburn, C. G., Agras, W. S., Walsh, B. T., & Kraemer, H. D. (2002). Cognitive behavior therapy for bulimia nervosa: Time course and mechanisms of change. *Journal of Consulting and Clinical Psychology, 70,* 267–274.

Wilson, G. T., Grilo, C. M., & Vitousek, K. M. (2007). Psychological treatment of eating disorders. *American Psychologist, 62,* 199–216.

Wilson, G. T., Loeb, K. L., Walsh, B. T., Labouvie, E., Petkova, E., Liu, X., et al. (1999). Psychological versus pharmacological treatments of bulimia nervosa: Predictors and processes of change. *Journal of Consulting and Clinical Psychology, 67,* 451–459.

Wilson, G. T., & Sysko, R. (2009). Frequency of binge eating episodes in bulimia nervosa and binge eating disorder: Diagnostic considerations. *International Journal of Eating Disorders, 42,* 603–610.

Wilson, G. T., Wilfley, D. E., Agras, W. S., & Bryson, S. W. (2010). Psychological treatments of binge eating disorder. *Archives of General Psychiatry, 67,* 94–101.

Wonderlich, S. A., Gordon, K. H., Mitchell, J. E., Crosby, R. D., & Engel, S. G. (2009). The validity and clinical utility of binge eating disorder. *International Journal of Eating Disorders, 42,* 687–705.

World Health Organization. (1978). *Mental disorders: Glossary and guide to their classification in accordance to the ninth revision of the International Classification of Diseases.* Geneva: Author.

Alcohol Use and Alcohol Use Disorders

Kenneth J. Sher, Julia A. Martinez, *and* Andrew K. Littlefield

Abstract

Alcohol use disorders (AUDs), alcohol abuse, and alcohol dependence, are among the most prevalent mental disorders in the United States and elsewhere. Considerable controversy exists concerning the optimal way of classifying these disorders and the boundaries between normal and abnormal drinking. Although AUDs can occur over much of the life span, from an epidemiological perspective, it is largely a disorder of adolescence and young adulthood. Many who experience AUDs are "mature out" of them as they age and acquire adult roles and, perhaps, as a function of normal personality. However, a significant minority of individuals fail to mature out, and some individuals develop AUDs later in adulthood. A number of etiological pathways are associated with developing an AUD; foremost among them, a pathway shared with other externalizing disorders such as conduct disorder, adult antisociality, and other substance dependence. However, pathways associated with internalizing disorders and with individual differences in alcohol effects also exist. All of these pathways likely involve major genetic and environmental determinants. Given the etiological pathways that have been documented, it is not surprising that AUDs are often comorbid with other mental disorders. A number of effective approaches to the prevention and treatment of AUDs have been developed. Additionally, basic research is setting the stage for further advances in both behavior and drug treatments of AUDs.

Keywords: Alcohol abuse, alcohol use disorders, assessment, comorbidity, epidemiology, etiology, personality, substance use disorders, treatment

Alcohol use disorders (AUDs) are among the most prevalent mental disorders in the United States, and are associated with significant consequences for the drinker, his or her friends and family, employers, the community, and the nation. Additionally, AUDs are also frequently associated with other psychiatric and medical conditions and, thus, their consequences can be far reaching.

Definitions of Alcohol-related Concepts
Alcohol Use Disorder
The *Diagnostic and Statistical Manual of Mental Disorders, Fourth Edition, Text Revision* (DSM-IV; American Psychiatric Association [APA], 2000) defines two major classes of substance use disorders,

substance dependence and substance abuse. The diagnostic criteria for AUDs follow those for substance use disorders more generally, with *alcohol dependence* defined as "a maladaptive pattern of use, leading to clinically significant impairment or distress, as manifested by three (or more) of the following symptoms occurring at any time within the same 12-month period: (1) tolerance; (2) withdrawal; (3) the substance is often taken in larger amounts or over a longer period than intended; (4) a persistent desire or unsuccessful efforts to cut down or control substance use; (5) a great deal of time is spent in activities necessary to obtain the substance, use the substance, or recover from its effects; (6) important social, occupational, or recreational activities are given up or reduced because of substance use; and (7) the substance use is continued despite knowledge of having a persistent or recurrent physical or psychological problem that is likely to have been caused or exacerbated by the substance" (p. 197). The DSM-IV defines alcohol abuse as "a maladaptive pattern of substance use leading to clinically significant impairment or distress as manifested by one (or more) of the following occurring within a 12-month period: (1) recurrent substance use resulting in a failure to fulfill major role obligations at work, school, or home; (2) recurrent substance use in situations in which it is physically hazardous; (3) recurrent substance-related legal problems; and (4) continued substance use despite having persistent or recurrent social or interpersonal problems caused or exacerbated by the effects of the substance" (pg. 198). According to the DSM-IV's diagnostic hierarchy, individuals who meet criteria for alcohol dependence do not receive diagnoses for alcohol abuse, thus implying that dependence is the more severe of the two AUDs.

The abuse/dependence distinction made its debut in the third edition of the DSM (APA, 1980), reflecting, in part, the distinction introduced by Edwards and Gross (1976) between the alcohol dependence syndrome and alcohol-related disabilities. The alcohol dependence syndrome reflected the degree to which alcohol has come to dominate the drinker's life, as evidenced by narrowing in the drinking repertoire, salience of drink-seeking behavior, increased tolerance to alcohol, repeated withdrawal symptoms, relief or avoidance of withdrawal symptoms by further drinking, subjective awareness of compulsion to drink, and/or reinstatement after abstinence. In contrast, the alcohol-related disabilities construct reflected the degree to which the drinker experienced a range of problems, such as physical ailments (e.g., developing cirrhosis), occupational impairment, marital discord, and hazardous use (e.g., drinking and driving). Unlike Edwards and Gross's conceptualization of the dependence syndrome and alcohol-related disabilities as distinct but related dimensions, the categorical diagnostic approach embraced by the DSM to date views abuse and dependence as mutually exclusive categories with a dependence diagnosis representing the more severe condition and precluding the ostensibly less severe abuse diagnosis. In the DSM-III, alcohol dependence was conceived as physiological, indicated by tolerance or withdrawal and reflecting "neuroadaptation." This narrow concept of dependence was broadened in the revised criteria of DSM-III (DSM-III-R; APA, 1987) and the

DSM-IV to include behavioral signs of dependence such as loss of control (i.e., drinking in larger amounts or longer than intended), inability to abstain, and other symptoms reflecting compulsive use.

Despite the widespread acceptance of the abuse/dependence distinction since its introduction, accumulating data are challenging the validity of this distinction. For example, Item-Response Theory (IRT)-based analyses that conceptualize diagnostic criteria as indicators of a latent trait of AUD demonstrate that some dependence criteria (e.g., tolerance, impaired control) are prevalent and thus statistically "less severe" than are some abuse criteria, which are comparatively rare (e.g., legal difficulties; Kahler & Strong, 2006; Saha, Stinson, & Grant, 2007). These results are inconsistent with the notion that abuse is a less severe condition than dependence and may be prodromal to it. Moreover, although some early factor analyses suggested that abuse and dependence items formed statistically distinct (albeit highly correlated) factors (e.g., Hasin, Muthén, Wisnicki, & Grant, 1994; Muthén, Grant, & Hasin, 1993), more recent data further suggest either unifactorial solutions (e.g., Proudfoot, Baillie, & Teeson, 2006) or two factors that do not clearly map onto abuse and dependence (e.g., Harford & Muthén, 2001). Additionally, the DSM-IVs requirement of three or more dependence symptoms for a diagnosis of dependence, but only one abuse symptom for a diagnosis of abuse, leads to the problematic situation in which someone who exhibits a pattern of hazardous use (which might reflect little more than a heedless drinking style) would meet criteria for an AUD but not someone who might experience one or two relatively severe dependence symptoms (Pollock & Martin, 1999). These "diagnostic orphans" pose a dilemma since they are likely more severe than individuals who have the single abuse criterion of hazardous use but, unlike those individuals, would not qualify for an AUD diagnosis.

The psychometric (i.e., IRT) analyses just cited indicate that current AUD criteria oversample moderate levels of pathology and are less accurate in scaling mild and severe levels of alcohol-related problems. Those interested in improving the diagnosis of AUDs must contend with findings questioning the empirical basis for the abuse/dependence distinction, as well as the dimensional nature of AUDs, which are clearly graded in intensity from those who are high functioning and developmentally limited (Sher & Gotham, 1999; Zucker, 1987; Zucker, Fitzgerald, & Moses, 1995) to those with severe and morbid courses. For these and other reasons, the validity of the current diagnostic system is coming under increasing criticism (Martin, Chung, & Langenbucher, 2008).

Martin et al. (2008) identify a number of additional problems regarding the DSM-IV substance use disorder criteria (including AUD criteria). Specifically, they note that the abuse category does not have a clear conceptual core and does not meet traditional standards for the concept of mental disorder (e.g., Spitzer, Endicott & Robins, 1978; Wakefield, 1992) that is based, in part, upon the notion of dysfunction. For example, it is not immediately clear why repeated hazardous use (a behavior that would qualify someone for a diagnosis of alcohol abuse in DSM-IV) is necessarily indicative of a *disorder* as opposed to, say, mere *heedlessness*. They also note a lack of empirical distinctions between exclusive criteria for substance abuse and dependence, and that current diagnostic algorithms produce unequal diagnostic coverage of those with similar levels of substance-problem severity.

Martin et al. suggested several solutions, including: (a) abandoning the category of substance abuse and defining a single category of substance dependence using revised DSM-IV substance use disorder (SUD) criteria and new symptoms (e.g., consumption criteria), (b) revising the definition of tolerance to require a minimum level of use in addition to the change-based definition, (c) defining the physiological features subtype of substance dependence by withdrawal only, (d) emphasizing specificity over sensitivity by removing mild alcohol withdrawal subcriteria (e.g., anxiety and vomiting) and/or increasing the threshold for symptom assignment, (e) clarifying that frequency and duration of use is due to compulsive behavior and not merely due to social reasons, (f) splitting quit/cut down into two separate criteria, (g) removing hazardous use and legal problems as diagnostic criteria, (h) integrating categorical and dimensional approaches to diagnosis, and (i) grouping SUDs with an externalizing spectrum of psychopathology that includes other substance use disorders, conduct disorder, antisocial personality disorder, and closely related traits and conditions (e.g., Krueger, Markon, Patrick, & Iacono, 2005).

Alcohol Consumption

It is important to note that current diagnostic criteria for AUDs fail to include direct measures of alcohol consumption, despite health concerns based on alcohol consumption patterns. For example, the U.S. government has recently, and for the first time, provided safe drinking guidelines as part of their Dietary Guidelines for Americans, 2005 (U.S. Department of Agriculture and U.S. Department of Health and Human Services, 2005). These guidelines discourage levels of consumption that exceed two drinks per day for men and one drink per day for women. Current estimates suggest that, among past-year drinkers 18 years of age and older, 46% of men and 32% of adult women in the United States exceed these safe drinking levels and are appropriate targets for interventions (Dawson, Grant, & Li, 2005).

In addition, there has been increasing concern in recent years over drinking patterns associated with high levels of consumption on drinking days (i.e., "binge" drinking). The National Institute of Alcohol Abuse and Alcoholism (NIAAA, 2004) defines binge drinking as "a pattern of drinking alcohol that brings blood alcohol concentration (BAC) to 0.08 gram percent or above. For the typical adult, this pattern corresponds to consuming five or more drinks (male), or four or more drinks (female), in about 2 hours.". These consumption-based limits have not been included in formal diagnostic algorithms, although psychometric analyses suggest that their inclusion would be useful in measuring a latent construct of AUD that has better lower-end resolution than does the DSM-IV (see Hasin, Hatzenbuehler, Keyes, & Ogburn, 2006; Saha, Stinson, & Grant, 2007).

Epidemiology

Multiple population-based, epidemiological surveys indicate that the prevalence rates of AUDs are high, especially among those in late adolescence and early adulthood. Over the past 25 years, five large-scale, population-based epidemiological surveys using structured diagnostic interviews have provided estimates of AUDs in the United States. These include the Epidemiologic Catchment Area (ECA) Survey (Helzer, Burnam, & McEnvoy, 1991; Robins & Price, 1991), the National Comorbidity Survey (NCS; Kessler, Crum, Warner, & Nelson, 1997; Kessler et al., 1994), the National Comorbidity Survey – Replication (NCS-R; Kessler, Berglund, Demler, Jin, & Walters, 2005; Kessler, Chiu, Demler, & Walters, 2005), the National Longitudinal Alcohol Epidemiologic Survey (NLAES; Grant, 1997; Grant, Harford, Dawson, Chou, Dufour, & Pickering, 1994; Grant & Pickering, 1996), and the National Epidemiologic Survey on Alcohol and Related Conditions (NESARC; Grant, Dawson, Stinson, Chou, Dufour, & Pickering, 2004; Grant, Stinson, et al., 2004). Each of these major studies indicate very high past-year and lifetime prevalence rates of AUDs in the U.S. population (13.8% lifetime and 6.8% past-year DSM-III in ECA; 23.5% lifetime and 7.7% past-year DSM-IIIR in NCS; 18.2 % lifetime and 7.41% past-year DSM-IV in NLAES; 30.3% lifetime and 8.46% past-year DSM-IV in NESARC; 18.6% lifetime and 4.4% past-year DSM-IV in NCS-R).

In general, men are much more likely to be diagnosed with past-year alcohol abuse (6.9%) or dependence (5.4%) than women (abuse: 2.6%; dependence: 2.3%; Grant, Dawson, et al., 2004). The prevalence of abuse is greater among whites (5.1%) than among blacks (3.3%), Asians (2.1%), and Hispanics (4.0%). The prevalence of dependence is higher in whites (3.8%), Native Americans (6.4%), and Hispanics (4.0%) than among Asians (2.4%).

Alcohol Use Disorders over the Life Course

If there is a single, salient phenomenon with respect to the epidemiology of AUDs, it is that their prevalence is highly age-graded. Using data from the NESARC, Figure 20.1 illustrates the dramatic age gradient, with peak prevalences for both abuse and dependence occurring early in the third decade of life, and with large decreases in prevalences clearly evident by age 30. These changes in prevalence rates of AUDs over the life course suggest AUDs, in part, should be considered as developmental phenomena. The period

intervening between adolescence and adulthood (known as "emerging adulthood"; Arnett, 2006) evidences the time when individuals are at the highest risk for manifesting an AUD, with the peak hazard for onset for both alcohol abuse and alcohol dependence occurring around the age of 20 in the United States (Grant, Moore, & Kaplan, 2003; Li, Hewitt, & Grant, 2004). This heightened risk is thought to reflect a time when individuals are relatively free of adult responsibilities but unrestrained by parental influence period. However, as individuals progress into adulthood, perhaps undertaking a number of novel adult responsibilities (e.g., marriage and parenthood), rates of AUDs typically decrease, a phenomenon which is known of as "maturing out" (Arnett, 2006; Bachman, Wadsworth, O'Malley, Johnston, & Schulenberg, 1997; Donovan, Jessor, & Jessor, 1983; Littlefield & Sher, 2010; Winick, 1962).

It is important to note that there is cultural variation in these developmental patterns. In particular, African-American men are likely to have later ages of onset of alcohol use disorder with increases during the third decade of life, while there is decreasing prevalence among whites of the same age (Grant, Dawson, et al., 2004; Herd & Grube 1996). These divergences in developmental paths may be due to cultural variation in education, labor market participation, drinking motives, and marriage and parenting (Cooper et al., 2008; Dawson, 1998).

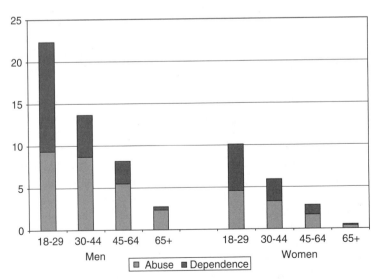

Fig. 20.1 Past 12-month prevalence of alcohol abuse and dependence for men and women (as defined by the Diagnostic and Statistical Manual of Mental Disorders, Fourth Edition. American Psychiatric Association, 1994). Data taken from the National Epidemiologic Survey on Alcohol and Related Conditions. Reproduced from Grant, B. F., Dawson, D. A., Stinson, F. S., Chou, P. S., Dufour, M.C., & Pickering, R. (2004). The 12-month prevalence and trends in DSM-IV alcohol abuse and dependence: United States, 1991-1992 and 2001-2002. *Drug and Alcohol Dependence, 74,* 223–234. With permission of the publisher, Elsevier.

Alcohol as a Drug
Acute Effects

The neuropharmacology of alcohol (specifically, ethanol, the form of alcohol contained in alcoholic beverages) is complex because it affects virtually all major neurotransmitter systems, especially at levels associated with intoxication. Indeed, alcohol operates both acutely and chronically with many central nervous system (CNS) neurotransmitter systems that play a key role in regulating cognition, affect, and behavior, as well as the subjective effects of alcohol, all of which may be factors in the development of alcohol addiction (Fromme & D'Amico, 1999; Vengeliene, Bilbao, Molander, & Spanagel, 2008). For purposes of discussion, the subjective effects of alcohol can be separated into three broad classes: (1) positive reinforcing effects (e.g., euphoric, arousing), (2) negative reinforcing effects (e.g., anxiolytic, anti-depressant), and (3) punishing effects (e.g., depressant and acute discomfort such as flushing, nausea, and vomiting).

Positively reinforcing effects of alcohol, such as euphoria and increased arousal, are thought to be largely associated with enhanced monoaminergic (especially dopaminergic) effects and related opioid peptide activity (NIAAA, 1997). Opiate antagonists or blockers, in particular naltrexone and nalmefene, have been found to suppress the subjective stimulating effects of alcohol and also craving, both in social drinkers and non–treatment-seeking alcoholics (Drobes, Anton, Thomas, & Voronin, 2004).

Negatively reinforcing acute subjective effects of alcohol, including anxiolysis and possibly some anti-depressant effects, are thought to be mediated by alcohol's effects on the γ-aminobutyric acid (GABA$_A$) receptor. It has been known for more than 50 years that alcohol has reliable effects on passive avoidance in rodents in a way quite similar to classic anxiolytic drugs such as the benzodiazepines (Harris, Mihic, & Valenzuela, 1998). Further, neuropharmacological studies have shown that alcohol works to enhance GABAergic activity through its action on the GABA$_A$ receptor. Drugs that have the opposite effect on this receptor (i.e., inverse agonists such as RO 15-4513) appear to reverse anxiolytic and related effects (Lister & Nutt, 1988), perhaps by competing for the same GABA$_A$ receptors as ethanol (Hanchar et al., 2006).

Some of the *punishing acute subjective effects of alcohol* (e.g., flushing) appear to be due to intermediary by-products of ethanol metabolism (specifically acetaldehyde, which is a toxic metabolite of alcohol; Eriksson, 1983; Eriksson, Mizoi, & Fukunaga, 1982).

Further, it appears that many of the effects of acetaldehyde are manifested in the periphery. Other presumably punishing effects (e.g., sedation) are likely mediated by central GABAergic mechanisms within the hippocampus, septum, cerebral cortex, and cerebellum, and are more likely to be observed at high doses and on the descending limb of the blood alcohol curve (Fromme & D'Amico, 1999).

Are Reinforcing and Punishing Effects of Alcohol Direct or Mediated via Cognitive Processes?

Until recently, there has been some disagreement as to the extent to which alcohol has anxiolytic properties similar to the benzodiazepines. For example, Lang, Patrick, and Stritzke (1999) reviewed the available human literature on the effects of alcohol and emotion and concluded that "evidence of intrinsic reward or selective stress reduction seems neither powerful enough nor reliable enough to account for the widespread appeal of alcohol and the prevalence of alcoholism" (p. 360). They also argued that most of alcohol's effects on affect and emotional responding were secondary to effects on cognition (and subsequent processing of relevant contextual cues and their relevance to the self).

One of the most influential cognitive processing theories of psychological vulnerability is Steele and Joseph's (1990) "alcohol myopia" theory, which proposes that the effect of alcohol is contingent upon information processing of more or less salient features of the drinking context. This theory has received support across multiple domains and can provide a coherent explanation as to how alcohol can lead to either an animated, euphoric, and celebratory experience (i.e., *reinforcement*) or to a depressive "crying in one's beer" experience (i.e., *punishment*). In several studies, Steele and colleagues have shown that alcohol consumption, followed by distracting pleasant or neutral stimuli, can attenuate stress responses. However, when no distraction is present, alcohol consumption either no longer reduces anxiety or produces anxiogenic effects (Josephs & Steele, 1990).

However, it has long been known that intermediate doses of alcohol have unpredictable effects on negative emotions, although as the dose of alcohol approaches those associated with "binge" levels of intoxication (e.g., BACs of approximately .08% or more), negatively and positively reinforcing effects tend to be observed reliably, independent of context (Sher, 1987). Consequently, it may be that it is only at intermediate doses where alcohol's effects are unreliable (Sher, 1987) and heavily dependent on context (Steele & Josephs, 1990) and appraisal (Sayette, 1993). This interpretation of the earlier literature is consistent with recent studies (e.g., Donohue, Curtin, Patrick, & Lang, 2007; Sher, Bartholow, Peuser, Erickson, & Wood, 2007) demonstrating unconditional salutary effects on negative emotions across diverse measures and experimental paradigms. Thus, existing data suggest that, particularly at low and intermediate levels, many affective consequences of consumption are cognitively mediated. As a corollary, these affective consequences are heavily context-dependent and moderated by individual differences related to appraisal processes. However, more direct effects of alcohol on brain centers responsible for mood and emotion are likely to be observed at higher doses.

Biphasic Effects of Alcohol

The reinforcing effects of alcohol typically are experienced on the ascending limb of the BAC curve (measured from the time that drinking is initiated until individuals reach their peak BAC), and the punishing effects typically occur on the descending limb of the BAC curve (measured at the time subsequent to that when individuals have reached their peak BAC), rendering the net effect of alcohol biphasic (Sher, Wood, Richardson, & Jackson, 2005). These biphasic effects are observable in the laboratory, and individuals also report expecting to experience such effects prior to drinking (Earleywine, 1994; Earleywine & Martin, 1993). Notably, heavier drinkers have been found more likely to experience stronger stimulant effects relative to sedative effects, whereas lighter drinkers have been found to experience the opposite (Earleywine, 1994). The biphasic effects of alcohol are subject to individual differences (Newlin & Thomson, 1990) as well as dosage (Holdstock & de Wit, 1998).

Chronic Adaptation to Alcohol

Chronic, heavy drinkers often experience a range of persistent changes relevant to acute withdrawal symptoms and resultant emotional functioning. First, alcohol withdrawal symptoms are often associated with affective disturbance, particularly anxiety (Sellers, Sullivan, Somer, & Sykora, 1991; Sullivan, Sykora, Schneiderman, Naranjo, & Sellers, 1989). These associations might create a vicious cycle whereby chronic alcohol use leads to affective disturbance, which in turn motivates further drinking. Second, some forms of anxiety and mood disorders appear to be "alcohol-induced" and, thus, the differential diagnosis of substance-induced mood

disorders is considered critical for nosology and treatment (APA, 1994, 2000; Schuckit, 1994). Anxiety and mood disorders that remit spontaneously after a short period (i.e., less than a month) of abstinence and that only appear in the context of ongoing substance use should be considered substance-induced and not "independent." Third, even ostensible "independent" anxiety and mood disorders often appear to temporally follow the occurrence of an AUD (especially true in the case of depression, Kessler, Crum, Warner, & Nelson, 1997). For example, in a multinational pool of five epidemiological studies (Merikangas et al., 1996), it was found that, among those with co-occurring alcohol dependence and depression, 20% reported that the onset of the disorders occurred together, 38% reported that depression came first, and 42% reported that alcohol dependence came first (the study did not compare order of onset for anxiety disorders and alcohol dependence).

A general perspective on changes associated with the chronic use of various drugs of abuse, including alcohol, is termed *allostasis* (i.e., adaptive homeostatic changes that occur in response to repeated drug challenges; e.g., Koob & Le Moal, 2001, 2008). According to this theory, an organism responds to drug challenges by producing counterdirectional (i.e., homeostatic) responses that increase over time. Thus, allostasis explains the phenomenon of *acquired tolerance*, the tendency for a given dose of a drug to elicit progressively less response over time, in a way similar to that proposed by Solomon and Corbit (1974) in their opponent-process theory and Siegel and colleagues (e.g., Siegel, Baptista, Kim, McDonald, & Weise-Kelly, 2000) in their Pavlovian account of tolerance development. However, the allostatic perspective goes further than these theories by specifically positing that repeated homeostatic challenges present an adaptive burden and result in a shift of a hedonic "set point" in the direction of the opponent process. Theoretically, such a process could explain intermediate- to long-term deviations in tonic emotional levels, resulting in a more depressed, irritable, and/or anxious alcohol-dependent person. Such a perspective is also consistent with the general principle that acute and chronic effects of alcohol are opposite in direction with respect to both neuropharmacological effects and their behavioral correlates. These allostatic, chronic adaptations are believed to be mediated by the hypothalamic-pituitary-adrenal (HPA) axis via effects of corticotrophin-releasing factor (CRF) (Koob & Le Moal, 2001, 2008), and current drug development efforts are targeting CRF antagonists to attempt to modulate these proposed allostatic influences.

Genetic and Environmental Factors Associated with Alcohol Use and Alcohol Use Disorders

The numbers of etiological factors contributing to alcohol use and AUDs are extensive, and both genetic and environmental factors—broadly construed—have been implicated, as well as their interactions.

Genetic Vulnerability

The existence of significant genetic influences on AUDs (among individuals who drink) has been firmly established in adoption studies (Cadoret, Yates, Troughton, Woodworth, & Stewart, 1995; Cloninger, Bohman, & Sigvardsson, 1981; Goodwin, Schulsinger, Hermansen, Guze, & Winokur, 1973; McGue, 1994) that show strong effects of biological parents independent of being reared with them. Moreover, classical twin studies (Heath, 1995; Heath et al., 1997; McGue, 1999) that compare concordance of alcohol-related phenotypes between monozygotic ("identical") and dizygotic ("fraternal") twins consistently show genes accounting for approximately half of the variance in AUD prevalence. Although the new era of molecular genetics has moved the focus from establishing the importance of genetic factors to identifying specific genes that are important in AUD etiology (Dick, Rose, & Kaprio, 2006), these twin and adoption studies remain useful in demonstrating both common genetic influences on AUDs and comorbid conditions, and the importance of gene–environment interaction in the absence of knowledge of specific genes involved.

For example, Slutske, Heath, Dinwiddie, Madden, Bucholz, Dunne, et al. (1998) showed that much of the comorbidity between childhood conduct disorder and AUDs can be attributed to shared, additive genetic effects and, further, that temperamental traits (especially those related to poor self-control) appear to represent common genetically mediated contributions to this disorder (Slutske, Cronk, Sher, Madden, Bucholz, & Heath, 2002). This suggests that, rather than looking for pure "alcohol genes," it might be fruitful to look for genes contributing to multivariate, spectrum phenotypes (Dick et al., 2008; Uhl et al., 2008) as well as for genes specific to alcohol dependence.

Similarly, genetically informative samples can be useful for identifying the presence of certain forms of gene–environment interactions. In behavior-genetic rodent models of drinking, cross-fostering designs (in which the genetic background and rearing environment are experimentally crossed) can be extremely informative (Randall & Lester, 1975). However, the comparable design in humans, the adoption design, is problematic for several reasons. Human adoptions tend to select for strong genetic effects (due to deviant biological parents) and low variance in rearing conditions (i.e., adoption agencies tend not to place adoptees in problem homes). Moreover, in the classic twin design, gene–environment interactions are confounded with additive genetic effects (in the case of genes–shared environment) and with unique environmental effects (in the case of genes–unique environment). However, extended twin-family designs that control for genetic background in parents while examining differences in rearing conditions can elucidate where some gene–environment interactions might occur. Specifically, the absence of parental alcoholism (a protective environmental factor) can reduce the impact of high genetic risk for the development of AUDs in the offspring of (discordant) twins (Jacob et al., 2003; but see Slutske et al., 2008).

In recent years, an increasing number of molecular genetic studies have sought to identify specific genes that confer risk. Much of this work focused on genes that play a role in alcohol metabolism and subsequent subjective responses to alcohol. For example, variations in alcohol dehydrogenase (ADH) and aldehyde dehydrogenase (ALDH), two of the major enzymes involved in alcohol metabolism, have been linked to individual differences in subjective and physiological responses to alcohol (Chen, Loh, Hsu, Chen, Yu, & Cheng, 1996; Luczak, Elvine-Kreis, Shea, Carr, & Wall, 2002; Nakamura, Iwahashi, Matsuo, Miyatake, Ichikawa, & Suwaki, 1996). The most widely studied of these is allelic variation in a gene that encodes for ALDH2. Individuals with one or two copies of the ALDH*2 allele have impaired acetaldehyde metabolism, resulting in elevated acetaldehyde levels that lead to an alcohol-induced flushing response (Higuchi, Matsushita, Murayama, Takagi, & Hayashida, 1995). This mutation, which is present in a large minority of several Asian groups, including Chinese, Japanese, and Koreans (but not Filipinos or Indians; Eng, Luczak, & Wall, 2007), is associated with a range of unpleasant effects such as facial flushing, heart palpitations, and nausea, and is therefore thought to be protective against the development of alcohol dependence (Higuchi et al., 1995; Takeshita, Morimoto, Mao, Hashimoto, & Furuyama, 1994; Wall, Thomasson, Schuckit, & Ehlers, 1992). In a recent meta-analysis, Luczak, Glatt, and Wall (2006) found that presence of one (or two) copies of these alleles (which are linked with impaired acetaldehyde metabolism) were associated with a greatly reduced risk of alcohol dependence in Asian populations.

Although subjective response to alcohol as a function of variability in ADH genotypes has only just begun to be explored in alcohol challenge studies, there is evidence suggestive of etiologically relevant variability. Specifically, the presence of the ADH1B *2 allele leads to more rapid metabolism of alcohol to acetaldehyde (Crabb, 1995), which may generate an altered subjective response to drinking. This genotype occurs at a high base rate in Asians (especially Chinese, Japanese, and Koreans; Eng et al., 2007) and is associated with lower rates of AUDs in these populations (Luczak et al., 2006). The presence of at least one ADH1B *2 allele was also observed to be significantly more prevalent among young adult African Americans who do not have a family history of AUDs (Ehlers, Gilder, Harris, & Carr, 2001). Furthermore, in the same population, the presence of the ADH1B*2 allele was linked with higher levels of alcohol expectancies, which could be associated with greater subjective responses to alcohol as well.

Perhaps more relevant for understanding genetic influences in individuals of European descent, a number of genes associated with central brain neurotransmitter systems have been found to be associated with alcohol dependence. For example, GABA is a neurotransmitter involved in many of the anxiolytic and sedative effects of alcohol, and GABA receptors are involved in alcohol tolerance. Recent studies have established associations between $GABA_A$ receptor genes, both on chromosome 4 (e.g., GABRA2, GABRB1) and on chromosome 15 (e.g., GABRB3), and AUDs across human and animal studies (Dick & Beirut, 2006). Although genes associated with alcohol and acetaldehyde metabolism and the GABRA2 gene show replicable links to AUDs, a number of less consistent links exist with candidate genes associated with neurotransmitter function. Because of the possible role of some of these genes in comorbidity, it is worthwhile to mention them while noting the weaker empirical basis for some of these findings.

Serotonin is a neurotransmitter that is important in mood regulation and is associated with decreased alcohol consumption; however, the short 5-HTT allele is less efficient in transcription than the long allele, and thus is thought to pose a risk for AUDs. There is also evidence for a relation between the short allele of the serotonin transporter (5-HTT)

encoding gene and AUDs (Dick & Beirut, 2006; Dick & Feroud, 2003). Because interaction between this gene and childhood adversity has been shown in a primate model of drinking (Barr et al., 2004), it seems possible that this gene, in combination with early stressors, predisposes individuals to alcohol-related problems later in life.

Due to the importance of the dopamine system to the rewarding properties of alcohol and other drugs of abuse, there has been interest in whether genotypes related to the dopamine system (e.g., polymorphisms related to dopamine receptors D_2 and D_4 and to the dopamine transporter) have also been linked to AUDs. Despite a number of findings associated with allelic variation in D_2 and, to a lesser extent, D_4 receptor genes, data in this area are inconsistent (Dick & Beirut, 2006).

It should also be noted that there is increasing evidence that one of the genes associated with the acetylcholine muscarinic receptor (CHRM2) is associated with a broad spectrum of pathology, including AUDs, other drug use disorders, and related nonsubstance pathology (Dick et al., 2008; Luo, Kranzler, Zuo, Wang, Blumberg, & Gelernter, 2005).

At present, a number of large-scale genome-wide association studies are under way that will likely reveal additional genes that are reliably associated with the AUD (or closely related) phenotypes. However, as is true for all psychological disorders (Kendler, 2005, 2006), it seems unlikely that any single gene will reveal a strong bivariate association with AUDs, given the long and complex causal chain between gene action and the manifestation of alcohol-related pathology (Kendler, 2005, 2006; Sher, 1991) and the failure of genome-wide scans to identify strong single-gene effects of complex disorders (Goldstein, 2009).

Environmental Factors Associated with Alcohol Use Disorders and Related Constructs

The range of potential environmental influences on the development of alcohol dependence is vast and ranges from the chemical environment (e.g., ethanol and other drug exposures) to broad social factors (e.g., cultural influences) to life-stage specific factors (e.g., various social roles that vary over the life course).

PRENATAL ALCOHOL EXPOSURE

From a developmental perspective, the first alcohol-related environment for the developing human is the womb. Prenatal alcohol exposure can cause fetal alcohol syndrome (FAS), which is a clinical syndrome characterized by growth retardation, facial dysmorphology, and CNS deficits, including tremors and visual irregularities (Larkby & Day 1997; Manning & Eugene-Hoyme, 2007). Studies examining school-aged outcomes for children affected by FAS reveal a range of cognitive and behavioral problems that often persist and/or worsen as children mature, leading to high rates of antisocial behavior and the development of AUDs (Baer, Sampson, Barr, Connor, & Streissguth, 2003; Streissguth et al. 1994; Steinhausen, Willms, & Spohr, 1993). These types of deficits and associated behavior problems are also common in children prenatally exposed to alcohol who are not diagnosed with full syndrome FAS (Streissguth, Barr, & Sampson, 1990; Testa, Quigley, & Eiden, 2003) but who have some subsyndromal spectrum disorder. Animal models suggest that fetal exposure to alcohol may lead to the development of specific drug sensitivities and preferences that may contribute to the development of AUDs (Abel, Bush, & Dintcheff, 1981; Dominguez, Lopez, & Molin, 1998; Osborn, Yu, Gabriel, & Weinberg, 1998).

ADOLESCENT ALCOHOL EXPOSURE

In addition to prenatal exposure to alcohol, there is increasing evidence to indicate that youthful exposure to alcohol may also be relevant to the development of AUDs. Accumulating evidence suggests that adolescents may be exquisitely sensitive to the neurotoxic effects of alcohol. Heavy exposure to alcohol in adolescence has been associated with structural and functional brain deficits, and also deficits in cognitive functioning (Clark, Thatcher, & Tapert, 2008; De Bellis et al., 2000; Hargreaves, Quinn, Kashem, Matsumoto, & McGregor, 2009; Tapert, Brown, Baratta, & Brown, 2004; Zeigler et al., 2005). The seemingly heightened sensitivity of the adolescent brain to alcohol-related insult is thought to be associated with neurodevelopmental vulnerability to the disruption of the normative extensive remodeling of the brain that takes place in adolescence (e.g., synaptic pruning; Clark, Thatcher, & Tapert, 2008). The associated neurocognitive deficits, especially those associated with deficits in executive functioning (Monti et al., 2005), could pose added risk for a range of externalizing behavior problems. Although a definite causal relation in humans has yet to be established, rodent models of adolescent ethanol exposure (Crews, Braun, Hoplight, Switzer, & Knapp, 2000; Spear, 2000; Swartzwelder, Wilson, & Tayyeb, 1995) demonstrate that adolescence appears to be a time of heightened sensitivity to persistent neurologic damage.

One of the most reliable findings in the epidemiology of AUDs is that early onset of drinking is associated with increased likelihood of developing an AUD (Grant & Dawson, 1997; Hingson, Heeren, & Winter, 2006). What is not clear is the extent that these findings represent a clear causal mechanism (perhaps because of increased sensitivity of the brain to alcohol or alcohol-related cues) or are an artifact of a common "third variable" associated with both early deviant behavior and the development of AUDs. Currently, the data are ambiguous, with some evidence suggesting that the early alcohol drinking $\rightarrow$ AUD link is a spurious effect of correlated conduct problems (Prescott & Kendler, 1999), although it is unclear if common third-variable causation is a sufficient explanation (McGue & Iacono, 2008; Odgers et al., 2008). Regardless of the mechanism of this association, early exposure, although associated with increased risk, does not appear to herald imminent alcohol dependence in younger adolescents. Indeed, Sartor, Lynskey, Heath, Jacob, and True (2007) and Hussong, Bauer, and Chassin (2008) found that, in early adulthood, earlier exposure is associated with longer duration from first drinking to dependence. This is likely due to limited opportunities for access and use in mid-adolescence, which constrains the dependence process (Sher, 2007).

PARENTAL INFLUENCE

Parental influences on drinking and AUDs are usually viewed along three dimensions: modeling, parenting practices (i.e., nurturance and control), and abuse and neglect.

Alcoholic parents have been thought to inadvertently model their problematic drinking to their children, so that these children may emulate their parents' behavior as they get older (Ellis, Zucker, & Fitzgerald, 1997). Although there is poorer psychosocial adjustment in children of alcoholics (COAs) whose parents are actively drinking heavily versus those who are abstinent (Andreas & O'Farrell, 2007), the extent to which parents' modeling increases the risk of later AUDs in COAs is unclear (Chassin, Pitts, DeLucia, & Todd, 1999). For example, adoption and children-of-twins studies tend to show little evidence of modeling. That is, rates of alcoholism in the adoptive COAs do not appear to be elevated (Hopfer, Crowley, & Hewitt, 2003), and the offspring of twin pairs (who are discordant for AUDs) are not statistically different in their risk for

AUDs after controlling for genetic and other environmental risk factors (Slutske et al., 2008).

Nonetheless, it might be less a matter of modeling and more a matter of general parenting practices that are of importance in considering the effects of parents on the development (or prevention) of AUDs. For example, parents who abuse alcohol are thought to demonstrate poor family management practices that are strongly linked with higher rates of internalizing and externalizing problems in children, such as lax and inconsistent discipline and inadequate supervision and monitoring. Also, poor parental monitoring puts children at risk for associating with substance-using peers. This peer association has been identified as a critical risk factor for early alcohol initiation and the development of alcohol problems (Hawkins, Catalano, & Miller, 1992). In addition to monitoring, a range of other familial factors have been found relevant to the familial transmission of AUDs. These include communication, cohesiveness, social support, parent and sibling attitudes toward alcohol use, familial conflict, parental loss through divorce or separation, disruption of family rituals, and unfair and harsh disciplinary practices (Leonard & Eiden, 2007).

In addition to these more general facets of parenting and their relation to the development of AUDs, child maltreatment and neglect are two risk factors for AUDs worth noting separately, given their increased severity as risk factors for a number of mental health issues. Child maltreatment is a correlate of substance use in families and poor parenting practices overall; thus, it is difficult to identify how maltreatment contributes to the development of AUDs beyond simply being an environmental risk factor (Lock & Newcomb, 2004). However, child neglect has been found to contribute to the development of AUDs by increasing children's vulnerability to being pressured by peers to use alcohol at early ages (Clark, Thatcher, & Maisto, 2004; Dunn et al., 2002; Leonard & Eiden, 2007).

PEER INFLUENCE

Peer influence is considered one of the strongest predictors of alcohol use, particularly in adolescence, with data suggesting near-perfect correlations between the alcohol use patterns of adolescent friends (Fowler et al., 2007). Peer influences on drinking may be stronger in adolescent girls than boys, although deviant peer associations have been found to exert influence on drinking behaviors in both boys and girls (Simons-Morton, Haynie, Crump, Eitel, & Saylor, 2001). This prompts the question of whether it is more often the case that peers socialize each other toward drinking behaviors, or whether it is more often that peers select into groups that are characterized by risky and heavy drinking behaviors (Sher, Grekin, & Williams, 2005). Data show that both selection and socialization effects are important aspects of peer influence on heavy drinking. Parental expectations moderate what types of peers children associate with and the amount to which the peers exert influence toward (or against) alcohol and substance use (Nash, McQueen, & Bray, 2005). As individuals move into adulthood, selection effects appear to become more important than socialization effects (Parra, Sher, Krull, & Jackson, 2007).

INTIMATE PARTNER INFLUENCE

Because of assortative mating, heavier drinkers (including those who are alcohol dependent) often marry heavier drinkers, and spouses appear to influence each others' drinking and likelihood of having an AUD (Leonard & Eiden, 2007). Earlier reports suggest that husbands' drinking prior to marriage increases the likelihood of wives' drinking in the first year of marriage (Leonard & Eiden, 1999), although wives' heavy drinking has a longitudinal predictive effect of husbands' heavy drinking later in the course of marriage (Leonard & Mudar, 2004). More recent evidence (Leonard & Homish, 2008) suggests that, for both husbands and wives, spousal heavy drinking, as well as post-marriage social networks (e.g., number of drinking buddies), are significant predictors of both partners' heavy drinking during the marriage. Decreased marital satisfaction and intimate partner violence are both causes and effects of heavy drinking in marriages, and heavy drinking has also typically been found to increase at the dissolution of a marriage (Leonard & Eiden, 2007). Further, higher levels of marital satisfaction appear to be protective against postmarital alcohol problems (Leonard & Homish, 2008). Thus, alcohol plays a role in the formation, maintenance, and dissolution of relationships, where inequalities in drinking between partners tend to forecast increases in discord in the relationship and continued or increased drinking. At a broader level, however, family systems' perspectives of alcoholism recognize decreases in heavy drinking, specifically when spouses become parents (Leonard & Eiden, 2007).

ADVERTISING AND MEDIA

Youth in the United States are heavily exposed to media promotions of alcohol. For example, it has been found that the average U.S. youth aged 10–14 years is exposed to, on average, 5.6 hours of alcohol use and 243.8 hours of alcohol brand appearances, mostly from the youth-rated movies that children report watching (Dal Cin, Worth, Dalton, & Sargent, 2008). The majority of media depictions of drinking show positive, rather than negative, consequences (Grube & Waiters, 2005). Thus, it is not surprising that modest associations have been found between exposure to television and magazine advertisements for beer and alcohol use in adolescents (Ellickson, Collins, Hambarsoomians, & McCaffrey, 2005). However, many studies are inconclusive, or show very weak effects (Grube & Waiters, 2005) and the extent to which advertising has a causal influence on consumption levels remains an area of controversy.

CULTURE

The prevalence of AUDs varies dramatically across nations and often equally dramatically across subcultural groups within countries. For example, a recent global status report on alcohol estimated the lifetime prevalence of alcohol dependence to be 0.2% in Egypt, 3.8% in China, 7.7% in the United States, 9.3% in Canada, 11.2% in Brazil, and 12.2% in Poland (World Health Organization, 2004). Perhaps due to this variation, culture has long been viewed an important correlate of the development of AUDs, as certain societal cultures appear to be more permissive of alcohol than others, or have drinking customs that might relate to the development of AUDS (Engs, 2001; MacAndrew & Edgerton, 1969).

Indeed, some have argued that one of the reasons that alcohol problems are so prevalent in the United States in comparison to certain Mediterranean countries (e.g., Italy) is that, in the United States, there is a 21-year-old minimum legal drinking age (MLDA). This restriction is thought to preempt the ability of youth to learn how to drink in a healthy way and thus creates a "forbidden fruit" phenomenon that leads to excess (Amethyst Initiative, 2008). However, recent research suggests rather comparable rates of drinking and alcohol problems in youth of different countries in Europe (which have lower MLDAs) and the United States (Grube, 2005), indicating that more research is necessary for understanding just how societal culture might play a role in the etiology of AUDs. In particular, with respect to effects of culture, the extent that alcohol is viewed as a drug versus a foodstuff or that intoxication represents a socially sanctioned "time out" from normal roles and responsibilities (MacAndrew & Edgerton, 1969) may be much more important than the age at which it is legal to consume alcohol (Heath, 1995).

Psychological Individual Differences in Risk for Alcohol Use Disorders

The genetic data cited earlier clearly indicate that there are important individual differences in susceptibility to AUDs. Some of this variability appears to be related to how ethanol and its metabolites are processed by individuals (e.g., pharmacokinetics). However, the link between AUDs and genes associated with major motivational systems suggests that some of these genetic effects are mediated by what are traditionally thought of as motivational and personality processes. Psychological individual difference variables that have been implicated in AUD etiology are wide ranging and include neurocognitive processing, personality-related vulnerabilities, and alcohol expectancies and motives for use.

Neurocognitive Deficits

Deficits in executive cognitive functioning (e.g., the regulation of goal-directed behavior, control of attention, planning, and cognitive flexibility) are associated with increased risk for AUDs (Giancola & Tarter, 1999). Such deficits are in evidence in children at elevated risk for alcoholism (Nigg et al., 2004). One particular endophenotypic measure of a neurocognitive deficit is reduced P300 amplitude, an electrophysiological index of inhibitory control. P300 amplitude has consistently been shown to be characteristic of individuals at high risk for AUDs (e.g., COAs) and is strongly associated with early-onset AUDs (Carlson, Iacono, & McGue, 2002; Carlson, McLarnon, & Iacono, 2007; Iacono, 1998), at least in boys and young men.

Personality

Personality traits have long been considered an important feature of psychological theories of alcoholism. However, despite the apparent conceptual appeal of an "addictive personality," decades of empirical research have failed to identify a unique constellation of personality traits that characterize alcoholics. Rather, broad-based personality constructs appear to have etiologic relevance to alcohol abuse and dependence, particularly within the context of larger psychosocial models (Sher, Trull, Bartholow, & Vieth, 1999). Three broad-band personality dimensions have received particular attention: Neuroticism/emotionality, impulsivity/disinhibition, and extraversion/sociability. For example, alcoholics exhibit significant elevations on measures of neuroticism/emotionality (Barnes, 1979, 1983; Sher et al., 1999), and many prospective studies have found neuroticism/emotionality to be predictive of subsequent alcohol involvement (Caspi et al., 1997; Chassin, Curran, Hussong, & Colder, 1996; Cloninger, Sigvardsson, & Bohman, 1988; Labouvie, Pandina, White, & Johnson, 1990; Sieber, 1981).

Impulsive/disinhibited traits appear to be some of the most etiologically significant personality dimensions for alcohol use and misuse, including such constructs as sensation seeking, aggressiveness, impulsivity, psychoticism, and novelty seeking (Sher & Trull, 1994). Prospective studies consistently indicate that traits such as aggression, conduct problems, impulsivity, unconventionality, and novelty seeking are strongly associated with the development of alcohol misuse, as well as with other forms of substance misuse (Bates & Labouvie, 1995; Caspi et al., 1997; Cloninger et al., 1988; Hawkins et al., 1992; Pederson, 1991; Schuckit, 1998; Zucker, Fitzgerald, & Moses, 1995). Whiteside and Lynam (2001) utilized factor analyses to identify four distinct personality facets associated with impulsive-like behavior: sensation seeking, lack of planning, lack of persistence, and urgency (acting rashly when distressed). Further work has distinguished among positive and negative urgency (Cyders, Smith, Spillane, Fischer, Annus, & Peterson, 2007), resulting in five personality facets of impulsivity. These facets were shown to account for different aspects of risky behaviors. Sensation seeking appeared to relate to the *frequency* of engaging in risky behaviors, including drinking-related behaviors, whereas urgency (particularly positive urgency, the tendency to act rashly while in a positive mood, see Cyders, Flory, Rainer, & Smith, 2009) appeared to relate to *problem levels* of involvement in those behaviors (e.g., Smith, Fischer, Cyders, Annus, Spillane, & McCarthy, 2007; see Cyders & Smith, 2008).

Although extraversion/sociability is considered a major personality dimension, reviews of the literature suggest that extraversion/sociability does not reliably distinguish alcoholic and nonalcoholic individuals (Barnes, 1983; Sher et al., 1999). However, there is some evidence from longitudinal studies to suggest that extraversion/sociability predict subsequent alcohol misuse (Jones, 1968; Kilbey, Downey, & Breslau, 1998; Sieber, 1981). Recent research (Park, Sher, Krull, & Wood, 2009) suggests that extraversion may be relevant to heavy consumption in late adolescence and early adulthood in that it is related to affiliation with certain types of highly sociable groups (e.g., Greek societies on college campuses) that often represent heavy drinking environments.

Alcohol Outcome Expectancies

Another important aspect of psychological vulnerability is alcohol outcome expectancies. Alcohol outcome expectancies can be defined as beliefs that people have about the affective, cognitive, and behavioral effects of drinking alcohol (Goldman, Brown, & Christiansen, 1987). Goldman, Del Boca, and Darkes (1999) suggest that outcome expectancies can be categorized along three basic dimensions: (a) positive versus negative expected outcomes (e.g., increased sociability versus increased aggressiveness), (b) positive versus negative reinforcement (e.g., social facilitation versus tension reduction), and (c) arousal versus sedation (e.g., stimulant versus depressant effects). Associations have been consistently found in cross-sectional studies between alcohol expectancies and both drinking behavior and drinking problems among children (Anderson et al., 2005; Dunn & Goldman, 2000), adolescents (Dunn & Goldman, 2000; Fromme & D'Amico, 2000), college students (Christiansen, Vik, & Jarchow, 2002; Palfai & Wood, 2001; Read, Wood, Lejuez, Palfai, & Slack, 2004) and adults (Lee, Greeley, & Oei, 1999; Pastor & Evans, 2003). These studies suggest that drinking behavior is positively associated with positive outcome expectancies (assessed both individually and as a composite) and negatively associated with negative outcome expectancies (assessed both individually and as a composite). Moreover, these associations are robust across a variety of drinking patterns and remain significant (although weaker) after controlling for demographics and previous drinking behavior (Carey, 1995; Jones, Corbin, & Fromme, 2001). Outcome expectancies tend to develop in childhood (Anderson et al., 2005; Christiansen, Goldman, & Inn, 1982; Dunn & Goldman, 2000; Jones, Corbin, & Fromme, 2001; Miller, Smith, & Goldman, 1990), strengthen during adolescence (Smith, Goldman, Greenbaum, & Christiansen, 1995), and weaken during early adulthood (presumably following extended experience with drinking; Sher, Wood, Wood, & Raskin, 1996). Moreover, several prospective studies demonstrate that expectancies uniquely predict future drinking over extended time periods (Kilbey, Downey, & Breslau, 1998; Leonard & Mudar, 2000; Sher et al., 1996; Smith et al., 1995;

Stacy, Newcomb, & Bentler, 1991). Although both cross-sectional and longitudinal studies suggest associations between expectancies and alcohol use, they do not necessarily implicate a causal relationship.

Longitudinal research (e.g., Sher et al., 1996) suggests reciprocal relations between alcohol outcome expectancies and drinking. Somewhat surprisingly, the question of how individual differences in alcohol expectancies relate to individual differences in alcohol effects has not yet been systematically explored (Sher, Wood, Richardson, & Jackson, 2005). However, recent research focusing on individuals who possess different genotypes associated with ALDH (e.g., Hahn et al., 2006), dopamine, and GABA receptors (e.g., Young, Lawford, Feeney, Ritchie, & Noble, 2004) suggests that pharmacogenomic interactions between ethanol and specific genotypes can contribute to individual differences in alcohol expectancies.

In recent years, there has been increasing interest in implicit cognitive processes and how they relate to alcohol involvement (Wiers & Stacy, 2006). In contrast to explicit alcohol expectancies, which are assessed by self-report questionnaires and assume that these expectancies are conscious, implicit expectancies are assessed by any of a variety of behavioral tasks that are assumed to be automatic and largely unconscious. Both of these levels of cognition are thought to act in concert in "dual-process" models. Dual-process models predict that both more reflective explicit and more reflexive, automatic implicit cognitive processes influence behavior (e.g., Fazio & Towles-Schwen, 1999). Implicit alcohol-related cognitions (e.g., implicit alcohol expectancies) are thought to represent individual differences in memory associations between alcohol-related cues, outcomes, and behavior (Thush, Wiers, Ames, Grenard, Sussman, & Stacy, 2008). Recent work has provided support for the utility of a range of assessments (e.g., Implicit Association Test; Greenwald, Nosek, & Banaji, 2003) of implicit alcohol-related cognitions by showing that these measures predict drinking behavior over and above the prediction afforded by explicit measures of similar constructs (e.g., Thush & Wiers, 2007). Dual-process models of addiction also posit that controlled self-regulatory processes interact with both implicit and explicit expectancies (e.g., Thush et al., 2008).

Motivations for Use
Individuals report a range of motives for consuming alcohol, and factor analyses of self-reported reasons

for drinking reliably yield a multidimensional, four-factor structure (Cooper, 1994) that can be described as (1) social motives (e.g., "to be sociable"), (2) enhancement motives (e.g., "to get high," "because it's fun"), (3) coping motives (e.g., "to forget your worries," "because it helps when you feel depressed or nervous"), and (4) conformity motives (e.g., "to fit in"). Notably, enhancement and coping motives (but not social or conformity motives) are strongly associated with drinking, heavy drinking, and drinking problems in both adolescents and adults (Cooper, 1994; Cooper, Frone, Russell, & Mudar, 1995). A growing body of literature indicates that the personality traits of extraversion and sensation-seeking tend to correlate with enhancement motives, and the personality traits of neuroticism tend to correlate with coping motives (Kuntsche, Knibbe, Gmel, & Engels, 2006). Notably, traits related to impulsivity have been linked to both coping and enhancement motives (Cooper, Agocha, & Sheldon, 2000; Littlefield, Sher, & Wood, 2010). These findings point to specific motivational pathways arising from individual differences in temperamental/personality traits and, thus, link broad dispositional traits to alcohol etiology.

Multiple Etiological Pathways
The literature on alcohol use motivations documents that AUDs are clearly multifactorial disorders and that there appear to be multiple pathways leading to the manifestation of an AUD (i.e., equifinality). These pathways are discussed below: *pharmacological vulnerability, general externalizing behavior,* and *affect regulation.* It is important to highlight the fact that these different pathways are not mutually exclusive and are likely additive or superadditive. In addition, they likely share common elements and so some constructs, such as executive functioning, could relate to all three of the pathways considered.

Pharmacological Vulnerability
The Pharmacological Vulnerability model (Sher, 1991) proposes that individuals differ in their responses to the acute and/or chronic effects of alcohol and that these individual differences are etiologically relevant. The model itself incorporates several submodels that would appear to offer opposing predictions. For example, it can be hypothesized that some individuals are at risk for alcohol-related difficulties because they are especially sensitive to reinforcement (either positive or negative) and are therefore more likely to use alcohol because they get a comparatively greater

effect from it (e.g., Finn & Pihl, 1987; Levenson, Oyama, & Meek, 1987). Alternatively, it can be hypothesized that some individuals are relatively insensitive to alcohol (either reinforcing or punishing effects). Such insensitivity can lead someone to higher consumption levels, either because he or she is seeking reinforcement or is less likely to be inhibited by punishing effects. These higher consumption levels are posited to increase the likelihood of inducing dependence processes (e.g., Schuckit & Smith, 2000).

Generalized Externalizing Behavior

Another perspective on AUD etiology is that it is just one manifestation of the types of generalized externalizing behavior problems that first appear in childhood and adolescence (e.g., Achenbach & Edelbrock, 1978; Jessor & Jessor, 1977). As noted earlier, there is a strong genetic correlation between conduct disorder and alcohol dependence (e.g., Slutske et al., 1998). Additionally, prospective studies indicate, for men (and probably for women), that early conduct problems predict subsequent alcohol and drug disorders and antisocial personality disorder (Hawkins, Catalano, & Miller, 1992; Nathan, 1988; Zucker & Gomberg, 1986). Factor analytic approaches to psychopathology indicate that all externalizing disorders (e.g., conduct disorder, adult antisocial behavior, drug use disorders, and AUDs) are highly correlated and form a distinct psychopathological factor of "externalizing disorder," with common personality correlates (e.g., Krueger et al., 2005; Krueger & Markon, 2006, 2008). Although popular models of generalized externalizing behavior (e.g., Jessor, Donovan, & Costa, 1991; Patterson, Reid, & Dishion, 1992) tend to highlight the importance of parenting and deviant peer groups, both twin studies (e.g., Slutske et al., 1998) and molecular genetics studies (e.g., Dick, 2007) suggest that common genetic influences are also contributing factors.

Affect Regulation

Another critical pathway involves using alcohol as an *affect regulation* strategy. Although the "self-medication" (e.g., Khantzian, 1985) view of the etiology of AUDs is widely held by both the lay public and many clinicians, the research literature indicates that alcohol can have variable effects on emotions and many, if not most, individuals do not drink to regulate negative moods. Some survey studies have found significant positive associations between stress and alcohol consumption and misuse (e.g., Cooper,

Russell, Skinner, Frone, & Mudar, 1992; Scheier, Botvin, & Miller, 1999). Findings indicate that the association is stronger and more consistent with alcohol problems than alcohol consumption (McCreary & Sadava, 2000), suggesting the alcohol–stress relation is more relevant for pathological drinkers. However, many studies find small or nonexistent relationships (Perreira & Sloan, 2001; Rohsenow, 1982; Welte & Mirand, 1995). Moreover, some research suggests that much of the alcohol–stressful event relation can be attributed to aversive events that directly result from drinking (e.g., losing a job due to alcohol use; Hart & Fazaa, 2004; O'Doherty, 1991).

Perhaps most critically, the research literature suggests that the alcohol–stress relation is highly conditional upon many factors such as individuals' coping styles, beliefs about the utility of alcohol as a coping device, and the availability of alternative coping strategies, among other things (e.g., Sher & Grekin, 2007). As noted earlier, individuals higher in neuroticism/negative affectivity tend to report drinking to regulate negative moods, and the endorsement of such reasons for drinking suggest a high likelihood for both heavy consumption and alcohol-related problems (Kuntsch et al., 2006). In addition, the literature on psychiatric comorbidity (discussed later) indicates that individuals with high levels of negative affect (as indicated by mood and anxiety disorder) are at high risk for the development of AUDs and, thus, directly implicates negative affect regulation as an important pathway into AUDs.

Psychiatric and Medical Comorbidity

Individuals who have AUDs frequently have multiple psychiatric diagnoses, as well as various medical illnesses. Given the focus of this volume, we do not consider the myriad health-damaging (and some health-promoting effects) of alcohol consumption in any depth but do bring attention to this issue because it has important implications for providing adequate health services to those individuals who have problematic alcohol use and AUDs.

Psychiatric Comorbidity

Individuals with AUDs are more than twice as likely to exhibit another psychiatric disorder than are persons without an alcohol abuse/dependence diagnosis (Regier et al., 1990), but the nature of these beyond-chance associations is difficult to assess. For example, (a) AUD can be secondary to a primary psychiatric disorder, (b) a psychiatric disorder can be secondary to primary AUD, (c) both disorders could arise from a common diathesis or underlying vulnerability, (d) bidirectional influence can occur, and (e) overlapping diagnostic criteria can create artifactual associations (Clark, Watson, & Reynolds, 1995; Schuckit, Irwin, & Brown, 1990; see Sher & Trull, 1996). Notably, comorbidity rates vary according to the population sampled, the diagnostic approach employed, the specific comorbid condition under consideration, gender, and the extent of other drug use (Ross, Glaser, & Stiasny, 1988; NIAAA, 1993). Here, the comorbidity of AUDs with drug use disorders, mood/anxiety disorders, and personality disorders is discussed.

DRUG USE DISORDERS

Perhaps not surprisingly, drug use disorders are the conditions that are most comorbid with AUDs. Although the co-occurrence of substance (alcohol or drug) use disorders (i.e., homotypic comorbidity) has been well documented in a number of large-scale surveys (e.g., the ECA Survey; Helzer, Burnam, & McEnvoy, 1991; Robins & Price 1991; NCS; Kessler, Crum, Warner, & Nelson, 1997; Kessler et al., 1994; NLAES; Grant, 1997; Grant, Harford, Dawson, Chou, et al., 1994; Grant & Pickering, 1996), only recently have data been published regarding the 12-month comorbidity of AUDs and drug use disorders in the general U.S. population. As shown in Table 20.1, data from Stinson et al. (2005) suggest that individuals with drug use disorders, compared to controls, have significantly higher odds to meet criteria for an AUD. The magnitude of these associations are especially noteworthy, as illustrated by the strong association between cocaine dependence and AUDs (OR = 43.0, 95% CI = 17.83–103.49). The high comorbidity among substance use disorders is important clinically in that it is often the case that the treatment of AUD is complicated by the presence of other substance use, abuse, and dependence. This comorbidity is also important etiologically because it suggests that there may be common causes or influences across diverse forms of substance use disorders.

However, data suggest (Stinson et al., 2005) that sociodemographic and psychopathologic correlates differ between individuals who (a) only meet criteria for AUDs (AUD-only), (b) only meet criteria for drug use disorders (drug use disorder [DUD]-only), and (c) meet criteria for both AUDs and drug use disorders (comorbid AUD/DUD). Compared to the AUD-only group, DUD-only and comorbid AUD/DUD individuals are more likely to be young,

Table 20.1 Adjusted odds ratios of 12-month DSM-IV alcohol use disorder and 12-month specific drug use disorders

Drug use disorder	OR (95% CI)b
Any drug use disorder	7.4 (6.00–9.03)
Any drug abuse	5.7 (4.49–7.30)
Any drug dependence	9.9 (6.47–15.01)
Sedative use disorder	3.4 (1.89–6.29)
Sedative abuse	5.3 (2.44–11.31)
Sedative dependence	1.8 (0.65–4.93)
Tranquilizer use disorder	5.7 (2.55–12.69)
Tranquilizer abuse	7.1 (2.52–20.17)
Tranquilizer dependence	4.0 (1.30–12.16)
Opioid use disorder	7.7 (5.18–11.41)
Opioid abuse	6.1 (3.76–9.91)
Opioid dependence	12.9 (6.18–26.89)
Amphetamine use disorder	8.8 (4.24–18.29)
Amphetamine abuse	5.2 (2.14–12.59)
Amphetamine dependence	20.3 (6.18–66.94)
Hallucinogen use disorder	12.8 (5.18–31.49)
Hallucinogen abuse	10.7 (4.24–26.80)
Hallucinogen dependence	–c
Cannabis use disorder	6.8 (5.36–8.75)
Cannabis abuse	6.2 (4.80–7.90)
Cannabis dependence	7.3 (3.92–13.72)
Cocaine use disorder	19.2 (10.71–34.56)
Cocaine abuse	10.5 (4.85–22.56)
Cocaine dependence	43.0 (17.83–103.49)
Solvent/inhalant abuse	3.6 (0.52–25.82)

[a] Odds ratios adjusted for sociodemographic factors, any personality disorder, any 12-month independent mood disorder and any independent anxiety disorder.
[b] 95% CI: 95% confidence interval.
[c] Unable to calculate OR because all respondents with hallucinogen dependence also had an alcohol use disorder.
Data taken from the National Epidemiologic Survey on Alcohol and Related Conditions (Stinson et al. 2005). Reprinted from *Drug and Alcohol Dependence*, 80, Stinson, F.S., Grant, B.F., Dawson, D.A., Ruan, W.J., Huang, B., & Saha, T., Comorbidity between *DSM-IV* alcohol and specific drug use disorders in the United States: Results from the National Epidemiologic Survey on Alcohol and Related Conditions, Copyright 2005, with permission from Elsevier.

male, never married, and of lower socioeconomic status. Furthermore, compared to the DUD-only group, comorbid AUD/DUD individuals were more likely to be male, young, and never married. Additionally, individuals in the AUD-only group were more likely to be white, 30–64 years old, and of higher socioeconomic status compared to those in the DUD-only and comorbid AUD/DUD groups, whereas blacks were over-represented in the DUD-only group when compared to those in the AUD-only group. Regarding treatment, individuals with comorbid AUD/DUD were more likely to seek treatment (21.76%) compared to DUD-only (15.63%) or AUD-only (6.06%) individuals, suggesting that combinations of alcohol and drug treatment services, as well as prevention and intervention efforts, may be profitable strategies for the management of substance use disorders. However, the study also revealed a new finding: AUD/DUD comorbidity did not significantly increase the likelihood of mood, anxiety, and personality disorder comorbidity above that found among DUD-only individuals. This intriguing finding warrants further study and replication (Stinson et al., 2005).

Alcohol use most commonly co-occurs with tobacco use (e.g., Jackson, Sher, & Schulenberg, 2005). As noted by Jackson et al. (2005), individuals with AUDs are more likely to smoke than individuals without AUDs (e.g., Martin, Kaczynski, Maisto, & Tarter, 1996); social drinkers are more likely to smoke than nondrinkers (Istvan & Matarazzo, 1984); and individuals with diagnosable tobacco use disorder exhibit greater risk for AUDs (Breslau, 1995). Further, concurrent alcohol and tobacco use appears to interact synergistically to produce elevated health risks (Bien & Burge, 1990), including oral (Blot et al., 1988), laryngeal (Flanders & Rothman, 1982), and esophageal (Muñoz & Day, 1996) cancers. Using nationally representative, prospective, multiwave data, Jackson et al. (2005) utilized a conjoint, developmental approach to examine alcohol–tobacco comorbidity, and identified seven co-occurring trajectories of alcohol and tobacco use. Associations between trajectory classes and risk factors were relatively unique to the substance being predicted. For example, the association of smoking with alcohol expectances and delinquency appeared to be attributed to smoking's comorbidity with drinking. These findings illustrate the ability of conjoint, developmental trajectory approaches to provide information regarding AUDs' co-occurrence with other psychiatric disorders that would otherwise remain "masked" by separately examining predictors of AUDs and other disorders. Such an approach could be applied to examine AUDs' co-occurrence with other substances (e.g., marijuana; Jackson, Sher, & Schulenberg, 2008) as well as other psychiatric disorders (e.g., mood and anxiety disorders, personality disorders [PD]).

MOOD AND ANXIETY DISORDERS

As with AUDs, mood and anxiety disorders are among the most prevalent psychiatric disorders in the United States, with prevalences of any 12-month DSM-IV independent mood (e.g., major depression) and anxiety (e.g., generalized anxiety disorder) disorders in the U.S. population estimated at 9.21% and 11.08%, respectively (Grant et al., 2004). Moreover, AUDs and independent mood and anxiety disorders commonly co-occur. Statistical associations between AUDs and independent mood and anxiety disorders are consistently positive and significant, with alcohol dependence exhibiting larger associations to both mood and anxiety disorders than alcohol abuse (see Grant et al., 2004). Alcohol use disorders also tend to exhibit stronger relations with independent mood disorders than with anxiety disorders. Further, of individuals with a current AUD who sought treatment during the same period, approximately 41% and 33% had a least one current independent mood or anxiety disorder, respectively (Grant et al., 2004), suggesting that mood and anxiety disorders should be addressed by substance abuse treatment providers.

At least one explanation of the significant co-occurrence between AUDs and mood/anxiety disorders are affect regulation models (see earlier discussion) that posit that individuals may be motivated to use alcohol in order to regulate negative and/or anxious emotions commonly associated with depression and anxiety. However, it should be noted that the relation between AUDs and mood/anxiety disorders is complex, and only a fraction of individuals with AUDs have a history of anxiety disorders (Schuckit & Hesselbrock, 2004). Indeed, in the NESARC data, only approximately 19% and 17% of individuals with a past-year AUD diagnosed with at least one mood and anxiety disorder, respectively. Thus, although individuals with an AUD are also more likely to diagnose with a mood or anxiety disorder compared to the general population, only a minority of individuals with AUDs experience co-occurring mood/anxiety disorder, suggesting that other factors (e.g., severity of AUD, motivation for alcohol use) may contribute to the likelihood of the co-occurrence of AUDs with mood/anxiety disorders.

PERSONALITY DISORDERS

In the *Diagnosis and Statistical Manual of Mental Disorders, Fourth Edition, Text Revision* (DSM-IV-TR), PDs are organized into three clusters—A, B, and C—based on descriptive similarities. Cluster A (characterized as odd or eccentric) includes paranoid, schizoid, and schizotypal PDs. Cluster B (dramatic, emotional, erratic PDs) includes antisocial, borderline, histrionic, and narcissistic. Cluster C (fearful, anxious PDs) includes avoidant, dependent, and obsessive-compulsive PDs. Although several studies have examined the prevalence of PDs (notably antisocial PD) among individuals with AUDs (e.g., Verheul, van den Brink, & Hartgers, 1995; see Sher & Trull, 2002; Trull, Sher, Minks-Brown, Durbin, & Burr, 2000), it is only recently that data have become available that systematically documents the co-occurrence of different PDs with

AUDs in the general population. Data from NESARC (Grant, Hasin, et al. 2004; Grant, Chou, Goldstein, Huang, Stinson, Saha, et al.,2008; Trull et al., in press) indicates that the co-occurrence of PDs with AUDs is pervasive in the U.S. population. As shown in Table 20.2, individuals with alcohol dependence are at increased risk to also meet diagnosis for a number of PDs, especially the Cluster B PDs such as antisocial, borderline, and histrionic PD. The strong relation between AUDs and Cluster B PDs is not surprising, given the association between impulsivity (see the earlier "Personality" section) and affective instability and the Cluster B PDs (see Trull et al., 2000).

Although several models explain the comorbidity between SUDs and PDs (see Sher & Trull, 2002; Trull et al., 2000), some research suggests that the development of PDs predicts the development of

Table 20.2 Odds Ratio (and 95% confidence interval) of document Personality Disorders (PDs) and Alcohol Dependence in the NESARC

Personality Disorder	NESARC – Original	NESARC – Strict
Any PD	3.58(3.44–3.73)	5.01(4.76–5.26)
Cluster A		
Paranoid	3.75(3.47–4.05)	4.53(4.11–4.99)
Schizoid	2.96(2.72–3.22)	4.30(3.70–4.99)
Schizotypal	3.12(2.87–3.39)	4.13(3.68–4.63)
Cluster B		
Antisocial (Wave 1)	7.76(7.26–8.30)	7.76 (7.26–8.30)
Antisocial (Wave 2)	6.80(6.33–7.31)	6.80(6.33–7.31)
Borderline	4.51(4.26–4.77)	5.37(5.02–5.75)
Histrionic	5.30(4.77–5.90)	6.98(5.79–8.42)
Narcissistic	2.65(2.52–2.79)	3.61(3.15–4.14)
Cluster C		
Avoidant	3.33(2.99–3.71)	3.84(3.39–4.35)
Dependent	3.34(2.67–4.19)	2.73(2.07–3.60)
Obsessive–compulsive	2.60(2.46–2.75)	3.38(3.13–3.64)

NESARC-Original refers to comorbidity estimates based upon the original scoring algorithms in the NESARC and NESARC-Revised refers to estimates based upon the more stringent requirement that each criterial personality disorder symptom be associated with impairment. Schizotypal, Borderline, and Narcissistic PD were assessed at Wave 2 only, Antisocial PD at Waves 1 and 2, and all other PDs assessed at Wave 1 only.

These data are drawn from Grant, B. F., Chou, S. P., Goldstein, R. B., Huang, B., Stinson, F. S., Saha, T. D., Smith, S. M., et al. (2008). Prevalence, correlates, disability, and comorbidity of DSM-IV borderline personality disorder: Results from the wave 2 National Epidemiological Survey on Alcohol and Related Conditions. *Journal of Clinical Psychiatry, 69,* 533-545; Grant, B. F., Hasin, D. S., Stinson, F. S., Dawson, D. A., Chou, S. P., Ruan, W. J., & Pickering, R. P. (2004). Prevalence correlates and disability of personality disorders in the *United States: Results from the National Epidemiological Survey on Alcohol and Related Conditions. Journal of Clinical Psychiatry, 65,* 948-958; Trull, T. J., Jahng, S., Tomko, R., Wood, P. K., & Sher, K. J. (in press). Revised NESARC Personality Disorder Diagnoses: Gender, Prevalence, and Comorbidity with Substance Dependence Disorders. *Journal of Personality Disorders.*

SUDs, including alcohol abuse and dependency symptoms (Cohen, Chen, Crawford, Brook, & Gordon, 2007; Stepp, Trull, & Sher, 2005), whereas other data suggest that adolescent AUDs predict later PDs (e.g., Thatcher, Cornelius, & Clark, 2005). With the perspective that certain PDs reflect extreme expressions of common personality traits (e.g., Widiger & Trull, 2007), recent research has posited and empirically examined drinking motives (see the earlier "Motivations for Use" section) as mediators in the relation between PD symptoms and AUDs. Several studies (Tragesser, Sher, Trull, & Park, 2007; Tragesser, Trull, Sher, & Park, 2008) suggest that enhancement (but not coping) motives mediate the relation between AUDs and PD symptoms, especially in regard to Cluster B PDs. These findings suggest that treatment of comorbid AUDs and PDs should focus on both developing strategies for positive emotion regulation and maintenance, as well as on interventions aimed at managing features related to impulsive/sensation-seeking personality traits (Tragesser et al., 2008).

Medical Consequences

Alcohol affects virtually all major organ systems, and considerable medical morbidity and mortality is directly related to alcohol consumption (Rehm, Room, Graham, Monteiro, Gmel, & Sempos, 2003) from both diseases (including cardiovascular diseases, gastrointestinal diseases, cancer) and injury (both intentional and unintentional; Rehm, Greenfield, & Rogers, 2001; Rehm et al., 2003). Given the clinical psychology focus of this volume, we discuss two of these areas that are important with respect to the role of behavior: neurological disease and injury.

NEUROLOGICAL DISEASE

Acute alcohol consumption has numerous effects on the brain (Peterson, Rothfleisch, Zelazo, & Pihl, 1990), including "blackouts" (a period of time when recollection is impaired; Vinson, 1989). Although alcoholic blackouts have been thought to be an important early sign of alcoholism, research suggests that blackouts only modestly predict future AUDs (e.g., Anthenelli, Klein, Tsuang, Smith, & Schuckit, 1994) and that alcohol-induced blackouts are relatively common, especially among college students (Wechsler, Dowdall, Maenner, Gledhill-Hoyt, & Lee, 1998).

There is little evidence of any lingering impairment in neuropsychological tests following acute intoxication (Lemon, Chesher, Fox, Greeley, & Nabke, 1993; see Yesavage, Dolhert, & Taylor, 1994 for an exception), and most studies show little apparent effect among those who drink infrequently or moderately (Hebert et al., 1993; Parker, Parker, & Harford, 1991), especially when baseline neuropsychological performance is controlled (Arbuckle, Chaikelson, & Gold, 1994). However, neuropsychological impairment becomes increasingly likely with heavier drinking patterns (>21 standard drinks/week; Parsons & Nixon, 1998). Moreover, increasing evidence suggests that adolescents may be at especially high risk for alcohol-related neuropsychological impairments, perhaps because of the rapid rate of neurodevelopment occurring during this stage of life (Monti et al., 2005).

Despite these findings, alcoholism is associated with chronic brain diseases, such as Wernicke encephalopathy (characterized by neurological signs such as ataxia, nystagmus, and confusion) and Korsakoff psychosis (a combination of retrograde and anterograde amnesia; Victor, 1993, 1994). Wernicke and Korsakoff syndromes typically co-occur and are thought to be due to nutritional deficiency related to alcoholism rather than the direct toxic effects of alcohol itself (Victor, 1993). Some symptoms of Wernicke-Korsakoff syndrome will resolve with improved nutrition and abstinence from alcohol, although the amnesia (classic Korsakoff syndrome) will resolve in only about 20% of patients (Victor, 1993). Further, predicting which patients with Wernicke-Korsakoff syndrome will improve is difficult (Berglund, 1991).

Ischemic strokes, in which blood flow to a part of the brain is stopped by a clot within an artery, and hemorrhagic strokes, in which bleeding in or around the brain occurs, are differentially related to alcohol. The association between alcohol and ischemic stroke risk appears to be J-shaped (Sacco et al., 1999), whereas the risk of hemorrhagic stroke increases monotonically with increasing alcohol consumption (Carmargo, Jr. 1989; Gorelick, 1989; Klatsky, Armstrong, & Friedman, 1989).

As noted in a recent review, the study of alcohol's effect on sleep dates back to the late 1930s (Roehrs & Roth, 2001). An extensive literature has been amassed since that time suggesting that alcohol has notable effects on sleep as well as daytime sleepiness. Acute high alcohol doses disturb the sleep in healthy subjects, but lower doses of alcohol appear to be beneficial for insomniacs. However, tolerance to alcohol's sedative effects can develop rapidly, resulting in potentially excessive hypnotic use and, for insomniacs, potentially excessive daytime use (Roehrs & Roth, 2001). Further, recent prospective studies suggest that initial sleep problems are a risk factor for subsequent AUD onset and other alcohol-related consequences (Crum, Storr, Chan, & Ford, 2004; Wong, Brower, Fitzgerald, & Zucker, 2004). Additionally, results suggest that individuals with sleep disturbances and co-occurring anxiety disorders or dysphoria are at the highest risk to develop alcohol-related problems (Crum et al., 2004).

INJURY

Acute alcohol consumption also contributes to unintended and intended alcohol-related injuries. Vehicular crashes are some of the most common unintentional alcohol-related injuries, and indeed, it is estimated that approximately half of traffic deaths in college-age youth in the United States are alcohol-related (see Hingson, Heeren, Winter, & Wechsler, 2005; Rehm et al., 2003). Other unintentional injuries occur as a result of falling, fires, sports activities, being hit by or against something, being cut/pierced, overdosing, or being poisoned—all of which can happen repeatedly to individuals (Rehm et al., 2003; Watt, Purdie, Roche, & McClure, 2006). For example, there is some evidence that recurrent traumatic brain injuries are associated with the first injury being alcohol-related (Winqvist, Luukinen, Jokelainen, Lehtilahti, Näyhä, & Hillbom, 2008).

Intentional alcohol-related injuries include self-inflicted injuries and homicides, with self-inflicted injuries being more common (Rehm et al., 2003). With regard to suicide, alcohol has been found to be involved in 10%–69% of completed suicides, and 10%–73% of suicide attempts (within literature published between 1991 and 2001; Cherpitel, Borges, & Wilcox, 2004). Homicides in which alcohol is involved are most likely to occur with the concurrent availability of firearms. Although stabbing and strangling are similarly common alcohol-related acts of violence, they are generally less fatal than alcohol-related shooting (Eckhardt & Pridemore, 2009; Roberts, 2009).

Assessment
Diagnostic Interviews

In the United States, several diagnostic interviews have been used to assess AUDs and other disorders, as they are defined by the DSM-IV of the American Psychiatric Association (1994). These include the Diagnostic Interview Schedule Version IV (DIS-IV: Robins, Cottler, Bucholz, & Compton, 1996), the Composite International Diagnostic Interview (WHO CIDI: Version 3.0: Kessler and Üstün, 2004), the Alcohol Use Disorder and Associated Disabilities

Interview Schedule-IV (AUDADIS-IV: Grant and Dawson, 2000), the Semi-Structured Assessment for the Genetics of Alcoholism (SSAGA), and the Structured Clinical Interview for DSM-IV (SCID: First, Spitzer, Gibbon, & Williams, 2002).

Grant, Dawson, Stinson, Chou, Kay, and Pickering (2003) assessed the test–retest reliability of selected DSM-IV diagnoses as well as (among others) modules for alcohol consumption, and alcohol abuse and dependence appearing in the National Institute on Alcohol Abuse and Alcoholism's (NIAAA) website. Based on their findings, Grant et al. (2003) suggest that alcohol consumption exhibited "good to excellent" reliability (Intraclass Correlation [ICC] = 0.69–0.84) whereas alcohol abuse and dependence exhibited "good reliability" (past-year diagnosis: κ = .74). Despite the high reliability associated with these interviews, a number of practical drawbacks exist, such as the personnel and time required for data gathering, leading researchers to employ other assessments, such as questionnaires.

Assessment of Consumption

Drinking questionnaires account for the variation in drinking styles by focusing on both drinking frequency and quantity of consumption on a given drinking occasion. Because many individuals exhibit high intraindividual variability in drinking quantity, some researchers measure volume/variability, in order to resolve drinking patterns further. More extensive assessments of drinking behavior, such as "graduated frequency" approaches (where individuals are queried as to how often they drink varying numbers of drinks per occasion [1–2 drinks, 3–4 drinks, 5–6 drinkers, etc.], Greenfield, 2000) are often employed to have sufficient data to measure intraindividual variability in drinking patterns. Another strategy is to measure typical quantity/frequency with supplementation using measures of heavy drinking to resolve drinking patterns that are likely to be associated with acute negative consequences, such as the 5/4 criteria (five drinks on an occasion for men and four drinks on an occasion for women) promoted by Wechsler and Austin (1998) as a measure of "binge drinking." Although this distinction appears somewhat crude, evidence suggests that this measure roughly corresponds to the NIAAA's (2004) recent definition of a "binge" episode as drinking that yields a BAC of .08% or more.

An alcohol timeline follow-back interview (TLFB: Sobell & Sobell, 1992, 1995, 2000, 2003) is a drinking assessment method that obtains detailed retrospective assessments of alcohol use.

By utilizing a calendar and memory aids to enhance recall (e.g., key dates that serve as anchors for reporting drinking), individuals provide retrospective estimates of their daily drinking over a specified time period that can vary up to 12 months from the interview date. The Alcohol TLFB has been shown to have good psychometric characteristics with a variety of drinker groups and can be flexibly scored to provide a range of measures relevant to drinking and abstention patterns (Sobell, Brown, Leo, & Sobell, 1996). Although originally developed to be used in face-to-face assessments with a trained technician or clinician, both telephone and computer-based administrations have been shown to be yield reliable results (Sobell et al., 1996).

Daily Diary and Ecological Momentary Assessment Approaches

Most questionnaire-based assessments of alcohol are cross-sectional and rely on retrospective reports of drinking. Cross-sectional, retrospective data suffer from several shortcomings, including potential reporting bias and the inability to address questions about the temporal order of cause-and-effect relationships. Although some approaches, such as retrospective TLFB assessments (Sobell & Sobell, 2003) and prospective panel studies resolve these issues to some degree, they fail to address shorter-term, dynamic associations between drinking and other variables of interest.

To address these issues, daily diary and ecological momentary assessment (EMA) methodologies have been developed. Participants in daily diary studies are instructed to record events or feelings that occurred during the day on structured nightly recording forms (Carney, Tennen, Affleck, Del Boca, & Kranzler, 1998), by providing daily reports via the Internet (e.g., Park, Armeli, & Tennen, 2004), or interactive voice response via telephone (Collins, Kashdan, & Gollnisch, 2003; Perrine, Mundt, Searles, & Lester, 1995). In EMA studies, however, drinkers are prompted several times per day to record drinking behaviors and other variables of interest in real time on palm-top computers. Thus, daily diary and EMA studies allow researchers to examine continually changing behaviors while utilizing naturalistic conditions and minimizing retrospective bias. In many clinical and research contexts, such assessments are burdensome but the value of obtaining real-time or near-real-time data is increasingly recognized (Piasecki, Hufford, Solhan, & Trull, 2007).

Biomarkers

Biomarkers of consumption derived from urine, blood, and expired air have traditionally been used to assess levels of alcohol use and treatment compliance (Allen, Litten, Strid, & Sillanauke, 2001; Lakshman & Tsutsumi, 2001; McClure, 2002), and biomarkers continue to be an active area of clinical research. Traditionally, blood markers such as mean corpuscular volume (MCV) and carbohydrate deficient transferring (CDT), and liver enzyme measures such as γ-glutamyl transferase (GGT), aspartate aminotransferase (AST), and alanine aminotransferase (ALT) have been the primary markers used both in clinical research, and to varying extent, in clinical practice (see Conigrave, Davies, Haber, & Whitfield, 2003). Existing blood markers of chronic exposure are limited in that they are relatively insensitive to many drinking patterns and can be nonspecific (Conigrave, Davies, Haber, & Whitfield, 2003), thus lacking both sensitivity and specificity. Additionally, they are not necessarily useful for assessing changes in patterns of drinking.

In recent years there has been increasing interest in more direct assessment of alcohol consumption such as the blood alcohol level (BAL). Although the BAL can be reliably estimated via simple devices that measure breath alcohol levels (e.g., Alcosensor IV, Intoximeters, Inc., St. Louis, MO) breath testing is only useful for assessing consumption when alcohol is still in the bloodstream. Given that the half-life of alcohol in the bloodstream is relatively brief, a legally intoxicated individual may show no blood alcohol several hours after reaching their peak BAL, thus limiting its use.

Although still in its infancy, wearable electrochemical devices that estimate BAC based on concentration of alcohol in sweat—referred to as transdermal ethanol sensors—provide objective real-time measures of substance use (Sakai, Mikulich-Gilbertson, Long, & Crowley, 2006; Swift, 2000). These devices can store data over days and thus provide a quantitative, continuous measure of BAL levels over an extended time frame.

Prevention

Alcohol misuse prevention efforts can be categorized into universal, selective, and indicated. Universal prevention strategies seek to address an entire population (e.g., all adults in a community). Selective prevention strategies target subsets of the entire population that are thought to be at risk for problematic alcohol involvement (e.g., fraternity/sorority members).

Indicated prevention efforts are designed to prevent the onset of a full-blown AUD in individuals who indicate early signs of dependence (e.g., mandated college students involved in problematic drinking).

Universal Prevention Approaches
POLICY INTERVENTIONS

Most public policies on alcohol are conceived and instituted with the express purpose of universally reducing alcohol use and related injuries and harms, either via penalties (sanctions) for risky behavior (e.g., drunk driving), or inducements (e.g., monetary appropriations) to support education and prevention efforts. Alcohol policies can be issued at federal, state, local, and institutional levels, and most commonly affect the pricing of alcohol (e.g., taxes, restrictions on happy-hour sales), how it is sold and its general availability (e.g., days of the week and hours that alcohol can be sold), where it is consumed (e.g., public places), enforcement (e.g., compliance checks, drunk driving laws), and underage access (Toomey & Wagenaar, 1999). Policies concerning the *price* and *taxation* of alcohol appear to be particularly effective. For example, a report of 112 studies on alcohol tax show a consistent moderately strong association between higher taxes on alcohol and lower heavy drinking rates (Wagenaar, Salois, & Komro, 2009). Notably, taxation is a somewhat difficult policy for U.S. citizens to endorse, as it is viewed by some as "punishing" moderate as well as heavy drinkers. Thus, such policies render the need for complicated tax formulas to achieve an optimal and agreeable tax rate for the general public (Pogue & Sgontz, 1989). Even if alcohol is not highly taxed however, restrictions on happy hours and alcohol specials (which utilize low alcohol prices as a means of increasing alcohol sales) can be effective in reducing heavy drinking in some populations, such as college students, who are particularly receptive to such advertising (Kuo, Wechsler, Greenberg, & Lee, 2003).

Restrictions on the availability of alcohol are also common deterrents of immoderate and problematic use, both in the general and underage population (Gruenwald, Ponicki, & Holder, 1993). For example, local policies that are placed on the *days and hours of operation* of premises that sell alcohol have been particularly effective in reducing alcohol-related traffic crashes (Ashe, Jernigan, Kline, & Galaz, 2003; McMillan & Lapham, 2006). Additionally, because adolescents and young adults have been found to be more likely to use alcohol if there is a higher local alcohol *outlet density* in the area in which they reside (Gruenwald, Johnson, & Treno, 2002; Treno, Ponicki, Remer, & Gruenwald, 2008; Weitzman, Folkman, Lemieux-Folkman, & Wechsler, 2003), local zoning limits on the density of alcohol outlets can help prevent alcohol use in these populations. Additionally, *server liability laws* (in which servers become liable for not responsibly "cutting off" drinkers) have also been shown to be slightly effective in reducing alcohol-related traffic crashes (Wagenaar & Holder, 1991). *Server training* is often suggested by researchers as an important potential prevention step; however, these policies are often created at the institutional level, and thus there is less evidence of their generalizable effectiveness (Toomey & Wagenaar, 1999).

Drunk driving laws are also popular sanctions put in place to prevent both heavy drinking, and also drinking and driving. Blood alcohol concentration limit laws are common internationally, and place a definable limit on one's BAC that is acceptable for driving (.08% in the United States). If the BAC is determined to be over this level, then the driver is punished, although the severity of such punishment differs widely by state (e.g., convictions, fines, and mandatory classes are common sanctions). Some states also institute zero-tolerance laws for underage drinkers, such that underage drivers are still liable for a BAC that is below .08%, yet over .02%, a law that has been found to be largely effective in reducing alcohol-related crashes (Voas, Tippetts, & Fell, 2003). With regard to punishment for repeat offenders, vehicle sanctions in particular (e.g., impoundment) have been shown to slightly reduce recidivism rates (Voas & DeYoung, 2002).

Perhaps one of the best known underage alcohol policies is the National Minimum Drinking Age Act, instituted in 1984. The act withheld highway funding from states that did not impose a minimum legal drinking age (MLDA) of 21, in effect making age 21 the standard MLDA across the nation. The age of 21 has historical value; it was the age that individuals could vote at the time that alcohol prohibition was repealed in 1933, and thus most states deemed it as their MLDA (NIAAA, 2008a). When the voting age was lowered to 18, most states followed suit with their MLDA. Due to the high prevalence of alcohol-related traffic fatalities in youth, and research showing that states with higher MLDAs suffered fewer fatalities, the Minimum Drinking Age Act was passed, resulting in vast reductions in alcohol-related traffic fatalities (American Medical Association, 2004; Mothers Against Drunk Driving, 2009; NIAAA, 2008a). However, there is recent interest to lower the MLDA, given that underage drinking continues to be a problem in the United States (Amethyst Initiative, 2008; Johnston, O'Malley, Bachman, & Schulenberg, 2007); although underage heavy drinkers tend to want younger MLDAs, other underage youth do not report a preference (Martinez, Muñoz, & Sher, 2009). Insurance companies have suggested that if citizens want the MLDA to be lowered to 18, the driving age should simultaneously be *raised* to 18 (Rubin, 2008).

School-based approaches are usually aimed at educating elementary school youth and adolescents about the ill effects of alcohol and drugs, and how to resist peer pressure to use. School-based approaches can be affect-based (i.e., focused on self-esteem and self-efficacy), skills-based (i.e., focused on interpersonal interactions), and knowledge-based (i.e., educating students about drugs and their effects), or a combination of the three (Tobler, 1986). Abstinence-only approaches that emphasize a "just say no" ideology toward alcohol consumption typically rely on education alone. Despite millions of dollars spent on programs that emphasize zero-tolerance approaches, such as Drug Abuse Resistance Education (DARE), a consensus of empirical studies indicate that these approaches fail to reduce alcohol use and related consequences (Lynam, Milich, Zimmerman, Novak, Logan, Martin, et al., 1999; Moskowitz, 1989). Such programs however, do successfully increase children's overall knowledge of drugs. Moreover, interventions that also incorporate skills training (e.g., Project ALERT) have been shown to reduce some hard drug use, and also improve self-efficacy and general decision making (Faggiano, Vigna-Taglianti, Versino, Zambon, Borraccino, & Lemma, 2008).

Community-based approaches are local efforts to prevent and reduce alcohol use and related problems. Much of what can be accomplished in a community-based approach is dependent on funding, and also on the environmental risks and strengths of a particular community. Common elements in many community-based approaches are media campaigns, citizen monitoring, youth outreach programs, server training programs, brief screening and/or counseling opportunities, and continuing education for professionals. Although evaluations of most of these locally based programs are unavailable, the evaluations that do exist show modest effectiveness (Giesbrecht & Haydon, 2006).

Selective Approaches

Selective approaches to prevention are common in college populations, which have characteristically high binge drinking rates. *Social norms marketing* (where information is disseminated to correct misperceptions regarding peer drinking behavior) and *expectancy challenge* interventions (that focus on perceptions of alcohol's effects and provide accurate information) are two approaches that appear to have garnered empirical support (Cruz & Dunn, 2004; Perkins, Haines, & Rice, 2005), although results are somewhat mixed (Wechsler, Nelson, Lee, Seibring, Lewis, & Keeling, 2003). Larimer and Cronce (2007) recently reviewed the literature on individual-focused prevention and treatment approaches for college drinking and found evidence for several similar efforts that appear to reduce drinking and/or related consequences, including normative reeducation programs, cognitive and behavioral skills-based interventions, motivational/feedback-based interventions, and brief motivational interventions. Notably, brief motivational interventions with personalized feedback were shown to be efficacious across a variety of modalities (e.g., delivered individually, in groups, or as stand-alone feedback with no in-person contact), thus highlighting the flexibility of implementing this approach.

In addition to these, *harm reduction approaches* (e.g., Marlatt & Gordon, 1985; Marlatt & Witkiewitz, 2002) promote strategies to avoid excessive levels of consumption and to minimize harmful consequences when intoxicated. Strategies that emphasize harm reduction approaches tailored to an individual's unique risk have been implemented for high school students, college students, and patients in medical settings (Neighbors, Larimer, Lostutter, & Woods, 2006). Interventions tailored to high school students that incorporate aspects of normative information and skill development for reducing risks associated with alcohol (specifically drunk driving) are linked to reductions in risky drinking and negative consequences from alcohol (Shope, Copeland, Marcoux, & Kamp, 1996). Similar programs that focus on drinking moderation skills and behavioral alternatives to high-risk alcohol-related behaviors have also been shown to result in reductions in risky drinking (D'Amico & Fromme, 2002).

Treatment Approaches

Depending upon the nature and extent of excessive consumption, physical dependence, and alcohol-related problems, a variety of treatment approaches to address these problems may be relevant. Beyond the treatment of AUDs and other behavioral aspects of drinking is the treatment of medical conditions that may be largely attributable to alcohol consumption (e.g., liver transplantation for alcohol cirrhosis; Beresford & Everson, 2000). In this section, we highlight those treatments that are most relevant to clinical psychologists.

Treatment of Alcohol Withdrawal

Withdrawal from alcohol in individuals with moderate to severe alcohol dependence is associated with a common abstinence syndrome characterized by cardiovascular overactivity, sweating, sleep problems, tremor, and anxiety (see Kosten & O'Connor, 2003). Detoxification treatment is designed to control the potential psychological and medical complications that may temporarily arise after a period of sustained, heavy use. Further, it is designed to do so in a way that is comfortable for the patient and to prepare the patient to make arrangements for future treatment of his or her dependence (Bayard, McIntyre, Hill, & Woodside., 2004; Kasser, Geller, Howell, & Wartenberg, 2004; Luty, 2006; Raistrick, 2000). A small minority of individuals who initially experience slight withdrawal reactions will progress to more severe reactions (e.g., alcohol withdrawal delirium, such as delirium tremens [Chick, 1989], hallucinosis, or seizure) that require skilled, hospital-based care.

Although the majority of individuals who are alcohol dependent can be withdrawn safely without medication (Whitfield et al., 1978), both human clinical and animal laboratory research suggests that a kindling-like process is associated with withdrawal. That is, the likelihood of damage to certain brain regions (and corresponding behavioral deficits) increases with greater numbers of detoxifications (Becker, 1998), thus highlighting the potential value of medical treatments that dampen the withdrawal process or provide neuronal protection. Detoxification typically consists of monitoring withdrawal symptoms and responding with appropriate psychopharmacological interventions, such as benzodiazepines (Raistrick, 2000) and/or other drugs (e.g., antiepileptic drugs to treat seizures).

For many years, it was assumed that medical detoxification (using benzodiazepines or similarly acting drugs) in an inpatient facility was necessary to prevent patients from progressing to major withdrawal. However, as discussed by Bischof, Richmond, and Case (2003), costs for inpatient treatment of alcohol abuse rose sharply during the 1980s, leading researchers to examine if outpatient services were as effective (Finney, Han, & Moos, 1996). As many of these less-expensive alternatives were found to be at least as effective as traditional inpatient detoxification (e.g., Alterman, Hayashida, & O'Brien, 1988; Bischof, Booker, Dyck, Graney, Hamblen, Hittinger, et al., 1991; Feldman, Pattison, Sobell, Graham, & Sobell, 1975; Hayashida, Alterman, McLellan, O'Brien, Purtill, Volpicelli, et al., 1989; Stinnett, 1982; see Bischof et al., 2003; Fleeman, 1997), other alternatives to hospital medical detoxification developed. These alternatives differed in both setting and in the use of medication. Some nonhospital medical detoxification programs moved treatment out of the more expensive hospital setting but continued to utilize medication routinely, whereas so-called social setting detoxification (Social Setting Detoxification, 1986) utilized a treatment process that provided a supportive, caring, and noninstitutional environment without the use of medication. Although several researchers concluded (based on empirical evidence) that social setting detoxification is an effective alternative to more costly hospital-based detoxification for most cases of withdrawal (e.g., O'Briant, Petersen, & Heacock, 1977), there may be concerns about the specific neurological sequelae of repeated unmedicated withdrawals.

Brief Interventions

Brief interventions, which can be as short as 10–15 minutes (e.g., Fleming, Mundt, French, Manwell, Stauffacher, & Barry, 2000; 2002), are often used in primary care settings with drinkers who have low levels of dependence and/or are unwilling to pursue more intensive treatment regimens. These interventions often involve motivational approaches designed to encourage drinkers to consider changing their drinking behavior (Wilk et al., 1997). Typically, the role of the clinician is to help the drinker set drinking goals, agree on a plan to reduce or stop consumption, and provide advice and educational materials. Follow-up sessions are scheduled to monitor progress and renegotiate drinking goals and strategies. Brief interventions can be administered by a wide variety of providers in a range of treatment modalities, and they are relatively less expensive than extended treatment (Heather 1986). The NIAAA (2007) has developed a treatment manual, *Helping Patients Who Drink Too Much,* and supporting materials to encourage clinicians to screen and intervene with patients they see in their practices. The NIAAA has also recently added online training materials (2008b).

Meta-analysis of controlled trials indicate that brief interventions reduce alcohol consumption and drinking-related outcomes (when compared to individuals who do not receive treatment) and appear to be as effective as extended treatment conditions (Moyer et al., 2002; Neighbors et al. 2006; Wilk et al., 1997). Further, these approaches appear to result in significant cost savings, compared to the utilization of other health-care services. Additionally, recent studies indicate that brief, motivational interventions delivered in an emergency room setting have been shown to reduce alcohol consumption, alcohol-related negative consequences, and recidivism (Bombardier & Rimmele, 1999; Gentilello, Ebel, Wickizer, Salkever, & Rivara, 2005; Monti et al., 1999). Thus, such brief motivational interventions are considered a "best-practice" recommendation in the United States (Neighbors et al., 2006).

Cognitive-Behavioral Approaches

Although numerous cognitive-behavioral interventions to treat alcohol dependence have been developed and assessed (Miller et al., 1995), a predominant model of cognitive-behavioral therapy (CBT) for AUDs is based on the work of Marlatt and Gordon (1985) regarding the relapse process. Marlatt's cognitive-behavioral model of relapse centers on high-risk situations and the individual's response in that situation (see Witkiewitz & Marlatt, 2008; Witkiewitz & Marlatt, 2004). Under this model, individuals who lack confidence to deal with the situation and/or lack an effective coping response are more likely to be tempted to drink. It is thought that the decision to use or not use is then mediated by the individual's outcome expectancies for the initial effects of using the substance (Jones, Corbin, & Fromme, 2001). This model provides the basis for relapse prevention interventions that are designed to prevent and manage relapse by identifying potential high-risk situations for relapse and challenging the individual's expectations for the perceived positive effects of a substance (Marlatt & Witkiewitz, 2008; Witkiewitz & Marlatt, 2004). A meta-analysis conducted by Irvin, Bowers, Dunn, and Wang (1999) suggested that relapse prevention was a successful intervention for substance use and improving psychosocial adjustment, especially for individuals with alcohol problems.

A related component of CBT is social skills training (Monti & O'Leary, 1999). This approach assumes that increasing the repertoire of coping skills will reduce the stress of high-risk situations and provide alternatives to drinking. Techniques include assertiveness training and role-playing skills related to alcohol refusal. Several studies suggest social skills training is effective in reducing drinking (see Chambless & Ollendick, 2001).

Despite the apparent effectiveness of cognitive-behavioral approaches to treat AUDs, little is known about the cognitive-behavioral processes that underlie current definitions of coping (Morgenstern & Longabaugh, 2000; Witkiewitz & Marlatt, 2004; Witkiewitz & Marlatt, 2008). Although numerous studies have examined possible mediators (e.g., changes in coping skills) of cognitive-behavioral treatment for AUDs, there is little empirical support for the hypothesized mechanisms of action of CBT (Morgenstern & Longabaugh, 2000).

Based on the notion that alcohol-related cues (e.g., the sight and smell of an alcoholic beverage) can trigger a relapse for alcoholics, cue-exposure therapy repeatedly exposes patients to alcohol-related cues while preventing the usual response (drinking alcohol), with the desired outcome to reduce or eliminate urges to drink in response to cues (Monti & Rohsenow, 1999). Cue exposure treatment draws from both classical learning models and social learning models of behavior. From the perspective of classical learning theory, environmental cues associated with past drinking elicit conditioned responses (e.g., Rohsenow, Monti, Rubonis, Sirota, Niaura, Colby, et al., 1994) that are thought to play a role in relapse. As a corollary, repeated exposure to substance-associated cues should lead to an extinction of conditioned reactions, resulting in decreases in the likelihood of craving and relapse, and also extend time to first relapse. Social learning theory suggests that the presence of cues increase the risk of relapse because cues increase the relevance (salience) to the drinker of the positive effects of alcohol, thus leading the drinker to want to consume more alcohol (Monti & Rohsenow, 1999). Alcohol cues may also trigger cognitive and neurochemical reactions that undermine the drinker's ability to use coping skills and the drinker's beliefs surrounding the use of skills (Monti et al., 1995). Various approaches to implement cue exposure exist (Rohsenow et al., 1994), with classical learning models that tend to focus on habituation and extinction of responses. Approaches based on social learning theory may incorporate coping skills training. Cue exposure is listed as a probably efficacious treatment for AUDs (Chambless & Ollendick, 2001), although some researchers have questioned the effectiveness of cue exposure for treating substance use disorders (e.g., Conklin & Tiffany, 2002).

Although traditional cue exposure techniques have focused on relatively passive exposures to alcohol cues (or various cues to drinking), it is possible that findings from recent research on implicit cognition in addiction can lead to techniques to enhance cue exposure (Wiers et al., 2006). For example, Fadardi and Cox (2007) showed that the tendency for alcohol cues to grab a drinker's attention can be altered by training excessive drinkers to gain more control over their attentional bias via behavioral training. Critically, these changes in attentional bias appear to correlate with changes in drinking behavior. Based on recent research on implicit cognition, other behavioral techniques that try to alter automatic reactions are also being evaluated. For example, Wiers et al. (2010) have exploited the finding that approach (pulling something toward oneself) and avoidance (pushing something away from oneself) are associated with more positive (pulling) and negative (pushing) emotions (e.g., Cacioppo et al., 1993). Specifically, they trained drinkers to "push" alcohol stimuli away. Preliminary data suggested reduced implicit positive attitudes toward alcohol, as well as reduced craving.

It should also be noted that there is growing evidence from research on treatment of anxiety disorders that pharmacological manipulations can enhance exposure-based fear reduction (Norberg, Krystal, & Tolin, 2008). Specifically, D-cycloserine has been used to enhance extinction of alcohol seeking in rats (Vengeliene, Kiefer, & Spanagel, 2008), suggesting that such pharmacological enhancement of exposure-based treatments could be useful clinically in the future. These innovative approaches that exploit new findings on implicit cognition and the pharmacology of learning potentially open up a new era of research on exposure-based approaches.

Generalized Self-regulation Training

Based on the perspective that (lack of) self-regulation (or self-control) contributes to AUDs, some researchers have recently suggested strengthening self-regulation as a treatment approach (e.g., Sher & Martinez, 2009). Recent research suggests that traits related to self-regulation, such as conscientiousness (Costa & McCrae, 1992), may be more mutable than previously thought (e.g., Roberts, Walton, & Viechtbauer, 2006). Experimental research has suggested that regular use of self-control will strengthen this attribute in a way akin to how muscles get stronger with regular use (Baumeister, Heatherton, & Tice, 1994; Muraven & Baumeister, 2000). This perspective provides novel approaches for training

or rehabilitating self-control in persons suffering from substance use disorders. For example, self-control "exercises," such as dietary monitoring, regular physical exercise, money management planning, and working on improving study habits (Baumeister, Gailliot, DeWall, & Oaten, 2006), have led to improvements in other self-regulatory behaviors, such as smoking fewer cigarettes and drinking less alcohol. Thus, there is now increased interest in the treatment (and preventive) potential of self-control training for a range of externalizing behavior problems, including AUDs.

The Question of Patient–Treatment Matching

It has long been recognized that individuals with AUDs are extremely heterogeneous with respect to etiology, symptomatology, and course of disorder. Because of this diversity, it has been speculated for many years that rather than a "one-size-fits-all" approach to alcohol treatment, treatment outcomes might be optimized if patients could be matched to specific treatments based on their personal characteristics. In a large, multisite, randomized control trial (RCT), this general hypothesis was put to the test by examining the interactions among three psychosocial treatments (i.e., Twelve-Step Facilitation, Cognitive-Behavioral Coping Skills, or Motivational Enhancement Therapy) and several individual difference variables hypothesized to be related to responsiveness to specific treatment approaches (e.g., sex, coping skills; Project MATCH Research Group, 1993). Although numerous papers and chapters have been published based on Project Match, the outcomes of the primary study hypotheses not only failed to find differences among treatments as a main effect but also failed to find much evidence for the hypothesized interactions (Project MATCH Research Group, 1997). It is possible that future research will provide more convincing evidence of patient–treatment matching strategies with psychological and behavioral treatments. For example, as discussed in the upcoming section on naltrexone, there appears to be evidence of patient–treatment matching for pharmacological treatments. It has also been suggested that the standard statistical approach to examining alcohol outcomes (e.g., relapse as a dichotomous outcome) may obscure important findings, compared to more sophisticated approaches that conceptualize relapse as a nonlinear, dynamical process (Witkiewitz & Marlatt, 2007; Witkiewitz, van der Maas, Hufford, & Marlatt, 2007). Thus, although Project Match (and the theory underpinning it) has been popularly viewed as a failed approach, it is clearly premature to jettison patient–treatment matching as a viable strategy.

Indeed, other researchers (e.g., Conrod et al., 2000) have examined important individual differences, such as personality and drinking motives, in order to develop individually tailored treatments predominantly targeted at substance use motivations associated with different personality dimensions. Preliminary empirical evidence suggests that approaches that focus on individual differences in drinking motives related to personality delay the growth of adolescent drinking and binge drinking, at least among individuals high in sensation seeking (Conrod, Castellanos, & Mackie, 2008).

Marital and Family Approaches

Alcohol use disorders often manifest themselves in the context of the family, and have considerable consequences for spouses and other family members, who often try to exert interpersonal influence over the drinker (Epstein & McCrady, 1998). Consequently, it is not surprising that a number of interventions involve couples and the family unit.

At the couples' level, the most extensively studied approach is Behavioral Couples Therapy (BCT). In addition to sharing many features of traditional cognitive-behavioral treatment for the drinker, BCT also targets partners' coping with drinking situations, reinforcing abstinence, and on improving the dyadic relationship. A recent meta-analysis of BCT in substance use disorders (where eight of the 12 studies reviewed were for treatment of AUDs; Powers, Vedel, & Emmelkamp, 2008) demonstrated that this treatment approach was more effective than control treatments in improving relationship satisfaction as well as substance-related outcomes. Interestingly, the comparatively stronger salutary effect of BCT on substance-related outcomes was not evident immediately after treatment, when all treatments fared well but, rather, the couples' treatment effect strengthened relative to control treatments over time. This suggests that improved interpersonal relationships fostered better alcohol-related outcomes. Importantly, there was no relation between the number of sessions and outcomes, suggesting that BCT could be delivered as a relatively brief treatment.

A number of treatment approaches that target the entire family and larger social networks have also been developed (Copello, Velleman, & Templeton, 2005). Arguably the most systematically studied of

these, the Community Reinforcement and Family Training approach (Smith & Meyers, 2004) is an extension of the Community Reinforcement Approach (CRA, Sisson & Azrin, 1986). Under this treatment, a friend or family member (e.g., spouse) either provides or removes agreed reinforcers (e.g., television access) to reward periods of sobriety and punish drinking for the targeted individual. Further, the agreed-upon friend or family member may also encourage the alcohol-dependent person to enter treatment and may supervise the use of disulfiram. Several studies suggest that CRA is an effective treatment for alcohol abuse and dependence (Carr, 2009; Chambless & Ollendick, 2001; Luty, 2006).

Self-help Groups

Perhaps the most widely recognized treatment approach for AUDs is Alcoholics Anonymous (AA; AA World Services, 1978), a self-help movement that has been in existence for 75 years. AA describes itself as:

> … a fellowship of men and women who share their experience, strength, and hope with each other that they may solve their common problem and help others to recover from alcoholism. The only requirement for membership is a desire to stop drinking. There are no dues or fees for AA membership; we are self-supporting through our own contributions. AA is not allied with any sect, denomination, politics, organization, or institution; does not wish to engage in any controversy, neither endorses nor opposes any causes. Our primary purpose is to stay sober and help other alcoholics to achieve sobriety.

Based upon a "disease model" of alcoholism that posits that alcoholism is a relapsing illness that requires complete abstinence (Luty, 2006), new members are encouraged to recruit support from a sponsor (an AA member who has been sober for at least 1 year) and to attend 90 meetings in the first 90 days of treatment. Several studies suggest that AA is as effective as alternative treatments (Tonigan, Toscova, & Miller, 1996), although many studies are small, unrandomized, and fail to account for the fact that many AA members are often concurrently involved in other forms of treatment.

Other self-help approaches have been developed that do not rely on abstinence goals. Specifically, Moderation Management (MM; Kishline, 1994) is based on the assumption that some individuals are problem drinkers yet not alcohol dependent, and these can learn to drink in nonproblematic ways. As noted by Humphreys (2003), both AA and MM share some assumptions. For example, both suggest that there is a difference between individuals who are alcohol dependent and less likely to be able to drink moderately and those who may have problems with alcohol not due to an underlying dependence on alcohol. However, the two approaches differ to the extent in which they believe the drinker is a good judge of how dependent he or she is and whether controlled drinking is a realistic outcome expectation. Specifically, AA and closely allied approaches embrace the notion that a hallmark symptom of alcoholism is denial (see Sher & Epler, 2004, for a discussion of this concept) and therefore an individual is unable to realistically appraise his or her drinking. Moderation Management, on the other hand, views the individual as capable of rationally evaluating the appropriateness of controlled drinking goals. Comparisons of those who affiliate with AA and MM suggest that the two approaches draw from very different subpopulations of those with AUDs, with MM affiliates being more socially stable and less alcohol dependent than those who affiliate with AA (Humphreys & Klaw, 2001). Thus, although there has been considerable antagonism between advocates of both AA and MM approaches, it appears that the two approaches are, to a large extent, serving different populations with different clinical needs and goals.

Pharmacotherapy

One of the most dramatic changes in the treatment of AUDs to have occurred in the past 15 years is the introduction of pharmaceuticals to curb craving and compulsive alcohol use. Although disulfiram (Antabuse) has been marketed for the treatment of alcohol dependence for more than 60 years, this medication (which causes an intense adverse reaction when the drinker consumes alcohol by blocking the enzyme that breaks down acetaldehyde, leading to a build-up of this toxic metabolite in the bloodstream) has not been shown to be effective as a major treatment modality by itself (although it may be useful as part of behavioral contracting).

In 1994, naltrexone (Revia) was the first new medication to get U.S. Food and Drug Administration (FDA) approval for the treatment of alcohol dependence since disulfiram. Naltrexone, which blocks opiate receptors in the brain, appears to be a fairly effective medication in reducing heavy consumption and reducing risk of relapse (Srisurapanont &

Jarusuraisin, 2005). Despite its apparent efficacy and low profile of side effects, many believe it is underutilized, perhaps because of physicians' reluctance to use medications to treat substance dependence. A long-acting, injectable form (Vivitrol) has recently been approved and appears to be effective as well (Garbutt et al., 2005). This long-acting form might prove useful in individuals who have difficulty in complying with oral pharmacotherapy. Additionally, recent findings (Kranzler et al., 2003) suggest that naltrexone can be taken on a targeted, as-needed basis (e.g., when a drinker wants to abstain or limit his drinking on a given occasion).

There appear to be important, genetically based individual differences in response to naltrexone (e.g., Oslin, Berttini, & O'Brien, 2006). Specifically, allelic variation in the μ-opioid receptor moderates treatment response to naltrexone in alcohol-dependent individuals. This finding may herald a new "pharmacogenomic" chapter in the history of patient–treatment matching attempts (e.g., Edenberg & Kranzler, 2005). It is hoped by many that advances in both genomics and neurobiology will lead to other forms of "personalized medicine" (Zerhouni, 2006) in the treatment of alcohol dependence, in which the characterization of one's own genetic makeup will guide treatment efforts.

It should also be noted that two other drugs have empirical support for their use in the treatment of alcoholism: acamprosate (Campral) and topiramate (Topamax). Acamprosate is FDA-approved for the treatment of alcohol dependence and is thought to work by restoring normal N-methyl-D-aspartic acid (NMDA) receptor tone in glutamate systems in the brain (Kiefer & Mann, 2005). However, in one recent, large, multicenter clinical trial in the United States, acamprosate was not found to be effective (Anton et al., 2006). Consequently, it has been speculated that this treatment only shows effectiveness in trials with patients with relatively severe dependence. Although topiramate has not received an indication for alcohol dependence from the FDA (it is approved for other conditions), this antiepileptic drug has been shown to be effective in a large, multisite, RCT (Johnson et al., 2007), presumably by facilitating GABA-ergic neurotransmission and inhibiting glutamatergic pathways in the brain, thus reducing alcohol-mediated reward. A number of drugs with different targets and methods of action are under investigation, and it seems likely that the range of treatment options for alcohol dependence will increase over the coming years.

Conclusion

It is difficult to imagine another health-related condition that provides more windows into varied aspects of the life sciences, the behavioral sciences, and the broader social sciences than do the AUDs. The noted 19th-century physician Sir William Osler is credited with claiming that to know syphilis was to know medicine, reflecting the diverse manifestations of this disease across multiple organ systems in the era before the introduction of antibiotics. It can probably be argued at this point in our history that to know AUDs is to know medicine as well as psychology and a host of allied disciplines including genetics, psychopathology, pharmacology, political science and sociology. Depending upon the intensity of use and when in the life course it is used, alcohol use can be a significant risk factor for a number of psychological and physical disorders. However, under some limited circumstances, it can also have significant health benefits. Similarly, a number of adverse social consequences stem from excessive alcohol use but, when used in moderation, many in our society value beverage alcohol as a means of facilitating social interactions and enhancing major celebrations. It is probably safe to state that American society holds strongly ambivalent attitudes surrounding the use of alcohol because of its combination of many valued effects coupled with its (often devastatingly) damaging effects. This ambivalence is longstanding, as evidenced by the 18th Amendment to the United States Constitution which, after passage in 1919, prohibited the manufacturing, sales, and transportation of beverage alcohol —and was subsequently repealed 14 years later, the only amendment of the U.S. Constitution to ever have been repealed.

Future Directions

There are many pressing areas for future alcohol research, a number of which have been discussed earlier. One of the most basic concerns nosology: How do we define disordered drinking, and where is the line when drinking moves from merely being incautious, risky, or foolish to being a mental disorder? Recent research has uncovered a number of serious problems with our current (DSM-IV) diagnostic system and casts serious doubt on the validity of the abuse-dependence distinction. Given problems with the construct of abuse as a distinct entity, we should focus our efforts in characterizing the dependence process more comprehensively. A more complete understanding of what dependence is and how it develops will help us to develop more valid criteria

sets and diagnostic algorithms. It could also help us to develop laboratory measures that can be used to assess dependence objectively, even during periods of abstinence (Sher, Wolf, & Martinez, 2009).

Another important area for research, and one in which we might expect to make significant progress in the coming years, is in understanding the reasons why most individuals are able to drink alcohol in a way that poses minimal risk to themselves and others, whereas others are not and go on to develop AUDs. A number of premorbid individual difference variables have been found to differentiate normal drinkers from those who have AUDs (e.g., certain genotypes, personality traits, and motives for use). Although sophisticated multivariate models have been put forth to describe how these individual difference variables might operate, we are still greatly limited in our ability to predict who will and who will not be able to control their consumption and how we might be able to intervene to prevent AUDs in those who are most vulnerable. The dream of "personalized medicine" that is "predictive, personalized, and preemptive" (Zerhouni, 2008) remains an elusive goal, but we are clearly getting closer to identifying critical vulnerabilities and how they influence the course and development of AUDs. Appropriate interventions will hopefully follow.

As noted earlier, one area of "personalized" medicine that is much closer is the selection of pharmacological treatment (i.e., naltrexone) based upon genetic testing (i.e., specific allele of the μ-opioid receptor). Presumably, the identification of more pharmacogenomic indicators will continue to be an active research area and represent the next phase of patient–treatment matching.

We also are moving toward developing and validating new treatment approaches that address both effortful self-regulatory processes (i.e., restraint or "will") and automatic approach tendencies (Sher & Martinez, 2009). Such new approaches hold the promise for having highly specific treatments that can be used individually or in combination with other behavioral and pharmacological treatments, based on an understanding of the motivational and regulatory structure of an individual's disordered drinking.

Although AUDs have been with human societies since antiquity, and it seems likely that they will represent significant health problems for the foreseeable future, our ability to identify, prevent, and treat these conditions continues to show constant improvement. Continued improvement rests on our ability to use new and existing research to design more effective assessments and interventions, and to validate them rigorously.

Acknowledgments

Preparation of this chapter was supported by NIH grants K05AA017242 and T32AA013526 to Kenneth J. Sher.

References

Alcoholics Anonymous. *Twelve steps, twelve traditions.* New York: AA World Services, 1978.

Abel, E. L., Bush, R., & Dintcheff, B. A. (1981). Exposure of rats to alcohol in utero alters drug sensitivity in adulthood. *Science, 212,* 1531–1533.

Achenbach, T. M., & Edelbrock, C. S. (1978). The classification of child psychopathology: A review and analysis of empirical efforts. *Psychological Bulletin, 85,* 1275–1301.

Allen, J. P., Litten, R. Z., Strid, N., & Sillanauke, P. (2001). The role of biomarkers in alcoholism medication trials. *Alcoholism: Clinical and Experimental Research, 25,* 1119–1125.

Alterman, A. I., Hayashida, M., & O'Brien, C. P. (1988). Treatment response and safety of ambulatory medical detoxification. *Journal of Studies on Alcohol, 49,* 160–166.

American Medical Association (2004). Minimum legal drinking age. Retrieved September 21, 2008, from http://www.ama-assn.org/ama/pub/category/print/13246.html

American Psychiatric Association. (1980). *Diagnostic and statistical manual of mental disorders* (3rd ed.). Washington DC: Author.

American Psychiatric Association. (1987). *Diagnostic and statistical manual of mental disorders* (3rd ed., revised). Washington DC: Author.

American Psychiatric Association. (1994). *Diagnostic and statistical manual of mental disorders* (4th ed.). Washington DC: Author.

American Psychiatric Association. (2000). *Diagnostic and statistical manual of mental disorders* (4th ed., Text Revision). Washington, DC: Author.

Amethyst Initiative. (2008). It's time to rethink the drinking age. Retrieved September 21, 2008, from http://www.amethystinitiative.org/statement/

Anderson, K. G., Smith, G. T., McCarthy, D. M., Fischer, S. F., Fister, S., Grodin, D., et al. (2005). Elementary school drinking: The role of temperament and learning. *Psychology of Addictive Behaviors, 19,* 21–27.

Andreas, J. B., & O'Farrell, T. J. (2007). Longitudinal associations between fathers' heavy drinking patterns and children's psychological adjustment. *Journal of Abnormal Child Psychology, 35,* 1–16.

Anthenelli, R. M., Klein, J. L., Tsuang, J. W., Smith, T. L., & Schuckit, M. A. (1994). The prognostic importance of blackouts in young men. *Journal of Studies on Alcoholism, 55,* 290–295.

Anton, R. F., O'Malley, S. S., Ciraulo, D. A., Cisler, R. A., Couper, D., Donovan, D. M., et al. (2006). Combined pharmacotherapies and behavioral interventions for alcohol dependence. The COMBINE study: A randomized controlled trial. *Journal of the American Medical Association, 295,* 2003–2017.

Arbuckle, T. Y., Chaikelson, J. S., & Gold, D. P. (1994). Social drinking and cognitive functioning revisited: The role of intellectual endowment and psychological distress. *Journal of Studies on Alcoholism,* 55, 352–361.

Arnett, J. J. (2006). Emerging adulthood: Understanding the new way of coming of age. In J. J. Arnett & J. L. Tanner (Eds.), *Emerging adults in America: Coming of age in the 21st century* (pp. 3–19). Washington, DC: American Psychological Association.

Ashe, M., Jernigan, D., Kline, R., & Galaz, R. (2003). Land use planning and the control of tobacco firearms, and fast food restaurants. *American Journal of Public Health, 93,* 1404–1408.

Bachman, J. G., Wadsworth, K. N., O'Malley, P.M., Johnston, L. D., & Schulenberg, J. E. (1997). *Smoking, drinking, and drug use in young adulthood: The impacts of new freedoms and new responsibilities.* Mahwah, NJ: Lawrence Erlbaum Associates.

Baer, J. S., Sampson, P. D, Barr, H. M., Connor, P. D., & Streissguth, A. P. (2003). A 21-year longitudinal analysis of the effects of prenatal alcohol exposure on young adult drinking. *Archives of General Psychiatry, 60,* 377–385.

Barnes, G. E. (1979). The alcoholic personality: A reanalysis of the literature. *Journal of Studies on Alcohol, 40,* 571–633.

Barnes, G. E. (1983). Clinical and prealcoholic personality characteristics. In B. Kissin and H. Begleiter, H. (Eds.), *The biology of alcoholism Vol. 6,* (pp. 113–195). New York: Plenum.

Barr, C. S., Newman, T. K., Lindell, S., Shannon, C., Champoux, M., Lesch, K. P., et al. (2004). Interaction between serotonin transporter gene variation and rearing condition in alcohol preference and consumption in female primates. *Archives of General Psychiatry, 61,* 1146–1152.

Bates, M. E., & Labouvie, E. W. (1995). Personality environment constellations and alcohol use: A process-oriented study of intraindividual change during adolescence. *Psychology of Addictive Behaviors, 9,* 23–35.

Baumeister, R. F., Gailliot, M., DeWall, C. N., & Oaten, M. (2006). Self-regulation and personality: How interventions increase regulatory success, and how depletion moderates the effects of traits on behavior. *Journal of Personality, 74,* 1173–1802.

Baumeister, R. F., Heatherton, T. F., & Tice, D. M. (1994). *Losing control: How and why people fail at self-regulation.* San Diego, Academic Press.

Bayard, M., McIntyre, J., Hill, K. R., & Woodside, J. (2004). Alcohol withdrawal syndrome. *American Family Physician, 69,* 1443–1450.

Becker, H. C. (1998). Kindling in alcohol withdrawal. *Alcohol, Health and Research World, 22,* 25–33.

Berglund, M. (1991). Clinical and physiological implications and correlations. *Alcohol and Alcoholism, 1,* 399–402.

Beresford, T. P., & Everson, G. T. (2000). Liver transplantation for alcoholic liver disease: Bias, beliefs, 6-month rule, and relapse—but where are the data? *Liver Transplantation, 6,* 777–778.

Bien, T. H., & Burge, J. (1990). Smoking and drinking: A review of the literature. *International Journal of Addiction, 25,* 1429–1454.

Bischof, G., Booker, J., Dyck, T., Graney, E., Hamblen, I., Hittinger, C., et al. (1991). Outpatient detoxification: An annotated bibliography. *Alcoholism Treatment Quarterly, 8,* 119–129.

Bischof, G. H., Richmond, C., & Case, A. (2003). Detoxification at home: A brief solution-oriented family systems approach. *Contemporary Family Therapy, 25,* 17–39.

Bischof, G., Rumpf, H. J., Hapke, U., Meyer, C., & John, U. (2003). Types of natural recovery from alcohol dependence: A cluster analytic approach. *Addiction, 98,* 1737–1746.

Blot, W. J., McLaughlin, J. K., Winn, D. M., Austin, D. F., Greenberg, R. S., Preston-Martin, S., et al. (1988). Smoking and drinking in relation to oral and pharyngeal cancer. *Cancer Research, 48*, 3282–3287.

Bombardier, C. H., & Rimmele, C. T. (1999). Motivational interviewing to prevent alcohol abuse after traumatic brain injury: A case series. *Rehabilitation Psychology, 44*, 52–67.

Breslau, N. (1995). Psychiatric comorbidity of smoking and nicotine dependence. *Behavior Genetics, 25*, 95–101.

Cacioppo, J. T., Priester, J. R., & Berntson, G. G., (1993). Rudimentary determinants of attitudes. II: Arm flexion and extension have differential effects on attitudes. *Journal of Personality and Social Psychology, 65*, 5–17.

Cadoret, R. J., Yates, M. D., Troughton, E., Woodworth, G., & Stewart, M. A. (1995). Adoption study demonstrating two genetic pathways to drug abuse. *Archives of General Psychiatry, 52*, 42–52.

Carey, K. B. (1995). Alcohol-related expectancies predict quantity and frequency of heavy drinking among college students. *Psychology of Addictive Behaviors, 9*, 236–241.

Carlson, S. R., Iacono, W. G., & McGue, M. (2002). P300 amplitude in adolescent twins discordant and concordant for alcohol use disorders. *Biological Psychology, 61*, 203–227.

Carlson, S. R., McLarnon, M. E., & Iacono, W. G. (2007). P300 amplitude, externalizing psychopathology, and earlier- versus later-onset substance use disorder. *Journal of Abnormal Psychology, 116*, 565–577.

Carmargo, C. A., Jr. (1989). Moderate alcohol consumption and stroke. *Stroke, 20*, 1611–1626.

Carney, M. A., Tennen, H., Affleck, G., del Boca, F. K., & Kranzler, H. R. (1998). Levels and patterns of alcohol consumption using timeline follow-back, daily diaries and real-time "electronic interviews." *Journal of Studies on Alcohol, 59*, 447–454.

Carr, A. A. (2009). The effectiveness of family therapy and systemic interventions for adult-focused problems. *Journal of Family Therapy, 31*, 46–74.

Caspi, A., Begg, D., Dickson, N., Harrington, H. -L., Langley, J., Moffitt, T. E., et al. (1997). Personality differences predict health-risk behaviors in adulthood: Evidence from a longitudinal study. *Journal of Personality and Social Psychology, 73*, 1052–1063.

Chambless, D. L., & Ollendick, T. H. (2001). Empirically supported psychological interventions: Controversies and evidence. *Annual Review of Psychology, 52*, 685–716.

Chassin, L., Curran, P. J., Hussong, A. M., & Colder, C. R. (1996). The relation of parent alcoholism to adolescent substance use: A longitudinal follow-up study. *Journal of Abnormal Psychology, 105*, 70–80.

Chassin, L., Pitts, S. C., DeLucia, C., & Todd, M. (1999). A longitudinal study of children of alcoholics: Predicting young adult substance use disorders, anxiety, and depression. *Journal of Abnormal Psychology, 108*, 106–119.

Chen, W. J., Loh, E. W., Hsu, Y. P., Chen, C. C., Yu, J. M., & Cheng, A. T. (1996). Alcohol-metabolizing genes and alcoholism among Taiwanese Han men: independent effect of ADH2, ADH3 and ALDH2. *British Journal of Psychiatry, 168*, 762–767.

Cherpitel, C. J., Borges, G. L. G., & Wilcox, H. C. (2004). Acute alcohol use and suicidal behavior: A review of the literature. *Alcoholism: Clinical and Experimental Research, 28*, 18–28.

Chick, J. (1989). Delirium tremens. *BMJ, 298*, 3–4.

Christiansen, B. A., Goldman, M. S., & Inn, A. (1982). Development of alcohol-related expectancies in adolescents: Separating pharmacological from social-learning influences. *Journal of Consulting & Clinical Psychology, 50*, 336–344.

Christiansen, M., Vik, P. W., & Jarchow, A. (2002). College student heavy drinking in social contexts versus alone. *Psychology of Addictive Behaviors, 27*, 393–404.

Clark, D. B., Thatcher, D. L., & Maisto, S. A. (2004). Adolescent neglect and alcohol use disorders in two-parent families. *Child Maltreatment, 9*, 357–370.

Clark, D. B., Thatcher, D. L., & Tapert, S. F. (2008). Alcohol, psychological dysregulation, and adolescent brain development. *Alcoholism: Clinical and Experimental Research, 32*, 375–385.

Clark, L. A., Watson, D., & Reynolds, S. (1995). Diagnosis and classification of psychopathology: Challenges to the system and future directions. In J. T. Spence, J. M. Darley, & D. J. Foss (Eds.), *The Annual Review of Psychology, 46*, (pp. 121–153). Palo Alto, CA: Annual Reviews Inc.

Cloninger, C. R., Bohman, M., & Sigvardsson, S. (1981). Inheritance of alcohol abuse: Cross-fostering analysis of adopted men. *Archives of General Psychiatry, 38*, 861–868.

Cloninger, C. R., Sigvardsson, S., Reich, T., & Bohman, M. (1988). Childhood personality predicts alcohol abuse in young adults. *Alcoholism: Clinical and Experimental Research, 12*, 494–505.

Cohen, P., Chen, H., Crawford, T. N., Brook, J. S., & Gordon, K. (2007). Personality disorders in early adolescence and the development of later substance use disorders in the general population. *Drug and Alcohol Dependence, 88*(Suppl 1), S71–84.

Collins, R. L., Kashdan, T. B., & Gollnisch, G. (2003). The feasibility of using cellular phones to collect ecological momentary assessment data: Application to alcohol consumption. *Experimental and Clinical Psychopharmacology, 11*, 73–78.

Conigrave, K. M., Davies, P., Haber, P., & Whitfield, J. B. (2003). Traditional markers of excessive alcohol use. *Addiction, 98*(Suppl 2), 31–43.

Conklin, C. A., & Tiffany, S. T. (2002). Applying extinction research and theory to cue-exposure addiction treatments. *Addiction, 97*, 155–167.

Conrod, P. J., Castellanos, N., & Mackie, C. (2008). Personality-targeted interventions delay the growth of adolescent drinking and binge drinking. *Journal of Child Psychology and Psychiatry, 49*, 181–190.

Conrod, P. J., Stewart, S. H., Pihl, R. O., Côté, S., Fontaine, V., & Dongier, M. (2000). Efficacy of brief coping skills interventions that match different personality profiles of female substance abusers. *Psychology of Addictive Behaviors, 14*, 231–242.

Cooper, M. L. (1994). Motivations for alcohol use among adolescents: Development and validation of a four-factor model. *Psychological Assessment, 6*, 117–128.

Cooper, M. L., Agocha, V. B., & Sheldon, M. S. (2000). A motivational perspective on risky behaviors: The role of personality and affect regulatory processes. *Journal of Personality, 68*, 1059–1088.

Cooper, M. L., Frone, M. R., Russell, M., & Mudar, P. (1995). Drinking to regulate positive and negative emotions: A motivational model of alcohol use. *Journal of Personality and Social Psychology, 69*, 990–1005.

Cooper, M. L., Krull, J. L., Agocha, V. B., Flanagan, M. E., Orcutt, H. K., Grabe, S., et al. (2008). Motivational pathways to alcohol use and abuse among black and white adolescents. *Journal of Abnormal Psychology, 117,* 485–501.

Cooper, M., Russell, M., Skinner, J. B., Frone, M. R., & Mudar, P. (1992). Stress and alcohol use: Moderating effects of gender, coping, and alcohol expectancies. *Journal of Abnormal Psychology, 101,* 139–152.

Copello, A.G., Velleman, R.D.B., Templeton, L. J. (2005). Family interventions in the treatment of alcohol and drug problems. *Drug and Alcohol Review, 24,* 369–385.

Costa, P. T., & McCrae, R. R. (1992). Normal personality assessment in clinical practice: The NEO personality Inventory. *Psychological Assessment, 4*(1), 5–13.

Crabb, D. W. (1995). Ethanol oxidizing enzymes: Roles in alcohol metabolism and alcoholic liver disease. *Progress in Liver Diseases, 13,* 151–172.

Crews, F. T., Braun, C. J., Hoplight, B., Switzer, R. C., & Knapp, D. J. (2000). Binge ethanol consumption causes differential brain damage in young adolescent rats compared with adult rats: Alcohol effects on the fetus, brain, liver, and other organ systems. *Alcoholism: Clinical and Experimental Research, 24,* 1712–1723.

Crum, R. M., Storr, C. L., Chan, Y. F., & Ford, D. E. (2004). Sleep disturbance and risk for alcohol-related problems. *American Journal of Psychiatry, 161,* 1197–1203.

Cruz, I. Y., & Dunn, M. E. (2003). Lowering risk for early alcohol use by challenging alcohol expectancies in elementary school children. *Journal of Consulting & Clinical Psychology, 71,* 493–503.

Cyders, M. A., Flory, K., Rainer, S., & Smith, G. T. (2009). The role of personality dispositions to risky behavior in predicting first-year college drinking. *Addiction, 104,* 193–202.

Cyders, M. A., & Smith, G. T. (2008). Emotion-based dispositions to rash action: positive and negative urgency. *Psychological Bulletin, 134,* 807–828.

Cyders, M. A., Smith, G. T., Spillane, N. S., Fischer, S., Annus, A. M., & Peterson, C. (2007). Integration of impulsivity and positive mood to predict risky behavior: development and validation of a measure of positive urgency. *Psychological Assessment, 19,* 107–118.

D'Amico, E. J., & Fromme, K. (2002). Brief prevention for adolescent risk-taking behavior. *Addiction, 97,* 563–574.

Dal Cin, S., Worth, K. A., Dalton, M. A., & Sargent, J. D. (2008). Youth exposure to alcohol use and brand appearances in popular contemporary movies. *Addiction, 103,* 1925–1932.

Dawson, D.A. (1998). Beyond black, white and Hispanic: Race, ethnic origin and drinking patterns in the United States. *Journal of Substance Abuse, 10,* 321–339.

Dawson, D. A., Grant, B. F., & Li, T. K. (2005). Quantifying the risks associated with exceeding recommended drinking limits. *Alcoholism: Clinical and Experimental Research, 29,* 902–908.

De Bellis, M. D., Clark, D. B., Beers, S. R., Soloff, P. H., Boring, A. M., Hall, J., et al. (2000). Hippocampal volume in adolescent-onset alcohol use disorders. *American Journal of Psychiatry, 157,* 737–744.

Dick, D. M. (2007). Identification of genes influencing a spectrum of externalizing psychopathology. *Current Directions in Psychological Science, 16,* 331–335.

Dick, D. M., Aliev, F., Wang, J. C., Grucza, R. A., Schuckit, M., Kuperman, S., et al. (2008). Using dimensional models of externalizing psychopathology to aid in gene identification. *Archives of General Psychiatry, 65,* 310–318.

Dick, D. M., & Beirut, L. J. (2006). The genetics of alcohol dependence. *Current Psychiatry Reports, 8,* 151–157.

Dick, D. M., & Feroud, T. (2003). Candidate genes for alcohol dependence: A review of genetic evidence from human studies. *Alcoholism: Clinical and Experimental Research, 27,* 868–879.

Dick, D. M., Rose, R. J., & Kaprio, J. (2006). The next challenge for psychiatric genetics: characterizing the risk associated with identified genes. *Annals of Clinical Psychiatry, 18,* 223–231.

Dominguez, H. D., Lopez, M. F., & Molin, J. C. (1998). Neonatal responsiveness to alcohol odor and infant alcohol intake as a function of alcohol experience during late gestation. *Alcohol, 16,* 109–117.

Donohue, K. F., Curtin, J. J., Patrick, C. J., & Lang, A. R. (2007). Intoxication level and emotional response. *Emotion, 7,* 103–112.

Donovan, J. E., Jessor, R., & Jessor, L. (1983). Problem drinking in adolescence and young adulthood: A follow-up study. *Journal of Studies on Alcohol, 44,* 109–137.

Drobes, D. J., Anton, R. F., Thomas, S. E., & Voronin, K. (2004). Effects of naltrexone and nalmefene on subjective response to alcohol among non-treatment-seeking alcoholics and social drinkers. *Alcoholism: Clinical and Experimental Research, 28,* 1362–1370.

Dunn, M. E., & Goldman, M. S. (2000). Validation of multidimensional scaling-based modeling of alcohol expectancies in memory: Age and drinking-related differences in expectancies of children assessed as first associates. *Alcoholism: Clinical and Experimental Research, 24,* 1639–1646.

Dunn, M. G., Tarter, R. E., Mezzich, A. C., Vanyukov, M., Kirisci, L., & Kirillova, G. (2002). Origins and consequences of child neglect in substance abuse families. *Clinical Psychology Review, 22,* 1063–1090.

Earleywine, M. (1994). Anticipated biphasic effects of alcohol vary with risk for alcoholism: A preliminary report. *Alcoholism: Clinical & Experimental Research, 18,* 711–714.

Earleywine, M., & Martin, C. S. (1993). Anticipated stimulant and sedative effects of alcohol vary with dosage and limb of the blood alcohol curve. *Alcoholism: Clinical & Experimental Research, 17,* 135–139.

Eckhardt, K., & Pridemore, W. A. (2009). Differences in female and male involvement in lethal violence in Russia. *Journal of Criminal Justice, 37,* 55–64.

Edenberg, H. J., & Kranzler, H. R. (2005). The contribution of genetics to addiction therapy approaches. *Pharmacology & Therapeutics, 108,* 86–93.

Edwards, G., & Gross, M. (1976). Alcohol dependence: Provisional description of a clinical syndrome. *British Medical Journal, 1,* 1058–1061.

Ehlers, C. L., Carr, L., Betancourt, M., & Montane-Jaime, K. (2003). Association of the ADH2*3 allele with greater alcohol expectancies in African-American young adults. *Journal of Studies on Alcohol., 64,* 176–181.

Ehlers, C. L., Gilder, D. A., Harris, L., & Carr, L. (2001). Association of the ADH2*3 allele with a negative family history of alcoholism in African American young adults. *Alcoholism: Clinical & Experimental Research., 25,* 1773–1777.

Ellickson, P. L., Collins, R. L., Hambarsoomians, K., & McCaffrey, D. F. (2005). Does alcohol advertising promote adolescent drinking?: Results from a longitudinal assessment. *Addiction, 100,* 235–246.

Ellis, D. A., Zucker, R. A., & Fitzgerald, H. E. (1997). The role of family influences in development and risk. *Alcohol Health & Research World, 21,* 218–226.

Eng, M. Y., Luczak, S. E., & Wall, T. L. (2007). ALDH2, ADH1B, and ADHIC genotypes in Asians: A literature review. *Alcohol Research & Health, 30,* 22–30.

Engs, R. C. (2001). Past influences, current issues, future research directions. In E. Houghton & A.M. Roche (Eds.), *Learning about drinking* (pp. 147–165). Philadelphia: Brunner-Routledge.

Epstein, E. E., & McCrady, B. S. (1998). Behavioral couples treatment of alcohol and drug use disorders: Current status and innovations. *Clinical Psychology Review, 18,* 689–711.

Eriksson, C. J. (1983). Human blood acetaldehyde concentration during ethanol oxidation (update 1982). *Pharmacology, Biochemistry & Behavior, 18*(Suppl 1), 141–150.

Eriksson, C.J., Mizoi, Y., & Fukunaga, T. (1982). The determination of acetaldehyde in human blood by the perchloric acid precipitation method: The characterization and elimination of artifactual acetaldehyde formation. *Analytical Biochemistry., 125,* 259–263.

Fadardi, J. S., & Cox, W. M. (2007). Alcohol attention-control training program. *The Addictions Newsletter, 14,* 16–17.

Faggiano, F., Vigna-Taglianti, F. D., Versino, E., Zambon, A., Borraccino, A., & Lemma, P. (2008). School-based prevention for illicit drugs use: A systematic review. *Preventive Medicine, 46,* 385–396.

Fazio, R. H., & Towles-Schwen, T. (1999). The MODE model of attitude–behavior processes. In S. Chaiken and Y. Trope (Eds.), *Dual-process theories in social psychology.* Guilford: New York, pp. 97–116.

Feldman, D., Pattison, E., Sobell, L., Graham, T., & Sobell, M. (1975). Outpatient alcohol detoxification: Initial findings on 564 patients. *American Journal of Psychiatry, 132,* 407–412.

Finn, P. R., & Pihl, R. (1987). Men at high risk for alcoholism: The effect of alcohol on cardiovascular response to unavoidable shock. *Journal of Abnormal Psychology, 96,* 230–236.

Finney, J. W., Hahn, A., & Moos, R. (1996). The effectiveness of inpatient and outpatient treatment for alcohol abuse: The need to focus on mediators and moderators of setting effects. *Addiction, 91,* 1773–1796.

First, M. B., Spitzer, R. L., Gibbon, M., & Williams, J. B. W. (2002). *Structured clinical interview for DSM-IV Axis I disorders, research version, non-patient edition (SCID-I/NP).* New York: Biometrics Research, New York State Psychiatric Institute.

Flanders, W. D., & Rothman, K. J. (1982). Interaction of alcohol and tobacco in laryngeal cancer. *American Journal of Epidemiology, 115,* 371–379.

Fleeman, N. D. (1997). Alcohol home detoxification: A literature review. *Alcohol and Alcoholism, 32,* 649–656.

Fleming, M. F., Mundt, M. P., French, M. T., Manwell, L. B., Stauffacher, E. A., & Barry, K. L. (2000). Benefit-cost analysis of brief physician advice with problem drinkers in primary care settings. *Medical Care, 38,* 7–18.

Fleming, M. F., Mundt, M. P., French, M. T., Manwell, L. B., Stauffacher, E. A., & Barry, K. L. (2002). Brief physician advice for problem drinkers: long-term efficacy and benefit-cost analysis. *Alcoholism: Clinical and Experimental Research, 26,* 36–43.

Fowler, T., Shelton, K., Lifford, K., Rice, F., McBride, A., Nikolov, I., et al. (2007). Genetic and environmental influences on the relationship between peer alcohol use and own alcohol use in adolescents. *Addiction, 102,* 894–903.

Fromme, K., & D'Amico E. J. (1999). Neurobiological bases of alcohol's psychological effects. In K.E. Leonard & H.T. Blane (Eds.), *Psychological theories of drinking and alcoholism* (pp. 422–455). New York: Guilford.

Fromme, K., & D'Amico, E. J. (2000). Measuring adolescent alcohol outcome expectancies. *Psychology of Addictive Behaviors, 14,* 206–212.

Garbutt, J. C., Kranzler, H. R., O'Malley, S. S., Gastfriend, D. R., Pettinati, H. M., Silverman, B. I., et al. (2005). Vivitrex Study Group. Efficacy and tolerability of long-acting injectable naltrexone for alcohol dependence: A randomized controlled trial. *Journal of the American Medical Association, 293,* 1617–1625.

Gentilello, L.M., Ebel, B.E., Wickizer, T.M., Salkever, D.S., & Rivara, F. P. (2005). Alcohol interventions for trauma patients treated in emergency departments and hospitals: A cost benefit analysis. *Annals of Surgery, 241,* 541–550.

Giancola, P. R., & Tarter, R. E. (1999). Executive cognitive functioning and risk for substance abuse. *Psychological Science, 10,* 203–205.

Giesbrecht, N., & Haydon, E. (2006). Community-based interventions and alcohol, tobacco, and other drugs: Foci, outcomes and implications. *Drug and Alcohol Review, 25,* 633–646.

Goldman, M. S., Brown, S. A., & Christiansen, B. A. (1987). Expectancy theory: Thinking about drinking. In H.T. Blane and K.E. Leonard (Eds.), *Psychological theories of drinking and alcoholism* (pp. 181–226). New York: Guilford Press.

Goldman, M. S., Del Boca, F. K., & Darkes, J. (1999). Alcohol expectancy theory: The application of cognitive neuroscience. In H.T. Blane and K.E. Leonard (Eds.), *Psychological theories of drinking and alcoholism* (pp. 203–246). New York: Guilford Press.

Goldstein, D. B. (2009). Common genetic variation and human traits. *New England Journal of Medicine, 360,* 1696–1698.

Goodwin, D. W., Schulsinger, F., Hermansen, L., Guze, S. B., & Winokur, G. (1973). Alcohol problems in adoptees raised apart from alcoholic biological parents. *Archives of General Psychiatry 28,* 238–243.

Gorelick, P. B. (1989). The status of alcohol as a risk factor for stroke. *Stroke, 20,* 1607–1610.

Grant, B. F. (1997). Prevalence and correlates of alcohol use and DSM-IV alcohol dependence in the United States: Results of the National Longitudinal Epidemiologic Survey. *Journal of Studies on Alcohol, 58,* 464–473.

Grant, B. F., Chou, S. P., Goldstein, R. B., Huang, B., Stinson, F. S., Saha, T. D., et al. (2008). Prevalence, correlates, disability, and comorbidity of DSM-IV borderline personality disorder: Results from the wave 2 National Epidemiological Survey on Alcohol and Related Conditions. *Journal of Clinical Psychiatry, 69,* 533–545.

Grant, B. F., & Dawson, D. A. (1997). Age at onset of alcohol use and its association with DSM-IV alcohol abuse and dependence: Results from the National Longitudinal Alcohol Epidemiologic Survey. *Journal of Substance Abuse, 9,* 103–110.

Grant, B. F., & Dawson, D. (2000). The Alcohol Use Disorder and Associated Disabilities Interview Schedule-IV (AUDADIS-IV), National Institute on Alcohol Abuse and Alcoholism, Rockville, MD.

Grant, B. F., Dawson, D. A., Stinson, F. S., Chou, P. S., Dufour, M.C., & Pickering, R. (2004). The 12-month prevalence and trends in DSM-IV alcohol abuse and dependence: United States, 1991-1992 and 2001-2002. *Drug and Alcohol Dependence, 74,* 223–234.

Grant, B. F., Dawson, D. A., Stinson, F. S., Chou, P. S., Kay, W., & Pickering, R. (2003). The alcohol use disorder and associated disabilities interview schedule-IV (AUDADIS-IV): Reliability of alcohol consumption, tobacco use, family history of depression and psychiatric diagnostic modules in a general population sample. *Drug and Alcohol Dependence, 71,* 7–16.

Grant, B. F., Harford, T. C., Dawson, D. A., Chou, P., Dufour, M., & Pickering, R. (1994). Prevalence of DSM-IV alcohol abuse and dependence: United States, 1992. *Alcohol Health & Research World, 18,* 243–248.

Grant, B. F., Hasin, D. S., Stinson, F. S., Dawson, D. A., Chou, S. P., Ruan, W. J., et al. (2004). Prevalence correlates and disability of personality disorders in the United States: Results from the National Epidemiological Survey on Alcohol and Related Conditions. *Journal of Clinical Psychiatry, 65,* 948–958.

Grant, B. F., Moore, T. C., & Kaplan, K. (2003). *Source and accuracy statement: Wave 1 National Epidemiologic Survey on Alcohol and Related Conditions (NESARC).* Bethesda, MD: National Institute on Alcohol Abuse and Alcoholism.

Grant, B. F., & Pickering, R. P. (1996). Comorbidity between DSM-IV alcohol and drug use disorders: Results from the National Longitudinal Alcohol Epidemiologic Survey. *Alcohol Health & Research World, 20,* 67–72.

Grant, B. F., Stinson, F. S., Dawson, D. A., Chou, P., Dufour, M. C., Compton, W., et al. (2004). Prevalence and co-occurrence of substance use disorders and independent mood and anxiety disorders: Results from the national epidemiologic survey on alcohol and related conditions. *Archives of General Psychiatry, 61,* 807–816.

Greenfield, T. K. (2000). Ways of measuring drinking patterns and the difference they make: experience with graduated frequencies. *Journal of Substance Abuse, 12,* 33–49.

Greenwald, A. G., Nosek, B. A., & Banaji, M. R. (2003). Understanding and using the implicit association test: I. An improved scoring algorithm. *Journal of Personality and Social Psychology, 85,* 197–216.

Grube, J. (2005). Youth drinking rates and problems: A comparison of European countries and the United States. Calverton, MD: Pacific Institute for Research and Evaluation and the Office of Juvenile Justice and Delinquency Prevention.

Grube, J. W., & Waiters, E. (2005). Alcohol in the media: Content and effects on drinking beliefs and behaviors among youth. *Adolescent Medicine Clinics, 16,* 327–343.

Gruenwald, P. J., Johnson, F. W., & Treno, A. J. (2002). Outlets, drinking and driving: A multilevel analysis of availability. *Journal of Studies and Alcohol, 63,* 460–468.

Gruenwald, P. J., Ponicki, W. R., & Holder, H. D. (1993). Relationship of outlet densities to alcohol consumption: A time series cross-sectional analysis. *Alcoholism: Clinical and Experimental Research, 17,* 38–47.

Hahn, C.Y., Huang, S.Y., Ko, H.C., Hsieh, C.H., Lee, I.H., Yeh, T.L., et al. (2006). Acetaldehyde involvement in positive and negative alcohol expectancies in Han Chinese persons with alcoholism. *Archives of General Psychiatry, 63,* 817–823.

Hanchar, H. J., Chutsrinopkun, P., Meera, P., Supavilai, P., Sieghart, W., Wallner, M., et al. (2006). Ethanol potently and competitively inhibits binding of the alcohol antagonist Ro15–4513 to $\alpha_{4/6}\,\beta_3\delta$ GABA$_A$ receptors. *Proceedings of the National Academy of Sciences, 103,* 8546–8551.

Harford, T. C., & Muthén, B. O. (2001). The dimensionality of alcohol abuse and dependence: A multivariate analysis of DSM-IV symptom items in the National Longitudinal Survey of youth. *Journal of Studies on Alcohol, 62,* 150–157.

Hargreaves, G. A., Quinn, H., Kashem, M. A., Matsumoto, I., & McGregor, I. S. (2009). Proteomic analysis demonstrates adolescent vulnerability to lasting hippocampal changes following chronic alcohol consumption. *Alcoholism: Clinical and Experimental Research, 33,* 86–94.

Harris, R. A., Mihic, S. J., & Valenzuela, C. F. (1998). Alcohol and benzodiazepines: Recent mechanistic studies. *Drug and Alcohol Dependence, 51,* 155–164.

Hart, K. E., & Fazaa, N. (2004). Life stress events and alcohol misuse: Distinguishing contributing stress events from consequential stress events. *Substance Use and Misuse, 39,* 1319–1339.

Hasin, D., Hatzenbuehler, M. L., Keyes, K., & Ogburn, E. (2006). Substance use disorders: Diagnostic and Statistical Manual of Mental Disorders, fourth edition (DSM-IV) and International Classification of Diseases, tenth edition (ICD-10). *Addiction, 101 Suppl 1,* 59–75.

Hasin, D. S., Muthen, B., Wisnicki, K. S., & Grant, B. (1994). Validity of the bi-axial dependence concept: A test in the US general population. *Addiction, 89,* 573–579.

Hawkins, J. D., Catalano, R. F., & Miller, J. Y. (1992). Risk and protective factors for alcohol and other drug problems in adolescence and early adulthood: implications for substance abuse prevention. *Psychological Bulletin, 112,* 64–105.

Hayashida, M., Alterman, A., McLellan, T., O'Brien, C., Purtill, J., Volpicelli, J., et al. (1989). Comparative effectiveness and costs of inpatient and outpatient detoxification of patients with mild-to-moderate alcohol withdrawal syndrome. *The New England Journal of Medicine, 320,* 358–365.

Heath, A. C. (1995). Genetic influences on alcoholism risk: A review of adoption and twin studies. *Alcohol Health & Research World, 19,* 166–171.

Heath, A. C., Bucholz, K., Madden, P., Dinwiddie, S., Slutske, W., Bierut, L., et al. (1997). Genetic and environmental contributions to alcohol dependence risk in a national twin sample: Consistency of findings in women and men. *Psychological Medicine, 27,* 1381–1396.

Heather, N. (1986). Minimal treatment intervention for problem drinkers. In G. Edwards (Ed.) *Current issues in clinical psychology* (Volume 4, pp. 171–186). London: Plenum.

Hebert, L. E., Scherr, P. A., Beckett, L. A., Albert, M. S., Rosner, B., Taylor, J. O., et al. (1993). Relation of Smoking and low-to-moderate alcohol consumption to change in cognitive function: A longitudinal study in a defined community of older persons. *American Journal of Epidemiology, 137,* 881–891.

Helzer, J.E., Burnham, A., &; McEvoy. L.T. (1991). Alcohol abuse and dependence. In L. N. Robins & D.A. Regier (Eds.), *Psychiatric disorders in America: The epidemiologic catchment area study* (pp. 81–115). New York: The Free Press.

Herd, D., & Grube, J. (1996). Black identity and drinking in the U.S.: A national study. *Addiction, 91,* 845–857.

Higuchi, S., Matsushita, S., Murayama, M., Takagi, S., & Hayashida, M. (1995). Alcohol and aldehyde dehydrogenase polymorphisms and the risk for alcoholism. *American Journal of Psychiatry, 152,* 1219–1221.

Hingson, R. W., Heeren, T., & Winter, M. R. (2006). Age of alcohol-dependence onset: Associations with severity of dependence and seeking treatment. *Pediatrics, 118,* 755–763.

Hingson, R., Heeren, T., Winter, M., & Wechsler, H. (2005). Magnitude of alcohol-related mortality and morbidity among U.S. college students ages 18–24: Changes from 1998 to 2001. *Annual Review of Public Health, 26,* 259–279.

Holdstock, L., & de Wit, H. (1998). Individual differences in the biphasic effects of ethanol. *Alcoholism: Clinical and Experimental Research, 22,* 1903–1911.

Hopfer, C. J., Crowley, T. J., & Hewitt, J. K. (2003). Review of twin and adoption studies of adolescent substance use. *Journal of the American Academy of Child & Adolescent Psychiatry, 42,* 710–719.

Humphreys, K. (2003). *Circles of recovery: Self-help organizations for addictions.* Cambridge: Cambridge University Press.

Humphreys, K., & Klaw, E. (2001). Can targeting non-dependent problem drinkers and providing internet-based services expand access to assistance for alcohol problems?: A study of the Moderation Management self-help/mutual aid organization. *Journal of Studies on Alcohol, 62,* 528–532.

Hussong, A., Bauer, D., & Chassin, L. (2008). Telescoped trajectories from alcohol initiation to disorder in children of alcoholic parents. *Journal of Abnormal Psychology, 117,* 63–78.

Iacono, W. G. (1998). Identifying psychophysiological risk for psychopathology: Examples from substance use and schizophrenia research. *Psychophysiology, 35,* 621–637.

Irvin, J.E., Bowers, C.A., Dunn, M.E., & Wang, M.C. (1999). Efficacy of relapse prevention: A meta-analytic review. *Journal of Consulting and Clinical Psychology, 67,* 563–570.

Istvan, J., & Matarazzo, J. D. (1984). Tobacco, alcohol, and caffeine use: A review of their interrelationships. *Psychological Bulletin, 95,* 301–326.

Jackson, K. M., Sher, K. J., & Schulenberg, J. (2005). Conjoint developmental trajectories of young adult alcohol and tobacco use. *Journal of Abnormal Psychology, 114,* 612–626.

Jackson, K. M., Sher, K. J., & Schulenberg, J. (2008). Conjoint developmental trajectories of young adult substance use. *Alcoholism: Clinical and Experimental Research, 32,* 723–737.

Jacob, T., Waterman, B., Heath, A., True, W., Bucholz, K. K., Haber, R., et al. (2003). Genetic and environmental effects on offspring alcoholism: New insights using an offspring-of-twins design. *Archives of General Psychiatry, 60,* 1265–1272.

Jessor, R., Donovan, J. E., & Costa, F. M. (1991). *Beyond adolescence: Problem behavior and young adult development.* New York: Cambridge University Press.

Jessor, R., & Jessor, S. L. (1977). *Problem behavior and psychosocial development: A longitudinal study of youth.* San Diego: Academic Press.

Johnson, B. A., Rosenthal, N., Capece, J. A., Wiegand, F., Mao, L., Beyers, K., et al. (2007). Topiramate for treating alcohol dependence: A randomized controlled trial. *The Journal of the American Medical Association, 298,* 1641–1651.

Johnston, L. D., O'Malley, P. M., Bachman, J. G., & Schulenberg, J. E. (2007). *Monitoring the Future national survey results on drug use, 1975-2006. Volume II: College students and adults ages 19-45* (NIH Publication No. 07-6206). Bethesda, MD: National Institute on Drug Abuse, 307 pp.

Jones, B. T., Corbin, W., & Fromme, K. (2001). A review of expectancy theory and alcohol consumption. *Addiction, 96,* 57–72.

Jones, M. C. (1968). Personality correlates and antecedents of drinking patterns in adult males. *Journal of Consulting and Clinical Psychology, 32,* 2–12.

Josephs, R. A., & Steele, C. M. (1990). The two faces of alcohol myopia: Attentional mediation of psychological stress. *Journal of Abnormal Psychology, 99,* 115–126.

Kahler, C. W., & Strong, D. R. (2006). A Rasch model analysis of DSM-IV Alcohol abuse and dependence items in the National Epidemiological Survey on Alcohol and Related Conditions. *Alcoholism: Clinical & Experimental Research, 30,* 1165–1175.

Kasser, C., Geller, A., Howell, E., & Wartenberg, A. (2004). Detoxification: principles and protocols. American Society of Addiction Medicine. Retrieved January 20, 2004, from http://www.asam.org/publ/detoxification.htm

Kendler, K. S. (2005). Psychiatric genetics: A methodologic critique. *American Journal of Psychiatry, 162,* 3–11.

Kendler, K. S. (2006). Reflections on the relationship between psychiatric genetics and psychiatric nosology. *American Journal of Psychiatry, 163,* 1138–1146.

Kessler, R. C., Berglund, P., Demler, O., Jin, R., & Walters, E. E. (2005). Lifetime prevalence and age-of-onset distributions of DSM-IV disorders in the national comorbidity survey replication. *Archives of General Psychiatry, 62,* 593–602.

Kessler, R. C., Chiu, W. T., Demler, O., & Walters, E. E. (2005). Prevalence, severity, and comorbidity in the national comorbidity survey replication. *Archives of General Psychiatry, 62,* 617–627.

Kessler, R. C., Crum, R. M., Warner, L. A., & Nelson, C. B. (1997). Lifetime co-occurrence of DSM-III-R alcohol abuse and dependence with other psychiatric disorders in the National Comorbidity Survey. *Archives of General Psychiatry, 54,* 313–321.

Kessler, R. C., McGonagle, K. A., Zhao, S., Nelson, C. B., Hughes, M., Eshleman, S., et al. (1994). Lifetime and 12-month prevalence of DSM-III-R psychiatric disorders in the United States: Results from the National Comorbidity Study. *Archives of General Psychiatry, 51,* 8–19.

Kessler, R.C., & Ustün, T.B. (2004). The World Mental Health (WMH) Survey Initiative Version of the World Health Organization (WHO) Composite International Diagnostic Interview (CIDI). *International Journal of Methods in Psychiatric Research, 13,* 93–121.

Khantzian, E. J. (1985). The self-medication hypothesis of addictive disorders: focus on heroin and cocaine dependence. *American Journal of Psychiatry, 142,* 1259–1264.

Kiefer, F., & Mann, K. (2005). New achievements and pharmacotherapeutic approaches in the treatments of alcohol dependence. *European Journal of Pharmacology, 526,* 163–171.

Kilbey, M. M., Downey, K., & Breslau, N. (1998). Predicting the emergence and persistence of alcohol dependence in young adults: The role of expectancy and other risk factors. *Experimental & Clinical Psychopharmacology, 6,* 149–156.

Kishline, A. (1994). *Moderate drinking: The moderation management guide for people who want to reduce their drinking.* New York: Crown.

Klatsky, A. L., Armstrong, M. A., & Friedman, G. D. (1989). Alcohol use and subsequent cerebrovascular disease hospitalizations, *Stroke, 20,* 741–746.

Koob, G. F., & Le Moal, M. (2001). Drug addiction, dysregulation of reward and allostasis. *Neuropsychopharmacology, 24,* 97–127.

Koob, G. F., & Le Moal, M. (2008). Addiction and the Brain Antireward System. *Annual Review of Psychology, 59,* 29–53.

Kosten, T. R., & O'Connor, P. G. (2003). Management of drug and alcohol withdrawal. *New England Journal of Medicine, 348,* 1786–1795.

Kranzler, H. R., Armeli, S., Tennen, H., Blomqvist, O., Oncken, C., Petty, N., et al. (2003). Targeted naltrexone for early problem drinkers. *Journal of Clinical Psychopharmacology, 23*, 294–304.

Krueger, R.F., & Markon, K.E. (2006). Reinterpreting comorbidity: A model-based approach to understanding and classifying psychopathology. *Annual Review of Clinical Psychology, 2*, 111–133.

Krueger, R.F., & Markon, K.E. (2008). Understanding psychopathology: Melding behavior genetics, personality, and quantitative psychology to develop an empirically based model. *Current Directions in Psychological Science, 15*, 113–117.

Krueger, R. F., Markon, K. E., Patrick, C. J., & Iacono, W. G. (2005). Externalizing psychopathology in adulthood: A dimensional-spectrum conceptualization and its implications for DSM-5. *Journal of Abnormal Psychology, 114*, 537–550.

Kuntsche, E., Knibbe, R., Gmel, G., & Engels, R. (2006). Who drinks and why? A review of socio-demographic, personality, and contextual issues behind the drinking motives in young people. *Psychology of Addictive Behaviors, 31*, 1844–1857.

Kuo, M., Wechsler, H., Greenberg, P., & Lee, H. (2003). The marketing of alcohol to college students: The role of low prices and special promotions. *American Journal of Preventive Medicine, 25*, 204–211.

Labouvie, E. W., Pandina, R. J., White, H. R., & Johnson V. (1990). Risk factors of adolescent drug use: An affect-based interpretation. *Journal of Substance Abuse, 2*, 265–285.

Lakshman, M. R., & Tsutsumi, M. (2001). Alcohol biomarkers: Clinical significance and biochemical basis. *Alcohol, 25*, 171–172.

Lang, A., Patrick, C., & Stritzke, W. (1999). Alcohol and emotional response: A multidimensional-multilevel analysis. In K.E. Leonard & H.T. Blane (Eds.). *Psychological theories of drinking and alcoholism* (2nd edition, pp. 328–371). New York: Guilford.

Larimer, M. E., & Cronce, J. M. (2007). Identification, prevention, and treatment revisited: Individual-focused college drinking prevention strategies 1999–2006. *Psychology of Addictive Behaviors, 32*, 2439–2468.

Larkby, C., & Day, N. (1997). The effects of prenatal alcohol exposure. *Alcohol, Health, and Research World, 2*, 192–198.

Lee, N. K., Greely, J., & Oei, T. P. (1999). The relationship of positive and negative alcohol expectancies to patterns of consumption of alcohol in social drinkers. *Psychology of Addictive Behaviors, 24*, 359–369.

Lemon, J., Chesher, G., Fox, A., Greeley, J., & Nabke, C. (1993). Investigation of the "hangover" effects of an acute dose of alcohol on psychomotor performance. *Alcohol: Clinical and Experimental Research, 17*, 665–668.

Leonard, K. E., & Eiden, R. D. (1999). Husbands and wives drinking: Unilateral or bilateral influences among newlyweds in a general population sample. *Journal of Studies on Alcohol Supplement, 13*, 130–138.

Leonard, K. E., & Eiden, R. D. (2007). Marital and family processes in the context of alcohol use and alcohol disorders. *Annual Review of Clinical Psychology, 3*, 285–310.

Leonard, K. E., & Homish, G. G. (2008). Predictors of heavy drinking and drinking problems over the first 4 years of marriage. *Psychology of Addictive Behaviors, 22*, 25–35.

Leonard, K. E., & Mudar, P. J. (2000). Alcohol use in the year before marriage: Alcohol expectancies and peer drinking as proximal influences on husband and wife alcohol involvement. *Clinical & Experimental Research, 24*, 1666–1679.

Leonard, K. E., & Mudar, P. (2004). Husbands influence on wives' drinking: Testing a relationship motivation model in the early years of marriage. *Psychology of Addictive Behaviors, 18*, 340–349.

Levenson, R. W., Oyama, O. N., & Meek, P. S. (1987). Greater reinforcement from alcohol for those at risk: Parental risk, personality risk, and sex. *Journal of Abnormal Psychology, 96*, 242–253.

Li, T. K., Hewitt, B., & Grant, B. F. (2004). Alcohol use disorders and mood disorders: A National Institute on Alcohol Abuse and Alcoholism perspective. *Biological Psychiatry, 56*, 718–720.

Lister, R. G., & Nutt D. J. (1988). RO 15-4513 and its interaction with ethanol. *Advances in Alcohol and Substance Abuse, 7*, 119–123.

Littlefield, A., & Sher, K. J. (2010). Alcohol use disorders in young adulthood. In J. E. Grant and M. N. Potenza (Eds.), *Young adult mental health.* pp. 292–310. New York: Oxford University Press.

Littlefield, A., Sher, K. J., & Wood, P. K. (2010). Do changes in drinking motives mediate the relation between personality change and "maturing out" of problem drinking?" *Journal of Abnormal Psychology, 119*, 93–105.

Locke, T. F., & Newcomb, M. D. (2004). Child maltreatment, parent alcohol- and drug-related problems, polydrug problems, and parenting practices: A test of gender differences and four theoretical perspectives. *Journal of Family Psychology, 18*, 120–134.

Luczak, S. E., Elvine-Kreis, B., Shea, S. H., Carr, L. G., & Wall, T. L. (2002). Genetic risk for alcoholism relates to level of response to alcohol in Asian-American men and women. *Journal of Studies on Alcohol, 63*, 74–82.

Luczak, S. E., Glatt, S. J., & Wall, T. L. (2006). Meta-analyses of ALDH2 and ADH1B with alcohol dependence in Asians. *Psychological Bulletin, 132*, 607–612.

Luo, X., Kranzler, H. R., Zuo, L., Wang, S., Blumberg, H. P., & Gelernter, J. (2005). CHRM2 gene predisposes to alcohol dependence, drug dependence and affective disorders: Results from an extended case-control structured association study. *Human Molecular Genetics, 14*, 2421–2434.

Luty, J. (2006). What works in alcohol use disorders. *Advances in Psychiatric Treatment, 12*, 13–22.

Lynam, D.R., Milich, R., Zimmerman, R., Novak, S.P., Logan, T.K., Martin, C., et al. (1999). Project DARE: no effects at 10-year follow-up. *Journal of Consulting and Clinical Psychology, 67*, 590–593.

MacAndrew, C., & Edgerton, R. B. (1969). *Drunken comportment: A social explanation.* Chicago: Aldine.

Manning, M.A., & Eugene-Hoyme, H. (2007). Fetal alcohol spectrum disorders: A practical clinical approach to diagnosis. *Neuroscience and Biobehavioral Reviews, 31*, 230–238.

Marlatt, G. A., & Gordon, J. R. (1985). Relapse prevention: Maintenance strategies in the treatment of addictive behaviors. New York: Guilford Press.

Marlatt, G.A., & Witkiewitz, K. (2002). Harm reduction approaches to alcohol use: Health promotion, prevention, and treatment. *Psychology of Addictive Behaviors, 27*, 867–886.

Martin, C. S., Chung, T., & Langenbucher, J. W. (2008). How should we revise diagnostic criteria for substance use disorders in the *DSM-5? Journal of Abnormal Psychology, 117*, 561–575.

Martin, C. S., Kaczynski, N. A., Maisto, S. A., & Tarter, R. E. (1996). Polydrug use in adolescent drinkers with and without *DSM–IV* alcohol abuse and dependence. *Alcoholism: Clinical and Experimental Research, 20*, 1099–1108.

Martinez, J. A., Muñoz, M. A., & Sher, K. J. (2009). A new minimum legal drinking age (MLDA)?: Some findings to inform the debate. *Psychology of Addictive Behaviors, 34,* 407–410.

McClure, J. B. (2002). Are biomarkers useful treatment aids for promoting health behavior change? An empirical review. *American Journal of Preventive Medicine, 22,* 200–207.

McCreary, D. R., & Sadava, S. W. (1998). Stress, drinking, and the adverse consequences of drinking in two samples of young adults. *Psychology of Addictive Behaviors, 12,* 247–261.

McCreary, D. R., & Sadava, S. W. (2000). Stress, alcohol use and alcohol-related problems: The influence of negative and positive affect in two cohorts of young adults. *Journal of Studies on Alcohol, 61,* 466–474.

McGue, M. (1994). Genes, environment, and the etiology of alcoholism. In *The development of alcohol problems: Exploring the biopsychosocial matrix of risk.* National Institute on Alcohol Abuse and Alcoholism Research Monograph 26, pp 1–40. Washington D.C.: N.I.H. Publication No. 94–3495.

McGue, M. (1999). Behavioral genetic models of alcoholism and drinking. In K.E. Leonard and H.T. Blane (Eds.), *Psychological theories of drinking and alcoholism* (2nd edition, pp. 372–421). New York: Guilford.

McGue, M., & Iacono, W. G. (2008). The adolescent origins of substance use disorders. *International Journal of Methods in Psychiatric Research, 17*(Suppl 1), S30-S38.

McMillan, G. P., & Lapham, S. (2006). Effectiveness of bans and laws in reducing traffic deaths: Legalized Sunday packaged alcohol sales and alcohol-related traffic crashes and crash fatalities in New Mexico. *American Journal of Public Health, 96,* 1944–1948.

Merikangas, K. R., Whitaker, A., Angst, J., Eaton, W., Canino, G., Rubio-Stipec, M., et al. (1996). Comorbidity and boundaries of affective disorders with anxiety disorders and substance misuse: Results of an international task force. *British Journal of Psychiatry, 168 Suppl. 30,* 58–67.

Miller, P.M., Smith, G.T., & Goldman, M.S. (1990). Emergence of alcohol expectancies in childhood: A possible critical period. *Journal of Studies on Alcohol, 51,* 343–349.

Miller, W. R., Zweben, A., DiClemente, C. C., & Rychtarik, R. G. (1995). *Motivational enhancement therapy manual: A clinical research guide for therapists treating individuals with alcohol abuse and dependence.* Rockville, MD: U.S. Department of Health and Human Services.

Monti, P.M., Colby, S.M., Barnett, N.P., Spirito, A., Rohsenow, D. J., Myers, M., et al. (1999). Brief intervention for harm reduction with alcohol-positive older adolescents in a hospital emergency department. *Journal of Consulting and Clinical Psychology, 67,* 989–994.

Monti, P. M., Miranda, R., Nixon, K., Sher, K. J., Swartzwelder, H. S., Tapert, S. F., et al. (2005). Adolescence: Booze, brains and behavior. *Alcoholism: Clinical and Experimental Research, 29,* 207–220.

Monti, P. M., & O'Leary, T. A. (1999). Coping and social skills training for alcohol and cocaine dependence. *Psychiatric Clinics of North America, 22,* 447–470.

Monti, P. M., & Rohsenow, D. J. (1999). Coping-skills training and cue-exposure therapy in the treatment of alcoholism. *Alcohol Research and Health, 23,* 107–115.

Monti, P. M., Rohsenow, D. J., Colby, S. M., & Abrams, D. B. (1995). Coping and social skills training. In R.K. Hester and W.R. Miller (Eds.), *Handbook of alcoholism treatment approaches: Effective alternatives* (2nd edition, pp. 2221–241). Needham Heights, MA: Allyn and Bacon.

Morgenstern, J., & Longabaugh, R. (2000). Cognitive-behavioral treatment for alcohol dependence: A review of evidence for its hypothesized mechanisms of action. *Addiction, 95,* 1475–1490.

Moskowitz, J. M. (1989). The primary prevention of alcohol problems: A critical review of the research literature. *Journal of Studies on Alcohol, 50,* 54–88.

Mothers Against Drunk Driving (2009). *The science behind the 21 law.* Retrieved, March 18, 2009 from http://www.madd.org/Parents/UnderageDrinking.aspx

Moyer, A., Finney, J. W., Swearingen, C. E., & Vergun, P. (2002). Brief interventions for alcohol problems: A meta-analytic review of controlled investigations in treatment-seeking and non-treatment seeking populations. *Addiction, 97,* 279–292.

Muñoz, N., & Day, N.E. (1996). Esophageal cancer. In D. Schoffenfield & J. F. Fraumani Jr. (Eds.), *Cancer epidemiology and prevention* (pp. 681–706). New York: Oxford University Press.

Muraven, M., & Baumeister, R. F. (2000). Self-regulation and depletion of limited resources: Does self-control resemble a muscle? *Psychological Bulletin, 126,* 247–259.

Muthén, B. O., Grant, B., & Hasin, D. (1993). The dimensionality of alcohol abuse and dependence: Factor analysis of DSM-III-R and proposed DSM-IV criteria in the 1988 National Health Interview Survey. *Addiction, 88,* 1079–1090.

Nakamura, K., Iwahashi, K., Matsuo, Y., Miyatake, R., Ichikawa, Y., & Suwaki, H. (1996). Characteristics of Japanese alcoholics with the atypical aldehyde dehydrogenase 2*2. I. A comparison of the genotypes of ALDH2, ADH2, ADH3, and cytochrome P-4502E1 between alcoholics and nonalcoholics. *Alcoholism: Clinical & Experimental Research, 20,* 52–55.

Nash, S. G., McQueen, A., & Bray, J. H. (2005). Pathways to adolescent alcohol use: Family environment, peer influence, and parental expectations. *Journal of Adolescent Health, 37,* 19–28.

Nathan, P. (1988). The addictive personality is the behavior of the addict. *Journal of Consulting and Clinical Psychology, 56,* 183–188.

National Institute on Alcohol Abuse and Alcoholism. (1993). *Eighth special report to the U.S. Congress on alcohol and health.* NIH Publication No. 94–3699. Washington DC: Author.

National Institute on Alcohol Abuse and Alcoholism. (1997). *Ninth special report to the U.S. Congress on alcohol and health from the secretary of health and human services.* Washington, DC: Author.

National Institute on Alcohol Abuse and Alcoholism. (2004). NIAAA Council Approves Definition of Binge Drinking, NIAAA Newsletter, No. 3. National Institute on Alcohol Abuse and Alcoholism, Bethesda, MD.

National Institute on Alcohol Abuse and Alcoholism. (2007). Helping patients who drink too much (2005 update). NIH Publication No. 07–3769. Rockville, MD.

National Institute on Alcohol Abuse and Alcoholism. (2008a). *Highlight on Underage Drinking.* Retrieved March 18, 2009 from http://alcoholpolicy.niaaa.nih.gov/index.asp?SEC={DA5E054D-FB8E-4F06-BBBC-6EED9F37A758}&Type=B_BASIC#_ftnref2

National Institute on Alcohol Abuse and Alcoholism. (2008b). NIAAA Clinician's Guide Online Training. Retrieved May 21st, 2009 from http://www.niaaa.nih.gov/Publications/EducationTrainingMaterials/VideoCases.htm

Neighbors, C., Larimer, M. E., Lostutter, T. W., & Woods, B. A. (2006). Harm reduction and individually focused alcohol prevention. *International Journal on Drug Policy, 17,* 304–309.

Newlin, D. B., & Thomson, J. B. (1990). Alcohol challenge with sons of alcoholics: A critical review and analysis. *Psychological Bulletin, 108,* 383–402.

Nigg, J. T., Glass, J. M., Wong, M. M., Poon, E., Jester, J. M., Fitzgerald, H. E., et al. (2004). Neuropsychological executive functioning in children at elevated risk for alcoholism: Findings in early adolescence. *Journal of Abnormal Psychology, 113,* 302–314.

Norberg, M. M., Krystal, J. H., & Tolin, D. F. (2008). A meta-analysis of d-cycloserine and the facilitation of fear extinction and exposure therapy. *Biological Psychiatry, 63,* 1118–1126.

O'Briant R.G., Petersen, N.W., & Heacock, D. (1977). How safe is social setting detoxification? *Alcohol Health and Research World, 1,* 22–27.

Odgers, C.L., Caspi, A., Nagin, D.S., Piquero, A.R., Slutske, W.S., Milne, B.J., et al. (2008). Is it important to prevent early exposure to drugs and alcohol among adolescents? *Psychological Science, 19*(10), 1037–1044.

O'Doherty, F. (1991). Is drug use a response to stress? *Drug and Alcohol Dependence, 29,* 97–106.

Osborn, J. A., Yu, C., Gabriel, K., & Weinberg, J. (1998). Fetal ethanol effects on benzodiazepine sensitivity measured by behavior on the elevated plus-maze. *Pharmacology Biochemistry and Behavior, 60,* 625–33.

Oslin, D. W., Berrettini, W. H., & O'Brien, C. P. (2006). Targeting treatments for alcohol dependence: The pharmacogenetics of naltrexone. *Addiction Biology, 11,* 397–403.

Palfai, T., & Wood, M. D. (2001). Positive alcohol expectancies and drinking behavior: The influence of expectancy strength and memory accessibility. *Psychology of Addictive Behaviors, 15,* 60–67.

Park, A., Sher, K. J., Krull, J. L., & Wood, P. K. (2009). Dual mechanisms underlying accentuation of risky drinking via fraternity/sorority affiliation: The role of personality, peer norms, and alcohol availability. *Journal of Abnormal Psychology, 118,* 241–245.

Park, C. L., Armeli, S., & Tennen, H. (2004). Appraisal-coping goodness of fit: A daily internet study. *Personality and Social Psychology Bulletin, 30,* 558–569.

Parker, E. S., Parker, D. A., & Harford, T. C. (1991). Specifying the relationship between alcohol use and cognitive loss: The effects of frequency of consumption and psychological distress. *Journal of Studies on Alcoholism, 52,* 366–373.

Parra, G., Sher, K. J., Krull, J., & Jackson, K. M. (2007). Frequency of heavy drinking and perceived peer alcohol involvement: Comparison of influence and selection mechanisms from a developmental perspective. *Psychology of Addictive Behaviors, 32,* 2211–2225.

Parsons, O.A., & Nixon, S.J. (1998). Cognitive functioning in sober social drinkers: A review of the research since 1986. *Journal of Studies on Alcohol, 59,* 180–190.

Pastor, A. D., & Evans, S. M. (2003). Alcohol outcome expectancies and risk for alcohol use problems in women with and without a family history of alcoholism. *Drug and Alcohol Dependence, 70,* 201–214.

Patterson, G. R., Reid, J. B., & Dishion, T. J. (1992). *Antisocial Boys.* Eugene, OR: Castalia.

Pederson, W. (1991). Mental health, sensation seeking and drug use patterns: A longitudinal study. *British Journal of Addiction, 86,* 195–204.

Perkins, H. W., Haines, M. P., & Rice, R. (2005). Misperceiving the college drinking norm and related problems: A nationwide study of exposure to prevention information, perceived norms and student alcohol misuse. *Journal of Studies on Alcohol, 66,* 470–478.

Perreira, K. M., & Sloan, F. A. (2001). Life events and alcohol consumption among mature adults: A longitudinal analysis. *Journal of Studies on Alcohol, 62,* 501–508.

Perrine, M. W., Mundt, J. C., Searles, J. S., & Lester, L. S. (1995). Validation of daily self-reported alcohol consumption using interactive voice response (IVR) technology. *Journal of Studies on Alcohol, 56,* 487–490.

Peterson, J. B., Rothfleisch, J., Zelazo, P. D., & Pihl, R. O. (1990). Acute alcohol intoxication and cognitive functioning. *Journal of Studies on Alcohol, 51,* 114–122.

Piasecki, T. M., Hufford, M. R., Solhan, M., & Trull, T. J. (2007). Assessing clients in their natural environments with electronic diaries: Rationale, benefits, limitations, and barriers. *Psychological Assessment, 19,* 25–43.

Pogue, T. F., & Sgontz, L. G. (1989). Taxing to control social costs: The case of alcohol. *The American Economic Review, 79,* 235–243.

Pollock, N. K., & Martin, C. S. (1999). Diagnostic orphans: Adolescents with alcohol symptom who do not qualify for DSM-IV abuse or dependence diagnoses. *American Journal of Psychiatry, 156,* 897–901.

Powers, M. B., Vedel, E., & Emmelkamp, P. (2008). Behavioral couples therapy (BCT) for alcohol and drug use disorders: A meta-analysis. *Clinical Psychology Review, 28,* 952–962.

Prescott, C. A., & Kendler, K. S. (1999). Age at first drink and risk for alcoholism: A noncausal association. *Alcoholism: Clinical and Experimental Research, 23,* 101–107.

Project MATCH Research Group. (1997). Matching alcoholism treatments to client heterogeneity: Project MATCH posttreatment drinking outcomes. *Journal of Studies on Alcohol, 58,* 7–29.

Proudfoot, H., Baillie, A. J., & Teesson, M. (2006). The structure of alcohol dependence in the community. *Drug and Alcohol Dependence, 81,* 21–26.

Raistrick, D. (2000). Management of alcohol detoxification. *Advances in Psychiatric Treatment, 6,* 348–355.

Randall, C. L., & Lester, D. (1975). Social modification of alcohol consumption in inbred mice. *Science, 189,* 149–151.

Read, J. P., Wood, M. D., Lejuez, C. W., Palfai, T. P., & Slack, M. (2004). Gender, alcohol consumption and differing alcohol expectancy dimensions in college drinkers. *Experimental and Clinical Psychopharmacology, 12,* 298–308.

Regier, D. A., Farmer, M. E., Rae, D. S., Locke, B. Z., Keith, S. J., Judd, L. L., et al. (1990). Comorbidity of mental disorders with alcohol and other drug abuse. Results from the Epidemiologic Catchment Area (ECA) Study. *Journal of American Medical Association, 264,* 2511–2518.

Rehm, J., Greenfield, T. K., & Rodgers, J. D. (2001). Average volume of alcohol consumption, patterns of drinking and all-cause mortality: Results from the US national alcohol survey. *American Journal of Epidemiology, 153,* 64–71.

Rehm, J., Room, R., Graham, K., Monteiro, M., Gmel, G., & Sempos, C. T. (2003). The relationship of average volume of alcohol consumption and patterns of drinking to burden of disease: An overview. *Addiction, 98,* 1209–1228.

Roberts, B. W., Walton, K. E., & Viechtbauer, W. (2006). Patterns of mean-level change in personality traits across the life course: A meta-analysis of longitudinal studies. *Psychological Bulletin, 132,* 1–25.

Roberts, D. W. (2009). Intimate partner homicide. *Journal of Contemporary Criminal Justice, 25,* 67–88.

Robins, L., Cottler, L., Bucholz, K., & Compton, W. (1996). *Diagnostic Interview Schedule, fourth version (DIS-IV).* St. Louis, MO: Washington University.

Robins, L. N., & Price, R. K. (1991). Adult disorders predicted by childhood conduct problems: Results from the NIMH Epidemiologic Catchment Area project. *Psychiatry: Journal for the Study of Interpersonal Processes, 54,* 116–132.

Robinson, T. E., & Berridge, K. C. (1993). The neural basis of drug craving: An incentive-sensitization theory of addiction. *Brain Research Reviews, 18,* 247–291.

Roehrs, T., & Roth, T. (2001). Sleep, sleepiness, and alcohol use. *Alcohol Research and Health, 25,* 101–109.

Rohsenow, D. J. (1982). Social anxiety, daily moods, and alcohol use over time among heavy social drinking men. *Psychology of Addictive Behaviors, 7,* 311–315.

Rohsenow, D. J., Monti, P. M., Rubonis, A. V., Sirota, A. D., Niaura, R. S., Colby, S. M., et al. (1994). Cue reactivity as a predictor of drinking among male alcoholics. *Journal of Consulting and Clinical Psychology, 62,* 620–626.

Ross, H. E., Glaser, F. B., & Stiasny, S. (1988). Sex differences in the prevalence of psychiatric disorders in patients with alcohol and drug problems. *Addiction, 83,* 1179–1192.

Rubin, R. (2008). Report makes a case for raising driving age. *USA Today.* Retrieved February 18, 2009 from http://www.usatoday.com/news/2008-09-0-teen-drivers_N.htm

Sacco, R. L., Elkind, M., Boden-Albala, B., Lin, I., Kargman, D. E., Hauser, W. A., et al. (1999). The protective effect of moderate alcohol consumption on ischemic stroke. *Journal of the American Medical Association, 281,* 53–60.

Saha, T. D., Stinson, F. S., & Grant, B. F. (2007). The role of alcohol consumption in future classifications of alcohol use disorders. *Drug and Alcohol Dependence, 89,* 82–92.

Sakai, J. T., Mikulich-Gilbertson, S. K., Long, R. J., & Crowley, T. J. (2006). Validity of transdermal alcohol monitoring: Fixed and self-regulated dosing. *Alcoholism: Clinical and Experimental Research, 30,* 26–33.

Sartor, C. E., Lynskey, M. T., Heath, A. C., Jacob, T., & True, W. (2007). The role of childhood risk factors in initiation of alcohol use and progression to alcohol dependence. *Addiction, 102,* 216–225.

Sayette, M. A. (1993). An appraisal-disruption model of alcohol's effects on stress responses in social drinkers. *Psychological Bulletin, 114,* 459–476.

Scheier, L. M., Botvin, G. J., & Miller, N. L. (1999). Life events, neighborhood stress, psychosocial functioning, and alcohol use among urban minority youth. *Journal of Child and Adolescent Substance Abuse, 9,* 19–50.

Schuckit, M. A. (1994). Substance-Related Disorders. *DSM-IV Sourcebook (Vol 1).* Washington, DC: American Psychiatric Association.

Schuckit, M. A. (1998). Biological, psychological and environmental predictors of the alcoholism risk: A longitudinal study. *Journal of Studies on Alcohol, 59,* 485–494.

Schuckit, M. A., & Hesselbrock, V. (1994). Alcohol dependence and anxiety disorders: What is the relationship? *American Journal of Psychiatry, 151,* 1723–1734.

Schuckit, M. A., Irwin, M., & Brown, S. A. (1990). The history of anxiety symptoms among 171 primary alcoholics. *Journal of Studies on Alcohol, 51,* 34–41.

Schuckit, M. A., & Smith, T. L. (2000). The relationships of a family history of alcohol dependence, a low level of response to alcohol and six domains of life functioning to the development of alcohol use disorders. *Journal of Studies on Alcohol, 61,* 827–835.

Sellers, E. M., Sullivan, J. T., Somer, G., & Sykora, K. (1991). Characterization of DSM-III-R criteria for uncomplicated alcohol withdrawal provides an empirical basis for DSM-IV. *Archives of General Psychiatry, 48,* 442–447.

Sher, K. J. (1987). Stress-response dampening. In K. E. Leonard & H. T. Blane (Eds.), *Psychological theories of drinking and alcoholism* (pp. 227–271). New York: Guilford Press.

Sher, K. J. (1991). *Children of alcoholics: A critical appraisal of theory and research.* A volume in the John D. and Catherine T. MacArthur Foundation Series on Mental Health and Development. Chicago: University of Chicago Press.

Sher, K. J. (2007). The road to alcohol dependence: Comment on Sartor et al. (2007). *Addiction, 102,* 185–187.

Sher, K. J., Bartholow, B. D., Peuser, K., Erickson, D. J., & Wood, M. D. (2007). Stress-Response dampening effects of alcohol: A systematic investigation of mediators, moderators, and outcomes. *Journal of Abnormal Psychology, 116,* 362–377.

Sher, K. J., & Epler, A. J. (2004). Alcoholic denial: Self-awareness and beyond. In B. D. Beitman & J. Nair, J. (Eds.), *Self-awareness deficits in psychiatric patients: Neurobiology, assessment and treatment.* (pp. 184–212). New York: W. W. Norton & Company.

Sher, K. J., & Gotham, H. J. (1999). Pathological alcohol involvement: A developmental disorder of young adulthood. *Development and Psychopathology, 11,* 933–956.

Sher, K. J., & Grekin, E. R. (2007). Alcohol and affect regulation. In J. Gross (Ed.). *Handbook of Emotion Regulation* (pp. 560–580). New York: Guilford.

Sher, K. J., Grekin, E., & Williams, N. (2005). The development of alcohol problems. *Annual Review of Clinical Psychology, 1,* 493–523.

Sher, K. J., & Martinez, J. A. (2009). The future of treatment for substance use: A View from 2009. In L. Cohen, F. L. Collins, A. M. Young, D. E. McChargue, & T. R. Leffingwell (Eds.), *The pharmacology and treatment of substance abuse: An evidence-based approach,* pp. 635–652. Mahwah, NJ: Lawrence Erlbaum Associates, Inc.

Sher, K. J., & Trull, T. J. (1994). Personality and disinhibitory psychopathology: Alcoholism and antisocial personality disorder. *Journal of Abnormal Psychology, 103,* 92–102.

Sher, K. J., & Trull, T. J. (1996). Methodological issues in psychopathology research. *Annual Review of Psychology, 47,* 371–400.

Sher, K. J., & Trull, T. J. (2002). Substance use disorder and personality disorder. *Current Psychiatry Reports, 4,* 25–29.

Sher, K. J., Trull, T. J., Bartholow, B. D., & Vieth, A. (1999). Personality and alcoholism: Issues, methods, and etiological processes. In K. Leonard & H. T. Blane (Eds.). *Psychological theories on drinking and alcoholism* (pp. 54–105). New York: Guilford Press.

Sher, K.J., Wolf, S.T., & Martinez, J.A. (2009). How can etiological research inform the distinction between normal drinking and disordered drinking? In L. M. Scheier (Ed.), *Handbook of drug use etiology,* pp. 225–246. Washington, DC: American Psychological Association.

Sher, K. J., Wood, M. D., Richardson, A. E., & Jackson, K. M. (2005). Subjective effects of alcohol I: Effects of the drink and drinking context. In M. Earleywine (Ed.), *Mind altering drugs: Scientific evidence for subjective experience* (pp. 86–134). New York: Oxford.

Sher, K. J., Wood, M. D., Wood, P. K., & Raskin, G. (1996). Alcohol outcome expectancies and alcohol use: A latent variable cross-lagged panel study. *Journal of Abnormal Psychology, 105*, 561–574.

Shope, J. T., Copeland, L. A., Marcoux, B. C., & Kamp, M. E. (1996). Effectiveness of a school-based substance abuse prevention program. *Journal of Drug Education, 26*, 323–337.

Sieber, M. F. (1981). Personality scores and licit and illicit substance abuse. *Personality and Individual Differences, 2*, 235–241.

Siegel, S., Baptista, M. A., Kim, J. A., McDonald, R. V., & Weise-Kelly L. (2000). Pavlovian psychopharmacology: The associative basis of tolerance. *Experimental and Clinical Psychopharmacology, 8*, 276–293.

Simons-Morton, B., Haynie, D. L., Crump, A. D., Eitel, P., & Saylor, K. E. (2001). Peer and parent influences on smoking and drinking among early adolescents. *Health Education and Behavior, 28*, 95–107.

Sisson, R. W., & Azrin, N. H. (1986). Family-member involvement to initiate and promote treatment of problem drinkers. *Journal of Behavior Therapy and Experimental Psychiatry, 17*, 15–21.

Slutske, W.S., Cronk, N.J., Sher, K.J., Madden, P.A.F., Bucholz, K.K., & Heath, A.C. (2002). Genes, environment and individual differences in alcohol expectancies among female adolescents and young adults. *Psychology of Addictive Behaviors, 16*, 308–317.

Slutske, W. S., D'Onofrio, B. M., Turkheimer, E., Emery, R. E., Harden, K. P., Heath, A. C., et al. (2008). Searching for an environmental effect of parental alcoholism on offspring alcohol use disorder: A genetically informed study of children of alcoholics. *Journal of Abnormal Psychology, 117*, 534–551.

Slutske, W. S., Heath, A. C., Madden, P. A., Bucholz, K. K., Statham, D. J., & Martin, N. G. (2002). Personality and the genetic risk for alcohol dependence. *Journal of Abnormal Psychology, 111*, 124–133.

Slutske, W. S., Heath, A. C., Dinwiddie, S. H., Madden, P. A., Bucholz, K. K., Dunne, M. P., et al. (1998). Common genetic risk factors for conduct disorder and alcohol dependence. *Journal of Abnormal Psychology, 107*, 363–374.

Smith, G. T., Fischer, S., Cyders, M. A., Annus, A. M., Spillane, N. S., & McCarthy, D. M. (2007). On the validity and utility of discriminating among impulsivity-like traits. *Assessment, 14*, 155–170.

Smith, G. T., Goldman, M. S., Greenbaum, P. E., & Christiansen, B. A. (1995). Expectancy for social facilitation from drinking: The divergent paths of high-expectancy and low expectancy adolescents. *Journal of Abnormal Psychology, 104*, 32–40.

Smith, J. E., & Meyers, R. J. (2004). *Motivating substance abusers to enter treatment: Working with family members*. New York: Guilford.

Sobell, L. C., Brown, J., Leo, G. I., & Sobell, M. B. (1996). The reliability of the Alcohol Timeline Followback when administered by telephone and by computer. *Drug and Alcohol Dependence, 42*, 49–54.

Sobell, L. C., & Sobell, M. B. (1992). Timeline follow-back: A technique for assessing self-reported alcohol consumption. In R.Z. Litten & J.P. Allen (Eds.), *Measuring alcohol consumption: psychosocial and biochemical methods* (pp. 41–72). Totowa, NJ: Humana Press.

Sobell, L. C., & Sobell, M. B. (2000). Alcohol Timeline Followback (TLFB). In American Psychiatric Association (Ed.), *Handbook of psychiatric measures* (pp. 477–479). Washington, DC: American Psychiatric Association.

Sobell, L. C., & Sobell, M. B. (2003). Alcohol consumption measures. In: P. Allen and V.B. Wilson, Editors, *Assessing alcohol problems: A guide for clinicians and researchers* (second edition), National Institute on Alcohol Abuse and Alcoholism, Bethesda, MD (2003), pp. 75–99.

Sobell, M. B., & Sobell, L. C. (1995). Controlled drinking after 25 years: How important was the great debate? *Addiction, 90*, 1149–1153.

Social Setting Detoxification (1986). A tailored training program. Available through Virginia Department of Mental Health and Mental Retardation Training Office, PO Box 1797, Richmond, VA 23214.

Solomon, R. L., & Corbit, J. D. (1974). An opponent-process theory of motivation: I. Temporal dynamics of affect. *Psychological Review, 81*, 119–145.

Spear, L. P. (2000). The adolescent brain and age-related behavioral manifestations. *Neuroscience and Biobehavioral Reviews, 24*, 417–463.

Spitzer, R.L., Endicott, J., & Robins, E. (1978). Research diagnostic criteria: Rationale and reliability. *Archives of General Psychiatry, 35*, 773–782.

Srisurapanont, M., & Jarusuraisin, N. (2005). Naltrexone for the treatment of alcoholism: A metaanalysis of randomized controlled trials. *International Journal of Neuropsychopharmacology, 8*, 267–280.

Stacy, A. W, Newcomb, M. D., & Bentler, P. M. (1991). Cognitive motivation and drug use: A 9-year longitudinal study. *Journal of Abnormal Psychology, 100*, 502–515.

Steele, C. M., & Josephs, R. A. (1988). Drinking your troubles away: II. An attention-allocation model of alcohol's effect on psychological stress. *Journal of Abnormal Psychology, 97*, 196–205.

Steele, C. M., & Josephs, R. A. (1990). Alcohol myopia: Its prized and dangerous effects. *American Psychologist, 45*, 921–933.

Steele, C. M., Southwick, L., & Pagano, R. (1986). Drinking your troubles away: The role of activity in mediating alcohol's reduction of psychological stress. *Journal of Abnormal Psychology, 95*, 173–180.

Steinhausen, H., Willms, J., & Spohr, H-L. (1993). Long-term psychopathological and cognitive outcome of children with fetal alcohol syndrome. *Journal of the American Academy of Child & Adolescent Psychiatry, 32*, 990–994.

Stepp, S. D., Trull, T. J., & Sher, K. J. (2005). Borderline personality features prospectively predict alcohol use problems. *Journal of Personality Disorders, 19*, 711–722.

Stinnett, J. L. (1982). Outpatient detoxification of the alcoholic. *The International Journal of the Addictions, 17*, 1031–1046.

Stinson, F.S., Grant, B.F., Dawson, D.A., Ruan, W.J., Huang, B., & Saha, T. (2005). Comorbidity between DSM-IV alcohol and specific drug use disorders in the United States: Results from the National Epidemiologic Survey on Alcohol and Related Conditions. *Drug and Alcohol Dependence, 80*, 105–116.

Streissguth, A. P., Barr, H. M., & Sampson, P. D. (1990). Moderate prenatal alcohol exposure: Effects on child IQ and learning problems at age 7 1/2 years. *Alcoholism: Clinical & Experimental Research, 14*, 662–669.

Streissguth, A. P., Sampson, P. D., Olson, H. C., Bookstein, F. L., Barr, H. M., Scott, M., et al. (1994). Maternal drinking during pregnancy: Attention and short–term memory in

14–year old offspring—a longitudinal prospective study. *Alcohol: Clinical and Experimental Research, 19,* 202–218.

Sullivan, J. T., Sykora, K., Schneiderman, J., Naranjo, C. A., & Sellers, E. M. (1989). Assessment of alcohol withdrawal: The revised clinical institute withdrawal assessment for alcohol scale (CIWA-Ar). *British Journal of Addiction, 84,* 1353–1357.

Swartzwelder, H.S., Wilson, W.A., & Tayyeb, M.I. (1995). Age-dependent inhibition of long-term potentiation by ethanol in immature versus mature hippocampus. *Alcoholism: Clinical and Experimental Research, 19,* 1480–1485.

Swift, R. (2000). Transdermal alcohol measurement for estimation of blood alcohol concentration. *Alcoholism: Clinical and Experimental Research, 24,* 422–423.

Takeshita, T., Morimoto, K., Mao, X., Hashimoto, T., & Furuyama, J. (1994). Characterization of the three genotypes of low Km aldehyde dehydrogenase in a Japanese population. *Human Genetics, 94,* 217–223.

Tapert, S. F., Brown, G. G., Baratta, M. V., & Brown, S. A. (2004). fMRI BOLD response to alcohol stimuli in alcohol dependent young women. *Addictive Behavior, 29,* 33–50.

Testa, M., Quigley, B. M., & Eiden, R. D. (2003). The effects of prenatal alcohol exposure on infant mental development: A meta-analytical review. *Alcohol & Alcoholism, 38,* 295–304.

Thatcher, D. L., Cornelius, J. R., & Clark, D. B. (2005). Adolescent alcohol use disorders predict adult borderline personality. *Psychology of Addictive Behaviors, 30,* 1709–1724.

Thush, C., & Wiers, R. W. (2007). Explicit and implicit alcohol-related cognitions and the prediction of future drinking in adolescents. *Psychology of Addictive Behaviors, 32,* 1367–1383.

Thush, C., Wiers, R. W., Ames, S. L., Grenard, J. L., Sussman, S., & Stacy, A. W. (2008). Interactions between implicit and explicit cognition and working memory capacity in the prediction of alcohol use in at-risk adolescents. *Drug and Alcohol Dependence, 94,* 116–124.

Tobler, N. S. (1986). Meta-analysis of 143 adolescent drug prevention programs: Quantitative outcome results of program participants compared to a control or comparison group. *Journal of Drug Issues, 16,* 537–567.

Tonigan, J. S., Toscova, R., & Miller, W. R. (1996). Meta-analysis of the literature on Alcoholics Anonymous: Sample and study characteristics moderate findings. *Journal of Studies on Alcohol, 57,* 65–72.

Toomey, T. L., & Wagenaar, A. C. (1999). Policy options for prevention: The case of alcohol. *Journal of Public Health Policy, 20,* 192–213.

Tragesser, S. L., Sher, K. J., Trull, T. J., & Park, A. (2007). Personality disorder symptoms, drinking motives, and alcohol use and consequences: Cross-sectional and prospective mediation. *Experimental and Clinical Psychopharmacology, 15,* 282–292.

Tragesser, S. L., Trull, T. J., Sher, K. J., & Park, A. (2008). Drinking motives as mediators in the relation between personality disorder symptoms and alcohol use disorder. *Journal of Personality Disorders, 22,* 525–537.

Treno, A. J., Ponicki, W. R., Remer, L. G., & Gruenwald, P. J. (2008). Alcohol outlets, youth drinking, and self-reported ease of access to alcohol: A constraints and opportunities approach. *Alcoholism: Clinical and Experimental Research, 32,* 1372–1379.

Trull, T. J., Jahng, S., Tomko, R. L., Wood, P. K., & Sher, K. J. (2010). Revised NESARC Personality Disorder Diagnoses: Gender, Prevalence, and Comorbidity with Substance Dependence Disorders. *Journal of Personality Disorders, 24,* 412–426.

Trull, T. J., Sher, K. J., Minks-Brown, C., Durbin, J., & Burr, R. (2000). Borderline personality disorder and substance use disorders: A review and integration. *Clinical Psychology Review, 20,* 235–253.

Uhl, G. R., Drgon, T., Johnson, C., Fatusin, O. O., Liu, Q. R., Contoreggi, C., et al. (2008). "Higher order" addiction molecular genetics: convergent data from genome-wide association in humans and mice. *Biochemical Pharmacology, 75,* 98–111.

U.S. Department of Agriculture and U.S. Department of Health and Human Services. (2005). *Dietary Guidelines for Americans,* 2005, 6th Edition. Washington, DC: U.S. Government Printing Office.

Vengeliene, V., Bilbao, A., Molander, A., & Spanagel, R. (2008). Neuropharmacology of alcohol addiction. *British Journal of Pharmacology, 154,* 299–315.

Verheul, R., van den Brink, W., & Hartgers, C. (1995). Prevalence of personality disorders among alcoholics and drug addicts: An overview. *European Addiction Research, 1,* 166–177.

Victor, M. (1993). Persistent altered mentation due to ethanol. *Neurology Clinic, 11,* 639–661.

Victor, M. (1994). Alcoholic dementia. *Canadian Journal of Neurological Science, 21,* 88–99.

Vinson, D. C. (1989). Acute transient memory loss. *American Family Physician, 39,* 249–254.

Voas, R. B., & DeYoung, D. J. (2002). Vehicle action: Effective policy for controlling drunk and other high-risk drivers? *Accident Analysis and Prevention, 34,* 263–270.

Voas, R. B., Tippetts, A. S., & Fell, J. C. (2003). Assessing the effectiveness of minimum legal drinking age and zero tolerance laws in the United States. *Accident Analysis and Prevention, 35,* 579–587.

Wagenaar, A. C., & Holder, H. D. (1991). Effects of alcoholic beverage server liability on traffic crash injuries. *Alcoholism: Clinical and Experimental Research, 15,* 942–947.

Wagenaar, A. C., Salois, M. J., & Komro, K. A. (2009). Effects of beverage alcohol price and tax levels on drinking: A meta-analysis of 1,003 estimates from 112 studies. *Addiction, 104,* 179–190.

Wakefield, J. C. (1992). Disorder as harmful dysfunction: A conceptual critique of DSM-III-R's definition of mental disorder. *Psychological Review, 99,* 232–247.

Wall, T. L., Thomasson, H. R., Schuckit, M. A., & Ehlers, C. L. (1992). Subjective feelings of alcohol intoxication in Asians with genetic variations of ALDH2 alleles. *Alcoholism: Clinical & Experimental Research, 16,* 991–995.

Watt, K., Purdie, D. M., Roche, A. M., & McClure, R. (2006). Acute alcohol consumption and mechanism of injury. *Journal of Studies on Alcohol, 67,* 14–21.

Wechsler, H., & Austin S. B. (1998). Binge drinking: The five/four measure. *Journal of Studies on Alcohol, 59,* 122–123.

Wechsler, H., Dowdall, G. W., Maenner, G., Gledhill-Hoyt, J., & Lee, H. (1998). Changes in binge drinking and related problems among American college students between 1993 and 1997: Results of the Harvard School of Public Health College Alcohol Study. *Journal of American College Health, 47,* 57–68.

Wechsler, H., Nelson, T. F., Lee, J. E., Seibring, M., Lewis, C., & Keeling, R. P. (2003). Perception and reality: A national evaluation of social norms marketing interventions to reduce college students' heavy alcohol use. *Journal of Studies on Alcohol, 64,* 484–494.

Weitzman, E. R., Folkman, A., Lemieux-Folkman, K., & Wechsler, H. (2003). The relationship of alcohol outlet density to heavy and frequent drinking and drinking-related problems among college students at eight universities. *Health & Place, 9,* 1–6.

Welte, J. W., & Mirand, A. L. (1995). Drinking, problem drinking and life stresses in the elderly general population. *Journal of Studies on Alcohol, 56,* 67–73.

Whiteside, S. P., & Lynam, D. R. (2001). The Five Factor Model and impulsivity: Using a structural model of personality to understand impulsivity. *Personality and Individual Differences, 30,* 669–689.

Whitfield, C. L., Thompson, G., Lamb, A., Spencer, V., Pfeifer, M., & Browning-Ferrando, M. (1978). Detoxification of 1,024 alcoholic patients without psychoactive drugs. *Journal of the American Medical Association, 239,* 1409–1410.

Widiger, T. A., & Trull, T. J. (2007). Plate tectonics in the classification of personality disorder: Shifting to a dimensional model. *American Psychologist, 62,* 71–83.

Wiers, R. W., & Stacy, A. W. (Eds.). (2006). *Handbook of implicit cognition and addiction.* Thousand Oaks: Sage.

Wiers, R. W., Rinck, M., Kordts, R., Katrijn Houben, K., & Strack, F. (2010). Retraining automatic action-tendencies to approach alcohol in hazardous drinkers. *Addiction, 105,* 279–287.

Wilk, A. I., Jensen, N. M., & Havighurst, T. C. (1997). Meta-analysis of randomized control trials addressing brief interventions in heavy alcohol drinkers. *Journal of General Internal Medicine, 12,* 274–283.

Winick, C. (1962). Maturing out of narcotic addiction. *Bulletin on Narcotics, 14,* 1–7.

Winqvist, S., Luukinen, H., Jokelainen, J., Lehtilahti, M., Näyhä, S., & Hillbom, M. (2008). Recurrent traumatic brain injury is predicted by the index injury occurring under the influence of alcohol. *Brain Injury, 22,* 780–785.

Witkiewitz, K., & Marlatt, G. A. (2004). Relapse prevention for alcohol and drug problems: That was Zen, this is tao. *American Psychologist, 59,* 224–235.

Witkiewitz, K., & Marlatt, G. A. (2007). Modeling the complexity of post-treatment drinking: It's a rocky road to relapse. *Clinical Psychology Review, 27,* 724–738.

Witkiewitz, K., & Marlatt, G. A. (2008). Why and how do substance abuse treatments work?: Investigating mediated change. *Addiction, 103,* 649–650.

Witkiewitz, K, van der Maas, H.L.J, Hufford, M.R, & Marlatt, G. A. (2007). Nonnormality and divergence in post-treatment alcohol use: Reexamining the Project MATCH data "another way" *Journal of Abnormal Psychology, 116,* 378–394.

Wong, M. M., Brower, K. J., Fitzgerald, H. E., & Zucker, R. A. (2004). Sleep problems in early childhood and early onset of alcohol and other drug use in adolescence. *Alcoholism: Clinical and Experimental Research, 28,* 578–587.

World Health Organization. (2004). *Global status report: Alcohol Policy.* Geneva, Switzerland: World Health Organization.

Yesavage, J. A., Dolhert, N., & Taylor, J. L. (1994). Flight simulator performance of younger and older aircraft pilots: Effects of age and alcohol. *Journal of the American Geriatric Society, 42,* 577–582.

Young, R. M., Lawford, B. R., Feeney, G. F., Ritchie, T., & Noble, E. P. (2004). Alcohol-related expectancies are associated with the D2 dopamine receptor and GABAA receptor beta3 subunit genes. *Psychiatry Research, 127,* 171–183.

Zeigler, D. W., Wang, C. C., Yoast, R. A., Dickinson, B. D., McCaffree, M. A., Robinowitz, C. B., et al. (2005). The neurocognitive effects of alcohol on adolescents and college students. *Preventive Medicine, 40,* 23–32.

Zerhouni, E. A. (2006). Clinical research at a crossroads: The NIH roadmap. *Journal of Investigative Medicine, 54,* 171–173.

Zerhouni, E. A. (March 5, 2008). Strategic vision for the future: From curative to preemptive medicine. National Institutes on Health. http://www.nih.gov/strategicvision.htm

Zucker, R. A. (1987). The four alcoholisms: A developmental account of the etiologic process. In P. C. Rivers (Ed.), *Alcohol and addictive behaviors: Nebraska symposium on motivation* (pp. 27–83). Lincoln, NE: University of Nebraska Press.

Zucker, R. A., Fitzgerald, H. E., & Moses, H. D. (1995). Emergence of alcohol problems and the several alcoholisms: A developmental perspective on etiologic theory and life course trajectory. In D. Cicchetti & D. J. Cohen (Eds.), *Developmental psychopathology, Vol. 2: Risk, disorder, and adaptation. Wiley series on personality processes* (pp. 677–711). New York: John Wiley & Sons.

Zucker, R. A., & Gomberg, E. S. L. (1986). Etiology of alcoholism reconsidered: The case for a biopsychosocial process. *American Psychologist, 41,* 783.

Sex and Gender Disorders

Andrea Bradford *and* Cindy M. Meston

Abstract

Sex and gender disorders are classified into three major categories. The *sexual dysfunctions* are problems that inhibit one's motivation or ability to engage in sexual activity. *Paraphilias* are recurrent patterns of sexual arousal and/or behavior involving inappropriate targets of sexual expression. *Gender identity disorder* is the experience of intense discomfort with one's assigned gender role, accompanied by the desire to live as a person of the opposite sex. Conceptualizations of sex and gender disorders are ever evolving in response to multiple cultural, scientific, political, and commercial influences. This chapter reviews current practice and emerging concepts in the diagnosis and treatment of sex and gender disorders, with emphasis on recent research findings and key unresolved questions.

Keywords: Gender dysphoria, gender identity disorder, orgasm, paraphilia, sexual arousal, sexual desire, sexual dysfunction

Although the behavior of many animal species suggests a "hard-wired," instinct-driven program for reproductive activity, other animals possess capabilities for a more flexible range of sexual behavior. The range of sexual behavior in humans is particularly diverse. As such, distinguishing "normal" from "abnormal" behavior for clinical purposes is problematic. The modern practice of classifying certain sexual behavior patterns as mental disorders has an ever-evolving and sometimes self-contradictory history. For example, although today hypoactive sexual desire disorder is the most common sexual dysfunction diagnosis assigned to women, earlier versions of the *Diagnostic and Statistical Manual of Mental Disorders* (DSM) reflected clinical concern about excessive sexual interest in women (nymphomania), which is no longer a defined diagnosis. Another prominent example is the diagnosis of homosexuality as a mental disorder, which was restricted to "ego dystonic homosexuality" in the third edition of the DSM and later removed altogether. Clearly, as norms for sexual behavior evolve, so do categories of psychopathology.

Classifying sexual behavior patterns as disorders has a variety of potential consequences. On one hand, viewing troublesome sexual behaviors as manifestations of clinical disorders rather than moral or volitional failings may open the door for education, support, and therapeutic intervention to improve the sufferer's quality of life. On the other hand, pathologizing sexual behavior that flouts cultural norms—however well-intentioned—may facilitate the stigmatization or exploitation of those with an identified "disorder." The tension between normative/affirming and pathologizing/medicalizing explanations of sexual and gender behavior is reflected even in the conventional nomenclature of the DSM, which makes most psychiatric diagnoses conditional upon personal distress or functional impairment associated with a sexual problem.

The goal of this chapter is to provide a brief overview of recent practices and theoretical perspectives on sex and gender disorders. Conventionally, these disorders are classified as sexual dysfunctions (problems related to initiation or resolution of sexual activity, generally with a partner), paraphilias (problems related to inappropriate targets of sexual arousal and behavior), and gender disorders (discomfort with the gender role behavior of one's sex at birth). As emerging opinion emphasizes sex and gender differences in the etiology and assessment of sexual dysfunctions, sexual dysfunctions affecting men and women will be discussed separately.

Sexual Dysfunctions in Women

The debut of sildenafil (Viagra) on the U.S. market in 1998, followed quickly by competitors tadalafil (Cialis) and vardenafil (Levitra), was met with both commercial success and increased popular attention to male sexual disorders. The search for a corresponding product for women's sexual problems has been less successful. Enthusiasm for a "pink Viagra" has been tempered by unremarkable clinical trial outcomes and pointed opposition to the medicalization of women's sexual problems (e.g., Moynihan, 2003; Tiefer, 2002). Although development of medical treatments for women's sexual dysfunction is ongoing, a lesson learned from the Viagra era is that models of male sexual function and dysfunction may not be readily applicable to women.

In 1999, Laumann, Paik, and Rosen published figures from the National Health and Social Life Survey indicating that 43% of women complained of a sexual problem in the past year. This frequently cited figure has been a subject of criticism as this estimate does not take into account the presence of personal distress and inflates the prevalence of clinically significant problems. More recent and conservative estimates of female sexual dysfunction, which take into account personal distress, range from 12.0% (Shifren, Monz, Russo, Segreti, & Johannes, 2008) to 24.4% (Bancroft, Loftus, & Long, 2003).

Sexual dysfunctions in women are often comorbid and may be related to multiple etiological factors. Thus, a multidimensional assessment and treatment strategy is often warranted. In addition to the assessment of the nature, severity, and course of current symptoms, a comprehensive assessment of sexual concerns should include a psychosocial history, a discussion of sexual attitudes in the family and culture of origin, a history of early sexual experiences (including, if applicable, unwanted sexual contact), assessment of general functioning in the current relationship, and a medical and psychiatric history. Validated instruments to assess sexual dysfunction in women include the Brief Index of Sexual Functioning for Women (BISF-W; Taylor, Rosen, & Leiblum, 1994), the Changes in Sexual Functioning Questionnaire

(CSFQ; Clayton, McGarvey, & Clavet, 1997), the Derogatis Interview for Sexual Functioning (DISF/DISF-SR; Derogatis, 1997), and the Female Sexual Function Index (FSFI; Rosen et al., 2000).

Sexual Desire and Arousal Disorders

The DSM-IV-TR (American Psychiatric Association, 2000) defines hypoactive sexual desire disorder (HSDD) as a persistent or recurrent deficiency (or absence) of sexual fantasies and desire for sexual activity that causes marked distress or interpersonal difficulty. The clinical judgment is made taking into consideration factors that affect sexual functioning such as age and the context of the person's life. The DSM-IV-TR criteria for HSDD are derived from an early model of sexual response introduced by Masters and Johnson (1966) and amended by Kaplan (1979), in which desire is assumed to precede arousal and orgasm in a unidirectional, sequential manner. However, this definition has elicited criticism (Basson et al., 2003) for its characterization of sexual fantasies as a primary trigger for sexual behavior in women. Although engaging in sexual fantasy may be characteristic of women in new relationships, research suggests that spontaneous sexual thoughts or fantasies occur far less frequently among women in longer-term relationships (e.g., Cawood & Bancroft, 1996). Basson (2001) proposed that, because women are often motivated to engage in sexual activity for reasons other than a desire for sexual stimulation, desire may follow *after* a woman has begun to experience sexual stimulation and arousal ("receptive" or "responsive" desire). Thus, there appears to be a close but not necessarily unidirectional association between sexual desire and sexual arousal in women. Laumann, Paik, and Rosen (1999) reported that 31% of women in the United States experienced a lack of interest in sex for at least several months during the prior year. Findings from clinic- and population-based studies indicated current prevalence rates of 10%–46% for sexual desire problems (Simons & Carey, 2001).

Commonly associated with low sexual desire is a lack of sexual arousal, which includes both feelings of subjective sexual excitement and physiological changes such as genital swelling and lubrication. Sexual arousal concerns seldom present outside of the context of other sexual disorders (Bancroft, Graham, & McCord, 2001; Heiman & Meston, 1997). Female sexual arousal disorder (FSAD) is defined in the DSM-IV-TR as a persistent or recurrent inability to attain or to maintain until completion of sexual activity an adequate genital lubrication and swelling response of sexual excitement that causes marked distress or interpersonal difficulty. Although the DSM-IV-TR definition of FSAD focuses exclusively on a genital response, it is widely recognized that women's sexual arousal includes a psychological component characterized by sexual excitement and that arousal may precede or enhance sexual desire (Basson, 2001). Moreover, vaginal lubrication appears to be an immediate "reflexive" response to any sexual stimuli—whether desired and enjoyed or not—and it does not always correlate closely with a woman's subjective experience of feeling "sexually turned on" (Basson et al., 2003).

Problems related to sexual desire and receptivity have been associated with negative or fearful beliefs and attitudes about sexuality and passive gender role identification (Nobre & Pinto-Gouveia, 2006; Sanchez, Crocker, & Boike, 2005). Assessment should include a psychosocial history to elicit family attitudes toward sexuality, early sexual experiences, and unwanted or otherwise upsetting sexual experiences. Depressed mood and anxiety are also associated with sexual desire and arousal difficulties and should be assessed. Anxiety that is specific to sexual concerns may play a central role in the development and maintenance of sexual arousal problems. Barlow (1986) proposed that the cognitive distraction of performance anxiety directs attention from sexual to nonsexual cues, interfering with arousal. Although performance anxiety in men is typically linked to the ability to attain and maintain an erection, "performance concerns" in women are more likely related to perceived sexual attractiveness and desirability than to genital function (Dove & Wiederman, 2000).

Problems with sexual desire and arousal may reflect not only intrapsychic factors but also problems in the relationship with the sexual partner. A presenting complaint of low sexual desire or responsiveness in the woman should therefore trigger several clinical hypotheses about both partners. Sexual problems may be epiphenomena of unresolved problems in the relationship or interpersonal dynamics between partners. Low desire or arousal may also represent a normative response to an unskilled partner or unsatisfactory conditions specific to the couple's sex life. Finally, sexual desire and arousal concerns may develop secondary to a *partner's* sexual dysfunction and may resolve with successful treatment of the partner (Goldstein et al., 2005).

Women's sexual desire and arousal appear to be influenced by levels of sex steroid hormones, particularly androgens and estrogens. Endocrinological disorders interfere with these synthesis of these hormones and have been linked to problems with sexual desire and arousal (for review, see Guay & Spark 2006). Decreased ovarian function during the menopausal transition also results in lower estrogen production and has also been associated with sexual desire and arousal problems. Recent epidemiological studies indicate that "surgical menopause" induced by oophorectomy (surgical removal of the ovaries) is a more prominent risk factor for HSDD than natural menopause, particularly in younger cohorts (Dennerstein, Koochaki, Barton, & Graziottin, 2006; Leiblum, Koochaki, Rodenberg, Barton, & Rosen, 2006). Testosterone has shown some efficacy in increasing sexual desire among surgically and naturally menopausal women, although further investigation is ongoing in light of concerns about side effects and long-term safety. Furthermore, testosterone therapy does not appear to influence sexual desire in women with testosterone levels in the typical range. Other contributing biological factors include the effects of medications, particularly selective serotonin reuptake inhibitors (SSRIs), and fatigue or neurological problems related to chronic illnesses.

The psychological treatment literature focuses primarily on HSDD. Few psychosocial treatment outcome studies have been directed specifically at FSAD. However, the behavioral sex therapy techniques pioneered by Masters and Johnson (1970) remain in widespread use among clinicians treating all types of sexual disorders. Traditional behavioral sex therapy emphasizes sexuality education, partner communication skills, and sensate focus exercises. Sensate focus is a core component of behavioral sex therapy and comprises a progressive series of touching exercises between partners (assigned as homework) to heighten partners' awareness of pleasurable experiences and enable communication of preferences for sexual touch. Prescribed sensate focus activities, completed by the couple at regular intervals throughout treatment, gradually progress from nongenital touching to mutual massage and masturbation to intercourse. An effectiveness study of behavioral sex therapy applied to couples in a real-world clinical setting demonstrated that these techniques were generally helpful across a range of sexual problems in both men and women (Sarwer & Durlak, 1997).

Despite early enthusiasm for Masters and Johnson's sex therapy program, contemporary sex therapies generally acknowledge the limitations of behavioral techniques for addressing the complex issues that often underlie sexual dysfunctions.

Relationship problems, issues related to past sexual trauma, and primary psychiatric conditions are a few of many potential concerns that may complicate sex therapy. Therefore, the contemporary clinical literature overwhelmingly emphasizes an integrative approach to treatment of sexual desire and arousal disorders. These approaches most often incorporate traditional sex therapy concepts with systems and/or cognitive-behavioral conceptualizations, as well as biomedical factors. Cognitive-behavioral techniques are distinguished from other sex therapy components by the use of cognitive techniques to challenge beliefs that undermine sexual desire and arousal, such as unrealistic expectations of performance, exaggerated fears of undesirable outcomes, and the notion that one is "innately" dysfunctional. Evidence from the relatively few systematic trials of psychotherapy for HSDD show varying levels of efficacy for both traditional sex therapy and cognitive-behavioral therapy (CBT) (Brotto, 2006). Limitations of the psychological treatment literature include heterogeneity of treatment methods and experimental designs that prevent the analysis of separate treatment components, precluding rigorous comparisons of studies. Evidence to support the efficacy of psychodynamic, systemic, and other types of treatment is at the level of clinical case reports. Thus, the relative efficacies of various psychosocial treatments for sexual desire and arousal disorders have not been clarified.

Sexual Aversion Disorder

Sexual aversion, the aversion to and avoidance of sexual contact with a partner, is a poorly understood phenomenon for which there has been little systematic research. Although sexual aversion disorder is commonly classified alongside hypoactive sexual desire disorder as a "desire disorder," the clinical literature describes sexual aversion both etiologically and symptomatically in terms more congruent with anxiety disorders. For instance, Kingsberg and Janata (2003) defined sexual aversion as "the acquisition of fear and anxiety, with accompanying symptoms of disgust, toward sexual activity with a partner." The diagnosis of sexual aversion disorder as defined in the DSM-IV-TR requires both the cognitive/affective experience of aversion and behavioral avoidance. Although it is not a requirement of diagnosis, sexual aversion is often discussed in terms of a panic-like response to sexual contact (e.g., Kaplan, 1988). It is not unusual for women with sexual aversion disorder to report a history of unwanted sexual contact, but it should not be assumed that sexual abuse is an etiological factor in all cases of sexual aversion.

Case reports support the use of cognitive-behavioral techniques in the treatment of sexual aversion disorder. As with phobias and other anxiety disorders, systematic desensitization to anxiety-provoking situations and stimuli is a common approach to treatment. Assessment of feared thoughts, images, and behaviors may be used to generate a hierarchy of anxiety-provoking stimuli and situations. Exposure to these stimuli, beginning with the least anxiety-provoking, is paired with relaxation techniques to reduce the fear response. Once a stimulus provokes minimal discomfort, exposure proceeds up the hierarchy to more intensely aversive stimuli. Imagined stimuli are often sufficient to provoke anxiety, although the usual treatment goal is to eventually engage in real-life sexual behaviors with little or no anxiety. Additional supportive treatment may be indicated when significant relationship or social problems are secondary to the disorder.

Female Orgasmic Disorder

For all its presumed importance in women's sexual lives, a precise definition of female orgasm is elusive. Even within the clinical and scientific literature, female orgasm is vaguely and variably defined, with over two dozen existing comprehensive definitions written by different authors (Mah & Binik, 2001). An attempt to clarify and reconcile definitions of female orgasm can be found in the report of the committee on female orgasm of the 2003 International Consultation on Urological Diseases as follows:

> An orgasm in the human female is a variable, transient peak sensation of intense pleasure, creating an altered state of consciousness, usually accompanied by involuntary, rhythmic contractions of the pelvic, striated circumvaginal musculature often with concomitant uterine and anal contractions and myotonia that resolves the sexually-induced vasocongestion (sometimes only partially), usually with an induction of well-being and contentment.
> (Meston, Hull, Levin, & Sipski, 2004)

The DSM-IV-TR defines Female Orgasmic Disorder (FOD) as the persistent or recurrent delay in, or absence of, orgasm following a normal sexual excitement phase, which causes marked distress or interpersonal difficulty. The diagnosis requires clinician judgment and careful assessment to determine whether the woman's ability to experience orgasm is less than would be reasonable for her age, sexual experience, and the adequacy of sexual stimulation she receives. Although not stated in the DSM-IV-TR, the clinical consensus is that a woman who can obtain orgasm during intercourse with manual stimulation but not intercourse alone would not meet criteria for clinical diagnosis unless her sexual response pattern is a significant source of distress.

In the National Health and Social Life Survey, 24% of women reported a lack of orgasm in the past year for at least several months or more (Laumann, Gagnon, Michael, & Michaels, 1994). Clinic-based studies have yielded comparable prevalence estimates for orgasm difficulties. In a sample of 329 healthy women attending an outpatient gynecological clinic, Rosen, Taylor, Leiblum, and Bachmann (1993) found that 29% reported orgasm problems. Similarly, 23% of women were found to report orgasm problems in a sample of 104 general practice patients (Read, King, & Watson, 1997). Because attaining a sufficient degree of sexual arousal usually precedes orgasm, factors that contribute to sexual arousal problems are indirectly implicated in FOD.

Important clinical distinctions exist between women who meet criteria for lifelong, generalized FOD ("primary anorgasmia"), who report having never experienced orgasm or only ever having experienced orgasm infrequently and with difficulty, and women who are orgasmic at least part of the time. Anorgasmia is more common in younger women and may be related to limited sexual experience (e.g., having never or seldom masturbated) or limited opportunities for intense sexual arousal. Other demographic factors associated with anorgasmia include low educational level and high religiosity, although explanatory mechanisms are largely speculative (for further review, see Meston et al., 2004). Women with situational and/or acquired orgasmic disorder make up a heterogeneous clinical population. For example, the definition is applicable to women who can experience orgasm through masturbation but not during sexual activity with a partner, women who were once able to experience orgasm but are no longer able to do so, or women who experience orgasm less frequently than desired. In general, treatment of this population is directed toward the factors that inhibit sexual arousal and/or orgasm in the particular contexts in which the dysfunction is present.

A well-studied and efficacious treatment for primary anorgasmia is directed masturbation, a multifaceted intervention that includes education, prescribed exploratory and experiential exercises in which a women learns to elicit pleasurable sensations through self-stimulation, and application of skills toward the attainment of orgasm. These experiences are first limited to the woman herself and are often facilitated with the use of aids such as vibrators, topical lubricants, and erotica. The partner is later included in the treatment once the woman has learned how to orgasm through solitary self-stimulation (for a detailed guide to directed masturbation, please refer to Heiman & LoPiccolo, 1988). Directed masturbation is efficacious in several treatment modalities including individual, group, and couples therapy and bibliotherapy (for review, see Meston, 2006). Directed masturbation for situational or acquired orgasmic disorders has received little study but appears to be less efficacious. Couple therapy, psychoeducation, and sex therapy techniques, such as those described in the previous section, may be of benefit in the case of situational or acquired orgasmic dysfunction. Anxiety reduction treatment may also be indicated in cases where sexual performance fears or similar concerns are present.

Sexual Pain Disorders

The DSM-IV-TR identifies two sexual pain disorders in women: vaginismus and dyspareunia. The defining criterion for the diagnosis of vaginismus is a persistent or recurrent involuntary spasm of the outer third of the vagina that interferes with sexual intercourse. This definition has been challenged on several grounds in recent years. For instance, although contraction of the pelvic floor musculature may prevent vaginal penetration, recent empirical work has demonstrated that vaginal spasms are neither sensitive nor specific to women who report difficulty with vaginal penetration (Reissing, Binik, Khalifé, Cohen, & Amsel, 2004). Furthermore, although vaginismus is classified as a sexual pain disorder and appears to be associated with genital pain in most cases (ter Kuile, van Lankveld, Vlieland, Willekes, & Weijenborg, 2005), the DSM-IV-TR diagnostic criteria do not specify that pain must be present to receive the diagnosis. The report of an international consensus conference on female sexual dysfunction classification (Basson et al., 2003) de-emphasizes the presence of muscle contraction and recommends a revised definition of vaginismus as follows:

> Persistent difficulties to allow vaginal entry of a penis, a finger, and/or any object, despite the woman's expressed wish to do so. There is a variable involuntary pelvic muscle contraction, (phobic) avoidance and anticipation/fear/experience of pain. Structural or other physical abnormalities must be ruled out/addressed.

In contrast to the DSM-IV-TR criteria, the proposed definition of vaginismus does not specify a muscle spasm localized exclusively to the vagina. The definition also emphasizes features of the disorder that suggest etiological mechanisms similar to those of anxiety disorders.

Dyspareunia is a broad term used to describe genital pain associated with sexual activity that causes distress or interpersonal difficulty. Although not a formal aspect of the definition, dyspareunia is typically described as either superficial (e.g., associated with the vulva and/or vaginal entrance) or deep (perceived in the abdomen or internal organs, often associated with penile thrusting); most cases fall into the former category. The DSM-IV-TR distinguishes dyspareunia from genital pain caused "exclusively" by vaginismus, lack of lubrication, or a medical condition. In practice, this criterion may be limiting and difficult to establish. Some researchers have argued that vaginismus and dyspareunia overlap in clinical presentation to the extent that it is questionable to regard them as distinct disorders (de Kruiff, ter Kuile, Weijenborg, & van Lankveld, 2000; Reissing, Binik, & Khalifé, 1999).

Many epidemiological studies exclude questions about vaginismus, and as such the prevalence of the disorder is not well established. The likely estimate is in the range of 1%–6% (Lewis et al., 2004). Laumann et al. (1999) reported that approximately 16% of American women reported persistent or recurrent sexual pain in the past year, with older age associated with a lower likelihood of sexual pain. In a community-based survey of 303 women, 12% reported a chronic history of pain provoked by *any* genital contact (Harlow, Wise, & Stewart, 2001).

There are multiple etiologies for sexual pain, including many medical conditions and anatomical variations. These potential factors necessitate a medical examination in any case of persistent sexual pain. Increased pelvic muscle tone and greater muscle weakness may distinguish sexual pain conditions with and without vaginal penetration difficulties (Reissing et al., 2004). Deep pain may result from uterine fibroids, endometriosis, urinary disease, and ovarian disease, among other conditions (for review, see Weijmar Schultz et al., 2005). Superficial pain may be a symptom of dermatological disorders affecting the external genitalia, vaginal atrophy, anatomical variations, urinary tract infections, injury, and other diseases and infections of the vulva. Many cases of superficial dyspareunia are associated with provoked vestibulodynia (PVD; formerly termed vulvar vestibulitis syndrome), a symptom pattern that includes sensitivity to touch and pressure of the vulvar vestibule. The etiology of PVD is uncertain, but several lines of research provide evidence of physiological hypersensitivity of the vulvar vestibule. Women with PVD often have a history of yeast infections and may have had significant hormonal events in adolescence, including early onset of menstruation and early use of oral contraceptives (Pukall, Payne, Kao, Khalifé, & Binik, 2005).

Regardless of origin, pain may persist after its initial provocation via a number of mechanisms, including psychological and neurological changes. When conceptualized as a pain disorder rather than a sexual disorder (Binik, Meana, Berkley, & Khalifé, 1999), sexual pain shares many etiological similarities with chronic low back pain and other chronic pain syndromes. To attempt to isolate the psychogenic and physiological components of chronic pain maintenance is a dubious exercise, as they are integral to one another. Research to date has not identified a reliable psychological "profile" associated with sexual pain disorders, although studies have reported increased anxiety and depressive symptoms, hostility, erotophobia, and psychotic features, albeit somewhat inconsistently, across the sexual pain disorders (Desrochers, Bergeron, Landry, & Jodoin, 2008; Weijmar Schultz et al., 2005). Although a past history of sexual trauma is commonly suspected as an etiological factor in the sexual pain disorders, findings are inconsistent and not sufficient to support a causal association (Desrochers et al., 2008; Weijmar Schultz et al., 2005).

Cognitive-behavioral interventions for sexual pain disorders typically focus on psychoeducation, anxiety reduction techniques (e.g., decatastrophizing pain), systematic desensitization to facilitate genital contact, and normalizing alternative forms of sexual activity (e.g., nonpenetrative sex) to enhance sexual pleasure. Eight- and twelve-session protocols of cognitive-behavioral treatment have been shown to reduce genital pain in populations of women with PVD (Bergeron et al., 2001; ter Kuile & Weijenborg, 2006). The use of systematic desensitization alone has a relatively long history in the treatment of sexual pain disorders, particularly vaginismus, but has surprisingly little empirical support.

Glazer and colleagues, observing a relationship between PVD and abnormal responding of the pelvic floor musculature, developed a novel treatment approach using electromyography (EMG) biofeedback to reduce hypertonicity and increase the strength and stability of the pelvic floor (Glazer, Rodke, Swencionis, Hertz, & Young, 1995). Clinical trial data indicate that the pelvic floor training approach significantly reduces vestibular pain and may occasionally eliminate it altogether (Bergeron et al., 2001; Glazer et al., 1995, McKay et al., 2001). Further collaboration with a physical therapist can enhance psychophysiological treatment with hands-on techniques informed by expertise on the muscular and connective tissue of the pelvic floor (Backman, Widenbrant, Bohm-Starke, & Dahlof, 2008; Rosenbaum, 2005).

Topical anesthetics and other medications are sometimes used to alleviate genital pain in the short-term, but there is no evidence supporting the use of topical treatments in long-term management of sexual pain disorders. Likewise, limited data are available to support the use of antidepressants and anticonvulsants for pain relief (Weijmar Schultz et al., 2005). Surgical treatment, on the other hand, may be a highly effective option for lasting pain relief in PVD, particularly when clients do not respond to psychosocial and physical therapies. Removal of vulvar vestibular tissue has been shown to significantly reduce or completely alleviate genital pain for the majority of recipients (Goldstein & Goldstein, 2006). Across treatment modalities, greater severity of pain at presentation predicts a poorer prognosis (Bergeron, Khalifé, Glazer, & Binik, 2008).

Sexual Dysfunctions in Men

In contrast to the conceptual shifts evident in emerging classifications of female sexual dysfunctions, the diagnostic classification of male sexual disorders has remained relatively uncontroversial in recent years. However, the clinical management of men's sexual problems was changed dramatically in 1998, with the advent of sildenafil (Viagra). The promise of Viagra is a safe, easy-to-use medical treatment for erectile dysfunction that requires no more than a trip to one's primary care physician—and little to no introspection. The reality is more complicated: a large minority (or perhaps even a majority) of men who are prescribed Viagra discontinue treatment, and the renewed ability to have a lasting erection may disrupt longstanding sexual equilibrium in a relationship (Leiblum, 2002; McCarthy & Fucito, 2005). Viewing erectile dysfunction strictly as a medical condition diverts attention from the contributing psychological factors that may continue to influence a man's sexual life. The relative ease of facilitating erection may also detract from assessment and treatment of more pervasive problems, such as diminished sexual interest or premature ejaculation. Moreover, a clinical focus on the attainment of erection reinforces narrow parameters and goals for sexual performance. Although sexologists have lamented a relative lack of data on women's sexual function, paradoxically, the failure of drug treatments for women's sexual dysfunctions has forced a more nuanced conceptualization of sexual problems that is not apparent in much of the literature on male sexual dysfunction. If today's theme is "women are complicated," it may be useful to add, "and so are men."

Hypoactive Sexual Desire Disorder

Research on sexual interest among adults in the general population suggests that males tend to have a higher level of sexual drive than females. Compared to women, men report greater desire for sexual activity, masturbate more frequently, and endorse a greater number of lifetime sexual partners (Jones & Barlow, 1990; Laumann et al., 1994; Regan & Atkins, 2006). The notion of a robust male libido is also deeply imbedded within many popular concepts of masculinity. As such, men may experience a lack of sexual interest as highly abnormal or unnatural, if not embarrassing or shameful. In the DSM-IV-TR, hypoactive sexual desire disorder is not differentiated by sex, so the diagnostic criteria are identical for men and women. However, there are several aspects of sexual desire disorders in men that distinguish their presentation from those in women. Complaints of low sexual desire are less frequent overall among men (Laumann et al., 1994), and, unlike low sexual desire in women, the incidence shows a steady and reliable increase with age (Maurice, 2007).

Low sexual desire in men is frequently associated with pharmacological treatments or medical conditions that affect testosterone. Sexual desire in the context of abnormally low testosterone levels is often amenable to treatment with testosterone supplementation (Buvat & Boujadoué, 2005). However, the dose-dependent effect of testosterone on sexual desire is limited. Above and beyond a normative threshold, additional testosterone does not further enhance sexual desire. Thus, men who experience low sexual desire but who do not show a testosterone deficiency are unlikely to benefit from testosterone supplementation.

Although there is a compelling case to investigate hormonal or other medical causes of low sexual desire, particularly in older men, careful assessment may reveal important information about underlying psychological causes. Bass (1985) cautioned that self-diagnosed "low sexual desire" may often represent a faulty attribution for infrequent sexual activity within conditions that are inconsistent with the individual's sexual preferences. Attributing low sexual desire to an innate medical condition rather than, for instance, a lack of sexual attraction to one's partner or an unsatisfying sexual repertoire, may be less threatening. Similarly, a loss of interest in sexual activity may reflect avoidance of sexual performance problems associated with another primary sexual dysfunction, such as erectile disorder or premature ejaculation. It is also important to investigate other sexual outlets that are preferred to partnered sexual activity, particularly the use of sexually explicit web sites and other media for masturbation, which suggest a situational lack of sexual interest in the context of an otherwise intact sexual drive (Maurice, 2007; Polonsky, 2003). As in women, psychiatric conditions—particularly mood disorders—are risk factors for low sexual desire and should be assessed.

The clinical literature offers little in the way of empirical study of psychotherapy for male hypoactive sexual desire disorder. The general consensus is that, as in women, sexual desire disorders in men are difficult to treat. Because low sexual desire is a symptom with multiple possible etiologies, a thorough assessment is necessary for appropriate treatment planning. Maurice (2007) recommends proceeding as follows:

• Men with lifelong, generalized low sexual interest have a poor prognosis in sex therapy and may be better served with supportive treatment to help the man and his partner adapt to his condition.
• Men with lifelong situational low sexual desire are unlikely to have a medical problem and therefore may be best treated with individual psychotherapy, although there is little guidance from the empirical literature on individual psychotherapy for male hypoactive sexual desire.
• If low sexual desire is acquired and generalized, a review of possible medical causes is warranted, although the etiology may or may not be organic. In any case, further assessment is usually indicated.
• If the problem is both acquired and situational, there is a lesser likelihood of medical causes, and a course of individual or couple therapy (depending on etiology) is most likely to be appropriate.

Erectile Disorder

Penile erection occurs when vascular smooth muscle relaxes and allows an increased volume of blood to flow into the corpora cavernosa. This process can be triggered by efferent or afferent nervous pathways. Older men tend to require a greater amount of tactile stimulation to attain an erection, whereas younger men more easily attain erection through fantasy or nontactile stimulation. Although a variety of chemical signals regulate erectile function, the most prominent effects on erectile function are mediated by the neurotransmitter nitric oxide. Nitric oxide is released from parasympathetic neurons in response to sexual stimulation and activates a metabolic pathway resulting in the production of cyclic guanosine monophosphate (cGMP), which in turn relaxes the vascular smooth muscle of the penis. Maintenance of the resulting erection depends on the ongoing production of nitric oxide, contingent on continued sexual stimulation. Normally, cGMP is broken down by enzymes known as phosphodiesterases (PDEs). However, this may be circumvented by inhibiting the activity of these enzymes. Viagra (sildenafil) and other drugs used to treat erectile disorder inhibit PDE type 5. In doing so, the PDE-5 inhibitors enhance the concentration of cGMP, allowing for greater smooth muscle relaxation and therefore improved erection.

Men of all ages have occasional difficulty obtaining or maintaining an erection. Common causes of transient erectile difficulty include fatigue, anxiety or other emotional distress, alcohol or drug intoxication, and (in older men) a long postejaculatory refractory period. Persistent or recurrent episodes of erectile problems are generally termed *erectile dysfunction*. The DSM-IV-TR defines *erectile disorder* as the inability to attain or maintain adequate erection of the penis through the completion of sexual activity. Importantly, the diagnosis cannot be given when the symptoms are attributable solely to a general medical condition. In practice, however, chronic disease and iatrogenic factors are common causes of erectile problems. Laumann et al. (1999) reported approximately 7% of men aged 18–29 years have erectile problems, whereas 18% of men aged 50–59 years experience difficulty with erection. Although the majority of cases of erectile disorder have an organic etiology, psychological and relationship factors can exacerbate the condition.

Barlow (1986) proposed a model of performance anxiety for psychogenic erectile dysfunction. The major psychological contributors to ED as identified by the model are anxiety, negative expectations, and spectatoring. In brief, men who are anxious about losing an erection tend to monitor the status of their erections and how they are "performing," which distracts from focusing on stimuli that are arousing and pleasurable. This "spectatoring" behavior is also associated with anxiety, which activates sympathetic nervous system arousal. Increased sympathetic activation inhibits the smooth muscle relaxation necessary for continued erection and contributes to continued negative affect and narrowed attentional focus on erectile performance. Eventually, the man is no longer able to maintain his erection, and the man's fears of not being able to perform are confirmed, thus increasing the likelihood that the process will repeat itself in subsequent sexual situations. Men without erectile dysfunction, on the other hand, tend to approach sexual situations with positive expectancies for performance and are able to focus on stimuli that are sexually arousing because they are not distracted by performance concerns. Consequently, these men become aroused easily and are able to obtain and sustain an erection. Repeated positive experiences shape expectancies for future sexual performance.

The assessment of ED includes identifying the situation(s) surrounding the onset of ED and the potential beliefs that were formed at that time. Beliefs may be specific to the relationship (i.e., a feeling of inadequacy with one specific partner) or may generalize to all situations. A medical evaluation is warranted when the problem is generalized or when the onset occurs in conjunction with an illness or medical treatment. Assays of free and bioavailable serum testosterone may be used to rule out abnormally low androgen levels. In cases where ED is the result of a vascular problem, laboratory assessments that measure genital blood inflow and outflow during sexual stimulation may be helpful. Measurement of nocturnal penile erections, which are expected to increase during the REM sleep cycle in sexually healthy men, is another commonly used technique for assessing potential vascular causes of ED.

Although PDE-5 inhibitors are now in widespread use, they are not effective for all men. Use of PDE-5 inhibitors is also contraindicated in men taking nitrates and should be monitored carefully in men taking α-blockers and certain other medications. Other medical treatments for erectile disorder include vacuum devices and constriction rings, intracavernosal injections, and intraurethral and topical pharmacotherapy. Lifestyle modifications, such as increasing exercise and eating a healthy diet,

may also be useful adjuncts to treatment (Esposito et al., 2004). As with PDE-5 inhibitors, these treatments are best introduced in conjunction with some form of sex or couple therapy. In a recent study that compared the effects of six months of treatment with Viagra alone, psychotherapy alone, or Viagra plus psychotherapy, psychotherapy alone outperformed Viagra alone in terms of improving erectile function (Melnik & Abdo, 2005). The psychotherapy aimed at developing realistic and positive expectations for the sexual relationship and encouraged patients to explore the emotional components linked to ED.

Penile implants are usually considered after other treatments have failed or when there is severe disease or damage to the penile tissue. There are several options for penile implants, including hydraulic, semirigid, and soft silicone cylinders that are surgically implanted into the space normally occupied by the spongy tissue in the penis. Surgery generally preserves the man's ability to ejaculate but can result in decreased penis size, which may dissuade some men from undergoing surgery.

Premature Ejaculation

The DSM-IV-TR defines premature ejaculation (PE) as a persistent or recurrent pattern of orgasm and ejaculation occurring with minimal stimulation before or shortly after penetration and sooner than desired. Although the latency period from intromission (or onset of sexual stimulation) to ejaculation is variable, men with PE have markedly and reliably shorter latencies than do men without PE. Patrick et al. (2005), for example, found that the average time to ejaculation from the start to sexual intercourse was 1.8 minutes for men with PE and 7.3 for non–sexually dysfunctional controls. Interestingly, men with PE tend to have a longer ejaculatory latency during masturbation. Rapid ejaculation is the most commonly reported sexual complaint in men, affecting approximately 1 out of every 3 to 5 men at some point during their lives, although the prevalence of severe and persistent PE is likely to be considerably lower (Waldinger, 2008). Prevalence estimates are somewhat unreliable across studies due to ambiguity in defining what exactly constitutes PE. Althof and Rowland (2008) identified seven different published definitions of PE, all of which were generated by opinion leaders and/or consensus within professional organizations, and noted that most of these definitions lacked measurable operational criteria. In practice, an ejaculatory latency time of less than 1 minute and perceived poor control over ejaculation, combined with personal distress or functional impairment, constitute a reasonably sensitive set of criteria for detection of PE.

Ejaculation occurs when sperm is emitted into the vas deferens through sympathetically mediated contraction of smooth muscle in the epididymis. This process is accompanied by a subjective perception that ejaculation is inevitable and followed by rhythmic contractions of smooth muscle in the penis and the pelvic floor. These contractions are associated with the experience of orgasm. Most men experience ejaculation and orgasm as interconnected events, although some men may experience orgasm without ejaculation.

Historically, PE has been associated with psychological etiological factors, especially anxiety, which has been thought lower the stimulus threshold required to trigger ejaculation. Although this hypothesis is intuitively appealing, empirical support is inconsistent at best. Perceived control over ejaculation is increasingly recognized as an important psychological factor that distinguishes men with and without PE. Although men with and without PE show comparable degrees of erectile response to sexual stimulation, men with PE report significantly less control over their ejaculation and may report a greater subjective experience of sexual excitement. Physiological factors may also contribute to some cases of PE. Researchers have postulated that men with PE have a lower sensitivity threshold such that less stimulation is needed to attain ejaculation. This explanation cannot account for all cases of PE, however, as studies show that PE exists in both men with high and with low sensory thresholds. It has also been proposed that men with PE may respond with a higher level of arousal to sexual stimuli (hyperarousability). Again, though, this cannot account for all cases of PE. One psychophysiological study that measured penile rigidity in the laboratory showed that men with PE had a weaker genital response to visual stimuli compared to men with no sexual dysfunction, but had a comparable genital response to men with no sexual dysfunction during tactile plus visual stimuli (Rowland & Slob, 1997).

Assessment of PE should include measurements of ejaculatory latency (length of time from intromission to ejaculation), perceived control over ejaculation, and any distress or interpersonal difficulty associated with the problem. These may be assessed through retrospective self-report questionnaires or by interview, although sometimes the patient (or his partner) is asked to time the interval between intromission and ejaculation to estimate the man's ejaculatory latency. The history of the condition is also important to assess; lifelong, global PE has a relatively poor prognosis (Waldinger, 2008).

The most commonly used psychotherapy techniques for increasing ejaculatory latency are the squeeze technique developed by Masters and Johnson (1970) and the pause technique (Kaplan, 1989). The squeeze technique consists of engaging in sexual stimulation alone or with a partner for as long as possible before ejaculation. Before reaching the "point of inevitable ejaculation," the man is instructed to stop the activity and apply tactile pressure to the glans to decrease the urge to ejaculate but not to the point that he completely loses his erection. When the urge has subsided, the man resumes masturbation or intercourse, stopping as many times as needed in order to delay ejaculation. The pause technique is similar to the squeeze technique with the exception that no pressure is applied to the penis. At times, clinicians may suggest using a PDE-5 inhibitor along with these techniques, so that the man can practice delaying ejaculation without worrying about maintaining an erection.

One promising medical treatment for premature ejaculatory is the off-label use of SSRIs to capitalize on their common side effect of delaying orgasm (e.g., Strassberg, de Gouveia Brazao, Rowland, Tan, & Slob, 1999; Waldinger, Hengeveld, & Zwinderman, 1994). In men with PE, there is some evidence that these drugs increase ejaculatory latency and sexual pleasure and satisfaction. Topical anesthetics have also been used to decrease penile sensitivity and prolong the duration of stimulation, although these are generally less acceptable among men with PE and their partners.

Male Orgasmic Disorder

Delayed or inhibited ejaculation following normal sexual arousal and adequate sexual stimulation is less common than premature ejaculation. Results of the National Health and Social Life Survey indicated that 3% of American men experience delay or difficulty in experiencing orgasm (Laumann et al., 1994). In a study of men over 40 in five English-speaking countries, the prevalence of this condition was estimated at 7% (Nicolosi et al., 2006).

A distinguishing feature of male orgasmic disorder is low subjectively perceived arousal during sexual stimulation despite an adequate erectile response (Rowland, Keeney, & Slob, 2004; Rowland, van Diest, Incrocci, & Slob, 2005). Impairments in orgasm and ejaculation have often been noted as a side effect of SSRI antidepressant use, and this has led some researchers to speculate that serotonin may play a role in the etiology of this disorder. Other medical causes of delayed orgasm or anorgasmia in men include spinal cord injury, diabetic neuropathy, infections of the genitourinary tract, and hypothyroidism (for review, see McMahon et al., 2004). In many cases, however, delayed or inhibited ejaculation is psychological rather than physiological in etiology. Like other sexual dysfunctions, male orgasmic disorder is commonly associated with relationship dissatisfaction and performance anxiety (Rowland et al., 2005). Poor sexual communication or discomfort between partners are typical relationship factors that may decrease enjoyment of sexual encounters and hinder attainment of high levels of arousal. Unlike other sexual dysfunctions, men with inhibited orgasm report better erections during masturbation than during intercourse with a partner and may strongly prefer masturbation to intercourse. Psychological treatment for delayed or inhibited ejaculation generally includes helping the couple to enhance sexual pleasure and intimacy, to address underlying hostility or other interpersonal problems, and to "retrain" the affected partner's sexual response using masturbation techniques that are more akin to the rhythm and intensity of intercourse.

Dyspareunia

Male dyspareunia is relatively uncommon and often ignored in the clinical literature, although the DSM-IV-TR diagnostic criteria for dyspareunia are applicable to both men and women. A recent population-based study of Australian men indicated that 5% of men reported pain associated with sexual activity (Pitts, Ferris, Smith, Shelley, & Richters, 2008). Most cases of male sexual pain are related to an underlying medical condition, anatomical defects, or iatrogenic factors. Thus, treatment is usually aimed at correcting physical causes through medical or surgical intervention. Medical/physiological causes include sexually transmitted infections, other diseases of the genitourinary tract, and pelvic floor hypertonicity. Anatomical features associated with sexual pain include curvature of the penis (e.g., from Peyronie disease) and an unusually short frenulum (a thin strip of tissue that attaches the penile foreskin to the glans). Primary male dyspareunia in the absence of any detectable physical cause is a rare condition, and very little work has examined contributing psychological factors involved in male sexual pain. Kaplan (1993) described postejaculatory pain in terms of intrapsychic conflict precipitating

involuntary muscle spasms. Pitts and colleagues (2008) reported that same-sex sexual experience and a history of experiencing sexual coercion were risk factors for male dyspareunia. The clinical literature on male dyspareunia is composed largely of case reports, and there are no published empirical studies of treatment for male sexual pain of presumed psychogenic origin.

Paraphilias

All paraphilias share the key feature of intense sexual interest and/or behavior directed toward an atypical target, which may be an inanimate object, a child or other nonconsenting individual, or the suffering or humiliation of oneself or someone else. Paraphilic disorders are categorized in the DSM-IV-TR with a relatively high degree of specificity, but they appear to co-occur frequently. Although prevalence estimates are most likely influenced by reporting bias, studies to date suggest that a single paraphilia diagnosis (i.e., with no coexisting paraphilias) is the exception rather than the rule. Accordingly, some theories of psychopathology cluster paraphilias that are presumed to share common psychological features (e.g., the "courtship disorder" hypothesis; Freund & Blanchard, 1986). Because of the high degree of overlap among paraphilias, and the fact that clinical research samples are often heterogeneous with respect to diagnosis, general treatment considerations will be discussed in this section after defining the specific paraphilias as listed in the DSM-IV-TR.

Many paraphilic behaviors are subject to attention not only from mental health professionals but also from the criminal justice system. Because such behaviors are socially unacceptable, if not illegal, those who engage in these behaviors seldom present voluntarily for treatment. Rather, referral for treatment is usually a consequence of being discovered by a loved one and/or apprehended by law enforcement officials. In the case of behaviors that constitute sex offenses, assessment and treatment have not only clinical implications but also potentially profound effects on the legal consequences for the sex offender.

The Internet plays a notable role in the world of paraphilias, providing a relatively anonymous forum for those with paraphilias to engage in their sexual interests. The Internet is also a tool for detecting persons with similar interests. Durkin, Forsyth, and Quinn (2006) described the potential for Internet-based communities organized around atypical sexual interests to shape paraphilic interests and/or behaviors. Online communities may, for instance, facilitate exchange of sexually explicit media, normalize atypical behaviors by connecting members with common sexual interests, or distribute carefully justified "manifestos" defending behaviors such as rape or sex with children or animals. On the other hand, the Internet may provide a safe outlet for sexual expression and satiety of sexual urges. The effects of sexually oriented Internet use on the development and course of paraphilias is unknown. The Internet has also greatly reduced barriers for access to mainstream sexually explicit materials, giving rise to a new generation of users whose exposure to pornography has largely existed within the confines of their homes.

Definitions and Features of the DSM-IV-TR Paraphilias

PEDOPHILIA

Pedophilia is the most prevalent disorder among the paraphilias and has attracted the greatest amount of attention from both the media and the scientific community. Pedophilia is defined as recurrent fantasies or desires involving sexual activity with a prepubescent child (usually 13 years or younger). The condition is diagnosed when the person acts on these urges or experiences distress or interpersonal difficulty related to these urges. The behavioral criterion is controversial as it can be misapplied in a criminal justice setting to any person who has engaged in sexual activity with a child, and meeting diagnostic criteria for a mental disorder may have legal implications in some jurisdictions (First & Frances, 2008).

Although many persons with pedophilia act upon their desires and engage in sexual behavior with children, sexual behavior with a child is not an absolute indicator of pedophilia. In other words, an incident of child molestation may or may not reflect a persistent sexual interest in children. Among those who have committed sexual offenses against children, only 30%–50% are considered pedophilic (Seto, 2004). Seto, Cantor, and Blanchard (2006) reported that, among sex offenders, a child pornography offense was a more reliable indicator of pedophilia than having committed a sexual offense against a child. Additionally, a person with pedophilia may or may not have concurrent sexual interest in adults. The targets of pedophilic interests may be male or female children, and this is not necessarily associated with the person's sexual preference for adult partners.

As with all of the paraphilias, the prevalence of pedophilia is difficult to estimate. The high prevalence of childhood sexual abuse suggests a significant number of adults who engage in sexual activity with children. In samples of college-aged men, 5–9% of respondents endorsed fantasizing about or desiring sex with young children (Briere & Runtz, 1989; Templeman & Stinnett, 1991). Although these figures indicate that adult–child sexual activity occurs frequently and that a small group of men are willing to endorse at least some degree of sexual interest in children, the numbers do little to help quantify the number of persons who have an enduring pattern of fantasies and urges that characterizes true pedophilia. It is known that pedophilia is largely a disorder of men, and female pedophiles are considered relatively uncommon. Data from sex offender samples indicates that victims are more often female than male, but Internet-based research with anonymous respondents does not reflect this trend.

Because assessment of pedophilia often occurs within a forensic setting, data gathered from interviews and other self-report assessment methods are interpreted with caution. The Clarke Sex History Questionnaire (Paitich, Langevin, Freeman, Mann, & Handy, 1977) and the Multiphasic Sex Inventory II (Nichols & Molinder, 2000), for instance, contain items expressly developed for the purpose of detecting socially desirable responding. Psychophysiological assessment methods are often used as adjuncts to the assessment process. Polygraph testing, in particular, is a popular method of authenticating sex offenders' self-reports despite a relatively weak evidence base and enduring concerns about its validity. Measurement of penile response (phallometry) is a controversial but common strategy used to measure men's sexual interest in stimuli depicting children and other types of people and activities. Phallometric devices measure either penile circumference (e.g., a strain gauge) or blood volume (e.g., a penile plethysmograph). Phallometry has been shown to distinguish between several types of sex offenders and men without a history of sexual offending (for review, see Seto, 2001), although its sensitivity for identifying sex offenders is modest. Methodological issues, including a lack of standards for the use of penile plethysmography and similar techniques, raise legitimate questions about the reliability and validity of phallometry. Research has also demonstrated that men may consciously manipulate their own erectile responses using cognitive distraction, which further detracts from the validity of this technique. Assessment of reaction time to sexual stimuli is an alternative, less-invasive psychophysiological assessment tool that has shown promise in differentiating sex offenders from nonoffenders (Abel, Huffman, Warberg, & Holland, 1998; Harris, Rice, Quinsey, & Chaplin, 1996), but this technique has not been widely adopted. Further study is needed to validate reaction time measures against other indicators of paraphilic interests.

Treatment of pedophilia and other sex offense–related paraphilias is distinguished from treatment of other sexual disorders in that the therapy is usually court-mandated (e.g., as a condition of probation or parole). Because typical limits of confidentiality do not hold when the client is an identified sex offender, the clinician adopts dual roles of both therapist and informant. Moreover, disclosure of sexual activity with children is generally not protected by confidentiality laws. Because of the unusual circumstances surrounding treatment, therapists working with sex offenders must be skilled in fostering trust and rapport. The development of a strong working alliance with court-referred sex offenders is a long-term and ongoing process.

FETISHISM

The defining feature of fetishism is a recurrent pattern of sexual interest or arousal involving a specific nonliving object. The fetish object is often used in masturbation, or it may be incorporated into sexual activity with a partner (for instance, asking the partner to wear a particular item of clothing). As the fetish object is often required or strongly preferred for sexual arousal, functional problems may arise when the affected person is unable to consistently use his or her preferred stimulus, or when the repeated use of the fetish object is a source of interpersonal conflict. However, if no distress or functional impairment is present, a diagnosis is not given. Fetishism is less frequently associated with criminal behavior than pedophilia and is more likely to create problems related to occupational, interpersonal, or social functioning.

The prevalence of fetishism is unknown, although a proliferation of Internet forums devoted to fetishes suggests that at least subclinical fetishism is not rare. Scorolli and colleagues attempted to quantify the prevalence of various subtypes of fetishes according to the number of fetish-themed Internet discussion groups and the level of membership and activity associated with these groups. Their review of 381 such discussion groups indicated that the majority were devoted to themes of either body parts or objects associated with the body (such as articles of clothing). Within this category, the most common themes were feet or foot-related objects such as footwear (Scorolli, Ghirlanda, Enquist, Zattoni, & Jannini, 2007).

Conditioning has been theorized to be important in the development of sexual fetishes and perhaps other paraphilias. There is some experimental evidence to support this hypothesis. Rachman (1966) famously "trained" healthy adult males to experience erection in response to an image of women's boots by repeatedly pairing this image with pictures of nude women in a classical conditioning paradigm. Additional studies have confirmed that sexual arousal in men can be conditioned through repeated pairing of nonsexual and sexually arousing stimuli (e.g., Hoffman, Janssen, & Turner, 2004; Rachman & Hodgson, 1968). The results of similar studies in women have been inconclusive at best (Hoffmann et al., 1997; Letourneau & O'Donohue, 1997). Some clinical reports are undoubtedly consistent with the conditioning hypothesis of fetish development, whereas others are more complicated. Case reports of persons with fetishes often identify highly salient childhood memories involving the fetish object or activity (e.g., Abel, Coffey, & Osborn, 2008), but these are not consistently associated with reports of sexual arousal at the time. The treatment literature specific to fetishism is sparse, and recent work is largely limited to case reports.

TRANSVESTIC FETISHISM

Transvestic fetishism is a particular type of fetish-like behavior in which the affected person (by DSM-IV-TR definition, a heterosexual male) engages in or fantasizes about dressing in women's clothing for the purpose of sexual excitement. As with fetishism, the behavior must be persistent and must cause distress or functional impairment in order to be considered a disorder. Few data are available to estimate the prevalence of this condition. A survey of 18- to 60-year-old adults in the Swedish general population found that 2.8% of men and 0.4% of women endorsed having ever experienced sexual arousal from cross-dressing (Långström & Zucker, 2005). The extent to which these behaviors would have met full diagnostic criteria, however, is unknown.

The etiology of transvestic fetishism is unclear, but it is notable that, in many cases, the cross-dressing behavior is accompanied by thoughts or fantasies of being a woman. This observation suggests that, at least in a portion of men, it is the adoption of a female identity, and not the feminine attire per se, that is sexually arousing. Blanchard (1989) labeled this behavior "autogynephilia"—the attraction to oneself as a woman—and has linked this pattern of sexual arousal to gender dysphoria and transsexualism (also see Lawrence, 2004). However, not all men with transvestic fetishism experience gender dysphoria, and not all male-to-female transsexuals endorse the autogynephilic arousal pattern (Veale, Clarke, & Lomax, 2008).

Treatment of men with transvestic fetishism should take into account the presence or absence of gender dysphoria, the functional areas that have been negatively affected by cross-dressing behavior (e.g., problems in the primary relationship), and the individual's goals for therapy. Cross-dressing in and of itself is not a disorder and is not associated with greater levels of psychopathology than in the general population. Thus, understanding the motivation for referral is key. Resolution of the problem may entail reducing or stopping cross-dressing behavior that is perceived as "out of control" or interfering with interpersonal relationships, in which case therapy is focused on achieving satisfaction with sexual expression as a male. Alternatively, the goal of therapy may be to help the man (and, if desired, his partner) incorporate his sexual preference more adaptively and attain greater comfort with cross-dressing activities. If gender dysphoria is persistent and continues despite greater acceptance and integration of cross-gender expression, more intensive treatment related to gender identity may be considered.

THE "COURTSHIP DISORDERS": EXHIBITIONISM, VOYEURISM, FROTTEURISM

Exhibitionism, voyeurism, and frotteurism are separately defined disorders in the DSM-IV-TR that share a common feature of sexual arousal or contact in the presence of a nonconsenting person. Exhibitionism is characterized by fantasies or urges to expose one's genitals to a stranger, whereas voyeurism is characterized by the desire to observe an unsuspecting person while nude, in the act of undressing, or while engaging in sexual activity. Frotteurism is defined by the urge to rub one's genitals against a nonconsenting person or to touch a nonconsenting person in a sexual way (sometimes referred to separately as "toucheurism"). In each case, the behavior or fantasy must be experienced as sexually arousing. These conditions meet the criteria for a disorder either when the person has acted on the desire to engage in the behavior or when these interests cause distress or interpersonal difficulty.

Although these behaviors represent distinct disorders in the DSM, they often co-occur. Freund and Blanchard (1986) interpreted the high comorbidity of exhibitionism, voyeurism, and frotteurism as evidence for a common etiological pathway for these disorders. They speculated that these behaviors represent a disturbance in the typical courtship behavior sequence of initial appraisal of a potential sex partner, "pretactile interaction" (e.g., smiling, talking) with a prospective partner, tactile interaction, and genital contact. A preference for nonconsensual intercourse (the "preferential rape pattern") was also considered to be a manifestation of courtship disorder. In a clinical sample of over 1,500 heterosexual males referred for treatment of a paraphilia, Freund and Watson (1990) found that exhibitionism co-occurred in 82.4% of cases of voyeurism and in 73.1% of cases of frotteurism/toucheurism, and only in 25.0% of cases was exhibitionism reported in the absence of another paraphilia. Rates of voyeurism and frotteurism/toucheurism occurring alone were even lower (10.1% and 16.8%, respectively).

SEXUAL SADISM AND MASOCHISM

The DSM-IV-TR defines sexual sadism with the key feature of "acts (real, not simulated) in which the individual derives sexual excitement from the psychological or physical suffering (including humiliation) of the victim." Phrased somewhat differently, sexual sadism—along with its counterpart, sexual masochism—can be viewed as the eroticized experience of a power differential between partners. To receive the diagnosis, the person must experience distress or interpersonal difficulty associated with sadism; alternatively, the diagnosis may be given when the person engages in sexual sadism with an nonconsenting person. Sexual masochism, conversely, is diagnosed when sexually arousing fantasies or sexual acts involving experiences of one's own humiliation or pain cause distress or interpersonal impairment.

The clinical literature describes sexual sadism largely in the context of two distinct populations: persons who are involved in BSDM (bondage-discipline/dominance-submission/sado-masochism) cultures and sexual assault perpetrators who torture, mutilate, and/or kill their victims. The former group of sexual sadists typically engage in consensual sexual activities and are not distressed by their preferences. Thus, the formal diagnosis of sexual sadism is perhaps most relevant to forensic settings. Because sex offenders may not be inclined to disclose sadistic fantasies or behaviors, the diagnosis requires considerable inference from the clinician. Even among mental health professionals with forensic training, the diagnosis of sexual sadism is unreliable (Marshall & Yates, 2004).

Very little literature addresses the prevalence of consensual sadomasochism. A population-based study of sexual practices among over 19,000 Australian adults revealed that 1.8% of respondents had engaged in some form of BDSM activity in the past year (Richters, de Visser, Rissel, Grulich, & Smith, 2008). Concern has been raised about the appropriateness of pathologizing behavior that, while atypical, does not appear to be associated with harm (there is a notable exception in the case of asphyxiation used to enhance arousal and orgasmic intensity, which is associated with risk of accidental death). As a group, persons who practice BDSM tend to be relatively well adjusted, with no greater-than-average risk of sexual problems or psychological distress (Connolly, 2006; Richters et al., 2008). Persons who engage in consensual BDSM practices are vulnerable to stigmatization, even from mental health professionals, and some have called for the elimination of sexual sadism and sexual masochism from the DSM, noting that their inclusion as "disorders" may contribute to unnecessary pathologizing and discrimination of BDSM practitioners (for primers on psychotherapeutic issues in BDSM/kink populations, see Moser & Kleinplatz, 2007; Nichols, 2006).

Paraphilia-related Behaviors and Hypersexuality

Sexual behavior that is typical in form or content may still be problematic when it occurs with atypical frequency or intensity or is subjectively difficult to control. Although there is now a considerable literature on nonparaphilic hypersexuality (examples of which include dependence on pornography or cybersex and excessive masturbation or promiscuity), such conditions are not defined in the DSM-IV-TR. Kafka (2007) has suggested the following definition of paraphilia-related disorders:

> Over a period of at least 6 months, recurrent, intense sexually arousing fantasies, sexual urges, or behaviors involving culturally normative aspects of sexual expression that increase in frequency or intensity so as to significantly interfere with the expression of the capacity for reciprocal, affectionate activity.

There is still considerable debate as to whether paraphilia-related disorders are best conceptualized as addictions, compulsions, or disorders of impulse control, whereas others reject this type of categorization. Although the focus of sexual interest is not atypical, the excessive or inappropriate sexual activity can cause substantial relational, social, and occupational problems. Excessive use of Internet pornography, in particular, is now a common cause for referral to mental health professionals and appears to be a factor in a surprisingly large number of recent divorce cases (Manning, 2006).

Treatment options for paraphilia-related disorders include individual, couple, and group psychotherapy. Group treatment is a popular option, as evidenced by the virtual explosion of 12-step treatment programs for self-described "sex addicts" (e.g., Sex Addicts Anonymous, Sex and Love Addicts Anonymous, Sexual Compulsives Anonymous, etc.). These programs may be of substantial benefit to individuals who are able and willing to participate in regular group meetings, maintain a relationship with a sponsor, and commit to long-term "abstinence" as variously defined by different programs. In addition to the 12-step recovery model of treatment, cognitive-behavioral group treatment is also likely to be beneficial to motivated participants. Behavioral and psychopharmacological treatments used to treat the paraphilias, as described later, may also be adapted for use in some persons with paraphilia-related disorders.

Treatment of Paraphilias

Unlike many individuals with mental disorders, persons with paraphilias and/or hypersexual behaviors do not necessarily wish to change their feelings or behavior. Some may desire change only after the consequences of their behavior have provoked a crisis, whereas others may not wish to change but are compelled by someone else to enter treatment. The individual's motivation for change is important to consider in treatment planning as it is a prognostic factor and may guide the goals of therapy. Research on the treatment of paraphilias is complicated by the fact that many research samples are heterogeneous with respect to diagnosis and (in forensic samples) types of offenses. However, given the high comorbidity of paraphilias it is both pragmatic and ecologically valid to examine treatment effects in diagnostically diverse groups. Many of the techniques described in the following sections have shown efficacy in multiple disorders.

Several behavioral techniques have been developed to reduce problematic sexual thoughts or behaviors, particularly among sex offenders but also for individuals with various paraphilic sexual interests. Aversion therapy, for instance, involves delivering an unpleasant stimulus (such as an electric shock) in combination with a sexually arousing stimulus until the sexual stimulus no longer elicits a response. Although there is some evidence to support the effectiveness of this treatment, high relapse rates have limited the use of aversion therapy over time (Kilman, Sabalis, Gearing, Bukstel, & Scovern, 1982; Rice, Quinsey, & Harris, 1991). More recent work has examined covert sensitization, a variant of aversive conditioning in which the person is asked to repeatedly *imagine* a scenario in which the inappropriate behavior is linked to an aversive consequence (e.g., McKibben, Proulx, & Lussier, 2001; Plaud & Gaither, 1997). An alternative technique is a form of "reconditioning," in which the individual masturbates to the unwanted sexual stimulus just to the point of orgasm, at which time the fantasy is turned to a more appropriate or acceptable target of sexual stimulation (such as a spouse or partner). Finally, masturbatory satiation is a technique in which the person is asked to fantasize about the inappropriate sexual behavior during the postorgasmic period, during which further sexual arousal is very difficult to attain. Relatively little research has been done to examine the effectiveness of these and related techniques (Laws & Marshall, 1991).

Cognitive-behavioral therapy is the current standard of care for paraphilias. Cognitive distortions have been found to play an important role in the maintenance of pedophilia (for review, see Navathe, Ward, & Gannon, 2008) and other paraphilias. Typical beliefs include those that justify one's own inappropriate sexual behavior (e.g., sexual behavior is out of one's control), distort the unwanted nature of the act (e.g., the victim implicitly consented to or was gratified by the act), or minimize the negative consequences of the behavior (e.g., the victim suffered no harm as a result of the act). Although cognitive distortions are acknowledged to be only one of multiple contributing factors for paraphilic behavior, they are an intensive focus of cognitive-behavioral treatment. Other goals of cognitive-behavioral treatment for pedophilia and other sex offenses are to accept responsibility for one's actions and their consequences, to foster improved social skills and relationships, to develop empathy toward victims and others (when applicable), and to better tolerate and cope with strong negative emotions that may precipitate inappropriate sexual behavior. Behavioral techniques such as those described in the preceding paragraph are also incorporated into therapy, and relapse prevention strategies may be used in long-term treatment. Much of the outcome research on CBT for paraphilias is conducted in populations of sex offenders, and there are few randomized clinical trials in this field, in part because of ethical problems involved in withholding treatment from willing participants. The evidence to date suggests that cognitive-behavioral treatment programs, often delivered in group format, have a modest positive effect on recidivism outcomes (Hanson et al., 2002), but further research in this area is needed.

Pharmacological treatment is usually reserved for the more severe criminal manifestations of paraphilias. These treatments are less invasive and less permanent alternatives to surgical castration, which is effective in reducing recidivism rates but fraught with ethical and legal problems. Most commonly used treatments work by reducing levels of androgen and other sex hormones that affect sexual drive and arousability (for review, see Bourget & Bradford, 2008). Currently used pharmacological treatments include medroxyprogesterone acetate, cyproterone acetate, and leuteinizing hormone-releasing hormone (LHRH) agonists such as leuprolide. However, these treatments are associated with a number of side effects, and recidivism rates have been found to increase on discontinuation of treatment. Selective serotonin reuptake inhibitors have also been used in the treatment of paraphilias due to their effects on erectile function and sexual desire, and have shown some efficacy in reducing problematic sexual thoughts and behaviors.

Gender Disorders

Although the terms *sex* and *gender* are frequently used interchangeably in lay language, they are distinct constructs. Whereas sex refers to genetic or anatomical features that define a person as male or female, gender refers to the subjective, internal experience of being female or male. Although a categorical and dualistic view of gender predominates, there are both sociocultural and biological arguments for more flexible conceptualizations of sex and gender. For instance, the extent to which gender is polarized varies with culture, and some cultures recognize more than two definable gender identities. From a biological standpoint, the processes of sexual differentiation and maintaining sex-linked characteristics are not all-or-none phenomena. Thus, considering a spectrum of both physiological/anatomical sex characteristics and gender identification is often helpful in conceptualizing gender variance and gender expression.

The Biological Basis of Sex and Gender

It is helpful to understand the multiple pathways that shape the development of sex-linked characteristics in the brain and elsewhere, and those that maintain sex differences in physiological function. At typical conception, the human egg contributes one X chromosome and the sperm cell contributes an X or Y chromosome. Females develop from a fertilized egg with two X chromosomes (XX) and males develop from a fertilized egg with an X and Y chromosome (XY), although other configurations of sex chromosomes such as XXY, XXX, XYY, and XX/XY mosaicism are possible. Regardless of chromosomal sex, human embryos begin development in a sexually undifferentiated state. Masculinization of the male embryo depends on the expression of Y chromosome genes that promote the development of the testes. The testosterone secreted from newly developed testes in turn influences the development of brain structures. If, for some reason, functional testes do not develop, or if the embryo's responsiveness to testosterone is abnormally low, a female-typical pattern of development results. These and other variations in development may affect the masculinization of brain structures including the hypothalamus, amygdala, and other areas of the limbic system (for review, see Keefe, 2002).

In addition to the early organizing effects of hormones (i.e., those that result in permanent developmental changes), circulating hormones continue to modify brain and nervous system pathways in reversible, temporary ways. Receptors for androgens and estrogens are located on the peripheral autonomic nerves, on nerves within the spinal cord, and in multiple structures in the brain. Sex hormones play a substantial role in regulating genital sexual function (Giuliano & Rampin, 2004; Min et al., 2003) and in cognition and emotion associated with sexual behavior (e.g., Anderson, Bancroft, & Wu, 1992; O'Connor, Archer, & Wu, 2004; Redouté et al., 2005).

Gender Identity Disorder

Discomfort with one's sex or with the gender role assigned to that sex (gender dysphoria), along with the desire to live as a member of the opposite sex, are the key symptoms of gender identity disorder (GID). In contrast to the typical presentation of other disorders identified in this chapter, GID may appear quite early in development. In children, the condition is marked by an expressed desire to be of the opposite sex, cross-gender role behavior or preferences, and/or preference for playmates of the opposite sex. Adolescents and adults with GID also identify strongly with the opposite sex and display a desire to live or be treated as the opposite sex. Among persons with GID, the genitals and other physical sex characteristics of one's natal sex are experienced as undesirable, "wrong," or even aversive. Atypical gender behavior, regardless of the extent of nonconformity, is not indicative of GID; a strong and persistent desire to *be* the opposite sex must be present to meet diagnostic criteria.

Few estimates of the prevalence of GID exist, given its relatively rare presentation and the stigma faced by gender variant individuals. One consistent finding from the literature is that GID occurs more frequently in males than in females, perhaps by as much as threefold (APA Task Force on Gender Identity and Gender Variance, 2008). Prevalence rates vary according to geographic location as well as survey methodology. The prevalence of male-to-female transsexuals reported in the literature ranges from 1:36,000 in Germany (Weitze & Osburg, cited in Sohn & Bosinski, 2007) to 1:2,900 in Singapore (Tsoi, 1988; cited in Sohn & Bosinski). The prevalence of female-to-male transsexuals ranges from 1:94,000 to 1:8,300 (Sohn & Boskinski).

Zucker et al. (1999) reported that children who develop GID tend to attain the concept of gender constancy, the understanding that gender is fixed and unchanging, later in development than is typical. Although children with GID display elevated rates of psychopathology relative to the general population, with about half meeting criteria for another psychiatric disorder, they do not differ in the number or type of comorbid conditions compared to other clinic-referred populations, such as children with attention-deficit hyperactivity disorder (Wallien, Swaab, & Cohen-Kettenis, 2007). The extent to which psychiatric comorbidity is a function of adjustment difficulties and not GID per se is unknown. Data from several studies suggest that GID resolves for the majority of persons diagnosed as children. Children with GID are substantially more likely than others to develop a bisexual or homosexual orientation in adulthood (Zucker, 2005). Many adults who present with gender dysphoria and/or GID have exhibited gender-atypical behavior from a very young age but, for various reasons, did not present for treatment earlier in life. However, some adult males with GID may have shown gender-typical behaviors in childhood and heterosexual preferences in adolescence but may have a history of cross-dressing behavior and/or fantasies about having a feminine appearance prior to developing gender dysphoria (Carroll, 2007).

The diagnosis of GID is controversial among clinicians and transgender advocates. Although transgender advocates generally view gender variance along a continuum of normative behavior, some support retention of a mental disorder diagnosis to provide a mechanism for medical referral and reimbursement. Others suggest that any disorder defined by atypical gender expression pathologizes the experience of gender-variant persons to their detriment. Of particular concern is the potential for health professionals to advocate "curing" gender dysphoria rather than affirming and supporting functional expressions of gender variance. Many advocates have drawn parallels between the diagnosis of GID and the history of pathologizing homosexuality. Although the availability of a formal diagnosis may or may not change a mental health professional's approach to the care of a person with GID, awareness of these issues is important due to their potential financial, legal, and professional ramifications.

Assessment of gender dysphoria at any age should include a history of gender identity from childhood to the present. Questionnaires such as the Gender Identity/Gender Dysphoria Questionnaire for Adolescents and Adults (Deogracias et al., 2007) and the Recalled Childhood Gender Questionnaire-Revised (Meyer-Bahlburg et al., 2006) may be useful tools to supplement a clinical interview. The person's past and current feelings about his or her own gender, cross-gender experiences and attempts to pass as the opposite sex, and desires regarding sex reassignment should also be assessed. It is also important for the mental health professional to determine early in the professional relationship whether the client with gender dysphoria intends to seek the provider's formal recommendation for hormone treatment and/or sex reassignment surgery. Although most individuals with GID do not have an intersex condition or another underlying medical cause, a medical evaluation may be indicated to rule out these factors in some cases.

The World Professional Association for Transgender Health (WPATH), formerly known as the Harry Benjamin International Gender Dysphoria Association, publishes a comprehensive set of guidelines for the mental health care of gender dysphoric individuals, with the stated goal of "lasting personal comfort with the gendered self in order to maximize overall psychological well-being and self-fulfillment" (WPATH, 2001). The most recent WPATH Standards of Care define several possible roles for the mental health professional in the care of persons with GID (see Table 21.1).

An early critical task in the psychotherapy of GID is to determine the most appropriate goal for treatment. One possible desired outcome is the acceptance of one's natal sex and its associated gender role. In this case, psychotherapy would approach the atypical gender behavior similarly to that of a paraphilia or related disorder. This type of gender acceptance may be a dubious treatment goal, however, particularly for clients whose gender dysphoria or gender-atypical behavior has been lifelong (Carroll, 2007). The alternative approach is to provide guidance in self-examination and formation of goals for gender expression, including a careful exploration of the client's options and a realistic appraisal of their ramifications. In some cases, the development of a "part-time" cross-gender role may best meet the client's needs, whereas in other cases the only satisfactory resolution of GID is to undergo full sex reassignment through hormone treatment and surgery. It should be noted that these options are not defined simply, and their particulars vary on

Table 21.1 Tasks for mental health professionals working with persons with gender identity disorder

- Accurately diagnose the individual's gender disorder.
- Accurately diagnose any comorbid psychiatric conditions and see to their appropriate treatment.
- Counsel the individual about the range of treatment options and their implications.
- Engage in psychotherapy.
- Ascertain eligibility and readiness for hormone and surgical therapy.
- Make formal recommendations to medical and surgical colleagues.
- Document their patient's relevant history in a letter of recommendation.
- Be a colleague on a team of professionals with an interest in the gender identity disorders.
- Educate family members, employers, and institutions about gender identity disorders.
- Be available for follow-up of previously seen gender patients.

Reprinted with permission from World Professional Association for Transgender Health (WPATH) Standards of Care (6th version; WPATH, 2001).

a case-by-case basis; for example, some clients may desire a "blended" gender identity and/or partial sex reassignment.

Whenever sex reassignment is desired, a psychological evaluation is indicated. Furthermore, the process of sex reassignment according to the WPATH Standards of Care includes a minimum of 1 year's full-time experience presenting and living in the desired gender (while using the appropriate hormones) before surgical treatment (WPATH, 2001). Although psychotherapy is not required during this transitional phase, it may be helpful to the client's adjustment in a new gender role and the decision-making process about whether to proceed to irreversible surgery. Although the WPATH Standards of Care discourage administration of cross-sex hormones until late adolescence, there has been a growing movement to delay the onset of puberty in younger adolescents with GID to prevent the development of undesired secondary sex characteristics (e.g., Cohen-Kettenis, Delemarre-van de Waal, & Gooren, 2008).

Conclusion

Psychological understanding of sex and gender disorders continues to evolve not only in response to research findings but also in concert with cultural and political shifts both internal and external to the behavioral sciences. Despite a tremendous amount of interest in sexual and gender disorders, the psychological treatment literature is somewhat sparse when compared to the body of work for many other types of mental health conditions. Political polarization among health care professionals and researchers, particularly in the case of gender identity disorder and, to a lesser extent, the paraphilias, further complicate the outlook for advances in empirically supported psychosocial treatments. Thus, the small number of high-quality clinical trials of psychotherapy for sex and gender disorders does not represent the sizeable amount of clinical wisdom and theory currently circulating in this field. On the other hand, research in the sexual disorders has contributed a substantial amount of data to guide the development of new treatments and the refinement of existing ones. Translation of laboratory and cross-sectional research to improved clinical care will be a major challenge in the coming decades.

Future Directions

SEXUAL DYSFUNCTIONS

Research on the treatment of sexual dysfunctions is at an interesting crossroads as the limitations of the biomedical model of sexual function come to light.

Meanwhile, there is a need for effective models of integrating medical and psychosocial treatments for certain disorders in both men and women. Emerging models of female sexual response, although intuitively appealing, have undergone little empirical scrutiny, and their ability to inform useful clinical practices remains unclear. Development of empirically supported treatments for low sexual desire in women is a particularly important priority area for future research given the high prevalence of this complaint.

PARAPHILIAS

The formal classification and conceptualization of paraphilia-related disorders may have an important impact on research and treatment. Although there is reason to believe that these disorders are quite prevalent, large-scale epidemiological work is needed to determine the prevalence and impact of these conditions. Meanwhile, sexual offenses against children continue to occur at alarming frequencies, and systematic efforts to examine the outcomes of sex offender treatment programs should be strengthened. High-quality efficacy trials and comparative outcome studies are needed to better determine the relative strengths of different treatment approaches and to refine prognostic indicators.

GENDER IDENTITY DISORDER

Gender identity disorder is a topic of great controversy, made more so by the many challenges to conducting high-quality research on this condition. Prospective longitudinal studies of psychological and functional outcomes of psychotherapy and gender reassignment, particularly among younger cohorts, are needed to evaluate existing standards of care for gender-variant persons. It is also important to examine models for broad dissemination of best practices in the assessment and treatment of gender dysphoria. Improving access to empirically supported care will likely go a long way toward repairing the transgender community's wary stance toward mental health care.

References

Abel, G. G., Coffey, L., & Osborn, C. A. (2008). Sexual arousal patterns: Normal and deviant. *Psychiatric Clinics of North America, 31,* 643–655.

Abel, G. G., Huffman, J., Warberg, B., & Holland, C. L. (1998). Visual reaction time and plethysmography as measures of sexual interest in child molesters. *Sexual Abuse: Journal of Research and Treatment, 10,* 81–95.

Althof, S. E., & Rowland, D. L. (2008). Identifying constructs and criteria for the diagnosis of premature ejaculation: Implication for making errors of classification. *BJU International, 102*, 708–712.

American Psychiatric Association. (2000). *Diagnostic and statistical manual of mental disorders* (4th ed., Text revision). Washington, DC: Author.

Anderson, R. A., Bancroft, J., & Wu, F. (1992). The effects of exogenous testosterone on sexuality and mood of normal men. *Journal of Clinical Endocrinology & Metabolism, 75*, 1503–1507.

APA Task Force on Gender Identity and Gender Variance. (2008). *Report of the Task Force on Gender Identity and Gender Variance*. Washington, DC: American Psychological Association.

Backman, H., Widenbrant, M., Bohm-Starke, N., & Dahlof, L. G. (2008). Combined physical and psychosexual therapy for provoked vestibulodynia – An evaluation of a multidisciplinary treatment model. *Journal of Sex Research, 45*, 378–385.

Bancroft, J., Graham, C. A., & McCord, C. (2001). Conceptualizing women's sexual problems. *Journal of Sex & Marital Therapy, 27*, 95–103.

Bancroft, J., Loftus, J., & Long, J. S. (2003). Distress about sex: A national survey of women in heterosexual relationships. *Archives of Sexual Behavior, 32*, 193–208.

Barlow, D. H. (1986). Causes of sexual dysfunction: The role of anxiety and cognitive interference. *Journal of Consulting and Clinical Psychology, 54*, 140–148.

Bass, B. A. (1985). The myth of low sexual desire: A cognitive behavioral approach to treatment. *Journal of Sex Education and Therapy, 11*, 61–64.

Basson, R. (2001). Using a different model for female sexual response to address women's problematic low sexual desire. *Journal of Sex & Marital Therapy, 27*, 395–403.

Basson, R., Leiblum, S., Brotto, L., Derogatis, L., Fourcroy, J., Fugl-Meyer, K., et al. (2003). Definitions of women's sexual dysfunction reconsidered: Advocating expansion and revision. *Journal of Psychosomatic Obstetrics and Gynecology, 24*, 221–229.

Bergeron, S., Binik, Y. M., Khalifé, S., Pagidas, K., Glazer, H. I., Meana, M., et al. (2001). A randomized comparison of group cognitive-behavioral therapy, surface electromyographic feedback, and vestibulectomy in the treatment of dyspareunia resulting from vulvar vestibulitis. *Pain, 91*, 297–306.

Bergeron, S., Khalifé, S., Glazer, H. I., & Binik, Y. M. (2008). Surgical and behavioral treatments for vestibulodynia: Two-and-one-half year follow-up and predictors of outcome. *Obstetrics & Gynecology, 111*, 159–166.

Binik, Y. M., Meana, M., Berkley, K., & Khalifé, S. (1999). The sexual pain disorders: Is the pain sexual or is the sex painful? *Annual Review of Sex Research, 10*, 210–235.

Blanchard, R. (1989). The concept of autogynephilia and the typology of male gender dysphoria. *Journal of Nervous and Mental Disease, 177*, 616–623.

Bourget, D., & Bradford, J. M. W. (2008). Evidential basis for the assessment and treatment of sex offenders. *Brief Treatment and Crisis Intervention, 8*, 130–146.

Briere, J., & Runtz, M. (1989). University males' sexual interest in children: Predicting potential indices of 'pedophilia' in a nonforensic sample. *Child Abuse & Neglect, 13*, 65–75.

Brotto, L. A. (2006). Psychologic-based desire and arousal disorders: Treatment strategies and outcome results. In I. Goldstein, C. M. Meston, S. R. Davis, & A. M. Traish (Eds.), *Women's sexual function and dysfunction: Study, diagnosis, and treatment* (pp. 441–448). New York: Taylor and Francis.

Buvat, J., & Boujadoué, G. (2005). Testosterone replacement therapy in the ageing man. *Journal of Men's Health & Gender, 2*, 396–399.

Carroll, R. A. (2007). Gender dysphoria and transgender experiences. In S. R. Leiblum (Ed.). *Principles and practice of sex therapy* (4th ed.), pp. 477–508. New York: Guilford Press.

Cawood, E. H., & Bancroft, J. (1996). Steroid hormones, the menopause, sexuality and well-being of women. *Psychological Medicine, 26*, 925–936.

Clayton, A. H., McGarvey, E. L., & Clavet, G. J. (1997). The Changes in Sexual Functioning Questionnaire (CSFQ): Development, reliability and validity. *Psychopharmacology Bulletin, 33*, 731–745.

Cohen-Kettenis, P., Delemarre-van de Waal, H., & Gooren, L. (2008). The treatment of adolescent transsexuals: Changing insights. *Journal of Sexual Medicine, 5*, 1892–1897.

Connolly, P. (2006). Psychological functioning of bondage/domination/sado-masochism (BDSM) practitioners. *Journal of Psychology & Human Sexuality, 18*, 79–120.

de Kruiff, M. E., ter Kuile, M. M., Weijenborg, P. T., & van Lankveld, J. J. (2000). Vaginismus and dyspareunia: Is there a difference in clinical presentation? *Journal of Psychosomatic Obstetrics and Gynecology, 21*, 149–155.

Dennerstein, L., Koochaki, P., Barton, I., & Graziottin, A. (2006). Hypoactive sexual desire disorder in menopausal women: A survey of Western European women. *Journal of Sexual Medicine, 2*, 212–222.

Deogracias, J., Johnson, L., Meyer-Bahlburg, H., Kessler, S., Schober, J., & Zucker, K. (2007). The gender identity/gender dysphoria questionnaire for adolescents and adults. *Journal of Sex Research, 44*, 370–379.

Derogatis, L. R. (1997). The Derogatis Interview for Sexual Functioning (DISF/DISF-SR): An introductory report. *Journal of Sex & Marital Therapy, 23*, 291–304.

Desrochers, G., Bergeron, S., Landry, T., & Jodoin, M. (2008). Do psychosexual factors play a role in the etiology of provoked vestibulodynia? A critical review. *Journal of Sex & Marital Therapy, 34*, 198–226.

Dove, N. L., & Wiederman, M. W. (2000). Cognitive distraction and women's sexual functioning. *Journal of Sex & Marital Therapy, 26*, 67–78.

Durkin, K., Forsyth, C. J., & Quinn, J. F. (2006). Pathological internet communities: A new direction for sexual deviance research in a post-modern era. *Sociological Spectrum, 26*, 595–605.

Esposito, K., Giugliano, F., Di Palo, C., Giugliano, G., Marfella, R., D'Andrea, F., et al. (2004). Effect of lifestyle changes on erectile dysfunction in obese men: A randomized controlled trial. *JAMA, 291*, 2978–2984.

First, M. B., & Frances, A. (2008). Issues for DSM-5: Unintended consequences of small changes: The case of paraphilias. *American Journal of Psychiatry, 165*, 1240–1241.

Freund, K., & Blanchard, R. (1986). The concept of courtship disorder. *Journal of Sex & Marital Therapy, 12*, 79–92.0

Freund, K., & Watson, R. (1990). Mapping the boundaries of courtship disorder. *Journal of Sex Research, 27*, 589–606.

Giuliano, F., & Rampin, O. (2004). Neural control of erection. *Physiology & Behavior, 83*, 189–201.

Glazer, H. I., Rodke, G., Swencionis, C., Hertz, B., & Young, A. W. (1995). Treatment of vulvar vestibulitis syndrome with electromyographic biofeedback of pelvic floor musculature. *Journal of Reproductive Medicine, 40*, 283–290.

Goldstein, A. T., & Goldstein, I. (2006). Sexual pain disorders within the vulvar vestibule: Current techniques. In I. Goldstein, C. M. Meston, S. R. Davis, & A. M. Traish (Eds.), *Women's sexual function and dysfunction: Study, diagnosis, and treatment* (pp. 587–596). New York: Taylor and Francis.

Goldstein I, Fisher WA, Sand M, Rosen RC, Mollen M, Brock, G., et al. (2005). Women's sexual function improves when partners are administered vardenafil for erectile dysfunction: A prospective, randomized, double-blind, placebo-controlled trial. *Journal of Sexual Medicine, 2,* 819–832.

Guay, A. T., & Spark, R. (2006). Pathophysiology of sex steroids in women. In I. Goldstein, C. M. Meston, S. R. Davis, & A. M. Traish (Eds.), *Women's sexual function and dysfunction: Study, diagnosis, and treatment* (pp. 218–227). New York: Taylor and Francis.

Hanson, R. K., Gordon, A., Harris, A. J., Marques, J. K., Murphy, W., Quinsey, V. L., et al. (2002). First report of the collaborative outcome data project on the effectiveness of psychological treatment for sex offenders. *Sexual Abuse: A Journal of Research and Treatment, 14,* 169–194.

Harlow, B. L., Wise, L. A., & Stewart, E. G. (2001). Prevalence and predictors of chronic lower genital tract discomfort. *American Journal of Obstetrics and Gynecology, 185,* 545–550.

Harris, G. T., Rice, M. E., Quinsey, V. L., & Chaplin, T. C. (1996). Viewing time as a measure of sexual interest among child molesters and normal heterosexual men. *Behaviour Research and Therapy, 34,* 389–394.

Heiman, J. R., & LoPiccolo, J. (1988). *Becoming orgasmic: A sexual and personal growth program for women* (Rev. ed.). New York: Prentice Hall.

Heiman, J. R., & Meston, C. M. (1997). Evaluating sexual dysfunction in women. *Clinical Obstetrics & Gynecology, 40,* 616–629.

Hoffmann, H., Janssen, E., & Turner, S. L. (2004). Classical conditioning of sexual arousal in women and men: Effects of varying awareness and biological relevance of the conditioned stimulus. *Archives of Sexual Behavior, 33,* 43–53.

Jones, J. C., & Barlow, D. H. (1990). Self-reported frequency of sexual urges, fantasies, and masturbatory fantasies in heterosexual males and females. *Archives of Sexual Behavior, 19,* 269–279.

Kafka, M. P. (2007). Paraphilia-related disorders: The evaluation and treatment of nonparaphilic hypersexuality. In S. R. Leiblum (Ed.), *Principles and practice of sex therapy* (4th ed., pp. 442–476). New York: Guilford Press.

Kaplan, H. S. (1979). *Disorders of sexual desire.* New York: Brunner/Mazel

Kaplan, H. S. (1988). Sexual panic states. *Sexual and Relationship Therapy, 3,* 7–9.

Kaplan, H. S. (1993). Post-ejaculatory pain syndrome. *Journal of Sex & Marital Therapy, 19,* 91–103.

Keefe, D. L. (2002). Sex hormones and neural mechanisms. *Archives of Sexual Behavior, 31,* 401–403.

Kilman, P. R., Sabalis, R. F., Gearing, M. L., Bukstel, L. H., & Scovern, A. W. (1982). The treatment of sexual paraphilias: A review of the outcome research. *Journal of Sex Research, 18,* 193–252.

Kingsberg, S. A., & Janata, J. W. (2003). The sexual aversions. In S. B. Levine, C. B. Risen, & S. E. Althof (Eds.), *Handbook of clinical sexuality for mental health professionals* (pp. 153–165). New York: Brunner-Routledge.

Långström, N., & Zucker, K. J. (2005). Transvestic fetishism in the general population: Prevalence and correlates. *Journal of Sex & Marital Therapy, 31,* 87–95.

Laumann, E. O., Gagnon, J. H., Michael, R. T., & Michaels, S. (1994). *The social organization of sexuality: Sexual practices in the United States.* Chicago: University of Chicago Press.

Laumann, E. O., Paik, A., & Rosen, R. C. (1999). Sexual dysfunction in the United States: Prevalence and predictors. *JAMA, 281,* 537–544.

Lawrence, A. A. (2004). Autogynephilia: A paraphilic model of gender identity disorder. *Journal of Gay & Lesbian Psychotherapy, 8,* 69–87.

Laws, D., & Marshall, W. (1991). Masturbatory reconditioning with sexual deviates: An evaluative review. *Advances in Behaviour Research & Therapy, 13,* 13–25.

Leiblum, S. R. (2002). After sildenafil: Bridging the gap between pharmacologic treatment and satisfying sexual relationships. *Journal of Clinical Psychiatry, 63*(Suppl. 5), 17–22.

Leiblum, S. R., Koochaki, P. E., Rodenberg, C. A., Barton, I. P., & Rosen, R. C. (2006). Hypoactive sexual desire disorder in postmenopausal women: US results from the Women's International Study of Health and Sexuality (WISHeS). *Menopause, 13,* 46–56.

Letourneau, E. J., & O'Donohue, W. (1997). Classical conditioning of female sexual arousal. *Archives of Sexual Behavior, 26,* 63–78.

Lewis, R. W., Fugl-Meyer, K. S., Bosch, R., Fugl-Meyer, A. R., Laumann, O., Lizza, E., et al. (2004). Definitions, classification, and epidemiology of sexual dysfunction. In T. F. Lue, R. Basson, R. Rosen, F. Giuliano, S. Khoury, & F. Montorsi (Eds.), *Sexual medicine: Sexual dysfunctions in men and women* (pp. 39–72). Paris: Health Publications.

Mah, K., & Binik, Y. M. (2001). The nature of human orgasm: A critical review of major trends. *Clinical Psychology Review, 21,* 823–856.

Manning, J. C. (2006). The impact of internet pornography on marriage and the family: A review of the research. *Sexual Addiction & Compulsivity, 13,* 131–165.

Marshall, W., & Yates, P. (2004). Diagnostic issues in sexual sadism among sexual offenders. *Journal of Sexual Aggression, 10,* 21–27.

Masters, W. H., & Johnson, V. E. (1966). *Human sexual response.* Boston: Little, Brown.

Masters W. H., & Johnson, V. E. (1970). *Human sexual inadequacy.* Boston: Little, Brown.

Maurice, W. L. (2007). Sexual desire disorders in men. In S. R. Leiblum (Ed.), *Principles and practice of sex therapy* (4th ed., pp. 181–211). New York: Guilford Press.

McCarthy, B. W., & Fucito, L. M. (2005). Integrating medication, realistic expectations, and therapeutic interventions in the treatment of male sexual dysfunction. *Journal of Sex & Marital Therapy, 31,* 319–328.

McKay, E., Kaufman, R. H., Doctor, U., Berkova, Z., Glazer, H., & Redko, V. (2001). Treating vulvar vestibulitis with electromyographic biofeedback of pelvic floor musculature. *Journal of Reproductive Medicine, 46,* 337–342.

McKibben, A., Proulx, J., & Lussier, P. (2001). Sexual aggressors' perceptions of effectiveness of strategies to cope with negative emotions and deviant sexual fantasies. *Sexual Abuse: A Journal of Research and Treatment, 13,* 257–273.

McMahon, C., Abdo, C., Incrocci, L., Perelman, M., Rowland, D., Waldinger, M., et al. (2004). Disorders of orgasm and ejaculation in men. *Journal of Sexual Medicine, 1,* 58–65.

Melnik, T., & Abdo, C. (2005). Psychogenic erectile dysfunction: Comparative study of three therapeutic approaches. *Journal of Sex & Marital Therapy, 31,* 243–255.

Meston, C. M. (2006). Female orgasmic disorder: Treatment strategies and outcome results. In I. Goldstein, C. M. Meston, S. R. Davis, & A. M. Traish (Eds.), *Women's sexual function and dysfunction: Study, diagnosis, and treatment* (pp. 449–461). New York: Taylor and Francis.

Meston, C. M., Hull, E., Levin, R. J., & Sipski, M. (2004). Women's orgasm. In T. F. Lue, R. Basson, R. Rosen, F. Giuliano, S. Khoury, & F. Montorsi (Eds.), *Sexual medicine: Sexual dysfunctions in men and women* (pp. 783–849). Paris: Health Publications.

Meyer-Bahlburg, H., Dolezal, C., Zucker, K., Kessler, S., Schober, J., & New, M. (2006, November). The Recalled Childhood Gender Questionnaire-Revised: A psychometric analysis in a sample of women with congenital adrenal hyperplasia. *Journal of Sex Research, 43,* 364–367.

Min, K., Munarriz, R., Kim, N. N., Choi, S., O'Connell, L., Goldstein, I., et al. (2003). Effects of ovariectomy and estrogen replacement on basal and pelvic nerve stimulated vaginal lubrication in an animal model. *Journal of Sex & Marital Therapy, 29,* 77–87.

Moser, C., & Kleinplatz, P. (2007). Themes of SM expression. In D. Langdridge & M. Barker (Eds.), *Safe, sane and consensual: Contemporary perspectives on sadomasochism* (pp. 35–54). New York: Palgrave Macmillan.

Moynihan, R. (2003). The making of a disease: Female sexual dysfunction. *BMJ, 326,* 45–47.

Navathe, S., Ward, T., & Gannon, T. (2008). Cognitive distortions in child sex offenders: An overview of theory, research & practice. *Journal of Forensic Nursing, 4,* 111–122.

Nichols, H. R., & Molinder, I. (2000). *Multiphasic Sex Inventory-II.* Tacoma, WA: Nichols & Molinder Assessments.

Nichols, M. (2006). Psychotherapeutic issues with 'kinky' clients: Clinical problems, yours and theirs. *Journal of Homosexuality, 50,* 281–300.

Nicolosi, A., Laumann, E., Glasser, D., Brock, G., King, R., & Gingell, C. (2006). Sexual activity, sexual disorders and associated help-seeking behavior among mature adults in five Anglophone countries from the Global Survey of Sexual Attitudes and Behaviors (GSSAB). *Journal of Sex & Marital Therapy, 32,* 331–342.

Nobre, P. J., & Pinto-Gouveia, J. (2006). Dysfunctional sexual beliefs as vulnerability factors for sexual dysfunction. *Journal of Sex Research, 43,* 68–75.

O'Connor, D. B., Archer, J., & Wu, F. C. (2004). Effects of testosterone on mood, aggression, and sexual behavior in young men: A double-blind, placebo-controlled, cross-over study. *Journal of Clinical Endocrinology & Metabolism, 89,* 2837–2845.

Paitich, D., Langevin, R., Freeman, R., Mann, K., & Handy, L. (1977). The Clarke SHQ: A clinical sex history questionnaire for males. *Archives of Sexual Behavior, 6,* 421–436.

Patrick, D., Althof, S., Pryor, J., Rosen, R., Rowland, D., Ho, K., et al. (2005). Premature ejaculation: An observational study of men and their partners. *Journal of Sexual Medicine, 2,* 358–367.

Pitts, M., Ferris, J., Smith, A., Shelley, J., & Richters, J. (2008). Prevalence and correlates of three types of pelvic pain in a nationally representative sample of Australian men. *Journal of Sexual Medicine, 5,* 1223–1229.

Plaud, J. J., & Gaither, G. A. (1997). A clinical investigation of the possible effects of long-term habituation of sexual arousal in assisted covert sensitization. *Journal of Behavior Therapy and Experimental Psychiatry, 28,* 281–290.

Polonsky, D. C. (2003). Young men who avoid sex. In S. B. Levine, C. B. Risen, & S. E. Althof (Eds.), *Handbook of clinical sexuality for mental health professionals* (pp. 201–216). New York: Brunner-Routledge.

Pukall, C. F., Payne, K. A., Kao, A., Khalifé, S., & Binik, Y. M. (2005). Dyspareunia. In R. Balon & R. T. Segraves (Eds.), *Handbook of sexual dysfunction* (pp. 249–272). New York: Taylor and Francis.

Rachman, S. (1966). Sexual fetishism: An experimental analogue. *Psychological Record, 16,* 293–296.

Rachman, S., & Hodgson, R. J. (1968). Experimentally-induced 'sexual fetishism': Replication and development. *Psychological Record, 18,* 25–27.

Redouté, J., Stoléru, S., Pugeat, M., Costes, N., Lavenne, F., Le Bars, D., et al. (2005). Brain processing of visual sexual stimuli in treated and untreated hypogonadal patients. *Psychoneuroendocrinology, 30,* 461–482.

Regan, P. C., & Atkins, L. (2006). Sex differences and similarities in frequency and intensity of sexual desire. *Social Behavior and Personality, 34,* 95–102.

Read, S., King, M., & Watson, J. (1997). Sexual dysfunction in primary medical care: Prevalence, characteristics and detection by the general practitioner. *Journal of Public Health Medicine, 19,* 387–391.

Reissing, E. D., Binik, Y. M., & Khalifé, S. (1999). Does vaginismus exist? A critical review of the literature. *Journal of Nervous and Mental Disease, 187,* 261–274.

Reissing, E. D., Binik, Y. M., Khalifé, S., Cohen, D., & Amsel, R. (2004). Vaginal spasm, pain, and behavior: An empirical investigation of the diagnosis of vaginismus. *Archives of Sexual Behavior, 33,* 5–17.

Rice, M. E., Quinsey, V. L., & Harris, G. T. (1991). Sexual recidivism among child molesters released from a maximum security psychiatric institution. *Journal of Consulting and Clinical Psychology, 59,* 381–386.

Richters, J., de Visser, R., Rissel, C., Grulich, A., & Smith, A. (2008). Demographic and psychosocial features of participants in bondage and discipline, 'sadomasochism' or dominance and submission (BDSM): Data from a national survey. *Journal of Sexual Medicine, 5,* 1660–1668.

Rosen, R. C., Brown, C., Heiman, J. R., Leiblum, S., Meston, C. M., Shabsigh, R., et al. (2000). The Female Sexual Function Index (FSFI): A multidimensional self-report instrument for the assessment of female sexual function. *Journal of Sex & Marital Therapy, 26,* 191–208.

Rosen, R. C., Taylor, J. F., Leiblum, S., & Bachman, G. A. (1993). Prevalence of sexual dysfunction in women: Results of a survey study of 329 women in an outpatient gynecological clinic. *Journal of Sex & Marital Therapy, 19,* 171–188.

Rosenbaum, T. Y. (2005). Physiotherapy treatment of sexual pain disorders. *Journal of Sex & Marital Therapy, 31,* 329–340.

Rowland, D. L., Keeney, C., & Slob, A. K. (2004). Sexual response in men with inhibited or retarded ejaculation. *International Journal of Impotence Research, 16,* 270–274.

Rowland, D. L., & Slob, A. K. (1997). Premature ejaculation: Psychophysiological theory, research, and treatment. *Annual Review of Sex Research, 8,* 224–253.

Rowland, D., van Diest, S., Incrocci, L., & Slob, A. (2005). Psychosexual factors that differentiate men with inhibited ejaculation from men with no dysfunction or another sexual dysfunction. *Journal of Sexual Medicine, 2,* 383–389.

Sanchez, D. T., Crocker, J., Boike, K. R. (2005). Doing gender in the bedroom: Investing in gender norms and the sexual experience. *Personality and Social Psychology Bulletin, 31,* 1445–1455.

Sarwer, D. B., & Durlak, J. A. (1997). A field trial of the effectiveness of behavioral treatment for sexual dysfunctions. *Journal of Sex & Marital Therapy, 23,* 87–97.

Scorolli, C., Ghirlanda, S., Enquist, M., Zattoni, S., & Jannini, E. A. (2007). Relative prevalence of different fetishes. *International Journal of Impotence Research, 19,* 432–437.

Seto, M. C. (2001). The value of phallometry in the assessment of male sex offenders. *Journal of Forensic Psychology Practice, 1,* 65–75.

Seto, M. C. (2004). Pedophilia and sexual offenses against children. *Annual Review of Sex Research, 15,* 321–361.

Seto, M. C., Cantor, J. M., & Blanchard, R. (2006). Child pornography offenses are a valid diagnostic indicator of pedophilia. *Journal of Abnormal Psychology, 115,* 610–615.

Shifren, J. L., Monz, B. U., Russo, P. A., Segreti, A., & Johannes, C. B. (2008). Sexual problems and distress in United States women: Prevalence and correlates. *Obstetrics & Gynecology, 112,* 970–978.

Simons, J. S., & Carey, M. P. (2001). Prevalence of sexual dysfunctions: Results from a decade of research. *Archives of Sexual Behavior, 30,* 177–219.

Sohn, M., & Bosinski, H. A. G. (2007). Gender identity disorders: Diagnostic and surgical aspects. *Journal of Sexual Medicine, 4,* 1193–1208.

Strassberg, D., de Gouveia Brazao, C., Rowland, D., Tan, P., & Slob, A. (1999). Clomipramine in the treatment of rapid (premature) ejaculation. *Journal of Sex & Marital Therapy, 25,* 89–101.

Taylor, J. F., Rosen, R. C., & Leiblum, S. R. (1994). Self-report assessment of female sexual function: Psychometric evaluation of the Brief Index of Sexual Function for Women. *Archives of Sexual Behavior, 23,* 627–643.

Templeman, T. L., & Stinnett, R. D. (1991). Patterns of sexual arousal and history in a 'normal' sample of young men. *Archives of Sexual Behavior, 20,* 137–150.

ter Kuile, M. M., van Lankveld, J. J., Vlieland, C. V., Willekes, C., & Weijenborg, P. T. (2005). Vulvar vestibulitis syndrome: An important factor in the evaluation of lifelong vaginismus? *Journal of Psychosomatic Obstetrics & Gynecology, 26,* 245–249.

ter Kuile, M. M, & Weijenborg, P. T. M. (2006). A cognitive-behavioral group program for women with vulvar vestibulitis syndrome (VVS): Factors associated with treatment success. *Journal of Sex & Marital Therapy, 32,* 199–213.

Tiefer, L. (2002). Sexual behaviour and its medicalisation. Many (especially economic) forces promote medicalisation. *BMJ, 325,* 45.

Veale, J. F., Clarke, D. E., & Lomax, T. C. (2008). Sexuality of male-to-female transsexuals. *Archives of Sexual Behavior, 37,* 586–597.

Waldinger, M. (2008). Premature ejaculation: Different pathophysiologies and etiologies determine its treatment. *Journal of Sex & Marital Therapy, 34,* 1–13.

Waldinger, M., Hengeveld, M., & Zwinderman, A. (1994). Paroxetine treatment of premature ejaculation: A double-blind, randomized, placebo-controlled study. *American Journal of Psychiatry, 151,* 1377–1379.

Wallien, M. S. C., Swaab, H., & Cohen-Kettenis, P. T. (2007). Psychiatric comorbidity among children with gender identity disorder. *Journal of the American Academy of Child and Adolescent Psychiatry, 46,* 1307–1314.

Weijmar Schultz, W., Basson, R., Binik, Y., Eschenbach, D., Wesselmann, U., & Van Lankveld, J. (2005). Women's sexual pain and its management. *Journal of Sexual Medicine, 2,* 301–316.

World Professional Association for Transgender Health (2001). *Standards of Care for Gender Identity Disorders.* Accessed January 2009. Available at: http://www.wpath.org/publications_standards.cfm.

Zucker, K. J. (2005). Gender identity disorder in children and adolescents. *Annual Review of Clinical Psychology, 1,* 467–492.

Zucker, K., Bradley, S., Kuksis, M., Pecore, K., Birkenfeld-Adams, A., Doering, R., et al. (1999). Gender constancy judgments in children with gender identity disorder: Evidence for a developmental lag. *Archives of Sexual Behavior, 28,* 475–502.

Kim T. Mueser *and* Stephanie Marcello Duva

Abstract

Schizophrenia

Schizophrenia is a severe mental illness marked by hallucinations, delusions, reduced social drive, apathy, and cognitive impairment. Schizophrenia tends to develop in early adulthood and has a major impact on all aspects of functioning, including work, school, social relationships, and self-care. The illness is thought to have a biological basis that interacts with environmental and psychological factors, including stress, social support, and social competence and coping skills. Schizophrenia was once thought to be a progressively deteriorating disorder. However, more recent perspectives on schizophrenia focus on helping people define the meaning of recovery for themselves, to set personally meaningful goals, and to become active participants in their own treatment. A broad range of effective treatments exist for schizophrenia, including antipsychotic medications and psychosocial interventions such as supported employment, family psychoeducation, social skills training, and cognitive-behavioral therapy for psychosis. Although most people with schizophrenia experience some symptoms and impairments throughout their lives, recent treatment advances enable them to live rewarding, fulfilling lives, and to make a contribution to society.

Keywords: Assertive Community Treatment, cognitive remediation, cognitive-behavioral therapy for psychosis, family psychoeducation, illness self-management, schizoaffective disorder, schizophrenia, schizophreniform disorder, schizotypal personality disorder social skills training, stress-vulnerability model, supported employment

Schizophrenia is a major psychiatric disorder that can have a profound effect on the individual, his or her family members, and society at large. Schizophrenia is characterized by a combination of psychotic symptoms, such as hallucinations and delusions, and negative (or deficit) symptoms, such as apathy, paranoia, and blunted affect. Although symptoms are critical to the diagnosis of schizophrenia, the hallmark of the disease is impaired functioning, including the ability to participate in meaningful and reciprocal relationships with others, to take care of oneself, and to function at work, school, or as a parent.

Because of the long-term impact of schizophrenia on functioning, and the episodic nature of psychotic symptoms that tend to vary in their presence and intensity—at times requiring temporary hospitalization to protect the individual or others—most people with schizophrenia rely on family members and disability benefits to meet their basic needs. The loss in functional capacity, combined with the intermittent need for inpatient psychiatric treatment, makes schizophrenia a costly disease to society (Rice, 1999; Samnaliev & Clark, 2008). In fact, due to the loss of productivity and premature death attributed to schizophrenia, it is considered one of the top ten of all diseases in the world contributing to disability burden (Murray & Lopez, 1996).

Schizophrenia is a biologically based disease that interacts with environmental factors such as stress and social support. Although the precise causes of schizophrenia remain unknown, substantial advances in the treatment of the disorder have been made over the past several decades. With a combination of pharmacological and psychosocial treatments, it is now possible for many people with schizophrenia to live rewarding and productive lives, despite continuing to experience some of the symptoms and characteristic impairments of the disorder. In this chapter, we review what is known about the nature and causes of schizophrenia, and describe the growing evidence base for the treatment of the disorder.

Epidemiology
Prevalence

Schizophrenia affects approximately 1% of the world population. In the United States alone, 3.7 million Americans or approximately 0.7% (ranging between.3% and 1.6%, depending on the study) have the disease (McGrath, Saha, Welham, Saadi, MacCauley, & Chant, 2004). Due to the chronic nature of schizophrenia, health-care costs are significant. It is estimated that 10% of all disabled persons meet criteria for schizophrenia (Goldman & Manderscheid, 1987). A significant percentage of people with this disorder are unemployed and typically have a lower quality of life, when compared to the rest of the population (Marwaha et al., 2007; Warner, Girolamo, & Bellini, 1998). Furthermore, the economic costs are considerable: people diagnosed with schizophrenia account for 75% of mental health care costs and approximately 40% of Medicaid reimbursements (Murray & Lopez, 1996). It is estimated that the overall U.S. cost of schizophrenia is $62.7 billion (Wu, Birnbaum, Shi, Ball, Kessler, & Moulis, 2005). This includes both the direct costs of treating the illness, as well as costs related to lost work productivity for clients and families, and costs associated with incarceration and the legal system. The substantial burden of the disease is a reflection of its early onset and persistent and fluctuating symptoms (American Psychiatric Association [APA], 1994).

Onset and Course

Schizophrenia is typically diagnosed in late adolescence or early adulthood, and infrequently after the age of 45. However, schizophrenia does develop through the adult lifespan, including past the age of 50 (Almeida, Howard, Levy, & David, 1995a, 1995b). The disease characteristically has a gradual onset that takes place over 5 years, starting with negative and depressive symptoms, followed by cognitive and social impairment, which is then followed by the emergence of psychotic symptoms (Häfner & an der Heiden, 2008; Häfner, Löffler, Maurer, Hambrecht, & an der Heiden, 1999).

Schizophrenia is a chronic, disabling disorder and, once it has developed, some impairment is present throughout most of life, although clients might experience times of remission (Häfner & an der Heiden, 2003). Between 50% and 70% of cases are associated with a chronic course, relapses, and permanent disability. However, despite past negativity about prognosis, recent studies suggest that early intervention and great advances in treatment can improve outcomes (Perkins, Gu, Boteva, & Lieberman, 2005). For example, Loebel et al. (1992) found that, in a state-of-the-art treatment program, 74% of people recovering from their first episode had achieved complete remission. Also, at a specialized clinic for high-risk youth in Australia, 91% of people with recent-onset psychosis were in remission after 1 year of assertive community treatment, medication, and cognitive-behavioral therapy (CBT) (Edwards, Maude, McGorry, Harrigan, & Cocks, 1998). Even among clients with a more chronic and disabling course (e.g., clients who have spent years in state psychiatric hospitals), recovery rates over 15–25 years can be promising. For example, several long-term studies have shown that approximately 25%–40% of people with schizophrenia lead relatively independent lives, or are even completely recovered and off all medication, after many years of comprehensive treatment (Ciompi, 1980; Harding, Brooks, Ashikaga, Strauss, & Breier, 1987a, 1987b; Harrison et al., 2001; Tsuang & Winokur, 1975).

Poor outcome is predicted by gender (male), early age of onset, severity of negative and cognitive symptoms, substance abuse, and sudden discontinuation of psychiatric medications (Emsley, Chiliza, & Schoeman, 2008). Lack of insight is present in 50% to 80% of people with schizophrenia and often contributes to poor medication adherence (Amador & Gorman, 1998; Lysaker, Lancaster, Davis, & Clements, 2003; Smith, Hull, Huppert, Silverstein, Anthony, & McClough, 2004). Also, a shorter duration of untreated psychosis is associated with greater response to treatment (Perkins et al., 2005).

Gender, Ethnicity, and Cultural Factors

Schizophrenia occurs equally in men and women, although symptoms typically appear earlier in men (20–28 years) than in women (26–32 years) (Murray & Van Os, 1998). Women also tend to have a more benign course of illness, including fewer hospital admissions and better social functioning (Angermeyer, Kuhn, & Goldstein, 1990; Canuso & Pandina, 2007; Riecher-Rössler & Häfner, 2000). The better outcome of women with schizophrenia compared to men is hypothesized to be the result of estrogen, which has antipsychotic properties and is associated with a later age at onset of the disorder and better psychosocial functioning due to having passed through more developmental milestones (Häfner, Maurer, Löffler, & Riecher-Rössler, 1993).

Substantial variations in the prevalence of schizophrenia across different countries and cultural groups have been reported (Institute of Medicine, 2001b). However, these differences are reduced when diagnostic criteria is controlled for (Jablensky, 1997). Research by the World Health Organization indicates similar rates of schizophrenia across cultures and countries, including developed and developing nations (Jablensky et al., 1992).

Risk Factors

Several forms of environmental stress and/or trauma may increase the likelihood of schizophrenia. Some research suggests that neglect and trauma during childhood increases the risk of developing this disorder later in life. The data indicate that childhood abuse is associated with increased rates of adult schizophrenia, and that high rates of neglect and physical and sexual abuse are found in the histories of people with schizophrenia (Read & Argyle, 1999; Read, van Os, Morrison, & Ross, 2005).

Some sociodemographic factors have been associated with increased risk for schizophrenia (van Os & Marcelis, 1998). Poverty (Bruce, Takeuchi, & Leaf, 1991), lower social class (Eaton, 1994; Hollingshead & Redlich, 1958), urban birth and upbringing (Torrey, Bowler, & Clark, 1997; Saha, Chant, Welham, & McGrath, 2005; van Os, 2004), and migration to urban areas are strongly correlated to higher rates of schizophrenia (Pedersen & Mortensen, 2001; van Os, 2004). Some hypotheses are that stressful environmental conditions increase the risk of schizophrenia, and schizophrenia results in a downward "social drift" due to a decline in social and occupational functioning (Fox, 1990). Although the incidence of the disorder is similar across different ethnic groups (Jablensky, 1999), increased rates are present in some monitory populations, such as second-generation Afro-Caribbean people in the United Kingdom (Boydell et al., 2001), Dutch Antillean and Surinamese immigrants in Holland (Selten, Slaets, & Kahn, 1997), and African American people (Rabkin, 1979). An additional environmental factor is international migration. A recent meta-analysis review (Cantor-Graae, Zolkowska, & McNeil, 2005) provides evidence that migration to a new country is correlated with increased rates of schizophrenia.

There is evidence that the prenatal environment and obstetric complications are related to increased risk of developing schizophrenia (Byrne, Agerbo, Bennedsen, Eaton, & Mortensen, 2007; Cannon, Jones, & Murray, 2002). Obstetric complications may disrupt early brain development, and several factors have been association with increased risk of developing schizophrenia; for example, maternal infection (Brown et al., 2004), maternal starvation (Hoek, Brown, & Susser, 1998), late winter birth (Hultman, Sparén, Takei, Murray, & Cnattingius, 1998), birth asphyxia (Dalman et al., 2001), and being born too small (Jones, Rantakallio, Hartikainen, Isohanni, & Sipila, 1998). Despite this growing body of evidence of the association between obstetric complications and later development of schizophrenia, there are some conflicting results. Haukvik et al. (2009) found that the number or severity of obstetric complications were not associated with brain cortical thickness in people with schizophrenia. Previous studies have found that people with schizophrenia have thinner brain cortices compared to controls (DeLisi et al., 2006).

There is some evidence that cannabis use can actually precipitate the onset of schizophrenia. In a meta-analysis, Henquet et al. (2005) found that cannabis use more than doubles the risk of developing schizophrenia. The risk of developing schizophrenia appears to be higher for individuals who smoke cannabis relatively early in adolescence (e.g., before the age of 16), with dose of use also associated with increased vulnerability to the disorder (Arseneault, Cannon, Witton, & Murray, 2004; Corcoran et al., 2008).

Psychopathology and Characteristic Impairments
Symptoms

Three types of symptoms are characteristic of schizophrenia: psychotic symptoms, negative symptoms, and disorganization symptoms. Common *psychotic symptoms* include delusions, hallucinations, and bizarre behavior. *Negative symptoms* are the absence or reduction of aspects of normal behavior, thinking, or feeling. Some examples are reduced facial emotional expressiveness (i.e., *flat affect*), poverty of speech (*alogia*), reduction in the experience of pleasure (*anhedonia*), and lack of motivation (*avolition, apathy*). Negative symptoms are sometimes subtyped into primary negative symptoms (symptoms that directly reflect a disease process) and secondary symptoms (symptoms due to the side effects of medication or other extraneous factors) (Carpenter, Heinrichs, & Wagman, 1988; Kirkpatrick & Galderisi, 2008; Mueser, Douglas, Bellack, & Morrison, 1991). Examples of disorganization symptoms include poorly planned behavior and difficult-to-understand speech due to disordered syntax (*word salad*) or making up new words (*neologisms*).

Depression in people with schizophrenia has been found to be more frequent and more severe than in the general population, and persistent over the course of the illness (Häfner et al., 1999). Depression during the acute phase of schizophrenia may be associated with a more favorable course and outcome (Vaillant, 1964), but during the chronic phase has been linked to greater risk of suicide (Cohen, 1995) and relapse (Johnson et al., 1998). The severity of depressive symptoms is correlated with positive symptoms and substance abuse, but not with age, gender, or negative symptoms (Brunette, Mueser, Xie, & Drake, 1997; Mueser et al., 1991b; Zisook et al., 1999).

Cognitive impairment is a core feature in people with schizophrenia that tends to remain stable after the onset of the disorder (Heaton et al., 1994). People with schizophrenia tend to show a broad spectrum of neurocognitive deficits, including in attention/vigilance, executive functioning, working memory, processing speed, verbal learning and memory, visual learning and memory, reasoning and problem solving, and social cognition. Large studies and meta-analyses suggest that neurocognitive functioning is compromised in a significantly large proportion of people with schizophrenia (Heinrichs & Zakzanis, 1998). Clinically, this is important because cognitive impairments in people with schizophrenia contribute to poor functional outcomes, including, difficulty maintaining work, independent living, and social networks, and reduced benefit from psychosocial treatments (Green, 1996, 2006; McGurk & Mueser, 2004; Mueser, 2000).

Functional Impairments

Psychosocial dysfunction, including impaired social relationships and role functioning, and poor self-care, are core behavioral features that distinguish schizophrenia (APA, 1994). Negative symptoms are significant contributors to poor social functioning (Puig et al., 2008), and have higher predictive value than do positive symptoms (Addington, Young, & Addington, 2003). Both have a negative impact on the quality of life for both clients and families. Chronic symptoms and cognitive impairments are the strongest predictors of psychosocial functioning (Puig et al., 2008).

Unemployment rates are higher than 20% in people with schizophrenia and are much higher when compared to the general population (Marwaha & Johnson, 2004). However, most people with schizophrenia indicate a desire to work (Mueser, Salyers, & Mueser, 2001). Work is associated with numerous favorable outcomes, including improved self-esteem, less severe symptoms, financial gain, and improved sense of recovery (Arns & Linney, 1993; Mueser, Becker, et al., 1997).

Self-care and community survival skills, such as grooming and hygiene, cooking, laundry, and home maintenance, are commonly impaired in people with schizophrenia (Holmberg & Kane, 1999), frequently requiring the involvement of family in getting basic needs met. Housing is often substandard, with high rates of homelessness (Fischer, Drake, & Breakey, 1992; Olfson, Mechanic, Hansell, Boyer, & Walkup, 1999; Susser, Struening, & Conover, 1989). Incarceration is common, and is often related to lack of treatment (Munetz, Grande, & Chambers, 2001; Teplin, 1985; Teplin, Abram, & McClelland, 1996) or increased rates of aggression and violence (Arseneault, Moffitt, Caspi, Taylor, & Silva, 2000; Brennan, Mednick, & Hodgins, 2000). Although schizophrenia is associated with an increased risk of violence, individuals with the disorder are significantly more likely to be victims of crime than perpetrators (Bebbington et al., 2004; Hiday, Swartz, Swanson, Borum, & Wagner, 1999; Teplin, McClelland, Abram, & Weiner, 2005).

Comorbidity

People with schizophrenia often have other comorbid psychiatric conditions or disorders. Depression is commonly found in people with this disorder. Lifetime estimates of clinically significant depression in people with schizophrenia range from 25% to 33% (Cohen, Talavera, & Hartung, 1996; Häfner et al., 2005; Sands & Harrow, 1999). Suicide is the leading cause of early death in people with schizophrenia. About 4.9% of people with schizophrenia commit suicide, frequently near the onset of their symptoms (Palmer, Pankratz, & Bostwick, 2005).

Substance use disorders occur in approximately 50% of individuals with schizophrenia, compared to approximately 15% in the general population (Kessler et al., 1996; Mueser, Bennett, & Kushner, 1995; Regier et al., 1990). Rates of abuse tend to be highest among younger males with lower educational level, antisocial personality disorder, and a family history of addiction (Kavanagh et al., 2004; Mueser, Crocker, et al., 2006; Noordsy, Drake, Biesanz, & McHugo, 1994). As described later in this chapter, substance abuse in people with schizophrenia is of particular concern and is an important focus of treatment because it leads to increases in severity of positive symptoms, treatment noncompliance, violence, human immunodeficiency virus (HIV) infection, homelessness, higher medical costs, and potential involvement with the legal system (Drake & Brunette, 1998).

Rates of conduct disorder in childhood and antisocial personality disorder in adulthood are also increased in persons with schizophrenia (Hodgins, Toupin, & Côté, 1996; Robins, 1966; Robins, Tipp, & Przybeck, 1991). Higher rates of antisocial personality disorder have been linked to increased aggression (Hodgins, Hiscoke, & Freese, 2002; Hodgins, Tiihonen, & Ross, 2005; Tengström, Hodgins, Grann, Långström, & Kullgren, 2004) and substance use disorders (Mueser, Crocker, et al., 2006; Mueser et al., 1997; Mueser, Rosenberg, et al., 1999). Hodgins and colleagues have hypothesized that the increased rate of violence in schizophrenia can be subtyped into one group of "early starters," with conduct disorder and a pattern of aggression that precedes the onset of schizophrenia; and another group of "late starters," whose violence is related to psychotic symptoms (Crocker et al., 2005; Hodgins et al., 1996; Moran & Hodgins, 2004; Tengström, Hodgins, & Kullgren, 2001).

Anxiety disorders are significant clinical problems in many people with schizophrenia and include panic disorder (Argyle, 1990; Hofmann, 1999), obsessive-compulsive disorder (Hwang, Morgan, & Losconzey, 2000; Tibbo, Kroetsch, Chue, & Warneke, 2000), social phobia (Penn, Hope, Spaulding, & Kucera, 1994), and post-traumatic stress disorder (PTSD) (Mueser, Goodman et al., 1998; Mueser, Salyers et al., 2004). Of particular concern, estimates of exposure to traumatic events for people with schizophrenia range from 34% to 98% (Goodman, Dutton, & Harris, 1995; Hatters Friedman & Loue, 2007), with rates of PTSD in people with schizophrenia of between 29% and 43% (Mueser, Rosenberg, Goodman, & Trumbetta, 2002). It has been suggested that the frequency of trauma among people with schizophrenia may also be *under*-estimated, due to clients' underreporting of traumatic experiences and insufficient assessments of traumatic events at mental health facilities (Rosenberg et al., 2001).

People with a serious mental illness die, on average (Pack, 2009), 25 years earlier than the general population, and medical comorbidity is largely to blame (Sokal et al., 2004). Suicide and injury account for about 30%–40% of deaths, but the high mortality and morbidity rates are not all accounted for by the higher rates of suicide (Harris & Barraclough, 1998). As many as 60% of premature deaths in people with schizophrenia are due to high rates of medical conditions, such as diabetes (Dixon et al., 2000), dyslipidemia (Meyer & Koro, 2004), obesity (Dickerson et al., 2006), cardiovascular and respiratory diseases (Druss, Bradford, Rosenheck, Radford, & Krumholz, 2000; Sokal et al., 2004), metabolic effects of antipsychotic medications (Meyer et al., 2008), and pulmonary and infectious diseases, such as hepatitis and acquired immune deficiency syndrome (AIDS) (Rosenberg et al., 2001). This is due to multiple factors including poor judgment about health needs (Felker, Yazel, & Short, 1996), receipt of fewer and poorer-quality health services (Desai, Rosenheck, Druss, & Perlin, 2002; Druss et al., 2000), poorer nutrition (Fontaine et al., 2001), high rates of smoking (de Leon & Diaz, 2005), lack of exercise (Daumit et al., 2005), "unsafe" sexual behavior (Cournos et al., 1994; Goodman & Fallot, 1998), and low socioeconomic standing and living in poor neighborhoods (Felker et al., 1996).

Diagnostic Systems and History

The characterization of schizophrenia as a single disorder dates back to Emil Kraepelin (1919/1971), who coined the term *dementia praecox* to mean "early dementia." This disorder was distinguished from manic-depression (now called bipolar disorder), which had a relapsing and remitting course. To Kraepelin, dementia praecox was a progressive disease involving deterioration in cognitive functioning and increased disability over time. The word *schizophrenia* was introduced in the early 20th century by the Swiss psychiatrist Eugen Bleuler (1911/1950). Bleuler changed the term because, he argued, many people with the disorder did recover, and, even when recovery did not occur, deterioration did not necessarily occur. The term *schizophrenia* is derived from the Greek words *skhiz* (split) and *phren* (mind), and refers to the fragmentation of thought, speech, emotion, and behavior found in the disorder. (It is often mistakenly assumed that people with schizophrenia have multiple personalities. However, that condition is known as dissociative identity disorder, and is unrelated to schizophrenia [APA, 1994].)

The *Diagnostic and Statistical Manual of Mental Disorders*, Fourth Edition (DSM-IV) (APA, 1994) and the *International Classification of Diseases*, 10th Edition (ICD-10) (World Health Organization, 1997) are the two sets of diagnostic criteria by which schizophrenia is most often diagnosed.

Schizophrenia-Spectrum Disorders

The symptoms of schizophrenia have historically been used to form different subtypes, including paranoid, disorganized, hebephrenic, undifferentiated, and catatonic. Although these subtypes are useful in describing some of the common patterns in which the symptoms of schizophrenia manifest themselves, the subtypes have not proven useful in identifying cohesive subgroups of individuals who differ in family history of the disorder, biological parameters, or response to treatments (Fenton & McGlashan, 1991). These subtypes of schizophrenia date back to the earliest descriptions of the disorder more than 100 years ago, but, given the lack of demonstrated utility, there is active debate about dropping the use of these subtypes in classifying the disorder.

Four disorders are commonly grouped together as schizophrenia-spectrum disorders based on family history, similarity in presenting symptoms, and response to available treatments: schizophrenia, schizoaffective disorder, schizophreniform disorder, and schizotypal personality disorder (Levinson & Mowry, 1991). Schizophreniform disorder differs from schizophrenia mainly with respect to the duration of symptoms and associated impairment in functioning. The diagnosis of schizophrenia requires a minimum 6 months' duration of either active symptoms or associated impairment. Individuals who meet symptom and functional impairment criteria for schizophrenia, but do not meet the 6 months' duration criterion, are diagnosed with schizophreniform disorder. Individuals whose symptoms and impaired functioning remit in less than a 6-month period are given the diagnosis of schizophreniform

disorder in remission. Individuals with schizophreniform disorder who continue to be symptomatic or impaired are diagnosed with schizophreniform disorder (provisional), which is then changed to schizophrenia when the symptoms or impairment have been present for a minimum of 6 months.

Schizoaffective disorder is defined by the presence of clear and prominent mood syndromes (meeting criteria for either major depressive episodes or hypomanic or manic episodes) in people who otherwise meet the diagnostic criteria for schizophrenia. The diagnosis of schizoaffective disorder is based on two primary criteria. First, the person much have experienced episodes of depression, hypomania, or mania during significant proportions of his or her life in terms of the overall duration of his or her psychiatric disorder. Second, the individual must show at least some of the prominent symptoms of schizophrenia (e.g., hallucinations, delusions) during periods when he or she was not experiencing an episode of abnormal mood. People who have psychotic symptoms only during a mood episode, but whose psychotic symptoms remit when the depression or mania remit, are diagnosed with a mood disorder (e.g., major depression, bipolar disorder) and are not classified with a schizophrenia-spectrum disorder (Pope & Lipinski, 1978).

Schizotypal personality disorder is defined by the long-term presence of milder symptoms of schizophrenia, including symptoms such as magical thinking, peculiar face-to-face report when interacting with others, social anxiety, and odd behavior. The symptoms of schizotypal personality disorder are typically milder and more stable compared to those in schizophrenia. Nevertheless, functioning is substantially impaired and often only marginally better than in schizophrenia (Ödéhn & Goulding, 2009). Paranoid personality disorder, which is characterized by suspiciousness and paranoid delusions, and schizoid personality disorder, which is defined in terms of aloofness and a lack of desire or need for social relationships, are also sometimes included in the schizophrenia spectrum (Kendler et al., 2006).

Etiology
Genetic Factors

Genetic and environmental factors appear to play a role in the development of schizophrenia. Structural brain abnormalities have consistently been found in clients with schizophrenia (Shenton, Dickey, Frumin, & McCarley, 2001) and at least some of these brain changes are progressive (Pantelis et al., 2005). The cause of the brain changes is still unclear, but have been associated with poorer long-term outcomes (van Haren et al., 2008). It appears that the severity of the illness and the medication used to treat it influence the progressive brain volume changes (Lieberman et al., 2001). However, genes may also be involved with these progressive brain changes. Brans et al. (2008) found that progressive brain volume loss found in clients with schizophrenia and their unaffected twin sibling are partly attributable to genetic factors. Rates of developing schizophrenia are higher among relatives of clients when compared to the general population, and the hereditable nature schizophrenia is estimated to be around 80% (Sullivan, Kendler, & Neale, 2003). The genetic risk of developing the disorder increases with each affected relative, to nearly 50% when both parents are affected, and 60%–84% when a monozygotic twin has the illness (Cardno et al., 1999). Multiple genes have been shown to be associated with schizophrenia (Harrison & Owen, 2003; Jianxin Shi et al., 2009).

Environmental Factors

Studies have found that higher rates of abuse and trauma (e.g., physical and sexual abuse) during childhood increase the chances of developing schizophrenia later in life (Read et al., 2005). Urban birth, upbringing, and migration to urban areas have been correlated with increased rates of developing schizophrenia (Torrey et al., 1997). Numerous studies have found that cannabis use more than doubles the risk of developing schizophrenia, with risk being highest in people with one variant of the COMT gene (Moore et al., 2008). Studies done in the Northern Hemisphere have shown small, but consistent correlations demonstrating that babies born in the winter and spring months develop schizophrenia to a greater extent than in the general population (Fritzsche & Schmidl, 2002). Data from the Southern Hemisphere, however, have not supported the hypotheses as consistently (McGrath & Welham, 1999).

The long-term effects of racism and stress associated with being an underprivileged minority are associated with the development of schizophrenia. Silverstein, Spalding, and Menditto (2006) suggest that, although social defeat is unlikely to be a sufficient cause of developing this disorder, it might interact with other factors to increase risk. For example, chronic stress can lead to anatomical changes in the hippocampus and produce biological changes that, in combination with other psychological, biological, and environmental factors, can facilitate expression of the illness.

Although the etiology of schizophrenia is unknown, several theories have gained support in the literature. Both biological and environmental factors can increase one's risk for developing schizophrenia. In people with a genetic predisposition, environmental factors can determine whether the person develops or does not develop the disorder. In people without a known family history, factors such as birth complications (Cannon et al., 2002; Geddes & Lawrie, 1995), viral infection of the mother during the second trimester of pregnancy (Brown et al., 2004), and paternal age of the father (Zammit et al., 2003) may create the same brain abnormalities associated with genetic forms of schizophrenia, thus increasing risk. Genetics have been found to contribute to 80% of the liability for developing schizophrenia, and eight chromosomal sites have been associated with increased risk. Having a parent with schizophrenia raises a person's risk from 1% to 10% of developing this disorder. Having an identical twin with the illness raises the risk to 50% (Gottesman, 1991). Three birth complications have been associated with increased risk for developing schizophrenia: pregnancy complications (e.g., bleeding), delivery complications (e.g., hypoxia), and abnormal fetal development (e.g., low birth weight) (Buchanan, 1995).

The dopamine hypothesis of schizophrenia attributes the disorder to a hyperactive dopaminergic system. It has been suggested that the dopamine pathways in the mesolimbic region may contribute to the positive symptoms of schizophrenia. The evidence to support this theory is the emergence of psychotic symptoms in people who used amphetamines, cocaine, and other drugs, which are known to increase dopamine in the brain, and the positive effects of antipsychotic medications, which block dopamine receptors and reduce psychotic symptoms of schizophrenia (Davis, Kahn, Ko, & Davidson, 1991). However, serotonin, γ-aminobutyric acid (GABA), glutamate, and other neurotransmitters have also been implicated in schizophrenia (Pantelis et al., 2005). Therefore, rather than trying to isolate one neurotransmitter, focusing on the interactions among neurotransmitter systems is important for understanding schizophrenia.

Stress–Vulnerability Model

The Stress–Vulnerability Model has become a framework for explaining how environmental factors interact with preexisting vulnerability in the etiology and course of schizophrenia (Liberman et al., 1986; Nuechterlein & Dawson, 1984; Zubin & Spring, 1977). The model posits that schizophrenia is caused by a psychobiological vulnerability, which is determined early in life by genetic and early environmental influences. Once the vulnerability is established, the onset and course of the illness is determined by both biological and psychosocial factors. An example of a biological factor that can worsen vulnerability is substance abuse, which can precipitate relapses and hospitalizations (Linszen, Dingemans, & Lenior, 1994). Stress, including normal or traumatic life events (Bebbington & Kuipers, 1992), exposure to high levels of interpersonal stress (Butzlaff & Hooley, 1998), or lack of meaningful structure (Wong et al., 1987) can impinge on vulnerability, precipitating relapses and contributing to impairments in other domains (e.g., social functioning). However, coping skills (e.g., social skills, problem-solving ability) and social support can minimize the effects of stress on relapse and functioning (Liberman et al., 1986; Norman et al., 2005).

The treatment implications of the Stress–Vulnerability Model are straightforward. The outcome of schizophrenia can be improved through interventions that reduce psychobiological vulnerability or stress, or that improve social support and coping skills. Increasing adherence to antipsychotic medication and reducing substance abuse can lower vulnerability and improve the course of the illness. Interventions that reduce stress in the environment and increase social support, such as family psycho-education, can minimize relapses and improve functioning. Providing meaningful structured activities that are not overdemanding can also reduce environmental stress. Additionally, people can be taught skills to enhance their ability to deal with internal sources of stress (e.g., coping skills for anxiety, depression, persistent hallucinations), to handle external sources of stress (e.g., social skills for managing interpersonal conflict), or to achieve personal goals (e.g., social skills, problem-solving skills).

Treatment

Because schizophrenia can have a major impact on all aspects of daily living, and the etiology of the illness remains a mystery, treatment is necessarily complex as it must address the broad range of different domains of functioning affected by the illness. In this section, we first address the recovery paradigm as a new model for conceptualizing the role of treatment and rehabilitation in the management of schizophrenia. We next discuss the targets of treatment in schizophrenia, followed by different systems of care involved in the treatment of the disorder. We then discuss the psychopharmacologic treatment of schizophrenia, followed by a review of evidence-based psychosocial treatment and rehabilitation approaches for schizophrenia.

The Recovery Paradigm

Over the past 15 years, a gradual change has occurred in the conceptualization of the goals in treatment for schizophrenia. At the core of this change has been an evolution in how *recovery* from mental illness is understood and defined. Traditional medical definitions of recovery have emphasized the elimination of psychopathology and remission of symptoms and functional impairments (Andreasen et al., 2005; Liberman, Kopelowicz, Ventura, & Gutkind, 2002). Because early conceptualizations of schizophrenia posited that the disorder had a deteriorating course over the lifetime (Kraepelin, 1919/1971), most experts believed that recovery from schizophrenia was impossible. However, longitudinal research studies on the long-term outcome of schizophrenia published over the last three decades have conclusively refuted this assumption and have demonstrated that, in fact, a significant proportion of people with schizophrenia experience a medical recovery from the disorder over their lifetime (Häfner & an der Heiden, 2008). The fact that medical recovery from schizophrenia does occur has been important to challenging stereotypes about the chronicity and poor prognosis of the disorder previously held by many treatment providers.

Even more important than research showing that medical recovery from schizophrenia occurs over the long-term has been the rise of the *consumer movement* (i.e., individuals with schizophrenia or other severe mental illnesses) in advocating for a new, more personally meaningful, and more hopeful definition of recovery (Chamberlin, 1978). Newer definitions of recovery have challenged the emphasis of the medical definition on psychopathology, and instead view recovery as the process of coming to grips with having a mental illness and then moving forward with one's life despite the presence of any continuing symptoms or impairments (Anthony, 1993; Corrigan, Giffort, Rashid, Leary, & Okeke, 1999; Davidson, Tondora, Lawless, O'Connell, & Rowe, 2009; Deegan, 1988; Ralph, Kidder, & Phillips, 2000; Silverstein & Bellack, 2008). When recovery is defined in this way, it is more akin to recovering something that one has lost, such as a sense of meaning and purpose in life, as opposed to recovery from a disease. Furthermore, the concept of recovery goes beyond coping and evokes personal growth, in which the experience of a mental illness presents an opportunity for personal transformation and development (Roe & Ben-Yishai, 1999; Roe & Chopra, 2003). Of greatest significance, this new definition means that recovery from schizophrenia is possible despite some persistent symptoms.

Defining recovery as a process involving the development of meaning and improved functioning has had dramatic effects on increasing the hope of clients, family members, and even professionals for improving the lives of people with this disease. As a result of this shift in the conceptualization of recovery, treatment approaches have also evolved to focus more on helping clients make personally meaningful changes in their lives and focus less on symptoms alone. In addition, since recovery is understood to be an individual process that varies from one person to the next, and that people differ in what they find meaningful and their personal goals, treatment approaches have been altered to be less prescriptive and hierarchical (i.e., "the doctor always knows best"), and based more on developing a collaborative relationship between treatment providers and clients and a shared-decision making approach to treatment decisions (Adams, Drake, & Wolford, 2007; Hamann, Leucht, & Kissling, 2003). Such an approach recognizes that the client is a vital participant in his or her own treatment and that treatment decisions are much more likely to be followed through on when they are arrived at in a collaborative fashion (Roe, Chopra, & Rudnick, 2004).

Systems of Care

A variety of different systems of care are involved in the treatment of persons with schizophrenia. Temporary inpatient psychiatric treatment may be periodically necessary during acute symptom exacerbations to protect the person or others. Acute inpatient treatment typically lasts between several days and several months, and has the primary goal of stabilizing the individual's symptoms, so they no longer pose a threat to themselves or others and can therefore be treated on an outpatient basis. A relatively small minority of people with schizophrenia have persistent symptoms that are so severe that they require long-term inpatient treatment, or treatment in residential facilities that provide close monitoring and ample assistance in getting daily needs met (Ciompi, 1980).

The most common system of care for people with schizophrenia is at local community mental health centers that serve geographic catchment areas and are publicly funded. These centers typically provide a wide range of services, including pharmacological treatment, psychosocial treatment and rehabilitation programs, housing supports, and assistance in obtaining disability benefits. Because of the complex array of needs and potential services, outpatients with schizophrenia are often provided case management at community mental health centers, which is aimed at identifying needs, providing services or connecting clients to other service providers, and evaluating receipt of services, improvement in targeted outcomes, and the need for further services (Kanter, 1989).

In addition to community mental health centers, a variety of other organizations or individuals may be involved in providing treatment to people with schizophrenia in the community. Freestanding psychiatric rehabilitation programs may provide an array of services to people who choose to use them. Psychosocial clubhouses that are based on the principles of self-help and responsibility for contributing to the program are another service in the community (Norman, 2006). In addition, people with schizophrenia may receive their treatment from private practitioners, including either primary care providers or psychiatrists, psychologists, or social workers.

Finally, because of the numerous social repercussions associated with schizophrenia, individuals with this disease are often involved in the criminal justice system (Abram, Teplin, & McClelland, 2003; Teplin, 1994) or are homeless (Susser et al., 1989). Although the criminal justice system was not designed to be a system of care, but rather to protect society from the transgressions of those who do not obey its laws, it has become a de facto system of care for many people with schizophrenia (Torrey, 1995). Similarly, services for homeless persons are needed to attend to the multiple needs of persons with severe mental illness because of their disproportionate numbers in this population (Peters, Kearns, Murrin, & Dolente, 1992).

Pharmacological Treatment

Since the discovery of antipsychotic medications in the late 1950s, these medications have been the mainstay of treatment in schizophrenia. Extensive research has shown that antipsychotic medications are effective at reducing the severity of psychotic symptoms of schizophrenia, and in preventing relapses and hospitalizations (Schatzberg, Cole, & DeBattista, 2007). However, antipsychotic medications do not have consistent effects on improving either negative symptoms or cognitive impairment in schizophrenia. Furthermore, these medications can produce a variety of undesirable side effects, such as tremors, involuntary movements, sedation, and restlessness.

Over the past 25 years, a variety of new antipsychotic medications have been developed with the intention of improving their efficacy and reducing the troubling side effects. Newer-generation antipsychotics have been successful at reducing some of the most subjectively distressing side effects of the traditional antipsychotics, but also tend to be associated with different problematic side effects, such as increased weight gain and other metabolic effects (Meyer et al., 2008). Research on the comparative efficacy of newer-generation and older antipsychotics indicates that they are of comparable efficacy in their impact on psychotic symptoms and preventing relapses, but do not significantly improve cognitive functioning or negative symptoms (Keefe et al., 2004; Lieberman et al., 2005).

One medication that should be distinguished from the other antipsychotics is clozapine, which was first developed in the 1970s (Matz, Rick, Thompson, & Gershon, 1974). Clozapine is more effective than other antipsychotics for the treatment of persistent psychotic symptoms and has also been shown to improve the severity of negative symptoms (Honigfeld, Patin, & Singer, 1984; Kane, Honigfeld, Singer, & Meltzer, 1988). Clozapine has also been shown to have a beneficial impact on suicidal thinking and behavior (Meltzer et al., 2003), to reduce aggression and violence (Volavka, 1999), and to reduce substance abuse (Drake, Xie, McHugo, & Green, 2000; Green, Zimmet, Strous, & Schildkraut, 1999; Volavka, 1999) in schizophrenia. The use of clozapine in schizophrenia needs to be carefully monitored because the medication can cause *agranulocytosis* (i.e., a lowering of white blood cells), which can be fatal if not detected and the medication reduced or withdrawn (de la Chapelle, Kari, Nurminen, & Hernberg, 1977). However, with appropriate monitoring of white blood cell count, clozapine can be a very safe and effective medication.

A wide range of other medications has been evaluated for the treatment of schizophrenia, especially antidepressants and mood stabilizers. Despite the widespread use of these medications, data from controlled trials do not support their efficacy at improving symptoms or reducing relapses in schizophrenia (Arey & Marder, 2008). Similarly, there has been a growing trend toward prescribing multiple classes of antipsychotic medication for schizophrenia (Clark, Bartels, Mellman, & Peacock, 2002), but data do not provide strong support for the efficacy of combining antipsychotics over the use of a single agent (Arey & Marder, 2008; Freudenreich & Goff, 2002).

Medication nonadherence is a common problem in schizophrenia that contributes to relapses and hospitalizations (Pratt, Mueser, Driscoll, Wolfe, & Bartels, 2006; Yamada et al., 2006). Several long-acting, injectable depot antipsychotic medications that can be administered every 2–4 weeks have been developed and shown to be clinically efficacious; these are viable alternatives for clients who forget to take oral medication but are willing to take injections (Kane et al., 2003; Schooler, 2003). A variety of other strategies have been developed and evaluated to improve medication adherence in schizophrenia (Zygmunt, Olfson, Boyer, & Mechanic, 2002), with illness self-management strategies and the Assertive Community Treatment model (described below) showing the most benefit.

Psychosocial Treatment

In addition to medications, a wide range of psychosocial treatments have been demonstrated to improve the outcome of schizophrenia. In this section, we first summarize effective psychosocial interventions for schizophrenia with a well-established evidence base (i.e., supported by multiple controlled trials). For each intervention, we provide a brief rationale for the targeted domain of the treatment, followed by a description of the intervention, and then research supporting it.

SUPPORTED EMPLOYMENT

Difficulty sustaining competitive work is one of the diagnostic criteria for the functional impairment characteristic of schizophrenia (APA, 1994). Although problems working are by definition common among people with schizophrenia, the majority of individuals express a desire for competitive work (Mueser, Salyers et al., 2001; Rogers, Walsh, Masotta, & Danley, 1991). However, rates of competitive work are typically low, usually between 10% and 20%, including part-time work (Marwaha et al., 2007). For these reasons alone, improving the competitive employment outcomes has been a major goal in the treatment of schizophrenia.

There are a number of advantages of helping people with schizophrenia return to work, either part- or full-time. Work is associated with self-esteem, and clients with schizophrenia report improvements in self-esteem when they obtain jobs (Torrey, Mueser, & Drake, 2000). Work has also been associated with modest reductions in symptoms severity (Bell, Lysaker, & Milstein, 1996; Bond et al., 2001), supporting the old adage that "work is good therapy" (Harding, Strauss, Hafez, & Liberman, 1987).

Work also provides clients with additional economic resources, an important consideration in light of the low incomes and need for disability entitlements that plague most people with schizophrenia. Finally, there is great social approval associated with work, and therefore helping people return to work can have destigmatizing effects both on how the individual sees himself or herself, as well as on how other people in society perceive the individual (Farina, 1998).

Description

The principles of supported employment for persons with severe mental illness were first established and standardized by Becker and Drake in a program called Individual Placement and Support (Becker & Drake, 1993, 2003). The focus of supported employment is on helping clients find competitive jobs that pay competitive wages in the community. Involvement in supported employment programs should be the client's choice, with no other exclusion criteria required in order to receive vocational services.

Supported employment emphasizes rapid job search and placement in favor of prevocational training and extensive assessment. For most clients, the job search commences within 1 month of joining a supported employment program. The goal is not only to help clients get jobs, but to help them keep jobs, or to help them transition from one job to another. Therefore, in contrast to traditional vocational rehabilitation approaches, in supported employment, follow-along supports are provided after a job has been successfully obtained. The nature of these supports varies from one client to another, and can include on-the-job training, consultation or a liaison with the client's supervisor, behind-the-scenes problem solving or skills training to address interpersonal or job performance issues, and temporary transportation assistance.

Another important feature of supported employment programs is the role of client preferences. Preferences are critical both in the nature of jobs that are sought, as well as in the types of supports provided by the employment specialist. Research has shown that client who obtain jobs in their preferred area of interest have job tenures approximately twice as long as those whose jobs do not match their interest (Becker, Drake, Farabaugh, & Bond, 1996; Mueser, Becker, & Wolfe, 2001). Client preferences are also important in terms of whether the person chooses to disclose their psychiatric disorder to a prospective employer. A final component of supported employment programs is

benefits counseling. All clients need information about how much they can work without loss of disability income, how much additional work will reduce their disability income, and the implications of work for maintaining insurance benefits.

Research

Multiple randomized controlled trials (RCTs) have been conducted to evaluate the effects of supported employment programs compared to other vocational programs. Comparison programs include traditional sheltered workshop approaches, transitional employment, and group skills training approaches. Across the broad range of different vocational models that it has been compared to, supported employment has been found to result in significantly better vocational outcomes (Bond, Drake, & Becker, 2008). This includes a greater likelihood of obtaining a competitive job, earning more wages, and working more hours. Although most of the research on supported employment has been conducted in the United States, several recent studies have replicated the effectiveness of the approach abroad (Burns et al., 2007; Killackey, Jackson, & McGorry, 2008; Latimer et al., 2006). Research on the clinical benefits of participating in supported employment in obtaining work indicates that work is associated with increases in self-sufficiency, modest decreases in symptoms, and improved satisfaction with economic standing (Bond et al., 2001; Mueser et al., 1997).

Research is under way in improving the effectiveness of supported employment. One approach with some recent empirical support has been to provide cognitive remediation, targeting cognitive impairments that interfere with vocational functioning in schizophrenia (McGurk, Mueser, Feldman, Wolfe, & Pascaris, 2007; McGurk, Mueser, & Pascaris, 2005). Cognitive remediation approaches are described in greater detail later.

SOCIAL SKILLS TRAINING

Similar to the reduced capacity to work, impairment in social relationships is a prominent feature of schizophrenia. Poor premorbid social functioning is a common precursor to schizophrenia that is also associated with a worsening course of the psychiatric illness, including more impaired psychosocial functioning, as well more frequent relapses and hospitalizations (Mueser, Bellack, Morrison, & Wixted, 1990; Zigler & Glick, 1986). Social support is an important mediator of the course of schizophrenia due to its role as a buffer against stress-induced relapses (Buchanan, 1995). Improving social functioning is also an important quality-of-life issue. Many people with schizophrenia desire close, intimate, and rewarding relationships (Ralph, 2000). Thus, improving social functioning is an important goal in the treatment research, with social skills training currently enjoying the strongest empirical support.

Description

Social skills training is a systematic approach to teaching interpersonal skills. It involves breaking down complex behaviors into smaller constituent elements or steps, and then teaching these skills through a combination of modeling (demonstrating the skill), role play rehearsal, positive feedback, corrective feedback, additional role play rehearsal, and home assignments to practice the skill outside of the training session (Bellack, Mueser, Gingerich, & Agresta, 2004; Liberman, DeRisi, & Mueser, 1989). Social skills training is usually conducted in groups of five to eight clients, with sessions conducted at least once or twice per week. The duration of the program is between 3 months to over 1 year. Sessions follow the highly structured teaching approach described earlier, with a wide range of curriculum taught, depending on the clients' needs and goals. Common target areas for social skills training include conversational skills, friendship and dating skills, conflict-resolution skills, assertiveness, interpersonal skills for the workplace, alcohol and drug refusal skills, and independent living/self-care skills. Standardized curriculum has been developed to facilitate the teaching of social skills to people with schizophrenia and other severe mental illnesses (Bellack et al., 2004).

Research

Extensive research has been conducted on social research training since the standardization of skills training methods in the 1960s and 1970s and the development of curriculum specifically geared to the needs of people with severe mental illness. Social skills training is hypothesized to improve functioning by improving the individual's social competence or ability to interact with others in a socially effective manner. Social skills training is also thought to improve the symptomatic outcome of schizophrenia, including relapses, through improved ability to cope with stress and increase social support (Liberman et al., 1986).

A recent meta-analysis confirmed the impact of social skills training on several different outcome domains (Kurtz & Mueser, 2008). As expected, social skills training had a large effect size on clients'

mastery of the information taught in skills training groups. Social skills training also had a moderate effect size on both social skills performance in role-play tests and on measures of community functioning and social adjustment. Skills training also had a somewhat smaller, but nevertheless significant, effect on reducing negative symptoms. Finally, social skills training had a small but significant effect size on reducing other symptoms and preventing relapses. These findings are consistent with those from another recently completed meta-analysis of social skills training conducted by an independent group of researchers (Pfammatter, Junghan, & Brenner, 2006). Thus, research supports the beneficial effects of social skills training on social functioning in schizophrenia.

FAMILY PSYCHOEDUCATION

Prior to the 1950s and the 1960s, some theories of the etiology of schizophrenia proposed that the origins of the disorder lay in disturbed family relationships characterized by problematic and contradictory communication patterns among the members (Fromm-Reichman, 1948). As family members were thought by many mental health professionals to be culprit in causing schizophrenia, collaborative relationships were rarely formed between treatment providers and the client's relatives, and families were usually left in the dark about the nature of the illness (Appleton, 1974).

However, psychogenic theories of the family causing schizophrenia were largely abandoned in the 1960s, for several reasons. First, research on the genetics of the disorder demonstrated that it was at least partly heritable, as indicated by facts such as the higher concordance rate of the disorder in monozygotic than dizygotic twins and increased rates of schizophrenia in the children of mothers with the disorder, even when they were raised by adoptive parents with no mental illness (Gottesman, 1991). Second, the dramatic effects of antipsychotic medications on the psychotic symptoms of schizophrenia made theories of the family as the causal agent increasingly implausible. Third, family therapy approaches that attempted to correct family pathology thought to be at the root of schizophrenia were largely unsuccessful (Terkelsen, 1983).

The discovery of antipsychotic medications in the late 1950s and their widespread use in the 1960s led to the deinstitutionalization of many people with schizophrenia (Johnson, 1990), with many others never being institutionalized and instead receiving treatment for their disorder in the community.

As a focus of the treatment for schizophrenia shifted from the hospital to the community, increasing numbers of clients either returned to their family's home or continued to live with them and depend on them for emotional and material support. Although families were heavily relied upon to provide support for a relative with schizophrenia, they were frequently ill-prepared to meet the challenge, and emotional turmoil was a common consequence. Research on family *express emotion* showed that the presence of strong negative emotional attitudes in the relatives of someone with schizophrenia acted as a stressor that could precipitate relapses and rehospitalizations (Butzlaff & Hooley, 1998). Furthermore, families began to demand better treatment from mental health professionals, both for themselves and their loved ones, thus giving birth to the family advocacy movement, as exemplified by organizations such as the National Alliance on Mental Illness (Hatfield & Lefley, 1993, 1987).

Description

Family psychoeducation programs were developed to address the needs of families to better understand the nature of schizophrenia and its treatment, to reduce stress in the family, and to foster a respectful and collaborative relationship with mental health treatment providers (Lefley, 2009). In the 1970s and the 1980s, several different models of family psychoeducation were developed and empirically validated (Anderson, Reiss, & Hogarty, 1986; Barrowclough & Tarrier, 1992; Falloon, Boyd, & McGill, 1984; Kuipers, Leff, & Lam, 2002; McFarlane, 2002; Mueser & Glynn, 1999). Although the programs differ in format (single family vs. multiple family groups), theoretical orientation (e.g., social learning, modified systems theory, etc.), and duration of treatment, they actually share more in common than they differ.

Effective family psychoeducation programs are led by professionals who assume a collaborative stance in working with families. In addition, family psychoeducation models for schizophrenia incorporate several other common characteristics, including (a) both the client and family members are included in treatment sessions; (b) the programs are long-term, lasting at least 9 months; (c) the focus of the programs is on the present and the future, rather than the past; (d) basic information is provided about schizophrenia, its treatment, and the role of the family in helping a loved one with the illness; (e) families are helped to develop strategies for addressing problems and reducing stress and conflict

among members; (f) family members have access to the treatment team to alert them to changes in clinical status or express other concerns; and (g) families are involved in treatment planning with other members of the treatment team.

Research

Extensive research has been conducted on family psychoeducation programs over the past 25 years. The most consistent impact of family psychoeducation is on the reduction of relapses and rehospitalizations (Pitschel-Walz, Leucht, Bäuml, Kissling, & Engel, 2001). This is presumably accomplished through a combination of reducing the effects of stress in the family on precipitating relapses, and improved monitoring of the illness by the family in collaboration with the treatment team, thereby permitting rapid intervention at the early stages of a relapse and the prevention of full-blown symptom exacerbations. Other effects of family psychoeducation include improved client functioning and the reduction of family stress and burden (Lefley, 2009).

ASSERTIVE COMMUNITY TREATMENT

The deinstitutionalization movement described earlier resulted in a shift in the locus of care for most people with schizophrenia from long-term state hospitals to local community mental health centers. With this shift, a subgroup of people with schizophrenia and other severe mental illnesses failed to access community-based services and were consequently prone to frequent relapses and hospitalizations for the management of their disorders. In addition, these clients usually had extremely impaired psychosocial functioning and often lived in impoverished conditions. As awareness grew about this subgroup of clients who did not access community-based psychiatric services, a new term was invented to describe their pattern of going in and out of hospitals for the treatment of acute exacerbations of their disorders: the *revolving door patient* (Bachrach, 1981; Harris & Bergman, 1984). Because of the high cost of inpatient treatment, there was a strong interest in developing a more effective approach to delivering mental health services to these clients.

Description

To address the problem of frequent relapses and hospitalizations for this subgroup of clients, Stein and Test (1985) developed the Assertive Community Treatment (ACT) model, based on the rationale that if clients did not go to local community mental health centers to receive their mental health services, the same services could be brought to the client, wherever he or she was in the community. The ACT model is a team-based approach to delivering mental health services that differs from traditional approaches in several ways. Members of an ACT team have lower caseloads, typically about one clinician for every ten clients, as compared to usual services in which each clinician may be responsible for 30 or more clients. Rather than each clinician on an ACT team having his or her own personal caseload, members of ACT teams share the responsibility for all the clients carried by an ACT team, thereby reducing the burnout associated with individual-based case management (Cook, Pickett-Schenk, & Nageotte, 2000). Consistent with the philosophy of assertive outreach, the majority of the services provided by an ACT team are conducted in the community, rather than in treatment setting such as a community mental health center. ACT teams assume 24-hour responsibility for clients, with different members of the ACT team taking turns being available for emergency calls during evenings and weekends. Another unique feature of ACT teams is that they focus on the direct provision of services to clients, rather than brokering services to other treatment providers. There are no time limitations placed on receiving services from an ACT team, although clients graduate from ACT teams to less intensive services as they improve their illness self-management and independent living skills (Salyers, Masterton, Fekete, Picone, & Bond, 1998). The principles of act have been standardized in several manuals (Allness & Knoedler, 1998; Stein & Santos, 1998).

Research
The ACT model has been extensively studied in RCTs. Most of the studies of ACT have been conducted in the United States, with the majority of participants including people with schizophrenia. Some successful replications of the ACT model have been reported from abroad (Rosen, Mueser, & Teeson, 2007), although there is also a question as to whether the ACT model is appropriate for some systems of care, such as in Great Britain (Johnson et al., 1998; McCrone et al., 1998; Thornicroft et al., 1998; Wykes, Leese, Taylor, & Phelan, 1998), where the fragmentation of services is not as great a problem as it is in the United States.

Research on ACT indicates that it has prominent effects on reducing hospitalizations and on stabilizing housing in people with schizophrenia (Bond, Drake, Mueser, & Latimer, 2001). The stabilization of housing is partly a reflection of reduced hospitalizations, but also reflects the effects of ACT on reducing homelessness in this population. Studies have found that clients express satisfaction with ACT services and report improved quality of life related to participation in the program. ACT treatment program have also been found to have modest effects on reducing symptom severity. However, the ACT model tends to have limited effects on social and vocational functioning, unless specific ACT team members are designated to focus on addressing these areas. For example, when an employment specialist is added to an ACT team to provide supported employment, competitive work outcomes improve (Gold, Meisler, Santos, Williams, Carnemolla, & Kelleher, 2004).

COGNITIVE-BEHAVIORAL THERAPY FOR PSYCHOSIS
Despite the growing variety of antipsychotic medications available for people with schizophrenia, a significant portion of clients continued to experience psychotic symptoms that are not the result of medication nonadherence. Estimates of the rate of persistent psychotic symptoms in people with schizophrenia vary, with most suggesting that between 20% and 35% of clients experience such symptoms (Mueser et al., 1991b; Silverstein & Harrow, 1978). Persistent psychotic symptoms are associated with high levels of distress (Mueser et al., 1991b), often related to the derogatory nature of auditory hallucinations or to the fear associated with paranoid delusions (Chadwick & Birchwood, 1994; Garety & Hemsley, 1994). In addition to the distress associated with psychosis, persistent psychotic symptoms increase vulnerability to relapses and contribute to poor psychosocial functioning (Racenstein et al., 2002). For these reasons, cognitive-behavioral therapy (CBT) for psychosis was developed to reduce the severity of psychotic symptoms or the distress associated with them.

Description
CBT for psychosis is based on the application of the same approach to other disorders, such as mood and anxiety disorders (Beck, Emery, & Greenberg, 1985; Beck, Rush, Shaw, & Emery, 1979). CBT for psychosis proposes that psychotic symptoms and associated distress in people with schizophrenia are related to clients' appraisals of events, which may be inaccurate due to illness-related biases in information processing, "normal" distortions in the interpretation

of events, and significant personal life experiences that may have influenced the person's perception of themselves or the world (e.g., childhood physical or sexual abuse) (Garety & Hemsley, 1994; Hemsley, 1996; Maher, 1988). In CBT, clients are taught how to identify and evaluate the evidence for and against upsetting thoughts or beliefs related to their psychotic symptoms and to modify them when the evidence does not support them.

The first applications of CBT for psychosis actually predated the use of the approach for depression, as described in a single case treated by Aaron Beck more than half a century ago (Beck, 1952). Following this initial case, little systematic work examined the utility of CBT for psychosis over the next several decades. Then, in the late 1980s and early 1990s, systematic efforts to apply CBT to psychosis began, with preliminary reports indicated promising effects (Chadwick & Birchwood, 1994; Garety, Kuipers, Fowler, Chamberlain, & Dunn, 1994). Since the 1990s, a number of manuals for CBT for psychosis have been developed, which share a range of common elements (Chadwick, Birchwood, & Trower, 1996; Fowler, Garety, & Kuipers, 1995; Kingdon & Turkington, 2004; Morrison, Renton, Dunn, Williams, & Bentall, 2004; Nelson, 1997).

CBT for psychosis emphasizes the importance of establishing a collaborative relationship between the therapist and the client, and of establishing treatment goals to work toward together. Information about the nature of psychotic symptoms is usually provided to clients, seeking to normalize these experiences as common reactions or responses to stress (Kingdon & Turkington, 1991). This makes it easier for clients with psychotic symptoms to talk about their symptoms without feeling shameful or embarrassed. Coping strategies for dealing with psychotic symptoms are usually taught, such as listening to the radio or other distraction techniques for auditory hallucinations. The heart of CBT for psychosis is in the use of cognitive restructuring to help clients examine the evidence for and against psychotic or otherwise distressing thoughts or beliefs, and changing those thoughts when the evidence does not support them. The exploration of evidence for and against thoughts or beliefs is conducted in a collaborative, nonconfrontational manner to avoid inadvertently reinforcing beliefs through psychological reactance (Milton, Patwa, & Hafner, 1978). When insufficient evidence exists for determining the correctness of the thought or believe, behavioral experiments may be conducted in which the client obtains additional information bearing on the question at hand (Hagen & Nordahl, 2008). Most CBT for psychosis programs last at least 3–6 months, and sometimes longer.

Research
Extensive research has been conducted on CBT for psychosis over the past 15 years, with the great preponderance of studies conducted in Great Britain. The most recent meta-analysis of CBT for psychosis reported moderate effects sizes on reducing the severity of psychotic symptoms (Wykes, Steel, Everitt, & Tarrier, 2008). Furthermore, CBT for psychosis was found to have significant effects on reducing the severity of negative symptoms and improving psychosocial functioning.

The success of research on CBT for psychosis has led it to be recommended in treatment guidelines for schizophrenia both in Great Britain (National Collaborating Centre for Mental Health, 2009) and the United States (Dixon et al., 2010). This strong research supporting CBT for psychosis is in contrast to the relative lack of access to this intervention in the United States. There have been calls to increase the access to CBT for psychosis for people with schizophrenia in the United States (Turkington, Kingdon, & Weiden, 2006) and for increased involvement of psychologists in the treatment of schizophrenia in the community (Mueser & Noordsy, 2005).

COGNITIVE REMEDIATION
Cognitive impairment increases the risk of developing schizophrenia (Zammit et al., 2004). Furthermore, the onset of schizophrenia is associated with a decline in cognitive functioning in almost all persons who develop the illness (Heaton et al., 1994). Cognitive impairment is strongly correlated with psychosocial functioning in schizophrenia (Green, 1996), and is predictive of an attenuated response to psychiatric rehabilitation approaches, such as supported employment (McGurk, Mueser, Harvey, Marder, & LaPuglia, 2003) and social skills training (Mueser, Bellack, Douglas, & Wade, 1991; Smith, Hull, Romanelli, Fertuck, & Weiss, 1999). For these reasons, improving cognitive functioning in schizophrenia is an important treatment goal. The importance of this goal is also underscored by the fact that currently available antipsychotic medications do not improve cognitive functioning, and other cognition-enhancing drugs have yet to be discovered.

Description

A variety of different methods have been developed and employed to remediate cognitive functioning in schizophrenia. Most of the approaches that have been developed involve a combination of practice and teaching cognitive strategies designed to improve cognitive performance. In addition to focusing directly on improving the quality of cognitive functioning, some programs also teach clients coping or compensatory strategies for managing persistent cognitive impairments that interfere with functioning. Thus, cognitive remediation programs seek both to improve cognitive functioning and to reduce the interference caused by cognitive impairments in psychosocial functioning.

Programs vary with respect to the actual strategies employed to remediate cognitive functioning. Many approaches include computer programs designed to help clients practice specific cognitive skills, such as attention, psychomotor speed, memory, and problem solving (Bell, Bryson, Greig, Corcoran, & Wexler, 2001; McGurk et al., 2005). Other programs utilize paper-and-pencil exercises (Brenner et al., 1994; Wykes & Reeder, 2005). Some programs also include a group format in which people practice different cognitive exercises together (Hogarty & Flesher, 1999). The length and intensity of cognitive remediation program also varies significantly. Many programs provide at least two or three training sessions per week, and most programs last at least several months, with some lasting over a year.

One other potentially important distinction between different cognitive remediation programs is whether they are integrated with a psychiatric rehabilitation program. Some cognitive remediation programs focus on cognitive remediation alone and do not attempt to integrate cognitive training with other rehabilitation methods (Medalia, Revheim, & Herlands, 2009; Wykes & Reeder, 2005). Other approaches integrate cognitive remediation with other psychiatric rehabilitation methods, such as social skills training (Silverstein et al., 2005) or vocational rehabilitation (Bell, Fiszdon, Greig, Wexler, & Bryson, 2007; McGurk et al., 2005).

An alternative approach to the remediation of cognitive impairments or the teaching of coping skills to minimize the effects of impaired cognitive functioning on adaptation is to modify the client's environment, so that it cues appropriate self-care behavior. *Cognitive adaptive therapy* was developed to facilitate the community functioning of former state psychiatric inpatients who were discharged into the community (Velligan, Mueller et al., 2006).

The program is implemented by staff members who regularly visit a client's apartment (e.g., weekly), and arrange his or her living space so that appropriate dressing, hygiene, and other self-care behaviors are cued by signs or other prompts. For example, the client's clothes may be selected for the following week with each day's clothes placed in a separate bag or plastic container. This approach to organizing the client's environment reduces the cognitive reserves necessary to sustain independent living in the community.

Research

Over the past several decades, numerous studies have been conducted on the effects of cognitive remediation. A meta-analysis of 26 studies of cognitive remediation in schizophrenia was recently completed (McGurk, Twamley, Sitzer, McHugo, & Mueser, 2007). This analysis found significant effects for cognitive remediation on improving cognitive functioning, psychosocial functioning, and negative symptoms. Exploration of possible factors that could influence the effect of cognitive remediation on cognitive functioning were not found. However, one significant factor was found to moderate the impact of cognitive remediation on psychosocial functioning. Specifically, cognitive remediation programs that provided adjunctive psychiatric rehabilitation had significant effects on improving psychosocial functioning, whereas cognitive remediation programs that were provided in isolation and did not provide ancillary psychiatric rehabilitation failed to demonstrate significant improvements in psychosocial functioning. The results are consistent with research showing that level of cognitive impairment is predictive of benefit from psychiatric rehabilitation (Bowen et al., 1994; Kern, Green, & Satz, 1992; Mueser et al., 1991a; Silverstein, Schenkel, Valone, & Nuernberger, 1998; Smith et al., 1999). These findings are in line with another meta-analysis that demonstrated significant effects on cognitive functioning and psychosocial adjustment of Integrated Psychological Therapy (Roder, Mueller, Mueser, & Brenner, 2006), a program developed in Switzerland by Brenner and colleagues (1994) that integrates cognitive remediation using group exercises with social skills training. Thus, cognitive remediation may be an effective way of increasing the ability of clients with schizophrenia to benefit from psychiatric rehabilitation approaches such as supported employment and social skills training.

Research on cognitive adaptive therapy is still in the relatively early stages. However, two RCTs provide support for the effectiveness of the program at improving community functioning, as well as some evidence that it increases medication adherence (Velligan et al., 2000; Velligan et al., 2008; Velligan, Diamond et al., 2006; Velligan et al., 2002). These results are encouraging, and suggest that modifying the environment is a viable approach to the management of debilitating cognitive impairments that often result in long-term institutionalization.

INTEGRATED TREATMENT FOR DUAL DISORDERS

Alcohol and drug use disorders are one of the most common comorbid disorders in people with schizophrenia, with approximately 50% of all clients meeting lifetime diagnostic criteria (Mueser, Bennett, & Kushner, 1995; Regier et al., 1990). Substance abuse is associated with a worse course of schizophrenia across the full spectrum of outcomes, including increased relapses and re hospitalizations, worse depression and suicidality, problems in social and role functioning, legal problems, housing problems, susceptibility to medical illnesses, and premature mortality. Thus, the treatment of substance abuse in people with schizophrenia is a high priority.

Traditional approaches to treating co-occurring psychiatric and substance use disorders (or dual disorders) have typically involved the provision of psychiatric and substance abuse services by different agencies and different clinicians who work either in a parallel or sequential fashion (Polcin, 1992). *Parallel treatment* involves the treatment of the psychiatric and the substance use disorders at the same time by different treatment providers. *Sequential treatment* involves attempting to first treat or stabilize one disorder before then attempting to treat or stabilize the other disorder. Research has clearly demonstrated that parallel or sequential treatment approaches for co-occurring disorders are ineffective (Ridgely, Goldman, & Willenbring, 1990). The most common problems with these approaches are the failure of clients to follow through on treatment referrals for their substance abuse due to a lack of insight into their substance use problems. Other problems with traditional treatment approaches include barriers to accessing both treatments, such as restrictive eligibility criteria, the use of confrontational and stressful treatment approaches in substance abuse programs (which can precipitate relapses in people with schizophrenia), high rates of dropout from either or both treatments due to lack of motivation, and the lack of integration between psychiatric and substance abuse treatment providers

when both disorders are treated simultaneously. The failure of traditional approaches in treating co-occurring disorders has led to the development of integrated treatment models for these disorders.

Description

Integrated treatment refers to the treatment of both the psychiatric and the substance use disorders at the same time, by the same treatment team, in which clinicians assume the responsibility for treating both disorders in an integrated fashion (Mueser, Noordsy, Drake, & Fox, 2003). The integration of substance abuse and psychiatric treatment in people with schizophrenia is important for schizophrenia because many of the symptoms and impairments related to the disorder contribute to the high vulnerability of clients for using and abusing substances. For example, common motives for using substances in people with schizophrenia include facilitating socialization, having something enjoyable to do, and coping with symptoms such as anxiety, depression, and demoralization (Addington & Duchak, 1997; Dixon, Haas, Weiden, Sweeney, & Frances, 1991; Mueser, Nishith, Tracy, DeGirolamo, & Molinaro, 1995). Effective integrated treatment for co-occurring disorders for people with schizophrenia involves both educating clients and their families about the effects of drugs and alcohol on the course of the illness, as well as using psychiatric rehabilitation approaches designed to address clients' motives for using (Mueser et al., 2003). For example, social skills training can be used to help clients develop more effective skills for establishing rewarding relationships with peers who do not abuse substances. Supported employment can enable clients to pursue their vocational goals and have something meaningful and purposeful to look forward to in their lives. Cognitive-behavioral therapy for psychosis or other approaches to helping clients cope with persistent symptoms can be used to reduce symptom distress and the motivation to use substances to cope with symptoms. Teaching clients new leisure and recreational skills can help them develop alternatives to drug and alcohol use as sources of pleasure.

A number of integrated treatment programs for co-occurring disorders have been developed over the past 15–20 years (Bellack, Bennet, & Gearon, 2007; Carey, 1996; Drake, Teague, & Warren, 1990; Minkoff, 1991; Mueser, Nishith et al., 1995; Roberts, Shaner, & Eckman, 1999). In addition to the shared focus on integration, effective treatment programs tend to incorporate similar elements as well. First, assertive outreach, which involves going into the community and meeting with individuals where they spend their time, such as in their apartments, a coffee shop, or a park, is a common practice used to engage those clients in treatment who do not otherwise come to mental health treatment settings. A second common feature of integrated treatment programs is the adoption of a harm reduction approach. *Harm reduction* refers to treatment that is initially aimed at reducing the harmful consequences of substance abuse without requiring the individual to endorse abstinence as a personal long-term goal (Marlatt, 1998). Harm reduction facilitates the development of a therapeutic relationship between the clinician and the client, and addresses immediately the most toxic effects of the client's substance abuse on health and functioning.

A third common feature of integrated treatment programs is the use of motivational enhancement strategies and the adoption of a stage-wise approach to treatment. People with schizophrenia often lack motivation to work on their substance use problems, and treatment must be geared according to the individual's level of motivation to change his or her behavior. The concept of *stages of change* has proven useful in developing treatments that are matched to the individual's motivation to change (DiClemente & Prochaska, 1998; Prochaska & DiClemente, 1984). The stages of change model posits that when people change their behavior, they progress through a series of discrete motivational states, including *pre-contemplation* (not thinking about change), *contemplation* (thinking about change), *preparation* (making plans to change), *action* (making changes), and *maintenance* (maintaining changes). The stages of change have been adapted to the *stages of treatment* for dual disorders, which describe the stages that individuals progress through when receiving professional treatment for their disorders, and identify treatment goals for each stage (Mueser et al., 2003; Osher & Kofoed, 1989). The stages of treatment include *engagement* (when the client is not receiving services for their co-occurring disorders, and the goal is to develop a therapeutic relationship with that person), *persuasion* (when a therapeutic relationship has been established but the client is not motivated to address substance use problems, and the goal of treatment is to instill such motivation), *active treatment* (when the client has demonstrated motivation to work on substance use problems, and the goal of treatment is to reduce substance use or achieve abstinence), and *relapse prevention* (when the client no longer has an active substance use problem, and the goal is to maintain sobriety while extending recovery to other areas of functioning, such as work, school, health, and social relationships). The stages of treatment construct helps clinicians optimize treatment by matching specific interventions to the client's stage of motivation to change.

Research
Extensive research has been conducted on the effectiveness of integrated treatment programs for co-occurring disorders. Early research was marred by methodological weaknesses and treatment programs that only included selected components of integrated dual-disorder programs (Mercer-McFadden, Drake, Brown, & Fox, 1997). More recently, however, rigorous research has been conducted evaluating well-defined integrated treatment programs for co-occurring disorders. Research on integrated dual-disorder treatment programs indicate that they are effective at reducing the severity of substance abuse and associated consequences, such as impaired functioning and psychiatric symptoms and hospitalizations (Drake, Mueser, Brunette, & McHugo, 2004; Drake, O'Neal, & Wallach, 2008).

ILLNESS SELF-MANAGEMENT TRAINING
Despite significant advances over the past several decades in the pharmacological treatment and psychiatric rehabilitation of schizophrenia, clients often know little about their psychiatric disorder or the principles of its treatment, lack basic illness self-management skills for using medication effectively, and are challenged by coping with stress and persistent symptoms. Many people with schizophrenia are not actively involved in establishing their treatment goals or making decisions with clinicians and family members about their own care (Fenton, 2003). All too often, people play a passive role in their own treatment, sometimes lacking awareness of their right to participate, and thus leading to dependency on others and low self-esteem (Oades et al., 2005). This lack of involvement and poor illness self-management skills often leaves people with schizophrenia prone to medication nonadherence, disruptive symptoms, and frequent relapses and rehospitalizations. Illness self-management programs have been developed to address these needs.

Description
Illness self-management programs are aimed at teaching people with schizophrenia information and skills that enable them to minimize their symptoms, reduce the distress and interference caused by

persistent symptoms, and prevent or limit the severity of relapses and hospitalizations. Teaching illness self-management can foster the development of a mutually respectful, collaborative therapeutic relationship by empowering the client to take an active role in his or her treatment. Several programs have been developed in recent years to teach illness self-management skills to clients with schizophrenia and other severe mental illnesses, including personal therapy (Hogarty, 2002; Hogarty, Greenwald et al., 1997; Hogarty, Kornblith et al., 1997), the UCLA Social and Independent Living Skills modules on symptom self-management and medication management (Liberman, 2007), and the Illness Management and Recovery (IMR) program (Gingerich & Mueser, 2005). These programs overlap in much of the information and skills taught to clients. We briefly describe here the IMR program, which is the most comprehensive illness self-management program, and the only program based on a comprehensive review of research on the topic.

The basic rationale underlying the IMR program is that people with schizophrenia can be most effectively taught how to manage their mental illness in the context of setting and pursuing personally meaningful, functional goals. The IMR program was designed as a curriculum-based approach that explicitly incorporates empirically supported practices for illness self-management into a single cohesive program. The program was designed to incorporate five practices found to improve the outcome of severe mental illness in a comprehensive review of 40 RCTs (Mueser, Corrigan et al., 2002). This review indicated that *psychoeducation* significantly improves knowledge about mental illness, but does not affect medication adherence, reduce relapse, or improve functioning (Macpherson, Jerrom, & Hughes, 1996). Medication adherence programs that utilize cognitive-behavioral techniques such *behavioral tailoring* (i.e., teaching clients how to incorporate taking medication into their daily routines by pairing medication adherence with another activity such as brushing one's teach) improve clients' ability to take medication as prescribed (Azrin & Teichner, 1998; Cramer & Rosenheck, 1999). Teaching *relapse prevention skills*, including identifying situations that have triggered relapses in the past, recognition of the early warning signs of relapse, and developing a written plan for responding to the early signs of relapse, have demonstrated decreases in relapses and rehospitalizations (Herz et al., 2000). Teaching people *coping skills* for how to manage symptoms such as hallucinations, depression, or anxiety has been shown to improve coping efficacy and to reduce the severity of symptoms or distress related to symptoms (Lecomte et al., 1999; Tarrier, Beckett, et al., 1993; Tarrier, Sharpe, et al., 1993). Finally, bolstering social support through *social skills training* can buffer the negative effects of stress on relapses and rehospitalizations (Bebbington & Kuipers, 1992; Kurtz & Mueser, 2008; Norman et al., 2005).

Motivation for learning how to manage one's illness in the IMR program is instilled by first helping individuals explore the concept of recovery, and then helping them develop personally meaningful goals based on what recovery means to them. Specific objectives are then set toward achieving these overall goals, with motivation to learn illness self-management harnessed by exploring how it could help them achieve their goals. The curriculum taught in the IMR program is organized into ten modules, including: Recovery Strategies, Practical Facts about Severe Mental Illness, Stress-Vulnerability Model and Treatment Strategies, Building Social Support, Using medications Effectively, Drug and Alcohol Use, Reducing Relapses, Coping with Stress, Coping with Problems and Persistent Symptoms, and Getting Your Needs Met in the Mental Health System. Between three and six sessions are usually spent teaching each module, in either an individual or group format, with the entire program requiring 9–10 months of weekly sessions (or 4–5 months of biweekly sessions) to complete.

Research
Limited research supports the efficacy of personal therapy (Hogarty, Greenwald et al., 1997; Hogarty et al., 1995; Hogarty, Kornblith et al., 1997) and the UCLA skills for independent living skills modules (Liberman, 2007) for improving the illness outcomes of schizophrenia. The feasibility and initial beneficial effects of the more recently developed IMR program were demonstrated in a three-site study conducted in the United States and Australia (Mueser et al., 2006), followed by a larger study demonstrating the feasibility of implementing the IMR program with good fidelity to the treatment model in 12 community mental health centers over a 2-year implementation and follow-up period (McHugo et al., 2007). In addition, two RCTs have indicated that participation in IMR improves illness self-management, including symptom severity and community functioning (Hasson-Ohayon, Roe, & Kravetz, 2007; Levitt et al., 2009). Thus, a growing body of research supports the benefits of training people with schizophrenia in illness self-management.

TOKEN ECONOMY

The role of inpatient treatment for schizophrenia has decreased dramatically since the discovery and widespread use of antipsychotics and the development of more effective approaches to outpatient management of the disorder, such as the ACT model. Inpatient treatment for the vast majority of persons with schizophrenia is limited to pharmacological intervention and stabilization for acute psychotic exacerbations, with most treatment episodes lasting 1–4 weeks. Despite the reduced role of inpatient treatment for schizophrenia, some clients with extremely severe symptoms, impaired psychosocial functioning, or aggression require intermediate or long-term inpatient treatment (Menditto, Baldwin, O'Neal, & Beck, 1991). The token economy was developed to address severely impaired social behavior in institutionalized persons with schizophrenia and other mental illnesses that are a barrier to community living.

Description

The token economy is based on the systematic manipulation of contingencies in a specific milieu (e.g., the inpatient setting, group home) that control disruptive behaviors, as well as reward socially appropriate behaviors. Clients participating in a token economy are rewarded for appropriate behaviors with tokens or points that can be exchanged for valued items or activities, such as food, listening to music, clothes, or personal hygiene products (Ayllon, 1968). Based on the principle of sharing, complex social behaviors are broken down into smaller component behaviors, with tokens provided for small steps toward the larger goal. Token economies typically include a store that stocks a wide range of desirable items that can be purchased, with additional items added upon request. Inappropriate behaviors can be reduced through either ignoring the behavior (i.e., *extinction*), fining the client tokens, or by imposing time-outs. Specific target behaviors and rewards are individually developed for each client and modified regularly to ensure that the person is making progress toward treatment goals. Token economy programs are most effective when all stakeholders, including staff and clients, are involved in the design of the program (Corrigan, McCracken, Edwards, Kommana, & Simpatico, 1997).

Research

The preponderance of research on the token economy was conducted in the 1960s and 1970s, when the deinstitutionalization movement was still largely under way. In a classic study conducted by Paul and Lentz (1977), "back ward" chronic patients were randomly assigned to one of three programs: an intensive token economy, an equally intensive milieu therapy program, and usual treatment. Clients who were randomized to the token economy program showed dramatically better improvements across a range of social and symptomatic behaviors, as well as better discharges into the community, compared to the two comparison programs.

In addition to the Paul and Lentz study, another 12 controlled studies have demonstrated the efficacy of the token economy for clients with schizophrenia and severely impaired social behavior (Dickerson, Tenhula, & Green-Paden, 2005). Although the token economy has been shown to be effective and is accepted as an evidence-based practice for schizophrenia (Dixon et al., 2010), the intervention is rarely used in inpatient treatment for schizophrenia, in part because it requires extensive coordination among the broad range of service providers in such settings (e.g., nurses, doctors, psychiatric technicians).

EMERGING PRACTICES

There are a number of treatment approaches for schizophrenia that are currently under development or for which preliminary evaluations suggest promise for improving the long-term course of the illness. We briefly describe these practices here.

Peer Support

There is a long history of peer support for persons with severe mental illness dating back to the Alleged Lunatic Friends Society in 1845 (Frese, 2008). More recently, in the 1940s, individuals who had been discharged from state psychiatric hospitals in New York City began to get together for mutual support and to talk about their experiences. From these meetings, the Psychosocial Clubhouse Model emerged as an approach to providing social support and assistance to people with severe mental illness in a context and setting in which individuals with mental illness themselves are involved in organizing and running the services (Beard, Propst, & Malamud, 1982). Since the development of the first psychosocial clubhouse in New York City, Fountain House, the clubhouse model has been standardized (Macias, Barreira, Alden, & Boyd, 2001; Propst, 1992) and hundreds of clubhouses have been created throughout the United States and abroad.

Clubhouse programs offer a variety of services, such as a place to hang out and socialize, recreational activities, vocational rehabilitation, and a role in running the clubhouse. An important component of the clubhouse model is the *work ordered day*, in which participants (referred to as *members*) are expected to fulfill tasks in the clubhouse necessary to its operation, such as cooking, washing dishes, giving guests tours, and assisting in event planning. Participation in the work ordered day is typically followed by involvement in transitional employment programs, in which members work temporarily at competitive jobs in the community that are secured by the clubhouse to build their work experience and help them move on to obtaining their own competitive jobs (McKay, Johnsen, Banks, & Stein, 2006; Schonebaum, Boyd, & Dudek, 2006).

In addition to the growth of psychosocial clubhouses throughout the world, the consumer movement of the 1970s challenged traditional, hierarchical approaches to treatment and psychiatry, and advocated for more patient voice in decision-making, respect for mental health professionals, and advocacy for the basic rights of persons with psychiatric disorders (Davidson et al., 2009). As a result of the consumer movement, and the growing acceptance of the recovery paradigm, other approaches to involving peers in the treatment of severe mental illness began to emerge. For example, peers are sometimes employed as mental health treatment providers at community mental health centers, such as on ACT teams (Solomon & Draine, 1995). The involvement of peers in delivering services is based on the expectation that the unique experience of peers may put them in a valuable position for forming relationships with others who are struggling to manage their psychiatric illness.

Research on peer support services has proved difficult to evaluate because, by its very nature, self-help organizations are difficult to evaluate in a controlled fashion. Nevertheless, the available evidence on peer support services suggests that persons with severe mental illness appreciate access to peers with similar experiences, and derive social support from their involvement in peer support activities (Davidson et al., 2009).

Supported Housing

Homelessness and poor housing conditions are significant problems for persons with schizophrenia and other severe mental illnesses (Lehman, 1983; Susser et al., 1989). Supported housing is an approach to addressing the housing needs of persons with severe mental illness, one that is aimed at helping clients obtain housing based on their personal preferences (Kloos, Zimmerman, Scrimenti, & Crusto, 2002; Siegel et al., 2006). Client choice with respect to roommates and type of housing situation is an important consideration, as such choice is expected to result in more stable long-term housing arrangements. In addition, supported housing approaches impose minimal exclusion criteria to obtain housing services, including substance abuse, with the expectation that stable housing is a critical ingredient for people with severe mental illness to learn how to more effectively manage their illness and to reduce their substance use habits.

Limited research has been conducted on supported housing approaches for people with severe mental illness. However, preliminary studies indicate that of supported housing has benefits, when compared to traditional approaches, in areas such as duration of time in stable housing in the community (McHugo et al., 2004; Rog, 2004; Tsemberis, Gulcur, & Nakae, 2004). More work is needed to evaluate the effectiveness of supported housing models and identify which clients are most likely to benefit from them.

Trauma Treatment

Those with schizophrenia have high rates of trauma, both in childhood, adolescence, and throughout the lifespan (Goodman, Rosenberg, Mueser, & Drake, 1997; Read et al., 2005). As a result of these high rates of trauma, post-traumatic stress disorder (PTSD) is a common comorbid disorder (Frueh, Cusack, Grubaugh, Sauvageot, & Wells, 2006; Mueser et al., 2002). PTSD is associated with a worse course of illness, high levels of subjective distress, and increased utilization of high-cost services such as emergency room visits and hospitalizations for acute symptom exacerbations (Switzer et al., 1999). To reduce the distress associated with trauma experiences and PTSD, different approaches have been developed in recent years that focus on either trauma or PTSD.

One approach to the treatment of trauma-related problems in people with schizophrenia and other severe mental disorders has been the development of a cognitive-behavioral program for PTSD that was specifically designed for persons with severe mental illness (Mueser, Rosenberg, & Rosenberg, 2009). This standardized, individual-based 12–16-week intervention was initially pilot tested in a sample of individuals with severe and persistent mental illness and found to be both feasible and associated with improvements PTSD and depression (Rosenberg, Mueser, Jankowski, Salyers, & Acker, 2004). The program incorporates three core elements of treatment commonly used in PTSD treatment programs in the general population: teaching breathing retraining as anxiety management skill; psychoeducation about trauma, PTSD, and associated problems; and cognitive restructuring. Cognitive restructuring is initially taught as a skill for managing negative feelings, with attention gradually shifting toward the identification and examination of thoughts and beliefs related to traumatic experiences that are believed to underlie PTSD symptoms. The treatment is coordinated with other treatments that the person is receiving in an integrated fashion. One RCT of this program was recently completed (Mueser, Rosenberg et al., 2008); it included 108 clients with severe mental illness (16% schizophrenia-spectrum) who were randomized to either the cognitive-behavioral treatment program for PTSD, or treatment as usual, with the assessments conducted at baseline, post-treatment, and at 3- and 6-month follow-ups. The results indicated high levels of retention in treatment for clients assigned to the cognitive-behavioral intervention, as well as greater improvement at post-treatment and at follow-ups in PTSD symptoms, depression, and other psychiatric symptoms. In addition, clients reported improvements in their working alliance with their case manager, who was different from the person who provided the treatment program. The findings provide encouragement for the treatment of PTSD in people with schizophrenia and other severe mental illnesses.

Several other treatment approaches for trauma and PTSD have been developed for people with severe mental illness. Frueh and colleagues (2004) have recently developed an intervention for people with schizophrenia and PTSD that involves first providing education and social skills training in a group format, followed by individual exposure-based methods (e.g., imaginal exposure). Preliminary work on the model supports its feasibility and suggests that it leads to clinical improvements in PTSD and related outcomes (Frueh et al., 2009). An alternative to the focus on treating PTSD symptoms in people with schizophrenia is to take a broader approach to addressing the consequences of trauma in this population, including skills deficits and poor self-esteem, such as the Trauma Recovery and Empowerment model developed by Harris and colleagues (1998).

Social Cognition
Social cognition refers to the cognitive processes involved in the recognition of emotions in other people, understanding the unwritten rules of social behavior, and *theory of mind*, or the ability to discern what is on another person's mind (Penn, Corrigan, Bentall, Racenstein, & Newman, 1997). Research on social cognition has demonstrated that it is both significantly associated with cognitive functioning and with social and community functioning, and that it mediates the relationship between the two (Addington & Addington, 2008; Brekke, Kay, Lee, & Green, 2005; Vauth, Rüsch, Wirtz, & Corrigan, 2004). Thus, treatment approaches aimed at improving social cognition skills have become a focus in recent years.

Social cognition interventions employ a variety of approaches to improving the ability of clients to recognize and understand important social information in different situations. Training in social cognition skills is typically done in groups, and employs a variety of exercises aimed at training social cognition skills. Preliminary research on social cognition programs indicate that they are feasible to conduct, and that clients who participate in such programs demonstrate expected improvements in social cognition skills (Combs et al., 2007; Penn et al., 2005).

Conclusion
Schizophrenia is a severe adult psychiatric disorder that contributes to functional impairment across the broad range of different life domains. Schizophrenia represents a major burden to clients, family, and society, and therefore its treatment is a high priority. Although schizophrenia is believed to be a biologically based disease, it interacts with the environment, as well as with social factors such as stress, social support, and social competence or coping skills. In addition, schizophrenia is known to be improved by antipsychotic medications and worsened by drug and alcohol abuse. Thus, there are a variety of ways in which the course and outcome of schizophrenia can be improved, including through the use of medication, reduction of substance abuse, building clients' competence at managing stress and persistent symptoms, and increasing social support.

Previously bleak expectations about the chronic and deteriorating course of schizophrenia, and the impossibility of recovery, have been replaced by more positive and personally meaningful definitions of recovery that emphasize improved functioning, well-being, and self-determination. Substantial progress has been made in the treatment of schizophrenia over the past several decades. New medications for the disorder continue to be developed, and although it remains unclear as to whether these medications are clinically more effective than the traditional antipsychotic medications, each medication has its own unique side-effect profile and the greater variety provides more choice for clients and treatment providers. In addition to advances in medication, a number of psychosocial treatment approaches have been developed and shown to be effective in improving the course and outcome of schizophrenia. These treatment approaches include supported employment, family psychoeducation, social skills training, CBT for psychosis, cognitive remediation, training in illness self-management, integrated treatment for co-occurring substance abuse, and the ACT program. There is now realistic hope, supported by a burgeoning treatment technology, that it is possible to live a personally meaningful, rewarding life in which one makes a contribution to society, despite continuing to have some symptoms and impairments of the illness.

Future Directions

A wide range of future research directions are possible for schizophrenia and its treatment. Extensive research is under way aimed at identifying the pathophysiological mechanisms that underlie the causes of schizophrenia and are responsible for its characteristic symptoms and impairments of the disorder. Drug development continues to be an active focus of research, primarily aimed at developing equally effective or more effective medications that have a more benign side-effect profile than those medications currently available. The discovery of medications that can ameliorate the severity of negative symptoms and cognitive impairment, for which effective medications do not currently exist, is also a high priority for research.

Psychosocial treatment development for schizophrenia is also needed, to address a variety of needs. Several promising treatment approaches were previously described, but many other treatments remain to be developed to address the stubborn features of schizophrenia. For example, although depression is one of the most consistent and debilitating features of schizophrenia (Häfner et al., 1999), the field still lacks a standardized and empirically validated intervention that targets depression in the illness. Cognitive-behavioral therapy for psychosis has been found to improve depression in some studies (Wykes et al., 2008), but has yet to be applied to depression as the primary focus. Similarly, anxiety disorders such as PTSD, obsessive-compulsive disorder, panic disorder, and social phobia are common in schizophrenia. However, with the exception of recent

work on treating PTSD (Frueh et al., 2009; Mueser et al., 2008), little work has focused on developing interventions that target other anxiety disorders in schizophrenia.

Another area in need of treatment development and research concerns the parenting needs of persons with schizophrenia. Although in Western countries the rate of fertility in men with schizophrenia is relatively low, among women with schizophrenia rates of fertility are close to that of the general population (Haukka, Suvisaari, & Lonnqvist, 2003; Howard, Kumar, Leese, & Thornicroft, 2002). However, women with schizophrenia often experience a broad range of problems in fulfilling their role as parent, and many must receive extensive help from relatives or give their children up for adoption or to foster care (Fox, 1999; Nicholson, Sweeney, & Geller, 1998). Because so many women with schizophrenia have children, the need exists to develop and standardized programs that address family planning (Coverdale & Grunebaum, 1998), as well as parent training programs designed to teach parenting skills to these women, potentially enabling them to continue to maintain their role as parents or to continue to have a positive role in relationship with their children who are being raised by another person or family.

Another potentially fruitful direction is the development of programs aimed at engaging in treatment those individuals experiencing their first episode of psychosis. People who are early in the stages of developing schizophrenia frequently have difficulty obtaining appropriate treatment, and in many cases remain untreated for years—until their behavior gets out of control and hospitalization is necessary. Strong evidence suggests that longer durations of untreated psychosis are associated with a reduced ability to successfully stabilize the key symptoms of the illness and lead to a worse overall prognosis (Perkins et al., 2005). Therefore, the identification and treatment of individuals in the early stages of psychosis has the potential to improve the long-term trajectory of schizophrenia.

Over the past 10–20 years, early psychosis identification and treatment programs been developed in a number of countries (Addington, Van Mastrigt, Hutchinson, & Addington, 2002; Leavey et al., 2004; Petersen et al., 2005). Studies based on these programs indicate that they are successful in engaging clients and families in treatment, and that early treatment is associated with positive outcomes in terms of psychosocial functioning in the minimization of relapses and rehospitalizations (Penn, Waldheter,

Mueser, Perkins, & Lieberman, 2005). However, well-controlled studies of the effectiveness of first-episode psychosis programs are limited at this point. Furthermore, no controlled studies of first-episode treatment programs have been conducted in the United States. Furthermore, most first-episode treatment programs developed in Europe and Australia are located in cities that serve a large population. These programs focus on recruiting clients into specialty first-episode clinics by drawing from the entire population in the city. In the United States., where mental health services are usually provided based on smaller geographic regions, there is a need to develop first-episode treatment approaches that can be implemented within the context of the U.S. mental health system.

The final consideration for future directions is increasingly access to evidence-based practices (EBPs) in the treatment of persons of schizophrenia. Despite the multitude of empirically validated psychosocial interventions for schizophrenia previously reviewed in this chapter, most clients of schizophrenia are not able to access these services at their local community mental health centers (Institute of Medicine, 2001a; Lehman & Steinwachs, 1998; President's New Freedom Commission on Mental Health, 2003). The need exists to develop more effective methods for disseminating EBPs for the treatment of schizophrenia to a broad range of mental health providers who serve this population. Recent research on the implementation of EBPs for severe mental illness indicates that standardized interventions can be successfully implemented with good fidelity to their treatment models for up to 2 years using routine mental health treatment settings (McHugo et al., 2007). However, all implementation efforts require training and a commitment to new practice standards.

Finally, there is a critical need to realign funding mechanisms for the provision of mental health services, so that they provide the incentive necessary to mental health centers to implement EBPs for their mental health population, including clients with schizophrenia. Current funding for mental health services for schizophrenia is not consistent with the evidence base of effective interventions, and in the absence of a realignment, the widespread implementation of efficacious treatments for schizophrenia is likely to remain an elusive goal.

References

Abram, K. M., Teplin, L. A., & McClelland, G. M. (2003). Comorbidity of severe psychiatric disorders and substance use disorders among women in jail. *American Journal of Psychiatry, 160*, 1007–1010.

Adams, J. R., Drake, R. E., & Wolford, G. L. (2007). Shared decision-making preferences of people with severe mental illness. *Psychiatric Services, 58*, 1219–1221.

Addington, J., & Addington, D. (2008). Social and cognitive functioning in psychosis. *Schizophrenia Research, 99*, 176–181.

Addington, J., & Duchak, V. (1997). Reasons for substance use in schizophrenia. *Acta Psychiatrica Scandinavica, 96*, 329–333.

Addington, J., Van Mastrigt, S., Hutchinson, J., & Addington, D. (2002). Pathways to care: Help seeking behaviour in first episode psychosis. *Acta Psychiatrica Scandinavica, 106*, 358–364.

Addington, J., Young, J., & Addington, D. (2003). Social outcome in early psychosis. *Psychological Medicine, 33*, 1199–1124.

Allness, D. J., & Knoedler, W. H. (1998). *The PACT model of community-based treatment for persons with severe and persistent mental illness: A manual for PACT start-up.* Arlington, VA: National Alliance for the Mentally Ill.

Almeida, O. P., Howard, R. J., Levy, R., & David, A. S. (1995a). Psychotic states arising in late life (late paraphrenia): Psychopathology and nosology. *British Journal of Psychiatry, 166*, 205–214.

Almeida, O. P., Howard, R. J., Levy, R., & David, A. S. (1995b). Psychotic states arising in late life (late paraphrenia): The role of risk factors. *British Journal of Psychiatry, 166*, 215–228.

Amador, X. F., & Gorman, J. M. (1998). Psychopathologic domains and insight in schizophrenia. *The Psychiatric Clinics of North America, 21*, 27–42.

American Psychiatric Association. (1994). *Diagnostic and statistical manual of mental disorders (DSM-IV)* (4th Edition ed.). Washington, DC: American Psychiatric Association.

Anderson, C. M., Reiss, D. J., & Hogarty, G. E. (1986). *Schizophrenia and the family.* New York: Guilford Press.

Andreasen, N. C., Carpenter, W. T., Jr., Kane, J. M., Lasser, R., Marder, S. R., & Weinberger, D. R. (2005). Remission in schizophrenia: Proposed criteria and rationale for consensus. *American Journal of Psychiatry, 162*, 441–449.

Angermeyer, M. C., Kuhn, L., & Goldstein, J. M. (1990). Gender and the course of schizophrenia: Differences in treated outcome. *Schizophrenia Bulletin, 16*, 293–307.

Anthony, W. A. (1993). Recovery from mental illness: The guiding vision of the mental health service system in the 1990s. *Psychosocial Rehabilitation Journal, 16*, 11–23.

Appleton, W. S. (1974). Mistreatment of patients' families by psychiatrists. *American Journal of Psychiatry, 131*, 655–657.

Arey, B. A., & Marder, S. R. (2008). Other medications. In K. T. Mueser & D. V. Jeste (Eds.), *Clinical handbook of schizophrenia* (pp. 186–195). New York: Guilford Press.

Argyle, N. (1990). Panic attacks in chronic schizophrenia. *British Journal of Psychiatry, 157*, 430–433.

Arns, P. G., & Linney, J. A. (1993). Work, self, and life satisfaction for persons with severe and persistent mental disorders. *Psychosocial Rehabilitation Journal, 17*, 63–79.

Arseneault, L., Cannon, M., Witton, J., & Murray, R. M. (2004). Causal association between cannabis and psychosis: Examination of the evidence. *British Journal of Psychiatry, 184*, 110–117.

Arseneault, L., Moffitt, T. E., Caspi, A., Taylor, P. J., & Silva, P. A. (2000). Mental disorders and violence in a total birth cohort. *Archives of General Psychiatry, 57*, 979–986.

Ayllon, T. (1968). *The token economy: A motivational system for therapy and rehabilitation*. New York: Appleton-Century-Crofts.

Azrin, N. H., & Teichner, G. (1998). Evaluation of an instructional program for improving medication compliance for chronically mentally ill outpatients. *Behaviour Research and Therapy, 36*, 849–861.

Bachrach, L. L. (1981). Continuity of care for chronic mental patients: A conceptual analysis. *American Journal of Psychiatry, 33*, 189–197.

Barrowclough, C., & Tarrier, N. (1992). *Families of schizophrenic patients: Cognitive behavioural intervention*. London: Chapman & Hall.

Beard, J. H., Propst, R. N., & Malamud, T. J. (1982). The Fountain House model of rehabilitation. *Psychosocial Rehabilitation Journal, 5*, 47–53.

Bebbington, P. E., Bhugra, D., Brugha, T., Singleton, N., Farrell, M., Jenkins, R., et al. (2004). Psychosis, victimisation and childhood disadvantage: Evidence from the second British National Survey of Psychiatric Morbidity. *British Journal of Psychiatry, 185*, 220–226.

Bebbington, P. E., & Kuipers, L. (1992). Life events and social factors. In D. J. Kavanagh (Ed.), *Schizophrenia: An overview and practical handbook* (pp. 126–144). London: Chapman & Hall.

Beck, A. T. (1952). Successful outpatient psychotherapy with a schizophrenic with a delusion based on borrowed guilt. *Psychiatry, 15*, 305–312.

Beck, A. T., Emery, G., & Greenberg, R. L. (1985). *Anxiety disorders and phobias: A cognitive perspective*. New York: Basic Books.

Beck, A. T., Rush, A. J., Shaw, B. F., & Emery, G. (1979). *Cognitive therapy of depression*. New York: Guilford Press.

Becker, D. R., & Drake, R. E. (1993). *A working life: The individual placement and support (IPS) program*. Concord, NH: New Hampshire-Dartmouth Psychiatric Research Center.

Becker, D. R., & Drake, R. E. (2003). *A working life for people with severe mental illness*. New York: Oxford University Press.

Becker, D. R., Drake, R. E., Farabaugh, A., & Bond, G. R. (1996). Job preferences of clients with severe psychiatric disorders participating in supported employment programs. *Psychiatric Services, 47*, 1223–1226.

Bell, M. D., Bryson, G., Greig, T., Corcoran, C., & Wexler, R. E. (2001). Neurocognitive enhancement therapy with work therapy. *Archives of General Psychiatry, 58*, 763–768.

Bell, M. D., Fiszdon, J., Greig, T., Wexler, B. E., & Bryson, G. J. (2007). Neurocognitive enhancement therapy with work therapy in schizophrenia: 6-month followup of neuropsychological performance. *Journal of Rehabilitation Research and Development, 44*.

Bell, M. D., Lysaker, P. H., & Milstein, R. M. (1996). Clinical benefits of paid work activity in schizophrenia. *Schizophrenia Bulletin, 22*, 51–67.

Bellack, A. S., Bennet, M. E., & Gearon, J. S. (2007). *Behavioral treatment for substance abuse in people with serious and persistent mental illness: A handbook for mental health professionals*. New York: Taylor and Francis.

Bellack, A. S., Mueser, K. T., Gingerich, S., & Agresta, J. (2004). *Social skills training for schizophrenia: A step-by-step guide* (2nd ed.). New York: Guilford Press.

Bleuler, E. (1911/1950). *Dementia praecox or the group of schizophrenias*. New York: International Universities Press.

Bond, G. R., Drake, R. E., & Becker, D. R. (2008). An update on randomized controlled trials of evidence-based supported employment. *Psychiatric Rehabilitation Journal, 31*, 280–290.

Bond, G. R., Drake, R. E., Mueser, K. T., & Latimer, E. (2001). Assertive community treatment for people with severe mental illness: Critical ingredients and impact on clients. *Disease Management and Health Outcomes, 9*, 141–159.

Bond, G. R., Resnick, S. G., Drake, R. E., Xie, H., McHugo, G. J., & Bebout, R. R. (2001). Does competitive employment improve nonvocational outcomes for people with severe mental illness? *Journal of Consulting and Clinical Psychology, 69*, 489–501.

Bowen, L., Wallace, C. J., Glynn, S. M., Nuechterlein, K. H., Lutzker, J. R., & Kuehnel, T. G. (1994). Schizophrenic individuals' cognitive functioning and performance in interpersonal interactions and skills training procedures. *Journal of Psychiatric Research, 28*, 289–301.

Boydell, J., van Os, J., McKenzie, K., Allardyce, J., Goel, R., McCreadie, R., et al. (2001). Incidence of schizophrenia in ethnic minorities in London: Ecological study into interactions with environment. *British Medical Journal, 323*, 1336–1338.

Brans, R. G. H., van Haren, N. E., van Baal, C. M., Schnack, H. G., Kahn, R. S., & Hulshoff, H. E. (2008). Heritability of changes in brain volume over time in twin pairs discordant for schizophrenia. *Archives of General Psychiatry, 65*, 1259–1268.

Brekke, J. S., Kay, D. D., Lee, K. S., & Green, M. F. (2005). Biosocial pathways to functional outcome in schizophrenia. *Schizophrenia Research, 80*, 213–225.

Brennan, P. A., Mednick, S. A., & Hodgins, S. (2000). Major mental disorders and criminal violence in a Danish birth cohort. *Archives of General Psychiatry, 57*, 494–500.

Brenner, H., Roder, V., Hodel, B., Kienzle, N., Reed, D., & Liberman, R. (1994). *Integrated psychological therapy for schizophrenic patients*. Seattle: Hogrefe & Huber Publishers.

Brown, A. S., Begg, M. D., Gravenstein, S., Schaefer, C. A., Wyatt, R. J., Bresnahan, M., et al. (2004). Serologic evidence of prenatal influenza in the etiology of schizophrenia. *Archives of General Psychiatry, 61*, 774–780.

Bruce, M. L., Takeuchi, D. T., & Leaf, P. J. (1991). Poverty and psychiatric status: Longitudinal evidence from the New Haven Epidemiologic Catchment Area Study. *Archives of General Psychiatry, 48*, 470–474.

Brunette, M. F., Mueser, K. T., Xie, H., & Drake, R. E. (1997). Relationships between symptoms of schizophrenia and substance abuse. *Journal of Nervous and Mental Disease, 185*, 13–20.

Buchanan, J. (1995). Social support and schizophrenia: A review of the literature. *Archives of Psychiatric Nursing, 9*, 68–76.

Burns, T., Catty, J., Becker, T., Drake, R. E., Fioritti, A., Knapp, M., et al. (2007). The effectiveness of supported employment for people with severe mental illness: A randomized controlled trial. *Lancet, 370*, 1146–1152.

Butzlaff, R. L., & Hooley, J. M. (1998). Expressed emotion and psychiatric relapse. *Archives of General Psychiatry, 55*, 547–552.

Byrne, M., Agerbo, E., Bennedsen, B., Eaton, W. W., & Mortensen, P. B. (2007). Obstetric conditions and risk of first admission with schizophrenia: A Danish national register based study. *Schizophrenia Research, 97*, 51–59.

Cannon, T. D., Jones, P. B., & Murray, R. M. (2002). Obstetric complications and schizophrenia: Historical and meta-analytic review. *American Journal of Psychiatry, 159*, 1080–1092.

Cantor-Graae, E., Zolkowska, K., & McNeil, T. F. (2005). Increased risk of psychotic disorder among immigrants in Malmö: A 3-year first-contact study. *Psychological Medicine, 35,* 1155–1163.

Canuso, C. M., & Pandina, G. (2007). Gender and schizophrenia. *Psychopharmacology Bulletin, 40,* 178–190.

Cardno, A., Marshall, E., Coid, B., Macdonald, A., Ribchester, T., Davies, N., et al. (1999). Heritability estimates for psychotic disorders: The Maudsley twin psychosis series. *Archives of General Psychiatry, 56,* 162–168.

Carey, K. B. (1996). Treatment of co-occurring substance abuse and major mental illness. In R. E. Drake & K. T. Mueser (Eds.), *Dual diagnosis of major mental illness and substance abuse: Volume 2: Recent research and clinical implications* (Vol. 70, pp. 19–31). San Francisco: Jossey-Bass Publishers.

Carpenter, W. T., Heinrichs, D. W., & Wagman, A. M. I. (1988). Deficit and nondeficit forms of schizophrenia: The concept. *American Journal of Psychiatry, 145,* 578–583.

Chadwick, P., & Birchwood, M. (1994). The omnipotence of voices: A cognitive approach to auditory hallucinations. *British Journal of Psychiatry, 164,* 190–201.

Chadwick, P., Birchwood, M., & Trower, P. (1996). *Cognitive therapy for delusions, voices and paranoia.* Chichester, West Sussex, England: John Wiley & Sons.

Chamberlin, J. (1978). *On our own: Patient-controlled alternatives to the mental Health system.* New York: Hawthorne.

Ciompi, L. (1980). Catamnestic long-term study on the course of life and aging of schizophrenics. *Schizophrenia Bulletin, 6,* 606–618.

Clark, R. E., Bartels, S. J., Mellman, T. A., & Peacock, W. J. (2002). Recent trends in antipsychotic combination therapy of schizophrenia and schizoaffective disorder: Implications for state mental health policy. *Schizophrenia Bulletin, 28,* 75–84.

Cohen, C. I. (1995). Studies of the course and outcome of schizophrenia in later life. *Psychiatric Services, 46,* 877–879.

Cohen, C. I., Talavera, N., & Hartung, R. (1996). Depression among aging persons with schizophrenia who live in the community. *Psychiatric Services, 47,* 601–607.

Combs, D. R., Adams, S. D., Penn, D. L., Roberts, D., Tiegreen, J., & Stem, P. (2007). Social Cognition and Interaction Training (SCIT) for inpatients with schizophrenia spectrum disorders: Preliminary findings. *Schizophrenia Research, 91,* 112–116.

Cook, J. A., Pickett-Schenk, S., & Nageotte, C. A. (2000). Dimensions of staff burnout in assertive community treatment and psychosocial rehabilitation programs for persons with severe mental illness. *International Journal of Mental Health Promotion, 2,* 6–12.

Corcoran, C. M., Kimhy, D., Stanford, A., Khan, S., Walsh, J., Thompson, J. et al. (2008). Temporal association of cannabis use with symptoms in individuals at clinical high risk for psychosis. *Schizophrenia Research, 106,* 286–293.

Corrigan, P. W., Giffort, D., Rashid, F., Leary, M., & Okeke, I. (1999). Recovery as a psychological construct. *Community Mental Health Journal, 35,* 231–240.

Corrigan, P. W., McCracken, S. G., Edwards, M., Kommana, S., & Simpatico, T. (1997). Staff training to improve implementation and impact of behavioral rehabilitation programs. *Psychiatric Services, 48,* 1336–1338.

Cournos, F., Guido, J. R., Coomaraswamy, S., Meyer-Behlburg, H., Sugden, R., & Horwath, E. (1994). Sexual activity and risk of HIV infection among patients with schizophrenia. *American Journal of Psychiatry, 151,* 228–232.

Coverdale, J. H., & Grunebaum, H. (1998). Sexuality and family planning. In K. T. Mueser & N. Tarrier (Eds.), *Handbook of social functioning in schizophrenia* (pp. 224–237). Needham Heights, MA: Allyn & Bacon.

Cramer, J. A., & Rosenheck, R. (1999). Enhancing medication compliance for people with serious mental illness. *Journal of Nervous and Mental Disease, 187,* 53–55.

Crocker, A. G., Mueser, K. T., Clark, R. E., McHugo, G. J., Ackerson, T., & Alterman, A. I. (2005). Antisocial personality, psychopathy and violence in persons with dual disorders: A longitudinal analysis. *Criminal Justice and Behavior, 32,* 452–476.

Dalman, C., Thomas, H. V., David, A. S., Gentz, J., Lewis, G., & Allebeck, P. (2001). Signs of asphyxia at birth and risk of schizophrenia: Population-based case-control study. *British Journal of Psychiatry, 179,* 403–408.

Daumit, G. L., Goldberg, R. W., Anthony, C., Dickerson, F., Brown, C. H., Kreyenbuhl, J. K.W., & Dixon, L. B. (2005). Physical activity patterns in adults with severe mental illness. *Journal of Nervous and Mental Disease, 193,* 641–646.

Davidson, L., Tondora, J., Lawless, M. S., O'Connell, M. J., & Rowe, M. (2009). *A practical guide to recovery-oriented practice: Tools for transforming mental health care.* New York: Oxford University Press.

Davis, K. L., Kahn, R. S., Ko, G., & Davidson, M. (1991). Dopamine in schizophrenia: A review and reconceptualization. *American Journal of Psychiatry, 148,* 1474–1486.

de la Chapelle, A., Kari, C., Nurminen, M., & Hernberg, S. (1977). Clozapine-induced agranulocytosis. *Human Genetics, 37,* 183–194.

de Leon, J., & Diaz, F. J. (2005). A meta-analysis of worldwide studies demonstrates an association between schizophrenia and tobacco smoking behaviors. *Schizophrenia Research, 76,* 135–157.

Deegan, P. E. (1988). Recovery: The lived experience of rehabilitation. *Psychosocial Rehabilitation Journal, 11,* 11–19.

DeLisi, L. E., Szulc, K. U., Bertisch, H., Majcher, M., Brown, K., Bappal, A., et al. (2006). Early detection of schizophrenia by diffusion weighted imaging. *Psychiatry Research, 148,* 61–66.

Desai, M. M., Rosenheck, R. A., Druss, B. G., & Perlin, J. B. (2002). Medical disorders and quality of diabetes care in the veterans health administration. *American Journal of Psychiatry, 159,* 1584–1590.

Dickerson, F. B., Brown, C. H., Daumit, G. L., Fang, L., Goldberg, R. W., Wohlheiter, K., & Dixon, L. B. (2006). Health status of individuals with serious mental illness. *Schizophrenia Bulletin, 32,* 584–589.

Dickerson, F. B., Tenhula, W. N., & Green-Paden, L. D. (2005). The token economy for schizophrenia: Review of the literature and recommendations for future research. *Schizophrenia Research, 75,* 405–416.

DiClemente, C. C., & Prochaska, J. O. (1998). Toward a comprehensive, transtheoretical model of change: Stages of change and addictive behaviors. In W. R. Miller & N. Heather (Eds.), *Treating addictive behaviors second edition* (pp. 3–24). New York: Plenum Press.

Dixon, L., Dickerson, F., Bellack, A. S., Bennett, M. E., Dickinson, D., Goldberg, R., et al. (in press). The 2009 PORT psychosocial treatment recommendations and summary statements. *Schizophrenia Bulletin, 36,* 48–70.

Dixon, L., Haas, G., Weiden, P. J., Sweeney, J., & Frances, A. J. (1991). Drug abuse in schizophrenic patients: Clinical correlates and reasons for use. *American Journal of Psychiatry*, *148*, 224–230.

Dixon, L., Weiden, P., Delahanty, J., Goldberg, R., Postrado, L., Lucksted, A., & Lehman, A. (2000). Prevalence and correlates of diabetes in national schizophrenia samples. *Schizophrenia Bulletin, 26*, 903–912.

Drake, R. E., & Brunette, M. F. (1998). Complications of severe mental illness related to alcohol and other drug use disorders. In M. Galanter (Ed.), *Recent developments in alcoholism: Consequences of alcoholism* (Vol. 14, pp. 285–299). New York: Plenum Publishing Company.

Drake, R. E., Mueser, K. T., Brunette, M. F., & McHugo, G. J. (2004). A review of treatments for clients with severe mental illness and co-occurring substance use disorder. *Psychiatric Rehabilitation Journal, 27*, 360–374.

Drake, R. E., O'Neal, E., & Wallach, M. A. (2008). A systematic review of psychosocial interventions for people with co-occurring severe mental and substance use disorders. *Journal of Substance Abuse Treatment, 34*, 123–138.

Drake, R. E., Teague, G. B., & Warren, R. S. (1990). Dual diagnosis: The New Hampshire Program. *Addiction and Recovery, 10*, 35–39.

Drake, R. E., Xie, H., McHugo, G. J., & Green, A. I. (2000). The effects of clozapine on alcohol and drug use disorders among schizophrenic patients. *Schizophrenia Bulletin, 26*, 441–449.

Druss, B. G., Bradford, D. W., Rosenheck, R. A., Radford, M. J., & Krumholz, H. M. (2000). Mental disorders and use of cardiovascular procedures after myocardial infarction. *Journal of the American Medical Association, 283*, 506–511.

Eaton, W. W., Jr. (1994). Residence, social class, and schizophrenia. *Journal of Health and Social Behavior, 15*, 289–299.

Edwards, J., Maude, D., McGorry, P. D., Harrigan, S. M., & Cocks, J. T. (1998). Prolonged recovery in first-episode psychosi. *British Journal of Psychiatry, 172 (Suppl)*, 107–116.

Emsley, R., Chiliza, B., & Schoeman, R. (2008). Predictors of long-term outcome in schizophrenia. *Current Opinion in Psychiatry, 21*, 173–177.

Falloon, I. R. H., Boyd, J. L., & McGill, C. W. (1984). *Family care of schizophrenia: A problem-solving approach to the treatment of mental illness*. New York: Guilford Press.

Farina, A. (1998). Stigma. In K. T. Mueser & N. Tarrier (Eds.), *Handbook of social functioning in schizophrenia* (pp. 247–279). Boston: Allyn and Bacon.

Felker, B., Yazel, J., & Short, D. (1996). Mortality and medical comorbidity among psychiatric patients: A review. *Psychiatric Services, 47*, 1356–1362.

Fenton, W. S. (2003). Shared decision making: A model for the physician-patient relationship in the 21st century? *Acta Psychiatrica Scandinavica, 107*, 401–402.

Fenton, W. S., & McGlashan, T. H. (1991). Natural history of schizophrenia subtypes I. Longitudinal study of paranoid, hebephrenic, and undifferentiated schizophrenia. *Archives of General Psychiatry, 48*, 969–977.

Fischer, P. J., Drake, R. E., & Breakey, W. R. (1992). Mental health problems among homeless persons: A review of epidemiological research from 1980 to 1990. In H. R. Lamb & L. L. Bachrach & F. I. Kass (Eds.), *Treating the homeless mentally ill*. Washington, DC: American Psychiatric Press.

Fontaine, K. R., Heo, M., Harrigan, E. P., Shear, C. L., Lakshminarayanan, M., Casey, D. E., & Allison, D. B. (2001). Estimating the consequences of anti-psychotic induced weight gain on health and mortality rate. *Psychiatry Research, 101*, 277–288.

Fowler, D., Garety, P., & Kuipers, E. (1995). *Cognitive behaviour therapy for psychosis: Theory and practice*. Chichester, West Sussex, England: John Wiley & Sons.

Fox, J. W. (1990). Social class, mental illness, and social mobility: The social selection-drift hypothesis for serious mental illness. *Journal of Health and Social Behavior, 31*, 344–353.

Fox, L. (1999). Missing out on motherhood. *Psychiatric Services, 50*, 193–194.

Frese, F. J. I. (2008). Self-help activities. In K. T. Mueser & D. V. Jeste (Eds.), *Clinical handbook of schizophrenia* (pp. 298–305). New York: Guilford Press.

Freudenreich, O., & Goff, D. C. (2002). Antipsychotic combination therapy in schizophrenia. A review of efficacy and risks of current combinations. *Acta Psychiatrica Scandinavica, 106*, 323–330.

Fritzsche, M., & Schmidl, J. (2002). Seasonal fluctuation in schizophrenia. *American Journal of Psychiatry, 159*, 499–500.

Fromm-Reichman, F. (1948). Notes on the development of treatment of schizophrenics by psychoanalytic psychotherapy. *Psychiatry, 1*, 263–273.

Frueh, B. C., Buckley, T. C., Cusack, K. J., Kimble, M. O., Grubaugh, A. L., Turner, S., et al. (2004). Cognitive-behavioral treatment for PTSD among people with severe mental illness: A proposed treatment model. *Journal of Psychiatric Practice, 10*, 26–38.

Frueh, B. C., Cusack, K. J., Grubaugh, A. L., Sauvageot, J. A., & Wells, C. (2006). Clinicians' perspectives on cognitive-behavioral treatment for PTSD among persons with severe mental illness. *Psychiatric Services, 57*, 1027–1031.

Frueh, B. C., Grubaugh, A. L., Cusack, K. J., Kimble, M. O., Elhai, J. D., & Knapp, R. G. (2009). Exposure-based cognitive-behavioral treatment of PTSD in adults with schizophrenia or schizoaffective disorder: A pilot study. *Journal of Anxiety Disorders, 23*, 665–675.

Garety, P., Kuipers, E., Fowler, D., Chamberlain, F., & Dunn, G. (1994). Cognitive behavior therapy for drug resistant psychosis. *British Journal of Medical Psychology, 67*, 259–271.

Garety, P. A., & Hemsley, D. R. (1994). *Delusions: Investigations into the psychology of delusional reasoning*. Oxford: Oxford University Press.

Geddes, J. R., & Lawrie, S. M. (1995). Obstetric complications and schizophrenia: A meta-analysis. *British Journal of Psychiatry, 167*, 786–793.

Gingerich, S., & Mueser, K. T. (2005). Illness management and recovery. In R. E. Drake & M. R. Merrens & D. W. Lynde (Eds.), *Evidence-based mental health practice: A Textbook* (pp. 395–424). New York: Norton.

Gold, P. B., Meisler, N., Santos, A. B., Williams, O. H., Carnemolla, M. A., & Kelleher, J. (2004). Randomized trial of supported employment integrated with Assertive Community Treatment in the rural south: Employment outcomes for persons with severe mental illness. *Schizophrenia Bulletin, 32*, 378–395.

Goldman, H. H., & Manderscheid, R. W. (1987). Epidemiology of chronic mental disorder. In W. W. Menninger & G. Hannah (Eds.), *The chronic mental patient II*. Washington, DC: American Psychiatric Press.

Goodman, L. A., Dutton, M. A., & Harris, M. (1995). Physical and sexual assault prevalence among episodically homeless women with serious mental illness. *American Journal of Orthopsychiatry, 65*, 468–478.

Goodman, L. A., & Fallot, R. (1998). HIV risk behaviors and poor urban women with severe mental disorders: Association with childhood physical and sexual abuse. *American Journal of Orthopsychiatry, 68*, 73–83.

Goodman, L. A., Rosenberg, S. D., Mueser, K. T., & Drake, R. E. (1997). Physical and sexual assault history in women with serious mental illness: Prevalence, correlates, treatment, and future research directions. *Schizophrenia Bulletin, 23*, 685–696.

Gottesman, I. I. (1991). *Schizophrenia genesis: The origins of madness.* New York: W.H. Freeman & Company.

Green, A. I., Zimmet, S. V., Strous, R. D., & Schildkraut, J. J. (1999). Clozapine for comorbid substance use disorder and schizophrenia: Do patients with schizophrenia have a reward-deficiency syndrome that can be ameliorated by clozapine? *Harvard Review of Psychiatry, 6*, 287–296.

Green, M. F. (1996). What are the functional consequences of neurocognitive deficits in schizophrenia? *American Journal of Psychiatry, 153*, 321–330.

Green, M. F. (2006). Cognitive impairment and functional outcome in schizophrenia and bipolar disorder. *Journal of Clinical Psychiatry, 67 Suppl 9*, 3–8.

Häfner, H., & an der Heiden, W. (2003). Course and outcome of schizophrenia. In S. R. Hirsch & D. R. Weinberger (Eds.), *Schizophrenia* (Second ed., pp. 101–141). Oxford: Blackwell Scientific.

Häfner, H., & an der Heiden, W. (2008). Course and outcome. In K. T. Mueser & D. V. Jeste (Eds.), *Clinical handbook of schizophrenia* (pp. 100–113). New York: Guilford Press.

Häfner, H., Löffler, W., Maurer, K., Hambrecht, M., & an der Heiden, W. (1999). Depression, negative symptoms, social stagnation and social decline in the early course of schizophrenia. *Acta Psychiatrica Scandinavica, 100*, 105–118.

Häfner, H., Maurer, K., Löffler, W., & Riecher-Rössler, A. (1993). The influence of age and sex on the onset and early course of schizophrenia. *British Journal of Psychiatry, 162*, 80–86.

Häfner, H., Maurer, K., Trendler, G., an der Heiden, W., Schmidt, M., & Könnecke, R. (2005). Schizophrenia and depression: Challenging the paradigm of two separate diseases—A controlled study of schizophrenia, depression and healthy controls. *Schizophrenia Research, 77*, 11–24.

Hagen, R., & Nordahl, H. M. (2008). Behavioral experiments in the treatment of paranoid schizophrenia: A single case study. *Cognitive and Behavioral Practice, 15*, 296–305.

Hamann, J., Leucht, S., & Kissling, W. (2003). Shared decision making in psychiatry. *Acta Psychiatrica Scandinavica, 107*, 403–409.

Harding, C., Strauss, J., Hafez, H., & Liberman, P. (1987). Work and mental illness I. Toward an integration of the rehabilitation process. *Journal of Nervous and Mental Disease, 175*, 317–326.

Harding, C. M., Brooks, G. W., Ashikaga, T., Strauss, J. S., & Breier, A. (1987a). The Vermont longitudinal study of persons with severe mental illness: I. Methodology, study sample and overall status 32 years later. *American Journal of Psychiatry, 144*, 718–726.

Harding, C. M., Brooks, G. W., Ashikaga, T., Strauss, J. S., & Breier, A. (1987b). The Vermont longitudinal study of persons with severe mental illness: II. Long-term outcome of subjects who retrospectively met DSM-III criteria for schizophrenia. *American Journal of Psychiatry, 144*, 727–735.

Harris, E. C., & Barraclough, B. (1998). Excess mortality of mental disorders. *British Journal of Psychiatry, 173*, 11–53.

Harris, M. (1998). *Trauma recovery and empowerment: A clinician's guide for working with women in groups.* New York: The Free Press.

Harris, M., & Bergman, H. (1984). Reassessing the revolving door: A developmental perspective on the young adult chronic patient. *American Journal of Orthopsychiatry, 54*, 281–289.

Harrison, G., Hopper, K., Craig, T., Laska, E., Siegel, C., Wanderling, J., et al. (2001). Recovery from psychotic illness: A 15- and 25-year international follow-up study. *British Journal of Psychiatry, 178*, 506–517.

Harrison, P. J., & Owen, M. J. (2003). Genes for schizophrenia: Recent findings and their pathophysiological implications. *Lancet, 361*, 417–419.

Hasson-Ohayon, I., Roe, D., & Kravetz, S. (2007). A randomized controlled trial of the effectiveness of the illness management and recovery program. *Psychiatric Services, 58*, 1461–1466.

Hatfield, A. B., & Lefley, H. P. (1993). *Surviving mental illness: Stress, coping, and adaptation.* New York: Guilford Press.

Hatfield, A. B., & Lefley, H. P. (Eds.). (1987). *Families of the mentally ill: Coping and adaptation.* New York: Guilford Publications.

Hatters Friedman, S., & Loue, S. (2007). Incidence and prevalence of intimate partner violence by and against women with severe mental illness. *Journal of Women's Health*, 471–480.

Haukka, J., Suvisaari, J., & Lonnqvist, J. (2003). Fertility of patients with schizophrenia, their siblings, and the general population: A cohort study from 1950 to 1959 in Finland. *American Journal of Psychiatry, 160*, 460–463.

Haukvik, U. K., Lawyer, G., Bjerkan, P. S., Hartberg, C. B., Jönsson, E. G., McNeil, T., & Agartz, I. (2009). Cerebral cortical thickness and a history of obstetric complications in schizophrenia. *Journal of Psychiatric Research, 43*, 1287–1293.

Heaton, R., Paulsen, J. S., McAdams, L. A., Kuck, J., Zisook, S., Braff, D., et al. (1994). Neuropsychological deficits in schizophrenics: Relationship to age, chronicity, and dementia. *Archives of General Psychiatry, 51*, 469–476.

Heinrichs, R. W., & Zakzanis, K. K. (1998). Neurocognitive deficit in schizophrenia: A quantitative review of evidence. *Neuropsychology, 12*, 426–445.

Hemsley, D. R. (1996). Schizophrenia: A cognitive model and its implications for psychological intervention. *Behavior Modification, 20*, 139–169.

Henquet, C., Krabbendam, L., Spauwen, J., Kaplan, C., Lieb, R., Wittchen, H. U., & van Os, J. (2005). Prospective cohort study of cannabis use, predisposition for psychosis, and psychotic symptoms in young people. *British Medical Journal, 330*, 11.

Herz, M. I., Lamberti, J. S., Mintz, J., Scott, R., O'Dell, S. P., McCartan, L., & Nix, G. (2000). A program for relapse prevention in schizophrenia: A controlled study. *Archives of General Psychiatry, 57*, 277–283.

Hiday, V. A., Swartz, M. S., Swanson, J. W., Borum, R., & Wagner, H. R. (1999). Criminal victimization of persons with severe mental illness. *Psychiatric Services, 50*, 62–68.

Hodgins, S., Hiscoke, U. L., & Freese, R. (2002). The antecedents of aggressive behavior among men with schizophrenia: A prospective investigation of patients in community treatment. *Behavioral Sciences & the Law, 21*, 523–546.

Hodgins, S., Tiihonen, J., & Ross, D. (2005). The consequences of conduct disorder for males who develop schizophrenia: Associations with criminality, aggressive behavior, substance use, and psychiatric services. *Schizophrenia Research, 78*, 323–335.

Hodgins, S., Toupin, J., & Côté, G. (1996). Schizophrenia and antisocial personality disorder: A criminal combination. In L. B. Schlesinger (Ed.), *Explorations in criminal psychopathology: Clinical syndromes with forensic implications* (pp. 217–237). Springfield, IL: Charles C. Thomas.

Hoek, H. W., Brown, A. S., & Susser, E. (1998). The Dutch famine and schizophrenia spectrum disorders. *Social Psychiatry and Psychiatric Epidemiology, 33*, 373–379.

Hofmann, S. G. (1999). Relationship between panic and schizophrenia. *Depression and Anxiety, 9*, 101–106.

Hogarty, G. E. (2002). *Personal therapy for schizophrenia & related disorders: A guide to individualized treatment.* New York: Guilford Press.

Hogarty, G. E., & Flesher, S. (1999). Practice principles of cognitive enhancement therapy for schizophrenia. *Schizophrenia Bulletin, 25*, 693–708.

Hogarty, G. E., Greenwald, D., Ulrich, R. F., Kornblith, S. J., DiBarry, A. L., Cooley, S., et al. (1997). Three year trials of personal therapy among schizophrenic patients living with or independent of family II: Effects of adjustment on patients. *American Journal of Psychiatry, 154*, 1514–1524.

Hogarty, G. E., Kornblith, S. J., Greenwald, D., DiBarry, A. L., Cooley, S., Flesher, S., et al. (1995). Personal therapy: A disorder-relevant psychotherapy for schizophrenia. *Schizophrenia Bulletin, 21*, 379–393.

Hogarty, G. E., Kornblith, S. J., Greenwald, D., DiBarry, A. L., Cooley, S., Ulrich, R. et al. (1997). Three year trials of personal therapy among schizophrenic patients living with or independent of family I: Description of study and effects on relapse rates. *American Journal of Psychiatry, 154*, 1504–1513.

Hollingshead, A. B., & Redlich, F. C. (1958). *Social class and mental illness: A community study.* New York: John Wiley & Sons.

Holmberg, S. K., & Kane, C. (1999). Health and self-care practices of persons with schizophrenia. *Psychiatric Services, 50*, 827–829.

Honigfeld, G., Patin, J., & Singer, J. (1984). Clozapine: Antipsychotic activity in treatment-resistant schizophrenics. *Advances in Therapy, 1*(2), 77–97.

Howard, L. M., Kumar, C., Leese, M., & Thornicroft, G. (2002). The general fertility rate in women with psychotic disorders. *American Journal of Psychiatry, 159*, 991–997.

Hultman, C. M., Sparén, P., Takei, N., Murray, R. M., & Cnattingius, S. (1998). Prenatal and perinatal risk factors for schizophrenia, affective psychosis, and reactive psychosis of early onset: a case-control study. *British Medical Journal, 318*, 421–426.

Hwang, M. Y., Morgan, J. E., & Losconzey, M. F. (2000). Clinical and neuropsychological profiles of obsessive-compulsive schizophrenia: A pilot study. *Journal of Neuropsychiatry and Clinical Neuroscience, 12*, 91–94.

Institute of Medicine. (2001a). *Crossing the quality chasm: A new health system for the 21st century.* Washington, DC: National Academy Press.

Institute of Medicine. (2001b). *Neurological, psychiatric, and developmental disorders: Meeting the challenges in the developing world.* Washington, DC: National Academy of Sciences.

Jablensky, A. (1997). The 100-year epidemiology of schizophrenia. *Schizophrenia Research, 28*, 111–125.

Jablensky, A. (1999). Schizophrenia: Epidemiology. *Current Opinion in Psychiatry, 12*, 9–28.

Jablensky, A., Sartorius, N., Ernberg, G., Anker, M., Korten, A., & Cooper, J. E. (1992). Schizophrenia: Manifestations, incidence, and course in different cultures: A World Health Organization ten-country study. *Psychological Medicine, Monograph Supplement 20*, 1–97.

Jianxin Shi, J., Levinson, D. R., Duan, J., Sanders, A. R., Zheng, Y., Pe'er, I., et al. (2009). Common variants on chromosome 6p22.1 are associated with schizophrenia. *Nature, 460*, 753–757.

Johnson, A. B. (1990). *Out of bedlam: The truth about deinstitutionalization.* New York: Basic Books.

Johnson, S., Leese, M., Brooks, L., Clarkson, P., Guite, H., Thornicroft, G., et al. (1998). Frequency and predictors of adverse events: PRiSM study 3. *British Journal of Psychiatry, 173*, 376–384.

Jones, P. B., Rantakallio, P., Hartikainen, A. L., Isohanni, M., & Sipila, P. (1998). Schizophrenia as a long term outcome of pregnancy, delivery, and perinatal complications: A 28-year follow-up of the 1966 north Finland general population birth cohort. *American Journal of Psychiatry, 155*, 355–364.

Kane, J., Honigfeld, G., Singer, J., & Meltzer, H. (1988). Clozapine for the treatment-resistant schizophrenic. *Archives of General Psychiatry, 45*, 789–796.

Kane, J. M., Eerdekens, M., Lindenmayer, J.-P., Keith, S. J., Lesem, M., & Karcher, K. (2003). Long-acting injectable risperidone: Efficacy and safety of the first long-acting atypical antipsychotic. *American Journal of Psychiatry, 160*, 1125–1132.

Kanter, J. (1989). Clinical case management: Definitions, principles, components. *Hospital and Community Psychiatry, 40*, 361–368.

Kavanagh, D. J., Waghorn, G., Jenner, L., Chant, D. C., Carr, V., Evans, M., et al. (2004). Demographic and clinical correlates of comorbid substance use disorders in psychosis: Multivariate analyses from an epidemiological sample. *Schizophrenia Research, 66*, 115–124.

Keefe, R. S. E., Seidman, L. J., Christensen, B. K., Hamer, R. M., Sharma, T., Sitskoorn, M. M., et al., & HGDH Research Group. (2004). Comparative effect of atypical and conventional antipsychotic drugs on neurocognition in first-episode psychosis: A randomized, double-blind trial of olanzapine versus low doses of haloperidol. *American Journal of Psychiatry, 161*, 985–995.

Kendler, K. S., Czajkowski, N., Tambs, K., Torgersen, S., Aggen, S. H., Neale, M. C., & Reichborn-Kjennerud, T. (2006). Dimensional representations of DSM-IV cluster A personality disorders in a population-based sample of Norwegian twins: A multivariate study. *Psychological Medicine, 36*, 1583–1591.

Kern, R. S., Green, M. F., & Satz, P. (1992). Neuropsychological predictors of skills training for chronic psychiatric patients. *Psychiatry Research, 43*, 223–230.

Kessler, R. C., Nelson, C. B., McGonagle, K. A., Edlund, M. J., Frank, R. G., & Leaf, P. J. (1996). The epidemiology of co-occurring addictive and mental disorders: Implications for prevention and service utilization. *American Journal of Orthopsychiatry, 66*, 17–31.

Killackey, E., Jackson, H. J., & McGorry, P. D. (2008). Vocational intervention in first-episode psychosis: A randomised controlled trial of individual placement and support versus treatment as usual. *British Journal of Psychiatry, 193*, 114–120.

Kingdon, D., & Turkington, D. (1991). The use of cognitive behavior therapy with a normalizing rationale in schizophrenia.

The Journal of Nervous and Mental Disease, 719(4), 207–211.

Kingdon, D. G., & Turkington, D. (2004). *Cognitive therapy of schizophrenia*. New York: Guilford Press.

Kirkpatrick, B., & Galderisi, S. (2008). Deficit schizophrenia: An update. *World Psychiatry, 7*, 143–147.

Kloos, B., Zimmerman, S. O., Scrimenti, K., & Crusto, C. (2002). Landlords as partners for promoting success in supported housing: "It takes more than a lease and a key". *Psychiatric Rehabilitation Journal, 25*, 235–244.

Kraepelin, E. (1919/1971). *Dementia praecox and paraphrenia* (R. M. Barclay, Trans.). New York: Krieger.

Kuipers, L., Leff, J., & Lam, D. (2002). *Family work for schizophrenia: A practical guide* (Second ed.). London: Gaskell.

Kurtz, M. M., & Mueser, K. T. (2008). A meta-analysis of controlled research on social skills training for schizophrenia. *Journal of Consulting and Clinical Psychology, 76*, 491–504.

Latimer, E. A., Lecomte, T., Becker, D. R., Drake, R. E., Duclos, I., Piat, M., et al. (2006). Generalisability of the individual placement and support model of supported employment: Results of a Canadian randomised controlled trial. *British Journal of Psychiatry, 189*, 65–73.

Leavey, G., Gulamhussein, S., Papadopoulos, C., Johnson-Sabine, E., Blizard, B., & King, M. (2004). A randomized controlled trial of a brief intervention for families of patients with a first episode of psychosis. *Psychological Medicine, 34*, 423–431.

Lecomte, T., Cyr, M., Lesage, A. D., Wilde, J., Leclerc, C., & Ricard, N. (1999). Efficacy of a self-esteem module in the empowerment of individuals with schizophrenia. *Journal of Nervous and Mental Disease, 187*, 406–413.

Lefley, H. (2009). *Family psychoeducation in serious mental illness: Models, outcomes, applications*. New York: Oxford University Press.

Lehman, A. (1983). The well-being of chronic mental patients. *Archives of General Psychiatry, 40*, 369–373.

Lehman, A. F., & Steinwachs, D. M. (1998). Patterns of usual care for schizophrenia: Initial results from the Schizophrenia Patient Outcomes Research Team (PORT) client survey. *Schizophrenia Bulletin, 24*, 11–20.

Levinson, D. F., & Mowry, B. J. (1991). Defining the schizophrenia spectrum: Issues for genetic linkage studies. *Schizophrenia Bulletin, 17*, 491–514.

Levitt, A., Mueser, K. T., DeGenova, J., Lorenzo, J., Bradford-Watt, D., Barbosa, A., et al. (2009). A randomized controlled trial of illness management and recovery in multi-unit supported housing. *Psychiatric Services, 60*, 1629–1636.

Liberman, R. P. (2007). Dissemination and adoption of social skills training: Social validation of an evidence-based treatment for the mentally disabled. *Journal of Mental Health, 16*, 595–623.

Liberman, R. P., DeRisi, W. J., & Mueser, K. T. (1989). *Social skills training for psychiatric patients*. Needham Heights, MA: Allyn & Bacon.

Liberman, R. P., Kopelowicz, A., Ventura, J., & Gutkind, D. (2002). Operational criteria and factors related to recovery from schizophrenia. *International Review of Psychiatry, 14*, 256–272.

Liberman, R. P., Mueser, K. T., Wallace, C. J., Jacobs, H. E., Eckman, T., & Massel, H. K. (1986). Training skills in the psychiatrically disabled: Learning coping and competence. *Schizophrenia Bulletin, 12*, 631–647.

Lieberman, J. A., Perkins, D., Belger, A., Chakos, M., Jarskog, F., Boteva, K., & Gilmore, J. (2001). The early stages of schizophrenia: Speculations on pathogenesis, pathophysiology, and therapeutic approaches. *Biological Psychiatry, 50*, 884–897.

Lieberman, J. A., Stroup, T. S., McEvoy, J. P., Swartz, M. S., Rosenheck, R. A., Perkins, D. O., et al., & Clinical Antipsychotic Trials of Intervention Effectiveness (CATIE) Investigators. (2005). Effectiveness of antipsychotic drugs in patients with chronic schizophrenia. *The New England Journal of Medicine, 353*, 1209–1223.

Linszen, D., Dingemans, P., & Lenior, M. (1994). Cannabis abuse and the course of recent onset schizophrenic disorders. *Archives of General Psychiatry, 51*, 273–279.

Loebel, A. D., Lieberman, J. A., Alvir, J. M. J., Mayerhoff, D. I., Geisler, S. H., & Szymanski, S. R. (1992). Duration of psychosis and outcome in first-episode schizophrenia. *American Journal of Psychiatry, 149*, 1183–1188.

Lysaker, P. H., Lancaster, R. S., Davis, L. W., & Clements, C. A. (2003). Patterns of neurocognitive deficits and unawareness of illness in schizophrenia. *Journal of Nervous and Mental Disease, 191*, 38–44.

Macias, C., Barreira, P., Alden, M., & Boyd, J. (2001). The ICCD benchmarks for clubhouses: A practical approach to quality improvement in psychiatric rehabilitation. *Psychiatric Services, 52*, 207–213.

Macpherson, R., Jerrom, B., & Hughes, A. (1996). A controlled study of education about drug treatment in schizophrenia. *British Journal of Psychiatry, 168*, 709–717.

Maher, B. A. (1988). Anomalous experience and delusional thinking: The logic of explanations. In T. F. Oltmanns & B. A. Maher (Eds.), *Delusional beliefs* (pp. 383–408). New York: Wiley.

Marlatt, G. A. (Ed.). (1998). *Harm reduction: Pragmatic strategies for managing high-risk behaviors*. New York: Guilford Publications.

Marwaha, S., & Johnson, S. (2004). Schizophrenia and employment: A review. *Social Psychiatry and Psychiatric Epidemiology, 39*, 337–349.

Marwaha, S., Johnson, S., Bebbington, P., Stafford, M., Angermeyer, M. C., Brugha, T., et al. (2007). Rates and correlates of employment in people with schizophrenia in the UK, France and Germany. *British Journal of Psychiatry, 191*, 30–37.

Matz, R., Rick, W., Thompson, H., & Gershon, S. (1974). Clozapine - A potential antipsychotic agent without extrapyramidal manifestations. *Current Therapeutic Research, 16*, 687–695.

McCrone, P., Thornicroft, G., Phelan, M., Holloway, F., Wykes, T., & Johnson, S. (1998). Utilisation and costs of community mental health services: PRiSM psychosis study 5. *British Journal of Psychiatry, 173*, 391–398.

McFarlane, W. R. (2002). *Multifamily groups in the treatment of severe psychiatric disorders*. New York: Guilford Press.

McGrath, J., Saha, S., Welham, J., Saadi, E., MacCauley, C., & Chant, D. (2004). A systematic review of the incidence of schizophrenia: The distribution of rates and influence of sex, urbanicity, migrant status and methodology. *BMC Medicine, 2*, 13.

McGrath, J. J., & JL, Welham. (1999). Season of birth and schizophrenia: A systematic review and meta-analysis of data from the Southern Hemisphere. *Schizophrenia Research, 35*, 237–242.

McGurk, S. R., & Mueser, K. T. (2004). Cognitive functioning, symptoms, and work in supported employment: A review and heuristic model. *Schizophrenia Research, 70*, 147–174.

McGurk, S. R., Mueser, K. T., Feldman, K., Wolfe, R., & Pascaris, A. (2007). Cognitive training for supported employment: 2–3 year outcomes of a randomized controlled trial. *American Journal of Psychiatry, 164*, 437–441.

McGurk, S. R., Mueser, K. T., Harvey, P. D., Marder, J., & LaPuglia, R. (2003). Cognitive and clinical predictors of work outcomes in clients with schizophrenia. *Psychiatric Services, 54*, 1129–1135.

McGurk, S. R., Mueser, K. T., & Pascaris, A. (2005). Cognitive training and supported employment for persons with severe mental illness: One year results from a randomized controlled trial. *Schizophrenia Bulletin, 31*, 898–909.

McGurk, S. R., Twamley, E. W., Sitzer, D. I., McHugo, G. J., & Mueser, K. T. (2007). A meta-analysis of cognitive remediation in schizophrenia. *American Journal of Psychiatry, 164*, 1791–1802.

McHugo, G. J., Bebout, R. R., Harris, M., Cleghorn, S., Herring, G., Xie, H., et al. (2004). A randomized controlled trial of integrated versus parallel housing services for homeless adults with severe mental illness. *Schizophrenia Bulletin, 30*, 969–982.

McHugo, G. J., Drake, R. E., Whitley, R., Bond, G. R., Campbell, K., Rapp, C. A., et al. (2007). Fidelity outcomes in the National Implementing Evidence-Based Practices Project. *Psychiatric Services, 58*, 1279–1284.

McKay, C. E., Johnsen, M., Banks, S., & Stein, R. (2006). Employment transitions for clubhouse members. *Work, 26*, 67–74.

Medalia, A., Revheim, N., & Herlands, T. (2009). *Cognitive remediation for psychological disorders: Therapist guide.* New York: Oxford University Press.

Meltzer, H. Y., Alphs, L., Green, A. I., Altamura, A. C., Anand, R., Bertoldi, A., et al., & International Suicide Prevention Trial Study Group. (2003). Clozapine treatment for suicidality in schizophrenia: International Suicide Prevention Trial (InterSePT). *Archives of General Psychiatry, 60*, 82–91.

Menditto, A. A., Baldwin, L. J., O'Neal, L. G., & Beck, N. C. (1991). Social-learning procedures for increasing attention and improving basic skills in severely regressed institutionalized patients. *Journal of Behavior Therapy and Experimental Psychiatry, 22*, 265–269.

Mercer-McFadden, C., Drake, R. E., Brown, N. B., & Fox, R. S. (1997). The community support program demonstrations of services for young adults with severe mental illness and substance use disorders 1987–1991. *Psychiatric Rehabilitation Journal, 20*, 13–24.

Meyer, J. M., Davis, V. G., Goff, D. C., McEvoy, J. P., Nasrallah, H. A., Davis, S. M., et al. (2008). Change in metabolic syndrome parameters with antipsychotic treatment in the CATIE Schizophrenia Trial: prospective data from phase 1. *Schizophrenia Research, 101*, 273–286.

Meyer, J. M., & Koro, C. E. (2004). The effects of antipsychotic therapy on serum lipids: A comprehensive review. *Schizophrenia Research, 70*, 1–17.

Milton, F., Patwa, V. K., & Hafner, R. J. (1978). Confrontation vs. belief modification in persistently deluded patients. *British Journal of Medical Psychology, 51*, 127–130.

Minkoff, K. (1991). Program components of a comprehensive integrated care system for serious mentally ill patients with substance disorders. In K. Minkoff & R. E. Drake (Eds.), *Dual diagnosis of major mental illness and substance disorders. new directions for mental health services* (Vol. 50, pp. 13–27). San Francisco: Jossey-Bass.

Moore, T. M., Stuart, G. L., Meehan, J. C., Rhatigan, D. L., Hellmuth, J. C., & Keen, S.M. (2008). Drug abuse and aggression between intimate partners: A meta-analytic review. *Clinical Psychology Review, 28*, 247–274.

Moran, P., & Hodgins, S. (2004). The correlates of comorbid antisocial personality disorder in schizophrenia. *Schizophrenia Bulletin, 30*, 791–802.

Morrison, A. P., Renton, J. C., Dunn, H., Williams, S., & Bentall, R. P. (2004). *Cognitive therapy for psychosis: A formulation-based approach.* New York: Brunner-Routledge.

Mueser, K. T. (2000). Cognitive functioning, social adjustment and long-term outcome in schizophrenia. In T. Sharma & P. Harvey (Eds.), *Cognition in schizophrenia: Impairments, importance, and treatment strategies* (pp. 157–177). Oxford: Oxford University Press.

Mueser, K. T., Becker, D. R., Torrey, W. C., Xie, H., Bond, G. R., Drake, R. E., & Dain, B. J. (1997). Work and non-vocational domains of functioning in persons with severe mental illness: A longitudinal analysis. *Journal of Nervous and Mental Disease, 185*, 419–426.

Mueser, K. T., Becker, D. R., & Wolfe, R. (2001). Supported employment, job preferences, and job tenure and satisfaction. *Journal of Mental Health, 10*, 411–417.

Mueser, K. T., Bellack, A. S., Douglas, M. S., & Wade, J. H. (1991a). Prediction of social skill acquisition in schizophrenic and major affective disorder patients from memory and symptomatology. *Psychiatry Research, 37*, 281–296.

Mueser, K. T., Bellack, A. S., Morrison, R. L., & Wixted, J. T. (1990). Social competence in schizophrenia: Premorbid adjustment, social skill, and domains of functioning. *Journal of Psychiatric Research, 24*, 51–63.

Mueser, K. T., Bennett, M., & Kushner, M. G. (1995). Epidemiology of substance abuse among persons with chronic mental disorders. In A. F. Lehman & L. Dixon (Eds.), *Double jeopardy: Chronic mental illness and substance abuse* (pp. 9–25). New York: Harwood Academic Publishers.

Mueser, K. T., Corrigan, P. W., Hilton, D., Tanzman, B., Schaub, A., Gingerich, S., et al. (2002). Illness management and recovery for severe mental illness: A review of the research. *Psychiatric Services, 53*, 1272–1284.

Mueser, K. T., Crocker, A. G., Frisman, L. B., Drake, R. E., Covell, N. H., & Essock, S. M. (2006). Conduct disorder and antisocial personality disorder in persons with severe psychiatric and substance use disorders. *Schizophrenia Bulletin, 32*, 626–636.

Mueser, K. T., Douglas, M. S., Bellack, A. S., & Morrison, R. L. (1991b). Assessment of enduring deficit and negative symptom subtypes in schizophrenia. *Schizophrenia Bulletin, 17*, 565–582.

Mueser, K. T., Drake, R. E., Ackerson, T. H., Alterman, A. I., Miles, K. M., & Noordsy, D. L. (1997). Antisocial personality disorder, conduct disorder, and substance abuse in schizophrenia. *Journal of Abnormal Psychology, 106*, 473–477.

Mueser, K. T., & Glynn, S. M. (1999). *Behavioral family therapy for psychiatric disorders* (Second ed.). Oakland, CA: New Harbinger.

Mueser, K. T., Goodman, L. A., Trumbetta, S. L., Rosenberg, S. D., Osher, F. C., Vidaver, R., Auciello, P., & Foy, D. W. (1998). Trauma and posttraumatic stress disorder in severe mental illness. *Journal of Consulting and Clinical Psychology, 66*, 493–499.

Mueser, K. T., Meyer, P. S., Penn, D. L., Clancy, R., Clancy, D. M., & Salyers, M. P. (2006). The Illness Management and

Recovery program: Rationale, development, and preliminary findings. *Schizophrenia Bulletin, 32 (Suppl. 1)*, S32-S43.

Mueser, K. T., Nishith, P., Tracy, J. I., DeGirolamo, J., & Molinaro, M. (1995). Expectations and motives for substance use in schizophrenia. *Schizophrenia Bulletin, 21*, 367–378.

Mueser, K. T., & Noordsy, D. L. (2005). Cognitive behavior therapy for psychosis: A call to action. *Clinical Psychology: Science and Practice, 12*, 68–71.

Mueser, K. T., Noordsy, D. L., Drake, R. E., & Fox, L. (2003). *Integrated treatment for dual disorders: A guide to effective practice.* New York: Guilford Press.

Mueser, K. T., Rosenberg, S. D., Drake, R. E., Miles, K. M., Wolford, G., Vidaver, R., & Carrieri, K. (1999). Conduct disorder, antisocial personality disorder, and substance use disorders in schizophrenia and major affective disorders. *Journal of Studies on Alcohol, 60*, 278–284.

Mueser, K. T., Rosenberg, S. D., Goodman, L. A., & Trumbetta, S. L. (2002). Trauma, PTSD, and the course of schizophrenia: An interactive model. *Schizophrenia Research, 53*, 123–143.

Mueser, K. T., Rosenberg, S. D., & Rosenberg, H. J. (2009). *Treatment of posttraumatic stress disorder in special populations: A cognitive restructuring program.* Washington, DC: American Psychological Association.

Mueser, K. T., Rosenberg, S. R., Xie, H., Jankowski, M. K., Bolton, E. E., Lu, W., et al. (2008). A randomized controlled trial of cognitive-behavioral treatment of posttraumatic stress disorder in severe mental illness. *Journal of Consulting and Clinical Psychology, 76*, 259–271.

Mueser, K. T., Salyers, M. P., & Mueser, P. R. (2001). A prospective analysis of work in schizophrenia. *Schizophrenia Bulletin, 27*, 281–296.

Mueser, K. T., Salyers, M. P., Rosenberg, S. D., Goodman, L. A., Essock, S. M., Osher, F. C., et al. (2004). Interpersonal trauma and posttraumatic stress disorder in patients with severe mental illness: Demographic, clinical, and health correlates. *Schizophrenia Bulletin, 30*, 45–57.

Munetz, M. R., Grande, T. P., & Chambers, M. R. (2001). The incarceration of individuals with severe mental disorders. *Community Mental Health Journal, 37*, 361–372.

Murray, C. J. L., & Lopez, A. D. (Eds.). (1996). *The global burden of disease: A comprehensive assessment of mortality and disability from diseases, injuries, and risk factors in 1990 and projected to 2020.* Cambridge, MA: Harvard School of Public Health on behalf of the World Health Organization and the World Bank, Harvard University Press.

Murray, R. M., & Van Os, J. (1998). Predictors of outcome in schizophrenia. *Journal of Clinical Psychopharmacology, 18*, 2S–4S.

National Collaborating Centre for Mental Health. (2009). *Schizophrenia: Core interventions in the treatment and management of schizophrenia in adults in primary and secondary care* (Updated ed. Vol. 82). London: National Institute for Health and Clinical Excellence.

Nelson, H. (1997). *Cognitive behavioural therapy with schizophrenia: A practice manual.* Cheltenham, United Kingdom: Nelson Thornes, Ltd.

Nicholson, J., Sweeney, E. M., & Geller, J. L. (1998). Mothers with mental illness: The competing demands of parenting and living with mental illness. *Psychiatric Services, 49*, 635–642.

Noordsy, D. L., Drake, R. E., Biesanz, J. C., & McHugo, G. J. (1994). Family history of alcoholism in schizophrenia. *Journal of Nervous and Mental Disease, 186*, 651–655.

Norman, C. (2006). The Fountain House movement, an alternative rehabilitation model for people with mental health problems, members' descriptions of what works. *Scandinavian Journal of Caring Sciences, 20*, 184–192.

Norman, R. M. G., Malla, A. K., Manchanda, R., Harricharan, R., Takhar, J., & Northcott, S. (2005). Social support and three-year symptom and admission outcomes for first episode psychosis. *Schizophrenia Research, 80*, 227–234.

Nuechterlein, K. H., & Dawson, M. E. (1984). A heuristic vulnerability/stress model of schizophrenic episodes. *Schizophrenia Bulletin, 10*, 300–312.

Oades, L. G., Deane, F. P., Crowe, T. P., Lambert, W. G., Lloyd, C., & Kavanagh, D. J. (2005). Collaborative recovery: An integrative model for working with individuals that experience chronic or recurring mental illness. *Australasian Psychiatry, 13*, 279–284.

Ödéhn, N., & Goulding, A. (2009). Schizotypy and mental health in the general population: A pilot study. *Personality and Mental Health, 3*, 193–202.

Olfson, M., Mechanic, D., Hansell, S., Boyer, C. A., & Walkup, J. (1999). Prediction of homelessness within three months of discharge among inpatients with schizophrenia. *Psychiatric Services, 50*, 667–673.

Osher, F. C., & Kofoed, L. L. (1989). Treatment of patients with psychiatric and psychoactive substance use disorders. *Hospital and Community Psychiatry, 40*, 1025–1030.

Pack, S. (2009). Poor physical health and mortality in patients with schizophrenia. *Nursing Standards, 23*, 41–45.

Palmer, B. A., Pankratz, V. S., & Bostwick, J. M. (2005). The lifetime risk of suicide in schizophrenia: A reexamination. *Archives of General Psychiatry, 62*, 247–253.

Pantelis, C., Yücel, M., Wood, S. J., Velakoulis, D., Sun, D., Berger, G., et al. (2005). Structural brain imaging evidence for multiple pathological processes at different stages of brain development in schizophrenia. *Schizophrenia Bulletin, 31*, 672–696.

Paul, G. L., & Lentz, R. J. (1977). *Psychosocial treatment of chronic mental patients: Milieu versus social-learning programs.* Cambridge, MA: Harvard University Press.

Pedersen, C. B., & Mortensen, P. B. (2001). Evidence of a dose-response relationship between urbanicity during upbringing and schizophrenia. *Archives of General Psychiatry, 58*, 1036–1046.

Penn, D. L., Corrigan, P. W., Bentall, R. P., Racenstein, J. M., & Newman, L. (1997). Social cognition in schizophrenia. *Psychological Bulletin, 121*, 114–132.

Penn, D. L., Hope, D. A., Spaulding, W., & Kucera, J. (1994). Social anxiety in schizophrenia. *Schizophrenia Research, 11*, 277–284.

Penn, D. L., Roberts, L. J., Munt, E. D., Silverstein, E., Jones, N., & Sheitman, B. (2005). A pilot study of social cognition and interaction training (SCIT) for schizophrenia. *Schizophrenia Research, 80*, 357–359.

Penn, D. L., Waldheter, E. J., Mueser, K. T., Perkins, D. O., & Lieberman, J. A. (2005). Psychosocial treatment for first episode psychosis: A research update. *American Journal of Psychiatry, 162*, 2220–2232.

Perkins, D. O., Gu, H., Boteva, K., & Lieberman, J. A. (2005). Relationship between duration of untreated psychosis and outcome in first-episode schizophrenia: A critical review and meta-analysis. *American Journal of Psychiatry, 162*, 1785–1804.

Peters, R. H., Kearns, W. D., Murrin, M. R., & Dolente, A. S. (1992). Psychopathology and mental health needs among drug-involved inmates. *Journal of Prison and Jail Health, 111,* 3–25.

Petersen, L., Jeppesen, P., Thorup, A., Abel, M. B., Ohlenschlager, J., Christensen, T. O., et al. (2005). A randomized, multi-center trial of integrated versus standard treatment for patients with a first episode of psychotic illness. *British Medical Journal, 331,* 602–609.

Pfammatter, M., Junghan, U. M., & Brenner, H. D. (2006). Efficacy of psychological therapy in schizophrenia: Conclusions from meta-analyses. *Schizophrenia Bulletin, 32, Suppl 1,* S64-S68.

Pitschel-Walz, G., Leucht, S., Bäuml, J., Kissling, W., & Engel, R. R. (2001). The effect of family interventions on relapse and rehospitalization in schizophrenia: A meta-analysis. *Schizophrenia Bulletin, 27,* 73–92.

Polcin, D. L. (1992). Issues in the treatment of dual diagnosis clients who have chronic mental illness. *Professional Psychology: Research and Practice, 23,* 30–37.

Pope, H. G., Jr., & Lipinski, J. (1978). Diagnosis in schizophrenia and manic-depressive illness: A reassessment of the specificity of "schizophrenic" symptoms in the light of current research. *Archives of General Psychiatry, 35,* 811–828.

Pratt, S. I., Mueser, K. T., Driscoll, M., Wolfe, R., & Bartels, S. J. (2006). Medication nonadherence in older people with serious mental illness: Prevalence and correlates. *Psychiatric Rehabilitation Journal, 29,* 299–310.

President's New Freedom Commission on Mental Health. (2003). *Achieving the promise: Transforming mental health care in America: Final report* (DHHS Pub. No. SMA-03-3832). Rockville, MD: Substance Abuse and Mental Health Services Administration.

Prochaska, J. O., & DiClemente, C. C. (1984). *The transtheoretical approach: Crossing the traditional boundaries of therapy.* Homewood, IL: Dow-Jones/Irwin.

Propst, R. N. (1992). Standards for clubhouse programs: Why and how they were developed. *Psychosocial Rehabilitation Journal, 16*(2), 25–30.

Puig, O., Penadés, R., Gastó, C., Catalán, R., Torres, A., & Salamero, M. (2008). Verbal memory, negative symptomatology and prediction of psychosocial functioning in schizophrenia. *Psychiatry Research, 158,* 11–17.

Rabkin, J. (1979). Ethnic density and psychiatric hospitalization: Hazards of minority status. *American Journal of Psychiatry, 136,* 1562–1566.

Racenstein, J. M., Harrow, M., Reed, R., Martin, E., Herbener, E., & Penn, D. L. (2002). The relationship between positive symptoms and instrumental work functioning in schizophrenia: A 10-year follow-up study. *Schizophrenia Research, 56,* 95–103.

Ralph, R. O. (2000). *Review of recovery literature: A synthesis of a sample of recovery literature 2000.* Portland, ME: Edmund S. Muskie Institute of Public Affairs, University of Southern Maine.

Ralph, R. O., Kidder, K., & Phillips, D. (2000). *Can we measure recovery? A compendium of recovery and recovery-related instruments.* Cambridge, MA: The Evaluation Center @ Human Services Research Institute.

Read, J., & Argyle, N. (1999). Hallucinations, delusions, and thought disorder among adult psychiatric inpatients with a history of child abuse. *Psychiatric Services, 58,* 1467–1472.

Read, J., van Os, J., Morrison, A. P., & Ross, C. A. (2005). Childhood trauma, psychosis and schizophrenia: A literature review with theoretical and clinical implications. *Acta Psychiatrica Scandinavica, 112,* 330–350.

Regier, D. A., Farmer, M. E., Rae, D. S., Locke, B. Z., Keith, S. J., Judd, L. L., & Goodwin, F. K. (1990). Comorbidity of mental disorders with alcohol and other drug abuse: Results from the Epidemiologic Catchment Area (ECA) study. *Journal of the American Medical Association, 264,* 2511–2518.

Rice, D. P. (1999). Economic burden of mental disorders in the United States. *Economics of Neuroscience, 1,* 40–44.

Ridgely, M. S., Goldman, H. H., & Willenbring, M. (1990). Barriers to the care of persons with dual diagnoses: Organizational and financing issues. *Schizophrenia Bulletin, 16,* 123–132.

Riecher-Rössler, A., & Häfner, H. (2000). Gender aspects in schizophrenia: Bridging the border between social and biological psychiatry. *Acta Psychiatrica Scandinavica, Suppl. 102,* 58–62.

Roberts, L. J., Shaner, A., & Eckman, T. A. (1999). *Overcoming addictions: Skills training for people with schizophrenia.* New York: W.W. Norton.

Robins, L. N. (1966). *Deviant children grown up.* Huntington, NY: Robert E. Krieger Publishing Company.

Robins, L. N., Tipp, J., & Przybeck, T. R. (1991). Antisocial personality disorder. In L. N. Robins & D. A. Regier (Eds.), *Psychiatric disorders in America: The epidemiologic catchment Area Study* (pp. 258–290). New York: Free Press.

Roder, V., Mueller, D. R., Mueser, K. T., & Brenner, H. D. (2006). Integrated Psychological Therapy (IPT) for schizophrenia: Is it effective? *Schizophrenia Bulletin, 32 (Suppl. 1),* S81-S93.

Roe, D., & Ben-Yishai, A. (1999). Exploring the relationship between the person and the disorder among individuals hospitalized for psychosis. *Psychiatry, 62,* 370–380.

Roe, D., & Chopra, M. (2003). Beyond coping with mental illness: Toward personal growth. *American Journal of Orthopsychiatry, 73*(3), 334–344.

Roe, D., Chopra, M., & Rudnick, A. (2004). Persons with psychosis as active agents interacting with their disorder. *Psychiatric Rehabilitation Journal, 28,* 122–128.

Rog, D. J. (2004). The evidence on supported housing. *Psychiatric Rehabilitation Journal, 27,* 334–344.

Rogers, E. S., Walsh, D., Masotta, L., & Danley, K. (1991). *Massachusetts survey of client preferences for community support services (final report).* Boston, MA: Center for Psychiatric Rehabilitation.

Rosen, A., Mueser, K. T., & Teeson, M. (2007). Assertive community treatment—Issues from scientific and clinical literature with implications for practice. *Journal of Rehabilitation Research & Development, 44,* 813–826.

Rosenberg, S. D., Goodman, L. A., Osher, F. C., Swartz, M., Essock, S. M., Butterfield, M. I., et al. (2001). Prevalence of HIV, hepatitis B and hepatitis C in people with severe mental illness. *American Journal of Public Health, 91,* 31–37.

Rosenberg, S. D., Mueser, K. T., Friedman, M. J., Gorman, P. G., Drake, R. E., Vidaver, R. M., et al. (2001). Developing effective treatments for post-traumatic disorders: A review and proposal. *Psychiatric Services, 52,* 1453–1461.

Rosenberg, S. D., Mueser, K. T., Jankowski, M. K., Salyers, M. P., & Acker, K. (2004). Cognitive-behavioral treatment of posttraumatic stress disorder in severe mental illness: Results of a pilot study. *American Journal of Psychiatric Rehabilitation, 7,* 171–186.

Saha, S., Chant, D., Welham, J., & McGrath, J. (2005). A systematic review of the prevalence of schizophrenia. *PLoS Medicine, 2*(5), e141.

Salyers, M. P., Masterton, T. W., Fekete, D. M., Picone, J. J., & Bond, G. R. (1998). Transferring clients from intensive case management: Impact on client functioning. *American Journal of Orthopsychiatry, 68,* 233–245.

Samnaliev, M., & Clark, R. E. (2008). The economics of schizophrenia. In K. T. Mueser & D. V. Jeste (Eds.), *Clinical handbook of schizophrenia* (pp. 507–515). New York: Guilford Press.

Sands, J. R., & Harrow, M. (1999). Depression during the longitudinal course of schizophrenia. *Schizophrenia Bulletin, 25,* 157–171.

Schatzberg, A. F., Cole, J. O., & DeBattista, C. (2007). *Manual of clinical psychopharmacology, third edition* (6th ed.). Washington, DC: American Psychiatric Publishing Group.

Schonebaum, A. D., Boyd, J. K., & Dudek, K. J. (2006). A comparison of competitive employment outcomes for the clubhouse and PACT models. *Psychiatric Services, 57,* 1416–1420.

Schooler, N. R. (2003). Relapse and rehospitalization: Comparing oral and depot antipsychotics. *Journal of Clinical Psychiatry, 64 (Suppl 16),* 14–17.

Selten, J. P., Slaets, J., & Kahn, R. S. (1997). Schizophrenia in Surinamese and Dutch Antillean immigrants to the Netherlands: Evidence of an increased incidence. *Psychological Medicine, 27,* 807–811.

Shenton, M. E., Dickey, C. C., Frumin, M., & McCarley, R. W. (2001). A review of MRI findings in schizophrenia. *Schizophrenia Research, 49,* 1–52.

Siegel, C., Samuels, J., Tang, D., Berg, I., Jones, K., & Hopper, K. H. (2006). Tenant outcomes in supported housing and community residences in New York City. *Psychiatric Services, 57,* 982–991.

Silverstein, M. L., & Harrow, M. (1978). First rank symptoms in the post acute schizophrenic: A follow-up study. *American Journal of Psychiatry, 135,* 1418–1426.

Silverstein, S. M., & Bellack, A. S. (2008). A scientific agenda for the concept of recovery as it applies to schizophrenia. *Clinical Psychology Review, 28,* 1108–1124.

Silverstein, S. M., Hatashita-Wong, M., Solak, B. A., Uhlhaas, P., Landa, Y., Wilkniss, S.M., et al. (2005). Effectiveness of a two-phase cognitive rehabilitation intervention for severely impaired schizophrenia patients. *Psychological Medicine, 35,* 829–837.

Silverstein, S. M., Schenkel, L. S., Valone, C., & Nuernberger, S. W. (1998). Cognitive deficits and psychiatric rehabilitation outcomes in schizophrenia. *Psychiatric Quarterly, 69,* 169–191.

Silverstein, S. M., Spaulding, W. D., & Menditto, A. A. (2006). *Schizophrenia.* Cambridge, MA: Hogrefe & Huber Publishers.

Smith, T. E., Hull, J. W., Huppert, J. D., Silverstein, S. M., Anthony, D. T., & McClough, J. F. (2004). Insight and recovery from psychosis in chronic schizophrenia and schizoaffective disorder patients. *Journal of Psychiatric Research, 38,* 169–176.

Smith, T. E., Hull, J. W., Romanelli, S., Fertuck, E., & Weiss, K. A. (1999). Symptoms and neurocognition as rate limiters in skills training for psychotic patients. *American Journal of Psychiatry, 156,* 1817–1818.

Sokal, J., Messias, E., Dickerson, F. B., Kreyenbuhl, J., Brown, C. H., Goldberg, R. W., & Dixon, L. B. (2004). Comorbidity of medical illnesses among adults with serious mental illness who are receiving community psychiatric services. *Journal of Nervous and Mental Disease, 192,* 421–427.

Solomon, P., & Draine, J. (1995). The efficacy of a consumer case management team: Two year outcomes of a randomized trial. *The Journal of Mental Health Administration, 22,* 135–146.

Stein, L., & Test, M. (1985). *The training in community living model: A decade of experience* (Vol. 26). San Francisco: Jossey-Bass.

Stein, L. I., & Santos, A. B. (1998). *Assertive community treatment of persons with severe mental illness.* New York: Norton.

Sullivan, P. F., Kendler, K. S., & Neale, M. C. (2003). Schizophrenia is a complex trait: Evidence from a meta-analysis of twin studies. *Archives of General Psychiatry, 60,* 1187–1192.

Susser, E., Struening, E. L., & Conover, S. (1989). Psychiatric problems in homeless men: Lifetime psychosis, substance use, and current distress in new arrivals at New York City shelters. *Archives of General Psychiatry, 46,* 845–850.

Switzer, G. E., Dew, M. A., Thompson, K., Goycoolea, J. M., Derricott, T., & Mullins, S. D. (1999). Posttraumatic stress disorder and service utilization among urban mental health center clients. *Journal of Traumatic Stress, 12,* 25–39.

Tarrier, N., Beckett, R., Harwood, S., Baker, A., Yusupoff, L., & Ugarteburu, I. (1993). A trial of two cognitive behavioural methods of treating drug-resistant residual psychotic symptoms in schizophrenic patients: I. Outcome. *British Journal of Psychiatry, 162,* 524–532.

Tarrier, N., Sharpe, L., Beckett, R., Harwood, S., Baker, A., & Yusupoff, L. (1993). A trial of two cognitive behavioural methods of treating drug-resistant residual psychotic symptoms in schizophrenia patients: II. Treatment-specific changes in coping and problem-solving skills. *Psychiatry and Psychiatric Epidemiology, 28,* 5–10.

Tengström, A., Hodgins, S., Grann, M., Långström, N., & Kullgren, G. (2004). Schizophrenia and criminal offending: The role of psychopathy and substance misuse. *Criminal Justice and Behavior, 31,* 1–25.

Tengström, A., Hodgins, S., & Kullgren, G. (2001). Men with schizophrenia who behave violently: The usefulness of an early versus late starters typology. *Schizophrenia Bulletin, 27,* 205–218.

Teplin, L. A. (1985). The criminality of the mentally ill: A dangerous misconception. *American Journal of Psychiatry, 142,* 593–598.

Teplin, L. A. (1994). Psychiatric and substance abuse disorders among male urban jail detainees. *American Journal of Public Health, 84,* 290–293.

Teplin, L. A., Abram, K. M., & McClelland, G. M. (1996). Prevalence of psychiatric disorders among incarcerated women. I. Pretrial jail detainees. *Archives of General Psychiatry, 53,* 505–512.

Teplin, L. A., McClelland, G. M., Abram, K. M., & Weiner, D. A. (2005). Crime victimization in adults with severe mental illness. *Archives of General Psychiatry, 62,* 911–921.

Terkelsen, K. G. (1983). Schizophrenia and the family: II. Adverse effects of family therapy. *Family Process, 22,* 191–200.

Thornicroft, G., Strathdee, G., Phelan, M., Holloway, F., Wykes, T., Dunn, G., et al. (1998). Rationale and design: PRiSM psychosis study 1. *British Journal of Psychiatry, 173,* 363–370.

Tibbo, P., Kroetsch, M., Chue, P., & Warneke, L. (2000). Obsessive-compulsive disorder in schizophrenia. *Journal of Psychiatric Research, 34,* 139–146.

Torrey, E. F. (1995). Editorial: Jails and prisons: American's new mental hospitals. *American Journal of Public Health*, *85*, 1611–1613.

Torrey, E. F., Bowler, A. E., & Clark, K. (1997). Urban birth and residence as risk factors for psychoses: An analysis of 1880 data. *Schizophrenia Research*, *25*, 169–176.

Torrey, W. C., Mueser, K. T., & Drake, R. E. (2000). Self-esteem as an outcome measure in vocational rehabilitation studies of adults with severe mental illness. *Psychiatric Services*, *51*, 229–233.

Tsemberis, S., Gulcur, L., & Nakae, M. (2004). Housing first, consumer choice, and harm reduction for homeless individuals with a dual diagnosis. *American Journal of Public Health*, *94*, 651–656.

Tsuang, M., & Winokur, G. (1975). The Iowa 500: Field work in a 35-year follow-up of depression, mania and schizophrenia. *Canadian Psychiatric Association Journal*, *20*, 359–365.

Turkington, D., Kingdon, D., & Weiden, P. J. (2006). Cognitive behavior therapy for schizophrenia. *American Journal of Psychiatry*, *163*, 365–373.

Vaillant, G. E. (1964). Prospective prediction of schizophrenia remission. *General Archives of Psychiatry*, *11*, 509–518.

van Haren, N. E., Hulshoff Pol, H. E., Schnack, H. G., Cahn, W., Brans, R., Carati, I., et al. (2008). Progressive brain volume loss in schizophrenia over the course of the illness: Evidence of maturational abnormalities in early adulthood. *Biological Psychiatry*, 106–113.

van Os, J. (2004). Does the urban environment cause psychosis? *British Journal of Psychiatry*, *184*, 287–288.

van Os, J., & Marcelis, M. (1998). The ecogenics of schizophrenia: A review. *Schizophrenia Research*, *32*, 127–135.

Vauth, R., Rüsch, N., Wirtz, M., & Corrigan, P. W. (2004). Does social cognition influence the relation between neurocognitive deficits and vocational functioning in schizophrenia. *Psychiatry Research*, *128*, 155–165.

Velligan, D. I., Bow-Thomas, C. C., Huntzinger, C., Ritch, J., Ledbetter, N., Prihoda, T. J., & Miller, A. L. (2000). Randomized controlled trial of the use of compensatory strategies to enhance adaptive functioning in outpatients with schizophrenia. *American Journal of Psychiatry*, *157*, 1317–1323.

Velligan, D. I., Diamond, P. M., Maples, N. J., Mintz, J., Li, X., Glahn, D. C., & Miller, A. L. (2008). Comparing the efficacy of interventions that use environmental supports to improve outcomes in patients with schizophrenia. *Schizophrenia Research*, *102*, 312–319.

Velligan, D. I., Diamond, P. M., Mintz, J., Maples, N., Li, X., Zeber, J., et al. (2006). The use of individually tailored environmental supports to improve medication adherence and outcomes in schizophrenia. *Schizophrenia Bulletin*, *32*, 483–489.

Velligan, D. I., Mueller, J., Wang, M., Dicocco, M., Diamond, P. M., Maples, N. J., & Davis, B. (2006). Use of environmental supports among patients with schizophrenia. *Psychiatric Services*, *57*, 219–224.

Velligan, D. I., Prihoda, T. J., Ritch, J. L., Maples, N., Bow-Thomas, C. C., & Dassori, A. (2002). A randomized single-blind pilot study of compensatory strategies in schizophrenia outpatients. *Schizophrenia Bulletin*, *28*, 283–292.

Volavka, J. (1999). The effects of clozapine on aggression and substance abuse in schizophrenic patients. *Journal of Clinical Psychology*, *60* (Suppl 12), 43–46.

Warner, R., Girolamo, G., & Bellini, G. (1998). The quality of life of people with schizophrenia in Boulder, Colorado and Bologna, Italy. *Schizophrenia Bulletin*, *24*, 559–568.

Wong, S. E., Terranova, M. D., Bowen, L., Zarate, R., Massel, H. K., & Liberman, R. P. (1987). Providing independent recreational activities to reduce stereotypic vocalizations in chronic schizophrenics. *Journal of Applied Behavior Analysis*, *20*, 77–81.

World Health Organization. (1997). *The composite international diagnostic interview (Version 2, 12 month)*. Geneva: Author.

Wu, E. Q., Birnbaum, H. G., Shi, L., Ball, D. E., Kessler, R. C., & Moulis, M. (2005). The economic burden of schizophrenia in the United States in 2002. *Journal of Clinical Psychiatry*, *66*, 1122–1129.

Wykes, T., Leese, M., Taylor, R., & Phelan, M. (1998). Effects of community services on disability and symptoms: PRiSM psychosis study 4. *British Journal of Psychiatry*, *173*, 385–390.

Wykes, T., & Reeder, C. (2005). *Cognitive remediation therapy for schizophrenia: Theory and practice*. London: Routledge.

Wykes, T., Steel, C., Everitt, B., & Tarrier, N. (2008). Cognitive behavior therapy (CBTp) for schizophrenia: Effect sizes, clinical models and methodological rigor. *Schizophrenia Bulletin*, *34*, 523–537.

Yamada, K., Watanabe, K., Nemoto, N., Fujita, H., Chikaraishi, C., Yamauchi, K., et al. (2006). Prediction of medication non-compliance in outpatients with schizophrenia: 2-year follow-up study. *Psychiatry Research*, *141*, 61–69.

Zammit, S., Allebeck, P., Dalman, C., Lundberg, I., Hemmingson, T., Owen, M. J., & Lewis, G. (2003). Paternal age and risk for schizophrenia. *British Journal of Psychiatry*, *183*, 405–408.

Zammit, S., Allebeck, P., David, A. S., Dalman, C., Hemmingsson, T., Lundberg, I., & Lewis, G. (2004). A longitudinal study of premorbid IQ score and risk of developing schizophrenia, bipolar disorder, severe depression, and other nonaffective psychoses. *Archives of General Psychiatry*, *61*, 354–360.

Zigler, E., & Glick, M. (1986). *A developmental approach to adult psychopathology*. New York: John Wiley & Sons.

Zisook, S., McAdams, L. A., Kuck, J., Harris, M. J., Bailey, A., Patterson, T. L., et al. (1999). Depressive symptoms in schizophrenia. *American Journal of Psychiatry*, *156*, 1736–1743.

Zubin, J., & Spring, B. (1977). Vulnerability: A new view of schizophrenia. *Journal of Abnormal Psychology*, *86*, 103–126.

Zygmunt, A., Olfson, M., Boyer, C. A., & Mechanic, D. (2002). Interventions to improve medication adherence in schizophrenia. *American Journal of Psychiatry*, *159*, 1653–1664.

Disorders of Impulse Control and Self-Harm

Matthew K. Nock, Christine B. Cha, *and* Halina J. Dour

Abstract

Disorders of impulse-control and self-harm are dangerous clinical problems that often present significant challenges for scientists and clinicians. In this chapter, we provide a comprehensive review of each disorder on the impulse-control spectrum. We begin by describing the clinical presentation and epidemiology of each disorder. Next, we discuss what is currently known about the etiology of these disorders, summarizing recent research on genetic/neurobiological factors, environmental factors, and psychological factors that appear to influence these disorders. The assessment and treatment of disorders of impulse-control and self-harm is complicated by the relatively low base-rate of these disorders, as well as by their dangerous and sensitive nature. Nevertheless, several evidence-based approaches to assessment and treatment have been developed and also are reviewed here. We conclude with recommendations for future scientific and clinical efforts aimed at better understanding, predicting, and preventing disorders of impulse-control and self-harm.

Keyword: suicide, self-injury, self-harm, impulse, impulsiveness, impulsivity

Everyone occasionally has an urge to do something that is harmful to himself, herself, or others. These urges may involve striking another person, taking something that does not belong to us, or even hurting oneself. Having an occasional urge, or even acting on such urges on rare occasions, is normal. However, some people have a problem inhibiting their behavior in response to such urges. When such failures of impulse control are severe, persistent, and impairing, they are considered to be a mental disorder. The harmful and potentially embarrassing or illegal nature of many of these behaviors often makes them difficult to study and treat. Fortunately, however, researchers and clinicians have been working to advance the understanding, assessment, and treatment of these challenging behavior problems. This chapter provides a review of what is currently

known about disorders of impulse-control or self-harm.[1]

Descriptive Psychopathology
Definitions, Epidemiology, and Phenomenology

The essential feature of impulse-control disorders (ICDs) is "the failure to resist an impulse, drive, or temptation to perform an act that is harmful to the person or to others" (American Psychiatric Association [APA], 2000, p. 663). In most cases, the behavior

---

[1] Although self-harm is not currently considered a disorder in the DSM, we use the term "disorders" in this chapter to refer to both ICDs and self-harm for ease of presentation.

is preceded by increased aversive arousal (i.e., "tension"), which dissipates following performance of the behavior. However, in many instances, the behavior is followed by the experience of pleasure or gratification, as we discuss in more detail later. The ICDs included in the *Diagnostic and Statistical Manual of Mental Disorders, Fourth Edition, Text Revision* (DSM-IV-TR) and reviewed in this chapter are trichotillomania, pathological gambling, pyromania, kleptomania, and intermittent explosive disorder.

The essential feature of self-harm (a term that includes both suicidal and nonsuicidal self-injury) is the performance of actions that are directly and deliberately harmful to the self. Self-harm is direct in that physical harm occurs without intervening steps (e.g., cutting oneself is direct, whereas cell death due to alcohol consumption is indirect). Such behaviors are deliberate, in that harm to the self is the intended outcome and is not incidental or accidental (e.g., accidentally cutting oneself while cooking). Like ICDs, self-harm can be conceptualized as resulting from a failure to resist an impulse, which in this case is an impulse to hurt oneself. Moreover, self-harm also is most often preceded by aversive arousal and followed by a tension release, and at times is followed by the experience of pleasure or gratification.

Although ICDs and self-harm appear to function quite similarly, they historically have been treated as two completely different classes of behaviors. Impulse-control disorders are included in the DSM-IV-TR, whereas self-harm behaviors are not. Literature on the two classes of behaviors has been fairly distinct and non-overlapping. Despite these historical differences, we propose that the similarities in function and in many other fundamental aspects of these behaviors support the placement of both ICDs and self-harm on a single impulse-control spectrum. We consider issues of classification and potential commonalities in etiology, assessment, and treatment later. However, before doing so, it is important to consider the definitions, epidemiology, and phenomenology of each of these behaviors.

In the following sections, we review each ICD and self-harm behavior and summarize what is known about their epidemiology and phenomenology. All of these disorders are characterized by a failure to control a harmful impulse—the outcome of which falls on a continuum representing "harm to self" on one end and "harm to others" on the other end. We begin by presenting each disorder in the order in which they appear on this continuum, starting with those that are directly harmful to the self (e.g., suicidal behaviors),

followed by those that are indirectly harmful to the self (e.g., pathological gambling) and others (e.g., kleptomania), and ultimately to those that are directly harmful to others (e.g., intermittent explosive disorder). Most important for clinicians and scientists to consider is the defining features, prevalence, average age of onset, course, and associated features (e.g., sex differences) of each disorder. These features are reviewed in detail below and summarized in Table 23.1.

Harm to Self
SUICIDAL BEHAVIORS
Defining Features and Subtypes
The term *suicidal behaviors* refers to a broad class of nonlethal behaviors in which a person directly and deliberately acts in a way intended to end one's own life. Suicidal behaviors can be conceptualized as being on a continuum of severity that begins with thoughts of suicide and ends with death by suicide. *Suicide ideation* refers to thoughts of engaging in behavior intended to end one's own life. Merely having thoughts of death is not considered suicide ideation (although this is sometimes referred to as "passive suicide ideation"). Having a *suicide plan* refers to the formulation of a specific method through which one intends to kill oneself. This involves more than simply thinking about suicide, but means that one has stopped short of actually attempting to kill oneself. A *suicide attempt* refers to potentially self-injurious behavior in which a person has at least some (i.e., nonzero) intent to die. The importance of using these terms clearly and consistently has been written about extensively (O'Carroll et al., 1996; Silverman, Berman, Sanddal, O'Carroll, & Joiner, 2007a, 2007b). Two relatively new terms have been introduced to more carefully characterize and classify behaviors that fall between suicide plans and suicide attempts. *Preparatory acts toward imminent suicidal behavior* refers to instances in which a person has taken steps toward making a suicide attempt but stops himself or herself before the potential harm has begun (Posner, Oquendo, Gould, Stanley, & Davies, 2007). This includes *interrupted suicide attempts,* in which a third party stops the attempt before the injurious behavior is performed, and *aborted suicide attempts,* in which the person stops himself or herself immediately before the injurious behavior is performed (Marzuk, Tardiff, Leon, Portera, & Weiner, 1997; Posner et al., 2007).

Prevalence
Suicidal behaviors are among the leading causes of death worldwide (Nock, Borges, Bromet, Cha,

Table 23.1 Characteristics of impulse control disorders and self-harm

	Definition	Prevalence	Sex difference	Average age of onset	Course
Harmful to self					
Suicidal behaviors	Direct, deliberate, nonlethal acts aimed at killing oneself	SI lifetime 8.0%–24.9% SP lifetime 1.5%–9.4% SA lifetime 1.3%–3.5%	F>M	Adolescence	33.6% SI cases transition to SP 15.4% SI (no SP) transition to SA 56.0% SP cases transition to SA
NSSI behaviors	Direct, deliberate, nonlethal acts of hurting oneself in the absence of intent to die	SG lifetime 1.9% NSSI community adult lifetime 4.0% NSSI community adol., lifetime 13.9%–46.5% NSSI clinical adult lifetime 19.0%–25.0% NSSI clinical adol. lifetime 40.0%–61.2%	F=M	Early Adolescence	Increase of NSSI in adolescence, decrease throughout adulthood
Trichotillomania	Repetitive pulling out of one's own hair resulting in noticeable hair loss	Community sample lifetime 1.0%–3.0% Clinical sample lifetime 3.4%–4.4%	F>M	Early Adolescence	Typically intermittent course, but could persist up to 17–21 years
Gambling	Betting or risking money on a game of chance in excess, leading to moderate (problem) or significant (pathological) distress or impairment	Problem gambling lifetime 2.3%–9.2% Pathological gambling lifetime 0.4%–3.4%	M>F	Gambling problems, Mid 20s; Pathological gambling, Earlier onset	Problem gambling persists on average for 3.6–9.4 years Pathological gamblers practice preferred gambling method on average for 13.0 years
Harmful to others					
Pyromania	Repetitive, deliberate, and purposeful fire-setting in the absence of other motivations (e.g., vengeance, political belief)	Clinical/forensic sample current diagnosis approx. 0%–39.0%	M>F	18.1 years	Course unknown. Fire-setting occurs approximately once every 6 weeks when present
Kleptomania	Repetitive, deliberate stealing, even though items are not needed for personal use or monetary value	General population <1%	F>M	Late adolescence, Early adulthood	Course unknown
IED	Repeated acts of assault and property destruction that are grossly out of proportion to precipitating triggers/events	Less severe IED General population lifetime, 7.3% More severe IED General population lifetime, 5.4% Clinical sample lifetime, 6.2%	M>F (Less severe IED)	14.8–18.3 years	Persists for 6.2–11.8 years

et al., 2008; World Health Organization [WHO], 2008). Suicide is the 14th leading of cause of death worldwide, accounting for 1.5% of all deaths (Nock, Borges, Bromet, Cha, et al., 2008; WHO, 2008). Cross-national mortality data are maintained by the World Health Organization (WHO) and indicate that suicide rates vary significantly across different regions and countries around the world (WHO, 2008). In the United States, suicide is the 11th leading cause of death, the fifth leading cause of years of life lost, and accounts for more deaths than homicides and more than twice as many deaths than HIV/AIDS (Centers for Disease Control [CDC], 2008a; Knox & Caine, 2005; Kung, Hoyert, Xu, & Murphy, 2008; Nock, Borges, Bromet, Cha, et al., 2008).

Nonlethal suicidal behaviors produce less severe outcomes than do suicide, but they occur much more frequently. A recent systematic review of the literature on suicidal behaviors revealed that the lifetime prevalence estimates of suicide ideation (3.1%–56.0%; Interquartile range [IQR]=8.0%–24.9%), plan (0.9%–19.5%; IQR=1.5%–9.4%), and attempt (0.4%–5.1%, IQR=1.3%–3.5%) differ substantially across studies (Nock, Borges, Bromet, Cha, et al., 2008). Part of this variability is likely due to variations in the method through which suicidal behaviors were assessed in each study. Studies requiring actual thoughts of suicide (i.e., rather than merely thoughts of death) to define suicide ideation and actual intent to die (i.e., rather than self-injury performed to communicate with others) to define suicide attempts yield lower estimates of each behavior (Nock & Kessler, 2006). One recent study examined the lifetime prevalence of suicide ideation, plans, and attempts across 17 different countries using the exact same assessment methods (Nock, Borges, Bromet, Alonso, et al., 2008). Substantial cross-national differences in the rates of each suicidal behavior were still observed, but with much less variability than obtained when comparing across prior studies, resulting in lifetime prevalence estimates of 9.2% for suicide ideation, 3.1% for suicide plans, and 2.7% for suicide attempts.

Onset and Course

Suicidal behaviors have been reported in children as young as 4 years of age (Pfeffer, 2001; Tishler, Reiss, & Rhodes, 2007), even though many authors suggest that children younger than 10 years of age are rarely capable of understanding the finality of death (Cuddy-Casey & Orvaschel, 1997; Pfeffer, 1997). Shortly after this point, at the onset of adolescence, the rates of each of the suicidal behaviors described

earlier increase dramatically. For instance, the rate of suicide death increases from 0.01 per 100,000 people per year among those 5–9 years of age to 1.29 in those 10–14 years old, and up to 12.35 among those 20–24 years old (CDC, 2008a). A similarly striking increase during adolescence is seen in the rates of suicide ideation, plans, and attempts (Kessler, Borges, & Walters, 1999; Nock, Borges, Bromet, Alonso, et al., 2008). Overall, adolescence is a time of significantly increased risk, and a major priority for research in this area is to better understand why this increased risk occurs during this particular developmental period.

Only a handful of studies have described the course of suicidal behaviors over time. Existing studies report that approximately 34% of people who experience suicide ideation go on to make a suicide plan, and 56% of those with a suicide plan go on to make an attempt, whereas only 15% of ideators without a plan go on to make an attempt (Nock, Borges, Bromet, Alonso, et al., 2008). Importantly, the majority of transitions from ideation to plan and attempt occur within the first year after the onset of suicide ideation (Nock, Borges, Bromet, Alonso, et al., 2008). Interestingly, the continued experience of suicide ideation in the absence of a suicide plan or attempt is associated with a *decreased* risk of suicide plan and attempt over time (Borges, Angst, Nock, Ruscio, & Kessler, 2008).

Associated Features

Sex- and ethnicity/race-related influences on suicide and suicidal behaviors have been reported consistently across studies. Regarding sex, in virtually every country around the world for which suicide rates are available (with the exception of only China and India), the suicide rate for men significantly exceeds that for women by a ratio of approximately 4:1 (WHO, 2008). In contrast, the rates of suicide ideation, plans, and attempts are 40%–70% higher among women than men (Nock, Borges, Bromet, Alonso, et al., 2008; Weissman et al., 1999). It is generally believed that men die by suicide much more often than women due to men's use of more lethal means for suicide attempts. For instance, in the United States, men are significantly more likely than women to die by suicide using firearms, whereas women overdose on poison at a much higher rate than men—a behavior less likely to have a lethal outcome (CDC, 2008a). The reason for the higher rate of nonlethal suicidal behavior among women is not well understood and represents another important question for future research.

Ethnic/racial influences on suicidal behavior are difficult to study cross-nationally, due to the obvious variability in how ethnicity/race is defined across countries and what groups constitute a minority group in each country. In the United States, 90.5% of those who die by suicide are white, and 71.9% are white men (CDC, 2008a). In contrast, there are no significant ethnic/racial differences in the rates of suicide ideation, plans, or attempts (Kessler, Berglund, Borges, Nock, & Wang, 2005). In addition to sex- and ethnicity/race-related factors, several factors have emerged as consistent predictors of suicidal behaviors, including being younger, less educated, unmarried (i.e., never married, divorced, or widowed), and having a mental disorder (Nock, Borges, Bromet, Alonso, et al., 2008; Nock, Borges, Bromet, Cha, et al., 2008). The presence of a mental disorder is one of the most often-studied correlates of suicidal behaviors, and work in this area has shown that more than 90% of those who die by suicide had a diagnosable mental disorder at the time of their death (Cavanagh, Carson, Sharpe, & Lawrie, 2003). Potential explanations for why mental disorders are associated with ICDs and self-harm are reviewed in greater detail in the section "Influences on ICDs and Self-Harm," later in this chapter.

NONSUICIDAL SELF-INJURY
Defining Features and Subtypes
Nonsuicidal self-injurious thoughts (NSSI) and behaviors can be classified into several distinct categories. A *suicide gesture* is a behavior performed to lead others to believe that one intends to kill oneself when one really has no intention of doing so (Nock & Favazza, 2009; Nock & Kessler, 2006). These behaviors occur in approximately 2% of the general population (Nock & Kessler, 2006). The term "suicide gesture" was originally used to describe behaviors in which soldiers self-inflicted injuries in order to escape from active military duty (Fisch, 1954; Tucker & Gorman, 1967), and as a result this term carries a negative connotation among some clinicians and researchers. *Nonsuicidal self-injurious thoughts* refer to episodes in which people consider engaging in NSSI, serving as a parallel to suicide ideation but in this case lacking any intent to die. *Nonsuicidal self-injury* refers to the deliberate destruction of one's own body tissue in the absence of any intent to die. The most common forms of NSSI include cutting (i.e., most often with a razor, knife, or other sharp object), burning, inserting objects under the skin, and scratching oneself until bleeding occurs.

Although researchers and clinicians agree on this definition of NSSI, and most use these terms, some use different terms to describe this behavior, including self-mutilation, deliberate self-harm, and parasuicide. Notably, some researchers also use the last two terms to refer to self-injury more generally, regardless of whether the person has intent to die from their behavior. Given evidence that self-injury performed with intent to die is associated with more lethal injury (Beck, Beck, & Kovacs, 1975; Brown, Henriques, Sosdjan, & Beck, 2004) and with a greater likelihood of subsequent death (Harriss & Hawton, 2005; Lonnqvist & Ostamo, 1991; Ostamo et al., 1991), it is wise to distinguish between suicidal self-injury and NSSI. The following paragraphs review what is currently known about NSSI, given that this is the most injurious and concerning of these three behaviors and the one for which most research is available.

Prevalence
As with suicidal behaviors, estimates of the rate of NSSI in the general population vary markedly across studies due to inconsistencies in the definitions and measurement methods used. In addition, because research on NSSI is relatively new, questions on NSSI have not been included in the large epidemiological studies that provide prevalence estimates for most mental disorders, such as the National Comorbidity Surveys (Kessler, Berglund, Demler, Jin, Merikangas, & Walters, 2005; Nock & Kessler, 2006) and the Epidemiologic Catchment Area Survey (Bourdon, Rae, Locke, Narrow, & Regier, 1992). These limitations notwithstanding, available studies suggest that 4% of adults (Briere & Gil, 1998; Klonsky, Oltmanns, & Turkheimer, 2003) and 13%–46% of adolescents (Lloyd-Richardson, Perrine, Dierker, & Kelley, 2007; Ross & Heath, 2002) in the community engage in NSSI at some point in their lifetime. The higher rates of NSSI among adolescents suggest that the rate of NSSI may be increasing, a fact also suggested by data from the Centers for Disease Control (CDC) on the increasing rate of nonfatal self-injury (although these figures include suicide attempts) (CDC, 2008b), or may reflect reporting biases among adults who deny their history of NSSI, or both. The rate of NSSI among clinical samples is much higher among both adults (outpatient rate=25%; inpatient rate=19%; combined=21%) (Briere & Gil, 1998) and adolescents (inpatient rate=40%–61%) (Darche, 1990; DiClemente, Ponton, & Hartley, 1991).

Onset and Course

Nonsuicidal self-injurious behavior typically has its onset during early adolescence (Jacobson & Gould, 2007; Nock & Prinstein, 2004), but it is important to note that this behavior has been reported to occur in 7%–8% of preadolescents in the community (Hilt, Nock, Lloyd-Richardson, & Prinstein, 2008). Little is known about the course of NSSI due to the absence of long-term longitudinal studies; however, studies on NSSI across age groups suggest that the rates of NSSI show an increase in adolescence and young adulthood, followed by a steady decline throughout later adulthood.

Associated Features

Nonsuicidal self-injurious behavior appears to occur at equal rates across different groups regardless of sex, ethnicity, or socioeconomic status (Hilt et al., 2008; Jacobson & Gould, 2007; Nock, Joiner, Gordon, Lloyd-Richardson, & Prinstein, 2006). People engaging in NSSI have significantly stronger family histories of suicide ideation, violence, and drug and alcohol abuse, but do not have higher rates of psychopathology more generally, thus suggesting that what may be transmitted within the family is a tendency to engage in impulsive aggression (Deliberto & Nock, 2008). Most people engaging in NSSI themselves meet criteria for a current mental disorder (87.6%), including internalizing disorders (51.7%), externalizing disorders (62.9%), substance use disorders (59.6%), and personality disorders (67.3%) (Nock et al., 2006). Self-injurers also are at significantly increased risk of suicidal behavior, as evidenced by the fact that 70% of self-injurious adolescents report at least one suicide attempt, and 55% report making multiple suicide attempts (Nock et al., 2006).

TRICHOTILLOMANIA

Defining Features and Subtypes

Trichotillomania, the first behavior reviewed in this chapter that is formally classified as an ICD in DSM-IV-TR, refers to the repetitive pulling out of one's own hair, resulting in noticeable hair loss. According to the DSM, trichotillomania also is characterized by the experience of increased tension immediately prior to episodes of hair-pulling, as well as relief or pleasure following hair-pulling. Consistent with all mental disorders, this behavior must be associated with significant distress or impairment in social, occupational, or other important areas, and the behavior cannot be better

explained by some other mental or medical disorder (APA, 2000).

The form and function of trichotillomania are quite similar to NSSI, and in fact, many researchers include hair-pulling in their definition of NSSI. However, the build-up and release of anxiety and tension involved in trichotillomania have led some to argue that it would be more appropriately classified on an anxiety or obsessive-compulsive spectrum (Swedo & Rapoport, 1991). Others have argued against such a move given that (a) trichotillomania is not characterized by the persistent and intrusive thoughts that occur in obsessive-compulsive disorder, (b) those with trichotillomania are more focused on the topography of their behavior than on mitigating their anxious thoughts, and (c) obsessive-compulsive behaviors are rarely if ever described as gratifying, as is often the case in trichotillomania (Franklin, Tolin, & Diefenbach, 2006; Grant, Odlaug, & Potenza, 2007). It also has been suggested that trichotillomania would be better classified on a spectrum of "unwanted repetitive species-typical behaviors," which, in the case of trichotillomania, consists of pathological grooming behaviors (Swedo & Rapoport, 1991). However, researchers specializing in the study of ICDs argue that trichotillomania should remain on the impulse-control spectrum, given its similarity to other behaviors on this spectrum in terms of characteristics and treatment response (Grant, Odlaug, & Potenza, 2007).

Disagreements about where to classify trichotillomania notwithstanding, research studies have provided a consistent clinical description of this behavior. Hair-pulling in trichotillomania most often occurs on the scalp, eyebrows, and eyelashes, but can occur anywhere on the body on which hair grows (Reeve, Bernstein, & Christenson, 1992; Stanley, Borden, Bell, & Wagner, 1994). Most people with trichotillomania (64%–93%) report pulling hair from more than one place on their body (Christenson, Mackenzie, & Mitchell, 1991; du Toit, van Kradenburg, Niehaus, & Stein, 2001), and the average number of pulling episodes reported ranges from 15 to 36 episodes per week (Christenson, Mackenzie, & Mitchell, 1991, 1994). Hair-pulling occurs most often following the experience of negative affect but also can occur in the context of positive affect a smaller percentage of the time (du Toit et al., 2001). Interestingly though, approximately 17%–36% of those who display chronic hair-pulling do not report the tension release or gratification thought to be diagnostic of trichotillomania

(Christenson, Mackenzie, & Mitchell, 1991, 1994). Complicating reports of the experience of trichotillomania is the fact that hair-pulling episodes often are classified into two subtypes, one of which involves hair-pulling as a deliberate response to negative affect (i.e., "focused pulling"), and the other of which involves hair-pulling outside of conscious awareness (i.e., "automatic pulling") (Flessner et al., 2008; O'Sullivan et al., 1997). The fact that automatic pulling occurs outside of awareness during times of sedentary activities requiring focused attention (e.g., television watching, reading) introduces obvious problems with relying on self-report to determine the factors that influence this behavior.

People with trichotillomania typically report experiencing little or no pain during hair-pulling, suggesting that there often are not immediate negative consequences for this behavior (Christenson, Mackenzie, & Mitchell, 1991). However, this behavior often leads to impairments in social and occupational functioning (e.g., du Toit et al., 2001; Franklin et al., 2006) in the form of shame, embarrassment, and attempts to conceal excessive hair loss (Christenson, Mackenzie, & Mitchell, 1991; du Toit et al., 2001). Despite this distress and impairment, as many as 40% of people with trichotillomania go undiagnosed, and 58% never receive treatment for this condition (Lejoyeux, McLoughlin, & Ades, 2000).

Prevalence
Studies of community and college student samples suggest that 1%–3% of people meet criteria for trichotillomania at some point in their lifetime (Christenson, Pyle, & Mitchell, 1991; King, Zohar, et al., 1995), with a slightly higher rate of 3.4%–4.4% obtained in inpatient psychiatric samples (Grant, Levine, Kim, & Potenza, 2005).

Onset and Course
Trichotillomania typically has its onset at 12–15 years of age (Christenson et al., 1994); however, an early-onset subgroup has been described in several studies with a mean age of onset of 6–9 years (King, Scahill, et al., 1995; Reeve et al., 1992). Once begun, trichotillomania typically persists for 17–21 years (Christenson, Mackenzie, Mitchell, & Callies, 1991; du Toit et al., 2001), with an intermittent course in which symptoms wax and wane over time (Christenson et al., 1994; King, Scahill, et al., 1995).

Associated Features
Trichotillomania typically is reported at higher rates among women than among men (Christenson,

Pyle, et al., 1991; du Toit et al., 2001). However, this difference may be partially explained by an unwillingness to report this potentially embarrassing behavior and by the increased likelihood that men can attribute the hair loss to male pattern baldness (Christenson, Mackenzie, & Mitchell, 1991). Interestingly, trichotillomania is associated with increased rates of "pathological grooming behaviors" (e.g., nail biting, skin picking) and anxiety disorders (especially obsessive-compulsive disorder) among first-degree relatives (Lenane et al., 1992; Swedo & Leonard, 1992).

PATHOLOGICAL GAMBLING
Defining Features and Subtypes
Gambling, which refers to betting or risking money on a game of chance, is not pathological and, when performed in moderation, is referred to as *social gambling* or *recreational gambling*. Researchers and clinicians use the term *problem gambling* to denote a pattern of gambling behavior that leads to some moderate (i.e., subclinical) level of distress and functional impairment. *Pathological gambling,* by contrast, refers to a persistent and maladaptive pattern of gambling behavior resulting in significant distress and impairment (APA, 2000). Essential features of pathological gambling include preoccupations with gambling, the need to risk increased amounts of money to achieve the desired level of excitement, repeated unsuccessful attempts to control one's gambling, chasing behavior (i.e., following up losses with more gambling in an attempt to get even), and engagement in deceitful and/or illegal activities in an effort to continue and finance one's gambling (APA, 2000). These thoughts and behaviors should not be better accounted for by another psychiatric disorder (e.g., manic episode). The impairment experienced as a result of this behavior often includes the loss of important relationships, jobs, and finances (e.g., bankruptcy) (Lesieur, 1984, 1998; W. N. Thompson, Gazel, & Rickman, 1996). Other terms, such as *disordered gambling* (Shaffer, Hall, & Vanderbilt, 1999) and *compulsive gambling* (Jacobs et al., 1989) have been used in the literature but generally have been discouraged in favor of "problem gambling" and "pathological gambling" (Moran, 1970). The most common forms of gambling reported include games played at casinos, lotteries, on- and off-track betting on horse-racing, and Internet gambling (Potenza, Kosten, & Rounsaville, 2001).

Prevalence
Approximately 80% of people in the U.S. general population report engaging in social/recreational

gambling at some point in their lifetime (Kessler et al., 2008). Rates of lifetime problem gambling (2.3%–9.2%) (Cunningham-Williams, Cottler, Compton, & Spitznagel, 1998; Kessler et al., 2008) and pathological gambling (0.4%–3.4%) (APA, 2000; Kessler et al., 2008; Shaffer et al., 1999) are much lower, but indicate that these are problems that occur in a significant number of people. Studies of adolescent (Shaffer et al., 1999) and clinical samples (Grant et al., 2005; Hall et al., 2000) suggest that the rates are even higher in these populations. In addition, the prevalence of pathological gambling appears to be increasing, perhaps due to greater social acceptability and accessibility of gambling in today's society (Petry & Armentano, 1999; Shaffer et al., 1999).

Onset and Course
Gambling problems typically begin in adolescence and early adulthood. A recent nationally representative survey of U.S. residents revealed that gambling problems typically begin during the mid-20s (Kessler et al., 2008). Age of onset is typically earlier for those who eventually develop pathological gambling, and for men (Kessler et al., 2008; Welte, Barnes, Tidwell, & Hoffman, 2008). Pathological gamblers report that they practice their preferred gambling method for an average of 13.0 years (Maccallum & Blaszczynski, 2003), but problems with gambling only persist for 3.6–9.4 years on average (Kessler et al., 2008; Maccallum & Blaszczynski, 2003).

Associated Features
Pathological gambling occurs at higher rates among men; adolescents and young adults; those who are divorced, separated, or widowed; and non-Hispanic African Americans (Kessler et al., 2008; Petry, Stinson, & Grant, 2005; Shaffer et al., 1999; Welte et al., 2008). Family and twin studies have suggested that gambling problems are transmitted across generations. For instance, 23% of pathological gamblers report that one or both parents are problem gamblers (Black & Moyer, 1998), and adolescents who report that their parents have problems with gambling display significantly higher levels of gambling (and other problems such as drinking, smoking, drug use, and over-eating) (Jacobs et al., 1989). Twin studies have demonstrated that these effects are not merely due to shared environment, as the risk of pathological gambling has been shown to be higher among monozygotic twins than among dizygotic twins, in men with problem gambling (Slutske et al., 2000).

Harm to Others
PYROMANIA
Defining Features and Subtypes
Pyromania refers to a persistent pattern of behavior in which a person deliberately and purposely sets fires (APA, 2000). As in the case of other ICDs, the person often experiences tension or affective arousal before the behavior and a sense of relief or pleasure following the behavior. Fire-setting motivated by criminal activity (i.e., arson, insurance fraud), political beliefs, or vengeance for a perceived wrong is not considered to be pyromania. Also excluded from the diagnosis of pyromania are instances of fire-setting in response to command hallucinations or in the context of conduct disorder or antisocial personality disorder. People diagnosed with pyromania often have a fascination or preoccupation with fire and fire-related objects and activities (e.g., matches, fire alarms), which leads many such people to regularly watch neighborhood fires they did not start or even to seek employment with the fire department (Lejoyeux, McLoughlin, & Ades, 2006). There are no accepted subtypes of pyromania. Some have proposed a classification system for pyromania based on the motives of the behavior (Prins, Tennent, & Trick, 1985); however, this system conflicts with the DSM-IV-TR requirement that pyromania must not be motivated by criminal or financial factors (APA, 2000).

Prevalence
The prevalence of pyromania in the general population is not known. Indeed, in the section on prevalence, the DSM-IV-TR states only that "pyromania is apparently rare" (APA, 2000, p. 670). There are no available data on pyromania from epidemiological studies, and studies carried out in clinical and forensic adult samples (e.g., those charged with arson) report rates ranging from 0% to 39% depending on the sample assessed (Grant et al., 2005; Koson & Dvoskin, 1982; Lewis & Yarnell, 1951). In addition to differences in sample selection, the definition used for pyromania (if not the formal diagnosis) likely contributes to this wide range of reported rates. For instance, Kolko and Kazdin (1988) reported that in a child and adolescent sample, 52.4% of their sample reported recurrent fire-setting, but only 9.1% led to serious enough consequences that fire fighters were called. Therefore, rates will vary widely depending on how one defines the behavior.

Onset and Course
The average age of onset for pyromania is 18.1 years (Grant & Kim, 2007), although fire-setting behavior

has been reported in children and young adolescents (Kolko & Kazdin, 1988). Studies of clinical samples diagnosed with pyromania reveal that fire-setting episodes occur approximately once every 6 weeks (Grant & Kim, 2007). The course or duration of pyromania is not known, although rates of recidivism for fire-setting have been reported to range between 4.5% and 28%.

Associated Features
As with prevalence, little is known about the associated features of pyromania. It has been suggested that pyromania occurs significantly more frequently among males than females (Lejoyeux et al., 2006), and that even when compared to clinical and forensic samples, those who engage in fire-setting are characterized by a history of more aggressive and antisocial behavior (Coid, Wilkins, & Coid, 1999; Kolko & Kazdin, 1991). Moreover, aggressive fire-setting also has been reported as a risk factor for future covert antisocial behavior, violence, and social problems (Del Bove, Caprara, Pastorelli, & Paciello, 2008).

KLEPTOMANIA
Defining Features and Subtypes
The defining feature of kleptomania is the recurrent failure to resist the urge to steal, even though the items are not needed for personal use or monetary value (APA, 2000). It is this lack of need for the stolen items that distinguishes kleptomania from nonpathological stealing or shoplifting. Consistent with other ICDs, this behavior is preceded by increased tension, followed by a tension release or feeling of pleasure, and is not performed due to financial need, vengeance, or in the context of another psychiatric disorder (e.g., not in response to command hallucinations or in the context of a manic episode). Most people with kleptomania report specific triggers for their urges to steal (e.g., stress), and the majority (68%) report intense shame or guilt following their behavior, suggesting that kleptomania is distressing (Grant & Kim, 2002a; Grant & Potenza, 2008).

Prevalence
The prevalence of kleptomania is not currently known. Most researchers who study this behavior suggest that it is relatively rare, occurring in less than 1% of the general population (Goldman, 1991; Grant, 2006).

Onset and Course
The average age of onset of kleptomania appears to be during late adolescence and early adulthood (Grant & Kim, 2002a; McElroy, Hudson, Pope, &

Keck, 1991), although onset has been reported after age 70 (McNeilly & Burke, 1998). People with kleptomania report an average duration of the disorder of 16–20 years and indicate that they steal an average of one or two times per week (Grant, 2004; Grant, Odlaug, & Wozniak, 2007; McElroy, Hudson, et al., 1991). Most of those diagnosed with kleptomania interviewed in research studies report that their stealing has resulted in arrest or incarceration at some point (e.g., Grant, Correia, & Brennan-Krohn, 2006); however, two-thirds of those arrested reported that their stealing persisted following the arrest(s) (McElroy, Pope, Hudson, Keck, & White, 1991).

Associated Features
Kleptomania occurs more frequently among women than men by a ratio of up to 3:1 (e.g., McElroy, Hudson, et al., 1991). No consistent age or racial/ethnic differences have been observed among people diagnosed with kleptomania. Although there is no evidence for a family or genetic basis for kleptomania itself, people diagnosed with kleptomania do report a higher rate of mental disorders among their first-degree relatives, especially other impulse-control problems like alcohol and substance use, as well as mood disorders (Dannon, Lowengrub, Iancu, & Kotler, 2004; Grant & Kim, 2002a).

INTERMITTENT EXPLOSIVE DISORDER
Defining Features and Subtypes
The defining feature of intermittent explosive disorder (IED) is the occurrence of repeated episodes of assault and property destruction that are grossly out of proportion to the precipitating triggers or events (APA, 2000). A diagnosis of IED also requires that these impulsive aggressive episodes are not better accounted for by another disorder, such as bipolar disorder, psychotic disorder, or conduct disorder. The key features of IED are that the aggressive behavior is both repetitive and unplanned. The anger and impulsive aggression that occurs in IED typically is brief (<30 minutes in duration) (Coccaro, 2003) and most often involves interpersonal violence (approximately 70% of the time) or threats of violence (approximately 15%–20% of the time) (Kessler et al., 2006)

Research on IED has been hampered by the fact that it was not included in the DSM until DSM-III (APA, 1980), and also because the criteria changed in both DSM-III-R (APA, 1987) and DSM-IV (APA, 1994). To help advance the scientific study of IED, research criteria for IED have been proposed that provide more specific criteria than those appearing in the current version of the DSM (APA, 2000). These research criteria also have undergone slight changes and were first presented as the research criteria for IED, Revised (IED-R) (Coccaro, Kavoussi, Berman, & Lish, 1998) and subsequently as the integrated research criteria for IED (IED-IR) (Coccaro, Schmidt, Samuels, & Nestadt, 2004; McCloskey, Berman, Noblett, & Coccaro, 2006). These integrated research criteria specify that diagnosing IED requires either verbal or physical aggression twice weekly, on average, for a period of 1 month or three episodes of physical assault or property destruction over 1 year (Coccaro & Danehy, 2006). They also state explicitly that the behavior cannot be premeditated and is not performed for tangible benefit (e.g., money, vengeance).

Prevalence

Prevalence estimates for IED differ slightly depending on which criteria are used. Using the DSM-IV criteria and requiring three lifetime IED episodes and one in the past 12 months yields an estimate of 7.3% for lifetime IED and 3.9% for the past 12 months (Kessler et al., 2006). When the more stringent criteria (i.e., three attacks in a 12-month period) are used, the prevalence estimates drop slightly to 5.4% lifetime and 2.7% for the past 12 months (Kessler et al., 2006). Rates of IED are approximately the same among clinical samples, with prior studies suggesting that 6.9% of psychiatric outpatients meet DSM-IV criteria for lifetime IED and 6.4% for current IED (e.g., Grant et al., 2005).

Onset and Course

Intermittent explosive disorder has an average age of onset of 14.8–18.3 years (Coccaro et al., 2004; Kessler et al., 2006). When present, IED persists for an average of 6.2–11.8 years (Kessler et al., 2006); however, the impulsive aggressive behaviors associated with IED reportedly occur throughout the lifespan, peaking in the fourth decade and decreasing over time from age 50 and beyond (Coccaro, Posternak, & Zimmerman, 2005; Coccaro et al., 2004). The average number of aggressive episodes in which a person with IED engages throughout his or her lifetime varies significantly depending on how IED is defined and ranges from 56 episodes for narrowly defined IED to seven episodes when a broader definition is used (Kessler et al., 2006).

Associated Features

More men than women are diagnosed with IED by a ratio of up to 3:1 (Coccaro, 2003); however, this difference appears to only be present when a broad definition of IED is used (i.e., requiring less frequent impulsive aggressive episodes) (Kessler et al., 2006). Those with lower levels of education and income are at increased risk of IED (Coccaro et al., 2005; Kessler et al., 2006), and these differences help to explain the relation sometimes observed between racial/ethnic minority status and IED (Coccaro et al., 2005). There appears to be familial transmission of IED, as approximately one-third of first-degree relatives of those with IED also have this disorder (McElroy, Soutullo, Beckman, Taylor, & Keck, 1998), and this increased likelihood of IED within families appears to be independent of comorbid diagnoses (see Coccaro, 2003).

Conceptualizing Impulse-Control Disorders and Self-Harm

Are These Behaviors "Mental Disorders?"

All of the behaviors reviewed in the previous section are clearly problematic, given that they result in harm to oneself or to others; however, should a failure to control one's behavioral impulses be considered a mental disorder? The answer to this question is not straightforward, given that no consensus yet exists about how the concept of mental disorder is best defined. The DSM-IV-TR defines a mental disorder as "a clinically significant behavioral or psychological syndrome or pattern that occurs in an individual and that is associated with present distress (e.g., a painful symptom) or disability (i.e., impairment in one or more important areas of functioning) or with a significantly increased risk of suffering, death, pain, disability, or important loss of freedom" (APA, 2000, p. xxxi). By this definition, behaviors that are harmful to the self, such as NSSI and trichotillomania would seem to clearly qualify as mental disorders. But what about behaviors characterized by harm to others, such as fire-setting (i.e., pyromania) or anger attacks (i.e., IED)? Questions about whether behaviors that involve harming others should be classified as mental disorders have been raised for many years, as captured in the frequent distinction that is raised between "the mad" versus "the bad" (Tucker, 1999). The approach of the DSM has been to not classify isolated acts of violence or self-harm as mental disorders, but instead to include only deliberate, repetitive, and unplanned aggressive behaviors that are grossly out of proportion to precipitating triggers.

Beyond the DSM-IV-TR, scholars have proposed definitions for what constitutes a mental disorder. One of the most widely discussed conceptualizations in the literature is the Harmful Dysfunction model proposed by Wakefield (1992, 1997). This model of mental disorders proposes that mental disorders require the presence of behaviors that have negative consequences for the individual as defined by socio-cultural standards (i.e., are harmful) and also by the failure of some internal mechanism to perform the function for which it was designed (i.e., are dysfunctional). This model makes sense intuitively; however, several concerns have been raised, such as the fact that the natural function of most behaviors is not clearly known, thus making it difficult to ascertain when a dysfunction has occurred (e.g., Houts, 2001; McNally, 2001). So, although an interesting and useful approach, the Harmful Dysfunction model leaves many questions unanswered and does not help to clearly define and classify most of the mental disorders currently included in the DSM-IV-TR.

An alternative approach to conceptualizing mental disorders has been proposed by McHugh (1992), who suggests that it is wise to consider several different perspectives on what it means to have a mental disorder. Such an approach suggests that no single definition or model exists for what it means to have a mental disorder, thus acknowledging the heterogeneity of disorders and the multiple influences on each disorder (i.e., not all disorders are caused solely by dysfunction of some internal mechanism). McHugh proposes four perspectives from which to view mental disorders. A *disease perspective* uses categorical logic (i.e., either you have it or you do not), and suggests that mental disorders are caused by some identifiable biological abnormality. Disorders best conceptualized from this perspective include schizophrenia, autism, and bipolar disorder. A *behavior perspective* uses the logic of teleology (i.e., consideration of the purpose or function of behavior), and suggests that mental disorders can occur when goal-directed behaviors that we all display are performed in excess (e.g., eating, drinking, aggression) or when our behavior is driven by abnormal goals (e.g., drug use). The final two perspectives described by McHugh (1992) are the *dimensional perspective*, which suggests mental disorders can represent an extreme position on a continuum of some common traits (e.g., personality disorders), and a *life-story perspective*, which suggests that past events in one's life can lead to the experience of subjective distress (e.g., post-traumatic stress disorder).

The disorders described in this chapter fit most closely with the *behavior perspective* of mental disorders described earlier. Each of these ICDs and self-harm behaviors involve performing a behavior in the service of achieving some purposeful goal, such as the relief of aversive arousal/tension, or the experience of pleasure or gratification, but they are considered pathological because they do so using behavior that is harmful to the self or others. Other mental disorders characterized by excessive engagement in otherwise normative behaviors, such as disorders of eating (e.g., anorexia, bulimia), drinking (e.g., alcohol use disorders), and drug use (i.e., substance use disorders) also are best conceptualized from this perspective. In fact, this may help to explain why ICDs, self-harm behaviors, and other behavior disorders, such as those related to eating, drinking, and drug use, have high rates of comorbidity (Beautrais et al., 1996; Hilt et al., 2008; Kessler et al., 1999). It may be that these behaviors all serve very similar functions (e.g., escape from aversive arousal, experience of pleasure or gratification) and etiological pathways (e.g., similar genetic/neurobiological influences) and differ only in the form of the behavior selected to achieve that function. Although one could conceptualize these disorders as sharing this commonality, some authors have proposed that there are important differences among these ICDs and self-harm behaviors, with some defined by their impulsiveness, others by their compulsiveness, and yet others by their addictive nature.

Clarifying the Nature of ICDs: Impulsiveness, Compulsiveness, and Addiction

The notion of an ICD spectrum in general and the placement of specific disorders on this spectrum in specific cases have been challenged over the years. One reason for this is that the disorders currently appearing on the ICD spectrum differ markedly in the form of the key behavior involved (e.g., fire-setting, stealing, hair-pulling, gambling). These differences have led some researchers and clinicians to suggest that several disorders currently classified on the ICD spectrum are not best conceptualized as representing problems with impulse-control, but would be more appropriately placed on another spectrum, such as that of compulsive disorders, addictive disorders, or even affective disorders. In this section, we briefly describe and attempt to synthesize these different perspectives.

In considering how the ICD spectrum should be defined and composed, it is most important to have a clear understanding of what it means to be impulsive. Although impulsiveness is a commonly used term, it is one for which there is a surprising lack of clarity and consistency in the definitions used by researchers and clinicians. Recent studies suggest that there are distinct dimensions of impulsiveness, such as *behavioral disinhibition, risky decision-making*, and *delay discounting* (Janis & Nock, 2009; Moeller, Barratt, Dougherty, Schmitz, & Swann, 2001; White et al., 1994). Behavioral disinhibition, sometimes referred to as behavioral impulsiveness, refers to a failure to inhibit an initiated response (e.g., failure to stop oneself from acting on an urge). Risky decision-making, sometimes referred to as cognitive impulsiveness, refers to making decisions that discount risk and increase the likelihood of negative consequences (e.g., choosing the riskiest of several alternatives). Delay discounting refers to a preference for smaller immediate rewards over larger later rewards (e.g., such as choosing to receive a small amount of money now rather than a larger amount of money later). Although risky decision-making and delay discounting are characteristic of some of the ICDs, it is the first dimension of behavioral disinhibition that is the central feature of each of the ICDs reviewed here. The differences in the form of the ICDs notwithstanding, they all involve a repeated failure to inhibit the urge to engage in a behavior that is harmful to oneself or to others and thus are appropriately classified together on the ICD spectrum.

Given that ICDs are characterized by a failure of behavioral inhibition, this raises the question of whether there also is consistency in the nature of the impulses experienced across different ICDs. As described in the preceding section, the behaviors performed in each ICD most commonly serve two functions: they lead to escape from, or decrease of, aversive arousal/tension (i.e., negative reinforcement); and they lead to a feeling of pleasure or gratification (i.e., positive reinforcement). Both of these processes appear among the DSM-IV-TR criteria for ICDs and have been implicated in the occurrence of self-harm (e.g., Nock & Prinstein, 2004, 2005) and therefore are considered central to these disorders. However, problems controlling behavioral impulses expected to help escape aversive affective or cognitive states, or to generate pleasurable states, also are characteristic of anxiety disorders and addictive disorders, respectively. This has led to debates about how best to conceptualize and classify ICDs and these related disorders.

Compulsions are "repetitive behaviors ... or mental acts ... the goal of which is to prevent or reduce anxiety or distress, not to provide pleasure or gratification" (APA, 2000, p. 457). The specific function that these behaviors play in reducing anxiety and distress has led some to argue that trichotillomania (Swedo, 1993; Swedo & Rapoport, 1991), pathological gambling (Decaria & Hollander, 1993), kleptomania (Dannon, 2002), and perhaps ICDs in general (McElroy, Phillips, & Keck, 1994) would be best conceptualized as obsessive-compulsive spectrum disorders. This argument has received further support from studies reporting common biological mechanisms between ICDs (e.g., trichotillomania) and obsessive-compulsive disorders (du Toit et al., 2001). However, ICDs are distinct from anxiety-related compulsions in that the former often are performed to obtain pleasure or gratification, which argues against placing ICDs and self-harm on the obsessive-compulsive spectrum.

Addiction has been defined as "compulsive drug use despite negative consequences" (Hyman, 2005, p. 1414) (although here the word "compulsive" means that a person is compelled to act on his or her urges). Addictive behaviors are most often performed in an effort to elevate one's mood. Similarly, kleptomania, pyromania, pathological gambling, and trichotillomania are characterized by attempts to obtain pleasure or gratification as a result of performing the behavior (APA, 2000). In addition, like ICDs and self-harm, addictive behaviors often are performed to decrease aversive states (e.g., drug-use in order to decrease the aversive symptoms of withdrawal). These similarities have led some to argue that ICDs and self-harm should be conceptualized as addictive disorders (Franklin et al., 2006; Grant & Potenza, 2006). Although there is clear overlap among addiction and ICDs/self-harm, they are distinct in that the former is driven primarily via dysregulation of the reward pathway and is characterized by the presence of tolerance and withdrawal, which do not appear to play a large role in ICDs or self-harm.

Finally, some researchers have proposed that disorders traditionally classified as compulsive or addictive behaviors should instead be classified within the ICD spectrum. For example, although currently conceptualized as compulsive disorders (APA, 1994), pedophilia and other forms of paraphilia have been described as ego syntonic and overlapping with ICDs (Barth & Kinder, 1987; Black, Kehrberg, Flumerfelt, & Schlosser, 1997). Some have highlighted the common co-occurrence of ICDs, self-harm, eating disorders, and substance use disorders, and have proposed that individuals who engage in one impulsive behavior are likely to engage in others (i.e., "multi-impulsive" patients) (Lacey & Evans, 1986).

We believe that the ICD spectrum, as currently defined and composed, should be retained, and as the structure of this chapter would suggest, we advocate adding self-harm behaviors to this spectrum. If any further change were made to this spectrum, we would propose expanding this spectrum to include disorders of eating, drinking, and drug use, given the many similarities across these different disorders. On one hand, such a move would be a clear break from the current DSM-IV-TR approach of classifying behaviors based on their topography rather than their etiology or function. On the other hand, however, the ICD spectrum as currently constituted already includes behaviors that are quite heterogeneous, and so this would not represent such a drastic change. Regardless of how these different disorders are classified in the DSM-5 (and beyond), an important focus for future research is to further examine the common etiologies of these disorders, and to elucidate the factors that determine which of these disorders develop among those characterized by problems with impulse-control.

Influences on Impulse-Control Disorders and Self-Harm

Impulse control disorders and self-harm are multi-determined behaviors that are influenced by a wide range of factors, including genetic, neurobiological, social, developmental, and psychological factors. In this section, we summarize what is known about the influences of each of these factors on ICDs and self-harm behaviors. Given that the vast majority of research in these areas has focused on self-harm (and on suicide in particular), we provide greater coverage of findings in this area, but highlight similarities and differences with analogous findings on ICDs.

Genetic and Neurobiological Factors

GENETIC FACTORS

Studies consistently have found that ICDs and self-harm occur at higher rates among the family members of those engaging in these behaviors than in the general population, as noted in the first section of this chapter. Evidence from twin and adoption studies suggests that a genetically heritable component is present in these disorders. For instance, studies of suicide among twins have revealed higher rates of concordance between monozygotic than dizygotic twins; and adoption studies have revealed higher concordance among biological compared to adoptive relatives (Baldessarini & Hennen, 2004; Brent & Mann, 2005, 2006). Importantly, the familial trans-

mission of suicide remains even after controlling for the presence of psychiatric disorders (Brent & Mann, 2005; Egeland & Sussex, 1985). Of course, it is unlikely that there is "a gene for" self-harm or ICDs, but instead that interactions between genetic and environmental factors contribute to biological and psychological processes that then have an impact on these ultimate outcomes of interest (Kendler, 2005; Moffitt, 2005; Moffitt, Caspi, & Rutter, 2006).

Although the exact mechanisms through which genetic factors might lead to self-harm and ICDs are not currently known, recent family studies have provided some leads about the key neurobiological and psychological processes involved. Although first-degree relatives of those who die by suicide are at increased risk for both suicide ideation and attempts, the risk of suicide ideation is reduced to a nonsignificant level when the presence of psychiatric disorders is controlled, whereas the risk of suicide attempts remains (Brent & Mann, 2005). This suggests that the familial transmission of suicide ideation is explained by the transmission of psychiatric disorders, but there is some tendency beyond this that must be passed on that increases the risk of acting on suicidal thoughts. This liability may be best conceptualized as behavioral disinhibition or a tendency to engage in impulsive aggression. This is consistent with the finding that there is a higher occurrence of suicidal behavior in the first-degree relatives of those who die by suicide characterized by impulsive aggression relative to those who do not (Brent, Bridge, Johnson, & Connolly, 1996; Brent & Mann, 2005), and also by recent findings indicating that a specific polymorphism of the serotonin transporter gene is associated with the subsequent experience of suicidality (Caspi et al., 2003). Research conducted over the past decade also has revealed evidence of familial transmission of ICDs such as trichotillomania (King, Scahill, et al., 1995), pathological gambling (Winters & Rich, 1998), and kleptomania (Grant & Kim, 2002a), further supporting the idea of familial transmission of behavioral disinhibition.

NEUROBIOLOGICAL FACTORS

Building nicely on the genetic studies mentioned earlier, research on the neurobiology of ICDs and self-harm has focused largely on potential problems in the serotonergic system of people with these disorders. Serotonin is an inhibitory neurotransmitter in the brain that plays an important role in the regulation of mood and behavior, and it has been shown to be particularly associated with the occurrence of impulsive and aggressive behavior. Low levels of serotonin and its primary metabolite (5-hydroxyindole acetic acid; 5-HIAA) have been found in the brainstems and cerebrospinal fluid of those who die by suicide (Asberg, Nordstrom, & Traskman-Bendz, 1986; Mann, Arango, Marzuk, Theccanat, & Reis, 1989) and also have been shown to predict suicide attempts and death (Cooper, Kelly, & King, 1992; Nordstrom et al., 1994). Serotonin abnormalities, such as low serotonin binding (e.g., New et al., 2002) and low levels of serotonin metabolite 5-HIAA (e.g., Virkkunen, Nuutila, Goodwin, & Linnoila, 1987) also have been found in patients with ICDs. Because serotonin has been implicated in the occurrence of many different mental disorders (and more general bodily functions, such as sleeping, eating, and others), it is important to identify *how* serotonergic dysfunction might lead to ICDs and self-harm in particular. Addressing this issue, Mann and colleagues recently have shown in a very illuminating series of studies that people who die by suicide have serotonergic dysfunction (i.e., fewer presynaptic serotonin transporter sites and upregulated postsynaptic serotonin receptors) in a specific brain region (i.e., ventromedial prefrontal cortex) that is associated with behavioral inhibition (see Mann, 2003; Mann, Brent, & Arango, 2001). Studies of serotonergic dysfunction in pathological gambling also have revealed decreased levels of platelet monoamine oxidase B (e.g., Blanco, Orensanz-Munoz, Blanco-Jerez, & Saiz-Ruiz, 1996), which has been associated with sensation-seeking and impulsiveness (Weyler, Hsu, & Breakefield, 1990). These findings have begun to elucidate the specific mechanisms through which genetic and neurobiological factors may lead to problems with impulse-control that are involved not only in suicidal behavior, but in ICDs and self-harm more broadly (Grant, Brewer, & Potenza, 2006).

The majority of research on the neurobiology of ICDs and self-harm has focused on dysfunction of the serotonergic system, given the links between this system and impulsive aggression. However, some interesting findings have been reported involving other aspects of neurobiological functioning, such as those involved in the experience of stress, depression, and reward processing. For instance, postmortem studies have revealed increased noradrenaline levels and decreased α-adrenergic receptor binding in the prefrontal cortex of the brains of people who have died by suicide (Arango, Ernsberger, Sved, & Mann, 1993; Mann, 2003). However, given that increased noradrenaline levels are associated with the experience of stress and depression (Heim & Nemeroff, 2001), it is not clear whether these findings are specific to suicide and other forms of ICDs and self-harm. In addition, the experience of strong urges to engage in ICDs and self-harm and the reported experience of pleasure after such behaviors has led researchers to examine the role of the dopaminergic and endogenous opioid systems in the occurrence of such behaviors (Blum et al., 2000; Grant, Brewer, et al., 2006).

Social and Developmental Factors

The development of ICDs and self-harm also is influenced by factors in a person's social environment. These influences include both distal factors that occur early in life, as well as more proximal factors present in the immediate environment. The distal factor most often associated with the development of ICDs and self-harm is the occurrence of early childhood maltreatment. Studies have consistently revealed evidence of an association between early childhood maltreatment and the occurrence of subsequent suicidal behavior (Joiner et al., 2007; Nock & Kessler, 2006), NSSI (Glassman, Weierich, Hooley, Deliberto, & Nock, 2007; Yates, 2004), and ICDs, such as trichotillomania (Boughn & Holdom, 2003; Lochner et al., 2002), pathological gambling (Petry & Steinberg, 2005; Scherrer et al., 2007), and pyromania (Root, MacKay, Henderson, Del Bove, & Warling, 2008). This association may be explained in part by the shared genetic and neurobiological characteristics of parent and offspring. That is, parents who are impulsive and aggressive by nature are more likely to have impulsive and aggressive children, and incidentally to act in an abusive way toward their offspring. However, evidence from studies of nonhuman primates reveals that early rearing experiences, such as being raised in a deprived social environment, contribute independently to the development of impulsive, aggressive, and self-injurious behavior via serotonergic dysfunction (Higley & Linnoila, 1997; Kraemer, Schmidt, & Ebert, 1997). Most recently, an exciting line of research has shown that not only do genetic factors and early environment independently influence the development of pathological behaviors, but that they interact to increase the likelihood of such outcomes (Caspi et al., 2003; Kaufman et al., 2004).

Proximal influences on the development of ICDs and self-harm include the experience of significant life stressors beyond childhood (e.g., Welte et al., 2008), social learning via interactions with peers (e.g., Prinstein, Boergers, & Spirito, 2001) or media (Whitlock, Purington, & Gershkovich, 2009), and access to the means required in the case of suicidal behavior (Miller & Hemenway, 2008). The experience of stressful events in one's environment appears to be a general risk factor for the occurrence of ICDs and self-harm, as studies of virtually all of these disorders have reported that social stressors are a proximal risk factor in each case (Flessner et al., 2008; Hawton & Harriss, 2006). In contrast, it is likely that social learning processes influence which ICD or self-harm behavior a person will perform. For instance, several recent studies have shown that media reporting of suicide deaths can influence the occurrence of subsequent suicidal behaviors (Gould, 2001), increasing media attention to NSSI may be contributing to increases in the prevalence of this behavior (Whitlock et al., 2009), and interactive media such as the Internet can provide a means of spreading information about engaging in NSSI across peers (Whitlock, Powers, & Eckenrode, 2006). Moreover, research on health risk behaviors more generally has shown that people's (adolescents in most of this research) engagement in behaviors such as self-harm, aggression, alcohol/drug use, and related behaviors is significantly associated with the perception that one's close friends also are engaging in these behaviors (Brent, Perper, Mortiz, & Allman, 1993; Vitaro, Tremblay, Kerr, Pagani, & Bukowski, 1997). Stated more simply, people are more likely to begin and continue engaging in a specific abnormal behavior (e.g., stealing, starting fires, self-injuring) if those around them are also doing so. Once initiated, it is likely that other intrapersonal/psychological factors help to explain whether and to what extent the behavior persists over time.

Psychological Factors

The psychological factors that lead to engagement in ICDs and self-harm emerge from the interaction of genetic/neurobiological and social/environmental factors. These psychological factors can be conceptualized and studied in myriad ways, and a full discussion of such factors could fill an entire volume (see Grant & Kim, 2003b; Hollander & Stein, 2006; Nock, 2009). Here, we provide a brief summary of the psychological factors most often associated with engagement in ICDs and self-harm.

Each of the ICDs and self-harm behaviors reviewed in this chapter represents problems in controlling behavioral impulses to engage in harmful behavior, and so perhaps not surprisingly, the psychological factors most often linked to these disorders are deficits in executive functions and high negative arousal. Executive functions refer to capacities for managing specific cognitive (e.g., attention,

planning, decision-making) and behavioral (e.g., response initiation, maintenance, and inhibition) processes (Lezak, 1995). Studies using brain-damaged patients and neuroimaging approaches suggest that the prefrontal cortex is the brain area most closely underlying such functions (e.g., Bechara & Van Der Linden, 2005). Integrating nicely with the findings on genetic (e.g., importance of serotonin transporter gene), neurobiological (e.g., serotonergic abnormalities in the prefrontal cortex), and environmental (e.g., maltreatment) factors reviewed earlier, studies on ICDs and self-harm have consistently revealed deficits in behavioral inhibition (Carlton & Manowitz, 1992; Grant, Correia, et al., 2006), decision-making (e.g., Best, Williams, & Coccaro, 2002; Cavedini, Riboldi, Keller, D'Annucci, & Bellodi, 2002), and problem-solving (e.g., Marazziti et al., 2008). Taken together, these findings provide an increasingly clear picture of the processes underlying problems with failure to inhibit the impulse to engage in maladaptive behaviors.

Studies of ICDs and self-harm also have consistently revealed problems with high negative arousal that may increase the likelihood of acting on behavioral impulses. This high arousal has been studied in the form of high emotion reactivity (Nock, Wedig, Holmberg, & Hooley, 2008), high levels of stress (Welte et al., 2008), elevated rates of psychological distress (Grant & Kim, 2002a), higher physiological arousal (Nock & Mendes, 2008), and high levels of neuroticism (Ashton, Marshall, Hassanyeh, & Marsh, 1994; Fernandez-Aranda et al., 2008). As mentioned in the first section of this chapter, each ICD and self-harm behavior is preceded most often by increased negative arousal, and the behavior is performed in an effort to decrease or escape from this arousal—highlighting the importance of this psychological factor in the occurrence of these disorders.

An important goal for future research on the psychological factors associated with ICDs and self-harm is to advance the understanding of what factors determine which particular ICD or self-harm behavior a person engages in and why. For instance, why does one person with poor impulse-control and high negative arousal decide to hurt himself or herself, whereas another person with this profile decides to set fires or steal items from a store? A wide range of psychological, genetic, neurobiological, and environmental factors likely contribute to such determinations, and gaining better clarity on this issue is important not only for improving our understanding of these disorders, but also for enhancing our ability to effectively assess and treat these problems.

Assessment and Intervention
Assessment

As in most areas of psychopathology, the assessment of ICDs and self-harm should incorporate the use of multiple measurement methods, including interviews, rating scales, and performance-based tests. The assessment methods used in any specific case will differ depending on whether the focus is on screening, diagnosis, or monitoring over the course of treatment. In each of these domains, many more assessment measures are available for suicidal behaviors (see Brown, 2000 for extensive reviews; Goldston, 2000; Nock, Wedig, Janis, & Deliberto, 2008) than for NSSI (Nock, Wedig, Janis, et al., 2008) and ICDs (Grant, 2008); however, these latter areas have received increased attention in recent years, and a number of excellent assessment tools currently are available for scientific and clinical use.

The first focus of assessment typically is to determine who in a population is most at risk for the outcomes of interest. As such, a range of assessment measures has been developed to enable scientists and clinicians to screen for ICDs and self-harm and their risk factors. For instance, the Columbia Suicide Screen (D. Shaffer et al., 2004) is a screening questionnaire designed to identify middle school and high school students at risk for suicide. Importantly, a related line of research has suggested that, despite common perceptions, asking teens questions about suicide does not increase their distress or likelihood of experiencing suicidal thoughts (Gould et al., 2005). Screening measures also are available for ICDs, such as the clinician-administered Minnesota Impulse Disorders Interview (Grant, 2008), which serves as an efficient method of screening for the presence of each of the ICDs reviewed in this chapter.

The next focus of assessment is making a determination about whether those who screen positive meet criteria for an ICD or are actually experiencing self-harm thoughts or behaviors. Unfortunately, ICDs and self-harm behaviors are not included in most used structured or semi-structured diagnostic interviews, such as the Structured Clinical Interview for DSM-IV (First, Spitzer, Gibbon, & Williams, 2002). However, specialized measures exist for in-depth assessment once the potential presence of an ICD or self-harm has been detected, such as the Self-Injurious Thoughts and Behaviors Interview (Nock, Holmberg, Photos, & Michel, 2007), Trichotillomania Diagnostic Interview (Rothbaum

& Ninan, 1994), and Structured Clinical Interview for Pathological Gambling (Grant, Steinberg, Kim, Rounsaville, & Potenza, 2004).

Once the presence of ICDs and self-harm are determined, monitoring of these disorders over time becomes especially important, given the potential harm to self and others involved in these problems and due to their persistence (as described earlier). Scientists and clinicians should conduct ongoing monitoring and risk assessment, following the currently available guidelines for such practices provided by professional organizations (American Academy of Child and Adolescent Psychiatry, 2001; APA, 2003) or individual experts in the field (Brown, 2000; Jacobs, Brewer, & Klein-Benheim, 1999).

In each phase of assessment, it is important to bear in mind several special issues that commonly arise in the measurement of ICDs and self-harm. First, given that ICDs and self-harm typically are comorbid with each other (e.g., Grant & Kim, 2003a) and with other DSM-IV-TR disorders (e.g., Christenson et al., 1994; Kessler et al., 2008), careful differential diagnosis is especially important. Second, because of the sensitive, embarrassing, and in some cases illegal nature of some ICDs and self-harm, many people fail to report such behaviors unless asked directly, and some still deny them on initial interview. For this reason, it is important to use a multi-method assessment approach, and to assess for the presence of these disorders more than once, in order to increase the likelihood of detecting such behaviors. Third, people with ICDs and self-harm often experience shame or guilt as a result of these disorders, and so the presence of such feelings should be assessed and, if present, they should be addressed as part of the intervention provided.

Intervention

Recent research has revealed both good and bad news about the treatment of ICDs and self-harm. The good news is that the percentage of people in the general population who receive treatment for mental disorders and self-harm has increased significantly over the past decade (Kessler, Berglund, Borges, et al., 2005). The bad news is that, despite this increase, the rates of these outcomes have not changed (Kessler, Demler, et al., 2005). Although this latter finding suggests that the treatments administered in many community settings may not be particularly effective, it is notable that several new psychological and pharmacological treatments have proven efficacious in decreasing the rates of ICDs and self-harm.

PSYCHOLOGICAL TREATMENT

Cognitive therapy (CT), which was initially developed to treat depression, has been adapted for a range of behavior problems, including self-harm and ICDs. Brown and colleagues (2005) recently modified CT specifically for suicide attempters and, through a randomized clinical trial, found that adult suicide attempters receiving CT, relative to treatment as usual, reported significantly lower reattempt rates and severity of depression throughout the 18-month follow-up period. This modified CT aimed to identify proximal thoughts and core beliefs that are activated before attempting suicide and to improve impulse control, problem solving and coping skills, degree of hopelessness, availability of social support, and compliance with treatment services (Brown et al., 2005; Henriques, Beck, & Brown, 2003). Cognitive therapy has also been developed and tested among small samples for pathological gambling (see Lopez Viets & Miller, 1997) and among adults for anger disorders (see Deffenbacher, 2003).

Cognitive-behavioral therapy (CBT), which is similar to CT but includes a more substantial focus on behavior change, also has been proven effective in the treatment of ICDs and self-harm. For instance, dialectical behavior therapy (DBT), a version of CBT that targets suicidal and nonsuicidal self-injurious behaviors (Linehan, 1993a, 1993b), has proven especially effective in the treatment of self-harm (Linehan, Armstrong, Suarez, Allmon, & Heard, 1991; Linehan et al., 2006). By validating the patient while simultaneously modifying his or her behavior, DBT focuses directly on reducing life-threatening behaviors (e.g., suicide attempts, NSSI), treatment-interfering behaviors (e.g., not returning clinician's phone calls), and quality-of-life interfering behaviors (e.g., homelessness), as well as on increasing behavioral skills. Dialectical behavior therapy clinicians use change strategies to improve mindfulness (i.e., nonjudgmental focus on present thoughts and feelings), distress tolerance, emotion regulation, and interpersonal effectiveness. These goals are achieved through multiple modes of service delivery (e.g., individual therapy, ingroup skills training, telephone consultation, therapist consultation meetings). Cognitive-behavioral therapy techniques and behavioral approaches have also been supported as efficacious means of treating trichotillomania (Franklin et al., 2006), kleptomania (Durst, Katz, Teitelbaum, Zislin, & Dannon, 2001; Gauthier & Pellerin, 1982), pathological gambling (Petry & Roll, 2001; Sylvain, Ladouceur, & Boisvert, 1997), pyromania (Bumpass, Fagelman, & Brix, 1983; McGrath, Marshall, & Prior, 1979), and IET (Edmondson & Conger, 1996).

Other psychological treatment strategies also have aimed to reduce disorders of self-harm and impulse control. For example, periodically contacting depressed or suicidal patients (e.g., through telephone calls, letters) discharged from a hospital emergency center has reduced the likelihood of reattempt relative to a group of discharged patients who did not receive any contact (Motto & Bostrom, 2001; Welu, 1977). Other interventions, such as the use of support groups (e.g., Gamblers Anonymous for pathological gambling) also have shown promise in the treatment of ICDs, although attrition rates are fairly high (Stewart & Brown, 1988). Future research must identify more effective treatments for these behavior problems, develop a clearer understanding of the mechanisms through which these treatments have their effects, and work to ensure that the most effective treatments possible are available to clinicians and patients in the community.

PHARMACOLOGICAL TREATMENT

Antidepressants

Some studies have reported positive results for antidepressant treatment of ICDs and self-harm. For instance, increased rates of antidepressant use in nationally representative (Gibbons, Hur, Bhaumik, & Mann, 2005) and adolescent (Olfson, Shaffer, Marcus, & Greenberg, 2003) samples have been associated with reduced rates of suicide. Selective serotonin reuptake inhibitors (SSRIs) in particular also have been shown to be effective in treating NSSI among severely to profoundly mentally retarded populations (Bodfish & Madison, 1993; Markowitz, 1992) and in adolescent populations when the treatment has been used in combination with CBT (Goodyer et al., 2007). Although the use of SSRIs in treating certain ICDs has not been as widely studied, SSRIs have been recommended as effective treatments for pathological gambling (Hollander et al., 1998; Kim, Grant, Adson, Shin, & Zaninelli, 2002) and IED (i.e., impulsive aggression; Coccaro & Kavoussi, 1997), based on what is known about serotonergic dysfunction contributing to ICDs. Results on the effectiveness of SSRIs for treating trichotillomania and kleptomania have been more controversial—with some studies demonstrating their efficacy (Dannon, 2002; Swedo & Rapoport, 1991) and other studies revealing no effects (Christenson, Mackenzie, Mitchell, et al., 1991). It has been suggested that SSRIs are more effective in treating ICDs when in combination with therapy (e.g., Lepkifker et al., 1999) and mood-stabilizing drugs

(Burnstein, 1992; Coccaro & Danehy, 2006) than when SSRIs are the only treatment implemented.

Despite reports of the effectiveness of antidepressants in the treatment of ICDs and self-harm, concerns about potential adverse effects of SSRIs have led to controversy. Some adverse effects (e.g., increased skin picking; Denys, van Megen, & Westenberg, 2003) have been reported when SSRIs have been used to treat NSSI. Similarly, studies on SSRI treatment of trichotillomania and kleptomania have reported relapse of symptoms (Bayle, Caci, Millet, Richa, & Olie, 2003; Stein & Hollander, 1992). The use of SSRI treatment for suicidal behaviors has been persistently debated. Several experimental studies have reported that those receiving SSRIs actually have a higher rate of suicidal thoughts and attempts than do those receiving placebo (e.g., Whittington et al., 2004). However, other studies report no such increase (e.g., Gibbons et al., 2005). It is likely that further study over the next several years will be required to resolve this debate.

Mood Stabilizers
Mood stabilizing anticonvulsants have been shown to significantly reduce suicide risk (Goodwin et al., 2003). Anticonvulsants have been shown to be effective in treating other forms of self-harm, such as NSSI (Cordas, Tavares, Calderoni, Stump, & Ribeiro, 2006). Mood stabilizers (Pallanti, Quercioli, Sood, & Hollander, 2002; Parks et al., 2005) alone have been recommended for some ICDs, but they should be used cautiously due to potential adverse effects (e.g., reduction in mood; Coccaro & Danehy, 2006; Cowdry & Gardner, 1988).

Antipsychotics
There have been mixed findings regarding the effectiveness of antipsychotic medication for ICDs and self-harm. Although some types of antipsychotic medications have been reported to reduce risk in suicide (e.g., clozapine) (Ernst & Goldberg, 2004), it has been suggested that neuroleptics could increase suicide risk in some cases due to subsequent akathisia (increased psychomotor agitation) and akinesia (apathy, difficulty initiating usual activities) (Drake & Ehrlich, 1985; Shaw, Mann, Weiden, Sinsheimer, & Brunn, 1986). Antipsychotics also have been reported to effectively reduce NSSI (Sandman, 2009), aggression (Schur et al., 2003), and trichotillomania (Stein, Harvey, Seedat, & Hollander, 2006); however, due to potential adverse effects, antipsychotics are not recommended as the first pharmacological treatment option for ICDs, nor are they recommended to be administered in large doses (Stein et al., 2006).

Opioid Antagonists
Opioid antagonists are another promising form of pharmacological treatment for ICDs and self-harm. Multiple studies, albeit consisting of small sample sizes, have demonstrated that opioid antagonists reduce NSSI (Sandman, Barron, & Colman, 1990; Symons, Thompson, & Rodriguez, 2004). Similar effects have been reported regarding ICDs (e.g., pathological gambling, kleptomania) (Grant & Kim, 2002b; Kim & Grant, 2001).

Prevention
Prevention programs for ICDs and self-harm have received much less scientific and clinical attention; however, some effective programs have been identified. Suicide prevention programs have been studied much more extensively than other ICDs and self-harm behaviors. In a systematic review of suicide prevention programs, primary care physician education programs and means restriction (e.g., increasing firearm restriction) were found to be the most effective in reducing suicide rates (Mann et al., 2005). Although substitution methods may emerge, means restriction could induce a transition from the use of more lethal means, such as firearms—which account for more than 50% of suicides in the United States—to less lethal means (Gould, Greenberg, Velting, & Shaffer, 2003). Other methods of suicide prevention, such as general public education, school-based awareness programs for youth, and media intervention efforts, lack sufficient research or have been found to be less effective (Gould et al., 2003; Mann et al., 2005). School-based awareness programs have demonstrated zero to negative effects (D. Shaffer, Garland, Vieland, & Underwood, 1991), whereas skills training (e.g., problem solving, coping) has produced more promising positive results (e.g., E. A. Thompson, Eggert, Randell, & Pike, 2001). Guidelines for reporting suicide in the media have been established to avoid a potential contagion effect (Gould et al., 2003; Mann et al., 2005), but the effectiveness of such guidelines is not currently known. Whitlock and Knox (2009) have suggested that since NSSI is a risk factor for suicide, NSSI prevention programs that resemble those for suicide may be useful in reducing rates of NSSI, although this also remains an open empirical question.

Prevention programs for ICDs have received the least amount of attention—a possible result of their low prevalence. Policy makers may exhaust valuable time and resources trying to prevent disorders that occur much less frequently than other behaviors, such as suicide. Although prevention programs for each of these disorders may exist, none have been systematically evaluated. Future prevention efforts could target behaviors that are often associated with ICDs. For example, prevention strategies that target violence may be helpful in reducing rates of ICDs (e.g., IED).

Conclusion

Disorders of impulse control and self-harm are characterized by a persistent inability to inhibit urges to engage in harmful behavior, to the point that such behavior causes significant distress and impairment. Disorders on the impulse control spectrum are somewhat heterogeneous, in the form of behaviors characterizing each disorder and in their prevalence, sex distribution, and course. Yet, these disorders also show several important commonalities beyond their defining features. They most often are preceded by aversive arousal that dissipates after the behavior and are followed by gratification or pleasure; they all typically have an onset during adolescence; and they appear to share genetic/neurobiological, environmental, and psychological influences that contribute to problems with heightened arousal and poor executive functioning. Most prior research in this area has focused on suicidal behaviors, but other disorders on this spectrum have received increased attention in recent years. The dangerous, sensitive, and often illegal aspects of disorders on this spectrum introduce problems for their assessment and treatment; however, significant advances have been made in this area, and currently a range of evidence-based approaches to assessment, intervention, and prevention are available to clinicians, researchers, and the public. Nevertheless, there is clearly much more work that must be done to increase understanding and decrease the prevalence and impact of these disorders.

Future Directions

As highlighted in this chapter, there is still much we do not know about the epidemiology, etiology, assessment, and treatment of ICDs and self-harm, and so research is needed on multiple fronts, each of which was mentioned earlier and so will not be reiterated here. We believe several additional and as yet unanswered questions are especially pressing and should guide future research in this area. First: Is persistent engagement in moderate-to-severe self-harm behaviors a mental disorder, and if so, should such disorders be placed on the impulse control spectrum? Compelling arguments have been made regarding why self-harm should be classified in DSM-5 (Muehlenkamp, 2005; Oquendo, Baca-Garcia, Mann, & Giner, 2008), and doing so would have significant implications for research, assessment, and treatment. We believe that, if such a classification is made, such behaviors should appear on the impulse control spectrum, given the similarities outlined in this chapter. Second, and related to the previous point: Given the commonalities and comorbidities among disorders characterized by behavioral dyscontrol, including ICDs, self-harm, eating disorders, alcohol and drug use disorders, and some anxiety disorders, should all of these disorders be placed on the same spectrum (or overlapping or intersecting spectra)? Doing so would result in a significant reorganization of existing DSM disorders, as well as a change from classifying behaviors based primarily on topography to classifying behaviors based more on the processes that produce and maintain these behaviors. Third, as research efforts continue to reveal the etiologic pathways that lead to each of these disorders, as well as uncover effective methods for assessing and treating these disorders, it will be important to consider commonalities and differences among different disorders and to map them onto common traits in order to more efficiently advance work in each area. Despite the many similarities between ICDs and self-harm, research on these two classes of behaviors rarely intersects. Greater communication among researchers and cross-fertilization of ideas and findings from these different areas of research are likely to lead to more rapid advances in each domain. Finally, surprisingly little is known about effective methods for assessing, treating, and preventing each of the disorders reviewed in this chapter. Therefore, it is especially important that researchers and clinicians focus intensively on developing more effective and efficient methods for assessing, predicting, and preventing these dangerous behaviors.

References

American Academy of Child and Adolescent Psychiatry. (2001). Practice parameter for the assessment and treatment of children and adolescents with suicidal behavior. *Journal of the American Academy of Child and Adolescent Psychiatry*, 40(Suppl. 2), 24S-51S.

American Psychiatric Association. (1980). *Diagnostic and statistical manual of mental disorders* (3rd ed.). Washington, DC: Author.

American Psychiatric Association. (1987). *Diagnostic and statistical manual of mental disorders* (3rd Rev. ed.). Washington, DC: Author.

American Psychiatric Association. (1994). *Diagnostic and statistical manual of mental disorders* (4th ed.). Washington, DC: Author.

American Psychiatric Association. (2000). *Diagnostic and statistical manual of mental disorders* (4th Rev. ed.). Washington, DC: Author.

American Psychiatric Association. (2003). Practice guideline for the assessment and treatment of patients with suicidal behaviors. *American Journal of Psychiatry, 160*(Suppl. 11), 1–60.

Arango, V., Ernsberger, P., Sved, A. F., & Mann, J. J. (1993). Quantitative autoradiography of alpha 1- and alpha 2-adrenergic receptors in the cerebral cortex of controls and suicide victims. *Brain Research, 630*, 271–282.

Asberg, M., Nordstrom, P., & Traskman-Bendz, L. (1986). Cerebrospinal fluid studies in suicide: An overview. *Annals of the New York Academy of Sciences, 487*, 243–255.

Ashton, C. H., Marshall, E. F., Hassanyeh, F., & Marsh, V. R. (1994). Biological correlates of deliberate self-harm behaviour: A study of electroencephalographic, biochemical and psychological variables in parasuicide. *Acta Psychiatrica Scandinavica, 90*, 316–323.

Baldessarini, R. J., & Hennen, J. (2004). Genetics of suicide: An overview. *Harvard Review of Psychiatry, 12*, 1–13.

Barth, R. J., & Kinder, B. N. (1987). The mislabeling of sexual impulsivity. *Journal of Sex and Marital Therapy, 13*, 15–23.

Bayle, F. J., Caci, H., Millet, B., Richa, S., & Olie, J. P. (2003). Psychopathology and comorbidity of psychiatric disorders in patients with kleptomania. *American Journal of Psychiatry, 160*, 1509–1513.

Beautrais, A. L., Joyce, P. R., Mulder, R. T., Fergusson, D. M., Deavoll, B. J., & Nightingale, S. K. (1996). Prevalence and comorbidity of mental disorders in persons making serious suicide attempts: A case-control study. *American Journal of Psychiatry, 153*, 1009–1014.

Bechara, A., & Van Der Linden, M. (2005). Decision-making and impulse control after frontal lobe injuries. *Current Opinion in Neurology, 18*, 734–739.

Beck, A. T., Beck, R., & Kovacs, M. (1975). Classification of suicidal behaviors: I. Quantifying intent and medical lethality. *American Journal of Psychiatry, 132*, 285–287.

Best, M., Williams, J. M., & Coccaro, E. F. (2002). Evidence for a dysfunctional prefrontal circuit in patients with an impulsive aggressive disorder. *Proceedings of the National Academy of Sciences of the United States of America, 99*, 8448–8453.

Black, D. W., Kehrberg, L. L., Flumerfelt, D. L., & Schlosser, S. S. (1997). Characteristics of 36 subjects reporting compulsive sexual behavior. *American Journal of Psychiatry, 154*, 243–249.

Black, D. W., & Moyer, T. (1998). Clinical features and psychiatric comorbidity of subjects with pathological gambling behavior. *Psychiatric Services, 49*, 1434–1439.

Blanco, C., Orensanz-Munoz, L., Blanco-Jerez, C., & Saiz-Ruiz, J. (1996). Pathological gambling and platelet MAO activity: A psychobiological study. *American Journal of Psychiatry, 153*, 119–121.

Blum, K., Braverman, E. R., Holder, J. M., Lubar, J. F., Monastra, V. J., Miller, D., et al. (2000). Reward deficiency syndrome: A biogenetic model for the diagnosis and treatment of impulsive, addictive, and compulsive behaviors. *Journal of Psychoactive Drugs,* (Suppl. 32), i-iv, 1–112.

Bodfish, J. W., & Madison, J. T. (1993). Diagnosis and fluoxetine treatment of compulsive behavior disorder of adults with mental retardation. *American Journal on Mental Retardation, 98*, 360–367.

Borges, G., Angst, J., Nock, M. K., Ruscio, A. M., & Kessler, R. C. (2008). Risk factors for the incidence and persistence of suicide-related outcomes: A 10-year follow-up study using the National Comorbidity Surveys. *Journal of Affective Disorders, 105*, 25–33.

Boughn, S., & Holdom, J. J. (2003). The relationship of violence and trichotillomania. *Journal of Nursing Scholarship, 35*, 165–170.

Bourdon, K. H., Rae, D. S., Locke, B. Z., Narrow, W. E., & Regier, D. A. (1992). Estimating the prevalence of mental disorders in U.S. adults from the Epidemiologic Catchment Area Survey. *Public Health Reports, 107*, 663–668.

Brent, D. A., Bridge, J., Johnson, B. A., & Connolly, J. (1996). Suicidal behavior runs in families: A controlled family study of adolescent suicide victims. *Archives of General Psychiatry, 53*, 1145–1152.

Brent, D. A., & Mann, J. J. (2005). Family genetic studies, suicide, and suicidal behavior. *American Journal of Medical Genetics Part C: Seminars in Medical Genetics, 133*, 13–24.

Brent, D. A., & Mann, J. J. (2006). Familial pathways to suicidal behavior–understanding and preventing suicide among adolescents. *New England Journal of Medicine, 355*, 2719–2721.

Brent, D. A., Perper, J. A., Mortiz, G., & Allman, C. (1993). Psychiatric sequelae to the loss of an adolescent peer to suicide. *Journal of the American Academy of Child and Adolescent Psychiatry, 32*, 509–517.

Briere, J., & Gil, E. (1998). Self-mutilation in clinical and general population samples: Prevalence, correlates, and functions. *American Journal of Orthopsychiatry, 68*, 609–620.

Brown, G. K. (2000). *A review of suicide assessment measures for intervention research with adults and older adults* (No. 263-MH914950). Bethesda, MD: National Institute of Mental Health.

Brown, G. K., Henriques, G. R., Sosdjan, D., & Beck, A. T. (2004). Suicide intent and accurate expectations of lethality: Predictors of medical lethality of suicide attempts. *Journal of Consulting and Clinical Psychology, 72*, 1170–1174.

Brown, G. K., Ten Have, T., Henriques, G. R., Xie, S. X., Hollander, J. E., & Beck, A. T. (2005). Cognitive therapy for the prevention of suicide attempts: A randomized controlled trial. *Journal of the American Medical Association, 294*, 563–570.

Bumpass, E. R., Fagelman, F. D., & Brix, R. J. (1983). Intervention with children who set fires. *American Journal of Psychotherapy, 37*, 328–345.

Burnstein, A. (1992). Fluoxetine-lithium treatment for kleptomania. *Journal of Clinical Psychiatry, 53*, 28–29.

Carlton, P. L., & Manowitz, P. (1992). Behavioral restraint and symptoms of attention deficit disorder in alcoholics and pathological gamblers. *Neuropsychobiology, 25*, 44–48.

Caspi, A., Sugden, K., Moffitt, T. E., Taylor, A., Craig, I. W., Harrington, H., et al. (2003). Influence of life stress on depression: Moderation by a polymorphism in the 5-HTT gene. *Science, 301*, 386–389.

Cavanagh, J. T., Carson, A. J., Sharpe, M., & Lawrie, S. M. (2003). Psychological autopsy studies of suicide: A systematic review. *Psychological Medicine, 33*, 395–405.

Cavedini, P., Riboldi, G., Keller, R., D'Annucci, A., & Bellodi, L. (2002). Frontal lobe dysfunction in pathological gambling patients. *Biological Psychiatry, 51*, 334–341.

Centers for Disease Control. (2008a). Fatal injuries: Mortality reports. *Web-based Injury Statistics Query and Reporting*

System (WISQARS). Retrieved March 7, 2008, from http://www.cdc.gov/nipc/wisqars

Centers for Disease Control. (2008b). Nonfatal injuries: Nonfatal injury reports. *Web-based Injury Statistics Query and Reporting System (WISQARS)*. Retrieved March 7, 2008, from http://www.cdc.gov/nipc/wisqars

Christenson, G. A., Mackenzie, T. B., & Mitchell, J. E. (1991). Characteristics of 60 adult chronic hair pullers. *American Journal of Psychiatry, 148*, 365–370.

Christenson, G. A., MacKenzie, T. B., & Mitchell, J. E. (1994). Adult men and women with trichotillomania: A comparison of male and female characteristics. *Psychosomatics, 35*, 142–149.

Christenson, G. A., Mackenzie, T. B., Mitchell, J. E., & Callies, A. L. (1991). A placebo-controlled, double-blind crossover study of fluoxetine in trichotillomania. *American Journal of Psychiatry, 148*, 1566–1571.

Christenson, G. A., Pyle, R. L., & Mitchell, J. E. (1991). Estimated lifetime prevalence of trichotillomania in college students. *Journal of Clinical Psychiatry, 52*, 415–417.

Coccaro, E. F. (2003). Intermittent explosive disorder: Taming temper in the volatile, impulsive adult. *Current Psychiatry, 2*, 42–60.

Coccaro, E. F., & Danehy, M. (2006). Intermittent Explosive Disorder. In E. Hollander & D. J. Stein (Eds.), *Clinical manual of impulse-control disorders* (pp. 19–37). Arlington, VA: American Psychiatric Publishing, Inc.

Coccaro, E. F., & Kavoussi, R. J. (1997). Fluoxetine and impulsive aggressive behavior in personality-disordered subjects. *Archives of General Psychiatry, 54*, 1081–1088.

Coccaro, E. F., Kavoussi, R. J., Berman, M. E., & Lish, J. D. (1998). Intermittent explosive disorder-revised: Development, reliability, and validity of research criteria. *Comprehensive Psychiatry, 39*, 368–376.

Coccaro, E. F., Posternak, M. A., & Zimmerman, M. (2005). Prevalence and features of intermittent explosive disorder in a clinical setting. *Journal of Clinical Psychiatry, 66*, 1221–1227.

Coccaro, E. F., Schmidt, C. A., Samuels, J. F., & Nestadt, G. (2004). Lifetime and 1-month prevalence rates of intermittent explosive disorder in a community sample. *Journal of Clinical Psychiatry, 65*, 820–824.

Coid, J., Wilkins, J., & Coid, B. (1999). Fire-setting, pyromania and self-mutilation in female remanded prisoners. *The Journal of Forensic Psychology, 10*, 119–130.

Cooper, S. J., Kelly, C. B., & King, D. J. (1992). 5-Hydroxyindoleacetic acid in cerebrospinal fluid and prediction of suicidal behaviour in schizophrenia. *Lancet, 340*, 940–941.

Cordas, T. A., Tavares, H., Calderoni, D. M., Stump, G. V., & Ribeiro, R. B. (2006). Oxcarbazepine for self-mutilating bulimic patients. *International Journal of Neuropsychopharmacology, 9*, 769–771.

Cowdry, R. W., & Gardner, D. L. (1988). Pharmacotherapy of borderline personality disorder: Alprazolam, carbamazepine, trifluoperazine, and tranylcypromine. *Archives of General Psychiatry, 45*, 111–119.

Cuddy-Casey, M., & Orvaschel, H. (1997). Children's understanding of death in relation to child suicidality and homicidality. *Clinical Psychological Review, 17*, 33–45.

Cunningham-Williams, R. M., Cottler, L. B., Compton, W. M., 3rd, & Spitznagel, E. L. (1998). Taking chances: Problem gamblers and mental health disorders–results from the St. Louis Epidemiologic Catchment Area Study. *American Journal of Public Health, 88*, 1093–1096.

Dannon, P. N. (2002). Kleptomania: An impulse control disorder? *International Journal of Psychiatry in Clinical Practice, 6*, 3–7.

Dannon, P. N., Lowengrub, K. M., Iancu, I., & Kotler, M. (2004). Kleptomania: Comorbid psychiatric diagnosis in patients and their families. *Psychopathology, 37*, 76–80.

Darche, M. A. (1990). Psychological factors differentiating self-mutilating and non-self-mutilating adolescent inpatient females. *The Psychiatric Hospital, 21*, 31–35.

Decaria, C., & Hollander, E. (1993). Pathological gambling. In E. Hollander (Ed.), *Obsessive-Compulsive Related Disorders* (pp. 155–178). Washington, DC: American Psychiatric Press.

Deffenbacher, J. L. (2003). Anger Disorders. In E. F. Coccaro (Ed.), *Aggression: Psychiatric assessment and treatment* (pp. 89–111). New York, NY: Marcel Dekker.

Del Bove, G., Caprara, G. V., Pastorelli, C., & Paciello, M. (2008). Juvenile fire setting in Italy: Relationship to aggression, psychopathology, personality, self-efficacy, and school functioning. *European Child and Adolescent Psychiatry, 17*, 235–244.

Deliberto, T. L., & Nock, M. K. (2008). An exploratory study of correlates, onset, and offset of non-suicidal self-injury. *Archives of Suicide Research, 12*, 219–231.

Denys, D., van Megen, H. J. G. M., & Westenberg, H. G. M. (2003). Emerging skin-picking behaviour after serotonin reuptake inhibitor-treatment in patients with obsessive-compulsive disorder: Possible mechanisms and implications for clinical care. *Journal of Psychopharmacology, 17*, 127–129.

DiClemente, R. J., Ponton, L. E., & Hartley, D. (1991). Prevalence and correlates of cutting behavior: Risk for HIV transmission. *Journal of the American Academy of Child and Adolescent Psychiatry, 30*, 735–739.

Drake, R. E., & Ehrlich, J. (1985). Suicide attempts associated with akathisia. *American Journal of Psychiatry, 142*, 499–501.

du Toit, P. L., van Kradenburg, J., Niehaus, D. J., & Stein, D. J. (2001). Characteristics and phenomenology of hair-pulling: An exploration of subtypes. *Comprehensive Psychiatry, 42*, 247–256.

Durst, R., Katz, G., Teitelbaum, A., Zislin, J., & Dannon, P. N. (2001). Kleptomania: Diagnosis and treatment options. *CNS Drugs, 15*, 185–195.

Edmondson, C. B., & Conger, J. C. (1996). A review of treatment efficacy for individuals with anger problems: Conceptual, assessment, and methodological issues. *Clinical Psychology Review, 16*, 251–275.

Egeland, J. A., & Sussex, J. N. (1985). Suicide and family loading for affective disorders. *Journal of the American Medical Association, 254*, 915–918.

Ernst, C. L., & Goldberg, J. F. (2004). Antisuicide properties of psychotropic drugs: A critical review. *Harvard Review of Psychiatry, 12*, 14–41.

Fernandez-Aranda, F., Pinheiro, A. P., Thornton, L. M., Berrettini, W. H., Crow, S., Fichter, M. M., et al. (2008). Impulse control disorders in women with eating disorders. *Psychiatry Research, 157*, 147–157.

First, M. B., Spitzer, R. L., Gibbon, M., & Williams, J. B. W. (2002). *Structured clinical interview for DSM-IV-TR Axis I disorders, Research Version, Non-Patient Edition (SCID-I/NP)*. New York, NY: Biometrics Research, New York State Psychiatric Institute.

Fisch, M. (1954). The suicidal gesture: A study of 114 military patients hospitalized because of abortive suicide attempts. *American Journal of Psychiatry, 111*, 33–36.

Flessner, C. A., Conelea, C. A., Woods, D. W., Franklin, M. E., Keuthen, N. J., & Cashin, S. E. (2008). Styles of pulling in trichotillomania: Exploring differences in symptom severity, phenomenology, and functional impact. *Behavior Research and Therapy, 46,* 345–357.

Franklin, M. E., Tolin, D. F., & Diefenbach, G. J. (2006). Trichotillomania. In E. Hollander & D. J. Stein (Eds.), *Clinical manual of impulse-control disorders* (pp. 149–173). Arlington, VA: American Psychiatric Publishing, Inc.

Gauthier, J., & Pellerin, D. (1982). Management of compulsive shoplifting through covert sensitization. *Journal of Behavior Therapy and Experimental Psychiatry, 13,* 73–75.

Gibbons, R. D., Hur, K., Bhaumik, D. K., & Mann, J. J. (2005). The relationship between antidepressant medication use and rate of suicide. *Archives of General Psychiatry, 62,* 165–172.

Glassman, L. H., Weierich, M. R., Hooley, J. M., Deliberto, T. L., & Nock, M. K. (2007). Child maltreatment, non-suicidal self-injury, and the mediating role of self-criticism. *Behaviour Research and Therapy, 45,* 2483–2490.

Goldman, M. J. (1991). Kleptomania: Making sense of the non-sensical. *American Journal of Psychiatry, 148,* 986–995.

Goldston, D. (2000). *Assessment of suicidal behaviors and risk among children and adolescents* (No. 263-MD-909995). Bethesda, MD: National Institute of Mental Health.

Goodwin, F. K., Fireman, B., Simon, G. E., Hunkeler, E. M., Lee, J., & Revicki, D. (2003). Suicide risk in bipolar disorder during treatment with lithium and divalproex. *Journal of the American Medical Association, 290,* 1467–1473.

Goodyer, I., Dubicka, B., Wilkinson, P., Kelvin, R., Roberts, C., Byford, S., et al. (2007). Selective serotonin reuptake inhibitors (SSRIs) and routine specialist care with and without cognitive behaviour therapy in adolescents with major depression: Randomised controlled trial. *British Medical Journal, 335,* 142–142.

Gould, M. S. (2001). Suicide and the media. *Annals of the New York Academy of Sciences, 932,* 200–224.

Gould, M. S., Greenberg, T., Velting, D. M., & Shaffer, D. (2003). Youth suicide risk and preventive interventions: A review of the past 10 years. *Journal of the American Academy of Child and Adolescent Psychiatry, 42,* 386–405.

Gould, M. S., Marrocco, F. A., Kleinman, M., Thomas, J. G., Mostkoff, K., Cote, J., et al. (2005). Evaluating iatrogenic risk of youth suicide screening programs: A randomized controlled trial. *Journal of the American Medical Association, 293,* 1635–1643.

Grant, J. E. (2004). Dissociative symptoms in kleptomania. *Psychological Reports, 94,* 77–82.

Grant, J. E. (2006). Kleptomania. In M. Hollander & D. J. Stein (Eds.), *Clinical manual of impulse-control disorders* (pp. 175–201). Washington, DC: American Psychiatric Publishing.

Grant, J. E. (2008). *Impulse control disorders: A clinician's guide to understanding and treating behavioral addictions.* New York, NY: W. W. Norton & Company, Inc.

Grant, J. E., Brewer, J. A., & Potenza, M. N. (2006). The neurobiology of substance and behavioral addictions. *CNS Spectrums, 11,* 924–930.

Grant, J. E., Correia, S., & Brennan-Krohn, T. (2006). White matter integrity in kleptomania: A pilot study. *Psychiatry Research, 147,* 233–237.

Grant, J. E., & Kim, S. W. (2002a). Clinical characteristics and associated psychopathology of 22 patients with kleptomania. *Comprehensive Psychiatry, 43,* 378–384.

Grant, J. E., & Kim, S. W. (2002b). An open-label study of naltrexone in the treatment of kleptomania. *Journal of Clinical Psychiatry, 63,* 349–356.

Grant, J. E., & Kim, S. W. (2003a). Comorbidity of impulse control disorders in pathological gamblers. *Acta Psychiatrica Scandinavica, 108,* 203–207.

Grant, J. E., & Kim, S. W. (2003b). *Stop me because I can't stop myself: Taking control of impulsive behavior.* New York, NY: McGraw-Hill.

Grant, J. E., & Kim, S. W. (2007). Clinical characteristics and psychiatric comorbidity of pyromania. *Journal of Clinical Psychiatry, 68,* 1717–1722.

Grant, J. E., Levine, L., Kim, D., & Potenza, M. N. (2005). Impulse control disorders in adult psychiatric inpatients. *American Journal of Psychiatry, 162,* 2184–2188.

Grant, J. E., Odlaug, B. L., & Potenza, M. N. (2007). Addicted to hair pulling? How an alternate model of trichotillomania may improve treatment outcome. *Harvard Review of Psychiatry, 15,* 80–85.

Grant, J. E., Odlaug, B. L., & Wozniak, J. R. (2007). Neuropsychological functioning in kleptomania. *Behavior Research and Therapy, 45,* 1663–1670.

Grant, J. E., & Potenza, M. N. (2006). Compulsive aspects of impulse-control disorders. *Psychiatric Clinics of North America, 29,* 539–551, x.

Grant, J. E., & Potenza, M. N. (2008). Gender-related differences in individuals seeking treatment for kleptomania. *CNS Spectrums, 13,* 235–245.

Grant, J. E., Steinberg, M. A., Kim, S. W., Rounsaville, B. J., & Potenza, M. N. (2004). Preliminary validity and reliability testing of a structured clinical interview for pathological gambling. *Psychiatry Research, 128,* 79–88.

Hall, G. W., Carriero, N. J., Takushi, R. Y., Montoya, I. D., Preston, K. L., & Gorelick, D. A. (2000). Pathological gambling among cocaine-dependent outpatients. *American Journal of Psychiatry, 157,* 1127–1133.

Harriss, L., & Hawton, K. (2005). Suicidal intent in deliberate self-harm and the risk of suicide: The predictive power of the Suicide Intent Scale. *Journal of Affective Disorders, 86,* 225–233.

Hawton, K., & Harriss, L. (2006). Deliberate self-harm in people aged 60 years and over: Characteristics and outcome of a 20-year cohort. *International Journal of Geriatric Psychiatry, 21,* 572–581.

Heim, C., & Nemeroff, C. B. (2001). The role of childhood trauma in the neurobiology of mood and anxiety disorders: Preclinical and clinical studies. *Biological Psychiatry, 49,* 1023–1039.

Henriques, G., Beck, A. T., & Brown, G. K. (2003). Cognitive therapy for adolescent and young adult suicide attempters. *American Behavioral Scientist, 46,* 1258–1268.

Higley, J. D., & Linnoila, M. (1997). Low central nervous system serotonergic activity is trait like and correlates with impulsive behavior: A nonhuman primate model investigating genetic and environmental influences on neurotransmission. *Annals of New York Academy of Sciences, 836,* 39–56.

Hilt, L. M., Nock, M. K., Lloyd-Richardson, E., & Prinstein, M. J. (2008). Longitudinal study of non-suicidal self-injury among young adolescents: Rates, correlates, and preliminary test of an interpersonal model. *Journal of Early Adolescence, 28,* 455–469.

Hollander, E., DeCaria, C. M., Mari, E., Wong, C. M., Mosovich, S., Grossman, R., et al. (1998). Short-term single-blind fluvoxamine treatment of pathological gambling. *American Journal of Psychiatry, 155,* 1781–1783.

Hollander, E., & Stein, D. J. (Eds.). (2006). *Clinical manual of impulse-control disorders.* Washington, DC: American Psychiatric Publishing.

Houts, A. C. (2001). The diagnostic and statistical manual's new white coat and circularity of plausible dysfunctions: Response to Wakefield, part 1. *Behavior Research and Therapy*, *39*, 315–345.

Hyman, S. E. (2005). Addiction: A Disease of Learning and Memory. *American Journal of Psychiatry*, *162*, 1414–1422.

Jacobs, D. F., Marston, A. R., Singer, R. D., Widaman, K., Little, T., & Veizades, J. (1989). Children of problem gamblers. *Journal of Gambling Studies*, *5*, 261–268.

Jacobs, D. G., Brewer, M., & Klein-Benheim, M. (1999). Suicide assessment: An overview and recommended protocol. In D. G. Jacobs (Ed.), *Harvard Medical School guide to suicide assessment and intervention* (pp. 3–39). San Francisco, CA: Jossey-Bass.

Jacobson, C. M., & Gould, M. (2007). The epidemiology and phenomenology of non-suicidal self-injurious behavior among adolescents: A critical review of the literature. *Archives of Suicide Research*, *11*, 129–147.

Janis, I. B., & Nock, M. K. (2009). Are self-injurers impulsive? Results from two behavioral laboratory studies. *Psychiatry Research*, *169*, 261–267.

Joiner, T. E., Jr., Sachs-Ericsson, N. J., Wingate, L. R., Brown, J. S., Anestis, M. D., & Selby, E. A. (2007). Childhood physical and sexual abuse and lifetime number of suicide attempts: A persistent and theoretically important relationship. *Behavior Research and Therapy*, *45*, 539–547.

Kaufman, J., Yang, B. Z., Douglas-Palumberi, H., Houshyar, S., Lipschitz, D., Krystal, J. H., et al. (2004). Social supports and serotonin transporter gene moderate depression in maltreated children. *Proceedings of the National Academy of Sciences of the United States of America*, *101*, 17316–17321.

Kendler, K. S. (2005). "A gene for…": The nature of gene action in psychiatric disorders. *American Journal of Psychiatry*, *162*, 1243–1252.

Kessler, R. C., Berglund, P., Borges, G., Nock, M. K., & Wang, P. S. (2005). Trends in suicide ideation, plans, gestures, and attempts in the United States, 1990–1992 to 2001–2003. *Journal of the American Medical Association*, *293*, 2487–2495.

Kessler, R. C., Berglund, P., Demler, O., Jin, R., Merikangas, K. R., & Walters, E. E. (2005). Lifetime prevalence and age-of-onset distributions of DSM-IV disorders in the National Comorbidity Survey Replication. *Archives of General Psychiatry*, *62*, 593–602.

Kessler, R. C., Borges, G., & Walters, E. E. (1999). Prevalence of and risk factors for lifetime suicide attempts in the National Comorbidity Survey. *Archives of General Psychiatry*, *56*, 617–626.

Kessler, R. C., Coccaro, E. F., Fava, M., Jaeger, S., Jin, R., & Walters, E. (2006). The prevalence and correlates of DSM-IV intermittent explosive disorder in the National Comorbidity Survey Replication. *Archives of General Psychiatry*, *63*, 669–678.

Kessler, R. C., Demler, O., Frank, R. G., Olfson, M., Pincus, H. A., Walters, E. E., et al. (2005). Prevalence and treatment of mental disorders, 1990 to 2003. *New England Journal of Medicine*, *352*, 2515–2523.

Kessler, R. C., Hwang, I., LaBrie, R., Petukhova, M., Sampson, N. A., Winters, K. C., et al. (2008). DSM-IV pathological gambling in the National Comorbidity Survey Replication. *Psychological Medicine*, *38*, 1351–1360.

Kim, S. W., & Grant, J. E. (2001). An open naltrexone treatment study in pathological gambling disorder. *International Clinical Psychopharmacology*, *16*, 285–289.

Kim, S. W., Grant, J. E., Adson, D. E., Shin, Y. C., & Zaninelli, R. (2002). A double-blind placebo-controlled study of the efficacy and safety of paroxetine in the treatment of pathological gambling. *Journal of Clinical Psychiatry*, *63*, 501–507.

King, R. A., Scahill, L., Vitulano, L. A., Schwab-Stone, M., Tercyak, K. P., Jr., & Riddle, M. A. (1995). Childhood trichotillomania: Clinical phenomenology, comorbidity, and family genetics. *Journal of the American Academy of Child and Adolescent Psychiatry*, *34*, 1451–1459.

King, R. A., Zohar, A. H., Ratzoni, G., Binder, M., Kron, S., Dycian, A., et al. (1995). An epidemiological study of trichotillomania in Israeli adolescents. *Journal of the American Academy of Child and Adolescent Psychiatry*, *34*, 1212–1215.

Klonsky, E. D., Oltmanns, T. F., & Turkheimer, E. (2003). Deliberate self-harm in a nonclinical population: Prevalence and psychological correlates. *American Journal of Psychiatry*, *160*, 1501–1508.

Knox, K. L., & Caine, E. D. (2005). Establishing priorities for reducing suicide and its antecedents in the United States. *American Journal of Public Health*, *95*, 1898–1903.

Kolko, D. J., & Kazdin, A. E. (1988). Prevalence of firesetting and related behaviors among child psychiatric patients. *Journal of Consulting and Clinical Psychology*, *56*, 628–630.

Kolko, D. J., & Kazdin, A. E. (1991). Motives of childhood firesetters: Firesetting characteristics and psychological correlates. *Journal of Child Psychology and Psychiatry*, *32*, 535–550.

Koson, D. F., & Dvoskin, J. (1982). Arson: A diagnostic study. *Bulletin of the American Academy of Psychiatry and the Law*, *10*, 39–49.

Kraemer, G. W., Schmidt, D. E., & Ebert, M. H. (1997). The behavioral neurobiology of self-injurious behavior in rhesus monkeys: Current concepts and relations to impulsive behavior in humans. *Annals of the New York Academy of Science*, *836*, 12–38.

Kung, H. C., Hoyert, D. L., Xu, J., & Murphy, S. L. (2008). Deaths: Final data for 2005. *National Vital Statistics Report*, *56*, 1–120.

Lacey, J. H., & Evans, C. D. (1986). The impulsivist: A multi-impulsive personality disorder. *British Journal of Addiction*, *81*, 641–649.

Lejoyeux, M., McLoughlin, M., & Ades, J. (2000). Epidemiology of behavioral dependence: Literature review and results of original studies. *European Psychiatry*, *15*, 129–134.

Lejoyeux, M., McLoughlin, M., & Ades, J. (2006). Pyromania. In E. Hollander & C. Stein (Eds.), *Clinical manual of impulse-control disorders* (pp. 229–250). Arlington, VA: American Psychiatric Publishing, Inc.

Lenane, M. C., Swedo, S. E., Rapoport, J. L., Leonard, H., Sceery, W., & Guroff, J. J. (1992). Rates of Obsessive Compulsive Disorder in first degree relatives of patients with trichotillomania: A research note. *Journal of Child Psychology and Psychiatry*, *33*, 925–933.

Lepkifker, E., Dannon, P. N., Ziv, R., Iancu, I., Horesh, N., & Kotler, M. (1999). The treatment of kleptomania with serotonin reuptake inhibitors. *Clinical Neuropharmacology*, *22*, 40–43.

Lesieur, H. R. (1984). *The chase: Career of the compulsive gambler*. Rochester, VT: Schenkman Books.

Lesieur, H. R. (1998). Costs and treatment of pathological gambling. *Annals of the American Academy of Political and Social Science*, *556*, 153–171.

Lewis, N. D. C., & Yarnell, H. (1951). *Pathological firesetting (pyromania)* (Vol. 82). New York, NY: Coolidge Foundation.

Lezak, M. D. (1995). *Neuropsychological assessment* (3rd ed.). New York, NY: Oxford University Press.

Linehan, M. M. (1993a). *Cognitive-behavioral treatment of borderline personality disorder*. New York, NY: Guilford Press.

Linehan, M. M. (1993b). *Skills training manual for treating borderline personality disorder*. New York, NY: The Guilford Press.

Linehan, M. M., Armstrong, H. E., Suarez, A., Allmon, D., & Heard, H. L. (1991). Cognitive-behavioral treatment of chronically parasuicidal borderline patients. *Archives of General Psychiatry, 48*, 1060–1064.

Linehan, M. M., Comtois, K. A., Murray, A. M., Brown, M. Z., Gallop, R. J., Heard, H. L., et al. (2006). Two-year randomized controlled trial and follow-up of dialectical behavior therapy vs therapy by experts for suicidal behaviors and borderline personality disorder. *Archives of General Psychiatry, 63*, 757–766.

Lloyd-Richardson, E. E., Perrine, N., Dierker, L., & Kelley, M. L. (2007). Characteristics and functions of non-suicidal self-injury in a community sample of adolescents. *Psychological Medicine, 37*, 1183–1192.

Lochner, C., du Toit, P. L., Zungu-Dirwayi, N., Marais, A., van Kradenburg, J., Seedat, S., et al. (2002). Childhood trauma in obsessive-compulsive disorder, trichotillomania, and controls. *Depression and Anxiety, 15*, 66–68.

Lonnqvist, J., & Ostamo, A. (1991). Suicide following the first suicide attempt: A five-year follow-up using a survival analysis. *Psychiatria Fennica, 22*, 171–179.

Lopez Viets, V. C., & Miller, W. R. (1997). Treatment approaches for pathological gamblers. *Clinical Psychology Review, 17*, 689–702.

Maccallum, F., & Blaszczynski, A. (2003). Pathological gambling and suicidality: An analysis of severity and lethality. *Suicide and Life Threatening Behaviors, 33*, 88–98.

Mann, J. J. (2003). Neurobiology of suicidal behaviour. *Nature Reviews Neuroscience, 4*, 819–828.

Mann, J. J., Apter, A., Bertolote, J., Beautrais, A., Currier, D., Haas, A., et al. (2005). Suicide prevention strategies: A systematic review. *Journal of the American Medical Association, 294*, 2064–2074.

Mann, J. J., Arango, V., Marzuk, P. M., Theccanat, S., & Reis, D. J. (1989). Evidence for the 5-HT hypothesis of suicide: A review of post-mortem studies. *British Journal of Psychiatry Supplement, 8*, 7–14.

Mann, J. J., Brent, D. A., & Arango, V. (2001). The neurobiology and genetics of suicide and attempted suicide: A focus on the serotonergic system. *Neuropsychopharmacology, 24*, 467–477.

Marazziti, D., Catena Dell'osso, M., Conversano, C., Consoli, G., Vivarelli, L., Mungai, F., et al. (2008). Executive function abnormalities in pathological gamblers. *Clinical Practice and Epidemiology in Mental Health, 4*, 7.

Markowitz, P. I. (1992). Effect of fluoxetine on self-injurious behavior in the developmentally disabled: A preliminary study. *Journal of Clinical Psychopharmacology, 12*, 27–31.

Marzuk, P. M., Tardiff, K., Leon, A. C., Portera, L., & Weiner, C. (1997). The prevalence of aborted suicide attempts among psychiatric in-patients. *Acta Psychiatrica Scandanavica, 96*, 492–496.

McCloskey, M. S., Berman, M. E., Noblett, K. L., & Coccaro, E. F. (2006). Intermittent explosive disorder-integrated research diagnostic criteria: Convergent and discriminant validity. *Journal of Psychiatry Research, 40*, 231–242.

McElroy, S. L., Hudson, J. I., Pope, H. G., & Keck, P. E. (1991). Kleptomania: Clinical characteristics and associated psychopathology. *Psychological Medicine, 21*, 93–108.

McElroy, S. L., Phillips, K. A., & Keck, P. E., Jr. (1994). Obsessive compulsive spectrum disorder. *Journal of Clinical Psychiatry*, (Suppl. 55), 33–51, 52–33.

McElroy, S. L., Pope, H. G., Jr., Hudson, J. I., Keck, P. E., Jr., & White, K. L. (1991). Kleptomania: A report of 20 cases. *American Journal of Psychiatry, 148*, 652–657.

McElroy, S. L., Soutullo, C. A., Beckman, D. A., Taylor, P., Jr., & Keck, P. E., Jr. (1998). DSM-IV intermittent explosive disorder: A report of 27 cases. *Journal of Clinical Psychiatry, 59*, 203–210, 211.

McGrath, P., Marshall, P. G., & Prior, K. (1979). A comprehensive treatment program for a fire setting child. *Journal of Behavior Therapy and Experimental Psychiatry, 10*, 69–72.

McHugh, P. R. (1992). A structure for psychiatry at the century's turn–the view from Johns Hopkins. *Journal of the Royal Society of Medicine, 85*, 483–487.

McNally, R. J. (2001). On Wakefield's harmful dysfunction analysis of mental disorder. *Behavior Research and Therapy, 39*, 309–314.

McNeilly, D. P., & Burke, W. J. (1998). Stealing lately: A case of late-onset kleptomania. *International Journal of Geriatric Psychiatry, 13*, 116–121.

Miller, M., & Hemenway, D. (2008). Guns and suicide in the United States. *New England Journal of Medicine, 359*, 989–991.

Moeller, F. G., Barratt, E. S., Dougherty, D. M., Schmitz, J. M., & Swann, A. C. (2001). Psychiatric aspects of impulsivity. *American Journal of Psychiatry, 158*, 1783–1793.

Moffitt, T. E. (2005). The new look of behavioral genetics in developmental psychopathology: Gene-environment interplay in antisocial behaviors. *Psychological Bulletin, 131*, 533–554.

Moffitt, T. E., Caspi, A., & Rutter, M. (2006). Measured gene-environment interactions in psychopathology: Concepts, research strategies, and implications for research, intervention, and public understanding of genetics. *Perspectives on Psychological Science, 1*, 5–27.

Moran, E. (1970). Varieties of pathological gambling. *British Journal of Psychiatry, 116*, 593–597.

Motto, J. A., & Bostrom, A. G. (2001). A randomized controlled trial of post crisis suicide prevention. *Psychiatric Services, 52*, 828–833.

Muehlenkamp, J. J. (2005). Self-injurious behavior as a separate clinical syndrome. *American Journal of Orthopsychiatry, 75*, 324–333.

New, A. S., Hazlett, E. A., Buchsbaum, M. S., Goodman, M., Reynolds, D., Mitropoulou, V., et al. (2002). Blunted prefrontal cortical 18fluorodeoxyglucose positron emission tomography response to meta-chlorophenylpiperazine in impulsive aggression. *Archives of General Psychiatry, 59*, 621–629.

Nock, M. K. (Ed.). (2009). *Understanding non-suicidal self-injury: Origins, assessment, and treatment*. Washington, DC: American Psychological Association.

Nock, M. K., Borges, G., Bromet, E. J., Alonso, J., Angermeyer, M., Beautrais, A., et al. (2008). Cross-national prevalence and risk factors for suicidal ideation, plans, and attempts in the WHO World Mental Health Surveys. *British Journal of Psychiatry, 192*, 98–105.

Nock, M. K., Borges, G., Bromet, E. J., Cha, C. B., Kessler, R. C., & Lee, S. (2008). Suicide and suicidal behaviors. *Epidemiologic Reviews, 30*, 133–154.

Nock, M. K., & Favazza, A. (2009). Non-suicidal self-injury: Definition and classification. In M. K. Nock (Ed.), *Understanding non-suicidal self-injury: Origins, assessment, and treatment*. Washington, DC: American Psychological Association.

Nock, M. K., Holmberg, E. B., Photos, V. I., & Michel, B. D. (2007). Self-Injurious Thoughts and Behaviors Interview: Development, reliability, and validity in an adolescent sample. *Psychological Assessment, 19*, 309–317.

Nock, M. K., Joiner, T. E., Jr., Gordon, K. H., Lloyd-Richardson, E., & Prinstein, M. J. (2006). Non-suicidal self-injury among adolescents: Diagnostic correlates and relation to suicide attempts. *Psychiatry Research, 144*, 65–72.

Nock, M. K., & Kessler, R. C. (2006). Prevalence of and risk factors for suicide attempts versus suicide gestures: Analysis of the National Comorbidity Survey. *Journal of Abnormal Psychology, 115*, 616–623.

Nock, M. K., & Mendes, W. B. (2008). Physiological arousal, distress tolerance, and social problem-solving deficits among adolescent self-injurers. *Journal of Consulting and Clinical Psychology, 76*, 28–38.

Nock, M. K., & Prinstein, M. J. (2004). A functional approach to the assessment of self-mutilative behavior. *Journal of Consulting and Clinical Psychology, 72*, 885–890.

Nock, M. K., & Prinstein, M. J. (2005). Clinical features and behavioral functions of adolescent self-mutilation. *Journal of Abnormal Psychology, 114*, 140–146.

Nock, M. K., Wedig, M. M., Holmberg, E. B., & Hooley, J. M. (2008). Emotion reactivity scale: Psychometric evaluation and relation to self-injurious thoughts and behaviors. *Behavior Therapy, 39*, 107–116.

Nock, M. K., Wedig, M. M., Janis, I. B., & Deliberto, T. L. (2008). Self-injurious thoughts and behaviors. In J. Hunsely & E. Mash (Eds.), *A guide to assessments that work* (pp. 158–177). New York, NY: Oxford University Press.

Nordstrom, P., Samuelsson, M., Asberg, M., Traskman-Bendz, L., Aberg-Wistedt, A., Nordin, C., et al. (1994). CSF 5-HIAA predicts suicide risk after attempted suicide. *Suicide and Life Threatening Behavior, 24*, 1–9.

O'Carroll, P. W., Berman, A. L., Maris, R. W., Moscicki, E. K., Tanney, B. L., & Silverman, M. M. (1996). Beyond the Tower of Babel: A nomenclature for suicidology. *Suicide and Life Threatening Behavior, 26*, 237–252.

O'Sullivan, R. L., Keuthen, N. J., Christenson, G. A., Mansueto, C. S., Stein, D. J., & Swedo, S. E. (1997). Trichotillomania: Behavioral symptom or clinical syndrome? *American Journal of Psychiatry, 154*, 1442–1449.

Olfson, M., Shaffer, D., Marcus, S. C., & Greenberg, T. (2003). Relationship between antidepressant medication treatment and suicide in adolescents. *Archives of General Psychiatry, 60*, 978–982.

Oquendo, M. A., Baca-Garcia, E., Mann, J. J., & Giner, J. (2008). Issues for DSM-5: Suicidal behavior as a separate diagnosis on a separate axis. *American Journal of Psychiatry, 165*, 1383–1384.

Ostamo, A., Lonnqvist, J., Heinonen, S., Leppavuori, A., et al. (1991). Epidemiology of parasuicides in Finland. *Psychiatria Fennica, 22*, 181–189.

Pallanti, S., Quercioli, L., Sood, E., & Hollander, E. (2002). Lithium and valproate treatment of pathological gambling: A randomized single-blind study. *Journal of Clinical Psychiatry, 63*, 559–564.

Parks, R. W., Green, R., Girgis, S., Hunter, M. D., Woodruff, P. W., & Spence, S. A. (2005). Response of pyromania to biological treatment in a homeless person. *Neuropsychiatric Disease and Treatment, 1*, 277–280.

Petry, N. M., & Armentano, C. (1999). Prevalence, assessment, and treatment of pathological gambling: A review. *Psychiatric Services, 50*, 1021–1027.

Petry, N. M., & Roll, J. M. (2001). A behavioral approach to understanding and treating pathological gambling. *Seminars in Clinical Neuropsychiatry, 6*, 177–183.

Petry, N. M., & Steinberg, K. L. (2005). Childhood maltreatment in male and female treatment-seeking pathological gamblers. *Psychology of Addictive Behaviors, 19*, 226–229.

Petry, N. M., Stinson, F. S., & Grant, B. F. (2005). Comorbidity of DSM-IV pathological gambling and other psychiatric disorders: Results from the National Epidemiologic Survey on Alcohol and Related Conditions. *Journal of Clinical Psychiatry, 66*, 564–574.

Pfeffer, C. R. (1997). Childhood suicidal behavior: A developmental perspective. *Psychiatric Clinics of North America, 20*, 551–562.

Pfeffer, C. R. (2001). Diagnosis of childhood and adolescent suicidal behavior: Unmet needs for suicide prevention. *Biological Psychiatry, 49*, 1055–1061.

Posner, K., Oquendo, M. A., Gould, M., Stanley, B., & Davies, M. (2007). Columbia Classification Algorithm of Suicide Assessment (C-CASA): Classification of suicidal events in the FDA's pediatric suicidal risk analysis of antidepressants. *American Journal of Psychiatry, 164*, 1035–1043.

Potenza, M. N., Kosten, T. R., & Rounsaville, B. J. (2001). Pathological gambling. *Journal of the American Medical Association, 286*, 141–144.

Prins, H., Tennent, G., & Trick, K. (1985). Motives for arson (fire raising). *Medicine, Science and the Law, 25*, 275–278.

Prinstein, M. J., Boergers, J., & Spirito, A. (2001). Adolescents' and their friends' health-risk behavior: Factors that alter or add to peer influence. *Journal of Pediatric Psychology, 26*, 287–298.

Reeve, E. A., Bernstein, G. A., & Christenson, G. A. (1992). Clinical characteristics and psychiatric comorbidity in children with trichotillomania. *Journal of the American Academy of Child and Adolescent Psychiatry, 31*, 132–138.

Root, C., MacKay, S., Henderson, J., Del Bove, G., & Warling, D. (2008). The link between maltreatment and juvenile firesetting: Correlates and underlying mechanisms. *Child Abuse and Neglect, 32*, 161–176.

Ross, S., & Heath, N. (2002). A study of the frequency of self-mutilation in a community sample of adolescents. *Journal of Youth and Adolescence, 31*, 67–77.

Rothbaum, B. O., & Ninan, P. T. (1994). The assessment of trichotillomania. *Behavior Research and Therapy, 32*, 651–662.

Sandman, C. A. (2009). Psychopharmacologic treatment of non-suicidal self-injury. In M. K. Nock (Ed.), *Understanding nonsuicidal self-injury: Origins, assessment, and treatment* (pp. 291–322). Washington, DC: American Psychological Association.

Sandman, C. A., Barron, J. L., & Colman, H. (1990). An orally administered opiate blocker, naltrexone, attenuates self-injurious behavior. *American Journal on Mental Retardation, 95*, 93–102.

Scherrer, J. F., Xian, H., Kapp, J. M., Waterman, B., Shah, K. R., Volberg, R., et al. (2007). Association between exposure to childhood and lifetime traumatic events and lifetime pathological gambling in a twin cohort. *Journal of Nervous and Mental Disease, 195*, 72–78.

Schur, S. B., Sikich, L., Findling, R. L., Malone, R. P., Crismon, M. L., Derivan, A., et al. (2003). Treatment recommendations for the use of antipsychotics for aggressive youth (TRAAY) part 1: A review. *Journal of the American Academy of Child and Adolescent Psychiatry, 42*, 132–144.

Shaffer, D., Garland, A., Vieland, V., & Underwood, M. (1991). The impact of curriculum-based suicide prevention programs for teenagers. *Journal of the American Academy of Child and Adolescent Psychiatry, 30*, 588–596.

Shaffer, D., Scott, M., Wilcox, H., Maslow, C., Hicks, R., Lucas, C. P., et al. (2004). The Columbia Suicide Screen: Validity and reliability of a screen for youth suicide and depression. *Journal of the American Academy of Child and Adolescent Psychiatry, 43*, 71–79.

Shaffer, H. J., Hall, M. N., & Vanderbilt, J. (1999). Estimating the prevalence of disordered gambling behavior in the United States and Canada: A research synthesis. *American Journal of Public Health, 89,* 1369–1376.

Shaw, E. D., Mann, J. J., Weiden, P. J., Sinsheimer, L. M., & Brunn, R. D. (1986). A case of suicidal and homicidal ideation and akathisia in a double-blind neuroleptic crossover study. *Journal of Clinical Psychopharmacology, 6,* 196–197.

Silverman, M. M., Berman, A. L., Sanddal, N. D., O'Carroll, P. W., & Joiner, T. E. (2007a). Rebuilding the tower of Babel: A revised nomenclature for the study of suicide and suicidal behaviors. Part 1: Background, rationale, and methodology. *Suicide and Life Threatening Behavior, 37,* 248–263.

Silverman, M. M., Berman, A. L., Sanddal, N. D., O'Carroll, P. W., & Joiner, T. E. (2007b). Rebuilding the tower of Babel: A revised nomenclature for the study of suicide and suicidal behaviors. Part 2: Suicide-related ideations, communications, and behaviors. *Suicide and Life Threatening Behavior, 37,* 264–277.

Slutske, W. S., Eisen, S., True, W. R., Lyons, M. J., Goldberg, J., & Tsuang, M. (2000). Common genetic vulnerability for pathological gambling and alcohol dependence in men. *Archives of General Psychiatry, 57,* 666–673.

Stanley, M. A., Borden, J. W., Bell, G. E., & Wagner, A. L. (1994). Nonclinical hair pulling: Phenomenology and related psychopathology. *Journal of Anxiety Disorders, 8,* 119–130.

Stein, D. J., Harvey, B., Seedat, S., & Hollander, E. (2006). Treatment of impulse-control disorders. In E. Hollander & D. J. Stein (Eds.), *Clinical manual of impulse-control disorders* (pp. 309–326). Arlington, VA: American Psychiatric Publishing.

Stein, D. J., & Hollander, E. (1992). Low-dose pimozide augmentation of serotonin reuptake blockers in the treatment of trichotillomania. *Journal of Clinical Psychiatry, 53,* 123–126.

Stewart, R. M., & Brown, R. I. (1988). An outcome study of Gamblers Anonymous. *British Journal of Psychiatry, 152,* 284–288.

Swedo, S. E. (1993). Trichotillomania. In E. Hollander (Ed.), *Obsessive-compulsive related disorders* (pp. 93–113). Washington, DC: American Psychiatric Publishing, Inc.

Swedo, S. E., & Leonard, H. L. (1992). Trichotillomania. An obsessive compulsive spectrum disorder? *Psychiatric Clinics of North America, 15,* 777–790.

Swedo, S. E., & Rapoport, J. L. (1991). Annotation: Trichotillomania. *Journal of Child Psychology and Psychiatry, 32,* 401–409.

Sylvain, C., Ladouceur, R., & Boisvert, J. M. (1997). Cognitive and behavioral treatment of pathological gambling: A controlled study. *Journal of Consulting and Clinical Psychology, 65,* 727–732.

Symons, F. J., Thompson, A., & Rodriguez, M. C. (2004). Self-injurious behavior and the efficacy of naltrexone treatment: A quantitative synthesis. *Mental Retardation and Developmental Disabilities Research Reviews, 10,* 193–200.

Thompson, E. A., Eggert, L. L., Randell, B. P., & Pike, K. C. (2001). Evaluation of indicated suicide risk prevention approaches for potential high school dropouts. *American Journal of Public Health, 91,* 742–752.

Thompson, W. N., Gazel, R., & Rickman, D. (1996). The social costs of gambling in Wisconsin. *Wisconsin Policy Research Institute Report, 9,* 1–44.

Tishler, C. L., Reiss, N. S., & Rhodes, A. R. (2007). Suicidal behavior in children younger than twelve: A diagnostic challenge for emergency department personnel. *Academic Emergency Medicine, 14,* 810–818.

Tucker, G. J., & Gorman, E. R. (1967). The significance of the suicide gesture in the military. *American Journal of Psychiatry, 123,* 854–861.

Tucker, W. (1999). The "mad" vs. the "bad" revisited: Managing predatory behavior. *Psychiatric Quarterly, 70,* 221–230.

Virkkunen, M., Nuutila, A., Goodwin, F. K., & Linnoila, M. (1987). Cerebrospinal fluid monoamine metabolite levels in male arsonists. *Archives of General Psychiatry, 44,* 241–247.

Vitaro, F., Tremblay, R. E., Kerr, M., Pagani, L., & Bukowski, W. M. (1997). Disruptiveness, friends' characteristics, and delinquency in early adolescence: A test of two competing models of development. *Child Development, 68,* 676–689.

Wakefield, J. C. (1992). The concept of mental disorder: On the boundary between biological facts and social values. *American Psychologist, 47,* 373–388.

Wakefield, J. C. (1997). Diagnosing DSM-IV–Part I: DSM-IV and the concept of disorder. *Behaviour Research and Therapy, 35,* 633–649.

Weissman, M. M., Bland, R. C., Canino, G. J., Greenwald, S., Hwu, H. G., Joyce, P. R., et al. (1999). Prevalence of suicide ideation and suicide attempts in nine countries. *Psychological Medicine, 29,* 9–17.

Welte, J. W., Barnes, G. M., Tidwell, M. C., & Hoffman, J. H. (2008). The prevalence of problem gambling among U.S. adolescents and young adults: Results from a national survey. *Journal of Gambling Studies, 24,* 119–133.

Welu, T. C. (1977). A follow-up program for suicide attempters: Evaluation of effectiveness. *Suicide and Life Threatening Behavior, 7,* 17–30.

Weyler, W., Hsu, Y. P., & Breakefield, X. O. (1990). Biochemistry and genetics of monoamine oxidase. *Pharmacology and Therapeutics, 47,* 391–417.

White, J. L., Moffitt, T. E., Caspi, A., Bartusch, D. J., Needles, D. J., & Stouthamer-Loeber, M. (1994). Measuring impulsivity and examining its relationship to delinquency. *Journal of Abnormal Psychology, 103,* 192–205.

Whitlock, J. L., & Knox, K. L. (2009). Intervention and prevention in the community. In M. K. Nixon & N. L. Heath (Eds.), *Self-injury in youth: The essential guide to assessment and intervention* (pp. 173–194). New York, NY: Taylor & Francis Group.

Whitlock, J. L., Powers, J. L., & Eckenrode, J. (2006). The virtual cutting edge: The internet and adolescent self-injury. *Developmental Psychology, 42,* 407–417.

Whitlock, J. L., Purington, A., & Gershkovich, M. (2009). Media and the internet and non-suicidal self-injury. In M. K. Nock (Ed.), *Understanding non-suicidal self-injury: Origins, assessment, and treatment.* Washington, DC: American Psychological Association.

Whittington, C. J., Kendall, T., Fonagy, P., Cottrell, D., Cotgrove, A., & Boddington, E. (2004). Selective serotonin reuptake inhibitors in childhood depression: Systematic review of published versus unpublished data. *Lancet, 363,* 1341–1345.

Winters, K. C., & Rich, T. (1998). A twin study of adult gambling behavior. *Journal of Gambling Studies, 14,* 213–225.

World Health Organization. (2008). World Health Organization: Suicide Prevention (SUPRE). Retrieved 2008 June 20, from http://www.who.int/mental_health/prevention/suicide/suicideprevent/en/

Yates, T. M. (2004). The developmental psychopathology of self-injurious behavior: Compensatory regulation in posttraumatic adaptation. *Clinical Psychology Review, 24,* 35–74.

CHAPTER 24

The Spectrum of Personality Disorders

Susan C. South, Thomas F. Oltmanns, *and* Robert F. Krueger

Abstract

The concept of personality disorder has existed throughout the history of psychology and psychiatry. The ten current personality disorders (PDs) listed in the DSM-IV are conceived of as distinct syndromes. Nevertheless, DSM-IV PDs overlap extensively with each other, with normal personality traits, and with Axis I psychopathology. Thus, many investigators suggest that, in DSM-5, the classification system for PDs should be revised to better reflect the closeness of the links between personality and psychopathology, perhaps by linking both constructs within broader spectrums of psychopathological variation. The most common and well-accepted suggestion is that the categorical diagnoses of DSM-IV should be replaced with a dimensional model of pathological personality traits, and the links between personality traits and more syndromal forms of psychopathology (Axis I disorders) should also be explicitly articulated. In this chapter, we review current research on how PDs are linked with broad spectrums of personality and psychopathology. Specifically, we examine (1) evidence relevant to the etiology and course of PDs, (2) how these disorders can best be assessed, and (3) evidence regarding the most effective practices in the treatment of PDs, with the aim of articulating how etiology, course, assessment, and treatment of PDs might be conceptualized in a spectrum-based classification system.

Keywords: Assessment, etiology, personality disorders, spectrum, treatment

The current *Diagnostic and Statistical Manual of Mental Disorders, Fourth Edition, Text Revision* (American Psychiatric Association [APA], 2000) identifies ten categorical disorders of personality, coded on Axis II, which are presumed to begin relatively early in life, follow a chronic and debilitating course, and result in significant personal, social, and occupational impairment or distress. The personality disorders (PDs) show considerable overlap with both "normal-range" personality traits and other forms of psychopathology (coded on Axis I). This has led some to suggest that PDs be reconceptualized as elements within broader spectrums of mental illness. From this vantage point, personality traits provide the underlying structures for understanding the full range of human variation, including the pathological range.

Both episodic (DSM-IV Axis I) psychopathologies, and relatively more enduring forms of psychopathology (DSM-IV Axis II) can then be understood as manifestations within spectrums organized by underlying personality-based risk for diagnosable mental disorders. Personality disorders are enduring, extreme manifestations of personality, and episodic mental disorders occur when persons with vulnerable personalities encounter circumstances that are beyond their ability to cope (e.g., a person with a propensity toward negative affect undergoes a significantly stressful life transition, resulting in a depressive episode). Indeed, this "spectrum perspective" is likely to have some impact on the organization and structure of the DSM, which is currently undergoing revision, with the publication of DSM-5 scheduled for 2013.

In this chapter, we review current research on where PDs fall within spectrums of personality and psychopathology. Specifically, we examine evidence relevant to the etiology and course of PDs, how these disorders can best be assessed by current techniques, and evidence regarding best practices in the treatment of PDs.

Conceptual Overview of Personality Disorders

With regard to the DSM, PDs have existed as discrete forms of mental illness since the first edition (APA, 1952). Conceptualizations of personality pathology arose from myriad clinical and theoretical formulations, from being viewed as *formes frustes* of more acute, debilitating pathology (e.g., schizotypal PD and schizophrenia) to Freudian notions of poor ego development (e.g., narcissistic PD; Frances & Widiger, 1986; Livesley, 2001). The first and second editions of the DSM listed descriptions of each main type of personality disorder (12 in the first edition, ten in the second), and a categorical diagnosis was made by use of these brief (one- to two-paragraph) descriptions. In the third edition of the DSM, the PDs were separated from more putatively acute disorders of mental functioning (e.g., major depressive disorder, schizophrenia) and placed on Axis II (APA, 1980); it was hoped that by placing the PDs on their own axis, clinicians would feel less of a pull between assigning *either* a more acute, transient condition, *or* a chronic, relatively stable character defect. Even more importantly, each of the disorders was now defined by a polythetic set of criteria, a certain number of which were required to meet a diagnosis.

Over the course of the four editions of the DSM, several disorders have been added (e.g., schizotypal, narcissistic, avoidant, and dependent in DSM-III), others have been removed (e.g., cyclothymic). Many have been present consistently since DSM-I (e.g., antisocial, paranoid, schizoid), although with various revisions to specific definitions and criteria (Coolidge & Segal, 1998). The current DSM-IV-TR (APA, 2000) includes ten PDs grouped into three, somewhat arbitrary (Sheets & Craighead, 2007), descriptive clusters: paranoid, schizoid, and schizotypal in Cluster A (odd-eccentric); antisocial, borderline, histrionic, and narcissistic in Cluster B (dramatic-erratic); and avoidant, dependent, and obsessive-compulsive in Cluster C (anxious-fearful).

All ten PD diagnoses are a collection of symptoms from one of four areas: affect, cognition, behavior, and interpersonal relations. A diagnosis is met if an individual meets enough criteria (e.g., four of seven paranoid symptoms) by demonstrating that symptom and by meeting the general provision of impairment or distress. As with any DSM disorder, it is presumed that each class or category of PD is at least somewhat unique in etiology, course, and treatment correlates (Widiger & Mullins-Sweatt, 2007). The PDs, therefore, are presumed to be nontrivially distinct from each other, from other forms of psychopathology (e.g., major depressive disorder, schizophrenia), and from general models of normal personality structure. We know from abundant research, however, that the ten PDs are highly comorbid with each other (Bornstein, 1998; Lilienfeld, Waldman, & Israel, 1994; Livesley, 2003) and with Axis I psychopathology (Dolan-Sewell, Krueger, & Shea, 2001), and they show high correlations with measures of normative personality traits (Costa & Widiger, 2002). The current diagnostic classification system for the PDs has been criticized on numerous other grounds, including poor reliability, poor convergent and discriminant validity, and inadequate coverage (Clark, Livesley, & Morey, 1997; First et al., 2002; Livesley, 2003; Millon, 2002; Widiger & Trull, 2007).

These criticisms have led to two interrelated lines of research. First, it has been suggested that the current conceptualization of PD should be revised, with a change from the current "yes/no" categorical system of diagnosis to a system whereby personality pathology is assessed on some type of dimensional scale (Widiger & Trull, 2007). Evidence in favor of a dimensional system includes better reliability and stability of personality assessment, the lack of a discrete boundary between normal and abnormal personal functioning, and empirical evidence that personality structure is similar across clinical and nonclinical samples (Clark & Watson, 1999; Livesley, 2003; Livesley, Jang, & Vernon, 1998; O'Connor, 2002). Second, researchers have investigated the different forms of interplay between PDs, normal personality, and psychopathology. Although there is mixed evidence for the various forms of relationships, the greatest support seems to be in favor of "spectrum" models that explain covariance of these constructs in terms of higher-order factors. A spectrum model would, in fact, pull together both dimensional conceptions of personality pathology and the ways in which personality traits form the basis for personality dysfunction and acute forms of psychopathology. We review evidence for both lines of research here.

Dimensional Conceptualizations of Personality Disorders

It was only with the third edition of the DSM that thresholds were delineated to identify the presence versus absence of a disorder per se (APA, 1980). This revision of PD diagnoses certainly helped with the ability to operationalize PDs in structured interviews and to thereby study their reliability and validity (e.g., Stangl et al., 1985). Categorical diagnoses have many benefits, including ease of conceptualization and communication among health professionals. Unfortunately, attempts to delineate discrete categories of pathology with clearly identified cut-points have instead resulted in inadequate coverage, as seen by the high prevalence of PDNOS (not otherwise specified); arbitrary thresholds (e.g., Is someone with five symptoms of borderline personality disorder truly different from someone with six symptoms? (see Asnaani, Chelminski, Young, & Zimmerman, 2007); and heterogeneity among individuals with the same diagnosis (there are 151 ways to earn a diagnosis of borderline PD; Skodol et al., 2002b; Widiger & Trull, 2007).

Given the numerous difficulties with a categorical model of PDs, there is now strong interest in moving toward a dimensional conceptualization of personality pathology (Trull & Durrett, 2005; Widiger & Simonsen, 2005; Widiger, Simonsen, Krueger, Livesley, & Verheul, 2006; Widiger & Trull, 2007). This push is based, at least in part, on the attempt to integrate research on PDs with basic science research on personality traits. Even though the current PDs originated in the clinical experiences of psychiatrists or psychoanalytically trained clinicians, with little input from normative personality trait research (Ball, 2001; Livesley, 2001; Millon et al., 1996), there appears to be a great deal of overlap between normal personality traits and abnormal personality traits (Markon, Krueger, & Watson, 2005).

One of the most prolific areas of research into dimensional conceptualizations of PDs has involved using one of the most popular models of normal personality, the Five Factor Model (FFM), to describe personality pathology. The FFM grew out of the lexical tradition of factor analytic models of trait theory, and includes the broad dimensions of extraversion, neuroticism, conscientiousness, agreeableness, and openness, each of which can be further divided into six separate facets (McCrae & Costa, 2008). Extensive empirical research supports the construct validity of the FFM. Factor analytic studies consistently find a similar underlying structure of the FFM (McCrae & Costa, 2008), behavior

genetic research supports the genetic basis of the five factors (Bouchard & Loehlin, 2001), and the five factors appear to be universally found across different races and cultures (Allik, 2005; Yamagata et al., 2006). Thus, the FFM appears to be appropriate to build a bridge between current PD diagnoses and normal personality traits.

Numerous studies have shown that DSM-defined PDs can be adequately represented with the FFM traits (Widiger & Costa, 2002), including the underlying facet dimensions (Axelrod, Widiger, Trull, & Corbitt, 1997; Dyce & O'Connor, 1998; Morey et al., 2002). For instance, the FFM description of borderline PD consists of high levels of many of the facets of neuroticism, plus low facets of agreeableness (i.e., trust, compliance; Mullins-Sweatt & Widiger, 2006). Meta-analysis of multiple independent samples has confirmed that the ten DSM-IV-TR PDs are related to the five higher-order factors in predictable and meaningful ways, with most lying in a quadrant formed by high neuroticism and low agreeableness (Samuel & Widiger, 2008; Saulsman & Page, 2004). Using ratings of hypothetical PD patients created by expert clinicians, Lynam and Widiger (2001) developed FFM prototypes of the PDs that largely accounted for covariation among PD symptoms.

The FFM does not stand alone as the only possible dimensional conceptualization of PDs. More than 18 different dimensional systems of classification have been proposed as alternatives to the current DSM classification (Widiger & Simonsen, 2005), and several of these dimensional systems have been operationalized with standardized assessment instruments. These systems differ in how they dimensionalize personality pathology. The Millon Clinical Multiaxial Inventory (MCMI, Millon, 1983; MCMI-II, Millon, 1987; MCMI-III, Millon, Millon, & Davis, 1994) uses the DSM PD constructs but presents scores dimensionally. In comparison, instruments like the Dimensional Assessment of Personality Pathology-Basic Questionnaire (DAPP-BQ; Livesley & Jackson, 2002) and the Schedule for Nonadaptive and Adaptive Personality (SNAP; Clark, 1993) were developed through structural modeling of personality traits thought to cover the range of personality pathology. The resulting factor structures of these different systems are not perfectly overlapping; for instance, the DAPP-BQ has four higher-order factors of emotional dysregulation, dissocial behaviour, inhibitedness, and compulsivity (Livesley et al., 1998), whereas the SNAP has three higher-order domains of positive affectivity, negative affectivity, and constraint (Clark, 1993). However, the SNAP and DAPP-BQ show a great deal of convergence at the specific trait level (Clark, Livesley, Schroeder, & Irish, 2002). In fact, a common hierarchical structure consistently appears across different measures of pathological personality, with four main factors emerging: extraversion (stimulus-seeking, exhibitionism, assertiveness, sociability, and detachment), antagonism (mistrust, aggression, suspiciousness, altruism, compliance, and submissiveness), constraint (dutifulness, achievement, ambitiousness, responsibility, and self-discipline), and emotional dysregulation (self-harm, dependency, alienation, depressiveness, and vulnerability) (Widiger & Simonsen, 2005).

A remaining issue pertains to "diagnosing" a PD using a dimensional model. One suggestion uses a four-step process within the FFM: (1) a comprehensive description using the 30 FFM facets; (2) identification of social and occupational impairments; (3) determination of the level of clinically significant impairment; and (4) matching the individual's FFM profile to diagnostic "prototypes" (Widiger, Costa, & McCrae, 2002; Widiger & Mullins-Sweatt, 2009; Widiger & Trull, 2007). Such a system would represent a paradigm shift, as it goes against the grain of the categorical system of psychiatric nomenclature; however, a dimensional system represents an opportunity to provide valid and reliable descriptions of personality pathology that are much richer in description than the current PD diagnoses. Numerous other advantages also accrue from a dimensional approach. We turn now to discuss how a dimensional approach can be helpful in handling the co-occurrence of putatively separable syndromes, a phenomenon traditionally known as comorbidity.

Comorbidity

One strong argument against the current categorical system of classification for personality pathology is the extreme comorbidity both within Axis II PDs, and between Axis I and Axis II disorders. The diagnosis of just one PD in an individual is rare; more common is the assignment of multiple PDs (Grant, Stinson, Dawson, Chou, & Ruan, 2005b; Zimmerman, Rothschild, & Chelminski, 2005), or the catch-all label of *personality disorder not otherwise specified* (PD-NOS; Verheul, Bartak, & Widiger, 2007; Verheul & Widiger, 2004). As much research attests, considerable overlap also exists between Axis I and Axis II psychopathology (Oldham et al., 1995). Dolan-Sewell and colleagues (2001) reported that between 66% and 97% of PD patients also

meet criteria for an Axis I disorder; in addition, between 13% and 81% of patients with a syndrome disorder can also be diagnosed with a PD. Certain patterns of comorbidity are more likely to be found, both in population-based and clinical samples. For instance, mood and anxiety disorders are often found in patients with PDs, particularly avoidant and dependent PD (Grant et al., 2005a). Substance use disorders are most commonly found in common with Cluster B PDs (Ball, 2005a; Compton, Conway, Stinson, Colliver, & Grant, 2005; Trull, Waudby, & Sher, 2004).

Currently, four models are used to explain Axis I–II connections (see Clark, Watson, & Mineka, 1994; Krueger & Tackett, 2003; Tackett, 2006; Watson, Clark, & Harkness, 1994; Widiger & Smith, 1999). These four models are known as the Vulnerability Model, the Complication/Scar Model, the Pathoplasty Model, and the Spectrum Model. The Predisposition or Vulnerability Model proposes that a PD acts as risk factor for the development of an Axis I clinical disorder. According to the Scar Model, the presence of an Axis I disorder "scars" an individual's preexisting personality, leading to the development of a PD. If an individual has both an Axis I and Axis II disorder that are etiologically distinct, the Pathoplasty Model suggests that the Axis II disorder will affect the course, severity, or treatment response to the Axis I disorder. Finally, the Spectrum Model states that that Axis I and Axis II disorders are comorbid because specific disorders can be well-conceptualized as being within the same psychopathology spectrums.

These models are not necessarily incompatible, and evidence supports a number of accounts of the ways in which Axis I and II disorders may be related. For instance, reports from the Children in the Community Study find support both for the influence of childhood MDD on the development of subsequent Axis II pathology (Kasen et al., 2001) and for adolescent PD symptoms as a risk factor for the development of later anxiety disorders (Johnson, Cohen, Kasen, & Brook, 2006b), eating disorders (Johnson, Cohen, Kasen, & Brook, 2006a), or unipolar depression (Johnson, Cohen, Kasen, & Brook, 2005a). Longitudinal studies have also found evidence for the influence of Axis I disorders in adolescence on presence of PDs (Rey, Morris-Yates, Singh, Andrews, & Stewart, 1995) and higher PD dimensional scores in young adulthood (Lewinsohn, Rohde, Seeley, & Klein, 1997). The general point is that Axis I and II disorders are related, as opposed to being entirely distinct. These relations need to be modeled and conceptualized in working toward a richer understanding of how personality phenomena are connected with the development of symptoms and syndromes that are more episodic.

Etiology and Development

Biological and genetic factors play important roles in personality pathology. The relevant literature ranges from comprehensive theories linking neurobiological substrates to specific forms of personality dysfunction, to behavior and molecular genetic research on specific PD diagnoses and latent factors underlying personality disorder traits. Cultural and psychosocial factors also play a role in the etiology and development of personality pathology, and longitudinal studies provide evidence of certain childhood predictors of adolescent and adult PDs. We turn now to review these literatures.

Biological and Genetic Basis of Personality Disorders

For decades, it was assumed that PDs were largely a result of psychosocial and environmental factors. The field of behavior genetics, which came to prominence in the latter half of the 20th century, changed many peoples' thinking by conclusively demonstrating a genetic basis to most forms of psychopathology, including PDs (e.g., Kendler et al., 2008).

The behavior genetic literature relies heavily on studies of twins. With advances in genotyping technology, however, many researchers are now moving toward molecular genetic studies of personality pathology. Unfortunately, molecular genetic work on personality has been stymied by poor replicability and small effect sizes (Krueger & Johnson, 2008). This situation is not unique to behavioral phenotypes and has also been observed with other disease phenotypes (e.g., Tuma, 2009).

With regard to the twin literature, there has been a wide range of estimates of genetic and environmental influences on the DSM PDs, varying by population sampled and the method of PD assessment used (see Livesley & Jang, 2008, for a recent review). Using a structured interview for the DSM-IV PDs, Torgersen and colleagues (2000) reported heritabilities ranging from 28% to 79%. Other research using structured interview assessments of PDs, found heritabilities at the lower end of the estimates that Torgersen and colleagues (2000) found for the cluster A and cluster C disorders (Kendler et al., 2006; Reichborn-Kjennerud et al., 2007).

Given the mixed results for DSM conceptualizations of PDs, researchers have turned to examine behavior genetic models of dimensional personality traits. As reviewed earlier, extensive overlap occurs between normal and pathological personality traits, to the point at which PD prototype descriptions have been created from normal models of personality (i.e., the FFM). The major dimensions of the FFM have consistently been shown to have heritabilities ranging from .4–.6 (Bouchard & Loehlin, 2001). And, indeed dimensional conceptualizations of pathological personality traits tend to have more consistent estimates in this range, for both more narrow, lower-order traits (Livesley, Jang, Jackson, & Vernon, 1993), as well as higher-order traits (Jang, Livesley, & Vernon, 1998). These data also support a hierarchical conceptualization of personality pathology, inasmuch as there is evidence for genetic influence on the higher-order broader factors (e.g., emotional dysregulation), as well as genetic influences specific to the lower-order traits, beyond influences on the higher-order factors (Livesley, Jang, & Vernon, 1998).

Psychosocial and Cultural Factors

Although PDs and pathological traits are moderately heritable, environmental factors also influence the development of PDs. Childhood risk variables that have been linked to the diagnosis of PD include low socioeconomic status in the family of origin, single-parent family, parental death, and childhood physical health problems (Cohen, 2008). Findings from several longitudinal studies have also uncovered other predictors of PD development, including childhood verbal, physical, and sexual abuse as well as other forms of family stress and trauma (see Clark, 2005, for a recent review).

In general, the psychosocial risk factors for adult personality psychopathology fall into one of three categories: maladaptive experiences in the family of origin; traumatic experiences, including childhood abuse; and social and interpersonal stressors (Pars, 2001). Problematic parenting behaviors evidenced by age 16 in offspring have been linked to elevated risk for offspring PDs (particularly antisocial, avoidant, borderline, histrionic, paranoid, and schizotypal) at age 22 and age 33 (Johnson, Cohen, Chen, Kasen, & Brook, 2006). Maladaptive parenting (e.g., harsh punishment, low amount of time spent with child, low affection, loud arguments with spouse) has also been significantly associated with PDs during adolescence and late adulthood (Johnson, Cohen, Kasen, Smailes, & Brook, 2001a).

One of the most researched psychosocial predictors of adult personality pathology is childhood abuse (Fossati, Madeddu, & Maffei, 1999; Grover et al., 2007). Childhood verbal abuse has been linked with presence of paranoid, narcissistic, borderline, and obsessive-compulsive PDs, and elevated symptom levels of borderline, narcissistic, paranoid, schizoid, schizotypal PDs (Johnson et al., 2001b), whereas Cluster A and Cluster B PDs were associated with physical and sexual abuse in adolescence and young adulthood (Cohen, Brown, & Smailes, 2001). Certainly the PD most strongly tied to child neglect and abuse is borderline PD (Zanarini, 2000). Data from the Collaborative Longitudinal PDs Study (CLPS) indicates that child maltreatment is in fact highly prevalent across all ten PDs; 34% of persons with a PD reported childhood sexual abuse, and 82% reported some type of childhood neglect (Battle et al., 2004). Borderline PD was the disorder most clearly linked with childhood maltreatment; obsessive-compulsive PD was also associated with sexual abuse, and individuals with antisocial PD showed elevated rates of verbal and sexual abuse.

With regard to cultural factors, given that the diagnosis of PD is dependent on dysfunction related to cultural norms—"an enduring pattern of inner experience and behavior that deviates markedly from the expectations of the individual's culture" (APA, 2000, p. 685)—it is possible that PDs may look different depending on the population studied. In general, the few studies to examine structural equivalence of PD pathology finds invariance across different cultures (Pukrop et al., 2001; Van Kampen, 2002; Zheng et al., 2002). Rigozzi et al. (2009) compared the structure of the International Personality Disorders Examination Screening Questionnaire (Loranger et al. 1994) in four French-speaking African subsamples and a subsample from Switzerland. They found that both a two-factor and four-factor solution replicated across the two cultures; further, the four-factor solution was similar to the four factors identified by Livesley (1998).

Longitudinal Course and Related Impairment

The DSM (APA, 2000) definition of PDs includes the provision that these disorders are "stable and of long duration," "inflexible and pervasive," and usually present by adolescence. Reports from the Children in the Community Study (CIC), which has collected data on more than 800 individuals beginning in childhood, have shown that mean levels of PD symptoms are highest in adolescence; a decline occurs from age 9 to age 27, but general

symptoms are relatively stable across all assessment ages (Cohen, Crawford, Johnson, & Kasen, 2005). The authors suggest that declines in PD symptoms over adolescence may represent a normative improvement in the types of maladaptive behaviors underlying PDs (e.g., impulsivity, rule breaking), whereas the most impaired individuals show increasingly deviant behavior beginning in adulthood. In the CLPS study, participants with diagnosable PDs tend to vary even from month to month on meeting threshold criteria and show high rates of remission, although they were more stable than individuals meeting a major depressive disorder diagnosis (Skodol et al., 2005). Dimensional conceptualizations of PDs were more stable over time, with some symptom dimensions (e.g., affective instability in borderline PD) showing greater stability than others (e.g., self-injury). Zanarini and colleagues (2005) also found relatively high rates of remission for borderline PD (73.5% over the 6-year study), suggesting that the road to health is slower for borderline PD patients than for patients with major mood disorders, but noting that recurrence is much rarer. Thus, across these three studies using community and clinical samples, evidence demonstrates a notable decline in PDs from adolescence into early adulthood.

One of the most consistent findings from these longitudinal studies is the greater stability found for dimensional conceptualizations of PDs versus categorical diagnosis. That is, the correlational stability of PD symptom counts over time is higher (Shea et al., 2002) than the stability of PD diagnoses per se (see McDavid & Pilkonis, 1996, for a review). This is further support for a reconceptualization of personality pathology, and another reason why researchers have turned to normal models of personality, particularly the FFM, as an alternative to current PD categories (i.e., such models provide constructs with greater temporal stability). A recent meta-analysis of longitudinal studies of the FFM found relatively good consistency of the traits, with stability coefficients increasing from .31 in childhood to .54 during older adolescence/young adulthood, with a high point of .74 in the 50–70 year age range (Roberts & DelVecchio, 2000). Utilizing data from the CLPS study, Warner and colleagues (2004) examined whether the stability of PD symptoms was attributable to the stability of normal personality traits (i.e., FFM dimensions) underlying the disorders. For three of the four PDs (schizotypal, borderline, and avoidant), FFM traits predicted change in the disorders over time, but change in the disorders did not predict change in the FFM factors. These results were consistent with the view that the same personality dimensions underlie both normal and pathological personality. Thus, PDs may in fact represent both biologically based temperaments and chronic and maladaptive behaviors that result as a function of interactions with the world (Clark, 2005).

Personality disorders are relatively common disorders that are related to personal distress and/or associated impairments that are not directly tied to a diagnostic criterion. Strong evidence now suggests that PDs impair functioning in multiple domains of life (Chen et al., 2006; Grant et al., 2004; Skodol et al., 2002; Skodol, Johnson, Cohen, Sneed, & Crawford, 2007), including strained family relationships (Johnson, Chen, & Cohen, 2004), poorly functioning marital relationships (South, Turkheimer, & Oltmanns, 2008), a greater likelihood of Axis I disorders (Johnson et al., 1999), and higher risk for violence and criminal behavior (Johnson et al., 2000). Using the Children in the Community sample, Chen et al. (2006) found that personality disorder diagnosis at age 22, particularly a Cluster B disorder, was associated with lower quality of life (i.e., a composite of physical health, psychological well-being, social relationships, role function, and contextual domain) at age 33, even after controlling for co-occurring Axis I disorders, demographics, and physical illness. In particular, the diagnosis of PDNOS appears to be strongly related to concurrent and future problems, including interpersonal difficulties, comorbid Axis I pathology, poor educational achievement, suicide attempts, and physical aggression (Johnson et al., 2005b).

Assessment

Several important issues must be considered with regard to the assessment of PDs, regardless of whether these problems are viewed in terms of the DSM-IV categorical definitions or in terms of a dimensional approach to personality pathology. These include the choice of measurement tools (e.g., interviews versus questionnaires) and the selection of a source of relevant information (e.g., the self versus other people who know the person well).

General Considerations

Disordered views of the self and others prevent many people with PDs from seeking help. When they do enter treatment, they may not describe their problems in a way that allows the therapist to recognize accurately the nature of their problems. Consider the example of paranoid personality disorder. Because they believe that all faults lie with others and not with the self, most paranoid individuals do not complain that they are unnecessarily suspicious, lacking in trust, or hypervigilant. Instead, they typically present with problems that reflect hostile and adversarial relationships with others. People who are narcissistic do not see themselves as being grandiose or entitled, but rather trace their problems to the failure of other people to appreciate their importance. People who meet the criteria for antisocial personality disorder often put a positive spin on their pathological personality traits and describe themselves as being adventuresome or fun-loving. Viewed from the perspective of the self, personality problems can easily be misconstrued or minimized.

An extended, comprehensive assessment process also requires a willingness to engage in an exchange of personal information that may be difficult for people with PDs to tolerate. Given their hypersensitivity to threat, direct confrontation may cause a paranoid person to become more guarded and less trusting of the therapist or to terminate therapy prematurely. People with antisocial personality disorder may view the process as an opportunity for manipulation and deception. Therefore, in discussing the information that is collected during the assessment process, the therapist must walk a fine line, balancing acceptance with objectivity.

The concept of social dysfunction plays an important role in the definition of PDs, as well as in their assessment. Subjective distress and social impairment provide a large part of the justification for defining these problems as mental disorders. If the personality characteristics identified in DSM-IV criterion sets typically interfere with a person's ability to get along with other people and perform social roles, they become more than just a collection of eccentric traits or peculiar habits. They can then be viewed as a form of harmful dysfunction (Kendell, 2002; Wakefield, 1999). In fact, most of the clusters of pathological personality traits that are described on Axis II do lead to impaired social functioning or occupational impairment (Oltmanns, Melley, Turkheimer, 2002; Skodol et al., 2007).

Unfortunately, the assessment of impairment in psychosocial functioning presents a difficult challenge for a number of reasons. One is that the criteria for social impairment have not been clearly defined (Ro & Clark, 2009). In some cases, specific criteria seem necessarily to imply interpersonal difficulties. For example, one criterion for obsessive-compulsive PD is: "excessively devoted to work and productivity to the exclusion of leisure activities and friendships." Other items require additional data gathering to indicate whether the feature in question, if present, actually causes a problem in the person's life (e.g., "shows rigidity and stubbornness"). Patients who are being treated in a clinical setting necessarily seem to suffer from distress or social impairment, but the assessment of these problems may be more difficult with regard to people who are not seeking treatment.

Questions about the impact of PD features also require the demonstration of self-knowledge. If a person does acknowledge the presence of a certain characteristic such as rigidity, he or she still might deny that it has any detrimental influence on daily activities. Should we accept that statement at face value? Are there other sources of information that might be consulted? The vast majority of studies that have examined psychosocial functioning and PDs have relied exclusively on self-report questionnaires to measure impairment. One example is the Social Functioning Questionnaire, an eight-item measure of general social functioning, e.g., "I have difficulties in getting and keeping close relationships" (Tyrer, 1993). The correlation between the SFQ and the Beck Depression Inventory in one study of 577 college students was .63 (Oltmanns et al., 2002). Clearly, mood has an important impact on subjective responses regarding psychosocial functioning.

Developmental issues also create challenges for the assessment of PDs, particularly with regard to the formal diagnostic categories defined in DSM-IV. One involves an assumption about age of onset for PDs (Tackett, Balsis, Oltmanns, & Krueger, 2009). According to DSM-IV, to assign a PD diagnosis "its onset can be traced back at least to adolescence or early adulthood." The manual does not allow for the possibility of a late-onset PD (Widiger & Seidlitz, 2002). How is that information collected for an older adult? If a 60-year-old person currently exhibits a sufficient number of features to qualify for a specific PD diagnosis, the clinician would need to establish that these symptoms were also evident many years ago. Should we rely on the person's recollections of long-past experiences to verify the diagnosis, recognizing that autobiographical memories are often flawed? The most practical solution is to focus on the person's recent experience, recognizing that it is difficult to create a completely accurate portrait of past experience.

Another important developmental issue involves the possibility of age bias in the DSM-IV diagnostic criteria (Balsis, Gleason, Woods, & Oltmanns, 2007; Balsis, Woods, Gleason, & Oltmanns, 2007). Some older adults with significant personality pathology may remain undiagnosed and untreated because the features listed in the manual were not chosen with the social context and physical condition of older adults in mind. For example, one criterion for avoidant personality disorder is met if the person "avoids occupational activities that involve significant interpersonal contact, because of fears of criticism, disapproval, or rejection." This criterion would be of little value in the consideration of people who are retired from their jobs. Formal psychometric assessments conducted with people from various age groups have demonstrated that a substantial proportion of the DSM-IV criteria may be inappropriate for use with older adults (Agronin & Maletta, 2000). It remains to be determined whether alternative descriptors can be identified that would be more useful in identifying constructs related to personality pathology in older adults (Tackett et al., 2009).

Assessment Instruments

The most widely recognized approach to the assessment of PDs, in both research and clinical practice, involves the use of interviews. Many different semistructured interviews have been developed for the diagnosis of PDs (Zimmerman, 1994). Examples include the Structured Interview for DSM-IV Personality (SIDP-IV; Pfohl, Blum, & Zimmerman, 1997) and the Personality Disorders Interview (PDI-IV; Widiger, Mangine, Corbitt, Ellis, & Thomas, 1995). Each of the interview schedules provides a list of opening questions on topics related to the diagnostic features, as well as suggested follow-up probes to be used whenever the person admits problems in a particular area. Clark and Harrison (2001) have described in detail the advantages and potential weaknesses of these instruments. Most efforts to evaluate empirically the utility of semistructured interviews have focused on the issue of reliability. Inter-rater reliability estimates in a joint interview format are higher (average $\kappa > .60$) than either short-interval test–retest or the long-interval test–retest. Reliability increases when PDs are computed using dimensional scores rather than categorical scores (Zimmerman & Coryell, 1989; Pilkonis, Heape, Proietti, & Clark, 1995). Less attention has been paid to the validity of diagnostic interviews in the assessment of PDs. Convergent validity (different interviews compared to each other or an interview compared to a self-report questionnaire) has been shown to be relatively poor (Clark, Livesley, & Morey, 1997). Clinicians should therefore consider the results of diagnostic interviews with some caution.

These instruments are considered to be the "gold standard" with regard to the diagnosis of PDs, but they depend largely on the ability or willingness of the person to recognize the nature of his or her problems.

Another popular approach to the assessment of PDs involves the administration of self-report questionnaires. Several different instruments are available. Some focus on symptoms of specific PDs, others focus on personality traits that are related to personality pathology. A final option is to collect information regarding interpersonal difficulties that follow as a consequence of PDs. Rather than focusing on diagnostic scales, with an emphasis on somewhat arbitrary thresholds and a categorical view regarding the presence or absence of specific PDs, some self-report instruments place greater emphasis on personality dimensions. Some of these focus exclusively on normal personality traits. One popular alternative of this type is the NEO-PI-R, a questionnaire that provides scores based on the FFM of personality (Costa & McCrea, 1989). Using this type of measure for the assessment of traits that are related to PDs, one might expect patterns of scores that have been shown to be associated with each of the different disorders (Lynam & Widiger, 2001; Miller, Pilkonis, & Clifton, 2005). For example, a person with antisocial personality disorder would be expected to produce scores that are high on some facets of neuroticism, such as angry hostility and impulsiveness, high on certain facets of extraversion, such as excitement seeking, low on certain facets of agreeableness, such as tendermindedness and straightforwardness, and low on certain facets of conscientiousness, such as self-discipline and dutifulness. A person who is pathologically dependent would also be expected to produce a high score on neuroticism (especially anxiousness and self-consciousness), as well as high scores on agreeableness (especially trust, compliance, and modesty). Many leading investigators favor this approach to the assessment of pathological personality characteristics (Samuel & Widiger, 2008; Widiger & Mullins-Sweatt, 2009).

The Schedule for Nonadaptive and Adaptive Personality (SNAP) is a factor analytically derived, self-report instrument that is designed to measure trait dimensions that are important in the domain of PDs (Clark, 1990; 1993; Simms & Clark, 2006). The instrument includes both obvious and more subtle items, which are intended to tap the high and low ends of all of the trait dimensions. The core of the SNAP is composed of 15 scales, including 12 trait scales associated with relatively specific forms of personality pathology and three more general "temperament" scales (negative temperament, positive temperament, and disinhibition). For example, the specific trait scales most related to paranoia include mistrust, aggression, and detachment. The SNAP also includes five validity scales that can be used to identify subjects who have responded carelessly or defensively. They are also sensitive to various other response sets that might contribute to an invalid profile. In addition to the 15 trait scales, the SNAP can also be used to derive scores on 13 diagnostic scales, which correspond to each of the specific PD categories included in DSM-IV. The combination of validity scales, trait scales, and diagnostic scales makes the SNAP an especially useful instrument to be used in an assessment aimed at the identification of personality problems related to paranoia.

The fact that semistructured interviews and self-report questionnaires have traditionally been used in the assessment of PDs should not imply that they are the best sources of information. Like everyone else, people with PDs are frequently unable to view themselves realistically and are unaware of the effects of their behavior on others (Oltmanns, Turkheimer, & Strauss, 1998; Westen & Schedler, 1999). Because realistic, accurate information about a client's behavior may not be obtained from the client's own report, it is often useful to collect information from other sources. Family members, friends, and other acquaintances may provide an important perspective. Studies that have examined the relation between self-report data and informant report data regarding personality pathology have found that the two sources often disagree (Klonsky, Oltmanns, & Turkheimer, 2002; Oltmanns & Turkheimer, 2009; Thomas, Turkheimer, & Oltmanns, 2003).

Comparisons between self- and peer reports reveal an interesting paradox regarding PDs. Take paranoia as an example. People who are viewed by their peers as being paranoid do not see themselves as being suspicious or lacking in trust. Rather, they described themselves as being angry and hostile (Clifton, Turkheimer, & Oltmanns, 2004). Research has shown that those who had thought of themselves as being paranoid were often regarded by others as cold and unfeeling. Although it has not yet been determined how the two very different types of information should be used, it is fair to state that patient and informant evaluation represent two different assessment approaches to personality that produce two different portrayals of a client's PD. Perhaps utilizing information from both sources may help a clinician gain a more comprehensive picture of a client's personality disorder than if the clinician were to rely solely on one source of information.

Treatment for Personality Disorders

A variety of different therapies have been proposed and developed for the PDs. These treatments vary in their goals, strategies, techniques, and objectives. Many of the assumptions of treatment for PDs were based on putative distinctions from Axis I clinical disorders. Because PDs were thought to begin at an earlier age and remain chronically stable through the life course, many assumed they would be more difficult to treat than clinical disorders. Conversely, it was also assumed that treatment would necessarily be in the form of psychotherapy, not pharmacotherapy. These assumptions have now been challenged (see e.g., Krueger, 2005, for a review). For instance, clinical lore suggested that people with PDs were less motivated for treatment because these disorders are egosyntonic; recent research disputes this stereotype, finding that people with PDs are more motivated for treatment than patients without PD pathology (van Beek & Verheul, 2008).

It is often difficult to decide what measures will be used to qualify a treatment as "efficacious," because the criteria for PDs vary widely both within a diagnosis and between diagnoses of different PDs. Some interventions focus on specific behaviors associated with PDs (see Piper & Joyce, 2001, for a review). Dialectical behavior therapy (DBT), for instance, was originally designed to treat parasuicidal behaviors and grew to encompass borderline PD (Linehan & Dexter-Mazza, 2008). Another complexity and limitation of intervention studies is the myriad outcome measures: Should treatment success be defined by absence of the PD diagnosis, symptom severity, general psychosocial functioning, or some other measure? According to these and other treatment outcome indicators, research now supports the efficacy of different manualized treatments for PDs. Most focus on one disorder (borderline), however, and the mechanism of action in most of these treatments is still uncertain. We focus here on manualized treatments supported by randomized clinical trials that are targeted at one or more of the ten DSM-IV PDs.

The Efficacy of Psychotherapy for Personality Disorders

Contrary to the clinical lore that PDs are chronic syndromes not amenable to therapeutic intervention, research seems to be converging on the effectiveness of psychotherapy for the treatment of PDs

(see Verheul & Herbrink, 2007, for a recent review). In a meta-analysis of the efficacy of therapeutic intervention for PDs, Perry, Banon, and Ianni (1999) found 15 studies that examined the outcome of short- or long-term psychotherapy for persons with PDs. They reported effect sizes of 1.11 and 1.29 for self-report and observer-rated outcome measures, respectively, of psychotherapy on PDs. Three of the fifteen studies included in the meta-analysis were randomized controlled treatment trials, and the average effect size for these three studies was .75. Further, the authors indicated that psychotherapy resulted in a recovery rate seven times greater than the natural recovery rate for borderline PD.

The different forms of psychotherapy that have been utilized for PDs can generally be grouped into four categories: psychodynamic/interpersonal, cognitive behavioral, supportive, and mixed (e.g., cognitive analytic therapy, a mixture of psychodynamic and cognitive behavioral; Ryle, 2001). These types of therapies can differ from other types grouped under the same general orientation. They also vary in duration, modality (group vs. individual vs. hospital-based), and focus. The forms that these interventions have taken when developed specifically for PD patients have, by and large, not been directed at any specific PD diagnosis per se. Certainly, borderline personality disorder is the most commonly studied disorder in the research literature, and DBT has become the industry standard for borderline PD. However, most PD treatments focus on the behaviors and skill deficits known to accompany one or more PDs (Piper & Joyce, 2001). These include relational patterns (Benjamin, 1993), maladaptive schemas (Beck et al., 1990), social skills deficits (Alden, 1989), or self-harming behaviors (Tyrer et al., 2003).

Several studies have examined the impact of one type of intervention for multiple PDs. Huband and colleagues (2007) examined the effectiveness of a social problem-solving therapy for PD patients in the community. Patients in the problem solving group (N = 87) attended psychoeducation sessions followed by 16 weekly group-based social problem-solving skills sessions. Compared to a waitlist control group, those in the intervention group had better problem-solving skills and lower overall anger expression. Abbass et al. (2008) investigated the efficacy and long-term effectiveness of intensive, short-term dynamic psychotherapy (ISTDP) for PDs. The goal of the ISTDP intervention was to develop awareness and expression of feelings and identify the psychic defenses that hinder exploration of early trauma and broken attachments. The ISTDP group ($N = 14$) was compared to a waitlist control group ($N = 13$), who eventually received treatment as well. The most prevalent PDs in both groups were borderline and avoidant. The ISTDP group improved relative to the control group on multiple outcome measures at post-treatment, including ratings on the Brief Symptom Inventory and Inventory of Interpersonal Problems, clinician-rated global assessment of functioning, employment rate, and hours worked per week.

To determine whether different forms of psychotherapy may be more efficacious, Leichsenring and Leibing (2003) conducted a meta-analysis to compare psychodynamic and cognitive-behavioral therapy (CBT) for PDs. They found 14 psychodynamic studies and 11 studies of CBT that met inclusion criteria. Of the psychodynamic studies, three were randomized controlled designs, whereas four included randomized comparison of two types of treatment; five of the CBT studies used a randomized controlled design. The authors reported an overall effect size of 1.46 for psychodynamic therapies and 1.00 for CBT. Effect sizes remained significantly different from zero when including only self-report outcome measures or observational outcome measure. For psychodynamic studies, including only randomized controlled studies still resulted in a significant effect size, whereas the active therapy condition was more effective than control for three of the five randomized controlled cognitive therapy studies. The authors concluded that both psychodynamic and CBT are efficacious treatments for PDs, with no apparent differences in efficacy between the two forms of intervention. Of note, this review was unable to compare directly the efficacy of these two types of interventions in the treatment of specific PDs. Future research is certainly needed that compares specific forms of psychotherapeutic intervention for the ten different types of PDs, or the full range of abnormal trait constructs that may frame DSM-5.

To date, the PD treatment literature is limited in several respects. Certainly, there is a need for more randomized controlled treatment trials, as too many effectiveness studies rely on case-comparison methods. Many studies are also conducted without manualized therapy; future work should strive to follow a manual that is then made widely available for replication studies and for community therapists who wish to implement the intervention. It would also be easier to compare results across studies if there was greater unanimity in (a) assessment of impairment

prior to and following treatment, (b) diagnostic tools for assessment of PDs, and (c) duration of follow-up period. Further, the research in this area should be extended to demonstrating that, in the long-run, psychotherapy for PDs is more cost-effective than no treatment at all (Bartak, Soeteman, Verheul, & Busschbach, 2007). In the era of managed health care, it is necessary to demonstrate that psychotherapy intervention will lower the disease-cost associated with PDs if it is to be widely implemented in community settings.

Interventions for Borderline Personality Disorder

Borderline PD, because of its high costs in terms of treatment utilization (Bender, 2001; Zanarini, Frankenburg, Hennen, & Silk, 2004) and associated impairment, including suicide attempts (e.g. Oldham, 2006), has been the focus of most research into efficacious and effective PD interventions. The American Psychiatric Association's practice guideline recommends psychotherapy as the primary treatment modality for borderline PD, supplemented by pharmacotherapy if needed (APA, 2001). Dialectical behavior therapy (Linehan, 1993) has emerged as the standard treatment for borderline PD. Dialectical behavior therapy is a variation of CBT that also incorporates aspects of meditation and Eastern philosophy. Originally developed to treat women with suicidal and self-harming behaviors, it was extended to the treatment of patients with borderline PD. Randomized clinical trials have shown that DBT is more effective than treatment as usual (Linehan, Armstrong, Suarez, Allmon, & Heard, 1991) and therapy by community experts (Linehan et al., 2006). However, DBT was no more effect than community therapy at reducing the frequency of self-mutilating, suicidal, and impulsive behaviors (Linehan et al., 2006), one of the primary targets for intervention as stated in the goals of DBT. Verheul and colleagues (2003) found that borderline PD patients in a DBT treatment condition demonstrated less attrition from therapy than treatment as usual and a reduction in self-mutilating and impulsive behaviors, but not suicidal behaviors. Other limitations of DBT include questions about its generalizability to non-clinical populations and the long-term stability of treatment gains, in addition to the drawbacks of such a time- and resource-intensive intervention (Paris, 2008).

Cognitive-behavioral therapy has also received empirical support in the treatment of borderline PD (Binks, 2006). The treatment focus of CBT, for PDs and other forms of psychopathology, is on maladaptive cognitive schemas which, in combination with affective, motivational, and social processes, determine behavior (Beck, Freeman, Davis, & Associates, 2004). For borderline PD in particular, CBT focuses on cognitive schemas of vulnerability and poor sense of self. Davidson and colleagues (2006) randomized 106 borderline PD patients to treatment as usual (TAU) or CBT plus TAU, with patients attending an average of 16 CBT sessions. Cognitive-behavioral therapy plus TAU resulted in fewer suicidal acts, a reduction in positive symptom distress index, and a decrease in dysfunctional core believes and state anxiety (Davidson, 2006). Blum et al. (2008) reported on the outcome of patients who completed the Systems Training for Emotional Predictability and Problem Solving (STEPPS) program, an adjunct to a patient's ongoing treatment. STEPPS is an outpatient, group-based treatment that includes cognitive-behavioral elements, skills training, and an educational component for primary mental health-care professionals and friends or family members of the patient. Patients in the STEPPS plus TAU group improved markedly over a comparison group of individuals receiving only TAU, according to several outcome measures (e.g., rating scale of borderline symptoms, global assessment of functioning, negative affectivity, Beck Depression Inventory, and social adjustment). Other CBT therapies that have shown improvement for borderline PD patients include a brief treatment (Weinberg, 2006) and schema-focused therapy, a hybrid of CBT and psychodynamic therapy (Giesen-Bloo, 2006).

Given that many PDs were initially identified by clinicians who were working in a psychodynamic conceptual framework, there has long been an interest in applying psychodynamic interventions to the treatment of PD patients. With the recent advent of manualized psychodynamic treatments, it has been possible to test the efficacy of this approach. One form of psychodynamic treatment, mentalization-based therapy (MBT), is incorporated into a partial hospital program and attempts to teach PD patients to observe and identify how their behaviors and the behaviors of others are linked to emotions and desires (Bateman, & Fonagy, 2006). Mentalization-based therapy has now been supported for the treatment of borderline PD (Bateman & Fonagy, 1999, 2001), although it has only been implemented in a hospital setting to this point. Another psychodynamically oriented therapy, transference-focused psychotherapy (TFP), uses the patient–therapist relationship to correct dysfunctional emotion regulation skills.

Clarkin and colleagues (2007) compared DBT, transference-focused psychotherapy, and a dynamic support treatment among 90 participants diagnosed with borderline PD. All three types of treatment were associated with improvement in multiple domains (e.g., suicidality, social adjustment, irritability, anger) over a 1-year time period. Of the three, TFP showed improvement in the greatest number of outcome variables.

Pharmacotherapy for Personality Disorders

As with psychotherapeutic interventions, most of the pharmacotherapies for PDs have focused on borderline PD. It is quite common for borderline PD patients to take multiple medications concurrently (Zanarini et al. 2004). A variety of different classes of drugs have been used, including neuroleptics, selective serotonin reuptake inhibitors (SSRIs), and mood stabilizers (Paris, 2008; Zanarini, 2004). In general, these pharmacological agents are relatively efficacious at reducing overall psychopathology, as well as anger and impulsivity, in patients with borderline PD. The lack of effectiveness for mood stabilizers in reducing the emotional dysregulation seen in borderline PD patients (but see Zanarini & Frankenburg, 2003, for a possible exception) suggests that the type of affective instability in these patients is quite different from that seen in patients with bipolar disorder (Paris, 2008).

Comorbid Personality Disorders and Axis I Disorders

Any discussion of treatment for PDs must also acknowledge the role that comorbidity plays in course and treatment of both Axis I and Axis II disorders. The rise in research on PDs following their move to Axis II in DSM-III (APA, 1980) exposed the high rates of comorbidity between PDs and Axis I clinical disorders; that is, the fact that one or more PDs are diagnosed in individuals with a clinical disorder at rates higher than would be expected by chance (see Verheul, Ball, & van den Brink, 1998). For instance, it is estimated that 20%–50% of inpatients and 50%–85% of outpatients with a current diagnosis of major depression also meet criteria for a PD (Corruble, Ginestet, & Guelfi, 1996). Comorbidity has many implications for the natural course, recovery, and treatment of psychopathology. Comorbid borderline PD and post-traumatic stress disorder (PTSD) is associated with increased risk for hospitalization and higher levels of dysfunction (Zlotnick et al., 2003). The presence of a PD diagnosis can also impair recovery and remission from an Axis I disorders. Viinamaki and colleagues (2003) compared patients' comorbidity for Cluster C and major depression (N = 30) with major depression-only patients (N = 60) over a 24-month follow-up period. The comorbid group was more likely to have a diagnosis of major depression at follow-up and less likely to have recovered.

For many years, it was a widely heralded truism that PDs affect the treatment of Axis I clinical disorders (Pilkonis, 2001; Reich, 2003b). However, more recent research suggests that PDs may not be as detrimental to treatment for Axis I clinical syndromes as previously thought. The most studied Axis I disorders in terms of comorbid PD and effects on intervention are depression, anxiety, and substance abuse/dependence. The evidence regarding the impact of comorbid PD pathology on treatment for depression is mixed. Research shows that cognitive treatment for depression is less effective for individuals with comorbid PDs than for individuals without PD pathology (Fournier et al., 2008; Newton-Howes, Tryer, & Johnson, 2006; Reich, 2003a). Patients with comorbid depression and Cluster C PDs show less improvement in response to treatment (Hardy et al., 1995), delayed recovery (Patience, McGuire, Scott, & Freeman, 1995), and quicker time to relapse (Ilardi, Craighead, & Evans, 1997). However, two recent meta-analyses showed only mixed support, at best, for the negative effect of PDs on depression outcome (Kool et al., 2005; Mulder, 2002). Further, a recent study found no impact of personality traits commonly associated with PDs (e.g., neuroticism; Blom et al., 2007) on interpersonal psychotherapy (IPT) for depression, whereas another study found that both personality traits (e.g., harm avoidance) and diagnosed PDs adversely impacted IPT but not CBT for depression (Joyce et al., 2007).

The impact of PDs on treatment for anxiety disorders also appears mixed. Cluster C PDs are related to poor treatment outcome in those comorbid for obsessive-compulsive symptoms (Cavedini, Erzegovesi, Ronchi, & Bellodi, 1997). Research also shows that borderline PD appears to impact treatment for people with PTSD (Feeny, Zoellner, & Foa, 2002) or depression (Goodman, Hull, Clarkin, & Yeomans, 1998; Meyer, Pilkonis, Proietti, Heape, & Egan, 2001). However, Feeny et al. (2002) found that patients with comorbid chronic PTSD and borderline PD did not differ in psychopathology, PTSD severity, social functioning, or diagnostic status from chronic PTSD-only patients following CBT for chronic PTSD. Moreover, patients with comorbid borderline PD improved to the same degree as non-comorbid PTSD patients even when treated in community settings, as opposed to CBT experts (Hembree, Cahill, & Foa, 2004). Based on a review and synthesis of the available literature at that time, Dreessen and Arntz (1998) concluded "there is no robust negative impact of personality disorders" on treatment of Axis I anxiety disorders (p. 493).

Finally, the impact of PDs on intervention for substance abuse and dependence has also been widely investigated. Personality disorders, particularly antisocial and borderline PDs, are highly prevalent among individuals with a substance abuse diagnosis (Sher & Trull, 1994; Trull, Sher, Minks-Brown, Durbin, & Burr, 2000; Trull et al., 2004). The presence of a comorbid PD in addition to a substance abuse disorder is also associated with myriad negative outcomes, including more pronounced abuse, greater psychiatric dysfunction, greater susceptibility to relapse, and increased risk for suicide and hospitalization (for a review, see Ball, 2005). One recent study found that individuals with comorbid substance use disorders and antisocial PD had higher levels of substance use symptom severity and related dysfunction (e.g., legal problems, family conflicts) than individuals with a substance use disorder and no comorbid antisocial PD (Westermeyer & Thuras, 2005). However, empirical research negates clinical lore, which suggests that individuals with a dual diagnosis of substance use and antisocial personality disorder have poorer outcomes (Brooner, Kidorf, King, & Stoller, 1998; Cacciola, Rutherford, Alterman, McKay, & Snider, 1996). In fact, patients with a diagnosis of alcohol abuse comorbid with antisocial PD responded to an abstinence-focused cognitive behavioral treatment as well as alcohol abuse-only patients (Longabaugh et al., 1994). A modified version of DBT has also been found to be efficacious in the treatment of patients with borderline PD comorbid with substance use disorder (Linehan et al., 1999).

Thus, although support exists for the negative effect of a PD diagnosis on the treatment for Axis I clinical disorders, there is also evidence failing to support this effect. It may be that the level of severity of personality pathology, as represented by number of diagnosable PDs, is a better indicator of treatment outcome than presence of a PD per se (Ogrodniczuk, Piper, Joyce, & McCallum, 2001). There is also evidence that, although patients with comorbid depression and PD pathology do not respond well to psychotherapy, they do respond to pharmacotherapy (Fournier et al., 2008; Newton-Howes et al., 2006).

Conclusion

Future Directions: Expanded Research Agenda for Complex Cases

Therapy for PDs is a challenging area of research, given the complex and multifaceted nature of these conditions. These are inherently heterogeneous disorders that may require flexible therapies that can be adapted to the myriad symptom presentations and related dysfunctions of persons with PDs. Much is still unknown about whether there is one "best" type of psychotherapy for any or all PDs. Some types of therapy have largely focused on one PD (e.g., DBT for borderline), whereas several PDs (e.g., Cluster C PDs) have been largely neglected in the research literature. If any one type of psychotherapy is to be refined and adapted for use with all PDs, it will be important to identify the core dysfunction that may lie at the heart of all PDs (Krueger, Skodol, Livesley, Shrout, & Huang, 2007); thus, a treatment that presumes to affect PDs in general might focus on the interpersonal difficulties that underlie all PDs.

Another option is to combine the principles and techniques of various treatments to form an integrated intervention best suited to the individual client. This may be the best option for adaptive treatments both across and within therapy patients. Certainly, different types of treatment may be necessary over the course of the disorder. Research shows that the symptoms of borderline PD that remit first are more acute symptoms (e.g., self-mutilation, quasi-psychotic thought), whereas temperament symptoms (e.g., chronic/major depression, intolerance of aloneness) are slower to remit over time (Zanarini et al., 2007). The success of treatments like DBT is their focus on abating the acute phase of borderline PD; future research may attempt to develop interventions on chronic symptoms that are more stable and enduring.

Adding one more layer of complexity to the treatment of PDs is the difficulty of comorbidity with Axis I clinical syndromes. Many controlled studies of the efficacy of psychotherapy for PDs exclude individuals with comorbid substance abuse problems. As noted, a great deal of comorbidity exists between Axis I and Axis II disorders (Dolan-Sewell et al., 2001), but only a handful of treatments that have been developed to focus on both at the same time. For instance, Ball (1998) developed dual-focus schema therapy (DFST), a manualized cognitive-behavioral intervention that focuses on relapse prevention and targeted interventions for maladaptive schemas and associated coping styles, specifically for substance-dependent patients with a comorbid PD. Whether using DFST or a combination of eclectic techniques, a therapist will need an overarching framework that provides guidelines for how to treat the complexities of cases with multiple Axis I and Axis II pathologies and related interpersonal and social difficulties. Livesley (2008) suggests a five-step process: safety, containment, control and regulation, exploration and change, and integration and synthesis. Thus, the therapist works with the patient to move from areas of crisis-management toward emotional regulation and finally a focus on establishing a stable and adaptive sense of self.

Reconceptualizing these entities in terms of dimensional spectrums of psychopathological variation may be helpful in clarifying these patterns. For example, a personality style with high neuroticism predisposes to a range of mood and anxiety (internalizing) disorders. Some presentations consistent with the idea of PD being present might then be understood as persons with unusually high levels of neuroticism, and hence, more severe personality pathology as well as more severe and more diverse internalizing problems. The magnitude of intervention needed to achieve symptom amelioration would then also be conceptualized dimensionally, as related to the overall extent of internalizing psychopathology. The question from this perspective is not, "What should we do when we treat a patient with a specific anxiety disorder and a specific PD?" Rather, the question is, "What kinds or intensities of intervention are appropriate for patients ranging in severity along an internalizing spectrum of problems?" For example, what intervention is appropriate for the mildly neurotic individual with a current depressive episode (lower in the spectrum)? How does this differ from the patient with extreme neuroticism, profound interpersonal difficulties likely attributable to neurotic worries (cf. avoidant PD in the current system), and various comorbid and often intense mood and anxiety symptoms that also wax and wane over time? Thinking more dimensionally about psychopathology opens up these novel possibilities for conceptualizing intervention strategies focused more on the complete history and current symptom picture, rather than trying to parse those phenomena in terms of categories of psychopathology that are known to have somewhat arbitrary and often overlapping boundaries.

References

Abbass, A., Sheldon, A., Gyra, J., & Kalpin, A. (2008). Intensive short-term dynamic psychotherapy for DSM-IV personality disorders. *Journal of Nervous and Mental Disease, 196*, 211–216.

Agronin, M.E., & Maletta G. (2000). Personality disorders in late life: Understanding and overcoming the gap in research. *American Journal of Geriatric Psychiatry, 8*, 4–18.

Alden, L. (1989). Short-term structured treatment for avoidant personality disorder. *Journal of Consulting and Clinical Psychology, 56*, 756–764.

Allik, J. (2005). Personality dimensions across cultures. *Journal of Personality Disorders, 19*, 212–232.

American Psychiatric Association. (1952). *Diagnostic and statistical manual of mental disorders*. Washington, DC.

American Psychiatric Association. (1980). *Diagnostic and statistical manual of mental disorders* (3rd ed.). Washington, DC.

American Psychiatric Association (2000). *Diagnostic and Statistical Manual of Mental Disorders (4th ed., Text Revision)*: Washington, D.C.: American Psychiatric Association.

American Psychiatric Association. (2001). Practice guideline for the treatment of patients with borderline personality disorder. *American Journal of Psychiatry, 158* (Suppl.), 1–52.

Asnaani, A., Chelminski, I., Young, D., & Zimmerman, M. (2007). Heterogeneity of borderline personality disorder: Do the number of criteria met make a difference? *Journal of Personality Disorders, 21*(6), 615–625.

Axelrod, S. R., Widiger, T. A., Trull, T. J., & Corbitt, E. M. (1997). Relationships of the five-factor model antagonism facets with personality disorder symptomatology. *Journal of Personality Assessment, 67*, 297–313.

Ball, S. A. (1998). Manualized treatment for substance abusers with personality disorders: Dual focus schema therapy. *Addictive Behaviors, 23*(6), 883–891.

Ball, S. A. (2001). Reconceptualizing personality disorder categories using personality trait dimensions: Introduction to special section. *Journal of Personality, 69*, 147–153.

Ball, S. A. (2005). Personality traits, problems, and disorders: Clinical applications to substance use disorders. *Journal of Research in Personality, 39*, 84–102.

Balsis, S., Gleason, M.E.J., Woods, C.M., & Oltmanns, T.F. (2007). An item response theory analysis of DSM-IV personality disorder criteria across younger and older age groups. *Psychology and Aging. 22*, 171–185.

Balsis, S., Woods, C.M., Gleason, M.E.J., & Oltmanns, T.F. (2007). The over and underdiagnosis of personality disorders in older adults. *American Journal of Geriatric Psychiatry, 15*, 742–753.

Bartak, A., Soeteman, D. I., Verheul, R., & Busschbach, J. J. V. (2007). Strengthening the status of psychotherapy for personality disorders: An integrated perspective on effects and costs. *The Canadian Journal of Psychiatry, 52*(12), 803–810.

Bateman, A., & Fonagy, P. (2006). *Mentalization-based treatment: A practical guide*. New York: John Wiley.

Bateman, A., & Fonagy, P. (1999). The effectiveness of partial hospitalization in the treatment of borderline personality disorder: A randomized controlled trial. *American Journal of Psychiatry, 156*, 1563–1569.

Bateman, A., & Fonagy, P. (2001). Treatment of borderline personality disorder with psychoanalytically oriented partial hospitalization: An 18-month follow-up. *American Journal of Psychiatry, 158*, 36–42.

Battle, C. L., Shea, M. T., Johnson, D. M., Yen, S., Zlotnick, C., Zanarini, M. C., et al. (2004). Childhood maltreatment associated with adult personality disorder: Findings from the collaborative longitudinal personality disorders study. *Journal of Personality Disorders, 18*(2), 193–211.

Beck, A. T., Freeman, A., Davis, D. D., & Associates (2004). *Cognitive therapy of personality disorders* (2nd ed.). New York: The Guilford Press.

Beck, A. T., Freeman, A., et al. (1990). *Cognitive therapy of personality disorders*. New York: Guilford.

Bender, D. S., Dolan, R.T., Skodol, A.E., Sanislow, C.A., Dyck, I.R., McGlashan,T.H., et al. (2001). Treatment utilization by patients with personality disorders. *American Journal of Psychiatry, 158*, 295–302.

Benjamin, L. S. (1993). *Interpersonal diagnosis and treatment of personality disorders*. New York: Guilford.

Binks, C. A., Fenton, M., McCarthy, L., et al. (2006). Psychological therapies for people with borderline personality disorder. *Cochrane Database Systematic Review, 1*, CD005652.

Blom, M. B. J., Spinhoven, P., Hoffman, T., Jonker, K., Hoencamp, E., Haffmans, P.M.J., & van Dyck, R. (2007). Severity and duration of depression, not personality factors, predict short term outcome in the treatment of major depression. *Journal of Affective Disorders, 104*, 119–126.

Blum, N., St. John, D., Pfohl, B., Stuart, S., McCormick, B., Allen, J., et al. (2008). Systems training for emotional predictability and problem solving (STEPPS) for outpatients with borderline personality disorder: A randomized controlled trial and 1-year follow-up. *American Journal of Psychiatry, 165*, 468–478.

Bornstein, R. F. (1998). Reconceptualizing personality disorder diagnosis in the *DSM-5*: The discriminant validity challenge. *Clinical Psychology: Science and Practice, 5*, 333–343.

Bouchard, T. J., Jr., & Loehlin, J. C. (2001). Genes, evolution, and personality. *Behavior Genetics, 31*, 243–273.

Brooner, R. K., Kidorf, M., King, V. L., & Stoller, K. (1998). Preliminary evidence of good treatment response in antisocial drug abusers. *Drug and Alcohol Dependence, 49*, 249–260.

Cacciola, J. S., Rutherford, M. J., Alterman, A. I., McKay, J. R., & Snider, E. C. (1996). Personality disorders and treatment outcome in methadone maintenance patients. *The Journal of Nervous and Mental Disease, 184*, 234–239.

Cavedini, P., Erzegovesi, S., Ronchi, P., & Bellodi, L. (1997). Predictive value of obsessive-compulsive personality disorder in anti obsessional pharmacological treatment. *European Neuropsychopharmacology, 7*, 45–49.

Chen, H., Cohen, P., Crawford, T. N., Kasen, S., Johnson, J. G., & Berenson, K. (2006). Relative impact of young adult personality disorders on subsequent quality of life: Findings of a community-based longitudinal study. *Journal of Personality Disorders, 20*(5), 510–523.

Clark, L. (1990). Toward a consensual set of symptom clusters for assessment of personality disorder. Advances in personality assessment, Vol. 8 (pp. 243–266). Hillsdale, NJ England: Lawrence Erlbaum Associates, Inc.

Clark, L. A. (1993). *Schedule for Nonadaptive and Adaptive Personality*. Minneapolis, MN: University of Minnesota Press.

Clark, L. A. (2005). Stability and change in personality pathology: Revelations of three longitudinal studies. *Journal of Personality Disorders, 19*(5), 524–532.

Clark, L. A. & Harrison, J. A. (2001). Assessment Instruments. In *Handbook of Personality Disorders: Theory, Research and Treatment* (pp. 277–306). New York: Guilford Press.

Clark, L. A., Livesley, W., & Morey, L. C. (1997). Personality disorder assessment: The challenge of construct validity. *Journal of Personality Disorders, 11*, 205–231.

Clark, L. A., Livesley, W. J., Schroeder, M. L., & Irish, S. L. (2002). Convergence of Two Systems for Assessing Specific Traits of Personality Disorder. 8(3), 294–303.

Clark, L. A., & Watson, D. (1999). Personality, disorder, and personality disorder: Towards a more rational conceptualization. *Journal of Personality Disorders*, 13(2), 142–151.

Clark, L. A., Watson, D., & Mineka, S. (1994). Temperament, personality, and the mood and anxiety disorders. *Journal of Abnormal Psychology*, 103(1), 103–116.

Clarkin, J. F., Levy, K.N., Lenzenweger, M.F., & Kernberg, O.F. (2007). Evaluating three treatments for borderline personality disorder: A multiwave study. *American Journal of Psychiatry*, 164, 922–928.

Clifton, A., Turkheimer, E., & Oltmanns, T.F. (2004). Contrasting perspectives on personality problems: Descriptions from the self and others. *Personality and Individual Differences*, 36, 1499–1514.

Cohen, P. (2008). Child development and personality disorder. *Psychiatric Clinics of North America*, 31(3), 477–493.

Cohen, P., Brown, J., & Smailes, E. (2001). Child abuse and neglect and the development of mental disorders in the general population. *Development and Psychopathology*, 13, 981–999.

Cohen, P., Crawford, T. N., Johnson, J. G., & Kasen, S. (2005). The children in the community study of developmental course of personality disorder. *Journal of Personality Disorders*, 19(5), 466–486.

Compton, W. M., Conway, K. P., Stinson, F. S., Colliver, J. D., & Grant, B. F. (2005). Prevalence, correlates, and comorbidity of DSM-IV antisocial personality syndromes and alcohol and specific drug use disorders in the United States: Results from the national epidemiologic survey on alcohol and related conditions. *Journal of Clinical Psychiatry*, 66(6), 677–685.

Coolidge, F. L., & Segal., D. L. (1998). Evolution of personality disorder diagnosis in the diagnostic and statistical manual of mental disorders. *Clinical Psychology Review*, 18(5), 585–599.

Corruble, E., Ginestet, D., & Guelfi, J. D. (1996). Comorbidity of personality disorders and unipolar major depression: A review. *Journal of Affective Disorders*, 37, 157–170.

Costa, P., & McCrae, R. (1989). Personality continuity and the changes of adult life. The adult years: Continuity and change (pp. 41–77). Washington, DC US: American Psychological Association

Costa, P.T., Jr., & Widiger, T. A. (Eds.). (2002). *Personality disorders and the five-factor model of personality* (2nd ed.). Washington, DC: American Psychological Association.

Davidson, K., Norrie, J., Tyrer, P., Gumley, A., Tata, P., Murray, H., & Palmer, S. (2006). The effectiveness of cognitive behavior therapy for borderline personality disorder: Results from the borderline personality disorder study of cognitive therapy (BOSCOT) trial. *Journal of Personality Disorders*, 20, 450–465.

Dolan-Sewell, R. T., Krueger, R.F., & Shea, M.T. (2001). Co-occurrence with syndrome disorders. In W. J. Livesley (Ed.), *Handbook of personality disorders: Theory, research, and treatment*. New York: Guilford.

Dreessen, L., & Arntz, A. (1998). The impact of personality disorders on treatment outcome of anxiety disorders: Best-evidence synthesis. *Behaviour Research and Therapy*, 36, 483–504.

Dyce, J. A., & O'Connor, B. P. (1998). Personality disorders and the five-factor model: A test of facet-level predictions. *Journal of Personality Disorders*, 12, 31–45.

Feeny, N. C., Zoellner, L. A., & Foa, E. B. (2002). Treatment outcome for chronic PTSD among female assault victims with borderline personality characteristics: A preliminary examination. *Journal of Personality Disorders*, 16, 30–40.

First, M.B., Bell, C.B., Cuthbert, B., Krystal, J.H., Malison, R., Offord, D.R. et al. (2002). Personality disorders and relational disorders: A research agenda for addressing crucial gaps in DSM. In D.J. Kupfer, M.B. First, & D.A. Regier (Eds.), *A research agenda for DSM-5* (pp. 123–199). Washington, DC: American Psychiatric Association.

Fossati, A., Madeddu, F., & Maffei, C. (1999). Borderline personality disorder and childhood sexual abuse: A meta-analytic study. *Journal of Personality Disorders*, 13, 268–280.

Fournier, J. C., DeRubeis, R.J., Shelton, R.C., Gallop, R., Amsterdam, J., & Hollon, S.D. (2008). Antidepressant medications v. cognitive therapy in people with depression with or without personality disorder. *British Journal of Psychiatry*, 192, 124–129.

Frances, A., & Widiger, T.A. (1986). Methodological issues in personality disorder diagnosis. In G.L. Klerman & T. Millon (Eds.), *Contemporary directions in psychopathology: Toward the DSM-IV* (pp. 381–400). New York: Guilford Press.

Giesen-Bloo, J., van Dyck, R., Spinhoven, P., van Tilburg, W., Dirksen, C., van Asselt, T., et al. (2006). Outpatient psychotherapy for borderline personality disorder-randomized trial of schema-focused therapy vs transference-focused therapy. *Archives of General Psychiatry*, 63, 649–658.

Goodman, G., Hull, J.W., Clarkin, J.F., & Yeomans, F.E. (1998). Comorbid mood disorders as modifiers of treatment response among inpatients with borderline personality disorder. *Journal of Nervous and Mental Disease*, 186, 616–622.

Grant, B. F., Hasin, D. S., Stinson, F. S., Dawson, D. A., Chou, S., Ruan, W., et al. (2005a). Co-occurrence of 12-month mood and anxiety disorders and personality disorders in the US: results from the national epidemiologic survey on alcohol and related conditions. *Journal of Psychiatric Research*, 39(1), 1–9.

Grant, B. F., Hasin, D. S., Stinson, F. S., Dawson, D. A., Chou, S. P., Ruan, W. J., et al. (2004). Prevalence, correlates, and disability of personality disorders in the United States: Results from the national epidemiologic survey on alcohol and related conditions. *Journal of Clinical Psychiatry*, 65, 948–958.

Grant, B. F., Stinson, F. S., Dawson, D. A., Chou, S., & Ruan, W. (2005b). Co-occurrence of DSM-IV personality disorders in the United States: Results from the national epidemiologic survey on alcohol and related conditions. *Comprehensive Psychiatry*, 46(1), 1–5.

Grover, K. E., Carpenter, L. L., Price, L. H., Gagne, G. G., Mello, A. F., Mello, M. F., et al. (2007). The relationship between childhood abuse and adult personality disorder symptoms. *Journal of Personality Disorders*, 21(4), 442–447.

Hardy, G. E., Barkham, M., Shapiro, D.A., Stiles, W.B., Rees, A., & Reynolds, S. (1995). Impact of cluster c personality disorders on outcomes of contrasting brief psychotherapies for depression. *Journal of Consulting and Clinical Psychology*, 63, 997–1004.

Hembree, E. A., Cahill, S. P., & Foa, E. B. (2004). Impact of personality disorders on treatment outcome for female assault survivors with chronic posttraumatic stress disorder. *Journal of Personality Disorders*, 18(1), 117–127.

Huband, N., McMurran, M., Evans, C., & Duggan, C. (2007). Social problem-solving plus psychoeducation for adults with personality disorder: Pragmatic randomised controlled trial. *British Journal of Psychiatry*, 190, 307–313.

Ilardi, S. S., Craighead, W.E., & Evans, D.D. (1997). Modelling relapse in unipolar depression: The effects of dysfunctional cognitions and personality disorders. *Journal of Consulting and Clinical Psychology, 65*, 381–391.

Jang, K. L., Livesley, W. J., & Vernon, P. A. (1998). A twin study of genetic and environmental contributions to gender differences in traits delineating personality disorder. *European Journal of Personality, 12*, 331–344.

Johnson, J. G., Chen, H., & Cohen, P. (2004). Personality disorder traits during adolescence and relationships with family members during the transition to adulthood. *Journal of Consulting and Clinical Psychology, 72*(6), 923–932.

Johnson, J. G., Cohen, P., Chen, H., Kasen, S., & Brook, J. S. (2006). Parenting behaviors associated with risk for offspring personality disorder during adulthood. *Archives of General Psychiatry, 63*(5), 579–587.

Johnson, J. G., Cohen, P., Kasen, S., & Brook, J. S. (2005a). Personality disorder traits associated with risk for unipolar depression during middle adulthood. *Psychiatry Research, 136*(2–3), 113–121.

Johnson, J. G., Cohen, P., Kasen, S., & Brook, J. S. (2006a). Personality disorder traits evident by early adulthood and risk for eating and weight problems during middle adulthood. *International Journal of Eating Disorders, 39*(3), 184–192.

Johnson, J. G., Cohen, P., Kasen, S., & Brook, J. S. (2006b). Personality disorders evident by early adulthood and risk for anxiety disorders during middle adulthood. *Journal of Anxiety Disorders, 20*(4), 408–426.

Johnson, J. G., Cohen, P., Kasen, S., Smailes, E., & Brook, J. S. (2001a). Association of maladaptive parental behavior with psychiatric disorder among parents and their offspring. *Archives of General Psychiatry, 58*(5), 453–460.

Johnson, J. G., Cohen, P., Skodol, A. E., Oldham, J. M., Kasen, S., & Brook, J. (1999). Personality disorders in adolescence and risk of major mental disorders and suicidality during adulthood. *Archives of General Psychiatry, 56*, 805–811.

Johnson, J. G., Cohen, P., Smailes, E., Kasen, S., Oldham, J. M., & Skodol, A. E. (2000). Adolescent personality disorders associated with violence and criminal behavior during adolescence and early adulthood. *American Journal of Psychiatry, 157*(9), 1406–1412.

Johnson, J. G., Cohen, P., Smailes, E. M., Skodol, A. E., Brown, J., & Oldham, J. M. (2001b). Childhood verbal abuse and risk for personality disorders during adolescence and early adulthood. *Comprehensive Psychiatry, 42*(1), 16–23.

Johnson, J. G., First, M. B., Cohen, P., Skodol, A. E., Kasen, S., & Brook, J. S. (2005b). Adverse outcomes associated with personality disorder not otherwise specified in a community sample. *American Journal of Psychiatry, 162*(10), 1926–1932.

Joyce, P. R., McKenzie, J.M., Carter, J.D., Rae, A.M., Luty, S.E., Frampton, C.M.A., & Mulder, R.T. (2007). Temperament, character and personality disorders as predictors of response to interpersonal psychotherapy and cognitive-behavioural therapy for depression. *British Journal of Psychiatry, 190*, 503–508.

Kasen, S., Cohen, P., Skodol, A. E., Johnson, J. G., Smailes, E., & Brook, J. S. (2001). Childhood depression and adult personality disorder: Alternative pathways of continuity. *Archives of General Psychiatry, 58*(3), 231–236.

Kendell, R.E. (2002). The distinction between personality disorder and mental illness. *British Journal of Psychiatry, 180*, 110–115.

Kendler, K. S., Aggen, S. H., Czajkowski, N., Roysamb, E., Tambs, K., Torgersen, S., et al. (2008). The structure of genetic and environmental risk factors for DSM-IV personality disorders: A multivariate twin study. *Archives of General Psychiatry, 65*, 1438–1446.

Kendler, K., Czajkowki, N., Tambs, K., Torgersen, S., Aggen, S. H., & et al. (2006). Dimensional representation of DSM-IV Cluster A personality disorders in a population-based sample of Norwegien twins: A multivariate study. *Psychological Medicine, 37*, 645–653.

Klonsky, E.D., Oltmanns, T.F., & Turkheimer, E. (2002). Informant reports of personality disorder: Relation to self-reports and future research directions. *Clinical Psychology: Science and Practice, 9*, 300–311.

Kool, S., Schoevers, R., de Maat, S., Van, R., Molenaar, P., Vink, A., et al. (2005). Efficacy of pharmacotherapy in depressed patients with and without personality disorders: A systematic review and meta-analysis. *Journal of Affective Disorders, 88*(3), 269–278.

Krueger, R. F. (2005). Continuity of Axis I and Axis II: Toward a unified theory of personality, personality disorders, and clinical disorders. *Journal of Personality Disorders, 19*(3), 233–261.

Krueger, R. F., & Johnson, W. (2008). Behavioral genetics and personality: A new look at the integration of nature and nurture. In O. P. John, R. W. Robins, & L. A. Pervin (Eds.), *Handbook of Personality: Theory and Research* (3rd ed., pp. 287–310). New York: Guilford.

Krueger, R. F., Skodol, A. E., Livesley, W. J., Shrout, P. E., & Huang, Y. (2007). Synthesizing dimensional and categorical approaches to personality disorders: Refining the research agenda for *DSM-5* Axis II. *International Journal of Methods in Psychiatric Research, 16*, S65-S73.

Krueger, R. F., & Tackett, J. L. (2003). Personality and psychopathology: Working toward the bigger picture. *Journal of Personality Disorders, 17*, 109–128.

Leichsenring, F., & Leibing, E. (2003). The effectiveness of psychodynamic therapy and cognitive behavior therapy in the treatment of personality disorders: A meta-analysis. *The American Journal of Psychiatry, 160*(7), 1223–1232.

Lewinsohn, P. M., Rohde, P., Seeley, J. R., & Klein, D. N. (1997). Axis II psychopathology as a function of Axis I disorders. *Journal of the American Academy of Child and Adolescent Psychiatry, 36*, 1752–1759.

Lilienfeld, S. O., Waldman, I. D., & Israel, A. C. (1994). A critical examination of the use of the term "comorbidity" in psychopathology research. *Clinical Psychology: Science and Practice, 1*, 71–83.

Linehan, M. M. (1993). *Cognitive-behavioral treatment of borderline personality disorder.* New York: Guilford.

Linehan, M. M., Armstrong, H. E., Suarez, A., Allmon, D., & Heard, H. (1991). Cognitive-behavioral treatment of chronically parasuicidal borderline patients. *Archives of General Psychiatry, 48*, 1060–1064.

Linehan, M. M., Comtois, K. A., Murray, A., Brown, M. Z., Gallop, R. J., Heard, H. L., et al. (2006). Two-year randomized controlled trial and follow-up of dialectical behavior therapy vs. therapy by experts for suicidal behaviors and borderline personality disorder. *Archives of General Psychiatry, 63*, 757–766.

Linehan, M. M., & Dexter-Mazza, E. T. (2008). Dialectical behavior therapy for borderline personality disorder. In D. H. Barlow (Ed.), *Clinical handbook of psychological disorders* (pp. 365–420). New York: Guilford.

Linehan, M. M., Schmidt, H. I., Dimeff, L. A., Craft, J. C., Kanter, J., Comtois, K. A., et al. (1999). Dialectical behavior therapy for patients with borderline personality disorder and drug-dependence. *Journal on Addictions, 8,* 279–292.

Livesley, W. J. (2001). Conceptual and taxonomic issues. In W. J. Livesley (Ed.), *Handbook of personality disorders. Theory, research, and treatment* (pp. 3–38). New York: Guilford Press.

Livesley, W. J. (2003). Diagnostic dilemmas in classifying personality disorder. In P. K.A, M. B. First & H. A. Pincus (Eds.), *Advancing DSM: Dilemmas in Psychiatric Diagnosis* (pp. 153–190). Washington, DC: American Psychiatric Association.

Livesley, W. J. (2008). Integrated therapy for complex cases of personality disorder. *Journal of clinical Psychology, 64,* 207–221.

Livesley, W. J., & Jackson, D. N. (2002). *Manual for the dimensional assessment of personality pathology-basic questionnaire (DAPP).* London, ON: Research Psychologists' Press.

Livesley, W. J., & Jang, K. L. (2008). The behavioral genetics of personality disorder. *Annual Review of Clinical Psychology, 4,* 247–274.

Livesley, W. J., Jang, K. L., Jackson, D. N., & Vernon, P. A. (1993). Genetic and environmental contributions to dimensions of personality disorder. *American Journal of Psychiatry, 150,* 1826–1831.

Livesley, W. J., Jang, K. L., & Vernon, P. A. (1998). Phenotypic and genetic structure of traits delineating personality disorder. *Archives of General Psychiatry, 55,* 941–948.

Longabaugh, R., Rubin, A., Malloy, P., Beattie, M., Clifford, P. R., & Noel, N. (1994). Drinking outcomes of alcohol abusers diagnosed as antisocial personality disorder. *Alcoholism: Clinical and Experimental Research, 18*(4), 778–785.

Loranger, A., Sartorius, N., Andreoli, A., & Berger, P. (1994). The International Personality Disorder Examination: The World Health Organization/Alcohol, Drug Abuse, and Mental Health Administration international pilot study of personality disorders. *Archives of General Psychiatry, 51,* 215–224.

Lynam, D. R., & Widiger, T. A. (2001). Using the five-factor model to represent the *DSM-IV* personality disorders: An expert consensus approach. *Journal of Abnormal Psychology, 110,* 401–412.

Markon, K. E., Krueger, R. F., & Watson, D. (2005). Delineating the structure of normal and abnormal personality: An integrative hierarchical approach. *Journal of Personality and Social Psychology, 88,* 139–157.

McCrae, R. R., & Costa, P. T., Jr. (2008). The five-factor theory of personality. In O. P. John, R. W. Robins & L. A. Pervin (Eds.), *Handbook of personality psychology: Theory and research* (3rd ed., pp. 159–181). New York: Guilford Press.

McDavid, J., & Pilkonis, P. (1996). The stability of personality disorder diagnoses. *Journal of Personality Disorders, 10,* 1–15.

Meyer, B., Pilkonis, P.A., Proietti, J.M., Heape, C.L., & Egan, M. (2001). Attachment styles and personality disorders as predictors of symptom course. *Journal of Personality Disorders, 15,* 371–389.

Miller, J.D., Pilkonis, P.A., & Clifton, A. (2005). Self- and other-reports of traits from the five-factor model: Relations to personality disorders. *Journal of Personality Disorders, 19,* 400–419.

Millon, T. (1983). *Millon clinical multiaxial inventory: Manual for the MCMI.* Minneapolis, MN: National Computer Systems.

Millon, T. (1987). *Millon clinical multiaxial inventory II: Manual for the MCMI-II.* Minneapolis, MN: National Computer Systems.

Millon, T. (2002). Assessment is not enough: The SPA should participate in constructing a comprehensive clinical science of personality. *Journal of Personality Assessment, 78,* 209–218.

Millon, T., Millon, C., & Davis, R. (1994). *MCMI-III manual.* Minneapolis, MN: National Computer Systems.

Millon, T., Davis, R. D., Millon, C. M., Wenger, A. W., Van Zuilen, M. H., Fuchs, M., et al. (1996). *Disorders of personality. DSM-IV and beyond.* New York: Wiley.

Morey, L. C., Gunderson, J. G., Quigley, B. D., Shea, M. T., Skodol, A. E., McGlashan, T. H., et al. (2002). The representation of borderline, avoidant, obsessive-compulsive, and schizotypal personality disorders by the five-factor model. *Journal of Personality Disorders, 16,* 215–234.

Mulder, R.T. (2002). Personality pathology and treatment outcome in major depression: A review. *American Journal of Psychiatry, 159,* 359–371.

Mullins-Sweatt, S. N., & Widiger, T. A. (2006). The five-factor model of personality disorder: A translation across science and practice. In R. F. Krueger & J. L. Tackett (Eds.), *Personality and Psychopathology.* New York: Guilford Press.

Newton-Howes, G., Tyrer, P., & Johnson, T. (2006). Personality disorder and the outcome of depression: Meta-analysis of published studies. *British Journal of Psychiatry, 188,* 13–20.

O'Connor, B. P. (2002). The search for dimensional structure differences between normality and abnormality: A statistical review of published data on personality and psychopathology. *Journal of Personality and Social Psychology, 83,* 962–982.

Ogrodniczuk, J. S., Piper, W.E., Joyce, A.S., & McCallum, M. (2001). Using DSM Axis II information to predict outcome in short-term individual psychotherapy. *Journal of Personality Disorders, 15,* 110–122.

Oldham, J. M. (2006). Borderline personality disorder and suicidality. *American Journal of Psychiatry, 163,* 20–26.

Oldham, J. M., Skodol, A. E., Kellman, H. D., Hyler, S. E., Doidge, N., Rosnick, L., et al. (1995). Comorbidity of Axis I and Axis II disorders. *American Journal of Psychiatry 152,* 571–578.

Oltmanns, T.F., Melley, A.H., & Turkheimer, E. (2002). Impaired social functioning and symptoms of personality disorders in a non-clinical population. *Journal of Personality Disorders, 16,* 438–453.

Oltmanns, T.F., & Turkheimer, E. (2009). Person perception and personality pathology. *Current Directions in Psychological Science. 18,* 32–36.

Oltmanns, T. F., Turkheimer, E., & Strauss, M.E. (1998). Peer assessment of personality traits and pathology. *Assessment, 5,* 53–65.

Paris, J. (2001). Psychosocial adversity. In W. J. Livesley (Ed.), *Handbook of personality disorders: Theory, research, and treatment* (pp. 231–241). New York: Guilford.

Paris, J. (2008). Clinical trials of treatment for personality disorders. *Psychiatric Clinics of North America, 31,* 517–526.

Patience, D. A., McGuire, R.J., Scott, A.I.F., & Freeman, C.P.L. (1995). The Edinburgh Primary Care Depression Study: Personality disorder and outcome. *British Journal of Psychiatry, 167,* 324–330.

Perry, J. C., Banon, E., & Ianni, F. (1999). Effectiveness of psychotherapy for personality disorders. *The American Journal of Psychiatry, 159*(9), 1312–1321.

Pfohl, B., Blum, N., & Zimmerman, M. (1997). *Structured Interview for DSM-IV Personality (SIDP-IV).* Washington, D.C.: American Psychiatric Association.

Pilkonis, P. A. (2001). Treatment of personality disorders in association with symptom disorders. In W. J. Livesley (Ed.), *Handbook of personality disorders: Theory, research, and treatment* (pp. 541–554). New York: The Guilford Press.

Pilkonis, P., Heape, C., Proietti, J., & Clark, S. (1995). The reliability and validity of two structured diagnostic interviews for personality disorders. Archives of General Psychiatry, *52*(12), 1025–1033.

Piper, W. E., & Joyce, A. S. (2001). Psychosocial treatment outcome. In W. J. Livesley (Ed.), *Handbook of Personality Disorders* (pp. 323–343). New York: Guilford.

Pukrop, R., Gentil, I., Steinbring, I., & Steinmeyer, E. (2001). Factorial structure of the German version of the Dimensional Assessment of Personality Pathology-Basic Questionnaire in clinical and nonclinical samples. *Journal of Personality Disorders, 15*, 450–456.

Reich, J. (2003a). The effect of axis II disorders on the outcome of treatment of anxiety and unipolar depressive disorders: A review. *Journal of Personality Disorders, 5*, 387–405.

Reich, J. (2003b). The effects of Axis II disorders on the outcome of treatment of anxiety and unipolar depressive disorders: A review. *Journal of Personality Disorders, 17*, 387–405.

Reichborn-Kjennerud, T., Czajkowki, N., Neale, M. C., Orstavik, R. E., Torgersen, S., & et al. (2007). Genetic and environmental influences on dimensional representations of DSM-IV Cluster C personality disorders: A population-based multivariate twin study. *Psychological Medicine, 37*, 645–653.

Rey, J. M., Morris-Yates, A., Singh, M., Andrews, G., & Stewart, G. W. (1995). Continuities between psychiatric disorders in adolescents and personality disorders in adults. *American Journal of Psychiatry, 152*, 895–900.

Rigozzi, C., Rossier, J., Dahourou, D., Adjahouisso, A., Ah-Kion, J., Amoussou-Yeye, D., et al. (2009). A cross-cultural study of the higher-order structures underlying personality disorders in French-speaking African and Switzerland. *Journal of Personality Disorders, 23*(2), 175–186.

Ro, E., & Clark, L. (2009). Psychosocial functioning in the context of diagnosis: Assessment and theoretical issues. *Psychological Assessment, 21*, 313–324.

Roberts, B. W., & DelVecchio, W. F. (2000). The rank-order consistency of personality from childhood to old age: A quantitative review of longitudinal studies. *Psychological Bulletin, 126*, 3–25.

Ryle, A. (2001). Cognitive analytic therapy. In W. J. Livesley (Ed.), *Handbook of personality disorders: Theory, research, and treatment* (pp. 400–413). New York: The Guilford Press.

Samuel, D. B., & Widiger, T. A. (2008). A meta-analytic review of the relationships between the five-factor model and DSM-IV-TR personality disorders: A facet level analysis. *Clinical Psychology Review, 28*(8), 1326–1342.

Saulsman, L. M., & Page, A. C. (2004). The five-factor model and personality disorder empirical literature: A meta-analytic review. *Clinical Psychology Review, 23*, 1055–1085.

Shea, M.T., Stout, R., Gunderson, J., Morey, L., Grilo, C., McGlashan, T., et al. (2002). Short-term diagnostic stability of schizotypal, borderline, avoidant, and obsessive-compulsive personality disorders. *The American Journal of Psychiatry, 159*, 2036–2041.

Sheets, E., & Craighead, W. E. (2007). Toward an empirically based classification of personality pathology. *Clinical Psychology: Science and Practice, 14*, 77–93.

Sher, K. J., & Trull, T. J. (1994). Personality and disinhibitory psychopathology: Alcoholism and antisocial personality disorder. *Journal of Abnormal Psychology, 103*, 92–102.

Simms, L., & Clark, L. (2006). The Schedule for Nonadaptive and Adaptive Personality (SNAP): A Dimensional Measure of Traits Relevant to Personality and Personality Pathology. Differentiating normal and abnormal personality (2nd ed.) (pp. 431–450). New York, NY US: Springer Publishing Co.

Skodol, A. E., Gunderson, J. G., McGlashan, T. H., Dyck, I. R., Stout, R. L., Bender, D. S., et al. (2002a). Functional impairment in patients with schizotypal, borderline, avoidant, or obsessive-compulsive personality disorder. *American Journal of Psychiatry, 159*, 276–283.

Skodol, A. E., Gunderson, J. G., Pfohl, B., Widiger, T. A., Livesley, W., & Siever, L. J. (2002b). The borderline diagnosis I: Psychopathology, comorbidity, and personality structure. *Biological Psychiatry, 51*(12), 936–950.

Skodol, A. E., Gunderson, J. G., Shea, M., McGlashan, T. H., Morey, L. C., Sanislow, C. A., et al. (2005). The Collaborative Longitudinal Personality Disorders Study (CLPS): Overview and implications. *Journal of Personality Disorders, 19*(5), 487–504.

Skodol, A. E., Johnson, J. G., Cohen, P., Sneed, J. R., & Crawford, T. N. (2007). Personality disorder and impaired functioning from adolescence to adulthood. *British Journal of Psychiatry, 190*, 415–420.

South, S. C., Turkheimer, E., & Oltmanns, T. F. (2008). Personality disorder symptoms and marital functioning. *Journal of Consulting and Clinical Psychology, 76*(5), 769–780.

Stangl, D. (1985). A structured interview for the DSM-III personality disorders: A preliminary report. *Archives of General Psychiatry, 42*, 591–596.

Tackett, J. L. (2006). Evaluating models of the personality-psychopathology relationship in children and adolescents. *Clinical Psychology Review, 26*, 584–599.

Tackett, J.L., Balsis, S.M., Oltmanns, T.F., & Krueger, R.F. (2009). A unifying perspective of personality pathology across the lifespan: Developmental considerations for DSM-5. *Development and Psychopathology, 21*, 687–713.

Thomas, C., Turkheimer, E., & Oltmanns, T. F. (2003). Factorial structure of pathological personality as evaluated by peers. *Journal of Abnormal Psychology, 112*(1), 81–91.

Torgersen, S., Lygren, S., Øien, P., Skre, I., Onstad, S., Edvardsen, J., et al. (2000). A twin study of personality disorders. *Comprehensive Psychiatry, 41*, 416–425.

Trull, T. J., & Durrett, C. A. (2005). Categorical And Dimensional Models Of Personality Disorder. *Annual Review of Clinical Psychology, 1*(1), 355–380.

Trull, T. J., Sher, K.J., Minks-Brown, C., Durbin, J., & Burr, R. (2000). Borderline personality disorder and substance use disorders: A review and integration. *Clinical Psychology Review, 20*, 235–253.

Trull, T. J., Waudby, C.J., & Sher, K.J. (2004). Alcohol, tobacco, and drug use disorders and personality disorder symptoms. *Experimental and Clinical Psychopharmacology, 12*, 65–75.

Tuma, R. S. (2009). Genome-wide association studies provoke debate and a new look at strategy. *Journal of the National Cancer Institute, 101*, 1041–1043.

Tyrer, P. (1993). Measurement of social function. In P. Tyrer & P. Casey (Ed.), *Social Function in Psychiatry. The Hidden Axis of Classification Exposed* (pp. 21–52). United Kingdom: Wrightson Biomedical Publishing Ltd.

Tyrer, P., Thompson, S., Schmidt, U., & al., e. (2003). Randomized controlled trial of brief cognitive behaviour therapy versus treatment as usual in recurrent deliberate self-harm: The POPMACT study. *Psychological Medicine, 33*, 969–976.

van Beek, N., & Verheul, R. (2008). Motivation for treatment in patients with personality disorders. *Journal of Personality Disorders, 22*(1), 89–100.

van Kampen, D. (2002). The DAPP-BQ in the Netherlands: Factor structure and relationship with basic personality dimensions. *Journal of Personality Disorders, 16*, 235–254.

Verheul, R., Ball, S., & van den Brink, W. (1998). Substance abuse and personality disorders. In H. R. Kranzler & B. J. Rounsaville (Eds.), *Dual diagnosis and treatment: Substance abuse and comorbid medical and psychiatric disorders* (pp. 317–363). New York: Marcel Dekker.

Verheul, R., Bartak, A., & Widiger, T. A. (2007). Prevalence and construct validity of personality disorder not otherwise specified (PDNOS). *Journal of Personality Disorders, 21*(4), 359–370.

Verheul, R., & Herbrink, M. (2007). The efficacy of various modalities of psychotherapy for personality disorders: A systematic review of the evidence and clinical recommendations. *International Review of Psychiatry, 19*(1), 25–38.

Verheul, R., Van den Bosch, L. M. C., Koeter, M. W. J., de Ridder, M. A. J., Stijnen, T., & Van den Brink, W. (2003). Dialectical behaviour therapy for women with borderline personality disorder: 12-month, randomised clinical trial in The Netherlands. *British Journal of Psychiatry, 182*, 135–140.

Verheul, R., & Widiger, T. A. (2004). A meta-analysis of the prevalence and usage of the personality disorders not otherwise specified (PDNOS) diagnosis. *Journal of Personality Disorders, 18*, 309–319.

Viinamäki, H., Tanskanen, A., Koivumaa-Honkanen, H., Haatainen, K., Honkalampi, K., Antikainen, R., Hintikka, J. (2003). Cluster C personality disorder and recovery from major depression: 24-month prospective follow-up. *Journal of Personality Disorders, 17*(4), 341–350.

Wakefield, Jerome C. (1999). Evolutionary versus prototype analyses of the concept of disorder. *Journal of Abnormal Psychology, 108*, 374–399.

Warner, M., Morey, L., Finch, J., Gunderson, J., Skodol, A., Sanislow, C., et al. (2004). The longitudinal relationship of personality traits and disorders. *Journal of Abnormal Psychology, 113*, 217–227.

Watson, D., Clark, L. A., & Harkness, A. R. (1994). Structures of personality and their relevance to psychopathology. *Journal of Abnormal Psychology, 103*, 18–31.

Weinberg, I., Gunderson, J.G., Hennen, J. et al. (2006). Manual assisted cognitive treatment for deliberate self-harm in borderline personality disorder patients. *Journal of Personality Disorders, 20*(5), 482–492.

Westen, D., & Shedler, J. (1999). Revising and assessing axis II, Part II: Toward an empirically based and clinically useful classification of personality disorders. *American Journal of Psychiatry, 156*, 273–285.

Westermeyer, J., & Thuras, P. (2005). Association of antisocial personality disorder and substance disorder morbidity in a clinical sample. *American Journal of Drug and Alcohol Abuse, 31*, 93–110.

Widiger, T. A., & Costa, P. T., Jr. (2002). Five-factor model personality disorder research. In P. T. Costa & T. A. Widiger (Eds.), *Personality disorders and the five-factor model of personality,* (2nd ed.). Washington, DC: American Psychological Association.

Widiger, T. A., Costa, P. T., & McCrae, R. R. (2002). A proposal for Axis II: Diagnosing personality disorders using the five factor model. In P. T. Costa & T. A. Widiger (Eds.), *Personality disorders and the five factor model of personality* (2nd ed., pp. 431–456). Washington, DC: American Psychological Association.

Widiger, T. A., Mangine, S., Corbitt, E. M., Ellis, C. G., & Thomas, G. V. (1995). *Personality Disorder Interview –IV: A Semistructured Interview for the Assessment of Personality Disorders.* Odessa, FL: Psychological Assessment Resources, Inc.

Widiger, T. A., & Mullins-Sweatt, S. (2007). Mental disorders as discrete clinical conditions: Dimensional versus categorical classification. In M. Hersen, S. M. Turner & D. Beidel (Eds.), *Adult psychopathology and diagnosis* (3rd ed., pp. 3–33). New York: Wiley.

Widiger, T. A., & Mullins-Sweatt, S. (2009). Five-Factor model of personality disorder: A proposal for DSM-5. *Annual Review of Clinical Psychology, 5,* 197–220.

Widiger, T.A., & Seidlitz, L. (2002). Personality, psychopathology, and aging. *Journal of Research in Personality, 36*, 335–362.

Widiger, T. A., & Simonsen, E. (2005). Alternative dimensional models of personality disorder: Finding a common ground. *Journal of Personality Disorders, 19*, 110–130.

Widiger, T. A., Simonsen, E., Krueger, R. F., Livesley, W. J., & Verheul, R. (2006). *Personality disorder research agenda for DSM-5.* Washington, DC: American Psychiatric Association.

Widiger, T. A., & Smith, G. T. (2008). Personality and psychopathology. In O. P. John, R. W. Robins & L. A. Pervin (Eds.), *Handbook of Personality* (Third ed.). New York: Guilford Press.

Widiger, T. A., & Trull, T. J. (2007). Plate tectonics in the classification of personality disorder: Shifting to a dimensional model. *American Psychologist, 62*(2), 71–83.

Yamagata, S., Suzuki, A., Ando, J., One, Y., Kijima, N., Yoshimura, K., et al. (2006). Is the genetic structure of human personality universal? Across-cultural twin study from North America, Europe, and Asia. *Journal of Personality and Social Psychology, 90*, 987–998.

Zanarini, M. C. (2000). Childhood experiences associated with the development of borderline personality disorder. *Psychiatric Clinics of North America, 23*, 89–101.

Zanarini, M. C. (2004). Update on pharmacotherapy of borderline personality disorder. *Current Psychiatry Reports, 6,* 66–70.

Zanarini, M. C., & Frankenburg, F. R. (2003). Omega-3 fatty acid treatment of women with borderline personality disorder: A double-blind, placebo-controlled pilot study. *American Journal of Psychiatry, 160*, 167–169.

Zanarini, M. C., Frankenburg, F. R., Hennen, J., Reich, D. B., & Silk, K. R. (2005). The McLean study of adult development (MSAD): Overview and implications of the first six years of prospective follow-up. *Journal of Personality Disorders, 19*(5), 505–523.

Zanarini, M. C., Frankenburg, F. R., Hennen, J., & Silk, K. R. (2004). Mental health service utilization by borderline personality disorder patients and axis II comparison subjects followed prospectively for 6 years. *Journal of Clinical Psychiatry, 65*, 28–36.

Zanarini, M. C., Frankenburg, F. R., Reich, D. B., Silk, K. R., Hudson, J. I., & McSweeney, L. B. (2007). The subsyndromal phenomenology of borderline personality disorder: A 10-year follow-up study. *American Journal of Psychiatry, 164*, 929–935.

Zheng, W., Wang, W., Huang, Z., Sun, C., Zhu, J., & Livesley, W. J. (2002). The structure of traits delineating personality disorder in a Chinese sample. *Journal of Personality Disorders, 16*, 477–486.

Zimmerman, M. (1994). Diagnosing personality disorders: A review of issues and research methods. *Archives of General Psychiatry, 51,* 225–245.

Zimmerman, M. & Coryell, W. (1989). The Reliability of personality disorder diagnoses in a non-patient sample. *Journal of Personality Disorders, 3,* 53–57.

Zimmerman, M., Rothschild, L., & Chelminski, I. (2005). The prevalence of DSM-IV personality disorders in psychiatric outpatients. *American Journal of Psychiatry, 162*(10), 1911–1918.

Zlotnick, C., Johnson, D.M., Yen, S., Battle, C.L., Sanislow, C.A., Skodol, A.E. et al. (2003). Clinical features and impairment in women with borderline personality disorder (BPD) with posttraumatic stress disorder (PTSD), BPD without PTSD, and other personality disorders with PTSD. *Journal of Nervous and Mental Disease, 191,* 706–713.

V. Mark Durand

Abstract

Disorders of development include a range of problems first evidenced in childhood. Although most disorders have their origins in childhood, a few fully express themselves before early adulthood. This chapter describes the nature, assessment, and treatment of the more common disorders that are revealed in a clinically significant way during a child's developing years. The disorders of development affect a range of functioning, from single skills deficits to more pervasive problems that negatively impact a child's ability to function. Included is coverage of several disorders usually diagnosed first in infancy, childhood, or adolescence, including *attention-deficit hyperactivity disorder, oppositional defiant disorder, conduct disorder, learning disorders, communication and related disorders, pervasive developmental disorders* (including autistic disorder and Asperger disorder), and *intellectual disabilities*. Recommendations for future research on the potential for advancing knowledge regarding spectrums within some of these disorders, as well as recommendations for treatment, are outlined.

Keywords: Attention-deficit hyperactivity disorder, autism spectrum disorders, conduct disorder, learning disorders, oppositional defiant disorder

Almost all psychological disorders are disorders of development in the sense that they change over time. Most disorders originate in childhood, although the full presentation of the problem may not manifest itself until much later. This chapter reviews the more common disorders that are revealed in a clinically significant way during a child's developing years and are of concern to families and educators. The disorders of development affect a range of functioning from narrow skills deficits (e.g., reading disorder) to more pervasive problems that negatively impact a child's ability to function (e.g., autistic disorder). This chapter includes coverage of several disorders usually diagnosed first in infancy, childhood, or adolescence, including attention-deficit hyperactivity disorder (ADHD), oppositional defiant disorder (ODD), conduct disorder (CD), learning disorders, pervasive developmental disorders (including autistic disorder and Asperger disorder) and intellectual

disabilities. Briefly discussed are communication and related disorders.

Spectrum Disorders

The disorders described in this chapter represent a broad range of problems first evident in childhood. Some of the disorders discussed may be considered part of a spectrum of disorders—a group of disorders that are thought to be related through the sharing of risk genes or pathophysiological mechanisms (Hyman, 2007). For instance, some of the pervasive developmental disorders are being studied under the category of "autism spectrum disorders." Autistic disorder and Asperger disorder are thought to be related in the spectrum, although research continues on the co-occurrence of childhood disintegrative disorder and pervasive developmental disorder—not otherwise specified (PDD-NOS) (Swedo, Thorsen, & Pine, 2008).

Two other major disorders—conduct disorder (CD) and ODD—may be part of a spectrum of disruptive behavior disorders, although this research is in a nascent stage (Shaffer, Leibenluft, Rohde, Sirovatka, & Regier, in press). There is also considerable comorbidity among attention deficit disorders, CD, and ODD, although any conclusion about their being part of a spectrum of disorders is premature (Shaffer et al., 2009). Where appropriate, research on comorbidity and the progress being made on identifying possible spectrum disorders is reviewed.

Attention-Deficit and Disruptive Behavior Disorders
Attention-Deficit Hyperactivity Disorder

The primary characteristics of ADHD include a pattern of inattention, and/or of hyperactivity and impulsivity. These deficits can significantly disrupt academic efforts, as well as social relationships. Attention-deficit hyperactivity disorder is one of the most common reasons children are referred for mental health services in the United States (Hechtman, 2005).

CLINICAL DESCRIPTION

The *Diagnostic and Statistical Manual of Mental Disorders, Fourth Edition, Text Revision* (DSM-IV-TR) differentiates three types of symptoms for ADHD. The first includes problems of *inattention*. People may appear not to listen to others; they may lose necessary school assignments, books, or tools; and they may not pay enough attention to details and make careless mistakes. The second type of symptom includes *hyperactivity*, which includes fidgeting, having trouble sitting for any length of time, always being on the go. The third general symptom is *impulsivity*, which includes blurting out answers before questions have been completed and having trouble waiting turns. Either the first (inattention) or the second and third (hyperactivity and impulsivity) domains of symptoms must be present for someone to be diagnosed with ADHD (Naglieri & Goldstein, 2006).

Inattention, hyperactivity, and impulsivity often lead to other problems that appear secondary to ADHD. Academic performance tends to suffer, especially as the child progresses in school. The cause of this poor performance is not known. It could be a result of the problems with attention and impulsivity characteristic of ADHD, and in some children this can be made worse by factors such as concurrent learning disabilities, which are common in boys with ADHD (Barkley, 2006b). Children with ADHD are likely to be unpopular and rejected by their peers (Hoza et al., 2004). Here, the difficulty appears to

be directly related to the behaviors symptomatic of ADHD. For example, one study found that young girls with ADHD in general were likely to be rejected by peers but that this likelihood was more pronounced in those with hyperactivity, impulsivity, and inattention when compared to girls who had only the inattentive type (Hinshaw, 2002). Evidence suggests that some children with ADHD (who are not also depressed) actually have an inflated sense of their own competence in areas such as social acceptance, physical appearance, and self-worth (Hoza et al., 2004).

EPIDEMIOLOGY

Attention-deficit hyperactivity disorder is estimated to occur in 3%–7% of school-age children in the United States, and an international analysis of prevalence suggests that the disorder is found in about 5.2% of the child populations across all regions of the world (Polanczyk, de Lima, Horta, Biederman, & Rohde, 2007). This finding of comparable international rates of ADHD is important because debates continue about the validity of ADHD as a disorder. Previously, there were historic differences in the number of people diagnosed with this disorder, with children in the United States being more likely to receive the label of ADHD. Based on this difference, some argue that ADHD in children is simply a cultural construct (Timimi & Taylor, 2004). However, with improvements in diagnosis, countries that previously reported lower rates of ADHD are now finding similar numbers of these children being brought to the attention of helping professionals (Barkley, 2006e).

Prevalence estimates suggest gender differences, with boys three times more likely to be diagnosed with ADHD than girls, and this discrepancy increases among clinic referrals (Spencer, Biederman, & Mick, 2007). The reason for this gender difference is largely unknown. It may be that adults are more tolerant of hyperactivity among girls, who tend to be less active than boys with ADHD. Boys tend to be more aggressive, which will more likely result in attention by mental health professionals (Barkley, 2006e). Girls with ADHD, on the other hand, tend to display more internalizing behaviors—specifically, anxiety and depression (Barkley, 2006e).

Children with ADHD are first identified as different from their peers around age 3 or 4; their parents describe them as active, mischievous, slow to toilet train, and oppositional (Conners, March, Frances, Wells, & Ross, 2001). The symptoms of inattention, impulsivity, and hyperactivity become increasingly obvious during the school years. It is estimated that about half of the children with ADHD have ongoing difficulties through adulthood (McGough, 2005). Over time, children with ADHD seem to be less impulsive, although inattention persists. During adolescence, the impulsivity manifests itself in different areas; for example, they are at greater risk for teen pregnancy and contracting sexually transmitted diseases. They are also more likely to have driving difficulties, such as crashes; to be cited for speeding; and to have their licenses suspended (Barkley, 2006a). Although the manifestations of ADHD change as people age, many of their problems persist (Weyandt & DuPaul, 2006).

Evidence for a spectrum of disorders—including ADHD—awaits empirical evidence. Up to 80% of children with ADHD are diagnosed with one or more other disorders (Wilens et al., 2002). Common comorbid disorders in children include anxiety, depression, and disruptive behavior (Barkley, 2006c). Similarly, almost 90% of adults with ADHD are likely to have at least one other disorder, including disruptive behavior, depression, anxiety, and substance use disorders (McGough, 2005).

Several other DSM-IV disorders, also found in children, appear to overlap significantly with this disorder. Specifically, ODD, CD, and bipolar disorder all have characteristics seen in children with ADHD (Shaffer et al., 2009). The impulsivity and hyperactivity observed in children with ADHD can manifest themselves in some of these symptoms. It has been estimated that at least half of those with ADHD could also be diagnosed with ODD (Barkley, 2006c).

ETIOLOGY

Attention-deficit hyperactivity disorder is considered to be highly influenced by genetics, with a relatively small role played by environmental influences in the cause of the disorder when compared to many other psychological disorders (Waldman & Gizer, 2006). The relatives of children with ADHD have been found to be more likely to have ADHD themselves than would be expected in the general population (Biederman et al., 1992). These families display an increase in psychopathology in general, including conduct disorder, mood disorders, anxiety disorders, and substance abuse (Faraone et al., 2000). This research and the comorbidity in the children themselves suggest that some shared genetic deficits may contribute to the problems experienced by individuals with these disorders (Faraone, 2003).

More than one gene is probably responsible for ADHD (Bobb, Castellanos, Addington, & Rapoport, 2006), with attention focusing on genes associated with the neurochemical dopamine, although norepinephrine, serotonin, and γ-aminobutyric acid (GABA) are also implicated in the cause of ADHD. More specifically, there is strong evidence that ADHD is associated with the dopamine D_4 receptor gene, the dopamine transporter gene (DAT1), and the dopamine D_5 receptor gene. DAT1 is of particular interest because methylphenidate (Ritalin)—one of the most common medical treatments for ADHD—inhibits this gene and increases the amount of dopamine available.

Researchers are looking for endophenotypes, those basic deficits—such as specific attentional problems—characteristic of ADHD. Specific areas of current interest for ADHD are the brain's executive attention system, working memory functions, inattentiveness, and impulsivity. Research is now focused on tying specific genetic defects to these cognitive processes to make the link between genes and behavior (Kim, Kim, & Cho, 2006).

The strong genetic influence in ADHD does not rule out any role for the environment (Sharp, Gottesman, Greenstein, Ebens, Rapoport, & Castellanos 2003; Waldman & Gizer, 2006). In one of the few gene–environment interaction studies of ADHD, researchers found that children with a specific mutation involving the dopamine system (DAT1 genotype) were more likely to exhibit the symptoms of ADHD if their mothers smoked during pregnancy (Kahn, Khoury, Nichols, & Lanphear, 2003). Prenatal smoking seemed to interact with this genetic predisposition to increase the risk for hyperactive and impulsive behavior.

Research on the neuroanatomy of ADHD suggests that the overall volume of the brain in those with this disorder is slightly smaller (3%–4%) than in children without this disorder. A number of areas in the brains of those with ADHD appear affected (Valera, Faraone, Murray, & Seidman, 2007).

A variety of such toxins as allergens and food additives have been considered as possible causes of ADHD over the years. The theory that food additives such as artificial colors, flavorings, and preservatives are responsible for the symptoms of ADHD remains controversial. There is some evidence that these substances have little or no effect on the symptoms of ADHD (Barkley, 1990; Kavale & Forness, 1983), however at least one clinical trial suggests that children *without* ADHD can become more active with the introduction of certain food colorings and additives (McCann et al., 2007).

Negative responses by parents, teachers, and peers to the affected child's impulsivity and hyperactivity may contribute to feelings of low self-esteem among children who are also depressed (Barkley, 2006c). Years of constant reminders by teachers and parents to behave, sit quietly, and pay attention may contribute to a negative self-image in these children, which, in turn, can negatively affect their ability to make friends. Thus, the possible biological influences on impulsivity, hyperactivity, and attention, combined with attempts to control these children, may lead to rejection and consequent poor self-image. An integration of the biological and psychological influences on ADHD suggests that both need to be addressed when designing effective treatments (Rapport, 2001).

ASSESSMENT AND TREATMENT

Evaluation of ADHD focuses on a number of areas, including an assessment of current social and academic concerns and differential diagnosis. Information from parents is important in assessing the child's behavior outside of school and how the family and school have collaborated on the problems (Thapar & Muñoz-Solomando, 2008). Findings from measures such as the ADHD rating scale-IV (DuPaul, Power, Anastopoulos, & Reid, 1998), the DSM-IV ADHD rating scale (Gomez, Harvey, Quick, Scharer, & Harris, 1999), the disruptive behavior rating scale (Barkley & Murphy, 1998), or the Conners' Parent Rating Scale (CRS-R; Conners, Sitarenios, Parker, & Epstein, 1998) provide more objective assessment of functioning that can be used to assess norms and to monitor treatment.

In addition, assessment extends to the functioning of the family and community resources, since parental behavior training and school intervention are often recommended. The use of assessment tools varies considerably across professionals, in part because assessors come from different disciplinary backgrounds (e.g., counseling, clinical or school psychology) and they work in varied settings (e.g., school, clinic, or university settings) (Handler & DuPaul, 2005).

Treatment for ADHD has proceeded on two fronts: biological and psychosocial interventions. Typically, the goal of biological treatments is to reduce the child's impulsivity and hyperactivity and to improve attention skills. Psychosocial treatments generally focus on broader issues such as improving academic performance, decreasing disruptive behavior, and improving social skills.

Since the use of stimulant medication with children with ADHD was first described (Bradley, 1937),

hundreds of studies have documented the effectiveness of this class of medication in reducing the core symptoms of the disorder. It is estimated that more than 2.5 million children in the United States are being treated with these medications (Centers for Disease Control and Prevention [CDC], 2005). Drugs such as methylphenidate (Ritalin, Metadate, Concerta) and D-amphetamine (Dexedrine, Dextrostat) have proved helpful for more than 70% of cases in at least temporarily reducing hyperactivity and impulsivity and improving concentration on tasks (Connor, 2006). Adderall, which is a longer-acting version of these psychostimulants, reduces the need for multiple doses for children during the day but has similar positive effects (Connor, 2006).

A newer drug—Strattera (or atomoxetine)—also appears effective for some children with ADHD, but it is a selective norepinephrine-reuptake inhibitor and therefore does not produce the same "highs" when used in larger doses—a recent concern due to the abuse of prescription drugs among teens. Research suggests that other drugs, such as one of the antidepressants (bupropion, imipramine) and a drug used for treating high blood pressure (clonidine), may have similar effects on people with ADHD (Spencer, 2006). All these drugs seem to improve compliance and decrease negative behaviors in many children, although their effects do not usually last once the drugs are discontinued.

Some portion of children with ADHD do not respond to medications, and most children who do respond show improvement in ability to focus their attention but do not show gains in the important areas of academics and social skills (Smith, Barkley, & Shapiro, 2006). In addition, the medications often result in unpleasant side effects, such as insomnia, drowsiness, or irritability (Connor, 2006). Because of these findings, researchers have applied various behavioral interventions to help these children at home and in school. In general, the programs set such goals as increasing the amount of time the child remains seated, improving academic performance, or engaging in appropriate play with peers. Other programs incorporate parent training to teach families how to respond constructively to their child's behaviors and how to structure the child's day to help prevent difficulties (Sonuga-Barke, Daley, Thompson, Laver-Bradbury, & Weeks, 2001). Social skills training for these children, which includes teaching them how to interact appropriately with their peers, also seems to be an important treatment component (de Boo & Prins, 2007). For adults with ADHD, cognitive-behavioral intervention for the distractibility and organizational skills problems appears quite helpful. Most clinicians typically recommend a combination of approaches designed to individualize treatments for those with ADHD, targeting both short-term management issues (decreasing hyperactivity and impulsivity) and long-term concerns (preventing and reversing academic decline and improving social skills).

To determine whether a combined approach to treatment is the most effective, a large-scale study initiated by the National Institute of Mental Health was conducted by six teams of researchers (Jensen et al., 2001). The Multimodal Treatment of Attention-Deficit Hyperactivity Disorder (MTA) study included 579 children who were randomly assigned to one of four groups. One group of the children received routine care without medication or specific behavioral interventions (community care). The three treatment groups consisted of medication management (usually methylphenidate), intensive behavioral treatment, and a combination of the two treatments. The study lasted 14 months. Initial reports from the study suggested that the combination of behavioral treatments and medication, and medication alone, were superior to behavioral treatment alone and community intervention for ADHD symptoms. For problems that went beyond the specific symptoms of ADHD, such as social skills, academics, parent–child relations, oppositional behavior, and anxiety or depression, results suggested slight advantages of combination over single treatments (medication management, behavioral treatment) and community care.

Some controversy surrounds the interpretation of these findings—specifically, whether the combination of behavioral and medical treatments is superior to medication alone (Biederman, Spencer, Wilens, & Greene, 2001; Pelham, 1999). One of the concerns surrounding the study was that, although medication continued to be dispensed, the behavioral treatment was faded over time, which may account for the observed differences. Reinterpretations of the data from this large-scale study continue, and more research likely will be needed to clarify the combined and separate effects of these two approaches to treatment (Smith et al., 2006).

Conduct Disorder

Conduct disorder is a DSM-IV-TR diagnosis for children who violate the basic rights of others or who engage in behaviors that violate society's norms. These children chronically engage in multiple and serious behavior problems (e.g., lying, cheating, truancy, theft, arson, etc.).

CLINICAL DESCRIPTION

A diagnosis of CD requires the presence of three or more criteria from the following general categories: aggression to people and animals, destruction of property, deceitfulness or theft, and serious violation of rules (American Psychiatric Association [APA], 2000). Clinicians can rate the severity of the disorder as mild (few if any conduct problems in excess of those required to make the diagnosis, and conduct problems cause only minor harm to others), moderate (number of conduct problems, and effect on others intermediate between "mild" and "severe"), or severe (many conduct problems in excess of those required to make the diagnosis, or conduct problems cause considerable harm to others). In addition, DSM-IV-TR provides for the designation of two subtypes; *childhood-onset type* (the onset of at least one criterion characteristic of CD prior to age 10 years) or *adolescent-onset type* (the absence of any criteria characteristic of CD prior to age 10 years).

The DSM-IV-TR criteria for CD focus almost entirely on observable behaviors (for example, "has used a weapon that can cause serious physical harm to others"). Underlying personality traits (for example, being self-centered or manipulative), which are also often an important aspect in this disorder, are not part of the diagnosis, in part to improve the reliability of the diagnosis.

EPIDEMIOLOGY

One population-based longitudinal study found that the presence of CD among children aged 4½–5 years was 6.6%, with 2.5% exhibiting problems in the moderate to severe range (Kim-Cohen, Arseneault, Caspi, Tomas, Taylor, & Moffitt, 2005). Many children with CD—most often diagnosed in boys (Eme, 2007)—become juvenile offenders (Eppright, Kashani, Robison, & Reid, 1993) and tend to become involved with drugs (Fergusson, Boden, & Horwood, 2008). For many of these children, rule violations, such as staying out late at night or truancy from school, begin at an early age (before 13 years of age) (Renk, 2008).

Early identification of this lifelong pattern of antisocial behavior is important because young children who display antisocial behavior are likely to continue these behaviors as they grow older (Soderstrom, Sjodin, Carlstedt, & Forsman, 2004). Data from long-term follow-up research indicate that many adults with antisocial personality disorder or psychopathy met the criteria for CD as children (Robins, 1978; Salekin, 2006); the likelihood increases if the child has both CD and ADHD

(Lynam, 1996). In many cases, the types of norm violations that an adult would engage in—irresponsibility regarding work or family—appear as younger versions in CD: truant from school, running away from home.

ETIOLOGY

Research on the influences affecting CD in children is evolving. It is clear that genetic factors are important in the development of these disruptive behaviors although there are relatively few well-conducted studies in this area. In part, this may be due to the apparent heterogeneity of symptoms of the disorder. One study, for example, found that symptoms such as breaking and entering and truancy showed limited evidence for heritability, while destruction of property, lying, stealing without confrontation, use of weapons, and fighting showed moderate heritability (Gelhorn, Stallings, Young, Corley, Rhee, & Hewitt, 2005). The same study found bullying, cruelty to animals, breaking and entering, truancy, and running away showed the effects of substantial shared environment (Gelhorn et al., 2005).

At the same time, familial environmental influences have received considerable attention. Patterson's influential work suggests that aggression in such children may escalate, partly as a result of their interactions with their parents (Granic & Patterson, 2006; Patterson, 1982). This research finds that the parents often give in to the problem behaviors displayed by their children. This "coercive family process" combines with other factors, such as parental depression, poor monitoring of their child's activities, and less parental involvement, to help maintain the aggressive behaviors (Chronis et al., 2007; Patterson, DeBaryshe, & Ramsey, 1989).

Biological influences appear to interact with environmental experiences such as early childhood adversity. In a family that may already be under stress because of divorce or substance abuse (Hetherington, Stanley-Hagan, & Anderson, 1989; Patterson et al., 1989), there may be an interaction style that encourages antisocial behavior on the part of the child (Wootton, Frick, Shelton, & Silverthorn, 1997). The child's disruptive and impulsive behavior—partly caused by the child's difficult temperament and impulsivity (Chronis et al., 2007; Kochanska, Aksan, & Joy, 2007)—alienates other children who might be good role models and attracts others who encourage disruptive behavior (Vuchinich, Bank, & Patterson, 1992). These behaviors may also result in the child dropping out of school and a poor occupational history in adulthood (Caspi, Elder, & Bem, 1987).

ASSESSMENT AND TREATMENT

A comprehensive evaluation is conducted with children with serious behavioral concerns and includes information about the behavior problems, family concerns, school concerns, and differential diagnosis with overlapping disorders such as ADHD, learning disorders, and ODD. Assessing the seriousness of behavior problems, especially in younger children, can be complicated by the tolerance thresholds of parents and teachers (Renk, 2008). The Child Behavior Checklist (CBCL) in its various forms for parents, teachers, and for self-report (Achenbach, 1991a-d), for example, is the most thoroughly researched assessment tool and provides norm-based information that is essential for decision-making.

The most common treatment strategy for children involves parent training (Patterson, 1986; Sanders, 1992). Parents are taught to recognize behavior problems early and how to use praise and privileges to reduce problem behavior and encourage prosocial behaviors. Treatment studies typically show that these types of programs can significantly improve the behaviors of many children who display antisocial behaviors (Harris & Rice, 2006). A number of factors, however, put families at risk either for not succeeding in treatment or for dropping out early; these include cases with a high degree of family dysfunction, socioeconomic disadvantage, high family stress, a parent's history of antisocial behavior, and severe CD on the part of the child (Dumas & Wahler, 1983; Kazdin, Mazurick, & Bass, 1993). Psychosocial intervention often extends to the school, and both approaches have significant empirical bases (Brown et al., 2008).

Oppositional Defiant Disorder

Children with ODD display uncooperative, defiant, and hostile behavior toward authority figures, although to a lesser degree when compared to children with CD. These types of problems are among most common causes of clinic referrals for children (Nock, Kazdin, Hiripi, & Kessler, 2006). Considerable heterogeneity exists in the behaviors that comprise ODD and CD, and research continues in order to identify distinguishing features to improve models that disentangle multiple pathways for these disorders (Biederman et al., 1996; Biederman, Petty, et al., 2008; Kolko, Dorn, Bukstein, & Burke, 2008).

Assessment mirrors the process and tools used for CD and includes a comprehensive evaluation formed after collecting information about the behavior problems, family concerns, school concerns, and differential diagnosis with overlapping disorders such as ADHD, learning disorders, and mood and anxiety disorders, as well as CD (Biederman, Ball, Monuteaux, Kaiser, & Faraone, 2008). Treatment also includes a heavy emphasis on psychosocial interventions that are home and school-based—also paralleling treatment for CD. Research on these treatments suggests that they produce moderate to large effect sizes for behavior problems (Brown et al., 2008; Eyberg, Nelson, & Boggs, 2008; McMahon, Kotler, Steele, Elkin, & Roberts, 2008).

Learning Disorders

This section describes learning disorders in reading, mathematics, and written expression—all characterized by performance that is substantially below what would be expected given the person's age, intelligence quotient (IQ) score, and education. Also briefly reviewed are disorders related to communication.

Clinical Description

According to DSM-IV-TR criteria, a reading disorder is defined as a substantial discrepancy between a person's reading achievement and what would be expected for someone of the same age—referred to by some as "unexpected underachievement" (Fletcher, Lyon, Fuchs, & Barnes, 2007). This is usually defined as a discrepancy of more than 2 standard deviations between achievement and IQ (APA, 2000). In addition, this disability cannot be caused by a sensory difficulty, such as trouble with sight or hearing, and should not be the result of poor or absent instruction. Similarly, the DSM-IV-TR defines a mathematics disorder as achievement below expected performance in mathematics, and a disorder of written expression as achievement below expected performance in writing. In each of these disorders, the difficulties are sufficient to interfere with the students' academic achievement and to disrupt their daily activities.

Epidemiology

Estimates of the prevalence of learning disorders range from 5% to 10% (Altarac & Saroha, 2007). It is currently believed that nearly 6 million children in the United States are diagnosed as having a specific learning disorder (Altarac & Saroha, 2007). There do appear to be racial differences in the diagnosis of learning disorders, with approximately 1% of white children and 2.6% of black children receiving services for problems with learning in 2001 (Bradley, Danielson, & Hallahan, 2002). This research suggests that the differences were related to the economic status of the child but not ethnic background.

Difficulties with reading are the most common of the learning disorders and occur in some form in 4%–10% of the general population (Tannock, 2005b). Mathematics disorder appears in approximately 1% of the population (Tannock, 2005a), but there is limited information about the prevalence of disorder of written expression among children and adults. Early studies suggested that boys were more likely to have a reading disorder than girls, although more contemporary research indicates that boys and girls may be equally affected by this disorder (Feinstein & Phillips, 2006). Students with learning disorders are more likely to drop out of school (Vogel & Reder, 1998), more likely to be unemployed (Shapiro & Lentz, 1991), and more likely to have suicidal thoughts and attempt suicide (Daniel et al., 2006).

A group of disorders loosely identified as *communication and related disorders* seems closely related to learning disorders. These disorders can appear deceptively benign, yet their presence early in life can cause wide-ranging problems later. For a brief overview of these disorders, which include stuttering, expressive language disorder, selective mutism, and tic disorder, see Table 25.1.

Etiology

Theories about the causes of learning disorders include genetic, neurobiological, and environmental factors. The genetic research in this area is particularly complex. It is clear that learning disorders run in families, and sophisticated family and twin studies bear this out (Fletcher et al., 2007). Yet, analyses of the genes involved suggest that many effects are not specific—meaning that different genes are not responsible for reading disorders and mathematics disorders. Instead, there are genes that affect learning, and these may contribute to problems across domains (reading, mathematics, writing) (Plomin & Kovas, 2005).

Children (and adults) often have very different problems associated with reading. Reading disorders are sometimes broken into problems with word recognition (difficulty decoding single words—sometimes called *dyslexia*), fluency (problems being able to read words and sentences smoothly and automatically), and comprehension (difficulty getting meaning from what is read) (Fletcher et al., 2007). Most research to date focuses on problems with word recognition, and there is evidence that some develop these problems primarily through biological processes, while others develop problems as a result of environmental factors (Shaywitz, Mody, & Shaywitz, 2006). Genes located

Table 25.1 Communication and related disorders

Stuttering

Clinical Description	Statistics	Etiology	Treatment
A disturbance in speech fluency that includes a number of problems with speech, such as repeating syllables or words, prolonging certain sounds, making obvious pauses, or substituting words to replace ones that are difficult to articulate.	Occurs twice as often among boys as among girls. Begins most often in children under the age of 3, and 98% of cases occur before the age of 10. Approximately 80% of children who stutter before they enter school will no longer stutter after they have been in school a year or so (Kroll & Beitchman, 2005).	Rather than anxiety causing stuttering, stuttering makes people socially anxious (Craig, Hancock, Tran, & Craig, 2003). Multiple brain pathways appear to be involved, and genetic influences may be a factor (Kroll & Beitchman, 2005).	Parents are counseled about how to talk to their children. *Regulated-breathing method* is a promising behavioral treatment in which the person is instructed to stop speaking when a stuttering episode occurs and then to take a deep breath (exhale, then inhale) before proceeding (Woods, Twohig, Fuqua, & Hanley, 2000). Altered auditory feedback (electronically changing speech feedback to people who stutter) can improve speech (Lincoln, Packman, & Onslow, 2006), as can using forms of self-monitoring, in which people modify their own speech for the words they stutter (Venkatagiri, 2005).

Expressive Language Disorders

Clinical Description	Statistics	Etiology	Treatment
Limited speech in *all* situations. *Expressive language* (what is said) is significantly below *receptive language* (what is understood); the latter is usually average.	Occurs in 10% to 15% of children younger than 3 years of age (Johnson & Beitchman, 2005) and is almost five times as likely to affect boys as girls (Whitehurst et al., 1988).	An unfounded psychological explanation is that the children's parents may not speak to them enough. A biological theory is that middle ear infection is a contributory cause.	May be self-correcting and may not require special intervention (Whitehurst et al., 1988).

Selective Mutism

Clinical Description	Statistics	Etiology	Treatment
Persistent failure to speak in specific situations—such as school—despite the ability to do so.	Occurs in less than 1% of children and most often between the ages of 5 and 7. More prevalent among girls than boys (Sharp, Sherman, & Gross, 2007).	Not much is known. Anxiety is one possible cause (Bergman & Piacentini, 2005).	*Contingency management:* Giving children praise and reinforcers for speaking while ignoring their attempts to communicate in other ways (Standart & Le Couteur, 2003).

Table 25.1 Communication and related disorders *(Cont'd)*

Tic Disorders

Clinical Description	Statistics	Etiology	Treatment
Involuntary motor movements *(tics),* such as head twitching, or vocalizations, such as grunts, that often occur in rapid succession, come on suddenly, and happen in idiosyncratic or stereotyped ways. In one type, *Tourette disorder,* vocal tics often include the involuntary repetition of obscenities.	Of all children, 12%–18% show some tics during their growing years, and 10–80 children out of every 10,000 have Tourette's disorder (Scahill & Leckman, 2005). Usually develops before the age of 14. High comorbidity between tics and ADHD, as well as obsessive-compulsive disorder (Scahill & Leckman, 2005).	Strong genetic component, but the nature of the genes are as yet unknown (Scahill & Leckman, 2005).	*Psychological:* Self-monitoring, relaxation training, and habit reversal. *Pharmacological:* Haloperidol; more recently, risperidone, and ziprasidone (Chowdhury, 2008).

Adapted from Barlow, D.H., & Durand, V.M. (2009). *Abnormal psychology: An integrative approach* (5th ed.). Belmont, CA: Wadsworth/ Cengage. Reproduced with permission from the publisher.

on chromosomes 2, 6, 15, and 18 have all been repeatedly linked to these difficulties (Paracchini et al., in press). At the same time, environmental influences such as the home reading habits of families can significantly affect outcomes—especially with skills such as word recognition—suggesting that reading to children at risk for reading disorders can lessen the impact of the genetic influence (Petrill, Deater-Deckard, Thompson, DeThorne, & Schatschneider, 2006).

Research suggests structural, as well as functional, differences in the brains of people with learning disabilities. Specifically, three areas of the left hemisphere appear to be involved in problems with dyslexia (word recognition)—Broca's area (which affects articulation and word analysis), an area in the left parietotemporal area (which affects word analysis), and an area in the left occipitotemporal area (which affects recognizing word form) (Shaywitz et al., 2006). A different area in the left hemisphere—the intraparietal sulcus—seems to be critical for the development of a sense of numbers and is implicated in mathematics disorder (Fletcher et al., 2007). In contrast, there is no current evidence for specific deficits responsible for disorders of written expression.

Disorders of reading have been diagnosed more often in English-speaking countries. Although some have thought that this may simply be a difference in diagnostic practices, biological research now suggests it may involve the relative complexity of the written word in English. Researchers tested individuals who displayed reading disorders and who spoke English, French, or Italian (Paulesu et al., 2001). Although those who spoke Italian did better on tests of reading, brain imaging (positron emission tomography) while all subjects were reading indicated each experienced the same reduced activity in the left temporal lobe. It was hypothesized that the complexity of reading English may account for these cultural differences.

Psychological and motivational factors that have been reinforced by others seem to play an important role in the eventual outcome of people with learning disorders. Factors such as socioeconomic status, cultural expectations, parental interactions and expectations, and child management practices, together with existing neurological deficits and the types of support provided in the school, seem to determine outcome (Fletcher et al., 2007).

Assessment and Treatment

Assessment for learning disorders is a complex process that involves ruling out medical explanations for learning difficulties and determining the nature of the specific learning problem(s). Typically, professionals conduct informal observations of the student in school settings and review academic work. Following medical screening, more focused assessments are conducted to assess general intellectual capabilities and specific deficit areas. There is some controversy over using the discrepancy between IQ and achievement as part of the process of identifying children with learning disorders. Part of the criticism involves the delay between when learning problems occur and when they finally result in a large enough difference between IQ scores and achievement scores—which may not be measurable until later in a child's academic life. An alternative approach—called "response to intervention"—is now being used by many clinicians. It involves identifying a child as having a learning disorder when the response to a known effective intervention (for example, an early reading program) is significantly inferior to the performance by peers (Compton, Fuchs, Fuchs, & Bryant, 2006). This provides an early warning system and focuses on providing effective instruction.

Treatment of learning disorders primarily requires educational intervention. Biological treatment is usually restricted to those individuals who may also have ADHD. Educational efforts can be broadly categorized into (a) specific skills instruction, including instruction on vocabulary, finding the main idea, and finding facts in readings; and (b) strategy instruction, which includes efforts to improve cognitive skills through decision making and critical thinking (Fletcher et al., 2007).

One of the approaches that has received considerable research support is *direct instruction* (Carnine, Silbert, Kame'enui, & Tarver, 2004). Among the components that make up this program are systematic instruction, using highly scripted lesson plans, placing students together in small groups based on their progress, and teaching for mastery (teaching students until they understand all concepts). In addition, children are constantly assessed and plans are modified based on progress or lack of progress. Direct instruction and a number of related training programs appear to significantly improve academic skills in children with learning disorders (Gajria, Jitendra, Sood, & Sacks, 2007).

One study used functional magnetic resonance imaging scanning to compare how children with and without reading disorders processed simple tasks (Temple et al., 2003). The children with reading difficulties were then exposed to 8 weeks of intensive training on a computer program that helped them work on their auditory and language processing skills. Not only did the children improve their reading skills, but their brains started functioning in a way similar to the brains of their peers who were good readers. This and similar studies (Simos et al., 2007) mirror results seen with other disorders—namely, that behavioral interventions can result in functional changes in the brain.

Pervasive Developmental Disorders

People with pervasive developmental disorders all experience problems with language, socialization, and cognition (Durand, 2005). Included under the heading of pervasive developmental disorders are autistic disorder (or autism), Asperger disorder, Rett disorder, childhood disintegrative disorder, and pervasive developmental disorder, not otherwise specified (PDD-NOS). This section focuses on two of the more prevalent pervasive developmental disorders—autistic disorder and Asperger disorder; the other disorders are highlighted in Table 25.2.

Autistic Disorder

Autistic disorder (autism) is a childhood disorder characterized by significant impairment in social interactions and communication and by restricted patterns of behavior, interest, and activities (Durand, 2005). Individuals have a puzzling array of symptoms.

Clinical Description

Three major characteristics of autism are expressed in DSM-IV-TR: impairment in social interactions, impairment in communication, and restricted behavior, interests, and activities (APA, 2000).

One of the defining characteristics of people with autistic disorder is that they do not develop the types of social relationships expected for their age (Durand, 2005). For young children, the signs of social problems usually include a failure to engage in skills such as joint attention (Dawson et al., 2004; MacDonald et al., 2006). When sitting with a parent in front of a favorite toy, young children will typically look back and forth between the parent and the toy, smiling, in an attempt to engage the parent with the toy. However, this skill in joint attention is noticeably absent or impaired in children with autism.

In one study, scientists showed an adult man with autism scenes from some movies and compared how he looked at social scenes with how a man without autism did so (Klin, Jones, Schultz, Volkmar, & Cohen, 2002). The man with autism scanned nonsocial aspects of the scene (an actors' mouth and jacket), while the man without autism looked at the socially meaningful sections (looking from eye to eye of the people conversing). This research suggests that people with autism may not be interested in important aspects of social situations, and this may interfere with their ability to develop meaningful relationships with others.

People with autism nearly always have severe problems with communicating. About one-third

Table 25.2 Additional pervasive developmental disorders

Rett Disorder

Clinical Description	Statistics	Etiology	Treatment
A progressive neurological disorder that primarily affects girls. It is characterized by constant hand-wringing, increasingly severe intellectual disabilities, and impaired motor skills, all of which appear *after* an apparently normal start in development (Van Acker, Loncola, & Van Acker, 2005). Motor skills seem to deteriorate progressively over time; social skills, however, develop normally at first, decline between the ages of 1 and 3, and then partially improve.	Rett disorder is relatively rare, occurring in approximately 1 per 10,000–15,000 live female births (Ham, Kumar, Deeter, & Schanen, 2005).	A mutation of a gene on the X chromosome (MECP2) appears responsible for the majority of cases (Ham, et al., 2005).	Focuses on teaching self-help and communication skills and on efforts to reduce problem behaviors.

Childhood Disintegrative Disorder

Clinical Description	Statistics	Etiology	Treatment
Involves severe regression in language, adaptive behavior, and motor skills after a 2–4-year period of normal development (Volkmar, Koenig, & State, 2005).	Rare, occurring in 1 of approximately every 100,000 births (Hendry, 2000).	Although no specific cause has been identified, several factors suggest an accumulation of a number of rare genetic mutations (Volkmar, Koenig, & State, 2005).	Typically involves behavioral interventions to regain lost skills and behavioral and pharmacological treatments to help reduce behavioral problems.

Pervasive Developmental Disorder, Not Otherwise Specified

Clinical Description	Statistics	Etiology	Treatment
Severe and pervasive impairments in social interactions, but without all criteria for autistic disorder. These individuals may not display the early avoidance of social interaction but still may exhibit significant social problems. Their problems may become more obvious after 3 years of age.	Little good evidence for prevalence at this time, although appears more common than autistic disorder (Lord, et al., 2006).	Some of the same genetic influences and neurobiological impairments common in autism are likely involved in these individuals as well (Towbin, 2005).	Focuses on teaching socialization and communication skills and on efforts to reduce problem behaviors.

Adapted from Barlow, D.H., & Durand, V.M. (2009). *Abnormal psychology: An integrative approach* (5th ed.). Belmont, CA: Wadsworth/ Cengage. Reproduced with permission of the publisher.

never acquire speech (Wetherby & Prizant, 2005). In those with some speech, much of their communication is unusual. Some repeat the speech of others, a pattern called *echolalia*. Some who can speak are unable or unwilling to carry on conversations with others.

The more striking characteristics of autism include *restricted patterns of behavior, interests,* and *activities.* This includes an intense preference for the status quo, which has been called *maintenance of sameness.* Often, people with autism spend countless hours in *stereotyped and ritualistic behaviors,* making such stereotyped movements as spinning around in circles, waving their hands in front of their eyes with their heads cocked to one side, or biting their hands.

Epidemiology

Recent estimates of the occurrence of autistic disorder seem to show an increase in its prevalence.

Previous estimates of autistic disorder are believed to be as high as 1 in every 500 births (Shattuck, 2006). The prevalence of autism spectrum disorders (which include autistic disorder, PDD-NOS, and Asperger disorder) is estimated as high as 1 in every 150 births (CDC, 2007). This rise in the rates may be the result of increased awareness on the part of professionals to distinguish the pervasive developmental disorders from intellectual disabilities. Gender differences for autism vary depending on the IQ level of the person affected. For people with IQs under 35, autism is more prevalent among females; in the higher IQ range, it is more prevalent among males. We do not know the reason for these differences (Volkmar, Szatmari, & Sparrow, 1993). Autistic disorder appears to be a universal phenomenon, identified in every part of the world (Chung, Luk, & Lee, 1990; Gillberg, 1984; Lebedinskaya & Nikolskaya, 1993; Sugiyama & Abe, 1989). Most people with autism develop the associated symptoms before the age of 36 months (APA, 2000).

Earlier estimates placed the rate of intellectual disabilities among children with autism as high as 75%, although more recent work—using more appropriate tests for these children—indicates a range between 40% and 55% (Chakrabarti & Fombonne, 2001; Edelson, 2006). Usually, language abilities and IQ scores are reliable predictors of how children with autistic disorder will fare later in life: the better the language skills and IQ test performance, the better the prognosis (Ben Itzchak, Lahat, Burgin, & Zachor, 2008).

Etiology
At present, workers in the field of autism do not believe that psychological or social influences play a major role in the development of this disorder. Autism has a genetic component (Volkmar, Klin, & Schultz, 2005), and families that have one child with autism have a 5%–10% risk of having another child with the disorder. This rate is 50 to 200 times the risk in the general population. There is evidence for some involvement with numerous chromosomes, and work is ongoing in this area (Autism Genome Project Consortium, 2007). However, it is generally accepted that there are different pathways to the behavioral symptomatology of autistic disorder, and it is expected that different causes of the disorders will be discovered.

Many neurobiological influences are being studied to help explain the social and communication problems observed in autism (Volkmar, Klin, & Schultz, 2005). Researchers studying the brains of people with autism note that adults with and without the disorder have amygdalae of about the same size but that those with autism have fewer neurons in this structure (Schumann & Amaral, 2006). Earlier research showed that young children with autism actually have a larger amygdala. The theory is that the amygdala in children with autism is enlarged early in life, causing excessive anxiety and fear (perhaps contributing to their social withdrawal). With continued stress, the release of the stress hormone cortisol damages the amygdala, causing the relative absence of these neurons in adulthood. The damaged amygdala may account for the different way people with autism respond to social situations.

An additional neurobiological influence involves the neuropeptide oxytocin, with some research on children with autism finding lower levels of oxytocin in their blood (Modahl et al., 1998). Providing oxytocin to people with autism improved their ability to remember and process information with emotional content (such as remembering happy faces), a problem that is symptomatic of autism (Hollander et al., 2007). This is one of a number of theories being explored as possible contributors to this puzzling disorder.

One highly controversial theory is that the mercury previously used as a preservative in childhood vaccines (thimerosal) is responsible for the increases seen in autism over the last decade. Large epidemiological studies conducted in Denmark show that there is no increased risk of autism in children who are vaccinated (Madsen et al., 2002). However, data in this area are sometimes contradictory (e.g., (Young, Geier, & Geier, 2008) suggesting that a very small number of children may be vulnerable to this preservative.

The study of autism is a relatively young field and still awaits an integrative theory. It is likely, however, that further research will identify the biological mechanisms that may explain the social aversion experienced by many people with the disorder. Also to be outlined are the psychological and social factors that interact early with the biological influences, producing deficits in socialization and communication, as well as the characteristic unusual behaviors.

Because of the overlap with all of the pervasive developmental disorders, assessment and treatment of autistic disorder is described at the end of this section.

Asperger Disorder
Asperger disorder involves a significant impairment in the ability to engage in meaningful social interaction, along with restricted and repetitive stereotyped

behaviors, but without the severe delays in language or other cognitive skills characteristic of people with autism (APA, 2000). First described by Hans Asperger in 1944, it is a separate disorder from autism, with an emphasis on the unusual and limited interests (such a train schedules) displayed by these individuals (Volkmar, Klin, & Schultz, 2005).

Clinical Description

People with Asperger disorder display impaired social relationships and restricted or unusual behaviors or activities (such as following airline schedules or memorizing ZIP codes), but unlike individuals with autism they can often be quite verbal. They have a tendency to be obsessed with esoteric facts over people, along with an often formal and academic style of speech. Individuals show few severe cognitive impairments and usually have IQ scores within the average range (Volkmar, Klin, & Schultz, 2005). They often exhibit clumsiness and poor coordination. Some researchers think Asperger disorder may be a milder form of autism rather than a separate disorder and, as described, is considered part of the autism spectrum.

Epidemiology

Until recently, most diagnosticians were relatively unfamiliar with this disorder, and it is generally believed that many individuals went undiagnosed. Current estimates of the prevalence are between 1 and 2 per 10,000, and it is believed to occur more often in boys than in girls (Volkmar, Klin, & Schultz, 2005).

Etiology

A small but growing literature on causal influences exists, and a possible genetic contribution is suspected (Woodbury-Smith & Volkmar, 2009). Asperger disorder does seem to run in families, and there appears to be a higher prevalence of both autism and Asperger disorder in some families. Because of the social–emotional disturbances observed in people with this disorder, researchers are looking at the amygdala for its possible role in the cause (Schultz, Romanski, & Tsatsanis, 2000), although, to date, there is no conclusive evidence for a specific biological or psychological model.

Assessment and Treatment of Pervasive Developmental Disorders

Assessment of the pervasive developmental disorders initially focuses on the diagnosis. Several assessment devices reliably diagnose these disorders (e.g., Autism Diagnostic Observation Schedule [ADOS], Autism Diagnostic Interview – Revised [ADI-R], and the Childhood Autism Rating Scale [CARS]; Charman, 2008). Given the range of problems posed by children with these disorders, a multidisciplinary team (including professionals in speech and language, physical therapy, education and psychology) is often required.

Most treatment research has focused on children with autism, so we primarily discuss treatment research for these individuals. However, because treatment for all of the pervasive developmental disorders relies on a similar approach, this research should be relevant across disorders. Like the approach to individuals with intellectual disabilities, most efforts at treating people with pervasive developmental disorders focus on enhancing their social, communication, and daily living skills, and on reducing problem behaviors, such as tantrums and self-injury (Durand, 2005).

One of the most striking features of people with autism is their unusual reactions to other people. Although social deficits are among the more obvious problems experienced by people with autism, they can also be the most difficult to teach. A number of approaches are now used to teach social skills (for example, how to carry on a conversation and ask questions of other people), including the use of peers who do not have autism as trainers, and there is evidence that those with autism can improve their socialization skills (Zager & Shamow, 2005).

Problems with communication and language are among the defining characteristics of this disorder. People with autism often do not acquire meaningful speech; they tend either to have limited speech or to use unusual speech, such as echolalia. For children with no or very limited speech, basic behavioral procedures of shaping and discrimination training are used to teach these nonspeaking children to imitate others verbally (Lovaas, Berberich, Perloff, & Schaeffer, 1966). Despite the success of some children in learning speech, other children do not respond to this training, and workers sometimes use alternatives to vocal speech, such as sign language, symbol systems, and vocal output devices (Wetherby & Prizant, 2005).

Early intensive behavioral intervention (EIBI) is generally recommended for very young children. Pioneered by Lovaas and his colleagues at University of California, Los Angeles, intensive behavioral treatment for communication and social skills problems involves 40 hours or more per week of intervention, which seemed to improve intellectual and educational functioning. Follow-up suggests that these improvements are long lasting for a percentage of children (Lord et al., 2005; McEachin, Smith, & Lovaas, 1993), although subgroups of children who are most successful have yet to be identified (Matson & Smith, 2008).

Medical intervention has had little success on the core symptoms of social and language difficulties. A variety of pharmacological treatments are used to decrease agitation, and the major tranquilizers and serotonin-specific reuptake inhibitors seem helpful here (Volkmar, Klin, & Schultz, 2005). Because the pervasive developmental disorders may result from a variety of deficits, it is unlikely that one biological approach will be effective for everyone with this disorder. Much current work is focused on finding pharmacological treatments for specific behaviors or symptoms.

Intellectual Disabilities

Intellectual disabilities (ID) (previously referred to as mental retardation) is a disorder evident in childhood as significantly below-average intellectual and adaptive functioning (King, Hodapp, & Dykens, 2005). People with ID experience difficulties with day-to-day activities to an extent that reflects both the severity of their cognitive deficits and the type and amount of assistance they receive. Perhaps more than any other group, people with ID have throughout history received treatment that can best be described as shameful (Scheerenberger, 1983). With notable exceptions, societies throughout the ages have devalued individuals whose intellectual abilities are deemed less than adequate.

Clinical Description and Epidemiology

People with ID display a broad range of abilities and personalities. Some individuals who have mild or moderate impairments, can, with proper preparation, carry out most day-to-day activities. Many can learn to use mass transportation, purchase groceries, and hold a variety of jobs. Those with more severe impairments may need help to eat, bathe, and dress themselves, although with proper training and support they can achieve a degree of independence. These individuals experience impairments that affect most areas of functioning. Language and communication skills are often the most obvious. In contrast, people with more severe forms of ID may never learn to use speech as a form of communication, requiring alternatives such as sign language or special communication devices to express even their most basic needs.

Intellectual disorder is included on Axis II of DSM-IV-TR, and the criteria are in three groups. First, a person must have *significantly subaverage intellectual functioning,* a determination made with one of several IQ tests, with a cutoff score set by DSM-IV-TR of approximately 70. Roughly 2%–3% of the population score at 70 or below on these tests. The American Association on Intellectual and Developmental Disabilities (AAIDD), which has its own, similar definition of ID, has a cutoff score of approximately 70–75 (King et al., 2005).

The second criterion of both the DSM-IV-TR and the AAIDD definitions for IDs calls for *concurrent deficits or impairments in adaptive functioning.* Scores from an IQ test are not sufficient for a diagnosis of ID; a person must also have significant difficulty in at least two of the following areas: communication, self-care, home living, social and interpersonal skills, use of community resources, self-direction, functional academic skills, work, leisure, health, and safety. This aspect of the definition is important because it excludes people who can function quite well in society but who, for various reasons, do poorly on IQ tests. For instance, someone whose primary language is not English may do poorly on an IQ test but may still function at a level comparable to peers. This person would not be considered to have ID even with a score of below 70 on the IQ test.

The final criterion for intellectual disabilities is the *age of onset.* The characteristic below-average intellectual and adaptive abilities must be evident before the person is 18. This cutoff is designed to identify affected individuals when the brain is developing and therefore when any problems should become evident. The age criterion rules out the diagnosis of ID for adults who suffer from brain trauma or forms of dementia that impair their abilities. The age of 18 is somewhat arbitrary, but it is the age at which most children leave school, when society considers a person an adult.

Perhaps the most controversial change in the AAIDD definition of ID is its description of different levels of this disorder, which are based on the level of support or assistance people need: *intermittent, limited, extensive,* or *pervasive* (Luckasson et al., 1992). The AAIDD system identifies the role of "needed supports" in determining level of functioning, whereas DSM-IV-TR implies that the ability of the person is the sole determining factor. The AAIDD system focuses on specific areas of assistance a person needs that can then be translated into training goals.

Approximately 90% of people with ID fall under the label of mild ID (IQ of 50–70), and when you add individuals with moderate, severe, and profound ID (IQ below 50), the total population of people with this disorder represents 1%–3% of the general population (King et al., 2005).

The course of ID is chronic; however, the prognosis for people with this disorder varies considerably. Given appropriate training and support, individuals with less severe forms can live relatively independent and productive lives. People with more severe impairments require more assistance to participate in work and community life.

Over the last century IQ scores have risen, a phenomenon known as the *Flynn effect* (Flynn, 1984). IQ tests are adjusted every decade or two to keep the average score around 100. For most people, these changes have no practical effect. However, for people hovering at the cutoff point for ID, this may mean the difference between receiving the diagnosis or not (Durand & Christodulu, 2006). In one study, the number of people scoring just below 70 (the cutoff for mild ID) tripled when they were administered one of the revised IQ tests (Kanaya, Scullin, & Ceci, 2003). These results emphasize the caution needed when interpreting who does or does not have ID.

Etiology

There are literally hundreds of known causes of ID, including environmental (e.g., deprivation, abuse, and neglect), prenatal (e.g., exposure to disease or drugs while in utero), perinatal (e.g., difficulties during labor and delivery), and postnatal (e.g., infections and head injury).

Heavy use of alcohol among pregnant women can produce *fetal alcohol syndrome,* a condition that can lead to severe learning disabilities. Other prenatal factors that can produce ID include the pregnant woman's exposure to disease and chemicals, and poor nutrition for the fetus. In addition, lack of oxygen (anoxia) during birth, and malnutrition and head injuries during the developmental period can lead to severe cognitive impairments. Despite the rather large number of known causes of ID, nearly 75% of cases either cannot be attributed to any known cause or are thought to be the result of social and environmental influences (King et al., 2005).

Almost 300 genes have been identified as having the potential to contribute to ID, and it is expected that there are many more (Inlow & Restifo, 2004). A portion of the people with more severe ID have identifiable single-gene disorders, involving a *dominant gene* (expresses itself when paired with a normal gene), a *recessive gene* (expresses itself only when paired with another copy of itself), or an *X-linked gene* (present on the X or sex chromosome).

Only a few dominant genes result in ID. One example of a dominant gene disorder, *tuberous sclerosis,* is relatively rare, occurring in 1 of approximately every 30,000 births. About 60% of the people with this disorder have ID, and most have seizures (uncontrolled electrical discharges in the brain) and characteristic bumps on the skin that, during their adolescence, resemble acne (Pulsifer, Winterkorn, & Thiele, 2007).

Phenylketonuria (PKU) affects 1 of every 14,000 newborns and is characterized by an inability to break down the chemical phenylalanine, found in normal human diets. Until the mid 1960s, the majority of people with this disorder had ID, seizures, and behavior problems resulting from high levels of this chemical. However, researchers developed a screening technique that identifies the existence of PKU; infants are now routinely tested at birth, and any individuals identified with PKU can be successfully treated with a special diet that avoids the chemical phenylalanine. Because untreated maternal PKU can harm the developing fetus, there is concern now that women with PKU who are of childbearing age may not stick to their diets and inadvertently cause PKU-related ID in their children before birth (Hanley, 2008). *Lesch-Nyhan syndrome,* an X-linked disorder, is characterized by ID, signs of cerebral palsy (spasticity or tightening of the muscles), and self-injurious behavior, including finger and lip biting (Nyhan, 1978). Only males are affected, because a recessive gene on the X chromosome is responsible.

Down syndrome, the most common chromosomal form of ID, was first identified by the British physician Langdon Down in 1866. The disorder is caused by the presence of an extra 21st chromosome and is therefore sometimes referred to as *trisomy 21.* During cell division, two of the 21st chromosomes stick together (nondisjunction), creating one cell with one copy that dies and one cell with three copies that divide to create a person with Down syndrome. People with Down syndrome have characteristic facial features, including folds in the corners of their upwardly slanting eyes, a flat nose, and a small mouth with a flat roof that makes the tongue protrude somewhat. Nearly *all* adults with Down syndrome past the age of 40 show signs of dementia of the Alzheimer type, a degenerative brain disorder that causes impairments in memory and other cognitive disorders (Prasher & Lawrence, 2006).

This disorder among people with Down syndrome occurs earlier than usual (sometimes in their early 20s) and has led to the finding that at least one form of Alzheimer disease is attributable to a gene on the 21st chromosome.

The incidence of children born with Down syndrome is related to maternal age. A woman at age 20 has a 1 in 2,000 chance of having a child with Down syndrome; at the age of 35, this risk increases to 1 in 500; and at the age of 45, it increases again to 1 in 18 births (Evans & Hammerton, 1985; Hook, 1982). Fortunately, there are now sophisticated tests of maternal blood that can be used to detect Down syndrome as early as the first trimester of pregnancy (Wax, 2007).

Fragile X syndrome is a second common chromosomally related cause of ID (King et al., 2005). This disorder is caused by an abnormality on the X chromosome, a mutation that makes the tip of the chromosome look as though it were hanging from a thread, giving it the appearance of fragility. As with Lesch-Nyhan syndrome, which also involves the X chromosome, fragile X primarily affects males because they do not have a second X chromosome with a normal gene to balance out the mutation. Unlike Lesch-Nyhan carriers, however, women who carry fragile X syndrome commonly display mild to severe learning disabilities (Koukoui & Chaudhuri, 2007). Men with the disorder display moderate to severe levels of ID and have higher rates of hyperactivity, short attention spans, gaze avoidance, and perseverative speech. In addition, such physical characteristics as large ears, testicles, and head circumference are common. Estimates are that 1 of every 1,000 males and 1 of every 3,000 females are born with fragile X syndrome (King et al., 2005).

Up to 75% of the cases of ID fall in the mild range and are not associated with any obvious genetic or physical disorders. People with these characteristics are thought to have cognitive impairments that result from a combination of psychosocial and biological influences, although the specific mechanisms that lead to this type of ID are not yet understood (Hammel et al., 2008). The cultural influences that may contribute to this condition include abuse, neglect, and social deprivation.

Assessment and Treatment of Intellectual Disabilities

Conducting a thorough assessment is essential to providing effective services for individuals with ID (Durand & Christodulu, 2006). Reliable and valid assessment protocols incorporate multiple methods and multiple sources in order to obtain the information needed to make an accurate diagnosis of ID. Areas of assessment include the assessment of cognitive, adaptive, and social-emotional behaviors. Commonly used intelligence tests include the Wechsler Preschool and Primary Scale of Intelligence – Third Edition (Wechsler, 1989); the Wechsler Intelligence Scale for Children – Fourth Edition (Wechsler, 2003); the Stanford-Binet – Fourth Edition (Thorndike, Hagen, & Sattler, 1986); the Kaufman Assessment Battery for Children – Second Edition (Kaufman & Kaufman, 2003); and the Bayley Scales of Infant Development – Third Edition (Bayley, 1993).

In addition to measuring cognitive development, it is also necessary to administer a measure of adaptive functioning to determine the presence of ID. Adaptive functioning refers to how effectively individuals cope with common life demands and how well they meet the standards of personal independence expected of someone in their age group, sociocultural background, and community setting (APA, 2000). The Vineland Adaptive Behavior Scales (Sparrow, Balla, & Cicchetti, 1984) and the Adaptive Behavior Scales – Revised (Lambert, Leland, & Nihira, 1992) are tests available to assess adaptive abilities in children. These scales typically provide a clinical cutoff score that is a composite of performance in a number of adaptive skill domains. Additional instruments, such as measures of academic achievement, are often administered when conducting a comprehensive battery in the assessment of children formulate a diagnosis of ID (Durand & Christodulu, 2006).

Individuals with ID have a higher prevalence of comorbid disorders and behavior problems than do the general population (Borthwick-Duffy, 1994; Matson & Barrett, 1993). Assessment procedures for specific emotional and behavioral problems are generally placed into the following categories: interviews, behavior rating scales, self-report measures, and direct observation procedures (American Association on Mental Retardation, 2000; Johnson, 1998).

Direct biological treatment of ID is currently not a viable option. Generally, the treatment of individuals with ID parallels that of people with pervasive developmental disorders, attempting to teach them the skills they need to become more productive and independent. For individuals with mild ID, intervention is similar to that for people with learning disorders. Specific learning deficits are identified and addressed to help the student improve such skills as reading and writing. At the same time, these individuals often need additional support to live in the community. For people with more severe disabilities, the general goals are the same; however, the level of assistance they need is often more extensive. Advances in electronic and educational technologies greatly enhance learning, even for people with profound ID.

People with ID can acquire skills through the many behavioral innovations first introduced in the early 1960s to teach such basic self-care as dressing, bathing, feeding, and toileting to people with even the most severe disabilities (Durand & Christodulu, 2006). Communication training is a core goal for people with ID. The goals of communication training differ, depending on the existing skills. For people with mild levels of ID, the goals may be relatively minor (for example, improving articulation) or more extensive (for example, organizing a conversation) (Sigafoos, Arthur-Kelly, & Butterfield, 2006). Some have communication skills that are already adequate for day-to-day needs.

For individuals with the most severe disabilities, this type of training can be particularly challenging, because they may have multiple physical or cognitive deficits that make spoken communication difficult or impossible. Alternative systems of communication may be easier for these individuals, including the teaching of sign language and *augmentative communication strategies*. Augmentative strategies may use picture books, teaching the person to make a request by pointing to a picture—for instance, pointing to a picture of a cup to request a drink (Beukelman & Mirenda, 2005). A variety of computer-assisted devices can be programmed so that the individual presses a button to produce complete spoken sentences (for example, "Would you come here? I need your help."). People with limited communication skills can be taught to use these devices, which helps them reduce the frustration of not being able to relate their feelings and experiences to other people (Durand, 2001).

A significant portion of people with ID can be physically or verbally aggressive, or may hurt themselves. Fortunately, our knowledge of the origins of these behaviors has increased over the past several decades, along with our ability to respond to these behaviors in a positive, constructive way (Durand & Hieneman, 2008). As a result of this expansion of knowledge, work on interventions with persons exhibiting severe challenging behavior has increased in a multitude of areas, such as environmental/curricular changes (Dunlap, Kern-Dunlap, Clarke, & Robbins, 1991; Evans & Meyer, 1985; Meyer & Evans, 1990) and teaching specific alternative skills

(Durand, 1990). Outcome data on these approaches suggest that significant improvements can be obtained at home, at school, and in the community.

In addition to ensuring that people with ID are taught specific skills, caretakers focus on the important task of supporting them in their communities. "Supported employment" involves helping an individual find and participate satisfactorily in a competitive job (Hall, Butterworth, Winsor, Gilmore, & Metzel, 2007). Research has shown not only that people with ID can be placed in meaningful jobs but also that, despite the costs associated with supported employment, it can be cost-effective (Sandys, 2007).

There is general agreement about *what* should be taught to people with ID. The controversy in recent years has been over *where* this teaching should take place. Should people with ID, especially the severe forms, be taught in specially designed separate classrooms or workshops, or should they attend their neighborhood public schools and work at local businesses? Increasingly, teaching strategies to help these students learn are being used in regular classrooms and in preparing them to work at jobs in the community (Frankel & Gold, 2007).

Conclusion

Taken together, the developmental disorders result in significant obstacles to providing many children with appropriate educational, social, and vocational opportunities. Fortunately, the rapid acquisition of knowledge regarding most of the developmental disorders offers great promise toward a greater understanding of the nature of these disorders, as well as toward improving treatments. Integrative approaches—combining biological, cognitive, and social factors—to both research on etiology and treatment provide a more optimistic view of these problems of childhood, holding out hope for these children, their families, and society.

Future Directions

The following questions represent just a handful of remaining issues that have the potential to further the research agenda for the major developmental disorders.

- There is a significant amount of treatment research for ADHD, and a growing amount that combines both medical and behavioral approaches. Given the practical limitations of both approaches (e.g., side effects of medication, time and skills required for behavioral approaches) there is a current need for "scale-up" research in this area.

This research would evaluate if these interventions are effective when they are implemented under conditions that would be typical if an educational setting or typical family were to implement them (i.e., without special support from a research team).

• Additional research on the nature of the disruptive behavior disorders (ODD and CD) is needed to address the spectrum of problems that are so troublesome for both families and educational settings. More information on the biological and psychosocial origins of these problems would aid future treatment efforts.

• The profound social deficits characteristic of the autism spectrum disorders continue to challenge current treatment efforts. An integrative theory of these disorders remains to be developed and could provide clues as to the underlying processes contributing to these social problems, which could guide improvements in current intervention efforts.

• Genetic research on the range of difficulties contributing to ID needs to be greatly expanded. This information will be invaluable in efforts to prevent the problems that lead to such profound cognitive impairments and interfere with independent functioning.

References

Achenbach, T. M. (1991a). *Integrative guide for the 1991 CBCL/4-18, YSR, and TRF profiles.* Burlington: University of Vermont, Department of Psychiatry.

Achenbach, T. M. (1991b). *Manual for the Child Behavior Checklist and 1991 profile.* Burlington: University of Vermont, Department of Psychiatry.

Achenbach, T. M. (1991c). *Manual for the Teacher's Report Form and 1991 profile.* Burlington: University of Vermont, Department of Psychiatry.

Achenbach, T. M. (1991d). *Manual for the Youth Self-Report and 1991 profile.* Burlington: University of Vermont, Department of Psychiatry.

Altarac, M., & Saroha, E. (2007). Lifetime prevalence of learning disability among US children. *Pediatrics, 119*(Suppl. 1), S77-S83.

American Association on Mental Retardation. (2000). Guideline 1: Diagnosis and assessment. *American Journal on Mental Retardation, 3,* 165-168.

American Psychiatric Association. (2000). *Diagnostic and statistical manual of mental disorders* (4th ed., text revision). Washington, DC: Author.

Autism Genome Project Consortium, The. (2007). Mapping autism risk loci using genetic linkage and chromosomal rearrangements. *Nature Genetics, 39,* 319-328.

Barkley, R. A. (1990). *Attention deficit hyperactivity disorder: A handbook for diagnosis and treatment.* New York: Guilford Press.

Barkley, R. A. (2006a). ADHD in adults: Developmental course and outcome of children with ADHD, and ADHD in clinic-referred adults. In R. A. Barkley (Ed.). *Attention-deficit hyperactivity disorder: A handbook for diagnosis and treatment,* 3rd ed. (pp. 248–296). New York: Guilford Press.

Barkley, R. A. (2006b). Associated cognitive, developmental, and health problems. In R. A. Barkley (Ed.). *Attention-deficit hyperactivity disorder: A handbook for diagnosis and treatment,* 3rd ed. (pp. 122–183). New York: Guilford Press.

Barkley, R. A. (2006c). Comorbid disorders, social and family adjustment, and subtyping. In R. A. Barkley (Ed.). *Attention-deficit hyperactivity disorder: A handbook for diagnosis and treatment,* 3rd ed. (pp. 184–218). New York: Guilford Press.

Barkley, R. A. (2006e). Primary symptoms, diagnostic criteria, prevalence, and gender differences. In R. A. Barkley (Ed.). *Attention-deficit hyperactivity disorder: A handbook for diagnosis and treatment,* 3rd ed. (pp. 76–121). New York: Guilford Press.

Barkley, R. A. & Murphy, K. R. (1998). *Attention-deficit hyperactivity disorder: A clinical workbook* (2nd ed.). NY: Guilford Press.

Barlow, D. H., & Durand, V. M. (2009). *Abnormal psychology: An integrative approach* (5th ed.). Belmont, CA: Wadsworth/Cengage.

Bayley, N. (1993). Bayley *Scales of Infant Development* (2nd ed.). San Antonio, TX: Psychological Corporation.

Ben Itzchak, E., Lahat, E., Burgin, R., & Zachor, A. D. (2008). Cognitive, behavior and intervention outcome in young children with autism. *Research in Developmental Disabilities, 29*(5), 447–458.

Bergman, R. L., & Piacentini, J. (2005). Selective mutism. In B. J. Sadock, & V. A. Sadock (Eds.), *Kaplan & Sadock's comprehensive textbook of psychiatry* (pp. 3302–3306). Philadelphia: Lippincott, Williams & Wilkins.

Beukelman, D. R., & Mirenda, P. (Eds.). (2005). *Augmentative and alternative communication supporting children and adults with complex communication needs* (3rd ed.). Baltimore: Paul H. Brookes.

Biederman, J., Ball, S. W., Monuteaux, M. C., Kaiser, R., & Faraone, S. V. (2008). CBCL Clinical Scales discriminate ADHD youth with structured-interview derived diagnosis of oppositional defiant disorder (ODD). *Journal of Attention Disorders, 12*(1), 76–82.

Biederman, J., Faraone, S. V., Keenan, K., Benjamin, J., Krifcher, B., Moore, C., et al. (1992). Further evidence for family-genetic risk factors in attention deficit hyperactivity disorder: Patterns of comorbidity in probands and relatives in psychiatrically and pediatrically referred samples. *Archives of General Psychiatry, 49,* 728–738.

Biederman, J., Faraone, S. V., Milberger, S., Garcia Jetton, J., Chen, L., Mick, E., et al. (1996). Is childhood oppositional defiant disorder a precursor to adolescent conduct disorder? Findings from a four-year follow-up study of children with ADHD. *Journal of the American Academy of Child and Adolescent Psychiatry, 35*(9), 1193–1204.

Biederman, J., Petty, C. R., Dolan, C., Hughes, S., Mick, E., Monuteaux, M. C., et al. (2008). The long-term longitudinal course of oppositional defiant disorder and conduct disorder in ADHD boys: Findings from a controlled 10-year prospective longitudinal follow-up study. *Psychological Medicine, 38*(7), 1027–1036.

Biederman, J., Spencer, T., Wilens, T., & Greene, R. (2001). Attention-deficit/hyperactivity disorder. In G. O. Gabbard (Ed.), *Treatment of psychiatric disorders* Vol. 1, 3rd ed. (pp. 145–176). Washington, DC: American Psychiatric Publishing.

Bobb, A. J., Castellanos, F. X., Addington, A. M., & Rapoport, J. L. (2006). Molecular genetic studies of ADHD: 1991 to 2004. *American Journal of Medical Genetics Part B (Neuropsychiatric Genetics), 141,* 551–565.

Borthwick-Duffy, S. A. (1994). Epidemiology and prevalence of psychopathology in people with mental retardation. *Journal of Consulting and Clinical Psychology, 62,* 17–27.

Bradley, R., Danielson, L., & Hallahan, D. P. (Eds.). (2002). *Identification of learning disabilities: Research to practice.* Mahwah, NJ: Erlbaum.

Bradley, W. (1937). The behavior of children receiving Benzedrine. *American Journal of Psychiatry, 94,* 577–585.

Brown, R. T., Antonuccio, D. O., DuPaul, G. J., Fristad, M. A., King, C. A., Leslie, L. K., et al. (2008). Oppositional defiant and conduct disorders. In R. T. Brown, D. O. Antonuccio, G. J. DuPaul, M. A. Fristad, C. A. King, et al. (Eds.), *Childhood mental health disorders: Evidence base and contextual factors for psychosocial, psychopharmacological, and combined interventions.* (pp. 33–41). Washington DC: American Psychological Association.

Carnine, D., Silbert, J., Kame'enui, E., & Tarver, S. (2004). *Direct instruction reading* (4th ed.). Upper Saddle River, NJ: Pearson.

Caspi, A., Elder Jr., G. H., & Bem, D. L. (1987). Moving against the world: Life-course patterns of explosive children. *Developmental Psychology, 23,* 308–313.

Centers for Disease Control and Prevention. (2005). Prevalence of diagnosis and medication treatment for attention-deficit/hyperactivity disorder — United States, 2003. *Morbidity and Mortality Weekly Report, 54,* 842–847.

Centers for Disease Control and Prevention. (2007). Prevalence of Autism Spectrum Disorders — Autism and Developmental Disabilities Monitoring Network, Six Sites, United States, 2000. Surveillance Summaries, 2002. *Morbidity and Mortality Weekly Report, 56,* 1–11.

Chakrabarti, S., & Fombonne, E. (2001). Pervasive developmental disorders in preschool children. *JAMA: Journal of the American Medical Association, 285,* 3093–3099.

Charman, T. (2008). Autism spectrum disorders. *Psychiatry, 7*(8), 331–334.

Chowdhury, U. (2008). Tourette syndrome. *Psychiatry, 7*(8), 345–348.

Chronis, A. M., Lahey, B. B., Pelham, J. W. E., Williams, S. H., Baumann, B. L., Kipp, H., et al. (2007). Maternal depression and early positive parenting predict future conduct problems in young children with attention-deficit/hyperactivity disorder. *Developmental Psychology, 43*(1), 70–82.

Chung, S. Y., Luk, S. L., & Lee, P. W. H. (1990). A follow-up study of infantile autism in Hong Kong. *Journal of Autism and Developmental Disorders, 20,* 221–232.

Compton, D. L., Fuchs, D., Fuchs, L. S., & Bryant, J. D. (2006). Selecting at-risk readers in first grade for early intervention: A two-year longitudinal study of decision rules and procedures. *Journal of Educational Psychology, 98,* 394–409.

Connor, D. F. (2006). Stimulants. In R. A. Barkley (Ed.), *Attention-deficit hyperactivity disorder: A handbook for diagnosis and treatment,* 3rd ed. (pp. 608–647). New York: Guilford Press.

Conners, C. K., March, J. S., Frances, A., Wells, K. C., & Ross, R. (Eds.). (2001). Treatment of attention deficit/hyperactivity disorder: Expert consensus guidelines. *Journal of Attention Disorders, 4*(Suppl. 1), S7-S128.

Conners, C. K., Sitarenios, G., Parker, J. D. A., & Epstein, J. N. (1998). The Revised Conners' Parent Rating Scale (CPRS-R): Factor structure, reliability, and criterion validity. *Journal of Abnormal Child Psychology, 26*(4), 257–268.

de Boo, G. M., & Prins, P. J. M. (2007). Social incompetence in children with ADHD: Possible moderators and mediators in social-skills training. *Clinical Psychology Review, 27,* 78–97.

Daniel, S. S., Walsh, A.K., Goldston, D.B., Arnold, E.M., Reboussin, B. A., & Wood, F.B. (2006). Suicidality, school dropout, and reading problems among adolescents. *Journal of Learning Disabilities, 39,* 507–514.

Dawson, G., Toth, K., Abbott, R., Osterling, J., Munson, J., Estes, A., & Liaw, J. (2004). Early social attention impairments in autism: Social orienting, joint attention, and attention to distress. *Developmental Psychology, 40,* 271–283.

Dunlap, G., Kern-Dunlap, L., Clarke, S., & Robbins, F. R. (1991). Functional assessment, curricular revision, and severe behavior problems. *Journal of Applied Behavior Analysis, 24,* 387–397.

DuPaul G. J., Power T. J., Anastopoulos A. D., & Reid R. (1998). *ADHD Rating Scale IV: Checklists, norms, and clinical interpretation.* New York: Guilford.

Dumas, J., & Wahler, R. G. (1983). Predictors of treatment outcome in parent training: Mother insularity and socioeconomic disadvantage. *Behavioral Assessment, 5,* 301–313.

Durand, V. M. (1990). *Severe behavior problems: A functional communication training approach.* New York: Guilford Press.

Durand, V. M. (2001). Future directions for children and adolescents with mental retardation. *Behavior Therapy, 32,* 633–650.

Durand, V. M. (2005). Past, present and emerging directions in education. In D. Zager (Ed.), *Autism spectrum disorders: Identification, education, and treatment,* 3rd ed. (pp. 89–109). Hillsdale, NJ: Lawrence Erlbaum Associates, Inc.

Durand, V. M., & Christodulu, K. V. (2006). Mental retardation. In M. Hersen (Ed.), *Clinician's handbook of child behavioral assessment* (pp. 459–475). Burlington, MA: Elsevier Academic Press.

Durand, V. M., & Hieneman, M. (2008). *Helping parents with challenging children: Positive family intervention, facilitator's guide.* New York: Oxford University Press.

Edelson, M. G. (2006). Are the majority of children with autism mentally retarded? *Focus on Autism and other Developmental Disabilities, 21,* 66–83.

Eme, R. F. (2007). Sex differences in child-onset, life-course-persistent conduct disorder: A review of biological influence. *Clinical Psychology Review, 27,* 607–627.

Eppright, T. D., Kashani, J. H., Robison, B. D., & Reid, J. C. (1993). Comorbidity of conduct disorder and personality disorders in an incarcerated juvenile population. *American Journal of Psychiatry, 150,* 1233–1236.

Evans, I. M., & Meyer, L. H. (1985). *An educative approach to behavior problems.* Baltimore: Paul H. Brookes.

Evans, J. A., & Hammerton, J. L. (1985). Chromosomal anomalies. In A. M. Clarke, A. D. B. Clarke, & J. M. Berg (Eds.), *Mental deficiency: The changing outlook,* 4th ed. (pp. 213–266). New York: Free Press.

Eyberg, S. M., Nelson, M. M., & Boggs, S. R. (2008). Evidence-based psychosocial treatments for children and adolescents with disruptive behavior. *Journal of Clinical Child and Adolescent Psychology, 37*(1), 215–237.

Faraone, S. V. (2003). Report from the 4th international meeting of the attention deficit hyperactivity disorder molecular genetics network. *American Journal of Medical Genetics, 121,* 55–59.

Faraone, S. V., Biederman, J., Spencer, T., Wilens, T., Seidman, L. J., Mick, E., et al. (2000). Attention-deficit/hyperactivity disorder in adults: An overview. *Biological Psychiatry, 48*, 9–20.

Fergusson, D. M., Boden, J. M., & Horwood, L. J. (2008). The developmental antecedents of illicit drug use: Evidence from a 25-year longitudinal study. *Drug and Alcohol Dependence, 96*(1–2), 165–177.

Feinstein, C., & Phillips, J. M. (2006). Developmental disorders of communication, motor skills, and learning. In M. K. Dulcan, & J. M. Wiener (Eds.), *Essentials of child and adolescent psychiatry* (pp. 203–231). Washington, DC: American Psychiatric Publishing.

Fletcher, J. M., Lyon, G.R., Fuchs, L. S., & Barnes, M. A. (2007). *Learning disabilities: From identification to intervention.* New York: Guilford Press.

Flynn, J. R. (1984). The mean IQ of Americans: Massive gains 1932 to 1978. *Psychological Bulletin, 95*, 29–51.

Frankel, E. B., & Gold, S. (2007). Principles and practices of early intervention. In I. Brown, & M. Percy (Eds.), *A comprehensive guide to intellectual & developmental disabilities* (pp. 451–466). Baltimore, MD: Paul H. Brookes.

Gajria, M., Jitendra, A. K., Sood, S., & Sacks, G. (2007). Improving comprehension of expository text in students with LD: A research synthesis. *Journal of Learning Disabilities, 40*, 210–225.

Gelhorn, H. L., Stallings, M. C., Young, S. E., Corley, R. P., Rhee, S. H., & Hewitt, J. K. (2005). Genetic and environmental influences on conduct disorder: Symptom, domain and full-scale analyses. *Journal of Child Psychology and Psychiatry, 46*(6), 580–591.

Gillberg, C. (1984). Infantile autism and other childhood psychoses in a Swedish urban region: Epidemiological aspects. *Journal of Child Psychology and Psychiatry, 25*, 35–43.

Gomez, R., Harvey, J., Quick, C., Scharer, I., & Harris, G. (1999). DSM-IV AD/HD: Confirmatory factor models, prevalence, and gender and age differences based on parent and teacher ratings of Australian primary school children. *Journal of Child Psychology and Psychiatry, 40*, 265–274.

Granic, I., & Patterson, G. R. (2006). Toward a comprehensive model of antisocial development: A dynamic systems approach. *Psychological Review, 113*, 101–131.

Hall, A. C., Butterworth, J., Winsor, J., Gilmore, D., & Metzel, D. (2007). Pushing the employment agenda: Case study research of high performing States in integrated employment. *Intellectual and Developmental Disabilities, 45*, 182–198.

Ham, A. L., Kumar, A., Deeter, R., & Schanen, N. C. (2005). Does genotype predict phenotype in Rett syndrome? *Journal of Child Neurology, 20*(8), 768–778.

Hammel, J., Jones, R., Smith, J., Sanford, J., Bodine, C., & Johnson, M. (2008). Environmental barriers and supports to the health, function, and participation of people with developmental and intellectual disabilities: Report from the State of the Science in Aging with Developmental Disabilities Conference. *Disability and Health Journal, 1*(3), 143–149.

Handler, M. W., & DuPaul, G. J. (2005). Assessment of ADHD: Differences across psychology specialty areas. *Journal of Attention Disorders, 9*(2), 402–412.

Hanley, W. B. (2008). Finding the fertile woman with phenylketonuria. *European Journal of Obstetrics & Gynecology and Reproductive Biology, 137*(2), 131–135.

Harris, G. T., & Rice, M. E. (2006). Treatment of psychopathy: A review of empirical findings. In C. J. Patrick (Ed.), *Handbook of psychopathy* (pp. 555–572). New York: Guilford Press.

Hetherington, E. M., Stanley-Hagan, M., & Anderson, E. R. (1989). Marital transitions: A child's perspective. *American Psychologist, 44*, 303–312.

Hechtman, L. (2005). Attention-deficit disorders. In B. J. Sadock, & V. A. Sadock (Eds.), *Kaplan & Sadock's comprehensive textbook of psychiatry* (pp. 3183–3198). Philadelphia: Lippincott, Williams & Wilkins.

Hendry, C. N. (2000). Childhood disintegrative disorder: Should it be considered a distinct diagnosis? *Clinical Psychology Review, 20*(1), 77–90.

Hollander, E., Bartz, J., Chaplin, W., Phillips, A., Sumner, J., Soorya, L., et al. (2007). Oxytocin increases retention of social cognition in autism. *Biological Psychiatry, 61*, 498–503.

Hook, E. B. (1982). Epidemiology of Down syndrome. In S. M. Pueschel, & J. E. Rynders (Eds.), *Down syndrome: Advances in biomedicine and the behavioral sciences* (pp. 11–88). Cambridge, MA: Ware Press.

Hinshaw, S. P. (2002). Preadolescent girls with attention-deficit/hyperactivity disorder: Part I. Background characteristics, comorbidity, cognitive and social functioning, and parenting practices. *Journal of Consulting and Clinical Psychology, 70*(5), 1086–1098.

Hoza, B., Gerdes, A. C., Hinshaw, S. P., Arnold, L. E., Pelham, W. E., Molina, B. S., et al. (2004). Self-perceptions of competence in children with ADHD and comparison children. *Journal of Consulting and Clinical Psychology, 72*, 382–391.

Hyman, S. E. (2007). Can neuroscience be integrated into the DSM-5? *Nature Reviews: Neuroscience, 8*(9), 725–732.

Inlow, J. K., & Restifo, L. L. (2004). Molecular and comparative genetics of mental retardation. *Genetics, 166*, 835–881.

Jensen, P. S., Hinshaw, S. P., Swanson, J. M., Greenhill, L. L., Conners, C. K., Arnold, L. E., et al. (2001). Findings from the NIMH Multimodal Treatment Study of ADHD (MTA): Implications and applications for primary care providers. *Journal of Developmental and Behavioral Pediatrics, 22*(1), 60–73.

Johnson, C. J., & Beitchman, J. H. (2005). Expressive language disorder. In B. J. Sadock, & V. A. Sadock (Eds.), *Kaplan & Sadock's comprehensive textbook of psychiatry* (pp. 3136–3142). Philadelphia: Lippincott, Williams & Wilkins.

Johnson, C. R. (1998). Mental retardation. In V. B. Van Hasselt, & M. Hersen (Eds.), *Handbook of psychological treatment protocols for children and adolescents* (pp. 17–46). Mahwah, NJ: Lawrence Erlbaum Associates, Inc.

Kahn, R. S., Khoury, J., Nichols, W. C., & Lanphear, B. P. (2003). Role of dopamine transporter genotype and maternal prenatal smoking in childhood hyperactive-impulsive, inattentive, and oppositional behaviors. *The Journal of Pediatrics, 143*(1), 104–110.

Kanaya, T., Scullin, M. H., & Ceci, S. J. (2003). The Flynn effect and U.S. policies: The impact of rising IQ scores on American society via mental retardation diagnoses. *American Psychologist, 58*, 778–790.

Kaufman, A. S., & Kaufman, N. L. (2003). *Kaufman Assessment Battery for Children* (2nd ed.). Circle Pines, MN: AGS Publishing.

Kavale, K. A., & Forness, S. R. (1983). Hyperactivity and diet treatment: A meta-analysis of the Feingold hypothesis. *Journal of Learning Disabilities, 16*, 324–330.

Kazdin, A. E., Mazurick, J. L., & Bass, D. (1993). Risk for attrition in treatment of antisocial children and families. *Journal of Child Clinical Psychology, 22*, 2–16.

Kim, J.-w., Kim, B.-n., & Cho, S.-c. (2006). The dopamine transporter gene and the impulsivity phenotype in attention deficit hyperactivity disorder: A case-control association study in a Korean sample. *Journal of Psychiatric Research, 40,* 730–737.

Kim-Cohen, J., Arseneault, L., Caspi, A., Tomas, M. P., Taylor, A., & Moffitt, T. E. (2005). Validity of DSM-IV conduct disorder in 4 1/2–5-year-old children: A longitudinal epidemiological study. *American Journal of Psychiatry, 162*(6), 1108–1117.

King, B. H., Hodapp, R. M., & Dykens, E. M. (2005). Mental retardation. In B. J. Sadock, & V. A. Sadock (Eds.), *Kaplan & Sadock's comprehensive textbook of psychiatry* (pp. 3076–3106). Philadelphia: Lippincott, Williams & Wilkins.

Klin, A., Jones, W., Schultz, R., Volkmar, F., & Cohen, D. (2002). Defining and quantifying the social phenotype in autism. *American Journal of Psychiatry, 159,* 895–908.

Kochanska, G., Aksan, N., & Joy, M. E. (2007). Children's fearfulness as a moderator of parenting in early socialization: Two longitudinal studies. *Developmental Psychology, 43,* 222–237.

Kolko, D., Dorn, L., Bukstein, O., & Burke, J. (2008). Clinically referred ODD children with or without CD and healthy controls: Comparisons across contextual domains. *Journal of Child and Family Studies, 17*(5), 714–734.

Koukoui, S. D., & Chaudhuri, A. (2007). Neuroanatomical, molecular genetic, and behavioral correlates of fragile x syndrome. *Brain Research Reviews, 53,* 27–38.

Kroll, R., & Beitchman, J. H. (2005). Stuttering. In B. J. Sadock, & V.A. Sadock (Eds.), *Kaplan & Sadock's comprehensive textbook of psychiatry* (pp. 3154–3159). Philadelphia: Lippincott, Williams & Wilkins.

Lambert, N., Leland, H., & Nihira, K. (1992). *AAMR adaptive behavior scales* (2nd edition). San Antonio, TX: Psychological Corporation.

Lebedinskaya, K. S., & Nikolskaya, O. S. (1993). Brief report: Analysis of autism and its treatment in modern Russian defectology. *Journal of Autism and Developmental Disorders, 23,* 675–697.

Lincoln, M., Packman, A., & Onslow, M. (2006). Altered auditory feedback and the treatment of stuttering: A review. *Journal of Fluency Disorders, 31,* 71–89.

Lord, C., Risi, S., DiLavore, P. S., Shulman, C., Thurm, A., & Pickles, A. (2006). Autism from 2 to 9 years of age. *Archives of General Psychiatry, 63*(6), 694–701.

Lord, C., Wagner, A., Rogers, S., Szatmari, P., Aman, M., Charman, T., et al. (2005). Challenges in evaluating psychosocial interventions for autistic spectrum disorders. *Journal of Autism and Developmental Disorders, 35,* 695–708.

Lovaas, O. I., Berberich, J. P., Perloff, B. F., & Schaeffer, B. (1966). Acquisition of imitative speech by schizophrenic children. *Science, 151,* 705–707.

Luckasson, R., Coulter, D. L., Polloway, E. A., Reiss, S., Schalock, R. L., Snell, M. E., et al. (1992). *Mental retardation: Definition, classification, and systems of supports* (9th ed.). Washington, DC: American Association on Mental Retardation.

Lynam, D. R. (1996). Early identification of chronic offenders: Who is a fledgling psychopath? *Psychological Bulletin, 120,* 209–234.

Matson, J. L., & Barrett, R. P. (1993). *Psychopathology in the mentally retarded* (2nd ed.). Boston, MA: Allyn and Bacon.

Matson, J. L., & Smith, K. R. M. (2008). Current status of intensive behavioral interventions for young children with autism and PDD-NOS. *Research in Autism Spectrum Disorders, 2*(1), 60–74.

MacDonald, R., Anderson, J., Dube, W. V., Geckeler, A., Green, G., Holcomb, W., et al. (2006). Behavioral assessment of joint attention: A methodological report. *Research in Developmental Disabilities, 27,* 138–150.

Madsen, K. M., Hviid, A., Vestergaard, M., Schendel, D., Wohlfahrt, J., Thorsen. P., et al. (2002). A population-based study of measles, mumps, and rubella vaccination and autism. *New England Journal of Medicine, 347,* 1477–1482.

McCann, D., Barrett, A., Cooper, A., Crumpler, D., Dalen, L., Grimshaw, K., et al. (2007). Food additives and hyperactive behaviour in 3-year-old and 8/9-year-old children in the community: A randomised, double-blinded, placebo-controlled trial. *The Lancet, 370*(9598), 1560–1567.

McEachin, J. J., Smith, T., & Lovaas, O. I. (1993). Long-term outcome for children with autism who received early intensive behavioral treatment. *American Journal on Mental Retardation, 97,* 359–372.

McGough, J. J. (2005). Adult manifestations of attention-deficit/hyperactivity disorder. In B. J. Sadock, & V. A. Sadock (Eds.), *Kaplan & Sadock's comprehensive textbook of psychiatry* (pp. 3198–3204). Philadelphia: Lippincott, Williams & Wilkins.

McMahon, R. J., Kotler, J. S., Steele, R. G., Elkin, T. D., & Roberts, M. C. (2008). Evidence-based therapies for oppositional behavior in young children *Handbook of evidence-based therapies for children and adolescents: Bridging science and practice.* (pp. 221–240). New York: Springer Science & Business Media.

Modahl, C., Green, L., Fein, D., Morris, M., Waterhouse, L., Feinstein, C., et al. (1998). Plasma oxytocin levels in autistic children. *Biological Psychiatry, 43,* 270–277.

Meyer, L. H., & Evans, I. M. (1989). *Nonaversive intervention for behavior problems: A manual for home and community.* Baltimore: Paul H. Brookes.

Naglieri, J. A., & Goldstein, S. (2006). The role of intellectual processes in the DSM-5 diagnosis of ADHD. *Journal of Attention Disorders, 10*(1), 3–8.

Nock, M. K., Kazdin, A. E., Hiripi, E., & Kessler, R. C. (2006). Prevalence, subtypes, and correlates of DSM-IV conduct disorder in the National Comorbidity Survey Replication. *Psychological Medicine, 36*(5), 699–710.

Nyhan, W. L. (1978). The Lesch-Nyhan syndrome. *Developmental Medicine and Child Neurology, 20,* 376–387.

Paracchini, S., Steer, C. D., Buckingham, L.-L., Morris, A. P., Ring, S., Scerri, T., et al. (in press). Association of the KIAA0319 dyslexia susceptibility gene with reading skills in the general population. *American Journal of Psychiatry.*

Patterson, G. R. (1982). *Coercive family process.* Eugene, OR: Castalia.

Patterson, G. R. (1986). Performance models for antisocial boys. *American Psychologist, 41,* 432–444.

Patterson, G. R., DeBaryshe, B. D., & Ramsey, E. (1989). A developmental perspective on antisocial behavior. *American Psychologist, 44,* 329–335.

Paulesu, E., Demonet, J. F., Fazio, F., McCrory, E., Chanoine, V., Brunswick, N., et al. (2001). Dyslexia: Cultural diversity and biological unity. *Science, 291*(5511), 2165–2167.

Pelham Jr., W. E. (1999). The NIMH Multimodal Treatment Study for attention-deficit hyperactivity disorder: Just say yes to drugs alone? *Canadian Journal of Psychiatry, 44,* 981–990.

Petrill, S. A., Deater-Deckard, K., Thompson, L. A., DeThorne, L. S., & Schatschneider, C. (2006). Reading skills in early readers: Genetic and shared environmental influences. *Journal of Learning Disabilities, 39*, 48–55.

Plomin, R., & Kovas, Y. (2005). Generalist genes and learning disabilities. *Psychological Bulletin, 131*, 592–617.

Polanczyk, G., de Lima, M. S., Horta, B. L., Biederman, J., & Rohde, L. A. (2007). The worldwide prevalence of ADHD: A systematic review and metaregression analysis. *American Journal of Psychiatry, 164*, 942–948.

Prasher, V. P., & Lawrence, D. (2006). Psychiatric morbidity in adults with Down syndrome. *Psychiatry, 5*(9), 316–319.

Pulsifer, M. B., Winterkorn, E. B., & Thiele, E. A. (2007). Psychological profile of adults with tuberous sclerosis complex. *Epilepsy & Behavior, 10*, 402–406.

Rapport, M. D. (2001). Bridging theory and practice: Conceptual understanding of treatments for children with attention deficit hyperactivity disorder (ADHD), obsessive-compulsive disorder (OCD), autism, and depression. *Journal of Clinical Child Psychology, 30*(1), 3–7.

Renk, K. (2008). Disorders of conduct in young children: Developmental considerations, diagnoses, and other characteristics. *Developmental Review, 28*(3), 316–341.

Robins, L. N. (1978). Sturdy childhood predictors of adult antisocial behavior: Replications from longitudinal studies. *Psychological Medicine, 8*, 611–622.

Salekin, R. T. (2006). Psychopathy in children and adolescents: Key issues in conceptualization and assessment. In C. J. Patrick (Ed.), *Handbook of psychopathy* (pp. 389–414). New York: Guilford Press.

Sanders, M. R. (1992). Enhancing the impact of behavioural family intervention with children: Emerging perspectives. *Behaviour Change, 9*, 115–119.

Sandys, J. (2007). Work and employment for people with intellectual and developmental disabilities. In I. Brown, & M. Percy (Eds.), *A comprehensive guide to intellectual & developmental disabilities* (pp. 527–543). Baltimore, MD: Paul H. Brookes.

Scahill, L., & Leckman, J. F. (2005). Tic disorders. In B. J. Sadock, & V. A. Sadock (Eds.), *Kaplan & Sadock's comprehensive textbook of psychiatry* (pp. 3228–3236). Philadelphia: Lippincott, Williams & Wilkins.

Scheerenberger, R. C. (1983). *A history of mental retardation*. Baltimore: Paul H. Brookes.

Schultz, R. T., Romanski, L. M., & Tsatsanis, K. D. (2000). Neurofunctional models of autistic disorder and Asperger syndrome: Clues from neuroimaging. In A. Klin, F. R. Volkmar, & S. S. Sparrow (Eds.), *Asperger syndrome* (pp. 172–209). New York: Guilford Press.

Schumann, C. M., & Amaral, D. G. (2006). Stereological analysis of amygdala neuron number in autism. *Journal of Neuroscience, 26*, 7674–7679.

Shaffer, D., Leibenluft, E., Rohde, L. A., Sirovatka, P., & Regier, D. A. (Eds.). (2009). *Externalizing disorders of childhood: Refining the research agenda for DSM-5*. Arlington, VA: American Psychiatric Association.

Shapiro, E. S., & Lentz, F. E. (1991). Vocational–technical programs: Follow-up of students with learning disabilities. *Exceptional Children, 58*, 47–59.

Sharp, W. G., Sherman, C., & Gross, A. M. (2007). Selective mutism and anxiety: A review of the current conceptualization of the disorder. *Journal of Anxiety Disorders, 21*(4), 568–579.

Sharp, W. S., Gottesman, R. F., Greenstein, D. K., Ebens, C. L., Rapoport, J. L., & Castellanos, F. X. (2003). Monozygotic twins discordant for attention-deficit/hyperactivity disorder: Ascertainment and clinical characteristics. *Journal of the American Academy of Child and Adolescent Psychiatry, 42*, 93–97.

Shattuck, P. T. (2006). The contribution of diagnostic substitution to the growing administrative prevalence of autism in US special education. *Pediatrics, 117*, 1028–1037.

Shaywitz, S. E., Mody, M., & Shaywitz, B. A. (2006). Neural mechanisms in dyslexia. *Current Directions in Psychological Science, 15*, 278–281.

Sigafoos, J., Arthur-Kelly, M., & Butterfield, N. (2006). *Enhancing everyday communication for children with disabilities*. Baltimore: Paul H. Brookes.

Simos, P. G., Fletcher, J. M., Sarkari, S., Billingsley-Marshall, R., Denton, C. A., & Papanicolaou, A. C. (2007). Intensive instruction affects brain magnetic activity associated with oral word reading in children with persistent reading disabilities. *Journal of Learning Disabilities, 40*, 37–48.

Smith, B. H., Barkley, R. A. & Shapiro, C. J. (2006). Combined child therapies. In R. A. Barkley (Ed.), *Attention-deficit hyperactivity disorder: A handbook for diagnosis and treatment*, 3rd ed. (pp. 678–691). New York: Guilford Press.

Soderstrom, H., Sjodin, A.-K., Carlstedt, A., & Forsman, A. (2004). Adult psychopathic personality with childhood-onset hyperactivity and conduct disorder: A central problem constellation in forensic psychiatry. *Psychiatry Research, 121*, 271–280.

Sonuga-Barke, E. J., Daley, D., Thompson, M., Laver-Bradbury, C., & Weeks, A. (2001). Parent-based therapies for preschool attention-deficit/hyperactivity disorder: A randomized, controlled trial with a community sample. *Journal of the American Academy of Child & Adolescent Psychiatry, 40*(4), 402–408.

Sparrow, S. S., Balla, D. A., & Cicchetti, D. V. (1984). *Vineland Adaptive Behavior Scales*. Circle Pines, MN: American Guidance Service.

Spencer, T. J. (2006). ADHD and comorbidity in childhood. *Journal of Clinical Psychiatry, 67*(Suppl. 8), 27–31.

Spencer, T. J., Biederman, J., & Mick, E. (2007). Attention-deficit/hyperactivity disorder: Diagnosis, lifespan, comorbidities, and neurobiology. *Ambulatory Pediatrics, 7*(1, Suppl. 1), 73–81.

Standart, S., & Le Couteur, A. (2003). The quiet child: A literature review of selective mutism. *Child and Adolescent Mental Health, 8*(4), 154–160.

Sugiyama, T., & Abe, T. (1989). The prevalence of autism in Nagoya, Japan: A total population study. *Journal of Autism and Developmental Disorders, 19*, 87–96.

Swedo, S., Thorsen, P., & Pine, D. (2008, February 3–5). *Autism and other pervasive developmental disorders conference*. Paper presented at The Future of Psychiatric Diagnosis: Refining the Research Agenda, Sacramento, CA.

Tannock, R. (2005a). Mathematics disorder. In B. J. Sadock, & V. A. Sadock (Eds.), *Kaplan & Sadock's comprehensive textbook of psychiatry* (pp. 3116–3123). Philadelphia: Lippincott, Williams & Wilkins.

Tannock, R. (2005b). Reading disorder. In B. J. Sadock, & V. A. Sadock (Eds.), *Kaplan & Sadock's comprehensive textbook of psychiatry* (pp. 3107–3116). Philadelphia: Lippincott, Williams & Wilkins.

Thapar, A., & Muñoz-Solomando, A. (2008). Attention deficit hyperactivity disorder. *Psychiatry, 7*(8), 340–344.

Thorndike, R. L., Hagen, E. P., & Sattler, J. M. (1986). *Stanford-Binet Intelligence Scale* (4th ed.). San Antonio: Psychological Corporation.

Towbin, K. E. (2005). Pervasive developmental disorder not otherwise specified. In F. R. Volkmar, R. Paul, A. Klin, & D. Cohen (Eds.), *Handbook of autism and pervasive developmental disorders: Volume one: Diagnosis, development, neurobiology, and behavior* (pp. 165–200). Hoboken, NJ: John Wiley & Sons.

Temple, E., Deutisch, G. K., Poldrack, R. A., Miller, S. L., Tallal, P., Merzenich, M. M., et al. (2003). Neural deficits in children with dyslexia ameliorated by behavioral remediation: Evidence from functional MRI. *Proceedings of the National Academy of Sciences, 100*, 2860–2865.

Timimi, S., & Taylor, E. (2004). ADHD is best understood as a cultural construct. *British Journal of Psychiatry, 184*, 8–9.

Valera, E. M., Faraone, S. V., Murray, K. E., & Seidman, L. J. (2007). Meta-analysis of structural imaging findings in attention-deficit/hyperactivity disorder. *Biological Psychiatry, 61*, 1361–1369.

Van Acker, R., Loncola, J. A., & Van Acker E. Y. (2005). Rett syndrome: A pervasive developmental disorder. In F. R. Volkmar, R. Paul, A. Klin, & D. Cohen (Eds.), *Handbook of autism and pervasive developmental disorders: Volume one: Diagnosis, development, neurobiology, and behavior* (pp. 126–164). Hoboken, NJ: John Wiley & Sons.

Venkatagiri, H. S. (2005). Recent advances in the treatment of stuttering: A theoretical perspective. *Journal of Communication Disorders, 38*, 375–393.

Vogel, S. A., & Reder, S. (1998). Educational attainment of adults with learning disabilities. In S. A. Vogel, & S. Reder (Eds.), *Learning disabilities, literacy, and adult education* (pp. 5–28). Baltimore: Paul H. Brookes.

Volkmar, F. R., Klin, A., & Schultz, R. T. (2005). Pervasive developmental disorders. In B. J. Sadock, & V. A. Sadock (Eds.), *Kaplan & Sadock's comprehensive textbook of psychiatry* (pp. 3164–3182). Philadelphia: Lippincott, Williams & Wilkins.

Volkmar, F. R., Koenig, K., & State, M. (2005). Childhood disintegrative disorder. In F. R. Volkmar, R. Paul, A. Klin, & D. Cohen (Eds.), *Handbook of autism and pervasive developmental disorders: Volume one: Diagnosis, development, neurobiology, and behavior* (pp. 70–87). Hoboken, NJ: John Wiley & Sons.

Volkmar, F. R., Szatmari, P., & Sparrow, S. S. (1993). Sex differences in pervasive developmental disorders. *Journal of Autism and Developmental Disorders, 23*, 579–591.

Vuchinich, S., Bank, L., & Patterson, G. R. (1992). Parenting, peers, and the stability of antisocial behavior in preadolescent boys. *Developmental Psychology, 28*, 510–521.

Waldman, I. D., & Gizer, I. R. (2006). The genetics of attention deficit hyperactivity disorder. *Clinical Psychology Review, 26*, 396–432.

Wax, J. R. (2007). Trends in state/population-based Down syndrome screening and invasive prenatal testing with introduction of first trimester combined Down syndrome screening, South Australia 1995–2005. *American Journal of Obstetrics and Gynecology, 196*, 285–286.

Wechsler, D. (1989). *WPPSI-R manual.* San Antonio, TX: Psychological Corporation.

Wechsler, D. (2003). *Wechsler Intelligence Scale for Children* (4th ed.) San Antonio, TX: The Psychological Corporation.

Wetherby, A. M., & Prizant, B. M. (2005). Enhancing language and communication development in autism spectrum disorders: Assessment and intervention guidelines. In D. Zager (Ed.), *Autism spectrum disorders: Identification, education, and treatment*, 3rd ed. (pp. 327–365). Hillsdale, NJ: Lawrence Erlbaum Associates, Inc.

Weyandt, L. L., & DuPaul, G. (2006). ADHD in college students. *Journal of Attention Disorders, 10*(1), 9–19.

Whitehurst, G. J., Fischel, J. E., Lonigan, C. J., Valdez-Menchaca, M. C., DeBaryshe, B. D., & Caulfield, M. B. (1988). Verbal interaction in families of normal and expressive-language-delayed children. *Developmental Psychology, 24*, 690–699.

Wilens, T. E., Biederman, J., Brown, S., Tanguay, S., Monuteaux, M. C., Blake, C., & Spencer, T. J. (2002). Psychiatric comorbidity and functioning in clinically referred preschool children and school-age youths with ADHD. *Journal of the American Academy of Child and Adolescent Psychiatry, 41*, 262–268.

Woodbury-Smith, M., & Volkmar, F. (2009). Asperger syndrome. *European Child & Adolescent Psychiatry.* 18(1), 2–11.

Woods, D. W., Twohig, M. P., Fuqua, R. W., & Hanley, J. M. (2000). Treatment of stuttering with regulated breathing: Strengths, limitations, and future directions. *Behavior Therapy, 31*, 547–568.

Wootton, J. M., Frick, P. J., Shelton, K. K., & Silverthorn, P. (1997). Ineffective parenting and childhood conduct problems: The moderating role of callous-unemotional traits. *Journal of Consulting and Clinical Psychology, 65*, 301–308.

Young, H. A., Geier, D. A., & Geier, M. R. (2008). Thimerosal exposure in infants and neurodevelopmental disorders: An assessment of computerized medical records in the Vaccine Safety Datalink. *Journal of the Neurological Sciences, 271*(1–2), 110–118.

Zager, D., & Shamow, N. (2005). Teaching students with autism spectrum disorders. In D. Zager (Ed.), *Autism spectrum disorders: Identification, education, and treatment*, 3rd ed. (pp. 295–326). Hillsdale, NJ: Lawrence Erlbaum Associates, Inc.

Cognitive Disorders in Adults

Roberta F. White

Abstract

This chapter provides an overview on cognitive disorders in adults from a neuropsychological perspective. It begins with a critical review of existing taxonomies for these disorders, especially those contained in the DSM-IV, and continues with a summary of neuropsychological terminology used in the chapter and the effects of focal brain lesions. A number of medical and neurological disorders are described, and their cognitive correlates are reviewed using data from clinical case studies and epidemiologic research. The conditions summarized include a brief consideration of medical disorders that do not involve primary central nervous system pathology, followed by extensive review of brain insults (trauma, infections, exposures) and primary neurological disorders (dementias, cerebrovascular disease, motor system disorders, structural lesions, epilepsy, autoimmune disorders). A concluding section describes current issues in understanding cognitive disorders and likely future approaches to research on them.

Keywords: Brain trauma, cognitive disorders, cognitive impairment, dementia, encephalopathy, neurocognition, neuropsychological assessment, subcortical dementia

This chapter reviews the behavioral manifestations of cognitive disorders in adults. The framework for the chapter and the contents of the discussion derive directly from a neuropsychological perspective. The chapter begins by considering what cognitive disorders are, how they are defined by the *Diagnostic and Statistical Manual of Mental Disorders, Fourth Edition* (DSM-IV) (American Psychiatric Association [APA], 1994), other possible taxonomies for defining and categorizing these disorders, and approaches to understanding the behavioral characteristics of them. The chapter then proceeds with descriptions of the behavioral characteristics of cognitive disorders in adulthood, including a brief consideration of medical diseases and an extensive review of external brain insults and primary neurological disorders. It ends by considering future directions in understanding these disorders and diseases.

What Are Cognitive Disorders?
The Universe of Disorders Affecting Cognition in Adults

For a neuropsychologist, writing a chapter on cognitive disorders is an exercise in focus and containment. Highly specific pathognomonic patterns of cognitive characteristics are associated with many diseases, disorders, and syndromes. More generalized, nonspecific findings are also seen across a number of disorders. Such characteristics and findings constitute the field of clinical neuropsychology. In general, the types of disorders and diseases with prominent cognitive manifestations include adult manifestations of conditions that occur or originate in childhood (developmental disorders), disorders that are generally classified as "psychiatric," exposures to exogenous drugs and chemicals, neurological diseases, and medical conditions. All of these categories of illness can also contribute to the occurrence of reversible acute or chronic confusional states characterized by generalized and shifting cognitive symptoms.

ADULT MANIFESTATIONS OF DEVELOPMENTAL CONDITIONS

These can arise from disorders of learning or attention, including learning disabilities (LD; e.g., disorders of reading, writing, arithmetic; nonverbal LDs) and attention-deficit hyperactivity disorder (ADHD, inattentive or hyperactive types). Extremes in intelligence quotient (IQ) dating from childhood also significantly affect cognitive function in adulthood (e.g., mental retardation, borderline IQ, superior IQ). These patterns of "native ability" or premorbid function are important because they persist and affect the patterns and types of cognitive changes that accompany the occurrence of central nervous system (CNS) insults and disorders in adulthood.

Before or after birth, children may also develop acute or chronic illnesses that affect CNS function, with manifestations extending to or even appearing in adulthood. There are too many of these to list exhaustively, but a few examples will be given along with their importance to lifelong patterns of cognitive abilities. Congenital disorders can affect cognition in a manner similar to that seen with LD and ADHD. For example, cerebral palsy and hydrocephalus are often associated with highly individual and specific cognitive anomalies. Some children are born with severe atrophy of the brain or a hemisphere of the brain, or unusual formations of the blood vessels in the brain (arteriovenous malformations or AVMs) that may have longstanding implications for cognitive function. Examples of important neuropsychiatric disorders with cognitive sequelae that are or can be longstanding include autism, schizophrenia, depression, post-traumatic stress disorder (PTSD), and personality disorders. Inherited and/or spontaneous medical disorders can also be associated with longstanding cognitive stigmata. Examples include thyroid diseases and other endocrine disorders, diabetes, heart disease, neoplasms outside of the CNS, respiratory illnesses affecting oxygenation of the brain, and renal failure. Epilepsy is a common chronic condition of childhood that can be associated with significant cognitive findings and changes, depending upon the etiology, type, and severity of the seizure disorder. Primary neurological insults and illnesses also occur in childhood or even in prenatal life, including traumatic brain injuries (TBIs), exposures to toxic chemicals such as metals or solvents, brain tumors, infections like meningitis, strokes, or even the childhood onset of diseases usually occurring in adulthood such as multiple sclerosis (MS) or Huntington disease (HD). The cognitive manifestations of disorders that can develop in both childhood and adulthood are an important area of concern because they are often distinctive at different developmental stages and have differing implications for future function. For example, neurological insults and diseases in childhood often produce a much more generalized pattern of cognitive changes than the more focal patterns in adults that will be described in this chapter. Interestingly, children often recover cognitive function better than do adults following brain insults, due to the plasticity of the developing brain.

Finally, it is important to consider late-appearing effects of childhood-onset conditions and CNS insults. Chronic medication use can affect brain function later in life; an example of this phenomenon involves drugs for epilepsy. Radiation treatment for cancers can also affect the brain on a permanent or even delayed basis. For example, leukemia was once treated with high doses of radiation that, in some patients, was associated with development of brain lesions in middle age. Even childhood lead exposure can manifest itself in behavior later in life. For example, the author saw an adult patient whose hyperthyroidism caused release of lead that had been stored in her bones during childhood, resulting in behavioral changes (Goldman, Kalis, White, & Hu, 1994).

NEUROPSYCHIATRIC AND PSYCHIATRIC DISORDERS

Many disorders that fall into the psychiatric domain are associated with anomalies of brain structure and of neurotransmitter function. These abnormalities are well documented for schizophrenic-spectrum diseases and for major affective disorders (Seidman, Cassens, Williams, & Pepple, 1992; Harvey & Keefe, 2009; Langenecker, Jin Lee, & Bieliauskas, 2009). Given the findings, these conditions might better be designated as "neuropsychiatric." The cognitive correlates of many other disorders that fall within the psychiatric domain have also been described. Examples include anxiety disorders and PTSD, personality disorders, and motivational states such as malingering and factitious disorders. Although not the primary focus of this chapter, the cognitive correlates of these disorders in individual patients must be considered when evaluating the impact of primary neurological and medical diseases on cognition.

MEDICAL AND NEUROLOGICAL DISORDERS AND CENTRAL NERVOUS SYSTEM INSULTS

Neurological diseases and disorders, and CNS insults from exogenous agents are the focus of this chapter. Primary neurological and neurodegenerative diseases with major cognitive sequelae include cerebrovascular disease, primary progressive dementia, MS, Parkinson disease (PD), brain tumors, and many other conditions. Central nervous system insults affecting cognition can arise from TBIs, chemical exposures of many types (medications, substances of abuse, industrial chemicals), and infection. Non-neurological medical diseases can affect cognition through both primary and secondary mechanisms. Conditions within this category include non-CNS neoplasms, immunological disorders, systemic infections, metabolic diseases, and symptom-based disorders such as fibromyalgia and chronic fatigue syndrome.

How Should Cognitive Disorders be Classified or Diagnosed?

DSM-IV TAXONOMY FOR COGNITIVE DISORDERS

The DSM-IV (APA, 1994) divides cognitive disorders into four categories as follows:

1. *Delirium* refers to acute confusional states associated with general medical conditions, substance-induced encephalopathies, multiple etiologies, and "not otherwise specified" etiologies.

2. *Dementia*, the second "cognitive disorder" included in the DSM-IV, is characterized as being remarkable for deficits in multiple cognitive domains, including "memory," attributable to "the direct physiological effects of a medical condition," the persisting effects of exposures to substances, or multiple etiologies. The manual lists four basic categories of dementia related to neuropathologically based "medical disorders:" Alzheimer disease (AD; further categorized as early vs. late onset), vascular dementia, human immunodeficiency virus (HIV), and "other" (traumatic brain injury, PD, HD, Pick disease, Creutzfeldt-Jacob disease, normal pressure hydrocephalus, hypothyroidism, vitamin B_{12} deficiency, intracranial radiation, substance-induced persisting dementias). Other categories of dementia relate to other general medical conditions, substance-induced persisting dementia (caused by exposure to substances of abuse, medications, or chemical toxicants), multiple etiologies, and etiology not otherwise specified.

3. *Amnestic disorders*, the third category of DSM-IV cognitive disorder, refer to conditions in which the patient cannot learn new information or is unable to remember previously learned information or events. The amnesias included in this category are due to general medical conditions or exposure to a substance, and are explicitly not diagnosable as delirium or dementia. They can be transient (less than 1 month in duration) or chronic (lasting more than 1 month). Examples of the medical conditions listed as possible etiologic bases for these amnesias include trauma, surgery, strokes, and brain infections that produce pathology in brain structures that subserve the functions mediating learning and memory. The category also includes *substance-induced persisting amnestic disorder*, which can be classified a secondary to alcohol, certain medications, and other or unknown substances (which include chemical toxicants).

4. *Cognitive disorder not otherwise specified (NOS)* is the fourth category. This diagnosis includes mild neurocognitive disorders identified through quantified assessment in patients who also have objective evidence of a systemic medical condition or CNS dysfunction. Postconcussional disorder with memory or attentional deficits is also included in this category.

The DSM-IV diagnostic system for cognitive disorders has several critical problems. First, it omits many disorders with prominent cognitive symptomatology (e.g., MS, progressive supranuclear palsy, epilepsy, lupus, and focal stroke, to name just a few). Second, the descriptions of the cognitive deficits accompanying each category overlap excessively, are vague, and are not as specific or complete as the state of knowledge about cognitive disorders allows. Especially notable is the frequent reference to "memory impairment," without specifying the type of memory problem and with the apparent assumption that memory problems are more or less universal in the progressive neurological disorders, an assumption that would be disputed by many clinicians and scientists who study these disorders (Bondi et al., 2009; Knopman et al., 2001). Finally, there is no consistent organizing principle underlying the diagnoses applied. Rather, the grouping of diagnoses includes at least three dimensions: acute versus chronic (acute event vs. persisting dementia), reversibility (delirium vs. dementia), and etiology (substances, genetics).

ALTERNATIVE APPROACHES TO CLASSIFYING COGNITIVE DISORDERS IN ADULTS

It is possible to consider classifying cognitive disorders in a more systematic fashion. For example, one classification principle could be based on the cognitive and behavioral manifestations of each disorder, organizing them by either observed types of behavioral and self-reported symptoms or by the typical domain- and process-specific patterns seen on neuropsychological assessment. For example, they could be classified as disorders most prominently involving language changes, memory dysfunction, visuospatial deficits, inattention, impairments in working memory/executive function, or diffuse dysfunction. Another possibility would be to organize them with regard to reversibility and progression (e.g., reversible confusional states, acute encephalopathies, static encephalopathies, progressive dementias).

Probably the most efficient organizational strategy for classifying cognitive disorders—and the one that forms the basis of this chapter—is to use etiology. Using this approach, cognitive disorders in adults can be divided into those emanating from medical disorders producing primary or secondary aberrations in brain function. Examples include metabolic, endocrine, respiratory, and other system-based medical conditions, as well as symptom-based disorders of unknown etiology such as fibromyalgia. A second group of cognitive disorders results from external insults to the brain. These can include open- and closed-head trauma, infections of the brain (e.g., HIV, herpes, meningitis, prion diseases), chemical exposures (medications, substances of abuse, industrial chemicals, environmental toxicants), radiation, and even the absence of critical elements (e.g., malnutrition). Finally, primary neurological, neurovascular, and neurodegenerative disorders also lead to disorders of cognition. These conditions include primary progressive dementias, stroke, vascular dementia, brain tumor, immune and autoimmune disorders of the CNS, motor system diseases, MS, epilepsy, and hydrocephalus, among many others.

What Evidence Is Used to Describe the Typical Behavioral Characteristics of Cognitive Disorders in Adults?

The cognitive impairments and dysfunctions associated with the conditions described in this chapter have been studied and defined in a variety of ways, including self-reported symptoms, deficits inferred by clinicians or family members based on patient behavior, and neuropsychological test performance.

The latter evidence has received the greatest weight and attention in the literature on cognitive disorders. Neuropsychological tests provide a quantified means of assessing domain-specific cognitive functions and specific kinds of cognitive processes, are standardized with regard to test administration and scoring (so that data from different sites provided by different examiners can be reliably compared), have normative values that allow inference of degree of impairment when comparing patients or groups of patients to referents with similar backgrounds (especially age, gender, education), and have been extensively validated with regard to the information that they provide about the functioning of specific brain structures and systems over many years of research in neuropsychology and cognitive neuroscience. In addition, the reliability, validity, and specificity of neuropsychological tests have been extensively studied and reported (Strauss, Sherman, & Spreen, 2006). This chapter describes findings from research using clinical case series methodology, as well as epidemiologic methods.

NEUROPSYCHOLOGICAL DOMAINS AND PROCESSES

Neuropsychological function is usually classified into domains, with specific tests generally assigned to one or more of these domains, depending upon the skills being assessed or the task demands of the test. A listing of the generally accepted domains follows, with examples of tests for each domain. For detailed descriptions of the tests and cognitive processing demands associated with each of these domains, the reader is referred to volumes by Lezak et al. (2004) and Strauss et al. (2006).

Attention

This domain refers to the capacity to monitor and process incoming stimuli; it is generally assessed by tasks such as the Continuous Performance Test (Rosvold, Mirsky, Sarason, Bransome, & Beck, 1956), which requires acknowledging a critical stimulus in a series of stimuli; Digit Span forward, which requires repeating back a series of numbers after they have been read by the examiner (Wechsler, 1997a); or Visual Span forward, requiring the correct replication of a series of blocks or boxes tapped by the examiner (Wechsler, 1997a).

Executive Function

This domain can be difficult to define, and there is some disagreement about what is included in it. However, it generally refers to the ability to develop strategies for solving novel problems or completing tasks, abstraction and reasoning, and capacity to inhibit responding to distracting stimuli. It is assessed by tasks such as the Similarities Test (correctly identifying the concept that makes two objects or concepts similar) (Wechsler, 1997b); Digit Span Backward (correct reversal of a string of numbers read aloud by the examiner) (Wechsler, 1997a); and the Stroop Task (ability to correctly identify the color of the ink in which color words are presented, with the ink a different color from the word) (Stroop, 1935). Another example is the Wisconsin Card Sorting Test (correctly inferring the implicit rules for categorizing visual stimuli and maintaining and switching sorting rules in response to examiner feedback) (Berg, 1948).

Working Memory

This domain refers to the ability to hold and process information in completing tasks. The Letter-Number Sequencing Test from the Wechsler scales (Wechsler, 1997b) is an example of a working memory test. For this task, the patient hears a sequence of letters and numbers in random order and then must repeat them back in the correct numerical and alphabetical order.

Language Skills

This domain encompasses basic linguistic processing, including naming, fluency, repetition of words and sounds, language comprehension, writing, and reading. Tests that assess this domain include the Boston Naming Test (correct identification of the name of an object depicted in a drawing) (Goodglass & Kaplan, 2000) and the Boston Diagnostic Aphasic Examination (includes many tests probing aspects of language) (Goodglass, Kaplan, & Barresi, 2000).

Visuospatial Abilities

Visuospatial processing includes mentally organizing visual percepts and visual constructions. An example of a nonmotor visuospatial task is the Hooper Visual Organization Test (Hooper, 1983), which requires correctly naming objects that have been depicted in cut-up form. Visual construction tasks include replications of drawings of visual designs using blocks that have sides that are red, white, or half red-half white (Block Design) (Wechsler, 1997b), drawing various objects to command (Boston Visuospatial Quantitative Battery) (Goodglass et al., 2000), or puzzle assembly (Object Assembly) (Wechsler et al., 1997b).

Learning and Memory

This complex domain includes the capacity to learn new material (encoding), store the material (retention), and recall it at will (retrieval). Types of tests that assess anterograde memory include story passages that must be learned and recalled on immediate and delayed recall (Wechsler Memory Scale Logical Memory) and visual designs that must be replicated from immediate and delayed recall (Wechsler Memory Scale Visual Reproduction) (Wechsler, 1997a). Memory for information that the patient has known for a long time (retrograde memory) can also be assessed. Tasks assessing this type of memory function include Albert's Famous Faces (Albert, Butters, & Levin, 1979), in which the examinee views famous faces from various decades and must identify the person depicted; there are also retrograde memory tests that are developed to test the individual's memory of her or his own life. Procedural memory refers to the ability to learn a new skill, such as reading writing that looks like it would in a mirror (mirror reading).

General Intellectual Function/Academic Skills

Neuropsychologists often use tests to estimate an examinee's cognitive ability level prior to a brain insult or development of a neurological disorder. For adults, these tests (called "hold tests") can be used to estimate premorbid verbal or visuospatial abilities. Such tests include single-word reading tasks such as the Wide Range Achievement Test Reading subtest (Wilkinson, 1993), vocabulary tests in which the examinee must define words, or tests requiring recall of information learned in school or through life experience (Wechsler Scales Information subtest) (Wechsler, 1997b). Premorbid visuospatial abilities can often be estimated in adults using the Wechsler Picture Completion subtest (identifying the missing detail in a picture) (Wechsler, 1997b) or the Arithmetic subtest of the Wide Range Achievement Test (Wilkinson, 1993).

Fine Manual Motor Skills

Motor abilities are generally assessed using techniques involving the hands, in which the examinee taps a tapping device with the index finger or inserts pegs into a pegboard. Outcomes are usually total correct responses or time to completion for each hand and both hands together (pegboards). These tests are not cognitive measures but can be used to assess motor contributions to test performance on visuospatial tasks that have a motor component and to gain clues about focal or lateralized brain damage.

Focal Cognitive Impairments

Structure–function relationships underlie a great deal of the inference process used in interpreting neuropsychological assessment results. A very general rendering of the domain-specific impairments associated with some major brain structures will be provided here. This section should be referred to in the descriptions of disease-associated cognitive deficits detailed later whenever *focal cognitive impairment* is mentioned.

Damage to the frontal lobes or that involves brain systems with frontal lobe components often results in deficits in the domains of attention, executive function, and working memory, sometimes also affecting learning and retrieval of newly learned information (but not true retention of it over time). Because the frontal lobes are richly connected to other parts of the brain, secondary frontal lobe dysfunction may be evident following damage to other brain areas, in which the domain-specific deficits just described are seen but are milder than those following primary insults to or disease of the frontal lobes.

Lesions affecting the lateral aspects of the temporal lobe on the dominant side of the brain (usually the left in right-handers) can result in language impairment, especially of naming ability. Mesial temporal lobe damage (hippocampal system) results in memory deficits for learning and retention of verbal (dominant hemisphere) or nonverbal information (nondominant hemisphere, usually the right hemisphere in right-handers).

The parietal lobes are involved in the processing of visuospatial information. Damage to them, especially the nondominant parietal lobe, may result in inability to organize visuospatial material. Inattention to one side of space can follow damage to the contralateral parietal lobe. Deficits in reading and arithmetic can also be seen following lesions in specific areas of the parietal lobes.

The occipital lobes also process visual information; dysfunction localized to these lobes can be manifested by profound inability to place objects in space.

The basal ganglia, which include structures that are important in motor function and are affected in disorders like PD, mediate visuospatial functions as well.

The cerebellum, also involved in motor function, appears to play a role in cognitive function, particularly visuospatial organization.

The white matter, which constitutes a large part of the brain under the gray matter, is important to cognitive function as well. Intact function of the myelin sheaths in the white matter allows effective information processing and transfer of information from one part of the brain to the other. White matter lesions can affect visuospatial processing, fine manual motor skills, retrieval of information from memory stores, and skills associated with the functioning of the frontal lobes.

Neuropsychology and behavioral neurology are rooted in studies of individuals with focal cerebral lesions, who demonstrate the kinds of deficits summarized earlier. These case study descriptions of individuals and case series provided the basis for research in cognitive neuropsychology, cognitive neuroscience, and clinical neuropsychological assessment. Clinical experience is also a key component of clinician-based inference concerning sites of brain damage in patients and associated neurological disorders (Filley, 2001; Luria, 1966; Mesulam, 2000; White, 1992).

Epidemiological evidence using case–control designs or exposure–outcome methodologies in populations of patients (population based case–control studies, exposure–outcome studies) are the basis for many of the conclusions about cognitive dysfunction associated with the specific disorders summarized in this chapter. Such studies are more objective and allow quantification of effect sizes and other parameters related to the severity of the specific cognitive deficits associated with the disorders described.

Often the evidence cited in a section describing a disease will include both case-based clinical inferences and epidemiological data. The two sources of information have very different advantages and disadvantages. Epidemiological studies can make it difficult to identify qualitative data or "pathognomonic signs" that indicate dysfunction associated with a disease or brain structure. They are, however, a very efficient means of identifying dose–effect relationships between degree of exposure to an agent and outcome (e.g., titers for infections, amount of tumor tissue, dosage of exposure to a drug). They are also better at identifying degree of deficit associated with different stages of a disease or degree of disease severity than clinical methodology. In fact, using epidemiological designs, it is much easier to confirm subtle dysfunction associated with brain disorders or insults. Clinical inference of dysfunction requires much greater impairment (scores 1–2 standard deviations below expectation on a test) than epidemiological methodology. Using case–control or exposure–outcome designs, it is possible to identify very subtle cognitive dysfunction that would not qualify as a clinical "impairment" or "deficit": group differences or dose–effect relationships can be found within the normal range of test performance. Identifying such dysfunction can provide valuable clues about cognitive changes in the earliest stages of an illness and provide markers for evidence of progression or type of dysfunction when patients develop clinically relevant impairments in cognition.

In the following sections of this chapter, reports on the types of cognitive dysfunction seen in neurodegenerative diseases and following exogenous brain insults and structural brain lesions will include epidemiological evidence, reports from clinicians on findings from cases, and the author's 30-plus years of experience in assessing thousands of patients with cognitive disorders in university hospital and Veterans Administration Hospital settings.

Medical Disorders

Medical disorders that are not neurodegenerative disorders and do not result from exogenous insults to the brain or structural brain lesions can be associated with cognitive dysfunction and deficits due to both primary and secondary effects on the brain or neurotransmitter systems. An example of primary effects is hypoxia from respiratory failure. Secondary effects can be associated with confusional states or delirium. For reviews of the impairments associated with medical diseases through these kinds of mechanisms, the reader is referred elsewhere (Brands & Kessel, 2009; Bruce, Aloia, & Ancoli-Israel, 2009; Lezak et al., 2004).

Brain Insults
Trauma
Head trauma is the most common form of brain injury. It ranges from mild TBI, defined in various ways, to severe TBI, with a wide variety in cognitive deficits apparent in both the acute stages and following medical recovery. Factors that determine the type and severity of cognitive dysfunction following TBI include severity of the brain injury, degree of deficit immediately following the injury, age, repeated brain injury, polytrauma involving other parts of the body, and preinjury alcohol abuse (Dikmen, Machamer, & Temkin, 2009; Hannay, Howieson, Loring, Fischer, & Lezak, 2004). Severity of injury has been defined in a number of ways, including score on the Glasgow Coma Scale, which quantifies quality of eye opening, motor, and verbal responsivity (see Dikman et al., 2009 for details on scale and scores) and length of post-traumatic amnesia (PTA) or time during which the patient is unable

to retain new information following the traumatic event (see Hannay et al., 2004 for severity estimates). Head injuries are often classified as penetrating head injuries, in which an object enters the brain; closed-head injuries, in which the brain sustains damage from primary contact to the head, as well as secondary injuries resulting from downstream neural processes initiated by the primary injury; and concussion, which can occur in the absence of a direct blow to the head but results from acceleration injuries such as those than can occur in whiplash. The primary brain injuries related to brain trauma include contusions at the site of the injury and on the opposite side of the brain (*contrecoups* injury), diffuse axonal injury resulting from acceleration/deceleration, and hematomas (Hannay et al., 2004). These kinds of injuries are important because long-lasting, even permanent residual impairments may be evident in patients with a history of TBI.

Cognitive impairment following TBI can be focal in nature (i.e., related to the site or sites of the brain injury) or diffuse, representing dysfunction from multiple brain sites. In their excellent review of the cognitive and behavioral consequences of TBI, Hannay and colleagues summarized the deficits associated with mild, moderate, and severe trauma. Mild TBI may result in subtle cognitive impairments that are not obvious to the observer, including attentional impairment and verbal retrieval problems accompanied by emotional distress and fatigue. Patients who have sustained moderate TBI may be able to work and live independently but may nevertheless demonstrate frontal lobe damage in their diminished capacity for or interest in planning and organizing, loss of spontaneity, impulsivity, and apathy. Focal cognitive deficits may also be apparent (see the section "Focal Cognitive Impairments" for a description of focal structural cognitive dysfunction). Severe TBI can be quite devastating, with permanent, severe effects in multiple cognitive domains that can include attention, short-term memory, working memory, and/or visuospatial abilities. The executive dysfunction associated with severe TBI can be especially devastating, affecting self-determination, awareness, and self-regulatory behavior (Hannay et al., 2004). This author has seen patients with histories of severe TBI and comas lasting months whose scores on tests of intelligence are normal but who cannot work because they are so apathetic and unable to organize and mobilize themselves. They can also have significant problems on tests assessing the ability to generate hypotheses, reason, develop strategies to solve problems or carry out tasks efficiently, and complete tasks when there is any kind of distraction. The behavioral and emotional correlates associated with these cognitive impairments and TBI-induced neuropathology can be severe (see Prigatano & Maier, 2009; Hannay et al., 2004).

Infections

Although many types of infections can affect the brain, three of the most common or cognitively interesting are described here.

HUMAN IMMUNODEFICIENCY VIRUS

Human immunodeficiency virus (HIV) primarily affects the immune system but can be neurovirulent, crossing the blood–brain barrier early in the disease (Davis et al., 1992). Brain structures that are particularly vulnerable to the neuropathological effects of HIV include the gray and white matter of the frontal lobes and the caudate nucleus and putamen. It is believed that approximately 30%–50% of HIV-infected individuals are cognitively impaired, although a substantial portion of these people may not show related deficits in their ability to carry out activities of daily living (Grant, Sacktor, & McArthur, 2005). Three levels of cognitive impairment have been defined for HIV, all of which exclude impairments related to delirium or other neurocognitive disorders. Asymptomatic cognitive impairment is defined as scores 1 standard deviation below the mean on standard neuropsychological tests assessing two or more domains of function without effects on activities of daily living; mild neurocognitive disorder is indicated by scores at least 1 standard deviation below the mean on tests assessing two or more domains accompanied by at least mild deficiencies in daily functioning; HIV-acquired dementia is characterized by marked impairment in at least two ability domains with scores at least 2 standard deviations below normal and marked impairment in daily functioning (Antinori et al., 2007). Woods and colleagues summarized domain-specific cognitive dysfunction. They emphasized deficits in attention, especially selective attention; working memory; executive function (planning and self-monitoring); learning and memory at the level of encoding and retrieval; prospective memory ("remembering to remember"); verbal fluency; and information processing speed. Visuospatial deficits were said to be probable but require further investigation (Woods et al., 2009).

PRION DISEASES

Four diseases caused by prion infections are known, two of which are very rare and hereditary and one of

which (kuru) was caused by cannibalism. The most common prion disease is subacute spongiform encephalopathy (SSE), often called Creutzfeldt-Jakob disease (CJD), although Victor and Ropper (2001) dispute this terminology. Two forms of SSE have been described: CJD, which generally occurs in the sixth decade of life, and "mad cow disease" or "new variant CJD," which occurs in people who are much younger. Subacute spongiform encephalopathy is characterized by changes in cognition and behavior, with visual and gait abnormalities. Myoclonic jerks are typically seen (Victor & Ropper, 2001). The dementia is rapidly progressive and involves multiple cognitive domains. In this author's experience, SSE can be distinguished from other neurodegenerative disorders by the rapidity of the cognitive decline and the co-occurrence of fasciculations.

HERPES ENCEPHALITIS

Brain infection from herpes simplex type 1 has been described as the most common form of acute encephalitis. The acute symptoms include fever, seizures, confusion, stupor, and coma, with characteristic hemorrhagic lesions in the temporal and medial orbital frontal lobes (Victor and Ropper, 2001). The cognitive sequelae can be quite severe, including a dense amnesia, language deficits, and severe problems with self-regulatory behavior, planning, and reasoning.

Chemicals

In its chapter on substance-related disorders, the DSM-IV (APA, 1994) describes the effects of a large number of substances along several dimensions (dependence, abuse, intoxication, withdrawal, intoxication delirium, withdrawal delirium, amnestic disorder, psychotic disorders, mood disorders, sexual dysfunction, and sleep disorders). The drugs listed include several substances of abuse (alcohol, cannabis, cocaine, hallucinogens, nicotine, phencyclidine) as well as medications that may also be abused (opioids, amphetamines, inhalants, sedatives/hypnotics/anxiolytics) and categories for polysubstance abuse and other substances. Of this list of drugs, we will briefly describe the cognitive deficits associated with alcohol use only; the reader is referred to the DSM-IV and elsewhere (Gonzalez, Vassileva, & Cobb Scott, 2009) for a detailed description of the cognitive impairments associated with acute and chronic use of cannabis, cocaine, benzodiazepines, methamphetamine, ecstasy, and opiates. Glue sniffing is associated with a specific neurobehavioral syndrome and results from exposure to toluene, an industrial chemical described later.

Prescribed medications that are not typically abused may also affect cognition through primary or secondary mechanisms. The reader is referred to the *Physician's Desk Reference* (PDR) and product material descriptions for details on these pharmaceuticals. We will follow our discussion on the cognitive effects of alcohol with a summary on the effects of industrial chemicals.

ALCOHOL

Because it is a neurotoxic chemical, alcohol has acute effects on brain function and cognition that are readily apparent to the most casual observer of people in bars and at parties who are partaking of the drug. However, for social drinkers, these effects appear to be temporary, at least as assessed by neuropsychological test measures (Rourke & Grant, 2009). Patients who meet DSM-IV criteria for alcohol dependence or alcohol-induced persisting amnestic disorder (APA, 1994), however, often exhibit cognitive deficits and cognitive dysfunction. Rourke and Grant summarized the literature on rates of cognitive disorders among alcoholics as follows. Among alcoholics, 10% meet criteria for alcohol-induced persisting amnestic disorder or alcohol-induced persisting dementia. Of the 90% of alcoholics who do not meet criteria for these two disorders, about 50% show no cognitive impairments after 2–3 weeks' abstinence. Of the remaining 50% with neuropsychological impairments evident 3 weeks after they stop drinking, 70%–90% show mild cognitive deficits that improve after several months or years of abstinence, whereas 10%–30% maintain mild cognitive dysfunction after a year of abstinence. The mild deficits seen in alcoholics who have recently stopped drinking include impairments in tests of attention (especially on tasks with high processing demands), abstraction and problems solving, visuospatial skills both with and without motor components, and learning and memory at the levels of learning, encoding, and possibly retrieval. These problems are often seen in the context of normal IQ and verbal skills. Patients with these mild cognitive problems tend to have prominent white and gray matter pathology in the frontal lobes. Rourke and Grant emphasize that the cognitive deficits seen in alcoholics may vary somewhat and are affected by a number of other factors, including age, genetic and developmental factors, hepatic dysfunction, history of head injury, nutritional deprivation, hypoxemia from cigarette smoking, sleep disturbances, seizures, repeated alcohol withdrawal, and antisocial personality disorder (Rourke & Grant, 2009).

Wernicke-Korsakoff encephalopathy (WK) is a distinctive disorder that begins with a set of acute symptoms that include confusion, abnormal eye movements, and ataxic gait secondary to thiamine deficiency (the Wernicke phase). As the acute confusional state abates, a dense amnesia is apparent in which the patient is profoundly impaired in ability to learn and retain new information and has trouble remembering information from the past. The domain-specific deficits associated with the mild form of cognitive deficits of alcoholism are also present (Rourke & Grant, 2009).

Dementia associated with alcoholism is characterized by impairments in learning and memory accompanied by frontal lobe dysfunction (deficits in planning, abstraction, reasoning, attention) (Hannay et al., 2004). The neuropathology appears to disproportionately involve white matter (Filley, 2001) and may reflect progressive brain atrophy (Rourke & Loberg, 1996).

INDUSTRIAL CHEMICALS

The effects of exposure to industrial chemicals in adulthood have been described for many substances (White & Janulewicz, 2009; White, Feldman, & Proctor, 1992a; Feldman, 1999; White, Feldman, & Travers, 1990). Chemicals that have been investigated most extensively include metals (lead, arsenic, mercury, thallium, aluminum, tin, manganese), solvents (trichloroethylene, tetrachloroethylene, 1,1,1-trichloroethane, toluene, xylene, n-hexane, Stoddard solvent, styrene), pesticides (e.g., organophosphates, carbamates), persistent organic pollutants (polychlorinated biphenyl), and gases (carbon dioxide, sarin, soman).

Because each chemical can exert specific and differing focal effects on brain structure and function, it is difficult to generalize about the cognitive effects of these substances. For example, toluene exposure has been studied rather intensively due to chronic abuse by glue sniffers. This chemical preferentially affects the white matter and cerebellum (Rosenberg et al., 1988; Filley, Rosenberg, & Heaton, 1990), with impairments in frontal lobe functions and visuospatial abilities, whereas solvents such as tetrachloroethylene (perchloroethylene, dry cleaning fluid) appear to especially affect frontal/limbic systems, with particular effects on reasoning and memory (White, 2001). Similarly, lead appears to affect frontotemporal lobe function, resulting in memory impairments and problems with sustained attention, whereas methylmercury is known to preferentially affect the motor strip, the visual cortex and the cerebellum, resulting in visuospatial and visual-motor deficits. Although most chemicals have the greatest effect on cognition and behavior at the time of exposure, with some recovery following absence of exposure, some chemicals, such as mercury and carbon dioxide, can have delayed effects on the brain and behavior.

However, adult exposure to industrial chemicals generally affects some combination of the domains of attention, executive function, working memory, visuospatial and visual-motor skills, anterograde memory, or retrograde memory, with sparing of basic language skills, such as naming. A classification system for diagnosing neurotoxic disorders from solvents developed by Baker and White (World Health Organization, 1985) characterized the conditions of exposure (acute vs. chronic) and permanency of outcomes (brief intoxication vs. chronic residual brain disorder) in terms of severity (mild, moderate, severe). This system has been applied to the diagnosis of encephalopathy following exposure to many types of industrial chemicals (White et al., 1992a).

Neurological Disorders
Primary Progressive Dementias
The primary progressive dementias are disorders that are notable for progressive cognitive and behavioral decline due to a degenerative neuropathological process.

ALZHEIMER DISEASE
Alzheimer disease is thought to be the most common form of dementia. Neuropathologically, it is characterized by the presence of neurofibrillary plaques and tangles in the brain, accompanied by neuronal atrophy and loss of synapses (Alzheimer, 1907). Medial temporal lobe structures, such as the hippocampus, are the first brain structures to be affected, followed by the association areas of the frontal, temporal, and parietal lobes (Braak & Braak, 1991), with relative sparing of the white matter and primary sensory and motor areas (Bondi, Salmon, & Kaszniak, 2009). These neuropathological changes are accompanied by acetylcholine depletion (Whitehouse et al., 1982). The greatest risk factor for the development of AD is advancing age, with dramatic increases in the incidence and prevalence of the disease through the 80s and 90s. Family history of AD in a first-degree relative is associated with about a four-fold increase in the risk for other family members (van Duijn, Stijnen, & Hofman, 1991), although the genetics of the disorder are quite complicated and several genes have been identified

as causative. The apolipoprotein E (ApoE) 4 allele on chromosome 19 has been repeatedly found to be more common in AD patients than in controls (Corder et al., 1993). Alzheimer disease may be more common in women and in people with lower occupational and educational attainments (Bondi et al., 2009) and is seen more frequently in persons with histories of head injury, especially those who carry the ApoE 4 allele (Mayeux et al., 1995).

The neuropathological progression of AD—from medial limbic structures to association areas in the frontal, temporal and parietal lobes—is associated with the cognitive changes expected, given the structure–function relationships subserved by these brain areas. The most remarkable initial cognitive finding in AD is a decline in anterograde memory function seen especially at the level of retention of newly learned information: Patients forget both information and events very quickly. They also have trouble learning new information and begin to forget information that they have known in the past (retrograde memory loss). In this author's experience, the retrograde memory loss appears to work backward, with forgetting of information from more recent decades followed eventually by loss of memories from youth and childhood. In addition, patients with AD begin to lose semantic memory relatively early in the course of the disease, with inability to name common objects or find words, accompanied by errors in the semantic and phonemic quality of speech. Problems with executive function—problem solving, inhibiting distractions, and working memory—also begin relatively early, as do deficits in visuospatial skills. As the disorder progresses, deficits in all domains of function co-occur, and the patient becomes profoundly cognitively impaired. Table 26.1 summarizes the cognitive deficits seen in AD and in vascular dementia, the other most common form of dementia in the elderly. Alzheimer disease is often used as the hallmark disorder representing a cortical dementia, which is characterized neuropathologically by lesions in gray matter and functionally by widespread cognitive deficits. In contrast, disorders that are characterized as subcortical dementias are notable for pathology deep in the brain, below the gray matter, and for functional deficits in attention and executive function, visuospatial skills, manual motor speed and dexterity, and capacity to learn new information and retrieve it from memory stores, with relative sparing of language skills (Albert et al., 1979). Table 26.4 (below) summarizes several neurodegenerative diseases along the cortical/subcortical continuum.

Table 26.1 Alzheimer disease (AD) vs. cerebrovascular dementia (CVD)

	AD	CVD
Attention	Intact digits forward; problems with anything complex	Slowed reaction time, errors
Executive/working memory	Impaired	Impaired
Motor	Mild impairment	Moderate impairment
Language	Naming deficit with phonemic and semantic errors; reading intact until late stages	Word retrieval problems*
Visuospatial	Moderate impairment	Moderate impairment
Anterograde Memory	Severely impaired learning and retention	Impaired learning and retrieval; recognition/retention relatively intact**
Mood/Personality	Paranoia may occur; loss of "personhood" as disease progresses	Anxiety/depression may appear very early; fatigue common
Retrograde Memory	Remote > recent; loss works backward	May see retrieval problems across decades; retrograde memory sometimes worse than anterograde on tests

Summary of findings in early to moderate stages of the two disorders
*Unless there is focal ischemia in speech areas, when naming and other language deficits may be present
**Unless there is involvement of structures mediating memory retention

Because cognitive decline is the hallmark symptom of AD, research has focused on the identification of cognitive changes in the elderly that indicate the earliest functional evidence of disease onset. Initially, this work focused largely on changes in memory but has expanded to include progressive declines in other cognitive domains as well, with complex and competing taxonomies for types of decline. The term *mild cognitive impairment* has been applied to these taxonomies and may represent the prodrome of AD or other neurological disorders.

OTHER PRIMARY PROGRESSIVE DEMENTIAS

Other primary progressive disorders have been described that are often difficult to distinguish from AD in living patients but have distinct neuropathological features. Often termed the frontotemporal or frontal lobe dementias (FTD), these disorders include Pick disease (Pick, 1898, 1906), progressive subcortical gliosis (Neumann & Cohn, 1967), and dementia of the frontal lobe type (Neary et al., 1986). The underlying neuropathology is found in the frontal and/or temporal lobes, without the presence of the neurofibrillary plaques and tangles found in AD and with gyral atrophy confined to the rostral temporal and frontal lobes (without the characteristic

parietal involvement see in AD) (Moss, Albert, & Kemper, 1992).

These disorders are often misdiagnosed as AD, with the correct diagnosis discovered at autopsy. Research attempts to differentiate AD from FTD using neuropsychological data from patients whose brains were later biopsied have been summarized by Bondi et al. (2009, pp. 175–178). Taken together, these studies indicate that patients with FTD show poorer executive skills in the context of better retained short-term memory and visuospatial abilities than AD patients.

A condition called *primary progressive aphasia* (Mesulam, 1982), which is characterized by rapid loss of meaningful fluent speech, has also been described. This appears to be a clinical diagnosis that, on autopsy, has been shown to accompany several types of neuropathological degeneration, including that of AD and FLD.

Cerebrovascular Disorders

Conditions that affect the cerebrovascular system of the brain are also extremely common and occur at about the same rates as AD—and at higher rates in some countries (Fratiglioni, De Ronchi, & Agüero-Torres, 1999). These conditions can be caused by occlusion of blood vessels in the brain or hemorrhage. They include common disorders such as ischemic stroke, transient ischemic attack (TIA), cognitive syndromes related to vascular dysfunction diagnosed as or related to vascular dementia (vascular cognitive impairment, vascular dementia, white matter disease), and rarer pathological conditions (AVMs, cerebral aneurysms, and cerebral autosomal dominant angiopathy with subcortical infarcts and leukoencephalopathy [CADASIL]). Each disorder will be described briefly in terms of its pathology, followed by a description of associated cognitive dysfunction. In cerebrovascular disorders, focal cognitive deficits confined to very specific functions are often apparent, as are aphasic disorders and specific constellations of symptoms related to pathology in certain tissue classes. These focal cognitive impairments have been described earlier as related to specific parts of the brain (see the section "Focal Cognitive Impairments") and will be discussed briefly as appropriate.

ISCHEMIC STROKE

Strokes are diagnosed following the rapid onset of neurological deficits that cannot be explained on the basis of convulsions. Ischemic stroke occurs when blood vessels are blocked, causing cell death. Embolism (occlusion of a blood vessel by an abnormal particle in the blood) and thrombosis (blood clots) can cause vessel blockages (Victor & Ropper, 2001). Stroke is a very common cause of death worldwide, with only heart disease more frequently occurring as a cause of death (Paul, Srikanth, & Thrift, 2007). The cognitive sequelae of stroke are dependent upon the site of the stroke and the brain functions mediated by the structures at the stroke site.

Cognitive effects of stroke can be primary; that is, as the result of pathology in specific brain structures. For example, patients with strokes in the third convolution of the frontal lobe on the side of the brain dominant for language (Broca's area) may exhibit expressive aphasia. However, secondary cognitive effects of stroke also occur, as when a stroke occurs in a brain pathway connecting two brain regions, with cognitive deficits related to the functional attributes of the disconnected brain region. An example of the latter from the author's experience is a stroke in the thalamus disrupting connections to the right parietal area, resulting in a syndrome in which the patient neglected the left side of space. Many strokes disrupt pathways to the frontal areas of the brain (which are the most richly connected to other brain structures), resulting in secondary frontal lobe dysfunction. The latter can

be seen especially clearly on tasks assessing executive function (working memory, novel problem solving, complex attention, inhibiting distractions) and is generally less extreme than that seen in patients with primary frontal pathology. It should be noted that patients with multiple strokes may exhibit more than one focal neurological syndrome and that strokes can occur in the context of other neurological or cerebrovascular disorders.

TRANSIENT ISCHEMIC ATTACK

Transient ischemic attacks are currently defined as brief episodes (less than 1 hour) of neurological deficit following presumed ischemia in the brain or eye when there is no imaging or other evidence of brain infarction (Albers et al., 2002). The occurrence of TIAs in many patients is associated with clinical stroke in the period immediately following (Wu et al., 2007).

In the acute phase of a TIA, the patient may exhibit focal cognitive deficits, of the type described earlier for ischemic stroke, that quickly resolve. For example, the patient may be quite aphasic for a few minutes, with inability to produce coherent words or sentences, unable to produce low-frequency words for a period after that, and then fully able to speak. Following resolution, neurological deficit of this type often disappears. However, many patients have multiple TIAs, and there is evidence that half of patients with histories of TIAs show deficits or dysfunction on neuropsychological testing, although these may not constitute focal neurobehavioral syndromes (Bakker et al., 2003).

VASCULAR DEMENTIA

Vascular dementia is diagnosed in patients who have cognitive deficits, and who have greater pathology than would be seen with single focal stroke or TIA. Often, these patients have a combination of clinical strokes and microinfarcts without obvious clinical symptomatology. At one time, it was believed that vascular dementia was characterized by a sudden onset of focal neurological deficit with step-wise progression. However, only 40% of patients diagnosed with vascular disease have focal neurological signs or a diagnosis of stroke (Bowler, 2002). It has been suggested that there may be two types of vascular dementia. The first is seen in patients with clinical infarction(s), sudden onset, and focal neuropsychological deficits. The second appears after a critical mass of subcortical small vessel pathology has occurred, develops slowly, and the clinical course is remarkable for slow progression and deficits in cognitive abilities associated with frontal-subcortical systems (Brown, Lazar, & Delano-Wood, 2009). Tatemichi (1990) pointed out that vascular dementia may develop for several reasons, including the critical location of a stroke or strokes, volume of cerebral injury resulting from infarction, numbers of strokes occurring, and co-occurrence of stroke with AD.

The neuropsychological deficits seen in patients with vascular dementia most commonly include reduced fine manual motor speed and coordination, executive dysfunction, and impaired visuospatial skills. Deficits in memory function are generally limited to slowed encoding or problems retrieving newly learned information (unless a focal stroke has occurred in medial temporal areas), and language dysfunction is most often manifested in word-finding or word retrieval deficit rather than frank aphasia (unless infarcts have occurred in primary language areas). Changes in mood may also occur, especially symptoms of agitated depression in patients who have not previously experienced depressive disorders.

Vascular dementia is included in the DSM-IV as a diagnostic entity (APA, 1994, p. 146). However, the diagnostic criteria include memory impairment, focal neurological signs, and specific neuropsychological syndromes that do not occur in many patients, especially those who have not had clinical strokes.

The differential diagnosis of vascular dementia and AD can be complex because there is some overlap in the cognitive profiles of the two disorders and also because some patients have both disorders. However, a few neuropsychological signs, based on the author's experience, provide clues for this differential diagnostic dilemma and are presented in Table 26.1. In vascular dementia, mental control skills (e.g., spelling *world* backward) are often more impaired than short-term memory (e.g., three-word recall on the Mini-Mental Status Examination).

Vascular Cognitive Impairment
Vascular cognitive impairment (VCI) refers to the early, subtle manifestations of vascular dementia, and is similar in concept to the mild cognitive impairment discussed earlier in relation to AD. It is thought to reflect dysfunction in the white matter (Brown et al., 2009).

White Matter Disease/White Matter Lesions
White matter (WM) pathology is thought to be a major determinant of the cognitive and behavioral changes seen in vascular dementia (Brown et al.,

2009; Filley, 2001). Because loss of white matter volume is a feature of "normal aging" (Filley, 2001), assessment of the pathological consequences of changes in the WM is complex. Overall, however, lesions in the WM associated with vascular dementia are, in our experience, clearly associated with the motor, visuospatial, and executive dysfunction found in patients with magnetic resonance imaging (MRI) lesions in the WM, history of TIAs or TIA-like episodes, and risk factors for stroke or microvascular pathology (e.g., hypertension, cardiac disease, diabetes).

ARTERIOVENOUS MALFORMATIONS
Arteriovenous malformations are malformations of the blood vessels, in which they appear as tangles of veins and arteries without a capillary bed (Arteriovenous Malformation Study Group, 1999; Stapf et al., 2001). In many patients, AVMs are asymptomatic until they rupture, resulting in brain hemorrhage, or cause seizures. Neuropsychological deficits have been identified in patients with AVMs compared to controls, although the literature on this issue is confusing because it has generally failed to differentiate the cognitive findings in AVM patients with and without history of hemorrhage (see Brown et al., 2009, for a review). Arteriovenous malformations are treatable with surgery. In this author's experience, patients with AVMs and no history of seizures or hemorrhage are unlikely to show cognitive deficit, whereas those with ruptured AVMs often show focal and more general cognitive deficits related to the site of the AVM in the patient's brain.

Dural Arteriovenous Fistulas
Dural arteriovenous fistulas are a form of vascular malformation similar to AVMs, but located in the dura (AVMs can be located anywhere in the brain or dura). However, a dementia syndrome has been described associated with the occurrence of these lesions (Hurst et al., 1998; Matsuda, Waragai, Shinotoh, Takahashi, Tagaki, & Hattori, 1999; Tanaka, Morooka, Nakagawa, & Shimizu, 1999).

CEREBRAL ANEURYSMS
Bulges in the walls of brain arteries, cerebral aneurysms (CAs) have weak walls and are highly susceptible to rupture, causing subarachnoid hemorrhages. They occur most commonly in the circle of Willis; the associated cognitive deficits depend upon the site of the rupture and tend to be focal in nature. For example, patients with rupture of the anterior cerebral artery often experience short-term memory deficits. Cerebral aneurysm ruptures are reportedly

the fourth most common cause of stroke (5%–10%) (Adams & Davis, 2004).

CEREBRAL AUTOSOMAL DOMINANT ANGIOPATHY WITH SUBCORTICAL INFARCTS AND LEUKOENCEPHALOPATHY

Cerebral autosomal dominant angiopathy with subcortical infarcts and leukoencephalopathy is an autosomal dominant disorder considered by some to be a variant of vascular dementia (Filley, 2001, pp 151–154), although the associated neurological and behavioral features are somewhat different from those described earlier for vascular dementia. First described in 1955, in two sisters (van Bogaert, 1955), data from several large cohorts show that the disorder is associated with several different mutations on chromosome 19q12 (Tournier-Lasserve et al., 1993). Other diagnoses found in patients or families of patients with CADASIL include mood disorders, stroke, dementia, and migraine (Filley, 2001). Imaging and neuropathological studies indicate that, early in the disorder, distinct lesions occur in the white matter and merge as the disease progresses into a generalized leukoencephalopathy (Harris & Filley, 2001). Although gray matter lesions occur in some cases, the dementia associated with the disorder appears to be explained by the white matter pathology (Hedera & Freidland, 1997). This disorder is remarkable for its behavioral manifestations, which can be seen in the absence of overt neurological deficit. Frequently, the initial symptoms involve mood and neuropsychiatric symptoms (Filley et al, 1999; Harris & Filley, 2001), with later cognitive decline. The cognitive dysfunction is notable for abulia, perseveration, impaired vigilance, and poor memory retrieval in the context of spared language (Filley, 2001).

Diseases of the Motor System

Many diseases involve brain systems that mediate motor movement. In this section, we focus on parkinsonian disorders and those with related pathology and similar symptomatology, and on HD.

PARKINSON DISEASE, PARKINSONISM, AND RELATED DISORDERS

These disorders, which involve motor movement and arise from neuropathology in the basal ganglia and deep motor neurons, and/or the presence of Lewy bodies in brain structures, are considered together because they are similar in their clinical features and underlying pathology. Table 26.2 summarizes the severity of domain-specific neuropsychological deficits observed clinically in the parkinsonian and related disorders, and Table 26.3 provides details concerning the types of cognitive processing problems that are apparent within each neuropsychological domain for each disorder. The cognitive disorders associated with these diseases tend to be subcortical in nature or to involve a mixture of symptoms that are both subcortical and cortical. These distinctions are summarized in Table 26.4, which compares several parkinsonian disorders on the cortical/subcortical dimension.

Parkinson Disease and Parkinsonism

The term *parkinsonism* refers to a constellation of motor signs and symptoms that include muscular rigidity, disequilibrium, masked face, problems initiating movement, slowed movement, postural abnormalities, gait disturbance, and motor impairments in speech. This group of symptoms is evident in parkinsonian disorders arising from a variety of brain insults and events, as well as in idiopathic PD.

Table 26.2 Severity of domain-specific dysfunction: Parkinsonian syndromes

	Attention	Executive	Visuospatial	Motor
PD	+	+	++	++
PSP	+	++	+++	+++
CBGD	+	++	++	+++
DLBD	++	+++	+	+
PD+AD	+	++	++	++
PD+DFLT	++	+++	++	++

PD, Parkinson disease; PSP, progressive supranuclear palsy; CBGD, cortical basal-ganglionic degeneration; DLBD, diffuse Lewy body disease; PD+AD, Parkinson disease and Alzheimer disease; PD+DFLT, Parkinson disease and frontal lobe dementia

Table 26.3 Domain-specific deficits in parkinsonian syndromes: Qualitative

	Naming/Language	Anterograde Memory	Comments
PD	Naming generally intact; can see retrieval deficits; right onset cases may have more problems	Impaired learning, retrieval; visuospatial <verbal; intact recognition	Micrographia; hypophonia; depression, fatigue
PSP	Intact lexicon; affected by motor problems	Like PD	Extreme expressive problems; ocular deficit; echolalia possible; extreme cognitive and behavioral rigidity
CBGD	Mild to moderate naming deficit; semantic paraphasias	Like PD	Light drawings; wandering hand; affect/personality varies
DLBD	Naming varies; often retrieval deficit	Impaired learning, retrieval	Diffuse multifocal disorder
Extrapyramidal onset AD	Impaired naming w/semantic paraphasias, phonemic paraphasias	Impaired learning, retrieval, retention	Visual hallucinations w/PD sx and memory loss

PD, Parkinson disease; PSP, progressive supranuclear palsy; CBGD, cortical basal-ganglionic degeneration; DLBD, diffuse Lewy body disease; AD, Alzheimer disease

Parkinsonism or parkinsonian syndromes can result from medications (e.g., tardive dyskinesia following use of antipsychotic medications like Haldol), exposure to chemical toxicants (MTPT, solvents, manganese), viral infections, trauma (e.g., dementia pugilistica in boxers), and strokes or lacunes in the basal ganglia and associated brain structures. Sometimes the course of the disorder is different. For example, patients with toxicant- or stroke-induced parkinsonism may progress extremely slowly or not at all in terms of symptoms and disability once their clinical picture has emerged.

Parkinson disease is a common neurodegenerative disorder associated with aging, although cases can occur before age 40 and even in childhood. Its clinical presentation includes the parkinsonian symptoms just described, accompanied by pill-rolling tremor when the patient is at rest, small handwriting (micrographia), soft stuttering speech, and neuro-ophthalmologic abnormalities. Steps are typically small in size, all movements are slowed, there is stiffness in muscle tone when moving a limb (cogwheel rigidity), and the patient may report depression (McPherson & Cummings, 2009; White, Au, Durso, & Moss, 1992d). Parkinson disease appears to have a genetic component, and certain genes are seen more often in the families of patients with PD, but the exact genetic determinants of the disease are not well understood. The stage of the disease is often described in terms developed by Hoehn and Yahr (1967). In the first stage, patients exhibit motor symptoms only on one side of the body, whereas in Stage 2 symptoms occur bilaterally but there is no gait disorder. In stage 3, mild gait disturbance is accompanied by mild to moderate disability. Stage 5 is characterized by confinement to wheelchair or bed (White et al., 1992d). The depletion of the neurotransmitter dopamine in PD has led to use of dopaminergic medications for treatment. In fact, PD can frequently be distinguished from parkinsonism because symptomatology in patients with PD typically improves with these medications, whereas it does not in patients whose parkinsonian symptoms arise from other causes. In addition, PD patients usually show tremor, which is not seen in other forms of parkinsonism.

Table 26.4 Cortical vs. subcortical dementia

PD	Subcortical
PSP	Subcortical
CBGD	Both
DLBD	Both
Extrapyramidal-onset AD	Cortical

PD, Parkinson disease; PSP, progressive supranuclear palsy; CBGD, cortical basal-ganglionic degeneration; DLBD, diffuse Lewy body disease; AD, Alzheimer disease

Terminology for cognitive dysfunction in PD is disputed and confusing. Patients with PD and parkinsonism typically show dysfunction in multiple domains when undergoing neuropsychological testing. This constellation of neuropsychological deficits is seen most prominently in slowed fine manual motor speed accompanied by incoordination (White et al., 1996), and impairment in tasks assessing visuospatial skills, inhibiting distractions and perseverations, developing strategies for carrying out a task, solving novel problems in a flexible manner, or holding information in short-term memory storage and manipulating it. On verbal memory tasks, patients typically have more difficulty learning and retrieving information that is not logically organized (word lists, word pairs) than on organized verbal learning tasks like recalling stories. Learning and retrieval of visual designs is typically particularly difficult. Multiple-choice recognition paradigms generally demonstrate better learning of information than when patients are asked to spontaneously recall information. Speech is often soft and sometimes stuttering or poorly paced, but the linguistic (semantic) aspects of speech are generally well retained (e.g., knowing the names of objects). Word-list generation is generally difficult for patients with PD and parkinsonism. Handwriting is typically small (micrographia). In unilateral parkinsonism or stage 1 PD, the cognitive profile sometimes appears to reflect the functioning of the contralateral hemisphere: For example, patients with right-sided onset of motor symptoms may have more trouble than others with verbal tasks, whereas left-onset patients may have disproportionate visuospatial dysfunction. Parkinson disease–associated neuropsychological findings are sometimes referred to as a *subcortical dementia* (see Table 26.4) or simply the neuropsychological profile accompanying PD or parkinsonism (White et al. 1992d).

The term "Parkinson disease dementia" (PDD) has been applied to patients with especially marked presentations of this just-described cognitive profile. Said to affect about 40% of PD patients (Emre, 2003), this syndrome was summarized by McPherson and Cummings (2009) as being characterized by especially severe deficits in executive and visuospatial function, accompanied by anterograde memory impairment that is more severe than in patients with PD without dementia but not as severe as seen in AD. This manifestation of cognitive decline in PD fits the DSM-IV description of dementia associated with a medical condition (PD) well.

Some PD and parkinsonism patients have concurrent AD. Our experience suggests that, in these cases, the cognitive profile of AD tends to predominate, although visuospatial and motor deficits are more prominent than those typically seen in AD. Patients with AD whose clinical course begins with an extrapyramidal motor onset are sometimes seen. In these patients, the correct diagnosis becomes apparent over time, the patient does not respond to dopaminergic medications, and the clinical course of AD predominates.

Lewy body disease

Lewy body disease (LBD) is neuropathologically related to the widespread occurrence of Lewy bodies in the brain. Lewy bodies are also present in both PD and AD, so that LBD can sometimes be difficult to differentiate from the other two disorders. It is remarkable for parkinsonian symptoms, visual hallucinations, and uneven alertness (McKeith et al., 2005). Impairments in attention and executive functions, as well as in visuospatial skills, are prominent, although confrontation naming and recognition memory are intact (see Table 26.3).

Progressive Supranuclear Palsy

Progressive supranuclear palsy (PSP) is characterized at onset by a tendency to fall and by a "doll's eye" gaze abnormality in which the patient loses volitional control of upward and downward gaze, as well as lateral eye movement. (Full eye movement can be obtained if the patient fixes on a target.) Tremor is unusual. Limbs are stiff and spastic, neck is stiff, and masked facies is common. Dysphagia and slurred speech are typical. The patient loses control of the voluntary musculature, eventually progressing to a "locked-in" state, with loss of voluntary speech despite consciousness and ability to process incoming information. The disease typically occurs in the sixth to seventh decade, with death following in 5–10 years (McPherson & Cummings, 2009). Neuropathologically, the disease is remarkable for loss of neurons in deep nuclei and loss of cholinergic neurons, along with characteristic neurofibrillary tangles that differ from those seen in AD (Victor & Ropper, 2001).

Progressive supranuclear palsy is the disorder from which the concept of subcortical dementia (Albert et al., 1974) was developed. The cognitive deficits associated with PSP are similar to those seen in PD, although the motor and visuospatial deficits tend to be much more remarkable. Speech is slurred, and echolalia may be seen, with anarthria in the later stages—however, naming appears to be intact but can be hard to evaluate given motor and retrieval deficits.

Learning of new information is possible but may be slowed, and verbal information is learned much more easily than visuospatial information; using recognition paradigms for assessment of memory functions shows better learning and retention than using recall paradigms. Mood is often depressed and anxious, characterized by sadness and isolation (see Tables 26.2, 26.3, 26.4).

Cortical Basal-ganglionic Degeneration

Cortical basal-ganglionic degeneration (CBDG) is a slowly progressive disorder with underlying neuropathology in the basal ganglia and cerebral cortex. It was first described by Rebiez and colleagues in a report on three cases in 1968 (Rebiez et al., 1968). This syndrome is remarkable for onset of various motor symptoms that appear most prominently on one side of the body and a distinctive syndrome in which the patient loses control of an arm or hand, so that it flies upward. Motor features of the disorder include rigidity, loss of kinesis, dystonia, myoclonus, and postural instability. Neuropathologically, the disease is marked by degeneration of the substantia nigra and motor nuclei, accompanied by posterior (parietal) cortical degeneration. The cognitive manifestations are quite interesting, because the patient may show lateralized brain dysfunction (especially in the early stages, when prominent lateralized motor symptomatology is present), and the dementia associated with the disorder includes elements of frontal-subcortical dysfunction that are similar to those seen in PD, accompanied by elements resembling Alzheimer dementia. Consistent with PD, patients show impaired visual-motor and visuospatial function and short-term memory deficits at the levels of encoding and retrieving new information, although they are able to retain substantial amounts of the information they learned, as demonstrated when their recall is tested using multiple-choice recognition probes. Like patients with AD, they often have trouble with naming objects or pictures of objects (confrontation naming) and make semantic paraphasias (substituting an incorrect word for the target word) in speech or on naming tasks. Like patients with both PD and AD, they demonstrate executive dysfunction (Mimura, White, & Albert, 1997). They differ from these other patient groups in that their drawings are frequently very light.

Cerebellar Disorders

Spontaneous or inherited cases of atrophy of the cerebellum and nearby structures occur, as do cerebellar lesions in MS and following brain insults, such as exposure to chemical toxicants (especially solvents and ethanol) (White et al., 1992a). The cognitive sequelae of cerebellar disease can involve many domains due to the connections of the cerebellum to other parts of the brain (Schmahmann, 1991). The classic cognitive dysfunction apparent with many types of cerebellar lesions and disease are described in the section "Focal Cognitive Impairments" on focal structural lesion effects.

HUNTINGTON DISEASE

Like PD, HD is a disorder neuropathologically involving the basal ganglia. However, neuronal degeneration in HD involves the head of the caudate nucleus and the putamen, and it cannot be effectively treated with dopaminergic medications. The disease is named after George Huntington, who first described the disorder in 1882. Long known to be inherited as an autosomal dominant trait, the chromosomal locus of the HD gene was identified in 1983 (Gusella et al., 1983), and the mutation itself described in 1993 (Huntington's Disease Collaborative Research Group, 1993). The genetics of HD are interesting in that the gene is characterized by a trinucleotide repeat (CAG). The number of CAG repeats occurring on the gene in a particular individual at risk for HD determines whether he or she will develop the disease (>36 repeats), and predicts the age at onset of HD symptomatology (larger number of repeats is associated with earlier age of onset, with typical onset in middle age) and speed of progression of the disease itself. Huntington disease is characterized by motor dysfunction remarkable for involuntary movements and impaired capacity for voluntary motor activity, a "frontal-subcortical" dementia with many features overlapping with the dementias seen in parkinsonian syndromes, and affective symptoms that include depression, apathy, and irritability (Brandt, 2009).

The cognitive dysfunction that develops in patients with HD is notable for relative sparing of ability to name objects and other aspects of language (except word-list generation) in the context of impaired attention, executive function, and visuospatial and visual-motor skills. The impairment in learning and memory includes diminished ability to learn word pairs and visuospatial information, with retrieval of newly learned information being especially problematic (White, Vasterling, Koroshetz, & Myers, 1992c; Brandt, 2009), although there is some disagreement about whether forgetting of newly learned information occurs over delays (deficit in retention) (Brandt, 2009). This author's experience and the limited research on the progression of cognitive change in HD suggest that it is slow (White et al., 1992c).

Because the onset of HD is often in middle age (or even later), and because there is a genetic test that allows identification of individuals who will develop the disease, it has been possible to study prodromal cognitive change in HD prior to onset of the neurological symptoms. Brandt (2009) has reviewed this literature, which is complex, concluding that persons close to diagnosis may show cognitive changes, although those far from diagnosis do not (Brandt, Shpritz, Codori, Margolis, & Rosenblatt, 2002).

Structural Lesions
BRAIN TUMORS
Brain tumors account for significant morbidity in cancer patients, about 25% of whom experience a primary tumor or metastatic tumor in the brain. Only stroke exceeds tumor as cause of death from intracranial disease (Victor & Ropper, 2001, p. 676). Primary brain tumors include the infiltrative gliomas (the most common form of brain tumor), meningiomas (which are not in the brain itself), and CNS lymphoma. Metastatic tumors also occur secondary to cancers in other physiological systems and structures. In addition, paraneoplastic disorders occur in which disease occurring in other parts of the body (especially cancers) have focal or generalized effects on brain structures. The cause of paraneoplasm is unclear but may be related to autoimmune mechanisms. For example, cerebellar degeneration can be seen following tumors in other parts of the body (Victor & Ropper, 2001, p. 724).

The cognitive sequelae of brain tumors can be focal and/or generalized. The location of the tumor may be important, causing focal cognitive deficits of the type described earlier (see the section "Focal Cognitive Impairments"). However, due to edema and vascular effects of some tumors, cognitive effects may be more generalized and include confusion. It has been hypothesized that rate of growth determines how generalized the cognitive consequences of brain tumor will be, with fast-growing tumors having the greatest pressure effects (Gleason & Meyers, 2002; Hom & Reitan, 1984; Meyers, 2000; Hannay et al., 2004). Despite the possibility of generalized as well as focal effects of tumors on cognition, Luria (1966) agreed with the clinical experience of this author that focal effects of tumors are usually apparent (especially if they are noninfiltrative).

HYDROCEPHALUS
Adult presentations of hydrocephalus include hydrocephalus ex vacuo, in which the individual presents with enlarged ventricles due to normal aging or the presence of a degenerative dementia such as Alzheimer disease (Filley, 2001), and the cognitive problems seen relate to the aging process or another disorder. Acute hydrocephalus can also occur in adults, which may be related to hemorrhages due to various types of vascular lesions (Victor & Ropper, 2001, p.662). Normal-pressure hydrocephalus (NPH) is a condition that is diagnosed following a triad of symptoms that include cognitive dysfunction, gait disturbance, and sphincter incontinence (Adams et al., 1965). Although sometimes linked to occurrence of TBI, multiple white matter strokes, or infections, NPH is generally idiopathic in etiology. Cognitive deficits are generally secondary to frontal lobe dysfunction and, in the author's experience, may include impairment in judgment and reasoning, perseverations, inattention, and executive dysfunction (see also Filley, 2001, Ch. 14).

CALLOSAL DISCONNECTIONS
Disruption of the corpus callosum, a bundle of fibers that connect the two hemispheres of the brain, can be seen following surgical resection of the corpus callosum (a treatment for epilepsy) and due to callosal agenesis that may be congenital or acquired. The major cognitive consequences of callosal disruption arise from ineffective transfer of signals from one side of the brain to the other. This can result in slowed or poor integration of information in carrying out tasks. In the author's experience, this may also lead to rather dramatic symptoms involving motor function, known as "alien hand" syndrome. The patient's two hands may "fight" or work in an uncoordinated manner when putting block designs or puzzles together or in which the patient's hand does not follow the patient's intent (e.g., refuses to let go of a chair or other object when the patient tries to move away from it).

Epilepsy
Like the parkinsonian syndromes and primary progressive dementias, the term "epilepsy" covers a wide variety of symptoms and results from multiple underlying causes. Buchtel and Selwa define epilepsy as a disorder that "results from hyperexcitability in neuronal circuits, resulting from structural, genetic, or fundamental neuronal function" (Buchtel & Selwa, 2009, p. 267). When neuronal circuits

become "hyperexited," electrical activity in the brain generates a seizure, which can be characterized by motor movements, sensory changes, cognitive dysfunction, change in consciousness, loss of consciousness, and amnesia for the event. The event itself is referred to as the *ictal* phase. Behavioral changes can also be observed in the *preictal* phase just before a seizure (an aura) and interictally, when the patient is not having seizures. Single seizures have a number of causes, including fever, alcohol withdrawal, overdose of a medication, or chemical exposure, but epilepsy is diagnosed when seizures are recurrent and the patient demonstrates abnormalities on electroencephalogram (EEG). *Symptomatic epilepsy* refers to a seizure disorder (with recurrent ictal events) that has a clear etiology such as trauma, stroke, infection, or chemical or pharmaceutical exposure in the brain. The term *idiopathic epilepsy* is used when there is no clear etiology to the seizure disorder.

Ictal events are termed *partial seizures* when they emanate from a particular area of the brain, and further classified as complex partial seizures if the patient loses consciousness or is unable to remember the seizure. *Generalized seizures* occur as a result of abnormal electrical activity involving the brain as a whole. For an exhaustive listing of seizure subtypes, see Buchtel and Selwa (2009, p. 278) or the link that they cite at http://www.ilae-epilepsy.org.

Patients with epilepsy often show cognitive dysfunction on neuropsychological assessment when they are not having seizures and EEGs are normal on the day of testing. In patients with partial and complex partial seizures, the evidence of cognitive dysfunction is often focal or lateralized (see the section "Focal Cognitive Impairments" on the domain-specific evidence of focal cognitive impairment). For example, a patient with a seizure focus in the frontal lobes might have deficits in attention and executive function. Cognitive dysfunction is less focal in patients with generalized epilepsy. The most common form of partial epilepsy is temporal lobe epilepsy. If the seizure focus is in the dominant temporal lobe (usually the left side of the brain), this form of epilepsy is associated with naming difficulties (with lateral temporal foci) and problems with verbal memory (mesial temporal involvement). Patients with nondominant temporal lobe foci are more likely to have problems with visual memory and visual constructions. Temporal lobe epilepsy (TLE) has been studied extensively with regard to interictal personality syndromes that are thought to typify nondominant and dominant TLE (Greenberg & Seidman, 1992; Schomer et al., 2000).

Autoimmune Disorders

Some disorders that occur through inflammatory autoimmune mechanisms exert significant direct effects on brain structures and functions, resulting in cognitive changes. Two of these disorders—MS and systemic lupus erythematosus (SLE)—will be described here. For a more exhaustive review of some relatively rare forms of autoimmune/inflammatory disorders affecting the CNS and their cognitive sequelae, the reader is referred to Filley (2001, Ch. 8).

MULTIPLE SCLEROSIS

The cognitive, behavioral and symptomatic presentations of MS have been studied quite extensively, perhaps due in part to the difficulty in definitively diagnosing MS prior to the availability of clinical MRI methodology, which provides direct evidence of MS lesions in the CNS. Positive imaging findings accompanied by laboratory findings of abnormalities in the cerebrospinal fluid (elevated immunoglobulin G index, evidence of oligoclonal bands) are now critical to the diagnosis of this disorder. Current clinical criteria for MS diagnosis include the occurrence of two or more episodes of MS symptoms accompanied by evidence of at least two separate CNS lesions (McDonald et al., 2001). Multiple sclerosis symptoms include visual changes (visual field cuts, blindness, diplopia), motor dysfunction, slurred speech (dysarthria), and paresthesias. Patients frequently report fatigue as a very early symptom (White, Nyenhuis, & Sax, 1992b; Thornton & DeFreitas, 2009). Neuropathologically, MS is most notable for plaques in the white matter that occur preferentially around the ventricles, corpus callosum, cerebellum, brainstem, optic nerves, and spinal cord (Noseworthy, Lucchinetti, Rodriguez, & Weinshenker, 2000; Victor & Ropper, 2001). The disease is known to have a genetic basis and is considered very likely to occur because of environmental exposures interacting with genetic vulnerability. The types of precipitating exposures have not been well defined, although viruses and exposures to certain neurotoxic chemicals have been considered. The disease is much more common in women and in people who live in the extreme northern and southern portions of the globe.

A taxonomy for types of MS has been developed based on the course of the illness, occurrence of acute symptoms, and progression. The most aggressive and rarest form of MS, malignant MS, is associated with rapid progression and death, whereas benign MS is remarkable for few and mild symptomatic episodes even over a long period of time. Relapsing-remitting MS is the most common form of the disease in the initial stages and is remarkable for the occurrence of symptomatic episodes interspersed with symptom-free intervals. However, this form often develops into secondary progressive MS as the disease progresses, at which time symptoms are always present and worsening. Primary progressive MS is diagnosed when the patient shows progressive decline without symptom-free interludes from the beginning (Thornton & DeFreitas, 2009). These differing clinical courses of MS are important because they appear to be related to the cognitive sequelae of the disease, as well as to prognosis and course.

The neuropsychological test performance characteristics of patients with MS have been studied in several meta-analytic investigations combining multiple studies (Wishart & Sharpe, 1997; Thornton & Raz, 1997; Zakzanis, 2000; Henry & Beatty, 2006; Prakash, Snook, Lewis, Motl, & Kramer, 2008). Thornton and DeFreitas (2009) provide an excellent tabulation of these findings, with a summary of the research on frequency of "cognitive impairment" (performance at least 2 standard deviations below average) (Nocentini et al., 2006; Rao, Leo, Bernardin, & Unverzagt, 1991). These findings and our own clinical experience (White et al., 1992b) and the experience of others (Filley, 2001) suggest that MS patients can differ quite markedly in the cognitive deficits/dysfunction that they show. This may be related to site of lesions, lesion load, intensity and duration of progression of the disease, and other factors. However, some cognitive findings are quite commonly encountered as subtle or severe findings on neuropsychological tests. Slowed information processing and deficits in working memory are typical, as are deficits in manual motor speed and dexterity and on visuospatial tasks (including those that do not require motor manipulations). Word-list generation is often diminished. Effects are also seen on memory tasks and sometimes naming tests because of problems retrieving information from memory storage, including newly learned information and facts that a person has learned over a lifetime. On formal testing, ability to learn and recall visuospatial information may be more affected than learning of verbal information. This general pattern of deficits is similar to that seen in frontal/subcortical dementia (Filley, 2001). Cognitive deficits may be especially severe and even appear to be generalized during an MS exacerbation, in patients with a long course, or in patients who have significant cerebral atrophy associated with the disease. Partial or apparently complete recovery from cognitive dysfunction/deficits often occurs following recovering from an acute episode of MS symptomatology, and it is important that testing done during exacerbations or periods of acute illness be repeated to get an accurate idea of how well the patient can function in daily life during asymptomatic intervals (White et al., 1992b).

SYSTEMIC LUPUS ERYTHEMATOSIS
Systemic lupus erythematosus can affect multiple body systems, and the CNS is involved in up to two-thirds (West, 1994) or 70% of cases (Johnson & Richardson, 1968), a condition known as lupus cerebritis. The cognitive and neurological manifestations of CNS lupus have been attributed to widespread microinfarcts in the cortex and cerebellum (Victor & Ropper, 2001, Ch. 34) and white matter disease pathology (Filley, 2001). The cognitive dysfunction associated with SLE varies in severity but, based on our clinical experience, most prominently involves attention and executive dysfunction, visuospatial deficits, and problems in retrieving newly learned information in the context of intact language skills such as naming.

Conclusion
As this chapter clearly shows, the cognitive deficits associated with a vast array of brain disorders have been described in both the clinical literature and through epidemiological and neurocognitive research methodology. Patterns of domain-specific dysfunction and cognitive processing deficits or dysfunction have been identified for damage to individual brain structures and brain systems. Focal dysfunction from damage to these structures and systems can occur with stroke, brain tumors, and other structural lesions; following brain insults such as infections or trauma; and during the neurodegeneration that occurs in disorders like AD, parkinsonian syndromes, and MS, especially in the early stages. Some of the patterns of dysfunction that can be seen in these neurological conditions have been described as cortical or subcortical dementias. This distinction provides clues about the neuropsychological domains that are affected in a disorder, although the specific cognitive processing deficits and pathognomonic signs accompanying cortical and subcortical dementias vary among the disorders. The patterns of cognitive dysfunction and deficit that accompany neurological disorders and insults allow the neuropsychologist or behavioral neurologist assessing patients to differentially diagnosis likely brain structures affected in patients who

suffer from CNS disease using behavioral findings, especially in combination with history and imaging results.

The patterns of focal and disorder-specific cognitive dysfunction described in this chapter are far more detailed than those listed in the DSM-IV under cognitive disorders. In some cases, there is outright disagreement between the DSM and the neuropsychological and neurobehavioral literature. This is especially true in the domain of memory, which is described by the DSM as being affected in virtually all disorders. For some of these disorders, the neuropsychological literature might support a deficit in learning, although not in memory when "memory" is defined as the capacity to retain information over time. Furthermore, the clinical and research evidence from neuropsychological approaches to CNS disorders addresses more domains of functional cognitive processing deficits with greater specificity than does the DSM, providing a clearer picture of the cognitive profiles expected with different diseases.

Cognitive dysfunction can also be generalized, occurring in most or all neuropsychological domains, in patients with neurological disorders. This occurs especially when the brain damage is widespread and in the later stages of neurodegenerative disorders, when atrophy and collapse of brain structures occur. Generalized cognitive dysfunction of this type is termed *dementia* and can be distinguished from delirium. In dementia, the dysfunction is permanent, with little fluctuation or relentless progression, whereas patients with delirium frequently show great variability in dysfunction and may recover completely from it once the cause is addressed. This distinction is in accord with DSM definitions.

Future Directions

The fields of cognitive neuropsychology and cognitive neuroscience have exploded in recent decades, examining the cognitive and behavioral effects of CNS diseases and pathology with regard to the cognitive determinants of domain-specific processing deficits, brain systems approaches to understanding CNS disorders, functional and structural brain imaging evidence concerning the structural and systems-based determinants of cognitive deficits, and nosology of subtypes of disorders. Many questions remain:

• Would it be possible to develop a DSM for cognitive disorders associated with neurological diseases that succinctly defines them in a manner similar to the DSM approach?

• What will we learn about the determinants of cognitive dysfunction, using imaging techniques in which the brain is visualized while patients and controls carry out cognitive tasks? Will the structural determinants of similar patterns of dysfunction that occur over several disorders become more apparent? Will the differences between these disorders also become clearer?

• Brain banks have increased in number, in which pathological tissue can be examined and compared to cognitive dysfunction that has been assessed during the lifetime of individuals. What will this tell us about the relationships between neuropathology and cognition?

• What role does genetics play in cognitive disorders? Do certain genes affect the expression of patterns of native abilities with which individuals are born (i.e., life-long tendencies for attentional dysfunction, problems with verbal expression or comprehension, or deficits in visuospatial or visual-motor function)? What genes play a role in the development of certain neurodegenerative disorders or vulnerability to brain insults? What are the interactions between genes that drive native ability patterns and those that cause or predispose individuals to CNS disorders and damage (gene–gene interactions)? Are there gene–environment or gene–environment–gene interactions that are important in the development of certain disorders?

• Finally, the behavioral evidence strongly suggests that there are subtypes of certain diseases. For example, patients with AD often present with different patterns of cognitive deficit, especially early in the disorder. Alzheimer disease caused by autosomal dominant inheritance has long been thought to differ from "spontaneous cases," which we now know are often associated with inherited differences in the ApoE allele. Similarly, brain bank data suggest that the pathological findings in patients who have been diagnosed with AD vary widely, as do the relationships between degree of measured pathology and severity of cognitive dysfunction seen in the patient during his or her lifetime. How will the combination of behavioral findings, genetic information, imaging, and neuropathological evidence drive new understandings of the definitions of cognitive disorders?

References

Adams, H. P., & Davis, P. H. (2004). Aneurysmal subarachnoid hemorrhage. (2005). In J. P. Mohr, D. W. Choi, I. C. Grotta, B. Weir, & P. A. Wolf (Eds.), *Stroke: Pathophysiology, diagnosis, and management*, 4th ed. (pp. 377–396). New York: Churchill Livingston.

Adams, R. D., Fisher, C. M., Hakim, S., et al. (1965). Symptomatic occult hydrocephalus with "normal" cerebrospinal fluid pressure: A treatable syndrome. *New England Journal of Medicine, 273*, 117.

Albers, G. W., Caplan, L. R., Easton, J. D., Fayad, P. B., Mohr, J. P., Saver, J. L., et al. (2002). Transient ischemic attack: Proposal for a new definition. *New England Journal of Medicine, 347*, 1713–1716.

Albert, M., Butters, N., & Levin, J. (1979). Temporal gradients in the retrograde amnesia of patients with alcoholic Korsakoff's disease. *Archives of Neurology, 36*, 211–216.

Albert, M., Feldman, R., & Willas, A. (1974). The 'subcortical dementia' of progressive supranuclear palsy. *Journal of Neurology, Neurosurgery, & Psychiatry, 3*, 121–130.

Alzheimer, A. (1907). Über eine eigenartige Ekrankung der Hirnrinde. *Allg Z Psychiatr Psychol-Gerichtl Med, 64*, 146–148.

American Psychiatric Association (APA). (1994). *Diagnostic and statistical manual of mental disorders* (4th ed.). Washington, DC.

Antinori, A., Arendt, G., Becker, J. T., Brew, B. J., Byrd, D. A., Cherner, M., et al. (2007). Updated research nosology for HIV-associated neurocognitive disorders. *Neurology, 69*, 1789–1799.

Arteriovenous Malformation Study Group, The. (1999). Arteriovenous malformations of the brain in adults. *The New England Journal of Medicine, 340*, 1812.

Bakker, F. C., Klijn, C. J., Jennekens-Schinkel, A., van der Tweel, I., Tullejen, C. A., & Kappelle, L. J. (2003). Cognitive impairment in patients with carotid artery occlusion and ipsilateral transient ischemic attacks. *Journal of Neurology, 250*, 1340–1347.

Berg, E. A. (1948). A simple objective treatment for measuring flexibility in thinking. *Journal of General Psychology, 39*, 15–22.

Bondi, M. W., Salmon, D. P., & Kaszniak, A. W. (2009). The neuropsychology of dementia. In I. Grant, & K. M. Adams (Eds.), *Neuropsychological assessment of neuropsychiatric and neuromedical disorders,* 3rd ed. (pp. 159–185). New York: Oxford University Press.

Bowler, J. V. (2002). The concept of vascular cognitive impairment. *Journal of the Neurological Sciences, 203–204*, 11–15.

Braak, H., & Braak, E. (1991). Neuropathological staging of Alzheimer-related changes. *Acta Neuropathologica, 82*, 239–259.

Brands, A. M. A., & Kessel, R. P. C. (2009). Diabetes and the brain: Cognitive performance in type 1 and type 2 diabetes. In I. Grant, & K. M. Adams (Eds.), *Neuropsychological assessment of neuropsychiatric and neuromedical disorders,* 3rd ed. (pp. 351–365). New York: Oxford University Press.

Brandt, J., Leroi, I., O'Hearn, E., Rosenblatt, A., & Margolis, R. L. (2004). Cognitive impairments in cerebellar degeneration: A comparison with Huntington's disease. *Journal of Neuropsychiatry and Clinical Neurosciences, 16*, 176–184.

Brandt, J., Shpritz, B., Codori, A. M., Margolis, R., & Rosenblatt, A. (2002). Neuropsychological manifestations of the genetic mutation for Huntington's disease in presymptomatic individuals. *Journal of the International Neuropsychological Society, 8*, 918–924.

Brandt, J., Shpritz, B., Munro, C. A., Marsh, L., & Rosenblatt, A. (2005). Differential impairment of spatial location memory in Huntington's disease. *Journal of Neurology, Neurosurgery and Psychiatry, 76*, 1516–1519.

Brandt, J. (2009). Huntington's disease. In I. Grant, & K. M. Adams (Eds.), *Neuropsychological assessment of neuropsychiatric and neuromedical disorders*, 3rd ed. (pp. 223–240). New York: Oxford University Press.

Brown, G. G., Lazar, R. M., Delano-Wood, L. Cerebrovascular disease. (2009). In I. Grant, & K. M. Adams (Eds.), *Neuropsychological assessment of neuropsychiatric and neuromedical disorders,* 3rd ed. (pp. 306–335). New York: Oxford University Press.

Bruce, A. S., Aloia, M. S., & Ancoli-Israel, S. (2009). Neuropsychological effects of hypoxia in medical disorders. In I. Grant, & K. M. Adams (Eds.), *Neuropsychological assessment of neuropsychiatric and neuromedical disorders*, 3rd ed. (pp. 336–349). New York: Oxford University Press.

Buchtel, H. A., & Selwa, L. M. (2009). The neuropsychology of epilepsy. In I. Grant, & K. M. Adams (Eds.), *Neuropsychological assessment of neuropsychiatric and neuromedical disorders*, 3rd ed. (pp. 267–305). New York: Oxford University Press.

Corder, E. H., Saunders A. M., Strittmatter, W. J., Schmechel, D. E., Gaskell, P. C., Small, G. W., et al. (1993). Gene dose of apolipoprotein E type 4 allele and the risk of Alzheimer's disease in late onset families. *Science, 261*, 921–923.

Davis, S. J., Schockmel, G. A., Somoza, C., Buck, D. W., Healey, D. G., Rieber, E. P., et al. (1992). Antibody and HIV-1 gp120 recognition of CD4 undermines the concept of mimicry between antibodies and receptors. *Nature, 358*, 76–79.

Dikmen, S., Machamer, J., & Temkin, N. (2009). Neurobehavioral consequences of traumatic brain injury. In I. Grant, & K. M. Adams (Eds.), *Neuropsychological assessment of neuropsychiatric and neuromedical disorders*, 3rd ed. (pp. 597–617). New York: Oxford University Press.

Emre, M. (2003). Dementia associated with Parkinson's disease. *The Lancet Neurology, 2*(4), 229–237.

Feldman, R. G. (1999). *Occupational and environmental neurotoxicology*. Philadelphia: Lippincott-Raven.

Filley, C. M. (1998). The behavioral neurology of cerebral white matter. *Neurology, 50*, 1535–1540.

Filley, C. M. (2001). *The behavioral neurology of white matter*. New York: Oxford University Press.

Filley, C. M., Rosenberg, N. L., Heaton, R. K. (1990). White matter dementia in chronic toluene abuse. *Neurology, 40*, 532–534.

Filley, C. M., Thompson, L. L., Sze, C-I., et al. (1999). White matter dementia in CADASIL. *Journal of the Neurological Sciences, 163*, 163–167.

Fratiglioni, L., De Ronchi, D., & Agüero-Torres, H. (1999). Worldwide prevalence and incidence of dementia. *Drugs and Aging, 15*, 365–375.

Gleason, A. C., & Meyers, C. A. (2002). Relationship between cognitive impairment and tumor grade in pre-surgical patients with primary brain tumors [abstract]. *Journal of the International Neuropsychological Society, 8*, 274.

Goldman, R. H., Kalis, S. N., White, R. F., & Hu, H. (1994). Lead poisoning from mobilization of bone stores during thyrotoxicosis. *American Journal of Industrial Medicine, 25*, 417–424.

Gonzalez, R., Vassileva, J., & Cobb Scott, J. (2009). Neuropsychological consequences of drug abuse. In I. Grant, & K. M. Adams (Eds.), *Neuropsychological assessment of neuropsychiatric and neuromedical disorders*, 3rd ed. (pp. 455–479). New York: Oxford University Press.

Goodglass, H., & Kaplan, E. (2000). *Boston Naming Test*. Philadelphia: Lippincott Williams & Wilkins.

Goodglass, H., Kaplan, E., & Barresi, B. (2000). *The Boston Diagnostic Aphasia Examination (BDAE-3)* (3rd ed.). Philadelphia: Lippincott.

Grant, I., & Adams, K. M. (2009). *Neuropsychological assessment of neuropsychiatric and neuromedical disorders* (3rd ed.). New York: Oxford University Press.

Grant, I., Sacktor, N., & McArthur, J. C. (2005). HIV neurocognitive disorders. In H. E. Gendelman, I. Grant, I. Everall, S. A. Lipton, and S. Swindells (Eds.), *The neurology of AIDS*, 2nd ed. (pp. 359–373) New York: Oxford University Press.

Greenberg, M. S., & Seidman, L. J. Temporal lobe epilepsy. (1992). In R. F. White (Ed.), *Clinical syndromes in adult neuropsychology: The practitioner's handbook* (pp. 345–379). Amsterdam: Elsevier Science Publishers B.V.

Gusella, J. F., Wexler, N. S., Conneally, P. M., Naylor, S. L., Anderson, M. A., Tanzi, R. E., et al. (1983). A polymorphic DNA marker genetically linked to Huntington's disease. *Nature*, *306*, 234–238.

Hannay, H. J., Howieson, D. B., Loring, D. W., Fischer, J. S., & Lezak, M. D. (2004). Neuropathology for neuropsychologists. In M. D. Lezak, D. B. Howieson, D. W. Loring, H. J. Hannay, & J. S. Fischer (Eds.), *Neuropsychological assessment*, 4th ed. (pp. 157–285). New York: Oxford University Press.

Harris, J. G., & Filley, C. M. (2001). CADASIL: Neuropsychological findings in three generations of an affected family. *Journal of the International Neuropsychological Society*, *7*, 768–774.

Harvey, P. D., & Keefe, R. S. E. (2009). Clinical neuropsychology of schizophrenia. In I. Grant, & K. M. Adams (Eds.), *Neuropsychological assessment of neuropsychiatric and neuromedical disorders*, 3rd ed. (pp. 507–522). New York: Oxford University Press.

Hedera, P., & Friedland, R. P. (1997). Cerebral autosomal dominant arteriopathy with subcortical infarcts and leukoencephalopathy: Study of the two American families with predominant dementia. *Journal of the Neurological Sciences*, *146*, 27–33.

Henry, J. D., & Beatty, W. W. (2006). Verbal fluency deficits in multiple sclerosis. *Neuropsychologia*, *44*(7), 1166–1174.

Hoehn, M. M., & Yahr, M. D. (1967). Parkinsonism: Onset, progression and mortality. *Neurology*, *1*, 427–442.

Hom, J., & Reitan, R. M. (1984). Neuropsychological correlates of rapidly vs. slowly growing intrinsic cerebral neoplasms. *Journal of Clinical and Experimental Neuropsychology*, *6*, 309–324.

Hooper, H. E. (1983). *Hooper Visual Organization Test Manual.* Lost Angeles: Western Psychological Services.

Huntington's Disease Collaborative Research Group. (1993). A novel gene containing a trinucleotide repeat that is expanded and unstable on Huntington's disease chromosomes. *Cell*, *72*, 971–983.

Hurst, R. W., Bagley, L. J., Galetta, S., Glosser, G., Lieberman, A. P., Trojanowski, J., et al. (1998). Dementia resulting from dural arteriovenous fistulas: The pathologic findings of venous hypertensive encephalopathy. *American Journal of Neuroradiology*, *19*, 1267–1273.

Johnson, R. T., & Richardson, E. P. (1968). The neurological manifestations of systemic lupus erythematosus. *Medicine*, *47*, 337.

Knopman, D. S., DeKosky, S. T., Cummings, J. L., Chui, H., Corey-Bloom, J., Relkin, N., et al. (2001). Practice parameter: Diagnosis of dementia (an evidence-based review). *Neurology*, *56*, 1143–1153.

Langenecker, S. A., Jin Lee, H., & Bieliauskas, L. A. (2009). Neuropsychology of depression and related mood disorders. In I. Grant, & K. M. Adams (Eds.), *Neuropsychological assessment of neuropsychiatric and neuromedical disorders*, 3rd ed. (pp. 523–559). New York: Oxford University Press.

Lezak, M. D., Howieson, D. B., Loring, D. W., Hannay, H. J., & Fischer, J. S. (Eds.). (2004). *Neuropsychological assessment* (4th ed.). New York: Oxford University Press.

Luria, A. R. (1966). *Higher cortical functions in man.* New York: Basic Books, Inc. and Consultants Bureau Enterprises.

Matsuda S., Waragai, M., Shinotoh, H., Takahashi, N., Tagaki, K., & Hattori, T. (1999). Intracranial dural arteriovenous fistula (DAVF) presenting progressive dementia and parkinsonism. *Journal of the Neurological Sciences*, *165*, 43–47.

Mayeux, R., Ottman, R., Maestre, G., Ngai, C., Tang, M-X., Ginsberg, H., et al. (1995). Synergistic effects of traumatic head injury and apolipoprotein ε4 in patients with Alzheimer's disease. *Neurology*, *45*, 555–557.

McDonald, W. I., Compston, A., Edan, G., Goodkin, D., Hartung, H. P., Lublin, F. D, et al. (2001). Recommended diagnostic criteria for multiple sclerosis: Guidelines from the International Panel on the Diagnosis of Multiple Sclerosis. *Annals of Neurology*, *50*(1) 121–127.

McKeith, I. G., Dickson, D. W., Lowe, J., Emre, M., O'Brien, J. T., Feldman, H., et al. (2005). Diagnosis and management of dementia with Lewy bodies: Third report of the DLB Consortium. *Neurology*, *65*(12), 1863–1872.

McPherson, S., & Cummings, J. (2009). Neuropsychological aspects of Parkinson's disease and Parkinsonism. In I. Grant, & K. M. Adams (Eds.), *Neuropsychological assessment of neuropsychiatric and neuromedical disorders*, 3rd ed. (pp. 199–222). New York: Oxford University Press.

Mesulam, M. M. (Ed.). (2000). *Principles of behavioral and cognitive neurology* (2nd ed.). New York: Oxford University Press.

Mesulam, M. M. (1982). Slowly progressive aphasia without generalized dementia. *Annals of Neurology*, *30*, 69–72.

Meyers, C. A. (2000). Neurocognitive dysfunction in cancer patients. *Oncology 14*, 75–78.

Mimura, M., White, R. F., & Albert, M. L. (1997). Corticobasal degeneration: Neuropsychological and clinical correlates. *Journal of Neuropsychiatry, 9*(1), 94–98.

Moss, M. B., Albert, M. S., & Kemper, T. L. (1992). Neuropsychology of frontal lobe dementia. In R. F. White. (Ed.), *Clinical syndromes in adult neuropsychology: The practitioner's handbook* (pp. 287–303). Amsterdam: Elsevier Science Publishers B. V.

Neary, D., Snowden, J. S., Bowen, D. M., Sims, N. R., Mann, D. M. A., Benton, J. S., et al. (1986). Neuropsychological syndromes in presenile dementia due to cerebral atrophy. *Journal of Neurology, Neurosurgery, & Psychiatry, 49*, 163–174.

Neumann, M. A., & Cohn, R. (1967). Progressive subcortical gliosis, a rare form of presenile dementia. *Brain*, *90*, 405–418.

Nocentini, U., Pasqualetti, P., Bonavita, S., Buccafusca, M., De Caro, M. F., Farina, D., et al. (2006). Cognitive dysfunction in patients with relapsing-remitting multiple sclerosis. *Multiple Sclerosis*, *12*(1), 77–87.

Noseworthy, J. H. Lucchinetti, C., Rodriguez, M., & Weinshenker, B.G. (2000). Multiple sclerosis. *The New England Journal of Medicine*, *343*(13), 938–952.

Paul, S. L., Srikanth, V. K., & Thrift, A. G. (2007). The large and growing burden of stroke. *Current Drug Targets*, *8*, 786–793.

Pick, A. (1898). *Beitrage zur pathologie und Pathologischen Anatomie des Zentralnervensystem*. Berlin: S Karger-Verlag.

Pick, A. (1906). Ueber die weiteren Symptomenkomplex im Rahmen der Dementia senilis, bedingt durch umschriebene stärkere Hirnatrophie (gemischte Apraxie). *Monatsschrift fur Psychiatrie und Neurologie 19*, 97–102.

Prakash, R. S., Snook, E. M., Lewis, J. M., Motl, R. W., & Kramer, A. F. (2008). Cognitive impairments in relapsing-remitting multiple sclerosis: A meta-analysis. *Multiple Sclerosis, 14*(9), 1250–1261.

Prigatano, G. P., & Maier, F. (2009). Neuropsychiatric, psychiatric, and behavioral disorders associated with traumatic brain injury. In I. Grant, & K. M. Adams (Eds.), *Neuropsychological assessment of neuropsychiatric and neuromedical disorders*, 3rd ed. (pp. 618–631.). New York: Oxford University Press.

Rao, S. M., Leo, G. J., Bernardin, L., & Unverzagt, F. (1991). Cognitive dysfunction in multiple sclerosis: Part I. Frequency, patterns, and prediction. *Neurology, 41*(5), 685–691.

Rebiez, J. J., Kolodny, E. H., & Richardson Jr., E. P. (1968). Corticodentatonigral degeneration with neuronal achromasia. *Archives of Neurology, 18*, 20–33.

Rosenberg, N. K., Kleinschmidt-DeMasters, B. K., Davis K. A., et al. (1988). Toluene abuse causes diffuse central nervous system white matter changes. *Annals of Neurology 23*, 611–614.

Rosvold, H., Mirsky, A., Sarason, I., Bransome, E., & Beck, L., (1956). A continuous test of brain damage. *Journal of Consulting and Clinical Psychology, 20*, 343–350.

Rourke, S. B., & Grant, I. (2009). The neurobehavioral correlates of alcoholism. In I. Grant, & K. M. Adams (Eds.), *Neuropsychological assessment of neuropsychiatric and neuromedical disorders*, 3rd ed. (pp. 398–454). New York: Oxford University Press.

Rourke, S. B., & L berg, T. (1996). Neurobehavioral correlates of alcoholism. In I. Grant, & K. M. Adams (Eds.), *Neuropsychological assessment of neuropsychiatric disorders*. New York: Oxford University Press.

Schmahmann, J. D. (1991). An emerging concept. The cerebellar contribution to higher function. *Archives of Neurology, 48*, 1178–1187.

Schomer, D. L., O'Connor, M., Spiers, P., Seeck, M., Mesulam, M. M., & Bear, D. (2000). Temporolimbic epilepsy and behavior. In M. M. Mesulam (Ed.), *Principles of behavioral and cognitive neurology*, 2nd ed. (pp. 373–405). New York: Oxford University Press.

Seidman, L. J., Cassens G. P., Williams, S. K., & Pepple, J. R. (1992). Neuropsychology of schizophrenia. In R. F. White (Ed.), *Clinical syndromes in adult neuropsychology: The practitioner's handbook* (pp. 381–449). Amsterdam: Elsevier Science Publishers B. V.

Stapf, C., Mohr, J. P., Pile-Spellman, J., Solomon, R. A., Sacco, R. L., & Connolly Jr., E. S. (2001). Epidemiology and natural history of arteriovenous malformations. *Neurosurgical Focus, 11*, 5:e1.

Strauss, E., Sherman E. M. S., & Spreen, O. (2006). *A compendium of neuropsychological tests: Administration, norms and commentary* (3rd ed.). New York: Oxford University Press.

Stroop, J. R. (1935). Studies of interference in serial verbal reactions. *Journal of Experimental Psychology, 18*, 643–662.

Tanaka, K., Morooka, Y., Nakagawa, Y., & Shimizu, S. (1999). Dural arteriovenous malformation manifesting as dementia due to ischemia in bilateral thalami. A case report. *Surgical Neurology, 51*, 489–493; discussion 493–484.

Tatemichi, T. K. (1990). How acute brain failure becomes chronic: A view of the mechanisms of dementia related to stroke. *Neurology, 40*, 1652–1659.

Thornton, A. E., & DeFreitas, V. G. (2009). The neuropsychology of multiple sclerosis. In I. Grant, & K. M. Adams (Eds.), *Neuropsychological assessment of neuropsychiatric and neuromedical disorders*, 3rd ed. (pp. 280–305). New York: Oxford University Press.

Thornton, A. E., & Raz, N. (1997). Memory impairment in multiple sclerosis: A quantitative review. *Neuropsychology, 11*(3), 357–366.

Tournier-Lasserve, E., Joutel, A., Melki, J., Weissenbach, J., Lathrop, G. M., Chabriat, H., et al. (1993). Cerebral autosomal dominant arteriopathy with subcortical infarcts and leukoencephalopathy maps to chromosome 19q12. *Nature Genetics, 3*, 256–259.

van Bogaert, L. (1955). Encéphalopathie sous corticale progressive (Binswanger) à évolution rapide chez des soeurs. *Méd Hellen, 24*, 961–972.

van Duijn, C. M., Stijnen, T., & Hofman, A. (1991). Risk factors for Alzheimer's disease: Overview of the EURODEM collaborative re-analysis of case-control studies. EURODEM Risk Factors Research Group. *International Journal of Epidemiology, 20*(Suppl. 2), S4-S212.

Victor, M., & Ropper A. H. (Eds.). (2001). *Adams and Victor's principles of neurology* (7th ed.). New York: McGraw-Hill.

Wechsler, D. (1997a). *Wechsler Memory Scale. Third edition manual*. San Antonio: The Psychological Corporation.

Wechsler, D. (1997b). *WAIS-III/WMS-III technical manual*. San Antonio: The Psychological Corporation.

West, S. G. (1994). Neuropsychiatric lupus. *Rheumatic Disease Clinics of North America, 20*, 129–158.

White, R. F. (Ed.). (1992). *Clinical syndromes in adult neuropsychology: The practitioner's handbook*. Amsterdam: Elsevier Science Publishers B. V.

White, R. F. (2001). Patterns of neuropsychological impairment associated with neurotoxicants. *Clinics in Occupational and Environmental Medicine: Neurotoxicology, 1*, 577–593.

White, R. F., Au, R., Durso, R., & Moss, M. B. (1992d). Neuropsychological function in Parkinson's disease. In R. F. White. (Ed.), *Clinical syndromes in adult neuropsychology: The practitioner's handbook* (pp. 253–286). Amsterdam: Elsevier Science Publishers B. V.

White, R. F., Diamond, R., Krengel, M., Lindem, K., Feldman, R. G., Letz, R., et al. (1996). Validation of the NES2 in neurologic patients. *Neurotoxicology and Teratology, 18*, 441–448.

White, R. F., Feldman, R. G., & Proctor, S. P. (1992a). Neurobehavioral effects of toxic exposures. In R. F. White. (Ed.), *Clinical syndromes in adult neuropsychology: The practitioner's handbook* (pp. 1–51). Amsterdam: Elsevier Science Publishers B. V.

White, R. F., Feldman, R. G., & Travers, P. H. (1990). Neurobehavioral effects of toxicity due to metals, solvents and insecticides. *Clinical Neuropharmacology, 13*, 392–412.

White, R. F., & Janulewicz, P. (2009). Neuropsychological, neurological, and neuropsychiatric correlates of exposure to metals. In I. Grant, & K. M. Adams (Eds.), *Neuropsychological assessment of neuropsychiatric and neuromedical disorders*, 3rd ed. (pp. 480–506). New York: Oxford University Press.

White, R. F., Krengel, M. H., & Thompson, T. A. (2009). Common neurological disorders associated with psychological-behavioral problems. In P. M. Kleespies (Ed.), *Behavioral emergencies: An evidence-based resource for evaluating and managing risk of suicide, violence, and victimization* (pp. 289–309). Washington DC: American Psychological Association.

White, R. F., Nyenhuis, D. S., & Sax, D. S. (1992b). Multiple sclerosis. In R. F. White (Ed.), *Clinical syndromes in adult neuropsychology: The practitioner's handbook* (pp. 176–212). Amsterdam: Elsevier Science Publishers B. V.

White, R. F., Vasterling, J. J., Koroshetz, W., & Myers, R. (1992c). Neuropsychology of Huntington's disease. In R. F. White (Ed.), *Clinical syndromes in adult neuropsychology: The practitioner's handbook* (pp. 213–251). Amsterdam: Elsevier Science Publishers B. V.

Whitehouse, P. J., Price, D. L., Struble, R. G., Clark, A. W., Coyle J. T., & DeLong, M. R. (1982). Alzheimer's disease and senile dementia: Loss of neurons in the basal forebrain. *Science, 215,* 1237–1239.

Wilkinson, G. S. (1993). *WRAT3: Wide Range Achievement Test.* Wilmington: Wide Range, Inc.

Wishart, H., & Sharpe, D. (1997). Neuropsychological aspects of multiple sclerosis: A quantitative review. *Journal of Clinical and Experimental Neuropsychology, 19*(6), 810–824.

Woods, S. P., Carey, C. L., Ludicello, J. E., Letendre, S.L., Fennema-Notestine, C., & Grant, I. (2009). Neuropsychological aspects of HIV infection. In I. Grant, & K. M. Adams (Eds.), *Neuropsychological assessment of neuropsychiatric and neuromedical disorders*, 3rd ed. (pp. 366–397). New York: Oxford University Press.

World Health Organization, Baker E. L., & White, R. F. (1985). *Chronic effects of organic solvents on the central nervous system and diagnostic criteria.* Copenhagen: World Health Organization and Oslo: Nordic Council of Ministers. Reprinted by the U.S. Department of Health and Human Services, Public Health Service.

Wu, C. M., McLaughlin, K., Lorenzetti, D. L., Hill, M. D., Manns, B. J., & Ghali, W. A. (2007). Early risk of stroke after transient ischemic attack. *Archives of Internal Medicine, 167,* 2417–2422.

Zakzanis, K. K. (2000). Distinct neurocognitive profiles in multiple sclerosis subtypes. *Archives of Clinical Neuropsychology, 15*(2), 115–136.

Further Reading

Filley, C. M. (2001). *The behavioral neurology of white matter.* New York: Oxford University Press. Outlines the cognitive correlates of many diseases affecting the white matter of the brain.

Grant, I., & Adams, K. M. (2009). *Neuropsychological assessment of neuropsychiatric and neuromedical disorders* (3rd ed.). New York: Oxford University Press. Covers neuropsychological assessment techniques, cognitive determinants of functions of daily living, and the cognitive manifestations of a number of neurological, medical and psychiatric disorders.

Lezak, M. D., Howieson, D. B., Loring, D. W., Hannay, H. J., & Fischer, J. S. (Eds.). (2004). *Neuropsychological assessment* (4th ed.). New York: Oxford University Press. Describes numerous neuropsychological tests, including findings for a variety of neurological, medical, and psychiatric disorders associated with the tests.

Luria, A. R. (1966). *Higher cortical functions in man.* New York: Basic Books, Inc. and Consultants Bureau Enterprises. Classic work describing the cognitive effects of focal brain damage.

Mesulam, M. M. (Ed.). (2000). *Principles of behavioral and cognitive neurology* (2nd ed.). New York: Oxford University Press. Systems-based approach to describing the relationships between brain damage and behavior. Covers a number of neurobehavioral disorders.

Strauss, E., Sherman E. M. S, & Spreen, O. (2006). *A compendium of neuropsychological tests: Administration, norms and commentary* (3rd ed.). New York: Oxford University Press. Details the psychometric properties of many neuropsychological tests, including some data involving neurological disorders and aging.

White, R. F. (Ed.). (1992). *Clinical syndromes in adult neuropsychology: The practitioner's handbook.* Amsterdam: Elsevier Science Publishers B. V. Describes the patterns of clinical deficit associated with a number of neurological diseases, including case studies and clinical case material (drawings, language samples, writing, etc.).

PART 4

Specialty Areas and Trends in Practice

Clinical Psychology Interventions in Primary Care

Leonard J. Haas

Abstract

This chapter reviews the need for clinical psychology services that are integrated into the primary health-care environment and covers in depth the issues that an effective primary care clinical psychologist must understand to function effectively in primary care. These are understanding the primary medical care environment, recognizing the unique characteristics of primary medical care patients who seek psychological services, and the key treatment tactics and strategies necessary for effective work in a primary care environment. Recommendations are illustrated with numerous case examples adapted from the experiences of a veteran primary care clinical psychologist.

Keywords: Boundaries, brief treatment, medication, patient perspectives on psychological treatment, physician–psychologist collaboration, problem-focused psychotherapy, somatic complaints, teamwork, therapeutic partnerships, underserved populations

The role of the clinical psychologist in primary care, and the need for such a role, can best be appreciated by considering the following facts:

• Most citizens in the United States (and arguably, in most other countries) obtain their health care in the primary medical care setting. In the United States, primary care is usually offered in outpatient clinics staffed by family physicians, general internists, pediatrics, obstetrician-gynecologists, or some combination of these specialties (Beardsley, Gardocki, Larson, & Hidalgo, 1988; Flocke, Frank, & Wenger, 2001; Green, Fryer, Yawn, Lanier, & Dovey, 2001; Katon et al., 1990; Kroenke et al., 1994; Mojtabai & Olfson, 2008). Not surprisingly, the primary care setting is also the one in which most psychosocial and psychiatric problems are first presented. Most individuals in need of mental health services will turn to their primary care physician as their first and sometimes only source of help (Cauce et al., 2002) and, indeed, most researchers suggest that

half or more of common mental disorders are treated exclusively in the primary care sector (Bea & Tesar, 2002). The prevalence of these disorders is substantial. Conservative estimates suggest that 18.5% of U.S. adults meet criteria for a mental health problem that significantly affects their functioning or well-being (Narrow, Rae, Robins, & Regier, 2002).

• The distinction between physical and mental health problems is increasingly problematic: The medical conditions seen in primary care frequently involve chronic diseases related to patients' behaviors, attitudes, relationships, and social environments, including physical inactivity, poor diet, obesity, smoking, and poor adherence to recommended medical regimens (Smedley & Syme, 2000; World Health Organization, 2003). For a variety of reasons, psychologically distressed patients experience increased physical symptomatology (Katon et al., 1990; Kroenke et al., 1994); patients with these "biopsychosocial" problems use medical resources at up to twice the baseline utilization rates (deGruy, 1996). In some cases, such as with somatization disorder, the increased utilization is extraordinary—up to nine times the national norm (Smith, 1994). There are also additional substantial numbers of patients with conditions such as hypertension, diabetes, functional gastrointestinal disorders, or low back pain who could benefit from clinical health psychology interventions (Trask et al., 2002) either because they need help making changes in their health behavior or they are distressed and stressed by having the illness.

• Primary care physicians have difficulty detecting and/or addressing these mental health or psychosocial issues effectively (Andersen & Harthorn, 1989; Christensen, Fetters, & Green, 2005; Kolbasovsky, Reich, Romano, & Jaramillo, 2005; Yeung et al., 2004). In cases of chronic diseases, which require self-management, primary care physicians have difficulty effectively addressing patients' motivations, behavior, and relationships, and particularly their seemingly irrational failures to adhere to medical recommendations (Katon et al., 2001). In cases of psychiatric disorders, those primary care clinicians who detect psychiatric issues frequently have difficulty informing the patient of their diagnosis: patients reject mental diagnoses since they strongly resist the idea that "this is all in my head" or "I have a mental illness" (Freidin, Goldman, & Cecil, 1980). Studies of time use in primary care visits (Deveugele, Derese, van den Brink-Muinen, Bensing, & De Maeseneer, 2002) suggest that when the physician considers the problem psychological but the patient does not, visits last longer.

• When the doctor and patient do agree that a psychological problem is the source of the patient's complaints, the primary care physician's preference is usually to offer a prescription, and less commonly a referral to a mental health specialist. Neither of these approaches is terribly effective: The nonadherence rate for psychiatric medications prescribed in such settings approaches 50%, and the percentage of patients who resist mental health referrals may be even higher (Forrest, Shadmi, Nutting, & Starfield, 2007; Gonzalez, Williams, Noel, & Lee, 2005).

• If referrals to mental health specialists were acted upon, problems of access would immediately become obvious. Specialty mental health care in the United States (as in most societies where it exists) has much more limited capacity than does primary care and, as a result, barriers to access are common: less flexibility in scheduling and access, and usually higher costs for patients. Ironically, patients who surmount these obstacles still drop out of treatment prematurely, at rates of 30%–60% (Johansson & Eklund, 2006; McFarland & Klein, 2005). Because the "patient capacity" of a traditional psychotherapist is approximately 300 patients per year, it is obvious that any sort of reasonable referral rate would quickly overwhelm the available resources (of note, the typical primary care physician carries a "panel" of 3,000–4,000 active patients).

This state of affairs has resulted in the emergence of a subspecialty of clinical psychology focused on providing psychological services within the primary care environment, collaborating closely with primary care clinicians, and providing rapid-access consultation to these physicians. First conceptualized as biopsychosocial care (Engel, 1980) as an approach to health, psychological practice in primary care settings has been called *integrated care* (McDaniel & Campbell, 1997), *collaborative care* (O'Donohue, 2004), or simply primary care psychology (Haas & DeGruy, 2004). Regardless of its name (and indeed some clinical health psychology and behavioral medicine practices are conceptually overlapping), psychological treatment provided in the primary care setting offers a number of benefits to patients (and, arguably, to the health-care system as a whole). Psychologists' presence in primary care has been shown to increase primary care physicians' awareness of and ability to respond to psychosocial aspects of their patients' problems (Craven & Bland, 2006). Anecdotally, the availability of primary care psychologists also reduces barriers to obtaining psychological treatment and may facilitate treatment at earlier junctures in the development of disorders. Additionally, when psychologists and physicians provide collaborative primary care, patients' unhealthy behavior choices, distorted beliefs about illness, and difficulty adhering to medical regimens are more effectively treated.

Practice as a primary care clinical psychologist differs in many ways from the type of practice for which most psychologists were prepared. Consider, as an example, a fictional morning clinic session derived from the author's primary care clinic practice (the rapid, thorough chart completion in particular may differ in reality):

8:30 a.m.: Initial visit for Sally Jones, aged 53, referred for smoking cessation. Getting an overview of her life circumstances, the psychologist learns that she is recently divorced after a 10-year marriage to a physically abusive man. She has never discussed the abuse with anyone other than her children, who were quite unsupportive of her and didn't believe that their father could have been abusive. Resisting the temptation to explore this aspect of her history further, the psychologist focuses on why her physician referred her. She acknowledges that her doctor has tried to get her to quit smoking several times, concerned about her family history of lung and heart disease and her frequent respiratory infections. Although she recognizes that she "should quit," Ms. Jones believes that "cigarettes are my friends," and relapses after short periods of abstinence. Much of the session is devoted to understanding her attraction to such "friends" (and, implicitly, husbands) who aren't good for her health, and she agrees to "sign on" for a few more such "interesting discussions."

9:30 a.m.: Followup visit for Rifqa Bordomi, a 32-year-old Somali woman who is having difficulty parenting her adolescent son; she emigrated to the United States to escape the violence of that nation's civil war, and she shows symptoms of post-traumatic stress disorder (PTSD). Despite these symptoms, her major concern is the upsetting changes she is seeing in her son, who is increasingly alienated from the family and Somali culture. The son, who is in the waiting room, is invited to join the session, and a productive, brief family therapy session ensues, and both agree to a least one follow-up session together.

10:15 a.m.: In the "break room" between scheduled patients, the psychologist encounters one of the clinic physician, Harriet Obsidian. Dr. Obsidian is a compassionate, skilled doctor with whom the psychologist has collaborated frequently. Today, she is frustrated and distressed by how tired and sad she becomes when working with a particular patient, and she asks if perhaps she should transfer care of this woman, a patient who has multiple unexplained physical ailments. They have a productive discussion on the relationship between this patient and the physician's hypochondriac, querulous mother, which helps the physician recognize her uncharacteristically intense response to the patient.

10:30 a.m.: Eliot Turgid is scheduled for a consultation visit; Mr. Turgid is a married 46-year-old man who seems unresponsive to the selective serotonin reuptake inhibitor (SSRI) that was prescribed for him. Since a consultation was requested, the psychologist asks a nearby medical assistant to find the man's physician, who is able to join them briefly for the visit. Because of the patient's history and the fact that SSRI medication "makes me angry all the time," the psychologist suspects that that the most appropriate diagnosis for this man may be bipolar disorder type II, and speculates with the

patient and physician whether a mood stabilizer might be more appropriate for such a condition than an SSRI. The physician concurs, decides to prescribe valproic acid, and moves on to the next patient. The psychologist must then help the patient cope with this new diagnosis of a "serious mental illness" (in the patient's words), and to understand the nature of the disorder and its treatment, as well as engage him in follow-up treatment. In this case, the patient opts for an online support group, but agrees to keep the option open to return.

11:30 a.m.: Follow-up visit with Jimmy Karp, a 28-year-old electrician. Mr. Karp believes he's "crazy," but his only evidence for this is that his physician referred him to a psychologist (for stress-induced headaches, as it turns out). After a productive discussion of what health psychology has to offer for his condition, he agreed to treatment, but only if it does not involve a psychiatric diagnosis. Since his medical diagnosis is "atypical tension headache," the psychologist is able to code the visits as a Health & Behavior intervention. This set of codes does not require a psychiatric diagnosis, and after this was explained to the patient, he was amenable to treatment. The present session reviews the patient's progress in applying progressive muscle relaxation and deep breathing techniques, and in charting possible triggers of his headaches.

11:45 a.m.: The psychologist is paged to an exam room in which Dr. Obsidian is seeing a patient with asthma who is resistant to quitting smoking; a 10-minute discussion of what the patient understands the doctor to be recommending, and why, reduces the patient's resistance somewhat. When the psychologist suggests that the doctor and patient try an "experiment" to reduce smoking to "only those cigarettes you really enjoy," and agrees to meet with them for a follow-up visit, both agree to the plan.

12:15 p.m.: The reception desk asks if the psychologist could fit in a few minutes to see a young mother of three whose husband has been deployed for military service; she had brought her youngest in for a "well-baby exam" but the medical assistant noted how distraught she seemed. The psychologist meets with her for a few minutes, legitimizes her distress, and assesses her support system. She reports that she has several close family members living nearby, and feels she can cope reasonably well; she just feels temporarily overwhelmed for unknown reasons. A quick review of her circumstances reveals that she has been getting very little sleep over the past 2 weeks, and that a neighbor's husband who is also deployed was just severely wounded. The psychologist acknowledges the sources of her distress, gives her some suggestions for improved sleep hygiene, *and information about a deployed families support group that is available online, and explains how she can make an appointment if she feels it is necessary.*

12:30 p.m.: The psychologist finishes his notes and charts, which are entered in an electronic health record shared with the physicians in the clinic. He reviews his upcoming patient appointments and notes from the chart that his first afternoon visit is with a patient who has just been discharged from the intensive care unit; he makes a mental note to inquire about this, completes the charting, makes a few follow-up phone calls, and walks to a nearby café for a late (and brief) lunch at 1:00 p.m.

Of course, almost all psychologists must practice flexibly, since patients' needs vary. However, I suggest that encounters such as those illustrated here are both common in primary care settings and unique to psychological primary care practice, for several reasons:

• Standard 50-minute appointment times are often unworkable; flexible scheduling related to specific goals is necessary.

• The demands on the psychologist's skills change dramatically and frequently, at unpredictable times. A patient who is struggling with impulse control and shame issues related to compulsive shopping may have accumulated sufficient credit card debt that this has become the biggest stressor for her; she may need help with debt management before the underlying issues can be addressed. Other patients may simply need information, such as the patient who was convinced she had bipolar affective disorder because of pronounced irritability; she was enormously relieved after a brief visit in which her symptoms and family history were reviewed, and the conclusion reached that her irritability stemmed from sleep disturbance and job stress.

• The patient's social network by definition includes another important professional relationship—that with their primary care physician (and sometimes others including pharmacist, medical assistant, nutritionist, nurse practitioner, and physician assistant), and part of primary care psychology treatment often involves helping to resolve impasses in those important relationships.

• The patient population spans an enormous range, including patients who might typically be seen by psychotherapists; patients who are chronically mentally ill, who might be seen in intensive outpatient settings; patients similar to those seen in behavioral medicine clinics and pain clinics; those who would typically be treated in substance abuse clinics; those in crisis who would typically first be in contact with crisis intervention specialists; those in need of information, who might be seen by health educators; and those who would ordinarily not be seen by any sort of mental health or psychoeducation specialist.

• Medication is almost always at issue in primary care; patients are either currently taking prescribed drugs, considering whether to take them, failing to take them, or unhappy with them and desirous of being prescribed a "better" medication.

• Problems are multisystemic—organic, behavioral, cultural, interpersonal, familial, legal, educational, vocational, residential, or some combination of these—and patients' most pressing concerns are not always those the psychologist most wants to address (Haas, Houchins, & Leiser, 2003).

Primary care practice offers clinical psychologists the opportunity to serve patients on the "front lines," and to offer psychological treatment for an enormous range of problems. In addition, primary care psychologists serve a translational role; they may help patients and physicians resolve difficulties in jointly managing patients' illnesses, they may help physicians understand the application of psychological principles to patient care, and they may help patients understand the links between mind, body, and behavior. In exchange for these opportunities, primary care clinical psychologists may sacrifice some degree of professional autonomy. For example, the record-keeping system, clinic schedule, billing practices, choice of support staff, and fee schedule may be arranged by nonpsychologist administrators. Ideally, the needs of the psychologist will be considered in a well-functioning primary care clinic, but they will certainly not be paramount.

To have the desired impact on the medical care system and the population of patients which it serves, the primary care clinical psychologist must understand the primary medical care environment, must recognize the unique characteristics of the patient population, and must be able to effectively apply a wide range of psychological treatment methods tailored to the needs of the patient and the constraints of the environment. Each of these topics is addressed in greater depth in the remainder of this chapter.

Understanding the Primary Care Environment

The primary care physician is what most patients would call their "regular doctor." More specifically, primary medical care has been defined by the Institute of Medicine (2003) as "integrated, accessible health-care services [provided] by clinicians who are accountable for addressing a large majority of personal health-care needs, developing a sustained partnership with patients, and practicing in the context of family and community" (p. 7).

There are four federally designated medical specialties in primary care: internal medicine, family practice, pediatrics, and obstetrics-gynecology. In addition, physician assistants (and less frequently, nurse practitioners) serve as patients' primary care providers. Of the 850,000 U.S. physicians, one-third are in the primary care specialties (Pasco & Smart, 2003). The typical primary care physician sees perhaps 16–30 patients per day, in visits of under 15 minutes in length (Balkrishnan, et al., 2002). Although primary care physicians often consider themselves generalists rather than specialists, almost all are credentialed in a medical specialty, which means that they have had 3–4 years of residency training after obtaining their medical degrees and have passed a specialty board certification exam (Haas & DeGruy, 2004).

Primary care has been called the de facto mental health system in the United States (Schurman, Kramer, & Mitchell, 1985). For psychiatric conditions, most primary care physicians' first choice of treatment is medication, most notably SSRI antidepressants. Primary care physicians write most of the prescriptions for psychoactive medications in the United States, by some estimates, up to 80% of such prescriptions (Beardsley et al., 1988). Despite criticism of primary care doctors' skill in prescribing for psychiatric conditions, the evidence comparing them to specialists (mainly psychiatrists), suggests that their skills are equivalent (Mojtabai & Olfson, 2008; van Rijswijk, Borghuis, van de Lisdonk, Zitman, & van Weel, 2007). In addition, some primary care physicians (primarily in the specialties of family medicine and pediatrics) also offer counseling, although this has become less common as reimbursement has decreased (Himelhoch & Ehrenreich, 2007).

Efforts to categorize the types of problems addressed in primary care have demonstrated that the majority of primary care patients have multiple problems (Flocke et al., 2001; Kroenke et al., 1994). Research that attempts to cluster primary care problems suggests that two highly prevalent clusters involve pain-related problems and chronic disease management (Stange, Zyanski, Jaen, & Callahan, 1998; Weiss, 1999), and further suggests that the primary care foci can be conceptualized in groups of problems centered on lifecycle-related issues (birth of child, retirement, death of spouse, etc.), risky behavior (uncontrolled hypertension, excessive drinking, smoking), caloric balance (obesity and more rarely, anorexia), pain, and a large proportion of "medically unexplained" (usually categorized as somatoform) symptoms. Although many symptoms can be related to psychological disorders, most primary care clinicians do not consider themselves to be providers of mental health care, and prefer to either refer such problems or disregard them in favor of "competing opportunities" (Stange, Woolf, & Gjeltema, 2002) to provide help they feel competent to offer. This is perhaps an unintended consequence of dichotomizing patients' problems into "mental" and "physical," since doing so helps primary care doctors think of themselves as "not psychological providers."

The presence of a clinical psychologist in the primary care setting allows physicians to address patients' psychological issues more effectively. However, this tells only half the story. The complementary issue is that patients with psychological disorders often have unmet medical needs or masked medical problems (Grace & Christensen, 2007). Two-thirds of primary care patients with a psychiatric diagnosis have a significant physical illness (Spitzer et al., 1995; Spitzer et al., 1994). Thus, the second benefit to patients seen in integrated primary care settings is that their psychologists are exposed to more information about the patients' overall health, and are thus more able to detect conditions that should be addressed medically.

Example: A patient referred for treatment of depression was evaluated by the primary care psychologist, who inquired carefully about the specific nature of the patient's sleep disturbance and found that the patient was likely suffering from untreated sleep apnea. Discussion with the patient's physician and appropriate testing showed this to be the case, and the patient's mood improved as the sleep apnea was treated.

Nonetheless, the more frequent issue addressed by the primary care clinical psychologist is that of psychological symptoms being expressed somatically (Kroenke, 1992). As noted earlier, pain complaints comprise an enormous proportion of primary care visits, and recent evidence suggests the close association of pain and depression (Freedland, Carney, & Skala, 2004). The amplification of cardiac risk posed by untreated depression (and conversely the improved recovery rates shown when cardiac patients are treated for depression) is significant—and often overlooked when no psychologists are involved (Bogner & de Vries, 2008; Wells et al., 1989). Part of the translational role that the psychologist plays is to treat these conditions without forcing patients to adopt psychological concepts first.

Example: A 45-year-old woman was referred for anxiety treatment, despite the fact that she insisted that her symptoms were the result of poorly treated cardiac arrhythmias; she was successfully engaged in treatment and helped with her symptoms by framing the issue as stress caused by her fears about her heart; a variety of cognitive-behavioral techniques aimed at "calming her nervous system so as not to trigger an arrhythmia" were used successfully without resolving the question of whether or not she had an anxiety disorder.

Rich as they are in opportunities for improved patient care, primary care environments are deficient in one key element: time in which to capitalize on these opportunities.

The duration of the average primary care visit in the United States has diminished from the standard "office visit" of 20 minutes to slightly under 13 minutes over the past few decades (Deveugele et al., 2002; Mechanic, McAlpine, & Rosenthal, 2001). An indirect illustration of this change is the fact that the second (and final) edition of a text on psychotherapy in medical contexts entitled *The Twenty-Minute Hour* (Castelnuovo-Tedesco, 1986) was published the same year as the first edition of a similar book on counseling for primary care physicians entitled *The Fifteen-Minute Hour* (Stuart & Leiberman, 1986) that is now in its third edition (Stuart & Leiberman, 2002). This is true as much for psychologists as it is for physicians.

For example, a 30-year-old mother of three young children who is seeing the primary care psychologist for treatment of PTSD arrives 30 minutes late to her session; she has been scheduled for 50 minutes, but since the psychologist has a full schedule that day, only 15 minutes of remaining time is available. Not only is transportation difficult for this young woman, but the delay was caused by her accomplishing one of the goals she and the psychologist had been discussing—resolving the conflict between the need to immunize her children and her anxious fears that she would thereby subject them to the risk of an adverse reaction. She and the psychologist were able to have a 10-minute worthwhile session focused on the changes in her thinking about the immunization, as well as noting several relatively less anxious periods during the previous 2 weeks and clarifying what led to their occurrence (the remaining

few minutes were spent scheduling a follow-up visit and discussing what information to provide to the primary care physician).

During primary care office visits, patients typically present multiple complaints, averaging three per visit, but sometimes as many as 12 (Flocke et al., 2001; Haas, Houchins, & Leiser, 2003). The pressure of time often leads the physician to interrupt patients after (or during) the description of the first complaint, redirect the conversation to biomedical rather than socioemotional areas, and leave patients with unexpressed needs, unanswered questions, and confusion about their responsibilities for follow-up (Bell, Kravitz, Thom, Krupat, & Azari, 2002; Kravitz & Callahan, 2000; Kroenke, 2003).

Primary health care is rife with obstacles to effective communication in addition to time pressure. Significant numbers of patients can be characterized as having "low health literacy," or difficulty understanding medical instructions and recommendations (Baker et al., 1996; Rudd, 2007; Wolf, Gazmararian, & Baker, 2007). In addition, patients often have explanatory models or perspectives on their illnesses that are discrepant with those of the physician (Lang, Floyd, & Beine, 2000; Lang, Floyd, Beine, & Buck, 2002). For example, one compelling study showed that as many as two-thirds of general (nonurgent) primary care patients were afraid that their symptoms indicated a serious illness (Jackson & Kroenke, 2001). Half of these patients left their visits still concerned about this, even though their physicians diagnosed them as having mild or benign conditions. For a surprisingly large number of "presenting problems"—even complaints as simple as "cough"—patients entertain a wide and often discrepant set of possible diagnoses that can differ widely from those considered by their physicians (Bergh, 1998). At an even more basic level of communication, there are discrepancies between doctor and patient regarding such apparently straightforward aspects of the visit as whether or not a prescription was given (Lapane, Dube, Schneider, & Quilliam, 2007).

Understanding the Primary Care Patient

Although many patients may be typical of those seen in specialty mental health care, the majority of primary care patients have characteristics that make them unique. These characteristics often have significant impact on the patient's reaction to seeing a primary care psychologist, and on their response to psychological treatment. As noted earlier, it is axiomatic that the primary care patient "has" a primary care physician, and it is almost axiomatic that the patient has been prescribed medication for the presenting condition. In addition:

• *Primary care patients often have multiple comorbid psychological and medical problems.* Primary care patients often have both medical and psychological conditions, and often more than one of each. As noted earlier, the primary care psychologist must be familiar and comfortable with addressing the reality of patients' medical conditions, particularly when the biomedical and psychosocial conditions affect each other.

With respect to psychopathology, problems may be even less clearly defined. For psychologists coming to primary care from specialty mental health settings or academic treatment settings, it may be startling to learn how multifaceted and interrelated patients' psychological disorders can be. For example, the initial research into the effectiveness of screening primary care patients for psychopathology (Spitzer et al., 1994) found that nearly one-third of the respondents had three or more mental diagnoses. In the World Health Organization primary care study, seven of the eight specific psychiatric diagnoses studied had comorbidity rates of 50% or higher, the sole exception being alcohol abuse (Ormel, et al., 1994). The extensive co-occurrence of depression and anxiety in the primary care patient has been well documented (Parkerson, Broadhead, & Tse, 1996; Sartorius, Ustun, Lecrubier, & Wittchen, 1996), as has the overlap of anxiety and panic disorder (Kroenke, Spitzer, Williams, Monahan, & Lowe, 2007; Simon, Gureje, & Fullerton, 2001), depression and panic disorder (Ronalds et al., 2002), and Axis I and Axis II problems (Sansone, Whitecar, Meier, & Murry, 2001). Relevant to this latter point, a significant prevalence of Axis II disorders, particularly borderline personality disorder, has been found in primary care populations—again much of it unrecognized and untreated by physicians (Gross et al., 2002).

Examples: A woman diagnosed (and well-treated for) schizophrenia who also has asthma and smokes (the referral problem was smoking cessation); a political refugee who has been tortured (the referral problem was gastrointestinal pain); a university faculty member suffering PTSD from the vicious academic politics that have resulted in the loss of a significant position (the referral problem was depression and alcohol abuse); a newly diagnosed diabetic patient who responds to the diagnosis by binge drinking (the referral problem was "poor decision making"); a young woman with nightmares who is helped to connect the onset of her symptoms to her decision to accept a marriage proposal (the referral problem was "panic attacks").

• *Primary care patients frequently come from marginalized, vulnerable, or traumatized populations.* Primary care patients as a population tend to be older, less educated, poorer, and members of underserved or marginalized groups (Wells et al., 1989; U.S. Dept. of Health and Human Services, 2001) and frequently have fewer resources and more common risk factors for disease and disability—what deGruy (1996) has termed "psychosocial vulnerabilities." The prevalence of abuse and trauma histories in primary care populations is significant and related to both overall levels of health, as well as both "somatic preoccupation" (Sansone, Wiederman, & Sansone, 2001) and depression (Walker & Townsend, 1998). Abuse histories, in particular, are prevalent in primary care populations, especially among women, although the presenting concerns in these patients are often fibromyalgia, chronic fatigue syndrome, and sexual disorders, particularly dyspareunia. It is noteworthy that pain plays a significant role in five of the 11 clusters of complaints identified by Stange and colleagues (Stange et al., 1998). Further, recent work has elucidated the relationship between what may be termed "subclinical trauma" or "adverse childhood experiences" and later difficulty practicing effective self-care among hypertensive, diabetic, and pain patients (Dong et al., 2004).

Example: The patient is a 53-year-old domestic violence victim who is struggling to establish a trustworthy social network, and who also suffers hypertension and joint pain. The primary care psychologist's treatment plan involves attempts to combine the goals of socializing and exercise by encouraging exercise classes, and resolving the self-blame, fear and anger resulting from the abuse. The patient, on the other hand, wants most to figure out how to get her teenage son to apply for a job so he'll contribute to the household and lower her resentment over the expenses he generates. It is only after this issue is addressed with at least partial success that she is ready to turn to the issue of protecting herself effectively and expanding her social network.

• *Primary care patients often believe that their problems are not "mental."* Patients may be unfamiliar with, hesitant about, or even resistant to psychological approaches to their problems. Primary care patients typically do not view their emotional disorders as something apart from their general health and a considerable number (up to half by some early estimates) will refuse referral to a mental health professional (Forrest et al., 2007). The stigma of mental illness and resistance to getting help in treating it are still common cultural features in the United States (Cole & Rajum, 1996). For example, Kessler and colleagues (Kessler et al., 2001) found that approximately 60% of adults with serious mental illness were not receiving regular treatment, the majority because they felt that they did not have a psychiatric problem. The most commonly reported reason that these seriously mentally ill individuals gave for failing to seek treatment (72%) and treatment dropout (58%) was "wanting to solve the problem on their own" (p. 201).

Patients (and sometimes doctors) have a primitive understanding of the meaning of a psychological referral. It is often difficult for the physician to explain to patients how psychological treatment will help them; it is also difficult and frequently not directly addressed that a referral does not mean the patient is insane, does not require that the patient must spend years of talking about their childhood, and does not mean that the physician is abandoning the patient (although it is sometimes the case that physicians refer patients they would rather not continue to see).

Example: A despondent 34-year-old man whose clinical picture included irritability, sleep disturbance, anhedonia, and suicidal thinking refused medication and referral to a mental health specialist when his physician recommended it; in fact, he left the physician's practice. When he was later seen by the primary care psychologist, at the insistence of his wife, he was questioned about whether his prominent depressive symptoms has been addressed by his previous primary care doctor. He responded that his previous doctor had told him he was depressed, but he didn't believe the diagnosis; he felt that the physician was just trying to minimize his complaints and get rid of him quickly, and was particularly skeptical because "the doctor didn't even examine me." It was only after the psychologist successfully explained the methods by which depression is diagnosed, and why direct physical examination does not help to rule out the common medical conditions can cause depressive symptoms that the man became engaged in treatment.

• *Primary care patients often need community support or education more than (or more urgently*

than) psychotherapy. The primary care psychologist must think beyond individual psychotherapy to such nontherapy interventions as psychoeducational classes and support groups (Caudill, Schnable, Zuttermeister, Benson, & Friedman, 1991; Lorig, Mazonson, & Holman, 1993) and such self-help materials as books (Kemper, Lorig, & Mettler, 1993) and videotapes to provide timely, cost-effective help. The effective primary care psychologist must also have an extensive awareness of community resources such as 12-step programs, self-help groups, and community education classes (Kates & Craven, 1998), and should be open to the possibility of helping to develop programs in coordination with community agencies (Schroeder, 1997)—and perhaps even help patients to understand and coordinate their benefits.

Sometimes disparaged as "social work," or avoided in preference to psychotherapeutic exploration, such linkage and advocacy efforts for patients can often be the demonstration of caring that a patient needs, and they rarely result in "boundary" issues with patients.

• *Primary care patients often neglect basic aspects of self-care, such as diet, sleep, social support, and exercise.* Unawareness of the role that healthy sleep, diet, relationships, exercise, and stress management play in maintaining health is a component of the link between psychosocial vulnerability and poor health (Dong et al., 2004). The primary care clinical psychologist must be comfortable or become comfortable with the rapidly expanding knowledge base of clinical health psychology in order to best serve the primary care population. The reciprocal effects of sleep disruption and psychological stress, obesity, hypertension, and perhaps even diabetic control and pain control are only now being better appreciated (Czajkowski, Casey, & Jones, 2004).

For example, a frustrated family physician referred a "noncompliant diabetic" to the primary care psychologist practicing in his clinic, requesting a consultation about behavior change; since the physician was able to simply have the patient walk down the hall after the medical visit to engage in a brief initial psychological session, it was easy to engage her. Empathic discussion of her illness and her life situation revealed that her noncompliance stemmed from her preoccupation with taking care of her toddler granddaughter, whose mother was a drug addict and currently in jail. Believing that every available moment and dollar should be spent on her granddaughter, the patient was neglecting her own health. One session of cognitive restructuring, focused on the need for better self-care in order to provider better grandparenting, served to help her resume her regimen. This change was reinforced by informing the physician of the discussion, so that ensuing changes in the diabetic regimen could be framed in the same manner, and suggestions for care-giving that were less burdensome to the patient could also be provided.

• *Primary care patients often expect psychological treatment to be similar to primary medical care: continuous, episodic, and brief.* Expectations of continuous, problem-focused, episodic care are in keeping with the model of practice in primary care, but may be somewhat foreign to the typical graduate of an American Psychological Association (APA)-accredited training program, who was likely trained to "complete a course of treatment" and then "discharge" the patient. Patients (and perhaps even psychologists) should not be blamed for resolving a focal problem within a few sessions and needing treatment at a later date, perhaps months or years later, for a new concern. Although it is certainly worth an inquiry about reasons for the absence (or for the return), the primary care psychologist should not overinterpret episodic appearances for care. Instead, he or she should make it easy for patients to return for additional treatment if necessary, by such means as complimenting them for proactively seeking helping before even more distress or disability occurs.

• *Primary care patients often expect "directive" care.* A considerable number of patients follow through on psychology referrals only because "the doctor told me to"; the primary care psychologist cannot take for granted that the patient understands or accepts the premises under which most psychological treatment is conducted, particularly the emphasis on the patient's responsibility for self-defined treatment goals and the need to focus on thoughts and feelings, as well as behaviors. Those patients who do engage in psychological treatment may expect brief, practical, directive, and pharmaceutical-based treatment that is "finished" within a session or two.

Most psychologists would be rather wary of setting goals for their patients, and rightly so; however, the idea of giving patients a "menu" of possible goals of treatment that can be accomplished relatively quickly may be suitable and ethical. In addition to focusing on rapid symptom resolution, the effective primary care

psychologist must be able to rapidly "engage" patients. At times, it is necessary to briefly explain psychotherapy and counseling to patients unfamiliar with it; another sometimes uncomfortable role for many psychologists is "selling" psychological treatment: It may be necessary to raise patients' motivation for participating (without promising unrealistic outcomes). It is also noteworthy how uncomfortable nondirective approaches can make many primary care patients; jointly interviewing a new patient with a trainee freshly arrived from a "traditional" counseling psychology program, the author (uncharacteristically) allowed long periods of silence during the initial visit, which prompted the patient to ask: "Is it always this quiet in here?" The "engagement" phase of treatment is crucial but not sufficient to guarantee effective service, and the substrate of a good therapeutic partnership—caring, attentive listening—is essential as well (Adler, 1997; Sobel, 2008). Agenda setting is also a crucial skill (Haas et al., 2003; Mauksch, Hillenburg, & Robins, 2001), since the primary care psychologist may be under greater time pressure and be faced with a wider range of concerns than the specialty mental health psychologist. Primary care patients may have difficulty organizing their visits and respond poorly to unstructured visits. Skills at helping patients to increase their awareness of symptomatic and especially of symptom-free periods is of critical importance in such cases (Fisher, Lichtenstein, Haire-Joshu, Morgan, & Rehberg, 1993). Ideally, the primary care psychologist should have the ability to focus on interventions that have fairly rapid effects (e.g., within a matter of days); this often involves helping the patient to appreciate the importance of small behavior changes.

• *Primary care patients may have difficulty with their physicians, and may need help negotiating that relationship (or they may try to get the primary care psychologist to ally with them against the doctor).* "Difficult patients" are present in every primary care practice, by some estimates comprising 15% of primary care physicians' caseload (Haas, Leiser, Magill, & Sanyer, 2005). This is particularly an issue with patients who complain of pain. Naïve psychologists can be manipulated into allying with a patient against an "insensitive" physician who refuses to provide effective pain-killers (e.g., narcotics) to the suffering patient. The common currency of medical settings is physical complaints, so it is not surprising that somatic symptoms and pain complaints, as well as "inadequate treatment" and "unsympathetic providers" form themes that constantly recur in work with primary care patients. Patients who present with somatization disorders and back pain, fibromyalgia and chronic fatigue syndrome, irritable bowel syndrome and other functional gastrointestinal disorders—all common somatic expressions of distress in primary care settings—must be helped to shift the focus of sessions to adaptive coping, symptom reduction, and efforts to improve quality of life and away from complaints about the failures of medical care (Bradley, Alarcon, Cianfrini, & McKendree-Smith, 2004). These are frequently considered "medically unexplained" (e.g., frustrating, bothersome, annoying) symptoms by physicians, and patients often get the message that the doctor doesn't like them. As one patient put it: "My doctor thinks I'm not sick enough to spend time on," or as another patient reported "My doctor told me he hates patients like me" (later discussion with the physician revealed that he was trying to communicate that he wanted to be helpful and felt inadequate to help her).

> *Other examples: A 57-year-old patient with diabetes and chronic pain is convinced that her doctor will stop seeing her if she engages in treatment with the psychologist; another patient isn't taking the medication that her doctor prescribed because of unpleasant side effects, but the doctor is "so nice" that the patient is too embarrassed to "confess" and has begun skipping follow-up appointments with her physician; a third is a 28-year-old woman with bipolar disorder whose agenda is to enlist the psychologist in an effort to get her physician to switch her from a mood stabilizer to a stimulant medication, since she is convinced she has attention-deficit hyperactivity disorder (ADHD).*

Psychological Treatment Skills

The primary care psychologist must have a number of skills in addition to the specialized knowledge and attitudes touched upon here. The skill set can be summarized as follows:

• *The primary care psychologist should be able to skillfully address shame and stigma issues.* One key issue that the primary care clinical psychologist must address early in working with a primary care patient is the issue of stigma. Although psychological disorders and their treatment are more accepted and understood in the United States than in many other developed nations, there is still considerable potential for shame and

stigmatization of the primary care psychologists' patients, even in the most cosmopolitan U.S. city. As one Pacific Islander patient in an urban primary care clinic put it when seeing the psychologist for an initial visit, "This is for white people." Another patient, certain that sitting in a waiting room with a variety of patients still marked her as a "head case," insisted that she be able to phone the psychologist from the parking lot so that she would be able to get right into the office without being forced to sit in the waiting room. Especially since time is short, stigma must be addressed early in the treatment of the primary care patient.

Another and equally challenging issue is the guilt experienced by patients who have concluded (from popularized psychosomatic theorizing, TV shows, or "new age" therapists) that they have "created their symptoms" and are sick either because they are unconsciously producing the condition or have failed to use their mental powers to overcome the symptoms. The effective primary care psychologist must first tease out these explanatory frameworks, then help the patient to take appropriate responsibility for his or her condition. It can be helpful to distinguish for patients the difference between responsibility for *causing* the condition and responsibility for taking the necessary self-management steps to *treat* it.

Conversely, the behaviorally trained psychologist must recognize the biological realities of organic pathology and not insist that everything can be modified or cognitively restructured. Somatoform disorders represent yet another condition common in primary care, and are likely to trigger humiliation in patients who get the message "it's all in your head" (Lazare, 1987). A sensitive yet effective method of "stress reduction" treatment, which does not require argument with the patient about the "reality" of his or her symptoms, is most effective (Servan-Schreiber, Tabas, Kolb, & Haas, 2004).

• *The primary care psychologist should be able to skillfully integrate multiple perspectives on medication use.* Regardless of psychologists' opinions on the role of medication in psychological treatment, involvement in primary care will mean involvement in a drug-saturated environment. Prescriptions are expected by most patients and are offered with regularity by most primary care physicians. The effective primary care psychologist must have a working knowledge of common medications, since patients don't always know whether they're taking a generic or branded medication, or what class of medication they have been prescribed (Small, 2004).

Two additional medication-related issues are easily overlooked: Nonpsychoactive medications may affect mental and behavioral functioning, and discontinuation of certain medications can have significant psychological effects (Gunning, 2004). Medication interactions, and the effects of drug or alcohol use on medication effects, are also issues that the psychologist should be able to assess, since patients are often more willing to disclose to psychologists than to their physicians. For example, a patient who liked and trusted his primary care doctor nonetheless kept from him the fact that the patient was drinking substantial amounts of alcohol, a fact he revealed to the primary care psychologist at the second session, and reluctantly allowed the psychologist to share with the physician. An early and comprehensive "medication history" may be important in setting the stage for effective psychological treatment. Even in integrated settings with electronic health records, which in theory make sure reconciliation easy, there are times when sequential prescriptions can cancel each other out. For example, a primary care patient being treated for depression (among other issues) was prescribed both modafinil (a wakefulness-producing medication with stimulant-like properties) and alprazolam (a benzodiazepine antianxiety agent with sedating properties); the net effect for this patient was drowsy days and sleepless nights, which she and her doctor attributed to treatment-resistant depression, for which she was prescribed increasingly high doses of antidepressants. The primary care psychologist's tactful questioning of the need for all these prescriptions led to a more rational regimen.

The psychologist who is skeptical of medication must be careful not to undermine the patients' (sometimes shaky) motivation to follow through with medication prescriptions. Direct and frank discussion with both physician and patient, in order not to unwittingly sabotage the patient–physician relationship and treatment plan, is crucial. For a number of psychological disorders, the combination of medication and psychotherapy is superior to either alone (Nathan, Gorman, & Salkind, 1999). Thus, even in cases in which the physician has not prescribed for the patient, either doctor or patient may ask the psychologist for recommendations about medications or dosage when a particular agent is being considered.

The primary care psychologist must be skilled at managing expectations and clarifying his or her role in such situations. This is especially true when the primary care psychologist may in fact have more familiarity with the effects of certain psychotropic medications than does the primary care physician; it is also an issue when he or she recognizes treatable psychopathology that the physician is not addressing and could usefully prescribe for. Unless he or she practices in a state that has granted prescriptive authority to psychologists, this information must be phrased carefully in question form, or as an observation about what the literature suggests, so that the psychologist's scope of practice is not exceeded (Haas & Malouf, 2005). Examples of "translational" and tactful approaches that are factual include: "I have read that—is useful in conditions like this; has that been your experience?," or "I saw a patient not long ago who was on—for symptoms similar to what this patient is experiencing, and he seemed to benefit from that medication."

- *The primary care psychologist should be able to skillfully use directive and prescriptive techniques.* Not only should the psychologist be able to help the patient set priorities for brief solution-focused behaviorally specific outcomes, it is frequently also the case that patients need help in changing their health-related behaviors. Adherence to long-term treatment and self-management of chronic disease is a well-known problem in primary care and behavioral medicine (World Health Organization, 2003); it is less well researched but certainly prevalent in psychological treatment. Useful advances in psychological approaches to these issues have been made by Prochaska and colleagues (Prochaska, 2005) and Rollnick (Rollnick, Mason, & Butler, 1999) among others. More recently, cognitive social psychologists have contributed usefully to self-regulation approaches (Baumeister & Vohs, 2004) than can help tailor behavior change programs to the patient's specific environment.

For example, a primary care patient with anxiety symptoms was also found to have disrupted and insufficient sleep. The primary care psychologist was able to negotiate a 1-week "experiment" with altered sleep hygiene and an "emergency" supply of alprazolam, with the result of the experiment being symptom reduction, increased energy, and no need to use the backup prescription. This change required the psychologist to overcome the patient's reluctance to risk another week of disrupted sleep (the patient wanted to rely on sedatives), and to do this in a way that was not authoritarian but was persuasive.

• *The primary care psychologist should have good teamwork skills.* The therapeutic frame often must be expanded to include the patient-therapist-family-physician network. As Drotar (1995) has described, developing effective collaboration is often time-consuming and requires sacrificing some of psychologists' hard-won independence. Yet, improved integration of psychological and primary care practice can be as simple for the psychologist as sending a copy of an intake report to a patient's family doctor. At the other extreme, efforts to integrate can be as far-reaching as full integration into primary care systems, with no difference in patients seen, time allocated, or problems addressed (Robinson & Strosahl, 2009). Primary care physicians expect confirmation regarding the patient having made the appointment, regarding the treatment plan, and regarding changes in the course of the problem. These communications should be concise and should focus in particular on a brief, comprehensible treatment plan. Patients should be informed about this, although most patients assume that their clinicians are in communication. It is also helpful to think about the frequency of treatment: A psychologist might see a psychotherapy patient four times in a month but the physician might evaluate the patient's progress once a month. Therefore, a monthly report might be reasonable unless you share a medical record. Unlike confidentiality in psychological practice, confidentiality in primary care is often taken to mean that all team members who are committed to professional expectations of confidentiality can share information. Typically, the specialists to whom a primary care physician refers a patient will send copies of the chart back to the referring doctor without asking the patient's permission. This practice would be quite unusual for a psychologist. Nonetheless, physicians usually want information about "their" patients. At the same time, psychologists' patients expect confidentiality, so clarity about what information will be shared is critical (Haas & Malouf, 2005).

The primary care psychologist should also take care not to under- or overestimate the physician's degree of knowledge about psychological treatment and psychopathology. It is not uncommon for the only exposure to formal teaching about

mental/behavioral health issues to have been during medical school, and it may have consisted of a few lectures on psychiatry. At the other extreme, some physicians read the psychosocial literature, have attended workshops/CME events about mental and behavioral health treatment, have had psychotherapy themselves, and fully recognize the connection between the mind and the body.

A third aspect of teamwork is the often unspoken "ownership" of the patient. Competition regarding who "cares more about the patient" can develop, with destructive consequences if boundaries and communications are not clear. The psychologist must be careful not to triangulate the patient (or be triangulated by the patient) if there is disagreement about treatment plans. Collaborative relationships are the key. Primary care physicians become understandably defensive when their rates of recognition and methods of management of mental health problems are criticized, arguing in part that without adequate resources and with pressure to respond to other needs, they make rational decisions about the allocation of their time and effort (deGruy, 1996; Schwenk, 2002). In fact, the societal demands on primary care physicians to address an ever-broader range of health-related issues requires constant, sometimes painful tradeoffs. For example, estimates of the time required to successfully address recommended preventive medicine screening elements is 7–8 hours per patient (Balkrishnan et al., 2002), which means that one patient per day could be seen rather than the 25–30 patients that primary care physicians typically need to schedule. In addition, the rate of malpractice actions against primary care physicians, largely based on failure to diagnose life-threatening medical conditions, is also increasing. As Hamberger and colleagues (Hamberger, Ovide, & Weiner, 1999) note, doctors get sued for missing biomedical diagnoses, not psychosocial ones. The doctor who practices "defensive medicine" may thus spend time and effort to carefully rule out rare but dangerous conditions, with accordingly less attention paid to "softer" psychosocial issues.

• *The primary care psychologist should be able to skillfully intervene in doctor–patient or patient–health-care system conflicts.* At times (and perhaps more frequently in cases involving patients who use their medical symptoms as symbolic or interpersonal messages) the doctor–patient relationship itself will be an issue. The patient may be affected more deeply than the physician, and may want to address the issue with the psychologist.

> For example, a patient who developed a "crush" on her doctor asked the psychologist if the doctor was married—this led to a useful discussion of her natural feelings of closeness to the doctor, and a productive exploration of the difference between devotion (which he was showing her since she was gravely ill) and romantic attraction. It helped that the psychologist and the physician worked closely enough together that they could discuss this issue.

Power issues are often present in medical care: For example, physicians may refuse to continue to treat patients who disagree with the treatment plan (or patients may fear that this will happen), and psychologists may hear complaints from patients about how their physicians dominate or intimidate them. Effectively balancing the competing demands of such a situation requires family therapy skills. It is noteworthy that more satisfactory relationships between patient and physician are predictive of improved health outcomes (Smedley & Syme, 2000). The patient may need help in resolving conflicts, especially if they are frightened that offending their doctor means loss of care. Although it is more common for patients to feel that their physicians do not care about them, it is also sometimes the case that physicians can become overinvolved with their patients; this can lead to insistent and even aggressive pressure on the patient to "get better".

The primary care psychologist should be able to take on somewhat of a consultant role with either patient or physician. Just as patients may need help with direct communication, physicians may need help in accurately assessing their communication and negotiation styles, or lack thereof (cf. Drotar, 1995). Accurate constructive feedback is a rare commodity in medical systems (Ende, 1983), and respectful colleagues who can help primary care physicians recognize their limits and perhaps expand them will be highly valued. Commonly, the primary care physician makes person-centered attributions about patients' behavior, and the psychologist can help to reframe these attributions to ones that are more productive.

• *The primary care psychologist should be able to skillfully manage his or her own boundaries and care for his or her own damaged ego.* Often, before an

effective working relationship has developed between the two clinicians, a frustrating patient will be sent to the psychologist. Certainly, such patients should be given all the help the psychologist can offer. It may also be necessary to help the patient recognize that his pathology may be difficult for his physician. In such cases, family therapy skills can be an asset, since the psychologist may be working to improve the physician–patient relationship, rather than to directly reduce the patient's distress. Regardless of the outcome of treatment, prompt and concise follow-up communication to the physician is appreciated. Pager messages, phone calls, and e-mails should be responded to quickly, as this is often a metacommunication of professional respect in medical settings. However, it is also important to recognize that the sense of urgency and time pressure inherent in these settings can be wearing. Professional support is essential; for some psychologists who practice exclusively in the primary care setting, the pressure to prove themselves to their medical colleagues can pose the risk of neglecting self-care strategies (Cole-Kelly & Hepworth, 1991). For example, the psychologist who never sets limits, seeing patients at home if they prefer, or on weekends, or at no charge if they claim indigence, needs peer support to develop better boundaries. As well, the psychologist must know very clearly the limits of his or her competence or capacity while remaining a generalist (Haas, 1993; Haas & Malouf, 2005). Ironically, a common way in which psychologists enhance their status among peers will detract from their effectiveness with primary care physicians—this being the display of theoretical sophistication. For example, explaining to a physician who is concerned about the patient's dependent "inner child" why such "pop psych" object relations theory adds unnecessary theoretical baggage to cognitive schema theory will bewilder and annoy most physicians. Differing approaches to treating medical conditions certainly exist (e.g., surgical vs. pharmaceutical treatment of cancer), although they are rarely as passionately held as are differing approaches in psychological treatment (e.g. behavioral vs. psychodynamic). The primary care physician is more likely to value practical, common-sense advice, and even suggestions for phrasing interventions (Stuart & Leiberman, 2002).

• *The primary care psychologist should have effective approaches to detecting and treating depression and substance abuse.* Most psychologists would probably consider themselves skilled in depression treatment. However, since depression is the most prominent mental health problem in primary care, and since many primary care doctors are quite comfortable managing mood disorders, especially mild and moderate unipolar depression (Brody et al., 1994, 1995), patients referred by such physicians are frequently suffering from treatment-resistant depression, from Axis II problems co-occurring with the depression, dysthymia, or all of the above.

It is also common to be referred patients who were initially sent to a psychiatrist, even when the physician believes psychotherapy is indicated. Many primary care physicians do not realize how little psychotherapy psychiatrists actually provide (Kainz, 2002). Other common referrals include patients with somatoform disorders, borderline personality disorder, panic disorders, addiction problems, and dependent personality disorders (Haas et al., 2005; Kainz, 2002). An additional significant issue common in primary care settings is alcohol and drug abuse. Specialty mental health is typically distinct from addiction treatment, but this luxury is not available to the primary care psychologist, who must at least have a working knowledge of treatment approaches and community resources.

Conclusion

Practicing in the primary care setting offers unique rewards and challenges to the clinical psychologist.

The physical location of the practice within or adjacent to a primary care clinic is often used as the defining characteristics of primary care clinical psychology, but primary care psychology is as much a point of view as it is a set of procedures or physical proximity to primary care physicians. In addition to endorsing the philosophy of primary care, the primary care psychology approach includes a special regard for generalism; an integrative, biopsychosocial orientation; an awareness that resources are limited and must be managed effectively; a perspective on psychopathology that searches for and builds on existing competencies; attentiveness to opportunities for educational and preventive interventions; and a population-based perspective.

Primary care needs psychology because alone it will never effectively address the enormous amount of untreated psychopathology, significant lifestyle and behavioral health problems, psychological impact

of chronic illness, and the combined psychological impact of being ill and being a member of a vulnerable population. The pressured and overburdened primary medical care system cannot easily meet these needs, nor can the often-inaccessible specialty mental health system.

The psychologist who intends to make a meaningful difference in the quality of health care for the population as a whole must be involved in the primary care setting. Medicine is based on the *biomedical* model, but there is a need for a more inclusive *biopsychosocial* model if we are to fully understand the person who is the patient. Psychology, too, to the extent that it relies narrowly on the *psychosocial* model, would benefit from explicitly adopting the more comprehensive biopsychosocial framework. The primary care psychologist's knowledge and skill base draws heavily from clinical health psychology, behavioral medicine, developmental psychology, cognitive psychology, family psychology, systems theory, learning theory, and educational psychology, as well as from the philosophy of primary care. The bridging and translating role, although challenging, can yield enormous benefits—for the psychologist himself or herself, the patients, the physicians, and the health-care system. To the extent that primary care clinical psychology can bridge some of the disciplinary and philosophical barriers, it can help to improve both patients' health and the health-care system.

References

Adler, H. M. (1997). The history of the present illness as treatment: Who's listening, and why does it matter? *The Journal of the American Board of Family Practice, 10*(1), 28–35.

Andersen, S. M., & Harthorn, B. H. (1989). The recognition, diagnosis, and treatment of mental disorders by primary care physicians. *Medical Care, 27*(9), 869–886.

Baker, D. W., Parker, R. M., Williams, M. V., Pitkin, K., Parikh, N. S., Coates, W., et al. (1996). The health care experience of patients with low literacy. *Archives of Family Medicine, 5*(6), 329–334.

Balkrishnan, R., Hall, M. A., Mehrabi, D., Chen, G. J., Feldman, S. R., & Fleischer Jr., A. B. (2002). Capitation payment, length of visit, and preventive services: evidence from a national sample of outpatient physicians. *The American Journal of Managed Care, 8*(4), 332–340.

Baumeister, R. F., & Vohs, K. D. (2004). *Handbook of self-regulation: Research, theory, and applications.* New York: Guilford Press.

Bea, S. M., & Tesar, G. E. (2002). A primer on referring patients for psychotherapy. *Cleveland Clinic Journal of Medicine, 69*(2), 113–114, 117–118, 120–112, 125–127.

Beardsley, R. S., Gardocki, G. J., Larson, D. B., & Hidalgo, J. (1988). Prescribing of psychotropic medication by primary care physicians and psychiatrists. *Archives of General Psychiatry, 45*(12), 1117–1119.

Bell, R. A., Kravitz, R. L., Thom, D., Krupat, E., & Azari, R. (2002). Unmet expectations for care and the patient-physician relationship. *Journal of General Internal Medicine, 17*(11), 817–824.

Bergh, K. (1998). The patient's differential diagnosis: Unpredictable concerns in visits for acute cough. *The Journal of Family Practice, 46*(2), 153–158.

Bogner, H. R., & de Vries, H. F. (2008). Integration of depression and hypertension treatment: a pilot, randomized controlled trial. *Annals of Family Medicine, 6*(4), 295–301.

Bradley, L. A., Alarcon, G. S., Cianfrini, L. R., & McKendree-Smith, N. (2004). Fibromyalgia and chronic fatigue syndrome. In L. Haas (Ed.), *Handbook of primary care psychology* (pp. 345–368). Oxford; New York: Oxford University Press.

Brody, D. S., Thompson, T. L. N., Larson, D. B., Ford, D. E., Katon, W. J., & Magruder, K. M. (1994). Strategies for counseling depressed patients by primary care physicians. *Journal of General Internal Medicine, 9*(10), 569–575.

Brody, D. S., Thompson, T. L. N., Larson, D. B., Ford, D. E., Katon, W. J., & Magruder, K. M. (1995). Recognizing and managing depression in primary care. *General Hospital Psychiatry, 17*(2), 93–107.

Castelnuovo-Tedesco, P. (1986). *The twenty-minute hour: A guide to brief psychotherapy for the physician* (2nd ed.). Washington, DC: American Psychiatric Press.

Cauce, A. M., Domenech-Rodriguez, M., Paradise, M., Cochran, B. N., Shea, J. M., Srebnik, D., et al. (2002). Cultural and contextual influences in mental health help seeking: A focus on ethnic minority youth. *Journal of Consulting and Clinical Psychology, 70*(1), 44–55.

Caudill, M., Schnable, R., Zuttermeister, P., Benson, H., & Friedman, R. (1991). Decreased clinic use by chronic pain patients: Response to behavioral medicine intervention. *The Clinical Journal of Pain, 7*(4), 305–310.

Christensen, R. E., Fetters, M. D., & Green, L. A. (2005). Opening the black box: cognitive strategies in family practice. *Annals of Family Medicine, 3*(2), 144–150.

Cole, S., & Rajum, A. (1996). Overcoming barriers to integration of primary care and behavioral health care: Focus on knowledge and skills. *Behavioral Health Care Tomorrow, 5*, 30–37.

Cole-Kelly, K., & Hepworth, J. (1991). Pressures for omnipotence, saner responses for family therapists in medicine. *Family Systems Medicine, 9*, 159–164.

Craven, M. A., & Bland, R. (2006). Better practices in collaborative mental health care: An analysis of the evidence base. *Canadian Journal of Psychiatry, 51*(6 Suppl 1), S7-S72.

Czajkowski, L. A., Casey, K. R., & Jones, C. R. (2004). Sleep disorders. In L. Haas (Ed.), *Handbook of primary care psychology* (pp. 511–526). Oxford, NY: Oxford University Press.

deGruy, F. V. (1996). Mental health care in the primary care setting. *Primary Care: America's health in a new era* (pp. 285–311). Washington DC: Institute of Medicine, National Academy Press.

Deveugele, M., Derese, A., van den Brink-Muinen, A., Bensing, J., & De Maeseneer, J. (2002). Consultation length in general practice: Cross sectional study in six European countries. *BMJ, 325*(7362), 472.

Dong, M., Giles, W. H., Felitti, V. J., Dube, S. R., Williams, J. E., Chapman, D. P., et al. (2004). Insights into causal pathways for ischemic heart disease: Adverse childhood experiences study. *Circulation, 110*(13), 1761–1766.

Drotar, D. (1995). *Consulting with pediatricians: Psychological perspectives.* New York: Plenum.

Ende, J. (1983). Feedback in clinical medical education. *JAMA: Journal of the American Medical Association, 250*(6), 777–781.

Engel, G. L. (1980). The clinical application of the biopsychosocial model. *American Journal of Psychiatry, 137*(5), 535–544.

Fisher Jr., E. B., Lichtenstein, E., Haire-Joshu, D., Morgan, G. D., & Rehberg, H. R. (1993). Methods, successes, and failures of smoking cessation programs. *Annual Review of Medicine, 44*, 481–513.

Flocke, S. A., Frank, S. H., & Wenger, D. A. (2001). Addressing multiple problems in the family practice office visit. *Journal of Family Practice, 50*(3), 211–216.

Forrest, C. B., Shadmi, E., Nutting, P. A., & Starfield, B. (2007). Specialty referral completion among primary care patients: Results from the ASPN Referral Study. *Annals of Family Medicine, 5*(4), 361–367.

Freedland, K., Carney, R., & Skala, J. (2004). Depression and mood disorders. In L. Haas (Ed.), *Handbook of primary care psychology* (pp. 279–298). Oxford, NY: Oxford University Press.

Freidin, R. B., Goldman, L., & Cecil, R. R. (1980). Patient-physician concordance in problem identification in the primary care setting. *Annals of Internal Medicine, 93*(3), 490–493.

Gonzalez, J., Williams Jr., J. W., Noel, P. H., & Lee, S. (2005). Adherence to mental health treatment in a primary care clinic. *The Journal of the American Board of Family Practice, 18*(2), 87–96.

Grace, G. D., & Christensen, R. C. (2007). Recognizing psychologically masked illnesses: The need for collaborative relationships in mental health care. *Primary Care Companion to the Journal of Clinical Psychiatry, 9*(6), 433–436.

Green, L. A., Fryer Jr., G. E., Yawn, B. P., Lanier, D., & Dovey, S. M. (2001). The ecology of medical care revisited. *New England Journal of Medicine, 344*(26), 2021–2025.

Gross, R., Olfson, M., Gameroff, M., Shea, S., Feder, A., Fuentes, M., et al. (2002). Borderline personality disorder in primary care. *Archives of Internal Medicine, 162*(1), 53–60.

Gunning, K. (2004). Could the symptoms be caused by the patient's medication: A guide to assessment. In L. Haas (Ed.), *Handbook of primary care psychology* (pp. 611–626). Oxford, NY: Oxford University Press.

Haas, L. (1993). Competence and quality issues in the performance of forensic psychologists. *Ethics & Behavior, 3*, 251–266.

Haas, L., & DeGruy, F. (2004). The discipline of primary care psychology. In L. Haas (Ed.), *Handbook of Primary Care Psychology* (pp. 17–49). New York: Oxford University Press.

Haas, L. J., Houchins, J., & Leiser, J. P. (2003). Changing family physicians' visit structuring behavior: A pilot study. *Family Medicine, 35*(10), 726–729.

Haas, L. J., Leiser, J. P., Magill, M. K., & Sanyer, O. N. (2005). Management of the difficult patient. *American Family Physician, 72*(10), 2063–2068.

Haas, L. J., & Malouf, J. L. (2005). *Keeping up the good work: A practitioner's guide to mental health ethics.* Sarasota, FL: Professional Resource Press.

Hamberger, L. K., Ovide, C. R., & Weiner, E. L. (1999). *Making collaborative connections with medical providers: A guide for mental health professionals.* New York: Springer.

Himelhoch, S., & Ehrenreich, M. (2007). Psychotherapy by primary-care providers: Results of a national sample. *Psychosomatics, 48*(4), 325–330.

Institute of Medicine. (2003). *Priority areas for national action: Transforming health care quality.* Washington, DC: National Academies Press.

Jackson, J. L., & Kroenke, K. (2001). The effect of unmet expectations among adults presenting with physical symptoms. *Annals of Internal Medicine, 134*(9 Pt 2), 889–897.

Johansson, H., & Eklund, M. (2006). Helping alliance and early dropout from psychiatric out-patient care: The influence of patient factors. *Social Psychiatry and Psychiatric Epidemiology, 41*(2), 140–147.

Kainz, K. (2002). Barriers and enhancements to physician-psychologist collaboration. *Professional Psychology: Research and Practice, 33*(2), 169–175.

Kates, N., & Craven, M. (1998). *Managing mental health problems: Practical guide for primary care.* Seattle: Hogrefe & Huber.

Katon, W., Rutter, C., Ludman, E. J., Von Korff, M., Lin, E., Simon, G., et al. (2001). A randomized trial of relapse prevention of depression in primary care. *Archives of General Psychiatry, 58*(3), 241–247.

Katon, W., Von Korff, M., Lin, E., Lipscomb, P., Russo, J., Wagner, E., et al. (1990). Distressed high utilizers of medical care. DSM-III-R diagnoses and treatment needs. *General Hospital Psychiatry, 12*(6), 355–362.

Kemper, D. W., Lorig, K., & Mettler, M. (1993). The effectiveness of medical self-care interventions: A focus on self-initiated responses to symptoms. *Patient Education and Counseling, 21*(1–2), 29–39.

Kessler, R. C., Aguilar-Gaxiola, S., Berglund, P. A., Caraveo-Anduaga, J. J., DeWit, D. J., Greenfield, S. F., et al. (2001). Patterns and predictors of treatment seeking after onset of a substance use disorder. *Archives of General Psychiatry, 58*(11), 1065–1071.

Kolbasovsky, A., Reich, L., Romano, I., & Jaramillo, B. (2005). Integrating behavioral health into primary care settings: A pilot project. *Professional Psychology: Research and Practice, 36*(2), 130–135.

Kravitz, R. L., & Callahan, E. J. (2000). Patients' perceptions of omitted examinations and tests: A qualitative analysis. *Journal of General Internal Medicine, 15*(1), 38–45.

Kroenke, K. (1992). Symptoms in medical patients: An untended field. *American Journal of Medicine, 92*(1A), S3–S6.

Kroenke, K. (2003). Patients presenting with somatic complaints: Epidemiology, psychiatric comorbidity and management. *International Journal of Methods in Psychiatric Research, 12*(1), 34–43.

Kroenke, K., Spitzer, R. L., Williams, J. B., Linzer, M., Hahn, S. R., deGruy, F. V., 3rd, et al. (1994). Physical symptoms in primary care. Predictors of psychiatric disorders and functional impairment. *Archives of Family Medicine, 3*(9), 774–779.

Kroenke, K., Spitzer, R. L., Williams, J. B. W., Monahan, P. O., & Lowe, B. (2007). Anxiety disorders in primary care: Prevalence, impairment, comorbidity, and detection. *Annals of Internal Medicine, 146*(5), 317–325.

Lang, F., Floyd, M. R., & Beine, K. L. (2000). Clues to patients' explanations and concerns about their illnesses. A call for active listening. *Archives of Family Medicine, 9*(3), 222–227.

Lang, F., Floyd, M. R., Beine, K. L., & Buck, P. (2002). Sequenced questioning to elicit the patient's perspective on illness: Effects on information disclosure, patient satisfaction, and time expenditure. *Family Medicine, 34*(5), 325–330.

Lapane, K. L., Dube, C. E., Schneider, K. L., & Quilliam, B. J. (2007). Misperceptions of patients vs. providers regarding medication-related communication issues. *American Journal of Managed Care, 13*(11), 613–618.

Lazare, A. (1987). Shame and humiliation in the medical encounter. *Archives of Internal Medicine, 147*(9), 1653–1658.

Lorig, K., Mazonson, P., & Holman, H. (1993). Evidence suggesting that health education for self-management in patients with chronic arthritis has sustained health benefits while reducing health care costs. *Arthritis and Rheumatology, 36*, 439–446.

Mauksch, L. B., Hillenburg, L., & Robins, L. (2001). The establishing focus protocol: Training for collaborative agenda setting and time management in the medical interview. *Families, Systems, and Health, 19*(2), 147–157.

McDaniel, S. H., & Campbell, T. L. (1997). Training health professionals to collaborate. *Families, Systems & Health, 15*(4), 353–359.

McFarland, B. R., & Klein, D. N. (2005). Mental health service use by patients with dysthymic disorder: Treatment use and dropout in a 7 1/2-year naturalistic follow-up study. *Comprehensive Psychiatry, 46*(4), 246–253.

Mechanic, D., McAlpine, D. D., & Rosenthal, M. (2001). Are patients' office visits with physicians getting shorter? *New England Journal of Medicine, 344*(3), 198–204.

Mojtabai, R., & Olfson, M. (2008). National patterns in antidepressant treatment by psychiatrists and general medical providers: Results from the national comorbidity survey replication. *Journal of Clinical Psychiatry, 69*(7), 1064–1074.

Narrow, W. E., Rae, D. S., Robins, L. N., & Regier, D. A. (2002). Revised prevalence estimates of mental disorders in the United States: Using a clinical significance criterion to reconcile 2 surveys' estimates. *Archives of General Psychiatry, 59*(2), 115–123.

Nathan, P. E., Gorman, J. M., & Salkind, N. J. (1999). *Treating mental disorders: A guide to what works.* New York: Oxford University Press.

O'Donohue, W. T. (2004). *Behavioral integrative care: Treatments that work in the primary care setting.* New York: Brunner-Routledge.

Ormel, J., VonKorff, M., Ustun, T. B., Pini, S., Korten, A., & Oldehinkel, T. (1994). Common mental disorders and disability across cultures. Results from the WHO Collaborative Study on Psychological Problems in General Health Care. *JAMA: Journal of the American Medical Association, 272*(22), 1741–1748.

Parkerson, G. R., Broadhead, W. E., & Tse, C. K. (1996). Anxiety and depressive symptom identification using the Duke Health Profile. *Journal of Clinical Epidemiology, 49*(1), 85–93.

Pasco, T., & Smart, D. R. (2003). *Physician characteristics and distribution in the United States: 2003–2004 edition.* Chicago: AMA Press.

Prochaska, J. O. (2005). Health behavior change research: A consortium approach to collaborative science. *Annals of Behavioral Medicine, 29*(Suppl), 4–6.

Robinson, P. J., & Strosahl, K. D. (2009). Behavioral health consultation and primary care: Lessons learned. *Journal of Clinical Psychology in Medical Settings, 16*(1), 58–71.

Rollnick, S., Mason, P., & Butler, C. (1999). *Health behavior change: A guide for practitioners.* Edinburgh, NY: Churchill Livingstone.

Ronalds, C., Kapur, N., Stone, K., Webb, S., Tomenson, B., & Creed, F. (2002). Determinants of consultation rate in patients with anxiety and depressive disorders in primary care. *Family Practice, 19*(1), 23–28.

Rudd, R. E. (2007). Health literacy skills of U.S. adults. *American Journal of Health Behavior, 31*(Suppl 1), S8-S18.

Sansone, R. A., Whitecar, P., Meier, B. P., & Murry, A. (2001). The prevalence of borderline personality among primary care patients with chronic pain. *General Hospital Psychiatry, 23*(4), 193–197.

Sansone, R. A., Wiederman, M. W., & Sansone, L. A. (2001). Adult somatic preoccupation and its relationship to childhood trauma. *Violence and Victims, 16*(1), 39–47.

Sartorius, N., Ustun, T. B., Lecrubier, Y., & Wittchen, H. U. (1996). Depression comorbid with anxiety: Results from the WHO study on psychological disorders in primary health care. *The British Journal of Psychiatry, 30*(Suppl), 38–43.

Schroeder, C. (1997). Conducting an integrated practice in a pediatric setting. In R. J. Illback, C. T. Cobb, & H. M. Joseph, Jr. (Eds.), *Integrated services for children and families,* (Vol. Ch. 10, pp. 221–255). Washington DC: American Psychological Association.

Schurman, R. A., Kramer, P. D., & Mitchell, J. B. (1985). The hidden mental health network. Treatment of mental illness by nonpsychiatrist physicians. *Archives of General Psychiatry, 42*(1), 89–94.

Schwenk, T. L. (2002). Diagnosis of late life depression: The view from primary care. *Biological Psychiatry, 52*(3), 157–163.

Servan-Schreiber, D., Tabas, G., Kolb, R., & Haas, L. J. (2004). Somatoform disorders. In L Haas (Ed.), *Handbook of primary care psychology* (pp. 551–562). Oxford, NY: Oxford University Press.

Simon, G. E., Gureje, O., & Fullerton, C. (2001). Course of hypochondriasis in an international primary care study. *General Hospital Psychiatry, 23*(2), 51–55.

Small, D. (2004). Psychotropic medications in primary care. In L. Haas (Ed.), *Handbook of primary care psychology* (pp. 591–610). Oxford, NY: Oxford University Press.

Smedley, B. D. & Syme, S. L. (2000). *Promoting health: Intervention strategies from social and behavioral research.* Washington, DC: National Academy Press.

Smith Jr., G. R. (1994). The course of somatization and its effects on utilization of health care resources. *Psychosomatics, 35*(3), 263–267.

Sobel, R. (2008). Beyond empathy. *Perspectives in Biology and Medicine, 51*(3), 471–478.

Spitzer, R. L., Kroenke, K., Linzer, M., Hahn, S. R., Williams, J. B., deGruy F. V., et al. (1995). Health-related quality of life in primary care patients with mental disorders. Results from the PRIME-MD 1000 Study [see comments]. *JAMA: Journal of the American Medical Association, 274*(19), 1511–1517.

Spitzer, R. L., Williams, J. B., Kroenke, K., Linzer, M., deGruy F. V., Hahn, S. R., et al. (1994). Utility of a new procedure for diagnosing mental disorders in primary care. The PRIME-MD 1000 study [see comments]. *JAMA: Journal of the American Medical Association, 272*(22), 1749–1756.

Stange, K. C., Woolf, S. H., & Gjeltema, K. (2002). One minute for prevention: The power of leveraging to fulfill the promise of health behavior counseling. *American Journal of Preventive Medicine, 22*(4), 320–323.

Stange, K. C., Zyanski, S., Jaen, C. R., & Callahan, E. J. (1998). Illuminating the 'black box': A description of 4454 patient visits to 138 family physicians. *Journal of Family Practice, 46*(5), 377–389.

Stuart, M. R., & Leiberman, J. A. (1986). *The fifteen minute hour: Applied psychotherapy for the primary care physician.* New York: Praeger.

Stuart, M. R., & Leiberman, J. A. (2002). *The fifteen minute hour: Practical therapeutic interventions in primary care* (3rd ed.). Philadelphia: Saunders.

Trask, P. C., Schwartz, S. M., Deaner, S. L., Paterson, A. G., Johnson, T., Rubenfire, M., et al. (2002). Behavioral medicine: The challenge of integrating psychological and behavioral approaches into primary care. *Effective Clinical Practice, 5*(2), 75–83.

U.S. Department of Health and Human Services. (2001). *Healthy people 2010: Understanding and improving health* (Rev. ed.). Boston: Jones and Bartlett Publishers.

van Rijswijk, E., Borghuis, M., van de Lisdonk, E., Zitman, F., & van Weel, C. (2007). Treatment of mental health problems in general practice: A survey of psychotropics prescribed and other treatments provided. *International Journal of Clinical Pharmacology and Therapeutics, 45*(1), 23–29.

Walker, Z., & Townsend, J. (1998). Promoting adolescent mental health in primary care: A review of the literature. *Journal of Adolescence, 21*(5), 621–634.

Weiss, B. D. (1999). *20 common problems in primary care.* New York: McGraw-Hill, Health Professions Division.

Wells, K. B., Stewart, A., Hays, R. D., Burnam, M. A., Rogers, W., Daniels, M., et al. (1989). The functioning and well-being of depressed patients. Results from the Medical Outcomes Study. *JAMA: Journal of the American Medical Association, 262*(7), 914–919.

Wolf, M. S., Gazmararian, J. A., & Baker, D. W. (2007). Health literacy and health risk behaviors among older adults. *American Journal of Preventive Medicine, 32*(1), 19–24.

World Health, Organization. (2003). *Adherence to long-term therapies: Evidence for action.* Geneva: World Health Organization.

Yeung, A., Kung, W. W., Chung, H., Rubenstein, G., Roffi, P., Mischoulon, D., et al. (2004). Integrating psychiatry and primary care improves acceptability to mental health services among Chinese-Americans. *General Hospital Psychiatry, 26*(4), 256–260.

Shifting Paradigms in Clinical Psychology: How Innovative Technologies Are Shaping Treatment Delivery

Linda A. Dimeff, Andrew P. Paves, Julie M. Skutch, *and* Eric A. Woodcock

Abstract

The accelerated expanse, affordability, and advances in technology, along with the ubiquitous Web, will continue to radically transform how we prevent and treat behavioral problems and reduce human suffering. These technologies have the potential to break down barriers and close the gap between empirically supported treatments (ESTs) and those who need them. This chapter attempts to capture the current use of technology to strengthen and disseminate ESTs. We focus on those areas that have or are expected to have the greatest reach and impact in the years to come. Web- or computer-based technology, virtual reality, mobile technology, and social networking will all be highlighted. We present innovative ideas, the evidence base for existing applications (when available), and future directions. The omnipresence of technology in our daily lives perfectly positions it to be a powerful agent of change in the science and practice of clinical psychology.

Keywords: Computer-based training, computerized CBT, dissemination, empirically supported treatments, innovative technology, mobile technology, social networking treatments, Twitter, virtual reality

We are in the midst of a major paradigm shift. The accelerating expanse, affordability, and advances in technology, along with the omnipresence of the Web, will continue to radically transform how we prevent and treat behavioral problems and reduce human suffering. The swift moving currents of technology will impact and redefine how we gather information, how treatment will be provided, and our roles as treatment professionals. We need to look no further than the Web to recognize the unimaginable transformation that results from and through technology. The Web, just 5,000 days old, was originally conceptualized as "TV but only better" (Kelly, 2007). In this brief window of time, the Web has transformed many aspects of our lives: how we communicate, find information and conduct research, plan our time and trips, and pay our bills. We are immobilized when Internet access fails or when we are "out of range" of connectivity. Our work comes

to a grinding halt, and we *feel* utterly disconnected. So intertwined are we with the Web that we can scarcely recall what life was like before its time.

Our enmeshed relationship with the Web is borne out by the statistics of its use: We collectively make 100 billion clicks per day accessing the more than 55 trillion links available on the Web, and we send two million e-mails and one million instant messages per second, resulting in total Web traffic running at 7 terabytes per second—the content equivalent of one-half of the holdings of the Library of Congress traversing the planet per second (Kelly, 2007). In less than 1,000 days, we have witnessed the explosive success of Web 2.0. We have found lost friends and new jobs on Facebook. And we have witnessed the rapid rise of Twitter—used for social and political purposes. Communications technology and innovation will continue to explode in dimension, reach, and impact.

The radical evolution of technology is but one factor accounting for the burgeoning of this new era in mental health services. The other important factor is the disturbing and seemingly intractable gap (Simon & Ludman, 2009) that continues to separate science from practice (Bebbington, Brugha, et al., 2000; Bebbington, Meltzer, et al., 2000; Kessler et al., 2003; Marks, 2004). We have developed, rigorously evaluated, and refined a number of powerful behavioral treatments for many Axis I and II problems over the past decades. In theory, clients now have treatment options when selecting an empirically supported therapy (EST) for many disorders. Yet, the likelihood that they will actually receive an EST is extremely low. In the United States, students working toward professional degrees in social work, psychology, and psychiatry seldom learn ESTs; when training is provided, it is cursory and insufficient to apply the treatment to adherence (Weissman et al., 2006). The prospects for learning do not improve after graduation, despite mandatory and ongoing continuing education (CE) as clinicians do not read textbooks or treatment manuals unless required to do so, and CE workshops seldom impact practice (Addis, 2002; Barlow, Levitt & Bufka, 1999; Davis et al., 1999). In contrast to the pharmaceutical industry, which spends millions annually on marketing their products, an analogous mechanism does not exist to promote the dissemination of behavioral and other efficacious psychosocial treatments.

The net effect of these factors is reflected in mental health treatment trends over the past two decades, where rates of psychotropic medication use continues to rise significantly while psychotherapy rates have held constant or have steadily declined (Olfson & Marcus, 2009; Olfson et al., 2002; Olfson, Marcus, Wan, & Geissler, 2004; Simon & Ludman, 2009). For example, the rate of antidepressant medication nearly doubled between 1996 and 2005, from 5.84% to 10.12%; however, the rate of those receiving psychotherapy in addition to psychotropic medications stayed constant (26.25% vs. 26.85%, respectively; Olfson & Marcus, 2009). Antidepressant medications now top the charts of the most common class of medications prescribed in the United States, surpassing hypertensive medications (Olfson & Marcus) despite the presence of three highly effective, short-term psychosocial treatments for depression (behavioral activation, cognitive therapy, and interpersonal psychotherapy; Cuijpers, van Straten, Anderson, & van Oppen, 2008).

Innovative applications of technology will provide the seismic force required to close the gap between research and practice. They are already being used to more efficiently and effectively deliver ESTs to a greater number of clients. Like the technology on which it is built, this area is expanding at a breathtaking pace. New research challenges arise in the process. How, for example, do we research application-based interventions when the technology morphs at a faster rate than our capacity to rigorously evaluate it? How "cutting edge" does the technology itself have to be when evaluating the efficacy of a technology-based intervention? For example, should investigators proposing high-impact and innovative clinical research involving technology be required to use empirically supported cutting edge technology? (We think, yes).

This chapter attempts to capture the transformation that is under way in how technology is already being used to strengthen behavioral ESTs and disseminate them. We focus on those areas that have or are expected to have the greatest reach and impact in the years to come. This chapter is divided into five sections. The first discusses the "dissemination problem" and how technology may be leveraged to close the gap between research and science. The second section examines the uses of computers and the Web to deliver treatments. This section spans the continuum from self-help to clinician-assist programs that structure and guide the treatment for novice clinicians. The third section explores the use of virtual reality (VR) in the treatment of anxiety disorders, as a method to offset the experience of pain through distraction during painful medical procedures, and to facilitate training in procedural learning in a fail-safe environment when hands-on practice is required. The fourth section examines one of the newest and fastest-moving areas of technology—mobile technologies in the prevention and treatment of behavioral problems. The fifth and final section reviews social networking, with a primary focus on Twitter, a micro-blog site that some believe may wield great powers, whereas others remain highly skeptical. We conclude with a discussion of the relevant issues that emerge from this paradigm shift.

Leveraging Technology to Close the Gap Between Research and Practice

Despite considerable attention to the importance of bridging the sizeable gap between research and practice (e.g., APA Presidential Task Force on Evidence-Based Practice, 2006; Insel, 2009; New Freedom Commission, 2003), ESTs continue to be widely underutilized in routine clinical practice. Numerous dissemination barriers have been identified (Addis,

2002; Barlow et al., 1999; Dimeff et al., 2009; Fixsen, Naoom, Blase, Friedman, & Wallace, 2005; Shafran et al., 2009; Street, Niederehe, & Lebowitz, 2000). These include:

1. *System-based factors impede EST delivery.* One common barrier to clinicians delivering ESTs to their clients begins with the systems within which clinicians practice. Competent and highly motivated clinicians may be blocked from delivering an EST by clinic policy or insurance provider, often in an effort to contain costs (Dimeff & Koerner, 2007). Further, clients may live in rural or frontier areas, where there is simply limited access to mental health services entirely, let alone clinicians providing specific EST protocols (e.g., Cook & Hoas, 2007; Brems, Johnson, Warner, & Roberts, 2006).

2. *Therapists do not know ESTs.* Another barrier is the lack of effective training opportunities available to clinicians (e.g., Becker, Zayfert, & Anderson, 2004; Weissman et al., 2006), as well as clinician reluctance to read and rely on treatment manuals on their own (Addis, 2002). To illustrate, despite extensive research that overwhelmingly supports the efficacy of exposure procedures for anxiety disorders, very few clinicians are familiar with exposure procedures. In a sample of over 350 participants with generalized anxiety disorder, panic disorder, and social phobia, only 19% and 11% reported receiving behavioral therapy in 1991 and 1995–1996, respectively (Goisman, Warshaw, & Keller, 1999). Freiheit, Vye, Swan, and Cady (2004) surveyed licensed doctoral-level psychologists who regularly treated anxiety disorder patients about their use of a variety of exposure and nonexposure procedures in their treatment of obsessive-compulsive disorder (OCD), panic disorder, and social phobia. Although a majority of the participants (71%) identified as cognitive-behavioral in orientation, and 88% indicated that they used cognitive-behavioral therapy (CBT) to treat anxiety disorders, very few used the key change agent: exposure interventions (Freiheit et al., 2004). In the treatment of OCD, 67% frequently used cognitive restructuring and 41% frequently used relaxation training, whereas only 38% frequently used exposure and response prevention. Participants reported frequently treating social phobia via cognitive restructuring (69%), relaxation training (59%), and breathing retraining (47%), and relatively few participants frequently used self-directed in vivo exposure

(31%) or clinician-directed in vivo exposure (7%). Even fewer participants (12%) frequently used interoceptive exposure to treat panic disorder; indeed, 76% indicated that they never or rarely used interoceptive exposure to treat panic disorder.

In the area of post-traumatic stress disorder (PTSD), Becker et al. (2004) surveyed licensed doctoral-level psychologists about their use of exposure procedures to treat PTSD and found that the most commonly endorsed reason for not using exposure was limited training (60%). Only 28.5% of participants reported receiving any training in imaginal exposure for PTSD, only 27.1% had been trained in in vivo exposure for PTSD, and only 12.5% had been trained in exposure for other anxiety disorders. Overall, 47% of participants reported that they were "not at all" or only "slightly" familiar with imaginal exposure for PTSD and only 20% reported being "very familiar" and 72% of respondents reported feeling "not at all" comfortable using imaginal exposure to treat PTSD. In another study involving clinicians designated as PTSD specialists, fewer than 20% conducted repeated exposure to traumatic memories or trauma-related stimuli, and fewer than 10% did so routinely (Rosen et al., 2004).

3. *Knowing an EST is no guarantee that a clinician will actually provide it.* Among clinicians who are trained in specific ESTs, many do not regularly apply the treatments to their clients with the specific disorders. To illustrate, Becker et al. (2004) found that only about half of those who had received adequate training reported using imaginal exposure to treat PTSD, and less than one-third used it to treat at least half of their PTSD clients. Moreover, almost one-third of those trained never used imaginal exposure to treat PTSD. The reasons provided by participants included a preference for individualized treatment over manualized therapy (25%) and a concern that clients would decompensate (22%) if provided the EST, a belief not supported by the empirical literature (Foa, Zoellner, Feeny, Hembree, & Alvarez-Conrad, 2002; Nishith, Resick, & Griffin, 2002).

4. *Drift happens.* Another significant problem involves clinician "drift" from the treatment protocol over time (Waller, 2009). Drift can occur intentionally (e.g., clinician is not inclined to follow the protocol, believes a blended approach is more effective for his or her client, or simply prefers to vary the approach) or inadvertently (e.g., the clinician is shaped by the client through

the use of contingencies to do something other that the protocol; she may be punished by client when properly administering the EST protocol and reinforced for drifting; Schulte & Eifert, 2002. Either way, treatment potency and effect may be compromised (e.g., Bright, Baker, & Neimeyer, 1999; Miller, Yahne, Moyers, Martinez, & Pirritano, 2004; Waller, 2009).

One clear advantage of technology-based approaches over traditional face-to-face treatment is that they bypass clinician and system (i.e., clinic, insurance) barriers to delivery of ESTs to fidelity. This is particularly the case with the computer-based self-help interventions described in the section "Delivering Treatments Using Personal Computers and the Internet," and virtual reality interventions described in the third section, "Virtual Reality." Assuming the intervention is selected wisely, and sufficient motivation and capability exist to follow its steps and procedures, clients can expect to receive the full dose of the intervention and, with it, the intended positive outcomes.

Delivering Treatments Using Personal Computers and the Internet

Since the groundswell in use of the Internet, innovative applications have been developed and launched to deliver evidence-based therapies over the Web. These tools vary widely, from pure self-help CBTs and clinician-guided self-help CBT to computer-assisted applications that guide treatment professionals in the delivery of efficacious CBTs. These approaches are new enough that naming conventions have not been codified. We use the most readily used of the term *computerized cognitive-behavioral therapy* (CCBT) to refer to these dynamic computer-based systems that deliver evidence-based CBTs directly to clients. (Other such terms include *computer-aided CBT* and *computer-assisted CBT*.) Computerized CBT refers to applications delivered via a personal computer, the Internet, interactive voice response systems (VRS), or mobile phones (National Institute for Health and Clinical Excellence, 2006). The distinguishing characteristic of CCBT compared to other technologies, such as video conference, standard phone contact, and e-mail, is the active engagement and interaction of the client in the CCBT environment (Marks, Shaw, & Parkin, 1998).

Computerized CBT was originally envisioned as an efficient, effective method of reaching the millions of untreated individuals who were suffering from behavioral problems and who were not already seeking and/or receiving adequate treatment (Marks et al., 2003). Computerized CBT was viewed as a first-line treatment for those with mild to moderate problems, one that could be accessed privately via the Internet or at one's primary health care provider. Nonresponders (i.e., those clients who did not achieve a sufficient clinical effect from the CCBT intervention) could then be "stepped up" to a higher level of care (Bower & Gilbody, 2005; Seekles, van Straten, Beekman, van Marwijk, & Cuijpers, 2009). More recently, the application of CCBT has been expanded for use by practitioners untrained in how to deliver a specific EST. Used in this way, clinician and client sit side by side and are mutually guided in treatment delivery by the CCBT (Craske et al., 2009). In this section, we will review the advantages of CCBT, highlight specific examples of different applications/types of CCBT for a variety of disorders, and discuss the research data to date.

Advantages of Computerized Cognitive-Behavioral Therapy

The advantages of CCBT are primarily two-fold. First, they significantly expand the menu of self-help options for clients wishing to (primarily) direct their own care and treatment. Second, they facilitate the dissemination and implementation of efficacious CBTs delivered to a high degree of fidelity by a large number of treatment providers who would not otherwise offer ESTs.

EXPANDING THE MENU OF SELF-HELP OPTIONS

Seeking one's own solutions to complicated behavioral health problems and managing one's own treatment plan is something that people have always done. Indeed, regardless of topic, self-help books typically occupy more shelf space at bookstores and libraries than empirically derived treatment manuals. Primary and secondary prevention health promotion campaigns to reduce the risk of major killers—from heart disease and cancer to motor vehicle accidents—rely extensively on self-directed actions to reduce risks. Examples are everywhere. We modify what we eat, increase our exercise, wear seat belts and helmets, and don't drink and drive. We brush and floss twice daily. In short, the majority of people self-manage or direct their behavior in the service of their long-term goals for health and well-being.

Within clinical psychology, the self-help empirical literature is equally vast and extensive, with meta-analytic studies reporting small to medium effect sizes on major outcome variables across a spectrum of disorders (Morgan & Jorm, 2008; van't Hoff, Cuijpers, & Stein, 2009; Ciujpers et al., 2009). To illustrate, a recent and exhaustive review of self-help treatments for subthreshold depression by Morgan and Jorm identified 38 diverse self-help treatments from St. John's wort (Pilkington, Boshnakova, & Richardson, 2006) and Korean ginseng (Kennedy & Scholey, 2003), to lavender (Akhondzadeh et al., 2003), lecithin (Benton & Donohoe, 2003), laughing (Berk, 2001; Newman & Stone, 1996), and light therapy (Golden et al., 2005; Tuunainen, Kripke, & Endo, 2004).

Self-help approaches, including self-help CCBT, offer a number of significant advantages over traditional face-to-face methods. First, they can be accessed around the clock and 365 days a year; their hours of operation are entirely client-determined. Services need not be temporarily delayed, postponed, or discontinued in the event of sickness, vacation, retirement, or clinic closure. Second, the direct and indirect costs to the client are significantly less than the cost of traditional methods. A number of CCBTs are free and freely accessed (e.g., http://www.psychologicalselfhelp.org, http://moodgym.anu.edu.au/welcome, http://www.beatingtheblues.co.uk/). Those that do require payment (e.g., www.myselfhelp.com) typically charge a nominal monthly subscription fee that is comparable to other monthly Internet subscriptions (e.g., Netflix, Audible books, etc.). Indirect costs associated with traditional methods are also saved, including transportation costs and loss of productivity while commuting and waiting. Third, self-help approaches require less motivation and commitment by the client before gaining access to treatment. In comparison to the extensive effort required to start traditional services (i.e., multiple calls to clinic, phone screen, initial paperwork, an initial session to assess "goodness of fit" between the clinician and client), self-help approaches are easily initiated. In the case of CCBT, gaining access often takes less than 5 minutes, the time it takes to create a user-name and password. The ease with which treatment can be sought has been identified as an important consideration, particularly in the treatment of depression (Harmen et al., 2001; Morey, Thacher, & Craighead, 2007). Finally, self-help approaches help eliminate the stigma that some individuals may associate with seeking out professional mental health services.

Computerized Cognitive-Behavioral Therapy Across the Treatment Continuum

Computerized CBT spans a continuum of use, from pure self-help and guided self-help to CCBT-augmented

therapy and use as a guide to treatment delivery (Craske et al., 2009). Differences in these approaches are discussed below.

PURE SELF-HELP COMPUTERIZED COGNITIVE-BEHAVIORAL THERAPY

As a *pure-self help* application, users navigate their own course through the CCBT, with minimal or no involvement from others. In the majority of cases, the CCBT is accessed via the Internet by the client, with no other human involvement. In some cases, the extent of involvement may be directing the client to a computer in a primary care setting and showing them how to use it. A number of self-administered CCBTs have been developed and evaluated for a variety of behavioral problems, including depression (Clarke et al., 2002; Clarke et al., 2005; Spek et al., 2007), anxiety disorders (Andersson, Bergstrom, Carlbring, & Lindefors, 2005; Anderson, Jacobs, & Rothbaum, 2004; Carlbring et al., 2005; Farvolden, Denisoff, Selby, Bagby, & Rudy, 2005; Kenwright & Marks, 2004; Schneider, Mataix-Cols, Marks, & Bachofen, 2005), insomnia (Ström, Pettersson, & Andersson, 2004), and smoking cessation (Cobb, Graham, Bock, Papandonatos, & Abrams, 2005; Etter, 2005).

GUIDED SELF-HELP COMPUTERIZED COGNITIVE-BEHAVIORAL THERAPY

Application of guided self-help CCBT typically involves pairing the CCBT with brief contact (by telephone, e-mail, instant message, or in person) with a clinician or coach. The extent of contact is often between 5 and 10 minutes, typically just before beginning the weekly CCBT module and/or upon session completion. Total coach/clinician time required for duration of the intervention is typically between 2 and 5 hours, significantly less than traditional face-to-face treatment. The functions of the guided approach are: (a) to increase motivation to use and complete the weekly CCBT session by "bookending" the session with scheduled (albeit brief) contact with the clinician or coach; (b) to ensure comprehension of content by providing clients with an opportunity to ask questions; (c) to assign and review homework; and (d) to overcome barriers to using the CCBT or completing the homework. Studies of guided self-help span depression (van Straten, Cuijpers, & Smits, 2008), social phobia (Andersson et al., 2006), panic disorder (Carlbring et al., 2006), pathological gambling (Carlbring & Smit, 2008), and obesity treatment (Micco et al., 2007). The evidence to date across multiple trials overwhelmingly supports the importance of having a clinician or coach involved in administering the CCBTs to facilitate user engagement and prevent dropout (Christensen, Griffiths, Korten, Brittliffe, & Groves, 2004; Clarke et al., 2002; Clarke et al., 2005; Kaltenthaler, Parry, Beverley, & Ferriter, 2008; Kaltenthaler, Sutcliffe, et al., 2008).

COMPUTERIZED COGNITIVE-BEHAVIORAL THERAPY ENHANCED THERAPY

Computerized CBTs are also used to augment traditional face-to-face treatment. When used in this way, routine psychoeducation and other standardized EST content is "outsourced" to the CCBT, thus reducing treatment costs (to clinic, system, and/or payee) by reducing the extent of face-to-face treatment by as much as 50%. Studies examining the efficacy of CCBT-enhanced therapy have been conducted with social phobics (Andersson et al., 2006), PTSD patients (Litz, Engel, Bryant, & Papa, 2007), anxious children (Spence, Holmes, March, & Lipp, 2006), and anxious youth (Kendall, Hudson, Gosch, Flannery-Schroeder, & Suveg, 2008).

COMPUTERIZED COGNITIVE-BEHAVIORAL THERAPY INTEGRATED WITHIN STEPPED CARE

Based on a public health model of care, the stepped care approach is characterized by different treatment steps arranged in order of increasing intensity, in which a specific level of care is not offered before it is needed or more intensely than is required and not later or at less intensely than is needed (Bower & Gilbody, 2005; Seekles et al., 2009). Clients start off with a low-intensity EST as the initial step, progress is monitored, and those who do not respond are then "stepped up" to a higher level of treatment. This process is continued until the therapeutic impact is achieved. When CCBTs are used in the context of stepped care, clients may start with the lowest level of care (pure self-help), then step up to guided CCBT, and then to traditional face-to-face treatment that may be enhanced by CCBT (MacGregor, Hayward, Peck, & Wilkes, 2009).

COMPUTERIZED COGNITIVE-BEHAVIORAL FACILITATED THERAPY

The newcomer to the CCBT approaches, the facilitated therapy method involves simultaneously guiding the client and the clinician who is unfamiliar with a specific treatment protocol through its full administration. The one study of CCBT-facilitated treatment conducted to date took place within the context of a primary care clinic where nurses were administering ESTs for clients with anxiety disorders (Craske et al., 2009). Here, the client has the benefit of sitting side by side with a "live" treatment professional who can aid the client in implementing the content of the EST; however, the nurse need not have specialized training in the specific treatment protocol.

Does Computerized Cognitive-Behavioral Therapy Work? A Summary of Research to Date

Marks and his colleagues recently concluded a systematic review of CCBTs that involved 97 applications from nine countries reported in 175 studies, 103 of which involved randomized controlled studies (RCTs) (Marks, Cavanagh, & Gega, 2007). They concluded that in comparison to waitlist (WL) controls or treatment as usual (TAU), CCBT is more effective, with small to medium effect sizes. Furthermore, in some, but not all studies comparing CCBT to traditional face-to-face treatment, CCBT performs comparably (Marks et al., 2007).

Kaltenthaler, Parry, et al. (2008) recently screened 445 references and reviewed 103 papers in their systematic review of CCBT for depression; of these, only three CCBTs were rigorously evaluated in RCTs: *Beating the Blues* (Proudfoot et al., 2004), *MoodGYM* (Christensen, Griffiths & Jorm, 2004), and *Overcoming Depression on the Internet* (*ODIN*; Clarke et al., 2002; Clarke et al., 2005). All studies compared CCBT to TAU; all included adults with mild to moderate depression. Participants across all four studies were predominantly female, ranging in age from 36 (SD = 9.4; Christensen et al., 2004) to 50 (SD = 10.8; Clarke et al., 2005). Computerized CBT was delivered alone or as part of an integrated package of care; control conditions included individual and group CBT, nondirective and primary care counseling, routine client management, and CBT therapy adjuncts, such as bibliotherapy. Results from their review provided "some evidence" to support the effectiveness of CCBT in the treatment of depression. Specifically, *Beating the Blues* was more effective than TAU for depression, *MoodGYM* and *BluePages* (a noninteractive website providing psychoeducational information on depression) were more effective in reducing depression compared to an attention control condition, and *ODIN* with staff reminders (guided) was more effective than TAU. Relatively high dropout rates were observed across all trials— 35% in *Beating the Blues*, 25.3% in *MoodGYM*, and 34% in *ODIN*.

Computerized CBTs have also been successfully implemented into large-sector systems, including four into a National Health Service self-help clinic in west London (Gega, Marks, & Mataix-Cols, 2004). These included: *COPE* for depression (Osgood-Hynes et al., 1998), *BTSteps* for OCD (Greist et al., 2002), *FearFighter* for panic and anxiety (Marks, Kenwright, McDonough, Whittaker, & Mataix-Cols, 2004), and *Balance* for generalized anxiety disorder (GAD) (Yates, 1996). *COPE* and *BTSteps* were both administered using interactive voice response (IVR) and a manual to guide clinician contacts with clients; *Balance* and *FearFighter* were initially delivered in the clinic (*FearFighter* was later placed on the Internet, where clients could access it from home). All CCBT participants first had a brief meeting with a clinician by phone (for those accessing CCBT at home) or in person (for those accessing CCBT in the office). Clinician contact with participants was limited to an initial brief screening and to provide brief advice if progress appeared slow. Results were very encouraging: CCBT participants improved significantly in distress and disability, and clinicians were able to manage four times more referrals by delegating routine treatment elements to the CCBT. In the United States, Kaiser Permanente Northwest has successfully implemented CCBTs in their system for the treatment of depression (Clarke et al., 2002). The early successes of CCBTs in public sector settings were among the factors that led to the 2006 landmark decision by the United Kingdom's National Institute for Health and Clinical Excellence (NICE) to approve the use of two CCBTs as part of their nationalized health care: *Beating the Blues* in the management of mild to moderate depression, and *FearFighter* (National Institute for Health and Clinical Excellence [NICE], 2006).

Review of Specific Computerized Cognitive-Behavioral Therapies

We showcase a number of CCBTs in an effort to demonstrate the range and diversity of CCBTs, how they are investigated, and their outcomes. Content is organized into three sections to illustrate the broad categories of CCBT: *pure and guided self-help CCBT, CCBT-enhanced therapy,* and *CCBT-facilitated therapy.* Whenever possible, we arrange CCBTs for specific problems together within each section. Our review is not exhaustive. These CCBTs were selected for one or more of the following reasons: (a) they are seminal works, (b) they illustrate the continuum of uses of CCBT, (c) the CCBT itself is highly innovative, and (d) the research design is novel and/or the outcomes

are particularly important in considering future directions. Additionally, CCBTs involving the use of mobile technologies are reviewed within the mobile technologies section of this chapter.

COMPUTERIZED COGNITIVE-BEHAVIORAL THERAPY FOR DEPRESSION
Beating the Blues (guided self-help)

Developed by U.K. researcher Judith Proudfoot and her colleagues, *Beating the Blues* was designed for use within a primary care setting and is now recognized by NICE as an efficacious, cost-effective treatment for mild to moderate depression (NICE, 2006). *Beating the Blues* consists of a 15-minute introductory video, and eight 1-hour interactive and customized computerized sessions (www.ultrasis.com). The CCBT was administered by a nurse at a primary care clinic who met briefly (no more than 5 minutes) with the participant at the start and at the conclusion of each session, for a maximum total of 10 minutes of face-to-face contact per CCBT session. The function of this contact was facilitative, intended solely to ensure that the participant was able to access the CCBT at the start and had completed each module (e.g., printed out the session summary, homework note, and the progress report at the end).

Clients with mild to moderate depression (*N* = 274) were randomly assigned to either the CCBT or TAU. Computerized CBT participants could also receive pharmacotherapy, practical assistance (e.g., case management services), and general support, as indicated by their physician, but no traditional face-to-face therapy. The TAU condition was structured to replicate naturalistic conditions of primary care settings, imposing few restrictions on the type or quality of services these participants could be provided, as deemed by their physician. Of the total sample, 35% dropped out of the study prior to completing the final assessment. In comparison to TAU, CCBT was efficacious in significantly reducing depressive symptoms and improving social and work adjustment. Importantly, no statistical interaction was found for drugs, severity of depression, or duration of preexisting depression, suggesting that *Beating the Blues* works for a broad spectrum of individuals with depression, with and without the use of antidepressant medications.

BluePages and MoodGYM (minimal guided)

Australian researcher Helen Christensen and colleagues (Christensen et al., 2004) developed and investigated two free Internet-delivered self-help programs (only one of which is a CCBT) designed for individuals with depression who were not otherwise seeking professional treatment. *BluePages* is a non-interactive psychoeducation website providing evidence-based information about depression that addresses what it is, how to prevent, and how to treat depression (http://bluepages.anu.edu.au/). Content is written at an eighth-grade literacy level to ensure accessibility. Resources include an online virtual support group for people with depression, recommended books, and how to find further help in New Zealand and Australia. *MoodGYM* (http://moodgym.anu.edu.au/welcome) is an interactive CCBT based on CBT and interpersonal therapy (IPT) that contains five interactive modules (Feelings, Thoughts, Unwarping, De-Stress, Relationships) provided sequentially on a week-by-week basis, with all modules available for review in the final sixth week. Topic titles are humorous and add to this nonstigmatizing, engaging program (i.e., Bad Hair Day, Three Encounters of an Emotional Kind, My Scores on My Warpy Thoughts Test, and Life Whacks). Mood questionnaires with feedback based on normative data are provided throughout.

Participants were recruited via a questionnaire posted to 27,000 individuals, ages 17–52 years, living in Canberra, a major metropolis in Australia. Of these, 6,122 returned the survey, 752 met study criteria, and 525 were eventually consented and provided baseline data. Participants were randomized to one of three conditions: *BluePages* (n = 166), *MoodGYM* (n = 182), or an attention control condition (n = 178) consisting of weekly contact with a lay interviewer to discuss lifestyle issues such as exercise, education, and health habits. To facilitate usage of both active interventions, participants assigned to *BluePages* and *MoodGYM* received weekly calls from an interviewer directing them to the website. *BluePages* participants visited the site an average of 4.5 (SD = 1.35) times and averaged 67.2 (SD = 24) hits; *MoodGYM* participants completed nearly half (M = 14.8; SD = 9.7) of the 29 exercises. Overall, 79% of participants completed their intervention, and 83% of the intent-to-treat sample provided follow-up data. A statistically significant attrition rate between the active conditions was observed, with higher rates of study completion by *BluePages* participants. Interestingly, post-hoc analyses revealed that participants who scored the highest on psychological distress and high knowledge of psychological treatments were more likely to drop out. Overall findings support the feasibility and effectiveness of the Internet tools to reduce depressive symptoms (Christensen et al., 2004). Specifically, both active conditions were superior to control in reducing depressive symptom; *MoodGYM*, but not *BluePages*, was superior to the study control in improving dysfunctional thinking.

Overcoming Depression on the Internet (ODIN) Developed at Kaiser Permanente Center for Health Research, *ODIN* was developed as a pure self-help intervention for mild to moderate depression that can also be used in conjunction with traditional face-to-face therapy (Clarke et al., 2002). Based on cognitive therapy, *ODIN* is comprised of self-guided and semi-interactive skills training tutorials emphasizing cognitive restructuring techniques. Like a brief booklet, ODIN is organized into seven "chapters" or lessons, each with didactic information and interactive practice exercises. For example, in one chapter, *Thought Helper*, users first learn to identify their negative thoughts and generate positive counter statements. Next, users type their negative or irrational thoughts into a text box, click *search*, and ODIN provides several close matches from its back-end database. Users then select those that appear to be the "best fit," click *submit*, then receive two to five possible counterthoughts for each dysfunctional thought selected. Built over a decade ago and at a time when video-streaming was no more than a distant fantasy, ODIN was largely text-based and lacked in rich visual media that is now industry standard.

Two RCTs of *ODIN* have been conducted to date. In the initial trial, clients identified as "depressed" (N = 6,994) were recruited from 430,000 enrollees of Kaiser Permanente Northwest (KPNW; Clarke et al., 2002). Only 526 individuals (3.8% of the total target sample) registered for more information, and only 223 consented to participate. Participants were randomized to *ODIN* or to a no-access control condition. Following online consent and completion of an online assessment, ODIN participants were advanced to ODIN; control participants were advanced to the non-interactive KPNW website, where they could obtain information about a variety of health concerns, including depression, and could submit a question to an online nurse or pharmacist. All participants were free to receive nonexperimental usual care services for depression, including psychotropic medication and face-to-face therapy. Use of ODIN was disappointingly low (potentially due to the lack of rich interactions and media): the modal number of participants only used ODIN one time (41%), the median was two, the mean was 2.6 (SD = 3.5), with a range of 0–20 sessions. Assessments were conducted at enrollment and at 4, 8, 16, and

32 weeks after enrollment. Assessment completion rates ranged from 53% (n = 148) at Week 4 to 66% (n = 196) at Week 16. Importantly, the most depressed participants were significantly less likely to participate in the follow-up assessments procedure. No differences were observed between conditions on depressive symptoms, and no dose effect was found among experimental participants. Investigators hypothesized that the null findings were due to low rates of CCBT completion.

With this hypothesis in mind, investigators sought to correct this problem in the second study by focusing on increasing participant use of the Internet (Clarke et al., 2005). A pool of participants were again recruited using the same methods as described in the original study (N = 6,030). Of these, 200 depressed individuals provided consent. Participants were then randomized to one of three conditions: *ODIN* + phone call reminders (n = 80), *ODIN* + postcard reminders (n = 75), and TAU control condition (n = 100). Sixty-six percent (n = 169) of participants completed the 16-week assessment. *ODIN* participants in both intervention conditions significantly outperformed control participants in reporting greater reductions in depression, with more severely depressed participants showing the greatest gains over time. By the study's end, 20% of *ODIN* participants no longer met criteria for depression. Interestingly, no differences were observed between the two *ODIN* conditions, suggesting that the less-expensive postcard reminder was as robust as the more labor-intensive phone calls made by study staff.

COMPUTERIZED COGNITIVE-BEHAVIORAL THERAPY FOR ANXIETY DISORDERS
FearFighter
Developed by Stuart Toole and Isaac Marks, *Fear-Fighter* (www.fearfighter.com) is based on 20 years of development and extensive testing in open clinical trials and RCTs. Designed to aid in the treatment of panic and other phobias, *FearFighter* has been demonstrated to reduce anxiety in individuals with comorbid depression and OCD. *FearFighter* is the only CCBT for anxiety approved by the National Institute of Clinical Excellence to date (NICE, 2006). *FearFighter* is delivered via the internet and is a ten-session exposure-based self-help treatment. Minimal human assistance is provided to users. Specifically, users receive approximately an hour of contact (either by phone or in person) with a nurse during the entire treatment, typically at the end of each CCBT session, for purposes of facilitating its use. Two RCTs have been conducted to date on

FearFighter by Marks and his colleagues (Marks et al., 2004; Schneider et al., 2005). Both involved the use of scheduled, brief clinician support for those receiving the CCBT, provided during weeks 1, 2, 4, 6, 8, and 10, and twice during the month-long follow-up. Clinician contact involved reviewing progress, gathering data on ratings of anxiety, and providing support and extra advice as needed. Clinician calls throughout the duration of the intervention were for 1 hour.

The first RCT (N = 93) involved outpatients with a phobia or panic disorder, who were randomized in a 2:2:1 ratio to the CCBT (based on exposure-based treatment strategies), traditional face-to-face exposure-based treatment, or to a placebo control computer-guided relaxation condition (Marks et al., 2004). Clinician support was administered to both the CCBT and control condition. All treatments were administered in a primary health care clinic. Dropout rates were significantly higher in both active treatment conditions compared to placebo (6%), with rates being nearly twice as high (43%) in CCBT than in traditional treatment (24%). Despite their higher dropout rate, both treatment conditions significantly outperformed control at post-treatment and at the 1-month follow-up. Mean effect sizes on the primary outcome measures were very large at post treatment and follow-up for CCBT (2.9 and 3.7, respectively) and traditional face-to-face treatment (3.5 and 3.5, respectively), whereas the control condition demonstrated medium effects (0.5 and 0.5, respectively).

Having demonstrated the efficacy of *FearFighter* (FF) when administered in a clinic setting, the second RCT sought to examine its effectiveness when provided off-site via the Internet (Schneider et al., 2005). Outpatients (N = 68) with a phobia or panic disorder were randomized in a 2:1 ratio to either *FearFighter* (n = 45) or to a minimal CBT without exposure (Managing Anxiety; n = 23). The Managing Anxiety (MA) program consisted of standard psychoeducation information about anxiety and panic and the importance of relaxation in controlling anxiety, as well as instruction in balancing worries with positive thoughts, diaphragmatic breathing, progressive muscle relaxation, and distracting. Both conditions were instructed to monitor behavior: FF participants compiled a daily diary of the self-exposures and MA participants completed homework sheets associated with the topics covered in the course. Both conditions received scheduled, brief clinician contacts, primarily by phone and, in two cases, by e-mail. The focus of these calls was again to reinforce their respective learning, answer questions, gather ratings, and provide support. Participants in both conditions improved equally over the 10-week trial, although FF participants improved significantly more on five out of ten measures at the final 1-month follow-up.

Free from Anxiety (Fri fran oro in *Swedish*)

In Sweden, Andersson, Carlbring, and their colleagues have also conducted a number of RCTs on *Free from Anxiety*, a ten-module self-help CCBT delivered via the Internet. The first study (N = 49) compared CCBT (n = 25) to ten individual weekly sessions of CBT (n = 24) for clients with panic disorder (PD; Carlbring et al., 2005). Both treatments consisted of standard CBT for PD, including psychoeducation, breathing retraining, interoceptive and in vivo exposure, and relapse prevention. Results found the CCBT equally effective as the traditional method. Composite within-group effect sizes were high in both groups and remained high at the 1-year follow-up (Cohen's d = 0.80 for CCBT and d = 0.93 for traditional face-to-face). Next, Carlbring et al. (2006) added brief weekly clinician contact to the CCBT and required subjects to send in their homework assignments before receiving the next treatment module. The brief calls were planned for no more than 10 minutes each and were for purposes of providing support. A total of 60 participants were randomized to either the multimodal treatment package or a WL control. Treatment participants averaged a total of 3.9 hours of clinician contact during the study's duration. Results revealed that, although all participants improved significantly with gains maintained at the 9-month follow-up, 77% of treated participants no longer met PD criteria at the end of treatment; all control participants continued to meet PD criteria.

Andersson and colleagues developed a multimodal Web-based self-help CCBT site for treatment of social phobia, with nine modules spanning 186 Internet pages (Andersson et al., 2006). The treatment was based on CBT protocols as described by self-help books (Antony & Swinson, 2000; Butler, 2001; Kaver, 1999; Rapee, 1998). Each module included psychoeducational material and exercises, with the culmination of the course being client-written essays describing their experience with the CCBT and their outcome. Investigators randomized individuals with social phobia (N = 64) to one of two conditions; the 9-week CCBT intervention (n = 32) or WL control (n = 32). Here, CCBT was combined with two live group sessions and minimal clinician contact. Results again demonstrated CCBT's

efficacy in that treated participants, but not controls, showed significant improvement on most outcome variables, and treatment gains were maintained at the 1-year follow-up. A second study for social phobia utilizing the same CCBT just described was conducted by Carlbring et al. (2007) that combined short weekly telephone calls, as they had in their earlier PD research, with a total duration of 95 minutes. Participants meeting diagnostic criteria for social phobia were randomized to either the treatment (n = 29) or a WL control (n = 28) condition. Compared to study controls, treated participants experienced significantly greater reductions in general and social anxiety, avoidance, and depression. Notably, adherence to treatment was high, with 93% completing treatment. Additionally, positive outcomes were maintained at the 1-year follow-up.

De-Stress

Litz et al. (2007) developed an 8-week clinician-assisted CCBT for PTSD and evaluated its efficacy on Department of Defense service members with PTSD resulting from 9/11 attacks on the Pentagon or combat in Iraq or Afghanistan. Participants (N = 45) were assigned to either CCBT (n = 24) or supportive counseling (n = 21), also delivered via a Web application. In addition to the CCBT, experimental participants had an initial meeting with an individual clinician to generate a fear hierarchy. Additionally, clinicians provided training in two stress management strategies and initial training in simple cognitive reframing techniques. Clinicians also provided assistance in generating a final personalized stress hierarchy (via e-mail). Results from this study are somewhat compromised by high dropout and attrition rates in both conditions (five dropped before treatment and seven during treatment). Only 18 of the original 45 participants completed the 6-month follow-up assessment. Despite high attrition, *De-Stress* completers had significantly greater reductions in PTSD, depression, and anxiety at 6 months compared to controls. One-third of *De-Stress* completers (a quarter of the intent-to-treat sample) achieved high end-state functioning 6 months after treatment.

BRAVE for Children

Australian researchers Spence et al. (2006) examined the feasibility and efficacy of traditional treatment combined with Internet-delivered CCBT in clinically anxious children (N = 72), ages 7–14. Participants were randomized to one of three conditions: standard clinic-based therapy ("CLINIC," n = 22), clinic plus CCBT ("CLIN-NET," $n = 27$), or a WL ($n = 23$) control. Both active conditions included the same treatment protocol over a 10-week period; the only difference was the mode of treatment delivery. Specifically, half the sessions for CCBT subjects were delivered via the Internet. The CCBT contained considerable use of animations, images, color, interactive elements, and self-assessment quizzes with immediate feedback. Each session contained approximately 20–30 Web pages and took around 1 hour to complete. Participants and their parents received an in-person tutorial on how to use the CCBT prior to the start of treatment, and CCBT compliance was monitored. Among completers at post treatment, 13 of 20 (65%) of CLINIC subjects, 14 of 25 (56%) of CLIN-NET participants, and three of 23 (13%) WL subjects no longer met criteria for their primary anxiety disorder, with both active conditions significantly outperforming WL. No difference was observed between the two active conditions. Importantly, treatment effects for both active conditions were consistent with other comparable treatment outcome studies of anxious children. At the 6-month follow-up, 78.9% of CLINIC subjects and 60.9% of CLIN-NET participants no longer met criteria for their primary anxiety diagnosis. By the 12-month follow-up, percentages of children free of their primary anxiety diagnosis increased in both conditions to 89.5% and 73.9%, respectively. Consistent with earlier findings, the differences between active conditions were not significant at either follow-up; however, both outperformed WL. Importantly, both active conditions earned high ratings of satisfaction from children and their parents, with no differences were observed between conditions, comparable rates of treatment retention, and comparable outcomes.

Extending their earlier work on BRAVE for children, March, Spence, and Donovan (2009) examined the efficacy of CCBT as a stand-alone intervention in the treatment of anxiety disorders in children. Clinically anxious children ($N = 73$), ages 7–12, were randomized to one of two conditions: CCBT via the Internet (NET; $n = 40$) or WL ($n = 33$). The 10-week intervention (BRAVE for Children-ONLINE) was adapted from the Internet course used in their prior research (Spence et al., 2006), in which each weekly module mirrored the clinic-provided traditional treatment and was designed to last approximately 60 minutes. In addition to the ten weekly modules, two bolster sessions were provided at 1 and 3 months post treatment to consolidate learning and emphasize relapse prevention

strategies. At post treatment, nine of the 30 NET participants (30%) and three of the 29 (10%) WL participants no longer met criteria for their primary anxiety disorder. The difference approached statistical significance. Five (16.7%) of the NET participants were fully free of any anxiety disorder, compared to one (3.4%) in the WL condition. NET participants however showed a significantly greater improvement in Clinician Severity Ratings and Children's Global Assessment Scale (Shaffer et al., 1983) over WL participants. The 6-month follow-up only involved reassessment of NET participants. The percentage of NET participants who no longer met diagnostic criteria for their primary disorder continued to increase, from 30% at post assessment to 75% at 6 months. Furthermore, 60.7% were free of all anxiety disorders at 6 months.

COMPUTERIZED CBT-FACILITATED TREATMENT FOR EST-NAÏVE CLINICIANS

The final type of CCBT we review involves the use of technology to support or guide a novice clinician in administering an evidence-based treatment protocol to a client while maintaining a high level of fidelity (Craske et al., 2009). Currently primarily used in primary care settings in the treatment of anxiety and depression, the potential applications of such an approach, if effective, are considerable and could radically impact dissemination of evidence-based therapies and how we provide effective training. Rather than passive diffusion methods, such as attending a workshop or reading a textbook, trainees and professionals could receive in vivo, on-the-job training.

Coordinated Anxiety Learning and Management (CALM): Tools for Living

Craske et al. (2009) have developed and begun investigating a CCBT that could be easily used in a variety of primary care contexts to support the delivery of CBT for anxiety disorders by novice clinicians. *CALM Tools for Living* singly addresses the four most common anxiety disorders that present in primary care settings: panic disorder, PTSD, GAD, and social anxiety disorder. One program (rather than four separate programs) navigates the clinician and client together through a treatment package for their primary anxiety disorder. CALM includes eight modules (i.e., self-monitoring, education, fear hierarchy, breathing retraining, cognitive restructuring, exposure to external cues, exposure to images, memories, sensations, and relapse prevention). Each module includes didactic text-based content (session goals, summaries, educational information, review of prior learning), homework review, in-session practice of new skills, instructions for homework practice, and video demonstration of specific client-relevant CBT strategies. Each module concludes with a self-rating of understanding, quizzes, and clinician rating of client's demonstrated skills knowledge. Finally, customized print-outs of session materials are provided to the client, and ideographic examples described by the client are entered into CALM for retrieval and tracking at subsequent meetings. Clinician and client sit side by side while viewing the same monitor, where prompts are provided to the clinician in specific tasks. The program is intended to be completed in six to eight visits.

Research findings from an uncontrolled trial of CALM supported feasibility of this innovative approach through both the acceptance and use of CALM by clinicians and its effectiveness with clients (Craske et al., 2009). CALM was tested at 13 clinics across four sites and involved 13 clinicians who provided CALM to clients ($N = 261$) in a primary care context. Although some suggestions for improvements were made (reduce amount of text, simplify language, eliminate redundancy), clinicians rated the program very highly across acceptability items. Study participants receiving CALM attended an average of 7.63 sessions (SD = 3.39; range = 1–19). Participants receiving at least one session of CALM reported high use of skills and strategies between their sessions. For example, participants reported using the breathing skills 6.5 times (SD = 3.6) and practiced in vivo exposure to feared stimuli 4.2 times (SD = 3.5) between the initial session when the strategy was introduced and the subsequent session. Assessment of self-reported levels of anxiety and depression, as well as outcome expectancies, indicated significant symptom reduction and clinical improvements that were not moderated by the presence or absence of psychotropic medication use.

Comments

At present, a number of CCBTs have been developed for a myriad of behavioral disorders, although primarily to treat anxiety disorders and depression. The research to date is strong. Generally, CCBT is superior to no treatment and to TAU; in many cases, it is as effective as traditional face-to-face treatment. These positive findings have paved the way for its use in large public and nonprofit healthcare systems, particularly when integrated within a broader stepped care approach. Computerized CBT

can be used in several different ways: as a "pure" self-help approach (requires no clinician involvement), a clinician-guided self-help approach (contact with clinician is made before and/or after engaging with the CCBT), to augment or enhance traditional treatment (psychoeducation is "outsourced" to CCBT), and to facilitate treatment delivery (Craske's CALM model).

Perhaps without intending to do so, CCBT can powerfully facilitate the dissemination of ESTs by reaching those individuals who may be unable or unwilling to seek out traditional psychotherapy. Additionally, CCBTs provide ESTs with fidelity; adhering to the treatment manual is implicit, as CCBTs do not inadvertently "drift" from the EST manual, dilute, or opt not to provide the EST. Computerized CBTs, however, are not without their limitations. Their primary challenge, particularly when used as a stand-alone option, is user-engagement. Just as psychotherapy may be the luxury of the rich or well-insured, CCBTs may be the luxury of the highly motivated, intelligent, and resourceful. Future research is still required to develop approaches that facilitate user engagement, and ultimately promote higher rates of CCBT use and completion. This research may be enhanced by applying empirically derived marketing and e-learning principles (Mayer, 2008).

Finally, CCBTs are unlikely to ever be sufficient for all clients with behavioral disorders. This may be particularly true for individuals with multiple, severe, and complex problems, such as those with borderline personality disorder (BPD). However, even in these cases, CCBTs can still be used to augment and facilitate the primary treatment.

Virtual Reality

Virtual reality (VR) is among the earliest of technologies used in the treatment of psychological problems. Virtual reality immerses and engages the client in a 3-D computer-simulated world. The quality of immersion and activation of one's sense of "being in it" separates VR from other multimedia applications and devices, like television and computer games. Its earliest application was in the treatment of anxiety disorders, in which clients faced their fears virtually. Like situational or in vivo exposure, VR exposure therapy (VRET) for anxiety disorders was based on the same emotional-processing-of-fear model used in standard exposure therapy (Foa & Kozak, 1986), namely cue exposure and response prevention (Baker, Patterson, & Barlow, 2002; Peñate, Pitti, Bethencourt, de la Fuente, & Gracia, 2008). Use of VRET has significantly increased in recent years as a treatment for PTSD in response to the President's Commission on Care for America's Returning Wounded Warrior (Dole & Shalala, 2007; Macedonia, 2009), which has further accelerated advances in technology, making VRET more affordable and more immersive. In addition to its use in the treatment of anxiety disorders, VR has also been successfully applied as a method of distraction to increase pain tolerance during painful medical procedures. Encouraging empirical support for its use as a pain analgesic during notoriously painful medical procedures, such as wound care with burn patients, makes it likely to have considerable reach and impact in the coming decade. In addition to these two well-researched areas of VR, other applications are beginning to emerge, including VR to aid in assessment of attention-deficit hyperactivity disorder (ADHD)-related deficits (Pollak et al., 2009) and to enhance street-crossing skills in the treatment of autism spectrum disorders (Goldsmith, 2009). In addition to these client-focused applications, VR has been used with considerable success as an effective method of training health professionals. We focus our review on those areas that currently have the greatest impact and evidence base to date, namely the application of VR in the treatment of anxiety disorders, as a method of distraction/pain analgesia, and as a training tool for new practitioners.

The Role of Presence in Virtual Reality

Virtual reality's success is achieved through *immersion*, in which awareness of actual reality is suspended and temporarily replaced by an engrossing artificial environment. Successful immersion facilitates *presence*, the extent to which the client *responds* and *reacts* as if he or she is "there," present in the alternative world. For example, does the spider phobic become similarly anxious when "encountering" a virtual spider as in real life? Do riders of a virtual roller coaster swerve, duck their heads, and experience butterflies in their stomach when "moving" through the virtual landscape? Contributing further to presence is *continuity*, the extent to which the client's experience of the virtual world is not interrupted (Strickland, Hodges, North, & Weghorst, 1997). Immersion and activation of presence in VR have relied primarily on visual sensory immersion, typically achieved through use of a computer screen or a stereoscopic head-mounted display (HMD), both paired with a computer mouse, joystick, or keyboard for navigation and/or engagement in the virtual world. Activation of other senses beyond vision contribute

to the extent of the client's immersion and can further facilitate presence. For example, tactile props, such as a furry toy to simulate spider hair, have been added in the VR treatment of spider phobia. More recently, the ability to activate a particular smell has been added to VR equipment, to further facilitate *presence,* thereby increasing the likelihood of the effectiveness of the VR experience (Rizzo et al., 2006).

Virtual Reality Exposure Therapy in Treatment of Anxiety Disorders

Virtual reality exposure therapy research for treatment of anxiety disorders has flourished over the past decade, beginning with the pioneering single-case design work of North and North in their treatment of a flying phobia (North & North, 1994; North, North, & Coble, 1997). Virtual reality exposure therapy has been investigated for a number of disorders, often using well-controlled research designs. These include the treatment of acrophobia (Emmelkamp et al., 2002; Krijn et al., 2004; Rothbaum et al., 1995), claustrophobia (Botella, Baños, Villa, Perpiñá, & García-Palacios, 2000), flying phobia (Botella, Osma, Garcia-Palacios, Quero, & Baños, 2004; Maltby, Kirsch, Mayers, & Allen, 2002; Mühlberger, Herrmann, Wiedemann, Ellgring, & Pauli, 2001; Mühlberger, Wiedemann, & Pauli, 2003; Rothbaum, Hodges, Anderson, Price, & Smith, 2002; Rothbaum, Hodges, Smith, Hwan, & Price, 2000; Wiederhold, 1999), spider phobia (García-Palacios, Hoffman, Carlin, Furness, & Botella, 2002), agoraphobia (Botella, et al., 2004; Choi et al., 2005; North et al., 1996; Peñate et al., 2008; Vincelli et al., 2003); and PTSD (Rothbaum et al., 1999). More recently, VRET has been used to address high rates of PTSD among active-duty soldiers, veterans, and U.S. service members (Reger & Gahm, 2008), as it is estimated that as many as 20% of returnees from Iraq and 11% of returnees from Afghanistan suffer from PTSD (Dole & Shalala, 2007).

Findings from this extensive body of research overwhelmingly provide empirical support for VRET in the treatment of anxiety disorders. Specifically, controlled trials have consistently found VRET to be superior to WL and placebo control conditions and equivalent, if not slightly superior to traditional exposure therapy-based CBT at post test and at follow-up. A recent meta-analysis by (Powers & Emmelkamp, 2008) involving 13 VRET studies (N = 397) found a large effect size for VRET compared to control conditions (Cohen's d = 1.11) (S.E. = 0.15, 95% CI: 0.82–1.39) across all primary and secondary outcome categories of analysis. As expected, standard in vivo exposure therapy was not significantly more effective than VRET. In fact, results from this meta-analysis slightly favored VRET over standard in vivo therapy, with a small effect size favoring VRET over in vivo conditions on major outcome variables (Cohen's d = 0.35) (S.E. = 0.15, 95% CI: 0.05–0.65).

A number of unique aspects of VRET make it a compelling alternative to standard in vivo or situational exposure. First, in contrast to standard exposure, clinicians are easily able to create and control precise and clinically relevant factors associated with the feared stimulus (cue) and its surrounding environment. For example, in the case of spider phobia, the clinician can control the look and "feel" of the spider, the proximity of the spider to the client, and the environment in which the client encounters the spider to maximize activation of presence. Additionally, VRET allows for repeated, gradual, and systematic exposure to the feared stimulus (Garcia-Palacios, Hoffman, Carlin, Furness, & Botella, 2002). Second, VRET is often more convenient to administer than standard exposure procedures. Clinicians, for example, are not required to leave their offices, nor do they need to create and/or control extraneous conditions for the exposure, whether it is finding an alley that is similar to the alley a woman was raped in, borrowing a snake from a local pet shop to aid in the treatment of a snake phobia, or finding a tall building with easy roof access for the client fearful of heights. Finally, it allows for exposure to specific situations and triggers that would otherwise be impossible to find and/or adequately recreate. For example, clinicians treating PTSD in military personnel returning from Iraq or Afghanistan can tailor exact conditions to those associated with the traumatic event when using VR. Here, the user can drive a Humvee down a desert highway alone or in a convoy through Iraq-like city streets while hearing the explosions and human cries, as well as smell burning rubber (Gerardi, Rothbaum, Ressler, Heekin, & Rizzo, 2008).

VIRTUAL REALITY EXPOSURE THERAPY ILLUSTRATED: THE FULL SPECTRUM VIRTUAL IRAQ PTSD APPLICATION

The Institute of Creative Technologies at University of Southern California recently brought together two other premier VR labs in the United States (Virtually Better, Inc. and Virtual Reality Medical Center) to develop a sophisticated VRET for PTSD among military personnel in Iraq (see Rizzo et al., 2006 for a thorough review). The *Full Spectrum Virtual Iraq* environment includes several diverse scenarios and is designed to be fully customized to the needs of the client. All scenarios can be adjusted for time of day, as well as weather and lighting conditions. Examples of the scenario settings include *city scenes* (a desolate city with low-populated streets, compromised old buildings, warehouses, factories, and a mosque and junk yard; and a highly populated city with bustling traffic, marketplaces, and monuments); *checkpoint* (includes a variety of moving vehicles that are arriving, stopping, and being inspected); *city building interiors* (users can navigate through the buildings; these buildings can be designed to be vacant or populated; characters populating the interior buildings can also be modified); *small rural village* (contains ramshackle structures, a village center, decaying garbage, and war-damaged vehicles); and a *desert military base* (includes tents, soldiers, and an array of military hardware). The VRET runs on two connected notebook computers: one used by the clinician to direct and control the exposure while the other drives the client's head-mounted device and orientation tracker. In addition to rich, complementary sounds matched to the visual animation, this VRET includes vibrations and a smell palette, both activated by specific triggers within the scene. Scents include burning rubber, cordite, garbage, body odor, smoke, diesel fuel, Iraqi spices, and gunpowder.

Virtual Reality Pain Reduction

Researchers have recently applied VR to distract patients from painful burn treatment procedures, such as physical therapy and wound care (Hoffman, Doctor, Patterson, Carrougher, & Furness, 2000). Because pain perception involves a strong psychological component, burn patients often report reliving the original burn incident during wound care and other medical procedures (http://www.hitl. washington.edu/projects/vrpain/). Investigators hypothesized that VR may provide sufficient distraction to interrupt the patient's ability to attend to pain, and thus decrease the experience of pain (Hoffman et al., 2008).

Virtual reality's efficacy as an analgesic for burn patients has been investigated in several trials. Using a within-subjects controlled trial, seven patients (ages 9–32 years, with an average of 24% total body surface area burned) received both conditions (VR experimental condition and no distraction control) during each trial; condition order was randomized and counterbalanced (Hoffman, Patterson, Carrougher, & Sharar, 2001). All participants received no less than three trials; VR sessions were limited to 3 minutes during physical therapy. Subjective pain ratings were significantly lower for participants receiving VR. Importantly, ratings of pain magnitude did not diminish with repeated use of VR. Later research applying a similar design with burn patients (N = 11) during wound care produced similar findings (Hoffman et al., 2008). In contrast to earlier studies, participants received VR while wounds were debrided in the hydrotherapy tank and then dressed. Reports of pain were significantly less—from "severe" to "moderate" (7.6 and 5.1, respectively) during VR. Importantly, participants with the strongest illusion of "going inside" the virtual world had the greatest analgesic effect (from severe pain without VR to only mild pain with VR, 7.2 vs. 3.7, respectively). Reductions in pain have also been verified through functional magnetic resonance imaging (fMRI) research that shows significant reductions in activity in the five brain regions associated with pain (i.e., anterior cingulated cortex, primary and secondary somatosensory cortex, insula, and thalamus) during VR (Hoffman et al., 2004). Importantly, the positive analgesic effects of VR distraction do not appear to diminish with repeated exposure (Hoffman, Patterson, Carrougher, Nakamura, et al., 2001; Hoffman, Patterson Carrougher, & Sharar, 2001; Rutter, Dahlquist, & Weiss, 2009).

ILLUSTRATION OF VIRTUAL REALITY IN TREATMENT OF BURN PATIENTS

SnowWorld, designed and created by Hunter Hoffman and his colleagues at the University of Washington, is the first immersive VR designed specifically for reducing pain via distraction. SnowWorld was built using Virtual World Development Software (www.virtools.com). Virtual reality is delivered using a HMD and headphones. (A water-friendly version of the head-mount has also been created and tested for use during the debriding process that occurs in specialized tubs in burn units.) Users of SnowWorld are transported into a visual world of snow-covered canyons filled with snowmen, penguins, swimming whales, and igloos. Users fly like fighter jets (controlled by a hand remote) through the seemingly vast world and launch snowballs at the snowmen, which explode on contact. Adding further dimension to the experience, *Graceland* (an upbeat, Grammy-award winning song by Paul Simon recorded in 1986 that is an eclectic mix of musical styles and that rose to the top of the charts in the U.K. and U.S.) plays in the background, providing the perfect accompaniment as the user experiences this imaginary virtual world.

Virtual Reality as a Method of Training Treatment Professionals

Virtual reality has also been used extensively in medical and dental training as a means of developing requisite skills within a simulated fail-safe environment that resembles real-world conditions (Mantovani, Castelnuovo, Gaggioli, & Riva, 2004). Virtual reality has been applied to teaching physicians debridement of gunshot wounds (Delp, Loan, Basdogan, & Rosen, 1997), temporal bone dissection (Kuppersmith, Johnston, Moreau, Loftin, & Jenkins, 1997), arthroscopic knee surgery (Mabrey et al., 2000), orthopedic surgery (Tsai, Hsieh, & Jou, 2001), training and assessment of laparoscopic skills (Katsavelis et al., 2009; Gurusamy, Aggarwal, Palanivelu, & Davidson, 2009; Rolfsson et al., 2002), esophageal intubation (Kesavadas, Joshi, Mayrose, & Chugh, 2002), microsurgical excision of cerebral arteriovenous malformations (Ng et al., 2009), and interventional neuroradiology procedures (Chui et al., 2002). Virtual reality has also been used to teach bedside manner, basic patient communication and history taking, decision-making, and treatment planning (Dickerson et al., 2005; Fleetwood et al., 2000; Janda et al., 2004; Johnsen et al., 2005; Johnsen, Dickerson, Raij, Harrison, & Lok, 2006; McGee, Neill, Goldman, & Casey, 1998; Stevens et al., 2006).

Use of VR and virtual patients (VP) to train mental health treatment providers has significantly lagged behind medicine; however, some studies are beginning to emerge (Kenny, Rizzo, Parsons, Gratch, & Swartout, 2007). Yellowlees and Cook (2006) developed a VR system that simulates the experience of auditory and visual hallucinations in schizophrenic patients as a means of increasing clinician empathy. Beutler and Harwood (2004) have used VR to prepare new clinicians for work with their first clients through the use of a computer-generated client that responds verbally and with corresponding emotional facial expressions to a trainee clinician. Similarly, using advanced VR, Kenny and his colleagues have developed a language-capable virtual client ("Justin") with conduct disorder to train novice therapists in clinical interviewing skills with a resistant client. The clinician meets the 16 year-old Justin, a life-like 3-D teenager, in a virtual therapy room. The interview can be recorded for supervision purposes.

Controlled trials examining the efficacy of VR and VP in training of professionals are, at this time, sparse. Janda and colleagues (2004) randomized 39 students to traditional instruction or an enhanced condition in which subjects practiced with a virtual client following the standard instruction. In comparison to those who received didactic instruction only, participants in the VR-enhanced condition asked more relevant questions, performed a more complete client history, and spent more time on client issues than did students who only received traditional instruction (Janda et al.). In an uncontrolled trial, Yellowlees and Cook (2006) found a significant training effect among medical students (n = 863) following use of the VR intervention in their understanding of visual hallucinations. By comparison, well-controlled trials within the field of medical research flourish and provide robust support for its efficacy as a supplemental method of training that provides the trainee with the benefits of hands-on training in a risk-free virtual environment (Gurusamy, Aggarwal, Palanivelu, & Davidson, 2008; Gurusamy et al., 2009).

Comments

There is no question that VR is efficacious for a variety of purposes in clinical psychology. These include the treatment of anxiety disorders, as an analgesic via distraction for painful medical procedures, and as a fail-safe method of training health professionals in specific procedures that require hands-on practice. Despite its efficacy, the application and dissemination of VR in real-world settings has significantly lagged behind the data and its utility. This may change as the cost of VR (now well over $20,000 for a high-quality head-mount) goes down and as systems and networks adopt it as a primary strategy, as the Veteran's Administration did for the treatment of PTSD.

Mobile Technologies

Fortune magazine-identified "guru" B.J. Fogg predicts that we are on the cusp of an "unstoppable revolution" (Reingold & Tkacyzk, 2008). Within 15 years, no other medium—from television and Web to word of mouth—will exert more influence on our behavior than our cell phones (Fogg & Eckles, 2007). His evidence? *We love our cell phones.* We dress them up, feel anxious when we can't find them, and spend more time with them than we do with our loved ones. *They are always with us,* often within range of an outstretched arm, whether we're working, flying, playing, or sleeping. Like magic wands, they are enchanting; they do almost everything imaginable and require little training. We can talk to a friend while rafting down the Colorado river, make reservations at a five-star restaurant for a dinner while

walking to the office, take photographs and upload them to a website, transfer money from one bank account to another, and get driving instructions using a global positioning system (GPS). The possibilities seem endless.

How have mobile technologies emerged as the "hottest" media expected to significantly shape human behavior? Three factors are at play. First, in less than 10 years, mobile phones have become affordable, and are faster and more powerful than the first several generations of the desktop computer. Multifunctional "smart" phones are now relatively inexpensive, some costing as little as $50. Between 2005 and 2008, usage expanded by 65%, from 2.14 billion phones to 3.3 billion (Wikipedia, December 16, 2009b). Cellular coverage has also substantially increased over the years. In 2006, 80% of the world's population had cell phone coverage; by 2010, coverage will exceed 90% worldwide (GSM Association, 2006). Second, Apple succeeded in crossing a critical threshold by making it easy for anyone to download applications to their phone. Such third-party applications are now ubiquitous (Tedeschi, 2009). By May 2009, over 1 billion applications had been downloaded from Apple's App Store (Apple, 2009). As of this writing, over 75,000 iPhone applications were available in 77 countries, reaching tens of millions of iPhone users. Apple's commercial success has ignited its competition to move in similar directions (Borden, 2009). Third, the use and integration of mobile phone functionality has the potential to radically improve the quality and cost-effectiveness of health care at a time when health-care costs are significantly rising (Tanguy & Heywood, 2007). For example, the integration of many of its functions—from camera, text messaging, and the Internet, to special add-on hardware monitoring devices (e.g., insulin levels in the diabetic, oxygen absorption in the asthmatic)—will allow patients to directly transmit data about their condition from any location with cellular coverage to their physician for analysis and instruction, thus improving care and decreasing needless office and/or emergency room visits (Perez et al., 2006).

Although mobile technologies are a relative neophyte to research, recent studies have emerged testing the use of mobile technologies in changing a wide range of behavior. These include promoting sexual health and decreasing sexually transmitted diseases (STDs) in youth (Hoffman, 2009; Levine, McCright, Dobkin, Woodruff, & Klausner, 2008), promoting smoking cessation (Haug et al., 2008; Obermayer, Riley, Asif, & Jean-Mary, 2004; Riley,

Obermayer, & Jean-Mary, 2008; Rodgers et al., 2005; Whittaker et al., 2008), facilitating weight loss (Joo & Kim, 2007; Kubota, Fujita, & Hatano, 2004; Morak et al., 2008; Tanguy & Heywood, 2007), increasing physical activity (Damen, 2007; Hurling et al., 2007), providing dialectical behavior therapy (DBT) skills coaching in substance-dependent patients with BPD (Rizvi, Dimeff, & Skutch, 2009), and monitoring and facilitating treatment of chronic diseases, including severe asthma (Ryan, Cobern, Wheeler, Price, & Tarassenko, 2005), diabetes (Carroll, Marrero, & Downs, 2007; Quinn et al., 2008), medication compliance in HIV/AIDs patients (Puccio et al., 2006), and side effects for antiepileptic medication treatment (Frings et al., 2008). Additionally, hardware attachments for cell phones are being used to monitor, record, and transmit peak flow levels in patients with severe asthma (Ryan et al., 2005), test and transmit to their doctors the blood glucose levels of diabetic patients (Carroll, Marrero, & Downs, 2007), and monitor blood alcohol levels in concerned drinkers (Chmielewski, 2008). In this section, we will review current research highlighting multiple modes of intervention delivery via mobile phones, several applications that have been the primary focus of research to date, and finally, discuss the future of this burgeoning field of clinical intervention research.

Thus far, short-message service (SMS; aka "text messaging" or "texting") is the most commonly investigated mobile application in the area of behavior change. Fjeldsoe, Marshall, and Miller (2009) recently conducted a review of studies published to date investigating the use of SMS as part of a behavioral intervention. Of the original 33 papers identified, 14 evaluated the use of SMS to change behavior. The majority of these ($n = 10$) focused on clinical care of health behaviors (e.g., diabetes); the remaining four focused on preventive health behaviors (e.g., smoking cessation). Positive outcomes were observed in 13 studies, leading investigators to conclude that SMS can be a powerful means of facilitating behavior change. Several key benefits of SMS were identified, including wide population reach; interactive, tailored, and individualized messages; and instant delivery with asynchronous receipt.

The following section reviews mobile phone interventions conducted to date with relevance to clinical psychology. Because this area of research is still in its infancy, yet is expanding rapidly, we also include novel, cutting-edge applications of mobile technologies that are or are soon to be available as products, but do not as yet have data to support their efficacy.

Smoking Cessation

To date, three RCTs and four open trials have been conducted evaluating the efficacy of six different mobile technologies systems for smoking cessation. The majority of mobile phone interventions (MPIs) in these trials were applied to young adults (Haug et al., 2008; Obermayer et al., 2004; Riley et al., 2008; Rodgers et al., 2005; Whittaker et al., 2008). The researchers universally commented that MPIs are an ideal fit for this population: Young adults who do wish to quit smoking seldom access traditional smoking cessation services, yet they commonly use mobile phones and rely on them as their primary means of communication. Of the two MPIs for adults, one was designed and evaluated for the specific needs of adults smokers with HIV/AIDS (Vidrine, Arduino, & Gritz, 2006; Vidrine, Arduino, Lazey, & Gritz, 2006); only one program (Happy Ending) was developed and tested for uncomplicated adults (Brendryen & Kraft, 2008; Brendryen, Drozd, & Kraft, 2008). The MPIs for smoking cessation range dramatically, from simple use of the telephone for weekly counseling calls (Vidrine, Arduino, & Gritz, 2006; Virdine, Arduino, Lazey, et al., 2006) to well-integrated Web and text-messaging system that tailor interventions to the user in real-time and foster social support from friends to facilitate and maintain cessation (Obermayer et al., 2004; Riley et al., 2008). Only those studies using an RCT or with replication are summarized below.

YOUNG ADULT STUDIES

Obermayer et al. (2004) developed and pilot tested a program for college students that integrates an interactive website and cell phone technology to deliver a customized smoking cessation intervention. Students first complete an online assessment that provides the basis for a personalized intervention. Although most of the intervention involves text messages received during the day, users are encouraged to go to the website daily to view a graph that depicts their smoking during the preparation phase through the present or to view the supportive text messages they have received earlier. The website also contains educational modules, such as handling withdrawal, coping with urges, and managing weight gain. A particularly novel innovation involves the use of social support: Users can opt to provide password-protected access to support people who can view their progress in quitting smoking and can leave a supportive message. Support persons receive a reminder e-mail prompting them to remember to leave a supportive message; tips are also provided on how to support the user who is attempting to give up smoking. Text interventions vary according to where the user is along the stages-of-change continuum (Prochaska & DiClemente, 1983, 1992), with messages increasing in frequency around the individual's quit date. Encouraging messages and tips to manage urges and other coping strategies are provided on the quit day. Users get no fewer than two texts per day, tailored to their progress; they can also communicate with the system should they desire additional assistance in managing a high-risk situation.

Obermeyer and colleagues have conducted two open trials to date, both with promising findings. In the first trial, college students ($N = 46$) who smoked on a regular, daily basis and desired to quit were recruited to participate (Obermayer et al., 2004). Seven participants formally dropped out of the study, and eight were lost at follow-up. At the 6-week follow-up, 43% made at least one 24-hour attempt at quitting; 22% quit. (These analyses were based on the intent-to-treat sample; those without follow-up data were presumed to be smoking.) The second trial sought to replicate the initial study (Riley et al., 2008). Thirty-one college students who were daily smokers wishing to quit were recruited and received the intervention. In comparison to the first sample, these participants were significantly heavier smokers. Four participants were lost at follow-up. After 6 weeks, 45% reported abstinence (42% on the basis of a biochemical validation); those who continued smoking reported significant reductions in their use and dependence.

Rodgers et al.'s (2005) MPI involved a complex back-end database with 1,000 responses for delivery of personally relevant text messages depending on the user's stage of change. Users received five text messages daily leading up to their quit day. Three types of messages were provided: advice (what to expect when you are quitting, how to avoid weight gain, ways to improve nutrition), motivation and support (success stories, feedback on money saved from not smoking), and distraction (topics of general interest such as sports, trivia, and travel). Other features included: TXT Quizzes (facts about smoking with answers provided the next day), Quit Buddy (participants with similar characteristics and quit days were put in touch with each other), and TXT Crave (users could "pull" for advice in managing

a high-risk situation). A total of 1,705 young adult daily smokers (median age = 22) from New Zealand were randomized to the text MPI or control condition (received a text message every 2 weeks thanking them for their participation). All participants were invited to access other standard services (Quitline and nicotine replacement medication). In comparison to the control condition, MPI participants were significantly more likely to quit smoking, with nearly twice the rate of quitting. The MPI participants were also significantly more successful at not smoking at 6- and 12-week follow-ups. By the 26-week follow-up, however, no between-group differences were detected, due to increased rates of nonsmoking reported by controls. Investigators concluded that the MPI may be particularly helpful at facilitating smoking cessation.

ADULT STUDIES

Brendryen and colleagues developed and evaluated *Happy Ending* (HE), an intensive multimedia 1-year smoking cessation program that uses the Internet and mobile phones to deliver SMSs, and provides interactive voice response, craving crisis help, and just-in-time phone assistance (Brendryen et al., 2008; Brendryen & Kraft, 2008). Happy Ending is fully automated, using a complex algorithm to deliver personalized and just-in-time responses. A two-arm RCT was conducted with daily smokers willing to quit on a prescribed day without the use of nicotine replacement therapy (NRT). Participants were either randomized to HE ($n = 144$) or a control condition ($n = 146$) consisting of a 44-page self-help booklet. The main outcome was repeated point abstinence (i.e., abstinence at all four time points). Happy Ending participants reported a clinically and statistically significant higher repeat point abstinence rates compared to controls (20% vs. 7%) and significantly higher levels of coping planning and precessation self-efficacy.

Vidrine et al. (2006a) examined the effectiveness of an 8-week MPI (telephone calls) for smoking cessation among individuals with HIV/AIDs. Proactive mobile phone counseling sessions were based on a CBT designed to increase coping and problem-solving strategies and build social support. Topics included preparing for and making a commitment to quit, withdrawal facts and effective coping, identifying triggers, and special health topics for HIV/AIDS-specific smokers. All participants received the Recommended Standard of Care (RSOC): physician advice, text-based self-help materials, and NRT. Participants were randomized to RSOC only (n = 47) or RSOC plus MPI (n = 48). Eighty-one percent completed the 3-month follow-up, at which experimental participants were 3.6 times more likely to quit smoking compared to TAU participants (36.8% vs. 10.3%, respectively). Additionally, RSOC + MPI participants experienced greater reductions in anxiety and depression and increases in self-efficacy, compared to RSOC-only participants. Investigators also identified that MPI's efficacy was at least partially mediated by its ability to decrease symptoms of distress while increasing self-efficacy (Vidrine et al., 2006a, 2006b).

Obesity and Weight Loss Interventions

Obesity has been described by the World Health Organization as a global epidemic (World Health Organisation, 1998). In 2000, the prevalence of obesity was 20% among U.S. adults, up 61% from 1991; 56% were overweight compared to 45% in 1991 (Mokdad et al., 2001). In their review of the successes and failures of public and behavioral health interventions to achieve weight loss, Tufano and Karras (2005) highlight a number of barriers that consistently appear in the literature. These include lack of treatment provider access to the latest, most efficacious interventions; lack of appropriate support services; and lack of motivation by treatment providers to work with heavy and obese patients (Frank, 1993). Tufano and Karras recommend leveraging robust mobile technologies to address the problem of obesity.

Hurling et al. (2007) evaluated the impact of a 9-week real-time assessment and personalized feedback delivered via the Internet and mobile phone on physical activity. Users began by completing an assessment to identify perceived barriers to physical activity, generate appropriate solutions, and identify the user's commitment to change. Users were then asked to record their exercise habits on a weekly basis and were then provided with constructive feedback relative to their own targets and the test group as a whole. A weekly scheduling tool for planning exercise was included. Users could opt to receive e-mail and/or mobile phone reminders. Through the use of an automated assessor, users received feedback on the rate of behavioral change (e.g., users are warned when their rate of change this week was significantly greater than in previous weeks, which may make it difficult to sustain in the weeks ahead). A text-based automated dialogue helped users identify perceived barriers and offers relevant solutions. Psychoeducational information with tips and suggestions, a library of information on the degree of strenuousness of different activities, and charts displaying real-time output of their physical activity were also available via technology.

Participants (N = 77) were randomly assigned to the intervention condition (n = 47) or to a no-treatment control condition (n = 30). Participants in both conditions wore an accelerometer on their wrists to objectively measure physical activity. Those in the intervention condition received access to a suite of technology-based services, including: an Internet-based message board to directly communicate with experimental subjects, an online scheduler to facilitate weekly planning of physical activity, and periodic assessments to provide solutions about perceived barriers to physical activity, as well as e-mails and periodic text messages based on real-time assessments of physical activity from the accelerometer. In comparison to study controls, experimental participants engaged in significantly more physical activity weekly (averaging 2 hours and 18 minutes more than controls each week) and lost more body fat compared to controls (−2.18 vs. −.17 pounds, respectively).

Joo and Kim (2007) investigated the use of a multimedia 12-week weight reduction program comprised of behavior modification, exercise, and nutritional education. A total of 927 individuals from the community participated in the study. Weight assessments were obtained at a public health clinic at both baseline and follow-up. Following the baseline assessment, participants received a randomly generated (without repetition) weekly motivational and informational text message (e.g., "Be proud of yourself for exercising!," "Be aware of snack!," "Did you exercise today? Have a light meal and end the day with some stretching?"). Additionally, participants received a weekly informational brochure about exercise and diet via standard post. Of the original sample, data were available for 534 participants, and 433 (47%) completed the entire program. Statistically significant differences were observed pre to post intervention in reduction of weight, waist circumference, and body mass index scores. Over two-thirds of participants had a reduction in waist circumference between 5–7.5 cm.

Morak et al. (2008) recently piloted a Web-based therapy management system with mobile phone access to support obese patients (N = 25). Participants initially received a face-to-face consultation with a clinician, from which an individualized program was established. Participants met with their clinician once monthly during the 3-month study period.

In between meetings, participants monitored their weight and other relevant health variables as a means of increasing their awareness and motivation regarding their physical activity. Self-monitoring was intentionally utilized as an intervention/change strategy, and not for the sole purpose of assessment. Additionally, participants received reminder prompts via SMS to enter their data and weekly feedback on their weight. On average, participants received a total of 14 reminder texts. At the study's end, investigators found significant reductions in abdominal girth (2.4 cm), in body weight (2.4 kg), and body mass index (0.78 kg/m²). Eighty percent of the sample indicated that they found the text reminder prompts helpful, 85% found it helpful to receive weekly feedback about their weight trend, and 100% would recommend it to a friend. Interestingly, only 60% could imagine using their own cell phone, but 80% could imagine using their PC to access the program over the Internet.

Lifestyle and Health Promotion Interventions

A highly innovative SMS intervention, *SEXINFO*, was recently developed and evaluated in a naturalistic setting in response to the growing rates of gonorrhea among inner city youth in San Francisco (Levine et al., 2008). With a primary goal of providing information and referrals to this at-risk population, researchers relied exclusively on the communication medium that most at-risk teens had in their possession: cell-phones. SEXIFNO was inspired by a similar program in London's Brook Centres' program (BBC News, 2004). Content for the SMS intervention was developed in an iterative process in which extensive end-user feedback was gathered via focus groups. Users were recruited through strategic placement of ads on city buses and Yahoo, and informational cards were distributed by outreach workers. In the first 25 weeks, 4,500 inquiries had been made and 2,500 led to provision of specific information. To gain access, users call a phone number, then type in SEXINFO. A list of codes is provided that users can then use to make selections for specific information or referrals. The top three messages accessed included: (1) "What 2 do if ur condom broke"; (2) "2 find out about STDs"; and (3) "If u think ur pregnant." (Additional information and access to text content is available at www.sexinfosf.org.)

MyFoodPhone (MFP) is the first-ever nutrition service that links individuals with their personal dietitian using a mobile phone. Its intent is to provide a fun and effective way of keeping a food journal, receiving feedback, and ultimately staying motivated to continue a difficult lifestyle change (Tanguy & Heywood, 2007). The program consists of three steps: taking a picture of the food you eat; sending the photos to a personalized online food journal where users can, if they wish, add additional information to each photo; and receive coaching and feedback from a dietitian in the form of a video message. MyFoodPhone also includes a community support tool and a location where friends, family members, and others with a shared goal can provide support (e.g., share food journals to get motivating feedback or suggestions, share ideas about managing chronic health conditions, recipes, etc.).

Although, to our best knowledge, no empirical studies supporting its efficacy are available, the service is available through Sprint and has received considerable attention in the media (Munoz, 2005). MyFoodPhone designers and promoters highlight several key elements they believe contribute to its success: receiving personalized, video-recorded feedback from a dietitian; making the experience fun and engaging; and ensuring that all aspects of its use are convenient and easy (e.g., MFP is integrated into a phone service, so does not require the individual to carry around a separate device).

Expanding the Use of Mobile Technologies: The DBT Field Coach 1.0

We are currently developing and evaluating a mobile phone application for use by clients with BPD who are receiving comprehensive DBT (Dimeff & Skutch, 2009; Rizvi et al., 2009). The primary purpose of the *DBT Field Coach* is to aid clients in using DBT skills in the context of their lives. Telephone consultation has always been a central treatment modality in standard outpatient DBT, intended to facilitate generalization of DBT skills to their natural environments—from the therapy room to the real world (Dimeff & Koerner, 2007). Rather than calling one's clinician *after* engaging in dysfunctional behavior, DBT encourages BPD clients to call for skills coaching should they have difficulty using their DBT skills. As an adjunct to standard treatment, the *Field Coach* can be used as an additional resource for clients, potentially before and/or instead of calling their primary clinician for coaching.

The hub of the *Field Coach* is the coaching device itself, which contains information about each DBT skill and instructions in their use. Upon activating the device, clients can choose to either be guided in a step-by-step fashion to select a specific skill to try, given the specific context (just as they might when calling their individual clinician for skills coaching); alternatively, clients can also go straight to a specific skill for information, just as they might flip through their DBT skills notebook. In addition to this essential feature, the *Field Coach* includes a number of other applications to facilitate skills use and skills generalization: (a) Skill of the Day, a feature to receive a randomly generated DBT Skill each day, including what it is, how to use it, and an ongoing tally of daily attempts to practice the skill during the day; (b) Skills Diary Card Log, a feature that allows the client to monitor use of all DBT skills across the course of the day; data can be downloaded for later use by the DBT clinician; (c) Rainy Day Recordings, in which clients can upload video and audio messages from their DBT clinician and supportive friends and family members whom they can index and access when needed (e.g., when feeling discouraged, demoralized, hopeless, and other mood states that make it difficult to take the needed action); (d) 100 Reasons, a feature intended to enhance clients' motivation to engage in effective behaviors during particularly rocky times by displaying particularly salient images that capture their most important reasons (personalized for the user) to engage in effective (vs. dysfunctional) behavior (e.g., pictures of one's children, images of junkies that remind clients of what they do not want to become, etc.); and (e) Survival Tools, a feature that includes an assortment of files the client can access when they need to survive a crisis without making it worse (e.g., games and music to distract oneself from high-intensity urges; previously effective skills individual used with success in similar past situations).

Just Around the Bend: Contextual Intelligence and Mobile Application Integration

We are at the tip of the iceberg in our understanding, design, and use of mobile technologies to treat behavioral problems. Thus far, interventions involve a single function or application running at a time (e.g., texting, taking a picture, sending a picture). Even the *Field Coach*, with its myriad of features and tools, barely scrapes the surface of what is possible. Just around the bend, new technology will make it possible for multiple applications to run concurrently in the background, and battery life will improve to support this functionality (Nokia, 2009). This advance will allow for the development of contextually intelligent programs—those that assess the relevance of new information based on

contextual factors (e.g., where a person is, who a person is calling or being called by, etc.). Use of such contextual intelligence, for example, could significantly expand the impact and reach of mobile technologies to facilitate behavior change. For example, the *DBT Field Coach 2.0* built using contextual intelligence could notice when users were nearing certain geographic high-risk hotspots using the GPS (and pre-identified GPS coordinates); *Field Coach* users could then receive a warning (e.g., "You are entering a high-risk area") and be asked if they need coaching. Images associated with their most cherished reasons for stopping a problem behavior could automatically appear on the screen. Similarly, incoming or outgoing calls and text messages could also include warnings, suggestions, and filters (built into the individual's contacts) based on preprogrammed information. For example, should a drug-using friend call, the phone could encourage the user to not pick up the call, but to instead use skills. The software could also be programmed to provide a special, prerecorded message for such callers (e.g., "I have stopped using drugs and am working hard to rebuild my life. Because of our history together, I cannot continue our friendship. Please do not call back. I wish you peace on your journey and all the best in life").

Comments

Mobile phones have already captured our hearts and, for scientists and technologists, are now captivating our attention. Preliminary studies have demonstrated both the feasibility and efficacy of mobile technologies in producing behavior change. Even when only the most basic elements of mobile technologies are utilized (e.g., text messaging, camera), mobile phones can be used effectively for a variety of purposes, including behavior change. Data to date has supported their use in facilitating quitting smoking, weight loss, exercise, and reducing STDs. Our own feasibility research of the *DBT Field Coach 1.0* indicates that even patients with severe and complex behavioral problems, such as BPD with concurrent substance dependence, positively view the use of mobile technology—in this particular case—as a helpful tool to facilitate skills generalization during trying times. Emerging innovations that facilitate contextual intelligence by allowing multiple applications to run concurrently ("silently") in the background will revolutionize what is possible. Our own planning for *DBT Field Coach* 2.0 hints at these possibilities. Recognition of the potential for future mobile technologies to radically promote behavior change provided the impetus for the National Institutes of Health to launch its first annual mobile health (m-Health) summit. Case studies for the summit are expected to examine how mobile technologies can be used to facilitate public health education, promote remote data collection and surveillance, facilitate diagnosis and health monitoring of patients in remote regions, and promoting healthy behavior change.

Social Networking

Social network service or "social networking" is the latest technological newcomer to impact behavior change. Social networking refers to the use of online communities to locate, interact with, and exchange information with other users. Social networks typically link people by common interests, activities, or people they know in common. These online communities have the ability to strengthen and generalize the known positive effects of social support on behavioral change (Olsen & Kraft, 2009). The most popular social networks worldwide include Facebook, MySpace, Twitter, and LinkedIn, with over 300 million active users of Facebook (Wikipedia, 2009a), and over 55 million Tweets sent daily via Twitter worldwide (biz, 2010). Within the area of psychology, QuitNet (www.quitnet.com), an Internet-based community that combines CCBT with social networking to stop cigarette smoking and support maintenance of abstinence, may be the oldest and most successful of such applications. Launched by developer Nathan Cobb in 1995, QuitNet includes a number of features intended to aid smokers in stopping and maintaining their goals, including: numerous forums, chat rooms, expert and medical support, and "buddies" (individuals users identify, track, and receive alerts when they are online). Each day, over 3,000 support messages are posted; over 60,000 members use QuitNet each month (QuitNet, n.d.).

Clinical research using popular social networking sites is currently in an embryonic stage. Yet efforts to begin examining ways in which social networking sites can be leveraged as tools to promote behavior change are furiously under way, and some empirical investigation have begun (Olsen & Kraft, 2009). Indeed, the National Institute on Drug Abuse (NIDA, 2009) recently convened a special conference of addictions treatment outcome researchers and technology experts to examine how Twitter can be used to facilitate smoking cessation (NIDA, 2009).

Twitter

Twitter, the popular social networking micro-blog, has rocketed in use since its introduction in 2006, and is beginning its emergence as a tool for changing chronic behaviors, such as cigarette smoking (NIDA, 2009). Simply, Twitter asks users, "What are you doing?" and provides 140 characters to respond. Users can subscribe to other users and become their "follower," allowing connection and increased social support. Many speculate that the brevity, along with its scope of reach (Comm, 2009; Israel, 2009; Morris, 2009), have made Twitter a powerful tool for political revolution (Grossman, 2009) and marketing (Comm), as well as an easy target for mockery (Stewart, 2009). With a monthly growth rate of 1,382% (McGiboney, 2009), over 6 million unique monthly visitors and 55 million visits per month (Kazeniac, 2009), Twitter is currently ranked third as the most used social network. Yet only 40% are retained (S. Hoffman, 2009).

Empirical data to date on the use of Twitter, either alone or with other more traditional tools as a treatment or intervention tool is lacking. However, its use in the context of behavioral change is being explored, and ideas for its application are proliferating quickly. For example, the Substance Abuse and Mental Health Services Administration (SAMHSA) has now begun using Twitter for its National Suicide Prevention Lifeline, to reach as many people as possible (Substance Abuse and Mental Health Services Administration [SAMHSA], 2009). SAMHSA is using TWITTER to provide didactic and prevention information.

Smoking cessation is another area in which Twitter is being used to reach large numbers of clients and to support behavior change. Prior to NIDA's efforts to investigate this application of Twitter, others had already begun to use the technology. The Moffitt Cancer Center Patient Smoking Cessation Program, a cancer center and research institute based in Florida, has added Twitter to its existing arsenal of online support. The Moffitt Center's Twitter account, Beaquitter, sends links to relevant, helpful articles, motivational statements, and tips and information (Smoking Cessation (beaquitter), 2009). Beaquitter also enhances social support by allowing the virtual connection of clients with the same behavioral goals. Many other similar Twitter accounts currently exist, some tied to larger online forums and groups, others not.

Although these are only two examples, use of the technology is widespread and growing at a rapid rate, making Twitter an especially well-poised social networking tool to reach people and make an impact in the field of behavior change. Indeed, in Olsen and Kraft's (2009) initial qualitative analysis of interview data with a small sample (*N* = 5) of social network users, they found that the personalized nature of Twitter coupled with the ease of staying connected to friends and family made the site very popular among participants. We expect a rapid increase in the uses of Twitter in the field of mental health to emerge, and with them a clearer empirical picture of its impact.

Conclusion

We have witnessed an explosion of advances in technology over the past decade that has produced a paradigm shift in how we consider and deliver psychosocial treatments for behavioral problems. In a relatively brief period, the Web, in particular, has made possible a kind of connectedness and sharing of information that was inconceivable just a generation ago. Its advance has made it possible for motivated individuals throughout the world to receive evidence-based therapies for specific behavioral problems and disorders. Mobile phones and mobile technologies, already ubiquitous in our lives, are expected to play an even greater role in shaping and influencing our behavior. This advance will put the clinician, as well as therapy itself, in the palm of the client's hand (and in his or her pocket, purse, backpack) 24/7; wherever the mobile phone is, so goes the efficacious treatment. The reliability, predictability, cost-effectiveness, efficiency, and global reach of technology will significantly close the gap between research and practice; its use and advance will significantly impact the dissemination problem.

Already innovative technologies are used to deliver ESTs, augment and enhance face-to-face treatment, and facilitate the delivery of ESTs in cases in which the clinician knows little about the treatment. Recent advances in VR make it possible to produce exposure to multiple sensory stimuli that transport the individual to the sights, smells, and sensations of the battlefield or to provide a powerful analgesic during painful procedures. Mobile technologies are being used to promote a number of health behaviors. Our own work moves the potential of its use a step further, by providing in vivo coaching to promote skills generalization in severely disordered individuals with BPD. The integration of contextual intelligence will produce another quantum leap forward in the use of innovative technologies to impact human behavior. The exponential growth of technology makes it

difficult to fully envision what is around the corner, and the limitless ways in which technology will impact the practice and scope of clinical psychology in the years to come. Most likely, we are at the tip of the iceberg.

Several things are certain. First, technology will play an ever-increasing role in how treatment is delivered. This force will be driven by an increased effort to improve efficiency, cost-effectiveness, and to ensure that treatments known to work are delivered fully and to fidelity. Technology's reach will impact all areas of clinical psychology, from assessment to treatment to long-term maintenance of treatment gains. We predict that within 10 years, the provision of most psychological treatment in the world will be significantly aided by technology. Second, although new technological innovations will significantly improve the quality and reach of service delivery, they will not replace people. Clinicians will continue to play a crucial role, particularly in motivating clients to engage in treatment. This will be particularly true for clients with multiple, severe, and complex problems, such as those with BPD. Third, there is more in store. Just as the Web created a myriad of possibilities impossible to imagine before its arrival, other technologies unknown today will emerge tomorrow. They will interact with existing technologies and be used in ways wholly independent of our present-day devices.

This chapter sought to provide a window into the major applications of technology currently used to aid in the provision of psychosocial treatments for behavioral problems. We initially reviewed the innovative use of computers to provide, augment, and facilitate the delivery of ESTs. In this discussion of CCBT, we sought to describe several examples of CCBTs for different disorders and review their current evidence base. Next, we explored the use of VR to facilitate exposure in the treatment of anxiety disorders and as a pain analgesic for individuals undergoing highly painful medical procedures, such as wound care following severe burns. We then turned to the burgeoning area of mobile technology, an area still in its infancy. Although most of the work relevant to clinical psychology conducted to date uses the most primitive elements of mobile technology (e.g., text messaging) and involves changing health behaviors (e.g., smoking, dieting, exercise), we described other around-the-corner applications. This included a review of our own recent work involving mobile phones to provide in vivo coaching in DBT skills for clients with BPD and who are engaged in a DBT program. We also illustrated several specific ways in which contextual intelligence may be used in the years to come. Finally, we reviewed the technology newcomer to psychology—use of social networking, and specifically the application of Twitter.

A final note: As the technology revolution continues to shape the new paradigm, new challenges to traditions emerge with great relevance to treatment developers, clinical outcome researchers, and those who rely on their research findings. First, how do we evaluate technology-based research proposals? Specifically, should proposals for technology-based treatment outcome research be required to earn exemplary critiques on both the scientific merit of the proposal *and* the innovation of the technology? Or, are traditional standards sufficient (i.e., the research is strong, investigators demonstrate a need for proposed trial, and area of research is innovative; however, the technology itself is not required to also be state-of-the art and built on empirically proven approaches). We strongly believe that the research is only as sound as the intervention it seeks to evaluate. In the case of technology-based research, innovation should be defined as both the *area* of technology (e.g., CCBT) and the extent to which the applied area of technology is innovative (e.g., the product itself is *also* innovative). It is not sufficient, in our view, for a research proposal to be built on dated technology, particularly when empirical research has demonstrated the new technology to be superior at changing behavior. Given the design and programming expense required to build highly engaging, interactive, and cutting-edge programs, it is imperative that grant proposal budget limits be expanded to allow investigators in this arena to build cutting-edge technology-based applications *and* conduct rigorous research. (Currently, budget amounts at the U.S. National Institutes of Health are sufficient to do one, but not both). Second, use of the commercial software industry standard in building technology-based tools and applications should be a requirement for public funding of technology-based research. Such an approach would involve an iterative process of prototype development, in which every element of the program is built and refined based on extensive feedback from target end-users. It is only through this careful, systematic (and expensive) process that the eventual product will achieve its intended purpose. Finally, given the usual many-year time lag from generation of an innovative idea to its funding and eventual publication of its research findings, *and* the swiftness with which technology advances, we must work to develop and use complementary and/or alternative methods to evaluate and disseminate findings involving cutting-edge technologies that maintain rigorous standards for scientific excellence. Greater use of within-subject and multiple-baseline designs may complement, for example, standard randomized controlled trials.

Acknowledgments

With the exception of the first author, the contribution of co-authors was equivalent; as such, authorship order is arranged in alphabetical order. The production of this chapter was supported by several Small Business Innovation Research (SBIR) grants from the National Institute on Drug Abuse (5R44DA016493, 5R44DA018049,4R44DA020975,1R43DA026244) and the National Institute of Mental Health (3R44MH082474, 5R44MH079525) awarded to the first author. We acknowledge and thank the following individuals for their support of our work and their contribution to it: Cecilia Spitznas, PhD, Enid Light, PhD, Adam Haim, PhD, and Shireen Rizvi, PhD. We gratefully thank our colleague Tim Kelly for his diligent research assistance in supporting the first author with final preparation of this manuscript.

References

Addis, M. E. (2002). Methods for disseminating research products and increasing evidence-based practice: Promises, obstacles, and future directions. *American Psychological Association, 9*(4), 367–378.

Akhondzadeh, S., Kashani, L., Fotouhi, A., Jarvandi, S., Mobaseri, M., Moin, M., et al. (2003). Comparison of Lavandula angustifolia Mill. tincture and imipramine in the treatment of mild to moderate depression: A double-blind, randomized trial. *Progress in Neuro-Psychopharmacology & Biological Psychiatry, 27*(1), 123–127.

Anderson, P., Jacobs, C., & Rothbaum, B. O. (2004). Computer-supported cognitive behavioral treatment of anxiety disorders. *Journal of Clinical Psychology, 60,* 253–267.

Andersson, G., Bergström, J., Carlbring, P., & Lindefors, N. (2005). The use of the internet in the treatment of anxiety disorders. *Current Opinion in Psychiatry, 18*(1), 73–77.

Andersson, G., Carlbring, P., Holmström, A., Sparthan, E., Furmark, T., Nilsson-Ihrfelt, E., et al. (2006). Internet-based self-help with therapist feedback and in vivo group exposure for social phobia: A randomized controlled trial. *Journal of Consulting and Clinical Psychology, 74*(4), 677–686.

Antony, M. M., & Swinson, R. P. (2000). *The shyness and social anxiety workbook: Proven techniques for overcoming your fears.* Oakland, CA: New Harbinger Publications.

APA Presidential Task Force on Evidence-Based Practice. (2006). Evidence-based practice in psychology. *American Psychologist, 61*(4), 271–285.

Apple. (2009, April 24). *Apple's revolutionary app store downloads top one billion in just nine months.* Retrieved October 15, 2009, from http://www.apple.com/pr/library/2009/04/24appstore.html

Baker, S. L., Patterson, M. D., & Barlow, D. H. (2002). Panic disorder and agoraphobia. In M. M. Antony & D. H. Barlow

(Eds.), *Handbook of assessment and treatment planning for psychological disorders.* (Vol. 1, pp. 67–112). New York: Guilford Press.

Barlow, D. H., Levitt, J. T., & Bufka, L. F. (1999). The dissemination of empirically supported treatments: A view to the future. *Behaviour Research and Therapy, 37*, 147–162.

BBC News. (2004, November 20). *Teenagers to get safe sex texts.* Retrieved October 15, 2009, from http://news.bbc.co.uk/2/hi/health/3993963.stm

Bebbington, P. E., Brugha, T. S., Meltzer, H., Jenkins, R., Ceresa, C., Farrell, M., et al. (2000). Neurotic disorders and the receipt of psychiatric treatment. *Psychological Medicine, 30*(6), 1369–1376.

Bebbington, P. E., Meltzer, H., Brugha, T. S., Farrell, M., Jenkins, R., Ceresa, C., et al. (2000). Unequal access and unmet need: neurotic disorders and the use of primary care services. *Psychological Medicine, 30*(6), 1359–1367.

Becker, C. B., Zayfert, C., & Anderson, E. (2004). A survey of psychologists' attitudes towards and utilization of exposure therapy for PTSD. *Behaviour Research and Therapy, 42*, 277–292.

Benton, D., & Donohoe, R. T. (2003). The influence on cognition of the interactions between lecithin, carnitine and carbohydrate. *Psychopharmacology, 175*(1), 84–91.

Berk, R. A. (2001). The active ingredients in humor: Psychophysiological benefits and risks for older adults. *Educational Gerontology, 27*, 323–339.

Beutler, L. E., & Harwood, T. M. (2004). Virtual reality in psychotherapy training. *Journal of Clinical Psychology, 60*(3), 317–330.

biz. (2010, April 14). Tweet preservation [Web log post]. Retrieved from http://blog.twitter.com/2010/04/tweet-preservation.html

Borden, M. (2009, September). iPhone envy? You must be joking. *Fast Company*, 67–106.

Botella, C., Baños, R. M., Villa, H., Perpiñá, C., & García-Palacios, A. (2000). Virtual reality in the treatment of claustrophobic fear: A controlled, multiple-baseline design. *Behavior Therapy, 31*(3), 583–595.

Botella, C., Martin, H. V., García-Palacios, A., Baños, R. M., Perpiñá, C., & Alcañiz, M. (2004). Clinically significant virtual environments for the treatment of panic disorder and agoraphobia. *CyberPsychology and Behavior, 7*(5), 527–535.

Botella, C., Osma, J., Garcia-Palacios, A., Quero, S., & Baños, R. M. (2004). Treatment of flying phobia using virtual reality: Data from a 1-year follow-up using a multiple baseline design. *Clinical Psychology and Psychotherapy, 11*(5), 311–323.

Bower, P., & Gilbody, S. (2005). Stepped care in psychological therapies: Access, effectiveness and efficiency. *The British Journal of Psychiatry, 186*, 11–17.

Brems, C., Johnson, M. E., Warner, T. D., & Roberts, L. W. (2006). Barriers to healthcare as reported by rural and urban interprofessional providers. *Journal of Interprofessional Care, 20*(2), 105–118.

Brendryen, H., Drozd, F., & Kraft, P. (2008). A digital smoking cessation program delivered through internet and cell phone without nicotine replacement (Happy Ending): Randomized controlled trial. *Journal of Medical Internet Research, 10*(5), 51.

Brendryen, H., & Kraft, P. (2008). Happy Ending: A randomized controlled trial of a digital multi-media smoking cessation intervention. *Addiction, 103*(3), 478–484.

Bright, J. I., Baker, K. D., & Neimeyer, R. A. (1999). Professional and paraprofessional group treatments for depression: A comparison of cognitive-behavioral and mutual support interventions. *Journal of Consulting and Clinical Psychology, 67*(4), 491–501.

Butler, G. (2001). *Overcoming social anxiety and shyness: A self-help guide using cognitive behavioral techniques.* London: Constable & Robinson.

Carlbring, P., Bohman, S., Brunt, S., Buhrman, M., Westling, B. E., Ekselius, L., et al. (2006). Remote treatment of panic disorder: A randomized trial of internet-based cognitive behavior therapy supplemented with telephone calls. *American Journal of Psychiatry, 163*, 2119–2125.

Carlbring, P., Gunnarsdottir, M., Hedensjo, L., Andersson, G., Ekselius, L., & Furmark, T. (2007). Treatment of social phobia: Randomized trial of internet-delivered cognitive–behavioural therapy with telephone support. *The British Journal of Psychiatry, 190*, 123–128.

Carlbring, P., Nilsson-Ihrfelt, E., Waara, J., Kollenstam, C., Buhrman, M., Kaldo, V., et al. (2005). Treatment of panic disorder: Live therapy vs. self-help via the Internet. *Behaviour Research and Therapy, 43*(10), 1321–1333.

Carlbring, P., & Smit, F. (2008). Randomized trial of internet-delivered self-help with telephone support for pathological gamblers. *Journal of Consulting and Clinical Psychology, 76*(6), 1090–1094.

Carroll, A. E., Marrero, D. G., & Downs, S. M. (2007). The HealthPia GlucoPack™ Diabetes Phone: A usability study. *Diabetes Technology & Therapeutics, 9*(2), 158–164.

Choi, Y. H., Vincelli, F., Riva, G., Wiederhold, B. K., Lee, J. H., & Park, K. H. (2005). Effects of group experiential cognitive therapy for the treatment of panic disorder with agoraphobia. *CyberPsychology and Behavior, 8*(4), 387–393.

Christensen, H., Griffiths, K., Korten, A., Brittliffe, K., & Groves, C. (2004). A comparison of changes in anxiety and depression symptoms of spontaneous users and trial participants of a cognitive behavior therapy website. *Journal of Medical Internet Research, 6*(4), e46.

Christensen, H., Griffiths, K. M., & Jorm, A. F. (2004). Delivering interventions for depression by using the internet: Randomised controlled trial. *British Medical Journal, 187*, 456–461.

Chmielewski, D. (2008, December 18). *New question for iPhone: Am iDrunk?* Retrieved October 16, 2009, from http://latimesblogs.latimes.com/technology/dawn_chmielewski/page/2/

Chui, C. K., Li, Z., Anderson, J. H., Murphy, K., Venbruz, A., Ma, X., et al. (2002). *Training and pretreatment planning of interventional neuroradiology procedures–initial clinical validation* (Vol. 85). Amsterdam: IOS Press.

Clarke, G., Eubanks, D., Reid, E., Kelleher, C., O'Connor, E., DeBar, L. L., et al. (2005). Overcoming Depression on the Internet (ODIN) (2): A randomized trial of a self-help depression skills program with reminders. *Journal of Medical Internet Research, 7*(2), e16.

Clarke, G., Reid, E., Eubanks, D., O'Connor, E., DeBar, L. L., Kelleher, C., et al. (2002). Overcoming Depression on the Internet (ODIN): A randomized controlled trial of an internet depression skills intervention program. *Journal of Medical Internet Research, 4*(3), e14.

Cobb, N. K., Graham, A. L., Bock, B. C., Papandonatos, G., & Abrams, D. B. (2005). Initial evaluation of a real-world internet smoking cessation system. *Nicotine and Tobacco Research, 7*(2), 207–216.

Comm, J. (2009). *Twitter power: How to dominate your market one tweet at a time.* Hoboken: John Wiley & Sons.

Cook, A. F., & Hoas, H. (2007). Hide and seek: The elusive rural psychiatrist. *Academic Psychiatry, 31,* 419–422.

Craske, M. G., Rose, R. D., Lang, A., Welch, S. S., Campbell-Sills, L., Sullivan, G., et al. (2009). Computer-assisted delivery of cognitive behavioral therapy for anxiety disorders in primary-care settings. *Depression and Anxiety, 26*(3), 235–242.

Cuijpers, P., Marks, I., van Straten, A., Cavanagh, K., Gega, L., & Andersson, G. (2009). Computer-aided psychotherapy for anxiety disorders: A meta-analytic review. *Cognitive Behaviour Therapy, 38*(2), 66–82.

Cuijpers, P., van Straten, A., Andersson, G., van Oppen, P. (2008). Psychotherapy for depression in adults: A meta-analysis of comparative outcome studies. *Journal of Consulting and Clinical Psychology, 76*(6), 909–922.

Damen, E. (2007). Simply persuasive: Using mobile technology to boost physical activity. In B. J. Fogg & D. Eckles (Eds.), *Mobile persuasion: 20 Perspectives on the future of behavior change* (pp. 39–45). Palo Alto: Stanford Captology Media.

Davis, D., O'Brien, M. A., Freemantle, N., Wolf, F. M., Mazmanian, P., & Taylor-Vaisey, A. (1999). Impact of formal continuing medical education: Do conferences, workshops, rounds, and other traditional continuing education activities change physician behavior or health care outcomes? *Journal of the American Medical Association, 282*(9), 867–74.

Delp, S. L., Loan, P., Basdogan, C., & Rosen, J. M. (1997). Surgical simulation: An emerging technology for training in emergency medicine. *Presence: Teleoperators and Virtual Environments, 6*(2), 147–159.

Dickerson, R., Johnsen, K., Raij, A., Lok, B., Stevens, A., Bernard, T., et al. (2005). *Virtual patients: Assessment of synthesized versus recorded speech.* Amsterdam: IOS Press.

Dimeff, L. A., & Koerner, K. (Eds.). (2007). *Dialectical behavior therapy in clinical practice: Applications across disorders and settings.* New York: The Guilford Press.

Dimeff, L. A., Koerner, K., Woodcock, E. A., Beadnell, B., Brown, M. Z., Skutch, J. M., et al. (2009). Which training method works best? A randomized controlled trial comparing three methods of training clinicians in dialectical behavior therapy skills. *Behavior Research and Therapy, 47,* 921–930.

Dimeff, L. A., & Skutch, J. M. (2009, September 21). *A tweet and a coach: Leveraging Twitter and mobile phone technology to produce behavior change.* In Developing a new mobile therapy: Twitter for tobacco "tweetment." Rockville, MD.

Dole, B., & Shalala, D. (2007). *Report of the President's Commission on Care for America's Returning Wounded Warriors.* Retrieved July 18, 2008, from http://www.pccww.gov/

Emmelkamp, P. M. G., Krijn, M., Hulsbosch, A. M., de Vries, S., Schuemie, M. J., & van der Mast, C. A. P. G. (2002). Virtual reality treatment versus exposure in vivo: A comparative evaluation in acrophobia. *Behaviour Research and Therapy, 40*(5), 509–516.

Etter, J. F. (2005). Comparing the efficacy of two internet-based, computer-tailored smoking cessation programs: A randomized trial. *Journal of Medical Internet Research, 7*(1), e2.

Farvolden, P., Denisoff, E., Selby, P., Bagby, R. M., & Rudy, L. (2005). Usage and longitudinal effectiveness of a Web-based self-help cognitive behavioral therapy program for panic disorder. *Journal of Medical Internet Research, 7*(1), e7.

Fixsen, D. L., Naoom, S. F., Blase, K. A., Friedman, R. M., & Wallace, F. (2005). *Implementation research: A synthesis of the literature.* Tampa, FL: University of South Florida, Louis de la Parte Florida Mental Health Institute, The National Implementation Research Network (FMHI Publication 231).

Fjeldsoe, B., Marshall, A., & Miller, Y. (2009). Behavior change interventions delivered by mobile telephone short-message service. *American Journal of Preventive Medicine, 36*(2), 165–173.

Fleetwood, J., Vaught, W., Feldman, D., Gracely, E., Kassutto, Z., & Novack, D. (2000). MedEthEx Online: A computer-based learning program in medical ethics and communication skills. *Teaching and Learning in Medicine, 12*(2), 96–104.

Foa, E. B., & Kozak, M. J. (1986). Emotional processing of fear: Exposure to corrective information. *Psychological Bulletin, 99,* 20–35.

Foa, E. B., Zoellner, L.A., Feeny, N.C., Hembree, E.A., & Alvarez-Conrad, J. (2002). Does imaginal exposure exacerbate PTSD symptoms? *Journal of Consulting and Clinical Psychology, 70*(4), 1022–1028.

Fogg, B. J., & Eckles, D. (Eds.). (2007). *Mobile persuasion: 20 perspectives of the future of behavior change.* Palo Alto: Stanford Captology Media.

Frank, A. (1993). Medical professionals in the treatment of obesity. *The Journal of the American Medical Association, 269*(16), 2132–2133.

Freiheit, S. R., Vye, C., Swan, R., & Cady, M. (2004). Cognitive-behavioral therapy for anxiety: Is dissemination working? *The Behavior Therapist, 27,* 25–32.

Frings, L., Wagner, K., Maiwald, T., Carius, A., Schinkel, A., Lehmann, C., et al. (2008). Early detection of behavioral side effects of antiepileptic treatment using handheld computers. *Epilepsy & Behavior, 13*(2), 402–406.

Garcia-Palacios, A., Hoffman, H., Carlin, A., Furness, T. A., & Botella, C. (2002). Virtual reality in the treatment of spider phobia: A controlled study. *Behaviour Research and Therapy, 40*(9), 983–993.

Gega, L., Marks, I. M., & Mataix-Cols, D. (2004). Computer-aided CBT self-help for anxiety and depressive disorders: Experience of a London clinic and future directions. *Journal of Clinical Psychology, 60*(2), 147–57.

Gerardi, M., Rothbaum, B. O., Ressler, K., Heekin, M., & Rizzo, A. (2008). Virtual reality exposure therapy using a virtual Iraq: Case report. *Journal of Traumatic Stress, 21*(2), 209–213.

Goisman, R. M., Warshaw, M. G., & Keller, M. B. (1999). Psychosocial treatments prescriptions for generalized anxiety disorder, panic disorder, and social phobia, 1991–1996. *American Journal of Psychiatry, 156,* 1819–1821.

Golden, R. N., Gaynes, B. N., Ekstrom, R. D., Hamer, R. M., Jacobsen, F. M., Suppes, T., et al. (2005). The efficacy of light therapy in the treatment of mood disorders: A review and meta-analysis of the evidence. *American Journal of Psychiatry, 162,* 656–662.

Goldsmith, T. R. (2009). Using virtual reality enhanced behavioral skills training to teach street-crossing skills to children and adolescents with autism spectrum disorders. *Dissertation Abstracts International: Section B: The Sciences and Engineering, 69*(7-B), 4421.

Greist, J. H., Marks, I. M., Baer, L., Kobak, K. A., Wenzel, K. W., Hirsch, M. J., et al. (2002). Behavior therapy for obsessive-compulsive disorder guided by a computer or by a clinician compared with relaxation as a control. *Journal of Clinical Psychiatry, 63*(2), 138–145.

Grossman, L. (2009, June 17). *Iran protests: Twitter, the medium of the movement.* Retrieved October 13, 2009, from http://www.time.com/time/world/article/0

GSM Association. (2006, October 17). *Mobile networks to cover 90% of the world's population by 2010.* Retrieved October 15, 2009, from http://gsmworld.com/newsroom/press-releases/2102.htm

Gurusamy, K., Aggarwal, R., Palanivelu, L., & Davidson, B. R. (2008). Systematic review of randomized controlled trials on the effectiveness of virtual reality training for laparoscopic surgery. *British Journal of Surgery, 95*(9), 1088–1097.

Gurusamy, K. S., Aggarwal, R., Palanivelu, L., & Davidson, B. R. (2009). Virtual reality training for surgical trainees in laparoscopic surgery. *Cochrane Database of Systematic Reviews, 21*(1), CD006575.

Harman, J. S., Mulsant, B. H., Kelleher, K. J., Schullberg, H. C., Kupfer, D. J., & Reynolds, C. F. (2001). Narrowing the gap in treatment of depression. *The International Journal of Psychiatry in Medicine, 31*, 239–253.

Haug, S., Meyer, C., Gross, B., Schorr, G., Thyrian, J. R., Kordy, H., et al. (2008). Continuous individual support of smoking cessation in socially deprived young adults via mobile phones: Results of a pilot study. *Gesundheitswesen, 70*(6), 364–371.

Hoffman, P. (2009, May 1). *When the cellphone teaches sex education.* Retrieved October 16, 2009, from http://www.nytimes.com/2009/05/03/fashion/03sexed.html?_r=1&scp=3&sq=hoffman%20When%20the%20Cellphone%20Teaches%20Sex%20Education&st=cse

Hoffman, S. (2009, April 29). *Twitter quitters outnumber those who stay, report finds.* Retrieved April 29, 2009, from http://www.crn.com/security/217200834;jsessionid=TMJW2UAT5QE4LQE1GHOSKHWATMY32JVN

Hoffman, H. G., Doctor, J. N., Patterson, D. R., Carrougher, G. J., & Furness, T. A. (2000). Virtual reality as an adjunctive pain control during burn wound care in adolescent patients. *Pain, 85*(1–2), 305–309.

Hoffman, H. G., Garcia-Palacios, A., Carlin, A., Furness, T. A., & Botella, C. (2003). Interfaces that heal: Coupling real and virtual objects to treat spider phobia. *International Journal of Human-Computer Interaction, 16*(2), 283–300.

Hoffman, H. G., Patterson, D. R., Carrougher, G. J., Nakamura, D., Moore, M., Garcia-Palacios, A., et al. (2001). The effectiveness of virtual reality pain control with multiple treatments of longer durations: A case study. *International Journal of Human-Computer Interaction, 13*(1), 1–12.

Hoffman, H. G., Patterson, D. R., Carrougher, G. J., & Sharar, S. R. (2001). Effectiveness of virtual reality-based pain control with multiple treatments. *The Clinical Journal of Pain, 17*(3), 229–235.

Hoffman, H. G., Patterson, D. R., Seibel, E., Soltani, M., Jewett-Leahy, L., & Sharar, S. R. (2008). Virtual reality pain control during burn wound debridement in the hydrotank. *The Clinical Journal of Pain, 24*(4), 299–304.

Hoffman, H. G., Richards, T. L., Coda, B., Bills, A. R., Blough, D., Richards, A. L., et al. (2004). Modulation of thermal pain-related brain activity with virtual reality: Evidence from fMRI. *NeuroReport, 15*(8), 1245–1248.

Hurling, R., Catt, M., De Boni, M., Fairley, B. W., Hurst, T., Murray, P., et al. (2007). Using internet and mobile phone technology to deliver an automated physical activity program: Randomized controlled trial. *Journal of Medical Internet Research, 9*(2), 7.

Insel, T. R. (2009). Translating scientific opportunity into public health impact: A strategic plan for research on mental illness. *Archives of General Psychiatry, 66*(1), 128–133.

Israel, S. (2009). *Twitterville: How businesses can thrive in the new global neighborhoods.* New York: Portfolio.

Janda, M. S., Mattheos, N., Nattestad, A., Wagner, A., Nebel, D., Färbom, C., et al. (2004). Simulation of patient encounters using a virtual patient in periodontology instruction of dental students: Design, usability, and learning effect in history-taking skills. *European Journal of Dental Education, 8*(3), 111–119.

Johnsen, K., Dickerson, R., Raij, A., Harrison, C., & Lok, B. (2006). Evolving an immersive medical communication skills trainer. *Presence: Teleoperators and Virtual Environments, 15*(1), 33–46.

Johnsen, K., Dickerson, R., Raij, A., Lok, B., Jackson, J., Shin, M., et al. (2005, March). *Experiences in Using Immersive Virtual Characters to Educate Medical Communication Skills.* Paper presented at the Proceedings of the 2005 IEEE Conference on Virtual Reality.

Joo, N. S., & Kim, B. T. (2007). Mobile phone short message service messaging for behaviour modification in a community-based weight control programme in Korea. *Journal of Telemedicine and Telecare, 13*, 416–420.

Kaltenthaler, E., Parry, G., Beverley, C., & Ferriter, M. (2008). Computerised cognitive-behavioural therapy for depression: Systematic review. *British Journal of Psychiatry, 193*(3), 181–184.

Kaltenthaler, E., Sutcliffe, P., Parry, G., Beverley, C., Rees, A., & Ferriter, M. (2008). The acceptability to patients of computerized cognitive behaviour therapy for depression: A systematic review. *Psychological Medicine, 38*, 1521–30.

Katsavelis, D., Siu, K. C., Brown-Clerk, B., Lee, I. H., Lee, Y. K., Oleynikov, D., et al. (2009). Validated robotic laparoscopic surgical training in a virtual-reality environment. *Surgical Endoscopy, 23*(1), 66–73.

Kaver, A. (1999). Social fobi: Att kanna sig granskad och bortgjord [Social phobia: Feeling scrutinized and make to feel like a fool]. Jyvaskyla, Finland: Cura Bokforlag.

Kazeniac, A. (2009, February 9). *Social networks: Facebook takes over top spot, Twitter climb.* Retrieved February 19, 2009, from http://blog.compete.com/2009/02/09/facebook-myspace-twitter-social-network/

Kelly, K. (2007, December). *The next 5,000 days of the Web.* Paper presented at the Entertainment Gathering, Los Angeles, CA.

Kendall, P. C., Hudson, J. L., Gosch, E., Flannery-Schroeder, E., & Suveg, C. (2008). Cognitive-behavioral therapy for anxiety disordered youth: A randomized clinical trial evaluating child and family modalities. *Journal of Consulting and Clinical Psychology, 76*(2), 282–297.

Kennedy, D. O., & Scholey, A. B. (2003). Ginseng: Potential for the enhancement of cognitive performance and mood. *Pharmacology, Biochemistry, and Behavior, 75*(3), 687–700.

Kenny, P., Rizzo, A. A., Parsons, T. D., Gratch, J., & Swartout, W. (2007). A virtual human agent for training novice therapist clinical interviewing skills. *Annual Review of CyberTherapy and Telemedicine, 5*, 77–83.

Kenwright, M., & Marks, I. M. (2004). Computer-aided self-help for phobia/panic via internet at home: A pilot study. *British Journal of Psychiatry, 184*(5), 448–449.

Kesavadas, T., Joshi, D., Mayrose, J., & Chugh, K. (2002). *A virtual environment for esophageal intubation training.* Amsterdam: IOS Press.

Kessler, R. C., Berglund, P., Demler, O., Jin, R., Koretz, D., Merikangas, K. R., et al. (2003). The epidemiology of major depressive disorder: Results from the national comorbidity survey replication (NCS-R). *Journal of the American Medical Association, 289*, 3095–3105.

Krijn, M., Emmelkamp, P. M. G., Biemond, R., de Wilde de Ligney, C., Schuemie, M. J., & van der Mast, C. A. P. G. (2004). Treatment of acrophobia in virtual reality: The role of immersion and presence. *Behaviour Research and Therapy, 42*(2), 229–239.

Kubota, A., Fujita, M., & Hatano, Y. (2004). Development and effects of a health promotion program utilizing the mail function of mobile phones. *Japanese Journal of Public Health, 51*(10), 862–873.

Kuppersmith, R. B., Johnston, R., Moreau, D., Loftin, R. B., & Jenkins, H. (1997). Building a virtual reality temporal bone dissection simulator. *Studies in Health Technology and Informatics, 39*, 180–186.

Levine, D., McCright, J., Dobkin, L., Woodruff, A. J., & Klausner, J. D. (2008). SEXINFO: A sexual health text messaging service for San Francisco youth. *American Journal of Public Health, 98*(3), 393–395.

Litz, B. T., Engel, C. C., Bryant, R. A., & Papa, A. (2007). A randomized, controlled proof-of-concept trial of an Internet-based, therapist-assisted self-management treatment for posttraumatic stress disorder. *The American Journal of Psychiatry, 164*, 1676–1683.

Mabrey, J. D., Cannon, W. D., Gillogly, S. D., Kasser, J. R., Sweeney, H. J., Zarins, B., et al. (2000). Development of a virtual reality arthroscopic knee simulator. *Studies in Health Technology and Informatics, 70*, 192–194.

Macedonia, M. (2009). Virtual worlds: A new reality for treating post-traumatic stress disorder. *IEEE Computer Graphics and Applications, 29*(1), 86–88.

MacGregor, A. D., Hayward, L., Peck, D. F., & Wilkes, P. (2009). Empirically grounded clinical interventions clients' and referrers' perceptions of computer-guided CBT (FearFighter). *Behavioral and Cognitive Psychotherapy, 37*(1), 1–9.

Maltby, N., Kirsch, I., Mayers, M., & Allen, G. J. (2002). Virtual reality exposure therapy for the treatment of fear of flying: A controlled investigation. *Journal of Consulting and Clinical Psychology, 70*(5), 1112–1118.

Mantovani, F., Castelnuovo, G., Gaggioli, A., & Riva, G. (2004). Virtual reality training for health-care professionals. *CyberPsychology and Behavior, 6*(4), 389–395.

March, S., Spence, S. H., & Donovan, C. L. (2009). The efficacy of an internet-based cognitive-behavioral therapy intervention for child anxiety disorders. *Journal of Pediatric Psychology, 34*(5), 474–487.

Marks, I. M., Cavanagh, K., Gega, L. (2007). *Hands-on help: Computer-aided psychotherapy.* New York: Psychology Press.

Marks, I., Mataix-Cols, D., Kenwright, M., Cameron, R., Hirsch, S., & Gega, L. (2003). Pragmatic evaluation of computer-aided self-help for anxiety and depression. *The British Journal of Psychiatry, 183*, 57–65.

Marks, I., Shaw, S., & Parkin, R. (1998). Computer-aided treatments of mental health problems. *Clinical Psychology: Science and Practice, 5*(2), 151–170.

Marks, I. M. (2004). Psychiatry in the future: Information technology can pull mental health care into the 21st century. *Psychiatric Bulletin, 28*, 319–320.

Marks, I. M., Kenwright, M., McDonough, M., Whittaker, M., & Mataix-Cols, D. (2004). Saving clinicians' time by delegating routine aspects of therapy to a computer: A randomized controlled trial in phobia/panic disorder. *Psychological Medicine, 34*(1), 9–17.

Mayer, R. E. (2008). Applying the science of learning: Evidence-based principles for the design of multimedia instruction. *American Psychologist, 63*(8), 760–769.

McGee, J. B., Neill, J., Goldman, J., & Casey, E. (1998). Using multimedia virtual patients to enhance the clinical curriculum for medical students. *Studies in Health Technology and Informatics, 52*(2), 732–735.

McGiboney, M. (2009, March 18). *Twitter's tweet smell of success.* Retrieved April 5, 2009, from http://blog.nielsen.com/nielsenwire/online_mobile/twitters-tweet-smell-of-success/

Micco, N., Gold, B., Buzzell, P., Leonard, H., Pintauro, S., & Harvey-Berino, J. (2007). Minimal in-person support as an adjunct to internet obesity treatment. *Annals of Behavioral Medicine, 33*(1), 49–56.

Miller, W. R., Yahne, C. E., Moyers, T. B., Martinez, J., & Pirritano, M. (2004). A randomized trial of methods to help clinicians learn motivational interviewing. *Journal of Consulting and Clinical Psychology, 72*(6), 1050–1062.

Mokdad, A. H., Bowman, B. A., Ford, E. S., Vinicor, F., Marks, J. S., & Koplan, J. P. (2001). The continuing epidemics of obesity and diabetes in the United States. *The Journal of the American Medical Association, 286*(10), 1195–1200.

Morak, J., Schindler, K., Goerzer, E., Kastner, P., Toplak, H., Ludvik, B., et al. (2008). A pilot study of mobile phone-based therapy for obese patients. *Journal of Telemedicine and Telecare, 14*(3), 147–149.

Morey, E., Thacher, J. A., & Craighead, W. E. (2007). Patient preferences for depression treatment programs and willingness to pay for treatment. *Journal of Mental Health Policy and Economics, 10*, 73–85.

Morgan, A. J., & Jorm, A. F. (2008). Self-help interventions for depressive disorders and depressive symptoms: A systematic review. *Annals of General Psychiatry, 7*, 13.

Morris, T. (2009). *All a twitter: A personal and professional guide to social networking with twitter.* Indianapolis: Que.

Mühlberger, A., Herrmann, M. J., Wiedemann, G., Ellgring, H., & Pauli, P. (2001). Repeated exposure of flight phobics to flights in virtual reality. *Behaviour Research and Therapy, 39*(9), 1033–1050.

Mühlberger, A., Wiedemann, G., & Pauli, P. (2003). Efficacy of a one-session virtual reality exposure treatment for fear of flying. *Psychotherapy Research, 13*(3), 323–336.

Muñoz, S. S. (2005, May 12). *A week with MyFoodPhone.* Retrieved October 15, 2009, from http://blog.myca.com/wp-content/uploads/2009/02/wsjcom-a-week-with-my-foodphone.pdf

National Institute for Health and Clinical Excellence (2006). *Computerised cognitive behaviour therapy for depression and anxiety.* London.

National Institute on Drug Abuse. (2009, September 21). *Developing a New Mobile Therapy: Twitter for Tobacco "Tweetment".* Rockville, MD.

New Freedom Commission (2003). New freedom commission on mental health, achieving the promise: Transforming mental health care in America. Final Report. (DHHS Pub. No. SMA-03-3832). Rockville, MD.

Newman, M. G., & Stone, A. A. (1996). Does humor moderate the effects of experimentally-induced stress? *Annals of Behavioral Medicine, 18*, 101–109.

Ng, I., Hwang, P. Y. K., Kumar, D., Lee, C. K., Kockro, R. A., & Sitoh, Y. Y. (2009). Surgical planning for microsurgical excision of cerebral arterio-venous malformations using virtual reality technology. *Acta Neurochirurgica, 151*(5), 453–463.

Nishith, P., Resick, P. A., & Griffin, M. G. (2002). Pattern of change in prolonged exposure and cognitive-processing therapy for female rape victims with posttraumatic stress disorder. *Journal of Consulting and Clinical Psychology, 70*(4), 880–886.

Nokia (2009). *Rich context modeling.* Retrieved October 14, 2009, from http://research.nokia.com/research/rich_context_modeling

North, M. M., & North, S. M. (1994). Virtual environments and psychological disorders. *Electronic Journal of Virtual Culture, 2*(4), 37–42.

North, M. M., North, S. M., & Coble, J. R. (1996). Effectiveness of virtual environment desensitization in the treatment of agoraphobia. *Presence: Teleoperators and Virtual Environments, 5,* 346–352.

North, M. M., North, S. M., & Coble, J. R. (1997). *Virtual reality therapy: An effective treatment for psychological disorders* (Vol. 44). Amsterdam: IOS Press.

Obermayer, J. L., Riley, W. T., Asif, O., & Jean-Mary, J. (2004). College smoking-cessation using cell phone text messaging. *Journal of American College Health, 53*(2), 71–78.

Olfson, M., & Marcus, S. C. (2009). National patterns in antidepressant medication treatment. *Archives of General Psychiatry, 66*(8), 848–856.

Olfson, M., Marcus, S. C., Druss, B., Elinson, L., Tanielian, T., & Pincus, H. A. (2002). National trends in the outpatient treatment of depression. *The Journal of the American Medical Association, 287,* 203–209.

Olfson, M., Marcus, S. C., Wan, G. J., & Geissler, E. C. (2004). National trends in the outpatient treatment of anxiety disorders. *Journal of Clinical Psychiatry, 65*(9), 1166–1173.

Olsen, E., & Kraft, P. (2009, April). *ePsychology: A pilot study on how to enhance social support and adherence in digital interventions by characteristics from social networking sites.* Poster session presented at the 4th International Conference on Persuasive Technology, Claremont, CA.

Osgood-Hynes, D. J., Greist, J. H., Marks, I. M., Baer, L., Henerman, S. W., Wenzel, K. W., et al. (1998). Self-administered psychotherapy for depression using a telephone-accessed computer system plus booklets: An open U.S.-U.K. study. *Journal of Clinical Psychiatry, 59*(358–365).

Peñate, W., Pitti, C. T., Bethencourt, J. M., de la Fuente, J., & Gracia, R. (2008). The effects of a treatment based on the use of virtual reality exposure and cognitive-behavioral therapy applied to patients with agoraphobia. *International Journal of Clinical and Health Psychology, 8*(1), 5–22.

Perez, F., Monton, E., Nodal, M. J., Vinoles, J., Guillen, S., & Traver, V. (2006). Evaluation of a mobile health system for supporting postoperative patients following day surgery. *Journal of Telemedicine and Telecare, 12*(Supplement 1), 41–43.

Pilkington, K., Boshnakova, A., & Richardson, J. (2006). St John's wort for depression: Time for a different perspective? *Complementary Therapies in Medicine, 14*(4), 268–281.

Pollak, Y., Weiss, P. L., Rizzo, A. A., Weizer, M., Shriki, L., Shalev, R. S., et al. (2009). The utility of a continuous performance test embedded in virtual reality in measuring ADHD-related deficits. *Journal of Developmental & Behavioral Pediatrics, 30*(1), 2–6.

Powers, M. B., & Emmelkamp, P. M. G. (2008). Virtual reality exposure therapy for anxiety disorders: A meta-analysis. *Journal of Anxiety Disorders, 22*(3), 561–569.

Prochaska, J. O., & DiClemente, C. C. (1992). Stages of change in the modification of problem behaviors. *Progress in Behavior Modification, 28,* 183–218.

Prochaska, J. O., & DiClemente, C. C. (1983). Stages and processes of self-change of smoking: Toward an integrative model of change. *Journal of Consulting and Clinical Psychology, 51*(3), 390–395.

Proudfoot, J., Ryden, C., Everitt, B., Shapiro, D. A., Goldberg, D., Mann, A., et al. (2004). Clinical efficacy of computerised cognitive–behavioural therapy for anxiety and depression in primary care: Randomised controlled trial. *The British Journal of Psychiatry, 185,* 46–54.

Puccio, J. A., Belzer, M., Olson, J., Martinez, M., Salata, C., Tucker, D., et al. (2006). The use of cell phone reminder calls for assisting HIV-infected adolescents and young adults to adhere to highly active antiretroviral therapy: A pilot study. *AIDS Patient Care and STDs, 20*(6), 438–444.

Quinn, C. C., Clough, S. S., Minor, J. M., Lender, D., Okafor, M. C., & Gruber-Baldini, A. (2008). WellDoc™ mobile diabetes management randomized controlled trial: Change in clinical and behavioral outcomes and patient and physician satisfaction. *Diabetes Technology & Therapeutics, 10*(3), 160–168.

QuitNet. (N.d.). *Expert FAQs.* Retrieved October 3, 2009, from http://www.quitnet.com/help/helpfaq.jtml?subjectID=925&section = Profile.

Rapee, R. M. (1998). *Overcoming shyness and social phobia: A step-by-step guide.* Northvale, NJ: Jason Aronson.

Reger, G. M., & Gahm, G. A. (2008). Virtual reality exposure therapy for active duty soldiers. *Journal of Clinical Psychology, 64*(8), 940–946.

Reingold, J., & Tkaczyk, C. (2008, November 13). *10 new gurus you should know.* Retrieved October 15, 2009, from http://money.cnn.com/galleries/2008/fortune/0811/gallery.10_new_gurus.fortune/

Riley, W., Obermayer, J., & Jean-Mary, J. (2008). Internet and mobile phone text messaging intervention for college smokers. *Journal of American College Health, 57*(2), 245–248.

Rizvi, S., Dimeff, L. A., & Skutch, J. M., (2009). Retrieved November 2, 2009, from http://crisp.cit.nih.gov/crisp/CRISP_LIB.getdoc?textkey=7611527&p_grant_num=1R43DA026244-01&p_query=&ticket=109685446&p_audit_session_id=507138700&p_keywords=

Rizzo, A., Pair, J., Graap, K., Manson, B., McNerney, P. J., Wiederhold, B., et al. (2006). A virtual reality exposure therapy application for Iraq war military personnel with post traumatic stress disorder: From training to toy to treatment. In M. Roy (Ed.), *NATO Advanced research workshop on novel approaches to the diagnosis and treatment of posttraumatic stress disorder* (pp. 235–250). Washington, DC: IOS Press.

Rodgers, A., Corbett, T., Bramley, D., Riddell, T., Wills, M., Lin, R. B., et al. (2005). Do u smoke after txt? Results of a randomised trial of smoking cessation using mobile phone text messaging. *Tobacco Control, 14,* 255–261.

Rolfsson, G., Nordgren, A., Bindzau, S., Hagström, J. P., McLaughlin, J., & Thurfjell, L. (2002). *Training and assessment of laparoscopic skills using a haptic simulator* (Vol. 85). Amsterdam: IOS Press.

Rosen, C. S., Chow, H. C., Finney, J. F., Greenbaum, M. A., Moos, R. H., Sheikh, J. I., et al. (2004). VA practice patterns and practice guidelines for treating posttraumatic stress disorder. *Journal of Traumatic Stress, 17,* 213–222.

Rothbaum, B. O., Hodges, L., Alarcon, R., Ready, D., Shahar, F., Graap, K., et al. (1999). Virtual reality exposure therapy for PTSD Vietnam veterans: A case study. *Journal of Traumatic Stress*, *12*(2), 263–271.

Rothbaum, B. O., Hodges, L., Anderson, P. L., Price, L., & Smith, S. (2002). Twelve-month follow-up of virtual reality and standard exposure therapies for the fear of flying. *Journal of Consulting and Clinical Psychology*, *70*(2), 428–432.

Rothbaum, B. O., Hodges, L. F., Kooper, R., Opdyke, D., Williford, J. S., & North, M. (1995). Effectiveness of computer generated (virtual reality) graded exposure in the treatment of acrophobia. *American Journal of Psychiatry*, *152*, 626–628.

Rothbaum, B. O., Hodges, L., Smith, S., Hwan, L., & Price, L. (2000). A controlled study of virtual reality exposure for the fear of flying. *Journal of Consulting and Clinical Psychology*, *68*(6), 1020–1026.

Rutter, C. E., Dahlquist, L., & Weiss, K. (2009). Sustained efficacy of virtual reality distraction. *The Journal of Pain*, *10*(4), 391–397.

Ryan, D., Cobern, W., Wheeler, J., Price, D., & Tarassenko, L. (2005). Mobile phone technology in the management of asthma. *Journal of Telemedicine and Telecare*, *11*, 43–46.

SAMHSA. (2009, March) *Tweets from the lifeline. SAMHSA News*, *17*(2). Retrieved September 15, 2009, from http://www.samhsa.gov/samhsaNewsletter/Volume_17_Number_2/Twitter.aspx

Schneider, A. J., Mataix-Cols, D., Marks, I. M., & Bachofen, M. (2005). Internet-guided self-help with or without exposure therapy for phobic and panic disorders. *Psychotherapy and Psychosomatics*, *74*(3), 154–164.

Schulte, D., & Eifert, G. H. (2002). What to do when manuals fail? The dual model of psychotherapy. *Clinical Psychology Science and Practice*, *9*(3), 312–328.

Seekles, W., van Straten, A., Beekman, A., van Marwijk, H., & Cuijpers, P. (2009). Stepped care for depression and anxiety: From primary care to specialized mental health care: A randomised controlled trial testing the effectiveness of a stepped care program among primary care patients with mood or anxiety disorders. *BMC Health Services Research*, *9*, 90

Shaffer, D., Gould, M. S., Brasic, J., Ambrosini, P., Fisher, P., Bird, H., et al. (1983). A children's global assessment scale (CGAS). *Archives of General Psychiatry*, *40*(11), 1228–1231.

Shafran, R., Clark, D., Fairburn, C., Arntz, A., Barlow, D., Ehlers, A., et al. (2009). Mind the gap: Improving the dissemination of CBT. *Behaviour Research and Therapy*, *47*(11), 902–909.

Simon, G., & Ludman, E. (2009). It's time for disruptive innovation in psychotherapy. *The Lancet*, *374*(9690), 594–595.

Smoking Cessation (beaquitter) on Twitter. (2009). Retrieved September 16, 2009, from http://twitter.com/beaquitter

Spek, V., Nyklicek, I., Smits, N., Cuijpers, P., Riper, H., Keyzer, J., et al. (2007). Internet-based cognitive behavioural therapy for subthreshold depression in people over 50 years old: A randomized controlled clinical trial. *Psychological Medicine*, *37*, 1797–1806.

Spence, S. H., Holmes, J. M., March, S., & Lipp, O. V. (2006). The feasibility and outcome of clinic plus internet delivery of cognitive-behavior therapy for childhood anxiety. *Journal of Consulting and Clinical Psychology*, *74*(3), 614–621.

Stevens, A., Hernandez, J., Johnsen, K., Dickerson, R., Raij, A., Harrison, C., et al. (2006). The use of virtual patients to teach medical students history taking and communication skills. *The American Journal of Surgery*, *191*(6), 806–811.

Stewart, J. (Host). (2009, March 2). The Daily Show. [Television Program]. United States: Comedy Central.

Street, L. L., Niederehe, G., & Lebowitz, B. D. (2000). Toward greater public health relevance for psychotherapeutic intervention research: An NIMH workshop report. *Clinical Psychology: Science and Practice*, *7*, 127–137.

Strickland, D., Hodges, L., North, M., & Weghorst, S. (1997). Overcoming phobias by virtual exposure. *Communications of the ACM*, *40*(8), 34–39.

Ström, L., Pettersson, R., & Andersson, G. (2004). Internet-based treatment for insomnia: A controlled evaluation. *Journal of Consulting and Clinical Psychology*, *72*(1), 113–120.

Tanguy, S., & Heywood, P. (2007). MyFoodPhone: The start of mobile health revolution. In B. J. Fogg & D. Eckles (Eds.), *Mobile persuasion: 20 perspectives in the future of behavior change* (pp. 19–29). Palo Alto: Stanford Captology Media.

Tedeschi, B. (2009, June 3). *At this price, Nokia's smartphone needs more and better apps.* Retrieved October 15, 2009, from http://www.nytimes.com/2009/06/04/technology/personaltech/04smart.html?_r=1

Tsai, M. D., Hsieh, M. S., & Jou, S. B. (2001). Virtual reality orthopedic surgery simulator. *Computers in Biology and Medicine*, *31*(5), 333–351.

Tufano, J. T., & Karras, B. T. (2005). Mobile eHealth interventions for obesity: A timely opportunity to leverage convergence trends. *Journal of Medical Internet Research*, *7*(5), e58.

Tuunainen, A., Kripke, D., & Endo, T. (2004). Light therapy for non-seasonal depression. *Cochrane Database System 2*, CD004050.

van't Hof, E., Cuijpers, P., & Stein, D. J. (2009). Self-help and internet-guided interventions in depression and anxiety disorders: A systematic review of meta-analyses. *CNS Spectrums*, *14*, 34–40.

van Straten, A., Cuijpers, P., & Smits, N. (2008). Effectiveness of a web-based self-help intervention for symptoms of depression, anxiety, and stress: Randomized controlled trial. *Journal of Medical Internet Research*, *10*(1), 7.

Vidrine, D. J., Arduino, R. C., & Gritz, E. R. (2006a). Impact of a cell phone intervention on mediating mechanisms of smoking cessation in individuals living with HIV/AIDS. *Nicotine and Tobacco Research*, *8*(Suppl 1), S103-S108.

Vidrine, D. J., Arduino, R. C., Lazev, A. B., & Gritz, E. R. (2006b). A randomized trial of a proactive cellular telephone intervention for smokers living with HIV/AIDS. *AIDS*, *20*(2), 253–260.

Vincelli, F., Anolli, L., Bouchard, S., Wiederhold, B. K., Zurloni, V., & Riva, G. (2003). Experiential cognitive therapy in the treatment of panic disorders with agoraphobia: A controlled study. *CyberPsychology and Behavior*, *6*(3), 321–328.

Waller, G. (2009). Evidence-based treatment and therapist drift. *Behaviour Research and Therapy*, *47*(2), 119–127.

Weissman, M. M., Verdeli, H., Gameroff, M. J., Bledsoe, S. E., Betts, K., Mufson, L., et al. (2006). National survey of psychotherapy training in psychiatry, psychology, and social work. *Archives of General Psychiatry*, *63*, 925–934.

Whittaker, R., Maddison, R., McRobbie, H., Bullen, C., Denny, S., Dorey, E., et al. (2008). A multimedia mobile phone–based youth smoking cessation intervention: Findings from content development and piloting studies. *Journal of Medical Internet Research*, *10*(5), e49.

Wiederhold, B. K. (1999). A comparison of imaginal exposure and virtual reality exposure for the treatment of fear of flying. *Dissertation Abstracts International: Section B: The Sciences y Engineering, 60*(4), 1837.

Wikipedia. (2009a). *List of social networking websites.* Retrieved October 16, 2009, from http://en.wikipedia.org/wiki/List_of_social_networking_websites

Wikipedia. (2009b). *Mobile telephony.* Retrieved October 16, 2009, from http://en.wikipedia.org/wiki/Mobile_telephony

World Health Organization. (1998). *Obesity: preventing and managing the global epidemic. Report of a WHO consultation on obesity.* Retrieved October 16, 2009, from http://whqlibdoc.who.int/hq/1998/WHO_NUT_NCD_98.1_(p1–158).pdf

Yates, A. (1996). Anxiety disorders in children and adolescents. In T. H. Guides (Ed.), *The Hatherleigh guide to child and adolescent therapy* (Vol. 5, pp. 1–21). New York: Hatherleigh Press.

Yellowlees, P. M., & Cook, J. N. (2006). Education about hallucinations using an internet virtual reality system: A qualitative survey. *Academic Psychiatry, 30,* 534–539.

Interventions in Forensic Settings: Juveniles in Residential Placement, Defendants in Drug Courts or Mental Health Courts, and Defendants in Forensic Hospitals as Incompetent to Stand Trial

Kirk Heilbrun, Naomi Goldstein, David DeMatteo, Allison Hart, Christina Riggs Romaine, *and* Sanjay Shah

Abstract

Interventions for criminal justice–involved populations have been an increasing focus of theoretical and research attention, and have also been recognized as among the "next frontier" of priorities for the forensic mental health professions. In this chapter, we present a description of three different kinds of interventions with criminal justice populations. These interventions—for adjudicated delinquents, defendants diverted into specialized courts, and defendants hospitalized as incompetent to stand trial—represent a range of population ages, traditional versus relatively new modalities, and stages of the juvenile/criminal justice systems. Perhaps surprisingly, the more established of these interventions (juvenile placement and forensic hospitalization) have relatively less empirical data regarding their effectiveness than do the newer drug and mental health court modalities. In this chapter, we summarize the evidence that does exist, describe existing and recommended practices where indicated (unfortunately, often without the assistance of effectiveness data), and draw conclusions regarding our future research needs in light of this discussion.

Keywords : Drug courts, forensic treatment, Incompetence to Stand Trial, juvenile delinquency, mental health courts

Forensic psychology is often associated with assessment. Psychological assessment and specialized measures have been important in the advances made in this area over the last 20–30 years (Melton, Petrila, Poythress, & Slobogin, 2007). But interventions for populations that are involved in the legal system have been an increasing focus of theoretical and research attention in some areas, such as violence risk assessment and treatment (see, e.g., Quinsey, Harris, Rice, & Cormier, 2006). They have also been recognized as among the "next frontier" of priorities for the forensic mental health professions (Otto & Heilbrun, 2002).

It is perhaps timely, therefore, to present in this chapter a description of three different kinds of interventions with criminal justice populations.

These interventions—for adjudicated delinquents, defendants diverted into specialized courts, and defendants hospitalized as incompetent to stand trial—represent a range of population ages, traditional versus relatively new modalities, and stages of the juvenile and criminal justice systems. It is perhaps ironic that the more established of these interventions, juvenile placement and forensic hospitalization, have relatively less empirical data regarding their effectiveness than do the newer drug and mental health court modalities. In this chapter, we summarize the evidence that does exist, describe existing and recommended practices where indicated (unfortunately, often without the assistance of effectiveness data), and draw conclusions regarding our future research needs in light of this discussion.

Interventions
Juveniles in Residential Placement

Since its inception at the turn of the 20th century, the U.S. juvenile justice system has struggled to balance the often competing demands of punishing and rehabilitating offending youth (Grisso, 1981). During the 1980s and 1990s, many states established punitive sanctions for youthful offenders. Recently, however, the majority of states have begun reforming their systems to keep more youth within the juvenile justice system and to provide much-needed mental health and aftercare services (Ziedenberg, 2006). Such changes have led to increasing demands for effective and replicable treatments that reduce recidivism.

In contrast to earlier reviews in the late 1970s and 1980s suggesting that "nothing works" in treating offending youth (Garrett, 1985), more recent research has demonstrated that treatments and interventions for juveniles can reduce recidivism (see, e.g., Alexander et al., 1998; Antonowicz & Ross, 1994; Henggeler, Schoenwald, Borduin, Rowland, & Cunningham, 1998). Studies have also suggested that treatment within the juvenile justice system may be more effective at reducing recidivism than placement within the adult correctional system (Bishop, Frazier, Lanza-Kaduce & Winner, 1996; Fagan, 1995). These effects remain even when selection bias (i.e., differences between youth who remain in the juvenile system and those who are sentenced in criminal court) is statistically controlled (Myers, 2003). Such findings are encouraging to treatment providers working with offending youth.

This section of the chapter will review the empirically supported treatments for juvenile offenders, focusing on treatment provided within residential juvenile justice settings. Empirical evidence does not support specific comprehensive programs for youth in custodial placement. However, meta-analytic results, as well as studies of risk and protective factors, identify treatment components that may reduce recidivism with delinquent youth in residential placement.

State of Empirically Supported Treatments for Juvenile Offenders

No comprehensive programming has yet been supported for use in custodial juvenile justice settings (Greenwood, 2005). In fact, based on the Office of Juvenile Justice and Delinquency Prevention (OJJDP) Model Programs' data, no programs have achieved even a "promising" level of empirical support for use in "correctional" settings (i.e., residential facilities that restrict the movement and activities of residents and serve as placements for adjudicated youth) (Office of Juvenile Justice Delinquency Prevention [OJJDP], 2008).

Research does support a number of community-based programs for reducing recidivism in juvenile offenders. For instance, multisystemic therapy (MST) has been shown to decrease delinquency and the incarceration rates of violent and chronic juvenile offenders for more than 2 years post-treatment (Henggeler et al., 1998). Multisystemic therapy is a community-based treatment that seeks to engage youth in treatment and reduce barriers to accessing services (Henggeler, Pickrel, Brondino, & Crouch, 1996). Master's level therapists provide about 60 hours of direct services over 3–6 months, working to empower the family to resolve and manage problems. Similarly, functional family therapy (FFT) (Alexander & Parsons, 1973) has been shown to reduce recidivism (Alexander et al., 1998). Unfortunately, both MST and FFT require intensive family participation that may be unrealistic with juvenile offenders in residential placements, where youth may be placed far from home, come from distressed families, or lack stable guardians (Guerra, Williams, Tolan, & Modecki, 2008). A family's ability and willingness to meaningfully participate in treatment may be severely limited for these youth. Thus, effective and empirically supported treatments are still needed within the highly structured, supervised, and treatment-intensive residential juvenile justice setting.

Promising Treatments in Residential Settings
TREATMENTS ASSOCIATED WITH REDUCTIONS IN RECIDIVISM

Although no comprehensive programs to reduce recidivism have been empirically evaluated for use in juvenile justice residential settings, some promising treatments have been identified for use in other types of residential settings. Like juvenile justice facilities, other types of residential settings provide 24-hour care, but they may or may not be secure.

Youth are often placed in such facilities for mental health and/or substance use needs, either voluntarily or by court order (OJJDP, 2008).

The OJJDP Model Programs database identifies three effective residential programs, empirically supported by quasi-experimental research, that are promising for adjudicated youth in placement (OJJDP, 2008). Two programs specifically target substance use (OJJDP, 2008). They include, but are not limited to, youth involved in the juvenile justice system. Although participation in both programs was associated with reductions in substance use, one program did not show reduced recidivism at 1-year follow-up (see Morral, McCaffrey, & Ridgeway, 2004) and the second did not consider recidivism as an outcome variable (see Morehouse & Tobler, 2000).

The third effective residential program identified by OJJDP—the Mendota Juvenile Treatment Center (MJTC) (see Caldwell & Van Rybroek, 2005)—combines the security provided in traditional correctional settings with the mental health treatment associated with psychiatric facilities. Adolescent males who have not responded favorably to traditional rehabilitative services in Wisconsin's juvenile justice system receive intensive, individualized therapy from experienced mental health professionals. The goal of treatment is to interrupt an escalating cycle of defiant behaviors and legal sanctions. The MJTC uses the Decompression Model (Monroe, Van Rybroek, & Maier, 1988) to keep youth from withdrawing or being withdrawn from treatment. Despite treatment-oriented intentions, staff members in many facilities focus primarily on behavioral control rather than treatment with aggressive youth (Caldwell & Van Rybroek, 2005). The MJTC seeks to maintain youth involvement in treatment by *increasing* individual treatment contact when additional security is required (Caldwell & Van Rybroek, 2005). Motivational interviewing approaches (see Miller & Rollnick, 2002) are used to foster change.

Youth in treatment at MJTC were significantly less likely to recidivate within 2 years than were youth who committed similar offenses and were referred for assessment, but not treatment, at MJTC. The MJTC youth were half as likely as these comparison youth to commit additional violent, serious offenses; there were no observed differences for misdemeanor offenses (Caldwell & Van Rybroek, 2005). This program may provide a useful model for the treatment of youth with substantial mental health needs. To date, however, it has not been extended to other centers or tested with female juvenile offenders.

Another OJJDP initiative, Blueprints for Change, identified promising mental health treatments for youth at different stages of the juvenile justice process (e.g., detention, residential treatment, aftercare) (Skowyra & Cocozza, 2007). Although Blueprints for Change primarily reviewed court liaison, mental health screening, and community reentry programs, it did identify one promising residential program. The Emotionally Disturbed Treatment Program (EDTP) in Corsicana, Texas, created and operated by the state's juvenile corrections agency, provides treatment for adjudicated youth with mental health disorders. Youth remain in placement for approximately 9 months, completing a 30-day evaluation period to verify the need for mental health treatment (Skowyra & Cocozza, 2007). Some 13.9% of youth who were enrolled in EDTP were incarcerated 1 year after they were released from secure confinement, compared with 25.6% of youth who were not enrolled (Texas Youth Commission [TYC], 2008). Youth who *completed* the EDTP had a lower rate of reincarceration at 1-year follow-up (8.5%) than did youth who did not complete treatment (17.2%; TYC, 2008). Smaller differences were observed in the cohort of youth followed for 3 years following release from secure confinement; 41.5% of youth enrolled in EDTP were reincarcerated, compared with 48.5% of youth who had not been enrolled (TYC, 2008). The mental health treatment at the EDTP includes "intensive psychiatric monitoring, increased psychological consultation, specialized counseling, and specially trained dorm staff" (TYC, 2008, p. 4). A detailed description of the actual treatment provided in the EDTP (i.e., the methods of psychiatric monitoring, the treatment techniques used in specialty counseling, and the training provided to dorm staff) was not available, illustrating one gap in the current juvenile justice treatment literature. The few programs with empirical support seldom provide the detailed treatment information that would allow other programs to integrate similarly effective techniques.

TREATMENTS ASSOCIATED WITH REDUCTIONS IN BEHAVIORS RELATED TO RECIDIVISM

Treatments for anger and aggression have been designed specifically for juvenile offenders, and researchers have begun examining the impact of these treatments when delivered within residential juvenile justice settings. Anger replacement training (ART) was designed for aggressive juvenile offenders. Anger replacement training groups meet three times per week, for 10 weeks, and emphasize the development of skills (e.g., thinking ahead, self-evaluation, self-rewarding, anger management, impulse control) and moral reasoning. Evaluations of program efficacy have shown positive effects for youth in many settings, including residential treatment facilities and secure confinement (Goldstein, 2004). To date, no studies have examined the effects of ART on recidivism.

Another anger management program designed specifically for girls in residential juvenile justice facilities is currently being evaluated. The juvenile justice anger management (JJAM) treatment for girls is an 8-week, 16-session, manualized, cognitive-behavioral group therapy program designed to teach girls anger-coping strategies, behavioral control techniques, and problem-solving skills to reduce physical and relational aggression. The JJAM uses role-plays, hands-on activities, and between-session practice assignments to help girls develop skills, solidify their learning, and use these skills when angry. The JJAM program addresses the hostile attribution biases often found in aggressive youth and provides girls with alternative methods of thinking about and reacting to anger-provoking events in their daily lives. The program was designed to address the needs of female juvenile offenders (e.g., abuse histories, low IQ and poor academic achievement, distress about unpredictable social support) and the frequency of co-occurring mental health problems in this population (e.g., substance abuse, attention-deficit hyperactivity disorder [ADHD], depression). A randomized, controlled pilot trial demonstrated significant reductions in anger, general aggression, verbal aggression, and indirect (relational) aggression for girls who completed the JJAM treatment in addition to the facility's treatment as usual (TAU); the control group completed only TAU. Medium to large effect sizes were observed for reductions in anger, verbal aggression, and indirect aggression. No recidivism data were collected in the pilot study (Goldstein, Dovidio, Kalbeitzer, Weil, & Strachan, 2007). Although these results appear promising, their interpretation from a small-scale pilot study requires caution. A full-scale, multisite, randomized controlled efficacy study is in progress and will include data on participants' recidivism rates.

Challenges to Conducting Juvenile Justice Research

Clearly, further research is needed to identify recidivism-reducing treatments for use in residential juvenile justice settings. Few empirically supported treatments are available for use in these settings, partly because of the difficulties inherent in performing research with juvenile offenders in placement. As both "children" and "prisoners," juvenile offenders are a doubly protected population under the U.S. Code of Federal Regulations (45 CFR 46.402; 45 CFR 46.303) used by Institutional Review Boards. As "children," such participants must receive permission from a parent or legal guardian to participate in research. Identifying and contacting the relevant parties can be prohibitively time-consuming and difficult, especially in large states where youth may be placed in facilities far from home. Many youth in residential settings may be "wards-of-the-state," based on the Office for Human Research Protections' regulations (45 CFR 46.407), thus raising complex questions about who can provide permission and which regulations granting authorizing participation may apply. Questions such as these can prevent many eligible youth from participating in treatment research and reduce studies' sample sizes.

Exacerbating these challenges to research, the length of stay for youths in placement is often unpredictable. Youth may be released earlier than anticipated for any number of reasons (e.g., good behavior, an unexpected decision by a judge during a review hearing, poor adjustment to a given placement), or may remain in a particular residential facility only until a bed is available elsewhere. Such variability makes it difficult to ensure that a youth completes an entire treatment protocol, and that the beginning group of youth completes a closed-group intervention.

Furthermore, youth involved in the juvenile justice system can be difficult to track after leaving residential placement. Such youth tend to come from distressed families that may often change locations (Scanlon & Devine, 2001). This inconsistency creates obstacles to tracking youth for post-treatment outcome periods. Similarly, moving between jurisdictions can interfere with accurate collection of official recidivism data—new charges might be unknown to officials in the original jurisdiction from which the recidivism data are collected.

Treatment outcome research is also limited by definitions of "success." Many program evaluations consider placement in a less restrictive setting to be one kind of successful outcome (see, e.g., Drais-Parrillo, 2004). Although this can provide a more complex view of improvement than simple recidivism, such information is typically provided *instead of* data on additional arrests and adjudications.

Measuring treatment success using only future juvenile justice placements may be misleading, as placement decisions are often heavily influenced by factors unrelated to the individual or the offense (e.g., bed availability) (Bender, 2004).

Empirically Supported Treatment Characteristics

Despite the challenges to conducting treatment outcome research within the juvenile justice system, many studies have examined the relationships between specific treatment characteristics and recidivism rates. Meta-analytic results have revealed several characteristics of treatment that appear related to recidivism.

TARGETING CRIMINOGENIC NEEDS

Consistent with intervention theory describing risk, need, and responsivity (Andrews & Bonta, 2006), meta-analyses of studies of adult and juvenile offenders have indicated that treatment programs directly addressing criminogenic needs (those empirically associated with the risk of recidivism) are more effective than programs that do not target recidivism-related factors (Antonowicz & Ross, 1994). In fact, the effect size of treatment tends to be associated with the number of criminogenic needs targeted in the treatment program (Dowden & Andrews, 2000). This is important for two reasons. First, not all programs explicitly focus on reducing the risk of future offending. Some facilities may simply remove the individual from the community for a designated period of time. For instance, many widely publicized "get tough" policies seek to deter potential offenders from committing future offenses and focus less on the rehabilitation of the adjudicated individual (Myers, 2003). Other programs may address issues (e.g., self-esteem) that may be helpful to the individual's emotional well-being but are not associated with criminal behavior (Bonta & Andrews, 2007). Approaches that focus on broad psychological change do not reduce the risk of delinquency (Lipsey, 1995); if the goal is recidivism reduction, resources are better invested by targeting criminogenic needs (Dowden & Andrews, 2000). Second, the application of this principle is far from straightforward because it requires identification of criminogenic needs and an understanding of how these needs are associated with juvenile offending.

Cottle, Lee, and Heilbrun (2001) examined 30 potential predictor variables in a meta-analysis of 22 studies reporting reoffending outcomes for juvenile offenders. The two variables with the strongest relationships to recidivism were younger age at first commitment and younger age at first contact with the law. These age-related variables are static risk factors that cannot be altered through planned intervention. Many other identified risk factors, such as history of physical and/or sexual abuse or significant family problems, are difficult or impossible to change through treatment at a post-adjudication residential facility. However, treatment within residential juvenile justice programs can target dynamic risk factors—modifiable characteristics that, if altered, may decrease youths' risks for future offending.

Nonsevere Psychopathology

Nonsevere psychopathology (e.g., stress, anxiety) was the strongest dynamic risk factor for reoffending found in Cottle, Lee and Heilbrun's (2001) meta-analysis. Notably, histories of severe psychopathology and psychiatric treatment were not significantly associated with reoffending. However, both nonsevere pathology and conduct problems were associated with reoffending. Studies involving large numbers of juvenile offenders and urban adolescents have noted that high impulsivity (Loeber, Farrington, Stouthamer-Loeber, Moffitt, & Caspi, 1998), as well as hyperactivity, concentration problems, and restlessness (Hawkins et al., 2000) were associated with delinquency. Attention deficits and irritability were also identified as risk factors for delinquency and crime, with moderate to large effect sizes (Agnew, 2005). Consequently, mental health treatment can address these symptoms as a potential mechanism for reducing recidivism.

There is an absence of empirically supported psychological treatments to address symptoms associated with hyperactivity, attention deficits, and irritability in juvenile offenders in residential facilities. However, empirically supported treatments (including psychopharmacological treatments) for many of these symptoms do exist for other populations in outpatient clinical settings. Later in this chapter, we will discuss ways to adapt non-psychopharmacological treatments for use within residential juvenile justice placements.

Poor Problem Solving Skills

In a study of adult males under federal supervision, Zamble and Quinsey (1997) observed that men who reoffended and were returned to federal prison had much poorer coping skills than did comparison samples of nonrecidivating and nonoffending males. In another study, poor social problem-solving skills served as a risk factor for delinquency, with a medium to large effect size observed (Agnew, 2005).

Not surprisingly, the abilities to seek social support, act in a nonimpulsive manner, and use flexible and reflective coping strategies have all been identified as protective factors (Hanna, 2001). Treatments involving problem-solving training can help participating youth develop these protective skills (see Kazdin, 2003), thereby potentially modifying this risk factor for recidivism.

Deviant Peers/Unstructured Time

Research has consistently found that youth with negative peer relations tend to be involved in more delinquent activity (Brendgen, Vitaro, & Bukowski, 2000; Chung & Steinberg, 2006; Hawkins et al., 2000; Haynie, 2002; Lipsey & Derzon, 1998). During adolescence, peer relationships become extremely important (see Guerra et al., 2008) and may become more influential than familial relationships (DeMatteo & Marczyk, 2005). Strained social relationships may cause youth to seek out accepting peer groups; if youth are not accepted by mainstream peers, they may become involved with delinquent peers (Patterson, Reid, & Dishion, 1992). Youth who value the opinions of their deviant peers may engage in delinquent activities to gain respect and become part of the group. Additionally, youth without meaningful peer relationships are at increased risk of engaging in delinquent behavior (Department of Health and Human Services, 2001). In sum, involvement with antisocial peers and lack of social ties between the ages of 12 and 14 has been identified as a critical risk factor for illegal behavior between the ages of 15 and 25 (Lipsey & Derzon, 1998).

Unstructured time also is a risk factor for delinquency (Agnew, 2005), whereas participation in structured, after-school, and community activities can serve as a protective factor for youth (DeMatteo & Marczyk, 2005). There is some evidence that involvement with prosocial peers decreases the likelihood of antisocial activities (Hawkins et al., 2000). However, the findings are mixed, with other studies finding no relationship between prosocial peers and antisocial activities (DHHS, 2001). Regardless, youth engaged in sports and other extracurricular activities have less unsupervised time in the community to engage in delinquent behavior. Although community reentry programs would be the most appropriate venues for promoting positive peer relationships and structured activities in youths' communities, these criminogenic risk factors can be targeted in residential placement as well. While in placement, youth can be encouraged to participate in prosocial activities (e.g., art, music, carpentry,

basketball) to promote interest in engaging in these types of activities post-release.

Substance Abuse

Substance abuse, but not substance use, has been identified as a significant predictor of juvenile recidivism (Cottle, Lee, & Heilbrun, 2001). Substance abuse is defined as the maladaptive use of a substance, as evidenced by significant and recurrent negative consequences (e.g., failure to fulfill obligations at home, work, school, or in interpersonal relationships). To meet diagnostic criteria, the substance must be used for a period of at least 12 months, with continued use despite negative consequences (American Psychiatric Association, 2000). One rigorous epidemiological study on the prevalence of mental health disorders in juvenile offenders estimated that 46% of offending youth may meet criteria for a substance abuse disorder (Teplin, Abram, McClelland, Dulcan, & Mericle, 2002; see Veysey, 2008, for a review of juvenile justice prevalence studies). Recent estimates suggest that only 50% of youth diagnosed with a substance use disorder receive any substance use treatment during their placement in a secure facility (Skowyra & Cocozza, 2007). Consequently, providing effective substance use treatment to the large proportion of juvenile offenders who qualify for substance abuse diagnoses could substantially reduce recidivism rates.

Beliefs Supporting Crime/Low Empathy

Beliefs about the acceptability of crime and low empathy have also been identified as risk factors for delinquency (Agnew, 2005). Youth who believe that crime is acceptable tend to show antisocial thinking that is often characterized by rationalizations about crime and negative attitudes about the law (Andrews & Bonta, 2006). Youth may acquire these antisocial attitudes and beliefs from parents, friends, or other cultural influences. For some youth, antisocial and illegal activities may be "normal" and preferred because of social ties and the perceived benefits of such a lifestyle (e.g., the youth sees neighborhood drug dealers obtaining money and respect) (Guerra et al., 2008).

It is very difficult to compete with youths' deeply imbedded beliefs about the acceptability of criminal lifestyles. If youth are ambivalent or unwilling to change, common didactic processes of teaching youth about the effects of crime on both perpetrator and victim may backfire and cause youth to defend their own beliefs about crime (Miller & Rollnick, 2002). Because of this strong adherence to beliefs, there has been a recent effort to introduce motivational interviewing (MI) principles into juvenile justice settings (Miller & Rollnick, 2002). Motivational interviewing theory characterizes this oppositional reaction as the normal response of a person whose personal choice is being challenged (Miller & Rollnick, 2002). If a person is ambivalent about choices A and B, and there is an external advocate for choice A (e.g., from a treatment provider), the person will naturally begin to think of the benefits of choice B. As such, well-intentioned directions from treatment providers may have the unintended effect of decreasing the likelihood of choice A. Motivational interviewing is an interactive process, not a specific treatment, and it can be used to engage youth in conversations about the acceptability of criminal behavior. It can also encourage youth to consider prosocial ideas and alternative behaviors without receiving pressure from treatment providers that can elicit defensiveness and solidify antisocial views.

MULTIFACETED AND STRUCTURED PROGRAMMING

Given the need to target a variety of criminogenic needs, it is not surprising that programs utilizing a variety of techniques are more effective than those using only a single method (Antonowicz & Ross, 1994). Multimodal programs that target concrete behaviors and skills, such as employment and problem solving, are more effective in reducing delinquency than are those that rely solely on individual and family counseling (Lipsey, 1992, 1995). Structured programming that focuses on skills and cognitions is also associated with better outcomes (Guerra, Kim, & Boxer, 2008). Although programs relying on individual or group therapy alone have not been found to be effective, counseling can be an important component of an effective, multimodal program. For example, counseling can help youth benefit from skills-building activities, case management, or educational and vocational training (Lee & McGinnis-Haynes, 1978). Incorporating structured therapy into wilderness programs can turn a previously ineffective approach into an effective one (Greenwood, 2005; Wilson & Lipsey, 2000).

COGNITIVE-BEHAVIORAL TREATMENT MODEL

Meta-analytic results have shown that effective programs for both juvenile and adult offenders are significantly more likely to have clearly specified theories of delinquency or crime than were noneffective programs (Antonowicz & Ross, 1994). Programs based on cognitive-behavioral models for treatment were most effective in reducing recidivism (Antonowicz & Ross, 1994). Cognitive-behavioral therapy (CBT)-based programming appears to be equally effective in correctional settings and community settings, and the specific type of CBT treatment does not seem to change the effectiveness of treatment (Landenberger & Lipsey, 2005). Notably, juvenile delinquency intervention programs that included a cognitive component were more than twice as effective as other programs (Izzo & Ross, 1990).

Programs using cognitive-behavioral therapeutic approaches seem to be particularly effective for several reasons. First, once youth learn to alter cognitions, they can generalize this skill to many settings and situations; purely behavioral techniques, however, rely on contingencies that tend to be situation-specific (Kazdin, Bass, Siegel, & Thomas, 1989). For example, if a youth is taught cognitive restructuring as part of problem-solving training, the youth can use this skill when facing problems at school, conflicts at home, tensions with friends, or difficulties at work. In contrast, the reinforcements and punishments that motivate behavior vary across these situations and can be unpredictable even within each situation. Despite this limitation of behavioral treatment, contingencies can be powerful motivators for behavior (Kronenberger & Meyer, 2001), and can thus be important in conjunction with the cognitive approach. A second strength of CBT-based programs is that they are inherently multifaceted. Cognitive-behavioral therapy–based treatments often integrate various tools and techniques, such as cognitive restructuring, behavioral activation, exposure, behavior prevention, problem solving, and psychoeducation (Brown, O'Leary, & Barlow, 2001; Ledley, Marx, & Heimberg, 2005). These techniques, combined with CBT's active and problem-focused approach to treatment (Ledley, Marx, & Heimberg, 2005), make CBT-based programs suitable for use in juvenile justice facilities. Several of the components frequently found in CBT-based programs are empirically supported for use within the juvenile justice system.

Changing Cognitions

Programs that include a cognitive component are more effective in reducing recidivism than are programs that do not attempt to alter thinking (Antonowicz & Ross, 1994). One key to changing juvenile delinquents' behavior seems to be changing their cognitions (Lipsey & Wilson, 1998), and programs that teach specific skills within the broader domain of cognitive change, such as social skills, anger control skills, or cognitive restructuring, seem to be more effective at reducing recidivism (Dowden & Andrews, 2000; Landenberger & Lipsey, 2005).

Responsivity to the Individual

Responsivity implies that interventions are tailored to the unique needs, strengths, abilities, and learning styles of the recipients (Dowden & Andrews, 2004). Responsive programs that match services to the needs of the offender and integrate various learning techniques are more likely to produce significant differences between treatment and control groups (Antonowicz & Ross, 1994). The "collaborative empiricism" approach of most CBT-based treatments is responsive to the needs of the individual youth; therapists and clients work together, in collaboration, to examine which thoughts and behaviors are helpful to the client, and which are not (Young, Weinberger, & Beck, 2001). By collaborating with the client, rather than imposing preformed rules or answers, the treatment provider is able to respond to the unique needs of the individual offender.

Effective Techniques

Juvenile offenders have many unique characteristics and differ from the general population of youth in several important ways that can affect treatment. Compared to nonoffending youth, juvenile offenders have lower IQ scores (Redding & Arrigo, 2005), higher rates of educational disabilities (approximately 45% of juvenile offenders, see Eggleston, 2008), and higher rates of ADHD (up to 68% of girls and 76% of boys in detention are estimated to meet criteria for ADHD, see Veysey, 2008). With the high rates of these problems, juvenile offenders receiving treatment are likely to have difficulties maintaining attention, organizing their thoughts and activities, and acquiring information taught didactically (Kronenberger & Meyer, 2001). The CBT treatment techniques of cognitive rehearsal (mentally practicing a behavior before performing it), role-playing (acting out real-life situations within the session), and scheduling (planning times to try new activities and behaviors) (Young, Weinberger, & Beck, 2001) can be used to work effectively with youth who may have intellectual, educational, and attentional deficits. These techniques can be used to help youth acquire specific skills and actively participate in treatment. Active learning techniques reduce the didactic portions of treatment and turn therapy from a passive experience into one involving active engagement in treatment.

Modeling is another component of many successful CBT-based interventions (see Kendall, Aschenbrand, & Hudson, 2003; Webster-Stratton & Reid, 2001). Effective programs for juvenile and adult offenders often use therapists and staff members to actively model the attitudes and behaviors taught in the program (Antonowicz & Ross, 1994; Dowden & Andrews, 2004). Through modeling, treatment providers can capitalize on the effects of social learning, demonstrating problem-solving skills, social skills, and prosocial attitudes for youth with limited exposure to these positive behaviors and conceptions of the world. Modeling is a common technique in CBT, with therapists often modeling desired activities and behaviors before asking youth to use new skills.

FAMILY INVOLVEMENT

Of the treatments that have been empirically examined with adjudicated youth, those involving families seem most often to be identified as effective (Guerra, Kim, & Boxer, 2008; Henggeler et al., 1998; Ryan & Yang, 2005; Washington State Institute for Public Policy, 2004). Whenever possible, it is particularly important to include families of younger offenders and those likely to return to the home environment when released from residential placement (Guerra, Kim, & Boxer, 2008). In one long-term residential facility, youth who received more on-site family visits, were permitted more home visits, or received in-home counseling were less likely to have reoffended 2 years after release (Ryan & Yang, 2005). It is possible that this improvement could have resulted from the interest, dedication, and superior functioning of families that were involved with their children while they were in placement. However, the consistent reduction in recidivism found in randomized controlled trials (RCTs) of interventions that specifically target family functioning (e.g., MST, FFT) suggest that inclusion of families in treatment, when feasible, may promote treatment success.

Empirically Supported Treatment Implementation Characteristics

In addition to identifying important treatment components, meta-analyses suggest several implementation issues that can alter the effect of treatments on recidivism.

LENGTH OF STAY

The length of time juvenile offenders remain in treatment can increase the effectiveness of the treatment, with longer residential treatments associated with lower recidivism rates (Billick & Mack, 2004;

Lipsey, 1992). In one study, youth who remained in treatment more than 11 months were less likely to recidivate than were those who received treatment for shorter periods of time (McMackin, Tansi, & Lafratta, 2004). Notably, however, there may be a curvilinear relationship between the length of treatment and treatment outcome. In one meta-analysis, the effect size associated with institutional treatment increased with the amount of treatment to a certain point, but then declined (Lipsey, 1992). It seems that enough (but not too much) treatment is needed. Further research is needed to establish the length of treatment that allows maximum benefits without resulting in iatrogenic effects. Additionally, this "ideal" length of stay may vary depending on characteristics of the youth, such as age, level of familial support, and access to prosocial activities and peers in the communities of origin.

TREATMENT INTEGRITY

Researcher involvement with the treatment program was strongly associated with the effect size of treatment (Lipsey, 1995). Researcher involvement did not appear to result in positive outcomes because of researcher bias or wishful thinking; rather, researcher involvement seems to be an indicator of treatment integrity (Lipsey, 1995). Generally, treatments that are designed and implemented as part of a research study are carefully monitored for consistency and fidelity to the model program. Studies involving treatments with such careful control and extensive training and supervision of treatment providers tend to produce larger effect sizes.

This finding is promising in that it demonstrates that well-trained, well-supervised, closely monitored treatments can result in recidivism reductions. However, it also suggests the need for caution when adopting treatments for standard use in juvenile justice programs. For instance, when Washington State attempted to implement MST with less oversight from the central training agency, MST was not associated with reductions in recidivism (Washington State Institute for Public Policy, 2004).

Consequently, the challenge for juvenile justice programs is to maintain treatment fidelity and integrity when using treatments outside of the research context. Procedures should be established for providing adequate supervision and ongoing checking to ensure that treatment is implemented as intended. It has been observed that it is easier to develop a valid instrument than to use it appropriately and effectively (Sarri et al., 2001), and the same can be said for treatment protocols.

Effective treatment implementation requires buy-in from staff at every level within the juvenile justice program, but particularly from the line staff who will deliver the treatment (Young, 2004; Young, Moline, Farrell, & Bierie, 2006). Additional research on successful implementation is needed to develop effective procedures for implementing treatment protocols in residential settings in which staff may be resistant to changes in programming and reluctant to deliver the newest treatments sent to them by program administrators (Young, 2004). Outcome studies rarely specify the strategies, components, and implementation issues that may be pivotal to delivering the same treatment in other residential facilities. Such "process evaluations" (Young, 2004) can provide detailed information about the implementation of the treatment protocol to guide treatment use following dissemination for clinical purposes.

Modifying Treatments Empirically Supported with Other Populations for Use Within Residential Juvenile Justice Facilities

Given the absence of empirically supported treatments for youth in residential juvenile justice placement, treatments that have been supported with other relevant populations (e.g., adult inmates, at-risk adolescents) can be modified for use with juvenile offenders in residential facilities. Full-scale assessment of needed revisions, through adaptation and randomized controlled outcome trials, would be ideal in developing and empirically evaluating treatments for this population. However, such a development and evaluation process requires substantial time and funding to identify needed changes, adapt activities, rewrite treatment manuals, create implementation protocols, and evaluate the resulting program. On a smaller scale, practitioners can make minor changes to empirically supported individual and group treatments to make them relevant for and accessible to adjudicated youth.

ACCESSIBILITY OF TREATMENT CONTENT

Given the high rates of ADHD (Veysey, 2008) and educational disabilities common among juvenile offenders (Eggleston, 2008), treatment content must be made accessible to delinquent youth. First, language and sentence structure may need to be simplified and made culturally relevant for participating youth. The amount of reading and writing involved in session and homework activities may need to be reduced or eliminated. Often, the treatment content can be maintained, but worksheets may need to be modified to include checklists that require less writing, or worksheets may need to be eliminated entirely and replaced with verbal statements or pictorial cues. Second, to engage youth with difficulties sustaining attention, treatment providers may need to reduce didactic portions of treatment and encourage learning through more interactive, hands-on activities that promote sustained attention. Allowing youth to have some control over what occurs in treatment (e.g., choosing a skill to practice or a situation to role-play) may also help to maintain attention and engage youth in treatment.

FOCUS ON SPECIFIC SKILLS

As suggested by meta-analytic findings on effective programs, treatments should focus on specific skills, such as problem-solving or anger coping. Treatments should be modified to allow ample time to learn, practice, and apply the concrete, practical skills (e.g., problem-solving steps, anger control techniques) taught in treatment. Role-plays and homework assignments may be particularly useful for engaging youth in practicing new skills.

BUILD IN PRAISE

Positive attention is a powerful reinforcement tool that is used in many empirically supported programs for children (see Weisz, 2004). Interest and attention from treatment providers may help to establish rapport and engage youth in treatment. Simple statements such as "Thanks for participating, John" and "Excellent example, Susan," should make youth more likely to repeat the desired behaviors. Such positive feedback can help provide the external motivation many youth with attentional difficulties require to remain engaged in activities (Anastopoulos & Barkley, 1990) or to complete homework assignments. To ensure that attention and praise are given, treatments for youth should include directions for treatment leaders to reward participation and desired behaviors.

PREPARE FOR OPPOSITIONALITY

Juveniles in residential care have generally been separated from their home environments involuntarily. This unwanted separation and restriction of freedom, combined with the developmentally appropriate process of developing independence during adolescence (Bolton Oetzel & Scherer, 2003), can yield resistance to ideas and activities suggested by treatment providers. Preparing for such opposition can help providers roll with resistance and engage

youth in treatment. First, it may be helpful for providers to simply be aware that this opposition may occur, so as not to be surprised in treatment. Adolescents in general, and especially those with histories of abuse and neglect, may require time to develop trusting, therapeutic relationships with adults and may test boundaries through their behavior (Pearce & Pezzot-Pearce, 2007). Treatment providers must be prepared for the defensive behaviors youth may exhibit, and respond with consistent empathy and availability (Bolton Oetzel & Scherer, 2003). In responding to oppositional behaviors, the therapist can respect the feelings expressed by the youth, while continuing to require a certain amount of participation (Pearce & Pezzot-Pearce, 2007). For example, if a youth in treatment refuses to role-play a scene involving his mother, the therapist can respond by acknowledging the youth's discomfort with and dislike of the activity, but ask him to give it a try, perhaps using a less sensitive topic such as an interaction with a teacher. The same tactic could work to prevent unsafe behaviors (e.g., throwing items, climbing on furniture) within treatment (Pearce & Pezzot-Pearce, 2007). That is, the treatment provider can acknowledge the feelings expressed by the youth (e.g., anger, frustration, sadness) but firmly maintain that the behavior is not allowable.

Allowing youth as much freedom and choice as possible while maintaining treatment integrity can prevent some opposition (Bolton Oetzel & Scherer, 2003). During treatment sessions, youth can choose the order to practice skills and the situations to use as examples for skills' practice. For example, in a group session reviewing anger-coping skills, each participant can choose which of the skills reviewed she most wants to practice. As group members role-play the various skills, she can describe a scenario in which the skill could be useful. Even small choices, such as the color of folder to use for homework assignments, may help youth become engaged in treatment. Juvenile justice facilities typically have strict rules that allow little room for individual choice; providing youth with some control over treatment-related decisions may reduce oppositionality and increase willingness to engage in treatment.

MODIFY ACTIVITIES TO BE
DEVELOPMENTALLY APPROPRIATE

Given the low IQs (Redding & Arrigo, 2005), academic difficulties (Eggleston, 2008), poor attentional abilities (Veysey, 2008), and immature social development (Bolton Oetzel & Scherer, 2003) of many juvenile offenders, some treatments designed for younger children may be cognitively appropriate for use with juvenile offenders. However, activities may need to be modified to make them developmentally appropriate to the interests of adolescents. For instance, activities using puppets to practice skills can be replaced with role-plays, and cartoon clips can be replaced with popular movie scenes as stimuli for discussion. Also, discussion topics may need to be altered, as adolescents may be more interested in talking about romantic relationships or problems with friends than about household chores or relationships with teachers.

ADD TOPICS RELEVANT TO THE POPULATION
Youth in the juvenile justice system show high rates of substance abuse (Teplin, Abram, McClelland, Dulcan, & Mericle, 2002), and most have experienced traumatic events (Veysey, 2008). These issues often arise in treatment and should be handled responsibly. Treatment providers should be aware of common symptoms of trauma, including physiological responses, intrusive images, and behavioral constriction (Veysey, 2008). Youth should never be forced to disclose traumatic experiences, and treatment should focus on specific problems while building on the strengths of the individual (Veysey, 2008). When adapting any treatment for use in juvenile justice facilities, treatment providers should consider how traumatic experiences may affect youths' participation in treatment. Because of the prevalence rates observed in juvenile offenders, explicit discussions of other topics, such as substance use and abuse, may need to be added to existing treatment programs. Additional topics may be needed, depending on the specific treatment audience. For example, it may be important to address relational aggression and sexual abuse with female juvenile offenders (Sondheimer, 2001). The lack of familial support and home stability may be important to address in treatments for youth in foster care.

MODIFY TREATMENT FOR CONFINES OF THE SETTING
Treatment providers may need to creatively adapt both the treatment structure and their implementation protocols for successful use in juvenile justice facilities.

Modifying Treatments
Certain components of treatment may need to be modified for use within the confines of a juvenile justice facility. Videotaping sessions, either for therapist supervision, for later review by the treatment participant, or for research purposes, may not be allowed because of confidentiality policies in residential juvenile justice settings. Instead, treatment providers may be able to audio-record sessions, or they may need to transcribe key information. Homework activities that would normally be completed with participation from parents or teachers can be modified to allow line-staff to assist youth. If staff participation is required, obtaining buy-in and participation from staff members is an important first step to implementing the treatment program.

Exposure-related activities present a unique challenge to implementing treatment in juvenile justice facilities. When treatment takes place in outpatient clinics, providers can arrange relevant practice situations or wait for such situations to arise. For instance, in anxiety treatments, therapists often take clients into the community to confront feared situations, such as standing atop a tall building or interacting with a waiter when ordering in a restaurant (Kendall, Aschenbrand, & Hudson, 2003). Treatment providers in juvenile justice facilities are more restricted, but they can create exposure activities for youth with the help of other program staff. When providing treatment within a residential setting, providers must also modify treatment to address both problems faced by youth within the facility (e.g., problems with facility peers and staff) and those they expect to confront upon return to the community (e.g., problems at home and school).

Modifying Treatment Implementation
Residential juvenile justice settings may have limited resources and space for treatment providers. With some creative planning, however, most treatment components can be successfully implemented. If a television/DVD is not available for showing movie clips, a laptop computer may be usable; if computers are not allowed, magazine pictures illustrating the key points can be shown to participants. Procedures common in outpatient therapy (e.g., carrying a paper and pencil for tracking homework assignments) must be carefully considered to ensure that youth are able to complete between-session assignments. Special access (e.g., permission to carry paper and a pencil) or procedures (e.g., having youth complete assignments with a staff member present) may need to be established, especially in facilities with strict security requirements. With careful consideration, between-session practice activities can still occur, and youth can benefit from the rehearsal of desired behaviors.

Conclusions

Contrary to earlier ideas that "nothing works" with juvenile offenders, research suggests that careful treatment can reduce recidivism. Treatment programs based in cognitive-behavioral theory that target criminogenic needs and specific skills within a structured setting can reduce youths' risk of future offending. Further research is needed on how to best treat criminogenic needs and effectively implement treatment protocols while maintaining treatment integrity. Until more programs are empirically supported for use within the juvenile justice system, treatment providers can carefully modify treatments designed for other settings to meet identified criminogenic needs of youth within juvenile justice facilities.

Defendants in Drug Courts or Mental Health Courts

Over the past 25 years, the number of drug-involved offenders entering the criminal justice system has increased dramatically. The "War on Drugs," which began in the 1970s and gained considerable momentum in the 1980s, contributed to an unprecedented expansion in the U.S. inmate population. Jail and prison admissions more than tripled in the ensuing years (Harrison & Karberg, 2003), with drug violations accounting for roughly 60% of the increase in the federal inmate population and over 30% of the increase in the state inmate population (Belenko & Peugh, 1998; Harrison & Beck, 2002). A review of recent data from the Bureau of Justice Statistics is informative. In 2004, an estimated 330,000 individuals were incarcerated for drug law violations, with drug offenders comprising 55% of federal prison inmates and roughly 20% of state prison inmates in the United States (Mumola & Karberg, 2006). Further, 17% of state inmates and 18% of federal inmates reported committing their crimes to obtain money for drugs (Mumola & Karberg, 2006). In 2004, 56% of state inmates and 50% of federal inmates reported using drugs in the 1 month prior to their offense, and 32% of state inmates and 26% of federal inmates reported being under the influence of drugs at the time of their offense (Mumola & Karberg, 2006). Finally, one in four violent offenders incarcerated as of 2004 reported committing their offenses while under the influence of drugs (Mumola & Karberg, 2006).

Given the documented relationship between drug use and criminal behavior, developing and implementing appropriate interventions for drug-involved criminal offenders has been a priority of the criminal justice system for decades. Historically, drug policy in the United States has vacillated between two competing approaches when dealing with drug-involved criminal offenders (Marlowe, 2002). On the one hand, drug use can be conceptualized as a *public safety* concern that requires a punitive correctional response. According to this view, drug use is illegal behavior, and illegal behavior should be met with a punitive response. Interventions consistent with this approach include imprisonment, in-prison rehabilitation programs, civil commitment, and community-based intermediate sanctions (e.g., electronic monitoring, house arrest, boot camps). On the other hand, drug use can be conceptualized as a *public health* concern that requires a treatment-oriented response. According to this view, drug addiction is a disease and, as such, the appropriate societal response is the provision of clinically appropriate treatment.

Unfortunately, neither the public safety approach nor the public health approach has resulted in meaningful reductions in drug use and criminal recidivism. Imprisonment, which is the mainstay of the public safety approach, has achieved little success. Roughly 50% of incarcerated drug-involved criminal offenders recidivate within 18 months of release from prison, and roughly 70% recidivate within 3 years of release (see Martin, Butzin, Saum, & Inciardi, 1999). The data concerning relapse to drug use are similarly disappointing. In some studies, approximately 85% of drug-abusing offenders returned to drug use within 1 year of being released from prison, and 95% returned to drug use within 3 years of being released from prison (e.g., Martin et al., 1999).

One could argue that imprisonment, by itself, should not be expected to necessarily lead to reductions in recidivism and drug use. As such, it may be informative to examine the effects of in-prison treatment programs specifically designed to reduce recidivism and drug use. Unfortunately, this approach has not fared much better. Most research suggests that in-prison rehabilitation programs are associated with small reductions in criminal recidivism and little to no reductions in relapse to drug use (see Marlowe, 2002, for a review of this research). A review of hundreds of studies of in-prison treatment programs found that these programs reduce criminal recidivism by, on average, 10 percentage points, from 55% for untreated offenders to 45% for treated offenders (Gendreau, Smith, & Goggin, 2001). Correctional treatment programs targeted specifically at drug-involved offenders have not produced encouraging results. For example, a large meta-analysis of over

1,600 program evaluations conducted between 1968 and 1996 found that group counseling interventions and boot camps had no appreciable effect on rearrest rates among drug offenders (Pearson & Lipton, 1999).

The limited success of the public safety approach led to a push for more treatment-oriented responses. Unfortunately, the public health approach has also failed to achieve meaningful results. Roughly one-half to two-thirds of individuals who schedule an intake appointment for drug use treatment fail to attend the intake session (Festinger, Lamb, Marlowe, & Kirby, 2002). For those who do show up for the intake session, research suggests that few will receive a sufficient dose of treatment. Between 40% and 80% of drug users drop out of treatment within 3 months (Stark, 1992), and 80%–90% drop out of treatment within 1 year (Satel, 1999). Research suggests that 3 months of treatment is the minimum threshold for observing dose-response effects, and 12 months may be necessary to observe clinically meaningful reductions in drug use, particularly for those with more severe drug use problems (see, e.g., Simpson, Joe, & Brown, 1997). Given that up to 90% of drug offenders drop out of treatment in less than 12 months, very few offenders are receiving an adequate dose of treatment. Moreover, even for those offenders who remain in treatment for at least 12 months, roughly 50% relapse to drug use within 1 year following termination of treatment (McLellan, Lewis, O'Brien, & Kleber, 2000).

Defendants in Drug Courts

Fortunately, a new approach for dealing with drug-involved offenders has achieved considerably more success. This approach is part of a new breed of interventions known as problem-solving courts, which combine elements of the public safety and public health approaches. Rather than simply punishing offenders, which contributes to an ongoing cycle of arrest, incarceration, release, and rearrest, these special jurisdiction courts emphasize dispositions such as drug treatment, mental health treatment, the provision of social services, and ongoing judicial monitoring of offenders' progress. Moreover, many problem-solving courts provide for the dismissal of criminal charges and expungement of the offender's arrest record upon successful completion of the treatment program, which allows offenders to have a fresh start without the stigma of an arrest record. The theory underlying problem-solving courts is that recidivism can be reduced if the problems presumed to underlie criminal behavior, such as

drug abuse and mental illness, are treated with a range of services under the watchful eye of a court.

The modern era of problem-solving courts began in the late 1980s, with the development of drug courts. Drug courts were created in response to the overwhelming numbers of drug-related cases that were inundating the court system due to the War on Drugs. The first drug court was opened in Dade County, Florida, in 1989, under the guidance of then-State Attorney Janet Reno. As of year-end 2007, there were 2,147 drug courts operating in the United States (National Association of Drug Court Professionals, 2008), with many more in advanced planning stages. In addition to having drug courts in all 50 states, the drug court model is being used in three U.S. territories and eight countries (Huddleston, Freeman-Wilson, Marlowe, & Roussell, 2005).

Drug courts are separate criminal court dockets that provide judicially supervised drug abuse treatment and case management services to nonviolent drug-involved offenders in lieu of prosecution or incarceration. Participation in a drug court is voluntary, and eligibility is typically determined by the local prosecutor based on an offender's current charges, criminal history, and drug problem severity. The key components of drug courts include ongoing status hearings in court before a designated drug court judge, mandatory completion of drug abuse treatment, random weekly urine drug screens, and escalating sanctions and rewards for program infractions and accomplishments (National Association of Drug Court Professionals, 1997). Drugs courts come in two main varieties. In pre-plea drug courts, offenders who complete the program have their charges dropped and may be eligible for expungement of their current arrest record, which permits them to respond truthfully on an employment application or similar document that they have not been arrested for a drug-related offense. In post-plea drug courts, graduates may avoid incarceration, reduce their probationary obligations, or receive a sentence of "time served."

Drug courts are primarily intended to reduce drug use (which is believed to lead to criminal recidivism), and they typically employ a multiphased treatment model consisting of stabilization, intensive treatment, and transition. Commonly employed strategies to reduce drug use include group counseling, individual and family counseling, and 12-step self-help groups (National Association of Drug Court Professionals, 1997). Although the primary focus of drug courts is reducing drug use, drug courts often provide comprehensive services, including educational and vocational training, CBT to address criminal thinking patterns, anger management, social services, and treatment for clients with co-occurring mental health disorders (National Association of Drug Court Professionals, 1997). Treatment is typically supplemented with case management services to assess the client's needs and progress.

Drug courts have served as the model for several other problem-solving courts, including mental health courts (for criminal offenders who have mental health needs), family dependency treatment courts (for child abuse, neglect, and dependency cases in which parental drug abuse is a key factor), community courts (for offenders charged with low-level "quality-of-life" offenses), domestic violence courts (for offenders charged with spousal abuse), and DWI courts (for alcohol-dependent or drug-dependent offenders charged with driving while impaired offenses). These problems-solving courts are firmly grounded in established principles of "therapeutic jurisprudence," which emphasize the law's ability to promote psychological well-being for those individuals who are subject to legal proceedings (see Wexler & Winick, 1996).

RESEARCH FINDINGS ON DRUG COURTS

Over the past 15 years, researchers have conducted a large number of studies on drug courts. Overall, the findings are encouraging. Research has reliably demonstrated that drug courts outperform virtually all other strategies that have been used with drug-involved criminal offenders (Marlowe, DeMatteo, & Festinger, 2003). Drug courts appear to be quite successful in reducing drug use and criminal recidivism (e.g., Belenko, 1998, 1999, 2001, 2002; Belenko, DeMatteo, & Patapis, 2007; Government Accountability Office [GAO], 2005).

Given the recent proliferation of drug courts, it is important that researchers, clinicians, administrators, and policy makers have a clear understanding of whether these courts are effective and, if so, how they achieve their results. In this section, we will summarize the existing research on drug courts. Given the large body of existing research on drug courts, it is not possible to review each study. Therefore, we will focus primarily on quantitative, large-scale studies that address either or both of the two major outcomes of drug courts (reductions in criminal recidivism and reductions in relapse to drug use). By reviewing the existing research in these important areas, we hope to clearly define areas in which more research is needed.

Several researchers have conducted comprehensive reviews of the effectiveness of drug courts in reducing criminal recidivism and relapse. In reviews of nearly 100 drug court evaluations, Belenko (1998, 1999, 2001) concluded that roughly 60% of drug court clients attended at least 1 year of treatment, and approximately 50% graduated from the drug court program. These figures represent a substantial improvement in treatment retention over most probationary programs, in which fewer than 10% of clients attend 1 year of treatment (e.g., Goldkamp, 2000; Satel, 1999). Belenko (1999, 2001) also reported favorable statistics for drug courts in terms of decreased recidivism and drug use while clients are enrolled in drug court programs. According to Belenko (1999, 2001), most program evaluations that reported data on drug test results noted that the percentage of positive urine screens was less than 10%, which is lower than the typical percentage of positive urine screens among probationers. Moreover, Belenko (1999, 2001) reported that drug court clients have significantly lower rates of criminal recidivism during the program compared to similar offender populations under other types of community supervision.

In the majority of evaluation studies that have included a suitable comparison condition, drug court clients achieved significantly greater reductions in drug use and criminal recidivism compared to individuals on standard probation or intensive supervised probation (see Belenko, 1999, 2001; Marlowe, DeMatteo, et al., 2003). The magnitudes of the during-treatment effects were typically in the range of 20–30 percentage points, and the magnitudes of the post-treatment effects were typically in the range of 10 to 20 percentage points. Although these figures are not ideal, they are about two to three times greater than what is commonly obtained from prison, intermediate sanctions, probation, or community-based drug treatment programs.

Two RCTs also support the effectiveness of drug courts compared to standard criminal justice approaches. In a study of the Maricopa County (Arizona) Drug Court, drug court clients exhibited roughly a 15 percentage-point reduction in rearrest rates at 3 years post-discharge, with 33% of drug court clients rearrested within that time period compared to 47% of drug-abusing offenders in various probationary conditions (Turner, Greenwood, Fain, & Deschenes, 1999). An RCT in the Baltimore City Drug Court found that 48% of drug court clients, versus 64% of traditionally adjudicated control clients, were rearrested within 1 year of admission (Gottfredson & Exum, 2002). The proportions of rearrested offenders were roughly the same within 2 years of admission (Gottfredson, Najaka, & Kearley, 2003).

The U.S. Government Accountability Office (GAO, 2005) recently completed a systematic review of 117 evaluations of adult drug courts published between May 1997 and January 2004 that reported criminal recidivism, substance use relapse, or program completion outcomes. Of the 117 studies, the GAO selected 27 evaluations of 39 drug courts that met its criteria for methodological soundness. Program completion rates varied considerably by program, from a low of 27% to a high of 66%. The GAO report focused heavily on the effectiveness of drug courts in reducing criminal recidivism and relapse to drug use. The GAO concluded that drug courts reduce during-treatment criminal recidivism to a greater degree than commonly used criminal justice alternatives, such as probation. The GAO also concluded that drug courts reduce post-program criminal recidivism (measured up to 1 year post completion), particularly for offenders who completed the drug court program. However, the GAO found mixed evidence supporting the effectiveness of drug courts in terms of reducing substance use relapse.

A recent meta-analysis by Wilson, Mitchell, and Mackenzie (2006) of 50 studies representing 55 drug court program evaluations is also informative. They included both published and unpublished studies that used experimental or quasi-experimental designs. The inclusion criteria specified that the studies had to use a comparison-group design and measure criminal activity. The meta-analysis revealed that the majority of studies found reductions in reoffending among drug court participants relative to participants in comparison groups. Of note, Wilson et al. (2006) found that the reduction in offending was 26% across all studies (and 14% in two high-quality RCTs). Interestingly, significantly larger effects were observed in the drug court programs that use either a pre-plea or post-plea model as opposed to a mixed/ad hoc approach (which lacks clear incentives for participation). There was also a (nonsignificant) trend in favor of drug courts that use a single treatment provider.

Wilson et al. (2006) concluded that the meta-analysis findings "tentatively suggest that drug offenders participating in a drug court are less likely to reoffend than similar offenders sentenced to traditional correctional options, such as probation" (p. 479). They labeled their conclusion as "equivocal" in light of the "weak" methodologies used in many of the studies (Wilson et al., 2006, p. 479). Of note, only five of the 55 studies included in the meta-analysis used an experimental design involving random assignment (and two of those studies had attrition rates of greater than 40%), whereas the remaining studies used quasi-experimental designs that suffered from serious methodological limitations. Nevertheless, Wilson et al. (2006) were optimistic because the experimental and higher-quality quasi-experimental studies provided evidence that drug courts produce desired outcomes beyond standard criminal justice system approaches.

Defendants in Mental Health Courts
Background
Recent statistics indicate that approximately half of all U.S. jail and prison inmates are suffering from a mental health problem (James & Glaze, 2006). According to the Bureau of Justice Statistics, at midyear 2005, 56% of state prison inmates, 45% of federal prison inmates, and 64% of jail inmates had identifiable mental health disorders, defined as a recent (within the previous 12 months) history of mental health symptoms (James & Glaze, 2006). The growing number of criminal offenders with mental health disorders has resulted in a revolving door characterized by arrest, incarceration, release, and rearrest (Steadman, Cocozza, & Veysey, 1999; Trupin & Richards, 2003). This disturbing cycle highlighted the lack of adequate treatment for offenders with mental health needs within the criminal justice system.

Mental Health Courts
Mental health courts emerged in the late 1990s to address the increasing numbers of mentally ill offenders who are entering the criminal justice system. Mental health courts function as a convenient point-of-entry through which criminal offenders with mental health problems can gain access to community-based mental health treatment services. The underlying belief is that treating an offender's mental health problems may be an effective way to improve clinical functioning and reduce criminal recidivism. Mental health courts borrowed their underling philosophy—therapeutic jurisprudence—from their successful predecessors, drug courts (Odegaard, 2007; Rottman & Casey, 1999; Wexler, 2001). Mental health courts follow the principle of

therapeutic jurisprudence by providing comprehensive and judicially supervised behavioral health treatment services to criminal offenders with mental health disorders.

The first mental health court in the United States was established in 1997 in Broward County, Florida, and many other jurisdictions have developed mental health courts since that time. A recent government report indicates that there are more than 150 mental health courts in the United States, with many more in the advanced planning stages (Thompson, Osher, & Tomasini-Joshi, 2007; see also Erickson, Campbell, & Lamberti, 2006). Mental health courts handle both misdemeanor and felony offenders (depending on the jurisdiction) (Redlich, Steadman, Monahan, Petrila, & Griffin, 2005), and several juvenile mental health courts have been developed in recent years (Cocozza & Shufelt, 2006; Thompson et al., 2007). The mental health court model has been adopted by several other countries, including Canada, Australia, and the United Kingdom.

Mental health courts differ considerably by jurisdiction, but they share one goal. Broadly stated, the purpose of mental health courts is to divert criminal offenders with mental health needs away from traditional criminal justice processing and into judicially supervised, community-based mental health treatment (Boothroyd, Poythress, McGaha, & Petrila, 2003). Clients in mental health courts receive mental health treatment typically delivered by community-based treatment providers, often consisting of individual and group counseling, the provision of psychotropic medications, and intensive case management. Mental health courts also offer many of the same services as drug courts, including drug treatment, social services, and case management. Importantly, the client's progress in treatment is monitored by the presiding mental health court judge, and a series of escalating sanctions and rewards are used to punish clients for program infractions and accomplishments.

Despite similarities, describing a prototypical mental health court is not easy because they exhibit greater variability than do drug courts (Bernstein & Seltzer, 2003; Erickson et al., 2006; Redlich, Steadman, Monahan, Robbins, & Petrila, 2006). For example, although some courts require offenders to meet criteria for a specific mental health diagnosis prior to entry, other courts simply confirm a previous diagnosis (Erickson et al., 2006). Some courts require clients to attend status hearings several times per week, whereas others require less frequent hearings. The sanctions used for noncompliance with

program requirements also differ (Griffin, Steadman, & Petrila, 2002), with some courts ratcheting up treatment requirements and other courts using brief incarceration or termination from the program (Erickson et al., 2006). Finally, after successfully completing the program, some courts dismiss the criminal charges, whereas other courts place the offenders on probation or impose a suspended sentence (Erickson et al., 2006; Griffin et al., 2002).

Despite variations in operation and structure, the majority of mental health courts share overlapping features. Some of more common features of mental health courts include: (a) a specialized court docket that employs a problem-solving approach for certain offenders with mental health needs, in lieu of more traditional criminal justice processing; (b) the provision of judicially supervised, community-based mental health treatment; (c) regularly scheduled judicial status hearings, during which each offender's progress in the program is evaluated, incentives are provided to reward adherence to program requirements, and sanctions are imposed to punish program infractions; and (d) the articulation of specific criteria indicating when a participant has successfully completed the program (Thompson et al., 2007). Moreover, research suggests that mental health courts are established for the same reasons as drug courts, which typically include a desire to increase public safety, facilitate the provision of mental health treatment to offenders with mental health needs, improve the quality of life for offenders with mental health needs, and make more efficient use of criminal justice and mental health treatment resources (Thompson et al., 2007).

Mental health courts follow one of three operational models. In the preadjudication model, the prosecution of the offender is deferred and, in exchange, the offender agrees to participate in a treatment program. In the post-plea model, the disposition of the offender's case is deferred while the offender participates in the treatment program. Finally, in the probation model, the offender is convicted and sentenced to probation, and participating in the treatment program is imposed by the court as a condition of the probation.

Research Findings on Mental Health Courts
The research literature on mental health courts has grown in recent years, but it still lags well behind the large and well-developed body of literature regarding drug courts. Moreover, most of the literature regarding mental health courts consists of either basic descriptive studies, process evaluations, or

nonempirical policy/theoretical papers. As such, we know considerably less about the operations and effectiveness of mental health courts. Moreover, differences among mental health courts make it difficult for researchers to examine the effectiveness of these interventions in an empirically defensible manner (see Wolff & Pogorzelski, 2005).

In this section, we will summarize the existing research on mental health courts by focusing on quantitative studies that address either or both of the two major outcomes of mental health courts: reductions in clinical symptoms (including increased access to and utilization of treatment services) and reductions in criminal recidivism. As with the review of the drug court literature, we hope that this review will highlight areas in which more research is needed.

Given the goals of mental health courts, an initial question is whether mental health courts increase the provision of behavioral health services and lead to meaningful clinical improvement. An early study by Boothroyd et al. (2003) compared 121 mental health court clients and 101 criminal court clients to determine whether the mental health court impacted offenders' access to behavioral health services. The results revealed that the percentage of mental health court clients who received behavioral health services increased significantly, from 36% during the 8 months prior to their initial court appearance to 53% during the 8 months after their initial court appearance. For the offenders in criminal court, the likelihood of receiving behavioral health services remained virtually unchanged during the same time periods (29% vs. 28%). More recent research by Herinckx, Swart, Ama, Dolezal, and King (2005) examined linkage to community mental health services among 368 misdemeanor offenders in the Clark County Mental Health Court. Results revealed that mental health court clients received more hours of case management and medication management services, and more days of outpatient service, in the 1 year following enrollment in the court. Mental health court clients also received fewer hours of crisis services and fewer days on inpatient treatment in the 1 year following enrollment.

Despite some research suggesting that mental health court clients have greater access to behavioral health services than do their counterparts in traditional criminal courts, few researchers have examined whether such treatment leads to clinical improvement. One study to address this issue involved the random assignment of 235 offenders to either a mental health court or criminal court (Cosden,

Ellens, Schnell, Yamini-Diouf, & Wolfe, 2003). All participants showed improvements in life satisfaction, psychological distress, and independent functioning, but mental health court clients showed greater gains in developing independent living skills and reducing their drug use. More recent research (Boothroyd, Mercado, Poythress, Christy, & Petrila, 2005) examined clinical improvement among 97 mental health court clients and 77 offenders in criminal court. All participants were assessed at 1, 4, and 8 months after their initial court appearances using the Brief Psychiatric Rating Scale. Results revealed no significant main effects for type of court or receipt of treatment, and no significant interaction effect between type of court and receipt of treatment. Overall, there were no significant changes in participants' clinical condition related to the receipt of treatment services or participation in mental health court. These counterintuitive results led Boothroyd et al. (2005) to hypothesize that the failure to observe meaningful clinical improvement was due to the absence of court control over the type and quality of treatment services provided to participants.

As previously noted, the primary goal of mental health courts is to reduce criminal recidivism by treating mental health disorders related to criminal behavior. Several researchers have examined whether mental health courts achieve this goal. Although one study (Trupin and Richards, 2003) found that mental health court clients had fewer arrests post-discharge (over 9 months) compared to criminal court clients, subsequent research (Christy, Poythress, Boothroyd, Petrila, & Mehra, 2005) cast doubt on this finding. The latter investigators used a within-group and between-group design to compare recidivism rates for mental health court clients and comparable defendants who did not participate in mental health court. Although they found that the number of arrests for mental health court clients significantly decreased from 1-year pre to 1-year post entry into the court, they also found that the mean number of rearrests, felony arrests, proportion rearrested, and survival time to rearrest were not significantly different from those defendants who did not participate in the mental health court.

One group of researchers used an experimental design to examine the effectiveness of mental health courts in reducing criminal recidivism. Cosden et al. (2003, 2005) randomly assigned 235 offenders to a mental health court in Santa Barbara, California, with assertive community treatment (*n* = 137) or to a traditional criminal court that offered less intensive case management services (n = 98). One-year post entry, mental health court participants had significantly fewer convictions for new offenses, and the charges of the mental health court participants were typically related to probation violations rather than to the commission of a new criminal offense (Cosden et al., 2003). Despite these positive findings, the outcomes at 2 years were less impressive. Participants in both groups increased arrests, and no change occurred in either the number of convictions or number of days in jail (Cosden et al., 2005).

In another study (Herinckx et al., 2005), investigators examined rearrest rates for 368 misdemeanor offenders participating in the Clark County Mental Health Court from April 2000 through April 2003. They compared rearrest rates in the 1 year preceding their enrollment in the court to rearrest rates in the 1 year following enrollment in the court. The results revealed significant reductions in arrests post-enrollment, with the mean number of arrests being significantly reduced from 1.99 pre-enrollment to .48 post-enrollment. Moreover, the overall crime rate was reduced by a factor of 4.0 at 1-year post-enrollment. Further, 54% of the clients had no arrests in the 1 year following enrollment, and probation violations were reduced by 62%. According to Herinckx et al. (2005), the most significant factor in determining the success of the mental health court clients was whether they graduated from the program. Graduates of the mental health court program were 3.7 times less likely to reoffend compared to nongraduates.

In more recent research, Moore and Hiday (2006) compared 82 offenders in a mental health court with 183 similar offenders processed in criminal court in the same county before the mental health court was established. Outcome variables examined included new arrests and offense severity from 1 year pre-entry to 1 year post-entry. The results of the between-group analyses revealed that the mental health court clients had significantly fewer new arrests and less severe criminal offenses during the 1-year follow-up period. Specifically, mental health court clients had a rearrest rate that was roughly one-fourth the rearrest rate of the offenders processed through the traditional criminal court. Interestingly, however, the rearrest rates for participants who did not complete the mental health court program did not significantly differ from the rearrest rates for participants who went through traditional criminal court.

Other research has also found mental health courts to effectively reduce recidivism. In a recent study, McNiel and Binder (2007) used a retrospective observational design to compare the occurrence of new criminal charges for 170 mental health court clients and 8,067 individuals with mental health disorders who were booked into an urban county jail after arrest during the same time period. Results revealed that participation in the mental health court was associated with longer time without any new criminal charges or new charges for violent crimes. As with the Moore and Hiday (2006) study, graduating from the mental health court was found to be an important correlate of reduced criminal recidivism. McNiel and Binder (2007) found that successful completion of the mental health court was associated with maintenance of reductions in criminal recidivism after the graduates were no longer under the supervision of the court.

Summary of the Research on Drug Courts and Mental Health Courts

A large body of research supports the effectiveness of drug courts in terms of reducing both criminal recidivism and relapse to drug use rates. The results of several large-scale studies and systematic reviews suggest that participating in drug courts is associated with reductions in recidivism and drug use both during treatment and post-treatment. Moreover, other research suggests that drug courts are associated with significant cost savings (e.g., Belenko, Patapis, & French, 2005; Bhati, Roman, & Chalfin, 2008). Although more research is needed (as discussed later in this chapter), there is good reason to be optimistic about drug courts.

The picture is less clear when it comes to mental health courts. Although some research suggests that mental health courts increase access to behavioral health services, the research is mixed in terms of whether treatment leads to measurable reductions in clinical symptoms. The picture is also mixed with respect to reductions in recidivism. Although some research supports the belief that mental health courts reduce recidivism, other research has found few differences in recidivism rates between offenders in mental health courts and offenders in traditional criminal courts. On the whole, however, there is reason to be cautiously optimistic about the effects of mental health courts (see Herman, 2005; Kuehn, 2007). The weight of the evidence appears to suggest that mental health courts can lead to increased provision of behavioral health treatment services, improvements in clinical functioning, and reductions in criminal recidivism. As such, mental health courts appear to be fulfilling their basic objectives.

Future Directions

Despite the large body of research supporting the effectiveness of drug courts, several important questions remain unanswered. Only a handful of studies have examined the impact of drug courts on post-program drug use and recidivism (Belenko, 2001; GAO, 2005; Harrell, Cavanagh, & Roman, 1999; Marlowe, Festinger, Dugosh, & Lee, 2005; Turner et al., 1999), and the limited results raise questions about the long-term effects of drug courts. For example, Marlowe et al. (2005) found that 10%–15% of drug court clients engaged in criminal behavior within 12 months of admission to drug court, and over 50% resumed drug use within that time period. Conducting studies with longer follow-up periods would enable us to draw more defensible conclusions regarding the long-term effects of drug courts.

Although we know that drug courts are effective, we know less about *how* they work. As such, more research is needed regarding the key components of drug courts. The essential elements of drug courts were described by the National Association of Drug Court Professionals in 1997, and several researchers have systematically examined some of these elements in an effort to get inside the "black box" of drug courts. For example, Marlowe and colleagues at the Treatment Research Institute at the University of Pennsylvania are conducting a program of experimental dismantling research examining the key components of drug courts, including the dosage of judicial status hearings and the administration of sanctions and rewards (Festinger, Marlowe, Lee, Kirby, Bovasso, & McLellan, 2002; Marlowe, Festinger, Dugosh, Lee, & Benasutti, 2007; Marlowe, Festinger, & Lee, 2003, 2004; Marlowe, Festinger, Lee, Dugosh, & Benasutti, 2006). Research regarding the appropriateness of the drug court intervention for all client types (e.g., low- vs. high-risk) would also be informative (DeMatteo, Marlowe, & Festinger, 2006).

The key limitation in drawing conclusions about mental health courts is the relatively small body of existing research. In contrast to drug courts, there is much less research on mental health courts, and most of the research consists of descriptive studies, process evaluations, program evaluations, and theory papers. The dearth of experimental studies is also noteworthy. As researchers seek to draw causal inferences about the effects of mental health courts, utilizing experimental designs will take on increased importance. Once the effectiveness of mental health courts is established through RCTs, it will be important to conduct a series of dismantling studies to

identify the active ingredients of the intervention. Further, because drug courts and mental health courts share many features, an examination of the key elements of drug courts may be instructive for mental health court researchers.

Conclusions

The development of drug courts and mental health courts has provided the criminal justice system with an integrated public safety/public health approach for handling the rising number of criminal offenders who have substance use problems and mental health disorders. There is reason to be optimistic about both of these strategies. A large body of research supports the effectiveness of drug courts, and a growing body of research supports the effectiveness of mental health courts. As more research is conducted in the coming years, researchers will be in a better position to draw empirically supported conclusions about these interventions.

Defendants in Forensic Hospitals as Incompetent to Stand Trial

Individuals adjudicated incompetent to stand trial (IST) represent a distinctive group treated in public mental health facilities. These individuals are committed by the court prior to conviction of criminal charges and have particular treatment needs. We will describe the frequency of IST adjudications, the treatment needs, and available empirical evidence regarding treatment effectiveness for these individuals in this section of the chapter.

Incompetence to Stand Trial

Competency to stand trial evaluations arise frequently in the criminal context. It was estimated in the 1980s that approximately 25,000 defendants were evaluated for competence to stand trial on an annual basis (Steadman, Monahan, Hartsone, Davis, & Robbins., 1982). There is apparently no more recent evidence regarding prevalence, but there is also no apparent reason to think this number of evaluations has decreased (Grisso, 2003). Some research (Poythress, Bonnie, Hoge, Monahan, & Oberlander, 1994) has suggested that attorneys formally raise the question of their clients' competence to stand trial in 5%–8% of cases, although they have concerns for as many as twice this number of individuals. Estimates for the number of individuals adjudicated IST has ranged from 10% (Melton et al., 2007) to 30% (Nicholson & Kugler, 1991). These individuals are suffering from a mental disorder or disability (most often a severe mental illness), which significantly impairs their ability to participate effectively in the adversarial trial process (Bullock, 2002). The notion that a criminal defendant must be competent in order to be tried stems from the idea that defendants must be present at their trials to confront their accusers, question witnesses, and otherwise act in their own defense (Bullock, 2002). The trial of a competent defendant ensures a fair trial of adversaries and maintains dignity and integrity in criminal proceedings.

The Legal Standard

The standard for determining a defendant's competency to stand trial that is used in most jurisdictions was set forth by the United States Supreme Court in *Dusky v. United States* (1960). The Court held that "the test must be whether [he] has sufficient present ability to consult with his lawyer with a reasonable degree of rational understanding—and whether he has a rational as well as factual understanding of the proceedings against him." Competency to stand trial refers to the defendant's mental state at the time of the adjudication of criminal charges. It is a legal decision, albeit one that is informed by clinical data. Defendants must be able to understand the charges against them and assist in their own defense (Melton et al., 2007).

Disposition

Following the formal consideration of a defendant's competence to stand trial, the court may determine that the defendant is competent. If so, the process for adjudication of charges continues. If the defendant is found to be incompetent, however, criminal proceedings are suspended and the defendant may receive treatment to restore competency. Treatment to restore competency may be provided on an outpatient basis, but typically incompetent defendants are involuntarily hospitalized in a secure setting and receive inpatient treatment to restore their competence to stand trial (Bullock, 2002). Such hospitalization may not be for an indefinite period; under *Jackson v. Indiana*, the U.S. Supreme Court limited the state's ability to confine those adjudicated IST can only be confined to a psychiatric hospital for a reasonable period of time necessary to determine whether competency can be restored (Melton et al., 2007). Depending on the jurisdiction, the patient is then treated until competency is restored, or the relevant *Jackson* period specified by the jurisdiction has lapsed, whichever occurs first (Marques, Hayes, & Nelson, 1993). If the specified time period expires, the court may initiate conservatorship proceedings or dismiss the criminal charges and release the patient (Marques, Hayes, & Nelson, 1993).

Characteristics of Incompetent Defendants

Competence to stand trial is the most frequently raised criminal issue in forensic mental health, involving defendants who often have extensive histories of involvement in both the legal and the mental health systems (Melton et al., 2007). A study of 539 men adjudicated IST revealed characteristically below-average education, few useful job skills, and few community ties (Steadman, 1979). Numerous studies have described the association between major mental disorders (typically schizophrenia and major affective disorders) and the adjudication of incompetence for trial (Riley, 1998; Rosenfeld & Wall, 1998). Certain symptom constellations in particular seem to interfere with the relevant functional legal capacities for assisting (higher levels of psychotic symptoms), whereas other domains of psychopathology (disorientation and low intellectual functioning) are more strongly associated with inability to understand charges and proceedings (Rosenfeld & Wall, 1998).

A study reviewing the competency evaluation reports for 468 defendants (Hubbard, Zapf, & Ronan, 2003) found that incompetent defendants significantly differed from competent defendants with respect to age, employment status, ethnicity, criminal charges, and diagnosis. Of the 468 defendants referred for competency, 19% were deemed incompetent by mental health evaluators. Most incompetent defendants were African American (67%), single (67%), and unemployed (59%). Some 72% of incompetent defendants had previous criminal histories, and 48% had previous psychiatric hospitalizations. Additionally, 34% of incompetent defendants were diagnosed with a psychotic disorder, and 40% were currently charged with a violent offense.

Medication and the Right to Refuse Treatment

Most incompetent defendants are committed to secure mental health facilities following adjudication as IST. Medication remains the most common form of treatment for IST individuals. However, little research has been done on the direct effects of medication on the decisional abilities relevant to the original findings of incompetence (Roesch, Ogloff, & Golding, 1993). Additionally, there is a need for research on clinicians' ability to predict medication response within a specified period.

In *Washington v. Harper* (1990), the U.S. Supreme Court considered the question of whether an inmate who was either gravely disabled or represented an active threat of harm to self or others could be involuntarily medicated. Although recognizing that persons have a liberty interest in being free from involuntary medication, the Court nonetheless cited the state's right to treat dangerous prison inmates with antipsychotic medication against their will (Appelbaum, 2003). A second Supreme Court decision, *Riggins v. Nevada* (1992) dealt with a case in which a prisoner who had been medicated involuntarily before trial, and who was later found guilty and sentenced to death, petitioned to have his conviction overturned on the grounds that treatment to restore his competence (antipsychotic medication) had been administered illegitimately. The Court held that "the state might have been able to justify medically appropriate, involuntary treatment with the drug by establishing that it could not obtain an adjudication of Riggins' guilt or innocence by using less intrusive means" (*Riggins v. Nevada*, 1992).

Following these decisions, many lower courts attempted to craft rules governing when incompetent defendants could be treated. *Harper* and *Riggins* implied that the government could medicate even nondangerous defendants under certain circumstances, but the nature of such circumstances was unclear. The U.S. Supreme Court clarified its position and applied a balancing test in *Sell v. United States* (2003), holding that a defendant who is hospitalized as IST may be involuntarily medicated under some circumstances but not others (Heilbrun & Kramer, 2005). In *Sell*, the Supreme Court considered the legality of involuntarily administering medication to a criminal defendant in order to render that defendant competent to stand trial. This is a particularly important question related to the treatment of defendants who are IST. Because of the high prevalence of severe mental disorder within this population, the prescription of psychotropic medication is a very common form of treatment. Consequently, we will pay particular attention in this section of the chapter to the circumstances under which *Sell* suggests such medication can be administered involuntarily.

In *Sell*, the Court ultimately held that medication may be administered involuntarily if it (a) is medically appropriate, (b) is the least intrusive means of restoring competency, and (c) does not infringe on trial rights (such as the ability to communicate with one's attorney and testify relevantly) (Melton et al., 2007). The Court recognized three situations in which the government's interest in medication might be necessary. First, *Sell* permits the forcible medication of any defendant who is dangerous to self or others, if the medication is necessary to reduce dangerousness.[1] Second, *Sell* implies that any defendant who is incompetent to make treatment decisions can be forcibly medicated. Finally, the Court indicated that even a nondangerous defendant who is competent to make treatment decisions may be forcibly medicated to restore competency to stand trial when the charges are "serious" (Melton et. al., 2007).

The Court in *Sell* cited a balancing test to consider the circumstances under which forced medication of an incompetent defendant is appropriate. The court of jurisdiction must (a) find important governmental interests at stake in this case; (b) conclude that taking medication will significantly further those state interests; (c) conclude that the involuntary medication is necessary to further those interests and that any alternative, less intrusive therapies are not likely to produce the same results; and (d) conclude that administration of the drugs is medically appropriate, and in the individual's best medical interests in light of their condition. If a mentally ill defendant agrees to take the prescribed medication and the individual is considered competent to make that decision, there should be no legal dispute (Heilbrun & Kramer, 2005). Clinically, however, the implications of the holding in *Sell* may be more complex.

Sell has a number of implications for the assessment and treatment of defendants who are IST. It suggests that the constructs of voluntariness, competence to consent to treatment, and dangerousness will be important for policy makers, clinical administrators, and clinicians to consider in determining whether a given patient falls under the auspices of this decision. *Sell* also underscores the important of the working relationship between treatment teams and defendants who are hospitalized as IST. One study suggested that IST defendants generally do not refuse treatment for rational reasons, but because they deny their mental illness or have delusions about the medications—whereas clinicians' decisions to seek forcible medication are typically made for clinical, not legal, reasons (Ladds & Convit, 1994).

---

[1] Such a circumstance would probably mean that involuntary medication would be appropriate under an emergency treatment order, consistent with *Washington v. Harper*, in correctional and quasi-correctional facilities. The *Sell* decision did not change this.

Additionally, *Sell* highlights the importance of nonmedical treatment strategies (discussed later in this section) for defendants who are IST. Programs treating IST defendants should develop and strengthen nonchemical interventions that are most likely to yield improvement in functional-legal deficits, such as communication, information retentions, and reasoning (Heilbrun & Kramer, 2005).

The relevant and accurate assessment of clinical symptoms, functional-legal capacities, and related issues are important for treatment decisions and for recommendations to the court. The assessment of competence to stand trial has improved substantially during the last two decades, assisted by major conceptual and empirical reviews (see, e.g., Grisso, 1986, 2003), regular reviews of the research literature (e.g., Grisso, 1992; Cooper & Grisso, 1997; Mumley, Tillbrook, & Grisso, 2003), and the development of specialized assessment tools (see, e.g., Grisso, 2003). One particularly important "related issue" for treatment decisions involves the response style of those declining medication; this is an important consideration for clinicians and should be well-documented. When patients respond in a fashion that is other than reliable/honest (either by under-reporting or over-reporting symptoms and capacities), it becomes extremely important to identify the style leading to the inaccuracy and appraise the functioning of such individuals in a reasonably accurate way. This may be accomplished through the combination of assessment approaches and tools focusing specifically on response style (see Rogers, 1997), as well as by gathering third-party information from multiple sources. The implications for assessment and treatment will be different for those who are not accurately reporting their own symptoms and experiences to their treatment teams—some may be more likely to need psychotropic medication, others less.

Skills-based Interventions for IST

Defendants who are IST constitute the majority of forensic patients receiving treatment in the United States. Under *Jackson v. Indiana* (1972), a defendant found IST cannot be hospitalized indefinitely. As a result, the treatment of incompetent defendants has become somewhat more focused in recent years. Several modes of treatment are being tried in various state hospitals. One trend currently observed involves the development of specialized forensic housing units for incompetent defendants, as contrasted with treating them within the larger forensic context (Cooper & Grisso, 1997). Initial phases of

treatment for this population tend to be psychopharmacological and focus on reduction and control of psychotic symptoms (Cooper & Grisso, 1997). Typically, this treatment is then followed by educational programs, focused on restoring competency, for those who do not appear to have regained competency following this initial phase.

Roesch et al. (1993) emphasized that, prior to treating an IST defendant, the expected level of competency should be delineated in a specific manner, so that the treatment can be targeted toward appropriate behaviors or capacities as they relate to the restoration of competency (Roesch et al., 1993). They emphasized that, before one can specify treatments, it is necessary to clearly understand the necessary knowledge and ability a defendant needs in order to be considered competent (Roesch et al., 1993).

Siegel and Elwork (1990) evaluated a skills-based treatment program for incompetent defendants. Using random assignment, they compared the impact of an experimental group (skills-based training in knowledge and interaction skills relevant to competence to stand trial) with a control group (treatment as usual). The experimental condition included use of a videotape that described the roles of courtroom personnel and court procedure, as well as group problem-solving sessions in which problems arising from a subject's actual legal case were presented and discussed. Results showed greater improvement on a measure of competency-relevant capacities for the experimental group, and a greater number of staff recommendations of competent to stand trial (43% of the treated group, but only 15% of the controls, were considered competent by staff 45 days after treatment) (Siegel & Elwork, 1990). This study highlighted the potential impact of a "second-stage" intervention (following stabilization of symptoms through medication), targeting legally relevant capacities as the primary focus of treatment.

Brown (1992) described a treatment group for IST individuals that was organized into modules on trial participation. Successful outcomes were related to defendants' attention, cooperation, and concentration, with the program being less successful for individuals with impairments in these areas and for individuals harboring idiosyncratic or paranoid delusions concerning their cases.

Characteristics of Treatment Approaches for IST

Treatment services for individuals who are IST can be divided into three categories: traditional, contemporary, and targeted (Heilbrun & Griffin, 1999).

Traditional mental health treatment services involve standard kinds of mental health interventions (e.g., diagnostic assessment for treatment planning purposes, medication, milieu therapy, and group and individual therapy for inpatients; medication, case management, and group and individual therapy for outpatients) that might be delivered to forensic patients in need of mental health intervention. Contemporary treatment services include psychoeducational, skills-based services and behavioral interventions, such as psychosocial rehabilitation. Finally, targeted treatment services include those interventions that are designed to address functional deficits relevant to legal standards (such as anger control or impulse control relevant to nonviolent behaviors, psychoeducational approaches to restore competency, and the teaching of responsible behavior required for legal compliance with conditional release criteria) (Heilbrun & Griffin, 1999).

Forensic treatment is directly affected by the law or the jurisdiction in which the forensic treatment takes place. Additionally, the setting in which the treatment is delivered is an important consideration. Typical settings include, but are not limited to hospital (high security and medium- to low-security), jail, and community. Finally, the goals for treatment of IST individuals could be clinical (focused on remission of symptoms and improvement in overall functioning), legal (designed to specifically address functional deficits that are directly relevant to legal standards), and hybrid (designed to improve both clinical symptomatology and functional deficits) (Heilbrun & Griffin, 1999).

APPROACHES TO TREATMENT
Various factors influence treatment approaches to individuals adjudicated IST. The first is the clinician's and/or facility's overall theoretical orientation and training model (Clark, Holden, Thompson, Watson, & Wightman, 1993). The second factor is the nature of the court order for which the patient is hospitalized; IST patients often require time-limited, active, and educative interventions, in concert with ongoing assessment of mental state and competency (Clark et al., 1993; Melton et al., 2007). Finally, the pathology of the patient will have an effect on the goals and objectives for treatment at the facility. Diagnostically, this patient population presents as more psychotic and severely disordered (Bullock, 2002; Heilbrun & Griffin, 1999). In addition to a number of other factors (e.g., severe personality disorders, substance abuse disorders, and subaverage intellectual functioning),

the combination of these clinical features with the status as criminal defendant result in an emphasis on medication and security concerns above standard treatment modalities.

For patients hospitalized as IST, the primary goal of treatment is to return the patient to the court as sufficiently improved to be considered competent for trial (Clark et al., 1993). Apart from the pharmacological intervention necessitated by the presenting symptoms, the treatment of such patients is largely psychoeducational (Clark et al., 1993; Marques et al., 1993; Wack, 1993). More traditional mental health goals, such as insight and the improvement of dysfunctional behavior, are considered in the context of how they relate to the needed legal capacities (Clark et al., 1993). Thus, symptoms or problems that would likely be the focus of treatment in other settings become more peripheral, and will only become the focus of treatment if they impinge directly on the patient's competency to stand trial (Clark et al., 1993; Wack, 1993).

Empirically Supported Treatment Characteristics
TRADITIONAL CLINICAL SERVICES
Traditional clinical services involve standard mental health treatment interventions and include diagnostic assessment for treatment planning purposes, medication, short- and long-term individual and group psychotherapy, family therapy, parenting skills groups, substance abuse treatment, anger control, and relaxation techniques, as well as assertiveness training (Heilbrun & Griffin, 1999; Clark et al., 1993; Marques et al., 1993; Wack, 1993). Additionally, the ongoing assessment and treatment of individuals presumed to be dangerous is a traditional clinical service. Traditional clinical services differ from contemporary treatment services, which often include psychoeducational skills-based services and behavioral interventions (Heilbrun & Griffin, 1999). Additionally, traditional clinical services differ from a strictly cognitive-behavioral approach; however, many facilities blend traditional clinical services with a more cognitive-behavioral approach. At some facilities, like the Kirby Forensic Psychiatric Center, program activities that can enhance confidence, skills, knowledge, creativity, and self-esteem, as well as more traditional treatment modalities, are offered (Wack, 1993). In addition, the Kirby Center provides many other supportive psychoeducational, as well as insight-oriented, approaches that are considered within the purview of their traditional clinical services (Wack, 1993). For neurologically impaired

individuals, cognitive restructuring, biofeedback, and psychoeducation and retraining in memory and attention should be considered (Marques, 1993). The effectiveness of these interventions has not been described through empirical research, however.

Substance Abuse Treatment

Substance abuse treatment is an important component of traditional clinical services. Many patients have histories of substance abuse, which can affect every aspect of a patient's life, and successful treatment requires the patient's ability to recognize relapse and maintain the recovery process. At one inpatient forensic facility, Atascadero State Hospital, the substance abuse treatment includes a three-phase intervention covering chemical dependency, recovery, and relapse, and takes about 9 months to complete (Marques et al., 1993).

At a second forensic hospital (Taylor Hardin Secure Medical Facility), the substance abuse group is recommended for patients who have a history of substance abuse/dependence of at least 1 year duration and who are not actively psychotic, aggressive, or significantly mentally retarded. Objectives in the group include helping patients to recognize and admit they have a substance abuse problem, promoting motivation for dealing with the problem, identifying variables that relate to the maintenance of substance abuse, and discussing attitudes toward addiction (Dixon & Rivenbark, 1993).

Restraints/Seclusion

Special management interventions that are designed to deal with crisis situations or with patients who require special attention due to agitated, threatening, self-destructive, or aggressive behavior should be in place for IST individuals (Clark et al., 1993; Marques et al., 1993). These interventions should be designed to prevent, deescalate, or control aggressive and self-destructive behavior (Wack, 1993). Most facilities limit the use of restraints and seclusion to instances in which they are necessary to prevent the patient from harming self or others or causing substantial property damage (Clark et al., 1993). In Michigan, a related treatment option is the "quiet room," involving the placement of a patient alone in a room with a closed but unlocked door (Clark et al., 1993).

Medication

The primary role of medication in the treatment of IST patients has been discussed earlier in this chapter. In the context of traditional interventions, pharmacological treatment is regarded as an approach to rapidly improving the capacities of actively psychotic individuals in the domains of thinking, reasoning, and communication. This not only addresses a number of potentially legally relevant deficits, but also allows some patients to participate more fully in other treatment modalities (Wack, 1993).

CONTEMPORARY MENTAL HEALTH SERVICES

Reality Orientation Groups

Reality orientation groups are often effective among fairly low-functioning patients who have significant cognitive impairment such as memory, concentration, or attention deficits, and low intellectual functioning (Dixon & Rivenbark, 1993). Patients are involved in over-learning practices to help maintain their awareness of important personal information such as name, birthday, current date, family information, and important and recent events. Treatment utilizes cognitive and reality therapy problem-solving techniques; and efforts are made to apply these techniques in analyzing daily problems that occur on the treatment unit. These techniques are also applied hypothetically in the discussion of characteristic styles of interacting with others, particularly those styles that have contributed to past difficulties. At Taylor Hardin, the emphasis of the group is for patients to learn how to evaluate, and then make appropriate changes in, nonproductive or destructive habits and attitudes, which might include nonproductive interactions with the attorney representing them (Dixon & Rivenbark, 1993).

Medication Education Group

One of the most important factors in keeping patients functioning effectively, both within the facility and following return to court, is medication compliance (Dixon & Rivenbark, 1993). A group that provides medication education to patients about the main therapeutic benefits and possible side effects of medications, while focusing on the importance of taking medication regularly and as prescribed, is quite important among this population. Among other considerations, it can help to anticipate the problem of declining to take prescribed medication while incarcerated in jail, following return from the hospital but prior to disposition of charges.

TARGETED LEGAL SERVICES

Some research suggests that targeted legal treatment services could have significant value for increasing relevant knowledge and decreasing length of hospitalization for IST defendants (Siegel & Elwork, 1990). Interventions that focus on the capacities and deficits relevant to understanding and assisting are among those most directly related to behaviors that will be considered in the subsequent legal decision of whether the defendant's competence to stand trial has been restored.

Restoration of Trial Competency Psychoeducational Groups

Commonly, patients adjudicated as IST display severe psychiatric-behavioral problems, with a significant proportion having symptoms of schizophrenic illness. Thus, in addition to medication and other traditional interventions addressing the symptoms of mental illness, competency education classes are utilized for patients hospitalized as IST. Behavioral approaches to restoring trial competence may include role-playing and mock trials in simulated courtroom settings to teach patients legal pleas, courtroom procedures, basic legal concepts, and how to cooperate with the defense counsel, and to increase understanding of the courtroom procedures (Pendleton, 1980). Verbal and written instructions, cartoons, mock trials, and video equipment can be used; as appropriate, individuals sessions can be held and the patient's lawyer included (Wack, 1993). Progress toward fulfilling the various fitness criteria should be evaluated and charted continually, and treatment interventions should be adjusted accordingly to ensure compliance with the individualized treatment plan (Wack, 1993).

TARGETED HYBRID TREATMENT

Targeted hybrid treatment refers to treatment that addresses both symptoms and legally relevant deficits. For example, at the Kirby Forensic Psychiatric Center, in addition to psychoeducational approaches to enhance competency, a patient may be taught stress management techniques to aid in coping with stress in the courtroom, or a patient may receive focused short-term psychotherapy or cognitive therapy to deal with a specific problem interfering with his or her fitness to stand trial (Wack, 1993).

TREATMENT MODALITIES

Over the past two decades, many forensic facilities treating IST patients have transitioned away from the insight-oriented verbal therapies and moved toward cognitive-behavioral, neurobehavioral, and skill-oriented approaches (Clark et al., 1993; Marques et al., 1993; Wack, 1993). The Kirby Forensic Psychiatric Center recommends a therapeutic community model, providing the patients with some self-governing functions within the "community" (Wack, 1993). At Atascadero State Hospital,

a wide range of treatment approaches are used by the staff (Marques et al., 1993).

Evaluation Component of Treatment Approaches Through Research

The past two decades have witnessed a trend toward more systematic and outcome-oriented approaches to IST treatment. At Taylor Hardin Secure Medical Facility, a treatment program is often evaluated with respect to measurable goals and objectives (Dixon & Rivenbark, 1993). The Trial Competency Program objectives include decreasing the length of stay and increasing the rate of concurrence between the hospital's dispositional recommendations and court decisions regarding competency. The effectiveness of this program is evaluated based on success of these goals (Dixon & Rivenbark, 1993).[2] For other programs, measurable goals and objectives may include length of stay, psychiatric symptomatology, levels of social and vocational functioning, and violent incidents (Wack, 1993).

Generally, it is important to integrate an evaluation component, both in measuring the attainment of in-treatment goals and objectives and to test the success of new and existing programs in reducing criminal recidivism. Studies to determine which offenders are most likely to respond to various hospital programs and particular treatment components should also be emphasized in future evaluation efforts. Finally, if treatment efforts are not effective after a reasonable period of time, clinicians need to render an opinion about restorability (or lack thereof) in light of *Jackson v. Indiana*, and proceed with initiating the process whereby the defendant may have charges dismissed and be considered for civil commitment (Roesch et. al., 1993).

Conclusion

The "evidence" available to support the interventions made in juvenile placements, drug courts, and forensic hospitals varies by setting and level of intervention. One important influence involves the way

---

[2] It should be noted that hospital reports making recommendations regarding competence to stand trial are not independent of judges' decisions. Indeed, there is evidence that courts render decisions consistent with the recommendations of experts in a very high percentage of cases (Melton et al., 2007). This notwithstanding, it is appropriate for hospitals to use concordance between recommendations and court decisions as one indicator of service effectiveness.

in which each of these settings is structured. Juvenile placements and forensic inpatient treatment of IST patients are standard justice settings in which adjudicated individuals are placed for both security and intervention purposes. Research on interventions at the single-modality level (e.g., an innovative anger control group) is more feasible than at the program level (combining multiple interventions) or at the broadest policy level (comparing different levels of placement). Single-modality interventions are less likely to have a substantial impact on individuals being treated than are programmatic or policy interventions, but good research on the latter interventions is very difficult among individuals with high-security requirements. This may help to explain why specialty courts, a more recent form of intervention in the criminal justice system, have received a relatively large amount of research attention: Designing a study in which individuals who meet certain criteria are diverted to drug court or mental court or processed as usual according to random selection means that carrying out the study is feasible with the cooperation of local judges and attorneys.

Whether this can explain the patterns observed across the three kinds of interventions described in this chapter is an open question. What is clear, however, is that good, programmatic research with juveniles in placement and adult IST defendants is inconsistent to nonexistent, whereas research on specialty courts is flourishing. Until juvenile and adult systems are willing to test innovation while maintaining security, this will probably continue into the indefinite future.

Future Directions

• Can in-program treatment of juvenile offenders be captured under a single umbrella, as MST has been for the community, to facilitate outcome research with careful attention to treatment integrity?

• Do a common set of principles govern the effective operation of drug courts and mental health courts?

• Can an effective "first stage" of treatment for IST defendants—focusing almost exclusively on medical stabilization—be developed in a community setting, and thereby substantially reduce the number of IST commitments to remote forensic hospitals?

References

Agnew, R. (2005). *Why do criminals offend?* Los Angeles: Roxbury Publishing.

Alexander, J., Barton, C., Gordon, D., Grotpeter, J., Hansson, K., Harrison, R., et al. (1998). *Blueprints for violence prevention: Book Three. Functional Family Therapy.* Boulder, CO: Center for the Study and Prevention of Violence.

Alexander, J., & Parsons, B. (1973). Short-term behavioral intervention with delinquent families: Impact on family process and recidivism. *Journal of Abnormal Psychology, 81,* 219–225.

American Psychiatric Association. (2000). *Diagnostic and statistical manual of mental disorders* (4th edition-Text revision). Washington, DC: Author.

Anastopoulos, A., & Barkley, R. (1990). Counseling and training parents. In R. Barkley (Ed.), *Attention-Deficit Hyperactivity Disorder: A handbook for diagnosis and treatment* (pp. 397–431). New York: Guilford Press.

Andrews, D., & Bonta, J. (2006). *The psychology of criminal conduct* (4th edition). Cincinnati, OH: Anderson.

Antonowicz, D., & Ross, R. (1994). Essential components of successful rehabilitation programs for offenders. *International Journal of Offender Therapy and Comparative Criminology, 38,* 97–104.

Appelbaum, P.S. (2003). Treating incompetent defendants: The Supreme Court's decision is a tough sell. *Law and Psychiatry, 54,* 1335–1341.

Belenko, S. (1998). Research on drug courts: A critical review. *National Drug Court Institute Review, 1,* 1–42.

Belenko, S. (1999). Research on drug courts: A critical review: 1999 update. *National Drug Court Institute Review, 2,* 1–58.

Belenko, S. (2001). *Research on drug courts: A critical review: 2001 update.* New York: National Center on Addiction and Substance Abuse at Columbia University.

Belenko, S. (2002). Drug courts. In C. Leukefeld, F. Tims, & D. Farabee (Eds.), *Treatment of drug offenders: Policies and issues* (pp. 301–318). New York: Springer.

Belenko, S., DeMatteo, D., & Patapis, N. (2007). Drug courts. In D. Springer & A. Roberts (Eds.), *Handbook of forensic mental health with victims and offenders: Assessment, treatment, and research* (pp. 385–423). New York: Springer Publishing Company.

Belenko, S., Patapis, N., & French, M. (2005). *Economic benefits of drug treatment: A critical review of the evidence for policy makers.* Philadelphia: Treatment Research Institute.

Belenko, S., & Peugh, J. (1998). *Behind bars: Substance abuse and America's prison population.* New York: National Center on Addiction and Substance Abuse at Columbia University.

Bender, E. (2004). Juvenile offenders languish while awaiting mental health services, Congress learns. *Psychiatric News, 39,* 1.

Bernstein, R., & Seltzer, T. (2003). The role of mental health courts in system reform. *University of the District of Columbia Law Review, 7,* 143–162.

Bhati, A., Roman, J., & Chalfin, A. (2008). *To treat or not to treat: Evidence on the prospects of expanding treatment to drug-involved offenders.* Washington, DC: Urban Institute.

Billick, S., & Mack, A. (2004). The utility of residential treatment programs in the prevention and management of juvenile delinquency. *Adolescent Psychiatry, 28,* 95–116.

Bishop, D., Frazier, C., Lanza-Kaduce, L., & Winner, L. (1996). The transfer of juveniles to criminal court: Does it make a difference? *Crime & Delinquency, 42,* 171–191.

Bolton Oetzel, K., & Scherer, D. (2003). Therapeutic engagement with adolescents in psychotherapy. *Psychotherapy: Theory, Research, Practice, Training, 40,* 215–225.

Bonta, J., & Andrews, D. (2007). Risk-Need-Responsivity model for offender assessment and rehabilitation 2007–06.

(Cat. No.: PS3-1/2007-6). Retrieved June 13, 2008, from http://www.publicsafety.gc.ca/res/cor/rep/risk_need_200706-eng.aspx

Boothroyd, R., Mercado, C., Poythress, N., Christy, A., & Petrila, J. (2005). Clinical outcomes of defendants in mental health court. *Psychiatric Services, 56,* 829–834.

Boothroyd, R., Poythress, N., McGaha, A., & Petrila, J. (2003). The Broward mental health court: Process, outcomes, and service utilization. *International Journal of Law & Psychiatry, 26,* 55–71.

Brendgen, M., Vitaro, F., & Bukowski, W. (2000). Stability and variability of adolescents' affiliation with delinquent friends: Predictors and consequences. *Social Development, 9,* 205–225.

Brown, D.R. (1992). A didactic group program for persons found unfit to stand trial. *Hospital and Community Psychiatry, 43,* 732–733.

Brown, T., O'Leary, T., & Barlow, D. (2001). Generalized anxiety disorder. In D. Barlow (Ed.), *Clinical handbook of psychological disorders* (pp. 137–188). New York: Guilford.

Bullock, J. (2002). Involuntary treatment of defendants found Incompetent to Stand Trial. *Journal of Forensic Psychology Practice, 2,* 1–33.

Caldwell, M., & Van Rybroek, G. (2005). Reducing violence in serious juvenile offenders using intensive treatment. *International Journal of Psychiatry and Law, 28,* 622–636.

Christy, A., Poythress, N., Boothroyd, R., Petrila, J., & Mehra, S. (2005). Evaluating the efficiency and community safety goals of the Broward County mental health court. *Behavioral Sciences & the Law, 23,* 1–17.

Chung, H., & Steinberg, L. (2006). Relations between neighborhood factors, parenting behaviors, peer deviance, and delinquency among serious juvenile offenders. *Developmental Psychology, 42,* 319–331.

Clark, C., Holden, C., Thompson, J., Watson, P., & Wightman, L. (1993). Treatment at Michigan's Forensic Center. *International Journal of Law and Psychiatry, 16,* 71–81.

Cocozza, J., & Shufelt, J. (2006, June). *Juvenile mental health courts: An emerging strategy.* Available from the National Center for Mental Health and Juvenile Justice at http://www.ncmhjj.com/pdfs/publications/JuvenileMentalHealth Courts.pdf.

Cooper, D., & Grisso, T. (1997). Five-year research update (1991-1995): Evaluations for competence to stand trial. *Behavioral Sciences and the Law, 15,* 347–364.

Cosden, M., Ellens, J., Schnell, J., & Yamini-Diouf, Y. (2005). Efficacy of a mental health treatment court with assertive community treatment. *Behavioral Sciences & the Law, 23,* 199–214.

Cosden, M., Ellens, J., Schnell, J., Yamini-Diouf, Y., & Wolfe, M. (2003). Evaluation of a mental health court with assertive community treatment. *Behavioral Sciences & the Law, 21,* 415–427.

Cottle, C., Lee, R., & Heilbrun, K. (2001). The prediction of criminal recidivism in juveniles: A meta-analysis. *Criminal Justice and Behavior, 28,* 367–394.

DeMatteo, D., & Marczyk, G. (2005). Risk factors, protective factors, and the prevention of antisocial behavior among juveniles. In K. Heilbrun, N. Sevin Goldstein, & R. Redding (Eds.), *Juvenile delinquency: Prevention, assessment, and intervention* (pp. 19–44). New York: Oxford University Press.

DeMatteo, D., Marlowe, D., & Festinger, D. (2006). Secondary prevention services for clients who are low risk in drug court: A conceptual model. *Crime & Delinquency, 52,* 114–134.

Department of Health and Human Services. (2001). *Youth violence: A report of the surgeon general.* Rockville, MD: Author.

Dixon, J., & Rivenbark, W. (1993). Treatment at Alabama's Taylor Hardin Secure Medical Facility. *International Journal of Law and Psychiatry, 16,* 105–116.

Dowden, C., & Andrews, D. (2000). Effective correctional treatment and violent reoffending: A meta-analysis. *Canadian Journal of Criminology, 42,* 449–467.

Dowden, C., & Andrews, D. (2004). The importance of staff practices in delivering effective correctional treatment: A meta-analysis of core correctional practices. *International Journey of Offender Therapy and Comparative Criminology, 48,* 203–214.

Drais-Parrillo, A. (2004). *The Odyssey Project: A descriptive and prospective study of children and youth in residential group care and therapeutic foster care.* Washington, DC: Child Welfare League of America.

Dusky v. United States. 362 U.S. 402 (1960).

Eggleston, C. (2008). Juvenile offenders with special education needs. In R. Hoge, N. Guerra, & P. Boxer (Eds.), *Treating the juvenile offender* (pp. 239–257). New York: Guilford Press.

Erickson, S., Campbell, A., & Lamberti, J. (2006). Variations in mental health courts: Challenges, opportunities, and a call for caution. *Community Mental Health Journal, 42,* 335–344.

Fagan, J. (1995). Separating the men from the boys: The comparative advantage of juvenile versus criminal court sanctions on recidivism among adolescent felony offenders. In J. Howell, B. Krisberg, J. Hawkins, & J. Wilson (Eds.), *A sourcebook: Serious, violent, and chronic juvenile offenders* (pp. 238–260). Thousand Oaks, CA: Sage.

Festinger, D., Lamb, R., Marlowe, D., & Kirby, K. (2002). From telephone to office: Intake attendance as a function of appointment delay. *Addictive Behaviors, 27,* 131–137.

Festinger, D., Marlowe, D., Lee, P., Kirby, K., Bovasso, G., & McLellan, A. (2002). Status hearings in drug court: When more is less and less is more. *Drug & Alcohol Dependence, 68,* 151–157.

Garrett, C. (1985). Effects of residential treatment on adjudicated delinquents: A meta-analysis. *Journal of Research in Crime and Delinquency, 22,* 287–308.

Gendreau, P., Smith, P., & Goggin, C. (2001). Treatment programs in corrections. In J. Winterdyk (Ed.), *Corrections in Canada: Social reactions to crime* (pp. 238–263). Toronto: Prentice Hall.

Goldkamp, J. (2000). The drug court response: Issues and implications for justice change. *Albany Law Review, 63,* 923–961.

Goldstein, A.P. (2004). Evaluations of effectiveness. In A.P. Goldstein, R. Nensen, B. Daleflod, & M. Kalt (Eds.), *New perspectives on aggression replacement training* (pp. 230–244). Chichester, UK: Wiley.

Goldstein, N.E.S., Dovidio, A., Kalbeitzer, R., Weil, J., & Strachan, M. (2007). An anger management intervention for female juvenile offenders: Results of a pilot study. *Journal of Forensic Psychology Practice, 7,* 1–28.

Gottfredson, D., & Exum, M. (2002). The Baltimore City Drug Treatment Court: One-year results from a randomized study. *Journal of Research in Crime & Delinquency, 39,* 337–356.

Gottfredson, D., Najaka, S., & Kearley, B. (2003). Effectiveness of drug courts: Evidence from a randomized trial. *Criminology & Public Policy, 2,* 171–196.

Government Accountability Office. (2005). *Adult drug courts: Evidence indicates recidivism reductions and mixed results for other outcomes.* Washington, DC: Author.

Greenwood, P. (2005). *Changing lives: Delinquency prevention as crime-control policy.* Chicago: University of Chicago Press.

Griffin, P., Steadman, H., & Petrila, J. (2002). The use of criminal charges and sanctions in mental health courts. *Psychiatric Services, 53,* 1285–1289.

Grisso, T. (1981). *Juvenile's waiver of rights: Legal and psychological competence.* New York: Plenum.

Grisso, T. (1986). *Evaluating competencies.* New York: Plenum Press.

Grisso, T. (1992). Five-year research update (1986–1990): Evaluations for competence to stand trial. *Behavioral Sciences and the Law, 10,* 353–369.

Grisso, T. (2003). *Evaluating competencies* (2nd edition). New York: Kluwer Academic/ Plenum Publishers.

Guerra, N., Kim, T., & Boxer, P. (2008). What works: Best practices with juvenile offenders. In R. Hoge, N. Guerra, & P. Boxer (Eds.), *Treating the juvenile offender* (pp. 79–102). New York: Guilford Press.

Guerra, N., Williams, K., Tolan, P., & Modecki, K. (2008). Theoretical and research advances in understanding the causes of juvenile offending. In R. Hoge, N. Guerra, & P. Boxer (Eds.), *Treating the juvenile offender* (pp. 33–53). New York: Guilford Press.

Hanna, A. (2001, June). *Risk and protective factors for delinquency.* Presented to the Virginia Juvenile Justice and Delinquency Prevention Advisory Committee, Richmond, VA.

Harrell, A., Cavanagh, S., & Roman, J. (1999). *Final report: Findings from the evaluation of the District of Columbia Superior Court Drug Intervention Program.* Washington, DC: Urban Institute.

Harrison, P., & Beck, A. (2002). *Prisoners in 2001.* Washington, DC: Bureau of Justice Statistics, U.S. Dept. of Justice.

Harrison, P., & Karberg, J. (2003). *Prison and jail inmates at midyear 2002.* Washington, DC: Bureau of Justice Statistics, U.S. Dept. of Justice.

Hawkins, J., Herrenkohl, T., Farrington, D., Brewer, D., Catalano, R., Harachi, T., & Cothern, L. (2000). *Predictors of youth violence.* Juvenile Justice Bulletin. Washington, DC: U.S. Department of Justice, Office of Justice Programs, Office of Juvenile Justice and Delinquency Prevention.

Haynie, D. (2002). Friendship networks and delinquency: The relative nature of peer delinquency. *Journal of Quantitative Criminology, 18,* 99–134.

Heilbrun, K. (1992). The role of psychological testing in forensic assessment. *Law and Human Behavior, 16,* 257–272.

Heilbrun, K., & Griffin, P. (1999). Forensic treatment: A review of programs and research. In R. Roesch, S. Hart, & J. Ogloff (Eds.), *Psychology and law: The state of the discipline* (pp. 241–274). New York: Kluwer Academic.

Heilbrun, K., & Kramer, G. (2005). Involuntary medication, trial competence, and clinical dilemmas: Implications of *Sell v. United States* for psychological practice. *Professional Psychology: Research and Practice, 36,* 459–466.

Henggeler, S., Pickrel, S., Brondino, M., & Crouch, J. (1996). Eliminating (almost) treatment dropout of substance abusing or dependent delinquents through home-based multisystemic therapy. *American Journal of Psychiatry, 153,* 427–428.

Henggeler, S., Schoenwald, S., Borduin, C., Rowland, M., & Cunningham, P. (1998). *Multisystemic treatment of antisocial behavior in children and adolescents.* New York: Guilford Press.

Herinckx, H., Swart, S., Ama, S., Dolezal, C., & King, S. (2005). Rearrest and linkage to mental health services among clients of the Clark County Mental Health Court Program. *Psychiatric Services, 56,* 853–857.

Herman, M. (2005). *Mental health court evaluations: An annotated review of the literature with commentary.* Williamsburg, VA: National Center for State Courts.

Hubbard, K.L., Zapf, P.A., & Ronan, K.A. (2003). Competency Restoration: An examination of the differences between defendants predicted restorable and not restorable to competency. *Law and Human Behavior, 27,* 127–139.

Huddleston, C. Freeman-Wilson, K., Marlowe, D., & Roussell, A. (2005, May). *Painting the current picture: A national report card on drug courts and other problem solving court programs in the United States.* Alexandria, VA: National Drug Court Institute.

Izzo, R., & Ross, R. (1990). Meta-analysis of rehabilitation programs for juvenile delinquents: A brief report. *Criminal Justice and Behavior, 17,* 134–142.

Jackson v. Indiana, 401 U.S. 715 (1972).

James, D., & Glaze, L. (2006). *Mental health problems of prison and jail inmates.* Washington, D.C.: Bureau of Justice Statistics, U.S. Dept. of Justice.

Kazdin, A. (2003). Problem-solving skills training and parent management training for conduct disorder. In A. Kazdin & J. Weisz (Eds.), *Evidence-based psychotherapies for children and adolescents* (pp. 241–262). New York: Guilford Press.

Kazdin, A., Bass, D., Siegel, T., & Thomas, C. (1989). Cognitive-behavioral therapy and relationship therapy in the treatment of children referred for antisocial behavior. *Journal of Consulting and Clinical Psychology, 55,* 76–85.

Kendall, P., Aschenbrand, S., & Hudson, J. (2003). Child-focused treatment of anxiety. In A. Kazdin & J. Weisz (Eds.), *Evidence-based psychotherapies for children and adolescents* (pp. 81–100). New York: Guilford Press.

Kronenberger, W., & Meyer, R. (2001). *The child clinician's handbook.* Boston: Allyn and Bacon.

Kuehn, B. (2007). Mental health courts show promise. *Journal of the American Medical Association, 297,* 1641–1643.

Ladds, B., & Convit, A. (1994). Involuntary medication of patients who are incompetent to stand trial: A review of empirical studies. *Bulletin of the American Academy of Psychiatry and the Law, 22,* 519–532.

Landenberger, N., & Lipsey, M. (2005). The positive effects of cognitive-behavioral programs for offenders: A meta-analysis of factors associated with effective treatment. *Journal of Experimental Criminology, 1,* 451–476.

Ledley, D., Marx, B., & Heimberg, R. (2005). *Making cognitive behavioral therapy work.* New York: Guilford Press.

Lee, R., & McGinnis Haynes, N. (1978). Counseling juvenile offenders: An experimental evaluation of Project Crest. *Community Mental Health Journal, 14,* 267–271.

Lipsey, M. (1992). Juvenile delinquency treatment: A meta-analytic inquiry into the variability of effects. In T. Cook, H. Cooper, S. Corday, H. Hartmann, L. Hedges, R. Light, T. Louis, & F. Mosteller (Eds.), *Meta-analysis for explanation: A casebook* (pp. 83–125). New York: Russell Sage Foundation.

Lipsey, M. (1995). What do we learn from 400 research studies on the effectiveness of treatment with juvenile delinquents? In J. McGuire (Ed.), *What works reducing reoffending: Guidelines from research and practice* (pp. 63–78). Hoboken, NJ: John Wiley & Sons.

Lipsey, M., & Derzon, J. (1998). Predictors of violent or serious delinquency in adolescents and early adulthood: A synthesis of longitudinal research. In R. Loeber & D. Farrington (Eds.), *Serious and violent juvenile offenders: Risk factors and successful interventions* (pp. 86–105). Thousand Oaks, CA: Sage.

Loeber, R., Farrington, D., Stouthamer-Loeber, M., Moffitt, T., & Caspi, A. (1998). The development of male offending: Key findings from the first decade of the Pittsburgh Youth Study. *Studies on Crime and Crime Prevention, 7,* 141–171.

Marlowe, D. (2002). Effective strategies for intervening with drug abusing offenders. *Villanova Law Review, 47,* 989–1025.

Marlowe, D., DeMatteo, D., & Festinger, D. (2003). A sober assessment of drug courts. *Federal Sentencing Reporter, 16,* 113–128.

Marlowe, D., Festinger, D., & Lee, P. (2003). The role of judicial status hearings in drug court. *Offender Substance Abuse Report, 3,* 33–46.

Marlowe, D., Festinger, D., & Lee, P. (2004). The judge is a key component of drug court. *Drug Court Review, 4,* 1–34.

Marlowe, D., Festinger, D., Dugosh, K., & Lee, P. (2005). Are judicial status hearings a "key component" of drug court? Six and twelve months outcomes. *Drug & Alcohol Dependence, 79,* 145–155.

Marlowe, D., Festinger, D., Dugosh, K., Lee, P., & Benasutti, K. (2007). Adapting judicial supervision to the risk level of drug offenders: Discharge and six-month outcomes from a prospective matching study. *Drug & Alcohol Dependence, 88S,* 4–13.

Marlowe, D., Festinger, D., Lee, P., Dugosh, K., & Benasutti, K. (2006). Matching judicial supervision to clients' risk status in drug court. *Crime & Delinquency, 52,* 52–76.

Marques, J., Hayes, R., & Nelson, C. (1993). Forensic treatment at Atascadero State Hospital. *International Journal of Psychiatry, 16,* 57–70.

Martin, S., Butzin, C., Saum, S., & Inciardi, J. (1999). Three-year outcomes of therapeutic community treatment for drug-involved offenders in Delaware: From prison to work release to after care. *Prison Journal, 79,* 294–320.

McLellan, A., Lewis, D., O'Brien, C., & Kleber, H. (2000). Drug dependence, a chronic medical illness: Implications for treatment, insurance, and outcomes evaluation. *Journal of the American Medical Association, 284,* 1689–1695.

McMackin, R., Tansi, R., & LaFratta, J. (2004). Recidivism among juvenile offenders over periods ranging from one to twenty years following residential treatment. *Journal of Offender Rehabilitation, 38,* 1–15.

McNiel, D., & Binder, R. (2007). Effectiveness of a mental health court in reducing criminal recidivism and violence. *American Journal of Psychiatry, 164,* 1395–1403.

Melton, G., Petrila, J., Poythress, N., & Slobogin, C. (2007). *Psychological evaluations for the courts: A handbook for mental health professionals and lawyers* (3rd edition). New York: Guilford Press.

Miller, W., & Rollnick, S. (2002). *Motivational interviewing: Preparing people for change.* New York: Guilford.

Monroe, C. Van Rybroek, G., & Maier, G. (1988). Decompressing aggressive inpatients: Breaking the aggression cycle to enhance positive outcome. *Behavioral Sciences and the Law, 6,* 543–557.

Moore, M., & Hiday, V. (2006). Mental health court outcomes: A comparison of re-arrest and re-arrest severity between mental health court and traditional court participants. *Law and Human Behavior, 30,* 659–674.

Morehouse, E., & Tobler, N. (2000). Preventing and reducing substance use among institutionalized adolescents. *Adolescence, 35,* 1–28.

Morral, A., McCaffrey, D., & Ridgeway, G. (2004). Effectiveness of community-based treatment for substance abusing adolescents: 12-month outcomes from a case-control evaluation of a phoenix academy. *Psychology of Addictive Behaviors, 18,* 257–68.

Mumley, D., Tillbrook, C., & Grisso, T. (2003). Five-year research update (1996–2000): Evaluations for competence to stand trial (adjudicative competence). *Behavioral Sciences and the Law, 21,* 329–50.

Mumola, C., & Karberg, J. (2006). *Drug use and dependence, state and federal prisoners, 2004.* Washington, DC: Bureau of Justice Statistics, U.S. Dept. of Justice.

Myers, D. (2003). The recidivism of violent youths in juvenile and adult court: A consideration of selection bias. *Youth Violence and Juvenile Justice, 1,* 79–101.

National Association of Drug Court Professionals. (1997). *Defining drug courts: The key components.* Washington, DC: Office of Justice Programs, U.S. Department of Justice.

National Association of Drug Court Professionals. (2008). *Drug courts today.* Retrieved March 28, 2008, from http://www.nadcp.org/whatis/.

Nicholson, R.A., & Kugler, K.E. (1991). Competent and incompetent criminal defendants: a quantitative review of comparative research. *Psychological Bulletin, 109,* 355–358.

Odegaard, A. (2007). Therapeutic jurisprudence: The impact of mental health courts on the criminal justice system. *North Dakota Law Review, 83,* 225–259.

Office of Juvenile Justice Delinquency Prevention. (2008). *Model programs guide.* Retrieved June 11, 2008, from OJJDP Model Programs Guide: http://www.dsgonline.com/mpg2.5/mpg_index.htm

Otto, R.K., & Heilbrun, K. (2002). The practice of forensic psychology: A look toward the future in light of the past. *American Psychologist, 57,* 5–18.

Patterson, G., Reid, J., & Dishion, T. (1992). *Antisocial boys.* Eugene, OR: Castalia.

Pearce, J., & Pezzot-Pearce, T. (2007). *Psychotherapy of abused and neglected children* (2nd edition). New York: Guilford Press.

Pearson, F., & Lipton, D. (1999). A meta-analytic review of the effectiveness of corrections-based treatments for drug abuse. *The Prison Journal, 79,* 384–410.

Pendleton, L. (1980). Treatment of persons found incompetent to stand trial. *American Journal of Psychiatry, 137,* 1098–1100.

Poythress, N., Bonnie, R., Hoge, S., Monahan, J., & Oberlander, L. (1994). Client abilities to assist counsel and make decisions in criminal cases: Findings from three studies. *Law and Human Behavior, 18,* 437–452.

Quinsey, V., Harris, G., Rice, M., & Cormier, C. (2006). *Violent offenders: Appraising and managing risk* (2nd edition). Washington, D.C.: American Psychological Association.

Redding, R., & Arrigo, B. (2005). Multicultural perspectives on juvenile delinquency: Etiology and intervention. In C. Frisby & C. Reynolds (Eds.), *Handbook of multicultural school psychology* (pp. 710–743). New York: Wiley.

Redlich, A., Steadman, H., Monahan, J., Petrila, J., & Griffin, P. (2005). The second generation of mental health courts. *Psychology, Public Policy, & Law, 11,* 527–538.

Redlich, A., Steadman, H., Monahan, J., Robbins, P., & Petrila, J. (2006). Patterns of practice in mental health courts: A national survey. *Law and Human Behavior, 30,* 347–362.

Riggins v. Nevada, 504 U.S. 127 (1992).

Riley, S.E. (1998). Competency to stand trial adjudication: A comparison of male and female defendants. *Journal of the American Academy of Psychiatry and the Law, 26,* 223–227.

Roesch, R., Ogloff, J.R., & Golding, S.L. (1993). Competency to stand trial: Legal and clinical issues. *Applied and Preventive Psychology, 2,* 43–51.

Rogers, R. (Ed.). (1997). *Clinical assessment of malingering and deception* (2nd edition). New York: Guilford.

Rosenfeld, B., & Wall, A. (1998). Psychopathology and competence to stand trial. *Criminal Justice and Behavior, 25,* 443–457.

Rottman, D., & Casey, P. (1999). Therapeutic jurisprudence and the emergence of problem-solving courts. *National Institute of Justice Journal,* July, 13–19.

Ryan, J., & Yang, H. (2005). Family contact and recidivism: A longitudinal study of adjudicated delinquents in residential care. *Social Work Research, 29,* 31–39.

Sarri, R., Shook, J. J., Ward, G., Creekmore, M., Alberston, C., Goodkind, S., & Chih Soh, J. (2001). *Decision making in the juvenile justice system: A comparative study of four states. Final report to the National Institute of Justice.* AnnArbor, MI: Institute for Social Research.

Satel, S. (1999). *Drug treatment: The case for coercion.* Washington, DC: American Enterprise Institute.

Scanlon, E., & Devine, K. (2001). Residential mobility and youth well-being: Research, policy, and practice issues. *Journal of Sociology and Social Welfare,* 28, 119–138.

Siegel, A.M., & Elwork, A. (1990). Treating incompetence to stand trial. *Law and Human Behavior, 14,* 57–65.

Sell v. United States, 123 S. Ct. 2174 (2003).

Simpson, D., Joe, G., & Brown, B. (1997). Treatment retention and follow-up outcomes in the Drug Abuse Treatment Outcome Study (DATOS). *Psychology of Addictive Behaviors, 11,* 294–307.

Skowyra, K., & Cocozza, J. (2007). *Blueprints for change: A comprehensive model for the identification and treatment of youth with mental health needs in contact with the juvenile justice system.* The National Center for Mental Health and Juvenile Justice Policy Research Associates: Author.

Sondheimer, D. (2001). Young female offenders: Increasingly visible yet poorly understood. *Gender Issues, 19,* 79–90.

Stark, M. (1992). Dropping out of substance abuse treatment: A clinically oriented review. *Clinical Psychology Review, 12,* 93–116.

Steadman, H. (1979). *Beating a rap? Defendants Found Incompetent to stand trial.* New York.

Steadman, H., Cocozza, J., & Veysey, B. (1999). Comparing outcomes for diverted and nondiverted jail detainees with mental illnesses. *Law and Human Behavior, 23,* 615–627.

Steadman, H., Monahan, J., Hartstone, E., Davis, S., & Robbins, P. (1982). Mentally disordered offenders: A national survey of patients and facilities. *Law and Human Behavior, 6,* 31–38.

Teplin, L., Abram, K., McClelland, G., Dulcan, M., & Mericle, A. (2002). Psychiatric disorders in youth in juvenile detention. *Archives of General Psychiatry, 59,* 1133–1143.

Texas Youth Commission. (2008). *2007 review of agency treatment effectiveness.* Retrieved June 18, 2008 from http://www.tyc.state.tx.us/research/TxmtEffect/01_index.html

Thompson, M., Osher, F., & Tomasini-Joshi, D. (2007). *Improving responses to people with mental illnesses: The essential elements of a mental health court.* New York: Council of State Governments Justice Center.

Trupin, E., & Richards, H. (2003). Seattle's mental health courts: Early indicators of effectiveness. *International Journal of Law & Psychiatry, 26,* 33–53.

Turner, S., Greenwood, P., Fain, T., & Deschenes, E. (1999). Perceptions of drug court: How offenders view ease of program completion, strengths and weaknesses, and the impact on their lives. *National Drug Court Institute Review, 2,* 61–85.

Veysey, B. (2008). Mental health, substance abuse, and trauma. In R. Hoge, N. Guerra, & P. Boxer (Eds.), *Treating the juvenile offender* (pp. 210–238). New York: Guilford Press.

Wack, R. (1993). Treatment services at Kirby Forensic Psychiatric Center. *International Journal of Psychiatry, 16,* 83–104.

Washington State Institute for Public Policy. (2004). *Outcome evaluation of Washington State's research-based programs for juvenile offenders.* Olympia, WA: Author.

Washington v. Harper. 494 U.S. 210 (1990).

Webster-Stratton, C., & Reid, M. (2001). The incredible years parent, teachers, and children training series: A multifaceted treatment approach for young children with conduct problems. In A. Kazdin & J. Weisz (Eds.), *Evidence-based psychotherapies for children and adolescents* (pp. 224–240). New York: Guilford Press.

Weisz, J. (2004). *Psychotherapy for children and adolescents.* Cambridge: Cambridge University Press.

Wexler, D. (2001). Robes and rehabilitation: How judges can help offenders "make good." *Court Review, 38,* 18–23.

Wexler, D., & Winick, B. (Eds.) (1996). *Law in a therapeutic key: Developments in therapeutic jurisprudence.* Durham, NC: Carolina Academic Press.

Wilson, D., Mitchell, O., & Mackenzie, D. (2006). A systematic review of drug court effects on recidivism. *Journal of Experimental Criminology, 2,* 459–487.

Wilson, S., & Lipsey, M. (2000). Wilderness challenge programs for delinquent youth: A meta-analysis of outcome evaluations. *Evaluation and Program Planning, 23,* 1–12.

Wolff, N., & Pogorzelski, W. (2005). Measuring the effectiveness of mental health courts: Challenges and recommendations. *Psychology, Public Policy, & Law, 11,* 539–569.

Young, D. (2004). First count to ten: Innovation and implementation in juvenile reintegration programs. *Federal Probation, 66,* 70–77.

Young, D., Moline, K., Farrell, J., & Bierie, D. (2006). Best implementation practices: Disseminating new assessment technologies in a juvenile justice agency. *Crime and Delinquency, 52,* 135–158.

Young, J., Weinberger, A., & Beck, A. (2001). Cognitive therapy for depression. In D. Barlow (Ed.), *Clinical handbook of psychological disorders* (pp. 264–308). New York: Guilford.

Zamble, E., & Quinsey, V. (1997). *The process of recidivism.* Cambridge, England: Cambridge University Press.

Ziedenberg, J. (2006). Models for change: Building momentum for juvenile justice reform (2006). Retrieved June 11, 2008 from http://www.macfound.org/site/apps/nlnet/content2.aspx?c=lkLXJ8MQKrH&b=1135955&ct=3279187

Further Reading

Andrews, D., & Bonta, J. (2006). *The psychology of criminal conduct* (4th edition). Cincinnati, OH: Anderson.

Bhati, A., Roman, J., & Chalfin, A. (2008). *To treat or not to treat: Evidence on the prospects of expanding treatment to drug-involved offenders.* Washington, DC: Urban Institute.

Cottle, C., Lee, R., & Heilbrun, K. (2001). The prediction of criminal recidivism in juveniles: A meta-analysis. *Criminal Justice and Behavior, 28,* 367–394.

Department of Health and Human Services (2001). *Youth violence: A report of the surgeon general.* Rockville, MD: Author.

Guerra, N., Kim, T., & Boxer, P. (2008). What works: Best practices with juvenile offenders. In R. Hoge, N. Guerra, & P. Boxer (Eds.), *Treating the juvenile offender* (pp. 79–102). New York: Guilford Press.

Heilbrun, K., & Kramer, G. (2005). Involuntary medication, trial competence, and clinical dilemmas: Implications of *Sell v. United States* for psychological practice. *Professional Psychology: Research and Practice, 36,* 459–466.

Redlich, A., Steadman, H., Monahan, J., Robbins, P., & Petrila, J. (2006). Patterns of practice in mental health courts: A national survey. *Law and Human Behavior, 30,* 347–362.

Wolff, N., & Pogorzelski, W. (2005). Measuring the effectiveness of mental health courts: Challenges and recommendations. *Psychology, Public Policy, & Law, 11,* 539–569.

Clinical Neuropsychology

Robert J. McCaffrey, Julie K. Lynch, *and* Holly James Westervelt

Abstract

The origins of clinical neuropsychology were founded in the diagnostic methods for identifying cerebral damage and, although this remains an important focus of the field, clinical neuropsychology is also focused upon understanding the functional consequences of neuropsychological dysfunction and on methods of treating or managing neuropsychological dysfunction. Neuropsychological research has also expanded beyond neurology to psychology, where delineating the neuropsychological correlates of psychological disorder has been of particular interest. Following a brief history of neuropsychology, this chapter discusses neuropsychiatric symptoms associated with neurological damage or disease. The discussion will then turn its focus to psychological disorders, with a review of the neuropsychological deficiencies that have been associated with various Axis I and Axis II disorders. The objective of this chapter is to provide information of potential utility to the psychotherapist or psychologist in understanding the neuropsychological underpinnings of psychological disorders, as well as the psychological and behavioral consequences of neurological conditions.

Keywords: Clinical neuropsychology, neuropsychiatric, neuropsychological correlates of psychological disorders, neuropsychological dysfunction, psychological/behavioral consequences of neurological conditions

A History of Clinical Neuropsychology

As with any new field of psychology, an organizational infrastructure facilitates the growth and development of the discipline through publication outlets and society meetings. The history of clinical neuropsychology has been detailed eloquently by the late Arthur Benton (2000) in his book *Exploring the History of Neuropsychology*. Those readers old enough to have had been assigned Edwin G. Boring's (1950) *History of Experimental Psychology* as a textbook in a history of psychology seminar will undoubtedly appreciate the depth of coverage of clinical neuropsychology by Dr. Benton. Although a detailed presentation of the history of clinical neuropsychology is beyond the scope of the current chapter, a brief history of the development of clinical neuropsychology into a full-fledged discipline is in order.

Formal Organizations

The founding of clinical neuropsychology as a discipline has been traced by Rourke and Murji (2000) back to the mid 1960s, through the formation of the International Neuropsychological Society (INS). Rourke and Murji (2000) outline the history of the INS into six phases: (1) 1965–1967 Conception and Gestation, (2) 1967–1973 Birth, (3) 1973–1976 Infancy and Toddlerhood, (4) 1976–1982 Early Childhood, (5) 1982–1985 Childhood, and (6) 1985–2000 Adolescence. Given the continued growth and development of clinical neuropsychology since 2000, we think it fair to say the field is well into early adulthood. The INS has a total worldwide membership of 4,500. It holds an annual North American meeting in February and a non-North American meeting in July. The society's journal is the *Journal of the International Neuropsychological Society.*

During the infancy period of the INS, other organizations were going through their own development. The National Academy of Neuropsychology (NAN) was founded in 1975. Currently, NAN has over 3,300 members in all 50 states and in 24 countries, representing the diverse interests of scientist-practitioners, clinicians, and researchers in the field of neuropsychology. The annual meeting draws both scientists and practitioners via a conference of workshops, scientific presentations, and updates on issues facing practitioners.

The Council of Representatives of the American Psychological Association (APA) approved the creation of Division 40 (Clinical Neuropsychology) in 1979. Today, Division 40 has 4,462 members and is active in all facets of clinical neuropsychology both within and outside of APA.

Training Issues

In the 1980s, clinical neuropsychology began to experience an identity crisis. What was the appropriate training in clinical neuropsychology? Who was a clinical neuropsychologist? How were the interest of the profession and the public best served? In 1981, a joint task force of the INS and Division 40 met to begin the arduous task of addressing these and other questions.

The late Manfred J. Meier proposed educational models for competency assurance in neuropsychology. Specifically, Meier (1981) presented four models:

- Model I. Clinical neuropsychology would be a subspecialty area in a traditional applied psychology program
- Model II. Clinical neuropsychology coursework would be provided through interdepartmental supporting programs in neuropsychology and the clinical neurosciences
- Model III. Clinical neuropsychology would be integrated in the scientist-practitioner curriculum for the PhD degree
- Model IV. Clinical neuropsychology would comprise a separate coordinated graduated curriculum with both PhD and PsyD components.

The most intensive training would occur in Model IV and would conclude with a competency based examination process (i.e., board certification). The issue of clinical neuropsychologist training was reexamined in 1997, during what has become known as the Houston Conference on Specialty Education and Training in Clinical Neuropsychology (Hannay,

Bieliauskas, Crosson, Hammeke, Hamsher, & Koffler, 1998). Although not without its critics (Reitan, Hom, Van De Voorde, Stanczak, & Wolfson, 2004), the conference did result in the publication of a set of aspirational training guidelines.

Board Certification

Presently, three primary organizations are involved in the process of board certification in clinical neuropsychology. These are the American Board of Clinical Neuropsychology, admitted through its parent the American Board of Professional Psychology in 1984 (Goldstein, 2001); the American Board of Professional Neuropsychology, founded in 1982 and reorganized in 1989 (Horton, Crown, & Reynolds, 2001); and the American Board of Pediatric Neuropsychology, founded in 1996 and reincorporated in 2004. It is noteworthy that the APA does not endorse nor recognize any specialty examining boards in psychology (Goldstein, 2001). Although clinical neuropsychology is a relatively new specialty within psychology, it is clearly a separate discipline that is now found in clinics and medical centers around the world. In addition to providing services across the lifespan, clinical neuropsychologists also provide expertise in forensic settings.

Clinical Neuropsychological Assessment

Neuropsychological evaluations are conducted for many reasons, including screening evaluations, diagnostic evaluations, assisting medical personnel with differential diagnosis, treatment planning, care planning, competency (i.e., the ability to make medical decisions, the ability to manage one's own finances, etc.), fitness-for-duty, and for forensic purposes both civil and criminal. The specific assessment tools used may vary according to the nature of the referral question and preferred approach of the clinician.

"Clinical neuropsychology is an applied science concerned with the behavioral expression of brain dysfunction" (Lezak, Howieson, & Loring, 2004, p. 3); hence, historically, clinical neuropsychologists have relied upon a fixed battery approach for general clinical use such as the Halstead-Reitan Neuropsychological Test Battery (HRNB; Reitan & Wolfson, 1993), the Luria-Nebraska Neuropsychological Battery (LNNB; Golden, Purisch, & Hammeke, 1991) and, more recently, the Neuropsychological Assessment Battery (NAB; Stern & White, 2003) (Table 30.1). Other batteries have been developed for assessing specific conditions such as the National Institute of Mental Health (NIMH) Core Neuropsychological Battery

Table 30.1 Criteria for a neuropsychological test battery

1. The battery should evaluate the full range of neuropsychological functions dependent upon the brain.
2. The battery should include tests of general brain functioning, as well as those that relate to specific areas of cerebral functioning.
3. The battery should employ "time-honored methods of clinical neuropsychology."
4. Each test in the battery must be validated for its sensitivity to brain damage/dysfunction.
5. The battery should provide a balanced sampling of behavior from each of the cerebral hemispheres.

for assessing HIV status (Butters et al.) and the Adult Environmental Neurobehavioral Test Battery (AENTB; Hutchinson et al., 1992) for assessing exposure to toxic substances. There are also screening batteries for general use when testing time is limited, for example, the Repeatable Battery for the Assessment of Neuropsychological Status (RBANS, Randolph, 1998) serves as a general-use battery for screening purposes. For a more detailed discussion of these batteries and others see Strauss, Sherman, and Spreen (2006).

Another approach to neuropsychological assessment has been characterized as a "flexible" battery approach. Generally, the battery contains a set of core tests applied within individual diagnostic categories (e.g., dementia, cerebral vascular accident) supplemented by other tests based upon the individual patient's condition or other examination-related issues (Lezak et al., 2004).

Particularly with a flexible battery approach, the length and components of the exam can vary considerably. Brief exams may focus assessment solely on the skills that are relevant to address the question at hand. For example, an inpatient assessment of an elderly patient's decisional capacity may involve a thorough interview and, at times, only brief testing of the patient's basic attention and language skills, judgment, daily problem-solving abilities, planning, and memory. Other areas that have little relevance to the referral question may not be assessed at all (e.g., visuospatial skills). In contrast, most comprehensive examinations will assess multiple "core" cognitive domains, regardless of the specific referral question, given that the patient and referrer may not have appreciated deficits that may be meaningful in providing diagnostic information (particularly for profile analyses) or functional recommendations. Most commonly, areas examined will include attention, executive functions, language, motor skills, visuospatial skills, and learning/memory. Although not an exhaustive list, Table 30.2 lists these domains with examples of the skills that comprise them. Of note, neuropsychologists are not always in agreement in terms of how these domains are most accurately

described, operationalized, and best measured. Although there is a tendency to reify these constructs, clearly these are made-up concepts, with the terms being used to help communicate among patients, professionals, and researchers, and to provide a framework for understanding how these diverse cognitive skills may group together and interrelate.

The interpretation of neuropsychological test scores must take into consideration a number of biopsychosocial factors known to impact an individual's test performance, including age, gender, educational level, cultural background, and the patient's native language. In addition, as discussed in greater detail later in this chapter, the presence of an Axis I or Axis II condition may have a direct impact on an individual's test performance above and beyond that of any brain-related pathology. Other factors to consider in the interpretation of test data are base rates, practice effects, and effort, as elaborated below.

Table 30.2 Commonly assessed cognitive domains

Domain	Exemplars of Associated Skills
Attention	Attentional capacity, sustained attention/sustained focus, divided attention, working memory/mental control, psychomotor speed
Executive Functions	Planning, organization, abstract reasoning, rapid word generation/verbal fluency, set shifting, multitasking, problem-solving, inhibition, judgment, concept formation
Language	Comprehension, repetition, naming, writing, reading, calculation, praxis
Motor Skills	Grip strength, fine motor coordination, fine motor speed
Visuospatial Skills	Construction, visuoperception
Learning/Memory	Encoding/storage, retrieval, recognition

Base Rates

The term *base rate* refers to the prevalence of an event, usually a sign, symptom, or disorder that exists within a given population. For example, the base rate for the symptom of fatigue among patients with a diagnosis of Epstein-Barr syndrome is 100%, whereas the base rate of visual disturbances among studies of patients with diabetes is approximately 7% (McCaffrey, Palav, O'Bryant, & Labarge, 2003). Similarly, the base rate of the symptom "easily distracted" reported in the general population of elementary school children is 49%, and the base rate of "eye tics" among the general population is 0.0% (McCaffrey, Bauer, O'Bryant, & Palav, 2006). The interpretation of test findings must consider issues such as base rates in an attempt to determine if an individual score represents normal variability or is indicative of underlying brain pathology. By way of example, the difference between an examinee's Verbal IQ (VIQ) and Performance IQ (PIQ) on any of the Wechsler Scales may be found to be *statistically significant* ($p < .05$); however, a statistically significant VIQ–PIQ discrepancy may not be *clinically significant* if the discrepancy commonly occurred in the normative sample (i.e., the base rate). Since many tests are accompanied by computer-generated score reports that contain detailed statistical comparisons of scores, the base rate data presented in these score reports must be considered in the interpretation of the data.

The importance of the base rates of impaired test scores on a battery of neuropsychological assessment instruments has been examined by Heaton, Miller, Taylor, and Grant (2004), who report that, on 25 measures administered to a group of 1,189 neurologically normal participants, 15% had at least one impaired score, 13% had two impaired scores, another 13% had three impaired scores, 9% had four impaired scores, approximately 7% had five impaired scores, and another 7% had six impaired scores. Binder, Iverson, and Brooks (2009) have also evaluated normative studies of variability in healthy adults on several neuropsychological batteries and conclude that abnormal performance on some portion of neuropsychological tests in a battery is psychometrically normal. These reports indicate that the presence of some abnormal test scores does not necessarily indicate the presence of acquired brain dysfunction, since both low scores and intraindividual variability are frequently found among healthy adults. As quoted by Binder et al. (2009), Schretlen et al. (2003) stated, "the findings reported underscore the importance of basing clinical neuropsychological inferences about cerebral dysfunction on clinically recognizable patterns of performance in the context of other historical, behavioral, and diagnostic information, rather than on psychometric variability alone." The interpretation of neuropsychological data requires a solid understanding of brain–behavior relationships and the neurocognitive patterns associated with specific neurological conditions. This is the neuropsychological assessment model that Ralph M. Reitan has advocated since the inception of the Halstead-Reitan Neuropsychological Test Battery. It appears that the field of clinical neuropsychology has come full circle, and that knowledge of base rates for false-positive and false-negative results will become increasing important in the future.

Repeat Assessment/Practice Effects

Practice effects refer to the change in an examinee's performance due to repeated exposure to an assessment instrument (McCaffrey, Duff, & Westervelt, 2000a, 2000b). For example, if the same group of patients were administered a memory test, such as the California Verbal Learning Test (CVLT), and then took the same test a week later, the performance on the second administration would be "better" due to having taken the same test 7 days earlier. The "better" performance on the second administration would not reflect any improvement in the groups' overall memory ability but rather practice effects. In some instances, practice effects are bothersome and need to be controlled for either experimentally or statistically in order to determine if an independent variable (e.g., medication X taken daily between administrations of the CVLT) actually was responsible for the groups' improved performance on the CVLT.

Although practice effects have been considered problematic by researchers and clinicians attempting to interpret changes in patients' performance across assessments, recent work has demonstrated that "practice effects" may have utility in the early diagnosis and/or prognosis of progressive neurological conditions. Specifically, Duff and colleagues in the Huntington's Study Group (2007) reported that, among three patient groups (older adults with mild cognitive impairment, individuals who were HIV positive, and individuals diagnosed with Huntington disease), practice effects accounted for as much as 31%–83% of the variance in the follow-up cognitive scores after controlling for baseline cognitive functioning. Therefore, the absence of the expected practice effect may be of prognostic value, and this is currently an active area of research. As an example, the presence of mild cognitive impairment has been confirmed by examining practice effects over a 1-week test–retest interval (Duff, Beglinger, Van Der Heiden, Moser, Arndt, Schultz, & Paulsen, 2008), as well as by using multiple assessments on a single day (Darby, Maruff, Collie, & McStephen, 2002). These studies indicate that practice effects data have significant implication for early diagnosis and treatment intervention.

Symptom Exaggeration/Examinee's Effort

The results of neuropsychological evaluations are used in making health-care decisions, as well as in civil and criminal legal proceedings, and these decisions may have a profound impact on an individual's life. As such, it is essential that the data upon which the clinician's opinions are based are rock solid, because if they are not, the opinion will lack a solid foundation and be of limited value to everyone involved. For example, will a 17-year-old high school junior who fell down an escalator at a local shopping mall and sustained a concussion be able to continue her educational and vocational dreams to become a pediatrician? Did the 15-year-old charged with capital murder have the ability to anticipate the consequences of his actions, in light of a history of developmental delays, limited formal schooling, and documented acquired brain injuries?

Clinical neuropsychologists cannot rely upon their clinical judgment alone when attempting to determine if the examinee participated fully in a neuropsychological evaluation. To determine if an examinee's level of effort was adequate to produce valid and reliable test scores, *symptom validity tests* have been developed. Although multiple symptom validity tests are available commercially, there are also a number in the development process. Regardless of the specific symptom validity test, they all contain a rich normative database, based upon both patient populations and analogue research studies.

Neurobehavioral and Neuropsychiatric Symptoms Associated with Neurological Conditions

A wide variety of neurologic insults can result in subtle to profound behavioral and emotional changes. Although alterations in cognition and movement/motor skills as a consequence of brain insults may be anticipated, often patients and families are not prepared for the resultant changes in mood and behavior. It is not unusual for laypeople to be unaware that the brain is responsible for emotional and behavioral regulation. The assumption may be that these factors are separable from "brain functioning," and that "mind" or "personality" somehow remains outside of the functions of cells and is attributable to something more intangible. As with other brain functions, however, emotion and behavior can be affected by brain insult, with the presence and nature of the symptoms being dependent on the location of injury. These changes may not occur solely in reaction to a potentially life-altering injury or disease, but by virtue of the injury itself. These alterations may be the most apparent and debilitating symptoms resulting from an injury or illness, even in a patient who is cognitively relatively unscathed. At other times, such changes can go unrecognized and hence untreated, either overshadowed by cognitive or physical deficits or misattributed to external or volitional factors.

It is important to note that *any* psychiatric symptom can occur as a function of central nervous system (CNS) dysfunction, and the *neuropsychiatric* symptoms displayed may be seemingly contradictory (see Cummings & Mega, 2003, for an excellent and thorough review of the principles of neuropsychiatry). For example, it is not unusual to see both impulsivity and apathy within the same patient as a consequence of a brain insult. As with disorders such as schizophrenia, the symptoms may include deficit syndromes (akin to "negative" symptoms of schizophrenia), in which expected behaviors are lacking, or productive syndromes (akin to "positive" symptoms of schizophrenia), in which unexpected behaviors are present. As stated earlier, it should be stressed that the particular symptoms that are displayed are largely dependent on the location of the injury. Neuropsychiatric changes are often attributable to the frontal lobes, particularly the right frontal lobe, limbic system insults, or regions/circuits connected to these areas. From a cognitive perspective, some of these areas, such as the right frontal lobe, can be among most challenging brain regions to assess using more traditional neuropsychological measures, despite fact that the frontal lobes comprise as much as a third of the brain. For this reason, careful psychodiagnostic assessment is an essential component to many neuropsychological evaluations, particularly for those patients with suspected frontal systems involvement.

Although this section is not intended to provide a neuroanatomic review of neuropsychiatric symptoms, some of the behavioral syndromes will be presented according to the affected brain regions, as the resulting symptoms may be likely to co-occur by virtue of their shared neuroanatomic and neurophysiologic underpinnings. It should be noted that disruption of the "frontal systems" circuits, involving primarily the frontal lobes, basal ganglia, and thalamus, can occur due to lesions anywhere along the circuits, although the syndromes are typically labeled according to their origins within the frontal lobe (i.e., dorsolateral circuit, orbitofrontal circuit, and medial frontal/anterior cingulate circuit; see Chow & Cummings, 1999 for a review of the frontal circuits).

Orbitofrontal Cortex

Symptoms involving damage to this circuit are primarily characterized by *disinhibition*. Patients may be lacking in social judgment, are apt to blurt out inappropriate comments, to act without considering the consequences of their actions, and may joke inappropriately. When more subtle, this may present as a patient seeming overly familiar with his or her clinician. At extremes, patients may be much more blatantly inappropriate. An example is a 53-year-old patient with a behavioral variant of frontotemporal dementia who noted that he had begun yelling out racial slurs in public, although he had never harbored such sentiments prior to the onset of his dementia. Patients with damage to this region may also show a pronounced lack of empathy and have very little insight into their behaviors. This can be a challenging combination of behaviors for the significant others of these patients, as the patients may be frequently making insensitive, embarrassing, or even hurtful comments without appreciating the inappropriateness of the comments or the impact on the receiver. In the case of the patient noted here with frontotemporal dementia, he reported often feeling embarrassed after blurting out a racial slur, noting that the sentiment was incongruent with his belief system. In most instances, however, he felt a sense of power and cathartic release after expressing his thoughts so freely, and he typically had no regret about the other remarks, which his partner found to be often tactless, if not frankly offensive. *Utilization behavior* may also be present with orbitofrontal damage, with patients attempting to use objects within their view (e.g., a comb, pen), even though they have no purpose for doing so. This behavior may be thought of as a form of disinhibition, with patients failing to inhibit the use of the objects for which they have no need and responding strongly to environmental rather than internal cues. Indeed, for patients with orbitofrontal injuries, external stimuli become highly influential in driving behavior, resulting in a strong dependency on the environment for behavioral response options.

Last, emotional changes as a result to damage to this region can include potentially significant mood lability, at times presenting as either *mania* or *depression*.

Dorsolateral Cortex

Damage to this circuit may result in symptoms that are typically considered to be more cognitive than behavioral in nature, and, hence, are more readily measurable by traditional neuropsychological assessment tools. These *executive deficits* can include problems with mental flexibility, planning, working memory, memory retrieval, problem-solving, and abstraction skills. Emotional changes may include *depression*.

Medial Frontal Cortex

Apathy is one of the most characteristic behavioral changes associated with damage to this circuit, with patients demonstrating difficulty with drive, initiation, and maintenance of behaviors. Patients may seem emotionally flat and indifferent, and family members can often mistake apathy for depression or willful "laziness." At the most extreme presentation, patients with damage to this region may display *akinetic mutism*, initiating neither speech nor movements, although they are not paralyzed nor, typically, aphasic. As an example, a 50-year-old, college-educated man with a stroke involving the thalamus and basal ganglia had relatively mild cognitive impairment on examination, but was unable to work or care for himself due to his extreme apathy. He sat on his couch all day, and only with strict implementation of a contingency management reward system for coffee (the only reward to which he responded) did he reach the point at which he would toilet himself without prompting. He rarely spoke unless first spoken to. His wife noted that, during the summer, if left alone, he would not get up from the couch to open a window or turn on the air conditioner, even if the temperature in the house was approaching 100° F.

Other Behavioral Disturbances

A number of other behavioral changes may be observed following frontal systems disruption, although they are not necessarily associated with any of the three neuroanatomic circuits noted earlier. Among those are:

ANOSOGNOSIA

Anosognosia refers to a lack of awareness of one's deficits. The term is derived from the Greek words "nosos," meaning disease, and "gnosis," meaning knowledge. Most medical definitions of the term will relate the condition to a lack of awareness of one's paralysis, typically involving insult to the nondominant, most often right hemisphere, and the typical left-sided paralysis. In this context, the patient may also neglect the entire affected side, not recognizing those body parts as belonging to him or her. Far more common (and typically less transient), is a lack of awareness of one's cognitive deficits or changes in one's behavioral regulatory control. Patients with Alzheimer's disease, for example, are often anosognosic. They may express rather fleeting awareness of their memory deficits, particularly in the moment of being confronted with a lapse in memory, but may otherwise have little awareness of even profound deficits. The degree of anosognosia exists along a continuum, with some patients appreciating that there has been some change in their cognition, but not appreciating the full extent of these changes. Other patients may be densely anosognosic and state very adamantly that there is nothing wrong with them, even when confronted with obvious, significant deficits. Although Alzheimer's disease may be the condition most commonly associated with anosognosia, it can occur with virtually any kind of brain insult. Family members often interpret this symptom as "denial," assuming that the patient is aware of the problem but is pretending there is no deficit, and it is often helpful for family to understand that the "denial" is actually a neurologically based phenomenon that prevents the patient from appreciating his or her deficits. This symptom can have a mixed impact on the patient and family. In some ways, the patient is spared from the distress associated with being more acutely aware of the often-devastating changes that are occurring. On the other hand, the lack of awareness of the deficits can lead to tremendous resistance once the family or the clinician attempts to impose appropriate restrictions (e.g., ceasing driving) on a patient who cannot appreciate the need for them.

CONFABULATION

Confabulation is sometimes referred to as "honest lying." Confabulation is often seen in conjunction with memory impairment, with patients "filling in the gaps" in their memories with false information. It should be stressed that this is not willful deception on the part of the patient; rather, the patient is not aware that the information supplied is false. The nature of the confabulations may be fantastical or mundane, and at times, family members may be bewildered as to why the patient is "lying" about seemingly inconsequential information. The content of the confabulation may be "stimulus-bound," in that ideas are irrationally linked solely because they are spatially or temporally contiguous (Lezak, 1995), although often the source of the confabulation is not readily apparent. As an example, a hospitalized 53-year-old patient with bilateral basal ganglia lesions had pronounced confabulation that could be readily elicited with very slight suggestion. Upon meeting the patient for the first time, the examiner said, "Good morning. Haven't we met before?" The patient readily replied, "Oh yes. We met in California at my brother's wedding last year." Although it was fairly early in the morning, when next asked, "Have you had lunch yet?" the patient responded, "Yes—we ate together. I had a hamburger, and you had the soup."

MISIDENTIFICATION SYNDROMES

This group of disorders is typically classified as a form of delusional syndromes and involves delusional misidentification of people or places. Among these are included *reduplicative paramnesia*, in which patients believe that there is one or more duplicate of a known person or place. An example is an 81-year-old woman with likely dementia with Lewy bodies who believed that there was more than one (perhaps as many as six) of her boyfriend, "Bob." She was never certain as to which "Bob" she would be encountering when they planned to meet—she described one as older and more stable, one as younger, more handsome and fun, and so forth, and she often referred to "Bob" as "they." A similar misidentification syndrome is *Capgras syndrome*, in which patients believe that someone known to them has been replaced by an imposter. With both Capgras syndrome and reduplicative paramnesia, some patients may believe that there are multiples of themselves. Another related misidentification is the *Frègoli syndrome*, in which the patient believes that someone well known to them is impersonating and taking on the appearance of an actual stranger. An example of the latter, a 60-year-old woman with a likely early degenerative condition believed that a stranger in her gym was actually a friend of hers from the past, disguised as another person. She remained adamant about this belief, despite the stranger (and several others) repeatedly providing her with convincing evidence to the contrary. With all of these misidentification syndromes, the symptoms may or may not be distressing to the patient, but are often distressing to the family. In the case of the latter patient, she was unconcerned by her belief that her friend was impersonating someone else at her gym, although the gym member felt harassed.

Other Delusions

Patients with brain insults can also present with other, perhaps more "typical" delusions, including unrealistic concerns about poverty, infidelity of their spouses, or their health status. As with other psychotic delusional states, the content of the delusion may be culturally dependent or driven by clear environmental or historical events relevant to the patient.

HALLUCINATIONS

As noted, any psychiatric symptom can result from brain insult, with hallucinations being no exception. In certain CNS disorders, such as dementia with Lewy bodies, hallucinations are common occurrences and may be fairly characteristic in nature (e.g., in dementia with Lewy bodies, the hallucinations are typically visual, and almost always of people or animals). Hallucinations caused by neurologic insult may be of any modality—auditory, visual, tactile, gustatory, or olfactory—which in some ways distinguishes some of these hallucinations from those more typically encountered in primary psychiatric disorders. For example, olfactory hallucinations are relatively unusual in schizophrenia, a disorder in which the hallucinations are often auditory, but may be seen as a result of certain brain tumors, migrainous or epileptic auras, ictal activity, and the like—again, with the nature of the symptom depending on the location of the lesion/event.

Treatment

Neuropsychiatric symptoms may not be immediately present or apparent after the causative insult. They may be overshadowed by more prominent deficits or pressing medical concerns, or they may emerge over time as the brain damage continues to evolve following the insult or with disease progression. Once present, the presence and intensity of the symptoms may fluctuate, but are unlikely to remit entirely (Cummings & Mega, 2003). These symptoms can obviously diminish the quality of life of the patient and may have a profound impact on his or her interpersonal relationships. Moreover, the presence of neuropsychiatric symptoms, particularly psychosis, is also often associated with increased morbidity and sometimes mortality in associated disease states (e.g., Almeida & Xiao, 2007). Thus, the need for careful assessment and thoughtful treatment of these symptoms is critical. The appropriate treatment may depend on the cause, nature, and

severity of the symptom, and may include medication, psychotherapy, family therapy, structuring of environment, psychosurgery, and, foremost, education. It is critical to educate the patient about the cause and prognosis of these symptoms, as well as to educate the patient's family about nature of neuropsychiatric symptoms as not necessarily reflecting willful behavior by the patient (e.g., appreciating apathy in a stroke patient rather than attributing the behavior to "laziness"). Of note, patients with neuropsychiatric disorders may be more likely to develop side effects from drug therapy (Cummings & Mega, 2003). This concern should not prohibit attempts at treatment, but may necessitate closer monitoring. It may also be necessary to ensure regular input from family or significant others regarding treatment response, especially if the patient does not have full insight into his symptoms or an appreciation of how his behavior impacts others. As noted, the cause of the symptom may also dictate appropriate treatment. For example, in dementia with Lewy bodies, which often presents with visual hallucinations, neuroleptic medications are contraindicated and should be used only very sparingly and with close monitoring, although there may not be similar concern with using neuroleptics in treating hallucinations originating from other brain insults. Last, attention to caregiver stress is critical. These significant others are faced with multiple challenges, which may include mourning the loss of a loved one as they once knew him or her, taking on the role of a caregiver, and managing difficult behaviors, potentially from a patient who may resent the caregiver's involvement. Although caregivers can often derive some clear rewards from their roles, helping them adjust to this role, providing the framework for understanding the patient's behavior, and monitoring for negative mood states in the caregiver is critical—for both the caregiver's and the patient's psychological well-being.

Psychologists or psychotherapists may become involved with neurologically impaired individuals in order to address some of the behavioral and/or emotional changes that are a direct result of the neurological condition, or to assist the individual and his or her family members in adjusting to changes in functioning and lifestyle that can follow neurological injury or disease. Psychotherapists who do not work with neurologically impaired individuals, however, also encounter patients with significant cognitive symptoms. Although associated with a psychological rather than neurological condition, the cognitive symptoms can present a significant functional disability. The next section will review the neuropsychological characteristics of several psychological disorders.

Neuropsychological Aspects of Psychological Disorders

Psychological disorders are often accompanied by cognitive symptoms. In the past, these cognitive symptoms were considered to be secondary to the psychological condition, with the expectation that cognitive difficulties would resolve as psychological symptoms remitted. In some cases, cognitive impairment was sufficiently severe to present as a dementia, and the term *pseudodementia* was used to refer to such psychologically based cognitive impairment. Over the years, however, it has become evident that cognitive impairment is not fully attributable to emotional symptoms. There is growing evidence that cognitive impairment persists after remission of psychological symptoms, and research has identified neuroanatomical abnormalities for some psychological disorders that could provide a neurological basis for the associated cognitive dysfunction. It has also become evident that the presence of cognitive impairment can significantly interfere with the psychological patient's functioning at home, school, and/or work. Therefore, neuropsychological impairment may be an important focus of treatment for some individuals with psychological disorders.

In this section, the neuropsychological correlates of anxiety disorders, mood disorders, somatoform disorders, and some of the personality disorders will be reviewed.

Personality Disorders

The personality disorders that have received the most research with regard to neuropsychological functioning are borderline personality disorder (BPD), antisocial personality disorder, and schizotypal personality disorder. Little if any research on the neuropsychological correlates of the remaining personality disorders has been completed and, therefore, these disorders will not be included in this discussion.

BORDERLINE PERSONALITY DISORDER

Individuals diagnosed with BPD frequently have cognitive difficulties, particularly memory difficulties. Their memory for recent events may be problematic, and they may have difficulty remembering information from therapy sessions. Additionally, long-term recall of autobiographical information may be distorted. These memory difficulties are often considered

to be psychologically based, reflecting motivated forgetting, denial mechanisms, or resistance. Research into the neuropsychological correlates of BPD, however, has explored whether these cognitive symptoms and the characteristic behavioral symptoms of affective dysregulation and impulsivity are related to underlying neuropsychological impairment.

The majority of the research has found that individuals with BPD perform lower on neuropsychological testing than comparison samples; however, a distinct profile of neuropsychological dysfunction has not emerged, and findings across studies have been inconsistent. A recent meta-analysis (Ruocco, 2005) of ten studies revealed that individuals with BPD performed significantly lower than did healthy comparison groups on tests of attention, processing speed, memory, cognitive flexibility, planning, and visuospatial abilities. Planning ability, as measured by performance on the Tower of London, was the greatest areas of cognitive weakness, with BPD patients requiring more time on planning tasks and making more errors (Bazanis et al., 2002). In another review of the literature, Monarch, Saykin, and Flashman (2004) reported that verbal memory, attention, and executive abilities were the most frequently found areas of cognitive deficiency in BPD, although several studies found no evidence of neuropsychological dysfunction. Legris and van Reekum (2006) reviewed 29 studies and found that the most commonly compromised areas of neuropsychological functioning in BPD was attention, response inhibition, and initiation; planning, intellectual abilities, and spatial working memory were the least commonly found deficient. The inconsistencies in this literature are evident in these reviews.

A weakness in this research is that the study participants have often had comorbid psychological disorders, including antisocial personality disorder and major depressive disorder (MDD), both of which commonly co-occur with BPD. Kunert, Druecke, Sass, and Herpertz (2003) found no evidence of neuropsychological dysfunction in a BPD group who did not have an Axis I disorder or evidence of antisocial personality. Further, individuals with co-morbid BPD and MDD, and individuals with MDD, have been found to perform similarly on neuropsychological measures, suggesting that MDD underlies any neuropsychological dysfunction in BPD (Fertuck et al., 2006). However, Monarch et al. (2004) found evidence of impaired levels of performance on tests of verbal memory and attention/vigilance, along with significantly lower but not impaired range scores on measures of visuomotor speed, visual memory, spatial organization, verbal intelligence, and language, in a BPD sample had no comorbid Axis I or Axis II disorders.

In summary of this clinical literature, there is growing evidence that BPD is associated with neuropsychological dysfunction, and there is some evidence that this is not entirely due to a comorbid psychological disorder or personality disorder. A specific pattern of neuropsychological deficits has not been identified, but it appears that attention, memory, and executive abilities are commonly compromised. It is important to recognize that, although the BPD groups perform at a significantly lower level than the comparison groups, test performances have not necessarily fallen within the impaired range. Further, not everyone with BPD has neuropsychological dysfunction. It is not clear whether neuropsychological dysfunction plays a causal role in BPD. There is some empirical work showing that children with borderline features evince weakness in attention/vigilance, cognitive flexibility, and abstraction. This suggests that neuropsychological dysfunction may be present early on in BPD, and has led to considerations that neuropsychological dysfunction is a feature BPD rather than a consequence of the disorder, and that it may underlie many of the symptomatic characteristics of BPD, including impulsivity and affective dysregulation. An association between neuropsychological dysfunction and self-injurious behavior has also been identified in BPD, although this requires further study (Bazanis et al., 2002; Legris et al., 2006; Monarch et al., 2004).

ANTISOCIAL PERSONALITY DISORDER

The neuropsychological functioning of individuals with antisocial behavior has received considerable research attention, primarily in an effort to develop an understanding of the etiology of this behavior. Clinical cases of individuals with brain injury who develop characteristics commonly associated with antisocial personality disorder and psychopathy have raised questions as to whether individuals with longstanding antisocial behavior or psychopathic personality have underlying neurological or neuropsychological dysfunction. The most famous clinical case of the development of socially deviant behavior following brain injury is Phineas Gage. Gage was a railroad worker who had an iron-tamping bar driven through the front of his head in a dynamite explosion. Following this injury, Gage, who had been a responsible and hard-working individual prior to injury, showed profound changes in his behavior, including impaired judgment, impaired planning

and organization, tactless and impulsive behavior, and emotional lability (Harlow, 1868). Subsequent clinical cases have revealed that marked personality changes of the type exhibited by Gage can occur with brain damage involving the prefrontal cortex, and these changes are commonly characterized by impaired decision making, impaired empathy/social insensitivity, social inappropriateness, emotional blunting, affective dysregulation, impaired goal-directed behavior, and lack of insight into the personality changes (Barrash, Tranel, & Anderson, 2000).

Much of the research on individuals with antisocial behavior that is not acquired from a brain injury has focused on executive functioning. This research has revealed a strong relationship between antisocial behavior and impairment in aspects of executive functioning including conceptual reasoning, response inhibition and impulse control, planning, mental flexibility, and initiation (Morgan & Lilienfeld, 2000). An emerging finding from this research is that the neuropsychological functioning varies among the different groups of individuals who exhibit antisocial behavior. There are a variety of groups of individuals with antisocial behavior, including individuals with antisocial personality disorder, conduct disorder, psychopathic personality traits, criminals, and juvenile delinquents. Inconsistencies in research findings appear to be due, in part, to variations in the antisocial behavior groups studied. This point was highlighted in a meta-analysis of 39 studies of executive functioning and antisocial behavior, which found that individuals with a history of criminal behavior or delinquency had greater impairment in executive abilities than did individuals with psychopathy, conduct disorder, or antisocial personality disorder. Individuals diagnosed with antisocial personality disorder tended to evidence the mildest level of executive dysfunction (Morgan & Lilienfeld, 2000).

The neuropsychological functioning of individuals with psychopathic personality appears to differ from individuals with antisocial personality disorder. Psychopathic personality is characterized by a lack of empathy and remorse, manipulativeness, fearlessness, impulsivity, superficial charm, shallow affect, and irresponsibility. Psychopaths appear to lack a conscience, and appear unconcerned about any punishment for their actions (Lykken, 2006). Although most psychopaths meet the diagnostic criteria for antisocial personality disorder, many individuals with antisocial personality disorder do not have psychopathic personalities. In terms of executive abilities, most of the research has identified a deficit in impulse control/behavioral inhibition, with other aspects of executive functioning unimpaired (Blair et al., 2006; Hiatt & Newman, 2006; Hiatt, Schmitt, & Newman, 2004; Mitchell, Colledge, Leonard, & Blair, 2002). In addition, a deficiency in attentional regulation has been identified, with psychopaths showing a reduced ability to allocate attention to peripheral information while focused on a task. Language deficits have also been identified. Psychopaths show difficulty using connotation and understanding the emotional content of language (Hiatt & Newman, 2006; Hiatt, Schmitt, & Newman, 2004).

There has also been considerable study of neuropsychological functioning of children and adolescents with antisocial behavior and/or conduct problems. This research has found deficits in verbal and executive abilities. Children and adolescents with significant conduct problems tend to have low verbal intelligence, impaired verbal memory, poor auditory processing, poor attention, and impairment in executive abilities that include conceptual/abstract reasoning, initiation, planning, and response inhibition. The presence of comorbid attention-deficit hyperactivity disorder (ADHD) is associated with greater neuropsychological impairment (Lynam & Henry, 2001). A more recent examination (Raine et al., 2005) of the neuropsychological functioning of adolescents with a history of antisocial behavior found that difficulties might also involve nonverbal abilities. They found that adolescents with a history of antisocial behavior performed significantly lower than the comparison group on measures of verbal and nonverbal intelligence, verbal and nonverbal memory, and attention. Of some interest was that these neuropsychological weaknesses remained even when the antisocial behavior was no longer present; that is, children with a prior history of antisocial behavior, but who no longer exhibited this behavior, continued to manifest neuropsychological weakness compared to controls. In summary, then, this research indicates that neuropsychological dysfunction is present in children and adolescents who exhibit antisocial behavior and may play a role in the development of this behavior. Those children and adolescents with comorbid ADHD tend to have more severe neuropsychological dysfunction and a greater risk for more severe antisocial behavior.

SCHIZOTYPAL PERSONALITY DISORDER
The schizophrenia spectrum disorders, which include schizophrenia, schizoaffective disorder, schizoid personality disorder, and schizotypal personality disorder, are associated with cognitive dysfunction.

Most research has been completed on schizophrenia and schizotypal personality disorder (SPD). In schizophrenia, there is severe and global neuropsychological impairment; that is, most aspects of cognitive functioning are severely compromised. In SPD, neuropsychological dysfunction is present but is more circumscribed and less severe than in schizophrenia. Some of the research has found that individuals with SPD, when compared to individuals without a psychological diagnosis, perform significantly lower across a broad range of neuropsychological abilities and, specifically, verbal intelligence (i.e., vocabulary, factual knowledge, word reading), spatial abilities, visuomotor abilities, attention, memory, working memory, abstract reasoning, and cognitive flexibility (Matsui, Sumiyoshi, Kato, Yoneyama, & Kurachi, 2004). Other studies, however, have found individuals with SPD to perform significantly lower than control subjects only on measures of verbal and/or visual memory, working memory, and abstract reasoning (Mitropoulou, Harvey, Maldari, et al., 2002; Mitropoulou, Harvey, Zegarelli, et al. 2005; Siever et al., 2002; Voglmaier et al., 2005), and the impairment in these areas is mild. There is some evidence that the neuropsychological functioning in SPD is characterized by deficits in working memory and information processing capacity, and that these deficits underlie all other cognitive symptoms/impairments found in this population (Barch et al., 2004; Harvey, Romero, Reichenberg, Granholm, & Siever, 2006; Mitropoulou et al., 2005; Moriarty et al., 2003).

Schizotypal personality disorder is characterized by impaired social and interpersonal functioning, with eccentric behavior and appearance, social discomfort, odd beliefs, and perceptual distortion. There may be an association between neuropsychological impairment and social/interpersonal dysfunction in this disorder, with greater working memory impairment and relatively lower intellectual abilities correlated with greater social difficulty (Mitropoulou et al., 2005; Trotman, McMillan, & Walker, 2006). Similar findings have been reported for individuals with schizophrenia (Trotman et al., 2006).

Somatoform Disorders
The somatoform disorders are characterized by the presence of physical symptoms that cannot be fully explained by a medical condition. The symptoms are not intentionally produced; that is, the individual believes that the physical symptoms are due to a medical cause and is unaware of the underlying psychological factors that could explain the symptoms.

Physical symptoms such as pain, paralysis, blindness, and seizures are considered the more classic presentation in somatoform disorder. It has become clear over the years, however, that individuals can also report significant cognitive symptoms that cannot be explained by an underlying a medical/neurological condition or another psychiatric condition. Although individuals with these presentations are sometimes diagnosed with a somatoform disorder, there has been discussion within the field of neuropsychology as to whether the current *Diagnostic and Statistical Manual of Mental Disorders, Fourth Edition, Text Revision* (DSM-IV-TR) diagnostic criteria are adequate to apply to these conditions. One problem that has been identified is that the current criteria specify the presence of "physical symptoms," and cognitive symptoms do not easily fit under this rubric (Binder, 2007; Boone, 2007; Delis & Wetter, 2007; Larrabee, 2007). Despite questions of the correct diagnostic label, however, the fact that an individual can manifest cognitive symptoms that are sometimes severe and debilitating and that are not associated with an underlying neurological or medical conditions is important to appreciate. Reinforcement of the individual's belief that he or she is experiencing severe deficits that are due to an underlying neurological condition can serve to perpetuate and perhaps worsen the individual's symptom.

The neuropsychological presentations of individuals with somatoform-like conditions fall into two general groups. In some cases, the individual will report cognitive difficulties and are preoccupied with cognitive and functional difficulties; however, there is no objective evidence of difficulties on psychometric testing or in daily living. The cognitive symptoms reported are typically common and perhaps associated with stress, fatigue, or normal age-related changes, but the individual interprets these symptoms as indicators of a serious neurological condition (Boone, 2007). The clinical presentation of these individuals is similar to hypochondrias. The other group of individuals with somatoform-like conditions has clinical presentations that are similar to somatization or conversion disorder. These individuals have marked cognitive symptoms and marked difficulty in daily functioning in the absence of any medical or neurological condition that could explain these symptoms. On psychometric testing, they may perform well despite severe cognitive and functional difficulties, or the test findings may show some areas of impaired ability, but the nature and extent of the impairment are not compatible with

severe disability. In other cases, there may be evidence of severe cognitive impairment on testing that cannot be accounted for neurological factors (Cicerone & Kalmar, 1995; Delis & Wetter, 2007). The symptoms may be unusual and, in some cases, incompatible with a brain-related disorder. An example of unusual symptoms would be an inability to recognize family members and inability to recall other autobiographical information following a mild cerebral concussion.

In both conversion disorders and somatization disorders, psychological factors are conceptualized as the underlying cause of the physical/cognitive symptomatology. In somatization disorder, the individual has a tendency to express psychological distress physically or cognitively. In conversion disorder, the classic conceptualization is that emotional distress associated with a trauma is unconsciously suppressed and converted into physical/cognitive symptomatology by the individual. In both disorders, the primary gain from the physical/cognitive symptoms is decreased emotional distress. The symptoms often elicit changes in the individual's lifestyle that may serve as positive reinforcement for these symptoms. These results are referred to as *secondary gains*. An inability to continue with employment or to complete household responsibilities, or the positive attention, nurturing and/or assistance gained from others as a result of the physical/cognitive symptoms are examples of secondary gains that can play a significant role in the continuance of physical symptoms and disability. The fact that the symptoms are due to psychological factors has implications for the information provided to the patient regarding etiology and prognosis, as well as the treatment approach but does not diminish the significance of the individual's perceived symptoms and difficulties. It is important to recognize that the symptoms are "real" to the individual.

There has been limited examination of the neurobiological and neuropsychological correlates of somatoform disorders. The research on conversion disorder has been completed with individuals with physical or sensory symptoms, such as paralysis or numbness, and therefore it is not clear if these findings generalize to cases involving cognitive symptoms. It has been proposed that individuals with conversion disorder have a deficit in higher-level information processing (Roelofs, vanGalen, Eling, Keijsers, & Hoogduin, 2003; Sierra & Berrios, 1999; Tallabs, 2005). This deficit is thought to be due to psychological stress, which disrupts higher-level processing but does not impact lower-level information processing. Lower-level information processing refers to the processing of information that occurs automatically, almost reflexively, with minimal cognitive effort or conscious awareness. Commonly referred to as *automatic processing*, this is the component of our information processing system involved when carrying out well-learned behavior or routines. Such tasks are completed effortlessly and without explicitly thinking about the behavior. In contrast, higher-level information processing requires explicit, effortful, conscious attention and processing. Higher-level information processing is required when involved in novel, nonroutine situations, where directed, effortful attention and processing is required to complete a task or carry out a behavior. A deficit in higher-level information processing with intact lower-level processing may explain the common observation that those individual with a conversion disorder may not have symptoms in situations where they are not thinking about the symptoms. More clearly, an individual with conversion paralysis of the arm may be observed to automatically move the arm to avoid hitting something or to reflexively catch a ball, but is unable to intentionally move the arm during a medical examination or physical therapy.

Brown (2004) has proposed a different conceptual model that subsumes both conversion disorder and somatization disorder. In this model, the automatic information processing system is the source of the problem. The automatic information processing system is the first level of processing at which various schemata are automatically activated, and this occurs without conscious awareness. In conversion and somatization disorder, it is theorized that a stimulus activates incorrect information regarding physical symptoms. Essentially, there is a mismatch between the current stimuli and the information that is activated and used to interpret the stimuli. The individual is unaware of the error in interpretation because the activation of the incorrect information occurs without his or her awareness. An important component of this model is self-focused bodily attention, as attention to bodily symptoms is necessary to activate the schema regarding physical symptoms. Self-focused bodily attention is often found in introspective individuals, individuals with depression or anxiety, or in the context of boredom. Self-focused bodily attention may also be a learned behavior developed within a family system, in which physical (or cognitive) symptoms were considered significant and likely reflective of serious illness. In addition, individuals encountering high levels of emotional distress associated with trauma can become focused on bodily symptoms to avoid thoughts or emotions associated with the trauma. Brown (2004) also discusses the various sources that contribute to our knowledge about physical symptoms, some of which may not be accurate. These include experiences when physically ill in the past, observations of others with a physical illness, or sociocultural conceptions of specific disorders and the symptomatology associated with these disorders, even if inaccurate. He notes that many individuals with a diagnosis of a somatoform disorder have a prior history of illness or exposure to other's illness, both of which have probably contributed to their beliefs regarding symptoms and disability associated with illness and/or injury.

Mood Disorders
BIPOLAR DISORDER

Neuropsychological dysfunction is associated with bipolar disorder. The most consistent findings across studies are impairment in attention, processing speed, verbal learning and memory, and executive abilities with respect to inhibitory control, conceptual reasoning/abstraction, cognitive flexibility, fluency, and working memory (Green, Cahill, & Malhi, 2007; Gruber, Rathgeber, Braunig, & Gauggel, 2007; Malhi et al., 2007). Some research has also found deficits in visual memory (Depp et al., 2007). There may be some variation in the pattern and severity of neuropsychological deficits during the depressed and manic/hypomanic phases of the disorder. Individuals with manic/hypomanic symptoms may have greater impairment in attention, processing speed, and inhibitory control than do individuals with depressed bipolar disorder (Gruber et al., 2007). Neuropsychological dysfunction appears to be present very early in bipolar disorder. A recent study of first-episode bipolar disorder patients found deficits in processing speed and executive abilities (i.e., poor abstraction/conceptual reasoning, poor mental flexibility, and poor inhibitory control). These researchers did not include a broad spectrum of neuropsychological functions, limiting their focus to executive functioning, so it is not known if other cognitive deficits are also present early (Gruber, Rosso, & Yurgelun-Todd, 2008). Although cognitive impairment is present at the onset of the disorder, there is some evidence that impairment is more pronounced in older individuals with bipolar disorder, particularly with respect to processing speed (Depp et al., 2007).

As symptoms remit, the cognitive functioning of bipolar patients improves, but there remains evidence of impairment even during the asymptomatic phase of the disorder (Gruber et al., 2007; Malhi et al., 2007). Recent meta-analytic reviews have found that euthymic bipolar patients perform significantly lower than do healthy controls on measures of sustained attention, processing speed, verbal learning and memory, delayed visual memory, and aspects of executive abilities and specifically, verbal fluency, working memory, conceptual reasoning, and mental control/flexibility (Arts, Jabben, Krabbendam, & van Os, 2008; Torres, Boudreau, & Yatham, 2007). Several variables may contribute to the findings of cognitive dysfunction in euthymic patients, and these require further exploration. Many of the studies have included medicated patients, which raises the possibility that the findings of neuropsychological dysfunction in asymptomatic bipolar patients is due to medication effects; although at least one study did not find any evidence of a significant medication effect on neuropsychological testing (Martinez-Aran et al., 2007). Another factor of consideration is that the euthymic patients included in these studies may have had subclinical mood symptoms that impacted testing. However, some research has found evidence of neuropsychological dysfunction even when subclinical symptoms are controlled, although the pattern of deficits may be more circumscribed. Specifically, Mur, Portella, Martinez-Aran, Pifarre, and Vieta (2007) reported deficits in processing speed, cognitive flexibility, inhibitory control, and working memory in a sample of individuals with either bipolar I or bipolar II disorder when subclinical mood symptoms were controlled. Attention, verbal memory, and visual memory abilities were not significantly different from a comparison group. These researchers also examined a subgroup of the sample whose medication was limited to lithium rather than multiple medications. In this group, neuropsychological deficits were limited to poor inhibitory control. This finding suggests that euthymic bipolar patients prescribed multiple medications may evidence more extensive neuropsychological dysfunction. There is also evidence that euthymic bipolar patients taking multiple medications have greater psychosocial impairment (Martinez-Aran et al., 2007). Whether this is due to medication effects or the severity of the illness is not clear.

In light of evidence of neuropsychological dysfunction during asymptomatic phases, cognitive impairment has been discussed as a possible trait of bipolar disorder. Further, findings of neuropsychological dysfunction in first-degree relatives of individuals with bipolar disorder have raised the possibility that cognitive impairment is a genetic risk factor for this disorder. A meta-analytic review of 14 studies found that first-degree relatives performed significantly lower than did controls on measures of verbal memory and mental control/flexibility. The effect sizes were small, indicating that the cognitive difficulties were not as great as those found in bipolar disorder patients (Arts et al., 2008). Finally, neuroimaging studies have also found abnormalities in the prefrontal and subcortical brain regions of bipolar patients, which appeared to be present at the onset of the disorder (Green, Cahill, & Malhi, 2007; Gruber et al., 2008).

Neuropsychological functioning is associated with functional outcome in bipolar disorder, and has been found to predict functional outcome better than clinical variables such as premorbid adjustment, symptom severity, or history of psychosis or substance use. Of particular relevance is verbal memory and executive abilities (i.e., working memory, inhibitory control, and verbal fluency), both of which have been shown to have the strongest relationship with the occupational and interpersonal functioning of bipolar disorder patients than other cognitive functions (Martinez-Aran et al., 2007; Tabares-Seisdedos et al., 2008).

MAJOR DEPRESSIVE DISORDER

Individuals with depressive disorders often complain of difficulty with concentration and memory. In some cases, neuropsychological evaluation reveals no objective evidence of cognitive impairment. In these cases, the cognitive difficulties appear to be secondary to emotional distress. In other cases, however, neuropsychological evaluation reveals areas of deficiency. It is well accepted that neuropsychological impairment can accompany MDD, but cognitive impairment has also been identified in individuals with other depressive disorders including dysthymia, depressive disorder not otherwise specified, and adjustment disorder with depressed mood. The severity and extent of neuropsychological impairment increases with an increase in the severity of the depressive disorder (Castaneda et al., 2008a; Elderkin-Thompson, Kumar, et al., 2003; Paelecke-Habermann, Phol, & Leplow, 2005). Although there has been some inconsistency in the research, the most commonly identified areas of cognitive impairment in depressive disorders are attention, psychomotor processing speed, and executive functioning involving cognitive flexibility, planning, problem solving, and fluency. Verbal and visual memory impairment has been identified as a correlate of depression in some studies (Castaneda et al., 2008a; Naismith et al.,

2003). Depressed individuals typically evince more difficulty on tasks requiring effortful attention and information processing, and there is some thought that poor performance on memory testing might reflect the effortful processing demands required for new learning, rather than impairment in memory ability per se (Gualtieri, Johnson, & Benedict, 2006). In addition, some research has linked memory impairment with illness chronicity, with those individuals who have a history of multiple depressive episodes showing memory impairment (Dotson, Resnick, & Zonderman, 2008).

Similar to the findings with bipolar disorder, neuropsychological dysfunction has been identified in asymptomatic individuals with MDD. Deficits may persist in executive functions (Castaneda, et al., 2008b; Clark, Sarna, & Goodwin, 2005), memory (Castaneda, et al., 2008b; Neu, Bajbouj, Schilling, Godemann, Berman, & Schlattmann, 2005), and attention (Paelecke-Habermann et al., 2005; Weiland-Fiedler et al., 2004) Additionally, neuropsychological dysfunction, and specifically impairment in cognitive flexibility, has been identified in unaffected first-degree relatives of individuals with MDD. These findings suggest that neuropsychological dysfunction may be a cognitive trait marker, or endophenotype, of MDD but this requires further scientific investigation (Clark et al., 2005).

Several factors have been found to be associated with an increased risk of cognitive impairment. Older individuals tend to have more prominent cognitive impairment in general, and particularly individuals with late-onset depressive illness, typically defined as having the first depressive episode after age 50. The chronicity of depressive episodes is also relevant in older individuals, with those having persistent depressive symptoms or multiple depressive episodes in later life showing greater decline in cognitive ability (Dotson et al., 2008; Elderkin-Thompson et al., 2003). Depression in older age groups can often be treatment resistant, and cognitive symptoms may not completely remit after depression subsides. The presence of an underlying neurodegenerative dementia is often raised in these cases. A concern about dementia is warranted, as depression can be an early sign of a neurodegenerative illness, such as Alzheimer disease (Dotson et al., 2008; Gualtieri et al., 2006).

Neuropsychological dysfunction is associated with functional disability in depressive illnesses. Cognitive impairment has been found to interfere with employment, education, and the ability to complete daily responsibilities in general (Jaeger, Berns, Uzelac, & Davis-Conway, 2006).

Anxiety Disorders

Research on the neuropsychological correlates of anxiety disorder has largely focused on obsessive-compulsive disorder (OCD) and post-traumatic stress disorder (PTSD), and therefore, this review will focus on these two disorders.

OBSESSIVE-COMPULSIVE DISORDER

The neuropsychological functioning of individual's diagnosed with OCD has received a great deal of research attention, primarily in the interest of identifying the neuropathological substrates of this disorder. Obsessive-compulsive disorder has been associated with frontal-subcortical dysfunction, and specifically with abnormalities involving the pre-frontal region, caudate nucleus, and the anterior cingulate cortex (Chamberlain, Blackwell, Fineberg, Robbins, & Sahakian, 2005; Kuelz, Hohagen, & Voderhlozer, 2004). The neuropsychological correlates of OCD vary across research studies, perhaps associated with factors such as medication, symptom severity, age of onset, and comorbid psychological disorder (Kim, Park, Shin, & Kwon, 2002; Kuelz, Hohagen, & Voderhlozer, 2004; Segalas et al., 2008). Among this variability, however, there have been fairly consistent findings of impairment in aspects of executive abilities and nonverbal memory. Visuospatial abilities and processing speed have also been identified as areas of deficiency in OCD, but these findings have been variable across studies (Anderson & Savage, 2004; Castaneda, et al., 2008b; Chamberlain et al., 2005; Greisberg & McKay, 2003; Harris & Dinn, 2003). In regard to executive impairment, the most commonly reported area of deficiency is response inhibition; that is, the ability to inhibit a well-learned or habitual response. Cognitive flexibility has also been identified as a common area of deficiency in the executive abilities of individual with OCD. There have been inconsistent findings showing impairment in other aspects of executive functioning, and specifically, conceptual skills, verbal fluency, and planning (Andres et al., 2008; Kim et al., 2002; Kuelz et al., 2004). Some research suggests that memory impairment in OCD may be associated with executive dysfunction. Analysis of the pattern of performance on memory testing has revealed a deficit in organizing information to facilitate learning. Individuals with OCD typically will not have difficulty with memory tasks involving organized or structured information (Anderson et al., 2004 Greisberg & McKay, 2003; Kuelz et al., 2004; Penades, Catalan, Andres, Salamero, & Gasto, 2005). Impairment on nonverbal memory tests have been the most frequent finding in OCD; however, verbal memory impairment has been identified in some studies, and this may emerge on those verbal learning tests that require application of organizational strategies for learning, such as word-list learning tests (Chamberlain et al., 2005; Greisberg & McKay, 2003; Kuelz et al., 2004). These findings suggest that memory techniques for organizing to-be-learned information may be an avenue for improving the memory functioning in individuals with OCD.

As with the mood disorders, there is growing evidence of persistence in neuropsychological dysfunction in individuals with OCD, even after symptoms are significantly reduced or have remitted. Although cognitive abilities improve, continued deficits in nonverbal memory and executive functioning during less symptomatic periods have been reported; however, persisting neuropsychological dysfunction has not been found in every study (Andres et al. 2008; Rao, Janardhan, Kumar, Kandavel, & Chandrashekar, 2008; Roh et al., 2005). Whether nonverbal memory and executive dysfunction are cognitive traits or endophenotypes of OCD remains an area of ongoing investigation.

POST-TRAUMATIC STRESS DISORDER

Individuals diagnosed with PTSD commonly report significant cognitive difficulties, usually involving concentration and memory. The frequency of cognitive symptoms in PTSD patients was a primary impetus for the scientific investigation of the underlying neuropsychological and neuropathological bases for these symptoms. Research has identified neuropathological abnormalities in PTSD involving the frontal and limbic regions of the brain (Dickie, Brunet, Akerib, & Armony, 2008; Vasterling & Brailey, 2005), and recent work suggests possible involvement of the parietal lobe (Weber et al., 2005). Neuropsychological dysfunction has also been associated with PTSD. Individuals with PTSD often evidence deficits in aspects of attention and specifically, sustained attention and working memory. Memory impairment is also a common neuropsychological correlate of this disorder and is characterized by deficiency in encoding and retrieval memory processes, but with generally intact storage (i.e., retention) ability. In addition, individuals with PTSD may be more susceptible to interference effects on learning (Koenen et al., 2001; Vasterling & Brailey, 2005). Executive dysfunction is also associated with PTSD involving response inhibition and verbal fluency (Castaneda et al., 2008b; Koenen et al., 2001; Vasterling & Brailey, 2005). There is some evidence

of a worsening of memory impairment in aging individuals with PTSD, which may be due to the chronicity of condition and/or aging effects (Golier, Harvey, Legge, & Yehuda, 2006; Yehuda, Golier, Halligan, & Harvey, 2004; Yehuda, Golier, Tischler, et al., 2005). Of some diagnostic importance is that retention processes remain uninvolved, which distinguishes this memory decline from the pattern typically associated with Alzheimer's disease.

The cause of the neuropathological and neuropsychological dysfunction in PTSD is an area of ongoing investigation (Vasterling & Brailey, 2005). Animal models have shown that stress can cause neurobiological and neuropsychological changes, and these findings support the view that PTSD is the cause of cognitive and neuropathological abnormalities identified in humans. There is also support, however, for the alternative viewpoint that neuropsychological dysfunction and neuropathological abnormalities are risk factors for PTSD. That is, those individuals who develop PTSD following trauma have pre-trauma cognitive and neurobiological compromise that increased their vulnerability to develop the disorder. Vasterling and Brailey (2005) suggests that neuropsychological dysfunction may be both a risk factor and a consequence of PTSD. Those who develop this disorder following a traumatic experience may have less cognitive resources to cope with the stress, and their cognitive functioning is further compromised with the onset of PTSD.

Neuropsychological Treatment in Psychiatric Disorders

Neuropsychological rehabilitation, also referred to as *cognitive rehabilitation*, concerns the treatment of cognitive, behavioral, and emotional changes that are due to a neurological injury or condition, such as a traumatic brain injury or stroke. The approaches to neuropsychological rehabilitation are varied, but most emphasize restoration of cognitive/behavioral functions and training in methods of compensating for impaired functions. Scientific evidence supports the efficacy of cognitive rehabilitation of neuropsychological impairments due to neurological insult, and practice recommendations have been proposed based upon this research (Cicerone et al., 2000; Cicerone et al., 2005; Laatsch et al., 2007).

Neuropsychological rehabilitation is not a typical component in the treatment of psychiatric disorders. There are, however, certainly exceptions, with schizophrenia being the best example of a psychiatric disorder for which cognitive remediation techniques are often employed, and it is the example that will be used here in describing the application of cognitive rehabilitation to psychiatric disorders.

Schizophrenia has been shown to impact virtually all cognitive domains. Although there may be tremendous variability among patients with regard to the extent and nature of the deficits, cognitive impairment can rightfully be considered a "core" aspect of the disease. Multiple studies have demonstrated that cognitive dysfunction in schizophrenia is strongly associated with poor psychosocial outcome, even more so than the clinical symptoms of the disease (Wexler & Bell, 2005). Cognitive deficits have also been shown to be strong predictors of response to psychiatric rehabilitation (McGurk, Twamley, Sitzer, McHugo, & Mueser, 2007), as well as predictors of work capacity and quality (Bell, Bryson, & Kaplan, 1999), independent living, social relationships/social skills, and ability to provide self-care (McGurk et al., 2007). Furthermore, current psychopharmacologic treatments have no notable benefit in treating the cognitive deficits associated with the disorder (Marder, 2006). As such, it is not surprising that cognitive functioning has been a target for intervention in schizophrenia, and there is a more than 40-year history of cognitive remediation programs in the treatment of the disorder (McGurk et al., 2007).

As in the treatment of cognitive deficits in neurologic disorders, two general strategies have been employed in the treatment of cognitive deficits in schizophrenia. These typically include compensatory strategies designed to circumvent deficits, and cognitive remediation techniques to enhance/restores deficient areas. Often, the latter involves extensive repetition of the same activity, under the assumption that this repetition leads to an increase in the number of active brain cells in regions of the brain that have been underutilized/avoided, and unrewarded (Wexler & Bell, 2005). Alternatively, programs may include "strategy coaching," in which patients are taught methods to facilitate memory recall (e.g., "chunking" information) and problem-solving skills, with the hope that the latter will provide better transfer of skills from the training setting to daily life (McGurk et al., 2007). Additional strategies include combining cognitive remediation with vocational rehabilitation, with the rationale that cognitive exercise may enhance vocational interventions, while in turn, work activity may provide appropriate opportunities for the practice and generalization of cognitive strategies (Wexler & Bell, 2005).

Some review papers that examined the impact of compensatory and restorative techniques have been discouraging, indicating that there appears to be minimal benefit beyond outcomes such as improvement on the trained task (without meaningful generalization) or on closely related but untrained measures (Wexler & Bell, 2005). A recent meta-analysis, however, more closely examined the impact of cognitive remediation on functional outcomes (McGurk et al., 2007). Results of the study showed highly consistent findings among studies, with a moderate effect of remediation on overall cognitive performance (0.41) despite notable variability in the setting, patients, and training methods. There was evidence of maintenance of those gains in the few studies that provided longitudinal follow-up. The effect size of remediation on improvement of clinical symptoms was smaller, but significant (0.28). The overall effect on psychosocial functioning was also small (0.35), but highly variable from study to study. For the latter outcome, McGurk et al. (2007) found that the impact on psychosocial outcomes was much greater in remediation programs that also provided adjunctive psychiatric rehabilitation (effect size = 0.47) than in those that did not (effect size = 0.05), or in programs that provide psychiatric rehabilitation alone (e.g., social skills training). They suggest that these findings challenge the assumption that improvement in cognition can lead to spontaneous improvement in psychosocial functioning, but, rather, that there may be some synergistic effect of these two treatment approaches.

Conclusion

Clinical neuropsychology is a field that is concerned with understanding the relationship between brain functioning and cognitive abilities, emotional functioning, personality, and behavior. As presented in this chapter, emotional and behavioral changes are often the direct result of neurological injury or disease, and these changes can mimic psychological disorders. Perhaps such clinical observations have led, in part, to the investigation of the neurobiological bases and neuropsychological correlates of psychological disorders. Neuropathological abnormalities and neuropsychological dysfunction have been identified for several Axis I and Axis II psychological disorders. Recent findings showing neuropsychological dysfunction in asymptomatic individuals with psychological disorders, as well as their asymptomatic family members, has introduced the possibility that neuropsychological dysfunction is a trait marker and/or risk factor for certain psychological disorders. Research has also shown that neuropsychological impairment is a substantial factor in the level of

Table 30.3 When is a neuropsychological consultation indicated?

- Forgetting that the topic has already been discussed
- Short-term memory problems
- Needing things repeated over and over again
- Confusion/disorientation
- Frequently losing/misplacing items (e.g., house keys, mail)
- Perseveration; behaviorally or verbally
- Problems with paying bills on time
- Problems managing/maintaining finances
- Problems with following step-wise instructions (e.g., sequence of a cooking recipe)
- Getting lost while driving, especially in familiar locations
- Failure to maintain an accurate debit card or checking account balance (e.g., over-the-limit or insufficient funds notification)
- Change in personal hygiene (e.g., not bathing, brushing teeth, etc.)
- Change in personality (e.g., blurting out socially inappropriate comments)
- Inappropriate behavior (e.g., touching others inappropriately)
- Deterioration in maintaining their household (e.g., dishes not washed, kitty litter not attended to, refrigerated food not put away properly)
- Unsafe behaviors (e.g., forgetting and burning food on the stove, not closing and locking entry doors)

functional disability experienced by the individual with a psychological disorder.

Clinical psychology plays an essential role in caring for the neurologically impaired patient. Behavioral and cognitive-behavioral techniques can have utility in managing and/or modifying problematic behavior and emotional dysregulation. Psychological support and treatment also play an important role in assisting the neurologically compromised individual and his or her family in adjusting to the changes in functioning and family life that often accompanies neurological injury or disease. Neuropsychology can play a role in the treatment of individuals with psychological disorders. In some cases, the psychotherapist or clinical psychologist may have concern about a neurological cause for an individual's psychological and/or behavioral difficulties. Such questions commonly arise in older individuals, in whom the typical concern is about the presence of a neurodegenerative illness in the context of significant memory decline. In addition to diagnostic issues, however, neuropsychology can also be of benefit in understanding the neuropsychological functioning of individuals with psychological disorders. Further, research linking neuropsychological impairment to functional disability in some psychological disorders has potential treatment implications. Specifically, incorporating training in strategies to compensate for cognitive difficulties into psychotherapy sessions may be beneficial (Table 30.3).

References

Almeida, O. P., & Xiao, J. (2007). Mortality associated with incident mental health disorders after stroke. *Australian and New Zealand Journal of Psychiatry, 41,* 474–481.

Anderson, K. E., & Savage, C. R. (2004). Cognitive and neurobiological findings in obsessive-compulsive disorder. *Psychiatric Clinics of North America, 27,* 37–47.

Andres, S., Lazaro, L., Salamero, M., Boget, T., Penades, R., & Castro-Fornieles, J. (2008). Changes in cognitive dysfunction in children and adolescents with obsessive-compulsive disorder after treatment. *Journal of Psychiatric Research, 42,* 507–514.

Arts, B., Jabben, N., Krabbendam, L., & van Os, J. (2008). Meta-analyses of cognitive functioning in euthymic bipolar patients and their first-degree relatives. *Psychological Medicine, 38,* 771–785.

Barch, D. M., Mitropoulou, V., Harvey, P. D., New, A. S., Silverman, J. M., & Siever, L. J. (2004). Context-processing deficits in schizotypal personality disorder. *Journal of Abnormal Psychology, 113,* 556–568.

Barrash, J., Tranel, D., & Anderson, S. W. (2000). Acquired personality disturbances associated with bilateral damage to the ventromedial prefrontal region. *Developmental Neuropsychology, 18,* 355–381.

Bazanis, E., Rogers, R. D., Dowson, J. H., Taylor, P., Meux, C., Staley, C., et al. (2002). Neurocognitive deficits in decision-making and planning with DSM-III-R borderline personality disorder. *Psychological Medicine, 32,* 1395–1405.

Bell, M., Bryson, G. J., & Kaplan, E. (1999). Work rehabilitation in schizophrenia: cognitive predictors of best and worse performance. *Schizophrenia Research, 36,* 211.

Benton, A. (2000). *Exploring the history of neuropsychology: Selected papers.* New York: Oxford University Press.

Binder, L. M., Iverson, G. L., & Brooks, B. L. (2009). To err is human: "Abnormal neuropsychological scores and variability are common in healthy adults. *Archives of Clinical Neuropsychology, 24,* 31–46.

Binder, L.M. (2007). Comment on cogniform disorder and cogniform condition: Proposed diagnoses for excessive cognitive symptoms. *Archives of Clinical Neuropsychology, 27,* 681–682.

Blair, K. S., Mitchell, D. G. V., Leonard, A., Newman, C., Richell, R. A., Morton, J., & Blair, R. J. R. (2006). Differentiation among prefrontal substrates in psychopathy: Neuropsychological test findings. *Neuropsychology, 20,* 153–165.

Boone, K. B. (2007). Commentary on "Cogniform disorder and cogniform condition: Proposed diagnoses for excessive cognitive symptoms" by D. C. Delis and S R. Wetter. *Archives of Clinical Neuropsychology, 27,* 675–679.

Boring, E. G. (1950). *A history of experimental psychology* (2nd ed.). New York: Appleton-Century-Crofts.

Brown, R. J. (2004). Psychological mechanisms of medically unexplained symptoms: An integrative conceptual model. *Psychological Bulletin, 130,* 793–812.

Butters, N., Grant, I., Haxby, J., Judd, L. L., Martin, A., McClelland, J., et al. (1990). Assessment of AIDS-related cognitive changes: Recommendations of the NIMH workgroup on neuropsychological assessment approaches. *Journal of Clinical and Experimental Neuropsychology, 12,* 963– 978.

Castaneda, A. D., Suvisaari, J., Marttunen, M., Peerala, J., Saarni, S. I., Aalto-Setala, T., et al. (2008a). Cognitive functioning in a population-based sample of young adults with a history of non-psychotic unipolar depressive disorders without psychiatric comorbidity. *Journal of Affective Disorders, 110,* 36–45.

Castaneda, A. E., Tuulio-Henriksson, A., Marttunen, M., Suvisaari, J., & Lonnqvist, J. (2008b). A review on cognitive impairments in depressive and anxiety disorders with a focus on young adults. *Journal of Affective Disorders, 106,* 1–27.

Chamberlain, S. R., Blackwell, A. D., Fineberg, N. A., Robbins, T. W., & Sahakian, B. J. (2005). The neuropsychology of obsessive-compulsive disorder: The importance of failures in cognitive and behavioural inhibition as candidate enophenotypic markers. *Neuroscience and Biobehavioral Reviews, 29,* 399–419.

Chow, T.W., & Cummings, J. L. (1999). Frontal-subcortical circuits. In Miller B. L., & Cummings J. L. (Eds.), *The human frontal lobes* (pp. 3–26). New York: Guilford Press.

Cicerone, K. D., Dahlberg, C., Kalmar, K., Langenbahn, D. M., Malec, J. F., Bergquist, T. F., et al. (2000). Evidence-based cognitive rehabilitation: Recommendations for clinical practice. *Archives of Physical Medicine and Rehabilitation, 81,* 1596–1615.

Cicerone, K. D., Dahlberg, C., Malec, J. F., Langenbahn, D. M., Felicetti, T., Kneipp, S., et al. (2005). Evidence-based cognitive rehabilitation: Updated review of the literature from 1998 through 2002. *Archives of Physical Medicine and Rehabilitation, 86,* 1681–1692.

Cicerone, K. D., & Kalmar, K. (1995). Persistent postconcussion syndrome: The structure of subjective complaints after mild traumatic brain injury. *Journal of Head Trauma Rehabilitation, 10,* 1–17.

Clark, L., Sarna, A., & Goodwin, G. (2005). Impairment of executive function but not memory in first-degree relatives of patients with bipolar I disorder and euthymic patients with unipolar depression. *American Journal of Psychiatry, 162,* 1980–1982.

Cummings, J. L., & Mega, M. S. (2003). *Neuropsychiatry and behavioral neuroscience. New York:* Oxford University Press.

Darby, D., Maruff, P., Collie, A., & McStephen, M. (2002). Mild cognitive impairment can be detected by multiple assessments in a single day. *Neurology, 59,* 1042–1046.

Delis, D. C., & Wetter, S. R. (2007). Cogniform disorder and cogniform condition: Proposed diagnosis for excessive cognitive symptoms. *Archives of Clinical Neuropsychology, 22,* 589–604.

Depp, C. A., Moore, D. J., Sitzer, D., Palmer, B. W., Eyler, L. T., Roesch, S., et al. (2007). Neurocognitive impairment in middle-aged and older adults with bipolar disorder: Comparison to schizophrenia and normal comparison subjects. *Journal of Affective Disorders, 101,* 210–209.

Dickie, E. W., Brunet, A., Akerib, V., & Armony, J. L. (2008). An fMRI investigation of memory encoding in PTSD: Influence of symptom severity. *Neuropsychologia, 46,* 1522–1531.

Dotson, V. A., Resnick, S. M., & Zonderman, A. B. (2008). Differential association of concurrent, baseline, and average depressive symptoms with cognitive decline in older adults. *American Journal of Geriatric Psychiatry, 16,* 318–330.

Duff, K., Beglinger, L. J., Schultz, S. K., Moser, D. J., McCaffrey, R. J., Haase, R. F., et al., & Huntington's Study Group. (2007). Practice effects in the prediction of long-term cognitive outcome in three patient samples: A novel prognostic index. *Archives of Clinical Neuropsychology, 22,* 15–24.

Duff, K., Beglinger, L. J., Vand Der Heiden, S., Moser, D. J., Arndt, S., Schultz, S. K., & Paulsen, J. S. (2008). Short-term practice effects in amnestic mild cognitive impairment: Implications for diagnosis and treatment. *International Psychogeriatrics, 20,* 986–999.

Elderkin-Thompson, V., Kumar, A., Bilker, W. B., Dunkin, J. J., Mintz, J., Moberg, P. J., et al. (2003). Neuropsychological deficits among patients with late-onset minor and major depression. *Archives of Clinical Neuropsychology, 18,* 529–549.

Fertuck, E. A., Marsano-Jozefowicz, S., Stanley, B., Tryon, W. W., Oquendo, M., Mann, J. J., & Keilp, J. G. (2006). The impact of borderline personality disorder and anxiety on neuropsychological performance in major depression. *Journal of Personality Disorders, 20,* 55–70.

Golden, C. J., Purisch, A. D., Hammeke, T. A. (1991). *Luria-Nebraska Neuropsychological Battery: Forms I and II.* Los Angeles: Western Psychological Services.

Goldstein, G. (2001). Board certification in clinical neuropsychology: Some history, facts and opinions. *Journal of Forensic Neuropsychology, 2,* 57–65.

Golier, J. A., Harvey, P. D., Legge, J., & Yehuda, R. (2006). Memory performance in older trauma survivors: Implications for the longitudinal course of PTSD. *Annals of the New York Academy of Sciences, 1071,* 54–66.

Green, M. J., Cahill, C. M., & Malhi, G. S. (2007). The cognitive and neurophysiological basis of emotion dysregulation in bipolar disorder. *Journal of Affective Disorders, 103,* 29–42.

Greisberg, S., & McKay, D. (2003). Neuropsychology of obsessive-compulsive disorder: A review and treatment implications. *Clinical Psychology Review, 23,* 95–117.

Gruber, S., Rathgeber, K., Braunig, P., & Gauggel, S. (2007). Stability and course of neuropsychological deficits in manic and depressed bipolar patients compared to patients with Major Depression. *Journal of Affective Disorders, 104,* 61–71.

Gruber, S. A., Rosso, I. M., & Yurgelun-Todd, D. (2008). Neuropsychological performance predicts clinical recovery in bipolar patients. *Journal of Affective Disorders, 105,* 253–260.

Gualtieri, C. T., Johnson, L. G., & Benedict, B. (2006). Neurocognition in depression: Patients off medication versus healthy comparison subjects. *Journal of Neuropsychiatry and Clinical Neurosciences, 18,* 217–225.

Hannay, J. J., Bieliauskas, L. A., Crosson, B. A., Hammeke, T. A., Hamsher, K., & Koffler, S. P. (1998). The Houston Conference on specialty education and training in clinical neuropsychology. *Archives of Clinical Neuropsychology, Special Issue. 13*, 157–250.

Harris, C. L., & Dinn, W. M. (2003). Subtyping obsessive-compulsive disorder: Neuropsychological correlates. *Behavioural Neurology, 14*, 75–87.

Harlow, J. M. (1868). Recovery from the passage of an iron bar through the head. *Publications of the Massachusetts Medical Society, 2*, 327–347.

Harvey, P. D., Romero, M., Reichenberg, A., Granholm, E., & Siever, L. J. (2006). Dual-task information processing in schizotypal personality disorder: Evidence of impaired processing capacity. *Neuropsychology, 20*, 453–460.

Heaton, R. K., Miller, W., Taylor, M. J., & Grant, I. (2004). *Revised comprehensive norms for an expanded Halstead-Reitan Battery: Demographically adjusted neuropsychological norms for African American and Caucasian adults. Professional manual.* Lutz, FL: Psychological Assessment Resources.

Hiatt, K. D., & Newman, J. P. (2006). Understanding psychopathy: The cognitive side. In C. J. Patrick (Ed.), *Handbook of Psychopathy* (pp. 334–352). New York: Guilford Press.

Hiatt, K. D., Schmitt, W. A., & Newman, J. P. (2004). Stroop tasks reveal abnormal selective attention among psychopathic offenders. *Neuropsychology, 18*, 50–59.

Horton, A. M., Crown, B. M., & Reynolds, C. R. (2001). American board of professional neuropsychology: An update–2001. *Journal of Forensic Neuropsychology, 2*, 67–78.

Hutchinson, L. J., Amler, R. W., Lybarger, J. A., & Chappell, W. (1992). *Neurobehavioral test battery for use in environmental health field studies.* Atlanta GA: Agency for Toxic Substances and Disease Registry, Public Health Service.

Jaeger, J., Berns, S., Uzelac, S., & Davis-Conway, S. (2006). Neurocognitive deficits and disability in major depressive disorder. *Psychiatry Research, 145*, 39–48.

Kim, M. S., Park S. J., Shin, M. S., & Kwon, J. S. (2002). Neuropsychological profile in patients with obsessive-compulsive disorder over a period of 4 month treatment. *Journal of Psychiatric Research, 36*, 257–265.

Koenen, D. C., Driver, K. L, Oscar-Berman, M., Wolfe, J., Folsom, S., Huang, M. T., & Schlesinger, L. (2001). Measures of prefrontal system dysfunction in posttraumatic stress disorder. *Brain and Cognition, 45*, 64–78.

Kuelz, A. K., Hohagen, F., & Voderhlozer, U. (2004). Neuropsychological performance in obsessive-compulsive disorder: A critical review. *Biological Psychiatry, 65*, 185–238.

Kunert, H. J., Druecke, H. W., Sass, H., & Herpertz, S. C. (2003). Frontal lobe dysfunction in borderline personality disorder? Neuropsychological findings. *Journal of Personality Disorders, 17*, 497–509.

Laatsch, L., Harrington, D., Hotz, G., Marcantuono, J., Mozzoni, M. P., Walsh, V., & Hersey, K. P. (2007). An evidence-based review of cognitive and behavioral rehabilitation treatment studies in children with acquired brain injury. *Journal of Head Trauma Rehabilitation, 22*, 248–256.

Larrabee, G. J. (2007). Commentary on Delis and Wetter, "Cogniform disorder and cogniform condition: Proposed diagnoses for excessive cognitive symptoms." *Archives of Clinical Neuropsychology, 27*, 683–687.

Legris, J., & van Reekum, R. (2006). The neuropsychological correlates of borderline personality disorder and suicidal behaviour. *Canadian Journal of Psychiatry, 51*, 131–142.

Lezak, M. D. (1995). *Neuropsychological assessment (3rd ed.).* New York: Oxford University Press.

Lezak, M. D., Howieson, D. B., & Loring, D. W. (2004). *Neuropsychological Assessment* (4th ed.). New York: Oxford University Press.

Lykken, D. T. (2006). Psychopathic personality: The scope of the problem. In C. J. Patrick (Ed.), *Handbook of psychopathy* (pp. 3–13). New York: Guilford Press.

Lynam, D. R., & Henry, B. (2001). The role of neuropsychological deficits in conduct disorders. In J. Hill & B. Maughan (Eds.), *Conduct disorders in childhood and adolescence* (pp. 235–263). New York: Cambridge University Press.

Malhi, G. S., Ivanovski, B., Hadzi-Pavlovic, D., Mitchell, P. B., Vieta, E., & Sachdev, P. (2007). Neuropsychological deficits and functional impairment in bipolar depression, hypomania and euthymia. *Bipolar Disorders, 9*, 114–125.

Marder, S. R. (2006). Initiatives to promote the discovery of drugs to improve cognitive function in severe mental illness. *Journal of Clinical Psychiatry, 67* (Suppl 9), 31–35.

Martinez-Aran, A., Vieta, E., Torrent, C., Sanchez-Moreno, J., Goikolea, J. M., Salamero, M., et al. (2007). Functional outcome in bipolar disorder: The role of clinical and cognitive factors. *Bipolar Disorder, 9*, 103–113.

Matsui, M., Sumiyoshi, T., Kato, K., Yoneyama, E., & Kurachi, M. (2004). Neuropsychological profile in patients with schizotypal personality disorder or schizophrenia. *Psychological Reports, 94*, 387–397.

McCaffrey, R. J., Bauer, L., O'Bryant, S. E., & Palav, A. (2006). *Practitioner's guide to symptom base rates in the general population.* New York: Springer.

McCaffrey, R. J., Duff, K., & Westervelt, H. J. (2000a). *Practitioner's guide to evaluating change with neuropsychological assessment instruments.* New York: Kluwer Academic/Plenum Publishers.

McCaffrey, R. J., Duff, K., & Westervelt, H. J. (2000b). *Practitioner's guide to evaluating change with neuropsychological intellectual assessment instruments.* New York: Kluwer Academic/Plenum Publishers.

McCaffrey, R. J., Palav, A., O'Bryant, S. E., Labarge, A. S. (2003). *Practitioner's guide to symptom base rates in clinical neuropsychology.* New York: Kluwer Academic/Plenum Publishers.

McGurk, S. R., Twamley, E. W., Sitzer, D. I., McHugo, G. J., & Mueser, K. T. (2007). A meta-analysis of cognitive remediation in schizophrenia. *American Journal of Psychiatry, 164*, 1791–1802.

Meier, M. J. (1981). Education for competency assurance in human neuropsychology: Antecedents, models, and directions. In S. B. Filskov & T. J. Boll (Eds.), *Handbook of clinical neuropsychology.* New York: Wiley.

Mitchell, D. G. V., Colledge, E., Leonard, A., & Blair, R. J. R. (2002). Risky decisions and response reversal: Is there evidence or orbitofrontal cortex dysfunction in psychopathic individuals? *Neuropsychologia, 40*, 2013–2022.

Mitropoulou, V., Harvey, P. D., Maldari, L. A., Moriarty, P. J., New, A. S., Silverman, J. M., & Siever, L. J. (2002). Neuropsychological performance in schizotypal personality disorder: Evidence regarding diagnostic specificity. *Biological Psychiatry, 52*, 1175–1182.

Mitropoulou, V., Harvey, P. D., Zegarelli, G., New, A. S., Silverman, J. M., & Siever, L. J. (2005). Neuropsychological performance in schizotypal personality disorder: Importance of working memory. *American Journal of Psychiatry, 162*, 1896–1903.

Monarch, E. S., Saykin, A. J., & Flashman, L. A. (2004). Neuropsychological impairment in borderline personality disorder. *Psychiatric Clinics of North America, 27*, 67–82.

Morgan, A. B., & Lilienfeld, S. O. (2000). A meta-analytic review of the relation between antisocial behavior and neuropsychological measures of executive function. *Clinical Psychology Review, 20*, 113–136.

Moriarty, P. J., Harvey, P. D., Mitropoulou, V., Granholm, E., Silverman, J. M., & Siever, L. J. (2003). Reduced processing resource availability in schizotypal personality disorder: Evidence from a dual-task CPT study. *Journal of Clinical and Experimental Neuropsychology, 25*, 335–347.

Mur, M., Portella, M. J., Martinez-Aran, A., Pifarre, J., & Vieta, E. (2007). Persistent neuropsychological deficit in euthymic bipolar patients: Executive function as a core deficit. *Journal of Clinical Psychiatry, 68*, 1078–1086.

Naismith, S. L., Hickie, I B., Turner, K., Little, C. L., Winter, V., Ward, P. B., et al. (2003). Neuropsychological performance in patients with depression is associated with clinical, etiological and genetic risk factors. *Journal of Clinical and Experimental Neuropsychology, 25*, 866–877.

Neu, P., Bajbouj, M., Schilling, A., Godemann, F., Berman, R. M., & Schlattmann, P. (2005). Cognitive function over the treatment course of depression in middle-aged patients: Correlation with brain MRI signal hyperintensities. *Journal of Psychiatric Research, 39*, 129–135.

Paelecke-Habermann, Y., Pohl, J., & Leplow, B. (2005). Attention and executive impairment in remitted major depression patients. *Journal of Affective Disorders, 89*, 125–135.

Penades, R., Catalan, R., Andres, S., Salamero, M., & Gasto, C. (2005). Executive function and nonverbal memory in obsessive-compulsive disorder. *Psychiatry Research, 133*, 81–90.

Raine, A., Loeber, R., Stouthamer-Loeber, M., Moffitt, T. E., Caspi, T. E., & Lynam, D. (2005). Neurocognitive impairments in boys on the life-course persistent antisocial path. *Journal of Abnormal Psychology, 114*, 38–49.

Randolph, C. (1998). *RBANS manual: Repeatable Battery for the Assessment of Neuropsychological Status*. San Antonio, TX: The Psychological Corporation.

Rao, N. P., Janardhan, Y. C., Kumar, K. J., Kandavel, T., & Chandrashekar, D. R. (2008). Are neuropsychological deficits trait markers of OCD? *Progress in Neuropsychopharmacology and Biological Psychiatry, 32*, 1574–1579.

Reitan, R. M., Hom, J., Van De Voorde, J., Stanczak, E. D., Wolfson, D. (2004). The Houston conference revisited. *Archives of Clinical Neuropsychology, 19*, 375–390.

Reitan, R. M., & Wolfson, D. (1993). *The Halstead-Reitan Neuropsychological Test Battery: Theory and clinical applications* (2nd ed.). Tucson, AZ: Neuropsychology Press.

Roelofs, K., van Galen, G. P., Eling, P., Keijsers, G. P. J., & Hoogduin, C. A. L. (2003). Endogenous and exogenous attention in patients with conversion paresis. *Cognitive Neuropsychology, 30*, 733–745.

Roh, K. S., Shin, M. S., Kim, M. S., Ha, T. H., Shin, Y. W., Lee, K. J., & Kwon, J. S. (2005). Persistent cognitive dysfunction in patients with obsessive-compulsive disorder: A naturalistic study. *Psychiatry and Clinical Neurosciences, 59*, 539–545.

Rourke, B. P., & Murji, S. (2000). A history of the international neuropsychological society: The early years (1965–1985). *Journal of the International Neuropsychological Society, 6*, 491–509.

Ruocco, A. C. (2005). The neuropsychology of borderline personality disorder: Meta-analysis and review. *Psychiatry Research, 137*, 191–202.

Schretlen, D. J., Munro, C. A., Anthony, J. C., & Pearlson, G. D. (2003). Examining the range of normal intraindividual variability in neuropsychological test performance. *Journal of the International Neuropsychological Society, 9*, 864–870.

Segalas, C., Alonso, P., Labad, J., Jauurrieta, N., Real, E., Jimenez, S., et al. (2008). Verbal and nonverbal memory processing in patients with obsessive-compulsive disorder: Its relationship to clinical variables. *Neuropsychology, 22*, 262–272.

Sierro M., & Berrios, G. E. (1999). Towards a neuropsychiatry of conversive hysteria. *Cognitive Neuropsychiatry, 4*, 267–287.

Siever, L. J., Koenigsberg, H. J., Harvey, P., Mitropoulou, V., Laruelle, M., Abi-Dargham, A., et al. (2002). Cognitive and brain function in schizotypal personality disorder. *Schizophrenia Research, 54*, 157–167.

Stern, R. A., & White, T. (2003). *Neuropsychological assessment battery*. Lutz, FL: Psychological Assessment Resources.

Strauss, E., Sherman, E. M. S., & Spreen. O. (2006). *A compendium of neuropsychological tests: Administration, norms, and commentary* (3rd ed.). New York: Oxford University Press.

Tabares-Seisdedos, R., Balanza-Martinez, V., Sanchez-Moreno, J., Martinez-Aran, A., Salazar-Fraile, J., Selva-Vera, G., et al. (2008). Neurocognitive and clinical predictors of functional outcome in patients with schizophrenia and bipolar I disorder at one-year follow-up. *Journal of Affective Disorders, 109*, 286–299.

Tallabs, F. A. (2005). Functional correlates of conversion and hypnotic paralysis: A neurophysiological hypothesis. *Contemporary Hypnosis, 22*, 184–192.

Torres, I. J., Boudreau, V. G., & Yatham, L. N. (2007). Neuropsychological functioning in euthymic bipolar disorder: A meta-analysis. *Acta Psychiatrica Scandinavica, 116*, 17–26.

Trotman, H., McMillan, A., & Walker, E. (2006). Cognitive function and symptoms in adolescents with schizotypal personality disorder. *Schizophrenia Bulletin, 32*, 489–497.

Vasterling, J. J., & Brailey, K. (2005). Neuropsychological findings in adults with PTSD. In J. J. Vasterling & C. R. Brewing (Eds.), *Neuropsychology of PTSD: Biological, cognitive and clinical perspectives* (pp. 178–207). New York: Guilford Press.

Voglmaier, M. M., Seidman, L. J., Niznikiewicz, M. A., Dickey, C. C., Shenton, M. E., & McCarley, R. W. (2005). A comparative profile analysis of neuropsychological function in men and woman with schizotypal personality disorder. *Schizophrenia Research, 74*, 43–49.

Weber, D. L., Clark, C. R., McFarlane, A. C., Moores, K. A., Morris, P., & Egan, G. F. (2005). Abnormal frontal and parietal activity during working memory updating in post-traumatic stress disorder. *Psychiatry Research, 140*, 27–44.

Weiland-Fiedler, P., Erickson, K., Waldeck, T., Luckenbaugh, D. A., Pike, D., Bonne, O., et al. (2004). Evidence of continuing neuropsychological impairments in depression. *Journal of Affective Disorders, 82*, 253–258.

Wexler, B. E., & Bell, M. D. (2005). Cognitive remediation and vocational rehabilitation for schizophrenia. *Schizophrenia Bulletin, 31*, 931–41.

Yehuda, R., Golier, J. A., Halligan, S. L., & Harvey, P. D. (2004). Learning and memory in holocaust survivors with post-traumatic stress disorder. *Biological Psychiatry, 55*, 291–295.

Yehuda, R., Golier, J. A., Tischler, L., Stavitsky, K., & Harvey, P. D. (2005). Learning and memory in aging combat veterans with PTSD. *Journal of Clinical and Experimental Neuropsychology, 27*, 504–515.

Psychological Interventions in Health-care Settings

Charles F. Emery, Derek R. Anderson, *and* Barbara L. Andersen

Abstract

Beginning in the 1980s, clinical psychologists have made significant contributions to the development, testing, and dissemination of psychological interventions for individuals undergoing stressful medical treatments or coping with chronic illness. This has been important, as there are elevated rates of mood and anxiety disorders among medical patients. Addressing the needs of patients with coronary heart disease (CHD), cancer, and cardio-pulmonary disease (COPD) is discussed. As is the case generally, cognitive behavior therapy (CBT), tailored to the specific medical illness/treatment circumstances of patients, plays a central role. More broadly, psychologists have been influential in contributing empirically based strategies to improve the health of all Americans. Effective behavior change methods for smoking cessation, dietary change, and increasing physical activity and improving fitness reduce morbidity and mortality and, of course, are key to reducing health-care costs. Thus, we urge psychological assessment and intervention as one element of standard, comprehensive, health care.

Keywords: Cancer, coronary, health behavior, psychological, stress

Medical advances of the 20th century have resulted in an increasing proportion of older adults (i.e., >65 years) in the United States. As the U.S. population ages, more and more health-care resources are needed for the management of chronic disease. In response, behavioral interventions in health-care settings have addressed psychological and behavioral correlates of chronic health problems. Coronary heart disease (CHD) and cancer are the leading causes of death, not only in the United States but also throughout the world. Long-term management of these and other conditions is required to reduce premature mortality and prevent associated morbidities. For example, comorbid mood and/or anxiety disorders are common among patients with either CHD or cancer. This chapter provides an overview of behavioral interventions used in health-care settings. We focus upon CHD and cancer and interventions designed to modify health behaviors (e.g., exercise, smoking) in any individual.

Coronary Heart Disease

From their astute clinical observations, cardiologists Friedman and Rosenman provided an early (1964) test of the role of behavioral/psychological factors and the progression of CHD in their Western Collaborative Group Study (Rosenman et al., 1964). Assessing over 3,500 men, their conception and operationalization of the Type A behavior pattern (TABP) was both novel and innovative. Their finding that individuals with TABP were subsequently found to have a significantly higher incidence of CHD directed the next three decades of behavioral medicine research. Behavioral interventions for cardiac patients began with a focus on the modification of cardiac risk factors and TABP. A large randomized clinical trial (RCT), the Recurrent Coronary Prevention Project (RCPP), compared a cognitive-behavioral intervention for TABP and relaxation training to no treatment with 862 post-myocardial infarction (MI) patients (Friedman et al., 1986).

Significantly lower rates of recurrent cardiac events were found for the intervention arm. Moreover, intervention participants showed decreases in TABP (i.e., reduced hostility, time urgency, impatience), improved mood, and increases in self-efficacy (Mendes de Leon, Powell, & Kaplan, 1991).

Subsequent RCTs of interventions to reduce hostility or psychological distress generally have revealed positive outcomes for CHD patients, reducing either cardiac symptoms or psychological distress. Gidron et al. (1999) found that a hostility-reduction intervention for men with CHD was associated with lower hostility and diastolic blood pressure when compared with a group receiving information only. Cowan and colleagues (2001) found that psychosocial therapy for 129 survivors of sudden cardiac arrest was associated with reduced risk of cardiac death. The intervention included 11 individual sessions with three components: physiologic relaxation with biofeedback training focused on altering autonomic tone; cognitive-behavioral therapy (CBT) aimed at self-management and coping strategies for depression, anxiety, and anger; and cardiovascular health education.

Interventions for Symptoms of Depression and Anxiety

During the past two decades, attention has shifted from TABP per se to the prognostic importance of stress and/or depression in CHD onset. Both epidemiologic and smaller RCTs have provided supporting data. The INTERHEART study of more than 30,000 adults worldwide, for example, indicated that psychosocial stress was associated with elevated risk of MI (Rosengren et al., 2004). Other data show that, among depressed individuals, there is a 65% increased risk of CHD; and among patients with CHD who are depressed, the risk of death is two to five times higher than normal risk estimates (Carney et al., 1988). It is not surprising that a high prevalence of anxiety disorders exists among patients with CHD (Todaro, Shen, Raffa, Tilkemeier, & Niaura, 2007), as the two disorders are often comorbid. In fact, anxiety symptoms alone have been found to predict MIs in men, independent of other psychological factors including depression, hostility, and TABP (Shen et al., 2008). Thus, treatment of depression and, more recently, anxiety has become a focus in rehabilitation efforts with CHD patients with the added possibility of preventing disease progression.

A second generation of trials has targeted post-MI patients who are at high risk for future events due to elevated depression or low social support. The Enhancing Recovery in Coronary Heart Disease (ENRICHD) trial enlisted 2,481 post-MI patients with elevated depressive symptom levels and/or low social support. Patients were randomized to receive CBT or usual medical care (Berkman et al., 2003). Cognitive-behavioral therapy was provided in individual sessions over a 6-month period (median of 11 sessions) or in a group format with relaxation training (approximately one-third of sample). Psychotropic medication (selective serotonin reuptake inhibitors, SSRIs) was also used for those with severe depressive symptoms at study entry or nonremission of symptoms during the initial 5 weeks. At 6 months post-treatment, patients in the intervention arm had significantly fewer symptoms of depression and increased social support. Longer follow-up (29 months average) showed no effect of the intervention on event-free survival. Several secondary analyses have been published. One, evaluating sex and racial group differences, showed a reduced incidence of cardiac death and nonfatal MI, but in white men only (Schneiderman et al., 2004). Another reported that patients with indicated low social support upon study entry had higher rates of death or recurrent MI, but the intervention was most effective for patients who entered the study with moderate levels of social support (Burg et al., 2005). Last, another secondary analysis indicated that standard components of CBT were effective in reducing depressive symptoms in the post-MI patients but did not appear to influence low social support (Cowan et al., 2008).

Rather than a psychological treatment, post-MI patients are often referred to exercise-based cardiac rehabilitation (CR), usually for 36 sessions (3 times a week for 12 weeks). As an adjunct, psychological interventions are also beneficial. Black and colleagues (1998) offered behavior therapy (one to seven sessions) to distressed patients entering cardiac rehabilitation following hospitalization for angina, MI, angioplasty, or coronary artery bypass graft (CABG) surgery ($N = 60$). Compared to no treatment (usual care) controls, intervention patients had significant reductions in depressive symptoms. Upon completion of CR, patients are routinely encouraged to maintain the lifestyle changes (e.g., increased physical activity, reduced fat intake, managing life stress) that have been instituted in CR, but there are few studies evaluating post-CR interventions. One multicenter, RCT evaluated patients at 3-year follow-up (Giannuzzi et al., 2008). MI patients ($N = 3,240$) were randomized to receive continued educational and behavioral intervention or usual care. Analyses showed the intervention arm to have significantly better health behaviors (i.e., exercise, diet), lower psychosocial stress, and less use of prescription drugs than did patients in the control arm.

Telephone-based Interventions

Telephone-based interventions may offer a less costly strategy for psychological treatment of cardiac patients. The Montreal Heart Attack Readjustment Trial (M-HART) (Frasure-Smith et al., 1997) was one of the first such trials. Post-MI patients ($N = 1,376$) were randomized to telephone intervention or standard care arms. Intervention participants received a call 1 week following hospital discharge and then monthly for 12 months. Any participant readmitted to the hospital or reporting significant psychological distress on the routinely administered General Health Questionnaire (GHQ) was then scheduled for a 1-hour home visit by a cardiology nurse who provided education, advice, reassurance, and referrals if necessary. The majority of patients (75%) in the intervention arm received five to six nurse visits. Outcome results indicated no study arm differences on cardiac mortality, all-cause mortality, or psychological outcomes. Oddly (and unfortunately), women in the intervention arm had higher all-cause mortality than did women in the control condition. Secondary analyses were conducted of 433 patients (36.0% women) from the M-HART treatment group who received two home visits after achieving a high psychological distress score (i.e., ≥ 5) on the GHQ. Patients with short-term reductions in GHQ scores were less likely to have high depression and anxiety at 1-year than were patients who did not experience short-term reductions (Cossette, Frasure-Smith, & Lesperance, 2001).

A pre-post, single-group study was conducted in Australia by Gallagher and colleagues (2003) among women ($N = 196$) who were hospitalized for coronary artery disease (myocardial infarction, CABG, coronary angioplasty, or unstable angina). During the 12-week intervention period, participants received telephone calls at 1, 2, 3, and 6 weeks after discharge from a nurse credentialed in cardiac rehabilitation and counseling. Analyses showed significant improvements in patients' psychosocial adjustment, as well as reductions in anxiety and depressive symptoms. Correlates of poor psychosocial outcomes included younger age (<55), being unemployed or retired, having poor psychosocial adjustment to illness at baseline, being readmitted to the hospital, or experiencing a stressful, personal event during follow-up.

Bambauer and colleagues (2005) enlisted 79 cardiac patients with mild to severe depression or anxiety (based on scores from the Hospital Anxiety and Depression Scale, HADS) 1 month following hospital discharge. Patients were randomized to usual care or to an intervention in which they received up to six 30-minute telephone counseling sessions focused on identifying cardiac-related fears. Results showed the intervention group had significantly greater improvements in self-rated health between baseline and 3 months post treatment, but there were no group differences at the 6-month follow-up.

Thus, the data regarding telephone interventions are equivocal. The M-HART data suggested that the telephone intervention may have inadvertently increased distress among some patients, especially women. The Gallagher et al. study indicates overall benefit, but notes lack of benefit in specific subgroups of patients who were relatively younger, unemployed, with low social support at study outset. The Bambauer data suggest that the benefits of a telephone-based intervention may be short-lived.

Additional Treatment Considerations Among Cardiac Patients

Other approaches to reducing physical and psychological symptoms and enhancing quality of life have been utilized. Relaxation training appears to benefit cardiac functioning (e.g., reduced heart rate, increased heart rate variability, increased exercise capacity, reduced angina) as well as reduce cardiac morbidity and mortality (van Dixhoorn & White, 2005). Stress management interventions are associated with reduced incidence of both fatal and nonfatal MI (Rees, Bennett, West, Davey, & Ebrahim, 2004). Blumenthal and colleagues (2005) found that stress management training was as effective as exercise training in enhancing cardiovascular response to stress among patients with ischemic heart disease. Manchanda and colleagues (2000) found that a short-term, intensive yoga intervention was associated with stabilization of coronary stenosis and reduction of cardiac morbidity among patients with CHD. In addition, musical stimulation during cardiac catheterization has been associated with reduced symptoms of anxiety in comparison to standard care (Argstatter, Haberbosch, & Bolay, 2006). Listening to music has been found to reduce symptoms of anxiety, as well as reduce heart rate and systolic blood pressure among patients awaiting cardiac catheterization (Hamel, 2001). However, among patients who had had cardiac surgery during the prior 24 hours, listening to music was found to have no effect on anxiety, pain, heart rate, respiratory rate, or oxygen saturation (Nilsson, 2009).

The preponderance of research in cardiac disease has been conducted with male samples. However, recent studies suggest gender differences in distress and social support that may be relevant to recovery (Emery et al., 2004; Janevic et al., 2004; Janz et al., 2001). Some studies suggest gender differences in response to behavioral treatments, whereas others do not. Michalsen and colleagues (2005) found that women were more likely than men to benefit from stress reduction/lifestyle modification on dimensions of depression and anger, and Janz and colleagues (2004) found reduced stress at 4-month follow-up among women with heart disease who had participated in a 6-week disease management intervention versus usual care. Yet, a RCT of a 1-year stress management program for 247 women with CHD found no effect of the intervention on depressive symptoms or vital exhaustion at the end of the intervention (Koertge et al., 2008). As noted earlier, the secondary analyses of ENRICHD data (Schneiderman et al., 2004) revealed that the intervention had no effect in reducing cardiac death and nonfatal MI among women. Thus, testing for the existence of gender differences (and exploring the biobehavioral mechanisms for such effects) is a fertile area for further research.

Illness knowledge may be another critical component associated with psychological well-being among cardiac patients. McKinley and colleagues (2009) conducted a randomized study of the effect of an educational counseling intervention on knowledge, attitudes, and beliefs about acute cardiac symptoms and their treatment among 3,522 patients with CHD. Results indicated that knowledge, attitudes, and beliefs scores increased significantly from baseline in the intervention group compared to the control group at 3 months and were sustained at 12 months. Higher perceived control over cardiac illness was associated with more positive attitudes, and higher state anxiety was associated with lower levels of knowledge, attitudes, and beliefs (McKinley et al., 2009). However, the effect of illness knowledge may be moderated by personality or coping style. Specifically, illness knowledge has been associated with greater distress among women with CHF who engage in repressive coping (i.e., tend to avoid experiencing negative emotions; Jackson & Emery, (in press) and with greater sleep disturbance, depression, and tension among post-MI men and women who engage in repressive coping (Shaw et al., 1985).

Conclusion

Stress management appears to be beneficial for improving cardiac function and reducing cardiac mortality. The data underscore the importance of evaluating depression and anxiety among patients with CHD, as well as instructing patients with depression and anxiety disorders that they may be at elevated risk of developing CHD. Cognitive-behavioral therapy is the most efficacious psychological treatment for depression, but studies suggest that other components, such as those for improving patients' social support networks, are important and need to be included. It is not clear if telephone-based supportive and educational interventions are beneficial and in fact, may be contraindicated for some. Only subgroups of patients may benefit, such as those receptive to receiving information. Adjunctive treatments, such as listening to music and relaxation training, also appear to be helpful. Thus, the data present a complex picture in which CBT is a central approach, which is then tailored to best meet patient needs.

Cancer

Psychological interventions are efficacious for reducing cancer stress (Andersen, 1992, 2002; Meyer & Mark, 1995). Interventions have varied from study to study (Goodwin et al., 2001; Spiegel, Bloom, Kraemer, & Gottheil, 1989); however, commonalities have included some form of active stress reduction (e.g., progressive muscle relaxation, guided imagery), information about the disease and treatment, an emotionally supportive context for treatment (with the "component" often being treatment in a group format), behavioral coping strategies (e.g., seeking information), cognitive-behavioral strategies (e.g., cognitive reframing, problem solving), and site-specific interventions (e.g., sun protection for melanoma patients). Despite their importance, components for improving health behaviors (Fawzy et al., 1990; Lepore, Helgeson, Eton, & Schulz, 2003) or adherence (Richardson et al., 1987) are usually not included.

Psychosocial Interventions

Randomized clinical trials have typically contrasted intervention and control arms (e.g., no intervention, waitlist, usual care) and accrued patients unscreened for psychiatric disorders. With such patients, meta-analyses show interventions to be generally effective, with larger effect sizes for patients with the greatest level of distress (Schneider et al., 2010) and for treating symptoms of anxiety versus depression (Sheard & Maguire, 1999). Using the Brief Symptom Inventory with over 8,000 patients newly diagnosed or beginning a new therapy (e.g. start of chemotherapy), BrintzenhofeSzoc and colleagues (2009) estimated that there were clinical levels of mood- or anxiety-related symptoms for approximately 30% of patients. Of the latter, they estimated depressive symptoms for 4%–9% and anxious symptoms for 8%–15%, with the largest percentage of patients, 10%–20%, having a mixed-symptom presentation. Other data show that both anxiety and depressive symptoms have independent, additive effects on impaired health-related quality of life (Brown, Kroenke, Theobals, Wu, & Tu, (2010).

Thus, mental health disorders among cancer patients occur at higher than expected base rates. In both early and recent surveys, it is estimated that 30% of patients studied met criteria for mood or anxiety disorders (Burgess et al., 2005; Derogatis & Melisaratos, 1983; Zabora, BrintzenhofeSzoc, Curbow, Hooker, & Piantadosi, 2001). Estimates for major depressive disorder (MDD) are 22%–29% for patients with early stage (stage I) disease (Raison & Miller, 2003) and 8%–40% for patients with advanced disease (stage II/III, or IV; Hotopf, Chidgey, Addington-Hall, & Ly, 2002), and the rates increase further with recurrence (Burgess et al., 2005). For the most common sites of disease, such as breast and gynecologic cancers for women, Zabora and colleagues (2001) found the prevalence of MDD to be 33% and 30%, respectively. Data suggest the numbers of patients with anxiety disorders to be lower, approximately 18%, with generalized anxiety disorder (GAD) being the most common disorder (Stark et al., 2002). As is the case for those without concurrent physical illness, depression and anxiety co-occur among cancer patients. Thirty-eight percent of cancer patients found to have anxiety disorders by Stark and colleagues (2002) also had MDD.

Intervention efficacy for cancer patients with comorbid depressive or anxiety disorders is unclear, due in part to the few trials conducted. To our knowledge, only seven of more than 200 RCTs either screened patients for clinical levels of distress or did not screen but did assess for psychiatric diagnoses. Across studies, the interventions were varied. A methodologically strong, early study was conducted by Telch and Telch (1986), who screened patients for high distress, and compared CBT to support group and control arms. The CBT group was most effective in reducing distress, and this was one of the few studies in the literature showing the control group to worsen. Moorey and colleagues (1998) enlisted patients diagnosed with an adjustment reaction and found problem-focused CBT to significantly reduce depressive and anxiety symptoms compared to supportive counseling. Simpson and colleagues (2002) provided group treatment combining stress management and goal setting for breast cancer patients, 26% of whom had depressive or anxiety disorders, and found no significant improvement. Using a psychosocial group intervention with stage I/II breast cancer patients, 36% of whom had depressive or anxiety disorders, Kissane and colleagues (2003) reported no improvement in depressive symptoms but a trend toward reductions in anxiety symptomatology when using the supportive expressive therapy described earlier by Spiegel and colleagues (1989).

However, Kissane and colleagues (2003) reported positive outcomes of supportive-expressive therapy offered to breast cancer patients with metastasis, 32% of whom had a comorbid mood disorder. The intervention significantly reduced hopelessness and traumatic stress, improved social functioning, and ameliorated some mood disorders and prevented the emergence of new ones. To treat insomnia, Savard and colleagues (2005) offered stimulus control/sleep hygiene and cognitive restructuring and reported significantly improved sleep patterns and reduced depressed moods for breast cancer patients, 56% of whom had a psychiatric disorder. Although not determining psychiatric diagnoses per se, Nezu and colleagues (2003) enlisted breast cancer patients scoring within the clinical range on the Hamilton Interview for depression. They found individual problem-solving therapy to have positive effects across depression, distress, and quality-of-life outcomes.

In summary, suggestive support exists for the effectiveness of general psychosocial interventions among cancer patients with psychopathology. These interventions are tailored to help patients with the immediate, overwhelming stress of cancer. Such interventions "normalize" patients' worries, fears, and concerns. They offer active, behavioral-change strategies to cope, such as encouragement to seek information or ask their oncologist questions about the disease or treatment. Coping strategies such as progressive relaxation are taught to reduce the psychological and physiologic manifestations of anxiety and to prevent or reduce symptoms, such as nausea or fatigue from cancer treatments. These strategies may have efficacy equaling standard therapy for mood or anxiety disorders, such as CBT, but no trials have tested this possibility.

Biobehavioral Interventions

More recent treatments emphasize stress reduction, inclusion of some CBT elements (e.g., problem solving, assertive communication), and cancer-specific interventions for improving health behaviors and compliance with cancer therapies (Andersen, Golden-Kreutz, Emery, & Thiel, 2009). Based on the Biobehavioral Model of Cancer Stress and Disease Course (Andersen, Kiecolt-Glaser and Glaser, 1994), an RCT showed breast cancer patients (N = 227) randomized to the biobehavioral intervention (BBI) to have significant reductions in emotional distress, increases in social support from family members, improved diet, reduced variability in chemotherapy dose intensity, improved immunity (increased T cell blastogenesis), fewer signs/symptoms and treatment toxicities, and higher functional status. This same intervention appears to have stemmed disease progression. After a median of 11 years of follow-up, analyses showed that the intervention arm had a reduced risk of breast cancer recurrence (hazard ratio [HR] 0.55, p = 0.034) compared to the assessment-only arm (Andersen et al., 2008). Follow-up analyses also showed a reduced risk of breast cancer death following recurrence (HR, 0.41; P=0.014) (Andersen et al., 2010).

According to data supporting the Biobehavioral model, the acute stress occurring at the time of cancer diagnosis, if left untreated, can contribute a stable, lower quality of life (Golden-Kreutz et al., 2005), depressive symptoms (Golden-Kreutz & Andersen, 2004), and less meaning in patients' lives (Jim, Richardson, Golden-Kruetz, & Andersen, 2006). Data have also consistently shown cancer stress to covary with biological effects. Early data showed stress at diagnosis (Andersen et al., 1998) to covary with downregulated T blastogenesis and natural killer cell cytotoxicity (NKCC). Longitudinal data showed that these relationships remained for as long as 2 years after diagnosis.

This stress–immune trajectory may be of even greater relevance for cancer patients with comorbid psychiatric disorders. In fact, stress-related biologic alterations can elicit symptoms consistent with depressive or anxiety disorders. Immune activation has been hypothesized as a causal factor in depression, as proinflammatory cytokines have been shown to produce "sickness behaviors," such as fatigue, lethargy, anorexia, and low mood (Anisman & Merali, 2003).

Anxiety, too, is correlated with immune and endocrine function (Stein, Keller, & Schleifer, 1988). Both depression and anxiety are believed to contribute to further dysregulation of the HPA axis, an overactive inflammatory response, and decreased cellular immunity (Elenkov, Iezzoni, Daly, Harris, & Chrousos, 2005; Pace, Hu, & Miller, 2007; Stein et al., 1988; Zorrilla et al., 2001). Thus, cancer patients facing diagnosis with a comorbid psychiatric disorder may show evidence of a robust downregulation of immunity.

Other aspects of depression may be additionally important in the context of cancer. Negative health behaviors, such as smoking, can increase during period of stress, and when increased, they covary with a downward trend in immunity (Jung & Irwin, 1999; McAllister-Sistilli et al., 1998). Alternatively, if depressed patients engage in positive health behaviors, such as exercise, immunity may be enhanced and mood improved (Blumenthal et al., 1999; Stathopoulou et al., 2006; Trivedi, Greer, Grannemann, Chambliss, & Jordan, 2006). Another behavioral factor of possible importance is treatment adherence, as depression is a correlate of low of compliance (Lebovits, Strain, Schleifer, Tanaka, Bhardwaj, & Messe, 1990; McDonough, Boyd, Varvares, & Maves, 1996). In summary, patients with comorbid disorders are at greater risk for high rates of negative and low rates of positive health behaviors and lowered treatment adherence. Moreover, they are at risk for higher levels of morbidity (Delgado-Guay, Parsons, Li, Palmer, & Bruera, 2009) and poorer survival (Chida, Hamer, Wardle, & Steptoe, 2008).

Secondary analyses from the biobehavioral trial just described examined the applicability of the BBI to patients with comorbid psychopathology. Approximately 25% (N = 45 of 227) of the patients reported clinically significant depressive symptoms (i.e., CES-D short-form scores $\geq$10). Twenty-two patients (54%) were randomized to the assessment arm and the remaining 23 (44%) to the intervention arm. Using linear mixed-effects models and controlling for baseline levels, the BBI significantly reduced depressive symptoms as well as measures of fatigue and impairments due to pain. The intervention was also associated with reductions in inflammation, as operationalized with measures of white blood cell (WBC) count, neutrophil count, and helper-to-suppressor ratio. Further analyses showed that reduced inflammation occurred via the reduction in depressive symptoms. Thus, the biobehavioral intervention effectively treated depressive symptoms, pain, and fatigue along with lowering inflammatory responses.

Conclusion

Depressive and anxiety disorders among cancer patients are prevalent, unrecognized, and untreated (Evans et al., 2005), and there is recent evidence of elevated suicide rates among cancer patients as well (Miller, Mogun, Azrael, Hempstead, & Solomon, 2008). In fact, data suggest that breast cancer patients have an increased risk of suicide for as long as 25 years following diagnosis (Schairer et al., 2006). Interventions exist for treating psychological distress among cancer patients. To the extent that both CBT and psychosocial treatments have independent, active components, a combination treatment may be most effective overall. The "cognitive" component (i.e., addressing the disorder-specific cognitive diathesis, identifying and evaluating depressive/anxious cognitions, etc.) of CBT has been most often missing from cancer interventions. To the extent that psychosocial treatments additionally address the cognitive diatheses underlying psychopathologies and to the extent that traditional treatments, such as CBT, might additionally include disease-specific elements, a combination treatment could be more efficacious than either treatment alone. Regardless of the therapeutic model chosen, however, it is important that the professional community better address needs of cancer patients with comorbid psychopathology.

Other Chronic Illnesses: Chronic Obstructive Pulmonary Disease and Diabetes

Although estimates vary, patients with chronic obstructive pulmonary disease (COPD) often have symptoms of depression (6%–42% of patients in the community) or anxiety (2%–50%; Dowson et al., 2001; van Ede, Yzermans, & Brouwer, 1999; Kim et al., 2000). Symptomatic of both types are limitations in functional abilities and activities of daily living (Graydon & Ross, 1995; Kim et al., 2000; Weaver, Richmond, & Narsavage, 1997). Fortunately, CBT interventions are efficacious in reducing distress and enhancing quality of life among patients with COPD. For example, Kunik et al. (2001) offered a 2-hour intensive CBT session incorporating cognitive intervention and relaxation training, followed by brief weekly telephone calls to prompt practice of skills over a 6-week interval and reported significant reductions in symptoms of anxiety and depression for their COPD participants.

A single-group study of CBT led by nurses found significant decreases in patients' distress and in medical service use (Heslop, De Soyza, Baker, Stenton, & Burns, 2009). Interestingly, an RCT found reduced symptoms of depression in patients receiving 20 sessions of acupressure over a 5-week period (Wu, Lin, Wu, & Lin, 2007). However, a study of patient case management (Egan, Clavarino, Burridge, Teuwen, & White, 2002) and another using patient education (Hesselink et al., 2004) found null effects on indicators of distress or well-being. In summary, the available data, although limited, suggest that CBT interventions may be more effective in reducing distress among patients with COPD than are educational or symptom-management interventions.

Similar findings have been reported for CBT offerings for patients with type 2 diabetes. A trial by Lustman and colleagues (1998) found a 10-week program of CBT efficacious for patients with comorbid depression. Other CBT trials have reported increased self-efficacy, reduced distress and mood (van der Ven et al., 2005), as well as enhanced well-being, reduced diabetes-related distress, and reduced anxiety and depressive symptoms (Amsberg et al., 2009). In sum, CBT interventions among diabetic patients with depression or disease-related distress demonstrate promise as a nonpharmacologic means of reducing distress and depression.

Conclusion

Data support the utility of CBT for treatment of comorbid depression and anxiety among patients with COPD and diabetes. Cognitive-behavioral therapy interventions also are associated with further beneficial changes in psychosocial functioning (e.g., increased self-efficacy) and in physical functioning (e.g., reduced health care utilization). Thus, CBT appears to be an important treatment consideration among patients with chronic health conditions and comorbid psychological distress. Educational interventions do not appear to be useful in reducing depression-related distress. Complementary therapies (e.g., acupressure) may be beneficial for reducing psychological distress, but further research is needed.

Cross-cutting Strategies
Health Behavior Interventions for Medical Populations

Psychological and behavioral interventions for health behaviors, especially physical activity and tobacco use, have been studied extensively. These interventions have a two-fold benefit: reducing patients' morbidity and mortality and, thereby, lowering health-care costs. For some patients, a new chronic illness diagnosis may be the impetus to change one's health behaviors (Keenan, 2009). Diagnosis offers a "teachable moment" to encourage positive health behavior change (Keenan, 2009; Pagoto & Ockene, 2009). Increasingly, physicians are using the "five A's—Assessing, Advising, Agreeing on goals, Assisting the patient to get support, and Arranging follow-up—to facilitate health behavior change (Ockene et al., 1996).

Smoking

The research literature on smoking cessation is extensive. Unfortunately, diagnosis with CHD, COPD, or similar serious illnesses is not, for some, a sufficient reason to stop smoking. Results from minimal-care smoking cessation interventions (e.g., brief bedside counseling with minimal or no follow-up) yield only small effects (Bolman, de Vries & van Breukelen, 2002a,b), suggesting that perhaps more intensive intervention and follow-up is needed. The majority of the research shows that offering cardiac patients relatively brief interventions during their inpatient surgery stay with perhaps a telephone follow-up over ensuing weeks or months produce stronger outcomes.

In an early study, a nurse-led intervention for hospitalized cardiac patients found 61% of intervention arm patients to be abstinent at 12 months versus 32% of patients receiving usual care (Taylor, Houston-Miller, Killen, & Debusk, 1990). Data on intention to stop smoking were revealing: Patients who resumed smoking within 3 weeks after infarction or who expressed little intention to quit were, not surprisingly, unlikely to have stopped at the 12-month follow-up. Comparable positive outcomes have been found with an intervention of education and a focus on fear arousal and relapse prevention, showing a quit rate of 57% at 12 months following hospital admission versus a 37% quit rate among usual care controls (Quist-Paulsen & Gallefoss, 2003). Even more intensive interventions, however, yield outcomes within the same range. For example, provision of 60 minutes of bedside counseling with a nurse and with seven follow-up counseling calls for the 2 months following discharge resulted in 12-month abstinence in 54% of patients receiving advice to quit from physicians and nurses along with cessation educational materials (Smith & Burgess, 2009). Similar strategies and outcomes are found in studies of patients with COPD (Efraimsson, Hillervik, & Ehrenberg, 2008). However, the addition of motivational interviewing and related techniques during hospitalization may be more facilitative, especially when followed by supportive counseling. Across strategies, however, cessation is more likely when patients have a positive attitude toward quitting (Christenhusz, Pieterse, Seydel, & van der Palin, 2007).

As among cardiac and pulmonary patients, many cancer patients continue to smoke after diagnosis. This is especially concerning because there is evidence that smoking reduces the efficacy of chemotherapy and radiotherapy (Tsao, Liu, Lee, Spitz, & Hong, 2006; Videtic et al., 2003), slows surgical recovery (Shimizu, Nakata, Hirami, Maeda, & Tanemoto, 2008), impairs nutritional status (Gritz, 1991), affects performance status (Baser et al., 2006), and, in turn, increases the cost of medical care (Slatore, Au, & Hollingworth, 2009). A significant impediment to changing smoking behavior among cancer patients (as well as other patients) is the continuation of smoking among one's family. Unfortunately, rates of smoking cessation among relatives of patients with serious smoking-related disorders (e.g., lung or head/neck cancers) are only in the range of 7%–10% (Goksel, Ozol, Bayindir, & Guzelant., 2002). Thus, future smoking cessation efforts among medical patients should consider not only motivation among patients, but also the considerable influence of patients' familial and social networks (Christakis, 2004).

Physical Activity

The encouragement of exercise (or even simple increases in physical activity) is seen as increasingly important to facilitate recovery and lower morbidity for many chronic illness groups. In addition to the cardiac rehabilitation studies described earlier, other studies have tested the utility of exercise, per se, for cardiac patients. Arrigo et al. (2008) found patients' monitoring of their physical activity, in combination with quarterly group meetings, led to significantly more regular physical activity at 1-year follow-up than was observed in a standard treatment control group. Intervention patients also achieved reductions in their body mass index (BMI) and blood lipid levels. Similarly, two behavioral counseling and goal-setting sessions plus use of a pedometer for the next 6 weeks for patients who were completing CR resulted in increases in number and duration of physical activity and walking at treatment's end, as well as after 6 months; psychosocial functioning was also improved (Butler, Furber, Phongsavan, Mark, & Bauman, 2009). A larger trial, the Extensive Lifestyle Management Intervention, offered to patients completing CR found reductions in overall cardiac risk, total cholesterol, low-density lipoprotein (LDL) cholesterol, and systolic blood pressure (SBP). Surprisingly, no lifestyle differences were found between the intervention group and the usual-care control group (Lear et al., 2006). A similar trial with patients in Germany found that post-CR training in self-regulatory skills (exercise planning) led to greater exercise activity at 4-month and 12-month follow-ups than found in the control arm. In addition, this trial achieved a reduction in depressive symptoms for the intervention group (Clark et al., 2000). Far fewer studies of health behavior interventions have been conducted among patients with COPD. However, the data to date generally indicate that exercise is associated with reduced symptoms of anxiety and depression, as well as significant increases in functional performance and quality of life (Emery, Leatherman, Burker, & MacIntyre, 1991; Griffiths et al., 2000). In addition, data suggest that exercise may have beneficial effects on cognitive performance among patients with COPD (Emery, Schein, Hauck, & MacIntyre, 1998; Kozora, Tran, & Make, 2002).

Numerous exercise interventions have been conducted with cancer patients. Literature reviews suggest that exercise is, in general, associated with reductions in cancer-related fatigue (Cramp & Daniel, 2008), as well as with increased quality of life and cardiovascular fitness (McNeely et al., 2006). Many studies have enlisted only breast cancer patients and, for them, physical activity has been associated with multiple positive outcomes (e.g., increased physical endurance, reduced fatigue, improved quality of life, reduced psychological distress; Courneya, 2003; Mock, Dow, Meares, & Grimm, 1997; Segar, Katch, & Roth, 1998; Valenti, Giampiero, & Aielli, 2008). For long-term survivors, moderate-intensity physical activity is associated with greater vigor as well as lower fatigue and fewer depressive symptoms (Trunzo & Pinto, 2004; Pinto, Frierson, Rabin, Trunzo, & Marcus, 2005). On the other hand, a Cochrane review found little evidence for beneficial effects of aerobic or resistance exercise for treatment-related side effects (e.g., fatigue, psychosocial distress, physiological changes) during adjuvant (chemotherapy) treatment (Markes, Brockow, & Resch, 2006). Similarly, a meta-analysis by Jacobsen and colleagues (2007) found limited evidence for the utility of psychological and activity-based interventions for treating cancer-related fatigue in cancer patients. Thus, the data regarding health and psychological benefits of exercise among cancer patients are not straightforward. It appears that physical activity is beneficial for survivors, especially breast cancer patients, but that fatigue may be especially difficult to reduce.

Lastly, exercise routines and benefits for patients with diabetes are moderated by the severity of the disease. For those with diabetes that can be managed via alterations in diet (type 2), exercise studies have documented reduced cholesterol levels and improved fitness for patients (Rimmer, Silverman, Braunschweig, Quinn, & Liu, 2002). For these same patients, physical exercise can be used for weight reduction and to achieve improved insulin sensitivity (Horton, 1988). However, for insulin-dependent (type 2) diabetics, exercise regimens require close physician monitoring, as patients may become hypoglycemic during or following exercise (Horton, 1988).

Multitarget Health Behavior Interventions

Health behavior interventions of the future will be designed to address multiple health behaviors. For example, studies will focus on the importance of energy balance, and include dietary and exercise components in tandem. Clark and colleagues (2009) found that a self-directed intervention group for cardiac patients reduced cardiac symptoms and contributed to weight loss at 18-month follow-up compared to the outcomes for the control group. The large Multisite Cardiac Lifestyle Intervention Program studied the interactions of health behavior changes influencing cardiac risk among more than 800 CHD patients. After 3 months, intervention patients were found to have significant reductions in overall coronary risk. Reductions in dietary fat intake predicted reductions in weight, total cholesterol, and LDL cholesterol, and interacted with increased exercise to predict reductions in perceived stress. Increases in exercise predicted improvements in total cholesterol and exercise capacity (for women). Increased stress management was related to reductions in weight, total cholesterol/high-density lipoprotein (HDL) cholesterol (for men), triglycerides, hemoglobin A1c (in patients with diabetes), and hostility. Schuler and colleagues (1992) found that a 12-month program of exercise and low-fat diet among coronary artery disease (CAD) patients was associated with reduced cardiac risk factors (e.g., body weight, cholesterol), as well as with less progression of coronary lesions. Other studies have documented that changes in diet, stress management, exercise, social support, and smoking contribute to reduced cardiac medication use, better quality of life, and reduced cardiac risk among postmenopausal women with CHD (Koertge et al., 2003).

Conclusion

Smoking cessation interventions have generated equivocal results, with more intensive interventions resulting in higher quit rates than brief interventions or usual care. Despite the greater success of intensive interventions, low motivation for quitting remains a barrier among cardiac and cancer patients, reflecting an ongoing need for enhanced motivational techniques among medical patients to increase positive attitudes toward smoking cessation. In addition, consideration of the environmental and social factors that may hinder patients' cessation may be especially important.

Exercise interventions among cardiac patients have resulted in increased functional capacity, reduced cardiac risk (including lower cholesterol levels), and less depressive symptomatology. Exercise interventions among cancer patients have revealed mixed results. Physical activity interventions have been associated with multiple positive outcomes among breast cancer patients and survivors. However, recent reviews have indicated limited benefits of exercise for the most common symptom, fatigue. Exercise interventions appear beneficial for other medical groups, such as patients with COPD or diabetes. Finally, interventions that target multiple problem behaviors, such as poor dietary habits and low physical activity rates, show considerable promise, as evidenced by the reduced risk of cardiac disease and improved quality of life.

Uptake of Behavioral Interventions: Trial Accrual, Retention, and Adherence

In the general case, psychosocial factors often covary with medical treatment adherence, with poor adherence hastening disease progression and/or death. Such is the case for patients with cardiac disease (Frasure-Smith, Lespérance, & Talajic, 1995; Ruberman, Weinblatt, Goldberg, & Chaudhary, 1984; Williams & Littman, 1996) or cancer (Ayres et al., 1994; Brown, Levy, Rosberger, & Edgar, 2003). This problem is not limited to medical treatments, as low accrual, high dropout, or inadequate adherence to the treatment protocol occurs for behavioral trials (Allison et al., 2004; Butler et al., 2009; Chang, Hendricks, Slawsky, & Locastro, 2004; Manne, Ostroff, & Winkel, 2007; Ostroff, Ross, Steinglass, Ronis-Tobin, & Singh, 2004). For example, Butler and colleagues (2009) recruited 212 cardiac patients into a behavioral intervention utilizing pedometer monitoring, behavior counseling, and goal-setting exercises. Of the 212 recruited, 90 (42%) refused randomization. After randomization, 32 out of

122 (26%) did not complete the intervention. Self-reported barriers to adherence included work commitments and medical problems. In a behavioral intervention study for chronic heart failure patients, Chang and colleagues (2004) found that 39 of 124 (31%) patients who consented to participate did not return for the baseline assessment. Studies of patients with cancer have documented similar difficulties.

The Multiple Family Group (MFG) intervention study for head and neck cancer patients implemented aggressive accrual and retention methods, but still had high dropout rates (Ostroff et al., 2004). Only 80 of 174 (46%) eligible families returned completed surveys. Of the remaining 80 families that returned surveys and were informed of the MFG workshops, only 15 (19%) completed the 6-hour workshop. Patients who did not participate in the study stated that they did not need family support, or they could not attend for practical reasons, such as living too far from the study site (Ostroff et al., 2004). In a couple-focused intervention for breast cancer patients and their caregivers, Manne, Ostroff & Winkel (2007) randomized 120 couples to the intervention group, 42 (35%) of whom became treatment dropouts.

As with treatments of any type, barriers exist, both practical and emotional, to enrolling in and completing psychological/behavioral interventions trials. Nonetheless, research demonstrates that, without intervention, psychological symptoms such as depression are associated with poorer compliance with medical treatment (McDonough et al., 1996; Richardson et al., 1987). The same is true for compliance with health-behavior change efforts. Kronish and colleagues (2006) found that depression was associated with lower rates of smoking cessation, exercise, and CR attendance in a study of 560 acute coronary syndrome patients. Glazer and colleagues (2002) found that depressive symptoms predicted dropout from CR.

According to Evenson and Fleury (2000), the commonly reported reasons for CR dropout or poor adherence include patient reports of low motivation, engagement in concurrent exercise programs or efforts, and/or lack of time. Work and financial concerns (including inadequate insurance coverage) have been reported by patients in other studies (Evenson & Fleury, 2000). Ostroff and colleagues (2004) reported that the need to travel a significant geographical distance was a major concern for patients who dropped out of the MFG study conducted at Memorial Sloan Kettering Cancer Hospital in New York City. Barriers such as the latter may spur alternative forms of delivering intervention content (e.g., telephone counseling, Internet websites).

In addition to understanding barriers to adherence, studies have also identified factors associated with participant retention. Leatham and colleagues (2009) found that providing more information to potential participants decreased the accrual rate, but if the participant consented to participate, retention was higher. Also, providing information (e.g., flyers or postings) to potential participants in advance provided additional time to consider participation and discuss the matter with family and friends, and ultimately led to higher accrual.

Conclusions

Although behavioral interventions have been associated with improved physical and emotional functioning among medical patients, participant retention in behavioral intervention trials is often problematic. Obstacles to low accrual and retention may include illness severity, employment or other time commitments, and the inconvenience of lengthy travel times; however, psychological symptoms, particularly depressive ones, also have been associated with lower rates of adherence. Thus, the data tentatively support the importance of conducting assessments of motivation, social support, and psychological well-being among medical patients entering a behavioral change program, with the goal of identifying patients who may require participation accommodations or additional support. Evaluation of barriers to behavioral change among medical patients, with the goal of modifying behavioral interventions to enhance adherence and success with behavioral change, is needed.

Conclusion

Elevated rates of mood and anxiety disorders among patients with CHD, cancer, and COPD highlight the importance of psychological assessment and intervention in health-care settings. Numerous meta-analyses suggest that highly distressed patients, particularly those with significant depressive symptomatology, are at risk for greater medical morbidity and hastened death, highlighting the need for psychological and/or behavioral assessment at critical points in illness trajectories (e.g., diagnosis, post MI, diagnosis of cancer recurrence).

Cognitive-behavioral therapy is an effective strategy for the treatment of clinical depression and anxiety disorders in the general population, and studies indicate that CBT is effective in reducing depression and anxiety among medical patients as well. However, CBT does not appear to be beneficial for improving perceived social support. Other interventions also have been useful in enhancing health and well-being. Among cancer patients, biobehavioral treatment strategies have been employed, and among cardiac patients stress management and relaxation techniques have been successful. The research literature has yet to identify the specific components of treatments that are responsible for reducing psychological distress or for influencing disease morbidity and mortality. Additionally, the tailoring of treatment to individual differences among patients is also needed. For example, studies of cardiac patients have identified interventions that do not appear to benefit women (e.g., telephone-based counseling from the M-HART study and psychosocial intervention in the ENRICHD trial), but the mechanisms for the apparent sex difference in treatment outcomes are not known. Further research is needed to provide evidence in support of specific intervention treatments, and to clarify the necessary components of treatment for producing specific outcomes (e.g., reduced depression, reduced physical symptoms, increased survival).

Mode of intervention delivery may be one determinant of treatment efficacy. To date, treatment delivery has primarily been through in-person group or individual treatment. However, telephone-based interventions appear to be beneficial for some cardiac patients. Use of the Internet for delivery of interventions has yet to be widely utilized. Prior studies indicate that telephone-based interventions may not be beneficial for all patients, and it is likely that Internet interventions too may benefit some but not all. In the area of health behavior change, cell phones may be useful in monitoring both positive (e.g., physical activity) and negative (e.g., smoking) health behaviors during the course of treatment. These technologies are providing new opportunities for both for intervention delivery and data collection.

Health-care providers are beginning to acknowledge that health behavior change (e.g., smoking, diet, physical activity) is central to effective chronic disease management. Psychologists can assist in the evaluation of both health behaviors and psychopathology, and also provide an awareness of environmental factors that may undermine patient efforts to initiate and maintain behavior change. If psychological assessment and intervention among medical patients are routine offerings in medical care, patients' hesitance to participate may be reduced, and they may be less reluctant to self-identify their unaddressed needs.

References

Allison, P. J., Nicolau, B., Edgar, L., Archer, J., Black, M., & Hier, M. (2004). Teaching head, neck cancer patients coping strategies: results of a feasibility study. *Oral Oncology, 40*, 538–544.

Amsberg, S., Anderbro, T., Wredling, R., Lisspers, J., Lins, P., Adamson, U., et al. (2009). A cognitive behavior therapy-based intervention among poorly controlled adult type 1 diabetes patients—a randomized controlled trial. *Patient Education and Counseling, 77*(1), 72–80.

Andersen, B. L. (1992). Psychological interventions for cancer patients to enhance the quality of life. *Journal of Consulting and Clinical Psychology, 60*(4), 552–568.

Andersen, B. L. (2002). Biobehavioral outcomes following psychological interventions for cancer patients. *Journal of Consulting and Clinical Psychology, 70*(3), 590–610.

Andersen, B. L., Farrar, W. B., Golden-Kreutz, D., Kutz, L. A., MacCallum, R., Courtney, M. E., et al. (1998). Stress and immune responses after surgical treatment for regional breast cancer. *Journal of the National Cancer Institute, 90*(1), 30–36.

Andersen, B. L., Golden-Kreutz, D. M., Emery, C. F., & Thiel, D. L. (2009). Biobehavioral intervention for cancer stress: Conceptualization, components, and intervention strategies. *Cognitive and Behavioral Practice, 16*(3), 253–265.

Andersen, B. L., Kiecolt-Glaser, J., & Glaser, R. (1994). A biobehavioral model of cancer stress and disease course. *The American Psychologist, 49*(5), 389–404.

Andersen, B.L., Thornton, L.M., Shapiro, C.L., Farrar, W.B., Mundy, B.L., Yang, H., et al.(2010). Biobehavioral, immune, and health benefits following recurrence for psychological intervention participants. *Clinical Cancer Research, 16*(12), 3270–3278.

Andersen, B.L., Yang, H.C., Farrar, W.B., Golden-Kreutz, D.M., Emery, C.F., Thornton, L.M., Young, D.C., Carson, W.E. III. (2008). Psychological intervention improves survival for breast cancer patients: A randomized clinical trial. *Cancer, 113*, 3450–3458.

Anisman, H., & Merali, Z. (2003). Cytokines, stress and depressive illness: Brain-immune interactions. *Annals of Medicine, 35*(1), 2–11.

Argstatter, H., Haberbosch, W., & Bolay, H. V. (2006). Study of the effectiveness of musical stimulation during intracardiac catheterization. *Clinical Research in Cardiology, 95*(10), 514–522.

Arrigo, I., Brunner-LaRocca, H., Lefkovits, M., Pfisterer, M., & Hoffmann, A. (2008). Comparative outcome one year after formal cardiac rehabilitation: The effects of a randomized intervention to improve exercise adherence. *European Journal of Cardiovascular Prevention and Rehabilitation, 15*(3), 306–311.

Ayres, A., Hoon, P. W., Franzoni, J. B., Matheny, K. B., Cotanch, P. H., & Takayanagi, S. (1994). Influence of mood and adjustment to cancer on compliance with chemotherapy among breast cancer patients. *Journal of Psychosomatic Research, 38*(5), 393–402.

Bambauer, K. Z., Aupont, O., Stone, P. H., Locke, S. E., Mullan, M. G., Colagiovanni, J., et al. (2005). The effect of a telephone counseling intervention on self-rated health of cardiac patients. *Psychosomatic Medicine, 67*(4), 539–545.

Baser, S., Shannon, V. R., Eapen, G. A., Jimenez, C. A., Onn, A., Lin, E., et al. (2006). Smoking cessation after diagnosis of lung cancer is associated with a beneficial effect on performance status. *Chest, 130*(6), 1784–1790.

Berkman, L. F., Blumenthal, J., Burg, M., Carney, R. M., Catellier, D., Cowan, M. J., et al. (2003). Effects of treating depression and low perceived social support on clinical events after myocardial infarction: The enhancing recovery in coronary heart disease patients (ENRICHD) randomized trial. *JAMA: The Journal of the American Medical Association, 289*(23), 3106–3116.

Black, J. L., Allison, T. G., Williams, D. E., Rummans, T. A., & Gau, G. T. (1998). Effect of intervention for psychological distress on rehospitalization rates in cardiac rehabilitation patients. *Psychosomatics, 39*(2), 134–143.

Blumenthal, J. A., Babyak, M. A., Moore, K. A., Craighead, W. E., Herman, S., Khatri, P., et al. (1999). Effects of exercise training on older patients with major depression. *Archives of Internal Medicine, 159*(19), 2349–2356.

Blumenthal, J. A., Sherwood, A., Babyak, M. A., Watkins, L. L., Waugh, R., Georgiades, A., et al. (2005). Effects of exercise and stress management training on markers of cardiovascular risk in patients with ischemic heart disease: A randomized controlled trial. *JAMA, 293*(13), 1626–1634.

Bolman, C., de Vries, H., & van Breukelen, G. (2002a). A minimal-contact intervention for cardiac inpatients: Long-term effects on smoking cessation. *Preventive Medicine, 35*(2), 181–192.

Bolman, C., de Vries, H., & van Breukelen, G. (2002b). Evaluation of a nurse-managed minimal-contact smoking cessation intervention for cardiac inpatients. *Health Education Research, 17*(1), 99–116.

BrintzenhoffSzoc, K. M., Levin, T. T., Li, Y., Kissane, D. W., & Zabora, J. R. (2009). Mixed anxiety/depression symptoms in a large cancer cohort: Prevalence by cancer type. *Psychosomatics, 50*(4), 383–391.

Brown, L. F., Kroenke, K., Theobald, D. E., Wu, J., & Tu, W. (2010). The association of depression and anxiety with health-related quality of life in cancer patients with depression and/or pain. *Psycho-Oncology, 19*(7), 734–741.

Brown, K. W., Levy, A. R., Rosberger, Z., & Edgar, L. (2003). Psychological distress and cancer survival: A follow-up 10 years after diagnosis. *Psychosomatic Medicine, 65*(4), 636–643.

Burg, M. M., Barefoot, J., Berkman, L., Catellier, D. J., Czajkowski, S., Saab, P., et al. (2005). Low perceived social support and post-myocardial infarction prognosis in the enhancing recovery in coronary heart disease clinical trial: The effects of treatment. *Psychosomatic Medicine, 67*(6), 879–888.

Burgess, C., Cornelius, V., Love, S., Graham, J., Richards, M., & Ramirez, A. (2005). Depression and anxiety in women with early breast cancer: Five year observational cohort study. *BMJ (Clinical Research Ed.), 330*(7493), 702–702.

Butler, L., Furber, S., Phongsavan, P., Mark, A., & Bauman, A. (2009). Effects of a pedometer-based intervention on physical activity levels after cardiac rehabilitation: A randomized controlled trial. *Journal of Cardiopulmonary Rehabilitation and Prevention, 29*(2), 105–114.

Carney R. M., Rich M. W., teVelde A., Saini J., Clark K., & Freedland K. E. (1988). The relationship between heart rate, heart rate variability and depression in patients with coronary artery disease. *Journal of Psychosomatic Research, 32*, 159–164.

Chang, B., Hendricks, A. M., Slawsky, M. T., & Locastro, J. S. (2004). Patient recruitment to a randomized clinical trial of behavioral therapy for chronic heart failure. *BMC Medical Research Methodology, 4*, 8–8.

Chida, Y., Hamer, M., Wardle, J., & Steptoe, A. (2008). Do stress-related psychosocial factors contribute to cancer incidence and survival? *Nature Clinical Practice. Oncology,* 5(8), 466–475.

Christakis, N. A. (2004). Social networks and collateral health effects. *British Medical Journal, 329,* 184–185.

Christenhusz, L., Pieterse, M., Seydel, E., & van der Palin, J. (2007). Prospective determinants of smoking cessation in COPD patients within a high intensity or a brief counseling intervention. *Patient Education and Counseling, 66(2),* 162–166.

Clark, N. M., Janz, N. K., Dodge, J. A., Schork, M. A., Fingerlin, T. E., Wheeler, J. R., et al. (2000). Changes in functional health status of older women with heart disease: Evaluation of a program based on self-regulation. *The Journals of Gerontology. Series B, Psychological Sciences and Social Sciences, 55(2),* S117–26.

Clark, N. M., Janz, N. K., Dodge, J. A., Lin, X., Trabert, B. L., Kaciroti, N., et al. (2009). Heart disease management by women: Does intervention format matter? *Health Education & Behavior, 36(2),* 394–409.

Cossette, S., Frasure-Smith, N., & Lespérance, F. (2001). Clinical implications of a reduction in psychological distress on cardiac prognosis in patients participating in a psychosocial intervention program. *Psychosomatic Medicine, 63(2),* 257–266.

Courneya, K. S. (2003). Exercise in cancer survivors: An overview of research. *Medicine and Science in Sports and Exercise, 35,* 1846–1852.

Cowan, M. J., Freedland, K. E., Burg, M. M., Saab, P. G., Youngblood, M. E., Cornell, C. E., et al. (2008). Predictors of treatment response for depression and inadequate social support—the ENRICHD randomized clinical trial. *Psychotherapy and Psychosomatics, 77(1),* 27–37.

Cowan, M. J., Pike, K. C., & Budzynski, H. K. (2001). Psychosocial nursing therapy following sudden cardiac arrest: Impact on two-year survival. *Nursing Research, 50(2),* 68–76.

Cramp, F., & Daniel, J. (2008). Exercise for the management of cancer-related fatigue in adults. *Cochrane Database of Systematic Reviews (Online), (2),* CD006145.

Delgado-Guay, M., Parsons, H. A., Li, Z., Palmer, L., & Bruera, E. (2009). Symptom distress in advanced cancer patients with anxiety and depression in the palliative care setting. *Support Care Cancer, 17(5),* 573–579.

Derogatis, L. R., & Melisaratos, N. (1983). The brief symptom inventory: An introductory report. *Psychological Medicine, 13(3),* 595–605.

Dowson, C., Laing, R., Barraclough, R., Mulder, R., Norris, K., Drennan, C. et al. (2001). The use of the Hospital Anxiety and Depression Scale (HADS) in patients with chronic obstructive pulmonary disease: A pilot study. *New Zealand Medical Journal, 114,* 447–449.

Efraimsson, E. O., Hillervik, C., & Ehrenberg, A. (2008). Effects of COPD self-care management education at a nurse-led primary health care clinic. *Scandinavian Journal of Caring Sciences, 22(2),* 178–185.

Egan, E., Clavarino, A., Burridge, L., Teuwen, M., & White, E. (2002). A randomized control trial of nursing-based case management for patients with chronic obstructive pulmonary disease. *Lippincott's Case Management: Managing the Process of Patient Care, 7(5),* 170–179.

Elenkov, I. J., Iezzoni, D. G., Daly, A., Harris, A. G., & Chrousos, G. P. (2005). Cytokine dysregulation, inflammation and well-being. *Neuroimmunomodulation, 12(5),* 255–269.

Emery, C. F., Frid, D. J., Engebretson, T. O., Alonzo, A. A., Fish, A., Ferketich, A. K., et al. (2004). Gender differences in quality of life among cardiac patients. *Psychosomatic Medicine, 66(2),* 190–197.

Emery, C. F., Leatherman, L. E., Burker, E. J., & MacIntyre, N. R. (1991). Psychological outcomes of a pulmonary rehabilitation program. *Chest, 100,* 613–617.

Emery, C. F., Schein, R. L., Hauck, E. R., & MacIntyre, N. R. (1998). Psychological and cognitive outcomes of a randomized trial of exercise among patients with chronic obstructive pulmonary disease. *Health Psychology, 17(3),* 232–240.

Evans, D. L., Charney, D. S., Lewis, L., Golden, R. N., Gorman, J. M., Krishnan, K. R., et al. (2005). Mood disorders in the medically ill: Scientific review and recommendations. *Biological Psychiatry, 58(3),* 175–189.

Evenson, K. R., & Fleury, J. (2000). Barriers to outpatient cardiac rehabilitation participation and adherence. *Journal of Cardiopulmonary Rehabilitation, 20(4),* 241–246.

Fawzy, F. I., Kemeny, M. E., Fawzy, N. W., Elashoff, R., Morton, D., Cousins, N., et al. (1990). A structured psychiatric intervention for cancer patients. II. changes over time in immunological measures. *Archives of General Psychiatry, 47(8),* 729–735.

Frasure-Smith, N., Lespérance, F., Prince, R. H., Verrier, P., Garber, R. A., Juneau, M., et al. (1997). Randomised trial of home-based psychosocial nursing intervention for patients recovering from myocardial infarction. *Lancet, 350(9076),* 473–479.

Frasure-Smith, N., Lespérance, F., & Talajic, M. (1995). Depression and 18-month prognosis after myocardial infarction. *Circulation, 91(4),* 999–1005.

Friedman, M., Thoresen, C. E., Gill, J. J., Ulmer, D., Powell, L. H., Price, V. A., et al. (1986). Alteration of type A behavior and its effect on cardiac recurrences in post myocardial infarction patients: Summary results of the recurrent coronary prevention project. *American Heart Journal, 112(4),* 653–665.

Gallagher, R., McKinley, S., & Dracup, K. (2003). Effects of a telephone counseling intervention on psychosocial adjustment in women following a cardiac event. *Heart & Lung: The Journal of Critical Care, 32(2),* 79–87.

Giannuzzi, P., Temporelli, P. L., Marchioli, R., Maggioni, A. P., Balestroni, G., Ceci, V., et al. (2008). Global secondary prevention strategies to limit event recurrence after myocardial infarction: Results of the GOSPEL study, a multicenter, randomized controlled trial from the Italian cardiac rehabilitation network. *Archives of Internal Medicine, 168(20),* 2194–2204.

Gidron, Y., Davidson, K., & Bata, I. (1999). The short-term effects of a hostility-reduction intervention on male coronary heart disease patients. *Health Psychology, 18(4),* 416–420.

Glazer, K. M., Emery, C. F., Frid, D. J., & Banyasz, R. E. (2002). Psychological predictors of adherence and outcomes among patients in cardiac rehabilitation. *Journal of Cardiopulmonary Rehabilitation, 22(1),* 40–46.

Goksel, T., Ozol, D., Bayindir, U., & Guzelant, A. (2002). Smoking habit among the relatives of patients with serious smoking-related disorders. *European Addiction Research, 8(3),* 118–121.

Golden-Kreutz, D., & Andersen, B. L. (2004). Depressive symptoms after breast cancer surgery: Relationships with global, cancer-related, and life event stress. *Psycho-Oncology, 13(3),* 211–220.

Golden-Kreutz, D., Thornton, L. M., Wells-Di Gregorio, S., Frierson, G. M., Jim, H. S., Carpenter, K. M., et al. (2005).

Traumatic stress, perceived global stress, and life events: Prospectively predicting quality of life in breast cancer patients. *Health Psychology, 24*(3), 288–296.

Goodwin, P. J., Leszcz, M., Ennis, M., Koopmans, J., Vincent, L., Guther, H., et al. (2001). The effect of group psychosocial support on survival in metastatic breast cancer. *The New England Journal of Medicine, 345*(24), 1719–1726.

Graydon, J. E., & Ross, E. (1995). Influence of symptoms, lung function, mood, and social support on level of functioning of patients with COPD. *Research in Nursing and Health, 18*, 525.

Griffiths, T. L., Burr, M. L., Campbell, I. A., Lewis-Jenkins, V., Mullins, J., Shiels, K. et al. (2000). Results at 1 year of outpatient multidisciplinary pulmonary rehabilitation: A randomized controlled trial. *The Lancet, 355*, 362–368.

Gritz, E. R. (1991). Smoking and smoking cessation in cancer patients. *British Journal of Addiction, 86*(5), 549–554.

Hamel, W. J. (2001). The effects of music intervention on anxiety in the patient waiting for cardiac catheterization. *Intensive & Critical Care Nursing, 17*(5), 279–285.

Heslop, K., De Soyza, A., Baker, C. R., Stenton, C., & Burns, G. P. (2009). Using individualised cognitive behavioural therapy as a treatment for people with COPD. *Nursing Times, 105*(14), 14–17.

Hesselink, A. E., Penninx, B. W. J. H., van der Windt, D. A. W. M., van Duin, B.,J., de Vries, P., Twisk, J. W. R., et al. (2004). Effectiveness of an education programme by a general practice assistant for asthma and COPD patients: Results from a randomised controlled trial. *Patient Education and Counseling, 55*(1), 121–128.

Horton, E. S. (1988). Role and management of exercise in diabetes mellitus. *Diabetes Care, 11*(2), 201–211.

Hotopf, M., Chidgey, J., Addington-Hall, J., & Ly, K. L. (2002). Depression in advanced disease: A systematic review part 1. prevalence and case finding. *Palliative Medicine, 16*(2), 81–97.

Jackson, J. L., & Emery, C. F. (in press). Illness knowledge moderates the influence of coping style on quality of life among women with congestive heart failure. *Heart & Lung.*

Jacobsen, P. B., Donovan, K. A., Vadaparampil, S. T., & Small, B. J. (2007). Systematic review and meta-analysis of psychological and activity-based interventions for cancer-related fatigue. *Health Psychology, 26*(6), 660–667.

Janevic, M. R., Janz, N. K., Dodge, J. A., Wang, Y., Lin, X., & Clark, N. M. (2004). Longitudinal effects of social support on the health and functioning of older women with heart disease. *International Journal of Aging & Human Development, 59*(2), 153–175.

Janz, N. K., Dodge, J. A., Janevic, M. R., Lin, X., Donaldson, A. E., & Clark, N. M. (2004). Understanding and reducing stress and psychological distress in older women with heart disease. *Journal of Women & Aging, 16*(3–4), 19–38.

Janz, N. K., Janevic, M. R., Dodge, J. A., Fingerlin, T. E., Schork, M. A., Mosca, L. J., et al. (2001). Factors influencing quality of life in older women with heart disease. *Medical Care, 39*(6), 588–598.

Jim, H. S., Richardson, S. A., Golden-Kreutz, D., & Andersen, B. L. (2006). Strategies used in coping with a cancer diagnosis predict meaning in life for survivors. *Health Psychology, 25*(6), 753–761.

Jung, W., & Irwin, M. (1999). Reduction of natural killer cytotoxic activity in major depression: Interaction between depression and cigarette smoking. *Psychosomatic Medicine, 61*(3), 263–270.

Keenan, P. S. (2009). Smoking and weight change after new health diagnoses in older adults. *Archives of Internal Medicine, 169*(3), 237–242.

Kim, H. F. S., Kunik, M. E., Molinari, V. A., Hillman, S. L., Petersen, N. J., Nahas, Z., et al. (2000). Functional impairment in COPD patients: The impact of anxiety and depression. *Psychosomatics, 41,* 465–471.

Kissane, D. W., Bloch, S., Smith, G. C., Miach, P., Clarke, D. M., Ikin, J., et al. (2003). Cognitive-existential group psychotherapy for women with primary breast cancer: A randomised controlled trial. *Psycho-Oncology, 12*(6), 532–546.

Koertge, J., Janszky, I., Sundin, O., Blom, M., Georgiades, A., Lszl, K. D., et al. (2008). Effects of a stress management program on vital exhaustion and depression in women with coronary heart disease: A randomized controlled intervention study. *Journal of Internal Medicine, 263*(3), 281–293.

Koertge, J., Weidner, G., Elliott-Eller, M., Scherwitz, L., Merritt-Worden, T., Marlin, R., et al. (2003). Improvement in medical risk factors and quality of life in women and men with coronary artery disease in the multicenter lifestyle demonstration project. *The American Journal of Cardiology, 91*(11), 1316–1322.

Kozora, E., Tran, Z. V., & Make, B. (2002). Neurobehavioral improvement after brief rehabilitation in patients with chronic obstructive pulmonary disease. *Journal of Cardiopulmonary Rehabilitation, 22*, 426–430.

Kronish, I. M., Rieckmann, N., Halm, E. A., Shimbo, D., Vorchheimer, D., Haas, D. C., et al. (2006). Persistent depression affects adherence to secondary prevention behaviors after acute coronary syndromes. *Journal of General Internal Medicine, 21*(11), 1178–1183.

Kunik, M. E., Braun, U., Stanley, M. A., Wristers, K., Molinari, V., Stoebner, D., et al. (2001). One session cognitive behavioural therapy for elderly patients with chronic obstructive pulmonary disease. *Psychological Medicine, 31*(4), 717–723.

Lear, S. A., Spinelli, J. J., Linden, W., Brozic, A., Kiess, M., Frohlich, J. J., et al. (2006). The extensive lifestyle management intervention (ELMI) after cardiac rehabilitation: A 4-year randomized controlled trial. *American Heart Journal, 152*(2), 333–339.

Leathem, C. S., Cupples, M. E., Byrne, M. C., O'Malley, M., Houlihan, A., Murphy, A. W., et al. (2009). Identifying strategies to maximise recruitment and retention of practices and patients in a multicentre randomised controlled trial of an intervention to optimise secondary prevention for coronary heart disease in primary care. *BMC Medical Research Methodology, 9*, 40–40.

Lebovits, A. H., Strain, J. J., Schleifer, S. J., Tanaka, J. S., Bhardwaj, S., & Messe, M. R. (1990). Patient noncompliance with self-administered chemotherapy. *Cancer, 65*(1), 17–22.

Lepore, S. J., Helgeson, V. S., Eton, D. T., & Schulz, R. (2003). Improving quality of life in men with prostate cancer: A randomized controlled trial of group education interventions. *Health Psychology, 22*(5), 443–452.

Lustman, P. J., Griffith, L. S., Freedland, K. E., Kissel, S. S., & Clouse, R. E. (1998). Cognitive behavior therapy for depression in type 2 diabetes mellitus. A randomized, controlled trial. *Annals of Internal Medicine, 129*(8), 613–621.

Manchanda, S. C., Narang, R., Reddy, K. S., Sachdeva, U., Prabhakaran, D., Dharmanand, S., et al. (2000). Retardation of coronary atherosclerosis with yoga lifestyle intervention. *The Journal of the Association of Physicians of India, 48*(7), 687–694.

Manne, S., Ostroff, J. S., & Winkel, G. (2007). Social-cognitive processes as moderators of a couple-focused group intervention for women with early stage breast cancer. *Health Psychology, 26*(6), 735–744.

Markes, M., Brockow, T., & Resch, K. L. (2006). Exercise for women receiving adjuvant therapy for breast cancer. *Cochrane Database of Systematic Reviews (Online), (4),* CD005001.

McAllister-Sistilli, C., Caggiula, A. R., Knopf, S., Rose, C. A., Miller, A. L., & Donny, E. C. (1998). The effects of nicotine on the immune system. *Psychoneuroendocrinology, 23*(2), 175–187.

McDonough, E. M., Boyd, J. H., Varvares, M. A., & Maves, M. D. (1996). Relationship between psychological status and compliance in a sample of patients treated for cancer of the head and neck. *Head & Neck, 18*(3), 269–276.

McKinley, S., Dracup, K., Moser, D. K., Riegel, B., Doering, L. V., Meischke, H., et al. (2009). The effect of a short one-on-one nursing intervention on knowledge, attitudes and beliefs related to response to acute coronary syndrome in people with coronary heart disease: A randomized controlled trial. *International Journal of Nursing Studies, 46*(8), 1037–1046.

McNeely, M. L., Campbell, K. L., Rowe, B. H., Klassen, T. P., Mackey, J. R., & Courneya, K. S. (2006). Effects of exercise on breast cancer patients and survivors: A systematic review and meta-analysis. *CMAJ: Canadian Medical Association Journal, 175*(1), 34–41.

Mendes de Leon, C. F., Powell, L. H., & Kaplan, B. H. (1991). Change in coronary-prone behaviors in the recurrent coronary prevention project. *Psychosomatic Medicine, 53*(4), 407–419.

Meyer, T. J., & Mark, M. M. (1995). Effects of psychosocial interventions with adult cancer patients: A meta-analysis of randomized experiments. *Health Psychology, 14*(2), 101–108.

Michalsen, A., Grossman, P., Lehmann, N., Knoblauch, N. T. M., Paul, A., Moebus, S., et al. (2005). Psychological and quality-of-life outcomes from a comprehensive stress reduction and lifestyle program in patients with coronary artery disease: Results of a randomized trial. *Psychotherapy and Psychosomatics, 74*(6), 344–352.

Miller, M., Mogun, H., Azrael, D., Hempstead, K., & Solomon, D. H. (2008). Cancer and the risk of suicide in older Americans. *Journal of Clinical Oncology, 26*(29), 4720–4724.

Mock, V., Dow, K. H., Meares, C. J., & Grimm, P. M. (1997). Effects of exercise on fatigue, physical functioning, and emotional distress during radiation therapy for breast cancer. *Oncology Nursing Forum, 24*(6), 991–1000.

Moorey, S., Greer, S., Bliss, J., & Law, M. (1998). A comparison of adjuvant psychological therapy and supportive counselling in patients with cancer. *Psycho-Oncology, 7*(3), 218–228.

Nezu, A. M., Nezu, C. M., Felgoise, S. H., McClure, K. S., & Houts, P. S. (2003). Project Genesis: Assessing the efficacy of problem-solving therapy for distressed adult cancer patients. *Journal of Consulting and Clinical Psychology, 71,* 1036–1048.

Nilsson, U. (2009). The effect of music intervention in stress response to cardiac surgery in a randomized clinical trial. *Heart & Lung: The Journal of Critical Care, 38*(3), 201–207.

Ockene, I. S., Hebert, J. R., Ockene, J. K., Merriam, P. A., Hurley, T. G., & Saperia, G. M. (1996). Effect of training and a structured office practice on physician-delivered nutrition counseling: The Worcester-area trial for counseling in hyperlipidemia (WATCH). *American Journal of Preventive Medicine, 12*(4), 252–258.

Ostroff, J., Ross, S., Steinglass, P., Ronis-Tobin, V., & Singh, B. (2004). Interest in and Barriers to Participation in Multiple Family Groups Among Head and Neck Cancer Survivors and Their Primary Family Caregivers. *Family Process, 43*(2), 195–208.

Pace, T. W. W., Hu, F., & Miller, A. H. (2007). Cytokine-effects on glucocorticoid receptor function: Relevance to glucocorticoid resistance and the pathophysiology and treatment of major depression. *Brain, Behavior, and Immunity, 21*(1), 9–19.

Pagoto, S., & Ockene, J. (2009). Windows of opportunity for smoking and weight loss counseling. *Archives of Internal Medicine, 169*(3), 217–218.

Pinto, B. M., Frierson, G. M., Rabin, C., Trunzo, J. J., & Marcus, B. H. (2005). Home-based physical activity intervention for breast cancer patients. *Journal of Clinical Oncology, 23*(15), 3577–3587.

Quist-Paulsen, P., & Gallefoss, F. (2003). Randomised controlled trial of smoking cessation intervention after admission for coronary heart disease. *BMJ (Clinical Research Ed.), 327* (7426), 1254–1257.

Raison, C. L., & Miller, A. H. (2003). Depression in cancer: New developments regarding diagnosis and treatment. *Biological Psychiatry, 54*(3), 283–294.

Rees, K., Bennett, P., West, R., Davey, S. G., & Ebrahim, S. (2004). Psychological interventions for coronary heart disease. *Cochrane Database of Systematic Reviews (Online), (2),* CD002902.

Richardson, J. L., Marks, G., Johnson, C. A., Graham, J. W., Chan, K. K., Selser, J. N., et al. (1987). Path model of multi-dimensional compliance with cancer therapy. *Health Psychology, 6*(3), 183–207.

Rimmer, J. H., Silverman, K., Braunschweig, C., Quinn, L., & Liu, Y. (2002). Feasibility of a health promotion intervention for a group of predominantly African American women with type 2 diabetes. *The Diabetes Educator, 28*(4), 571–580.

Rosengren, A., Hawken, S., Ounpuu, S., Sliwa, K., Zubaid, M., Almahmeed, W. A., et al. (2004). Association of psychosocial risk factors with risk of acute myocardial infarction in 11119 cases and 13648 controls from 52 countries (the INTERHEART study): Case-control study. *Lancet, 364*(9438), 953–962.

Rosenman, R. H., Friedman, M., Straus, R., Wurm, M., Kositchek, R., Hahn, W., et al. (1964). A predictive study of coronary heart disease. *JAMA, 189,* 15–22.

Ruberman, W., Weinblatt, E., Goldberg, J. D., & Chaudhary, B. S. (1984). Psychosocial influences on mortality after myocardial infarction. *The New England Journal of Medicine, 311*(9), 552–559.

Savard, J., Simard, S., Ivers, H., Morin, C. M. (2005). Randomized study on the efficacy of cognitive-behavioral therapy for insomnia secondary to breast cancer, part I: Sleep and psychological effects. *Journal of Clinical Oncology, 23,* 6083–6096.

Schairer, C., Brown, L. M., Chen, B. E., Howard, R., Lynch, C. F., Hall, P., et al. (2006). Suicide after breast cancer: An international population-based study of 723,810 women. *Journal of the National Cancer Institute, 98*(19), 1416–1419.

Schneider, S., Moyer, A., Knapp-Oliver, S., Sohl, S., Cannella, D., & Targhetta, V. (2010). Pre-intervention distress moderates the efficacy of psychosocial treatment for cancer patients: A meta-analysis. *Journal of Behavioral Medicine, 33*(1), 1–14.

Schneiderman, N., Saab, P., Catellier, D., Powell, L., DeBusk, R., Williams, R., et al. (2004). Psychosocial treatment within sex by ethnicity subgroups in the enhancing recovery in coronary heart disease clinical trial. *Psychosomatic Medicine, 66*(4), 475.

Schuler, G., Hambrecht, R., Schlierf, G., Niebauer, J., Hauer, K., Neumann, J., et al. (1992). Regular physical exercise and low-fat diet: effects on progression of coronary artery disease. *Circulation, 86*, 1–11.

Segar, M. L., Katch, V. L., & Roth, R. S. (1998). The effect of aerobic exercise on self-esteem and depressive and anxiety symptoms among breast cancer survivors. *Oncology Nursing Forum, 25*(4), 654.

Shaw, R. E., Cohen, F., Doyle, B., & Palesky, J. (1985). The impact of denial and repressive style on information gain and rehabilitation outcomes in myocardial infarction patients. *Psychosomatic Medicine, 47*(3), 262–273.

Sheard, T., & Maguire, P. (1999). The effect of psychological interventions on anxiety and depression in cancer patients: Results of two meta-analyses. *British Journal of Cancer, 80*(11), 1770–1780.

Shen, B., Avivi, Y. E., Todaro, J. F., Spiro, A., 3rd, Laurenceau, J., Ward, K. D., et al. (2008). Anxiety characteristics independently and prospectively predict myocardial infarction in men the unique contribution of anxiety among psychologic factors. *Journal of the American College of Cardiology, 51*(2), 113–119.

Shimizu, K., Nakata, M., Hirami, Y., Maeda, A., & Tanemoto, K. (2008). Recent results regarding the clinical impact of smoking history on postoperative complications in lung cancer patients. *Interactive Cardiovascular and Thoracic Surgery, 7*(6), 1001–1006.

Simpson, J. S., Carlson, L. E., Beck, C. A., & Patten, S. (2002). Effects of a brief intervention on social support and psychiatric morbidity in breast cancer patients. *Psycho-Oncology, 11*(4), 282–294.

Slatore, C. G., Au, D. H., & Hollingworth, W. (2009). Cost-effectiveness of a smoking cessation program implemented at the time of surgery for lung cancer. *Journal of Thoracic Oncology, 4*(4), 499–504.

Smith, P. M., & Burgess, E. (2009). Smoking cessation initiated during hospital stay for patients with coronary artery disease: A randomized controlled trial. *CMAJ: Canadian Medical Association Journal, 180*(13), 1297–1303.

Spiegel, D., Bloom, J. R., Kraemer, H. C., & Gottheil, E. (1989). Effect of psychosocial treatment on survival of patients with metastatic breast cancer. *Lancet, 2*(8668), 888–891.

Stark, D., Kiely, M., Smith, A., Velikova, G., House, A., & Selby, P. (2002). Anxiety disorders in cancer patients: Their nature, associations, and relation to quality of life. *Journal of Clinical Oncology, 20*(14), 3137–3148.

Stathopoulou, G., Powers, M. B., Berry, A. C., Angela, C., Smits, J. A., & Otto, M. W. (2006). Exercise Interventions for Mental Health: A Quantitative and Qualitative Review. *Clinical Psychology: Science and Practice, 13*(2), 179–193.

Stein, M., Keller, S. E., & Schleifer, S. J. (1988). Immune system. relationship to anxiety disorders. *The Psychiatric Clinics of North America, 11*(2), 349–360.

Taylor, C. B., Houston-Miller, N., Killen, J. D., & Debusk, R. F. (1990). Smoking cessation after acute myocardial infarction: effects of a nurse-managed intervention. *Annals of Internal Medicine, 113*(2), 118–123.

Telch, C. F., & Telch, M. J. (1986). Group coping skills instruction and supportive group therapy for cancer patients: A comparison of strategies. *Journal of Consulting and Clinical Psychology, 54*(6), 802–808.

Todaro, J. F., Shen, B., Raffa, S. D., Tilkemeier, P. L., & Niaura, R. (2007). Prevalence of anxiety disorders in men and women with established coronary heart disease. *Journal of Cardiopulmonary Rehabilitation and Prevention, 27*(2), 86–91.

Trivedi, M. H., Greer, T. L., Grannemann, B. D., Chambliss, H. O., & Jordan, A. N. (2006). Exercise as an augmentation strategy for treatment of major depression. *Journal of Psychiatric Practice, 12*(4), 205–213.

Trunzo, J., & Pinto, B. (2004). Body esteem and mood among sedentary and active breast cancer survivors. *Mayo Clinic Proceedings, 79*(2), 181–186.

Tsao, A. S., Liu, D., Lee, J. J., Spitz, M., & Hong, W. K. (2006). Smoking affects treatment outcome in patients with advanced nonsmall cell lung cancer. *Cancer, 106*(11), 2428–2436.

Valenti, M., Giampiero, P., & Aielli, F. (2008). Physical exercise and quality of life in breast cancer survivors. *International Journal of Medical Sciences, 5*, 24–28.

van der Ven, N. C. W., Hogenelst, M. H. E., Tromp-Wever, A., Twisk, J. W. R., van der Ploeg, H. M., Heine, R. J., et al. (2005). Short-term effects of cognitive behavioural group training (CBGT) in adult type 1 diabetes patients in prolonged poor glycaemic control. A randomized controlled trial. *Diabetic Medicine, 22*(11), 1619–1623.

van Dixhoorn, J., & White, A. (2005). Relaxation therapy for rehabilitation and prevention in ischaemic heart disease: A systematic review and meta-analysis. *European Journal of Cardiovascular Prevention and Rehabilitation, 12*(3), 193–202.

van Ede, L., Yzermans, C. J., & Brouwer, H. J. (1999). Prevalence of depression in patients with chronic obstructive pulmonary disease: A systematic review. *Thorax, 54*, 688–692.

Videtic, G. M. M., Stitt, L. W., Dar, A. R., Kocha, W. I., Tomiak, A. T., Truong, P. T., et al. (2003). Continued cigarette smoking by patients receiving concurrent chemoradiotherapy for limited-stage small-cell lung cancer is associated with decreased survival. *Journal of Clinical Oncology, 21*(8), 1544–1549.

Weaver, T. E., Richmond, T. S., & Narsavage, G. L. (1997). An explanatory model of functional status in chronic obstructive pulmonary disease. *Nursing Research, 46*, 26.

Williams, R. B., & Littman, A. B. (1996). Psychosocial factors: Role in cardiac risk and treatment strategies. *Cardiology Clinics, 14*(1), 97–104.

Wu, H., Lin, L., Wu, S., & Lin, J. (2007). The psychologic consequences of chronic dyspnea in chronic pulmonary obstruction disease: The effects of acupressure on depression. *The Journal of Alternative and Complementary Medicine, 13*(2), 253–261.

Zabora, J., BrintzenhofeSzoc, K., Curbow, B., Hooker, C., & Piantadosi, S. (2001). The prevalence of psychological distress by cancer site. *Psycho-Oncology, 10*(1), 19–28.

Zorrilla, E. P., Luborsky, L., McKay, J. R., Rosenthal, R., Houldin, A., Tax, A., et al. (2001). The relationship of depression and stressors to immunological assays: A meta-analytic review. *Brain, Behavior, and Immunity, 15*(3), 199–226.

Behavioral Interventions in Public Health Settings: Physical Activity, Weight Loss, and Smoking

Beth A. Lewis, Eric Statt, *and* Bess H. Marcus

Abstract

This chapter discusses three health behaviors that significantly impact public health. Specifically, physical activity behavior, weight loss, and smoking cessation are associated with many health benefits, including decreased risk of cardiovascular disease, type 2 diabetes, and cancer. These three health behaviors are important modifiable risk factors that can have a significant impact on health. Unfortunately, only half of Americans are physically active at the recommended levels. Additionally, 66.3% of Americans are overweight or obese. Finally, despite the health problems related to smoking, about one-fifth of Americans continue to smoke cigarettes. We provide an overview of the theoretical models commonly used in intervention studies and summarize the research evidence from randomized trials. Finally, we review three different intervention approaches for improving health behaviors, including an individual-level approach for physical activity, a community-level approach for weight loss, and a group-based approach for smoking cessation.

Keywords: Cigarette use, exercise, interventions, obesity, overweight, physical activity, smoking cessation

In this chapter, we discuss three health behaviors— physical activity, weight loss, and smoking cessation— that significantly impact public health (Centers for Disease Control [CDC], 2005; National Heart, Lung, and Blood Institute/National Institute of Diabetes and Digestive and Kidney Diseases [NHBLI/NIDDK], 1998; Renehan, Tyson, Egger, Heller, & Zwahlen, 2008; U.S. Department of Health and Human Services [USDHHS], 2001a, b). These health behaviors are associated with many health benefits, including decreased risk of cardiovascular disease, type 2 diabetes, and cancer. Therefore, modifying these health behaviors can have a significant public health impact. For each behavior, we will review the prevalence, recommendations, health benefits, theoretical models commonly used in interventions, evidence from randomized controlled efficacy trials, and applied application examples. The theoretical models section will not include an exhaustive

summary of all of the available models, but will summarize the models most frequently used for the particular health behavior.

Physical Activity
Physical Activity Prevalence and Recommendations
The American College of Sports Medicine (ACSM) recommends that adults participate in 30 minutes or more of moderate-intensity physical activity on 5 or more days per week or 20 minutes or more of vigorous-intensity physical activity on 3 or more days per week (Haskell et al., 2007). Moderate- and vigorous-intensity physical activity can be combined to meet the above recommendations. Only 45%–50% of Americans meet or exceed this recommendation (USDHHS, 2001b). Therefore, approximately half the U.S. population is at an increased risk of cardiovascular disease, cancer, type 2 diabetes, and other

health problems. Consequently, promoting physical activity participation is an important public health issue.

Health Benefits of Physical Activity

Physical activity is associated with decreased rates of all-cause mortality among both men and women (USHHS, 2001a). Specifically, physically active individuals have a 30% lower risk of mortality than inactive individuals. The leading cause of death among Americans is cardiovascular disease. One-third of Americans have some form of cardiovascular disease, including hypertension, coronary heart disease, heart failure, or stroke (Rosamond et al., 2008). In recent years, cardiovascular disease has decreased due to decreased cholesterol levels, a decline in cigarette use, and better controlled blood pressure levels. Unfortunately, one modifiable risk factor for cardiovascular disease that has remained relatively constant is physical activity participation (USDHHS, 2001b). Research indicates a strong relationship between physical activity and reduced rates of cardiovascular disease (USDHHS, 2001b). Therefore, increasing physical activity among Americans has the potential to make a significant public health impact on decreasing rates of cardiovascular disease.

The leading cause of death among men and women below 80 years of age is cancer (Jemal et al., 2008). It is estimated that 38% of women and 45% of men will be diagnosed with cancer during their lifetime (USDHHS, 2001b). Participation in regular physical activity has been shown to reduce the risk of certain types of cancers, especially breast and colon cancer. For example, individuals who participate in 3–4 hours of physical activity per week that is at least of moderate intensity, have a 20%–40% reduced risk of breast cancer and a 30% reduced risk of colon cancer (USHDDS, 2001b). Additional research is needed to determine if greater amounts of physical activity are associated with greater risk reductions.

Physical activity is also important for preventing and treating *metabolic syndrome*, which refers to a combination of medical disorders that increases the risk of diabetes and cardiovascular disease (USDHHS, 2001b). Physical activity has also been shown to prevent type 2 diabetes and plays a significant role in its treatment. The role of physical activity for treating type 1 diabetes is less clear, although it appears that physical activity may be helpful. Finally, physical activity has also been shown to be helpful in preventing and treating gestational diabetes (i.e., diabetes during pregnancy) (USDHHS, 2001b).

Physical activity can be helpful for weight loss and for weight maintenance following weight loss. However, the amount of physical activity needed for weight loss is significantly higher than the recommendations listed earlier (USDHHS, 2001b). For a modest weight loss of 1%–3%, it is estimated that individuals need to walk for 4 miles per hour for 150 minutes or more or jog for 75 minutes per week at a pace of 6 miles per hour. However, a higher duration of physical activity is recommended for individuals seeking weight losses greater than 1%–3%. Regarding weight maintenance following weight loss, it is estimated that individuals would need to walk 54 minutes per day at a pace of 4 miles per hour or jog 26 minutes per day at a pace of 6 miles per hour. Calorie restriction is also a very important component of weight loss and weight maintenance, and this component will be explored more thoroughly in the weight management section.

Physical activity has been shown to improve mental health. For example, Blumenthal and colleagues (2007) found that physical activity participation was just as effective as antidepressant medication in a randomized controlled trial in reducing the incidence of depression. Interestingly, studies indicate that moderate and high levels of physical activity are just as effective as low levels of physical activity in combatting depression (USDHHS, 2001b). Physical activity is also associated with a reduced risk of anxiety disorders (USDHHS, 2001b).

Finally, physical activity is associated with musculoskeletal and functional health. For example, physical activity reduces the risk of hip fractures (USDHHS, 2001b). Additionally, resistance training, such as weight-lifting, improves bone mineral density (USDHHS, 2001b). Regarding functional health, research indicates that physical activity delays the cognitive decline associated with aging and the onset of dementia. Studies suggest that physical activity may also be helpful in treating symptoms of Alzheimer disease.

Theoretical Models

SOCIAL COGNITIVE THEORY

Social cognitive theory (SCT) is one of the most common theories used in physical activity intervention studies (e.g., Marcus et al., 2007a,b; Wilcox et al., 2008). Social cognitive theory postulates that there are multiple influences on behavior, including both cognitive and social variables (Bandura, 1986). One construct frequently associated with SCT is self-efficacy. Bandura (1986) conceptualizes self-efficacy as one's confidence in being able to carry out a specific behavior. Related to physical activity, self-efficacy refers to one's confidence to be physically active in certain situations (Marcus, Selby, Niaura, & Rossi, 1992). For example, an individual may have high self-efficacy to be physically active during manageable work weeks but low self-efficacy during busy work weeks. Other theoretical constructs related to SCT include outcome expectations, enjoyment, and decisional balance. Outcome expectancy refers to an individual's estimate that participating in physical activity will lead to a particular outcome. Examples of expectancies include improved mood, increased energy, and better sleep. Enjoyment of physical activity is an individuals' ratings of various attributes of physical activity (Kendzierski & DeCarlo, 1991). Examples include physical activity leading to gratification, exhilaration, and/or invigoration.

Social support is also considered part of SCT. Social support has been defined as feeling loved, cared for, and valued, as well as having a sense of belonging (Cobb, 1976). Three constructs of social support theory that relate to physical activity include supportive climates, support networks, and social integration (Laireiter & Baumann, 1992). Support networks include specific individuals who can provide support for the individual adopting and maintaining physical activity, such as family members, co-workers, and friends. For example, social support persons can remind the individual about the importance of physical activity or even participate in physical activity with the individual. Research indicates that high social support from family members is related to increases in physical activity (Courneya & McAuley, 1995; Oka, King, & Young, 1995). Supportive climates refer to the quality of the social relationships. For example, this could refer to how committed the support person is in assisting the person adopting increased physical activity. Finally, social integration refers to being integrated with a social group that has the same objective as the client, such as physical activity adoption.

THE TRANSTHEORETICAL MODEL

The transtheoretical model (TTM) is another common model utilized in physical activity intervention studies (e.g., Dunn et al., 1997; Marcus et al., 2007a,b). This theory posits that individuals move through a series of stages as they adopt and maintain physical activity (Marcus & Lewis, 2003; Prochaska & DiClemenete, 1983). Specific stages include: precontemplation (not intending to become physically active), contemplation (intending to become physically active in the next 6 months), preparation

(physically active sometimes, but not at the recommended levels), action (physically active at the recommended levels, but for less than 6 months), and maintenance (physically active at the recommended levels for 6 or more months). The TTM also posits that individuals use different processes of change as they progress through the stages. Specific behavioral processes include: (1) committing oneself; (2) reminding oneself; (3) enlisting social support; (4) rewarding oneself; and (5) substituting alternatives (Marcus, Rossi et al., 1992). Specific cognitive processes include: (1) comprehending benefits; (2) increasing knowledge; (3) increasing healthy opportunities; (4) being aware of risks; and (5) caring about consequences to others. Additionally, the TTM conceptualizes that the importance of the theoretical constructs may vary across time. For example, it is assumed that cognitive processes change prior to behavioral processes, based on the assumption that individuals modify their cognitions before engaging in behavioral strategies to change a behavior. Another construct related to the TTM is decisional balance. Decisional balance refers to weighing the pros and cons of becoming physically active. It is hypothesized that the pros and cons change as individuals progress through the stages of change (Marcus, Rakowski, & Rossi, 1992).

Efficacy of Physical Activity Interventions

Studies indicate that theory-based physical activity interventions are efficacious for increasing physical activity. A variety of types have been tested using randomized controlled trials including face-to-face interventions (e.g., Dunn et al., 1999), Internet (Marcus, Lewis, et al., 2007), telephone (e.g., King, Haskell, Young, Oka, & Stefanick, 1995), and tailored print (e.g., Marcus, Napolitano et al., 2007). Below we provide a brief summary of the evidence for each type of intervention.

FACE-TO-FACE

Research indicates that face-to-face interventions are effective for increasing physical activity; however, there is some evidence that non face-to-face interventions may be more effective. For example, Dishman and Buckworth (1996) conducted a review of 127 studies published between 1965 and 1995 and found larger effect sizes for interventions using non face-to-face methods (e.g., print mailings, telephone) when compared to completely face-to-face interventions. Furthermore, face-to-face interventions have several limitations. First, face-to-face interventions are costly, given the staff time involved in delivering the interventions. Additionally, unlike non face-to-face interventions, such as telephone calls, face-to-face interventions present time, child-care, and transportation barriers to participation. The authors of this review reported an overall success rate of 70%–88% regarding the percentage of individuals increasing their physical activity.

INTERNET-BASED INTERVENTIONS

The support for Internet-based intervention is mixed. Some studies show positive results, whereas other have found no effect of the intervention (for a review see Ciccolo, Lewis, & Marcus, 2008). One problem is that many of these studies did not use control groups and compared the Internet intervention to other types of interventions. In many of these studies, change in physical activity was found over time, but no differences were found between groups. For example, Marcus and colleagues randomized 249 sedentary participants to one of three interventions: Internet-based, print-based, or physical activity websites that were currently available to the public (e.g., American Heart Association, American College of Sports Medicine). Participants in the tailored Internet arm were regularly prompted to access a physical activity intervention website and received tailored feedback based on responses to questionnaires. The print intervention received the same tailored feedback, and this was an approach that has been shown to be effective (Marcus et al., 1998; Marcus, Napolitano, et al., 2007). Participants in all three arms self-monitored their physical activity using an Internet-based or paper log, depending on the arm, and were given incentives for self-monitoring. Results indicated that participants in all three arms of the study significantly increased their physical activity from baseline to 6 and 12 months; however, no differences were found among groups. Specifically, the Tailored Internet group increased from a median of 0 minutes per week at baseline to 120 minutes per week at 6 months and 90 minutes per week at 12 months. The Standard Internet group increased from a median of 10 minutes per week at baseline to 90 minutes per week at 6 months and 80 minutes per week at 12 months. The Tailored Print Group increased from a median of 0 minutes per week at baseline to 112.5 minutes per week at 6 months and 90 minutes per week at 12 months. It is possible that the self-monitoring alone was the efficacious component for the Standard Internet arm.

TELEPHONE AND PRINT INTERVENTIONS

Research indicates that telephone and print interventions are efficacious for increasing physical activity (Eakin, Lawler, Vandelanotte, & Owen, 2007; Marcus, Napolitano et al., 2007). For example, Eakin and colleagues (2007) conducted a review of telephone-based interventions for physical activity and dietary behavior change and found that 69% of the telephone-based physical activity interventions were efficacious. There is some evidence that tailored print-based interventions may be more efficacious than telephone-based interventions. For example, Marcus, Napolitano, and colleagues (2007) randomly assigned 239 sedentary participants to one of three conditions: telephone, tailored print mailings, and contact control condition. Participants in the telephone and print interventions significantly increased their physical activity relative to the contact control condition at 6 months; however, at 12 months, the print-based intervention was more efficacious than the telephone-based intervention. Specifically, the print group increased from a mean of 20.19 minutes per week at baseline to 129.49 minutes per week at 6 months and 162.37 minutes per week at 12 months. The telephone group increased from a mean of 19.75 minutes per week at baseline to 123.32 minutes per week at 6 months and 100.59 minutes per week at 12 months. The contact control group increased from a mean of 19.36 minutes per week at baseline to 77.67 minutes per week at 6 months and 81.92 minutes per week at 12 months. It is possible that as the number of contacts decreased between 6 and 12 months, participants in the print-based intervention made an easier transition to maintaining physical activity with fewer contacts than did participants in the telephone intervention. More research is needed to better understand the relative efficacy and cost-efficacy of print and telephone interventions.

Application of Physical Activity Interventions: Individual-level Approach

The following summarizes a physical activity intervention that could be applied at an individual level. This particular intervention could be administered in face-to-face sessions or via the telephone. The overall concepts of the intervention are based on the Transtheoretical Model (Prochaska & DiClemenete, 1983; Marcus & Lewis, 2003) and SCT (Bandura, 1986), both described earlier. More information regarding individual-level approaches can be found in Marcus and Forsyth, 2008.

PHYSICAL ACTIVITY ASSESSMENT

The first component of the intervention is to assess how much physical activity the client is currently participating in. The best strategy for assessing physical activity is to ask the client to think back over the previous week and recall how many minutes of physical activity he or she engaged in each day. If the previous week was not a typical week in terms of physical activity, then the previous week should be assessed. If 2 weeks prior is still not typical, then the client should recall how much physical activity he or she does in a typical week on average during the previous 3 months. Taken together, both the frequency (number of times per week) and duration (number of minutes per session) should be documented.

Physical activity should be defined to the client as anything that feels as hard, or harder than a brisk walk. It can also be described as something that feels like being late for an appointment, trying to catch a bus, or trying to get out of the rain. Basically, physical activity is any activity that elevates heart rate. Additionally, the activity should be done for at least 10 continuous minutes to be considered physical activity. Once the baseline level of physical activity is determined, the physical activity prescription can be generated by the counselor.

PHYSICAL ACTIVITY PRESCRIPTION

The physical activity prescription will depend upon the client's current level of physical activity. If the client is participating in no physical activity, he or she should start with two 15-minute brisk walks done during a 1-week timeframe. The frequency of the physical activity should first be increased, followed by increases in duration. More specifically, the number of days should gradually increase to 5, followed by an increase in the duration to 20, 25, and finally 30 minutes. The client can also divide his or her physical activity into 10 minute bouts throughout the day, or perform it all at once.

The client can choose the type of physical activity; however, many clients will choose brisk walking, given it is inexpensive, convenient, special equipment is not needed, and it is medically appropriate for almost everyone. Clients should be instructed to walk briskly enough to feel their heart rate increase (typically, a pace of 3 to 4 mph). In cases of inclement weather, walking at the mall is often a good option. Also, clients may want to consider purchasing a treadmill if possible, which offers various settings, including inclining the walking deck to create more challenging workouts. In general, it is the client's decision regarding the type of physical activity.

MONITORING INTENSITY

Clients should be instructed to perform their physical activity in the moderate or harder range. The counselor calculates their target heart rate by taking 220 minus their age and then multiplying that number by 60%–70% for the moderate range. If the client wishes to be physically active in the vigorous range, the number should be multiplied by 75%–80%. Clients should check with their doctor before stepping up the intensity of their workouts to the vigorous level. The easiest and most accurate way to monitor heart rate is by using a heart rate monitor watch. The watch displays the current heart rate of the client by detecting heart rate using a band that is worn right below the chest. However, if a heart rate monitor is not worn, heart rate can be assessed manually by placing the index and middle finger on one side of the neck. The client should monitor his or her heart rate for 15 seconds and multiple by 6. This should be done every 15 minutes during physical activity.

When being physically active outside, another way to monitor progress is by using a global positioning system (GPS) watch. The GPS watch uses satellites to monitor distance walked or jogged. On the watch, the time, heart rate, current pace, and calculated mileage is displayed. This watch can be motivating to clients to increase their intensity by increasing their pace and overall mileage. Many clients find it useful to obtain the same feedback provided by a treadmill while being able to enjoy the outdoors.

SAFETY ISSUES

There are safety issues to consider when participating in physical activity. First, it is important to do a 5-minute warm-up and end with 5 minutes of cooldown. On extremely hot or cold days, it is important to walk inside (such as at a mall), do an exercise video, use home equipment, or go to the gym. If the client's preference is to always do outdoor activities, encourage him or her to do the physical activity in the early morning or evening during hot, humid weather. Clothing should be loose fitting, and staying hydrated is very important. In cold weather, outdoor activities should be avoided if it is icy due to the risk of falling. However, if it is not icy, it is fine to do physical activity outside as long as the client dresses in layers and wears protective clothing such as a scarf, hat, and mittens. Many running stores offer special clothing that can be worn in cold weather.

It is important to wear safety equipment during certain types of physical activity. For example, a bicycle helmet when bicycling is always recommended. It is also recommended to do physical activity during the daylight hours; however, this may not always be feasible. If doing physical activity outdoors at dawn, dusk, or evening, the client should wear bright-colored clothing equipped with reflectors. It is also important to have at least one physical activity partner when engaging in physical activity at night. Clients often report that they "zone out" while being physically active. Remind the client to stay alert to passing traffic, especially at intersections; never assume that drivers can see pedestrians. Finally, it is important for the client to listen to his body. If he experiences pain, tightening of the chest, or a pain down one side of the arm, physical activity should be discontinued immediately and medical personnel should be alerted.

For clients who plan to walk, run, or bicycle outside, the general rules of the road should be discussed. For example, walkers and runners should walk or run against traffic, and bicyclists should stay on the side of the road that follows the flow of traffic. Obviously, walkers and runners should use the sidewalks whenever possible. Given the foot traffic on sidewalks, it is sometimes safer for bicyclists to ride on the road rather than on the sidewalk.

SELF-MONITORING AND GOAL SETTING

Two of the most important components of a physical activity intervention are goal setting and self-monitoring. Participants should be given a log to document their physical activity. It is useful to have the log look like a calendar, so that the client can write down the duration and type of activity done each day. Clients may also find it useful to put stars on a posted calendar so others can see their achievements.

Progress toward goals should be assessed at the beginning of each session, and a new goal should be set at the end of the session. If goals were met, the client should be reinforced for meeting those goals, and he should reward himself for meeting his goal. If goals were not met, an assessment of what particular barriers interfered with accomplishing the goal should be conducted. It is important to give the client feedback on how she is doing and identify any ups and downs regarding achieving goals. The counselor and client should strategize regarding how to attain the goals.

The goals should be specific, attainable, and measurable. For example, vague goals such as "I will do my best" should be avoided. If the client is currently doing no activity, he or she should avoid setting a goal of jogging five times per week for 30 minutes each time. As an example, a more attainable and specific goal might be, "I will walk for 15 minutes at lunch and 15 minutes after dinner, 3 days this week." It is important to remember that achieving a goal is important for increasing confidence.

Both short- and long-term goals should be set. The short-term goal should include specific goals for the next week, and long-term goals should include the next 6 months. The ultimate goal should be to engage in physical activity five or more times per week for 30 minutes or more each session, and this should likely be the long-term goal. The weekly short-term goals should gradually increase activity in order to eventually reach the long-term goal.

It is often helpful to compare physical activity adoption with some other behavior the client has successfully adopted or stopped previously. The client should be asked why he or she was able to make that particular change, and what helped with her success. Also, assess what factors interfered with success in the long term. What had to be given up to make time for physical activity and how much value was placed on what was given up should also be assessed. Overall, it is important to help the client find more time in the day to be physically active.

BENEFITS OF PHYSICAL ACTIVITY

The many benefits of physical activity should be discussed with the client. It will be important to discuss the benefits that are particularly relevant for the client. For example, if the client has a family history of cardiovascular disease, the fact that physical activity significantly reduces the risk of cardiovascular disease should be emphasized. As discussed previously, other long-term benefits of physical activity include reduced risk for some types of cancer (e.g., colon, breast), stroke, osteoporosis, obesity, and type 2 diabetes. Although it is important to discuss the long-term benefits of physical activity, many clients find the immediate benefits of physical activity more rewarding and therefore, it is important to also emphasize these benefits. For example, many clients find that physical activity improves mood, sleep, anxiety, energy level, and overall functioning. Many clients report that, after beginning a physical activity program, they have less fatigue and are more energized throughout the day. This should be emphasized with the client, given that one of the barriers to physical activity is often feeling fatigued. The client should be reminded that on days when he or she feels tired, although it may seem counterintuitive, physical activity may actually help give him or her a boost of energy.

SOCIAL SUPPORT

Social support is one of the key factors in helping a client adopt physical activity. The counselor should assess if a spouse or significant other can support physical activity, and if there are specific things they can do to encourage physical activity. This could include engaging in physical activity with the client, reminding them to be physically active, or taking care of household responsibilities, such as childcare, while the client engages in physical activity. If the spouse or significant other is not supportive, the counselor should assess why they are not supportive. Some common reasons include taking away time from the significant other, expenses related to physical activity, and difficulty completing household tasks. It is sometimes helpful to do a joint session with both the client and significant other to assess any resistance to the client's becoming physically active.

Social support can also come from other family members, friends, and the work environment. For example, some work environments encourage physical activity by offering on-site facilities, release time from work for physical activity (especially during lunch), and reimbursement for gym memberships. Friends can also be an important source of support for physical activity. Physical activity can become a social event, by meeting a friend at the mall to walk or exercising at the gym with a friend next to you on the elliptical trainer. Clients can also be encouraged to tell their friends about their plan for adopting physical activity, so that these friends can encourage and reward the client for meeting his or her goals.

ENJOYMENT

To increase the likelihood of maintaining physical activity, it important to make physical activity as enjoyable as possible, and to ensure it is not aversive. The counselor should assess what the client likes and dislikes about physical activity. For example, changing the type of physical activity that the client does on a monthly basis can help decrease boredom. Changing the environment can also be helpful; for example, engaging in physical activity outside if physical activity is normally done inside. If the client is physically active at a gym, listening to music or watching television can be helpful. Other tips include engaging in physical activity with other people, buying an exercise video, trying a new exercise

class, or buying a new piece of exercise home equipment.

SELF-EFFICACY

Self-efficacy for physical activity refers to one's confidence for being physically active in challenging situations. Self-efficacy can be assessed by asking how confident the client feels about engaging in physical activity during the following five situations (rated on a 5-point Likert scale ranging from not at all confident to extremely confident): (1) Feeling tired; (2) in a bad mood; (3) not having time; (4) on vacation; and (5) when it is raining or snowing (Marcus, Selby, Niaura, & Rossi, 1992). The counselor should regularly convey to the participant that she believes the client will succeed in adopting physical activity. The counselor can discuss specific strategies for overcoming low self-efficacy for physical activity during one or more of the situations listed. If the client rates his confidence at a 1 or a 2, think about why he does not feel confident and discuss ways to increase confidence. If the rating is a 3, talk about what he likes the most and least about physical activity and consider ways to make physical activity more enjoyable. If the rating is a 4 or a 5, make plans for making sure physical activity becomes a habit. It is important to instill confidence that, if clients are not physically active for a short period of time, they can resume their physical activity as soon as possible. Instill confidence that the client can continue her physical activity program despite difficult times (e.g., increased stress, poor mood, busy work week).

MAKING PHYSICAL ACTIVITY A HABIT

Once the client successfully adopts physical activity, it is time to start talking about making physical activity a habit. The counselor should discuss any benefits the client may have noticed as a result of physical activity, such as more energy, better weight management, and improved mood. Encourage the client to periodically remind herself about how she benefits from continuing with the physical activity program. The counselor should also discuss what the participant had to give up for physical activity and how important the things are that she had to give up. The client and counselor can think about any obstacles that might arise in the future that could interfere with her ability to stay active. A plan for how to deal with these potential issues should be created. Work with the client to instill confidence that she can start up the physical activity program, if she should stop for any reasons. Remind the client how far she has come, and continue to praise her for her effort.

The counselor might make a suggestion to try a new activity or to ask someone else to do physical activity with them. The client might want to think of someone he or she would like to serve as a role model to. Another good strategy is to decide on the number of miles to accumulate from now until the next session. Agree on a small gift for accomplishing goals, and set up a plan for significant others to reward the participant for physical activity. The client's environment should include posted reminders about physical activity. Finally, "all or none thinking" should be avoided. If he or she misses a session or two, the program is not lost, and the client should hurry to get back in the habit.

RELAPSE PREVENTION

The counselor should discuss the possibility that a lapse will occur when maintaining physical activity over the long term. It is important to prevent the lapse from turning into a relapse, which refers to not being physically active for more than 1 week. Discuss how the client will get back on track and identify the trigger(s) for lapse. For example, many individuals stop being physically active when they get sick, and once physical activity is discontinued, an individual fails to begin the program again once he or she feels better. In this situation, the counselor would discuss with the client the importance of getting back to the physical activity program after being sick. Also, discuss with the client what will keep him or her motivated to get back on track. In summary, the counselor and client should make a plan for preventing a lapse or relapse from occurring.

Weight Loss
Prevalence of Obesity

The prevalence of obesity and being overweight has steadily increased in recent years, especially among men (Ogden et al., 2006). Specifically, 66.3% of adults are overweight or obese, and 32.2% are obese. The prevalence of extreme obesity (body mass index [BMI] of ≥40) is 2.8% in men and 6.9% among women. It appears that obesity increases with age, in that 36.8% of adults ages 40–59 are obese, which is higher than the 32.2% observed in the general public. Obesity is defined as a BMI of 30 or above, overweight is a BMI between 25–30, and normal weight is considered between 18.5 and 25. Body mass index is calculated by assessing weight in relation to height. The specific calculation is weight in

kilograms divided by the square root of height in meters. Other indicators of obesity commonly used in the literature are waist-to-hip ratio and waist circumference.

Health Consequences of Obesity

Overweight and obesity are associated with numerous health problems, including type 2 diabetes, dyslipidemia (i.e., disruption in the amount of lipids in the blood), coronary heart disease, hypertension, gall bladder disease, stroke, sleep apnea, respiratory problems, osteoarthritis, and cancers, especially endometrial, prostate, and postmenopausal breast cancer (NHBLI, NIDDK, 1998; Renehan et al., 2008). Research indicates that the most significant health risk associated with obesity is type 2 diabetes. For example, in the Nurses Health Study, BMI was the most significant predictor of type 2 diabetes after adjusting for age (Colditz, Willett, Rotnisky, & Mason, 1995). When compared to women with a BMI of 21, women who had a BMI of 25 had a five-fold increased risk of diabetes, a 28-fold increase for those with a BMI of 30, and a 93-fold increase among those with a BMI of 35 or greater. Additionally, women who gained between 8–10.9 kg during the time of the study had a 2.7-fold increased in the risk of diabetes when compared to women whose weight did not change. Regarding men, after adjusting for age, the increased risk was 2.2-fold for a BMI between 25 and 26.9, 6.7-fold for a BMI between 29 and 30, and 42-fold for men whose BMI was 35 or greater, when compared to men with a BMI of less than 21 (Chan, Rimm, Colditz, Stampfer, & Willett, 1994). Additionally, a waist circumference of more than 40 inches is associated with an increased risk of diabetes by 3.5-fold after controlling for BMI (Lean, Han, & Seidell, 1998).

Research indicates that obesity is a significant predictor of coronary heart disease among both women and men. In the Women's Health Study (prospective cohort study of 38,987 women), both physical inactivity and higher BMI were individual predictors of coronary heart disease (Weinstein et al., 2008). The increased risk was 54% for overweight-active women, 87% for obese-active, 8% for normal weight-inactive, 88% for overweight-inactive, and 253% for obese-inactive. In a study among men, after adjusting for age, men who had a waist-to-hip ratio greater than or equal to .95 or a waist circumference of greater than or equal to 36.8 had a significantly increased risk of coronary heart disease (Rexrode, Buring, & Mason, 2001). Men in the highest quintile of waist circumference had a 60%

increase in coronary heart disease, and those in the highest waist-to-hip ratio quintile (.99) had a 50% increased risk. It should be noted that when BMI was controlled for, these relationships were significantly attenuated. Among men in the highest BMI quintile, the risk of coronary heart disease was 200% and was 252% for myocardial infarction.

Polednak (2008) recently published a study estimating that 50,535 of new cancers among women and 33,966 of new cancers among men diagnosed in 2007 were attributed to obesity. Therefore, obesity accounts for 6% of all new cancer cases. The association between obesity and cancer was observed for endometrial cancer, kidney cancer, gallbladder cancer, breast cancer, adenocarcinoma of the esophagus, liver cancer, and colorectal cancer (Polednak, 2008). The estimates of this recent study are larger than what has been observed in previous studies; however, previous studies have included fewer types of cancers than those in the Polednak study.

Finally, obesity is a significant predictor of sleep problems. For example, one study found that 50% of men and 33% of women with a BMI above 35 reported snoring and sleep apnea, compared to 15.5% of the normal-weight participants (Grunstein, Stenlof, Hedner, & Sjostrom, 1995). This is important, given that sleep apnea is associated with myocardial infarction and stroke. Additionally, snoring is a significant risk factor for sleep-related strokes (Palomaki, Partinen, Erkinjuntti, & Kaste, 1992).

Theoretical Models

LEARNING THEORY

Learning theory forms the basis for many weight loss interventions (Brownell, 1998). One component of learning theory is *operant conditioning,* in which individuals receive positive reinforcement, which in turn increases a particular behavior. Specifically related to weight loss, participants who change their diet and increase physical activity are typically rewarded with weight loss. Other important components of learning theory that are commonly applied to weight loss include goal setting, self-monitoring (i.e., documenting everything one eats during the day and documenting physical activity), and stimulus control (e.g., keeping junk food out of the house). Feedback is also a common component of weight loss interventions. For example, research indicates that a higher rate of self-weighing is associated with greater weight loss and therefore, daily weighing is recommended (Linde, Jeffery, French, Pronk, & Boyle, 2005).

ECOLOGICAL MODEL FOR HEALTH PROMOTION

McLeroy and colleagues (1988) proposed the Ecological Model for Health Promotion, which has been applied to weight loss interventions. This theory postulates that five factors influence behavior change. The first component includes interpersonal factors, which refer to characteristics of the individual such as behavior, attitudes, self-concept, and knowledge. Interpersonal intervention strategies include mass media, educational programs, organizational incentives, and support groups. This intervention strategy focuses on changing behavior at the individual level, including changing attitudes, intention to comply with behavioral norms, and knowledge. The second component is interpersonal processes, which refer to social networks and social support systems. These could include friends, families, co-workers, neighbors, and acquaintances. Interpersonal intervention strategies focus on changing the individual's behavior through social influences. The third component of the ecological model is institutional or organizational factors, which refer to social institutions. This is an important component, given that a majority of people spend much of their time in organizational settings ranging from daycare, primary and secondary school, university, and the workplace. The intervention focus should be on how characteristics of the organization can be used to instill behavioral changes. The fourth component is community factors, which are relationships among institutions, informal networks, and organizations. The community can include families, neighbors, friendship networks, voluntary agencies, schools, health providers, and/or political entities. The final component is public policy, which refers to laws and policies at the local, state, and national level. Specifically, policy development activities can include increasing public awareness, creating advocacy groups to lobby for obesity-related laws and policies, and/or passing legislation related to obesity.

NEW MODEL FOR BEHAVIORAL MAINTENANCE

Several models have been applied to weight loss, including the theory of reasoned action (Ajzen & Fishbein, 1980), the Health Belief Model (Rosenstock, Strecher, & Becker, 1988), and the theory of planned behavior (Ajzen, 1991). These tend to focus on the premise that positive expectations about the outcome of behavior change predict weight loss. The problem with these models is that they focus on the initiation of a behavior and do not explain how behavior is maintained.

Rothman (2000) postulates that the factors involved in behavioral maintenance are different from the factors involved in behavioral initiation. Specifically, Rothman theorizes that individuals will maintain a behavior if they are satisfied with their accomplishments. Therefore, the feeling of satisfaction as a result of changing a behavior suggests that initially changing the behavior was the correct decision. Individuals maintain the behavior to maintain the positive situation and to avoid a negative state. Specifically related to weight loss, individuals work to maintain their weight loss because they are happy with their decision to lose weight and the weight loss results.

Efficacy of Weight Loss Interventions

BEHAVIORAL GROUP-BASED INTERVENTIONS

Structured group behavior weight loss programs are the most efficacious nonmedical intervention for overweight and obesity (Wing, 2004). These interventions include cognitive restructuring (i.e., restructuring thoughts that are more consistent with weight loss), stress management, physical activity, self-monitoring (e.g., writing type of food and related calories into a food diary each day), social support, and relapse prevention. Participants typically eat a low-fat, balanced diet (1,200–1,800 calories per day depending on starting weight) and engage in physical activity (30–60 minutes per day). The groups are typically run by trained behavioral counselors. The weight loss typically reported by the behavioral group interventions is 10% of baseline weight over approximately 6 months (Wing, 2004). One limitation of the group-based intervention is that it is expensive and typically not reimbursed by health insurance. Other barriers to group-based interventions are time, childcare and transportation. Therefore, researchers have begun to examine other non face-to-face interventions, such as Internet interventions, for weight loss.

INTERNET-BASED INTERVENTIONS

Saperstein and colleagues (2007) recently completed a review examining the efficacy of Internet-based interventions for weight loss. Five of the six studies reviewed indicated that Internet-based weight loss interventions were efficacious. There is also some evidence that more intensive interventions lead to better efficacy. For example, Tate and colleagues (2001) randomly assigned participants to either a 6-month Internet behavior therapy intervention or an Internet education intervention. The education intervention participants received access to links for Internet weight loss resources. Participants in the behavior therapy intervention received access to the links plus lessons via e-mail, self-monitored, and received individualized therapist feedback. Participants in the Internet behavior intervention lost significantly more weight than did individuals in the Internet education intervention (4.1 kg vs. 1.6 kg at 6 months). In a follow-up study, Tate and colleagues (2003) randomized participants to either basic Internet or to Internet plus behavior e-counseling. Both groups were instructed to submit weekly weights. Again, the behavior counseling group lost significantly more weight than the basic Internet group (4.4 kg vs. 2.0 kg at 12 months). Given the high cost of individualized Internet-based feedback, more research is needed regarding how to better automate Internet interventions without reducing efficacy.

TYPE OF DIET

Nordmann and colleagues (2006) conducted a meta-analysis that included studies that have compared traditional low-fat high-carbohydrate diets to low-carbohydrate diets. Findings from this meta-analysis indicated that low-carbohydrate, non–calorie restriction diets were at least as efficacious as traditional low-fat, higher-carbohydrate diets that did restrict calorie intake. Unfortunately, there were several limitations to these studies, including high attrition rates, short duration, and small sample sizes. Recently, Gardner and colleagues (2007) randomized female participants to one of four conditions: (1) Atkins (≤20 grams of carbohydrates for the first 2–3 months and then ≤50 grams of carbohydrates); (2) Zone (40% carbohydrate, 30% protein, and 30% fat); (3) LEARN (55%–60% of food from carbohydrates and <10% of food from saturated fat, increased physical activity, caloric restriction, behavior modification strategies); and (4) Ornish (10% of energy from fat). The LEARN and Zone diets had specific goals for caloric intake, whereas the Atkins and Ornish diets did not. The LEARN and Atkins diets emphasized multiple strategies, such as preparation and relapse prevention strategies. The LEARN diet had the greatest emphasis on behavior modification. Results indicated that weight loss was greatest for women on the Atkins diet when compared with the other diets at 12 months. Specifically, participants in the Atkins diet lost 4.7 kg, the Zone 1.6 kg, LEARN 2.6 kg, and Ornish 2.2 kg.

MAINTENANCE

Despite the positive effects of weight loss interventions, the evidence for maintaining weight loss in the long-term is discouraging. For example, Fappa and colleagues (2008) recently conducted a weight loss intervention review and concluded that support for long-term weight loss maintenance is weak. Based on this review, it appears that booster sessions following the conclusion of the weight loss interventions may be an important component for weight loss maintenance. Additional research is needed to better understand effective strategies for long-term weight loss maintenance.

COMMUNITY-BASED INTERVENTIONS

Given the widespread obesity epidemic (Ogden et al., 2006), researchers and policy makers have called for community-based interventions that have the potential to make a significant public health impact (Horowitz et al., 2008). Byers and Sedjo (2007) recently reviewed community-based interventions for obesity and concluded that there is little evidence regarding the efficacy of these types of interventions. However, the lack of efficacy is likely due to the lack of large-scale intervention trials in this area. Therefore, despite the lack of efficacy, community-based interventions should be implemented and evaluated in the real-world setting to establish their effectiveness. The U.S. Surgeon General has released a "call to action" regarding community-based interventions (USDHHS, 2001b). The remaining part of this section will therefore focus on community intervention strategies and this "call to action."

Application of Weight Intervention: Community-level Approach

The following community-level approach will be based on the social ecological model in that the environment will be an important component of the intervention. We will summarize strategies that can be used in a variety of settings, including schools, community centers, worksites, health-care centers, and health insurance companies. We will address what community leaders, policy makers, school administrators, and health-care providers can do to address the obesity epidemic.

LEVERAGING COMMUNITY ORGANIZATIONS

Several community-level organizations are in a position to influence community member eating behaviors, including churches, local organizations, fitness centers such as the YMCA, daycare centers, and community centers. For example, healthy lifestyle education classes could be offered to community members of these organizations. Experts in nutrition and physical activity participation could hold

sessions within these organizations and encourage community members to enlist each other's support for making healthy lifestyle choices. This model works best when community members are already involved with one another and are, therefore, able to provide support to one another. It is also possible to leverage events like harvest parties, community field days, and festivals to disseminate healthy-eating messages and to foster community efforts for healthy lifestyle changes (Economos & Irish-Hauser, 2007).

CHANGING THE BUILT ENVIRONMENT

Many neighborhoods are designed for motorists rather than bicyclists and walkers, which is important given that research indicates that higher levels of "walkability" (defined as higher density, pedestrian-friendly design, proportion of residents walking to work, and land-use diversity) is correlated with a decreased risk of overweight and obesity (Smith et al., 2008). Additionally, research indicates that land layout is significantly related to overweight and obesity (Ewing, Schmid, Killingsworth, Zlot, & Raudenbush, 2003). Many suburbs that were built in previous decades are subject to what has been termed "suburban sprawl," in which it is necessary for community members to own an automobile. The "suburban sprawl" effect makes it difficult for community members to bicycle or walk to their local grocery store or library. Additionally, research indicates that individuals who live near wooded walking paths and sidewalks containing shops are more likely to be physically active than are individuals not living near these amenities (Corti, Donovan, & Holman, 1997). Therefore, increasing access to walking paths and sidewalks with shops may increase physical activity, which in turn may play a role in decreasing obesity.

The Prevention Institute profiled 11 different case examples of implementing changes to the built environment for purposes of improving health (Prevention Institute, 2004). Many of these case examples were directly related to leading a healthier lifestyle. One case example was the Evergreen Cemetery Jogging Path. In this example, a predominately Latino, urban community in California rallied community-wide support to create a safe, 1.5 mile walking/jogging path. Previously, community members did not have access to open spaces or parks in their neighborhood. In another example, community members of Rochester, New York, increased access to healthy food by organizing the building of a full-service supermarket into a community that lacked a single grocery store. In Denver, Colorado, a community/academic organization transformed vacant lots into a community garden in an urban neighborhood. Finally, 20 well-respected arts, culture, and academic institutions formed the Fenway Alliance and revitalized the culture district by improving walkability through major infrastructure projects in Boston, Massachusetts.

U.S. SURGEON GENERAL'S CALL TO ACTION

The U.S. Surgeon General published a report outlining community-level strategies to prevent obesity in five settings (USDHHS, 2001b). These are outlined in more detail below.

Family and Communities

Communities and families are at the foundation of adopting and maintaining a healthy lifestyle. Families can share their knowledge with their friends, children, and community members. It is important to increase consumer awareness of the health problems related to being overweight and/or obese. Community coalitions should be formed to developed opportunities for healthy food choices and opportunities to engage in physical activity. Community members should encourage the food industry to provide reasonable beverage and food portion sizes. The availability of nutritious foods that are prepared away from home should be increased. More community-based obesity prevention and treatment programs should be created. It is important to empower families to manage weight within their own family through skill building in parenting, behavioral management, and meal planning. The efforts to encourage health eating patterns that are consistent with the Dietary Guidelines for Americans should be expanded. Demonstration grants should be provided to inner cities, where healthy affordable foods are often not available. The consumption of at least five servings of fruits and vegetables should be supported. Community environments that promote and support breast-feeding should be created to decrease weight retention during the postpartum phase. Time spent watching television and other sedentary behaviors should be decreased at the family level. Demonstration grants should be given to community leaders who address the lack of public access to safe places in which to be physically active and the lack of affordable physical activity programs. Finally, community leaders should pass important public policy regarding increasing accessible sidewalks, stairs, and walking and bicycle paths.

Schools

A majority of children spend a large portion of their time each day in school and therefore, this is an ideal setting to prevent overweight and obesity. Schools have a unique opportunity to engage children in healthy eating and physical activity, and to communicate important healthy eating and physical activity messages. Public schools should not simply focus on health and physical education, but also modify the school's physical and social environment so that it is conducive to healthy lifestyles. It is important for schools to ensure that meals offered for breakfast and lunch are nutritious. It is also important that health education helps students develop the skills necessary to enjoy healthy eating and physical activity. Schools should also adopt policies ensuring that beverages and foods available on school grounds are consistent with a healthy lifestyle. This can be a complex issue, given that many schools bring in substantial revenue via vendors of sugared drinks. Schools that provide choices in addition to the main school lunch offerings should have healthy options presented through school stores and vending machines. Schools may consider prohibiting vending machines and school stores that compete with healthy school lunches. It is important to have adequate time for students to eat their school lunches, as well as adequate time for physical activity during recess. All children should receive regular physical education that will help develop the knowledge, skills, and behaviors essential for lifelong physical activity. Extracurricular physical activity programs should also be included. Finally, schools should encourage after-school programs that implement time for physical activity and healthy snacks.

Health-care

The health-care industry provides a unique opportunity to intervene on healthy eating and physical activity. Many individuals look to their health-care providers for advice regarding health and therefore, these providers are in a unique situation to help individuals achieve their weight loss goals. It is important that health-care providers and health-care students are trained in prevention and treatment strategies for obesity. Partnerships among health-care providers, schools, faith-based groups, and other community organizations should be formed to target the environmental and social causes of obesity. Additionally, obesity should be clarified as a disease for reimbursement coding. Currently, most nutrition and physical activity interventions for obesity are not reimbursed by insurance companies, and classifying them as a disease may be the first step in changing health insurance reimbursement policies.

Media and Communications

One strategy recommended by the U.S. Surgeon General's report is to conduct a national campaign that fosters public awareness of the health benefits of healthy diet choices and the importance of maintaining a healthy weight. It is also important to encourage reasonable consumer goals for weight management programs and products. Via media outlets, many products promise lofty weight loss goals, and this leads to frustrations and dropout by participants in the programs when the goals are not attained. It is important to incorporate healthy eating and regular physical activity messages into television programming targeting youth. For example, a recent magazine advertisement, asks, "Which do you think your kid will think is cooler?" The advertisement goes on to show a picture of an apple and a juice box. This type of advertising needs to be examined by policy makers to determine if it is potentially harmful to children. Finally, media professionals should be encouraged to utilize actors' influences as role models for healthy eating and physical activity.

Worksites

A majority of Americans spend most of their day at work and, therefore, the worksite has the potential to make a significant impact on lifestyle choices. Workers can benefit from flexible work hours that allow them to create opportunities for regular physical activity. It is important to have protected time for lunch, so that time is available for physical activity, and healthy food options also should be available. Worksites can create incentives for workers maintaining a healthy body weight. Health insurance companies, offered through the worksite, should offer physical activity and weight management programs. For example, many health insurance companies are beginning to offer subsidies for health club memberships, as long as the members visits the gym a certain number of times (Lewis, Martinson, Anderson, & Sherwood, 2006). Finally, it is important for the work environment to promote and support breast-feeding, given that this can lead to effective weight loss for some individuals during the postpartum phase.

Smoking Cessation
Smoking Prevalence

The Centers for Disease Control (CDC) estimates that 20.8% of adults (45.3 million) in the United States smoke cigarettes (CDC, 2007a). Approximately, 23.9 % of 18- to 24-year-olds smoke cigarettes, 23.5% of 25- to 44-year-olds, 21.8% of 45- to 64-year-olds, and 10.2% of individuals over the age of 65. Regarding ethnicity, 32.4% of Native Americans smoke cigarettes, 23.0% of African Americans, 21.9% of Caucasians, 15.2% of Hispanics, and 10.4% of Asians. For educational levels, the highest prevalence is among adults with a general education development (GED) diploma (46.0%) or 9–11 years of education (35.4%), and the lowest prevalence is among individuals with an undergraduate degree (9.6%) or a graduate degree (6.6%; CDC, 2007b).

Health Consequences of Cigarette Use

Smoking is the number one preventable cause of death in the United States (USDHHS, 2001a). Each year, over 438,000 people die from smoking related illness. Of the 438,000 people who die prematurely from smoking-related illness, approximately 59.5% are male and 40.5% are female (CDC, 2005). In data collected by the CDC from 1995 through 1999, the American Cancer Society (ACS) reports on average male smokers lost 13.2 years of life expectancy and female smokers lost 14.5 years. Smokers also experience a decrease in quality of life as a result of smoking (American Cancer Society [ACS], 2007a).

In a review of CDC data compiled since 2000, the ACS indicates that both disease and quality-of-life issues are prevalent for smokers. It is estimated that 8.6 million people had at least one chronic disease related to a history or prevalence of smoking (ACS, 2008). Disease issues for this group include chronic bronchitis, emphysema, coronary heart disease, strokes, and cancer. Additionally, smokers can find managing daily activities challenging due to limitations in breathing and moving.

Smoking and Morbidity

Cigarette smoking is responsible for approximately 90% of lung cancer deaths in men and 80% in women. Since 1950, lung cancer for women has increased 600%. By 1987, it became the leading cause of cancer-related death among women (USDHHS, 2001a). Novotny and colleagues (1998) indicate that the risk of dying from lung cancer is 22 times greater for men and 12 times greater for women who smoke than for nonsmokers. Cigarette smoking also increases the risk of dying from coronary heart disease by two- to three-fold. In relation to chronic obstructive lung diseases, approximately 90% are attributable to cigarette smoking. Smoking is responsible for more deaths each year than the combined effects of human immunodeficiency virus (HIV), illegal drug use, alcohol use, motor vehicle injuries, suicides, and murders (CDC, 2005).

Smoking cessation is associated with significant health benefits. For example, the U.S. Surgeon General (2004) published the following sequence of benefits that begin immediately upon quitting:

- *20 minutes after quitting*: Heart rate and blood pressure drop.
- *12 hours after quitting*: Carbon monoxide levels in blood drop to normal.
- *Between 2 weeks and 3 months after quitting*: Heart attack risk drops, circulation improves, and lung function increases.
- *Between 1 month and 9 months after quitting*: Coughing and shortness of breath decrease.
- *1 year after quitting*: Risk of coronary heart disease is half of that of a smoker's.
- *Between 5 years and 15 years after quitting*: Risk of stroke is reduced to that of a nonsmoker.
- *10 years after quitting*: Lung cancer death rate is about half that of a smoker; risk of cancers of the mouth, throat, esophagus, bladder, kidney, and pancreas decrease.
- *15 years after quitting*: Risk of coronary heart disease is back to that of a nonsmoker.

Using data collected from 1997–2001, the CDC determined that the annualized health-related economic loss to the United States was $167 billion dollars due to cigarette smoking, with $75 billion attributed to direct medical costs and $92 billion dollars to lost productivity (CDC, 2005). This calculates to approximately $3,561 per adult smoker per year (CDC, 2000, 2003, 2007). In summary, given the strong relationship between smoking and premature death, low quality of life, and the costs associated with cigarette use, smoking cessation initiatives are necessary to improve public health in the United States. It is also important to focus on programs that prevent smoking initiation among adolescents and young adults.

Theoretical Models
TRANSTHEORETICAL MODEL
The TTM has been described previously in this chapter and therefore, this section will focus solely on the TTM as applied to smoking cessation. Fava and colleagues (1995) postulate that the TTM's five stages of change "provide temporal organization"

for monitoring the individual's progress through a smoking cessation program. The five stages of change are precontemplation (smoker has no intention of quitting within the next 6 months), contemplation (smoker is considering quitting within the next 6 months), preparation (smoker is planning on quitting within the next 30 days, and has made one attempt to quit within the last year), action (the smoker has been continuously abstinent from 1 day to 6 months), maintenance (smoker has been continuously abstinent for more than 6 months). The behavioral and cognitive processes described in the physical activity section can also be applied to smoking cessation.

COGNITIVE-BEHAVIORAL THERAPY
Cognitive behavior therapy is the leading type of intervention for treating psychological conditions (David & Szentagotai, 2006). The cognitive component of CBT has roots in Albert Ellis' ABCDE model (Ellis, 1962). According to this model, "A" refers to an individual perceiving an event as either rational or irrational, which then creates a belief or cognition. This belief will then lead to "B," which are the emotional and cognitive consequences. The rational beliefs will lead to "C," the functional consequences or irrational and dysfunctional consequences. Next, "D" refers to the individual actively disputing his or her irrational beliefs (restructuring the thought). Finally, "E" refers to assimilating the more rational thoughts with the outcome and has a positive impact on the individual's cognitive, emotional, and behavioral responses (David & Szentagotai, 2006; Ellis 1994). The cognitive component of CBT emphasizes the human condition and the effect of changing dysfunctional thoughts. There is a focus on making a fundamental shift in the way an individual perceives, reflects upon, and processes his or her life circumstances (Dobson & Kahtri, 2000). Cognitive-behavioral therapy assumes that an individual's behavior is significantly mediated by his or her process of cognition, and therefore changing dysfunctional cognition will lead to change in behavior.

The behavioral component of CBT for smoking cessation has its foundations in operant conditioning, which is the premise that adding something positive (i.e., positive reinforcer) or taking away something negative (i.e., negative reinforcer) following a behavior will lead to increases in that behavior. Specifically related to smoking, the relaxed feelings resulting from smoking can serve as a positive reinforcer and the alleviation of stress can serve as a negative reinforcer, with both leading to an increase in smoking behavior. Specific behavior strategies for smoking cessation will be discussed later in the application section.

RELAPSE PREVENTION

Relapse prevention strategies are key to long-term smoking cessation. Relapse prevention theorists differentiate between lapses and relapses. A *lapse* refers to a single event in which a smoker consumes tobacco following a period of recovery. Some individuals may be able to effectively cope with this "slip" and quickly return to smoking cessation. Others may continue to use tobacco and move closer to relapsing. A *relapse* refers to the smoker who has been unable to maintain his or her therapeutic gains and returns to smoking (Marlatt & Gordan, 1985). Much of the success or failure regarding relapse rests in the individual's ability to demonstrate his or her new skills acquired through therapy.

Three factors play a role in relapse prevention: lifestyle factors, intrapersonal factors, and interpersonal factors. Lifestyle factors include having a poor image of roles regarding social functions, such as school, work, and/or church. Intrapersonal factors involve negative physical states, poor mood, impulsive decision making, and temptations. Interpersonal factors could include lack of support from peer groups, social pressure, relationship conflicts, and poor social skills (Daley & Salloum, 1999). To effectively avoid the transition of a lapse into a relapse, the therapeutic plan must include strategies that identify, interrupt, and reverse episodes of lapses. For example, the counselor could identify factors, such as stress, that may trigger a relapse and strategize alternative ways to deal with this smoking trigger. Additionally, ongoing stress may result in a lapse becoming a relapse and, therefore, stress reduction strategies to use during a lapse should be emphasized.

Efficacy of Smoking Cessation Programs
NICOTINE REPLACEMENT THERAPY

Stead and colleagues (2008) recently conducted a Cochrane review evaluating the efficacy of nicotine replacement therapy (NRT). Based on the 111 qualifying studies, they concluded that all commercially available forms of NRT (i.e., transdermal patch, nasal spray, gum, inhaler, tablets/lozenges) increase the chances of a successful quit attempt. Specifically, they estimated that NRT increases quit rates by 50%–70%. This was found regardless of setting, and efficacy appears to be independent of the intensity of additional support for smoking cessation. The exact quit rates vary depending on the type of

sample. As an example, if the quit rate without pharmacotherapy was estimated at 15%, the authors of the review concluded that NRT would add an additional 8%, to make the total quit rate 23%.

COMPUTER-BASED INTERVENTIONS

Walters and colleagues (2006) conducted a review of 19 studies examining the efficacy of computer- and Internet-based interventions. Forty-seven percent of the studies demonstrated long-term smoking cessation success. The quit rates were highly variable across studies, with a majority ranging from 21% to 26%; however, a few studies reported quit rates as low as 4%. The heterogeneity of the methods across the studies makes it difficult to determine consistent predictors of efficacy. However, based on this review, the first-generation intervention, which included mailing tailored computer-generated feedback reports, was associated with better outcomes (57% of the studies reported better efficacy for the intervention group vs. the comparison group).

Bock and colleagues (2009) recently conducted a review assessing the content and quality of smoking cessation websites available to the public. Of the 23 websites meeting their inclusion criteria, these websites scored significantly higher in quality ratings when compared to their review published in 2004 (Bock et al., 2004). Specifically, the websites had significantly improved on practical counseling, providing advice to quit, motivational strategies to quit, and recommending pharmacotherapy. Fifty-nine percent of the studies offered at least one interactive feature. Overall, it appears that quality websites are currently available to the public; however, the authors concluded that additional improvements are still needed.

GROUP AND INDIVIDUAL-LEVEL THERAPIES

Stead and Lancaster (2005) conducted a Cochrane review evaluating the efficacy of group-based therapies relative to self-help materials or no intervention and compared group therapy to individual therapy. Fifty-five trials met the criteria for inclusion. The authors concluded that group therapy was superior to self-help and other less intensive therapies. However, there was no adequate evidence to determine whether group therapies were more efficacious than individual-level therapies. However, it is important to note that group therapies have advantages over individual-level therapy in that more clients can be managed by a given facilitator, which results in lower cost.

Fiore and colleagues (2000) conducted a meta-analysis examining the effectiveness of interventions using various types of behavioral therapies. Interventions that had statistically significant abstinence rates tended to include practical counseling, such as skills training, problem solving, relapse prevention, and stress management (odds ratio [OR] = 1.5); support during a client's treatment phase (OR = 1.3); focus on increasing social support for the client (OR = 1.5); and use of adverse smoking procedures (OR = 1.7).

Application of Smoking Cessation Intervention: Group-level Approach

The following applied intervention example focuses on delivering the intervention to a group of approximately 8–12 participants. However, the basic concepts could also be applied at an individual level. Nicotine replacement therapy is recommended as an adjunct to any therapy (Fiore et al., 2000; Stead & Lancaster, 2005), and therefore we will discuss this therapy prior to the group-level approach. It is also important to note that motivational interviewing is another popular intervention for smoking cessation. The general principles of motivational interviewing are giving advice, removing barriers, providing choice, decreasing desirability, practicing empathy, providing feedback, clarifying goals, and actively helping. More information on motivational interviewing is available elsewhere (Miller & Rollnick, 1991).

NICOTINE REPLACEMENT THERAPY

Nicotine replacement therapy can increase the success rate of any intervention by treating the withdrawal symptoms following smoking cessation. The NRT instructions should be read carefully, given that side effects can be unpleasant when used inappropriately. The FDA has approved five types of NRT, including the nicotine patch (transdermal nicotine systems), nicotine gum (nicotine polacrilex), nicotine nasal spray, nicotine inhalers, and nicotine lozenges (ACS, Guide to Quitting Smoking, 2007b). Nicotine replacement therapy can be used effectively for a set period of time, and discontinuing NRT should be done gradually as instructed. Some individuals may experience withdrawal symptoms as NRT is discontinued. Physicians commonly prescribe adjunct medications to help with the smoking cessation process. For example, bupropion (Zyban) is an extended-release antidepressant specifically used to treat nicotine withdrawal. Another example, varenicline (Chantix), interferes with nicotine receptors in the brain to decrease the pleasure of nicotine and lessen withdrawal symptoms (ACS, Guide to Quitting Smoking, 2008). It is important

to note that varenicline and NRT should not be used at the same time.

COGNITIVE-BEHAVIORAL THERAPY

The following intervention is based on the Commit to Quit (CTQ) program (Marcus et al., 1999), which uses CBT for smoking cessation that can be applied at the group level. The Substance Abuse and Mental Health Services Administration (SAMHSA), which is part of the U.S. Health and Human Services Department, has deemed the Commit to Quit program an evidence-based program. Therefore, the complete Commit to Quit manual is available through the SAMHSA website at http://nrepp.samhsa.gov/. The program emphasizes stress management, developing self-awareness regarding cues that trigger smoking desire, reconfiguring habitual smoking environments, acquiring skills to avoid lapses, improving body image, and managing weight.

The program operates on the assumption that smoking is a learned addiction, the habit is learned over time, and addiction may lead to withdrawal. Goals for the program include the gradual elimination of smoking, the reduction of present nicotine levels in the body, the elimination of the need for cigarette smoking by teaching relaxation and self-talk to deal effectively with stressful situations, and the elimination of excessive weight gain associated with smoking cessation. Components of the program include self-monitoring, the daily recording of smoking habits, the establishment of a quit date (i.e., date smoking cessation will occur), stress management training, development of a set of self-instructions to help counter maladaptive thoughts that may lead to smoking, learning relaxation techniques to handle everyday stress in a more positive manner, and weight management, which includes increasing activity and making better food choices to decrease the likelihood of gaining weight.

Various modalities are used to increase the breadth of learning. For example, home activities create awareness of real-time issues associated with smoking. Group activities are done on-site to reinforce cognition surrounding the positive rationale for quitting. Handouts are also used to increase learning. Additionally, physical activity and general wellness (e.g., good nutrition) are also emphasized to help with the weight gain commonly following smoking cessation.

BEGINNING STRATEGIES FOR SMOKING CESSATION

Three basic strategies are used for the reduction of the number of cigarettes smoked per day; these include temporal control, situational control, and access to cigarettes. *Temporal control* is a time-based technique in which the goal is to limit the number of cigarettes smoked over a set period of time. *Situational control* involves limiting smoking to specific situations. *Access to cigarettes* refers to changing the place where cigarettes are stored in one's surroundings. All of these strategies are designed to increase awareness of the habits involved with smoking and to delay the smoking process. This delay will, in turn, create a moment for the client to evaluate the need for the cigarette and make a choice to resist the urge to smoke. These strategies are often combined to increase their effectiveness.

SELF-MONITORING

Self-monitoring cards are used to record information around smoking while the client is at home. There is a card for each day of the week, and the cards are placed around the package of cigarettes with a rubber band. The cards allow the client to quickly and effectively categorize his or her smoking tendency. The card includes time of day, activity at time of smoking, an emotion rating (i.e., bored, depressed, happy, relaxed, etc.), and a "need rating" of 1, 2, or 3 (1 being high need). This process increases personal awareness and understanding of the smoking patterns. It also adds the component of "hassle" to smoking, given that the client is required to take an extra step to have a cigarette. The self-monitoring cards are utilized throughout the group sessions as discussion and learning points.

SOCIAL SUPPORT

Developing social support involves enlisting the aid of others to help the individual quit. There are two ways to use social support. The first involves enlisting current support from friends, family, and co-workers in the quitting process. The second is through the use of a buddy system, in which both individuals are attempting to quit smoking. In this situation, there are five central points: (1) stay in regular contact; (2) praise success and problem-solve together; (3) do not use time together to complain; (4) offer encouragement, understanding, and empathy; and (5) commit to holding each other as capable and to a high standard.

PREPARATION FOR QUITTING

Starting the process of quitting begins with date selection. Initially, morale will be high, as there are positive feelings surrounding this change. As the date draws closer and withdrawal symptoms may begin to become prominent, morale will wane. It is at this point that the strategies learned will become important to success. Lapses can become compounded with a failure to recognize the moment and to intervene in a positive manner. Thoughts of failure based on unrealistic expectations can overtake one and lead to failure across the board, as opposed to a simple mis-step. It is especially important at this moment that connection to the program is maintained. Failure to do so isolates the individual and will lead to forces that may become too strong to overcome. Recognizing this prior to the actual quit date, and thus creating contingencies and scripts to follow in this event, will create the opportunity for greater success in the cessation program. In the end, lapses are learning tools, not failures. Another technique used by many is the replacement of cigarettes with snacks. Although this can be effective, it is important to reach for a low-fat, low-calorie snack versus a high-fat, high-calorie snack. Reading labels is an important skill here, as many low-fat snacks can be high in sugar and thus high in caloric content.

RELAPSE AVOIDANCE

Relapse is both a physiological and psychological phenomena. As nicotine clears the system in a few days, the physiological component can be overcome rather quickly. However, relapse can also occur much later, and this involves the psychological component. It is important for participants to determine what situations will potentially lead to a lapse, and having a plan for dealing with high-risk situations should be discussed. Triggers can include times of emotional distress as well as positive situations. Removing potential triggers is an important strategy for avoiding relapse. Alcohol may be associated, as well. It does not take long for a relapse to become too strong to overcome. Negative self-talk associated with failure to keep the "oath of abstinence" can creep in and overtake the individual, leading to giving up altogether. Anticipation of high-risk situations should assist in reducing this likelihood. This awareness is developed through the close use of self-monitoring cards, which allow the smoker to create scenarios likely to engender temptations and urges. These can lead to the development of a personalized relapse plan.

Limiting access to cigarettes is also an effective process for avoiding relapse. Rules for this behavior are: (1) Do not keep any cigarettes in the home, car, or office; (2) never smoke a cigarette that is given to you; (3) never buy cigarettes in the place you are about to relapse in, for instance a restaurant; and (4) after buying a pack a cigarettes and smoking one, throw the rest away.

SMOKING AS A LEARNED ADDICTION

Over many years, smoking becomes associated with specific situations, thoughts, and feelings, which are referred to as triggers. Situations (drinking coffee), thoughts (I need a break from this work), and feelings (tension) will become strong cues to smoke. Therefore, developing coping mechanisms will assist the client in his or her pursuit of a smoke-free life. The client should list specific triggers, which starts the process of creating new coping mechanisms. Relaxation techniques become important at this phase to combat nervousness from withdrawal and psychological dependency. Other coping skills include changing behavior, such as walking instead of smoking; changing thoughts, by using positive self-talk instead of negative self-talk; and altering bodily reactions by using relaxation techniques to relieve stress. Activity is stressed as a positive replacement for smoking.

MANAGING WITHDRAWAL

Most withdrawal symptoms will be dramatically reduced by the third and fourth week of cessation. Continued development of strategies and identification of triggers is necessary. Awareness of negative self-talk can lead to the ability to reframe this through positive imagery and relaxation techniques. Making lifestyle changes, such as changing to tea from coffee, will help in managing situational triggers. Reinterpretation of withdrawal symptoms as the body's natural correction will also reframe the discomfort on a cognitive level. Development of a written plan for both situational and bodily reaction triggers and the associated coping mechanism will assist in successful retraining.

NEGATIVE SELF-TALK

Negative self-talk should also be addressed. The use of thought-stopping and positive thinking is a learned skill and must be practiced to be effective. One example of negative self-talk is rationalization, "I feel worse now than when I was smoking." The response could be, "STOP, this is withdrawal and will only last a few days. I will survive." Another example is nostalgia, "This cup of coffee would taste much better with a smoke." The response could be, "STOP, those times are gone now. It won't be long until I enjoy my good health even more." The group can use written materials to better understand the thought-stopping process.

SLIP CARDS

Slip cards are also useful tools at this stage of the program. They allow detailed information to be gathered when an individual has a lapse. They also offer possible delays in the smoking process, given that they contain a set of instructions to be read prior to smoking. Continuing to practice the process of "letting go" through relaxation techniques should be stressed.

MAPS: MULTIPLE APPROACHES FOR THE PREVENTION OF SMOKING

For a lapse to not become a relapse, strategies must be established to create a successful environment once a lapse has occurred. It is important to understand that, even in the face of a relapse, specific steps can be followed to continue the work that has been accomplished. Specific steps include: (1) Start self-monitoring immediately; (2) limit access to cigarettes; (3) set another quit date; and (4) implement the strategies that the individual has learned during this program. Connection to the program is vital in this circumstance.

Weight gain is also an area that should be addressed. The first strategy to address weight gain is to increase activity to offset the reduction in metabolic rate that follows nicotine elimination. The second is to be aware that snacking may replace the old habit of smoking. Strategies to avoid high-sugar snacks, often craved when quitting smoking, should be implemented.

STRESS AS A TRIGGER

Stress can serve as a significant trigger for smoking. Awareness of the level of life stress will allow the client to make choices as to how much he or she is willing to take on while going through this important behavior modification. Opportunities to reduce life stress should be identified and explored.

FOCUS ON TIME MANAGEMENT

Time management is a skill that will allow the client a better opportunity to manage everyday stress that may trigger relapse. Seven steps have been identified to help manage time appropriately: (1) Create time every day to organize and plan your day; (2) break big tasks into small steps and prioritize them; (3) utilize categories to describe prioritization such as "must do," "hope to do," and "do if there is time";

(4) beware of peak energy times and use them to your advantage; (5) concentrate on one task at time; (6) take short breaks when you feel fatigue coming on; and (7) celebrate the finishing of tasks for the day and find positive rewards for meeting smoking cessation goals.

PROBLEM-SOLVING SKILLS

Developing problem-solving skills is a behavior that can replace the need to smoke. Once rational skills are in place, stress can be reduced, given that there is a sense of control over life events. Steps in the development of these skills are (1) Identify the problem or trigger; (2) brainstorm solutions; (3) evaluate the solutions and rate them; (4) pick the best solution; and (5) use the chosen solution the next time a trigger appears. Using a worksheet to practice this skill will provide a framework for the client. In this phase of the program, skill development is essential for success once the program has completed. At this point, it is important to continue to review all materials and constructs to ensure a full understanding of their use and power for the client.

PROGRAM REVIEW

At the end of the intervention, it is important to remember that this is just the beginning for the group members. Fears surrounding the idea of no longer smoking may arise and therefore, it is important to stress the "one day at a time" model. It is important to review the basic concepts of the program with the group members and discuss triggers that may occur in the future. Additionally, it is important to encourage the client to seek out ways to become more physically active, given that this may help alleviate the weight gain that commonly occurs following smoking cessation, and that physical activity may be a useful strategy for coping with urges to smoke. The earlier physical activity section offers some practical tips for helping clients adopt and maintain physical activity. Finally, as mentioned previously, all of the preceding subsections are derived from the Commit to Quit program. More information regarding this program can be found at http://nrepp.samhsa.gov/.

References

Ajzen, I. (1991). The theory of planned behavior. *Organizational Behavior and Human Decision Processes, 50*, 179–211.

Ajzen, I., & Fishbein, M. (1980). *Understanding Attitudes and Predicting Social Behavior.* Prentice-Hall: Englewood Cliffs, NJ.

American Cancer Society. (2007a). *Prevention and early detection: Cigarette smoking.* Retrieved September 17, 2008, from http://www.cancer.org/docroot/PED/content/PED_10_2X_Cigarette_Smoking.asp?siteare=PED.

American Cancer Society. (2007b). *Prevention and early detection: Guide to quit smoking.* Retrieved September 17, 2008, from http://www.cancer.org/docroot/PED/content/PED_10_13X_Guide_for_Quitting_Smoking.asp?siteare=PED

Bandura, A. (1986). *Social foundations of thought and action: A social cognitive theory.* Englewood Cliffs, NJ: Prentice-Hall.

Blumenthal, J. A., Babyak, M. A., Doraiswamy, P. M., Watkins, L., Hoffman, B. M., Barbour, K. A., et al. (2007). Exercise and pharmacotherapy in the treatment of major depressive disorder. *Psychosomatic Medicine, 69*, 587–96.

Bock, B., Lewis, B., Jennings, E., Marcus-Blank, J., & Marcus, B. H., (2009). Women and smoking cessation: Challenges and opportunities. *Current Cardiovascular Risk Reports, 3*, 205–210.

Bock, B., Graham, A., Sciamanna, C., Krishnamoorthy, J., Whiteley, J., Carmona-Barros, R., et al. (2004). Smoking cessation treatment on the Internet: Content, quality, and usability. *Nicotine & Tobacco Research, 6*(2), 207–219.

Brownell, K. D. (1998). *The LEARN program for weight control* (7th ed.). Dallas: American Health Publishing Company.

Byers, T., & Sedjo, R. L. (2007). Public health response to the obesity epidemic: Too soon or too late? *The Journal of Nutrition, 137*(2), 488–492.

Centers of Disease Control and Prevention. (2000). Cigarette smoking among adults-United States 1998. *Morbidity and Mortality Weekly Report* [serial online]; 49(39): 882–884. Retrieved 18 September 2008 from http://www.cdc.gov/mmwr/preview/mmwrhtml/mm4939a1.htm

Centers of Disease Control and Prevention. (2003). Cigarette smoking among adults-United States 2000. *Morbidity and Mortality Weekly Report* [serial online]; 51(29): 642–245. Retrieved 18 September 2008 from http://www.cdc.gov/mmwr/preview/mmwrhtml/mm5129a3.htm

Centers of Disease Control and Prevention. (2005). Annual smoking-attributable mortality, year, of potential life lost, and productivity losses-United States, 1997–2001. *Morbidity and Mortality Weekly Report* [serial online]; 54(25): 625–628. Retrieved 18 September 2008 from http://www.cdc.gov/mmwr/preview/mmwrhtml/mm5425a1.htm

Centers of Disease Control and Prevention. (2007a). Cigarette smoking among adults – United States, 2006. *Morbidity and Mortality Weekly Report* [serial online]; 56(44): 1157–1161. Retrieved 18 September 2008 from http://www.cdc.gov/mmwr/preview/mmwrhtml/mm5644a2.htm

Centers of Disease Control and Prevention. (2007b). Number of adults who were current, former, or never smokers, overall and by sex, race, Hispanic origin, age, and education: National health interview surveys-United States, 1965–2006. *Morbidity and Mortality Weekly Report* [chart online]. Atlanta, GA: Centers for Disease Control and Prevention, Office of Smoking Health. Updated 2007 Feb 28. Retrieved 17 September 2008 from http://www.cdc.gov/tobacco/data_statistics/tables/adult/table_3.htm

Chan, J. M., Rimm, E. B., Colditz, G. A., Stampfer, M. J., & Willett, W. C. (1994). Obesity, fat distribution, and weight gain as risk factors for clinical diabetes in men. *Diabetes Care, 17*(9), 961–969.

Ciccolo, J. T., Lewis, B. A., & Marcus, B. H. (2008). Internet-based physical activity interventions. *Current Cardiovascular Risk Reports, 2* 299–304.

Cobb, S. (1976). Social support as a moderator of life stress. *Psychosomatic Medicine, 3B,* 300–314.

Colditz, G. A., Willett, W. C., Rotnitsky, A., & Manson, J. E. (1995). Weight gain as a risk factor for clinical diabetes in women. *Archives of Internal Medicine, 122,* 481–486.

Corti, B., Donovan, R. J., & Holman, C. D. J. (1997). Factors influencing the use of physical activity facilities. Results from qualitative research. *Health Promotion Journal of Australia, 7,* 16–21.

Courneya, K. S., & McAuley, E. (1995). Cognitive mediators of the social influence-exercise adherence relationship: A test of the theory of planned behavior. *Journal of Behavioral Medicine, 18,* 499–515.

Daley, D. C., & Salloum, I. (1999). Relapse prevention. In P. Ott, R. E. Tarter, & R. T. Ammerman (Eds.), *Sourcebook on substance abuse: Etiology, epidemiology, assessment and, treatment* (pp. 255–263). Needham Heights, MA: Allyn & Bacon.

David, D., & Szentagotai, A. (2006). Cognitions in cognitive-behavioral psychotherapies; toward an integrative model. *Clinical Psychology Review, 26,* 284–298.

Dishman, R. K., & Buckworth, J. (1996). Increasing physical activity: A quantitative synthesis. *Medicine & Science in Sports & Exercise, 28*(6), 706–719.

Dobson, K. S., & Khatri, N. (2000). Cognitive therapy: Looking backward, looking forward. *Journal of Clinical Psychology, 56,* 907–923.

Dunn, A. L., Marcus, B. H., Kampert, J. B., Garcia, M. E., Kohl 3rd, H. W., & Blair, S. N. (1997). Reduction in cardiovascular disease risk factors: 6-month results from Project Active. *Preventive Medicine, 26*(6), 883–892.

Dunn, A. L., Marcus, B. H., Kampert, J. B., Garcia, M. E., Kohl 3rd, H. W., & Blair, S. N. (1999). Comparison of lifestyle and structured interventions to increase physical activity and cardiorespiratory fitness: a randomized trial. *JAMA: The Journal of the American Medical Association, 281*(4), 327–334.

Eakin, E. G., Lawler, S. P., Vandelanotte, C., & Owen, N. (2007). Telephone interventions for physical activity and dietary behavior change: A systematic review. *American Journal of Preventive Medicine, 32*(5), 419–434.

Economos, C. D., & Irish-Hauser, S. (2007). Community interventions: A brief overview and their application to the obesity epidemic. *Journal of Law, Medicine, & Ethics,* 131–137.

Ellis A. (1994). *Reason for emotion in psychotherapy* (2nd ed.). Secaucus, NJ: Birch Lane.

Ellis, A. (1962). *Reason for emotion in psychotherapy.* New York: Lyle Stuart.

Ewing, R., Schmid, T., Killingsworth, R., Zlot, A., & Raudenbush, S. (2003). Relationship between urban sprawl and physical activity, obesity, and morbidity. *American Journal of Health Promotion, 18*(1), 47–57.

Fappa, E., Yannakoulia, M., Pitsavos, C., Skoumas, I., Valourdou, S., & Stefanadis, C. (2008). Lifestyle intervention in the management of metabolic syndrome: Could we improve adherence issues? *Nutrition, 24*(3), 286–291.

Farmer, R. F., & Chapman A. L. (2008). *Behavioral interventions in cognitive therapy.* Washington DC: American Psychology Association.

Fava, J. L., Verlicer, W. F., & Prochaska, J. O. (1995). Applying the transtheoretical model to a representative sample of smokers. *Addictive Behaviors, 20*(2), 189–203.

Fiore, M. C., Bailey W. C., Cohen, S. J., et al. (2000). *Treating tobacco use and dependence. Clinical Practice Guideline,* Rockville, MD: U. S. Department of Health and Human Services. Public Health Service.

Gardner, C. D., Kiazand, A., Alhassan, S., Kim, S., Stafford, R. S., Balise, R. R., et al. (2007). Comparison of the Atkins, Zone, Ornish, and LEARN diets for change in weight and related risk factors among overweight premenopausal women: the A TO Z Weight Loss Study: A randomized trial. *JAMA: The Journal of the American Medical Association, 297*(9), 969–977.

Grunstein, R. R., Stenlof, K., Hedner, J., & Sjostrom, L. (1995). Impact of obstructive apnoea and sleepiness on metabolic and cardiovascular risk factors in the Swedish Obese Subjects (SOS) Study. *International Journal of Obesity, 19,* 410–418.

Haskell, W. L., Lee, I. M., Pate, R. R., Powell, K. E., Blair, S. N., Franklin, B. A., et al. (2007). Physical activity and public health: updated recommendation for adults from the American College of Sports Medicine and the American Heart Association. *Medicine & Science in Sports & Exercise, 39*(8), 1423–1434.

Horowitz, C. R., Goldfinger, J. Z., Muller, S. E., Pulichino, R. S., Vance, T. L., Arniella, G., et al. (2008). A model for using community-based participatory research to address the diabetes epidemic in East Harlem. *The Mount Sinai Journal of Medicine, 75*(1), 13–21.

Jemal, A., Siegel, R., Ward, E., Hao, Y., Xu, J., Murray, T., & Thun, M. J. (2008). Cancer statistics. *CA: A Cancer Journal for Clinicians, 58*(2), 71–96.

Kendzierski, D., & DeCarlo, K. J. (1991). Physical Enjoyment Scale: Two validation studies. *Journal of Sport and Exercise Psychology, 13,* 50–64.

King, A. C., Haskell, W. L., Young, D. R., Oka, R. K., & Stefanick, M. L. (1995). Long-term effects of varying intensities and formats of physical activity on participation rates, fitness, and lipoproteins in men and women aged 50 to 65 years. *Circulation, 91*(10), 2596–2604.

Laireiter, A., & Baumann, U. (1992). Network structures and support functions-theoretical and empirical analyses. In H. O. F. Veiel & U. Baumann (Eds.), *The meaning and measurement of social support* (pp. 33–55). New York: Hemisphere.

Lean, M. E., Han, T. S., & Seidell, J. C. (1998). Impairment of health and quality of life in people with large waist circumference. *Lancet, 351*(9106), 853–856.

Lewis, B. A., Martinson, B. C., Anderson, L. H., & Sherwood, N. E. (2006, April). *The evaluation of a healthclub physical activity reimbursement program among members of a health plan.* Presented at the 27th annual meeting of the Society of Behavioral Medicine, San Francisco, CA, April, 2006.

Linde, J. A., Jeffery, R. W., French, S. A., Pronk, N. P., & Boyle, R. G. (2005). Self-weighing in weight gain prevention and weight loss trials. *Annals of Behavioral Medicine, 30*(3), 210–216.

Marcus, B., & Forsyth, L. (2008). *Motivating people to be physically active.* Champaign, IL.: Human Kinetics.

Marcus, B. H., Bock, B. C., Pinto, B. M., Forsyth, L. H., Roberts, M. B., & Traficante, R. M. (1998). Efficacy of an individualized, motivationally-tailored physical activity intervention. *Annals of Behavioral Medicine, 20*(3), 174–180.

Marcus, B. H., Albrecht, A. E., King, T. K., Parisi, A. E., Pinto, B. M., Roberts, M. et al. (1999). The efficacy of exercise as an aid for smoking cessation in women: A randomized controlled trial. *Archives of Internal Medicine, 159,* 1229–1234.

Marcus, B. H., & Lewis, B. A. (2003). Stages of motivational readiness to change physical activity behavior. *Research Digest, 4,* 1–8.

Marcus, B. H., Lewis, B. A., Williams, D. M., Dunsiger, S., Jakicic, J. M., Whiteley, J. A., et al. (2007a). A comparison of Internet and print-based physical activity interventions. *Archives of Internal Medicine, 167*(9), 944–949.

Marcus, B. H., Napolitano, M. A., King, A. C., Lewis, B. A., Whiteley, J. A., Albrecht, A., et al. (2007b). Telephone versus print delivery of an individualized motivationally tailored physical activity intervention: Project STRIDE. *Health Psychology, 26*(4), 401–409.

Marcus, B. H., Rakowski, W., & Rossi, J. S. (1992). Assessing motivational readiness and decision making for exercise. *Health Psychology, 11*(4), 257–261.

Marcus, B. H., Rossi, J. S., Selby, V. C., Niaura, R. S., & Abrams, D. B. (1992). The stages and processes of exercise adoption and maintenance in a worksite sample. *Health Psychology, 11*(6), 386–395.

Marcus, B. H., Selby, V. C., Niaura, R. S., & Rossi, J. S. (1992). Self-efficacy and the stages of exercise behavior change. *Research Quarterly for Exercise and Sport, 63*(1), 60–66.

Marcus, B. H., King, T. K., Albrecht, A. E., Parisi, A. F., & Abrams, D. B., (1997). Rationale, design, and baseline data for commit to quit: An exercise efficacy trial for smoking cessation among women. *Preventive Medicine, 26,* 586–597.

Marlatt, G. A., & Gordon, J. (Eds.). (1985). *Relapse Prevention: A self-control strategy for the maintenance of behavior change.* New York: Guilford Press.

McLeroy, K. R., Bibeau, D., Steckler, A., & Glanz, K. (1988). An ecological perspective on health promotion programs. *Health Education Quarterly, 15,* 351–377.

Miller, W. R., & Rollnick, S. (1991). *Motivational Interviewing: Preparing People to Change Addictive Behavior.* Guilford Publications, Inc: New York, NY.

National Heart, Lung, and Blood Institute, National Institute of Diabetes and Digestive and Kidney Diseases. (1998). *Clinical guidelines on the identification, evaluation, and treatment of overweight and obesity in adults: the evidence report.* Bethesda, MD: National Institutes of Health, National Heart, Lung, and Blood Institute.

Nordmann, A. J., Nordmann, A., Briel, M., Keller, U., Yancy, W. S., Jr., Brehm, B. J., et al. (2006). Effects of low-carbohydrate vs low-fat diets on weight loss and cardiovascular risk factors: A meta-analysis of randomized controlled trials. *Archives of Internal Medicine, 166*(3), 285–293.

Novotny, T. E., & Giovani, G. A. (1998). Tobacco use. In R. C. Brownson, P. L. Remington, & J. R. Davis (Eds.), *Chronic disease epidemiology and control,* 2nd ed. (pp. 117–148). Washington D. C.: American Public Health Association.

Ogden, C. L., Carroll, M. D., Curtin, L. R., McDowell, M. A., Tabak, C. J., & Flegal, K. M. (2006). Prevalence of overweight and obesity in the United States, 1999–2004. *JAMA: The Journal of the American Medical Association, 295*(13), 1549–1555.

Ogden, C. L., Carroll, M. D., Curtin, L. R., McDowell, M. A., Tabak, C. J., & Flegal, K. M. (2006). Prevalence of overweight and obesity in the United States, 1999–2004. *JAMA: The Journal of the American Medical Association, 295*(13), 1549–1555.

Oka R., King, A. C., Young, D. R. (1995). Sources of social support as predictors of exercise adherence in women and men ages 50 to 65 years. *Women's Health: Research on Gender, Behavior, and Policy, 1,* 161–175.

Palomaki, H., Partinen, M., Erkinjuntti, T., & Kaste, M. (1992). Snoring, sleep apnoea syndrome, and stroke. *Neurology, 42*(Suppl. 6), 75–81.

Physical Activity Guidelines Advisory Committee. (2008). *Physical Activity Guidelines Advisory Committee Report.* Washington, DC: U. S. Department of Health and Human Services.

Polednak, A. P. (2008). Estimating the number of U.S. incident cancers attributable to obesity and the impact on temporal trends in incidence rates for obesity-related cancers.. *Cancer Detection and Prevention, 32,* 190–199.

Prevention Institute. (2004). *The built environment and health: 11 profiles of neighborhood transformation.* Oakland, CA: Prevention Institute.

Prochaska, J. O., & DiClemente, C. C. (1983). Stages and processes of self-change of smoking: toward an integrative model of change. *Journal of Consulting & Clinical Psychology, 51*(3), 390–395.

Renehan, A. G., Tyson, M., Egger, M., Heller, R. F., & Zwahlen, M. (2008). Body-mass index and incidence of cancer: a systematic review and meta-analysis of prospective observational studies. *Lancet, 371,* 569–578.

Rexrode, K. M., Buring, J. E., & Manson, J. E. (2001). Abdominal and total adiposity and risk of coronary heart disease in men. *International journal of obesity and related metabolic disorders, 25*(7), 1047–1056.

Rosamond, W., Flegal, K., Furie, K., Go, A., Greenlund, K., Haase, N., et al. (2008). Heart disease and stroke statistics–2008 update: A report from the American Heart Association Statistics Committee and Stroke Statistics Subcommittee. *Circulation, 117*(4), e25–146.

Rosenstock, I. M., Strecher, V. J., & Becker, M. H. (1988). Social learning theory and the Health Belief Model. *Health Education Quarterly, 15*(2), 175–183.

Rothman, A. J. (2000). Toward a theory-based analysis of behavioral maintenance. *Health Psychology, 19*(1 Suppl), 64–69.

Saperstein, S. L., Atkinson, N. L., & Gold, R. S. (2007). The impact of Internet use for weight loss. *Obesity Reviews, 8*(5), 459–465.

Smith, K. R., Brown, B. B., Yamada, I., Kowaleski-Jones, L., Zick, C. D., & Fan, J. X. (2008). Walkability and body mass index density, design, and new diversity measures. *American Journal of Preventive Medicine, 35*(3), 237–244.

Stead, L. F., & Lancaster, T. (2005). Group behaviour therapy programmes for smoking cessation. *Cochrane Database Systematic Review, 2,* CD001007.

Stead, L. F., Perera, R., Bullen, C., Mant, D., & Lancaster, T. (2008). Nicotine replacement therapy for smoking cessation. *Cochrane Database of Systematic Reviews, 1,* Art. No.: CD000146. DOI: 10.1002/14651858.CD000146.pub3.

Tate, D. F., Jackvony, E. H., & Wing, R. R. (2003). Effects of Internet behavioral counseling on weight loss in adults at risk for type 2 diabetes: a randomized trial. *JAMA: The Journal of the American Medical Association, 289*(14), 1833–1836.

Tate, D. F., Wing, R. R., & Winett, R. A. (2001). Using Internet technology to deliver a behavioral weight loss program. *JAMA: The Journal of the American Medical Association, 285*(9), 1172–1177.

U. S. Department of Health and Human Services. (2001a). *Women and smoking: a report of the surgeon general.* Atlanta, GA: U. S. Department of Health and Human Services, CDC, National Center for Chronic Disease Prevention and Health Promotion, Office of Smoking and Health. Retrieved 17 September 2008 from http://www.cdc.gov/tobacco/data_statistics/sgr/sgr_2001/index.htm.

U. S. Department of Health and Human Services. (2004). *The health consequences of smoking: What it means to you.* U. S.

Department of Health and Human Services, Centers for Disease Control and Prevention, National Center for Chronic disease Prevention and Health Promotion, Office of Smoking Health.

U.S. Department of Health and Human Services. Office of the Surgeon General. (2001b). *The Surgeon General's call to action to prevent and decrease overweight and obesity.* Rockville, MD: U. S. Department of Health and Human Services, Public Health Service, Office of the Surgeon General; Available from: U. S. GPO, Washington.

Walters, S. T., Wright, J. A., & Shegog, R. (2006). A review of computer and internet-based interventions for smoking behavior. *Addictive Behaviors, 31,* 264–277.

Weinstein, A. R., Sesso, H. D., Lee, I. M., Rexrode, K. M., Cook, N. R., Manson, J. E., et al. (2008). The joint effects of physical activity and body mass index on coronary heart disease risk in women. *Archives of Internal Medicine, 168*(8), 884–890.

Wilcox, S., Dowda, M., Leviton, L. C., Bartlett-Prescott, J., Bazzarre, T., Campbell-Voytal, K., et al. (2008). Active for life final results from the translation of two physical activity programs. *American Journal of Preventive Medicine, 35*(4), 340–351.

Wing, R. R. (2004). *Behavioral approaches to the treatment of obesity.* In G. A. Bray & C. Bouchard C, Eds. *Handbook of obesity: Clinical applications.* New York: Marcel Dekker.

Behavioral Emergencies and Crises

Phillip M. Kleespies *and* Justin M. Hill

Abstract

This chapter illustrates the mental health clinician's relationship with behavioral emergencies. The chapter begins by distinguishing the terms *behavioral emergency* and *behavioral crisis,* and underlying themes among all behavioral emergencies are identified. Given that most clinicians will face a behavioral emergency in their careers, the importance of enhancing the process of educating and training practitioners for such situations far beyond the minimal training that currently exists is highlighted. The chapter continues by exploring various aspects of evaluating and managing high-risk patients (i.e., those who exhibit violent tendencies toward themselves or others, and those at risk for victimization). It includes a discussion of the benefits and limitations to estimating life-threatening risk factors and specific protective factors. The chapter concludes by discussing the emotional impact that working with high-risk patients has on clinicians, and an emphasis is placed on the importance of creating a supportive work environment.

Keywords: Behavioral crisis, behavioral emergency, high-risk, risk factors, suicide, victimization, violence

A couple in their late 20s has come to you because they have been having intense arguments that seem to revolve around the wife's desire to have some independent activities in her life. She complains that her husband is too controlling and gets upset when she engages in activities that do not include him, such as going out with her girlfriends. He states that she is neglectful of their life together at home. After a session or two, it is revealed that there have been times when their arguments have led to physical abuse, in which the husband has beaten his wife. It also becomes clear that the young woman now wants out of the marriage, but she is frightened by her husband's violent temper. In the context of a session, she brings up the possibility of a trial separation. The husband is obviously upset and does not agree. At the end of the meeting, you counsel them about how such a difficult and emotional topic could lead to an escalation of anger and further physical abuse. They both say that they will not let anything like that happen.

Two days later, you receive a phone call from the wife. She reports that, in fact, they had a terrible argument after the therapy session and her husband threatened her with a knife, saying that he would kill her and himself if she left him. She fled to her sister's house, where she has been staying, but she now believes that she has seen her husband sitting outside in his car watching the house. She is not sure what to do.

As we shall see later in this chapter, there is evidence that such a high-risk scenario, or one similar to it, could occur to any clinician with an active practice. If you were that clinician, how might you evaluate and manage such a situation? Clearly, your response could have very serious consequences for your patients or clients, as well as for yourself. It is a situation that we refer to as a potential *behavioral emergency.*

In our view, a behavioral emergency exists (a) when a patient or client is at *imminent* risk of intentionally behaving in a way that will result in serious harm or death to self or others, or (b) when a patient or client is at *imminent* risk of being a victim of serious harm or death. Fortunately, there are relatively few situations in clinical practice that would be considered behavioral emergencies. They include serious suicidal states, potential violence to others, situations of grave risk to a relatively defenseless victim (e.g., a severely battered spouse or an abused child), and states of very impaired judgment in which the individual is endangered.

As used in the definition above, the term *imminent risk* means that, in the clinician's opinion, there is a risk that the patient will harm or kill him- or herself, or others, "in the next few minutes, hours, or days" (Pokorny, 1983, p. 249). It has been pointed out, however, that, since patients who appear to be at imminent risk are usually excluded, or removed, from research studies for ethical and clinical reasons, there are actually no empirical investigations of imminent risk (Kleespies, Niles, Kutter, & Ponce, 2005). Simon (2006), in discussing the risk of suicide, has recently made this point in a more pronounced way by maintaining that the term *imminence* defies definition (at least in any measurable terms), and that there are, in fact, no known short-term risk factors that identify when, or if, a patient will attempt or complete suicide.

Despite this state of affairs, potential behavioral emergencies (such as the one described earlier) happen, and, when they happen, the mental health clinician's skill and coping resources can be seriously tested. One would hope that the clinician forms an opinion of the likelihood of imminent risk based on the available evidence known about the individual patient. It should be clear, however, that a statement implying that a patient or client is at imminent risk for harm to self or others is a clinical judgment; and, as Simon (2006) has pointed out, such judgments should not be taken as implying prediction. As will be discussed later, the prediction of statistically rare events such as suicide, violence, or victimization is beyond our current capabilities.

In this chapter, we will further illustrate what is meant by a behavioral emergency by contrasting it with the concept of a *behavioral crisis*, a term with which it has often been confused. We will then contend that an inter-relatedness exists among the major behavioral emergencies that goes beyond the simple fact that they can be life-threatening events. Next, we will present evidence that virtually any

mental health practitioner can, from time to time, have a behavioral emergency to deal with in his or her clinical practice. A case will be made that, therefore, all psychology practitioners should receive education and training in evaluating and managing such situations. We will then offer a framework for estimating the risk of life-threatening behaviors, and proceed to discuss the evaluation and management of the suicidal patient, the potentially violent patient, and the patient who is vulnerable to victimization. We will conclude with a discussion of the emotional impact that work with high-risk patients can have on the clinician and the need for a work environment that supports the practitioner when managing such cases.

Behavioral Emergencies Versus Behavioral Crises

As Callahan (1998, 2009) and Kleespies (1998, 2000) have pointed out, the concepts of behavioral emergency and behavioral crisis have been frequently confused or erroneously used interchangeably. They further note that it is important to understand the distinction between these concepts because it frequently drives our thinking, our decision-making, and our interventions when dealing with potential emergencies. A behavioral crisis is a serious disruption of the individual's baseline level of functioning, such that his or her usual coping mechanisms are inadequate to restore equilibrium. It is an emotionally significant event in which there may be a turning point for better or worse. It does not necessarily imply danger of serious physical harm or life-threatening danger (as in an emergency). Working for an emergency service or in an emergency room, however, one is asked to assess a variety of psychological crises, and sometimes these crises can contribute to the development of emergencies. An important part of the work is attempting to distinguish between crises that may lead to emergencies and those that, in all likelihood, will not.

As alluded to earlier, the confusion between the concepts of *crisis* and *emergency*, of course, extends to the level of intervention. Callahan (1998) has found that many clinicians seem to think that crisis intervention is needed when an individual is suicidal or potentially violent. Although this could be the case in situations of low risk, when risk is high, the most appropriate response is not crisis intervention, but *emergency intervention*. An emergency intervention implies three things: (1) an immediate response to perceived imminent risk, (2) management to prevent harm or death, and (3) resolution of the immediate risk within a single encounter. Crisis intervention, on the other hand, typically implies (1) a response within 24–48 hours, (2) therapy to develop or reestablish the ability to cope, and (3) resolution within four to six sessions. In clinical practice, there seems to be a heuristic value in making a distinction between these concepts.

The Inter-relatedness of Behavioral Emergencies

For many years, Plutchik and his colleagues (e.g., Plutchik, Botsis, & van Praag, 1995) have theorized that suicide and violence reflect an underlying aggressive impulse that is modified by variables that they have referred to as *amplifiers* and *attenuators*. To support their theory, they have cited evidence of the overlap of suicidal and violent behavior in hospitalized psychotic adolescents and in incarcerated juvenile delinquents, as well as in adult psychiatric inpatients. In this same vein, Mann, Waternaux, Haas, and Malone (1999) conducted a study in which they interviewed 347 consecutive admissions to a psychiatric hospital and found that rates of lifetime aggression and impulsivity were significantly greater in suicide attempters than in those who had never attempted suicide. They concluded that, in estimating the risk of future suicidal acts, clinicians should factor in lifetime impulsivity and/or aggression. Similarly, Apter et al. (1995) assessed 163 consecutive admissions to an adolescent psychiatric inpatient unit for depression, suicidal behaviors, and violent behaviors. They found that both depression and violent behavior correlated significantly with suicidal behavior scores, but there was no significant correlation between violent behaviors and depressive symptoms. The authors hypothesized that two types of suicidal behavior may occur during adolescence: (1) a planned desire to die secondary to depression, and (2) behavior related to problems with aggression and impulse control.

Of course, it is obvious that violence begets victims; but, as Kilpatrick (2005) has pointed out, victimization can also contribute to suicidality and to the perpetration of violence in the future. In analyzing the data from a National Survey of Adolescents (Kilpatrick et al, 2003) involving more than 4,000 interviewees ranging in age from 12 to 17, Kilpatrick (2005) noted that victimization increased the risk of suicide attempts after controlling for risk of depression, post-traumatic stress disorder (PTSD), and drug use disorders. It was also found that, after controlling for other mental health problems, victimization increased risk for the perpetration of violence.

Finally, in a 7- to 8-year follow-up with this study, it was found that young women who were victimized as adolescents and developed PTSD were at high risk for revictimization. In addition, Ehrensaft et al. (2003) examined data gathered prospectively on a community sample of 543 children over a period of 20 years to test the relationship between childhood maltreatment, power-assertive punishment in childhood, and exposure to violence between parents on subsequent risk for adult partner violence. Among other things, they found that physical injury by a caretaker directly increased the probability of using similar violent tactics of conflict resolution in future intimate relationships. They also found that exposure to violence between parents posed the greatest independent risk for being a victim of any act of partner violence. Although the development of a conduct disorder in adolescence mediated the effect of child abuse, exposure to violence between parents and power-assertive punishment were nonetheless additional and potent predictors of the perpetration of violence on partners.

The findings of Kilpatrick et al. (2003) and of Ehrensaft et al. (2003) are supported by the extensive literature reviews of Kolko (2002) on child physical abuse, and of Berliner and Elliott (2002) on the sexual abuse of children. Kolko has summarized many studies demonstrating that a history of physical abuse in childhood puts individuals at greater risk of future aggression, poor anger modulation, impulsivity, and violent behavior; whereas Berliner and Elliott have noted numerous studies showing that a history of sexual abuse in childhood can lead to greater risk of depression, anxiety, lower self-esteem, and suicidal behavior. Thus, interpersonal victimization (particularly in childhood and adolescence), in addition to at times being a behavioral emergency itself, also appears to be a distal contributing factor in the development of other, future behavioral emergencies.

Despite these findings, the inter-relatedness of behavioral emergencies has not been a major focus of clinical or research attention until very recently. Rather, as Lutzker and Wyatt (2006) have pointed out, suicide research, violence research, and research on interpersonal victimization have been regarded as relatively independent areas of study. These authors further note that, for truly effective clinical service and research, one area should inform the other, and collaborative efforts are more likely to lead to more effective outcomes. One of the objectives of the current chapter is to promote such collaborative thinking, clinical service, and research.

The Incidence of Behavioral Emergencies

Behavioral emergencies are clearly not limited to events that occur in an emergency room. As stated earlier, they can occur in any mental health clinician's practice. In this section, we present data relevant to the incidence of such events in practice.

Patient Suicidal Behavior

Investigators have found that it is likely that a mental health professional will experience some form of client or patient suicidal behavior at some point in his or her career. McAdams and Foster (2000), for instance, reported that 23% of professional counselors who were surveyed experienced at least one client who committed suicide. Specifically among psychologists, Pope and Tabachnick (1993) found that approximately 29% of their national sample reported experiencing a completed suicide by one of their clients or patients; and the rate among psychiatrists has been reported to be as high as 51% (Chemtob, Hamada, Bauer, Kinney, & Torigoe, 1988). Similarly, a study surveying social workers found that approximately 53% reported experiencing a suicide attempt or completion by a client at least once in their careers (Jacobsen, Ting, Sanders, & Harrington, 2004).

As would be expected, mental health trainees are also not immune to experiencing issues related to client suicidal behavior. In a study surveying psychology graduate students about their predoctoral training years, Kleespies, Penk, and Forsyth (1993) found that 97% had at least one patient (and sometimes many more) who reported suicidal ideation at some point during their graduate training. Further, 29% reported having had a client make a suicide attempt, and 11% experienced having a client commit suicide. In the aforementioned study by McAdams and Foster (2000), of the 23% of professional counselors who reported having had a client commit suicide, approximately one-quarter of them were student counselors. Moreover, in surveys of psychiatric residents, Brown (1987), and, more recently, Ruskin, Sakinofsky, Bagby, Dickens, and Souza (2004) found that 31%–33% (or 1 in 3) residents reported having a patient who completed suicide during their residency years.

Patient Violent Behavior

In addition to having a client or patient who engages in behaviors that could result in self-harm, many mental health professionals experience being victims of threats and sometimes physical violence themselves. Statistics gathered by the Bureau of Justice between 1992 and 1996 revealed that 80 of every 1,000 mental health professionals was the victim of some form of nonfatal workplace victimization each year (Arthur, Brende, & Quiroz, 2003). According to Warchol (1998), this rate of victimization is higher only for police officers, security guards, taxi drivers, prison guards, and bartenders.

MacDonald and Sirotich (2001) have suggested that clinicians under-report patient aggressive behavior, yet studies continue to support the fact that mental health professionals are at significant risk of being verbally and/or physically assaulted by those whom they are treating. For instance, a survey of 1,131 mental health professionals revealed that 61% reported being verbally and/or physically assaulted by a client or patient, and 29% reported that they had feared for their lives at least once during their professional careers (Arthur et al., 2003). Further, from a national survey of 340 psychologists, Guy, Brown, and Poelstra (1990) reported that almost 50% of their sample had been threatened with physical attack by a client or patient, and 40% reported actually being attacked. It is notable that 41% of the physical attacks reportedly occurred in public psychiatric hospitals and 22% in private psychiatric facilities. Of those who were attacked, 30% reported suffering some form of mild physical injury, and 10% reported moderate injury (Guy et al., 1990).

Further analysis of those who reported being victimized in the study by Guy et al. (1990) revealed that 46% of all attacks on therapists involved graduate students and trainees, and another 33% took place during the clinician's first 5 years after completing the doctoral degree. Guy and Brady (1998) offer some potential explanations for these findings. They include the suggestion that new therapists may be less apt to identify cues of violence, they may allow aggressive behavior to escalate as a result of setting and enforcing fewer limits or boundaries, and clinicians early in their careers may be more likely to work in inpatient settings with more severely impaired patients.

Patients As Victims of Violence

It is not unlikely for a patient to have a history of some type of victimization, often beginning in childhood. For instance, the prevalence rates of childhood sexual assault (CSA) among women tend to consistently range between 15% and 33% (Polusny & Follette, 1995). Tewksbury and Mustaine (2001) reported that 22% of male undergraduates across 12 universities reported having been a victim of sexual assault at some point in their lives, and approximately 27% of college-aged women reported having a history of CSA (Arata, 2002). In a study consisting of 941 participants, approximately 22% of women and 4% of men reported that they were a victim of at least one sexual assault after the age of 15, with 61% of these women and 59% of these men also reporting an experience of at least one CSA (Elliott, Mok, & Briere, 2004). Studies of gay/bisexual men reveal a prevalence of sexual victimization between 12% and 28% (Tewksbury, 2007). Further, in a survey of psychologists and family therapists, 42% of the clients being seen reported a history of CSA (Follette, Polusny, & Milbeck, 1994).

The prevalence of physical assault victimization in childhood, as well as in adulthood, is also remarkably high. MacMillan et al. (1999) reported that 24% of children surveyed reported experiencing some form of physical assault (e.g., biting, kicking, punching, beating, burning, shaking, or other form of physical harm). Among adults in a relationship, a national survey reported that 22.1% of women and 7.4% of men report that they had been a victim of intimate partner assault at some point in their lifetime (Tjaden & Thoennes, 2000), and the prevalence of physical aggression among treatment-seeking couples has been as high as 74% (Ehrensaft & Vivian, 1996).

The Need for Training in Evaluating and Managing Behavioral Emergencies

Consistent with the findings just noted, a Task Force Report on Education and Training in Behavioral Emergencies[1] (Kleespies et al., 2000) has emphasized that virtually all psychologists who are active clinicians have behavioral emergencies of one type or another in their practice. The Task Force Report also recommended that all psychology practitioners be educated and trained to deal with such emergency situations.

Despite the Task Force Report and the data on the incidence of patient life-threatening behaviors presented earlier, the profession of psychology appears to have done little of a systematic nature to prepare clinicians specifically to cope with these critical events. As noted in the report, a study by Kleespies et al. (1993) found that only an estimated

55% of a sample of former graduate students in clinical psychology had some form of didactic instruction on suicide during their graduate school years. The instruction (when given) was quite limited (i.e., one or two lectures). In a subsequent survey of psychology internships and psychiatry residency programs, Ellis and Dickey (1998) found that psychology programs seemed to lag behind psychiatry programs in suicide-related training in most formats (e.g., seminars, journal clubs, case conferences, and assigned readings). Even in a format that psychology utilized to a greater extent (i.e., workshops), the overall utilization rate was low. In an earlier study, Bongar and Harmatz (1991) conducted national surveys of the Council of University Directors of Clinical Psychology Programs and the National Council of Schools of Professional Psychology and found that, when all the efforts of these groups were combined, only 40% of all graduate programs in clinical psychology offered some form of training in the study of suicide.

In their survey of patient violence, Guy et al. (1990) reported that the psychologists in their sample had a mean of 1 hour of clinical training on the management of patient violence during their predoctoral training years. After graduation, the mean was 2.3 hours. Could it be that lack of adequate training is related to the findings that less experienced therapists are at greater risk from patient violence?

In terms of working with victims of violence, such as sexually abused children, Alpert and Paulson (1990) reported that most professional degree programs in psychology did not incorporate CSA as an area of training. Moreover, in a national sample of psychologists, Pope and Feldman-Summers (1992) reported that *very poor* was the rating most frequently given to graduate training in the areas of sexual and physical abuse.

Twenty years ago, Covino (1989) suggested that psychology graduate and professional school programs were deficient in teaching the skills needed for dealing with behavioral emergencies. The survey of after-hours coverage in psychology training clinics by Bernstein, Feldberg, and Brown (1991) provided support for his contention. Twenty-five percent of the clinics in their sample provided no emergency coverage. Among those that did, there were reports of disarray in the emergency policies and procedures, concern that the services would not be sufficiently responsive, and uncertainty about continuity of student and supervisor availability, particularly during vacations and semester breaks.

---

[1] This Task Force Report was completed for the Section on Clinical Emergencies and Crises, Section VII of Division 12 (Society of Clinical Psychology) of the American Psychological Association.

The authors suggested that this state of affairs reflected a general inattention to emergency services in the field of professional psychology.

As noted earlier, behavioral emergencies confront the clinician with the need to make decisions that can have very serious, possibly irreversible, consequences. There can be far-reaching emotional, ethical, and legal repercussions. Society at large, through our legal system, holds psychologists responsible for observing a reasonable standard of care in managing behavioral emergencies. They can be held liable for negligence in malpractice litigation if their emergency care is found to be substandard. In this regard, if psychologists are to have a sound basis for fulfilling the duties attendant on their professional role, it seems crucial that they be provided with specific education and training on the evaluation and management of emergency situations.

It is very important to acquire a knowledge base about suicide risk and the risk of violence and victimization. Kleespies (2009) has proposed a curriculum for such a knowledge base. Applying a knowledge base in practice and with good supervision, however, leads to skill development and true clinical competency. When a patient or client is threatening suicide or is potentially violent, the situation can be anxiety arousing for the seasoned professional, let alone for those who are in training and less confident of their clinical abilities and status. A *mentor model* for learning under such conditions seems advisable, and the clinical internship seems to be an ideal site in which it can be applied. In this model, an experienced clinician and an intern are paired in settings such as an emergency room or an urgent care clinic or on a mobile crisis team. The intern then has the opportunity to observe and work with a professional who has been successfully engaged in this type of clinical work. Cases can be discussed on site and subsequently in a supervisory session. While the intern initially is more of an observer, the supervisor can gradually shift greater responsibility for the evaluation and management of cases to the professional-in-training. It is during this process of gradually increasing skill and responsibility that some inoculation to the stress involved in these emergency situations occurs—and stress inoculation is so very important to clear decision-making in situations where tensions can run high.

As Driskell and Johnston (1998) have pointed out, it is important to distinguish between *training* and *stress training*. These authors indicate that most training, which is focused on skill acquisition and retention, takes place under conditions designed to maximize learning—a quiet classroom, practice under predictable conditions, uniformity of presentation, and so forth. Some tasks, however, must be performed under conditions that are very different from a training classroom (e.g., conditions that include time pressure, ambiguity, a heavy task load, and distractions). The evaluation and management of behavioral emergencies can involve such circumstances, and it can be difficult to maintain effective performance and decision-making when there has been no training under such high-stress conditions.

A Framework for an Evidence-based Approach to Estimating the Risk of Life-threatening Behaviors

Although it was suggested as an approach to estimating the risk of suicidal behavior, the framework proposed by Rudd and his associates (Rudd and Joiner, 1998; Rudd, Joiner, & Rajab, 2001) can be extended to organizing risk factors and estimating the risk of life-threatening behaviors more generally. Rudd and his colleagues proposed that the clinician think in terms of predisposing or distal risk factors, acute or proximal risk factors, and protective factors. Extended to life-threatening behaviors more broadly, distal risk factors form the groundwork upon which suicidal or violent behavior can take root. They are what make the individual vulnerable when proximal risk factors occur. Proximal risk factors, on the other hand, are closer in time to the life-threatening behavior itself, and tend to act as precipitants. They are not, however, in most circumstances sufficient in themselves to explain the occurrence of life-threatening behavior. Rather, in combination with a significant set of distal factors, they can create the conditions needed for life-threatening behavior to occur. Protective factors are conditions or characteristics (such as good social support or value-based inhibitions) which, if present, may decrease the risk of life-threatening behavior, but, if absent or diminished, may increase it. Although these are factors that might help the clinician be more specific about who may not engage in suicidal or violent behavior, research on them, as we shall see, has unfortunately been underdeveloped.

Rudd and Joiner (1998) suggested that the degree of risk for suicide can be estimated by weighing these three types of factors. They presented a gradation of suicide risk ranging from minimal to extreme that we propose may also be a fruitful way of estimating risk for violence or victimization. A person at minimal risk for life-threatening behavior might have no known distal risk factors or proximal risk factors and multiple protective factors, whereas someone at moderate risk might have some distal factors, some proximal factors, and some protective factors that are beginning to weaken. Those in the extreme range, who may have multiple distal and proximal risk factors and lack protective factors, are more likely to be at imminent risk.

The Limitations of Risk Estimation

This framework obviously provides only a *rough* guide for risk estimation in a clinical setting. As mentioned earlier in this chapter, the prediction of such rare events as suicide or homicide is not possible with the knowledge base and methodology currently available, and it would be misleading to imply that we can be more precise. Suicide, for example, has a base rate of approximately 11.0 per 100,000 in the general U.S. population (U.S.A. Suicide: 2005 Official Final Data, 2008), whereas the homicide rate tends to be far lower at approximately 5.9 per 100,000 (as of 2004) (U.S. Bureau of Justice Statistics, 2008). Estimates of the suicide rate in the psychiatric population have been about five- or six-fold that of the general population, or approximately 55–66 per 100,000 (Tanney, 1992). Our clinical acumen as mental health practitioners and the existing assessment instruments at our disposal are simply not sensitive and specific enough to detect such infrequent events so that we might know with any degree of certainty which patients will actually commit suicide or homicide.

To further illustrate the difficulties of risk estimation, let us look at what is generally acknowledged as our best single predictor of suicide, a past suicide attempt. The problem with this predictor is that *only* an estimated 10%–15% of suicide attempters ever complete suicide, whereas an estimated 60%–70% of suicide completers commit suicide on the first known attempt (Maris, 1992). Thus, although a history of a suicide attempt heightens risk, the absence of such a history clearly cannot be taken as diminishing it. Possibly making suicide prediction still more difficult, Maris (1992) has argued that suicide completers and suicide attempters may represent separate but overlapping populations, as evidenced by the fact that the ratio of male-to-female completers is approximately 4:1, but the ratio of male-to-female attempters is approximately 1:4.

Evaluating the Acute Risk of Suicide

In presenting risk and protective factors in the sections that follow, space does not permit an exhaustive review. We have therefore limited ourselves to some of the major factors that have been supported by the empirical evidence in the literature. For more extensive reviews of suicide risk and protective factors, please see Kleespies and Dettmer, 2000a; Miller and Emanuele, 2009; Miller and Glinski, 2000; and Sullivan and Bongar, 2009.

Distal Risk Factors
DEMOGRAPHIC FACTORS
The elderly (≥75) have consistently had the highest rate of suicide in the United States. Youth suicide (ages 15–24 and 25–34) rose through the 1980s and early 1990s, then seemed to peak in the mid-90s and to decline significantly compared to the previous decade (U.S.A. Suicide: 2005 Official Final Data, 2008). As noted earlier, men are nearly four times more likely than women to complete suicide, whereas women are four times more likely than men to engage in nonfatal suicidal behavior. In terms of race/ethnicity, Native Americans have the highest suicide rates in the United States. Whites typically have a suicide rate that is two to three times higher than blacks, and white males account for approximately 70% of all suicides in the United States. Socioeconomic status is not a strong predictor of suicide.

SERIOUS MENTAL ILLNESS
Serious mental illness has emerged as one of the strongest distal predictors of suicide; and, of course, certain mental illnesses can be both distal and proximal risk factors (as, e.g., when there is an acute exacerbation of depression in a patient with a pre-existing diagnosis of chronic or recurrent depression). Literature reviews have summarized findings that over 90% of adults and adolescents who commit suicide suffer from a major psychiatric disorder (Kleespies & Dettmer, 2000a; Miller & Emanuele, 2009; Miller & Glinski, 2000; Sullivan & Bongar, 2009). Further investigation has found that only certain diagnoses are associated with a significantly elevated risk. The above-noted reviews identified mood disorders (primarily depression), alcohol abuse, and schizophrenia as diagnoses most strongly associated with a heightened risk in adults. An estimated 80%–85% of adults who complete suicide suffer from at least one of these diagnoses, and comorbidity only heightens risk. Other diagnoses that have been empirically associated with an increased risk of suicide include combat-related PTSD (Bullman & Kang, 1994), bipolar II disorder (Rihmer & Kiss, 2002), and several personality disorders, most prominently borderline personality disorder (Duberstein & Witte, 2009). In adolescents, suicide attempts

have been associated with major depression, substance use disorders, and conduct disorders, as well as with psychological characteristics such as impulsivity and poor affect regulation (Lewinsohn, Rohde, & Seeley, 1996; Miller & Emanuele, 2009).

FAMILY-RELATED FACTORS

A family history of suicide and suicidal behavior has been found to be a significant predictor of suicide attempts (Brent, Bridge, Johnson, & Connolly, 1996; Moscicki, 1997). The families of suicidal individuals often exhibit impaired communication and problem-solving skills (McLean & Taylor, 1994), and suicidal behavior might, in some cases, be a learned strategy for communicating with family members or coping with difficult situations. With adolescents, investigators have identified poor parent–child communication and negative family interactions as risk factors (King, Segal, Naylor, & Evans, 1993). In addition to transmitting a direct risk for suicidal behavior, elevated risk of suicide in family members might also be due to the genetic or environmental transmission of characteristics associated with suicidal behavior, such as depression or impulsivity (Brent, 2001).

Proximal Risk Factors

ACUTE RISK FACTORS WITHIN
HIGH RISK DIAGNOSES

There has been some evidence that suicide risk profiles vary across different high-risk diagnoses (Clark & Fawcett, 1992; Clark, 1998). Kleespies and Dettmer (2000a) outlined the acute risk factors for each of these diagnoses. In terms of the diagnosis of depression, Fawcett et al. (1987), in a large prospective study, identified several symptoms that heighten risk for the depressed person. These symptoms include severe anhedonia, global insomnia, severe anxiety (and/or panic), and current alcohol abuse. The clinician would do well to observe caution when a depressed patient presents with some or all of these symptoms. Among individuals with schizophrenia, prospective studies have found suicide risk most associated with feelings of hopelessness, depression, obsessive-compulsive features, paranoid ideation, and subjective distress (Cohen, Test, & Brown, 1990; Peuskins et al., 1997). Risk is greatest for male schizophrenic patients under the age of 40, and occurs when these patients are not acutely psychotic but have a heightened awareness of the debilitating aspects of their illness and suffer with depression.

The findings of retrospective studies examining risk factors for suicide among individuals with alcohol abuse disorders have suggested that comorbid depression and the recent loss of a significant relationship are acute risk factors for suicide in this population (Murphy, 1992). Suicide among individuals with alcoholism is generally more likely in mid-life and after a prolonged history of alcohol abuse and dependence. As Murphy (1992) has also noted, it occurs predominantly during an active phase of drinking. Among drug abusers, cocaine abuse has been associated with an elevated risk of suicide (Marzuk et al., 1992). Clinical reports have suggested that cocaine abusers are at highest risk if they have been heavy users and experience depression during withdrawal.

ACUTE RISK FACTORS FOR ADOLESCENTS

An acute crisis can usually be identified in the lives of adolescents who exhibit suicidal behavior. As noted earlier, these crises typically elevate risk in the context of a mental or emotional disorder. Precipitants to suicidality include family problems (e.g., physical abuse, sexual abuse, disciplinary action, argument with parent), problems in social relationships (e.g., breakup with a romantic partner, argument with a friend), the loss of a relative or friend (e.g., through moving or death), the suicide or suicide attempt of a friend or relative, legal problems, substance abuse, and serious medical illness (Lewinsohn et al., 1996; Miller & Emanuele, 2009; Wagner, 1997).

Protective Factors

Many individuals who would seem to be at heightened risk for suicide based on a review of risk factors such as those noted manage to cope successfully without becoming suicidal. Observations of such resilience have stimulated interest in identifying protective factors (i.e., characteristics of the individual or the environment that may buffer the impact of distressing symptoms or stress). When present, these characteristics increase resilience and decrease the risk of suicidal behavior; when they are absent, the risk is increased. Protective factors are thus important considerations in assessing suicide risk. Although the research on protective factors for suicide is underdeveloped relative to research on risk factors, several factors have received some empirical support.

FAMILY RELATIONSHIPS

Good family relationships appear to offer significant protection against suicidal ideation and behavior. In adults, strong family relationships, being married or in a committed relationship, and having children under the age of 18 living at home have been found to reduce suicide risk (Lester, 1987; Fawcett et al., 1987). In studies of adolescents, family connectedness and cohesion have been identified as strong protective factors, significantly lowering the risk of suicidal ideation and behavior (Resnick et al., 1997; Rubenstein, Heeren, Housman, Rubin, & Stechler, 1989). With adolescents in particular, it can be preventive if family relationships can be strengthened or improved.

SOCIAL SUPPORT NETWORK
OUTSIDE OF THE FAMILY

Supportive relationships outside of the family seem to confer protection against suicide risk. Friendships have been found protective in adults as well as in adolescents. Although supportive relationships with a few close friends have been found protective in adults, acceptance and integration into a social group has been found more protective for adolescents (Rubenstein et al., 1989). In addition, an adolescent's sense of connectedness to school has been identified as protective against suicide (Resnick et al., 1997).

REASONS FOR LIVING

Linehan, Goodstein, Nielsen, and Chiles (1983) identified a set of beliefs that differentiate individuals with and without suicidal ideation. They developed a scale to assess these *reasons for living* (e.g., responsibility toward family and children, moral objections to suicide, fears of social disapproval, and fears of pain involved in suicide). The results of subsequent studies have offered support for the assertion that reasons for living, such as those just identified, serve as protective factors against suicidal behavior in adolescents and adults (Gutierrez et al., 2002; Jobes & Mann, 1999). Other studies have identified additional protective factors, including hopefulness and spiritual well-being, a purpose for living, and employment (Stack, 2000).

Managing the Acute Risk of Suicide

There is no absolute rule for when a suicidal patient can be managed and treated on an outpatient basis or when one must make an emergency intervention and hospitalize the patient. The clinician needs to be guided by a carefully considered estimate of the level of risk. The sections that follow offer some guidance for making the difficult decision to proceed on an outpatient basis or to hospitalize.

When Is Outpatient Management Feasible?

Clinicians may be inclined to hospitalize patients with suicidal ideation because they feel it is safer,

and because they have a high index of concern about liability issues. Many patients with suicidal ideation, however, can be treated successfully on an outpatient basis, and level of risk is the key issue in making this decision. Generally, outpatient management for patients at either mild or moderate risk has been found to be feasible and safe (Rudd et al., 2001; Sullivan & Bongar, 2009). An example of a patient at moderate risk might be someone with a few distal risk factors (e.g., a diagnosis of chronic schizophrenia, male gender, age <40), some proximal risk factors (e.g., discouragement about difficulties in functioning, mild to moderate hopelessness, episodic suicidal ideation with a plan but no immediate intent), and some protective factors that are beginning to weaken (e.g., the patient lives with supportive parents who are aging and having health problems). For such patients, Rudd and Joiner (1998) have suggested the following contingencies in outpatient management: (1) an increase in outpatient visits and/or in telephone contacts; (2) frequent assessment of suicide risk; (3) recurrent evaluation for hospitalization while the risk continues; (4) 24-hour availability or coverage; (5) reevaluation of the treatment plan as needed; (6) consideration for a medication evaluation or change in regimen; and (7) use of professional consultation as warranted. For patients at milder risk, recurrent evaluation and monitoring of suicide potential may suffice.

There is some accumulating evidence that cognitive-behavioral approaches to treatment have been successful in reducing suicidal ideation and the risk of suicide attempts (Rudd, Joiner, Trotter, Williams, & Cordero, 2008). These approaches tend to emphasize the learning of problem-solving and adaptive coping skills. Linehan (1993) has advocated an approach oriented toward changing patterns of dichotomous thinking and learning skills to help regulate strong emotions. She has reported that, with such treatment, patients with borderline personality disorder who are suicidal can be treated as outpatients without a high frequency of hospitalization (Linehan, Armstrong, Suarez, Allmon, & Heard, 1991).

When Is Emergency Intervention Necessary?

Emergency intervention is necessary when the level of suicide risk becomes severe. It often begins with an effort to resolve or reduce a crisis that has precipitated an increase in suicidal intent. At times, it is possible to achieve such a resolution and have the patient continue to pursue outpatient follow-up. As Comstock (1992) has pointed out, however, hospitalization is indicated when it is not possible to establish or reinstate a treatment alliance, when crisis intervention techniques fail, and when the patient continues to voice intent to commit suicide in the immediate future. Although there is no evidence that hospitalization ultimately prevents suicide, it does provide a relatively safer environment during a period of heightened suicide risk. Typically, 1 or 2 hours with a patient who maintains imminent suicidal intent are sufficient to convince clinicians to hospitalize.

Since most suicidal patients seem to have ambivalence about taking such a final action as suicide, the majority who require hospitalization agree to voluntary admission. When patients evaluated at imminent risk refuse to be hospitalized, however, the clinician is confronted with a decision about involuntary commitment. This decision can be difficult because we know that the estimation of suicide risk is not always reliable, and involuntary hospitalization may create barriers to effective treatment in the form of heightened resistance to forming or maintaining a therapeutic alliance (Comstock, 1992). As Kleespies, Deleppo, Gallagher, and Niles (1999) have pointed out, however, it nonetheless remains the clinician's responsibility to decide if hospitalization is needed. In the final analysis, the decision to hospitalize involuntarily must be based on sound clinical judgment that considers the risk–benefit ratio and the estimated imminence and severity of the suicide risk. In making such trying decisions, it may be helpful to keep in mind that, once hospitalization has occurred, resistant patients often begin to perceive the caring nature of the clinician's actions and reestablish a treatment alliance.

Evaluating the Acute Risk of Violence
Distal Risk Factors
DEMOGRAPHIC FACTORS
It is well known that violence is more common among adolescents and young adults, but, as McNiel (2008) has pointed out, this is not exclusively the case. Elderly patients who suffer from dementia, for example, have an increased risk of violence (Kalunian, Binder, & McNiel, 1990). It is also commonly known that, in the general population, males are far more likely to be violent than females (U.S. Bureau of Justice Statistics, 2008). Among patients with acute mental illness, however, women have been found to be as likely as men to become violent, whereas males with mental illness remain more likely to engage in more injurious forms of violence (Monahan et al., 2001). When other factors, such as socioeconomic status are controlled, race/ethnicity

has not been found to be a strong predictor of violence. Lower socioeconomic status, however, is associated with increased risk (Swanson, Holzer, Ganju, & Jono, 1990).

SERIOUS MENTAL ILLNESS
In general, the diagnosis of a major mental illness is a risk factor for violence. It is important to qualify that statement, however, by noting that most violence in our society is not committed by the mentally ill (Fazel & Grann, 2006), and we should be careful not to demonize those with mental illness as extremely violent. As is the case with risk for suicide, certain mental illnesses are both distal and proximal risk factors for violence. With regard to the risk for violence, these diagnoses include schizophrenia, schizoaffective disorder, bipolar disorder, and major depression (McNiel, Gregory, Lam, Binder, & Sullivan, 2003). In addition, military veterans with PTSD (Beckham, Feldman, Kirby, Hertzberg, & Moore, 1997; Kulka et al., 1990), especially those with a history of war zone violence (Hiley-Young, Blake, Abueg, Rozynko, & Gusman, 1995), and patients with cognitive disorders secondary to brain injury (Monahan et al., 2001) have been found to be at increased risk.

Certain personality disorders, particularly antisocial personality disorder and, to a lesser degree, borderline personality disorder, have been associated with violent behavior (Moran et al., 2003). These disorders are marked by an impulsive lifestyle and poor behavioral control. Conduct disorders in adolescents, as well as attention deficits and hyperactivity, have been found to predict violence in adolescence and adulthood (Satterfield & Schell, 1997).

HISTORICAL AND DISPOSITIONAL FACTORS
It is well known that the best single predictor of future violence is a history of violent behavior (Gardner, Lidz, Mulvey, & Shaw, 1996; Monahan, 2006; Monahan et al., 2001). In addition to inquiring about a history of violence, McNiel (2009) has recommended evaluating for seriousness of past violence, frequency of past violence, and whether there is an escalating pattern of violence. Other relevant factors include whether past violence was planned or impulsive, the circumstances under which past violence was likely to occur, and whether there were particular precipitants to past violence.

The risk level for future violence increases when there has been an early onset of violent and aggressive behavior. Individuals who have engaged in violent acts, delinquent offenses, and substance abuse before the age of 12 are more likely to engage in violent and criminal activities over the course of their lifespan (Farrington, 1991; Tolan & Thomas, 1995). It is important to note that many adolescents (and particularly male adolescents) have incidents of minor violence (e.g., one or two fights) in their teenage years, but do not go on to become violent adults. In general, the greater the number of violent acts, the greater the likelihood of future violence. Borum (1996) has noted that a recent history of five or more acts of violence indicates a 50% probability of future violence.

It has been noted earlier in this chapter that childhood maltreatment, physical abuse, and exposure to violence between parents increase the risk of perpetration of violence in adulthood (Ehrensaft et al., 2003; Kilpatrick et al., 2003). It is thought that these experiences model, reward, or reinforce the use and display of violence (Otto, 2000). Others have hypothesized that they disrupt bonding or socialization during childhood (Klassen & O'Connor, 1994). Smith and Thornberry (1995) have cited some evidence that the seriousness of antisocial behavior varies proportionally with the severity of childhood maltreatment.

A constellation of affective, interpersonal, and behavioral characteristics referred to as *psychopathy* has been found to be a clear risk factor for violence in a number of studies (e.g., Forth, Hart, & Hare, 1990; Harris, Rice, & Quinsey, 1993; Quinsey, Rice, & Harris, 1995) Psychopathy, as defined by Hare (1998), is said to refer to characteristics that include "egocentricity; impulsivity; irresponsibility; shallow emotions; lack of empathy, guilt, or remorse; pathological lying; [and] manipulativeness" (p. 188). Hare (1991) developed a 20-item measure of the concept called the Hare Psychopathy Checklist – Revised (or PCL-R). The PCL-R has been found to be a good predictor of violence in diverse populations (i.e., not only among criminal offenders, but also among schizophrenic and personality disordered individuals) (Harris et al., 1993). Psychopathy is said to be overlapping but distinct from antisocial personality disorder (which tends to be defined more exclusively by antisocial acts or behaviors). It is considered a static factor since treatment programs have not been effective in making substantial changes in psychopathic individuals.

Proximal Risk Factors

ACUTE MENTAL ILLNESS AND SUBSTANCE ABUSE

As pointed out by McNiel et al. (2003) and Tardiff (2003), schizophrenic patients are at most risk of violence when they are having a psychotic episode, and bipolar patients are at most risk when they are having a manic episode. In this regard, schizophrenic patients and manic patients are at elevated risk during the time period immediately preceding hospitalization, whereas manic patients continue to be at risk during the initial days after hospitalization. With manic patients, it is thought that, in the initial days of hospitalization, they react with aggression when efforts are made at containment and limit setting.

Monahan et al. (2001), in the MacArthur Violence Risk Assessment Study, sampled admissions to acute civil inpatient facilities that were preceded by violent incidents. They found that, of the many hundreds of violent incidents studied, 54.1% were preceded by drinking just before the incident and 23.0% were preceded by use of illegal drugs. They concluded that alcohol was a major predictor of violent assaults on the part of the patients studied. They also reported that more men than women in their sample had histories of violent acts along with concomitant alcohol dependence issues, and that men were more likely than women to be using alcohol and drugs prior to committing a violent act.

Wallace, Mullen, and Burgess (2004) have noted that active substance abuse significantly increases the risk of violence when it co-occurs in persons with serious mental illness. Swanson (1994), for example, studied mental illness, substance abuse, and community violence in a sample of 10,000 people. He found that mental disorder alone was twice as likely to be present in violent individuals as compared to those who were nonviolent. He also found that substance abuse alone and in combination with a co-morbid mental illness was five times as likely to be present in the violent as opposed to the nonviolent group.

CLINICAL SYMPTOMS AS PROXIMAL RISK FACTORS

McNiel (2009) has noted that certain clinical symptoms are relevant as factors for estimating short-term risk for violence. In a sample of decompensating patients who were evaluated at the time of admission to a psychiatric unit, McNiel and Binder (1994) found that the symptoms described as hostile-suspiciousness, agitation-excitement, and disturbed thinking (unusual thought content/hallucinations) were associated with aggressive behavior in the first hours or days after admission. Not surprisingly, others have reported that patients who had difficulty managing their anger were at elevated acute risk for violence (Doyle & Dolan, 2006). Link and Steuve (1994) identified a delusional state that they referred to as *threat/control override*. This term refers to a delusional state in which the person feels personally threatened to the point that he or she feels justified in overriding self-control to eliminate the threat. Such beliefs have been found to predict violent behavior by male patients in the community (Teasdale, Silver, & Monahan, 2006). Finally, so-called *command hallucinations* (i.e., a voice telling the patient to harm or kill someone) have been found to increase the acute risk of violence, particularly if the command is consistent with a delusional belief (e.g., a patient who hears a voice telling him to attack one of his former teachers whom he believes has plotted to ruin his life) (Monahan et al., 2001).

SITUATIONAL OR CONTEXTUAL FACTORS

As Otto (2000) has pointed out, it is important to consider victim specificity and victim availability when assessing risk for violence. Especially in cases where the risk of violence is limited to one or two people, whether the individual or individuals live in close proximity or somewhere across the country can make a difference when the patient has limited means or ability to travel. In patients with major mental illness who become violent, family members are at high risk. Stranickas, McNiel, and Binder (1993) found that, of 113 acute psychiatric patients admitted after a violent event, 56% of them had assaulted a family member. It has long been known that mothers who live with adult children who have schizophrenia have an increased risk for violent victimization by their children (Estroff, Swanson, Lachiotte, Swartz, & Bolduc, 1998).

Although there is no empirical evidence linking weapon availability and risk for violence in individual cases, it can clearly be said that most homicides in the United States are by firearm (U.S. Department of Justice Statistics, 2008). It seems sensible to assume that those who have ready access to weapons, if they become violent, are more likely to engage in more serious forms of violence. Indirect support for this position can be found in the study by Kaplan and Gelig (1998), in which higher rates of gun-related violence were reported in locales with greater access to guns.

Protective Factors

As noted in an earlier section of this chapter, research on protective factors for suicide risk is an underdeveloped area. Hart (2001) has pointed out that such is also the case with violence risk assessment. In fact, inquiry into protective factors for violence may be even less developed than research into protective factors for suicidal behavior. There has been an effort to examine treatments that might result in violence "risk reduction" (Monahan & Applebaum, 1999), but there has been little emphasis on "personal strengths, resources, and protective or 'buffer' factors" (Hart, 2001, p. 21). Certainly, good personal and family support have been viewed as protective factors, as has involvement in a treatment and support program (Estroff & Zimmer, 1994). Some studies have noted factors that are, in essence, the reverse of known risk factors and might, therefore, reduce risk. Thus, in their large-scale study including a community sample, Hanson, Cadsy, Harris, and LaLonde (1997) reported that nonabusive men were less likely to have experienced violence during childhood, to have antisocial personality features, to be experiencing subjective distress and marital maladjustment, to have attitudes tolerant of spouse abuse, and to engage in impulsive behaviors. Clearly, further research on protective factors is needed and might prove helpful in improving the specificity of who is less likely to engage in violence.

Managing the Acute Risk of Violence

If an evaluator has made an informed clinical judgment that a patient or client is at acute risk of becoming violent to others, he or she must formulate a plan for managing the risk. The plan will, of course, depend on the immediacy of the risk and the capacity of the patient to exercise or gain self-control. Monahan (1993) has suggested three types of intervention for dealing with the patient or client who is a risk to others: intensifying treatment, hardening the target, and incapacitation of the patient or client. Given that incapacitation usually means hospitalization, the decision to use one or the other (or more) of these interventions generally parallels the decision, discussed earlier, to manage the suicidal patient either on an outpatient or inpatient basis.

Interventions to Manage Risk

INTENSIFYING TREATMENT

With the patient or client who does not appear to pose an imminent risk of violence, and who has some capacity to modulate or modify his or her behavior, it is possible to intensify treatment in the community as a way of managing risk. Thus, the clinician can increase the frequency of therapy sessions, have telephone safety checks with the patient, have the patient enter a more structured outpatient or partial hospitalization program, have the patient enter a substance abuse treatment program (if needed), develop a plan for 24-hour emergency coverage, and make frequent reassessments of the level of risk. The focus of therapy sessions should be on techniques or methods that might reduce the likelihood of violence (e.g., increasing insight, anger management techniques, increasing frustration tolerance, improving affect regulation, and so forth).

Of course, as VandeCreek and Knapp (2000) have cautioned, it behooves the clinician to be aware of his or her state statutes that may regulate what actions a treatment provider is to take in managing a patient's or client's risk of violence. Some may require that the intended victim be warned, in addition to intensification of treatment.

HARDENING THE TARGET
Warning the intended victim(s) and/or alerting law enforcement has become known as *hardening the target*. In the case of the potential victim, it makes it possible for him or her to take protective measures. After the Tarasoff case in California, warning the intended victim became known to clinicians as the "duty to warn" (*Tarasoff v. Regents of University of California*, 1974). The California court, however, reviewed the case 2 years later and revised their opinion to what has now become known as the "duty to protect" (*Tarasoff v. Regents of University of California*, 1976). In effect, the Court's revised opinion was that therapists have a duty to protect the intended victim or victims of their clients or patients, and there can be a number of ways to do so. Warning the individual in question may be one way, but it is not the only way or, depending on the circumstances, necessarily the best way.

Borum (2009) has noted that warning the intended victim can be frightening to the individual and should be reserved for those times when other interventions have been rejected by the patient or are not feasible. If a warning is given, his advice is that the clinician be careful in reviewing the nature and seriousness of the threat, and then work with the individual to find sources of assistance and develop protective measures.

INCAPACITATION
Incapacitating a patient or client means utilizing measures that directly decrease the person's ability to act out in a violent manner. These measures can include involuntary hospitalization, sedating medication, and physical restraints or seclusion. These are obviously very intrusive interventions and should only be used in situations where the danger of serious harm is great and less restrictive means

have failed or will not be effective. The use of these means is typically regulated by law and institutional or agency policy. Their use is sometimes necessary to avoid a worse alternative (i.e., serious harm or death of an intended victim). They are not a solution to the longer-term risk of violence, but prevent immediate harm. They may also allow a diagnostic evaluation and initiation of treatment that may have longer lasting benefit.

When There Is Immediate Risk to the Clinician
If a clinician works with patients who have the potential to lose control in his or her practice setting, the safety of the patient, the clinician, other patients, and colleagues are all of critical importance. Particular attention should be given to the environment in which such patients are seen. Objects that could easily be used as weapons should be removed. As Kleespies and Richmond (2009) have pointed out, the office or interview room should be arranged so that, in the event of a serious threat to safety, the clinician will have easy access to an exit, or can obtain help quickly. In a clinic or hospital setting, a panic button that alerts the police or security service can be very helpful when a patient seems on the verge of losing control. Under such circumstances, those in private practice should have a means by which to quickly notify a receptionist or colleague for assistance.

In addition to aggressive verbal statements or threats, clinical experience has informed us that there are certain behavioral signs of potential loss of control or dangerousness. These may include psychomotor restlessness, such as pacing, fidgeting, clenching fists, startle response, grinding teeth, or inability to sit down; affective and facial changes that reflect either hostility, fear, or paranoia; and the tone and loudness of the patient's speech. The clinician should pay careful attention to such behaviors. It may be helpful to develop an internalized algorithm for how one will respond if levels of aggression or threat increase.

An initial response might be to observe that the patient or client seems upset; then ask if he or she can talk about it. If such an empathic approach fails, the clinician might ask if he or she should be worried about his or her safety. Another approach might be to inform the patient that you would like to help him or her, but it's difficult to do so if his or her behavior is making you concerned and nervous. At times, taking a break can also reduce tension.

If a patient or client is not responsive to verbal efforts to reduce tension or set limits, the next level of response will probably depend on the environment and the availability of assistance. Those who work in a counseling center or private practice setting may wish to terminate the session (if it is safe to do so) or contact security officers. If the situation is serious enough, the clinician might complete a temporary involuntary commitment so that local police can take the patient to a more secure setting, such as an emergency room, where he or she can be evaluated further. In such instances, the assistance of a colleague who can make the appropriate phone calls, or stay with the patient while the clinician calls, can be invaluable.

There are typically more options for response for those who work in more secure settings such as an emergency room, a hospital, or an urgent care clinic. In these settings, medical staff can offer the patient tranquilizing medication (if appropriate), or the patient might agree to voluntary hospitalization. If the patient is losing control, there is typically a code team that can be called, and, if worse comes to worse, the patient can be incapacitated as noted earlier (see Kleespies and Richmond [2008] for a more complete discussion of this topic).

Evaluating the Risk of Interpersonal Victimization
Distal Risk Factors
DEMOGRAPHIC FACTORS
As McCart, Fitzgerald, Acierno, Resnick, and Kilpatrick (2009) have pointed out, there are age, gender, and racial differences in the prevalence of interpersonal victimization. Findings from the National Crime Victimization Survey (Catalano, 2006) have indicated that nearly half (47%) of those victimized by rape, robbery, aggravated assault, and simple assault are between the ages of 12 and 24. Yet, this segment of the population is less than 25% of the total U.S. population. The risk of victimization by violent crime decreases after age 24.

Young women are more likely to be victims of rape and other sexual assault, whereas men are more likely to be victims of robbery and physical assault (Hapke, Schumann, Rumpf, John, & Meyer, 2006). Women are more likely to be assaulted by an intimate partner, friend, or acquaintance, whereas men are more likely to be assaulted by a stranger (Catalano, 2006).

In terms of race, the CDC (2003) has reported that African American men and women constitute 28% of all nonfatal crime victims while constituting only 12% of the population. They constitute 47% of all homicide victims. Further, the CDC has noted that African American men and women and Hispanic American men and women, across all age groups, are approximately 60% more likely to be victims of violent crime than are European American men and women. Native Americans, however, have the highest rate of violent crime victimization of any ethnic group in the United States (Greenfield & Smith, 1999).

SERIOUS MENTAL ILLNESS
Patients with serious mental illness (SMI) tend to be vulnerable to victimization. In fact, Teplin, McClelland, Abram, and Weiner (2005) compared rates of violence against adults with SMI to general population rates reported in the National Crime Victimization Survey and found that violent crime against those with SMI was nearly 12 times higher. Some of the most common experiences of victimization were assault and theft, and approximately 25% of those with SMI reported being victimized in the year preceding the study. Lifetime history of victimization reportedly reaches 88% among persons with SMI (McFarlane, Schrader, Bookless, & Browne, 2006).

FAMILY AND HISTORICAL FACTORS
Experiences of violence in the family of origin have been linked to victimization in adult relationships in a number of studies (Desai, Arias, Thompson, & Basile, 2002; Ornduff, Kelsay, & O'Leary, 2001). In the study by Desai et al. (2002), data from a nationally representative sample of men and women indicated that male and female victims of childhood physical and sexual abuse were two to five times more likely to experience a physical or sexual assault in adulthood. Despite these findings, there has been considerable debate about this issue. Schumacher, Feldbau, Slep, and Heyman (2001), for example, did a review of studies and concluded that, at most, physical victimization as a child was only weakly related to adult, intimate partner victimization, but emotional victimization as a child may have a more significant effect.

Witnessing violence between parents has also been linked to being a victim of intimate partner violence in adulthood (Hotaling & Sugarman, 1986). Reviews, however, have not been consistent in this regard, and Schumacher et al. (2001) concluded that witnessing interparental violence had only a small effect on the risk of victimization in adult relationships. In spite of the controversy, the frequency with which an association between the experience of violence in childhood and adult victimization has been reported suggests that these experiences be taken advisedly as "red flags" that the patient may be vulnerable to becoming a victim.

Quigley and Leonard (2000) have noted that violence early in marriage appears to be predictive of subsequent marital violence. Likewise, Kemp, Rawlings, and Green (1991) reported that a history of being victimized in an adult relationship was related to revictimization in violent relationships. In fact, Kilpatrick, Acierno, Resnick, Saunders, and Best (1997) found that, compared to women who had never been physically or sexually assaulted, risk of a new assault increased in a linear fashion for those with a history of one assault, two assaults, and three or more assaults. Further, prior violence by the same partner has been found to be related to an increased risk of physical injuries sustained by abused women (Thompson, Saltzman, & Johnson, 2001).

Proximal Risk Factors
Several factors have been identified as proximal risk factors for victimization in intimate partner relationships (Riggs, Caulfield, & Fair, 2009).

CURRENT CONFLICT AND VERBAL AGGRESSION IN THE RELATIONSHIP
It is not surprising that there have been a number of studies in which it has been found that conflict or argument often preceded violence in an intimate relationship (e.g., Cascardi & Vivian, 1995). In a study by Hyden (1995), 90% of couples reported that the violence in their relationships happened during an argument or verbal altercation, and data from the U.S. Department of Justice has presented very similar findings (Greenfield et al., 1998). Moreover, Murphy and O'Leary (1994) conducted a longitudinal study on spousal abuse that indicated that there was an increase in arguments prior to the initiation of physical violence.

TERMINATION OF A RELATIONSHIP
The termination of a relationship, especially a relationship that has been marked by violence, may be a situation during which a woman is at increased risk of victimization at the hands of her former partner. Women who are estranged from their partners, as opposed to those who are in intact couples, have been found to be at increased risk of abuse and even murder (Wilson & Daly, 1993; Wilson, Daly, & Wright, 1993). Ellis and Wright (1997) also found a positive association between conjugal violence and estrangement. In a 1998 report, the U.S. Department of Justice stated that women who are separated from their husbands have a rate of victimization that is three times higher than divorced women, and it is 25% higher for separated women relative to married women (U.S. Department of Justice, 1998).

ALCOHOL USE
In a sample of domestically violent men seeking treatment for either domestic violence or for alcohol abuse, Fals-Stewart (2003) found that male-to-female aggression was eight to 11 times more likely to occur on days when men drank than on days of no alcohol consumption. This same study also found that violence was more likely to occur during male partners' drinking or shortly after drinking episodes as compared to long after the drinking had ceased. The exact mechanism by which alcohol use contributes to violent behavior remains a matter of speculation. Some have suggested that it disinhibits the perpetrator, whereas others have thought that it erodes relationship satisfaction. O'Farrell, Fals-Stewart, Murphy, and Murphy (2003) have found that partner violence decreased substantially after alcoholism treatment (from 56% to 25%) and that those patients who remained abstinent were only half as likely (15%) to engage in domestic violence as those who resumed some alcohol use (32%).

PERCEIVED DANGER
It has been suggested that a woman's previous experiences of violence perpetrated by her male partner are likely to have given her a sense of when she is in danger. Weisz, Tolman, and Saunders (2000) have provided evidence to support this position. They studied a sample of women whose partners had been arrested for domestic violence and found that the women's predictions of risk were strongly associated with subsequent violence during a period of 4 months. In fact, the women's ratings were better than ratings generated through the use a list of established risk markers.

Protective Factors
As with protective factors for violence, there have been few studies of protective factors for interpersonal victimization. In a study by Rickert, Wieman, Kissoon, Berenson, and Kolb (2002), physical violence against women seen in a public family planning clinic was found to be less likely if the women had a higher education level and were older when they first gave birth. Among a sample of Mexican American women, Lown and Vega (2001) reported that good social support was associated with less risk of physical abuse. Such limited empirical data,

however, does not provide a great deal of guidance for the clinician who is attempting to be more specific about whether or not his or her patient is likely to become a victim of domestic or intimate partner violence. Until such time as research on protective factors develops, practitioners must use their best judgment on a case-by-case basis about factors that may attenuate risk.

Managing Incidents of Interpersonal Victimization

A number of therapeutic approaches have been suggested as acute interventions for dealing with the reactions of victims following a violent or traumatic event. Critical incident stress debriefing (CISD; Mitchell & Everly, 1996) was one such intervention but many now consider it to be contraindicated. It was originally developed for emergency first responders such as firefighters and police officers, who were required to meet in a group immediately after a traumatic incident to talk about their emotional reactions. Education about coping techniques was also provided. The effort was intended to diminish distress and prevent the development of PTSD. Unfortunately, randomized controlled trials of CISD have not found it to be beneficial (Mayou, Ehlers, & Hobbs, 2000; Rose, Brewin, Andrews, & Kirk, 1999) and some studies have raised questions about it being harmful or of exacerbating symptoms (Bisson, Jenkins, Alexander, & Bannister, 1997). Moreover, given some of the recent findings on how the majority of people who experience trauma are resilient and do not develop PTSD (Bonanno, 2004), it hardly seems wise to attempt to require CISD for every victim of trauma.

The apparent failures of CISD have led clinicians and researchers to recommend a less invasive and more supportive approach during the initial aftermath of trauma or violent victimization. It is termed "psychological first aid" and it was developed by the National Child Traumatic Stress Network and the National Center for PTSD (NCTSN and NCPTSD, 2006). The National Institute of Mental Health (NIMH, 2002) has now adopted this type of intervention as a best practice. It is regarded as more in keeping with the empirical findings on risk and resilience after trauma. It is only provided for those who request help, and it has four components: information gathering, safety planning, practical assistance, and offering information on coping.

If the trauma survivor requests help and is willing to talk about the incident, *information gathering* focuses on identifying the victim's immediate needs

(e.g., for safety and shelter) and on screening for incident-related and psychological factors that might suggest an increased risk of developing longer-term emotional problems. It is, of course, important to create a supportive relationship and environment in which the victim can feel safe in revealing details about events that may have been experienced as embarrassing and degrading.

Once the victim's needs have been identified, *safety planning* and *practical assistance* can be offered. The clinician and the victim need to work together to ensure that the victim has a safe place to stay (e.g., a safe house for victims of domestic violence) and to identify any potentially dangerous situations that the victim may encounter in the community. They can then formulate plans for how the victim might keep himself or herself safe if dangerous situations arise. Emergency phone contacts should, of course, be a part of the plan. Since some victims can become suicidal or may wish to retaliate in a violent way against a perpetrator, it is important to inquire about such thoughts or plans, and, if necessary, work to prevent harm to self or others.

Offering practical assistance can help to counter the feelings of helplessness and hopelessness that victims often experience. Assistance with contacting social service agencies that can offer financial aid, information about accessing legal services, or information about housing can help to relieve many worries and concerns. Any victim with physical injuries or possible physical injuries should be encouraged to seek medical attention, whereas those who have suffered sexual assault should be informed about the importance of being evaluated for the risk of sexually transmitted diseases or pregnancy.

The victim should also be provided with information on the emotional reactions he or she might experience, as well as with *information on coping* with stress. Thoughts about being at fault or to blame for what happened can be discussed and countered. Good self-care, such as getting rest and engaging in enjoyable activities, can be encouraged. Relaxation techniques can be taught. By actively coping in these ways, the victim can start to regain a sense of control in his or her life.

As noted earlier, most people who suffer trauma seem to have coping resources and are resilient in the face of these very difficult experiences. If, however, after 4–6 weeks, the individual has shown no improvement in the distress and symptoms that he or she has been experiencing, or his or her condition has grown worse, the clinician should consider doing a more thorough diagnostic evaluation, so that appropriate treatment might be recommended. A discussion of the assessment instruments that might best be used, and of the empirically based treatments that are available, is beyond the scope of this chapter. For such a discussion, the interested reader is referred to Fitzgerald, McCart, and Kilpatrick (2009).

Coping with the Impact of Negative Events

Earlier in this chapter, we discussed the incidence of patient suicide, of patient violence toward clinicians, and of patients as victims of violence. The findings indicate that, given our current state of knowledge and skill and, at times, despite the best of care, we are not able to prevent all such negative outcomes. Moreover, as Kleespies and Dettmer (2000b) have suggested, the very sensitivity that enables individuals to become excellent clinicians may also leave them vulnerable to the emotional distress that can follow in the aftermath of such events. The potential impact on the treating clinician has been well documented (e.g., Chemtob, Bauer, Hamada, Torigoe, & Kinney, 1988; Guy, Brown, & Poelstra, 1991; Hendin, Haas, Maltsberger, Szanto, & Rabinowicz, 2004; Kleespies & Ponce, 2009; Kleespies, Penk, & Forsyth, 1993; McCann & Pearlman, 1990; Pope & Tabachnick, 1993).

When there is a patient suicide, it is not uncommon for the clinician to report feelings of shock, disbelief, failure, self-blame, guilt, shame, helplessness, anxiety, and/or depression. He or she may also have concerns about responsibility, malpractice suits, censure from colleagues, and damage to reputation (i.e., concerns that can complicate dealing with one's personal reactions to the death). Clinicians who were assaulted by a patient often state that they experienced a dramatically increased sense of vulnerability in the aftermath. The greater the extent of any physical injury, the greater the sense of fear and vulnerability that followed. Working with individuals who have been the victims of interpersonal violence can lead therapists to be concerned about their competency and ability to help those who are suffering (Astin, 1997). They may develop anxiety, intrusive thoughts about the client's experiences, and emotional numbing. They may also employ avoidance strategies to minimize discussion of traumatic material in sessions (McCann & Pearlman, 1990).

There is a need for clinicians who work with patients or clients who present with the behavioral emergencies noted earlier to reflect upon how they might cope with their feelings and reactions should a negative event occur. There have been a number of single case reports of what proved helpful to clinicians coping with the aftermath of a patient suicide (e.g., Alexander, 1991; Berman, 1995; Spiegelman & Werth, 2005). Kleespies et al. (1993) sought data from a larger sample on this topic and found that psychology interns found it most beneficial to seek emotional support and opportunities to review the case with their supervisor. For those at the professional level, talking with a colleague who knew the patient or who had had a similar experience has been reported as helpful in reducing isolation and providing support. Kolodny, Binder, Bronstein, and Friend (1979) have written about how meaningful it was for four therapists to meet over the course of a year to discuss their reactions to patient suicides that each had experienced.

Many of the suggestions for coping with the aftermath of patient suicidal behavior apply as well to coping with the aftermath of violent patient behavior. Some clinicians who are threatened or actually assaulted are either resilient (Bonanno, 2004) or seem to go through a natural recovery process and prefer to cope on their own. Others may wish to do as suggested by Guy and Brady (1998)—find a trusted colleague with whom to discuss the issues and sort through any feelings of guilt or responsibility for the patient's behavior. If issues of personal vulnerability and safety seem to be affecting the victim–clinician's ongoing clinical work, an alternative is to enter or reenter personal therapy to work through the issues. In the state mental health system in Massachusetts, Flannery and his colleagues (Flannery, Fulton, Tausch, & DeLoff, 1991) have developed a program that has been used by clinical staff who have been assaulted by patients. It is referred to as the Assaulted Staff Action Program (ASAP), and it provides support and "psychological first aid" to those staff who wish to utilize it. If a patient assault occurs, an ASAP team member contacts the individual staff member to offer support and see if the person is receiving any needed medical care. The team member discusses whether the victim feels able to manage his or her feelings and continue to work. He or she also offers to check back in 3 days and 10 days to see how the person is doing.

In terms of coping with the impact of work with patient victims, some experts in the field have emphasized the need to attend to professional needs like continuing education, ongoing supervision, and consultation with colleagues who are sensitive to the difficulties of dealing with traumatized patients or clients (Deiter, Nicholls, & Pearlman, 2000; Trippany, White Kress, & Wicoxin, 2004).

They have also recommended balancing this type of work with other, less stressful work, and with play and rest. Bober and Regehr (2006), however, did not find an association between trauma clinicians' stress scores and time devoted to leisure, self-care, or supervision. They recommended having a focus on structural changes to protect trauma therapists. Thus, a significant structural change might include distributing caseloads in a manner that limits exposure to trauma patients.

Conclusion

Evaluating and managing patients or clients who engage in life-threatening behaviors, or whose lives are threatened, is a complex and trying part of clinical practice. In the preceding section, we have noted some of the ways that clinicians have found to deal with negative outcomes when they occur. Efforts to work with cases in which such destructive or self-destructive behavior can occur can be supported or made difficult by the environment or system within which the clinician functions. That is to say, clinical sites and training programs can be more or less sensitive or insensitive to the needs of clinicians who undertake the stressful work of dealing with patients or clients who are at high risk. They can foster a health-promotive environment (Stokols, 1992) in which clinicians feel supported and protected by the administration in their efforts to work with and learn from difficult cases; or they can focus on defending narrowly defined institutional interests, thereby creating an environment in which clinicians feel isolated and left to fend for themselves (as, for example, with a patient suicide). It seems clear to us that those health-care systems that take the former approach will reap the benefit of having clinicians who feel less stressed and better able to pursue what they perceive as the best interests of their patients.

Future Directions

From a clinical perspective, there is a need to have the evaluation and management of behavioral emergencies recognized as an area of practice in which all psychology practitioners should achieve competency. Training in this area should begin with the teaching of a knowledge base through graduate coursework and should be followed (on internship) by the type of *stress training* discussed earlier in this chapter. From a research perspective, it has been noted that suicide research, violence research, and research on interpersonal victimization have, to a large degree, developed along independent lines. There appears to be a need to explore the inter-relatedness of these

behavioral emergencies to see if collaboration and cross-fertilization might lead to greater progress in understanding and preventing life-threatening behaviors.

References

Alexander, V. (1991). *Words I never thought to speak: Stories of life in the wake of suicide.* New York: Lexington Books.

Alpert, J., & Paulson, A. (1990). Graduate-level education and training in child sexual abuse. *Professional Psychology: Research and Practice, 21,* 366–371.

Apter, A., Gothelf, D., Orbach, I., Weizman, R., Ratzoni, G., Har-Even, D., & Tyano, S. (1995). Correlation of suicidal and violent behavior in different diagnostic categories in hospitalized adolescent patients. *Journal of the Academy of Child and Adolescent Psychiatry, 34,* 912–918.

Arata, C. M. (2002). Child sexual abuse and sexual revictimization. *Clinical Psychology: Science and Practice, 9,* 135–164.

Arthur, G. L., Brende, J. O., & Quiroz, S. E. (2003). Violence: Incidence and frequency of physical and psychological assaults affecting mental health providers in Georgia. *Journal of General Psychology, 130*(1), 22–45.

Astin, M. (1997). Trauma therapy: How helping rape victims affects me as a therapist. *Women & Therapy, 20,* 101–109.

Beckham, J., Feldman, M., Kirby, A., Hertzberg, M., & Moore, S. (1997). Interpersonal violence and its correlates in Vietnam veterans with chronic Posttraumatic Stress Disorder. *Journal of Clinical Psychology, 53,* 859–869.

Berliner, L., & Elliott, D. (2002). Sexual abuse of children. In J. Myers, L. Berliner, J. Briere, C. Hendrix, C. Jenny, & T. Reid (Eds.), *The APSAC handbook on child maltreatment* (2nd ed., pp. 55–78). Thousand Oaks, CA: Sage Publications.

Berman, A. (1995). "To engrave herself on all our memories; to force her body into our lives": The impact of suicide on psychotherapists. In B. Mishara (Ed.), *The impact of suicide* (pp. 85–99). New York: Springer Publishing.

Bernstein, R., Feldberg, C., & Brown, R. (1991). After-hours coverage in psychology training clinics. *Professional Psychology: Research and Practice, 22,* 204–208.

Bisson, J. L., Jenkins, P. L., Alexander, J., & Bannister, C. (1997). Randomised controlled trial of psychological debriefing for victims of acute burn trauma. *British Journal of Psychiatry, 171,* 78–81.

Bober, T., & Regehr, C. (2006). Strategies for reducing secondary or vicarious trauma: Do they work? *Brief Treatment and Crisis Intervention, 6,* 1–9.

Bongar, B., & Harmatz, M. (1991). Clinical psychology graduate education in the study of suicide: Availability, resources, and importance. *Suicide and Life-Threatening Behavior, 21,* 231–244.

Bonanno, G. A. (2004). Loss, trauma, and human resilience. Have we underestimated the human capacity to thrive after extremely aversive events? *American Psychologist, 59,* 20–28.

Borum, R. (2009). Children and adolescents at risk of violence. In P. Kleespies (Ed.), *Behavioral emergencies: An evidence-based resource for evaluating and managing risk of suicide, violence, and victimization.* Washington, DC: APA Books.

Borum, R. (1996). Improving the clinical practice of violence risk assessment: Technology, guidelines, and training. *American Psychologist, 51,* 945–956.

Brent, D. (2001). Assessment and treatment of the youthful suicidal patient. *Annals of the New York Academy of Sciences, 932,* 106–131.

Brent, D., Bridge, J., Johnson, B., and Connolly, J. (1996). Suicidal behavior runs in families: A controlled family study of adolescent suicide victims. *Archives of General Psychiatry, 41,* 888–891.

Brown, H. (1987). Patient suicide during residency training: Incidence, implications, and program response. *Journal of Psychiatric Education, 11,* 201–216.

Bullman, T., & Kang, H. (1994). Posttraumatic stress disorder and the risk of traumatic deaths among Vietnam veterans. *The Journal of Nervous and Mental Disease, 182,* 604–610.

Callahan, J. (1998). Crisis theory and crisis intervention in emergencies. In P. Kleespies (Ed.), *Emergencies in mental health practice: Evaluation and management.* New York: Guilford Press.

Callahan, J. (2009). Emergency intervention and crisis intervention. In P. Kleespies (Ed.), Behavioral emergencies: An evidence-based resource for evaluatingand managing risk of suicide, violence, and victimization. Washington, DC: APA Books.

Cascardi, M. A., & Vivian, D. (1995). Context for specific episodes of marital aggression. *Journal of Family Violence, 10,* 265–293.

Catalano, S. (2006). Criminal victimization, 2005. (U.S. Department of Justice Report NCJ 214644). Washington, DC: Office of Justice Programs.

Centers for Disease Control and Prevention. (2003). Costs of intimate partner violence against women in the United States. Retrieved August 22, 2008 from http://www.cdc.gov/ncipc/pub-res/ipv_cost/ipv.htm

Chemtob, C., Hamada, R., Bauer, G., Kinney, B., & Torigoe, R. (1988). Patients' suicides: Frequency and impact on psychiatrists. *American Journal of Psychiatry, 145,* 224–228.

Chemtob, C., Hamada, R., Bauer, G., Torigoe, R., & Kinney, B. (1988). Patient suicide: Frequency and impact on psychologists. *Professional Psychology: Research and Practice, 19*(4), 416–420.

Clark, D. (1998). The evaluation and management of the suicidal patient. In P. Kleespies (Ed.), *Emergencies in mental health practice: Evaluation and management (pp. 75–94). New York: Guilford Press.*

Clark, D., & Fawcett, J. (1992). Review of empirical risk factors for evaluation of the suicidal patient. In B. Bongar (Ed.), *Suicide: Guidelines for assessment, management, and treatment.* (pp. 16–48). New York: Oxford University Press.

Cohen, L., Test, M., & Brown, R. (1990). Suicide and schizophrenia: Data from a prospective community study. *American Journal of Psychiatry, 147,* 602–607.

Comstock, B. (1992). Decision to hospitalize and alternatives to hospitalization. In B. Bongar (Ed.), *Suicide: Guidelines for assessment, management, and treatment.* (pp. 204–217). New York: Oxford University Press.

Covino, N. (1989). The general hospital emergency ward as a training opportunity for clinical psychologists. *The Journal of Training and Practice in Professional Psychology, 3,* 17–32.

Deiter, P., Nicholls, S., & Pearlman, L. (2000). Self-injury and self-capacities: Assisting an individual in crisis. *Journal of Clinical Psychology, 56,* 1173–1191.

Desai, S., Arias, I., Thompson, M. P., & Basile, K. C. (2002). Childhood victimization and subsequent adult revictimization assessed in a nationally representative sample of women and men. *Violence and Victims, 17,* 639–653.

Doyle, M., & Dolan, M. (2006). Evaluating the validity of anger regulation problems, interpersonal style, and disturbed mental state for predicting inpatient violence. *Behavioral Sciences and the Law, 24,* 783–798.

Driskell, J., and Johnston, J. (1998). Stress exposure training. In J. Cannon-Bowers & E. Salas (Eds.), *Making decisions under stress: Implications for individual and team training.* Washington, DC: APA Books.

Duberstein, P., & Witte, T. (2009). Suicide risk in personality disorders: An argument for a public health perspective. In P. Kleespies (Ed.), *Behavioral emergencies: An evidence-based resource for evaluating and managing risk of suicide, violence, and victimization. Washington, DC: APA Books.*

Ehrensaft, M., & Vivian, D. (1996). Spouses' reasons for not reporting existing marital aggression as a marital problem. *Journal of Family Psychology, 10,* 443–453.

Ehrensaft, M., Cohen, P., Brown, J., Smailes, E., Chen, H., & Johnson, J. (2003). Intergenerational transmission of partner violence: A 20-year prospective study. *Journal of Consulting and Clinical Psychology, 71,* 741–753.

Elliott, D., Mok, D., & Briere, J. (2004). Adult sexual assault: Prevalence, symptomatology, and sex differences in the general population. *Journal of Traumatic Stress, 17,* 203–211.

Ellis, D., & Wight, L. (1997). Estrangement, interventions, and male violence toward female partners. *Violence and Victims, 12,* 51–67.

Ellis, T., & Dickey, T. (1998). Procedures surrounding the suicide of a trainee's patient: A national survey of psychology internships and psychiatry residency programs. *Professional Psychology: Research and Practice, 29,* 492–497.

Estroff, S., Swanson, J., Lachiotte, W., Swartz, M., & Bolduc, M. (1998). Risk reconsidered: Targets of violence in the social networks of people with serious psychiatric disorders. *Social Psychiatry and Psychiatric Epidemiology, 33,* S95-S101.

Estroff, S., & Zimmer, C. (1994). Social networks, social support, and violence among persons with severe, persistent mental illness. In J. Monahan and H. Steadman (Eds.), *Violence and mental disorder: Developments in risk assessment* (pp. 259–295). Chicago: University of Chicago Press.

Fals-Stewart, W. (2003). The occurrence of partner physical aggression on days of alcohol consumption: A longitudinal diary study. *Journal of Consulting and Clinical Psychology, 71,* 41–52.

Farrington, D. (1991). Childhood aggression and adult violence: Early precursors and later life outcomes. In D. Pepler and K. Rubin (Eds.), *The development and treatment of childhood aggression* (pp. 5–29). Hillsdale, NJ: Erlbaum.

Fawcett, J., Scheftner, W., Clark, D., Hedeker, D., Gibbons, R., & Coryell, W. (1987). Clinical predictors of suicide in patients with major affective disorder. *American Journal of Psychiatry, 144,* 1189–1194.

Fazel, S., & Grann, M. (2006). The population impact of severe mental illness on violent crime. *Hospital and Community Psychiatry, 163,* 1397–1403.

Fitzgerald, M., McCart, M., & Kilpatrick, D. (2009). Psychological/behavioral treatment with victims of interpersonal violence. In P. Kleespies (Ed.), *Behavioral emergencies: An evidence-based resource for evaluating and managing risk of suicide, violence, and victimization. Washington, DC: APA Books.*

Flannery, R., Fulton, P., Tausch, J., & DeLoffi, A. (1991). A program to help staff cope with psychological sequelae of assaults by patients. *Hospital and Community Psychiatry, 42,* 935–938.

Follette, V., Polusny, M., & Milbeck, K. (1994). Mental health and law enforcement professionals: Trauma history, psychological symptoms, and impact of providing services to child sexual abuse survivors. *Professional Psychology: Research and Practice, 25,* 275–282.

Forth, A., Hart, S., & Hare. R. (1990). Assessment of psychopathy in male young offenders. *Psychological Assessment: A Journal of Consulting and Clinical Psychology, 2,* 342–344.

Gardner, W., Lidz, C., Mulvey, E., & Shaw, E. (1996). A comparison of actuarial methods for identifying repetitively violent patients with mental illness. *Law and Human Behavior, 20,* 35–48.

Greenfield, L. A., & Smith, S. K. (1999). *American Indians and crime* (U.S. Department Of Justice Report NCJ 173386). Washington, DC: Office of Justice Programs.

Greenfeld, L. A., Rand, M. R., Craven, D., Klaus, P. A., Perkins, C. A., Ringel, C., Warchol, G., Maston, C., & Fox, J. A. (1998). *Violence by intimates: Analysis of data on crimes by current or former spouses, boyfriends, and girlfriends.* Washington, D.C.: U. S. Department of Justice.

Gutierrez, P., Osman, A., Barios, F., Kopper, B., Baker, M., & Haraburda, C. (2002). Development of the Reasons for Living Inventory for young adults. *Journal of Clinical Psychology, 58,* 339–357.

Guy, J., & Brady, J. L. (1998). The stress of violent behavior for the clinician. In P. Kleespies (Ed.), Emergencies in mental health practice: Evaluation and management. New York: Guilford Press.

Guy, J., Brown, C., & Poelstra, P. (1990). Who gets attacked? A national survey of patient violence directed at psychologists in clinical practice. *Professional Psychology: Research and Practice, 21,* 493–495.

Hanson, R., Cadsy, O., Harris, A., & LaLonde, C. (1997). Correlates of battering among 997 men: Family history, adjustment, and attitudinal differences. *Violence and Victims, 12,* 191–208.

Hapke, U., Schumann, A., Rumpf, H., John, U., & Meyer, C. (2006). Posttraumatic stress disorder: The role of trauma, pre-existing psychiatric disorder, and gender. *European Archives of Psychiatry and Clinical Neuroscience, 256,* 299–306.

Harris, G., Rice, M., & Quinsey, V. (1993). Violent recidivism of mentally disordered offenders: The development of a statistical prediction instrument. *Criminal Justice and Behavior, 20,* 315–335.

Hare, R. (1991). *Manual for the Hare Psychopathy Checklist – Revised.* Toronto: Multi- Health Systems.

Hare, R. (1998). Psychopaths and their nature: Implications for the mental health and criminal justice systems. In T. Milton, E. Simonsen, M. Birkett-Smith, & R. Davis (Eds.), *Psychopathy: Antisocial, criminal, and violent behavior* (pp. 188-223). New York: Guilford Press.

Hart, S. (2001). Assessing and managing violence risk. In K. Douglas, C. Webster, S. Hart, D. Eaves, & J. Ogloff (Eds.), *HCR-20: Violence risk management companion guide* (pp. 13–25). Burnaby, British Columbia: Mental Health, Law, and Policy Institute, Simon Fraser University.

Hendin, H., Haas, A., Maltsberger, J., Szanto, K., & Rabinowicz, H. (2004). Factors contributing to therapists' distress after the suicide of a patient. *American Journal of Psychiatry, 161,* 1442–1446.

Hiley-Young, B., Blake, D., Abueg, F., Rozynko, V., & Gusman, F. (1995). Warzone violence in Vietnam: An examination of premilitary, military, and postmilitary factors in PTSD inpatients. *Journal of Traumatic Stress, 8,* 125–141.

Hotaling, G. T & Sugarman, D. B. (1986). An analysis of risk markers in husband to wife violence: The current state of knowledge. *Violence and Victims, 1,* 101–124.

Hyden, H. (1995). Verbal aggression as prehistory of woman battering. *Journal of Family Violence, 10,* 55–71.

Jacobsen, J., Ting, L., Sanders, S., & Harrington, D. (2004). Prevalence and reactions to fatal and nonfatal client suicidal behavior: A national study of mental health social workers. *Omega, 49,* 237–248.

Jobes. D., & Mann, R. (1999). Reasons for living versus reasons for dying: Examining the internal debate of suicide. *Suicide and Life-Threatening Behavior, 29,* 97–104.

Kalunian, D., Binder, R., & McNiel, D. (1990). Violence by geriatric patients who need psychiatric hospitalization. *Journal of Clinical Psychiatry, 51,* 340–343.

Kaplan, M., & Gelig, O. (1998). Firearm suicides and homicide in the United States: Regional variations and patterns of gun ownership. *Social Science and Medicine, 46,* 1227–1233.

Kemp, A., Rawlings, E., & Green, B. (1991). Post-traumatic stress disorder (PTSD) in battered women: A shelter sample. *Journal of Traumatic Stress, 4,* 137–148.

Kilpatrick, D. (2005). The role of trauma in behavioral emergencies: Implications for policy and practice. Presidential address for Section VII of Division 12. Presented at 113th Annual Convention of the American Psychological Association. Washington, DC, August 19, 2005.

Kilpatrick, D. G., Acierno, R., Resnick, H. S., Saunders, B. E., & Best, C. L. (1997). A two year longitudinal analysis of the relationship between violent assault and alcohol and drug use in women. *Journal of Consulting and Clinical Psychology, 65,* 834–847.

Kilpatrick, D., Ruggiero, K., Acierno, R., Saunders, B., Resnick, H., & Best, C. (2003). Violence and risk of PTSD, major depression, substance abuse/dependence, and comorbidity: Results from the National Survey of Adolescents. *Journal of Consulting and Clinical Psychology, 71,* 692–700.

King, C., Segal, H., Naylor, M., & Evans T. (1993). Family functioning and suicidal behavior in adolescent inpatients with mood disorders. *Journal of the American Academy of Child and Adolescent Psychiatry, 32,* 1198–1206.

Klassen, D., & O'Connor, W. (1994). Demographic and case history variables in risk assessment. In J. Monahan and H. Steadman (Eds.), *Violence and mental disorder: Developments in risk assessments* (pp. 229–258). Chicago: University of Chicago Press.

Kleespies, P. (2000). Behavioral emergencies and crises: An overview. *Journal of Clinical Psychology, 56,* 1103–1108.

Kleespies, P. (2009). *Behavioral emergencies: An evidence-based resource for evaluating and managing risk of suicide, violence, and victimization* (in press). Washington, DC: APA Books.

Kleespies, P. (Ed.). (1998). *Emergencies in mental health practice: Evaluation and management.* New York: Guilford Press.

Kleespies, P., Berman, A., Ellis, T., McKeon, R., McNiel, D., Nock, M., et al. (July, 2000). Report on education and training in behavioral emergencies: Abridged version APPIC Newsletter, pp. 10, 33–38.

Kleespies, P., Deleppo, J., Gallagher, P., & Niles, B. (1999). Managing suicidal emergencies: Recommendations for the practitioner. *Professional Psychology: Research and Practice, 30,* 454–463.

Kleespies, P., & Dettmer, E. (2000a). An evidence-based approach to evaluating and managing suicidal emergencies. *Journal of Clinical Psychology, 56,* 1109–1130.

Kleespies, P., & Dettmer, E. (2000b). The stress of patient emergencies for the clinician: Incidence, impact, and means of coping. *Journal of Clinical Psychology, 56,* 1353–1369.

Kleespies, P., Niles, B., Kutter, C., & Ponce, A. (2005). Managing behavioral emergencies. In R. Coombs (Ed.), *Family therapy review: Preparing for comprehensive and licensing exams* (pp. 213–231). NJ: Lawrence Erlbaum Associates.

Kleespies, P., Penk, W., & Forsyth J. (1993). The stress of patient suicidal behavior during clinical training: Incidence, impact, and recovery. *Professional Psychology: Research and Practice, 24*, 293–303.

Kleespies, P., & Ponce, A. (2009). The stress and emotional impact of clinical work with the patient at risk. In P. Kleespies (Ed.), *Behavioral emergencies: An evidence-based resource for evaluating and managing risk of suicide, violence, and victimization.* Washington, DC: APA Books.

Kleespies, P., & Richmond, J. (2009). Evaluating behavioral emergencies: The clinical interview. In P. Kleespies (Ed.), *Behavioral emergencies: An evidence-based resource for evaluating and managing risk of suicide, violence, and victimization.* Washington, DC: APA Books.

Kolko, D. (2002). Child physical abuse. In J. Myers, L. Berliner, J. Briere, C. Hendrix, C. Jenny, & T. Reid (Eds.), *The APSAC handbook on child maltreatment* (2nd ed., pp. 21–54). Thousand Oaks, CA: Sage Publications.

Kolodny, S., Binder, R., Bronstein, A., & Friend, R. (1979). The working through of patients' suicides by four therapists. *Suicide and Life-Threatening Behavior, 9*, 33–46.

Kulka, R., Schlenger, W., Fairbank, J., Hough, R., Jordan, B., Marmar, C., et al. (1990). *Trauma and the Vietnam War generation: Report of findings from the National Vietnam Veterans Readjustment Study.* New York: Bruner/Mazel.

Lester, D. (1987). Benefits of marriage for reducing risk of violent death from suicide and homicide for white and non-white persons: Generalizing Gove's findings. *Psychological Reports, 61*, 198.

Lewinsohn, P.M., Rohde, P., Seeley, J.R., & Klein, D.N. (1997). Axis II psychopathology as a function of Axis I disorders in childhood and adolescence. *Journal of the American Academy of Child and Adolescent Psychiatry, 36*, 1752–1759.

Linehan, M. (1993). *Skills training manual for treating borderline personality disorder.* New York: Guilford Press.

Linehan, M., Armstrong, H., Suarez, A., Allmon, D., & Heard, H. (1991). Cognitive-behavioral treatment of chronically parasuicidal borderline patients. *Archives of General Psychiatry, 48*, 1060–1064.

Linehan, M., Goodstein, J., Nielsen, S., & Chiles, J. (1983). Reasons for staying alive when you are thinking of killing yourself: The Reasons for Living Inventory. *Journal of Clinical and Consulting Psychology, 51*, 276–286.

Link, B., & Steuve, A. (1994). Psychotic symptoms and the violent/illegal behavior of mental patients compared to community controls. In J. Monahan and H. Steadman (Eds.), *Violence and mental disorder: Developments in risk assessment* (pp. 137–159). Chicago: University of Chicago Press.

Lown, E., & Vega, W. (2001). Prevalence and predictors of physical partner abuse among Mexican American women. *American Journal of Public Health, 91*, 441–445.

Lutzker, J., & Wyatt, J. (2006). Introduction. In J. Lutzker (Ed.), *Preventing violence: Research and evidence-based intervention strategies* (pp. 3–15). Washington, DC: APA Books.

MacDonald, G., & Sirotich, F. (2001). Reporting client violence. *Social Work, 46*(2), 107–114.

MacMillan, H. L., Fleming, J. E., Trocme, N., Boyle, M. H., Wong, M., Racine, Y. A., Beardslee, W. R., & Offord, D. R. (1999). Prevalence of child physical and sexual abuse in the community. *Journal of the American Medical Association, 278*(2), 131–135.

Mann, J., Waternaux, C., Haas, G., & Malone, K. (1999). Toward a clinical model of suicidal behavior in psychiatric patients. *American Journal of Psychiatry, 156*, 181–188.

Maris, R. (1992). The relationship of non-fatal suicide attempts to completed suicides. In R. Maris, A. Berman, J. Maltsberger, & R. Yufit (Eds.), *Assessment and prediction of suicide* (pp. 362–380). New York: Guilford Press.

Marzuk, P., Tardiff, K., Leon, A., Stajic, M., Morgan, E., & Mann, J. (1992). Prevalence of cocaine use among residents of New York City who committed suicide during a one year period. *American Journal of Psychiatry, 149*, 371–375.

Mayou, R., Ehlers, A., & Hobbs, M. (2000). Psychological debriefing for road traffic accident victims: Three-year follow-up of a randomized controlled trial. *British Journal of Psychiatry, 176*, 589–593.

McAdams, C., & Foster, V. (2000). Client suicide: Its frequency and impact on counselors. *Journal of Mental Health Counseling, 22*, 107–121.

McCann, I. L., & Pearlman, L. A. (1990). Vicarious traumatization: A framework for understanding the psychological effects of working with victims. *Journal of Traumatic Stress, 3*, 131–149.

McCart, M., Fitzgerald, M., Acierno, R., Resnick, H., & Kilpatrick. D. (2009). Evaluation and acute intervention with victims of violence. In P. Kleespies (Ed.), *Behavioral emergencies: An evidence-based resource for evaluating and managing risk of suicide, violence, and victimization.* Washington, DC: APA Books.

McFarlane, A., Schrader, G., Bookless, C., & Browne, D. (2006). Prevalence of victimization, posttraumatic stress disorder and violent behaviour in the seriously mentally ill. *Australian and New Zealand Journal of Psychiatry, 40*, 1010–1015.

McLean, P., & Taylor, S. (1994). Family therapy for suicidal people. *Death Studies, 18*, 409–426.

McNiel, D. (2009). Assessment and management of acute risk of violence in adult patients. In P.Kleespies (Ed.), Behavioral emergencies: An evidence-based resource for evaluating and managing risk of suicide, violence, and victimization. Washington, DC: APA Books.

McNiel, D., & Binder, R. (1994). The relationship between acute psychiatric symptoms, diagnosis, and short-term risk of violence. *Hospital and Community Psychiatry, 45*, 133–137.

McNiel, D., Gregory, A., Lam, J., Binder, R., & Sullivan, G. (2003). Utility of decision support tools for assessing acute risk of violence. *Journal of Consulting and Clinical Psychology, 71*, 945–953.

Miller, A., & Emanuele, J. (2009). Children and adolescents at risk of suicide. In P. Kleespies (Ed.), *Behavioral emergencies: An evidence-based resource for evaluating and managing risk of suicide, violence, and victimization.* Washington, DC: APA Books.

Miller, A., & Glinski, J. (2000). Youth suicidal behavior: Assessment and intervention. *Journal of Clinical Psychology, 56*, 1131–1152.

Mitchell, J. T., & Everly, G. S. (1996). *Critical incident stress debriefing: An operations manual for the prevention of traumatic stress among emergency services and disaster workers* (2nd ed.). Ellicott, MD: Chevron Publishing.

Monahan, J. (2006). A jurisprudence of risk assessment: Forecasting harm among prisoners, predators, and patients. *Virginia Law Review, 92*, 391–435.

Monahan, J. (1993). Limiting therapist exposure to Tarasoff liability: Guidelines for risk containment. *American Psychologist, 48*, 242–250.

Monahan, J., & Applebaum, P. (1999). Reducing violence risk: Diagnostically based clues from the MacArthur Violence Risk Assessment Study. In S. Hodgins (Ed.), *Violence among the mentally ill: Effective treatments and management strategies*. Boston: Kluwer Academic Publishers.

Monahan, J., Steadman, H., Silver. E., Appelbaum, P., Robbins, P., Mulvey, E., et al. (2001). *Rethinking risk assessment: The MacArthur Study of mental disorder and violence*. New York: Oxford University Press.

Moran, P., Walsh, E., Tryer, P., Burns, T., Creed, F., & Fahy, T. (2003). Impact of comorbid personality disorder on violence in psychosis: Report from the UK 700 trial. *British Journal of Psychiatry, 182*, 129–134.

Moscicki, E. (1997). Identification of suicide risk factors using epidemiologic studies. *Psychiatric Clinics of North America, 20*, 499–517.

Murphy, C. M., & O'Leary, K. D. (1994). Research paradigms, values, and spouse abuse. Journal of Interpersonal Violence, 9, 207–223.

Murphy, G. (1992). *Suicide in alcoholism*. New York: Oxford University Press.

National Child Traumatic Stress Network & National Center for PTSD. (2006). *Psychological first aid: Field operations guide, 2nd edition*. Available at www.nctsnet.org and www.ncptsd.org.

National Institute of Mental Health (2002). *Mental health and mass violence: Evidence-based early psychological intervention for victims/survivors of mass violence. A workshop to reach consensus on best practices* (NIH Publication No. 02-5138). Washington, DC: U.S. Government Printing Office.

O'Farrell, T., Fals-Stewart, W., Murphy, M., & Murphy, C. (2003). Partner violence before and after individually based alcoholism treatment for male alcoholic patients. *Journal of Consulting and Clinical Psychology, 71*, 92–102.

Ornduff, S., Kelsey, R., & O'Leary, K. (2001). Childhood physical abuse, personality, and adult relationship violence: A model of vulnerability to victimization. *American Journal of Orthopsychiatry, 71*, 322–331.

Otto, R. (2000). Assessing and managing violence risk in outpatient settings. *Journal of Clinical Psychology, 56*, 1239–1262.

Peuskins, J., DeHert, M., Cosyns, P., Pieters, G., Theys, P., & Vermotte, R. (1997). Suicide in young schizophrenic patients during and after inpatient treatment. *International Journal of Mental Health, 25*, 39–44.

Plutchik, R., Botsis, A., & van Praag, H. (1995). Psychopathology, self-esteem, sexual and ego functions as correlates of suicide and violence risk. *Archives of Suicide Research, 1*, 27–38.

Pokorny, A. (1983). Prediction of suicide in psychiatric patients. *Archives of General Psychiatry, 40*, 249–259.

Polusny, M., & Follette, V. (1995). Long-term correlates of child sexual abuse: Theory and review of the empirical literature. *Applied & Preventive Psychology, 4*(3), 143–166.

Pope, K., & Feldman-Summers, S. (1992). National survey of psychologists' sexual and physical abuse history and their evaluation of training and competence in these areas. *Professional Psychology: Research and Practice, 23*, 353–361.

Pope, K., & Tabachnick, B. (1993). Therapists' anger, hate, fear, and sexual feelings: National survey of therapist responses, client characteristics, critical events, formal complaints, and training. *Professional Psychology: Research and Practice, 24*, 142–152.

Quigley, B., & Leonard, K. (2000). Alcohol and the continuation of early marital aggression. Alcoholism: Clinical and Experimental Research, 24, 1003–1010.

Quinsey, V., Rice, M., & Harris, G. (1995). Actuarial prediction of sexual recidivism. *Journal of Interpersonal Violence, 10*, 85–105.

Resnick, M., Bearman, P., Blum, R., Bauman, K., Harris, K., Jones, J., et al. (1997). Protecting adolescents from harm: Findings from the National Longitudinal Study on Adolescent Health. *Journal of the American Medical Association, 278*, 823–832.

Rickert, V., Wiemann, C., Kissoon, S., Berenson, A., & Kolb, E. (2002). The relationship among demographics, reproductive characteristics, and intimate partner violence. *American Journal of Obstetrics and Gynecology, 187*, 1002–1007.

Riggs, D., Caulfield, M., & Fair, K. (2009). Risk for intimate partner violence: Factors associated with perpetration and victimization. In P. Kleespies (Ed.), *Behavioral emergencies: An evidence-based resource for evaluating and managing risk of suicide, violence, and victimization*. Washington, DC: APA Books.

Rihmer, Z., & Kiss, K. (2002). Bipolar disorders and suicidal behavior. *Bipolar Disorder, 4 (Suppl 1)*, 21–25.

Rose, S., Brewin, C. R., Andrews, B., & Kirk, M. (1999). A randomized controlled trial of individual psychological debriefing for victims of violent crime. *Psychological Medicine, 29*, 793–799.

Rubenstein, J., Heeren, T., Housman, T., Rubin, C., & Stechler, G. (1989). Suicidal behavior in "normal" adolescents: Risk and protective factors. *American Journal of Orthopsychiatry, 59*, 59–71.

Rudd, M. D., & Joiner, T. (1998). The assessment, management, and treatment of suicidality: Toward clinically informed and balanced standards of care. *Clinical Psychology: Science and Practice, 5*, 135–1150.

Rudd, M. D., Joiner, T., & Rajab, M. H. (2001). *Treating suicidal behavior: An effective, time-limited approach*. New York: Guilford Press.

Rudd, M. D., Joiner, T., Trotter, D., Williams, B., & Cordero, L. (2009). The psychological and behavioral treatment of suicidal behavior: A critique of what we know (and don't know). In P. Kleespies (Ed.), *Behavioral emergencies: An evidence-based resource for evaluating and managing risk of suicide, violence, and victimization*. Washington, DC: APA Books.

Ruskin, R., Sakinofsky, I., Bagby, R., Dickens, S., & Sousa, G. (2004). Impact of patient suicide on psychiatrists and psychiatry trainees. *Academic Psychiatry, 28*, 104–110.

Satterfield, J., & Schell, A. (1997). A prospective study of hyperactive boys with conduct problems and normal boys: Adolescent and adult criminality. *Journal of the American Academy of Child and Adolescent Psychiatry, 36*, 1726–1735.

Schumacher, J. A., Feldbau. S., Smith Slep, A. M., & Heyman, R. E. (2001). Risk factors for male-to-female partner physical abuse. *Aggression and Violent Behavior, 6*, 281–352.

Simon, R. (2006). Imminent suicide: The illusion of short-term prediction. *Suicide and Life-Threatening Behavior, 36*, 296–301.

Smith, C., & Thornberry, T. (1995). The relationship between childhood maltreatment and adolescent involvement in delinquency. *Criminology, 33*, 451–481.

Spiegelman, J., & Werth, Jr., J. (2005). Don't forget about me: The experiences of therapists-in-training after a client has attempted or died by suicide. In K. Weiner (Ed.), *Therapeutic and legal issues for therapists who have survived a client suicide: Breaking the silence*. Bingampton, NY: Hawthorn Press.

Stack,S. (2000). Work and the economy. In R. Maris, A. Berman, and M. Silverman (Eds.): *Comprehensive textbook of suicidology* (pp. 193–221). New York: Guilford Press.

Stokols, D. (1992). Establishing and maintaining healthy environments: Towards a social ecology of health promotion. *American Psychologist, 47,* 6–22.

Stranickas, K., McNiel, D., & Binder, R. (1993). Violence toward family caregivers by mentally ill relatives. *Hospital and Community Psychiatry, 44,* 385–387.

Sullivan, G., & Bongar, B. (2009). Assessing suicide risk in the adult patient. In P. Kleespies (Ed.), *Behavioral emergencies: An evidence-based resource for evaluating and managing risk of suicide, violence, and victimization.* Washington, DC: APA Books.

Swanson, J. (1994). Mental disorder, substance abuse, and community violence: An epidemiological approach. In J. Monahan & H. Steadman (Eds.), *Violence and mental disorder: Developments in risk assessment* (pp. 101–136). Chicago: University of Chicago Press.

Swanson, J., Holzer, C., Ganju, V., & Joni, R. (1990). Violence and psychiatric disorder in the community. Evidence from the Epidemiologic Catchment Area surveys. *Hospital and Community Psychiatry, 41,* 761–770.

Tanney, B. (1992). Mental disorders, psychiatric patients, and suicide. In R. Maris, A. Berman, J. Maltsberger, & R. Yufit (Eds.), *Assessment and prediction of suicide* (pp. 270–320). New York: Guilford Press.

Tarasoff v. Regents of University of California (1974). S29 P. 2d 553, 118 Cal Rptr. 129.

Tarasoff v. Regents of University of California (1976). 17 Cal. 3d 425, 551 P. 2d 334, 131 Cal Rptr, 14.

Tardiff, K. (2003). Violence. In R. Hales, S. Yudofsky, & J. Talbot (Eds.), *Textbook of Clinical Psychiatry* (4th edition, pp. 1485–1509). Washington, DC: American Psychiatric Publishing.

Teasdale, B., Silver, E., & Monahan, J. (2006). Gender, threat/control override delusions and violence. *Law and Human Behavior, 30,* 649–658.

Teplin, L. A., McClelland, G. M., Abram, K. M., & Weiner, D. A. (2005). Crime victimization in adults with severe mental illness: Comparison with the National Crime Victimization Survey. *Archives of General Psychiatry, 62,* 911–921.

Tewksbury, R. (2007). Effects of sexual assaults on men: Physical, mental, and sexual consequences. *International Journal of Men's Health, 6*(1), 22–35.

Tewksbury, R., & Mustaine, E. E. (2001). Lifestyle factors associated with the sexual assault of men: A routine activity theory of analysis. *The Journal of Men's Studies, 9*(2), 153–182.

Thompson, M., Saltzman, L., & Johnson, H. (2001). Risk factors for physical injury among women assaulted by current or former spouses. *Violence Against Women, 7,* 886–899.

Tjaden, P., & Thoennes, N. (2000). Prevalence and consequences of male-to-female and female-to-male intimate partner violence as measured by the National Violence Against Women Survey. *Violence Against Women, 6*(2), 142–161.

Tolan, P., & Thomas, P. (1995). The implications of age of onset for delinquency risk: II. Longitudinal data. *Journal of Abnormal Child Psychology, 23,* 157–181.

Trippany, R. L., White Kress, V. E., & Wilcoxin, S. A. (2004). Preventing vicarious trauma: What counselors should know when working with trauma survivors. *Journal of Counseling & Development, 82,* 31–37.

U.S.A. Suicide: 2005 Official Final Data. (2008, January 24). Retrieved June 8, 2008, from http://www.suicidology.org.

U.S. Bureau of Justice Statistics. (2008). Retrieved June 27, 2008, from http://www.ojp.usdoj.gov/bjs/glance/tables/hmrttab.htm

U.S. Department of Justice. (1998). Violence by intimates: Analysis of data on crimes by current or former spouses, boyfriends, or girlfriends. Washington, DC: Bureau of Justice Statistics.

VandeCreek, L., & Knapp, S. (2000). Risk management and life-threatening behaviors. *Journal of Clinical Psychology, 56,* 1335–1351.

Wagner, B. (1997). Family risk factors for child and adolescent suicidal behavior, *Psychological Bulletin, 121,* 246–298.

Wallace, C., Mullen, P., & Burgess, P. (2004). Criminal offending in schizophrenia over a 25-year period marked by deinstitutionalization and increasing prevalence of co-morbid substance use disorders. *American Journal of Psychiatry, 161,* 716–727.

Warchol, G. (1998). *Workplace violence, 1992-1996.* (Bureau of Justice Statistics Special Report on World Wide Web). Retrieved from http://www.ojp.usdoj.gov/bjs/pub/ascii/wv96.txt.

Weisz, A. N., Tolman, R. M., & Saunders, D. G. (2000). Assessing the risk of severe domestic violence: The importance of survivors' predictions. *Journal of Interpersonal Violence, 15,* 75–90.

Wilson, M., & Daly, M. (1993). Spousal homicide risk and estrangement. *Violence and Victims, 8,* 3–16.

Wilson, M., Daly, M., & Wright, C. (1993). Uxoricide in Canada: Demographic risk patterns. *Canadian Journal of Criminology, 35,* 263–291.

Clinical Interventions with Children and Adolescents: Current Status, Future Directions

Thomas H. Ollendick *and* Stephen R. Shirk

Abstract

This chapter on clinical interventions with children and adolescents has four primary goals: (1) to review early efforts to identify evidence-based psychosocial treatments for youth and their families; (2) to provide an overview of current evidentiary support for the treatment of the four most prevalent psychiatric disorders in youth: anxiety disorders, mood disorders, attentional disorders, and oppositional/conduct disorders; (3) to examine relational and developmental factors that qualify and potentially moderate these efficacious treatments; and (4) to speculate on the future of psychotherapy research and practice with youth. Our review indicates that several evidence-based interventions are available, although with few exceptions they are cognitive-behavioral ones. However, we conclude that the evidence base even for these interventions is not overly robust at this time, and that we must evaluate other commonly practiced interventions such as play therapy, family systems therapy, and psychodynamic-based therapies before their routine use can be endorsed. We also identify important developmental, contextual, and relationship variables that qualify these efficacious findings and encourage the pursuit of additional process and outcome research. We conclude our discourse by suggesting that we must move beyond reliance upon manual-based treatments to the development of principle-based interventions that draw upon these specific evidence-based interventions but move beyond and unify them. Although much progress has occurred in the past 50 years, much work remains to be done. This is an exciting time in the child and adolescent psychotherapy arena.

Keywords: Behavioral and emotional disorders, child and adolescent psychotherapy, cognitive behavioral treatment, evidence-based treatment, process and outcome research

Over 50 years ago, Eysenck (1952) published his now (in)famous review of the effects of adult psychotherapy. Boldly, he proclaimed that psychotherapy practices at that time were no more effective than the simple passage of time. Subsequently, Levitt (1957, 1963) reviewed the child and adolescent psychotherapy literature and arrived at the same conclusion. These reviews were disquieting, and they led many clinicians, researchers, and policy analysts to question the continued viability of the psychotherapy enterprise for children, adolescents, and adults.

Fortunately, as noted by Kazdin (2000), these reviews also served as a wake-up call to the profession of clinical psychology and related mental health disciplines. In the clinical child and adolescent arena, significant advances in the study of developmental psychopathology, refinements in the psychiatric diagnostic nomenclature, attention to evidence-based assessment and treatment practices, and improved experimental designs for the study of treatment process and outcome have all occurred in the ensuing years. These developments, in turn, have resulted in well over 1,500 treatment studies (Durlak, Wells, Cotton, & Johnson, 1995; Kazdin, 2000) and seven major meta-analyses examining the effects of child and adolescent psychotherapy (Casey & Berman, 1985; Durlak, Fuhrman, & Lampman, 1991;

Kazdin, Bass, Ayers, & Rodgers, 1990; Miller, Wampold, & Varhely, 2008; Weisz, Jensen-Dose, & Hawley, 2006; Weisz, Weiss, Alicke, & Klotz, 1987; Weisz, Weiss, Han, Granger, & Morton, 1995). As noted by Weersing and Weisz (2002), there is little doubt that psychotherapy—as it is practiced these days—produces beneficial outcomes for youth and their families. Consistently, reviews show that psychotherapies for youth and their families outperform waiting list and attention-placebo control conditions; moreover, in several studies, it is becoming clear that some forms of psychotherapy work better than others. As a result, much progress has been made, and we can conclude that the field of clinical child and adolescent psychology has moved beyond the simple question, "Does psychotherapy work for youth?" to identify the efficacy of *specific* treatments for youth who present with *specific* behavioral, emotional, and social problems. Clearly, the field has moved beyond the generic question of whether psychotherapy "works" for youth and their families to a more specific one that seeks to determine the evidence base for various treatments and the conditions under which those treatments are effective. This is an exciting time in the field of psychotherapy research and practice with youth.

This chapter has four major goals: (1) to review efforts to identify evidence-based psychosocial treatments for youth and their families; (2) to provide an overview of the evidentiary support for the treatment of the four most prevalent psychiatric disorders in youth (anxiety disorders, mood disorders, attentional disorders, and oppositional/conduct disorders); (3) to examine relational and developmental factors that qualify and potentially moderate these efficacious treatments; and (4) to look to the future of psychotherapy research and practice with youth.

On the Nature of Evidence-based Treatments

The development and identification of evidence-based treatments (EBTs) is part of a larger zeitgeist labeled *evidence-based medicine* (Sackett, Richardson, Rosenberg, & Haynes, 1997, 2000). At its core, evidence-based practice is an approach to knowledge and a systematic strategy for improving treatment outcomes (Ollendick & King, 2004). The evidence-based approach is not wedded to any one theoretical position or orientation. Rather, it holds that treatments, of whatever theoretical orientation, need to be based on objective and scientifically credible evidence—evidence that is obtained largely

through randomized clinical trials (RCTs). In an RCT, youth with a specific presenting problem or disorder are randomly assigned to one treatment or another treatment, or to some control condition, such as a waiting list or an attention-placebo condition, and the effects of these conditions are evaluated. Although such a design is not without problems, it appears to be the best scientific strategy for ruling out biases and expectations (on the part of the youth, the youth's parents, *and* the therapist) that can result in misleading research findings. Evidence-based practice also values information or opinions obtained from observational studies, logical intuition, personal experiences, and the testimony of experts. However, such information is viewed as less acceptable from a scientific, evidentiary-based standpoint. It is not discounted; it simply occupies a lower rung on the ladder of evidentiary support.

In 1995, the Society of Clinical Psychology Task Force on Promotion and Dissemination of Psychological Procedures issued its report on "empirically validated" psychosocial treatments (see also Chambless, 1996; Chambless & Hollon, 1998). The task force committee was comprised of members from different theoretical orientations, including psychodynamic, interpersonal, family systems, and cognitive-behavioral points of view. This diversity in membership was intentional, in as much as the committee wished to emphasize a commitment to identifying *all* psychotherapies of proven worth, not just those emanating from one particular school of thought. However, defining empirically validated treatments proved to be a difficult task. Of course, from a scientific standpoint, no treatment is ever fully validated and, as noted in the task force report, there are always more questions to ask about any treatment, including questions about the essential ingredients of treatment, moderator variables that predict treatment outcome, and the mechanisms or processes associated with behavior change. In recognition of this state of affairs, the term "empirically supported" was adopted subsequently to describe treatments of scientific value—a term that many agreed was more felicitous than "empirically validated." Herein, we will use the more generic term, "evidence-based" treatment.

Three categories of treatment efficacy were proposed in the 1995 report: *well-established treatments*, *probably efficacious treatments*, and *experimental treatments*. Subsequent to that initial report, Chambless and Hollon (1998) proposed a fourth category, *possibly efficacious treatments*. The primary distinction between well-established and probably efficacious treatments was that a well-established treatment should be shown to be superior to a psychological placebo, pill, or another treatment, whereas a probably efficacious treatment need only be shown to be superior to a waiting list or no treatment control condition. In addition, effects supporting a well-established treatment should be demonstrated by at least two different investigatory teams, whereas the effects of a probably efficacious treatment need not (for example, the effects might be demonstrated in two studies from the same investigatory team). For both types of empirically supported treatments, it was posited that characteristics of the clients should be well specified (e.g., age, sex, ethnicity, diagnosis), and the clinical interventions should be conducted with treatment manuals. Furthermore, it was required that the outcomes of treatment be demonstrated in "good" group design studies or a series of controlled single-case design studies. "Good" designs were those in which it was reasonable to conclude that the benefits observed were due to the effects of treatment and not due to chance or confounding factors such as passage of time, the effects of psychological assessment, or the presence of different types of clients in the various treatment conditions. Randomized clinical trials—group designs in which patients were assigned randomly to the treatment of interest or one or more comparison conditions—and carefully controlled and executed single-case experiments were recommended as good designs. The additional category suggested by Chambless and Hollon (1998), *possibly efficacious treatment*, possessed all the characteristics of a probably efficacious treatment with the exception that the treatment only need to be shown to be effective in one study, not the two studies associated with the probably efficacious category of evidence. *Experimental treatments* were those treatments not yet shown to be at least possibly efficacious. This category was intended to capture treatments frequently used in clinical practice but that have not yet been fully evaluated, or newly developed ones not yet put to the test of scientific scrutiny. The development of new treatments was strongly encouraged. It was also noted that treatments could "move" from one category to another depending on the empirical support available for that treatment *over time*. For example, an experimental treatment might move into probably efficacious or well-established status as new findings become available. The categorical system was intended to be dynamic, not static or fixed.

Evidence-based treatments for Child and Adolescent Behavior Problems and Disorders

The 1995 Task Force Report on Promotion and Dissemination of Psychological Procedures (1995) identified 18 well-established treatments and seven probably efficacious treatments using the criteria just described. Of these 25 efficacious treatments, only three well-established treatments for youth (behavior modification for developmentally disabled individuals, behavior modification for enuresis and encopresis, and parent management training programs for children with oppositional defiant behavior) and one probably efficacious treatment for children (habit reversal and control techniques for children with tics and related disorders) were identified. As noted in that report, the list of empirically supported treatments was intended to be representative of efficacious treatments, not necessarily exhaustive. In recognition of the need to identify additional psychosocial treatments that were potentially effective with children, task forces were set up by the Society of Clinical Psychology (Division 12 of the American Psychological Association) and its offspring, the Society of Clinical Child and Adolescent Psychology (Division 53 of the American Psychological Association). The two independent task forces joined efforts and, in 1998, published their collective reviews in the *Journal of Clinical Child Psychology*. Reviews of empirically supported treatments for children with autism, anxiety disorders, attention-deficit hyperactivity disorder (ADHD), mood disorders, and oppositional and conduct problem disorders were included in the special issue. As noted by Lonigan, Elbert, and Johnson (1998), the goal was not to generate a comprehensive list of treatments that met criteria for empirically supported treatments for *all* disorders; rather, the goal was to focus on a number of high-frequency problems encountered in clinical settings serving children with mental health problems. As such, a number of problem areas were not reviewed (e.g., eating disorders, substance use, reactive attachment disorder, childhood psychosis).

In a subsequent review of empirically supported psychological interventions for adults and youth published in the *Annual Review of Psychology*, Chambless and Ollendick (2001) noted that other work groups had been instrumental in identifying empirically supported treatments as well. Namely, books edited by Roth and Fonagy (1996) and Nathan and Gorman (1998) identified other treatments and evaluated many of the same treatments identified by the Society of Clinical Psychology and the Society of Clinical Child and Adolescent Psychology. In general, the criteria used by the various groups were similar to those used by Division 12, although some relatively minor differences were evident (see Chambless & Ollendick for details). At that time, Chambless and Ollendick identified 108 empirically supported treatments (including both well-established and probably efficacious treatments) for adults and 37 for children and adolescents—an obvious increase over those reported in 1995. Yet, Chambless and Ollendick suggested considerable caution in as much as no well-established treatments had been identified for the treatment of such common problems as the mood and anxiety disorders in youth (although probably efficacious treatments were evident for these disorders). Moreover, rarely did any one treatment have more than the two requisite studies to support its well-established or probably efficacious status (with the exception of parenting programs for oppositional and conduct problem youth and for youngsters with ADHD). It was also evident that *all* of the probably efficacious and well-established treatments were based on behavioral and cognitive-behavioral principles at that time. As a result, using these criteria, evidentiary support for frequently practiced treatments from other theoretical orientations (e.g., play therapy, family systems therapy, psychodynamic therapy) was notably lacking.

More recently, under the auspices of the Society of Clinical Child and Adolescent Psychology, the evidentiary support for the most prevalent psychiatric disorders in youth has been reexamined once again (Silverman & Hinshaw, 2008). Of significance, the evidence base has increased substantially since that reported by the Task Force (1995), the early Society report (1998), and the review by Chambless and Ollendick (2001). We now turn our attention to the evidence base for psychosocial interventions that exist at this time.

Anxiety Disorders

Anxiety disorders are among the most common mental health problems in youth, with prevalence rates approximating 12% in community samples and 36% in clinical samples (cf., Kessler, Berglund, Demler, Jin, Merikangas, & Walters, 2005). The *Diagnostic and Statistical Manual of Mental Disorders, Fourth Edition* (DSM-IV) specifies that all of the anxiety disorders of adulthood can be identified in youth (i.e., generalized anxiety disorder [GAD],

specific phobia [SP], social phobia [SOC], panic disorder [PD], agoraphobia [AG], obsessive-compulsive disorder [OCD], and post-traumatic stress disorder [PTSD]), as well as one "childhood" disorder that occurs prior to age 18 (separation anxiety disorder [SAD]). In addition, past research based on earlier versions of the DSM included two additional diagnoses (i.e., overanxious disorder [OAD] and avoidant disorder [AD]) that have been subsumed under GAD and SOC in DSM-IV, respectively.

Surprisingly, no controlled between-group design outcome studies examining the efficacy of psychosocial treatments for youth experiencing anxiety disorders, other than simple or specific phobia, existed until recent years. However, several early controlled case studies provided preliminary support for the likely efficacy of behavioral and cognitive-behavioral interventions with these youth (Eisen & Silverman, 1993; Ollendick, 1995; Ollendick, Hagopian, & Huntzinger, 1991). Cognitive-behavioral treatment for anxiety disorders in youth, as used by Kendall and his colleagues (e.g., Kendall et al., 1992), is based on these early studies and is focused on both cognitive and behavioral interventions. Cognitive strategies are used to assist the youth to recognize anxious thoughts, to use awareness of such cognitions as a cue for managing anxiety, and to help them cope more effectively in anxiety-provoking situations. In addition, behavioral strategies such as modeling, in vivo exposure to the anxiety cues, role play, relaxation training, and reinforced practice are used. In the first manualized between-group study, Kendall (1994) compared the outcome of a 16-session treatment to a waitlist control condition. Forty-seven 9- to 13-year-old youth were assigned randomly to treatment or waitlist conditions. All the youth met diagnostic criteria for one of the anxiety disorders, and over half of them were comorbid with at least one other psychiatric disorder. Treated children improved on a number of dimensions; perhaps the most dramatic difference was the percentage of children not meeting criteria for an anxiety disorder at the end of treatment—64% of treated cases versus 5% of the waitlist children. At follow-up 1, 3, and 7 years later, improvements were maintained (Kendall, Safford, Flannery-Schroeder, & Webb, 2004; Kendall & Southam-Gerow, 1996). In a second RCT, Kendall et al. (1997) reaffirmed the efficacy of this procedure with 94 youth (also 9–13 years of age) randomly assigned to cognitive-behavioral and waitlist control conditions. Seventy-one percent of the treated children did not meet diagnostic criteria at the end of treatment, compared to 5% of those in the waitlist condition. Very recently, the efficacy of this approach has been further validated in the Child-Adolescent Anxiety Multimodal Study (Walkup et al., 2008). In this study involving 488 youth between 7 and 17 years of age, 60% of youth receiving cognitive-behavioral treatment were diagnosis-free at the end of treatment, compared to 55% of youth receiving sertraline and 24% of youth receiving a drug placebo. In addition, 81% of youth receiving both sertraline and cognitive-behavioral treatment were diagnosis-free, suggesting the additive effects of combinatorial treatment.

Subsequent to Kendall's first randomized clinical trial, his cognitive-behavioral therapy (CBT) approach was evaluated independently by a different investigatory team in Australia (Barrett, Dadds, & Rapee, 1996). Youth (between 7 and 14 years of age) were assigned randomly to one of three groups: cognitive-behavioral treatment, cognitive-behavioral treatment plus a family intervention, and a waitlist control. The cognitive-behavioral treatment was intended to be a replication of that used by Kendall (although it was shortened to 12 sessions). At the end of treatment, 57% of the anxious children in the cognitive-behavioral treatment were diagnosis-free, compared to 26% of the waitlist children; at 6-month follow-up 71% of the treated children were diagnosis-free (waitlist children were treated in the interim). In the cognitive-behavioral plus family anxiety management treatment condition, parents were trained in how to reward courageous behavior and how to extinguish reports of excessive anxiety in their children. More specifically, parents were trained in reinforcement strategies including verbal praise, privileges, and tangible rewards to be made contingent on facing up to feared situations. Planned ignoring was used as a method for dealing with excessive complaining and anxious behaviors; that is, the parents were trained to listen and respond empathetically to the children's complaints the first time they occurred but then to withdraw attention if the complaints persisted. In this treatment condition, 84% of the children were diagnosis-free immediately following treatment, a rate that was maintained at 6-month follow-up. The augmented parent condition was found to be superior to cognitive-behavioral treatment directed toward the child alone at post-treatment and 6-month follow-up. However, in more recent studies, parent involvement has not always shown superior outcomes (Ollendick, Davis, & Muris, 2004).

Following these early studies, a large number of RCTs have been undertaken, with all of them examining the efficacy of CBT interventions in various formats and with different anxiety disorders (e.g., individual vs. group, child vs. family, GAD, SOP, SP, OCD, PTSD). Most of the studies have shown comparable outcomes regardless of the format of treatment or the specific anxiety disorders treated. Overall, significant reductions in symptoms or diagnoses have been observed in about 60%–70% of youth, compared with about 5%–20% of youth in waitlist comparison groups. In their recent review, Silverman, Pina, and Viswesvaran (2008) concluded that these CBT interventions meet the criteria for probably efficacious status in as much as they have been shown to be superior to waitlist control conditions. Moreover, they identified a host of other variations on these standard procedures that possess possibly efficacious status. Surprisingly, no interventions were found to enjoy well-established status even at this time—none was shown to be superior to another efficacious treatment or a placebo condition in two well-controlled studies conducted by different investigatory teams.

Mood Disorders

Mood disorders evidenced by children and adolescents include major depressive disorder (MDD) and dysthymia. Epidemiological studies suggest the prevalence of these affective disorders in youth to be between 1.5% and 8.0% (Angold, Costello, & Erkanli, 1999; Costello et al., 1996). The diagnostic criteria for MDD and dysthymia in youth are similar to those specified for adults, with the exception that youth may experience irritability instead of depressed mood. In addition, weight and appetite disturbances may be manifested by failure to make developmentally appropriate weight gains (rather than loss of weight) and dysthymia can be diagnosed in youth after 1 year of symptoms, in contrast to the 2 years required for adults (APA, 1994). Overwhelmingly, research suggests that depression in youth is characterized by significant distress and interference and, left untreated, negative long-term outcomes.

The efficacy of psychosocial interventions in the treatment of youth with affective disorders was reviewed early on by Kaslow and Thompson (1998). Psychodynamic, interpersonal, cognitive-behavioral, and family systems interventions were examined for child and adolescent samples. Seven treatment outcome studies with children with elevated levels of depressive symptoms (but not a diagnosis of depression) were identified. All of the interventions were conducted in a group format and in school settings. Most treatments entailed less than 20 sessions and all were cognitive-behavioral or psychoeducational in nature. Commonly used interventions included social skills and social competency training, self-control therapy, cognitive restructuring, and problem-solving approaches. Collectively, these studies revealed that these similar although not identical approaches were efficacious in reducing depressive symptoms in children who were not formally diagnosed as depressed. In addition, treatment gains were maintained at follow-up intervals ranging from 4 weeks to 2 years. The majority of the studies adequately described the characteristics of the samples, used treatment manuals, and showed that the treatments were superior to waiting list control conditions and, in at least one study conducted by Stark and colleagues, superior to an alternative treatment (traditional school counseling groups). Although positive outcomes were noted in these seven studies, only the self-control behavioral treatment program developed by Stark and colleagues (Stark, Reynolds, & Kaslow, 1987; Stark, Rouse, & Livingston, 1991) reached the criteria for probably efficacious status, as defined by the 1995 Task Force. No treatments met criteria for well-established status at that time.

In their early review, Kaslow and Thompson (1998) also examined the status of psychosocial treatments for adolescents with depression. As with children, seven treatment outcome studies were identified, five of which examined variants of CBT (self-control therapy, problem solving, relaxation training, social skills, and cognitive restructuring); one examined interpersonal psychotherapy (which addresses the interpersonal, social, and developmental issues common to adolescents with special attention to problems associated with depression); and the other compared cognitive-behavioral approaches to systemic-behavioral family therapy (which combined techniques from functional family therapy and a problem-solving model and included a focus on parenting and developmental concerns) and to a nondirective supportive control condition. Adolescents ranged in age from 13 to 18 years and were in the ninth to twelfth grades. Six of the seven treatments were delivered in a group format (one used individual therapy), and four of the interventions were conducted in a school setting (three were administered in outpatient clinic settings). As with the child studies, all seven studies showed positive outcomes for the various treatments, reflecting superiority of the active treatments over waitlist control conditions. However, none of the active interventions proved to be superior to one another, reflecting both the absence of differences in the few studies that made

such comparisons and the dearth of treatment outcome studies conducted at that time. Furthermore, only the Adolescents Coping with Depression (CWD-A) program conducted by Lewinsohn, Clarke, and colleagues (Lewinsohn, Clarke, Hops, & Andrews, 1990; Lewinsohn, Clarke, Rohde, Hops, & Seeley, 1996; see also Clarke, Rohde, Lewinsohn, Hops, & Seeley for long-term follow-up of these treated youth) provided an indication of the replicability of findings associated with any one treatment, and then only within the same group of investigators. No treatments for adolescents met criteria for well-established status at that time, but the CWD-A treatment by Lewinsohn and colleagues was determined to be a probably efficacious one.

In their recent review, David-Fernon and Kaslow (2008) provide a more optimistic, albeit still guarded, picture of the treatment of child and adolescent depression. As with the earlier review, the self-control program of Stark and colleagues continued to meet probably efficacious status for children. In addition, they reported that the Penn Prevention Program (cf., Jaycox, Reivich, Gillman, & Seligman, 1994; Yu & Seligman, 2002) also possessed probably efficacious status at this time. This intervention, also based on a CBT model, was designed to address depressive symptoms (although not necessarily depressive disorders) in at-risk children and early adolescents. It too is a school-based program, although one recent trial has examined it in a primary care setting (Gillham, Hamilton, Freres, Patton, & Gallop, 2006). The program consists of two primary components: a cognitive component and a problems-solving component. The cognitive component teaches the youth to identify negative beliefs, evaluate the evidence for them, and to generate more realistic alternatives. The social problem-solving component focuses on goal setting, perspective taking, decision making, and self-instruction. Overall, the program has been shown to be more effective than waitlist or no intervention control programs.

Although the number of treatment studies for adolescents has greatly increased in recent years, no treatment has emerged as a well-established one at this time (David-Ferdon & Kaslow, 2008). Both CWD-A and a relatively new treatment, interpersonal psychotherapy for adolescents (IPT-A; Mufson et al., 1999; Mufson, Weissman, Moreau, & Garfinkel, 2004; Roselló & Bernal, 1999; Young, Mufson, & Davies, 2006), enjoy probably efficacious status. Interpersonal psychotherapy for adolescents addresses a variety of adolescent problem areas, such as interpersonal disputes and conflicts, role transitions, grief, and family and relational problems. The program helps youth develop effective strategies (e.g., improved communication, expression of affect related to changes in relationships, development of new social support systems) to deal with their problems areas. The treatment usually consists of 12 individual sessions conducted over a 12- to 16-week period. In most trials, recovery rates (i.e., percent diagnosis free) for the CWD-A and IPT-A treatments range from 50% to 85%, very similar to those found in the treatment of anxiety disorders in youth. Follow-up studies demonstrate that these programs produce lasting effects up to 2 years in duration. In addition to these two probably efficacious interventions, David-Ferdon and Kaslow (2008) also identified a number of possibly efficacious programs including attachment-based family therapy (Diamond, Reis, Diamond, Siqueland, & Issacs, 2002).

Attention-Deficit Hyperactivity Disorder

Attention-deficit hyperactivity disorder is also a prevalent psychological disorder in childhood, with studies typically showing prevalence rates ranging from 3% to 7% (APA, 2000). In addition, the DSM-IV delineates three subtypes of the disorder based on the two symptom dimensions of inattention and hyperactivity-impulsivity: ADHD, predominantly inattentive type (ADHD-I), ADHD, predominantly hyperactive/impulsive type (ADHD-H/I), and ADHD, combined type (ADHD-C; APA, 2000). Attention-deficit hyperactivity disorder is often associated with significant short- and long-term impairment and is a risk factor for the development of additional psychological problems across the lifespan.

In 1998, as part of the Society of Clinical Child and Adolescent Psychology report, Pelham, Wheeler, and Chronis (1998) reviewed the status of psychosocial treatments for ADHD in children (very few studies were conducted with adolescents at that time) and concluded that behavioral parent training (BPT) programs and behavior contingency management (BCM) programs in the classroom met criteria for well-established treatments, as specified by the 1995 Task Force; however, cognitive therapy, standard cognitive-behavioral interventions, and their variants (e.g., social skills training) failed to meet such criteria. In fact, these latter treatments failed to show significant improvements and were not recommended as front-line interventions. Moreover, other interventions such as play therapy, family therapy, and psychodynamic therapy had not been systematically evaluated in RCTs.

Pelham et al. (1998) noted further that, although psychostimulant medications possessed relatively immediate and positive effects on many domains of functioning in children with ADHD and are well-established interventions, they did not produce long-term changes in academic achievement, classroom deportment, and peer relationships. Moreover, consistent with other EBTs, about 60%–80% of children with ADHD respond positively to a central nervous system stimulant regimen; the remainder shows either no response or an adverse response. Furthermore, of those children who do respond, the behavior of the majority is not normalized. That is, they continue to display relatively high rates of problematic behaviors. Given these findings, Pelham et al. (1998) recommended the inclusion of behavioral programs aimed at addressing these persistent and refractory behaviors. As noted earlier, BPT and BCM programs have been recommended either to supplement the gains observed with stimulant medication or to use on their own accord.

Behavioral parent training and BCM programs are frequently combined in comprehensive behavioral programs. In typical BPT programs, parents are given a series of readings about the principles of behavior modification and are taught standard behavior management techniques, such as time-out, response-cost, point systems, and contingent attention. Usually, these techniques are taught in a series of outpatient sessions lasting 10–20 weeks. At the same time, therapists work closely with the child's teachers to develop similar BCM strategies that can be implemented in the classroom by the teachers; in addition, they assist the teachers in developing daily report cards that provide feedback to parents about their child's performance in the classroom. Typically, parents are asked to provide consequences for targeted classroom behavior at home (e.g., special rewards, time-out, response cost). Such programs consistently show mild to moderate improvements in both classroom and home settings. Pelham et al. (1998) further noted that these positive findings are enhanced when a consulting professional is available (in addition to the therapist) to work closely with the teachers and parents. Under such conditions, greater control (and fidelity) is obtained over treatment implementation. Finally, these effects are enhanced even more when the peer relationships of ADHD children are specifically addressed. For a number of years, Pelham and his colleagues (e.g., Pelham & Hoza, 1996) have conducted an intensive Summer Treatment Program that has as a major purpose the improvement of social relationships in these children.

The program is in effect 9 hours a day for 6–8 weeks and combines behavior management techniques with academic activities and sports skills training in a summer camp format.

Until recently, the question of whether treatments should be administered individually or in combination with one another remained unanswered. In the largest RCT ever conducted for the treatment of ADHD, the Multimodal Treatment Study of Children with ADHD (MTA Study; MTA Cooperative Group, 1999) attempted to answer this question by comparing behavioral treatment alone (primarily consisting of BPT and BCM, along with the summer program), stimulant medication alone, a combined treatment, and a community control treatment. Overall, the study found that stimulant medication alone and the combined treatment were significantly more effective than the behavioral treatment alone and the community control, which did not differ from one another. In addition, the combined treatment did not significantly differ from the stimulant medication alone condition for core ADHD symptoms.

Since the time of this initial publication, data from two follow-up points have been published (2 years after treatment and 3 years after treatment; MTA Cooperative Group, 2004; Jensen et al., 2007). Although the groups involving MTA medication management (i.e., medication alone and combined) continued to show advantages at the first follow-up, the effect sizes were approximately half of what they were at the time of the initial outcome analyses. Interestingly, results recently published from the 3-year follow-up found no differences between treatment conditions, although remarkable improvements were seen in all four of the groups, suggesting that any form of treatment may result in relatively long-term treatment gains (Jensen et al., 2007).

In a recent review of this literature, Pelham and Fabiano (2008) affirmed the earlier conclusions of Pelham et al. (1998): namely, BPT and BCM remain well-established psychosocial treatments, and stimulant medications remain a well-established pharmacological intervention. They also showed that behavioral peer interventions (BPI) were well-established at this time. Behavioral peer intervention programs are typically implemented as part of summer treatment programs that are typically day-long programs conducted for 6–8 weeks, delivering 200–400 hours of treatment. Daily activities in these programs include intensive social skills training, coached group play in recreational activities, concurrent contingency management systems (e.g., point

systems, time-out), and home-based report cards (see Pelham, Fabiano, Gnagy, Greiner, & Hoza, 2005). These programs also focus on teaching sports skills and team membership skills. Frequently, BPI programs are embedded in BCM and BPT programs. As a result, it is difficult to disentangle the effects of each of these programs; nonetheless, their combined effects are well-established.

Pelham and Fabiano (2008) reaffirmed earlier findings related to the inadequacy of cognitive therapies, CBTs, and other more traditional therapies. They could find no evidence that these treatments were effective in treating ADHD. They recommended strongly against their routine use. As a result, none of these interventions was described as probably efficacious or even possibly efficacious for children with ADHD.

Oppositional/Conduct Problems

Youth with oppositional and conduct problems comprise a heterogeneous group who engages in a broad array of behavior problem ranging from relatively minor defiance and temper tantrums to more serious violations such as physical aggression, destructiveness, stealing, and juvenile delinquency. Oppositional defiant disorder (ODD) refers to a recurrent pattern of developmentally inappropriate levels of negativistic, defiant, disobedient, and hostile behavior toward authority figures. Conduct disorder (CD) consists of more severe antisocial and aggressive behavior that involves serious violations of others' rights or deviations from age-appropriate norms. The prevalence of these disorders is estimated to be between 2% and 16%, depending on the population, ascertainment methods, and diagnostic measures used (Greene & Doyle, 1999; Loeber, Burke, Lahey, Winters, & Zera, 2000). In the absence of effective treatment, a significant subset of these youth become delinquent, and a significant minority become antisocial adults.

In their early review of the efficacy of psychosocial treatments for these youth, Brestan and Eyberg (1998) identified one well-established treatment and a host of probably efficacious treatments for these youth. Parent management training (PMT, very similar to BPT as defined by Pelham et al., 2008) was found to have strong empirical support and to warrant well-established status. Parent management training based on Patterson and Gullion's book, *Living with Children*, is derived from operant principles of behavior change and is designed to teach parents to monitor targeted deviant behaviors, observe and reward incompatible behaviors, and ignore or punish deviant behaviors. This program has been shown to be more effective than psychodynamic and client-centered therapy interventions, in addition to no-treatment control groups. Overall, this approach was shown to possess robust effects in studies conducted with youth referred by schools, family physicians, and juvenile courts; in addition, these positive effects were obtained by several different investigatory teams.

Several programs were viewed as probably efficacious by Brestan and Eyberg (1998) including Webster-Stratton's (1984, 1990, 1994) parent training program, which is similar to that of Patterson and Gullion (1968); however, it is used primarily with very young, oppositional children who are at risk for developing more serious conduct problems. It includes a videotape series of parent-training "lessons" based in developmental and social learning theory. It is typically delivered to parents in small groups with therapist-led group discussion of the videotape lessons. The treatment has been tested in several studies, but all by the same investigatory team. It has been compared to waitlist control groups and to alternative parent training formats and found to be successful. For the most part, these studies have typically included children between 4 and 8 years of age.

In addition to these two treatments, Brestan and Eyberg (1998) identified a host of other treatments that met criteria for probably efficacious status. Some of these were variants of parent training, whereas others included child-centered and context-relevant treatments such as anger control training, anger coping training, parent–child interaction therapy, problem-solving skills training, rational-emotive therapy, and multisystemic therapy (MST). Most of these treatments were evaluated in well-controlled and well-designed outcome studies and simply awaited systematic replication by a second research team before advancing to well-established status.

In their more recent review, Eyberg, Nelson, and Boggs (2008) reported on a large number of additional studies that have been conducted in the past 10 years. Surprisingly, however, only PMT based on Patterson and Gullion's book was found to enjoy well-established status at this time. No new treatments were found to be well established. However, 15 treatments were found to possess probably efficacious status and a handful to possess possibly efficacious status. It is evident that much research remains to be conducted before we have an armamentarium of well-established treatments for youth with conduct problems. Considerably more research on a wide range of youth who live in a variety of familial and community contexts is required. The pioneering work conducted by Henggeler and colleagues on MST (Borduin et al., 1995; Henggeler & Lee, 2003; Henggeler, Melton, & Smith, 1992; Henggeler et al., 1986) and the work by Sanders and colleagues (Bor, Sanders, & Markie-Dadds, 2002; Sanders, 1999; Sanders, Markie-Dadds, Tully, & Bor, 2000) on the positive parenting program (Triple P) represent the kind of work that will likely yield the best pay-off. MST is provided in the family's natural environment (e.g., home, school, community) and generally lasts up to 6 months in duration. Usually, the families are in contact with the therapists several times a week (both in person and by phone), and therapists are available at all hours to assist the family. Sanders's (1999) Triple P program is a multilevel system of treatment, with five levels of treatment designed to match child and family needs based on the problem severity of any one family. The levels range from a universal prevention program for all youth and families to a parent training program for clinically diagnosed youth to programs that target stressors in the family, such as parental depression or marital problems associated with child behavior problems.

Summary Comments: Evidence-based Treatments with Youth

It is evident that only a few well-established treatments have been identified for the treatment of child behavior disorders at this time. No well-established treatments have been identified for the treatment of depression or anxiety in youth. Moreover, only one treatment has been shown to possess well-established status in the treatment of youth with oppositional and conduct problems, and only two treatments have been shown to possess well-established status in the treatment of children with ADHD. Although a stable of interventions can be described as probably efficacious, it is evident that support for even these interventions is often meager. Rarely does any treatment have more than the two requisite studies that support its well-established or probably efficacious status (with the exception of parenting programs for oppositional and conduct problem children and for children with ADHD). It should also be evident that most of these probably efficacious and well-established treatments are based on behavioral and cognitive-behavioral principles, with the exception of interpersonal psychotherapy for adolescents with depression. To some extent, however, we do not really know whether frequently practiced treatments from other orientations work or do not work (e.g., play therapy, family systems therapy, psychodynamic therapy); in many instances, they simply have not been evaluated.

Developmental Context of Evidence-based Treatments for Youth

Clinicians working with children and adolescents are faced with a daunting challenge not shared by their adult therapist counterparts. Between preschool and late adolescence, children undergo enormous developmental changes in their cognitive, linguistic, emotional, interpersonal, and biological systems. Clinicians are faced, not only with individual differences, but with developmental differences as well. Over two decades ago, Kendall, Lerner, and Craighead (1984), and Ollendick and Hersen (1984) suggested that the "same" intervention delivered to children at different ages could produce dramatically different results owing to developmental differences in child capacities. In this respect, one class of change processes—interventions—could be constrained or facilitated by another class—developmental processes (Shirk, 1988).

Increasingly, research on child and adolescent treatment has drawn on basic principles of *developmental psychopathology* (Cicchetti & Rogosch, 2002; Silverman & Ollendick, 1999; Toth & Cicchetti, 1999). In their framework for developing EBTs for youth, Kazdin and Kendall (1998) proposed that the starting point for treatment development is research in developmental psychopathology that clarifies the nature and origin of mechanisms of dysfunction. Treatment, then, is geared toward remediating or compensating for pathogenic mechanisms that contribute to maladjustment. Similarly, a developmental psychopathology perspective is essential for the identification of boundaries of treatment effectiveness. A basic tenet of developmental psychopathology is that most forms of maladjustment result from the dynamic interplay among multiple developmental systems (Toth & Cicchetti, 1999). Insofar as children and adolescents present to treatment with different developmental capacities, social environments, and genetic liabilities, the same treatment should not be expected to produce uniform effects, even for youth with the same disorder (Shirk & Russell, 1996; Shirk, Talmi, & Olds, 2000; Silverman & Ollendick, 1999).

How might developmental processes impact treatment response to youth EBTs? A number of alternatives can be identified. First, children's developing capacities could limit (or facilitate) their ability to utilize specific treatment interventions. For example, children's emerging cognitive capacities, such as the capacity for self-monitoring, could impact their ability to identify emotional or situational cues that are critical for self-instructions. Consistent with this view, an early meta-analysis of CBT for children and adolescents (Durlak et al., 1991) found rather substantial age-related treatment effects. Cognitive-behavioral therapy with adolescents, presumably at a relatively advanced level of cognitive development, produced effects that were twice as large as those with younger children. Alternatively, typical social development could lead to a different pattern of age-related treatment effects. Developmental changes in autonomy and peer influence could mitigate the effects of interventions that rely on parent influence, such as parent management training, as in the treatment of ADHD or ODD, and in parent-augmented treatment in the mood and anxiety disorders. In this case, one might expect an inverse relationship between developmental level and effect sizes for PMT or the augmented conditions. In fact, an early review of parent training interventions reported diminished effects with increasing age (Strain, Young, & Horowitz, 1981) and, in the Barrett et al. (1996) study of anxious youth, the augmented treatment was found to be less effective for adolescents than for children.

A second alternative involves developmental differences in age of *onset* of a specific disorder. For example, research has supported the distinction between early-onset versus adolescent-onset conduct disorder (McMahon, Wells, & Kotler, 2006). These developmental patterns are associated with different liabilities (e.g., neuropsychological impairments that could impact treatment response). Similarly, negative cognitions may play a very different role in childhood-onset depressive disorders than in adolescent depression. For example, there is evidence that cognitions operate as *mediators* between stressful life events and depressive symptoms in childhood, but function as *moderators* during adolescence (Turner & Cole, 1994). Given this difference in function, one might expect interventions that target negative thinking to have different effects for children and adolescents.

A third and related alternative is that *duration* of emotional or behavioral problems could impact treatment outcome. By virtue of their age, older children have greater risk for disorders of longer duration than do younger children. Problems can become increasingly entrenched over time as a function of environmental contingencies or neurobiological changes. In addition, parents who have lived with child problems for a longer time may become less optimistic about change and, in turn, less motivated to continue treatment (Dishion & Patterson, 1992). Thus, treatment response is likely to be inversely related to problem duration. To the degree that older children are more likely to have problems of longer duration than are younger children, treatment effects might be expected to decrease with age.

For the most part, the search for potential developmental predictors or moderators of treatment outcome has focused on child age. Age represents a proxy for developmental processes, a stand-in for adaptive or maladaptive processes that take time to develop and unfold. And, as the foregoing alternatives suggest, age could be a proxy for processes that either facilitate or impede treatment efficacy. In the next section, age-related patterns in EBT outcomes for anxiety and depressive disorders, ADHD, and conduct problems are reviewed. Age trends are considered in terms of alternative developmental processes.

Age as a Predictor or Moderator of Evidence-based Treatment Effects with Youth

Age can function as either a predictor or moderator of treatment outcomes. As a predictor, age would be associated with outcomes, change in symptoms, or loss of diagnosis, regardless of treatment condition. For example, in a comparative trial involving several treatment conditions, age would be a predictor of outcome if it were significantly related to changes across treatment conditions. If, however, age were to be differentially related to treatment outcomes, that is, the magnitude or direction of effect varied as a function of treatment condition, then age would be a moderator of treatment outcome. Given the limited number of comparative outcome studies in the EBT literature, age is most typically conceptualized as a predictor of treatment response.

AGE AND THE TREATMENT OF ANXIETY DISORDERS

A "family" of CBT interventions has been shown to be probably efficacious across a range of anxiety disorders in children and adolescents (Ollendick & March, 2004; Silverman et al., 2008). Most research has concentrated on children between the ages of 7 and 14, with fewer studies of young children or adolescents. Nevertheless, a number of studies suggest potential age-related trends in response to CBT for anxiety. Southam-Gerow, Kendall, and Weersing

(2001) examined predictors, including child age, of treatment response among children ages 7–14 who received CBT for anxiety disorders in a specialty clinic. Poor treatment response was operationalized as the presence of any anxiety diagnosis following a full course of CBT. Analyses revealed a number of predictors of poor response, including higher levels of internalizing symptoms at pretreatment, higher maternal depression, and older child age. Child age continued to predict poor response even when analyses controlled for the other predictors.

Unlike the meta-analysis of CBT by Durlak and colleagues (1991), increasing age was not associated with greater treatment benefit among youth with anxiety disorders. As such, these results are inconsistent with a developmental facilitation perspective (e.g., increasing age is associated with greater capacity to utilize and benefit from interventions). It is possible that the facilitating effects of development on treatment response are unique to disruptive problems, in which deficits in cognitive processes such as self-monitoring and perspective-taking are prominent. However, because CBT, especially Kendall's Coping Cat approach to anxiety reduction, involves both cognitive and behavioral components, it is possible that children at different ages respond to different facets of the intervention (e.g., relaxation training versus restructuring or modifying self-talk). Further, as Southam-Gerow et al. (2001) point out, it is not clear if the diminished response of older children is a function of poor developmental fit between the activities that comprise Coping Cat or the result of anxiety problems of longer duration.

In a second study, Barrett et al. (1996) examined age as a potential moderator of treatment outcome in CBT for child anxiety. Children between the ages of 7 and 14 received either individual CBT or CBT with an additional family anxiety management (FAM) component. Results indicated that younger children responded more favorably (fewer retained their anxiety diagnosis) to CBT + FAM than did older children. A similar pattern was not obtained with individual CBT alone. Thus, age moderated the association between treatment and outcome. It appears that the inclusion of a family component was especially useful for younger children. From a developmental perspective, these results might be attributed to greater parent influence over younger than older children, or possibly to the greater importance of parent-assisted coping among younger children. Although this pattern of results clearly needs to be replicated, it raises an important developmental question: Might greater treatment benefits be expected from the addition of family or parent components in EBTs for younger compared to older youth? Unfortunately, studies comparing individual treatments with individual plus family or parent components have not evaluated this possibility.

AGE AND THE TREATMENT
OF DEPRESSION

In their meta-analysis of 34 RCTs for youth depression, Weisz, McCarty, and Valerie (2006) compared treatment effects for children under the age of 13 with outcomes for adolescents. Their results did not indicate differential efficacy across the two age groups, with overall effects in the small to medium range for both groups. It should be noted, however, that the meta-analysis included all randomized trials for child and adolescent depression, and not just studies of well-established or probably efficacious treatments. Based on their review of EBTs for youth depression, David-Feron and Kaslow (2008) reached a rather different conclusion; they concluded "the limited data suggest that psychosocial interventions are more effective for adolescents than for children and for younger adolescents than older adolescents." It is not clear if these discrepant conclusions stem from non-overlapping samples of outcome studies or from a differential focus on diagnostic response versus symptom change. Of equal importance, a comparison of effects for children and adolescents is complicated by the fact that the "same" treatment, for example, CBT, is not the "same" (i.e., identical) for child and adolescent depression. An evaluation of developmental effects at the level of specific treatment components (e.g., cognitive restructuring), is likely to yield less ambiguous results than are broad comparisons of multicomponent treatments (Shirk & Russell, 1996).

There is some evidence to suggest that younger adolescents respond more favorably to CBT for depression than do their older counterparts (Brent, Kolko, Birmaher, Baugher, Bridge, Roth, & Holden, 1998; Clarke, Hops, Lewinsohn, & Andrews, 1992; Curry et al., 2006). As in the case of CBT for anxiety disorders, this pattern is not consistent with a developmental facilitation perspective that would predict greater capacity to utilize cognitive interventions, and consequently better outcomes, with increasing cognitive maturity. Other predictors of treatment response may shed light on this age trend. A number of studies have shown that symptom severity, hopelessness, suicidal ideation, and cognitive distortions

are related to poor treatment response. These risk factors appear to accumulate with number of depressive episodes; by virtue of their age, older adolescents have a greater chance to experience more or longer episodes of depression.

AGE AND THE TREATMENT OF ATTENTION-
DEFICIT HYPERACTIVITY DISORDER

Behavioral interventions, including behavioral parent training, behavioral classroom management, and intensive social skills training, have been shown to produce reductions in ADHD-related behaviors (Pelham & Fabiano, 2008). Most of the research on these treatments, however, has focused on school-aged children, with substantially fewer studies of preschoolers and adolescents available (Pelham & Fabiano, 2008). Overall, the bulk of the evidence suggests that behavioral interventions for ADHD are effective across the elementary school-age years (Pelham & Fabiano, 2008). Continuity in beneficial effects into adolescence is less well-established.

Two studies by Barkley and colleagues (Barkley, Guevremont, Anastopoulos, & Fletcher, 1992; Barkley, Edwards, Laneri, Fletcher, & Metevia, 2001) provide some evidence for efficacy of family-based programs for adolescents with ADHD. In the first study, families were assigned to one of three conditions: behavioral management training (BMT), problem-solving communication training (PSCT), or structural family therapy. All three treatments produced reductions in negative communication, conflict, and anger during conflict, as well as improvements in ratings of school adjustment. Despite these positive outcomes, clinically significant change was very low across all groups, including the behavior management condition in which only 10%–29% of adolescents showed significant change depending on outcome measure. In a second study, Barkley et al. (2001) compared BMT with PSCT for adolescents with ADHD. Again, both treatments produced significant improvements in family conflict but with no differences between therapies. Using a measure of reliable change as an index of clinical significance, only 23% of families showed clinically significant benefits.

Results from these two studies suggest that behaviorally oriented therapies that focus on parent management skills or family communication are associated with behavioral improvements at home and at school. However, the limited magnitude of change indicates that these treatments are far from optimal for adolescents. It is certainly possible that developmental differences in the duration of ADHD problems and family patterns associated with such problems make change more difficult with adolescents than with children. Although symptoms of hyperactivity and impulsivity often improve with age, it may be the case that the cumulative effect of persistent attention symptoms engenders high levels of academic and social impairment, or that adolescents with ADHD, compared to children, present with greater comorbidity that complicates treatment progress. Alternatively, it may be the case that parent-focused interventions, such as BMT, are less effective with teens owing to developmental changes in autonomy and a corresponding reduction in response to parent reinforcement.

AGE AND THE TREATMENT OF OPPOSITIONAL/CONDUCT PROBLEMS

Although only one treatment, PMT, has met criteria as a well-established treatment for conduct problems (ODD/CD), a number of treatments have been found to be probably efficacious, including problem-solving skills training and MST. It is noteworthy that these treatments have been constructed with development in mind; that is, PMT and problem-solving skills training have concentrated on elementary school-age children, whereas MST has targeted adolescents.

Results for age-related trends in parent management training are mixed. In their analysis of 26 studies of PMT, Serketich and Dumas (1996) found somewhat larger treatment effects for elementary school-aged children than preschool-aged children. However, neither McMahon and colleagues (1985) nor Beauchaine and colleagues (2005) found age-related effects for Helping the Noncompliant Child or the Incredible Years interventions, respectively. In one large-scale study of PMT, Ruma, Burke, and Thompson (1996) found that adolescents had a lower rate of clinical recovery from disruptive behavior problems than did preadolescents.

As reflected by these discordant results, a clear pattern of age effects is difficult to discern, although some evidence suggests that adolescents might be less responsive to parent management interventions. It is certainly possible that poorer response by adolescents results from developmental changes in autonomy and peer influence that diminish parent behavioral leverage. However, evidence also indicates that adolescents present with more severe and long-lasting conduct problems than do younger children seen in PMT (Kazdin, Holland, & Crowley, 1997; Ruma et al., 1996). Age effects in treatment response may reflect developmental changes in the nature and severity of disruptive problems that emerge during adolescence.

Summary Comments: Development and Youth Evidence-based Treatments

Across all four clinical disorders, there is some evidence for age trends in treatment response. In general, results suggest that younger children respond more favorably than older children or adolescents to CBT for anxiety, PMT for conduct problems, and possibly to behavioral interventions for ADHD. Age trends for depression are less clear, although emerging results suggest that younger adolescents respond more favorably to CBT than do older adolescents. Overall, there is relatively little evidence for a developmental facilitation perspective. In general, younger children appear to respond better to EBTs than do older children, especially when adolescents are considered. But this tentative conclusion must be tempered by the existence of inconsistent findings, variations across disorders, and the absence of clear data for some age groups. Where age trends do exist, they appear to be more consistent with developmental models that consider age of onset, problem duration, or the accumulation of liabilities as explanatory variables. In general, although not in all cases, problems of long duration and high severity are associated (confounded) with child age, thus reflecting the adage that age is a proxy for processes that take time to develop and unfold.

As the current review suggests, simple clinical formulations such as *younger children respond more favorably to behavioral interventions whereas older children respond better to cognitive interventions* must be qualified by both disorder and treatment specifics. Although such "rules of thumb" make intuitive sense, existing data provide relatively little support for such a principle. Of course, given that many EBTs involve multicomponent packages, and given the dearth of dismantling studies, it is not evident which components, be they cognitive, behavioral, or relational, actually account for treatment changes.

On a more positive note, most EBTs have been developed for specific age groups, most commonly preschoolers, school-aged children, or adolescents. In fact, the absence of robust age effects may be due to the attenuation of age range in most EBT outcome studies. This is by no means a criticism, but rather a virtue. Most youth EBTs have been constructed with development in mind. Consequently, modest or mixed findings for age-related treatment effects should not be viewed as a license to use a specific empirically supported treatment with youth of widely varied ages, but rather as an indication to use EBTs with the specific age group for which they were designed.

Relational Context of Evidence-based Treatment for Youth

Perhaps it goes without saying that all of the foregoing EBTs are delivered through face-to-face contact with a therapist. Although bibliotherapy and internet-mediated programs have been developed, especially in the prevention area, most current EBTs for youth and their families occur in the context of an interpersonal relationship. The importance of the therapeutic relationship has long been recognized by child and adolescent clinicians of different theoretical orientations (Axline, 1947; A. Freud, 1946, Kendall, 1991; Ollendick & Cerny, 1981; Patterson & Chamberlain, 1994), however most research over the last 25 years has focused on the identification, manualization, and evaluation of specific treatment procedures. The search for EBTs has been based on the assumption that "specific factors," those procedures that distinguish one form of therapy from another, are likely to account for greater improvements in youth treatments than variations in "nonspecific factors," those features that are common across therapies. Indeed, recent meta-analytic results showing the superiority of EBTs over usual-care treatments are consistent with this perspective (Weisz et al., 2006).

Other reviews, however, have presented a more cautious portrayal of youth EBTs. For example, in their review of studies comparing youth EBTs with active control conditions, Jensen, Weersing, Hoagwood, and Goldman (2005) found that EBTs were superior to active control conditions of similar intensity in only about half of the reviewed studies. Similarly, results were equivocal when differences in "dose" of putatively active ingredients were compared. More recently, Miller et al. (2008) conducted a meta-analysis of direct comparisons of treatment modalities for the same four youth disorders reviewed here—anxiety, depression, ADHD, and conduct problems. In this review, they included only comparisons between EBTs and active, bona fide treatments, that is, not placebo or attention controls. Consistent with the narrative review, this study revealed small comparative effects ($d = .22$). The combined results of these reviews suggest that the impact of EBTs cannot be fully attributed to specific factors that are unique to these treatments. Instead, it is very likely that features that are common across bona fide therapies account for significant outcome

variation, a finding that is consistent with results from the adult therapy literature (see Luborsky et al., 2002; Messer & Wampold, 2002).

Of all the nonspecific factors, the therapeutic relationship has received the most attention in the child and adolescent research literature (Shirk & Karver, 2003; Karver, Handelsman, Fields, & Bickman, 2006), and a review of treatment manuals, whether for youth- or parent-focused interventions, reveals a common concern with building a collaborative, working relationship. Our aim, then, is not to argue that nonspecific factors are more important than specific factors in youth treatment, but rather to rise above this traditional polarity to draw attention to emerging "relational principles" that could complement the focus on treatment procedures. To this end, the empirical literature on the therapeutic alliance and treatment participation in youth therapy were examined for common themes.

Therapeutic Alliance in Child and Adolescent Treatment

Evidence indicates that the alliance between client and therapist is one of the most consistent predictors of treatment outcome across types of problems and types of therapies (Martin, Graske, & Davis, 2000). A small but growing set of studies shows that therapeutic relationship variables are associated with outcomes in child and adolescent therapy as well (Shirk & Karver, 2003; Karver et al., 2006). Specifically, Shirk and Karver (2003) found modest but comparable associations between measures of therapeutic relationship and outcomes across behavioral and nonbehavioral, manualized and nonmanualized, and adolescent and child therapies.

Consistent with the adult literature (Bordin, 1976; Horvath & Luborsky, 1993), the alliance in child and adolescent therapy has been conceptualized as a multidimensional construct (Shirk & Karver, 2006; Shirk & Saiz, 1992). Across self-, therapist, and observer reports two dimensions—emotional bond and task collaboration— have emerged as core features of the alliance (Estrada & Russell, 1999; Shirk & Saiz, 1992). A third dimension found in the adult literature, agreement on treatment goals, has received less attention, perhaps because of the low rate of goal consensus found in child and adolescent therapy (Hawley & Weisz, 2003). In brief, the alliance in youth treatment has been viewed as a *collaborative bond* between patient and therapist (Kazdin, Marciano, & Whitley 2005). Of course, because youth are rarely self-referred and typically reside with adult caregivers, youth treatment involves multiple alliances, that is, between therapist and youth, as well as between therapist and parent(s). In fact, for some forms of youth therapy, such as PMT, the child's problems may be targeted by working directly with the parent. In such cases, the critical alliance, then, is between therapist and parent. In other cases, parents can be involved as consultants, co-therapists, or collateral patients (Kendall, 1991), and typically parents are at least involved as the transporter of the child to the clinic. The alliance in child treatment, then, is both multidimensional and multirelational. Typically, therapists are faced with establishing and maintaining a collaborative bond with both youth and adult caregivers.

Early research on the therapeutic relationship, including the alliance, focused on nonbehavioral therapies delivered in usual-care contexts (Shirk & Karver, 2003; Shirk & Russell, 1996). Although such treatments were widely practiced, few had received empirical scrutiny. Recently, there has been growing interest in the contribution of the alliance to outcome in EBTs. Specifically, the alliance has been examined in CBT for child anxiety disorders and adolescent depression, and in behavioral PMT for children with disruptive behavior disorders.

Two published studies have examined the contribution of the alliance to outcome in CBT for child anxiety disorders. In the first study, Kendall (1994) examined associations between the children's perceptions of the therapeutic relationship and a broad set of outcome variables. Although Kendall found a pattern of significant correlations between child-reported alliance and child-reported anxiety outcomes, these results were not found across different sources of outcome data. In fact, the vast majority of correlations were small and nonsignificant. As Kendall noted (1994), children gave therapists very positive alliance ratings overall, which may have limited associations. In a second study, Kendall et al. (1997) found a similar pattern of results in their replication study of CBT for child anxiety disorders. Again, results revealed very modest and nonsignificant associations between child-reported alliance and outcomes, with an average correlation of less than .01. Thus, in both studies of alliance–outcome relations for childhood anxiety disorders, results provide minimal evidence for the contribution of the alliance to outcome. It should be noted, however, that in both studies, the alliance was assessed at post-treatment, which could have truncated the range of alliance scores thereby limiting associations with outcomes.

Two studies have reported on alliance–outcome relations in CBT for adolescent depression. In the first, Kaufman, Rohde, Seeley, Clarke, and Stice (2005) examined the mediating role of the alliance in group CBT. Their results showed higher alliance scores in the more effective CBT condition, compared to a life skills training condition, but alliance was not significantly predictive of outcome in either condition. In contrast, Shirk, Gudmundsen, Kaplinski, and McMakin (2008) found significant associations between alliance and change in depressive symptoms in their study of individual CBT for adolescent depression. Results were stronger for associations between adolescent-reported alliance and outcomes than for therapist-reported alliance; however, the average association between alliance and outcome across sources was very similar to results obtained in the meta-analysis by Shirk and Karver (2003). It is not clear if the discrepant findings of these two studies are the result of differences in modality (group vs. individual CBT), alliance measure, or some other factor.

In the area of disruptive behavior disorders, Kazdin and colleagues (Kazdin, Holland, & Crowley, 1997; Kazdin & Wassell, 1999; Kazdin & Whitley, 2006; Kazdin, Marciano, & Whitley, 2006) have conducted a series of studies on alliance–outcome relations in PMT and problem-solving skills training with youth. These studies have consistently demonstrated links between parents' alliance with their therapists and reductions in externalizing problems. In their most recent study, Kazdin et al. (2006) found that child–therapist alliance predicted treatment progress in youth problem-solving skills training. In addition, parent–therapist alliance in PMT predicted improvements in parenting, as well as child improvements in externalizing behavior. Importantly, Kazdin and Whitley (2006) showed that alliance–outcome relations in PMT could not be explained by variations in pretreatment client characteristics, such as parents' level of social functioning. Although this finding clearly needs to be replicated, it suggests that the alliance is a relational construct that emerges through the course of interactions between patient and therapist.

Taken together, then, results are mixed on alliance–outcome relations in youth EBTs. The most consistent findings come from research on youth with disruptive behavior disorders. Notably, the most consistent results have been obtained with parents rather than youth. It is possible that the use of self-report alliance measures is a less optimal assessment strategy with youth than with parents, perhaps due to positive biases that truncate the range of alliance scores among youth. In addition to predicting outcomes, parent–therapist alliance also predicts treatment dropout (Kazdin et al., 1997). A similar result has been obtained in usual-care therapy delivered in community clinics (Hawley & Weisz, 2005). In this study, parent–therapist alliance predicted premature termination, whereas youth–therapist alliance predicted changes in youth symptoms. Overall, then, emerging results suggest that cultivating a strong working alliance with parents may be essential for successful delivery of EBTs to youth. Perhaps this is not surprising, given the important role of parents in youth treatment. Typically, parents make decisions about initiating and terminating treatment, and often they are responsible for transporting children and adolescents to sessions even when they are not being seen themselves (Ollendick & Cerny, 1981).

Thus, an emerging evidence-based principle is that the alliance in youth treatment is multirelational. Initial evidence indicates that alliance formation with adult caregivers may be as, if not more, important than alliance formation with youth for the delivery of EBTs. Specifically, the formation of a working alliance with adult caregivers appears to be critical for treatment continuation and, in turn, the delivery of an adequate dose of EBT.

It is noteworthy that most research on alliance–outcome relations in child and adolescent therapy has focused on the youth rather than on their caregivers. As a result, we know relatively little about the best methods for building alliances with parents. There is some evidence to suggest that parent–therapist alliance may be related to parent perceptions of treatment relevance, credibility, and effectiveness (Kazdin et al. 1997; Nock, Ferriter, & Holmberg, 2007; Nock & Kazdin, 2001), but most of this work has focused on treatment attendance and adherence rather than alliance per se. Although a number of studies have shown that parent attendance and adherence can be enhanced through brief preparatory interventions or ongoing enhancement strategies, such as contingencies for homework adherence or collateral supportive parent sessions (see Nock & Ferriter, 2005, for a review), there is a dearth of research on specific therapist strategies for building and maintaining a positive parent alliance. Research on the alliance in child and adolescent treatment should be expanded to include both youth patients, as well as their adult caregivers.

Treatment Participation in Child and Adolescent Therapy

A second nonspecific factor that has received some attention in the child and adolescent therapy literature is treatment participation. Although participation has been equated with session attendance in some studies—and clearly exposure to efficacious treatment protocols is essential—virtually all EBTs demand more than session attendance and exposure to treatment components. Across diverse therapies, EBTs involve both an active therapist and an active patient. The efficacy of EBTs does not reside in the manual or merely in the therapist's fidelity to the manual, but rather in the client's active participation in the tasks or procedures specified by the manual. For example, the impact of homework assignments in most EBTs presumably is less about its assignment by the therapist and more about its completion by the patient. Similarly, a therapist can be exceptionally skilled in the construction of an exposure hierarchy, but if the patient fails to engage in exposure trials, it is unlikely that he or she will attain the benefits of the evidence-based procedure. It is the patient who changes, consequently, any comprehensive account of change processes must include patient behavior as well as therapist behavior over the course of therapy. As a broad construct, treatment participation provides a window on the patient's contribution to the beneficial effects of EBTs. A review of EBT manuals for children and adolescents reveals a consistent principle—children and adolescents are not passive recipients of therapy, but rather active participants in their own treatment. Although interventions that exclusively target parent behavior represent an exception to this pattern, youth-focused EBTs require active child and adolescent participation in sessions. Presumably variations in this common factor could account for substantial differences in treatment outcomes.

A substantial body of evidence from the adult psychotherapy literature indicates that patient participation, typically defined as patient self-disclosure, initiation of difficult topics, and verbal elaboration in response to therapist prompts or inquiries, is predictive of patient-, therapist-, and evaluator-reported outcomes across therapeutic approaches (Eugster & Wampold, 1996; Gomes-Schwartz & Schwartz, 1978; O'Malley, Suh, & Strupp, 1983). In light of results suggesting treatment equivalence for some adult disorders, it has been suggested that the specific form of treatment may be less important for successful outcomes than the patient's active participation in whatever treatment is offered (Eugester & Wampold, 1996; Luborsky, Rosenthal, Diguer, Andrusy, Levitt, Seligman, & Krause, 2002).

In their meta-analysis of relationship variables in youth and family therapy, Karver et al. (2005) identified ten studies that examined associations between youth treatment participation and outcome. Overall, their results showed a modest effect for treatment participation, with estimates ranging widely between null and large effects. Given the wide range of measures, heterogeneity of therapies and patients, and varied designs (controlled vs. uncontrolled), such a broad range is not unusual. As an example, one study of eclectic therapy delivered in a usual-care setting to children with varied disorders showed that youth participation accounted for 20% of outcome variance. Although such a finding is very promising, it does not appear that any of the studies included in the meta-analysis involved the evaluation of treatment participation in an EBT.

A study by Chu and Kendall (2004) appears to be the only study to have examined the role of treatment participation in an EBT for youth, in this case, CBT for children with anxiety disorders. Patient participation was defined as the child's behavioral involvement in therapy tasks, self-disclosure, verbal initiation, and task-relevant verbal elaboration. Negative indicators of participation included child withdrawal, avoidance, and passivity. Level of child involvement measured at mid-treatment was predictive of positive treatment outcomes, as indexed by the absence of an anxiety disorder diagnosis and reductions in impairment. Involvement in early sessions did not predict positive outcomes, but positive shifts in involvement between early and mid-treatment were highly predictive of diagnostic improvement. Interestingly, most youth showed a negative shift in involvement over the course of treatment (perhaps because treatment moved toward participating in exposure trials). Children who showed a large negative shift were far more likely to retain their anxiety diagnosis. As Chu and Kendall (2004) observed, "growing signs of withdrawal, avoidance, and diminished participation may signal to the therapist that strategies to reengage the child may be required." Although prospective correlations between child involvement and outcome are a necessary step toward establishing a causal relation, they are by no means sufficient. However, the case is somewhat strengthened by the absence of associations between pre-treatment child characteristics and level of involvement. Nevertheless, it remains

possible that early symptom change could affect children's level of treatment involvement.

The contribution of parent participation to outcome has been examined in the youth literature as well. In their meta-analysis, Karver et al. (2005) identified six studies that examined the contribution of parent participation to outcome. Again, participation was assessed with a wide variety of instruments, but unlike the research on child participation, five of the six studies were conducted in the context of behavioral or cognitive-behavioral therapy. All five studies showed significant positive association between participation and outcomes. In general, these results reflected the importance of the level of parent participation in parent-focused treatments such as PMT. Systematic research on parent "resistance" in PMT by Patterson and colleagues (see Patterson & Chamberlain, 1994) are consistent with these results. Their research indicates that parent nonadherence within and between sessions accounted for as much as 40% of change in parenting behavior, which was strongly associated with subsequent improvement in child behavior. Thus, once again, we find stronger evidence for parent relationship predictors than for child predictors in youth EBTs, essentially due to the absence of research on youth participation in EBTs.

A common feature of most EBTs for youth, and an important index of treatment participation, is between-session homework. Research with adults has revealed consistent relations between homework adherence and positive treatment outcomes. In their meta-analysis of the effects of homework on treatment response, Kazantzis, Ronan, and Deane (2000) found that interventions that included homework were more effective than interventions that did not. Similarly, Thase and Callan (2006) reported in their review of the literature on homework adherence in cognitive-behavioral treatment of adult depression that adherence was a moderate, but consistent, predictor of improvement. Remarkably, research on homework adherence in youth treatment is virtually nonexistent. This is especially surprising given that academic difficulties, including homework completion, are a common form of impairment among referred youth. Thus, homework completion in treatment, as in school, might be especially challenging for children and adolescents with significant mental health problems.

In one of the few studies to examine the role of homework adherence in a youth EBT, Clarke, Hops, Lewinsohn, Andrews, Seeley, and Williams (1992) examined the association between homework completion and outcome in group CBT for adolescent depression. Homework completion was assessed for each session and correlated with diagnostic recovery and change in self-reported depressive symptoms. Although both correlations were in the expected direction, both were very small and failed to attain statistical significance. In a second study with a very small sample of depressed adolescents in group CBT, Gaynor, Lawrence, and Nelson-Gray (2006) found associations that were more consistent with results from the adult literature. However, the small sample size of eight indicates the importance of replication.

In summary, despite substantial evidence from the adult therapy literature for the importance of treatment participation, research on participation in youth therapy, including EBTs, is quite limited. Given that children and adolescents rarely self-refer, often minimize their problems, and frequently fail to acknowledge a need for change, substantial variation in treatment participation might be expected among youth. Yet the contribution of in-session involvement and between-session adherence largely has been ignored, despite the possibility that it could account for significant outcome variance. Demonstration of the contribution of treatment participation to treatment outcome could open a new avenue for strengthening EBTs by improving treatment participation and adherence. Although the idea is intuitively appealing, it currently lacks an empirical foundation with youth.

Summary Comments: Relational Context of Evidence-based Treatments for Youth

Emerging evidence suggests that the beneficial effects of EBTs for youth are the result of both specific treatment procedures that are unique to evidence-based interventions and of nonspecific factors that are common across a wide range of therapies. The relative contribution of these factors has yet to be clearly established. Relational processes, such as the therapeutic alliance and treatment participation, have received some consideration in the empirical literature, but the evidence base is so thin that it is difficult to derive evidence-based principles. Across virtually all empirically supported protocols for youth, the importance of establishing a strong therapeutic alliance and engaging children, adolescents, or their parents in active participation in the tasks of therapy are clearly recommended. Yet, research on the contribution of these factors to treatment outcome in EBTs for youth is only beginning to emerge.

Currently, existing research suggests that it is important to view the alliance in youth therapy as multirelational. Initial results indicate that clinicians need to attend, not only to their alliance with the youth, but also to the alliance with adult caregivers. Neglect of the parent–therapist alliance could have grave implications for treatment continuation and, in turn, adequate exposure the effective components of EBTs. And while exposure to evidence-based procedures is necessary for therapeutic benefits, active participation by youth and/or parents is likely to be critical as well. However, this second principle—effective treatment involves an active therapist *and* an active patient—is currently "on loan" from the adult literature. Although it is built into the structure of evidence-based protocols through specific therapist–patient activities, variations in youth or parent participation have received very limited consideration. Hopefully, the next generation of treatment research will consider such process variables, as they may reveal new alternatives for strengthening EBTs.

Conclusion

The last 50 years has witnessed a remarkable change in the field of child and adolescent psychotherapy. An inadequate and unsteady empirical foundation has been replaced by a firm (and deep) base of outcome studies. Across multiple meta-analyses of this literature, results indicate that child and adolescent psychotherapy produces significant change in emotional, social, and behavioral problems. Accordingly, a relatively dismal view has been replaced by a more optimistic and well-grounded perspective. In turn, the field has redirected its attention to identifying efficacious treatments for specific disorders. The question for youth therapy researchers has shifted from "does child and adolescent therapy work" to "what works for youth with different types of problems?"

As our review indicates, substantial progress has been made toward addressing this question. Across four prevalent child and adolescent disorders, a number of treatments are now considered to be probably efficacious and many more as possibly efficacious. Although these results are promising, it is evident that only a handful of interventions have been shown to be well-established, and that more work needs to be done to establish the efficacy of interventions for other understudied problems such trauma reactions, eating disorders, childhood psychosis, self-injurious behavior, and complicated patterns of comorbidity that frequently present in community clinics (Ollendick, Jarrett, Grills-Taquechel, Seligman, & Wolff, 2008; Weisz et al., 1987).

Despite the growth in child and adolescent outcome studies over the last five decades, remarkably few studies have been designed to address specific mechanisms of therapeutic action. As a result, research on mediators of youth treatment effects is in a nascent state. Thus, although it is evident that many youth treatments produce beneficial effects, there is much less certainty about what actually produces these effects. In part, this ambiguity stems from a focus on the evaluation of full treatment packages that typically include multiple therapeutic components, and from the tendency to assess change or response at the end of treatment rather than at multiple points during the course of therapy.

Although some might argue that the identification of mechanism is relatively unimportant as long as treatments "work," the fact that virtually all existing youth therapies produce substantial variability in treatment response, including 30%–40% of youth who fail to respond, identification of active therapeutic ingredients could provide the basis for treatment refinement and enhancement. Initial patterns might be detected by evaluating associations between variations in therapist delivery of and youth involvement in specific therapy components and measures of treatment outcome (Shirk & Karver, 2006). Of course, this strategy would need to be followed by dismantling studies that experimentally vary specific components across randomized groups.

Similarly, research on moderators of outcome is relatively limited. Our review of one important moderator, developmental level, revealed that few studies actually test for moderation, but rather are limited to predictors of change. With regard to developmental level, exclusively defined in the literature as child age, the pattern of age-related trends in treatment response appears to depend on the type of treatment, type of disorder, and the age range evaluated. Importantly, however, many EBTs have been devised with development in mind; that is, most manual-guided therapies have been developed specifically for either elementary school children or adolescents. With the exception of conduct problems, fewer treatments have been developed and tested with preschool children.

Of course, other potentially important moderators of treatment outcome remain to be examined (see Ollendick et al., 2008). Some that have received limited attention in the youth literature are gender, ethnicity, family disadvantage, comorbidity, and parental psychopathology. Although studies are very limited at this time, suffice it to indicate that, as with age, the few findings available are mixed and highly complex, with some studies demonstrating the effects of moderation for these variables and others failing to do so. Unfortunately, firm conclusions cannot be drawn at this time.

Implications for Clinical Research and Practice

Typically, current effectiveness trials compare treatment-as-usual (TAU) with a manual-guided therapy, and emerging evidence suggests that such structured therapies outperform an eclectic blend of youth treatments (Weisz et al., 2006). A reasonable inference, then, is that clinical outcomes will be improved when youth practitioners abandon TAU and adopt manual-guided therapies that have been shown to be effective. Of course, this conclusion implies that effective youth therapists will need to master a vast library of treatment protocols, or will need to specialize in the treatment of a limited set of disorders in order to manage information and skill overload. Thus, while the expansion of youth outcome studies and the emergence of EBTs clearly represent major advances in the field, the sheer number of "possibly efficacious," "probably efficacious," and "well-established" treatments presents a significant challenge for both therapists-in-training, as well as for seasoned practitioners.

Given the information and skill acquisition demands inherent in mastering multiple treatment manuals, it is not evident that improvement of youth treatment outcomes will follow from the proliferation of treatment manuals. Instead, it might be worth revisiting the role of treatment manuals in both clinical research and practice. Manuals were developed to homogenize treatment and reduce within-(treatment) condition variability across therapists, supervisors, and sites. Although most manuals lend themselves to flexible application, the aim of manualized therapy is to provide a consistent treatment at a "set" dose analogous to pharmacological therapy. Thus, manuals represent a means to an end. Specifically, they operationalize specific treatment principles (for example, principles of reinforcement, exposure, or cognitive restructuring)through a set of recommended activities or interactions—what might be called *implementation guidelines*. In brief, a manual is a means for bringing specific change principles to life.

We propose that what is critical for the improvement of child and adolescent therapy is less about mastery of manuals, and more about understanding and applying core change principles inherent in manuals with known efficacy. To this end, it may be time to redirect attention to core principles that are captured in empirically supported protocols (see Barlow, Allen, & Choate, 2004 and Moses & Barlow, 2006). Recently, Woody and Ollendick (2006) summarized the core principles of effective treatments for anxiety disorders. In conducting evidence-based treatment for the anxiety disorders, they proposed that therapists should:

- Challenge misconceptions through discussion and explicitly question the evidence.
- Actively test the validity of erroneous and maladaptive beliefs through behavioral experiments.
- Use repeated exposure to the feared situation to reduce the intensity of the fear response.
- Eliminate avoidance of feared situations.
- Improve skills for handling feared situations.

Our review of EBTs across commonly occurring disorders reveals significant overlap in treatment principles, albeit significant variation in treatment protocols. As an initial effort to refocus attention on change principles, we highlight some of the common features and cross-cutting principles inherent in evidence-based protocols. This account is not intended to be exhaustive, but rather illustrative of emerging principles of change in youth treatment.

Principle 1: Treatments Are Focused and Time-limited

Perhaps the most striking difference between EBTs and traditional child therapies involves level of structure. Traditionally, child therapy has been open-ended and guided by the principle of "following the lead of the child." To a great degree, the agenda was defined by whatever the child or family presented in a specific session. Thus, the content and focus of sessions could range widely over successive weeks of treatment. In contrast, EBTs provide a structure for the course of therapy. Although the client's concerns are elicited and incorporated into ongoing therapy, treatments are focused on specific treatment targets that are viewed as relevant for the reduction of a class of symptoms. For example, in the treatment of adolescent depression, the target could be the acquisition of effective coping strategies (typical of CBT) or the restructuring of problematic relationships (central to IPT). Once the treatment target has been identified, therapy remains focused on its modification.

Some years ago, Weisz, Donenberg, Han, and Kauneckis (1995) used a gardening metaphor to describe this important difference across therapies. To extend their metaphor, EBT therapists tend to "water their gardens" (conduct therapy) with the hose set to "stream," whereas traditional therapists set the nozzle to "spray." Evidence-based treatments target specific skills, processing deficits, or cognitive, emotional, or behavioral patterns, including interpersonal patterns, and attend to their modification sequentially, rather than simultaneously addressing multiple problems. Consequently, therapy is structured in a relatively orderly manner. Manuals undoubtedly enhance structure, but the core principle embodied in the manual involves systematic focus on single treatment targets and an orderly progression to new targets following improvement in the initial target. Although most EBTs involve multiple components, all involve a sequential approach to change.

Similarly, EBTs tend to be time-limited in duration. It is possible that this feature is an artifact of the constraints of conducting clinical trials, and very little evidence exists on dose–response relations in youth EBTs. However, it is also possible that a time-limited approach prevents therapist drift, sharpens treatment focus, and increases client participation. Based on this common feature of EBTs, it may be wise for therapists to structure treatment in time-limited segments rather than presenting it as an open-ended process. In turn, therapist and client can renegotiate additional segments based on treatment progress.

Principle 2: Therapists Are Active

As noted earlier, traditional child and adolescent therapy is structured, in large part, by the youth's lead. To a great degree, then, therapists are in a *responsive* mode. In contrast, a review of EBT manuals indicates that therapists are cast in a very different role. Although therapists are expected to respond to concerns or situations presented by clients, therapists also are expected to actively guide patients through therapy tasks. In this respect, EBT therapists share a number of important characteristics with coaches. Like coaches, therapists are expected to form a good working relationship with their players, prepare them for the challenges of a game or performance, and help them develop the skill repertoire for, or overcome the impediments to, successful execution in a game or show (live-performance conditions). Therapy is not simply didactic. Good therapists identify the relevant skills, capacities, or patterns that are essential for successful performance and provide clients with relevant opportunities and motivation to practice or rehearse. In brief, therapists don't just talk about the skills, just as a good dance instructor doesn't just describe a ballet. Evidence-based treatment therapists break down the "dance" into specific components, model "moves," provide ample opportunities for practice (e.g., in role-plays), and ultimately conduct "dress rehearsals" (e.g., in behavioral experiments, exposure trials, or prescribed interactions).

As Woody and Ollendick (2006) noted, effective EBT therapists do not just "direct" clients as to what to do, when to do it, where to do it, and how to do it. Rather, a collaborative process is enlisted in which the therapist draws upon clients' input to shape the content of sessions. This collaboration is most evident in such activities as constructing a hierarchy for exposure, planning homework assignments, or devising relevant role-plays. Importantly, in the context of skill training, effective EBT therapists attempt to integrate clients' immediate concerns or situations, often elicited at the beginning of sessions, into modeling or practicing relevant components. In this respect, therapists are actively responding to child or adolescent material while maintaining therapeutic focus.

A limited number of studies have compared EBTs to nondirective approaches. Perhaps the best evidence for the importance of therapist activity comes from a series of studies comparing trauma-focused CBT (TF-CBT) to nondirective supportive therapy for sexually abused children. Across four randomized controlled trials, results consistently showed greater improvements among children treated in TF-CBT compared to nondirective therapy (see Cohen, Mannarino, Murray, & Igleman, 2006 for a review). Similar findings have been obtained in the area of adolescent depression. Brent et al. (1997) found that CBT produced a lower rate of major depressive disorder at the end of treatment than nondirective supportive therapy, as well as a higher rate of remission. Of course, level of therapist activity and direction is only one dimension of difference between these two treatments, but clearly results favor treatments with a more active and directive therapist. Additional studies comparing EBTs to nondirective supportive therapy will strengthen the evidence base for EBTs and help isolate the contribution of specific factors to treatment outcomes.

Principle 3: Clients Are Active Participants
Evidence-based treatment manuals consistently prescribe an active role for clients. Children and adolescents are not passive recipients of treatment, but rather they are active participants in therapy.

Treatment involves much more than exposure to the components in a manual; instead, EBTs call for active youth involvement in the activities, procedures, and interactions outlined by the manual. For example, skill acquisition is predicated on active practice of new skills in and between sessions. Exposure requires active encounters with actual or imagined anxiety-evoking situations. Reworking emotional reactions in IPT for adolescent depression hinges on the client's presentation of relevant emotional events in sessions. As these examples suggest, EBTs require both an active therapist and an active client.

As noted earlier, surprisingly few studies have examined the role of client involvement in EBTs. Research by Chu and Kendall (2004) yielded results that are consistent with this treatment principle. Higher levels of child participation produced better response to CBT for anxiety disorders. But, for the most part, this finding stands alone in the EBT literature. Despite the importance ascribed to active client participation in EBT manuals, very little has been done to evaluate this assumption or to identify what constitutes an adequate level of participation. Research on EBTs would be advanced by identifying how much participation is needed to which treatment components.

Given the importance of active participation in EBTs, the identification of therapist strategies or behaviors that promote or undermine treatment involvement is critical. A number of studies have examined therapist behaviors as predictors of working alliance in youth EBTs (Creed & Kendall, 2005; Russell, Shirk, & Jungbluth, 2008), but this line of research is in an early stage of development. It is likely that effective engagement strategies will vary as a function of client characteristics, for example, initial level of motivation or conversely hostility, and that one set of strategies will not fit all.

Principle 4: Therapy Extends Beyond the Therapy "Hour" and Setting
In virtually all EBTs, the assignment of between-session activities (homework) is a common feature. Between session assignments provide opportunities for practicing newly acquired skills, for generalization of concepts and skills to new situations, for behavioral experimentation, and for potentially greater integration of therapy content with "live" emotional reactions than can be attained in session. Thus, therapy extends well beyond the office setting.

Again, despite the importance ascribed to homework in EBTs, evidence for the impact of homework completion by youth is virtually nonexistent.

Initial results with depressed adolescents are mixed. In fact, it has been suggested that homework completion might be less important with youth since noncompleted homework is typically completed in session (Clarke et al., 1992). Yet, given the putative functions of homework, completion of assignments in sessions barely approximates its presumed goals. As a core component of EBTs, the contribution of homework completion to treatment outcome is clearly in need of evaluation across child and adolescent disorders. If, for example, homework completion is unrelated to outcomes, or only related to outcomes for a subset of youth, then time allocated to homework assignment and review could be reallocated to other therapy components that may be more strongly related to beneficial effects.

The foregoing principles cut across widely divergent EBT protocols. It is likely that other principles will emerge with further scrutiny of diverse manuals. In many ways, the foregoing principles represent *formal* rather than *content* features of EBTs. It may be that core change principles will need to be anchored to specific classes of disorders, as enumerated by Woody and Ollendick (2007) for anxiety disorders. However, the identification of general principles may not be out of reach. To this end, we offer the following examples as potential core change principles in youth EBTs.

- *A significant portion of behavior is regulated by environmental consequences.* Contingent reinforcement of desired behavior is critical for change.
- *A significant portion of behavior, including maladaptive emotional reactions, is maintained by avoidance.* Graded exposure to challenging situations can reduce avoidance and improve behavior.
- *Stress is associated with many psychological disorders and can amplify symptoms.* Methods to reduce stress either through improved coping or environmental change (e.g., reduce family conflict) will decrease symptoms.
- *Cognitive processing problems or maladaptive beliefs often are associated with specific disorders.* An important focus of treatment is the identification and remediation of such cognitive features.

Admittedly, these examples are highly consistent with a cognitive-behavioral approach to treatment—and not by accident! Cognitive-behavioral therapy and behavior therapy have been the most commonly examined approaches in the EBT literature. A growing number of studies have examined interpersonal therapy and family-based approaches, and it is likely that accumulating evidence will point to additional change principles. An area that has received less attention in the youth treatment literature involves the role of emotion in therapeutic change. A comprehensive model of therapeutic change may ultimately include cognitive, behavioral, emotional, and relational principles derived from different therapeutic perspectives.

Future Directions

As is evident, the field of child and adolescent psychotherapy has reemerged in recent years. Not that many years ago, the practice was in danger of becoming extinct and relegated to dinosaur status. Fortunately, advances in the study of developmental psychopathology have occurred that have been accompanied by exciting and far-reaching developments in evidence-based assessment and treatment practices. These advances have placed clinical child and adolescent interventions on more sure footing. However, our legs are not strong, and we cannot rest on our laurels. Much more remains to be accomplished in terms of developing well-established interventions for a variety of child and adolescent problems and disorders, and in identifying the core principles that underlie these interventions. We have our work cut out for us!

References

American Psychiatric Association. (1994). *Diagnostic and Statistical Manual of Mental Disorders,* (4th ed.). Washington, DC: Author.

American Psychiatric Association. (2000). *Diagnostic and statistical manual of mental Disorders: Text revision* (4th ed.). Washington, DC: American Psychiatric Press.

Angold, A., Costello, E. J., & Erkanli, A. (1999). Comorbidity. *Journal of Child Psychology and Psychiatry and Allied Disciplines, 40,* 57–87.

Axline, V. (1947). *Play therapy.* Boston: Houghton Mifflin.

Barkley, R., Guevremont, A., Anastopoulos, A., & Fletcher, K. (1992). A comparison of three family therapy programs for treating family conflicts in adolescents with attention-deficit hyperactivity disorder. *Journal of Consulting and Clinical Psychology, 60,* 450–462.

Barkley, R., Edwards, G., Laneri, M., Fletcher, K., & Metevia, L. (2001). The efficacy of problem-solving communication training parent management training alone, and their combination for parent adolescent conflict in teenagers with ADHD. *Journal of Consulting and Clinical Psychology, 69,* 926–944.

Barlow, D. H., Allen, L. B., & Choate, M. L. (2004). Toward a unified treatment for emotional disorders. *Behavior Therapy, 35,* 205–230.

Barrett, P., Dadds, M., & Rapee, R. (1996). Family treatment of childhood anxiety: A controlled trial. *Journal of Consulting and Clinical Psychology, 64,* 333–342.

Beauchaine, T., Webster-Stratton, C., & Reid, M. (2005). Mediators, moderators and predictors of one year outcomes of children treated for early-onset conduct problems. *Journal of Consulting and Clinical Psychology, 73,* 371–388.

Bor, W., Sanders, M. R., & Markie-Dadds, C. (2002). The effects of the triple p-positive parenting program on preschool children with co-occurring disruptive behavior and attentional/hyperactive difficulties. *Journal of Abnormal Child Psychology, 30,* 571–587.

Bordin, E. (1979). The generalizability of the psychoanalytic concept of working alliance. *Psychotherapy, Theory, Research, and Practice, 16,* 252–260.

Borduin, C. M., Mann, B. J., Cone, L. T., Henggeler, S. W., Fucci, B. R., Blaske, D. M., & Williams, R. A. (1995). Multisystemic treatment of serious juvenile offenders: Long-term prevention of criminality and violence. *Journal of Consulting and Clinical Psychology, 63,* 569–578.

Brent, D., Holder, D., Kolko, D., Birmaher, B., Baugher, M., Roth, C., Iyengar, S., & Johnson, B. (1997). A Clinical Psychotherapy Trial for Adolescent Depression Comparing Cognitive, Family, and Supportive Therapy. *Archives of General Psychiatry, 54,* 877–885.

Brent, D., Kolko, D., Birmaher, B., Baugher, M., Bridge, J., Roth, C., & Holder, D. (1998). Prediction of treatment efficacy in a clinical trial of three psychosocial treatments for adolescent depression. *Journal of the American Academy of Child and Adolescent Psychiatry, 37,* 906–914.

Brestan, E., & Eyberg, S. (1998). Effective psychosocial treatment of conduct-disordered children and adolescents: 29 years, 82 studies, and 5,272 kids. *Journal of Clinical Child Psychology, 27,* 180–189.

Casey, R. J., & Berman, J. (1985). The outcome of psychotherapy with children. *Psychological Bulletin, 98,* 388–400.

Chambless, D. L. (1996). In defense of dissemination of empirically supported psychological interventions. *Clinical Psychology: Science and Practice, 3,* 230–235.

Chambless, D. L., & Hollon, S. D. (1998). Defining empirically supported therapies. *Journal of Consulting and Clinical Psychology, 66,* 7–18.

Chambless, D. L., & Ollendick, T. H. (2001). Empirically supported psychological interventions: Controversies and evidence. *Annual Review of Psychology, 52,* 685–716.

Chorpita, B. F., Yim, L. M., Donkervoet, J. C., Arensdorf, A., Amundsen, M. J., McGee, C., et al. (2002). Toward large-scale implementation of empirically supported treatments for children: A review and observations by the Hawaii empirical basis to services task force. *Clinical Psychology: Science and Practice, 9,* 165–190.

Chu, B.C., & Kendall, P.C. (2004). Positive association of child involvement and treatment outcome within a manual-based cognitive-behavioral treatment for children with anxiety. *Journal of Consulting and Clinical Psychology, 72,* 821–829.

Cicchetti, D., & Rogosch, F. (2002). A developmental psychopathology perspective on adolescence. *Journal of Consulting and Clinical Psychology, 70,* 6–20.

Clarke, G., Hops, H., Lewinsohn, P., Andrews, J., Seeley, J., & Williams, J. (1992). Cognitive behavioral group treatment of adolescent depression: Prediction of outcome. *Behavior Therapy, 23,* 341–354.

Clarke, G. N., Rohde, P., Lewinsohn, P. M., Hops, H., & Seeley, J. R. (1999). Cognitive-behavioral treatment of adolescent depression: Efficacy of acute group treatment and booster sessions. *Journal of the American Academy of Child and Adolescent Psychiatry, 38,* 272–279.

Cohen, J., Mannarino, A., Murray, L., & Igelman, R. (2006). Psychosocial interventions for maltreated and violence-exposed children. *Journal of Social Issues, 62,* 737–766.

Costello, E. J., Angold, A., Burns, B. J., Erkanli, A., Stangl, D. K., & Tweed, D. L. (1996). The Great Smoky Mountains Study of Youth: Functional impairment and serious emotional disturbance. *Archives of General Psychiatry, 53,* 1137–1143.

Creed, T., & Kendall, P. (2005). Therapist Alliance-Building Behavior Within a Cognitive-Behavioral Treatment for Anxiety in Youth. *Journal of Consulting and Clinical Psychology, 73,* 498–505.

Curry, J., Rohde, P., Simons, A., Silva, S., Vitiello, B., Kratochvil, C., et al., & The TADS Team. (2006). Predictors and moderators of acute outcome in the treatment for adolescents with depression study (TADS). *Journal of the American Academy of Child and Adolescent Psychiatry, 45,* 1427–1439.

David-Ferdon, C., & Kaslow, N. J. (2008). Evidence-based psychosocial treatments for child and adolescent depression. *Journal of Clinical Child and Adolescent Psychology, 37,* 62–104.

Diamond, J. A., Reis, B. F., Diamond, G. M., Siqueland, L., & Issacs, L. (2002). Attachment-based family therapy for depressed adolescents: A treatment development study. *Journal of the American Academy of Child and Adolescent Psychiatry, 41,* 1190–1196.

Dishion, T., & Patterson, G. (1992). Age effects in parent training outcomes. *Behavior Modification, 23,* 719–729.

Durlak, J. A., Wells, A. M., Cotton, J. K., & Johnson, S. (1995). Analysis of selected methodological issues in child psychotherapy research. *Journal of Clinical Child Psychology, 24,* 141–148.

Durlak, J. A., Fuhrman, T. & Lampman, C. (1991). Effectiveness of Cognitive Behavior Therapy for Maladapting Children: A Meta-Analysis. *Psychological Bulletin, 110,* 204–214.

Eisen, A. R., & Silverman, W. K. (1993). Should I relax or change my thoughts? A preliminary examination of cognitive therapy, relaxation training, and their combination with overanxious children. *Journal of Cognitive Psychotherapy: An International Quarterly, 7,* 265–279.

Estrada, A., & Russell, R. L. (1999). Child and child therapist psychotherapy process scales. *Psychotherapy Research, 9,* 154–166.

Eugster, S.L., & Wampold, B.E. (1996). Systematic effects of participant role on evaluation of the psychotherapy session. *Journal of Consulting and Clinical Psychology, 64,* 1020–1028.

Eyberg, S. M., Nelson, M. M., & Boggs, S. R. (2008). Evidence-based psychosocial treatments for children and adolescents with disruptive behavior. *Journal of Clinical Child and Adolescent Psychology, 37,* 215–237.

Eysenck, H. J. (1952). The effects of psychotherapy: An evaluation. *Journal of Consulting Psychology, 16,* 319–324.

Freud, A. (1946). *The psychoanalytic treatment of children.* New York: International Universities Press.

Gaynor, S., Lawrence, P., & Nelson-Gray, R. (2006). Measuring homework compliance in cognitive-behavioral therapy for adolescent depression: Review, preliminary findings, and implications for theory and practice. *Behavior Modification, 30,* 647–672.

Gillham, J. E., Hamilton, J., Freres, D. R., Patton, K., & Gallop, R. (2006). Preventing depression among early adolescents in the primary care setting: A randomized controlled study of the

Penn Resiliency Program. *Journal of Abnormal Child Psychology, 34,* 203–219.

Gomes-Schwartz, B., & Schwartz, J. (1978). Psychotherapy process variables distinguishing the inherently helpful person from the professional psychotherapist. *Journal of Consulting and Clinical Psychology, 46,* 196–197.

Greene, R.W., Doyle, A. E. (1999). Toward a transactional conceptualization of oppositional defiant disorder: Implications for assessment and treatment. *Clinical Child and Family Psychology Review, 2,* 129–147.

Hawley, K., & Weisz, J. (2003). Child, Parent, and Therapist (Dis)Agreement on Target Problems in Outpatient Therapy: The Therapist's Dilemma and Its Implications. *Journal of Consulting and Clinical Psychology, 71,* 62–70.

Hawley, K., & Weisz, J. (2005). Youth versus parent working alliance in usual clinical care: Distinctive associations with retention, satisfaction, and treatment outcome. *Journal of Clinical Child and Adolescent Psychology, 34,* 117–128.

Henggeler, S. W., & Lee, T. (2003). Multisystemic treatment of serious clinical problems. In A. E. Kazdin & J. R. Weisz (Eds.), *Evidence-based psychotherapies for children and adolescents* (pp. 301–322). New York: Guilford Press.

Henggeler, S. W., Melton, G. B., & Smith, L. A. (1992). Family preservation using multisystemic therapy: An effective alternative to incarcerating serious juvenile offenders. *Journal of Consulting and Clinical Psychology, 60,* 953–961.

Henggeler, S. W., Rodick, J. D., Bourdin, C. M., Hanson, C. L., Watson, S. M., & Utey, J. R. (1986). Multisystemic treatment of juvenile offenders: Effects on adolescent behavior and family interaction. *Developmental Psychology, 22,* 132–141.

Horvath, A., & Luborsky, L. (1993). The role of the therapeutic alliance in psychotherapy. *Journal of Consulting and Clinical Psychology, 61,* 561–573.

Jaycox, L., Reivich, K., Gillman, J. E., & Seligman, M. E. P. (1994). Prevention of depressive symptoms in school children. *Behavioral Research and Therapy, 32,* 801–816.

Jensen, P. S., Arnold, L. E., Swanson, J. M., Vitiello, B., Abikoff, H. B., Greenhill, L. L., et al. (2007). 3-year follow-up of the NIMH MTA Study. *Journal of the American Academy of Child and Adolescent Psychiatry, 46,* 989–1002.

Jensen, P., Weersing, R., Hoagwood, K., & Goldman, E. (2005). What is the evidence for evidence-based treatments? A hard look at our soft underbelly. *Mental Health Services Research, 7,* 53–74.

Kaslow, N. J., & Thompson, M. P. (1998). Applying the criteria for empirically supported treatments to studies of psychosocial interventions for child and adolescent depression. *Journal of Clinical Child Psychology, 27,* 146–155.

Karver, M., Handelsman, J., Fields, S., & Bickman, L. (2005). A Theoretical Model of Common Process Factors in Youth and Family Therapy. *Mental Health Services Research, 7,* 35–51.

Karver, M., Handelsman, J., Fields, S., & Bickman, L. (2006). Meta-analysis of relationship variables in youth and family therapy: Evidence for different relationship variables in the child and adolescent treatment literature. *Clinical Psychology Review, 26,* 50–65.

Kaufman, N., Rohde, P., Seeley, J., Clarke, G., & Stice, E. (2005). Potential mediators of cognitive-behavioral therapy for adolescents with co-morbid major depression and conduct disorder. *Journal of Consulting and Clinical Psychology, 73,* 38–46.

Kazantzis, N., Ronan, K., & Deane, F. (2000). Concluding Causation from Correlation: Comment on Burns and Spangler. *Journal of Consulting and Clinical Psychology, 69,* 1079–1083.

Kazdin, A. E. (2000). Developing a research agenda for child and adolescent psychotherapy. *Archives of General Psychiatry, 57,* 829–836.

Kazdin, A. E., Bass, D., Ayers, W. A., & Rodgers, A. (1990). Empirical and clinical focus of child and adolescent psychotherapy research. *Journal of Consulting and Clinical Psychology, 58,* 729–740.

Kazdin, A.E., Holland, L., & Crowley, M. (1997). Family experience of barriers to treatment and premature termination from child therapy. *Journal of Consulting and Clinical Psychology, 65,* 453–463.

Kazdin, A., & Kendall, P. (1998). Current progress and future plans for developing effective treatments: Comments and perspectives. *Journal of Clinical Child Psychology, 27,* 217–226.

Kazdin, A., Marciano, P., & Whitley, M. (2005). The therapeutic alliance in cognitive-behavioral treatment of children referred oppositional, aggressive, and antisocial behavior. *Journal of Consulting and Clinical Psychology, 73,* 726–730.

Kazdin, A., & Wassell, G. (2000). Predictors of barriers to treatment and therapeutic change in outpatient therapy for antisocial children and their families. *Mental Health Services Research, 2,* 27–40.

Kazdin, A., & Whitley, M. (2006). Comorbidity, Case Complexity, and Effects of Evidence-Based Treatment for Children Referred for Disruptive Behavior. *Journal of Consulting and Clinical Psychology, 74,* 455–467.

Kendall, P. (Ed.). (1991). *Child and adolescent therapy: Cognitive behavioral procedures.* New York: Guilford Press.

Kendall, P. (1994). Treating anxiety disorders in youth: Results of a randomized clinical trial. *Journal of Consulting and Clinical Psychology, 61,* 235–247.

Kendall, P., Chansky, T. E., Kane, M. T., Kim, R. S., Kortlander, E., Ronan, K. R., et al. (1992). *Anxiety disorders in youth: Cognitive-behavioral interventions.* Needham Heights, MA: Allyn & Bacon.

Kendall, P., Flannery-Schoeder, E., Panichelli-Mindell, S., Southam-Gerow, M., Henin, A., & Warman, M. (1997). Therapy for youth with anxiety disorders: A second randomized trial. *Journal of Consulting and Clinical Psychology, 64,* 209–220.

Kendall, P., Lerner, R., & Craighead, W.E. (1984). Human Development and Intervention in Childhood Psychopathology. *Child Development, 55,* 71–82.

Kendall, P. C., Safford, S., Flannery-Schroeder, E., & Webb, A. (2004). Child anxiety treatment: Outcomes in adolescence and impact on substance use and depression at 7.4-year follow-up. *Journal of Consulting and Clinical Psychology, 72,* 276–287.

Kendall, P. C., & Southam-Gerow, M. A. (1996). Long-term follow-up of a cognitive-behavioral therapy for anxiety-disordered youth. *Journal of Consulting and Clinical Psychology, 64,* 724–730.

Kessler, R., Berglund, P., Demler, O., Jin, R., Merikangas, K., & Walters, E. (2005). Lifetime Prevalence and Age-of-Onset Distributions of *DSM-IV* Disorders in the National Comorbidity Survey Replication. *Archives of General Psychiatry, 62,* 593–602.

Lewinsohn, P. M., Clarke, G. N., Hops, H., & Andrews, J. A. (1990). Cognitive-behavioral treatment for depressed adolescents. *Behavior Therapy, 21,* 385–401.

Lewinsohn, P. M., Clarke, G. N., Rohde, P., Hops, H., & Seeley, J. (1996). A course in coping: A cognitive-behavioral approach to the treatment of adolescent depression. In E. D. Hibbs, & P. S. Jensen (Eds.), *Psychosocial treatments for child and adolescent disorders: Empirically based strategies for clinical practice* (pp. 109–135). Washington, DC: American Psychological Association.

Levitt, E. E. (1957). The results of psychotherapy with children: An evaluation. *Journal of Consulting and Clinical Psychology, 21,* 189–196.

Levitt, E. E. (1963). Psychotherapy with children: A further evaluation. *Behaviour Research and Therapy, 60,* 326–329.

Loeber, R., Burke, J., Lahey, B., Winters, A., & Zera, M. (2000). Oppositional defiant disorder and conduct disorder: A review of the past 10 years, Part I. *Journal of the American Academy of Child and Adolescent Psychiatry, 39,* 1468–1484.

Lonigan, C. J., Elbert, J. C., & Johnson, S. B. (1998). Empirically supported psychosocial interventions for children: An overview. *Journal of Clinical Child Psychology, 27,* 138–145.

Luborsky, L., Rosenthal, R., Diguer, L., Andrusyna, T., Berman, J., Levitt, J., Seligman, D., & Krause, E. (2002). The dodo verdict is alive and well – mostly. *Clinical Psychology: Science and Practice, 9,* 2–12.

Martin, D., Graske, J., & Davis, M. (2000). Relation of therapeutic alliance with outcomes and other variables: A meta-analytic review. *Journal of Consulting and Clinical Psychology, 68,* 438–450.

McMahon, R., Forehand, R., & Tiedmann, G. (1985). *Relative effectiveness of a parent training program with children of different ages.* Poster presented at annual meeting of Association for the Advancement of Behavior Therapy. Houston.

McMahon, R., Wells, K., & Kotler, J. (2006). Conduct problems. In E. Mash, & R. Barkley (Eds.), *Treatment of childhood disorders,* 3rd ed. (pp. 137–268). New York: Guilford Press.

Messer, S., & Wampold, B. (2002). Let's face facts: Common factors are more potent than specific therapy. *Clinical Psychology: Science and Practice, 9,* 21–25.

Miller, S., Wampold, B., & Varhely, K. (2008). Direct comparisons of treatment Modalities for youth disorders: A meta-analysis. *Psychotherapy Research, 18,* 5–14.

Moses, E. B., & Barlow, D. H. (2006). A new unified treatment approach for emotional disorders based on emotion science. *Current Directions in Psychological Science, 15,* 146–150.

MTA Cooperative Group (1999). A 14-month randomized clinical trial of treatment strategies for attention-deficit/hyperactivity disorder. *Archives of General Psychiatry, 56,* 1073–1086.

MTA Cooperative Group (2004). The NIMH MTA follow-up: 24-month outcomes of treatment strategies for attention-deficit/hyperactivity disorder (ADHD). *Pediatrics, 113,* 754–761.

Mufson, L., Dorta, K. P., Wickramaratne, P., Nomura, Y., Olfson, M., & Weissman, M. M. (2004). A randomized effectiveness trial of interpersonal psychotherapy for depressed adolescents. *Archives of General Psychiatry, 61,* 577–584.

Mufson, L., Weissman, M. M., Moreau, D., & Garfinkel, R. (1999). Efficacy of interpersonal psychotherapy for depressed adolescents. *Archives of General Psychiatry, 56,* 573–579.

Nathan, P. E., & Gorman, J. M. (Eds.). (2002). *A guide to treatments that work* (2nd ed.). New York: Oxford University Press.

Nock, M. K., & Ferriter, C. (2005). Parent management of attendance and adherence in child and adolescent therapy: A conceptual and empirical review. *Clinical Child and Family Psychology Review, 8,* 149–166.

Nock, M., Ferriter, C., & Holmberg, E. (2007). Parent beliefs about treatment credibility and effectiveness: Assessment and relation to subsequent treatment participation. *Journal of Child and Family Studies, 16,* 27–38.

Nock, M., & Kazdin, A. (2001). Parent expectancies for child therapy: Assessment and relation to participation in treatment. *Journal of Child and Family Studies, 10,* 155–180.

Ollendick, T. H. (1995a). Cognitive-behavioral treatment of panic disorder with agoraphobia in adolescents: A multiple baseline design analysis. *Behavior Therapy, 26,* 517–531.

Ollendick, T. H. (1995b). AABT and empirically validated treatments. *The Behavior Therapist, 18,* 81–82.

Ollendick, T. H., & Cerny, J. A. (1981). *Clinical behavior therapy with children.* New York: Plenum Press.

Ollendick, T. H., Davis III, T. E., & Muris, P. (2004). Treatment of specific phobias in children and adolescents. In P. Barrett, & T. H. Ollendick (Eds.), *Handbook of interventions that work with children and adolescents: From prevention to treatment* (pp. 273–300). London: John Wiley & Sons, Inc.

Ollendick, T. H., Hagopian, L. P., & Huntzinger, R. M. (1991). Cognitive-behavior therapy with nighttime fearful children. *Journal of Behaviour Therapy and Experimental Psychiatry, 22,* 113–121.

Ollendick, T. H., & Hersen, M. (Eds.). (1984). *Child behavioral assessment: Principles and procedures.* New York: Pergamon Press.

Ollendick, T. H., Jarrett. M. A., Grills-Taquechel, A. E., Hovey, L. D., & Wolff, J. C. (2008). Comorbidity as a predictor and moderator of treatment outcome in youth with anxiety, affective, ADHD, and oppositional/conduct disorders. *Clinical Psychology Review, 28,* 1447–1471.

Ollendick, T. H., & King, N. J. (2004). Empirically supported treatments for children and adolescents: Advances toward evidence-based practice. In P. M. Barrett, & T. H. Ollendick (Eds.), *Handbook of interventions that work with children and adolescents: Prevention and treatment* (pp. 1–26). Chichester: John Wiley & Sons, Ltd.

Ollendick, T. H., & March, J. S. (Eds.). (2004). *Phobic and anxiety disorders in children and adolescents: A clinician's guide to effective psychosocial and pharmacological interventions.* New York: Oxford University Press.

O'Malley, S., Suh, C., & Strupp, H. (1983). The Vanderbilt Psychotherapy Process Scales: A report on the scale development and a process-outcome study. *Journal of Consulting and Clinical Psychology, 51,* 581–586.

Patterson, G., & Chamberlain, P. (1994). A functional analysis of resistance during parent training therapy. *Clinical Psychology: Science and Practice, 1,* 53–70.

Patterson, G., & Guillion, M. (1968). *Living with children: New methods for parents and teachers.* Champaign, IL: Research Press.

Pelham, W. E., & Fabiano, G. A. (2008). Evidence-based psychosocial treatments for attention-deficit/hyperactivity disorder. *Journal of Clinical Child and Adolescent Psychology, 37,* 184–214.

Pelham, W. E., Fabiano, G. A., Gnagy, E. M., Greiner, A. R., & Hoza, B. (2005). The role of summer treatment programs in the context of comprehensive treatment for ADHD. In E. Hibbs, & P. Jensen (Eds.), *Psychological treatments for child and adolescent disorders: Empirically based strategies for clinical practice* (pp. 377–410). Washington, DC: APA Press.

Pelham, W. E., & Hoza, B. (1996). Intensive treatment: A summer treatment program for children with ADHD.

In E. Hibbs, & P. Jensen (Eds.), *Psychosocial treatments for child and adolescent disorders: Empirically based strategies for clinical practice* (pp. 311–340). New York: APA.

Pelham, W. E., Wheeler, T., & Chronis, A. (1998). Empirically supported psychosocial treatments for attention deficit hyperactivity disorder. *Journal of Clinical Child Psychology, 27,* 190–205.

Rosselló, J., & Bernal, G. (1999). The efficacy of cognitive-behavioral and interpersonal treatments for depression in Puerto Rican adolescents. *Journal of Consulting and Clinical Psychology, 67,* 734–745.

Roth, A. D., & Fonagy, P. (1996). *What works for whom? A critical review of psychotherapy research.* New York: Guilford Press.

Ruma, P., Burke, R., & Thompson, R. (1996). Group parent training: Is it effective for children of all ages? *Behavior Therapy, 27,* 159–169.

Russell, R., Shirk, S., & Jungbluth, N. (2008). Erratum: First-session Pathways to the Working Alliance in Cognitive-Behavioral Therapy for Adolescent Depression. *Psychotherapy Research, 18,* 237.

Sackett, D., Richardson, W., Rosenberg, W., & Haynes, B. (1997). *Evidence-based medicine.* London: Churchill Livingston.

Sackett, D., Richardson, W., Rosenberg, W., & Haynes, B. (2000). *Evidence-based medicine* (2nd ed.). London: Churchill Livingston.

Sanders, M. R. (1999). Triple P Positive Parenting Program: Towards an empirically evaluated multilevel parenting and family support strategy for the prevention of behavior and emotional problems in children. *Clinical Child and Family Psychology Review, 2,* 71–90.

Sanders, M. R., Markie-Dadds, C., Tully, L. A., & Bor, W. (2000). The Triple P Positive Parenting Program: A comparison of enhanced, standard, and self-directed behavioral family intervention for parents of children with early onset conduct problems. *Journal of Consulting and Clinical Psychology, 68,* 624–640.

Serketich, W., & Dumas, J. (1996). The effectiveness of behavioral parent training to modify antisocial behavior in children: A meta-analysis. *Behavior Therapy, 27,* 171–186.

Shirk, S. (Ed.). (1988). *Cognitive development and child psychotherapy.* New York: Plenum Press.

Shirk, S., Gudmundsen, G., Kaplinski, H., & McMakin, D. (2008). Alliance and outcome in cognitive-behavioral therapy for adolescent depression. *Journal of Clinical Child and Adolescent Psychology, 37,* 631–639.

Shirk, S., & Karver, M. (2003). Prediction of treatment outcome from relationship variables in child and adolescent therapy: A meta-analytic review. *Journal of Consulting and Clinical Psychology, 71,* 462–471.

Shirk, S., & Karver, M. (2006). Process issues in cognitive-behavioral therapy for youth. In P. C. Kendall (Ed.), *Child and adolescent therapy: Cognitive-behavioral procedures* (pp. 465–491). New York: Guilford Press.

Shirk, S., & Russell, R. (1996). *Change processes in child psychotherapy.* New York: Guilford Press.

Shirk, S., & Saiz, C. (1992). Clinical, empirical, and developmental perspectives on the therapeutic relationship in child psychotherapy. *Development and Psychopathology, 4,* 713–728.

Shirk, S., Talmi, A., & Olds, D. (2000). A developmental psychopathology perspective on child and adolescent treatment policy. *Development and Psychopathology, 12,* 835–855.

Silverman, W. K., & Hinshaw, S. P. (2008). The second special issue on evidence-based psychosocial treatments for children and adolescents: A 10-year update. *Journal of Clinical Child and Adolescent Psychology, 37,* 1–7.

Silverman, W. K., & Ollendick, T. H. (Eds.). (1999). *Developmental issues in the clinical treatment of children.* Boston: Allyn and Bacon.

Silverman, W. K., Pina, A. A., & Viswesvaran, C. (2008). Evidence-based psychosocial treatments for phobic and anxiety disorders in children and adolescents. *Journal of Clinical Child and Adolescent Psychology, 37,* 105–130.

Southam-Gerow, M., Kendall, P., & Weersing, V. (2001). Examining outcome variability: Correlates of treatment response in a child and adolescent anxiety clinic. *Journal of Clinical Child Psychology, 30,* 422–436.

Stark, K. D., Reynolds, W. R., & Kaslow, N. J. (1987). A comparison of the relative efficacy of self-control therapy and a behavioral problem-solving therapy for depression in children. *Journal of Abnormal Child Psychology, 15,* 91–113.

Stark, K., Rouse, L., & Livingston, R. (1991). Treatment of depression during childhood and adolescence: Cognitive-behavioral procedures for the individual and family. In P. Kendall (Ed.). *Child and adolescent therapy* (pp. 165–206). New York: Guilford Press.

Strain, P., Young, C., & Horowitz, J. (1981). Generalized behavior change during oppositional child training: An examination of child and family demographic variables. *Behavior Modification, 5,* 15–26.

Task Force on Promotion and Dissemination. (1995). Training in and dissemination of empirically validated treatments: Report and recommendations. *The Clinical Psychologist, 48,* 3–23.

Thase, M., & Callan, J. (2006). The Role of Homework in Cognitive Behavior Therapy of Depression. *Journal of Psychotherapy Integration, 16,* 162–177.

Toth, S., & Cicchetti, D. (1999). Developmental psychopathology and child psychotherapy. In S. Russ, & T. Ollendick (Eds.), *Handbook of psychotherapies with children and families* (pp. 15–44). New York: Kluwer Academic/Plenum.

Turner, J., & Cole, D. (1994). Development differences in cognitive diatheses for child depression. *Journal of Abnormal Child Psychology, 22,* 15–32.

Walkup, J. T., Albano, A. M., Piacentini, J., Birmaher, B., Compton, S. N., Sherrill, J. T., et al. (2008). Cognitive behavioral therapy, sertraline, or a combination in childhood anxiety. *New England Journal of Medicine, 1056,* 1–14.

Young, J. F., Mufson, L., & Davies, M. (2006). Impact of comorbid anxiety in an effectiveness study of interpersonal psychotherapy for depressed adolescents. *Journal of the American Academy of Child and Adolescent Psychiatry, 45,* 904–912.

Yu, D. L., & Seligman, M. E. P. (2002). Preventing depressive symptoms in Chinese children. *Prevention and Treatment, 5(9).*

Webster-Stratton, C. (1984). Randomized trial of two parent training programs for families with conduct-disordered children. *Journal of Consulting and Clinical Psychology, 52,* 666–678.

Webster-Stratton, C. (1990). Enhancing the effectiveness of self-administered videotape parent training for families with conduct-problem children. *Journal of Abnormal Child Psychology, 18,* 479–492.

Webster-Stratton, C. (1994). Advancing videotape parent training: A comparison study. *Journal of Consulting and Clinical Psychology, 62,* 583–593.

Weersing, V. R., & Weisz, J. R. (2002). Mechanisms of action in youth psychotherapy. *Journal of Child Psychology and Psychiatry, 43,* 3–29.

Weisz, J., Donenberg, G., Han, S., & Kauneckis, D. (1995). Child and adolescent psychotherapy outcomes in experiments versus clinics: Why the disparity? *Journal of Abnormal Child Psychology, 23*, 83–106.

Weisz, J., Jensen-Doss, A., & Hawley, K. (2006). Evidence-based youth psychotherapies versus usual clinical care: A meta-analysis of direct comparisons. *American Psychologist, 61*, 671–689.

Weisz, J. R., McCarty, C. A., & Valeri, S. M. (2006). Effects of psychotherapy for depression in children and adolescents: A meta-analysis. *Psychological Bulletin, 132*, 132–149.

Weisz, J. R., Weiss, B., Alicke, M. D., & Klotz, M. L. (1987). Effectiveness of psychotherapy with children and adolescents: A meta-analysis for clinicians. *Journal of Consulting and Clinical Psychology, 55*, 542–549.

Weisz, J. R., Weiss, B., Han, S. S., Granger, D. G., & Morton, T. (1995). Effects of psychotherapy with children and adolescents revisited: A meta-analysis of treatment outcome studies. *Psychological Bulletin, 117*, 450–468.

Woody, S. R., & Ollendick, T. H. (2006). Technique factors in treating anxiety disorders. In L. Castonguay, & L. E. Beutler (Eds.), *Principles of therapeutic change that work* (pp. 167–186). New York: Oxford University Press.

Couple Therapy: Theoretical Perspectives and Empirical Findings

Donald H. Baucom, Norman B. Epstein, Jennifer S. Kirby, *and* Mariana K. Falconier

Abstract

Whereas most couples enter into marriage or similar committed, romantic relationships with the full expectation that they will live their lives together in a happy and rewarding manner, the divorce rate in the United States and many Western countries continues to be alarmingly high—in the United States hovering around 50%. As a result, mental health practitioners have focused energy on ways to alleviate relationship distress. Many approaches for assisting distressed couples have been developed, yet few have been evaluated to demonstrate that they actually help couples. The current chapter provides an overview of the major models of couple therapy that have been evaluated in well-controlled research studies and have demonstrated that they benefit couples. The models included are: behavioral couple therapy, cognitive-behavioral couple therapy, integrative behavioral couple therapy, emotionally focused couple therapy, and insight-oriented couple therapy. For each model, the theoretical approach, overall interventions, and effectiveness are discussed.

Keywords: Cognitive-behavioral therapy, couple therapy, marriage, relationship distress

Most adults across cultures are involved in committed, intimate couple relationships at some point in their lives, whether it be in the form of marriage or cohabitation (Buss, 1995). Since 1970, marriage rates have declined in most Western countries, the average age at marriage is increasing, and the rate of cohabitation is growing. Even with these delays in committing to a relationship, intimate couple relationships continue to be viewed as the best forum for meeting individual needs for affection, companionship, loyalty, and emotional and sexual intimacy, even among those individuals who have experienced previous relationships as unsatisfactory (Halford, Kelley & Markman, 1997). And marriage continues to be the most common means of expressing commitment in a couple's relationship. Based on data from the 1990s, within 5 years of cohabitation, 82% of couples in the United States and between 50% and 66% of couples in most European countries have married (Kiernan, 2004). By the age

of 50, approximately 90% of the population in Western countries has been married at least once (McDonald, 1995); the great value placed on marriage also can be seen in widespread efforts among same-sex couples to enact legislation to legalize marriage for them.

As common as committed intimate relationships and marriage are, approximately 55% of American and 40%–45% of Australian, English, German, or Swiss first marriages end in divorce (Halford et al., 1997), and approximately 50% of the divorces occur early in the relationship, during the first 7 years of marriage. An additional 10%–25% of couples live in stable but unhappy relationships (Gallup, 1990; Hahlweg, 2004). And, as painful as the experience of divorce is for many people, approximately 75% of divorced men and 66% of divorced women remarry within 3 years. Unfortunately, the divorce rate in second marriages is even higher than in first marriages (Cherlin, 1992).

Given the alarming rate of both marital distress and dissolution, it is fortunate that clinicians and researchers have devoted considerable effort to developing and evaluating interventions for treating marital and relationship problems. In the current chapter, we provide an overview of the major models of couple therapy[1] that currently have accumulated empirical support demonstrating that the interventions are of help to couples when applied in well-controlled research studies, what the field refers to as "empirically supported interventions." This decision to include only approaches with empirical support is not intended to imply that other widely used approaches such as structural family therapy (Minuchin & Nichols, 1998), narrative therapy (Freedman & Combs, 2002), and brief strategic therapy (Shoham & Rohrbaugh, 2001) are not useful for couples. In fact, investigators interested in some other couple therapy approaches such as solution-focused therapy (a brief approach centered on finding solutions with clients rather than discussing the history of their problems, Hoyt, 2008) have begun to conduct well-controlled treatment investigations to evaluate their efficacies, but at present such studies are limited. In addition, the field awaits evaluation of the efficacy of interventions for individuals who are in committed relationships but who are not married; thus, the research described throughout this chapter applies to legally married couples only.

In discussing the efficacy of various approaches to couple therapy, we have adopted criteria set forth by Chambless and Hollon (1998) for empirically supported interventions. Briefly, for a treatment to be evaluated as efficacious for a given population, these authors propose that the treatment needs to be superior to a waitlist condition (i.e., couples not receiving treatment) or equivalent to another efficacious treatment (i.e., as helpful to couples as another intervention that has already been shown to be of assistance to couples); all of these criteria must be met within the context of an otherwise well-conducted scientific investigation. Successful implementation of treatments by therapists other than the originators

of the treatment is another prerequisite for defining an intervention as efficacious; that is, persons other than those who developed the treatment must be able to conduct it successfully as well. Thus, Chambless and Hollon require that the efficacy of a treatment must be corroborated by at least two independent teams of investigators, and that the preponderance of the evidence must support the treatment's utility for distressed couples. If the type of treatment has been successful in only one study or in multiple studies by the same investigator, then it is described as "possibly efficacious" (see Chambless & Hollon, 1998 and the special issue of the *Journal of Consulting and Clinical Psychology* [Kendall & Chambless, 1998] for an in-depth discussion of the strengths and weaknesses of this approach to evaluating psychotherapy research). Whereas these criteria might seem highly technical, they are important in the current context because they serve as the basis for identifying the treatments that are discussed in this chapter, based on the research support for them. Based on these criteria, we will discuss three broad approaches to couple therapy with sufficient current empirical support: (a) behavioral couple therapy (BCT) and its variants, including cognitive-behavioral and integrative BCT; (b) emotionally focused couple therapy (EFCT); and (c) insight-oriented couple therapy (IOCT).

Just as different theoretical approaches to individual therapy vary in a wide variety of ways, different forms of couple therapy vary in numerous ways. However, many of these differences among couple therapy approaches can be captured by exploring three dimensions that characterize the treatment. First, theoretical approaches vary in the degree to which they focus on overt behavioral patterns versus on internal experiences such as cognitions and emotions. That is, some approaches emphasize how partners communicate or act toward each other, whereas other approaches give greater focus to a partner's internal experience of how safe it feels to be close to another person. Second, approaches vary in whether they focus on the roles that the individual members play in the development and functioning of the relationship (e.g., a good relationship requires two well-adjusted individuals) or on the couple's dyadic interaction patterns and other relationship characteristics (e.g., the couple's problem is that, as a unit, they cannot communicate well with each other). Third, approaches differ in the extent to which they focus on the present or more proximal factors (e.g., the couple spends little time together enjoying themselves) versus more

---

[1] The term "couple therapy" is employed in this chapter because it is the term commonly used in the field at present. However, the reader should be aware that in almost all of the empirical investigations to date, couples receiving intervention have been married; thus, the applicability of the findings to unmarried, committed couples is unclear.

historical or distal factors in addressing relationship distress (e.g., the husband has learned from early experiences in his family of origin that even caring relationships always end in pain; thus, he stays distant from his wife). Therefore, we will describe how each approach addresses each of these three dimensions. No approach focuses exclusively on one pole of these dimensions, but there are notable differences in their relative emphases that shape how a therapist understands a couple's difficulties and intervenes to be of assistance to them.

Models Based on Behavioral Perspectives
Behavioral Couple Therapy

As suggested by the title of the model, BCT takes a systematic approach to the assessment and modification of couples' *behaviors* (e.g., Jacobson & Margolin, 1979; Stuart, 1980). Behavioral couple therapy was developed in the 1960s and 1970s, from the theoretical models of social exchange theory (Thibaut & Kelley, 1959) and social learning theory (Bandura, 1977). Social exchange theory proposes that a person's level of relationship satisfaction depends on his or her ratio of positive to negative experiences in that relationship; that is, few people are likely to be satisfied in a relationship that has a high rate of negative interactions between the partners while few positive interactions occur. Social learning theory suggests that members of a couple shape each other's behavior by providing positive or negative consequences for each other's actions. Thus, whether intended or not, often partners teach each other how to behave within the relationship by what behaviors are rewarded or punished. For example, if a husband puts down the newspaper to talk only when his wife finally yells at him, he has inadvertently reinforced her yelling, which he greatly dislikes.

BASIC CONCEPTS
Behavior

Empirical investigations have supported the social exchange conceptualization of intimate relationships focusing on rates of positive and negative behaviors, such that self-reported relationship satisfaction is correlated (a) positively with the frequencies of partners' positive actions, and (b) negatively, to an even stronger degree, with the frequencies of the partners' negative actions (Weiss & Heyman, 1990). Thus, distressed couples are more likely to demonstrate a high rate of negative behaviors and a low rate of positive behaviors; conversely, non-distressed spouses are more likely to engage in more

positive behaviors toward their partners than negative ones (Gottman, 1994). In accordance with social learning theory, other findings indicate that distressed married couples are more prone than non-distressed couples to aversive, destructive patterns of communication, such as a demand–withdraw pattern in which one partner pursues an issue while the other withdraws, often resulting in an escalation of these roles over time (Christensen & Heavey, 1990; Christensen & Shenk, 1991). Furthermore, distressed couples are more likely to engage in exchanges in which one person's hurtful comment is reciprocated with greater intensity by the receiving partner. Consequently, there are not only high rates of negative communication behaviors among distressed couples, but there are long continuous strings of negative behaviors between the two partners, with one person's negative behavior leading to the other person being negative as well.

Cognition

As will be discussed subsequently, BCT has evolved into cognitive-behavioral couple therapy, a therapeutic modality that places significant emphasis on partners' cognitions about each other and their relationship. Even from a more behavioral perspective, however, cognitions are important because of their relationship to behavior. First, the impact of a partner's behaviors as positive or negative depends, in part, on the recipient's subjective experience and evaluation of these behaviors (Baucom & Epstein, 1990). For example, a husband may buy his wife a new blouse as a gift for no particular occasion. The wife may either interpret this behavior as a loving and thoughtful act, based on her inference that he was thinking of her and thought the blouse would look good on her, or she may interpret his gesture as an indication of his dissatisfaction with her wardrobe and an attempt to improve her appearance. These different interpretations of the same behavior likely would have differing impacts on the wife's feelings and subsequent behavior toward her husband. Behavioral couple therapists also assume that people choose to engage in a particular behavior because of their expectancies about the rewards and punishments they will receive from their partners. Therefore, when partners think about their relationships in distorted or extreme ways, it is likely to influence their behavior.

Affect

In addition to cognition, behavioral couple therapists have noted that emotional responses or affect has a great influence on couples' behaviors and relationship satisfaction. Studies of couples' conversations have shown that distressed partners are more likely to respond negatively to each other's expressions of negative affect than are members of nondistressed couples (negative reciprocity); furthermore, these expressions of negative affect are not as likely to be offset by high levels of positive affect as they are in nondistressed relationships (Gottman, 1994). Thus, the expression of emotion, both negative and positive, is an important form of communication between partners. At times, a couple experiences difficulties as a function of the degree and manner in which emotion is expressed. At one end of the continuum, some individuals express little emotion, which can contribute to a lack of understanding from the other partner and a lack of closeness between the partners in particular. At the other end of the spectrum, some individuals express a great deal of emotion, and particularly when the emotions expressed are negative, such expression can be overwhelming to the other partner, who will often withdraw in an attempt to stop or escape from the strong emotions.

CONTRIBUTION OF THE COUPLE VERSUS THE INDIVIDUAL IN COUPLE DISTRESS

With a major focus on interactive processes as a primary source of couple distress, behavioral couple therapists place a strong emphasis on the contribution of the couple as a dyad, rather than the individual's unique characteristics. Although partners bring learned behaviors from the past into their current relationships, social learning theory emphasizes that a spouse's behavior is both learned and influenced by the other partner's behavior. Over time, spouses' influences on each other become a stronger predictor of current behavior than the influences of previous close relationships. The behavioral approach also is based on social exchange theory principles that link the couple's satisfaction to higher ratios of pleasing versus displeasing behaviors that the partners exchange. Thus, the behavioral model suggests that a couple's ability to maintain a satisfying relationship is based on their skills for providing each other with pleasing and effective behavioral exchanges. As a result, therapeutic interventions are focused primarily on altering behavioral exchanges between the partners and developing more effective communication skills. In early behavioral models, little attention was given to understanding the unique characteristics of each partner, and how individual factors, including both strengths and vulnerabilities, contribute to marital adjustment.

PROXIMAL VERSUS DISTAL FACTORS IN UNDERSTANDING RELATIONSHIP DISCORD

Behavioral couple therapy places a strong emphasis on the present, exploring how partners interact with each other and communicate with each other. Historical perspectives are addressed primarily in terms of understanding how well entrenched a behavioral interaction pattern might be and the various contexts in which it has occurred over time.

APPROACHES TO TREATMENT
Behavior

Because a central tenet of the behavioral model is that distress is caused by a low ratio of positive to negative exchanges, behavioral couple therapists have used behavior-exchange procedures such as "love days" (Weiss, Hops, & Patterson, 1973) or "caring days" (Stuart, 1980) to alter this ratio. More precisely, these procedures involve each partner agreeing to enact certain positive behaviors requested by his or her partner in order to increase the percentage of positive exchanges. Similarly, couples have been taught to develop behavioral contracts in which each person agrees to behave in specific ways desired by the partner, and then receives reinforcement for these actions. Although behavioral contracting appears to be less emphasized in current behavioral approaches to assisting distressed couples, it served as a major intervention strategy in many of the treatment outcome investigations that have been conducted. In addition, to increase the likelihood that couples will experience more positive interactions, behavior therapists teach couples specific communication skills and guidelines for (a) expressing thoughts and feelings, (b) engaging in empathic listening, and (c) problem-solving or decision-making. It is assumed that, by developing these skills, couples will enhance their abilities to negotiate more satisfying solutions to conflicts, as well as their abilities to experience more intimacy through skillful expression of feelings. As a result, couples will decrease negative reciprocity and increase positive reciprocity in their communication and overall relationship.

Cognition

In the early texts on BCT, Jacobson and Margolin (1979) recommended that therapists instruct couples to monitor and record their cognitions at home, and Stuart (1980) promoted the concept of *relabeling*, which involves challenging the partners to alter their negative interpretations of ambiguous actions on each other's part. Unfortunately, descriptions of cognitive restructuring in early behavioral texts were quite brief, and they typically did not give therapists a great deal of guidance in how to accomplish this goal. It also should be noted that cognitive interventions were not systematically employed in the treatment outcome studies that were conducted, which we discuss subsequently. Thus, despite the theoretical recognition of the role of cognitions in influencing the behaviors of spouses, the original BCT interventions did not address cognitions directly.

Affect

Behavioral approaches to couple relationships have viewed emotions (e.g., joy, anger, sadness) as reactions to specific behavioral interactions. That is, distress is viewed as resulting from particular behavioral patterns that are repetitive, ingrained, and reciprocal, which then lead to negative emotions. Consequently, behaviorists' approaches to modifying emotion typically have depended on the behavioral interventions described previously; once the behaviors change, affect will follow as well. However, this approach of altering affect through changing behavior may be problematic for some distressed couples (Epstein & Baucom, 2002). Specific behavior changes may not be powerful enough to overcome existing negative feelings toward the partner due to "sentiment override," or overall negative feelings about the partner and relationship that have developed over time. Indeed, research findings indicate limited associations between partner behaviors and overall relationship satisfaction (e.g., Halford, Sanders, & Behrens, 1993; Iverson & Baucom, 1990), suggesting that the original behavioral model might be too limited to explain and intervene with the complexities of relationship distress.

Theoretical models of relationship distress and related interventions continue to evolve over time, and this has been the case with behavioral perspectives on relationship functioning. As a result, two noteworthy enhanced behaviorally oriented approaches have evolved: cognitive-behavioral couple therapy (CBCT) and integrative behavioral couple therapy (IBCT).

Cognitive-Behavioral Couple Therapy

Cognitive-behavioral couple therapy evolved from BCT and is consistent with trends in the overall field of behavior therapy to incorporate cognitive factors into behavioral conceptualizations of maladaptive responses. Consequently, most of the BCT theoretical perspectives and interventions described previously have been incorporated into CBCT. The much greater emphasis on cognition in the original formulation of CBCT (e.g., Baucom & Epstein, 1990) is its primary difference from BCT. Whereas BCT practitioners noted the importance of cognitions to behavior change without explicitly targeting cognitions in treatment, the CBCT model also proposes that cognitive change is important in its own right. That is, in many instances, a couple might *not* need to change their behavior to increase their relationship satisfaction; instead, if they develop more positive interpretations of each other's behavior, then positive relationship adjustment might result. For example, a woman who holds an extreme standard for her husband's behavior (e.g., that if he is committed to the family, he should want to spend of all his nonwork hours with them) might be dissatisfied if he does not meet this standard, perhaps interpreting his involvement in individual hobbies as indicating a lack of commitment to the family. Helping her to reevaluate and reduce the stringency of her standard might be the intervention of choice, rather than a behavior change on either person's part. Thus, CBCT builds on the behavioral model by proposing that increasing relationship satisfaction involves a balance of behavioral and cognitive changes, both of which hold the potential for important emotional change.

BASIC CONCEPTS

Overall, CBCT incorporates basic behavioral perspectives on the role of behavior and affect in relationship functioning. Its major contribution involves the development and elaboration of the role of cognitions in relationship distress. Thus, a brief description of the cognitive perspective is provided.

Cognition

CBCT researchers have identified five major types of cognitions involved in couple relationship functioning (Baucom, Epstein, Sayers, & Sher, 1989). Empirical studies suggest that these cognitions are associated with, or even lead to, partners' negative affective and behavioral responses to each other (Epstein & Baucom, 1993, 2002; Fincham, Bradbury, & Scott, 1990; Noller, Beach, & Osgarby, 1997). The first three cognitions involve partners' thoughts about specific events in their relationship. *Selective attention* involves how each member of a couple idiosyncratically notices, or fails to notice, particular aspects of relationship events. Selective attention contributes to distressed couples' low rates of agreement about the occurrence and quality of specific events, as well as to negative biases in perceptions of each other's messages (Noller et al., 1997). Thus, if a husband does not notice his wife's attempts to be more caring, then her behaviors are unlikely to have an effect on him. *Attributions* are inferences that an individual makes about the determinants of a partner's positive and negative behaviors. The tendency of distressed partners to attribute each other's negative actions to global, stable traits has been referred to as making "distress-maintaining attributions" because they leave little room for future optimism that one's partner will behave in a more pleasing manner in other situations or in the future (Holtzworth-Munroe & Jacobson, 1985). For example, if a husband attributes his wife's difficulties in completing all of her tasks (while she serves as the major caregiver to their three children and pursues a graduate degree) to her lack of intelligence, then he is unlikely to believe that there is much hope for change in the future. Bradbury and Fincham (1990) reviewed and noted the empirical support for the importance of partners' attributions in relationship functioning, and a growing body of research (e.g., Sanford, 2006) has continued to demonstrate the significant impact of partners' attributions on their emotional responses and behavior toward each other. *Expectancies*, or predictions that each member of the couple makes about particular relationship events in the immediate or more distant future, are the last type of cognitions involving specific events. Negative relationship expectancies have been associated with lower satisfaction, stemming from pessimism about improving the relationship (Fincham & Bradbury, 1989; Pretzer, Epstein, & Fleming, 1991).

The fourth and fifth categories of cognition are forms of what cognitive therapists have referred to as basic or core beliefs shaping one's experience of the world. These include (a) *assumptions*, or beliefs that each individual holds about the characteristics of individuals and intimate relationships, and (b) *standards*, or each individual's personal beliefs about the characteristics that an intimate relationship and its members "should" have (Baucom & Epstein, 1990; Baucom et al., 1989). Couples' assumptions and standards are associated with current relationship distress, either when these beliefs are unrealistic or when the partners are not satisfied with how their personal standards are being met in their relationship (Baucom, Epstein, Rankin, & Burnett, 1996; Halford, Kelly & Markman, 1997). For example, if a wife has an assumption that men simply cannot deal with emotions, then she might be unlikely to share her feelings with her husband, which leads to a sense of distance and lack of

intimacy, something that is very important to her. In such a circumstance, her assumption led her to behave in ways that rob her of what she greatly desires.

CONTRIBUTIONS OF THE COUPLE VERSUS THE INDIVIDUAL IN COUPLE DISTRESS

Cognitive-behavioral couple therapists see relationship problems as developing not only from behavioral excesses and deficits within the couple, but also from each individual's cognitions that either elicit distress or impede the resolution of conflicts (Epstein, Baucom, & Rankin, 1993). Thus, some of the problematic cognitions that the therapist identifies may have developed from each individual's history, including previous romantic relationships, a person's family of origin, and society at large, as well as from their current relationship. For example, depending on how a husband experienced his mother's domination and control over his father's daily activities, he might overgeneralize and predict that his wife will eventually try to control his every move, even if she presently exhibits no overt signs of making such attempts. He might then react defensively to any suggestions from his wife regarding how he might behave more effectively, even when her ideas have considerable merit. Thus, many of the problematic behavioral interactions between spouses may evolve from their relatively stable cognitions about the relationship. Unless these cognitions are taken into account, successful intervention with the couple's behavioral interactions is likely to be compromised. Therefore, cognitive behavioral couple therapists attend to how each person thinks about and experiences the relationship. In this way, the unique characteristics, learning histories, and current thoughts and cognitions of each partner are integrated into the couple's ongoing interactions.

PROXIMAL VERSUS DISTAL FACTORS IN UNDERSTANDING RELATIONSHIP DISCORD

Given that CBCT derived from BCT, it also emphasizes the present relative to the past. However, to the degree that an individual's distorted cognitions are rooted in the past, such historical precedents are noted, so that an individual can learn to differentiate between what he or she learned in the past versus what is occurring in the present. It is important to identify instances in which a cognition may have been accurate regarding past experiences but does not fit the current relationship.

APPROACHES TO TREATMENT

The various interventions described in BCT apply to CBCT as well, again with the major contribution of CBCT being an increased focus on interventions to directly alter cognitions.

Cognition

The cognitive behavioral approach (Baucom & Epstein, 1990; Epstein & Baucom, 2002; Rathus & Sanderson, 1999) has integrated assessment and intervention procedures from cognitive therapies (Beck, Rush, Shaw, & Emery, 1979; Meichenbaum, 1985) with traditional skills-oriented behavioral strategies. CBCT teaches partners to monitor and test the appropriateness of their cognitions. It incorporates some standard cognitive restructuring strategies, such as: (a) considering alternative attributions or explanations for a partner's negative behavior; (b) asking for behavioral data to test a negative perception concerning a partner (e.g., that the partner never complies with requests); and (c) evaluating extreme standards by generating lists of the advantages and disadvantages of trying to live up to a highly stringent standard.

Integrative Behavioral Couple Therapy

Christensen and Jacobson developed IBCT (Christensen, Jacobson, & Babcock, 1995; Jacobson & Christensen, 1996) to build on BCT by emphasizing acceptance of the characteristics of one's partner and the relationship. IBCT includes a core assumption that there are genuine incompatibilities in all couples that are not amenable to change and that partners' emotional reactions, based on a lack of acceptance of each other's behavior, are as problematic, or more so, than the behavior itself. Attempting to cajole or force one's partner to change often can lead to a resistance to change. Therefore, IBCT interventions focus on a balance between systematically changing partners' behavior and the achievement of acceptance between partners regarding behavior that is unlikely to change.

BASIC CONCEPTS

IBCT incorporates many of the concepts from BCT and CBCT but places an increased focus on emotional reactions that partners have in response to the difficulties they encounter in their relationships. The importance of constructive behavioral interactions and cognitively viewing each other's behaviors in realistic ways remain central to IBCT. IBCT primarily differs from BCT in its emphasis on partners accepting incompatibilities that are unlikely to be responsive to behavioral change efforts. Whereas Christensen and Jacobson describe acceptance as a largely emotional process, it is difficult to differentiate between the cognitive and affective changes that are necessary in the acceptance process. Unless such differentiations can be demonstrated empirically, it might be best to refer to an emphasis on an internal, subjective affective/cognitive shift that is critical for accepting one's partner.

CONTRIBUTIONS OF THE COUPLE VERSUS THE INDIVIDUAL IN COUPLE DISTRESS

IBCT continues to incorporate the BCT emphasis on couples' maladaptive behavioral interaction patterns, and thus, places a significant focus on the couple as a unit. Although these couple-level interaction patterns might be a notable aspect of what needs to be accepted by both partners, acceptance itself is an internal, subjective experience that exists on an individual level. Thus, IBCT attempts to promote acceptance in each partner and the couple as a unit as a means for reducing maladaptive interaction patterns that have been caused by a lack of acceptance.

PROXIMAL VERSUS DISTAL FACTORS IN UNDERSTANDING RELATIONSHIP DISCORD

Given its derivation from BCT, IBCT also emphasizes present circumstances in the couple's relationship. However, an individual's achievement of greater acceptance of a partner can involve being aware of the vulnerabilities that the partner developed in the past, perhaps prior to the current relationship.

APPROACHES TO TREATMENT

Affect

In addition to the use of the typical behavioral interventions described earlier to promote behavior change, IBCT employs three major strategies to promote acceptance: empathic joining around the problem, unified detachment from the problem, and tolerance building (Christensen et al., 1995; Jacobson & Christensen, 1996). During empathic joining, the IBCT therapist elicits vulnerable feelings (such as sadness) that may underlie partners' observed negative emotional reactions (such as anger) about an area of concern, encourages expression and elaboration of these vulnerable feelings, and communicates empathy for these understandable reactions. As a result, the therapist attempts to build empathy between the partners for each other. During unified detachment from the problem, the therapist helps the couple step back from the problem and assume a more descriptive and less evaluative stance toward the problem. The therapist may engage the couple in an effort to describe (without evaluating) the common sequences that they go through, to specify the triggers that activate each other and escalate negative emotions, to create a name for their problematic pattern, and to consider variations in their interaction pattern and factors that might account for these variations. The therapist then might encourage the couple to engage deliberately in the problematic sequence in the session or at home, so that they can become more aware of their pattern and take it less personally. In tolerance building, the therapist helps the couple remember the positive aspects and benefits of their individual differences, as well as the negative implications of their differences.

Empirical Support for Behaviorally Oriented Interventions

BEHAVIORAL COUPLE THERAPY

Behavioral couple therapy is the most widely evaluated couple treatment, having been a focus of approximately two-dozen well-controlled treatment outcome studies. Behavioral couple therapy has been reviewed in detail in several previous publications, including findings from specific investigations (e.g., Alexander, Holtzworth-Munroe, & Jameson, 1994; Baucom & Epstein, 1990; Baucom, Shoham, Mueser, Daiuto, & Stickle, 1998; Bray & Jouriles, 1995) as well as meta-analyses (Baucom, Hahlweg, & Kuschel, 2003; Dunn & Schwebel, 1995; Hahlweg & Markman, 1988; Shadish et al., 1993; Shadish & Baldwin, 2002, 2003). All of these reviews reach the same conclusion: BCT is an efficacious intervention for distressed couples.

A large number of investigations have satisfied efficacy criteria by comparing BCT to waitlist control conditions in which couples do not receive treatment, consistently finding that BCT is more efficacious than the absence of systematic treatment. Several early investigations of BCT also have compared it to nonspecific or placebo treatment conditions (in which couples were seen for treatment but the specific components focal to behavioral interventions were omitted), with BCT generally being more efficacious than nonspecific treatment conditions (Azrin et al., 1980; Crowe, 1978; Jacobson, 1978). Researchers also can conduct what are called *meta-analyses,* in which the findings across all investigations are placed on a common metric or unit of measurement, so that findings across studies can be averaged even when different measures are employed. The results of meta-analyses have confirmed the previous findings that behaviorally oriented treatments are of help to distressed couples (Dunn & Schwebel, 1995; Hahlweg & Markman, 1988; Shadish et al., 1993; Shadish & Baldwin, 2002, 2003). Baucom et al. (2003) concluded that, compared to waiting list control groups, BCT has an average effect size[2] of 0.72 (which would generally be viewed as a moderate effect), and is consistent among studies conducted in several countries.

Another way in which the usefulness of psychotherapeutic interventions is assessed is to evaluate the frequency with which clients receiving treatment move from the distressed to the nondistressed range, in what is regarded as clinically significant change (Jacobson, Follette, & Revenstorf, 1984). Findings suggest that between one-third and two-thirds of couples will be in the nondistressed range of marital satisfaction after receiving BCT. Most couples appear to maintain these gains for short time periods (6–12 months); however, long-range follow-up results are not as encouraging. In a 2-year follow-up of BCT, for example, Jacobson, Schmaling, and Holtzworth-Munroe (1987) found that approximately 30% of couples who had recovered during therapy had relapsed subsequently. In addition, Snyder, Wills, and Grady-Fletcher (1991) reported that 38% of couples receiving BCT had divorced during a 4-year follow-up period. Thus, brief BCT improvements are not maintained for many couples over a number of years, although some couples maintain and even improve upon their gains.

COGNITIVE-BEHAVIORAL COUPLES THERAPY

The efficacy of cognitive interventions has been explored in two ways—as the sole intervention, or as part of a broader set of therapeutic strategies to assist distressed couples. Huber and Milstein (1985) compared cognitive couple therapy with a waiting list control condition. Their cognitive couple therapy focused primarily on irrational relationship standards and assumptions that were highlighted by Epstein and Eidelson (1981), along with specific irrational marital beliefs noted by Ellis (1978).

---

[2] A between-group effect size is merely the difference in means between two treatment conditions expressed in standard score form; that is, it can be derived by calculating the difference between the means of the two interventions, divided by the standard deviation of the control group. Glass, McGraw, and Smith (1981) propose the following guidelines for different sizes of effect sizes: 0.2–0.49 = small; 0.5–0.79 = medium; 0.8 and above = large.

Six weeks of cognitive couple therapy was more effective in assisting couple than was the waiting list condition. Applying the Chambless and Hollon criteria (1998), conjoint cognitive therapy would be classified as a possibly efficacious treatment for marital distress.

In current practice, cognitive interventions are typically used with a variety of behavioral interventions, as well as with interventions focusing on couples' emotions. Based on the description of CBCT provided earlier, Baucom and colleagues (Baucom & Lester, 1986; Baucom, Sayers, & Sher, 1990) supplemented traditional BCT with cognitive restructuring interventions targeted at couples' marital attributions and their marital standards. In these two studies, both traditional BCT and CBCT were more effective than a waiting list condition in improving the couples' marital adjustment and communication. However, there were no significant differences between the two treatment conditions. These results were replicated in a similar investigation by Halford et al. (1993). Furthermore, the magnitude of change produced for various dependent measures appears to be consistent with what has been found in a number of BCT investigations. Compared to a waiting list control group, Baucom et al. (1990) found in their larger study that CBCT has an effect size of 0.52. They also found that approximately 43% of the couples had moved into the nondistressed range following treatment. Thus, the findings to date suggest that CBCT is as efficacious as BCT alone and shows more improvement than waitlist conditions, but it does not produce enhanced treatment outcomes. In interpreting these findings, it is important to note that couples were randomly assigned to treatment conditions. Some couples might benefit more from a central focus on cognitive change, whereas others may need extensive alterations in how they behave toward each other. At present, no reported investigations have addressed this matching issue.

INTEGRATIVE BEHAVIORAL COUPLE THERAPY

Christensen et al. (2004) have completed the first large-scale randomized, controlled trial of IBCT, comparing it to BCT as described by Jacobson and Margolin (1979). This study, including 134 couples, is the largest trial of therapy to date for distressed couples and has adequate power to detect treatment differences, compared to the small sample sizes included in most other treatment studies. The findings indicated that, in terms of improving marital adjustment, both treatments resulted in gains from pre- to post-test, and there were no overall differences

between the two conditions at post-test. However, couples in the two treatments demonstrated different patterns of change over the course of treatment. Couples in BCT improved more quickly than did couples in IBCT, but their level of improvement flattened out near the end of treatment. Meanwhile, IBCT couples showed slow but steady improvement during treatment, with no flattening out over time. The proportion of couples showing clinically significant improvement into the nondistressed range was not different for the two treatments (52% and 44% for IBCT and BCT, respectively) and was similar to what has been demonstrated for BCT in other investigations. Likewise, the within-group effect size of IBCT was $d = 0.86$, almost identical to the average within-group effect size of BCT ($d = 0.82$), seen across 17 investigations of BCT (Baucom et al., 2003). Thus, similarly to CBCT, IBCT appears to be of benefit to couples, and the magnitude of its effects is similar to those of BCT. At 5-year follow-up, separation/divorce rates for couples in the two treatment conditions were virtually identical at slightly over 25% (Christensen, personal communication, July, 2007).

Emotionally Focused Couple Therapy

Emotionally focused couple therapy, developed by Johnson and Greenberg (1985; Greenberg & Johnson, 1988), has its roots in experiential therapies and emphasizes understanding individuals' subjective experiences, in particular their emotional responses, in their intimate relationships. Johnson and Denton (2002) have noted that EFCT represented an important shift away from the prevailing emphasis on behavior and cognition in the marital field. Emotionally focused couple therapy draws substantially from attachment theory (Bowlby, 1989), which describes how humans have an innate need for emotional attachment to nurturant others, beginning in infancy and continuing throughout life. Based on the degree to which an individual's early caretakers are physically and psychologically available, a child develops either a secure or an insecure attachment style. Empirical evidence has lent support to the concept that the attachment style or pattern that an individual develops during childhood tends to be stable into adulthood, although significant experiences in adult relationships are capable of altering an individual's attachment pattern (Berman, Marcus, & Berman, 1994; Davila, Burge, & Hammen, 1997; Rothbard & Shaver, 1994; Waters, Hamilton, & Weinfeld, 2000). Instances in which an individual's partner was unavailable to meet his or her attachment needs can result in what are labeled "attachment injuries." Memories of such experiences of abandonment can make the individual highly sensitive to feeling abandoned by the partner in future situations (Johnson, 1996; Johnson & Denton, 2002).

Theory and research have identified up to three types of insecure adult attachment: dismissing-avoidant, preoccupied (anxious-ambivalent), and fearful-avoidant (Ainsworth, Blehar, Waters, & Wall, 1978; Bartholomew & Horowitz, 1991; Hazan & Shaver, 1987), but all of them involve a cognitive component or "working model" in which the individual is sensitive to the likelihood that significant others will not meet his or her needs for emotional attachment. According to attachment theory, when an individual perceives that a significant other, such as a spouse, is not available, this elicits internal, vulnerable "primary" emotions such as anxiety but also may elicit "secondary" emotions such as anger expressed toward the spouse. Johnson and Greenberg (1985) developed EFCT as a means of helping partners to understand their own and each other's emotional responses due to attachment concerns, especially identifying the more vulnerable primary emotions underlying partners' expressed anger toward each other, and to find more constructive forms of behavior to increase intimacy and fulfill attachment needs.

Basic Concepts

BEHAVIOR

The EFCT model draws on family systems theory in positing that often a couple responds to one or both partners' attachment needs in a dysfunctional manner, which leads to a negative interaction pattern (Johnson, 1996; Johnson & Denton, 2002). On the one hand, each person attempts to elicit caring responses from the other in ways that backfire (e.g., nagging, clinging, criticism) or withdraws from the other in a self-protective manner to avoid hurt or rejection. On the other hand, the recipient of these maladaptive actions responds negatively (counterattacking, withdrawing) rather than providing nurturance. Emotionally focused couple therapy focuses on these negative interaction cycles between partners, as well as the two individuals' emotional experiences associated with attachment needs—how those needs are met or not met.

COGNITION

Attachment theory, which forms a key part of the foundation of EFCT, describes fairly stable "working models" or cognitive schemas that individuals hold about themselves (as lovable or not) and about significant others (as available for nurturance or not). However, the proponents of EFCT (Johnson, 1996; Johnson & Denton, 2002; Johnson & Greenberg, 1985) emphasize that emotions organize partners' perceptions and attachment behaviors toward each other. Johnson and Denton (2002) state that change does not occur through insight but rather through new emotional experiences involving attachment interactions between partners. Thus, an individual comes to view a partner more as a secure source of nurturance based on interactions with the partner that elicit more positive emotions.

AFFECT

In couples' relationships, insecure partners use a variety of strategies to cope with their primary emotions, such as fear or sadness concerning being neglected or abandoned. Some coping strategies involve the expression of anger or other secondary emotions (that cover up the primary emotions that, for some reason, seem too vulnerable or unacceptable) and attempts to coerce the partner to provide intimacy, whereas other strategies involve emotional states such as apathy or contempt and behavior such as distancing. It also is assumed that as long as individuals are experiencing strong fear of not having their attachment needs met, they will be unable to communicate constructively with each other. However, EFCT proposes that when partners have opportunities to feel emotionally soothed in interactions with each other, they will be less likely to respond with negative emotions and behavior toward each other. When an individual expresses primary attachment emotions such as sadness and anxiety, this communicates the individual's needs to the partner, who is the potential caregiver, which in turn should elicit comforting responses from the caregiver.

Contributions of the Couple Versus the Individual in Couple Distress

The central role of attachment needs in the theoretical base of EFCT clearly identifies characteristics of the individual partners that contribute to marital distress. Kobak, Ruckdeschel, and Hazan (1994) note that when individuals' internal working models are secure, they expect that caregivers will attend to their attachment needs. Consequently, secure individuals are more likely to express their emotions so as to facilitate attachment (e.g., expressing anger as a reflection of concern about distance in the relationship rather than as a personal attack on the caregiver). In contrast, individuals with insecure attachment working models commonly expect that direct expressions of attachment needs and emotions will lead to negative responses from a significant other, which results in a high level of anxiety about their ability to maintain the attachment. As described earlier, strategies for coping with attachment fears, such as detachment or hypervigilance and exaggerated expressions of emotion, are unlikely to elicit the desired nurturing responses, and the partner is unlikely to correctly interpret the vulnerable attachment needs underlying such behavior. The individual's insecure working model is reconfirmed when the caregiver does not respond in a comforting, nurturing manner.

Thus, the characteristics of the two individuals shape the couple's interactions, but the dyadic pattern that arises between partners also plays a crucial role in maintaining marital distress. Research studies have found that adults with insecure attachment patterns tend to use less constructive conflict-resolution tactics in intimate relationships, as well as more negative conflict management behavior, including psychological and physical abuse (Bookwala, 2002; Bookwala & Zdaniuk, 1998; Creasey, 2002; Dutton, Saunders, Starzomski, & Bartholomew, 1994; Roberts & Noller, 1998). Furthermore, EFCT's focus on dyadic couple interaction patterns is supported by studies indicating the combinations of two partners' attachment styles that are associated with levels of marital distress. For example, Fisher and Crandell (2000) found that clinic couples in which one partner had a preoccupied attachment style (anxious about losing the other's nurturance) and the other had a dismissing-avoidant style (more comfortable when distant) were characterized by conflict and a demand–withdraw interaction pattern.

Proximal Versus Distal Factors in Understanding Relationship Discord

Emotionally focused couple therapy acknowledges that attachment concerns in the current relationship might be greatly influenced by historical factors and experiences that an individual had in earlier relationships, including family-of-origin interactions with parents, for example, and earlier romantic relationships. However, the focus within treatment is on the current relationship and attachment issues that are operating in the present.

Approaches to Treatment

BEHAVIOR

Emotionally focused couple therapy proponents suggest that adults' perception of threats to their attachment relationships elicits natural negative behavioral responses. To change such problematic responses, the therapist creates a safe setting in sessions for each person to explore, understand, and reveal his or her primary (insecure) emotions and gain empathy for the partner's attachment needs. The therapist assists individuals in developing more constructive interactions with their partners, such as direct, nonhostile communication, that increase the probability of receiving reassuring responses and greater intimacy (Johnson & Denton, 2002; Johnson & Greenberg, 1995). Although the therapist and couple may set general goals of improving communication and relationship functioning, they typically do not identify and focus on specific behavioral targets or skills-training. The therapist "reframes" negative behavior in terms of vulnerabilities and attachment needs and encourages further expressions of vulnerability. Presumably, understanding oneself and one's partner more clearly and experiencing an honest expression of emotion and needs for nurturance provide the context for adaptive behavior change.

COGNITION

Emotionally focused therapists believe that relationship distress is caused by insecure attachment styles that include cognitive schemas in the form of "working models" of self in relation to a significant other, and that these schemas typically are formed in the individuals' earlier attachment relationships. However, in EFCT, little attention is paid to fostering insight about earlier origins of attachment responses; rather, the focus is on the partners understanding each other's adaptive needs for closeness and nurturance within the current relationship, so that they can seek and provide for these needs in more positive ways. Each person's expressions of vulnerability should foster empathy from the other partner. The empathic shift toward viewing the partner's negative behavior as arising from attempts to cope with vulnerable feelings, rather than from malicious motives, results in a significant cognitive change in the individual's attributions about the partner and potentially a greater willingness to provide comfort to that partner.

AFFECT

A central goal of EFCT is to access the partners' insecure attachment styles through identifying the secondary emotions typically expressed to each other and the underlying vulnerable primary emotions associated with attachment insecurity. The therapist not only reflects back an individual's expressions of emotion regarding the partner and relationship, but also probes for vulnerable feelings (Johnson & Denton, 2002). By increasing partners' mutual empathy for each other's attachment fears and understanding of the more benign reasons for each other's misguided and negative strategies that are intended to provide security, therapists help soothe the individuals and create opportunities for them to meet each other's attachment needs better (Johnson, 1996; Johnson & Denton, 2002; Kobak et al., 1994). Thus, affect is the therapist's window into the partners' attachment styles and the means for increasing more mutually satisfying interactions between partners.

Empirical Support for Emotionally Focused Couple Therapy

Several investigations of EFCT have addressed its efficacy, and the findings to date indicate that it is of significant benefit to distressed couples (Baucom et al., 1998; Johnson, Hunsley, Greenberg, & Schindler, 1999). Approximately a half-dozen controlled studies have found EFCT to be superior to a waitlist control group (e.g., Denton, Burleson, Clark, Rodriguez, & Hobbs, 2000), with one study finding greater marital satisfaction for EFCT couples than BCT couples at post-treatment and at 8-week follow-up (Johnson & Greenberg, 1985). Johnson (2002) describes a meta-analysis of the four most methodologically rigorous outcome studies on EFCT and reports that EFCT produced recovery rates from relationship distress (into the nondistressed range) of 70%–73%, as well as an effect size of 1.3, all higher than has been found for BCT, CBCT, and ICBT (note that, as described below, Shadish and Baldwin [2003] concluded that there are no differences in the efficacy of behaviorally oriented couple interventions and EFCT). Also, most studies on EFCT have treated couples who range from nondistressed to moderately distressed, so further studies are needed to test the efficacy of EFCT with more highly distressed couples. In the one study with more distressed couples, Goldman and Greenberg (1992) found that the 14 couples in EFCT and 14 couples in systemic couple therapy were not different from each other at post-test, but at a 4-month follow-up the systemic therapy was superior to EFCT, due to the EFCT couples experiencing significant relapse during the follow-up period.

Goldman and Greenberg (1992) caution that, with severely distressed couples, a time-limited course of EFCT might not be sufficient to create a level of intimacy between partners necessary to maintain post-treatment gains. Considering the overall results from these empirical investigations, Baucom et al. (1998) classified EFCT as an efficacious treatment in assisting moderately distressed couples.

Insight-Oriented Couple Therapy

Just as there is no singular behavioral approach to understanding relationship distress or conducting couple therapy, there is no one approach to understanding and treating relationship distress that focuses on the role of insight in fostering change. In general, these approaches are labeled psychodynamic and share a common emphasis on exploring the effects of relationship experiences early in an individual's life and their impact on current adult intimate relationships such as marriage (in contrast to EFCT, which emphasizes the couple's current relationship). Although psychodynamic approaches continue to be popular among couple therapists, little empirical research has been conducted on their efficacy, with one notable exception—Snyder's IOCT (Snyder & Wills, 1989). Insight-oriented couple therapy is based on the notion that current relationship problems result from partners' difficult or painful experiences in prior relationships. These negative experiences from the past intensify the effects of current challenging relationship interactions; within this context, partners react to current conflict by using defensive strategies that are designed to protect them from further hurt. In IOCT, individuals are helped to see how their negative emotional and behavioral responses within their current relationship are influenced by distressing experiences that they had in prior relationships, and that the coping strategies that were adaptive in those earlier relationships are inappropriate for achieving emotional intimacy and other personal needs in their current committed relationship. These interventions contribute to insight into one's interpersonal conflicts and coping patterns, including distortions and inappropriate solutions for achieving intimacy in one's relationship that are rooted in the past.

Basic Concepts

BEHAVIOR

Insight-oriented couple therapy is based on the premise that adults' negative behavioral responses in their relationships are influenced by previous relationship experiences that compromise an individual's ability to respond adaptively to the present relationship. As in other insight-oriented approaches, the individual's internalized views of relationships, or their relationship schemas, create a tendency to behave in particular ways to cope with perceived relationship conflict or dangers. Marital distress is increased by the partners' previously developed behavioral strategies for protecting themselves from relationship injuries, often in ways that do not fit the current relationship context. In essence, to a significant degree the individual is behaving as he or she did in the past, rather than responding to the present.

COGNITION

Insight-oriented couple therapy views individuals' cognitions regarding intimate relationships as a system of internalized representations that function as models of how relationships should and do work. These internalized representations are comprised of characteristics that the client either observed or experienced in early relationships with parents or similar significant caregiving figures; again, the experience of the present is seen as largely due to the past, particularly if there were earlier relationship difficulties or traumas that greatly impacted the individual. These representations from the past may be beyond awareness but are still influential in how the person interacts with his or her partner in the present and how the individual interprets current situations in the relationship. For example, a man whose parents devalued his artistic abilities because such behaviors were not perceived by the parents as masculine while he was growing up may subsequently develop limited self-esteem and believe that significant others view him as an inadequate male. Subsequently, he may perceive any disagreement from his wife as a devaluation of him as a male and respond with hurt feelings and withdrawal.

AFFECT

Insight-oriented couple therapists propose that emotions experienced within the context of interacting with a partner have a major impact on the overall relationship. The individual's developmental history presumably influences many of these emotional responses to one's mate. Although a couple's distress also may be due to current stressors in their life together and inadequate skills for coping with them, negative emotions tied to past relationship injuries tend to color present interactions and make them more difficult. In "affective reconstruction," these emotions and their origins must be identified, so that the partners can differentiate between past

and present relationship experiences and develop more constructive strategies for interacting with a partner in the present.

Contributions of the Couple and the Individual in Couple Distress

Of all the models presented in this chapter, IOCT places the greatest emphasis on the *individual's* positive and negative contributions to the relationship. Although insight-oriented couple therapists pay considerable attention to the couple's interaction patterns, they largely focus on the personal histories that the individual partners bring to the relationship and how those histories influence the current interactions. A major goal of therapy is to make each partner's emotionally charged beliefs about relationships and their associated strategies for coping with significant others (typically developed during past relationships) clearer to both members of the couple. Through becoming aware of past injuries and hurts that have influenced an individual's view of relationships and how they behave currently, partners have the potential to develop empathy for each other as both partners struggle to correct these distorted schemas. Insight-oriented couple therapy capitalizes on the likelihood that each person's dysfunctional patterns of relating to significant others will be elicited in couple sessions more than in individual therapy, making them more apparent to the therapist and couple and available for therapeutic intervention.

Proximal Versus Distal Factors in Understanding Relationship Discord

As noted earlier, IOCT assumes that current relationship difficulties often derive from earlier relationship traumas or difficulties. Thus, a major emphasis is placed on exploring and attempting to understand these earlier difficulties, consistent with the psychodynamic priority placed upon insight into the role of the past and how the past influences current functioning.

Approaches to Treatment
BEHAVIOR

In IOCT, the therapist identifies for the couple how their current negative affect and interaction patterns are emotional responses and coping strategies developed in response to emotional injuries in past relationships. The therapist reframes these negative responses as understandable based on those past events and encourages the partners to view them in a more benign manner and to self-disclose their more vulnerable feelings within their relationship. A primary emphasis is placed on gaining insight into how previous relationship injuries contribute to current interaction patterns. Hopefully, this awareness of the past will allow the partner to behave differently in the present, recognizing that past hurts and injuries need not dictate how to interact with one's current mate.

COGNITION

Insight-oriented couple therapists and other relatively psychodynamically oriented therapists believe that much of a couple's distress results from underlying processes and schemas that are generally accessible with effort, but often are beyond the individual's day-to-day awareness. Therefore, therapy focuses on identifying the content of these internalized representations derived from distressing experiences in past relationships and then interpreting them to clients in order to create insight into the effects of their relationship histories on their current maladaptive reactions to their partners. It is assumed that this insight then helps the individuals to modify their schemas and their continuing problematic relationship patterns in light of current awareness. The focus is on producing more realistic views of each other in the present relationship rather than focusing on resolving old issues with significant others, such as parents, from past relationships (Snyder & Schneider, 2002).

AFFECT

Insight-oriented couple therapists consider clients' emotional responses to be a key source of information about partners' internal dynamics and views of relationships. Moments in which an individual experiences emotion toward the partner during therapy sessions are viewed as potential windows into unconscious material from earlier relationships. These earlier experiences are presumed to have contributed to the current distressing emotions and associated dysfunctional behavior toward a partner. When appropriate, the therapist attempts to identify and interpret the meaning of these emotional responses derived from the person's early history and encourages the individual to self-disclose vulnerable feelings. Each person is encouraged to identify relationship themes involving past disappointments and injuries. By helping the couple understand the significance of their negative emotional responses to each other and their developmental origins, the therapist helps the partners tolerate distress from the past without acting on it in the present. Furthermore, each partner becomes

better able to provide for the other's personal needs because of their increased understanding of, and empathy for, each other.

Empirical Support for Insight-Oriented Couple Therapy

Snyder and Wills (1989) compared the relative efficacy of IOCT and traditional BCT, both delivered for a mean of 19 sessions, and found both treatments to be efficacious relative to a waiting list condition at post-test. In terms of marital adjustment, the IOCT versus waiting list control comparison effect size was 1.15, and the BCT versus control group effect size was .85. There were no differences between IOCT and BCT, however, in altering marital adjustment. Furthermore, at post-test, the two therapies had similar percentages of couples who moved from the distressed range of relationship functioning to the nondistressed range (40% of IOCT couples and 55% of BCT couples, compared with only 5% of waiting-list couples). Whereas IOCT and BCT were comparable on marital adjustment at a 6-month follow-up, Snyder et al. (1991) recontacted 96% of the treated couples 4 years after the completion of therapy and found that significantly more of the BCT couples (38%) had experienced divorce relative to the IOCT couples (3%). In the longest follow-up period of any couple therapy intervention to date, IOCT couples also reported significantly higher levels of marital adjustment than BCT at the 4-year follow-up. Because finding meaningful differences between active treatment conditions is rare in the field of couple therapy, Snyder et al.'s findings call for replication to determine whether the long-term impact of IOCT is consistently superior to skills-based behavioral interventions. Based on the results from this one investigation, IOCT can be classified as possibly efficacious.

The Overall Efficacy of Couple Therapy Across Theoretical Orientations

When the previously described approaches to couple therapy are compared, meta-analyses of couple therapy affirm that various approaches to treating couple distress produce statistically and clinically significant improvement for a substantial proportion of couples, with the average couple receiving therapy being better off at termination than 80% of couples not receiving treatment (Shadish & Baldwin, 2003). However, tempering enthusiasm from this overall conclusion are additional findings that in only 50% of treated couples do both partners show significant improvement in relationship satisfaction, and that

30%–60% of treated couples show significant deterioration at 2 years or longer after termination (Snyder, Castellani, & Whisman, 2006). Meta-analyses provide little evidence of differential efficacy across different theoretical orientations to couple therapy, particularly once other factors are controlled (Shadish & Baldwin, 2003). Thus, there appear to be several efficacious approaches to helping distressed couples with little data to suggest that, overall, one approach is more beneficial to couples than others. Of course, there is the possibility that specific couples might benefit most from a particular type of couple therapy, but so far no research has explored this important set of questions.

Processes of Change

As discussed throughout the chapter to this point, each theoretical approach to couple therapy proposes that relationship distress results from specific factors and, therefore, that creating certain specific changes is necessary to improve the overall relationship adjustment or satisfaction for couples. However, there has been little research that confirms that these mechanisms proposed by each therapeutic approach are responsible for the overall therapeutic improvement that has been observed (Snyder et al., 2006). For example, investigations of BCT do result in improvement in communication and relationship satisfaction but fail to find an association between the magnitude of changes in communication behaviors and gains in relationship satisfaction. Similarly, although CBCT has been shown to produce positive change in targeted cognitions (e.g., expectancies and attributions), changes in these cognitions have not been linked to couples' gains in overall relationship satisfaction following CBCT (see Whisman & Snyder, 1997, for a summary of relevant studies).

More encouraging results have been reported by Doss and colleagues (Doss, Thum, Sevier, Atkins, & Christensen, 2005), who examined mechanisms of change in Christensen and colleagues' (2004) clinical trial comparing traditional BCT with IBCT. Both therapies were effective in increasing emotional acceptance and improving communication behaviors across the course of therapy; however, these changes differed by treatment in a manner that was consistent with their respective presumed change mechanisms. That is, as expected, acceptance increased significantly more for couples in IBCT than for couples in BCT, whereas couples in BCT showed larger initial gains in positive communication. Similarly, in an initial pilot study comparing IBCT with BCT, Cordova, Jacobson, and Christensen

(1998) found that couples in IBCT showed relatively more unified detachment (a component of acceptance) over the course of therapy, and that these changes predicted couples' gains in relationship satisfaction.

Effectiveness Investigations

All of the treatment research thus described has been conducted in university settings under highly controlled conditions with carefully selected couples and well-trained therapists working under close supervision. Whereas the findings from these types of investigations are promising and important, one cannot assume that similar treatment effects are obtained in real-world clinical settings, where a broader range of couples might be seen by therapists who have greater diversity of training and likely less supervision. Whereas treatments conducted in these highly controlled conditions are typically referred to as *efficacy* studies, intervention in less-controlled real-world settings are labelled as *effectiveness* investigations. The effectiveness of couple therapy in the field, outside of research settings, has not been researched sufficiently. In two uncontrolled prospective studies, Hahlweg and Klann (1998) and Klann (2002) investigated the effectiveness of marital counseling in Germany. In total, 139 counselors recruited 1,152 clients into the study. The interpretation of the results is difficult because the attrition rate was high: Only about 50% of the clients participated in the post-assessment 6 months later. Pre-post comparisons resulted in significant improvements in several scales. The effect size for overall marital adjustment was 0.45, a medium effect size. About 26% reported happy relationships after couple counseling—considerably less than in the efficacy study conducted by Christensen et al. (2006). Although much is still to be learned about the utility of couple therapy in typical clinical settings, the initial findings suggest it might be less effective than in the highly controlled contexts of efficacy studies.

Conclusion
Integrated Approaches

Considering the centrality that marriage holds in the lives of most adults and the high divorce rate, it is striking that controlled outcome studies have been conducted with only a few of the major theoretical approaches to treating relationship distress, as described in this chapter. The outcome evidence for behavioral (and its derivatives), emotionally focused, and insight-oriented approaches tends to be encouraging. The positive impacts demonstrated in investigations of behavioral, cognitive, and affective interventions of BCT, CBCT, IBCT, EFCT, and IOCT need not be the basis for competition among approaches, but rather the grounds for seeking integration of models and procedures, to maximize our ability to be of help to couples who are struggling with the most significant relationships in their lives. At times, the concepts and terms used by different approaches seem to be incompatible, but our review suggests that the areas of overlap are substantial. The functioning of an intimate relationship includes behavioral interactions between the two individuals (including ingrained patterns), the often idiosyncratic cognitions that each person holds regarding the other, and a range of positive and negative emotional responses that influence cognitive appraisal, as well as types of behavior toward the partner. Consequently, all of the approaches reviewed here have much to offer the researcher who is attempting to understand couple functioning and the clinician whose goal is to alleviate conflict and distress, because they all address behavior, cognition, and emotion. Furthermore, they vary in their focus on the two individuals' characteristics versus influences of the couple as a dyad, but they all attend to both realms.

Some significant steps toward theoretical and procedural integration in couple therapy have been developed in recent years. Epstein and Baucom (2002) described an enhanced CBCT that incorporates a greater focus on containing or eliciting emotions and broadens the focus of assessment and intervention to include relatively equal attention to characteristics of the two individuals, their dyadic interaction patterns, and the interpersonal and physical environments that comprise the context within which the couple functions. The individual level includes each person's developmental history, personality characteristics, needs and motives, and any psychopathology that he or she brings to the relationship. At the dyadic level, the couple's communication and problem-solving skills, which have long been foci of BCT practitioners, still are staples of enhanced CBCT. Environmental factors, such as extended family members, jobs, and social institutions (e.g., schools), commonly present in close relationships have not previously been incorporated into the empirically supported couple interventions discussed here and require attention in future treatment research. Although environmental demands may challenge a couple's ability to adapt, they also may be vital sources of resources to help the couple cope with life stressors.

Similarly, Snyder and Schneider's (2002) recent pluralistic approach to affective reconstruction broadens Snyder's earlier IOCT and assumes that relationship problems are influenced by multiple factors and require a multidimensional conceptual model and varied interventions. This pluralistic approach combines insight into developmental processes with behavioral, cognitive, and structural interventions intended to improve couples' relationship skills, enhance intimacy, reduce stressors in the partners' lives, and eliminate negative defensive coping strategies. Snyder and Schneider describe a hierarchical model of intervention that includes the components of (a) developing a collaborative alliance with the couple; (b) containing disabling relationship crises; (c) strengthening the marital dyad through positive interactions and increased goodwill; (d) promoting relationship skills for expressiveness, empathic listening, conflict resolution, parenting, financial management, and time management; (e) challenging partners' cognitive distortions contributing to relationship distress; and (f) exploring the individuals' psychological injuries in past relationships that affect their current negative emotional and behavioral responses to each other. In-depth exploration of negative impacts that psychological injuries from earlier relationships have on current emotional and behavioral responses to a partner are combined with practical training in behavioral skills to reduce stress on the couple and enhance intimacy (which can reduce the effects of old emotional wounds). Emotionally focused therapy proponents have not pursued integration with other approaches to a significant extent, but there seems to be great potential for using concepts and methods from other theoretical approaches in the service of modifying problematic responses to insecure attachments.

Christensen (2009) proposes a set of common elements that cut across those various couple therapy approaches that have demonstrated efficacy. Building on the work of Barlow and colleagues (Allen, McHugh, & Barlow, 2008; Barlow, Allen, & Choate, 2004) related to general principles of therapeutic change for individual psychopathology, Christensen suggests that all of the empirically supported couple therapies have five common elements: (a) alteration of cognitive distortions regarding the bases for relationship distress; (b) decreases in negative, destructive behaviors between partners; (c) increases in positive behaviors and an emphasis on strengths; (d) encouragement for couples to address difficult issues that have been avoided; and (e) the teaching of effective communication to assist in these goals.

The employment of broad principles might contribute to an even more pervasive effect that cuts across different theoretical approaches. The listed principles might make couples more relationally attuned and aware, and provide them with novel ways to think about how to improve their relationship. Baucom and colleagues (Sullivan & Baucom, 2004, 2005) have addressed this issue from the perspective of *relationship schematic processing* (RSP), which refers to the degree to which an individual processes information in terms of relationship processes. An individual who is high on RSP thinks about his or her own behavior and its impact on the other person and the relationship, along with anticipating the other partner's needs and preferences and balancing the partner's needs with one's own needs. Sullivan and Baucom (2004; Sullivan & Baucom, 2005) proposed that increasing RSP might be a common mechanism of change that cuts across theoretical approaches, such that any effective couple therapy teaches individuals to think more appropriately in relationship terms. Consistent with this notion, they demonstrated (a) that CBCT does increase the quantity and quality of men's RSP and (b) that women's increases in marital satisfaction in response to CBCT were correlated with the degree to which their male partners increased in RSP. Stated differently, women became more satisfied with the marriage when men learned to process more effectively in relationship terms. Likewise, they demonstrated that couples receiving insight-oriented couple therapy in Snyder's outcome study (Sullivan, Baucom, & Snyder, 2002) increased in RSP as well. Whether the education of couples to think more effectively in relationship terms or the use of the principles suggested by Christensen (2009) turn out to be common mechanisms of change that are central to all efficacious forms of couple therapy is not known at present, but it will be important to continue to explore whether the specific interventions that therapists employ are the critical variables, or whether therapeutic change can be accounted for in other ways as well.

Future Directions

The integrative efforts described here focus primarily on theoretical approaches that have received empirical support for their efficacy. In addition, a number of other couple therapy approaches have not yet been evaluated empirically, yet are widely practiced and have many elements in common with the approaches described in detail in this chapter. For example, as the name implies, de Shazer (1985,

1988) developed solution-focused couple therapy, a brief approach centered on finding solutions with clients rather than discussing the history of their problems. Central to this approach is the notion that language constructs people's reality; therefore, a heavy emphasis is placed in therapy on the content of clients' language and how their choices of terms influence their experiences. Solution-focused therapy emphasizes the here and now, focusing on the concerns that clients bring to therapy regarding issues currently existing in their relationship. To work toward solutions, practitioners of this approach emphasize setting goals with a couple that are important to the clients; clear; described in specific concrete behavioral terms; workable; and involve what needs to happen rather than what needs to be avoided (Hoyt, 2008), an approach similar in many ways to BCT in its emphasis on solutions for the here-and-now. Consistent with the focus on language in solution-focused therapy, narrative therapy involves the belief that our behavior, emotions, and perceptions are shaped by the way we "story" or conceptualize themes in our lives (White & Epston, 1990). The issues that couples bring to therapy involve narratives about their relationship that are limited, in the sense that they incorporate only some experiences from the partners' lives and also are influenced by broader cultural values about what constitute appropriate and healthy characteristics of individuals and relationships. It is assumed that distressed couples have developed "problem-saturated stories" about their relationship (e.g., that they cannot meet each other's basic emotional needs). The focus of narrative couple therapy is on uncovering alternative narratives about the couple and their relationship that open up new meanings and possible ways for the partners to relate to each other—stories with themes in which problems are overcome and in which the partners have more positive identities as individuals and as a couple. Narrative therapists help couples actively search for "unique outcomes" or evidence of exceptions to their negative story about their relationship and collaboratively develop a new narrative, strategies that are consistent with those in CBCT.

Whereas the preceding discussion of common elements of efficacious treatment highlights the issues that should be emphasized in couple therapy, this might not be all that is essential for efficacious treatment. In addition, the overall quality of the couple–therapist relationship (i.e., the therapeutic alliance) might be an important factor in efficacious treatment. Although the quality of the therapeutic alliance in explaining treatment effects has not been investigated empirically in couple therapy, the therapeutic alliance has received considerable attention in psychotherapy research more generally. A recent meta-analysis of psychotherapy concluded that the therapeutic alliance explains between 38% and 77% of the variance in treatment outcome, whereas specific techniques account for only 0%–8% of the variance (Wampold, 2001). Furthermore, Fitzpatrick, Stalikas, and Iwakabe (2001) demonstrated that the impact of specific techniques was dependent on the quality of the therapeutic alliance. Thus, focusing on certain issues within the couple's relationship within the context of a positive, safe therapeutic relationship might provide an optimal context for couples to relate to each other in a more constructive manner.

References

Ainsworth, M. S., Blehar, M. C., Waters, E., & Wall, S. (1978). *Patterns of attachment: A psychological study of the Strange Situation.* Hillsdale, NJ: Erlbaum.

Alexander, J. F., Holtzworth-Munroe, A., & Jameson, P. B. (1994). The process and outcome of marital and family therapy: Research review and evaluation. In A. E. Bergin, & S. L. Garfield (Eds.), *Handbook of psychotherapy and behavior change*, 4th ed. (pp. 595–630). New York: Wiley.

Allen, L. B., McHugh, R. K., & Barlow, D. H. (2008). Emotional disorders: A unified protocol. In D. H. Barlow (Ed.), *Clinical Handbook of Psychological Disorders*, 4th ed. (pp. 216–249). New York: Guilford.

Australian Bureau of Statistics. (2001). *Marriage and divorces, Australia.* Canberra, Australia: Australian Bureau of Statistics.

Azrin, N. H., Besalel, V. A., Betchel, R., Michalicek, A., Mancera, M., Carroll, D., et al. (1980). Comparison of reciprocity and discussion-type counseling for marital problems. *American Journal of Family Therapy, 8,* 21–28.

Bandura, A. (1977). *Social learning theory.* Englewood Cliffs, NJ: Prentice-Hall.

Barlow, D. H., Allen, L. B., & Choate, M. L. (2004). Toward a unified treatment for emotional disorders. *Behavior Therapy, 35,* 205–230.

Bartholomew, K., & Horowitz, L. M. (1991). Attachment styles among young adults: A test of a four-category model. *Journal of Personality and Social Psychology, 61,* 224–226.

Baucom, D. H., & Epstein, N. (1990). *Cognitive-behavioral marital therapy.* New York: Brunner/Mazel.

Baucom, D. H., Epstein, N., Rankin, L., & Burnett, C. K. (1996). Understanding and treating marital distress from a cognitive-behavioral orientation. In K. S. Dobson, & K. D. Craig (Eds.), *Advances in cognitive-behavioral therapy* (pp. 210–236). Thousand Oaks, CA: Sage.

Baucom, D. H., Epstein, N., Sayers, S. L., & Sher, T. G. (1989). The role of cognitions in marital relationships: Definitional, methodological, and conceptual issues. *Journal of Consulting and Clinical Psychology, 57,* 31–38.

Baucom, D. H., Hahlweg, K., & Kuschel, A. (2003). Are waiting list control groups needed in future marital therapy outcome research? *Behavior Therapy, 34,* 179–188.

Baucom, D. H., & Lester, G. W. (1986). The usefulness of cognitive restructuring as an adjunct to behavioral marital therapy. *Behavior Therapy, 17,* 385–403.

Baucom, D. H., Sayers, S. L., & Sher, T. G. (1990). Supplementing behavioral marital therapy with cognitive restructuring and emotional expressiveness training: An outcome investigation. *Journal of Consulting and Clinical Psychology, 58,* 636–645.

Baucom, D. H., Shoham, V., Mueser, K. T., Daiuto, A. D., & Stickle, T. R. (1998). Empirically supported couples and family therapies for adult problems. *Journal of Consulting and Clinical Psychology, 66,* 53–88.

Beck, A. T., Rush, A. J., Shaw, B. F., & Emery, G. (1979). *Cognitive therapy of depression.* New York: Guilford Press.

Berman, W. H., Marcus, L., & Berman, E. R. (1994). Attachment in marital relations. In M. B. Sperling, & W. H. Berman (Eds.), *Attachment in adults: Clinical and developmental perspectives* (pp. 204–231). New York: Guilford Press.

Bischof, G. H., & Helmeke, K. B. (2003). Couple therapy. In L. L. Hecker, & J. L. Wetchler (Eds.), *An introduction to marriage and family therapy* (pp. 297–336). New York: Haworth Press.

Bookwala, J. (2002). The role of own and perceived partner attachment in relationship aggression. *Journal of Interpersonal Violence, 17,* 84–100.

Bookwala, J., & Zdaniuk, B. (1998). Adult attachment styles and aggressive behavior within dating relationships. *Journal of Social and Personal Relationships, 15,* 175–190.

Bowlby, J. (1989). The role of attachment in personality development. In S. Greenspan, & G. Pollock (Eds.), *The course of life: Vol. 1. Infancy* (pp. 229–270). Madison, CT: International Universities Press.

Bradbury, T. N., & Fincham, F. D. (1990). Attributions in marriage: Review and critique. *Psychological Bulletin, 107,* 3–33.

Bray, J. H., & Jouriles, E. N. (1995). Treatment of marital conflict and prevention of divorce. *Journal of Marital and Family Therapy, 21,* 461–473.

Buss, D. H. (1995). Psychological sex differences: Origins through sexual selection. *American Psychologist, 50,* 164–168.

Chambless, D. L., & Hollon, S. (1998). Defining empirically supported therapies. *Journal of Consulting and Clinical Psychology, 66,* 7–18.

Cherlin, A. (1992). *Marriage, divorce, and remarriage.* Cambridge, MA: Harvard University Press.

Christensen, A. (2009). A "unified protocol" for couple therapy. In K. Hahlweg, M. Grawe, & D. H. Baucom (Eds.), *Enhancing couples: The shape of couple therapy to come* (pp. 33–46). Göttingen: Hogrefe.

Christensen, A., & Heavey, C. L. (1990). Gender and social structure in the demand/withdraw pattern of marital conflict. *Journal of Personality and Social Psychology, 59,* 73–81.

Christensen, A., & Shenk, J. L. (1991). Communication, conflict, and psychological distance in nondistressed, clinic, and divorcing couples. *Journal of Consulting and Clinical Psychology, 59,* 458–463.

Christensen, A., Atkins, D., Berns, S., Wheeler, J., Baucom, D. H., & Simpson, L. (2004). Traditional versus integrative behavioral couple therapy for significantly and chronically distressed married couples. *Journal of Consulting and Clinical Psychology, 72,* 176–191.

Christensen, A., Jacobson, N. S., & Babcock, J. C. (1995). Integrative behavioral couple therapy. In N. S. Jacobson, & A. S. Gurman (Eds.), *Clinical handbook of couple therapy* (pp. 31–64). New York: Guilford Press.

Cordova, J. V., Jacobson, N. S., & Christensen, A. (1998). Acceptance versus change interventions in behavioral couple therapy: Impact on couples' in-session communication. *Journal of Marital and Family Therapy, 24,* 437–455.

Creasey, G. (2002). Associations between working models of attachment and conflict management behavior in romantic couples. *Journal of Counseling Psychology, 49,* 365–375.

Crowe, M. J. (1978). Conjoint marital therapy: A controlled outcome study. *Psychological Medicine, 8,* 623–636.

Davila, J., Burge, D., & Hammen, C. (1997). Why does attachment style change? *Journal of Personality and Social Psychology, 73,* 826–838.

de Shazer, S. (1985). *Keys to solutions in brief therapy.* New York: Norton.

de Shazer, S. (1988). Clues: Investigating solutions in brief therapy. New York: Norton.

Denton, W. H., Burleson, B. R., Clark, T. E., Rodriguez, C. R., & Hobbs, B. V. (2000). A randomized trial of emotionally focused therapy for couples in a training clinic. *Journal of Marital and Family Therapy, 26,* 65–78.

Denton, W. H., Burleson, B. R., Clark, T. E., Rodriguez, C. R., & Hobbs, B. V. (2000). A randomized trial of emotionally focused therapy for couples in a training clinic. *Journal of Marital and Family Therapy, 26,* 65–78.

Doss, B. D., Thum, Y. M., Sevier, M., Atkins, D. C., & Christensen, A. (2005). Improving relationships: Mechanisms of change in couple therapy. *Journal of Consulting and Clinical Psychology, 73,* 624–633.

Dunn, R. L., & Schwebel, A. I. (1995). Meta-analytic review of marital therapy outcome research. *Journal of Family Psychology, 9,* 58–68.

Dutton, D. G., Saunders, K., Starzomski, A., & Bartholomew, K. (1994). Intimacy-anger and insecure attachment as precursors of abuse in intimate relationships. *Journal of Applied Social Psychology, 24,* 1367–1386.

Ellis, A. (1978). Family therapy: A phenomenological and active directive approach. *Journal of Marital and Family Therapy, 4,* 43–50.

Epstein, N., & Baucom, D. H. (1993). Cognitive factors in marital disturbance. In K. S. Dobson, & P. C. Kendall (Eds.), *Psychopathology and cognition* (pp. 351–385). San Diego, CA: Academic Press.

Epstein, N., & Baucom, D. H. (2002). *Enhanced cognitive-behavioral therapy for couples: A contextual approach.* Washington, DC: American Psychological Association.

Epstein, N., Baucom, D. H., & Rankin, L. A. (1993). Treatment of marital conflict: A cognitive-behavioral approach. *Clinical Psychology Review, 13,* 45–57.

Epstein, N., & Eidelson, R. J. (1981). Unrealistic beliefs of clinical couples: Their relationship to expectations, goals and satisfaction. *American Journal of Family Therapy, 9*(4), 13–22.

Fincham, F. D., & Bradbury, T. N. (1989). The impact of attributions in marriage: An individual difference analysis. *Journal of Social and Personal Relationships, 6,* 69–85.

Fincham, F. D., Bradbury, T. N., & Scott, C. K. (1990). Cognition in marriage. In F. D. Fincham, & T. N. Bradbury (Eds.), *The psychology of marriage: Basic issues and applications* (pp. 118–149). New York: Guilford Press.

Fisher, J., & Crandell, L. (2000). Patterns of relating in the couple. In C. Clulow (Ed.), *Adult attachment and couple psychotherapy: The 'secure base' in practice and research* (pp.15–27). London: Brunner-Routledge.

Fitzpatrick, M. R., Stalikas, A., & Iwakabe, S. (2001). Examining counselor interventions and patient progress in the context of the therapeutic alliance. *Psychotherapy, 38,* 160–170.

Freedman, J. H., & Combs, G. (2001). Narrative couple therapy. In A.S. Gurman, & N. S. Jacobson (Eds.), *Clinical handbook of couple therapy,* 3rd ed. (pp. 308–334). New York: Guilford Press.

Gallup Jr., G. (1990). *The Gallup poll: Public opinion 1990.* Wilmington, DE: Scholarly Resources.

Glass, G. V., McGraw, B., & Smith, M. L. (1981). *Meta-analysis in social research.* Beverly Hills: Sage Publications.

Goldman, A., & Greenberg, L. (1992). Comparison of integrated systemic and emotionally focused approaches to couples therapy. *Journal of Consulting and Clinical Psychology, 60,* 962–969.

Gottman, J. M. (1994). *Why marriages succeed or fail.* New York: Simon and Schuster.

Greenberg, L. S., & Johnson, S. M. (1988). *Emotionally focused therapy for couples.* New York: Guilford Press.

Hahlweg, K. (2004). Strengthening partnerships and families. In P. L. Chase-Lindale, K. Kiernan, & R.J. Friedman (Eds.), *Human development across lives and generations* (pp. 204–238). Cambridge: Cambridge University Press.

Hahlweg, K., & Klann, N. (1998). The effectiveness of marital counseling in Germany: Contribution to health services research. *Journal of Family Psychology, 11,* 410–421.

Hahlweg, K., & Markman, H. J. (1988). Effectiveness of behavioral marital therapy: Empirical status of behavioral techniques in preventing and alleviating marital distress. *Journal of Consulting and Clinical Psychology, 56,* 440–447.

Halford, W. K., Kelly, A., & Markman, H. J. (1997). The concept of a healthy marriage. In W. K. Halford, & H. J. Markman (Eds.), *Clinical handbook of marriage and couples interventions* (pp. 3–12). Chichester, UK: Wiley.

Halford, W. K., Sanders, M. R., & Behrens, B. C. (1993). A comparison of the generalisation of behavioral martial therapy and enhanced behavioral martial therapy. *Journal of Consulting and Clinical Psychology, 61,* 51–60.

Hazan, C., & Shaver, P. (1987). Romantic love conceptualized as an attachment process. *Journal of Personality and Social Psychology, 52,* 511–524.

Holtzworth-Munroe, A., & Jacobson, N. S. (1985). Causal attributions of married couples: When do they search for causes? What do they conclude when they do? *Journal of Personality and Social Psychology, 48,* 1398–1412.

Hoyt, M. F. (2001). Solution-focused couple therapy. In A. S. Gurman, & N. S. Jacobson (Eds.), *Clinical handbook of couple therapy,* 3rd ed. (pp. 335–369). New York: Guilford Press.

Hoyt, M. F. (2008). Solution-focused couple therapy. In A. S. Gurman (Ed.), *Clinical handbook of couple therapy,* 4th ed. (pp. 259–295). New York: Guilford.

Huber, C. H., & Milstein, B. (1985). Cognitive restructuring and a collaborative set in couples' work. *American Journal of Family Therapy, 13*(2), 17–27.

Iverson, A., & Baucom, D. H. (1990). Behavioral marital therapy outcomes: Alternative interpretations of the data. *Behavior Therapy, 21,* 129–138.

Jacobson, N. S. (1978). Specific and nonspecific factors in the effectiveness of a behavioral approach to the treatment of marital discord. *Journal of Consulting and Clinical Psychology, 46,* 442–452.

Jacobson, N. S., & Christensen, A. (1996). *Integrative couple therapy: Promoting acceptance and change.* New York: Norton.

Jacobson, N. S., & Margolin, G. (1979). Marital therapy: Strategies based on social learning and behavior exchange principles. New York: Brunner/Mazel.

Jacobson, N. S., Follette, W. C., & Revenstorf, D. (1984). Psychotherapy outcome research: Methods for reporting variability and evaluating clinical significance. *Behavior Therapy, 15*, 336–352.

Jacobson, N. S., Schmaling, K. B., & Holtzworth-Munroe, A. (1987). Component analysis of behavioral marital therapy: 2-year follow-up and prediction of relapse. *Journal of Marital and Family Therapy, 13*, 187–195.

James, P. S. (1991). Effects of a communication training component added to an emotionally focused couples therapy. *Journal of Marital and Family Therapy, 17*, 263–275.

Johnson, S. M. (1996). The practice of emotionally focused marital therapy: Creating connection. New York: Brunner/Mazel.

Johnson, S. M. (2002). Marital problems. In D. H. Sprenkle (Ed.), *Effectiveness research in marriage and family therapy* (pp. 163–190). Alexandria, Virginia: American Association for Marriage and Family Therapy.

Johnson, S. M., & Denton, W. (2002). Emotionally focused couple therapy: Creating secure connections. In A. S. Gurman, & N. S. Jacobson (Eds.), *Clinical handbook of couple therapy*, 3rd ed. (pp. 221–250). New York: Guilford Press.

Johnson, S. M., & Greenberg, L. S. (1985). Differential effects of experiential and problem-solving interventions in resolving marital conflict. *Journal of Consulting and Clinical Psychology, 53*, 175–184.

Johnson, S. M., & Greenberg, L. S. (1995). The emotionally focused approach to problems in adult attachment. In N. S. Jacobson, & A. S. Gurman (Eds.), *Clinical handbook of couple therapy* (pp. 121–141). New York: Guilford Press.

Johnson, S. M., Hunsley, J., Greenberg, L., & Schindler, D. (1999). Emotionally focused couples therapy: Status and challenges. *Clinical Psychology: Science and Practice, 6*, 67–79.

Kendall, P.C., & Chambless, D. L. (Eds.). (1998). Empirically supported psychological therapies [Special issue]. *Journal of Consulting and Clinical Psychology, 66*, 3–167.

Kerr, M., & Bowen, M. (1988). *Family evaluation*. New York: Norton.

Kiernan, K. (2004). Cohabitation and divorce across nations and generations. In P. L. Chase-Lansdale, K. Kiernan, & R. J. Friedman (Eds.), *Human development across lives and generations: The potential for change* (pp. 139–170). New York: Cambridge University Press.

Klann, N. (2002). *Institutionelle Beratung – ein erfolgreiches Angebot* (Counselling in institutions – an effective offer). Freiburg, Germany: Lambertus.

Kobak, R., Ruckdeschel, K., & Hazan, C. (1994). From symptom to signal: An attachment view of emotion in marital therapy. In S. M. Johnson, & L. S. Greenberg (Eds.), *The heart of the matter: Perspectives on emotion in marital therapy* (pp. 46–71). New York: Brunner/Mazel.

McDonald, P. (1995). *Families in Australia: A socio-demographic perspective*. Melbourne, Australia: Australian Institute of Family Studies.

Meichenbaum, D. (1985). *Stress inoculation training*. New York: Pergamon Press.

Minuchin, S., & Nichols, M. P. (1998). Structural family therapy. In F. M. Dattilio (Ed.), *Case studies in couple and family therapy: Systemic and cognitive perspectives* (pp. 108–131). New York: Guilford Press.

Noller, P., Beach, S. R. H., & Osgarby, S. (1997). Cognitive and affective processes in marriage. In W. K. Halford, & H. J. Markman (Eds.), *Clinical handbook of marriage and couples interventions* (pp. 43–71). Chichester, UK: Wiley.

Pretzer, J., Epstein, N., & Fleming, B. (1991). Marital Attitude Survey: A measure of dysfunctional attributions and expectancies. *Journal of Cognitive Psychotherapy: An International Quarterly, 5*(2), 131–148.

Rathus, J. H., & Sanderson, W. C. *Marital distress: Cognitive behavioral interventions for couples*. Northvale, NJ: Jason Aronson.

Roberts, N., & Noller, P. (1998). The association between adult attachment and couple violence. In J. A. Simpson, & W. S. Rholes (Eds.), *Attachment theory and close relationships* (pp. 317–350). New York: Guilford Press.

Rothbard, J. E., & Shaver, P. (1994). Continuity of attachment across the lifecourse: An attachment-theoretical perspective on personality. In M. B. Sperling, & W. H. Berman (Eds.), *Attachment in adults: Theory, assessment and treatment* (pp. 31–71). New York: Guilford Press.

Sanford, K. (2006). Communication during marital conflict: When couples alter their appraisal, they change their behavior. *Journal of Family Psychology, 20*, 256–265.

Shadish, W. R., & Baldwin, S. A. (2002). Meta-analysis of MFT interventions. In D. H. Sprenkle (Ed.), *Effectiveness research in marriage and family therapy* (pp. 339–370). Alexandria, VA: The American Association for Marriage and Family Therapy.

Shadish W. R., & Baldwin, S. A. (2003). Meta-analysis of MFT interventions. *Journal of Marital and Family Therapy, 29*, 547–570.

Shadish, W. R., Montgomery, L. M., Wilson, P., Wilson, M. R., Bright, I., & Okwumabua, T. (1993). Effects of family and marital psychotherapies: A meta-analysis. *Journal of Consulting and Clinical Psychology, 61*, 992–1002.

Shoham, V., & Rohrbaugh, M. J. (2001). Brief strategic couple therapy. In A. S. Gurman, & N. S. Jacobson (Eds.), *Clinical handbook of couple therapy*, 3rd ed. (pp. 5–25). New York: Guilford Press.

Snyder, D. K., Castellani, A. M., & Whisman, M. A. (2006). Current status and future directions in couple therapy. *Annual Review of Clinical Psychology, 57*, 317–344.

Snyder, D. K., & Schneider, W. J. (2002). Affective reconstruction: A pluralistic, developmental approach. In A. S. Gurman, & N. S. Jacobson (Eds.), *Clinical handbook of couple therapy*, 3rd ed. (pp. 151–179). New York: Guilford Press.

Snyder, D. K., & Wills, R. M. (1989). Behavioral versus insight-oriented marital therapy: Effects on individual and inter-spousal functioning. *Journal of Consulting and Clinical Psychology, 57*, 39–46.

Snyder, D. K., Wills, R. M., & Grady-Fletcher, A. (1991). Long-term effectiveness of behavioral versus insight-oriented marital therapy: A 4-year follow-up study. *Journal of Consulting and Clinical Psychology, 59*, 138–141.

Stuart, R. B. (1980). Helping couples change: A social learning approach to marital therapy. New York: Guilford.

Thibaut, J. W., & Kelley, H. H. (1959). *The social psychology of groups*. New York: Wiley.

United States Census Bureau. (2002). *Number, timing and duration of marriages and divorces: 1996*. Washington DC: United States Census Bureau.

Wampold, B. E. (2001). *The great psychotherapy debate: Models, methods, and findings*. Mahwah, NJ: Lawrence Erlbaum.

Waters, E., Hamilton, C. E., & Weinfield, N. S. (2000). The stability of attachment security from infancy to adolescence and early adulthood: General information. *Child Development, 71*, 678–683.

Weiss, R. L., & Heyman, R. E. (1990). Observation of marital interaction. In F. D. Fincham, & T. N. Bradbury (Eds.), *The psychology of marriage: Basic issues and applications* (pp. 87–117). New York: Guilford Press.

Weiss, R. L., Hops, H., & Patterson, G. R. (1973). A framework for conceptualizing marital conflict, a technology for altering it, some data for evaluating it. In M. Hersen, & A. S. Bellack (Eds.), *Behavior change: Methodology, concepts and practice* (pp. 309–342). Champaign, IL: Research Press.

Whisman, M. A., & Snyder, D. K. (1997). Evaluating and improving the efficacy of conjoint couple therapy. In W. K. Halford, & H. J. Markman (Eds.), *Clinical handbook of marriage and couples interventions* (pp. 679–693). New York: Wiley.

White, M., & Epston, D. (1990). *Narrative means to therapeutic ends*. New York: Norton.

Interventions for Mental Health Problems in Later Life

Jason M. Holland *and* Dolores Gallagher-Thompson

Abstract

Older adults are increasingly making up a larger segment of the worldwide population, which presents both challenges and opportunities for the clinical psychologist in the 21st century. In this chapter, we address some of the unique aspects of working with this population, focusing on general guidelines for tailoring interventions for older adults, specific treatments for particular problems commonly faced in later life, as well as issues of diversity and how they might impact psychotherapy with older clients. We also outline several areas in geropsychology that are in need of further investigation, namely the use of technology, post-traumatic stress, and family therapy, and offer some recommendations for future directions in this field of study.

Keywords: Age difference, diversity, geropsychology, interventions, older adults

In the midst of a long-term caregiving relationship with her husband who was suffering from a terminal cancer, Rosa, a Latino woman of 67 years of age accompanied her husband during his final weeks in an inpatient hospice unit. Although her demeanor conveyed a profound sense of emotional fatigue and at times hopelessness, Rosa maintained that she was "managing," and night after night sat by her husband's side, often neglecting her own health by only sleeping a few hours each night, skipping meals, refusing staff assistance, and only allowing herself sporadic 5- to 10-minute breaks during the day. Despite efforts on the part of staff to persuade Rosa to take better care of herself and rest more frequently, she maintained that she must stay with her husband around the clock, as it was of the utmost importance to him that only she would assist with "private matters," such as helping him go to the bathroom. Likewise, both Rosa and her husband expressed a sense of mistrust of staff, at times noting that if she left the room no one will be monitoring him. These tensions were aggravated by the presence of Rosa's American-born children, who tended to grieve more expressively and were confused by their mother's stoic presentation. At the time of her husband's death, however, Rosa exhibited clear signs of depression, complaining of fatigue, sleeplessness, lack of appetite, and a deep sense of being misunderstood.

In many ways, this clinical vignette exemplifies the shifting demographics of our society and the new challenges and demands these changes will bring for clinical psychologists in the 21st century. Indeed, in 2006, an estimated 37 million people in the United States (12% of the population) were 65 and older, and this figure is anticipated to grow to approximately 71.5 million people (nearly 20% of the total U.S. population) by 2030. Far from being a homogenous group, racial and ethnic diversity is increasing among seniors as well—a trend that is literally and figuratively changing the face of geropsychology (see www.aging-stats.gov, for additional U.S. aging statistics). Notably, with improving health-care interventions and longer life expectancies, these U.S. figures also parallel a larger pattern worldwide, in which older adults are progressively representing a larger and larger segment of the population (Kinsella & Velkoff, 2001).

Inextricably linked to these demographic trends are a host of unique biological, psychological, and social issues faced by older adults that might often call for specialized skills, knowledge, and sensitivity on the part of clinical psychologists (American Psychological Association, 2004). Although most older adults are resilient and lead active/productive lives even in the face of developmental challenges, such as increasing health problems and interpersonal losses (Bonanno et al., 2002; Davis, Zautra, Johnson, Murray, & Okvat, 2007), the combination of these factors can make for a complex clinical picture when an older adult presents for treatment. Notably, many clinicians may feel somewhat unprepared for work with these clients, as few doctoral programs in clinical psychology offer specialized training in gerontology (DeVries, 2005). As illustrated by Rosa and her struggle to cope with the increasing demands of caregiving, clinicians who are working with older adults must often attend to issues related to bereavement, physical health, and cultural diversity, as well as generational differences—all of which are interwoven within a long and rich personal history.

Given these unique issues and increasing demand for geriatric services, it is the purpose of the present chapter to: (a) orient the reader to important differences between older adults and younger adults and provide general recommendations on how psychologists might appropriately modify their assessments and interventions with older clients, (b) outline some of the most common problems faced by this population and describe specific treatments and assessment strategies that have been shown to have strong empirical support, (c) discuss issues of diversity as applied to psychotherapeutic work with older adults, and (d) describe some promising new directions in geropsychology and propose areas for future work.

Tailoring Assessments and Interventions for Older Adults

Although older adult clients pose unique challenges to clinicians, we propose that most psychological interventions need not be significantly "adapted" for this population, which would imply that psychotherapies in their current forms are somehow insufficient and require alterations at a fundamental level. Indeed, studies have consistently shown that treatments, such as cognitive-behavioral therapy (CBT), are applicable and efficacious with older clients even when few substantive changes are made to the basic protocol (Gatz et al., 1998; Laidlaw, 2001; Scogin & McElreath, 1994). Rather than reinventing one's

therapeutic approach, Laidlaw and colleagues (2003) suggest that clinicians would do well to simply consider how existing approaches might be "modified" for older adults by attending to client-specific variables and making subtle changes in the delivery, timing, or pace of interventions to maximize efficacy. Of course, we believe that these modifications work best when tailored to the individual client as closely as possible and when they take into account the tremendous heterogeneity among older adults (Nelson & Dannefer, 1992). For example, many often consider anyone over the age of 65 years to be an older adult. However, this broad definition encompasses individuals who might differ in age by 20 to 30 years, have diverse experiences as members of a unique generational cohort (e.g., World War II, the Great Depression), and face vastly different developmental challenges. As a way of partially addressing this issue, distinctions have been made between the *young-old* (65–74 years), *old-old* (75–84 years), and *oldest old* (85 years and over).

General Assessment Issues

Notwithstanding the diversity among older adults, some general guidelines can be applied to work with this population, starting with the initial assessment (Edelstein et al., 2008). Because of the stigma associated with mental illness for earlier-born cohorts, older persons might often come into contact with a psychologist only after being referred by a family member or other health-care providers, such as a primary care physician (Heath, Grant, Kamps, & Margolin, 1991). In these cases, the initial stages of an assessment with an older adult would ideally involve communicating with the referring provider, in order to gain a full understanding of the reason for the referral and gather other relevant information about the client's history from the medical records (La Rue, 1992; Storandt, 1994). Likewise, it also becomes important to include family members as part of the assessment to gain collateral information about their understanding of the presenting problem(s) and how their perceptions align with (or differ from) the client's own self-report (La Rue & Watson, 1998).

Assessment with an older client should also involve some evaluation of his or her cognitive functioning, as the cognitive changes associated with aging will vary from client to client. Memory impairments in older adults can signal different problems, such as mild cognitive impairment, dementia, or depression, and neuropsychological testing can often help provide a clearer diagnostic picture (Kaszniak & Christenson, 1994).

In many cases, a cognitive assessment might simply take the form of a brief screening instrument, such as the Mini Mental Status Examination (MMSE; Folstein, Folstein, & McHugh, 1975) or the Cognistat Evaluation (Kiernan, Mueller, Langston, & Van Dyke, 1987). However, because these brief assessments are often not sensitive enough to accurately and reliably diagnose problems such as Alzheimer disease (Galasko et al., 1990), a more refined and thorough neuropsychological assessment would likely be necessary if the goal were to arrive at a differential diagnosis (see Morris, Worsley, & Matthews, 2000; Storandt & Vandenbos, 1994, for reviews).

The assessment of psychological symptomatology might also take a different course when working with older adults. Although many common assessment instruments, like the Minnesota Multiphasic Personality Inventory (MMPI; Butcher et al., 1991), have been shown to yield similar results with different age groups, clinicians would do well to be cognizant of potential differences in the way symptoms might manifest themselves among older and younger adults and tailor their assessments accordingly (Jeste, Blazer, & First, 2005). For example, depressed older adults are less likely to endorse cardinal symptoms of depression, such as feelings of sadness, and instead often report a variety of somatic complaints (e.g., sleep disturbance, weight loss, and/or fatigue) unrelated to any medical problem (Gallo, Anthony, & Muthén, 1994). As a result, primary care clinics often miss elevated depressive symptoms among older adults (Lebowitz et al., 1997). Thus, when available, clinicians might prefer to rely on assessments that take into account the unique clinical presentation of older adults (Edelstein et al., 2008). In the case of depressive symptoms, instruments like the Geriatric Depression Scale (GDS) have been devised that specifically target those symptoms of depression more typically endorsed by older adults (Yesavage et al., 1983).

Clinicians working with older adults should also be aware that the elderly are at heightened risk for suicide, and about one-fifth of all completed suicides are carried out by people over the age of 65 (Florio, Hendryx, Jensen, & Rockwood, 1997; Hall, Platt, & Hall, 1999; Hirschfeld & Russell, 1997). Indeed, older clients' suicide attempts, particularly those of elderly men, are more likely to be lethal, as these individuals are less likely to make suicidal gestures as a cry for help, often have access to lethal doses of medications, and frequently use more lethal methods (e.g., shooting) (Hall et al.,

1999; NIH Consensus Conference; 1992). Risk factors for suicide among older adults include mental health problems (e.g., depression, anxiety), physical health problems (e.g., cancer, renal failure, congestive heart failure), and moderate to heavy alcohol use (Adams, 1999; Fiske, O'Riley, & Widoe, 2008; Grabbe et al., 1997; Heisel & Flett, 2008; Moore & Bona, 2001).

Given these alarming trends, at a minimum, assessment should involve some screening for suicidal ideation and intent. This assessment would ideally include collateral contact with family, given that the majority of older adults who commit suicide do not divulge this information to a health professional but do make suicidal ideations known to their spouse (Moore & Bona, 2001). The topic of suicide should also be raised directly with the older client, to gauge suicidal ideation/intent and also express openness to discussing difficult topics of this sort. Such conversations might also be supplemented with more formal assessments such as the Geriatric Suicide Ideation Scale, which has been validated with older adult samples and includes age-appropriate items dealing with reactions to loss of physical functioning, social relationships, and status (Heisel & Flett, 2006).

General Intervention Issues

Beyond the initial assessment, researchers and practitioners have also proposed models to help clinicians make decisions about how to modify their interventions for work with this population. One model that has remarkable practical value is the Contextual, Cohort-Based, Maturity, Specific Challenge (CCMSC) model (Knight & McCallum, 1998). This model applies knowledge from scientific gerontology to a psychotherapy context and takes into account the fact that older adults are in many ways more mature than younger adults but are often facing some of life's most arduous challenges (e.g., bereavement, caregiving, chronic illness, and disability). The CCMSC model also considers the unique social context of older adults as a population of individuals who were raised within a different sociocultural environment (as members of an earlier-born cohort) and are potentially immersed within age-specific communities (e.g., assisted living communities, senior centers).

From a maturational standpoint, the CCMSC model emphasizes that older adults bring a variety of valuable strengths to the table when presenting for psychotherapy. In particular, older adults have a vast storehouse of knowledge about how things are and how things work, based on years of work, family, and other interpersonal experiences. Thus, existing problems that become a focus of clinical intervention will often share some similarities with past experiences an older adult has already encountered, which might serve as important parallels to enhance understanding and possibly reframe current challenges. For instance, in the case of Rosa presented in the opening vignette, treatment involved discussing past experiences with loss and how these experiences might relate to her present circumstances. Through this exploration, Rosa was able to normalize some of her reactions to the loss of her husband after considering her father's death, nearly 30 years prior, and how she and her mother had grieved intensely at first but later recovered and even came to value life more as a result of the experience.

Despite misconceptions that memory impairment is a normal part of aging, the memory performance of older adults has been found to be comparable to that of younger adults in most domains, especially when the material is relevant and motivation is high (Hultsch & Dixon, 1990). However, the aging process is typically associated with declines in some specific areas of cognition, such as processing speed (i.e., timed tasks) and working memory, which is where memories are temporarily held and processed before being stored within long-term memory (Light, 1990; Salthouse, 1985). Given these cognitive changes, the CCMSC model suggests that therapy might be appropriately modified by slowing the pace of speech, simplifying sentences, and breaking down complex information into smaller parts (Knight & McCallum, 1998). Growing older is also often associated with decrements in sensory perception (i.e., hearing and vision), and this might require adjustments in terms of providing written materials and questionnaires in large print, decreasing excess noise, or respecting clients' preferred modes of communication (e.g., speaking into one's "good ear") (Desai, Pratt, Lentzner, & Robinson, 2001; Hays, 1996). Clinicians would do well to apply these general guidelines flexibly, though, as cognitive and sensory changes could be rather subtle, particularly among the young-old.

Beyond the effects of maturation, the CCMSC model also proposes that older adults' experiences as members of a particular generational cohort, as well as their unique social context, has an influence on the process of psychotherapy, perhaps more so than aging itself (Knight & McCallum, 1998). Having matured within a different period of time, earlier-born cohorts have different skills, viewpoints (e.g., about marriage, divorce, or gender roles), and life experiences compared to later-born cohorts—all of which come to bear on the psychotherapeutic endeavor. For instance, members of earlier-born cohorts, on average, tend to have less formalized education compared to later-born cohorts (Stoops, 2004), which could translate into less reliance on abstract thinking, unfamiliarity with complex terms, and less psychological-mindedness. The particular settings where seniors live, socialize, and receive services—which may or may not be age-specific—can also operate as distinctive subcultures that shape older adults' experiences and potentially put parameters around what is possible in terms of resources, support, and opportunities for growth. Thus, in many ways, psychotherapy with an older client is analogous to working with individuals from another culture, in that the therapist will ideally gain knowledge of the idioms, values, and mores unique to this population and, at a minimum, be appropriately sensitive to differences and willing to ask questions and learn.

As an example of how a specific therapeutic approach might be modified for older adults, Laidlaw and colleagues (2004) have developed a comprehensive conceptualization of CBT for late-life depression (Figure 36.1). Consistent with Knight and McCallum's (1998) CCMSC model, this conceptualization considers cohort effects, maturation, physical health, and the unique sociocultural context of older adults. However, in keeping with the principles of CBT, this conceptual framework primarily emphasizes how these factors might work in combination to influence core beliefs and potentially lead to automatic negative thoughts that would become the focus of a cognitive-behavioral intervention. For instance, *cohort beliefs* that one should be strong and independent may impact one's reaction to a change in physical health (e.g., "I should not be a burden on my family") and may also affect an older adult's *sociocultural beliefs* (internalized societal beliefs) about the aging process (e.g., "Growing old equals frailty and weakness") (Laidlaw, Thompson, & Gallagher-Thompson, 2004).

Laidlaw and colleagues' (2004) also encourage CBT therapists working with older adults to be mindful of *transitions in role investments* and the challenges many older adults face to remain invested in meaningful roles after life transitions like retirement. In addition, this model emphasizes *intergenerational linkages* and the importance that older generations place on the continuity and transmission

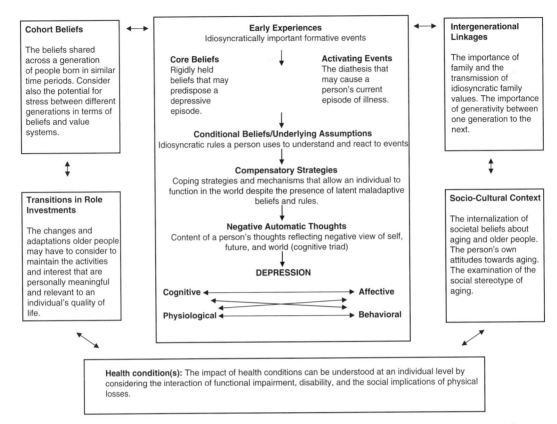

Fig. 36.1 Cognitive-behavioral conceptual framework for older adults. Adapted from Laidlaw, K., Thompson, L. W., & Gallagher-Thompson, D. (2004). Comprehensive conceptualization of cognitive behaviour therapy for late life depression. *Behavioural and Cognitive Psychotherapy, 32,* 389–399. Used with permission of the publisher, Cambridge Journals.

of values within the family. Notably, intergenerational relationships with younger generations, who may tend to place more value on autonomy/independence, may become a source of distress and confusion for older adults, and it is not uncommon for older adults to report strained relations with their adult children as the source of a depressive episode (Bengtson et al., 2000; Floyd & Scogin, 1998; Thompson, 1996). Given the universality of these themes for many older adults, clinicians working with geriatric clients should be mindful of disruptions in role transitions and intergenerational relationships when conducting their initial assessments.

Empirically Supported Interventions for Specific Problems

Beyond these general guidelines for how the process of psychotherapy might be tailored for older adults, specific psychosocial interventions that aim to target particular problems or symptoms experienced by older adults have been developed and tested. It is to these specific treatments that we now turn our attention. Before doing so, however, it should be

noted that many of these psychological interventions for older adults are used in tandem with psychotropic medications. Although our primary focus is on psychologically based treatments in later life, clinical psychologists would do well to have some base knowledge of psychopharmacology with older adults and be able to play an active role in coordinating care with providers from different disciplines.

Notably, the psychopharmacology of younger adults does not necessarily apply to older adults and having this specialized knowledge puts clinicians in a better position to offer informed recommendations and act as an additional safeguard against dangerous drug interactions and other medication problems. For example, although benzodiazepines are often used as antianxiety medications, this class of drugs has been known to have paradoxical effects when used with older adults and could actually increase elderly clients' agitation (Kyomen & Whitfield, 2008). Additional information about geriatric psychopharmacology has been comprehensively reviewed in previous works (e.g., Jacobson, Pies, & Katz, 2007).

Notwithstanding the important role of psycho-pharmacology in later life, in this section, we focus on specific psychosocial treatments that have been shown to have empirical support with older adults for a number of problems often faced by this population, namely depression, anxiety, alcohol and drug misuse, insomnia, behavior problems associated with dementia, caregiver stress, and complications in the grieving process.

Depression

Depression is one of the most commonly occurring psychological problems in late life. In particular, the prevalence of major depressive disorder (MDD) ranges from 1% to 4% among community-dwelling elders, from 5% to 10% among primary care patients, from 10% to 12% among older adults hospitalized for medical and surgical services, and to about 13% among home health-care patients (Blazer, 2003; Bruce et al., 2002). Of course, these figures likely underestimate the impact of depression among older adults, as 8%–16% of community-dwelling elders tend to report elevated levels of depressive symptoms, which may or may not meet criteria for MDD (Blazer, 2003).

Elevated levels of depression are a serious concern for older adults and have been shown to hasten the progression of a number of health conditions and also increase the likelihood of hospital admission and nursing home placement (Harris & Cooper, 2006; Rumsfeld et al., 2005; van Gool et al., 2005). Thus, assessment and screening for these symptoms becomes all the more important, and several instruments have been shown to have validity with older samples, including the Geriatric Depression Scale (Yesavage et al., 1983), the Beck Depression Inventory (Beck, Steer, & Brown, 1996), and the Center for Epidemiological Studies Depression Scale (Radloff, 1977). As mentioned previously, clinicians should be aware that depression can manifest differently among older adults compared to younger individuals, in that depressed elders might be less likely to endorse affective symptoms, such as depressed mood, and instead exhibit more somatic complaints, anxiety, memory loss, or cognitive impairments (Gottfries, 1998).

Fortunately, clinicians have a range of treatments for geriatric depression to select from that have been shown to have strong empirical support. Generally speaking, meta-analyses of outcome studies for depression among older adults have revealed substantial treatment effects, with those in a treatment condition being between .61 and .78 of a standard deviation better off than controls on measures of depression (Cuijpers, van Straten, & Smit, 2006; Engels & Vermey, 1997; Scogin & McElreath, 1994). More specifically, Scogin and colleagues (2005) have identified several evidence-based psychological treatments (EBTs) for geriatric depression (Scogin, Welsh, Hanson, Stump, & Coates, 2005). In this evidence-based review, a treatment was regarded as an EBT if at least two methodologically strong studies (e.g., randomized controlled trials) were identified with a minimum of 30 participants across studies (60 years or older) that showed a given treatment to be "(a) better than the control or comparison groups or (b) equivalent to an existing EBT" for the same targeted problem, in this case geriatric depression (Scogin et al., 2005, p. 225).

Using this set of criteria, six different treatments were identified as EBTs, namely behavioral therapy, CBT, cognitive bibliotherapy, problem-solving therapy, brief psychodynamic therapy, and reminiscence therapy (Scogin et al., 2005). Behavioral therapy typically views depressed mood as stemming from a lack of pleasant events and/or an overload of unpleasant events, and hence treatment involves helping clients to incorporate more pleasant activities into their daily lives, in order to improve mood (Lewinsohn, 1974). Cognitive-behavioral theory, whether applied in a psychotherapy or bibliotherapy context, tends to emphasize the role of unhelpful, negative thoughts in maintaining depressive symptoms and aims to gently challenge these cognitions in an effort to promote more rational thinking and improved mood (Gallagher-Thompson, Steffan, & Thompson, 2008). Notably, CBT treatments also tend to incorporate behavioral strategies (e.g., increasing pleasant activities, relaxation), and protocols have been developed that are specifically designed for older adults (Laidlaw, Thompson, Dick-Siskin, & Gallagher-Thompson, 2003).

In contrast to these approaches, problem-solving therapy typically teaches skills for adaptively approaching problems and encourages older adults to view problem-solving as a coping strategy for dealing with situations that promote a depressed mood (Nezu, Nezu, & Perri, 1989). Brief psychodynamic approaches to treating geriatric depression emphasize the role of internal conflicts and unresolved issues, particularly around issues of independence and dependence, and focus on how these processes play out in the therapeutic relationship, which is often viewed as a driving mechanism of change (Rose & DelMaestro, 1990). Finally, reminiscence therapy involves having depressed older adults review their life histories, concentrating on the significant positive and negative life events, in an effort to promote an enhanced understanding of these events and a greater sense of acceptance about life accomplishments and disappointments (Birren & Deutchman, 1991).

Anxiety

Although anxiety disorders are common in later life, the prevalence has been shown to be somewhat lower than that of younger age groups (Sheikh & Salzman, 1995). In a review of epidemiological research examining anxiety disorders among the elderly, Flint (1994) found prevalence rates of diagnosable anxiety disorders among older adults spanning from 0.7% to 18.6%. In terms of specific disorders, prevalence rates ranged from 0% to 10% for phobic disorder, 0.7% to 7.1% for generalized anxiety disorder (GAD), 0% to 1.5% for obsessive-compulsive disorder, and 0.1% to 1.0% for panic disorder.

However, these figures likely do not provide a complete picture of the role of anxiety in later life, and clinicians would be well advised to use caution and flexibility when applying present diagnostic criteria for anxiety disorders with older adults (Jeste et al., 2005). For example, older adults are less likely than their younger counterparts to report their own symptoms of anxiety and, interestingly, less likely to report symptoms of anxiety in others as well (Levy, Conway, Brommelhoff, & Merikangas, 2003). Hence, it is not uncommon for older adults to experience considerable distress even when reporting subthreshold levels of anxiety (Wetherell, Le Roux, & Gatz, 2003). Current diagnostic criteria might also fail to distinguish between true anxiety symptoms and anxiety secondary to physical illness and/or loss of function (e.g., fears about being out at night that coincide with the onset of visual problems) (Jeste et al., 2005).

It is also notable that anxiety symptoms might manifest differently in older adults. In particular, some research suggests that the anxiety disorders are more likely to co-occur with depression (and vice versa) among older adults compared to younger adults (Palmer, Jeste, & Sheikh, 1997; Parmelee, Katz, & Lawton, 1993). It has also been suggested that the content of phobias could differ as a function of age, with older adults possibly being more likely to fear inanimate objects, such as heights or lightning, and younger adults being more likely to have fears related to tangible entities like animals (Jeste et al., 2005).

Given the potentially unique presentation of anxiety among older adults, clinicians working with elder clients would do well to rely on assessment instruments that have been tested with this population when assessing for these symptoms. Fortunately, a broad range of clinician-administered and self-report measures of anxiety symptoms have demonstrated adequate reliability and validity with older samples, including the Anxiety Disorders Interview Schedule (DiNardo, Brown, & Barlow, 1994), the State Trait Anxiety Inventory (Spielberger, Gorsuch, Lushene, Vagg, & Jacobs, 1983), and the Beck Anxiety Inventory (Beck, Epstein, Brown, & Steer, 1988), just to name a few. The Worry Scale, in particular, deserves mention as it was specifically designed to gauge worries that are often salient to older adults (e.g., worries about finances, physical health, and social matters; Wisocki, Handen, & Morse, 1986).

Recent reviews of the psychotherapy outcome literature on late-life anxiety have also revealed that several treatment approaches appear to be effective at ameliorating anxiety symptoms with this population. Overall, psychosocial treatments for late-life anxiety have been shown to reduce anxiety symptoms by .55 of a standard deviation unit compared to controls (Nordhus & Pallesen, 2003). However, a more recent review of the current empirical literature supported four treatment approaches as EBTs, using criteria similar to that of Scogin and colleagues (2005; see Yon & Scogin, 2007, for the updated criteria). In particular, this review found support for CBT, cognitive therapy, relaxation training, and supportive therapy (Ayers, Sorrell, Thorp, & Wetherell, 2007). Cognitive-behavioral therapy for late-life anxiety involved many of the same treatment components as CBT for depression (e.g., cognitive restructuring, relaxation techniques) but often also included exposure interventions designed to habituate clients to feared stimuli. Interestingly, cognitive therapy (e.g., cognitive restructuring) and relaxation training (e.g., progressive muscle relaxation, meditation) were also found to be effective stand-alone strategies for addressing late-life anxiety. In addition to these treatments, supportive therapy was also found to be efficacious and involved reflective listening, empathic communication, and support.

Alcohol and Drug Misuse

Alcohol and drug misuse among older adults is often unrecognized by health providers, as older adults are often hesitant to acknowledge these difficulties due to concerns about the social stigma attached to such problems (e.g., being labeled an "alcoholic") (Substance Abuse and Mental Health Services Administration [SAMHSA], 1998). In addition, obvious markers for substance abuse/dependence among younger adults (e.g., impairments at work or school, concerns of a spouse) might not apply for older adults, who could be retired and/or widowed (Dupree, Schonfeld, Dearborn-Harshman, & Lynn, 2008; Oslin, 2005). Yet, the best evidence suggests that alcohol and drug misuse is a problem faced by many older adults. For example, among participant 65 years or older who completed SAMHSA's (2004) annual survey, 6.9% reported binge drinking (i.e., five or more drinks on the same occasion) in the last month, and 1.8% reported heavy drinking (i.e., binge drinking for 5 or more days during the last 30 days). Other studies have also found that 2%–15% of older adults exhibit symptoms consistent with alcoholism (Adams, Barry, & Fleming, 1996; Gomberg, 1992).

Notably, depending on the specific clinical population and setting, these figures could vary. For example, it has been estimated that 10%–15% of primary care patients meet criteria for problem drinking (i.e., drinking levels leading to social, emotional, or health difficulties) (Callahan & Tierney, 1995; Oslin, 2004). Also, among veterans with substance abuse diagnoses being treated in Veterans Affairs (VA) hospitals, 23% are over the age of 55 (Moos, Mertens, & Brennan, 1993). Schonfeld and colleagues (2000) also reported fairly high rates (38%) of recent illicit substance use in a VA substance abuse treatment program for older adults. Consistent with these findings, it appears that substance abuse problems are generally more prevalent among older men compared to older women. One study found that 2.75% of elderly men met criteria for alcohol abuse or dependence; whereas, only .51% of women of the same age met these diagnostic criteria (Grant et al., 2004). The Epidemiologic Catchment Area Study also revealed that the lifetime prevalence of drug abuse and dependence among older men was .12% compared to .06% for elderly women (Anthony & Helzer, 1991).

Because substance abuse problems are often overlooked in older adults, psychologists and other health-care providers would do well to regularly screen older adults for these problems. In particular, markers that might prompt an alcohol and/or drug screening include recently experiencing a major psychosocial transition (e.g., loss of a spouse, retirement), the presence of physical symptoms often associated with substance use (e.g., sleep complaints, cognitive impairments), abnormality in liver functioning, and/or slurred speech (Dupree et al., 2008). Three brief screening instruments have been recommended

by the Center for Substance Abuse Treatment (2006). In particular, the older adult–specific measure, the Short-Michigan Alcoholism Screening Test–Geriatric (Blow et al., 1992), has been recommended, as well as the Alcohol Use Disorders Identification Test (AUDIT; Babor, de la Fuenta, Saunders, & Grant, 1992) and the CAGE screening instrument (Mayfield, McLeod, & Hall, 1974)—both of which have shown adequate sensitivity and specificity with older samples (O'Connell et al., 2004).

In general, older adults who have been identified as having problems with substance abuse/dependence are amenable to treatment but tend to prefer interventions that are nonconfrontive, supportive, and focus broadly on coping with depression, loneliness, and loss (SAMHSA, 1998). Although some studies have suggested that older adults do best in age-specific substance use treatment programs (Kashner, Rodell, Ogden, & Guggenheim, 1992; Kofoed, Tolson, Atkinson, & Toth, 1987), more recent findings indicate that older adults can have good outcomes in mixed-age programs when the treatment itself is compatible with older adults' needs and preferences (Oslin, Pettinati, & Volpicelli, 2005).

With regard to specific interventions, SAMHSA (1998) recommends that the least intensive treatment choices be considered first with older substance abusers. In keeping with this guideline, two randomized clinical trials have been conducted with older problem drinkers that tested the efficacy of brief interventions in primary care settings, which for the most part consisted of an expression of concern, feedback regarding the implications of their drinking, and an explicit recommendation to reduce alcohol consumption (Copeland, Blow, & Barry, 2003; Fleming, Manwell, Barry, Adams, & Stauffacher, 1999). The collective outcomes of these trials revealed that brief counseling is an acceptable strategy for this population and might reduce alcohol use and increase service utilization among at-risk drinkers who received treatment, compared to those in the control conditions.

Preliminary evidence also suggests that, when appropriate, more intensive interventions, such as motivational interviewing (MI) and CBT, are effective with older adults dealing with substance-related problems. For example, in one drug trial comparing naltrexone (used to prevent cravings for alcohol) to a placebo medication among older adult alcohol abusers, participants in both conditions received a 3-month motivational counseling intervention, which involved exploring ambivalent feelings about change and meeting the client where they were in terms of their readiness for change (Oslin et al., 2005). Notably, compared to the younger adults in this study, older adults attended more therapy sessions, had greater medication adherence, and experienced less relapse—providing preliminary support for the utility of an MI approach with this population. In another investigation, problem drinkers were randomly assigned to one of three conditions, namely CBT, relationship enhancement, or relationship enhancement plus vocational enhancement (Rice, Longabaugh, Beattie, & Noel, 1993). Among the older adults in this sample, CBT proved to be the most beneficial treatment option and consisted of standard CBT interventions that particularly emphasized cultivating skills for dealing with personal problems. Other CBT interventions for alcohol abuse, specifically tailored for older adults, have also been used with success (see Dupree et al., 2008, for a full description).

Insomnia

Older adults tend to experience insomnia more frequently and more intensely compared to younger adults (Lichstein, Durrence, Riedel, Taylor, & Bush, 2004). Indeed, somewhere between 20% and 40% of older adults experience clinical levels of insomnia, which is the most prevalent sleep disorder among individuals of this population (Ancoli-Israel, Pat-Horenczyk, & Martin, 2001; Foley, Monjan, Brown, & Simonsick, 1995; Mellinger, Balter, & Uhlenhuth, 1985). The increased susceptibility of older adults to insomnia has been attributed to factors such as an increase in stressors, environmental changes, and physical and emotional difficulties—all of which can prompt and/or exacerbate sleep problems (Stone, Booth, & Lichstein, 2008). However, it is notable that normal aging by itself is associated with some changes in sleeping patterns and might results in decreased sleep efficiency, variable and earlier sleep time, less deep sleep, and waking up more frequently during the night (Nau, McCrae, Cook, & Lichstein, 2005). Thus, clinicians might often have difficulty distinguishing between normal developmental sleep changes and insomnia, highlighting the importance of assessment with this population.

Assessment might take the form of sleep diaries or psychometrically sound questionnaires, such as the Pittsburgh Sleep Quality Index (PSQI; Buysse, Reynolds, Monk, Berman, & Kupfer, 1989), which provide cutoff scores that can aid in differential diagnosis. Objective measures are also available that do not rely on self-report and are often preferable,

particularly if memory impairments are suspected. For example, a device known as an *actigraph* can be worn on the wrist to measure movement, in order to make inferences about whether or not a person is asleep or awake (Ancoli-Israel et al., 2003). More sophisticated and comprehensive objective measures are also available, such as polysomnography, which might provide more accurate data with older adults and help to differentiate between the overlapping symptoms of many sleep, mental, and physical disorders (Sivertsen et al., 2006).

Once an older adult has been identified as experiencing elevated symptoms of insomnia, clinicians have several empirically supported psychological treatments to choose from that have been shown to significantly enhance the sleep quality of older adults (McCurry, Logsdon, Teri, & Vitiello, 2007). In particular, using the criteria for identifying EBT's for older adults (Yon & Scogin, 2007), McCurry and colleagues (2007) concluded that both sleep restriction-sleep compression interventions as well as multicomponent CBT treatments are efficacious for this population. Sleep restriction therapy is based on the notion that a discrepancy often exists between *perceptions* of the amount of sleep needed and *actual* sleep need, and this discrepancy can be dealt with by encouraging clients to spend time in bed based on actual sleep needs instead of desired sleep (Spielman, Saskin, & Thorpy, 1987). Specifically, in this treatment, clients are instructed to limit the time spent in bed to match the amount of time they actually spend sleeping (gauged by sleep diaries or other assessments), and clients can gradually increase the time spent in bed by 15–20 minutes until an optimal sleep duration is attained. Sleep compression therapy is based on the same psychological principles but instead gradually decreases time in bed (Riedel, Lichstein, & Dwyer, 1995).

Multicomponent CBT interventions include a variety of strategies, most often education about sleep hygiene, relaxation, sleep restriction, and stimulus control. Sleep hygiene education involves discussion about the contribution of a variety of factors—sleep schedule, diet, physical environment, and activity—that often contribute to and maintain sleep difficulties (Stepanski & Wyatt, 2003). Relaxation techniques, such as diaphragmatic breathing and progressive muscle relaxation, are also frequently used to lessen physiological arousal and increase the likelihood of getting to sleep (Manber & Kuo, 2002).

Stimulus control interventions typically involve providing a list of instructions that aim to establish bed as a prompt for sleep, avoid pairing time in bed with activities inconsistent with sleep (e.g., watching television, reading), and help individuals acquire a consistent sleep pattern (Bootzin, 1977). These instructions typically involve advising clients to only use the bed for sleep (or sex); go to bed only when sleepy; leave the bed and bedroom after 20 minutes of sleeplessness and only return after feeling sleepy (to be repeated as many times as necessary); regardless of sleep quantity, wake up at the same time each morning; and avoid daytime napping (Bootzin & Epstein, 2000). With older adults, this intervention should be applied flexibly, as it potentially involves getting in and out of bed repeatedly, which could be challenging in the presence of physical limitations. In these cases, clients could instead sit up in bed and initiate a relaxing or soothing activity (e.g., listening to music) until they get tired, as a way to avoid further tossing and turning (Stone et al., 2008).

Behavior Problems Associated with Dementia

Epidemiological studies suggest that roughly 6% of community-dwelling older adults over the age of 70 suffer from some form of dementia, and this figure rises to about 50% for individuals over the age of 85 (Evans et al., 1989; Kukull et al., 2002). Likewise, in long-term care settings (e.g., nursing homes), about half of the residents carry a dementia diagnosis (Magaziner et al., 2000). As dementia progresses, it is often associated with a variety of behavioral problems, such as verbal and physical aggression, wandering, and opposition to care (Cohen-Mansfield & Billig, 1986; Mega, Cummings, Fiorella, & Gornbein, 1996). Notably, these behaviors increase the risk of caregiver stress, falls, or other accidents, and ultimately they are often the primary reason for institutionalization (Yaffe et al., 2002).

Because of the potential emotional, physical, and financial costs of dementia-related behavioral problems, behavioral management of these symptoms becomes an important part of a care recipient's treatment plan. However, before intervening, it is important to conduct a comprehensive assessment. This assessment is often done idiographically and involves interviewing the caregiver or residential staff members to generate hypotheses about what antecedents (e.g., boredom, hunger, having to go the bathroom) could be triggering problematic behaviors and what consequences of the behavior (e.g., increased attention) might be reinforcing its reoccurrence. Other more formal assessments include the Behavioral Pathology in Alzheimer's Disease Rating Scale (Reisberg et al., 1989), which

asks caregivers to rate their level of distress related to 25 possible problem behaviors, and the Pittsburgh Agitation Scale (Rosen, Burgio, Kollar, & Cain, 1994), which measures aggression and agitation based on 1–8 hours of direct observation. Since depressive symptoms can also contribute to behavioral disturbances, an assessment of these symptoms might also be warranted using the Cornell Scale for Depression in Dementia. This 19-item instrument gauges behavioral symptoms of depression through interview and observational methods and collects information from both the patient and a family caregiver or nursing staff member (Alexopoulos, Abrams, Young, & Shamoian, 1988).

Intervention for behavior problems related to dementia often involves pharmacological treatment in the form of antipsychotic, antidepressant, and/or anticonvulsant medication (see Bharani & Snowden, 2005, for a review of specific medications). However, treatment would ideally involve some combination of pharmacology and behavioral management. Medications for the management of these behaviors are not without risk (e.g., fatigue, sedation, increased disorientation/confusion) and a behavioral approach represents a safe and effective supplement (or in some cases perhaps an alternative) to these interventions. Notably, a recent empirically based review concluded that two approaches to behavioral management of these symptoms have strong empirical support (Logsdon, McCurry, & Teri, 2007), namely treatments based on the progressively lowered stress threshold (PLST; Hall & Buckwalter, 1987) and behavioral problem-solving (Teri et al., 1998) theoretical models. Generally speaking, both of these treatment approaches involve training family caregivers or nursing staff members to identify targeted behaviors, generate hypotheses about possible antecedents, make appropriate changes to the care recipient's physical environment or schedule, and/or modify interpersonal interactions to reduce the occurrence of these behaviors.

Caregiver Stress

There are an estimated 44.4 million caregivers in the United States (roughly 21% of the adult population) who offer unpaid care to another adult suffering from a physical or mental disability. Although the typical caregiver in the United States is a Caucasian woman in her mid-forties, it is notable that 39% of caregivers are men, 43% are 50 years of age or older, and 27% represent ethnic minorities (12% African American, 10% Hispanic/Latino, 4% Asian American)—highlighting the rich diversity among these individuals (National Alliance for Caregiving & AARP, 2004). Caregiving of any kind can be a source of stress that affects physical and psychological functioning; however, evidence suggests that caring for a loved one with Alzheimer disease or other form of dementia presents unique challenges and often results in higher levels of stress compared to other caregiving circumstances (Ory, Hoffman, Yee, Tennstedt, & Schulz, 1999). Indeed, caring for a loved one with dementia has been associated with higher levels of depression as well as physiological outcomes, such as high blood pressure and heart problems (Gallagher, Rose, Rivera, Lovett, & Thompson, 1989; Schulz & Martire, 2004; Vitaliano, Scanlan, Zhang, Savage, & Hirsch, 2002; Vitaliano, Young, & Zhang, 2004).

Given the prevalence of depression among dementia caregivers (estimated at roughly 20%; Cuijpers, 2005), the assessment of a caregiver presenting for treatment would ideally include an evaluation of current depressive symptoms. Notably, the instruments recommended for depressed older adults would also be applicable for caregivers. Two caregiving-specific measures also deserve mention and provide useful information beyond an assessment of depression. The Revised Memory and Behavior Problem Checklist gauges the frequency of disruptive behaviors and memory-related behaviors, such as asking questions repeatedly, on the part of the care recipient and asks caregivers to indicate the amount of stress experienced as a result of these behaviors (Teri et al., 1992). Another useful instrument is the 22-item self-report measure, the Zarit Burden Interview, which assesses the total physical, emotional, and financial tolls of caregiving (Zarit, Todd, & Zarit, 1986).

The last 10 years have seen tremendous growth in the number of high-quality treatment outcome studies for distressed caregivers. For example, in Gatz and colleagues' (1998) review of psychological treatments for older adults, only four caregiver intervention studies met EBT criteria. In contrast, in an updated review of this literature using similar inclusion criteria (Yon & Scogin, 2007), 19 studies were identified that supported the efficacy of a variety of caregiver interventions, including psychoeducational skill building programs, psychotherapy and counseling, and multicomponent interventions (Gallagher-Thompson & Coon, 2007).

With regard to psychoeducational skill building programs, four approaches were found to warrant EBT status (Gallagher-Thompson & Coon, 2007). They include behavioral management skills training

(e.g., Bourgeois, Schulz, Burgio, & Beach, 2002), depression management (e.g., Coon, Thompson, Steffen, Sorocco, Gallagher-Thompson, 2003), anger management skill training (e.g., Steffen, 2000), and the PLST model (e.g., Huang, Shyu, Chen, Chen, & Lin, 2003). Behavioral, depression, and anger management programs typically adhere to CBT principles and involve interventions such as training individuals to increase pleasant activities, challenge automatic thoughts, and identify triggers for anger and frustration. Rather than directly targeting caregiver symptoms, programs based on the PLST model typically focus on teaching skills to manage stressors, such as changes in routine or multiple and competing stimuli, that might interact with the care recipient's physical condition to exacerbate problem behaviors (Hall & Buckwalter, 1987).

This empirically based review also supported the use of psychotherapy as well as multicomponent interventions (Gallagher-Thompson & Coon, 2007). Of the three studies that tested formal psychotherapy or counseling and met EBT criteria, all used CBT or were strongly CBT based. Two studies that tested a multicomponent intervention (made up of two or more distinct theoretical perspectives) were labeled as EBTs. These studies included one treatment that involved individual and family counseling sessions, participation in support groups, and ad hoc follow-up counseling (Mittelman, Ferris, Shulman, & Steinberg, 1995), and another treatment that incorporated family therapy with a computerized phone system, which allowed for support group participation, as well as access to information about caregiving and community resources (Eisdorfer et al., 2003).

Prolonged Grief

The loss of loved ones is perhaps one of the most challenging psychosocial transitions in later life (Thompson, Tang, DiMario, Cusing, & Gallagher-Thompson, 2007). Notably, by the age of 65, one half of all women and 10% of all men experience the loss of a spouse, and these figures rise to 80% and 40%, respectively, by age 85 (Rosenzweig, Prigerson, Miller, & Reynolds, 1997). Of course, the cumulative losses experienced by older adults dramatically surpass these figures, as the loss of siblings and friends exceed spousal bereavement by factors of 3:1 and 9:1, respectively (Hays, Gold, & Peiper, 1997). Despite the ubiquity of loss in later life, recent evidence suggests that most successfully adjust to these trying circumstances. In particular, the Changing Lives of Older Couples (CLOC) project, a prospective study of spousal bereavement among older couples, found that about 40% of widows and widowers were resilient in the face of loss and 6 months afterward exhibited minimal depressive and grief symptomatology (Bonanno et al., 2002).

For a subset of 10%–15% of bereaved older adults, however, the loss of a loved one prompts a prolonged grief reaction—a chronic and severe form of grieving lasting longer than 6 months that is characterized by intense separation distress, intrusive thoughts about the deceased, a sense of purposelessness and meaninglessness about life, and impairments in everyday functioning (Bonanno et al., 2002; Prigerson, Bierhals, Kasl, & Reynolds, 1997; Prigerson & Maciejewski, 2006). The proposed diagnostic criteria for Prolonged Grief Disorder (PGD) are presented in Table 36.1. Although PGD is still being considered for inclusion in the *Diagnostic and Statistical Manual of Mental Disorders*, this cluster of symptoms has been shown to uniquely predict a variety of detrimental outcomes (after accounting for the impact of depressive and anxiety symptoms), such as heart problems, cancer, hypertension, and changes in eating and smoking habits (Prigerson et al., 1997).

Given the potential impact of PGD, clinicians would do well to screen for the presence of these symptoms using validated self-report and/or clinician-administered instruments, such as the Inventory of

Complicated Grief (Prigerson & Jacobs, 2001). Importantly, this type of assessment could identify bereaved older adults who are most likely to benefit from treatment. For example, in a recent meta-analysis of bereavement intervention research, it was found that interventions generally did not promote improvements on measures of depression, grief, and other relevant outcomes, and this trend held across all age groups (Currier, Neimeyer, & Berman, 2008). However, when efforts were made to specifically include only bereaved individuals who were particularly distressed, the effects of treatment were substantial, underscoring the importance of assessing for complications in the grieving process (Currier et al., 2008).

Tests of psychosocial treatments for PGD are just beginning to emerge; however, several recent studies support the efficacy of CBT-based interventions. Generally speaking, these interventions often involve gently challenging negative grief-related beliefs (e.g., "Life will never hold meaning again") and facilitating gradual exposure to the painful details of the loss experience in order to promote less avoidance and new understandings of the loss that allow for a more hopeful future. For example, a 6-week therapy, complicated grief treatment (CGT), was recently tested against interpersonal psychotherapy (IPT) in a randomized clinical trial with

Table 36.1 Criteria for prolonged grief disorder proposed for DSM-5

Criterion A. Chronic and disruptive yearning, pining, longing for the deceased

Criteria B. The person must have four of the following eight remaining symptoms at least several times a day or to a degree intense enough to be distressing and disruptive:

1. Trouble accepting the death

2. Inability to trust others

3. Excessive bitterness or anger related to the death

4. Uneasiness about moving on (e.g., making new friends, pursuing new interests)

5. Numbness/detachment (e.g., feeling disconnected from others)

6. Feeling that life is empty or meaningless without deceased

7. Feeling bleak about the future

8. Agitation (e.g., jumpiness or edginess)

Criterion C. The above symptom disturbance causes marked and persistent dysfunction in social, occupational, or other important domains.

Criterion D. The above symptom disturbance must last at least 6 months.

Adapted from Prigerson, H. G., & Maciejewski, P. K. (2005–2006). A call for sound empirical testing and evaluation of criteria for complicated grief proposed for DSM-5. *Omega: Journal of Death and Dying, 52*(1), 9–19. Reprinted with permission of the publisher, Baywood Publishing.

95 participants who met criteria for PGD (Shear, Frank, Houck, & Reynolds, 2005), many of whom were older adults. The CGT condition included therapeutic procedures such as *revisiting*, in which participants retold, recorded, and reviewed their stories of loss, and *imaginal conversations*, which facilitated a renewed bond to the deceased through imaginary dialogue. In this study, CGT was shown to be better than IPT at ameliorating symptoms of PGD and improving participants' work and social adjustment. Complicated grief treatment also yielded a more rapid rate of recovery with regard to PGD symptoms, although the two treatments generated similar outcomes on measures of depression and anxiety. Notably, other recent studies that have tested the efficacy of CBT-based interventions for PGD have also produced favorable results (Boelen, de Keijser, van den Hout, & van den Bout, 2007; Wagner, Knaevelsrud, & Maercker, 2006).

Diversity Among Older Adults

Recent years have shown an increase in the ethnic and racial diversity among older adults in the United States, and this trend is expected to continue over the next several decades. In particular, in 1990, ethnic minorities made up 13% of individuals over the age of 65 years. Notably, this figure rose to 16% in 2000, and is anticipated to grow to 23% by 2020, and to 36% by 2050 (U.S. Census Bureau, 2003). These demographic shifts are likely to have an impact on the health-care system as a whole, and for psychologists working with older clients, in particular, signal the importance of culturally sensitive clinical practice. Thus, beyond having a general understanding of how interventions might be tailored for older adults and knowledge about the specific empirically based treatments for this population, geropsychologists of the 21st century will increasingly need to have an understanding of cultural differences and be able to respond to older clients' varying needs. Given the relevance of these issues to older adults, in this section we will explore important ethnic/racial differences in later life and discuss how these relate to (a) the clinical presentation of emotional distress and its assessment, as well as (b) treatment usage, treatment preferences, and treatment outcome.

Clinical Presentation of Emotional Distress

In many ways, mental illness itself represents a culturally created construct. Notwithstanding tremendous within-culture variation, the signs and symptoms of emotional disruption are undoubtedly influenced by the collective expectations and beliefs of a culture about the etiology of psychological problems and the appropriateness of different ways of expressing these problems. Indeed, it is interesting to note that psychological difficulties like eating disorders that are prevalent in Westernized, technologically advanced societies are virtually nonexistent in less industrialized cultures, highlighting the crucial role of culture in defining mental illness (Horwitz, 2002).

Not surprisingly, culture and ethnicity seem to operate in a similar fashion with older adults and have a palpable effect on the ways in which emotional distress is manifested in this population. Although some investigations have failed to find substantial differences in the symptom profiles of older adults on the basis of ethnicity or race (Blazer, Landerman, Hays, Simonsick, & Saunders, 1998; Mouton, 1997), other studies have revealed subtle variations and provide clinicians with a roadmap (albeit an incomplete one) for understanding how culture might intersect with psychological problems in later life. For example, with regard to ethnic differences in geriatric depressive symptoms (which have been researched most extensively), depressed African American elders have been found to be less likely to report symptoms of dysphoria (Gallo, Cooper-Patrick, Lesikar, 1998), as well as feelings of helplessness or worthlessness (Karel & Moye, 2002), compared to Caucasian older adults. Other studies have also suggested that older African Americans might be more likely than Caucasians to endorse having thoughts about death (Gallo et al., 1998) and fatigue-like symptoms (i.e., reporting that "everything was an effort") (Mills, Alea, & Cheong, 2004, p. 224).

In studies with adults of mixed age groups, possible differences in the expression of depressive symptoms have also been noted among individuals of Latino and Asian cultures. For example, some studies suggest that depressed individuals from Asian cultures might be less likely to endorse symptoms from the psychological realm, such as sadness, irritability, or rumination, and more likely to report somatic complaints like headaches, insomnia, or fatigue (Cheung, 1980; Kleinman, 1982; Lin & Cheung, 1999). These global trends should be considered cautiously, however, especially in light of the fact that other studies have failed to identify elevated levels of somatization among Asian participants (Mackinnon, McCallum, Andrews, & Anderson, 1998). Beyond these findings pertaining to Asian cultures, one investigation of Latino and Caucasian individuals found that Latinos were more likely than Caucasians to endorse items related to tearfulness and punishment and less likely to endorse an inability to work (Azocar, Areán, Miranda, Muñoz, 2001).

These potential differences in symptom presentation are likely due to a variety of culturally influenced factors, such as the degree of stigmatization placed on mental illness, as well as to beliefs about aging and the cause of psychological problems. For example, studies of African American and Caucasian elders have found that African Americans tend to be more likely to view depression as a sign of personal weakness (Mills et al., 2004) and are more likely to hold negative beliefs about aging (Foos, Clark, & Terrell, 2006). It is also notable that ethnic minority older adults vary in their degree of identification with traditional cultural norms, and the extent to which someone has adopted the folkways of the dominant culture appears to have an impact on their expression of emotional distress. Specifically, one study of Mexican American elders found that acculturation was associated with pervasive differences in the way items were endorsed on the Center for Epidemiological Studies – Depression (CES-D) scale (Chiriboga, Jang, Banks, & Kim, 2007). Another study of more than 1,500 elderly Chinese-Canadian immigrants revealed that higher levels of identification with traditional Chinese cultural values resulted in a greater likelihood of being depressed (Lai, 2004).

Cultural differences are also likely to influence the prevalence of psychological problems. Although less is known about the relative incidence of mental disorders among older adults of different ethnicities, studies of adults in general have shown some differences. For example, one large multisite epidemiological study suggested that, after accounting for socioeconomic status, African Americans were less likely than Caucasians to meet diagnostic criteria for major depression, obsessive-compulsive disorder, drug and alcohol abuse or dependence but were more likely to experience phobias and somatization (Zhang & Snowden, 1999). Another investigation specific to older adults found the prevalence rate of suicide among Caucasian elders to be greater than that of African American elders by a factor of more than three (15.8 suicides per 100,000 compared to 5). Notably, Asians and Hispanic/Latino older adults were also shown to be less likely to commit suicide than Caucasians (with 10.6 and 7.9 suicides per 100,000, respectively; National Institute of Mental Health, 2007).

There are, of course, a multitude of possible explanations for these differences in prevalence rate.

In the case of suicide, it is notable that, compared to Caucasians, African American elders tend to have higher levels of religiosity, which often plays an important role in coping with depressive symptoms and also likely strengthens cultural prohibitions against suicide (Consedine, Magai, & Conway, 2004; Jang, Borenstein, Chiriboga, & Mortimer, 2005). Beyond the possibility that ethnic differences in prevalence are due to true variation in the expression of psychological distress, it has also been noted that practitioners may be influenced by cultural biases when diagnosing older adults of ethnic minority groups. For example, one study found that African American and Hispanic/Latino individuals with bipolar disorder were more likely to be misdiagnosed with schizophrenia (Mukherjee, Shukla, Woodle, Rosen, & Olarte, 1983). Notwithstanding these worrisome findings, it is notable that many of these studies have yielded mixed results, and two recent investigations using a case vignette design (where participants of a different ethnicity/gender portray the exact same clinical presentation) suggest that psychiatrists and primary care physicians diagnose geriatric depression similarly regardless of race and gender (Kales, Neighbors, Blow et al., 2005; Kales Neighbors, Valenstein et al., 2005).

Given these cultural differences in clinical presentation and prevalence, as well as the possibility of clinician bias in diagnostic practices, it is imperative that clinical psychologists be mindful of culturally sensitive practices when assessing and conceptualizing cases involving diverse older adults. Hays (1996) suggests that one helpful model for conducting a culturally responsive assessment with older adults is the ADRESSING framework, which takes into account the influences of Age, Disability, Religion, Ethnicity, Social status, Sexual orientation, Indigenous heritage, National origin, and Gender. Notably, such an approach acknowledges the rich heterogeneity within cultural groups and discourages inaccurate generalizations, in that within any given ethnic group (or other ADRESSING factor) individuals are represented as varying across all other factors proposed by the ADRESSING paradigm. When clinicians have knowledge and interest in the unique experience of diverse older adults, and apply it to their therapeutic work, treatment and assessment will likely be improved by enhancing rapport and fostering greater understanding of clients' identity and heritage, as well as by improving the assessment of clients' circumstances, needs, and unique strengths (Hays, 1996).

Beyond these general guidelines, culturally sensitive assessment can also be supplemented with standardized instruments that have been translated into different languages and shown to be reliable and valid with diverse groups of older adults. For example, the CES-D is available in English and Spanish and has been shown to be a useful tool for assessing geriatric depression among diverse older adults, although norms and factor structures might vary across different groups (Mui, Burnette, & Chen, 2001). Clinicians can also make use of the GDS, which is also available in 28 different languages at http://www.stanford.edu/~yesavage/GDS.html. Likewise, the commonly administered cognitive screening instrument, the MMSE, is available in 57 different languages at www.minimental.com, and has generally been shown to be a fair test of mental status with older adults of different ethnicities, although some ethnic groups might be more likely to have errors for certain items (Escobar et al., 1986; Espino, Lichtenstein, Palmer, Hazuda, 2001). Other measures have also been devised that specifically tap into culturally relevant factors, such as level of acculturation and cultural mistrust, and could provide a useful supplement to traditional measures of psychopathology (see Sabnani & Ponterotto, 1992, for a review).

Treatment Usage, Preferences, and Outcome

The collective experiences, beliefs, and attitudes of different cultural groups about psychotherapy and other health services undeniably has an impact on the way in which these services are utilized and, in some cases, might influence treatment adherence and outcome. Generally speaking, minority populations tend to underuse mental health services, regardless of age or insurance status (Pingatore, Snowden, Sansone, & Klinkman, 2001; Yeo & Gallagher-Thompson, 2006). After accounting for confounding factors, such as socioeconomic status, older African Americans have also been shown to visit a physician less frequently, which statistically accounts for the higher mortality rates observed among this population compared to Caucasians (Sherkat et al., 2007). Thus, these service utilization patterns are certainly reason for concern and can potentially have fatal implications.

A variety of reasons have been proposed for these disparities among ethnic minority older adults, including lack of financial resources, knowledge deficits, perceived insensitivity of practitioners, and/or fear of unnecessary hospitalization or other intrusive interventions (Alvidrez, Areán, & Stewart, 2005; Mills & Edwards, 2002; Unützer, Katon,

Sullivan, & Miranda, 1999). With regard to knowledge deficits, studies have shown that ethnic minority older adults tend to possess less knowledge about Alzheimer disease and perhaps depression too, which could partially explain why services addressing these issues might be underutilized (Ayalon & Areán, 2004; Zylstra & Steitz, 1999). Another investigation points to an additional contributing factor and showed that African American elders were more likely than Caucasians to believe that doctors do not display enough compassion or respect toward older adults (Jackson & George, 1998). Similarly, Strakowski and colleagues (1995) found that African Americans were in fact more likely to be hospitalized than Caucasians when presenting for emergency psychiatric services, irrespective of insurance coverage or suicidal/homicidal ideation—likely adding to a general sense of mistrust held by many African Americans.

Another culturally influenced factor that has been found to impact the utilization of mental health services among older adults is treatment preference. In particular, African Americans and Hispanics/Latinos have been found to be less likely to view depression as being biologically-based and often indicate a preference for psychotherapy over antidepressant medications (Cooper et al., 2003; Givens, Houston, Van Voorhees, Ford, & Cooper, 2007). Numerous studies have shown that older ethnic minorities are less likely than Caucasians to receive an adequate trial of antidepressants (Blazer, Hybels, Simonsick, & Hanlon, 2000; Fyffe, Sirey, Heo, & Bruce, 2004; Strothers et al., 2005), and it seems likely that this association is at least partially explained by differences in treatment preference. Indirect evidence for such a claim is offered from a handful of studies that have shown that ethnic minorities are just as likely as Caucasians (or in some cases more likely) to receive an adequate trial of psychotherapy, contrasting with the literature on antidepressants (Brown, Schulberg, Sacco, Perel, & Houck, 1999; Harman, Edlund, & Fortney, 2004).

One simple tactic for handling issues of preference would, of course, be to offer the preferred treatment if it is available and has been shown to be effective. However, in some cases, treatment options may be limited, due to financial constraints, insurance, or lack of resources. In addition, the empirical evidence in support of the preferred treatment might be insufficient. Encouragingly, one study suggests that the preferences of older adults for counseling or antidepressants do not appear to predict subsequent satisfaction with treatment or outcome, regardless of whether or not the preferred treatment was received (Gum et al., 2006).

Given the lack of association between treatment preference and outcome, clinicians may opt to provide psychoeducation to older ethnic minority clients to enhance adherence and reduce treatment dropouts when a preferred treatment is not available or indicated. For example, one study found that older African Americans who received a brief psychoeducational meeting attended significantly more psychotherapy sessions compared to those in the control group (Alvidrez et al., 2005). Notably, this psychoeducational intervention involved addressing issues, such as (a) how a medical-model conceptualization of mental illness could reduce stigma, (b) the specific circumstances that would prompt an involuntary hospitalization, (c) the importance of the patients' input and feedback in the process of therapy, and (d) the receptivity of the therapist to discussing issues of spirituality or religion, just to name a few. These preliminary results are encouraging, and provide clinicians with some direction on how issues of treatment preference and nonadherence might be addressed with older ethnic minority clients. Although Alvidrez and colleagues' (2005) psychoeducational intervention was specifically tailored to increase adherence to a psychotherapeutic intervention, it could likely be altered to address concerns about antidepressant or other psychotropic medications. Of course, more work is needed in this area before any definitive claims can be made.

Notwithstanding the importance of attending to cultural differences among older adults and making appropriate treatment modifications, several studies suggest that psychotherapeutic approaches that are effective with older adults generally appear to be applicable to ethnic minority elders as well. For instance, one randomized controlled trial tested the efficacy of a combined antidepressant and/or problem-solving treatment with 1,801 older adults experiencing symptoms of depression, many of whom were African American and Latino (Areán et al., 2005). This study found that those in the intervention condition exhibited significantly less depressive symptoms than controls, regardless of their ethnicity. Notably, minimal efforts were made to tailor this intervention to ethnic minority groups, highlighting the efficacy of this treatment approach even in a virtually unmodified form (Areán et al., 2005). In another randomized clinical trial, the efficacy of a home-based CBT intervention was tested with a sample of 134 diverse rural older adults, predominantly African American, and those who received

CBT exhibited significantly greater improvements in quality of life and reductions in psychological symptoms (Scogin et al., 2007). Taken together, these studies provide preliminary evidence supporting the use of CBT and problem-solving techniques with diverse groups of older adults.

The Resources for Enhancing Alzheimer Caregiver Health (REACH) projects also incorporated a large proportion of ethnic minority groups and in many ways represent a model for culturally sensitive intervention. The first phase of the REACH project included 1,222 caregivers at seven different sites, many of whom were African American or Hispanic/Latino (Schulz et al., 2003). Although the specific treatments varied across each location, most included psychoeducation/skill building interventions, often combined with efforts intended to improve caregiver social support. Despite differences across sites, overall findings demonstrated that active interventions were superior to control conditions at ameliorating symptoms of caregiver burden. Notably, these improvements were most prominent for women and those with lower levels of education. With regard to depressive symptoms, Hispanic caregivers, nonspouses, and individuals with less education exhibited the most treatment-induced gains. These different effects observed for subgroups of REACH I participants underscore the varying needs of diverse caregivers as well as the potential benefit of an intervention that could flexibly attend to the distinctive combinations of problems faced by individual caregivers (Gallagher-Thompson et al., 2003).

In an attempt to better handle these varying needs, a second phase (REACH II) administered a structured, yet customized, multicomponent intervention (mostly based on CBT principles) to 642 Hispanic/Latino, Caucasian, and African American caregivers across five sites (REACH II Investigators, 2006). Depending on a caregiver's level of symptomatology on baseline measures, the actual intervention that a caregiver received could be molded to concentrate on five potential target areas; depression, burden, self-care, social support, and problem behaviors. For most participants, these interventions decreased symptomatology (as assessed by measures that corresponded to each of the five target areas) compared to controls, particularly among Caucasian and Hispanic/Latino caregivers and African American spousal caregivers. In both REACH projects, all interventions and assessment materials were offered in Spanish, bilingual/bicultural staff were hired, and substantial efforts were made to individualize the interventions to make them more amenable to varying cultural views of dementia and caregiving (Gallagher-Thompson et al., 2003).

Future Directions in Geropsychology

Although a wealth of information is now available about psychological problems among diverse groups of older adults and the efficacy of interventions for this population, some gaps in the empirical literature are still in need of further investigation. It is, of course, not feasible to cover all of these topics. However, in this section we will discuss several "high-priority" areas for further research and offer some recommendations for what this future work might look like.

Technology

Recent years have seen vast improvements in elder care through the advancement of a variety of technologies. One of the most prominent advances has been the advent of the Internet and its use with older adults to improve mental and physical health. Indeed, a recent survey of more than 2,000 adults in the United States found that 22% of individuals over the age of 65 reported having access to the Internet and were as enthusiastic about online resources as younger users (Fox, 2004). This trend is encouraging, given the salutary effects of Internet use among older adults. For instance, one study of 293 bereaved older adults found that Internet use predicted lower levels of prolonged grief and post-traumatic stress symptomatology after a loss (Vanderwerker & Prigerson, 2004). Other investigations have revealed that Internet use among older adults is associated with lower levels of social loneliness and higher levels of global psychological well-being (Chen & Persson, 2002; Sum, Mathews, Hughes, & Campbell, 2008).

Given these encouraging trends, clinicians and researchers have increasingly looked to the Internet as a potential modality for intervention. Although there are certainly drawbacks to this mode of delivery (e.g., lack of face-to-fact contact), Internet-administered interventions might overcome many barriers to treatment faced by older adults, such as lack of transportation and/or physical disability. One of the most successful and promising advancements in this area has been the online adaptation of Lorig and colleagues' (2006) self-management program for chronic diseases, such as arthritis, diabetes, and heart disease. The core of this intervention involves enhancing self-efficacy, which is viewed as a crucial mechanism for improving coping, communication, and control in the context of chronic illness (Marks, Allegrante, & Lorig, 2005). Encouragingly, a recent

randomized clinical trial that tested the efficacy of the online adaptation of this brief intervention revealed that those receiving the self-management program had significantly improved health statuses at a 1-year follow-up compared to controls. The proposed mechanism of change for this intervention was also supported by a significant positive association between improved self-efficacy at 6 months and improved health status at 1 year (Lorig, Ritter, Laurent, & Plant, 2006).

With the success of this Internet-administered self-management program for chronic illness, interventionists have sought to adapt it to other contexts, such as caregiving. Specifically, the Powerful Tools for Caregivers program is based on similar self-management concepts and aims to provide caregivers with tools for managing self-care, coping with common stressors, and improving communication. This program is available as an Internet-administered intervention, in addition to an in-person group format, and preliminary evidence from an uncontrolled pilot study suggests that it increases caregivers' level of confidence, reduces depressive symptoms, and improves reactions to care recipients' memory and behavior problems (see www.matherlifeways.com; www.rosalynncarter.org/ptchistory, for additional information).

Randomized clinical trials are beginning to emerge that demonstrate the utility of computer-mediated interventions for caregivers (e.g., Marziali & Donahue, 2006). However, more methodologically sound interventions studies of this kind are needed to investigate the efficacy of these treatments in the context of caregiving, as well as other problems commonly faced by older adults. Notably, improved quality control of Internet resources for older adults is sorely needed, as one investigation of Internet geriatric health information found that much of the publicly available materials are of suboptimal quality with regard to credibility and educational value (Hajjar, Gable, Jenkinson, Kane, & Riley, 2005). Future studies would also do well to consider visual presentation of these Web-based materials and whether or not age-specific modifications (e.g., in layout, organization, or font size) enhance participation or outcome (Echt, 2002).

Beyond the Internet, technologies such as artificial intelligence (AI) and robotics will also likely play a larger role in improving elder care in the future (Marling, 2007; Roy & Pineau, 2007). For instance, repetitive and mechanical tasks, such as medication reminding, walking assistance, and monitoring, can likely be performed with technological assistance, which could free caregivers to focus on more demanding tasks and potentially reduce burnout (Roy & Pineau, 2007). Importantly, assistive technology already appears to be having a substantial impact on elder care, and one study found that the use of assistive technologies dramatically increased in the 1990s, which accounted for the observed declines in personal care needs of older adults during this time (Freedman, Agree, Martin, & Cornman, 2006). Of particular relevance to clinical psychologists, future work that examines the psychological benefits of this kind of assistance in terms of reducing caregiver burnout or improving the quality of life of physically impaired older adults would certainly enhance our knowledge about the total impact of these technological changes.

Post-traumatic Stress

Post-traumatic stress reactions (i.e., characterized by hyperarousal, avoidance, and reexperiencing symptoms following a negative life event) among older adults have increasingly become a focus of concern over recent years. Indeed, older adults may possess unique risk factors for post-traumatic stress, as the transitions associated with growing older (e.g., bereavement, caregiving, and retirement) combined with cognitive, physical, and functional declines could aggravate the stress related to a traumatic event (Bonwick & Morris, 1996; Schnurr, 1996). In addition, in one of the largest studies of Vietnam veterans, 30% of male veterans met criteria for lifetime post-traumatic stress disorder (PTSD), and 15% met criteria for current PTSD (Kulka et al., 1990). Notably, this cohort of veterans are approaching old age, underscoring the need for more work in the area of PTSD and aging.

The best available evidence suggests that older adults have a 6-month prevalence rate of 0.9% for PTSD. However, it appears that a larger subset of older adults (13.1%) experiences elevated levels of post-traumatic stress that do not necessarily meet all of the criteria for a full PTSD diagnosis, emphasizing the importance of not focusing on diagnostic criteria too narrowly when working with this population (Van Zelst, de Beurs, Beekman, Deeg, & van Dyck, 2003). Although more work is clearly still needed, the existing literature also suggests that PTSD in older adults might manifest differently compared to younger or middle-aged adults. For example, compared to younger male veterans with PTSD, older male veterans with PTSD have been found to be less likely to have a comorbid major depression episode or current substance abuse

diagnosis (Frueh et al., 2004). Furthermore, other research has shown that older adults who experience a traumatic life event during later life tend to experience more avoidance, sleep problems, crying spells, and hyperarousal compared to middle-aged or younger adults who experienced similar traumas (Goenjian, Najarian, Pynoos, & Steinberg, 1994; Hagström, 1995).

Studies like these that point to potential differences in the expression of PTSD among older and younger adults highlight the need for age-appropriate assessment instruments. Several investigations of older adult veterans have demonstrated the reliability and validity of some of the more widely used measures of post-traumatic stress, such as the Clinician-Administered PTSD Scale (Hyer, Summers, Boyd, Litaker, & Boudewyns, 1996), the Mississippi Scale for Combat-Related PTSD (Hyer, Walker, Swanson, & Sperr, 1992), and the Impact of Events Scale (Summers, Hyer, Boyd, & Boudewyns, 1996). However, two of these studies recommended using lower cutoff scores for older veterans (Hyer et al., 1992; Summers et al., 1996). Future studies would do well to further examine the sensitivity and specificity of existing PTSD instruments and consider the usefulness of age-specific measurement as more is learned about the unique presentation of PTSD among older adults.

With regard to treatment, it is sobering to note that, to the best of our knowledge, there have been no randomized controlled intervention studies for the treatment of PTSD among older adults. However, several case studies and single-subject investigations have provided researchers with some promising directions for future studies. In particular, these preliminary reports describe the potential usefulness of a variety of approaches, namely anger management therapy, eye movement desensitization reprocessing (Hyer & Woods, 1998), and life-review techniques (Maercker, 2002), as well as exposure-based treatments (Russo, Hersen, & Van Hasselt, 2001). Nevertheless, randomized controlled trials that test the efficacy of these interventions for the treatment of PTSD in later life are badly needed to establish the relative effectiveness of different treatment approaches with this population.

Marital and Family Therapy

In many ways, marital and family therapy represents an ideal framework for approaching older adults, in that the family is often the most important social context for these individuals (Qualls, 1999, 2000). Although it is not without its drawbacks (e.g., Qualls,

1996; potentially increasing concerns about stigma and privacy), a family-focused approach makes sense, given that multiple family members of different generations are often impacted by the life transitions faced by an older adult (Doka, 1997; Kriegsman, Penninx, & van Eijk, 1994; Ronch & Crispi, 1997). Indeed, transitions such as illness, disability, or retirement can disrupt traditional family and martial roles, often shifting the balance of responsibility and independence (Qualls, 1993).

In spite of the applicability of such an approach, only 8.9% of marriage and family therapy (MFT) programs have reported incorporating topics relevant to gerontology (Barber & Lyness, 2001). Likewise, as of 1996, only 2.3% of conference sessions and 3.2% of articles in the MFT literature were found to focus on issues specific to aging. This content analysis of the MFT literature also revealed a dearth of empirical studies and theoretical papers related to retirement, widowhood, and sexual dysfunction in later life (Van Amburg, Barber, & Zimmerman, 1996).

Although this disparity in coverage of late-life topics in MFT training programs and scholarly works is likely due to a number of factors, one possible explanation might stem from biases of practitioners about their own self-efficacy in changing such longstanding and ingrained family patterns. In particular, one survey of doctors', nurses', and social workers' attitudes toward family therapy for older adults revealed that, although these professionals were open to the possibility of family therapy with this population, many had concerns about the potential for change in older families (Gilleard, Lieberman, & Peeler, 1992).

Despite these possible concerns, there is growing awareness that enhanced communication and functioning within the family of an older adult can have a reciprocal effect. Notably, it seems that improved relationships positively impact the physical and mental health status of elderly clients dealing with difficult life transitions and, in turn, often also lead to better adjustment of the family as a whole— further supporting the potential utility of family therapy for this population. In particular, one recent study found that higher levels of caregiver burden experienced by a spouse or adult child negatively impacted an older adult's response to antidepressant treatment for geriatric depression (Martire et al., 2008). Other investigations have also shown that a high degree of support from family and friends can have a profound impact on health outcomes and improve adjustment to disability and chronic illness (McIlvane & Reinhardt, 2001; Seeman, 2000).

It appears that the effects of positive relationships within the family work both ways and can also serve to buffer the impact of a difficult late-life transition on the family unit. For example, in their review of the impact of chronic illness on elderly patients' families, Kriegsman and colleagues (1994) found that these medical problems generally had a significant negative impact on both spouses and adult children. However, based on their review of this literature, it was concluded that the most salient factor affecting the health of the family members appeared to be the strength of the patient's marriage and the degree of social support the patient was able to provide to his or her spouse (Kriegsman et al., 1994).

Considering the impact of familial relationships in the context of older adults' medical and mental health problems, future studies would do well to focus on the potential benefits of marital and family therapy for older adults. Given the longstanding relationships within families of older adults, core family therapy strategies and techniques, like genograms, transmission of family histories, and exploration of cyclical patterns of interacting would likely have great relevance for this population (Tisher & Dean, 2000). Theorists and practitioners have also proposed other techniques, such as narrative therapy and expressive arts (Caldwell, 2005), life validation, and life review (Hargrave & Anderson, 1997), as well as solution-focused and behavioral interventions (Bonjean, 1997).

Despite the promise of many of these treatments, the present empirical evidence does not appear to be strong enough to support any of these interventions as an EBT. With regard to randomized clinical trials, several multicomponent caregiver stress interventions have successfully implemented a family therapy module, offering some preliminary support for this approach (Eisdorfer et al., 2003; Mittelman et al., 1995; Schulz et al., 2003). However, more studies are needed to shed light on the unique impact of family therapy and provide information about the relative efficacy of different approaches.

Conclusion

We believe this is an exciting time to be working in the area of clinical geropsychology. Medical advances and increased knowledge about healthy life practices (e.g., diet, exercise, emotional health) have increased the adult life span and, as a result, older adults are making up an increasingly larger proportion of the worldwide population. As clinical psychologists, we are in a unique position to improve the lives of these individuals, and a wealth of resources is now available to aid clinicians in conducting empirically based practice with older adults. In this chapter, we relied on the best available evidence to provide both general and specific recommendations for handling a variety of problems often encountered in later life, including depression, anxiety, substance abuse, insomnia, dementia, caregiver stress, and prolonged grief. Although more work is, of course, still needed—particularly in the areas of cultural diversity, technology, post-traumatic stress, and family therapy—we have offered a preliminary roadmap for approaching older adults in a psychotherapeutic context and hopefully have demystified some of the idiosyncrasies of working with this population.

References

Adams W. L. (1999). Alcohol and the health of aging men. *Medical Clinics of North America, 83,* 1195–1211.

Adams, W. L., Barry, K. L., & Fleming, M. F. (1996). Screening for problem drinking in older primary care patients. *JAMA: Journal of the American Medical Association, 276*(24), 1964–1967.

Alexopoulos, G. S., Abrams, R. C., Young, R. C., & Shamoian, C. A. (1988). Cornell Scale for Depression in Dementia. *Biological Psychiatry, 23*(3), 271–284.

Alvidrez, J., Areán, P. A., & Stewart, A. L. (2005). Psychoeducation to increase psychotherapy entry for older African-Americans. *American Journal of Geriatric Psychiatry, 13*(7), 554–561.

American Psychological Association. (2004). Guidelines for psychological practice with older adults. *American Psychologist, 59,* 236–260.

Ancoli-Israel, S., Cole, R., Alessi, C., Chambers, M., Moorcroft, W., & Pollak, C. P. (2003). The role of actigraphy in the study of sleep and circadian rhythms. *Sleep: Journal of Sleep and Sleep Disorders Research, 26*(3), 342–392.

Ancoli-Israel, S., Pat-Horenczyk, R., & Martin, J. (2001). Sleep disorders. In A. S. Bellack, M. Hersen (Series Eds.), & B. Edelstein (Vol. Ed.), *Comprehensive clinical psychology: Clinical geropsychology* (Vol. 7, pp. 307–326). Oxford, England: Elsevier Science, Ltd.

Anthony, J. C., & Helzer, J. E. (1991). Syndromes of drug abuse and dependence. In L. N. Robins, & D. A. Regier (Eds.), *Psychiatric disorders in America: The Epidemiologic Catchment Area Study.* New York: Free Press.

Areán, P. A., Gum, A., McCulloch, C. E., Bostrom, A., Gallagher-Thompson, D., & Thompson, L. (2005). Treatment of depression in low-income older adults. *Psychology and Aging. Special Issue: Emotion-Cognition Interactions and the Aging Mind, 20*(4), 601–609.

Ayalon, L., & Areán, P. A. (2004). Knowledge of Alzheimer's disease in four ethnic groups of older adults. *International Journal of Geriatric Psychiatry, 19*(1), 51–57.

Ayers, C. R., Sorrell, J. T., Thorp, S. R., & Wetherell, J. L. (2007). Evidence-based psychological treatments for late-life anxiety. *Psychology and Aging, 22*(1), 8–17.

Azocar, F., Areán, P., Miranda, J., & Muñoz, R. F. (2001). Differential item functioning in a Spanish translation of the Beck Depression Inventory. *Journal of Clinical Psychology, 57*(3), 355–365.

Babor, T. F., de la Fuenta, J. R., Saunders, J., & Grant, M. (1992). *AUDIT: The Alcohol Use Disorders Identification Test: Guidelines for its use in primary health care.* Geneva, Switzerland: World Health Organization.

Barber, C. E., & Lyness, K. P. (2001). Gerontology training in marriage and family therapy accredited training program: Prevalence of aging issues and later-life family concerns. *Gerontology & Geriatrics Education, 22*(1), 1–12.

Beck, A. T., Epstein, N., Brown, G., & Steer, R. A. (1988). An inventory for measuring clinical anxiety: Psychometric properties. *Journal of Consulting and Clinical Psychology, 56*(6), 893–897.

Beck, A. T., Steer, R. A., & Brown, G. K. (1996). *Beck Depression Inventory – II.* San Antonio: The Psychological Corporation.

Bengtson, V., Biblarz, T., Clarke, E., Giarusso, R., Robers, R., Richlin-Klonsky, J., & Silverstein, M. (2000). Intergenerational relationships and aging: Families, cohorts, and social change. In J. M. Clair, & R. Allman (Eds.), *The gerontological prism: Developing interdisciplinary bridges.* New York: Baywood.

Bharani, N., & Snowden, M. (2005). Evidence-based interventions for nursing home residents with dementia-related behavioral symptoms. *Psychiatric Clinics of North America. Special Issue: Evidence-Based Geriatric Psychiatry, 28*(4), 985–1005.

Birren, J. E., & Deutchman, D. E. (1991). *Guiding autobiography groups for older adults.* Baltimore, MD: Johns Hopkins University Press.

Blazer, D. G. (2003). Depression in late life: Review and commentary. *Journals of Gerontology: Series A: Biological Sciences and Medical Sciences, 58*(3), 249–265.

Blazer, D. G., Hybels, C. F., Simonsick, E. M., & Hanlon, J. T. (2000). Marked differences in antidepressant use by race in an elderly community sample: 1986–1996. *American Journal of Psychiatry, 157*(7), 1089–1094.

Blazer, D. G., Landerman, L. R., Hays, J. C., Simonsick, E. M., & Saunders, W. B. (1998). Symptoms of depression among community-dwelling elderly African-American and white older adults. *Psychological Medicine, 28*(6), 1311–1320.

Blow, F. C., Brower, K. J., Schulenberg, J. E., Demo-Dananberg, L. M., Young, J. P., & Beresford, T. P. (1992). The Michigan Alcoholism Screening Test – Geriatric Version (MAST-G): A new elderly-specific screening instrument. *Alcoholism: Clinical and Experimental Research, 16,* 372.

Boelen, P. A., de Keijser, J., van den Hout, Marcel A., & van den Bout, J. (2007). Treatment of complicated grief: A comparison between cognitive-behavioral therapy and supportive counseling. *Journal of Consulting and Clinical Psychology, 75*(2), 277–284.

Bonanno, G. A., Wortman, C. B., Lehman, D. R., Tweed, R. G., Haring, M., Sonnega, J., et al. (2002). Resilience to loss and chronic grief: A prospective study from preloss to 18-months postloss. *Journal of Personality and Social Psychology, 83*(5), 1150–1164.

Bonjean, M. J. (Ed.). (1997). Solution-focused brief therapy with aging families. In T. D. Hargrave, & S. M. Hanna (Eds.), *The aging family: New visions in theory, practice, and reality* (pp. 81–100). Philadelphia, PA: Brunner/Mazel.

Bonwick, R. J., & Morris, P. L. P. (1996). Post-traumatic stress disorder in elderly war veterans. *International Journal of Geriatric Psychiatry, 11*(12), 1071–1076.

Bootzin, R. (1977). Effects of self-control procedures for insomnia. In R. B. Stuart (Ed.), *Behavioral self-management: Strategies, techniques and outcomes* (pp. 176–195). New York: Brunner/Mazel.

Bootzin, R. R., & Epstein, D. R. (2000). *Stimulus control.* Thousand Oaks, CA: Sage Publications, Inc.

Bourgeois, M. S., Schulz, R., Burgio, L. D., & Beach, S. (2002). Skills training for spouses of patients with Alzheimer's disease: Outcomes of an intervention study. *Journal of Clinical Geropsychology, 8*(1), 53–73.

Brown, C., Schulberg, H. C., Sacco, D., Perel, J. M., & Houck, P. R. (1999). Effectiveness of treatments for major depression in primary medical care practice: A post hoc analysis of outcomes for African-American and white patients. *Journal of Affective Disorders, 53*(2), 185–192.

Bruce, M. L., McAvay, G. J., Raue, P. J., Brown, E. L., Meyers, B. S., Keohane, D. J., et al. (2002). Major depression in elderly home health care patients. *American Journal of Psychiatry, 159*(8), 1367–1374.

Butcher, J. N., Aldwin, C. M., Levenson, M. R., Ben-Porath, Y. S., Spiro, A., & Bossé, R. (1991). Personality and aging: A study of the MMPI-2 among older men. *Psychology and Aging, 6*(3), 361–370.

Buysse, D. J., Reynolds, C. F., Monk, T. H., & Berman, S. R. (1989). The Pittsburgh Sleep Quality Index: A new instrument for psychiatric practice and research. *Psychiatry Research, 28*(2), 193–213.

Caldwell, R. L. (2005). At the confluence of memory and meaning— life review with older adults and families: Using narrative therapy and the expressive arts to re-member and re-author stories of resilience. *The Family Journal, 13*(2), 172–175.

Callahan, C. M., & Tierney, W. M. (1995). Health services use and mortality among older primary care patients with alcoholism. *Journal of Geriatric Psychiatry and Neurology, 13,* 106–114.

Center for Substance Abuse Treatment. (2006). *Alcohol use among older adults: Pocket screening instruments for health care and social service providers.* Retrieved July 27, 2008, from http://kap.samhsa.gov/products/brochures/pdfs/Pocket_2.pdf

Chen, Y., & Persson, A. (2002). Internet use among young and older adults: Relation to psychological well-being. *Educational Gerontology, 28*(9), 731–744.

Cheung, F. K. (1980). The mental health status of Asian Americans. *Clinical Psychologist, 34*(1), 23–24.

Chiriboga, D. A., Jang, Y., Banks, S., & Kim, G. (2007). Acculturation and its effect on depressive symptom structure in a sample of Mexican-American elders. *Hispanic Journal of Behavioral Sciences, 29*(1), 83–100.

Cohen-Mansfield, J., & Billig, N. (1986). Agitated behaviors in the elderly: I. A conceptual review. *Journal of the American Geriatrics Society, 34*(10), 711–721.

Considine, N. S., Magai, C., & Conway, F. (2004). Predicting ethnic variation in adaptation to later life: Styles of socioemotional functioning and constrained heterotypy. *Journal of Cross-Cultural Gerontology, 19*(2), 97–131.

Coon, D. W., Thompson, L., Steffen, A., Sorocco, K., & Gallagher-Thompson, D. (2003). Anger and depression management: Psychoeducational skill training interventions for women caregivers of a relative with dementia. *The Gerontologist, 43*(5), 678–689.

Cooper, L. A., Gonzales, J. J., Gallo, J. J., Rost, K. M., Meredith, L. S., Rubenstein, L. V., et al. (2003). The acceptability of treatment for depression among African-American, Hispanic, and white primary care patients. *Medical Care, 41*(4), 479–489.

Copeland, L. A., Blow, F. C., & Barry, K. L. (2003). Health care utilization by older alcohol-using veterans: Effects of a brief intervention to reduce at-risk drinking. *Health Education & Behavior, 30*(3), 305–321.

Cuijpers, P. (2005). Depressive disorders in caregivers of dementia patients: A systematic review. *Aging & Mental Health, 9*(4), 325–330.

Cuijpers, P., van Straten, A., & Smit, F. (2006). Psychological treatment of late-life depression: A meta-analysis of randomized controlled trials. *International Journal of Geriatric Psychiatry, 21*(12), 1139–1149.

Currier, J. M., Neimeyer, R. A., & Berman, J. (2008). The effectiveness of psychotherapeutic interventions for bereaved individuals: A comprehensive quantitative review. *Psychological Bulletin, 134,* 648–661.

Davis, M. C., Zautra, A. J., Johnson, L. M., Murray, K. E., & Okvat, H. A. (2007). *Psychosocial stress, emotion regulation, and resilience among older adults.* New York, NY: Guilford Press.

Desai, M., Pratt, L. A., Lentzner, H., & Robinson, K. N. (2001). Trends in vision and hearing among older Americans. *Aging Trends, 2,* 1–8.

DeVries, H. M. (2005). Clinical geropsychology training in generalist doctoral programs. *Gerontology & Geriatrics Education. Special Issue: Clinical Geropsychology Training, 25*(4), 5–20.

DiNardo, P. A., Brown, T. A., & Barlow, D. H. (1994). *Anxiety disorders interview schedule for DSM-IV (ADIS-IV).* New York: Oxford University Press.

Doka, K. J. (Ed.). (1997). The effect of parental illness and loss on adult children. In I. Deitch, & C. W. Howell (Eds.), *Counseling the aging and their families. The family psychology and counseling series* (pp. 147–155). Alexandria, VA: American Counseling Association.

Dupree, L. W., Schonfeld, L., Dearborn-Harshman, K. O., & Lynn, N. (2008). A relapse prevention model for older alcohol abusers. In D. Gallagher-Thompson, A. M. Steffen, & L. W. Thompson (Eds.), *Handbook of behavioral and cognitive therapies with older adults* (pp. 61–75). New York: Springer.

Edelstein, B. A., Woodhead, E. L., Segal, D. L., Heisel, M. J., Bower, E. H., Lowery, A. J., et al. (2008). Older adult psychological assessment: Current instrument status and related considerations. *Clinical Gerontologist, 31,* 1–35.

Echt, K. V. (Ed.). (2002). Designing web-based health information for older adults: Visual considerations and design directives. In R. W. Morrell (Ed.), *Older adults, health information, and the World Wide Web* (pp. 61–87). Mahwah, NJ: Lawrence Erlbaum Associates Publishers.

Eisdorfer, C., Czaja, S. J., Loewenstein, D. A., Rubert, M. P., Argüelles, S., Mitrani, V. B., et al. (2003). The effect of a family therapy and technology-based intervention on caregiver depression. *The Gerontologist, 43*(4), 521–531.

Engels, G. I., & Vermey, M. (1997). Efficacy of nonmedical treatments of depression in elders: A quantitative analysis. *Journal of Clinical Geropsychology, 3*(1), 17–35.

Escobar, J. I. (1986). Use of the Mini-Mental State Examination (MMSE) in a community population of mixed ethnicity: Cultural and linguistic artifacts. *Journal of Nervous and Mental Disease, 174*(10), 607–614.

Espino, D. V., Lichtenstein, M. J., Palmer, R. F., & Hazuda, H. P. (2001). Ethnic differences in Mini-Mental State Examination (MMSE) scores: Where you live makes a difference. *Journal of the American Geriatrics Society, 49*(5), 538–548.

Evans, I. A., Funkenstein, H., Albert, M. S., Scherr, P. A., Cook, N. R., Chown, M. J., et al. (1989). Prevalence of Alzheimer's disease in a community population of older persons: Higher than previously reported. *JAMA: Journal of the American Medical Association 262*, 2551–2556.

Fiske, A., O'Riley, A. A., & Widoe, R. K. (2008). Physical health and suicide in late life: An evaluative review. *Clinical Gerontologist, 31*, 31–50.

Fleming, M. F., Manwell, L. B., Barry, K. L., Adams, W., & Stauffacher, E. A. (1999). Brief physician advice for alcohol problems in older adults: A randomized community-based trial. *The Journal of Family Practice, 48*(5), 378–384.

Flint, A. J. (1994). Epidemiology and comorbidity of anxiety disorders in the elderly. *American Journal of Psychiatry, 151*(5), 640–649.

Florio, E. R., Hendryx, M. S., Jensen, J. E., & Rockwood, T. H. (1997). A comparison of suicidal and nonsuicidal elders referred to a community mental health center program. *Suicide and Life-Threatening Behavior, 27*(2), 182–193.

Floyd, M., & Scogin, F. (1998). Cognitive-behavior therapy for older adults: How does it work? *Psychotherapy: Theory, Research, Practice, Training. Special Issue: Psychotherapy and Older Adults, 35*(4), 459–463.

Foley, D. J., Monjan, A. A., Brown, S. L., & Simonsick, E. M. (1995). Sleep complaints among elderly persons: An epidemiologic study of three communities. *Sleep: Journal of Sleep Research & Sleep Medicine, 18*(6), 425–432.

Folstein, M. F., Folstein, S. E., & McHugh, P. R. (1975). Mini-mental state: A practical method for grading the cognitive state of patients for the clinician. *Journal of Psychiatric Research, 12*(3), 189–198.

Foos, P. W., Clark, M. C., & Terrell, D. F. (2006). Adult age, gender, and race group differences in images of aging. *Journal of Genetic Psychology, 167*(3), 309–325.

Fox, S. (2004). *Older Americans and the Internet.* Washington, DC: Pew Internet & American Life Project.

Freedman, V. A., Agree, E. M., Martin, L. G., & Cornman, J. C. (2006). Trends in the use of assistive technology and personal care for late-life disability, 1992–2001. *The Gerontologist, 46*(1), 124–127.

Frueh, B. C., Elhai, J. D., Hamner, M. B., Magruder, K. M., Sauvageot, J. A., & Mintzer, J. (2004). Elderly veterans with combat-related posttraumatic stress disorder in specialty care. *Journal of Nervous and Mental Disease, 192*(1), 75–79.

Fyffe, D. C., Sirey, J. A., Heo, M., & Bruce, M. L. (2004). Late-life depression among black and white elderly homecare patients. *American Journal of Geriatric Psychiatry, 12*(5), 531–535.

Galasko, D., Klauber, M. R., Hofstetter, C. R., & Salmon, D. P. (1990). The Mini-Mental State Examination in the early diagnosis of Alzheimer's disease. *Archives of Neurology, 47*(1), 49–52.

Gallagher, D., Rose, J., Rivera, P., Lovett, S., & Thompson, L. W. (1989). Prevalence of depression in family caregivers. *The Gerontologist, 29*(4), 449–456.

Gallagher-Thompson, D., Steffen, A. M., & Thompson, L. W. (2008). *Handbook of behavioral and cognitive therapies with older adults.* New York: Springer.

Gallagher-Thompson, D., & Coon, D. W. (2007). Evidence-based psychological treatments for distress in family caregivers of older adults. *Psychology and Aging, 22*(1), 37–51.

Gallagher-Thompson, D., Haley, W., Guy, D., Rupert, M., Argüelles, T., Zeiss, L. M., et al. (2003). Tailoring psychological interventions for ethnically diverse dementia caregivers. *Clinical Psychology: Science and Practice, 10*(4), 423–438.

Gallo, J. J., Anthony, J. C., & Muthén, B. O. (1994). Age differences in the symptoms of depression: A latent trait analysis. *Journals of Gerontology, 49*(6), P251-P264.

Gallo, J. J., Cooper-Patrick, L., & Lesikar, S. (1998). Depressive symptoms of whites and African-Americans aged 60 years and older. *Journals of Gerontology: Series B: Psychological Sciences and Social Sciences, 53*(5), P277–P286.

Gatz, M., Fiske, A., Fox, L. S., Kaskie, B., Kasl-Godley, J. E., McCallum, T. J., et al. (1998). Empirically validated psychological treatments for older adults. *Journal of Mental Health and Aging, 4*(1), 9–46.

Gilleard, C., Lieberman, S., & Peeler, R. (1992). Family therapy for older adults: A survey of professionals' attitudes. *Journal of Family Therapy, 14*(4), 413–422.

Givens, J. L., Houston, T. K., Van Voorhees, B. W., Ford, D. E., & Cooper, L. A. (2007). Ethnicity and preferences for depression treatment. *General Hospital Psychiatry, 29*(3), 182–191.

Goenjian, A. K., Najarian, L. M., Pynoos, R. S., & Steinberg, A. M. (1994). Posttraumatic stress disorder in elderly and younger adults after the 1988 earthquake in Armenia. *American Journal of Psychiatry, 151*(6), 895–901.

Gomberg, E. S. L. (1992). Medication problems and drug abuse. In F. J. Turner (Ed.), *Mental health and the elderly* (pp. 355–374). New York: Free Press.

Gottfries, C. G. (1998). Is there a difference between elderly and younger patients with regard to the symptomatology and aetiology of depression? *International Clinical Psychopharmacology, 13*(Suppl 5), S13–S18.

Grabbe, L., Demi, A., Camann, M. A., et al. (1997). The health status of elderly persons in the last year of life: A comparison of deaths by suicide, injury, and natural causes. *American Journal of Public Health, 87*, 434–437.

Grant, B. F., Dawson, D. A., Stinson, F. S., et al. (2004). The 12-month prevalence and trends in DSM-IV alcohol abuse and dependence: United States, 1991–1992 and 2001–2002. *Drug and Alcohol Dependence, 74*, 223–234.

Gum, A. M., Areán, P. A., Hunkeler, E., Tang, L., Katon, W., Hitchcock, P., et al. (2006). Depression treatment preferences in older primary care patients. *The Gerontologist, 46*(1), 14–22.

Hagström, R. (1995). The acute psychological impact on survivors following a train accident. *Journal of Traumatic Stress, 8*(3), 391–402.

Hajjar, I., Gable, S. A., Jenkinson, V. P., Kane, L. T., & Riley, R. A. (2005). Quality of Internet geriatric health information: The Geriatric Web project. *Journal of the American Geriatrics Society, 53*(5), 885–890.

Hall, G., & Buckwalter, K. (1987). Progressively lowered stress threshold: A conceptual model for care of adults with Alzheimer's disease. *Archives of Psychiatric Nursing, 1*, 399–406.

Hall, R. C. W., Platt, D. E., & Hall, R. C. W. (1999). Suicide risk assessment: A review of risk factors for suicide in 100 patients who made severe suicide attempts: Evaluation of suicide risk in a time of managed care. *Psychosomatics: Journal of Consultation Liaison Psychiatry, 40*(1), 18–27.

Hargrave, T. D., & Anderson, W. T. (Eds.). (1997). Finishing well: A contextual family therapy approach to the aging family. In T. D. Hargrave, & S. M. Hanna (Eds.), *The aging family: New visions in theory, practice, and reality* (pp. 61–80). Philadelphia, PA: Brunner/Mazel.

Harman, J. S., Edlund, M., & Fortney, J. C. (2004). Disparities in the adequacy of depression treatment in the United States. *Psychiatric Services, 55*(12), 1379–1385.

Harris, Y., & Cooper, J. K. (2006). Depressive symptoms in older people predict nursing home admission. *Journal of the American Geriatrics Society, 54*(4), 593–597.

Hays, J. C., Gold, D. T., & Peiper, C. F. (1997). Sibling bereavement in late life. *Omega: Journal of Death and Dying, 35*(1), 25–42.

Hays, P. A. (1996). Culturally responsive assessment with diverse older clients. *Professional Psychology: Research and Practice, 27*(2), 188–193.

Heath, J. M., Grant, W. D., Kamps, C. A., & Margolin, E. G. (1991). Outpatient geriatric assessment: Associations between referral sources and assessment findings. *Journal of the American Geriatrics Society, 39*(3), 267–272.

Heisel, M. J., & Flett, G. L. (2006). The development and initial validation of the Geriatric Suicide Ideation Scale. American Journal of Geriatric Psychiatry. *Special Issue: Theme: Progress in Identifying Risk and Protective Factors in Older Suicidal Adults, 14*(9), 742–751.

Heisel, M. J., & Flett, G. L. (2008). Psychological resilience to suicide ideation among older adults. *Clinical Gerontologist, 31*, 51–70.

Hirschfeld, R. M. A., & Russell, J. M. (1997). Current concepts: Assessment and treatment of suicidal patients. *New England Journal of Medicine, 337*(13), 910–915.

Horwitz, A. V. (2002). *Creating mental illness.* Chicago, IL: University of Chicago Press.

Huang, H., Shyu, Y. L., Chen, M., Chen, S., & Lin, L. (2003). A pilot study on a home-based caregiver training program for improving caregiver self-efficacy and decreasing the behavioral problems of leaders with dementia in Taiwan. *International Journal of Geriatric Psychiatry, 18*(4), 337–345.

Hultsch, D. E., & Dixon, R. A. (1990). Learning and memory in aging. In J. E. Birren, & K. W. Schaie (Eds.), *Handbook of the psychology of aging,* 3rd ed. (pp. 259–274). San Diego, CA: Academic Press.

Hyer, L., Summers, M. N., Boyd, S., & Litaker, M. (1996). Assessment of older combat veterans with the clinician-administered PTSD scale. *Journal of Traumatic Stress, 9*(3), 587–594.

Hyer, L., Walker, C., Swanson, G., & Sperr, S. (1992). Validation of PTSD measures for older combat veterans. *Journal of Clinical Psychology, 48*(5), 579–588.

Hyer, L., & Woods, M. G. (Eds.). (1998). *Phenomenology and treatment of trauma in later life.* In V. M. Follette, J. I. Ruzek, & F. R. Abueg (Eds.), *Cognitive-behavioral therapies for trauma* (pp. 383–414). New York, NY: Guilford Press.

Jackson, P. B., & George, L. K. (1998). Racial differences in satisfaction with physicians: A study of older adults. *Research on Aging, 20*(3), 298–316.

Jacobson, S. A., Pies, R. W., & Katz, I. R. (2007). *Clinical manual of geriatric psychopharmacology.* Washington, DC: American Psychiatric Publishing, Inc.

Jang, Y., Borenstein, A. R., Chiriboga, D. A., & Mortimer, J. A. (2005). Depressive symptoms among African-American and white older adults. *Journals of Gerontology: Series B: Psychological Sciences and Social Sciences, 60*(6), P313–P319.

Jeste, D. V., Blazer, D. G., & First, M. (2005). Aging-related diagnostic variations: Need for diagnostic criteria appropriate for elderly psychiatric patients. *Biological Psychiatry, 58*(4), 265–271.

Kales, H. C., Neighbors, H. W., Blow, F. C., Taylor, K. K. K., Gillon, L., Welsh, D. E., et al. (2005). Race, gender, and psychiatrists' diagnosis and treatment of major depression among elderly patients. *Psychiatric Services, 56*(6), 721–728.

Kales, H. C., Neighbors, H. W., Valenstein, M., Blow, F. C., McCarthy, J. F., Ignacio, R. V., et al. (2005). Effect of race and sex on primary care physicians' diagnosis and treatment of late-life depression. *Journal of the American Geriatrics Society, 53*(5), 777–784.

Karel, M. J., & Moye, J. (2002). Assessing depression in medically ill elderly male veterans: Item-scale properties across and within racial groups. *Journal of Mental Health and Aging, 8*(2), 121–138.

Kashner, T. M., Rodell, D. E., Ogden, S. R., & Guggenheim, F. G. (1992). Outcomes and costs of two VA inpatient treatment programs for older alcoholic patients. *Hospital & Community Psychiatry, 43*(10), 985–989.

Kaszniak, A. W., & Christenson, G. D. (1994). *Differential diagnosis of dementia and depression.* Washington, DC: American Psychological Association.

Kiernan, R. J., Mueller, J., Langston, J. W., & Van Dyke, C. (1987). The Neurobehavioral Cognitive Status Examination: A brief but quantitative approach to cognitive assessment. *Annals of Internal Medicine, 107,* 481–485.

Kinsella, K., & Velkoff, V. (2001). *An Aging World: 2001.* Washington, DC: U.S Government Printing Office.

Kleinman, A. (1982). Neurasthenia and depression: A study of somatization and culture in China. *Culture, Medicine and Psychiatry, 6*(2), 117–190.

Knight, B. G., & McCallum, T. J. (1998). Adapting psychotherapeutic practice for older clients: Implications of the contextual, cohort-based, maturity, specific challenge model. *Professional Psychology: Research and Practice, 29*(1), 15–22.

Kofoed, L. L., Tolson, R. L., Atkinson, R. M., & Toth, R. L. (1987). Treatment compliance of older alcoholics: An elder-specific approach is superior to "mainstreaming." *Journal of Studies on Alcohol, 48*(1), 47–51.

Kriegsman, D. M. W., Penninx, B. W. J. H., & van Eijk, J. T. M. (1994). Chronic disease in the elderly and its impact on the family: A review of the literature. *Family Systems Medicine, 12*(3), 249–267.

Kukull, W. A., Higdon, R., Bowen, J. D., McCormick, W. C., Teri, L., Schellenberg, G. D., et al. (2002). Dementia and Alzheimer disease incidence: A prospective cohort study. *Archives of Neurology, 59*(11), 1737–1746.

Kulka, R. A., Schlenger, W. E., Fairbank, J. A., Hough, R. L., Jordan, B. K., Marmar, C. R., et al. (1990). *Trauma and the Vietnam war generation: Report of findings from the national Vietnam veterans readjustment study.* Philadelphia, PA: Brunner/Mazel.

Kyomen, H. H., & Whitfield, T. H. (2008). Agitation in older adults. *Psychiatric Times, 25.* Retrieved on August 28, 2008, from http://www.psychiatrictimes.com/display/article/10168/1166790

La Rue, A. (1992). *Aging and neuropsychological assessment.* New York, NY: Plenum Press.

La Rue, A., & Watson, J. (1998). Psychological assessment of older adults. *Professional Psychology: Research and Practice, 29*(1), 5–14.

Lai, D. W. (2004). Impact of culture on depressive symptoms of elderly Chinese immigrants. *The Canadian Journal of Psychiatry / La Revue Canadienne De Psychiatrie, 49*(12), 820–827.

Laidlaw, K. (2001). An empirical review of cognitive therapy for late life depression: Does research evidence suggest adaptations are necessary for cognitive therapy with older adults? *Clinical Psychology and Psychotherapy, 8,* 1–14.

Laidlaw, K., Thompson, L. W., Dick-Siskin, L., & Gallagher-Thompson, D. (2003). *Cognitive behaviour therapy with older people.* New York, NY: John Wiley & Sons, Ltd.

Laidlaw, K., Thompson, L. W., & Gallagher-Thompson, D. (2004). Comprehensive conceptualization of cognitive behaviour therapy for late life depression. *Behavioural and Cognitive Psychotherapy, 32,* 389–399.

Lebowitz, B. D., Pearson, J. L., Schneider, L. S., Reynolds, C. F., Alexopoulos, G. S., Bruce, M. L., et al. (1997). Diagnosis and treatment of depression in late life: Consensus statement update. *JAMA: Journal of the American Medical Association, 278*(14), 1186–1190.

Levy, B. R., Conway, K., Brommelhoff, J., & Merikengas, K. (2003). Intergenerational differences in the reporting of elders' anxiety. *Journal of Mental Health and Aging, 9*(4), 233–241.

Lewinsohn, P. M. (1974). *A behavioral approach to depression.* Oxford, England: John Wiley & Sons.

Lichstein, K. L., Durrence, H. H., Riedel, B. W., Taylor, D. J., & Bush, A. J. (2004). *Epidemiology of sleep: Age, gender, and ethnicity.* Mahwah, NJ: Lawrence Erlbaum Associates Publishers.

Light, L. L. (1990). *Interactions between memory and language in old age.* San Diego, CA: Academic Press.

Lin, K., & Cheung, F. (1999). Mental health issues for Asian-Americans. *Psychiatric Services, 50*(6), 774–780.

Logsdon, R. G., McCurry, S. M., & Teri, L. (2007). Evidence-based psychological treatments for disruptive behaviors in individuals with dementia. *Psychology and Aging, 22*(1), 28–36.

Lorig, K. R., Ritter, P. L., Laurent, D. D., & Plant, K. (2006). Internet-based chronic disease self-management: A randomized trial. *Medical Care, 44,* 964–971.

Mackinnon, A., McCallum, J., Andrews, G., & Anderson, I. (1998). The center for epidemiological studies depression scale in older community samples in Indonesia, North Korea, Myanmar, Sri Lanka, and Thailand. *Journals of Gerontology: Series B: Psychological Sciences and Social Sciences, 53*(6), P343–P352.

Maercker, A. (2002). Life-review technique in the treatment of PTSD in elderly patients: Rationale and three single case studies. *Journal of Clinical Geropsychology. Special Issue: Traumatic Exposure and PTSD in Older Adults, 8*(3), 239–249.

Magaziner, J., German, P., Zimmerman, S. I., Hebel, J. R., Burton, L., Gruber-Baldini, A. L., et al. (2000). The prevalence of dementia in a statewide sample of new nursing home admissions aged 65 and older: Diagnosis by expert panel. *The Gerontologist, 40*(6), 663–672.

Manber, R., & Kuo, T. F. (2002). Cognitive-behavioral therapies for insomnia. In T. L. Lee-Chiong, M. J. Sateia, & M. A. Carskadon (Eds.), *Sleep medicine* (pp. 177–185). Philadelphia: Hanley & Belfus.

Marks, R., Allegrante, J. P., & Lorig, K. (2005). A review and synthesis of research evidence for self-efficacy-enhancing interventions for reducing chronic disability: Implications for health education practice: Part I. *Health Promotion Practice, 6*(1), 37–43.

Marling, C. R. (2007). Intelligent system technology for enhancing the quality of life. In G. Lesnoff-Caravaglia (Ed.), *Gerontechnology: Growing old in a technological society* (pp. 182–205). Springfield, IL: Charles C. Thomas Publisher.

Martire, L. M., Schulz, R., Reynolds, C. F., III, Morse, J. Q., Butters, M. A., & Hinrichsen, G. A. (2008). Impact of close family members on older adults' early response to depression treatment. *Psychology and Aging, 23*(2), 447–452.

Marziali, E., & Donahue, P. (2006). Caring for others: Internet video-conferencing group intervention for family caregivers

of older adults with neurodegenerative disease. *The Gerontologist, 46*(3), 398–403.

Mayfield, D., McLeod, G., & Hall, P. (1974). The CAGE questionnaire: Validation of a new alcoholism screening instrument. *American Journal of Psychiatry, 131*(10), 1121–1123.

McCurry, S. M., Logsdon, R. G., Teri, L., & Vitiello, M. V. (2007). Evidence-based psychological treatments for insomnia in older adults. *Psychology and Aging, 22*(1), 18–27.

McIlvane, J. M., & Reinhardt, J. P. (2001). Interactive effect of support from family and friends in visually impaired elders. *Journals of Gerontology: Series B: Psychological Sciences and Social Sciences, 56*(6), P374–P382.

Mega, M. S., Cummings, J. L., Fiorello, T., & Gornbein, J. (1996). The spectrum of behavioral changes in Alzheimer's disease. *Neurology, 46*(1), 130–135.

Mellinger, G. D., Balter, M. B., & Uhlenhuth, E. H. (1985). Insomnia and its treatment: Prevalence and correlates. *Archives of General Psychiatry, 42*(3), 225–232.

Mills, T. L., Alea, N. L., & Cheong, J. (2004). Differences in the indicators of depressive symptoms among a community sample of African-American and Caucasian older adults. *Community Mental Health Journal, 40*(4), 309–331.

Mills, T. L., & Edwards, C. D. A. (2002). A critical review of research on the mental health status of older African-Americans. *Ageing & Society, 22*(3), 273–304.

Mittelman, M. S., Ferris, S. H., Shulman, E., & Steinberg, G. (1995). A comprehensive support program: Effect on depression in spouse-caregivers of AD patients. *The Gerontologist, 35*(6), 792–802.

Moore, J. D., & Bona, J. R. (2001). Depression and dysthymia. *Medical Clinics of North America, 85,* 631–644.

Moos, R. H., Mertens, J. R., & Brennan, P. L. (1993). Patterns of diagnosis and treatment among late-middle-aged and older substance abuse patients. *Journal of Studies on Alcohol, 54*(4), 479–487.

Morris, R.G., Worsley, R., & Matthews, D. (2000). Neuropsychological assessment in older people: Old principles and new directions. *Advances in Psychiatric Treatment, 6,* 362–372.

Mouton, C. P. (1997). Special health considerations in African-American elders. *American Family Physician, 55,* 1243–1253.

Mui, A. C., Burnette, D., & Chen, L. M. (2001). Cross-cultural assessment of geriatric depression: A review of the CES-D and the GDS. *Journal of Mental Health and Aging, 7*(1), 137–164.

Mukherjee, S., Shukla, S., Woodle, J., Rosen, A. M., Olarte, S. (1983). Misdiagnosis of schizophrenia in bipolar patients: A multiethnic comparison. *American Journal of Psychiatry, 140,* 1571–1574.

National Alliance for Caregiving & AARP. (2004). *Caregiving in the U. S.* Retrieved July 18, 2008, from http://www.caregiving.org/data/04finalreport.pdf

National Institute of Health Consensus Conference. (1992). Diagnosis and treatment of depression in late life. *JAMA: Journal of the American Medical Association, 268,* 1018–1024.

National Institute of Mental Health. (2007). *Older Adults: Depression and Suicide Facts.* Retrieved July 15, 2008, from http://www.nimh.nih.gov/health/publications/older-adults-depression-and-suicide-facts.shtml

Nau, S. D., McCrae, C. S., Cook, K. G., & Lichstein, K. L. (2005). Treatment of insomnia in older adults. *Clinical Psychology Review. Special Issue: Insomnia and Behavioral Sleep Medicine, 25*(5), 645–672.

Nelson, E. A., & Dannefer, D. (1992). Aged heterogeneity: Fact or fiction? The fate of diversity in gerontological research. *The Gerontologist, 32*(1), 17–23.

Nezu, A. M., Nezu, C. M., & Perri, M. G. (1989). *Problem-solving therapy for depression: Theory, research, and clinical guidelines*. Oxford, England: John Wiley & Sons.

Nordhus, I. H., & Pallesen, S. (2003). Psychological treatment of late-life anxiety: An empirical review. *Journal of Consulting and Clinical Psychology, 71*(4), 643–651.

O'Connell, H., Chin, A., Hamilton, F., Cunningham, C., Walsh, J. B., Coakley, D., et al. (2004). A systematic review of the utility of self-report alcohol screening instruments in the elderly. *International Journal of Geriatric Psychiatry, 19*(11), 1074–1086.

Ory, M., Hoffman, R. R., Yee, J. L., Tennstedt, S., & Schulz, R. (1999). Prevalence and impact of caregiving: A detailed comparison between dementia and nondementia caregivers. *The Gerontologist, 39*(2), 177–185.

Oslin, D. W. (2004). *Late life alcoholism in primary care*. Reno, NV: Context Press.

Oslin, D. W. (2005). Evidence-based treatment of geriatric substance abuse. *Psychiatric Clinics of North America. Special Issue: Evidence-Based Geriatric Psychiatry, 28*(4), 897–911.

Oslin, D. W., Pettinati, H., & Volpicelli, J. R. (2005). Alcoholism treatment adherence: Older age predicts better adherence and drinking outcomes. *American Journal of Geriatric Psychiatry, 10*, 740–747.

Palmer, B. W., Jeste, D. V., & Sheikh, J. I. (1997). Anxiety disorders in the elderly: DSM-IV and other barriers to diagnosis and treatment. *Journal of Affective Disorders. Special Issue: Ageing, 46*(3), 183–190.

Parmelee, P. A., Katz, I. R., & Lawton, M. P. (1993). Anxiety and its association with depression among institutionalized elderly. *American Journal of Geriatric Psychiatry, 1*(1), 46–58.

Pingatore, D., Snowden, L., Sansone, R. A., & Klinkman, M. (2001). Persons with depression symptoms and the treatments they receive: A comparison of primary care physicians and psychiatrists. *International Journal of Psychiatry in Medicine, 31*, 41–60.

Prigerson, H., & Jacobs, S. C. (2001). *Traumatic grief as a distinct disorder: A rationale, consensus criteria, and a preliminary empirical test*. Washington, DC: American Psychological Association.

Prigerson, H. G., Bierhals, A. J., Kasl, S. V., & Reynolds, C. F. (1997). Traumatic grief as a risk factor for mental and physical morbidity. *American Journal of Psychiatry, 154*(5), 616–623.

Prigerson, H. G., & Maciejewski, P. K. (2005–2006). A call for sound empirical testing and evaluation of criteria for complicated grief proposed for DSM-5. *Omega: Journal of Death and Dying, 52*(1), 9–19.

Qualls, S. H. (1993). Family therapy with older adults. *Generations: Journal of the American Society on Aging, 17*(1), 73–74.

Qualls, S. H. (Ed.). (1996). Family therapy with aging families. In S. H. Zarit, & B. G. Knight (Eds.), *A guide to psychotherapy and aging: Effective clinical interventions in a life-stage context* (pp. 121–137). Washington, DC: American Psychological Association.

Qualls, S. H. (1999). Family therapy with older adult clients. *Journal of Clinical Psychology, 55*(8), 977–990.

Qualls, S. H. (2000). Therapy with aging families: Rationale, opportunities, and challenges. *Aging & Mental Health, 4*, 191–199.

Radloff, L. S. (1977). The CES–D Scale: A self-report depression scale for research in the general population. *Applied Psychological Measurement, 1*, 385–401.

REACH II Investigators. (2006). Enhancing the quality of life of dementia caregivers from different ethnic or racial groups: A randomized, controlled trial. *Annals of Internal Medicine, 145*, 727–738.

Reisberg, B., Borenstein, J., Salob, S. P., Ferris, S. H., Franssen, E., & Georgotas, A. (1989). Behavioral symptoms in Alzheimer's disease: Phenomenology and treatment. *Journal of Clinical Psychiatry, 48*, 9–15.

Rice, C., Longabaugh, R., Beattie, M. C., & Noel, N. (1993). Age group differences in response to treatment for problematic alcohol use. *Addiction, 88*(10), 1369–1375.

Riedel, B. W., Lichstein, K. L., & Dwyer, W. O. (1995). Sleep compression and sleep education for older insomniacs: Self-help versus therapist guidance. *Psychology and Aging, 10*(1), 54–63.

Ronch, J. L., & Crispi, E. L. (Eds.). (1997). Separation and loss in Alzheimer's disease: Impact on the family. In I. Deitch, & C. W. Howell (Eds.), *Counseling the aging and their families. The family psychology and counseling series* (pp. 105–119). Alexandria, VA: American Counseling Association.

Rose, J. M., & DelMaestro, S. G. (1990). Separation-individuation conflict as a model for understanding distressed caregivers: Psychodynamic and cognitive case studies. *The Gerontologist, 30*(5), 693–697.

Rosen, J., Burgio, L., Kollar, M., & Cain, M. (1994). The Pittsburgh Agitation Scale: A user-friendly instrument for rating agitation in dementia patients. *American Journal of Geriatric Psychiatry, 2*(1), 52–59.

Rosenzweig, A., Prigerson, H., Miller, M. D., & Reynolds, C. F. (1997). Bereavement and late-life depression: Grief and its complications in the elderly. *Annual Review of Medicine, 48*, 421–428.

Roy, N., & Pineau, J. (2007). Robotics and independence for the elderly. In G. Lesnoff-Caravaglia (Ed.), *Gerontechnology: Growing old in a technological society* (pp. 209–242). Springfield, IL: Charles C. Thomas Publisher.

Rumsfeld, J. S., Jones, P. G., Whooley, M. A., Sullivan, M. D., Pitt, B., Weintraub, W. S., et al. (2005). Depression predicts mortality and hospitalization in patients with myocardial infarction complicated by heart failure. *American Heart Journal, 150*, 961–967.

Russo, S. A., Hersen, M., & Van Hasselt, V. B. (2001). Treatment of reactivated post-traumatic stress disorder: Imaginal exposure in an older adult with multiple traumas. *Behavior Modification, 25*(1), 94–115.

Sabnani, H. B., & Ponterotto, J. G. (1992). Racial/ethnic minority-specific instrumentation in counseling research: A review, critique, and recommendations. *Measurement and Evaluation in Counseling and Development, 24*(4), 161–187.

Salthouse, T. A. (1985). Speed of behavior and its implications for cognition. In J. E. Birren, & K. W. Schaie (Eds.), *Handbook of the psychology of aging*, 2nd ed. (pp. 400–426). New York: Van Nostrand Reinhold.

Schnurr, P. P. (1996). Trauma, PTSD, and physical health. *PTSD Research Quarterly, 7*, 1–3.

Schonfeld, L., Dupree, L. W., Dickson-Fuhrmann, E., Royer, C. M., McDermott, C. H., Rosansky, J. S., et al. (2000). Cognitive-behavioral treatment of older veterans with substance abuse problems. *Journal of Geriatric Psychiatry and Neurology, 13*(3), 124–129.

Schulz, R., Burgio, L., Burns, R., Eisdorfer, C., Gallagher-Thompson, D., Gitlin, L. N., et al. (2003). Resources for enhancing Alzheimer's caregiver health (REACH): Overview, site-specific outcomes, and future directions. *The Gerontologist, 43*(4), 514–520.

Schulz, R., & Martire, L. M. (2004). Family caregiving of persons with dementia: Prevalence, health effects, and support strategies. *American Journal of Geriatric Psychiatry, 12*(3), 240–249.

Scogin, F., & McElreath, L. (1994). Efficacy of psychosocial treatments for geriatric depression: A quantitative review. *Journal of Consulting and Clinical Psychology, 62*(1), 69–73.

Scogin, F., Morthland, M., Kaufman, A., Burgio, L., Chaplin, W., & Kong, G. (2007). Improving quality of life in diverse rural older adults: A randomized trial of a psychological treatment. *Psychology and Aging, 22*(4), 657–665.

Scogin, F., Welsh, D., Hanson, A., Stump, J., & Coates, A. (2005). Evidence-based psychotherapies for depression in older adults. *Clinical Psychology: Science and Practice, 12*(3), 222–237.

Seeman, T. E. (2000). Health promoting effects of friends and family on health outcomes in older adults. *American Journal of Health Promotion, 14*(6), 362–370.

Shear, K., Frank, E., Houck, P. R., & Reynolds III, C. F. (2005). Treatment of complicated grief: A randomized controlled trial. *JAMA: Journal of the American Medical Association, 293*(21), 2601–2608.

Sheikh, J. I., & Salzman, C. (1995). Anxiety in the elderly: Course and treatment. *Psychiatric Clinics of North America, 18*(4), 871–883.

Sherkat, D. E., Kilbourne, B. S., Cain, V. A., Hull, P. C., Levine, R. S., & Husaini, B. A. (2007). The impact of health service use on racial differences in mortality among the elderly. *Research on Aging, 29*(3), 207–224.

Sivertsen, B., Omvik, S., Havik, O. E., Pallesen, S., Bjorvatn, B., Nielsen, G. H., et al. (2006). A comparison of actigraphy and polysomnography in older adults treated for chronic primary insomnia. *Sleep: Journal of Sleep and Sleep Disorders Research, 29*(10), 1353–1358.

Spielberger, C. D., Gorsuch, R., Lushene, R., Vagg, P. R., & Jacobs, G. A. (1983). *STAI manual for the State-Trait Anxiety Inventory.* Palo Alto, CA: Consulting Psychologists Press.

Spielman, A. J., Saskin, P., & Thorpy, M. J. (1987). Treatment of chronic insomnia by restriction of time in bed. *Sleep: Journal of Sleep Research & Sleep Medicine, 10*(1), 45–56.

Steffen, A. M. (2000). Anger management for dementia caregivers: A preliminary study using video and telephone interventions. *Behavior Therapy, 31*(2), 281–299.

Stepanski, E. J., & Wyatt, J. K. (2003). Use of sleep hygiene in the treatment of insomnia. *Sleep Medicine Reviews, 7*, 215–225.

Stone, K. C., Booth, A. K., & Lichstein, K. L. (2008). Cognitive-behavioral therapy for late-life insomnia. In D. Gallagher-Thompson, A. M. Steffen, & L. W. Thompson (Eds.), *Handbook of behavioral and cognitive therapies with older adults* (pp. 48–60). New York: Springer.

Stoops, N. (2004). *Educational attainment in the United States: 2003.* United States Census Bureau. Retrieved on July 19, 2008, from www.census.gov/prod/2004pubs/p20-550.pdf

Storandt, M. (1994). *General principles of assessment of older adults.* Washington, DC: American Psychological Association.

Storandt, M., & VandenBos, G. R. (1994). *Neuropsychological assessment of dementia and depression in older adults: A clinician's guide.* Washington, DC: American Psychological Association.

Strakowski, S. M., Lonczak, H. S., Sax, K. W., & West, S. A. (1995). The effects of race on diagnosis and disposition from a psychiatric emergency service. *Journal of Clinical Psychiatry, 56*(3), 101–107.

Strothers III, H. S., Rust, G., Minor, P., Fresh, E., Druss, B., & Satcher, D. (2005). Disparities in antidepressant treatment in Medicaid elderly diagnosed with depression. *Journal of the American Geriatrics Society, 53*(3), 456–461.

Substance Abuse and Mental Health Services Administration (SAMHSA). (1998). *Substance abuse among older adults: Treatment improvement protocol* (TIP; Series 26). Rockville, MD: U.S. Department of Health and Human Services.

Substance Abuse and Mental Health Services Administrations (SAMHSA). (2004). *National survey on drug use and health.* Rockville, MD: U.S. Department of Health and Human Services.

Sum, S., Mathews, R. M., Hughes, I., & Campbell, A. (2008). Internet use and loneliness in older adults. *CyberPsychology & Behavior, 11*(2), 208–211.

Summers, M. N., Hyer, L., Boyd, S., & Boudewyns, P. A. (1996). Diagnosis of later-life PTSD among elderly combat veterans. *Journal of Clinical Geropsychology, 2*(2), 103–115.

Teri, L., Logsdon, R. G., Whall, A. L., Weiner, M. F., Trimmer, C., Peskind, E., et al. (1998). *Psychotherapy, 35*, 436–443.

Teri, L., Truax, P., Logsdon, R., Uomoto, J., Zarit, S., & Vitaliano, P. P. (1992). Assessment of behavioral problems in dementia: The revised memory and behavior problems checklist. *Psychology and Aging, 7*(4), 622–631.

Thompson, L. W. (1996). Cognitive-behavioral therapy and treatment for later life depression. *Journal of Clinical Psychiatry, 57*, 29–37.

Thompson, L. W., Tang, P., DiMario, J., Cusing, M., & Gallagher-Thompson, D. (2007). Bereavement and adjustment disorders. In D. Blazer, D. C. Steffens, & E. W. Busse (Eds.), *Essentials of geriatric psychiatry* (pp. 219–239). Arlington, VA: American Psychiatric Publishing, Inc.

Tisher, M., & Dean, S. (2000). Family therapy with the elderly. *Australian and New Zealand Journal of Family Therapy, 21*(2), 94–101.

Unützer, J., Katon, W., Sullivan, M., & Miranda, J. (1999). Treating depressed older adults in primary care: Narrowing the gap between efficacy and effectiveness. *Milbank Quarterly, 77*(2), 225–256.

U.S. Census Bureau. (2003). *The older population in the United States: March 2002.* Issued April 2003.

Van Amburg, S. M., Barber, C. E., & Zimmerman, T. S. (1996). Aging and family therapy: Prevalence of aging issues and later family life concerns in marital and family therapy literature (1986–1993). *Journal of Marital & Family Therapy, 22*(2), 195–203.

van Gool, C. H., Kempen, G. I. J. M., Penninx, B. W. J. H., Deeg, D. J. H., Beekman, A. T. F., & van Eijk, J. T. M. (2005). Impact of depression on disablement in late middle aged and older persons: Results from the longitudinal aging study Amsterdam. *Social Science & Medicine, 60*(1), 25–36.

van Zelst, W. H., de Beurs, E., Beekman, A. T. F., Deeg, D. J. H., & van Dyck, R. (2003). Prevalence and risk factors of post-traumatic stress disorder in older adults. *Psychotherapy and Psychosomatics, 72*(6), 333–342.

Vanderwerker, L. C., & Prigerson, H. G. (2004). Social support and technological connectedness as protective factors in bereavement. *Journal of Loss & Trauma. Special Issue: Risk and Resiliency Following Trauma and Traumatic Loss, 9*(1), 45–57.

Vitaliano, P. P., Scanlan, J. M., Zhang, J., Savage, M. V., & Hirsch, I. B. (2002). A path model of chronic stress, the metabolic syndrome, and coronary heart disease. *Psychosomatic Medicine, 64*(3), 418–435.

Vitaliano, P. P., Young, H. M., & Zhang, J. (2004). Is caregiving a risk factor for illness? *Current Directions in Psychological Science, 13*(1), 13–16.

Wagner, B., Knaevelsrud, C., & Maercker, A. (2006). Internet-based cognitive-behavioral therapy for complicated grief: A randomized controlled trial. *Death Studies, 30*(5), 429–453.

Wetherell, J. L., Le Roux, H., & Gatz, M. (2003). DSM-IV criteria for generalized anxiety disorder in older adults: Distinguishing the worried from the well. *Psychology and Aging, 18*(3), 622–627.

Wisocki, P. A., Handen, B., & Morse, C. K. (1986). The Worry Scale as a measure of anxiety among homebound and community active elderly. *The Behavior Therapist, 9*(5), 91–95.

Yaffe, K., Fox, P., Newcomer, R., Sands, L., Lindquist, K., Dane, K., et al. (2002). Patient and caregiver characteristics and nursing home placement in patients with dementia. *JAMA: Journal of the American Medical Association, 287*(16), 2090–2097.

Yeo, G., & Gallagher-Thompson (2006). *Ethnicity and the dementias* (2nd ed.). New York: Routledge/Taylor & Francis Group.

Yesavage, J. A. (1983). Development and validation of a geriatric depression screening scale: A preliminary report. *Journal of Psychiatric Research, 17*(1), 37–49.

Yon, A., & Scogin, F. (2007). Procedures for identifying evidence-based psychological treatments for older adults. *Psychology and Aging, 22*(1), 4–7.

Zarit, S. H., Todd, P. A., & Zarit, J. M. (1986). Subjective burden of husbands and wives as caregivers: A longitudinal study. *The Gerontologist, 26*(3), 260–266.

Zhang, A. Y., & Snowden, L. R. (1999). Ethnic characteristics of mental disorders in five U. S. communities. *Cultural Diversity and Ethnic Minority Psychology, 5*(2), 134–146.

Zylstra, R. C., & Steitz, J. A. (1999). Public knowledge of late-life depression and aging. *Journal of Applied Gerontology, 18*(1), 63–76.

Working with Sexual-Minority Individuals

Lisa M. Diamond, Molly R. Butterworth, *and* Ritch C. Savin-Williams

Abstract

The present chapter provides a review of some of the primary psychological issues confronting sexual minorities (i.e., individuals with same-sex attractions and relationships). Our goal is to provide a flexible set of preliminary questions that can be used to help sexual-minority clients to articulate their own idiosyncratic experiences and give voice to their own unique needs. We begin by addressing two of the most common and important clinical issues faced by sexual minorities: generalized "minority stress" and acceptance and validation from the family of origin. We then turn attention to the vast—and vastly underinvestigated—population of individuals with bisexual attractions and behavior, who actually constitute the majority of the sexual-minority population, despite having been systematically excluded from most prior research. We review the increasing body of research suggesting that individuals with bisexual patterns of attraction and behavior actually face greater mental health risks than those with exclusive same-sex attractions and behavior, and we explore potential processes and mechanisms underlying this phenomenon, focusing particular attention on issues of identity development and transition over the life span. We conclude by outlining a number of areas for future clinically oriented research.

Keywords: Bisexuality, identity development, minority stress, sexual orientation, stigmatization

One of the most notable developments in clinical psychology over the past 20 years has been the explosion of attention to the lives of men and women with same-sex attractions and relationships—which we collectively denote *sexual minorities*. After a long history of denigration and stigmatization, during which such individuals were viewed as fundamentally and necessarily maladjusted (for example Krafft-Ebing, 1882; Socarides, 1996), psychologists now generally adopt a balanced and thoughtful approach to these populations, attending to their unique and ordinary strengths, as well as to their unique and ordinary challenges. This has not only improved our basic understanding of the sexual-minority life course, but has also contributed to mainstream research on mental health by highlighting how individuals' private experiences of love and desire, and their resulting sexual

self-concepts, profoundly shape their day-to-day and long-term well-being.

Perhaps the single most important recent change in our understanding of sexual-minority populations concerns their size and composition. A decade ago, a chapter such as this would have probably been called "Working with Lesbian and Gay Individuals," and would have focused exclusively on men and women who were exclusively attracted to the same sex and who openly claimed a lesbian or gay identity. These characteristics were presumed prototypical of individuals with same-sex attractions and relationships. Although there were clearly some men and women who identified as bisexual or who rejected sexual identity labels, these individuals were typically considered exceptional and were often suspected to be struggling with confusion, denial, and/or internalized homophobia.

We now know that these assumptions were woefully inaccurate. Studies using random, representative samples have demonstrated that the most common type of individual with same-sex attractions is actually *not* an openly identified lesbian or gay man, but someone who considers himself or herself to be heterosexual *despite* same-sex desires and/or behaviors. The most common type of individual with same-sex attractions actually experiences attractions to *both* sexes and not just the same sex; the most common type of individual with same-sex attractions does *not* report tidy correspondences among his or her desires, fantasies, love relationships, and sexual behaviors, but instead experiences mild to moderate discrepancies among these domains (i.e., desires that are never acted upon; same-sex sexual liaisons in the absence of lesbian-gay-bisexual identification). The most common type of individual with same-sex attractions has *not* been unambiguously certain of these attractions since early childhood, but has experienced discontinuities—sometimes slight, sometimes drastic—between childhood, adolescent, midlife, and late-life experiences of love, desire, fantasy, behavior, and identification.

Unfortunately, psychological research has been slow to match this expanded picture. Practically all scientific knowledge regarding clinical issues facing individuals with same-sex attractions is based on fairly narrow samples of openly identified lesbians and gay men (and historically, far more men than women). Compounding the problem, studies have long underrepresented bisexual, ethic-minority, rural, and working-class individuals. As a result, we face significant obstacles in providing accurate guidelines to clinical psychologists on the needs and experiences of individuals with same-sex attractions and behaviors. Our state of knowledge regarding their needs and experiences is currently being revolutionized as psychologists increasingly come to terms with the startling breadth and diversity of sexual minorities.

How, then, to proceed? We could certainly adhere closely to the published literature on lesbians and gay men, acknowledging its limitations but nonetheless using it as the basis for extrapolation to other sexual minorities. Yet, the usefulness and validity of such a strategy is dubious—now that we realize just how much of the iceberg lies beneath the surface, it is difficult to justify focusing only on the tip. Accordingly, our review proceeds as follows. We begin by providing an overview of sexual-minority populations and two of the most common and important clinical issues they face: generalized "minority stress," and acceptance and validation from the family of origin. We then turn attention to the vast—and vastly underinvestigated—population of individuals with *bisexual* attractions and behavior, who actually constitute somewhere between 75% and 90% of the sexual-minority population, despite having been systematically excluded from the majority of research on sexual minorities over the past several decades. We address the increasing body of research suggesting that individuals with bisexual patterns of attraction and behavior actually face *greater* mental health risks than those with exclusive same-sex attractions and behavior, and we explore potential processes and mechanisms underlying this phenomenon, focusing particular attention on issues of identity development and transition over the lifespan. We conclude by outlining a number of areas for future research. The goal is to provide clinicians not with a static model of "lesbian-gay-bisexual concerns" but a flexible set of preliminary questions that they can use to help their sexual-minority clients to articulate their own idiosyncratic experiences and give voice to their own unique needs.

Defining the Population

First, foundational and definitional issues deserve attention. Most notably, what exactly does it mean to talk about sexual minorities? Who is included in this population, and what is the rationale for considering them a distinct subgroup? The term *sexual minority* refers to all men and women with same-sex attractions and/or experiences. It is used here instead of "lesbian-gay-bisexual" because research has resoundingly demonstrated that not all individuals with same-sex attractions and experiences identify as lesbian, gay, or bisexual. In fact, very few of them do. A random, representative survey of American adults found that the number of individuals with same-sex attractions or experiences was more than double the number of individuals who actually identified as lesbian-gay-bisexual (Laumann, Gagnon, Michael, & Michaels, 1994). Similar findings have emerged from surveys conducted in other countries (Wichstrom & Hegna, 2003) and in studies of adolescents (reviewed later). Despite the diversity of these individuals' experiences, one thing they undeniably share is that their same-sex attractions and/or experiences place them squarely outside conventional norms prescribing uniform and universal heterosexuality, potentially exposing them to multiple personal and social ramifications, such as self-stigmatization, denigration by others, harassment or victimization, lack of social support, and lack of public acknowledgment of their relationships. This is why they are considered sexual *minorities*.

Unfortunately, many of our observations about the experiences of this broad group are hampered by the fact that the majority of psychological research on same-sex sexuality has adopted a much narrower focus, recruiting participants on the basis of their open identification as lesbian or gay. Hence, the inevitable result is that practically everything psychologists currently know about the sexual-minority life course is based on an extremely small and arguably unrepresentative subset of sexual-minority populations as a whole. This, of course, raises the larger question, exactly *why* are the lives of sexual minorities distinctive to begin with? After all, there has certainly been plenty of psychological research conducted during the past 20 years focused on demonstrating just how "normal" (i.e., similar to heterosexuals) sexual minorities are, in a variety of psychological and social domains. Hence, in contrast to historical notions of homosexuals as psychologically sick and therefore fundamentally different from heterosexuals, the trend over the past several decades has been for psychologists to emphasize that lesbian-gay-bisexual individuals are healthy individuals who are actually quite similar to heterosexuals in practically all domains of psychological health and functioning (Kitzinger, 1987).

The key difference, of course, is their desire for and participation in same-sex intimate relationships, despite the widespread cultural condemnation of such relationships. This exposes such individuals to a range of unique psychosocial challenges from early childhood through adulthood, potentially including confusion and self-doubt, denigration and stigmatization from peers, rejection from family members, social stereotyping, employment and housing discrimination, difficulties accessing health care, and outright physical violence. A national survey by the Kaiser Foundation found that three-fourths of lesbian-gay-bisexual adults reported some form of prejudice or discrimination as a result of their sexuality, one-third of gay men and one-half of lesbians reported experiencing rejection by a friend or family member, and one-third said that they had actually suffered violence against them or their property (Kaiser Foundation, 2001, November). Attitudes can be particularly pernicious in rural, suburban, and other more isolated environments. Lynch (1992) found that, compared to sexual minorities living in urban centers with large and visible lesbian-gay-bisexual populations, suburban sexual minorities were more circumspect, more fearful of exposure,

and anticipated more intolerance and discrimination. The same is true for some ethnic communities (reviewed in Greene, 1997, 1998).

Although attitudes toward same-sex marriage have become increasingly positive over the past decade, about half of American adults oppose legal recognition for same-sex marriages (Polling Report. com, 2008). Reflecting this view, in 1996, Congress passed the Defense of Marriage Act, allowing the Federal government to override any state legal recognition of same-sex marriage. Opposition to same-sex marriage is mainstream, endorsed by all major candidates for president in the 2000, 2004, and 2008 elections—although some candidates support non-marriage alternatives, such as civil unions or domestic partnerships. Six months after Massachusetts began issuing marriage licenses to same-sex couples in November 2004, 11 states passed ballot measures denying any formal recognition of same-sex marriages. That trend continued in 2006, when seven more states passed same-sex marriage bans. Currently, 45 states have either a constitutional amendment or a state law restricting marriage to one man and one woman.

Minority Stress and Mental Health

The end result of the social stigmatization, rejection, and legal disenfranchisement that some sexual minorities face is "minority stress," defined as the unique strain experienced as a result of occupying a socially marginalized category (Meyer, 2003). As comprehensively reviewed by Meyer, the fundamental tenet underlying the conceptualization of minority stress is that individuals learn about themselves and develop their self-concepts partly on the basis of how they are treated and perceived by others (Allport, 1954; Crocker, Major, & Steele, 1998; Goffman, 1963; Pettigrew, 1967). Hence, chronic negative evaluations, at the level of both concrete interpersonal interactions and broad-based cultural norms, have detrimental effects on sexual minorities' self-evaluations and, accordingly, their mental well-being. Meyer (2003) discussed four key mechanisms through which minority stress operates. The first and perhaps most obvious includes objective, external stressors, which may be either chronic or acute. Examples include harassment and victimization (Balsam, Rothblum, & Beauchaine, 2005; D'Augelli, Pilkinton, & Hershberger, 2002), workplace discrimination (Badgett, 1998; Waldo, 1999), the lack of institutional resources such as marriage (Brewer & Wilcox, 2005; Lannutti & Lloyd, 2005; Rothblum, Balsam, & Solomon, 2008), and experiences such as chronic neglect or rude treatment at restaurants, hotels, and shops (D. A. Jones, 1996; A. S. Walters & Curran, 1996). The second includes *expectations* of such events and hence might include phenomena such as personal discomfort in certain settings, such as family events, where disapproval and poor treatment is expected (Caron & Ulin, 1997; Oswald, 2002). The third includes the internalization of negative social attitudes toward same-sex sexuality, often called "internalized homophobia" (Igartua, Gill, & Montoro, 2003; Meyer & Dean, 1998), and the fourth includes active and vigilant concealment of one's same-sex sexuality in an attempt to avoid external stressors (DiPlacido, 1998; Herek & Capitanio, 1996; McKenna & Bargh, 1998).

Minority stress has been advanced as an explanation for the fact that, on the whole, both adolescents and adults reporting same-sex attractions and/or identifying as lesbian-gay-bisexual tend to show disproportionately high rates of anxiety, depression, suicidality, self-injurious behavior (including eating problems), substance use, and use of mental health services. These findings are based on studies using large, nationally representative populations (Austin et al., 2004; Case et al., 2004; Cochran, Sullivan, & Mays, 2003; Jorm, Korten, Rodgers, Jacomb, & Christensen, 2002; Paul et al., 2002; Ziyadeh et al., 2007), as well as on studies using heterosexual siblings as a comparison group to control for potential confounds of family background and even the heritability of psychological distress (Balsam, Beauchaine, Mickey, & Rothblum, 2005). The notion that minority stress may account for the link between same-sex sexuality and mental health is supported by the fact that studies have found that sexual-minority youth with the highest mental health risks are those who have been exposed to the greatest levels of stigmatization and victimization (Balsam, Rothblum, & Beauchaine, 2005; Bontempo & D'Augelli, 2002; D'Augelli, Grossman, & Starks, 2006; Russell & Joyner, 2001).

These data, however, highlight a critical point: Stigma, discrimination, and minority stress are *not* uniform experiences. Not only do sexual-minority individuals face vastly different exposure to minority stress, depending on their individual family background, social class, geographic environment, etc., but they are also equipped with vastly different coping resources, due to personality characteristics, social support resources, and institutional protections from harassment and discrimination. This helps to explain why some studies have not found significantly greater mental health problems among sexual-minority individuals than among their heterosexual counterparts. Because different studies capture different subgroups of sexual-minority men and women, with different psychosocial risk factors, different degrees of exposure to prejudice and discrimination, different sets of family issues, and different coping mechanisms, such variability in the findings is to be expected (Anderson, 1998; Fitzpatrick, Euton, Jones, & Schmidt, 2005; Konik & Stewart, 2004; Meyer, 2003; Rutter & Soucar, 2002; Savin-Williams, 2001c).

Furthermore, social attitudes toward same-sex sexuality have been gradually changing over the years (reviewed in Loftus, 2001; Savin-Williams, 2005; S. D. Walters, 2001), thus reducing some sexual-minority individuals' exposure to minority stress. For example, the proportion of Americans who think homosexuality is an "acceptable alternative lifestyle" has steadily increased from 34% in the early 1980s to 57% in 2008 (Polling Report.com, 2008). Nearly all Fortune 500 companies include sexual orientation in their nondiscrimination policies, and about half offer same-sex domestic partner benefits to their employees (Graham, 2005; Gunther, 2006; Weinstein, 2007). This pattern of increased acceptance appears to be linked to increased familiarity with sexual-minority individuals in day-to-day life. Approximately four in ten Americans report having a close friend or a family member who is lesbian, gay, or bisexual (Neidorf & Morin, 2007), and those who befriend sexual minorities tend to have more positive perceptions of them. Among adolescents and young adults, attitudes toward sexual minorities are especially positive (Savin-Williams, 2005). For example, two-thirds of high school seniors supported the right of same-sex couples to adopt, and a recent study found that more than three-fourths of high school seniors favored legalized same-sex marriage or civil unions (Broverman, 2006; Buchanan, 2008). Such historically high levels of acceptance can be attributed in part to the growing visibility of same-sex sexuality in the national media. As one cultural observer noted, "During the course of the '90s homosexuality went from being largely invisible to shockingly visible to fairly pedestrian" (Doig, 2007). As a result of such changes, we can expect increased variability in sexual-minority individuals' exposure to minority stress. Although some gay/lesbian/bisexual individuals continue to face unrelenting stigma in their local communities as a result of their same-sex sexuality, others are able to live lives that are relatively free of harassment, shame, and denigration, and may enjoy full support, validation, and acceptance from friends, family members, and co-workers. Clearly, the task for clinicians is to sensitively attend to the unique constellation of risk and resiliency factors characterizing each of their sexual-minority clients. Critical factors to assess include their overall exposure to the four forms of minority stress outlined earlier *and* to the combination of individual and cultural factors (coping mechanisms, access to social support, cultural norms that permit or forbid open discussion of personal problems, etc.) that moderate their responses to such stressors. This approach will yield more effective clinical interventions than an approach that presumes that an individual's sexual-minority status automatically confers a relatively automatic and uniform degree of psychological strain.

Sexual-Minority Youth

The same factors that introduce mental health risks for sexual-minority adults—stigmatization, internalized homophobia, victimization, and minority stress—may be particularly problematic for sexual-minority adolescents. Studies documenting the specific effects of these phenomena on sexual-minority youth have been beset by the same methodological problems that have plagued research on adults, namely misspecification of the target population and over-reliance on small, nonrepresentative samples. With respect to specifying the target population, one chronic limitation of previous research has been that investigators often discount same-sex sexuality when it occurs during the adolescent years, presuming that youth who engage in same-sex contact are simply experimenting and will eventually identify as heterosexual. For example, Maccoby (1998, p. 191) asserted that "a substantial number of people experiment with same-sex sexuality at some point in their lives, and a small minority settle into a life-long pattern of homosexuality." Maccoby is certainly correct in that adolescent same-sex contact is not a reliable predictor of future same-sex sexuality, but the problem is that there is no definitive way at the time to differentiate between youth who will "settle into a lifelong pattern" of same-sex sexuality and those who will not. Longitudinal research on adolescent and young adult sexual-minority women (Diamond, 2000b, 2003a, 2005b) has found that factors such as age of first same-sex attractions, age at first sexual questioning, and age of first same-sex contact failed to distinguish women who ended up, by their mid 30s, maintaining lesbian-bisexual versus heterosexual identities. The only significant predictor of future identity was a woman's

initial ratio of same-sex to other-sex attractions, which remained relatively stable over time (Diamond, 2008b). In the absence of such information, *all* same-sex sexuality during the adolescent years deserves careful attention. Even for youth who end up identifying as heterosexual, adolescent expressions of same-sex sexuality might prove to be developmentally significant, and hence have implications for their adjustment and well-being (both positive and negative).

Just how common is adolescent same-sex sexuality? The National Longitudinal Study of Adolescent Health found that 13% of American girls and 6% of American boys reported same-sex attractions, a same-sex relationship, or a nonheterosexual identity (Savin-Williams, 2005). For comparison, Laumann et al.'s (1994) similarly random, representative survey of American adults found that nearly 9% of women and 10% of men reported same-sex attractions or behaviors. Focusing specifically on same-sex behavior, a recent representative survey found that 5% of male teenagers and 11% of female teenagers reported same-sex sexual contact (Mosher et al., 2005). Notably, estimates of adolescent same-sex sexual contact increase dramatically when one restricts the sample to youth who have also pursued heterosexual sexual contact (DuRant, Krowchuk, & Sinal, 1998), demonstrating that most adolescents pursue same-sex contact in addition to—rather than instead of—other sexual contact. Also, youth reporting same-sex attractions or same-sex contact overwhelmingly identify as heterosexual (Garofalo, Wolf, Wissow, Woods, & Goodman, 1999; Mosher, Chandra, & Jones, 2005; Remafedi, Resnick, Blum, & Harris, 1992).

Do youth with same-sex attractions, behaviors, or identities show greater mental health problems than their heterosexual counterparts, similar to the findings regarding sexual-minority adults? The answer is *perhaps*—it depends on which populations are being sampled. Numerous studies have found that sexual-minority youth, lumped together as a unitary unit, often report heightened feelings of stress, loneliness, anxiety, and depression, and heightened use of drugs and alcohol (Consolacion, Russell, & Sue, 2004; French, Story, Remafedi, Resnick, & Blum, 1996; Garofalo et al., 1999; Remafedi, 1999; Remafedi, French, Story, Resnick, & Blum, 1998; Rosario, Schrimshaw, & Hunter, 2004b, 2006; Russell & Consolacion, 2003; Russell, Franz, & Driscoll, 2001; Russell & Seif, 2002; Savin-Williams, 2001c). As with adults, stigmatization and victimization play a critical role in these problems (Balsam, Rothblum et al., 2005; Bontempo & D'Augelli,

2002; D'Augelli et al., 2006; D'Augelli, Pilkington, & Hershberger, 2002; Horn & Nucci, 2006; Mallon, 2001; Rivers & D'Augelli, 2001; Safe Schools Coalition of Washington, 1999; T. Williams, Connolly, Pepler, & Craig, 2003, 2005).

Perhaps the greatest amount of research and popular attention has focused on sexual-minority youths' risks for suicidality. Numerous studies over the past 20 years have provided ample evidence for elevated suicide attempts and suicidal thoughts among lesbian-gay-bisexual-identified youth sampled from community support groups, university groups, Internet respondents, and high schools across the United States (Garofalo et al., 1999; Halpert, 2002; Kulkin, Chauvin, & Percle, 2000; McDaniel, Purcell, & D'Augelli, 2001; Morrison & L'Heureux, 2001; Remafedi et al., 1998; Russell & Joyner, 2001; Saulnier, 1998). This conclusion has been articulated in major clinical, medical, and public health journals, and is based on research with numerous adolescent populations using a variety of research designs and conducted across time and various cultures (Faulkner & Cranston, 1998; Fergusson, Horwood, & Beautrais, 1999; Fergusson, Horwood, Ridder, & Beautrais, 2005; Garofalo, Wolf, Kessel, Palfrey, & DuRant, 1998; Garofalo et al., 1999; Jorm et al., 2002; Pinhey & Millman, 2004; Ploderl & Fartacek, 2005; Remafedi et al., 1998; Russell & Joyner, 2001; Silenzio, Pena, Duberstein, Cerel, & Knox, 2007). The proportion of such youth reporting suicide attempts ranges from slightly elevated upward to 70%, considerably above the attempt rates of youth who do not identify as gay.

Rethinking Sexual-Minority Youth Suicidality

There are, however, exceptions to this blanket conclusion, and the research on sexual-minority youth suicide actually provides an important cautionary lesson in making inferences about the mental health "consequences" of sexual-minority status. Specifically, a number of empirical studies over the years have failed to find sexual orientation differences in suicide risk between young adult heterosexuals and nonheterosexuals (Eskin, Kaynak-Demir, & Demir, 2005; Fitzpatrick et al., 2005; Jorm et al., 2002; Norlev, Davidsen, Sundaram, & Kjoller, 2005; Robin et al., 2002; Rutter & Soucar, 2002; Savin-Williams, 2001c; Skegg, Nada-Raja, Dickson, Paul, & Williams, 2003; van Heeringen & Vincke, 2000; Whitbeck, Chen, Hoyt, Tyler, & Johnson, 2004; Yoder, Hoyt, & Whitbeck, 1998). In trying to explain these discrepancies, investigators have focused on the different subpopulations that have been represented in different studies (Muehrer, 1995; Savin-Williams, 2001a). For example, some studies have sampled youth almost exclusively from "nonrepresentative settings such as crisis centers, runaway shelters, or support groups" (Muehrer, 1995, p. 75), which tend to over-represent a specific, help-seeking fraction of the sexual-minority youth population that is most likely to suffer from pronounced physical, psychological, and social problems.

Furthermore, research on sexual-minority youth suicide—like research on sexual minorities more generally—rarely includes individuals with same-sex attractions or experiences who do not identify as lesbian/gay/bisexual. One study that did include these "unidentified" sexual-minority youth found relatively lower rates of suicide attempts during the past year than have been found in other studies: 5% among young men and 11% among young women (Russell & Joyner, 2001). This raises the possibility that elevated rates of suicide attempts may be specifically linked to lesbian-gay-bisexual identification rather than to same-sex sexuality in and of itself. Importantly, the link between identification and increased suicidality could operate in a number of ways. Perhaps for some youth, identification increases their exposure to victimization and harassment; for other youth, being targeted and teased by other kids (perhaps because of gender nonconformity) might prompt them to question their sexuality and identify as lesbian, gay, or bisexual at a relatively early age.

Thus, it is more accurate to conclude that *certain subsets* of sexual-minority youth face increased risks for suicide than to conclude that all sexual-minority adolescents face increased risks. Of course, some might argue that the distinction is functionally irrelevant: What does it matter if the suicide risk applies to only a subset of the sexual-minority youth population? After all, any elevated risk certainly deserves serious attention. The problem, however, is that, in order to intervene effectively with the most troubled youth, clinicians must understand exactly *who* is at greatest risk, and why. Does it have to do with prior adjustment problems? Gender nonconformity? Family strife? The lack of social support? Research has not yet provided definitive answers to these questions. There is, however, sufficient evidence to indicate that certain factors should be treated as "red flags": dysregulated impulse control and a propensity for intense psychological pain (Joiner, Brown, & Wingate, 2005); persistent social stigmatization and victimization; feelings of self-loathing and rejection by either peers or family (Garofalo et al., 1999; Hershberger, Pilkington, & D'Augelli, 1997; Remafedi et al., 1998); and a history of depression or anxiety, substance use, victimization, impulsivity, delinquency, homelessness, and previous suicide of friends or family members (Brent, 1995, 2001; Joiner et al., 2005; Kisch, Leino, & Silverman, 2005; Miller & Taylor, 2005; Norlev et al., 2005; Silenzio et al., 2007; Weissman et al., 1999; Yip et al., 2004).

It bears noting that one of the inadvertent "downsides" of focusing so much attention on the potential for suicidality among sexual-minority youth is that the large but generally invisible population of well-adjusted sexual-minority youth is routinely ignored in much contemporary research. In trying to identify and help the most troubled youth, we have generally failed to make use of the indispensable information afforded by the "success stories" in this population: What accounts for their resilience? Why do some youth escape a "risk" trajectory while others do not? From a clinical perspective, it is important to remember that many of the most pressing psychosocial problems facing sexual-minority youth have little to do with their sexual identity. Rather, they may be struggling with routine adolescent concerns regarding maturity, schoolwork, relationships with parents, resisting peer pressure, and dating.

Finally, it is important to note that the persistent focus on suicidality risks may become a self-fulfilling prophecy. Sexual-minority youth may come to internalize the widely disseminated image of the long-suffering, suicidal gay adolescent (Savin-Williams, 1990). For example, one youth told an interviewer that he did not believe he was truly gay because he had not yet attempted suicide (Savin-Williams, 1998). Clearly, clinicians need to remain mindful of the potential for suicidality among sexual-minority youth, yet still take full account of each individual youth's particular mix of risk and resiliency, challenges and strengths.

Family Ties

Another of the most common topics of clinically oriented research on sexual minorities concerns family relationships. It is commonly assumed that sexual minorities are uniformly alienated or ostracized from their families of origin, yet this is not the case. Rather, research has demonstrated incredible diversity in sexual minorities' family ties. These relationships can provide support *or* shame; acceptance *or* rejection, joy *or* distress, comfort *or* alienation.

Perhaps the only generalization that can safely be made is that the family relationships of sexual minorities pose a unique set of challenges for all members. Unfortunately, rigorous empirical research in this area has lagged behind other topics in sexual-minority psychology. For example, although many studies of sexual-minority youth have investigated their ties to parents (reviewed in Crosbie Burnett, Foster, Murray, & Bowen, 1996; Savin-Williams, 2001b), this is less so for studies of sexual-minority adults. This leaves us with an incomplete picture of sexual-minority individuals' socioemotional development, given that immediate and extended family members clearly have powerful influences on one another's opinions, feelings, choices, and well-being across the entire life course, as reviewed later.

Initial Disclosure

How many sexual minorities are completely open about their sexuality to family members? How long does it typically take for them to come out? Reliable answers to these questions are practically impossible to obtain, and estimates vary dramatically depending on how samples are recruited (Green, 2000). For example, sexual minorities recruited from lesbian-gay-bisexual social activities and organizations tend to report relatively higher rates of family disclosure than do individuals recruited from support groups. Overall, however, studies suggest that about 80% of self-identified lesbian-gay-bisexual individuals have disclosed their sexuality to one or more family member (Kaiser Foundation, 2001, November), with about 60%–77% of respondents reporting that they are "out" to their parents (Bryant & Demian, 1994).

Disclosure of one's sexuality to some family members, but not others, is fairly common (reviewed in Green, 2000). In general, mothers and sisters are told more often—and earlier—than are other family members, largely because they are perceived as being more potentially accepting (reviewed in Savin-Williams, 2001b). Other factors that shape the timing and breadth of sexual minorities' disclosure to family members include the degree of predisclosure intimacy, openness, support, contact, and conflict in these relationships; issues of economic dependence; the family's cultural background and religious values; and overall appraisals of the costs and benefits, for both continued secrecy versus the inevitable disruption brought about by disclosure (Bryant & Demian, 1994; Green, 2000).

Of course, simply revealing one's same-sex sexuality to family members is not the same as establishing an open and honest dialogue about it. Surveys indicate that even among lesbian-gay-bisexual individuals who are "out" to their parents, many do not discuss the issue directly (Kaiser Foundation, 2001). In some cases, parents may know and quietly tolerate the situation (Brown, 1989; D'Augelli, Grossman, & Starks, 2005; Herdt & Beeler, 1998), and yet make their disapproval subtly known, for example by refusing to acknowledge or validate the sexual-minority individual's romantic relationships. Much remains unknown about the long-term process through which families—and particularly parents—gradually progress from initial disapproval of a family member's same-sex sexuality to increasing acceptance and tolerance, and how issues of disclosure and openness are managed over time in the course of ongoing day-to-day interactions. The dynamics introduced by selective disclosure also warrant greater attention. When sexual minorities choose to reveal their sexuality to some family members, but not others, they inadvertently create "ingroups" and "outgroups" within the family who maintain starkly different perceptions and expectations of the sexual-minority family member (Crosbie Burnett et al., 1996). Over time, these differences may hinder family cohesion.

Is Openness Beneficial?

Some families never accept a family member's same-sex sexuality, which raises an important question: *Why disclose at all?* It is easy to assume that openness is preferable to secrecy, and that sexual minorities who choose never to share their identity, their community, and their romantic lives with family members are less well-adjusted and less psychologically connected to family members.

Yet, researchers have increasingly called this assumption into question (Green, 2000; Green & Mitchell, 2002; Laird, 2003; LaSala, 2000b). It is certainly true that many sexual-minority individuals derive distinct benefits from being open about their sexuality with family members, including increased intimacy and communication, heightened connectedness and support, and feelings of validation and legitimacy of one's identity and relationships (Herdt & Beeler, 1998; LaSala, 2000a, 2000b; Weston, 1991).

However, these effects are largely dependent on the type of family relationships that existed prior to the disclosure. If a sexual-minority individual has a history of conflict and poor communication with family members and anticipates that they will sharply disapprove of his or her same-sex sexuality, then secrecy might make more sense than disclosure

(Green & Mitchell, 2002). In such cases, secrecy might actually prove psychologically adaptive because it allows the individual to protect and cherish his or her own personal truth and integrity (Laird, 1993, 1998; Ponse, 1978). Hence, instead of uniformly encouraging full disclosure, it may be preferable for friends, activists, and clinicians to encourage sexual-minority individuals to carefully evaluate their goals and expectations regarding disclosure and to realistically assess whether—given their own particular family dynamics—these expectations are likely to be met (Green, 2000).

Issues of disclosure also take on a different meaning for sexual minorities at later stages of the life course. As Herdt and Beeler (1998) indicated, when young adults disclose their same-sex sexuality to parents and other family members, family reactions often revolve around thoughts of the future, sometimes involving grieving for lost expectations and fantasies, as well as fears about their loved one's risk for harassment and victimization. Yet, when the family member making the disclosure is in his or her 50s or early 60s, many of these concerns about the future are largely moot. The sexual-minority family member has already traversed major milestones involving career, intimate relationships, and, potentially, even children. Hence, disclosure to family members raises more issues about the past than the future. Family members may have to substantially revise and reconsider their narratives of family history (Beeler & DiProva, 1999). Was *everything* involving this person a fabrication? What else might be unknown—not only about this particular individual, but all other family members? How can something so important go unnoticed? As Herdt and Beeler (1998) pointed out, reckoning with and undoing decades of duplicity may prove to be a more pressing issue in such cases than wrestling with the fact of same-sex sexuality itself.

Unique Issues for Ethnic-Minority Families

Culture and ethnicity play important roles in structuring sexual minorities' family-of-origin relationships. As noted earlier, reliable estimates are difficult to obtain, but extant research suggests that ethnic minorities are often less likely to disclose their sexuality to family members, largely because they expect more negative responses (reviewed in Green, 2000). Same-sex sexuality obviously has drastically different meanings in different cultures (Blackwood, 2000; Murray, 2000; W. L. Williams, 1998), and families with highly traditional or religious backgrounds might have more negative conceptions of same-sex sexuality—or less knowledge about it altogether—than more mainstream Western families (Chan, 1992; Collins, 1990; Espin, 1984; Greene, 1998; Hidalgo, 1984; Icard, 1986; Morales, 1992). For example, some languages do not have positive or neutral terms for "lesbian," "gay," or "bisexual" (Espin, 1997).

Importantly, the nature, parameters, and underlying reasons for the stigmatization of same-sex sexuality vary considerably across different ethnic groups, and these differences have correspondingly distinct implications for sexual-minority individuals' experiences, both in terms of initial decisions to disclose and also with respect to long-term adjustment. For example, Latino, African American, Asian-Pacific Islander, and South Asian communities typically place considerable emphasis on family ties, and same-sex sexuality is often construed as a violation and betrayal of familial cohesion and loyalty (Amaro, 1978; Chan, 1992; Espin, 1984, 1987; Hidalgo, 1984; Jayakar, 1994; Smith, 1997; Tremble, Schneider, & Appathurai, 1989; Vasquez, 1979; Wooden, Kawasaki, & Mayeda, 1983).

In addition, many South Asian families continue to arrange their children's marriages (Jayakar, 1994), and the social ties created by these marriages may have important implications for the family's integration into other social networks. Men and women whose same-sex sexuality leads them to withdraw from this tradition may be viewed by their parents as making a selfish choice that impacts negatively upon the family's entire social system. Within African American communities, same-sex sexuality is often associated with longstanding cultural stereotypes of African Americans as hypersexual and morally bankrupt (Clarke, 1983; Collins, 1990; Greene, 1986; Icard, 1986). Thus, sexual minorities often feel pressured to hide their same-sex sexuality in order present an image of normalcy to larger Anglo society and contradict these racist stereotypes (Clarke, 1983; De Monteflores, 1986; Gomez & Smith, 1990; Mays & Cochran, 1988).

For these reasons, ethnic-minority men and women may express their sexuality in distinctive ways that run counter to common conceptions of "the lesbian-gay-bisexual experience." For example, some ethnic-minority men might pursue exclusively sexual same-sex behavior with strangers to avoid identifying as gay, and maintain their most important romantic ties to women (Carballo-Dieguez, 1989; Carballo-Dieguez & Dolezal, 1994; Vasquez, 1979). Others might identify as lesbian or gay and regularly pursue same-sex behavior, but might resist larger participation in gay culture, choosing to

emphasize the cultural component of their identity in order to maintain their strong cultural and family ties (Icard, 1986; Mays & Cochran, 1988; Mays, Cochran, & Rhue, 1993). These factors must be carefully considered by researchers investigating how sexual minorities from different ethnic groups manage their sexual-minority identity in the context of broader family and community ties.

From the Family's Point of View

In considering how sexual minorities maintain functioning relationships with their families of origin, it is important not to lose sight of the fact that adjustment to a family member's disclosure of same-sex sexuality may be experienced quite differently from the family's point of view than from the point of view of the sexual-minority individual. Overall, there has been far more research from the latter than the former perspective (Crosbie Burnett et al., 1996). Yet, we know from the small amount of qualitative, clinically oriented accounts available (Beeler & DiProva, 1999; Griffin, Wirth, & Wirth, 1986; C. Jones, 1978; Oswald, 2000; Strommen, 1989; Walsh, 2003) that many of the psychological hurdles faced by sexual minorities—feelings of invisibility, fears of marginalization and social stigmatization, uncertainty and confusion about the future, and feelings of loss for the old, ostensibly "normal" self—are shared by their parents, siblings, aunts, uncles, and grandparents. Family members also face many of the same practical decisions: Should they hide this information from colleagues? Can anyone "tell?" Which friends of the family are likely to be supportive, and which are likely to be judgmental and rejecting? Will people think that it is the family's "fault" and that they somehow provided a dysfunctional childhood environment that "caused" this to happen? It is also not uncommon for some family members—especially siblings—to question their *own* sexuality. Especially given the public visibility of scientific findings about the potential genetic underpinnings of same-sex sexuality, it is perhaps natural for siblings and even parents to wonder if they are carrying the much-touted "gay gene," and what that might mean for them.

Overall, then, one way to summarize these issues is to note that such families face an extended period of vulnerability during which they gradually reconstruct a new sense of themselves as a unit and during which they must revise their own individual relationships with the sexual-minority family member (Beeler & DiProva, 1999; Walsh, 2003). This vulnerability, as noted earlier, need not be interpreted as necessarily dramatic or negative. Some families experience these transitions as positive events that bring them together, whereas others wrestle with significant feelings of anger, resentment, and betrayal (Crosbie Burnett et al., 1996; Savin-Williams, 2001b; Strommen, 1989). Perhaps the only reliable predictions that can be made are that families with high-quality ties before the disclosure, characterized by mutual intimacy, support, cohesion, and warmth, generally fare better (Patterson, 2000; Savin-Williams, 2001b), and that the family's adjustment must be considered in light of contextual factors such as their local community, their values, religious background, economic status, and cultural beliefs (Crosbie Burnett et al., 1996; Rostosky et al., 2004; Savin-Williams, 2001b; Strommen, 1989).

Stepping Back: Whose Experiences Are We Missing?

As the foregoing review attests, both adolescents and adults with same-sex attractions and behaviors face a number of psychosocial challenges stemming from their minority status with respect to the culture at large. Yet, moving from this broad-based view to a more specific, process-oriented strategy for addressing the clinical needs of this population is exceedingly difficult because our present knowledge—improved as it may be compared to a decade ago—remains incomplete. Quite simply, nearly all extant research on the well-being of sexual minorities under-represents the largest subset of sexual minorities—those with same-sex *and* other-sex attractions and behavior. Some of these individuals may identify as bisexual, others as "mostly heterosexual," and still others may attach no label to their sexuality whatsoever (Diamond, 2008b). All of these individuals are overlooked when researchers specifically recruit only lesbian- and gay-identified participants.

With respect to individuals who actually identify as bisexual, some researchers have deleted such respondents from their research samples on the basis that it was impossible to know whether they were "actually" confused heterosexuals versus closeted lesbian-gay individuals (reviewed in Rust, 2000d). Even researchers willing to study bisexual individuals have faced definitional problems. If one broadly conceives of bisexuality as a pattern of erotic responsiveness to both sexes (Rust, 2002), then just how *much* erotic responsiveness to each sex is necessary to qualify one as bisexual rather than either heterosexual or lesbian-gay? One attraction? Several fantasies? What about individuals who claim that they do

not currently experience attractions to both sexes but have so in the past, or expect that they might have the potential to do so in the future?

Rather than wrestling directly with these questions, researchers have tended to take the easy route of simply excluding bisexuals or, more frequently, lumping them with gays and lesbians. The end result is a literature on sexual minorities that implicitly posits lesbian and gay experiences as prototypical. For example, between 1975 and 1985, only 3% of the journal articles published on same-sex sexuality specifically included the word "bisexual" or "bisexuality" in the title, abstract, or subject headings. Between 1985 and 1995, this figure increased to 16%, reflecting the emerging acknowledgment of bisexuality as a legitimate sexual identity. In the past 10 years, however, that percentage has climbed only 3 more percentage points, demonstrating that the empirical under-representation of bisexuality persists (with some notable exceptions, such as Firestein, 1996, 2007; Paul, 1985, 1996; Rust, 1992, 1993, 2000c).

The implications of this systematic omission would not be so dire if bisexuals constituted only a small subgroup of sexual minorities, but this is not the case, as a number of representative studies have demonstrated (Bailey, Dunne, & Martin, 2000; Garofalo et al., 1999; Kirk, Bailey, Dunne, & Martin, 2000; Laumann et al., 1994; Mosher et al., 2005; Remafedi et al., 1992; Savin-Williams & Ream, 2006). Not only do bisexuals constitute a rather large group, but they are in fact the largest subset of individuals with same-sex attractions and experiences. For example, Laumann's research team (1994) found that approximately 4% of American men and 4% of American women described themselves as attracted to both men and women, whereas only 2.4% of men and .3% of women described themselves as exclusively attracted to the same sex. Another large-scale representative study of American adults (Mosher et al., 2005), conducted more than a decade later, found that 5.6% of American men and nearly 13% of American women were attracted to both sexes, whereas only 1.5% of men and .8% of women were exclusively attracted to the same sex. Similar results have been found internationally. Analyses of the self-reported sexual attractions of 3,000 twins in the Australian Twin Registry (Bailey et al., 2000) found that 8% of men and women reported same-sex attractions and, of these individuals, 75% of men and over 90% of women also reported experiencing other-sex attractions. A random representative sample of New Zealanders (Dickson,

Paul, & Herbison, 2003) found that approximately 6.8% of men and 18% of women reported some degree of attraction to the same sex, but only 1.2% of men and .8% of women were exclusively attracted to the same sex. Hence, directly contrary to the conventional wisdom that lesbian and gay men and women represent the prototypical "types" of sexual minorities and that bisexuals are unusual exceptions, the data clearly show that bisexuals are the prototypical sexual minorities, and lesbian-gay individuals represent the exceptions.

The specific distribution of attractions to both sexes also warrants attention. In every large-scale representative study, the single largest group of individuals with same-sex attractions are predominantly—but not exclusively—attracted to the other sex. We might think of these individuals as "Kinsey 1's" or the "mostly heterosexuals." On the Kinsey scale, zero represents exclusive heterosexuality and 6 represents exclusive same-sex sexuality. What is particularly interesting about this finding—and its consistency across different studies conducted in different countries—is that this group of "mostly-heterosexual" men and women has historically been treated with the *most* skepticism and denigration from scientists and laypeople alike. When it comes time to eliminate questionable cases from research samples, Kinsey 1's are the first to go (e.g., Bos, Sandfort, de Bruyn, & Hakvoort, 2008; Rahman & Hull, 2005; Tiggemann, Martins, & Kirkbride, 2007). Most researchers would not consider them sexual minorities at all. Yet, this has the unintended result of eliminating the vast majority of individuals with some degree of same-sex sexuality. Our failure to examine their experiences has important implications, as recent research suggests that they may vary in several key outcomes from heterosexuals *and* from gays/lesbian individuals (Austin et al., 2004; Busseri, Willoughby, Chalmers, & Bogaert, 2008; Busseri, Willoughby, Chalmers, & Bogaert, 2006; Diamond, 2008b; Ellis, Robb, & Burke, 2005; Thompson & Morgan, 2008). For example, in terms of commitment to a sexual identity, "mostly heterosexual" women have been found to be more likely to explore their sexual identity than are heterosexual women (Thompson & Morgan, 2008), manifested through their increased interest in same-sex romantic and sexual relationships and their openness in the future to these endeavors. Thompson and Morgan argued that these were not women on their way to "becoming something else"; rather, they occupied a behaviorally unique space and did not aspire to being heterosexual, bisexual, or lesbian.

In other domains, the research findings are conflicting, underscoring the need for future research. For example, some studies find that "mostly heterosexual" individuals score higher than all other groups on mental health problems (Austin et al., 2004), whereas other studies find that they score lower, or show no significant differences (Austin et al., 2004; Busseri et al., 2008; Busseri et al., 2006).

The underinvestigation of bisexual, "nonidentified," and "mostly-heterosexual" youth has begun to change in recent years. Investigators have increasingly adopted broader inclusion criteria for studying sexual minorities and have attempted to understand the unique experiences of men and women with attractions to both sexes (Dickson et al., 2003; Hoburg, Konik, Williams, & Crawford, 2004; Kinnish, Strassberg, & Turner, 2005; Savin-Williams, 2005). One troubling result of these efforts has been a growing number of studies suggesting that individuals with bisexual patterns of attraction and behavior may actually have *higher* mental and physical health risks than lesbian, gay, mostly heterosexual, or heterosexual individuals (Marla Eisenberg & Wechsler, 2003; Galliher, Rostosky, & Hughes, 2004; Jorm et al., 2002; Moon, Fornili, & O'Briant, 2007; Robin et al., 2002; Russell, Seif, & Truong, 2001; Udry & Chantala, 2002). The mechanisms underlying these greater risks have not been specified, although extant findings support the possibility that bisexual individuals simply face more extreme and prolonged versions of the stressors that are common to all sexual minorities, due to the invisibility and stigmatization of bisexuality and the lack of social support resources targeted specifically to bisexuals.

Hence, in the next section, we focus specifically on what is currently known about the mental health of bisexual men and women. Following the practice of most studies reviewed, we use the descriptor "bisexual" to describe individuals who report sexual attractions and/or behavior with both men and women, regardless of whether they openly identify as bisexual. We take a broader review of the collected findings, adopting a process-oriented approach to discern reasons as to why bisexual individuals face distinct risks and what their experiences can tell us about the clinical concerns of sexual minorities more generally.

Anxiety, Depression, and Generalized Mental Health

Comparing bisexuals to other sexual identity groups on anxiety, depression, or general mental health, bisexuals typically score significantly worse (Jorm et al., 2002; Rothblum & Factor, 2001; Savin-Williams & Joyner, 2007) than gay men and lesbians, who may or may not score significantly worse than heterosexuals. Some studies find no statistically significant differences between groups, but nonetheless report that bisexuals typically have the most elevated scores on these measures (Balsam, Beauchaine et al., 2005; Tjepkma, 2008). For example, in a representative sample of Canadian adults, including hundreds of self-identified bisexual men and women, Tejpkema (2008) found that, in comparison with heterosexuals, all four sexual-minority groups (bisexual men, gay men, bisexual women, lesbians) reported significantly more mood and anxiety disorders. Although they did not specifically compare bisexuals to lesbians and gay men, the data clearly indicate higher rates among both male and female bisexuals, especially bisexual women. For example, 25% of bisexual women reported being diagnosed with a mood disorder, compared with 11% of lesbian women and 8% of heterosexual women. Similarly, in a nationally representative sample of youth, Udry and Chantala (2002) found that girls who had both male and female sexual partners were more than twice as likely to be depressed as were those who had exclusively male partners; boys with both male and female partners were also at significantly greater risk. In contrast, girls and boys with exclusively same-sex partners were not at increased risk. Thus, with few exceptions (Sandfort, Bakker, Schellevis, & Vanwesenbeeck, 2006), bisexual women are consistently found to be at greater risk than women with exclusively same-sex or exclusively other-sex attractions and behavior; among males, the only difference is that, in some studies, males with exclusively same-sex attractions and behaviors have mental health risks equal to or greater than those of bisexual men.

Substance Use

Consistent with findings for anxiety and depression, studies directly comparing bisexuals with heterosexuals and with lesbians and gay men have generally found that bisexuals report significantly greater use of alcohol and drugs, although findings are often moderated by age of the sample. Among adolescents, those with both same-sex and other-sex sexual partners consistently report greater use of alcohol and illegal drugs than do adolescents with exclusively other-sex partners (Robin et al., 2002; Udry & Chantala, 2002), and they are also at greater risk for binge drinking (Robin et al., 2002). In large population-based studies of high school students

conducted by Robin and colleagues (2002), approximately 45% of bisexually behaving adolescents had tried cocaine, compared with approximately 20% of youth with same-sex partners and approximately 13% of youth with other-sex partners. Similar findings have emerged from studies using convenience samples of youth recruited from sexual-minority youth centers. One recent study found that bisexually behaving youth were significantly more likely to be current smokers and to report having currently or previously used hard alcohol, marijuana, crack, and heroin (Moon et al., 2007).

Among adults, findings have been more mixed. Jorm and colleagues (2002) found that self-identified bisexuals had the highest rates of alcohol use, followed by gay and lesbian individuals. Consistent with this, the Dutch population-based survey conducted by Sandfort and colleagues (2006) found that bisexually attracted adults were more likely than heterosexuals to have ever used marijuana or hashish, although they did not differ regarding alcohol or hard drugs. As with the research on anxiety and depression, there is some evidence for sex differences, with bisexual women demonstrating increased risk more consistently than bisexual men. For example, in a study using a national random sample of college students on 119 college campuses, Eisenberg and Wechsler (2003) reported that bisexually behaving women were approximately twice as likely to smoke, binge drink, and use marijuana in comparison to women with exclusively other-sex partners. Yet, bisexually behaving men were actually less likely to binge drink than were men with exclusively other-sex partners, similar to other findings regarding alcohol and drug use among bisexual versus gay men (Warner et al., 2004).

Suicidality

Bisexual individuals frequently have the highest rates of suicidal ideation and suicide attempts when compared to heterosexuals and to men and women with exclusively same-sex patterns of attraction and behavior, both during adolescence and adulthood (Jorm et al., 2002; Ploderl & Fartacek, 2005; Robin et al., 2002; Savin-Williams & Joyner, 2007). For example, in Robin et al.'s population-based study, approximately 45% of youth with both male and female sexual partners reported suicide attempts, compared to approximately 17% of those with exclusively same-sex partners and 12% of those with exclusively other-sex partners. Moon et al.'s (2007) study of youth center participants found that bisexually behaving adolescents were more than four times as likely to have attempted suicide than were lesbian and gay youth, and bisexual youth were less likely to endorse the statement, "I am a good person worthy of being alive" (Moon et al., 2007). Again, however, findings are moderated by sex differences, with bisexual females showing particularly high risk, reporting, in some cases, twice as many suicidal thoughts as heterosexual girls (Udry & Chantala, 2002), and exclusively gay young men showing risks that are sometimes equal to and sometimes greater than young bisexual men.

Making Sense of the Findings: Sexual-Minority "Subtypes?"

Taken together, findings have been so striking that it is somewhat surprising that there has not been more open and explicit discussion of the potential mechanisms underlying the apparent risks associated with bisexuality. Some scholars have interpreted these findings to suggest that bisexuals, particularly youth, are disproportionately likely to engage in a wide range of risk-taking behavior and that their pursuit of sexual behavior with both male and female partners reflects a generalized tendency toward experimentation and risk-taking (Moon et al., 2007; Robin et al., 2002). This interpretation is consistent with Eisenberg's (2001) data that women with both same-sex and other-sex sexual partners were disproportionately likely to report having multiple sexual partners in the past 30 days. Although this at first appears to confirm the negative stereotype of bisexuals as sexually unrestrained, it is important to remember that Eisenberg's study—as is the case with many others—operationally defined the "bisexual" category so that it only included individuals who had pursued recent sexual contact with *both* male and female partners. Bisexually attracted individuals who had no recent sexual partners, or only one sexual partner, were not considered "bisexual." Hence, in such cases, bisexuality is confounded with having multiple sexual partners. Such sampling considerations must be carefully considered when interpreting all aforementioned findings.

Another common explanation offered for the mental health risks associated with bisexuality is that men and women with bisexual patterns of attraction and behavior are generally mired in the process of transitioning from a heterosexual to a gay or lesbian identity, and that the attendant confusion and ambiguity accounts for their greater mental health problems. Certainly, some bisexual individuals, particularly youth, report confusion and self-doubt about their identities (Hillier, Dempsey, Harrison,

Beale, & Matthews, 1998), describing reasons for bisexual identification such as, "Confused because I'm in love with my best friend, but I've only had sex with boys," "How do I explain the fact that I just got drunk and kissed a boy/girl at a party?," and "What if it's only this girl/boy and not any others?" However, Hillier and colleagues also noted that many bisexually identified youth "were quite comfortably assuming this label, did not appear at all confused, and described supportive and progressive family and friendship networks" (p. 29). Among adults, some studies have found greater identity confusion among bisexuals than among lesbians and gay men, but associations between identity confusion and mental health typically disappear after controlling for "outness" and connection to lesbian-gay-bisexual communities (Balsam & Mohr, 2007). Hence, in these cases, it is not "identity confusion" that places bisexuals at greater risk but the fact that bisexuals who are doubtful about their sexual identity tend to be more secretive and to have less access to social support. It also bears emphasizing that the global characterization of bisexuals as "in transition" or "confused" is increasingly dubious, especially as the phenomenon of bisexuality gains greater cultural legitimacy and visibility as a distinct sexual-minority identity unto itself (reviewed in Diamond, 2008a; Rust, 2000e). Certainly, some bisexuals have been observed to transition to gay or lesbian identity labels (Kinnish et al., 2005; Rosario et al., 1996; Rosario, Schrimshaw, Hunter, & Braun, 2006), and often report improved psychological health thereafter (Paul et al., 2002; Stokes, Damon, & McKirnan, 1997). Yet, recent long-term longitudinal research suggests that, over long stretches of time, sexual-minority women are actually more likely to switch to bisexual from lesbian labels than vice versa (Diamond, 2008b).

A third possible explanation for the greater mental health risks reported by bisexuals centers on the aforementioned minority stress model (Herek, 2007; Meyer, 2003), which maintains that bisexual men and women are more detrimentally affected by chronic and acute stressors associated with their sexual-minority status than are gays and lesbians. Is there evidence to suggest that this is the case? Some research suggests that there is. Bisexuals not only face many of the same forms of stigma and discrimination as do gay and lesbian individuals, but they are often subjected to additional prejudice—specifically targeted to bisexuals—from both the heterosexual and gay-lesbian communities (Hillier et al., 1998; Morris & Rothblum, 1999). This additional stigma, commonly denoted *biphobia,* may contribute to the elevated mental health problems observed in bisexual individuals. Indeed, Herek (2002) found that bisexuals elicited more negative responses from heterosexual individuals than *any other minority group*, with the exception of injecting drug users. Other surveys have found that bisexuals are significantly more likely than gay and lesbian individuals to be judged "unacceptable" (Eliason, 1997), and are perceived as being likely to cheat on their relationship partners, potentially infecting them with sexually transmitted infections as a result (Spalding & Peplau, 1997).

A particular form of minority stress unique to bisexuality is the fact that many individuals—scientists and laypeople alike—believe that bisexuality does not really exist (Ochs, 1996; Rieger, Bailey, & Chivers, 2005; Rust, 2002). As a result, many bisexual individuals lack support and validation not only from the mainstream heterosexual community, but also from the lesbian-gay community. Even in purportedly inclusive sexual-minority groups and organizations, bisexuals may be distinctly excluded. Similarly, sexual-minority youth with bisexual patterns of attraction and behavior often report feeling isolated within gay and lesbian communities (Ault, 1996; Ochs, 1996), noting that their sexual-minority peers think they are just going through a phase, or a temporary state of confusion or denial (Hillier et al., 1998). For youth who find their identities invalidated by sexual-minority peers, forming connections with such peers may not provide the same psychological benefits that have been observed among conventionally identified lesbian and gay youth. For example, one young bisexual woman noted that, after joining a gay and lesbian support group, she was criticized for not being a "real lesbian," and therefore failed to find the support and acceptance that she was seeking (Hillier et al., 1998). Rothblum and Factor (2001) suggested that because bisexuals are often denigrated by both heterosexuals and gay and lesbian individuals, they end up being "doubly oppressed," and as a result may be more likely to remain closeted and to feel disconnected from lesbian and gay communities (Balsam & Mohr, 2007). Prolonged secrecy and isolation among bisexual individuals may keep them from accessing forms of social support and solidarity that have been observed to buffer sexual-minority individuals from the negative effects of minority stress (Lewis, Derlega, Griffin, & Krowinski, 2003; Luhtanen, 2003). The end result is that bisexual individuals have fewer opportunities and resources for replacing negative

and stigmatizing self-concepts with positive affirmations of their sexual selfhood (Morris, Waldo, & Rothblum, 2001).

Bisexual Subtypes?

Given the diverse mechanisms that may account for various mental health risks facing bisexual individuals, one potential interpretation of the extant data is that there is no global "type" of bisexual individual who faces heightened psychosocial challenges, but rather a number of different "subtypes" of bisexual men and women who face either greater or lesser risks, and that the key to understanding a particular bisexual individual's mental health status is to figure out the subtype to which he or she belongs.

For example, it bears noting that, in contrast to the relatively dire portrait painted by some of the large-scale studies comparing bisexual to lesbian, gay, and heterosexual individuals, some studies have found that there are undoubtedly many bisexual men and women who proudly embrace their enduring patterns of attraction to both sexes and take steps to affiliate with other bisexuals and bolster their social support (Firestein, 2007). These are arguably the "healthiest" bisexual individuals possible, and they stand in sharp contrast to bisexual men and women who may "actually" be gay or lesbian but are identifying as bisexual as an irrational defense against acknowledging their same-sex sexuality to themselves and others (Paul et al., 2002; Stokes et al., 1997). Presumably, such individuals should be at risk for higher levels of self-loathing, have little access to social support, and be persistently fearful of victimization and stigmatization. One might further imagine that there is a group of bisexuals who are most accurately described as "curious heterosexuals," dabbling in bisexual attractions or relationships because it has become relatively "cool" in the current cultural context (Diamond, 2005a; Hegna & Larsen, 2007).

The notion of "subtypes" is a tempting one. After all, psychologists have long gravitated toward categorizing sexual-minority individuals with respect to their specific degrees of same-sex and other-sex attractions and behavior, the triggers and contexts for these attractions and behaviors, expressions of masculinity versus femininity, and preferences for social contact with men versus women (Blumstein & Schwartz, 1977; Klein, 1993; MacDonald, 1981; Stokes, Miller, & Mundhenk, 1998; Taywaditep & Stokes, 1998; Weinberg, Williams, & Pryor, 1994). Importantly, there is no empirical evidence that such sexual-minority types *actually exist*—they are fundamentally human creations, born of our own attempts to impart order and coherence on a vast and complex phenomenon. On one hand, subtypes might prove to be useful heuristics, assisting clinicians in quickly grasping a client's key issues. An individual who reports only one instance of "experimental" same-sex behavior obviously does not face the same risks of social stigmatization as an individual with a long-term pattern of bisexual behavior. On the other hand, such heuristics risk drawing attention away from a particular client's unique and fundamentally individual concerns and risks reifying distinctions that end up doing more harm than good.

In particular, typologies that distinguish between presumably enduring versus transient forms of bisexuality are problematic, as they set up an implied hierarchy of authenticity that deems some individuals' same-sex sexuality more legitimate than others. Such hierarchies have a long history in the psychological literature. Researchers have historically contrasted "constitutional" same-sex sexuality, attributed to an intrinsic predisposition for the same sex, with "facultative" or "opportunistic" same-sex sexuality, attributed to reduced opportunities for other-sex contact or prolonged sex-segregation (Bell, Weinberg, & Hammersmith, 1981; Klein, 1993; Money, 1988; Rust, 2000a; Zinik, 1985). Individuals with "constitutional" same-sex sexuality have been expected to periodically seek same-sex partners even when other-sex partners are available, whereas those with "facultative" same-sex sexuality are expected to seek same-sex partners only when other-sex partners are unavailable. An example of facultative same-sex sexuality might be adolescent boys at same-sex boarding schools, who have been found to engage in more same-sex behavior than those at mixed-sex schools, but to return to other-sex behavior on leaving such environments (Wellings, Field, Johnson, & Wadsworth, 1994). The same phenomenon at all-female colleges has been jokingly called "LUG," or "lesbian until graduation" (Davis, 1999; Kyrakanos, 1998; Rimer, 1993).

Are such distinctions meaningful? It depends on their use. Certainly, the clinical issues facing individuals who have consistently pursued bisexual behavior from adolescence through adulthood are different from the clinical issues facing individuals whose expression of same-sex sexuality is more dependent on situational factors. Yet, the problem with sorting sexual minorities into "constitutional/facultative" categories or other, similar, categories, such as "born/primary lesbians" versus "elective/political lesbians" (Golden, 1996), is that such distinctions,

once invoked, tend to take on a life of their own. They also presume that we understand much more about the etiology of different expressions of same-sex sexuality than is actually the case. For example, despite the widespread assumption that self-identified lesbians with stable and enduring patterns of same-sex sexuality probably express those attractions at an early age (theoretically reflecting the essential, "constitutional" origin of those attractions), whereas bisexuals with more variable, situationally based expressions of same-sex sexuality probably express their attractions much later, this does not appear to be the case (Diamond, 1998, 2005b). Hence, invoking such distinctions in the absence of solid data regarding the factors that do and do not differentiate between diverse experiences and expressions of same-sex sexuality may be more misleading than helpful.

In the end, researchers have come to view all same-sex and other-sex behavior as governed by varying degrees of constitutional and situational components (Kirkpatrick, 2000, p. 390). Instead of implicitly dismissing any individual's same-sex sexuality as "transient" or "opportunistic" on the basis of certain surface features such as its duration, its age of onset, or its situational context, we should focus on asking relevant questions about the ways in which *all* individuals' sexual desires, motives, and self-concepts have unfolded in diverse ways, across diverse contexts, and according to diverse timetables, and should probe the implications of such variability for current and future behavior, self-concept, and well-being.

Taking a Process-oriented Approach

For this reason, it is preferable to parse the complex phenomenon of same-sex sexuality, especially bisexuality, in terms of underlying processes and mechanisms that shape individual experience and adjustment, rather than shoehorning individuals into predefined categories. This approach guards against reifying inaccurate typologies, highlights important sources of diversity within sexual-minority populations, and prevents exaggerating differences between heterosexuals and sexual minorities. This last point is particularly important from a clinical perspective. Historically, when researchers describe distinctive or salient characteristics of sexual minorities, the implicit presumption is that such characteristics are attributable to their sexual-minority status. In other words, despite the voluminous psychological literature detailing hundreds of individual difference dimensions that moderate social, sexual, emotional, cognitive, and moral development, researchers frequently frame investigations of sexual-minority men and women as studies of "the impact of sexual orientation" or "the consequence of a stigmatized sexual identity" without testing or even questioning whether something other than the individual's same-sex sexuality might be responsible for the phenomenon of interest.

The critical point is that clinicians should not presume that sexual-minority status is the most important influence on a client's well-being, simply because it might be the most salient and distinctive. Even when sexual-minority status *is* a critical issue for an individual's mental health, clinicians must remain mindful of the many different processes and mechanisms through which it potentially exerts its effects. For one person, sexual-minority status might prove significant because it introduces chronic self-doubt and anxiety; another might be completely confident and well-adjusted on an individual level but find that his or her sexual-minority status introduces a chronic source of tension and distrust within the family of origin. One study (Diamond & Lucas, 2002) of adolescent peer relationships found that sexual-minority adolescents had significantly higher levels of anxiety, depression, and loneliness than their heterosexual counterparts, but mediational analyses found that these differences were entirely attributable to the fact that sexual-minority adolescents had significantly more pessimistic expectations when it came to future romantic relationships. The majority of these youth—even those who had successfully managed to date a number of same-sex partners—reported fearing that they would never find the type of romantic relationship that they wanted. Hence, in this case, it was not prejudice, stigmatization, bullying, or self-loathing that was responsible for these youth' psychological difficulties. It was, instead, a particularly acute version of a relatively common adolescent worry: Will I find someone to really and truly love me?

Similarly, studies of same-sex couples have repeatedly found that their most characteristic features often have less to do with being sexual minorities than with distinctive interpersonal dynamics that arise when two women or two men are combined in a romantic relationship, providing a "double dose" of conventionally socialized patterns of gender-specific interpersonal behavior. For example, Kurdek (1998) detected a small but significant tendency for lesbian couples to report greater intimacy with their partners, assessed by self-reported factors such as shared time and the degree to which

partners maintained a "couple" identity (see also Roisman, Clausell, Holland, Fortuna, & Elieff, 2008). Yet, the degree to which such heightened intimacy is beneficial to the relationship is unclear. For example, it does not necessarily promote relationship longevity (Kurdek, 1998), and some clinicians have argued that it might actually prove detrimental to same-sex female couples by promoting excessive psychological "fusion" or "merger" (Biaggio, Coan, & Adams, 2002; Nichols, 1987). This psychological fusion might play a role in the finding that long-term female couples show sharper declines in sexual frequency over time than either heterosexual or male couples (Iasenza, 2002; Peplau, Fingerhut, & Beals, 2004), along with the tendency for women to to desist from taking the lead in initiating sexual activity as a result of conventional female socialization (Blumstein & Schwartz, 1983; Nichols, 1988, 1990). These examples demonstrate the fundamental importance of taking a process-oriented approach to unearthing both *whether* and *why* sexual-minority individuals might present a distinctive range of issues to clinicians.

With this in mind, we now adopt a process-oriented approach to one particular issue that is psychologically significant for all sexual minorities, but which has particular and enduring relevance for those with bisexual patterns of attraction and behavior—identity development and transition over the lifespan. In addition to the general issue of minority stress discussed earlier, issues of identity transition remain among the most preeminent clinical issues facing sexual minorities. Furthermore, our understanding of these issues has arguably undergone more dramatic transformation in the past decade than any other aspect of sexual-minority psychology, especially in light of the accumulating evidence for stark gender differences in same-sex sexuality and in the phenomenon of sexual fluidity. This latter is particularly fundamental to our understanding of the antecedents and implications of bisexuality. For this reason, issues of identity development and transition merit particularly close attention.

Identity Development and Transition

The process by which same-sex attracted individuals come to acknowledge those attractions, question their meaning, and potentially adopt a gay, lesbian, or bisexual identity has received extensive attention by social scientists over the past three decades. Initially, researchers were primarily concerned with charting a normative timetable of sexual identity "milestones" through which all sexual minorities were presumed to progress from uncertainty and confusion to self-knowledge and self-acceptance (Diamond, 2005c; Savin-Williams, 2005). Although diverse in conceptual underpinnings, sexual identity models are nearly universal in their linear stage sequences (Cohen & Savin-Williams, 1996; Sophie, 1986). For example, most models mark the onset of sexual identity development as the individual's first awareness of same-sex attractions, presumed to occur in late childhood or early adolescence. This is followed some years later by a period of testing and exploration, during which youth seek information about gay, lesbian, and bisexual individuals and communities and/or engage in experimentation with same-sex sexual contact. Succeeding stages of identity development entail adopting a sexual-minority label, disclosing this sexual identity to others, becoming involved in a same-sex romantic relationship, celebrating one's sexual identity within a larger social context (e.g., the political arena), and, finally, integrating sexuality within a personal identity.

Although such a linear progression is intuitively appealing, extant research suggests it is simply inaccurate. Rather, considerable diversity exists among sexual-minority youth of different backgrounds, cohorts, and ethnicities regarding the paths taken to sexual-minority identification, particularly regarding the relative ordering of first same-sex sexual contact and self-labeling among young gay and bisexual males (Dubé, 2000; Rosario, Hunter, Maguen, Gwadz, & Smith, 2001; Rosario, Schrimshaw, Hunter et al., 2006; Savin-Williams & Diamond, 2000). Perhaps, the most notable deviations from the standard model have been documented among lesbians and bisexual women (Diamond, 1998, 2000b, 2003a, 2005b, 2008a, 2008b; Golden, 1996; Rust, 1992, 1993). This is perhaps to be expected, given that most sexual identity models were originally derived from exclusively male samples. Not only do women typically initiate sexual identity development at later ages than men, but they appear to do so for different reasons, often referencing emotional rather than sexual feelings for women. In some cases, the order in which they complete stages of sexual identity development is reversed (Diamond, 1998). For example, whereas same-sex activity typically occurs 1 to 2 years prior to a gay or bisexual identification among males (Herdt & Boxer, 1993; Rosario et al., 1996; Savin-Williams & Diamond, 2000), sexual-minority females often have their first same-sex contact after identifying as lesbian or bisexual (Diamond, 1998; Savin-Williams & Diamond, 2000), perhaps reflecting the fact that interpersonal and situational

factors exert a greater press on women's than men's psychosexual development more generally (Baumeister, 2000; Diamond, 2008b; Udry & Billy, 1987; Udry, Talbert, & Morris, 1986).

In critiquing traditional sexual models, numerous researchers (Cass, 1990; Eliason, 1996, 1997; Morris, 1997; Rust, 2000b) have called for a more nuanced approach that examines the multiple antecedents and implications of sexual identity transitions across the entire life course, and not simply when an individual *first* comes to grips with same-sex sexuality. One of the primary weaknesses of previous sexual identity research is its longstanding reliance on retrospective data, which (by default) defines the outcome of sexual identity development to be whatever identity an individual claims when he or she happens to be surveyed. This has led to the widespread supposition that sexual identity development is a "one-time-only" event that begins in early adolescence and finishes in early adulthood. Yet, numerous studies suggest that individuals may begin, suspend, and revisit the process at multiple points in the life course, particularly as their social environments, developmental tasks, and intimate relationships undergo change (Diamond, 2007; Peplau, 2001; Peplau, Garnets, Spalding, Conley, & Veniegas, 1998; Rosario, Schrimshaw, Hunter et al., 2006). Longitudinal studies have found that continued questioning and change in sexual identity is particularly common among individuals with bisexual patterns of attraction and behavior (Diamond, 2008b; Stokes et al., 1997; Weinberg et al., 1994), due to the fact that bisexual attractions create, ipso facto, a broader range of possibilities for individuals' sexual and romantic experiences over time (Weinberg et al., 1994).

Overall, this phenomenon has received little substantive attention because it has been viewed the same way that bisexuality has been defined—exceptional rather than normative. Furthermore, because individuals are highly motivated to construct coherent and consistent life histories (Boxer & Cohler, 1989; Cass, 1990), those who periodically re-question their sexual identities are likely to edit these experiences from the retrospective identity narratives they tell to researchers, or to dismiss them as artifacts of protracted denial of their true sexual orientation (Blumstein & Schwartz, 1977). Yet, research increasingly suggests that multiple transitions in identity are not indicative of psychological dysfunction or denial; they may simply reflect an individual's honest and straightforward reckoning with a continually changing landscape of intimate relationships whose meaning is fundamentally context specific. Particularly for individuals with bisexual patterns of attraction and behavior, a single, fixed identity label may never completely succeed in representing the complicated, situation-specific, and sometimes relationship-specific nature of their sexual self-concepts. Given the complexities of their desires, the healthiest identity outcome might not be a stable identity—even if it is a bisexual identity—but rather openness to multiple identities in different contexts.

A Case Study of Multiple Identity Transitions

In the only long-term longitudinal study of sexual-minority women's sexual identity development, approximately one-third of women changed their sexual identity labels in the 2 years between the first and second waves of data collection (Diamond, 2000b). Some of these changes involved women in the "questioning-unlabeled" category deciding to adopt lesbian or bisexual labels, which was certainly consistent with traditional coming-out models. Yet, there were numerous additional "switches" between lesbian and bisexual labels and, perhaps most unexpectedly, five women actually *gave up* their lesbian or bisexual labels in favor of "unlabeled" identities, and an additional five women gave up their lesbian-bisexual labels in favor of a *heterosexual* label! Yet, all of these women continued to acknowledge attractions to women. The women who switched to heterosexual typically reported that their same-sex attractions simply were not sufficiently strong or frequent enough to justify identifying as lesbian or bisexual.

In the ensuing 2 years, an additional one-quarter of women switched labels (Diamond, 2003a). This time, three lesbians switched to bisexual labels, one bisexual and one unlabeled woman switched to a lesbian label, three lesbian and three bisexual women "unlabeled" themselves, six bisexuals now identified as heterosexual, and three of the women who had adopted heterosexual labels at the previous interview changed their minds and now considered themselves nonheterosexual, but unlabeled. The next two assessments brought more of the same (Diamond, 2005b, 2008a): about one-third of women changed identities between the third and fourth interviews, and another third changed identities between the fourth and fifth assessments. Furthermore, it was not the same subset of women who changed each time. Although some women changed their label more than once over the decade, most changes were "one-time-only" transitions. By the 10-year point, *over two-thirds* of the women had changed their identity label at least once after the first interview. Whereas traditional sexual-developmental models (based on *men's* memories of their pasts) presume that it is fairly atypical for individuals to undergo any additional identity questioning after they first come out, this study found exactly the opposite. The women who kept the same label for the whole decade turned out to be the smallest and most atypical group.

The specific patterns of change observed were also telling. The majority of identity changes undertaken during the 10 years of the study (over 80%) accommodated other-sex attractions and relationships. That is, women switched *to* a bisexual, unlabeled, or heterosexual label. Thus, when women reconsidered and changed their identities, they typically did so in a way that broadened rather than narrowed their potential range of attractions and relationships. Notably, this pattern corresponded to observations made in the 1960s, in which women's sexual experiences were viewed as "broadening" as they aged, whereas men's tended to become narrow and more specialized (McIntosh, 1968). In the final analysis, two groups could be identified. The first included self-identified lesbians who had been fairly exclusively attracted to and involved with women throughout the study, and who were least likely to change their identities. The second group included everyone else: They reported consistently bisexual patterns of attraction and behavior over time, and they were the most likely to change their identities. Their experiences demonstrate just how much researchers have been missing by failing to include bisexual women in previous studies of identity development. Clearly, individuals who are drawn to both men and women face a more complex set of issues when adopting an identity label—and maintaining that label over time—than do individuals with exclusive same-sex attractions and relationships. In order to settle on the "right" identity, individuals with nonexclusive attractions must go beyond acknowledging their same-sex attractions and must consider exactly how strongly they lean toward women versus men, whether sexual and emotional feelings are equally important, whether behavior trumps fantasy or vice versa, and whether social networks and ideological beliefs should play a role.

Importantly, the undertaking of multiple identity transitions introduces its own set of complexities and challenges. Individuals who undertake such changes may face confusion, disdain, and anger from friends and family members, perhaps even from gay and lesbian friends, many of whom may have internalized negative stereotypes about bisexuals and may interpret the change in terms of betrayal and/or abandonment. Thus, individuals with bisexual attractions often find, ironically, that participating in a "socially desirable" heterosexual romance suddenly garners more scorn and anger than did their previous same-sex relationships. Their gay and lesbian friends might accuse them of "selling out" and trying to pass as heterosexual. Family members may claim that their other-sex attractions prove that their same-sex attractions were a phase, or that they can "give up" their same-sex interests if they so desire. Hence, even when undertaken thoughtfully, and with sound reasons, post–sexual identity transitions can introduce a number of psychosocial hurdles for sexual minorities.

It also bears noting that the aforementioned findings regarding women's long-term patterns of identity change clearly demonstrate that bisexuality is not a transitional stage for most women. Few women adopt bisexuality "on the way" to lesbian identification; neither is it common for heterosexual women to adopt bisexuality as an experimental phase (Diamond, 2008a). Although women who entered the study with bisexual or unlabeled identities were significantly more likely to subsequently change their identities than were lesbians, most of these changes were between bisexual and unlabeled identities, and there was no evidence for large-scale shifts toward either lesbianism or heterosexuality. By the 10-year point, only one of the women who had initially identified as bisexual, and only five of the women who had initially been unlabeled, had identified as lesbian. A similarly small number of women who had initially identified as bisexual eventually settled on a heterosexual label by the 10-year point. Furthermore, none of these women showed evidence of progressive changes in their ratio of same-sex to other-sex attractions over the 10 years of the study. They were—and remained—sexually attracted to both men and women consistently over time.

Additional evidence against the "transitional stage" model of bisexuality comes from the fact that the overall number of women adopting bisexual or unlabeled identities did not decline over the course of the study. If bisexuality were a temporary stage or phase, one would expect that, as women moved into adulthood, fewer and fewer would maintain these identities. Yet, to the contrary, the percentage of women claiming a bisexual or unlabeled identity hovered between 50% and 60% at each study wave. By the 10-year point, more than 75% of participants had spent at least some time identifying as bisexual or unlabeled. These results do not rule out the possibility that some women adopt "bisexual" as a temporary, transitional label, but they do suggest that this appears to be an exceptional rather than a normative pattern, especially as "bisexual" gains increasing cultural visibility as a legitimate sexual orientation in and of itself (Rust, 2000e).

Rejecting All Identities

Another notable finding from the longitudinal research on women's identity development was the large number of women who consciously rejected lesbian or bisexual labels in favor of "unlabeled" identities. This pattern flies in the face of traditional sexual identity models, which presume that the process of sexual questioning inevitably and uniformly culminates in the adoption of a lesbian, gay, or bisexual label. Yet, an increasing number of studies report that some individuals conclude, or temporarily suspend, the questioning process without claiming *any* identity label, sometimes as a thoughtful challenge to the notion of sexual categorization and sometimes because they simply find that none of the existing identity labels aptly describes the way in which they experience their sexuality (Diamond, 2008b; Golden, 1987; Savin-Williams, 2005). For example, many of these individuals claim that they "fall in love with the person, not the gender," and that current sexual identity labels fail to adequately describe such a phenomenon (Blumstein & Schwartz, 1990; Diamond, 2008b).

According to conventional sexual identity models, "unlabeled" identities are necessarily dysfunctional. All existing sexual identity models posit a final stage involving the synthesis, resolution, integration, and consolidation of a clearly defined lesbian, gay, or bisexual identity (Cass, 1979; Coleman, 1981/1982; Lee, 1977; Minton & McDonald, 1983; Mohr & Fassinger, 2000; Troiden, 1979), and this final stage is presumed to be critical for future healthy development. Ambivalence or uncertainty about claiming a lesbian, gay, or bisexual label is typically taken as a sign that the individual continues to suffer from internalized homophobia and self-stigmatization. To be sure, studies conducted in the 1980s and 1990s have reliably found that sexual-minority individuals with positive, well-defined lesbian, gay, or bisexual identities had greater ego strength, self-esteem, general adjustment, and overall well-being compared to those who did not claim positive lesbian-gay-bisexual self-concepts (Brady & Busse, 1994; Levine, 1997; Miranda & Storms, 1989; K. L. Walters & Simoni, 1983; Wells & Kline, 1987).

Yet, much of this research failed to tease out whether such benefits were attributable to the acceptance and integration of a sexual *identity* or to the acceptance and integration of one's *same-sex sexuality*, labeled or not. For example, one of the items that Mohr and Fassinger (2000) used to assess identity synthesis among lesbians was, "I am at the point where I feel a deep contentment about my love for other women." Mohr and Fassinger implicitly suggest that any woman agreeing with this statement would identify as lesbian or bisexual, yet the present research shows that this is not necessarily the case. Another problem in interpreting previous research is that there has been considerable historical change in attitudes toward sexual self-identification. A growing number of sexual-minority youth are intentionally challenging notions of sexual categorization and adopting alternative self-concept such as "queer," "questioning," and "none of the above" (Savin-Williams, 2005). For this newest cohort, being "unlabeled" means something drastically different than for a sexual minority 20 years ago.

For all of these reasons, clinicians should avoid making assumptions about the meaning of identity rejection or relinquishment without carefully attending to the individual's reasons and reasoning. There is no single pathway for healthy sexual identity development and no prototypical outcome. Men and women with different peer environments, different families, different ethnic and cultural backgrounds, and different personalities face markedly different options and constraints in crafting healthy identities and relationships. The goal should be to help them weigh these multiple options rather than prescribing one particular goal.

Are Women Distinctive?

The findings reviewed here regarding the phenomenon of identity change and the adoption of "unlabeled" identities concern women. Although similar phenomena have been observed among men (Rosario, Schrimshaw, Hunter et al., 2006; Savin-Williams, 2005), they appear to be less common. Why is this the case? Over the years, researchers have begun to gravitate toward the notion that female same-sex sexuality is intrinsically more flexible and variable than male same-sex sexuality (Baumeister, 2000; Diamond, 2003b, 2005b; Peplau, 2001), perhaps best reflected in the fact that bisexual patterns of attraction appear more common in women than in men (Baumeister, 2000; French et al., 1996; Laumann et al., 1994; Russell & Consolacion, 2003; Russell & Seif, 2002). Notably, this phenomenon

has recently been validated using physiological, as well as self-report measures (Chivers, Rieger, Latty, & Bailey, 2005; Rieger et al., 2005). Specifically, researchers found that, although self-identified bisexual men reported sexual attractions to both women and men, they tended to become physiologically aroused by either one or the other (Rieger et al., 2005). In direct contrast, the majority of lesbian and heterosexual women showed physiological arousal to *both* male and female sexual stimuli, regardless of sexual orientation (Chivers et al., 2005).

There is also evidence that women's attractions—whether bisexual or "monosexual"—show a greater capacity for change over time and across situations (Diamond, 2003a, 2005b; Weinberg et al., 1994). Perhaps for this reason, women are more likely than men to ascribe a role for choice, circumstance, chance, and change in their sexual orientation and identity (Golden, 1996; Whisman, 1996), not only during adolescence but also well into adulthood. Thus, whereas many gay- or bisexual-identified men recall experiencing their first same-sex attractions a few years prior to puberty (similar to the age at which most heterosexual children recall their first other-sex desires, as pointed out by McClintock & Herdt, 1996), many women report that they did not experience same-sex attractions until adulthood, often as a result of encountering gay, lesbian, or bisexual individuals, ideas, or opportunities for same-sex contact (Cass, 1990; Diamond, 1998; Golden, 1987, 1994; Kitzinger & Wilkinson, 1995; Silber, 1990). This is often the case for "political lesbians," who typically report that they chose to orient their lives around women for social and political reasons, and then found their sexual desires following suit (Ettore, 1980; Golden, 1987, 1994; Kitzinger & Wilkinson, 1995; Silber, 1990; Whisman, 1993, 1996). Women are also more likely than men to pursue sexual behavior that runs counter to their avowed attractions and identities—that is, women with predominantly heterosexual attractions pursuing sex with women and women with nearly exclusive same-sex attractions engaging in sex with men (Bell et al., 1981; Diamond, 2003a, 2005b; Rust, 1992; Weinberg et al., 1994).

In many such cases, the impetus for these "atypical" encounters is an intense emotional bond (reviewed in Diamond, 2003b), and in fact, numerous sexual-minority women have reported that their feelings for women are predominantly emotional, or that their sexual desires are triggered or enhanced by feelings of emotional connection (Blumstein & Schwartz, 1990; Esterberg, 1994; Gramick, 1984;

Hedblom, 1973; Nichols, 1987; Ponse, 1978; Savin-Williams, 1998; Vance & Green, 1984; Weinberg et al., 1994). In extreme examples of this phenomenon, some women report having fallen in love with one—and only one—woman, and experiencing same-sex desires exclusively in this context (Blumstein & Schwartz, 1990; Cass, 1990; Cassingham & O'Neil, 1993; Diamond, 2000a). Women also appear more likely than men to report that their desires are not so much directed toward *women* at all, but rather to "the person" they happen to fall in love with (Blumstein & Schwartz, 1990; Cassingham & O'Neil, 1993; Diamond, 2002, 2008b; Golden, 1987).

This is consistent with the fact that the aforementioned 10-year study of women's sexual identity development found that self-identified lesbians who *fell in love* with a man over the course of the study found it far more difficult to continue identifying as lesbian than did women who simply engaged in periodic sexual contact with men (Diamond, 2008b). In fact, all of the women who had initially identified as lesbian, but who developed full-blown romantic relationships with men (which amounted to 30% of the lesbians) eventually switched to bisexual or unlabeled identities. Most notably, they undertook these changes even if they felt that their true orientation was still lesbian. Taken altogether, then, the accumulated evidence suggests that variable patterns of same-sex and other-sex desire and behavior may emerge in any woman over time, and this might simply be more pronounced among the subset of women who consciously identify as bisexual. Accordingly, the distinction between lesbianism and bisexuality may be a matter of degree rather than kind, and a woman's adoption of a bisexual or lesbian identity may have more to do with her self-concept, ideology, and intimate relationships than with her sexual "essence" (Golden, 1996; Rust, 1993, 1995, 2001).

What about men? Importantly, we simply lack sufficient data to determine the specific degree of sexual fluidity among men largely because there have been no long-term longitudinal studies of sexual variability in men. Evidence suggests some degree of fluidity (Rosario, Schrimshaw, Hunter et al., 2006; Stokes et al., 1997; Weinberg et al., 1994), although not as much as has been documented in women. Hence, although clinicians might find the concept of sexual fluidity more broadly applicable to female than male clients, it proves useful in guarding against reductionistic assumptions regarding same-sex behavior in *both*

men and women. Quite simply, the phenomenon of sexual fluidity reminds us that not all individuals who experience same-sex desires or relationships at any one point in time, within any particular relationship, will continue to do so in the future. Of course, this fact creates somewhat of a quandary for clinicians. On one hand, individuals who describe their same-sex experiences as uncharacteristic, "one-time-only" events, attributable to the unusual features of a particular same-sex relationship, might be making a truthful and accurate assessment, or they might be attempting to discount and deny their own capacity for same-sex sexuality. Although it is important for clinicians to avoid prematurely categorizing their clients' sexual identities, it is also important to prompt individuals to honestly reflect on the nature of their same-sex feelings and determine their personal relevance. Because there is no bona fide way, at a single moment in time, to differentiate an enduring pattern of same-sex sexuality from a highly circumscribed, relationship-specific experience triggered by sexual fluidity, the best strategy is to remain open and nonjudgmental, so that individuals can reflect openly and honestly about the quality and personal relevance of their same-sex *and* other-sex experiences in a safe, pressure-free environment. Clinicians might remind clients struggling with these issues that no single sexual or romantic experience can "prove" one's true sexual identity or place a definitive end to the sexual questioning process. Given that individuals with ambiguous, fluid, or bisexual attractions often feel abnormal by heterosexual, gay, and lesbian standards, such individuals need to be reassured that such inconsistencies and ambiguities are actually far more common than they realize.

Conclusion
Future Directions
In considering directions for future research on sexual-minority individuals, it is important to remain mindful of the weaknesses that have plagued previous research, particularly failures to represent the full range of individuals with same-sex attractions, behaviors, identities, and relationships. In addition to the underrepresentation of bisexuals, "mostly heterosexuals," and unlabeled individuals, studies have also underrepresented ethnic minorities, rural and working-class individuals, and those in the later stages of the life course. Greater research on these underrepresented subpopulations is critical for accurately understanding how the unique strengths and challenges of sexual-minority individuals interact with various

individual and contextual factors to shape their life trajectories. Contextual influences are also likely to be particularly important in understanding the unique experiences of individuals with bisexual patterns of attraction and behavior. A growing body of research has demonstrated that issues of ethnicity, culture, and social class influence the meaning that such individuals ascribe to their experiences, and their decisions about behavior, disclosure, and identification (Chung & Katayama, 1999; Greene, 1997; Grov, Bimbi, NanÁn, & Parsons, 2006; Jayakar, 1994; McLean, 2003; Nazario, 2003; Rosario, Schrimshaw, & Hunter, 2004a; Savin-Williams, 1996). The clinical implications of these decisions bear close attention.

Another important direction for future research concerns intersections between sexual identity and *gender* identity (the latter referring to an individual's psychological sense of being female or male, whereas the former refers to one's sense of being heterosexual, lesbian-gay, or bisexual). Research has found that a subset of sexual-minority adolescents and adults report significantly more gender-atypical (i.e., violating conventional cultural standards for appropriate masculinity or femininity) ideation and/or behavior—both in childhood and in adulthood—than do heterosexuals (Bailey, Nothnagel, & Wolfe, 1995; Bailey & Zucker, 1995; Lippa, 2000; Phillips & Over, 1992, 1995). Hence, although gender identity and sexual identity are fundamentally distinct constructs, many individuals wrestle with questions about both domains simultaneously, largely owing to the fact that they have absorbed cultural stereotypes suggesting that all sexual-minority individuals are "inverted" with respect to gender. As a result of these pervasive cultural stereotypes, gender-atypical men and women are not only frequently suspected of being lesbian, gay, or bisexual, but often wonder themselves whether this is the case, even in the absence of same-sex attractions (Hunter, 1993; McGann, 1999). This reflects the fact that there is more cultural "space" for a notion of gender-*typical* sexual minorities than gender-atypical *heterosexuals* (Hunter, 1993). In other words, although people may no longer unilaterally presume that all gay men are hyperfeminine, it is still commonly presumed that any man who *is* hyperfeminine is necessarily gay. Thus, in addition to confronting the same risks for stigmatization, isolation, and harassment that are confronted by sexual-minority youths, gender-atypical men and women also face the problem of having their sexual identity defined for them, often before they have even had a chance to reflect upon it, and often erroneously.

We know little about the internal psychological sequelae of gender atypicality over the life course and how it may differ for individuals with different patterns of same-sex and other-sex attractions. Some individuals, notably, may face greater stigma for gender-atypicality than for same-sex sexuality. Hence, in considering the phenomenon of "minority stress," the unique experiences of gender-atypical men and women must be borne in mind. Even individuals who do not face explicit condemnation for their gender atypical interests or behavior may wrestle with ongoing concerns about the nature of their gender and sexual identity. Women may be wrestling with painful realizations of the pervasive social constraints that continue to be placed upon them in contemporary society, and which limit their interpersonal and occupational aspirations. Men may wrestle with the realization that, to maintain status as appropriately masculine men, they must adopt behaviors and attitudes that some find intrinsically distasteful, such as aggressiveness, dominance, and often outright misogyny. Some have argued, in fact, that one reason "sissy" behavior is so virulently denigrated is that conventional masculinity is so restrictive, distasteful, and difficult to attain that boys could not be counted on to fully adopt it unless the penalties for *not* adopting it were severe (Gilmore, 1990; Hart & Richardson, 1981; Herek, 1986; Hunter, 1993).

Given how little is known about the etiology and ontology of gender atypicality, it is important to avoid making assumptions about the motives for and long-term implications of a particular individual's gendered ideation, appearance, or behavior. On this point, it is important to acknowledge that there has long been considerable debate over whether extreme forms of gender atypicality, including actual cross-gender identification, should be treated as correctable psychological problems or natural forms of human variation (Bradley & Zucker, 1997; Corbett, 1998, 1999; Halderman, 2000). At present, there is no uniform answer to this question, and most researchers and clinicians have taken a case-by-case approach to this issue. Certainly, there has been growing awareness and appreciation of the unique experiences of individuals with fluid, ambiguous, changing notions of their own gender, just as there has been growing appreciation of individuals with fluid, ambiguous, changing notions of their own sexuality (Diamond & Butterworth, 2008). The important point is to recognize the unique *and diverse* developmental experiences of gender-atypical men and women, to appropriately assess the relevance (or lack of relevance) of sexual orientation to different individual's cases, and to take active steps to promote their physical and psychological well-being.

Finally, it is important that future studies counteract the negative cast of most prior research on sexual minorities by closely investigating the positive attributes, strengths, and skills of individuals with same-sex attractions and behaviors (Savin-Williams, 2005). One unexplored possibility, for example, is that individuals who actively wrestle with questions about their sexuality end up developing a healthier sense of sexual agency, better able "to know their sexuality as feelings as well as actions, feelings to which they are entitled" (Tolman, 1994, p. 268). Even individuals who experiment with same-sex sexuality, but end up identifying as heterosexual, might benefit from temporarily broadening their definitions and conceptualizations of sexuality. In particular, participation in same-sex activity necessarily disrupts widespread cultural assumptions about the "naturalness" of heterosexuality, as well as the "naturalness" of female and male gender roles. Participation in same-sex relationships and consideration of same-sex attractions might prompt all individuals to ask themselves important, useful questions about how they conceive of their sexuality, and what types of relationships they desire in the future. This has the potential to create altogether new and healthy trajectories of sexual and gender development.

Perhaps the most important recommendation for clinicians serving sexual-minority men and women is to take seriously the incredible diversity of these individuals' sexual profiles. This entails acknowledging and communicating to sexual-minority men and women that the categories "heterosexual," "gay/lesbian," "bisexual," and even "female" and "male" do not represent the full range of feelings, fantasies, and relationships they may find themselves experiencing throughout the life span. Clinicians can play a critically important role in sexual-minority individuals' well-being by simply providing them with a safe and supportive context within which they can consider the personal meaning of same-sex sexuality for their current and future relationships and identity. In contrast to early research on sexual minorities, which emphasized commonalities in their experiences due to their shared experience of stigmatization, we are now faced with the task of charting the multiple, interacting factors producing diversity in their developmental pathways. A fuller understanding of such diversity will clearly advance our capacity to foster sexual minorities' well-being over the life span.

References

Allport, G. W. (1954). *The nature of prejudice*. Reading, MA: Addison-Wesley.

Amaro, H. (1978). *Coming out: Hispanic lesbians, their families and communities*. Paper presented at the National Coalition of Hispanic Mental Health and Human Services Organization, Austin, TX.

Anderson, A. L. (1998). Strengths of gay male youth: An untold story. *Child and Adolescent Social Work Journal, 15*, 55–71.

Ault, A. (1996). Ambiguous identity in an unambiguous sex/gender structure: The case of bisexual women. *Sociological Quarterly, 37*, 449–463.

Austin, S. B., Ziyadeh, N., Kahn, J. A., Camargo, C. A. J., Colditz, G. A., & Field, A. E. (2004). Sexual orientation, weight concerns, and eating-disordered behaviors in adolescent girls and boys. *Journal of the American Academy of Child & Adolescent Psychiatry, 43*, 1115–1123.

Badgett, M. V. L. (1998). The economic well-being of lesbian, gay, and bisexual adults' families. In C. Patterson, & A. R. D'Augelli (Eds.), *Lesbian, gay, and bisexual identities in families: Psychological Perspectives* (pp. 231–248). New York: Oxford University Press.

Bailey, J. M., Dunne, M. P., & Martin, N. G. (2000). Genetic and environmental influences on sexual orientation and its correlates in an Australian twin sample. *Journal of Personality and Social Psychology, 78*, 524–536.

Bailey, J. M., Nothnagel, J., & Wolfe, B. A. (1995). Retrospectively measured individual differences in childhood sex-typed behavior among gay men: A correspondence between self and maternal reports. *Archives of Sexual Behavior, 24*, 613–622.

Bailey, J. M., & Zucker, K. J. (1995). Childhood sex-typed behavior and sexual orientation: A conceptual analysis and quantitative review. *Developmental Psychology, 31*, 43–55.

Balsam, K. F., Beauchaine, T. P., Mickey, R. M., & Rothblum, E. D. (2005). Mental health of lesbian, gay, bisexual, and heterosexual siblings: Effects of gender, sexual orientation, and family. *Journal of Abnormal Psychology, 114*, 471–476.

Balsam, K. F., & Mohr, J. J. (2007). Adaptation to sexual orientation stigma: A comparison of bisexual and lesbian/gay adults. *Journal of Counseling Psychology, 54*, 306–319.

Balsam, K. F., Rothblum, E. D., & Beauchaine, T. P. (2005). Victimization over the life span: A comparison of lesbian, gay, bisexual, and heterosexual siblings. *Journal of Consulting and Clinical Psychology, 73*, 477–487.

Baumeister, R. F. (2000). Gender differences in erotic plasticity: The female sex drive as socially flexible and responsive. *Psychological Bulletin, 126*, 247–374.

Beeler, J., & DiProva, V. (1999). Family adjustment following disclosure of homosexuality by a member: Themes discerned in narrative accounts. *Journal of Marital & Family Therapy, 25*, 443–459.

Bell, A. P., Weinberg, M. S., & Hammersmith, S. K. (1981). *Sexual preference: Its development in men and women*. Bloomington: Indiana University Press.

Biaggio, M., Coan, S., & Adams, W. (2002). Couples therapy for lesbians: Understanding merger and the impact of homophobia. *Journal of Lesbian Studies, 6*, 129–138.

Blackwood, E. (2000). Culture and women's sexualities. *Journal of Social Issues, 56*, 223–238.

Blumstein, P., & Schwartz, P. (1977). Bisexuality: Some social psychological issues. *Journal of Social Issues, 33*, 30–45.

Blumstein, P., & Schwartz, P. (1983). *American couples: Money, work, sex*. New York: Morrow.

Blumstein, P., & Schwartz, P. (1990). Intimate relationships and the creation of sexuality. In D. P. McWhirter, S. A. Sanders, & J. M. Reinisch (Eds.), *Homosexuality/heterosexuality: Concepts of sexual orientation* (pp. 307–320). New York: Oxford University Press.

Bontempo, D. E., & D'Augelli, A. R. (2002). Effects of at-school victimization and sexual orientation on lesbian, gay, or bisexual youths' health risk behavior. *Journal of Adolescent Health, 30*, 364–374.

Bos, H. M. W., Sandfort, T. G. M., de Bruyn, E. H., & Hakvoort, E. M. (2008). Same-sex attraction, social relationships, psychosocial functioning, and school performance in early adolescence. *Developmental Psychology, 44*, 59–68.

Boxer, A., & Cohler, B. (1989). The life course of gay and lesbian youth: An immodest proposal for the study of lives. *Journal of Homosexuality, 17*, 315–355.

Bradley, S. J., & Zucker, K. J. (1997). Gender identity disorder: A review of the past 10 years. *Journal of the American Academy of Child and Adolescent Psychiatry, 36*, 872–880.

Brady, S., & Busse, W. J. (1994). The gay identity questionnaire: A brief measure of homosexual identity formation. *Journal of Homosexuality, 26*, 1–22.

Brent, D. A. (1995). Risk factors for adolescent suicide and suicidal behavior: Mental and substance abuse disorders, family environmental factors, and life stress. *Suicide and Life-Threatening Behavior, 25*, 52–63.

Brent, D. A. (2001). Assessment and treatment of the youthful suicidal patient. In H. Hendin, & J. J. Mann (Eds.), *The clinical science of suicide prevention* (pp. 106–131). New York, NY: New York Academy of Sciences.

Brewer, P. R., & Wilcox, C. (2005). The polls-trends: Same-sex marriage and civil unions. *Public Opinion Quarterly, 69*, 599–616.

Broverman, N. (2006, February 14). By the numbers: Gay rights. *The Advocate, 36.*

Brown, L. (1989). Lesbians, gay men, and their families: Common clinical issues. *Journal of Gay and Lesbian Psychotherapy, 1*, 65–77.

Bryant, A. S., & Demian. (1994). Relationship characteristics of American gay and lesbian couples: Findings from a national survey. *Journal of Gay and Lesbian Social Services, 1*, 101–117.

Buchanan, W. (2008). Poll finds US warming to gay marriage. Retrieved October 3, 2008, from http://www.sfgate.com/cgi-bin/article.cgi?file=/c/a/2006/03/23/MNGAOHSE4I1.DTL

Busseri, M. A., Willoughby, T., Chalmers, H., & Bogaert, A. F. (2008). On the association between sexual attraction and adolescent risk behavior involvement: Examining mediation and moderation. *Developmental Psychology, 44*, 69–80.

Busseri, M. A., Willoughby, T., Chalmers, H., & Bogaert, A. R. (2006). Same-sex attraction and successful adolescent development. *Journal of Youth and Adolescence, 35*, 563–575.

Carballo-Dieguez, A. (1989). Hispanic culture, gay male culture, and AIDS: Counseling implications. *Journal of Counseling and Development, 68*, 26–30.

Carballo-Dieguez, A., & Dolezal, C. (1994). Contrasting types of Puerto Rican men who have sex with men (MSM). *Journal of Psychology and Human Sexuality, 6*, 41–67.

Caron, S. L., & Ulin, M. (1997). Closeting and the quality of lesbian relationships. *Families in Society, 78*, 413–419.

Case, P., Austin, S. B., Hunter, D. J., Manson, J. E., Malspeis, S., Willett, W. C., et al. (2004). Sexual orientation, health risk factors, and physical functioning in the Nurses' Health Study II. *Journal of Women's Health, 13*, 1033–1047.

Cass, V. (1979). Homosexual identity formation: A theoretical model. *Journal of Homosexuality, 4*, 219–235.

Cass, V. (1990). The implications of homosexual identity formation for the Kinsey model and scale of sexual preference. In D. P. McWhirter, S. A. Sanders, & J. M. Reinisch (Eds.), *Homosexuality/heterosexuality: Concepts of sexual orientation* (pp. 239–266). New York: Oxford University Press.

Cassingham, B. J., & O'Neil, S. M. (1993). *And then I met this woman.* Freeland, WA: Soaring Eagle Publishing.

Chan, C. S. (1992). Cultural considerations in counseling Asian-American lesbians and gay men. In S. H. Dworkin, & F. J. Gutierrez (Eds.), *Counseling gay men and lesbians: Journey to the end of the rainbow* (pp. 115–124). Alexandria, VA: American Association for Counseling and Development.

Chivers, M. L., Rieger, G., Latty, E., & Bailey, J. M. (2005). A sex difference in the specificity of sexual arousal. *Psychological Science, 15*, 736–744.

Chung, Y. B., & Katayama, M. (1999). Ethnic and sexual identity development of Asian-American lesbian and gay adolescents. In K. S. Ng (Ed.), *Counseling Asian families from a systems perspective* (pp. 159–169). Alexandria, VA: American Counseling Association.

Clarke, C. (1983). The failure to transform: Homophobia in the Black community. In B. Smith (Ed.), *Home girls: A Black feminist anthology* (pp. 197–208). New York: Kitchen Table Press.

Cochran, S. D., Sullivan, J. G., & Mays, V. M. (2003). Prevalence of mental disorders, psychological distress, and mental services use among lesbian, gay, and bisexual adults in the United States. *Journal of Consulting and Clinical Psychology, 71*, 53–61.

Cohen, K. M., & Savin-Williams, R. C. (1996). Developmental perspectives on coming out to self and others. In R. C. Savin-Williams, & K. M. Cohen (Eds.), *The lives of lesbians, gays, and bisexuals: Children to adults* (pp. 113–151). Fort Worth, TX: Harcourt Brace.

Coleman, E. (1981/1982). Developmental stages of the coming out process. *Journal of Homosexuality, 7*, 31–43.

Collins, P. H. (1990). Homophobia and Black lesbians. In P. H. Collins (Ed.), *Black feminist thought: Knowledge, consciousness, and the politics of empowerment* (pp. 192–196). New York: Routledge.

Consolacion, T. B., Russell, S. T., & Sue, S. (2004). Sex, race/ethnicity, and romantic attractions: Multiple minority status adolescents and mental health. *Cultural Diversity & Ethnic Minority Psychology, 10*, 200–214.

Corbett, K. (1998). Cross-gendered identifications and homosexual boyhood: Toward a more complex theory of gender. *American Journal of Orthopsychiatry, 68*, 352–360.

Corbett, K. (1999). Homosexual boyhood: Notes on girlyboys. In M. Rottnek (Ed.), *Sissies and tomboys: Gender nonconformity and homosexual childhood* (pp. 107–139). New York: New York University Press.

Crocker, J., Major, B., & Steele, C. (1998). Social stigma. In D. T. Gilbert, S. T. Fiske & G. Lindzey (Eds.), *The handbook of social psychology, Vols. 1 and 2*, 4th ed. (pp. 504–553). New York, NY: McGraw-Hill.

Crosbie Burnett, M., Foster, T. L., Murray, C. I., & Bowen, G. L. (1996). Gays' and lesbians' fam ilies-of-origin: A social-cognitive behavioral model of adjustment. *Family Relations, 45*, 397–403.

D'Augelli, A. R., Grossman, A. H., & Starks, M. T. (2005). Parents' awareness of lesbian, gay, and bisexual youths' sexual orientation. *Journal of Marriage & Family, 67*, 474–482.

D'Augelli, A. R., Grossman, A. H., & Starks, M. T. (2006). Childhood gender atypicality, victimization, and PTSD among lesbian, gay, and bisexual youth. *Journal of Interpersonal Violence, 21*, 1462–1482.

D'Augelli, A. R., Pilkington, N. W., & Hershberger, S. L. (2002). Incidence and mental health impact of sexual orientation victimization of lesbian, gay, and bisexual youths in high school. *School Psychology Quarterly, 17*, 148–167.

Davis, A. (1999). Confessions of a LUG. *Flagpole Magazine Online, October 25, 1999*.

De Monteflores, C. (1986). Notes on the management of difference. In T. Stein, & C. Cohen (Eds.), *Contemporary perspectives on psychotherapy with lesbians and gay men* (pp. 73–101). New York: Plenum.

Diamond, L. M. (1998). Development of sexual orientation among adolescent and young adult women. *Developmental Psychology, 34*, 1085–1095.

Diamond, L. M. (2000a). Passionate friendships among adolescent sexual-minority women. *Journal of Research on Adolescence, 10*, 191–209.

Diamond, L. M. (2000b). Sexual identity, attractions, and behavior among young sexual-minority women over a 2-year period. *Developmental Psychology, 36*, 241–250.

Diamond, L. M. (2002). "Having a girlfriend without knowing it": The relationships of adolescent lesbian and bisexual women. *Journal of Lesbian Studies, 6*, 5–16.

Diamond, L. M. (2003a). Was it a phase? Young women's relinquishment of lesbian/bisexual identities over a 5-year period. *Journal of Personality and Social Psychology, 84*, 352–364.

Diamond, L. M. (2003b). What does sexual orientation orient? A biobehavioral model distinguishing romantic love and sexual desire. *Psychological Review, 110*, 173–192.

Diamond, L. M. (2005a). "I'm straight, but I kissed a girl": The trouble with American media representations of female-female sexuality. *Feminism and Psychology, 15*, 104–110.

Diamond, L. M. (2005b). A new view of lesbian subtypes: Stable vs. fluid identity trajectories over an 8-year period. *Psychology of Women Quarterly, 29*, 119–128.

Diamond, L. M. (2005c). What we got wrong about sexual identity development: Unexpected findings from a longitudinal study of young women. In A. Omoto, & H. Kurtzman (Eds.), *Sexual orientation and mental health: Examining identity and development in lesbian, gay, and bisexual people* (pp. 73–94). Washington, DC: American Psychological Association Press.

Diamond, L. M. (2007). A dynamical systems approach to female same-sex sexuality. *Perspectives on Psychological Science, 2*, 142–161.

Diamond, L. M. (2008a). Female bisexuality from adolescence to adulthood: Results from a 10-year longitudinal study. *Developmental Psychology, 44*, 5–14.

Diamond, L. M. (2008b). *Sexual fluidity: Understanding women's love and desire*. Cambridge, MA: Harvard University Press.

Diamond, L. M., & Butterworth, M. (2008). Questioning gender and sexual identity: Dynamic links over time. *Sex Roles, 59*, 365–376.

Diamond, L. M., & Lucas, S. (2002). *Close relationships and well-being among sexual-minority and heterosexual youths.* Paper presented at the biennial meeting of the Society for Research on Adolescence, New Orleans, LA.

Dickson, N., Paul, C., & Herbison, P. (2003). Same-sex attraction in a birth cohort: Prevalence and persistence in early adulthood. *Social Science & Medicine, 56*, 1607–1615.

DiPlacido, J. (1998). Minority stress among lesbians, gay men, and bisexuals: A consequence of heterosexism, homophobia, and stigmatization. In G. M. Herek (Ed.), *Stigma and sexual orientation: Understanding prejudice against lesbians, gay men, and bisexuals* (pp. 138–159). Thousand Oaks, CA: Sage.

Doig, W. (2007, July 17). America's real first family. *The Advocate,* 46–50.

Dubé, E. M. (2000). *Same- and cross-gender romantic relationships: Mediating variables between female presence and relationship quality (Doctoral dissertation, Cornell University, 1990). Dissertation Abstracts International, 60*(8-B), 4273. Unpublished manuscript.

DuRant, R. H., Krowchuk, D. P., & Sinal, S. H. (1998). Victimization, use of violence, and drug use at school among male adolescents who engage in same-sex sexual behavior. *Journal of Pediatrics, 133*, 113–118.

Eisenberg, M. (2001). Differences in sexual risk behaviors between college students with same-sex and opposite-sex experiences: Results from a national survey. *Archives of Sexual Behavior, 30*, 575–589.

Eisenberg, M., & Wechsler, H. (2003). Substance use behaviors among college students with same-sex opposite sex-experience: Results from a national study. *Addictive Behaviors, 28*, 899–913.

Eliason, M. J. (1996). Identity formation for lesbian, bisexual and gay persons: Beyond a 'minoritizing' view. *Journal of Homosexuality, 30*, 31–58.

Eliason, M. J. (1997). The prevalence and nature of biphobia in heterosexual undergraduate students. *Archives of Sexual Behavior, 26*, 317–326.

Ellis, L., Robb, B., & Burke, D. (2005). Sexual orientation in United States and Canadian college students. *Archives of Sexual Behavior, 34*, 569–581.

Eskin, M., Kaynak-Demir, H., & Demir, S. (2005). Same-sex sexual orientation, childhood sexual abuse, and suicidal behavior in university students in Turkey. *Archives of Sexual Behavior, 34*, 185–195.

Espin, O. M. (1984). Cultural and historical influences on sexuality in Hispanic/Latina women: Implications for psychotherapy. In C. Vance (Ed.), *Pleasure and danger: Exploring female sexuality* (pp. 149–163). London: Routledge & Kegan Paul.

Espin, O. M. (1987). Issues of identity in the psychology of Latina lesbians. In Boston Lesbian Psychologies Collective (Ed.), *Lesbian psychologies: Explorations and challenges* (pp. 35–51). Urbana: University of Illinois Press.

Espin, O. M. (1997). Crossing borders and boundaries: The life narratives of immigrant lesbians. In B. Greene (Ed.), *Ethnic and cultural diversity among lesbians and gay men* (pp. 191–215). Thousand Oaks, CA: Sage.

Esterberg, K. G. (1994). Being a lesbian and being in love: Constructing identities through relationships. *Journal of Gay and Lesbian Social Services, 1*, 57–82.

Ettore, E. M. (1980). *Lesbians, women, and society*. London: Routledge.

Faulkner, A. H., & Cranston, K. (1998). Correlates of same-sex sexual behavior in a random sample of Massachusetts high school students. *American Journal of Public Health, 88*, 262–266.

Fergusson, D. M., Horwood, L. J., & Beautrais, A. L. (1999). Is sexual orientation related to mental health problems and suicidality in young people? *Archives of General Psychiatry, 56*, 876–880.

Fergusson, D. M., Horwood, L. J., Ridder, E. M., & Beautrais, A. L. (2005). Sexual orientation and mental health in a birth cohort of young adults. *Psychological Medicine, 35*, 971–981.

Firestein, B. A. (Ed.). (1996). *Bisexuality: The psychology and politics of an invisible minority*. Thousand Oaks, CA: Sage Publications, Inc.

Firestein, B. A. (Ed.). (2007). *Becoming visible: Counseling bisexuals across the lifespan*. New York: Columbia University Press.

Fitzpatrick, K. K., Euton, S. J., Jones, J. N., & Schmidt, N. B. (2005). Gender role, sexual orientation and suicide risk. *Journal of Affective Disorders, 87*, 35–42.

French, S. A., Story, M., Remafedi, G., Resnick, M. D., & Blum, R. W. (1996). Sexual orientation and prevalence of body dissatisfaction and eating disordered behaviors: A population-based study of adolescents. *International Journal of Eating Disorders, 19*, 119–126.

Galliher, R. V., Rostosky, S. S., & Hughes, H. K. (2004). School belonging, self-esteem, and depressive symptoms in adolescents: An examination of sex, sexual attraction status, and urbanicity. *Journal of Youth and Adolescence, 33*, 235–245.

Garofalo, R., Wolf, R. C., Kessel, S., Palfrey, S. J., & DuRant, R. H. (1998). The association between health risk behaviors and sexual orientation among a school-based sample of adolescents. *Pediatrics, 101*, 895–902.

Garofalo, R., Wolf, R. C., Wissow, L. S., Woods, E. R., & Goodman, E. (1999). Sexual orientation and risk of suicide attempts among a representative sample of youth. *Archives of Pediatrics and Adolescent Medicine, 153*, 487–493.

Gilmore, D. D. (1990). *Manhood in the making: Cultural concepts of masculinity*. New Haven, CT: Yale University Press.

Goffman, I. (1963). *Stigma*. Englewood Cliffs, NJ: Prentice-Hall.

Golden, C. (1987). Diversity and variability in women's sexual identities. In Boston Lesbian Psychologies Collective (Ed.), *Lesbian psychologies: Explorations and challenges* (pp. 19–34). Urbana: University of Illinois Press.

Golden, C. (1994). Our politics and choices: The feminist movement and sexual orientation. In B. Greene, & G. M. Herek (Eds.), *Lesbian and gay psychology: Theory, research, and clinical applications* (pp. 54–70). Thousand Oaks, CA: Sage.

Golden, C. (1996). What's in a name? Sexual self-identification among women. In R. C. Savin-Williams, & K. M. Cohen (Eds.), *The lives of lesbians, gays, and bisexuals: Children to adults* (pp. 229–249). Fort Worth, TX: Harcourt Brace.

Gomez, J., & Smith, B. (1990). Taking the home out of homophobia: Black lesbian health. In E. C. White (Ed.), *The Black women's health book: Speaking for ourselves* (pp. 198–213). Seattle, WA: Seal.

Graham, C. (2005, October 11). Good news at the 500. *The Advocate*, 60.

Gramick, J. (1984). Developing a lesbian identity. In T. Darty, & S. Potter (Eds.), *Women-identified women* (pp. 31–44). Palo Alto, CA: Mayfield.

Green, R.-J. (2000). 'Lesbians, gay men, and their parents': A critique of LaSala and the prevailing clinical 'wisdom.' *Family Process, 39*, 257–266.

Green, R.-J., & Mitchell, V. (2002). Gay and lesbian couples in therapy: Homophobia, relational ambiguity, and social support. In A. S. Gurman (Ed.), *Clinical handbook of couple therapy*, 3rd ed. (pp. 546–568). New York, NY: Guilford Press.

Greene, B. (1986). When the therapist is white and the patient is Black: Considerations for psychotherapy in the feminist heterosexual and lesbian communities. *Women and Therapy, 5*, 41–66.

Greene, B. (1997). Ethnic minority lesbians and gay men: Mental health and treatment issues. In B. Greene (Ed.), *Ethnic and cultural diversity among lesbians and gay men* (Vol. 62, pp. 216–239). Thousand Oaks, CA: Sage.

Greene, B. (1998). Family, ethnic identity, and sexual orientation: African-American lesbians and gay men. In C. Patterson, & A. R. D'Augelli (Eds.), *Lesbian, gay, and bisexual identities in families: Psychological perspectives* (pp. 40–52). New York: Oxford University press.

Griffin, C. W., Wirth, M. J., & Wirth, A. G. (1986). *Beyond acceptance: Parents of lesbians and gays talk about their experience*. New York: St. Martin's Press.

Grov, C., Bimbi, D. S., NanÂn, J. E., & Parsons, J. T. (2006). Race, ethnicity, gender, and generational factors associated with the coming-out process among gay, lesbian, and bisexual individuals. *Journal of Sex Research, 43*, 115–121.

Gunther, M. (2006). Queer Inc.: How corporate America fell in love with gays and lesbians. It's a movement. Retrieved April 25, 2010 from http://money.cnn.com/magazines/fortune/fortune_archive/2006/12/11/8395465/index.htm

Halderman, D. C. (2000). Gender atypical youth: Clinical and social issues. *School Psychology Review, 29*, 192–200.

Halpert, S. C. (2002). Suicidal behavior among gay male youth. *Journal of Gay & Lesbian Psychotherapy, 6*, 53–79.

Hart, J., & Richardson, D. (1981). *The theory and practice of homosexuality*. London: Routledge & Kegan Paul.

Hedblom, J. H. (1973). Dimensions of lesbian sexual experience. *Archives of Sexual Behavior, 2*, 329–341.

Hegna, K., & Larsen, C. J. (2007). Straightening out the queer? Same-sex experience and attraction among young people in Norway. *Culture, Health & Sexuality, 9*, 15–30.

Herdt, G., & Beeler, J. (1998). Older gay men and lesbians in families. In C. Patterson, & A. R. D'Augelli (Eds.), *Lesbian, gay, and bisexual identities in families: Psychological perspectives* (pp. 177–196). New York: Oxford University Press.

Herdt, G., & Boxer, A. M. (1993). *Children of Horizons: How gay and lesbian teens are leading a new way out of the closet*. Boston: Beacon Press.

Herek, G. M. (1986). On heterosexual masculinity: Some psychical consequences of the social construction of gender and sexuality. *American Behavioral Scientist, 29*, 563–577.

Herek, G. M. (2002). Heterosexuals' attitudes toward bisexual men and women in the United States. *Journal of Sex Research, 39*, 264–274.

Herek, G. M. (2007). Confronting sexual stigma and prejudice: Theory and practice. *Journal of Social Issues, 63*, 905–925.

Herek, G. M., & Capitanio, J. P. (1996). "Some of my best friends": Intergroup contact, concealable stigma, and heterosexuals' attitudes toward gay men and lesbians. *Personality and Social Psychology Bulletin, 22*, 412–424.

Hershberger, S. L., Pilkington, N. W., & D'Augelli, A. R. (1997). Predictors of suicide attempts among gay, lesbian, and bisexual youth. *Journal of Adolescent Research, 12*, 477–497.

Hidalgo, H. (1984). The Puerto Rican lesbian in the United States. In T. Darty, & S. Potter (Eds.), *Women identified women* (pp. 105–150). Palo Alto, CA: Mayfield.

Hillier, L., Dempsey, D., Harrison, L., Beale, L., & Matthews, L. (1998). Writing themselves in: A national report on the sexuality, health and well-being of same-sex attracted young people. Monograph Series No. 7, Australian Research Centre in Sex, Health & Society, National Centre in HIV Social Research, La Trobe University.

Hoburg, R., Konik, J., Williams, M., & Crawford, M. (2004). Bisexuality among self-identified as heterosexual college students. *Journal of Bisexuality, 4*, 25–36.

Horn, S. S., & Nucci, L. (2006). Harassment of gay and lesbian youth and school violence in America: An analysis and directions for intervention. In C. Daiute, Z. Beykont, C. Higson-Smith, & L. Nucci (Eds.), *International perspectives on youth conflict and development* (pp. 139–155). New York: Oxford University Press.

Hunter, A. (1993). Same door, different closet: A heterosexual sissy's coming-out party. In S. Wilkinson, & C. Kitzinger (Eds.), *Heterosexuality: A feminism and psychology reader* (pp. 150–168). London: Sage.

Iasenza, S. (2002). Beyond "lesbian bed death": The passion and play in lesbian relationships. *Journal of Lesbian Studies, 6*, 111–120.

Icard, L. (1986). Black gay men and conflicting social identities: Sexual orientation versus racial identity. *Journal of Social Work and Human Sexuality, 4*, 83–93.

Igartua, K. J., Gill, K., & Montoro, R. (2003). Internalized homophobia: A factor in depression, anxiety, and suicide in the gay and lesbian population. *Canadian Journal of Community Mental Health, 22*, 15–30.

Jayakar, K. (1994). Women of the Indian subcontinent. In L. Comas-Diaz, & B. Greene (Eds.), *Women of color: Integrating ethnic and gender identities in psychotherapy* (pp. 161–181). New York: Guilford.

Joiner, T. E. J., Brown, J. S., & Wingate, L. R. (2005). The psychology and neurobiology of suicidal behavior. *Annual Review of Psychology, 56*, 287–314.

Jones, C. (1978). *Understanding gay relatives and friends.* New York: Seabury Press.

Jones, D. A. (1996). Discrimination against same-sex couples in hotel reservation policies. *Journal of Homosexuality, 31*, 153–159.

Jorm, A. F., Korten, A. E., Rodgers, B., Jacomb, P. A., & Christensen, H. (2002). Sexual orientation and mental health: Results from a community survey of young and middle-aged adults. *British Journal of Psychiatry, 180*, 423–427.

Kaiser Foundation. (2001, November). *Inside-out: Report on the experiences of lesbians, gays and bisexuals in America and the public's view on issues and policies related to sexual orientation.* Mento Park, CA: Kaiser Foundation.

Kinnish, K. K., Strassberg, D. S., & Turner, C. W. (2005). Sex differences in the flexibility of sexual orientation: A multidimensional retrospective assessment. *Archives of Sexual Behavior, 34*, 173–183.

Kirk, K. M., Bailey, J. M., Dunne, M. P., & Martin, N. G. (2000). Measurement models for sexual orientation in a community twin sample. *Behavior Genetics, 30*, 345–356.

Kirkpatrick, R. C. (2000). The evolution of human homosexual behavior. *Current Anthropology, 41*, 385–413.

Kisch, J., Leino, E. V., & Silverman, M. M. (2005). Aspects of suicidal behavior, depression, and treatment in college students: Results from the Spring 2000 National College Health Assessment Survey. *Suicide and Life-Threatening Behavior, 35*, 3–13.

Kitzinger, C. (1987). *The social construction of lesbianism.* London: Sage.

Kitzinger, C., & Wilkinson, S. (1995). Transitions from heterosexuality to lesbianism: The discursive production of lesbian identities. *Developmental Psychology, 31*, 95–104.

Klein, F. (1993). *The bisexual option* (2nd ed.). New York: Harrington Park Press.

Konik, J., & Stewart, A. (2004). Sexual identity development in the context of compulsory heterosexuality. *Journal of Personality, 72*, 815–844.

Krafft-Ebing, R. (1882). *Psychopathia sexualis* (M. E. Wedneck, Trans.). New York: Putnams.

Kulkin, H. S., Chauvin, E. A., & Percle, G. A. (2000). Suicide among gay and lesbian adolescents and young adults: A review of the literature. *Journal of Homosexuality, 40*, 1–29.

Kurdek, L. A. (1998). Relationship outcomes and their predictors: Longitudinal evidence from heterosexual married, gay cohabiting, and lesbian cohabiting couples. *Journal of Marriage and the Family, 60*, 553–568.

Kyrakanos, J. (1998). LUGgin' It. *InsideOUT Magazine, 9*.

Laird, J. (1993). Women's secrets – women's silences. In E. Imber-Black (Ed.), *Secrets in families and family therapy* (pp. 331–362). New York: Norton.

Laird, J. (1998). Theorizing culture: Narrative ideas and practice principles. In M. McGoldrick (Ed.), *Revisioning family therapy: Race, class, and gender in clinical practice* (pp. 20–36). New York: Guilford.

Laird, J. (2003). Lesbian and gay families. In F. Walsh (Ed.), *Normal family processes: Growing diversity and complexity,* 3rd ed. (pp. 176–209). New York, NY: Guilford Press.

Lannutti, P. J., & Lloyd, S. (2005). For better or worse: Exploring the meanings of same-sex marriage within the lesbian, gay, bisexual and transgendered community. *Journal of Social and Personal Relationships, 22*, 5–18.

LaSala, M. C. (2000a). Gay male couples: The importance of coming out and being out to parents. *Journal of Homosexuality, 39*, 47–71.

LaSala, M. C. (2000b). Lesbians, gay men, and their parents: Family therapy for the coming-out crisis. *Family Process, 39*, 67–81.

Laumann, E. O., Gagnon, J. H., Michael, R. T., & Michaels, F. (1994). *The social organization of sexuality: Sexual practices in the United States.* Chicago: University of Chicago Press.

Lee, J. A. (1977). Going public: A study in the sociology of homosexual liberation. *Journal of Homosexuality, 3*, 47–78.

Levine, H. (1997). A further exploration of the lesbian identity development process and its measurement. *Journal of Homosexuality, 34*, 67–78.

Lewis, R. J., Derlega, V. J., Griffin, J. L., & Krowinski, A. C. (2003). Stressors for gay men and lesbians: Life stress, gay-related stress, stigma consciousness, and depressive symptoms. *Journal of Social & Clinical Psychology, 22*, 716–729.

Lippa, R. A. (2000). Gender-related traits in gay men, lesbian women, and heterosexual men and women: The virtual identity of homosexual-heterosexual diagnosticity and gender diagnosticity. *Journal of Personality, 68*, 899–926.

Loftus, J. (2001). America's liberalization in attitudes toward homosexuality. *American Sociological Review, 66*, 762–782.

Luhtanen, R. K. (2003). Identity, stigma management, and well-being: A comparison of lesbians/bisexual women and gay/bisexual men. *Journal of Lesbian Studies, 7*, 85–100.

Lynch, F. R. (1992). Nonghetto gays: An ethnography of suburban homosexuals. In G. Herdt (Ed.), *Gay culture in America: Essays from the field* (pp. 165–201). Boston: Beacon Press.

Maccoby, E. M. (1998). *The two sexes: Growing up apart, coming together.* Cambridge, MA: Harvard University Press.

MacDonald, A. P. (1981). Bisexuality: Some comments on research and theory. *Journal of Homosexuality, 6*, 21–35.

Mallon, G. P. (2001). Sticks and stones can break your bones: Verbal harassment and physical violence in the lives of gay and lesbian youths in child welfare settings. *Journal of Gay & Lesbian Social Services: Issues in Practice, Policy & Research, 13,* 63–81.

Mays, V. M., & Cochran, S. D. (1988). The black women's relationships project: A national survey of black lesbians. In M. Shernoff, & W. A. Scott (Eds.), *The sourcebook on lesbian/gay health care* (pp. 54–62). Washington, DC: National Lesbian and Gay Health Foundation.

Mays, V. M., Cochran, S. D., & Rhue, S. (1993). The impact of perceived discrimination on the intimate relationships of black lesbians. *Journal of Homosexuality, 25,* 1–14.

McClintock, M. K., & Herdt, G. (1996). Rethinking puberty: The development of sexual attraction. *Current Directions in Psychological Science, 5,* 178–183.

McDaniel, J. S., Purcell, D., & D'Augelli, A. R. (2001). The relationship between sexual orientation and risk for suicide: Research findings and future directions for research and prevention. *Suicide and Life-Threatening Behavior, 31,* 84–105.

McGann, P. J. (1999). Skirting the gender normal divide: A tomboy life story. In M. Romero, & A. J. Stewart (Eds.), *Women's untold stories: Breaking silence, talking back, voicing complexity* (pp. 105–124). New York: Routledge.

McIntosh, M. (1968). The homosexual role. *Social Problems, 16,* 182–192.

McKenna, K. Y. A., & Bargh, J. A. (1998). Coming out in the age of the Internet: Identity "demarginalization" through virtual group participation. *Journal of Personality and Social Psychology, 75,* 681–694.

McLean, R. (2003). Deconstructing Black gay shame: A multicultural perspective on the quest for a healthy ethnic and sexual identity. In G. Roysircar, D. S. Sandhu, & V. E. S. Bibbins (Eds.), *Multicultural competencies: A guidebook of practices.* (pp. 109–118). Alexandria, VA: Association for Multicultural Counseling & Development.

Meyer, I. H. (2003). Prejudice, social stress, and mental health in lesbian, gay, and bisexual populations: Conceptual issues and research evidence. *Psychological Bulletin, 129,* 674–697.

Meyer, I. H., & Dean, L. (1998). Internalized homophobia, intimacy, and sexual behavior among gay and bisexual men. In G. M. Herek (Ed.), *Stigma and sexual orientation: Understanding prejudice against lesbians, gay men, and bisexuals* (pp. 160–186). Thousand Oaks, CA: Sage.

Miller, T. R., & Taylor, D. M. (2005). Adolescent suicidality: Who will ideate, who will act? *Suicide and Life-Threatening Behavior, 35,* 425–435.

Minton, H. L., & McDonald, G. J. (1983). Homosexual identity formation as a developmental process. *Journal of Homosexuality, 9,* 91–104.

Miranda, J., & Storms, M. (1989). Psychological adjustment of lesbians and gay men. *Journal of Counseling and Development, 68,* 41–45.

Mohr, J., & Fassinger, R. (2000). Measuring dimensions of lesbian and gay male experience. *Measurement and Evaluation in Counseling and Development, 33,* 66–90.

Money, J. (1988). *Gay, straight, and in-between: The sexology of erotic orientation.* New York: Oxford University Press.

Moon, M. W., Fornili, K., & O'Briant, A. L. (2007). Risk comparison among youth who report sex with same-sex versus both-sex partners. *Youth & Society, 38,* 267–284.

Morales, E. (1992). Latino gays and Latina lesbians. In S. H. Dworkin, & F. J. Gutierrez (Eds.), *Counseling gay men and lesbians: Journey to the end of the rainbow* (pp. 125–139).

Alexandria, VA: American Association for Counseling and Development.

Morris, J. F. (1997). Lesbian coming out as a multidimensional process. *Journal of Homosexuality, 33,* 1–22.

Morris, J. F., & Rothblum, E. D. (1999). Who fills out a "lesbian" questionnaire? The interrelationship of sexual orientation, years out, disclosure of sexual orientation, sexual experience with women, and participation in the lesbian community. *Psychology of Women Quarterly, 23,* 537–557.

Morris, J. F., Waldo, C. R., & Rothblum, E. D. (2001). A model of predictors and outcomes of outness among lesbian and bisexual women. *American Journal of Orthopsychiatry, 71,* 61–71.

Morrison, L. L., & L'Heureux, J. (2001). Suicide and gay/lesbian/bisexual youth: Implications for clinicians. *Journal of Adolescence, 24,* 39–49.

Mosher, W. D., Chandra, A., & Jones, J. (2005). *Sexual behavior and selected health measures: Men and women 15–44 years of age, United States, 2002.* Advance data from vital and health statistics, no. 362. Hyattsville, MD: National Center for Health Statistics.

Muehrer, P. (1995). Suicide and sexual orientation: A critical summary of recent research and directions for future research. *Suicide and Life-Threatening Behavior, 35*(Suppl.), 72–81.

Murray, S. O. (2000). *Homosexualities.* Chicago: University of Chicago Press.

Nazario, A. (2003). Latino cross-cultural same sex male relationships: Issues of ethnicity, race, and other domains of influence. In V. Thomas, T. A. Karis, & J. L. Wetchler (Eds.), *Clinical issues with interracial couples: Theories and research* (pp. 103–113). Binghamton, NY: Haworth Press, Inc.

Neidorf, S., & Morin, R. (2007). Four-in-ten Americans have close friends or relatives who are gay. Retrieved October 3, 2008, from http://pewresearch.org/pubs/485/friends-who-are-gay

Nichols, M. (1987). Lesbian sexuality: Issues and developing theory. In Boston Lesbian Psychologies Collective (Ed.), *Lesbian Psychologies* (pp. 97–125). Urbana: University of Illinois Press.

Nichols, M. (1988). Low sexual desire in lesbian couples. In S. R. Leiblum, & R. C. Rosen (Eds.), *Sexual desire disorders* (pp. 387–412). New York: Guilford.

Nichols, M. (1990). Lesbian relationships: Implications for the study of sexuality and gender. In J. C. Gonsiorek, & J. D. Weinrich (Eds.), *Homosexuality: Research implications for public policy* (pp. 350–364). Newbury Park, CA: Sage.

Norlev, J., Davidsen, M., Sundaram, V., & Kjoller, M. (2005). Indicators associated with suicidal ideation and suicide attempts among 16–35-year-old Danes: A national representative population study. *Suicide and Life-Threatening Behavior, 35,* 291–308.

Ochs, R. (1996). Biphobia: It goes more than two ways. In B. A. Firestein (Ed.), *Bisexuality: The psychology and politics of an invisible minority* (pp. 217–239). Thousand Oaks, CA: Sage Publications, Inc.

Oswald, R. F. (2000). Family and friendship relationships after young women come out as bisexual or lesbian. *Journal of Homosexuality, 38,* 65–83.

Oswald, R. F. (2002). Inclusion and belonging in the family rituals of gay and lesbian people. *Journal of Family Psychology, 16,* 428–436.

Patterson, C. J. (2000). Family relationships of lesbians and gay men. *Journal of Marriage and the Family, 62,* 1052–1069.

Paul, J. P. (1985). Bisexuality: Reassessing our paradigms of sexuality. In F. Klein, & T. Wolf (Eds.), *Two lives to lead: Bisexuality in men and women* (pp. 21–34). New York: Harrington Park Press.

Paul, J. P. (1996). Bisexuality: Exploring/exploding the boundaries. In R. C. Savin-Williams, & K. M. Cohen (Eds.), *The lives of lesbians, gays, and bisexuals: Children to adults* (pp. 436–461). Orlando, FL: Harcourt Brace College Publishers.

Paul, J. P., Catania, J., Pollack, L., Moskowitz, J., Canchola, J., Mills, T., et al. (2002). Suicide attempts among gay and bisexual men: Lifetime prevalence and antecedents. *American Journal of Public Health, 92*, 1338–1345.

Peplau, L. A. (2001). Rethinking women's sexual orientation: An interdisciplinary, relationship-focused approach. *Personal Relationships, 8*, 1–19.

Peplau, L. A., Fingerhut, A., & Beals, K. P. (2004). Sexuality in the relationships of lesbians and gay men. In J. H. Harvey, A. Wenzel, & S. Sprecher (Eds.), *Handbook of sexuality in close relationships*. Mahway, NJ: Lawrence Erlbaum Associates, Inc.

Peplau, L. A., Garnets, L. D., Spalding, L. R., Conley, T. D., & Veniegas, R. C. (1998). A critique of Bem's "Exotic Becomes Erotic" theory of sexual orientation. *Psychological Review, 105*, 386–394.

Pettigrew, T. F. (1967). Social evaluation theory: Convergences and applications. *Nebraska Symposium on Motivation, 15*, 241–311.

Phillips, G., & Over, R. (1992). Adult sexual orientation in relation to memories of childhood gender conforming and gender nonconforming behaviors. *Archives of Sexual Behavior, 21*, 543–558.

Phillips, G., & Over, R. (1995). Differences between heterosexual, bisexual, and lesbian women in recalled childhood experiences. *Archives of Sexual Behavior, 24*, 1–20.

Pinhey, T. K., & Millman, S. R. (2004). Asian/Pacific Islander adolescent sexual orientation and suicide risk in Guam. *American Journal of Public Health, 94*, 1204–1206.

Ploderl, M., & Fartacek, R. (2005). Suicidality and associated risk factors among lesbian, gay, and bisexual compared to heterosexual Austrian adults. *Suicide and Life-Threatening Behavior, 35*, 661–670.

Polling Report.com. (2008). Law and civil rights. Retrieved October 2, 2008, from http://www.pollingreport.com/civil.htm

Ponse, B. (1978). *Identities in the lesbian world: The social construction of self.* Westport, CT: Greenwood Press.

Rahman, Q., & Hull, M. S. (2005). An empirical test of the kin selection hypothesis for male homosexuality. *Archives of Sexual Behavior, 34*, 461–467.

Remafedi, G. (1999). Sexual orientation and youth suicide. *JAMA: Journal of the American Medical Association, 282*, 1291–1292.

Remafedi, G., French, S., Story, M., Resnick, M. D., & Blum, R. (1998). The relationship between suicide risk and sexual orientation: Results of a population-based study. *American Journal of Public Health, 88*, 57–60.

Remafedi, G., Resnick, M., Blum, R., & Harris, L. (1992). Demography of sexual orientation in adolescents. *Pediatrics, 89*, 714–721.

Rieger, G., Bailey, J. M., & Chivers, M. L. (2005). Sexual arousal patterns of bisexual men. *Psychological Science, 16*, 579–584.

Rimer, S. (1993, June 5). Campus lesbians step into unfamiliar light. *New York Times*, pp. A2.

Rivers, I., & D'Augelli, A. R. (2001). The victimization of lesbians, gay, and bisexual youths. In A. R. D'Augelli, & C. J. Patterson (Eds.), *Lesbian, gay, and bisexual identities and youth: Psychological perspectives* (pp. 199–223). New York: Oxford University Press.

Robin, L., Brener, N. D., Donahue, S. F., Hack, T., Hale, K., & Goodenow, C. (2002). Associations between health risk behaviors and opposite-, same-, and both-sex sexual partners in representative samples of Vermont and Massachusetts high school. *Archives of Pediatrics and Adolescent Medicine, 156*, 349–355.

Roisman, G. I., Clausell, E., Holland, A., Fortuna, K., & Elieff, C. (2008). Adult romantic relationships as contexts of human development: A multimethod comparison of same-sex couples with opposite-sex dating, engaged, and married dyads. *Developmental Psychology, 44*, 91–101.

Rosario, M., Hunter, J., Maguen, S., Gwadz, M., & Smith, R. (2001). The coming-out process and its adaptational and health-related associations among gay, lesbian, and bisexual youths: Stipulation and exploration of a model. *American Journal of Community Psychology, 29*, 113–160.

Rosario, M., Meyer-Bahlburg, H. F., Hunter, J., Exner, T. M., Gwadz, M., & Keller, A. M. (1996). The psychosexual development of urban lesbian, gay, and bisexual youths. *Journal of Sex Research, 33*, 113–126.

Rosario, M., Schrimshaw, E. W., & Hunter, J. (2004a). Ethnic/racial differences in the coming-out process of lesbian, gay, and bisexual youths: A comparison of sexual identity development over time. *Cultural Diversity & Ethnic Minority Psychology, 10*, 215–228.

Rosario, M., Schrimshaw, E. W., & Hunter, J. (2004b). Predictors of substance use over time among gay, lesbian, and bisexual youths: An examination of three hypotheses. *Addictive Behaviors, 29*, 1623–1631.

Rosario, M., Schrimshaw, E. W., & Hunter, J. (2006). A model of sexual risk behaviors among young gay and bisexual men: Longitudinal associations of mental health, substance abuse, sexual abuse, and the coming-out process. *AIDS Education and Prevention, 18*, 444–460.

Rosario, M., Schrimshaw, E. W., Hunter, J., & Braun, L. (2006). Sexual identity development among lesbian, gay, and bisexual youths: Consistency and change over time. *Journal of Sex Research, 43*, 46–58.

Rostosky, S. S., Korfhage, B. A., Duhigg, J. M., Stern, A. J., Bennett, L., & Riggle, E. D. B. (2004). Same-sex couple perceptions of family support: A consensual qualitative study. *Family Process, 43*, 43–57.

Rothblum, E. D., Balsam, K. F., & Solomon, S. E. (2008). Comparison of same-sex couples who were married in Massachusetts, had domestic partnerships in California, or had civil unions in Vermont. *Journal of Family Issues, 29*, 48–78.

Rothblum, E. D., & Factor, R. (2001). Lesbians and their sisters as a control group: Demographic and mental health factors. *Psychological Science, 12*, 63–69.

Russell, S. T., & Consolacion, T. B. (2003). Adolescent romance and emotional health in the U.S.: Beyond binaries. *Journal of Clinical Child and Adolescent Psychology, 32*, 499–508.

Russell, S. T., Franz, B. T., & Driscoll, A. K. (2001). Same-sex romantic attraction and experiences of violence in adolescence. *American Journal of Public Health, 91*, 903–906.

Russell, S. T., & Joyner, K. (2001). Adolescent sexual orientation and suicide risk: Evidence from a national study. *American Journal of Public Health, 91*, 1276–1281.

Russell, S. T., & Seif, H. (2002). Bisexual female adolescents: A critical analysis of past research, and results from a national survey. *Journal of Bisexuality, 2*, 73–94.

Russell, S. T., Seif, H., & Truong, N. L. (2001). School outcomes of sexual minority youth in the United States: Evidence from a national study. *Journal of Adolescence, 24*, 111–127.

Rust, P. C. R. (1992). The politics of sexual identity: Sexual attraction and behavior among lesbian and bisexual women. *Social Problems, 39*, 366–386.

Rust, P. C. R. (1993). Coming out in the age of social constructionism: Sexual identity formation among lesbians and bisexual women. *Gender and Society, 7*, 50–77.

Rust, P. C. R. (1995). *Bisexuality and the challenge to lesbian politics: Sex, loyalty, and revolution*. New York: New York University Press.

Rust, P. C. R. (2000a). Academic literature on situational homosexuality in the 1960s and 1970s. In P. C. R. Rust (Ed.), *Bisexuality in the United States: A reader and guide to the literature* (pp. 221–249). New York: Columbia University Press.

Rust, P. C. R. (2000b). Alternatives to binary sexuality: Modeling bisexuality. In P. C. R. Rust (Ed.), *Bisexuality in the United States* (pp. 33–54). New York: Columbia University Press.

Rust, P. C. R. (2000c). *Bisexuality in the United States: A reader and guide to the literature*. New York: Columbia University Press.

Rust, P. C. R. (2000d). Criticisms of the scholarly literature on sexuality for its neglect of bisexuality. In P. C. R. Rust (Ed.), *Bisexuality in the United States: A reader and guide to the literature* (pp. 5–10). New York: Columbia University Press.

Rust, P. C. R. (2000e). Popular images and the growth of bisexual community and visibility. In P. C. R. Rust (Ed.), *Bisexuality in the United States: A reader and guide to the literature* (pp. 537–553). New York: Columbia University Press.

Rust, P. C. R. (2001). Two many and not enough: The meanings of bisexual identities. *Journal of Bisexuality, 1*, 31–68.

Rust, P. C. R. (2002). Bisexuality: The state of the union. *Annual Review of Sex Research, 13*, 180–240.

Rutter, P. A., & Soucar, E. (2002). Youth suicide risk and sexual orientation. *Adolescence, 37*, 289–299.

Safe Schools Coalition of Washington. (1999). Selected findings of eight population-based studies as they pertain to anti-gay harassment and the safety and well-being of sexual minority students. Retrieved May 15, 2006, from http://www.safe-schoolscoalition.org/83000youth.pdf

Sandfort, T. G. M., Bakker, F., Schellevis, F. o. G., & Vanwesenbeeck, I. (2006). Sexual orientation and mental and physical health status: Findings from a dutch population survey. *American Journal of Public Health, 96*, 1119–1125.

Saulnier, C. F. (1998). Prevalence of suicide attempts and suicidal ideation among lesbian and gay youth. *Journal of Gay and Lesbian Social Services, 8*, 51–68.

Savin-Williams, R. C. (1990). *Gay and lesbian youth: Expressions of identity*. Washington, DC: Hemisphere.

Savin-Williams, R. C. (1996). Ethnic- and sexual-minority youth. In R. C. Savin-Williams, & K. M. Cohen (Eds.), *The lives of lesbians, gays, and bisexuals: Children to adults* (pp. 152–165). Fort Worth, TX: Harcourt Brace.

Savin-Williams, R. C. (1998). *"… And then I became gay": Young men's stories*. New York: Routledge.

Savin-Williams, R. C. (2001a). A critique of research on sexual-minority youths. *Journal of Adolescence, 24*, 5–13.

Savin-Williams, R. C. (2001b). *Mom, Dad. I'm gay*. Washington, DC: APA Press.

Savin-Williams, R. C. (2001c). Suicide attempts among sexual-minority youths: Population and measurement issues. *Journal of Consulting & Clinical Psychology, 69*, 983–991.

Savin-Williams, R. C. (2005). *The new gay teenager*. Cambridge, MA: Harvard University Press.

Savin-Williams, R. C., & Diamond, L. M. (2000). Sexual identity trajectories among sexual-minority youths: Gender comparisons. *Archives of Sexual Behavior, 29*, 607–627.

Savin-Williams, R. C., & Joyner, K. (2007). Sexual identity and suicide attempts: Research and clinical implications of differentiating sexual subgroups. Manuscript under review.

Savin-Williams, R. C., & Ream, G. L. (2006). Pubertal onset and sexual orientation in an adolescent national probability sample. *Archives of Sexual Behavior, 35*, 279–286.

Silber, L. J. (1990). Negotiating sexual identity: Non-lesbians in a lesbian feminist community. *Journal of Sex Research, 27*, 131–139.

Silenzio, V. M. B., Pena, J. B., Duberstein, P. R., Cerel, J., & Knox, K. L. (2007). Sexual orientation and risk factors for suicidal ideation and suicide attempts among adolescents and young adults. *American Journal of Public Health, 97*, 2017–2019.

Skegg, K., Nada-Raja, S., Dickson, N., Paul, C., & Williams, S. (2003). Sexual orientation and self-harm in men and women. *American Journal of Psychiatry, 160*, 541–546.

Smith, A. (1997). Cultural diversity and the coming-out process: Implications for clinical practice. In B. Greene (Ed.), *Ethnic and cultural diversity among lesbians and gay men* (pp. 279–300). Thousand Oaks, CA: Sage.

Socarides, C. W. (1996). *Homosexuality: A freedom too far*. Phoenix, AZ: Adam Margrave Books.

Sophie, J. (1986). A critical examination of stage theories of lesbian identity development. *Journal of Homosexuality, 12*, 39–51.

Spalding, L. R., & Peplau, L. A. (1997). The unfaithful lover: Heterosexuals' perceptions of bisexuals and their relationships. *Psychology of Women Quarterly, 21*, 611–625.

Stokes, J. P., Damon, W., & McKirnan, D. J. (1997). Predictors of movement toward homosexuality: A longitudinal study of bisexual men. *Journal of Sex Research, 34*, 304–312.

Stokes, J. P., Miller, R. L., & Mundhenk, R. (1998). Toward an understanding of behaviourally bisexual men: The influence of context and culture. *Canadian Journal of Human Sexuality, 7*, 101–113.

Strommen, E. F. (1989). "You're a what?": Family members' reactions to the disclosure of homosexuality. *Journal of Homosexuality, 18*, 37–58.

Taywaditep, K. J., & Stokes, J. P. (1998). Male bisexualities: A cluster analysis of men with bisexual experience. *Journal of Psychology and Human Sexuality, 10*, 15–41.

Thompson, E. M., & Morgan, E. M. (2008). 'Mostly straight' young women: Variations in sexual behavior and identity development. *Developmental Psychology, 44*, 15–21.

Tiggemann, M., Martins, Y., & Kirkbride, A. (2007). Oh to be lean and muscular: Body image ideals in gay and heterosexual men. *Psychology of Men & Masculinity, 8*, 15–24.

Tjepkma, M. (2008). Health care use among gay, lesbian, and bisexual Canadians. *Health Reports, 19*, 53–64.

Tolman, D. L. (1994). Daring to desire: Culture and the bodies of adolescent girls. In J. Irvine (Ed.), *Sexual cultures: Adolescents, communities and the construction of identity* (pp. 250–284). Philadelphia: Temple University Press.

Tremble, B., Schneider, M., & Appathurai, C. (1989). Growing up gay or lesbian in a multicultural context. *Journal of Homosexuality, 17*, 253–267.

Troiden, R. R. (1979). Becoming homosexual: A model of gay identity acquisition. *Psychiatry, 42*, 362–373.

Udry, J. R., & Billy, J. O. G. (1987). Initiation of coitus in early adolescence. *American Sociological Review, 52*, 841–855.

Udry, J. R., & Chantala, K. (2002). Risk assessment of adolescents with same-sex relationships. *Journal of Adolescent Health, 31*, 84–92.

Udry, J. R., Talbert, L. M., & Morris, N. M. (1986). Biosocial foundations for adolescent female sexuality. *Demography, 23*, 217–230.

van Heeringen, C., & Vincke, J. (2000). Suicidal acts and ideation in homosexual and bisexual young people: A study of prevalence and risk factors. *Social Psychiatry and Psychiatric Epidemiology, 35*, 494–499.

Vance, B. K., & Green, V. (1984). Lesbian identities: An examination of sexual behavior and sex role acquisition as related to age of initial same-sex encounter. *Psychology of Women Quarterly, 8*, 293–307.

Vasquez, E. (1979). Homosexuality in the context of the Mexican-American culture. In D. Kukel (Ed.), *Sexual issues in social work: Emerging concerns in education and practice* (pp. 131–147). Honolulu: University of Hawaii, School of Social Work.

Waldo, C. R. (1999). Working in a majority context: A structural model of heterosexism as minority stress in the workplace. *Journal of Counseling Psychology, 46*, 218–232.

Walsh, F. (2003). *Normal family processes: Growing diversity and complexity* (3rd ed.). Guilford Press.

Walters, A. S., & Curran, M. C. (1996). "Excuse me, sir? May I help you and your boyfriend?": Salespersons' differential treatment of homosexual and straight customers. *Journal of Homosexuality, 31*, 135–152.

Walters, K. L., & Simoni, J. M. (1983). Lesbian and gay male group identity attitudes and self-esteem: Implications for counseling. *Journal of Counseling Psychology, 40*, 94–99.

Walters, S. D. (2001). *All the rage: The story of gay visibility in America*. Chicago: University of Chicago Press.

Warner, J., McKeown, A., Griffin, M., Johnson, K., Ramsay, A., Cort, C., et al. (2004). Rates and predictors of mental illness in gay men, lesbians and bisexual men and women: Results from a survey based in England and Wales. *British Journal of Psychiatry, 185*, 479–485.

Weinberg, M. S., Williams, C. J., & Pryor, D. W. (1994). *Dual attraction: Understanding bisexuality*. New York: Oxford University Press.

Weinstein, S. (2007, June 19). Their best foot forward. *The Advocate*, 69–70.

Weissman, M. M., Bland, R. C., Canino, G. J., Greenwald, S., Hwu, H.-G., Joyce, P. R., et al. (1999). Prevalence of suicide ideation and suicide attempts in nine countries. *Psychological Medicine, 29*, 9–17.

Wellings, K., Field, J., Johnson, A., & Wadsworth, J. (1994). *Sexual behavior in Britain: The national survey of sexual attitudes and lifestyles*. London: Penguin Books.

Wells, J. W., & Kline, W. B. (1987). Self-disclosure of homosexual orientation. *Journal of Social Psychology, 127*, 191–197.

Weston, K. (1991). *Families we choose: Lesbians, gays, kinship*. New York: Columbia University Press.

Whisman, V. (1993). Identity crisis: Who is a lesbian anyway? In A. Stein (Ed.), *Sisters, sexperts, queers: Beyond the lesbian nation* (pp. 47–60). New York: Penguin.

Whisman, V. (1996). *Queer by choice: Lesbians, gay men, and the politics of identity*. New York: Routledge.

Whitbeck, L. B., Chen, X., Hoyt, D. R., Tyler, K. A., & Johnson, K. D. (2004). Mental disorder, subsistence strategies, and victimization among gay, lesbian, and bisexual homeless and runaway adolescents. *Journal of Sex Research, 41*, 329–342.

Wichstrom, L., & Hegna, K. (2003). Sexual orientation and suicide attempt: A longitudinal study of the general Norwegian adolescent population. *Journal of Abnormal Psychology, 112*, 144–151.

Williams, T., Connolly, J., Pepler, D., & Craig, W. (2003). Questioning and sexual minority adolescents: High school experiences of bullying, sexual harassment and physical abuse. *Canadian Journal of Community Mental Health, 22*, 47–58.

Williams, T., Connolly, J., Pepler, D., & Craig, W. (2005). Peer victimization, social support, and psychosocial adjustment of sexual minority adolescents. *Journal of Youth and Adolescence, 34*, 471–482.

Williams, W. L. (1998). Social acceptance of same-sex relationships in families: Models from other cultures. In C. Patterson, & A. R. D'Augelli (Eds.), *Lesbian, gay, and bisexual identities in families: Psychological perspectives* (pp. 53–71). New York: Oxford University press.

Wooden, W. S., Kawasaki, H., & Mayeda, R. (1983). Lifestyles and identity maintenance among gay Japanese-American males. *Alternative Lifestyles, 5*, 236–243.

Yip, P. S. F., Liu, K. Y., Lam, T. H., Stewart, S. M., Chen, E., & Fan, S. (2004). Suicidality among high school students in Hong Kong. *Suicide and Life-Threatening Behavior, 34*, 284–297.

Yoder, K. A., Hoyt, D. R., & Whitbeck, L. B. (1998). Suicidal behavior among homeless and runaway adolescents. *Journal of Youth and Adolescence, 27*, 753–771.

Zinik, G. (1985). Identity conflict or adaptive flexibility? Bisexuality reconsidered. *Journal of Homosexuality, 11*, 7–19.

Ziyadeh, N. J., Prokop, L. A., Fisher, L. B., Rosario, M., Field, A. E., Camargo, C. A. J., et al. (2007). Sexual orientation, gender, and alcohol use in a cohort study of U.S. adolescent girls and boys. *Drug and Alcohol Dependence, 87*, 119–130.

Interventions with Culturally Diverse Populations

Lillian Comas-Díaz

Abstract

This chapter addresses the need for cultural competence in the delivery of clinical psychological services. It advocates for cultural integrity in the adaptation of mainstream psychological practice. The role of cultural mirrors in the psychotherapeutic process is examined, namely, how worldviews, the therapeutic relationship, and communication affect therapy. The centrality of a sociocentric worldview in the delivery of psychological interventions for culturally diverse individuals is emphasized. The chapter discusses the role of cross-cultural therapeutic relationships, including racial identity developmental theories and ethnoracial bias, in addition to communication styles and their impact on clinical practice. The author advocates for the incorporation of ethnic specific therapies into psychological practice, and concludes with a discussion of ethnocultural psychological practice, an approach developed to integrate culture and ethnicity into the delivery of interventions with culturally diverse individuals.

Keywords: Cultural competence, liberation, sociocentric worldview, resilience

Treating culturally diverse populations can be a challenge and an opportunity. Many multicultural scholars and practitioners have questioned the cross-cultural effectiveness of mainstream psychological practice (Hall, 2001; Sue, Bingham, Porche-Burke, & Vasquez, 1999; Zane, Hall, Sue, Young, & Nunez, 2004). Some clinicians have examined the need to maintain cultural integrity within diverse psychological interventions. For instance, several psychoanalysts have incorporated clients' social, communal, and spiritual orientations into their practices (Foster, Moskowitz, & Javier, 1996). To illustrate, Altman (1995) modified an object relations framework to examine his clients' progress by their ability to use relationships to grow, rather than by the insights gained. Such adaptation appears to be consistent with the relational orientation of culturally diverse individuals. Likewise, Kakar (1985) adapted his psychoanalytic approach by educating, empathizing, and actively expressing interest and warmth toward

his East Indian clients. Moreover, several multicultural clinicians have recommended adapting evidence-based practice (EBP) to culturally diverse populations (Muñoz & Mendelson, 1995). Certainly, EBP contains elements congruent with culturally diverse individual' values, such as the importance of education in healing, the role of thoughts in maintaining health, the mind and body connection, and the relevance of making meaning out of adversity.

The gap between mainstream psychotherapists and culturally diverse individuals is beginning to narrow as the understanding between these two groups improves. A promise of an efficacious and ethical application of psychological services to culturally diverse individuals is on the horizon. In this chapter, I discuss psychological interventions with culturally diverse individuals. First, I advocate for cultural integrity in the delivery of psychological practice. Then, I examine the cultural adaptations of EBP practice.

Afterward, I discuss cultural variables that affect the therapeutic process with culturally diverse individuals. Furthermore, I examine the application of ethnic therapies and indigenous healing to multicultural individuals. I conclude with a discussion of an ethnocultural approach to delivery of psychological services. Finally, I offer recommendations for future research.

Cultural Competence in Clinical Practice

Cultural competence is a process that provides the clinical skills needed to work effectively with culturally diverse individuals and communities (Cross, Bazron, Dennis, & Isaacs, 1989). This development enables practitioners to work effectively in a cross-cultural or multicultural situation. Since every therapeutic encounter is cross-cultural in nature (Comas-Díaz & Griffith, 1988), culturally competent psychotherapists enhance their clinical effectiveness. Likewise, clients who perceive their clinicians as being culturally competent tend to complete treatment and be satisfied with it. A set of congruent behaviors, attitudes, and policies, cultural competence reflects an understanding of how cultural and sociopolitical influences shape individuals' worldviews and related health behaviors, and how such factors interact at multiple levels of psychological practice (Betancourt, Green, Carrillo, & Ananch-Firempong, 2003). Culturally competent clinicians are specially trained in specific behaviors, attitudes, and policies that recognize, respect, and value the cultural uniqueness of individuals and groups (Hansen, Pepitone-Arreola-Rockwell, & Greene, 2000). These therapists develop the clinical skills needed to work effectively with culturally diverse populations and have the capacity to value diversity, manage dynamics of difference, acquire and incorporate cultural knowledge into their interventions and interactions, develop multicultural skills, conduct self- reflection and assessment, and adapt to diversity and to the cultural contexts of their clients. Needless to say, cultural competence enhances clients' treatment engagement, adherence, and completion.

However, cultural competence extends beyond clinical skills. In addition to practitioners' self-assessment, cultural competence requires an understanding of the historical and sociopolitical contexts of individuals and groups. Many culturally diverse individuals view mainstream psychotherapy as being monocultural, ethnocentric, and insensitive to their cultural and spiritual experiences (Hall, 2001; Sue, Bingham, et al., 1999). As such, dominant psychotherapy tends to support mainstream cultural values and consequently, neglects multicultural worldviews. In its extreme form, dominant psychotherapy can promote cultural imperialism by dismissing indigenous and spiritual beliefs. According to Young (1990), cultural imperialism universalizes and establishes as a norm the dominant group's experience and culture while ignoring multicultural perspectives. Furthermore, the history of service delivery to under-represented populations has been fraught with obstacles and missed opportunities. In particular, people of color in the United States have been subjected to neglect, discrimination, and even exploitation. For example, a medical apartheid—the history of medical experimentation on African Americans—offers a dark lens into the delivery of health services to this population (Washington, 2007). Also referred as America's Nuremberg, the history of gross injustices through medical research imparted upon African Americans has reduced their likelihood of seeking help for many treatable conditions, as well as their participation in clinical research (Caldwell-Colbert, Daniel, & Dudley-Grant, 2003). The Tuskegee project is a case in point. To illustrate, African American men were given a placebo, but were led to believe that they were receiving curative medication (penicillin), despite the fact that a cure for syphilis was found during the course of the research and administered to white men (Washington, 2007).

The legacy of the medical apartheid and America's Nuremberg has caused a psychopolitical reaction among many African Americans. Consequently, many African Americans tend to distrust clinical research protocols and established treatment facilities. Other people of color share a similar distrust or psychopolitical paranoia. Moreover, some researchers have used flawed and fraudulent methodologies and interventions with Native American individuals to the detriment of the community's well-being (Duran, 2006). Likewise, many Puerto Rican women were involuntarily sterilized when they received medical treatment (Comas-Díaz, 2008). Called *la operacion* (the operation), this medical procedure was a consequence of the U.S. policy to decrease overpopulation and unemployment among Puerto Ricans (Garcia, 1982). Such an oppressive medical legacy is relevant to psychological practice because many people of color seek treatment for emotional distress via their primary care practitioner. Thus, these clients frequently transfer their psychopolitical paranoia to psychological practitioners.

Interestingly, an empirical study showed that African Americans who endorsed positive expectations about seeking mental health services found treatment less positive than their European American counterparts after utilizing such services (Diala et al., 2000). Moreover, when people of color seek mental health care, many receive poor psychopharmacological treatment. Clinicians' lack of recognition of racial and ethnic differences in drug metabolism and responses has resulted in psychopharmacological mistreatment of many people of color (Melfi, Croghan, Hanna, & Robinson, 2000). For example, although African Americans with affective disorders are often inappropriately treated with antipsychotic medications (Lawson, 1996; Strickland, Ranganeth, & Lin, 1991), many Latinos are treated inappropriately with other psychopharmacology, party due to their variable rate of drug metabolism (Jacobsen & Comas-Díaz, 1999; Mendoza & Smith, 2000). Moreover, due to ethnoracial differences in drug metabolism, Asian clients require lower doses of haloperidol than do whites to produce similar clinical effects (Pi & Gray, 2000). As a result, clinicians unaware of people of color's ethnopharmacological needs further add to their clients' mistreatment.

Another source of distrust among numerous people of color is what Duran (2006) called the "soul wound." According to these authors, many Native people need to heal the wound that is product of historical trauma, ungrieved losses, internalized oppression, suffering, and learned helplessness. Furthermore, many people of color's discomfort with mental health treatment may be strengthened by their suspicion that dominant psychotherapy is an instrument of acculturation (Ramirez, 1991) and of cultural imperialism. As a result, several mental health organizations examined impediments to the delivery of cultural competent services. The need for cultural competence emerged out of such examination.

Cultural Competence in Mental Health Practice: Responses from Mental Health Organizations

In this section, I examine how two professional associations, namely the American Psychiatric Association and the American Psychological Association, addressed the need to infuse cultural competence into the delivery of psychological services to culturally diverse populations. The American Psychiatric Association (1994, 2000) developed the *cultural formulation*, a process-oriented assessment that grounds diagnosis in a cultural context. As a clinical tool, the cultural formulation examines (a) an individual's cultural identity, (b) cultural explanations for individual illnesses, (c) cultural factors related to the psychosocial

environment and levels of functioning, (d) cultural elements of the therapist–patient relationship, and (e) overall cultural assessment for diagnosis and treatment (APA, 1994). It also acknowledges the expression of distress through a glossary of culture-bound syndromes (APA, 1994). Such culture-bound syndromes are not restricted to unsophisticated, unacculturated individuals. I have witnessed several educated, intelligent, and achieving clients exhibit culture-bound syndromes in my clinical practice. As many of these clients suffer from anxiety and disconnection, an element of their treatment is to help them reconnect with their cultural and ethnic roots. Although the development of the cultural formulation is an impressive initial step, it is limited in its scope. Anchored in a medical model, the cultural formulation tends to emphasize individual pathology rather than strengths. Notwithstanding this limitation, the cultural formulation can be used as a model to increase the practitioner's cultural competence (Comas-Díaz, 2001; Lewis-Fernandez, & Díaz, 2002).

The development of the cultural formulation provided the impetus for the incorporation of *cultural analysis* into treatment. Based on ethnographic and anthropological research, cultural analysis aims to uncover the cultural knowledge people use to organize their behaviors and interpret their experiences (Spradley, 1990). When used in clinical practice, a cultural analysis relies on an object-relation model, with an emphasis on the importance of self and its relationships with others and with the environment. Lo and Fung (2003) identified the self, relations, and treatment as the three domains of the cultural analysis. The self domain entails the cultural influences on the self that may be relevant in psychological practice. These include affect, cognition, behavior, body, and self-concept, plus individual goals and motivations. The relations domain examines the cultural influence on clients' relationships with family, groups, others, society, possessions, environment, spirituality, and time. Finally, the treatment domain highlights therapy elements influenced by culture, such as communication (both verbal and nonverbal), problem–solution models, and the clinician–client relationship.

American Psychological Association

The American Psychological Association formulated its *Guidelines for Providers of Psychological Services to Ethnic, Linguistic, and Culturally Diverse Clients* (APA, 1990) to guide culturally sensitive treatment. In essence, these guidelines exhorted practitioners to recognize cultural diversity; understand the central role culture, ethnicity, and race play in culturally diverse individuals; appreciate the significant impact of socioeconomic and political factors on mental health; and help clients understand their cultural identification (APA, 1990). Following this development, the American Psychological Association (2003) published its *Guidelines on Multicultural Education, Training, Research, Practice and Organizational Change*. Both documents highlight the importance of psychologists' commitment to cultural competence. In brief, the multicultural guidelines encourage psychologists to recognize that we are cultural beings; value cultural sensitivity and awareness; use multicultural constructs in education; conduct culture-centered and ethical psychological research with culturally diverse individuals; use culturally appropriate skills in applied psychological practices; and implement organizational change processes to support culturally informed organizational practices and policy (APA, 2003).

Cultural Adaptation of Evidence-based Psychological Practice

A challenge in the delivery of effective psychotherapy to clients from other cultures is to balance clinical expertise with the use of treatments that are informed by science in a culturally appropriate manner (Comas-Díaz, 2006a). Unfortunately, there is a lack of cultural and ecological validity in empirically supported treatment (EST) studies (Chambless at al, 1996; Hall, 2001; Roselló & Bernal, 1999; Sue et al., 2006). To address these concerns, practitioners and researchers have suggested adapting EST to multicultural populations (Bernal & Scharron del Rio, 2001). Such cultural adaptation has been proposed through the development of generic cross-cultural skills or the integration of culture-specific skills. *Generic cultural competence* refers to knowledge and skills required to work effectively in any cross-cultural psychotherapy (Lo & Fung, 2003). As every therapeutic encounter is cross-cultural in nature, the development of generic cultural competences is just plain good clinical practice. On the other hand, specific cultural competence enables therapists to work with particular ethnocultural groups. Nonetheless, EST tends to emphasize decontextualized manualized treatments (Carter, 2006; Wampold, 2007) and to restrict access to treatments of choice (Norcross, Koocher, & Garofalo, 2006; Rupert & Baird, 2004). In response to these concerns, the American Psychological Association established a Presidential Task Force on Evidence-based Practice (2006) to develop complementary frameworks for the integration of research evidence into practice. In turn, the task force members extended the definition of EBP to include contextual factors. More specifically, they defined EBP as the integration of the best available research, clinical expertise, and clients' culture, characteristics, and preferences (APA, 2006).

Therapeutic gains are reported in the application of EBP to culturally diverse populations (Voss Horrell, 2008). Researchers of color found that cognitive-behavioral therapy (CBT) was effective in treating depression among Latinos (Comas-Díaz, 1981; Organista, Munoz, & Gonzales, 1994) and African Americans (Kohn, Oden, Muñoz, Robinson, & Leavitt, 2002). Research also found efficacious results in the application of EBP to clients of color suffering from anxiety (Sanderson, Rue, & Wetzler, 1998) and obsessive disorder (Hatch, Friedman, & Paradis, 1996). Furthermore, Huey and Polo (2008) reported research findings providing evidence of EBP success with youth of color in the areas of attention-deficit hyperactivity disorder (ADHD), depression, conduct disorder, substance use, trauma-related disorders, and other clinical problems. The caveat of these research findings is that, to be effective, EBP needs to be culturally adapted to clients' contexts. To illustrate, Bernal and Scharron del Rio (2001) recommended the addition of multicultural awareness and culture-specific strategies, not only to cognitive-behavioral treatment, but also to other types of psychotherapy. Similarly, Comas-Díaz and Duncan (1985) provided an example of a successful cultural adaptation of an assertiveness training. Their empirical findings suggested that the intervention helped Latinas to express their assertiveness in a culturally relevant manner, while exploring the cultural consequences of their actions.

Notwithstanding these accomplishments, many clients of color tend to drop out of CBT as compared to European American counterparts (Miranda, et al., 2005; Organista et al., 1994). This finding seems to reaffirm the need to culturally adapt EBP for diverse populations. As Bigfoot (2008, March 13) stated, EBP is different from practice-based evidence. Thus, treating culturally diverse clients implies that cultural evidence needs to inform practice. For example, Lopez and his associates (2002) explored when and how to culturally adapt CBT. Bernal, Bonilla, and Bellido (1995) examined this issue and identified eight dimensions to increase cultural sensitivity and ecological validity in treatment outcome research. Moreover, they stated that these dimensions—language, persons, metaphors, content, concepts, goals, method, and context—additionally serve as a guide for culturally adapting existing treatments. According to Bernal and his associates, the *language* used in therapy needs to be culturally appropriate to the client's worldview and life experiences. The dimension of *persons* refers to the therapeutic relationship. The *metaphors* dimension involves symbols and concepts shared by members of a cultural group. Moreover, the dimension of *content* comprises the therapist's cultural knowledge (i.e., does the client feel understood by the therapist?). The role of the *concepts* dimension is to examine whether the treatment concepts are consonant with the client's culture. *Goals* inquire whether therapeutic objectives are congruent clients' adaptive cultural values. *Methods* refer to the cultural adaptation and validation of methodology and instruments. Last, *context* considers the clients' environment, including sociopolitical and historical circumstances.

Evidence-based practice has not fully incorporated all of these dimensions. In particular, it has not taken into consideration the sociopolitical context. Moreover, mainstream psychotherapy has been silent regarding the role of history and sociopolitical contexts in people's lives (Brown, 1997). More specifically, EST modalities have underemphasized the role of cultural and social contexts in the delivery of clinical care to people of color (Rogers, 2004). The omission of sociocultural and political contexts is particularly detrimental for people of color, whose history of trauma and oppression differs from the experience of most majority group members (Vasquez, 1998). Dominant psychotherapy tends to overlook the effects of *racial microaggressions* on clients of color. Defined as the assaults inflicted upon individuals on a regular and acute basis solely due to their race, color, and/or ethnicity (Pierce, 1995) racial microaggressions also occur within therapeutic encounters in the form of color blindness, denial of individual racism, the myth of meritocracy, and pathologizing multicultural values and styles, among others (Sue et al., 2007). Moreover, fame and privilege do not protect people of color from microaggressions (Rivera, 1999). Indeed, racial microaggressions can lead to *ethnocultural allodynia*, a disturbance in individuals' ability to judge perceived ethnic and racial insults, and subsequently, discern defiant and maladaptive responses from adaptive and resilient ones (Comas-Díaz & Jacobsen, 2001). Since a decontextualized and ahistorical psychotherapy may lead marginalized people to internalize their oppression, such internalization compromises their agency (Freire, 1973) and mastery. As a result, clinicians

need to consider the sociopolitical context and examine oppression when working with culturally diverse clients.

Muñoz (1996) highlighted the sociopolitical context in his cultural adaptation of CBT by targeting both internal and external realities in Latinos' lives. Muñoz's recommendations included (a) the involvement of culturally diverse people in the development of psychological interventions, (b) inclusion of sociocentric worldview values, (c) consideration of religion/spirituality, (d) relevance of acculturation, and (e) acknowledgment of the effects of oppression on mental health (Muñoz & Mendelson, 2005). However, Muñoz's cultural adaptations need to be tailored to specific ethnic groups. For example, Muñoz identified the development of a positive meaning in life under adversity as a core belief within his CBT cultural adaptation. Such recommendation may need to be modified when working with some African Americans. Partly due to their history of trauma, slavery, and oppression, many African Americans are distrustful of "too much" positive thinking, in that they believe that this type of outlook may be unrealistic (hooks, 1993). A potential strategy to counteract this belief is to foster the development of resistance against oppression. For instance, in my clinical practice with African Americans, I culturally translate "positive thinking" into hope. When appropriate, I use my clients' spiritual and ideological beliefs to cognitively reframe their distrust of positive thinking. Indeed, I have found that hope—along with other positive values—is culturally contextualized. As an example, I associate hope with resilience. In short, the limitations of the adaptations of empirically supported practice point out to the influence of culture on the psychotherapeutic process.

Cultural Mirrors in the Therapeutic Process

Culture reflects the psychological and spiritual factors that affect people's lives. Consequently, these "cultural mirrors" are reflected in the clinical practice. Indeed, cultural mirrors influence assessment and treatment, as well as the psychotherapeutic process. To illustrate, cultural mirrors reflect factors such as client's expectations, perception of clinician credibility, self-disclosure, trust, engagement, and development of therapeutic alliance. Whaley and Davis (2007) reviewed the empirical literature on EBP with people of color and concluded that culture affects the psychotherapeutic process more than it affects psychotherapeutic outcome. Therefore, the examination of cultural mirrors can enhance clinicians' cultural competence and treatment effectiveness. For the purpose of this discussion, I concentrate on three cultural mirrors that affect the therapeutic process. They are worldview, therapeutic relationship, and communication.

Worldview

Worldview informs behavior. The term *worldview* refers to the total system of ideas and beliefs that an individual holds of the universe and how it is constructed (Maduro, 1982). To illustrate, many people of color's interpersonal styles reflect the interactive influence of race, culture, ethnicity, gender, socioeconomic class, amount of acculturation to the mainstream, and sociopolitical factors. Within this context, the American Psychological Association Multicultural Guideline 1 endorses a commitment to a cultural understanding of the worldview of self and other. Furthermore, it encourages psychologists to appreciate how, as cultural beings, our worldviews (both clients' and psychologists') affect psychotherapy. This is necessary since client and therapist's differences in worldview can limit collaboration in treatment.

Many culturally diverse individuals adhere to a sociocentric or collectivistic worldview (Comas-Díaz, 2006b). Within a collectivistic orientation, members tend to endorse affiliation; understand themselves through others; emphasize family, social, emotional, and spiritual bonds; and prefer communal goals above individual ones (Triandis, 1995). Furthermore, they favor relational values such as interdependence, holism, and balance (Shweder & Bourne, 1982). Practitioners unaware of their clients' sociocentric worldview can violate personal and family norms by asking clients to prematurely disclose intimate information, soliciting the expression of emotion and affect, and requesting them to air family disputes—all before achieving credibility and earning their trust (Varma, 1988). Next, I discuss three sociocentric values, namely *familismo*, saving face, and contextualism.

SOCIOCENTRIC WORLDVIEW VALUES:
FAMILISMO
An example of a sociocentric worldview, *familismo* extends family relations beyond bloodlines. *Familismo* is a Latino cultural mandate that designates as family members those individuals who have a significant role in the person's life. For example, people adhering to *familismo* often consider godparents, friends, mentors, teachers, close co-workers, and even neighbors as family members. Within this context, therapists and other health providers fit into the role of extended family members (Comas-Díaz, 1989). Moreover, clients endorsing *familismo* tend to translate individual treatment into family therapy with one person. For example, many Latinos frequently bring their relatives to therapy sessions. This means that clinicians need to be knowledgeable of family and group dynamics. Moreover, due to *familismo*, many clients are likely to share therapeutic knowledge and even medications with significant others (Jacobsen & Comas-Díaz, 1999). Along these lines, Roselló and Bernal (1999) identified the need to incorporate sociocentric values into psychological practice. Their empirical investigation found both CBT and interpersonal psychotherapy (IPT) to alleviate depression among Latinos. However, these researchers reported that participants in the IPT condition had an added advantage because the clients improved their self-concept and social adaptation. Rossello and Bernal noted that IPT is culturally congruent with *familismo*, since IPT can be culturally sensitive for collectivistic clients who experience losses, relational difficulties, and cultural role transitions. Interestingly, in a similar study published in 2008, Roselló, Bernal, and Rivera-Medina found CBT to be significantly superior to IPT. The researchers explained their contradictory 1999 and 2008 findings as a result of methodological flaws. The discrepancy in the two studies suggests the need for further research in the cultural adaptation of EBP.

Latinos who adhere to *familismo* tend to value relationships that bear mutuality. Within the mutuality context, some Latino clients may express gratitude toward their therapist by giving a gift. Indeed, gift-giving is an expression of sociocentric relations. Moreover, this practice has indigenous roots. As individual survival is linked to a communal survival, gift-giving solidifies gratitude within an interdependent context. Adherence to *familismo* can lead clients to present their therapist with small gifts such as folkloric expressions, souvenirs, food, beverage, art, and other small tokens of appreciation. *Familismo* gifts can be facilitated by the information available through the Internet. For example, clients can search their therapist's personal information through Google (Zur, 2008), LinkedIn, and others. Therefore, clients can find out the therapist's birthday and give a card (or small gift) for the occasion. Nonetheless, therapists' management of gift-giving requires a blend of cultural skills with cultural sensitivity.

SOCIOCENTRIC WORLDVIEW
VALUES: SAVING FACE

The concept of saving or losing "face" is central to a traditional Asian interpersonal orientation. Among many Asians, *face* refers to an interpersonal orientation within relationships and thus, represents social position gained through behavior that is recognized by others. According to Zane (2008, March 13), face entails the person's social presentation of values, attitudes, and traits that comprise his or her character. When behavior seems to reify this set of attributions, others recognize the person's face. *Saving face* is a motivator in behavior, not only socially, but also during therapy. Zane (2008) reported research that found loss of face among Asian clients as affecting self-disclosure in treatment. Based on this research, Zane identified the prevention of the threat to face as (a) direct avoidance of certain relationships, (b) use of intermediaries, (c) monitoring of conversation, (d) self-restraint in expression, and (e) modesty and self-effacing to reduce the possibility of being discredited. These recommendations can also be extended to Latinos coping with *verguenza*. As a cultural concept, *verguenza* is a type of socioemotional shame and/or absence of pride that is elicited when individuals lose face. The relevance of the cultural values of face and *verguenza* can be exemplified by Confucius' maxim: "Without shame you are not human" (Ji Xuesong, personal communication, 2007). A person's *verguenza* extends from the individual to the family and even to the ethnic community. Indeed, "being a credit to your ethnic group" entails pride and thus, is the opposite of *verguenza*. Moreover, *verguenza* can act as self-censorship in therapy. Zane suggested that to manage face (and I add *verguenza*) clinicians can (a) use protective maneuvers (such as respect and politeness), (b) depersonalize face-threatening incidents through the provision of warnings and explanations, (c) minimize the face-threatening episode, and (d) conceal or hide the incident when the client has lost control of his or her emotions.

SOCIOCENTRIC WORLDVIEW VALUES: TRANSPERSONALITY

Transpersonality is a sociocentric way of relating. The term *transpersonal* refers to the development of identity beyond personal and individual levels (Scotton, 1996). Therefore, transpersonality involves people's ability to transcend their individual self into a self-other-environment identity to foster the interpenetration of cosmic influences in people's lives. As an illustration, many people of color endorse a transpersonal agency in which they see themselves as co-creators of their reality (Comas-Díaz, 2006b). That is, they share their agency with a transpersonal entity—a spiritual, religious, material, and or cosmic force (fate, destiny, fortune). Indeed, transpersonality can help people of color to enhance their cultural resilience and deepen their sense of meaning and purpose in life. For example, Ricardo Muñoz identified (1996) the development of a positive meaning in life under difficult circumstances as a core belief within his CBT cultural adaptation. Likewise, practitioners can explore clients' meaning-making and how they learn from adversity. Assigning meaning to a painful situation can cognitively reframe the event as a transformative experience. Along these lines, research has found that an ideological understanding of discriminatory events coupled with social activism facilitates recovery from oppressive trauma (Landrine & Klonoff, 1994).

SOCIOCENTRIC WORLDVIEW VALUES: CONTEXTUALISM

Many culturally diverse individuals are immersed in their contexts. Consequently, they tend to take into consideration contextual factors in their behavior. Such style has been named *contextualism*, or the tendency to describe the self and other using more contextual references and fewer dispositional references (Choi, Nisbett, & Norenzayan, 1999). Individuals with a contextual cognitive style tend to process information while paying attention to their surrounding context, as opposed to individuals with a context-independent style, who tend to process stimuli as if they were unaffected by the context (Kuhner, Hannover, & Shubert, 2001). Berry (1991) empirically found that persons with individualistic worldviews on average score higher on context independence, whereas collectivistic persons tend to score higher on context dependence. For many people of color, contextualism is accompanied by a combined locus of control—a blend of internal and external locus of control, in which the context determines which locus of control will prevail (Comas-Díaz, 2006b).

Life experiences, history, and sociopolitical factors nurture people of color's contextualism. As discussed previously, African Americans' history of medical establishment abuses may result in a mistrust of treatment. Consequently, such mistrust hinders the development of the psychotherapeutic alliance among African American clients. Thus, practitioners need to expect, recognize, and address this mistrust as a healthy paranoia. In response, clinicians need to prove credibility beyond their professional credentials, in order to earn their clients' trust. When working with clients of color, therapists need to exercise clinical acumen. Similarly, when compared to novice clinicians, experienced therapists tend to have better alliances with clients who are not comfortable with intimacy (Kivlighan, Patton, & Foote, 1998). Therefore, therapists working with people of color need to actively earn their trust. A way to accomplish this goal is to facilitate a therapeutic environment in which clients feel comfortable addressing contextual factors such as racism, sexism, and oppression. To initiate a therapeutic dialogue, clinicians can assess individuals' worldviews.

ASSESSING WORLDVIEWS

Clients' worldviews and life experiences affect how they perceive, interpret, and present their problems to their practitioners. Moreover, worldviews shape the meaning that clients attribute to their illness, their help-seeking behavior, identification of their of social support, and their behavior in treatment (Anderson, 1995). The explanatory model is an effective clinical tool to elicit clients' expectations and perspectives on their illness (Kleinman, 1980). Clinicians can use this culture-centered assessment based on an anthropological method to begin unfolding their clients' worldviews. They can ask the following questions (Callan & Littlewood, 1998; Kleinman, 1980):

- What do you call your problem (distress or illness)?
- What do you think your problem (illness) does?
- What do you think the natural course of your illness is?
- What do you fear?
- Why do you think this illness or problem has occurred?
- How do you think the distress should be treated?
- How do want me to help you?
- Who do you turn to for help?
- Who should be involved in decision-making?

As many culturally diverse individuals endorse a sociocentric worldview, they require relational approaches to assessment and treatment. As examples of relational interventions, family and group therapy are particularly central to individuals' sense of well-being. Indeed, genealogical trees or genograms (McGoldrick, Gerson, & Shellenberger, 1999) and

cultural genograms (Hardy & Laszloffy, 1995) are congruent with a sociocentric worldview. In addition to family dynamics, cultural genograms map information such as cultural translocation, adaptation, acculturation, ethnic/racial identity development, historical and current trauma, racial socialization, oppressive experiences, in-group/out-group member dynamics, relations with members of dominant society, geopolitics, and many other contextual factors. When working with immigrant families, clinicians can use a culturagram to assess specific immigration issues and stages, such as reasons for relocation, legal status, languages spoken both at home and at the community, time in community, health beliefs, crisis events, holidays and special events, contact with cultural spiritual and religious organizations, values about education and work, and values about family structure power, hierarchy, rules, subsystems, and boundaries (Congress, 2002). Moreover, therapists can use these tools to chart their own cultural locations, as well as examine similarities and differences vis-a-vis their clients' contexts. Effective management of the therapeutic relationship is a significant way for clinicians to earn credibility, enhance trust, and cement a therapeutic alliance.

Therapeutic Relationship

If the therapeutic relationship carries the treatment (Norcross & Lambert, 2005), culture is the steering wheel. Like other interpersonal relationships, therapists and clients negotiate psychotherapy not merely in terms of theoretical frameworks, but also in terms of cultural meanings. Successful clinical work with ethnic minorities depends on the therapist's skill in establishing and managing the therapeutic relationship (Jenkins, 1985). It also depends on the therapist's self-awareness and understanding of how ethnocultural and racial factors affect both therapist and client. The development of a therapeutic alliance, therefore, acquires inordinate importance within multicultural encounters. The strength of the early therapeutic relationship has been associated with positive therapeutic outcomes (Horvath, 2001). However, therapists need to obtain clients' *permission* to develop a multicultural alliance (Duran, 2006). In other words, the therapeutic alliance cannot emerge until the client feels comfortable with the clinician's trustworthiness, credibility, and cultural competence. Culture's influence ranges from treatment expectations, trust, credibility, and rapport, to the development of a therapeutic alliance. However, expectations about a therapeutic relationship vary cross-culturally (Portela, 1971). For instance, many Native American clients expect their therapist to exemplify empathy, genuineness, availability, respect, warmth, congruence, and connectedness (Trimble et al., 1996). Traditional Asian clients may be overly deferential and inhibited (Sakauye, 1996), and lose face when revealing certain information. Likewise, many Latinos expect their therapist to act as a member of their extended family. Furthermore, some African Americans may wonder if their clinician is racist until proven otherwise.

Research suggests that many clients of color expect their practitioner to be active by giving advice, teaching, and guiding, as well as helping them to explore their lives and to grow emotionally (Comas-Díaz, Geller, Melgoza, & Baker, 1982). These complex expectations seem consistent with Atkinson, Thompson, and Grant's (1993) recommendations. Atkinson and his colleagues advised clinicians to integrate the intersecting roles of advisor, advocate, facilitator, and change agent into their function of psychotherapist when working with culturally diverse clients. Within this framework, acculturation levels and sources of the client's problem are less rigidly defined. For instance, a highly acculturated client may require the therapist's involvement as an advisor, advocate, and facilitator.

Similarly, a directive therapeutic style can facilitate the development of trust during the initial stages of therapy (Comas-Díaz 2006a). Many sociocentric clients interpret this therapeutic method as a sign of caring. Such an approach may be crucial for clients of color who expect instrumental help from their clinician. For instance, the term *ethno-underclass* describes low-income African Americans, American Indians, and Latinos who are chronically isolated from the mainstream (Fuchs, 1990). During psychotherapy, they may present ethno-underclass issues such as inadequate employment, housing, and food, as well as issues of personal safety, violence, and physical health. Therapists who acknowledge and respond to these concerns validate the client's reality and help to establish and cement the therapeutic relationship. The client's presentation of environmental issues should not be perceived as resistance to treatment. Furthermore, instrumental help can be broadly translated, as in modeling and psychoeducation. To illustrate, I often add the function of mentor to my psychotherapist's role when working with high-achieving women of color. Most of my therapeutic mentoring aims to facilitate clients' successful navigation of racism and sexism. Similarly, Seeley (2000) suggested flexibility in the therapist's role when working with culturally diverse individuals.

Likewise, Kakar (1985) modified his psychoanalytic approach with Southeast Indians by being active and didactical, as well as feeling and expressing pity, interest, and warmth. Flexibility in a clinician's role is also prevalent among mainstream psychotherapists. For example, therapists act as a combination of philosopher, teacher, and scientist in rational emotive therapies (Prochaska & Norcross, 1994).

Racial Identity Development

Racial and ethnic identity development is salient in multicultural psychotherapy and relevant for the cross-cultural therapeutic relationship. The racial identity developmental theories offer a lens for understanding how clients of color process, as well as how they present to treatment, and even how they select their practitioner. Like levels of acculturation, racial identity stages speak about people of color's relationship with the dominant society. Racial identity theories propose that members of racial and ethnic minority groups initially value the dominant group and devalue their own group, then move to value their own group while devaluing the dominant group, and, in a final stage, integrate a value for both groups (Cross, 1991). According to Atkinson, Morten, and Sue (1998), the different minority identity development stages include (a) conformity (clients aspire to assimilate as they choose values and role models from the dominant group), (b) dissonance (individuals' begin to question and suspect the dominant group's cultural values), (c) resistance-immersion (individuals endorse minority-held views and reject the dominant culture's values), (d) introspection (individuals establish their racial ethnic identity without following all cultural norms), and (e) synergistic (individuals experience a sense of self-fulfillment towards their racial/ethnic/cultural identity without having to categorically accept their minority group's values). Other groups have proposed diverse cultural identity development theories. For example, mixed-race individuals develop their identity from personal identity, choice of group categorization, enmeshment/denial, appreciation, and integration (Poston, 1990).

Moreover, an European American identity developmental model also exists. According to Helms (1995), the white identity developmental stages include (a) contact (unaware of their own racial identity; white Americans tend to believe that the system in the United States is fair when considering race), (b) disintegration (individuals begin to acknowledge their white identity), (c) reintegration (individuals tend to idealize their racial group and minimize the qualities and conditions of other racial groups), (d) pseudo-independence (individuals tend to intellectualize the acceptance of their own and others' race), (e) immersion-emersion (individuals question their racial status and privileges), and (f) autonomy (individuals develop flexible standards and internalize a multicultural identity without racism).

Racial identity formation is an active process; it does not necessarily follow a course of linear stages. Indeed, minority development is a fluid process that may change according to one's context, the emergence of new challenges, adult developmental stages, ego statuses, and sociopolitical circumstances. Clients' racial identity development can have a direct effect on the therapeutic relationship. For instance, individuals at the conformity stage may prefer a clinician from the dominant group, as opposed to a therapist from their own cultural group. Conversely, clients at the synergistic stage may not be overly concerned about their practitioner's ethnic or racial group. Racial identity developmental stages potentially interact with client and therapist ethnoracial match. Some research suggests that clients working with clinicians of similar ethnoracial backgrounds and languages tend to remain in treatment longer than those clients whose practitioners are not ethnically or linguistically matched (Sue, 1998). Furthermore, an empirical study showed that clients of color in race-similar therapeutic dyads participate more in their care than do those in race-dissimilar dyads (Cooper-Patrick et al., 1999).

Nevertheless, ethnic and racial client–practitioner matching is not always realistic. Additionally, some culturally diverse clients are concerned about confidentiality and stigma associated with psychological treatment. These individuals may prefer a therapist who is not a member of their ethnocultural group. Moreover, there are contradictory results regarding provider–client ethnic matching (Hall, 2001). A review of the research on ethnic matching between psychotherapists and clients found inconclusive results and low validity for ethnic matching (Karlsson, 2005). Furthermore, research on the effects of ethnic matching on treatment satisfaction among Mediterranean migrant patients showed that they did not value ethnic matching as relevant, and considered clinical competence, compassion, and sharing their worldview as important (Knipscheer & Kleber, 2004). These findings can potentially be extended to other ethnic groups. Regardless of ethnicity, race, gender, sexual orientation, class, physical ability, or other diversity variables, therapists who are culturally competent enhance their clients' satisfaction with treatment. As an illustration, Fuertes and Brobst (2002) empirically examined European American and ethnic minority (Asian American, African American, Hispanic/Latinos, and American Indian) respondents' perceptions of the impact of cultural competency in psychotherapy. Their findings suggested that the participants' perceptions of a clinician's cultural competence correlated significantly with their perceptions of a therapist's trustworthiness and expertise. The researchers concluded that counselor cultural competence increased client satisfaction in therapy.

Ethnocultural Transference and Countertransference

The contradictory results in the client–therapist ethnic match may reflect the effects of racial, ethnic, and cultural identification and disidentification. Indeed, clients and clinicians often bring their imprinting of cultural, ethnic, and racial experiences into treatment. Such imprinting plays a significant role in the therapeutic relationship, since the reactions based on ethnocultural factors offer a roadmap for the relationship between self and other. Regardless of theoretical orientation, therapists working with culturally diverse individuals need to understand transference and countertransference, including the ethnocultural determinants of these phenomena (Zaphiropoulos, 1982). Racial and ethnic factors are easy and available targets for projection in therapy, which may be manifested in transference and countertransference. For example, Comas-Díaz and Jacobsen (1991) discussed ethnocultural transference and countertransference in both inter-ethnocultural dyads as well as in intra-ethnocultural dyads. These authors identified inter-ethnocultural transference as overcompliance and friendliness (predominant under a therapist–client societal power differential); denial (denial of ethnicity and/or culture); mistrust, suspiciousness, and hostility; and ambivalence.

The intra-ethnocultural transferential reactions include omnipotence (idealization of the therapist frequently promoted by the ethnic similarity), treason (client exhibits resentment and envy at therapist's successes), autoracism (client projects the strong negative feelings about him- or herself onto the ethnically similar therapist, and ambivalence. Some countertransferential reactions within the inter-ethnic dyad include denial of cultural differences, the clinical anthropologist's syndrome (excessive curiosity about clients' ethnocultural backgrounds at the expense of their psychological needs, guilt (around working with lower societal-status clients, pity (expression of political impotence within the therapeutic hour), aggression, and ambivalence (toward the client's culture as well as toward the therapist's own culture). The intra-ethnocultural countertransferential manifestations include overidentification, *Us and Them* mentality (shared victimization due to racial discrimination), distancing, survivor's guilt (surviving harsh circumstance can impede professional growth and may lead to denying their clients' psychological needs), cultural myopia (inability to see clearly due to cultural factors that obscure therapy), ambivalence (working through the therapist's own ethnic ambivalence), and anger (being too ethnoculturally close to a client may uncover painful, unresolved emotions). Ethnocultural transference and countertransference tend to serve as catalysts for major therapeutic issues, such as trust, ambivalence, anger, identity, and others. As an initial step to initiate a discussion of ethnocultural transference and countertransference, Comas-Díaz (2001) suggested asking clients: "How do you feel about my being from a different culture from yours?" or conversely, "How do you feel about our being from similar cultures?" This type of examination can help to unfold the existence of unconscious racial bias.

Therapist's Bias

Clinical work provides a fertile ground for the manifestation of ethnocultural and racial factors in the therapeutic process (Comas-Díaz & Griffith, 1988). These manifestations involve the conscious and/or unconscious acknowledgment of clients' and therapists' feelings and attitudes about their own ethnic and cultural identities, as well as their conscious and unconscious messages about racial, ethnic, and cultural differences in the therapeutic dyad (Comas-Díaz & Jacobsen, 1987). Indeed, empirical research has documented the existence of therapists' bias toward culturally different clients. To illustrate, Wampold and his associates (1981) studied the attitudes of psychotherapists toward African Americans, Chinese Americans, Japanese Americans, Jews, and Mexican Americans. They found that over 79 % of the sample of therapists' responses demonstrated the presence of subtle stereotypic attitudes, whereas 22.6% indicated highly blatant stereotypic attitudes. Therefore, as part of being culturally competent, therapists may want to examine their own biases. According to Laura Brown (1997), European Americans who grow up as members of a majority group are likely to be either covertly or overtly racist to some degree.

Cognitive psychology research has confirmed Brown's observation. Through the use of a response latency measure of bias, research has shown individuals who appear as nonprejudiced in self-report measures generally have negative attitudes toward African Americans (Dovidio & Gaertner, 1998). Moreover, in addition to the existence of unconscious and aversive negative racial feelings and beliefs toward people of color, studies have documented a widespread dissociation between implicit and explicit social stereotyping. (Dovidio, Gaertner, Kawakami, & Hodson, 2002). Research suggests that once stereotypic impressions are formed, these notions are often resistant to change (Gilbert, 1998). Therapists who do not examine their implicit and unconscious biases contribute to the development of pernicious effects on their clients (Vasquez, 2007). Self-reflection can help clinicians to recognize their attitudes toward others, and examine their impressions by unlearning and relearning information that has been socially taught about self and others (i.e., cultural, racial, and ethnic stereotypes, white privilege, internalized oppression, and other factors; Comas-Díaz & Caldwell-Colbert, 2006). This approach can allow for a deeper understanding of self and other.

Indeed, the American Psychological Association's Multicultural Guideline 2 encourages psychologists to understand how minority groups' history of oppression influences people of color's worldviews. In addition to recognizing historical factors, this understanding includes becoming aware of the effects of ongoing discrimination within the interaction of racism, sexism, elitism, xenophobia, and other forms of discrimination. Therapists can examine their biases through self-reflection, genograms, and power analysis. A power analysis compares the client's cultural group's social status with the practitioner's. This comparison entails the identification and challenge of internalized privilege and oppression. While conducting a power analysis, therapists examine their own areas of privilege and oppression, and compare their findings with their client's. According to Worrell and Remer (2003), clinicians can write down under a column headed by the letter "O" their areas of oppression. Next, they write their areas of privilege in a column under the letter "P" for privilege. After following the same procedure for their client's areas of oppression and privilege, therapists can compare their own results with those of their client's. In completing a power analysis, clinicians may want to include areas of historical oppression and privilege. Power analysis can help to unfold areas of similarities and differences between clinicians and their clients. This process can help psychologists to take the perspective of their clients. When therapists are able to take the perspective of the "other," they can reduce their stereotypic and ethnocentric attitudes (Galinsky & Moskowitz, 2000). This process facilitates the development of empathy (Finlay & Stephan, 2000). Nonetheless, clinicians working with culturally diverse clients have to go beyond developing cognitive and affective empathy; furthermore, they need to engage in cultural empathy. A process of perspective taking by using a cultural framework as a guide for understanding the client from the outside-in, cultural empathy (Ridley & Lingle, 1996) helps to recognize the self in the other. Therapists can use explanatory models of distress, cultural genograms, self-awareness, and power differential analysis, among other methods, to develop cultural empathy.

Communication

Communication is an integral component of culture. Likewise, language and cultural nuances transform the psychotherapeutic process. However, worldview differences between therapist and client can result in the clinician "hearing" but not "listening to" the client's narrative. As indicated previously, differing worldviews interfere with communication, the development of a therapeutic alliance, and therapist–client collaboration in decision making. Thus, an integral part of the therapeutic work is the "translation" of worldviews into a communication bridge that connects client and therapist. Being understood by another person can be intrinsically therapeutic because it eases the distress of isolation. Clinical lore proclaims that communication is to the psychotherapist what the scalpel is to the surgeon. Hence, when working with culturally diverse individuals, therapists need to expand their communication repertoire. Regardless of their use of language, culturally diverse clients often communicate in a sociocentric style. In other words, sociocentric members tend to communicate implicitly and indirectly. Such style helps to maintain harmonious relationships, relies on a substantial amount of nonverbal communication, and pays high attention to contextual factors. Hall (1983) identified this style as context-rich, in which communication adheres to a rich web of cultural nuances and meaning. In a similar vein, many people of color raise racial, ethnic, gender, socioeconomic, ideological, and political issues as a means of evaluating their therapist's credibility. For example, many Latino clients might engage in

plática to check out their therapist (Comas-Díaz, 2006a). A social lubricant, plática is a light conversation used prior to the discussion of serious issues. As such, plática helps to address potential conflicts, desensitize painful reactions, and offers a safety net for delving into deeper issues in therapy. Consequently, effective interventions with culturally diverse individuals require an understanding of context-rich communication. Beyond words, a context-rich communication comprises nonverbal signs such as body language, voice pitch and intonation, and other kinesthetic messages. An example of a nonverbal process, intuition can illuminate cross-cultural encounters. As a way of communicating and understanding, intuition relies on internal cues, hunches, and vibes (Butler, 1985). In a similar vein, I adhere to cultural resonance, the ability to understand clients through intuition, clinical skill, and cultural competence (Comas-Díaz, 2006a). Cultural resonance can provide information beyond those messages that are communicated verbally, such as clients' internal emotional state.

Psychotherapy language is culturally constructed and thus reflects the power differential inherent in the therapeutic relationship. Indeed, clinicians need to avoid eliciting what Duran (2006) called historical transference. In other words, historical transference entails a power differential resulting from the replication of the colonizer and colonized dynamic. An example of this power differential is the therapist's attitude toward the client's language. With its English-only movement, the United States government does not value bilingualism (Comas-Díaz & Padilla, 1992). Likewise, psychotherapy has not paid proper attention to language issues (Claus, 1998). For example, monolingual therapists do not appreciate, nor fully understand, bilingual and polyglot clients' experiences (Santiago Rivera & Altarriba, 2002). Such an attitude underestimates the multiple layers of meaning that language and bilingualism provide to people's lives. Javier (1995) studied bilingual individuals and gave them the choice to express their thoughts in English or Spanish. Most of them preferred to switch languages, and the researcher followed the lead of the participants. Based on these findings, Javier recommended that researchers who work with bilingual participants should integrate both languages to provide more reliable and descriptive data. Similarly, Luna, Ringberg, and Peracchio (2008) empirically found that bilingual bicultural individuals have incorporated two cultures within themselves, and consequently, have distinct sets of culture-specific concepts and mental frameworks that activate aspects of their identities. In brief, bilingual bicultural individuals may be different persons, according to the language they speak. Clinicians unaware of these processes may be addressing only one identity when they communicate with bicultural clients in English.

Furthermore, clinical practice does not frequently speak to the realities or special needs of linguistic minorities. To enhance client and clinician communication, the American Psychological Association's Multicultural Guideline 5 urges psychologists to respect clients' language preferences and ensure accurate translation of documents by providing informed consent about the language in which assessment, therapy, and other procedures will be conducted (APA, 2003). Multicultural Guideline 5 also encourages psychologists to respect clients' privacy by not using interpreters who are significant others, relatives, community authorities, and/or unskilled in the area of mental health. The unaddressed psychotherapeutic needs of culturally and linguistically diverse individuals have fomented the examination of ethnic-specific modalities.

Ethnic-specific Psychological Practice

The common elements in a psychotherapeutic process include a shared worldview, the healing qualities of the therapist, the client's expectations, and an emerging sense of mastery (Torrey, 1986). However, these elements may be interpreted differently across cultures. Some multicultural scholars have asked if there is any role for the development of culture-specific approaches to psychotherapy (López, Kopelowicz, & Cañive, 2002). As a response, various clinicians looked into the ancient wisdom of their ethnic communities (Comas-Díaz, 2006a; Duran, 2006). Ethnic psychological practice offers a culturally relevant framework, validates racial and ethnic meanings, and recognizes the importance of historical and political contexts of oppression (Comas-Díaz, 2007). Indeed, many ethnic psychologies adhere to a social justice perspective that promotes the construction and transformation of a more egalitarian future. Moreover, ethnic psychologies are anchored in a liberation discourse because they provide resources for rescuing ancestry and archetypes by reaffirming and grounding ethnic identity into a collective self. Certainly, indigenous practices and ethnic psychologies can be a source of healing and liberation. The Surgeon General concluded that Western psychological interventions could benefit from incorporating the core assumptions and practices of indigenous healing (Surgeon

General, 2000). Similarly, the American Psychological Association's Multicultural Guideline 5 encourages psychologists to recognize that culture-specific treatment may require ethnic and indigenous interventions. When suitable, this guideline encourages psychologists to acknowledge and solicit the assistance of recognized helpers (community leaders, clergy) and traditional healers (shamans, santeros, medicine women/men, curandero(a)s, astrologers, psychics, espiritistas, and others). Psychologists can learn about helping practices and healing traditions used in non-Western cultures that may be appropriately incorporated into psychological practice.

Many traditional healing practices are based on indigenous sources of knowledge such as intuition, spirituality, experience, observation, nature, balance, harmony, ancestors, history, humor, and others (Bigfoot, 2008). This knowledge is obtained through specific ways of being in the world. Hence, these ways of knowing include honoring, listening, respecting, being humble, accepting, revering, collaborating, teaching, and learning, among others. These meaning-making processes are used to create awareness, foster healing, encourage liberation, and promote development. For instance, the family structure among many people of color honors ancestors by including the deceased, since relationships don't necessarily end with death (Council of National Psychological Associations, 2003; Shapiro, 1994). Dominant psychological models seldom address the domain of relationships with the deceased in psychological assessment and/or treatment (Comas-Díaz & Caldwell-Colbert, 2006). In the next section, I present a few illustrations of ethnic psychological practices.

Bicultural Approaches

Bicultural effectiveness training (BET) and family effectiveness training (FET) target intergenerational conflicts elicited by acculturation and adaptation problems among Latinos (Szapocznik, Santisteban, Kurtines, Perez-Vidal, & Hervis, 1984). The Strengthening of Intergenerational/Intercultural Ties in Immigrant Chinese American Families (SITICAF) is an example of addressing cultural adaptation issues among Chinese Americans (Ying, 1999).

Dichos therapy

Dichos psychotherapy, an ethnic psychology, involves Spanish proverbs or idiomatic expressions that capture folk wisdom (Aviera, 1996; Zuñiga, 1991). Also known as refranes, these Spanish language proverbs are a type of flash therapy that offers the therapist a window into many Latinos' worldview

(Comas-Díaz, 2006b). Muñoz used *dichos* in his cultural adaptation of CBT. Likewise, de Rios (2001) recommended *dichos* as a cognitive restructuring tool to facilitate flexibility, manage anger, and address interpersonal conflicts.

Family Constellation Therapy

Developed by Bert Hellinger, and based on Zulu cultural and spiritual beliefs, family constellation therapy views individual and family dynamics in a larger context (Hellinger, Weber, & Beaumont, 1998). A former Catholic priest and missionary in South Africa, Hellinger conceptualizes the family energy field or family soul as the principle for understanding and treatment. The family soul, according to Hellinger, includes ancestors and future generations. Specifically, family constellation treatment entails becoming conscious of unconscious loyalties toward ancestors and generational burdens. A classic example is a woman who rejects her cold and distant mother and cannot get pregnant. Through constellation work, the client becomes conscious that her mother's distance was a protection against the loss of her first child.

Liberation Psychology

Psychology of liberation emerged in Latin America as a response to sociopolitical oppression (Aron & Corne, 1994). It is intimately linked to Paulo Freire's (1970) *concientization* or the critical consciousness that involves the process of personal and social transformation that oppressed Latin Americans experienced while they alphabetized themselves in a dialectic discourse with their world. Within this context, psychology of liberation integrates an indigenous psychological perspective within an emancipatory paradigm (Comas-Díaz, Lykes, & Alarcon, 1998). Thus, psychology of liberation attempts to work with people in their contexts to enhance their awareness of oppression and the inequalities that have kept them subjugated. Through these means, liberation practitioners collaborate with the oppressed in developing critical analysis and engaging in a transforming practice.

Morita and Naikan therapies

Morita therapy (Morita, 1998) and Naikan therapy (Reynolds, 1980) are psychological interventions developed in Japan, which infuse Japanese and Asian values (such as face) into clinical practice. Both therapies are sociocentric in nature and use relationships, beliefs, and milieu approaches in healing. Chinese mental health practitioners are using Morita therapy to treat inpatient clients (Xin Ke, personal communication 2007).

Network Therapy

Carolyn Attneave (Attneave, 1990) developed network therapy. Using Native American values, network therapy is an extended family/group psychotherapy approach that involves the client's network (Speck & Attneave, 1973). It entails recreating the clan's network to activate and mobilize a person's family, kin, and relationships in the healing process.

TEMAS and Cuento therapy

Tell Me a Story (TEMAS) is a projective psychological test developed with culturally relevant stimuli (Costantino, Dana, & Malgady, 2007). Multicultural in nature, this test comprises two sets of structured stimulus cards with pictorial problem solving—one for minorities (African Americans and Latino/Hispanics) and the other for nonethnic minorities. As a narrative assessment tool, TEMAS evolved into *cuento* therapy. According to Costantino, Malgady, and Rogler (1994) *cuento* therapy uses folktales with ethnic and culturally relevant stimuli in a social learning approach. It is designed to present models of adaptive interpersonal behavior. Through storytelling, this therapy uses modeling to promote a new synthesis of bicultural symbols and foster adaptive personality growth among Latino youngsters who live in two cultures (Costantino, Malgady, & Rogler, 1986). In this approach, clients are asked to focus on a culturally relevant hero or heroine and to use them as idealized but achievable figures (Costantino, Malgady, & Rogler, 1988). *Cuento* therapy provides a strong psychoeducational component. Research found *cuento* therapy to be effective with Puerto Rican children (Costantino, Malgady, & Rogler, 1986).

Testimonio

Testimonio or testimony is a Latin American way of bearing witness that chronicles one's traumatic experiences and how these have affected the individual, family, and community (Cienfuegos & Monelli, 1983). Due to many people of color's history of distress, *testimonio* has successfully been used in trauma therapy (Aron, 1992). This verbal healing journey to the past honors the historically situated reality of culturally diverse individuals and anchors healing in a sociopolitical context.

Ethnocultural Psychological Practice

To address the needs of culturally diverse clients—particularly clients of color—I suggest an ethnocultural psychological approach. This theoretical and practical orientation integrates ethnic, cultural, racial, class, and other diversity variables into clinical practice. An ethnocultural practice aims to incorporate cultural competence and cultural integrity into the delivery of services to culturally diverse people (Comas-Díaz & Jacobsen, 2004). It integrates ethnicity and culture into clinical practice by infusing mainstream practice with multicultural values, ethnic/indigenous practices, critical analysis, and empowering approaches. Ethnocultural practice facilitates a transcultural analysis that aims at critical consciousness, or the process of transformation that oppressed individuals experience while educating themselves in a dialectical conversation with the world. Through this process, clients learn to read their condition and author their reality. Within this approach, the therapeutic relationship encourages the dialogue that helps clients express their truth, assert their identity, heal, and achieve agency.

Ethnocultural psychotherapy proposes an extensive evaluation—the ethnocultural assessment (Jacobsen, 1988). The ethnocultural assessment stages are heritage, saga, niche, self-adjustment, and relationships (Comas-Díaz & Jacobsen, 2004). To explore clients' heritage, therapists look at clients' ethnocultural ancestry, genealogy, history, genetics, and sociopolitical contexts. During this stage, clinicians examine clients' cultural trauma, psychopolitical mistrust, and soul wounds. To explore clients' saga, clinicians examine clients' family, clan, and group story through the history of immigration and other significant transitions. Exploration of the niche stage reveals the post-transition analysis, in which clinicians pay attention to clients' cognitive and emotional interpretation of their family saga. Next, therapists evaluate clients' self-adjustment separate from their family adaptation. Of relevance to this stage is the examination of clients' cultural resilience and creativity. Finally, the last stage of the ethnocultural assessment explores clients' significant affiliations, including the therapeutic relationship.

An essential aspect of ethnocultural therapeutic approach is an ethnopolitical perspective. As indicated before, many people of color require emancipatory approaches since the pain of oppression can be unbearable for individuals residing in a society that prides itself on being classless and open. This psychopolitical lens promotes conscientization, decolonization, social justice, and global solidarity. Consequently, ethnocultural approaches facilitate people of color's identification, acceptance, and celebration of their ethnicity and culture, as they help

to rescue ancestry and cultural resources (Comas-Díaz, 2007). It facilitates the development of cultural consciousness—a critical awareness of ancestry that encourages a reconnection to cultural resources to empower, heal, and redeem (Comas-Díaz, 2007). One of these resources is resilient creativity. Many people of color have used creativity as a resilient and subversive mechanism against oppression. Examples range from flamenco (*canto hondo* music from the Gypsy or Roma people), Hip Hop music, to Spoken Word or the original Nuyorican Poets Café (Algarín. & Piñero, 1975). *Arpilleras*, a colorful weaving depicting the stories of oppressed and traumatized Latin Americans, is a subversive creative response (Agosin, 1996). Interestingly, Leung, Maddux, Galinsky, and Chiu (2008) empirically showed that the relationship between multicultural experiences and creativity is stronger when people adapt (i.e., are culturally resilient), are open to new experiences, and when the creative context emphasizes flexibility over rigidity. This ethnopolitical approach depathologizes, affirms cultural strengths, encourages cultural consciousness, and facilitates resilience. It clinically addresses issues such as ethnocultural allodynia and exposure to racial microaggressions. Additionally, it examines postcolonization stress disorder, soul wound, and postslavery trauma, among other kinds of historical oppression. A goal of the ethnopolitical approach is to promote liberation, enhance group solidarity, sustain collective continuity, and promote the development of a just society.

Conclusion
Collective Cultural Competence
Dominant psychological practice tends to endorse an individualistic worldview, frequently ignoring collective, systemic, and sociopolitical contexts. Therefore, to effectively work with culturally diverse individuals, clinicians need to expand their scope of interventions. Adding a sociocentric lens to their clinical practice can enhance therapists' cultural competence. The development of cultural competence is a life-long process. To help this process, clinicians need to extend their cultural competence into collective contexts. Therefore, cultural competence requires the inclusion of systemic, organizational, and communal strategies. Likewise, Cross, Bazron, Dennis, and Issacs (1989) identified cultural competence as the encouragement of organizational change and growth. They suggested that the development of organizational cultural competence evolves from (a) *cultural destructiveness* (characterized by attitudes, policies, and practices that are destructive

to individuals' cultures, such as the prohibition against speaking individuals' mother tongue); (b) *cultural incapacity* (characterized by attitudes, policies, and practices that support the racial dominance of the dominant group and assume a paternalistic mode toward the ethnic groups); (c) *cultural blindness* (characterized by attitudes, policies, and practices that support the belief that all people are the same and that members of minority groups have some cultural deficiency); (d) *cultural precompetence* (characterized by attitudes, policies, and practices that convey awareness of limitations in multicultural communication and desire to provide a culturally sensitive treatment, but that have a simplistic view of cultural competence, and believe that a single act fulfills any perceived obligation to all ethnic groups); and finally, to (e) *cultural competence* (characterized by attitudes, policies, and practices that value and respect cultural differences, support continuing self assessment regarding culture, pay attention to the dynamics of difference, and continue to expand their knowledge and resources).

Individuals need to promote cultural competence in their communities. Indeed, social progress emerges when communities appreciate diversity (Fuentes, 1992), and thus, develop cultural competence. Moreover, communal cultural competence enhances society's civic benefits. The development of communal cultural competence emerges through the following stages: (a) *exclusionary* (communities are monocultural and have a civic disengagement); (b) *oblivious* (communities are mostly monocultural and have a civic detachment); (c) *naïve* (communities have civic amnesia, are ahistorical and acultural; (d) *charitable* (communities are multicultural and have civic altruism, but the norm is the giver's perspective); (e) *reciprocal* (communities are multicultural, address the legacies of inequalities and value partnering and cultural competence, and focus on the present society), finally, (f) *generative* (communities are multicultural; value interconnectedness, multiple perspectives, and cultural competence; and focus on everyone in the present and in the future) (Bordewich, 2005; Musil, 2003). Although the generative stage may be aspirational at this time, collaboration between researchers, clinicians, clients, and community shareholders is an initial step toward the promotion of community cultural competence.

Future Directions

As the development of cultural competence is a life-long process, maintaining cultural integrity in the delivery of psychological interventions also requires a life-long commitment. Therefore, to increase cultural competence and preserve cultural integrity in the delivery of interventions to culturally diverse populations, clinical psychologists need to systematically examine the following areas:

• Operational definition of cultural competent behaviors
• Connection between cultural competence and improved mental health functioning
• Relevance of sociopolitical contexts to clinical practice
• Incorporation of indigenous and ethnic psychology into psychological practice
• Examination of the role of spirituality and faith
• Cross-cultural studies of language and nonverbal communication
• Studies on transculturation/borderland issues and their effects on mental health
• Examination of ethnobiological and neurohormonal factors in psychopharmacological and psychological treatment
• Combinations of qualitative and quantitative methods
• Studies of resilience and cultural strengths among culturally diverse populations

Furthermore, we continue to face the following outstanding questions:

• What is the effect of globalization on clinical psychological practice?
• How does transnational mobility impact on clinical practice?
• How does multiculturalism influence dominant psychological effect practice?
• How does language (bilingualism, being a polyglot, nonstandard English) affect delivery of psychological services?
• How do we develop creative resilience, and how can we teach it?

As clinical psychology continues to improve the services to culturally diverse individuals and communities, the whole field will enhance its competence and integrity.

References

Agosin, M. (1996). *Tapestries of hope, threads of love: The arpillera movement in Chile, 1974–1994.* Albuquerque: University of New Mexico Press.

Algarín, M., & Piñero, M. (Eds.). (1975). *Nuyorican poetry: An anthology of Puerto Rican words and feelings.* New York: William Morrow & Co.

Altman, N. (1995). *The analyst in the inner city: Race, class and culture through a psychoanalytic lens.* New York: Analytic Press.

American Psychiatric Association. (1994). *Diagnostic and statistical manual of mental disorders* (4th ed.). Washington, DC: Author.

American Psychiatric Association. (2000). *Diagnostic and statistical manual of mental disorders* (4th ed.). Text Revision. Washington, DC: Author.

American Psychological Association. (2003). Guidelines on multicultural education, training, research, practice, and organizational change for Psychologists. *American Psychologist, 58,* 377–402.

American Psychological Association Presidential Task Force on Evidence-Based Practice. (2006). Evidence-based practice in psychology. *American Psychologist, 6*(4), 271–285.

Anderson, N. (1995). Behavioral and sociological perspectives on ethnicity and health: Introduction to the special issue. *Health Psychology, 14,* 589–591.

APA (1990). *Guidelines for providers of psychological services to ethnic, linguistic, and culturally diverse populations.* Washington, DC: Office of Ethnic Minority Affairs, American Psychological Association.

Aron, A. (1992). Testimonio, a bridge between psychotherapy and sociotherapy. *Women & Therapy, 13*(3), 173–189.

Aron, A., & Corne, S. (Eds.). (1994). *Writings for a liberation psychology: Ignacio Martín-Baró.* Cambridge, MA: Harvard University Press.

Atkinson, D. R. Morten, G. & Sue, D. W. (Eds.). (1998). *Counseling American Minorities (5th Edition).* Boston: McGraw-Hill.

Atkinson, D. R., Thompson, C. E., & Grant, S. K. (1993). A three dimensional model for counseling racial/ethnic minorities. *Counseling Psychologist, 21,* 257–277.

Attneave, C. (1990). Core networks intervention: An emerging paradigm. *Journal of Strategic and Systemic Therapies, 9,* 3–10.

Aviera, A. (1996). "Dichos" therapy group: A therapeutic use of Spanish language proverbs with hospitalized Spanish-speaking psychiatric patients. *Cultural Diversity and Mental Health, 2*(2), 73–87.

Bernal, G. Bonilla, J, & Bellido, C. (1995). Ecological validity and cultural sensitivity for outcome research: Issues for cultural adaptation and development of psychosocial treatments with Hispanics. *Journal of Abnormal Child Psychology, 23* (1), 67–82.

Bernal, G., & Scharron del Rio, M. R. (2001). Are empirically supported treatments valid for ethnic minorities: Toward an alternative approach for treatment research. *Cultural Diversity and Ethnic Minority Psychology, 7,* 328–342.

Berry, J. W. (1991). Cultural variations in field dependence-independence. In S. Wapner & J. Derrick (Eds.), *Field dependence-independence cognitive style across the life span* (pp. 289–308). Hillsdale, NJ: Laurence Earlbaum Associates Publishers.

Betancourt, J. R., Green, A. R., Carrillo, J. E., & Ananch-Firempong, O. (2003). Defining cultural competence: A practical framework for addressing racial/ethnic disparities in health and health care. *Public Health Reports, 118, July-August,* 293–302.

Bigfoot, D. (2008, March 13). *Adaptations and implementations for American Indians: Lessons learned.* Presentation made at the Culturally Informed Evidence Based Practice: Translating Research and Policy for the Real World. Bethesda: MD.

Bordewich, F. M. (2005). *Bound for Canaan: The Underground Railroad and the war for the soul of America.* New York: Amistad Press.

Brown, L. S. (1997). The private practice of subversion: Psychology as Tikkun Olam. *American Psychologist, 52,* 449–462.

Butler, L. (1985). Of kindred minds: The ties that bind. In M. A. Orlandi (Ed.), *Cultural competence for evaluators: A guide for alcohol and other drug abuse prevention practitioners working with ethnic/racial communities* (pp. 23–54). Rockville, MD: U.S. Department of Health and Human Services.

Brown, L. S. (1997). The private practice of subversion: Psychology as Tikkun Olam. *American Psychologist, 52,* 449–462.

Caldwell-Colbert, A. T., Daniel, J. H., & Dudley-Grant, G. R. (2003). The African Diaspora: Blacks in the therapeutic relationship. In J. D. Robinson, & L. C. James (Eds.), *Diversity in human interactions: The tapestry of America* (pp. 33–61). New York: Oxford University Press.

Callan, A., & Littlewood, R. (1998). Patient satisfaction: Ethnic origin or explanatory model? *International Journal of Social Psychiatry, 44,* 1–11.

Carter, J. (2006). Theoretical pluralism and technical eclecticism. In C. Goodheart, R. J. Sternberg, & A. Kazdin (Eds.), *Evidence-based Psychotherapy: Where practice and research meet* (pp. 63–79). Washington, DC: American Psychological Association.

Chambless, D. L., Sanderson, W. C., Shoham, V., Johnson, S. B., Pope, K. S., Cris-Christoph, P., et al. (1996). An update on empirically validated therapies. *The Clinical Psychologist, 49,* 5–18.

Choi, I., Nisbett, R. E., & Norenzayan, A. (1999). Causal attribution across cultures: Variations and universality. *Psychological Bulletin, 125,* 47–63.

Cienfuegos, A. J., & Moneli, C. (1983). The testimony of political repression as a therapeutic instrument. *American Journal of Orthopsychiatry, 53,* 43–51.

Clauss, C. S. (1998). Language: The unspoken variable in psychotherapy practice. *Psychotherapy, 35,* 188–196.

Comas-Díaz, L. (1981). Effects of cognitive and behavioral group treatment in the depressive symptomatology of Puerto Rican women. *Journal of Consulting and Clinical Psychology, 49*(5), 627–632.

Comas-Díaz, L. (1989). Culturally relevant issues and treatment implications for Hispanics. In D. R. Koslow, & E. Salett (Eds.), *Crossing cultures in mental health.* Washington, DC: Society for International Education Training & Research (SIETAR).

Comas-Díaz, L. (2001). Building a multicultural private practice. *The Independent Practitioner, 21(4),* 220–223.

Comas-Díaz, L. (2006a). Cultural variation in the therapeutic relationship. In C. Goodheart, R. J. Sternberg, & A. Kazdin (Eds.), *Evidence-based Psychotherapy: where practice and research meet* (pp. 81–105). Washington, DC: American Psychological Association.

Comas-Díaz, L. (2006b). Latino healing: The integration of ethnic psychology into psychotherapy. *Psychotherapy: Theory, Research, Practice & Training, 43(4),* 436–453.

Comas-Díaz, L. (2007). Ethnopolitical psychology: Healing and transformation. In E. Aldarondo (Ed.), *Promoting social justice in mental health practice.* New Jersey: Lawrence Earlbaum Associates.

Comas-Díaz, L. (2008). *Spirita:* Reclaiming womanist sacredness in feminism. *Psychology of Women Quarterly, 32,* 13–21.

Comas-Díaz, L., & Caldwell-Colbert, A. T. (2006). Applying the APA multicultural guidelines to psychological practice. Online course and Primer. American Psychological Association Division of Psychologists in Independent Practice.

Comas-Díaz, L., & Duncan, J. (1985). The cultural context: A factor in assertiveness training with mainland Puerto Rican women. *Psychology of Women Quarterly, 9*(4), 463–475.

Comas-Díaz, L., & Griffin, E. H. E. (Eds.). (1988). *Clinical guidelines in cross cultural mental health.* New York: John Wiley and Sons.

Comas-Díaz, L., Geller, J., Melgoza, B., & Baker, R. (1982, August). Ethnic minority patients' expectations of treatment and of their therapists. Presentation made at the American Psychological Association Annual Meeting.

Comas-Díaz, L., & Jacobsen, F. M. (1991). Ethnocultural transference and countertransference in the therapeutic dyad. *American Journal of Orthopsychiatry, 61*(3), 392–402.

Comas-Díaz, L., & Jacobsen, F. M. (2001). Ethnocultural allodynia. *The Journal of Psychotherapy Practice and Research, 10*(4), 1–6.

Comas-Díaz, L., & Jacobsen, F. M. (2004). Ethnocultural psychotherapy. In E. Crighead, & C. Nemeroff (Eds.), *The concise Corsini encyclopedia of psychology and behavioral science* (pp. 338–339). New York: Wiley.

Comas-Díaz, L., Lykes, B., & Alarcon, R. (1998). Ethnic conflict and psychology of liberation in Guatemala, Perú, and Puerto Rico. *American Psychologist, 53*(7), 778–792.

Comas-Díaz, L., & Padilla, A. M. (1992). The English-only movement: Implications for mental health. *American Journal of Orthopsychiatry, 62*(1), 6.

Congress, E. (2002). Using culturagrams with culturally diverse families. In A. Roberts, & G. Greene (Eds.), *Social desk reference* (pp. 57–61). New York: Oxford University Press.

Cooper-Patrick, L., Gallo, J., Gonzales, J. J., Vu, H. T., Powe, N. E., Nelson, C., & Ford, D. (1999). Race, gender and partnership in the patient–physician relationship. *JAMA: Journal of the American Medical Association, 282*, 583–589.

Costantino, G., Dana, R. H., & Malgady R. (2007). *TEMAS (tell-me-a-story) Assessment in Multicultural Societies.* Clifton, NJ: Lauwence Earbaum Associates.

Council of National Psychological Associations (2003, November). *Psychological treatment of ethnic Minority Populations.* Washington, DC: The Association of Black Psychologists.

Cross, T., Bazron, B., Dennis, K., & Issacs, M. (1989). *Towards a Culturally Competent System of Care: A Monograph on Effective Services for Minority Children Who are Severely Emotionally Disturbed* (pp. 13–17). Washington, DC: CASPP Technical Assistance Center, Georgetown University Child Development Center.

Cross, W. E. Jr. (1991). *Shades of Black: Diversity in African American Identity.* Philadelphia: Temple University Press.

de Rios, M. D. (2001). *Brief psychotherapy with the Latino immigrant client.* New York: Harworth Press.

Diala, C., Muntaner, C., Walrath, C., Nickerson, K., LaVeist, T., & Leaf, P. (2000). Racial differences in attitudes toward professional mental health care in the use of services. *American Journal of Orthopsychiatry, 70*(4), 455–456.

Dovidio, J. F., & Gaertner, S. L. (1998). On the nature of contemporary prejudice: The causes, consequences and challenges of aversive racism. In J. L. Eberhardt, & S. T. Fiske (Eds.), *Confronting racism: The problem and the response* (pp. 3–32). Thousand Oaks, CA: Sage.

Dovidio, J. F., Gaertner, S. L., Kawakami, K., & Hodson, G. (2002). Why can't we just get along? Interpersonal biases and interracial distrust. *Cultural Diversity and Ethnic Minority Psychology, 8*, 88–102.

Duran, E. (2006). *Healing the Soul Wound: Counseling with American Indians and other Native People.* New York: Teachers College Press.

Finlay, K. A., & Stephan, W. G. (2000). Improving intergroup relations: The effects of empathy on racial dyads. *Journal of Applied Social Psychology, 30*, 1720–1737.

Foster, R. F., Moskowitz, M., & Javier, R. (Eds.). (1996). *Reaching across the boundaries of culture and class: Widening the scope of psychotherapy.* New York: Jason Aronson.

Freire, P. (1973). *Education for critical consciousness.* New York: Seabury.

Fuentes, C. (1992). *The buried mirror: Reflections on Spain and the new world.* New York: Houghton Mifflin Company.

Fuchs, L. H. (1990). *The American kaleidoscope: Race, ethnicity, and the civic culture.* Middletown, Connecticut: Wesleyan University Press.

Fuertes, J. N., & Brobst, K. (2002). Clients' ratings of counselor multicultural competency. *Cultural Diversity and Ethnic Minority Psychology, 8*, 214–223.

Garcia, A. M. (1982). *La Operacion.* Latin American Film Project. New York: Cinema Guild. (documentary; Ana Maria Garcia, director and producer).

Galinsky, A. D., & Moskowitz, G. B. (2000). Perspective-taking: Decreasing stereotype expression, stereotype accessibility, and in-group favoritism. *Journal of Personality & Social Psychology, 78*, 708–724.

Gilbert D. T. (1998). Ordinary personalogy. In D. T. Gilbert, & S. T. Fiske (Eds.), *The Handbook of Social Psychology*, 4th ed. (Vol. 2, pp. 89–150). New York: McGraw-Hill.

Hall, E. T. (1983). *The Dance of Life: The Other Dimension of Time.* Garden City, NY: Anchor Press/Doubleday.

Hall, G. C. N. (2001). Psychotherapy research with ethnic minorities: Empirical, ethical, and conceptual issues. *Journal of Consulting and Clinical Psychology, 69*, 502–510.

Hansen, N. D., Pepitone-Arreola-Rockwell, F., & Greene, A. F. (2000). Multicultural competence: Criteria and case examples. *Professional Psychology: Research & Practice, 31*, 652–660.

Hatch, M. L., Friedman, S., & Paradis, C. M. (1996). Behavioral treatment of obsessive disorder in African-Americans. *Cognitive and Behavioral Practice, 3*, 303–315.

Hardy, K. V., & Laszloffy, T. (1995). The cultural genogram: Key to training culturally competent family therapists. *Journal of Marital and Family Therapy, 21*(3), 227–237.

Hellinger, B., Weber, G., & Beaumont, H. (1998). *Love's Hidden Symmetry: What Makes Love in Relationships.* Phoenix, AZ: Zeig, Tucker, & Theisen.

Helms, J. (1995). An update of Helm's White and people of color racial identity models. In J. G. Ponterotto, J. M. Casas, L. A. Suzuki, & C. M. Alexander (Eds.), *Handbook of multicultural counseling* (pp. 181–198). Thousand Oaks, CA: Sage.

Hooks, b. (1993). *Sister of the Yam: Black Women and Self-recovery.* Cambridge, MA: South End Press.

Horvath, A. O. (2001). The alliance. *Psychotherapy Research, 38*(4), 365–373.

Huey, S. J., & Polo, A. J. (2008). Evidence-based psychosocial treatments for ethnic minority youth. *Journal of Clinical Child and Adolescent Psychology, 37*, 262–301.

Jacobsen, F. M. (1988). Ethncoultural assessment. In L. Comas-Díaz, & E. H. Griffith (Eds.), *Clinical Guidelines in Cross Cultural Mental Health.* New York: Wiley.

Jacobsen, F. M., & Comas-Díaz, L. (1999). Psychopharmacological treatment of Latinas. *Essential Psychopharmacology, 3*(1), 29–42.

Javier, R. A. (1995). Vicissitudes of autobiographical memories in bilingual analysis. *Psychoanalytic Psychology, 12*, 429–438.

Jenkins, A. H. (1985). Attending to self-activity in the Afro-American client. *Psychotherapy, 22*(2), S335–S348.

Ji X. (2007, September 20). Personal Communication.

Kakar, S. (1985). Psychoanalysis and non-Western cultures. *International Review of Psychoanalysis, 12*, 441–448.

Karlsson, R. (2005). Ethnic matching between therapist and patient in psychotherapy: An overview of findings, together with methodological and conceptual issues. *Cultural Diversity and Ethnic Minority Psychology, 11*(2), 113–129.

Kivlighan, D. M., Patton, M. J., & Foote, D. (1998). Moderating effects of client attachment on the counselor experience-working alliance relationship. *Journal of Counseling Psychology, 45*, 274–278.

Kleinman, A. (1980). *Patients and Healers in the Context of Culture: An Exploration of the Borderland Between Anthropology, Medicine, and Psychiatry.* Berkeley: University of California Press.

Knipscheer, J. W., & Kleber, R. J. (2004). A need for ethnic similarity in the therapist-patient interaction? Mediterranean Migrants in Dutch mental health care. *Journal of Clinical Psychology, 60*(6), 543–554.

Kohn, L., Oden, T., Muñoz, R. F., Robinson, A., & Leavitt, D. (2002). Adapted cognitive behavioral group therapy for depressed low-income African-American women. *Community Mental Health Journal, 38*(6), 497–504.

Kuhner, U., Hannover, B., & Shubert, B. (2001). The semantic-procedural interface model of the self: The role of self-knowledge for context-dependent versus context-independent modes of thinking. *Journal of Personality and Social Psychology, 80*(3), 397–409.

Landrine, H., & Klonoff, E. (1997). *Discrimination Against Women: Prevalence, Consequences, Remedies.* Thousand Oaks, CA: Sage.

Lawson, W. B. (1996). Clinical issues in pharmacotherapy of African-Americans. *Psychopharmacological Bulletin, 32*, 275–281.

Leung, A. K-y., Maddux, W., Galinsky, A., Chiu, C-y. (2008). Multicultural experience enhances creativity: The when and how. *American Psychologist, 63*(3), 169–181.

Lewis-Fernandez, R., & Díaz, N. (2002). The cultural formulation: A method for assessing cultural factors affecting the clinical encounter. *Psychiatric Quarterly, 73*, 271–295.

Lo, H-T., & Fung, K. P. (2003). Culturally competent psychotherapy. *Canadian Journal of Psychiatry, 48*(3), 161–170.

López, S. R., Kopelowicz, A., & Cañive, J. M. (2002). Strategies in developing culturally congruent family interventions for schizophrenia: The case of Hispanics. In H. P. Lefley, & D. L. Johnson (Eds.), *Family interventions in mental illness: International perspectives* (pp. 61–90). Westport, CT: Praeger.

Luna, D., Ringberg, T., & Peracchio, L. A. (2008). One individual, two identities: Frame-switching among biculturals. *Journal of Consumer Research, 35*(2), 279–293.

Maduro, R. J. (1982). Working with Latinos and the use of dream analysis. *Journal of the American Academy of Psychoanalysis, 10*(4), 609–628.

Mendoza, R. & Smith, M. W. (2000). The Hispanic response to psychotropic medications. In P. Ruiz (Ed), *Ethnicity and Psychopharmacology* (pp. 55–89). Washington, DC: American Psychiatric Press.

McGoldrick, M., Gerson, R., & Shellenberger, S. (1999). *Genograms: Assessment and intervention.* New York: Norton W. W. Company.

Melfi, C. A., Croghan, T. W., Hanna, M. P., & Robinson, R. (2000). Racial variation in antidepressant treatment in a Medication population. *The Journal of Clinical Psychiatry, 61*(1), 16–21.

Miranda, J., Bernal, G., Lau, A., Kohn, L., Hwang, W-C., & La Framboise, T. (2005). State of the science on psychosocial interventions for ethnic minorities. *Annual Review of Clinical Psychology, 1*, 113–142.

Miranda, J., Green B. L., Krupnick, J. L., Chung, J., Siddique, J., Beslin, T., & Revicki, D. (2006). One-year outcome of a randomized clinical trial treating depression in low-income minority women. *Journal of Consulting and Clinical Psychology, 74*, 99–111.

Morita, S. (1998). *Morita Therapy and the True Nature of Anxiety-based Disorders (Shinkeishitsu).* Thousand Oaks, CA: Sage Publications, Inc.

Muñoz, R. F. (1996). The healthy management of reality. Retrieved April 25, 2010 from http://www.medschool.ucsf.edu/latino/pdf/healthy_management.pdf

Muñoz, R. F., & Mendelson, T. (2005). Toward evidence-based interventions for diverse populations: The San Francisco General Hospital Prevention and Treatment Manuals. *Journal of Clinical and Consulting Psychology, 73*(5), 790–799.

Musil, C. M. (2003). Educating for citizenship. *Peer Review, 5*(3), 4–8.

Norcross, J. C., & Lambert, M. J. (2005). The therapy relationship. In J. Norcross, L. Beutler, & R. Levant (Eds.), *Evidence-based Practices in Mental Health: Debate and Dialogue on Fundamental Questions* (pp. 208–218). Washington DC: American Psychological Association.

Norcross. J. C., Koocher, G. P., & Garofalo, A. (2006). Discredited psychological treatments and tests: A Delphi poll. *Professional Psychology: Research and Practice, 37*, 515–522.

Organista, K. C., Muñoz, R. F., & Gonzales, G. (1994). Cognitive behavioral therapy for depression in low income and minority medical outpatients: Description of a program and exploratory analyses. *Cognitive Therapy and Research, 18*, 241–259.

Pierce, C. M. (1995). Stress analogs of racism and sexism: Terrorism, torture and disaster. In C. V. Willie, P. P. Reiker, & B. S. Brown (Eds.), *Mental health, racism and sexism* (pp. 277–293). Pittsburgh: University of Pittsburgh Press.

Pi, E. H., & Gray, G. E. (2000). Ethnopharmacology for Asians. In P. Ruiz (Ed.), *Ethnicity and Psychopharmacology* (pp. 91–113). Washington, DC: American Psychiatric Press.

Portela, J. M. (1971). Social aspects of transference and counter-transference in the patient–psychiatrist relationship in an underdeveloped country: Brazil. *International Journal of Social Psychiatry, 17*, 177–188.

Poston, W. C. (1990). The biracial identity development model: A needed addition. *Journal of Counseling and Development, 69*(2), November-December, 152–155.

Prochaska, J. O., & Norcross, J. C. (1994). *Systems of Psychotherapy: A Transtheoretical Analysis (3rd Ed.).* Pacific Grove, CA: Brooks/Cole.

Ramirez, M. (1991). *Psychotherapy and Counseling with Minorities: A Cognitive Approach to Individual and Cultural Differences.* New York: Pergamon.

Reynolds, D. K. (1980). *The Quiet Therapies: Japan Pathways to Personal Growth.* Honolulu: The University Press of Hawaii.

Ridley, C., & Lingle, D. W. (1996). Cultural empathy in multicultural counseling: A multidimensional process model. In P. B. Pedersen, J. G. Draguns, W. J. Lonner, & J. E. Trimble

(Eds.), *Counseling Across Cultures, 4th Ed.* (pp. 21–46). Thousand Oaks, CA: Sage.

Rivera, G. (1999, May 26). Police brutality against minorities (Geraldo Rivera interviewed by Katie Curic). *The Today Show.* New York: NBC.

Rogers, W. A. (2004). Evidence medicine and justice: A framework for looking at the impact of EBM upon vulnerable and disadvantage groups. *Journal of Medical Ethics, 30,* 141–145.

Roselló, J., & Bernal, G. (1999). The efficacy of cognitive-behavioral and interpersonal treatments for depression in Puerto Rican adolescents. *Journal of Consulting and Clinical Psychology, 67,* 734–745.

Roselló, J., Bernal, G., & Rivera-Medina, C. (2008). Individual and group CBT and IPT for Puerto Rican adolescents with depressive symptoms. *Cultural Diversity and Ethnic Minority Psychology, 14,* 234–245.

Rupert, P., & Baird, R. (2004). Managed care and the independent practice of psychology. *Professional Psychology: Research and Practice, 35,* 185–193.

Sakauye, K. (1996). Ethnocultural aspects. In J. Sadavoy, L. W. Lazarus, L. F. Jarvik, & G. T. Grossberg (Eds.), *Comprehensive review of geriatric psychiatry,* 2nd ed. (pp. 197–221). Washington, DC: American Psychiatric Press.

Sanderson, W. C., Rue, P. J., & Wetzler, S. (1998). The generalization of cognitive behavior therapy for panic disorder. *Journal of Cognitive Psychotherapy, 12,* 323–330.

Santiago-Rivera, A. L., & Altarriba, J. (2002). The role of language in therapy with the Spanish-English bilingual client. *Professional Psychology: Research and Practice, 33,* 30–38.

Scotton, B. W. (1996). Introduction and definition of transpersonal psychiatry. In B. W. Scotton, A. B. Chinen, & J. R. Battista (Eds.), *Textbook of transpersonal psychiatry and psychology* (pp. 3–8). New York: Basic Books.

Seeley, K. M. (2000). *Cultural psychotherapy: Working with culture in the clinical encounter.* Northvale, NJ: Jason Aronson, Inc.

Shapiro, E. R. (1994). *Grief as a Family Process: A Developmental Approach to Clinical Practice.* New York: Guilford.

Shweder, R. A., & Bourne, E. J. (1982). Does the concept of person vary cross culturally? In A. J. Marsella, & G. M. White (Eds.), *Cultural Conceptions of Mental Health and Therapy.* Dordrecht, Holland: Reidel.

Speck R, V., & Attneave, C. L. (1973). *Family Networks.* New York: Panthenon Books.

Spradley, J. P. (1990). *Participant Observation.* New York: Holt, Rinehart and Winston.

Strickland, T. L., Ranganeth, V., & Lin, K. M. (1991). Psychopharmacologic considerations in the treatment of Black American populations. *Psychopharmacology Bulletin, 27,* 441–448.

Sue, D. W., Bingham, R. P., Porche-Burke, L., & Vasquez, M. (1999). The diversification of psychology: A multicultural revolution. *American Psychologist, 54*(12), 1061–1069.

Sue, D., Capodilupo, C. M., Torino, G. C., Bucceri, J. M., Holder, A. M., Nadal, K. L., & Esquilin M. (2007). Racial microaggressions in everyday life: Implications for clinical practice. *American Psychologist, 62*(4), 271–286.

Sue, S. (1998). In search of cultural competence in psychotherapy and counseling. *American Psychologist, 53,* 440–448.

Sue, S., Zane, N., Levant, R. F., Silverstein, L. B., Brown, L. S., Olkin, R. et al. (2006). How well do both evidence-based practices and treatment as usual satisfactorily address the various dimensions of diversity? In J. C. Norcross, L. E. Beutler, and R. F. Levant (Eds.), *Evidence-based Practices in Mental Health: Debate and Dialogue on the Fundamental Questions*

(pp. 329–337). Washington, DC: American Psychological Association.

Surgeon General. (2000). *Mental Health, Culture, Race and Ethnicity: A Supplement to Mental Health – A Report of the Surgeon General Disparities in Mental Health Care for Racial and Ethnic Minorities.* Rockville, MD: Office of the Surgeon General.

Szapocznik, J., Santistekan, D., Kurtines, W., Perez-Vidal, A., & Harvis, O. E. (1984). Bicultural effectiveness training: A treatment intervention for enhancing intercultural adjustment. *Hispanic Journal of Behavioral Sciences, 6,* 317–344.

Torrey, E. F. (1986). *Witchdoctors and psychiatrists: The common roots of psychotherapy and its future.* New York: Harper Row.

Triandis, H. (1995). *Individualism and Collectivism.* Boulder, CO: Westview.

Trimble, J. E., Fleming, C. M., Beauvais, F. & Jumper-Thurman, P. (1996). Essential cultural and social strategies for counseling Native American Indians. In P. B. Pedersen, G. G. Draguns, P. B. Lonner, & Trimble, J. E. (Eds.). *Counseling Across Cultures (4th Edition).* (pp. 177–209). Thousand Oaks, CA: Sage.

Varma, V. K. (1988). Culture personality and psychotherapy. *International Journal of Social Psychiatry, 43*(2), 142–149.

Vasquez, M. J. T. (1998). Latinos and violence: Mental health implications and strategies for clinicians. *Cultural Diversity and Mental Health, 4,* 319–334.

Vasquez, M. J. T. (2007). Cultural difference and the therapeutic alliance: An evidence based analysis. *American Psychologist, 62*(8), 878–885.

Voss Horrell, S. C. (2008). Effectiveness of cognitive-behavioral therapy with adult ethnic minority clients: A review. *Professional Psychology, Research and Practice, 39,* 160–168.

Wampold, B. E. (2007). Psychotherapy: The humanist (and effective) treatment. *American Psychologist, 62*(8), 857–873.

Wampold, B. E., Casas, J. M., & Atkinson, D. R. (1981). Ethnic bias in counseling: An information processing approach. *Journal of Counseling Psychology, 28,* 498–503.

Washington, H. A. (2007). *Medical Apartheid: The Dark History of Medical Experimentation on Black Americans from Colonial Times to the Present.* New York: Doubleday.

Whaley, A. L., & Davis, K. E. (2007). Cultural competence and evidence-based practice in mental health services: A complementary perspective. *American Psychologist, 62*(6), 563–574.

Worrell, J., & Remer, P. (2003). *Feminist Perspectives in Therapy (2nd Ed.).* New York: Wiley.

Xin, K. (2007). Personal communication. September 20.

Ying, Y. (1999). Strengthening intergenerational/Intercultural ties in immigrant families: A new Intervention for parents. *Journal of Community Psychology, 27*(1), 89–96.

Young, M. I. (1990). *Justice and the Politics of Difference.* Princeton, NJ: Princeton University Press.

Zane, N. (2008, March 13). *Cultural Competence Issues and Evidence Based Psychological Practices.* Presentation made at the Culturally Informed Evidence Based Practice: Translating Research and Policy for the Real World. Washington, DC.

Zane, N., Hall, G. C. N., Sue, S., Young, K., & Nunez, J. (2004). Research on psychotherapy with culturally diverse populations. In M. J. Lambert (Ed.), *Handbook of Psychotherapy and Behavior Change, 5th Ed.* (pp. 767–804). New York: Wiley.

Zaphiropoulos, M. L. (1982). Transcultural parameters in the transference and countertransference. *Journal of the American Academy of Psychoanalysis, 10*(4), 571–584.

Zuñiga, M. E. (1991). "Dichos" as metaphorical tools for resistant Latino clients. *Psychotherapy, 28,* 480–483.

Zur, O. (2008). The Google factor: Therapists' self-disclosure in the age of the Internet. *Independent Practitioner, 28*(2), 82–89.

PART 5

Conclusion and Future Directions

The Future of Clinical Psychology: Promises, Perspectives, and Predictions

David H. Barlow *and* Jenna R. Carl

Abstract

In this chapter, we speculate on near to immediate future trends in clinical psychology and make ten predictions in the broad areas of training, diagnosis and assessment, and treatment. These include: (1) an increased focus on competencies in training; (2) the implications of evidence-based practice as a new major focus of training; (3) changes in the accreditation of training programs; (4) a move to dimensional conceptions of diagnosis; (5) clinical outcomes assessment as an integral part of practice, as well as a more individual focus in clinical research; (6) the increasing recognition and dissemination of psychological treatments; (7) the end of single-diagnosis psychological treatment manuals; (8) the development of drugs that specifically enhance the mechanisms of action of psychological treatments; (9) an expanded role for technology in service delivery; and (10) a clearer delineation of the terms "psychological treatments," referring to interventions directed at psychopathology and pathophysiology in the context of our health-care delivery system, and, "psychotherapy," increasingly based on data from positive psychology, but directed at enhancing personal adjustment and growth.

Keywords: Assessment, clinical psychology, diagnosis, future trends, training, treatment

In the first chapter of this handbook, I (DHB) recount two 40-year odysseys in the profession of clinical psychology: The first is David Shakow's 1969 look back at the first 40 years of his career; and the second is my own 40-year odyssey that coincidently began in 1969. Chapter 1 examines Shakow's predictions made in 1969 for the coming years in clinical psychology, focusing on three broad areas: training, diagnosis and assessment, and treatment. My own 40-year odyssey has played out in the context of a realization of Shakow's vision in most of these areas, but with many surprises and unexpected twists along the way, as detailed in Chapter 1. In this chapter, I am joined by a young colleague (JRC) beginning her own odyssey in clinical psychology, and together we briefly outline likely trends and developments over the coming decades. Many of these trends and developments are articulated in some detail in other chapters of

this handbook, and, in that sense have already begun. Others represent predictions that are more implicit than explicit in the book, but seemed important enough to us to note. In a very arbitrary manner and reflecting a popular organizational scheme of the day, we have grouped our predictions in a "top ten" list and emulate Shakow in covering the areas of training, diagnosis and assessment, and intervention (see Table 39.1), but without any intent to suggest that one topic is more important than another. Of course, the list could have been much longer and some of the themes could have been grouped together or separated into more specific issues, but this seemed as reasonable a way as any to venture into the realm of visions for the future. It will remain for someone else (perhaps JRC) to reflect on the fate of these themes at some future time, much as we have done with Shakow's predictions presented in Chapter 1.

Table 39.1 Top predictions in clinical psychology by area

Training	1. A Focus on Competencies	Clinical training goals will be assessed and indexed by outcomes in applied settings.
	2. Evidence-based Practice	Strategies of evidence-based practice will join psychopathology, assessment, and interventions as foundational foci in training.
	3. Accreditation	The face of accreditation will change to reflect distinct competencies.
Diagnosis & Assessment	4. Diagnoses as Dimensions	A theoretically based dimensional system of nosology for mental disorders will gradually replace the current prototypical, categorical classification system.
	5. Clinical Outcomes Assessment	Clinicians will be evaluated and differentially compensated based on treatment outcomes, and clinicians and clinical scientists will return to a more individual, idiographic focus to guide future clinical research and practice.
Treatment	6. The Growth of Psychological Treatments and a Focus on Dissemination and Implementation	As new psychological treatments are developed and existing treatments become more efficacious, the focus will shift to currently underdeveloped efforts on dissemination and implementation.
	7. Moving Beyond Single-Diagnosis Treatment Manuals	Modular transdiagnostic interventions will replace treatment protocols applicable to only a single diagnostic category.
	8. Drugs That Enhance Psychological Treatments	Pharmacological agents that specifically bolster the effectiveness of mechanisms of action of psychological interventions will become increasingly common.
	9. Technology-based Service Delivery	Digital technologies will become increasingly integrated into service delivery systems and will lead to more personalized care.
	10. Psychological Treatments or Psychotherapy?	Psychological treatments will be a term reserved for evidence-based practices appropriate for addressing pathology in the context of health care systems. Psychotherapy will be a term reserved for procedures directed at enhancing personal adjustment and growth, but administered outside of health care systems and based increasingly on data emerging from the field of positive psychology.

Training

A Focus on Competencies

Clinical training goals will be assessed and indexed by outcomes in applied settings.

In Chapter 1, and also in Chapter 8 by Catherine Grus, we find that the long-desired goal of measuring competencies, eloquently articulated by Shakow 40 years ago, is beginning to be realized. As described by Grus, and based to a large extent on work by Nadine Kaslow and colleagues, these initiatives are currently developing along several fronts. First, much has been achieved recently in the definition of competencies. The American Psychological Association's Competency Benchmarks Document (American Psychological Association [APA], 2007) outlines

a competency framework with two domains of core competencies—foundational and functional—that are defined in detail at specific levels of professional development, such as entry to practicum, internship, and practice. The foundational competencies put forth by the APA (2007) comprise 12 core competencies that are then further delineated by "essential components" (defining skills) and "behavioral anchors" (behavioral benchmarks for assessing readiness). Specific assessment methods are suggested for each set of behavioral anchors. For example, the foundational competency "Relationships" is defined as, "Capacity to relate effectively and meaningfully with individuals, groups, and/or communities," and has three subcategories: Interpersonal Relationships;

Affective Skills; and Intradisciplinary Relationships. At the entry to practicum level, Interpersonal Relationships has the essential component "interpersonal skills" and behavioral anchors such as "listens and is empathic with others" and "respects and shows interest in others' cultures, experiences, values, points of view, goals and desires, fears, etc." Assessment methods recommended include: "performance and behavior in course(s) or evaluation milestones" and "examination of performance in interviews." Whereas, at the entry to practice level for Interpersonal Relationships, the essential component is "to develop and maintain effective relationships with a wide range of clients, colleagues, organizations, and communities" and behavioral anchors are "negotiates conflictual, difficult, and complex relationships including those with individuals and groups that differ significantly from oneself" and "maintains satisfactory interpersonal relationships with clients, peers, faculty, allied professionals, and the public." Here assessment methods proffered are "360 evaluation" (which refers to an evaluation that includes feedback from all levels of co-workers, supervisors and supervisees, clients, and sometimes self-feedback) and "self-evaluation."(APA, 2007; for further discussion of competencies see Grus, Chapter 8, this volume).

Second, efforts are under way aimed at developing more rigorous methods to assess competence. In 2004, the APA Board of Educational Affairs formed a Task Force on Assessment of Competence in Professional Psychology charged with researching and developing competency assessment methods. In 2008, the Task Force released "The Competency Assessment Toolkit for Professional Psychology," which provides information on 15 different assessment practices to help educate and guide users (APA, 2009). These assessment methods are also listed in the Competency Benchmarks Document (APA, 2007) mentioned earlier, and they include practices such as Client/Patient Process and Outcome Data, Case Presentation Review, and Simulation/Role Plays. The toolkit includes a grid that displays ratings of the usefulness of each assessment method for particular competencies and a fact sheet that describes each method, how it can be used, and the challenges involved in implementation for practicing clinicians (APA, 2009).

Third, there are increasing efforts between education/training organizations and regulatory/credentialing bodies to collaborate on developing competencies and assessment methods. Historically, these groups have functioned fairly independently, but a mutual interest in developing consistent competencies has encouraged cooperation. As Grus notes, several national competency initiatives, like the Competencies Conference and the APA Benchmarks and Toolkit work groups, recently brought these groups together (Chapter 8, this volume), and there is evidence that this trajectory of cooperation will continue. The Association of State and Provincial Psychology Licensing Boards (ASPPB) has made a concerted effort to include education and training advocates in its work on competencies "to ensure that the proposed regulations used language and constructs consistent with models of professional psychology education and training" (Grus, Chapter 8, this volume). Both sides understand the advantages of having a competency framework that is integrated across the education, licensing, and practicing continuum, and is simultaneously reflective of the needs of each of these systems. With consistent competency requirements in place, these uniform measures of knowledge and skills can replace complicated one-off licensing systems, as in the example of Canada's pioneering Mutual Recognition Agreement (MRA). This agreement foreshadows future possibilities enabled by competencies; it establishes five core competencies (interpersonal relationships, assessment and diagnosis, intervention and consultation, research, and ethics and standards) as the basis for recognition of practitioner licenses across territories (see Grus, Chapter 8, this volume).

A future development will be extending these learning objectives and strategies for assessing competencies directly into applied settings. In other words, it is not enough to simply ascertain learning outcomes in training programs; we also need to understand whether these outcomes, in the form of competencies, can be applied in such a way that they make a measurable difference in outcomes in the setting in which they are implemented—with an individual patient, within a clinic, or more broadly in the context of a community intervention.

To take one example, in the United Kingdom, Roth and Pilling (2007) have developed a competency framework for the use of cognitive-behavioral therapy (CBT) in the treatment of depression and anxiety. They identified which competencies to include in the framework through retrospective analysis of clinical trials outcomes data. That is, they reviewed clinical trials that tested CBT for depression and anxiety; identified those treatments with the greatest efficacy; studied the CBT manuals of those successful treatments; and deduced the underlying competencies necessary for effectively applying these treatments. Examples include knowledge of the common cognitive biases relevant to CBT, ability to explain and demonstrate rationale for CBT to client, ability to adhere to an agreed-upon agenda, ability to use thought records, capacity to adapt interventions in response to client feedback, and knowledge of up-to-date research on each anxiety disorder. Grounding clinical competencies in the evidence base of treatment outcomes data is a promising beginning for developing competencies relevant to an applied setting. In addition, it will be important to conduct regular assessments of the quality of services provided, and the effectiveness of such assessment procedures will be contingent on the development of appropriate outcomes measures in each setting (described later). Although we still have more work to do, it seems very clear that we are on the road to setting standards for competency that will be more than grades on an exam and will extend into actual measured performance in clinical settings. A new book series entitled "Specialty Competencies in Professional Psychology," edited by Art and Christine Nezu and published by Oxford University Press, will take up these themes.

Evidence-based Practice

Strategies of EBP will join psychopathology, assessment, and interventions as foundational foci in training.

At the time of the writing of this chapter, every health-care profession has accepted the fundamental concept of EBP. Policies have been developed articulating the principles of EBP as they would be operative ideally in each health profession (e.g., APA, 2006). Despite the widespread recognition of the importance of EBP, there is continuing ambiguity and uncertainty on the specific directions training programs must take to prepare students to be fully competent in implementing EBP. To take one example, the mental health field clearly recognizes the existence of empirically supported psychological treatments, and, as detailed later, governments and health-care policy makers around the world have committed over $2 billion to government agencies to disseminate evidence-based psychological treatments throughout systems of health care as of 2009. These agencies include the Substance Abuse and Mental Health Services Administration (SAMHSA), particularly in its National Registry of Evidence-based Programs and Practices (NREPP), as well as the Veterans Health Administration (VHA) and various state departments of mental health. In the United Kingdom, the National Health Service, through its National Institute for Health and Clinical Excellence (NICE), is also promulgating evidence-based

psychological treatments. Each of these groups is developing its own strategies and dissemination program for identifying and disseminating these interventions. The end result is that a large number of groups are frequently updating EBP approaches after a thorough search and analysis of the evidence, as outlined in some detail in Chapter 7 (Spring & Neville, this volume), Chapter 9 (Zeiss & Karlin, this volume), and Chapter 11 (Chorpita, Bernstein, & Miranda, this volume).

But how can the interested clinician find this information? At present, one would be hard-pressed to find one clinical psychology doctoral program that incorporates training in identifying up-to-date evidence-based interventions for its clinicians. However, well-articulated strategies for navigating the network of existing evidence-base resources have begun to appear in recent books on EBP (e.g., Norcross, Hogan, & Koocher, 2008; Spring & Neville, Chapter 7, this volume). More importantly, the National Institutes of Health (NIH) is funding a Council for Training in Evidence-based Behavioral Practice (EBBP) whose sole mission is to develop learning modules to facilitate the development of evidence-based behavioral practice at the level of the individual clinician. The Council is working toward granting continuing education credits for completion of these modules, but a step in the near future will be to incorporate these training procedures, or very similar strategies, into the curricula of training programs in clinical psychology (Spring & Neville, Chapter 7, this volume).

Three training modules have been developed by the Council: the EBBP Process Module, the Search for Evidence Module, and the Systematic Review Module (EBBP, 2007). These modules describe the foundation of what EBBP is; why it is advantageous for practitioners, clients, and the community; and how it can be implemented. The first module explains the EBBP five-step process: Ask, Acquire, Appraise, Apply, Analyze & Adjust—and then provides two simulated case examples, one with an individual client and one as a community intervention, through which the user gains practice applying this technique. Each of the five steps is a cue to the practitioner. "Ask" reminds the practitioner to formulate pertinent questions about health status and relevant environmental or cultural factors. "Acquire" prompts the practitioner to gather the best evidence related to the question. "Appraise" cues the practitioner to critically assess the evidence for "validity and applicability to the problem at hand." "Apply" calls for the practitioner to integrate the "context, values, and preferences of the recipient of the health intervention, as well as available resources, including [his or her own professional] expertise" and to collaborate with the client in selecting and implementing the treatment. "Analyze & Adjust" entreats the practitioner to assess the process and outcomes and to modify the practices as necessary to improve outcomes.

The final two training modules focus on describing the resources available for EBBP and how to use them. The second module offers guidelines on searching for evidence, including describing differences between types of evidence, sources, and search resources; it also suggests strategies for improving search results. The third module describes systematic reviews and explains how they differ from traditional reviews; it also provides instruction for how to evaluate and conduct systematic reviews. These modules are designed to provide both an efficient and effective training tool. Although the information is intended to be accessible to users with little or no research training, even those with advanced research experience will likely improve their search techniques and use of existing resources.

This effort is pioneering and fills a critical gap, given that many training programs have not yet fully and systematically incorporated training in EBP into their curricula. However, in consideration of the growing top-down emphasis on EBP, it will not be long before accreditation bodies put forth standardized EBP training requirements (which may be based on the EBBP system described earlier) that can then be more fully integrated into each institution's training curricula. In addition, navigating EBP treatment guidelines will undoubtedly become simpler as existing resources expand their coverage of EBP and improve the quality of treatment guidelines. Most likely, one or two resources will emerge as the standards for the field. This has already happened in certain areas of medicine. UpToDate, for example, is an online resource that provides the latest treatment recommendations for physicians in 14 medical specialties. The information provided is evidence-based, extensive (covering 7,700 clinical topics), frequently updated with relevant new findings from peer-reviewed journals, and easy to use and access (by hand-held devices or computer) (UpToDate, 2009). Probably for all of these reasons, this resource has become a leading secondary source of reference for physicians seeking recommendations on clinical care. Development of a similar resource for psychological treatments will allow training programs to focus more on teaching the principles and frameworks of EBP and less on the more technical skills of searching the evidence. Thus, immersion in the principles of EBP will be a foundational component of training in clinical psychology.

Accreditation
The face of accreditation will change to reflect distinct competencies.

Accreditation systems for clinical psychology in the years to come will identify clinical psychologists with overlapping but also distinct training and competencies. One set of competencies will be appropriate to service delivery, and with EBP as a context, will reflect Shakow's (1969) vision of a Scientist-Practitioner model of training in which science is integrated into practice. The second set of competencies will reflect the geometrically increasing complexity of actually conducting clinical science, in contrast to applying it to clinical problems. Scientist-practitioner programs concerned mostly with applying scientific findings in a clinical or applied context will likely continue to be accredited by the longstanding and widely accepted Committee on Accreditation (CoA) of the APA, with its well-established procedures for evaluating doctoral training programs and internships in clinical psychology and closely related fields. However, CoA's accreditation criteria will undergo change. As agreement is reached upon guidelines for EBP training, CoA will develop requirements that reflect these objectives. But for those programs charged with instilling an additional set of competencies focused on actually conducting "big" science in the form of large clinical trials, brain imaging technology, clinical behavioral genetics, and the like, a different system of accreditation may be required. Of course, it is also possible that CoA could accommodate this new development.

But some psychologists think that a new accrediting agency is needed for research-focused programs. The Academy of Psychological Clinical Sciences ("the Academy") was formed in 1995 as a coalition of research-focused (primarily clinical scientist model) doctoral programs to advocate for their interests in the accreditation process and in the development of the field. By the early 2000s, this group concluded that CoA's all-encompassing accreditation system was hindering scientific training and research within clinical psychology programs. The major impediment was the proliferation of courses and other requirements stipulated by CoA that greatly diminished the amount of time available for conducting science, with its requisite time-intensive individual mentoring.

Another factor was the slow pace at which CoA was requiring the integration of EBP as a training requirement. To resolve this dilemma, in 2006, the Academy created the Psychological Clinical Science Accreditation System (PCSAS), designed specifically to meet the needs of clinical science doctoral programs (PCSAS, 2009). The PCSAS is charged with the two-fold goals of "promot[ing] high-quality science-oriented doctoral education and training" and "enhanc[ing] the knowledge base for disseminating and delivering the safest, most cost-effective mental and behavioral health services to the public" (2009). Only doctoral clinical psychology programs that sit within "nonprofit, research-intensive universities" and that profess a "primary mission" of providing "high-quality, science-centered education and training" are eligible to apply for accreditation with PCSAS. There are five general areas that programs are evaluated on for accreditation: conceptual foundations, design and resources, quality of the science, quality improvement, and outcomes. The PCSAS aims to foster training in the most scientifically advanced research techniques possible and to continue to push research to the cutting edge by instilling methods of "quality improvement," continuously examining feedback and program results, making ongoing changes to the program as needed, and assessing "outcomes"—valuations of training based on results rather than on checklists of criteria.

A debate is under way regarding the value of a new accreditation system for research-focused programs. PCSAS proponents argue that this new accreditation system will set a higher standard for clinical science research training, to distinguish these programs from those with decreased emphasis on science and research. However, this point is contested by scientifically oriented clinical psychologists who believe that the emphasis should be on a better integration of the principles of EBP into existing programs. They also argue that pursuit of high-quality scientific research in academic programs historically has not been dictated by accreditation requirements, citing examples in other areas of science, such as biology, sociology, and the like, and therefore that an accreditation system focused on advancing scientific research is unnecessary.

Assuming that the PCSAS continues to grow, questions that remain include the relative value placed on matriculating in programs accredited by one organization or the other among health-care agencies and state licensing boards. Given the initial response from major health-care agencies such as the VHA and the NIH, it is likely that trainees from programs accredited by either organization would be seen as competent to deliver services and work in one setting or the other. The reaction of state licensing boards remains to be seen.

Looking toward the future, we project that both accreditation systems will remain relevant. The CoA accreditation will continue to identify programs meeting all criteria for training clinicians with competency in the practice of clinical psychology. This information, of course, will continue to be very relevant to state licensing boards. But, as noted earlier, and consistent with the vision of Shakow and the rise of EBP, the true realization of the Scientist-Practitioner model of training, which is a clinician who integrates science into his or her practice, will likely occur in both types of programs, including those whose training goals primarily focus on producing competent practitioners. These practitioners will also be capable of participating in the production of new knowledge as part of practice-research networks (Borkovec, 2004; Borkovec, Echemendia, Ragusea, & Ruiz, 2001) or through using more idiographic methods of assessment and evaluation (see Section 5). The introduction of EBP and outcomes assessment will facilitate this change, a trend that may have been underestimated by the Academy.

Accreditation by the PCSAS, on the other hand, will signify training that will produce competent practitioners, albeit with a different set of skills. These clinical scientists will be focused primarily on producing new knowledge, utilizing the full range of scientific methods (developing new treatments or assessment procedures, or delving in depth into the nature of psychopathology or psychological problems). A rather different set of skills is required for this endeavor, including grant preparation and writing, training in the conduct of large clinical trials, brain imaging technology and increasingly sophisticated data analytic strategies that would go well beyond the Scientist-Practitioner model as heretofore envisioned (Barlow, Hayes, & Nelson, 1984; Hayes, Barlow, & Nelson-Gray, 1999; Shakow, 1969). We expect that the majority of clinical psychologists will come from CoA-accredited scientist-practitioner programs. These programs will include current professional schools as well as some university-based doctoral programs that traditionally have produced clinical psychologists who engage primarily in service delivery. But, in view of the full tuition remission and stipends traditionally accorded in scientifically based PhD programs, we predict that fewer slots in the future will be available on this track and the competition will remain keen. Much as Craighead and Craighead (2006) envisioned, these individuals will be dually competent in clinical practice and "big science," but, given support in the form of tuition remissions and stipends from mostly government sources targeted for training new scientists, these individuals will be increasingly expected to play out their careers in the context of providing the basic scientific underpinnings of our health-care delivery systems.

Diagnosis and Assessment
Diagnoses as Dimensions
A theoretically based dimensional system of nosology for mental disorders will gradually replace the current prototypical, categorical classification system.

The classification and diagnosis of pathology has its origins in medicine dating back to the time of Hippocrates. Traditionally, the goal was to identify pathologies that were somehow distinctly and qualitatively different from normality and from each other, thereby forming non-overlapping categories (Barlow, 1991; Widiger & Edmundson, Chapter 13, this volume; Kendall, 1975; Millon, 1991). When dealing with certain kinds of pathophysiology, such as neoplasms or bacterial infection, this model fits well. But a consensus has now emerged that the application of categorical classification to mental disorders is unsatisfactory and, in fact, has not been followed since the publication of the third edition of the *Diagnostic and Statistical Manual of Mental Disorders, Third Edition* (DSM III; American Psychiatric Association, 1980). At that time, the framers of the DSM III and subsequent editions, such as DSM III-R (American Psychiatric Association, 1987) and DSM-IV (American Psychiatric Association, 1994), adopted a modified categorical or "prototypical" model of classification in which it was recognized that clear-cut boundaries among the disorders did not exist, but that we could create "prototypes" and assess to what degree psychopathology in individuals approximates the prototype. Thus, diagnostic prototypes listing various symptoms and characteristics were created with the provision that individuals must present with some of the core features, as well as a certain subset of the remaining prototypical symptoms of a particular disorder. This led to a state of affairs in which two individuals diagnosed with, for example, major depressive disorder (MDD), might meet diagnostic criteria for the requisite five

of eight symptoms of MDD, but have only two of them in common, and thereby look very different from one another. One patient might have symptoms 1, 2, 3, 4, and 5, while the other has 1, 2, 6, 7, and 8.

Difficulties with this approach have been detailed elsewhere (e.g., Widiger & Edmundson, Chapter 13, this volume), but include such issues as extensive comorbidity among existing diagnoses, questionable reliability of some prototypical categories, and difficulties in ascertaining categorical thresholds for the number, severity, or duration of symptoms. In fact, it seems that this problem in discerning when someone has reached a threshold in diagnostic criteria may be one of the major causes of diagnostic unreliability (Brown, Di Nardo, Lehman, & Campbell, 2001). It is also the case that there are many individuals who are, for example, clearly depressed or anxious at a clinically severe level, but who do not happen to meet prototypical criteria for one or another of the existing disorders. These individuals must then fall into a category "not otherwise specified" (NOS). In eating disorders, individuals categorized as eating disorder NOS comprise a sizable portion of those presenting for treatment (Fairburn, Cooper, Shafran, & Wilson, 2008). Finally, imposing what are essentially categories, even if just prototypes, on dimensional phenomenon leads to a substantial loss of valuable clinical information.

A consensus has also developed that adopting the more traditional method of organizing psychopathology along dimensions on various psychopathological features will provide a more conceptually satisfying system of classification. This approach would also avoid many of the difficulties inherent in the prototypical system, which is, of course, an attempt at a compromise between a strictly categorical and a fully dimensional approach. The research underlying dimensional approaches to diagnosis draws on decades of research on temperaments and has now advanced to the point at which it can be more broadly integrated into systems of nosology. To take just one example, over 40 years ago, Achenbach (1966) produced data on classifying psychopathology in children that led to what are now widely accepted dimensions of internalizing disorders and externalizing disorders (Achenbach & Edelbrock, 1978). This system became widely used as a more practical and valid approach to dealing with psychopathology in children, but did not, over the previous decades, seriously impact the categorical or prototypical system of diagnosis present in the DSM.

The historical and conceptual development of systems of diagnosis are thoroughly reviewed in Chapter 13 of this volume by Widiger and Edmundson.

As briefly noted in Chapter 1, the DSM-5 working groups, with substantial input from psychological scientists, have begun to move more systematically away from a psychometrically unsatisfactory categorical (or prototypical) approach to a more dimensional approach (Brown & Barlow, 2009; Leyfer & Brown, Chapter 14, this volume; Widiger & Edmundson, Chapter 13, this volume). This progress is furthest along for the personality disorders, in which categorical approaches are the least satisfactory (South, Oltmanns, & Krueger, Chapter 24, this volume). It also seems clear that the fullest realization of a dimensional approach in any official system of nosology will not be complete in time for DSM-5, but that it does represent the future, and the future of nosology will rest on increasingly sophisticated, empirically based psychological approaches incorporating rapidly developing information on the nature of psychopathology.

As one example, we (Brown & Barlow, 2009) have recently proposed a dimensional classification system based on the shared features of the DSM-IV anxiety and mood disorders. This proposal is based on research that has demonstrated substantial cross-sectional covariation in DSM-IV emotional disorders (mood and anxiety disorders). Much of the covariation is accounted for by the common higher-order dimensions that we refer to as neuroticism/behavioral inhibition (N/BI) and behavioral activation/positive affect (BA/P). We argue that N/BI presents as trait anxiety or chronic generalized distress, and can be more accurately referred to as anxiety/neuroticism/behavioral inhibition (A/N), which is a substantial component of all negative emotional disorders. This temperament, which is strongly associated with activation of the hypothalamic-pituitary-adrenocortical (HPA) axis, is characterized by perceptions of uncontrollability regarding future threatening events, low self-confidence or low self-efficacy over one's ability to cope with these events, and excessive vigilance. Low positive affect on the other hand, reflecting low enthusiasm, an overriding pessimistic sense, and relative lack of interest is more specifically associated with the DSM-IV disorders of MDD and social phobia (SOC). Thus, A/N contributes to all of the emotional disorders, but (low) BA/P makes particular contributions to only some of them (Brown, Chorpita, & Barlow, 1998).

In addition to these two temperaments, individuals with emotional disorders present with varying levels of depressive mood. Some also present with manic features representing a pathological excess of positive affect. Several other key features are found across the emotional disorders, mostly having to do with the specific focus of A/N. That is, A/N can be focused on somatic symptoms (as in hypochondriasis), panic attacks and related autonomic surges (as in panic disorder), intrusive cognitions (as in obsessive-compulsive disorder [OCD]), social evaluation (as in social anxiety disorder), or past traumatic experiences (as in post-traumatic stress disorder [PTSD]). Finally, each individual experiencing the temperament of high A/N displays a pattern of avoidance behaviors manifested in various behavioral and cognitive dimensions. In summary, all individuals presenting with emotional disorders present with patterns reflecting dimensions of higher-order temperaments, dysregulated affective state, avoidance behaviors, and various foci of anxiety.

An example of a case from our clinic with a principal diagnosis of PTSD organized according to this dimensional system of nosology is presented in Figure 39.1. As illustrated in the figure, this individual evidenced an elevated focus of anxiety on past trauma, but also on social evaluation and panic (flashbacks). Various manifestations of avoidance were also elevated (see Brown & Barlow, 2009 for a fuller explication).

Although the transition to a dimensional nosology has already begun, the fullest realization of this approach will be slow to develop, and some have pointed out new problems that will arise (First, 2005). Among these difficulties, the "user friendliness" for clinicians who are accustomed to categorical labels (e.g., "she is depressed" or "he suffers from hypochondriasis") is perhaps the most serious, and presents a barrier that must be overcome. It is also clearly the case that clinical scientists have not yet reached full consensus on optimal ways to organize dimensional approaches, or in some cases such as personality disorders, just what the principal dimensions should be (see South, Oltmanns, & Krueger, Chapter 24, this volume). Nevertheless, barring some unanticipated radical new discovery on the nature of psychopathology by clinical scientists, systems of nosology will become increasingly dimensional.

Clinical Outcomes Assessment
Clinicians will be evaluated and differentially compensated based on treatment outcomes, and clinicians and clinical scientists will return to a more individual, idiographic focus to guide future clinical research and practice.

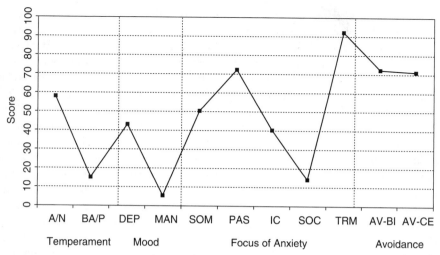

Fig. 39.1 Example Patient Profile with a Dimensional Classification System.

A/N, anxiety/neuroticism/behavioral inhibition; BA/P, behavioral activation/positive affect; DEP, unipolar depression; MAN, mania; SOM, somatic anxiety; PAS, panic and related autonomic surges; IC, intrusive cognitions; SOC, social evaluation; TRM, past trauma; AV-BI, behavioral and interoceptive avoidance; AV-CE, cognitive and emotional avoidance. Higher scores on the *y*-axis (0–100) indicate higher levels of the *x*-axis dimension, but otherwise the *y*-axis metric is arbitrary and is used for illustrative purposes. From Brown, T. A., & Barlow, D. H. (2009). A proposal for a dimensional classification system based on the shared features of the DSM-IV anxiety and mood disorders: Implications for assessment and treatment. *Psychological Assessment, 21*(3), 256–271. Reprinted with permission of the publisher, American Psychological Association.

Clinical outcomes assessment, a strategy clearly anticipated and called for by David Shakow 40 years ago (see Chapter 1), is at the heart of EBP across all areas of applied psychology, but, as with most new initiatives, it is off to a rocky start. Although government agencies and policy makers are unanimous that we should be moving to outcomes assessment in almost every area of service provision, in many cases they have not settled on the best methods for accomplishing this. This is a process that will play itself out over the next several years, until consensus develops on the best ways to integrate outcome measurements in health and educational systems, and this consensus should and will be based on the full participation of all stake holders. This development will then get us past the problem of yet another unfunded mandate on practitioners. Nevertheless, outcomes measurement will ultimately highlight competence and quality among clinical psychologists.

Recent evidence of the promise of outcomes measurement has been eloquently highlighted in the field of cystic fibrosis (Gawande, 2004). This devastating medical condition is ordinarily treated in specialty clinics around the country. Policy makers and third-party payers persuaded these clinics several years ago to begin administering more uniform and valid outcomes measures under strict provisions of confidentiality (as requested by the clinics), such that individual clinics providing the services not

be identified. These confidentiality provisions were motivated, of course, by fear among clinicians of the possible fall-out of misinterpretation of data indicating less than optimal outcomes in a given clinic. As data were collected and shared among the clinics, it became clear that one clinic was doing far better than the others in terms of increasing quality of life and survival time. This was a considerable shock to the other clinics, all of which were under the impression that they were delivering state-of-the-art treatment in an effective manner. At this point, the remaining clinics (still operating under anonymity) requested that the identity of the leading clinic be revealed, so that they could ascertain why and how this clinic was achieving such superior results. A clinic in Minnesota was identified, and remaining clinics quickly arranged to compare notes, visit, and learn how current practices differed from other clinics, and how these differing procedures could be rapidly incorporated into clinics across the country. The result was improved patterns of care for all patients and closer collaboration and cooperation among the clinics on new advances.

A number of state psychological association officials in the United States have noted that outcomes measurement holds the promise of highlighting the superior services provided by doctoral-level clinical psychologists, since these findings are increasingly evident in research settings. Evidence has also begun to appear that outcomes assessment changes the practice of mental health professionals. For example, Lambert and colleagues (2003) conducted a meta-analysis of three large treatment studies (each included over 1,000 clients) that showed that providing periodic feedback on patient progress to the clinician during the course of treatment, based on repeated ongoing objective assessment, improves treatment outcomes. Ideally, sophisticated outcomes assessment practices would be established, but in the meantime, therapists do not even know if their results are better or worse than average (see Hunsley & Mash, Chapter 5, this volume).

In view of various state and federal mandates on the implementation of EBP, there seems little question that outcomes assessment will become required and will lead, ultimately, to clinician profiling, as it has in some areas of medicine and surgery. This development, in turn, will facilitate the dissemination of evidence-based psychological (and drug) treatments as clinics and clinicians attempt to increase positive outcomes and meet developing "pay for performance" standards proposed for health-care systems. But, once again, developing a consensus of specific assessment procedures will prove difficult and contentious.

Clinical outcomes assessment focuses on change in the individual and, as we pointed out recently (Barlow & Nock, 2009), psychology has a long tradition of research that focuses on the individual rather than on the group average. These two emphases in establishing knowledge are referred to as *idiographic* and *nomothetic*. In 1962, Gordon Allport quoted Edward Tolman as saying "I know I should be more idiographic in my research, but I just don't know how to be." To which Allport replied "Let's learn" (Allport, 1962, p. 414). This longstanding aspiration reflects an understanding by most psychologists that the individual organism is the principal unit of analysis in psychology, whether the efforts be laboratory-based research with animals or the establishment of new interventions or assessments procedures with patients in the clinic. Indeed, some of the founders of experimental psychology, such as Wundt and Pavlov, focused their research on the study of individual organisms without sacrificing the scientific validity of their findings. When it came to establishing generality of results for their findings, they relied on replication in additional individuals (Barlow, Nock, & Hersen, 2009).

The funding of large randomized clinical trials (RCTs) to establish the efficacy of drug and psychological treatments, which began in earnest in the 1970s and 1980s, was one reason for a renewed emphasis on a more nomothetic approach to assessing change in clinical research. All psychologists, of course, whether working in the clinic or in a large clinical trial, are interested in the effects of treatment. But nomothetic and idiographic strategies approach the subject of variability among individuals and generality of findings across individuals in very different ways. Patients responding to a treatment in a clinical trial often show a range of outcomes from substantial improvement, to no improvement, or even deterioration. But the clinical trial, as with any nomothetic approach, assumes that much of this intersubject variability is intrinsic to the patient or due to uncontrollable external events. As a result, sophisticated data-analytic procedures are employed to look for treatment effects over and above this "error." If significant treatment effects are found, it is assumed that the results will be generalizable, at least to individuals similar to those patients included in the treatment group of the large clinical trial, if not to the population of all individuals presenting with the problem under study, such as depression. A more idiographic approach, on the other hand, would highlight why one individual differed from another after a given treatment by conducting some functional analyses in the context of a case formulation that might pinpoint reasons why one patient improved and the other did not. This information would be of considerable value to the clinician delivering services.

Randomized clinical trials are the gold standard for assessing the efficacy of our treatments (Kendall & Comer, Chapter 4, this volume). But it seems that a developing trend, which should be more fully realized in the years to come, is to enrich these methodologies with a complementary focus on the individual. We do have a good idea of how to be more idiographic in our research (e.g., Barlow & Nock, 2009; Barlow et al., 2009), and many of these more individualized strategies do not necessarily manipulate independent variables but rather are closer to the clinic. That is, assessment of a patient's progress over time is observed, and, based on the educated hypotheses of experienced clinicians, is functionally related to internal or external events that can then be addressed in therapy (McCullough, 2002; Shapiro, 1961). Furthermore, with the advent of outcomes assessment, these kinds of observations will be more common and our clinical science will be enriched.

Clinical replication is one example of a well-established idiographic assessment method that may become more frequently utilized in applied settings in view of the growing emphasis on tracking treatment outcomes. Clinical replication is a form of field testing whereby a new treatment or treatment component is repeatedly administered by the same investigator or clinician within a specific setting across a series of patients with similar symptom presentations (Barlow & Hersen, 1984; Barlow et al., 2009; Hersen & Barlow, 1976). During treatment, and with the assistance of ongoing outcomes assessment, a clinician would carefully follow each individual's progress and document response, partial response, or nonresponse in patients. Since these clinicians are close to the situation, they are in the best position to formulate educated hypotheses on reasons for individual variation (success, partial success, or failure). These hypotheses could initially be evaluated by clinicians themselves and also fed back to clinical research centers for more systematic testing. Obviously, this information on generality of findings at the individual level would be extremely helpful both for future clinicians in selecting and applying similar treatments and for clinical scientists in investigating more systematically ways of improving treatments by making them more generally applicable. This strategy is eminently feasible and adds little, if any, cost. As mentioned earlier, the move toward instituting outcomes assessment will likely support an increase in data collected from clinical replication efforts, as will the rise of practice research networks (Borkovec, 2004; Borkovec et al., 2001). In these networks, as noted in Section 3, clinicians systematically collect data on individual patients, and do so in close collaboration with clinical research centers, with the goal of mutually explicating the individual outcomes of interventions across a large number of individuals and settings.

Treatment
The Growth of Psychological Treatments and a Focus on Dissemination and Implementation

As new psychological treatments are developed and existing treatments become more efficacious, the focus will shift to currently underdeveloped efforts on dissemination and implementation.

When it became clear over the past decade that psychological treatments targeting various presentations of psychopathology were at least the equal of pharmacological approaches, and in some cases superior (Barlow, 2004; Nathan & Gorman, 2007), health-care systems began to take action. Health-care policy makers and government agencies around

the world committed several billion dollars to facilitate the dissemination of these treatments through a series of financial and regulatory incentives and mandates. For example, the VHA is the largest organized system of health care in the United States. In 2004, the VHA created a Mental Health Strategic Plan calling for the integration and improvement of mental health care (Zeiss & Karlin, Chapter 9, this volume). One of the principal goals of this plan was the dissemination and implementation of evidence-based psychological treatments throughout the system. Committees appointed by the VHA targeted a number of these treatments that seem most relevant to their mission, such as cognitive processing therapy (CPT) (Resick, Monson, & Chard, 2007) and prolonged exposure therapy (Foa, Hembree, & Rothbaum, 2007) for PTSD. Over a billion dollars has already been committed to initial efforts to roll out these treatments systemwide. Going forward, the intent is to identify additional treatments that would be particularly relevant to clinical care in the VHA, with the goal of making evidence-based psychological treatments available to all who need them.

Another major U.S. agency, SAMHSA has introduced the National Child Traumatic Stress Network (NCTSN), funded by the Center for Mental Health Services within SAMHSA. Congress has committed approximately $150 million thus far to the NCTSN to identify and disseminate evidence-based psychological treatments for traumatized children and adolescents. SAMHSA also supports 14 Addiction Technology Transfer Centers (ATTCs) across the United States to disseminate evidence-based assessments and treatments for substance use disorders.

Similar programs are ongoing at the level of state mental health systems in the United States, with a number of states actively implementing the dissemination of psychological treatments throughout their systems. For example, in the state of Hawaii, a task force entitled "The Empirical Bases to Services" was created by the Child and Adolescent Mental Health Division of the Hawaii Department of Mental Health. The purpose of this task force was to identify evidence-based psychological treatments for dissemination throughout their health-care system. Evidence-based family therapy programs for externalizing disorders in youth were seen as particularly relevant for the types of problems encountered by the state mental health system, and training ensued (Nakamura, Higa-McMillan, & Chorpita, in press).

In the United Kingdom, where health service delivery is nationalized, broader availability of evidence-based psychological interventions is now a matter of health policy and has been mandated and funded (Clark, in press). This recognition has resulted in an unprecedented boom in the job market for clinical psychology in that country.

Given the enormous amount of clinical research on the efficacy and effectiveness of psychological treatments and procedures in the pipeline, it is likely that the number of these treatments will increase, as will their efficacy. But it is also likely that these interventions will undergo systematic modifications and developments, some of which are suggested in upcoming sections of this chapter. And an increasing emphasis will be placed on developing programs to prevent the onset of psychopathology and increase resilience as our knowledge of risk factors for various disorders grows. Preliminary efforts along these lines for depression, to take one example, look promising (Horowitz & Garber, 2006).

Yet, in the coming years, questions remain as to the implications of increased recognition of psychological treatments along with the pioneering but preliminary efforts at dissemination noted earlier. For example, in other health systems that are either less organized or less advanced than that in the United Kingdom, such as the U.S. health-care system, it is not clear that greater recognition of these treatments will be sufficient to translate into greater availability for the population in need. For example, Olfson and Marcus (2009) recently reported that, in the United States, the rate of treatment of depression with antidepressant medications approximately doubled over the most recent decade in which these data were collected, while the rate of "psychotherapy" diminished. Without more effective efforts at implementation and dissemination, it is not clear that greater recognition of psychological treatments will have a long-term impact. Thus, dissemination and implementation programs will become increasingly important.

Many of the dissemination programs in the United Kingdom and VHA were created with a distinct sense of urgency (McHugh & Barlow, 2010; McHugh & Barlow, in press). The difficulty is that this sense of urgency precluded the deliberate development of a consensus on how to best to implement the dissemination process. For example, dissemination science (Fixsen, Naoom, Blase, Friedman, & Wallace, 2005; Gladwell, 2000; Rogers, 2003) has long recognized a set of relatively consistent barriers to the adoption of innovations in almost any field of endeavor, such as agriculture, education, and communication. Some of these problems are eloquently detailed by Gawande (2007) in his discussions of the difficulties in implementing consistent hand-washing procedures in hospitals, despite very clear empirical evidence on the health benefits of this approach and a "common sense" appreciation of the realistic nature of this policy.

So, for example, prior to successful implementation, several steps must be undertaken based on the wisdom of dissemination science. These steps include a comprehensive assessment of the nature of the stakeholders involved, a structured assessment of needs, and a plan for proceeding. Beyond that, potential outcomes of the implementation procedures, particularly training efforts in which individuals involved in service delivery acquire new skills, require close attention. Most dissemination projects recognize the need for didactic training, usually in the form of workshops, and more recently, in terms of Web-based interactive training. And most include some kind of assessment of the knowledge acquired from these efforts. But the evidence very clearly shows that these steps alone are inadequate to actually change the behavior of service delivery personnel (McHugh & Barlow, 2010; McHugh & Barlow, in press). In addition to didactic training, the necessity of training to a predefined level of competence and assessing the level of competence attained is crucial. The fact is that current efforts often stop there, assuming that, armed with this new knowledge and trained to a level of competence, evidence-based procedures will be successfully disseminated and implemented. But a number of additional issues must be considered in determining the success of a program of dissemination. For example, what percent of the clinicians who entered the program complete the training modules? What percent of the clinicians beginning the training program actually achieve a predefined level of competence, and what happens if they don't? After training efforts have been completed, how many patients are actually administered evidence-based procedures, and, most importantly, how many have benefited from the introduction of these new procedures, not only in terms of symptomatic reductions but also in increases in quality of life? Finally, and reflecting one of the most difficult issues in the dissemination of any innovation, has the implementation of EBPs been sustained over the long-term, and what procedures have been put in place to foster the sustainability of these innovations and to continue to assess outcomes?

Very few programs have considered the full range of barriers relevant to dissemination and implementation, and many often restrict their efforts to didactic information with an assessment of knowledge gain.

At present, it is an empirical question to decide which combination of procedures may prove to be the most useful to attain the kinds of outcomes desired. Obviously, it will be to the advantage of organizations to ascertain and adopt the minimum number of procedures necessary to achieve high levels of adoption, competence, and sustainability in the introduction of evidence-based psychological treatments into health delivery systems. Such an evaluation will need to include potential mediators of successful adoption, which could involve factors such as the length of supervision to achieve competence, as well as the best means to achieve long-term sustainability from among the several options currently available.

It seems clear that the demand for evidence-based psychological (and drug) treatments is increasing rapidly both at the level of individuals suffering from psychological problems as well as governments and public health authorities charged with improving the health of the population. But, at present, this demand has gotten ahead of our knowledge of the optimal ways to achieve the dissemination of these practices. An area of substantial growth for the immediate future will be addressing these pressing problems.

Moving Beyond Single-diagnosis Treatment Manuals

Modular transdiagnostic interventions will replace treatment protocols applicable to only a single diagnostic category.

A number of significant limitations to current psychological treatments exist. Obviously, there are still a considerable number of patients who do not respond well to this type of remedy, and the reasons for their lack of response are not yet known. Thus, although treatment is effective for many people, there is plenty of room for improvement. Another problem that has become apparent with manualized treatments is that there are simply too many of them. Multiple manuals and protocols have been developed for most DSM-IV disorders, many of them with their own flavors or twists, but most of them reflecting the "copycat" phenomena present in pharmacological development in that they all rely on a core set of principles. For example, within the anxiety disorders, over 15 published manuals exist for panic disorder alone, most with simply trivial alterations and no empirical support justifying these alterations, and it is sometimes difficult to choose among them. Manuals for other disorders are proliferating as quickly, and it can take a significant amount of training to become adequately familiar

with even a few of the protocols. In addition, and as noted earlier, because the protocols require both didactic training and supervised training to competence, dissemination of even one treatment protocol to providers is an obstacle to the delivery of evidence-based treatment (Barlow, Levitt, & Bufka, 1999; McHugh & Barlow, 2010). Despite the allocation of billions of dollars to train and disseminate these protocols, when a clinician completes the required months of training, they are certified to treat only one diagnostic category (e.g., panic disorder, PTSD), with uncertain abilities to treat or even address common patterns of accompanying comorbidity (e.g., depression, OCD).

It is also clear that the presence of extensive comorbidity among various classes of disorders would clearly be better served through transdiagnostic unified treatment protocols that target several disorders simultaneously by focusing on common underlying factors. Considerable advances in understanding the nature of psychopathology have resulted in the identification of substantial overlap and common factors among disorders within a larger grouping. This overlap is evidenced through common patterns of neural activation, as well as through quantitative structural equation modeling, all of which suggest underlying factors in various classes of disorders that may be amenable to a single set of therapeutic principles. Within the anxiety and mood disorders, as we have detailed elsewhere (Fairholme, Boisseau, Ellard, Ehrenreich, & Barlow, 2010), some of these common factors include avoidance of emotional experience, pathological attributions and appraisals, the use of inappropriate emotion regulation skills, and the presence of emotion-driven behaviors or "action tendencies" associated with maladaptive and intense emotional experience.

Similar issues exist within other classes of disorders, such as the eating disorders (see Sysko & Wilson, Chapter 19, this volume). For example, and as noted earlier, Fairburn and colleagues (2008) have noted that as many as 40% of those presenting with eating disorders fall under the category of eating disorders not otherwise specified (NOS). Thus, whereas single-diagnosis protocols for eating disorders, such as bulimia and binge eating, are fully developed and have good evidence for efficacy, data on the efficacy of these protocols with eating disorder NOS patients has not been entirely clear. Fairburn et al.'s (2008) solution has also been to extract the core psychopathological principles present in all eating disorders and target them in a transdiagnostic protocol (Fairburn, Cooper, & Shafran, 2003).

In fact, it has become clear that existing treatment protocols for the full range of various classes of disorders, such as anxiety and eating disorders, contain a common set of therapeutic procedures. For anxiety disorders, this would include encouraging reappraisal and reattribution of perceived threat or danger both external and internal (interoceptive), the prevention of avoidance behavior, and exposure-based procedures that differ only in the situations, cognitions, and behaviors that provide the context for the application of the procedures (Allen, McHugh, & Barlow, 2008; Barlow, Allen, & Choate, 2004; Moses & Barlow, 2006). There is some evidence that these same fundamental therapeutic principles would be applicable to mood disorders, as well as to many of the somatoform and dissociative disorders that have anxiety, depression, and emotion dysregulation as key elements.

Other investigators are also working to identify evidence-based components of treatment that can be arranged in a modular fashion. For example, Chorpita and colleagues (Chapter 11, this volume), working closely with the State of Hawaii, have identified sets of psychological principles of change that comprise a menu of modules that can then be individually adapted for clients by trained providers in that state's mental health system. Mastering this set of principles and its implementation is a far more parsimonious and cost-effective method for reaching the largest number of people in need, when compared to mastering multiple single-diagnosis protocols.

Drugs That Enhance Psychological Treatments

Pharmacological agents that specifically bolster the effectiveness of mechanisms of action of psychological interventions will become increasingly common.

What are the optimal ways of combining of psychological and pharmacological treatments for various mental disorders? Until recently, there has been a widespread belief that concurrent combinations of psychological treatments with pharmacological treatments produce a better outcome than either treatment alone. Of course, this has been true for psychotic disorders such as schizophrenia, in which psychological treatments directed at both positive and negative symptoms as well as social skill deficits may double the beneficial effects of medications. On the other hand, for the emotional disorders, data on the beneficial effects of concurrently combining treatments are surprisingly sparse. For the anxiety disorders specifically, most studies report no beneficial effects from combining treatments concurrently, although sequential strategies are proving effective in some cases (Barlow, 2008; Nathan & Gorman, 2007). In fact, some anxiolytic drugs, such as benzodiazepines, actually reduce or eliminate the beneficial effects of psychological treatments (Barlow, 2002).

To date, there has been no good theoretical reason why combining drugs and psychological treatments in the anxiety disorders would be effective. But now, based on exciting new translational research from neuroscience isolating brain circuits active in the learning and unlearning of fear and anxiety, new developments have occurred. To take one example, a drug called D-cycloserine (DCS), an old antibiotic, has been found to be synergistic with psychological procedures that enhance the extinction of fear and anxiety responses. Based on solid research from animal laboratories on neural circuitry involved in extinction learning (Hofmann, 2008; Myers & Davis, 2002), we now know this drug acts as a partial agonist of the glutamatergic N-methyl-D-aspartate (NMDA) neurotransmitter system that plays a major role in this type of learning. Unlike most anxiolytics, DCS is administered acutely, meaning that it is only taken just before the psychological treatment (exposure-based session) begins. Several clinical trials have demonstrated that DCS does enhance competently administered psychological exposure-based treatments for the anxiety disorders, such as social phobia (e.g., Hofmann et al., 2006) and OCD (Kushner et al., 2007; Wilhelm et al., 2008). Research is now rapidly expanding to other anxiety disorders. In view of the fact that this drug must be skillfully integrated with psychological treatments, a strong case can be made for prescription privileges for psychologists to best administer this combined treatment approach.

A more recent development is based on new neurobiological studies focused on understanding how fear memories are controlled. Gogolla, Caroni, Lüthi, and Herry (2009) noticed that, although extinction of fear memories was very difficult in adult rats, the extinction of fear acquired in young rats was much more successful in eliminating the fear memory. Since it is known that fear extinction involves neuronal circuits in the amygdala, the question became: What changes might occur during development of the amygdala that are responsible for making extinction of fear memories more difficult? Prior research had determined that maturation of a matrix of surrounding cells in the visual cortex occurred during development, and that eliminating this matrix (which is composed of chondroitin sulfate proteoglycans [CSPGs]) from the cortex in the adult rat could enhance neuroplasticity to a level that is close to that found in a very young rat. This elimination can be accomplished by injecting the enzyme chondroitinase ABC. Building on this basic information from neuroscience, based on previous experiments on the visual cortex, Gogolla et al. (2009) demonstrated that acquired fear could also be eliminated in adult rats during extinction trials when these rats were injected with chondroitinase ABC. Although this has not been attempted in humans, it is representative of a trend that is almost certain to increase. That is, neurobiological research into brain function associated with psychopathology may lead to pharmacological agents that can augment the effects of psychological treatments, but that may have little or no effect in isolation from psychological treatments.

Other research has demonstrated that the neuropeptide oxytocin is fundamentally associated with trust and interpersonal closeness. The neural circuitry of trusting behavior seems to be associated with reduced activation of several brain structures, including the amygdala, the midbrain regions, and the dorsal-striatum. Now investigators are wondering whether this particular substance might augment psychological treatments for social anxiety and avoidance, as well as for autism. Thus, Guastella, Mitchell, and Mathews (2008) demonstrated that nasal administration of oxytocin enhanced the encoding of positive social information such that it was more memorable. The authors inferred that this could enhance the tendency to bond with other humans and experience greater intimacy and a stronger tendency to approach others. Another finding indicated that oxytocin acts specifically to increase gazing toward the eye region of human faces (Guastella, Mitchell, & Dadds, 2008). The authors speculate that this tendency may enhance emotional recognition and therefore interpersonal communication. All of these findings suggest that this substance could very well augment treatment for social difficulties. Now one preliminary study suggests that individuals with social anxiety disorder treated with a psychological intervention augmented by oxytocin evaluated their appearance more positively and performed somewhat better in a public speaking scenario than did those not receiving oxytocin (Guastella, Howard, Dadds, Mitchell, & Carson, 2009). Although this substance has not yet been demonstrated to be clinically useful in any definitive way, it is yet another example of where integrated research in neuroscience and psychological interventions is going.

Technology-based Service Delivery

Digital technologies will become increasingly integrated into service delivery systems and will lead to more personalized care.

Advances in digital technologies have already enabled the development of many creative new approaches to mental health interventions, service delivery, and clinician training. These emerging practices include computerized training and interventions and service delivery via telephone, e-mail, text messages, instant messages, videoconferences, and the Internet. In Chapter 28 of this volume, Linda Dimeff and colleagues provide a thorough account of current technology-based interventions and highlight the wide range of application formats and their corresponding capabilities as interventions based on varying levels of interactivity, richness of media, social connectivity, and automation or live support. From a public health perspective these approaches potentially serve several objectives: they serve to increase dissemination of and access to high-quality, evidence-based treatments; and they serve to extend mental health care to rural and remote locations and to underserved populations, including populations who either cannot access mental health facilities (due to disability or time constraints, for instance) or who choose not to access such care due to perceived stigma associated with mental health treatment. It is also anticipated that technology-based service delivery would have the secondary benefit of reducing overall treatment costs (although it is yet to be determined how cost savings would be distributed along the patient-provider-payer continuum).

Translating traditional training models for evidence-based treatments into high-quality computerized training programs may be the most feasible and cost-effective way to provide continuing education for clinicians. Dimeff and colleagues (2009) have demonstrated with their Panic Control Treatment Online Training (PCT OLT) for clinicians that Web-based interactive training can have better learning outcomes in terms of acquiring information on the principles of interventions than traditional didactic methods, and may also facilitate competence in the administration of an intervention. In addition, interactive computerized programs ensure a certain standardization of quality and may be easier to disseminate.

The computerization of psychological interventions extends evidence-based treatment a step further—into the hands of patients themselves. These interventions take many forms, utilizing different psychological modalities, targeting different diagnoses, and comprising different media and sensory components (for additional information see Dimeff, Paves, Skutch, & Woodcock, Chapter 28, this volume). They can be accompanied by varying levels of clinician guidance and support, and administered in treatment settings or at home. To date, the most tested and efficacious computerized therapies have been CBTs, which also comprise the majority of leading evidence-based interventions and have the advantage of a structured format that translates easily into a computer program (Proudfoot, 2004). Several studies have found computerized CBTs for depression or anxiety disorders to be comparable to or even better than individualized CBT treatment with a therapist (Proudfoot, 2004; Reger & Gahm, 2009). However, there are limitations to these findings (Reger & Gahm, 2009), and these limitations are discussed later in the context of future directions.

One exciting example of the potential offered by computerized interventions is a treatment program developed by Craske and colleagues (2009) called Coordinated Anxiety Learning and Management (CALM). This interactive, computer-based CBT intervention aims to "singly address … the four most common anxiety disorders in primary-care settings: panic disorder (PD) with or without agoraphobia, generalized anxiety disorder (GAD), social anxiety disorder (SAD), and post-traumatic stress disorder (PTSD)" (Craske et al., 2009, p. 236). Customarily, in this setting, the primary care clinician refers patients to mental health professionals who are often not trained in evidence-based interventions, and, as a result, treatment outcomes are often unsatisfactory (Craske et al., 2009). Craske's program provides these mental health professionals with a tool to guide the patient through a structured evidence-based treatment modality while assisting the clinician in delivering the treatment with fidelity. This hybrid approach—that is, the combination of clinician assistance along with self-administered computer treatment—has been found to have higher rates of patient retention than computer-based treatment packages with no in-person support (Craske et al., 2009; Proudfoot, 2004). Preliminary data from an RCT for CALM indicate that clinicians have rated it positively and that patients have demonstrated understanding of the learning objectives, with concomitant reductions in clinical symptoms (Craske et al., 2009).

Another recent development is an expansion of service delivery mechanisms to include cell phones, e-mail, text messages, instant messages, videoconferences, and Internet applications. The telephone has made possible remote continuation of care for at least 50 years (Richardson, Frueh, Grubaugh, Egede, & Elhai, 2009), and for the most part, other new communication mechanisms are simply providing alternative and possibly enhanced options for the same treatment approach. An exception is the innovative use of remote sensing software and cell phones to monitor health signals and medication adherence, and to send updates to physicians via text messages (Koocher, 2009). Perhaps other novel treatment paradigms via these technologies await us. In the meantime, videoconferencing has significantly improved remote psychotherapy delivery by enhancing patient perception of the therapeutic alliance and allowing clinicians to observe some behavioral cues. Australia has widely implemented videoconferencing-based assessments and interventions and found that this type of service delivery may be as efficacious as face-to-face treatment as usual (TAU), although they are still grappling with how to best compare these methods (Richardson et al., 2009). Although each of these methods has limitations as a stand-alone therapy, if viewed as an extension of mental health service that can be applied and combined flexibly, depending on the patient's circumstances and preferences, there is considerable promise that these techniques will increase mental health-care coverage (Mohr, 2009).

A much-discussed area of research entails undertaking studies to target specific underserved populations with limited access to health-care providers, who may benefit significantly from computerized delivery of care (Mohr, 2009; Richardson et al., 2009). Policies will also be required to address the legal and ethical issues that will arise with wider dissemination of technology-based interventions and telemental health practices. For example, new standards of care will need to be determined, and a new governing body will likely be necessary to regulate interstate and international mental health care delivery (Koocher, 2009). Another area of future research involves the development of novel therapeutic modalities predicated on emerging digital technologies. As Mohr (2009) perceptively points out, most of the current technology-enabled treatments are merely traditional treatments applied via new technologies. He suggests that, in addition to optimizing current services, we should be asking how these technologies might enable new treatment paradigms.

In the future, continued improvement in the knowledge of individual predictors of treatment outcomes should allow the adaptive or "branching" capabilities of computer programming to far more efficiently and accurately individualize treatments for specific patients. It is conceivable that computer-based assessment programs could at once triage, recommend personalized treatments, and where appropriate, provide part or all of a treatment package. Consider the following scenario: A treatment-seeker accesses an online or brick-and-mortar clinic where he or she completes a computerized, adaptive assessment module that poses questions regarding his or her areas of distress, symptomatology, health history, treatment preferences, demographic and psychosocial factors, behavioral tendencies, learning style, and other factors that may be deemed to have predictive value for treatment outcomes. With each response provided by the individual to a particular question, the computer adapts and refines the subsequent questions to increasingly hone in on the individual's specific needs and preferences. This assessment could even incorporate genetic information if the individual provided a DNA sample in advance of the assessment. Integrating all of this information into the assessment would allow the computer program to triage the case and recommend a treatment package with the most empirical support for that individual based on his or her predictive factors. For one individual, the prescribed treatment package could be purely self-administered, at-home, online treatment exercises; for another it could be a combination of medication, plus at-home online homework modules, plus bimonthly videoconference support with a specialty mental health provider. Obviously, for a more urgent case, the program would refer the individual for a live consultation with a clinician, but, even in this case, the individual could be immediately referred to the most appropriate clinical specialist rather than just any physician or mental health professional. This type of integrative computerized assessment process would support the National Institute of Mental Health (NIMH) priority of providing personalized care (Insel, 2009), as well as free up mental health professionals to provide other, perhaps more specialized services. Of course, there are still many details to be worked out, and rapidly emerging technologies will continue to change the format and capabilities of these interventions. No matter what form they take, it is clear that digital technologies will be increasingly integrated into the health-care delivery system.

Psychological Treatments or Psychotherapy?

Psychological treatments *will be a term reserved for EBPs appropriate for addressing pathology in the context of health-care systems. Psychotherapy will be a term reserved for procedures directed at enhancing personal adjustment and growth, but administered outside of health-care systems and based increasingly on data emerging from the field of positive psychology.*

Thus far, we have outlined as likely future trends in clinical psychology the further development of outcomes measurement, psychological treatments, EBP, and the role of these developments in emerging health-care systems. An implication of these predictions is that clinical psychology is becoming ever more integrated into our health-care systems and is seen as having an increasingly important role to play in the remediation and prevention of both psychopathology and pathophysiology. In addition, the American Psychological Association has recently made it a matter of policy that psychology is a health-care profession (American Psychological Association, 2001; Johnson, 2001), and recent policy initiatives have focused on a greater integration of clinical psychology into primary care settings (Bray, 2009). Clearly, this is a very important initiative that is already coming to pass and that will have an impact on training programs and the way we practice. But one residual source of confusion going forward is an understanding by the lay public and health-care policy makers alike on the meaning of the term "psychotherapy." Elsewhere (Barlow, 2004; Barlow, 2006) it was noted that *psychotherapy* reflects such a heterogeneous set of activities that the term has lost its ability to communicate any precise meaning. Furthermore, the variety of procedures currently subsumed under the label of psychotherapy would be all but unrecognizable from one therapist to another (or one profession to another), encompassing such procedures as Web-based interactive behavior-change programs and long-term in-depth individual psychoanalysis. We have noted that this ambivalence and ambiguity can be resolved to some extent by delineating two different approaches to therapy that would be fundamentally identified by the problems addressed. The term "psychological treatments" and its synonyms, such as "psychological interventions," terms that are increasingly used today in health-care systems, would be reserved for those treatments that are part of health-related EBPs with a target of ameliorating psychopathology or pathophysiology; in other words, mental or physical disorders that would be eligible for treatment in organized health-care systems. Labeling these procedures as "psychological treatments" also identifies their origins in the psychological behavioral and cognitive science laboratories, and brands them in a manner that distinguishes clinical psychologists as the most qualified profession to administer these procedures. Thus, clinical psychology would at last lay claim to its own set of procedures, a primary goal of any health-care profession. Of course, the debate over problems or disorders that are eligible for treatment, and therefore reimbursement by third-party payers within health-care systems, is a controversial one that is playing out both federally and state by state in the United States, with definitions tending to be relatively conservative. For example, despite parity legislation, even disorders widely accepted in diagnostic schemes of mental disorders (such as the DSM) are not necessarily gaining entrance into the health-care system if they are not somehow judged to be severe enough or "biologically based." But it is a reasonably good bet that, as parity legislation increases, most forms of psychopathology identifiable in accepted systems of nosology will likely gain coverage.

But remediation of pathology is not always the principal goal of psychotherapy. In fact, as pointed out previously (Barlow, 2006), psychotherapy has often been directed at problems in adjustment and growth. For thousands of years, this has been a very noble undertaking. In an Op-Ed contribution to the *New York Times* entitled "A Mind Is a Terrible Thing to Measure," Phillips (2006, February 26), addressing the current state of psychotherapy, notes that Western societies have been "divided between religious truth and scientific truth" as a basis for understanding human nature, and that perhaps psychotherapy should "inhabit the middle ground of arts in which truth and usefulness have traditionally been allowed certain latitude (nobody measures Shakespeare or tries to prove his values)." As Socrates noted thousands of years ago, "an unexamined life is not worth living" (Plato, 1996). And there are many people, perhaps most of us, who are searching generally for greater meaning in life, the resolution of problems in living, working out relationships, learning how to love and be loved, and personal growth. It is no accident that these goals are also addressed from an epistemological point of view by a variety of the humanities that do in fact occupy "the middle ground of the arts." But the fact of the matter is that these approaches will never be part of conservatively defined health-care systems and be reimbursed by health-care dollars, even if arguments are made noting the correlation of better adjustment with longevity and health. Health-care systems will always have difficulty paying for the direct treatment and prevention of pathology and are unlikely to fund the pursuit of happiness. Nevertheless, a very large

market will continue to exist for these services, and psychologists may well continue to play a major role. However, these services will operate on a self-pay basis, and psychologists will not have a unique prerogative in the delivery of psychotherapy, as is now the case. Thus, psychological treatments or interventions will come to delineate those procedures with an accumulating evidence base as appropriate for treating pathology. The term "psychotherapy" would then refer to a heterogeneous set of approaches to personal growth and adjustment. Psychological treatments and psychotherapy would not necessarily be distinguished on the basis of theory, techniques, or even evidence, but rather on the types of problems addressed. But is an evidence-base for "psychotherapy" defined in this manner? The explosive growth in the field of positive psychology in recent years (Diener, 2000; Seligman, 2002) may well prove to be the emerging evidence base for psychotherapy that aims to facilitate personal growth and the pursuit of happiness. In this way, psychotherapy (as defined here) could become every bit as evidence-based as psychological treatments addressing psychopathology. And substantial confusion existing in the mind of the public on what we do will be clarified.

Conclusion

In this chapter, we have speculated on ten themes or areas that are likely to reflect changes in the field of clinical psychology in the near to intermediate future. As noted at the beginning of the chapter, some of these changes have already begun, and we speculate more on how they will play out in the coming years. Other projected trends have not yet occurred, and time will tell whether our predictions come true or not. But the goal of this chapter is not necessarily to come out with the highest percentage of correct predictions among the large number of prognosticating psychologists willing to take these conceptual (and some would say foolish) leaps of faith. Rather, the overarching goal is to convey the current intellectual ferment, creativity, and vision that exist in clinical psychology today. To those who will be pursuing these goals and bearing witness to these changes, we can only say that we would be hard-pressed to think of a more exciting time to play out a career in clinical psychology. The longstanding potential of clinical psychology to relieve human suffering and enhance human functioning will become increasingly evident, and anyone participating in the realization of trends outlined in this chapter and other developments not yet envisioned will be very fortunate indeed to be a part of it.

References

Achenbach, T. M. (1966). The classification of children's psychiatric symptoms: A factor-analytic study. *Psychological Monographs, 80*(7), 1–37.

Achenbach, T. M., & Edelbrock, C. S. (1978). The classification of child psychopathology: A review and analysis of empirical efforts. *Psychological Bulletin, 85*(6), 1275–1301.

Allen, L. B., McHugh, R. K., & Barlow, D. H. (2008). Emotional disorders: A unified protocol. In D. H. Barlow (Ed.), *Clinical handbook of psychological disorders: A step-by-step treatment manual*, 4th ed., (Vol. pp. 578–614). New York: Guilford Press.

Allport, G. D. (1962). The general and the unique in psychological science. *Journal of Personality, 30*, 405–422.

American Psychiatric Association . (1980). *Diagnostic and statistical manual of mental disorders* (3rd ed.). Washington, DC: Author.

American Psychiatric Association. (1987). *Diagnostic and statistical manual of mental disorders* (3rd ed, revised). Washington, DC: Author.

American Psychiatric Association. (1994). *Diagnostic and statistical manual of mental disorders* (4th ed.). Washington, DC: Author.

American Psychological Association. (2001). Amendment to bylaws accepted. *Monitor on Psychology, 32*.

American Psychological Association. (2006). Evidence-based practice in psychology. *American Psychologist, 61*(4), 271–285.

American Psychological Association. (2007). Competency Benchmarks Document. Retrieved from http://www.apa.org/ed/graduate/competency.html

American Psychological Association. (2009). Competency Assessment Toolkit for Professional Psychology. Retrieved April 25, 2010 from http://www.apa.org/ed/graduate/competency.html

Barlow, D. H. (1991). Introduction to the special issue on diagnosis, dimensions, & DSM-IV: The science of classification. *Journal of Abnormal Psychology, 100*, 243–244.

Barlow, D. H. (2002). *Anxiety and its disorders: The nature and treatment of anxiety and panic* (2nd ed.). New York: The Guilford Press.

Barlow, D. H. (2004). Psychological treatments. *American Psychologist, 59*(9), 869–878.

Barlow, D. H. (2006). Psychotherapy and psychological treatments: The future. *Clinical Psychology: Science & Practice, 13*, 216–220.

Barlow, D. H. (2008). *The power of psychological treatments: Implications for the future.* Paper presented at the 5th World Congress Psychotherapy.

Barlow, D. H., Allen, L. B., & Choate, M. L. (2004). Toward a unified treatment for emotional disorders. *Behavior Therapy, 35*, 205–230.

Barlow, D. H., Hayes, S. C., & Nelson, R. O. (1984). *The scientist-practitioner: Research and accountability in clinical settings.* New York: Pergamon Press.

Barlow, D. H., & Hersen, M. (1984). *Single case experimental designs: Strategies for studying behavior change* (2nd ed.). New York: Pergamon Press.

Barlow, D. H., Levitt, J. T., & Bufka, L. F. (1999). The dissemination of empirically supported treatments: A view to the future. *Research and Therapy, 37*(Suppl. 1), S147–S162.

Barlow, D. H., & Nock, M. K. (2009). Why can't we be more idiographic in our research? *Perspectives on Psychological Science, 4*(1), 19–21.

Barlow, D. H., Nock, M. K., & Hersen, M. (2009). *Single case experimental designs: Strategies for studying behavior change* (3rd ed.). Boston: Pearson Allyn & Bacon.

Borkovec, T. D. (2004). Research in training clinics and practice research networks: A route to the integration of science and practice. *Clinical Psychology: Science and Practice, 11*(2), 211–215.

Borkovec, T. D., Echemendia, R. J., Ragusea, S. A., & Ruiz, M. (2001). The Pennsylvania Practice Research Network and future possibilities for clinically meaningful and scientifically rigorous psychotherapy effectiveness research. *Clinical Psychology, Science & Practice, 8*, 155–167.

Bray, J. H. (2009). President's column: Collaborating for a change. *Monitor on Psychology, 40*(7), 5.

Brown, T. A., & Barlow, D. H. (2009). A proposal for a dimensional classification system based on the shared features of the DSM-IV anxiety and mood disorders: Implications for assessment and treatment. *Psychological Assessment, 21*(3), 256–271.

Brown, T. A., Chorpita, B. F., & Barlow, D. H. (1998). Structural relationships among dimensions of the DSM-IV anxiety and mood disorders and dimensions of negative affect, positive affect, and autonomic arousal. *Journal of Abnormal Psychology, 107*(2), 179–192.

Brown, T. A., Di Nardo, P. A., Lehman, C. L., & Campbell, L. A. (2001). Reliability of DSM-IV anxiety and mood disorders: Implications for the classification of emotional disorders. *Journal of Abnormal Psychology, 110*(1), 49–58.

Clark, D. (in press). Improving access to psychological therapies programs. In R. K. McHugh, & D. H. Barlow (Eds.), *Dissemination and implementation of evidence-based interventions.* New York: Oxford University Press.

Craighead, L., & Craighead, W. E. (2006). Ph. D. training in clinical psychology: Fix it before it breaks. *Clinical Psychology: Science & Practice, 13*(3), 235–241.

Craske, M. G., Rose, R. D., Lang, A., Welch, S. S., Campbell-Sills, L., Sullivan, G., et al. (2009). Computer-assisted delivery of cognitive behavioral therapy for anxiety disorders in primary-care settings. *Depression and Anxiety, 26*(3), 235–242.

Diener, E. (2000). Subjective well-being: The science of happiness, and a proposal for a national index. *American Psychologist, 55*, 34–43.

Dimeff, L. A., Koerner, K., Woodcock, E. A., Beadnell, B., Brown, M. Z., Skutch, J. M., Harned, M.S. (2009). Which training method works best? A randomized controlled trial comparing three methods of training clinicians in dialectical behavior therapy skills. *Behaviour Research and Therapy, 47*(11), 921–930.

Evidence-Based Behavioral-Practice. (2007). Online Training Modules. Retrieved September 25, 2009, from http://www.ebbp.org/training.html

Fairburn, C. G., Cooper, Z., & Shafran, R. (2003). Cognitive behaviour therapy for eating disorders: A "transdiagnostic" theory and treatment. *Behaviour Research and Therapy, 41*, 509–528.

Fairburn, C. G., Cooper, Z., Shafran, R., & Wilson, G. T. (2008). Eating disorders: A transdiagnostic protocol. In D. H. Barlow (Ed.), *Clinical handbook of psychological disorders: A step-by-step treatment manual*, 4th ed. (pp. 578–614). New York: Guilford Press.

Fairholme, C. P., Boisseau, C. L., Ellard, K. K., Ehrenreich, J. T., & Barlow, D. H. (2010). Emotions, emotion regulation, and psychological treatment: A unified perspective. In A. M.

Kring, & D. M. Sloan (Eds.), *Emotion regulation and psychopathology*. New York: Guilford Press.

First, M. B. (2005). Clinical utility: A prerequisite for the adoption of a dimensional approach in DSM. *Journal of Abnormal Psychology, 114*(4), 560–564.

Fixsen, D. L., Naoom, S. F., Blase, K. A., Friedman, R. M., & Wallace, F. (2005). *Implementation research: A synthesis of the literature*. Tampa, FL: University of South Florida, The Louis de la Parte Florida Mental Health Institute, Department of Child and Family Studies.

Foa, E., Hembree, E., & Rothbaum, B. (2007). *Prolonged exposure therapy for PTSD: Emotional processing of traumatic experiences, therapist guide*. New York: Oxford University Press.

Gawande, A. (2004, December 6). The bell curve. *The New Yorker*, (80). Retrieved from Academic OneFile via Gale.

Gawande, A. (2007). *Better: A surgeon's notes on performance*. New York: Metropolitan Books.

Gladwell, M. (2000). *The tipping point: How little things can make a big difference*. New York: Little, Brown and Company.

Gogolla, N., Caroni, P., Luthi, A., & Herry, C. (2009). Perineuronal nets protect fear memories from erasure. *Science, 325*(5945), 1258–1261.

Guastella, A. J., Howard, A. L., Dadds, M. R., Mitchell, P., & Carson, D. S. (2009). A randomized controlled trial of intranasal oxytocin as an adjunct to exposure therapy for social anxiety disorder. *Psychoneuroendocrinology, 34*(6), 917–923.

Guastella, A. J., Mitchell, P. B., & Dadds, M. R. (2008). Oxytocin increases gaze to the eye region of human faces. *Biological Psychiatry, 63*(1), 3–5.

Guastella, A. J., Mitchell, P. B., & Mathews, F. (2008). Oxytocin enhances the encoding of positive social memories in humans. *Biological Psychiatry, 64*(3), 256–258.

Hayes, S. C., Barlow, D. H., & Nelson-Gray, R. O. (1999). *The scientist-practitioner: Research and accountability in the age of managed care* (2nd ed.). Boston: Allyn & Bacon.

Hersen, M., & Barlow, D. H. (1976). *Single case experimental designs: Strategies for studying behavior change*. New York: Pergamon Press.

Hofmann, S. G. (2008). Cognitive processes during fear acquisition and extinction in animals and humans: Implications for exposure therapy of anxiety disorders. *Clinical Psychology Review, 28*, 200–211.

Hofmann, S. G., Meuret, A. E., Smits, J. A. J., Simon, N. M., Pollack, M. H., Eisenmenger, K., et al. (2006). Augmentation of exposure therapy with d-cycloserine for social anxiety disorder. *Archives of General Psychiatry, 63*(3), 298–304.

Horowitz, J., & Garber, J. (2006). The prevention of depressive symptoms in children and adolescents: A meta-analytic review. *Journal of Consulting and Clinical Psychology, 74*, 401–415.

Insel, T. R. (2009). Translating scientific opportunity into public health impact: A strategic plan for research on mental illness. *Archives of General Psychiatry, 66*(2), 128–133.

Johnson, N. G. (2001). President's column: Psychology's mission includes health: An opportunity. *Monitor on Psychology, 32*(4), 5.

Kendall, R. E. (1975). *The role of diagnosis in psychiatry*. Oxford, England: Blackwell.

Koocher, G. P. (2009). Any minute now but far away: Electronically mediated mental health. *Clinical Psychology: Science & Practice, 16*(3), 339–342.

Kushner, M. G., Kim, S. W., Donahue, C., Thuras, P., Adson, D., Kotlyar, M., et al. (2007). D-cycloserine augmented exposure therapy for obsessive-compulsive disorder. *Biological Psychiatry, 62*(8), 835–838.

Lambert, M. J., Whipple, J. L., Hawkins, E.J., Vermeersch, D. A., Nielsen, S. L., & Smart, D. W. (2003). Is it time for clinicians to routinely track patient outcome? A meta-analyses. *Clinical Psychology: Science & Practice, 10*, 288–301.

McCullough, Jr., J.P. (2002). The scientist-practitioner schism in clinical psychology: A fifty year problem. *Virginia Academy of Clinical Psychology Psychogram, 27*(2), 4–25.

McHugh, R. K., & Barlow, D. H. (2010). Dissemination and implementation of evidence-based psychological treatments: A review of current efforts. *American Psychologist, 65*(2), 73–84.

McHugh, R. K., & Barlow, D. H. (Eds.). (in press). *Dissemination and implementation of evidence-based interventions*. New York: Oxford University Press.

Millon, T. (1991). Classification in psychopathology: Rationale, alternatives, and standards. *Journal of Abnormal Psychology, 100*(3), 245–261.

Mohr, D. C. (2009). Telemental health: Reflections on how to move the field forward. *Clinical Psychology: Science & Practice, 16*(3), 343–347.

Moses, E. B., & Barlow, D. H. (2006). A new unified treatment approach for emotional disorders based on emotion science. *Current Directions in Psychological Science, 15*, 146–150.

Myers, K. M., & Davis, M. (2002). Behavioral and neural analysis of extinction. *Neuron, 36*, 567–684.

Nakamura, B. J., Higa-McMillan, C. K., & Chorpita, B. F. (in press). Sustaining Hawaii's evidence-based service system in children's mental health. In R. K. McHugh, & D. H. Barlow (Eds.), *Dissemination and implementation of evidence-based interventions*. New York: Oxford University Press.

Nathan, P. E., & Gorman, J. M. (Eds.). (2007). *A guide to treatments that work* (3rd ed.). New York: Oxford University Press.

Norcross, J. C., Hogan, T. P., & Koocher, G. P. (2008). *Clinician's guide to evidence based practices: Mental health and the addictions*. New York: Oxford University Press.

Olfson, M., & Marcus, S. C. (2009). National patterns in antidepressant medication treatment. *Archives of General Psychiatry, 66*(8), 848–856.

PCSAS. (2009). PCSAS home page. Retrieved on September 25, 2009, from http://www.pcsas.org/index.html

Phillips, A. (2006, February 26). A mind is a terrible thing to measure. *The New York Times*.

Plato. (1996). *Apology*. (H. N. Fowler, Trans.). Cambridge, MA: Harvard University.

Proudfoot, J. G. (2004). Computer-based treatment for anxiety and depression: Is it feasible? Is it effective? *Neuroscience and Biobehavioral Reviews, 28*(3), 353–363.

Reger, M. A., & Gahm, G. A. (2009). A meta-analysis of the effects of internet- and computer-based cognitive-behavioral treatments for anxiety. *Journal of Clinical Psychology, 65*(1), 53–75.

Resick, P. A., Monson, C. M., & Chard, K. M. (2007). *Cognitive processing therapy: Veteran/Military version*. Washington, DC: Department of Veterans' Affairs.

Richardson, L. K., Frueh, B. C., Grubaugh, A. L., Egede, L., & Elhai, J. D. (2009). Current directions in videoconferencing tele-mental health research. *Clinical Psychology: Science & Practice, 16*(3), 323–338.

Rogers, E. M. (2003). *Diffusion of innovations* (5th ed.). New York: Free Press.

Roth, A. D., & Pilling, S. (2007). The competences required to deliver effective cognitive and behavioural therapy for people with depression and with anxiety disorders. Retrieved April 25, 2010 from http://www.ucl.ac.uk/clinical-psychology/CORE/CBT_Competences/CBT_Competence_List.pdf

Seligman, M. E. P. (2002). *Authentic happiness: Using the new positive psychology to realize your potential for lasting fulfillment.* New York: Free Press/Simon & Schuster.

Shakow, D. (1969). *Clinical Psychology as science and profession: A 40-year odyssey.* Chicago: Aldine.

Shapiro, M. B. (1961). The single case in fundamental clinical psychological research. *British Journal of Medical Psychology, 34,* 255–262.

UpToDate. (2009). About UpToDate webpage. Retrieved on October 29, 2009, from http://www.uptodate.com/home/about/index.html

Wilhelm, S., Buhlmann, U., Tolin, D. F., Meunier, S. A., Pearlson, G. D., Reese, H. E., et al. (2008). Augmentation of behavior therapy with D-cycloserine for obsessive-compulsive disorder. *American Journal of Psychiatry, 165*(3), 335–341; quiz 409.

INDEX

Note: Page references followed by "f" and "t" denote figures and tables, respectively.

Hawaii Psychological Association (HPA), 37–38
Hawaii's health care initiatives, 40, 44
HD. *See* Huntington disease (HD)
Head trauma, 580–81
Health and Behavior Assessment and Intervention (H&B) CPT codes, 181
Health Belief Model, 725
Health care
  broadened conceptualization of, 46
  policy initiatives, in clinical psychology, 164–65
Health Resources and Services Administration (HRSA), 35, 45
Helmholtz, Hermann, 24
Hermeneutic of suspicion, 100
Herpes encephalitis, 581
"Hierarchy of needs," 108
High-potency tranquilizers, 16
Hippocrates, 23–25, 98, 897
Hippocratic Oath, 194
Historical transference, 879
History of clinical psychology
  early clinical psychologists, 23–31
  modern era, 31
Hobbs, Nicholas, 187
Hollingworth, Leta, 27–28
Home Based Primary Care (HBPC), 176
Homeless services, 177
Hooper Visual Organization Test, 578
Hopelessness, 239
Hot cognitions, 106
HRSA. *See* Health Resources and Services Administration (HRSA)
Human immunodeficiency virus (HIV), 576, 581
Humanistic/experiential therapies
  empirical support, 111–12
  models of function and dysfunction, 108–10
  neo-humanistic process view, 109
  process of, 110–11
  strategies and interventions, 110–11

Huntington, George, 590
Huntington disease (HD), 575, 590
Hydrocephalus, 591
  normal pressure, 576
Hyperarousal symptoms, 361
Hypersexuality, 460
HyperText Markup Language (HTML), 215
Hypnosis, 29
Hypoactive sexual desire disorder, 452–53
Hypochondriasis
  defined, 343
  diagnostic criteria and prevalence, 343–44
  psychosocial treatments, 344–45
Hypomania, 302
Hypomanic episodes, 294
Hypothalamic-pituitary-adrenocortical (HPA) axis, 410, 898
  mobilization, 372
Hypothyroidism, 576
Hysteria, 26

I
ICD. *See* Impulse-control disorders (ICDs)
ICT. *See* Integrative cognitive treatment
Ictal events, 592
Idiopathic epilepsy, 592
Idiosyncratic negative cognitive schemas, 104
Illusory correlation, 241
Imipramine, 296
Imminent risk, 740
Implied question, 242
Impulse-control disorders (ICDs)
  assessment, 519
  behavioral inhibition, 515
  characteristics, 506t
  compulsions and addiction, 515
  conceptualizing, 513–16
  essential features, 504
  genetic factors, 516
  harm to others, 511–13
  neurobiological factors, 516–17
  nonsuicidal self-injurious thoughts (NSSI) and behaviors, 508–9

pharmacological treatment strategies, 520–21
  prevention programs, 521–22
  psychological factors, 518–19
  psychological treatment strategies, 519–20
  social and developmental factors, 517–18
  spectrum, 514
  treatment of, 519–21
Individualized case conceptualization, 106
InfoPOEMS, 131
Information variance, 231
Informed consent, 228
  in cognitive psychology, 195
  as a continuing process, 196
  forms for, 195–96
  helpful information, 194–95
  legal cases, 194
  patient competence, 194
  patient's decision-making process, 195
Inherent organismic tendency, 108
Inhibition, 257
In-session markers, 111
Insight-oriented couple therapy (IOCT), 790, 795–96
  approaches to treatment, 801–2
  basic concepts, 800–801
  contributions, 801
  empirical support, 797, 802
  proximal vs. distal factors, 801
Insight-oriented marital therapy, 115
Integrated clinical settings, 5, 8–10
Integrated Psychotherapy Consortium (IPC), 214
Integrative behavioral couple therapy (IBCT), 115
Integrative cognitive treatment (ICT), 119
Intellectual disabilities (ID), 259
  assessment, 566–67
  clinical description and epidemiology, 564–65
  etiology, 565–66
  treatment, 566–67
Intelligence, 258
Intelligence quotient (IQ), 27, 80–81, 258–59, 559–60, 575

Male libido, 452
Male orgasmic disorder, 455–56
Manic-depressive disorder, 24
Marital and family therapy, 827–28
Masters and Johnson's sex therapy program, 448
Masturbation, 450
Maudsley family therapy, 389
McGuire, Margaret, 26
MDFT. *See* Multidimensional family therapy (MDFT)
Medicaid, 41, 180, 211
Medical and neurological disorders, 576
Medical apartheid, 869
Medically unexplained physical symptoms (MUPS), 334
Medicare Improvements for Patients and Providers Act (2008), 181
Medicare Prescription Drug, Improvement, and Modernization Act (2003), 181
Medicare Program, 180–82
"Medigap" insurance, 180
MEDLINE, 141
Medroxyprogesterone acetate, 461
Mental health courts
    functions, 663–64
    research findings, 664–66
Mental Health Intensive Care Management (MHICM), 174
Mental health issues, 24
Mental Health Policy Research, 214
Mental health problems interventions
    alcohol and drug misuse, 816–18
    anxiety disorders, 816
    behavior problems associated with dementia, 819
    caregiver stress, 819–20
    depression, 815–16
    diversity among older adults, 822–26
    empirical support, 814–22
    future directions in geropsychology, 826–28
    general assessment issues, 811–12

general intervention issues, 812–13
    insomnia, 818–19
    marital and family therapy, 827–28
    post-traumatic stress reactions, 827
    prolonged grief, 820–22, 821t
Mental Health's Measurement and Treatment Research to Improve Cognition in Schizophrenia (MATRICS), 82
Mental Illness Research, Education, and Clinical Centers (MIRECCs), 179
Mentalization, 102
Mental retardation in DSM-IV-TR, 258
Mental status examination (MSE), 230
Meta-analytic procedures, 66–67
M-HART. *See* Montreal Heart Attack Readjustment Trial (M-HART)
MHICM. *See* Mental Health Intensive Care Management (MHICM)
Microcephaly, 259
Military sexual trauma (MST), 177–78
Mind–Body Interactions, 214
MINI. *See* Mini-International Neuropsychiatric Interview (MINI)
Mini-depressions, 303
Mini-International Neuropsychiatric Interview (MINI), 234–35, 323
Minimum legal drinking age (MLDA), 415
Minnesota Multiphasic Personality Inventory-2 (MMPI-2), 81, 86, 235
Minor depressive disorder, 264
MIRECCs. *See* Mental Illness Research, Education, and Clinical Centers (MIRECCs)
Mixed anxiety-depressive disorder, 256
MLDA. *See* Minimum legal drinking age (MLDA)

MMPI-2. *See* Minnesota Multiphasic Personality Inventory-2 (MMPI-2)
Mobile technologies, in health care
    cellular coverage, 633
    evolution, 633
    increasing physical activity, 634
    lifestyle and health promotion interventions, 637
    medication compliances, 634
    monitoring of blood alcohol levels, 634
    obesity weight loss interventions, 636–37
    in promoting sexual health, 633
    providing dialectical behavior therapy (DBT) skills, 634, 637–38
    SEXINFO, 637
    short-message service (SMS), 634
    smoking cessation, 634–36
    TXT Quizzes, 635
    video and audio messages, 637–38
Modules, 215
Monoamine oxidase inhibitor (MAO-I) pharmacology, 303
Monotherapy, 296
Montreal Heart Attack Readjustment Trial (M-HART), 703
Mood and Anxiety Symptoms Questionnaire, 245
Mood disorders, 257
MoodGYM, 623–24
Mood intolerance, 393
Mood stabilizers, 295–96, 521, 541
Morgan-Russell criteria, 391
Morita therapy, 881
Mosaicism, 259
Mowrer's two-factor model of fear, 316
MS. *See* Multiple sclerosis (MS)
MST Services, Inc., 217
Multidimensional family therapy (MDFT), 115
Multimodal Treatment of Attention- Deficit Hyperactivity Disorder (MTA), 555